ISBN 978-1-5285-3328-7
PIBN 10922735

1 MONTH OF
FREE
READING

at
www.ForgottenBooks.com

By purchasing this book you are eligible for one month membership to ForgottenBooks.com, giving you unlimited access to our entire collection of over 1,000,000 titles via our web site and mobile apps.

To claim your free month visit:
www.forgottenbooks.com/free922735

English
Français
Deutsche
Italiano
Español
Português

www.forgottenbooks.com

Mythology Photography **Fiction**
Fishing Christianity **Art** Cooking
Essays Buddhism Freemasonry
Medicine **Biology** Music **Ancient
Egypt** Evolution Carpentry Physics
Dance Geology **Mathematics** Fitness
Shakespeare **Folklore** Yoga Marketing
Confidence Immortality Biographies
Poetry **Psychology** Witchcraft
Electronics Chemistry History **Law**
Accounting **Philosophy** Anthropology
Alchemy Drama Quantum Mechanics
Atheism Sexual Health **Ancient History**
Entrepreneurship Languages Sport
Paleontology Needlework Islam
Metaphysics Investment Archaeology
Parenting Statistics Criminology
Motivational

ANNALS

OF

THE CONGRESS OF THE UNITED STATES.

SIXTEENTH CONGRESS—SECOND SESSION.

THE·

DEBATES AND PROCEEDINGS

IN THE

CONGRESS OF THE UNITED STATES;

WITH

AN APPENDIX,

CONTAINING

IMPORTANT STATE PAPERS AND PUBLIC DOCUMENTS,

AND ALL

THE LAWS OF A PUBLIC NATURE;

WITH A COPIOUS INDEX.

SIXTEENTH CONGRESS.—SECOND SESSION:

COMPRISING THE PERIOD FROM NOVEMBER 13, 1820, TO MARCH 3, 1821, INCLUSIVE.

COMPILED FROM AUTHENTIC MATERIALS.

WASHINGTON:

PRINTED AND PUBLISHED BY GALES AND SEATON.
....
1855.

PROCEEDINGS AND DEBATES

OF

THE SENATE OF THE UNITED STATES,

AT THE SECOND SESSION OF THE SIXTEENTH CONGRESS, BEGUN AT THE CITY OF WASHINGTON, MONDAY, NOVEMBER 13, 1820.

MONDAY, November 13, 1820.

The second session of the Sixteenth Congress commenced this day, at the City of Washington, conformably to the act, approved the thirteenth of May, one thousand eight hundred and twenty, entitled "An act fixing the time for the next meeting of Congress," and the Senate assembled.

PRESENT:

DAVID L. MORRIL and JOHN F. PARROTT, from the State of New Hampshire.

JAMES BURRILL, jr., from Rhode Island.

ISAAC TICHENOR, from Vermont.

RUFUS KING and NATHAN SANFORD, from New York.

MAHLON DICKERSON and JAMES J. WILSON, from New Jersey.

JONATHAN ROBERTS and WALTER LOWRIE, from Pennsylvania.

OUTERBRIDGE HORSEY and NICHOLAS VAN DYKE, from Delaware.

JAMES BARBOUR and JAMES PLEASANTS, from Virginia.

NATHANIEL MACON, from North Carolina.

JOHN GAILLARD and WILLIAM SMITH, from South Carolina.

RICHARD M. JOHNSON, from Kentucky.

JOHN HENRY EATON, from Tennessee.

BENJAMIN RUGGLES and WILLIAM A. TRIMBLE, from Ohio.

JAMES BROWN and HENRY JOHNSON, from Louisiana.

WALLER TAYLOR and JAMES NOBLE, from Indiana.

THOMAS H. WILLIAMS and DAVID HOLMES, from Mississippi.

NINIAN EDWARDS and JESSE B. THOMAS, from Illinois.

WILLIAM R. KING and JOHN W. WALKER, from Alabama.

JOHN CHANDLER and JOHN HOLMES, from Maine.

JOHN GAILLARD, President *pro tempore*, resumed the Chair.

The new members having qualified and taken their seats, they were classed, by lot, as is usual.

The result was, that the term of service of Mr. HOLMES will expire on the 3d March next, and that of Mr. CHANDLER on the 3d of March two years thereafter.

Mr. KING, of Alabama, moved the appointment of a committee to acquaint the President of the United States of the organization of the Senate, and of its readiness to receive any communication from him; whereupon, Messrs. KING, of Alabama, and MACON were appointed.

On motion of Mr. MORRIL,

Resolved, That two Chaplains, of different denominations, be appointed to Congress, during the present session, one by each House, who shall interchange weekly.

The orders usual at the commencement of the session having been made, the Senate adjourned.

TUESDAY, November 14.

WILLIAM A. PALMER, from the State of Vermont, and JOHN WILLIAMS, from the State of Tennessee, severally attended.

The PRESIDENT communicated a copy of the constitution, as adopted for the government of the State of Missouri, which was read.

Whereupon, on motion of Mr. SMITH,

Resolved, That a committee be appointed to inquire whether any, and if any, what, legislative measures may be necessary for admitting the State of Missouri into the Union.

Messrs. SMITH, BURRILL, and MACON, were appointed the committee.

The Senate adjourned to two o'clock, to await the organization of the House of Representatives, and met again, but finding the House of Representatives had not yet elected a Speaker, they adjourned until to-morrow.

WEDNESDAY, November 15.

SAMUEL W. DANA, from the State of Connecticut, attended.

Mr. BURRILL communicated a resolution, passed by the Legislature of the State of Rhode Island and Providence Plantations, instructing their Senators, and requesting their Representatives in Congress, to exert their influence to reduce the compensation of members of Congress to six dollars per day; and the resolution was read.

On motion by Mr. WALKER, of Alabama, the Senate adjourned to one o'clock in the afternoon.

One o'clock in the afternoon.

A message from the House of Representatives informed the Senate that a quorum of the House of Representatives is assembled, and have elected JOHN W. TAYLOR, one of the Representatives from the State of New York, their Speaker, in the place of Henry Clay, resigned, and are ready to proceed to business; and that they have appointed a committee on their part to join the committee appointed on the part of the Senate, to wait on the President of the United States, and inform him that a quorum of the two Houses is assembled, and ready to receive any communications he may be pleased to make to them.

Mr. KING, of Alabama, reported, from the joint committee, that they had waited on the President of the United States, and that the President informed the committee that he would make a communication to the two Houses forthwith.

PRESIDENT'S MESSAGE.

The following Message was received from the PRESIDENT OF THE UNITED STATES:

Fellow-citizens of the Senate
and of the House of Representatives:

In communicating to you a just view of public affairs, at the commencement of your present labors, I do it with great satisfaction; because, taking all circumstances into consideration which claim attention, I see much cause to rejoice in the felicity of our situation. In making this remark, I do not wish to be understood to imply that an unvaried prosperity is to be seen in every interest of this great community. In the progress of a nation, inhabiting a territory of such vast extent and great variety of climate, every portion of which is engaged in foreign commerce, and liable to be affected, in some degree, by the changes which occur in the condition and regulations of foreign countries, it would be strange if the produce of our soil and the industry and enterprise of our fellow-citizens received at all times, and in every quarter, an uniform and equal encouragement. This would be more than we would have a right to expect, under circumstances the most favorable. Pressures on certain interests, it is admitted, has been felt; but allowing to these their greatest extent, they detract but little from the force of the remarks already made. In forming a just estimate of our present situation, it is proper to look at the whole, in the outline, as well as in the detail. A free, virtuous, and enlightened people know well the great principles and causes on which their happiness depends; and even those who suffer most, occasionally, in their transitory concerns, find great relief under their sufferings, from the blessings which they otherwise enjoy, and in the consoling and animating hope which they administer. From whence do these pressures come? Not from a Government which is founded by, administered for, and supported by the people. We trace them to the peculiar character of the epoch in which we live, and to the extraordinary occurrences which have signalized it. The convulsions with which several of the Powers of Europe have

been shaken, and the long and destructive wars in which all were engaged, with their sudden transition to a state of peace, presenting, in the first instance, unusual encouragement to our commerce, and withdrawing it in the second, even within its wonted limit, could not fail to be sensibly felt here. The station, too, which we had to support through this long conflict, compelled as we were finally to become a party to it with a principal Power, and to make great exertions, suffer heavy losses, and to contract considerable debts, disturbing the ordinary course of affairs, by augmenting, to a vast amount, the circulating medium, and thereby elevating, at one time, the price of every article above a just standard, and depressing it at another below it, had likewise its due effect.

It is manifest that the pressures of which we complain have proceeded, in a great measure, from these causes. When, then, we take into view the prosperous and happy condition of our country, in all the great circumstances which constitute the felicity of a nation—every individual in the full enjoyment of all his rights: the Union blessed with plenty, and rapidly rising to greatness, under a national Government, which operates with complete effect in every part, without being felt in any, except by the ample protection which it affords, and under State governments which perform their equal share, according to a wise distribution of power between them, in promoting the public happiness—it is impossible to behold so gratifying, so glorious a spectacle, without being penetrated with the most profound and grateful acknowledgments to the Supreme Author of all good for such manifold and inestimable blessings. Deeply impressed with these sentiments, I cannot regard the pressures to which I have adverted otherwise than in the light of mild and instructive admonitions; warning us of dangers to be shunned in future; teaching us lessons of economy, corresponding with the simplicity and purity of our institutions, and best adapted to their support; evincing the connexion and dependence which the various parts of our happy Union have on each other, thereby augmenting daily our social incorporation, and adding, by its strong ties, new strength and vigor to the political; opening a wider range, and with new encouragement, to the industry and enterprise of our fellow-citizens at home and abroad; and more especially by the multiplied proofs which it has accumulated of the great perfection of our most excellent system of government, the powerful instrument, in the hands of our all-merciful Creator, in securing to us these blessings.

Happy as our situation is, it does not exempt us from solicitude and care for the future. On the contrary, as the blessings which we enjoy are great, proportionably great should be our vigilance, zeal, and activity, to preserve them. Foreign wars may again expose us to new wrongs, which would impose on us new duties, for which we ought to be prepared. The state of Europe is unsettled, and how long peace may be preserved is altogether uncertain; in addition to which, we have interests of our own to adjust, which will require particular attention. A correct view of our relations with each Power will enable you to form a just idea of existing difficulties, and of the measures of precaution best adapted to them.

Respecting our relations with Spain, nothing explicit can now be communicated. On the adjournment of Congress in May last, the Minister Plenipotentiary of the United States, at Madrid, was instructed to inform the Government of Spain that, if His

Catholic Majesty should then ratify the treaty, this Government would accept the ratification, so far as to submit to the decision of the Senate, the question, whether such ratification should be received in exchange for that of the United States. heretofore given By letters from the Minister of the United States to the Secretary of State, it appears that a communication, in conformity with his instructions, had been made to the Government of Spain, and that the Cortes had the subject under consideration. The result of the deliberations of that body, which is daily expected, will be made known to Congress as soon as it is received. The friendly sentiment which was expressed on the part of the United States, in the Message of the 9th of May last, is still entertained for Spain. Among the causes of regret, however, which are inseparable from the delay attending this transaction, it is proper to state that satisfactory information has been received, that measures have been recently adopted, by designing persons, to convert certain parts of the Province of Florida into depots for the reception of foreign goods, from whence to smuggle them into the United States. By opening a port within the limits of Florida, immediately on our boundary, where there was no settlement, the object could not be misunderstood. An early accommodation of differences will, it is hoped, prevent all such fraudulent and pernicious practices, and place the relations of the two countries on a very amicable and permanent basis.

The commercial relations between the United States and the British colonies in the West Indies, and on this continent, have undergone no change; the British Government still preferring to leave that commerce under the restriction heretofore imposed on it, on each side. It is satisfactory to recollect that the restraints resorted to by the United States were defensive only, intended to prevent a monopoly, under British regulations, in favor of Great Britain; as it likewise is to know that the experiment is advancing in a spirit of amity between the parties.

The question depending between the United States and Great Britain, respecting the construction of the first article of the Treaty of Ghent, has been referred, by both Governments, to the decision of the Emperor of Russia, who has accepted the umpirage.

An attempt has been made with the Government of France, to regulate, by treaty, the commerce between the two countries, on the principle of reciprocity and equality. By the last communication from the Minister Plenipotentiary of the United States at Paris, to whom full power had been given, we learn that the negotiation had been commenced there; but, serious difficulties having occurred, the French Government had resolved to transfer it to the United States, for which purpose the Minister Plenipotentiary of France had been ordered to repair to this city, and whose arrival might soon be expected. It is hoped that this important interest may be arranged on just conditions, and in a manner equally satisfactory to both parties. It is submitted to Congress to decide, until such arrangement is made, how far it may be proper, on the principle of the act of the last session, which augmented the tonnage duty on French vessels, to adopt other measures for carrying more completely into effect the policy of that act.

The act referred to, which imposed new tonnage on French vessels, having been in force from and after the first day of July, it has happened that several vessels of that nation which had been despatched from France before its existence was known, have entered the ports of the United States, and been subject to its operation, without that previous notice which the general spirit of our laws gives to individuals in similar cases. The object of that law having been merely to countervail the inequalities which existed to the disadvantage of the United States, in their commercial intercourse with France, it is submitted, also, to the consideration of Congress, whether, in the spirit amity and conciliation which it is no less the inclination than the policy of the United States to preserve in their intercourse with other Powers, it may not proper to extend relief to the individuals interested in those cases, by exempting from the operation of law all those vessels which have entered our ports without having had the means of previously knowing the existence of the additional duty.

The contest between Spain and the Colonies, cording to the most authentic information, is maintained by the latter with improved success. unfortunate divisions which were known to exist time since, at Buenos Ayres, it is understood, prevail. In no part of South America has Spain more any impression on the colonies, while, in many parts and particularly in Venezuela and New Granada, colonies have gained strength and acquired reputation both for the management of the war, in which they have been successful, and for the order of the internal administration. The late change in the Government of Spain, by the re-establishment of the constitution of 1812, is an event which promises to be favorable the Revolution. Under the authority of the Congress the Congress of Angostura was invited to open a gotiation for the settlement of differences between parties, to which it was replied, that they would lingly open the negotiation, provided the acknowledgment of their independence was made its basis not otherwise. Of further proceedings between us we are uninformed. No facts are known to this Government, to warrant the belief, that any of the Powers of Europe will take part in the contest; whence may be inferred, considering all circumstances, we must have weight in producing the result, that an justment will finally take place, on the basis proposed by the colonies. To promote that result, by friendly counsels, with other Powers, including Spain herself, has been the uniform policy of this Government.

In looking to the internal concerns of our country, you will, I am persuaded, derive much satisfaction from a view of the several objects to which, in the charge of your official duties, your attention will drawn. Among these, none holds a more important place than the public revenue, from the direct operation of the power, by which it is raised, on the people, by its influence in giving effect to every other of the Government. The revenue depends on the sources of the country, and the facility by which amount required is raised, is a strong proof of the extent of the resources, and the efficiency of the Government. A few prominent facts will place this great interest in a just light before you. On the 30th of September 1815, the funded and floating debt of the United States was estimated at one hundred and nineteen million six hundred and thirty-five thousand five hundred fifty-eight dollars. If to this sum be added the amount of five per cent. stock subscribed to the Bank of United States, the amount of Mississippi stock, of the stock which was issued subsequently to date, the balances ascertained to be due to

States, for military services, and to individuals, for supplies furnished, and services rendered during the late war, the public debt may be estimated as amounting, at that date, and as afterwards liquidated, to one hundred and fifty-eight millions seven hundred and thirteen thousand forty-nine dollars. On the 30th of September, 1820, it amounted to ninety-one millions nine hundred and ninety-three thousand eight hundred and eighty-three dollars, having been reduced in that interval, by payments, sixty-six millions eight hundred and seventy-nine thousand one hundred and sixty-five dollars. During this term, the expenses of the Government of the United States were likewise defrayed, in every branch of the civil, military, and naval establishments; the public edifices in this city have been rebuilt, with considerable additions; extensive fortifications have been commenced, and are in a train of execution; permanent arsenals and magazines have been erected in various parts of the Union; our Navy has been considerably augmented, and the ordnance, munitions of war, and stores, of the Army and Navy, which were much exhausted during the war, have been replenished.

By the discharge of so large a proportion of the public debt, and the execution of such extensive and important operations, in so short a time, a just estimate may be formed of the great extent of our national resources. The demonstration is the more complete and gratifying, when it is recollected that the direct tax and excise were repealed soon after the termination of the late war, and that the revenue applied to these purposes has been derived almost wholly from other resources.

The receipts into the Treasury, from every source, to the 30th of September last, have amounted to sixteen millions seven hundred and ninety-four thousand one hundred and seven dollars and sixty-six cents; whilst the public expenditures, to the same period, amounted to sixteen millions eight hundred and seventy-one thousand five hundred and thirty-four dollars and seventy-two cents; leaving in the Treasury, on that day, a sum estimated at one million nine hundred and fifty thousand dollars. For the probable receipts of the following year, I refer you to the statement which will be transmitted from the Treasury.

The sum of three millions of dollars, authorized to be raised by loan, by an act of the last session of Congress, has been obtained upon terms advantageous to the Government, indicating, not only an increased confidence in the faith of the nation, but the existence of a large amount of capital seeking that mode of investment, at a rate of interest not exceeding five per centum per annum.

It is proper to add, that there is now due to the Treasury, for the sale of public lands, twenty-two millions nine hundred and ninety-six thousand five hundred and forty-five dollars. In bringing this subject to view, I consider it my duty to submit to Congress, whether it may not be advisable to extend to the purchasers of these lands, in consideration of the unfavorable change which has occurred since the sales, a reasonable indulgence. It is known that the purchases were made when the price of every article had risen to its greatest height, and that the instalments are becoming due at a period of great depression. It is presumed that some plan may be devised, by the wisdom of Congress, compatible with the public interest, which would afford great relief to these purchasers.

Considerable progress has been made, during the present season, in examining the coast and its various bays and other inlets; in the collection of materials, and in the construction of fortifications for the defence of the Union, at several of the positions at which it has been decided to erect such works. At Mobile Point and Dauphin Island, and at the Rigolets, leading to Lake Pontchartrain, materials to a considerable amount have been collected and all the necessary preparations made for the commencement of the works. At Old Point Comfort, at the mouth of James river, and at the Rip-Rap, on the opposite shore, in the Chesapeake Bay, materials to a vast amount have been collected; and at the Old Point some progress has been made in the construction of the fortification, which is on a very extensive scale. The work at Fort Washington, on this river, will be completed early in the next Spring; and that on the Pea Patch, in the Delaware, in the course of the next season. Fort Diamond, at the Narrows, in the harbor of New York, will be finished this year. The works at Boston, New York, Baltimore, Norfolk, Charleston, and Niagara, have been in part repaired; and the coast of North Carolina, extending south to Cape Fear, has been examined, as have likewise other parts of the coast eastward of Boston. Great exertions have been made to push forward these works with the utmost despatch possible; but, when their extent is considered, with the important purposes for which they are intended, the defence of the whole coast, and in consequence of the whole interior, and that they are to last for ages, it will be manifest that a well-digested plan, founded on military principles, connecting the whole together, combining security with economy, could not be prepared without repeated examinations of the most exposed and difficult parts, and that it would also take considerable time to collect the materials at the several points where they would be required. From all the light that has been shed on this subject, I am satisfied that every favorable anticipation which has been formed of this great undertaking will be verified, and that when completed it will afford very great, if not complete, protection to our Atlantic frontier in the event of another war; a protection sufficient to counterbalance in a single campaign with an enemy powerful at sea the expense of all these works, without taking into the estimate the saving of the lives of so many of our citizens, the protection of our towns and other property, or the tendency of such works to prevent war.

Our military positions have been maintained at Belle Point, on the Arkansas, at Council Bluffs, on the Missouri, at St. Peter's, on the Mississippi, and at Green Bay, on the Upper lakes. Commodious barracks have already been erected at most of these posts, with such works as were necessary for their defence. Progress has also been made in opening communications between them, and in raising supplies at each for the support of the troops by their own labor, particularly those most remote.

With the Indians peace has been preserved, and a progress made in carrying into effect the act of Congress, making an appropriation for their civilization, with the prospect of favorable results. As connected equally with both these objects, our trade with those tribes is thought to merit the attention of Congress. In their original state, game is their sustenance and war their occupation: and if they find no employment from civilized Powers, they destroy each other. Left to themselves, their extirpation is inevitable. By a judicious regulation of our trade with them, we supply

HISTORY OF CONGRESS.

their wants, administer to their comforts, and gradually, as the game retires, draw them to us. By maintaining posts far in the interior, we acquire a more thorough and direct control over them; without which it is confidently believed that a complete change in their manners can never be accomplished. By such posts, aided by a proper regulation of our trade with them, and a judicious civil administration over them, to be provided for by law, we shall it is presumed be enabled not only to protect our own settlements from their savage incursions, and preserve peace among the several tribes, but accomplish also the great purpose of their civilization.

Considerable progress has also been made in the construction of ships of war, some of which have been launched in the course of the present year.

Our peace with the Powers on the coast of Barbary has been preserved, but we owe it altogether to the presence of our squadron in the Mediterranean. It has been found equally necessary to employ some of our vessels for the protection of our commerce in the Indian sea, the Pacific, and along the Atlantic coast. The interests which we have depending in those quarters, which have been much improved of late, are of great extent, and of high importance to the nation, as well as to the parties concerned, and would undoubtedly suffer if such protection was not extended to them. In execution of the law of the last session, for the suppression of the slave trade, some of our public ships have also been employed on the coast of Africa, where several captures have already been made of vessels engaged in that disgraceful traffic.

JAMES MONROE.
WASHINGTON, *November* 14, 1820.

The Message was read, and three thousand copies thereof ordered to be printed for the use of the Senate.

THURSDAY, November 16.

Mr. JOHNSON, of Kentucky, submitted the following motion for consideration:

Resolved, That it is expedient to make provision, by law, to authorize any person who has purchased public lands, and not made full payment for the same, to relinquish to the United States so much thereof as may not be paid for, and retain such portion of the original purchase as may amount to the sums of money actually paid, at the price for which the land was purchased.

Mr. WALKER, of Alabama, gave notice that, to-morrow, he should ask leave to bring in a bill to provide for altering the times of holding the district courts in the State of Alabama.

Mr. BURRILL submitted the following motion for consideration:

Resolved, That the act, entitled "An act allowing compensation to the members of the Senate, members of the House of Representatives of the United States, and to the delegates of the Territories, and repealing all other laws on the subject," passed at the first session of the fifteenth Congress, ought to be so altered and amended that the compensation to the members and delegates aforesaid, shall hereafter be six dollars for each day's attendance, and six dollars for every twenty miles travel, instead of the compensation now allowed by said act, and that it be referred to a committee to prepare and report a bill for altering and amending said act accordingly.

Mr. DICKERSON submitted the following motion for consideration:

Resolved, That a committee of three members be appointed, who, with three members of the House of Representatives, to be appointed by that House, shall have the direction of the money appropriated to the purchase of books and maps for the use of the two Houses of Congress.

On motion, by Mr. ROBERTS,
Resolved, That the Senate will, on Monday next, at twelve o'clock, proceed to the appointment of the Standing Committees.

FRIDAY, November 17.

JAMES LANMAN, from the State of Connecticut, arrived yesterday, and attended this day.

Mr. SANFORD submitted the following motions for consideration:

Resolved, That so much of the Message of the President of the United States as concerns our relations with Spain and with France, be referred to the Committee of Foreign Relations.

Resolved, That so much of the Message of the President of the United States as relates to Finance, be referred to the Committee of Finance.

Resolved, That so much of the Message of the President of the United States as relates to the debt due for the sale of public lands, be referred to the Committee on Public Lands.

Resolved, That so much of the Message of the President of the United States as relates to the Indian tribes, be referred to the Committee on Indian Affairs.

Mr. WALKER, of Alabama, asked and and obtained leave to bring in a bill to alter the terms of the district court in Alabama, and the bill was twice read by unanimous consent, and referred to a select committee to consider and report thereon; and Messrs. WALKER, of Alabama, BURRILL, and KING, of Alabama, were appointed the committee.

The Senate resumed the consideration of the motion of the 16th instant, respecting the compensation of the members and delegates of Congress, and the further consideration thereof was postponed until next Monday week.

The Senate resumed the consideration of the resolution for the appointment of a joint committee on the arrangements for the Library of Congress, and having agreed thereto, Messrs. DICKERSON, DANA, and HUNTER, were appointed the committee.

A message from the House of Representatives informed the Senate that the House concur in the resolution of the Senate for the appointment of Chaplains, and have appointed the Rev. J. N. CAMPBELL, Chaplain on their part.

On motion by Mr. WILSON, the Senate proceeded to the election of a Chaplain on their part; and, on counting the ballots, it appeared that the Rev. WILLIAM RYLAND was duly elected.

The PRESIDENT communicated a letter from the Commissioner of the General Land Office, transmitting copies of the reports of the Land Commissioners at Jackson Courthouse, and a copy of a letter, dated 17th August, 1820, which accompanied them; which were read.

The PRESIDENT also communicated a report of the Secretary of the Treasury, made in obedience to a resolution of the Senate of the 3d April, 1820, directing him to "cause to be prepared, and laid before the Senate, at the commencement of the next session of Congress, a statement of money annually appropriated, and paid, since the Declaration of Independence, for purchasing from the Indians, surveying, and selling the public lands, showing, as near as may be, the quantities of land which have been purchased, the number of acres which have been surveyed, the number sold, and the number which remain unsold; the amount of sales, the amount of forfeitures, the sums paid by purchasers, and the sums due from purchasers and from receivers in each land district;" and the report was read.

The PRESIDENT also communicated a report of the Secretary of the Treasury, made in obedience to a resolution of the Senate, directing him to "cause to be prepared, and laid before the Senate, at the commencement of the next session of Congress, a statement of the money which has been annually appropriated and paid, since the year seventeen hundred and seventy-five, for surveying the seacoast, bays, inlets, harbors, and shoals, and for erecting, and keeping in repair, lighthouses, beacons, buoys, and for the purchase of ground for lighthouses, distinguishing the places where they have been erected, and the sums annually expended for keeping and supplying the same;" and the report was read.

Adjourned to Monday.

MONDAY, November 20.

JOHN ELLIOTT, and also, FREEMAN WALKER, from the State of Georgia, severally arrived, on the 17th instant, and attended this day.

Mr. WALKER, of Alabama, from the committee to whom was referred the bill to alter the terms of the district court in Alabama, reported the same without amendment, and it was considered as in Committee of the Whole, and no amendment having been proposed thereto, it was reported to the House; and ordered to be engrossed and read a third time.

Mr. WALKER, of Alabama, submitted the following motions for consideration:

Resolved, That it is expedient to provide for the relief of purchasers of the public lands, by dividing the sums now severally unpaid, exclusive of interest, into —— equal instalments; each instalment bearing interest only from the time at which it shall be made payable.

Resolved, That it is expedient to permit such purchasers of the public lands as may elect that mode, to surrender. within —— months from and after the —— day of —— next, their certificates, which shall be cancelled, and the lands shall be taken to have reverted and become forfeited to the United States, and shall be advertised, and sold for cash at public auction, to the highest bidder, in the same manner as other public lands. They shall not be sold for less than one dollar and twenty-five cents per acre, which sum shall go to the use of the United States, in addition to the sums already paid; but if said lands should be so re-

sold for more than one dollar and twenty-five cents per acre, the excess shall be paid to the person surrendering the certificate, provided such excess shall never be greater than the amount actually paid on such lands before such surrender.

Resolved, That it is expedient to permit such purchasers of the public lands as may elect that mode, to extinguish their debt, complete their titles, and demand and receive patents, by paying, within the period of one year from and after the —— day of —— next, into their respective land offices, five-eighths of the original price at which their lands were purchased, including interest, and computing the moneys already paid as part of the said final payment of five-eighths.

Resolved, That it is expedient, in addition to the privilege contemplated in the preceding resolution, to permit such purchasers of the public lands as may elect that mode, at any time within the said period of one year from and after the —— day of —— next, to forfeit and abandon to the United States such fractions, quarter sections, and half quarter sections, as they may deem fit; and to transfer and apply the moneys already paid on the tract or tracts so forfeited to the payment for such other fraction, quarter section, or half quarter section as they may choose to retain; and in cases where the purchaser has bought only one quarter section, he shall be permitted to divide it, and make his election between its halves—such division being made by a north and south line according to law.

The PRESIDENT communicated a letter from the Secretary of State of the United States, requesting an additional supply of documents, printed by order of the Senate; and the letter was read, and referred to the Committee on the Judiciary.

The Senate resumed the consideration of Mr. SANFORD's motions of the 17th instant, for referring to various committees the Message of the President of the United States; and agreed thereto.

STANDING COMMITTEES.

The Senate then, pursuant to the order of the day, proceeded to the appointment, by ballot, of the standing committees, which resulted in the distribution of the members, as follows:

On the Committee of Foreign Relations—Messrs. BARBOUR, MACON, BROWN, HUNTER, and KING of New York.

On Finance—Messrs. SANFORD, MACON, DANA, EATON, and HOLMES of Maine.

On Commerce and Manufactures—Messrs. DICKERSON, RUGGLES, BURRILL, HORSEY, and SANFORD.

On Military Affairs—Messrs. WILLIAMS of Tennessee, TRIMBLE, TAYLOR, ELLIOTT, and JOHNSON of Kentucky.

On the Militia—Messrs. NOBLE, TICHENOR, STOKES, LANMAN, and CHANDLER.

On Naval Affairs—Messrs. PLEASANTS, PARROTT, WILLIAMS of Mississippi, WALKER of Alabama, and WALKER of Georgia.

On the Public Lands—Messrs. THOMAS, TAYLOR, LOWRIE, EATON, and VAN DYKE.

On Indian Affairs—Messrs. HOLMES of Mississippi, JOHNSON of Kentucky, JOHNSON of Louisiana, KING of Alabama, and LOWRIE.

On *Claims*—Messrs. WILSON, ROBERTS, MORRIL, RUGGLES, and VAN DYKE.

On the *Judiciary*—Messrs. SMITH, BURRILL, PINKNEY, WALKER of Georgia, and HOLMES of Maine.

On the *Post Office and Post Roads*—Messrs. STOKES, WILSON, PALMER, CHANDLER, and EDWARDS.

On *Pensions*—Messrs. NOBLE, ELLIOTT, WILSON, EATON, and TICHENOR.

On the *District of Columbia*—Messrs. HORSEY, LANMAN, LLOYD, BARBOUR, and HUNTER.

On *Accounts*—Messrs. ROBERTS, BURRILL, and LANMAN.

On *Roads and Canals*—Messrs. KING of New York, TRIMBLE, LOWRIE, MACON, and DANA.

TUESDAY, November 21.

Mr. WILLIAMS, of Tennessee, presented the memorial of William Kelly, on behalf of himself and divers others, claimants of land in the Territory of Arkansas, under Elisha and William Winter, deceased; and the memorial was read, and referred to the Committee on Public Lands.

Mr. HOLMES, of Maine, presented the memorial of the delegates from the commercial and agricultural sections of the State of Maine, met in convention at Portland, protesting against the proposed tariff; and the memorial was read, and referred to the Committee on Commerce and Manufactures.

The PRESIDENT communicated the memorial of Matthew Lyon, of Eddyville, Kentucky, praying compensation for certain losses and sufferings under the act commonly called the Sedition law; and the memorial was read, and referred to a select committee; and Messrs. BARBOUR, JOHNSON of Kentucky, and BURRILL, were appointed the committee.

Mr. PLEASANTS presented the memorial of the merchants and other inhabitants of the town of Petersburg, in the State of Virginia, in opposition to the proposed tariff; and the memorial was read, and referred to the Committee on Commerce and Manufactures.

Mr. HOLMES, of Mississippi, presented the petition of Clarissa Scott, widow of the late Colonel William Scott, of the State of Mississippi, praying the confirmation of her title to a certain tract of land, as stated in the petition; which was read, and referred to the Committee on Public Lands.

Mr. JOHNSON, of Kentucky, presented the petition of Rufus Easton, for himself and heirs of James Bruff, praying the confirmation of their title to a certain tract of land, as stated in the petition; which was read, and referred to the same committee.

The bill to alter the terms of the district court in Alabama was read a third time, and passed.

Mr. DICKERSON, after a few remarks reiterating his desire for the passage of the measure, and his continued confidence in its importance and utility, gave notice that he should, on to-morrow, ask leave to introduce a joint resolution proposing an amendment to the Constitution, in relation to the appointment of Electors of President and Vice President of the United States, and members of the House of Representatives, [which was introduced by Mr. D., and passed the Senate at the last session; and was introduced yesterday in the House of Representatives by Mr. SMITH, of North Carolina.]

WEDNESDAY, November 22.

Mr. NOBLE presented the petition of sundry citizens of the Western States, purchasers of public lands, praying that a law may be passed enabling them to apply the payments already made, to such portions of their entries as those payments will cover, at two dollars an acre, agreeably to the law under which the entries were made, relinquishing the residue to the United States. And also allowing those purchasers who have purchased but one tract, the privilege of retaining it entire, with a reasonable extension of credit without interest, or otherwise relinquishing a part of it; and the petition was read, and referred to the Committee on Public Lands.

Mr. THOMAS presented two memorials of the Legislature of the State of Missouri, praying of Congress some legislative provisions for the relief of indigent actual settlers on the public lands, particularly widows and orphans; and the memorials were severally read, and respectively referred to the same committee.

Mr. DICKERSON obtained leave to introduce a resolution, proposing an amendment to the Constitution of the United States, as it respects the election of Representatives in Congress, and the choice of Electors of President and Vice President of the United States; and the resolution was read, and passed to the second reading.

Mr. EATON obtained leave to introduce a bill for the relief of Robert Purdy; and the bill was read, and passed to the second reading.

The Senate resumed the consideration of the motions of Mr. WALKER of the 20th instant, in relation to purchasers of the public lands; and they were referred to the Committee on Public Lands.

The Senate resumed the consideration of the motion of Mr. JOHNSON of the 16th instant, in relation to the same subject; and it was referred to the same committee.

THURSDAY, November 23.

Mr. NOBLE submitted the following motion for consideration:

Resolved, That the Committee on Public Lands be instructed to inquire into the expediency of permitting such purchasers of the public lands, prior to the 1st of July, 1820, to demand and receive patents, who have paid into their respective land offices the first, second, and third instalments, on each tract purchased.

Mr. THOMAS submitted the following motion for consideration:

Resolved, That the Committee on Public Lands be instructed to inquire into the expediency of providing, by law, for granting to actual settlers on the public lands the right of pre-emption in becoming the purchasers of lands, including their improvements.

The resolution proposing an amendment to the Constitution of the United States, as it respects the election of Representatives in Congress, and the choice of Electors of President and Vice President of the United States, was read the second time, and referred to a select committee, to consist of five members, to consider and report thereon; and Messrs. DICKERSON, BARBOUR, MACON, HOLMES, of Mississippi, and HOLMES, of Maine, were appointed the committee.

The bill for the relief of Robert Purdy was read the second time, and referred to the Committee on Military Affairs.

Mr. KING, of New York, presented the memorial of Ebenezer Stevens and others, praying that Congress would afford them relief, on account of a demand against the United States, arising out of certain contracts entered into with Robert Morris, Esq., for the supply of provisions to the Army of the United States during the Revolutionary war; and the memorial was read, and referred to the Committee of Claims.

RESTRICTION OF SLAVERY.

Mr. SANFORD communicated the following resolutions, passed by the Legislature of the State of New York; which were read.

STATE OF NEW YORK,
In Assembly, November 13, 1820.

Whereas the Legislature of this State, at the last session, did instruct their Senators and request their Representatives in Congress to oppose the admission, as a State into the Union, of any Territory not comprised within the original boundaries of the United States, without making the prohibition of slavery therein an indispensable condition of admission: And whereas this Legislature is impressed with the correctness of the sentiments so communicated to our Senators and Representatives; therefore,

Resolved, (if the honorable the Senate concur herein,) That this Legislature does approve of the principles contained in the resolutions of the last session; and, further, if the provisions contained in any proposed constitution of a new State deny to any citizens of the existing States the privileges and immunities of citizens of such new State, that such proposed constitution should not be accepted or confirmed; the same, in the opinion of this Legislature, being void by the Constitution of the United States. And that our Senators be instructed, and our Representatives in Congress be requested, to use their utmost exertions to prevent the acceptance and confirmation of any such constitution.

Resolved, (if the honorable the Senate concur herein,) That the President of the Senate and the Speaker of the Assembly do cause copies of these resolutions, duly certified by them, to be transmitted to the Senators and Representatives in Congress from this State.

Ordered, That the clerk deliver a copy of the preceding resolutions to the honorable the Senate, and request their concurrence to the same.

PETER SHARPE, *Speaker.*

Attest—DL. VAN DU WEYDEN,
Clerk of Assembly.

STATE OF NEW YORK,
In Senate, November 15, 1820.

Resolved, That the Senate do concur with the honorable the Assembly, in their said resolutions and recitals.

Ordered, That the clerk deliver a copy of said resolution of concurrence to the honorable the Assembly.

JOHN TAYLER, *President.*

Attest—JOHN F. BACON,
Clerk of the Senate.

FRIDAY, November 24.

Mr. WILSON presented the memorial of James Leander Cathcart, praying the passage of a law directing the accounting officers of the Treasury to allow his claim upon the Government, in the settlement of his accounts, as stated in the memorial; which was read, and referred to the Committee of Claims.

Mr. WALKER, of Alabama, submitted the following motion for consideration:

Resolved, That the Committee on the Public Lands be instructed to inquire into the expediency of securing to actual settlers, in all cases where the lands they occupy shall be sold after the first day of March, in any year, the right of remaining on the same until they shall have gathered their growing crop.

Mr. HORSEY presented the petition of the President and Directors of the Farmers' Bank of Alexandria, in the District of Columbia, praying the extension of their charter for twenty years, from and after the 1st day of June, 1822; and the petition was read, and referred to the Committee on the District of Columbia.

Mr. TRIMBLE presented the petition of Major Charles Larrabee, of the Army of the United States, praying remuneration for losses sustained while in the service of the United States, as stated in the petition; which was read, and referred to the Committee of Claims.

The Senate resumed the consideration of the motion of the 23d instant, in relation to actual settlers on the public lands, and agreed thereto.

The Senate also resumed the consideration of the motion of the 23d instant, in relation to certain purchasers of the public lands, and agreed thereto.

The Senate adjourned to Monday.

MONDAY, November 27.

HARRISON GRAY OTIS, from the State of Massachusetts, arrived on the 25th instant; and WILLIAM HUNTER, from the State of Rhode Island and Providence Plantations, arrived on the 24th instant, severally attended this day.

ISHAM TALBOT, appointed a Senator by the Legislature of Kentucky, to supply the vacancy occasioned by the resignation of William Logan, produced his credentials, was qualified, and he took his seat in the Senate.

The PRESIDENT communicated the memorial of a convention of Delegates, representing the merchants and others interested in commerce, assembled at Philadelphia, against the proposed tariff; and the memorial was read, and referred to the Committee on Commerce and Manufactures.

The PRESIDENT also communicated the memorial of Joseph Wheaton, late deputy quartermaster general, and major of cavalry, praying relief in the settlement of his accounts against the Government, as stated in the memorial; which was read, and referred to the Committee on Military Affairs.

The following Message was received from the PRESIDENT OF THE UNITED STATES:

To the President of the Senate:

In conformity with a resolution of the Senate, passed the 28th of January, 1818, I communicate herewith to the Senate the report of the Commissioner of Public Buildings, required by that resolution.

JAMES MONROE.

NOVEMBER 23, 1820.

The Message and report were read.

Mr. WALKER, of Alabama, presented the petition of John Holmes, of Alabama, praying compensation for the loss of a horse, as stated in the petition; which was read, and referred to the Committee of Claims.

Mr. WALKER, of Alabama, also presented the petition of Dr. David Moore, praying relief in the settlement of his account for medical services rendered certain sick soldiers, under the command of Colonel John Coffee, engaged in an expedition against the Creek Indians in the year 1813; which was read, and referred to the same committee.

Mr. JOHNSON, of Louisiana, presented the petition of Presly Kemper, of the State of Ohio, praying compensation for services rendered in the capacity of principal wagonmaster, in the year 1812, under General William Hull; and also payment of the balance due for a horse and accoutrements, taken by the enemy at Detroit; which was read, and referred to the same committee.

Mr. JOHNSON, of Louisiana, gave notice that to-morrow he should ask leave to bring in a bill granting to the people of the county of Point Coupee, in the State of Louisiana, for the purposes therein mentioned, two tracts of land.

Mr. EATON gave notice that to-morrow he should ask leave to bring in a bill for the relief of the officers and volunteers engaged against the Seminole Indians in the year 1818.

The Senate resumed the consideration of the motion of the 16th instant, relating to the compensation to the members and delegates to Congress; and the further consideration thereof was postponed until Monday next.

The Senate resumed the consideration of the motion of the 24th instant, for instructing the Committee on Public Lands to inquire into the expediency of securing to certain actual settlers, when the lands they occupy shall be sold, the right of remaining on the same until they shall have gathered their growing crops; and agreed thereto.

A message from the House of Representatives informed the Senate that the House have passed a bill entitled "An act to provide for paying to the State of Illinois three per cent. of the net proceeds arising from the sale of the public lands within the same;" in which bill they request the concurrence of the Senate.

The bill was read, and passed to the second reading.

And the Senate then adjourned.

TUESDAY, November 28.

Mr. NOBLE submitted the following motion for consideration:

Resolved, That the Committee on the Judiciary be instructed to inquire into the expediency of authorizing by law so much of the western and northern boundaries of the State of Indiana to be surveyed, marked, and designated, as divides said State from the State of Illinois and Territory of Michigan, agreeably to the boundaries as established by the act, entitled "An act to enable the people of the Indiana Territory to form a constitution and State government, and for the admission of such State into the Union on an equal footing with the original States," passed April 19, 1816.

Mr. NOBLE presented the memorial of Eliza Dill, Jane Jervis, and Louisa St. C. Robb, daughters of the late General Arthur St. Clair, praying the payment of the balance stated to be due to their deceased father; and the memorial was read, and referred to the Committee of Claims.

Mr. CHANDLER presented the petition of Moses Wing, of Maine, praying an increase of his pension; and the petition was read, and referred to the Committee on Pensions.

Mr. NOBLE presented the petition of Alexander Irvine, of Indiana, praying an increase of pension; and the petition was read, and referred to the same committee.

The bill entitled "An act to provide for paying to the State of Illinois three per cent. of the net proceeds arising from the sale of the public lands within the same," was read the second time, and referred to the Committee on Public Lands.

Mr. EATON obtained leave to bring in a bill for the relief of the officers and volunteers engaged in the late campaign against the Seminole Indians; and the bill was read, and passed to the second reading.

WEDNESDAY, November 29.

EDWARD LLOYD, from the State of Maryland, attended.

Mr. SMITH, from the committee to whom was referred the constitution, as adopted for the government of the State of Missouri, reported a resolution declaring the admission of the State of Missouri into the Union; and the resolution was read, and passed to the second reading.

Mr. LANMAN presented the petition of Park Avery, stating that he has been erroneously placed on the pension list as a private soldier, and praying the pension, to which by law he is entitled, as a commissioned officer; and the petition was read, and referred to the Committee on Pensions.

Mr. JOHNSON, of Kentucky, gave notice that, to-morrow, he should ask leave to bring in a bill to incorporate the Columbian Society for literary purposes.

The Senate resumed the consideration of the motion of the 28th instant, relating to the western and northern boundaries of the State of Indiana, and agreed thereto.

Mr. WILSON, from the Committee of Claims, to whom the subject was referred, reported a bill for the relief of Ebenezer Stevens and Austin L.

States, for military services, and to individuals, for supplies furnished, and services rendered during the late war, the public debt may be estimated as amounting, at that date, and as afterwards liquidated, to one hundred and fifty-eight millions seven hundred and thirteen thousand forty-nine dollars. On the 30th of September, 1820, it amounted to ninety-one millions nine hundred and ninety-three thousand eight hundred and eighty-three dollars, having been reduced in that interval, by payments, sixty-six millions eight hundred and seventy-nine thousand one hundred and sixty-five dollars. During this term, the expenses of the Government of the United States were likewise defrayed, in every branch of the civil, military, and naval establishments; the public edifices in this city have been rebuilt, with considerable additions; extensive fortifications have been commenced, and are in a train of execution; permanent arsenals and magazines have been erected in various parts of the Union; our Navy has been considerably augmented, and the ordnance, munitions of war, and stores, of the Army and Navy, which were much exhausted during the war, have been replenished.

By the discharge of so large a proportion of the public debt, and the execution of such extensive and important operations, in so short a time, a just estimate may be formed of the great extent of our national resources. The demonstration is the more complete and gratifying, when it is recollected that the direct tax and excise were repealed soon after the termination of the late war, and that the revenue applied to these purposes has been derived almost wholly from other resources.

The receipts into the Treasury, from every source, to the 30th of September last, have amounted to sixteen millions seven hundred and ninety-four thousand one hundred and seven dollars and sixty-six cents; whilst the public expenditures, to the same period, amounted to sixteen millions eight hundred and seventy-one thousand five hundred and thirty-four dollars and seventy-two cents; leaving in the Treasury, on that day, a sum estimated at one million nine hundred and fifty thousand dollars. For the probable receipts of the following year, I refer you to the statement which will be transmitted from the Treasury.

The sum of three millions of dollars, authorized to be raised by loan, by an act of the last session of Congress, has been obtained upon terms advantageous to the Government, indicating, not only an increased confidence in the faith of the nation, but the existence of a large amount of capital seeking that mode of investment, at a rate of interest not exceeding five per centum per annum.

It is proper to add, that there is now due to the Treasury, for the sale of public lands, twenty-two millions nine hundred and ninety-six thousand five hundred and forty-five dollars. In bringing this subject to view, I consider it my duty to submit to Congress, whether it may not be advisable to extend to the purchasers of these lands, in consideration of the unfavorable change which has occurred since the sales, a reasonable indulgence. It is known that the purchases were made when the price of every article had risen to its greatest height, and that the instalments are becoming due at a period of great depression. It is presumed that some plan may be devised, by the wisdom of Congress, compatible with the public interest, which would afford great relief to these purchasers.

Considerable progress has been made, during the present season, in examining the coast and its various bays and other inlets; in the collection of materials, and in the construction of fortifications for the defence of the Union, at several of the positions at which it has been decided to erect such works. At Mobile Point and Dauphin Island, and at the Rigolets, leading to Lake Pontchartrain, materials to a considerable amount have been collected and all the necessary preparations made for the commencement of the works. At Old Point Comfort, at the mouth of James river, and at the Rip-Rap, on the opposite shore, in the Chesapeake Bay, materials to a vast amount have been collected; and at the Old Point some progress has been made in the construction of the fortification, which is on a very extensive scale. The work at Fort Washington, on this river, will be completed early in the next Spring; and that on the Pea Patch, in the Delaware, in the course of the next season. Fort Diamond, at the Narrows, in the harbor of New York, will be finished this year. The works at Boston, New York, Baltimore, Norfolk, Charleston, and Niagara, have been in part repaired; and the coast of North Carolina, extending south to Cape Fear, has been examined, as have likewise other parts of the coast eastward of Boston. Great exertions have been made to push forward these works with the utmost despatch possible; but, when their extent is considered, with the important purposes for which they are intended, the defence of the whole coast, and in consequence of the whole interior, and that they are to last for ages, it will be manifest that a well-digested plan, founded on military principles, connecting the whole together, combining security with economy, could not be prepared without repeated examinations of the most exposed and difficult parts, and that it would also take considerable time to collect the materials at the several points where they would be required. From all the light that has been shed on this subject, I am satisfied that every favorable anticipation which has been formed of this great undertaking will be verified, and that when completed it will afford very great, if not complete, protection to our Atlantic frontier in the event of another war; a protection sufficient to counterbalance in a single campaign with an enemy powerful at sea the expense of all these works, without taking into the estimate the saving of the lives of so many of our citizens, the protection of our towns and other property, or the tendency of such works to prevent war.

Our military positions have been maintained at Belle Point, on the Arkansas, at Council Bluffs, on the Missouri, at St. Peter's, on the Mississippi, and at Green Bay, on the Upper lakes. Commodious barracks have already been erected at most of these posts, with such works as were necessary for their defence. Progress has also been made in opening communications between them, and in raising supplies at each for the support of the troops by their own labor, particularly those most remote.

With the Indians peace has been preserved, and a progress made in carrying into effect the act of Congress, making an appropriation for their civilization, with the prospect of favorable results. As connected equally with both these objects, our trade with those tribes is thought to merit the attention of Congress. In their original state, game is their sustenance and war their occupation: and if they find no employment from civilized Powers, they destroy each other. Left to themselves, their extirpation is inevitable. By a judicious regulation of our trade with them, we supply their wants, administer to their comforts, and gradually, as the game retires, draw them to us. By maintaining posts far in the interior, we acquire a more thorough and direct control over them; without which it is confidently believed that a complete change in their manners can never be accomplished. By such posts, aided by a proper regulation of our trade with them, and a judicious civil administration over them, to be provided for by law, we shall it is presumed be enabled not only to protect our own settlements from their savage incursions, and preserve peace among the several tribes, but accomplish also the great purpose of their civilization.

Considerable progress has also been made in the construction of ships of war, some of which have been launched in the course of the present year.

Our peace with the Powers on the coast of Barbary has been preserved, but we owe it altogether to the presence of our squadron in the Mediterranean. It has been found equally necessary to employ some of our vessels for the protection of our commerce in the Indian sea, the Pacific, and along the Atlantic coast. The interests which we have depending in those quarters, which have been much improved of late, are of great extent, and of high importance to the nation, as well as to the parties concerned, and would undoubtedly suffer if such protection was not extended to them. In execution of the law of the last session, for the suppression of the slave trade, some of our public ships have also been employed on the coast of Africa, where several captures have already been made of vessels engaged in that disgraceful traffic.

JAMES MONROE.

WASHINGTON, *November* 14, 1820.

The Message was read, and three thousand copies thereof ordered to be printed for the use of the Senate.

THURSDAY, November 16.

Mr. JOHNSON, of Kentucky, submitted the following motion for consideration:

Resolved, That it is expedient to make provision, by law, to authorize any person who has purchased public lands, and not made full payment for the same, to relinquish to the United States so much thereof as may not be paid for, and retain such portion of the original purchase as may amount to the sums of money actually paid, at the price for which the land was purchased.

Mr. WALKER, of Alabama, gave notice that, to-morrow, he should ask leave to bring in a bill to provide for altering the times of holding the district courts in the State of Alabama.

Mr. BURRILL submitted the following motion for consideration:

Resolved, That the act, entitled "An act allowing compensation to the members of the Senate, members of the House of Representatives of the United States, and to the delegates of the Territories, and repealing all other laws on the subject," passed at the first session of the fifteenth Congress, ought to be so altered and amended that the compensation to the members and delegates aforesaid, shall hereafter be six dollars for each day's attendance, and six dollars for every twenty miles travel, instead of the compensation now allowed by said act, and that it be referred to a committee to prepare and report a bill for altering and amending said act accordingly.

Mr. DICKERSON submitted the following motion for consideration:

Resolved, That a committee of three members be appointed, who, with three members of the House of Representatives, to be appointed by that House, shall have the direction of the money appropriated to the purchase of books and maps for the use of the two Houses of Congress.

On motion, by Mr. ROBERTS,

Resolved, That the Senate will, on Monday next, at twelve o'clock, proceed to the appointment of the Standing Committees.

FRIDAY, November 17.

JAMES LANMAN, from the State of Connecticut, arrived yesterday, and attended this day.

Mr. SANFORD submitted the following motions for consideration:

Resolved, That so much of the Message of the President of the United States as concerns our relations with Spain and with France, be referred to the Committee of Foreign Relations.

Resolved, That so much of the Message of the President of the United States as relates to Finance, be referred to the Committee of Finance.

Resolved, That so much of the Message of the President of the United States as relates to the debt due for the sale of public lands, be referred to the Committee on Public Lands.

Resolved, That so much of the Message of the President of the United States as relates to the Indian tribes, be referred to the Committee on Indian Affairs.

Mr. WALKER, of Alabama, asked and obtained leave to bring in a bill to alter the terms of the district court in Alabama, and the bill was twice read by unanimous consent, and referred to a select committee to consider and report thereon; and Messrs. WALKER, of Alabama, BURRILL, and KING, of Alabama, were appointed the committee.

The Senate resumed the consideration of the motion of the 16th instant, respecting the compensation of the members and delegates of Congress, and the further consideration thereof was postponed until next Monday week.

The Senate resumed the consideration of the resolution for the appointment of a joint committee on the arrangements for the Library of Congress, and having agreed thereto, Messrs. DICKERSON, DANA, and HUNTER, were appointed the committee.

A message from the House of Representatives informed the Senate that the House concur in the resolution of the Senate for the appointment of Chaplains, and have appointed the Rev. J. N. CAMPBELL, Chaplain on their part.

On motion by Mr. WILSON, the Senate proceeded to the election of a Chaplain on their part; and, on counting the ballots, it appeared that the Rev. WILLIAM RYLAND was duly elected.

The PRESIDENT communicated a letter from the Commissioner of the General Land Office, transmitting copies of the reports of the Land Commissioners at Jackson Courthouse, and a copy of a letter, dated 17th August, 1820, which accompanied them; which were read.

The PRESIDENT also communicated a report of the Secretary of the Treasury, made in obedience to a resolution of the Senate of the 3d April, 1820, directing him to "cause to be prepared, and laid before the Senate, at the commencement of the next session of Congress, a statement of money annually appropriated, and paid, since the Declaration of Independence, for purchasing from the Indians, surveying, and selling the public lands, showing, as near as may be, the quantities of land which have been purchased, the number of acres which have been surveyed, the number sold, and the number which remain unsold; the amount of sales, the amount of forfeitures, the sums paid by purchasers, and the sums due from purchasers and from receivers in each land district;" and the report was read.

The PRESIDENT also communicated a report of the Secretary of the Treasury, made in obedience to a resolution of the Senate, directing him to "cause to be prepared, and laid before the Senate, at the commencement of the next session of Congress, a statement of the money which has been annually appropriated and paid, since the year seventeen hundred and seventy-five, for surveying the seacoast, bays, inlets, harbors, and shoals, and for erecting, and keeping in repair, lighthouses, beacons, buoys, and for the purchase of ground for lighthouses, distinguishing the places where they have been erected, and the sums annually expended for keeping and supplying the same;" and the report was read.

Adjourned to Monday.

MONDAY, November 20.

JOHN ELLIOTT, and also, FREEMAN WALKER, from the State of Georgia, severally arrived, on the 17th instant, and attended this day.

Mr. WALKER, of Alabama, from the committee to whom was referred the bill to alter the terms of the district court in Alabama, reported the same without amendment, and it was considered as in Committee of the Whole, and no amendment having been proposed thereto, it was reported to the House; and ordered to be engrossed and read a third time.

Mr. WALKER, of Alabama, submitted the following motions for consideration:

Resolved, That it is expedient to provide for the relief of purchasers of the public lands, by dividing the sums now severally unpaid, exclusive of interest, into —— equal instalments; each instalment bearing interest only from the time at which it shall be made payable.

Resolved, That it is expedient to permit such purchasers of the public lands as may elect that mode, to surrender. within —— months from and after the —— day of —— next, their certificates, which shall be cancelled, and the lands shall be taken to have reverted and become forfeited to the United States, and shall be advertised, and sold for cash at public auction, to the highest bidder, in the same manner as other public lands. They shall not be sold for less than one dollar and twenty-five cents per acre, which sum shall go to the use of the United States, in addition to the sums already paid; but if said lands should be so re-

sold for more than one dollar and twenty-five cents per acre, the excess shall be paid to the person surrendering the certificate, provided such excess shall never be greater than the amount actually paid on such lands before such surrender.

Resolved, That it is expedient to permit such purchasers of the public lands as may elect that mode, to extinguish their debt, complete their titles, and demand and receive patents, by paying, within the period of one year from and after the —— day of —— next, into their respective land offices, five-eighths of the original price at which their lands were purchased, including interest, and computing the moneys already paid as part of the said final payment of five-eighths.

Resolved, That it is expedient, in addition to the privilege contemplated in the preceding resolution, to permit such purchasers of the public lands as may elect that mode, at any time within the said period of one year from and after the —— day of —— next, to forfeit and abandon to the United States such fractions, quarter sections, and half quarter sections, as they may deem fit; and to transfer and apply the moneys already paid on the tract or tracts so forfeited to the payment for such other fraction, quarter section, or half quarter section as they may choose to retain; and in cases where the purchaser has bought only one quarter section, he shall be permitted to divide it, and make his election between its halves—such division being made by a north and south line according to law.

The PRESIDENT communicated a letter from the Secretary of State of the United States, requesting an additional supply of documents, printed by order of the Senate; and the letter was read, and referred to the Committee on the Judiciary.

The Senate resumed the consideration of Mr. SANFORD's motions of the 17th instant, for referring to various committees the Message of the President of the United States; and agreed thereto.

STANDING COMMITTEES.

The Senate then, pursuant to the order of the day, proceeded to the appointment, by ballot, of the standing committees, which resulted in the distribution of the members, as follows:

On the Committee of Foreign Relations—Messrs. BARBOUR, MACON, BROWN, HUNTER, and KING of New York.

On Finance—Messrs. SANFORD, MACON, DANA, EATON, and HOLMES of Maine.

On Commerce and Manufactures—Messrs. DICKERSON, RUGGLES, BURRILL, HORSEY, and SANFORD.

On Military Affairs—Messrs. WILLIAMS of Tennessee, TRIMBLE, TAYLOR, ELLIOTT, and JOHNSON of Kentucky.

On the Militia—Messrs. NOBLE, TICHENOR, STOKES, LANMAN, and CHANDLER.

On Naval Affairs—Messrs. PLEASANTS, PARROTT, WILLIAMS of Mississippi, WALKER of Alabama, and WALKER of Georgia.

On the Public Lands—Messrs. THOMAS, TAYLOR, LOWRIE, EATON, and VAN DYKE.

On Indian Affairs—Messrs. HOLMES of Mississippi, JOHNSON of Kentucky, JOHNSON of Louisiana, KING of Alabama, and LOWRIE.

On Claims—Messrs. WILSON, ROBERTS, MORRIL, RUGGLES, and VAN DYKE.

On the Judiciary—Messrs. SMITH, BURRILL, PINKNEY, WALKER of Georgia, and HOLMES of Maine.

On the Post Office and Post Roads—Messrs. STOKES, WILSON, PALMER, CHANDLER, and EDWARDS.

On Pensions—Messrs. NOBLE, ELLIOTT, WILSON, EATON, and TICHENOR.

On the District of Columbia—Messrs. HORSEY, LANMAN, LLOYD, BARBOUR, and HUNTER.

On Accounts—Messrs. ROBERTS, BURRILL, and LANMAN.

On Roads and Canals—Messrs. KING of New York, TRIMBLE, LOWRIE, MACON, and DANA.

TUESDAY, November 21.

Mr. WILLIAMS, of Tennessee, presented the memorial of William Kelly, on behalf of himself and divers others, claimants of land in the Territory of Arkansas, under Elisha and William Winter, deceased; and the memorial was read, and referred to the Committee on Public Lands.

Mr. HOLMES, of Maine, presented the memorial of the delegates from the commercial and agricultural sections of the State of Maine, met in convention at Portland, protesting against the proposed tariff; and the memorial was read, and referred to the Committee on Commerce and Manufactures.

The PRESIDENT communicated the memorial of Matthew Lyon, of Eddyville, Kentucky, praying compensation for certain losses and sufferings under the act commonly called the Sedition law; and the memorial was read, and referred to a select committee; and Messrs. BARBOUR, JOHNSON of Kentucky, and BURRILL, were appointed the committee.

Mr. PLEASANTS presented the memorial of the merchants and other inhabitants of the town of Petersburg, in the State of Virginia, in opposition to the proposed tariff; and the memorial was read, and referred to the Committee on Commerce and Manufactures.

Mr. HOLMES, of Mississippi, presented the petition of Clarissa Scott, widow of the late Colonel William Scott, of the State of Mississippi, praying the confirmation of her title to a certain tract of land, as stated in the petition; which was read, and referred to the Committee on Public Lands.

Mr. JOHNSON, of Kentucky, presented the petition of Rufus Easton, for himself and heirs of James Bruff, praying the confirmation of their title to a certain tract of land, as stated in the petition; which was read, and referred to the same committee.

The bill to alter the terms of the district court in Alabama was read a third time, and passed.

Mr. DICKERSON, after a few remarks reiterating his desire for the passage of the measure, and his continued confidence in its importance and utility, gave notice that he should, on to-morrow, ask leave to introduce a joint resolution proposing an amendment to the Constitution, in relation to the appointment of Electors of President and Vice President of the United States, and members of the House of Representatives, [which was introduced by Mr. D., and passed the Senate at the last session; and was introduced yesterday in the House of Representatives by Mr. SMITH, of North Carolina.]

WEDNESDAY, November 22.

Mr. NOBLE presented the petition of sundry citizens of the Western States, purchasers of public lands, praying that a law may be passed enabling them to apply the payments already made, to such portions of their entries as those payments will cover, at two dollars an acre, agreeably to the law under which the entries were made, relinquishing the residue to the United States. And also allowing those purchasers who have purchased but one tract, the privilege of retaining it entire, with a reasonable extension of credit without interest, or otherwise relinquishing a part of it; and the petition was read, and referred to the Committee on Public Lands.

Mr. THOMAS presented two memorials of the Legislature of the State of Missouri, praying of Congress some legislative provisions for the relief of indigent actual settlers on the public lands, particularly widows and orphans; and the memorials were severally read, and respectively referred to the same committee.

Mr. DICKERSON obtained leave to introduce a resolution, proposing an amendment to the Constitution of the United States, as it respects the election of Representatives in Congress, and the choice of Electors of President and Vice President of the United States; and the resolution was read, and passed to the second reading.

Mr. EATON obtained leave to introduce a bill for the relief of Robert Purdy; and the bill was read, and passed to the second reading.

The Senate resumed the consideration of the motions of Mr. WALKER of the 20th instant, in relation to purchasers of the public lands; and they were referred to the Committee on Public Lands.

The Senate resumed the consideration of the motion of Mr. JOHNSON of the 16th instant, in relation to the same subject; and it was referred to the same committee.

THURSDAY, November 23.

Mr. NOBLE submitted the following motion for consideration:

Resolved, That the Committee on Public Lands be instructed to inquire into the expediency of permitting such purchasers of the public lands, prior to the 1st of July, 1820, to demand and receive patents, who have paid into their respective land offices the first, second, and third instalments, on each tract purchased.

Mr. THOMAS submitted the following motion for consideration:

Resolved, That the Committee on Public Lands be instructed to inquire into the expediency of providing, by law, for granting to actual settlers on the public lands the right of pre-emption in becoming the purchasers of lands, including their improvements.

The resolution proposing an amendment to the Constitution of the United States, as it respects the election of Representatives in Congress, and the choice of Electors of President and Vice President of the United States, was read the second time, and referred to a select committee, to consist of five members, to consider and report thereon; and Messrs. DICKERSON, BARBOUR, MACON, HOLMES, of Mississippi, and HOLMES, of Maine, were appointed the committee.

The bill for the relief of Robert Purdy was read the second time, and referred to the Committee on Military Affairs.

Mr. KING, of New York, presented the memorial of Ebenezer Stevens and others, praying that Congress would afford them relief, on account of a demand against the United States, arising out of certain contracts entered into with Robert Morris, Esq., for the supply of provisions to the Army of the United States during the Revolutionary war; and the memorial was read, and referred to the Committee of Claims.

RESTRICTION OF SLAVERY.

Mr. SANFORD communicated the following resolutions, passed by the Legislature of the State of New York; which were read.

STATE OF NEW YORK,
In Assembly, November 13, 1820.

Whereas the Legislature of this State, at the last session, did instruct their Senators and request their Representatives in Congress to oppose the admission, as a State into the Union, of any Territory not comprised within the original boundaries of the United States, without making the prohibition of slavery therein an indispensable condition of admission: And whereas this Legislature is impressed with the correctness of the sentiments so communicated to our Senators and Representatives; therefore,

Resolved, (if the honorable the Senate concur herein,) That this Legislature does approve of the principles contained in the resolutions of the last session; and, further, if the provisions contained in any proposed constitution of a new State deny to any citizens of the existing States the privileges and immunities of citizens of such new State, that such proposed constitution should not be accepted or confirmed; the same, in the opinion of this Legislature, being void by the Constitution of the United States. And that our Senators be instructed, and our Representatives in Congress be requested, to use their utmost exertions to prevent the acceptance and confirmation of any such constitution.

Resolved, (if the honorable the Senate concur herein,) That the President of the Senate and the Speaker of the Assembly do cause copies of these resolutions, duly certified by them, to be transmitted to the Senators and Representatives in Congress from this State.

Ordered, That the clerk deliver a copy of the preceding resolutions to the honorable the Senate, and request their concurrence to the same.

PETER SHARPE, *Speaker.*

Attest—DL. VAN DU WEYDER,
Clerk of Assembly.

STATE OF NEW YORK,
In Senate, November 15, 1820.

Resolved, That the Senate do concur with the honorable the Assembly, in their said resolutions and recitals.

Ordered, That the clerk deliver a copy of said resolution of concurrence to the honorable the Assembly.

JOHN TAYLER, *President.*

Attest—JOHN F. BACON,
Clerk of the Senate.

FRIDAY, November 24.

Mr. WILSON presented the memorial of James Leander Cathcart, praying the passage of a law directing the accounting officers of the Treasury to allow his claim upon the Government, in the settlement of his accounts, as stated in the memorial; which was read, and referred to the Committee of Claims.

Mr. WALKER, of Alabama, submitted the following motion for consideration:

Resolved, That the Committee on the Public Lands be instructed to inquire into the expediency of securing to actual settlers, in all cases where the lands they occupy shall be sold after the first day of March, in any year, the right of remaining on the same until they shall have gathered their growing crop.

Mr. HORSEY presented the petition of the President and Directors of the Farmers' Bank of Alexandria, in the District of Columbia, praying the extension of their charter for twenty years, from and after the 1st day of June, 1822; and the petition was read, and referred to the Committee on the District of Columbia.

Mr. TRIMBLE presented the petition of Major Charles Larrabee, of the Army of the United States, praying remuneration for losses sustained while in the service of the United States, as stated in the petition; which was read, and referred to the Committee of Claims.

The Senate resumed the consideration of the motion of the 23d instant, in relation to actual settlers on the public lands, and agreed thereto.

The Senate also resumed the consideration of the motion of the 23d instant, in relation to certain purchasers of the public lands, and agreed thereto.

The Senate adjourned to Monday.

MONDAY, November 27.

HARRISON GRAY OTIS, from the State of Massachusetts, arrived on the 25th instant; and WILLIAM HUNTER, from the State of Rhode Island and Providence Plantations, arrived on the 24th instant, severally attended this day.

ISHAM TALBOT, appointed a Senator by the Legislature of Kentucky, to supply the vacancy occasioned by the resignation of William Logan, produced his credentials, was qualified, and he took his seat in the Senate.

The PRESIDENT communicated the memorial of a convention of Delegates, representing the merchants and others interested in commerce, assembled at Philadelphia, against the proposed tariff; and the memorial was read, and referred to the Committee on Commerce and Manufactures.

The PRESIDENT also communicated the memorial of Joseph Wheaton, late deputy quartermaster general, and major of cavalry, praying relief in the settlement of his accounts against the Government, as stated in the memorial; which was read, and referred to the Committee on Military Affairs.

The following Message was received from the PRESIDENT OF THE UNITED STATES:

To the President of the Senate:

In conformity with a resolution of the Senate, passed the 28th of January, 1818, I communicate herewith to the Senate the report of the Commissioner of Public Buildings, required by that resolution.

JAMES MONROE.

NOVEMBER 23, 1820.

The Message and report were read.

Mr. WALKER, of Alabama, presented the petition of John Holmes, of Alabama, praying compensation for the loss of a horse, as stated in the petition; which was read, and referred to the Committee of Claims.

Mr. WALKER, of Alabama, also presented the petition of Dr. David Moore, praying relief in the settlement of his account for medical services rendered certain sick soldiers, under the command of Colonel John Coffee, engaged in an expedition against the Creek Indians in the year 1813; which was read, and referred to the same committee.

Mr. JOHNSON, of Louisiana, presented the petition of Presly Kemper, of the State of Ohio, praying compensation for services rendered in the capacity of principal wagonmaster, in the year 1812, under General William Hull; and also payment of the balance due for a horse and accoutrements, taken by the enemy at Detroit; which was read, and referred to the same committee.

Mr. JOHNSON, of Louisiana, gave notice that to-morrow he should ask leave to bring in a bill granting to the people of the county of Point Coupee, in the State of Louisiana, for the purposes therein mentioned, two tracts of land.

Mr. EATON gave notice that to-morrow he should ask leave to bring in a bill for the relief of the officers and volunteers engaged against the Seminole Indians in the year 1818.

The Senate resumed the consideration of the motion of the 16th instant, relating to the compensation to the members and delegates to Congress; and the further consideration thereof was postponed until Monday next.

The Senate resumed the consideration of the motion of the 24th instant, for instructing the Committee on Public Lands to inquire into the expediency of securing to certain actual settlers, when the lands they occupy shall be sold, the right of remaining on the same until they shall have gathered their growing crops; and agreed thereto.

A message from the House of Representatives informed the Senate that the House have passed a bill entitled "An act to provide for paying to the State of Illinois three per cent. of the net proceeds arising from the sale of the public lands within the same;" in which bill they request the concurrence of the Senate.

The bill was read, and passed to the second reading.

And the Senate then adjourned.

TUESDAY, November 28.

Mr. NOBLE submitted the following motion for consideration:

Resolved, That the Committee on the Judiciary be instructed to inquire into the expediency of authorising by law so much of the western and northern boundaries of the State of Indiana to be surveyed, marked, and designated, as divides said State from the State of Illinois and Territory of Michigan, agreeably to the boundaries as established by the act, entitled "An act to enable the people of the Indiana Territory to form a constitution and State government, and for the admission of such State into the Union on an equal footing with the original States," passed April 19, 1816.

Mr. NOBLE presented the memorial of Eliza Dill, Jane Jervis, and Louisa St. C. Robb, daughters of the late General Arthur St. Clair, praying the payment of the balance stated to be due to their deceased father; and the memorial was read, and referred to the Committee of Claims.

Mr. CHANDLER presented the petition of Moses Wing, of Maine, praying an increase of his pension; and the petition was read, and referred to the Committee on Pensions.

Mr. NOBLE presented the petition of Alexander Irvine, of Indiana, praying an increase of pension; and the petition was read, and referred to the same committee.

The bill entitled "An act to provide for paying to the State of Illinois three per cent. of the net proceeds arising from the sale of the public lands within the same," was read the second time, and referred to the Committee on Public Lands.

Mr. EATON obtained leave to bring in a bill for the relief of the officers and volunteers engaged in the late campaign against the Seminole Indians; and the bill was read, and passed to the second reading.

WEDNESDAY, November 29.

EDWARD LLOYD, from the State of Maryland, attended.

Mr. SMITH, from the committee to whom was referred the constitution, as adopted for the government of the State of Missouri, reported a resolution declaring the admission of the State of Missouri into the Union; and the resolution was read, and passed to the second reading.

Mr. LANMAN presented the petition of Park Avery, stating that he has been erroneously placed on the pension list as a private soldier, and praying the pension, to which by law he is entitled, as a commissioned officer; and the petition was read, and referred to the Committee on Pensions.

Mr. JOHNSON, of Kentucky, gave notice that, to-morrow, he should ask leave to bring in a bill to incorporate the Columbian Society for literary purposes.

The Senate resumed the consideration of the motion of the 28th instant, relating to the western and northern boundaries of the State of Indiana, and agreed thereto.

Mr. WILSON, from the Committee of Claims, to whom the subject was referred, reported a bill for the relief of Ebenezer Stevens and Austin L.

consolatory to the suffering patriot, what better calculated to inspire constancy and courage, than a conviction, founded on fact, that his wrongs, on the restoration of sound principles, will attract the regard of the successful asserters of freedom, and who will cheerfully indemnify him for the injuries he has sustained? Such examples are not wanting in Governments less beneficent than ours—that of England is replete with instances of this kind. Acts of Parliament, passed in times of heat and excitement, are frequently reversed, and the individuals on whom they had operated are restored to the rights of which they had been deprived. Succeeding Parliaments do not hesitate to indemnify the victims of oppression, because they had suffered under the forms of law. Acts of their Legislature, whose power is omnipotent, form no obstacle with those to whom their injustice is made manifest, in granting relief. An American Congress will not suffer itself to be exceeded by any Government in acts of justice or beneficence.

The committee have only further to remark, that the Executive interposed its authority in various cases, and granted a full pardon to those convicted under the act in question, by which their fines were either remitted, or restored; relief, therefore, to the petitioner, would be only a common measure of justice. According to information received from the Department of State, no money has ever been paid into the Treasury by the officer who received the fines imposed under the sedition act. It is submitted to the discretion of the Senate, whether provision shall be made by law to indemnify the petitioner, by directing the amount of his fine to be paid out of the Treasury, or to reclaim it from the delinquent officer or officers; and, in the latter event, to be at liberty to use the name of the United States in any prosecution to which resort may be had, with a view to that end.

Inasmuch, however, as the relief proposed to be given in this case is on general principles, the committee are of opinion it should be afforded also to every sufferer under the law.

They, therefore, beg leave to submit the following resolutions:

Resolved, That so much of the act, entitled "An act for the punishment of certain crimes against the United States," approved the 14th of July, 1798, as pretends to prescribe and punish libels, is unconstitutional.

Resolved, That the fines collected under that act ought to be restored to those from whom they were exacted; and that these resolutions be recommitted to the committee who brought them in, with instructions to report a bill to that effect.

WEDNESDAY, December 6.

Mr. TRIMBLE presented three memorials, signed by a number of individuals concerned directly or indirectly, as purchasers of public lands, prior to the law "making further provision for the sale of the public lands," stating that said law operates injuriously on them, and praying that they may be permitted to apply the payments already made to such portions of their entries as such payments will cover, at two dollars per acre, and that the residue may revert to the United States; and the memorials were read, and severally referred to the Committee on Public Lands.

Mr. EATON presented the petition of Thomas Hardiman, of Missouri, praying to be confirmed in his title to a tract of land in Missouri; and the petition was read, and referred to the Committee on Public Lands.

Mr. HOLMES, of Mississippi, from the Committee on Indian Affairs, to whom the subject was referred, reported a bill to continue in force, for a further time, the act entitled "An act for establishing trading-houses with the Indian tribes;" and the bill was read, and passed to a second reading.

Mr. TRIMBLE gave notice, that, to-morrow, he would ask leave to bring in a bill to authorize the appointment of commissioners to lay out a canal in the State of Ohio.

The Senate proceeded to consider the motion of yesterday, requesting information of the President of the United States respecting the execution of the act "authorizing the purchase of fire engines and for building houses for the safe-keeping of the same;" and agreed thereto.

The Senate proceeded to consider the motion of yesterday, instructing the Committee on Military Affairs to inquire into the expediency of allowing to officers a specific sum monthly in lieu of their present pay, rations, and other emoluments; and agreed thereto.

The Senate proceeded to consider the motion of yesterday, instructing the Committee on Public Lands to inquire into the expediency of establishing an additional land office in Indiana; and agreed thereto.

The Senate proceeded to consider the report of the select committee on the petition of Matthew Lyon; and the further consideration thereof was postponed to and made the order of the day for Wednesday next.

The Senate proceeded to consider, as in Committee of the Whole, the bill entitled "An act to provide for paying to the State of Illinois three per cent. of the net proceeds arising from the sale of the public lands within the same;" and the consideration thereof was postponed until to-morrow.

The Senate took up the motion of the fourth instant, requesting an inquiry into the expediency of extending the time for locating military land warrants in Ohio; which was amended and agreed to, as follows:

Resolved, That the Committee on Public Lands be requested to inquire into the expediency of extending the time for locating military land warrants in the State of Ohio.

COLUMBIAN SOCIETY.

The Senate resumed the consideration of the bill to incorporate "the Columbian Society for Literary purposes."

Mr. JOHNSON, of Kentucky, submitted a general view of the character of the association and its objects, to establish its laudable and unobjectionable nature; and, by comparing it with other incorporations created by Congress, argued to show that it was entirely unexceptionable, being merely the incorporation of the managers of a college erected purely for the promotion of those branches of education which were taught in other institutions of learning. The same bill, Mr. J. remarked, had been defeated at the last session, merely because the title, which had been inadvertently and without reflection given to it, had been construed by gentlemen into an indication that the bill was for the incorporation of an exclusive religious society for religious objects alone. Mr. J. concluded by moving to postpone the bill to Friday next, that it might not now interfere with business of more importance, and to give time for considering it.

Mr. HORSEY avowed himself willing to vote for the incorporation of this society, under certain limitations and restrictions, in which the bill was now defective. He would confine the society, by express provisions, to objects strictly collegiate and literary. The bill was defective in not defining the mode of electing its principal, its trustees, professors, &c., and he would provide especially that no person should be excluded from an office in the college, or from its benefits, on account of his religious opinions. These were objects he wished to provide for in the bill, and therefore would wish it to be recommitted to the Committee on the District of Columbia.

Mr. JOHNSON, of Kentucky, concurred entirely in the views of Mr. HORSEY, and acquiesced in its recommitment; and the bill was recommitted accordingly.

The other intervening subjects on the orders of the day being, on motion of Mr. BARBOUR, postponed for that purpose—

The Senate resumed the consideration of the resolution declaring the admission into the Union of the

STATE OF MISSOURI.

Mr. BARBOUR, of Virginia, rose merely to suggest, as there was no doubt the mind of every gentleman was fully made up on the subject, that the question should be decided without consuming the time of the Senate in further debate.

Mr. EATON, of Tennessee, said, before the question was taken, he would ask leave to offer the following proviso to the resolution:

Provided, That nothing herein contained shall be so construed as to give the assent of Congress to any provision in the constitution of Missouri, if any such there be, which contravenes that clause in the Constitution of the United States, which declares that "the citizens of each State shall be entitled to all privileges and immunities of citizens in the several States."

Mr. KING, of New York, thought this amendment of too much importance to be decided without a moment's reflection. Some little time, he thought, ought to be allowed to see its bearing; to see whether it meant any thing or nothing, and, if any thing, what that was. He hoped the question would be postponed at least until to-morrow.

Mr. EATON observed, that there was a feature in the constitution of Missouri which presented a difficulty to the minds of some gentlemen, and to his among the number. Doubts were entertained whether that constitution was not repugnant to the Constitution of the United States, and some might not be willing to adopt the unconditional terms of the resolution which declared the new constitution to be republican, and in conformity to the Constitution of the United States. It was to obviate difficulty on this point, by avoiding a declaration one way or the other on the questionable clause, that he offered the amendment.

Mr. KING, of New York, confessed himself at some loss how to decide on this amendment. If he voted in the affirmative, it might seem as if the Senate could pass a resolution contrary to the Constitution; if in the negative, it would declare that a clause should have no effect which could have none, and must be nugatory. He thought a day, at least, should be given to consider the matter. For himself, he had asked no delay of the resolution; he was ready to vote on it; and he took this occasion to say he had not desired the subject to be reopened in the Senate; he believed it would do no good, but, on the contrary, that the public tranquillity would be promoted by deciding it quietly; the subject, he conceived, had been exhausted, and his opinion had undergone no change. He regretted that these sentiments had not been felt elsewhere, and where he thought they ought to have been felt. As to the amendment, he thought a moment's delay should be allowed to examine it, and he moved its postponement until to-morrow.

Mr. BURRILL was in favor of a longer postponement, but hoped until to-morrow at least would be permitted. He, too, expressed his regret that the question had been reopened, and added a few remarks on the propriety of giving some time to consider this amendment, which was certainly of an important character.

Mr. MORRIL moved a postponement of the question to Monday, and spoke a few words in favor of that course.

Messrs. SMITH and BARBOUR opposed so long a postponement as to Monday, but were willing to allow until to-morrow.

The motion to postpone the subject to Monday was lost; and the resolution and amendment were postponed until to-morrow.

THURSDAY, December 7.

The PRESIDENT communicated a report of the Secretary of the Treasury, made in pursuance of the resolution of the Senate of the third of April last, directing that the Secretary of the Treasury "cause to be prepared and laid before the Senate, at the commencement of the next session of Congress, a statement of the money expended in each year, since the Declaration of Independence, in holding conferences and making treaties with the Indian tribes; specifying grants and presents, whether in money or goods; annuities paid, and now payable to the Indian tribes; the money annually appropriated and paid for the Indian trade, including the sums allowed for salaries, and allowances to superintendents, clerks, factors, commissioners, agents, interpreters, and all other persons employed under the authority of the United States, in nego-

mittee of the Whole, the bill for the relief of Robert Purdy; and the further consideration thereof was postponed to Thursday next.

The Senate proceeded to consider, as in Committee of the Whole, the bill for the relief of the officers and volunteers engaged in the late campaign against the Seminole Indians, together with the amendments reported thereto by the Committee on Military Affairs; and the further consideration thereof was postponed to Thursday next.

Mr. JOHNSON, of Kentucky, submitted the following motion for consideration:

Resolved, That the Committee on Military Affairs be instructed to inquire into the expediency of extending the time for locating military land warrants in the State of Ohio.

COMPENSATION OF MEMBERS.

The Senate, according to the order of the day, took up the resolution submitted by Mr. BURRILL on the 16th ultimo, to reduce the compensation of members of Congress to six dollars a day.

Mr. JOHNSON, of Kentucky, observed that he had no doubt the ultimate fate of this proposition would be indefinite postponement. As he did not, however, desire a discussion of the subject at present, he would not make that motion, but would move its postponement until next Monday week, the 18th instant; which motion was agreed to, and the resolution was postponed accordingly.

PUNISHMENT OF PIRACY.

The resolution submitted by Mr. BARBOUR, on Friday last, was taken up, and having been modified by the mover, so as to direct an inquiry into the expediency of authorizing the President of the United States to commute the capital punishment of piracy by confinement in penitentiary houses, in such cases as he may deem expedient—

Mr. BARBOUR proceeded to give, at considerable length, his views in support of the object of his motion. He entered into a general defence of the superiority of the penitentiary system of punishment over the old code, contrasting the mildness and good effects of the one, with the cruelty, yet ineffectual operation, of the other—maintaining the great superiority of the former, not only in its humanity, but in its salutary effects on the subject of the punishment, as well as in its example on society—and referring to facts and experience in some of the States, Virginia particularly, compared with the effects of the bloody code in England and this country, to sustain his opinions.

The resolution was agreed to without objection.

ADMISSION OF MISSOURI.

The Senate, according to the order of the day, proceeded to the consideration of the resolution declaring the admission of the State of Missouri into the Union on an equal footing with the original States.

Mr. SMITH, of South Carolina, (chairman of the select committee which reported the resolution,) observed that the resolution was conformable to those adopted on similar occasions heretofore, and he hoped there would be no difficulty or delay in its passage. The constitution of the new State was republican, and no objection, he presumed, could arise to it: it was unnecessary to detain the Senate with any remarks on the subject, unless any explanations were desired by gentlemen, which he would with pleasure afford, so far as he was able. He trusted the resolution would now be acted on, and the members from the new State, who had been waiting for a considerable time, be admitted to their seats in the National Councils.

Mr. EATON, of Tennessee, disclaimed any disposition to create delay on this subject; but it was proper, Mr. E. said, that the mind of every member should be satisfied on a question of so much importance before he was called on to give his vote. His own mind, he confessed, was not satisfied; and, to obtain time for reflection, and to mature his opinion on it, he should move to postpone the resolution to a future day. At present, he repeated, he was not prepared to vote either in the affirmative or negative, with the conviction of being right. There were controverted points in the constitution presented by the new State, and he wished to see whether it was in all respects conformable to the Constitution of the United States. Another reason which Mr. E. offered in favor of a postponement of the question here, was, that the House of Representatives (if he might refer to its proceedings without being out of order) had fixed on Wednesday next for going into the consideration of the subject, and he did not consider it expedient or proper for both Houses to be discussing the same question contemporaneously. He deemed it a more eligible course that the subject should be acted on in one House first, and then be taken up in the other. To obtain time for himself, however, as he at first intimated, he should ask the Senate to postpone the resolution to Wednesday next only, and accordingly made a motion to that effect.

Mr. SMITH would not oppose the motion, but he objected to that reason of the gentleman, for postponement, which referred to the purposes of the other House. There was no such comity due to that House from this, as to wait until it had decided a question before it should be taken up here. This opinion was not incompatible with perfect respect for the other House; and such an argument ought not to govern the Senate or any other body. This question, Mr. S. remarked, had, in another shape, at the last session occupied a vast portion of the time of the Senate, and there was no authority for believing that the present would be a debated question. If gentlemen had any objections to the constitution, let them state them at once, and it would then be known whether any discussion was to ensue. Heretofore, States had come into the Union without being stopped at the threshold. He referred to the State of Indiana, in 1816; while the resolution for the admission of Indiana was under progress in the Senate, the House of Representatives had the member from that State in his seat debating and voting. There was no reason why the Senate, in the present case, should wait for the other House; let this branch go on and decide whether the new members have a right to their seats. It was only when this ill-fated Missouri presented itself for admission, that a desire was expressed for procrastination and delay. He hoped the Senate would not agree to the motion, unless divested of the reason given by the mover in relation to the other House.

Mr. Eaton replied that the argument objected to by the gentleman from South Carolina, had been merely thrown out by him from an impression that it was not proper for both Houses to be acting on the subject at one and the same moment. It was strange, however, he thought, that the gentleman should object to the motion solely because in his opinion one bad argument was offered in its favor. It was singular that a proposition admitted to have sufficient good reasons in its support, should be opposed by the gentleman merely because the arguments for it concluded with a bad one. He had stated that he entertained doubts on the question, and he only desired one or two days for reflection, and to make up an opinion. He concluded by varying his motion for postponement to Thursday next.

Mr. Johnson, of Kentucky, felt no reluctance to postpone the subject for the gentleman's accommodation, but he would not consent to the postponement for the reason that the Senate ought to wait the decision of the other House, because the latter reason might operate to the postponement of the question here altogether, or at least for a considerable period beyond the time now proposed. His only motive for objecting to the motion was on account of the latter argument urged by the gentleman from Tennessee. If the gentleman wanted time merely to mature his opinion, let him move the postponement from day to day, until he had made up his mind on the question. Mr. J. said the question to be decided was one of great importance; it swallowed up, in fact, every other, and until it was settled, they could not well go on with the ordinary business of the session. He was unwilling, therefore, to postpone it on a motion accompanied by a reason that might call for still further delay. He was not willing to wait for the other House, as he deemed it right and proper for the Senate to decide the question as early as possible; sufficient delay had already taken place, and he hoped the gentleman would change his motion to a postponement until to-morrow only. If he should not then be prepared for the question, Mr. J. said he would agree to give him further time.

Mr. Barbour, of Virginia, was never opposed to allowing gentlemen time to make up their opinions on all matters of deliberation; but in this case he concurred with Messrs. Smith and Johnson, in their opposition to the motion, for the reasons they had assigned. The argument used by Mr. Eaton, that it was proper to wait the decision of the other House, amounted almost to an indefinite postponement of the subject here. He was averse to delay on that ground. The question, he thought, had been forever sealed at the last session; so fully was he persuaded of this, that he had supposed accursed would have been the hand that should again open this fountain of bitter waters. Mr. B. then proceeded into a brief argument to show that it was right and proper, under every consideration

of courtesy towards the members from the new State, now kept waiting at the bar for admission, and towards the State itself, to decide the question without more delay. A contrary course, he urged, would be a departure from the proceeding in all pre-existing cases; and he could not believe that a mere technical exception could operate on the wisdom of the Senate, of which he entertained the most exalted opinion, to prevent it from eternally burying the brand of discord which had been lighted up at the last session. Mr. B. said, as there was no good reason for the postponement asked for, he must vote against it. He hoped the time would never come when the opinion of this body, solemnly expressed, would not have a great moral effect out of doors as well as in doors. This question was looked at by the nation with much anxiety and some degree of alarm, and he hoped the Senate would not keep the public mind in suspense, but decide it without delay.

Mr. Eaton having again varied his motion to its original shape, for Wednesday—

Mr. Johnson, of Kentucky, said, as the gentleman had placed his motion on the ground of personal indulgence, he would cheerfully withdraw his opposition to the postponement, as he was always ready to accord to any gentleman reasonable time for preparation.

Mr. Smith concurred with Mr. Johnson in this sentiment, and, for the same reason, would not oppose the postponement to Wednesday.

Mr. Eaton added a few words explanatory of his reasons for asking a short delay. His health had not been good, and he had not possessed the opportunity of satisfying his mind on some points involved in the decision of the question. He thought opposition to such a motion was unusual, and that when any gentleman asked further time it was always granted, even when the question was one of inconsiderable importance; but, on a question of such acknowledged magnitude, it was still more extraordinary that the indulgence he asked should have been opposed. He wanted no time to prepare a great harangue, for he should probably pass over the question silently; but it was to see if a measure which he was called to vote on would violate the instrument which he had sworn to observe.

Mr. Smith rose again, merely to correct the gentleman as to a fact. The gentleman had stated that time was never refused to a member when he asked for it; but Mr. S. recollected, on one occasion, he himself, late in the day, asked the Senate to postpone the question on the bank only to the next day, and was refused; and, so far from indulging him, they took the question over his head, while he was in the midst of a speech on the subject.

The question was then taken on postponing the resolution to Wednesday, and was agreed to, *nem. con.*

Tuesday, December 5.

The President communicated a report of the Secretary of the Treasury, prepared in obedience

of an act of Congress. The constitution of Missouri is entirely silent on this point, although some of its language could not be understood without referring to the act of Congress authorizing a convention; they declare that they establish, ratify, and confirm, certain boundaries, but they nowhere recognise the authority which prescribed these boundaries to them. Mr. B. repeated, that he thought Congress ought not to vary from the former mode of declaring its assent to the admission of new States. They would have to admit other States hereafter, and a departure now from the practice of the Government in receiving the constitutions of new States, would form a precedent which might in future cases be deplored.

But proceeding to the question, whether this constitution was such an one as ought to be accepted, Mr. B. said his objection to it arose on the following clause, which he found in the 26th section of the 3d article: "That it shall be the duty ' of the General Assembly of the State, as soon as ' may be, to pass such laws as may be necessary ' (among other things) to prevent free negroes and ' mulattoes from coming to and settling in this ' State, under any pretext whatsoever." This clause Mr. B. conceived to be entirely repugnant to the Constitution of the United States. It prohibits a very large class of persons from entering the State at all; it does not say what shall be done when they get there, but it peremptorily prohibits their entering it under any pretext whatsoever. Even if soldiers of the United States, people of this proscribed class cannot enter Missouri without violating the constitution of the State. It was well known, Mr. B. said, that we have colored soldiers and sailors, and good ones, too, but under no pretext, whether of duty or any other motive, can they enter Missouri. He did not suppose if people of this description, in the service of the country, should enter the State, it would be attempted by the State authorities to exclude them; but it was sufficient, he thought, to show the unconstitutionality of the clause.

Great difficulty seemed to arise in deciding the question, as to what constituted citizens in the different States. Citizens of one State were entitled to the rights of citizens of all the States; yet the different States exercised the power of prescribing certain probationary rules to those coming from another State, to entitle them to all the privileges. If a citizen of Massachusetts removes to another State, he cannot vote as soon as he enters it—a certain residence is required of him—and the people of Missouri were competent by law to impose a residence of one or more years on a citizen going there, to entitle him to all the privileges of citizens of the State; he complies with no more than is exacted of all, and which the State has a right to require. This was a question, however, which they did not touch; they avoided it altogether, and have declared that a certain class shall not come into their State at all, even though they may be citizens of other States, enjoying all the privileges of such.

Mr. B. did not himself conceive it difficult to define what constituted a citizen. If a person was not a slave or a foreigner—but born in the United States, and a free man—going into Missouri, he has the same rights as if born in Missouri; after complying with the conditions prescribed by the laws to qualify him for the exercise of these rights, he stands precisely on the same footing, and his rights are in every respect the same as if he had been born there. The question then was, Mr. B. said, had the people of Missouri the Constitutional right to prohibit from entering that State a large class of persons who were citizens of the Commonwealth of Massachusetts? To establish the negative of this proposition, Mr. B. adduced various other arguments in addition to the preceding, and endeavored to show that even many laws of the United States would become inoperative in Missouri, if the clause which he opposed could be maintained in force; and, as an instance, he referred to the laws against kidnapping. In regard to this crime of kidnapping, Mr. B. remarked, the constitution of Missouri had done nothing; for, according to it, all people of color who are carried there must, *ipso facto*, be slaves, inasmuch as a free negro could in nowise go there, admitting the clause to have its full effect.

Mr. B. said he was not prepared at present to affirm that Missouri might not pass laws to prohibit persons from carrying there negro or mulatto convicts, or perhaps foreigners from coming into the State; this was a question on which no opinion now was necessary; but he contended that the clause as it stood prohibited the entrance of a large portion of people who were, to all intents and purposes, citizens in other States. Admit the legality of this clause, and, Mr. B. said, the Legislature of Missouri might, with the same right, go still further, and pass laws to exclude citizens born in certain portions or districts of the United States. This was a measure, he argued, which one independent nation could not adopt towards another. England could not pass such a law against the people of France, or of any other friendly nation; such a measure would be too offensive to be borne, and would be considered to amount almost to a declaration of war. If distinct and independent nations dare not enact such laws towards each other, how was it possible, Mr. B. said, that the power could be exercised by one of these States towards other States of the Union?

All the distinctions among citizens which arise from color, rested, Mr. B. said, on State laws alone—there was nothing in the Constitution of the United States which recognised distinctions. In Massachusetts there was no distinction; a man of color possessed there precisely and identically the same rights as a white man born in the same State, and he asked if it was possible for Missouri, consistently with the Constitution of the United States, to exclude any of those people from that State, who should think proper to remove from Massachusetts to Missouri? The States of this Union were not distinct and independent nations—they are, said Mr. B., a confederacy of kindred republics; when they formed their constitution of government, they used the language, "we, the people of the United States," and it is not in the

this day to enter into an elaborate disquisition to sustain the correctness of this opinion. They will content themselves by referring to the history of the times in which the law originated, when both its constitutionality and expediency underwent the strictest scrutiny. The opponents of the law challenged its advocates to point out the clause of the Constitution which had armed the Government with so formidable a power as the control of, or interference with, the press. A Government, said they, of limited powers, and authorized to execute such only as are expressly given by the Constitution, or such as are properly incident to an express power, and necessary to its execution, has exercised an authority over a most important subject, which, so far from having been delegated, has been expressly withheld. That the patriots contemporary with the adoption of the Constitution, not content with the universally received opinion, that all power not granted had been withheld, to obviate all doubt on a point of such moment, insisted that an amendment to that effect should be inserted in the Constitution; and still jealous of that propensity, incident to all Governments, no matter what may be the form of its organization, or by whom administered, to enlarge the sphere of its authority, they, by express provisions, guarded from violation some of the cardinal principles of liberty; among these, as most important, they placed the liberty of conscience and of the press. Profoundly versed in the history of human affairs, whose every page made known that all Governments had seized on the altar and the press, and prostituted them into the most formidable engines against the liberty of mankind, they resolved, and most wisely so, as the sequel has evinced, to surround these great, natural, and inalienable rights by impassable barriers; and, to that end, have expressly declared, that Congress should have no power to legislate on them; and, notwithstanding these great obstacles, you have passed this act. The advocates of the law vainly endeavored to defend themselves by a technical discrimination between the liberty and licentiousness of the press. The American people, by overwhelming majorities, approaching, indeed, unanimity, denounced the law as a palpable and an alarming infraction of the Constitution; and, although no official record of that decision can be produced, it is as notorious as a change of their public servants, which took place at that time, and to which this obnoxious measure so essentially contributed.

The committee cannot withhold an expression of regret, that, upon the restoration of sound principles, the Congress of the times should have omitted to leave some memorial on their records, of their disapprobation of this unjustifiable assumption of power; and none would have been more satisfactory than an ample indemnity to those who had suffered by its operation. In the fluctuating conflicts between power and liberty, which exist everywhere, in a greater or lesser degree, where any portion of liberty is to be found, it is believed, by the committee, to be a most solemn duty imposed on the defenders of the latter, in every triumph it may acquire over the encroachments of the former, to make certain every doubtful point, to which resort had been had as a pretext for such encroachment; to repair every breach made in the Constitution; and, if practicable, to surround liberty with new ramparts. That having been omitted by our predecessors, in the instance of the sedition act, the task devolves on us. And although it has been long delayed, the regret arising therefrom is, in some

degree, lessened by the reflection that the decision now to be pronounced, when the angry passions of party have subsided, will be dictated by an exclusive regard to the intrinsic merits of the question, and the interesting consideration it involves.

The committee are aware, that, in opposition to this view of the subject, the decision of some of the judges of the Supreme Court, sustaining the constitutionality of the law, has been frequently referred to, as sovereign and conclusive of the question.

The committee entertain a high respect for the purity and intelligence of the judiciary. But it is a rational respect, limited by a knowledge of the frailty of human nature, and the theory of the Constitution, which declares, not only that judges may err in opinion, but also may commit crimes, and hence has provided a tribunal for the trial of offenders.

In times of violent party excitement, agitating a whole nation, to expect that judges will be entirely exempt from its influence, argues a profound ignorance of mankind. Although clothed with the ermine, they are still men, and carry into the judgment seat the passions and motives common to their kind. Their decisions, on party questions, reflect their individual opinions, which frequently betray them unconsciously into error. To balance the judgment of a whole people, by that of two or three men, no matter what may be their official elevation, is to exalt the creature of the Constitution above its creator, and to assail the foundation of our political fabric, which is, that the decision of the people is infallible, from which there is no appeal, but to Heaven.

Taking it, therefore, as granted, that the law was unconstitutional, we are led to the next question, growing out of the inquiry, is the petitioner entitled to relief? This question, as a general one, is not susceptible of that precise answer, which might establish a uniform rule, applying equally to all times, and to all occasions. On the contrary, it must be decided by the peculiar circumstances of every case to which its application is attempted.

The committee, for instance, would themselves decide that relief was impracticable, where, from a long course of tyranny, attended with a rapacity far and wide, society had become so impoverished that the attempt to relieve might blight every prospect of future prosperity. Nor could they advocate relief, where the authority exercised admitted of a rational doubt as to its constitutionality, upon powers not expressly inhibited, nor in cases, perhaps, where the amount of the injuries complained of could not be ascertained with a reasonable precision. None of these difficulties, however, present themselves in this case. The law under which the petitioner suffered, as has been previously asserted, and attempted to be shown, was palpably unconstitutional, as being directly in opposition to an express clause of the Constitution. The amount of the injury sustained, in so far as relates to the fine paid by the petitioner, is fixed and certain, and the sum equal to a reimbursement is insignificant to the nation. In this case, therefore, the committee think the Government is under a moral obligation to indemnify the petitioner. An indemnity as consistent with policy as with justice, inculcating an instructive lesson to the oppressor and the oppressed. Successful usurpation yields, indeed, to but few checks; among the few is the justice to posterity, who take cognizance equally of the crimes of the usurper, and of the sufferings and the virtue of his victim—condemning the former, and administering relief to the latter. And what more consolatory to the suffering patriot, what better calculated to inspire constancy and courage, than a conviction, founded on fact, that his wrongs. on the restoration of sound principles, will attract the regard of the successful asserters of freedom, and who will cheerfully indemnify him for the injuries he has sustained? Such examples are not wanting in Governments less beneficent than ours—that of England is replete with instances of this kind. Acts of Parliament, passed in times of heat and excitement, are frequently reversed, and the individuals on whom they had operated are restored to the rights of which they had been deprived. Succeeding Parliaments do not hesitate to indemnify the victims of oppression, because they had suffered under the forms of law. Acts of their Legislature, whose power is omnipotent, form no obstacle with those to whom their injustice is made manifest, in granting relief. An American Congress will not suffer itself to be exceeded by any Government in acts of justice or beneficence.

The committee have only further to remark, that the Executive interposed its authority in various cases, and granted a full pardon to those convicted under the act in question, by which their fines were either remitted, or restored; relief, therefore, to the petitioner, would be only a common measure of justice. According to information received from the Department of State, no money has ever been paid into the Treasury by the officer who received the fines imposed under the sedition act. It is submitted to the discretion of the Senate, whether provision shall be made by law to indemnify the petitioner, by directing the amount of his fine to be paid out of the Treasury, or to reclaim it from the delinquent officer or officers; and, in the latter event, to be at liberty to use the name of the United States in any prosecution to which resort may be had, with a view to that end.

Inasmuch, however, as the relief proposed to be given in this case is on general principles, the committee are of opinion it should be afforded also to every sufferer under the law.

They, therefore, beg leave to submit the following resolutions:

Resolved, That so much of the act, entitled "An act for the punishment of certain crimes against the United States," approved the 14th of July, 1798, as pretends to prescribe and punish libels, *is* unconstitutional.

Resolved, That the fines collected under that act ought to be restored to those from whom they were exacted; and that these resolutions be recommitted to the committee who brought them in, with instructions to report a bill to that effect.

WEDNESDAY, December 6.

Mr. TRIMBLE presented three memorials, signed by a number of individuals concerned directly or indirectly, as purchasers of public lands, prior to the law "making further provision for the sale of the public lands," stating that said law operates injuriously on them, and praying that they may be permitted to apply the payments already made to such portions of their entries as such payments will cover, at two dollars per acre, and that the residue may revert to the United States; and the memorials were read, and severally referred to the Committee on Public Lands.

Mr. EATON presented the petition of Thomas Hardiman, of Missouri, praying to be confirmed in his title to a tract of land in Missouri; and the petition was read, and referred to the Committee on Public Lands.

Mr. HOLMES, of Mississippi, from the Committee on Indian Affairs, to whom the subject was referred, reported a bill to continue in force, for a further time, the act entitled "An act for establishing trading-houses with the Indian tribes;" and the bill was read, and passed to a second reading.

Mr. TRIMBLE gave notice, that, to-morrow, he would ask leave to bring in a bill to authorize the appointment of commissioners to lay out a canal in the State of Ohio.

The Senate proceeded to consider the motion of yesterday, requesting information of the President of the United States respecting the execution of the act "authorizing the purchase of fire engines and for building houses for the safe-keeping of the same;" and agreed thereto.

The Senate proceeded to consider the motion of yesterday, instructing the Committee on Military Affairs to inquire into the expediency of allowing to officers a specific sum monthly in lieu of their present pay, rations, and other emoluments; and agreed thereto.

The Senate proceeded to consider the motion of yesterday, instructing the Committee on Public Lands to inquire into the expediency of establishing an additional land office in Indiana; and agreed thereto.

The Senate proceeded to consider the report of the select committee on the petition of Matthew Lyon; and the further consideration thereof was postponed to and made the order of the day for Wednesday next.

The Senate proceeded to consider, as in Committee of the Whole, the bill entitled "An act to provide for paying to the State of Illinois three per cent. of the net proceeds arising from the sale of the public lands within the same;" and the consideration thereof was postponed until to-morrow.

The Senate took up the motion of the fourth instant, requesting an inquiry into the expediency of extending the time for locating military land warrants in Ohio; which was amended and agreed to, as follows:

Resolved, That the Committee on Public Lands be requested to inquire into the expediency of extending the time for locating military land warrants in the State of Ohio.

COLUMBIAN SOCIETY.

The Senate resumed the consideration of the bill to incorporate "the Columbian Society for Literary purposes."

Mr. JOHNSON, of Kentucky, submitted a general view of the character of the association and its objects, to establish its laudable and unobjectionable nature; and, by comparing it with other incorporations created by Congress, argued to show that it was entirely unexceptionable, being merely the incorporation of the managers of a college

ported on it. (1) On the 19th of February, 1803, Congress passed a law "to provide for the due ' execution of the laws of the United States with- ' in the State of Ohio." In this last law it is de- clared that, by the law of 30th April, 1802, author- izing the people of the Territory of Ohio to form a constitution and State government, Ohio had become one of the United States of America. This law says nothing about her being admitted into the Union on an equal footing with the origi- nal States; but simply says, "whereby the said State has become one of the United States of America."

Louisiana was authorized, by an act of Congress of the 20th of February, 1811, to form a constitu- tion and State government, and formed her con- stitution on the 28th January, 1812. (2) On the 8th of April, 1812, was admitted into the Union by a law. This was the first State admitted with formality. The new mode of declaring this State to be admitted, by law, seems to have been dicta- ted from motives of interest. Louisiana had with- in her limits the Mississippi and other valuable navigable rivers. By that law, which admits her into the Union, the free navigation of all those rivers is secured forever to all the old States, free from "any tax, duty, impost, or toll;" whilst the old States retain the right to these exactions, and some of them do actually exact it. The State of New York now exacts, as a toll, one dollar upon every passenger in the steamboats that go up the North river, and derives from that source an im- mense revenue, laying the whole United States under contribution; whilst her own citizens are navigating the Mississippi and its waters, under the act of Congress, without being subjected to any such duty. And this is what they have been pleased to call admitting her "into the Union upon an equal footing with the original States, in all respects whatsoever."

Indiana was admitted into the Union by a joint resolution of both Houses of Congress, on the 11th of December 1816; but its history proves beyond a doubt that it was considered a State, to all intents and purposes, before the resolution passed. An act in the usual form had passed for its admission; and it had, by a convention, formed a constitution on the 20th of June, 1816. Congress assembled on the 2d of December, 1816; on that day the House of Representatives admitted Mr. Hen- dricks, the member elect, to take the oath of office, and take his seat in the House. On the 4th, the resolution originated in the Senate; on the 6th it passed; was sent to the House on the 9th, and passed that day—eight days after the member had been admitted to his seat; nor had the House of Representatives ever taken up the subject at all. On the 11th, the resolution was approved. Here, it is evident there was a great falling off in vigi- lance; but, it is to be remarked, we were going north about. Louisiana could not be admitted by any thing less solemn than a law. Indiana did not require a resolution, for the House of Repre-

(1) Laws U. S. page 524.
(2) Laws U. S. vol. 4, page 407.

sentatives at least. On the 12th of February, 1817, the Presidential votes were counted in the Repre- sentatives' Chamber, whither the Senate, in a body, had gone for that purpose. All the votes of the several States were counted, except the votes of Indiana. Here Mr. S. said, he would read from the Journals of the House of Representatives, what passed on that occasion, as there were several gen- tlemen of the Senate who had taken their seats since. (1)

Mr. S. said, in consequence of this proceeding, the Senators had a very solemn procession down the stairs and up again, and there it ended; for they unanimously concurred in considering it so frivolous that they forbid it a place on the Jour- nals. The Electors of President and Vice Presi- dent were elected by the State of Indiana, and the electoral votes given before the resolution was of- fered for its admission into the Union. This act was solemnly sanctioned by both Houses of Con- gress. It was the highest act which a State, in its political capacity, can perform. Who, then, can doubt for a moment that Indiana was a State, as perfect as it is possible for this Government to make? If Indiana was so, why should not Mis- souri be so, under the same circumstances? It cannot be doubted. She is a State, and you can- not disfranchise her. But, it is said she cannot be admitted into the Union, because her constitu- tion is repugnant to the Constitution of the United

(1) Journal H. R. 2d session, 14th Congress, pages 385, 386, 387.

"When the President of the Senate was about to open the votes of that State, for the purpose of having the same counted,

"Mr. Taylor, one of the Representatives from the State of New York, rose, and objected to the same, and stated that, in his opinion, the votes of the Elect- ors of Indiana, for President and Vice President, ought not to be received.

"Upon which objection being made, the Senate, on motion of one of its members, withdrew; and, being absent, a resolution was then submitted by Mr. Sharp, in the following words:

"Resolved, by the Senate and House of Representa- tives, &c., That the votes of the Electors *for the State of Indiana for President and Vice President of the United States*, were properly and legally given, and ought to be counted.

"A motion was made by Mr. Taylor, of New York, to amend the said resolution, by striking out all thereof after the enacting clause, and inserting the following: 'That the votes of the Electors of the State of Indiana, for President and Vice President of the United States, having been given previous to the admission of that State into the Union, *ought not to be received and counted.*' And debate arising thereon, a motion was made by Mr. Ingham, that the resolution be postponed indefinitely. And the question being taken thereon, it passed in the affirmative.

"The Senate again attended, &c. And the Presi- dent of the Senate, in the presence of both Houses, proceeded to open the certificates of the Electors of the State of Indiana, which he delivered to the tellers, by whom it was read, and who took lists of the votes therein enclosed."

States, and is not republican; and that Congress, by the Federal Constitution, is to guaranty to every State a republican form of Government; therefore, it is the province of Congress to examine for this quality in the constitution of any State which applies for admission into the Union.

If, sir, Congress has to decide upon the republican form of government of the new States, it has also to decide upon it for all the old States. The language of the Constitution is, "the United States shall guaranty to every State in this Union a republican form of government." This applied immediately to the old States; and, if it is the duty of Congress, why did not Congress examine all the constitutions of the several States? Why not require each State, when it alters or new-models its constitution, to submit it to that tribunal to decide whether it is republican? Nine of the States have altered their constitutions since the adoption of the Constitution of the United States. New Hampshire, in February, 1792; Connecticut, in September, 1818; Vermont, in July, 1793, or rather formed one; Pennsylvania, in September, 1792; Delaware, in June, 1792; Maryland, at sundry times; South Carolina, in June, 1790; Georgia, in May, 1798; and Kentucky, in August, 1799. None of these States have ever submitted their renewed constitutions to Congress for its approbation. It is the duty of Congress, under the term "guaranty," to look into any constitution. Who will be bold enough to say it is not its duty to see that no State shall alter its constitution, but by its permission and authority? It would be to little purpose to say the United States shall guaranty the republican form of government, unless its control can be continued. Every State has the power to revise its constitution whenever it shall think proper. And, if you look at the constitution of Missouri to-day, and pass it as republican, and that State should alter it to-morrow, and destroy its republican features, and defy your control, this power has been given to very little purpose, and had much better been withheld.

Mr. S. said, upon looking into the constitution of the thirteen original States, he had discovered that Rhode Island had no constitution; nor had she ever any. She has what the good people of that State call the "charter of Rhode Island," granted by King Charles the Second; in which he has made certain reservations, as an acknowledgment of his sovereignty. And throughout the whole instrument, the people are treated of, and called subjects. They can have no claim to a republican form of government under such a charter.

Why, then, does not Congress issue its writ of *quo warranto* to the Governor or the Legislature of Rhode Island, calling on them to show by what authority they claim to be one of the United States? Or to show cause, if any they can, why that State should not be disfranchised for holding her government under a foreign Prince? Or else issue some process to compel her to form such a constitution as shall guaranty to her a republican form of government? Congress has as much power to do this as it has to reject the constitution of Missouri.

If Congress has the power to guaranty the republican form of government, and it can only be exercised when a State presents itself for admission into the Union, there ought to be an uniformity in its course. The same State of Rhode Island refused to adopt the Federal Constitution for some time after the organization of this Government. Then Rhode Island stood precisely on the ground on which Missouri now is said to stand. Missouri is a State, but it is said is not in the Union; Rhode Island was a State, and acknowledged on all hands to be out of the Union at that time. Why did not Congress exercise this salutary control when Rhode Island came into the Union; and abrogate her English charter, and give her a constitution, with at least some semblance of a republican form of government in it, and blot out the odious words, sovereign and subject, monarchical vestiges which still characterize it? It is evident, to a demonstration, that Congress is not the tribunal to decide this Constitutional question. It must be left to the judicial department, whose province alone it is to judge the private rights of individuals. There are no governmental rights to be involved, but the rights of persons only, if any; and shall Congress erect itself into a tribunal to investigate whether by chance some free negro or mulatto, fifty years hence, might suffer, and put this whole Union in jeopardy? He viewed such a crisis with awe. Mr. S. said he would be amongst the last to invoke it, but we could not shut our eyes upon what was going on in the northern section of this Union. At the time they were fulminating their threats to dissolve the Union, if Missouri should be admitted into it, they were declaring to the world that the Southern States were endeavoring to intimidate, but would not dare to disturb the Confederacy. One printer, of Philadelphia, tired of waiting for some post of honor or profit under the old government, has divided the Union on paper, and laid out a snug government for himself and his friends, under which, perchance, he may be better provided for. Another fellow has called himself Patrick Henry, and writes as if it belonged to him to dissolve this empire, if he should so will it. He intends to bring about in this country a succession of Patrick Henrys, in imitation of the Cæsars of the Roman world; and he is to be Patrick Henry the second. This Patrick Henry the second has declared if Missouri with her constitution is received, it is of itself a dissolution of the Union. If ever this Union is disturbed, it will be by such monsters as these. It is not here that revolution is to commence; it is to begin with the people, by means of misrepresentations. By imposing on their honesty. Let those who are fanning this flame beware of the consequences. If the torrent begins to roll, there is no telling where it is to stop.

We are told this constitution is not republican; therefore it cannot be sanctioned, because it is the duty of the Government to guaranty to every State of this Union a republican form of government. The evidence of this, it is said, is manifested in the third and fourth clauses of the twenty-sixth section of the third article of the constitution of Missouri, which authorizes the Legislature to pass laws "to prevent free negroes and mulattoes from coming to and settling in this State under any pretext whatsoever."

The Convention, which formed our Federal Constitution, has not been as explicit as we could wish in defining what a republican form of government is. But we have always understood that sort of government which is administered by the people to be a republican form of government, and does not obtain nor lose this form when the free negroes and mulattoes are excluded from a participation. This is a case *sui generis.* The history of the ancient world furnishes no precedent. The Grecian Republics abounded in slaves; but they had no share in the political concerns of the nation. Sparta was said to approach nearer to a pure democracy than any other Government that ever existed. Yet they had slaves in thousands and hundreds of thousands, who had no share in political affairs. They were white, and what of them were not sold to foreign nations, or butchered by their masters, who had the absolute control over their persons and lives, without account, were finally suffered to mingle with the free men, and became one people. But the difference of color forbids that course with us, and will operate as a perpetual barrier, until time shall overcome it. Although they are not slaves themselves, who were prohibited by this constitution to settle in Missouri; yet they are the late offspring of slaves, and have been placed and considered in the body politic upon the same footing and no other. Their parents were slaves during the Revolutionary war. They were in a state of slavery from Boston to the St. Mary's, laboring in your fields. It was not then slaveholding States and non-slaveholding States, but all were slaveholding States. It is true since that time the Northern States, finding it their interest to do so, have sold the greater part of them to the Southern people, and have freed the rest. These freed negroes and mulattoes are now, for the first time, called citizens of the United States; and are, it is said, by the Constitution of the United States, entitled to all the privileges and immunities of citizens of the several States.

As no example is to be found in the history of any other nation, and this being the first time which this question has occurred in our own Government, whether free negroes and mulattoes are, as such, citizens, must be ascertained by such evidences as, from the nature of things, we are compelled to give the highest credence to. Mr. S. said this was to be found in the Constitution and laws of the United States, and in the constitutions or laws of the several States. They furnish a mass of evidence, which nobody could doubt but a sceptic, that free negroes and mulattoes have never been considered as a part of the body politic; neither by the General Government nor the several State governments. All their laws, and all their constitutions, contain marked distinctions by which this class of people are excluded from all partici-

pation in your political institutions; not in the Southern States, but in the Eastern States, the Northern States, and the Western States. Almost all the States in the Union have excluded them from voting in elections. There is no State that admits them into the militia. Very few States admit them to give evidence. No State had passed any law constituting them citizens. Mr. S. said he would not inquire in what department the power existed, if it existed anywhere, whether in the State governments or in the General Government, to naturalize them; but at present neither the one nor the other had done so; and, until some supreme power should do so, they could not claim "the privileges and immunities of citizens of the several States." He would now ask the Senate for their further indulgence, till he could examine this subject more minutely, from the written documents themselves, which he would beg leave to read severally. In doing so, he would begin with the Declaration of Independence itself. This sacred instrument says: "We hold these truths 'to be self-evident: that all men are created 'equal; that they are endowed by their Creator 'with certain inalienable rights; that among 'these are life, liberty, and the pursuit of happi-'ness."

If this was a declaration of independence for the blacks as well as the whites, why did you not all emancipate your slaves at once, and let them join you in the war. But we know this was not done. We know that slavery was as much cherished in Massachusetts, and the other New England States, as it was anywhere else in the Union. In fine, there was an universal consent, at that day, that these people were slaves, and were our personal property, and had no share in the body politic. No gentleman will now be bold enough to say otherwise. New York is yet seeking for remuneration from the British Government for their slaves, by that name, which were plundered from that State during the Revolutionary war. The very Constitution under which we are now assembled, which was formed for the better cementing the Government, derived from that Declaration of Independence, has not only sanctioned the slavery which then existed in the United States, but, by the ninth section of the first article, expressly permitted the whole of the States, twelve years after this Declaration of Independence, to open their ports to the African slave trade for a succession of twenty years. But it is said these free negroes and mulattoes are citizens. The most of them were born slaves, and the act of manumission by the masters could not constitute them citizens. If the master can make a citizen, it must be by some other process than his sign manual on paper. By the act of Congress, passed on the 14th of April, 1802, to establish an uniform rule of naturalization, the Congress itself has guarded against naturalizing any but white population. The first clause of the act is these words: * "That any alien, be-'ing a free white person, may be admitted to 'become a citizen of the United States, or any of

---

* Laws of the United States, 3d volume, page 475.

' them, on the following conditions," &c. The Government of Hayti was then an independent Empire; and why were they excluded this privilege, if all men were created equal?

Mr. SMITH said he would now examine the constitutions of those States which had been admitted into the Union since the adoption of the Federal Constitution. The most of which had passed under the eye of Congress, and had their solemn sanction; and would show how assiduously they had kept up the distinction between the white and black population, and how carefully the colored people were excluded from all share in the affairs of the body politic in the State governments.

In the eighth section of the second article of the constitution of Kentucky, are these words: "In ' all elections for Representatives, every free male ' citizen, (negroes, mulattoes, and Indians, ex- ' cepted,) &c., shall enjoy the right of an elector."

In the first section of the seventh article of that constitution it is said: "The General Assembly ' shall have no power to pass laws for the eman- ' cipation of slaves without the consent of their ' owners, or without paying their owners a full ' equivalent in money for the slaves so emanci- ' pated."

In the first section of the fourth article of the constitution of Ohio, it is said: "In all elections, ' all white male inhabitants, &c., shall enjoy the ' right of an elector."

In the constitution of Louisiana, it is said: "No ' person shall be a Representative who, at the time ' of his election, is not a free white male citizen ' of the United States."

This constitution was submitted to Congress, and was examined with more than ordinary vigilance. So much so, that the State could not gain admittance into the Union without passing a very special and a very rigid law; in which Louisiana was laid under injunctions imposed on no other State, before or since. Yet, with all this vigilance, she is suffered to exclude from the right of representing the State, all colored people. If there are black and yellow citizens, how could Congress permit that constitution to exclude from so valuable a privilege men who, perhaps, had all the requisites of a representative except that of color? Who can estimate the difference between being denied a residence in a State, or denied the valuable privilege of being a representative, or even the right of being represented.

In the 1st section of the 3d article of the constitution of the State of Mississippi, you find the same in substance. The words are, "Every free white male person, &c., shall be deemed a qualified elector."

In the 1st section of the 2d division, of the 6th article of the same constitution, are the words: "The General Assembly shall have no power to pass laws for the emancipation of slaves without the consent of their owners." Mr. S. observed, that he read this last part of that constitution because it was nearly in the same words as the 26th section of the 3d article of the constitution of Missouri, to which he had heard great objections because it

prevented the desirable work of emancipation. When the constitution of Mississippi was before the Senate, only three years ago, there was not a dissenting voice, nor a murmur in the community.

In the constitution of Indiana, which passed the scrutiny of the Senate only four years ago, in the 1st section of the 1st article, it is said, "That all ' men are born equally free and independent, and ' have certain natural, inherent, and inalienable ' rights; among which are the enjoying and de- ' fending life and liberty, and of acquiring, pos- ' sessing, and protecting property, and pursuing ' and obtaining happiness and safety."

How very incompatible would these two clauses of that constitution appear, if it were not for that universal assent which prevails throughout the Union, that free negroes and mulattoes are not known in your political institutions. This is a more marked distinction than any of the preceding. They, for the most part, say, "free white male," &c., but this is simply a distinction between white and black, with the utter exclusion of the colored man. What citizen of the United States would prefer this degrading distinction to exile? The people of Indiana had been eulogized by a gentleman of the Senate, (Mr. KING, of New York,) on this very question, at the last session of Congress, and, Mr. S. said he believed, very deservedly, as a wise and prudent people. These people could have had no prejudices from habitual slavery. They had been nursed in the lap of freedom. When that territory was ceded by Virginia to the United States, there was a stipulation to exclude slavery; notwithstanding which, their men of color are excluded from any portion of political rights. As a further evidence of the degraded condition of free negroes and mulattoes, in Indiana, below that of a citizen, he would beg leave to read a law of that State, passed about two years after it was elevated from its territorial government. He read as follows: " No negro, mulatto, or Indian, shall be a witness, ' except in pleas of the State against negroes, ' mulattoes, or Indians, or in civil cases where ne- ' groes, mulattoes, or Indians, alone, shall be parties." They have, by another clause of the same law, graduated the mulatto. It says, "Every person ' other than a negro, of whose grandfathers or grand- ' mothers any one is, or shall have been a negro, ' although all his other progenitors, except that ' descending from a negro, shall have been white ' persons, shall be deemed a mulatto, and so every ' person who shall have one-fourth part or more ' of negro blood, shall in like manner be deemed ' a mulatto." Can any possible doubt exist that the people of Indiana consider that free negroes and mulattoes are not citizens?

Mr. S. said he would now beg leave to advert to some laws of Congress, of recent dates, which would show, as strongly as can be shown, that Congress has not only believed them to be degraded below the level of citizens, but have actually placed them there, by their laws. Congress required all territorial laws to come under its revision, and particularly so the laws of the Territory of Orleans, before it became the State of Louisiana. By one of the territorial laws of Orleans, of the 7th of June, 1806, it is enacted, (1) " That free people ' of color ought never to insult or strike white peo- ' ple, nor presume to conceive themselves equal to ' the white; but, on the contrary, that they ought ' to yield to them on every occasion, and never ' speak or answer to them but with respect, under ' the penalty of imprisonment, according to the ' nature of the offence." This is a law which passed under the immediate inspection of Congress.

He would now turn to the act of Congress, of last session, which passed on the 15th of May, 1820, and not long after the heated debate upon the bill for admitting Missouri into the Union, when the minds of all the members were filled with this subject, for incorporating the inhabitants of the City of Washington, &c., by which they were continued to be a body politic and corporate. In this act is to be found these words :(2) "Any person shall be eligible to the office of Mayor who is a free white male citizen of the United States." In another part of the same act it says, "That no ' person shall be eligible to a seat in the Board of ' Aldermen, or Board of Common Council, unless ' he shall be more than twenty-five years of age, a ' free white male citizen of the United States, &c. In another part of that act, in enumerating the powers of the corporation, it is said it shall have full power and authority " to prescribe the terms and conditions upon which free negroes and mu- lattoes may reside in the city."

Mr. Smith observed, that, when this law was before the Senate, it was thoroughly investigated by an honorable gentleman from the East, (Mr. Burrill.) Seeing it in such hands, he paid but little attention to it himself; but he found, upon examining it, free negroes and mulattoes were not only excluded from all share in the offices, but were placed under the inspection of the corporation, to prescribe the terms and conditions upon which they may reside in the city. Giving power to pre- scribe the terms, is, in effect, giving power to expel. This is an unanswerable proof of the de- graded condition in which Congress consider free negroes and mulattoes ought to be placed. With this strong and peculiar example before their eyes, well might the people of Missouri conceive they had a right to provide against this evil. The ex- ample is peculiar, because Congress have sat here for the last twenty years; during which time, he had understood, a swarm of mulattoes had been reared in the city; many of whom, no doubt, had as illustrious fathers as any in the nation. These mulattoes have been under the parental care of Congress, until some of them have nearly arrived to the years of maturity; and, if their education has been equal to their parentage, might, in a few years, fill the mayoralty with great dignity. Instead of which, they are now to be placed at the disposal of a petty corporation. All their hopes are blasted, and themselves drove to seek their fortunes in the wilds of Missouri, on account of their color. And shall a mulatto to whom Congress will deny a residence in the City of Washington, unless he is

specially licensed by the corporation, be considered, by that same Congress, if he will only emigrate to the State of Missouri, entitled to all the privi- leges and immunities of the most distinguished citizens of the United States?

He supposed gentlemen who contended for the rights of these sable brethren in Missouri, and who had denied them a residence at Washington, could have no objection to see one of them returned as a member of this honorable body. And if they are entitled to all privileges and immunities of the cit- izens of the several States, wheresoever they would go, it would be infringing much upon the republi- can principle to refuse them this honor. Had Christophe, the famous chief of Hayti, came to some sections of our country, before he blew his own brains out, if he could have obtained the nat- uralization which our free negroes and mulattoes have done, by a residence merely, he might, under the spirit of these times, soon have found his way here. He had seen in this morning's paper some high encomiums on his rival and successor Boyer, his present Majesty of Hayti, by a correspondent of his, in the State of Connecticut, who seems to invite an alliance with his Excellency. This cor- respondent thinks it would be very useful to this country.

In the very law which authorized Missouri to elect the convention which formed the constitu- tion now before you, is the following provision, (1) "that all free white male citizens of the United ' States, &c., shall be qualified to be elected, and ' they are hereby qualified and authorized to vote ' and choose representatives to form a convention." We find nothing in that law for the free negroes and mulattoes. Mr. S. said he had not been able to obtain the statute laws of Ohio and Illinois, but was informed that both those States had laws im- posing penalties upon, and degrading free negroes and mulattoes. So far he had confined his ober- vations and references to the Declaration of Inde- pendence, the Constitution and laws of the United States, and to the constitutions and laws of such of the separate States as had been formed, under the authority, and since the adoption, of the Federal Constitution. He had done so for the purpose of showing the uniformity of sentiment and of action, which had so invariably prevailed, on every polit- ical occasion, to give a decisive character to the degraded condition of free negroes and mulattoes. He had, as yet, offered no evidence derived from the laws and constitutions of the original States. He would now do so, and see how far they main- tained the arguments of the gentleman from Rhode Island (Mr. Burrill) that the constitution of Mis- souri is repugnant to the Constitution of the Uni- ted States, and wants the republican form, which it is the duty of Congress to guaranty; because it provides for prohibiting free negroes and mulattoes from going to, and settling in that State. We were taught to believe that no State in the Union, besides Missouri, had had the boldness to restrain the ingress or egress of any citizen; or that any distinction had been made between the white citi-

(1) Territorial Laws of Orleans, vol. 1, p. 188 190.
(2) Acts 1st session 16th Congress, page 14.

(1) Laws 1st session 16th Congress, page 14.

of an act of Congress. The constitution of Missouri is entirely silent on this point, although some of its language could not be understood without referring to the act of Congress authorizing a convention; they declare that they establish, ratify, and confirm, certain boundaries, but they nowhere recognise the authority which prescribed these boundaries to them. Mr. B. repeated, that he thought Congress ought not to vary from the former mode of declaring its assent to the admission of new States. They would have to admit other States hereafter, and a departure now from the practice of the Government in receiving the constitutions of new States, would form a precedent which might in future cases be deplored.

But proceeding to the question, whether this constitution was such an one as ought to be accepted, Mr. B, said his objection to it arose on the following clause, which he found in the 26th section of the 3d article: "That it shall be the duty ' of the General Assembly of the State, as soon as ' may be, to pass such laws as may be necessary ' (among other things) to prevent free negroes and ' mulattoes from coming to and settling in this ' State, under any pretext whatsoever." This clause Mr. B. conceived to be entirely repugnant to the Constitution of the United States. It prohibits a very large class of persons from entering the State at all; it does not say what shall be done when they get there, but it peremptorily prohibits their entering it under any pretext whatsoever. Even if soldiers of the United States, people of this proscribed class cannot enter Missouri without violating the constitution of the State. It was well known, Mr. B. said, that we have colored soldiers and sailors, and good ones, too, but under no pretext, whether of duty or any other motive, can they enter Missouri. He did not suppose if people of this description, in the service of the country, should enter the State, it would be attempted by the State authorities to exclude them; but it was sufficient, he thought, to show the unconstitutionality of the clause.

Great difficulty seemed to arise in deciding the question, as to what constituted citizens in the different States. Citizens of one State were entitled to the rights of citizens of all the States; yet the different States exercised the power of prescribing certain probationary rules to those coming from another State, to entitle them to all the privileges. If a citizen of Massachusetts removes to another State, he cannot vote as soon as he enters it—a certain residence is required of him—and the people of Missouri were competent by law to impose a residence of one or more years on a citizen going there, to entitle him to all the privileges of citizens of the State; he complies with no more than is exacted of all, and which the State has a right to require. This was a question, however, which they did not touch; they avoided it altogether, and have declared that a certain class shall not come into their State at all, even though they may be citizens of other States, enjoying all the privileges of such.

Mr. B. did not himself conceive it difficult to define what constituted a citizen. If a person was

not a slave or a foreigner—but born in the United States, and a free man—going into Missouri, he has the same rights as if born in Missouri; after complying with the conditions prescribed by the laws to qualify him for the exercise of these rights, he stands precisely on the same footing, and his rights are in every respect the same as if he had been born there. The question then was, Mr. B. said, had the people of Missouri the Constitutional right to prohibit from entering that State a large class of persons who were citizens of the Commonwealth of Massachusetts? To establish the negative of this proposition, Mr. B. adduced various other arguments in addition to the preceding, and endeavored to show that even many laws of the United States would become inoperative in Missouri, if the clause which he opposed could be maintained in force; and, as an instance, he referred to the laws against kidnapping. In regard to this crime of kidnapping, Mr. B. remarked, the constitution of Missouri had done nothing; for, according to it, all people of color who are carried there must, *ipso facto*, be slaves, inasmuch as a free negro could in nowise go there, admitting the clause to have its full effect.

Mr. B. said he was not prepared at present to affirm that Missouri might not pass laws to prohibit persons from carrying there negro or mulatto convicts, or perhaps foreigners from coming into the State; this was a question on which no opinion now was necessary; but he contended that the clause as it stood prohibited the entrance of a large portion of people who were, to all intents and purposes, citizens in other States. Admit the legality of this clause, and, Mr. B. said, the Legislature of Missouri might, with the same right, go still further, and pass laws to exclude citizens born in certain portions or districts of the United States. This was a measure, he argued, which one independent nation could not adopt towards another. England could not pass such a law against the people of France, or of any other friendly nation; such a measure would be too offensive to be borne, and would be considered to amount almost to a declaration of war. If distinct and independent nations dare not enact such laws towards each other, how was it possible, Mr. B. said, that the power could be exercised by one of these States towards other States of the Union?

All the distinctions among citizens which arise from color, rested, Mr. B. said, on State laws alone—there was nothing in the Constitution of the United States which recognised distinctions. In Massachusetts there was no distinction; a man of color possessed there precisely and identically the same rights as a white man born in the same State, and he asked if it was possible for Missouri, consistently with the Constitution of the United States, to exclude any of those people from that State, who should think proper to remove from Massachusetts to Missouri? The States of this Union were not distinct and independent nations—they are, said Mr. B., a confederacy of kindred republics; when they formed their constitution of government, they used the language, "we, the people of the United States," and it is not in the power of one of the members of this confederacy to enforce the clause Missouri has adopted, and it is the duty of Congress to reject it.

Mr. B. said he would add nothing more about the right of Congress to decide this question; he would merely say, Congress must from necessity decide it; it must admit the members of Missouri; in that act the question was involved, and they were obliged, therefore, to decide it. It was useless, therefore, to talk of referring the question to the judiciary. As Congress "might admit new States" into the Union, it was clear to his mind that Congress must determine the conditions on which they should come in.

Mr. B. said he would offer a few words as to the dangers which were apprehended by some gentlemen from a rejection of the constitution offered by Missouri. What were the consequences, Mr. B. asked, which would follow the rejection? The only one which he could perceive was, that Missouri must remain one year longer out of the Union. Was this such a hardship? And to avoid this trifling consequence, must we, said Mr. B., give a vote which will violate the Constitution we have sworn to support, and which we are all so deeply interested in maintaining? As a Territory the people of Missouri had gone on, he said, very prosperously, and no great inconvenience could result from continuing in the territorial condition one year longer. It is said they have formed a constitution, and under it have elected a Governor and Legislature, and, having assumed the functions and character of a State, if they are not now admitted into the Union, they will go on without our consent. Mr. B. said he presumed the people of Missouri felt the same attachment to the Union, and to the tranquillity, and honor, and glory of it as we do; and he would not believe, he would not do them the injustice to believe, that rather than endure the small inconvenience of retaining the territorial character a few months more, they would rashly throw away all the interest they had in the greatness and glory of their country. They might possibly still think that their constitution ought not to have been rejected on account of this offensive clause, and may feel some excitement on the occasion; yet they must see the necessity and propriety of some sacrifice to the conscientious opinion of Congress, and would consent to qualify their constitution in the objectionable feature. But, said Mr. B., if we ratify it as it is, we establish a precedent and admit a point that the judiciary will never be able to overthrow; do not then leave to another tribunal the decision of a question which belongs to us, but let us meet and decide it ourselves.

If the constitution were not accepted, Mr. B said it would be easy to obviate any difficulty by passing an additional act authorizing the people of Missouri to form another convention and revise their constitution; and he was confident this odious feature would be expunged. These people, Mr. B. said, were not Missourians, properly so distinguished, but were Americans, collected there from all the States, the same people as ourselves. They would appreciate the motives of Congress,

and do them justice; they would recollect, also, that this act passed in a spirit of compromise and accommodation, from a desire to preserve peace and quietness in every part of the Union; and re-assembling with such views, finding the clause could do no good, they would repeal it. Sanction this improper clause now, said he, and you sanction it for all time to come; and however we may desire hereafter to avoid it, it will be irrevocably established.

Mr. B. said, the little he had spoken had exhausted his strength, and he could add nothing more if he wished to do so.

When Mr. B. had concluded—

Mr. SMITH, of South Carolina, intimated an intention of replying to Mr. B.; but, as he would have to refer to several constitutions and other authorities, in the course of his argument, he asked a short time to prepare them, and moved the postponement of the subject until to-morrow; which motion prevailed, and it was postponed accordingly.

FRIDAY, December 8.

Mr. PLEASANTS presented the memorial of Charlotte I. Bullus, widow of John Bullus, deceased, late navy agent for the port of New York, praying that the accounting officer of the Navy Department may be directed to credit the account of the deceased at the rate of $2,000 per annum during the time he performed the extra duties of navy agent on the Lakes; and the memorial was read, and referred to the Committee on Naval Affairs.

Mr. SMITH presented the memorial of the citizens of Charleston, South Carolina, protesting against any increase of the duties at present imposed on imported goods; and the memorial was read, and referred to the Committee on Commerce and Manufactures.

Mr. ROBERTS presented the memorial of Paul Beck, junior, and Thomas Sparks and others, of Philadelphia, manufacturers of, and dealers in, shot, praying that an additional duty may be laid on imported shot; and the memorial was read, and referred to the Committee on Commerce and Manufactures.

Mr. HOLMES, of Mississippi, presented the petition of John M. Whitney and John Snodgrass, in behalf of the legal representatives of Alexander Montgomery, deceased, praying that a law may be passed directing a warrant to be issued to them for a quantity of land in Mississippi, as an indemnity for a like quantity of their land improperly disposed of by the Register and Receiver of the Land Office west of Pearl river; and the petition was read, and referred to the Committee on the Public Lands.

Mr. PINKNEY presented the petition of Rebecca Hodgson, widow of Joseph Hodgson, deceased, praying remuneration for the loss of the house burnt in the year 1800, whilst occupied by the Government as the War Office; and the petition was read, and referred to the Committee on Military Affairs.

Mr. THOMAS, from the Committee on Public

(1) "That no person by this act authorized to
' marry, shall join in marriage any white person
' with any negro, Indian, or mulatto, on penalty of
' the sum of fifty pounds, two-third parts thereof
' to the use of the county wherein such offence
' shall be committed, and the residue to the prose-
' cutor, to be recovered by the treasurer of the
' county, &c., and the said marriage shall be null
' and void," &c.

Massachusetts emancipated her slaves, what she
had not sold off, at a pretty early period after the
Revolutionary war. Those alluded to must be
free negroes and mulattoes. Massachusetts we all
know to be a Republican State, and to have a
Republican form of government. She had been
called the cradle in which the Revolution had
been rocked. Her early achievements in that Revolution had been conspicuous. The battles of
Bunker Hill and Concord would be spoken of by
posterity with delight. She had been famed for
her men of eloquence, and he had the pleasure to
say, without flattery or irony, that he believed
justly. She had the most numerous legislative
body of any State in the Union—her number of
representatives was about six hundred. Amidst
such a multitude of council, is it possible for one
member to believe, for a moment, that such a law
could have passed, to prohibit a citizen to marry
whomsoever he could gain the affections of? Or
is there a man in Massachusetts who will say that
marriage is not an essential happiness? If it is
not secured to every citizen, where is their declaration of rights? We must look for the reason of
this law, as in all the other States, in the universal assent to the degraded condition of that class
of people, and from which none of the States
would, perhaps, ever think it expedient to raise
them. From the ranting of some enthusiasts, and
the jeerings of some politicians, Mr. S. said, he had
been led to believe there were no mulattoes in the
New England States. But looking into their
statute books, he found they were numerous; so
much so, as to become the subjects of legislative
control, and that a long time ago. It appears
they were breeding them as far back as 1788, and
he did not know how much earlier, but he supposed as long ago as when they began to import
the Africans into Portsmouth, in the State of New
Hampshire.

As the laws and constitution of Connecticut
would give some aid in illustrating this question,
he would refer to them.

In the first section of the first article of that constitution are the following words:

"That all men, when they form a social com-
' pact, are equal in rights."

In the second section of the sixth article of that
constitution it is said: "Every white male citizen
' of the United States, &c., shall be an elector."

This constitution was formed on the 15th of
September, 1818. The good people of that State
called the convention which formed that constitution, for the express purpose of making it Republican. Nor will any one doubt but that the citizens

of Connecticut and their constitution are Republican. But how can the constitution be Republican, if their free negroes and mulattoes are citizens,
and not entitled to all the privileges and immunities of citizens in the several States? All men
cannot be equal in rights, and be deprived of all
these rights, or any of them, and still be called
equal, without a gross violation of the rights it
declares to be sacred. Such absurdities cannot be
ascribed to the wise men of Connecticut, who so
recently formed this constitution. And they must
be ascribed to them, if the free negroes and mulattoes are citizens, and deprived of the elective franchise. We have been taught to consider it the
highest privilege of a freeman. Some extracts
from the laws of that cautious and prudent people
will throw much light on the question of State
sovereignty, and the powers of a State to prohibit
the ingress of persons from other States. By a law
of the State, published in 1792, and which was
since the adoption of the Constitution of the United States, they have carried their powers much
further than those assumed by Missouri for excluding the free negroes and mulattoes. He would
read the extracts, which he had taken from their
statute books. The first was in these words:

(1) "That when an inhabitant of any of the
' United States (this State excepted) shall come
' to reside in any town in this State, the civil au-
' thority, or major part of them are authorized,
' upon the application of the selectmen, if they
' judge proper, by warrant under their hands, di-
' rected to either of the constables of said town, to
' order said persons to be conveyed to the State
' from whence he or she came," &c.

Another part of the same law, in further execution of the foregoing principle, says:

(2) "The selectmen of the town are author-
' ized to warn any person, not an inhabitant of
' this State, to depart such town, and the person so
' warned, if he does not depart, shall forfeit and
' pay to the treasurer of such town one dollar and
' sixty-seven cents per week. If such person re-
' fuses to depart, or pay his fine, such person shall
' be whipped on the naked body, not exceeding ten
' stripes, unless such person departs in ten days."

"If any such person returns, after warning, he
' is to be whipped again, and sent away again, and
' as often as there is occasion."

No argument can be drawn from the facts that
Missouri makes Constitutional provisions to deprive a citizen of his right of residence, and that
of Connecticut is only by law. There is no man
of sense and honesty, too, who will venture to say
a State may prohibit by a law those whom the
Constitution protects. It would be nugatory to
protect a right by the Constitution, if you can destroy it by law. The constitution of a State is
paramount to all other of its laws. Then, if Connecticut can prohibit the citizens of other States
from remaining or residing in that State, by a law,
they will certainly permit Missouri to exclude
free negroes and mulattoes by their constitution.

_____
(1) Laws of Massachusetts, vol 1, pp. 323-4.

(1) Laws of Connecticut, page 240.
(2) Laws of Connecticut, page 241,

Nor could he be easily brought to believe that a citizen of Connecticut would not rather be entirely forbidden to reside in any State to which he might remove, than to be whipped out of it after he had got there. Is it not absurd, to a demonstration, for the people of a State to say the constitution of Missouri is not republican, because it provides for excluding free negroes and mulattoes from a residence, when their own laws, recently enacted, exclude all the citizens of all the rest of the Union? South Carolina, some years ago, passed a law to prohibit slaves from the Northern States, when they were selling them to the Southern people, from coming into that State; but there was an exception in favor of the servants of public functionaries and members of Congress. The laws of Connecticut do not exempt the members of Congress themselves, much less their servants. A member of Congress, going from the Southern States to Connecticut, would not conceive himself very highly honored if put under an escort of town constables; nor could he well suppose the honor enhanced by being whipped on the naked body if he should happen to return that way.

Another law of that State, published in 1796, concerning free negroes, mulattoes, and negro, mulatto, and Indian servants, is worth notice. One clause says:

"Whatsoever negro, mulatto, or Indian servant, 'shall be found wandering out of the bounds of 'the town or place to which they belong, without 'a ticket, or pass, in writing, to be taken up," &c.

By another clause there is a distinct and degrading restraint laid upon free negroes. It says:

"No free negro is to travel without a pass from 'the selectmen or justices."

So careful have they been to restrain this degraded class of people, in the same law it is provided:

"That every free person shall be punished by 'fine, &c., for buying or receiving any thing from 'a free negro, mulatto, or Indian servant," &c.

If free negroes and mulattoes are citizens, why this distinct restraint on their right of locomotion more than on a white citizen? If citizens, why restrained from travelling without a pass? Who is authorized by the Constitution of the United States to prescribe the terms to a particular class of citizens, by what means they shall be suffered to pass? And who shall interdict the rest of the community from buying or receiving from a particular portion of citizens, if they are citizens?

The great and respectable State of New York would afford us some light also upon this subject. In the 42d article of the constitution of that State we find the following words:

"And this convention doth further, in the name 'and by the authority of the good people of this 'State, ordain, determine, and declare, that it shall 'be in the discretion of the Legislature to natural-'ize all such persons, and in such manner, as they 'shall think proper."

This remains a prominent part of the constitution of New York. She has reserved to herself, or to her Legislature, the sole right to naturalize all such persons as they shall think proper. They, perhaps, may have the power to do so; but they ought to be candid enough, at least, to allow Missouri to naturalize such persons, and in such manner as they may think proper, also. Her powers are co-ordinate. But, so far is the Legislature of New York from this, that whilst she retains the power herself, she not only denies it to the State of Missouri, but has sent her resolutions of instructions to her Senators, which now lie on your table, to endeavor, by all means, to disfranchise her for attempting to exercise this right upon free negroes and mulattoes only. With what grace she can do so, let the world judge. Her citizens, too, are declaring in their bulletins that, for this defect in the Missouri constitution, she ought to be rejected, and if admitted it will, of itself, be a complete dissolution of the union of the States.

By a law of New York, passed the 8th of April, 1801, they have shown, in the most emphatic words, the power which each State retains, of excluding from their limits all and every person who shall come therein. Nor are their means for imposing this power the least energetic. This power they have not limited to exclusion of free negroes and mulattoes only, as Missouri has done, but they have extended it to every class of citizens, of every age, sex, and denomination. He would read the several clauses. The first is in these words:

(1) "If a stranger is entertained in the dwel-'ling-house or out-house of any citizen for fifteen 'days, without giving notice to the overseers of 'the poor, he shall pay a fine of five dollars."

This clause goes to punish any hospitable man who shall have the rashness to entertain a stranger. Whatever may be the custom of the people of that State, the laws deny to a stranger even the rights of hospitality. The next clause comes a little closer to the stranger. He would read it. It is in these words:

(2) "If such person continues above forty days, 'the justices can call on all the inhabitants of the 'town or city, and the person may be sent to jail, '&c. And the justices may cause such stranger 'to be conveyed from constable to constable, until 'transported into any other State, if from thence 'he came."

This stranger may be a man of the purest morality, the most accomplished manners, extensive fortune, or most finished education; or he may be an object for the exercise of charity; it is immaterial which—he is put into the hands of a constable, who hands him to his brother constable, and so he goes on, until they hand him out of the State of New York. This is the first legal entertainment which a gentleman or lady, for they are to be entertained pretty much alike, are subjected to when they visit the State of New York, if they remain forty days. There was another clause, if they made a second visit, which entertains them in a different style. It is in the following words:

(3) "If such person returns, the justices, if they 'think proper, may direct him to be whipped by

(1) Laws of New York, vol. 1, p. 568.
(2) Laws of New York, vol. 1, p. 563.
(3) Laws of New York, vol. 1, pp. 568, 569.

' every constable into whose hands he shall come; ' to be whipped, if a man not exceeding thirty-nine ' lashes, and if a woman not exceeding twenty-five ' lashes. And so as often as such person shall ' return."

It may be said, this law was only intended to guard against transient poor from other States. The rights of a poor man are and ought to be held, if he is a citizen of the United States, as sacred as the rights of the rich man. But this law itself has made no distinction. The constitution authorizes the Legislature to naturalize in such manner as they shall think proper. If this was the manner of naturalizing, and no other appeared yet to have been adopted, to be whipped at the public whipping post by every town constable into whose hand he should come, it was not so very inviting to foreigners; and it was more than probable that but few would like the certificate, as the registry is to be made, on the back of the man, by thirty-nine lashes, (Moses's Law;) of the woman, by twenty-five lashes. It has been remarked by enlightened travellers, that the attention to ladies is in proportion to the civilization and refined manners of nations. New York has given in this law a proof of *her* refinement of manners by *their* marked attention to ladies, as they are to receive fourteen lashes less than the gentlemen.

However romantic this may all appear, it is literally true that such a law is not only to be found in the statute books of New York, but has been enacted twelve years since the adoption of the Constitution of the United States, is now in full force, and is constantly practised upon; by which they can drag from the State the most worthy gentleman or lady of the United States, by the rude hand of town constables; and, if they should dare to return, can make them hug the whipping post. Yet, with this gigantic stretch of power in full exercise by their own State, the people of that State are riding foremost in the cause of the wandering vagabond free negroes and mulattoes with a view to thrust them upon others, or with some other more unkind view.

If this concatenation of Constitutional and legal authorities, beginning with the Declaration of Independence itself, and running through the Constitution and every law of the United States, wherever the subject could occur, or be acted on, as well as a voluminous concurrence of the State constitutions and State laws, all bearing directly on this question, without a solitary case to be found to contravene them, when combined with that universal sentiment and universal rule of action of the whole of the white population of the whole nation, denying positively all the precious and valuable privileges of citizenship to free negroes and mulattoes, would not demonstrate that they were not citizens, he knew no human proof which could comprehend it.

Mr. SMITH said he should offer no more legal or Constitutional authorities. What he had offered were within the statute books and constitutions of the several States, sent here by authority of those States, as an evidence of their State policy. Therefore, those authorities could not be question-

ed. He had been thus tedious that he might give them chapter and verse. He had done so, because he believed the policy of the States throughout the Union, on this subject, had heretofore been but little known, and which, he thought, on this occasion, ought to be elicited. More time would, he had no doubt, have enabled him to have shown many other State regulations relating to the same purpose. Such as he had been able to obtain he had submitted, in the humble hope that they would be useful, and enable other gentlemen to improve. He knew he had consumed much time already, and more than he wished to have done; but the subject would not suffer him to abridge it, for which he begged pardon. But he had yet a little bundle for Rhode Island, which some gentlemen might not think quite applicable; but, as he had heretofore spoken of the facts contained in it, when in debate on the same subject, he would rely upon the favor of the Senate to be indulged.

What he had to read and say was nothing more than paying a compliment to Rhode Island. That State had not only been very bitter against slaveholders generally, but had been particularly so, at the last session of Congress, against Missouri, unless negro slavery should be restricted there. This he believed, however, could not have been the opinion or temper of the majority. He was warranted in this opinion by the late election, by the Legislature of that State, of a Senator to Congress. Mr. James D'Wolf was the successful candidate, and this gentleman had accumulated an immense fortune by the African slave trade. In the year of 1804 the ports of South Carolina, by an act of its Legislature, under the permission of the Constitution of the United States, were opened for the importation of Africans. They remained open four years. During that time there were two hundred and two vessels entered the port of Charleston, with African slaves. Ten of these vessels, and their African cargoes, belonged to Mr. D'Wolf. [Here Mr. BURRILL, of Rhode Island, called Mr. SMITH to order, because it was out of order to mention the name of a member, and because he was approaching the State of Rhode Island. The PRESIDENT of the Senate decided that Mr. SMITH was not out of order, as Mr. D'Wolf was not a member of the Senate, and Mr. S. proceeded.] Mr. SMITH said his object was not to reproach that respectable State, but to eulogize it. But, sir, said Mr. S., look into your archives, and you will find many memorials and remonstrances from the town meetings of the people of that State last year, not only against slavery in Missouri, but aiming at its total abolition; and reproaching the States which tolerate it. See the resolutions just laid on your table from New York, to influence your decision against Missouri. And he would here remark, that when a bill was offered by a gentleman from New York, (Mr. ROOT,) for the purpose of declaring that slavery did not exist in that State, it was objected to by the gentleman who offered the resolutions for rejecting Missouri, (Mr. J. C. SPENCER,) because, he said, it did not apply. Mr. S. observed, that he had been informed that that gentleman was the owner of several slaves himself. If that was the fact, it would not apply very well until he could find means to dispose of them. Then no doubt the thing would apply very handsomely. We are reproached for our dealing in slaves and human flesh, whenever gentlemen chose to indulge themselves, but become very fastidious when you mention facts that apply to their side of the House.

Mr. D'WOLF, he said, was trading under the authority of the laws of this Government, and it could be no reproach. He would say nothing about the African trade which he had been engaged in since it was prohibited by law, because that would very deservedly subject him to a criminal prosecution.

This subject had been forgotten in Carolina. It was supposed to be at an end. However, hearing late in the Summer that the storm was gathering to the north, and that the admission of Missouri into the Union would be opposed on account of slavery, or something springing from that source, he wrote to a friend in Charleston, to apply to the custom-house officer for a full statement of all the ships engaged in that trade during the four years, together with their owners, consignees, their places of residence, country, nation to which they belonged, &c., that he might be able to show the public who were engaged in it. In answer to his request, he had received from the custom-house books, from the hand of the collector, the following authentic documents. He would present to the Senate, in the first place, the documents which contained the years of arrival, the names of the vessels, the place to which the vessel belonged, the names of the proprietors, the names of the consignees, their country, and to where they belonged.

[*Explanation*—B. *British*, F. *French*, R. I., *R. Island*.]

Vessels' names.	Proprietors—of what country.
1804.	
Aurora, Charleston, A.	S. E. Turner, New Eng'd
Ann, British	W. M'Cleod, Scotland
Easter, do.	W. Boyd, do.
Brilliant, do.	Bixby, Rhode Island.
Armed Neutrality, Chas'n	Napier, Smith & Co. G. B.
Argo, R. I.	James Miller, Ireland
Thomas, B.	Janus & Price, G. B.
Horizon, Charleston	A. & J. M'Clure, do.
Harriot, F.	James Broadfoot, do.
Eliza, R. I.	James Miller, do.
Alexander, Charleston	W. Broadfoot, do.
Francis, do.	J. Potter, do.
Christopher, B.	Wm. Boyd, do.
Favorite, R. I.	James Millar, do.
M'Leapine, B.	Gibson & Broadfoot, do.
Susanna, Charleston	S. E. Turner, New Eng.
Active, B.	I. Campbell, G. Britain
Hamilton, B.	W. Boyd, do.
Ruby, Charleston	do do.
Mary, Norfolk	J. Broadfoot, do.
1805.	
Perseverance, B.	Turner & Price, do.
Kitty, Charleston	G. Parker, Charleston
Lupin, B.	Bixby, Rhode Island
Mary Huntley, B.	Wm. Boyd, Great Britain
Gov. Wentworth, B.	Turner & Price, do.
Experiment, B.	W. Boyd, do.
Eagle, R. I.	Gardner & Phillips, R. I
Neptune, do.	E. Cook, do.
Fanny, B.	Turner & Price, G. B.
Thomas, Charleston	do. do.
Nile, do.	Wm. Boyd, do.
Recourse, B.	Gibson & Broadfoot, do.
Isabella, B.	I. S. Allen, do.
Armed Neutrality, Chas'n	Napier & Smith, do.
Susans, do.	J. Duncan, do.
Love and Unity, B.	S. Adams, R. I.
Jack Park, B.	John Price, Great Britain
Manning, B.	Tunno & Cox, do.
Juliet, R. I.	Phillips & Gardner, R. I.
Margaret, B.	W. Boyd, Great Britain
Louisa, R. I.	Phillips & Gardner, R. I.
Ariel, B.	W. Boyd, Great Britain
Estor, B.	do. do.
Margaret, B.	do. do.
Hiram, R. I.	Phillips & Gardner, R. I.
Louisiana, B.	Eddy, R. I.
Maria, B.	Cooper, Great Britain
Hambleton, B.	Wm. Boyd. do.
Rambler, R. I.	E. Sayer, Rhode Island
William, B.	Turner & Price, G. B.
1806.	
Ariel, B.	W. Boyd, Great Britain
Mary, B.	Gibson & Broadfoot, do.
Daphne, Charleston	W. Boyd, do.
Carie, B.	Tunno & Cox, do.
America, B.	James Broadfoot, do.
Davis, Charleston	John Davidson, do.
Lydia, do.	Everingham, N. Jersey
Dudton, B.	Gibson & Broadfoot, G. B.
Amazon, B.	Tunno & Cox, do.
Fair American, Charlest.	J. S. Adam, R. I.
Miller, do.	J. Queen, Ireland
Edward & Edmund do.	Cooper, Great Britain
Factor, Rhode Island	Sherman, R. I.
Louisa, do.	Phillips & Gardner, R. I.
Commerce, do.	Seeson, do.
Gustavus, Swede	Spencer Man, Charleston
Neptune, R. I.	C. Cook, R. I.
Robert, B.	Gibson & Broadfoot, G. B.
Polly, Rhode Island	Benson, R. I.
Hiram, do.	Phillips & Gardner, R. I.
Samuel, B.	Gilchrist, New Jersey
Love and Unity, B.	J. S. Adams, R. I.
Three Sisters, R. I.	W. Champlain, do.
Hector, B.	John Watson, G. Britain
Ruby, Charleston	W. Boyd, do.
Farmer, do.	John Carr, do.
Maria, R. I.	Phillips & Gardner, R. I.
Ceres, B.	Gibson & Broadfoot, G. B.
Independence, Baltimore	Churchill, R. I.
Hibernia, B.	Pratt, Great Britain
Alert, B.	Wm. Boyd, do.
Agent, R. I.	Eddy, R. I.
Mary, Charleston	W. Boyd, Great Britain
Three Friends, B.	J. Calligan, do.
Fair Eliza, R. I.	J. Metter, do.
Fox, Charleston	J. S. Adams, R. I.
Kitty, do.	G. Parker, Charleston
Hope, R. I.	W. Lyon, R. I.
Hope, Charleston	Wm. McCormic, Ireland
Nantasket, do.	Boohorod, Great Britain
John Watson, B.	Tunno & Price, do.
Governor Dodsworth, B.	W. Boyd, do.
Mary Ann, B.	J. Kennedy, do.
Diana, B.	P. Mooney, do.

SENATE.   *Admission of Missouri.*   DECEMBER, 1820.

Davenport, B.	J. Everingham, N. Jersey
Corydon, B.	W. Boyd, Great Britain
Kate, B.	Watson & Co. do.
Mercury, Charleston	W. Kelly, do.
Union B.	W. Boyd, do.
Washington, R. I.	D. McKelvey, do.
Louisa, R. I.	Phillips & Gardner, R. I.
Nicholson, B.	W. C. Tarmed, G. Britain
Edw'd & Edmund, Charl'n	J. Calligan, do.
Mercury, B.	J. Watson & Co. do.
Little Ann, R. I.	Christian, Charleston
Margaret, B.	T. Rowlinson, G. Britain

1807.

Katy, Charleston	T. Cassin, Great Britain
James, B.	A. Holmes, do.
Eliza, Charleston	Christian & D'Wolf, R. I.
Cleopatra, do.	W. Boyd, Great Britain
Union, R. I.	Phillips & Gardner, R. I.
Tartar, B.	J. Hambleton, G. Britain
Maria, B.	J. Cooper, do.
James, Baltimore	N. Ingraham, Mass.
Mary, B.	J. S. Adams, R. I.
Aspinal, B.	Hamilton & Co., G. Brit'n
James, R. I.	C. Christian, Charleston
Norfolk, Charleston	Cushman, Ireland
Fourth of July, B.	G. Parker, Charleston
Dudder, B.	Gibson & Broadfoot, G. B.
Habit, F.	Delan & Co., France
Agent, R. I.	T. Eddy, R. I.
Eliza, Charleston	T. Ogin, Great Britain
Ann, B.	Tunno & Cox, do.
Ellis, B.	James & Price, do.
Andromache, R. I.	Drown, R. I.
Gov. Clairborn, R. I.	T. Depau, France
Hiram, R. I.	Phillips & Gardner, R. I.
Semiramis, R. I.	do. do.
Neptune, R. I.	C. Cook, do.
Nancy, R. I.	Phillips & Gardner, do.
Minerva, Charleston	T. Depau, France
Columbia, R. I.	Phillips & Gardner, R. I.
Factor, R. I.	C. Cook, do.
Lavinia, R. I.	Christian & D'Wolf, do.
Leander, Charleston	T. Vincent, do.
Daphney, do.	W. Broadfoot, G. Britain
Vulture, R. I.	Christian & D'Wolf, R. I.
Africa, B.	W. Boyd, Great Britain
Three Friends, B.	J. Calligan, do.
Eliza, R. I.	J. Christian & D'Wolf, R. I.
Lark, R. I.	W. Bradford, do.
Alfred, R. I.	Phillips & Gardner, do.
Louisa, Charleston	J. Duncan, Great Britain
Hiram, R. I.	Norris, R. I.
Concord, do.	Christian & D'Wolf, R. I.
Friendship, do.	Phillips & Gardner, do.
Flora, do.	D'Wolf, do.
Ann and Harriot, do.	Phillips & Gardner, do.
Monticello, do.	D'Wolf, do.
Amazon, B.	Bennet, Great Britain
Baltimore, R. I.	Church, R. I.
Juliet, do.	Phillips & Gardner, do.
Miriam, B.	Depau, France
Heron, Connecticut	C. Fitzimons, Ireland
Ruby, Charleston	W. Boyd, Great Britain
Three Sisters, R. I.	D'Wolf, R. I.
Betsey and Sally, do.	do. do.
Armed Neutrality, Charl'n	Boyd, Britain
Anna, do.	Depau, France
John, B, do.	Tunno & Price, Britain
Nantasket, do.	Bousroyd, do.

George Clinton, Britain	Delai & Clement, France
Eagle, R. I.	D'Wolf, R. I.
Port Mary, Charleston	W. Boyd, Britain
Eliza, do.	Christy, Charleston
Mary, R. I.	Phillips & Gardner, R. I.
Eagle, R. I.	do. do.
Actor, Charleston	P. Kennedy, Ireland
Hanna Bartlet, do.	Phillips & Gardner, R. I.
Mary, do.	J. Eglistin, R. I.
Edward and Edmund, do.	Hilton, do.
Charleston, do.	Bailey & Wailer, Britain
Experience, Boston	Fisher, R. I.
Rambler, R. I.	Phillips & Gardner, R. I.
Eliza, B.	J. B. Cotton, do.
Cleopatra, Charleston	W. Hoyd, Britain
Hope, R. I.	D'Wolf R. I.
Charlotte, do.	do. do.
Albert, Charleston,	W. Timmon, S. Carolina
Commerce, R. I.	W. Lyon, R. I.
Hope, Charleston	N. Ingram, Massachusetts
Wealthy Ann, do.	D'Wolf, R. I.
Columbia, R. I.	Phillips & Gardner, do.
Agenora, R. I.	D'Wolf, do.
Mercury, B.	M. Kelly, Ireland
Venus, Charleston	Preble, R. I.
Agent, do.	Depau, French
General Claiborne, do.	do. do.
James, R. I.	D'Wolf, R. I.
Resolution, Charleston	J. S. Adams, Britain
William and Mary, do.	H. Kerr, do.
Caroline, F.	Synagal, French
Polly, Charleston	J. Stoney, Charleston
Jupiter, Norfolk	J. Willick, Britain
Heart of Oak, Baltimore	J. S. Adams, R. I.
Horizon, B.	do. do.
Mary Ann, Charleston	S. Miller, do.
Mary Ann, Baltimore	Dallas
Rio, Charleston	O'Harra, Charleston
Sally, B.	C. Graves, do.

[Dates in the above statement are omitted.]

Mr. SMITH then read the recapitulation in the following words and figures:

RECAPITULATION

Of the African trade, and by what nation supported, from January 1, 1804, to December 31, 1807.

VESSELS BELONGING TO

Charleston.	Rhode Island.	Baltimore.	Boston.	Norfolk.	Connecticut.	Swede.	British.	French.	Consignees, natives of Charleston.	Consignees, natives of Rhode Island.	Consignees, natives of Britain.	Consignees, natives of France.	Total.
61	59	4	1	2	1	1	70	3	13	88	91	10	202

This paper, sir, contains the whole number of slaves imported, and the particular number imported by each foreign nation, and each of the United States. It is in the following words and figures:

Slaves imported at Charleston, from the 1st January, 1804, to 31st December, 1807, and by what nation.

British - - - - -	19,949
French - - - - -	1,078
	21,027

In American Vessels.

Charleston, South Carolina - -	7,723	
Of this number there were, belonging to foreigners - - - -	5,717	—5,717
Leaving, imported by merchants and planters of Charleston and vicinity	2,006	
Bristol, Rhode Island	3,914	
Newport, do.	3,488	7,958
Providence, do.	556	
Baltimore - - - - -	750	
Savannah - - - - -	300	
Norfolk - - - - -	287	
Warren - - - - -	280	
Hartford - - - - -	250	
Boston - - - - -	200	
Philadelphia - - - -	200	
New Orleans - - - -	100	
		26,744
		39,075

Here, sir, ends the black catalogue. It would show to the Senate, that those people who most deprecate the evils of slavery and traffic in human flesh, when a profitable market can be found, can sell human flesh with as easy a conscience as they sell other articles. The whole number imported by the merchants and planters of Charleston and its vicinity were only two thousand and six. Nor were the slaves imported by the foreigners, and other American vessels and owners, sold to the Carolinians, only in a small part. They were sold to the people of the Western States; Georgia, New Orleans, and a considerable quantity were sent to the West Indies, especially when the market became dull in Carolina.

When Mr. SMITH had concluded, on motion, the House adjourned.

SATURDAY, December 9.

Mr. THOMAS presented a memorial, signed by a number of individuals concerned directly or indirectly as purchasers of public lands, prior to the law "making further provision for the sale of the public lands," stating that said law operates injuriously on them, and praying that they may be permitted to apply the payments already made to such portions of their entries as such payments will cover at two dollars per acre, and that the residue may revert to the United States; and the memorial was read, and referred to the Committee on Public Lands.

The bill for the relief of Morgan Brown was read the second time.

The Senate proceeded to the third reading of the bill, entitled "An act to amend the act entitled 'An act for the relief of the legal representatives of Henry Willis;'" and, on motion by Mr. KING, of Alabama, it was ordered to lie on the table.

The Senate proceeded, as in Committee of the Whole, to the consideration of the bill for the

relief of Robert Purdy; and the consideration thereof was postponed to Monday next.

The Senate resumed, as in Committee of the Whole, the consideration of the bill for the relief of the officers and volunteers engaged in the late campaign against the Seminole Indians; and the consideration thereof was further postponed to Monday next.

RESTRICTION OF SLAVERY.

Mr. TICHENOR communicated the following resolutions of the Legislature of the State of Vermont; which were read:

STATE OF VERMONT,
In General Assembly, Nov. 15, 1820.

The committee, to whom was referred so much of his Excellency's speech as relates to the admission of the Territory of Missouri into the Union as a State, submit the following report:

The history of nations demonstrates that involuntary servitude not only plunges the slave into the depths of misery, but renders a great proportion of community dependent and wretched, and the remainder tyrannic and indolent.

Opulence, acquired by the slavery of others, degenerates its possessors, and destroys the physical powers of government. Principles so degrading are inconsistent with the primitive dignity of man, and his natural rights.

Slavery is incompatible with the vital principles of all free governments, and tends to their ruin. It paralyzes industry, the greatest source of national wealth, stifles the love of freedom, and endangers the safety of the nation.

It is prohibited by the laws of nature, which are equally binding on governments and individuals. The right to introduce and establish slavery in a free government does not exist.

The Declaration of Independence declares, as self-evident truths, "that all men are created equal; that they are endowed by their Creator with certain inalienable rights; that among these are life, liberty, and the pursuit of happiness; that, to secure these rights, governments are instituted among men, deriving their just powers from the governed; that whenever any form of government becomes destructive of these ends, it is the right of the people to alter or abolish it."

The Constitution of the United States, and of the several States, have recognised these principles as the basis of their Governments, and have expressly inhibited the introduction or extension of slavery, or impliedly disavowed the right.

The powers of Congress to require the prohibition of slavery in the constitution of a State, to be admitted as one of the United States, is confirmed by the admission of new States according to the ordinance of 1787, and by a Constitutional "guarantee to every State in the Union of a republican form of government." This power in Congress is also admitted in the act of March 6, 1820, which declares that, in all that territory ceded under the name of Louisiana, which lies north of thirty-six degrees thirty minutes north latitude, "slavery and involuntary servitude shall be forever prohibited."

Where slavery existed in the States, at the time of the adoption of the Constitution of the United States, a spirit of compromise, or painful necessity, may have excused its continuance; but can never justify its introduction into a State to be admitted from the Territories of the United States.

Though slavery is not expressly prohibited by the Constitution, yet that invaluable instrument contains powers, first principles, and self-evident truths, which bring us to the same result, and lead us to Liberty and Justice, and the equal rights of man, from which we ought never to depart. "In it is clearly seen a deep and humiliating sense of slavery," and a cheering hope that it would, at some future period, be abolished—and even a determination to do it.

It is apparent that servitude produces, in the slaveholding States, peculiar feelings, local attachments, and separate interests ; and, should it be extended into new States, "it will have a tendency to form a combination of power which will control the measures of the General Government," and which cannot be resisted, except by the physical force of the nation.

The people of the United States adopted the Constitution " to form a more perfect union of the several States, to establish justice, to secure domestic tranquillity, provide for the common defence, promote the general welfare, and secure the blessings of liberty ;" and have thereby blended, and inseparably connected the interests, the safety, and welfare, of every State in the Union. We, therefore, become deeply concerned in the fundamental principles of the constitution of any new State to be admitted into the Union. Whatever powers are necessary to carry into effect the great objects of the Union are implied in the Constitution, and vested in the several departments of the General Government.

The act of the United States authorizing a provisional admission of Missouri into the Union as a State, does not pledge the faith of the Government to admit whatever may be its constitution or system of State government; for that constitution, by the act, must be republican, and not repugnant to the Constitution of the United States.

From information, it is to be seriously apprehended that Missouri will present to Congress, for their approbation, a constitution which declares, that "the General Assembly shall have no power to pass laws—first, for the emancipation of slaves, without the consent of their owners, or without paying them, before emancipation, a full equivalent for such slaves so emancipated ;" and, "secondly," to prevent emigrants from bringing slaves into said State, so long as slavery is legalized therein.

It is also made the imperious duty of its Legislature to pass laws, as soon as may be, " to prevent free negroes and mulattoes from coming to, and settling in, that State, under any pretence whatever."

These powers, restrictions, and provisions, to legalize and perpetuate slavery, and to prevent citizens of the United States, on account of their origin, color, or features, from emigrating to Missouri, are repugnant to a republican government, and in direct violation of the Constitution of the United States.

If Missouri be permitted to introduce and legalize slavery by her constitution, and we consent to her admission, we shall justly incur the charge of insincerity in our civil institutions, and in all our professions of attachment to liberty. It will bring upon the Constitution and Declaration of Independence a deep stain, which cannot be forgotten or blotted out. "It will deeply affect the Union in its resources, political interests, and character."

The admission of another new State into the Union with a constitution which guaranties security and protection to slavery, and the cruel and unnatural traffic of any portion of the human race, will be an error which the Union cannot correct, and an evil which may endanger the freedom of the nation.

Congress never ought, and we trust never will, plant the standard of the Union in Missouri, to wave over the heads of involuntary slaves, "who have nothing they can call their own, except their sorrows and their sufferings," and a life beyond the grave, and who can never taste the sweets of liberty, unless they obtain it by force or by flight. Nor can a community made up of masters and slaves ever enjoy the blessings of liberty, and the benefits of a free government; these enjoyments are reserved for a community of freemen, who are subject to none, but to God and the laws.

The committee, therefore, submit for the consideration of the General Assembly the following resolutions, viz :

Resolved, That, in the opinion of this Legislature, slavery, or involuntary servitude, in any of the United States, is a moral and political evil, and that its continuance can be justified by necessity alone.

That Congress has a right to inhibit any further introduction or extension of slavery, as one of the conditions upon which any new State shall be admitted into the Union.

Resolved, That this Legislature views with regret and alarm the attempt of the inhabitants of Missouri to obtain admission into the Union, as one of the United States, under a constitution which legalizes and secures the introduction and continuance of slavery ; and also contains provisions to prevent freemen of the United States from emigrating to and settling in Missouri, on account of their origin, color, and features. And that, in the opinion of this Legislature, these principles, powers, and restrictions, contained in the reputed constitution of Missouri, are anti-republican, and repugnant to the Constitution of the United States, and subversive of the inalienable rights of man.

Resolved, That the Senators from this State, in the Congress of the United States, be instructed, and the Representatives requested, to exert their influence and use all legal means to prevent the admission of Missouri, as a State, into the Union of the United States, with those anti-republican features and powers in their constitution.

Resolved, That the Secretary of State be requested to transmit a copy of the foregoing report and resolutions to each of the Senators and Representatives from this State in the Congress of the United States.

ADMISSION OF MISSOURI.

The Senate resumed the consideration of the resolution declaring the consent of Congress to the admission of the State of Missouri.

Mr. HOLMES, of Maine, addressed the Chair as follows:

Mr. President, it is not my intention to trouble the Senate with any remarks on that part of the constitution of Missouri which recognises the right to hold slaves. The act of the last session has settled that question ; and, in spite of the reasoning in the Vermont memorial just read, and the authority from whence it emanates, I feel bound by a solemn compact to admit Missouri, unless it is manifest that her constitution is repugnant to that of the United States. The honorable gentleman from Rhode Island (Mr. BURRILL) who opposed this resolution, gives up the ground of restriction; and I understand that he, and other gentlemen who think with him on that subject, would consent to the admission of Missouri, if her constitution does not contravene any provision of the Constitution of the United States, nor the act of last session which authorizes her admission. The honorable gentleman from Rhode Island did, to be sure, suggest some objections not strictly consistent with this admission, on which he did not seem to place much reliance, and which probably were not, in his mind, insuperable. He thinks it was improper, and somewhat indecorous, that the act was not incorporated in the constitution, or at least referred to by the convention as the ground of their proceedings. But, if they have complied with the provisions and conditions of the act, it is equally binding as if they had recited the whole, and the constitution itself is more concise, explicit, and intelligible.

Another objection is, that the constitution of Missouri allows emigration from the State, but prohibits free blacks and mulattoes from coming in and settling. This is charged upon Missouri as an inconsistency. But surely there can be nothing inconsistent in this. The people are forming a compact, and one of its provisions is, that those members of the State who shall become dissatisfied may abandon it. "Go," they say, "when ‘ you please, and where you can. We give you no ‘ warrant to break open the doors of our neigh- ‘ bors and force them to receive you against their ‘ consent. We allow no such liberties to be taken ‘ with us." This is the substance of the provision. It surely is neither inconsistent nor illiberal.

Passing by these objections, which were not urged with much confidence or zeal, I come to that which is principally relied on. Free negroes and mulattoes are to be prohibited by law from coming to and settling in the State; and this, it is contended, contravenes that clause of the Constitution of the United States which provides that " the citizens of each State shall be entitled to all privileges and immunities of citizens in the several States."

The honorable gentleman from Rhode Island contends that this prohibition would exclude them from entering the State, even without an intent to settle. This construction makes the clause consist of two distinct prohibitions, the one against entering, the other settling; and this absurdity would result—that the legislature should prohibit free blacks without from coming in, and free blacks within from settling. The true construction is—that they are not to be permitted to come in and settle.

It is true that it is made imperative on the legislature to exclude free blacks and mulattoes, and they are not to be admitted to settlement in the State, under any pretext whatever. Had the expression been *all* free blacks and mulattoes, the legislature could have made no exceptions. But the omission of the word "all" leaves them a discretion; and other provisions in their constitution limit the extent of the prohibition, and expound its meaning.

All purchasers of lands in Missouri, previous to the law enacted under this clause, are expressly provided for. A purchase of lands by deed is "a contract executed." The covenants in the deed secure to the purchaser the right to hold, possess, and enjoy. Should the purchaser be lawfully excluded from the possession, the covenant or "contract" is broken. If the State by law excludes a purchaser from his possession, it impairs the obligation of the contract. In the celebrated Georgia case in relation to the Yazoo purchase, it was determined that a law annulling a precedent sale was void, as impairing the obligation of a contract. And whatever law takes from a purchaser the benefit of any covenant in his deed is void, being repugnant to the Constitution of the United States. Now, there is the same clause in the constitution of Missouri as in that of the United States. Any law, therefore, which should exclude a precedent purchaser from the enjoyment of his purchase would be contrary to a provision in the bill of rights of Missouri. Wherefore, taking these two provisions together, the meaning is this: "the legislature shall exclude free blacks and mulattoes, provided they are not purchasers of lands within the State."

This reasoning will apply to all soldiers who hold under the United States, and all subsequent purchasers under them will be also excepted by another provision in the constitution of Missouri. Among the terms and conditions in the act of last session, Missouri is never to interfere with the primary disposal of the soil by the United States, nor with any regulations Congress may find necessary for securing the title in such soil to the *bona fide* purchasers. Now, a title is never perfected, or "secured," unless the purchaser has, not only the rights of property and possession, but the possession itself. To prohibit a purchaser under the United States from enjoying the possession, would most unquestionably interfere with those regulations which Congress might adopt to secure the title to the purchaser. But it is still more manifest that it would be an interference with the " primary disposal " of the soil. Could Missouri, without a violation of this compact, provide that no purchaser of the United States' lands in the State should possess or enjoy it? If not, how can she prohibit any portion of purchasers from this possession or enjoyment? If, in the sale of a dwelling-house, which I had the right to prevent, I should covenant not to interfere, should I fulfil my covenant by prohibiting the purchaser from entering and inhabiting it? Here, then, is a positive stipulation made a part of the constitution of Missouri, and unalterable without the consent of Congress, which expressly excepts from the prohibition all purchasers of the United States. The whole power given, then, taken in connexion with the rest of the constitution, is to exclude free blacks and mulattoes from the State, except purchasers of every description, before the act of exclusion, and purchasers of the United States, whether before or after. Inasmuch, then, as we find express limitations to this power, and the word "all" not inserted in the prohibition, and the members of the legislature bound by oath to support the Constitution of the United States, would it not be fair to expound this clause to extend to those cases only which are not repugnant to this Constitution?

Having, as it is believed, ascertained the extent and meaning of the clause objected to, let us, before we proceed to a discussion of the part of the Constitution of the United States said to be infringed, glance for a moment at some of the inconveniences which would result from denying to a State the power to exclude free blacks and mulattoes.

These are an unfortunate class. They, or their ancestors, having been subjected to the control of a master, are most of them ignorant and poor, and many of them infirm, decrepid, and vicious. Their vices and frailties render them an encumbrance, if not a nuisance, wherever they reside. It is just that the evils arising from such a population should be sustained by those who have had the benefit of their labor, and who have contributed in some measure to their degradation. To confine them to the State by whose laws they or their ancestors were enslaved, and compel that State to administer to their relief without imposing a burden on their neighbors, comports as well with justice as humanity. These reasons have prevailed in almost every State in the Union, and have produced exclusion laws of the same character and principle, and of greater extent, than the offensive clause in the constitution of Missouri. The people of Missouri, possessing a territory whose soil and products would not admit of a numerous slave population, whose extent and climate would afford facilities to emigrants, and whose vicinity to States and Territories having a crowded black population, would induce an inundation of this description of people, have thought it prudent, the better to facilitate the emancipation of their own slaves, and to improve the condition of their own free blacks and mulattoes, to prohibit their emigration from other States.

If a State does not possess this power, the condition of the non-slaveholding States is most alarming. A free black population is fast increasing and gaining upon the whites, in the slaveholding States. An asylum for these unfortunate people is now become important, and will be more so. This has been an object of solicitude with all the colonization and abolition societies, and all the friends of freedom and humanity. Slaves would be manumitted if they could be transported. But to let them loose among an already crowded free black population, would make them miserable and dangerous. Send them to St. Domingo, you subject them to the disposal of a cruel tyrant; transport them to Africa, and they are food for pestilence; colonize them on the Columbia river, and they will be butchered and eaten by the Indians. To this time, no suitable place has been found which afforded a safe and comfortable retreat for the emancipated slave. But this doctrine has solved the doubt and removed the difficulty. Free blacks are citizens and may go where they will, or

where their emancipators shall please to send. All the slaves in a State may be made free at once, on condition of their removal to a non-slaveholding State, and this State cannot prevent it. The New England States are probably in little danger from this principle. It is the States bordering on the slaveholding States which will experience its tendency and effect. Ohio, Indiana, and Illinois, are now thinly populated and little cultivated. Vast tracts of land in them are owned by the United States. The State of Virginia, for example, might purchase some millions of acres and parcel them out in small lots, as gratuities to her free blacks who should emigrate and settle them. Such an event would probably create no uneasiness at first, in a State which had the power at any time to prevent it. The non-slaveholding States might even for the sake of humanity encourage it, having a discretion at all times to check it when it should become dangerous. But to be forced, against our will, to receive free blacks from the slaveholding States, is a doctrine that I, as a northern man, do not so fully relish, and to which I cannot subscribe without the fullest examination and strongest necessity. This effect has been perceived, and some have attempted to avoid it by making a distinction between free and *freed* blacks. The former only having been born free, it is said, are citizens. The latter are a degraded class, not entitled to the privileges and immunities of citizens, and can therefore be prohibited from entering and settling in a State. This distinction is entirely visionary. It neither comports with reason nor humanity. It is the local authority, the State sovereignty which makes a slave. The same supreme power which deprives a man of his freedom can restore it, and restore it, too, in its highest perfection. The same power which makes a slave can make him free, and advance him to the highest privileges of a citizen. If this power does not exist in the States, it exists nowhere; and this absurdity would necessarily follow, that there is no power in this country to convert a slave into a citizen. The Constitution of the United States gives no such right to Congress. They have the power to establish uniform rules of naturalization; but naturalization is the converting a foreigner into a citizen. To suppose an emancipated negro, whose ancestors had resided here ever since the settlement of the country, and who had never quitted the plantation where he was born, could be made a citizen by naturalization, and in no other way, is an absurdity too gross and palpable to be seriously entertained. It hence follows, inevitably, that an emancipated slave may, if the State will it, be placed on the same footing as any other free black, and one may be a citizen as well as the other. The State which gave them their freedom for purposes of emigration would take care to obtain its object by breaking down this distinction if it ever existed.

The honorable gentleman from Rhode Island disregards this distinction, and takes broader ground still. His definition of a citizen comprehends all the inhabitants except slaves and foreigners. With free blacks and mulattoes, he includes convicts, dissolute persons, paupers, and vagabonds. Yet he seems to admit that a State may exclude for personal demerit. And who establishes the standard of merit, and makes the discrimination? The State. By what rule is it governed? Discretion, policy, expediency. It is the State law which defines who are worthy of a residence within the State. What, then, becomes of his definition, but that it includes all but those which a State may, in its discretion, except? If a State can fix a name of disgrace or demerit on any population, and exclude them, the point is yielded that free blacks may be excluded.

If this definition of the honorable gentleman be correct, it would be much the safest inference that one State might exclude all the population of another, except those which the Constitution of the United States specially authorizes. Self-protection seems to require that a State should retain the power to prevent a troublesome or dangerous population. In doing this, they might exclude those who are useful and respectable. Of this there is no danger. The State from which they would emigrate would not wish to spare them; and that to which they would come, would always find it for its interest to receive them. The Constitution of the United States would provide for all who have a duty to perform under that Constitution, and the laws; members of Congress, and judges of courts, must perform federal duties. The President must command the Army and Navy and the Militia, when in service; the soldiers must be called to suppress insurrection and repel invasion. To all these and others, having federal duties to perform, the Constitution says "go;" and a State cannot oppose. The clause of the Constitution of the United States said to be infringed by this of Missouri, by no means repels this construction. The citizens of one State are to enjoy "all the privileges and immunities of citizens" when "in" another. The State is left at its option whether it will receive the citizens of another as residents. It may impose restrictions which amount to prohibition; but if the citizen does come, by express or implied consent, this clause secures him "the privileges and immunities," and subjects him to the duties and disabilities of citizens.

I do not say that this construction admits of no doubts or difficulties. But I do say, that, upon this broad definition, it is the safest and most consistent with the practice and rights of the States. And I can never admit the principle that free blacks of any description, and to any extent, may fix their residence in a State against its consent.

The honorable gentleman from South Carolina, (Mr. SMITH,) with much talent and industry, has given us a history of the practice, and proved that this power claimed by Missouri has been exercised by nearly every State in the Union, and the right has never before been questioned. The subject has been so fully and ably presented, that no further time need be occupied in discussing it.

Permit me now to take a different view of the subject, and endeavor to present a construction of the Constitution which will avoid the difficulties.

Gentlemen, I apprehend, reason from wrong premises. In the broad and comprehensive definition of citizen, lies the error. Let us endeavor to select a meaning for the word which will comport with the Constitution, the practice, and the convenience. The Constitution of the United States has nowhere defined it; it occurs on five different occasions in that Constitution—in prescribing the qualification of Representative, Senator, and President, in giving jurisdiction to the Federal Court, and in the controverted clause. In the three first cases, no one will pretend that it is to be taken in this unlimited sense. That the framers of the Constitution intended that blacks and mulattoes might be members of Congress or Presidents, is a supposition too absurd to be for a moment entertained. Gentlemen, with all their humanity, to be obliged to sit in this Senate by a black man, would consider their rights invaded. The section of the Constitution which gives jurisdiction to the courts, uses it in a different sense, but gives it no precise definition. If all entitled to be parties to suits are citizens, and those only, then a large and respectable portion of the community are excluded, and probably resident foreigners included. The word here is inaptly used, and intended in this case to mean the same as inhabitant. The laws of Congress are as deficient in furnishing a meaning as the Constitution. But, as the naturalization laws have uniformly restricted the right to become citizens to free *white* persons, so far as practice is to influence a decision, it is in favor of the constitutionality of the objectionable clause.

The word was never used by the ancient Republics, but to include privileges and immunities of a high character. In the Grecian States, these privileges were preserved with much tenacity, and conferred with much solemnity. The Romans divided their inhabitants into citizens, subjects, freedmen, and slaves. To be a Roman citizen was a proud distinction, and carried with it privileges and immunities of the highest order. After the subversion of the Roman Empire, and some time in the eleventh century, cities began to be established or incorporated in Europe, and first in Italy, and the inhabitants entitled to their freedom and liberties were called citizens. These, principally, were to elect and be elected, and to bear arms in their own defence, under commanders of their own choice.

The best definition of citizen, according to European writers, which I have been able to find, is "a native or inhabitant of a city, vested with its freedom and liberties." The "freedom and liberties," or "privileges and immunities" essential to a citizen, were those I have mentioned; and, although the name was originally confined to the inhabitant of a *city*, yet when these principles were diffused among and conferred on the inhabitants of the *country*, they, having the same attributes, took the same name.

The rights of an American citizen are essentially the same: to elect, be elected, and bear arms in his defence; they are essential, for, divest him of these, and you divest him of his citizenship. He has other essential rights, such as those of property and personal security under the protection of laws fairly administered; but he has these in common with foreigners, and in some respects with slaves. No person can be said to be entitled to the privileges of an American citizen, unless he can have an agency in the formation or administration of the laws; that agency may be prospective, but a perpetual exclusion from this deprives him of the essential attributes of a citizen; but these attributes are conferred or withheld by the will of the State, legally or constitutionally expressed; a citizen, therefore, has his character from the State of which he is a member; the State may deprive him of it, and again restore it back; as it can totally destroy it, so it can create it in its highest perfection. It would seem, then, inevitable that, inasmuch as the privileges of citizenship are conferred or withheld by each State at its will, they may be and almost unavoidably must be different in different States. The question then presents, what "privileges and immunities of citizens have the free blacks of Missouri? And we see at once they have none. By the charter which you made for them, free blacks can neither elect nor be elected, and this disability is made perpetual by their constitution. By the existing territorial laws they cannot bear arms without being housekeepers and having a license from the civil authority; nor act as jurors in any case, nor testify as witnesses, except in suits between persons of their own color. The free black of Missouri, then, has no privileges of citizenship there. Then, can a free black citizen of Maine have any greater privileges or immunities in Missouri, than her own free blacks? Does a citizen of one State going to another carry his political condition with him or assume that of the State where he goes? The former principle breaks down every qualification required by a constitution of a State, and authorizes one State to confer privileges for the whole. No gentleman has, I believe, pretended to insist on such a construction. A citizen of Maine entitled to elect and be elected, goes to Virginia; the constitution of Maine made him an elector without property and with a year's residence; that of Virginia requires a freehold and further residence; does he instantaneously become an elector in Virginia, or must he be subjected to the disabilities of Virginians conditioned like him? He must submit of course to the laws of the State to which he goes. But in Maine a free black is a citizen; he goes to Virginia—can he there have any other privileges and immunities than the free blacks of Virginia? By the same rule, certainly not; if he could, the free blacks of Virginia might emigrate to Maine, tarry a year, become electors there, and return, bringing with them the elective franchise, which they could exercise in spite of the constitution of Virginia. A person, then, going from one State to another, takes all the privileges and immunities, and is subject to all the restraints and disabilities as to residence, property, age, and *color*, of the people of the State where he goes. If, then, free blacks and mulattoes going into Missouri could have no privileges and immunities of citizens when there, she has a right to exclude them.

Their right to go is only by inference. They are entitled, you say, to certain privileges and immunities when there; and therefore they have a right to go. We answer, they are entitled to no privileges and immunities of citizens, when there; and therefore Missouri has a right to exclude them.

A contrary decision would moreover be against all precedent, and the constant practice of most of the States in the Union. When a contest for power between the United States and a State occurs, it becomes this Senate jealously to guard those rights which it was constituted to preserve. The tendency of the Federal Government is to acquire by slow and imperceptible encroachments on the rights of the States—one acquisition may succeed another until there shall be nothing left.

It is, furthermore, unusual strictly to scrutinize every clause of a constitution of a new State, on her admission into the Union. Reject a State for one objectionable clause, and, if you err, the error cannot be easily corrected. Admit her, and, if a clause is repugnant to the Constitution of the United States, it is inoperative and void, and would be annulled by a judicial decision. The State would be, in the Union, pruned of the offensive limb, and the residue of her constitution would remain.

This is a question which may be very safely trusted with the Judiciary. Who are the parties to the compact in the act of last session? The United States and Missouri. Missouri contends that she has complied with the terms, and demands a fulfilment on our part. We refuse, and charge her with a failure to fulfil her stipulations. Who is to decide? Will we insist on deciding our own case, or will we consent to the decision of an umpire? There is no risk on *our* part in submitting the question to the Supreme Court. In questions of State and Federal powers, they have, I believe, never been suspected of leaning very far in favor of the former. Indeed, it is not in the nature of men placed as they are to do it. Their origin, compensation, responsibility, and pride, all forbid it. If the people of Missouri are willing to submit to this tribunal, we act not as an honorable man would act with his neighbor if we refuse.

But suppose you insist on the objection. Is it by any means certain that you may not produce a state of things perplexing, if not dangerous? I do not pretend that Missouri will resist your authority. My fear is, that you cannot agree to exercise it.

Suppose a case, not improbable,—suppose Missouri rejected by a disagreement between the two Houses of Congress—one branch believing that she has complied with the conditions, is a State, and entitled to admission; the other believing that she has failed to comply, and must retire back to her territorial condition. You promised Missouri two things—a State government, and admission into the Union. She is in the enjoyment of one, and demands the other. One House of Congress is willing she should enjoy the other, and the other House refuses, and demands that she should yield up what she has obtained. One House having a negative on the other, what could be done? The necessity should be strong, and the case clear, before I would hazard such a state of things. But, so far from the case being clear, and the necessity strong, it is manifest, I think, that you have no power, and, if you had, it is not only unnecessary, but impolitic and unsafe, to exercise it. The propositions upon which I have insisted, and endeavored to maintain, are these:

The "privileges and immunities" of citizens are nowhere extended to free blacks and mulattoes, by the Constitution of the United States nor laws of Congress.

The constitution and laws of the States are alone capable of conferring them.

The State of Missouri has not conferred them on this class of her population.

Black citizens of other States acquire no other privileges and immunities there than her own black population.

But the latter are not citizens there, nor are the former; and, as the former could have no privileges and immunities of citizens there, they may be excluded.

Mr. OTIS, of Massachusetts, said that, in presenting to the Senate a few general observations upon the question before them, he would take leave to begin where the honorable gentleman, (Mr. HOLMES,) who had just sat down, had left off. That gentleman had enlarged upon the consequences to be apprehended from the rejection of Missouri, under her present constitution, in terms adapted to excite alarm. But while he admitted that, in all cases, where discretion can be exercised, the consequences of measures, as they might affect not only the welfare but the feelings of the people, and their disposition to execute the laws, should justly be regarded; yet when the dictates of conscience, and the obligation of oaths, and language of the Constitution, left no alternative, it was the part of those who had duties to perform to discharge them with firmness, after due deliberation, and to trust to the consequences and effects. This would be his course, under any view to be imagined, of the reception of the fate of their application for admission by the good people of Missouri. But he did not permit himself to indulge any fears of such results as had been intimated. His respect for that people, and his persuasion of their knowledge of their true interests, banished from his mind every suspicion of a temper that would lead them to adopt rash and violent measures, and embroil themselves with the Union upon a question of Constitutional law, which it would be so much easier to settle by an amicable adjustment. He was sorry that the question had arisen, and had presumed that the people of Missouri would have placed themselves in a condition to claim their admission, upon the ground of a compliance with the terms held forth to them by Congress; and thus to have disarmed the opposition of such of the former minority as might have considered those terms binding on the public faith. But this they had not done, and, although some inconvenience might be attached to the course they had taken, the only remedy could be found in

a course of reasonable and moderate measures on the part of themselves and their friends.

The resolution upon the table, said Mr. O., contains a proposition, which Congress is either bound to adopt of course, as a ministerial act, or upon which they are entitled to exercise a sound discretion. But propositions of the first description, calling upon Congress to register the acts of another State, and to do, *pro forma*, what was already done in substance without their consent, were, as he humbly conceived, anomalies entirely unknown to the Constitution, and not recognised by any rules or proceedings of this House.

Under the sanction of an act of Congress, the people of Missouri have been authorized to form a constitution, subject to certain limitations and conditions, and thereupon to become an integral part of the Union. How, then, is it possible to advance a step without reading and examining their constitution, and deciding upon the fact whether or not they have complied with these terms? To a certain extent, he presumed, this investigation would be admitted on all sides to be indispensable; without it, who can tell whether she has confined herself within the prescribed territorial limits? Who would know that she had not extended her claim of jurisdiction to the Rocky mountains? We may also be entitled to ascertain whether she has established a republican or a monarchical government; whether she arrogates the power of making peace and war, regulating commerce, collecting imposts, or other powers inhibited in express terms of the Constitution to the several States. If, then, we not only may carry our researches thus far, but should be bound in duty not to shut our eyes against these flagrant assumptions of power, who will say where the line of discrimination begins, and class under their proper heads those invasions of the Constitution which we are held to notice, and those at which it behooves us to wink?

Gentlemen who deny this right of Congress to decide upon a question placed before them for decision, insist with great vehemence that Missouri is a State, and, of consequence, that her members are entitled to their seats; and if she be not a State, they call upon us to describe her actual condition, and to say what she is. But, to say nothing of the inference which seems unavoidable, that, upon this hypothesis, the proceedings of Congress are superfluous, and the foundation for all debate is removed, and the members need only offer themselves to be qualified; it might with equal truth be affirmed that Missouri would be a State, if she had made a Governor for life, or instituted an hereditary Senate, or claimed the public lands, or, in many other particulars, trenched upon the rights of the General Government, and held the terms of the proffered admission in contempt. But the assumption of her being a State is a fallacy—a begging of the question—and an illusion, arising from the repetition of a high-sounding word. In truth, the people of the United States, by their Congress, are parties to an executory contract. The people of Missouri are the other parties. The former have granted to the latter the faculty of becoming a

State, when, among other things, they shall have formed a constitution not repugnant to the Constitution of the United States. Now, by what law or usage, or principle of natural equity, does a party, who, by certain acts to be performed on his part, is to be entitled to the benefit of a subsequent act to be performed by another party, become the sole judge of his own fulfilment and perfect claim? Has not the party who is called upon to make the last concession a right to be satisfied? If there be a controversy and a tribunal, will not this last mentioned party stand upon his defence? In the ordinary transactions of civil life there could be no doubt. Why, then, is it expected that Congress should surrender an advantage which every individual would retain? Congress, it may be said, cannot be arraigned before any tribunal, neither can it be impleaded upon any of the innumerable private pecuniary claims that are constantly made upon its justice. In these cases it invariably makes a law for itself. Doubtful claims are always rejected; and there could be no consistency in reserving scrupulously the power of deciding upon demands for money and services, which are often paltry and insignificant, and shrinking from decisions which involve the civil or political rights of any portion of the people, however poor and humble their condition. It is, then, entirely fallacious to insist that Missouri, by taking advantage of her own wrong, has become a State, and precluded your right of inquiring into her condition. The fallacy is apparent when the inquiry is made, is she a State of that description which is entitled to be admitted into the Union? This involves the further questions, Is her constitution republican? Is it conformable to the Constitution of the United States? Has she complied with the precedent conditions annexed to her grant? If in these points her constitution is defective, it is not incumbent on those who oppose her admission to waive their objections in consequence of the change of name or organization; neither is it essential to give her a name, or to define the heteroclite condition in which she has placed herself; though he saw no difficulty in saying she was yet a Territory, in her transit towards the condition of one of the United States, and none in providing by law (especially with a kindly concurrence on the part of that people) for an adaptation of the present form of her government to her territorial condition, until that should be approved.

The honorable gentleman from South Carolina had asserted, with great confidence, that several States had been admitted into the Union without any evidence to be found on record of an examination into the provisions of their constitution. "Several of those States were without constitutions," and, "why," exclaimed the gentleman, triumphantly, "do you not issue a *quo warranto* against Rhode Island and other States?" To this, said Mr. O., the answer is most obvious. Rhode Island, Vermont, and North Carolina, had the option, at the time of the formation of the Federal Government, of becoming parties to it at pleasure. They were independent States, acting as such, and their constitutions or forms of government were

subjects of notoriety to the other States with whom they had united under the Old Confederation. They did not adopt the Constitution of the United States at the same epoch with the other States, but there was a perfect understanding of their being at liberty to send in their adhesion; and, when they did so, nothing was wanting but laws extending to them the jurisdiction of the Union. In respect to every other State, it was manifest that their several constitutions had been submitted to the inspection of Congress, as would be demonstrated by a recurrence to its acts, and although the form of the resolutions adopted of late years had not been originally observed. The State of Virginia, by an act of December, 1789, authorized Kentucky to become a State at some period subsequent to 1791, at a time to be fixed by the people. They accordingly formed a constitution, and determined that the era of its active supremacy should be in June, 1792. Meanwhile Congress convened, and determined on the same time for its admission into the Union, and, by necessary intendment, must have had before them the constitution as it had been adopted. In the act extending to Ohio the benefit of certain laws of the Union, there is an express recognition of her having framed a republican form of government. In the instance of Tennessee, there was a debate upon a clause in her constitution, which shows that the instrument was before Congress; and, since the time of her admission, a more precise formality has been observed in every instance. Nothing, therefore, he contended, was to be gained by the gentleman's reliance upon precedents, which were all against him. Having thus, (continued Mr. O.,) established it to be the right and duty of Congress to examine this instrument, he should proceed to state and to support his objection arising upon the face of it, and it was shortly to the clause which made it the duty of the Legislature of the new State to prevent the ingress and settlement of free people of color, under any pretext whatsoever, within its boundaries. This requisition being, at first blush, in palpable collision with the clause of the United States' Constitution which provides for a community of rights for the citizens of one State with those of any other State into which we may go, there is no refuge from the objection but in a bold denial of the fact, that free persons of color may be citizens of some one State. And, to do justice to the candor of gentlemen, it must be allowed they enter the lists with manly frankness, and, in so many words, deny to people of color this capacity of citizenship; and it follows as a corollary, that they deny also the right of any one State to confer that capacity upon them. They call upon us to show what constitutes a citizen, and especially to prove that persons of color were at all considered as coming under that denomination, in any compact made with each other by the people of the United States. It would require more time than could be fairly claimed by any individual, to do justice to this subject under all its aspects, but he trusted a very few remarks would be sufficient for a satisfactory confutation of this novel theory. For his greater security, however, he would confine himself to the circumstances which would give to a man the right of citizenship in Massachusetts; for if a man of color could be a citizen there, he would carry his privilege elsewhere. In that State, he said, at the time of the Revolution, the people were considered as retaining all such portions of the common law of England as were applicable to their circumstances. By that law, the people of England were distinguished into citizens, denizens, and aliens. In Massachusetts, they were also either citizens or aliens; and he had no doubt he might safely contend that in all the States they were either citizens, aliens, or slaves. All persons born within the realm of England were citizens. All persons born in Massachusetts, of free parents, were citizens; and all persons in that State, not aliens or slaves, (and there could be none of the latter, though perhaps a fugitive slave might have been considered as an alien prior to the federal stipulations on that point,) were of consequence free citizens.

To this relationship of a free citizen to his State, protection and allegiance were the necessary incidents, and these imply, of necessity, a right to reside within the jurisdiction, and to be secure of life, liberty, and property, under the guardianship of the laws. Every citizen is held to serve the State in time of public danger and of war, and to contribute to the public burdens. He is entitled to redress when injured by a foreign Power; to be reclaimed when unjustly captured or detained; and when he brings an action for land, alienage cannot be pleaded in bar to his demand. If he possesses these rights, and stands in this relation to the State, he is a citizen. In Massachusetts, many persons of color existed in this relation to the State, and he should believe, until the contrary was shown, that the same was true in every State in the nation. To strengthen this construction, he quoted the 4th article of the first Confederation, which ordains that the "free inhabitants of each 'of these States, paupers, vagabonds, and fugitives 'from justice excepted, shall be entitled to all priv-'ileges and immunities of free citizens in the sev-'eral States," and "shall have free ingress and 'regress," &c. He also quoted, from the Journals of the Old Congress, the resolve which formed the basis of the new constitution, and which recommends the apportionment of taxes upon the numbers of "white and other free citizens," and made comments upon them, which he considered as conclusive in favor of his construction. Pursuant to these principles, it was familiar to all that persons of this description had received grants of land for serving in your army, and had been reclaimed among your impressed seamen.

Now, against these facts and plain reasoning, he was aware of but one objection adduced by gentlemen who had preceded him. These men were not citizens, it is said, in every State, because in nearly all, if not in every State, they are, or have been, made liable to certain disabilities not common to the free white citizens. All the arguments of gentlemen upon this point, however diversified, and the immensely voluminous citations from the statute books of the different States,

terminated in this one objection. It was, therefore, the soundness of this single foundation stone, and that alone, which he was called upon to examine. To this, then, his first answer was, that a class of citizens may, under certain circumstances, be subjected to particular disqualifications, without being thereby disfranchised.[*] In every country women and minors are subject to disqualifications—the former are such as are perpetual. In some, large classes are debarred from the power of electing, or being elected, to office. An unjust Government may create many odious distinctions between its privileged orders and other citizens; and a just Government, from motives of sound policy, may exclude a minor class of the community from certain civil and political rights, enjoyed by the rest, and yet leave the excluded or restricted class in the condition of citizens. The right of protection in life, liberty, and property; of residence, and of inheritable blood; of taking and transmitting, by descent, lands, and chattels, may all be unimpaired, and, while they remain so, it is impossible to say that a man ceases to be a citizen. Certainly, Republics formed upon the model of the United States will abstain from all permanent distinctions among their citizens, not founded in unavoidable necessity, or the all-controlling force of public opinion; and perhaps the case in contemplation is the only one that can ever arise to authorize or induce the annexation of perpetual disqualifications for political or civil trusts to qualities which are in themselves innocent and personal. But it might be otherwise; and if a State, by its constitution, were empowered to restrain its citizens from wearing arms or killing game, or discharging certain political or civil functions, laws made pursuant to such authority would not operate an extinguishment of the rights of the citizen, hateful and oppressive as they would be in themselves. Again, cases may be supposed to exist in which one description of citizens may have assented, either expressly or by implication, to enjoy the rights of citizenship under some limitations. And, perhaps, the consent of the colored free people who remained in our country at the epoch of our Independence, or who, being born within the United States, have since become the voluntary inhabitants of any State, in which such limitations have prevailed from time immemorial, may fairly be presumed to have acquiesced in the legality of such limitations, and to be concluded

---

[*] An act of Parliament, in the time of William III., provides, in substance, that "no person, born out of the kingdom of England, Scotland, or Ireland, or the dominions thereto belonging, although he be naturalized and made a denizen, (except such as are born of English parents,) shall be capable to be of the privy council, or a member of either House of Parliament, or to enjoy any office or place of trust, either civil or military, or to have any grant of lands, tenements, or hereditaments, from the Crown, to himself, or others in trust for him." Each State, prior to the Confederation, and subsequent to the Revolution, had the same powers, in regard to this subject, as the British Parliament.

by their own consent. Still they may be citizens. Modifications of the rights of citizenship were familiar to the laws of Rome prior to the time of Justinian; and, in fact, most of the distinctions of the privileged orders in modern Governments, when fairly examined, may be referred to the same principles, and are neither more nor less than rights of citizenship differently graduated. Believing, therefore, in the correctness of this exposition, he considered all arguments drawn from the laws of the several States, respecting free people of color, to be entirely irrelevant to the subject, unless it could be made manifest that these laws had not merely been confined to a limitation of their political or civil privileges, but had entirely annulled all that portion of them which were essential to constitute the relation of citizen. In no State, he contended, had they yet been carried to this extreme; and, while any one of them could be found, in whose jurisdiction these persons were citizens, it would follow that they could not be disentitled to become citizens in any other State. The honorable gentleman from South Carolina had occupied an entire day, principally in reading and commenting upon the laws of the respective States, from North to South, discriminating between the white and colored people, in support of his broad denial of the capacity of citizenship to the latter. However amusing and enlivening those researches might have been in the hands of that gentleman, Mr. O. was convinced they would lose their charm in his hands, and should therefore abstain from following them in detail. He persuaded himself, however, that all the inferences from these laws might be reduced to a few points, and disposed of in a few general remarks. As to one, and that by far the greater portion of the statutes cited by the honorable gentleman, they applied exclusively to paupers, vagabonds, and fugitives. Either the purview of each statute, or other statutes found in the same code, and constituting a part of one system, proved these to be the only objects of those laws, and as, in many instances, they applied to white persons equally with others, the argument built upon them proved too much.

Another portion of these statutes affected merely qualifications for electing, or being elected, to office. These also might be laid aside. By the constitution or laws of several States, the political rights of the white citizen are abridged. It is so in Massachusetts; in Virginia, where freeholders only vote; in Mississippi, where a creed (or the want of it) disqualifies a man for office, and where clergymen are not eligible to the Legislature. This species of exclusion is, therefore, no test of the character of citizen. Indeed, some of the instances mentioned by the honorable gentleman might be regarded as exemptions from burdensome duties with more propriety than as restrictions of civic privileges; and persons who are dispensed from obligations to serve in the militia, and on juries, by law, do not generally complain of their condition.

When the laws and quotations, introduced with such profusion by the honorable gentleman, were arranged with reference to these two general heads, they would leave but a small remnant for any other. He did not recollect but one case which would not fall under them, and that was the statute of Massachusetts prohibiting intermarriages between white and colored people. With respect to that law, it was proper to remark, that marriage was a civil contract regulated by the policy of every State, according to its own views of public utility, and subject to greater or less ceremonials and restraints by the sovereign authority. It would not be pretended that laws creating temporary disabilities for matrimonial alliances, requiring age, consent of parents, or forms of marrying, would impair the quality of citizenship. And if the policy of a State might justify one denomination of restrictions upon the marriage contract which did not disfranchise those who became subject to them, why could not the same policy interpose other impediments to marriage without drawing after them disfranchisement as a necessary consequence? Why was a black person disqualified as a citizen by being inhibited from marrying a white person, more than a white person was so under a reverse of the rule? There was no necessary connexion between an incapacity created by law, in one description of persons, to contract marriage with those of another description, and an incapacity of all the rights of a citizen. It was difficult to illustrate this position by supposing examples, without seeming to disparage the unfortunate persons who were the objects of the exclusion. Hardly any other probable case could be imagined, that would call for the establishment of permanent legal distinctions between classes of citizens, in the exercise of the right to form matrimonial connexions, and yet the policy of such a distinction in the state of our society, in this one instance, may be very unquestionable. The free people of color being everywhere a very small minority of individuals, under particular circumstances, are not entitled to complain of special restrictions and exclusions, which the vast majority, by high considerations connected with their ideas of sound policy, and invincible predilections for their own race, and the desire of transmitting to posterity its blood pure and unmixed, and for no other reason, may have seen fit to impose. If leprosy, or any other disease attended with a decidedly hereditary and incurable taint, were known to prevail in a State, laws might be passed to prevent marriage with the infected persons without touching any other rights. He meant, however, only to exemplify, and not to assimilate the cases—this, he repeated, being a peculiar case, and entire *sui generis*. He had thus far proceeded upon the supposition that all the statutes of the several States adduced upon the occasion, were in themselves Constitutional. But, his second answer to this objection from the State laws was, that if any of them went so far as to disfranchise all free persons of color, such laws were void in themselves. He had heard of none that did go that length. Let us next, said he, advert for a moment to the suggestion of gentlemen, that if the clause of the constitution of Missouri should be found in discordance with that of the United States, a remedy would be found in the judicial department. It was, however, the first time he had ever heard it urged as a sound or safe principle that the rights, or even the claims of any portion of the people might be abandoned by the Legislature, because the courts could do them justice. It was, indeed, curious to observe the fluctuations of opinion relative to the judicial power occasioned by the different circumstances under which it was called forth. There was now upon the table a resolution declaring null and void the sedition act, which had received the sanction of two Congresses and many judicial decisions. In this case of Missouri, however, he insisted that the judiciary could give no adequate relief. The justice here sought was not remedial but preventive—not to restore to an individual violated rights, but to place numbers beforehand in a condition to exercise them. It was to retain (so far as the expression of the opinion of Congress could do it) to all free colored citizens the right of going to Missouri, if they thought fit, and settling therein, and not to redress the injury of one or more individuals who might be driven from its limits. Congress was to settle a principle, not to try a cause—and if the principle was abandoned, no cause would ever be tried. What individual would ever be found to journey through the immeasurable wilderness, "with lingering steps and slow," and set his foot in Missouri with a certainty of being driven back, for the privilege of having recourse to the courts of the United States, at an expense entirely beyond his compass, and beyond the value of the object of his journey? And if such a person could be found, what is the situation of others who might wish to settle there while the cause is pending? It had, indeed, been often urged, that the Legislature of Missouri might enact laws to the end provided for in their constitution, even if that instrument had been silent. Certainly they might do so, but it was equally certain they might forbear thus to legislate. But, by passing this resolution, and thus giving efficacy to their constitution, you communicate to the State and to its constitution the whole power of the Union for giving effect to this policy, and compel their Legislature to pass laws which they might otherwise omit, or which, if enacted, they might afterwards repeal. The honorable gentleman from Maine had favored the Senate with an exposition of his ideas of the term citizen, as found in the Constitution, which . O. said he was not able to comprehend, but which, if he did understand it, would enable a Legislature to disfranchise all her citizens of all colors and complexions.

He would not pause to consider that doctrine, nor, indeed, to notice all the suggestions of that gentleman. There was, however, one topic unfolded by him to which he would for a moment advert. The gentleman contended that our opposition to the power of the States to exclude persons of color from settlement in their jurisdictions would operate in favor of the slaveholding States sending away their freed blacks into other States, and that the Northern States would be thus overrun with their swarms. He could not believe, however, that the North would realize their obli-

gation to the gentleman for wishing to prevent that quarter of the country from this inconvenience, by shutting up Missouri, which would leave them no other resort but the white peopled States. But further, if a colored man may become a free citizen, he cannot be sent away; and, if not a citizen, other States are not bound to receive him when he is sent away. Mr. O., however, did not admit that the mere manumission of a slave would make him a citizen. This was a very different question from any which he had considered, and it might be far from true that manumission would produce any such effect, and yet every principle advanced by him remains impregnable.

On the whole, he said, he had no ambition to be distinguished as a zealot in the cause of emancipation, or an advocate for a sudden change of condition in that unfortunate class of persons who were held in servitude. Much less was he inclined to adopt any language or measures tending to excite among them a spirit of discontent, or to wound the feelings or rouse the irritation or resentment of their owners. The evil of slavery was too profoundly rooted for him to indicate or even imagine its cure.

No circumstances led him to regret discussions affecting the people of color in the United States more than their unavoidable tendency to elicit observations which might be misunderstood, and aggravate the troubles of slavery by adding discontent and vain hopes of freedom to the number. The actual condition of slaves in the old States was not a subject for the cognizance of Congress. And until those whom it immediately concerned could make some discovery whereby the abolition of slavery could be effected, he feared that the efforts of others, however well intended, would be worse than nugatory. So far was he from wishing it to be understood by the slaves that the people of the North would hold them justified in any violent measures to attempt the attainment of freedom, he was desirous of their realizing, what he believed to be true, that all considerate persons in every section of the Union would unite with one accord with their masters in putting down every species of revolt and insurrection, as pregnant with dreadful calamities to the whole nation. This had ever been his feeling and his language. But, with these convictions, he would strenuously and for ever oppose the extension of slavery, and all measures which should subject a freeman, of whatever color, to the degradation of a slave. Believing, therefore, that every free citizen of color in the Union was joint tenant with himself in the public lands of Missouri, and of the jurisdiction possessed by the United States in that Territory until it should be elsewhere vested; and that, however humble and disadvantageous might be his sphere, he was entitled to his protection equally with those born to a happier destiny, he could not consent to an act which should divest him of his property and rights, and interdict him from even passing into a country of which he was a legitimate co-proprietor with himself.

When Mr. OTIS had concluded—

Mr. BARBOUR, of Virginia, presuming that some

other gentleman might desire to deliver his sentiments on the question, moved an adjournment; and the Senate adjourned.

MONDAY, December 11.

Mr. BARBOUR gave notice that, to-morrow, he would ask leave to bring in a bill concerning the collection of the public moneys.

Mr. PINKNEY submitted the following motion for consideration:

Resolved, That the Committee on the Judiciary be instructed to inquire into the expediency of passing a law amending or explaining the judiciary laws in such manner as to authorize, under such restrictions as may be thought proper, the prosecution of writs of error, in criminal cases, from the judgments of the highest court of judicature in a State, in which any question has arisen under the Constitution or laws of the Union, to the Supreme Court of the United States; and that the said committee report by bill or otherwise.

A message from the House of Representatives informed the Senate that the House have passed a bill, entitled "An act for the relief of Nicholas Jarrott;" a bill, entitled "An act to alter the time of holding the district court in the district of Mississippi;" and a bill, entitled "An act to amend the act entitled 'an act to alter the times of the session of the circuit and district courts in the District of Columbia;'" in which bills they request the concurrence of the Senate.

The three last bills brought up for concurrence were read, and severally passed to the second reading.

Mr. HORSEY, from the Committee on the District of Columbia, to whom was recommitted the bill to incorporate the Columbian Society for literary purposes, reported the same with an amendment.

Mr. HORSEY presented the memorial of Thomas Law and others, citizens of Washington, praying that so much of that portion of the public ground in the city of Washington, known by the name of "Reservation No. 10," as now remains to the public, may be sold on condition of improvement; and the memorial was read, and referred to the Committee on the District of Columbia.

Mr. WALKER, of Alabama, presented the memorial of the Legislature of the State of Alabama, in behalf of certain petitioners, inhabitants of that State, who are purchasers of public lands, and who, from the great diminution of the circulating medium, and the operation of the law reducing the price of the public lands, are unable to comply with the terms of their purchases, soliciting for said purchasers such relief as to Congress may seem meet; and the memorial was read, and referred to the Committee on the Public Lands.

The Senate resumed, as in Committee of the Whole, the consideration of the bill for the relief of Robert Purdy; and, on motion of Mr. LLOYD, it was ordered to lie on the table.

The Senate resumed, as in Committee of the Whole, the consideration of the bill for the relief of the officers and volunteers engaged in the late campaign against the Seminole Indians, together with the amendments reported thereto by the Committee on Military Affairs, and, having agreed to the amendments, the further consideration of the bill was postponed until to-morrow.

The Senate proceeded to consider, as in Committee of the Whole, the bill, entitled "An act to incorporate the managers of the National Vaccine Institution in the District of Columbia;" and the further consideration thereof was postponed until to-morrow.

The Senate proceeded to consider, as in Committee of the Whole, the bill to continue in force for a further time the act, entitled "An act for establishing trading-houses with the Indian tribes;" and the further consideration thereof was postponed to Thursday next.

The Senate proceeded to consider, as in Committee of the Whole, the resolution authorizing Mountjoy Bayly to employ a person to attend the furnace, and no amendment having been proposed thereto, the PRESIDENT reported it to the House, and the resolution was ordered to be engrossed and read a third time.

The Senate proceeded to consider, as in Committee of the Whole, the bill for the relief of John Holmes, and no amendment having been proposed thereto, the PRESIDENT reported it to the House, and it was ordered to be engrossed and read a third time.

The Senate proceeded to consider, as in Committee of the Whole, the bill for the relief of Morgan Brown, and no amendment having been proposed thereto, the PRESIDENT reported it to the House, and it was ordered to be engrossed and read a third time.

ADMISSION OF MISSOURI.

The Senate then resumed the consideration of the resolution declaring the assent of Congress to the admission of the State of Missouri into the Union.

Mr. EATON, of Tennessee, said, before the Senate proceeded to a final vote upon the resolution, he would ask permission again to offer the amendment which had heretofore been submitted, and rejected. This, he believed, was strictly in order. The rejection of the proviso being before the Senate, in Committee of the Whole, did not prevent it from being considered, now that the resolution was reported to the Senate. Mr. E. then offered the following amendment to the resolution:

"*Provided,* That nothing herein contained shall be so construed as to give the assent of Congress to any provision in the constitution of Missouri, if any such there be, which contravenes that clause in the Constitution of the United States which declares that "the citizens of each State shall be entitled to all privileges and immunities of citizens in the several States."

Mr. KING, of New York, said, as the amendment had already been considered, and rejected by the Senate, he regretted that it had been deemed expedient to offer it again. I object now, said Mr. K., as I have done before, to this amendment, because it declares that, in the admission of Missouri, the Senate have not considered, and do not pronounce any opinion, concerning the clause of the Missouri constitution which makes it the duty of the Legislature thereof to pass laws to exclude free negroes and mulattoes from coming to, and settling in, Missouri. This declaration ought not to be made, because it would exhibit the Senate in this singular situation, (if his construction of the constitution of Missouri was correct,) that, in passing the act of admission, the Senate omits to consider and to allow its due weight to the only provision in that Constitution upon which the obligation to admit, or not admit, Missouri depends. Mr. K. said he considered this proposition of much more importance than the mover of it appeared to do; and he was not willing to decide on it instanter at any rate.

Mr. EATON replied at some length. He said he certainly would be as unwilling as any one to press the consideration of what he had submitted, before gentlemen had fully made up their minds, and were prepared to vote. He doubted not, however, but that upon this subject all were prepared. It would be borne in mind by the Senate that this was not now an original proposition, but one that had before been considered and voted upon. When he had first the honor of submitting it, the gentleman from New York (Mr. KING) had urged his want of preparation, and on an application for postponement by himself, the postponement had been granted. Under this state of things, Mr. E. could not perceive any necessity for further procrastination, more especially when it seemed to be the wish of all to put an end, in some way, to this unpleasant question. Mr. E. said as to the constitutionality of the subject, however other gentlemen might be fully satisfied, yet with him, and with others he believed, the fact was otherwise. He was not willing either to affirm or to deny, that the constitution of Missouri was in strict conformity to the Constitution of the United States; he should have doubts were he to be required affirmatively to vote either way. But of this he did not pretend to doubt that, thus situated, thus doubting, it was his duty to lean to the side of the Constitution, and by his vote to support that instrument which he and every member had sworn to maintain inviolate. The proviso ventured an opinion neither way; it was a *protestando* in the true signification of the term—the exclusion of a conclusion—a waiver on the part of Congress to give an opinion either one way or the other. This being the object which he wished to attain, he trusted the Senate would excuse his again pressing on their consideration that which had been before acted and voted upon. Encouraged by the information that some gentlemen who had before voted against the proviso had changed their opinions, and were now disposed to vote for it, was with him the inducement for again venturing to offer it. Time had been afforded to think fully on it, and further delay he thought ought not to be requested.

Mr. BARBOUR declined engaging in the debate, not, he said, that he was unwilling to meet the question, but with a hope and under the expectation that the question would be immediately taken.

Mr. TRIMBLE, of Ohio, said it was not his wish to detain the Senate; that if he had entertained a wish to engage in the discussion, the present state of his health was such, that he could not express himself so as to be heard by the Senate, nor could he speak at all without great pain. He rose, he said, to state an objection to the constitution of Missouri, which had not been alluded to in the debate on this resolution—an objection of more force, and, in his view, involving principles more important to the interests of the nation, than the provision which had been so much discussed. The eighth article of the constitution of Missouri authorizes the establishment of a bank with a capital not to exceed five millions of dollars, at least one-half of which shall be reserved for the use of the State. Mr. T. said he considered this provision a direct and palpable violation of that part of the tenth section of the Federal Constitution, which provides that "no State shall coin money, emit bills of credit, [or] make any thing but gold and silver coin a tender in payment of debts." This important provision of the Federal Constitution, said Mr. T., was intended to guard against evils which might embarrass the Federal·Government, and prove destructive to the best interests of the people of the United States. An immaterial change in the form did not change the substance. Whether a bill of credit is signed by an auditor, a treasurer, an officer of a State, or a president of a bank created for that purpose, the evils are the same. The power to coin money, regulate the value thereof, and of foreign coin, and fix the standard of weights and measures, has been exclusively given to Congress. It was never contemplated or anticipated that these important powers should be rendered nugatory by bank machinery, put in operation either by Federal or State power. Mr. T. said it was also his opinion that banks, as established in the United States, are anti-republican institutions, which tend inevitably to aristocracy.

Mr. SMITH said he would refer the gentleman to the journals of the last session, to show that a resolution admitting Alabama into the Union had passed without opposition, and that the constitution of Alabama contained a provision for the establishment of a bank.

The Senate then divided on the amendment, and there rose in its favor twenty-three members, and it was agreed to.

The question then being on ordering the resolution to a third reading, as amended—

Mr. MORRIL, of New Hampshire, arose and thus addressed the Senate:

Mr. President: It cannot be said by the honorable Senate that I am in the practice of consuming much of their time in debate, or of frequently asking their attention to my remarks. When the honorable gentleman from Virginia, (Mr. BARBOUR,) immediately after this resolution was reported by your committee, intimated a wish that the question might·be taken *sub silentio*, I was gratified with the hope that the unpleasant subject would pass off in that way. But as several gentlemen have occupied your attention, and have presented an unexpected view of the subject, I am inclined to offer my opinion also. In doing this, I am not influenced from an anxiety to make a speech before the Senate, nor from the pride of having the event announced in the public papers simply for the perusal of my constituents. I would assure the Senate I am not stimulated either by pleasure or ambition on this occasion ; neither will my remarks arise from any peculiar hostility to the admission of Missouri into this Union, on such principles, and with such a constitution, as coincide with the provisions of the Constitution of the United States. I disclaim sinister motives and sectional partialities on this subject, and declare myself actuated by more noble and important views; and, solemnly impelled by a sense of duty I owe to my constituents and my country, I will endeavor to divest myself of preconceived opinions on the subject of slavery, and avoid any expression which may tend to revive those unpleasant sensations which so evidently prevailed in this body during the last session, and through the country, and examine the subject as involving a great Constitutional question. The inquiry is not, in this case, whether slavery shall exist or be tolerated in Missouri. I am ready to admit, for the moment, that this has been so far settled by the vote of the last session as not to come into the present debate ; but the passing of the resolution recognises a principle materially affecting the rights of other States and the privileges of their citizens. This principle, and the consequences of admitting it, will be the subject of my remarks.

Sir, I must be permitted to state that this debate is not courted by Congress; it is from imperious necessity that any are compelled to protest against the adoption of the resolution; to save the Constitution of the nation inviolate, and preserve harmony and union.

To present my view more fully on this subject, it may be useful to recur to the objects of the Confederation. These I discover, in part, in the preamble of the Constitution :

" We, the people of the United States, in order to form a more perfect union, establish justice, insure domestic tranquillity, provide for the common defence, promote the general welfare, and secure the blessings of liberty to ourselves and our posterity, do ordain and establish this Constitution for the United States of America."

" Union, justice, domestic tranquillity, common defence, general welfare, and the blessings of liberty secured to posterity," were the grand and primary objects in establishing this Constitution, under which, and for these purposes, the Government was organized. The guardianship and protection of this, the charter of our rights, is now committed to the people and their representatives in Congress. It is, then, our duty, with vigilance and a watchful eye, to mark the progress of events, and arrest, at the threshold, the unhallowed hand which may be raised to pervert its meaning, misuse its provisions, or tarnish its glory. After reflecting upon the solemn obligations which devolve upon the members of this body, to examine with solicitude the principles and provisions of the Constitution, and faithfully and impartially apply them to the ex-

isting circumstances of the country, it would not seem strange if a peculiar anxiety were manifest on their application to a case pregnant with doubts and fearful apprehensions.

Sir, the first thing when I entered this chamber, to become a member of the Senate, was, to approach your chair, and take a solemn oath to support the Constitution. This I consider more than a mere formality—an obligation by which I am bound, in my own conscience, to guard with vigilance the general and particular rights guarantied by that instrument to this privileged nation. It is not necessary to refer you to the toils and privations of past periods to show their value. A moment's reflection upon the time that Sir Walter Raleigh visited the banks of the Roanoke; Captain Smith explored the Eastern shore from Penobscot to Cape Cod, or our ancestors landed upon the Rock of Plymouth, with some of the succeeding events, will furnish the mind with evidence of the estimate we ought to put upon the Constitution, and the blessings it secures to our country. Forty years successful experience of the enjoyment of equal rights, under a free Government, demonstrate the advantages of republican institutions. But, sir, I waive all other considerations, and proceed to examine one point which attracts our attention and merits particular notice.

Is there any paragraph in the constitution of Missouri which contravenes any provision in the Constitution of the United States ? This will be a subject of inquiry.

We find in the Constitution of Missouri that, " it shall be the duty of the General Assembly, as ' soon as may be, to pass such laws as may be ne- ' cessary to prevent negroes and mulattoes from ' coming to, and settling in this State, under any ' pretext whatsoever. No comment upon this can be necessary to render its meaning perfectly intelligible.

This will lead me to inquire into the duty and power of Congress, and then recur to this provision again.

"The United States, in Congress assembled, shall ' guaranty to every State in this Union a republi- ' can form of Government, and protect each of ' them against invasion." This is necessary, to " insure domestic tranquillity, promote the gen- ' eral welfare, and secure the blessings of liberty ' to ourselves and our posterity."

It is the duty of Congress to see " that full faith ' and credit are given in each State to the public ' acts, records, and judicial proceedings of every ' other State." This is essential " to perfect the Union, establish justice," cement the bonds of harmony, and secure the rights and privileges of the existing States.

By this, a mutual friendship would be encouraged, a unity of sentiment extended, and a confidence in the whole concentrated.

Congress have power to receive new States into the Confederacy. "New States may be admitted by the Congress into this Union." In doing this, they are bound to see that the rights and privileges of the individual States are not infringed. They are not only expected to secure inviolate the rights of States, but "the privileges and immunities" of their citizens. Among these, the following is a very essential one. "The citizens of each State shall be entitled to all the privileges and immunities of citizens in the several States."

Sir, by this I understand that a citizen in any State in the Union may pass into any other State in the Union, and there enjoy "all the privileges and immunities of citizens" in the State to which he removes.

The same principle I find engrafted in the Articles of Confederation; by having recourse to that I find my exposition confirmed, and the same sentiment more fully and particularly expressed.

" The better to secure and perpetuate mutual friendship and intercourse among the *people* of the different States in this Union, the free *inhabitants* of each of these States shall be entitled to all the privileges and immunities of free *citizens* in the several States; and the people of each State shall have free ingress and regress to and from any other State, and shall enjoy therein all the privileges of trade and commerce, subject to the same duties, impositions, and restrictions, as the inhabitants thereof respectively."

The express language of this section so perfectly coincides with the opinion I have ventured to advance, that a comment could add nothing to its perspicuity. Could the term citizen need exposition, I would offer one, which, however, I could scarcely have imagined, had it not been for the novel and fallacious remarks of the honorable gentleman from Maine (Mr. Holmes.) In the foregoing extract we find the terms "inhabitants, citizens, and people," used as synonymous.

These are perfectly well understood in our community, and, I will only add, take from the inhabitants slaves and aliens, and the remainder are citizens.

Color does not come into the consideration, and it has no share in characterizing an inhabitant or a citizen. On this exposition I shall rest my argument.

I will now pass to inquire what are the provisions of the Constitution of the United States respecting the powers of the several States. These are all uniform and equal. They have certain powers, and are prohibited certain acts.

" The times, places, and manner of holding elec-
' tions for Senators and Representatives, shall be
' prescribed in each State by the Legislature there-
' of;" and, when vacancies occur, the State authority may fill them. But "no State shall enter
' into any treaty, alliance, or confederation; coin
' money, or make any thing but gold and silver
' coin a tender in payment of debts; or grant any
' title of nobility; or keep troops or ships of war
' in time of peace."

The reason is, by agreement, it is prohibited in the Constitution, and in the same manner by agreement, it is provided, that "the citizens of each State
' shall be entitled to all the privileges and immuni-
' ties of citizens in the several States;" and they
" shall have free ingress and regress to and from
' any other State, and shall enjoy therein all the
' privileges of the inhabitants thereof, subject to no
' other restriction than they respectively" endure.

As I before observed, I must now, for the purpose of comparison, recur to the provision of the constitution of Missouri, which makes it the duty of "the General Assembly to pass laws to prevent
' free negroes and mulattoes from coming to, and
' settling in, this State, under any pretext whatso-
' ever."

Believing it fully demonstrated, that free persons of color are citizens, and conceiving it equally clear that some States in the Union have citizens of this description, and that the Constitution of the United States secures to all the citizens in all the States the unmolested liberty of migrating to any State in the Union, and there to enjoy unrestrained, the "privileges and immunities" of the citizens of that State, I ask, is this restrictive clause in the constitution of Missouri compatible with the express provisions of the Constitution of the United States?

I distinctly answer the question. Sir, it is not. But, say gentlemen, "we must not examine this subject;" there may be difficulties, and there may not be. If there should be any, submit them to the Judiciary.

Sir, I do not accede to this doctrine. Congress have the power to examine, and I shall venture to exercise it. "New States may be admitted by the Congress into this Union." How? By guess, or by lot, without knowledge or reflection; or by examination and legislation? " The United States shall guaranty to every State in this Union a republican form of government." How are the republican features of the Constitution to be ascertained but by examination? It can be done neither by weight nor by measure.

I would seriously ask, for what purpose was the constitution of Missouri presented to Congress? We are led to presume, for examination and approbation, as this has been the general practice from the organization of the Government to the present time. .

If this were not the case, why did not the convention of Missouri inform Congress by letter, or its delegate, they had made a constitution, and must now be admitted into the Union? Surely this would have been a very summary and novel course, but no more exceptionable than to offer a constitution without admitting the liberty of examining it.

The condition of Vermont was materially different from that of any other State. In consequence of difficulties subsisting between her and New York, respecting territorial limits, her constitution was formed, and her government organized, some years previous to her admission into the Union. But on her application by commissioners, she was admitted by an act of Congress, approved February 18, 1791. " The State of Vermont hav-
' ing petitioned the Congress to be admitted a
' member of the United States, Be it enacted, &c.,
' That, on the 4th day of March, 1791, the said
' State, by the name and style of ' the State of
' Vermont,' shall be received and admitted into
' this Union, as a new and entire member of the
' United States of America."   . .

The district of Kentucky, being originally a part

of Virginia, applied to that Commonwealth for permission to form herself into a new State, and petitioned Congress for admission into the Union; whereupon an act passed for that purpose. "Where-
' as the Legislature of the Commonwealth of Vir-
' ginia, by an act entitled, &c., have consented that
' the district of Kentucky, &c., should be formed
' into a new State; and whereas a convention of
' delegates, &c., have petitioned Congress to con-
' sent, &c., that the said district should be formed
' into a new State, and be received into the Union,
' by the name of 'the State of Kentucky'—Be it
' enacted, &c., That the Congress doth consent
' that the said district of Kentucky, &c., shall,
' upon the first day of June, 1792, be formed into
' a new State; and, upon the aforesaid first day of
' June, 1792, the said new State, by the name and
' style of the State of Kentucky, shall be received
' and admitted into this Union, as a new and en-
' tire member of the United States of America."

Thus we see the formality which has been observed in admitting new States into the Union. In no instance has this diminished, but in all instances it has increased. We will pass the admission of all intermediate States, and come to that of Louisiana, which is directly in point. The Territory of Orleans applied for admission into the Union, and Congress passed an act authorizing them to call a convention and form a constitution, enumerating certain conditions upon which she should be received; among which were the following: "That, in case the convention shall de-
' clare its assent, in behalf of the people of the
' said territory, to the adoption of the Constitu-
' tion of the United States, and shall form a con-
' stitution and State government for the people of
' the said territory, the said convention is hereby
' required to cause to be transmitted to Congress
' the instrument by which its assent to the Con-
' stitution of the United States is thus given and
' declared; and also a true and attested copy of
' such constitution as shall be formed by said con-
' vention; and, if the same shall not be disapprov-
' ed by Congress at their next session, the said
' State shall be admitted into the Union upon the
' same footing with the original States."

Here we distinctly see that Congress required, previous to her admission, and as pre-requisites, that the convention should declare its assent to the adoption of the Constitution of the United States, and transmit the instrument of their assent to them; and, also, an attested copy of their constitution, "and, if the same should not be disapproved by Congress," they should be admitted.

With respect to Missouri the law says, Section 7, "And be it further enacted, That, in case a con-
' stitution and State government shall be formed
' for the people of the said Territory of Missouri,
' the said convention, or representatives, as soon as
' may be, shall cause a true and attested copy of
' such constitution or frame of State government,
' as shall be formed or provided, to be transmitted
' to Congress."

Here, then, we learn Congress prescribed conditions; required the constitution to be presented; reserved the privilege of examination, and the

power of approving or disapproving. For this I contend; and these remarks are made to show the propriety and reasonableness of my claim. This privilege has been claimed, and this power has been exercised by an authority no more competent than that of the present Congress.

But, say gentlemen, you must not examine into this subject, but turn it over to the judiciary.

Sir, I choose to examine for myself. This being my right, I conceive a different course needless and improper. Needless, because Congress have the power and ability. This is delegated to this department of the Government; in the first instance, by the Constitution; and Congress have no right to surrender it. "New States may be admitted by the Congress," and no other body.

It is improper, because it would perplex a certain class of proprietors. Apply this to the poor yellow man who owns land in Missouri. They pass a law prohibiting free negroes and mulattoes from settling "in the State, under any pretext whatsoever." This is in force till nullified by the judiciary, which cannot be effected without an action at law. Is he able to endure this excessive burden? Who would undertake it to get into Missouri? The barrier is equal to an armed force, extending around the whole territory of the State. It would keep any citizen in the Union out, and this was the design of it. Surely, if they were to say, (which they could with equal propriety,) that no citizen with a *gray head* should settle in Missouri, I would never make the attempt. Hence, then, this provision in the constitution of Missouri is in direct hostility to the Constitution of the United States.

This, sir, is distinctly admitted in the report of the committee of the House, to whom the constitution was referred. They say, "the committee
' are not unaware that a part of the 26th section of
' the 3d article of the constitution of Missouri, by
' which the legislature of that State has been direct-
' ed to pass laws 'to prevent free negroes and mu-
' lattoes from coming to, and settling in, the State,'
' has been construed to apply to such of that class
' as are citizens of the United States; and that
' their exclusion has been deemed repugnant to the
' Federal Constitution." Here the fact for which we contend is conceded; and, also, that there are some "of that class who are citizens of the United States." If this is not the case, why your provisos? Why submit nothing to the judiciary? Why must there be a *protestando* introduced?

Mr. President, I proceed to show the consequences of this provision.

Some States have free citizens of color. This is the case in Vermont, New Hampshire, and Massachusetts. In Vermont, there is a mulatto man by the name of Haines, who is a regular ordained minister in Rutland. He is pastor of a church and society of white people; has frequently been moderator of the Theological Association to which he belongs, and also of ecclesiastical councils convened for the ordination of ministers. In fact, his abilities, education, moral character, and standing in society, are such that he has received an honorary degree of Master of Arts from the University. But this man and his family, although of high standing in community, and possessing all the faculties of citizens, are proscribed, and, by the constitution of Missouri, are prohibited settling in the State.

In New Hampshire, there was a yellow man by the name of Cheswell, who, with his family, were respectable in point of abilities, property, and character. He held some of the first offices in the town in which he resided, was appointed justice of the peace for that county, and was perfectly competent to perform with ability all the duties of his various offices in the most prompt, accurate, and acceptable manner. But, this family are forbidden to enter and live in Missouri.

In Boston, is a mulatto man by the name of Thomas Paul, a regularly ordained Baptist Minister, pastor of a church of people of color, at whose meeting many white people attend, and who preaches by exchange or otherwise, with all the neighboring ministers of his denomination.

Sir, you not only exclude these citizens from their Constitutional "privileges and immunities," but also your soldiers of color, to whom you have given patents for land. You had a company of this description. They have fought your battles; they have defended your country; they have preserved your privileges, but have lost their own. What did you say to them on their enlistment? We will give you a monthly compensation, and at the close of the year, 160 acres of good land, on which you may settle, and, by cultivating the soil, spend your declining years in peace, and in the enjoyment of those immunities for which you have fought and bled. Now, sir, you restrict them, and will not suffer them to enjoy the fruit of their labor. Where is the public faith in this case? Did they suppose, with a patent in their hand, declaring their title to land in Missouri, with the seal of the nation and President's signature affixed thereto, it would be said to them, by any authority, you shall not possess the premises? This could never have been anticipated.

But, says the honorable gentleman from Maine, (Mr. HOLMES,) "they are perfectly secured by a saving clause in the constitution of Missouri," which must be taken in connexion with that part which prohibits their settling in the State. It must, therefore, be read: "it shall be the duty of ' the General Assembly to pass laws, to prevent free ' negroes and mulattoes from coming to and settling ' in this State, under any pretext whatsoever: ' *Provided, however,* The General Assembly shall ' never interfere with the primary disposal of the ' soil by the United States, nor with any regula- ' tion Congress may find necessary for securing ' the title in such soil to the bona fide purchasers.'' My humble opinion is, this does not reach the case. Were it to protect patentees of the Government, this would be only a part of that class of citizens who are liable to suffer. But the fact is, it will not do that. The law says, a mulatto man shall not settle in Missouri "under any pretext whatsoever." This provision says, "the Assembly shall never [interfere with the primary disposal of the soil." What has this to do with his settling in

that State? It will afford him no relief. But "the ' Assembly shall not interfere with any regulation ' Congress may find it necessary for securing the ' title in such soil to the bona fide purchasers." What security will this afford to the yellow man desirous of settling in Missouri? They will not destroy his title, but they will not permit him to come into the State. The gentleman's argument goes upon the ground, that a title and possession are the same. This I do not admit. It is a principle laid down in the books, that one person may hold the title and another the possession; and this is proved from daily experience. If this were not the case, what gives origin to a writ of ejectment? It grows out of the very circumstance that one person may hold the title and another the possession; and the title may be good, but possession cannot be obtained without an action at law. The quality of the title in this case may be inferred from the fact, that, although the yellow man may not enter and possess the premises, he can transfer his title to a white citizen, who may, without molestation, enter and enjoy the premises.

Then, on a critical examination of the Constitution, we find no relief, but are compelled to yield to the fact, that free citizens of some States are precluded the privilege of settling in Missouri; by which their rights are abridged, contrary to the provisions of the Constitution of the United States.

Mr. President, can we suffer one, even the meanest of our citizens, to be unconstitutionally deprived of his privileges? No. We are the guardians of his rights, and, in the performance of our duty, we cannot permit them to be infringed.

How was it with Mr. Meade, who was unjustly retained in prison in Spain? He was deprived of his liberties and immunities. Congress took notice of the circumstance, and that very justly. Executive interference was exercised, and his liberty was regained. This manifested a suitable regard to the rights of our citizens. When our citizens are taken and retained by the Algerines, you retake or negotiate and redeem them. In this case you make no distinction between the white man and negro—they are both redeemed with your money. When Commodore O'Brien was consul at Algiers, there were six negroes redeemed at the same price as white men; and one slave, who was restored to his owner, but not made free. When your soldiers are captured, black or white, you redeem them. It is proper that you should. These are only the infringement of other rights, than those abridged by the constitution of Missouri. The question is not what privileges may be violated, nor how many, nor to what degree, nor whether the citizen be black or white; but can we tamely suffer one State to deprive any citizen of any of his Constitutional rights and privileges?

If Missouri can do this, why not keep a standing army, enter into a treaty, coin money, and grant titles of nobility? She is a frontier State—the Indians are near; it may be very convenient to keep an army or make a treaty. The reason is, the Constitution of the United States distinctly says she shall not. And in the other case it expressly declares, "the citizens of each State shall be en-

' titled to all the privileges and immunities of the ' citizens of Missouri; and they shall have as free ' ingress and regress as her own citizens now ' have." This is the only consistent construction that can be given to the Constitution of the United States, and the only safe principle which can be adopted to secure the provisions of the Constitution from infraction, and the rights and privileges of the citizens of the several States from the most destructive violation. Admit the contrary principle, and each State becomes a monarchy, or is transformed to despotism. Our dearest privileges are wrested from our hands; and those very rights by which our national union, domestic tranquillity, and general welfare are secured, are forever annihilated. If you can proscribe one class of citizens, you may another. Color no more comes into consideration to decide who is a citizen than size or profession. You may as well say a tall citizen shall not settle in Missouri, as a yellow citizen shall not. If one State can do this all may. The consequence will be, that size, profession, age, shape, color, or any disgusting quality in a citizen, would be a sufficient reason why he should be precluded settling in any State, which, from its pride, caprice, or vanity, are disposed to keep him out. Sir, under such a state of things, where are our liberties and privileges? They are fled. They are absorbed in the caprice of a State. Where is your "free ingress and regress from State to State?" Your national existence is lost; the Union is destroyed; the objects of confederation annihilated, and your political fabric demolished.

Sir, I have endeavored to point out the objects of the American confederacy; the duty and power of Congress; the duty, power, and privileges of States; who are citizens of some States, and the rights of our citizens, and the provisions of the Constitution of the United States, by which those rights are secured, and the provisions of the constitution of Missouri; and have come to this irresistible conclusion, that the Constitution of the United States secures to the citizens of all the States in the Union, "the privileges and immunities of the citizens" of each State in the Union; but Missouri, in her constitution, precludes certain citizens, in certain States, the "privileges and immunities" of her own citizens; therefore, the constitution of Missouri contravenes the express provisions of the Constitution of the United States. For these reasons I vote against the resolution.

Sir, a few more words, and I close my argument. I regret that I feel compelled to offer an opinion of the complexion of this business. I lament that it has the appearance of defiance. I have endeavored to put the most favorable construction possible upon it, and it amounts to a challenge. Oppose us if you dare! I am driven to this result from knowledge and reflection. On examining this constitution, I am sure it was not penned by uninformed men. Aside from a few exceptionable parts, it is one of the best constitutions I have ever seen. The Convention were not unapprized of the feelings excited last session. The particular exceptionable clause was not in the original draught. They were informed by their honorable Delegate, and one of the gentlemen who appears here as a Senator, that this paragraph would be objectionable. But it is here, not inadvertently nor from necessity. If they had intended to pass a law similar to that directed by this paragraph in the constitution, they could have done it without this provision.

Mr. President: Before I take my seat, I must be permitted to make a few strictures upon some remarks which fell from the honorable gentleman from South Carolina, (Mr. SMITH.) He observed that "negroes and mulattoes are not citizens of the United States." It is not my intention to consume your time to demonstrate the contrary of this; because it would not, in the least degree, vary the subject. Our inquiry is, and it is the point which settles the question, are they citizens of any particular State? This point I have proved, and on the other hand it is admitted; and if they are citizens of any one State in the Union, this is enough for our purpose. I would ask my friend, what *is* the man in his country who is neither a *slave* nor an *alien*? In mine he is a citizen. The gentleman argued largely to show "that slavery was tolerated in Republics." He need not have gone to Rome, Greece, nor Sparta, to have proved this; it is evident from our daily observation, and, of course, admitted. But what is this to the point in debate? What has this to do with the question whether Missouri has a Constitutional right to prohibit free citizens from settling in her Territory? Does it follow, because slavery is tolerated in Republics, therefore Missouri may proscribe free citizens? This reasoning is neither conclusive nor convincing.

The gentleman says: "Missouri is now a State to all intents and purposes." This is not admitted. What has made her a State? What is the language of your resolution? Not that she now *is*, but that she *shall be*, a State, when this resolution is passed by both Houses, and approved by the President.

"Be it resolved, &c., that the State of Missouri ' *shall be*, and is hereby declared to be, one of the ' United States of America." But, were it true that she is a State, there is nothing gained by it. Vermont was a State a long time before she was received into the Union. The question is, shall Missouri be admitted with a constitution which conflicts with the Constitution of the United States?

My friend argues, "we are bound by the Treaty of Cession to receive her." Admit this. But in that treaty there are terms and conditions. "The ' inhabitants of the ceded territory shall be incor- ' porated in the Union of the United States, and ' admitted as soon as possible, according to the ' principles of the Federal Constitution." Hence, in her admission, the principles of the Federal Constitution must be observed and maintained inviolate. This was the ground on which Louisiana was received, and Missouri being a part of the same purchase, she must be admitted on the same principles, and in the same way, and no other.

But the gentleman says, " States were admitted

without presenting their constitution." This may have been the case. Circumstances have been different, especially with Vermont; and the manner of this transaction less formal and correct than at the present time. Because another State has been received, which did not present her constitution, does it follow that Congress must not examine the constitution of Missouri? It matters not in this case what has been done; the constitution is here presented to Congress. "But you have no power to control a constitution." For what purpose, then, is it sent here. To lie on our table? Congress had power to control the constitution of Louisiana. Have they less power than they then had? In this case they said to the Convention, send a true and attested copy of your constitution here, and if the same shall not be disapproved by Congress at their next session, the said State shall be admitted into the Union. This is all the power for which we contend; and this is a privilege which Congress has had, and still has, a right to exercise.

"Louisiana, Ohio, and other States, declare how persons coming into them shall obtain a residence." This we readily admit; and against such regulation have no objection. But does it follow, because certain States prescribe conditions on which emigrants shall gain a residence, therefore Missouri has a Constitutional right to prohibit the citizens of other States from settling in her territory? Really I do not see the force of the argument.

"States have made a distinction between white people and blacks." This is very true; so they have between white people. South Carolina has distinguished that gentleman in giving him a seat here, and that very justly; and he has nobly distinguished himself. And what is this to the point? "But in the Eastern States, they whip black people—not only once and twice, but ten times, and every ten days." This may be true; and equally true, that they whip white people when they violate their laws; and continue to whip, black or white, as long as they continue to violate wholesome laws; and I suspect will persevere in the practice until they reform or emigrate to South Carolina, where they may receive better treatment. Does this prove any thing with respect to the constitutional power of Missouri?

But, says the gentleman, "New Hampshire excludes negroes from training." This is very true; and so they excuse many white people. This only places them among the exempts; generally, the first class in society. And from this very circumstance, they have the privilege of walking about with the other gentlemen and seeing the soldiers train. It neither deprives them or any other person of citizenship or any other privilege.

Blacks, then, are not degraded in New Hampshire. Custom has made a distinction between them and other men; but the Constitution and laws make none.

Mr. President, a few words in reply to what has fallen from the gentleman from Maine, (Mr. HOLMES,) and I shall have done. He observed, purchasers under the United States are not re-

stricted. To maintain this position, he took occasion to explain the Constitution of the United States, and that of Missouri, the incorrectness of which will more fully appear in his after remarks, in the application of the principle. As my former argument had a particular allusion to these opinions, any further refutation is unnecessary.

This gentleman says, "the doctrine that free blacks have a right to enter free States, is dangerous." I am a little surprised to hear a gentleman of so much acuteness in disquisition upon Constitutional law, calculating upon consequences which have no immediate connexion with the subject. He might as well argue, that a commercial enterprise to the Euxine sea, would be detrimental to Massachusetts, and therefore Missouri must keep all free citizens of color out of her territory, as to argue that if free blacks may enter any free State, Maine will be infested with them; and therefore, Missouri must prohibit their settling in that State.

"A State may exclude any person." Here we are at issue. I by no means admit the doctrine. Any State may regulate the terms upon which emigrants shall become residents; but no State has any right to exclude them. To utterly prohibit, and regulate by law the terms of inhabitancy, are materially and essentially different; and one within the municipal power of every State, the other expressly prohibited by the Constitution of the United States.

But, says the gentleman, "the Constitution *means,* when they get *in,* they shall have privileges, but they may be kept *out.*" This is a little curious, for a gentleman learned in the law. Then, if a person were to ascend in an air balloon, at a small distance from the line of Missouri, and safely land within her territory, the constitution secures to him "privileges and immunities;" but it makes no provision for his crossing the line by *land.* Under this exposition, where is the "free ingress and regress" of the citizens of each State guarantied by the Constitution? Sir, your constitution is like a nose of wax. Your liberties and privileges are a bubble. Your union, domestic tranquillity, and prospect of common defence, are prostrated to the ground. But, says the gentleman, this doctrine is certainly correct, and to test his principle, he adds, "send a mulatto man here, should *we* not feel our rights invaded? This has no connexion with the question. It is possible some gentleman might feel his rights invaded. But I would inquire, in my turn, *what* rights are invaded? And I would seriously ask the Senate, if any State in the Union were duly to elect a yellow man Constitutionally qualified, commission and send him here with his credentials, you can exclude him a seat? You have a right to decide on the qualifications of your members; but color is no more a qualification than height, profession, or nation. The gentleman observes, "a mulatto, though a citizen in one State, going into Missouri, has no other rights than a mulatto has in Missouri." Here we are at issue again. This doctrine I flatly deny. The salubrious air and fertile soil of Missouri can never metamorphose a free citizen into a slave;

neither can the constitution and law of Missouri do it. Were the proposition true, then a black or yellow free citizen of Maine, going into Virginia, would be a slave. As I before intimated, it is *citizen* only, and *not* color, that comes into consideration, in deciding this question.

But the gentleman, in a very *affecting* tone, enlists all our sympathies, in view of the consequences of rejecting this unconstitutional instrument from Missouri. For these, sir, I conceive Congress is not accountable; and, therefore, such imaginary phantoms are not proper subjects of discussion, nor suitable beacons to direct our course. Missouri was permitted, under a law of Congress, to form a constitution, "republican, and not repugnant to the Constitution of the United States," and "transmit an attested copy of such constitution to Congress." It was expected she would perform this in good faith. If she has utterly failed—formed and presented a constitution repugnant to the Constitution of the United States, and unpleasant consequences result, the fault is her own. There can be no provision in the constitution of Missouri inadvertently introduced; of course, all the consequences rest upon Missouri. These, however, are not to come into our consideration; the Constitution of the United States alone is to direct our course.

But the gentleman discovers another difficulty, in case this constitution is rejected: he is unable to determine in what condition Missouri will be, whether Territory, or State, or neither. With respect to this, sir, I have only to observe, if that gentleman cannot divine, I presume it is within the scope of Congress, and merely that circumstance would not convince me the object is unattainable.

I would also add, that every difficulty of this kind which could possibly have arisen might have been avoided by precautions similar to those observed by Maine. She, in the first place, petitioned the Legislature of Massachusetts for leave to form a constitution and independent State. This was granted. She then formed her constitution, and fixed her election for State officers after the probable time of the adjournment of the then next session of Congress. She presented her constitution for the approbation of Congress and admission into the Union. This was done. After she became, by an act of Congress, a State in the Union, she elected her officers, and organized her government. If Missouri had pursued the same moderate and consistent course, there could have been no possible difficulty with respect to her character or condition.

Mr. President, these being my views of the subject, I close my remarks, after presenting my thanks to the honorable Senate for the great candor and attention with which they have indulged me while I have occupied their time.

Mr. MACON followed the above speech with a motion to recommit the resolution to the select committee which reported it, with instructions to strike out the proviso adopted to-day on the motion of Mr. EATON. Mr. M. had no doubt whatever of the propriety of the naked resolution as

reported, and was opposed to the proviso; he therefore proposed this mode of getting rid of it.

The question on recommitting the resolution was decided in the negative, by yeas and nays, as follows:

YEAS—Messrs. Burrill, Dickerson, King of New York, Lanman, Lowrie, Macon, Mills, Morril, Noble, Palmer, Roberts, Ruggles, Sanford, Smith, Tichenor, Williams of Tennessee, and Wilson—17.

NAYS—Messrs. Barbour, Brown, Chandler, Dana, Eaton, Edwards, Elliott, Gaillard, Holmes of Maine, Holmes of Mississippi, Horsey, Hunter, Johnson of Kentucky, Johnson of Louisiana, King of Alabama, Lloyd, Parrott, Pinkney, Pleasants, Talbot, Taylor, Thomas, Trimble, Van Dyke, Walker of Alabama, Walker of Georgia, and Williams of Mississippi—27.

The question was then taken on ordering the resolution, as amended, to be engrossed and read a third time, and was decided in the affirmative, by yeas and nays, as follows:

YEAS—Messrs. Barbour, Brown, Chandler, Eaton, Edwards, Elliott, Gaillard, Holmes of Maine, Holmes of Mississippi, Horsey, Johnson of Kentucky, Johnson of Louisiana, King of Alabama, Lloyd, Parrott, Pinkney, Pleasants, Smith, Talbot, Taylor, Thomas, Van Dyke, Walker of Alabama, Walker of Georgia, Williams of Mississippi, and Williams of Tennessee—26.

NAYS—Messrs. Burrill, Dana, Dickerson, Hunter, King of New York, Lanman, Lowrie, Macon, Mills, Morril, Noble, Palmer, Roberts, Ruggles, Sanford, Tichenor, Trimble, and Wilson—18.

TUESDAY, December 12.

Mr. THOMAS presented the memorial of the register of the land office and receiver of public moneys at Shawneetown, praying compensation for extra services rendered in the execution of the act "granting the right of pre-emption in the purchase of lands to certain settlers in the Illinois Territory," and of the acts concerning Shawneetown; and the memorial was read, and referred to the Committee on Public Lands.

Mr. TRIMBLE presented four memorials, signed by a number of individuals concerned directly or indirectly as purchasers of public lands prior to the law "making further provision for the sale of the public lands," stating that said law operates injuriously on them, and praying that they may be permitted to apply the payments already made to such portions of their entries as such payments will cover at two dollars per acre, and that the residue may revert to the United States; and the memorials were read, and severally referred to the Committee on Public Lands.

Mr. NOBLE presented two memorials, signed by a number of individuals, of the same import and object as the preceding; which were read, and severally referred to the last mentioned committee.

On motion by Mr. WILLIAMS, of Tennessee, that the Committee on Military Affairs, to whom was referred the petition of Rebecca Hodgson, be discharged from the further consideration thereof; the said motion was ordered to lie on the table.

The Senate proceeded to consider the motion of yesterday, to inquire into the expediency of amending the judiciary laws in relation to writs of error in criminal cases; and agreed thereto.

The bill from the House of Representatives, entitled "An act for the relief of Nicholas Jarrott," was read the second time, and referred to the Committee on Public Lands.

The bill from the House of Representatives, entitled "An act to alter the time of holding the district court in the district of Mississippi," was read the second time, and referred to the Committee on the Judiciary.

The bill from the House of Representatives, entitled "An act to amend the act, entitled 'An act to alter the times of the session of the circuit and district courts of the District of Columbia," was read the second time, and referred to the Committee on the District of Columbia.

The Senate resumed, as in Committee of the Whole, the consideration of the bill for the relief of the officers and volunteers engaged in the late campaign against the Seminole Indians, and no further amendment having been proposed thereto, the President reported it to the House amended; and the bill was ordered to be engrossed and read a third time.

The Senate resumed, as in Committee of the Whole, the consideration of the bill, entitled "An act to incorporate the managers of the National Vaccine Institution in the District of Columbia;" and the consideration thereof was further postponed until to-morrow.

The Senate resumed, as in Committee of the Whole, the consideration of the bill to incorporate the Columbian Society for literary purposes; and, on motion, by Mr. JOHNSON of Kentucky, it was laid on the table.

The resolution authorizing Mountjoy Bayly to employ a person to attend the furnace, was read the third time, and passed.

The bill for the relief of John Holmes, was read the third time, and passed.

The bill for the relief of Morgan Brown, was read the third time, and passed.

ELECTORAL VOTES.

Mr. WILSON, of New Jersey, submitted the following resolution:

Resolved, That the Committee on the Judiciary be instructed to inquire whether any, and, if any, what provisions are necessary or proper to be made by law to meet contingencies which may arise from unlawful, disputed, or doubtful votes under that part of the 12th article of amendments to the Constitution of the United States, which relates to counting the votes of the Electors for the President and Vice President of the United States.

Mr. WILSON said, it would be found, on referring to the article in the Constitution alluded to in this resolution, that the provision in relation to counting the votes for President and Vice President is very general. The words are, " the Presi- 'dent of the Senate shall, in presence of the Sen- 'ate and House of Representatives, open all the 'certificates, and the votes shall then be counted." It is not said who shall count the votes, nor who shall decide what votes shall be counted. In con-

sequence of this defect, as the Senate would well remember, some difficulty occurred four years ago, in relation to the votes from Indiana. Objections were made to receiving these votes; the counting was interrupted; the two Houses separated; and although on that occasion they again came together, and proceeded on, and completed the business before them, so happy a result might not always be produced. Cases might occur where stronger doubts might exist, or more excitement prevail; debates be protracted, and decisions deferred, and serious inconveniences or evils follow. Was it not probable such a case would occur during the present session? Would it not at least be prudent to guard against danger from such a contingency? Congress has unquestionably the power, under the last clause of the 8th section of the first article of the Constitution, and he thought they ought to exercise it, by vesting the authority to decide upon doubtful, disputed, or unlawful votes, either in the President of the Senate, the Senate itself, the House of Representatives, or in the two Houses, conjointly or separately. At least, Mr. W. deemed the subject of sufficient importance to justify the inquiry proposed in the resolution which he had submitted.

Mr. WILSON submitted also the following resolution:

Resolved, That the Committee on the Judiciary be instructed to inquire whether any, and, if any, what amendments are necessary and proper to be made to the act, entitled "An act relative to the election of a President and Vice President of the United States, and declaring the officer who shall act as President, in case of vacancies in the offices both of the President and Vice President," passed March 1, 1792.

Both resolutions lie on the table one day of course.

ADMISSION OF MISSOURI.

The resolution declaring the consent of Congress to the admission of the State of Missouri into the Union was read a third time, and the question stated " Shall the resolution pass ?"

Mr. TRIMBLE observed, in reference to some remarks between himself and Mr. SMITH yesterday, that he had not voted for the admission of Alabama, because he could not reconcile the provision in relation to banks, (with all the checks and guards which had been introduced into the constitution of Alabama on that subject,) with the Federal Constitution. In relation to that provision he had entertained doubts which were at the time expressed to some of his friends. Mr. T. said it was true that he had not made a formal opposition to the admission of Alabama, because he had just taken his seat in the Senate, and was unaccustomed to legislative proceedings; nor did he then suppose that it was so important that he should record his name, in opposition to the measures which he thought violated the spirit and true meaning of the Federal Constitution. But, had the gentleman, said Mr. T., no other defence to set up for that article of the constitution of Missouri? If, said he, the Federal Constitution has been violated, in one instance, is that any reason that it should be violated in another? Can precedent sanctify a violation of the Constitution which we are sworn to support?

The question being then put, the resolution was passed and sent to the House of Representatives for concurrence.

WEDNESDAY, December 13.

Mr. RUGGLES presented the petition of Philander Chase, President of Worthington College, in the State of Ohio, praying a donation in land for the use of said college; and the memorial was read, and referred to the Committee on Public Lands.

The following Message was received from the PRESIDENT OF THE UNITED STATES:

To the Senate of the United States:

In compliance with a resolution of the Senate of the 6th of December, requesting that the agent employed under the act, entitled "An act authorizing the purchase of fire engines and building houses for the safe keeping of the same," should report in the manner stated in the said resolution his conduct in execution of the said act, I now transmit to the Senate a report from the agent, which communicates all the information which has been desired.

JAMES MONROE.

DECEMBER 12, 1820.

The Message and report were read, and referred to a select committee, to consider and report thereon; and Messrs. MORRIL, ROBERTS, and LANMAN, were appointed the committee.

Mr. NOBLE presented the petition of George Love, only son of Thomas Love, deceased, praying compensation for certain services rendered by his father in the Revolutionary war; and the petition was read, and referred to the Committee of Claims.

Mr. ROBERTS presented the petition of Julia Plantou, of the city of Philadelphia, representing that she has designed and executed an allegorical painting of the Treaty of Ghent, which she solicits Congress to purchase; and the petition was read, and referred to the Committee on the Public Buildings.

Mr. ROBERTS presented the memorial of Jane Baker, widow of Thomas Baker, late a Post Captain in the Navy, praying that the pension which was granted to her husband may be continued to her; and the memorial was read, and referred to the Committee on Naval Affairs.

Mr. TRIMBLE presented the petition of George Jackson, of Ohio, praying compensation for the use of a wagon and team, and for four horses which were lost in the service of the United States during the late war; and the petition was read and referred to the Committee of Claims.

Mr. LLOYD presented a petition, signed by a number of the citizens of Georgetown, remonstrating against the passage of the bill from the House of Representatives, entitled "An act to amend the act, entitled 'An act to alter the times of the session of the circuit and district courts in the District of Columbia;'" and the petition was read, and referred to the Committee on the District of Columbia.

Mr. HOLMES, of Mississippi, communicated a letter to him from the Superintendent of Indian Trade, enclosing a copy of his report in relation to Indian trade; and the letter and report were read.

Mr. JOHNSON, of Louisiana, gave notice, that to-morrow he should ask leave to bring in a bill for the relief of the legal representatives of Gabriel Berzat, deceased.

The bill for the relief of the officers and volunteers engaged in the late campaign against the Seminole Indians, was read a third time, and passed.

The Senate resumed, as in Committee of the Whole, the consideration of the bill to incorporate the Columbian Society for literary purposes, together with the amendment last reported thereto by the Committee on the District of Columbia; and the said amendment having been amended, the further consideration of the bill and amendment was postponed to Monday next.

The Senate proceeded to consider the motion of yesterday, instructing the Committee on the Judiciary to inquire if any provisions are necessary to be made by law to meet contingencies, which may arise from unlawful, disputed, or doubtful votes, under that part of the twelfth article of amendments to the Constitution, which relates to counting the votes of the Electors for President and Vice President; and agreed thereto.

The Senate proceeded to consider the motion of yesterday, instructing the Committee on the Judiciary to inquire what amendments are necessary to be made to the act "relative to the election of President and Vice President, and declaring the officer who shall act as President in case of vacancies in the offices both of President and Vice President;" and agreed thereto.

The resolutions reported by Mr. BARBOUR, from the select committee to which was referred the petition of Matthew Lyon relative to the late sedition law and the fines and penalties incurred under it, were, on motion of Mr. SMITH of South Carolina, with the consent of Mr. BARBOUR, postponed to the 1st of January.

THURSDAY, December 14.

Mr. THOMAS presented the memorial of E. B. Clemson, praying compensation for certain services rendered in the commissary's department, and in other stations in the Army, and also remuneration for certain expenses incurred therein; and the memorial was read, and referred to the Committee of Claims.

Mr. WILSON presented the petition of Thomas L. Ogden of New York, on behalf of himself and others, owners of certain real estate at Sackett's Harbor, in the State of New York, which, during the late war with Great Britain, was used for public purposes, praying compensation and indemnity therefor; and the petition was read, and referred to the Committee of Claims.

Mr. WILSON, from the Committee of Claims, to whom was referred the bill, entitled "An act for the relief of Elias Parks," reported it with an amendment; which was read.

Mr. WILSON, from the same committee, to whom was referred the memorial of Eliza Hill, Jane Jervis, and Louisa St. Clair Robb, daughters of the late General St. Clair, made a report, accompanied by a resolution, that the prayer of the petitioners ought not to be granted. The report and resolution were read.

Mr. WILSON, from the same committee, to whom was referred the petition of Charles Larabee, made a report, accompanied by a resolution, that the petitioner have leave to withdraw his papers. The report and resolution were read.

Mr. VAN DYKE presented the memorial of the President and Directors of the Chesapeake and Delaware Canal Company, praying the aid of the Government; and the memorial was read, and referred to the Committee on Roads and Canals.

Mr. JOHNSON, of Louisiana, obtained leave to bring in a bill for the relief of the legal representatives of Gabriel Berzat, deceased; and the bill was twice read by unanimous consent, and referred to the Committee on Public Lands.

Mr. LANMAN, from the Committee on the District of Columbia, to whom was referred the bill, entitled "An act to amend the act, entitled 'An act to alter the times of the session of the circuit and district courts in the District of Columbia;'" reported the same without amendment.

The Senate resumed, as in Committee of the Whole, the consideration of the bill, entitled "An act to incorporate the Managers of the National Vaccine Institution in the District of Columbia;" and the further consideration thereof was postponed to Tuesday next.

The Senate resumed, as in Committee of the Whole, the consideration of the bill to continue in force, for a further time, the act, entitled "An act for establishing trading-houses with the Indian tribes;" and the further consideration thereof was postponed to Tuesday next.

Mr. TRIMBLE gave notice that, on Monday next, he should ask leave to bring in a bill to organize a Law Department.

Mr. NOBLE submitted the following motion for consideration:

Resolved, That the Committee on Public Lands be instructed to inquire into the expediency of authorizing the sale, and to reduce the price of certain sections of land, heretofore reserved for the future disposal of Congress, situate and being within that part of the Cincinnati district which lies in Indiana.

On motion by Mr. KING, of New York, to reconsider the vote of the 12th instant, on the resolution authorizing the Sergeant-at-Arms of the Senate to employ a person to attend the furnace. The said motion was laid on the table.

The Senate adjourned to Monday.

MONDAY, December 18.

Mr. HOLMES, of Maine, presented the petition of Samuel Tucker, praying compensation for services rendered as a captain in the Navy, prior to the adoption of the Federal Constitution; and the petition was read, and referred to the Committee on Naval Affairs.

Mr. SANFORD presented the petition of Jacob Barker, of New York, praying the interposition of Congress in the settlement of his accounts, under his contracts of the 2d of May, 1814, with the Secretary of the Treasury, for a portion of the ten million loan, being part of the twenty-five millions authorized by the act of the 24th of March, 1814; and the petition was read, and referred to the Committee of Claims.

Mr. HOLMES, of Mississippi, presented the petition of Horatio Stark, of Mississippi, praying that, in consideration of long military services, the right of entry of one thousand acres of land in Mississippi, which may become forfeited for non-payment by those who made the original entries, may be granted to him at the present or former price; and the petition was read, and referred to the Committee on Military Affairs.

Mr. ELLIOTT presented the memorial of the Savannah Poor House and Hospital Society, praying that the proper officer of the Government may be authorized to take, in behalf of the United States, an interest of one-half in the buildings erected by them for the accommodation of sick and disabled seamen; and the memorial was read, and referred to the Committee on Commerce and Manufactures.

Mr. PLEASANTS presented the petition of the delegates of the United Agricultural Societies of Prince George, Sussex, Surry, Petersburg, Brunswick, Dinwiddie, and Isle of Wight, in Virginia, protesting against any increase of the duties at present imposed on imported goods; and the petition was read, and referred to the Committee on Commerce and Manufactures.

Mr. SANFORD, from the Committee on Finance, to whom was referred the bill, entitled "An act for the relief of Perley Keys and Jason Fairbanks," reported it with an amendment; which was read.

Mr. WILSON, from the Committee on Claims, to whom was referred the petition of George Love, made a report, accompanied by a resolution, that the prayer of the petitioner ought not to be granted. The report and resolution were read.

Mr. NOBLE, from the Committee on Pensions, to whom was referred the petition of Park Avery, made a report, accompanied by a resolution, that the prayer of the petitioner ought not to be granted. The report and resolution were read.

The Senate resumed the consideration of the motion of the 16th of November, to amend the act allowing compensation to the members of Congress, so as to reduce the per diem to six dollars; and it was further postponed until to-morrow.

The Senate proceeded to consider the motion of the 14th instant, instructing the Committee on Public Lands to inquire into the expediency of authorizing the sale, and to reduce the price of certain sections of land, and agreed thereto.

The Senate proceeded to consider the report of the Committee of Claims, to whom was referred the petition of Charles Larabee; and the further consideration thereof was postponed to Wednesday next.

The Senate proceeded to consider the report of

the Committee of Claims, to whom was referred the memorial of Eliza Dill, Jane Jervis, and Louisa St. Clair Robb, daughters of the late General Arthur St. Clair; and in conformity therewith resolved, that the prayer of the petitioners ought not to be granted.

The Senate resumed, as in Committee of the Whole, the consideration of the bill to incorporate the Columbia Society for literary purposes, together with the amendment last reported thereto by the Committee on the District of Columbia; and the consideration thereof was further postponed until to-morrow.

The Senate proceeded to consider, as in Committee of the Whole, the bill, entitled "An act for the relief of Elias Parks," together with the amendment reported thereto by the Committee of Claims; and, having agreed to the amendment, the President reported it to the House amended accordingly; and the amendment being concurred in, it was ordered to be engrossed, and the bill read a third time as amended.

The Senate resumed, as in Committee of the Whole, the consideration of the bill, entitled "An act to amend the act, entitled 'An act to alter the times of the session of the circuit and district courts in the District of Columbia;'" and the consideration thereof was postponed to Wednesday next.

A message from the House of Representatives announced to the Senate the death of NATHANIEL HAZARD, late a member of the House of Representatives from the State of Rhode Island and Providence Plantations, and that his funeral will take place this day at two o'clock.

On motion of Mr. HUNTER, it was

Resolved, unanimously, That the Senate will attend the funeral of Nathaniel Hazard, late a member of the House of Representatives from the State of Rhode Island and Providence Plantations, this day at two o'clock; and as a testimony of respect for the memory of the deceased, they will go into mourning, and wear a black crape round the left arm for thirty days.

TUESDAY, December 19.

Mr. WILSON presented the petition of Elisha Gordon, of New Jersey, legal representative of Patience Gordon, deceased, praying payment of a loan office certificate issued to the said Patience in her life time, by the loan officer of New Jersey, and which is now lost; and the petition was read, and referred to the Committee of Claims.

Mr. WILSON, from the Committee of Claims, to whom was referred the petition of Thomas L. Ogden, in behalf of himself and others, reported a bill for the relief of Thomas L. Ogden and others; which was read, and passed to a second reading.

Mr. DICKERSON, from the Joint Library Committee, made a report; which was read.

Mr. JOHNSON, of Louisiana, submitted the following motions for consideration:

Resolved, That the Committee on Public Lands be instructed to inquire into the expediency of confirming to the inhabitants of the counties of Attakapas, Opelousas, and Avoyelles, in the State of Louisiana, their claim to the common use of all cypress and cypress swamps within the limits of those counties.

Resolved, That the Committee on the Public Lands be instructed to inquire into the causes which have occasioned the delay in surveying the public lands and private claims within the State of Louisiana, and into the expediency of modifying existing laws on that subject, so as to facilitate the surveying of those lands.

Resolved, That the same Committee inquire into the expediency of making, by law, such provision as may be deemed essential, to cause patents to be issued for all private land claims within the State of Louisiana, which have been legally confirmed; and into the expediency of making further provision for compensating the principal deputy surveyors of Louisiana, for the services required of them.

Mr. THOMAS, from the Committee on Public Lands, to whom was referred the bill for the relief of the legal representatives of Gabriel Berzat, deceased, reported it without amendment.

A message from the House of Representatives informed the Senate that the House have passed the bill, entitled "An act for the relief of Margaret Perry," and the bill, entitled "An act for the relief of William McIntosh;" in which bills they request the concurrence of the Senate.

The two bills last brought up for concurrence were read, and severally passed to a second reading.

The amendment to the bill entitled "An act for the relief of Elias Parks," having been engrossed, the bill was read the third time as amended, and passed.

CONGRESSIONAL COMPENSATION.

The Senate, agreeably to the order of the day, proceeded to the consideration of the following resolution, introduced by Mr. BURRILL, of Rhode Island, on the 16th ultimo:

Resolved, That the act entitled "An act allowing compensation to the members of the Senate, members of the House of Representatives of the United States, and to the delegates of the Territories, and repealing all other laws on the subject," passed at the first session of the fifteenth Congress, ought to be so altered and amended that the compensation to the members and delegates aforesaid shall hereafter be six dollars for each day's attendance, and six dollars for every twenty miles' travel, instead of the compensation now allowed by said act; and that it be referred to a committee, to prepare and report a bill for altering and amending said act accordingly.

Upon the merits of the proposition, and of the several motions made in the course of its consideration, a spirited, good tempered, and interesting debate took place, occupying more than three hours. The following embraces a statement simply of the proceedings and of the names of those gentlemen who took part therein:

The resolution was supported by Messrs. BURRILL and ROBERTS, and was opposed by Messrs. JOHNSON, of Kentucky, and DANA; and Mr. J. concluded his remarks by moving to postpone the resolution to the second Monday of January next.

The postponement was supported by the mover, and was opposed by Messrs. MACON, DANA, and

BURRILL; and negatived by yeas and nays: For the postponement 16; against it 20.

Mr. MORRIL moved to postpone the resolution to Monday next, for reasons which he stated; and it was opposed by Mr. WILSON. The motion was negatived, without a division.

Mr. DANA moved to amend the resolution by striking out all after the word *Resolved*, and inserting the following substitute:

" That a committee be appointed to inquire into the propriety of reducing the allowances authorized by the act entitled ' An act allowing compensation to the members of the Senate, the members of the House of Representatives of the United States and to the delegates of the Territories, and repealing all other laws on the subject,' with the allowances to the officers of the respective Houses of Congress; and also reducing the allowances made by law to the principal and other officers in each of the Executive Departments; and that the committee have leave to report by bill or otherwise."

Mr. ROBERTS required a division of the question; and it being accordingly first taken on striking out, it was determined in the affirmative—ayes 23.

Considerable debate followed on the relative merits of this amendment and the original resolution, in which the amendment was advocated by Messrs. DANA, JOHNSON, of Kentucky, and CHANDLER, and was opposed by Messrs. BURRILL and ROBERTS; in the course of which

Mr. BURRILL moved to strike out of the amendment so much as relates to the salaries of the executive officers, wishing to encumber, and therefore endanger, the main object as little as possible.

The motion, after considerable discussion, was decided in the negative, as follows:

YEAS—Messrs. Burrill, Dickerson, Eaton, Hunter, Johnson of Louisiana, King of New York, Lowrie, Roberts, Ruggles, Sanford, Smith, Thomas, and Wilson—14.

NAYS—Messrs. Chandler, Dana, Edwards, Elliott, Gaillard, Holmes of Maine, Holmes of Mississippi, Johnson of Kentucky, King of Alabama, Macon, Morril, Noble, Palmer, Parrott, Pleasants, Talbot, Taylor, Tichenor, Trimble, Walker of Alabama, Walker of Georgia, and Williams of Tennessee—22.

The question being taken on the amendment of Mr. DANA, it was agreed to; and the resolution, as amended, was then agreed to by the following vote:

YEAS—Messrs. Burrill, Chandler, Dana, Dickerson, Edwards, Elliott, Gaillard, Holmes of Maine, Holmes of Mississippi, Hunter, Johnson of Kentucky, Johnson of Louisiana, Lowrie, Macon, Morril, Noble, Palmer, Parrott, Pleasants, Roberts, Ruggles, Sanford, Smith, Talbot, Taylor, Thomas, Tichenor, Trimble, Walker of Alabama, Walker of Georgia, and Williams of Tennessee—32.

NAYS—Messrs. Eaton, King of Alabama, King of New York, and Mills—4.

Messrs. DANA, BURRILL, JOHNSON, of Kentucky, ROBERTS, and SMITH were appointed the committee; and the Senate adjourned.

WEDNESDAY, December 20.

Mr. JOHNSON, of Kentucky, presented the petition of William Pancoast, representing that, in consequence of there being no land office in the District of Columbia for that purpose, he is unable to obtain a right to certain vacant lands discovered by him within said District in the year 1799, and praying relief; and the petition was read, and referred to the Committee on the Judiciary.

Mr. JOHNSON, of Louisiana, presented the memorial of Thomas Shields, a purser in the Navy, praying remuneration for certain losses sustained by him whilst in the New Orleans station, in the Winter of 1814 and 1815; and the memorial was read, and referred to the Committee on Naval Affairs.

Mr. NOBLE presented four memorials, signed by a number of individuals, concerned directly or indirectly as purchasers of public lands prior to the law " making provision for the sale of the public lands," stating that said law operates injuriously upon them, and praying that they may be permitted to apply the payments already made, to such portions of their entries as such payments will cover at two dollars per acre, and that the residue may revert to the United States; and the memorials were read, and referred to the Committee on Public Lands.

The PRESIDENT communicated a report of the Secretary of War, made in obedience to a resolution of the Senate of the 30th of November, on the petition of Eleanor Lawrence; which was read, and referred to the Committee on Military Affairs.

Mr. ROBERTS, from the Committee of Claims, to whom was referred the petition of Presley Kemper, made a report, accompanied by the following resolution:

Resolved, That the prayer of the petitioner ought not to be granted.

The report and resolution were read.

Mr. HOLMES, of Mississippi, from the Committee on Indian Affairs, to whom the subject was referred, reported a bill for the better regulation of the trade with the Indian tribes; and the bill was read, and passed to a second reading.

Mr. TRIMBLE, from the Committee on Roads and Canals, to whom was referred the bill to authorize the appointment of commissioners to lay out a canal in the State of Ohio, reported it without amendment.

Mr. HOLMES, of Maine, submitted the following motion for consideration:

Resolved, That the Committee of Finance be instructed to inquire what diminutions and alterations may be made in the compensations to officers of the customs.

Mr. WILLIAMS, of Tennessee, from the Committee on Military Affairs, made an unfavorable report on the petition of Horatio Stark, late an officer in the Army, praying to be allowed to enter one thousand acres of public land at the minimum price, in consideration of his military services from 1801 to 1815, when he was disbanded without receiving more advance than officers of younger standing.

The Senate took up the bill to amend the act for the relief of the legal representatives of Henry Willis.

Mr. KING, of Alabama, offered some amendments, intended to secure more completely the reservations made by the United States of public lands, from the location intended by the act to be allowed to the persons concerned; when, on motion of Mr. EATON, the bill was recommitted to the Committee on the Public Lands.

BANK OF THE UNITED STATES.

Mr. SANFORD, from the Committee on Finance, to which was referred the petition of the President and Directors of the Bank of the United States, reported the following bill, which received the first reading:

Be it enacted, &c., That it shall be lawful for the Directors of the Bank of the United States to appoint an agent and a register; and that all bills and notes of the said corporation, issued after the first appointment of such agent and register, shall be signed by the agent, and countersigned by the register; that such bills and notes shall have the like force and effect as the bills and notes of the said corporation which are now signed by the president, and countersigned by the cashier, thereof; and that, as often as an agent or a register of the said corporation shall be appointed, no note or bill, signed by an agent, or countersigned by a register, shall be issued, until public notice of the appointment of such agent or register shall have been previously given, for ten days, in two gazettes printed at the City of Washington.

SEC. 2. *And be it further enacted,* That if any president, director, cashier, or other officer or servant of the Bank of the United States, or of any of its offices, shall fraudulently convert to his own use any money, bill, note, security for money, evidence of debt, or other effects whatever, belonging to the said bank, such person shall, upon due conviction, be punished by imprisonment, not exceeding three years, and by standing in a pillory not more than three times in open day, in some public place, during one hour at a time; which standing in a pillory, when inflicted more than once, shall be on different days.

THURSDAY, December 21.

MONTFORT STOKES, from the State of North Carolina, attended.

Mr. EATON, from the Committee on Public Lands, to whom was recommitted the bill, entitled "An act to amend the act entitled 'An act for the relief of the legal representatives of Henry Willis," reported the same with amendments, which were read, and taken up as in Committee of the Whole; and having been agreed to, the bill was reported to the House, amended accordingly; and the amendments having been concurred in, they were ordered to be engrossed, and the bill be read a third time as amended.

A message from the House of Representatives announced to the Senate the death of JESSE SLOCUMB, late a member of the House of Representatives from the State of North Carolina, and that his funeral will take place this day at 3 o'clock.

On motion, by Mr. MACON, it was

Resolved, unanimously, That the Senate will attend the funeral of Jesse Slocumb, late a member of the House of Representatives from the State of North Carolina, this day at three o'clock; and, as a testimony of respect for the memory of the deceased, they will go into mourning, and wear a black crape round the left arm for thirty days.

FRIDAY, December 22.

Mr. PLEASANTS presented the memorial of the Roanoke Agricultural Society, praying that no additional duties may be imposed on imported goods; and the memorial was read, and referred to the Committee on Commerce and Manufactures.

Mr. CHANDLER presented the petition of Nathan McWarren, praying to be allowed pay for the time he was detained as a prisoner by the enemy in the late war; and the petition was read, and referred to the Committee of Claims.

Mr. WILLIAMS, of Tennessee, from the Committee on Military Affairs, to whom was referred the petition of Eleanor Lawrence, and the report of the Secretary of War thereon, reported the following resolution:

Resolved, That the claim of the petitioner ought to be liquidated and paid by the War Department, and for that purpose no act of Congress is necessary.

The resolution was read, and concurred in.

Mr. MORRIL submitted the following motion for consideration:

Resolved, That the Committee of Pensions be directed to inquire into the expediency of so amending the law regulating pensions, that the heirs of non-commissioned officers and soldiers in the Army of the United States, who have deceased while in actual service, since the close of the last war, or who may hereafter decease while in actual service, shall be entitled to receive five years half pay, under such regulations as the Secretary of War may prescribe.

Mr. LOWRIE, from the Committee on Public Lands, to whom was referred the petition of Daniel W. Coxe, made a report, accompanied by a bill confirming the title of the Marquis de Maison Rouge; and the report and bill were read, and the bill passed to a second reading.

The Senate proceeded to consider the report of the Committee of Claims, on the petition of George Love, and, in concurrence therewith, resolved that the prayer of the petitioner ought not to be granted.

The Senate proceeded to consider the report of the Committee on Pensions, on the petition of Park Avery; and, in concurrence therewith, resolved, that the prayer of the petitioner ought not to be granted.

The Senate proceeded to consider the report of the Committee on Military Affairs, on the petition of Horatio Stark; and, in concurrence therewith, resolved, that the prayer of the petitioner ought not to be granted.

The Senate proceeded to consider the report of the Committee of Claims on the petition of Presly Kemper; and the further consideration thereof was postponed to Tuesday next.

The Senate proceeded to consider the motion of the 19th instant, instructing the Committee on Public Lands to inquire into the expediency of confirming to certain inhabitants of Louisiana the use of the cypress and the cypress swamps; and agreed thereto.

The Senate proceeded to consider the motion of the 19th instant, instructing the Committee on Public Lands to inquire into the causes of the delay in surveying the public and private land claims, and into the expediency of modifying the existing laws on that subject, so as to facilitate the surveying of those lands in Louisiana; and the consideration thereof was postponed until to-morrow.

The Senate proceeded to consider the motion of the 19th instant, instructing the Committee on Public Lands to inquire what provisions are necessary to cause patents to be issued for all confirmed private land claims, and what further provision is necessary for compensating the principal deputy surveyors in Louisiana, and agreed thereto.

The Senate proceeded to consider the motion of the 20th instant, instructing the Committee on Finance to inquire what diminutions or alterations may be made in the compensation to officers of the customs; and agreed thereto.

The bill to amend the act, entitled "An act to incorporate the subscribers to the Bank of the United States," was read the second time and referred to the Committee on Finances.

The bill for the relief of Thomas L. Ogden and others was read the second time.

The bill, entitled "An act for the relief of Margaret Perry," was read the second time, and referred to the Committee on Public Lands.

The bill, entitled "An act for the relief of William McIntosh," was read the second time, and referred to the Committee on Public Lands.

The bill for the better regulation of the trade with the Indian tribes was read the second time.

The amendments to the bill, entitled "An act to amend the act, entitled 'An act for the relief of the legal representatives of Henry Willis,'" having been reported by the committee correctly engrossed, the bill was read the third time as amended, and passed.

The bill from the other House, to amend the act to alter the terms of the circuit court of Washington county, in the District of Columbia, (to intermit the December term thereof, in consequence of the new arrangement of the terms,) was taken up.

Some debate took place on this bill; in which Mr. LANMAN stated the facts coming within the knowledge of the committee to which the bill had been referred. Mr. ROBERTS opposed, and Messrs. OTIS, HOLMES, and DANA favored the bill. After an unsuccessful motion by Mr. ROBERTS, to postpone the bill indefinitely, it was ordered to a third reading by a large majority.

Mr. LANMAN moved that the bill be read a third time to-day, inasmuch as the term to be suspended would commence on Monday next, and the bill therefore would be ineffectual unless passed promptly.

Mr. ROBERTS objected to this motion, and it was therefore negatived, the rules of the Senate

requiring an unanimous consent to a third reading to-day.

A motion was made to adjourn to Tuesday, but it was negatived, (with the view, it was understood, of meeting to-morrow, for the purpose of passing the bill just under consideration;) and then the Senate adjourned until to-morrow.

SATURDAY, December 23.

Mr. WILLIAMS, of Tennessee presented the memorial of the Senate and House of Representatives of the State of Missouri, in behalf of the purchasers of public lands in Missouri, praying that a law may pass authorizing all persons who have purchased a quarter section or more of land to apply the payments made to any one or more sections, quarter or half-quarter sections, so as to complete the payments for said sections or parts of sections, and to release the purchasers from the remainder; and the memorial was read, and referred to the Committee on Public Lands.

Mr. SANFORD presented the petition of Jacob Barker, of the city of New York, praying that the existing differences with the Treasury Department, in relation to his contract for a portion of the loan of 1814, may be referred to the Supreme Court; and the petition was read, and referred to the Committee of Claims.

Mr. JOHNSON, of Louisiana, gave notice that, on Tuesday next, he should ask leave to bring in a bill for the relief of John Hoffman.

The Senate resumed the consideration of the motion of the 19th instant instructing the Committee on Public Lands to inquire into the causes of the delay in surveying the public and private land claims, and into the expediency of modifying the existing laws on that subject, so as to facilitate the surveying of those lands in Louisiana, and it was amended and agreed to as follows:

Resolved, That the Committee on Public Lands be instructed to inquire into the expediency of modifying the existing laws in relation to the surveying of the public lands and private claims within the State of Louisiana, so as to facilitate the surveying of those lands.

The bill, entitled "An act to amend the act, entitled 'An act to alter the times of the session of the circuit and district courts in the District of Columbia," was read the third time and passed.

The Senate adjourned to Tuesday next.

TUESDAY, December 26.

DEATH OF MR. BURRILL.

The Journal of Saturday having been read—

Mr. HUNTER, of Rhode Island, rose, and, with much emotion, said, he had to perform a melancholy, and, to him, truly distressing duty. His friend and worthy colleague, the Honorable JAMES BURRILL, Jr., had departed this life about ten o'clock last night, and it devolved upon him to announce the painful event to the Senate.

Mr. DANA, of Connecticut, said, the serious loss which had just been announced must be extremely felt by the Senate, and he could not doubt its disposition to manifest every regard for the memory of the deceased, and every respect towards his remains. He therefore offered the following resolution:

Resolved, That a committee be appointed to take order for superintending the funeral of the Honorable James Burrill, Jr., and that the Senate will attend the same; and that notice of the event be given to the House of Representatives.

The resolution was unanimously adopted, and Messrs. MACON, DANA, CHANDLER, HOLMES, of Maine, and PARROTT, were appointed the committee accordingly.

On the further motion of Mr. DANA, it was—

Resolved, unanimously, That the members of the Senate, from a sincere desire of showing every mark of respect due to the memory of the Honorable James Burrill, Jr., deceased, late a member thereof, will go into mourning for him one month, by the usual mode of wearing crape round the left arm.

On motion of Mr. DANA, it was—

Resolved, unanimously, That, as an additional mark of respect for the memory of the Hon. James Burrill, Jr., the Senate do now adjourn.

And the Senate adjourned accordingly, to one o'clock to-morrow.

WEDNESDAY, December 27.

On motion, by Mr. HUNTER—

Resolved, That the President of the Senate be requested to notify the Executive of the State of Rhode Island and Providence Plantations, of the death of James Burrill, Jr., late a Senator of the United States from that State.

THURSDAY, December 28.

Mr. SANFORD presented the memorial of the Mayor, Aldermen, and Commonalty of the city of New York, praying that the land ceded by them in the year 1808, to the United States, for the purpose of erecting military works thereon, may revert to the Corporation, and that the said works may be removed at the expense of the United States; and the memorial was read, and referred to the Secretary of War.

Mr. WILLIAMS, of Tennessee, presented the petition of John W. McGirk, of Missouri, praying to be allowed the right of pre-emption to certain public lands; and the petition was read, and referred to the Committee on Public Lands.

Mr. RUGGLES presented two memorials signed by a number of individuals concerned directly or indirectly as purchasers of public lands prior to the law "making further provision for the sale of the public lands," stating that said law operates injuriously on them, and praying that they may be permitted to apply the payments already made to such portions of their entries as such payments will cover at two dollars per acre, and that the residue may revert to the United States; and the memorials were read, and referred to the Committee on Public Lands.

Mr. THOMAS presented a memorial signed by a number of individuals, of the same import and

object as the preceding; which was read, and referred to the Committee on Public Lands.

Mr. JOHNSON, of Louisiana, presented the memorial of Paul Lanusse, and F. Bailly Blanchard, merchants of the city of New Orleans, praying that a law may pass granting to them the benefit of drawback on certain merchandise exported by them in 1819, which is withheld from them in consequence of their having neglected to take the "export oath," within the prescribed time; and the memorial was read, and referred to the Committee on Finance.

Mr. SMITH presented the petition of William Smith, junior, of Charleston, praying to be released from the payment of the interest accrued on a debt due the United States by N. Ingraham and Son, late navy agents at Charleston, and for which he is responsible as one of their sureties; and the petition was read, and referred to the Committee on Finance.

Mr. JOHNSON, of Kentucky, presented a petition signed by certain inhabitants of Kentucky, holders of land warrants to be located in the Virginia military district in the State of Ohio, praying an extension of the time for locating said warrants; and the petition was read, and laid on the table.

Mr. WALKER, of Alabama, presented the petition of Thomas H. Boyles, praying that a law may be passed directing a patent to be issued to him for certain lands; and the petition was read, and referred to the Committee on Public Lands.

Mr. HOLMES, of Mississippi, presented the petition of William Doak, keeper of a public house on the road through the Indian nations between Natchez and the State of Tennessee, praying that the right of pre-emption may be granted to him for a tract of land of one mile square so as to include his improvements; and the petition was read, and referred to the Committee on Public Lands.

Mr. WALKER, of Alabama, presented the memorial of the Mayor and Aldermen of the city of Mobile, praying the grant of certain public grounds therein for the use of the Corporation; and the memorial was read and referred to the Committee on Public Lands.

Mr. PLEASANTS, from the Committee on Naval Affairs, to whom was referred the memorial of Thomas Shields, made a report, accompanied by a bill authorizing the payment of a sum of money to Thomas Shields; and the report and bill were read, and the bill passed to a second reading.

Mr. JOHNSON, of Louisiana, obtained leave to bring in a bill for the relief of John Hoffman; which was read, and passed to a second reading.

Mr. WALKER, of Alabama, gave notice, that, to-morrow, he should ask leave to bring in a bill for the relief of John Coffee.

Mr. JOHNSON, of Kentucky, submitted the following motion for consideration:

Resolved, That the Committee on Public Lands be instructed to inquire into the expediency of providing by law a map to be annexed to the patent of each soldier, designating the survey in which his portion is located, provided the same shall not cost the Government more than twenty-five cents per map.

The Senate proceeded to consider the motion of the 22d instant, directing the Committee on Pensions to inquire into the expediency of granting to the heirs of non-commissioned officers and soldiers, who have deceased while in actual service, five years half pay; and disagreed thereto.

The Senate resumed the consideration of the report of the Committee of Claims on the petition of Presley Kemper; and the consideration thereof was further postponed until to-morrow.

The bill confirming the title of the Marquis de Maison Rouge was read the second time.

The Senate resumed, in Committee of the Whole, the consideration of the bill to incorporate the Columbian Society for literary purposes, together with the amendment last reported thereto by the Committee on the District of Columbia; and the consideration thereof was further postponed to Tuesday next.

The Senate proceeded to consider, as in Committee of the Whole, the bill, entitled "An act for the relief of Perley Keyes and Jason Fairbanks," together with the amendment reported thereto by the Committee of Finance, and the said amendment having been agreed to, the bill was reported to the House amended accordingly; and the amendment having been concurred in, was ordered to be engrossed, and the bill read a third time as amended.

The Senate resumed, as in Committee of the Whole, the consideration of the bill, entitled "An act to incorporate the managers of the National Vaccine Institution in the District of Columbia;" and the consideration thereof was postponed to Wednesday next.

PUBLIC LANDS.

Mr THOMAS, from the Committee on Public Lands, to whom the subject was referred, reported a bill for the relief of the purchasers of public lands prior to the first day of July, 1820; which was read, and passed to a second reading.

The bill is as follows:

Be it enacted, &c., That, in all cases where lands have been purchased from the United States prior to the 1st day of July, 1820, it shall be lawful for any such purchaser, on or before the —— day of ——, 1821, to file with the register of the land office where any tract of land has been purchased, a relinquishment in writing, of any legal subdivision of the land so purchased, upon which the whole purchase money has not been paid; and all sums paid on account of the part relinquished shall be applied to the discharge of any instalments which may be, or shall hereafter become due and payable upon such part of land so purchased, as shall not have been relinquished under the foregoing provision: *Provided,* That the right of relinquishment hereby given shall in no case be exercised so as to require any repayment from the United States.

Sec. 2. *And be it further enacted,* That in all cases where the payment of the whole sum due from the purchaser of any tract of land from the United States, aforesaid, shall be made on or before the —— day of ——, eighteen hundred and twenty-one, a deduction at the rate of —— per cent. shall be allowed upon such payments.

Sec. 3. *And be it further enacted,* That all sums due, or which may hereafter become due, to the United States, on account of any purchase of public land, heretofore made, after the —— day of ——, eighteen hundred and twenty-one, may be discharged by —— equal annual instalments, which shall be paid on or before the day and month in each successive year, upon which the several purchases were made: *Provided,* That any purchaser of public land, who shall accept of the foregoing condition, shall, on or before the —— day of ——, eighteen hundred and twenty-one, file, with the register of the land office where any tract of land has been purchased, subject to the said condition, a written declaration of his acceptance of the terms therein prescribed: *And provided, also,* That if any purchaser of public land who shall have filed such declaration, shall fail to make the payments required in this section, in conformity with the provisions thereof, he shall be subject to all the conditions of the original contract and purchase; and if such failure shall occur after the time within which the whole purchase money should have been paid to the United States, the tract or tracts of land upon which the instalments aforesaid shall not have been paid, shall be deemed and held to be forfeited to the United States, and the same proceedings shall be had that are prescribed by the existing laws in relation to lands forfeited to the United States.

Sec. 4. *And be it further enacted,* That any purchaser of public land as aforesaid, who shall comply with the conditions prescribed by either of the foregoing sections of this act, shall not be liable to pay any interest which shall have accrued to the United States on the purchase of any tract of public land, but the same, in all such cases, shall be, and is hereby declared to be, remitted.

FRIDAY, December 29.

A message from the House of Representatives informed the Senate that the House of Representatives have passed a bill, entitled "An act for the relief of Daniel McDuff;" and, also, a bill entitled "An act to authorize the President of the United States to establish a port of entry in the district of Sandusky, in the State of Ohio, and for other purposes;" in which bills they request the concurrence of the Senate.

The two bills last brought up for concurrence were read, and severally passed to a second reading.

Mr. OTIS presented the petition of Alexander Gardner, of Massachusetts, praying an increase of his pension; and the petition was read, and referred to the Committee on Pensions.

Mr. MILLS presented the memorial of sundry officers of the Revolutionary army, praying that the half pay granted by a resolve of the Revolutionary Congress to the officers and soldiers of that army may be continued to them during life; and the memorial was read, and referred to the Committee on Pensions.

Mr. TRIMBLE presented three memorials signed by a number of individuals concerned directly or indirectly as purchasers of public lands prior to the law "making further provision for the sale of the public lands," stating that said law operates injuriously on them, and praying that they may be permitted to apply the payments already made to such portions of their entries as such payments will cover at two dollars per acre, and that the residue may revert to the United States; and the memorials were read, and laid on the table.

Mr. THOMAS, from the Committee on Public Lands, to whom was referred the petition of the Trustees of the Worthington College, in the State of Ohio, made a report, accompanied by a resolution, that the prayer of the petitioners ought not to be granted. The report and resolution were read.

Mr. THOMAS, from the same committee, to whom was referred the bill, entitled "An act for the relief of Nicholas Jarrott," reported it with amendments; which were read.

Mr. WALKER, of Alabama, asked and obtained leave to bring in a bill for the relief of John Coffee; and the bill was read, and passed to a second reading.

Mr. ROBERTS, from the Committee of Claims, to whom was referred the petition of Joseph Janney, made a report accompanied by a resolution, that the prayer of the petitioner ought not to be granted. The report and resolution were read.

Mr. VAN DYKE gave notice that, on Tuesday next, he should ask leave to bring in a bill to establish an uniform system of bankruptcy throughout the United States.

The Senate resumed the consideration of the report of the Committee of Claims, on the petition of Presley Kemper, and, in concurrence therewith, resolved that the prayer of the petitioner ought not to be granted.

The bill authorizing the payment of a sum of money to Thomas Shields, was read the second time.

The bill for the relief of the purchasers of public lands prior to the first day of July, 1820, was read the second time.

The bill for the relief of John Hoffman was read the second time, and referred to the Committee of Claims.

The amendment to the bill, entitled "An act for the relief of Perley Keyes and Jason Fairbanks," having been engrossed, the bill was read the third time as amended, and passed.

On motion by Mr. ROBERTS, the Senate proceeded to consider the motion of the 14th instant to reconsider the vote of the 12th instant, on the resolution authorizing the Sergeant-at-Arms to employ a person to attend the furnace, and agreed thereto; and, on motion by Mr. CHANDLER, the resolution was laid on the table.

The Senate adjourned to Tuesday.

TUESDAY, January 2, 1821.

Mr. EATON presented the petition of Nicholas Perkins, of Tennessee, praying to be confirmed in his title to a tract of land in Alabama; and the petition was read, and referred to the Committee on Public Lands.

Mr. WILLIAMS, of Tennessee, presented the petition of Richard G. Waterhouse, of Tennessee, praying to be compensated for a quantity of wood consumed by a brigade of militia that encamped on his land in December, 1814; and the petition was read, and referred to the Committee of Claims.

Mr. TRIMBLE presented a petition signed by a number of individuals concerned directly or indirectly as purchasers of public lands prior to the law "making further provision for the sale of the public lands," stating that said law operates injuriously on them, and praying that they may be permitted to apply the payments already made to such portions of their entries as such payments will cover at two dollars per acre, and that the residue may revert to the United States; and the petition was read, and laid on the table.

Mr. JOHNSON, of Louisiana, presented the memorial of John B. Chatard, of New Orleans, praying a pension for Revolutionary services; and the memorial was read, and referred to the Committee on Pensions.

Mr. HOLMES, of Mississippi, presented the petition of the Choctaw nation of Indians, praying that Silas Dinsmoor, late Indian agent to the said nation, may be confirmed in his title to a tract of land granted to him by them; and the petition was read, and referred to the Committee on Public Lands.

Mr. WILLIAMS, of Tennessee, from the Committee on Military Affairs, to whom was referred the petition of Joseph Wheaton, made a report, accompanied by a resolution, that the prayer of the petitioner ought to be rejected. The report and resolution were read.

The Senate proceeded to consider the report of the Committee of Claims on the petition of Joseph Janney; and the further consideration thereof was postponed to Friday next.

The Senate resumed the consideration of the report of the select committee on the petition of Matthew Lyon; and the consideration thereof was further postponed to Monday the 15th instant.

The bill for the relief of John Coffee was read the second time, and referred to the Committee on Public Lands.

The bill, entitled "An act for the relief of Daniel McDuff," was read the second time, and referred to the Committee of Claims.

The bill, entitled "An act to authorize the President of the United States to establish a port of entry in the district of Sandusky, in the State of Ohio, and for other purposes," was read the second time, and referred to the Committee on Commerce and Manufactures.

The Senate resumed, as in Committee of the Whole, the consideration of the bill to continue in force, for a further time, the act, entitled "An act for establishing trading-houses with the Indian tribes;" and, on motion by Mr. TRIMBLE, it was postponed to, and made the order of the day for, Thursday next.

The bill for the relief of the representatives of Gabriel Berzat, and the bill for the relief of Thomas L. Ogden and others, were severally considered and passed to a third reading.

The Senate proceeded to consider, as in Committee of the Whole, the bill to authorize the appointment of commissioners to lay out a canal in the State of Ohio; and it was postponed to, and made the order of the day for, Friday next.

The Senate proceeded to consider, as in Committee of the Whole, the bill for the better regulation of the trade with the Indian tribes; and, on motion by Mr. HOLMES of Mississippi, it was laid on the table.

The Senate proceeded to consider, as in Committee of the Whole, the bill confirming the title of the Marquis de Maison Rouge, and it was postponed until to-morrow.

The Senate proceeded to consider, as in Committee of the Whole, the bill for the relief of the purchasers of public lands prior to the first day of July, 1820, and it was postponed until to-morrow.

The Senate proceeded to consider, as in Committee of the Whole, the bill authorizing the payment of a sum of money to Thomas Shields, and it was postponed to Thursday next.

The Senate proceeded to consider, as in Committee of the Whole, the bill, entitled "An act for the relief of Nicholas Jarrott," together with the amendments reported thereto by the Committee on Public Lands, and it was postponed to Monday next.

The Senate resumed, as in Committee of the Whole, the consideration of the bill to incorporate the Columbian Society for literary purposes, together with the amendment last reported thereto by the Committee on the District of Columbia, and it was postponed to, and made the order of the day for, to-morrow.

Mr. VAN DYKE, agreeably to notice, and having obtained leave, introduced a bill to establish an uniform system of bankruptcy. [This bill embraces only the bankrupt principle, and, with some modifications, not affecting its main principle, is the same as the original bill before the Senate at the last session.] The bill passed to a second reading.

The Senate proceeded to supply the place of the late Mr. Burrill, in the Judiciary Committee, and Mr. MILLS, of Massachusetts, was appointed.

The resolution submitted some days ago by Mr. JOHNSON, of Kentucky, directing an inquiry into the expediency of providing, by law, that a map be annexed to the land patent of each soldier, designating the survey in which his portion is located, was taken up, and, after some discussion, was agreed to.

MISSOURI.

Mr. WILLIAMS, of Tennessee, submitted the following resolution for consideration:

Resolved, That the Committee on the Judiciary be instructed to report a bill extending the judicial authority of the United States over the State of Missouri.

The resolution having been read—

Mr. WILLIAMS said it was highly important that the judicial authority of the United States should be extended over Missouri, with the least possible delay. The Territorial courts no longer existed in that Territory, having been superseded by the courts of the State. The State courts had no jurisdiction of offences committed against the United States. Several Indian tribes, said Mr. W., live within the limits of Missouri; our treaty stipulations, and the laws regulating intercourse with the Indian tribes, prohibit intrusion on their territory, and subject the intruders to criminal prosecution. This is an offence of almost daily occurrence, and none but a federal court can try such offences. If, in the Indian country, a white man should kill a red one, the federal court alone can take cognizance of the offence. In answer to such a complaint, it would be but a poor apology to say we had provided no court to try the cause. The Indians would not understand this excuse, and it would lead to retaliation, and perhaps to an Indian war. It is essential, therefore, said Mr. W., to enable us to execute in good faith our engagements with the aborigines of the country, that federal courts should be organized in Missouri. We have other and perhaps more important interests in that country, which alone can be protected by the extension of the judicial authority of the Union. If, said he, the mail should be robbed, or the public funds purloined, the offender at this moment would go without punishment, although there was abundant proof to establish his guilt. Nay, if treason should be committed, the traitors would escape with impunity, for the want of a court to take cognizance of such crimes. In whatever point of view this subject is considered, said Mr. W., it is important that no time should be lost in establishing the federal authority in that State.

The resolution, by the rules of the Senate, lies on the table one day, of course.

WORTHINGTON COLLEGE.

The Senate took up the report of the Committee of Public Lands unfavorable to the petition of the trustees of Worthington College, in Ohio, who pray for a grant of the public lands in their vicinity for the benefit of the college.

Mr. RUGGLES said, as he had been charged with the care of the petition of the trustees of Worthington College, he could not consent to let the report of the committee pass without making some opposition to it. He regretted that the committee had not taken a different view of the subject, and recommended a resolution favorable to the prayer of the petitioners. Mr. R. said he did not propose now to go at large into the subject, but he would state succinctly to the Senate the grounds upon which he meant to rely in opposing this report, and conclude with a motion to postpone the further consideration of the report until Friday. The Committee on Public Lands, in their report, had recapitulated the reasons and arguments used in the petition, which is some evidence that they do not consider them without foundation. Mr. R. said he did not understand the committee as making a decision directly against the claim of the petitioners; the report merely states "that the 'committee have not been able to discover any 'thing in this case which gives the petitioners 'any stronger claim to the bounty of Government 'than other respectable seminaries of learning." If there was an objection to designating any particular seminary, Mr. R. said, he would not object to have the resolution so modified as to have the grant made to the State, for the use of such institutions as the Legislature thereof might think proper to apply it to. Mr. R. said, as it might possibly be contended that the State of Ohio has had her share of the public lands for the purposes of education, he would state the facts as they existed. No grant of any townships of land has been made to the State of Ohio since the adoption of the Federal Constitution. All the other States which have been admitted into the Union have received two townships. Under the old Confederation, Congress made a private contract with the Ohio Company for the sale of a tract of land in the Northwestern Territory; and, as an inducement for said company to comply with their propositions, Congress offered number sixteen in each township, for the support of schools, number twenty-nine for the purposes of religion, and two townships of land for the support of a college, which was to be established in the centre of the tract. The resolutions of Congress, the contract made under them, and the deed of conveyance which grants the two townships for the use of the company and their associates, all go to show that it was a mere private transaction, and that it was not intended for the State at large. The contract with John Cleves Symmes rests upon the same principles, and must receive the same construction. It therefore appears that Ohio has never received, as a State, the same advantages in this respect as the other new States which have been admitted into the Union. Mr. R. said he would say no more at present, but move that the further consideration of the report be postponed until Friday next.

Mr. R.'s motion was agreed to, and the report postponed accordingly.

WEDNESDAY, January 3.

The PRESIDENT communicated a letter from the Secretary of War, transmitting a copy of the Army Register for each member of the Senate, conformably to a resolution of the 13th December, 1815; and the letter was read.

Mr. THOMAS presented the memorial of the House of Representatives of the State of Missouri, praying that the right of pre-emption may be granted to the settlers on the public lands within said State, who have made improvements thereon; and the memorial was read, and referred to the Committee on Public Lands.

Mr. SANFORD presented the petition of Matthew McNair, praying to be compensated for a boat impressed into the service of the United States by Robert Swartwout, Quartermaster General, and lost; and the petition was read, and referred to the Committee of Claims.

Mr. SANFORD presented the petition of Robert Swartwout, of New York, praying to be indemnified against a judgment obtained against him for the loss of a boat impressed by him into the public service, whilst acting as quartermaster general of the northern army, in the year 1813; and the petition was read, and referred to the Committee on Military Affairs.

Mr. PLEASANTS presented the petition of Thomas Oxley, now of Virginia, by birth a foreigner, and not entitled to citizenship, praying to be enabled, by a special law, to take out letters patent for certain useful inventions; and the petition was read, and referred to the Committee on the Judiciary.

Mr. ROBERTS presented the petition of H. Catlett, a post surgeon in the Army, praying compensation for a negro boy who was drowned in June, 1814, whilst ascending the Ohio with the United States troops; and the petition was read, and referred to the Committee of Claims.

Mr. HOLMES, of Maine, presented the petition of E. Cousens, and others, praying compensation for Revolutionary services; and the petition was read, and referred to the Committee on Pensions.

Mr. HOLMES, of Mississippi, from the Committee on Indian Affairs, to whom the subject was referred, reported a bill to authorize the appointment of certain Indian agents; and the bill was read, and passed to a second reading.

Mr. ROBERTS, from the Committee of Claims, to whom was referred the petition of James Leander Cathcart, reported a bill explanatory of the act for the relief of James Leander Cathcart, passed May the fifteenth, in the year 1820; and the bill was read, and passed to a second reading.

The Senate proceeded to consider the motion of yesterday, instructing the Committee on the Judiciary to extend the judicial authority of the United States over the State of Missouri; and it was postponed to, and made the order of the day for, Monday next.

The Senate proceeded to consider the report of the Committee on Military Affairs, to whom was referred the petition of Joseph Wheaton; and in concurrence therewith resolved, that the prayer of the petition ought to be rejected.

The bill for the relief of the legal representatives of Gabriel Berzat, deceased, was read the third time, and passed.

Resolved, That this bill pass, and that the title thereof be, "An act for the relief of the legal representatives of Gabriel Berzat, deceased."

The bill for the relief of Thomas L. Ogden, and others, was read the third time, and passed.

Resolved, That this bill pass, and that the title thereof be, "An act for the relief of Thomas L. Ogden, and others."

The Senate resumed, as in Committee of the Whole, the consideration of the bill, entitled "An act to incorporate the Managers of the National Vaccine Institution in the District of Columbia;" and it was postponed to Monday next.

The Senate resumed, as in Committee of the Whole, the consideration of the bill confirming the title of the Marquis de Maison Rouge; and it was postponed to Wednesday next.

The Senate resumed, as in Committee of the Whole, the consideration of the bill for the relief of the purchasers of public lands prior to the first day of July, 1820; and it was postponed to Monday next.

The PRESIDENT communicated a letter from the

Commissioner of the General Land Office, transmitting a copy of the report of the land commissioners at St. Helena, dated 18th November, 1820, with lists of claims and a list of settlers; and the letter and report were read.

Mr. EATON submitted the following motion for consideration:

Resolved, That the President of the United States be requested to communicate to the Senate any information he may have as to the power and authority which belonged to Don John Beneventure Morales, and to the Baron Carondelet, to grant and dispose of the lands of Spain in Louisiana, previously to the year 1803.

COLUMBIAN SOCIETY.

The Senate resumed the consideration of the bill to incorporate the Columbian Society for Literary purposes; on which there arose a debate of some length, in the course of which Messrs. KING, of New York, and OTIS, explained their objections to the bill, on the ground that it proposed the incorporation of an institution, one of the objects of which was the cultivation of the tenets of a particular sect; that, at any rate, the means and whole object of the institution had not been properly developed; that the capacity of its founders for establishing a college on a proper basis was not known; that the disposition of the people of the District of Columbia towards the establishment of such an University was not known, &c.

To these objections Messrs. BARBOUR, JOHNSON, of Kentucky, and MORRIL, replied, that these objections were not founded on the provisions of the bill, but on supposed features not to be found in it; that the bill had nothing of a religious character about it; that, if it could be made more clear on that point, they wished it might be so by any amendment which could be proposed to the bill; that persons of every religious denomination were subscribers to the fund for establishing the institution; that it was no reason, moreover, against the institution that its establishment was undertaken by religious persons; that, though there was no petition before the House, there were all the facts that the Senate could wish, &c.

The bill was postponed to Monday next.

THURSDAY, January 4.

Mr. NOBLE presented the memorial of the General Assembly of the State of Indiana, praying permission to tax all lands sold by the United States on, and subsequent to the first day of July, 1820, and all lands whereon the payments have been completed; and the memorial was read, and referred to the Committee on Public Lands.

Mr. NOBLE presented the petition of a number of the inhabitants of Indiana, residing in that part of the State called the New Purchase, in the Brookville district, praying that the right of pre-emption to a quarter section of land may be granted to Isaac M. Johnson, for the purpose of erecting a mill thereon; and the petition was read, and referred to the Committee on Public Lands.

Mr. NOBLE presented two petitions, signed by a number of individuals, concerned directly or indirectly in the purchase of public lands prior to the law "making further provision for the sale of the public lands," stating that said law operates injuriously on them, and praying that they may be permitted to apply the payments already made to such portions of their entries as such payments will cover at two dollars per acre, and that the residue may revert to the United States; and the petitions were read, and laid on the table.

Mr. KING, of New York, presented the memorial of the National Institution for the promotion of Industry, praying that a duty of ten per cent. may be imposed on sales at auction; that the credits allowed on duties on foreign merchandise may be abolished, and that the tariff of duties may be so modified as to protect the labor and resources of the nation; and the memorial was read.

Mr. HUNTER presented the petition of John Cahoone, commander of the United States revenue cutter "Vigilant," praying to be allowed a portion of the proceeds of the ship Caledonia and cargo, condemned, on his information, for a breach of the revenue laws of the United States; and the petition was read, and referred to the Committee on the Judiciary.

Mr. TRIMBLE presented the petition of Dean Weymouth, praying an increase of pension; and the petition was read, and referred to the Committee on Pensions.

Mr. SANFORD presented the memorial of the auctioneers of the city of New York, remonstrating against the imposition of legislative restrictions on their occupation; and the memorial was read.

Mr. SANFORD presented the petition of Nathan Ford, of New York, praying compensation for certain houses and other property destroyed by the enemy in the late war, while in the military service of the United States; and the petition was read, and referred to the Committee of Claims.

Mr. HUNTER presented the petition of John Slocum, surveyor of the port of Newport, praying to be allowed a portion of the proceeds of the brig "Langdon Cheves" and cargo, condemned, on his information, for a breach of the revenue laws of the United States; and the petition was read, and referred to the Committee on the Judiciary.

On motion by Mr. JOHNSON, of Louisiana, the report and documents of the land commissioners at St. Helena, which were yesterday received from the Commissioner of the General Land Office, were referred to the Committee on Public Lands.

Mr. SMITH, from the Committee on the Judiciary, to whom was referred the bill, entitled "An act to alter the time of holding the district court in the district of Mississippi," reported the same without amendment.

Mr. SANFORD, from the Committee on Finance, to whom was referred the bill to amend the act, entitled "An act to incorporate the subscribers to the Bank of the United States," reported it without amendment.

The Senate proceeded to consider the motion of yesterday, requesting the President to communicate to the Senate the power and authority under which Don John Beneventure Morales, and the Baron Carondelet, granted and disposed of the lands of Spain in Louisiana ; and agreed thereto.

The bill explanatory of the act for the relief of James Leander Cathcart, passed May the 15th, in the year 1820, was read the second time.

The bill to authorize the appointment of certain Indian agents was read the second time.

The Senate resumed, as in Committee of the Whole, the consideration of the bill to continue in force, for a further time, the act, entitled "An act for establishing trading-houses with the Indian tribes ;" and, on motion by Mr. HOLMES, of Mississippi, the bill was laid on the table.

The Senate resumed, as in Committee of the Whole, the consideration of the bill authorizing the payment of a sum of money to Thomas Shields ; and, on motion by Mr. PARROTT, it was laid on the table.

FRIDAY, January 5.

Mr. THOMAS, from the Committee on Public Lands, to whom was referred the bill, entitled "An act for the relief of Margaret Perry," reported it without amendment.

Mr. EATON, from the same committee, to whom was referred the bill, entitled "An act for the relief of William McIntosh," made a report thereupon, which was read.

The Senate resumed the consideration of the report of the Committee of Claims on the petition of Joseph Janney ; and it was postponed to Monday next.

The Senate resumed the consideration of the report of the Committee on Public Lands on the petition of the Trustees of Worthington College in Ohio ; and, on motion by Mr. THOMAS, it was postponed to Monday, the 15th instant.

A message from the House of Representatives informed the Senate that the House have passed a bill, entitled "An act making a partial appropriation for the military service of the United States for the year 1821 ;" a bill, entitled "An act to extend the time for locating Virginia military land warrants, and returning surveys thereon to the General Land Office ;" and a bill, entitled "An act for the relief of Daniel Seward ;" in which they request the concurrence of the Senate.

The said bills were severally read, and passed to a second reading.

The bill, entitled "An act making a partial appropriation for the military service of the United States for the year 1821," was read the second time by unanimous consent, and referred to the Committee on Finance.

The Senate took up and considered, as in Committee of the Whole, the bill for the relief of Robert Purdy ; and, no amendment having been proposed thereto, the President reported it to the House, and it was ordered to be engrossed, and read the third time.

The Senate proceeded to consider, as in Committee of the Whole, the bill, entitled "An act to alter the time of holding the district court in the district of Mississippi," and no amendment having been proposed thereto, the President reported it to the House ; and it passed to a third reading.

The Senate proceeded to consider, as in Committee of the Whole, the bill to amend the act, entitled "An act to incorporate the subscribers to the Bank of the United States ;" and, on motion by Mr. SANFORD, it was postponed to Wednesday next.

The Senate proceeded to consider, as in Committee of the Whole, the bill to authorize the appointment of certain Indian agents; and, on motion by Mr. TRIMBLE, it was postponed to Thursday next.

The Senate proceeded to consider, as in Committee of the Whole, the bill explanatory of the act for the relief of James Leander Cathcart, passed May the 15th, in the year 1820 ; and it was postponed to Wednesday next.

OHIO AND ERIE CANAL.

The Senate took up the bill to authorize the appointment of commissioners to lay out a canal from Lake Erie to the navigable waters of the Ohio river.

Mr. TRIMBLE, of Ohio, submitted his views in support of the bill, referring to the general advantages of improved internal intercourse ; the necessity of a canal through the country contemplated, for the convenience of the people; the great advantages which would thereby accrue to the United States, by enhancing the value of the public lands in that quarter, &c.; to show the expediency of at least authorizing the course or line of a canal to be laid out, as proposed by the bill.

Mr. MACON was opposed to the bill on general grounds, as well as for the further reasons that it would encourage a spirit of speculation among the people, which it was the duty of the Government to discountenance—not to encourage; that all works undertaken by the public became mere jobs ; that canals, &c., ought to be made by individual enterprise, or private associations, &c.

Mr. OTIS was also opposed to this bill. He was not in favor of holding out any temptation to purchasers of public lands, which might never be realized. The bill was supported on the ground that it would give additional value to the public lands in that quarter of the country; but if the route of a canal were laid out, the canal itself might never be completed ; and Mr. O. was opposed to giving an artificial value to those lands, merely as a lure to people to become purchasers. He argued against affording additional inducements to the purchase of public lands ; the land of the United States was sold with sufficient rapidity already, and he wished those sales to go on steadily, but gradually. Besides these reasons, Mr. O. was not in favor of going into the unpeopled region designated by this bill, and there beginning the system of internal improvement. It was beginning at the wrong end. There was a committee appointed on the subject of internal improvement. He wished to leave the subject to this committee; let them extend their views over the whole Union, and see where it would be better to begin this great work, before a blow be struck in it.

Mr. TRIMBLE replied to Mr. OTIS, and went into a description of the present and prospective condition of that part of Ohio, its population, &c., to show the expediency of adopting this measure. He referred to the great extent of the land transportation, which was so heavy a burden on the agriculture of the country that there was no inducement to raise more than sufficient for the consumption of the people there, and that it would be useless to produce any thing for a foreign market; also the burdens on imports, such as salt and other heavy articles. He stated these facts to show the peculiar necessity for affording water transportation by a canal, to the vast population which would certainly spread over that country. The general advantages of such an improvement were too obvious to require illustration from him, and he abstained from touching on them. He argued that this bill would not give an artificial, but a real and intrinsic additional value to the public lands there. A great part of those lands were now reserved from sale, and might continue to be reserved until they should receive their full value from this improvement; and speculation might be thus prevented, as they would then sell for what they were worth. The expense to be incurred by this measure, if authorized, would be inconsiderable, the advantages of it to the Union incalculable. If the bill passed, Congress would not be concluded on the subject, and were expressly not pledged to make the canal. He referred to facts to show, however, that a canal there was very practicable; that there was water sufficient for all its purposes, &c.

Mr. HOLMES, of Maine, wished, before he could support this bill, more information on the subject than he now possessed. In all incipient measures it was natural to inquire, what next? He desired to know what was to follow this bill. He wanted to know whether this canal was to be made, by whom it was to be made, in whom the property of it or interest would be, &c. It was to go through the lands of the United States; but, he asked, in substance, could the United States have jurisdiction over it when completed? Would the State consent? Would the United States have exclusive jurisdiction without, or even with, the consent of the State? And could the State give exclusive jurisdiction, &c.? These were questions which admitted doubt; though on some of them he himself had none. Suppose the State should choose, for any cause, to stop this canal up, could the United States prevent it, &c.? If not, was it worth while to make a canal over which they might not have complete control? If the State or individuals were to own the canal, were the United States to have no more interest in it than the additional value which it might give to their lands, &c.? He had no doubt the United States could construct roads or canals in the States, but the exclusive control and jurisdiction over the property of them was another question, not so clear, &c.

Mr. JOHNSON, of Louisiana, moved the post-

ponement of the bill to Wednesday, as there appeared many doubtful questions connected with this subject, which he wished some little time to examine.

Mr. TRIMBLE spoke at some length, to afford the information required by Mr. HOLMES, and to obviate the objections which he had suggested against the bill; and the bill was then postponed to Wednesday.

The Senate adjourned to Monday.

MONDAY, January 8.

The PRESIDENT communicated a letter from the Clerk of the House of Representatives, transmitting a resolution of that House, announcing to the Senate the death of JOHN LINN, late a member of the House of Representatives from the State of New Jersey, and the letter and resolution were read.

On motion by Mr. DICKERSON,

Ordered, That the said letter and resolution be entered at large on the journal of the Senate, which is done accordingly in the following words:

CLERK'S OFFICE, HOUSE OF REP'S U. S.,
January 6, 1821.

SIR: The House of Representatives of the United States having received intelligence of the death of John Linn, late a member of that House from the State of New Jersey, and having taken order for superintending and attending his funeral, have also directed me to communicate the same to the Senate. The recess in that body to-day rendering it impossible to make such communication in the ordinary way, I have, therefore, the honor to transmit you, enclosed, the resolution adopted by the House on that subject.

I have the honor to be, &c.

THOMAS DOUGHERTY,
Clerk of the House of Rep's.

Hon. JOHN GAILLARD,
President of the Senate.

IN THE HOUSE OF REP'S OF THE U. S.,
January 6, 1821.

Resolved, That a message be sent to the Senate to notify them of the death of John Linn, late a member of this House from the State of New Jersey, and that his funeral will take place this day at three o'clock from the Hall of the House of Representatives.

Attest,   TH. DOUGHERTY, C. H. R.

On motion by Mr. DICKERSON,

Resolved, unanimously, That the Senate, as a testimony of respect for the memory of the honorable John Linn, late a member of the House of Representatives from the State of New Jersey, will go into mourning and wear a black crape round the left arm for thirty days.

The PRESIDENT communicated a letter from JAMES J. WILSON, a member of the Senate from the State of New Jersey, resigning his seat in the Senate; which was read.

The PRESIDENT also communicated a letter from the Secretary of the Navy, transmitting statements exhibiting the names of the clerks employed in the Navy Department and in the office of the commissioners of the Navy for the year 1820, and the amount of compensation paid to each; and the letter and statements were read.

· Mr. HORSEY presented the memorial of the President and Cashier of the Bank of the Metropolis, on behalf of the Directors and Stockholders of said bank, praying a renewal of their charter; and the memorial was read, and referred to the Committee on the District of Columbia.

Mr. SANFORD presented the petition of Terrence Clark, of New York, praying to be confirmed in his title to certain land; and the petition was read, and referred to the Committee on Public Lands.

Mr. WALKER, of Alabama, presented the petition of P. P. Saint Guirons and others, members of the French association established in the State of Alabama, by virtue of an act, entitled "An act to set apart and dispose of certain public lands for the encouragement of the cultivation of the vine and olive;" praying certain modifications of said act; and the petition was read, and referred to the Committee on Public Lands.

Mr. WALKER, of Alabama, also presented the petition of the citizens of Lawrence and Franklin counties, in the State of Alabama, praying that all persons who have purchased lands for actual settlement, and who have settled upon and improved the same, may be authorized to obtain a patent for a limited quantity, to be ascertained by law, on paying the sum of one dollar and twenty-five cents per acre, at any time within five years from the date of the sales; and the petition was read, and laid on the table.

Mr. PLEASANTS, from the Committee on Naval Affairs, to whom was referred the petition of John Gooding and James Williams, made a report, accompanied by a bill authorizing the payment of a sum of money to John Gooding and James Williams; and the report and bill were read, and the bill passed to a second reading.

The Senate proceeded to fill the vacancies occasioned in several Committees, by the death of Mr. BURRILL and the resignation of Mr. WILSON, when the following appointments were made:

On the Committee of Commerce, Mr. LANMAN.

On the Committee of Accounts, Mr. WILLIAMS, of Mississippi.

On the Committee of Claims, Mr. PALMER.

On the Committee of the Public Buildings, Mr. TALBOT.

On the Committee on the Post Office and Post Roads, Mr. KING, of Alabama.

And Mr. JOHNSON of Kentucky, having, on his request, been excused from serving on the Committee on Enrolled Bills, Mr. MORRIL was appointed in his place.

Mr. EATON submitted the following motion for consideration:

Resolved, That the Committee of Claims inquire into the expediency of allowing the claim of Matthew B. Carthey, for two horses lost in the public service, at Pensacola and at New Orleans.

The bill, entitled "An act to extend the time for locating Virginia military land warrants and returning surveys thereon to the General Land Office," was read the second time, and referred to the Committee on Public Lands.

The bill, entitled "An act for the relief of Daniel Seward," was read the second time, and referred to the Committee of Claims.

The bill for the relief of Robert Purdy was read the third time, and passed.

The bill from the House of Representatives, entitled "An act to alter the time of holding the district court in the district of Mississippi," was read the third time, and passed.

The Senate resumed the consideration of the motion of the second instant, instructing the Committee on the Judiciary to report a bill extending the laws of the United States over the State of Missouri; and it was postponed to Monday next.

The Senate resumed the consideration of the report of the Committee of Claims on the petition of Joseph Janney; and it was postponed until to-morrow.

The Senate proceeded to consider, as in Committee of the Whole, the bill, entitled "An act for the relief of Margaret Perry;" and, no amendment having been proposed thereto, the PRESIDENT reported it to the House, and it passed to a third reading.

The Senate proceeded to consider, as in Committee of the Whole, the bill, entitled "An act for the relief of William McIntosh," together with the report of the Committee of Public Lands thereon; and, on motion, by Mr. EDWARDS, it was laid on the table.

The bill "to incorporate the Columbian Society, for literary purposes," was taken up in Committee of the Whole.

On the numerous provisions of this bill, and the various amendments proposed to it in the course of its consideration, much discussion arose, and much time was consumed. The bill was not disposed of nor got through with; and, the usual hour of adjournment having arrived, the Senate adjourned.

TUESDAY, January 9.

Mr. HOLMES, of Maine, presented the petition of Josiah Hook, jr., collector of the port of Penobscot, praying to be indemnified for his losses, and for the money he has paid, with interest thereon, in satisfaction of a judgment obtained against him for an act done by him in his official capacity; and the petition was read, and referred to the Committee on the Judiciary.

Mr. SANFORD, from the Committee on Finance, to whom was referred the bill, entitled "An act making a partial appropriation for the military service of the United States for the year 1821," reported the same with an amendment, which was read.

Mr. HOLMES, of Maine, submitted the following motion for consideration:

Resolved, That a committee be appointed to inquire into the expediency of diminishing, equalizing, and establishing the fees of district attorneys, clerks, and marshals, and other officers.

On motion, by Mr. WILLIAMS, of Mississippi, the letter received from the Commissioner of the General Land Office, with the copies of the reports of the land commissioners at Jackson courthouse, and other documents therewith transmitted, were referred to the Committee on Public Lands.

Mr. EATON, from the Committee on Public Lands, to whom was referred the petition of Nicholas Perkins, made a report accompanied by a bill for the relief of Nicholas Perkins; and the report and bill were read, and the bill passed to a second reading.

Mr. SMITH, from the Committee on the Judiciary, to whom was referred the letter from the Secretary of State, requesting to be supplied with an additional number of the documents printed by order of the Senate, reported the following resolution, which was read:

Resolved, That twenty-five copies of all documents printed for the use of the Senate, except bills and amendments, including the number now furnished, shall be furnished to the Secretary of State.

The Senate proceeded to consider the motion of yesterday, instructing the Committee of Claims to inquire into the expediency of allowing the claim of Matthew B. Carthey, and agreed thereto.

The Senate resumed the consideration of the report of the Committee of Claims on the petition of Joseph Janney; and, on motion of Mr. PLEASANTS, it was laid on the table.

The bill to establish an uniform system of bankruptcy throughout the United States was read the second time, and referred to the Committee on the Judiciary.

The bill from the House of Representatives, entitled "An act for the relief of Margaret Perry," was read the third time, and passed.

COLUMBIAN SOCIETY.

The Senate resumed, as in Committee of the Whole, the consideration of the bill to incorporate the Columbian Society for literary purposes, together with the amendment last reported thereto by the Committee on the District of Columbia, and the said amendment having been further amended and agreed to, the bill was reported to the House amended accordingly, and the said amendments, except the seventh and tenth sections, having been concurred in, on the question to concur in the said seventh section, as follows:

"SEC. 7. *And be it further enacted,* That persons of every religious denomination shall be capable of being elected trustees; nor shall any person, either as president, professor, tutor, or pupil, be refused admittance into said college, or denied any privileges, immunities, or advantages thereof, for, or on account of, his sentiments in matters of religion."

It was determined in the affirmative, as follows:

YEAS—Messrs. Brown, Chandler, Dickerson, Eaton, Elliott, Gaillard, Holmes of Maine, Horsey, Hunter, Johnson of Louisiana, Lanman, Lloyd, Mills, Otis, Roberts, Ruggles, Sanford, Stokes, Talbot, Van Dyke, Walker of Alabama, Walker of Georgia, and Williams of Mississippi.

NAYS—Messrs. Barbour, Johnson of Kentucky, King of Alabama, Lowrie, Macon, Morril, Palmer, Pleasants, Smith, Taylor, Thomas Tichenor, and Trimble.

And the said tenth section having been amended, it was concurred in.

The bill was then ordered to be engrossed and read a third time.

WEDNESDAY, January 10.

The PRESIDENT communicated a letter from the Secretary of State, transmitting a list of the American seamen registered in the several ports of the United States for the three first quarters of the year 1820, made in pursuance of "An act to revive and continue in force certain parts of the 'act for the relief and protection of American seamen;" and the letter and list were read.

The PRESIDENT communicated a letter from the Secretary of the Navy, transmitting a statement of the expenditure and application of the moneys drawn from the Treasury on account of the Navy, from the first day of October, 1819, to the 30th of September, 1820; and of the unexpended balances of former appropriations remaining in the Treasury on the first of October, 1820; and the letter and statement were read.

The PRESIDENT communicated a letter from the Secretary of the Navy, transmitting a report of the Commissioners of the Navy Pension Fund, made in obedience to the act for the better government of the Navy of the United States; and the letter and report were read.

The PRESIDENT communicated a letter from the Secretary of War, transmitting a statement prepared in conformity with the fifth section of the "Act to amend the several acts for the establishment and regulation of the Treasury, War, and Navy Departments," showing the expenditure of the moneys appropriated for the contingent expenses of the military establishment for the year 1820; and the letter and statement were read.

The PRESIDENT also communicated a letter from the Secretary of the Treasury, transmitting a report of the register of the district of Edwardsville, made in conformity with the provisions of the "Act for the relief of the inhabitants of the village of Peoria, in the State of Illinois," upon the claims exhibited under the said act; and the letter and report were read.—Referred to the Committee on Public Lands.

Mr. PLEASANTS presented the petition of Thomas W. Todd, praying to be reimbursed in the expenses incurred by him in consequence of a suit wrongfully instituted against him by the United States; and the petition was read, and referred to the Committee of Claims.

Mr. HORSEY presented, severally, the memorials of the President and Directors of the Bank of Washington, of the Bank of Alexandria, and of the Bank of Potomac, praying a renewal of their respective charters; and the memorials were read, and referred to the Committee on the District of Columbia.

Mr. BARBOUR obtained leave to bring in a bill concerning the collection of public moneys; and the bill was twice read by unanimous consent, and referred to the Committee on Finance.

Mr. NOBLE, from the Committee on Pensions, to whom was referred the petition of Moses Wing, made a report, accompanied by a resolution, that the prayer of the petitioner ought not to be granted. The report and resolution were read.

Mr. LLOYD submitted the following motion for consideration:

Resolved, That the Committee on Public Lands be instructed to inquire into the justice and expediency of granting land for the purpose of education within the limits of the old States, corresponding with the appropriations which have been made for the same object within the limits of the new States.

Mr. NOBLE, from the Committee on Pensions, to whom was referred the petition of Alexander Irwin, made a report, accompanied by a resolution, that the prayer of the petitioner ought not to be granted. The report and resolution were read.

Mr. THOMAS, from the Committee on Public Lands, to whom was referred the bill granting to the Governor of the State of Louisiana, for the time being, and his successors in office, two tracts of land in the county of Point Coupee, reported the same with amendments; which were read.

Mr. THOMAS, from the same committee, to whom was referred the bill for the relief of John Coffee, reported the same with an amendment; which was read.

Mr. ROBERTS, from the Committee of Claims, to whom was referred the petition of Richard G. Waterhouse, communicated a letter from the Secretary of the Treasury, transmitting to the committee a report of the Third Auditor on said petition; and the letter and report were read.

On motion, by Mr. ROBERTS, the committee were discharged from the further consideration of said petition, and had leave to withdraw his petition and papers.

The Senate proceeded to consider the motion of yesterday, for the appointment of a committee to inquire into the expediency of diminishing, equalizing, and establishing, the fees of attorneys, clerks, and marshals, and it was amended and agreed to as follows:

Resolved, That the Committee on the Judiciary be instructed to inquire into the expediency of diminishing, equalizing and establishing, the fees of district attorneys, clerks, and marshals, and other officers.

The Senate proceeded to consider the resolution yesterday reported by the Committee on the Judiciary, on the application of the Secretary of State, for an additional supply of the documents printed by order of the Senate; and agreed thereto.

The bill authorizing the payment of a sum of money to John Gooding and James Williams was read the second time.

The bill for the relief of Nicholas Perkins was read the second time.

The bill to incorporate the Columbian Society for literary purposes, was read the third time.

Resolved, That this bill pass; and the title thereof be "An act to incorporate the Columbian College in the District of Columbia."

The Senate resumed, as in Committee of the Whole, the consideration of the bill, entitled "An act for the relief of Nicholas Jarrott," together with the amendments reported thereto by the Committee on Public Lands; and it was postponed until to-morrow.

The Senate resumed, as in Committee of the Whole, the consideration of the bill for the relief of the purchasers of public lands prior to the first day of July, 1820; and it was postponed to, and made the order of the day for, to-morrow.

The Senate proceeded to consider, as in Committee of the Whole, the bill, entitled "An act making a partial appropriation for the military service of the United States for the year 1821," together with the amendment reported thereto by the Committee on Finance; and the said amendment having been agreed to, the President reported the bill to the House amended accordingly; and the amendment was concurred in, and ordered to be engrossed, and the bill read a third time as amended.

NATIONAL VACCINE INSTITUTION.

The Senate proceeded to the consideration of the bill from the House of Representatives to incorporate the National Vaccine Institution.

On this bill there arose a short debate.

Messrs. ROBERTS and TALBOT opposed the bill, on the ground that it was not necessary to the object avowed, which could be easily accomplished without it; that, if necessary, an act of incorporation could be obtained from the State of Maryland sufficient for all useful purposes; that the bill proposed to incorporate an institution without limiting it to the District; that there were within the District so many corporations that the number ought not to be increased, unless under an urgent necessity, &c.

Messrs. HORSEY and LLOYD supported the bill, on the ground of its importance to the proper accomplishment of an object of great interest to humanity, which could not be in any other way so well accomplished. The same explanation of the bill was substantially given as was given of its merits when pending in the House of Representatives.

Mr. ROBERTS had moved a general postponement of the bill; but, with a view to allow gentlemen favorable to the bill to amend it, if they desired, he withdrew his motion; and, on motion of Mr. LLOYD, the bill was postponed to Monday next.

OHIO AND ERIE CANAL.

The Senate then resumed the consideration of the bill to authorize the appointment of commissioners to lay out a canal between the navigable waters of the Ohio and Lake Erie.

Mr. RUGGLES moved to strike out the clause which provides that nothing in the bill shall be construed as pledging the United States to defray any part of the expense of making the said canal, and to insert, in lieu thereof, a provision that, on the canal being laid out, so much of the proceeds of the sales of public lands in the Delaware district, in Ohio, as shall exceed the minimum cash price of one dollar and twenty-five cents per acre, should be applied to the purpose of making this canal.

Mr. LOWRIE required a division of the question, so as to take it first on striking out.

Mr. HOLMES, of Maine, moved to amend the

amendment, by adding to the end of it the words, "When the said canal shall have been completed to the satisfaction of Congress."

There grew out of these motions a debate, which was interrupted only by the arrival of the usual hour for adjournment.

Mr. Trimble was opposed in opinion, with regard to this amendment, to his colleague who moved it, because he was favorable to the bill, which he apprehended the proposed amendment might defeat.

With the exception of Mr. Trimble, the other gentlemen who spoke were *pro* or *con* the whole scheme of the bill, as well as of the amendment. The bill was supported and opposed by the following gentlemen:

For the bill—Messrs. Ruggles and Trimble.
Against the bill—Messrs. Otis, Brown, Macon, and Chandler.

The argument in favor of the general objects of the bill, besides the obvious one of promoting public convenience and private comfort, was, principally, that it would greatly increase the value of the public lands, by facilitating intercourse between them and other parts of the country.

The argument against the bill was not against the policy of such improvements, so much as against any partial measures in regard to internal improvements of this description. If canals were to be made at the expense of the United States, as it was evident this was intended to be, it was suggested that the experiment should begin in improved and populous parts of the country, rather than in the wilderness, &c.

Before any question was decided in regard to the bill, the Senate adjourned.

Thursday, January 11.

The President communicated a letter from the Postmaster General, transmitting a statement showing the names and salaries of the clerks employed in his office during the year 1820; and the letter and statement were read.

The bill making a partial appropriation for the military service for the year 1821, was read the third time and passed, with a small amendment requiring the concurrence of the House of Representatives.

Mr. Edwards presented a petition, signed by a number of individuals, concerned directly or indirectly as purchasers of public lands prior to the law "making further provision for the sale of the public lands," stating that said law operates injuriously on them, and praying that they may be permitted to apply the payments already made to such portions of their entries as such payments will cover at two dollars per acre, and that the residue may revert to the United States; and the petition was read, and laid on the table.

Mr. Noble presented four petitions, signed in like manner, and of the same import and object as the preceding; which were read, and laid on the table.

Mr. Roberts, from the Committee of Claims, to whom was referred the petition of Nathan Ford,

reported a bill for the relief of Nathan Ford; and the bill was read, and passed to a second reading.

Mr. Smith, from the Committee on the Judiciary, to whom was referred the bill to establish an uniform system of bankruptcy throughout the United States, reported it without amendment.

Mr. Smith, from the same committee, to whom the subject was referred, reported a bill to authorize the President of the United States to ascertain and designate certain boundaries; and the bill was read, and passed to a second reading.

Mr. Lanman submitted the following motion for consideration:

Resolved, That the Committee on Naval Affairs be instructed to inquire whether there are any obstructions to the navigation of the river Thames, in the State of Connecticut, which were placed there by the American ships blockaded during the late war; and, if any, what measures ought to be adopted for the removal of such obstructions.

The Senate proceeded to consider the motion of yesterday, instructing the Committee on Public Lands to inquire into the expediency of granting lands for the purpose of education within the limits of the old States, and agreed thereto.

The Senate proceeded to consider the report of the Committee on Pensions on the petition of Moses Wing; and on motion, by Mr. Chandler, it was postponed indefinitely.

The Senate proceeded to consider the report of the Committee on Pensions, on the petition of Alexander Irwin; and, in concurrence therewith, resolved that the prayer of the petitioner ought not to be granted.

On motion, by Mr. Holmes, of Mississippi, the Senate took up and considered, as in Committee of the Whole, the bill to continue in force, for a limited time, the act, entitled "An act for establishing trading-houses with the Indian tribes;" and it was postponed to, and made the order of the day for, Monday next.

OHIO AND ERIE CANAL.

The Senate resumed the consideration of the bill to authorize the appointment of commissioners to lay out the route of a canal from the navigable waters of the Ohio to Lake Erie—the motion made by Mr. Ruggles to pledge certain proceeds of the sales of the public lands to making the canal being the question under consideration.

Mr. Walker, of Alabama, spoke against the bill, grounding his objections—without examining at all the Constitutional question, but only the question of expediency—on the belief that such a work ought not to be undertaken unless as part of a great system of internal improvement; that this, for several reasons which he adduced, was not the point at which such a system ought to be commenced; that the enhancement of the value of the public lands was not a good argument in favor of the bill, unless the Government meant, in good faith, to make the canal after its course was laid out, and therefore the amendment offered by Mr. Ruggles was fair and commendable, &c. In order, however, to test the sense of the Senate at once on the bill, which had been fully discussed

at the last session, he moved its indefinite postponement.

Mr. TRIMBLE followed, and spoke in answer to the arguments used by gentlemen yesterday, and by Mr. WALKER to-day, against the bill—reasoning to show that people would buy the neighboring public lands under a fair calculation of the chances in favor of the making of the canal, formed on a view of the law, and, consequently, no deception would mislead them; and reasoning also against the various local interests and jealousies which opposed this bill, and the commencement of the contemplated work; and arguing that it was only by adopting a plan of this kind by the General Government that the public interest could be promoted, and the improper influence of private interest, which might operate if the work were left to the State, could be avoided, &c.

Mr. MORRIL was opposed to the bill as well on account of its inexpediency, as from well founded doubts of the Constitutional power of Congress to authorize the work, and also from the inability of the Treasury at this time to defray extraordinary expenses, presuming that the cost of the work would be derived indirectly if not directly from the public funds. He viewed it also as a lure held out to the purchasers of the public lands, which he could not support; and thinking that when a business of this kind was commenced it ought to be part of a general plan, the expense defrayed out of a general fund, each State receiving its proportion of it; that this, moreover, was not the suitable place to begin the plan; that it would probably cost a great deal more, judging from other public works, than was now estimated.

Mr. RUGGLES spoke in favor of his amendment and also of the bill, and argued to show that the canal would be made if now authorized; and also to show the vast commerce which would be carried on through the canal, from and to a great part of the Western country; its extensive advantages to that quarter of the Union, and the salutary policy generally of authorizing such a work.

Mr. TRIMBLE again spoke to show that the expense of the canal would never have to be defrayed out of the funds of the General Government; that the expense of the survey would be a mere trifle, and the value of it to Ohio and the whole Western country incalculable. He was particularly desirous that the bill should now pass, because the advantages of it would otherwise be soon lost to the State and the Union, inasmuch as the Indian title being extinguished to the lands, they would be in the market, and would pass into the hands of individuals, &c.

Mr. BARBOUR viewed the question strictly as one of internal improvement, and involving all the considerations connected with that question. It appeared to be the settled sense of the country, though absurd and preposterous in his opinion, that the public funds may be appropriated to works of internal improvement, but that as soon as any work was completed it became derelict and beyond the control of the National Government. He gave a history of the attempts in Congress to authorize and commence a system of internal improvements, and their failure; especially the last serious effort, made in the most unexceptionable aspect, rejected by the veto of President Madison, and which had not the necessary majority in Congress to make the bill a law; and arguing that if that decision were correct, this measure was improper. On the policy of that bill the public sentiment seemed to be about equally divided; and he had at a subsequent session offered a resolution to give the General Government the desired power, which also failed. He would therefore not support a measure now which conflicted with the settled opinion that there existed no power in the General Government to make roads and canals in the States. At any rate, he hoped, if the system were commenced, it would not be in an insulated, narrow, partial manner, but on a great, equitable, and impartial system.

Mr. JOHNSON, of Kentucky, was decidedly against the indefinite postponement of the bill. He insisted that the sentiment of Congress had been expressed by a large majority in favor of making internal improvements; and, without fearing any ill consequences from such a policy, he viewed it as of vital importance to the convenience, the happiness, the harmony, and lasting union of the Republic. But this bill, he argued, did not touch the question referred to by Mr. BARBOUR; and its legality had been settled by the law authorizing the continuation of the Cumberland road to Missouri. He controverted the opinion that this canal would be a local work. It was a great national object, as were all works which brought the different parts of the country together, and promoted their comfort and union; and he was ready to support similar objects in other quarters. He maintained the right of the West to expect some expenditure of the public funds in that quarter of the Union, and thereby aid in some sort the moneyed institutions of that part of the country, &c.; in support of which opinions he spoke at some length.

Mr. MORRIL subjoined a remark or two in support of the opinions he had previously expressed; after which

The question was put on the indefinite postponement of the bill, and decided in the affirmative, by yeas and nays, as follows:

YEAS—Messrs. Barbour, Brown, Chandler, Eaton, Elliot, Gaillard, Hunter, Johnson of Louisiana, King of Alabama, Lanman, Lloyd, Macon, Mills, Morril, Otis, Palmer, Parrott, Pleasants, Roberts, Smith, Taylor, Tichenor. Walker of Alabama, Walker of Georgia, Williams of Mississippi, and Williams of Tenn.—26.

NAYS—Messrs. Dana, Dickerson, Edwards, Johnson of Kentucky, Lowrie, Noble, Ruggles, Sanford, Stokes, Talbot, Thomas, Trimble, and Van Dyke—13.

So the bill was rejected.

RELIEF TO LAND PURCHASERS.

The Senate then, agreeably to the order of the day, took up in Committee of the Whole, the bill for the relief of the purchasers of public lands prior to the first day of July, 1820.

Mr. THOMAS, of Illinois, said, that, by the laws in operation before the 1st of July, 1820, the minimum price of the public land was two dollars an acre, payable one-fourth down, one-fourth at the end of two years, and one-fourth at the end of each of the two succeeding years; one year of grace was allowed to the purchaser after the last payment became due. If the payments were not completed within that period, the land was offered at public sale; if it sold for more than was due, the surplus was paid to the purchaser, If it would not sell for the amount due, it reverted to the United States. Interest, in case of non-payment of any instalment when it became due, was charged upon such payment. A deduction of eight per cent. was allowed to purchasers for prompt payment.

By the act of the 24th April, 1820, credit was abolished, and the minimum price of the public land reduced to one dollar and twenty-five cents an acre. The probable consequence of that measure, said Mr. T., if no provision is made to counteract it. will be the forfeiture of all the land purchased prior to the 1st of July, 1820, upon which the first payment only has been made, except where valuable improvements have been made, upon a quarter or half-quarter section. On all purchases at the minimum price, in that situation, the purchaser will save, by the forfeiture, twenty-five cents an acre, unless competition at the resale should increase the price. Where a higher price has been given, the saving will be increased in proportion to that price, unless competition at the resale should be as great as at the original sale. When the situation of the country, at the time the great mass of debt was contracted for the public lands, is considered, and contrasted with the present circumstances of those disposed to become purchasers of those lands, it will be readily perceived that the idea of increased competition, at any sale which may be made of lands that may be forfeited, will not be realized. The immense quantity of land which the Government has in the market, of itself, independent of the unfavorable change which has occurred in the capacity of the community to purchase, would greatly diminish the fear of competition, which is the only inducement on the part of the public debtor not to suffer the land purchased by him to revert to the United States.

It is, therefore, the interest of the Government, in a pecuniary point of view, to afford that measure of relief which will diminish the motive with purchasers to suffer their lands to revert to the United States.

But it is conceived, said Mr. T., that considerations of a higher nature are involved in this investigation. All governments ought to act so as to command the love and confidence of the governed. In this country, where the people are sovereign, the Government will always act in conformity to their sovereign will. The question, then, ought to be decided upon considerations of policy, of justice, and equity, and not by those of interest alone.

Independent of the motive to a liberal and magnanimous conduct to the public debtors, resulting from the act of the Government diminishing the minimum price, other circumstances present themselves and press with irresistible force upon the consideration of the Legislature. It is matter of general notoriety, that, when the greatest portion of this debt was contracted, the price of produce of every description was more than an hundred per cent. higher than at present.

Banks which had multiplied, and, apparently, in some instances, been located with the express view of furnishing facilities to the purchasers of public lands, had rendered money, or what was then deemed money, so plenty, that a momentary frenzy seized upon the purchasers of public lands. Prices were bid for lands wholly unimproved greatly beyond what lands of equal quality, and highly improved, in the neighboring States, would have commanded.

Shortly after these purchases were made, produce fell to less than half the price which it then commanded; the facilities afforded by banks were suddenly withdrawn, by the drain of specie from their vaults, or notes ceasing to be receivable in consequence of their bankruptcy.

The public debtor, by these occurrences, found himself embarrassed by engagements which it would have been difficult for him to fulfil, and which the change in the price of the public land has considerably aggravated. It is unnecessary to charge the Government with having contributed to the error which has been committed by the purchasers of the public lands, to induce it to afford relief. It is sufficient, for that purpose, to show that great loss will inevitably fall upon their purchasers unless relief is granted, and, that no benefit will inure to the Government from that loss. In all governments, even the most despotic, the resources of the Government consist of the surplus means of the Government. If the people are impoverished, the revenues of the Government are dried up, and all its operations enfeebled; this is the true reason why free States are always more powerful and fruitful in their resources than despotic States.

It is, however, admitted, that, if the Government should exact the penalty of the law, it would apparently be benefited in a pecuniary view. It would retain the whole of the money received on the improvident purchases which have been described, and have the land which would revert at its disposition. This benefit, however, would be apparent only, and not real. The state of destitution to which this exaction would reduce the purchasers would destroy all competition among the purchasers at the resale of those lands; and a sense of the extreme rigor which had been exercised towards them, would restrain the citizens of other States disposed to purchase from entering into the competition. Sympathy, even among those disposed to better their situation by removal from the place of their nativity, would afford that relief which the equity and magnanimity of the Government ought to have promptly granted. But if this opinion should be deemed erroneous, still, any pecuniary benefit which the Government might be supposed to derive from the rigid exaction of the conditions, would be more than balanced by the increased payments in the Treasury, which the relief to which the purchasers are equitably entitled would produce, in the year 1821, and by the uniformity of the receipts from that source of revenue during the eight succeeding years.

The right to relinquish, proposed by the bill, would probably diminish the debt $4,000,000. The prompt payments which would be produced by the discount tendered in the bill would probably further reduce it $3,000,000. There would then remain $15,000,000 which would, according to the third proposition in the bill, produce an annual revenue of $1,875,000.

This sum, with the amount of new purchases made during that term, could not fail to produce an annual revenue of $2,500,000. From these general considerations, Mr. President, I shall proceed to a particular examination of the provisions of the bill.

1st. The right to relinquish is an equitable consequence of the change which the Government has made in the minimum price of the public land.

If the purchaser should, by any cause whatever, be under the necessity of selling a part of his land to discharge his debt to the Government, the price which he will be able to obtain for it will be affected by that change, and his ability to make the payment diminished in the proportion which two hundred bears to one hundred and twenty-five. It is rational to presume that such will be the consequence, as the quantity of land which the Government has for sale will, for a much longer term than that proposed in the bill for the final extinguishment of the debt, greatly exceed the demand for it for settlement, or for speculation. The exorbitant price given for a portion of the public lands, and the inability of the purchasers to pay that price, appeals strongly to the equity and magnanimity of Congress. The first section of the bill does not propose to reduce the price of the land retained by the purchaser; it only releases him from what it is impracticable to perform.

The Government receives back its property, which will again by it be sold for what it is really worth. The right of relinquishment cannot be exercised so as to release the purchaser from his bargain, as far as the purchase-money has been paid.

2. To excite to prompt payment, as well as to grant equitable relief to the purchasers of public land, the second section provides that when the full purchase-money for any tract of land shall be paid on a certain day, a deduction shall be made. This provision is almost a necessary consequence of the change which has been made in the minimum price of the public lands by the act of the 24th April, 1820. Nothing can be more equitable than the tender to the former purchaser of the option of paying, on a given day, the whole sum for any tract of land, subject to a deduction equal to the proportion which the former minimum price bears to the present. Considering the state of the Treasury, any measure which will increase the payments on account of the debt due for the public land ought to receive due consideration. For the want of punctuality in the payment of this debt, the Government is compelled to borrow money. A reduction for prompt payment, not inconsistent with the equity, would greatly increase the payments into the Treasury during the present year, and correspondently diminish the amount necessary to be obtained by loan. It may appear, upon first consideration, that the foregoing provisions present all the relief to which the parties are equitably entitled, and which the Government can, consistently with due regard to justice, grant. It may be urged that, after the parties have been permitted to relinquish such part of the land purchased by them as they may think proper, and a reasonable deduction made for prompt payment has been tendered to them, that no cause of complaint can exist, no case of oppression can occur. To this it may be answered, that cases may still exist in which it may be the interest of the parties to suffer the lands purchased by them to revert. Under the former system tracts of not less than one hundred and sixty acres were sold, with the exception of sections numbers two, five, twenty, twenty-three, and thirty, in each township, which were divided into half-quarters, in the former case, where but a single tract has been purchased by an individual, the right of relinquishment cannot in many instances be exercised without great loss to the purchaser; and in the latter it would be inconvenient and impolitic to admit of the right to relinquish. In such cases the parties are presumed, from the quantity purchased, to be poor. Their poverty will probably disable them from making prompt payment. They will therefore be driven to the necessity of suffering their small farms to revert. If saved from this necessity, it will be by the compliance with terms from which they see their wealthy neighbors exempt. But it has been shown to be their interest to suffer their lands to revert, and run the risk of repurchasing, when the land shall be again offered for sale. It certainly never can be sound policy in any Government to act in such a manner as to make it the interest of its citizens voluntarily, and from a regard to their pecuniary interests, to incur forfeitures, and to fail in the fulfilment of engagements which, though not legally, ought always to be considered morally binding. Such an example could not fail to have a baleful influence upon the public morality. Such an example will be exhibited by the act of the 24th of April, 1820, reducing the minimum price of the public land from two dollars to one dollar and twenty-five cents an acre, if the third section of the bill, or one analogous to it in principle, shall not be adopted by the National Legislature. By that act it is clearly made the interest of the purchaser to fail in his engagements with the Government, and run the risk of purchasing at a cheaper rate when the lands shall be reoffered for sale. The third provision is clearly an alternative offered to those who cannot accept of the second. All those whose pecuniary means will not enable them to avail themselves of the second, will consider that justice is inequitably distributed between the poor and the rich, if by the rejection of the third they are compelled, from a regard to their interest, to suffer their small farms to revert to the United States.

But the third section of the bill is strongly recommended to the attention of the Senate—1. Because it will prevent reversions; 2. Will secure a greater revenue from the land retained than if it was suffered to revert; and, 3. Will produce a greater degree of punctuality in the payments into the Treasury, during the time of its operation, than can be obtained by any other provision in the power of the Legislature to adopt. If there was no other recommendation in its favor, this ought to command the unqualified assent of the Senate. The purchaser will see, in the conditions tendered, a sufficient inducement to avoid a reversion, and inducements not less strong will impel him to the most rigid punctuality in making the payments required by the provisions of the section.

In favor of the term of eight years, which has been fixed upon by a majority of the committee, it may be urged that the indulgence which has been heretofore granted by Congress has in some degree directed its decision. It is admitted that the situation of the parties which will be affected by it is different, and that if it was practicable to adapt the provisions of the section to their various cases, it would have been done; but, considering this measure as an act of liberality, and at the same time calculated to have a salutary influence upon the fiscal operations of the Government, it was considered more important to introduce a uniform rule, the operation of which would be easily comprehended, than to encumber the section with the complex provisions which otherwise would have been indispensable.

For these reasons, I think the provisions of the bill are such as to be entitled to the consideration of the Senate.

I cannot close my remarks on a question so interesting to the people I have the honor to represent, without reminding the Senate that the attention of Congress was called to this subject by the President of the United States in his Message to both Houses of Congress at the commencement of the present session, and that a plan for the relief of the purchasers of public lands under the ancient system was submitted by the Secretary of the Treasury in his annual report, not different in principle from the bill under consideration.

It is my duty to state, Mr. President, that there was some difference of opinion in the committee in relation to this bill, but all were in favor of granting relief to those concerned in its provisions.

Mr. EDWARDS, of Illinois, rose, and expressing a hope that the great importance of the subject then under discussion to the nation, and more particularly the deep interest which the people of the State he had the honor in part to represent had in it, would be a sufficient apology for his asking the attention of the Senate to the remarks he felt it his duty to offer to its consideration, proceeded to notice certain defects in the bill, and, among others, suggested that, by its phraseology, the relief which it proposed to grant was limited, and confined to the direct purchasers from the Government, to the entire exclusion of those who had purchased from individuals lands subject to the lien of the Government, for the instalments that are still due upon them; which latter class, he contended, if they

16th Con. 2d Sess.—6

were not the most numerous, were in general the most deserving of relief, because they were principally composed of persons who, having gone to the respective States in which the public lands lie, strangers, and not knowing where to find vacant land, or being desirous of settling in the vicinities of friends and acquaintances who had preceded them, had generally purchased at an advanced price, and of course would, in proportion to their purchases, be the greatest sufferers. But, said he, what is still worse, by the provisions of the bill as it now reads, the original purchasers have the right to relinquish the very lands which they have sold, in many instances, at an exorbitant profit, and to appropriate to themselves the benefit of all the instalments that have been paid by their assignees. These objections, however, said he, may be easily obviated by substituting the word holders in the place of purchasers. Other amendments he thought most obviously necessary; but, said he, in this stage of the bill, it may be most advisable to discuss its general objects, which, by eliciting the views of different gentlemen, may enable us to ascertain with the more certainty and precision what provisions and amendments will be most acceptable to the majority of the Senate.

All agree that relief is necessary. Much diversity of opinion, however, may exist as to what it should be. And, in order justly to appreciate the claims which the debtors for public land have upon the humanity and justice of this Government, it seems to be necessary to advert to the times of artificial and fictitious prosperity that are recently past, and to contrast them with the present disastrous turn of affairs which we see every day more and more realized; and this for the double purpose of accounting for the causes that have seduced that class of our fellow-citizens into a condition which renders the beneficent interposition of Congress necessary to them; and at the same time to demonstrate the expediency, on the part of Congress, of extending to them such relief as their situation requires, and as is not forbidden by the dictates of a liberal and enlightened policy, and a just regard to the public interest.

Mr. President, said Mr. E., I discard from my view of this subject all mercenary considerations of profit to the Government, from granting the relief proposed by this bill. Narrow considerations of interest, nice calculations of pecuniary profit, when the great question is one of legislative grace and relief, to a considerable and suffering portion of the community, seem to me to be out of place on this floor. I never can ask this Senate to do what I consider wrong, because it may produce a profit to the nation. Nor will I ask it to do what I consider right in itself by appealing to any such contracted and mercenary considerations. A course like this may suit the superannuated, corrupt, and tottering monarchies on the other side of the Atlantic, living from hand to mouth by the expedients of the day, and hastening their downfall by the very food on which they feed; but such a course is, in my opinion, as unsuited to the meridian as it is inconsistent with the dignity of a great, a youthful, a vigorous, and magnanimous Republic—a Republic founded on the affections of the people; flowing from them as the great fountain of power—*instituted solely for their happiness, and, consequently, ever ready to administer, from the purest motives, a just relief to their sufferings.* This Government, sir, depends for its successful operations on the affections of the people. They can never have affection for a Government which they cannot respect. And what respect can be felt for a Government which, professing to do an act of grace, founds that act on a cold calculation of a return of profit? Charity is certainly one of the most amiable of virtues; yet, what would be thought of that charity which should be bestowed on an arithmetical estimate of usurious interest? Considerations of this sort, Mr. President, are, in my opinion, unworthy of the grave and enlightened deliberations of this Senate. I will not urge them. I cannot rely on them. No, sir, any measure of relief which may be afforded by the National Legislature, should bear the *general stamp* of an act of grace to the individuals interested; it should also be a measure of wise and just policy in relation to the Union. I am no advocate, Mr. President, for the romantic and ostentatious display of generosity on the part of this Government; and this case would not receive the support of my poor abilities, did I not believe that relief is necessary to prevent real, extensive, eminent, and, in my opinion, at least, unmerited suffering. The debt is of such magnitude, that, in point of fact, it cannot possibly be paid in the present state of affairs. Had the people of the West incurred this debt by any imprudence peculiar to themselves, they might have had no claims to your sympathy. But there was no peculiar imprudence in this case. It was no malady confined to that country. It was the general mania that raged universally throughout the land; and, even if the fever was hotter there, it was only because the pabulum which fed it was more copious and tempting.

That these people have erred, miscalculated, and purchased public land greatly beyond their ability to pay for it, is evident enough from the enormous sum which, from the Message of the President of the United States, referred to by the gentleman who has just resumed his seat, (Mr. THOMAS,) it appears that they now owe on that account. But, taking into view the frailties and imperfections of human nature, the want of sufficient foresight, which is the common lot of man, and the illusions of hope, which too easily cheat us into the belief of the practicability of that which we wish to accomplish, the case makes a strong appeal to our compassion. There are, indeed, also, some circumstances in this case, with a part of which the Government has been so intimately connected as ought not only to prevent it from regarding those people with the sternness of stoic indifference, and leaving them to all the unmitigated consequences of the errors into which they have been betrayed, but loudly appeal to the sympathies, clemency, and magnanimity, and even the justice of the National Legislature, and demand the utmost alleviation which it can reasonably grant.

Infatuated as all classes of our fellow-citizens have been, by a short-lived prosperity, which, though depending wholly upon temporary causes, too many believed would be permanent, and too few supposed would end so soon, it is hardly to be supposed that our free representative Government should have been totally exempt from the influence of the general delusion, or that it should not have participated in it, and even given rise to a portion of it.

In all such Governments as ours, the people and Government must necessarily, to a certain extent, at least, reciprocally act upon and influence each other; and therefore, in intimating the opinion that the Government itself did contribute to the delusion which misled our fellow-citizens into excessive purchase of public lands, I do not wish to be understood as imputing any blame or censure whatever, but merely as speaking of things as they actually have been; and as, from the intimate connexion between the people and Government, they must necessarily have been.

The long convulsions in Europe, which grew out of the French Revolution, by furnishing us with a ready and most extraordinary market for our produce, and by the advantages which they afforded to our navigation and commerce, had produced such unparalleled prosperity that the whole nation had become so intoxicated with its ephemeral success as to overlook the causes from whence its prosperity sprung, and upon which its continuance depended.

The late war, so far from abating in the least degree the fallacious calculations that were but too generally indulged, produced a train of events which inspired new and more extravagant hopes and expectations, the causes of which I will endeavor briefly to explain.

In the prosecution of the war, the exigencies of the Government became so pressing that it found itself reduced to the expediency of borrowing large sums of money of the local banks, which it was well known they could not lend without suspending specie payments. And, although the value of bank notes in general must depend upon their convertibility into specie, yet, seeing that the war could not be prosecuted with effect without those loans, public opinion, co-operating with the Government, so far sanctioned the consequent suspensions of specie payments that few men would venture to refuse to take the paper of these banks, lest they should be denounced as enemies to their country. The Government used it to support the war and pay its debts. Public creditors were obliged to receive it, and, to render it as current as possible, it was made receivable in the land offices —all of which circumstances combined to give to it the character of a fair representative of so much real coin. And thus were those banks tempted and seduced to issue a most unexampled and unjustifiable profusion of paper, from which exorbitant profits were made, that generated a spirit of banking which operated like a contagion, and produced a vast multiplication of such institutions— some of which were fortunate enough to have their paper also made receivable in payment for public lands.

These banks were anxious to loan money. The facilities with which it could be obtained could not fail to allure the enterprising citizens of this free and aspiring Republic into almost every species of active adventure and bold speculation, as well as many of them into inconsiderate extravagance. And hence there were many borrowers, and finally an issue of paper so greatly exceeding the whole amount of the current coin of the United States as to beget an infatuation little if any thing short of that which was produced in France and England about a century ago by the memorable Mississippi and South-Sea schemes.

In addition to this monstrous augmentation of our circulating medium, a large number of claims for land on the northwest side of the Ohio, which had been recognised by the Old Congress in 1787, had been converted into certificates, which, as well as the Mississippi stock, were made receivable in payment for public lands—thereby increasing the facilities of paying for, and the temptation to buy, those lands.

It was during this tide of visionary prosperity, which innocent credulity fondly hoped would never ebb, that the most of those purchases were made; and indeed the delusion continued so long, that the hopes and expectations of the most sanguine seemed to acquire strong confirmation of their fancied practicability.

Nor was this infatuation confined to the purchasers of public land, nor to the ignorant, uninformed, and inconsiderate part of the community. It affected all classes of society, and even the Government itself. It gave to every species of property a fictitious value; produced an entire revolution in the manners and habits of our fellow-citizens; substituted in the place of that republican simplicity which had heretofore characterized us, all the extravagant pomp and pageantry of Royalty itself; and gave birth to a multitude of the wildest projects and most visionary speculations.

Our means were thought adequate to accomplish all that the imagination could suggest, or that art could execute, to minister to the comforts, convenience, interest, or pride, of individuals; or to the improvement, embellishment, and aggrandizement, of our country; and of all the various improvements, adventures, or undertakings, by individuals or corporations, which distinguish those times, nothing was attempted but upon the most magnificent scale.

The excessive importations of foreign goods that were made immediately succeeding the peace, and which have proved so ruinous to those who were concerned in them, had so greatly augmented the public revenue, that it was deemed expedient to abolish all internal taxation. The greatest difficulty that seemed to present itself, even to our wisest politicians, was to devise ways and means of disposing of the vast sums which it was supposed would overflow the national coffers. And hence, among other things, was that rage for internal improvements which, agitating the nation from North to South and from East to West, put in requisition the highest order of talents, and produced the most powerful arguments and splendid displays of eloquence which this or any other country can boast, to demonstrate that this Government either had or ought to have delegated power to accomplish this great national object. And yet not one of those keen-sighted politicians and distinguished orators could have imagined that at this early day we should not only be without a single cent to appropriate to such purposes; but that the state of our Treasury should be relied upon as affording the most powerful argument for overthrowing valuable institutions and suspending measures which recent and melancholy experience has evinced to be necessary for our future protection.

The miscalculations and indiscretions of the purchasers of public land, therefore, are not to be wondered at. Even that able statesman, who now so honorably to himself, and so advantageously to his country, fills the first station in the Government, after visiting the Western country, considered the purchase of public land at the minimum price so advantageous to the purchasers, and so injurious to the public interest, that he felt it his duty to recommend to Congress an augmentation of the price. In consequence of which an immense quantity of public land was immediately purchased, with the firm belief that the measure recommended by the President would be adopted. At length, however, those splendid and bewitching visions began to disappear. The paper in circulation, no longer supported by the exigencies of the Government, began to lose its credit, and much of it ceased to answer the purposes of a circulating medium; to supply the want of which was one of the most powerful arguments for the establishment of the Bank of the United States, whose operations soon annihilated many of the local banks, and crippled and prostrated the balance, to the incalculable injury of those who had been induced to rely upon them, by the credit and currency which the Government itself had given to their notes. And thus, after using those banks for the payment of its debts, and seducing our fellow-citizens to rely upon them for the payment of theirs, the Government became instrumental in accelerating the overthrow and ruin of those institutions, to which they had principally exposed themselves by the very loans which they had made to the Government.

The Bank of the United States was, however, relied upon as the great panacea that was to restore to healthful vigor our expiring prosperity. Wise men contended, and good ones sincerely believed, that it would effectually remedy evils that were in themselves incurable, and which nothing but time, with the utmost industry, prudence, and economy, could even alleviate. But if it has not verified all the predictions of its enemies, it has certainly so far disappointed the hopes, expectations, and prom ses of its most reasonable and intelligent friends; for, notwithstanding all the promised amelioration of our condition by this expedient, it most unquestionably aggravated the distress and embarrassments of the whole Western country, at least by prematurely destroying, with rash and inconsiderate hostility, the local currency, without substituting any adequate medium in its place.

The circulating medium of the Union was soon reduced from one hundred and ten to forty-five millions of dollars, of which residue the Western country neither did nor could participate, in proportion either to its numbers or its wants, as must be evident from the immense sums which have been drawn from it on account of public lands; from the balance of trade, as proved by the rate of exchange having been constantly against it, and from the disproportionate expenditure of public money in the Atlantic States.

Money, therefore, with us, became scarce, and within the last two years has almost entirely disappeared. No sound currency remains. Every species of property has lost its value. The products of agriculture have ceased to reward the labor employed in growing them. Commerce languishes. Our manufactures have gone to decay; and nothing is now to be seen but the hopeless despair and ruin which these portentous vicissitudes have occasioned. And hence it is that we have heard so much of the various efforts of several of the most respectable State Legislatures to relieve the embarrassments, alleviate the distress, and avert the ruin, that threatens to overwhelm their fellow-citizens. And, although we may not approve of all the expedients that have been resorted to for that purpose, yet the disposition which they manifest is worthy of our imitation, and ought to be most seriously regarded by us as proof that public sentiment demands of us the utmost relief which it is in our power, consistently with our duty, to extend to a suffering community.

Mr. President, said Mr. E., the records of history furnish no instances of an infatuation so universal, with consequences so much to be deplored, as that which has pervaded our own country, unless they are to be found in the famous Mississippi and South Sea schemes, to which I have already alluded, and which were not more disastrous to the people of France and England than would be the situation of the debtors for public land, if, with all their other engagements to pay money, the Government should continue to hold them bound to pay the prodigious sum of near twenty-three millions of dollars, which they now owe, or lose all the instalments that they have already paid.

It is true, sir, that those cases are not precisely analogous to our own, but they are not without some traits of similitude, for the agency and influence of Government is visible in all of them; and the evils produced in each case primarily resulted from the countenance afforded by Government to incorporated companies, by using them for the payment of public debts, and giving to them a credit which they never otherwise could have acquired. And, although our Government was not, like those of France and England, directly interested in and connected with those moneyed corporations by whose aid it paid its debts, yet there cannot be a doubt that, to the loans which it made from them, to the countenance it afforded to their suspension of specie payments, and to the credit and currency which it gave to their notes, under such circumstances, are justly to be attributed that undue multiplication of banks, and that superabundant issue of paper which have caused the distress that afflicts and the ruin that threatens our suffering fellow-citizens.

Mr. E. dilated upon the conduct of the Government in relation to those banks, and declared that he did verily believe that, but for the loans which it had made from them, and its consequent conduct, we should have escaped the fatal consequences which we all now so sincerely deplore, and which, though they were doubtless not designed, might have been foreseen, because they are the natural consequences of the conduct of the Government, for which it could have no apology except that which is to be found in its necessities at that particular period.

Mr. President, said Mr. E., France and England did not hesitate, in the cases referred to, to extend to their subjects the most prompt and effectual relief that was practicable. Have you less sympathy for the sufferings of your free and patriotic fellow-citizens? Will you hesitate to relieve them when the most that is asked of you is to forbear to take advantage of the indiscretions into which they have been decoyed? To relinquish a mere speculation, which a liberal-minded individual would not hesitate to cancel under similar circumstances?

Mr. President, were the debtors for public lands entirely free from all other embarrassments, it is evident that so small a portion of the community must be utterly unable, in the present state of affairs, to pay the enormous sum which they now owe the Government; a sum that exceeds one-half of the whole amount of the circulating medium of the United States, and is constantly increasing by the accumulation of interest. But, sir, the same causes that have embarrassed others have most certainly equally operated upon them; and there is no part of your population, who, in proportion to their means of payment, have probably contracted a greater mass of other engagement—none whose situation required a greater expenditure of money, as must be obvious to all those who will reflect upon the cost of moving to and making improvements in a new country; the length of time that is necessary to render farms productive, and the necessity, in the mean time, of purchasing every article of husbandry, clothing, and subsistence, with cash.

Besides a great variety of other debts, which the temporary success of themselves, or others, in land speculations, seduced many of those persons to contract, in the vain hope of discharging them with the profits which they expected to realize from the land purchasers, a vast proportion of them are doubtless still indebted to banks or individuals for the very money with which they paid the first instalments upon those lands, whilst, in addition to all the other causes which have contributed to produce their inability to fulfil their engagements, you have depreciated their lands, and destroyed all hopes of resource from the sale of them, by reducing the price of the residue of that part of your own which you have purchased of the Indians, amounting to one hundred and seventy-two millions of acres, to one dollar and twenty-five cents an acre; and immediately bringing into competition with them upwards of fifty-four millions of acres, that are now actually surveyed and in the market; which are events that could not have been foreseen, and certainly were not anticipated by those debtors.

As, then, it is absolutely impossible for them to complete their payments for the lands which they have purchased, it follows that, without the relief which Congress alone can afford them, they must forfeit all that they have already paid on that account, which, if no one of them has paid more than one instalment, cannot be less than between seven and eight millions of dollars; for, as has been correctly stated by my colleague, the law required payments for public lands to be divided into four equal instalments, one of which must have been paid down at the time of making each respective purchase, and, therefore, it is impossible that those debtors can owe the amount reported to be due, without having paid the sum which I have stated. So, if they have paid two instalments, the amount liable to forfeiture is precisely equal to that which is due. And, as many of them have paid two or more instalments, there can be no doubt that the amount greatly exceeds the minimum which I have mentioned.

But, were the sum to be forfeited, only eight millions of dollars, which, if every one who is able, should complete his payments, is, I am sure, the very least that it could possibly be, it surely cannot be difficult to conceive of the individual distress that would be produced, and the dangerous ferments and commotions that might be excited by such a prodigious sacrifice as the total forfeiture of that amount, being nearly equal to one-fifth of our whole circulating medium.

This, however, sir, is an aspect of the case upon which I forbear all further remark, lest I should seem to expect from your fears that which I am very certain would be much more readily yielded to the superior claims upon your humanity and justice. And, indeed, sir, I have no hesitation in saying that, whatever may be your ultimate decision upon the case now under consideration, it will be as likely to be acquiesced in, and submitted to, in the West, as it would be, under similar circumstances, in any other part of the United States; for the people of the Western country, not less patriotic than brave, are second to none in the most devoted attachment to the Union; whose advantage to themselves they duly appreciate, well knowing, among other things, that, with but one single outlet for the products of their country, of such vast extent and unrivalled fertility, they must look to the Atlantic States for that naval protection which, from the peculiarity of their own situation, they are unable to create for themselves. They also believe that their Atlantic brethren, who must become the carriers of their produce, cannot fail to see in their prosperity the best means of increasing their own, by the additional encouragement which it would afford

to their navigation and commerce—objects of great national importance, which the Western people have not been backward in assisting to cherish and to protect.

They have, moreover, seen, with great satisfaction, in some recent measures, a pledge of those liberal feelings towards them, which has allayed all former fears, and forbids the belief that any motive of hostility or jealousy could, in the least degree, influence your decision on the present occasion; and I flatter myself that there is no gentleman of this honorable Senate who, under any circumstances, could find so much cruelty in his heart as to be willing to take from those people even eight millions of dollars, and at the same time keep all the lands for which those dollars were given, together with all the improvements that have been made upon the lands. No, sir; humanity, justice, and sound policy, equally forbid it. ·

The only real difficulty, therefore, that presents itself is, to decide upon the relief which it is expedient and proper to grant. In considering which, the obvious policy of making it so liberal as to prevent all hopes of advantage from future applications to Congress upon the subject, ought not to be overlooked; for experience proves, that where relief in such cases is frequently granted, which must always be likely to happen when it has been inadequate in the first instance, it never fails to beget an habitual dependence upon it, which prevents the necessary exertions to make payment, and often creates a state of things that renders it difficult to refuse, and sometimes necessary to grant, further indulgence, than would have been necessary had sufficient liberality been dispensed in the first instance.

With this view of the subject, it appears to me that the first great object should be to diminish the debt, which can be accomplished justly in two ways—

1st. By permitting purchasers who are unable to pay for the whole of their lands, to relinquish a part of them, upon equitable terms.

2d. By offering just and proper inducements to make prompt payment.

It is the object of the bill now under consideration, to accomplish the first of these measures, by permitting the holders of a plurality of half-quarter sections of land, upon which the whole instalments have not been paid, to relinquish as many entire half-quarter sections as they please, with the privilege of having the money paid thereon applied to their credit, upon such as they may retain.

It is scarcely necessary to remind the Senate, that, as the public lands were required by law to be sold in tracts not exceeding a quarter section in any case, and a half-quarter section in some cases, the sale of each quarter or half-quarter section, as the case may have been, is to be considered as a distinct contract, and therefore the practical effects of the indulgence asked for would be but little, if any thing, more than to enable those unfortunate and distressed public debtors to get rid of so many separate and distinct contracts with the Government as they are unable to comply with, and admits of no arbitrary selections, contrary to the subdivisions which Congress itself has created.

And, besides the inutility and folly of requiring men to perform impossibilities, the Government, in granting this indulgence, will still be in as good a situation as if those improvident contracts had never been made; for, if it does not get the money most imprudently contracted to be paid for its land, it gets back the land itself, without any deterioration, while the purchasers cannot get a single acre for which they will not have paid the Government a full equivalent; and thus the evils which have their origin in an excess of those contracts will be most naturally corrected by diminishing their number, upon such terms as will leave both parties in as good a situation as they would have been in if such excess had never existed.

This measure is greatly to be preferred to any plan of indulgence, whose object is a mere extension of the times of payment; for, embarrassed as those debtors now are, in common with the rest of their fellow citizens, by other engagements, and deprived of all resource in the sale of their lands, by the conduct of the Government in reducing the price of its own; the entire change in our commercial relations, and the permanent loss of foreign markets for all, or nearly all, the great staples of our country, leave no ground to hope that they will be able at any future time, whatever indulgence may be granted to them, to pay the amount which they now owe the Government.

But, even if they should be able to pay, it is not reasonable to suppose that they will do so, since Congress has made it the interest of a great majority of them to forfeit all that they have already paid, rather than to pay the balance that is due. This is particularly the case with all those who have paid one instalment only; for, supposing them to have purchased at the minimum price, they still have to pay one dollar and fifty cents an acre, with interest, while they can purchase as good or better land of the Government, at one dollar and twenty-five cents an acre, without interest; at which price they will be able to repurchase the very lands that may be forfeited when they shall be again offered for sale.

Therefore, taking it for granted that the Government would not wish, under the circumstances that have been mentioned, like a ruthless, heartless sharper, to take advantage of forfeitures which its own conduct had rendered it the interest of a large and meritorious class of citizens to subject themselves to, and seeing that these contracts neither can nor will be complied with, there seems to be no reasonable motive to refuse, and the strongest inducements to grant, to those debtors the privilege of relinquishing a part of their lands, upon the terms proposed, whereby the debt would be diminished. The lands would immediately revert to the Government, and could be disposed of for its benefit, to persons who would improve them. The debtors would be relieved from a debt which, pressing upon them like an *incubus*, paralyzes all their energies, and destroys their enterprise; and the prosperity of the States in which they reside would be greatly promoted—for it can-

not be disguised, that almost all the citizens in some of those States have purchased more land than they can pay for; and, while the fear of losing their lands prevents many from improving them, the desire of others to save as much of the money which they have already advanced as possible, induces them to lay up every cent that they can command for that purpose, and prevents other improvements that would greatly enhance the value of the public lands, and are absolutely necessary to those States.

Strong as these considerations recommend and enjoin the adoption of the measure now under consideration as one of necessary and just relief to those debtors, and of wise and correct policy in relation to the Union, there is an additional view of the subject which exhibits claims to relief which no court of chancery, were it a case between individuals, could refuse to decree and enforce. And I trust that the high character for good faith and honor which this Government has so deservedly acquired at home and abroad is a sufficient pledge that it would not in any case disregard those principles of moral justice which, under precisely similar circumstances, would be obligatory upon individuals.

In order to understand correctly the mutual obligations between the Government and those purchasers, in relation to those contracts, reference must be had to the law under which they were made. It may safely be premised that all the terms offered, and inducements held out to the purchasers by the law, when acceded to by them, became, upon every fair principle of legal construction, as well as of moral justice, obligatory upon the Government, and consequently that the latter could not, without a palpable violation of such obligations, deprive those purchasers of any advantages which the positive declarations of the law at the time of contracting promised them, and which may fairly be considered as having constituted a part (and no inconsiderable either) of the inducements to enter into those contracts.

By the law it was explicitly declared that no public land should be sold for a less price than two dollars per acre. The payments were divided into four equal instalments—one of which was to be paid down at the time of making the purchase. On completing his payments, any purchaser was entitled to his patent; but, if he did not choose to pay within five years from the date of his purchase, the land was to be sold, and all that it might sell for above what was due upon it was to be returned to the first purchaser. Thus every one in purchasing had the two alternatives presented to him, either to purchase with a view to obtain his patent, or to receive the profits upon his money, arising from the enhanced value of the land within five years. Both alternatives were equally fair and legitimate objects of contract, because equally authorized by it. The latter alternative was doubtless presented by the Government to promote sales. Its acceptance therefore by purchasers was a fair and authorized speculation, consistent with the views of the Government, whose object has always been to sell as much land as possible, without any

173   HISTORY OF CONGRESS.   174

JANUARY, 1821.   *Relief to Land Purchasers.*   SENATE.

discrimination with regard to the objects of purchasers. It cannot therefore excuse itself from granting relief to those persons by affecting to consider them as the less entitled to it for being speculators, in yielding to the very temptations with which it seduced them, if indeed there were any thing wrong in the speculation itself. There are however a vast number of persons who have been induced to rely wholly upon the latter alternative from necessity, not choice. No one who purchased with such objects, particularly at the minimum price, and made judicious selections, could have lost by it, and many would have made a considerable profit, had not the price of public land been reduced, contrary to the plighted faith of the Government.

The adoption of this measure has not only depreciated the lands heretofore sold, impaired the ability of purchasers to pay for their lands, and made it their interest to surrender them, but, in relation to all those who relied upon the sale of the lands according to law for the reimbursement of the instalments paid upon them, with a reasonable profit upon their money, it has most injuriously affected their condition; deprived them of advantages connected with their contracts; subjected them to great losses, that could not have been anticipated at the time those contracts were entered into; and would most unquestionably, were it a case between individuals, render it the duty of a court of equity to decree that those contracts should be set aside altogether.

Let me suppose, sir, that the public lands had belonged to an individual who under similar circumstances had sold a part of them, not barely with an understanding, but with a positive, unequivocal declaration, that he would not reduce the price of the residue. Can it, I ask, be doubted, that if he had totally disregarded that declaration, as the Government has done, with so much injury to the purchasers, a court of equity would hesitate to grant relief? These purchasers are *ex æquo et bono* entitled to a return of their money, and the Government ought, for its own sake, be glad to compromise with them upon the terms proposed by the measure now under consideration.

Mr. E. further contended that this measure, by enabling the Government to cause to be settled a large quantity of lands now held by persons who can never pay for them, and therefore will not improve them, would have a tendency to consolidate our settlements, and impart additional strength to our inland frontier; and that it would give a spring to industry which, by increasing our stock of national wealth, would be felt advantageously by the whole Union. But, said he, Mr. President, though those public debtors may see but little prospect of ever paying for or disposing of their lands to advantage, yet, if they cannot be permitted to relinquish a part of them upon equitable terms, the hope of some favorable occurrence—some auspicious turn of affairs, or more propitious fortune—will induce them to retain the whole of those lands, not only as long as the law now allows, but as long as the utmost indulgence of Congress (for which you will be constantly importuned) will permit.

So that you will ultimately have to compromise upon terms not better than those proposed, or to resort to the odious alternative of enforcing forfeitures, and taking from those people an immense sum of money, without rendering them the slightest equivalent for it. This, sir, would indeed be so much like a parent robbing his own children, and so repugnant to the best feelings of the human heart, as well as to all the maxims of justice, that it would be very difficult to persevere in it against the constant petitions of those people, backed and supported as they now are, and hereafter will be, by their respective States, whose influence, if it should bear any proportion to their rapidly increasing population, will not be altogether unavailing, in a just cause, some ten years hence.

Mr. President, depend upon it, sir, public sentiment never will, under the whole circumstances of the case, sanction the exaction of such forfeitures from the brave and patriotic defenders of our frontiers, when the necessity for them can be avoided without any real sacrifice, and upon such just and equitable terms. And, though the time may not yet have arrived, I am persuaded it is not distant when relief will be granted to those upon whom forfeitures have already been enforced. I confess that, for one, I am prepared to grant it at any time, believing, as I sincerely do, that, while liberality and justice recommend it, good policy does not forbid it, because it is as intrinsically wrong in a Government as it would be in an individual unnecessarily to take, or to keep, something for nothing. The sum forfeited is a serious punishment for so slight an indiscretion. The object of punishment itself is not vindictive. The necessity of example has ceased, since the law upon which it was intended to operate has been repealed; and the aggregate amount of those forfeitures is a serious loss to the Western country itself, which contributes so largely to the public revenue, and participates so little in the expenditure of public money. I therefore would not hesitate, particularly in times of such universal distress, which the Government has unquestionably contributed to produce, to grant to these persons certificates receivable in payment for public land, to the amount which they have respectively forfeited; whereby they would get only the value of their money, while the Government would not part with an acre of land for which it would not have received a full equivalent. But, be this as it may, the solicitude which the Western States now feel, and are most strongly manifesting upon this subject, as appears by the petitions now upon your table, sufficiently indicates that, unless suitable relief should be granted, you may annually expect petitions, memorials, and remonstrances, against all future forfeitures; and it is not to be doubted that nothing less than the most judicious management can prevent this enormous debt from becoming the fruitful source of much future difficulty and trouble, intermingling itself in all elections, and producing political effects which no one could regret more than myself.

I therefore trust that enough has been said to demonstrate the expediency of diminishing the debt, not only by permitting the relinquishment of a part of the land, but by offering just and proper inducements to make prompt payment for the balance.

This being a measure of sound policy, as well as of justice, its objects will be most effectually attained by making those inducements as liberal as the public interest will permit. And, as the success of the measure must depend upon the ability as well as the inclination of the debtors, they should not only be allowed suitable deductions to create the necessary incentives to make prompt payment, but reasonable time to render it practicable for them to do so.

I can see no difficulty in deciding what deduction ought, in sheer justice, to be made; for, if the Government, by the reduction of the price of its own lands, has imposed upon itself any equitable obligation whatever in favor of those debtors, (which all admit,) it is to allow them a deduction equal to the difference between the price contracted to be paid to the Government for those lands, and the value to which they have been reduced by the Government, which, whether considered in reference to the actual depreciation of the land, or appreciation of money, cannot be less than 37½ per cent.; for the land heretofore sold at two dollars an acre will not now command more than the present minimum price, while the latter will purchase the same quantity of as good land as could heretofore have been purchased at the former minimum; and it would seem to be unreasonable, if not unjust, that the Government, having the power to do so, should, by its own act, reduce the land which it has heretofore sold, to a certain value, and yet demand more than that value of it.

With this view of the subject, and taking into consideration the difficulties and embarrassments of the present times, it appears to me to be both just and expedient to allow a deduction of 37½ per cent. to all who shall pay up on or before the 31st December next, without interest, and with interest to those who shall pay up at any time between that day and the 30th September, 1822; at which latter period, the indulgence for such as may be unable to avail themselves of those proffered inducements should commence. By these means, every cent that could be commanded for that purpose would be paid into your Treasury, and this awful subject would be finally put to rest.

Let it not be supposed that the success of the two first measures proposed will be, in the least degree, affected by the indulgence which is asked for those whose peculiar situation will prevent them from relinquishing their lands, and who may not be able to avail themselves of the proffered inducements to make prompt payments.

You have, in the personal interest of the debtors for public land, the most efficient guarantee against any such consequences, unless you can suppose that that energetic spring of human action has much less influence upon them than upon all the rest of mankind.

It has been correctly assumed by the honorable Secretary of the Treasury, in his annual report,

that the extent of the national domain will, for ages, enable the Government to determine the price of unimproved land, similarly situated. The effects produced by the practical demonstration of such a power, in the reduction of the price of public land, and the quantity brought into market, as has been stated by my colleague, and as I have already endeavored to show, would of themselves be sufficient to induce a great majority of those debtors to surrender their lands, even though no relief whatever should be afforded them.

There can be no rational motive to induce them, under existing circumstances, to wish to keep unimproved lands, for which they could not make prompt payment upon the terms proposed. It would be madness itself to retain them for the purposes of speculation, since such an immense quantity of as good or better land can be purchased at a lower price; and therefore it may be fairly presumed that none would wish to avail themselves of the latter measure of relief, except such as have made improvements upon their lands, and may be unable, from the pressure of the present times, to make prompt payment. These being the actual cultivators of the soil, the most needy, and at the same time the most meritorious and deserving of relief, will not relinquish their lands, though they may not be able to pay for them within the time prescribed by law—but they will rely upon your future mercy. The longer time you allow for the operation of the proposed inducements to make prompt payments, the more of them will be made, and the fewer of these cases will remain. Some, however, will necessarily still exist, and therefore such cases ought to be provided for at this time, so as to prevent the necessity of our having to legislate again upon the subject.

Mr. President, said Mr. E., were any reasoning wanting to prove that no system of coercion ought to be resorted to in less than two years, it is to be found in the late annual Treasury Report; for if, as is therein contended, the condition of the currency in several of the States in the Union; the exclusion from circulation in all the States west and south of the seat of Government, of the notes of the Bank of the United States and its branches; and there being no sound paper in circulation in several of those States, prove "that a resort to internal taxation, under such circumstances, would be to require of the citizens of those States what would be impossible for them to perform," and did last year, and do this year, justify a resort to loans to support the Government in a time of profound peace. If, I say, these circumstances are sufficient to prove the inability of the whole people of the United States to pay the amount of the loan of the last year, or the amount of the reported balance against the Treasury on the first day of the present year, *a fortiori,* they prove that the debtors for public land, being a part only of the population of a few of the very States in which those causes of embarrassment have operated, and continue to operate, most powerfully, must be utterly unable to pay the estimated sum that is proposed to be drawn from them, which is but little short of the amount of the loan of the last year, or the reported deficit in the revenue at the commencement of the present year.

Mr. President, said Mr. E., the population of the United States, I presume, may be safely estimated at ten millions ; if so, the loan of last year would be at the rate of thirty cents for each one of our whole population ; the amount of the balance against the Treasury at the commencement of the present year would require still less ; but even supposing the loan to be seven millions of dollars, as proposed by the honorable Secretary of the Treasury, (and I flatter myself we shall not want half that amount,) it would only be at the rate of seventy cents each. And can it be conceded to be "impossible" for the whole population of the Union, or even that of the Southern and Western States in general, to pay at the rate of seventy cents each, and, at the same time, be supposed that a part of the population of Ohio, Indiana, Illinois, Alabama, Mississippi, and two land districts in Missouri, with the few purchasers of public land which the present year may produce, will be able to pay two and a half millions of dollars, which is the sum estimated to be received from them ?

There must, indeed, sir, be a fallacy in supposing that the whole people of the Union are unable to do so little, or that so considerable a part of our whole population will be able to do so much : and I hope you will not adopt the latter opinion in the present case, and the former one when we come to act upon the proposition for a loan, whatever may be the amount required ; for I deem it all-important that we should not mistake in our estimate of what it is in the power of the debtors of public land to perform.

The debt of Alabama, divided among her white population, would not be less than one hundred and twenty dollars each, which, divided into ten annual instalments, would be twelve dollars per annum to be paid by each. Deduct one-half the debt, it would reduce the proportion, as before stated, to six dollars ; but strike off three-fourths of the debt, (and, I presume, a greater reduction could not be safely calculated on,) it would still leave to be paid, for ten years in succession, at the rate of three dollars per annum for each one of her whole white population. And can it be supposed that Alabama, which has no sound paper circulation at all, is capable of doing more, and yet that it is impossible for the whole population of the Union to pay at the rate of seventy cents even for one year only ? But I will not pursue the subject further.

I had, indeed, sir, intended to have availed myself much more at large of the reasoning and statements contained in the Treasury report ; but the fatigue which I myself feel, admonishes me not to trespass longer upon the patience of the Senate, which I fear is already exhausted. Therefore, hoping that every member of this honorable body feels the importance of putting this momentous subject to rest, I will conclude by barely remarking that this truly desirable object can only be accomplished by duly considering what those debtors for public land are capable of performing, with

reasonable exertions, and requiring no more of them : for, without this, they will be encouraged to petition you again and again ; while you yourselves will not, cannot be inflexible, unless you should feel the most perfect conviction that you had done all, or rather more than ought to have been expected of you ; and if, for the want of due liberality on the present occasion, it should become necessary to grant further relief at some future session of Congress, God only knows when the business will end. Were I to judge from what I have witnessed in a similar case, I should certainly suppose, not until a large majority of this House shall have taken their exit for another world. Therefore, as well to discourage and prevent future applications for relief, as to fortify your own determination to adhere to the measures you are now about to adopt, believe me, sir, it is better to require too little than too much.

When Mr. Edwards had concluded, the bill was laid on the table till to-morrow.

FRIDAY, January 12.

The PRESIDENT communicated a report of the Secretary of the Navy, made in obedience to a resolution of the Senate of the first of May last, requesting the Secretary of the Navy to cause to be revised the rules, regulations, and instructions, for the naval service ; and the report was read, and referred to the Committee on Naval Affairs.

Mr. DANA presented the memorial of David Mallory, of Connecticut, praying a pension in consideration of Revolutionary services ; and the memorial was read.

On motion by Mr. DANA,

Ordered, That it be referred to the Committee on Pensions, to consider and report thereon.

Mr. OTIS, from the Committee on the Public Buildings, to whom was referred the petition of Julia Plantou, made a report, accompanied by the following resolution :

Resolved, That the petitioner have leave to withdraw her petition.

The report and resolution were read.

Mr. WALKER, of Georgia, from the Committee on Naval Affairs, to whom was referred the petition of Samuel Tucker, made a report, accompanied by a bill for the relief of Samuel Tucker, late a captain in the Navy of the United States ; and the report and bill were read.

Ordered, That the bill pass to a second reading.

The Senate proceeded to consider the motion of yesterday, instructing the Committee on Naval Affairs to inquire whether there are any obstructions to the navigation of the river Thames, in the State of Connecticut, which were placed there by the American ships during the late war, and what measures ought to be adopted to remove them if any there are ; and agreed thereto.

The bill for the relief of Nathan Ford was read the second time.

The bill to authorize the President of the United States to ascertain and designate certain boundaries, was read the second time.

Mr. EDWARDS gave notice that, on Monday

179   **HISTORY OF CONGRESS.**   180

SENATE.   *Road—Miami of the Lakes—Bank of the United States.*   JANUARY, 1821.

next, he should ask leave to bring in a bill confirming certain claims to land in the State of Illinois.

Mr. NOBLE submitted the following motion for consideration :

Resolved, That the Committee on the Public Lands be instructed to inquire into the expediency of authorizing by law a patent to issue to James Nickles, senr., for the southwest quarter of section nine in township No. 11 north, range No. 5 east, which said southwest quarter has been located by the said James Nickles, senr., in the State of Indiana, by virtue of a warrant from the War Department, No. 245.

Mr. JOHNSON, of Kentucky, submitted the following motion for consideration :

Resolved, That the Committee on Pensions be instructed to inquire into the expediency of increasing the pension of Willis Tandy.

Mr. EATON submitted the following motion for consideration :

Resolved, That the Committee on Finance inquire into the expediency of so amending the act of last session " to provide for the publication of the laws of the United States, and for other purposes," that the private acts of Congress and Indian treaties shall be published in some one newspaper in the District of Columbia.

ROAD—MIAMI OF THE LAKE.

Mr. TRIMBLE communicated the following resolutions of the General Assembly of the State of Ohio; which were read:

" The committee, to whom was referred so much of the Governor's message as relates to the roads contemplated by the Treaty of Brownstown, have had the same under consideration, and have collected all the information on that subject within their reach ; and find that, on the 26th of January last, a select committee was appointed in the House of Representatives of the Congress of the United States, to inquire whether any, and, if any, what, further provisions were necessary to give effect to the provisions of the Treaty of Brownstown, in the Territory of Michigan. That to that committee, the resolution on that subject, passed by the General Assembly of this State, at their last session, was referred, together with other documents on the same subject. That that committee, on the 12th day of May last, made a long and elaborate report, accompanied by a resolution, which resolution the committee have thought proper to transcribe, and make a part of this report, which is as follows, viz :

" *Resolved,* That the Committee on Roads and Canals be instructed to bring in a bill to authorize the Secretary of the Treasury to contract with any person or persons to construct a permanent and suitable road, to extend from the foot of the rapids of the Miami of the Lake, to the western line of the Connecticut Western Reserve, according to the plan contemplated by the Treaty of Brownstown ; and, on such route passing through the reserve (so called) at Lower Sandusky, as the President may direct, in consideration of the whole of the tracts on each side of the contemplated road, which were granted by the Treaty of Brownstown, or so much thereof, as, in the opinion of the Secretary of the Treasury, may be adequate to the object. And in which bill shall also be inserted, among other things, a provision or provisions, that the person or persons so contracted with, do complete the said road within a reasonable time in said bill to be limited : That such person or persons do stipulate to keep said road in good repair for and during a number of years, to be in said bill defined ; and, also, that the person or persons so contracted with, do also give bond, with sufficient sureties, for the faithful performance of his or their contract ; and, also, a provision defining the time and manner in which the title to said land may be conveyed.

" The committee, from an examination of the report and resolution above alluded to, are of opinion, that the plan contemplated therein is the best, under existing circumstances, that can be devised. The committee would, therefore, recommend the adoption of the following resolution :

" *Resolved by the General Assembly of the State of Ohio,* That they do concur in the afore-mentioned report made, and resolution reported to the Congress of the United States : And that our Senators and Representatives in Congress be requested to use their best endeavors to procure the passage of the law contemplated thereby.

" *Resolved further,* That the Governor of this State be, and he is hereby, requested to send a copy of the foregoing report and resolutions to each of our Senators and Representatives in Congress.

        " JOSEPH RICHARDSON,
           " *Speaker of the House of Rep's.*
        " ALLEN TRIMBLE,
           " *Speaker of the Senate.*
" DECEMBER 26, 1820."

The resolutions were referred to the Committee on Roads and Canals.

RELIEF TO LAND PURCHASERS.

The Senate resumed, as in Committee of the Whole, the consideration of the bill for the relief of the purchasers of public lands prior to the first day of July, 1820 ; and, on motion by Mr. EATON, that the bill be recommitted to the Committee on Public Lands, with instructions to—

1st. Make the provisions of the bill applicable to those purchasers of public lands only who have purchased at public sale since the 30th day of December, 1816.

2d. And with instructions to extend the contemplated relief to none but those who, on or before the 30th day of October last, had made a settlement on the lands by them so purchased, defining and considering the settlement of any quarter section, a settlement of all contiguous and adjoining land, not exceeding two entire sections.

3d. And with instructions to extend the contemplated relief to no section on which any town may have been laid off, and the lots sold by any individual or company of individuals :

On motion by Mr. OTIS, the further consideration of the bill was postponed to Monday next.

BANK OF THE UNITED STATES.

The Senate took up the bill reported by the Committee on Finance, to amend the act to incorporate the subscribers to the Bank of the United States, (proposing penal enactments against violations of their trust by officers of the bank or its branches ; and authorizing the appointment of two officers to sign the notes of the bank, instead of the president and cashier.)

Mr. SANFORD laid before the Senate, in a speech of some length, the views which operated on the Committee on Finance in recommending this bill; the reasons in favor of its provisions, and those which induced the committee not to recommend the other two objects petitioned for by the bank.

Mr. ROBERTS moved to amend the bill by adding thereto the following sections:

SEC. 3. *Be it further enacted,* That the bills or notes of the offices of discount and deposite of the said bank, excepting those of the office in the District of Columbia, originally made payable, or which shall have become payable on demand, shall be receivable in all payments to the United States, only in the States and Territories in which they are made payable, and in the States and Territories in which no office of discount and deposite shall be established; any thing in the fourteenth section of the act incorporating the subscribers to the Bank of the United States to the contrary notwithstanding: *Provided,* That all notes of the denomination of five dollars, issued either by the bank or any of its offices of discount and deposite, made payable on demand, shall be receivable at the bank or any of its offices: *And provided, further,* That it shall not be lawful for the directors of the said bank to establish more than one office of discount and deposite in any State, without the consent of the Legislature thereof first had and obtained.

SEC. 4. *Be it further enacted,* That so much of the second and fourteenth fundamental article of the constitution of said bank, contained in the eleventh section of the act incorporating the subscribers thereto, as provides that no director of the said bank or any of its offices of discount and deposite, shall hold his office more than three years out of four in succession, be, and the same is hereby, repealed.

SEC. 5. *Be it further enacted,* That the directors of the said corporation shall cause a list of the stockholders of the said bank, together with their places of residence, to be kept in the banking house, at Philadelphia, open to the inspection of any and every stockholder of said bank, who may apply for the same within hours of business, for at least ninety days previously to every annual election of directors; and no person who may be entitled to vote at any election for directors of said bank, as attorney, proxy, or agent, for any other person, copartnership, or body politic, shall, as such, give a greater number than —— votes, under any pretence whatsoever; and no letter of proxy shall be of any force or effect longer than —— years, or until it shall have been revoked.

SEC. 6. *Be it further enacted,* That, whenever the said corporation assent to the provisions of this act, and certify such assent to the Secretary of the Treasury Department, by writing, duly authenticated, this act shall be of full force and effect, and not otherwise.

Some debate ensuing on this proposition, as well as on the bill itself, a motion prevailed to postpone the bill to Wednesday, that the amendment might be printed; and the bill was postponed accordingly.

Mr. SANFORD, having laid before the Senate sundry papers connected with the subject of this bill, which had been communicated to the Committee on Finance by the Bank of the United States, to enforce the expediency of granting the objects prayed for in their memorial—

Mr. OTIS moved that these papers be printed for the use of the Senate.

Mr. BARBOUR moved that all the papers submitted to the Committee on Finance by the bank be printed.

[This motion was understood, by the debate which ensued on it, to refer to a particular paper which had been communicated to the committee by the bank, with a request that it might be received confidentially; which paper is understood to contain a statement of frauds committed on the bank, and the names of those persons or officers who committed them.]

A good deal of discussion took place on this motion, and many gentlemen entered into it. The debate turned principally on the propriety of making public information of this personal character, which had been confidentially communicated to a committee of the body to whom the subject had been referred, simply to show the expediency of granting to the bank the security of penal sanctions against violations of trust by its officers, and the reason which existed for asking of Congress this additional guard against such treacherous spoliations, some gentlemen being in favor of making the information public, as a just punishment of the offenders, and a warning to the world against them; and others being opposed to disclosing it, under the circumstances in which it came to the knowledge of the Senate. In the course of the debate, it appeared that the document was not now in possession of the committee, and part of the discussion referred to the propriety of taking measures to obtain it, the proper mode of proceeding with that object, &c. The debate was terminated by a motion by Mr. SMITH to postpone the subject to Monday, with the view of then submitting a resolution on the subject; and the subject was postponed—ayes 21; and the Senate adjourned to Monday.

MONDAY, January 15.

The PRESIDENT communicated a letter from the Secretary of the Treasury, transmitting statements of the payments made according to law during the year 1820, for miscellaneous claims of such demands of a civil nature as are not otherwise provided for; of contracts made relative to oil, lighthouses, buoys, stakeages, &c.; of contracts and purchases made by the collectors for the revenue service during the year 1819; and of expenditures on account of sick and disabled seamen during the year 1819; and the letter and statements were read.

The PRESIDENT also communicated a letter from the Secretary of the Treasury, transmitting a statement exhibiting the amount received by each clerk in the several offices of the Treasury Department for services rendered during the year 1820; and the letter and statement were read.

Mr. KING, of Alabama, presented ten petitions, severally signed by a number of the merchants, and citizens, shipmasters, and shipowners, of the town of Blakeley, and of the merchants of the interior towns in the State of Alabama, praying that the town of Blakeley may be made a port of entry; and the petitions were read, and severally referred to the Committee on Commerce and Manufactures.

Mr. WALKER, of Alabama, presented a petition, signed by a number of individuals concerned directly or indirectly in the purchase of public lands prior to the law "making further provision for the sale of the public lands," stating that said law operates injuriously on them, and praying that they may be permitted to apply the payments already made to such portions of their entries as such payments will cover at two dollars per acre, and that the residue may revert to the United States; and the petition was read, and laid on the table.

Mr. THOMAS presented a petition, signed by a number of the inhabitants of the village of Cote Sans Dessein, in the Territory of Missouri, praying to be confirmed in their title to certain lands in said Territory; and the petition was read, and referred to the Committee on Public Lands.

Mr. SMITH submitted the following motion for consideration:

Resolved, That, the better to enable Congress, in considering a bill to amend the act, entitled "An act to incorporate the subscribers to the Bank of the United States," to apportion the punishment to be inflicted upon the Presidents, Directors, Cashiers, and other officers or servants of the Bank of the United States, and its several offices, or branch banks, the President of the Bank be requested to transmit to the Senate, if any such exist, a statement of any and all fraudulent conversions by the said Presidents, Directors, Cashiers, officers, or servants, of any of them, of any moneys, bills, notes, securities for money, evidences of debt, or other effects whatsoever, belonging to the said bank, to his or their own use; and in what offices these frauds have been practised, and to what extent, and by whom committed, and at what times; and likewise to state what facilities each of those several officers have, by means of their stations respectively, to commit frauds of this character.

Mr. TRIMBLE submitted the following motions for consideration:

1. *Resolved,* That the Committee on Roads and Canals be instructed to inquire into the expediency of authorizing by law the employment of the Topographical engineers, under the direction of the President of the United States, in surveying roads and canals through the public lands, in such places and upon such plan as will best promote the general interest, and improve the military defence of the United States.

2. *Resolved,* That the Committee on Roads and Canals be instructed to inquire into the expediency of authorizing by law the employment of the Topographical engineers in surveying, under the direction of the President of the United States, canals to connect the navigable waters between Boston Harbor, in the State of Massachusetts, and Pamlico Sound, in the State of North Carolina, in such direction and on such plan as will best promote the interests and military and naval defence of the United States.

On motion by Mr. THOMAS, the Committee on Public Lands were discharged from the further consideration of the resolution of the 2d instant, instructing them to inquire into the expediency of authorizing a map of the military bounty lands to be annexed to the patent to be granted to each soldier.

On motion by Mr. MORRIL, the committee to whom was referred the Message of the President of the United States of the 13th December, transmitting information relative to the execution of the "Act authorizing the purchase of fire engines, and building houses for the safe-keeping of the same," were discharged from the further consideration thereof.

Mr. THOMAS, from the Committee on Public Lands, to whom was referred the memorial of the General Assembly of the State of Missouri, in behalf of settlers on public lands, made a report, accompanied by a resolution that the prayer of the memorialist be rejected.

Mr. THOMAS, from the same committee, to whom was referred the petition of the inhabitants of that part of the State of Indiana called the Brookville land district, made a report, accompanied by a resolution that the prayer of the petitioners ought not to be granted.

Mr. EDWARDS obtained leave to bring in a bill confirming certain claims to lands in the State of Illinois; and the bill was passed to a second reading.

Mr. ROBERTS, from the Committee of Claims, to whom was referred the petition of Elisha Gordon, reported a bill for the relief of the representatives of Patience Gordon, widow, deceased; and the bill was read, and passed to a second reading.

Mr. ROBERTS laid on the table a letter from the Secretary of the Treasury in relation to the claim of Elisha Gordon.

The Senate having proceeded to fill the vacancy occasioned by the death of Mr. BURRILL, in the committee appointed to inquire into the expediency of reducing the pay of the members of Congress and officers of the Executive departments, Mr. STOKES was appointed to supply said vacancy.

Mr. MACON was appointed to supply the vacancy in the Committee of Pensions, occasioned by the resignation of Mr. WILSON.

The bill for the relief of Samuel Tucker, late captain in the Navy of the United States, was read the second time.

The Senate proceeded to consider the report of the Committee on the Public Buildings on the petition of Julia Plantou; and, on motion by Mr. ROBERTS, it was laid on the table.

The Senate proceeded to consider the motion of the 12th instant, instructing the Committee on Public Lands to inquire into the expediency of granting a patent to James Nickles, sr., for a quarter section of land; and agreed thereto.

The Senate proceeded to consider the motion of the 12th instant, instructing the Committee on Pensions to inquire into the expediency of increasing the pension of Willis Tandy; and agreed thereto.

The Senate proceeded to consider the motion of the 12th instant, instructing the Committee on Finance to inquire into the expediency of directing the publication of the private acts of Congress and Indian treaties; and agreed thereto.

The PRESIDENT communicated a letter from the

Secretary of the Navy, transmitting an abstract of the expenditures on account of the contingent expenses of the Navy during the year ending on the 30th of September last; and the letter and abstract were read.

Mr. LANMAN laid on the table certain depositions in relation to the obstructions of the navigation of the river Thames; which were referred to the Committee on Naval Affairs.

MATTHEW LYON.

The Senate then proceeded to consider the report of the select committee on the petition of Matthew Lyon, who prays to be indemnified for the damages which were inflicted on him under the former Sedition law. The report concludes with the following resolutions:

Resolved, That so much of the act, entitled "An act for the punishment of certain crimes against the United States," approved the 14th July, 1798, as pretends to prescribe and punish libels, is unconstitutional.

Resolved, That the fines collected under that act ought to be restored to those from whom they were exacted; and that these resolutions be recommitted to the committee who brought them in, with instructions to report a bill to that effect.

The resolutions having been read, Mr. BARBOUR rose in support of them, and spoke about two hours; when (not having finished his argument) he gave way for a motion to postpone the subject until tomorrow; which prevailed.

TUESDAY, January 16.

Mr. THOMAS presented the petition of the inhabitants and settlers in that part of the State of Illinois, commonly called the *Sangamo country,* praying the right of pre-emption to the lands settled by them; and the petition was read, and referred to the Committee on Public Lands.

Mr. EATON, from the Committee on Finance, to whom the subject was referred, reported a bill supplementary to an act passed on the 11th of May, 1820, entitled "An act to provide for the publication of the laws of the United States, and for other purposes;" and the bill was read, and passed to the second reading.

On motion, by Mr. HORSEY, the Secretary of the Treasury was directed to lay before the Senate the latest statements he may have received, showing the state of the several incorporated banks in the District of Columbia.

On motion, by Mr. VAN DYKE, the Senate proceeded to consider, as in Committee of the Whole, the bill to establish an uniform system of bankruptcy throughout the United States; and it was postponed to, and made the order of the day for, Monday next.

The bill for the relief of the representatives of Patience Gordon, widow, deceased, was read the second time.

The bill confirming certain claims to land in the State of Illinois was read the second time, and referred to the Committee on Public Lands.

The Senate resumed the consideration of the report of the Committee of Public Lands on the petition of the trustees of Worthington College, in Ohio; and it was postponed to Monday next.

MATTHEW LYON.

The Senate then resumed the consideration of the report of the select committee on the case of Matthew Lyon.

Mr. BARBOUR concluded the argument which he left unfinished yesterday, in support of the resolutions.

Mr. WALKER, of Georgia, next rose and spoke some time against the resolutions.

Mr. JOHNSON of Kentucky replied to Mr. W. and advocated the resolutions.

WEDNESDAY, January 17.

Mr. WALKER, of Alabama, presented the petition of William Dick, of Alabama, praying that he may be permitted to surrender the certificate for a quarter section of land erroneously entered in his name, and that the amount paid therefor may be credited in payment for other lands; and the petition was read and referred to the Committee on Public Lands.

Mr. NOBLE presented the petition of Isaac M. Johnson and others, inhabitants of that part of the State of Indiana called the "New Purchase," in the Brookvill Land District, praying that the pre-emption right to a quarter section of land may be granted to Moses Finch, senr., for the purpose of building a bridge over Blue River; and the petition was read and referred to the Committee on Public Lands.

Mr. JOHNSON, of Louisiana, presented the memorial of the General Assembly of that State, praying that a military road may be made on each side of the Mississippi river, from Fort St. Philip to the English Turn; and the memorial was read and referred to the Secretary for the Department of War.

Mr. HOLMES, of Maine, from the Committee on Finance, to whom the subject was referred, reported a bill further to establish the compensation of the officers employed in the collection of duties on imports and tonnage, and for other purposes; and the bill was read, and passed to a second reading.

Mr. WILLIAMS, of Tennessee, from the Committee on Military Affairs, to whom was referred the petition of Robert Swartwout, reported a bill for the relief of General Robert Swartwout; which was read, and passed to a second reading.

Mr. PARROTT gave notice, that, to-morrow, he should ask leave to bring in a bill authorizing the repair of a sea-wall at the Isles of Shoals, and for other purposes.

The Senate resumed the consideration of the motion of the second instant instructing the Committee on the Judiciary to report a bill extending the judicial authority of the United States over the State of Missouri; and, on motion by Mr. EATON, it was laid on the table.

Mr. RUGGLES communicated the following resolutions of the General Assembly of the State of Ohio; which were read:

" *Resolved by the General Assembly of the State of Ohio*, That our Senators and Representatives in Congress be requested to use their exertions to procure the passage of a law, granting and allowing, out of the United States' lands lying within this State, now unlocated, and to which the Indian title has been recently extinguished, so much land for the use of schools in that part of the State known by the "Connecticut Reserve," as shall, with such lands as have heretofore been granted, amount to one thirty-sixth part of the land on said reserve.

" *Resolved*, That the Governor be requested to transmit a copy of this resolution to each of our Senators and Representatives in Congress.

"JOSEPH RICHARDSON,
" *Speaker of the House of Rep's.*
" ALLEN TRIMBLE,
" *Speaker of the Senate.*

" JANUARY 1, 1821."

The resolutions were referred to the Committee on Public Lands.

The Senate proceeded to consider the report of the Committee on Public Lands on the petition of the inhabitants of that part of the State of Indiana called the Brookville Land District; and, in concurrence therewith, resolved that the prayer of the petitioner ought not to be granted.

The Senate proceeded to consider the motion of the 15th instant instructing the Committee on Roads and Canals to inquire into the expediency of employing the topographical engineers in surveying roads and canals through the public lands; and agreed thereto.

The Senate proceeded to consider the motion of the 15th instant instructing the Committee on Roads and Canals to inquire into the expediency of employing the topographical engineers in surveying canals to connect the navigable waters between Boston Harbor and Pamlico Sound; and it was postponed until to-morrow.

The bill supplementary to an act passed on the eleventh of May, 1820, entitled "An act to provide for the publication of the laws of the United States, and for other purposes," was read the second time.

Mr. THOMAS, from the Committee on Public Lands, to whom was referred the memorial of the General Assembly of the State of Missouri, representing the injurious operation of the act of Congress, requiring prompt payment for the public lands, on the actual settlers thereon, submitted the following report:

That, by an act of Congress, of the 12th April 1814, every person, or the legal representative of every person, who had actually inhabited and cultivated a tract of land lying in the Missouri Territory, which tract was not rightfully claimed by any other person, and who had not removed from the said Territory, was entitled to a preference in becoming the purchaser from the United States of such tract of land, at private sale, at the same price and on the same terms and conditions, in every respect, as were or might be provided by law for the sale of other lands sold at private sale in said Territory at the time of making such purchase, under other restrictions prescribed by the said act. The committee are of opinion that, inasmuch as the right of pre-emption was granted to those settlers upon the express condition that the lands should be paid for on the same terms and conditions in every respect, that were or might be provided by law for the sale of their lands sold at private sale, in said Territory, at the time of making the purchase; and, moreover, as, by the act requiring prompt payment, the minimum price of the public land is reduced from two dollars to one dollar and twenty-five cents an acre, they have no just cause of complaint; and therefore recommend that the prayer of the memorialists be rejected.

The report was taken up and concurred in by the Senate.

BANK OF THE UNITED STATES.

The Senate proceeded to consider the motion made on Friday, by Mr. SANFORD, to print sundry papers connected with, or illustrative of, the bill reported by the Committee of Finance to amend the charter of the Bank of the United States—Mr. BARBOUR's motion to print *all* the papers communicated by the bank to the committee (including the private statement of frauds and the names of the defrauders) being the first question for decision.

Mr. BARBOUR's motion was negatived, and the original motion was agreed to.

The Senate then took up the resolution offered by Mr. SMITH, on Monday, to call on the president of the bank for a list, as far as it could be furnished, of all frauds committed on the bank by any of its officers, the names of the defrauders, at what offices committed, the facilities possessed by the officers for committing them, &c.

On motion of Mr. SANFORD, the resolution was amended by adding a request for "a statement ' of the number of bank notes issued by the bank, ' signed by the president and countersigned by the ' cashier thereof, of every different amount or de-' nomination; and also a statement of the amount ' of notes heretofore issued and made payable at the ' principal bank, and the amount of notes made ' payable at the different offices "

The question being then put on the resolution as amended, it was decided in the negative, and the resolution rejected.

MATTHEW LYON.

The Senate then resumed the consideration of the report and resolutions in the case of Matthew Lyon.

Mr. SMITH delivered a speech of near two hours, principally against the expediency of legislating on the subject.

Mr. TALBOT followed in a speech of nearly the same length, in support of the resolutions. When he concluded, the Senate adjourned.

THURSDAY, January 18.

The PRESIDENT communicated a letter from the Secretary of the Treasury, transmitting a report of the Director of the Mint; and the letter and report were read.

Mr. ROBERTS presented the memorial of the merchants, traders, manufacturers, mechanics, landlords, and others, of the city of Philadelphia, praying that a duty of ten per cent. may be imposed on all merchandise when disposed of t auction in the original packages, and fifteen pe.

189   HISTORY OF CONGRESS.   190

JANUARY, 1821.   *Case of Matthew Lyon—Roads and Canals.*   SENATE.

cent. when so disposed of in less quantities, with certain exceptions; and the memorial was read, and referred to the Committee on Commerce and Manufactures.

Mr. THOMAS, from the Committee on Public Lands, to whom was referred the petition of the chiefs of the Choctaw nation of Indians in behalf of Silas Dinsmore, made a report, accompanied by a resolution, that the prayer of the petitioners ought not to be granted. The report and resolution were read.

Mr. ROBERTS, from the Committee of Claims, to whom was referred the bill for the relief of John Hoffman, reported it without amendment.

Mr. PARROTT asked and obtained leave to bring in a bill authorizing the repair of a sea-wall at the Isles of Shoals, and for other purposes; and the bill was read, and passed to a second reading.

Mr. KING, of Alabama, submitted the following motion for consideration:

Resolved, That the Committee on Public Lands be instructed to inquire into the expediency of authorising Jared E. Groce to enter a fraction of seventy-four acres of land situate on the Alabama river, township five, range four east, at such price as they may deem proper.

Mr. JOHNSON, of Kentucky, submitted the following motion for consideration:

Resolved, That the Committee on Public Lands be instructed to inquire into the expediency of amending an act, entitled "An act for the relief of the inhabitants of the late county of New Madrid, in the Missouri Territory, who suffered by earthquakes," passed on the 17th February, 1815.

The bill further to establish the compensation of the officers employed in the collection of duties on imports and tonnage, and for other purposes; and, also, the bill for the relief of General Robert Swartwout, were severally read the second time.

ROADS AND CANALS.

The Senate proceeded to consider the resolution submitted by Mr. TRIMBLE, on the 15th inst., which is in the following words:

Resolved, That the Committee on Roads and Canals be instructed to inquire into the expediency of authorizing by law the employment of the topographical engineers, in surveying, under the direction of the President of the United States, canals to connect the navigable waters between Boston harbor, in the State of Massachusetts, and Pamlico Sound, in the State of North Carolina, in such direction and on such plan as will best promote the interest, and the military and naval defence of the United States.

Mr. CHANDLER moved to amend it by adding thereto the following:

"And a military and post road from some part of the Penobscot river, in the State of Maine, to the Schodiac river, in said State, on the Eastern line of the United States."

Mr. CHANDLER made a few remarks in support of his proposed amendment, to show how necessary such a road is to the military defence of that part of the Union, &c.

Mr. HOLMES, of Maine, seconded his colleague, adding, as a further reason in favor of the meas-

ure, that, as far as the line had been run under the fifth article of the Treaty of Ghent, it was found to include a much more extensive portion of territory than was supposed to belong to the United States in that quarter.

Mr. TRIMBLE said he had no further objection to the amendment than that it embraced an object totally distinct from the original proposition, and which should therefore be separately proposed.

To which Mr. CHANDLER replied, that, though the objects were geographically distinct, the power to be exercised in regard to both was the same, and the inquiry as to both was properly referable to the same committee.

The amendment of Mr. CHANDLER was agreed to, as was the resolution as amended.

MATTHEW LYON.

The Senate then again proceeded to the consideration of the report of the select committee in the case of Matthew Lyon.

Mr. OTIS rose, and, in a speech of considerable length, delivered his views in opposition to the report.

Mr. MACON followed, in a speech which occupied some time in the delivery, in favor of the report.

Mr. DANA then spoke against it, and the Senate adjourned.

FRIDAY, January 19.

The PRESIDENT communicated a letter from the Secretary of the Navy, transmitting a statement of the contracts made by the Commissioners of the Navy during the year 1820; and the letter and statement were read.

On motion, by Mr. RUGGLES, the Committee of Claims were discharged from the further consideration of the bill from the House of Representatives, entitled "An act for the relief of Daniel Seward;" and it was referred to the Committee on Public Lands.

Mr. JOHNSON, of Louisiana, presented the petition of L. B. Macarty, of Louisiana, praying to be compensated for the injury and losses sustained in consequence of the military occupancy of his plantation by order of General Jackson in the Winter of 1814 and 1815; and the petition was read, and referred to the Committee of Claims.

Mr. HORSEY, from the Committee on the District of Columbia, to whom the subject was referred, reported a bill authorizing the sale of certain grounds belonging to the United States in the City of Washington; and the bill was read, and passed to a second reading.

On motion, by Mr. THOMAS, the Committee on Public Lands were discharged from the further consideration of the petition of Isaac M. Johnson and others.

The Senate proceeded to consider the motion of yesterday, instructing the Committee on Public Lands to inquire into the expediency of authorizing Jared E. Groce to enter a fraction of land; and agreed thereto.

The bill authorizing the repair of a sea-wall at

the Isles of Shoals, and for other purposes, was read the second time; and referred to the Committee on Commerce and Manufactures.

MATTHEW LYON.

The Senate resumed the consideration of the report of the select committee on the petition of Matthew Lyon, together with the motion to postpone the same indefinitely.

Mr. DICKERSON, of New Jersey, rose, and expressed himself as follows:

In addressing the Senate upon the subject of the resolutions for the relief of Matthew Lyon, I shall, said Mr. D., make some preliminary observations upon a few remarks that fell from the honorable gentleman from Massachusetts, (Mr. OTIS,) which seem not intended as any solid part of his argument, but were introduced by way of embellishment to his very ingenious and very eloquent speech.

The honorable gentleman seems much annoyed by the thunders from the West, and the roaring of the lion.   *

By the thunders from the West, I understand the torrent of eloquence which we have heard with delight from the honorable gentleman from Kentucky (Mr. TALBOT.) That thunder, sir, was not a mere *brutum fulmen ;* it was a succession of electric shocks, attended with the most vivid lightnings. Such thunder tends to purify the political atmosphere, and to invigorate our languid systems.

The honorable gentleman says, the lion will come again, and, if he does, he will heed him not, but say, *encore, let him roar, once more.* Sir, the lion will come again and again, unless we restore him the money we have taken from him; but, give him that, and then, if I may borrow a line from Pyramus and Thisbe, as that gentleman has done—and he always keeps within the pale of senatorial decorum—give him the money, and then he *will roar you as gently as any sucking dove.* And this, I am confident, would be the cheaper way of getting rid of him. I have other reasons for believing it would be the better way.

The honorable gentleman conducted the correspondence between himself and one of his constituents, with great address, and brought it to a happy conclusion; which is the less to be wondered at, as he managed on both sides, and composed the answer as well as the letter. But, when he informed his correspondent that the case of Matthew Lyon was obtruded upon our notice, at a time when we were crowded with a great variety of important business, I wish he had added, by way of postscript, that the Senate had adjourned from Friday to the Monday following, every week this session, except one, and then I think there would be a postscript to the answer, that, on the score of want of time, or press of business, there could be no excuse for refusing to hear the case of Matthew Lyon. In which opinion I most heartily concur.

The honorable gentleman seems to doubt as to the numbers said to have been arrayed against the sedition act. There were eighteen thousand petitioners against that act, from Pennsylvania alone,

and several thousands from other States; but before that Congress, this multitude were as grasshoppers, and their noise was as the chirping of grasshoppers.

The honorable gentleman informs us, that the grasshoppers in the field make more noise than the beasts which graze the pasture. I understand the application, but the figure is an unfortunate one, notwithstanding it has the authority of Mr. Burke for its support. Surely Mr. Burke could never have heard the tremendous bellowings of the lordly leader of the herd, or the nasal, harsh, ear-rending note of one of the descendants of Sancho's Dapple. Why, sir, a single jack will bray more noise in a minute than could be made in the same time by all the grasshoppers that ever hopped. Believe me, it was an egregious error to mistake the voice of the people for the chirping of grasshoppers.

The honorable gentleman thinks that most of us must have been too young in 1798, to have formed accurate opinions of the transactions of that time, insinuating that those who were not young then must be old now. Whether I was old enough then, or even now, to form accurate opinions of the transactions of that time, is not so certain; but I have perfect recollection of what happened then, within the sphere of my own observation. I have a painful recollection that my mind was irritated, my indignation excited, my passions roused, by what I thought a systematic attempt to impair the liberties of my country. But time cures all things. In twenty years I have cooled down to what my former associates think much below the temperate point, and, even on the measure now before the Senate, the propriety or expediency of which I never doubted, I have embarked with great reluctance, as those know who first presented the petition of Matthew Lyon. I do not wish to throw Congreve rockets into the ranks of this corps of invalids, as the gentleman chooses to designate himself and friends. I do not wish to revive the feuds of 1798; but I did hope that, at this time, when we are all federalists, all republicans; when not a breath disturbs the harmony of this amalgamation, the good feelings which we perceive every day would not be exercised exclusively on one side, but that there would be some degree of reciprocity; that, as that gentleman allows that the sedition act was inexpedient, and had been pronounced to be so by the people, it was also hoped, that the punishing of Matthew Lyon under the act would be deemed inexpedient; that it would be deemed inexpedient to raise money by such means; that it would be deemed inexpedient to retain moneys thus raised, in our Treasury, and therefore that it would be deemed quite expedient to return the moneys thus obtained; or, at least, it was hoped that no very determined opposition would be given to this measure. But so far from this, the honorable gentleman admonishes us not to press him and those with whom he acts; not to irritate them, for, although nobody was disposed to attack the present administration, comparisons might be made; comparisons of the expenses of former times, with those of the present; expenses of the war, with the advantages gained by it. Besides, our political concerns were not of the most flattering kind; there was a great deficit in our revenue; our foreign relations were not in the most prosperous train; some troubles with France. This, to be sure, is not threatening, but looks a little like it. For one, I do not fear, but rather court, such comparisons; for, if the results of such comparisons should sometimes turn out unfavorably to those who have the expenditure of public moneys, or of those who authorize those expenditures, it would operate as an excellent corrective; it might do much good, but no hurt.

I regret that the merits or demerits of Matthew Lyon should be called up in deciding a principle, involving consequences much more important than the character or sufferings of any individual. I am aware that Matthew Lyon is unpopular in Congress, but that want of popularity should have no unfavorable effect in fixing a principle in which the citizens of the United States are deeply interested. We are not to try the man; we are to decide his cause, which is one of general interest. Why, we are triumphantly asked by the honorable gentleman from Georgia (Mr. WALKER) has this question been suffered to sleep for twenty years? Why are its slumbers now disturbed? Frequent attempts have been made to disturb its slumbers, but in vain; an attempt is now made, but that gentleman seems resolved to perpetuate those slumbers, by this motion for indefinite postponement. Perhaps there have been in Congress too many who believe, with that gentleman, that no injury has been done to Matthew Lyon; who think that the eulogiums which have been bestowed upon him, have been a sufficient compensation for his sufferings; for eulogiums have been poured out upon him in great profusion, from the time he became an object of persecution. If he could be paid for his sufferings in this way, he might be overpaid; and it may be thought that, upon a fair reckoning, there may be found a balance against Mr. Lyon, and that it would be but fair that he should suffer a little more; but, trust me, that honorable gentleman, who seems to envy the happy estate of Mr. Lyon, would not suffer what he did for all the eulogiums which fame herself, with her hundred trumpets, could pour out upon him for the rest of his life.

But why, says the honorable gentleman, is this time, when our Treasury is empty, selected for voting money to Mr. Lyon—why was not this done in the time of Mr. Jefferson's Administration, when we had an overflowing Treasury—and we were at a loss for the means of disposing of the public money? In the first place, there was really not so much difficulty in disposing of the public money as seems to be imagined—emptying the Treasury was a very simple business then, as we have found it to be in latter days. In the next place, a full Treasury was no good reason for paying M. Lyon a thousand dollars then, any more than a bare Treasury is, for withholding it now. The merits of the case do not depend on the state of the Treasury; if they did, those merits

would sometimes be very great, at other times very small, but generally rather small. I trust, however, in voting on this resolution, we shall not stop to inquire how much money there may be in the Treasury; if we do, sure I am, the gentleman's motion, the indefinite postponement, must prevail.

If the friends of the liberty of the press have heretofore neglected to urge this subject upon the consideration of Congress, let the reproach rest with them; their apathy affords no apology to us for refusing to act. If we have been negligent, let us now redeem our character. Those who consider the sedition act constitutional, and called for by the circumstances of the times, must consider this inquiry as altogether unnecessary and improper—and those who believe that the act was unconstitutional and oppressive, I fear, feel satisfied that much good has resulted to themselves from the sufferings of those who were fined and imprisoned under that act—and that the party with whom it originated, not only failed to accomplish the object they had in view, but in fact by this very measure lost the power which it was intended to perpetuate. Under such comfortable, but selfish reflections, I fear we are disposed to forgot the victims of the law.

We cannot but feel some reluctance at entering upon the investigation of a question, which, by many, has long been considered at rest; more especially when that question is calculated to call up feelings that once painfully agitated the public mind. Under such circumstances, a love of ease will prevail, where a strong sense of duty does not impel to action.

The present case, however, comes before us, in a way that demands, and must receive a serious consideration. One of our citizens has brought his claim before us in the usual form of petition. The Constitution, laws, and usages, by which this body is governed, make it imperative upon us to decide for or against the petitioner; and whatever gentlemen may think, as to the merits of the individual, his case involves consequences of the highest importance, such as cannot be decided but with great responsibility, a responsibility which I trust will insure a correct decision.

Some who think the sedition act unconstitutional may be of opinion that it is not necessary, nor even consistent with the dictates of sound policy, after a lapse of twenty years, to relieve the sufferers under that law. With such it will remain to devise a better mode of restoring and reviving, as far as it can be done by Congress, the first article of the amendments to the Constitution, which was practically suspended by the sedition act, and which may be considered as null and void if the constitutionality of the act shall now receive the sanction of Congress.

If it were known with absolute certainty that a result, similar to that which attended the passing of the sedition act, would inevitably attend every similar attempt—that part of our Constitution which respects the liberty of the press would remain secure from further violation. But, such a result is by no means certain—and we deceive ourselves if we suppose that the rage and fury of party are no more to prevail in this country.

Should an attempt hereafter be made to revive the sedition law, Constitutional objections would have but little avail, as coming too late. It would be said the sedition act of ninety-eight was not repealed, although every effort was made to procure its repeal, expressly on Constitutional grounds. It was suffered to expire by its own limitation. Its constitutionality was sanctioned by two decisions of Congress; and those decisions corroborated by all the force which the judiciary could give them.

If those who raised their voice from one extremity of the Union to the other against the constitutionality of this act, when it was passed, and when an attempt was made to repeal it, will not now, when they have the power, make an effort to repair the breach in the Constitution, it will be yielding the point, and acknowledging that all their clamor was raised to gain power, which they did gain; not to preserve the Constitution, which is left mutilated, without an effort at reparation. And this precedent, thus sanctioned by one party and acquiesced in by the other, will be considered as the legislative and judicial construction of the Constitution; and, by this process, the Constitution will practically be altered, and the liberty of the press be as completely within the control of Congress and the Judiciary of the United States, as if the first amendment to the Constitution had declared Congress shall have power to abridge the liberty of the press.

For my part, I have never doubted that the sedition act, so far as it respects the printing and publishing of libels, was a direct, open, and unequivocal breach of the Constitution. And, although I do not hold the United States responsible for all the losses sustained under that act, I would not willingly retain in our Treasury a single dollar of the money iniquitously acquired under it. The whole forms but a small sum, but if it were large, it should be returned to those from whom it was taken. I should not stop to inquire whether it was a thousand or a hundred thousand dollars.

The friends of the sedition act aver that it was no breach of the Constitution—no infringement, but rather an enlargement of the liberty of the press. It ought, they say, to be considered:

1st. Mitigating the rigor of the common law on the subject of libels, inasmuch as it limits the punishment under it to two thousand dollars fine and two years' imprisonment, and allows the truth to be given in evidence, while those guilty of the same offences might be punished at common law, by fine and imprisonment, at the discretion of the court.

2d. That it is merely declaratory of the common law, making nothing penal that was not penal before.

3d. That it did not abridge the liberty of the press, inasmuch as it imposed no previous restraint upon publications—established no censorship or system of licensing.

4th. That it was necessary for carrying into effect the powers vested by the Constitution in the Government, and, therefore, required under the eighth section of the first article of the Constitution.

5th. That it was a part of a system of national defence, adopted at a crisis of extraordinary difficulty and danger.

Most of those arguments we have heard upon this floor, and all of them are contained in a very celebrated report of a committee of the House of Representatives, made on the 21st of February, 1799, in which report the committee condensed whatever they supposed could be urged in favor of the sedition act, and against its repeal. This received the sanction of the House of Representatives, and was published in many journals of the day as proof positive of the unerring wisdom of Congress.

It was to be hoped that the dangerous doctrine that the common law was the prop and support of the sedition act, would long since have been formally abandoned, but I see nothing like it. The honorable gentleman from Massachusetts, two years ago, when the subject was under discussion, did say, in justification of the sedition act, that every Government had an inherent right to punish offences which endanger its existence—which sentiment he now reiterates. Such rights, if not derived from the Constitution, must be derived from the broad principles of the common law—such principles as were assumed by the committee in their celebrated report. He seems to have abated nothing in his reverence for the common law; he considers the stigma cast upon it by gentlemen, particularly by gentlemen of the bar, as a species of profanation. The eulogium he has pronounced upon this common law is such as to leave no doubt as to his opinion that it ought to be ingrafted upon our system, if it does not already form the vital part of it. He informs us that the common law, I quote his words, is a system in which, under God, we live, and move, and have our being.

Was the sedition act passed in mitigation of the common law? If it was, it will conclusively follow that the press was more free during the existence of that act than it was before it passed, or has been since it expired. And that period, which has been called the reign of terror, should be recorded and remembered as the golden days of the publishers of pamphlets and newspapers.

In investigating a proposition so extraordinary as this, we are led to inquire into the motives of those by whose means the act passed. Why should the party in power, who had everything to fear from the press at this time of difficulty and danger, pertinaciously insist upon mitigating the rigor of the law upon the subject of libels, while those for whom all this kindness was meant as pertinaciously refused to receive the boon? Had the Legislatures of any of the States instructed their Senators and Representatives to obtain any such mitigation of the common law? Had the printers asked this as a favor? Had any meetings of the citizens presented memorials to Congress upon this subject? Had the cries of any convicted for libels, and sentenced to a fine of more than two thousand dollars, and imprisonment more than two years, moved the tender mercies of the majority in Congress? Nothing of all this appears upon the record.

If this act was in truth meant to extend the liberty of the press, these publishers of pamphlets and newspapers have been guilty of the vilest ingratitude towards their benefactors. For, so far from puffing them in their publications, or toasting them at their feasts, or giving them dinners for their patriotic exertions, they have poured out upon them innumerable streams of invective, which, with the aid of some other causes, not necessary to be detailed, have deprived them of the power of further mitigating the rigor of the common law.

But I believe the charge of ingratitude will not lie against these publishers of pamphlets and newspapers. They judged correctly, and some of them know by sad experience the exact nature of the good things intended for them by the dominant party in Congress.

If Congress by this act meant to mitigate the rigor of the common law, they most certainly missed their aim. But I hope it will not be thought uncharitable to suspect that nothing was further from their intention. If such was indeed their intention, it should have appeared in the bill; the evils to be remedied should have been pointed out, and such parts of the common law as were deemed too severe should have been expressly abrogated; otherwise the courts might have gone on to indict and punish offenders at common law, the sedition act notwithstanding, and in this way have entirely defeated the benevolent intentions of Congress.

But Congress should have been very sure that they had this common law before they undertook to mitigate it.

How far can the sedition act be considered as declaratory of the common law?

If it is declaratory of the common law of England, and not of this country, it is idle, as much so as if it was declaratory of the common law of France or China.

It is impossible that it could be declaratory of the common law of the individual States, for the laws upon the subject of libels were not probably alike in any two of them. And Congress never stopped to inquire whether, in all the States, authors of libels upon the Government of the United States were punishable by fine and imprisonment, at common law, whether any had been punished for such offences to an extent beyond two thousand dollars fine and two years imprisonment; and, if so, whether the States might not have been left to mitigate their own common law.

If the State courts had power to punish at common law, or any other law, those guilty of the offences mentioned in the sedition act, that act did not take away such power, and the offenders might have been punished both in the State and Federal courts; for, in such a strange complexity of jurisdictions, the plea of *autre fois acquit* would not have been available on the second indictment, more especially as one prosecution would be for an offence against the State, the other for an offence against the United States. Such a divi-

ded empire in matter of jurisdiction cannot be tolerated. If Congress have power to provide for the punishment of the offences mentioned in the sedition act, they must have the exclusive power, uncontrolled by the States. For, if the States have such control, they might mitigate the rigor of the sedition act, by providing that the punishment for offences mentioned in that act should be merely nominal, and thus render that act inoperative, except in the District of Columbia.

The United States and individual States can have no concurrent jurisdiction in the trial of criminal prosecutions. If the United States have jurisdiction in such cases, it must be exclusive jurisdiction. And Congress cannot declare what is the law of the States; the States must be left to declare for themselves.

If, therefore, the sedition act was declaratory of any common law, it must have been the common law of the United States. The United States, it will be allowed, could have had no common law from immemorial usage. If they had it at all, it must have been by adoption. But, where do we find, in the Constitution, the power to adopt the common law as a part of our criminal code? With such a power, the Constitution itself would never have been adopted. That such a power exists, is a doctrine the most extraordinary and the most dangerous that has ever been urged in Congress or in our courts of justice.

Yet the committee who made the celebrated report I have already mentioned declare that " the 'act in question (sedition act) cannot be unconsti- 'tutional, because it makes nothing penal that was 'not penal before; gives no new powers to the 'courts, but is merely declaratory of the common 'law; libels against the Government are offences 'arising under the Constitution, (second section of 'the third article,) and consequently punishable at 'common law by the courts of the United States."

This report has been sanctioned by a vote of a majority of the House of Representatives, and by an acquiescence on the part of the then minority of more than twenty years. And yet, if the committee were right, the same common law still exists, and the Federal courts can now take cognizance of the offences mentioned in the sedition act, and try the offenders without allowing them the privilege of giving the truth in evidence, for Mr. Fox's bill can form no part of the common law, and punish them by fine and imprisonment at their discretion. Can we tolerate such doctrines? Will we now by our decision give currency and effect to such damnable heresies?

The discussion upon this point alone would form a long argument. Whatever can be said upon it has been said by Mr. Madison and other members of the Virginia Legislature in their debates upon this subject, which have been published. For the present, I will satisfy myself with quoting the opinion of Judge Chase, in the case of the United States against Worral, 2 Dallas's rep. 398. In the term of April, 1798, three months before the passing of the sedition act, the defendant was tried and convicted at common law, in the circuit court for the Pennsylvania district, for an attempt to bribe Tench Coxe, the commissioner of the revenue. A motion was made in arrest of judgment, and it was alleged that the circuit court could not take cognizance of this offence, inasmuch as it was not a crime against any of the statute laws of the United States, and that the common law could give no jurisdiction to the court in this case.

Chase, Justice: "This is an indictment for an offence highly injurious to morals, and deserving the severest punishment; but, as it is an indictment at common law, I dismiss at once every thing that has been said about the Constitution and laws of the United States." "In my opinion, the United States, as a Federal Government, have no common law; and, consequently, no indictment can be maintained in their courts for offences merely at the common law. If, indeed, the United States can be supposed for a moment to have a common law, it must, I presume, be that of England; and yet it is impossible to trace when or how the system was adopted or introduced."

The Judge supported this opinion by sound argument, but not such as to convince his brother Peters, who dissented.

Peters, Justice: "Whenever a Government has been established, I have always supposed that a power to preserve itself was a necessary and inseparable concomitant. But the existence of the Federal Government would be precarious; it could no longer be called an independent Government, if, for the punishment of offences of this nature, tending to obstruct and pervert the administration of its affairs, an appeal must be made to the State tribunals, or the offenders must escape with absolute impunity.

"The power to punish misdemeanors is originally and strictly a common law power; of which I think the United States are constitutionally possessed. It might have been exercised by Congress as a legislative act; but it may also, in my opinion, be enforced in a course of judicial proceeding. Whenever an offence aims at the subversion of any federal institution, or at the corruption of its public officers, it is an offence against the well-being of the United States. From its very nature, it is cognizable under their authority, and consequently is within the jurisdiction of the court, by virtue of the eleventh section of the judicial act."

If this opinion was correct, then, indeed, Congress had nothing further to do in a criminal code, but to soften the rigor of the common law. I must call the attention of the Senate for a moment to the extraordinary termination of this case. The court being divided, the motion in arrest of judgment failed; but, being so divided, it became a matter of doubt whether sentence could be pronounced upon the defendant. Those doubts were removed, I know not how, and the defendant sentenced to an imprisonment of three months and a fine of two hundred dollars; and thus was punished at common law, the opinion of Judge Chase to the contrary notwithstanding.

These opinions, thus judicially expressed, must have been well known to the majority in Congress who passed the sedition act, and well known to the committee who drew up the celebrated report, and to the majority in the House of Representatives who sanctioned that report; and they have given all the validity which they possibly could to the broad and sweeping doctrine of the common law under which Worral was punished. Further comment, as to this point, is unnecessary.

It is said that the sedition act is no abridgment of the liberty of the press, inasmuch as it imposes no previous restraint upon publications—establishes no censorship, or system of licensing.

And can we admit that no law can abridge the liberty of the press, unless it subject publications to a system of licensing? Did the first amendment to the Constitution mean only to provide against such a system? A system which no administration in England has dared to enforce since the time of William III. A system that would no sooner be tolerated in this country than would the holy inquisition. A system against which it would be wholly useless to provide by the Constitution. For, whenever Congress shall be so utterly lost to every principle of liberty as to wish for such a system, be assured no Constitution will stand in their way. Some pretext will easily be found for prostrating the liberty of the press, by some new and more rigid sedition act. If all other pretexts should fail, that of introducing it as a part of the system of national defence will be deemed satisfactory.

If a law to punish the authors of libels with a fine of two thousand dollars and an imprisonment of two years be not to abridge the liberty of the press, because it imposes no previous restraint upon publications, then, by a parity of reasoning, to punish with ten thousand dollars fine and ten years' imprisonment would be no abridgment of the liberty of the press. No, not even if the offence should be made capital, as was done under Augustus Cæsar.

The importance of a free press in preventing the abuses of Government, was well understood at the adoption of the Constitution and its amendments, and much more justly appreciated than now. And such was the extreme jealousy of the people upon this subject, that, although no power was given to Congress to interfere with the liberty of the press, and all powers not given were reserved, yet, fearing that Congress might, by implication, arrogate this power to themselves, they provided this prohibitory amendment, that Congress should not abridge the liberty of the press.

If, in consequence of passing the sedition act, it was more dangerous to investigate and expose the abuses of Government, than it was before the act passed, then was the liberty of the press abridged.

To subject the publisher of what might be deemed a libel, to punishment by indictment, when before he was only answerable in damages to the party injured; or to be tried in two courts when before he could be tried but in one; or to be tried in a court in which he could not be tried before, is to increase the hazard and danger of such publication. But to make him, for an alleged libel on the President and Senate of the United States indictable before judges appointed by the President and Senate; by a grand jury chosen by a marshal, and before a traverse jury selected by the same marshal, holding his office at the pleasure of the President; the prosecution to be urged by the zeal of a district attorney, also holding his office at the will of the President; is so far a restraint upon the liberty of the press, that none but the most intrepid would dare to arraign the conduct of the President before the bar of the public.

But the practice under this act, whatever was intended by it, was made to produce the effect of previous restraint. A person charged with publishing a libel against the provisions of this act, would be bound under recognizance, himself in a thousand dollars, and two good sureties in a thousand more, to appear and answer; and also to keep the peace and be of good behavior. If, before the session of the court, he publishes that Congress have passed an unconstitutional act, this, by the vigilant prosecuting officer, would be deemed a new libel and a forfeiture of the former recognizance. The offending party would be bound over again, with sureties, to appear and answer, and also to keep the peace and be of good behavior— and suits immediately commenced on the first recognizance against the party and his sureties; and so on *toties quoties*, till the party would be silent. This is not merely hypothesis, but matter of fact. Two suits were depending against the editor of the Aurora and his sureties, on recognizances thus forfeited, when Mr. Jefferson came into office; I need hardly add that, soon after this, they were discontinued, and thus was Mr. Duane saved from serious embarrassment, if not ruin, and his sureties from heavy losses. It was generally a part of the sentence on conviction, that the party should find surety for his good behavior for a limited time. Those who were intrepid enough to meet the consequences of such a process in their own property and persons, were not willing to expose their friends to vexatious lawsuits and ruinous losses. They would, therefore, be as much restrained as they would be under a law requiring a license for publication—nay, more so, for any one could publish without license, subjecting himself to the penalty of the law, in which case he would not be punished through his friends; a kind of punishment much more mortifying to a man of an ingenuous mind, than fine or imprisonment in his own person. What could—what did prevent a total prostration of the liberty of the press, under such a system?—Public opinion; a tribunal which I hope no party or administration in this country will ever be able to put at defiance; a tribunal which has pronounced on this law, and the makers of it.

To ascertain how far this act was an abridgment of the liberty of the press, let us examine a little further into its practical operation. It is unnecessary to add any thing to what has already been said upon the trial of Matthew Lyon. The trial of Thomas Cooper, in 1800, in the Circuit Court of the United States, for the Pennsylvania District, will furnish a complete illustration of the views of those who made, and of those who administered this law.

I select this case because I was a witness of the whole trial: a trial which, at the time, filled my mind with horror and indignation. I saw a man whom it was my pride then, as it is now, to call my friend; a man of the most honorable feelings; a man whose name is identified with science and literature; the constant study of whose life it has been to render himself useful to his fellow beings; I saw this man dragged before a criminal court, arraigned, tried, and punished, for publishing words which nothing but the violence and blindness of party rage could have construed into crime. In the year '97 Mr. Cooper had asked of the President, Mr. Adams, to be appointed an agent for American claims; the request was made through Dr. Priestley directly to Mr. Adams, with a frankness warranted on the part of the Doctor by the intimacy which had long existed between them. As the application was thus personal, it was supposed to be confidential. It was unsuccessful, and there it should have rested. But, by some means never explained, two years afterwards this application was made public, and afforded the editor of a paper in Reading, an opportunity of inserting a scurrilous paragraph against Mr. Cooper. Irritated at being thus held up as a subject of ridicule, Mr. Cooper, in justification of his own conduct, published the address for which he was indicted. The words contained in the indictment, stripped of the inuendoes, are the following:

"Nor do I see any impropriety in making this request of Mr. Adams: at that time he had just entered into office; he was hardly in the infancy of political mistake; even those who doubted of his capacity, thought well of his intentions. Nor were we yet saddled with the expense of a permanent navy, or threatened, under his auspices, with the existence of a standing army. Our credit was not yet reduced quite so low as to borrow money at eight per cent. in time of peace, while the unnecessary violence of official expressions might justly have provoked a war. Mr. Adams had not yet projected his embassies to Prussia, Russia, and the Sublime Porte; nor had he yet interfered, as President of the United States, to influence the decisions of a court of justice; a stretch of authority which the monarch of Great Britain would have shrunk from; an interference without precedent, against law, and against mercy! The melancholy case of Jonathan Robbins, a native citizen of America, forcibly impressed by the British, and delivered up, with the advice of Mr. Adams, to the mock trial of a British court martial, had not yet astonished the republican citizens of this free country; a case too little known, but which the people ought to be fully apprised of before the election, and they shall be."

I have the highest veneration for the exalted statesman and revolutionary patriot against whom this censure was levelled; but he was not infallible—much less so were those around him, by whose advice, at this particular period, he was too much influenced. But, however exalted his station, he had accepted it with a full knowledge that it was the disposition and practice, and a salutary one too, in this country, to examine and censure, with great freedom, the conduct of those in power. To be censured freely, and sometimes unjustly, is a tax which every one must pay who holds the highest station in our Government. Laws which should completely prevent this, would as completely prostrate the liberties of the people.

However much Mr. Adams might have been hurt at the asperity of the language applied to him, I am confident he never intimated a wish in favor of a prosecution. Most probably this took place in consequence of the advice of those who advised that Robbins should be given up. About this time Mr. Adams thought proper to repress the zeal of his political friends by pardoning Fries, who had been guilty of a misdemeanor, but was convicted of treason, and by other acts evincing a disposition to pursue a more moderate system than that which had prevailed for two preceding years. It will also be remembered, that, not long after this period, he dismissed some of his advisers, in whom he had probably placed too much confidence.

At the present time of good feelings it seems incredible, that what Mr. Cooper said of the expenses of a permanent navy—of the standing army—the eight per cent. loan, and the projected embassies to Prussia, Russia, and the Sublime Porte, should have been considered as the subject of indictment. What was said as to the case of Jonathan Robbins, otherwise called Thomas Nash, was of a more serious character, and should have been answered, if it could have been answered, by a true history of that transaction—not by punishing Mr. Cooper; for, if this interference on the part of the President, was without precedent and against law and against mercy, fining and imprisoning Mr. Cooper could not make it otherwise.

It has never been pretended that there was any precedent for delivering up Robbins. He had been charged with piracy and murder on board the British sloop Hermione, and demanded by the British minister. His case was depending before Judge Bee, of South Carolina. He alleged that he was a native citizen of the United States, and that he had been forcibly impressed on board the Hermione. If his story had been true, it will not be pretended by those who recollect the history connected with that transaction that he ought to have been given up. But, as he averred it to be true, and produced his passport under the authority of the United States, in support of his assertion, the proof that he stated a falsehood should have been so complete as to leave no loop to hang a doubt upon, before he should ever have been given up to certain death. The proof, if it deserves the name, was of a very doubtful character as to this point. While the case was thus before the Judge, Mr. Pickering, then Secretary of State, wrote a letter to the Judge, containing, among others, this expression:

"The President has, in consequence hereof, authorized me to communicate to you his advice and request that Thomas Nash should be delivered up to the consul or other agent of Great Britain, who shall appear to receive him."

Whether Robbins, or, as he is called in this letter, Nash, was or was not a native citizen, will probably never be known with certainty. After he was hung in chains, a strong disposition was discovered to try his case, and great pains were taken to prove that he was not a native of the town in which he said he was born. Probably he

was not a native of this country; I hope to Heaven he was not.

But, if it had been otherwise; if it had turned out upon this posthumous trial, that his story was true, it would have been a source of lasting regret to Mr. Adams; and, had he known precisely how the case stood before Judge Bee, sure I am he would not have interfered in the manner he did. He was governed, no doubt, by a rigid sense of justice, and a regard for the conditions of our treaty with Great Britain. But I have ever thought, and still think, the act was precipitate, and peculiarly unfortunate. Mr. Cooper, without doubt, thought this interference was without precedent, because no such case had happened before. He thought it against law, because the facts alleged by Robbins, as to his birth and impressment, should have been ascertained with certainty before he was delivered up. He thought it against mercy, because the man was delivered up to certain death. Such were the opinions of Mr. Cooper; opinions which, under our free system of Government, he ought to have been allowed to express and publish, without being dragged before a criminal court, or sentenced to a loathsome prison. Yet for this he was sentenced to pay a fine of four hundred dollars, to be imprisoned for the term of six months, and to enter into recognizance for his good behavior after that period, himself in one thousand dollars, with two sureties in five hundred dollars each. And was this no abridgment of the liberty of the press? The press is more free under the monarchy of Great Britain.

A further examination of this trial will show that the difficulty of proving facts and opinions of common notoriety, under this law, was such as to leave no chance of escape to any one indicted under it; and, accordingly, I believe none did escape. Judge Chase, in his charge to the jury, observed, that:

"The traverser, in his defence, must prove every charge he has made to be true. He must prove it to the marrow. If he asserts three things, and proves but one, he fails; if he proves two, he fails in his defence, for he must prove the whole of his assertions to be true. If he were to prove that the President had done every thing charged against him in the first paragraph of the publication; though he should prove to your satisfaction, that the President had interfered to influence the decisions of a court of justice; that he had delivered up Jonathan Robbins without precedent, against law and against mercy, this would not be sufficient unless he proved, at the same time, that Jonathan Robbins was a native American, and had been forcibly impressed and compelled to serve on board a British ship of war."

According to this, the most trivial mistake in point of fact or opinion would deprive the party indicted of all the advantages of that part of the law which allows the truth to be given in evidence. Indeed, that part of the act appears a mere mockery, when we read this trial, and see the difficulty of proving facts and opinions of common notoriety, by the technical nicety of the common law.

If the Government in 1798 had been sufficiently strong, as, thank Heaven! they were not, to give permanency to such a law, and such an administration of the law, there would have been an end to our boasted liberty of the press. The silence of despotism would have pervaded the Union, communicating a palsy to every part of our Constitution, which was intended to retard the march of aristocracy, or to defend the just rights of the great body of the people.

The friends of the sedition act say that Congress were authorized to pass it, as a law necessary and proper for carrying into effect the powers vested by the Constitution in the Government, under the 8th section of the 1st article of the Constitution.

This part of the Constitution is very elastic, and some gentlemen discovered that under it Congress may do what they please, by simply making the word *necessary* mean *convenient*. But I cannot imagine what power vested by the Constitution in the Government it was necessary to carry into effect by the sedition act. That no such necessity as is alleged did exist is evident from this circumstance, that the Government went on very well before that act passed, and quite as well since it has expired. However convenient, therefore, the law might have been, it certainly was not necessary. If it was necessary in the meaning of the Constitution, it was indispensably necessary—not partly necessary. If necessary then, it must be necessary now, and Congress must of course be neglecting their duty in not reviving that law.

But the most extraordinary reason offered for passing that law is, that it was part of a system of national defence. If so, it must be required by that part of our Constitution which imposes it as a duty upon Congress to provide for the common defence. Whether this bill was recommended by the Secretary of War, or reported by the Committee on Military Affairs, I have not inquired; but, if it was intended as a part of our system of national defence, it should have been incorporated into the bill for establishing a navy, or for raising a standing army, or for arming the whole body of the militia of the United States. If national defence was the object of the bill, it should have appeared in some of its sections, or in its preamble, or in its title; its duration should have been limited to the period of the just and necessary war which it was then intended if posssible to get up against France; instead of which it was limited, with an aspect somewhat ominous, to the third of March, 1801—the very day on which the Administration which it was meant to support ceased to exist. From all which it has been suspected that this act was no part of a system of defence for the nation, but for a party—a defence of the *ins* against the *outs*—a defence of a falling administration against the people who had determined to change their public servants.

We are now in effect to declare this act to have been Constitutional or unconstitutional. If we do the latter, we correct not the errors of the court, but of Congress. If the law was not Constitutional when passed, the decisions of the court could not make it so. Probably the court did not think that a question for them to decide. The act was a legislative construction of the Constitution expressly.

It was opposed and supported on Constitutional grounds, and is a declaration of the three branches of the Legislature of the meaning of the Constitution in this particular. And it is not yet ascertained that, in construing the Constitution, Congress is subordinate to the Judiciary. Probably the first decisive experiment upon this subject will prove the contrary.

The honorable gentleman from Georgia (Mr. WALKER) informed us that, as long as the act was in force, Constitutional or unconstitutional, it was the law of the land, and we were bound to obey its dictates. If it was the law of the land, it was the duty of the judges to see it enforced. The act, though not declaratory of the common law, was declaratory of the Constitution, or meant to be so. And the Judiciary considered that they were bound to carry it into effect, leaving those by which it was enacted to be responsible for its consequences.

If Congress infringe the Constitution, can they not heal the breach? If not, this is the most unfortunate instrument ever devised by man as a system of Government—subject indeed to the laws of decay and dissolution, without the possibility of redemption. If such be the case, our delightful anticipations of transmitting this instrument unimpaired to the latest posterity are idle dreams—the baseless fabric of a vision. But I trust, sir, there is a redeeming spirit, by which this sacred charter of our liberties, when violently and insidiously invaded, may be restored to its pristine purity.

If the last Congress had passed an act limited to the duration of the Congress, levying a duty on articles exported from the United States, with proper and penal clauses to enforce obedience; and if some individual with the spirit of Hampden had refused obedience to the law, and had been fined by the court for such disobedience one thousand dollars, and that fine had gone into our Treasury; can any one doubt that the present Congress would restore the money, and by that act virtually declare the former to have been unconstitutional?

We do not assume an appellate jurisdiction over the courts, but declare the law under which they acted null and void—the proceedings under it to have been *coram non judice*—the fines to have been levied in direct violation of our Constitution, and consequently no part of the lawful revenue of the country. We restore the money to those from whom it was extorted, agreeably to the dictates of common honesty.

The honorable gentleman from Georgia wishes to know in what part of the Constitution we are authorized to make donations. I leave that to be discovered by those who so frequently vote for donations. At present, no donation is contemplated. If we restore the money to Matthew Lyon, it will be an act of justice, not of favor.

But, the honorable gentleman makes himself somewhat merry with what he calls the *modesty* of Matthew Lyon. This petitioner, he says, very *modestly* asks, not only for the thousand dollars, but for interest, costs, and damages, and his pay as a member of Congress; and he apprehends the petitioner has a design to drain our Treasury. Most of those, sir, who make applications to Congress, take especial care never to lose any thing by not asking for enough. But I can see nothing so unreasonable in the petition of Matthew Lyon; for, if we should grant all he asks, it would fall far short of an indemnity for all his losses. But we are bound to restore what we have taken from him, with interest. Perhaps he will consider the eulogiums he has received as a sort of set-off against the residue of his claim; if not, he seems to be without remedy.

If Congress had repealed the law as unconstitutional, would they not have restored the money levied under it? Those who consider that the act should never have passed, as being unconstitutional, must be of opinion that our Treasury should not be replenished by such means; and, if so, can we conscientiously consider the money thus acquired as ours, unless indeed long possession has made it so, and we are to profit by our own neglect to do justice?

I do not think it necessary to search for precedents to justify us in the measure now proposed. If we have no precedent let us make one that may be a memento to dominant parties not to abuse their power. But if precedents were necessary, we may find enough in the history of England, not in that of our own country; for, fortunately for us, our history affords but a few instances of the abuse of power. For such precedents we need not go back to the heavy time of York and Lancaster, when the triumphant party constantly reversed all that had been done by the party subdued. We may look into a later period, when the Stuarts and their immediate successors were upon the throne, when the principles of liberty were much better understood than practised.

The attainder of the Earl of Strafford, who had been treacherously given up by a cowardly King to the indignation of Parliament, was reversed.

The attainders against Algernon Sidney and against Lord Russell were reversed.

The attainder against Alderman Cornish was reversed, as also that against Lady Lisle, and many others. In these cases, it is true, the Parliament only reversed their own proceedings. But they sometimes reversed the proceedings of other courts, as in the case of Bastwick, Burton, and Prynne, who were tried in the court of Star Chamber, for libels, and sentenced to lose their ears, to pay a fine of five thousand pounds each, and to be imprisoned for life. This is a very strong case, and in point; for the Parliament not only reversed the sentence, but remitted the fine, and ordered satisfaction for damages to the parties injured.

I must ask the indulgence of the Senate while I read a few passages from the proceedings in this extraordinary case. I shall read them for the edification of those who are, who have been, or who hereafter may be, in favor of a sedition act.

Dr. Bastwick, Mr. Burton, and Mr. Prynne, had written some religious books, in which were contained some reflections on the Bishops, which were deemed libellous. Mr. Prynne, three years before this time, had written a book in which he censured stage plays, music, and dancing, for which he was punished by the loss of his ears. "Between eight and nine o'clock in the morning, 'the fourteenth of June, [1637,] the Lords being 'set in their places, in the said court of Star 'Chamber, and casting their eyes at the prisoners, 'then at the bar, Sir John Finch, Chief Justice of 'the Common Pleas, began to speak after this 'manner:*

"I had thought Mr. Prynne had no ears, but methinks he hath ears; which caused many of the Lords to take a stricter view of him; and, for their better satisfaction, the usher of the court was commanded to turn up his hair and show his ears; upon the sight whereof, the Lords were displeased that they had been formerly no more cut off, and cast out some disgraceful words of him.

"To which Mr. Prynne replied, My Lords, there is never a one of your honors but would be sorry to have your ears as mine are.

"The Lord Keeper replied again, In good faith, he is somewhat saucy.

"I hope, said Mr. Prynne, your honors will not be offended; I pray God to give you ears to hear.

"The business of the day, said the Lord Keeper, is to proceed on the prisoner at the bar.

"Mr. Prynne then humbly desired the court to give him leave to make a motion or two; which being granted, he moves:

"First, that their honors would be pleased to accept of a cross bill against the prelates, signed with their own hands, being that which stands with the justice of the court, which he humbly craved, and so tendered it.

"*Lord Keeper.* As for your cross bill, it is not the business of the day; hereafter, if the court should see just cause, and that it savors not of libelling, we may accept of it; for my part, I have not seen it, but have heard somewhat of it.

"*Mr. Prynne.* I hope your honors will not refuse it, being, as it is, on His Majesty's behalf. We are His Majesty's subjects, and therefore require the justice of the court.

"*Lord Keeper.* But this is not the business of the day.

"*Mr. Prynne.* Why then, my Lords, I have a second motion, which I humbly pray your honors to grant, which is, that your Lordships will please to dismiss the prelates, here now sitting, from having any voice in the censure of this cause, being generally known to be adversaries, as being no way agreeable with equity or reason, that they who are our adversaries should be our judges; therefore I humbly crave they may be expunged out of the court.

"*Lord Keeper.* In good faith it is a sweet motion; is it not! Herein you are become libellous; and if you should thus libel all the Lords and reverend judges as you do the reverend prelates, by this your plea, you would have none to pass sentence upon you for your libelling, because they are parties."

The whole trial is very interesting. I proceed to the sentence.

"Thus the prisoners, desiring to speak a little more for themselves, were commanded to silence. And so the Lords proceed to censure.

"The Lord Cettington's censure :—I condemn these three men to lose their ears, in the palace-yard

─────
* *Harleian Miscellany,* vol. 4, p. 220.

at Westminster, to be fined five thousand pounds a man to His Majesty, and to perpetual imprisonment, in three remote places in the kingdom, namely, the castles of Caernarvon, Cornwall, and Lancaster.

"The Lord Finch addeth to this censure:

"Mr. Prynne to be stigmatized in the cheeks with two letters, S and L, for seditious libeller. To which all the Lords agreed."

I omit what is said of the punishment of Dr. Bastwick and Mr. Burton, which was inflicted with great cruelty, but that of Mr. Prynne deserves a particular notice:

"Now the executioner being come to sear him and cut off his ears, Mr. Prynne said these words to him: Come, friend, come burn me, cut me; I fear not; I have learned to fear the fire of hell, and not what man can do unto me. Come, sear me, sear me; I shall bear in my body the marks of the Lord Jesus; which the bloody executioner performed with extraordinary cruelty, heating his iron twice to burn one cheek, and cut one of his ears so close that he cut off a piece of his cheek. At which exquisite torture he never moved with his body, or as much as changed his countenance, but still looked up as well as he could towards Heaven, with a smiling countenance, even to the astonishment of all the beholders, and uttering, as soon as the executioner had done, this heavenly sentence: "The more I am beaten down, the more I am lift up."

What protection was afforded to these wretched men by the common law, the law in which they lived, and moved, and had their being?

The honorable gentleman from Georgia admonishes us not to destroy the independence of the judiciary, the bulwark of the liberties of the people. We shall not, in the measure now proposed, in the slightest degree, interfere with the independence of the judiciary. It must be a matter of indifference to them what we do with the sedition act; it cannot affect their emoluments. I have understood that the independency of the judiciary was regulated by the greater or less permanency in the tenure of their office, and the greater or less certainty in the payment of their fixed salaries.

But I must beg leave to differ from the honorable gentleman when he informs us that our independent judiciary is the bulwark of the liberties of the people. By which he must mean, defenders of the people against the oppressions of the Government. From what I witnessed in the years 1798, 1799, and 1800, I never shall, I never can, consider our judiciary as the bulwark of the liberties of the people. The people must look out for other bulwarks for their liberties. I have the most profound respect for the learning, talents, and integrity, of the honorable judges who fill our Federal bench. But, if those who carried into effect the sedition act are to be called the people's defenders, it must be for nearly the same reason that the Fates were called *Parcæ—quia non parcebant.* It would be a subject of curious investigation, how far the judiciary, from the earliest times to the present, have been the defenders of the people's liberties against the oppressions of Government; how much their zeal has been increased or

diminished by the certainty or uncertainty in the tenure of office; how far by an increase or diminution of salary; how much it has been affected by a fear of loss of office or salary on one side, or the hope of further promotion or increase of salary on the other. But such speculations at present are unnecessary.

An observation or two more, and I will trespass no longer upon the patience of the Senate.

I hope the motion for indefinite postponement will not prevail. I hope that we shall pass the resolution; that we shall restore to Matthew Lyon the money that has been extorted from him; and, more especially, I hope we shall, as far as in us lies, repair the breach made in our Constitution by the sedition act. But the honorable gentleman from Georgia sees no such breach, but thinks we shall make one by adopting the present resolution; and he now implores us not to disturb this sacred instrument of our Union, which he considers as the sun of our political firmament. We gaze upon the meridian sun till we are dazzled with his splendors, and can see none of his imperfections. But, if we view him through a misty atmosphere, or, in imitation of children, through a smoked glass, we have a less splendid, but more distinct view of this luminary. We see the dark spots which deform his disk. So the honorable gentleman, taking a lofty view of the sun of our political firmament, through an attenuated atmosphere, is dazzled with its splendor—sees nothing but light and perfection. But, if he would condescend to view it through a more obscure and dense medium, he would see in this luminary certain dark spots, indicative of decay. He would perceive, sir, that its first amendment, once its most resplendent limb, is now obscured in dim eclipse, shorn of its beams, shedding around "disastrous twilight."

When Mr. D. had concluded—

Mr. MORRIL spoke at length against the resolutions.

Mr. ROBERTS spoke in favor of the resolutions.

Mr. DANA replied to Mr. R. and others; and the Senate adjourned.

SATURDAY, January 20.

The PRESIDENT communicated a letter from the Secretary of the Navy, transmitting, for the use of the members of the Senate, sixty copies of the Naval Register for the year 1821; and the letter was read.

The following Message was received from the PRESIDENT OF THE UNITED STATES:

To the Senate of the United States :

In compliance with a resolution of the Senate of the 4th instant, "requesting the President of the United States to communicate to the Senate any information he may have, as to the power or authority which belonged to Don John Bonaventure Morales and to the Baron Carondelet, to grant and dispose of the lands of Spain in Louisiana, previously to the year 1803"—I transmit a report from the Secretary of the Treasury, submitting a letter of the Commissioner of the General Land Office, with the document to which it refers.

JAMES MONROE.

JANUARY 18, 1821.

The Message and accompanying documents were read.

NEHEMIAH R. KNIGHT, appointed a Senator by the Legislature of the State of Rhode Island and Providence Plantations, to supply the vacancy occasioned by the death of James Burrill, jr., produced his credentials, was qualified, and took his seat in the Senate.

The credentials of JAMES NOBLE, appointed a Senator by the Legislature of the State of Indiana, for the term of six years, commencing on the fourth day of March next, were read, and laid on file.

Mr. KING, of New York, presented the memorial of Archibald Gracie, and sons, and others, shipowners and merchants of the city of New York, praying an extension of the time allowed by law for unlading ships and vessels arriving in the ports of the United States; and the memorial was read and referred to the Committee on Finance.

The bill, reported yesterday by Mr. HORSEY, from the Committee on the District of Columbia, authorizing the sale of certain lots on the public reservation numbered 10, in the city of Washington, (the lots on C and on 4½ streets,) was read a second time.

SEDITION LAW—MATTHEW LYON.

The Senate then resumed the consideration of the resolutions declaring the late sedition law unconstitutional, and to indemnify those who suffered damages under it—the motion of Mr. WALKER, of Georgia, made some days ago, to postpone the resolutions indefinitely, being still under consideration.

Mr. BARBOUR again addressed the Senate in support of the resolutions, and in reply to their opponents.

Mr. SMITH also again spoke in reply to Mr. BARBOUR and others who advocated the resolutions.

Mr. MACON likewise spoke again in support of the resolutions, and in defence of the opinions he had previously advanced.

Mr. HOLMES, of Maine, spoke at length against postponing the resolutions, though he preferred legislating for the particular case of Matthew Lyon.

Mr. WALKER, of Georgia, spoke again to vindicate his opposition to these resolutions.

The question was then taken on the indefinite postponement of the resolutions, and was decided in the affirmative, as follows:

YEAS—Messrs. Chandler, Dana, Eaton, Elliott, Gaillard, Horsey, Hunter, Johnson of Louisiana, King of New York, Lanman, Lloyd, Mills, Morril, Noble, Otis, Palmer, Parrott, Pinkney, Smith, Taylor, Tichenor, Van Dyke, Walker of Georgia, and Williams of Tennessee—24.

NAYS—Messrs. Barbour, Brown, Dickerson, Holmes of Maine, Holmes of Mississippi, Johnson of Kentucky, King of Alabama, Lowrie, Macon, Pleasants, Roberts, Ruggles, Sanford, Stokes, Talbot, Thomas, Trimble, Walker of Alabama, and Williams of Mississippi—19.

So the report and resolutions were rejected.

Mr. BARBOUR then gave notice that he should on Monday ask leave to bring in a bill for the relief of Matthew Lyon.

PUBLIC LANDS.

Mr. TALBOT communicated the following preamble and resolutions of the Legislature of the State of Kentucky, which were read:

" Whereas many of the citizens of this Commonwealth, allured by the prospect of increasing their wealth, or procuring a more desirable home for themselves or their posterity, which the uninterrupted growth of the Western country presented to activity and enterprise, became purchasers of the public lands of the United States, under a well-founded confidence that the earnings of honest labor, the profits of fair trade, or the sale of their other property, would speedily enable them to fulfil their engagements to the public: Whereas the unexpected depression in the price of labor and of property, the stagnation of trade, and the derangement of the local currency in the Western States, rendering it unfit for the payment of dues at the several land offices, have darkened the fairest prospects, deprived the public debtors of their power to fulfil engagements made in good faith, and thrown upon them and their country an accumulated load of debt and distress, which no foresight could avert and no exertion can remove: Whereas, in addition to all these events, the Congress of the United States have, by the act of April, 1820, reducing the price of public lands, deprived the debtors of their last resource, and rendered them unable to sell any part of their purchases, and thereby raise the means to fulfil their engagements ; by which events and act the said purchasers are in danger not only of forfeiting their whole purchases, but of losing the money already paid, and are reduced to the humble necessity of resigning themselves to their fate, or soliciting indulgence for an indefinite period at the hand of their Government, with expense to themselves and injury to their country : And whereas it is not the interest or policy of a free Government to push the citizen beyond his ability, nor rigidly exact a forfeiture of his property when such penalty is neither merited by any wilful delinquency, nor useful in affording a salutary public example, it is, in the opinion of this General Assembly, the duty of the Congress of the United States, as it is within their power, to relieve the purchasers of public lands from this oppressive debt, on terms equitable to them and just to the Government: Wherefore,

"Resolved by the Senate and House of Representatives of the Commonwealth of Kentucky, That our Senators in Congress be instructed, and our Representatives requested, to use their exertions to procure the passage of a law permitting the purchasers of public lands at private sale to apply the instalments already paid to the payment in full for such portion of their purchases as such instalments may be adequate to pay for, at the price of two dollars per acre, and to relinquish the balance of their purchases to the United States.

"Resolved, That our Senators and Representatives in Congress be, and they are hereby, requested to present the foregoing preamble and resolution to the

213   HISTORY OF CONGRESS.   214

JANUARY, 1821.   *Relief to Land Purchasers.*   SENATE.

Senate and House of Representatives, of which they are members.

 " Attest : J. C. BRECKENRIDGE,
        " *Secretary.*"

MONDAY, January 22.

Mr. ROBERTS presented the memorial of John Bioren, of Philadelphia, and Fielding Lucas, jr., of Baltimore, booksellers, proposing to sell to Government a certain number of copies of the edition of the laws of the United States, published by said Bioren and others, and to print a sixth volume, to contain all subsequent laws, to the close of the present session of Congress, under the authority and patronage of Congress; and the memorial was read, and referred to the Committee on the Judiciary.

Mr. ROBERTS presented the petition of Ann Hodge, relict of George Hodge, deceased, late a boatswain in the Navy of the United States, praying to be remunerated for the loss of household furniture, occasioned by the burning of the navy yard at Washington, in the year 1814; and the petition was read, and referred to the Committee of Claims.

Mr. LOWRIE presented the petition of Thomas Dobson and son, booksellers of Philadelphia, praying that an act may be passed authorizing the purchase from them of six hundred copies of "Seybert's Statistical Annals of the United States," for the use of Government; and the petition was read, and referred to the Committee on Commerce and Manufactures.

Mr. PLEASANTS, from the Committee on Naval Affairs, to whom was referred the petition of Thomas Shields, made a report, accompanied by a bill concerning Thomas Shields and others; and the report and bill were read, and the bill passed to a second reading.

Mr. KING, of Alabama, gave notice that, to-morrow, he should ask leave to bring in a bill to establish a port of entry at Blakeley, in the State of Alabama.

The Senate proceeded to consider the motion of the 18th instant, instructing the Committee on Public Lands to inquire into the expediency of amending the act for the relief of the inhabitants of the late county of New Madrid, in the Missouri Territory, who suffered by earthquakes; and agreed thereto.

RELIEF TO LAND PURCHASERS.

The Senate resumed the consideration of the bill to extend relief to the purchasers of the public lands prior to the 1st of July, 1820.

When the bill was last under consideration, Mr. EATON moved to recommit the bill to the Committee on the Public Lands, with instructions to—

1st. Make the provisions of the bill applicable to those purchasers of public lands only who have purchased at public sale since the 30th day of December, 1816.

2d. And with instructions to extend the contemplated relief to none but those who, on or before the 30th day of October last, had made a settlement on the lands by them so purchased, defining and considering the settlement of any quarter section, a settlement of all contiguous and adjoining land, not exceeding two entire sections.

3d. And with instructions to extend the contemplated relief to no section on which any town may have been laid off, and the lots sold by any individual or company of individuals.

Mr. EATON spoke at some length in support of his motion, and to show that the bill, unamended in the mode he proposed, would be defective.

Mr. THOMAS briefly opposed the recommitment, because it would produce delay.

Mr. JOHNSON, of Kentucky, opposed the motion to recommit, and advocated the bill at considerable length. Mr. J. spoke as follows:

The system of relief, said Mr. JOHNSON, which the bill provides, is embraced in two propositions: First, the power to relinquish that portion of the land which is entered, but not paid for, and to obtain a patent for what is paid for; secondly, indulgence for eight or ten years, by annual instalments, without interest, to those who prefer retaining the whole amount purchased. In the former case, it is so constructed as not to derange the surveys, or to produce any loss or inconvenience by interfering with the system upon which sales are now made. Under the present laws, our public lands are surveyed in ranges of six miles wide, and, by transverse lines, at the same distances, divided into townships, as they are technically called, of six miles square, numbered from a line of latitude taken for the basis, and a meridian of longitude. These townships are each subdivided into thirty-six sections, of a mile square, or six hundred and forty acres, and these sections again subdivided into oblong rectangles of one-eighth of a section, or eighty acres each, and all divided by lines running with the four cardinal points. When the sales are made for which moneys are now due, the smallest sub-division was one hundred and sixty acres, the fourth part of a section; and, if a purchaser is now indebted for the smallest purchase which he could then make, he may now relinquish one-half of that purchase, without derangement to the present system. The provision made in the bill which is now proposed, carefully guards this point. If the purchaser shall choose to avail himself of the provision, he can relinquish only such aliquot part of a section as shall form the proper division, agreeably to the present system. The purchases made, which this bill will embrace, are either a section, six hundred and forty acres; three-fourths of a section, four hundred and eighty acres; a half section, three hundred and twenty acres; or a quarter section, one hundred and sixty acres. In every case, at least one-fourth part of the purchase money was paid within forty days of the time of application; another fourth part was required to be paid in two years; another in three years; the remainder in four years: and, in case any part shall be delayed till the expiration of five years from the day of application, the land is re-sold; and, unless some person shall advance cash in hand for what is due, the land reverts to the United States, and the whole of the money paid upon it, improvements and all, are forfeited, and the industrious, frugal, but more unfortunate husbandman, sent adrift with his family, and deprived of all the fruits of his honest labors. Now, sir, the bill before you proposes, that, in such cases, the purchaser may still be rescued from the grasp of penury and famine, in a land of plenty, by permitting him to retain so much of the land as the moneys paid by him will actually purchase, at the price of the original entry, not varying in quantity or form from the present legal sub-division, and to relinquish the remainder—a proposition that every honorable member of this House would accede to, under similar circumstances, in his own individual transactions with a poor and unfortunate debtor.

The second proposition is equally necessary to screen the purchaser from loss, and will equally secure the Government against any sacrifice. If a purchaser shall have entered a quarter section, (one hundred and sixty acres,) and shall have paid thereon only eighty dollars, the first instalment, it will not entitle him to a patent for any part of his purchase, as it will not have paid for eighty acres; or, if he shall have entered three-quarter sections, (four hundred and eighty acres,) and paid thereon only one instalment, two hundred and forty dollars, he will be entitled to a patent for eighty acres, amounting to one hundred and sixty dollars; but the remaining eighty dollars must be lost to him, unless relief be extended, by granting him time to complete his payment for an additional quantity of land. But most of these purchasers have paid more than the first instalment. They are generally an industrious, economical class of citizens, who, when they have been fortunate enough to collect small sums in return for their labor, pay them over to the land offices, as partial liquidations of the instalments due, or becoming due, for their lands, cheered by the animating prospect of being able one day to call that little portion of the wilderness on which their industry is creating perpetual smiles, their own. But all payments which either exceed or fall short of equal sums of one hundred and eighty dollars, the amount of purchase money for the smallest legal division of public land, must be forever lost to them and their families, unless the time shall also be extended, by which they may complete their payment for these aliquot parts of a section. One other course, it is true, might secure these over payments, which would be, to grant them certificates for such surpluses, receivable in payment for public lands; but no such provision is contained in the bill, and the relief proposed will be more for the interest of the Government, and quite as accommodating to the generality of those interested.

Let us have some regard to the character of those who need this relief. I mean the great body of this population, which must suffer without it. The question may seem to be local, from the particular interests which it involves; but no subject can, in reality, have a more extensive operation. It embraces the citizens of every section of every State in the Union; and the most useful and virtuous class of citizens, the honest, industrious farmers, by whose labors life and vigor are imparted to every other, and from whose persevering enterprise our country derives all its treasures. These citizens have left their homes, to subdue the wilderness, and make it subservient to the welfare of man, there to provide a home for themselves and their numerous offspring. With this class of citizens the security of our liberties, and the energies of the Government rest. To them we owe our national safety and prosperity. Virtue and independence, when exiled from every other class, find an asylum with them. They already form an impregnable barrier against territorial invasion; and it is a duty which the Government owes no less to itself than to them, to protect them from injustice, from injury, from ruin. Withhold the relief which their peculiar necessities now demand, and you give a deadly blow to the brightest hopes of the nation. It will be like refusing the kind offices of paternal care to a perishing child, who, if nourished, is destined to be your support and comfort in declining age.

There may be some exceptions to this description of character, but the proportion is very small; and a good man will not leave all his children to starve, lest the sons of strangers eat their crumbs. All have paid their money, all are citizens, and we can make no discrimination. None will receive relief beyond what justice warrants; the Government will lose nothing by any, and the measure, even in relation to the least meritorious, is founded in reason and equity. If any difficulty shall seem to exist in correctly designating the part to be relinquished, it is easily surmounted by the proposition which I have the honor to make; that when actual settlements are made, the part retained shall include the improvements, or such part of them as shall be contained within a regular legal division of the section; and when no improvements are made the division to be decided by lot. This will remove every difficulty which might arise from submitting the decision to either of the parties.

Those citizens have a claim to the consideration of the Government founded in equity. The amount due to the Government for sales of public lands is something less than twenty-four millions of dollars. For lands on which that amount is due, there cannot have been paid less than eight millions of dollars—one-fourth part of the purchase-money. And if one-half has been paid, then the money actually received is equal to the whole amount due. It is most probable that at least twelve millions have been paid; and if the relief shall be denied, this amount—the fruit of honest industry, drawn from the most virtuous and useful class of the community, the laboring husbandmen, into the public Treasury—must be forfeited and lost forever. Now, sir, let me inquire who among us is so lost to justice—so hardened against the cries of suffering innocence—that he would give his voice thus to fill the cup of misery, by replenishing the national coffers with twelve millions of dollars from this meritorious class of citizens, and then deprive them of the very lands which were designed to be purchased by that money? Let us bring this to a case betwixt individuals. Suppose one man sells to another a tract of land for four thousand dollars, to be paid in four annual instalments. The purchaser pays the two first instalments, (two thousand dollars,) and is unable to pay the balance. In such a case, what would be the course of an honorable man—one who loved justice—who acted upon the golden rule, "Whatsoever ye would that men should do unto you, do ye even so unto them?" Would he deprive the honest laborer of the hard-earned money which he had paid him, and triumphing in the misfortune of his neighbor, drive him, with his helpless babes, a houseless, homeless vagrant, upon the charities of an unfriendly world? No, sir; he would first inquire whether the failure to pay the residue had operated so as to subject him to any considerable loss. He would next inquire whether the land could be divided, without injury, so as to convey to the purchaser the worth of the money he had actually paid. He would then investigate the cause of the failure—whether it had originated in a fraudulent design of the purchaser. Being satisfied on all these points, that no special injury had arisen to himself in consequence of the failure; that the premises might be divided without injury or inconvenience; that the purchaser had failed to complete the payment through pure misfortune,—he would, without a moment's hesitation, either return him the money or divide the land, and convey so much as the payment made would cover. Such, sir, is precisely the case before us. The purchasers of public lands do not solicit our charity. Donations are not called for. Abatement in the price of the land is not expected. But they *implore* what they have a moral right to demand—they *implore* your justice. Confirm them in the possession of what they have paid for, at the price stipulated in the purchase, and give them the privilege of relinquishing the remainder; and where their payments do not exactly cover the legal rectangle, for where they have extended improvements over the different parts of the purchase, that they may receive *quid pro quo* for their moneys, or, that they may enjoy the benefit of their improvements, extend the time for paying the balance. This is what justice warrants them to expect, and is only continuing the principle which the Government has acted upon in former cases.

When times were more propitious than at present, relief has been repeatedly extended to others. Purchasers of lands between the Miami rivers, to whom a right of preëmption was given in consideration of their contract with John Cleves Symmes, were at first required to pay the whole purchase-money in three annual instalments. The inability of many to comply, rendered it necessary to forfeit their claims, or extend the time. The liberal course was adopted; and, after several years had elapsed, and relief more than once had been granted them, a law was passed which permitted them to hold the lands and liquidate the balances by six annual instalments, without interest. On several occasions, relief has been granted to other purchasers, by extending the time of payment, when their claims to indulgence were far less than at present. But why should we withhold relief

at this hour of unparalleled pressure and distress? On a more auspicious day, these citizens became purchasers of the public domain, when the prospect of a fair remuneration invited to industry. They cheerfully endured the toils and privations incident to their undertakings, in prospect of happier days. Returning to their shelter, from the labors of the day, gladness sparkled in their eyes, and the smile of hope beamed in their countenances, as their little ones hailed their approach, because fortune promised them a long and comfortable abode. Shall these smiles of innocence be followed with tears of anguish and disappointment? Shall the labor of the parent be forfeited and the hope of infancy be blasted forever, when we can, without detriment to the public interest, still fan the heavenly flame? The voice of justice, the voice of mercy, the voice of God, forbid it. The times are now changed. The products of their labor and their lands find no place in market, or will command no money, in comparison with what they once would do. It would be the height of injustice and oppression to seize upon this occasion to deprive them of their homes, and reduce them to all the horrors of wretchedness and despair. They can still live, and exhibit all the joys of contentment, if you will afford them this relief. If they cannot get money, they can furnish the comforts of life without it, and cheerfulness will still rest in their bosoms. They are now waiting in awful suspense the result of this proposition—in anxious solicitude, betwixt hope and despair, whether the arrival of the courier will sound the trump of their jubilee, or ring the knell of their departed happiness.

It is necessary for us to look into the reasons for fixing this penalty to the law under which these purchases were made. It originated in a policy to influence punctuality on the part of purchasers, and to prevent an accumulation of the debts due from individuals to the Government. That reason exists no longer. The old system of credit is abolished, and the debts, therefore, never can accumulate. In doing away this reason, you have also diminished the means of payment; by requiring prompt payment for all lands sold, which drains the money from those sections of the country, and by diminishing the price of lands in reducing the minimum from two dollars to one dollar and twenty-five cents per acre. Thus you have at once renewed the objections to relief, and by the same act increased the necessity of that relief.

When the purchases were made, there existed a stronger pretext for the enforcing of the penalty. The law provides, that when those lands shall be offered for sale, if they fetch more than the balance due the United States, including interest and costs, the surplus shall be repaid to the original purchaser; and when the circulating medium was great, and but few forfeitures were made, the lands might command a price which would partially remunerate him for his improvements; but now, when the circulating medium is almost entirely withdrawn, nearly all the lands must be forfeited, and there is not one-twentieth part of the money in all the States and territories together, where these lands lie, necessary to pay the balances due upon them.

The Government is bound in justice to grant the relief; and these citizens have a moral right to demand it. It may be classed among the imperfect rights; imperfect, only because they have not the legal nor physical power to enforce the demand; but the right, in its binding efficacy upon the conscience, is perfect and complete; the same as a father's perfect right, in morality and religion, to demand honor and gratitude from his son; but the right is imperfect in law, because he cannot legally enforce it.

In the case of the purchaser of the public land, there is an equity of redemption in his favor. This word is technical in the language of the law, and is referred to a principle established between mortgagers and mortgagees. In the case of a mortgage between citizens, a court of equity will not consider the mortgaged premises vested in the mortgagee, though the party who has given the mortgage fails to pay the money on a day certain, fixed by express contract in writing. So uniform have been the decisions of courts of equity in these cases, that the principle is universally established, even beyond controversy, that whatever number of years may have elapsed, the party has a right to redeem his mortgaged premises, by paying the principal and interest of the sum for which the mortgage was given; and in no case, can the property mortgaged be sold, nor the fee simple vested in the mortgagee, but by a foreclosure of the mortgage, and a decree of the court of chancery. The cases may not be exactly similar; but the resemblance is sufficiently strong to show that the equity of redemption, if we may use the expression, is as great in favor of the purchasers of public lands, and against the right of the Government to deprive them of their domains.

According to the former system of our land laws, the purchaser had the right to purchase by prompt payment, or by instalments; but he could not purchase even the smallest subdivision by prompt payment, so as to procure a patent for his land, and thus secure it to himself and his heirs, for less than $264 40, exclusive of discount. The poor man, then, who could command but a little sum, was under the necessity of purchasing upon the terms of credit which the law provided. Now he can purchase the amount of a legal subdivision, 80 acres, so as to obtain his patent, for $100. Suppose, sir, the poor man, four years since, entered the smallest quantity which could then be purchased, 160 acres, and paid upon it 80 dollars at the time of entry, and two years thereafter he paid the second instalment, 80 dollars more, making together 160 dollars; there is no doubt that, could he have the right of bringing his case into a court of equity, as he might do against an individual, the court would establish this principle— that the failure, being without fraud, and the point being ceded, as in this case, that the division was neither injurious nor inconvenient to the seller, the unfortunate purchaser should be confirmed in his claim to 80 acres, the amount which he had actually paid for at the original price. The chancellor would say, " as no fraud has been committed by the purchaser; as the means of payment ' are cut off by the withdrawal of the circulating ' medium, producing great calamity and distress, ' beyond both the control and foresight of either ' party; and as the Government, by changing the ' system and reducing the price of lands, has contributed much more than the purchaser to his ' inability to pay, the loss to the purchaser is still ' sufficiently great; for, had he saved his money ' till this time, one hundred dollars would have ' purchased all that he now claims for the payment of 160 dollars; he shall therefore be confirmed in his claim."

The provision for extending the time of payment might be more doubtful in a court of equity, but not less necessary to secure to the honest laborer the reward of his industry, and measure out to him the full cup of justice. The Government will thereby receive a higher price for the lands thus obtained than to suffer them to revert, and at the same time promote the interests of the most deserving class of the community. In many cases injustice will be done to the purchasers, and ruin will fall upon their families without it. The benefit will be almost exclusively in favor of the poor, whom it is a public duty to protect. A person has purchased one hundred and sixty acres, and paid the first instalment, according to law, at the time of purchase. By the sweat of his brow he has since raised forty dollars, with which he has made a partial payment upon the second instalment. The price was two dollars per acre, and he has paid one hundred and twenty. The pressure of the times renders it impossible for him to procure money; and as the sum paid will not cover the purchase of eighty acres, he must lose all that he has paid, unless you extend the time. This, sir, is not an imaginary, but a real case: not a solitary case, for hundreds, and even thousands, of such cases do exist; and tens of thousands of our fellow citizens, of every age and sex, must inevitably be reduced to misery and ruin, if the provision shall be denied them.

If their own imprudence had brought these disasters upon them, they would have a slighter claim to consideration; but, unless we ascribe to them angelic foresight, or more sagacity than has ever yet fallen to the lot of man, we cannot justly charge them with imprudence. If no change had taken place in the circulating medium of the country; if our markets had remained the same at home and abroad; if the price of labor had not depreciated; if the same amount of exportation and importation had continued; their ability to meet the instalments would have continued, and the forfeitures would have been in as small a ratio to the purchasers as at any former period. The disorders in our currency, and the consequent depression of all our moneyed concerns, originated in the struggles of the late war—events which no human sagacity could foresee. Before that event, no general pecuniary embarrassments threatened us, and we could anticipate no extraordinary fluctuations. The banks had the confidence of the people; and in all their operations they maintained the specie standard. Contracts were sacredly executed, or the remedy was within our own control; and confidence between citizens was unimpaired. But war was proclaimed, and our national expenditures were necessarily increased to an amount beyond the power of taxation to meet. Loans were resorted to, which were confined principally to New York, Philadelphia, Baltimore, and Washington, the greater part of which was drawn from banks disposed to aid the Government in its efforts to sustain the independence and glory of the nation. An excessive issue of notes was the consequence; and as confidence began to be shaken on account of the internal divisions which existed, the circulation of those notes became local, and caused them to return upon the banks. At this moment, as by a kind of inspiration, to sustain their own credit and their country's cause, the banks simultaneously suspended the payment of specie; and the causes which produced this suspension were so identified with the honor, the rights, and the independence of the country, that there was a general and almost universal acquiescence in the measure.

When peace returned, the whole country became impatient for the resumption of specie payments; and, to satisfy the general call which was unfortunately pressed upon the banks, specie payments were resumed at least five years too soon for the general good, unless it had been very gradually introduced, so as to give time for loans to have been collected more leisurely and as the people could meet the calls. At the same moment Europe was laboring to effect the same object. France and the United States were the only specie countries in all our commercial relations. The general peace of Europe had produced a total revolution in the labor and commercial intercourse of the civilized world. Russia was making bonfires of her paper. England was making every exertion to substitute a specie currency for her paper, and inundating this country with her merchandise to supply her coffers with bullion; and the nation was almost drained of specie to supply other countries with which we had intercourse. Such was the state of affairs when the vaults of our banks were opened to sustain their solvency. The thirteen millions of surplus money in the Treasury was soon exhausted in payment of the floating debt. Paper flowed like torrents into the banks, by which the circulating medium was almost entirely withdrawn; and, to meet the demand, the banks called upon their debtors, who were by that very circumstance deprived of the means of payment. Property was sacrificed for want of purchasers, because the means of raising funds were at an end. The banks were crushed, individuals were ruined, and the community has sustained a loss of not less than fifty millions of dollars. In this state of things, there is an utter impossibility of the purchasers of public land meeting claims against them. Coercion will be fruitless; and by tearing from them their lands you will only fill up to them the cup of misery without relieving others.

As their claim is founded in justice; as they are among the most valuable of our citizens; as the relief will not injure the Government, while it will impart happiness to thousands and contribute to increase the wealth and resources of the nation, it is devoutly hoped that the unanimous voice of the Senate will sanction the measure.

Mr. NOBLE followed in a short speech on the same side of the question, and of the same purport.

Mr. KING, of Alabama, also opposed the recommitment, at some length, and incidentally defended the object and general provisions of the bill.

Mr. WALKER, of Alabama, addressed the Chair as follows:

Mr. President: I can see no sufficient reason for recommitting th s bill, especially at this stage of the discussion. If the Senate concur in opinion with the honorable gentleman from Tennessee, all his objects may be obtained in the usual mode, and in the shape of amendments. At any rate, a recommitment should not take place until some general principles are fixed, until we have agreed on the leading features of that system of relief which we may deem it expedient to grant. That some relief is necessary, seems to be universally conceded; we differ only as to the mode and the degree.

Let us notice the objects for which a recommitment is asked. The first is, to limit the relief proposed by the bill to those purchasers of the public land who have bought since the 30th December, 1816, leaving those who bought lands before that day to abide as they may the terms of their contracts, and the tender mercies of the law of forfeiture. In support of this proposition it is said, that they have had sufficient indulgence already; that they have repeatedly had the advantages of relief; that their years of grace have been many, and that they have no reasonable claim to more. Let us inquire a little into this matter. Why have you given time heretofore? Because these persons were unable to comply with their engagements, and because you did not deem it politic to drive them from the lands which they had improved, and for which they had made partial payment; because, in short, you would not involve them in distress and ruin. But this indulgence was merely an extension of time, and these purchasers paid the price of it. You exacted interest still, and a portion of the principal annually. Those who could not pay this price, reaped not the benefit of your indulgence. On this unfortunate class the law of forfeiture took its course, and was consummated; and those who had the means made final payment, for the purpose of freeing themselves from the increasing load of interest. It would seem then that the purchasers anterior to the year 1817, are not so clearly beyond the pale of an equitable clemency, as the gentleman supposes. They have paid the price of the indulgence which they have received; and it should be shown that they are in a condition now to do what they were confessedly unable to do heretofore. I say nothing of the situation of those who bought only a short time before this golden era of mercy—in the year 1816 for instance, and whose year of grace, even according to the contract, is not expired. It is evident that *they* have received no indulgence, and can receive none, if this proposition should succeed. Would this be fair? would it be equal? would it be just? I think not. Their condition would be worse than that of those going before or coming after them. It would be an odious anomaly, marring the harmony and beauty of your system.

The gentleman from Tennessee contends that the late purchasers, particularly those in Alabama, are better entitled to relief than others, because they have purchased at enormous prices. This is very true, and I concur entirely in his opinion. Sir, the situation of Alabama is peculiar, is critical, is deplorable. Relief that will be efficient and adequate for the other new States, would be much less so for her. Time alone would do nothing for her, except in the cases of the fortunate few who made their purchases at reasonable rates. For others we must resort to very different provisions, which I shall take the liberty to suggest in the further progress of this bill.

But, Mr. President, this is a great national question, which, however deeply and pre-eminently it may concern Alabama, does not concern Alabama alone; it embraces the Union. When we act on it, we must look at the paramount interests of the entire Confederacy. We must frame a system which shall be general, which shall take in the whole, and particular hardships are incident to all such general measures. They may be deplored, but they must be submitted to. But I shall have more to say on this point in its proper place. Meantime, I content myself with repeating that this object of the honorable gentleman from Tennessee may be obtained directly by an amendment, more conveniently than by the circuitous process of recommitment.

The second object of a recommitment is to confine the relief proposed by the bill to *actual settlers only*—to those who had made an actual settlement before the 30th October, 1820. Those who have not made such settlement are denounced as *speculators*, and speculators are entitled to no redress. Speculation ought to be repressed and discountenanced, and subjected to the ban of penalty and forfeiture. I know this Senate too well; I have too high a respect for its intelligence and liberality to suppose, for a moment, that it is in danger of being misled by a *name*. I can see nothing in the nature and reason of the thing which calls upon Congress, acting for the United States at large, to make the discrimination proposed. It is in the nature of a premium on actual settlement, a bounty for removing from the old States to the new. It supposes that there is something of positive merit in such removal, which is entitled to reward. If this be so, why not proclaim the fact? Why not embody it in your system? Why not make the advantage known before the sale? Why not draw your line of distinction prospectively, and not retrospectively? Why hold out the same terms to *all*, if you do not intend to mete out to all the same equal measure of justice? Sir, it seems to me that you are foreclosed, in all equity and good conscience, from making this distinction. It is not

"in the bond." Your faith is pledged, and you are bound, in all fair construction of the contract, to make no such distinction. I speak now of the Union. With regard to the new States, the question assumes a totally different aspect and character. Population is their strength. They desire, for the most obvious and cogent reasons, to increase it. Every immigrant not only adds to their numerical force, but he brings from abroad an accession to their wealth. He improves the soil; he supports the local government; he imparts new vigor to the body politic; he gives new value to every thing around him. Well may the new States, therefore, be ready to welcome him. They, indeed, might very naturally be willing to make distinctions in his behalf. But can they do so? Have you left them at liberty to pursue a course so obviously advantageous to them? You have done no such thing. As if foreseeing th.. very result, you have taken the precaution .. ' .. s in you lay, to tie up their hands. You ... ve :.. 'ed at the interest of the whole, and no: ... ' ... '. You have regarded the public lands as t... ! .. of the nation. Your object has been to . for the highest price. You invite all the w ... ' the auction. The only condition of the s.. ... that the highest bidder shall be the purch. You do not inquire whether he live in Maine .. on the lakes, on the Gulf of Mexico, or at the f. . of the Stony mountains. He may reside in *terr.. incognita*, or the moon. You ask not, you cannot. All you ask is his money. You want a chapman, who will give the highest price for your commodity. You do not limit the quantity which an individual may buy. His purse and his judgment are left to fix the limit. You do not require him to erect a cabin, or girdle a tree. The property is his, and he is allowed "to manage his own concern in his own way." But do you stop here? Do you content yourselves with this negative legislation? You do not, sir. You go still further, and, lest the new States, in their sovereign capacities, and for their local interests, should make discriminations in the burdens which they may see proper to impose on the soil, you cautiously restrain them, and you declare "that the lands of non-residents shall never be taxed higher than the lands of residents." This article enters into every act by which any of your Territories has been authorized to become a State. It is part of the consideration of admission into the federal family. It is of permanent obligation, and cannot be rescinded without your consent. Thus careful have you been to protect the rights of purchasers, let them live where they may; and this policy increased the number of bidders, and enhanced the value of your lands. But when have you required actual settlement as a condition of the purchase? When have you made distinctions in favor of actual settlers? How often have you refused any particular advantages to *squatters*? And will you make a difference after the sale which you did not make before? And will you tie the hands of the new States, lest they should follow their particular interests, to your prejudice, while you yourselves commit a gratuitous injustice—an injustice the more cruel, from the very pains which you have taken to mask it? But, whatever may be the decision of the Senate on this point, it should not be forgotten that a recommitment is not necessary to attain it.

The third object of a recommitment is, to exclude town sites from the operation and benefits of the bill. These, again, have been matter of speculation and profit, and ought to be beyond the pale of relief; and the gentleman tells us that the town companies and other companies of speculators, bid up the lands to enormous prices, and excessively enhanced their value in the market. And he quotes a case, in Alabama, where a town company gave upwards of eighty thousand dollars for less than three thousand acres. Here, then, the speculators gave more than twenty-four dollars the acre; and must have paid for the first instalment only, upwards of twenty thousand dollars—when the fee-simple, at the minimum price, would have been less than six thousand. And who was the receiver of this enormous sum? Your Treasury, sir. It has already in its vaults more than the entire value of the land. Yes, sir, the Government is, in reality, the great land speculator. Your system is built upon speculation. You have encouraged and fostered it; you have lent it aid and inducement; you have shared in its gains; your cryers have set forth your commodity with all the art and eloquence of auctioneers. All the blandishments of description have been lavished; the eager excitement of public competition has been employed; and now you stigmatize your dupes and repel them from your clemency. But, if it shall be the good pleasure of the Senate to exclude town sites from the benefits of the bill, I shall acquiesce. I do not object. But let this be done by a direct amendment; and do not send back the bill to a committee for such a purpose. This is, in fact, but a trifling matter—a mere affair of detail; and I am ashamed to have occupied your attention on it so long. I will pass to considerations of higher import.

Let us look, then, Mr. President, at the bill itself; let us examine, a little more nearly, the system of relief which it proposes; let us inquire into its inducements and its objects, and estimate the force of the motives by which it appeals to our support. This is the more necessary at this time, since to recommit with specific instructions is to pass on its merit or demerit; is to fix principles; is, in short, to decide the fate of the bill. I consider the whole question as now fairly and fully before us; and I am encouraged to go on by the wish of certain gentlemen near me, to whom the subject of the public lands, in its multiform character and interest, is not very familiar.

The national domain is of immense extent, and stretches over regions of every variety of soil. I shall not enter into the history of its acquisition. It is with your mode of disposing of it, that we have to do. This was, for a considerable period, variant and irregular. But in 1802 you adopted a regular, well-defined, and comprehensive system, which continued to be in operation until the 1st of July, 1820. By this system, the lands were laid

off in townships of six miles square, each containing thirty-six sections; which, again, were subdivided into quarters, of one hundred and sixty acres each. This was the smallest subdivision known to your law until 1817, when six sections in each township were made divisible, at the option of the purchaser, into tracts of eighty acres, or half-quarter sections. So much for the mode of survey, and the size of the tracts: and so far your system was beautiful and excellent. It still remains without alteration, except that every section is now divisible into half quarters: an alteration which, while it did not impair the beauty and harmony of the system, was of the highest political importance, as tending directly to increase the number of freeholders—the strength and glory of a nation.

The land, so divided, was sold at public auction to the highest bidder. One fourth of the purchase money was paid in hand, and the residue was payable in three instalments, of two, three, and four years, bearing interest from the date of the purchase, if not punctually paid; and, if any portion of the purchase money remained unpaid at the expiration of five years from the date of the purchase, the land became forfeited to the United States, and was re-sold for their benefit. It could not be sold for less than the whole sum remaining unpaid, including interest: but if sold for more than that sum, the excess was paid to the former purchaser. I forbear to mention other particulars of detail, as unnecessary to my present purpose.

What was the practical result of this system? An enormous debt, sir, continually accumulating, growing with the growth of the new States, until, on the 30th of September, 1819, it had amounted up to the frightful sum of upwards of twenty-two millions of dollars! Half of which had been added during the last two years immediately preceding that date. This was the radical defect of the system. The debt was always growing, with an accelerating ratio, at an average of more than a million a year, until it hung like an ugly excrescence over half the Republic. You began to regard it with an eye of apprehension. You saw in the relation of debtor and creditor something unbefitting the relation of the citizen towards the Government. Too much might be expected on the one hand, and too much or too little refused or granted on the other. The very magnitude of the debt was alarming, especially when considered in connexion with its inherent vice of continual increase. Its locality, too, was not without interest. It was not diffused in equal ratio over all parts of the Union. It was confined to the new States. These, standing in the same situation, must be supposed to have a common feeling, as well as a common interest, on this subject. Their number was increasing, their population augmenting with unparalleled rapidity. Their representation in the councils of the Union were increasing, *pari passu*, with their population. Already it was nearly one-third of this body. What might not be feared from this debt when it should have reached a hundred millions, when the debtors should constitute half your numerical force, and occupy the largest and fairest portion of your empire? The apprehension of evil seemed natural and reasonable; and rational patriots, loving the Union, and desiring to perpetuate it, could not but wish to arrest the march of a system carrying in its bosom so much of inquietude and danger for the future. This you have done. You have performed your duty. You have accomplished the first great object of your wishes. You abolished the system; and you have instituted a new one, which excludes credit altogether from all future purchasers of the public lands. Cash, and cash alone, is received in payment. The danger from the further increase of the debt no longer exists. The debt has reached its maximum. We must look at the debt, then, as it now exists, divested of its most odious features. It is a monster still; but it is no longer dangerous to you; it threatens, now, only those who are its subjects, on whom it presses with a mountainous weight, and whom it must crush as victims unless they shall be rescued from impending ruin by some timely act of clemency on your part.

What, then, is the measure now proposed by the Committee on the Public Lands? The bill allows to purchasers, 1st, a right to surrender any legal subdivision of their purchases, to transfer the money paid on the part surrendered, and apply it to the discharge of the sum due or unpaid on such legal subdivisions as they may choose to retain; 2d, a deduction for prompt payment; 3d, instalments for the sums due or unpaid; and, 4th, remission of interest to all who comply with the terms proposed. Its objects seem to be to hasten the extinction of the debt, to get money, and to grant adequate relief.

The privilege of transfer is of the first importance. It is an admirable expedient for lessening the debt, without sacrificing the interest of either party; and it will be worth more, especially to Alabama, than all the other provisions of the bill. It will afford great relief to thousands. It will enable them to save some portion of their lands; it will release them from debt, by abandoning what they cannot pay for; it will save their money from being swallowed up for nothing; it will prevent forfeiture, and the distress and odium attendant on forfeiture—distress to the citizen and odium to the Government; while it puts at once into the hands of the United States land which will bring its fair value in cash, and which may thus be resold without exciting public sympathy for the first purchaser, who would always profit by it in cases of involuntary forfeiture; and, above all, it will diminish the great land debt more than any other feature of the bill. This principle, I shall hope, then, will receive the unanimous sanction of the Senate.

But the privilege of transfer merely—of removing payments made on a tract surrendered, and applying them to the discharge of the debt on the tract retained—does not equalize conditions, and put purchasers under the old system on the footing of those who buy for cash, because each and every purchase was bottomed on the indefinite credit allowed for the three last instalments; and because the minimum price, and consequently the current

value, was greater than it is now, in the proportion of eight to five. But transfer and *deduction* of three-eighths from the original price would do this in a great degree; and purchasers would only get the same quantity and the same tracts which they would have bought originally, had the sales been made for cash only. I shall therefore at a proper time move an amendment combining these principles.

The second section of the bill allows a deduction for prompt payment. It is to be observed that a very large portion of this enormous sum of twenty-five millions outstanding and unpaid is not yet due, especially in Alabama. The day of grace is still distant—in many cases several years. The object of this section is to hasten the extinction of these future debts, by holding out to your debtors inducements to make such a course desirable to them on the score of interest. They may "owe you a debt, but they would be loth to pay you before your day." If you wish to anticipate that day, you must appeal to their interest; you must offer some consideration—some motive—and this is presented in the shape of this allowance or discount. This is still in blank. It is obvious that the amount to be derived immediately from this section will depend very much upon the rate of discount. The more liberal the deduction, the greater the prompt payments. This is the opinion of the Secretary of the Treasury, who proposes the principles of this bill in aid of the finances. Of one thing I am convinced—that more money will be obtained by the bill than ever would be obtained without it. Five-eighths of the purchase-money is much more than Alabama lands could be sold for. The amount of the first payment—the first instalment, as it is popularly called—could not, in innumerable instances, be had for them. This is not an idle conjecture; it is a fact proved recently by actual sales. The lands in Colbert's reserve were sold at Huntsville last autumn under your new cash law; and, although their situation is superior to any in the Tennessee valley, they did not on the average bring so much as the first instalment of adjoining lands of equal quality sold two years before. In very many cases, indeed, I have no doubt that it would be more advantageous to purchasers to incur a forfeiture, and buy again, rather than seek relief under this bill. They would make money by it in the end. But this course would require patience and courage. It must encounter the vexation of delay and suspense—the most tormenting state of the mind. It would arrest improvement, and it would not be unmixed with apprehension. Great exertions, therefore, under the operation of proper inducements, would be made to prevent forfeiture. Men form attachments to the chosen spots—they are endeared by a thousand agreeable and powerful associations—and much would be sacrificed to preserve them from risk. Yes, sir, the settler has fixed his heart on the spot of his choice. It is his home. It is improved by his labor, em llished by his taste, in part paid for by his money. It contains the cabin which shelters his wife and children, and which may have been their tower of refuge from the tomahawk and scalping-knife.

The little orchard is of his own planting; the little garden smiles from the culture of his wife; his old friends, who have followed him to the wilderness, neighbor around him. These are items of that strong passionate predilection with which you have to deal; but this predilection has its limits. These ties are strong, but they may be broken.

Mr. President, Congress can fix the value of lands in the new States and Territories. You can raise and depress it at pleasure. The price between individuals must bear some relation to that of the Government. Mr. Crawford admits this frankly, and argues from it, with truth and force, proving that this immense domain of the Union must leave this power for a long time to come in your hands. Of that immense domain, what a small speck has been sold! How little, comparatively, has been even surveyed! Vast regions remain still covered by Indian title. Your official agents estimate the total number of acres to which the Indian title has been extinguished at 191,978,-536! the number of acres surveyed at 72,805,092! and the number sold at 18,601,930! The difference in these aggregates is prodigious. You are still, and must long remain, a mighty monopolist. You can regulate the price of your commodity at will. You do so regulate it. The entire minimum now is less by one-sixth than three-fourths of the old minimum; and, where the lands are of equal value, must effectually disable the credit purchaser from entering the market as your competitor, unless at the absolute loss of three-eighths of his capital. Can individuals sell their land for two dollars, when your price is one dollar and a quarter? Their certificates, with the first payment made, would not be received as a present, under the condition of completing the purchase according to the terms of the original contract, as there would remain to be paid one dollar and a half, and the donee would be a clear loser by twenty-five cents the acre! The same relation of prices exists, whatever may be the cost of the land. The diminution of actual current value is real and absolute, and universal. And this diminished value proceeds from the act of the Government. Yes, sir, from your own act. Will you thus vitally affect the condition of your debtor, and afford him no redress? Will you suddenly lessen the value of the article, after the sale, and still exact the full price? Will you lessen his ability to pay, and yet require "the utmost mite?" Will you insist on "the pound of flesh," because it is so written "in the bond?" I think you will not: I am sure you ought not.

In this view, the remission of interest now proposed, cannot be more than equivalent to the diminished value effected by the change of system from credit to cash; and that, even on low priced lands; on others, it is nothing like an equivalent. Sir, the remission of interest is not a new principle. It is only an extension of the principle on which Congress has long acted. At first the interest accrued, by the term of the contract, on each instalment, from the date of the purchase, absolutely; afterwards this principle was relaxed, and interest accrued only on failure of punctual payment. Here was a great change, highly favorable to the purchaser, and certainly not demanded by such powerful motives as now cry aloud for a further change. The former was matter of mere grace: the latter grows out of a strong equity, fastening itself upon you in consequence of your own subsequent act, for your own advantage.

We come now, sir, to the credit. And what was the credit under the old system? We have seen that it was nominally for five years, in the first instance. Then three more were granted: then three more: then forfeitures were suspended from year to year: and there the matter rests at present. The credit was, in fact, indefinite. Congress never refused indulgence: and lands are still in part unpaid for, which were sold soon after the credit system was adopted.

In Alabama, for instance, eight years from the date of the purchase, had been already granted to debtors in Madison county, and on the Tombigbee; and at the unfortunate sales of 1817 and 1818 no man calculated on a shorter term. Congress was considered to be pledged, in good faith and equal dealing, to indulge them as much as it had indulged others. This cry was in everybody's mouth. This was regarded as a tacit condition of the contract; and it was a consideration which, whether true or false, operated powerfully and universally: I need not say how ruinously, if you now refuse what you never refused before. But this you will not do. You will not subject yourselves to the imputation of hard-heartedness and partiality. To refuse time now to those who have had no indulgence, would be unequal and unjust; and this is the case with nearly all Alabama, who needs relief the most, and has the strongest claims upon you for it.

The credit purchasers calculated on the indefinite continuance, if not the perpetuity, of the system. At any rate, they were innocent purchasers, for a fair consideration, and they have a fair equitable claim to be relieved and protected against an act of the other party to the contract, which lessens directly and necessarily, in their hands, the value of the property which they had purchased.

What sort of comparison, then, can there be between the motives to afford relief heretofore, and those which call for it now? Then, there was no chance of system, no reduction of price, no diminution of value; and the amount of the debt was annually increasing; yet you never refused relief. Now, the system is changed by your act; the price is reduced by your act; the value of the article sold is diminished in the hands of the purchaser, by your act; and the debt cannot be further increased; it has reached its maximum; and will you now, for the first time, refuse relief?

This, Mr. President, is a general view of the subject, and these arguments will reach and cover the case of the debtors in all the new States. But, I have said, that the situation of Alabama was peculiar. Sir, it is deeply distressing and deplorable. It stands out from the canvass in bold relief. Suffer me to call your attention to a few facts, by way of verification:

Total number of acres of land sold, up to 30th of September, 1819 - - - - 18,601,930

Deduct number of acres sold in Alabama - - - - -		$3,646,857
Leaves number sold in all other States and Territories - -		14,955,073
Total amount of sales - -	$44,054,452 83¾	
Deduct amount of sales in Alabama - -	15,312,565 19¼	
Leaves for am'nt of sales in all other States, &c. - -	28,741,886 92½	
Total amount actually paid by purchasers - - - - - -		22,229,180 63¾
Deduct amount paid by purchasers in Alabama - - - - -		4,469,626 19½
Leaves amount paid by purchasers in all other States - - - -		$17,759,553 44¼
Total amount of debt outstanding -		22,000,657 64
Deduct amount due in Alabama -		10,834,270 76
Leaves am'nt due in all other States		$11,166,386 88

According to the returns, there has been actually paid in other States, per acre, not quite one dollar and twenty cents: and there remains due, per acre, in those States, not quite seventy-five cents.

There has been paid, per acre, in Alabama, not quite one dollar and twenty-five cents; and remains due there, per acre, not quite two dollars and seventy-five cents.

It appears, then, that 14,955,073 acres in other States, have been sold for -	$28,741,886
While only 3,646,857 acres in Alabama, have been sold for - - -	15,312,565
Leaving a difference in amount of only - - - - - - -	$13,429,321

But, if lands in Alabama had been sold at the same average price per acre, as in other States, the amount of sales there would have been only about $6,650,000; nothing like half the actual amount; and making the enormous difference of eight millions and a half of dollars. For the debt of Alabama, according to the returns up to 30th September, 1819, is $10,834,270, being less than the debt of all the other States and Territories only by the trifling sum of $332,116. But, had only equal prices been given, the debt of Alabama would be only about $2,180,000, making a difference of debt in the two cases, as before, of eight millions and a half.

This, according to the returns up to September, 1819. But, it is proper to remark, that a portion of the lands sold at St. Stephens, lie in the State of Mississippi. The amount, however, due for them in that State is not very great, and the lands sold at that office are by far the lowest in Alabama. The price given there is, on the average, only about two dollars and thirty-eight cents the acre; while at Cahawba it is about three dollars and seventy cents; and, at Huntsville, about five dollars and ninety cents! A single township in the Tennessee valley was sold for half a million of dollars—upwards of twenty dollars the acre.—Many tracts, for actual settlement, were sold at thirty and forty dollars, and one as high as seventy-eight dollars; sites for towns, still higher.

Nine hundred and fifty-one thousand one hundred and thirty-one acres have been sold, at St. Stephens, for $2,266,076. Suppose that, of this sum, there is due, in Mississippi, $834,270; and this is perhaps near the truth, it certainly does not exceed it. This would reduce the debt of Alabama, in round numbers, to ten millions of dollars, and would reduce the number of acres sold in Alabama to three thousand two hundred and ninety-six thousand, six hundred and ninety-three; calculating all lands sold at St. Stephens at the same average price, while, in fact, the portion which lies in Mississippi was sold before the era of distraction, and at scarcely more than the old minimum price. Could we speak in exact terms, the number of acres sold lying in Cahawba would be still fewer, and the relative price greater; and the excess of price which has been given and promised there, over that for an equal number of acres elsewhere, would be still further increased. Say, however, that it is eight millions, and it cannot be made less, from the tables, by any practical calculation, and what shall be said of it? A debt of ten millions from a single State—of which eight millions is mere excess of price—a sum given, or rather promised, in Alabama, beyond the sum given or promised, anywhere else, for the same number of acres. Does it not make a strong claim upon your clemency? And will you refuse all manner of relief? You will not, you cannot. But this bill is general. It affords no special relief to Alabama.

I fear, sir, that I have already trespassed too long on the patience of the Senate, fatiguing others even more than I fatigue myself. But the deep interest of my constituents in the subject must plead my apology. Indulge me, therefore, a few moments longer, and let us see if we cannot unravel the mystery of these high prices in Alabama—the causes of this enormous debt. Sir, there is no mystery in it; the causes are obvious, and the finger of the Government is visible throughout the whole transaction.

Almost the whole of the debt of Alabama has been contracted since the war, and during the period of our highest apparent prosperity. The first sales took place in August, 1817, and in February and March, 1818. It was an era, not merely of plenty, but of superabundance; and it begat a thousand wild schemes of every sort and character. The spirit of speculation possessed almost the entire mass of society. You yourselves were infected with the contagion of extravagance. The national coffers were overflowing, and you busied yourselves in devising new modes of expending your excessive wealth. You gave the tone, the people caught and echoed it. Everywhere visions of magnificence occupied and created the public mind. The circulating medium was everywhere unnaturally abundant, but nowhere so much so as in Alabama. About seventy banks were just instituted in the neighboring States of Tennessee and Kentucky. If they were without capital what did that signify? Their paper was receivable in your land offices where it was as good as gold or silver. They were anxious to lend. Everybody who could muster a couple of endorsers could borrow. Capital was not necessary either to the banks or their customers. Credit was all, and credit was universal. Everything was fictitious. No man was without money, or the representative of money. Cotton was selling at twenty-five cents the pound, and all other articles in proport on—that being there the common standard of appraisement, the measure of value. This state of things was naturally calculated to produce the most unhappy results. But there was another circumstance which must not be forgotten. It aggravated these evils unspeakably. It had a prime agency in the events which followed; of which agency you were directly the authors. This was the Mississippi stock, the fruit of the Yazoo compromise, upwards of four millions of which were issued by you, and made receivable in payment for lands in Alabama and Mississippi, and nowhere else. This stock, bearing no interest and owned chiefly in the East, was bought up at a large discount for the purpose of being invested in lands. It doubled the money of Alabama. It destroyed the salutary proportion between the circulating medium and the commodity in the market. It produced an artificial scarcity of land, and the high prices induced by scarcity. The holder of the stock thought himself warranted to bid beyond the specie value, to the extent of his discount, forgetting that the remaining instalments must, after the absorption of the stock, be paid in cash. Those who had no stock were compelled to go up to the stock price, or lose the lands on which they had fixed their affections.

The madness was general, it was epidemic. The most prudent and calculating men were carried away with the rest. Land was the philosopher's stone. To buy it was to be rich. Alas! the mines which it promised to the distempered fancy of the purchaser have proved to be like those of the fable on which repose the ends of the boy's rainbow. We have seen the consequence of this excessive excitement, this paroxysm of speculation —an enormous debt which never will be paid, which never can be paid. Yes, sir, I say it cannot be paid. The white population is about one hundred thousand. The debt is one hundred dollars each. Say that the sexes are equal, and the debt is two hundred dollars for every male. Say that the heads of families, the real buyers of the land, and the actual debtors, are twenty thousand, and the debt is five hundred each! And what is the situation of Alabama now, and what are her means of payment? Sir, it is a fearful question for her. Remember that you are told from high authority that the total currency of the Union has been suddenly reduced from one hundred and ten to forty-five millions of dollars, fifty-four per cent. more than

one-half. The seventy banks whose paper inundated Alabama have shut up shop, or are curtailing their discounts, and pressing for payment of those very loans which they were so eager to make, What is left floating of Mississippi stock is nearly at par. Cotton has fallen to ten cents, and every thing else in the same proportion. But the paper which buys cotton at ten cents will not pay the debt of Alabama. You have repudiated the seventy banks. You will not receive their notes; and the planter who owes you must exchange one hundred dollars in these vile rags for eighty-five dollars of such as will pass muster at the land office. You must have specie or the paper of specie paying banks, and these are at a premium of fifteen per cent. This fact you have in a memorial on your table, and it is indisputably true. To expect payment of ten millions from a people so distressed is to expect impossibilities, is to call for a miracle which will not be wrought in our day. The Senate cannot have forgotten the strong expression of an eloquent gentleman, (Mr. King, of New York,) whose long experience, rich and various attainments, and great abilities are so well known and appreciated, and whose opinions in regard to all questions touching the public lands, have always commanded respect and influence. Speaking on this subject at the last session, he said that the debt of Alabama grew out of "a contract which never ' would be enforced, which never could be en- ' forced, and which never ought to be enforced; ' and that, as an individual, if the case were his ' own, he could not, in equity and good conscience, ' enforce it." I rejoiced to hear him add, frankly and emphatically, that relief of some sort must be granted; and that, at the proper time, he would go all reasonable lengths to make that relief effective and ample. The time has arrived, and I call upon him to redeem his pledge, and I have no doubt that he will redeem it.

Once more, sir, to the bill. Without transfer, no reasonable man can expect a speedy extinguishment of the Alabama debt. To pay ten millions, according to the contract, is out of the question. Nor will your second section, which offers a premium for prompt payment, accomplish that object, because the money is not to be had. The committee contemplate a deduction of three-eighths from the balance due. The debt being $10,000,000, this discount would reduce it to $7,500,000, a sum certainly not within the power of the State to command by the 30th September next. It is clear to me that the principle on which the committee proceed, demands that the deduction should be made from the original price, the entire purchase money, since the current value of the whole land is lessened in that proportion by the change of system. If you legislate on that principle at all, as I think you ought, you should give it full scope; and I shall, at a proper time, move to amend the section accordingly. But, even suppose the amendment made, and a discount of thirty-seven and a half per cent. allowed on the original price, there would then remain to be paid upwards of six millions of dollars, a sum still far beyond the reach of the State within the limited period. You must resort, then, to other principles, or expect general forfeiture and distress. Transfer is one of those principles. It is best for you and for your debtor. Let us look at its operation. Let us assume that one-fourth only has been paid; and let us suppose, for the sake of illustration, what, however, is certainly not the fact, that all the lands are of equal value, and have cost the same price. Suppose half to be surrendered to the United States. This would reduce the debt one-half, viz : to five million dollars, and that without any deduction of price. Transfer the payment of one-fourth already made on the part surrendered, and apply it towards a discharge on the part retained, and the debt would then amount to $3,750,000, a prodigious difference, certainly; but even this sum could not be reasonably expected by the 30th September. This shows the necessity of calling in the last principle of the bill—the prolonged credit by instalments. And this is the more necessary for that meritorious class who have not the means of transfer, owning but one tract, and who will not be able to make prompt payment.

Sir, I repeat that the change of system imperatively calls upon you to grant relief. Many of the Representatives of the debtor States approved the change, and contributed by their votes to effect it. They thought the credit system injurious to the communities whose interests it was their peculiar province to guard. That system exhausted the new States, and kept them poor and in debt. Men laid out all their money in the first instalment, and staked their hopes and mortgaged their future earnings for the payment of the residue. The system quadrupled the power and inducement to buy, without increasing adequately the ability to pay. The quantity purchased was almost always measured by the amount of the first instalment. The new system deals not in hopes and fears ; it leaves no man in suspense ; it offers no check to the march of improvement. The purchaser feels erect and independent; he dreads no accident ; he dreams not of forfeiture. He has the patent at once in his pocket ; and the soil he tills is emphatically his own. He erects his cabin with a sturdy delight, and he sows in the confident hope of reaping the increase. Happy had it been for Alabama, in particular, had the change been made before August, 1817. How vastly different would have been her situation! She could have laid out no more money, for she laid out all; but she would have had her lands for the same money, and been free from debt; she would have had patents instead of certificates. The Representatives of the new States, therefore, gave their sanction to the change of system. But they warned you at the same time of the immediate and necessary effects of that change. The abolition of credit was not all. You reduced the price of your lands from two dollars to one dollar and twenty-five cents the acre. They pointed out to you how this would affect former purchasers, and reduce the value of their lands; and they contended that this reduction gave those purchasers a fair and equitable claim to relief to the full extent of that deduction. The justness of the claim was not denied.

Mr. President, a word or two more, and I have done. It was proposed at the last session to incorporate the principles of relief in the bill then before the Senate. Gentlemen said, "No, it is not time yet. Change the system, and we will give you relief—reasonable, adequate, full relief. Put a stop to the further increase of the debt, and you shall have your own terms ; but we will not embarrass the bill with any thing extraneous to the change, lest we endanger its passage. Call upon us next year, and your griefs shall be healed." Well, sir, we now make the call ; we set forth our case. The President recommends relief; your Minister of Finance advises ; your committee reports ; the nation expects it. Individuals petition ; nay, whole States supplicate your clemency, invoke your magnanimity, and demand the measure of a just and liberal equity at your hands. Their prosperity is also that of the Union, of which they are the fruit, and which they have gallantly defended with their blood. Nothing can give to foreign nations so grand and imposing an idea of your extent, your strength, and your resources, as this rapid expansion of the Republic, and the almost magical filling up of so many new States, won from the savage and the wilderness, for the use and habitation of freemen—your sons and brothers. Seven of these new States and two Territories await with solicitude the fate you are preparing for them. Your decree can make them flourish, or make them fade ; can cripple them for a long series of years, or strike off the bonds which fetter them ; cramping their young limbs, and retarding their free growth. It is for you now to determine whether they shall be stifled by the horrible incubus of this debt, which presses upon their vitals, paralyzing their energies, and arresting the wholesome play of their organs : whether they shall be crushed by this gigantic Colossus, which bestrides the vast and fertile region of the West, with one foot in the Gulf of Mexico, and the other I know not where—on the shores of the lakes, on the summit of the Stony Mountains, under whose "huge legs" your fellow citizens in that quarter "must peep about" to find the grave of their hopes and fortunes !

When Mr. W. had concluded—

Mr. MORRIL spoke briefly in support of the bill as it stood, and against recommitment.

On the question to agree to the above motion, Mr. SMITH asked to be excused from voting on this, and all other questions that may arise on said bill in the Senate, and stated as a reason why he should be excused, that, being a purchaser of public lands in Alabama, and not residing therein, he was interested in the provisions of the bill; and on the question to grant the leave asked, it was determined in the negative.

The question being taken on the motion to recommit the bill, it was negatived without a division.

Mr. THOMAS then offered a substitute for the first section of the bill, (not affecting any principle of the bill, but intended to render its meaning clearer,) which was ordered to be printed; and the Senate adjourned.

Tuesday, January 23.

On motion by Mr. WILLIAMS, of Tennessee, the Senate took up and considered the motion of the 12th of December, to discharge the Committee on Military Affairs from the consideration of the petition of Rebecca Hodgson, and agreed thereto; and it was referred to a select committee, to consider and report thereon; and Messrs. PINKNEY, WILLIAMS of Tennessee, and MACON, were appointed the committee.

Mr. HORSBY presented the petition of the President and Directors of the Union Bank of Georgetown, in behalf of the stockholders, praying an extension of the charter of said bank; and the petition was read, and referred to the Committee on the District of Columbia.

Mr. ROBERTS presented the memorial of the merchants, traders, manufacturers, mechanics, landlords, and others, of the city of Philadelphia, praying that a duty of ten per cent. may be imposed on all merchandise sold at auction, when disposed of in original packages, and fifteen per cent. when so sold in less quantities, with certain exceptions; and the memorial was read, and referred to the Committee on Commerce and Manufactures.

Mr. EATON presented the petition of George Harpole; and, also, the petition of Drury Bettis, severally praying to be compensated for a horse lost while in the military service of the United States; and the petitions were severally read, and referred to the Committee on Claims.

Mr. THOMAS, from the Committee on Public Lands, to whom was referred the bill, entitled "An act to extend the time for locating Virginia Military Land Warrants, and returning surveys thereon to the General Land Office," reported the same without amendment.

Mr. ROBERTS, from the Committee of Claims, to whom was referred the petition of Nathaniel McWarren, made a report, accompanied by a resolution, that the petitioner have leave to withdraw his petition. The report and resolution were read.

Mr. JOHNSON, of Louisiana, submitted the following motion for consideration:

Resolved, That the Committee on Public Lands be instructed to inquire into the expediency of granting to every person now residing on, and to those who may hereafter settle on the public lands on the bank of the Mississippi river, within the State of Louisiana, the right of pre-emption to a tract of such land at the minimum price fixed by law for the sale of the public lands of the United States, on condition that such persons shall make and keep up a substantial levee in front of the same.

The Senate proceeded to consider the report of the Committee on Public Lands on the petition of the chiefs of the Choctaw Indians, praying that Silas Dinsmore may be confirmed in his title to a tract of land; and, in concurrence therewith, resolved that the prayer of the petitioners ought not to be granted.

The Senate resumed the consideration of the report of the Committee on Public Lands on the petition of the trustees of Worthington College, in the State of Ohio; and it was further postponed until to-morrow.

The bill concerning Thomas Shields and others was read the second time.

The Senate took up and considered, as in Committee of the Whole, the bill for the relief of the purchasers of the public lands prior to the first day of July, 1820, together with the proposed amendment; and, on motion, by Mr. KING, of New York, the bill was laid on the table.

The Senate resumed, as in Committee of the Whole, the consideration of the bill to continue in force, for a further time, the act, entitled "An act for establishing trading houses with the Indian tribes;" and, on motion, by Mr. HOLMES, of Mississippi, it was laid on the table.

A message from the House of Representatives informed the Senate that the House have passed a bill, entitled "An act to reduce and fix the Military Peace Establishment of the United States;" and, a bill, entitled "An act to continue in force an act, entitled 'An act to provide for persons who were disabled by known wounds received in the Revolutionary war, and for other purposes;" in which bills they request the concurrence of the Senate.

***

Wednesday, January 24.

Mr. JOHNSON, of Louisiana, presented the petition of Louis Lauret, a native of Orthez, in France, an alien, residing in Louisiana, praying to be admitted to the privileges of a citizen of the United States at an earlier period than is authorized by existing laws; and the petition was read, and referred to the Committee on the Judiciary.

Mr. DANA presented the petition of Ezekiel P. Belden, of Connecticut, who was a captain of cavalry in the Revolutionary army, praying to be allowed half pay; and the petition was read, and referred to the Committee on Military Affairs.

Mr. SANFORD presented the petition of Nathaniel Allen, of New York, praying to be allowed, in the settlement of his accounts as paymaster of the New York militia, on the northern and western frontiers, in the year 1812, the disbursements made by him by virtue of orders from Governor Tompkins to said militia, for clothing; and the petition was read, and referred to the Committee on Military Affairs.

Mr. SANFORD, from the Committee on Finance, to whom was referred the memorial of Paul Lanusse and F. Bailly Blanchard, made a report, accompanied by a resolution, that the prayer of the memorial be not granted. The report and resolution were read.

The two bills from the House of Representatives yesterday brought up for concurrence were severally read the first and second time by unanimous consent; and the bill, entitled "An act to reduce and fix the Military Peace Establishment of the United States," was referred to the Committee on Military Affairs.

On motion, the bill, entitled "An act to continue in force an act entitled 'An act to provide for persons who were disabled by known wounds received in the Revolutionary war, and for other purposes;" was referred to the Committee on Pensions.

HISTORY OF CONGRESS.

Marquis de Maison Rouge.

The Senate proceeded to consider the motion of yesterday, instructing the Committee on Public Lands to inquire into the expediency of granting to actual settlers on the public lands on the bank of the Mississippi, in Louisiana, the right of pre-emption on certain conditions; and agreed thereto.

The Senate proceeded to consider the report of the Committee of Claims on the petition of Nathaniel McWarren; and, in concurrence therewith, resolved that the petitioner have leave to withdraw his petition.

The Senate resumed the consideration of the report of the Committee on Public Lands on the petition of the trustees of Worthington College, in Ohio; and, on motion by Mr. RUGGLES, it was laid on the table.

The Senate took up and considered, as in Committee of the Whole, the bill to continue in force the act, entitled "An act for establishing trading-houses with the Indian tribes; and the consideration thereof was postponed to Friday next.

The Senate took up and considered, as in Committee of the Whole, the bill for the better regulation of the trade with the Indian tribes; and, on motion by Mr. TRIMBLE, to amend the bill by striking out all after the enacting clause and inserting a new draught, the consideration of the bill was postponed to Friday next.

The Senate proceeded to consider, as in Committee of the Whole, the bill authorizing the payment of a sum of money to John Gooding and James Williams; and it was postponed until to-morrow.

The bill explanatory of the act of the last session for the relief of James L. Cathcart; the bill for the relief of John Coffee; and the bill for the relief of Nicholas Perkins, were severally considered in Committee of the Whole, and were ordered to a third reading.

The bill granting to the Governor of Louisiana, (for the time being) two tracts of land in the county of Point Coupee, (for the benefit of the people of that county, for the purpose of establishing thereon a public seminary of education,) was taken up.

The bill was explained and supported by Mr. JOHNSON, of Louisiana, and, having been amended, was postponed until to-morrow.

MARQUIS DE MAISON ROUGE.

The Senate next took up the bill reported by the Committee on the Public Lands, confirming the title of the Marquis de Maison Rouge to a tract of land on the Washita river, in the State of Louisiana, granted to him by the Spanish Government, on the 20th of June, 1797. [The title covers a tract of thirty square leagues, and comes before Congress for confirmation by petition from Daniel W. Coxe, who claims under the title of de Maison Rouge, and holds the greater part of the immense tract which that title embraces.]

The bill was accompanied by a long report from the committee, setting forth the facts of the case, and the principles on which the bill was predicated.

Mr. EATON spoke at some length against the bill, and the reasoning of the report.

The bill and report were supported by Mr. LOWRIE and Mr. VAN DYKE.

Mr. JOHNSON, of Louisiana, offered an amendment to the bill, expressly to prevent its interference with any of the Spanish grants, which have been recommended for confirmation by the board of commissioners of the western land district of Louisiana, and since confirmed by Congress—and he spoke to show the necessity of such a provision in the bill. Whereupon, the bill was, on motion of Mr. KING, of Alabama, postponed to Friday.

The Senate again took up the bill granting relief to the purchasers of public lands prior to the 1st of July, 1820.

A good deal of discussion again took place on this bill, principally on amendments offered to it; none of which, however, of a material character, were agreed to. The bill was, after some time, again laid on the table.

THURSDAY, January 25.

A message from the House of Representatives informed the Senate that the House have passed a bill, entitled "An act for the relief of the family of the late Oliver Hazard Perry, Esq.," a bill, entitled "An act for the relief of Jacob Hunsinger;" a bill, entitled an act extending the time for issuing and locating military land warrants to officers and soldiers of the Revolutionary army;" a bill, entitled "An act for the relief of Joseph McNiel;" a bill, entitled "An act for the relief of Alexander Milne;" a bill, entitled "An act for the relief of Lewis H. Guerlain;" a bill, entitled "An act for the relief of John Rodriguez;" a bill, entitled "An act to regulate the location of land warrants, and the issuing of patents in certain cases;" a bill, entitled "An act for the relief of Francis B. Languille;" a bill, entitled "An act for the relief of James Brady;" a bill, entitled "An act for the relief of Bartholomew Duverge;" and a bill, entitled "An act to alter the times of holding the District Court in the northern District of New York;" and also, a "Resolution to suspend the recruiting service for a limited time;" in which bills and resolution they request the concurrence of the Senate.

The said bills and resolution were severally read the first and second times by unanimous consent.

The bill, entitled "An act for the relief of Jacob Hunsinger;" the bill, entitled "An act extending the time for issuing and locating military land warrants to officers and soldiers of the Revolutionary army;" the bill, entitled "An act to regulate the location of land warrants, and the issuing of patents in certain cases;" and the bill, entitled "An act for the relief of James Brady," were severally referred to the Committee on Public Lands.

The bill, entitled "An act for the relief of the family of the late Oliver Hazard Perry, Esq.," was referred to the Committee on Naval Affairs.

The bill, entitled "An act for the relief of Joseph McNiel;" the bill, entitled "An act for the relief of Alexander Milne;" the bill, entitled "An act for the relief of Lewis H. Guerlain;" the bill, entitled "An act for the relief of John Rodriguez;" the bill, entitled "An act for the relief of Francis B. Languille;" and the bill, entitled "An act for the relief of Bartholomew Duverge;" were severally referred to the Committee of Claims.

The bill, entitled "An act to alter the times of holding the District Court in the northern District of New York," was referred to the Committee on the Judiciary.

The "Resolution to suspend the recruiting service for a limited time," was referred to the Committee on Military Affairs.

Mr. TRIMBLE presented the memorial of Bartholomew Shaumburg, of the city of New Orleans, praying to be repaid the sum of $3,000, intrusted to him by the paymaster of the 8th regiment of infantry at New Orleans in June, 1817, to be delivered to James P. Harrison, for the payment of a detachment of the said regiment at Fort Selden, and which was by him delivered to Major Riddle, then acting as quartermaster at said fort, to be conveyed for that purpose, and by him lost; and the memorial was read, and referred to the Committee of Claims.

Mr. CHANDLER presented the petition of Job Shurborn, of the State of Maine, praying a pension in consideration of Revolutionary services; and the petition was read, and referred to the Committee on Pensions.

Mr. OTIS presented the petition of Joshua Aubin, of Boston, the petition of William. Whitehead, of New York; and the petition of James Graham, also of New York, praying the restitution of certain moneys paid by them respectively for duties wrongfully exacted on goods imported by them into Castine in the year 1814; and the petitions were severally read, and referred to the Committee on Finance.

Mr. HORSEY presented the memorial of the Mayor, members of the Board of Aldermen, and of the Common Council, of the City of Washington, soliciting Congress to direct astronomical observations to be made in the said city, with a view to the establishment of a principal meridian for the United States; and he also presented the memorial of the President and Directors of the Farmers and Mechanics' Bank of Georgetown, praying an extension of the charter of said bank; and the memorials were read, and severally referred to the Committee on the District of Columbia.

Mr. JOHNSON, of Louisiana, gave notice that, to-morrow, he should ask leave to bring in a bill to authorize the clerk of the district court of the United States for the district of Louisiana, to appoint a deputy to aid him in discharging the duties of his office.

Mr. EATON gave notice that, to-morrow, he should ask leave to bring in a bill supplementary of an act passed at the last session of Congress, for the relief of John Harding and others.

Mr. KING, of Alabama, obtained leave to bring in a bill to establish the district of Blakeley; and the bill was read, and passed to a second reading.

Mr. VAN DYKE, from the same committee, to whom was referred the petition of Jacob Barker, made a report, accompanied by a resolution, that the prayer of the petitioner ought not to be granted. The report and resolution were read.

Mr. ROBERTS, from the same committee, to whom was referred the bill from the House of Representatives, entitled "An act for the relief of Daniel McDuff," reported it without amendment.

The bill explanatory of the act for the relief of James Leander Cathcart, passed May the 15th, in the year 1820, was read the third time, and passed.

The bill for the relief of John Coffee was read the third time, and passed.

The bill for the relief of Nicholas Perkins was read the third time, and passed.

The Senate proceeded to consider the report of the Committee on Finance, on the memorial of Paul Lanusse and F. Bailly Blanchard; and it was postponed to Monday next.

The Senate resumed, as in Committee of the Whole, the consideration of the bill to authorize the appointment of certain Indian agents; and, on motion by Mr. HOLMES, of Mississippi, it was laid on the table.

The bill for the relief of Nicholas Jarrott, passed through a Committee of the Whole, was amended, and ordered to a third reading.

The Senate took up the bill authorizing the President of the United States to cause to be surveyed, marked, and designated, a portion of the northern and western boundaries between Indiana, Illinois, and the Territory of Michigan, agreeably to the act authorizing Indiana to become a State.

A good deal of discussion took place on the merits of this bill, its constitutionality in its present shape, the circumstances which were conceived to render it necessary or inexpedient, and on its details; in which discussion, Messrs. SMITH, NOBLE, THOMAS, LOWRIE, HOLMES, of Maine, TRIMBLE, MILLS, EDWARDS, and TALBOT, principally engaged. The debate ended by postponing the bill, with the view of attempting some amendment to obviate the objections urged against it.

The bill for the relief of Nathan Ford, passed through a Committee of the Whole, and was ordered to a third reading.

NATIONAL VACCINE INSTITUTION.

The Senate next took up the bill from the other House to incorporate the Managers of the National Vaccine Institution.

Mr. LLOYD moved so to amend the bill as to reserve to Congress the power at any time to repeal the act, and to give it duration until Congress should so repeal it—instead of incorporating it unconditionally and positively for the term of thirty years, as the bill stood. Mr. L. also adverted to the anticipated utility of the institution, and to some of the reasons in its support.

After some debate between Mr. ROBERTS, (who was opposed to the bill altogether, and not satisfied with the proposed amendment) and Mr. LLOYD, the amendment was adopted.

On the motion also of Mr. LLOYD, the bill was

further so amended, as to require from the President of the Institution on oath an annual report of their property, funds, receipts, expenditures, &c., to the Secretary of the Treasury, and by him to be laid before Congress.

On motion of Mr. LLOYD, several other amendments were made to the details of the bill—amongst them an obligation on the managers to provide for the vaccination of indigent persons, free of any charge. Mr. L. having gone through the bill,

Mr. ROBERTS entered into a very general review of the provisions of the bill, to show their inadequacy to the objects contemplated by the friends of the measure, as well as their objectionable character in some respects; and having some doubts of the constitutionality of the bill in its present shape, which question, however, he did not discuss.

Mr. LLOYD rose to reply to Mr. R., when, on motion of Mr. TALBOT, the bill was laid on the table.

GRANT OF LAND TO LOUISIANA.

The Senate resumed the consideration of the bill for granting to the State of Louisiana a piece of public land in the county of Point Coupee, whereon to establish a school for the use of the people of that county. The bill was so amended yesterday as to grant to the State the pre-emption right only.

Mr. LLOYD moved to lay the bill on the table, that it might be taken up in connexion with the proposition to grant to the old States donations of the public lands for the benefit of education, corresponding to those which have been conferred on the new States, deeming the two subjects similar in their character.

Mr. BROWN spoke to show that the present bill had no connexion in principle with the important proposition referred to; that this was a small isolated piece of land necessary to the people of the county of Point Coupee for the purpose contemplated; that the State would be willing to pay for it the small sum which the minimum price would amount to, but that it would not be worth the cost of sending a United States surveyor one hundred miles to survey it, make out a plat, and set it up to sale, &c. He thought Congress might safely make a donation of it to the State, without danger of establishing any litigated principle; but that there could be no objection to the bill now, he thought, as it proposed simply to give the State a pre-emption right to the land, &c.

Mr. LLOYD replied to Mr. BROWN, and argued in support of the objections which he had at first suggested against acting on this bill now, which, if it were passed in its present shape, would be used as an argument against the proposition he had referred to.

The question being taken, the bill was ordered to lie on the table—ayes 22.

FRIDAY, January 26.

The PRESIDENT communicated a report of the Secretary of War, to whom was referred, by resolution of the Senate of the 29th December last, the memorial of the Mayor, Aldermen, and Commonalty of the city of New York; and the report was read, and together with the memorial referred to the Committee on Military Affairs.

The PRESIDENT also communicated a letter from the Secretary of the Treasury, transmitting, in obedience to a resolution of the 16th instant, statements showing the state of the several banks in the District of Columbia; and the letter and statements were read.

Mr. WILLIAMS, of Tennessee, presented the memorial of Kon-na-noo-lus-kee or Chalange, a native of the Cherokee nation of Indians, praying that the *life* estate to a reservation of land in the State of Alabama, secured to him by the treaty with said nation in 1817, may be extended to a *fee-simple* estate, or that he may be permitted to purchase the same at the minimum price, with a reasonable time to accomplish the payment; and the memorial was read, and referred to the Committee on Public Lands.

Mr. BARBOUR presented the memorial of Richard S. Hackley, late Consul of the United States at Cadiz, praying to be remunerated for certain disbursements made by him in the discharge of his official duties; and the memorial was read, and referred to the Committee of Claims.

Mr. LANMAN presented the petition of Abel Sholes, of Connecticut, praying an increase of his pension; and the petition was read, and referred to the Committee on Pensions.

Mr. SMITH presented the petition of John Lowden, of South Carolina, praying to be refunded the amount of an export bond paid at the custom house at Charleston, for reasons stated in the petition; which was read, and referred to the Committee on Finance.

Mr. THOMAS, from the Committee on Public Lands, to whom was referred the memorial of the General Assembly of the State of Indiana, praying permission to tax the lands sold by the United States; made a report, accompanied by a resolution, that the prayer of the memorialists ought not to be granted. The report and petition were read.

Mr. JOHNSON, of Louisiana, obtained leave to bring in a bill to authorize the clerk of the District Court of the United States for the District of Louisiana to appoint a deputy to aid him in the discharge of the duties of his office; and the bill was twice read by unanimous consent; and referred to the Committee on the Judiciary.

On motion by Mr. THOMAS, it was agreed to reconsider the vote of yesterday on ordering the bill entitled "An act for the relief of Nicholas Jarrott," to be read a third time; and it was recommitted to the Committee on Public Lands.

The Senate proceeded to consider the report of the Committee of Claims on the petition of Jacob Barker; and it was postponed to Monday next.

The bill for the relief of Matthew McNair, and the bill to establish the district of Blakeley, were severally read the second time.

The bill for the relief of Nathan Ford was read the third time, and passed.

The Senate proceeded to consider, as in Committee of the Whole, the bill for the relief of

Samuel Tucker, late a captain in the Navy of the United States; and it was postponed to, and made the order of the day for, Monday next.

The Senate proceeded to consider, as in Committee of the Whole, the bill further to establish the compensation of the officers employed in the collection of duties on imports and tonnage, and for other purposes; and it was postponed to, and made the order of the day for, Monday next.

The Senate proceeded to consider, as in Committee of the Whole, the bill for the relief of General Robert Swartwout; and it was postponed to Monday next.

The Senate proceeded to consider, as in Committee of the Whole, the bill for the relief of John Hoffman; and on motion by Mr. JOHNSON, of Louisiana, it was laid on the table.

The Senate proceeded to consider, as in Committee of the Whole, the bill concerning Thomas Shields and others; and it was postponed to, and made the order of the day for, Monday next.

The Senate resumed, as in Committee of the Whole, the consideration of the bill authorizing the payment of a sum of money to John Gooding and James Williams; and it was postponed to Monday next.

The Senate proceeded to consider, as in Committee of the Whole, the bill entitled "An act for the relief of Daniel McDuff;" and it was postponed to Friday next.

Mr. HORSEY, from the Committee on the District of Columbia, to whom was referred the resolution from the House of Representatives, authorizing the President of the United States to cause astronomical observations to be made to ascertain the longitude of the Capitol, in the city of Washington, from some known meridian in Europe, reported the same without amendment.

Mr. DICKERSON, from the committee to which was referred the resolution proposing an amendment of the Constitution of the United States, as it respects the election of President and Vice President of the United States, and Representatives to Congress, reported the same with an amendment, (to make it imperative on the Electoral Colleges to fill vacancies, instead of merely authorizing them to do so;) which report was read.

The bill for the relief of the legal representatives of Patience Gordon passed through a Committee of the Whole, and was ordered to a third reading.

Mr. VAN DYKE, from the Committee on Public Lands, to which was referred the petition of Thos. Sloo and John Caldwell, the register and receiver of public moneys at Shawneetown, praying an increase of compensation, made an unfavorable report thereon; which was read.

The bill to authorize the publication of private acts of Congress and Indian treaties in some one newspaper in the city of Washington, was taken up in the Committee of the Whole, where it was explained by Mr. EATON; and the bill was ordered to be engrossed for a third reading.

The bill to authorize the sale of certain lots in the public reservation No. 10, in Washington city, being taken up, it was, on motion of Mr. HORSEY, ordered to lie on the table, with the view of allowing to an individual who conceives his private rights affected by the bill, time to make his representation to the Senate on the subject.

Mr. EATON, having obtained leave, introduced a bill supplementary to the act of last session, for the relief of John Harding, Giles Harding, John Shute, and John Nichols; which was read.

VIRGINIA MILITARY LANDS.

The bill from the other House for extending the time for locating Virginia military land warrants (for two years longer) was taken up in Committee of the Whole.

This subject gave rise, as usual when under consideration heretofore, to a good deal of discussion.

Mr. THOMAS briefly explained to the Senate the considerations in favor of extending the indulgence proposed by the bill.

Mr. KING, of New York, thought it was time that something explicit was done, as to the time when this subject should be closed, and some report made of the lands located, and those which remained for the disposal of the United States, &c. He gave a brief narrative of the circumstances which produced the reservation by Virginia, of the country between the Sciota and Little Miami, for satisfying her military land warrants. The body of land in Ohio, reserved by Virginia for this purpose, was of great extent, and the surplus belonged as much to the United States as any other land in that State; and it was time, he thought, that something was done to show what quantity was left—how this matter stood—and to begin to think of some termination to this long standing subject. Instead of passing this bill with an extension of two or three years; he would give but one year, with an understanding, that it would not be extended longer, unless some explanation should be given to justify it.

Mr. BARBOUR entered into a history of the subject, to show the difficulties which had impeded a final adjustment of this whole subject. He adverted to the cession made by Virginia to the Union, of all her immense northwestern possessions, presumed then to extend to the Pacific ocean, out of which territory she had reserved a tract for satisfying the pledge she had given to her Revolutionary officers and soldiers. This pledge was made as well to those of the State line as of the Continental line, but in the contract of cession and reservation, by some unknown means, the word *State* was omitted; and the Congress of the United States had taken advantage of this omission, in the face of the most conclusive circumstances, even its recognition of the principle, in one of the articles, to reject all applications to satisfy warrants of the State line. Mr. B. animadverted on this conduct, which he would not characterize by the epithet which would be applied to it in private life. Leaving this part of the subject, Mr. B. argued to show that most of the persons originally possessing these unlocated titles, being scattered far and wide, were either ignorant, or their descendants or heirs were ignorant, of their title; many of these were orphans, who would sooner or later learn their right, and claim it; that it would be cruel and unjust to foreclose them, &c., and he defended the bill as it stood.

Mr. TRIMBLE made some remarks explanatory of the circumstances of this reservation, and the course heretofore pursued by Congress, as well as by Virginia; the difficulties which had grown out of the conduct of Virginia herself, from turning out the surveyor appointed by the officers, &c., and to show the reasons why all the locations had not been made; one of which was that the Indian title to a great part of the tract between the Sciota and Miami had not until recently (a part of it as late as 1818) been extinguished, and which of course could not previously be located. He was decidedly of opinion that it would be great injustice in Congress to refuse ample time for the location of those warrants.

Mr. JOHNSON, of Kentucky, thought this a question simply whether Congress would enforce the principles of the statute of limitations against the just claims of the poor war-worn soldier, or his friendless orphans. Against such a course he protested and reasoned. These claims had lost no part of their validity by delay; much less had they been forfeited; and he did not believe it could, he hoped it could not, ever become a serious question in Congress whether time should be allowed for them to be brought in.

Mr. THOMAS referred to the several acts of Congress on the subject, and spoke as to the legislative history of this subject, illustrative of the propriety and justice of extending the full time proposed.

Mr. RUGGLES, of Ohio, moved to strike out *two* years, and insert *one* year as the time of extension. He argued that those lands which were not taken up by the warrants, remained unsettled; and that the further extension of indulgence operated to prevent the populating of the country in question; that there ought to be some limit established to this indulgence, and he thought one year more would enable Congress to judge when this limit could be fixed, and a termination be put to this drawback on the settlement of the country.

The motion was opposed by Messrs. BARBOUR, TALBOT, and TRIMBLE; and it was negatived without a division.

The bill was then reported to the Senate, and ordered to a third reading.

MONDAY, January 29.

The PRESIDENT communicated a letter from the Secretary of War, transmitting statements exhibiting the contracts which were made by the quartermaster general, commissary general of subsistence, the ordnance department, the commissary general of purchases, and the engineer department, in the year 1820; and the letter and statements were read.

Mr. HORSEY presented the petition of the president and directors of the Bank of Columbia, and the petition of the directors of the Patriotic Bank

of Washington, severally praying an extension of the charters of the said banks respectively; and the petitions were read, and severally referred to the Committee on the District of Columbia.

Mr. SANFORD presented the petition of Harriet Shackerley and others, surviving children of Peter Shackerley, who was slain on board the frigate Chesapeake, in the rencounter with the British frigate Leopard, in 1807, praying to be allowed a stipend equal to that proffered by the British Government, to the families of those killed on that occasion; and the petition was read, and referred to the Committee on Naval Affairs.

Mr. KING, of New York, presented the memorial of the Chamber of Commerce of the city of New York, praying that such an increase of the naval force of the United States on the southwestern coast of America may be made, as will afford sufficient protection to the commerce of the United States in that quarter; and the memorial was read, and referred to the Committee on Foreign Relations.

Mr. HUNTER presented the petition of Stephen F. Northam and others, of Rhode Island, merchants, representing that they took out license in the year 1815, for distilling spirits from molasses for one year; that a few days after their distillery was inundated, and so much injured by the violent gale of wind and flood of tide, which at that time happened, as to suspend its operation nearly half the year, and praying that so much of the money paid for said license may be restored to them, as will be equal to the time the distillery remained inoperative; and the petition was read, and referred to the Committee on Commerce and Manufactures.

Mr. JOHNSON, of Kentucky, presented the petition of Watson Brown, of Louisiana, praying a grant of land in consideration of military services; and the petition was read, and referred to the Committee on Public Lands.

Mr. ROBERTS, from the Committee of Claims, to whom was referred the petition of George Jackson, made a report, accompanied by a resolution, that the prayer of the petitioner ought not to be granted. The report and resolution were read.

Mr. ROBERTS, from the same committee, to whom were referred the petition of J. L. B. Macarty, made a rep~~~t, accompanied by a bill for the relief of J. L. B. Macarty; and the report and bill were read, and the bill passed to a second reading.

Mr. ROBERTS, from the same committee, to whom was referred the petition of James Villere, made a report, accompanied by a resolution, that the prayer of the petitioner ought not to be granted. The report and resolution were read.

Mr. ROBERTS, from the same committee, to whom the subject was referred by resolution of the Senate of the 19th instant, made a report on the claim of Matthew B. Cathey, accompanied by a resolution, that the petitioner's claim ought not to be allowed. The report and resolution were read.

Mr. ROBERTS, from the same committee, to whom was referred the memorial of E. B. Clemson, made a report, accompanied by a resolution, that the prayer of the petitioner ought not to be granted. The report and resolution were read.

Mr. VAN DYKE, from the last mentioned committee, to whom was referred the petition of Hanson Catlett, made a report, accompanied by a resolution, that the prayer of the petitioner ought not to be granted. The report and resolution were read.

Mr. SANFORD, from the Committee on Finance, to whom was referred the petition of William Smith, jr., made a report, accompanied by a resolution, that the prayer of the petitioner be refused. The report and resolution were read.

The Senate proceeded to consider the report of the Committee on Public Lands, on the memorial of the General Assembly of the State of Indiana, praying permission to tax certain lands; and on motion by Mr. THOMAS, it was laid on the table.

The Senate proceeded to consider the report of the Committee on Public Lands, on the memorial of the register and receiver of the Land Office at Shawneetown; and, in concurrence therewith, resolved that the prayer of the memorialists ought not to be granted.

The Senate resumed the consideration of the report of the Committee on Claims, on the petition of Jacob Barker; and, on motion by Mr. KING of New York, it was laid on the table.

The bill supplementary to an act passed on the 5th of April, 1820, entitled "An act for the relief of John Harding, Giles Harding, John Shute, and John Nichols," was read the second time, and referred to the Committee of Claims.

The bill for the relief of the representatives of Patience Gordon, widow, deceased, was read the third time, and passed.

The bill supplementary to the act passed on the 11th of May, 1820, entitled "An act to provide for the publication of the laws of the United States and for other purposes," was read the third time, and passed.

The bill from the House of Representatives, entitled "An act to extend the time for locating Virginia military land warrants, and returning surveys thereon to the General Land Office," was read the third time, and passed.

The Senate spent some time in considering the bill for the relief of Commodore Samuel Tucker; which bill was advocated at some length by Mr. WALKER of Georgia. The bill' was then postponed to Wednesday.

The Senate resumed, as in Committee of the Whole, the consideration of the bill further to establish the compensation of the officers employed in the collection of imports and tonnage, and for other purposes; and having amended the same, the Senate adjourned.

TUESDAY, January 30.

Mr. NOBLE presented the petition signed by a number of individuals, concerned, directly or indirectly, as purchasers of public lands prior to the law "making further provision for the sale of public lands," stating, that said law operates in-

juriously upon them, and praying that they may be permitted to apply the payments already made to such portion of their entries as such payments will cover at two dollars per acre, and that the residue may revert to the United States; and the petition was read, and laid on the table.

Mr. KING, of New York, laid on the table sundry resolutions adopted at an assemblage of the citizens of the city of New York, consisting of the most respectable merchants, landlords, and others, declaring the pernicious and injurious effects upon commerce from sales at auction, under the existing system; which were read, and referred to the Committee on Commerce and Manufactures.

Mr. SANFORD, from the Committee on Finance, to whom was referred the bill concerning the collection of public moneys, reported the same with amendments; which were read.

Mr. THOMAS, from the Committee on Public Lands, to whom was referred the bill, entitled "An act for the relief of Daniel Seward," reported it without amendment.

Mr. THOMAS, from the same committee, to whom was referred the bill, entitled "An act to regulate the location of land warrants, and the issuing of patents in certain cases;" reported it with amendments, which were read.

The bill for the relief of J. L. B. Macarty was read the second time.

Mr. WILLIAMS, of Tennessee, from the Committee on Military Affairs, to whom was referred the resolution from the House of Representatives, to suspend the recruiting service for a limited time; reported it without amendment.

The Senate proceeded to consider the report of the Committee of Claims, on the petition of George Jackson; and it was postponed to Monday next.

A message from the House of Representatives informed the Senate that the House of Representatives have passed a bill, entitled "An act for the relief of John Webster;" a bill, entitled "An act to establish the district of Pearl river;" and a bill, entitled "An act further to regulate the entry of merchandise imported into the United States from any adjacent territory;" in which bills they request the concurrence of the Senate.

The three bills last brought up for concurrence were read, and severally passed to a second reading.

Mr. VAN DYKE, from the Committee of Claims, made an unfavorable report on the petition of Thomas Hardeman, which was read.

The reports of the Committee of Claims unfavorable to the petitions of Matthew B. Cathey, of E. B. Clemson, of Hanson Catlett, and that of the Committee of Finance against the petition of William Smith, jun., were severally considered and agreed to.

The Senate took up the bill further to establish the compensation of the officers employed in the collection of the customs, and spent some time in maturing its details.

In the course of its consideration, Mr. HOLMES, of Maine, submitted the views which governed him in proposing this measure, and referred to various facts touching probable abuses, in the illegal conversion of public funds to private emolument, to show the expediency of the bill, as well in regard to the prevention of these abuses, as to the object of retrenchment and economy. Before the bill was gone through—

On motion of Mr. LLOYD, who wished a little further time to examine its important provisions, the bill was postponed to Thursday.

The bill concerning Thomas Shields and others, passed through a Committee of the Whole, in which it was explained by Mr. PLEASANTS, and was ordered to be engrossed for a third reading.

RELIEF TO LAND PURCHASERS.

The Senate resumed, as in Committee of the Whole, the consideration of the bill for the relief of the purchasers of public lands. The question under consideration was an amendment offered by Mr. THOMAS, in substance, to extend the provisions of the bill to those who hold lands under the original purchasers from the public.

Mr. KING, of New York, submitted at large his views of the policy of this bill, and the reasons which claimed his support of it—stating his ideas of the mode and measure of relief proper to be granted to the different classes of purchasers, &c.

The amendment proposed by Mr. THOMAS was agreed to without a division.

Various other amendments were adopted on successive motions of Mr. THOMAS, making its provisions more extensively applicable to the various classes of purchasers; as well as in other features of its detail.

Mr. WALKER, of Alabama, moved an amendment going to extend the proposed discount to the whole amount of purchase money, instead of merely on the sum remaining due: in support of which he referred to the reasons submitted by him some days ago in favor of such a provision.

A debate of some length took place on this proposition; in which it was opposed by Messrs. VAN DYKE, LOWRIE, and KING, of New York, and was defended by Mr. WALKER, of Alabama.

The proposed amendment was ultimately rejected without a division.

The blank in which to insert the discount contemplated to be allowed to these purchasers on their payments, Mr. THOMAS moved to fill with "thirty-seven and a half" per cent.

This motion produced likewise some debate, touching the proper deduction to be allowed, &c., Messrs. LOWRIE, and KING, of New York, opposing this amount.

The amendment was agreed to—19 to 11.

Mr. VAN DYKE moved an amendment, going to limit the extension of the credit to those who have purchased no more than two contiguous half quarter sections of land.

On this motion considerable discussion arose, in which Messrs. VAN DYKE, KING of Alabama, EDWARDS, KING of New York, and WILLIAMS of Mississippi, took part.

Before the question was taken on the motion the usual hour of adjournment had arrived; and, about 4 o'clock, the Senate adjourned.

WEDNESDAY, January 31.

The PRESIDENT communicated a letter from the Postmaster General, transmitting a statement of all contracts made by the Post Office Department during the last year, and a statement of contracts made in a former year; and the letter and statements were read.

The following Message was received from the PRESIDENT OF THE UNITED STATES:

To the Senate of the United States :

I transmit to Congress a report from the Secretary of the Treasury, submitting copies of the instructions given to the commissioners appointed under the act of the 15th of May, 1820, authorizing the location of a road from Wheeling, in the State of Virginia, to a point on the left bank of the Mississippi river, between St. Louis and the mouth of the Illinois river; and copies of the report made by the said commissioners to the Treasury Department, of the progress they have made in the execution of the duties prescribed by the said act, together with maps of the country through which the location is to be made.

                  JAMES MONROE.

WASHINGTON, *January* 31, 1821.

The Message and report were read, and referred to the Committee on Roads and Canals.

Mr. ROBERTS, from the Committee of Claims, to whom were referred the bill, entitled "An act for the relief of Joseph McNiel ;" the bill, entitled "An act for the relief of Alexander Milne," the bill entitled "An act for the relief of Lewis H. Guerlain ;" the bill, entitled "An act for the relief of John Rodriguez ;" the bill, entitled "An act for the relief of Francis B. Languille ;" and the bill, entitled "An act for the relief of Bartholomew Duverge ;" reported them severally without amendment.

Mr. THOMAS, from the Committee on Public Lands, to whom was recommitted the bill, entitled "An act for the relief of Nicholas Jarrott," reported it with amendments; which were read.

Mr. HORSEY presented the petition of the President and Directors of the Central Bank of Georgetown and Washington, in behalf of the stockholders, praying that the charter of said bank may be continued, until they can effectually close the concerns thereof; and the petition was read, and referred to the Committee on the District of Columbia.

The bill, entitled "An act for the relief of John Webster ;" the bill, entitled "An act to establish the district of Pearl river ;" and the bill, entitled "An act further to regulate the entry of merchandise imported into the United States from any adjacent territory ;" were severally read the second time, and the bill, entitled "An act for the relief of John Webster," was referred to the Committee of Claims.

The bill, entitled "An act to establish the district of Pearl river ;" was referred to the Committee on Commerce and Manufactures.

The bill, entitled "An act further to regulate the entry of merchandise imported into the United States from any adjacent territory," was referred to the Committee on Finance.

The Senate proceeded to consider the report of

the Committee of Claims, on the petition of James Villeré; and it was postponed to Friday next.

The Senate proceeded to consider the report of the Committee on Public Lands, on the petition of Thomas Hardeman; and it was postponed until to-morrow.

Mr. SMITH, from the Committee on the Judiciary, obtained leave to be discharged from the further consideration of the petition of John Bioren and Fielding Lucas, booksellers; and also (after some discussion on the practicability of maturing any thing on so intricate a subject during the present session) from the further consideration of the inquiry referred to that committee, into the expediency of diminishing, equalizing, and establishing, the fees of district attorneys, clerks, and marshals, and other officers.

The engrossed bill concerning Thomas Shields and others was read the third time, passed, and sent to the other House for concurrence.

COMPENSATION OF MEMBERS.

Mr. DANA, from the select committee appointed to inquire into the propriety of reducing the compensation of the members of Congress, and also the salaries of the principal and other officers of the Executive Departments, at the Seat of Government, stated, that the committee had made all the necessary inquiries, and collected all requisite information from the different departments comprehended in the scope of their inquiry, from the year 1790 to the year 1820; that the committee had duly deliberated on the whole matter referred to them, and that not being able to agree on any specific report, embracing any system or measure of reduction, partial or general, it only remained to state this fact to the Senate, which he was instructed to do, and ask to be discharged from the further consideration of the subject, that the Senate might be enabled thus early to take such further order on it as should to it appear expedient.

A good deal of debate arose on the question of thus discharging the committee from the subject.

It was opposed by Messrs. ROBERTS and SMITH, chiefly on the ground that, as a specific inquiry had been referred, a specific report, either for or against the object, ought to be made; that this mode of disposing of such an inquiry was an innovation on legislative custom; that, as the Chairman had, with great industry, collected a mass of information on the subject, it was proper to submit it to the Senate, with an opinion, no matter how concise, of the committee; that, as the committee had come to a decision on the subject-matter referred to them, that decision ought to be reported, &c. Mr. MACON thought the documents, at any rate, ought to be laid before the Senate, that it might have the same light on the subject as the committee had.

The motion to discharge the committee was supported by Messrs. DANA, STOKES, OTIS, and JOHNSON, of Kentucky, for the reasons, generally, that, as the committee could agree upon no plan of reduction, they could come to no practical conclusion, and therefore could make no specific report or recommendation; that the committee had tried the question on one salary and amount of compensation after another, but a majority could not unite on any one point of reduction; that the information possessed by the committee would be (and was after the discussion commenced) laid before the Senate; that the mode now proposed, of discharging a committee which could do nothing, was the most proper, under the circumstances, the most Parliamentary and logical; that there was an incongruity in the committee's reporting it expedient to do nothing; that it would be competent still for any gentleman, who was dissatisfied with the result, to make any specific motion for reduction in any branch of the Government, &c.

The question being taken on discharging the committee from the further consideration of the subject, it was decided in the negative, by yeas and nays, as follows:

YEAS—Messrs. Dana, Edwards, Johnson of Kentucky, Johnson of Louisiana, King of Alabama, Mills, Noble, Otis, Parrott, Stokes, Talbot, Taylor, Walker of Georgia, and Williams of Tennessee.

NAYS—Messrs. Barbour, Brown, Chandler, Dickerson, Eaton, Elliott, Gaillard, Holmes of Maine, Holmes of Mississippi, Horsey, Hunter, King of New York, Knight, Lanman, Lloyd, Lowrie, Macon, Morril, Palmer, Pinkney, Pleasants, Roberts, Ruggles, Sanford, Smith, Thomas, Tichenor, Trimble, Van Dyke, Walker of Alabama, and Williams of Mississippi—31.

Mr. DANA delivered in the following report:

The committee appointed to inquire into the propriety of reducing the allowances authorized by law for the two Houses of Congress, and for the Executive Departments, report: That they have made inquiry according to the resolution for their appointment, and do not consider it advisable at the present time to propose any reduction of legal allowances in the cases to them referred. The following resolution is accordingly submitted:

Resolved, That it is not expedient to reduce the compensation allowed by law for the respective Houses of Congress, and for the principal and other officers in the Executive Departments.

The report was read.

THE RELIEF BILL.

The Senate, resumed, as in Committee of the Whole, the consideration of the bill for the relief of the purchasers of public lands—Mr. VAN DYKE's motion to amend the bill by limiting the credit to those whose purchases have not exceeded two contiguous half-quarter sections, being still under consideration.

The question was taken on this amendment without debate, and it was agreed to—16, to 12.

The Senate spent much much time in considering other amendments, as well of the original provisions as of additional provisions proposed to be inserted, with the view of rendering its enactments more clear, of guarding them against abuse, &c.; in the proposition and discussion of which Messrs. VAN DYKE, WALKER, of Georgia, KING, WALKER, of Alabama, EATON, KING, of New York, and TALBOT, took part. Of these propositions, the following, offered by Mr. EATON, as a new section, was the only one which affected or embraced any important principle:

And be it further enacted, That any purchaser of public lands who, previous to the —— day of —— last, had actually made a settlement on the same, shall be allowed a remission of all interest; and twenty-five per cent. discount on the amount yet unpaid, and shall pay for the residue in instalments of one, two, —— years without interest: *Provided,* That the settlement of any one quarter section or legal subdivision of a fractional section, shall be deemed and held a settlement of all contiguous and adjoining quarter sections or legal subdivisions of fractional section, so by him, in his own right, held, and possessed, not exceeding one section.

This amendment was opposed for various reasons by Messrs. KING, of New York, TALBOT, VAN DYKE, and EDWARDS, as inexpedient, and incompatible with the original views which produced the bill, which it might endanger; and was advocated by Messrs. EATON, and JOHNSON, of Kentucky, on the general ground that the actual settlers and cultivators of public lands ought to be relieved, as well as the very large and very small purchasers, now only in the contemplation of the bill. Mr. TALBOT was in favor of confining the amendment to a half section; and Mr. JOHNSON, of Kentucky, was in favor of one section. Mr. LOWRIE thought the amendment unnecessary, and was willing to extend the class of small purchasers to half a section of land. Mr. EATON modified his amendment so as to extend it to one section of land. Before the question was taken on the amendment, it was with the bill laid on the table and ordered to be printed.

The Senate then according to the order of the day took up the Bankrupt bill; but before any progress was made in it, the Senate adjourned.

———

THURSDAY, February 1.

Mr. OTIS presented the petition of Samuel Parker, of Massachusetts, praying that the patent heretofore granted to him for certain improvements in machinery, the limitation of which is about to expire, may be renewed; and the petition was read, and referred to the Committee on the Judiciary.

Mr. WILLIAMS, of Tennessee, from the Committee on Military Affairs, to whom was referred the petition of Nathaniel Allen, reported a bill for passing to the credit of Nathaniel Allen certain moneys by him disbursed in the public service; and the bill was read, and passed to a second reading.

Mr. WALKER, of Georgia, gave notice, that, to-morrow, he should ask leave to bring in a bill concerning the process of execution issuing from the sixth circuit court of the United States for the district of Georgia.

Mr. NOBLE, from the Committee on Pensions, to whom was referred the bill, entitled "An act to continue in force an act, entitled 'An act to provide for persons who were disabled by known wounds received in the Revolutionary war, and for other purposes," reported it without amendment.

Mr. HORSEY, from the Committee on the District of Columbia, to whom the subject was referred, reported a bill to extend the charters of certain banks in the District of Columbia; and the bill was read, and passed to a second reading.

Mr. JOHNSON, of Louisiana, submitted the following motion for consideration:

Resolved, That the Committee on Commerce and Manufactures be instructed to inquire into the expediency of providing by law for the erection of a marine hospital at, or near to, the city of New Orleans, for the admission of sick and disabled seamen of the United States, and for the accommodation of sick and disabled boatmen who may descend the Mississippi river.

A message from the House of Representatives informed the Senate that the House have passed a bill, entitled "An act for the relief of Rosalie P. Deslonde;" a bill, entitled "An act for the relief of Pierre Dennis De La Ronde; a bill, entitled "An act confirming the location of the seat of government of the State of Illinois, and for other purposes;" and a bill, entitled "An act authorizing the President of the United States to remove the land office in the district of Lawrence county, in the Territory of Arkansas;" in which bills they request the concurrence of the Senate.

The four bills last brought up for concurrence were read, and severally passed to a second reading.

The bill entitled "An act for the relief of Rosalie P. Deslonde" was read the second time by unanimous consent, and referred to the Committee of Claims.

Mr. EATON, from the Committee on Pensions, to whom was referred the memorial of Andrew Peters and others, made a report, accompanied by a resolution that the prayer be not granted. The report and resolution were read.

The Senate proceeded to consider the report of the Committee on Public Lands on the petition of Thomas Hardeman; and, on motion by Mr. EATON, it was laid on the table.

The Senate resumed the consideration of the bill to establish an uniform system of bankruptcy throughout the United States; and it was postponed to, and made the order of the day for, Monday next.

The Senate resumed, as in Committee of the Whole, the consideration of the bill to amend the act, entitled "An act to incorporate the subscribers to the Bank of the United States;" and it was postponed to, and made the order of the day for, Monday next.

The Senate resumed, as in Committee of the Whole, the consideration of the bill for the relief of Samuel Tucker, late a Captain in the Navy of the United States; and it was postponed to, and made the order of the day for, to-morrow.

Mr. SMITH, from the Committee on the Judiciary, made an unfavorable report on the petition of Louis Lauret, of New Orleans, praying to be admitted to the rights of citizenship earlier than is prescribed by law.

Mr. SMITH, from the same committee, to which was referred the resolution to inquire whether any, and if any what, amendments are necessary and proper to be made to the act, entitled "An act relative to the election of President and Vice President of the United States, and declaring the officer

257   **HISTORY OF CONGRESS.**   258

FEBRUARY, 1821.   *Bank of the United States—Drawback—Relief Bill.*   SENATE.

who shall act as President in case of a vacancy in the offices both of President and Vice President," passed March 1, 1792, made a report that it is inexpedient at this time to legislate further on the subject.

Mr. SMITH from the same committee, to which was also referred the resolution to inquire whether any, and if any what, provisions are necessary or proper to be made by law to meet contingencies which may arise from unlawful, disputed, or doubtful votes, under that part of the twelfth article of amendments to the Constitution of the United States which relates to counting the votes of the Electors for President and Vice President of the United States, made a report that it is inexpedient at this time to legislate on the subject.

The resolution offered yesterday by Mr. CHANDLER was taken up and agreed to.

BANK OF THE UNITED STATES.

The PRESIDENT laid before the Senate a letter from the Governor of the State of Ohio, transmitting a report of the joint committee of the two Houses of the Legislature of that State on the proceedings of the Bank of the United States against the officers of the State in the United States circuit court.

Mr. RUGGLES moved that the letter and report be printed for the use of the Senate.

This motion was opposed by Messrs. WILLIAMS, of Tennessee, and EATON, for the reasons that it was a document out of which no legislation could be expected to grow; that the Senate had no more to do with the report, or the case to which it related, than any other legislative proceedings of the States; that it came not from any branch of the General Government, but was in the nature merely of a private paper, which, however curious members might be to peruse, the Senate in its public capacity had nothing to do with it, &c. Mr. EATON moved, however, that it be referred to the Committee of Finance, to see if it was of a nature to make the printing of it necessary, it being so long that it had not been read in the Senate.

The motion to print was supported by Messrs. RUGGLES, TALBOT, and BARBOUR, on the ground generally that the report was transmitted directly from the government of the State of Ohio to the Senate, and that respect for that State required that the document should be treated in the usual way and be printed; that it was a document of an important character, relating to a subject of great national interest—one concerning which severe animadversions on the State of Ohio had been made throughout the Union; that it was a most able and ingenious argument of a great Constitutional question, deeply involving State rights, as well as the interest of the General Government.

The letter and report were finally referred to the Committee on Finance, and ordered to be printed.

ALLOWANCE OF DRAWBACKS.

The report of the Committee of Finance unfavorable to the petitions of Paul Lanusse and of F. Bailly Blanchard, of New Orleans, (praying to be allowed certain drawbacks,) was taken up.

Mr. JOHNSON, of Louisiana, moved to reverse the report, and to instruct the Committee on Finance to bring in a bill conformable to the prayer of the petitioners.

Mr. BROWN supported the motion by recapitulating the circumstances of the case, and offering several arguments to show that it was justly and reasonably entitled to the relief prayed. Mr. JOHNSON, of Louisiana, also spoke in support of his motion, and in favor of relief for the petitioners.

Messrs. DANA, HOLMES of Maine, and LANMAN, defended the report, and maintained the expediency of enforcing the rules prescribed by the laws.

The motion to reverse the report was negatived—18 votes to 15.

Mr. JOHNSON, of Louisiana, then moved to separate the two cases, by instructing the Committee of Finance to report a bill for the relief of F. Bailly Blanchard only.

After considerable debate, in which the motion was supported by Messrs. BROWN, JOHNSON of Louisiana, and MILLS, and was opposed by Messrs. LANMAN and HOLMES, this amendment was also negatived—19 to 16—and the report of the committee was concurred in.

RELIEF BILL.

The Senate went into a Committee of the Whole on the bill for the relief of the purchasers of public land—the following additional section, offered yesterday by Mr. EATON, being still under consideration:

"*And be it further enacted,* That any purchaser of public lands, who, previous to the —— day of ——— last, had actually made a settlement on the same, shall be allowed a remission of all interest, and twenty-five per centum discount on the amount yet unpaid; and shall pay for the residue in instalments of one, two, ——— years, without interest: *Provided,* That the settlement of any one quarter section, or legal subdivision of a fractional section, shall be deemed and held a settlement of all contiguous and adjoining quarter sections, or legal subdivision of fractional sections, so by him in his own right held and possessed, not exceeding one section."

This amendment was again debated at some length—Messrs. KING of New York, NOBLE, TALBOT, and VAN DYKE, opposing it for various reasons as impolitic, and at variance with the main object in view—the diminution of the debt;—and Messrs. EATON, RUGGLES, and SMITH, advocating it, as essential to render the bill just and impartial in its provisions. Mr. SMITH and Mr. KING of New York, entered more largely into this question, as well as into the policy of the bill generally, and of the proper mode and extent of relief.

Mr. KING, of Alabama, spoke in favor of the principle of the amendment, to which the only objection, in his opinion, was the difficulty of the discrimination.

The amendment was ultimately negatived without a division.

On motion of Mr. WALKER, of Alabama, a proviso was inserted in the bill substantially to make the new instalments of credit commence at the expiration of ——— years respectively from the days of purchase, in the cases of those whose final payments are not yet due.

The amendment adopted yesterday to confine the proposed extension of credit to those whose purchases have "not exceeded two contiguous half quarter sections," was, on motion of Mr. RUGGLES, reconsidered; and then

Mr. TALBOT moved to modify the amendment, so as to read "not exceeding *four* contiguous half quarter sections," and supported his motion by sundry arguments.

The modification was agreed to, and, in this shape, the amendment was again agreed to.

Some other amendments were offered, but, before any one of consequence was acted on, it had become late, and the Senate adjourned.

FRIDAY, February 2.

The PRESIDENT communicated a letter from the Postmaster General, transmitting a list of unproductive post roads; and the letter and list were read.

Mr. SANFORD presented the petition of William Vaughan, sailingmaster in the Navy, praying to be allowed prize-money for the destruction of two vessels of the enemy in the late war; and the petition was read, and referred to the Committee on Naval Affairs.

Mr. THOMAS, from the Committee on Public Lands, to whom were referred the bill, entitled "An act for the relief of Jacob Hunsinger, and the bill, entitled 'An act extending the time for issuing and locating military land warrants to officers and soldiers of the Revolutionary army," reported them severally without amendment.

Mr. LOWRIE, from the same committee, to whom was referred the bill, entitled "An act for the relief of James Brady," reported it with an amendment; which was read.

Mr. SANFORD, from the Committee on Finance, to whom was referred the memorial of Archibald Gracie & Sons, and others, reported a bill to extend the time for unlading vessels arriving from foreign ports in certain cases; and the bill was read, and passed to a second reading.

Mr. HORSEY, from the Committee on the District of Columbia, to whom was referred the memorial of the Bank of Potomac, reported a bill to extend the charter of the Bank of Potomac; which was read, and passed to a second reading.

Mr. DICKERSON, from the Committee on Commerce and Manufactures, to whom was referred the bill, entitled "An act to establish the district of Pearl river," reported the same without amendment.

Mr. WILLIAMS, of Mississippi, gave notice that, on Monday next, he should ask leave to bring in a bill to establish a new land office in the State of Mississippi, and for the better regulation of certain land districts in the States of Alabama and Mississippi.

The bill for passing to the credit of Nathaniel Allen certain moneys by him disbursed in the public service, and the bills from the House of Representatives, entitled "An act for the relief of Pierre Dennis De La Ronde;" "An act authorizing the President of the United States to remove the land office in the district of Lawrence county, in the Territory of Arkansas;" and "An act confirming the location of the seat of government of the State of Illinois, and for other purposes," were severally read the second time.

The bill entitled "An act for the relief of Pierre Dennis De La Ronde" was referred to the Committee of Claims.

The bill entitled "An act authorizing the President of the United States to remove the land office in the district of Lawrence county, in the Territory of Arkansas," and the bill, entitled "An act confirming the location of the seat of government of the State of Illinois, and for other purposes," were severally referred to the Committee on Public Lands.

The Senate proceeded to consider the report of the Committee on the Judiciary on the memorial of Louis Lauret; and, in concurrence therewith, resolved that the prayer of the memorialist be not granted, and that he have leave to withdraw his papers.

The Senate proceeded to consider the report of the Committee on the Judiciary on the resolution of the 13th of December, directing them to inquire if any, and what, provisions are necessary to be made by law to meet contingencies which may arise from unlawful votes under that part of the twelfth article of the amendment to the Constitution which relates to counting the votes of the Electors for President and Vice President, and concurred therein.

The Senate proceeded to consider the report of the Committee on the Judiciary on the resolution of the 13th of December, directing them to inquire if any, and what, amendments are necessary to be made to the act "relative to the election of President and Vice President of the United States, and declaring the officer who shall act as President in case of vacancies in the offices both of President and Vice President," and concurred therein.

The Senate proceeded to consider the motion of yesterday, instructing the Committee on Commerce and Manufactures to inquire into the expediency of establishing a marine hospital at New Orleans; and agreed thereto.

The Senate proceeded to consider the report of the Committee on Pensions on the memorial of Andrew Peters, and others, officers of the Revolutionary army; and, in concurrence therewith, resolved that the prayer be not granted.

The Senate resumed the consideration of the report of the Committee of Claims on the petition of James Villere; and it was postponed to Monday next.

The Senate took up and considered, as in Committee of the Whole, the bill authorizing the sale of certain grounds belonging to the United States in the City of Washington, which was amended, and the PRESIDENT reported it to the House accordingly; and, the amendments having been concurred in, the bill was ordered to be engrossed, and read a third time.

Mr. SMITH, from the Committee on the Judiciary, to whom was referred the bill to authorize the clerk of the district court of the United States for the district of Louisiana, to appoint a deputy to aid him in the discharge of the duties of his office; and the bill from the House of Representatives, entitled "An act to alter the times of holding the district court in the northern district of New York," reported them severally without amendment.

On motion, by Mr. HOLMES, of Mississippi, it was agreed to reconsider the vote of yesterday on the report of the Committee on Finance on the memorial of Paul Lanusse and F. Bailly Blanchard; and it was laid on the table.

On motion, by Mr. VAN DYKE, the Secretary of the Treasury was directed to report to the Senate what proceedings have been had in relation to the claim of John H. Piatt, authorized to be liquidated and settled by an act of the 8th day of May, 1820; and that he report how, and upon what principles, reasons, and construction of the law, the said claimant attempts to support his claim.

Mr. WILLIAMS, of Tennessee, from the Committee on Military Affairs, to which was referred the bill from the other House, to fix the Peace Establishment of the Army, reported a substitute for the whole bill.

Mr. WILLIAMS also laid on the table an estimate of the comparative expenses of the army, under the organization of the last mentioned bill, as it passed the House of Representatives, and that of the proposed substitute, which was read.

RELIEF TO LAND PURCHASERS.

The Senate resumed, in Committee of the Whole, the consideration of the bill to relieve the purchasers of public lands.

Mr. KING, of New York, after some remarks on the details of the bill, and explanatory of his ideas of the proper principles on which the proposed relief ought to be granted, and stating the great object in view—the prospective abolition of the land debt, and the complete payment for all that portion of the land which shall be retained by the purchasers—suggested a substitute for the first section of the bill (which he had heretofore informally submitted to the Senate.)

Mr. OTIS stated the perplexity under which he labored, owing to the various principles that had been inserted in the bill, and the different doctrines which had been urged in the course of its protracted consideration; he therefore moved that the bill be recommitted to a select committee, that its details might be so digested as to promise the early and general concurrence of the Senate in the plan to be adopted.

Mr. LOWRIE and Mr. KING, of Alabama, thought certain points in the bill, yet undecided, ought to have the sense of the Senate expressed thereon before it should be recommitted; and Mr. WALKER, of Alabama, considered that all the principles of the bill ought to be previously settled by the Senate, and proceeded at some length to controvert in part the opinions advanced by Mr. KING, of New York. Messrs. RUGGLES, NOBLE, JOHNSON, of Kentucky, and EDWARDS, opposed any

recommitment, as promising nothing valuable in smoothing the way of the bill; and the certain effect would be delay. Messrs. KING, of New York, and VAN DYKE advocated the recommitment, from a belief that it would accelerate its consummation, and produce a greater degree of unanimity in its passage, &c.

The motion to recommit the bill was negatived: ayes 13, noes 20.

Mr. THOMAS moved that the number of annual instalments by which the debt remaining due shall be discharged, be *eight.*

Mr. EATON was opposed to so long a credit, and argued to show the propriety of a more limited number of instalments. Messrs. RUGGLES, JOHNSON, of Kentucky, NOBLE, and EDWARDS, advocated the motion to fill the blank with *eight* years, as an extent of credit, under the circumstances of the times, and the condition of forfeiture annexed, no more than proper.

The motion to fill the blank with *eight,* was agreed to without a division.

On motion of Mr. TALBOT, a new section was inserted in the bill, (similar to a provision offered previously by Mr. VAN DYKE,) principally further to secure the terms of the act from evasion or imposition.

Mr. SMITH moved to add the following section to the bill:

And be it further enacted, That all sums due, or which may hereafter become due, to the United States, on account of any purchase of public lands heretofore made, may be discharged by —— equal annual instalments, which shall be paid on the first day of December in each successive year, together with so much interest as shall have accrued on each instalment from the time such instalment became due, according to the terms of the original sale. And upon the failure of any such purchaser to pay any of the aforesaid instalments on the day that such instalment shall become due, the said land on which such instalment shall be due shall be forfeited to the United States: *Provided,* That any person or persons taking the benefit of this provision shall be excluded from all other benefits offered by this act.

Mr. S. deemed this the only legitimate or salutary provision which could be made by Congress for the alleviation of the public land debtors, and argued at some length in support of his proposition.

The question was taken on this amendment, without further debate, and was negatived— ayes 10.

The blank in the bill, left to fix the period at which payment of any sum due, or becoming due, must be made, to entitle the purchaser to the discount of thirty-seven and a half per cent. on such payment, was, after some debate as to the time most expedient, filled with the *first day of April, eighteen hundred and twenty-two.*

The bill was then reported to the Senate, as amended, and all the amendments agreed to without objection, except that one which fixes the discount to be allowed for the prompt payment at *thirty-seven and a half* per cent.

This amendment Mr. LOWRIE moved to substitute with the deduction of *twenty-five* per cent.

This motion was negatived, by yeas and nays, as follows:

YEAS—Messrs. Chandler, Dickerson, Horsey, Hunter, King of New York, Knight, Lanman, Lowrie, Macon, Mills, Morril, Otis, Palmer, Parrott, Pleasants, Roberts, Sanford, Smith, Tichenor, and Van Dyke—20.

NAYS—Messrs. Brown, Eaton, Edwards, Elliott, Gaillard, Holmes of Maine, Holmes of Mississippi, Johnson of Kentucky, King of Alabama, Lloyd, Noble, Ruggles, Stokes, Talbot, Taylor, Thomas, Trimble, Walker of Alabama, Walker of Georgia, and Williams of Mississippi—21.

The bill was then, on motion of Mr. MACON, recommitted to the Land Committee, with the view of revising merely its phraseology, and to report any corrections of form which may be rendered necessary therein by the various modifications which it has undergone in the Senate.

The Senate adjourned to Monday.

MONDAY, February 5.

The PRESIDENT communicated a letter from the Secretary of the Navy, transmitting a statement of the Second Comptroller of the Treasury, showing the amount of the appropriations for the Navy Department for the year 1820; and the balances remaining unexpended in the Treasury on the 31st of December last; and the letter and statement were read.

Mr. SANFORD presented the petition of James Duffie, executor of Captain William Sloo, deceased, praying payment of three certificates issued to the deceased by the Quartermaster General, for services rendered in the Revolutionary war; and the petition was read, and referred to the Committee on Claims.

Mr. DANA presented the petition of William Sizer, one of the surviving officers of the Revolutionary army, praying that the benefit of the late act of Congress, granting pensions to the indigent surviving officers and soldiers of that army, may be extended to him; and the petition was read, and referred to the Committee on Pensions.

Mr. SANFORD, from the Committee on Finance, made an unfavorable report on the petition of John Lowden; which was read.

Mr. PLEASANTS, from the Committee on Naval Affairs, to which was referred the bill from the other House, for the relief of the family of the late Commodore Oliver Hazard Perry, reported the same without amendment.

Mr. THOMAS, from the Committee on the Public Lands, made an unfavorable report on the petition of Thomas H. Boyles; which was read.

Mr. T., from the same committee, reported a bill for the relief of the legal representatives of Clarissa Scott; which was read, and passed to the second reading.

The bill authorizing the sale of certain public lots in the City of Washington, was read the third time, passed, and sent to the other House for concurrence.

The bill to extend the charters of certain banks in the District of Columbia; the bill to extend the charter of the Bank of Potomac; and the bill to extend the time for unlading vessels arriving from foreign ports, in certain cases, were severally read the second time.

The Senate resumed the consideration of the report of the Committee of Claims, on the petition of George Jackson; and it was postponed until to-morrow.

Mr. DICKERSON, from the Committee on Commerce and Manufactures, to whom was referred the bill authorizing the repair of a sea wall at the Isles of Shoals, and for other purposes, reported it with an amendment; which was read.

Mr. THOMAS, from the Committee on Public Lands, to whom was recommitted the bill for the relief of the purchasers of public lands, prior to the first day of July, 1820, reported it with amendments; which were read.

Mr. WILLIAMS, of Tennessee, from the Committee on Military Affairs, to which was referred the petition of the corporation of the city of New York on the subject, reported a bill authorizing the President of the United States to retrocede to the city of New York the piece of ground therein called the Battery; which bill was read.

The Senate resumed the consideration of the bill further to establish the compensation of the officers of the customs, and for other purposes, and spent some time in maturing its details; after which, it was further postponed until to-morrow.

COMPENSATION TO MEMBERS.

The Senate took up the report of the select committee, appointed on the subject, adverse to the propriety of at this time making any reduction in the compensation of the members of Congress, or officers of the Executive Departments.

Mr. ROBERTS moved to amend the report by striking out the resolution of the committee, and inserting the following matter as a substitute:

"*Resolved*, That hereafter the compensation of the members of the Senate and House of Representatives, and the delegates from territories, ought to be —— dollars for every day they shall respectively attend on their duties, and —— dollars for every twenty miles they may necessarily travel, respectively, in going to and returning from any session of Congress; and that the compensation of the President *pro tempore* of the Senate and the Speaker of the House of Representatives ought to be —— dollars for each and every day they may perform the duties of their respective offices.

"*Resolved*, That, from and after the thirty-first day of March next, the salaries of the Secretaries of the Departments of State, of the Treasury, of War, and of the Navy; the Attorney General of the United States; the Register; the first and second Comptrollers; the first, second, third, fourth, and fifth Auditors of the Treasury; the Commissioner of the General Land Office; the Board of Commissioners for the Navy; the Postmaster General; the Assistant Postmasters General; and the salaries of all clerks employed in the several Executive departments of the Government, including those in the General Post Office, which amount annually to a sum exceeding eleven hundred and fifty dollars, ought to be reduced —— per centum on the said annual amount."

The amendment was ordered to be printed, and the further consideration of the report was then, after some debate, postponed to Monday the 19th instant.—Ayes 23, noes 18.

JAMES VILLERE.

The Senate took up the report of the Committee of Claims, unfavorable to the petition of James Villere, who prays remuneration for the destruction of his sugar crop, and other damages sustained, by the operations of the American army in defence of New Orleans in 1814 and 1815.

Mr. JOHNSON, of Louisiana, moved to reverse the report, and to direct the Committee of Claims to bring in a bill for the relief of the petitioner. Mr. J. spoke at some length in opposition to the report, and in favor of his motion.

Mr. ROBERTS supported, in a speech of considerable length, the correctness and justice of the report.

Mr. BROWN opposed the report, and argued some time to show that the relief claimed by the petitioner was entirely reasonable and just, and ought to be granted.

The question being taken on the proposed amendment, it was decided in the negative, without a division; and the report of the Committee of Claims was concurred in by the Senate.

COMMODORE TUCKER.

The Senate then again took up the bill for the relief of Commodore Samuel Tucker, authorizing him to be placed on the list of invalid pensioners, at $50 a month; on which bill a long and wide debate took place.

Mr. SMITH opposed this bill on principle; admitting the merits of Captain T., but arguing that, if really an invalid and unable to maintain himself, there was already provision made by law to embrace his case and afford relief; that, if not an invalid, this bill ought not to pass, the system of pensioning for public services merely being bad in itself, and still worse in its tendency. Mr. S. also went into an examination of the circumstances alleged in the case of the applicant, to show that they did not justify the passage of the bill; that the applicant had been already, long since, uncommonly well provided for by the public, to support which he referred to resolves of Congress, &c.; that, affording this gratuitous relief to the applicant, would be treading on the rights of thousands of other citizens equally meritorious, &c.

Mr. HOLMES, of Maine, replied to Mr. S., and submitted a number of arguments, in addition to those which he used when the bill was before under consideration, in support of it; referring to the long and singularly successful services, and the highly gallant conduct of Commodore T. during the Revolutionary war, and his present reduced circumstances and great age, to establish the justice of granting him a maintenance out of the navy pension fund; that fund being expressly pledged to afford relief in such cases as the present.

Mr. SMITH replied, and contended that this very pension fund was intended to provide for disabled seamen, and not for those who were not disabled; that Commodore T. did not come within the description, and therefore was not entitled to be dis-tinguished from all the other honorable and brave men who have grown old since they signalized themselves in the Revolution. He argued also, (in reply to a remark of Mr. WALKER, of Georgia, the other day,) that the statute of limitations was a just law, as well as a wise and prudent one.

Mr. CHANDLER made a remark or two in reply to Mr. SMITH.

Mr. KING, of New York, placed this case on a footing with a few others of the Revolutionary class, particularly that of General Stark, for whom a bill passed at a recent session. He adverted to some of the prominent features of Commodore T.'s Revolutionary services, and contended that it was not just or equitable that a veteran of the Revolution such as he, in want now of the means of support, should ask relief in vain. There was no danger, he argued, from such a course; for, however natural the prejudices in this country which existed against the pension system, they arose from the abuses practised in Great Britain, where pensions were lavished by the Crown upon favorites of every kind, often without regard to public services or private virtues. There was no danger of such an abuse in this country. The justice of military pensions had been settled in this country; it was a power delegated to the Government by the Constitution; and there was no risk of its abuse in a Government constituted as ours, as the people, holding the corrective, would always apply a remedy if the practice was ever carried beyond its just and proper limits.

Mr. SMITH, after subjoining a few remarks, moved to postpone the bill indefinitely.

Mr. MACON observed, that nothing would be more curious than a history of the pensions of this country; the practice was constantly getting wider and wider; but it had been well said, the history of the country was lost. He referred to the circumstances of the first pensions and those granted since, to show the regular extension of the principle beyond the limits at first deemed right. A rule was always found for a new case, and the case gave rise to a new rule, so that the principle was constantly stretching. He was opposed to this course, and argued briefly against it.

Mr. DANA spoke to show that there was no principle opposed to the case of Commodore T., and that the relief ought to be granted, as it might be done without danger of exceeding the just limits to which Congress were authorized to go by the spirit and principles of our Government.

Mr. ROBERTS opposed this pension on principle, for the same reasons that he opposed the pension of General Stark. He observed, that if pensions were granted for military services, without disability, it was not far removed, and would not long be distinguished from civil pensions, which would probably follow; and argued to show the evil tendency of authorizing pensions in cases like the present, which could not justly be distinguished from a civil pension.

Mr. PLEASANTS stated the ground on which the Naval Committee reported the bill, which was intended to give Commodore T. the amount of half-pay for a certain period, to which he was strictly

267   HISTORY OF CONGRESS.   268

SENATE.   *Proceedings.*   FEBRUARY, 1821.

entitled; to show which Mr. P. adduced the facts of the case.

Mr. OTIS maintained that the case of Commodore T. entitled him, strictly, to avail himself of the benefits of the navy pension fund; that the bill called for no new grant of money out of the Treasury; that it violated no principle; and that it did not become a magnanimous legislature to withhold this boon from him, to which he was so signally entitled in justice and gratitude.

Messrs. SMITH and MACON added a few remarks, and Mr. WALKER, of Georgia, also a few, in addition to what he had said the other day in support of the claim, declining to go again at large into the case, as it had been so ably supported.

The motion to postpone the bill indefinitely was negatived—yeas 13, nays 24.

After an unsuccessful attempt of Mr. ROBERTS to reduce the proposed allowance to $20 a month, the bill was ordered to be engrossed for a third reading.

TUESDAY, February 6.

The PRESIDENT communicated a letter from the Secretary of War, transmitting a statement by the Second Comptroller, of the appropriations for the service of the year 1820, showing the amount expended, and the balance remaining unexpended, on the 31st of December last; and the letter and statement were read.

Mr. THOMAS communicated a resolution of the General Assembly of the State of Illinois; which was read, as follows:

"*Resolved by the Senate and House of Representatives of the General Assembly of the State of Illinois,* That our Senators and Representatives in Congress be requested to endeavor to obtain the passage of a law, so amending the act of the last session of Congress, entitled 'An act to authorize the appointment of commissioners to lay out the road therein mentioned,' as that the said road may be surveyed and laid out through the seats of government of the States of Ohio, Indiana, and Illinois; *Provided,* The commissioners to have been appointed by that act have not yet performed the duties enjoined upon them by the same; but that, if in case they *have* made the survey contemplated by said act, they endeavor to obtain the passage of one authorizing a new survey, and lay out the said road through the seats of government of the said States.

"JOHN McLEAN,
"*Speaker of the House of Reps.*
"GEO. CALDWELL,
"*Speaker of the Senate, pro tem.*"

Mr. BARBOUR submitted the following motion for consideration:

Resolved, That a committee be appointed, to join such committee as may be appointed by the House of Representatives, to ascertain and report a mode of examining the votes for President and Vice President of the United States, and of notifying the persons elected of their election.

On motion of Mr. THOMAS, the Committee on the Public Lands was discharged from the consideration of the reports of the land commission-

ers at St. Helena Courthouse in Louisiana, and at Jackson Courthouse in Mississippi.

Mr. JOHNSON, of Louisiana, said he had not opposed the motion, knowing the mass of business the committee had before them; but he sincerely regretted that the committee had not time to act on the subject. He entered into an examination of the nature of the reports, and the character of the claims embraced in them; and urged the importance of acting on the subject at the present session. With that aim, Mr. J. moved that the reports be referred to a select committee.

The reference was opposed by Messrs. EATON, LOWRIE, and ROBERTS, principally on the ground, that it was now too late in the session to act definitively on a subject of such difficulty and importance.

Mr. JOHNSON of Louisiana, Mr. BROWN, and Mr. EDWARDS, replied, and pressed the reference.

The motion was adopted, and the following committee appointed: Mr. JOHNSON of Louisiana, Mr. WALKER of Alabama, Mr. WILLIAMS of Mississippi, Mr. EATON, and Mr. LOWRIE.

Mr. THOMAS, from the Committee on Public Lands, to whom was referred the bill, entitled "An act authorizing the President of the United States to remove the land office in the district of Lawrence county, in the Territory of Arkansas;" and the bill, entitled "An act confirming the location of the seat of government of the State of Illinois, and for other purposes;" reported them severally without amendment.

Mr. RUGGLES submitted the following motion for consideration:

Resolved, That the Committee of Claims be instructed to inquire into the expediency of making provision by law for the allowance and payment of the claim of David Cooper, for property taken for military services during the late war, by order of Captain O. H. Holden.

Mr. HOLMES, of Mississippi, submitted the following motion for consideration:

Resolved, That the Committee on Public Lands be instructed to inquire into the expediency of complying with the request made by the chiefs of the Choctaw tribe of Indians, to grant tracts of land to certain individuals named in the documents which accompanied the Message of the President of the United States, transmitting to the Senate the treaty concluded at Doakes, on the 18th day of October, in the year 1820.

The bill for the relief of Samuel Tucker, late a Captain in the Navy of the United States, was read a third time, and passed.

The bill for the relief of the legal representatives of Manuel and Isaac Monsanto, deceased; and the bill to authorize the reconveyance of a tract of land to the city of New York; were severally read the second time.

The Senate proceeded to consider the report of the Committee on Finance on the petition of John Lowden; and it was postponed until to-morrow.

The Senate proceeded to consider the report of the Committee on Public Lands on the petition of Thomas H. Boyles; and, in concurrence therewith, the Committee on Public Land were discharged from the further consideration of the subject, and the petitioner had leave to withdraw his petition and papers.

The Senate resumed the consideration of the report of the Committee of Claims on the petition of George Jackson ; and it was postponed until to-morrow.

A message from the House of Representatives informed the Senate that the House have passed a bill, entitled "An act making appropriations for the public buildings," in which they request the concurrence of the Senate.

THE BANKRUPT BILL.

The Senate resumed the consideration of the bill to establish a uniform system of bankruptcy throughout the United States.

Mr. VAN DYKE spoke in exposition of the principles of the bill.

Mr. ROBERTS having moved to strike out the first section of the bill, rose, and said, that he ought to offer an apology for entering into this debate, if it could be supposed at all proper, in the situation he now stood. He was about to discuss a subject with which he was little familiar; one to which, until very lately, his inquiries had not extended. When the subject had been up in former sessions, he had waited for light from those who were movers of it. Having at all times entertained impressions of great doubt as to the propriety of adopting a bankrupt system, he had been led hesitatingly to countenance a proposition from his honorable friend from Delaware, (Mr. VAN DYKE,) at the last session, calculated to operate on all insolvents above a very small amount. The friends of such a bill as this, then joined in opposition, and it fell : but why my friend should have abandoned a scheme so liberal and congenial with the principles of equal justice, for such an one as that now before us, I have yet to learn. If I had doubts about that, I have none about this. I think it utterly repugnant to the first principles of our Government, as indeed I do every system of bankruptcy that will impair the obligation of contracts, in any shape or form. I give the gentleman full credit, when he assures us he thinks the interests of the country call for this measure. Knowing his correct feelings and great moral worth, I cannot ascribe the change of his opinions since the former session to a less solemn conviction. With equal sincerity, I believe the most mischievous consequences must flow from this project. The first object of which is, we are told, to protect the right of creditors ; and, second, to shield the innocent though unfortunate debtor. If, with a proper exercise of legitimate legislative authority, these ends could be consistently obtained, it would be desirable to proceed. It becomes my duty to show they cannot be obtained either by the bill or by adopting such a bankrupt system as gentlemen seek by any the most ingenious exercise of the legislative power.

Gentlemen may talk as much as they please about the protecting of the rights of creditors; that has never been, nor never can be, the object of a system that intends to discharge the debtor from the obligation of his contract without fulfilling it, or without the free concurrence of all his creditors. Originally, bankrupt laws went merely to seize and apply the property of insolvents, summarily to the payment of their creditors, before it should be wasted entirely. Bankrupt laws were introduced into England in innovation of the common law, and, for the first two hundred years of their operation, no idea ever occurred of applying them to release the debtor from his contracts. The insolvent laws, also an innovation upon the common law, of a century later introduction, were, from the beginning, allowed to work this effect. The first English bankrupt act that provided for entire discharges was not enacted till about 1708. From that time the original purpose of the law has been lost in effect, and almost abandoned in purpose. I owe these to the obliging suggestions of my honorable friend from Rhode Island, (Mr. HUNTER,) whose views on these subjects, in the case of Sturgis *vs.* Crowninshield, I have read with equal profit and approbation. But I contend this bill promises little to the creditor, while the debtor is secure of his discharge from his contracts, whether a dividend be made or not. We had a right to anticipate strong appeals to the generous sympathies of our nature in favor of the innocent and unfortunate trader. That there are cases highly compassionable, I am bound to suppose ; as bad as men may be generally, there are still some consolatory exceptions. If the gentleman will present me a scheme to relieve such, that shall not carry in its train as certainly as cause follows effect, an increase of, and impunity to, knavery, perjury, and the most atrocious iniquities, I will co-operate with him with alacrity. The scheme he proposes will discharge ten villains for one honest man. I say it will do it, because it has done it. On this point we have history, not theory ; and demonstration, not hypothesis. The system offered us is substantially the English system, and of the results of that system, after a trial of three centuries, I shall have occasion presently to speak. It becomes men legislating for a great community not to be betrayed too easily, even by the syren song of compassion, into the most baneful expedients. We are told, on this measure, there is no Constitutional difficulty. Certainly we have substantial powers to establish uniform laws on the subject of bankruptcy. But, whether or not it is necessary to use that power, we are left soberly to judge. It is equally in our discretion in what form we shall apply that power. It certainly is not indispensable in the establishment of uniform laws of bankruptcy, that the debtor should be discharged from future liability for his contracts. This, I have shown, was not the purpose of such laws originally, nor is it necessarily to be concluded that this was an object with the framers of the Constitution. Though wise and experienced men, there was scarcely any experience of bankrupt laws in the country. On the most extended construction, it is but barely possible. They left it entirely optional with Congress to mould these laws by such enactments as wisdom might dictate. The States are not restrained from passing bankrupt laws, so far as Congress may not exercise the power; though they are restrained from passing laws impairing the obligation of contracts. Congress are charged with the highest conservatory powers delegated by the Constitution. The defence of the country, for example, against foreign aggression and domestic violence. It was well understood, that, in the progress of time, emergencies might arise when all would have to submit to the law of necessity. The Constitution is therefore wisely silent on some points of power in the General Government. The citizen is secured against bills of attainder, corruption of blood, and *ex post facto* laws. While the States are denied the power of impairing the obligation of contracts, emitting bills of credit, coining money, or making tender laws, these, with the power of raising armies and navies, loaning and appropriating moneys for their support, are left in the discretion of Congress. This discretion ought always to be regulated by the great laws of moral obligation. What powers are forbidden to the States ought to be used with the greatest caution by the United States. Nothing in ethics is more strictly enjoined than the inviolability of contracts; and the case must be very strong indeed that will justify the Congress in impairing them. Considering them consecrated by the most sacred moral sanction, it is our duty to inquire whether, by justly perhaps providing for the releasing of an innocent man from a pressure of obligation he has neither hope nor faculty to extinguish himself, you will not inundate the country with fraud and villainy. It is my conscientious opinion it will be the result. Though this bill is substantially the former law of the United States, it is more ambiguous as to when and to what extent it is to go into effect. If it is to affect transactions past, I not only doubt, but deny, its constitutionality. It proceeds on the ground that bankruptcy is a criminal act; in its nature it often is so.

This bill is avowed to be intended to take immediate effect, and of course so far as a commission of bankruptcy is a punishment, the law will be *ex post facto*. But, what will be the confusion and injustice this kind of legislation will produce? Look at the details of the bill; not only will the bankrupt be discharged from his contracts, but men who have dealt with him with equal fairness, will, some, be allowed to prove (for recovery) their debts, while others, merely from the retrospective character of the law, will be denied. I can see nothing but the most monstrous injustice, likely to result from making such a law close upon dealings already had. All laws affecting rights ought to be prospective. Every thing ought to have time to conform to them, especially those which enter most deeply into the transactions of trade. Mere remedial laws may sometimes wisely and salutarily apply to the existing state of things. But even those will be found most frequently to promise much more benefit applied prospectively. We are told " the principles of this bill are happily adapted ' to the situation of the country. That it is confined ' to proper traders; to such as incur risks other

' classes are exempted from." This will be found I think otherwise. It is confined to traders in merchandise of every kind, and exchange, while large classes of dealers, in equally hazardous business, are absolutely excluded. What risk does the mere retailer incur that the builder of ships and houses, or the manufacturer of leather, shoes, hats, clothes, and manufacturers generally, do not incur; to say nothing of a variety of other professions? Credit is as necessary in business to one as to the other. The principles of our Government are opposed to this sort of immunity. Why, let me ask, are a particular profession to be provided with the means of an entire escape from their debts, a comparatively few in number, even of insolvents, while the great mass, at least equally meritorious, are to be chained to perpetual liability? Why is this beneficent system you offer, only applicable to a favored few? for, when you leave the narrow confines of navigation and maritime commerce, and foreign exchange, no reason exists why the middle-man, retailer, factor, and broker, should have a boon you do not extend to other more meritorious classes, who of necessity accept and give credit. If your system does not reach all, it does not suit us; as we are not a people of castes and classes. Gentlemen must show some better reason than alleged extraordinary risks for a claim of partial legislation. The truth is, the whole system is unsound. It is intrinsically vicious, and it is feared to attempt it on a general scale. These we must take for the reasons of the proposed limitation of its benefits until better reasons are assigned than we have yet heard. We are told our unfortunate merchants are rendered useless. Many of them hold property that ought to be given up. Human nature must very much change before it is reasonable that men who now fraudulently withhold property from their creditors will, under the proposed system, freely yield it up. Exemption from liability for debts, where there is no disposition to fraud, is a great boon, but a greater when it can be obtained with assured opulence. We know that it has long been proverbial that at the custom-house a peculiar doctrine of ethics prevails. The legal sanctions are not always sufficient to restrain perjuries. High duties we are told will not always increase the revenue. These are found to work a premium for fraud. You now propose the highest temptation to cupidity, and my word for it there are the seeds in this bill for a plentiful harvest. Relief is contemplated for the innocent, but to get at him you must pass the imprudent, extravagant, and vicious one. Do not tell me that your commissioners, your searches, your examinations, your oaths, and your sanctions, will purify and refine youth into virtue and innocence. On the one hand we are told if we do not act we shall give up the blameless to depravity and despair; but if we do act, the inevitable result must be to reward and protect the dissolute. The gentleman reminds us we prospered by a state of neutrality in a belligerent world, but that the scene is changed. Look, says he, at the list of sufferers from seizures and confiscations abroad, and embargoes and restrictions at home; from bank accommodations, and endorsements, which have produced wide-spread ruin. The panacea for all these evils is a bankrupt law. But, then, this compassionate appeal extends only to a small class of traders, while the thousands of insolvents, involved in the vortex of ruin by the intemperate speculators in trade, are consigned over to the "confusion of insolvent laws," as the gentlemen terms them, to uselessness and despair. We are asked if the confusion of State legislation on insolvencies is a fit situation for a commercial people. Certainly, till we are shown a better. I am free to say I greatly prefer it to the scheme now proposed; to any scheme which shall not extend to insolvents generally; indeed to any bankrupt scheme that shall vest such arbitrary powers in a few men, sitting, as it were, in private, and where the security against fraud lies in oaths, the abuse of which is opposed by feeble because uncertain sanctions.

We are reminded that we deal much with nations where bankrupt laws prevail—where American creditors are paid, *pro rata*, while the foreign merchant has it in his power perpetually to harass the American debtor. To talk of dividends in bankruptcies, where the certificate is the object, as it must ever be, where discharges are provided for, is mockery. The American insolvent, when released, personally, has little to fear of trouble or cost from his foreign creditor, however vindictive. Distance and the unprofitableness of the attempt will preclude it. But, we are informed, bankrupt laws make men honest. It happens, though these laws are somewhat a novelty among us, that this assertion can be tested and denied by stubborn history.

The country, whose system it is desired we should adopt, has had a long trial of it. I shall recur presently to the tests of her experience. As to the decision of the courts of law of the United States, on the subject of the power of the States to discharge from liability, prospectively, I consider it as yet very far from being the settled law of the land. But, suppose it be granted: I still hold, no mode of discharge but one fairly and voluntarily granted by the creditor ought to be allowed. The attempt has been abundantly proved to be an embarkation on the sea of iniquity, without rudder or compass. My friend from Delaware anticipates objections to his system: that it will tempt the dishonest debtor to fraud and cover him with impunity. But he says the bill shuns the shock of the British system, the great error of which is in the severity of its sanctions. Humanity, he says, revolts at punishment so disproportioned. In this country, penalty of death is scarcely applied to any crime but that of taking human life or putting it in imminent jeopardy. The fraudulent taking of property can never justify it. But the gentleman will find, in the evidence taken before the committee of the House of Commons, in 1818, that it is very far from being supposed the unfrequency of prosecutions, for crimes committed under the bankrupt laws, is wholly due to aversion to see the penalty inflicted. It arises from the discouragements a loss of time and incurment of expense presents, together with the uncertainty of conviction. These things will be found to attend prosecutions where convictions would incur a milder punishment. But I will touch this subject further in the examination of the bill. But, says the gentleman, the committee of the House of Commons do not recommend a repeal of the bankrupt laws. Ay, and I will add, they forbear even to recommend all the changes they think are necessary. Need I tell the gentleman that systems of three hundred years' standing are not easily rooted up when they are found to be evil. There is a great difference, let me tell him, between abolishing systems and adopting them. We go upon the principle of equality of privilege among the citizens, of keeping the civil power above the military, of separating civil from religious establishments. What other country has done this? We have found all the blessings to result from following these great maxims we expected. You would, even in these days of revolution, be surprised to see a British House of Commons recognising them, not because they are not true, but because, before she could, she must reform her whole Constitution of Government, which the boldest would hardly dare to attempt, but from dire necessity. I confess I do not like a bankrupt system, from the machinery which seems necessarily to belong to it. You must have a chancellor, commissioners, solicitors, clerks, assignees, messengers, and a long train of persons armed with monstrous powers, and absorbing such an amount of fees as must necessarily, in nine cases out of ten, leave nothing for the creditors. This is an objection to a bankrupt system that no legislation can obviate, and a much better alternative is presented in not legislating at all, but to let every man take care of his own business, under the laws regulating property, which surely no country ever had more abundant or safer means of enacting. The defects of the British system, says the gentleman, are healed in the bill before you. This we shall be better able to judge when we have reviewed the bill. We find, however, after three hundred years' trial in that country, and multiplied modifications by the legislative power, so late as 1818, an inquiry into the administration of the British bankrupt laws results in the most perfect demonstration that its whole history is a continued scene of increasing iniquities and enormities. An entire change is deemed desirable; an essential one is earnestly urged. It is true the bill differs from the British system; the difference in the situation of the two countries does not admit of all the principles that apply there.

This bill, as I have before said, rests substantially on British precedent, and is very nearly a copy of the law of 1800. The minutes which I shall presently recur to are of recent date, and will illustrate the effects which must inevitably flow from such a system. The scheme will be found unsound at bottom; what is evil in principle cannot, by any exercise of legislation, be turned to good. The system before us will be found liable to many objections intrinsically belonging to it, and altogether incurable. The bill is, in many parts, vague and ambiguous; its sanctions are not definite; and a variety of trusts are reposed which cannot be enforced. The innocent, though unfortunate trader, may be persecuted and ruined with impunity, where the fraudulent one can hardly fail to get his discharge from all liability for his debts. If this is not found to be the case, then, indeed, am I very far from having read the bill profitably. Your former law was limited to five years; it went off by euthansia in three. No voice was raised in defence of it. It is true it was not repealed by a Congress of the same politics that enacted it. Its blessings could not have been very apparent, or its repeal would hardly have anticipated its limitation. It failed as a bankrupt system everywhere had failed. They belong to the lumber of other species of Governments, and are of the same family with privileged orders and State religion. Now, let us take a brief review of the bill. On the face of the first clause no certain construction can be had, as to when it is to go into operation, or how it is to effect existing insolvencies.

The purpose of the bill is avowed to be, to relieve existing insolvencies. All the confessions of judgment and assignments to favored creditors which have been made are to be confirmed and sanctioned. Can it be pretended that a man who has notoriously paid some creditors to the prejudice of the rest, can ever be entitled to a certificate of bankruptcy discharging him from future liability, when a *pro rata* dividend, the great object of a commission of bankruptcy, is impossible? Yet, by this bill, such will surely get it; and it is intended for that purpose, as we shall presently see. Persons owing debts to a certain amount, using the trade of merchandise by buying and selling, dealing in exchange or marine insurance, are, by this bill, made the subjects of a commission of bankruptcy; but then, farmers, graziers, drovers, dyers, bleachers, shoemakers, carpenters, ship-carpenters, butchers, tailors, bakers, schoolmasters, inn-keepers, or any artificer whose living is got with some mixture of buying and selling, are excluded. These exclusions are as unjust as they are capriciously grouped. A man must suppose himself insolvent before he will commit or be involved involuntarily in a charge of bankruptcy. What will then be his object or hope from it? Exoneration from his debts at best; but, if he be not honest, exoneration and the retention of all he can. The certificate is the legitimate object of all. Now, why shall the middle man, the retailer, the factor, have the boon of exoneration denied to drovers, graziers, bleachers, carpenters, ship-carpenters, farmers, schoolmasters, &c.? Must not all these professions necessarily often take and give extensive credits? Much more so than some of the included classes. In fact, many of these are not only buyers and sellers, but factors of very extensive dealings. Why is that most important class, the manufacturers of flour, not even mentioned, and the dealer in lands, though brokers in other business are? I have known a large capital embarked in the establishment of a school, which, from the turn of times, has failed; and a person

so failing is, surely, not less worthy of sympathy from the nature of his undertaking. There is no ground of justification for these exclusions. Every body must suffer from the exoneration of bankrupts; why, then, is one class to be favored more than another? Are gentlemen afraid of their own principles? The bill admits no other inference. The President is to appoint as many general commissioners of bankruptcy in each judicial district as he may deem necessary. The President, *remark*, without check or control. The Governor of Pennsylvania so appoints justices of the peace, and the consequence is, that, by a late report, they are multiplied to a most injurious extent. In these times, I expect the President will have applications enough. He cannot know the applicants, and the appointments will not be the better for that. The number, too, is in his discretion. With all the virtue and prudence I rejoice to believe he possesses, I look for nothing from him above good intentions, under the common frailties of man. The commissioners are to receive a per diem allowance for their services. The object of the office must be profit, rather than honor; and here you have a pledge that business will not be turned away. Concerted bankruptcies will afford as good profit as any others, as the commissioners are to be assured of their fees, whether there be a dividend or not. Well, the commissioners are to be sworn; they are then "to proceed, as soon as may be, to execute the commission, and, upon sufficient cause appearing, declare the bankruptcy." The party charged is to have notice, and may have, on demand, a trial by jury. This is pretended to be a security against malicious petitions, for concerted ones will never involve a wish to contest. The party may, before or at the time of examination, demand a trial of the fact by a jury. What situation will he be in while this is in contest? His business is suspended; he is threatened with ruin. He obtains a verdict; and what then? Has he any remedy against his prosecutor? The bill does not provide it, however, against the commissioners from wrong intent or error; his only redress seems to be the verdict. This wrong will have emanated from a tribunal sitting in a by-place, whose proceedings are not exposed to the purifying eye of public observation. Next comes the power of this secret commission to issue their warrant of seizure against the bankrupt, and his doors, and the doors of any dwelling-house supposed to contain him, are to be forced, on demand first being made. The exercise of these powers, by the regular judicial authority in criminal cases, is not without features of objection in the eyes of a free people. But they must be odious when resorted to by a tribunal which never can have the respect and confidence of the American public. Again, these three commissioners—and the chances are much against their being always the wisest or most discreet men—may, on what they deem probable cause, shown on oath, direct any person—mind, it is *any person*—in the day time, to break open houses, chests, trunks, &c., to come at the bankrupt's goods and writings. Now, if resistance be made, is there any power to call out the posse,

277   HISTORY OF CONGRESS.   278

FEBRUARY, 1821.   *The Bankrupt Bill.*   SENATE.

and what is to be done with those who resist? The bill is silent. If this power be put in operation, the public feeling will not sustain it; without it, your tribunal is an object of contempt. The bankruptcy being declared, the commissioners are to take possession of his property, &c., and shall cause them to be safely kept until assignees be chosen, in manner hereinafter provided; that is, as often as they shall see fit, shall appoint one or more assignees to take care of the property until the meeting of the creditors. They shall then deliver it over, or forfeit five thousand dollars. I apprehend the commissioners will rarely see fit to appoint such assignee; because few men will be found willing, without fee or reward, to incur the risk. A man worth nothing might be induced to accept; for the forfeiture is the only consequence of embezzlement, which he will laugh to scorn; therefore, all the evils of embezzlement may be expected in the English system. Legislation cannot devise remedies against these abuses. Three principal things are to be done in commissions of bankruptcy; the appointment of assignees, the proving of debts, and granting the certificates. We have now come to the appointment of assignees. They are to be appointed by the major part, in value, of the creditors who have proved their debts. The debts may be proved any where, on oath or affirmation, and the party proving can vote by proxy, and, notwithstanding judicial investigation may be resorted to on every paper, much, if not all, of the evils of British practice will take place. Objects much at variance with the fair distribution of the estate among the creditors will often govern. Frauds will advance upon justice with steady pace, from this fruitful soil of temptation.

Fictitious debts will be proved, and the conspiracies appear that disgrace the English system. Assignees may be removed, and they are required to deliver over under a penalty of $5,000. The assignee has wasted the estate, together with his own; and where is your remedy? Executors and administrators are held to account. How can you make them account for what never came into their hands? The commissioners are to make assignments of the estate of the bankrupt. Will this operate an eviction of tenants in possession, or produce a surrender of personal property? Certainly not. Look at the scene of litigation which must occur, or what frauds must be confirmed. On information given, if the commissioners have good reason to believe or suspect that any of the property of the bankrupt is in the possession of any person, they shall have power to summon, (and ere they attach, too, by consequence;) yes, by such process or other means, as they think convenient, and examine them, &c.; and if they shall not declare the whole truth touching the subject-matter, then the commissioners may commit, &c. Tell me, now, are you serious in conferring such powers on those persons appointed by the President, whom he cannot know? Could they exercise these powers in this free community? If they could, I should doubt its fitness for freedom. We shall presently see how this power of

commitment, for not declaring the whole truth, has worked in the country we are about to imitate. Perjury committed by others than the bankrupt is to be punished with a fine not exceeding $4,000, and imprisonment not exceeding two years, and by incapacity to give witness in any court of record. Every man is susceptible of imprisonment, but few, comparatively, of those who may be the subject of this punishment will be likely to have means of paying this fine. Is he to be discharged at the end of his term, whether payment or not can be made, or is he to be continued on a contempt? The bill is silent. How is he to be fed and clothed—where is the police of your prisons in this frightful bill, where so many crimes are to be engendered, most of which are to be punished with imprisonment? You have none. You have neither prison nor prison-keepers, and no provision is made for the treatment of the prisoner. The wealthy or fortunate culprit may have every comfort of life but liberty, while the indigent one must languish under hunger and nakedness. Such penal legislation as is here proposed is shocking to reflection. There is a vagueness of expression in the bill that seems to indicate the supposed existence of a common law jurisdiction, that, by judicial legislation, will fill up the chasms in the statute. I doubt very much if the judiciary will venture on so hardy an experiment in administering a penal statute. It follows, then, that no expectation is had of the penalties closing on delinquents. They are just put for show, and to eke out the system. I ask the gentleman from Delaware to say, if he thinks we have the power to say who shall be a competent witness in the courts of Delaware? Lands or goods assigned by the bankrupt to children or other persons, to defraud creditors, shall be assignable by the commissioners as effectually as if the bankrupt stood seized of them. This opens a wide avenue to litigation, and promises nothing to creditors.

We next come to the forty-two days within which surrender and disclosure is to be made of the bankrupt's person and affairs, which is to be prolonged to fifty more, on application to the judge, which, as in the English law, "will be quite a matter of course." And in this lapse of time, as there, a great amount of property will disappear. The oath requires he should purge himself of concealing any property, either before or after the commission issued, for his own benefit, or "except it had been really disposed of in the way of his dealings or trade, and family expenses—an item that will no doubt make a heavy draught on the estate." Such an oath would be about as effectual to obtain a fair disclosure as a sieve to lade water. Apparently, moral men might save a great deal under this oath. It is, in fact, offering temptation to perjury, and a sort of premium for it. If the bankrupt can only swear through successfully, his fortune is made, though he may have entered business but a little while before, without capital. There is little danger of the penalty; if it falls, it may be only twelve months, it cannot exceed ten years, confinement. Imprisonment may be mitigated by what money will purchase, and the pardoning power is ever ready to hear. But the chances are great in favor of escape and triumph, as we shall see in the sequel. There is to be a first dividend day, when the assignees shall be allowed to retain all sums of money they have expended prosecuting the commission, and all other just allowances on account of, or by reason or means of, being assignees. This does not promise much dividend. It promises nothing but business and fees to the officers and agents concerned. It is no wonder dividends so seldom occur! A second is to succeed in eighteen months after the issuing of the commission, which is to be final, unless any suit in law or equity be depending, or any of a variety of contingencies exist, some of which will, mostly where it is the interest of the assignees to keep their accounts unclosed. All the evils of delayed settlements, as under the British system, will result, doubtlessly. It is provided, certain liens shall not be impaired by the bankruptcy. I am not lawyer enough to say if mortgage creditors are to be paid a portion rate, as they are not in the exceptions. The assignees are to keep books, and have them for inspection of the creditors. Suppose they do not; no remedy is provided. The bill provides, a second bankruptcy shall not discharge contracts, and a third shall not even discharge the person of the debtor.

No provision, however, sir, seems to bar those who were discharged under the former law from being discharged under this; such persons can have two full benefits, and none others. The bill admits that those excluded may be tempted to become bankrupts in the hope of a discharge. But, if he be not found within the true intent and meaning of the act, he shall not be entitled to a certificate, nor, if granted, shall it avail him.

Gentlemen talk of the benefits the bill is to be to creditors. Its whole purpose is the release of the debtor from his contracts, and with invidious and unjust discriminations, and odious and unreasonable exclusions. After wading to the 35th section, we come to the last act of the drama—the certificate of bankruptcy that is to regenerate and disenthral the bankrupt from all his contracts. A district judge, sitting as grand chancellor, must issue this amulet, but the commissioners' must certify the bankrupt has acted fairly, and two-thirds, in value and number, of his creditors above $50 must sign the certificate, and he must make oath he has surrendered his effects fairly. Any of his creditors may be heard before the judge, who may allow the certificate peremptorily, or have a summary hearing, and make a final decree. There is no jury here—it is all chancery. If a corporation be a creditor, and that only be-wanting to make the two-thirds in number and value, it shall be considered as nothing. Now it may happen frequently that these proscribed corporations may be almost the sole creditor, but it shall have no control over the certificate. A bankrupt may owe $20,000, and $19,049 may be due to a corporation, and $51 to an individual; that individual signing will release the debtor from his contracts. This extraordinary feature is a new one—it was not in the law of 1800. The debtor is to be released at all events—that is the object of the bill. It is the first time, I venture to say, such a feature was ever proposed. It is departing from all the principles of bankrupt laws. They seem to have gone a great length of time before they were discharged at all. Till now, even in Britain they have not ventured to disregard the rights of more than one-quarter or one-fifth; but this is at one leap reversing all former ideas.

I think, sir, it is pretty clear, a certificate under these provisions will always issue. It is only for the bankrupt stoutly to swear through. He is to have family maintenance, three dollars a day for his attendance, and a dividend, too, if he be honest enough to surrender his property. But a certificate and maintenance are secured alike to honest and dishonest. If a bankrupt does not discover fraudulent demands, he loses his dividend and his certificate. This only points out where frauds will occur—it offers no preventive. A jailer is to forfeit $3,000 if he suffers a bankrupt committed on the commissioner's warrant to escape; a forfeiture of $3,000 for a jailer! It might just as well have been a million. The assignees are to sell at auction, free of any tax. I doubt the wisdom of hazarding this provision. I believe it would be found difficult to resist a State law, that should levy a tax on such auctions. The petitioning creditor is to give bond to pay the costs and charges of the commission. This would be very convenient in a concerted commission; if the commissioners get their fees, we shall not see them care much if there be a dividend or not. The poor man who may not have enough to pay the costs, may lie in jail till the laws of insolvency release him. He is not worthy of the boon of a certificate of bankruptcy, though he may have been an eminent and honest merchant. The creditors are to direct the deposite of the moneys in some bank; but if the assignees do not choose to comply, there is an end to it. By the 59th section the State insolvent laws are reserved, and any person imprisoned remaining therein one month, and not prosecuted as a bankrupt, is to be relievable under these laws. Taking all these provisions into view, and what must be the inevitable conclusion as to their effect? A very small class of our insolvent citizens can have the benefit of a certificate. Those who are within its purview are the class whose insolvency has very much been produced by extravagance and desperate adventure; among whom the strongest temptation to fraud will exist. An honest merchant, of whatever extent of business, and however a victim of misfortune not to have been foreseen, if he has surrendered his all, and no petitioning creditor can expect reimbursement of costs and charges of the commission, is without the scope of the bill's benevolence; is turned over to the State insolvent laws—to withering despair; while he who risked nothing, having nothing, who has failed full-handed, and withholds from his creditors, may, by a concerted commission, obtain a release almost to a certainty. This law is to close immediately. Do you not believe those who are anxious for its benefit are prepared to realize it?

281   HISTORY OF CONGRESS.   282

FEBRUARY, 1821.   *The Bankrupt Bill.*   SENATE.

Yes, sir; we must know little of human nature if we do not believe it; and they will be sought by all the means human experience has matured in England, or by the former law here, of which this is substantially a copy, so far as relates to temptations to frauds and perjuries. The old maxim of the merchant was, that, if he became opulent by a life devoted to business, it was the success that founded his wishes. But, in later times, it was accounted nothing unless four or five years' business did not realize a splendid fortune, and in the mean time allow the indulgence in splendid extravagance. No doubt there will always be, among insolvent trading men, many of merit; but the mass of those whom this bill compassionates and seeks to relieve, are very far from being of the class of insolvents most to be pitied and most worthy of relief. The great defect of all bankrupt laws, and of this in particular, is, that it does not discriminate between the innocent and blamable insolvent. They are equally entitled to relief, on a surrender of their property; equally entitled to daily pay, family maintenance, &c.; though the one by misfortune may have lost fairly and honorably a solid fortune, and the other never had owned a solid dollar. No law can be safe or useful that consolidates such extremes, and extends equal benefit to men of so very different aspects of character. Bankruptcy will hardly cure the rash and desperate adventurer. He has the impulse from nature, and habit has confirmed it on him. Certificate him and make him a new man, and we shall soon see the meteor reappear in the precincts of trade.

In the 63d section, a chancery jurisdiction is gotten up, that is to extend to all cases arising under bankrupt laws. It is not easy to conceive the consequences that are thence to flow. This, too, is the English system, only there there is a single head, but here we are to get up a hydra, with as many heads as there are circuit and district judges; every one being a tribunal of the last resort. So monstrous an innovation on all the just principles of jurisprudence has, I believe, never been adventured upon by any the most despotic Governments. Every pretence will justify a chancery suit.

The evil passions will be ever ready to seize this mean of gratification, and professional ingenuity will be taxed to spread the evil. Chancery is chancery every where. It is one of those modes of administering distributive justice not compatible with a free country. Bills can be filed in the scheme here presented, where no decision is sought or wished. He who may be thus assailed will be happy if he lives long enough to get clear of his defence. The decree is to be according to equity and good conscience, and shall be conclusive, and forced by attachment or other process in the discretion of the judge—"the law of tyrants." You may call him who has power such as this a judge, but he is in essence a tyrant, and you can have no security against his abusing his powers but public opinion, a poor, though the only check upon tyrants. You will have by this bill at once thirty independent and uncontrolled chancellors, holding

their office by permanent tenure, of every degree of intellect and professional capacity, who cannot always be known when appointed, but whom you must take for better or worse, in sickness or in health, through good and evil report. From such a system, what can we expect but the fruits of a tyranny erected by folly?

It was not, till within a few days, that I determined to examine this bill, and the principles on which it is founded. It was a subject I was not (as I before noted) conversant with. I went into your library to search for information. I found plenty of law, but I could find nothing in the history of the administration of it. I was led to inquire of my experienced friend from North Carolina, (Mr. MACON,) upon what ground the former had been repealed. He referred me to the chairman of the Committee of Commerce of the House of Representatives, (Mr. NEWTON,) who had been active in proposing the repeal. He very kindly informed me that law had, in three years, produced universal disgust, from the enormous evils it had originated. He obligingly added, I can put into your hands the minutes of evidence taken before a committee of the British House of Commons, on the subject of their bankrupt laws, reported in the year 1818. I found, subsequently, the document had been in the hands of my friend from South Carolina, (Mr. SMITH,) and his notices have facilitated my examination of it much. At one time I resigned the task into his hands I am now executing, but a multiplicity of engagements has induced him to refer it back to me. I have thus lost some time, and have not been able to speak in a manner so well digested as I wished. I shall recur to the minutes of evidence; they are derived from commissioners of bankruptcy of the best standing, solicitors, members of Parliament, and men in business. I shall not read the extracts in a digested order. They go directly to illustrate and sustain the observations I have made generally. They prove, conclusively, that, after a trial of three centuries, in England, and frequent statutory modifications, the system has at last resulted in multiplying crimes and most extensive evils. In fine, that it has failed. Mr. Montague, a commissioner, says: "The advantages of being solicitor are 'almost obvious; all the litigation with which 'the estate may be properly or improperly burden-'ed—litigation not checked by the fear of expense 'to the individual on whose behalf the process is 'instituted, and not subjected to any control, ex-'cept by the assignee, with whom there may be 'such an understanding as not to render investi-'gation expedient." "Assignees seek the appoint-'ment to conceal transactions which others might 'detect, as a case of usury. I once knew a case 'where a bankrupt reluctantly disclosed an usuri-'ous transaction, conscious of the control of the 'creditor, as assignee, without success, as the de-'linquent would not sign the certificate, and of 'course he was not a competent witness. A credi-'tor who has obtained a preference in payment is 'often anxious to become an assignee, to prevent 'a disclosure. Assignees often offer themselves 'to favor the bankrupt in concerted commissions.

'Men in the same trade will offer to learn who 'were the bankrupt's customers. Another motive 'to become assignee is, to purchase the bankrupt's 'estate in collusion with him. Another is to re- 'tain the unclaimed dividends or undivided re- 'sidue. The last motive which induces a wish to 'be assignee, is to obtain dominion over the bank- 'rupt's property, which may result in entire em- 'bezzlement. With regard to the proof of accom- 'modation bills, I believe them to exist to a very 'considerable and alarming extent. I believe con- 'clusive proof of this might be obtained from ex- 'amining what creditors have proved debts, under 'different commissions. In a case before the 10th 'list of commissioners, I was counsel against the 'proof of certain debts; almost all of them were 'brought forward by persons who were or had 'been bankrupts. They were defeated, and the 'parties, as is usual in such cases, compromised, 'and I heard no more of it. In 1809 a bankrupt, 'for whom I was retained in counsel, told me that 'he could obtain the signature of any number of 'persons to his certificate; that nothing was more 'easy than to obtain the proof of fictitious debts, 'and that there were persons who lived by proving 'debts and signing certificates. There are many 'men in the city of London who obtain capital 'for extensive business out of the trust of assignee. 'When the creditors become very clamorous, and 'they have been summoned two or three times 'before the commissioners, at the end of two years, 'or perhaps longer, they will declare a first dividend, 'taking care to keep a considerable sum on hand, 'and this they will do by entering claims against 'the estate, to be proved at the next dividend, and 'reserve the amount of such claims in hand at the 'first dividend. After a lapse of another two or 'three years, they will declare a second dividend. 'The creditors being thus wearied out, a third or 'final dividend is seldom obtained of assignees of 'this description. Sir, says a correspondent to 'me, could you see those numerous cases of mal- 'versation, misapplication, and shameful neglect 'of assignees, that perpetually meet the eye of the 'solicitor, you would be satisfied, with me, they 'are a great cause of bankruptcy itself. The 'practice has now got to such a pitch, that I verily 'believe barely one assignee in a dozen, fairly, in- 'dustriously, and honestly, performs his duty." After a tedious detail of abuses, which your pa- tience will not allow me to read, Mr. Montague pro- poses, as a remedy, "that there should be an Ac- 'countant General, charged with the disposing of 'the effects, collecting the debts, and making divi- 'dends pertaining to all bankruptcies." The bill before us goes upon the old British system of as- signees. It is in vain gentlemen hope to escape these abuses. Are Americans less acute than Britons; or have they shown less address in every branch of trade? These abuses grow out of the spirit of trade; they intrinsically belong to it, and no legislation can avoid the evils if you adopt a bankrupt system. Again, Mr. Montague says: "In forty thousand bankruptcies, I doubt whether 'there have been ten prosecutions. I believe there 'have only been three executions, and yet fraudu-

'lent bankrupts and concealments of property are 'proverbial; are so common as to be supposed al- 'most to have lost the nature of crime." Mr. Montague proposes "to assist prosecuting creditors with funds out of the bankrupt's estate." This shows that it is not the severity of the punish- ment only that discourages prosecutions, but the difficulty of conviction, trouble and expense, which operate alike under milder or severer punishments. Your bill, like the British system, supposes that an act of bankruptcy shall be done with intent to de- fraud or delay a creditor; therefore, an act to benefit him cannot be an act to defraud or delay him. This, says Mr. Montague, "is the whole foundation of concerted commissions." The bill will, I have no doubt, produce a plentiful harvest of the abuses accompanying them, and growing out of them. The evidence proceeds: "The credi- 'tor sustains by the bankrupt a loss of property, 'his feelings are also wounded by the improper 'conduct of one in whom he confided. He ought, 'therefore, to have control over the certificate. It 'is impossible he should explain to any tribunal 'the nature of the injury he may have sustained 'by abuse of his confidence. I propose three-fifths 'in number and value of the creditors should con- 'trol the certificate." In the bill before us the creditor may be heard, but the judge has power to give the certificate peremptorily, and without ap- peal from his decision. Ought such a power to release any man from the obligation of contracts, to be rested any where? The bill proposes two- thirds of the creditors, but it seems designed to dispense with them altogether. Mr. Montague was asked, "Do you not think 'it extremely common for the most undeserving 'bankrupts to obtain their certificates? I do be- 'lieve that it is most common for the most unde- 'serving bankrupts to obtain their certificates by 'fraudulent and improper means, to the great injury 'of the good creditor, and to the great injury of 'public justice; and I do think that it frequently 'happens that dishonest bankrupts, from having 'recourse to means from which honesty would 'recoil, have greater facility in obtaining their 'certificates than honest men possess." Mr. Mon- tague, from the 6th volume of Vesey's Reports, read the following declaration of the Lord Chan- cellor: "He expressed his strong indignation at 'the frauds committed under cover of the bankrupt 'laws. The abuses of it are a disgrace to the 'country. It would be better to repeal at once all 'the statutes than to suffer them to be applied to 'such purposes. There is no mercy to the estate; 'nothing is less thought of than the commission. 'As they are frequently conducted in the country, 'they are little more than a stock in trade for the 'commissioners, the assignees, and the solicitor. 'Instead of solicitors attending to their duties as 'ministers of the court, for they are so, commis- 'sions of bankruptcy are treated as matter of traf- 'fic. A taking up the commission, B and C acting 'as commissioners. They are considered as stock 'in trade, and calculations are made how many 'commissions can be brought into the partnership. 'Unless the court holds a strong hand over a

' bankruptcy, particularly as administered in the
' country, it is itself necessary to as great a nuisance
' as any known in the land, and known too to pass
' under the forms of its laws." This opinion expressed in 1809, Mr. Montague "conceives to have
been greatly strengthened by cases which have
arisen since." The Chancellor, in one case, concludes his judgment thus: "It comes round to this,
' whether in a case where one partner is petition-
' ing creditor, another partner the acting commis-
' sion, another partner the solicitor to the com-
' mission, and the remaining partner the sole
' assignee, the commission can be permitted to
' stand." It is the Chancellor speaks. Is this a system
we ought to copy? In the evidence of Mr. Vandercorn, a solicitor, he was asked, "If in his ex-
' perience the greater number of the acts of bank-
' ruptcy had not been concerted? Answer. I
' think they have, the greatest part of them. Do
' you not think the majority of commissions are
' issued with the concurrence, and at the request
' of the bankrupt? I think they are." He was
asked, "Is it not in the power of an insolvent to
' delay his bankruptcy, and in the interim misap-
' ply property in payment of favored creditors?
' It certainly is. Have you not known, in the
' course of your professional experience, a great
' many dishonorable and worthless bankrupts ob-
' tain their certificates? I certainly have. I may
' venture to say, I have hardly known an unfortu-
' nate man who was altogether deprived of his
' certificate, or a dishonest one that did not find the
' means of procuring it." "The man goes with
' the warrant of seizure," says Mr. Vandercorn; "he
' is placed below stairs, and knows nothing of what
' is going on above. This I believe to be the time
' when the greatest peculation prevails. Relations
' and friends attend for condolence. I believe
' most of them take something away. They live
' upon the house and the produce so long as they
' are permitted." Mr. Lavie, a soliciter, on evidence, says: "The business of bankruptcy is not
' sought for eagerly by solicitors of eminence and
' character. As the bankrupt laws are at present
' managed, they afford advantage to no one except
' the bankrupt. If solicitors do their duty, they
' get neither credit nor profit. With regard to
' creditors, any means short of bankruptcy in hon-
' est cases is preferable, and I consider the criterion
' of a person subject to the bankrupt laws, being
' desirous of acting fairly by his creditors, is, whe-
' ther he seeks a bankruptcy, or is desirous to avoid
' it. Those desirous of making up their affairs
' without a bankruptcy, are certainly to be com-
' mended; and those anxious to go into the Gazette
' evidently have in view their own relief, not the
' interests of their creditors. Upon all occasions
' I have considered it for the interest of my em-
' ployers, whether bankrupts or creditors, to en-
' deavor, in the first instance, by every possible
' means, to prevent a commission from issuing.
' The settlement of the affairs of insolvents in my
' office have been very numerous. Compositions
' and other modes of arrangements have very much
' increased. The increase of bankruptcies being,
' in my opinion, solely of petty traders, so long as

' the bankrupt laws continue as they are now, any
' thing, as I have said before, short of bankruptcy,
' is desirable." Again, Mr. Lavie answers: "If
' the solicitor, assignee, and the bankrupt, should
' be in collusion together, proving debts by oath,
' where the creditor does not appear, would afford
' facility for frauds." This avenue is left entirely
open in the bill. Sir Samuel Romilly states, in
his evidence, "There is an offence often committed
' under the bankrupt laws, more serious than not
' surrendering, or concealing property, for which
' there is appointed a much slighter punishment,
' to wit: the procuring of a commission, in order,
' by means of false and fictitious debts proved under
' it, to obtain a relief from real debts. This has
' become very common. This fraud can only be
' perpetrated, by numerous, repeated, and flagrant
' perjuries. This is an intrinsic vice in the system,
' not curable. When you tempt men by your le-
' gislation to commit crimes, your penalties avail
' nothing. The greatest moral evils must flow from
' any law which offers the hope of a release from
' debts to a man who is not able or willing to pay."
Mr. Waithman, a man of great experience in
trade, says: "The great defect in the system has
' arisen from the want of discrimination between
' the honest and dishonest debtors. They are on
' precisely the same footing. I seldom find a bank-
' rupt fails to get his certificate. I have witnessed
' property passing away before the eyes of the
' creditor, and he has not been able to lay his
' hands on it. I pursued a bankrupt, and had
' above twenty meetings; fictitious debts to a large
' amount were proved. The property all disap-
' peared in a moment. A vast number of bills
' were fabricated; they chose assignees, and car-
' ried all before them. I had twenty meetings at
' my own expense; he swore himself out of one
' thing into another; I at last obtained consent for
' his commitment; some doubts as to form defer-
' red it until next day, and the man ran away, and
' there was end to it." "I have observed, there is
' hardly ever a man, however atrocious his con-
' duct, who cannot contrive to get his certificate,
' and go into business again. I have observed,
' nine times out of ten, the commission is worked
' for the benefit of the bankrupt, not the creditors."
"Do you not, it was asked, think the bankrupt
' law, as it now exists in this country, is a scandal
' and disgrace to it? I have long considered it so;
' and that it has induced much dishonesty. Major
' Simple said to a Bow-street officer, why I have
' been a fool all my lifetime. I have not known
' how to go to work; I have been running the risk
' of my life for a trifling thing; but, if I were to
' begin again, I would open a shop as a trader, be-
' come a bankrupt, and make my fortune at once."
Mr. Cullen, a commissioner: "The bankrupt law
' was introduced to prevent and punish frauds of
' debtors, and distribute their property equally
' among their creditors; but it has not succeeded.
' However wise at first, and modified since, it
' effects neither of these objects, the property is
' not forthcoming, or it is wasted. The same
' frauds still exist, neither diminished nor punish-
' ed; and a new class has sprung up, engendered

'by the very proceedings instituted to prevent
'them, so that the prominent evil of the present
'day appears to be the bankrupt law itself. With-
'out it, individual creditors would have the or-
'dinary chance, by better luck, or greater diligence
'to recover their particular debts. But, the bank-
'rupt law, while it defeats individual right, pro-
'duces the loss of all under the precious forms of
'proceeding at the common expense for the com-
'mon benefit. I am convinced that a majority
'of commissions that issue, may be considered as
'a sort of conspiracies between the debtor, and
'one or more of his creditors, to plunder the rest.
'Concerted commissions must arise out of this law
'from the nature of its provisions. I would sug-
'gest whether the certificate should discharge the
'future property, except the estate paid 75 per
'cent. ?" In the evidence of Mr. Grote, a banker,
it is stated : " That the improvidence of the bank-
'rupt ; the false statement he gives in at the third
'examination ; the want of making the most of his
'effects ; (the account of which he gives in on his
'third examination.) The assignees seldom pay
'any dividend whatever. I applied within the last
'six months for dividend in three instances. In
'the first £30,000 were proved to exist two years
'after the commission issued. The assignee had
'collected barely £200, which was absorbed in ex-
'penses. In a second case I got seven farthings
'in the pound ; and in the third, a dividend of
'nine pence. I have perfectly made up my mind
'that I would rather take an offer of two shillings
'and six pence in the pound than my chance for
'a dividend if it went to the Gazette. I suggest
'that no bankrupt should have his certificate un-
'less he paid a dividend." Mr. Montague says :
"Bankrupts are induced to conceal their property
'in order to bribe their creditors ; they buy goods
'upon credit, after the last act of bankruptcy, in
'order, either to make partial payments to hostile
'creditors, or to fail full handed ; and if the hon-
'esty of the bankrupt renders him unable to bribe
'his creditors, they have another resource, by ob-
'taining security from him, or by extorting from
'the compassion of his friends, what they cannot
'procure from his poverty.
Mr. Lockhart, a member of the committee,
stated : " that, in almost every commission in
'which he had been named, he found the bank-
'rupt had acted with great injustice towards his
'creditors, generally with dishonesty and fraud,
'and always with imprudence and carelessness of
'the wreck of his substance, which is not his, but
'theirs. The cause is found in the facility with
'which the bankrupt goes through his commis-.
'sion. It is proved from the situation he is gen-
'erally found in after his last examination, the
'appearance he makes, and the connexions he re-
'news. The want of a due investigation to dis-
'criminate between innocent insolvents and fraud-
'ulent ones appears to be a radical defect of our
'law. It is difficult at present to prevent the proof
'of unfounded claims, and which are generally
'attempted to be proved with a view to the choice
'of assignees, and the granting of the certificate.
'There are laws now in force to prevent these
'practices, but they are of little effect ; and the
'bankrupt, who might detect and expose them, is
'the party most interested in concealment and
'silence. The committee have already abundant
'evidence of those criminal combinations and
'perjuries, and of the fictitious bills of exchange
'which are drawn and circulated in order to give
'them effect."

I shall forbear further remark ; neither your
patience nor my own strength allow me to proceed. I look for the argument to be supported by
friends much better qualified than I am to do it
justice.

When Mr. Roberts concluded, Mr. Barbour
moved that the bill be postponed indefinitely.

On motion of Mr. Roberts, it was agreed to
take this question by yeas and nays.

The Senate then adjourned.

WEDNESDAY, February 7.

The PRESIDENT communicated a report of the
Commissioners of the Sinking Fund, stating that
the measures which have been authorized by the
board subsequent to the report of the 5th of February, 1820, so far as the same have been completed, are fully detailed in the report of the Secretary of the Treasury to that board, also communicated as part of the report of said Commissioners ;
and the report was read.

Mr. WILLIAMS, of Mississippi, presented the
memorial of the General Assembly of that State,
praying that the right of pre-emption may be
granted to certain settlers on the public lands within said State ; and the memorial was read, and
referred to the Committee on Public Lands.

Mr. JOHNSON, of Kentucky, presented the petition of Joseph G. Roberts, of that State, and late
a surgeon in the Navy, praying to be allowed a
share of certain prize money ; and the petition was
read, and referred to the Committee on Naval
Affairs.

Mr. WALKER, of Georgia, obtained leave to
bring in a bill concerning the process of execution
issuing from the sixth circuit court of the United
States, for the district of Georgia ; and the bill
was read, and passed to a second reading.

Mr. ROBERTS, from the Committee of Claims,
to whom was referred the bill, entitled "An act for
the relief of Rosalie P. Deslonde," and the bill,
entitled "An act for the relief of Pierre Dennis
De La Ronde," reported them severally without
amendment.

The bill from the House of Representatives, entitled "An act making appropriations for the public buildings," was twice read by unanimous consent, and referred to the Committee on the Public
Buildings.

The Senate proceeded to consider the motion of
yesterday to appoint a joint committee to ascertain
and report a mode of examining the votes of President and Vice President, and of notifying the persons elected of their election, and agreed thereto ;
and Messrs. BARBOUR and MACON were appointed
the committee on the part of the Senate.

The Senate proceeded to consider the motion of

yesterday, instructing the Committee on Public Lands to inquire into the expediency of complying with the request of the Choctaw Indians to grant tracts of land to certain individuals, and agreed thereto.

The Senate proceeded to consider the motion of yesterday, instructing the Committee of Claims to inquire into the expediency of allowing the claim of David Cooper, and agreed thereto.

The Senate resumed the consideration of the report of the Committee of Claims on the petition of George Jackson, and it was postponed to Monday next.

The Senate resumed the consideration of the report of the Committee on Finance on the petition of John Lowden; and, on motion by Mr. Johnson, of Louisiana, it was laid on the table.

RELIEF TO LAND PURCHASERS.

The Senate proceeded to consider again the bill for the relief of purchasers of public lands; and

Mr. King, of New York, moved further to amend the same by substituting for a part of the bill the following new sections:

Sec. 2. *And be it further enacted,* That the interest which shall have accrued before the —— day of ——, upon any debt of the United States, for public land, shall be, and the same is hereby, remitted and discharged.

Sec. 3. *And be it further enacted,* That on all debts to the United States, which may have arisen from the purchase of public land, at a price less than three dollars the acre, a discount at the rate of twenty-five per cent. shall be allowed and made; and that on all such debts, which may have arisen from the purchase of public land at or above three dollars the acre, a discount, at the rate of thirty-three and one-third per cent., shall be allowed and made; and the persons indebted to the United States, as aforesaid, shall be divided into three classes: the first class to include all such persons as shall have paid to the United States only one-fourth part of the original price of the land by them respectively purchased or held; the second class to include all such persons as shall have paid to the United States only one-half part of such original price; and the third class to include all such persons as shall have paid to the United States three-fourth parts of such original price; and the debts of the persons included in the first class shall be paid in eight equal annual instalments; the debts of the persons included in the second class shall be paid in six equal annual instalments; and the debts of the persons included in the third class shall be paid in four equal annual instalments; the first of which instalments, in each of the classes aforesaid, shall be paid on the —— day of ——, and the whole of the debt aforesaid shall bear an annual interest at the rate of six per cent: *Provided, always,* That the same shall be remitted upon each and every of the instalments aforesaid, which shall be punctually paid when the same shall become payable as aforesaid.

Sec. 4. *And be it further enacted,* That for failure to pay the several debts aforesaid, in manner aforesaid, and for the term of three months after the day appointed for the payment of the last instalment thereof, in each of the classes aforesaid, the land so purchased, or held by the respective persons indebted to the United States as aforesaid, shall, *ipso facto,* become forfeited and revert to the United States.

Sec. 5. *And be it further enacted,* That no person shall be deemed to be included within, or entitled to the benefit of, any of the provisions of this act, who shall not, on or before the —— day of ——, sign, and file in the office of the register of the land office of the district where the land was purchased, a declaration in writing, expressing his consent to the same.

And then, on motion of Mr. King, of New York, the bill and amendments were recommitted to the Committee on Public Lands.

BANKRUPT BILL.

The Senate then resumed the consideration of the bill to establish an uniform system of bankruptcy.

Mr. Barbour delivered his sentiments in opposition to the bill.

Mr. Otis said, that, in rising to address the Senate upon the subject of a bankrupt act, he felt, equally with the honorable gentleman from Virginia (Mr. Barbour) the difficulty of obtaining the attention of those who were called to decide upon the question: That gentleman, however, had succeeded in giving to the inquiry an interest which he could not aspire to excite. The subject had grown familiar to the public and to the Legislature. It was dry in its nature and voluminous, and to appearance complicated in its details. In the observations which it was his present intention to offer, he should avoid details and confine himself to an explanation of some general and leading principles, and even in performing this duty he feared he might fail to engage the attention of the Senate. Yet he was firmly persuaded that the claim of those interested in the result of the question, was exceeded in importance by none but those subjects, a decision upon which was at all times indispensable to the support of Government. With that exception, he insisted they were of equal rank with any other question that could be agitated, whether considered in reference to the magnitude of the interested party, the long standing of their pretensions, the extent of the benefit to be derived from the relief contemplated, the happiness and comfort which would attend success, and on the chagrin and misery that awaited a failure of the measure. A calamity affecting specially one class of the community, spread over the whole extent of the nation, sometimes made less impression on the mind, than an evil, which, though involving a much less considerable number of individuals, was felt by the whole society of a particular place—and though every wind which blows from the various quarters of the Union, comes laden with the sighs of the unfortunate insolvent, and the groans of the imprisoned debtor, as well as with the regrets of his creditor, yet are they disregarded, and die upon the ear before they reach the heart.

If, said he, the fire which last night broke out in the city had extended its desolation far and wide—if the torch of the incendiary had been applied in various quarters to the habitations, and thousands of tenants had been turned houseless into the streets—or if the Great Disposer of events had permitted the baleful pestilence in the course of the past season to sweep over its population; and under these circumstances, the survivors of these disasters this morning filled your galleries and lobbies with their complaints and petitions for assistance; with what alacrity would you proceed to administer whatever relief could be had at your hands, possessing as you do exclusive jurisdiction in this District! Yet those who are now before you with petitions for your humane aid, are sufficiently numerous, if collected together, to form a population very many times exceeding that of this city—their accumulated wretchedness would be found to exceed that of the visitations just supposed, and they are equally the subjects of your exclusive guardianship under the Constitution of the United States.

The time, he said, had now arrived in which the parties interested in the passing of a bankrupt act, were entitled not merely to request it as a favor, but with all due respect to demand it as a right. It might be affirmed as a universal proposition, that the acceptance of a trust imposed upon the trustee an obligation to discharge its duties. A sound discretion as to the time and mode of performing such duties were certainly of course implied, but the trustee cannot object to the nature of his trust. Now the objections of the honorable gentleman from Virginia (Mr. BARBOUR) go to the very essence of the trust itself. His hostility is to a bankrupt act at all times and in all places, and to such objections thus openly avowed, the true answer is, they come too late. You have accepted the trust, and are bound by the Constitution. But the honorable gentleman from Pennsylvania (Mr. ROBERTS) resorts to the old system of opposition to the measure, and while he objects to the details of the bill, in other words to the mode of executing the trust, he contends still for the discretionary power of Congress in the selection of the proper time. There is, however, no real difference between objections to the nature of the trust, and such objections to the time and mode of execution, as show that he makes them will never be reconciled to any time or any mode. Will he pledge himself to any fixed time or to any substitute for the proposed plan? If he will not, he deceives himself, (for it is not to be said that he is insincere to others) in assailing the details of the bill, when his enmity applies to its principle; and in objecting to the exercise of a discretion at this time, which he in his conscience wishes and means should be forever suspended. Thus, the two honorable gentlemen are agreed in their object, and arrive by different routes to the same issue. It is the bankrupt system, under all its aspects, and in every imaginable form, to which they are opposed. It is to the nature of the trust—to the execution of a power conferred by the Constitution, for the benefit of a great class of the citizens of the Union, whose trustees you are. This trust, previously to the adoption of the Federal Government, was vested in the separate States. It was a necessary and inseparable incident of State authority claiming to be sovereign. It is a power indispensable to the exigencies of a commercial people. It was

always exercised, permanently or occasionally, by the Legislatures or subordinate magistrates, by standing or by special laws in the separate States. Now it can be no longer enforced to any useful end by the State jurisdiction—it has been transferred to Congress as trustees for all persons, whether creditor or debtor, who have or may have an interest in such a system. The Supreme Tribunal of the Union has decided that the States can make no laws discharging an insolvent person from the demands of his creditors. Of consequence, Congress is bound to execute this trust at some time; otherwise the States which have surrendered that power are caught in a snare and disqualified from relieving the distress of their own citizens—while vast numbers of unfortunate persons are converted into outlaws and deprived of the benefits and protection afforded to the citizen by all civilized communities. This high obligation to execute a trust for the use of all who have the beneficiary interest is a fundamental of all public as well as of all municipal law. Neither the executive or judiciary departments can dispense with the performance of their several duties, constantly and indefinitely, under the pretext of discretion in regard to time and means.

Nor can the right of Congress to withhold relief from the urgent claims of a great portion of their constituents be inferred from their power. It was for the purpose of giving activity and energy to the powers vested in the General Government that the Constitution was framed, and not to the end that such as could not be efficaciously employed by the separate States, but were nevertheless of vital importance, should be thrown into a general reservoir of national authority, and therein be permitted to remain entirely stagnant. It was not, he repeated, his intention, on the present occasion, to go into an investigation of the special provisions of the bill upon the table. Should this be thought requisite, after the attention of Congress had been so frequently called to that examination, he doubted not it would be undertaken and performed by others to the perfect satisfaction of the Senate. He professed that his object would be merely to illustrate, by general remarks, the points to which he had adverted, namely, the condition and numbers of the applicants for relief—the duty of Congress to provide for it, and to obviate some of the principal objections now urged by the opponents of the measure. Let us first, then, bestow a cursory consideration upon the circumstances, condition, and numbers of those who are interested in the fate of this question.

The debtors may, for this purpose, be divided into three classes. First, persons in actual confinement for debt. These are either such as, in a state of extreme and unqualified pauperism, drag out their wretched existence in the charnel-houses of living misery, waiting for the advantage, so called, of State insolvent laws; or others who are one degree removed from the immediate dangers of hunger and nakedness, by having concealed some paltry remnant of the wreck of their little • fortunes, preferring the durance of bolts and bars to the iron grasp of the laws which authorize the seizure of the last trifle for the benefit of the first plaintiff.

The next description of persons consists of those to whom the calculating or relenting mercy of their creditors has spared the last bitter portion of actual imprisonment, but who are stripped nearly or entirely of their all, and turned out naked upon the world. This class is more numerous than the other, includes a greater mass of misery, and calls upon your humanity and your policy in a still louder tone for commiseration and relief.

Leaving, then, for the present, all considerations of humanity, surely it is not a matter of light moment, that this numerous body of individuals are, in their present circumstances, disqualified for the performance of the most important duties of the man and the citizen. Of what value is a distressed and harassed insolvent debtor to his country? His mind is distracted, his energies are paralyzed, his heart is broken. He feels as if all his relations to society were extinguished. His sensibility to the happiness or misery, to the honor or wrongs of his country, are merged in the agony of his own wretchedness. Selfishness is the offspring of a sense of desolation which tells him he has no friends. He goes forth in the morning under the languid impulse of some vague and undefinable hope; and wanders through the streets busy with occupations in which he has no share, in quest of he knows not what. He encounters the frown of his offended creditor, the "proud man's contumely," the averted countenance of the friend of happier days. At night he returns to a habitation of which he is tenant by sufferance from hour to hour. He meets the companion of his sorrows and the partner of his fate, without any tidings of comfort even in prospect. His children turn towards him with the instinct of the nestling, for the food which he has not brought. To hide the anguish of his soul, he flies to the bed which the pity of his creditor may have left to him, but not to repose. Or if perchance tired nature yields for a time to the conflict with suffering, and the tear which blisters on his cheek permits him to doze, instead of peaceful visions, poverty and famine, "in execrable shape," disturb his dreams, and the sad reality of his waking hours is exchanged for the aggravated torments of his doubtful slumbers. This is an epitome of the days of thousands—too often varied by recourse to the miserable comforts which idleness and despair are so apt to embrace. Here, then, are fathers and heads of families! What, in this state, is to be the destiny and utility of their children? What the effect upon the public morals, wealth, and prosperity of the nation? Entire generations, constantly multiplying, are to be brought up in pauperism and idleness, destitute of education, untaught in civil duties, and insensible to the love of country.

There was still a third class of debtors, whose case would be reached by this bill. Those who, having actually become insolvent, or, being in failing circumstances, had concealed or otherwise secured property, either for themselves alone, or for favored creditors. In this class are comprehended, not merely those who have taken this step

in a spirit of fraud, but great numbers who would willingly surrender their effects under a bankrupt system, but who, for want of it, make their consciences conform to their exigency, and live at the expense of their creditors upon a fund which is daily melting away.

Now, sir, as the wives and children of these unfortunate persons are manifestly parties in interest to the provisions of the bill not less than themselves, you have before you a mass of distressed persons seeking for relief, which, whatever difference of opinion may prevail respecting their aggregate number, could not be regarded with indifference if they alone were the petitioners for the act. But they are far enough from being destitute of auxiliaries who have a different, but still a most valuable interest, in its success. The creditor class of the whole nation may fairly be regarded as uniting in the support of this bill. Not only had numerous petitions, some from meetings of merchants, and others signed by individuals, been preferred to Congress, but expressions of public sentiment in favor of it were reiterated from all quarters of the Union, with one accord, through all ordinary vehicles of intelligence and opinion, in newspapers, and pamphlets, and circular letters. Never did a more general and longing expectation of a measure prevail. This was not counteracted, so far as he could learn, by any meeting, remonstrance, or opposition, whatsoever, except in one instance by a portion of his constituents—of whom, some had informed him subsequently to the signature of their remonstrance, that they had changed their opinion and been converted to a belief of the necessity of the act.

Taking, then, in connexion this great union of men and interest in favor of the measure, he was warranted in asserting that no application could be made to Congress more entitled to attention. Some uncertainty attended every estimate of their numbers. He had been assured that, on a former occasion, his computation was quite short of the sum total. From his best means of information, he now was induced to think that the number of insolvent debtors and their families in the United States, (of appalling magnitude in itself,) when added to that of their creditors, amounted to at least half a million of persons. After every allowance for erroneous data, it was doubtless very great—a number, beyond all controversy, equal to the population of several States in the Union, reckoned collectively. If the honorable gentleman from Alabama, (Mr. King,) who was on his right, and the other honorable gentleman from Tennessee, (Mr. Eaton,) on his left, were authorized to represent any particular grievance bearing down to the dust the entire population of their respective States, which it was competent to Congress to redress; with what importunate eloquence should we hear from them, until redress was obtained! Yet the population represented by the friends of the bill interested in its fate, greatly exceeded that of both those States; and, strictly speaking, had a more legitimate claim on the national Government for relief, than any State could ever set up, inasmuch as a universal calamity always outweighs a local grievance. Then, sir, wherefore shall not these persons be gratified in a reasonable request? What requisite is wanting to their claim? They combine numbers, wealth, misfortune, interest in the country, political rights, and a special right to a Constitutional protection, intended expressly for their circumstances and condition. So far as the debtors are concerned, their happiness or misery is involved.

With a wise Government the happiness of the citizens will always be regarded as its principal aim. The happiness of each class constitutes the welfare of all. The "*salus populi,*" which is the "*suprema lex,*" means not merely the safety of the people, but their felicity, for the promotion of which, only, is their safety of any value. You may have safety, and glory, and splendor, and what is commonly, though falsely, called national prosperity, in monarchies, and under despotic forms. But happiness and comfort belong to, or ought to emanate from, the depositories of a mild, paternal, popular authority, which feels the sympathies, consults the interests, listens to the petitions, and obviates the complaints, of all the various classes of the people. Some great defect of wisdom or attention, or of enlarged and liberal views, is always to be suspected in a Republic where any one great portion or interest in society is permitted to remain for years together in a state of discontent and misery, without a single public measure adopted for its relief.

Having thus stated his views of the number and pretensions of those for whose benefit, as creditors and debtors, the bill was intended, he said, he would offer a few remarks explanatory of the true intent of the Constitution, to which he had already alluded. He had, indeed, indulged a hope that the Senate had come to the consideration of one public bill, which might proceed without the embarrassment of Constitutional difficulties. But the objections of honorable gentlemen, if they do not proceed to the whole extent of a denial of the power of Congress to legislate upon the affair of bankruptcy, go far enough to render the power nugatory, and to show that it ought to remain a dead letter. Yet it is worthy of observation, that, in that number of the Federalist which treats of the Constitutional provisions concerning bankruptcy, (and which in the edition possessed by him was ascribed to Mr. Madison,) the fitness of vesting the whole power of making laws regulating that subject, is considered as so palpable and almost self-evident, that, for that express reason, the writer forbears to illustrate and maintain it by any arguments, resting its propriety upon the obvious dictates of common sense, and leaving it to the understanding of his readers. By the light of this common sense it will be easy to discern the reason, and, indeed, the necessity, of reposing this power in the General Government, as contracts are governed by the laws of the place or State where they are made. The tribunals either of the State or of the United States are competent to do complete justice to a creditor against a debtor, while he continues to be solvent. Each creditor acts for himself, and if, by any legal process, he can obtain payment of

his own demand when due, he has no further concern in the funds of his debtor, nor in any arrangements or negotiations between him and other creditors. But the relations of the creditor of the bankrupt towards him, and among each other, are entirely changed by his insolvency. He becomes by the very act, conformably to the principles of natural justice, a trustee of a common fund for the use of all his creditors, in a just proportion to their demands. They are in equity, and should be in law, converted into one party, and compelled to submit to an average loss, and to be precluded from all priorities and preferences in favor of one or more of their number. When they have become entirely possessed of such fund, it is still in furtherance of the same just and equitable principles that they should be restrained from further legal process, in every part of the nation, against the person or future earnings of the bankrupt. His creditors, however, may be citizens of different. States. He may have occasion to go, or to place his future earnings beyond the limits of his own State. If any of his debtors, residing in another State, should become bankrupt, it is just that he should be entitled to the same measure of assets which his creditors in such other State will be empowered to obtain from him. There is then no one State whose courts or laws could, by any possibility, make adjudications, or enforce regulations, embracing these objects and innumerable collateral circumstances and requisites attending a system of bankruptcy. This impossibility was realized by the framers of the Constitution. They knew that bankruptcy was incident to commerce at all times and in all places. They perceived that an uniform system only would be capable of securing equal and impartial justice to all the citizens, in every part of the nation, and of controlling the monstrous extravagancies and collisions of the State insolvent laws, which they knew were not. to be endured among the citizens of the same nation. Pursuant to these convictions, they clothed Congress with the entire power; and it is quite worthy of observation, that, while in all cases of controversy between citizens of the same State, (unless bankruptcy has happened,) the jurisdiction is left exclusively in the State courts, yet, in the event of bankruptcy, and in that event alone, an act of Congress regulating that subject would operate directly upon all controversies to which the bankrupt might be a party, (no matter with whom,) and consequently draw them into the sphere of the national judiciary. Well then might the author of the Federalist, just now cited, rely, upon the full and unequivocal concession of this power to Congress, and assume for it a character of fitness and expediency which required the support of no commentary whatever. And why, sir, should this most urgent and necessary measure be delayed—a measure which forms a distinguished feature in the code of every civilized commercial nation? If the time has not arrived for the experiment, in what disastrous juncture shall it be expected? In what country, and at what period, has commerce been exposed to the tremendous, sudden, and total vicissitudes which it has under-

297   HISTORY OF CONGRESS.   298

February, 1821.   *The Bankrupt Bill.*   SENATE.

gone in our own nation, and in our own time? When was ever known a spirit of enterprise so ardent, impelled by such prospects, rewarded by such success, tempted to such dangers, and suddenly checked by a reaction so overwhelming and unexpected? The whole world of commerce is shaken to its centre. And with us all the elements and means of commerce are disturbed and impaired. In many parts of the country an unsound currency has supplanted a valuable medium, and the depreciation of capital in land, produce, ships, and merchandise, is universal. No reliance can be placed on the foreign or domestic market, and the want of confidence has caused the precious metals to be withdrawn from circulation, and to be hoarded in the coffers of the rich.— Surely, then, (if ever,) you are now bound to extend a Constitutional relief to citizens who are suffering under these sad reverses, and to qualify them by active occupation to attempt to retrieve, not only their own affairs, but the general prosperity. Many, very many, of these persons are ready and anxious to resort to industrious callings, and to relieve the nation from the weight of their support. And it is certain that those who are not supported by their own industry and resources, must subsist, in some way or other, upon the labor or resources of others, and are a dead weight on society. They eat the bread of others, as was expressed by the honorable gentleman from Delaware, and are "*nati consumere fruges;*" the fruits which they consume belong to their creditors.

Sir, all these suggestions are again met by the old objection to the power of Congress to enact retrospective laws, and it would seem as if the distinction between retrospective and *ex post facto* laws, instead of being manifest and clear, was without reality.

He was then compelled to repeat, what was familiar to every civilian, that an *ex post facto* law created the crime which it punished, but a retrospective law had no necessary relation to crimes or offences. Every *ex post facto* law is retrospective, but the converse of the proposition, that every retrospective law is *ex post facto*, cannot be sustained. Of these, the first description is repugnant to the fundamental principles of humanity and justice, and is expressly prohibited by the Constitution. But retrospective laws, in their correct and general signification, are applicable to civil contracts, controversies, and concerns. Even these should be passed with great caution, and in cases only of indispensable necessity. Insolvent laws fall under this rigorous character of necessity. And, therefore, although they do effect what in ordinary cases would be a violation of private right by extinguishing the obligation of contracts, yet this power was undoubtedly vested in the several States, and exercised, under some modification, by most of them in this particular instance. Many other examples of this species might be adduced from the practice of the States, all of which could not be justified by this plea of necessity.

This right of regulating the affair of insolvency, so far as it was claimed and applied in acts impairing the obligation of contracts, was taken from the States and transferred to the General Government. The entire argument is comprehended in the following propositions: A bankrupt act, *ex vi termini*, may be retrospective. Congress has the exclusive power of framing such an act; and, of consequence, Congress may, and the several States may not, make acts in relation to bankruptcy, the operation of which may be retrospective. The present bill, he said, defined the various delinquencies which were intended to constitute acts of bankruptcy. These must be committed subsequently to the passing of the act. In regard to them, the law would be in no respect *ex post facto* or retrospective. But he would not disguise his expectation and intention that its operation should be retrospective upon all contracts existing at the time of its passing. So that, though the delinquency constituting a bankrupt should be posterior, the salutary influence of the provisions of the law should reach back to those children of misfortune who were not the less entitled to relief because their trouble was of long duration. A law which would not extend to antecedent cases would lose its principal value in his estimation. His object was to set free from their shackles all honest debtors of the classes designated in the act, who could bring themselves within its provisions, with the consent of the competent number of their creditors. Nothing short of this was worthy of effort.

The next objection (said Mr. O.) to the bill, urged as well by those who do, as those who do not entertain the Constitutional doubt, is the liability of the bankrupt system to the danger of frauds. To this it was easy to anticipate the general answer, that the objection was not peculiar to this bill, but lay at the bottom of all legislation upon nearly every subject. Laws against murder might give birth to frauds and perjuries also. Those against theft and the receiving of stolen goods were frequently the sources of fraudulent practices of various descriptions. The revenue laws of the country might be considered as a fertile soil, in which frauds were produced in perennial crops. The great volume of balances not accounted for by the receivers of public moneys (which, being too huge to lie upon his table, he had been obliged to place under it) would furnish materials for a history of all sorts of frauds, without including the accounts of individuals whose balances were merely apparent, and those who had been prevented by inevitable casualties from closing their accounts. It was no objection to a law, that it was susceptible of fraudulent evasion; and, though nothing more certainly roused the jealousies and prejudices of honest minds than the cry of fraud, yet it was an ingredient dyed in the wool, and spun in the yarn, and woven into the texture, of all the laws to be found in the statute book. But, in order to show the peculiar exposure of a bankrupt system to the evasions of fraud, resort is had to the experience of foreign nations, and of our own country.

The honorable gentleman from Pennsylvania has occupied nearly a day in reading passages from minutes of evidence taken before a committee of the British House of Commons, appointed to inquire into the operation and defects of their laws; and the honorable gentleman from Virginia has adopted the same course, though not to the same extent. They have cited detached opinions, and partial extracts bearing upon the abuses and imperfections of the system, and those only. Sir, to all examples of this species, it would seem sufficient to reply, that this same committee, upon a full view of all this evidence, made a report of certain improvements of which they thought the system to be susceptible, but were far enough from recommending its abolition; and the British Parliament, swayed no doubt in this instance by the prevalent sentiments of the mercantile interest, have not yet adopted even those improvements. It was then, he believed, a novelty in legislation, that the evidence taken before the committee of a foreign legislature should be adduced in the Congress of the United States, to the end of inducing them to come to a result precisely the reverse of that which had been attained by the constituent body to whom the report of such committee had been made. This was inviting the Senate to do, upon very limited information, what the Parliament had refused to do with a full knowledge of the subject. The conclusion was undeniable that Parliament, after long experience, deemed an adherence to the system with all its imperfections to be preferable to its renunciation, and considered it, on the whole, better than any substitute that had been matured. He had for some time been possessed of a copy of the documents introduced by those gentlemen. They had been sent to him by an English merchant, eminently conversant with the course of trade between this country and England, and with the operations of the bankrupt system there, and our mongrel systems here, at his request, to furnish him with materials for the defence of the act, and accompanied by a letter strongly expressive of his assurance that it would elevate the credit of the American merchants, and of the hope that this Government would perceive the utility and necessity of the English bankrupt act, or something like it.

Mr. O. then proceeded to a brief examination of the contents of some of the depositions taken before the British committee, and in particular to that of Sir Samuel Romilly, (who, as he contended, was the best informed and most competent judge of the whole merits of the system,) and repeated and enforced the assertion, that it was not the aim of those intelligent persons to abolish, but to reform the bankrupt system. That the principal defect of that system, as has been stated by his honorable friend from Delaware, was its revolting severity, which, being capital, prevented the punishment of the fraudulent bankrupt; and that a careful comparison of the entire testimony of the witnesses before the committee of Parliament with this bill, (which he should not now undertake,) would demonstrate that many of the minor defects were obviated. He entirely dissented from the doctrine of the honorable gentleman from Virginia, maintaining that France, Holland, and other commercial nations, had rejected the bankrupt

system, as a scourge and a curse; and he had yet to learn that any commercial nation had persevered in doing without one. So much, sir, said he, for the general objection of fraud, and the report of the committee of the House of Commons. Let us approach nearer to particulars.

It would be admitted that the sources of fraud, so far as the bankrupt was concerned, were twofold—concerted acts of bankruptcy and concealment of property. As to the first, he had no doubt that if the bill should pass, it would give rise to manifold acts of concerted bankruptcy, and he was ready to declare his persuasion, that such a concert was not immoral nor injurious in its own nature. It became so only when accompanied by unjust priorities, given to favored creditors, or by an exhibition of fictitious debts, to facilitate the obtaining of a certificate. If a man were in failing circumstances, and honestly disposed to surrender his effects for the use of all his creditors, an agreement between him and one or two bona fide creditors to do, for that purpose, an act which, if done without such agreement, might be (against his consent) converted to the same purpose, was in itself certainly neither a shame or a sin. Sometimes it would be wickedly and fraudulently perverted. Sometimes the best systems will be abused; but the act was intended to guard against malpractices, undue preference, and fictitious claims—and much would depend upon the fidelity of those employed to give it effect. In any event, relief would be given to thousands of honest and suffering victims to misfortune, and the maxim would be found substantially applicable, that it is better for the guilty to escape than the innocent to be punished—especially as the creditors of the ill-disposed will get nothing whether they become bankrupt or not—and consequently sustain no real injury, even when fraud takes place.

With respect to the danger of fraud from the concealment of effects, it was hardly possible to imagine that any system could be more prolific of abuses of that description than already prevail under the various and conflicting laws of the different States. Frauds in all shapes and varieties that human ingenuity could devise were perpetrated in every State, and under such disguise as defied the scrutiny of State laws, or State courts. These had furnished topics for eloquence on many former occasions, and their frequency was familiar to every individual whose attention had been called to the subject. The absurdities and inconveniences incident to the collision of State laws, would suffice to furnish a theme that might well occupy more time than was reasonably to be employed by any one member who attempted merely to present a general view of the question. But he would refer those who were inclined to bestow upon that part of the subject a special attention to a most luminous and learned argument in the case of Sturgis and Crowninshield, by an honorable member of the Senate, (Mr. HUNTER,) which might justly be regarded as a model of classical taste and forensic eloquence.

That argument, taken in connexion with the

decision of the case, whereby it appears that the right of the States to establish systems of bankruptcy is expressly disaffirmed, demonstrates the absolute necessity of a national system for the more effectual prevention of fraudulent concealments, and defeating the contrivances and combinations to cheat creditors, for which the State laws, in truth, at present operate as a bounty and strong inducement. The real difference in the account of fraudulent practices with and without the proposed system, would be found principally to consist in this, namely, that a dishonest debtor, in order to avail himself of the advantage of the act, might be guilty of a single prevarication, or make, once for all, a fraudulent arrangement to cover his property, exposed, however, to the risk of detection by the vigilance of those who would be interested to unmask him; but, without this system, he would find the greatest motives for t.king up fraud as a profession for life; it becomes his only resource and vocation, and, by the aid of friends, he can pursue it with impunity. Nay, in one event, those who are tempted to be guilty of one deviation from the path of rectitude, may be left to return to it, and make some amends to society, by a confidence that the fruits of their future industry will be their own; while, in the other event, they will proceed in their career of fraud, consuming the property of their creditors, and finding in the perpetual thraldom to which they are doomed, apologies and salvos for honor and conscience, until all sense of them is extinct.

If these suggestions are correct, a bankrupt act, under its least favorable aspect, will be auspicious to the public morals in the same proportion that occasional frailties, with a chance of reformation, are preferable to habitual and unrepented vice. It was, however, not only to the frauds of the bankrupt, but the expense, delay, and detention of money by assignees, that objections had been made. He did not remember that, under the experiment of the former act, grievances of this kind had been the subject of complaint. Without doubt assignees, like other agents, were sometimes guilty of mismanagement. Here again the comparison of evils must be taken into view, as in all human institutions, and the choice lay between leaving all in the hands of a debtor or a favored creditor, from whom nothing could be obtained, or placing all in the hands of an assignee, chosen by the creditors, and accountable at their pleasure.

He would next advert to the very formidable objection pressed with so much earnestness by the honorable gentleman from Virginia, and which, being indeed the basis of his argument, was entitled to a distinct consideration. He, Mr. B., alluded to the experience of this nation under the former act. It was taken for granted, that this act, after a fair trial, had been condemned by the deliberate sense of the nation, and repealed at the solicitation of those by whose procurement it had been enacted; that it was a disgraced and pernicious system, and held in universal reprobation. But this view of that subject was much too strong. The apparent disfavor into which that system fell, was not a true test of the sober opinion of the

mercantile community at that time. In the first stage of its operation, it was calculated to excite great attention and animadversion. Great numbers of individuals were seen rushing towards this new avenue to freedom at the same time. The process of deliverance was generally rapid and easy to all who undertook it. Very many were seen emerging from an obscurity in which they had pined until their misfortunes, and sometimes their names, had been forgotten. Some appeared whose characters and conduct were held in no estimation, and others whose circumstances were not suspected. How was it possible that a sight of all the insolvent merchants and traders in a great nation, suddenly brought together in public array, should not produce a great sensation among friends and enemies? From the nature of the case, they must have had both enemies and friends: by enemies, he meant persons hostile to their discharge. Unless two-thirds of the creditors were friendly, they could not have obtained their certificate. Unless some individuals were averse, they would have had no occasion to adopt this mode of obtaining their deliverance. Among these adverse creditors of course would be found much of vexation and disappointment, and of open and clamorous censure and crimination of the debtor's contract, and justification of their own rigor and opposition. Thus the consenting creditors, feeling no interest in a concern which they had abandoned, would no longer make it an object of thought or conversation, while the dissenting creditors would be stimulated, by the irritation of their feelings, to make loud and constant complaints against the operation of the act, and to become active in their endeavors to effect its repeal.

Under these circumstances, the great mass of insolvent persons, having accomplished their object, could not be expected to unite their efforts in any strenuous opposition to such repeal. The still greater number of assenting creditors would be equally passive, as their bad debts were now spunged, and their motives for an active interference were exceedingly diminished. So that the old set was thus left in the hands of its zealous and bitter opponents, and fell, without a struggle, under the odium of one part of the mercantile community, and indifference of the other.

He would not deny, however, that there were to be found everywhere many highly respectable and impartial merchants who were originally opposed in principle to the old system, and who were for a time confirmed in their prejudices by observation of its effects. But, so far as his information extended, those very individuals had generally become the friends and advocates of another trial. The tables of both Houses had been covered with petitions from merchants and traders of unsuspected credit, from every quarter. He knew only of the single remonstrance against it to which he had before alluded. The petition in its favor, from Boston and its vicinity, was first signed by a gentleman (Mr. Gray) who had long been ranked as the first merchant and ship-owner in the United States, and by far the greater number of eminent merchants and established traders in his part of the country. Indeed, he held in his hand a letter that day received from an association of persons of known worth and credit, in the opulent town of Salem, distinguished for commerce and enterprise, and the sound judgment of its citizens, zealously urging upon him to lend his feeble aid to the good work. The sentiment in its favor is indeed universal; consequently, the honorable gentlemen could take nothing by his argument from experience, for experience was in its favor.

He would not allow that a single experiment deserved to be dignified with the name of experience, which he admitted to be the best and only sure guide in the political as well as the physical world. Experience was the result of an impression made by a succession of events in a course of time, and of circumstances and of benefits and evils to be weighed off and balanced against each other. And, as the opinion of the mercantile community had at length settled down in favor of a bankrupt act, and surmounted and laid aside their own objections after a fair trial, both with one and without one, it was now strictly correct to say that experience was not against it, but proclaimed with a loud voice and final decision in its favor.

But, if any doubt remains of the beneficial effect, even of the old act, with all its imperfections and all the malversation ascribed to it, let those who entertain it take an enlarged view of its consequences. Has society, on the whole, lost or gained by the extinguishment of the debts of the thousand who availed themselves of its benefits? Were not the means and fruits of industry increased by restoring them from the idle to the laborious and productive classes? Has any great inconvenience or public calamity grown out of the system? Would it be advantageous to their creditors, or in any respect desirable to replace them in their late state of embarrassment, were this practicable? These are the inquiries to be made by statesmen. Let them ask, what on the great scale is for the good of the nation? and not whether here and there will be found cheats, and swindlers, and fraudulent bankrupts; nor whether, in some instances, cunning devices and sham bankruptcies will not be carried on under the umbrage of the proposed bill. Objections, he regretted to say, were again presented in behalf of the landed interest; indeed, he might say, in behalf of all those who were not expressly comprehended within the purview of the statute. Nothing could exceed the embarrassment which had always been made to involve the friends to this measure. When they attempted to frame the bill in the words of the former act, an outcry was raised against the generality of its provisions. All classes, it was then said, were to be subjected to this odious law, in order to please the merchants; when they offered a bill embracing the yeomanry, and other trades and professions, it was still less graciously received. It was stigmatized, then, not as a bill of privilege, but of penalties, not at all desired by any but merchants, and which, if they wanted it, should be confined to their own order. Twenty years ago its friends were placed in this dilemma;

it is now the same. A bankrupt act was not, in ordinary cases, adapted to the circumstances of farmers and planters; but, if honorable gentlemen would admit that this part of their constituents were ready for it, and if the comprising of them in the bill would reconcile them to it, he was ready at a word, for his part, to say, put them all in. But he knew that gentlemen would consent to no such thing, and that farmers would regard a bill of universal application to the landed interest as a Pandora's box, and not as a boon. He therefore implored them not to preclude others from a benefit which they did not want for themselves, nor to urge objections which they did not wish to remove, nor to suggest, as amendments, provisions which they would not agree to adopt by the friends of the bill. Although planters and farmers were not made subject to the penalties of the act, they would partake of all its benefits, in their capacity of creditors, equally with merchants, and certainly would be placed upon a footing of greater security than they at present stand. They would be dispensed from all trouble, vigilance, and anxiety, to prevent the near and favorite creditors of a failing person from availing themselves of their better means of information and knowledge of his circumstances, and securing themselves to his exclusion. At present a country creditor had little chance of saving any part of a debt from the property of a failing debtor in a seaport or trading town. He was commonly at a distance, and precluded from all opportunity of inspecting his course of business and deviation from punctuality. He depended for his advices on those who were sometimes interested to deceive him, and when, in the event of failure, he came to look after his debt, he found every shilling taken by the nearest creditors. But, on the contrary, under this act, the vigilance and attempts at security of the most zealous and best informed of the creditors must be exerted for the benefit of the planter and farmer, in common with their own. He appropriates to his own use the advantages of their agency, without additional expense or trouble. A favorite creditor can do nothing fairly for himself which does not redound to the benefit of all, and unfair proceedings are more liable to detection and abrogation by remedies growing out of the statute, and pursued by the united efforts of all the creditors, than by the solitary zeal of a single person.

Sir, said he, these are some of the general and prominent principles of a measure recommended to the attention of the Senate by the most urgent calls of humanity and justice, by the wants and sufferings of thousands who are deprived, by the construction given to the Constitution by the Supreme Court, of every other hope and resource. He would not exhaust the patience of his hearers by even touching upon the details of the bill, for which, if it was sustained, ample opportunity would be afforded, not only to himself, but friends who would do them more justice. He relied upon a magnanimous spirit of liberality, to extend aid and protection to every class of people without favor or partial affection. They had just passed an act for the relief of public debtors—an act of unprecedented generosity, and passed with unexampled harmony. Reciprocity of legislation, among the various interests of the country, ought not to be introduced into legislative bodies as the sole motive for the support of a measure. But without reciprocal candor and good will among the representatives of those various interests, and a just attention and respect to mutual circumstances and necessities, while every thing would be conceded to a predominating interest, all other and minor claims would be sacrificed.

In this view, it was the duty of those whose constituents were relieved by the act just passed for the ease of the purchasers of public lands, to look abroad upon the exigencies of their fellow-citizens. The one had experienced the parental kindness of Government, in anticipating their day of trouble, and been delivered from all fear of the future, while the last are groaning under a weight of realized and long continued affliction, with a prospect of interminable wretchedness, without your assistance. It was impossible to remain blind to the least evil consequences of a rejection of the bill. No man can be insensible to the manifold mischiefs which follow in the train of insolvency and pauperism. These will be infinitely multiplied by the general state of embarrassment pervading the country, and indeed their natural tendency is to multiply themselves. A scene will be presented, in this free country, which will be without parallel—thousands of slaves for life, and each with a number of masters; and these slaves our brethren and fellow-citizens, and doomed to this condition as a penalty for misfortune! And, if this be the least, what will be the greatest evil arising from this state of things? What may be expected when their numbers shall be increased, and they seriously commence a system of measures for obtaining that relief, by their active efforts, which is denied to their supplications? What could be more appalling and inauspicious to men of property, and to Government itself, than to see organized, self-created corporations of debtors, embodied in all the great commercial towns, and formed into one vast combination, to influence elections! What state of things more dangerous than an universal alliance among all classes of debtors, public and private, to effectuate their own freedom, through the instrumentality of persons chosen into Congress, with no other recommendation! How should you be pleased, sir, to see the great commercial States represented in Senate by delegates from an established order of insolvent debtors?

He wished not to enlarge upon the topic, nor to assign reasons, satisfactory to his own mind, for believing that these hints were not merely visionary. He earnestly implored gentlemen not to drive these persons to despair, by again postponing their petitions. No language could describe the longing expectations, and eager hopes, and distressing fears, of the vast population that are awaiting your decision. Upon it depends the fate of fathers and of families; and the notice of further delay will overwhelm them with sorrows too heavy to be borne. He therefore trusted that

the Senate would not consent longer to protract this state of disquietude, which it was so easy to relieve, and that the motion to postpone would be rejected.

THURSDAY, February 8.

The PRESIDENT communicated a report of the Secretary of War, exhibiting the names of the clerks employed in the several offices attached to the Department of War, and the sums paid to each; and the report was read.

Mr. RUGGLES presented the petition of David Chambers, of Ohio, praying to be allowed, in payment for any public land he may enter, a credit for three hundred and twenty dollars, being the first payment made by him for a quarter section of land, which has become forfeited to the United States; and the petition was read, and referred to the Committee on Public Lands.

Mr. WILLIAMS, of Mississippi, obtained leave to bring in a bill to establish a new land office in the State of Mississippi, and for the better regulation of certain land districts in the States of Alabama and Mississippi; and the bill was read, and passed to a second reading.

Mr. PARROTT, from the Committee on Naval Affairs, to whom was referred the petition of William Vaughan, reported a bill to reward Lieutenant Gregory, his officers and companions; and the bill was read, and passed to a second reading.

The bill concerning the process of execution issuing from the sixth circuit court of the United States, for the district of Georgia, was read the second time.

Mr. HOLMES, of Maine, from the Committee on Finance, made reports unfavorable to the petitions of James Graham, of Joshua Aubin, and of William Whitehead.

BANKRUPT BILL.

The Senate resumed the consideration of the bill to establish an uniform system of bankruptcy.

Mr. MILLS, of Massachusetts, delivered his views at large, and at great length, in support of the bill; and

Mr. HOLMES, of Maine, addressed the Senate as follows:

Mr. President, when a claim is urged with ability and perseverance, and, when, moreover, it is presented in the name of humanity, whoever opposes it speaks with reluctance, and is heard with impatience. And if reliance is to be placed on the prophetic suggestions of the two honorable members from Massachusetts, there may be some danger in opposing a bankrupt system. According to these gentlemen, such is the power, influence, and combination of the applicants and their connexions, that unless we prudently yield all they ask they will conspire, not only to control your elections and embarrass your Government, but even to dissolve the Union.

Sir, it has more than once been my misfortune to be obliged to oppose the wishes and interests of some of my best and dearest friends. I do it with extreme regret. But I have established my maxim: Let a man deliberate well, settle the principle with himself, and then march up to his duty, and if he falls a victim to popular excitement, he has the consolation that he falls for his country.

I know very well the unwillingness of gentlemen to examine a bill consisting of sixty-four sections and fifty-three folio pages. You take up this volume with a view of particular examination, and every member is chilled to his fingers' ends. The able and eloquent advocates of this system perceive this, and very adroitly profit by it. Finding that sober reason has no relish for this subject, they appeal to the passions, and, displaying their brilliant parts, so dazzle our eyes that we can neither seek after the truth, nor distinguish it when we have found it. The honorable member from Massachusetts who first addressed you, (Mr. OTIS,) seems determined that our feelings shall get the better of our understandings. Quitting the matter and merits he leads you to the prison, and "through the twilight of its grated door" presents you a captive, "half wasted away with long expectation and confinement," and you witness "the sickness of the heart which arises from hope deferred." You see him "pale and feverish; for twenty years the western breeze has not once fanned his blood; he has seen no sun nor moon in all that time, nor has the voice of friend, of kinsman, breathed through his lattice." He is seated on a "little straw, which is alternately his chair and bed; a little calendar of small sticks is laid by his side, notched all over with the dismal days and nights he has lingered there. He has one of those little sticks in his hand, and with a rusty nail is etching another day of misery to add to the heap." "As you darken the little light he has, he lifts up a hopeless eye towards the door, casts it down, shakes his head, and goes on with his work of affliction." Your sensibility is roused, and breathless you wait for the proposed relief. The orator pauses; here, he exclaims, here, pointing to the bill, is the remedy! This is the physician who can bind up his wounds, and apply the balm of comfort to his aching heart. This is the apostle of liberty. He unlocks the prison door, the captive comes to the light. You see him restored to his family, witness the ecstatic embrace, the convulsive sob, the agony of joy. In a moment, and as rapid as lightning, the sun of prosperity bursts upon him, the bounties of Providence are poured into his bosom, he is surrounded with ease and affluence, wife, children, and friends! Who can descend from these regions of fancy to grope and grovel through fifty-three folio pages of verbose and barbarous statute law?

But, sir, as much reason as there is to despair of a patient examination of the subject, I shall proceed, without preamble or apology, to state my objections to the bill, and endeavor to maintain the following propositions:

1. To regulate the relation between debtor and creditor is the peculiar province of the State government.

2. A bankrupt system is opposed to the genius of our Government and interests of the people.

3. This bill is particularly objectionable, as its operations would be expensive, unequal and unjust.

The power to establish uniform laws on the subject of bankruptcies is, with one exception, the only municipal power granted to the Congress of the United States. The exterior concerns of the United States and the relations between the several States were very properly confided to Congress. The local interests of the people of a State, and their relations with each other, were as properly reserved to themselves. This rule of distinction ought to have been observed without exception, and the peculiar condition of the people at the time the Constitution was framed, is the only apology for granting this State power to the Congress of the United States. At that time public and private credit were low, the Government was without funds or credit, and private confidence was nearly destroyed. The best funds could be purchased at a discount of fifty per cent.

To restore public credit Congress may levy and collect taxes; to restore private confidence they may regulate commerce. Should these means fail, and the people be oppressed with debts and unable to pay, as a last resort, they may exercise this municipal power, and pass uniform laws on the subject of bankruptcies. So far is this grant of power from making it imperative on Congress to exercise it, that it is only to be resorted to in the extremest necessity. If all the powers granted to Congress were to exclude a discretion on the propriety of their exercise, we must then have constant direct taxes and perpetual wars.

I had been taught to believe that one of the greatest excellencies of our Government consisted in the adaptation of local legislation to the peculiar wants, necessities, and interests of the people. Congress will find enough to do in regulating the foreign concerns of the States, and in passing and executing laws for this purpose, adapted to the condition of twenty-four, and, perhaps, thirty different sovereignties. All these local authorities have different manners, habits, and institutions. Their codes of laws on the subject of contract vary as they are old or young, commercial or agricultural, or as exigencies may require.

Now, while the powers of creating, executing, and discharging contracts belong to the several States so long as the parties remain solvent, it seems absurd to suppose that, after a man fails, his affairs may be transferred to, and be regulated and disposed of by, the United States, with any prospect of a correct result.

The differences in the State laws, so much complained of, are far from being a blemish in our institutions. Every State understands its interest, and will take care that its laws shall be calculated to promote it. To invite an efficient population; to encourage an influx of active capital, and to rival a neighbouring State, will be the objects of the local legislatures. The differences, therefore, in the institutions of States, are a constant source of instruction and competition. The citizen of one State, in giving credit to one of another, very well understands that he must enforce his demand according to the laws of the State where his debtor lives. There, the laws, it is to be presumed, will be wise, and not so much calculated to tempt runaway debtors, always a nuisance, as to invite creditors and capitalists, whose wealth and energies will promote the interest of the State.

The difference, too, as to the frequency and magnitude of frauds, and the kind and degree of punishment arising out of the manners, habits, and employments of the people, would prevent the operation of any general law, but with partiality and injustice.

This system is urged because the States have attempted and failed. And how does this reason bear upon the subject? If the States have tried and failed, what better prospect of success have you? You have learned nothing from experience. The State of Pennsylvania had a bankrupt system so long ago as 1785. That State is distinguished for its civilians and statesmen. It is the land of Penn and Franklin. The people are proverbial for their simplicity and unvarnished morality. And, yet, with all these talents and virtues, and this experience, they have totally failed to devise any practicable way to discharge a debtor on delivering up his effects. New York has been equally unfortunate; a State great, commercial, enterprising, and ambitious; a State which has furnished men who would have honored Rome in her proudest days. But even New York, with all these "appliances and means to boot," has failed, totally failed, in a bankrupt system. Connecticut, too, which claims more morality and religion than any other people ever did or will possess, has met with no better success; and other States, equally respectable, have been equally unfortunate. Yet, in other branches of jurisprudence, they are all pre-eminent. Political and civil rights are well defined; fraud and oppression prevented, and crimes punished. The judiciary of some of them would not suffer by a comparison with that of the United States or any other country. And, yet, a law to divide an insolvent's effects and discharge him from his debts, can be no where equitably enforced. Sir, the reason is in the system itself. You increase the temptation to fraud, and attempt to prevent it by laws cruel in their character, unequal in their operation, and uncertain in their application. It savors of vanity to expect that, after so many unsuccessful attempts by the local authorities, with power to adapt their laws to their condition, we could invent a system that would remove all former obstacles, and equitably apply to so many different interests. Have you been, hitherto, very successful in enforcing laws against strong temptation? Let experience, during the non-intercourse, and embargo, and war, answer the question.

This grant of power to the United States is not exclusive. No federal power is exclusive, unless by expression or necessary implication. This grant is not expressly prohibited to the States, nor is it prohibited by necessary implication. Where Congress has power to pass uniform laws, in the exercise of this power, they can control the State laws on the same subject. They can make uniform rules of naturalization, a uniform standard of weights and measures, and uniform laws on the subject of bankruptcies. The rules, standard, and laws, when established, will control or modify every State law that stands in the way of their uniformity. But, until Congress shall have legislated on the subject, these powers remain dormant and inoperative, and the States can exercise them. They can neither be said to be exclusive nor concurrent, but alternate. When those of the United States are exercised, those of the States must be suspended; and, when the former are suspended, the latter revive. This was yielded by the court in the celebrated case of Sturgis and Crowninshield; and, although I am not disposed to give implicit confidence to those decisions of the court which settle the limits of federal powers, yet, as this is an admission against the extension of those powers, I would regard it as the testimony of a witness who swears against his interest.

In the case to which I have just alluded, the court decide that a State insolvent law, which discharges a debtor from a debt existing at the time the law was passed is void, as being repugnant to that clause of the Constitution of the United States which prohibits a State from passing any law "impairing the obligation of contracts." Although I do not consider myself as a legislator, bound by judicial exposition of the Constitution of the United States, and am by no means satisfied that this prohibition upon a State was ever intended to extend to insolvent laws, still, as it is not necessary to my purpose, I am not disposed to contest the doctrine. A State law then, discharging a debtor from an existing contract, is unconstitutional. This decision creates little or no necessity for us to legislate on the subject. Those States which have found it for their interest, have long since enacted such laws. In some of them these have existed thirty, and in none less than twelve or fifteen years. There are few contracts existing at the time of their passage, which could now be enforced against their statutes of limitations.

The States which have made no provision for a debtor's discharge, have deemed it inexpedient, and, consequently, have no wish that you should exercise a power which, until very lately, they had no doubt they possessed, and which they would have exercised had the interest of their people required it.

But, if a State law discharging a debtor from an existing debt, is void, for the single reason that it impairs the obligation of a contract, what right have you to pass such a law? Have you a power given in the Constitution of the United States to pass a law so odious and tyrannical? Will it be said that, because a State is expressly prohibited, and the United States are not, this power is consequently granted? I have not yet come to the conclusion, that every thing not prohibited in the Constitution is granted. The converse of the proposition is true, that whatever is not expressly granted, is prohibited. Do you suppose, sir, that, had there been no prohibition, Congress could have passed a bill of attainder or *ex post facto* law? Or, because these are prohibited, and the prohibition to impair the obligation of contracts omitted, that Congress now possesses this power? If so, we might make a grant of land to-day to A, and to-morrow rescind it, and grant to B, and on through the alphabet, so long as we could find any one foolish enough to buy.

If the power is expressly granted, it is in the clause which authorizes us to pass uniform laws on the subject of bankruptcies. This power is, like every other to pass laws, prospective, but not to operate on acts already done. Congress can define and punish piracies, regulate commerce, and punish counterfeits; but the laws for these and all other purposes must be prospective. We have power to establish a system of bankruptcy which shall operate to discharge future contracts, but never to violate the faith of those existing at the times it was made. It is not essential, or incidental, to the exercise of this power more than any other, that it should be retrospective; and, as that to impair or violate existing contracts, is odious and tyrannical, it cannot be exercised by the Congress of the United States. It is then manifest that you have no more power than a State to pass a retrospective bankrupt law.

The right of a State to pass a prospective bankrupt law has been no where exclusively surrendered. Here I am aware that I shall be met by another decision of the Supreme Court, which goes to clip the wings of States even in this particular, and to establish a principle which disrobes them of almost their last attribute of sovereignty. In the case of McMillan vs. McNeil, from the State of Louisiana, in a very defective and clumsy report, the court are made to say, that, whether the contract existed at the time the law was enacted, or not, it made no difference. There must have been some mistake, for I deem it impossible that the court could ever have gone this length. But, whether they made this decision or not, it is one to which I will never subscribe, or make the basis of legislation, and against which I will forever most solemnly protest.

If this decision is to prevail, it indeed becomes Congress, and especially this Senate, the guardians of State rights, to look about them, gather up the fragments, and see if those that remain are worth preserving.

The grand objects of the framers of the Constitution were " to form a more perfect union, establish justice, insure domestic tranquillity, provide for the common defence, promote the general welfare, and secure the blessings of liberty to ourselves and our posterity." To carry into effect these benevolent and patriotic purposes, they established the Federal Constitution, granting certain defined and specified powers; and, lest the States, in their sovereign capacity, should interpose to prevent the accomplishment of these purposes, certain restraints and prohibitions were imposed on them. That "a more perfect union," may be formed, the States were prohibited to enter into " any treaty, alliance, or confederacy." That the " peace, welfare, or defence" of the Union may not be impaired, they could not "declare war;" nor do acts leading to, or provoking it. That " justice" should be "established," they are to "pass no bill of attainder, *ex post facto* law, nor

law impairing the obligation of contracts ;" all of which are retrospective, and therefore unjust.

Sir, what is the obligation of a contract ? It is the law itself, in existence at the time the contract is made, and forms the basis of the contract. Without a law a contract could have no obligation. It is the tie which binds the parties, the power of enforcing a contract, which is its obligation. There may be contracts without obligation, that is, without a law to enforce them. It is preposterous and absurd to speak of a present obligation of a future contract. You may as well speak of a quality without supposing a substance. You may as well imagine the roundness of a ball, the smoothness of a surface, or the beauty of a woman, without the existence of those objects, as an obligation without a contract.

There can be no obligation until the contract is made, and then the existing law becomes its obligation, its basis, and the rule by which it is to be enforced and discharged. Take the clause in connexion, and its object admits of no doubt. It was to prevent retrospective laws. You shall "pass no law of attainder." This is a legislative conviction and judgment, and thereby retrospective. Nor any " *ex post facto* law." This makes that act criminal which was innocent when done, or increases its criminality. It is, therefore, retrospective. Nor a " law impairing the obligation of a contract." This makes that contract bad which was good at its creation, and is therefore retrospective. But break down this line of distinction, and where will this prohibition end? It is essential to every well-regulated community that it should have power to control parties in the formation and execution of their contracts. To deny to some an obligation or law to enforce their contracts is essential to the morals of the State; to prescribe to others the rule by which they are to be created is essential to its commerce; and to define the terms and condition of their discharge is no less important to prevent injustice and oppression. A law making gambling, wagering, or usurious contracts, void, would, so far as it should operate upon existing contracts, legally created, be repugnant to this clause in the Constitution. But no one, I presume, has yet pretended that such a law might not operate on all contracts thereafter made. A law which makes certain contracts voidable, by a less or different consideration from that agreed on, or on a contingency not stipulated, if retrospective, would be void, but not otherwise. That a State can prescribe that, if it is agreed to pay above a certain interest, the party promising may discharge himself by paying a lesser sum, has hitherto, I believe, admitted of no doubt. The same may be said of those laws which extend an equity of redemption, or relieve from the penalty of a bond.

The plain reason of the distinction is this: The law existing at the time the contract is made is the known rule which is to govern its discharge. Why, then, I ask, if an insolvent law exists at the time the contract is made, by which the parties understand that, in case of insolvency, and a disclosure, and dividend, the contract is to be discharged, is it not a perfectly fair transaction, and completely within the scope of ordinary legislation? If this prohibition extends to this case, it must unquestionably extend to that of usury, and all the others which I have mentioned. This extension of this prohibition is unwarrantable and alarming. It is usurping the powers of the States, and robbing them of nearly their last vestige of sovereignty. And, sir, allow me to say, that the pretension is novel and unprecedented. In a case decided not long after the adoption of the Federal Constitution, the distinction for which I contend is clearly recognised. Judge Wilson, who was one of the Convention, regrets that this prohibition did not " extend to all retrospective laws," admitting that it was limited exclusively to such. The expression was probably borrowed from the celebrated ordinance of 1787. And, it is remarkable that the prohibition there is against an interference with contracts, &c., " previously formed." Sir, the expression itself, the reason, the precedents, and the policy, are all against the construction of the court.

I know it is the fashionable doctrine, that the court are exclusive expositors of the Constitution, and that, by our oath, to support it, we swallow every exposition, however absurd. But I never did, and I never will, swear to support a glaring absurdity, nor dangerous usurpation. *Est boni judicis ampliare jurisdictionem,* is a maxim very well understood by judges. With this maxim, the right of exclusive exposition, and this broad construction of prohibitions upon States, judges of less integrity and more ambition might, at some future period, trample on the States, and annihilate their sovereignty. Look at the constant encroachments of the Federal on the State Governments, the executive, legislative, and judicial pretensions, and, I ask, how long, at this rate, will your local authorities have an existence? Sir, such is the progress of power; it is like our progress in vice, and we do that at last, with firmness of nerve, from which we should shrink with horror at the commencement of our course. The advance of power is not only *onward* but *upward.* " With an eye that never winks, and a wing that never tires," it soars above. Casting all human rights beneath its feet, its course is among the stars. Nor is it satisfied until it can scale heaven, and seize upon the throne of Almighty God. Let the gentleman from Virginia, who sits by me, the peculiar guardian of State rights, now invoke them. It must be like the invocation of departed spirits. He may call them from the vasty deep, but they wont come. He may speak of them, and speak to them, but it must be, not of something that *is,* but of something that *was:* " Like the memory of joys that are past, pleasant and painful to the soul." Like the recollection of some dear departed friend who visits you in visions, and embraces you in dreams. You awake—the vision is gone; the endearing phantom is escaped from your arms.

But, I beg pardon, my province is to reason, not to declaim. I trust I have proved, as I intended, that a State has still a power to pass a prospective bankrupt law, and you have no more.

But, suppose the power to be exclusive and unlimited in the Congress of the United States, I still maintain that its exercise is inexpedient, and will be pernicious. The individual distress which gentlemen so feelingly describe is unquestionably magnified. I wish they could all be presented here, and each individual case could be scrutinized and exposed. I would first select all who were fraudulently secreting their property to be used after their discharge, and arrange them by themselves. As another class, I would then take the smugglers and swindlers, who, in attempting to defraud the Government or individuals, had failed of success. The next class should be composed of spendthrifts and prodigals, who had long been knowingly wasting money, not their own, but which had been intrusted to their use, by the confidence and charity of friends. And, last, but not least, all those who, too indolent, and too proud, or too impatient to seek a living by honest industry, had undertaken a business which they did not understand, and had experienced the fate which usually awaits every unskilful pretender. Then, from the prudent, skilful, honest, and unfortunate trader, deduct all those whose creditors are disposed to grant them relief, and I ask, will not your army of insolvents be much diminished? But, would you not pardon the vicious and imprudent, and relieve them? Yes, could I do this without encouraging them to vice and extravagance again, and tempting others, by witnessing their success, to imitate their example. I scarcely know on what ground to meet the honorable gentleman. At one time, it is compassion for the debtor that absorbs all other considerations; at another, the system is a punishment upon the debtor, and is demanded only by the creditor. The honorable gentleman from Delaware (Mr. Van Dyke) has probably taken the only fair and rational ground; that it is intended for the relief and benefit of both. Assuming this as his basis, it must follow, that a bankrupt system is to increase the confidence and security of the creditor. When his money is loaned, he is better satisfied to be sure of a part, under this act, than to risk the whole under the existing laws. The lender is safer, and will be encouraged to lend. If the borrower fails, he is sure to be discharged from his debt; and, if he succeeds, he may make his fortune. He, then, will be encouraged to borrow. The facility of credit, then, is doubly increased. It then resolves itself into a question of national policy; is it expedient or prudent, at this time, to encourage people in running in debt?

There is scarcely a country in the world where enterprise is so much encouraged. With a Government imposing no restraints, and a population intelligent, enterprising, and avaricious, the spirit of speculation has become general and extravagant. There is probably not a nation on earth whose trade, in proportion to its wealth and population, exceeds that of the United States. It is double that of Great Britain, treble that of Holland, and six times that of France. In these times of depression even, our annual exports are greater than were those of Great Britain the years immediately succeeding the American Revolution. There seems to be in man an irresistible propensity to speculation. The aversion to labor, its slow returns, avarice, and the fascinations of chance, all conspire to lure us into its vortex. In this country are superadded the facilities of freedom, the prospect of success, and the ardor of a bold, daring, and restless population. Add, further, the ultimate safety which a bankrupt system affords, and you are at once overwhelmed with extravagance and prodigality.

The arch usurer is all this while cherishing this spirit, spreading his snare, and exhibiting the bait to lure the ardent and unsuspecting youth within his gripe. A victim to these temptations, the son of an honest farmer, bred to the plough, sets out with a fictitious capital, without skill and without experience. Provided he can trade, he thinks little of his pay. The allurements of long credit, cheap goods, and a new trader, soon exhaust his store. His debtors, when too late, have found the truth of the maxim, that if a man is tempted to buy what he don't want, he may soon want what he can't buy. His day of remittance has arrived; his goods are all out on credit; he becomes bankrupt. He is subjected to the order of the commissioners; the farce is played, and the gentleman bankrupt is discharged of all his debts, and ready to impose on some other people in some other village. But what is the fate of his debtors? Thousands of petty demands must be transferred to the lawyers, and each of them prosecuted in the Federal courts. Yes, sir, in the district or circuit courts, which alone can have jurisdiction under this act; and a debtor to the amount of five dollars may be summoned or attached to appear at the distance of two or three hundred miles, and eventually be compelled to take up his residence in a loathsome prison, while the gentleman bankrupt trader is at his liberty and his ease.

This is not all. This forced, unnatural state of things awakes the cupidity of the prudent, quicksighted, and avaricious, and, from the avails of these wrecks of extravagance and folly, immense fortunes will be accumulated. The economy of consumption will be impaired, and productive labor diminished, and in both ways will the revenues of the country be reduced. The few will be rich, and the many poor; wealth will accumulate, and population deteriorate. And here the economist and poet agree that—

"Ill fares the land, to hastening ills a prey,
Where wealth accumulates, and men decay;
Princes and Lords may flourish and may fade;
A breath can make them, as a breath has made;
But a bold yeomanry, their country's pride,
If once destroyed, can never be supplied."

This bill, sir, will provoke enterprise, even to madness. A young, bold, adventurous American wants nothing to urge, but much to restrain him. He launches into the ocean of life; reason should be his helm, and experience his compass. His passions are his sails, good or bad fortune, prosperous or adverse winds; and the wiles and delusions of an artful and treacherous world, are the rocks, shoals, and quicksands, which lie concealed at the bottom. By this act you urge him into unknown regions, amid dangerous seas and tempestuous skies; you give him a life boat by which he can preserve himself; but you expose his owners to ruin, and his crew to destruction.

Is this all? Would to Heaven it were. But dangers and difficulties increase as we proceed. Our way seems to lead through a dismal and dreary desert, where there is nothing to enliven, cheer, or exhilarate; where every step we take is attended with peril and disaster.

Sir, the Constitution is a charter of limited powers. Congress can do little, but by individual example, to improve the morals or religion of the community. Our business is to regulate the condition and instruct the understanding, but not to improve the heart. As we can do little to inculcate virtue, let us take care to do nothing to encourage vice. Is it not enough that you tempt man to become the sport of capricious fortune? Is it not enough that you delude him to rank speculation, which beggars him and his family? But will you superadd an irresistible inducement to perjury and fraud? "Lead us not into temptation," is an invocation prescribed by one who well knew the frailty and depravity of the human heart. And he illustrated the necessity of this invocation, by showing that one of his favorite disciples, in the face of a solemn admonition, and in spite of the most endearing attachments, in an hour, too, when his love seemed to be most needed, could deny his lord and master with an oath! We need not the aid of inspiration to perceive that man is inclined to evil as the sparks are to ascend, and that the hearts of very many are "deceitful above all things, and desperately wicked;" every day's experience proves the melancholy truth. Few of the best, perhaps, are proof against strong temptation. We have all a weak side—a favorite propensity. Some love of wealth, power, or fame, or some other love, interposes to detach us from duty, and operates as a Syren to lure us upon the Scylla and the Charybdis while we navigate the dangerous channel of human life. The idol of the merchant is his love of speculation. This is so irresistible that even disaster and ruin will not abate, but rather increase it. And does not your bill add to the temptation? If it does not, I admit freely that these remarks are inapplicable. Take, then, two men, equally insolvent, equally moral, and having equal means to conceal property from the eye of the creditor. One is subject to the existing laws, and the other to your bankrupt law; and which has the strongest temptation? The concealment of the first must be perpetual. He must be always upon his guard; he constantly imagines that he is suspected or betrayed; his trustee or confidant may become false, or death may throw the deposite into other hands; and, last of all, the property can never increase, but must constantly diminish, and he is forever debarred from indulging in his favorite employment. The other is subjected to a severer ordeal; but the trial is short. In a few weeks, perhaps, he is discharged; the concealed treasure comes to the light; he proceeds with an effective capital. No one knows from whence it came, and no one has a right to inquire. Sir, the difference is beyond comparison.

And will you tempt men to fraud, and then restrain them by sanguinary laws? Your attempt will be worse than fruitless. The difficulty of detection and discrimination, the disproportion between the crime and the punishment, our abhorrence of cruelty, and our charity and compassion, will all combine, and form an insuperable barrier to conviction. But your law will have another and most deleterious effect upon the community. A law so obnoxious and unequal will become unpopular, and impair your attachment to all your laws. While other nations are bowing in adoration to a man or a family, it is our glory that our idol is our Constitution and laws. Weaken this affection, and it will take a different direction, and attach to some other object dangerous to your liberties. And, sir, there is another principle which ought to be remembered, that if a law is too sanguinary for the genius of your Government or habits of your people, you must either abandon your law or change your Government and habits, to make them conform.

But I would not obtrude my sentiments upon this Senate, on this or any other subject, were I not supported, much lest were I contradicted, by experience. Experience is our best instructor, and without it the calculations and predictions of the wisest statesman fail. Our inclination to imitate is so strong that, finding other nations have bankrupt laws, we, without considering the differences in the necessity and power of enforcing them, conclude they are also expedient for us. If honorable gentlemen would adduce England or France in proof of their expediency, they must compare those nations with ours at the time their bankrupt systems were invented and built up. From 1543, the time of the statute of Henry 8th, to 1571, when that of Eliza, justly considered the foundation of the British system, was passed, what was the condition of the commerce of England? It was literally in its infancy, and carried on principally in foreign ships, navigated by foreigners.

The passage to India by the Cape of Good Hope, and the discovery of the rich mines of America, had given commerce a new impetus and new channels. The Dutch prohibited a second hand India trade with the Portuguese, had pursued it to its source, and wrested it, in a measure, from these monopolizers, and had monopolized it in their turn. Lisbon had succeeded Venice, as the emporium of the East, and Cadiz had become the emporium of the West. The republics of Venice and Genoa, rivals in commerce, as in arms, had wasted their mutual strength in fruitless contests; and the former was now no longer a barrier to the Turks, who were pressing hard upon Christendom. Five hundred hostile ships were approaching each other, and the fate of the commerce of the Mediterranean seemed suspended on the event of a single battle. Elizabeth saw, at her own door, Antwerp, the resort and grand exchange of the North, and Amsterdam, treading fast upon its heels. Her own tonnage, then engaged in foreign trade, was less than that of a second-rate port of the United States

at this day. Her circulating medium was short of four millions sterling; her interest was then established at ten per cent., and there was not an insurance office, nor a bank, in the kingdom. The merchants of the Steelyard, a company of foreigners, had monopolized the commerce, as had the Jews of Lombard street the money transactions of the kingdom, and her own merchants were obliged to seek employment abroad.

This wise but arbitrary monarch was determined to correct these evils, and wrest commerce from the hands of her neighbors. Among other regulations to prevent her subjects from emigrating, and to encourage their creditors, and give them a preference, she established a bankrupt system to divide the effects of an absconding British subject exclusively among British creditors. This act of Eliza, intended to punish and restrain a British debtor, held his future effects liable for his debts. A final discharge was given by the statutes of James, and perfected by those of Anne. It is not till then that a bankrupt system becomes emphatically an inducement to speculation, and an instrument of fraud, and then it is the cause and effect of extravagance. Prodigality is its parent, and prodigality its offspring. How nearly contemporaneous the wild speculations of England and France with the improvements in their bankrupt systems! The acts of Anne were in 1706–7–'18. The ordinances of France were in 1702, 1716, and in 1720. The South Sea and Mississippi bubbles had burst, involved thousands, nay, millions, in ruin, and brought the two nations to the verge of destruction.

Why, sir, should we, in every thing, become the humble copyers of Great Britain? Her Government and policy may require what would be pernicious to us. Distinctions and discriminations are the basis of her Government—equality is the basis of ours. There sanguinary punishments are familiar, and may be enforced; here it is impossible. There the system has been in progress for centuries, and has become familiar, and interwoven with her code on contracts. The United States have no such code, and never can have; and, after all, it is far from being certain that a bankrupt system has benefited the nation, or that, were it now for the first time proposed, it would be adopted. We have seen, by the report of the committee of the House of Commons, the operation of the law, and its defects. The evils are not corrected, nor is the system abandoned. But we very well know, such is the structure of their Government, that abuses cannot always be corrected, or mischiefs removed, and that the courts are often obliged to devise means to evade laws which are opposed to the interest of the nation, but of which the monarchy or aristocracy prevents the repeal.

You go abroad, then, and the lessons of experience are either equivocal or against you. At home, you admit that the experiments by the States have totally failed. As every resemblance may be more or less imperfect, reasoning from analogy is seldom or never conclusive. Could we find an experiment of our own, it might be made the basis of a correct result. Let us then see what has been our own experience.

The subject was brought before the House of Representatives at the first session of the first Congress, and committed. At the second session a petition of the merchants of Charleston, South Carolina, for a bankrupt law, was presented, committed, and a bill reported, and made the order of the day. At the first and second sessions of the third Congress the same proceedings were had, and at the first session of the fourth Congress a bill was reported, acted on, matured, and rejected, by ayes and noes. The subject was not revived until the second session of the fifth Congress, 1798 and 1799, when a bill was brought in, and at the next session, on the 4th of April, 1800, finally passed.

The passage of this bill could scarcely be considered as the voice of the nation. It was in party times, and, as all the gentlemen of one political sect voted against it, and all the others, with very few exceptions, in its favor, it is not improbable that political considerations had some influence on the decision. When we consider, moreover, that it was near the time of a new apportionment of Representatives, and perceive that those who voted against the bill actually represented a majority of the people, and that the House was divided, forty-eight and forty-eight, and its passage was effected by the casting vote of the Speaker, it will not, I trust, be even pretended that it was called for by public opinion.

Such was its birth, and its advent was hailed as a jubilee by some honest and unfortunate men, and by all the spendthrifts and swindlers in the community. What was its progress? The monster came forth, fraud his companion, supported by perjury. Justice threw away her scales, modesty covered her face with her mantle, and innocence fled in a fright. What was its end? Like the rest of the wicked, it scarcely lived out half its days. It was limited to five years, and thence to the end of the next session of Congress, and, when a little more than half that period had expired, it had become so odious and detestable, that all parts, all parties, all professions, and all classes, united against it, and it was repealed by the almost unprecedented unanimity of 99 to 13!

Let me not be told that it was most unpopular at first, because it embraced numerous existing cases. If its operations were as intended, the greater number of objects the more necessary, and therefore the more popular, the law. A law, armed with all the terrors of sanguinary penalties, would not be infringed, nor evaded at first. The timid would stand aloof, waiting for the ingenuity of counsel, or the decision of courts, to point out the weak places, and prescribe the manner of evasion. The frauds committed under any bankrupt system will continue to increase until they shall become familiar, and matters of course.

What then says experience? It speaks with a loud and emphatic voice, "This is a way in which ye shall not go. On one side is vice in affluence, on the other virtue in misery. Here criminal levity, there sanguinary cruelty, and at the end you will inevitably meet confusion and in-

famy." But gentlemen imagine that experience has pointed out the dangers, and they are prepared to shun them.

We hear much of the perfection of this bill, and, as it is too long to be read, its excellencies are taken for granted. Much expectation has, to be sure, been excited. The bill was prepared by two of the most learned and cunning lawyers in the United States, and at the first session of the last Congress it underwent, in the other House, the scrutiny of a very learned Judiciary Committee. The Speaker was distinguished for his power of discrimination, and his discretion had a wide range, as the selection was made from one hundred and twenty lawyers. It was reported, discussed, and postponed. It was revised at the succeeding session, by a committee equally respectable—at the last endured the ordeal of this Senate, and now it comes to us, reported by your Judiciary Committee, aided by the additional industry, and experience, and wisdom, of the honorable gentleman from Delaware. And, after all this, what have they brought forth? It has the same form and features, and, with very few and trifling exceptions, is the very image and superscription of the odious and detestable act of 1800.

This, sir, would bring me, where I assure the Senate I am not disposed to go—into a particular examination of this tedious bill. I shall take a shorter, and, I trust, better course. I have collated this with the act of 1800, and in about five minutes will show you the result. They both include the same persons. With two trifling variances, the acts of bankruptcy are the same. The petitioning creditors have the same qualifications, and are subjected to the same proceedings; the appointment, number, power, and duties, of the commissioners are the same; the creditors are to appoint the assignees, in the same manner, and by the same majority of interest; they are alike removeable and responsible, and their powers and duties are alike; the bankrupt is subjected to the same ordeal; he is entitled to come in three times within the forty-two days, and incurs the same penalties for refusal; he must surrender and disclose his estate; what he has sold, and if he expects any profits; must assign all and deliver up all; the powers of the commissioners over him are alike, and he is subject to like proceedings and punishments: he is entitled to the same support for his family pending the process, and the same per centage in the distribution; and the same persons or tribunals must consent before he obtains his discharge, and his certificate is to have the same effect. The two acts vary in a few particulars. This commences presently, that commenced at a future day; this fixes the pay of the commissioners, that left it to the judge; this excludes farmers, graziers, &c., expressly, that by implication. This has a few provisions not found in the other. It excl⁻⁻des persons becoming merchants, &c., with design to take the benefit of the act; prevents a bank corporation from unreasonably withholding a certificate, and gives the United States' courts jurisdiction in all cases. It omits obliging a wife to swear against her husband. This is a bird's eye view of the two: and what have you gained by these trifling variations? That this should commence presently, I do not object; for the sooner it begins to operate, the sooner the people will be disgusted with it, and demand its repeal. Paying the commissioners by the day will promote procrastination. The difference, however, is trifling, but the change is for the worse.

The express exclusion of certain persons is an unquestionable blemish. You define who are included, and particularize others who are excluded; and what is to be the condition of those who are neither embraced by the provision nor the exception? Is it the intent to embrace all not expressly excepted? Such would seem to be the principle, and yet its operation would be utterly unjust. There are both injustice and obscurity in the proviso, and it is an unquestionable defect. And the exclusion of those who become merchants to partake of its benefits is still worse. How are you to decide on the intent? Were it a question ever to be in contest between the parties, it is a fact of difficult proof. But, here both the parties will be agreed against the proof of such intent. The petitioning creditor is for bringing the debtor within the description, or else he would not petition. The debtor who designs to make himself a merchant or trader, is of the same opinion, and the commissioners are to decide a question where both parties agree. You have then no other way to detect an infraction of this provision, but by contesting the validity of the certificate after it is granted, when all the property is consumed by commissioners, assignees, officers, agents, and lawyers. Your provision, as to bank corporations, amounts to nothing—it might as well extend to any other creditor. And the jurisdiction given to the United States' courts is an evil of such magnitude, that I have neither time nor patience to discuss it.

There is, however, the omission of a usual provision which I approve. You will not compel a wife to disclose the fraud of her husband. Indeed! And is it a merit that this Senate, so distinguished for their gallantry, should have refrained from a provision so barbarous? Is it not rather a source of mortification that such a rude and savage provision should ever have disgraced our statute book? Sir, we live in the nineteenth century, and have some claims, I hope, to civilization. A man was once in affluence, "the candle of God shone on his head, and by his light he walked through darkness. His children were about him; he washed his steps with butter, and the rock poured him out rivers of oil." But, the storm of adversity began to beat upon him, and in an unlucky and inconsiderate moment he conceived the design to shelter himself from the impending danger, and lay aside a portion for the protection and sustenance of his family; and his wife is called to disclose the fraud. On the one hand, she must call upon her God to witness a falsehood—on the other, she consigns herself and children to misery, and her husband to a perpetual dungeon. What would an affectionate wife do? What ought she to do? She would swear him innocent. And "the accusing spirit which should fly to Heaven's chancery with the oath, would blush as he gave it in, and the record-

ing angel, as he should write it down, would drop a tear upon the word and blot it out forever." But still, sir, the omission adds nothing to the efficacy of your system. Nay, it rather shows the defectiveness of a system, for whose support you have been obliged to resort to principles at which the soul of a civilized man would revolt. No, sir, take all your deviations from the act of 1800 together, and, instead of helping the matter, they make it worse.

But, the most odious principle in the bill is that of discrimination. You desire uniformity, and make the most invidious distinctions. A merchant or trader in Louisiana must be put on the same footing with one in Maine. Yet a person in either of those places, living in the same neighborhood, and even in the same house with another as good as himself, is entitled to different laws for the protection of his liberty and prosperity. And yet we are told the farmer and manufacturer do not want it. If either of these is utterly insolvent, what policy should hold him forever liable any more than the merchant? When gentlemen tell us of the inability of these to make prompt payment, and that to subject them to this process against their will would be cruel and oppressive, and expect us to receive this as an insuperable objection, they pay us no compliment. It really appears that gentlemen were disposed to pacify us, no matter how. Your objection is answered in a word. Let the same process be had against the farmer and manufacturer, with this simple addition only, that on being summoned he should not be held to further proceedings without his consent. The apology for excluding him is frivolous, indeed.

Is not the farmer subject to equal risks? He has his perils by water, and his perils by fire, and adopt this discriminating principle, and he will have his perils too among false brethren. Droughts, inundations, diseases, insects, and fires, are his ministers of destruction. Suppose, sir, some of these children of adversity now before you, and applying for relief. The first is a dealer in bank and other stocks. He purchased United States' Bank stock to an amount ten times more than he was worth, while it stood at only one hundred and fifty per cent. It fell. He failed, and he tells you that as this bank facilitates commerce you ought to relieve him for its sake; and his claim is allowed. The next is a manufacturer, who has withstood a change of times, and foreign and domestic competition; but, in consequence of the failure of the first gentleman, he must fail too, and he prays you to put him on the same footing. But, no; he purchases his stock, applies the labor, and sells the manufactured article; he gets his living chiefly by labor, and is, therefore, excluded.

The broker comes next. He tells you that he commenced business a year ago. He was then worth nothing, but his friends put money into his hands, and his speculations were profitable. But, unfortunately, as the large sums were constantly passing through his hands, some occasionally stopped by the way. He took the funds of his patron, and converted them to purposes of speculations of his own, and he failed. This worthy, faithful, honest, useful citizen is entitled to your relief. A fisherman immediately succeeds him. He built his vessels, employed and furnished his men, sent them to the straits or banks, received, cured, and disposed of the cargoes. But the tempest sunk and destroyed his ships, while cultivating the nursery of your seamen, and he asks relief. But he does not get his living by buying and selling. He builds his vessels, but not to sell. He catches his fish, but does not buy them; he is excluded. A merchant comes and he tells you that while you were engaged in that wicked war against Great Britain, goods were scarce and the wants of the community required that he should attempt to import some in spite of your laws. The prospect was so tempting, and the war so unjust, his interest and conscience both agreed that it would be right. His importations were large, and he was on the eve of independence, when your revenue officers like so many harpies, pounced upon him, seized his goods, and your unrelenting courts condemned them. A man so worthy and patriotic is entitled to your first consideration, and you grant him all he asks.

The plain unvarnished farmer comes next. His family was large, his sons were growing up, he sold and went into the wilderness, purchased and expected to pay for his lands with their aid, and make farms for all; but unforeseen misfortunes assailed him. His crops were destroyed, his cattle died, the fires in the woods caught and burnt up his dwelling, and sickness and death deprived him of the anticipated help of his family. The pay day is come, he is insolvent, and he claims your interposition. But you are a farmer, and farmers don't want the act. Yet, nevertheless, as your case is hard, we can tell you how you may contrive to get within its provisions. Purchase a barrel of rum or whiskey, become a trader, keep secret the design, and, by the time the barrel is out, you may apply to some friendly creditor—he will petition against you, you will be declared a bankrupt, and be punished by a discharge from all your debts. These men would undoubtedly go away feeling the highest respect for your laws and the profoundest reverence for the makers.

There is an excellent story of a father whose son wished for his portion of the estate; it was assigned to him; he went away, wasted his substance in riotous living, was in misery, came back, was penitent, and his father relieved his distresses and forgave him. With a little alteration this story would illustrate our case. Let us then suppose that the father had two sons who wished for their portions that they might depart—the one a merchant, the other a farmer—they receive their property and take their journey into a far country. The farmer purchases his land and cattle, and goes to work, but the merchant wastes his substance in rank speculation, and riotous living. He applies to his brother for relief, and he loans him even all he has. This, too, is wasted in the same prodigal manner, and there is a famine in the land, and they both begin to be in want; and they join themselves to a citizen who sends them into the field to feed swine, and they fain would have

satisfied their hunger with the husks which the swine did eat, and no one gave unto them. When they came to reflect, (for hunger will produce reflections,) they say, how many hired servants of our father have bread enough and to spare, and we perish with hunger! Let us arise and go to him and confess that we are not worthy to be his sons, and beg to be received as his hired servants. They go; and while they are yet a great way off, their father sees and comes out to meet them. On the merchant he has compassion, falls on his neck and embraces him, orders a new robe to be put on him, and the fatted calf to be killed, and the music to strike up to announce and welcome his return. The farmer waits until the merchant has received his blessing, as farmers are usually obliged to do. But the father turns to him, and, with an angry look and vindictive voice, exclaims, begone, thou credulous charitable fool, begone! I have given thee all I ever intend; thou hast wasted it upon that prodigal. I have forgiven him, but if I ever do thee, may God never forgive me. Go starve and be forgotten. Would not you denounce such a father as a monster? Just such a father this bill makes you.

But this is not the least odious feature in the bill. Its effects upon an honest and fair debtor will be cruel and oppressive, and, in most cases, the expense of the process will exhaust the whole estate. The commissioners are designated—they appoint their clerk, organize their court, and take care to take bond for their own compensation, and then proceed with all the prudence, economy, and deliberation, of the commissioners under the Treaty of Ghent, whose very modest bill of $194,000 has been presented to you this session, and who intend probably to get another $194,000 before they let you go. It is not to be expected that your commissioners will very much exceed these in integrity, ability, or character. The danger of delay is, then, by no means visionary. Within three or four years an act has passed to revive a commission under the old bankrupt act, some of the commissioners having died, and the business being unfinished after a continuance of fifteen years. And, although I do not expect that one board of these Ghent Treaty commissioners will finish within fifteen years, yet this case shows that those under the Treaty of Ghent are not the only ones who understand the art of procrastination. The outstanding debts placed for collection often in unfaithful or dilatory hands, the right of the assignee to retain to satisfy contingent demands, the power of making demands appear contingent for the sake of retaining the money, the fees of lawyers, judges, clerks, commissioners, assignees, and other expenses, will be enough to absorb a very good estate. You give, moreover, to the commissioners a dangerous, unusual, and unconstitutional power over the secret transactions and personal rights of the debtor. If there is any one personal right that we value more than another, it is that "a man's house is his castle." This invaluable inheritance secures us from violence under color of law, and preserves our own secret concerns from the scrutiny and inspection of unhallowed eyes. Nothing but a crime should authorize an invasion of a private dwelling. The fourth article of the amendments to the Constitution has secured to the people this right to be exempt from all unreasonable searches and seizures, not only in their "persons," but in their "houses, papers, and effects." What are unreasonable searches and seizures? Those which are unusual and contrary to precedent. But you, in the face of this provision, would subject a man's person to be seized, his house broken open, and his trunks and papers ransacked and inspected, for the crime of being in jail for debt, or unable to discharge an attachment. And his remedy is a jury at the discretion of the court!

How is it with the dishonest debtor? Not one additional impediment to fraud. If there be any difference, the restraints are less and the inducements stronger than in the act of 1800. And the ultimate tribunal is an assemblage of creditors—a mixture of parents, brothers, children, friends, enemies, competitors, and rivals. This fair, impartial tribunal, possessing coincident feelings and co-ordinate virtue, are, by a complicated majority of number and interest, to give or refuse the last sanction. The doctrine of impartial justice, it seems, has become too common and insipid for modern refinement, and the best tribunal is one the most partial.

I think I perceive in the countenance of the honorable gentleman from Massachusetts, (Mr. OTIS,) an intimation that my argument in this particular is a little inconsistent. I complain, at the same time, that the act has too much severity and not enough. Sir, there is an inconsistency, but it is not mine; it is in your system itself. It is a perfect chapter of contradictions. It does give too much power to the creditor, and it does not give enough; it is too severe upon the debtor, and it is not severe enough. To the crafty, evasive, or vindictive creditor, it gives too much power; to the liberal and just, not enough. Upon the honest and fair, but unfortunate debtor, it is too severe; upon the fraudulent, not enough: and the mischief is here—that you have no means, nor is there any power, short of omniscience, that can make the discrimination.

I shall vote against the indefinite postponement, not that I have any hope that any system can be matured so as to obviate my objections, but because the petitioners are entitled to a decision. It is with the utmost regret that I have been obliged to take this stand against the wishes of many good friends whom I desire to relieve; and, when humanity seems to urge, and justice and policy forbid, we oppose with reluctance. But, describe the distresses as you will, magnify and color them with all the power and embellishments of eloquence, and they fall short of the reality, and still I maintain that this remedy is worse than the disease. Nay, more; the remedy itself will produce a relapse which will rage like a pestilence, and sweep like a whirlwind. But I have done. Pass this bill, and I conjure you to alter its title by striking out "uniform system of," and inserting "universal." It will then be, "An act to establish an universal bankruptcy throughout the United States," and the tendency and effect will be apparent in the title. Pass this bill, and it will blight like a mildew; it will corrode like a canker; it will pollute like a leprosy. Pass this bill, and you "smite the land with a curse."

FRIDAY, February 9.

The credentials of the honorable JAMES BARBOUR, appointed a Senator by the Legislature of the State of Virginia, for the term of six years, to commence on the fourth day of March next, were read, and laid on the file.

Mr. DANA presented the petition of William Plumbe, of Connecticut, praying to be allowed a pension of twenty five dollars per month during life, in consideration of Revolutionary services and sacrifices; and the petition was read, and referred to the Committee on Pensions.

Mr. SMITH, from the Committee on the Judiciary, to whom was referred the petition of Josiah Hook, Jr., made a report, accompanied by a bill for the relief of Josiah Hook, Jr., and the report and bill were read; and the bill passed to a second reading.

Mr. RUGGLES presented the petition of Levi Chadwick, praying the renewal of a land warrant issued to him for Revolutionary services, and which is now lost; and the petition was read, and referred to the Committee on Public Lands.

Mr. SMITH, from the Committee on the Judiciary, to whom was referred the petition of Thomas Oxley, reported that "the prayer of the petitioner ought not to be granted;" and the report was read.

Mr. THOMAS, from the Committee on Public Lands, to whom was recommitted the bill for the relief of the purchasers of public lands prior to the first day of July, 1820, reported the same with amendments; which were read.

Mr. SANFORD, from the Committee on Finance, to whom was referred the bill, entitled "An act further to regulate the entry of merchandise imported into the United States from any adjacent territory," reported the same with amendments; which were read.

PUNISHMENT OF PIRACY.

Mr. SMITH, from the Committee on the Judiciary, to whom was referred the resolution of the 4th of December, "to inquire into the propriety of so modifying the law punishing piracy as to authorize the President of the United States, in such cases as he may deem expedient, to commute capital punishments for confinement in penitentiary houses," reported that it is inexpedient to make the modification suggested; and the report was read. It is as follows:

The object of the resolution is to alter the criminal code of the United States so far as to place within the power of the President of the United States the complete control over the punishment now affixed by law to the crime of piracy, and to soften it down from death to the less rigorous punishment of confinement in penitentiary houses.

As we have drawn most of our impressions of the

utility and efficacy of penitentiaries from the practical operations of this system in the several States where it has been adopted, it may not be thought improper to give the result of certain official inquiries into the condition, usefulness, and advantages of some of these institutions in States where much zeal and diligence had been displayed to cherish them.

Some time in the year 1817 the grand jury of Philadelphia visited the penitentiary in that city, upon which they made the following presentment :

"That, while they notice with pleasure the high degree of order and cleanliness, they are compelled by a sense of duty to present, as an evil of considerable magnitude, the present very crowded state of the penitentiary ; the number of prisoners of all classes continues to increase, so that from twenty to forty are lodged in rooms eighteen feet square. So many are thus crowded together, that the institution already begins to assume the character of a European prison and seminary for every vice, in which the unfortunate being who commits the first offence, and knows none of the arts of methodised villany, can scarcely avoid the contamination which leads to extreme depravity." The same grand jury further stated "that, of four hundred and fifty-one convicts now in the penitentiary of Pennsylvania, one hundred and sixty-one have been confined there before." It is believed that no institution of this character ever received more attention as respects its comforts and means of promoting the reformation of offenders.

The commissioners appointed to examine into the state of the New York prison, not long since, in their report say : "It has for some time past not only failed of effecting the object chiefly in view, but has subjected the treasury to a series of disbursements too oppressive to be continued if they can in any way be prevented."

The commissioners of the prison of Massachusetts, in a report, complain "that the prison is so crowded as to defeat the object for which the institution was created." These commissioners, after enumerating what they consider to be the advantages arising to the Commonwealth, say : "But there appears great reason to suppose that the advantage first mentioned is more than counterbalanced by the greater hardihood and more settled corruption which a promiscuous association among the convicts must produce, particularly the young."

These appear to be fair and impartial representations made by men whose duty it was to represent things as they were, in order to bring to the public view their true character; and if this is the state and effect of those prisons, after twenty years of experience and prudent management, upon convicts whose offences are not of the most atrocious class, but little hope can be entertained that pirates can be reformed by such means.

In the catalogue of human offences, if there is any one supremely distinguished for its enormity over others, it is piracy. It can only be committed by those whose hearts have become base by habitual depravity. It is called by jurists an offence against the universal laws of society. A pirate is *hostis humani generis*. He is at war with his species, and has renounced the protection of all civilized Governments, and abandoned himself again to the savage state of nature. His flag consists of a "black field, with a death's head, a battle axe, and an hour-glass." These are the ensigns of his profession. He does not select the enemies of his native country as the only objects of his conquest, but attacks indiscriminately the defenceless of every nation ; prowls every ocean in quest of plunder ; and murders or jeopardizes the lives of all who fall within his power, without regard to nation, to age, or to sex. With such a blood-stained front, a pirate can have no claim to the clemency of a Government, the protection of which he has voluntarily renounced, and against which he has so highly offended.

Our general policy and politcal institutions are administered so mildly, that we seem to have forgotten the protection due to the public ; and call that punishment which the law prescribes for offences, however enormous they may be against the public safety and public morals, cruel and degrading to our national character. The laws punishing piracy with death have had from the legislative department all the consideration due to so important a subject at a time when no undue influence could interpose.

The Executive clemency has more than sufficient range for its exercise, without the aid sought for by this resolution. Whatever may be the public feeling against a pirate previous to his trial and conviction, as soon as that takes place that feeling subsides and becomes enlisted on the part of the criminal. There is not a favorable trait in his case but what is brought up and mingled with as many circumstances of pity and compassion as his counsel can condense in a petition, which everybody subscribes without any knowledge of the facts ; and this is presented to the Executive, upon which alone he is to judge the case. All the atrocious circumstances are kept out of view. There is no one hardy enough to tell that this criminal and his associates had boarded a defenceless ship, and, after plundering all that was valuable, had, with the most unrelenting cruelty, butchered the whole crew and passengers ; or crowded them into a small boat, in the midst of the sea, without provisions or clothing, and set them adrift, where their destruction was inevitable ; or, the better to secure their purpose, had shut all, both male and female, under deck, and sunk the ship, to elude detection, or to indulge an insatiable thirst for cruelty.

The object of capital punishment is to prevent the offender from committing further offences, or to deter others from doing so by the example. If it be commuted for temporary confinement, it can effect neither to any valuable purpose. The temptation is so strong, and detection so difficult and so rare, that but few, it is feared, can be deterred. The punishment of death is inflicted upon pirates by all civilized nations, notwithstanding which it is a growing evil ; every sea is now crowded with them, which, instead of diminishing, ought to increase the reasons for inflicting capital punishment.

The committee are of opinion that capital punishment is the appropriate punishment for piracy, and that it would be inexpedient to commute it for confinement in penitentiary houses.

PROMOTION OF EDUCATION.

Mr. THOMAS, from the Committee on Public Lands, to whom was referred the resolution of the 11th of January, "to inquire into the justice and expediency of granting land for the purposes of education within the limits of the old States," reported that it is inexpedient to grant lands to the extent contemplated in the resolution, but that it is just and expedient to grant a per centum on the sales of public lands to a reasonable extent, for promoting education in the old States, and to grant an equivalent to the new States; and the report was read. It is as follows:

That, under the laws of the United States, lands have been granted for the purposes of education in the States of Ohio, Louisiana, Indiana, Mississippi, Illinois, and Alabama, in the proportion of one thirty-sixth part of all the public lands within the State, with the addition of two townships, or forty-six thousand and eighty acres in each State, and to Louisiana an additional township, or twenty-three thousand and forty acres. The quantity which is already vested in each of the above States by the operation of this system, and which will vest in them when the Indian title shall have been extinguished, and the whole of the lands are surveyed, will be exhibited with sufficient accuracy for all practical purposes by the annexed estimate of the Commissioner of the General Land Office, and is a part of this report. The committee also remark that, by an act of the eighteenth of April, 1806, a donation of two hundred thousand acres of land was made to the State of Tennessee, for the use of two colleges and academies in each county in the State, to be established by the Legislature thereof, and six hundred and forty acres in each six miles square, where it was practicable, for the use of schools; and that a township, or twenty-three thousand and forty acres, was, on the 3d of March, 1819, granted by the United States to the Connecticut Asylum for the education of deaf and dumb persons.

The lands thus granted to the States for the above purposes are not subject to taxation by the State government, and can only be settled in the manner pointed out by the States in which they lie. If, therefore, correspondent quantities for the purposes of education are to be granted to all the old States, (under which term the committee believe all States will be included which have not received donations of land for that purpose,) it would seem that the States and Territories which now contain public land would have an excessive proportion of their superfices taken up with such donations, leaving but a small part of the land in each subject to taxation, or to settlement, except at the will of other sovereign States. In receiving donations of land for the purposes of promoting education in the States in which they have been granted, in the opinion of the committee, a consideration has been rendered therefor, on the part of those States, by the increased value which the population and improvement of the State gave to the unsold public lands, and by the compact not to tax the lands of the United States at any time before they were sold, nor until the lapse of five years thereafter.

The lands, therefore, granted to some of the new States, for the purposes of education, though distinguished in common parlance by the name of *donations*, were in fact sales bottomed upon valuable considerations, in which the new States surrendered their right of sovereignty over the remaining public lands, and gave up the whole amount which might have been received in taxes before such lands were sold, and for five years thereafter.

The committee are therefore of opinion, that it is inexpedient to grant lands to the extent contemplated in the resolution; but that it is just and expedient to grant a per centum, to a reasonable extent, on the amount of sales of public lands, for the purpose of promoting education in such of the States as have not received the aid of the General Government, distrib-

uting the amount among the several States, according to the population of each; and that justice would require an equivalent from the United States to the States and Territories which contain public lands, if it should be deemed advisable to make the donation to the old States recommended in this report; and they are of opinion that, in that event, it will be entirely just to subject to taxation, by such State or Territory, all lands sold by the United States therein, from and after the day on which they may be sold.

GENERAL LAND OFFICE, *Feb. 2, 1821.*

SIR: Agreeably to your letter of 30th ultimo, I transmit herewith an estimate of the quantity of lands in Ohio, Indiana, Louisiana, Mississippi, Illinois, and Alabama, showing the quantity surveyed in each, the quantity unsurveyed, and the amount of one thirty-sixth part of the surveyed and unsurveyed lands.

I am, very respectfully, &c.

JOSIAH MEIGS.

Hon. J. B. THOMAS,
    Chairman Com. Public Lands.

Estimate of the quantity of Public Lands in the following States; showing the quantity surveyed and unsurveyed; also the amount of one thirty-sixth part of each.

States.	Public Lands in the State.	Quantity surveyed.	Thirty-sixth part.	Quantity unsurveyed.	Thirty-sixth part.
Ohio	13,824,000	13,043,000	351,166	1,182,000	32,683
Indiana	21,565,440	9,926,020	275,722	11,639,430	398,317
Illinois	34,560,000	9,330,600	259,183	25,229,400	700,815
Louisiana	26,486,000	1,964,720	54,631	24,529,380	681,369
Mississippi	26,000,000	9,040,960	251,137	16,959,040	471,094
Alabama	26,448,000	12,948,480	359,680	13,499,580	374,986

N. B.—The estimate of the quantity in each State is obtained by calculations from printed maps, and cannot be relied on for accuracy.

GENERAL LAND OFFICE, *February 2, 1821.*

JOSIAH MEIGS.

On motion, by Mr. JOHNSON, of Louisiana, that the message of the President of the United States of the 13th of May last, transmitting a report of the Secretary of State on the subject of claims of citizens of the United States for Spanish spoliations, be printed for the use of the Senate; on motion, by Mr. LOWRIE, it was postponed until to-morrow.

The bill to reward Lieutenant Gregory, his officers and companions; and the bill to establish a new land office in the State of Mississippi, and for the better regulation of certain land districts in the States of Alabama and Mississippi, were severally read the second time.

The last mentioned bill was referred to the Committee on Public Lands.

The Senate proceeded to consider the report of the Committee on Finance, on the petition of James Graham; and, on motion, by Mr. SANFORD, it, together with the reports of the same committee on the petitions of Joshua Aubin and William Whitehead were postponed to Monday next.

A message from the House of Representatives informed the Senate that they have passed a bill, entitled "An act for the relief of Robert Buntin;" and a bill, entitled "An act to authorize the collectors of the customs to pay debentures issued on the exportation of loaf sugar and spirits distilled from molasses;" in which bills they request the concurrence of the Senate.

THE BANKRUPT BILL.

The Senate then resumed the consideration of the bill to establish a uniform system of bankruptcy.

Mr. HOLMES, of Maine, concluded his speech against the bill; Mr. HUNTER spoke in favor of it; Mr. MACON against it; and Mr. VAN DYKE concluded the debate by some remarks in favor of the bill.

The question on the motion to postpone the bill indefinitely was then decided as follows:

YEAS—Messrs. Barbour, Eaton, King of Alabama, Macon, Morril, Pleasants, Roberts, Smith, Walker of Alabama, and Williams of Tennessee—10.

NAYS—Messrs. Brown, Chandler, Dana, Dickerson, Edwards, Elliott, Gaillard, Holmes of Maine, Holmes of Mississippi, Horsey, Hunter, Johnson of Kentucky, Johnson of Louisiana, King of New York, Knight, Lanman, Lloyd, Lowrie, Mills, Otis, Palmer, Parrott, Pinkney, Sanford, Stokes, Talbot, Taylor, Thomas, Tichenor, Trimble, Van Dyke, and Williams of Mississippi—32.

So the Senate refused to postpone the bill indefinitely; in other words, to reject it.

SATURDAY, February 10.

Mr. CHANDLER presented the petition of Job Sherborn, of Maine, praying to be reimbursed in certain expenses incurred, and compensated for services rendered, in the army, during the late war; and the petition was read, and referred to the Committee of Claims.

Mr. HOLMES, of Maine, submitted the following motion for consideration:

Resolved, That the Committee on Finance be instructed to inquire into the expediency of altering the act, entitled "An act for enrolling and licensing ships or vessels to be employed in the coasting trade and fisheries, and for regulating the same."

The bill from the House of Representatives, entitled "An act for the relief of Robert Buntin,"

and the bill, entitled "An act to authorize the collectors of customs to pay debentures issued on the exportation of loaf sugar, and spirits distilled from molasses," were severally read, and passed to a second reading.

The bill for the relief of Josiah Hook, Jr. was read the second time.

The Senate proceeded to consider the report of the Committee on the Judiciary on the resolution of the 4th December last, to commute the punishment of the crime of piracy; and, on motion, by Mr. BARBOUR, it was laid on the table.

The Senate proceeded to consider the report of the Committee on Public Lands on the resolution of the 11th January last, to grant lands for the purposes of education within the limits of the old States; and it was postponed to Monday next.

The Senate resumed the consideration of the bill to establish an uniform system of bankruptcy throughout the United States, as amended; and it was laid on the table.

A message from the House of Representatives informed the Senate that the House have passed a bill, entitled "An act making appropriations for the support of Government for the year 1821;" and a bill, entitled "An act to alter and establish certain post roads;" in which bills they request the concurrence of the Senate.

The two bills last brought up for concurrence were severally read twice, by unanimous consent; and the first mentioned bill was referred to the Committee on Finance; and the last mentioned bill was referred to the Committee on the Post Office and Post Roads.

Mr. RUGGLES, from the Committee of Claims, made an unfavorable report on the petition of Thomas W. Todd; which was read.

Mr. THOMAS, from the Committee on the Public Lands, reported a bill for the relief of the legal representatives of Alexander Montgomery; and the bill was read.

Mr. NOBLE, from the Committee on Pensions, made an unfavorable report on the petition of Dean Weymouth; which was read.

The motion made by Mr. JOHNSON, of Louisiana, on yesterday, to reprint the Message of the President of the United States of the last session, respecting claims for Spanish spoliations, was taken up and agreed to.

The report of the Committee on the Judiciary, unfavorable to the petition of Thomas Oxley, was considered, and concurred in.

RELIEF TO LAND PURCHASERS.

The Senate resumed the consideration of the bill for the relief of the purchasers of public lands.

The amendments reported by the Committee on the Public Lands, to which the bill was recommitted on Wednesday last, including the amendment offered by Mr. KING, of New York, were considered in Committee of the Whole; and, having been severally agreed to, were reported to the Senate.

Mr. LOWRIE moved to strike out of the new 3d section (as proposed by Mr. KING) the words, "at a price less than three dollars," and also, out of the same section, the words "and that, on all such debts which may have arisen from the purchase of public land, at or above three dollars the acre, at the rate of 33⅓ per cent. shall be allowed."

This proposition was negatived by yeas and nays—28 votes to 12, as follows:

YEAS—Messrs. Chandler, Dana, Dickerson, Knight, Lanman, Lloyd, Lowrie, Macon, Roberts, Sanford, Talbot, and Trimble.

NAYS—Messrs. Barbour, Eaton, Edwards, Elliott, Gaillard, Holmes of Maine, Holmes of Mississippi, Hunter, Johnson of Kentucky, Johnson of Louisiana, King of Alabama, King of New York, Mills, Morril, Noble, Otis, Parrott, Pleasants, Ruggles, Smith, Stokes, Thomas, Tichenor, Van Dyke, Walker of Alabama, Walker of Georgia, Williams of Mississippi, and Williams of Tennessee.

The several amendments were then concurred in by the Senate, with some additional provisions, amongst them one offered by Mr. WALKER, of Alabama, to extend the relief to purchasers who have laid off towns on their land, and those who hold lots or contiguous land under them.

The bill was then ordered to be engrossed for a third reading—36 to 5, as follows:

YEAS—Messrs. Barbour, Dickerson, Eaton, Edwards, Elliott, Gaillard, Holmes of Maine, Holmes of Mississippi, Horsey, Hunter, Johnson of Kentucky, Johnson of Louisiana, King of Alabama, King of New York, Lanman, Lloyd, Mills, Morril, Noble, Otis, Parrott, Pleasants, Ruggles, Sanford, Smith, Stokes, Talbot, Taylor, Thomas, Tichenor, Trimble, Van Dyke, Walker of Alabama, Walker of Georgia, Williams of Mississippi, and Williams of Tennessee.

NAYS—Messrs. Chandler, Dana, Lowrie, Macon, and Roberts.

The Senate took up and considered the bill to establish an uniform system of bankruptcy throughout the United States, as amended; and, on motion, the Senate adjourned.

MONDAY, February 12.

Mr. LLOYD presented the memorial of the merchants and underwriters of the city of Baltimore, suggesting to Congress the expediency of augmenting the naval force of the United States in the Pacific ocean, to an extent equal to the protection of our commerce there; and the memorial was read, and referred to the Committee on Foreign Relations.

The bill, entitled "An act for the relief of Robert Buntin" was read the second time, and referred to the Committee on Public Lands.

The bill, entitled "An act to authorize the collectors of customs to pay debentures issued on the exportation of loaf sugar, and spirits distilled from molasses," was read the second time, and referred to the Committee on Commerce and Manufactures.

The bill for the relief of the legal representatives of Alexander Montgomery, deceased, was read the second time.

The Senate proceeded to consider the report of the Committee of Claims, on the petition of Thomas W. Todd; and, on motion by Mr. PLEASANTS, it was laid on the table.

Mr. LOWRIE communicated the following resolutions of the General Assembly of the State of Pennsylvania; which were read.

" In the General Assembly of the Commonwealth of Pennsylvania :

" Resolved by the Senate and House of Representatives, That our Senators and Representatives in Congress be requested to use their exertions in procuring the passage of a law, providing for the removal of the obstructions in the entrance of Erie harbor; and that this Commonwealth will co-operate with the United States in the accomplishment of that object.

" Resolved, That the Governor be requested to transmit a copy of the foregoing resolution to each of our Senators and Representatives in the Congress of the United States.

"JOHN GILMORE,
" Speaker of the House of Representatives.
" WM. MARKS, JR.,
" Speaker of the Senate.
"Approved February 1, 1821.
"JOSEPH HIESTER."

The Senate proceeded to consider the report of the Committee on Pensions, on the petition of Dean Weymouth; and, on motion by Mr. HOLMES, of Maine, it was laid on the table.

The Senate resumed the consideration of the report of the Committee of Claims, on the petition of George Jackson; and it was postponed until to-morrow.

The Senate resumed the consideration of the report of the Committee on Public Lands on the resolution of the 11th January last, to grant lands for the purposes of education within the limits of the old States; and, on motion, by Mr. THOMAS, it was laid on the table.

A resolution submitted by Mr. HOLMES, of Maine, on Saturday, to instruct the Committee on Finance to inquire into the expediency of altering the act for enrolling and licensing ships or vessels to be employed in the coasting trade and fisheries, &c., was taken up and agreed to.

REMISSION OF DUTIES.

The Senate took up successively the reports of the Committee on Finance unfavorable to the petitions of James Graham, William Whitehead, and Joshua Aubin.

[The petitioners state that, in the month of October, 1814, they, being subjects of Great Britain, imported certain British goods into Castine, a port of the United States, then in the possession of the British, with whom the United States were at war; that they entered the goods at the British custom-house, and paid the duties; that at the time the United States regained the possession, the collector demanded the duties and that they paid them; and they pray that the duties so paid may be refunded.]

Mr. OTIS moved to reverse the reports of the committee and instruct it to bring in bills for the relief of the petitioners; and after a long debate in which the reports were defended by Messrs. HOLMES, of Maine, EATON, and MACON, and were opposed by

Messrs. OTIS, MILLS, DANA, SANFORD, KING, of New York, and LANMAN,

The motion was agreed to; and the committee were directed to report bills accordingly.

BANKRUPT BILL.

The Senate resumed the consideration of the bill to establish a system of bankruptcy. A number of amendments were made to its details, and others were offered, on which, as well as on the merits of the bill, a good deal of debate took place, in which Messrs. VAN DYKE, TALBOT, OTIS, MILLS, and HOLMES, of Maine, chiefly participated.

Mr. TALBOT closed his remarks against the bill by offering the following motion:

Resolved, That the bill to establish an uniform system of bankruptcy throughout the United States be committed to the Committee on the Judiciary, with instructions to report amendments thereto which shall secure to all classes of the community, other than the descriptions of persons contained in the first section of the bill, the privilege, at their election, of becoming voluntary bankrupts, with the consent and approbation of a major part in value of all the creditors of such voluntary bankrupt, previously obtained and duly certified; and further providing that such bankrupt shall be subjected to the same proceedings, and liable to the same penalties, fines, and forfeitures, and be entitled to all the privileges, benefits, and advantages, as are provided for, and made applicable to, all other bankrupts by the regulations of the said bill.

To allow this motion, and an amendment offered by Mr. HOLMES, of Maine, (not affecting the principle of the bill,) to be printed, the bill was laid on the table.

RELIEF TO LAND PURCHASERS.

The engrossed bill for the relief of the purchasers of public lands, was read the third time.

Mr. LOWRIE observed, that, from the course this bill had taken, he found himself placed in a situation in which his views without some explanation might be misunderstood. He asked the attention of the Senate, while he compared the provisions of the bill just read, with the one reported by the Committee on Public Lands.

This subject was brought before Congress by the President's Message—by the report of the Secretary of the Treasury, and by a large number of petitions, as well as by resolutions offered by gentlemen in both Houses. All these were referred to the Committee on Public Lands. Being a member of that committee, I know something of the difficulty and embarrassment they experienced in coming to a conclusion, and in digesting a system, that, without going too far, would give such equitable relief as the situation of the country required. At that time, sir, I was among the warmest friends of this measure; and few gentlemen, except those whose constituents were immediately interested, were willing to give relief to the same extent that appeared to me equitable; I am still willing to go as far as was at first proposed.

The bill reported by the committee has been very ably elucidated by the observations of the two members from Illinois, and by the gentle-

man from Kentucky, (Mr. JOHNSON.) I had also gleaned some arguments which escaped those gentlemen, and which were intended to have been presented to the Senate in favor of that bill if it had been necessary. It would have given me great pleasure to have done so, because the provisions of that bill had the sanction of my judgment, and was in accordance with the feelings of my heart. That bill contained three principles, which, in my view, covered the whole justice and equity of the case. The first was the permission to surrender any portion of the land, and apply the payments to the part retained. The second offered an inducement for prompt payment by giving a discount, which was afterwards fixed by the Senate at 37½ per cent. The third authorized the payment by eight annual instalments, without interest, and without limitation as to quantity. This provision was afterwards so limited by the Senate as to apply to 320 acres only, and an oath was required from each person embracing this provision, stating that he held no more land unpaid for than 320 acres. A section was also added releasing all interest now due. Now, I beg leave to remind the Senate that it was in support of this bill, with these provisions, that the able speeches of the gentlemen, to whom I have alluded, were made. With them I acted in concert until they abandoned the bill they had so ably supported.

But, sir, that bill has been postponed. We have now to pass upon another and a very different one, to which I call the attention of the Senate while I examine its provisions.

The first section contains the principle of the first bill word for word. Connected as it is, however, with the subsequent provisions, it promises no practical effects. Before I resume my seat, I will show that this principle, great and valuable as it was in the former bill, will, in this one, be almost entirely inoperative. The second section releases the amount due; in this it coincides with the first bill. The third section contains the following provisions:

To purchasers at the rate of three dollars and upwards per acre, a discount of 33⅓ per cent. is given, and to those who purchased at a rate less than three dollars, a discount of 25 per cent.

The residue of the debt thus reduced, is divided into three classes. Those purchasers who have made one payment form the first class; the second comprises those who have made two payments; and those who have made three payments, form the third.

The debt of the first class is made payable in eight, the second class in six, and the third class in four annual instalments respectively. The debt on each instalment bears interest, but it is provided that this interest shall be remitted, on the instalments being punctually paid.

Now, sir, it is to me matter of astonishment that, with these provisions, the Senate are about to pass this bill.

The principle of discrimination between the purchasers above and those below three dollars is to me peculiarly objectionable. I cannot reconcile it with any sound principle of legislation. If any discrimination be made, it should be the reverse of this—the preference should be given to the man who cultivates the land. It cannot be denied that the great majority of the poorer class purchased their land at the minimum price—while your land merchant (I do not use the word speculator) attended your sales and bought the choice land, with a view to his own profit. I know, by our regulations for the sale of public lands, no distinction has been made heretofore, and, therefore, none is now expedient; but my feelings towards these two classes are very different, and, if an extra favor is now to be given, I would bestow it on the man who earns his bread by the sweat of his face.

Sir, this point was discussed last Saturday, and it is not necessary to repeat the arguments then used. In support of the principle, it was stated, that this provision was for the benefit of those who purchased at a high rate south of the Mississippi river. But high prices were also given north of the Ohio river. In the States of Ohio, Indiana, Illinois, and Missouri, the sum received, up to the 30th September, 1819, above minimum price, was $1,179,179; there can be no doubt that much of this was at a price above three dollars the acre, and thus it appears that, in the last mentioned States, you carry this invidious distinction. It is a singular fact, also, that the purchaser at $275 per acre, will, where three payments are now due, owe a larger sum than if he had purchased at three dollars.

But these objections are of minor importance, when compared with the other provisions. After reducing the debt by 33⅓ and 25 per cent. you propose to give eight, six, and four years credit, and release the interest on the instalments, if paid when due. If we take the interest which will become due on these instalments, it brings us to the following results: eight years, 27; six years, 21; and four years, 15 per cent. If the discount is taken, we find the following: eight years, 20⅓; six years, 16⅓; four years, 12⅓ per cent. Neither of these modes of calculation, however, is the proper one to be applied to this subject. I have therefore taken the mean between the two, which produces the following: eight years, 23⅔; six years, 18⅔; four years, 13⅔ per cent. By adding these respective sums to the discount given in the bill, the extent of the reduction is ascertained:

1st class	8 years	23⅔	+	33⅓	=	57
2d	6	18⅔	+	33⅓	=	52
3d	4	13⅔	+	33⅓	=	47

In the first class, three original payments are due; in the second class, two; and in the third class, one. The average reduction on each original payment, therefore, is 53⅔ per centum.

1st class	8 years	23⅔	+	25	=	48⅔
2d	6	18⅔	+	25	=	43⅔
3d	4	13⅔	+	25	=	38⅔

In these cases the average reduction on the original payments is 45⅓ per cent. The mean between 43⅔ and 45⅓ is 49 per cent., which is the average reduction on the whole debt due from the purchasers of public land. Besides all this, the interest now due is remitted. These results cannot be disputed; they are as certain as figures themselves.

With these facts in view, let me ask the Senate of what use is the first section of this bill? Will any individual surrender part of his land to pay for the residue, when he can pay his debts with 51 cents in the dollar. If this principle has any operation, it will only be when the land is not worth half the price at which it was originally purchased; and land only of the most inferior quality will be surrendered to the Government.

Mr. L. observed, if this bill is passed, more will be done than any person has yet asked for. He referred to the petitions signed by thousands. All that was asked or expected was a reduction of the existing debt to the present minimum price. But, pass this bill, and you lay the ground for present discontent among the inhabitants, and of future application for relief to other classes. Will A be satisfied to pay you $1 25 per acre, when you have reduced the debt of B from $2 to $1? Will the Legislature of the Nation refuse to hear the man who tells them, that, with great sacrifice and exertion, he paid his debt to the last farthing; that his neighbor, who made no such exertion or sacrifice, has been relieved of half his burden? But, suppose this class rejected; will you, after passing this bill, refuse to hear those whose lands have been forfeited? They will show by the records of the Treasury, that from them you have received $412,670. In the Cincinnati district alone, they will show you $130,756. They will plead the provisions of this bill; and I do not see on what principle you can refuse them.

In this bill you have entirely lost sight of the system of prompt payment. That part of the system is at this time one of no ordinary importance. The Secretary of the Treasury estimates the receipts from land, for the ensuing year, at not more than $1,600,000, unless some inducement for prompt payment should be offered. With proper inducements, he estimates the receipts at $2,500,000. The difference between these two, in the present embarrassed situation of the Treasury, is not to be disregarded. This advantage was strongly relied upon in pressing the first bill on the favorable attention of the Senate. In the bill now before us nothing is retained that will be of immediate advantage to the Treasury, and the estimate of the officer at the head of that Department is disregarded.

It would have given me great pleasure to have voted for a bill giving relief on this subject. Had the first bill been sustained by the Senate, I would have given it all the support in my power. It is not a common or a cold feeling I have for the persons interested in this measure. Many of my neighbors and acquaintances have removed to, and settled in the States concerned. My best wishes are for their prosperity; and, if the whole subject should fall by its own weight, which is at least a probable event, I am not to blame—my course on this measure has been a liberal one; it has been consistent and uniform.

The bill was passed and sent to the House of Representatives for concurrence.

TUESDAY, February 13.

The credentials of ELIJAH H. MILLS, appointed a Senator by the Legislature of the State of Massachusetts for the term of six years, commencing on the fourth day of March next, were read, and laid on file.

Mr. LANMAN presented the memorial of John Parish and others, inhabitants of the county of Windham, in the State of Connecticut, praying for the establishment of a certain post route; and the memorial was read, and referred to the Committee on the Post Office, &c.

Mr. RUGGLES presented the petition of Robert Caldwell and others, inhabitants of Morgan and Guernsey counties, in the State of Ohio, praying for the establishment of a certain post route; and the petition was read, and referred to the Committee on the Post Office, &c.

Mr. SMITH, from the Committee on the Judiciary, to whom was referred the petition of William Pancoast, made a report refusing the prayer of the petitioner; which was read.

On motion, by Mr. PLEASANTS, the Committee on Naval Affairs were discharged from the consideration of the resolution of the 12th of January, "to inquire whether there are any obstructions to the navigation of the river Thames, in the State of Connecticut, which were placed there by the American ships blockaded during the late war, and, if any, what measures ought to be adopted for the removal of such obstructions;" and it was referred to the Committee on Finance.

Mr. MILLS, from the Committee on the Judiciary, to whom was referred the petition of Samuel Parker, made a report, accompanied by a bill to extend the term of Samuel Parker's patents, for his improvement in currying and finishing leather of all kinds; and the report and bill were read, and the bill passed to a second reading.

Mr. THOMAS, from the Committee on Public Lands, to whom was referred the bill to establish a new land office in the State of Mississippi, and for the better regulation of certain land districts in the States of Alabama and Mississippi; reported it without amendment.

The Senate resumed the consideration of the report of the Committee of Claims on the petition of George Jackson; and, on motion, by Mr. BARBOUR, it was laid on the table.

THE BANKRUPT BILL.

The Senate resumed the consideration of the bill to establish an uniform system of bankruptcy, the question being on the motion, made by Mr. TALBOT, to recommit the bill, with instructions so to modify it as to allow all other classes, as well as merchants, to become bankrupts, on their voluntary application to avail themselves of the provisions of the act.

Messrs. VAN DYKE and LANMAN opposed the motion, the latter at some length; and Mr. TALBOT advocated it.

The question being taken on agreeing to the motion, it was decided in the negative, by the following vote:

YEAS—Messrs. Barbour, Chandler, Holmes of Maine, Johnson of Kentucky, Macon, Morril, Pleasants, Ruggles, Smith, Stokes, Talbot, Walker of Alabama, and Walker of Georgia—13.

NAYS—Messrs. Dickerson, Elliott, Gaillard, Holmes of Mississippi, Horsey, Hunter, King of New York, Knight, Lanman, Lloyd, Lowrie, Mills, Noble, Otis, Palmer, Parrott, Roberts, Sanford, Thomas, Tichenor, Trimble, Van Dyke, Williams of Mississippi, and Williams of Tennessee—24.

So the proposition to recommit and amend the bill was rejected.

The question then was stated on the following amendment, submitted yesterday by Mr. HOLMES, of Maine, as a new section:

"SEC. 3. *And be it further enacted,* That whenever any person, resident within the United States, not being a merchant or person actually using the trade of merchandise by buying and selling in gross or by retail, nor dealing in exchange, nor as a banker, broker, factor, underwriter, or marine insurer, shall do or suffer any act or thing which is herein described, or declared to be an act of bankruptcy, any one creditor, or a greater number, being partners, whose single debt shall amount to five hundred dollars, or any two or more creditors whose debts shall amount to one thousand dollars, may petition, in writing, against such person in the same manner, and the same proceedings shall be had therein, as directed and prescribed in the second section of this act; and the commissioners' designated by the said judge shall, moreover, issue a summons under their hands and seal, notifying and commanding such person to appear at a certain time and place before said commissioners, to show cause why he or she may not be declared a bankrupt, and the same commissioners shall cause personal service to be made on such person, and reasonable notice of the time and place to be given; and if such person shall not appear, or, appearing, shall consent to a commission of bankruptcy, then, and not otherwise, such person may be declared a bankrupt, and shall be subject to all the provisions of this act."

Mr. VAN DYKE deemed the argument against Mr. TALBOT's proposition as applicable to this amendment, and therefore did not conceive it necessary to add any thing on this question, except to say that, were he a farmer, he should not desire to place this power in the hands of his creditors.

Mr. HOLMES defended his amendment in detail, and at some length.

Mr. KING, of New York, spoke against the proposition, and in support, briefly, of the expediency and constitutionality of a single bankrupt system, applicable only to the trading class.

Mr. BARBOUR replied to Mr. KING, and argued in support of the justice of extending the bill to farmers and other classes, as well as traders, to which the consent of the debtor being rendered necessary, obviated all objection; stating, in conclusion, that if the amendment did not prevail, he should attempt an amendment, to confine the operation of the bill entirely to dealings between merchant and merchant, and to leave the claims of others on them unimpaired.

Mr. VAN DYKE argued to show that the amendment would produce an incongruity in the system, and was in principle inexpedient.

The question was then put on the amendment,

and was decided in the negative, by yeas and nays, as follows:

YEAS—Messrs. Barbour, Chandler, Eaton, Holmes of Maine, Holmes of Mississippi, Knight, Macon, Pleasants, Ruggles, Smith, Walker of Alabama, Walker of Georgia, and Williams of Tennessee—13.

NAYS—Messrs. Dickerson, Elliott, Gaillard, Horsey, Hunter, Johnson of Kentucky, Johnson of Louisiana, King of Alabama, King of New York, Lanman, Lloyd, Lowrie, Mills, Otis, Parrott, Roberts, Sanford, Stokes, Talbot, Thomas, Tichenor, Trimble, Van Dyke, and Williams of Mississippi—24.

So this amendment was also rejected.

Mr. BARBOUR then moved the amendment which he had intimated, and which was to insert a clause providing that, in the dividend of a bankrupt's estate, the debts due to those whose occupation excluded them from the operation of the act, should first be paid. Mr. B. spoke briefly, to show that, as other classes were not to have the benefits of the law, they ought not to suffer by it, and that, therefore, it ought to be confined to debts between merchants, and not affect the lien of the farmer.

Mr. LLOYD argued that this amendment, so far from having the effect to preserve or guard the interest of the farmers, would destroy all the chance which the bill now gave them of deriving any good from it, and would, in fact, be absolutely injurious to their interest.

Mr. BARBOUR replied, and Mr. LLOYD rejoined, in illustration and support of their opinions on the effect of the amendment.

Mr. VAN DYKE contended that the amendment was totally inconsistent with the principles of a bankrupt system.

The amendment was negatived—yeas 11.

The bill was then laid on the table, for the purpose of receiving a report necessary to be acted on to-day.

ELECTION OF PRESIDENT.

Mr. BARBOUR then, from the joint select committee appointed on the subject, reported the following resolutions:

Resolved, That the two Houses shall assemble in the Chamber of the House of Representatives on Wednesday next, at 12 o'clock, and the President of the Senate shall be the presiding officer; that one person be appointed a Teller on the part of the Senate, to make a list of the votes as they shall be declared; that the result shall be delivered to the President of the Senate, who shall announce the state of the vote, and the persons elected, to the two Houses assembled as aforesaid; which shall be deemed a declaration of the persons elected President and Vice President of the United States, and, together with a list of the votes, be entered on the Journals of the two Houses.

Resolved, That if any objection be made to the votes of Missouri, and the counting or omitting to count which shall not essentially change the result of the election; in that case they shall be reported by the President of the Senate in the following manner: Were the votes of Missouri to be counted, the result would be for A. B., for President of the United States, —— votes; if not counted, for A. B., as President of the United States, —— votes; but, in either event, A. B. is elected President of the United States; and in the same manner for Vice President.

Mr. BARBOUR explained, in detail, the reasons which influenced the committee in adopting the resolutions which it recommended.

Mr. KING, of New York, spoke in particular reference to what he deemed the correct course of proceeding in joint meetings; thinking it consistent with the Constitution, and with propriety, that the House should come to the Senate, if the apartment had not rendered it inconvenient; and that, when a convenient plan should be completed for joint meetings, he hoped the practice heretofore prevailing would not be considered in the light of a precedent, but that they should repair thither, and the President of the Senate preside in the joint meeting, &c. He was opposed to the settlement of any litigated question in joint meeting, where the Senate, as a body, would be lost; and argued that, whenever any such should arise, it would be always proper that the two Houses should separate.

Mr. MACON offered some remarks, explanatory of the views of the committee on the points before them—some thinking the votes of Missouri ought to be received and counted, and others that they ought to be rejected; that they had agreed on the second resolution as the most likely course to reconcile any difficulty. As to the place of meeting, the Chamber of the Senate would have been recommended, (he was understood to say,) but for the reason that it could not accommodate comfortably the two Houses.

The question being put on the first resolution, it was agreed to, *nem. con.*

On the second resolution a long debate took place. It was opposed by Messrs. SMITH, TALBOT, WILLIAMS, of Tennessee, and LANMAN, on various grounds; principally, for the reasons that it was not competent in the Senate to decide such a question in anticipation; that the proper time to consider and settle it was the day appointed by the Constitution; that the two Houses would not be bound to-morrow by this report; that it was useless to touch the question now, whether Missouri was a State or not, or had a right to vote; that her votes could not be legally known now, &c.

The resolution was defended by Messrs. BARBOUR, OTIS, and JOHNSON, of Kentucky, on the grounds that, as the question would certainly arise to-morrow in joint meeting, it was much better to adjust it now, and prevent all difficulty or trouble; that it was wrong to allow the pleasure and good feelings growing out of the event of to-morrow, a great and pleasing incident illustrative of our free institutions, to be disturbed by a question which could be so well settled previously, &c.

Mr. KING, of New York, in accordance with the opinions he had submitted, wished some amendment introduced to prevent the mode of proceeding from being quoted as a precedent hereafter—an amendment declaring that, if any question should arise relative to any votes, in joint meeting, that the two Houses would separate to consider the case, and not decide it jointly.

Mr. BARBOUR said that, on the present occasion,

as the election could not be affected by the votes of any one State, no difficulty could arise; and that it was his intention hereafter to bring the subject up, to remedy what he considered a *casus omissus* in the Constitution, either by an act of Congress, if that should appear sufficient, or, if not, by proposing an amendment to the Constitution itself.

The second resolution was then also agreed to; and the Senate adjourned.

WEDNESDAY, February 14.

The Senate proceeded to the appointment of a Teller on their part, in pursuance of the report of the joint committee appointed to consider and report a mode of examining the votes for President and Vice President of the United States; and Mr. BARBOUR was appointed.

Mr. KNIGHT presented the petition of Lemuel White, of Rhode Island, praying a pension; which was read, and referred to the Committee on Pensions.

Mr. JOHNSON, of Louisiana, presented the memorial of François Dufossat, son of Guy Dufossat, representing that certain forts have been erected and established on his land in Orleans county, in said State, and praying that other lands may be granted to him of equal value in lieu thereof; and the memorial was read, and referred to the Secretary of War.

Mr. SANFORD, from the Committee on Finance, in pursuance of instructions of the 12th instant, reported a bill for the relief of William Whitehead, Joshua Aubin, and James Graham; and the bill was read, and passed to the second reading.

Mr. VAN DYKE, from the Committee on Public Lands, to whom was referred the petition of P. P. Saint Guirons and others, French emigrants, engaged in the cultivation of the vine and olive, made a report, accompanied by a resolution, that the prayer of the petitioners ought not to be granted. The report and resolution were read.

Mr. ROBERTS, from the Committee on the Public Buildings, to whom was referred the bill, entitled "An act making appropriations for the public buildings," reported it with amendments; which were read.

Mr. JOHNSON, of Kentucky, laid on the table the copy of a letter from him to the President of the Bank of the United States, and the answer thereto; which were read, and laid on file.

The bill to extend the term of Samuel Parker's patents, for his improvement in currying and finishing leather of all kinds, was read the second time.

The Senate proceeded to consider the report of the Committee on the Judiciary on the petition of William Pancoast; and it was laid on the table.

BANKRUPT BILL.

The Senate took up and considered the bill to establish an uniform system of bankruptcy throughout the United States, as amended.

A motion was made by Mr. KNIGHT, of Rhode Island, to include manufacturers in the operation of the system. On which, Mr K. made the following remarks:

Mr. KNIGHT said, it had been stated by the honorable mover of the bill, (Mr. VAN DYKE,) that it is intended particularly for those who are subject to risks and losses, in their lawful business; for those who intrust their property out of their control and on the ocean. In this provision, I perfectly agree with the honorable gentleman, said Mr. K. And, as the bill does not provide for every class of our citizens, who are subject to great risks and losses in their business, I now move, sir, to amend the bill, by inserting in the —— line of the first section, after the word merchant, the word manufacturer. The bill will then read, that, if any merchant, manufacturer, or other persons.

In order to show that manufacturers are entitled to the benefit of the provisions of this bill, permit me to state a few facts. It is well known to gentlemen living in the Eastern section of the United States, that the freshets occasioned by the breaking up of one of our Northern Winters, often do great damage to the mills, mill-dams, and other property belonging to manufacturing establishments. I have known, sir, many persons nearly ruined by these disasters, their labor, toil, and savings for many years, entirely swept away by one of those freshets.

But, sir, water is not the only element to which they are exposed; fire, too, hath made its ravages. I believe, sir, a larger proportion of this kind of property has been destroyed by fire within the last fifteen years than of any other species within the United States. In fact, so frequent has been the destruction of manufacturing establishments by fire, that no prudent person will insure against it. The offices to the East totally reject all applications for insurance on cotton mills. They would not be taken even at what would be called by the merchant a war risk—a premium that no regular business can give in this or any other country. If this amendment is adopted, it will not only include cotton manufacturers, but the manufacturer of hats, woollen, hemp, powder, &c. I would ask, sir, who among us would insure on a powder mill? I presume, nobody, at any premium that could be afforded by the proprietor, unless it was a person willing to be blown up. Then, sir, the manufacturer is compelled to risk and endure all losses that may happen; and, if so unfortunate as to lose his property by fire or other casualty, he is doomed to everlasting misery while on earth; while the merchant, who can be insured, and thereby divide his loss among the community, you exonerate from responsibility; you set him free to seek new fortunes, and to provide for himself and family the means of a comfortable subsistence—

[Here it was observed by Mr. VAN DYKE, that the manufacturer, who gets his living by buying and selling, was embraced in the bill.]

It is now suggested by the honorable mover of the bill, that manufacturers are embraced in the operations of the bill. Be it so. But, if they are embraced in the bill by implication, why object to the amendment? Why not have it clearly expressed? I admit there is no music in the word, yet it will not destroy the harmony of the bill if it should be inserted. Besides, sir, I have been taught to believe that statutes are to be construed strictly, that little is to be taken by implication; and unless manufacturers are particularly mentioned, as such, they cannot participate in the benefits, nor be subject to the operations of the law. Can it be said, sir, that the manufacturer, who merely purchases the raw material, manufactures it into cloth or other commodity, sends it to his factor or agent to sell, is a trader within the meaning of the bill? He does not make a living by buying and selling, and in my mind does not come within the purview of the law. I hope, sir, the amendment will prevail.

Mr. MILLS, of Massachusetts, replied, that he believed the object of the gentleman was now attained; that the manufacturer did carry on trade in such a manner as to be clearly within the meaning of the bill. And to insert manufacturer, was too broad a term; that not only the persons designed by the gentleman would be embraced, but shoemakers, carpenters, and all mechanics, would come in under that provision.

Mr. VAN DYKE repeated, that the manufacturer who gets his living by buying and selling, was now embraced in the bill.

The question being taken on Mr. KNIGHT's motion, it was lost; but ten rising in its favor. The bill was laid on the table.

ELECTORAL VOTES FOR PRESIDENT.

A message from the House of Representatives informed the Senate that the House of Representatives have rejected the resolution of the Senate declaring the admission of the State of Missouri into the Union. The House of Representatives concur in the report of the joint committee appointed to make arrangements upon the subject of counting the votes for PRESIDENT and VICE PRESIDENT of the UNITED STATES, and have appointed tellers on their part, and are now ready to receive the Senate to perform that ceremony.

Whereupon, the two Houses of Congress, agreeably to the joint resolution, assembled in the Representatives' Chamber, and the certificates of the Electors of the several States, beginning with the State of New Hampshire, were, by the President of the Senate, opened and delivered to tellers appointed for the purpose, by whom they were read, except the State of Missouri; and, when the certificate of the Electors of that State was opened, an objection was made by Mr. LIVERMORE, a member of the House of Representatives from the State of New Hampshire, to counting said votes. Whereupon on motion, by Mr. WILLIAMS, of Tennessee, the Senate returned to their own Chamber.

A message from the House of Representatives informed the Senate that the House of Representatives is now ready to receive the Senate in the Chamber of the House of Representatives for the purpose of continuing the enumeration of the votes of the Electors for President and Vice President, according to the joint resolutions agreed upon between the two Houses.

On motion, by Mr. BARBOUR, it was

Resolved, That the Senate proceed to meet the House of Representatives in order to conclude the counting of the votes for President and Vice President of the United States, according to the last of the joint resolutions adopted for that purpose.

Whereupon, the two Houses having again assembled in the Representatives' Chamber, the certificate of the Electors of the State of Missouri was, by the President of the Senate, delivered to the tellers, who read the same, and who, having examined and ascertained, the whole number of votes, presented a list thereof to the President of the Senate, by whom it was read, as follows:

		President.		Vice President.				
Number of votes to which each State is entitled.	STATES.	James Monroe, of Virginia.	John Quincy Adams, of Mass.	Daniel D. Tompkins, of N. Y.	Richard Stockton, of N. Jersey.	Robert G. Harper, of Maryland.	Richard Rush, of Pennsylvania.	Daniel Rodney, of Delaware.
8	New Hampshire -	7	1	7	-		1	
15	Massachusetts -	15	-	7	8			
4	Rhode Island -	4	-	4				
9	Connecticut -	9	-	9				
8	Vermont -	8	-	8				
29	New York -	29	-	29				
8	New Jersey -	8	-	8				
25	Pennsylvania -	24	-	24				
4	Delaware -	4	-	-	-	-	-	4
11	Maryland -	11	-	10	-	1		
25	Virginia -	25	-	25				
15	North Carolina -	15	-	15				
11	South Carolina -	11	-	11				
8	Georgia -	8	-	8				
12	Kentucky -	12	-	12				
8	Tennessee -	7	-	7				
8	Ohio -	8	-	8				
3	Louisiana -	3	-	3				
3	Indiana -	3	-	3				
3	Mississippi -	3	-	2				
3	Illinois -	3	-	3				
3	Alabama -	3	-	3				
9	Maine -	9	-	9				
3	Missouri -	3	-	3				
		228	1	215	8	1	1	4

The whole number of the Electors appointed being 235, including those of Missouri, of which 118 make a majority; or, excluding the Electors of Missouri, the whole number would be 232, of which 117 make a majority; but, in either event, JAMES MONROE, of Virginia, is elected PRESIDENT, and DANIEL D. TOMPKINS, of New York, is elected VICE PRESIDENT of the United States.

Whereupon,

The President of the Senate declared JAMES

MONROE, of Virginia, duly elected President of the United States, commencing with the fourth day of March next; and DANIEL D. TOMPKINS Vice President of the United States, commencing with the fourth day of March next.

The votes of the Electors were then delivered to the Secretary of the Senate; the two Houses separated, and the Senate returned to their own Chamber, and then adjourned.

THURSDAY, February 15.

The following Message was received from the PRESIDENT OF THE UNITED STATES:

To the Senate of the United States :

I transmit to Congress a report from the Director of the Mint, enclosing a statement of the Treasurer, submitting the operations of the Mint for the last year.

JAMES MONROE.

WASHINGTON, *February* 14, 1821.

The Message and report were read.

Mr. SANFORD presented the petition of Charlotte Read, widow of Thomas M. Read, deceased, late a Captain in the Army, praying to be allowed a pension, in consideration of the military services of her late husband; and the petition was read, and referred to the Committee on Pensions.

Mr. SANFORD, from the Committee on Finance, to whom was referred the bill, entitled "An act making appropriations for the support of Government for the year 1821," reported it with an amendment; which was read.

Mr. ROBERTS gave notice that, to-morrow, he should ask leave to bring in a resolution declaring the admission of the State of Missouri into the Union.

Mr. HORSEY gave notice that, to-morrow, he should ask leave to bring in a bill concerning divorces and alimony in the District of Columbia.

On motion, by Mr. NOBLE, the Committee on Pensions were discharged from the consideration of the petitions of John B. Chatard, David Mallory, William Sizer, and William Plumbe; and John B. Chatard and William Plumbe had leave, respectively, to withdraw their petitions and papers.

On motion, by Mr. BARBOUR, the Committee on Foreign Relations were discharged from the consideration of the memorials of the Chamber of Commerce of the city of New York, and the merchants and underwriters of the city of Baltimore; and they were respectively referred to the Secretary of the Navy.

On motion, by Mr. TRIMBLE, the Senate took up and considered the report of the Committee on Pensions on the petition of Dean Weymouth; and the resolution accompanying the same was amended, and agreed to as follows:

Resolved, That the prayer of the petitioner ought to be granted, and that the committee be instructed to report a bill allowing him a pension at the rate of twelve dollars and fifty cents per month.

Mr. SMITH submitted the following motion for consideration:

Resolved, That the President of the United States be requested to cause to be laid before the Senate the original order for building the barracks at Sackett's Harbor, together with all the communications between the War Department and Major General Brown relative thereto, and the amount of public moneys expended thereon.

The bill for the relief of William Whitehead, Joshua Aubin, and James Graham, was read the second time.

The Senate proceeded to consider the report of the Committee on Public Lands on the petition of P. P. St. Guirons and others; and, in concurrence therewith, resolved that the pra er of the petitioners ought not to be granted. y

BANKRUPT BILL.

The Senate resumed the consideration of the bill to establish an uniform system of bankruptcy.

Mr. CHANDLER moved to amend the bill by inserting in the first section the following additional proviso:

And provided, also, That no discharge which may be given to a bankrupt, under this act, shall operate so as to discharge the bankrupt from debts which may be due to any persons, except those debts which may be due to merchants, bankers, brokers, factors, underwriters, or marine insurers.

This proposition gave rise to some debate, in which the amendment was supported by Messrs. LLOYD, CHANDLER, TRIMBLE, and ROBERTS, and was opposed by Messrs. VAN DYKE, OTIS, MILLS, and KING, of Alabama.

The discussion resulted in the rejection of the amendment by the following vote:

YEAS—Messrs. Barbour, Chandler, Eaton, Holmes of Maine, Johnson of Kentucky, Lloyd, Macon, Morril, Noble, Pleasants, Roberts, Smith, Talbot, Trimble, Walker of Alabama, Walker of Georgia, and Williams of Tennessee—17.

NAYS—Messrs. Dana, Dickerson, Edwards, Elliott, Horsey, Hunter, Johnson of Louisiana, King of Alabama, King of New York, Lanman, Lowrie, Mills, Otis, Palmer, Parrott, Sanford, Stokes, Taylor, Thomas, Tichenor, Van Dyke, and Williams of Mississippi—22.

Mr. HOLMES, of Maine, moved to strike out the 21st section of the bill, which provides that the commissioners shall, on probable cause shown, have authority to issue their warrant to any person or officer, authorizing him to break open, in the day time, the houses, chambers, shops, trunks, &c., of the bankrupt, where any of his goods, or estate, deeds, writings, books, &c., may be, and take possession thereof.

This motion was decided also in the negative, by yeas and nays—yeas 14, nays 27, as follows:

YEAS—Messrs. Chandler, Eaton, Holmes of Maine, Johnson of Kentucky, Lloyd, Macon, Morril, Pleasants, Roberts, Smith, Stokes, Talbot, Walker of Georgia, and Williams of Tennessee.

NAYS—Messrs. Barbour, Dana, Dickerson, Edwards, Elliott, Gaillard, Horsey, Hunter, Johnson of Louisiana, King of Alabama, King of New York, Knight, Lanman, Lowrie, Mills, Noble, Otis, Palmer, Parrott, Sanford, Taylor, Thomas, Tichenor, Trimble, Van Dyke, Walker of Alabama, and Williams of Mississippi.

On motion of Mr. HOLMES, of Maine, the sixty-third section of the bill was so amended as to provide that the facts of any case shall be tried by a jury, at the election of either party, instead of at the discretion of the court or judge.

Mr. LOWRIE then, with the view, as he remarked, of making the system entirely prospective in its operations, and not touch existing debts at all, moved to add a provision to the sixty-first section, declaring that the act should "release no person who may hereafter be declared a bankrupt from any debt existing at the passage of this act."

On this proposition a long debate ensued; in which Mr. LOWRIE and Mr. ROBERTS maintained the amendment, on the ground of its expediency, without reference to the Constitutional question; and Mr. EDWARDS spoke briefly on the proper construction of the bill as it now stood. Mr. HOLMES, of Maine, and Mr. WALKER, of Alabama, argued th at a discharge of debts existing at the passage of the act would be unconstitutional; which opinion was answered and opposed by Messrs. MILLS, OTIS, and VAN DYKE.

Mr. WALKER, of Georgia, though opposed to the bill altogether, was opposed to the amendment, and advocated an entire discharge of the debtor, if the system passed at all.

The question being taken on the amendment, it was negatived by the following vote:

YEAS—Messrs. Barbour, Chandler, Eaton, Holmes of Maine, King of Alabama. Lloyd, Lowrie, Macon, Morril, Pleasants, Roberts, Talbot, Trimble, and Walker of Alabama—14.

NAYS—Messrs. Dana, Dickerson, Edwards, Elliott, Gaillard, Horsey, Hunter, Johnson of Kentucky, Johnson of Louisiana, King of New York, Knight, Lanman, Mills, Noble, Otis, Palmer, Parrott, Sanford, Stokes, Taylor, Thomas, Tichenor, Van Dyke, Walker of Georgia, Williams of Mississippi, and Williams of Tennessee—26.

Mr. TALBOT moved to strike out of the bill that clause of the sixty-third section, which gives to the circuit courts of the United States jurisdiction of all cases in law or equity arising under the act.

This motion was assented to by the friends of the bill, and was agreed to.

Mr. TALBOT next moved to reduce the term to which the duration of the bill is limited, from five years (the time with which the blank had been filled) to two years.

Mr. OTIS proposed to split the difference with the gentleman, and make it four years.

Mr. TALBOT agreed to change his proposition to three years, and in that shape it was adopted.

After one or two unsuccessful attempts by Mr. ROBERTS to amend certain features of the bill, to which he objected; and no other amendment being offered—

The question was then taken on ordering the bill to be engrossed, as amended, and read a third time, and it was decided in the affirmative by yeas and nays, as follows:

YEAS—Messrs. Dana. Dickerson, Edwards, Elliott, Gaillard, Horsey, Hunter, Johnson of Louisiana, King of New York, Knight, Lanman, Mills, Otis, Parrott, Stokes, Thomas, Tichenor, Van Dyke, and Williams of Mississippi—19.

NAYS—Messrs. Barbour, Chandler, Eaton, Holmes of Maine, Johnson of Kentucky, King of Alabama, Lloyd, Lowrie, Macon, Morril, Palmer, Pleasants, Roberts, Talbot, Trimble, Walker of Alabama, Walker of Georgia, and Williams of Tennessee—18.

FRIDAY, February 16.

The PRESIDENT communicated a letter from the Secretary of War, transmitting, in compliance with a resolution of the Senate, of the 15th of May last, statements exhibiting the number of militia from each State, that were called into the public service by orders of the President of the United States; the number furnished by each State; the number recognised by the United States from each State, and the period of their service; the amount of fines imposed for neglect of duty, distinguishing the number of persons on whom fines have been imposed, the sums collected, and the sums paid into the Treasury; and the expenses of courts martial in the several States; and the letter and statements were read.

Mr. PINKNEY presented the petition of Nathaniel W. and C. H. Appleton, merchants, and late copartners in Baltimore, praying for the restitution of certain moneys illegally exacted from them for duties on goods imported into Castine, whilst in possession of the British, and the petition was read, and referred to the Committee on Finance.

Mr. HORSEY obtained leave to bring in a bill concerning divorces and alimony in the District of Columbia; and the bill was twice read by unanimous consent, and referred to the Committee on the District of Columbia.

Mr. H. laid on the table a communication from the vaccine agent in Baltimore, exhibiting the present state of the vaccine institution.

The Senate proceeded to consider the motion of yesterday, requesting the President of the United States to lay before the Senate the original order for building the barracks at Sackett's Harbor, and other documents connected therewith; and agreed thereto.

SAMUEL L. SOUTHARD, appointed a Senator by the Legislature of the State of New Jersey, to supply the vacancy occasioned by the resignation of James J. Wilson, produced his credentials, was qualified, and took his seat in the Senate.

The Senate, according to the order of the day, took up the bill from the other House, to reduce the Military Peace Establishment; when,

On motion by Mr. SMITH, who wished to offer some remarks on the subject, for which he was not prepared to-day, the bill was postponed to and made the order of the day for Monday next.

BANK OF THE UNITED STATES.

The Senate then resumed the consideration of the bill to amend the charter of the Bank of the United States, the question pending being on the amendments offered by Mr. ROBERTS; first to make the notes of the bank and its branches receivable by the United States only in the States where they are made payable, except notes of the amount of five dollars, which shall be receivable at the bank or any of its branches. Secondly, that it shall not be lawful for the bank to establish more than one branch in any State without the consent of the Legislature of such State, &c.

Much discussion took place of these propositions, and the others embraced in the amendments, in the course of which,

Mr. RUGGLES moved so to amend the amendment as to make the consent of the Legislature of a State necessary to the establishment of any branch of the bank in such State.

This motion was negatived without a division, and, soon after the bill was laid on the table for the purpose of acting on the message which was received from the other House.

MISSOURI.

Mr. ROBERTS asked and obtained leave to bring in a resolution declaring the admission of the State of Missouri into the Union.

The resolution is as follows:

Resolved by the Senate and House of Representatives of the United States of America, in Congress assembled, That the State of Missouri shall be, and is hereby declared, one of the United States of America, and is admitted into the Union on an equal footing with the original States in all respects whatever: *Provided,* That the following be taken as fundamental conditions and terms upon which the said State is admitted into the Union, namely: that the fourth clause of the twenty-sixth section of the third article of the constitution, submitted by the people of Missouri to the consideration of Congress, shall, as soon as the provisions of said constitution will admit, be so amended, that it shall not be applicable to citizens of any State in this Union; and that, until so amended, no law, passed in conformity thereto, shall be construed to extend to any citizen of either State in this Union.

Mr. VAN DYKE, of Delaware, said he hoped the gentleman would not understand him, in making the motion which he was about to make, as offering any disrespect towards him or his proposition; but, Mr. VAN DYKE said, he should consider it unfortunate for the Senate now to take any step in this business. The Senate ought to recollect the course this subject had taken; they had at an early period sent to the other House a resolution for the admission of the State into the Union, containing a proviso which it was hoped would obviate all objection to it. That resolution, however, had been rejected by the House of Representatives. They have informed us, by message, of its rejection, without any indication of what would be acceptable to them; and that message is scarcely cold before we have a proposition to bring forward another resolution. He thought the Senate had better not stir in the subject again so soon; but that it would be more expedient to wait a while at least, and see what the other House should do, if it did any thing. He had no objection to make another effort to get the State admitted, but to make it so soon after the fate of the first proposition had been announced from the other House, would be premature, he thought, and unwise. If the Senate had not moved first in this business, but had now its reso-

lution to send to the other House as an original proposition, he thought it highly probable it would prevail there. With the best intentions, that resolution had been sent there; it had been rejected; and the Senate was as yet ignorant of the form of admission which would be acceptable to that body. He hoped the Senate would keep back, a little longer at least, any new proposition; and therefore moved that the motion to grant the leave asked for, be postponed until Monday next.

Mr. ROBERTS was of opinion that the Senate might, without the slightest departure from propriety or dignity, receive the resolution; and then he should have no objection to laying it on the table for some days; it would then be before the Senate, and gentlemen could give it due reflection. Mr. R. said he offered this resolution from a strong and serious conviction of duty; and, as the session was near its end, he trusted that the Senate would not allow any punctilio to interfere with an object so important. He was one who had been unable to vote for the former resolution which passed the Senate; that having failed in the other branch, he now offered such a one as he could support. He earnestly desired the admission of the State into the Union; it was an object all important to the nation and to its public councils, and he hoped the Senate would so far indulge him at least as to entertain his proposition, and then, if it saw fit, lay it by for future decision.

Mr. WALKER, of Georgia, viewed this proposition as a kind of peace offering on the part of those gentlemen of the Senate who had opposed the former resolution. He was extremely anxious that the question should be settled, and that nothing should be left undone to effect a settlement of it. He therefore acknowledged himself much obliged to the gentleman from Pennsylvania for bringing this proposition forward. Whatever may be the decisions of the other branch, said Mr. W., let us do all we can to preserve the peace and harmony of the Union. He hoped no point of etiquette would interfere with the motion, but that the leave would be granted; that the proposition would be ultimately adopted, and the tranquillity of the nation be restored by the admission of the State without more delay.

Mr. MORRIL, of New Hampshire, adverted to the unpleasant feelings and effects of this long agitated Missouri question; the great portion of time which it consumed of the last and of the present session; the embarrassment it produced in the public business. It pursues us, said he, every where in the House, and from one House to the other, into the committee rooms and out of doors. He sincerely hoped that it might be terminated at the present session, and was a little surprised that his friend from Delaware should make an objection to receiving a proposition which might bring the subject to a favorable issue. The act of the last session concerning Missouri, Mr. M. said, passed both Houses of Congress, and received the Executive sanction. Had that act been properly met by Missouri, there would have been no difficulty in her admission; the former question was considered as settled, and, but for the clause now objected to, her admission would have met with no serious opposition. He thought every effort ought to be made to bring the subject to an amicable issue, and hoped it would be ended by the passage of this resolution. There was nothing, among the numerous subjects before Congress, of more importance, and he thought the Senate ought to receive, without postponement, the proposition now offered.

Mr. JOHNSON, of Kentucky, could not see, because the Senate had done its duty once, that it was to do nothing more. He, for one, was ready to embrace every opportunity of performing it. How, he asked, were the Senate to ascertain the sentiments of the other House, or of each other, but by proceeding in this way? Caucussing was no longer fashionable here, and the distance over which members were scattered completely prevented an interchange of opinions in private. It was the best course to do what they could when the opportunity offered. This subject was of more importance than any other before Congress; it distracted the legislative councils and impeded all other business. An immense quantity of business of the deepest concern to the nation continued before them, to be done during the short remainder of the session—more than he had ever known, even at the commencement of some sessions; yet none of this would or could be done until this all-devouring subject of Missouri was settled. Every other subject was put in jeopardy by it. The relief of our land debtors is endangered—the army is endangered—the Union itself is endangered—those ties which have bound us together as a nation of brothers, have been weakened by this all-distracting question. He would therefore meet it, and continue to meet it, until the 4th of March; he would discard all other subjects to make an effort to terminate and adjust it. We see, said he, that nothing else can be done; we send to the other House bill after bill, but in vain; we hear of nothing there but Missouri, Missouri, Missouri! and thus will it continue until we can end it. Mr. J. avowed that he felt under obligations to the gentleman from Pennsylvania for bringing this proposition forward; and, unless some member would get up and say he was not ready to vote on granting the leave, he should oppose the postponement.

Mr. BARBOUR, of Virginia, said he would vote against the postponement, because it was an unusual course, and he was inclined to advance, under the hope that this resolution would receive the sanction of the Senate and of the House of Representatives, and put an end to this painful contest. This proposition would either obtain with the other House, or it would not, and though there might be something in its passage now, like a surrender of etiquette on the part of the Senate, yet he would not consider a little matter of form as more important than the adjustment of this all important question. If it should finally fail, a great responsibility would rest somewhere. Gentlemen might smile, he said, but they who treated the subject lightly were far removed from the scene of real excitement. Could they witness the

sensations which it produced in that part of the Union where its effects were most to be dreaded, they would think more gravely of it. When the Senate, said Mr. B., shall have manifested a desire, an anxious desire, to settle the question by one more effort, and shall still fail, our skirts will be clear; and let what consequences ensue that may, our records will show that *we* have done what we could to prevent them. If nothing serious ensue, still we shall have nothing to regret. Mr. B. hoped the proposition would at least be received, if then laid on the table.

Mr. HOLMES, of Maine, was willing to grant the leave requested, but merely as a matter of courtesy—not from a hope of its doing any good. The Senate had passed a resolution to admit the State; it was sent to the other House, where it was amended, and then rejected. Was it for the Senate immediately to shape another and send to them, or to wait and see if that House would agree on any proposition of its own? If they send us none, it will be evidence that they are not disposed to do any thing. The public mind, Mr. H. said, had been much excited on this subject, but a change was taking place, and the people were beginning to say, let Missouri into the Union—if you do not, let the responsibility rest where it belongs.

Mr. VAN DYKE disclaimed being influenced in his motion by motives of etiquette. He acted from a conviction of its expediency in regard to the object in view—the admission of the State. He believed Missouri would be admitted into the Union before the 4th of March, on a footing with the other States; but he thought it impolitic for the Senate again to take up the subject so hastily, and that he was walking in the plain path of his duty towards Missouri, in regard to her admission, in making his motion to postpone the introduction of this resolution. The proposition was the same in substance as the former resolution, and if there was no difficulty apprehended here, on it, why should it be pressed again so soon; why not allow the other House some time to act on a plan of its own, or at least wait a short time and observe the indications there? The strength of Missouri was increasing in this House at least, and it was prudent to rest awhile, and discover what course the other House was likely to take. The proposition could sustain no injury by the delay; it was before the Senate, in fact, though not in form, for it had been printed and was on the table of each member. All he asked was, that the Senate would hold its hand until Monday next, before it entertained the proposition.

Mr. WALKER, of Alabama, concurred in the opinions of the gentleman from Delaware. The Senate had evinced, at all times, a disposition to admit Missouri. It had at an early period of the session, passed a resolution declaring her admission, and sent it to the other House, where it was finally rejected. The Senate knew that many propositions had been before that House on this subject; none of them had succeeded, and there was, consequently, no evidence of a disposition there to admit the State. Nothing would be gained by this resolution but affording to the House of

Representatives another opportunity of having the subject before them at large; for this identical proposition, with the exception of perhaps a single word, had already been considered in that House, and been rejected by it. He was of opinion that it would be much better for the Senate now to wait until the other House took some step of its own in the business, as it had rejected the resolution sent down by the Senate. He could perceive no probable good likely to result from the Senate's again acting on the subject; its disposition was undoubted; it had done its duty; and he was for giving the House an opportunity of adopting its own plan if it had any.

Mr. CHANDLER, of Maine, conceived that the Senate had done every thing, so far, that was proper on the subject. If it entertained this proposition, it might prevent the other House from proceeding in its endeavors to agree on some plan of its own; and he was in favor, therefore, of deferring any other step on the part of the Senate for some time at least.

The question being then taken on postponing the motion for leave, it was decided in the negative—18 rising in favor of the postponement, and 20 against it.

The question then being on granting the leave, Mr. SMITH, of South Carolina, made a point of order. The 13th of the joint rules of the two Houses inhibited the re-introduction, in either House, without a notice of ten days, of any bill or resolution which should have been passed by one House and sent to the other, and there rejected. Mr. S. conceived that this rule would oppose the introduction of this resolution at this time, ten days' notice not having been given by the mover; and Mr. S. was proceeding to support his objection with some arguments; when

The PRESIDENT overruled the objection taken, referring to the practice of the Senate in former cases.

The question being then put on granting the leave, it was carried without a division, and the resolution received its first reading.

A message having been received from the House of Representatives, announcing the death of the Hon. WM. A. BURWELL, a member of that House from the State of Virginia—

On motion of Mr. PLEASANTS, it was

Resolved, unanimously, That the members of the Senate will attend the funeral of the Hon. Wm. A. Burwell, late a member of the House of Representatives from the State of Virginia, to-morrow, at ten o'clock, A. M.; and, as a testimony of respect for the memory of the deceased, will go into mourning, and wear crape for thirty days.

The Senate adjourned to Monday.

MONDAY, February 19

The PRESIDENT communicated a report of the Secretary of the Treasury, complying with the resolution of the Senate of the 2d instant, relative to the liquidation and settlement of the claims of John H. Piatt at the Treasury; and the report was read.

Mr. SANFORD presented the memorial of Jacob Barker, of New York, representing that the report of the Committee of Claims made on his former memorial is erroneous; exhibiting additional evidence in support of the claim, and praying a revision thereof; and the memorial was read, and referred to the Committee of Claims.

Mr. THOMAS presented the memorial of John Caldwell and others, purchasers of certain lots in Shawneetown, which they presented to the county of Gallatin, for the purpose of erecting a courthouse and jail, praying that the balance of the purchase money due may be remitted; and the memorial was read, and referred to the Committee on Public Lands.

Mr. ROBERTS presented the petition of Daniel Carroll, of Duddington, and others, proprietors of the House occupied by the Senate and House of Representatives during the fourteenth and fifteenth Congresses, praying that the damages which the House sustained during the said occupancy may be repaired; and the petition was read, and referred to the Committee on Public Buildings.

Mr. LOWRIE presented the petition of Henry S. Tanner, praying the aid of the Government to enable him to publish an atlas, to embrace the whole territory of the United States, with its relative importance with respect to other portions of the world; and the petition was read and laid on the table.

Mr. KING, of New York, presented the memorial of Gurdon Buck, and others, citizens of the United States, praying that additional lights may be authorized for greater safety in navigating the "Sound," between the continent and Long Island; and the memorial was read, and referred to the Committee on Commerce and Manufactures.

Mr. SANFORD presented the petition of Samuel S. Baldwin and others, of New York, praying the establishment of certain post routes; and the petition was read, and referred to the Committee on the Post Office and Post Roads.

Mr. THOMAS, from the Committee on Public Lands, to whom was referred the resolution of the 19th of January, instructing said committee to inquire into the expediency of authorizing Jared E. Groce to enter a fraction of land, made a report accompanied by a resolution that the Committee on Public Lands be discharged from the further consideration of this subject.

Mr. EATON, from the same committee, to whom was referred the petition of Kon-na-noo-lus-kee, or Chalenge, of the Cherokee tribe of Indians, made a report accompanied by a bill for the relief of Kon-na-noo-lus-kee or Chalenge, one of the tribe of the Cherokee Indians; and the report and bill were read, and the bill passed to a second reading.

Mr. DICKERSON, from the Committee on Commerce and Manufactures, to whom was referred the petition of Thomas Dobson and Son, made a report accompanied by a resolution that the petitioners have leave to withdraw their petition.

Mr. KING, of New York, from the Committee on Roads and Canals, reported a bill supplemental to the act of last session, authorizing the appointment of commissioners to lay out a road from Wheeling to the Mississippi; and the bill was read. [This bill provides that the said road shall be so laid out as to pass through Columbus, Indianopolis, and Vandalia, (the seats of government of Ohio, Indiana, and Illinois,) and making an additional appropriation of ten thousand dollars for that object.]

Mr. Johnson, of Louisiana, from the select committee to whom the subject was referred, reported a bill supplementary to the several acts for adjusting the claims to land, and establishing land offices in the districts east of the island of New Orleans; and the bill was read, and passed to a second reading.

The resolution declaring the admission of the State of Missouri into the Union was read the second time.

COMPENSATION TO MEMBERS.

The report of the committee, adverse to the reduction of the compensation of members of Congress, with the amendment, going to alter the tenor of that report, was next on the orders of the day.

Mr. Barbour moved to lay the resolution on the table.

Mr. Roberts, considering this motion as proposing a final disposition of the subject for the present session, required the yeas and nays on the question; and the yeas and nays on the question were taken accordingly, as follows:

Yeas—Messrs. Barbour, Eaton, Elliott, Gaillard, Holmes of Maine, Hunter, Johnson of Louisiana, King of New York, Lanman, Mills, Otis, Pleasants, Sanford, Stokes, Walker of Georgia, and Williams of Tennessee—17.

Nays—Messrs. Dana, Dickerson, Holmes of Mississippi, Knight, Lowrie, Macon, Morril, Noble, Palmer, Roberts, Ruggles, Smith, Southard, Talbot, Taylor, Thomas, Trimble, Walker of Alabama, and Williams of Mississippi—19.

So the Senate refused to lay the report on the table, and proceeded to consider it.

Subsequently, on motion of Mr. Barbour, supported by an argument on the merits of the proposition, the report was postponed to Thursday next.

BANK OF THE UNITED STATES.

The Senate resumed the consideration of the bill to amend the charter of the Bank of the United States, the question still being on the following amendment, proposed by Mr. Roberts:

Sec. 3. *And be it further enacted,* That the bills or notes of the Offices of Discount and Deposite of the said bank, excepting those of the office in the District of Columbia, originally made payable, or which shall have become payable on demand, shall be receivable in all payments to the United States, only in the States and Territories in which they are made payable, and in the States and Territories in which no Office of Discount and Deposite shall be established, any thing in the fourteenth section of the act incorporating the subscribers to the Bank of the United States, to the contrary notwithstanding: *Provided,* That all notes of the denomination of five dollars, issued either by the bank or any of its Offices of Dis-

count and Deposite, made payable on demand, shall be receivable at the bank or any of its offices: *And provided further,* That it shall not be lawful for the directors of the said bank to establish more than one Office of Discount and Deposite in any State, without the consent of the Legislature thereof, first had and obtained.

Sec. 4. *And be it further enacted,* That so much of the second and fourteenth fundamental articles of the constitution of said bank, contained in the eleventh section of the act incorporating the subscribers thereto, as provides that no director of the said bank, or any of its Offices of Discount and Deposite, shall hold his office more than three years out of four in succession, be, and the same is hereby repealed.

Sec. 5. *And be it further enacted,* That the directors of the said corporation shall cause a list of the stockholders of the said bank, together with their places of residence, to be kept in the banking house at Philadelphia, open to the inspection of any and every stockholder of said bank who may apply for the same within the hours of business, for at least ninety days previously to every annual election of directors, and no person who may be entitled to vote at any election for directors of said bank, as attorney, proxy, or agent, for any other person, copartnership, or body politic, shall, as such, give a greater number than —— votes, under any pretence whatsoever, and no letter of proxy shall be of any force or effect longer than —— years, or until it shall have been revoked.

Sec. 6. *And be it further enacted,* That whenever the said corporation assent to the provisions of this act, and certify such assent to the Secretary of the Treasury Department by writing, duly authenticated, this act shall be of full force and effect, and not otherwise.

The question being taken on the first section of this amendment, it was rejected by the following vote:

Yeas—Messrs. Dana, Dickerson, Edwards, Elliott, Roberts, Taylor, and Williams of Mississippi—7.

Nays—Messrs. Barbour, Brown, Chandler, Eaton, Gaillard, Holmes of Maine, Holmes of Mississippi, Horsey, Hunter, Johnson of Louisiana, King of New York, Lanman, Lowrie, Macon, Mills, Noble, Otis, Palmer, Pleasants, Ruggles, Sanford, Smith, Southard, Stokes, Talbot, Tichenor, Trimble, Walker of Alabama, Walker of Georgia, and Williams of Tennessee—30.

The remainder of the amendment was then also rejected.

On motion of Mr. Lowrie, the following provision, being the last in the bill, and among the penalties for defrauding the bank, was stricken out, viz:

"And by standing in a pillory not more than three times, in open day, in some public place, during one hour at a time, which standing in a pillory, when inflicted more than once, shall be on different days."

The bill was then ordered to be engrossed, as amended, and read a third time, by the following vote:

Yeas—Messrs. Barbour, Dana, Dickerson, Eaton, Edwards, Elliott, Gaillard, Holmes of Maine, Holmes of Mississippi, Hunter, Johnson of Kentucky, Johnson of Louisiana, King of New York, Mills, Morril, Otis, Parrot, Pleasants, Roberts, Sanford, Southard, Stokes, Tichenor, Walker of Alabama, Walker of Georgia, and Williams of Mississippi—26.

NAYS—Messrs. Chandler, Lanman, Lowrie, Macon, Noble, Palmer, Ruggles, Smith, Talbot, and Trimble—10.

At the request of Mr. KNIGHT, who stated that he is a stockholder in the Bank of the United States, he was excused from voting on the preceding questions.

BANKRUPT BILL.

The engrossed bill to establish an uniform system of bankruptcy throughout the United States was read the third time.

On the question, "Shall this bill pass?" it was determined in the affirmative—yeas 23, nays 19, as follows:

YEAS—Messrs. Brown, Dana, Dickerson, Edwards, Elliott, Gaillard, Horsey, Hunter, Johnson of Louisiana, Knight, Lanman, Mills, Noble, Otis, Parrott, Sanford, Southard, Stokes, Taylor, Thomas, Van Dyke, and Williams of Mississippi.

NAYS—Messrs. Barbour, Chandler, Eaton, Holmes of Maine, Holmes of Mississippi, Johnson of Kentucky, King of Alabama, Lowrie, Macon, Morril, Pleasants, Roberts, Ruggles, Smith, Talbot, Trimble, Walker of Alabama, Walker of Georgia, and Williams of Tennessee.

So it was *Resolved*, That the said bill do pass; and that the title thereof be "An act to establish a uniform system of bankruptcy throughout the United States."

TUESDAY, February 20.

The PRESIDENT communicated a letter from the Secretary of State, with a transcript of all the lists of passengers taken on board ships and vessels in foreign ports and places, which arrived in the United States from the first of October, 1819, to the 30th September, 1820, inclusive; and the letter and transcript were read.

Mr. HORSEY presented the petition of John Threlkeld and Joseph Brooks, of Georgetown, in the District of Columbia, praying authority to close a certain public road in the county of Washington, in said district; and the petition was read, and referred to the Committee on the District of Columbia.

Mr. TICHENOR presented the petition of Josephus B. Stuart, late paymaster of the 29th regiment of infantry, praying that certain lots of land in Ohio may be received in discharge of a balance due by him to the United States; and the petition was read, and referred to the Committee of Claims.

Mr. RUGGLES, from the Committee of Claims, to whom the subject was referred by a resolution of the Senate of the 7th instant, reported a bill for the relief of David Cooper; which was read, and passed to a second reading.

Mr. SANFORD, from the Committee on Finance, to whom the subject was referred by a resolution of the Senate of the 12th instant, reported a bill concerning vessels employed in the fisheries; it was read, and passed to a second reading.

Mr. THOMAS, from the Committee on Public Lands, to whom was referred the bill from the House of Representatives, entitled "An act for the relief of Robert Buntin," reported it with an amendment; which was read.

The bill supplemental to an act, entitled "An act to authorize the appointment of commissioners to lay out the road therein mentioned," and the bill for the relief of Koo-na-noo-lus-kee, or Challenge, one of the tribe of the Cherokee Indians, were severally read the second time.

The report of the Committee on Public Lands unfavorable to the petition of Jared E. Groce, was taken up and agreed to.

The report of the Committee of Commerce and Manufactures, unfavorable to the petition of T. Dobson & Son, was taken up and concurred in.

The bill to extend the charters of certain banks in the District of Columbia, was postponed to and made the order of the day for Thursday next.

The bill "further to establish the compensation of the officers employed in the collection of duties on imports and tonnage, and for other purposes," as amended, was taken up; and the bill having been further amended, was ordered to be engrossed for a third reading.

The bill to amend the act "to incorporate the subscribers to the Bank of the United States," was read a third time, passed, and sent to the House for concurrence.

The Senate resumed, as in Committee of the Whole, the consideration of the bill, entitled "An act to reduce and fix the Military Peace Establishment of the United States," together with the amendment reported thereto by the Committee on Military Affairs; and it was postponed to and made the order of the day for to-morrow.

The resolution instructing the Judiciary Committee to bring in a resolution extending the laws of the United States to the State of Missouri was taken up, and then Mr. WILLIAMS, of Tennessee, the mover of it, so modified it as to include also the territory of Florida; and then the resolution was again ordered to lie on the table.

Mr. BARBOUR submitted the following motions for consideration:

Resolved, That a committee be appointed to join such committee as may be appointed by the House of Representatives to wait on the President of the United States, and to notify him of his re-election to the office of President of the United States.

Resolved, That the President of the United States be requested to cause to be transmitted to Daniel D. Tompkins, Esquire, of New York, Vice President of the United States, a notification of his re-election to that office.

MISSOURI.

The Senate proceeded to consider, as in Committee of the Whole, the resolution declaring the admission of the State of Missouri into the Union.

The resolution of Mr. ROBERTS was taken up, and was modified by the mover, so as to read as follows:

Resolved, by the Senate and House of Representatives of the United States of America in Congress assembled, That the State of Missouri shall be and is hereby declared one of the United States of America, and is admitted into the Union on an equal footing with the original States in all respects whatever: *Provided*, That the following be taken as fundamental conditions and terms upon which the said State is admitted into the Union, namely: that the fourth clause of the twenty-sixth section of the third article of the constitution, submitted by the people of Missouri to the consideration of Congress, shall, as soon as the provisions of the said constitution will admit, be so modified that it shall not be applicable to any description of persons who may now be or hereafter shall become citizens of any State in this Union; and that, until so modified, no law passed in conformity thereto shall be construed to exclude any citizen of either State in this Union from the enjoyment of any of the privileges and immunities to which such citizen is entitled under the Constitution of the United States.

After some debate, this resolution was, on the motion of Mr. EATON, seconded by Mr. VAN DYKE and Mr. SOUTHARD, postponed to and made the order of the day for to-morrow. Mr. TALBOT and Mr. JOHNSON, of Kentucky, at first opposed the postponement, but, when time was asked by members in order to examine more fully the resolution, they ceased their opposition.

WEDNESDAY, February 21.

Mr. SMITH presented the petition of John B. Lemaitre, of South Carolina, merchant, praying the restitution of the amount of an export bond paid by him, for reasons stated in the petition; which was read, and referred to the Committee on Finance.

Mr. EDWARDS presented the petition of the inhabitants of, and settlers on, the military bounty lands in the State of Illinois, praying the establishment of post offices and post routes therein; and it was referred to the Committee on the Post Office and Post Roads.

On motion, by Mr. SANFORD, the Committee on Finance were discharged from the consideration of the "report of the joint committee of the General Assembly of Ohio, on the subject of the suit of the Bank of the United States against the officers of the State."

Mr. DICKERSON, from the Committee on Commerce and Manufactures, to whom was referred the bill from the House of Representatives, entitled "An act to authorize the collectors of customs to pay debentures issued on the exportation of loaf sugar, and spirits distilled from molasses," reported it without amendment.

Mr. THOMAS, from the Committee on Public Lands, to whom was referred the petition of William Doak, made a report, accompanied by a bill giving the right of pre-emption to William Doak and Noble Osborne; and the report and bill were read, and the bill passed to a second reading.

Mr. THOMAS, from the same committee, to whom was referred the petition of John Caldwell and others, purchasers of lots in Shawneetown, made a report, accompanied by a bill to authorize the Commissioner of the General Land Office to remit the instalments due on certain lots in Shawneetown, in the State of Illinois; and the report and bill were read, and the bill passed to a second reading.

Mr. ROBERTS, from the Committee on Claims, to whom was referred the memorial of Bartholomew Shaumburg, made a report accompanied by a resolution, that the prayer of the petitioner ought not to be granted.

The Senate proceeded to consider the motion of yesterday, to appoint a joint committee to wait on the President of the United States, and to notify him of his re-election, and agreed thereto; and Messrs. BARBOUR and KING, of New York, were appointed the committee on the part of the Senate.

The Senate proceeded to consider the motion of yesterday, requesting the President of the United States to notify the Vice President of his re-election; and agreed thereto.

The bill supplementary to the several acts for adjusting the claims to land and establishing land offices in the districts east of the island of New Orleans; the bill for the relief of David Cooper; and the bill concerning vessels employed in the fisheries; were severally read the second time.

The bill further to establish the compensation of the officers employed in the collection of duties on imports and tonnage, and for other purposes, having been reported by the committee correctly engrossed, was read the third time, and passed.

Mr. TALBOT gave notice that to-morrow, he should ask leave to bring in a bill to extend the judicial authority of the United States over the State of Missouri.

MISSOURI.

The Senate resumed, as in Committee of the Whole, the consideration of the following resolution, offered by Mr. ROBERTS:

Resolved, by the Senate and House of Representatives of the United States of America in Congress assembled, That the State of Missouri shall be, and is hereby declared, one of the United States of America, and is admitted into the Union on an equal footing with the original States in all respects whatever: *Provided,* That the following be taken as fundamental conditions and terms upon which the said State is admitted into the Union, namely: that the fourth clause of the twenty-sixth section of the third article of the constitution submitted by the people of Missouri to the consideration of Congress, shall, as soon as the provisions of said constitution will admit, be so modified, that it shall not be applicable to any description of persons who may now be, or hereafter shall become, citizens of any State in this Union; and that, until so modified, no law, passed in conformity thereto, shall be construed to exclude any citizens of either State in this Union from the enjoyment of any of the privileges and immunities to which such citizen is entitled under the Constitution of the United States.

Much debate took place on the merits of the resolution, as well as on the expediency of now acting on it, in the course of which Mr. BARBOUR moved to strike out the proviso, but subsequently withdrew the motion. The resolution was advocated by Messrs. ROBERTS, LOWRIE, and BARBOUR, and was opposed by Messrs. SMITH and VAN DYKE.

Mr. LOWRIE, after observing that the resolution had been brought forward by those who had opposed the former resolution of the Senate, from a sincere desire to see the State admitted, and with the view of meeting gentlemen on the other side, as far as they could; but, as the proposition appeared not to be acceptable to them, he, for one, would not press it on them, and therefore moved its indefinite postponement.

This motion was negatived—yeas 24, nays 18, as follows:

YEAS—Messrs. Brown, Chandler, Dickerson, Eaton, Horsey, King of New York, Lanman, Lowrie, Macon, Mills, Noble, Otis, Sanford, Smith, Southard, Tichenor, Van Dyke, and Williams of Mississippi.

NAYS—Messrs. Barbour, Dana, Edwards, Elliott, Gaillard, Holmes of Maine, Holmes of Mississippi, Johnson of Kentucky, Johnson of Louisiana, King of Alabama, Knight, Morril, Palmer, Parrott, Pleasants, Roberts, Stokes, Talbot, Taylor, Thomas, Trimble, Walker of Alabama, Walker of Georgia, and Williams of Tennessee.

Mr. WILLIAMS, of Tennessee, made an unsuccessful motion to lay the resolution on the table, with the view of taking up the Army bill.

Mr. KING, of New York, renewed the motion previously made and withdrawn by Mr. BARBOUR, to strike from the resolution all the proviso, as follows:

"*Provided*, That the following be taken as fundamental conditions and terms upon which the said State is admitted into the Union, namely: that the fourth clause of the twenty-sixth section of the third article of the constitution, submitted by the people of Missouri to the consideration of Congress, shall, as soon as the provisions of said constitution will admit, be so modified, that it shall not impair the privileges or immunities of any description of persons who may now be, or hereafter shall become, citizens of any State in this Union; and that, until so modified, no law, passed in conformity thereto, shall be construed to exclude any citizen of either State in this Union, from the enjoyment of any of the privileges and immunities to which such citizen is entitled under the Constitution of the United States."

The motion was decided, without debate, in the negative, by yeas and nays, as follows:

YEAS—Messrs. Brown, Gaillard, Holmes of Mississippi, King of Alabama, King of New York, Macon, Mills, Otis, Sanford, Smith, Tichenor, Van Dyke, Walker of Alabama, Williams of Mississippi, and Williams of Tennessee—15.

NAYS—Messrs. Barbour, Chandler, Dana, Dickerson, Eaton, Edwards, Elliott, Holmes of Maine, Horsey, Johnson of Kentucky, Johnson of Louisiana, Knight, Lanman, Lowrie, Morril, Noble, Palmer, Parrott, Pleasants, Roberts, Southard, Stokes, Talbot, Taylor Thomas, Trimble, and Walker of Georgia—27.

Mr. BROWN moved to amend the proviso so as to deprive it of its injunction on the State of Missouri to amend its constitution in the clause referred to, and leave it to read, that the clause "should not be so construed as to impair the privileges of citizens of other States," &c.

Mr. ROBERTS objected to this amendment, as it would change the whole principle of the proviso, and give the resolution such a shape as would compel him to oppose it.

Mr. BROWN maintained his motion at some length. Had the resolution come from the other

House in the shape it now was, he should perhaps vote for it, for the sake of closing this long standing and disagreeable question, to accomplish which he was willing to make great sacrifices; but he was not ready to play so bold a game as to volunteer to the other House a surrender of the whole principle for which they contended; especially as the Senate had already tendered to it one proposition, which had been there rejected. A compromise to the extent the proviso went would be time enough when it came from the other House.

Mr. TALBOT conceived that the amendment proposed by Mr. BROWN would be mischievous and produce no good. On so great a subject, and to settle a question so momentous, he was willing to give up something, and hold out to the other side the hand of compromise; but it was certainly a question which every one was to settle with his own conscience.

The question being taken on Mr. BROWN's motion, it was negatived without a division.

Mr. TRIMBLE moved to amend the proviso, by adding thereto the following clause:

And provided, also, That the 8th article of the said constitution [the article authorizing the establishment of banks,] shall be annulled as soon as said constitution, in conformity with the provisions thereof, is subject to amendment.

This amendment was rejected without debate, and without division.

The question was then put on ordering the resolution to be engrossed and read the third time; and was decided by yeas and nays as follows:

YEAS—Messrs. Barbour, Edwards, Elliott, Holmes of Maine, Horsey, Johnson of Kentucky, Johnson of Louisiana, Lowrie, Morril, Parrott, Pleasants, Roberts, Southard, Stokes Talbot, Taylor, Thomas, Walker of Georgia, and Williams of Tennessee—19.

NAYS—Messrs. Brown, Chandler, Dana, Dickerson, Eaton, Gaillard, Holmes of Mississippi, King of Alabama, King of New York, Knight, Lanman, Macon, Mills, Noble, Otis, Palmer, Ruggles, Sanford, Smith, Tichenor, Trimble, Van Dyke, Walker of Alabama, and Williams of Mississippi—24.

So the resolution was rejected.

MILITARY PEACE ESTABLISHMENT.

The Senate then resumed the consideration of the bill from the other House to reduce the Army, and the amendments proposed thereto by the Committee on Military Affairs.

Mr. WILLIAMS, of Tennessee, submitted to the Senate the considerations which induced the committee to recommend the modifications which they had reported to the bill. He went into a detailed view of the subject, of the posts necessary to be maintained, the proper distribution of the forces, &c., to show that the service required the number of regiments proposed by the substitute; also to show that the staff ought to be constituted as proposed by the amendment; that the cost of the organization proposed by the substitute would be but a small sum more than that proposed by the other House; that they had varied from the bill of the other House only in features which they deemed of importance, leaving others, to some of

HISTORY OF CONGRESS.

which there was some objections, as the other House had passed them.

The principal objection which Mr. WALKER, of Georgia, had to the details of this bill, or the amendment, was the amalgamation of the ordnance corps with that of the artillery ; to show the inexpediency of which, he offered a few arguments, and added some observations on the impolicy of the whole plan of reduction, to which he was opposed, conceiving it incompatible with considerations of true economy, and for which he should vote with reluctance.

Mr. TICHENOR offered his views at large on the subject of reduction, and of the modes proposed ; and also submitted a number of remarks on the present organization of the Army, in its supply department particularly, to show its great and unexampled excellence, both in efficiency and economy ; also, to prove the inexpediency of consolidating the ordnance and artillery corps; and in favor of leaving the system established in 1815 relative to the ordnance department untouched.

Mr. DANA objected to that clause of the amendment which proposes to merge the ordnance department in the artillery, as it proposed to abolish a separate superintendence and control of the public military property, and the responsibility which ought to attach to those officers discharging those duties, and explained his views at some length ; he preferred the provision in the bill of the other House.

Mr. WALKER, of Georgia, moved to strike out the 4th section of the amendment which merges the ordnance in the artillery, giving the President power to select artillery officers to perform the present ordnance duties, giving them extra pay therefor, &c., and to insert in lieu thereof a clause to retain the ordnance corps as at present established.

Mr. TRIMBLE opposed this motion, and spoke to obviate the objections which had been urged by Messrs. DANA and WALKER against the proposed consolidation of the two corps, and referred to its operation and effect to show its expediency in the organization of our Army.

Mr. OTIS advocated the motion to amend, being always in favor of maintaining existing establishments which there were not strong and clear reasons for changing, which reasons did not exist for the present change, but on the contrary they were adverse to it ; he would therefore prefer the provision of the other House in preference to the amendment.

Mr. WILLIAMS, of Tennessee, explained the difference of cost in the two plans, showing that the mode pr   sed b   the committee would make a saving o $882,00 ; that, besides this reason, the ordnance corps wanted revision, and spoke to show that the duties would be better discharged by an amalgamation ; that it would practice the artillery officers in the performance of those duties, &c.

Messrs. WALKER, of Georgia, TICHENOR, and TRIMBLE, severally spoke repeatedly to enforce their views of this matter of detail.

The question being taken first on striking out the 4th section, it was negatived—yeas 18, nays 19.

The bill was then laid on the table.

THURSDAY, February 22.

Mr. WALKER, of Alabama, presented the memorial of the convention convened pursuant to the act of Congress " to enable the people of the Alabama territory to form a constitution and State government," in behalf of the people of the State of Alabama, suggesting the expediency and policy of annexing to that State so much of the country lately ceded by Spain as lies west of the Appalachicola river, and declaring their consent to such annexation; and the memorial was read, and laid on the table.

Mr. THOMAS, from the Committee on Public Lands, to whom the subject was referred, by resolution of the 6th December, reported a bill to designate the boundaries of a land district and for the establishment of a land office in the State of Indiana ; and the bill was read, and passed to a second reading.

Mr. RUGGLES, from the Committee of Claims, to whom was referred the bill supplementary to an act passed on the 5th of April, 1820, entitled "An act for the relief of John Harding, Giles Harding, John Shute, and John Nichols," reported the same without amendment.

Mr. NOBLE, from the Committee on Pensions, in pursuance of a resolution of the 15th instant, reported a bill for the relief of Dean Weymouth; which was read, and passed to a second reading.

Mr. SMITH, from the Committee on the Judiciary, to whom was referred the petition of John Slocum, made a report, acompanied by a resolution, that the prayer of the petitioner be not granted, and that he have leave to withdraw his petition.

Mr. SMITH, from the same committee, to whom was referred the petition of John Cahoone, made a report, accompanied by a resolution, that the prayer of the petition be not granted, and that the petitioner have leave to withdraw his papers.

Mr. SMITH, from the same committee, to whom was referred the resolution of the 12th of December to inquire into the expediency of amending the judiciary laws, so as to authorize writs of error in criminal cases, reported that it is inexpedient to legislate on the subject; and the report was read.

The bill to authorize the Commissioner of the General Land Office to remit the instalments due on certain lots in Shawneetown, in the State of Illinois ; and the bill giving the right of pre-emption to William Doak and Noble Osborne ; were severally read the second time.

The Senate proceeded to consider the report of the Committee of Claims on the memorial of Bartholomew Shaumburg ; and in concurrence therewith, resolved that the prayer of the petitioner ought not to be granted.

The Senate resumed the consideration of the report of the select committee on reducing the allowances authorized by law for the two Houses of Congress, and for the Executive Departments ; and, on motion by Mr. BARBOUR, it was laid on the table.

A message from the House of Representatives informed the Senate that they have passed the bill which originated in the Senate, entitled "An act for the relief of Samuel Tucker, late a Captain in the

Navy of the United States ;" with an amendment. They have also passed a bill, entitled "An act to fix and equalize the pay of the officers in the Army of the United States;" a resolution providing for jails in certain cases, for the safe custody of persons committed under the authority of the United States ; and a resolution for the appointment of a joint committee to report the subjects proper to be acted on during the present session; in which amendment, bill, and resolutions, they request the concurrence of the Senate.

MILITARY PEACE ESTABLISHMENT.

The Senate resumed, as in Committee of the Whole, the consideration of the bill, entitled "An act to reduce and fix the Military Peace Establishment of the United States," together with the amendment reported thereto by the Committee on Military Affairs.

Mr. DICKERSON proposed to amend the said amendment by striking out of section nine, lines one, two, and three, the words "that there shall be one judge advocate with an annual salary of two thousand dollars.

Mr. DICKERSON said, if the amendment of the Committee on Military Affairs, to the bill sent from the House of Representatives, proposed an equal reduction of the army with that bill, and an equal reduction of the officers of the army, he should prefer it to the bill, because it proposed some improvement in the organization of the force to be retained ; but this, said he, is far from being the case. The army, as proposed by the bill, is composed of skeleton regiments, but that proposed by the amendment is a much nearer approach to an army of officers. The reduction is to fall chiefly upon the non-commissioned officers and privates. The nearest approach we can make to the bill, except in organization, the better. Retrenchment is the object, and it ought to fall in due proportion upon the most expensive part of the army. But, sir, we know that a considerable part of the Senate is opposed to any reduction of the army, and we have just heard a gentleman say, upon this floor, he would willingly vote for an indefinite postponement of the bill.

The army which it is proposed by the amendment to retain in the service, although unnecessarily large, and calculated to add to the embarrassments of our exhausted Treasury, is not such as to excite any alarm as to the liberties of our country, although history furnishes us with numerous instances of revolutions, effected by armies of no greater numbers. But, the exertions which have been made, and I fear successfully made, to produce a revolution in the public mind, upon the subject of standing armies in time of peace, I will confess, fill me with apprehension that our liberties after a war or two more are to be controlled by our standing armies. The apathy of the people upon this subject, to judge from their silence, would indicate that their former jealousies of permanently standing armies, by some strange influence, had been put to rest forever ; and if so, the fundamental principles of our free Government

will soon be abandoned for something more splendid. The presses, once the guardians of our liberties, are now silent upon this subject, or advocate the present establishment of the army ; and not a breath is heard against it except upon the floor of Congress.

A respectable army in time of peace, by which at present we are to understand a force of about 12,664 men, is spoken of with as little concern as if such an establishment was of the essence of our Government.

Parents calculate to educate their sons to the profession of arms, as a provision for life, as they would do to the profession of medicine, law, or divinity.

Many who have provided for their sons in the army, and many who wish to provide for their sons in the army, find their minds strangely altered upon this subject; and they begin to view as chimerical and ridiculous their former fears of a military government. If we may judge of the future by the past, the standing army is to make a most rapid progress in this country. Every circumstance attending the army indicates this, but excites little apprehension in the minds of the people, who must bear the burden. In thirty years from this time an army of 50,000 men will be considered as a very moderate peace establishment.

If we succeed in reducing the army now, it will not be because it is against the genius of our Government to keep up such an establishment in time of peace, but because our revenues fail us ; it will be because a resort to measures calculated to save the army, as at present established, would not be exactly calculated to save ourselves. Loans, if frequently repeated in time of peace, are pernicious and dangerous expedients. Direct taxes would lead to certain inquiries which might be extremely troublesome to us who are responsible for the expenditure of the public moneys. We shall be told, that, with a surplus of five millions in our Treasury four years ago, we have, in time of profound peace, been obliged to borrow three millions last session, and must borrow more this—for no taxes can save us from this necessity.

I should wish to see the army reduced to five thousand men in time of peace, when no enemy threatens to molest us, even if our finances were in the most prosperous train. But a reduction which principle would render proper, our empty Treasury will render necessary; and but for this necessity no reduction would take place. If our country was not in distress—if our finances were not embarrassed, the army, as at present established, would be permanently fixed upon us. No efforts of those who think such a force unnecessary for our defence, or dangerous to our liberties, would have the least avail. The peace establishment would go on to increase, but never to decrease, from this time forward.

The time was, about twenty years ago, when a certain party made prodigious clamors against standing armies in time of peace; but times have altered, and I fear we have altered with them.

For my own part, however, I like to look back

to the period when our Government was first established—when its fundamental principles were more duly appreciated than they are now—when we were swayed by political maxims that had been rendered sacred by the Revolution.

And if, by comparison and examination, we find that we have deviated from the courses then pursued; that we have advanced in measures then condemned as dangerous to our Government, a retrograde movement should be prescribed. An approach to first principles should be attempted. But in nothing is this more necessary than in a rigid economy in the expenditure of public moneys, and a proper and necessary jealousy to be observed towards a standing army in time of peace. These sentiments, I know, are somewhat unfashionable at present; they are considered as illiberal, contracted, calculated only for the short-sighted politicians of the early stages of our Government—not suited to the lofty and expanded views of the statesmen of the present day. But these are sentiments of which I am very tenacious. Former principles (perhaps I should say prejudices) have taken deep root in my mind. I delight in the simplicity and economy of our early establishments. And, as good old fashions sometimes revive, I cannot but hope that these discarded principles, now covered with obloquy and ridicule, may again become the favorites of those at least who cherished them twenty years ago.

Sir, the present embarrassed condition of our finances, and the general distress of our country, will produce a salutary change in the minds and views of our citizens generally, which could not have been hoped for in times of prosperity. The most beneficial effects result, not unfrequently, as well from national as individual calamity. It is the part of wisdom to profit by the lessons such times afford.

In order to form a just estimate of what may be expected from a standing army in this country, it will be well to consider what has happened in the land from which we derive our origin. Charles II., after his restoration, when he found it necessary to disband his army, retained in his service one thousand horse and four thousand foot under Monk, who had betrayed the commonwealth. This force was retained for guards and garrisons. And this was the first appearance of a regular standing army in England, under a monarchy. I do not speak of the very ingenious plans of Oliver Cromwell to fix an army on that nation.

James II. was anxious to increase his army, and in his speech to Parliament, immediately after Monmouth's rebellion, he says: "but when I re-
'flect what an inconsiderable number of men be-
'gan it, (the rebellion,) and how long they car-
'ried it on without any opposition, I hope eve-
'ry body will be convinced that the militia, which
'hath hitherto been so much depended on, is not
'sufficient for such occasions, and that there is
'nothing but a good force of well disciplined
'troops, in constant pay, that can defend us from
'such as, either at home or abroad, are disposed
'to disturb us!" Here we have royal doctrine, as well in favor of the army as against the militia.

This speech, says the historian, equally surprised both Houses of Parliament and the whole kingdom, when it came to be published; notwithstanding which, the Parliament enabled him to increase his army from seven thousand to fifteen thousand men; and subsequently to thirty thousand men, when his kingdom was invaded by his dear nephew and son-in-law, the Prince of Orange. His army, then, in imitation of other armies, deserted him; and, having no confidence in his subjects, he abdicated his throne.

King William, after establishing himself upon the throne, was obliged to disband his army; but he was extremely anxious to retain a large peace establishment; in this he was opposed by his own friends, the whigs, who had brought him over. And, notwithstanding he was the best monarch that nation ever imported to rule over them; notwithstanding his remonstrances and even entreaties, in favor of his army; notwithstanding the cry excited and kept up from one end of the kingdom to the other, that the church and the monarchy were in danger; the Parliament were inflexible, and obliged him to reduce his forces to ten thousand men, and subsequently to seven thousand. If I should attempt to point out the most brilliant period in the parliamentary history of Great Britain, I should select this, when the Parliament thus obliged the King to reduce his army, and, what was still more mortifying to him, to send home his favorite Dutch guards. Let it be remembered, however, that, when they thus reduced the army, they made a larger provision for the sea service; they did not consider an increased navy as at all dangerous to their liberties.

In the reign of Queen Anne, the military glory acquired by the English, reconciled them to a standing army, which was unnecessarily kept up, with all its corruptions and abuses, under the most fortunate, the most mean, and the most mercenary of mortals, the Duke of Marlborough.

During the two succeeding reigns, the constant cry of the Pope and the Pretender, seems to have deprived the people of that kingdom of their senses; and they went on from period to period to increase the army, which was to enslave them.

The circumstances which have led to a large increase of their standing army, since that period, are too familiar to need recital. It is a melancholy fact which we should constantly keep in view, that that nation which, a little more than one century ago, looked with the greatest jealousy upon a standing army of ten thousand men, now groans under the curse of a military Government.

Our progress, I fear, will be still more rapid. In the year 1790, General Knox, then the Secretary of War, made a report upon the subject of the militia, which will afford a just test of the sentiments of those who were most favorable to a standing army in time of peace at that day; for, it can hardly be supposed that General Knox, a distinguished officer of the Revolution, had not a strong partiality for the army. In this report he says:

"A small corps of well disciplined and well informed

artillerists and engineers, and a legion for the protection of our frontiers, and the magazines and arsenals, are all the military which may be required for the use of the United States. The privates of the corps to be enlisted for a certain period, and, after the expiration of which, to return to the mass of citizens. An energetic national militia is to be regarded as the capital security of a free Republic, and not a standing army, forming a distinct class in the community.

"It is the introduction and diffusion of vice and corruption of manners into the mass of the people, that renders a standing army necessary. It is when public spirit is despised, and avarice, indolence, and effeminacy of manners, predominate, and prevent the establishment of institutions which would elevate the minds of the youth in the paths of virtue and honor, that a standing army is formed and rivetted forever."

This report was examined, and strongly recommended to the attention of Congress, by General Washington, the then President of the United States. Eight months after this, it was enacted by Congress that the whole number of non-commissioned officers, musicians, and privates, to be in the service of the United States at any one time, should not exceed 1,216 men, to be raised for three years, unless sooner discharged, to be organized into one regiment of infantry, to consist of three battalions, and one battalion of artillery.

In 1802, the Peace Establishment was fixed at 3,284 officers, non-commissioned officers, musicians, and privates, exclusive of a few military agents.

In 1815, it was enacted by Congress, that the Peace Establishment of the United States should consist of such portions of artillery, infantry, and riflemen, not exceeding in the whole ten thousand men, as the President of the United States should judge proper, and that the corps of engineers should be retained, which consisted of 140 men, making, in the aggregate, 10,140 men ; yet, such is the construction given to this law, that, by the present organization, our army amounts, in the aggregate, to 12,664.

After the next war in which we may be engaged shall be finished, I have no doubt our Peace Establishment will be fixed at 20,000 or more.

We had for the head of our first Peace Establishment a colonel ; for the second, a brigadier general ; for the third, two major generals and four brigadiers. If such has already been the progress of our army, what may we not expect in future?

I think, with General Knox, that an energetic national militia is to be regarded as the capital security of a free Republic. The navy has grown up to a degree of importance that could not have been anticipated thirty years ago. It is now looked upon, and justly so, as our strong defence against European enemies ; and it has this important circumstance to recommend it, that it has no tendency to endanger the liberties of the country. It was the policy of the party of the De Witts, who were Republicans, to encourage the navy, but of the Orange party, to encourage the army, because, says Mr. Hume, the army were in favor of monarchy ; and a large army must at all times, from its organization, be anti-republican.

The Military Academy at West Point is a valuable institution, inasmuch as it leads to a diffusion of correct military science throughout the United States, to be called into requisition whenever wanted, and thus renders it proper to reduce the standing army to a point below what it would otherwise be expedient to do. There is but one thing to be feared from this academy, which is, that it may enlist too many friends in favor of standing armies.

In time of war we must have armies sufficient for the exigencies of the war ; most of the fighting should be done by regular forces ; but the first onset in all our wars must be sustained by our militia, and, during the war, they must be prepared at all points to defend the country ; and, in order that they may be enabled so to do, the greatest attention should be paid to their organization and discipline, which never will be the case while we rely upon a standing army.

The policy of keeping up skeleton regiments, so much reduced as to consist of no more than 440 rank and file, with a full complement of officers, will not be understood, except by gentlemen of the army. To show the propriety of reducing the army to the lowest point proposed, both as to officers and men, I will read some statements made and calculated from documents laid on our tables:

Expense of the army for pay, subsistence, forage, bounties, premiums, expenses of recruiting, hospital department, and Military Academy, for

the year 1818 - - - - -	-	$3,748,445
For the year 1819 - - - -	-	3,351,363
Eleven months in 1820	$2,616,526	
Add for one month, estimate	218,044	
		2,834,570
		$9,934,378

The average of three years	-	$3,311,457

Which would give for our six years of peace, nineteen millions eight hundred and sixty-eight thousand, seven hundred and forty-two dollars. It will be observed, that this is exclusive of expenses for fortifications, and a variety of other charges attending the defence of the country by land.

Expense for transportation for officers amounted, in three years, 1816, 1817, 1818, to $92,564, and their charges for the same time, for fuel and quarters, amounted to $14,263.

For the recruiting service:

Recruits in the year 1817	-	-	-	3,939
" 1818	-	-	-	4,238
" 1819	-	-	-	4,304
" 1820	-	-	-	3,211
			15,692

Average of four years -	-	-	-	3,923

This would give for our six years of peace, 23,538, which, at fourteen dollars for each recruit, would amount to $315,532. So much for recruiting, besides large sums for taking up deserters, at thirty dollars a head, and for shooting deserters thirty dollars each; at least, that was the sum ordered by Colonel King to be paid to Sergeant Childress for shooting Neil Cameron, a deserter, who begged for his life, and that he might be tried by a court martial. And are the people of the United States to be taxed to keep up an army of such materials, which is crumbling away at the rate of about one-third annually? Of what use can such an army be to the country? If there were no other reason, this would be sufficient to justify a reduction of the army to the lowest point proposed. As these calculations are made from scanty materials, they may, in some instances, be above, and in some below, the truth.

Great as the disposition is to increase the body of the army, there is still a greater disposition to increase the head.

The staff of the army, as established by Congress in 1815, was not satisfactory; and, in 1816, Congress created the offices of one Adjutant and Inspector General, one Adjutant General, one Inspector General, three Topographical Engineers, and one Quartermaster General. In 1818, a bill was introduced for reducing the staff of the army; and, under that imposing name, it passed on till its last stage, when it was discovered that it increased the staff, and its title was changed to a bill regulating the staff of the army. By this reduction of the staff, we gained one Surgeon General, with a salary of two thousand five hundred dollars; but, as he is allowed, notwithstanding his being a salary officer, thirty-six dollars per month for quarters, and thirteen dollars per month for fuel, by some rule I do not understand, his allowance amounts to three thousand and eighty-eight dollars a year. And now, sir, when we are about to reduce the army, we are called upon to create a new staff officer, to be called a Judge Advocate—a bureau officer—a subordinate head of department, to be located at Washington, with a salary of two thousand dollars a year. We have now two Judge Advocates, one for the Northern, and one for the Southern division; who, for a long time past, have had nothing to do, that I can discover, but to draw their pay. They are not necessary to the service, and such must be the opinion of the Military Committee, for they have not provided for continuing them. But, if a judge advocate is not wanted where the troops are, how can he be wanted here? Is he to attend the courts martial that may take place at the Marine Barracks or Fort Warburton? Surely, he is not to be sent round to the different regiments located at separate and distant points, from the Niagara frontier to the Council Bluffs? When courts martial are detailed for the service, judge advocates may be detailed to attend the trials; and that will be done even if we have a Judge Advocate General here. The honorable chairman of the committee has been called upon to state, as far as the same may have come to his knowledge, what are to be the duties of this Judge Advocate General. He informs us that he is to keep a record of the proceedings of the courts martial to be held for the army, and to compile a system of

martial law for the United States. As to the first, it is the duty of all Judge Advocates in the service of the United States, or who may be detailed to attend courts martial, to transmit all the documents, and papers, and proceedings, of the courts which they may respectively attend, to the War Department, where they are to be carefully filed and preserved; under the immediate care, I presume, of the Adjutant General, and where they are to remain as records. Surely, these papers and documents are not all to be recorded in a book; but, if they are, it can be done by a common clerk. As to compiling a system of martial law, I would not employ an officer with a permanent salary to perform such a service, even if we wanted it, but we do not; we have such a system reported to us within a few days, and laid upon our tables, chiefly copied from a former system, which was copied from one still earlier, adopted about the commencement of our Revolutionary war. A Judge Advocate General is altogether unnecessary. I will, therefore, move to strike out so much of the amendment as relates to this officer; and I hope and trust that in this solemn farce of reduction, we shall not create an officer whose services are not wanted, and whose duties no one can define.

Mr. DICKERSON's motion was determined in the affirmative—yeas 21, nays 18, as follows:

YEAS—Messrs. Barbour, Chandler, Dana, Dickerson, Gaillard, Holmes of Maine, Horsey, King of Alabama, Knight, Lanman, Macon, Noble, Palmer, Ruggles, Sanford, Smith, Southard, Tichenor, Van Dyke, Walker of Alabama, and Williams of Mississippi.

NAYS—Messrs. Eaton, Edwards, Elliott, Holmes of Mississippi, Hunter, Johnson of Kentucky, King of New York, Lowrie, Mills, Otis, Parrott, Roberts, Stokes, Taylor, Thomas, Trimble, Walker of Georgia, and Williams of Tennessee.

On motion, by Mr. SMITH, further to amend the said amendment, by striking out of section five, lines two and three, the words "Major General with two Aids-de-Camp, two Brigadier Generals each," and inserting *Brigadier General ;* and also, by striking out of the third line, the words " Aids-de-Camp," and inserting *Aid-de-Camp*—a division of the question was called for, and the question was taken on striking out the words "Major General with two Aids-de-Camp ;" and it was determined in the negative—yeas 16, nays 24, as follows :

YEAS—Messrs. Barbour, Dana, Dickerson, Gaillard, King of Alabama, Knight, Lanman, Lowrie, Macon, Noble, Palmer, Ruggles, Smith, Southard, Tichenor, and Van Dyke.

NAYS—Messrs. Chandler, Eaton, Edwards, Elliott, Holmes of Maine, Holmes of Mississippi, Horsey, Hunter, Johnson of Kentucky, Johnson of Louisiana, King of New York, Mills, Otis, Parrott, Roberts, Sanford, Stokes, Talbot, Thomas, Trimble, Walker of Alabama, Walker of Georgia, Williams of Mississippi, and Williams of Tennessee.

And the question being taken on the residue of the proposed amendment to the said amendment, it was also determined in the negative—yeas 9, nays 31, as follows :

YEAS—Messrs. Barbour, Dana, Gaillard, Lowrie, Macon, Noble, Palmer, Ruggles, and Smith.

NAYS—Messrs. Chandler, Dickerson, Eaton, Edwards, Elliott, Holmes of Maine, Holmes of Mississippi, Horsey, Hunter, Johnson of Kentucky, Johnson of Louisiana, King of Alabama, King of New York, Knight, Lanman, Mills, Otis, Parrott, Roberts, Sanford, Southard, Stokes, Talbot, Thomas, Tichenor, Trimble, Van Dyke, Walker of Alabama, Walker of Georgia, Williams of Mississippi, and Williams of Tennessee.

And the said amendment having been further amended, it was agreed to, and the bill was reported to the House, amended accordingly; and the Senate adjourned.

FRIDAY, February 23.

The following Message was received from the PRESIDENT OF THE UNITED STATES:

To the Senate and House of
Representatives, of the United States :

The Treaty of Amity, Settlement, and Limits, between the United States and Spain, signed on the 22d of February, 1819, having been ratified by the contracting parties, and the ratifications having been exchanged, it is herewith communicated to Congress, that such legislative measures may be taken as they shall judge proper for carrying the same into execution.

JAMES MONROE.
WASHINGTON, *Feb.* 22, 1821.

The Message and treaty were read, and referred to the Committee on Foreign Relations.

The following Message was also received from the PRESIDENT OF THE UNITED STATES:

To the Senate of the United States :

In compliance with a resolution of the Senate of the 16th instant, requesting "the President of the United States to cause to be laid before the Senate, the original order for building the barracks at Sackett's Harbor, together with all communications between the War Department and Major General Brown relative thereto, and the amount of public moneys expended thereon," I now transmit a report from the Secretary of War, with the papers enclosed, which contain the information desired.

JAMES MONROE.
WASHINGTON, *Feb.* 22, 1821.

The Message and report were read.

The PRESIDENT communicated a report of the Secretary of State, upon weights and measures, prepared in conformity with a resolution of the Senate of the 3d of March, 1817; and the report was read, and six hundred copies thereof ordered to be printed; five hundred of which shall be for the use of the Senate, and one hundred for the use of the Department of State.

The PRESIDENT communicated a letter from the Commissioner of the General Land Office, transmitting the reports of the land officers at Jackson Courthouse, on claims for land; and the letter and reports were read.

Mr. KING, of New York, presented the memorial of the merchants of the city of New York, representing that, by the construction given to the thirteenth section of the act supplementary to an act to regulate the collection of duties on imports and tonnage at the custom-house, and which they believe is erroneous; they are subjected to great inconvenience and frequent penalties; and praying that an act may be passed explanatory thereof, and that the penalties incurred may be remitted; and the memorial was read, and referred to the Committee on Finance.

The credentials of SAMUEL L. SOUTHARD, appointed a Senator by the Legislature of the State of New Jersey for the term of six years, commencing on the fourth day of March next, were read, and laid on file.

Mr. ROBERTS presented the petition of the inhabitants of thirteen counties in the State of Pennsylvania, praying that such a reorganization of the circuit court of the United States in that State may be made, as to the time and place of holding said court, as will conduce more to their convenience; and the petition was read, and laid on the table.

On motion by Mr. WALKER, of Alabama, the memorial of the convention that formed the constitution of Alabama, yesterday presented to the Senate, was referred to the Committee on Foreign Relations.

Mr. SANFORD gave notice that, to-morrow, he should ask leave to bring in a bill to revive and continue in force "An act fixing the compensations of the Secretary of the Senate and Clerk of the House of Representatives, of the clerks employed in their offices, and of the Librarian;" approved April 18, 1818.

Mr. ROBERTS, from the Committee on Public Lands, to whom was referred the memorial of the Mayor and Aldermen of the city of Mobile, made a report, accompanied by a bill granting to the corporation of the city of Mobile, in the State of Alabama, certain lots of ground in the said city; and the report and bill were read, and the bill passed to a second reading.

Mr. THOMAS, from the same committee, made an unfavorable report on the petition of Watson Brown.

Mr. TALBOT obtained leave to bring in a bill to provide for the due execution of the laws of the United States within the State of Missouri; which was read, and passed to a second reading.

Mr. BARBOUR submitted the following motion for consideration:

Resolved, That the President of the United States be requested to cause to be laid before the Senate, at their next session, whatever information he may possess in relation to the execution or violation of the laws, entitled "An act concerning navigation," passed April 18th, 1818; and an act, entitled "An act supplementary to an act, entitled 'An act concerning navigation,'" passed May 15th, 1820; whether any, and if any what, additional measures be necessary to give full effect to the laws aforesaid.

The Senate proceeded to consider the amendment of the House of Representatives to the bill, entitled "An act for the relief of Samuel Tucker, late a captain in the Navy of the United States;" and concurred therein.

The bill from the House of Representatives, entitled "An act to fix and equalize the pay of the officers in the Army of the United States," was twice read by unanimous consent, and referred to the Committee on Military Affairs.

The resolution from the House of Representatives, providing for jails in certain cases for the safe custody of persons committed under the authority of the United States, was read, and passed to a second reading.

The resolution from the House of Representatives, for the appointment of a joint committee to report the subjects proper to be acted on during the present session, was read three times by unanimous consent, and concurred in; and Messrs. Sanford and Smith were appointed the committee on the part of the Senate.

The Senate proceeded to consider the report of the Committee on the Judiciary, on the petition of John Slocum; and, in concurrence therewith, resolved, that the prayer of the petitioner be not granted, and that he have leave to withdraw his petition.

The Senate proceeded to consider the report of the Committee on the Judiciary, on the petition of John Cahoone; and, in concurrence therewith, resolved, that the prayer of the petition be not granted, and that the petitioner have leave to withdraw his papers.

The Senate proceeded to consider the report of the Committee on the Judiciary, on the expediency of extending to the Supreme Court appellate jurisdiction in criminal cases, and concurred therein.

A message from the House of Representatives informed the Senate that the House have passed a bill, entitled "An act making appropriations for the support of the Navy of the United States, for the year 1821;" and a bill, entitled "An act to authorize the building of lighthouses on Cross and Pond islands, in the harbor of Boothbay, and at the mouth of Oswego river, and placing buoys on the shoals of Nantucket and Vineyard Sound, near the harbor of Wickford, and on the Altamaha river, and for other purposes;" in which bills they request the concurrence of the Senate.

MILITARY PEACE ESTABLISHMENT.

The Senate resumed the consideration of the bill to reduce the Military Peace Establishment, and the substitute proposed therefor by the Military Committee of the Senate.

Mr. Tichenor moved to strike out the 4th section of the substitute, which proposes, in substance, to merge the ordnance corps in the artillery, and giving the President authority to select artillery officers to perform the present ordnance duties, to receive extra pay therefor, and to be subject only to the orders of the Secretary of War; and to insert, in lieu of said section, another, making provision for a separate corps of ordnance.

This proposition again gave rise to a debate of more than an hour's continuance, in which Messrs. Tichenor, Williams, of Tennessee, Trimble, Chandler, Dana, and Johnson, of Kentucky, took part.

In the end the amendment was negatived, without a division.

After some further motions and discussion on the minor details of the bill, Mr. Smith moved to strike out of the 14th section of the committee's amendment that part which directs that all vacancies which may occur in the Army prior to June, 1822, "shall be filled by selection from the officers disbanded by virtue of this act, provided a sufficient number of suitable character apply for the same".—Mr. S. considering such a provision an encroachment on the unconditional right of nomination conferred on the President of the United States by the Constitution, and in effect a violation of the Constitution, as it went to take from the President the right of appointing, with the consent of the Senate, whomsoever he pleases to office.

After some discussion on the part of the mover, and Messrs. Trimble, Chandler, Williams, of Tennessee, Johnson, of Louisiana, Macon, and Lanman, in which it was urged by those in favor of the provision, that, as there would be a number of valuable officers disbanded under the act, this was only a promise on the part of Congress, the President concurring, that they should have a preference in filling future vacancies. Mr. Williams, however, consented, not deeming it material that the whole section should be stricken out, considering that the practice would be that which the provision contemplated. The debate ended in rejecting the whole section.

Mr. Otis moved to restore the provision for a Judge Advocate, with a salary of two thousand dollars, which was yesterday stricken out in Committee of the Whole.

The proposition was earnestly opposed by Mr. Dickerson, and also by Mr. Smith, and was supported by Messrs. Otis and Trimble.

The motion was agreed to—yeas 20, nays 17; and the bill was then ordered to be engrossed as amended, and read a third time.

Saturday, February 24.

The two bills from the House of Representatives yesterday brought up for concurrence, were severally read twice by unanimous consent, and referred.

Mr. Horsey, from the Committee on the District of Columbia, to whom was referred the bill concerning divorces and alimony in the District of Columbia, reported it with amendments; which were read.

Mr. Horsey, from the same committee, to whom was referred the petition of John Threlkeld and Joseph Brooks, reported a bill to empower the Levy Court for the county of Washington to discontinue a certain road therein mentioned; and the bill was read, and passed to a second reading.

Mr. Ruggles, from the Committee of Claims, to whom was referred the bill, entitled "An act for the relief of John Webster," reported it without amendment.

Mr. Sanford obtained leave to bring in a bill to revive and continue in force "An act fixing the compensations of the Secretary of the Senate and Clerk of the House of Representatives, of the clerks employed in their offices, and of the Librarian," approved the 18th day of April, 1818; which was read, and passed to a second reading.

Mr. JOHNSON, of Louisiana, submitted the following motion for consideration:

Resolved, That the Committee on the Judiciary be instructed to inquire into the expediency of modifying the laws organizing the district court of the United States for the State of Louisiana, so as to require the judge of said district to hold a court at Opelousas or at Alexandria, in the western district of the State, during the months of August and September in every year.

Mr. EATON submitted the following motion for consideration:

Resolved, That the President of the United States be requested to communicate to the Senate, if any, and what, proceedings have been had in relation to any person holding an office under the authority of this Government, charged with being concerned in the introduction of any slave or slaves into the United States, contrary to existing laws upon the subject; and that he report such evidences and opinions connected therewith, not confidentially communicated to him, as may be in his possession.

On motion, by Mr. EATON, the report of the Secretary of the Treasury, made in obedience to a resolution of the Senate of the 2d instant, relative to the claim of John H. Piatt, was referred to the Committee of Claims.

The bill to designate the boundaries of a land district, and for the establishment of a land office in the State of Indiana; the bill for the relief of Dean Weymouth; the bill granting to the corporation of the city of Mobile, in the State of Alabama, certain lots of ground in the said city; and the bill to provide for the due execution of the laws of the United States within the State of Missouri; were severally read the second time.

The Senate proceeded to consider the last mentioned bill, as in Committee of the Whole; and it was postponed to, and made the order of the day for, Monday next.

The resolution from the House of Representatives providing for jails in certain cases for the safe custody of persons imprisoned under the authority of the United States, was read the second time, and referred to the Committee on the Judiciary.

The Senate proceeded to consider the motion of yesterday, for information relative to the execution or violation of the navigation laws; and agreed thereto.

The Senate proceeded to consider the report of the Committee on Public Lands on the petition of Watson Brown; and, in concurrence therewith, resolved, that the prayer of the petitioner ought not to be granted.

The amendment to the bill, entitled "An act to reduce and fix the Military Peace Establishment of the United States," having been reported by the committee correctly engrossed, the bill was read a third time as amended, and passed.

The bill to continue the charters of certain banks in the District of Columbia was taken up, and having been amended so as to provide for the consolidation of the Bank of Alexandria and the Bank of Potomac into one bank (according to their own request) the bill was ordered to be engrossed for a third reading.

Mr. BARBOUR, from the Committee on Foreign Relations, to whom the subject was referred, reported a bill providing for the adjudication and payment of claims arising under the Treaty of Amity, Settlement, and Limits, between the United States and His Catholic Majesty; and the bill was twice read by unanimous consent.

On motion by Mr. SANFORD, the Committee on Finance were discharged from the memorial of the merchants of the city of New York, which was yesterday presented to the Senate.

A message from the House of Representatives informed the Senate that the House have passed a bill, entitled "An act authorizing the Secretary of State to issue a patent to Thomas Oxley," in which they request the concurrence of the Senate.

The Senate resumed, as in Committee of the Whole, the consideration of the bill for the better regulation of the trade with the Indian tribes; and, on motion by Mr. TRIMBLE, it was postponed indefinitely.

A message from the House of Representatives informed the Senate that the House have passed a resolution for the appointment of a joint committee to report whether it be or not expedient to admit Missouri into the Union on an equal footing with the original States, and to provide for the due execution of the laws therein, and, if not, whether any other, and what, provision adapted to her actual condition ought to be made by law.

The bill to confirm the claim of the Marquis de Maison Rouge to a tract of land in Arkansas, was taken up; and after a short time spent in its consideration, it was ordered to be engrossed for a third reading, by yeas and nays—yeas 22, nays 9, as follows:

YEAS—Messrs. Barbour, Elliott, Gaillard, Horsey, Hunter, Johnson of Kentucky, Johnson of Louisiana, Lowrie, Mills, Otis, Pleasants, Ruggles, Sanford, Southard, Stokes, Taylor, Thomas, Trimble, Van Dyke, Walker of Alabama, Williams of Mississippi, and Williams of Tennessee.

NAYS—Messrs. Chandler, Eaton, Holmes of Maine, Holmes of Mississippi, King of New York, Lanman, Macon, Palmer, and Smith.

INDIAN TRADE.

The Senate resumed the consideration of the bill further to continue in force, (until June, 1822,) the act for establishing trading-houses with the Indian trades.

Mr. TRIMBLE, of Ohio, opposed the bill and the present system of Indian trade, at much length; and the bill was defended by Messrs. HOLMES, of Mississippi, and JOHNSON, of Kentucky, principally on the ground that it was too late now to go into a revision of the system of Indian trade at the present session.

Mr. TRIMBLE proposed to amend the bill by adding thereto the following section:

"SEC. 2. *And be it further enacted,* That the Superintendent of Indian trade shall not hereafter purchase

381   HISTORY OF CONGRESS.   382

FEBRUARY, 1821.   *Admission of Missouri.*   SENATE.

any goods for the Indian Department, except for such factories as the United States are bound by treaty to continue; and that the President of the United States be, and he is hereby, authorized to adopt such measures as may be necessary and proper to have the funds and the property employed in the Indian trade to be paid into the Treasury of the United States."

The amendment was negatived by yeas and nays—23 votes to 12; as follows:

YEAS—Messrs. Eaton, King of New York, Lanman, Macon, Ruggles, Sanford, Smith, Taylor, Trimble, Walker of Alabama, Williams of Mississippi, and Williams of Tennessee.

NAYS—Messrs. Barbour, Chandler, Dana, Elliott, Gaillard, Holmes of Maine, Holmes of Mississippi, Horsey, Hunter, Johnson of Kentucky, Johnson of Louisiana, King of Alabama, Knight, Lowrie, Mills, Palmer, Parrott, Pleasants, Southard, Stokes, Thomas Van Dyke, and Walker of Georgia.

The bill was then ordered to be engrossed and read a third time.

MISSOURI.

On motion of Mr. HOLMES, of Maine, the Senate proceeded to consider the message from the House, announcing their appointment of a committee to meet such committee as may be appointed by the Senate, on the subject of the admission of Missouri into the Union; and the question was on concurring with the other House in the course proposed.

Mr. SMITH, of South Carolina, observed, that, from the hasty glance he could give the subject, he saw no good reason for such a proceeding on the part of the Senate. There was no doubt or difficulty here on the subject of Missouri. If there was any in the other House, he had no objection to give them the advice of the Senate, if necessary, but it could be no reason for the appointment of a committee on the part of this body to consult with them. Not being able to see the expediency of the course proposed, Mr. S. moved that the message lie on the table.

Mr. BARBOUR, of Virginia, remarked that the time left to act on this matter was so short that a little delay might defeat the object. The subject was one of great importance, Mr. B. said, and he hoped the Senate would act on it immediately. The course proposed by the other House was not a novelty in the proceedings of Congress or of the English Parliament, whence most of our rules were drawn. Committees of conference were frequently appointed on subjects of much less importance than the present; and it was proper that, when the two Houses do not agree on the principles of a public act, there should be a joint committee to see if they can devise any course in which the two branches would probably meet. This was a mere proposition for such an inquiry, and he hoped the Senate would accede to it.

Mr. SMITH said he had no opportunity to see what the proposition from the other House actually was, as it had just been received, and once read. If the Senate were straitened for time, it was a reason for not acting precipitately, and the importance of the subject, which had been urged

in favor of an immediate decision, was a reason for acting with caution. As to the mode of proceeding in Parliament, it did not apply to this case. If the other House had sent back the resolution of the Senate for the admission of Missouri, with an amendment, on which the two Houses could not agree, a committee of conference would be proper on the disagreeing votes; but a committee of conference to settle original principles was a novelty. He hoped, at any rate, that the Senate would allow a little time—even a half an hour—to think of this proposition.

Mr. HOLMES, of Maine, hoped that the message would not be laid on the table. The subject involved in it was sufficiently embarrassed and difficult already, and he should be sorry to see any additional impediments thrown in the way. It was simply a proposition from the other House for a committee of inquiry into an all-important matter; and would it, he asked, be proper for the Senate to refuse it?

The motion to lay the message on the table was negatived.

The Senate then concurred in the proposition—yeas 29, nays 7, as follows:

YEAS—Messrs. Barbour, Chandler, Eaton, Elliott, Gaillard, Holmes of Maine, Holmes of Mississippi, Horsey, Hunter, Johnson of Kentucky, Johnson of Louisiana, King of Alabama, Knight, Lanman, Lowrie, Morril, Palmer, Parrott, Pleasants, Roberts, Southard, Stokes, Talbot, Taylor, Trimble, Van Dyke, Walker of Alabama, Walker of Georgia, and Williams of Mississippi.

NAYS—Messrs. Dana, King of New York, Mills, Otis, Ruggles, Sanford, and Smith.

Messrs. HOLMES, of Maine, BARBOUR, ROBERTS, MORRIL, SOUTHARD, JOHNSON, of Kentucky, and KING, of New York, were appointed the committee on the part of the Senate.

MONDAY, February 26.

The following Message was received from the PRESIDENT OF THE UNITED STATES:

To the Senate of the United States:

I transmit to Congress a letter from the Secretary of War, enclosing " an annual return of the militia of the United States," prepared by the Adjutant and Inspector General., conformably to the militia laws on that subject.

       JAMES MONROE.

WASHINGTON, *Feb.* 24, 1821.

The Message and accompanying documents were read.

Mr. SANFORD presented the petition of the inhabitants of that part of the State of New York residing on the turnpike road from Catskill to Ithaca, praying the establishment of a certain post route; and the petition was read, and referred to the Committee on the Post Office and Post Roads.

Mr. LANMAN presented the memorial of Elisha Denison and others, of New London; and, also, the memorial of W. Heaton and others, of New Haven and Hartford, in Connecticut, severally praying the establishment of additional lights on the Sound, between the continent and Long

Island, for the better security to vessels navigating the same; and the memorials were read, and referred to the Committee on Commerce and Manufactures.

Mr. HOLMES, of Maine, from the Joint Committee of the two Houses of Congress, appointed on the subject, reported a resolution providing for the admission of Missouri into the Union on a certain condition; which was read, and laid on the table.

On motion by Mr. BARBOUR, the Committee on Foreign Relations were discharged from the consideration of the memorial of the Alabama convention, presented to the Senate on the 22d inst.

Mr. BARBOUR, from the Committee on Foreign Relations, to whom the subject was referred, reported a bill to authorize the President of the United States to take possession of East and West Florida, and establish a temporary government therein; and the bill was twice read by unanimous consent.

The twenty-fourth rule for conducting business in the Senate having been suspended for the purpose, on motion by Mr. KING, of New York, he asked and obtained leave to bring in a bill to amend the act entitled "An act supplementary to an act entitled 'An act to regulate the collection of duties on imports and tonnage,' passed the 2d day of March, 1799;" and the bill was twice read by unanimous consent.

Mr. ROBERTS, from the Committee of Claims, to whom was referred the report of the Treasury Department, in relation to the claim of John H. Piatt, made a report, accompanied by a bill explanatory of the act for the relief of John H. Piatt; and the report and bill were read, and the bill passed to a second reading.

Mr. ROBERTS, from the same committee, to whom was referred the petition of Richard S. Hackley, made a report, accompanied by a resolution that the prayer of the petitioner ought not to be granted.

On motion, by Mr. ROBERTS, the Committee of Claims were discharged from the consideration of the memorial of Jacob Barker, presented to the Senate on the 19th instant.

The bill from the House of Representatives, entitled "An act authorizing the Secretary of State to issue a patent to Thomas Oxley," was twice read by unanimous consent.

The bill to revive and continue in force "An act fixing the compensations of the Secretary of the Senate and Clerk of the House of Representatives, of the clerks employed in their offices, and of the librarian," approved the 18th day of April, 1818; and the bill to empower the Levy Court for the county of Washington to discontinue a certain road therein mentioned; were severally read the second time.

The Senate proceeded to consider the motion of the 24th instant, instructing the Committee on the Judiciary to inquire into the expediency of making certain modifications to the law organizing the district court in Louisiana; and agreed thereto.

The Senate proceeded to consider the motion of

the 24th instant, requesting the President of the United States to communicate what proceedings, if any, have been had in relation to persons holding offices under the Government charged with being concerned in the introduction of slaves into the United States, contrary to existing laws; and agreed thereto.

The Senate proceeded to consider, as in Committee of the Whole, the bill to provide for the due execution of the laws of the United States within the State of Missouri; and, on motion, by Mr. HOLMES, of Mississippi, it was laid on the table.

The Senate resumed, as in Committee of the Whole, the consideration of the bill to authorize the appointment of certain Indian agents; and the same having been amended, the PRESIDENT reported it to the House accordingly; and the amendment being concurred in, it was ordered to be engrossed and read a third time.

The engrossed bill further to extend the act establishing trading-houses with the Indian tribes, and the engrossed bill to extend the charters of certain banks in the District of Columbia, were severally read the third time, passed, and sent to the other House for concurrence.

Mr. PINKNEY communicated to the Senate a report adopted by the Legislature of Maryland, in favor of allowing to those States which have had no appropriations of public land, for the purposes of education, such appropriations as will correspond, in a just proportion, with those heretofore made in favor of the other States, with resolutions requesting the Senators and Representatives of Maryland in Congress to endeavor to procure the passage of an act to carry the views of the report into effect; and the said document was laid on the table.

The bill to authorize the President of the United States to have certain boundaries designated and marked, (between the States and Territories northwest of the Ohio,) was taken up in Committee of the Whole, where it underwent some amendment, and was ordered to be engrossed for a third reading.

The bill for the relief of Matthew McNair was considered and discussed in Committee of the Whole, and was ordered to be engrossed for a third reading; as was also the bill to establish a port of entry at Blakely.

Mr. ROBERTS gave notice that, to-morrow, he should ask leave to bring in resolutions for an allowance for extra services, to the assistants to the doorkeeper of the Senate, and for compensating a temporary clerk in the office of the Secretary of the Senate.

Mr. DICKERSON, from the Committee on Commerce and Manufactures, to whom was referred the bill, entitled "An act to authorize the President of the United States to establish a port of entry in the district of Sandusky, in the State of Ohio, and for other purposes," reported it with an amendment; which was read.

The Senate proceeded to consider, as in Committee of the Whole, the resolution proposing an amendment to the Constitution of the United

385   HISTORY OF CONGRESS.   386

FEBRUARY, 1821.   *Treaty with Spain—Marquis de Maison Rouge.*   SENATE.

States as it respects the election of Representatives in Congress, and the choice of Electors of President and Vice President of the United States, together with an amendment reported thereto by the select committee; and it was laid on the table.

TREATY WITH SPAIN.

The Senate then went into Committee of the Whole on the bill providing for the adjudication and payment of claims arising under the treaty with Spain; and proceeded to fill the blanks therein.

In moving to fill the blank left for the compensation of the commissioners to be appointed under the act, Mr. BARBOUR said it appeared to be the common impression that men of the first standing for character and abilities ought to be selected, and to induce such men to accept the office, a liberal salary ought to be allowed. He therefore moved that the sum be fixed at three thousand dollars each; which motion was agreed to without objection. The salary for the secretary of the commissioners was fixed at two thousand dollars; and, on motion of Mr. KING, of New York, an amendment was inserted requiring that the person filling the office of secretary shall be skilled in the French and Spanish languages.

Mr. KING, of New York, deeming three thousand dollars not a sufficient salary to induce suitable persons to undertake the highly important duties devolving on the commissioners, moved to reconsider the vote on filling the blank with three thousand dollars, with the view of filling it with three thousand five hundred dollars; but the motion was negatived—ayes 12, noes 16.

The bill was then reported to the Senate, and was ordered to be engrossed for a third reading.

MARQUIS DE MAISON ROUGE.

The engrossed bill to confirm the title of the Marquis de Maison Rouge, on the application of Daniel W. Coxe, to a tract of land, (held by him under a Spanish grant, recommended by the American Commissioners to confirmation, and covering a tract of about thirty leagues square,) in Louisiana, west of the Mississippi, was read the third time.

Mr. LANMAN made an ineffectual motion to lay the bill on the table with the view of examining the claim more fully; after which a debate of considerable length took place on the merits of the title, the validity of the facts on which it rested, &c. The bill was opposed by Mr. LANMAN, and advocated by Messrs. JOHNSON, of Louisiana, (on whose motion an amendment had been adopted reserving from its operation all claims which it might conflict with or affect,) OTIS, VAN DYKE, and DANA. Mr. KING, of New York, without giving any opinion on the justice of the claim, said he could not vote for the bill, for the reason that he did not conceive this to be the tribunal to decide such a question.

The question being taken on the passage of the bill, it was decided by yeas and nays, in the affirmative—ayes 26, noes 8, as follows:

YEAS—Messrs. Barbour, Dana, Dickerson, Elliott, Gaillard, Holmes of Mississippi, Hersey, Hunter, Johnson of Kentucky, Johnson of Louisiana, Knight, Lowrie, Mills, Otis, Parrott, Pleasants, Roberts, Ruggles, Sanford, Talbot, Taylor, Thomas, Trimble, Van Dyke, Williams of Mississippi, and Williams of Tennessee.

NAYS—Messrs. Chandler, Eaton, Holmes of Maine, King of New York, Lanman, Macon, Pinkney, and Tichenor.

TUESDAY, February 27.

Mr. DANA presented the memorial of Wolcott and Kilbourn and others, inhabitants of sundry towns in Connecticut, praying the establishment of additional lights on the Sound, between the continent and Long Island, for the better security to vessels navigating the same; and the memorial was read, and referred to the Committee on Commerce and Manufactures.

Mr. SANFORD, from the joint committee of the Senate and House of Representatives, appointed to consider what subjects before the two Houses are proper to be acted on during the present session of Congress, made a report, which was read.

Mr. SANFORD, from the Committee on Finance, to whom was referred the bill, entitled "An act making appropriations for the support of the navy of the United States for the year 1821," reported it without amendment.

On motion, by Mr. SANFORD, the Committee on Finance were discharged from the consideration of the petition of John B. Lemaitre.

On motion, by Mr. THOMAS, the Committee on Public Lands were discharged from the consideration of the petition of Rufus Easton; and from the consideration of the resolution of the 22d January, instructing said committee to inquire into the expediency of amending the "Act for the relief of the inhabitants of the late county of New Madrid, in the Missouri Territory, who suffered by earthquakes, passed on the 17th February, 1815."

Mr. BARBOUR, from the joint committee appointed for the purpose, reported that, pursuant to the resolution, the joint committee of the Senate and House of Representatives yesterday waited on the President of the United States and notified him of his re-election to that office; and that he informed the committee he would take the oath prescribed by the Constitution on Monday next.

Mr. STOKES, from the Committee on the Post Office and Post Roads, to whom was referred the bill, entitled "An act to alter and establish certain post roads," reported it with amendments, which were read.

The bill explanatory of the act for the relief of John H. Piatt, was read the second time.

The Senate proceeded to consider the report of the Committee of Claims on the petition of Richard S. Hackley; and it was laid on the table.

The Senate proceeded to consider, as in Committee of the Whole, the resolution from the House of Representatives authorizing the President of the United States to cause astronomical observations to be made to ascertain the longitude of the Capitol, in the City of Washington, from some known meridian in Europe; and, on motion of Mr. BARBOUR, it was laid on the table.

The following engrossed bills were severally read the third time, passed, and sent to the other House for concurrence, viz:

The bill to authorize the President to cause to be surveyed and designated certain boundaries;

The bill providing for the settlement and payment of certain claims arising under the treaty with Spain;

The bill to establish the district of Blakeley; and

The bill authorizing the appointment of certain Indian agents.

Mr. ROBERTS obtained leave to bring in the following resolutions; which were read:

Resolved, That Robert Tweedy, Tobias Simpson, and George Hicks, assistants to the Sergeant-at-Arms and Doorkeeper of the Senate, be paid out of the contingent fund two dollars a day for each day they may have attended the Senate during the present session of Congress, and that Henry Tims be allowed one hundred dollars for his attendance the present session.

Resolved, That there be paid out of the contingent fund to Robert Tweedy, Tobias Simpson, and George Hicks, the sum of one hundred and fifty dollars for extra services.

Resolved, That the Secretary be authorized to pay R. B. Washburn, out of the contingent fund of the Senate, at the rate of an engrossing clerk for the time during which he has been and shall be employed in the Secretary's office.

Ordered, That the said resolutions severally pass to a second reading.

The Senate proceeded to consider, as in Committee of the Whole, the bill concerning the collection of public moneys, together with the amendments reported thereto by the Committee on Finance; and the said amendments having been agreed to, on motion, by Mr. HOLMES of Maine, it was laid on the table.

The Senate resumed, as in Committee of the Whole, the bill, entitled "An act for the relief of Daniel Seward;" and it was laid on the table.

Mr. DICKERSON, from the Committee on Commerce and Manufactures, to whom was referred the bill, entitled "An act to authorize the building of lighthouses on Cross and Pond Islands, in the harbor of Boothbay, and at the mouth of Oswego river, and placing buoys on the Shoals of Nantucket and Vineyard Sound, near the harbor of Wickford, and on the Altamaha river, and for other purposes," reported it with amendments; which were read.

The Senate proceeded to consider, as in Committee of the Whole, the bill, entitled "An act to regulate the location of land warrants and the issuing of patents in certain cases, together with the amendments reported thereto by the Committee on Public Lands; and it was postponed to Saturday next.

The Senate proceeded to consider, as in Committee of the Whole, the bill, entitled "An act for the relief of Bartholomew Duverge;" and it was laid on the table.

The Senate proceeded to consider, as in Committee of the Whole, the bill, entitled "An act to continue in force an act, entitled 'An act to provide for persons who were disabled by known wounds received in the Revolutionary war, and for other purposes;'" and, on motion, by Mr. EATON, it was laid on the table.

The Senate proceeded to consider, as in Committee of the Whole, the bill, entitled "An act for the relief of Daniel McDuff;" and it was postponed until to-morrow.

The following bills successively passed through Committees of the Whole, and were severally ordered to be read a third time, viz:

The bill for the relief of John Gooding and James Williams; the bill for the relief of General Robert Swartwout; the bill for the relief of J. L. B. McCarty; the bill for the relief of Alexander Milne; the bill for the relief of Joseph McNeil; the bill for the relief of Nicholas Jarrott; the bill for the relief of Lewis H. Guerlain; the bill for the relief of Francis B. Languille; the bill for the relief of John Rodriguez; the bill for the relief of James Brady; the bill for passing to the credit of Nathaniel Allen certain moneys by him disbursed in the public service; the bill to authorize the clerk of the District Court of Louisiana to appoint a deputy to aid him in his duties; the bill to establish the district of Pearl river.

The bill for the relief of Jacob Hunsinger was discussed, and finally rejected by indefinite postponement.

The resolution from the other House to suspend the recruiting service was considered, and ordered to be read a third time.

MISSOURI.

A message from the House of Representatives informed the Senate that the House have passed a resolution providing for the admission of the State of Missouri into the Union on a certain condition, in which they request the concurrence of the Senate.

The Senate then proceeded to consider the said resolution.

After an unsuccessful attempt by Mr. MACON to strike out the condition and proviso, which was negatived by a large majority, and a few remarks by Mr. BARBOUR in support of the expediency of harmony and concession on this momentous subject.

The question was taken on ordering the resolution to be read a third time, and was decided in the affirmative, by the following vote:

YEAS—Messrs. Barbour, Chandler, Eaton, Elliott, Gaillard, Holmes of Maine, Holmes of Mississippi, Horsey, Hunter, Johnson of Kentucky, Johnson of Louisiana, King of Alabama, Lowrie, Morril, Parrott, Pleasants, Roberts, Southard, Stokes, Talbot, Taylor, Thomas, Van Dyke, Walker of Alabama, Williams of Mississippi, and Williams of Tenn.—26.

NAYS—Messrs. Dana, Dickerson, King of New York, Knight, Lanman, Macon, Mills, Noble, Otis, Palmer, Ruggles, Sanford, Smith, Tichenor, and Trimble—15.

A motion was made to read the resolution a third time forthwith, but it was objected to, and, under the rule of the Senate, of course it could not be done.

WEDNESDAY, February 28.

A message from the House of Representatives informed the Senate that they concur in the amendment of the Senate to the bill, entitled "An act to reduce and fix the Military Peace Establishment of the United States," with an amendment. They have passed a bill, entitled "An act to release French ships and vessels entering the ports of the United States prior to the 30th of September, 1820, from the operation of the act, entitled "An act to impose a new tonnage duty on French ships and vessels, and for other purposes;" in which bill and amendment they request the concurrence of the Senate.

The bill last mentioned was twice read by unanimous consent, and referred to the Committee on Foreign Relations.

Mr. KING, of New York, from the Committee on Foreign Relations, reported the last mentioned bill with an amendment; which was read.

The Senate proceeded to consider the amendment of the House of Representatives to their amendment to the bill, entitled "An act to reduce and fix the Military Peace Establishment of the United States," and concurred therein.

Mr. PLEASANTS, from the Committee on Naval Affairs, to whom was referred the memorial of Jane Baker, made a report, accompanied by a resolution that the prayer of the petitioner ought not to be granted.

On motion, by Mr. PLEASANTS, the Committee on Naval Affairs were discharged from the consideration of the petition of John B. Timberlake, the petition of Charlotte J. Bullus, the petition of Harriet Shackerly, and the petition of Joseph G. Roberts; and, also, from the report of the Secretary of the Navy on the rules and instructions of the naval service.

On motion, by Mr. VAN DYKE, the Committee on Public Lands were discharged from the consideration of the petition of Terrence Clark.

On motion by Mr. THOMAS, the said committee were discharged from the consideration of the memorials of the Legislature of the State of Missouri, the petition of the inhabitants of Illinois, and the memorial of the Legislature of the State of Mississippi; and, also, from the resolutions of the 24th of November and 24th of January last, to grant the right of pre-emption in certain cases.

On motion of Mr. NOBLE, the Committee on Pensions were discharged from the consideration of the petition of Job Sherburne, the petition of Lemuel Wight, and the petition of Charlotte Read; and, also, from the resolution of the 15th of January, to grant a pension to Willis Tandy.

Mr. ROBERTS communicated a letter from the Third Auditor of the Treasury, relative to the report on the claim of John H. Piatt, which was read.

Mr. SMITH, from the Committee on the Judiciary, to whom was referred the resolution from the House of Representatives, providing for jails in certain cases for the safe custody of persons imprisoned under the authority of the United States, reported it without amendment.

On motion by Mr. SMITH, the Committee on the Judiciary were discharged from the consideration of the resolution of the 26th instant, relative to a reorganization of the district court in Louisiana, and it was laid on the table.

Mr. WILLIAMS, of Tennessee, from the Committee on Military Affairs, to whom was referred the bill, entitled "An act to fix and equalize the pay of the officers of the Army of the United States," reported it without amendment.

The resolutions to compensate certain attendants on the Senate were severally read the second time.

The Senate resumed, as in Committee of the Whole, the consideration of the bill, entitled "An act to continue in force an act, entitled 'An act to provide for persons who were disabled by known wounds received in the Revolutionary war, and for other purposes;" and it was postponed indefinitely.

The Senate proceeded to consider, as in Committee of the Whole, the bill to extend the charter of the Bank of Potomac; and it was laid on the table.

The Senate proceeded to consider, as in Committee of the Whole, the bill authorizing the repair of a sea-wall at the Isles of Shoals, and for other purposes; and, on motion by Mr. DICKERSON, it was laid on the table.

The Senate proceeded to consider, as in Committee of the Whole, the bill for the relief of the legal representatives of Manuel and Isaac Monsanto, deceased; and it was laid on the table.

The resolution from the House of Representatives for the suspension of the recruiting service, was read the third time, and, on motion, was ordered to lie on the table.

Bills entitled as follows, viz : For the relief of Joseph M'Neil ; for the relief of Alexander Milne ; for the relief of Lewis H. Guerlain ; for the relief of John Rodriguez ; for the relief of Francis B. Languille ; to establish the district of Pearl River ; for the relief of James Brady ; for the relief of Nicholas Jarrott ; were severally read a third time and passed.

The resolution from the House of Representatives for the admission of the State of Missouri into the Union on a certain condition, was read the third time.

On the question, " Shall this resolution pass ?" it was determined in the affirmative—yeas 28, nays 14, as follows :

YEAS—Messrs. Barbour, Chandler, Eaton, Edwards, Gaillard, Holmes of Maine, Holmes of Mississippi, Horsey, Hunter, Johnson of Kentucky, Johnson of Louisiana, King of Alabama, Lowrie, Morril, Parrott, Pinkney, Pleasants, Roberts, Southard, Stokes, Talbot, Taylor, Thomas, Van Dyke, Walker of Alabama, Walker of Georgia, Williams of Mississippi, and Williams of Tennessee.

NAYS—Messrs. Dana, Dickerson, King of New York, Knight, Lanman, Macon, Mills, Noble, Otis, Ruggles, Sanford, Smith, Tichenor, and Trimble.

The bill, from the House of Representatives, for the relief of the family of O. H. Perry, was resumed; and, after debate, in the course of which the bill was eloquently supported by Mr. HUNTER, the bill was ordered to a third reading by the following vote:

YEAS—Messrs. Dana, Dickerson, Edwards, Elliott, Gaillard, Holmes of Maine, Holmes of Mississippi, Horsey, Hunter, Johnson of Kentucky, Johnson of Louisiana, King of New York, Knight, Lanman, Lowrie, Mills, Morril, Otis, Parrott, Pleasants, Sanford, Smith, Southard, Stokes, Talbot, Thomas, Tichenor, Trimble, Van Dyke, Walker of Georgia, and Williams of Tennessee—31.

NAYS—Messrs. Eaton, King of Alabama, Macon, Roberts, Ruggles, Taylor, Walker of Alabama, and Williams of Mississippi—8.

And the bill was immediately read a third time and passed.

The Senate proceeded to consider, as in Committee of the Whole, the bill concerning the process of execution issuing from the sixth circuit court of the United States for the district of Georgia; and it was laid on the table.

The Senate proceeded to consider, as in Committee of the Whole, the bill to reward Lieutenant Gregory, his officers, and companions; and it was laid on the table.

The Senate proceeded to consider, as in Committee of the Whole, the bill for the relief of Josiah Hook, jr.; and it was laid on the table.

The Senate proceeded to consider, as in Committee of the Whole, the bill for the relief of the legal representatives of Alexander Montgomery, deceased; and it was laid on the table.

Bills of the following titles, to wit: Authorizing the payment of a sum of money to John Gooding and James Williams; for the relief of General Robert Swartwout; to authorize the clerk of the district court of the United States for the district of Louisiana to appoint a deputy to aid him in the discharge of the duties of his office; for the relief of J. L. B. Macarty; for passing to the credit of Nathaniel Allen certain moneys disbursed by him for the use of the United States; for the relief of Bartholomew Duverge; to alter the time of holding the district court in the northern district of the State of New York; to extend the time for unlading vessels arriving from foreign ports, in certain cases; to authorize the reconveyance of a tract of land to the city of New York; to authorize the President of the United States to remove the land office in Lawrence county, in Arkansas; confirming the location of the seat of government of the State of Illinois, and for other purposes; for the relief of Rosalie P. Deslonde; for the relief of P. D. De La Ronde; further to regulate the entry of merchandise imported into the United States from any adjacent territory; to establish a new land office in the State of Mississippi, and for the better regulation of certain land districts in the States of Alabama and Mississippi; and to extend the term of Samuel Parker's patent.

These bills, some of which originated in this House, and some of them in the House of Representatives, were severally considered, and ordered to be read a third time to-morrow.

A message from the House of Representatives

informed the Senate that they have passed the bill which originated in the Senate, entitled "An act to extend the charters of certain banks in the District of Columbia;" and also the bill, entitled "An act for the relief of the purchasers of public lands prior to the first day of July, 1820," with amendments. They have passed a bill, entitled "An act further to amend the several acts relative to the Treasury, War, and Navy Departments;" in which amendments and bill they request the concurrence of the Senate.

The bill last mentioned was read, and passed to a second reading.

The Senate proceeded to consider the amendments of the House of Representatives to the bill, entitled "An act for the relief of the purchasers of public lands prior to the first day of July, 1820," and concurred therein.

THURSDAY, March 1.

The credentials of JOHN HOLMES, appointed a Senator by the Legislature of the State of Maine for six years, commencing on the fourth instant, were read, and laid on file.

The following Message was received from the PRESIDENT OF THE UNITED STATES:

To the Senate and House of
Representatives of the United States:

I herewith transmit to Congress certain extracts, and a copy of letters received by the Secretary of State from the Marshal of the United States for the eastern district of Virginia, in relation to the execution of the act of the 14th of March, 1820, to provide for taking the Fourth census, together with the answers returned to that marshal by the Secretary of State. As the time within which the assistants of the marshals can legally make their returns expired on the first Monday of the present month, it would appear, by the information from the marshal at Richmond, that the completion of the Fourth census, as it respects the eastern district of Virginia, will have been defeated, not only as it regards the period contemplated by law, but during the whole of the current year, unless Congress, to whom the case is submitted, should, by an act of the present session, allow further time for making the returns in question.

As connected with this subject, it is also submitted for the consideration of Congress, how far the marshals ought to be liable to the payment of postage on the conveyance of the papers concerning the census and manufactures by the mail. In one instance it has been already ascertained that this item of contingent expense will amount to nearly a moiety of the compensation of the marshal for the whole of his services. If the marshals are to be relieved from this charge, provision will be necessary by law, either for the admission of it in their accounts, or the refunding of it by the respective postmasters.

JAMES MONROE.

WASHINGTON, *Feb. 28, 1821.*

The Message and documents therein referred to were read.

Mr. BARBOUR, by unanimous consent, asked and obtained leave to bring in a bill to amend the act, entitled "An act to provide for taking the Fourth census or enumeration of the inhabitants of the United States, and for other purposes;" and the bill was twice read by unanimous consent, and referred to the Committee on the Judiciary.

Mr. SMITH, from the Committee on the Judiciary, reported the last mentioned bill with an amendment, which was read, and the bill was considered as in Committee of the Whole; and, the amendment having been agreed to, the bill was reported to the House accordingly; and, the amendment being concurred in, the bill was ordered to be engrossed, and read the third time. It was then read the third time by unanimous consent, and passed.

On motion by Mr. THOMAS, the Committee on Public Lands were discharged from the consideration of the petition of David Chambers, the petition of William Dick, the petition of the inhabitants of the village of Cote Sans Dessein, in Missouri, and the petition of John W. McGirk; and also from the resolution of the Assembly of Ohio, respecting the appropriations of lands for the support of schools.

Mr. JOHNSON, of Louisiana, submitted the following motion, which was read, considered, and disagreed to:

Resolved, That the President of the United States be requested to lay before the Senate such information as he may possess, in relation to the decision of the Emperor of Russia on the question depending between the United States and Great Britain, respecting the construction of the first article of the Treaty of Ghent, as relates to the restitution of slaves, which has been referred to his umpirage by both Governments.

On motion by Mr. MACON, the President of the United States was requested to cause to be laid before the Senate, in the first week of the next session, a copy of the survey of the coast of North Carolina, made in pursuance of the resolution of Congress of the 19th day of January, in the year 1819.

The Senate proceeded to consider the report of the Committee on Naval Affairs, on the memorial of Jane Baker; and, in concurrence therewith, resolved, that the prayer of the petitioner ought not to be granted.

The bill entitled "An act further to amend the several acts relative to the Treasury, War, and Navy Departments," was read the second time.

The bill to extend the time for unlading vessels arriving from foreign ports in certain cases, was read the third time, and passed.

The bill to authorize the reconveyance of a tract of land to the city of New York, was read the third time, and passed.

The bill to establish a new land office in the State of Mississippi, and for the better regulation of certain land districts in the States of Alabama and Mississippi, was read the third time, and passed.

The bill to extend the term of Samuel Parker's patents, for his improvement in currying and finishing leather of all kinds, was read the third time, and passed.

The amendments to the bill, entitled "An act further to regulate the entry of merchandise imported into the United States from any adjacent territory," having been reported by the committee correctly engrossed, the bill was read the third time as amended, and passed.

The bill entitled "An act extending the time for issuing and locating military land warrants to officers and soldiers of the Revolutionary Army," was read the third time, and passed.

The bill entitled "An act for the relief of Pierre Dennis De La Ronde," was read the third time, and passed.

The bill entitled "An act for the relief of Rosalie P. Deslonde," was read the third time, and passed.

The bill entitled "An act confirming the location of the seat of government of the State of Illinois, and for other purposes," was read the third time, and passed.

The bill entitled "An act authorizing the President of the United States to remove the land office in the district of Lawrence county, in the Territory of Arkansas," was read the third time, and passed.

The bill entitled "An act for the relief of Bartholomew Duverge," was read the third time, and passed.

The bill entitled "An act to alter the times of holding the district court in the northern district of New York," was read the third time, and passed.

The Senate took up and considered, as in Committee of the Whole, the bill to provide for the due execution of the laws of the United States within the State of Missouri; and the bill having been amended, it was reported to the House accordingly; and the amendments being concurred in, it was ordered to be engrossed and read the third time.

The Senate proceeded to consider, as in Committee of the Whole, the bill, entitled "An act making appropriations for the public buildings," together with the amendments reported thereto by the Committee on the Public Buildings; and, the amendments having been agreed to, the bill was reported to the House accordingly; and, the amendments being concurred in, they were ordered to be engrossed, and the bill read a third time as amended.

The Senate proceeded to consider, as in Committee of the Whole, the bill for the relief of William Whitehead, Joshua Aubin, and James Graham; and, the same having been amended, it was reported to the House accordingly; and, the amendment being concurred in, the bill was ordered to be engrossed and read a third time.

It was read the third time by unanimous consent, and passed.

The Senate proceeded to consider, as in Committee of the Whole, the bill, entitled "An act making appropriations for the support of Government for the year 1821," together with the amendment reported thereto by the Committee on Finance; and the amendment being agreed to, the bill was reported to the House accordingly, and the amendment was concurred in, and ordered to be engrossed, and the bill be read a third time as amended.

The bill was then read the third time as amended, by unanimous consent, and passed.

On motion by Mr. KING, of New York, the Senate proceeded to consider, as in Committee of the Whole, the bill, entitled "An act to release French ships and vessels entering the ports of the United States prior to the 30th day of June, 1820, from the operation of the act, entitled "An act to impose a new tonnage duty on French ships and vessels, and for other purposes," together with the amendment reported thereto by the Committee on Foreign Relations; and the said amendment having been amended, it was agreed to, and the bill was reported to the House accordingly, and the amendment was concurred in, and ordered to be engrossed, and the bill be read a third time as amended.

It was then read the third time as amended by unanimous consent, and passed.

The Senate proceeded to consider, as in Committee of the Whole, the bill to authorize the President of the United States to take possession of East and West Florida, and to establish a temporary government therein; and, no amendment having been proposed, it was reported to the House, and ordered to be engrossed and read a third time.

It was then read the third time by unanimous consent, and passed.

The Senate proceeded to consider, as in Committee of the Whole, the bill supplemental to an act, entitled "An act to authorize the appointment of commissioners to lay out the road therein mentioned;" and, no amendment having been made, it was reported to the House, and ordered to be engrossed and read a third time.

The Senate proceeded to consider, as in Committee of the Whole, the bill to amend the act, entitled "An act supplementary to an act, entitled 'An act to regulate the collection of duties on imports and tonnage,' passed the second day of March, 1799;" and the same having been amended, it was reported to the House; and, the amendments being concurred in, the bill was ordered to be engrossed and read a third time.

The Senate proceeded to consider, as in Committee of the Whole, the bill, entitled "An act to alter and establish certain post roads," together with the amendments reported thereto by the Committee on the Post Office and Post Roads; and, the amendments having been amended, they were agreed to, and the bill was reported to the House accordingly, and the amendments being concurred in, the bill was further amended; and on the question, "Shall the amendments be engrossed, and the bill be read a third time as amended?" it was determined in the affirmative.

FRIDAY, March 2.

On motion, by Mr. ROBERTS, the Committee on Finance were instructed to inquire into the expediency of providing for the payment of the balance found to be due on the settlement of the accounts of Alexander James Dallas, paymaster of the Pennsylvania militia, on the 30th of June, 1808.

On motion by Mr. RUGGLES, the Committee of Claims were discharged from the consideration of the petition of James Duffee, the petition of Ann Hodge, the petition of George Harpole, the petition of Drury Bettis, and the petition of Elderkin Potter.

On motion by Mr. HORSEY, the Committee on the District of Columbia were discharged from the consideration of the memorial of the inhabitants of said District in favor of a penitentiary.

On motion by Mr. ROBERTS, the Committee on the Public Buildings were discharged from the consideration of the petition of Daniel Carroll and others.

On motion by Mr. KING, of New York, the Committee on Roads and Canals were discharged from the consideration of the memorial of the Chesapeake and Delaware Canal Company.

The Senate took up and considered, as in Committee of the Whole, the resolution from the House of Representatives authorizing the President of the United States to cause astronomical observations to be made to ascertain the longitude of the Capitol, in the City of Washington, from some known meridian in Europe; and, no amendment having been proposed, it was reported to the House, and passed to a third reading.

The resolution was then read the third time by unanimous consent, and passed.

The Senate proceeded to consider, as in Committee of the Whole, the bill for the relief of Koo-na-noo-lus-kee, or Challenge, one of the tribe of the Cherokee Indians; and it was laid on the table.

The Senate proceeded to consider, as in Committee of the Whole, the bill supplementary to the several acts for adjusting the claims to land and establishing land offices in the districts east of the island of New Orleans; and, on motion by Mr. HORSEY, it was laid on the table.

The Senate proceeded to consider, as in Committee of the Whole, the bill for the relief of David Cooper; and, on motion by Mr. WILLIAMS, of Mississippi, it was laid on the table.

The Senate proceeded to consider, as in Committee of the Whole, the bill concerning vessels employed in the fisheries; and it was laid on the table.

The Senate proceeded to consider, as in Committee of the Whole, the bill, entitled "An act to authorize the collectors of customs to pay debentures issued on the exportation of loaf sugar, and spirits distilled from molasses;" and, no amendment having been proposed, it was reported to the House, and passed to a third reading. The bill was then read the third time by unanimous consent, and passed.

The Senate proceeded to consider, as in Committee of the Whole, the bill to authorize the Commissioner of the General Land Office to remit the instalments due on certain lots in Shawneetown, in the State of Illinois; and it was laid on the table.

The Senate proceeded to consider, as in Committee of the Whole, the bill to revive and continue in force "An act fixing the compensations of the Secretary of the Senate and Clerk of the House of Representatives, of the clerks employed in their offices, and of the Librarian," approved the 18th day of April, 1818; and, the same having been amended, it was reported to the House accordingly; and, the amendment being concurred in, the bill was ordered to be engrossed and read a third time. It was then read the third time by unanimous consent, and passed.

The bill supplemental to "An act to authorize the appointment of commissioners to lay out the road therein mentioned," was read the third time, and passed.

The bill to provide for the due execution of the laws of the United States within the State of Missouri, was read the third time, and passed.

The bill to amend the act, entitled "An act supplementary to an act, entitled 'An act to regulate the collection of duties on imports and tonnage," passed the 2d day of March, 1799, was read the third time, and passed.

The bill entitled "An act making appropriations for the public buildings," was read the third time as amended, and passed.

The amendments to the bill, entitled "An act to alter and establish certain post roads," having been reported by the committee correctly engrossed, the bill was further amended by unanimous consent, and was read the third time as amended, and passed.

The Senate proceeded to consider, as in Committee of the Whole, the bill, entitled "An act for the relief of John Webster;" and no amendment having been proposed, it was reported to the House, and passed to a third reading. The bill was then read the third time by unanimous consent, and passed.

The Senate proceeded to consider, as in Committee of the Whole, the bill, entitled "An act to authorize the President of the United States to establish a post of entry in the district of Sandusky, in the State of Ohio, and for other purposes," together with the amendment reported thereto by the Committee on Commerce and Manufactures; and the amendment having been agreed to, the bill was reported to the House accordingly, and the amendment being concurred in, it was ordered to be engrossed, and the bill read a third time as amended. The bill was then read the third time as amended, and passed.

The Senate proceeded to consider, as in Committee of the Whole, the bill, entitled "An act authorizing the Secretary of State to issue letters patent to Thomas Oxley;" and no amendment having been proposed, it was reported to the House, and passed to a third reading. The bill was then read the third time by unanimous consent, and passed.

The Senate proceeded to consider, as in Committee of the Whole, the bill, entitled "An act making appropriations for the support of the Navy of the United States for the year 1821;" and the same having been amended, it was reported to the House accordingly; and the amendment being concurred in, it was ordered to be engrossed and the bill be read a third time as amended. The bill was then read the third time as amended by unanimous consent, and passed.

The Senate resumed, as in Committee of the Whole, the consideration of the bill, entitled "An act for the relief of Daniel McDuff;" and, on motion by Mr. ROBERTS, it was laid on the table.

The Senate proceeded to consider, as in Committee of the Whole, the bill, entitled "An act to fix and equalize the pay of the officers in the Army of the United States;" and, on motion by Mr. WILLIAMS, of Tennessee, it was laid on the table.

The Senate proceeded to consider, as in Committee of the Whole, the resolution from the House of Representatives providing for jails in certain cases for the safe custody of persons imprisoned under the authority of the United States; and, no amendment having been proposed, it was reported to the House, and passed to a third reading. The resolution was then read the third time by unanimous consent, and passed.

The Senate proceeded to consider, as in Committee of the Whole, the bill, entitled "An act further to amend the several acts relative to the Treasury, War, and Navy Departments;" and, on motion by Mr. MILLS, it was laid on the table.

The Senate proceeded to consider, as in Committee of the Whole, the bill, entitled "An act for the relief of Robert Buntin;" and the same having been amended, it was reported to the House accordingly, and the amendment being concurred in, was ordered to be engrossed and the bill be read a third time as amended.

Mr. THOMAS, from the Committee on Public Lands, to whom was referred the bill confirming certain claims to land in the State of Illinois, reported it without amendment; and it was laid on the table.

Ordered, That the following bills which originated in the Senate severally lie on the table, viz: A bill giving the right of pre-emption to William Doak and Noble Osborne; a bill supplementary to an act passed on the 5th of April, 1820, entitled "An act for the relief of John Harding, Giles Harding, John Shute, and John Nichols;" a bill concerning divorces and alimony in the District of Columbia; a bill to designate the boundaries of a land district and for the establishment of a land office in the State of Indiana; a bill for the relief of Dean Weymouth; a bill granting to the corporation of the city of Mobile, in the State of Alabama, certain lots of ground in said city; a bill to empower the Levy Court for the county of Washington to discontinue a certain road therein mentioned; a bill explanatory of the act for the relief of John H. Piatt.

A message from the House of Representatives informed the Senate that they have passed a bill, entitled "An act authorizing the Secretary of the Treasury of the United States to sell and convey a certain tract of land in Northumberland county, in the State of Virginia;" in which bill they request the concurrence of the Senate.

The bill last brought up for concurrence was twice read by unanimous consent; and referred to the Committee on Finance.

Mr. SANFORD, from the Committee on Finance, reported the last mentioned bill without amendment.

The Senate proceeded to consider, as in Committee of the Whole, the last mentioned bill; and no amendment having been proposed, it was reported to the House; and passed to a third reading. The bill was read the third time by unanimous consent, and passed.

Mr. HOLMES, of Mississippi, communicated a letter signed by a number of chiefs of the Choctaw nation of Indians, addressed to Andrew Jackson and Thomas Hinds, requesting to be permitted by law to become citizens of the United States; and the letter was read, and laid on the table.

The Senate proceeded to consider, as in Committee of the Whole, the three resolutions of the 27th February, to compensate certain attendants on the Senate; and the last of them having been amended, they were reported to the House accordingly; and, the amendments being concurred in, the resolutions were ordered to be engrossed and read a third time.

The Senate proceeded to consider, as in Committee of the Whole, the bill, entitled "An act to authorize the building of lighthouses on Cross and Pond Island, in the harbor of Boothbay, and at the mouth of Oswego river, and placing buoys on the Shoals of Nantucket and Vineyard Sound, near the harbor of Wickford, and on the Altamaha river, and for other purposes," together with the amendments reported thereto by the Committee on Commerce and Manufactures; and the said amendments having been amended, they were agreed to, and the bill was reported to the House accordingly; and, the amendments being concurred in, they were ordered to be engrossed, and the bill be read a third time as amended. The bill was then read the third time as amended by unanimous consent, and passed, and the title was amended to read "An act to authorize the building of lighthouses therein mentioned, and for other purposes."

SATURDAY, March 3.

The credentials of BENJAMIN RUGGLES, appointed a Senator by the Legislature of the State of Ohio, for the term of six years, commencing on the fourth instant, were read, and laid on file.

The following Message was received from the PRESIDENT OF THE UNITED STATES:

To the Congress of the United States:

I communicate to the two Houses of Congress copies of a treaty, this day duly ratified on the part of the United States, concluded and signed at the Indian Springs, on the 8th of January last, with the Creek nation of Indians, in order to such legislative measures as may be necessary for giving effect to it.

JAMES MONROE.

WASHINGTON, *March* 2, 1821.

The Message was read.

On motion, by Mr. THOMAS, the Committee on Public Lands were discharged from the consideration of the petition of Levi Chadwick; and, also, from the consideration of the resolution of the 24th January, to grant the right of pre-emption in certain cases.

On motion, by Mr. SANFORD, the Committee on Finance were discharged from the consideration of the resolution of the first instant, to provide for the payment of a balance due on the settlement of the accounts of Alexander James Dallas.

On motion, by Mr. RUGGLES, the Committee of Claims were discharged from the consideration of the petition of Josephus B. Stuart.

The Senate resumed, as in Committee of the Whole, the consideration of the bill, entitled "An act to regulate the location of land warrants and the issuing of patents in certain cases," together with the amendments reported thereto by the Committee on Public Lands; and, the amendments being agreed to, the bill was reported to the House amended; and, the amendments being concurred in, were ordered to be engrossed, and the bill be read a third time as amended. The bill was then read the third time as amended by unanimous consent, and passed.

The following resolutions were respectively read a third time, and passed:

Resolved, That Robert Tweedy, Tobias Simpson, and George Hicks, assistants to the Sergeant-at-arms and Doorkeeper of the Senate, be paid out of the contingent fund two dollars a day for each day they may have attended the Senate during the present session of Congress; and that Henry Tims be allowed one hundred dollars for his attendance during the present session.

Resolved, That there be paid out of the contingent fund to Robert Tweedy, Tobias Simpson, and George Hicks, the sum of one hundred and fifty dollars each for extra services.

Resolved, That the Secretary be authorized to pay R. B. Washburn, out of the contingent fund of the Senate, at the rate of four dollars per day for the time during which he has been employed in the Secretary's office during the present session.

The bill entitled "An act for the relief of Robert Buntin," was read the third time as amended, and passed.

A message from the House of Representatives informed the Senate that they have passed a bill, entitled "An act making appropriations for the military service of the United States for the year 1821;" in which they request the concurrence of the Senate.

The bill last brought up for concurrence was twice read by unanimous consent; and referred to the Committee on Finance.

Mr. SANFORD, from the Committee on Finance, reported the last mentioned bill with amendments, which were read. Whereupon the Senate proceeded to consider, as in Committee of the Whole, the last mentioned bill, together with the amendments reported thereto by the Committee on Finance; and the amendments having been agreed to, the President reported the bill to the House accordingly; and, the amendments being concurred in, they were ordered to be engrossed, and the bill be read a third time as amended.

The Senate adjourned to seven o'clock, P. M.

Seven o'clock, P. M.

A message from the House of Representatives informed the Senate that the House have passed bills of the following titles, viz: "An act to authorize the President of the United States to borrow a sum not exceeding four millions five hundred thousand dollars;" "An act for carrying into execution the treaty between the United States and Spain, concluded at Washington on the 22d day of February, 1819;" "An act to amend the act, entitled 'An act for the gradual increase of the Navy of the United States;" "An act to amend an act, entitled 'An act for regulating process in the courts of the United States;" and "An act to establish an additional land office in the Territory of Michigan;" in which they request the concurrence of the Senate.

The five bills last mentioned were severally read twice by unanimous consent.

The bill, entitled "An act to authorize the President of the United States to borrow a sum not exceeding four millions five hundred thousand dollars," was referred to the Committee on Finance.

Mr. SANFORD, from the Committee on Finance, reported the last mentioned bill with amendments; which were read.

The Senate proceeded to consider the said bill and amendments, as in Committee of the Whole; and, the amendments having been agreed to, the bill was reported to the House accordingly; and the amendments being concurred in, were ordered to be engrossed, and the bill be read a third time as amended. The bill was read the third time as amended by unanimous consent, and passed.

On motion, the title was amended, so as to read "An act to authorize the President of the United States to borrow a sum not exceeding *five millions of dollars.*"

The amendments to the bill from the House of Representatives, entitled "An act making appropriations for the military service of the United States for the year 1821," having been reported by the committee correctly engrossed, the bill was further amended, and read the third time by unanimous consent, and passed. On motion the title was amended by adding thereto the words *and for other purposes.*

The bill, entitled "An act for carrying into execution the treaty between the United States and Spain, concluded at Washington on the 22d day of February, 1819," was referred to the Committee on Foreign Relations.

Mr. BARBOUR, from the Committee on Foreign Relations, reported the last mentioned bill without amendment.

The Senate proceeded to consider the said bill, as in Committee of the Whole, and no amendment having been made thereto, it was reported to the House, and read a third time by unanimous consent, and passed.

The Senate proceeded to consider, as in Committee of the Whole, the bill, entitled "An act to amend the act, entitled 'An act for the gradual increase of the Navy of the United States;" and no amendment having been made thereto, it was reported to the House, and read the third time by unanimous consent, and passed.

The Senate proceeded to consider, as in Committee of the Whole, the bill, entitled "An act to amend the act, entitled 'An act for regulating process in the courts of the United States;" and no amendment having been made thereto, it was reported to the House, and read the third time by unanimous consent, and passed.

The bill from the House of Representatives, entitled "An act to establish an additional land office in the Territory of Michigan," was ordered to lie on the table.

A message from the House of Representatives informed the Senate that they have passed a bill, entitled "An act to continue in force an act, entitled 'An act regulating the currency within the United States of the gold coins of Great Britain, France, Portugal, and Spain,' passed on the 29th day of April, 1816, so far as the same relates to the crowns and five franc pieces of France;" in which they request the concurrence of the Senate.

The bill last mentioned was read twice by unanimous consent, and it was considered by the Senate, as in Committee of the Whole; and the bill having been amended, it was reported to the House accordingly; and, the amendment being concurred in, was ordered to be engrossed, and the bill be read a third time as amended. The bill was then read the third time as amended, and passed.

A message from the House of Representatives informed the Senate that the House have passed a bill, entitled "An act establishing the salaries of the commissioners and agents appointed under the Treaty of Ghent," in which they request the concurrence of the Senate.

They disagree to the amendments proposed by the Senate to the bill, entitled "An act making appropriations for the military service of the United States for the year 1821."

The Senate proceeded to consider their amendments to the bill last mentioned, disagreed to by the House of Representatives; and,

Resolved, That they do *insist* on their said amendments, except the last paragraph of the fourth amendment, from which they *recede.*

The bill from the House of Representatives, entitled "An act establishing the salaries of the commissioners and agents appointed under the Treaty of Ghent," was twice read by unanimous consent, and considered by the Senate, as in Committee of the Whole; and,

On motion, by Mr. BARBOUR, to strike out after the word "that," in the third line of the first section, the following words:

From and after the first day of January, one thousand eight hundred and twenty-one, each commissioner now appointed, or who may be appointed agreeably to the provisions of the Treaty of Ghent, shall be entitled to receive at the rate of twenty-five hundred dollars per annum ; and each agent appointed, or who may be appointed as aforesaid, shall be entitled to receive at the rate of twenty-five hundred dollars per annum ; which said sums so allowed to said officers respectively, shall be a full compensation for services and all personal expenses incurred while in the performance of the duties of their respective offices : *Provided,* That the compensation by this section allowed, shall not be continued longer than two years from the said first day of January, 1821.

"SEC. 2. *And be it further enacted,* That each

commissioner and agent shall not be entitled to receive for services performed in their respective offices, before the said first day of January, 1821, any greater sum than the rate of four thousand four hundred and forty-four dollars per annum, which shall be considered a full compensation for services and all personal expenses incurred while in the discharge of their respective duties.

"SEC. 3. *And be it further enacted,* That"

It was determined in the negative—yeas 14, nays 19, as follows:

YEAS—Messrs. Barbour, Chandler, Eaton, Elliott, Gaillard, Holmes of Mississippi, Hunter, Johnson of Kentucky, King of New York, Otis, Parrott, Stokes, Trimble, and Walker of Alabama.

NAYS—Messrs. Dana, Dickerson, Edwards, Holmes of Maine, Johnson of Louisiana, Knight, Lanman, Lowrie, Macon, Pleasants, Roberts, Sanford, Smith, Southard, Talbot, Taylor, Thomas, Tichenor, and Williams of Tennessee.

And no amendment having been made to the said bill it was reported to the House, read the third time by unanimous consent, and passed.

On motion, by Mr. BARBOUR, the Senate proceeded to the appointment of a printer or printers on their part, to execute the printing of the Senate for the Seventeenth Congress, pursuant to the resolution of the 3d of March, 1819, on the subject; and, the ballots having been counted, it appeared that Messrs. GALES & SEATON had a majority, and were elected.

A message from the House informed the Senate that they disagree to the first and second, and agree to the third of the amendments of the Senate to the bill, entitled "An act to authorize the President of the United States to borrow a sum not exceeding four millions five hundred thousand dollars;" and they insist on their disagreement to the amendments insisted on by the Senate to the bill, entitled "An act making appropriations for the military service of the United States for the year 1821."

The Senate proceeded to consider the amendments disagreed to by the House of Representatives to the bill, entitled "An act to authorize the President of the United States to borrow a sum not exceeding four millions five hundred thousand dollars;" and on motion, by Mr. BARBOUR, it was resolved, that the Senate do insist on their said amendments, and ask a conference on the disagreeing votes of the two Houses.

Ordered, That Messrs. BARBOUR and KING, of New York, be the managers at the said conference on the part of the Senate.

The Senate again considered their amendments to the bill, entitled "An act making appropriations for the military service of the United States for the year 1821," disagreed to by the House of Representatives; and on motion, by Mr. BARBOUR, that the Senate further insist on their said amendments, and ask a conference, a division of the question was called for; and on the question again to insist on the first of the said amendments as follows:

Section 1, line 40, strike out "two hundred and two thousand," and insert "four hundred thousand,"

It was determined in the affirmative—yeas 20, nays 12, as follows:

YEAS—Messrs. Barbour, Eaton, Edwards, Elliott, Holmes of Maine, Holmes of Mississippi, Hunter, Johnson of Kentucky, Johnson of Louisiana, King of New York, Lanman, Macon, Otis, Parrott, Pleasants, Sanford, Stokes, Talbot, Thomas, and Trimble.

NAYS—Messrs. Chandler, Dana, Dickerson, Gaillard, Knight, Lowrie, Roberts, Ruggles, Smith, Taylor, Tichenor, and Williams of Tennessee.

Whereupon, *Resolved,* That the Senate do further insist on their said amendments, and ask a conference on the disagreeing votes of the two Houses.

Ordered, That Mr. BARBOUR, and Mr. KING, of New York, be the managers at the said conference on the part of the Senate.

A message from the House of Representatives informed the Senate that they agree to the conference asked by the Senate on the disagreeing votes of the two Houses, on the amendments of the Senate to the bill, entitled "An act making appropriations for the military service of the United States for the year 1821," and have appointed managers at the same on their part; and they have passed a bill, entitled "An act authorizing the settlement of the accounts of the late Le Roy Opie;" in which they request the concurrence of the Senate.

The bill last brought up for concurrence was twice read by unanimous consent, and considered by the Senate as in Committee of the Whole; and no amendment having been made, it was reported to the House, read the third time by unanimous consent, and passed.

Mr. BARBOUR, from the managers on the part of the Senate at the conference on the amendments of the Senate disagreed to by the House of Representatives to the bill, entitled "An act making appropriations for the military service of the United States for the year 1821," reported that they had met the managers on the part of the House of Representatives, and conferred freely on the subjects committed to them, but that they could come to no agreement thereupon.

On motion, by Mr. LOWRIE, that the Senate recede from their said amendments, it was determined in the affirmative—yeas 17, nays 16, as follows:

YEAS—Messrs. Chandler, Dana, Dickerson, Elliott, Gaillard, Hunter, Knight, Lowrie, Macon, Roberts, Ruggles, Smith, Southard, Taylor, Van Dyke, Walker of Tennessee.

NAYS—Messrs. Barbour, Eaton, Edwards, Holmes of Maine, Holmes of Mississippi, Johnson of Kentucky, King of New York, Lanman, Otis, Parrott, Pleasants, Sanford, Stokes, Talbot, Taylor, and Trimble.

So it was *Resolved,* That the Senate do recede from their amendments to the said bill.

On motion, by Mr. BARBOUR,

Resolved, unanimously, That the thanks of the Senate be presented to JOHN GAILLARD, for the impartial, able, and dignified manner in which he has discharged the duties of President of the Senate during the present session. Whereupon,

Mr. GAILLARD addressed the Senate as follows:

GENTLEMEN: In the approbation of my conduct as presiding officer, expressed by this honorable body, by those with whom I have been so long and so happily associated, for many of whom I entertain a warm personal attachment, and for all a sincere respect and esteem, I have received an ample and gratifying reward for the solicitude I have felt to merit their favorable opinion. If various and repeated acts of kindness; if an indulgent and liberal support in the discharge of my official duties, present claims on gratitude, then am I largely and truly your debtor; and the more especially so, when it may be emphatically added, that, whatever of public consideration I may enjoy, if indeed I possess any, has been derived more, much more, from the confidence and favor you have bestowed on me, than from any merit of my own. Under such strong obligations, obligations which will ever be recollected and acknowledged with pride and pleasure, I now tender to you gentlemen, collectively, as well as individually, my grateful thinks, wishing you a safe and happy return to your homes and families, and the enjoyment of health, happiness, and prosperity.

On motion, by Mr. HOLMES, of Maine, a committee was appointed on the part of the Senate, jointly with such committee as may be appointed on the part of the House of Representatives, to wait on the President of the United States, and notify him that, unless he may have other communications to make to the two Houses of Congress, they are ready to adjourn.

Mr. HOLMES, of Maine, and Mr. HUNTER, were appointed the committee on the part of the Senate.

A message from the House of Representatives informed the Senate that the House, having finished the business before them, are about to adjourn.

Mr. HOLMES, of Maine, from the joint committee, reported that they had waited on the President of the United States, who informed them that he had no further communication to make to the two Houses of Congress.

Whereupon, the PRESIDENT adjourned the Senate without day.

SUPPLEMENTAL SPEECHES.

SPEECH OF MR. SMITH, OF S. C.

IN THE SENATE, JAN. 17, 1821.

On the Report of the Committee on the Petition of Matthew Lyon.

Mr. SMITH, of South Carolina, addressed the Senate as follows:

He thought this subject had been brought before the Senate at a very unseasonable time. He likewise felt a reluctance in taking any part in the debate, and had intended to content himself with giving a silent vote when the resolutions were first submitted; but his honorable friend from Virginia (Mr. BARBOUR) had, in a very unprovoked manner, laid him under the necessity of entering the lists in self-defence. That gentleman had told the Senate the great object of the resolutions was, to declare by a law, to be passed by the present Congress, that the act of Congress which was passed on the 14th day of July, 1798, and which expired by its own limitation on the 3d day of March, 1801, commonly called the sedition law, under which the petitioner, Matthew Lyon, and several other worthy citizens, had been at different times indicted for libels, was an unconstitutional law; and, therefore, all the fines and forfeitures which had been received in consequence of the convictions under those indictments ought to be refunded. In discussing this subject he would not attempt to follow the gentleman through all the arguments with which he had with so much eloquence entertained the Senate; because very many of them had no sort of application to the question before us. Upon an inquiry by Congress into their powers to look back upon a law which had expired twenty years ago by its own limitation, and to revive it for no other purpose but to declare that this expired law, at the time of its operation, was unconstitutional, but little aid could be derived from being told, as the gentleman had done in a strain of eloquence which no one could reach but himself, that Mathew Lyon was a very poor man, and to return him his fine of one thousand dollars would profit him, and not impoverish the United States; and that it would tend to restore his injured reputation; that he had been sent fifty miles from the place of his conviction through a populous country for the purpose of exposing him to public view; that he had been confined in a dreary dungeon, during the whole Winter months, without the privilege of fire; and denied at the same time the privilege of pen, ink, and paper, lest he should communicate his privations and his agonies to his friends. These were arguments addressed to our feelings, and not to our judgments. If Matthew Lyon has been oppressed by those who have been intrusted with the execution of this law, in the manner stated by the honorable gentleman, it would excite the utmost contempt for such unrelenting tyrants. But, he hoped, for the honor of the public officers, as well as for the honor of the citizens of the State of Vermont, and for the honor of humanity itself, that the charge was, unfounded. It was substantiated by no testimony, or document of any description whatever, except the petition; and that coming from the person immediately concerned, uncorroborated by any one circumstance whatsoever, was a ground too slender to gain our credence, and he would discard it from his mind. But, if true to the full extent, as represented by the petitioner himself, it could only excite our pity and indignation, but could arm us with no power to decide, in our legislative capacity, upon the Constitutionality of a law which had been extinct for twenty years.

The gentleman from Virginia had asserted that the sedition law was unconstitutional, and that we had the power to declare it so by a law, even now. He has gone so far as to say that no other competent power exists by which a law can be declared unconstitutional.

Mr. S. observed, that what he was about to say on this question, should not be said as an advocate for the sedition law; on the contrary, he wished it to be explicitly understood that he should not speak a single word to prove it Constitutional. He would not even go into the inquiry. If a proposition was now before the Senate to re-enact that law, it would then be his duty to do so, and he would fulfil that duty. And if it would in the least degree gratify his friends, he had no hesitation in saying that he held the sedition law in as utter contempt as any man in this nation could do. Nor had he the least possible doubt but that the Federal party, which then held the reins of Government, had no other object in view when they passed this law, than that of securing their power and putting down the Republican party. However, he denied what gentlemen had said, who advocated the resolutions, that the sedition law had such an effect upon the public sentiment as to produce a revolution in the political parties, by which the Republican party got possession of the Government. The Republican party stood in need of no such aid. It was founded on correct principles, and such as could stand the test of experience and trial; and had obtained such a strong hold on the public mind, that Federalism was giving way to it, and the sedition law was passed with a hope of bolstering up the Federal cause. But, what has all this to do with the question now under consideration? The motives for passing the law, and the effect upon the public mind, could neither give to, nor take from you, the power of declaring that law unconstitutional. If you have the power, it exists independent of any such circumstances; if you have it not, no circumstances whatever can give it to you. You must derive your power from the Constitution itself; if that does not give it to you, nothing foreign can give it to you.

Mr. S. observed, that Congress had the power to pass laws, but had no power to declare such laws unconstitutional after they had passed. That function belonged exclusively to the judges. Congress could repeal any law, whilst it was in operation, but that was the only control it had over a law. As soon as a law becomes extinct, the powers of Congress to exercise a control over it become extinct also. It has been asked, if one Congress should pass an unconstitutional law, and should refuse to repeal it, as in the case of the sedition law, and the judges should pronounce it Constitutional, what course were the people to pursue to redress such a grievance? The answer is a plain one; the people have the power to hurl from their seats such perverse members who should pass an unconstitutional law, and refuse afterwards to repeal it. They have this control, and this only, over their members. Over the judges they had the power of impeachment, but no other Constitutional control. If these two departments should continue to abuse the powers in them vested, and pervert the Constitution, and bring on such oppression as could not be borne, the sovereign people would resort to first principles, and new model their Government. No human institutions were free from imperfections; no human actions exempt from error; and if one abuse had crept into your Government, and had nearly passed into oblivion, and not likely to be repeated, it was better to let it rest than to attempt to remedy it by a violent infraction of the Constitution, by assuming to yourselves the powers of reviewing the decisions of your courts of justice.

The Constitution of the United States is not the production of Congress—it is not the property of Congress. It is the production of the people, and the property of the people. It is their shield against the abuse of powers, as well as against the usurpation of powers both by Congress and the judges. Your powers are limited. All legislative powers are granted to Congress, and all judicial powers are granted to the judges. You have, therefore, the power to enact laws, but no power to sit in judgment upon those laws. It is expressly and exclusively given to the judges to construe the laws, and to decide upon their constitutionality. The judges are an independent and co-ordinate branch of the Government; deriving their authority from the Constitution, and not from Congress. They are accountable to the sovereign people; and if guilty of malpractice in administering the laws, they can, and ought to be impeached; and you are the tribunal before which they are to answer; but there your powers cease. You have powers to punish judges for corruption, but none to revise and correct their decisions.

Mr. S. said, of the whole number of the Senators which he then had the honor to address, he was happy to know that three-fourths of them were, or had been practising lawyers, and the greater part of them statesmen of much experience; and, as he had once done when this question was before the Senate at a former session, he would call on gentlemen to point out that part of the Constitution which gives to Congress the power to declare a law unconstitutional, and to revoke a solemn judicial decision, made by judges constitutionally authorized, and competent to decide twenty years after the decision had had its complete operation, and twenty years after the law itself had expired by its own limitation. No gentleman would attempt it. Such a power nowhere exists—such a decision was unheard of in the annals of legislation. There was not a deliberative body in the whole civilized world that had ever claimed this right.

Mr. S. observed, that the gentleman from Virginia (Mr. BARBOUR) had indulged in many observations upon the judges, and the conduct of the judges. In doing so he had said "Kings can do no wrong; but your judges have not that attribute —they are fallible, like other men." The gentleman then observed, that "those who had been ' judges themselves, would, no doubt, take part ' with those who had decided upon the constitu- ' tionality of the sedition law to maintain the fra- ' ternity." And, whilst the gentleman thus addressed the Senate, he, in the most significant manner, Mr. S. said, had pointed at himself, so as to leave no doubt but he was the subject of this animadversion, as he had once had the honor to hold the appointment of an associate judge in the State in which he resided. To relieve himself from the imputation, he would beg leave to compare his own course, since he had held a seat in the Senate, with that of the gentleman himself, as respected partiality for the judges. When one of the judges, from South Carolina, too, at a former session, asked to be paid a sum of money for extra services, he had himself objected to that claim, because he was of opinion it was wrong. The gentleman from Virginia voted for that claim. Three years ago the gentleman originated a bill to increase the salary of the heads of departments, and, along with them, to raise the salary of the circuit judges from $3,500 to $4,500. He opposed it himself, believing the then salary was adequate to the services; the gentleman maintained it. Finally the bill passed, and the associate judges are now on a salary of $4,500, by his exertions. Why give to the judges this increase of salary, if they are not to be confided in? And he would ask, on whose side the strongest partiality had been evinced?

As his honorable friend from North Carolina (Mr. MACON) would probably give his opinion to the Senate on this subject, Mr. S. would anticipate what he would say concerning judges. He would say that, appointing a man a judge, would by no means change his principles. If he had settled his political opinion, the appointment could not change him; if he was corrupt, he would continue corrupt. That judges were always on the side of the Administration, and dependent upon those who gave them their places, and, upon a question where the Government was concerned, they always went with the Government; and withal, that judges were no more to be trusted than other men. Mr. S. said he was willing to admit all this. He was by no means an advocate for the rights of judges beyond those of other men. Indeed he would allow more than that; judges not only had their prejudices when grand political questions agitated the public mind, but sometimes became partisans, and endeavored to influence the

public sentiment. Some of the United States judges, and likewise some of the State judges, about the time this sedition law passed, and during its continuance, were in the habit of preaching political sermons in the courts of justice, in the shape of what they called a charge to the grand jury. In these charges they availed themselves of their official stations to disseminate their own political creeds. They preached much against French politics, and the danger of French influence, and against the growing democracy in our own country. He had in his library one of those political sermons, which was delivered to the grand juries by one of the associate judges of South Carolina. He kept it as a memento of the times.

Mr. S. observed, there was a story in circulation, but whether a true story he could not tell, that one of your judges had descended from his high station during the last session of Congress, and mingled in the strife; and endeavored, with no little zeal, to influence, by his arguments, both within and without the Congress, the decision of a political question to a result that would shake this Union to its centre; and, not content with this, he had likewise taken up the trade of political preaching to grand juries, upon the same subject. Although he acknowledged that a judge, who should forget that it was his duty to administer the laws, but not to make laws, and should, by his vanity or his ambition, thrust himself into this House, to whisper his political tenets into your ears, was intermeddling beyond his Constitutional sphere, and would justly incur the execrations of every independent man, yet he had still to learn, however profligate the judges might be, that Congress could assume powers not delegated by the Constitution.

His friend from Virginia (Mr. BARBOUR) had said, that "the judges had refused to declare this ' sedition law unconstitutional, and, unless Con- ' gress will do so, the Government is in danger, ' and it is the only means by which your Consti- ' tution can be brought back to its original purity."

Amongst many other grounds to impress a belief that the law is unconstitutional, and that you ought to declare it so, he gives us the opinions of President Madison and Chief Justice Marshall; and, the better to enforce it, tells you to look into the Journals of the Federal Convention, lately published for your use, and you will find that Mr. Madison furnished more of the materials for that Constitution than any other member of that Convention. Mr. S. said, he did not wish to take from that venerable patriot, nor from Virginia, any of their just honors, of which they were really entitled to so great a portion; nor was he willing to ask for any for the citizens of his own State; where they had no claim; but, from the Journals of that Convention, it must be acknowledged that Mr. Charles Pinckney of South Carolina, had submitted propositions upon which almost all the important provisions of the Constitution were based. This, however, had but little to do with the subject under consideration, nor would he have mentioned it but to correct what he considered a mistake in his friend from Virginia. As to the opinions of President Madison and Chief

Justice Marshall, although he believed them to rank with the greatest statesmen living, nevertheless, as they were offered as authority, they, like other authorities, were subject to be examined on both sides; and, so far as regards bringing the Constitution back to its original purity, their opinions on another occasion would leave some doubt. Within three years after the adoption of the Federal Constitution, Mr. President Madison, in debate upon a proposition to incorporate the former Bank of the United States, opposed it on the ground of its being unconstitutional—he said:

"In making these remarks on the merits of the bill, he had reserved to himself the right to deny the authority of Congress to pass it. He had entertained this opinion from the date of the Constitution. His impression might perhaps be stronger, because he well recollected that a power to grant charters to incorporations had been proposed in the General Convention, and rejected."

But, when a bill to incorporate the present Bank of the United States was submitted for his approval, and when he could have put it down forever, he found means to get over all his Constitutional scruples, and approved the act. This afforded him proper occasion to restore the Constitution. There was no overwhelming majority in Congress in its favor, and but a few sessions before it had been negatived by a majority of Congress, upon the express ground of its unconstitutionality. There was no war to impose any thing like necessity for establishing such a bank. But the era of good feelings had began to dawn. We had never heard that the Chief Justice Marshall had said the bank was unconstitutional, but, to prove the converse, upon the question of right in the States to tax that bank, the opinion he gave must be admitted to be a very labored one, destitute of authority, and only maintained upon the ground of implication and experience.

The gentleman from Virginia had said, "that 'the defenders of the sedition law had found the 'authority for Congress to pass such a law, in 'that part of the eighth section of the first article 'of the Constitution, which provides for calling 'forth the militia to execute the laws of the Union, 'suppress insurrection, and repel invasions." Mr. SMITH said, he had adverted to this remark of the gentleman, not with a view of defending the sedition law, but to show that the gentleman had drawn from the same fruitful source himself on several occasions, and to caution the gentleman, if he wishes to bring the Constitution back to its original purity, and maintain it in that purity, to touch that 8th section with a sparing hand. In 1816 the gentleman had stood foremost with the friends of the bank. The bank sprung from the same fountain, the 8th section. The gentleman now acknowledged he had erred in that vote, but says it was a time of imperious necessity. He says, "the house was on fire, and no alternative but to extinguish it in this way." If he meant by the house being on fire, the pressure of the war, he was mistaken. The bank charter was not granted till 1816, and peace had been proclaimed in 1815, more than a year before. This institution

had sprung up in the era of good feeling too; and was now convulsing the Union. It was a brand of discord between the States and the General Government. In 1817 the road and canal *mania* raged. The gentleman was one of its zealous advocates, and voted for it. He had since found he was wrong, and that it was unconstitutional. The gentleman, in speaking of the sedition law springing from the 8th section, takes occasion to say, the alien law was a twin from the same mother. He could tell the gentleman that his road and canal law had descended from the 8th section also, but its mother could not be ascertained. One gentleman derived the power to Congress to make roads and canals from that clause of this 8th section which gives Congress power "to pay the debts and provide for the common defence and general welfare of the United States." Another could see it in the clause which gives Congress the power "to regulate commerce with foreign nations." Another, in that clause which authorizes Congress "to establish post offices and post roads;" another in that clause which authorizes Congress "to raise and support armies;" and another class could perceive it in the wisdom of the Convention. They could not believe that so wise an assemblage of men could have intended to forget making provision for improvements so desirable, although they had actually forgotten it. We could, from this diversity of opinions, perceive that the mother of this road and canal law could not be accurately traced. Nor was the father of it known, and it was of course an illegitimate.

If gentlemen wished to restore the Constitution to its original purity, and preserve it inviolate, it was not to be done by retrospective operations upon expired laws, and long past legal decisions. If you wish to preserve your Constitution pure, you must, when questions of policy of a doubtful character arise, first examine for your Constitutional powers to act upon them. If the power is not delegated, it is reserved to the States or to the people, and you can go no further. But, instead of resorting to an inquiry of this sort, the usual mode is, when a gentleman of the Senate wishes to carry a favorite point, he tells you what you have done heretofore; he gives you a precedent. These precedents are produced very often, because, gentlemen say, the object is of little importance, or their friends are concerned, and they do not like to oppose it. And he had been told, on a very important occasion, when he, Mr. S., was urging the propriety of adhering to the Constitution, that, "if the meas-'ure was unconstitutional, it was, nevertheless, 'safe, whilst we had it in our own hands; that we 'would take care not to abuse it." So your own precedents, which you are daily accumulating, to suit the convenience of one to-day, and of another to-morrow, and your own infallibility, now seem to form the measure of your Constitutional powers. The gentleman from Virginia has not contented himself with this, but has gone to the Parliament of Great Britain for precedents, and gives you some cases of attainder. The cases referred to were cases of attainder by the Parliament itself, and not the decisions of a court of justice. There

Supplemental Speeches.

was no parallel between the Parliament of Great Britain and the Congress of the United States. The Parliament of Great Britain was omnipotent. By its fundamental principles that Parliament is a court of judicature to hear cases in the last resort; they can do any thing which the wisdom of its members may deem right. It can depose a king, or raise one to the throne; or it can change the royal descent at pleasure. The will of Parliament is the Constitution alone by which its powers are limited. It is not so in our Government. Your powers are prescribed, and you cannot act beyond that limit. Can Congress remove a Chief Magistrate at its mere will and pleasure, and place another in the chair? You have not thought so yet, perhaps, but if you are to take the Parliament of Great Britain, with all its gigantic and omnipotent powers for your guide, and conceive your powers to be equally gigantic and omnipotent, you may do so whenever you think a fit occasion presents itself. Whilst the whole civilized world is gazing upon our political course, and admiring the simplicity of our Government, not more on account of the powers retained by the people and by the States, than for the well defined and precise limits that are prescribed to the powers given to each branch of the Government, we are looking for foreign precedents to authorize us to go beyond our limits, and lay hold on powers not delegated by the Constitution.

The gentleman from Virginia (Mr. BARBOUR) had declared, "it was against the theory of our institutions to control the liberty of the press by tolerating a prosecution for a libel, even in a State." And then, the gentleman avows, "it is a business between individuals only."

Mr. S. observed, although the people of the United States, for wise purposes, may have denied this power to the General Government, and probably it was wise to do so, yet the gentleman had most egregiously mistaken the powers as well as the practice of the States to carry on prosecutions for libels. The English common law of libels was said to have originated in the Star Chamber, in the times of high-handed political oppression. But it became a part of the common law, and was transferred to this country, and adopted by all the old States, some of which still retain it, and others have ameliorated by it, their constitutions or by statute. There was not a State in the Union, either old or new, where a prosecution for libels was not authorized, either by the common law, by statute, or by the State constitution. In the States of New Hampshire, Massachusetts, Rhode Island, New Jersey, Vermont, Georgia, and New York, the common law had been relaxed by statute so far as to allow the defendant to give the truth in evidence. But these States still retain the common law punishment of fine, imprisonment, pillory, and whipping, at the discretion of the judge who shall pass the sentence upon conviction.

Virginia itself retained the common law, but by a forced construction suffered the truth to be given in evidence, and punished by the common law rule of fine, imprisonment, pillory, and whipping, if the judge should so order. All these States

which have noticed the subject at all, have protected the liberty of the press. Virginia had been silent on that important privilege in her constitution. Maryland had adopted the common law, and punished and prosecuted according to its rules.

The State of North Carolina had formed for herself, immediately after the declaration of independence, perhaps the best constitution of any State in the Union. In that constitution the liberty of the press was better protected than in any other State. Its language is stronger and more explicit. It is in these words: "That the freedom of the press is one of the great bulwarks of liberty, and, therefore, ought never to be restrained." Notwithstanding this, the common law of libels is in full force in that State. And it would appear as if it was universally approved; and, as his authority for believing so, he read from the *Richmond Enquirer* the following passage: "The House of 'Commons of North Carolina has unanimously 'directed that prosecution be commenced against 'John Wright, (formerly of this town,) printer 'and proprietor of the Halifax Compiler, for a 'libellous publication contained in a late number 'of that paper against the Legislature of North 'Carolina." This appears to have been at the last session of that Legislature. From this course of proceeding, by that respectable body, it would seem, whatever protection the constitution of that State had given to the liberty of the press, it was not intended to give protection to the publication of libels, or this prosecution could not have been ordered.

The State of South Carolina has said, in the 6th section of the 9th article of her constitution, "the trial by jury, &c., and the liberty of the press, shall be forever inviolably preserved." Yet, in that State, the common law is in full force, with all its absurdities, that the truth cannot be given in evidence, "the greater the truth, the greater the libel," &c.; and, not only in force, but in constant practice; and, what is more, it is likely to remain in force. Two years ago, a bill was brought before the Legislature of that State to relax the common law, so far as to authorize the defendant to give truth in evidence on the trial; and this bill was supported by unrivalled eloquence, and yet it was negatived by a large majority.

The State of Connecticut has said, in the 5th section of the 1st article of her declaration of rights, "every citizen may freely speak, write, and publish, his sentiments on all subjects, being responsible for the abuse of that liberty."

The States of Pennsylvania and Delaware both declare in their constitutions, that the press shall be free to every citizen to write and print what he pleases, being responsible for the abuse of that liberty; but do not authorize the truth to be given in evidence, except in cases for prosecutions for publications of papers investigating the official conduct of public officers.

The States of Kentucky, Tennessee, Louisiana, Ohio, Indiana, Mississippi, Illinois, Alabama, and Maine, have all declared by their constitutions that the presses shall be free, and every citizen may freely write, speak, and print, on any subject, being responsible for the abuse of that liberty. Some of those States have authorized the defendant to give the truth in evidence in a prosecution for the publication of papers examining the proceedings of the Legislature, or the official conduct of public officers; but others do not go so far. And all the constitutions of those States of Kentucky, Tennessee, Ohio, Louisiana, Indiana, Mississippi, Illinois, Alabama, and Maine, have been within your control, and all but two or three of them have actually passed under your revision, and not a single objection offered to one of them. Five or six of these very exceptionable constitutions had passed under the inspection of the gentleman from Virginia; and the mildest feature any of them presented was, that the truth might be given in evidence on a prosecution for a libel, and yet he supposes a prosecution cannot be maintained under the authority of any of the States.

His very worthy friend from Kentucky (Mr. JOHNSON) had enumerated many offences committed by the Federal party in the course of the late war, such as impeding the enlistment of soldiers, saying the President of the United States ought to be hanged, or that he ought to be removed to make way for some other who knew the interests of the people, and would administer the Government for the public good; that it was a war dictated by the Emperor of France, and carried on for his aggrandizement, &c. He says all these impediments, and may others, for the purpose of favoring the enemy, were carried on, yet your war succeeded; and asks what would you do with such persons as those? And then replies, that he had forgiven them; and the country had forgiven them; and it was much better than to punish them. Mr. S. said he knew the goodness of that gentleman's heart would almost overcome public justice itself, to embrace an opportunity to indulge his native benignity. But, were he to answer the gentleman's question, "what would you do with such persons as those?" he would answer, without any impassioned feelings, or any desire or wish whatever to offend, that he would have hanged them; because, by doing so, he would have terminated the war at a much earlier period, and have saved the lives of many valuable citizens of the United States, and prevented the effusion of much blood.

Gentlemen have said much about the liberty of the press; that it was the scourge of tyrants, and the bulwark of our civil liberty, as well as of our holy religion. Mr. S. observed, that he had said nothing in opposition to the liberty of the press. He was as friendly to the liberty of the press as any gentleman who had favored the resolutions before the Senate. He hoped the liberty of the press would always be protected, both by the Constitution and by the public sentiment. But, whilst he entertained this hope, he could not, for a moment, believe that the public sentiment of the American people would protect the propagation of falsehood, by any means, in any shape, or for any purpose. He knew much had been done for the cause of civil liberty, and of religion, since the art of printing had been discovered; but it was by the means of works of religion, of science, and of philosophy, which it

had given to the world, and by which the mind of man had been enlightened and expanded. It was this which had paved the way to civil liberty; it was this which had subverted the despotisms that prevailed in the dark ages of antiquity; and it was this alone which had given freedom to the civilized world. In this great work, it was not your newspaper presses that were useful; tyrants could wield these as well as the friends of liberty. Nor was it the indiscriminate publication of truth and falsehood, for which gentlemen so much contended, that ever aided the cause of freedom. It is impossible to admit that the well-earned reputation of any citizen, whether he be a President, a member of Congress, or a private citizen, should be suffered to be assailed by falsehood, and that the spoiler should plead the liberty of the press to cover his malignity. Should this principle succeed, an honest reputation would be but a name, and the cut-throat and philanthropist would have equal claims upon your patronage and protection.

In these United States, there are about four hundred newspaper presses. There is, perhaps, amongst them, about one-tenth part that are impartial, and would do equal justice to both sides of any political question, and perhaps to the political character of public men. The rest are ready for any thing that may promote their own emolument, and serve themselves and their friends. Some of them have been ready for the highest bidder. They have become the channels through which themselves and friends are to glide into office. An office-hunter has nothing to do but enclose a fifty dollar bill to the editor, and he becomes pre-eminently qualified to fill the first office in the State, or the nation, without perhaps a single qualification for either, unless it is his talents for intrigue, for which there is now so large a demand in our country. If an editor cannot obtain sufficient supplies of slander from his customers, to keep the community in an uproar, he will supply the deficiency by his editorial remarks. If a single word is uttered which an *editor* supposes to be aimed at *him*, however true it may be, he then considers himself at liberty to name the rash offender, and to make his own press the vehicle through which he may vent his malignity and defamation. He considers this the rod of terror, by which he can awe into obedience any who should dare to call in question his conduct. Some of them have the vanity to believe they can write a man into power, and then write him out again; some make it a matter of conscience to go with the party in power; others take part with the party in power as long as they see any hope to share in the public favors; but, if the prospects darken, they become the bitter enemies of those they supposed they had put into power, and endeavor to change the dynasty, in hope of a better fortune for themselves under the new order of things. Some cannot subsist without falsehood: it is the food that nourishes and gives life to their presses. During the late war, many of your presses were kept up for the sole purpose of distracting your councils, and aiding your enemies; and protracted your war, and did you more essential injury than the enemy. These presses, instead of being the guides to the true character of political men, have become the sordid channels of intrigue, in which every scribbler can puff his patron, whether he has merit or not, provided he has secured the affections of the editor. This is so truly the character of many of your newspapers, that little or no credit is given to any thing they detail, even if it be the truth. Yet these are the presses which gentlemen consider to be the ark of your political safety, and the shield to your holy religion.

We are told that the voice of the people of this nation had passed judgment upon this law, and now demanded at your hands that you declare it unconstitutional. We are also cautioned to beware how we oppose public opinion. Mr. S. said, no gentleman had more respect for public opinion than he had, or would yield with more obedience to its mandate, whenever it was his duty, or became respectful for him to do so; but, in forming an opinion upon a Constitutional question, the Constitution itself should be his guide, not public opinion. The people whom he had the honor to represent were a magnanimous people, and intended him to form his own opinion upon Constitutional law, or they ought not, as they would not, have sent him here.

Gentlemen speak of party, and have denounced those who oppose the resolutions as apostates from the republican cause. Mr. S. observed, that apostacy could not be ascribed to himself, for he had enlisted under no party banner. Nor was he emulous to belong to any party, if he must sacrifice his honest opinion as the price of such a privilege.

The judges are said to be tyrants, and, if not controlled, may demolish your Government. Your judges may become ambitious of power, and aspire after dominion, but it is not in the nature of their avocations that they should obtain that sort of influence in the Government, which could render them dangerous to its peace. There is not an instance recorded in history of the common law judges having subverted the liberties of a nation. Whenever the civil liberties of this nation are destroyed, it must be by one of the other departments; and, if the opinion of Congress is to be the standard of right, instead of the Constitution of your country, it may unfortunately fall there. If Congress is not bound by the Constitution, it is under the control of no law but the law of opinion, which is the law of tyrants. Your judges may err, and very often do; sometimes from a want of capacity, sometimes from corruption, and sometimes from interest; but they are circumscribed by law, and subject to its penalties. If it is too difficult to reach them by impeachment, change your Constitution. It would be better for the nation that the judges should be subject to the control of one-third of the Senate, upon a case of impeachment, than that Congress should assume the power of revising their decisions. If you can organize yourselves into a high court of appeal, upon no other authority than that justice cannot be done without your interference, there can be no limits to your usurpation. The pure ermine may be stained; your judges may become corrupt; but

these are evils against which the Government can protect itself. A well-regulated judiciary, with the right of trial by a jury, is the great palladium of civil liberty; it will hover round the temple of justice after it shall have forsaken these walls.

SPEECH OF MR. TALBOT, OF KENTUCKY.

IN THE SENATE, JANUARY 17, 1621.

On the report of the Committee on the petition of Matthew Lyon.

Mr. TALBOT, of Kentucky, addressed the Senate as follows:

Mr. Chairman, it is with some hesitation I rise to address this honorable body, on the present important subject of their deliberations; a subject which involves in its decision questions of the highest moment; of Constitutional principles and constructions; of the character and merits of a former, as well as of the present, administration of our Government, as well as considerations of justice, as applied to the claim of the petitioner, who has appealed to the justice and liberality of his country for redress. I have waited long, during the protracted discussion of these various topics, with much anxiety and some impatience, to hear from some gentleman qualified for such a task, a development of the causes, either in the peculiar condition of the country; the sentiments, feelings, or opinions of the people; the dangers to which the Government may have been exposed, either from external or domestic enemies; or the actual state of parties at this important and alarming crisis, we are to ascribe this extraordinary act of national legislation. I have waited for this information with more anxiety, from the consideration that we are fortunately honored with the presence of more than one gentleman, who, as members of the Senate, are now in their seats on this floor, who were also members of the National Councils at the enaction of the sedition law; but a development of the policy, scope, and object, of the extraordinary act, the cause of so much terror and alarm, and the instrument of so much oppression and injustice, was most emphatically to have been expected from an honorable gentleman from Massachusetts, (Mr. OTIS) who, if my recollection of the history of the times does not deceive me, not only gave his voice in favor of the passage, but, as a warm and able advocate, most signally contributed to the success of this obnoxious measure. But my expectations have been in vain. A silence the most profound, a discretion the most circumspect and refined, has kept the friends and advocates of this measure mute. In vain has this sedition act been denounced by my honorable friend from Virginia, (Mr. BARBOUR,) as an usurpation on the Constitution; as oppressive, tyrannical, and unjust. This denunciation, Mr. Chairman, I take the liberty to repeat—declaring it as my most sincere conviction, that the sedition act is not only, in its principle and enactions, without warrant or authority to be deduced from the Constitution of the United States, amongst the defined and enumerated powers there contained; nor is such authority to be deduced by any fair rule of argument or construction, as the execution of a power conferred on the Congress of the United States, as subsidiary to the powers expressly delegated; and I challenge honorable gentlemen who are the advocates or apologists for this measure, to point out, to put their finger on the clause or section of the Constitution, which confers such power, or from which it can be rationally, or even plausibly, inferred. If this be true, and I have a right to assume it, no honorable gentleman opposed to the resolution on your table, though repeatedly called on to do so, having come forward to controvert it, need I even advert to that article in the amendments to the Federal Constitution, emphatically called the Bill of Rights, (amendments, dictated by the cautious and jealous spirit of liberty, the watchful guardian of the people's rights,) which contains an inhibition, positive and express, to the Congress of the United States, to enact any law "concerning an establishment of religion, or abridging the freedom of the press."

The general frame and scope, as well as the subject and intent, of our national compact, the Constitution of the United States, affords no argument, or even countenance, for such a course of legislation; the whole frame and organization of the Federal Constitution, in the power delegated to the National Government, embracing only objects of national concern, connected with the national defence, and such as are placed beyond the scope and limits of the powers belonging to the individual States, to which was intended to be left the exercise of all the sovereign powers connected with internal government and municipal regulation. In illustration of this view, it is to be remarked, that the Constitution of the United States has, in no part of that instrument, vested Congress with the power to enact a criminal code for the restraint and punishment of crimes within the limits of the respective States. The absurdity, as well as dangerous consequences, of conferring such power, is obvious, and must obtrude itself on the mind of every man. That this power belongs to the sovereignty of the individual States, will not be controverted. A power in the National Government, to be exercised over the same subject, operating on each and every citizen in the United States, to be exercised simultaneously by each of these sovereign powers, by prosecutions and convictions in their respective courts, would produce a conflict of jurisdictions and of powers, which must hasten, by rapid strides, to a dissolution of that Government, which could not long endure.

But no warrant is to be found in the Constitution of the United States for a construction which would lead to consequences so disastrous. The power in Congress to enact a criminal code for the government of the citizens of the several States is repelled by every view which can be taken of its principles and provisions. Why did the framers of this sacred instrument, this charter of our rights and liberties, employ an entire section of the Constitution in defining treason against the United States, and prescribing what should be the limits of the punishment to be inflicted on the culprit? The answer is obvious: this crime being committed against the nation, and not against a State, the authority of the nation is alone concerned in, and competent to, its punishment; and besides, not only the peace and happiness, but the very existence of the nation essentially depend on the possession and exercise of such a power. Why has the Constitution of the United States, after delegating, in the most explicit and ample terms, to Congress, power over the currency and coins of the United States, in the very next and succeeding paragraph, conferred the additional, and therefore not merely an incidental power, of providing for the punishment of those who should be guilty of counterfeiting such currency or coin? Can we deem so irreverently of the wisdom of the framers of this glorious instrument, as for a moment to indulge the supposition, that they would have taken the pains, by an express provision, to delegate the power to provide for the punishment of the crime alluded to, if they had contemplated, by any other provision in the Constitution, either to confer a general power to provide for the punishment of crimes, the perpetration of which might be deemed to affect the prosperity of the nation, or the quiet and tranquil operation of the General Government? Yet such is the supposition on which arguments must be based which are employed to vindicate the power of Congress to punish political libels by the enaction of sedition laws, to be enforced by the powers and intervention of a Federal judiciary. But when it must be conceded by the advocates of this sedition act, that there is no express power to be found in the Constitution for its enaction; that, if it can be claimed at all, it must be supported on the ground that it is amongst the subsidiary powers necessary and proper for the execution of expressly delegated powers, when it is answered that no such expressly delegated power has or can be shown to which this power of enchaining the freedom of the press, and closing up the avenues to a full and free investigation of the characters and measures of public men, who are the delegates and servants of the people, as necessary and proper. When it is further answered, that the amendment to the Constitution, inhibiting all abridgment of the freedom of the press; an amendment dictated by the jealous and watchful caution of the Legislatures of the States, by which it was recommended; a jealousy springing from a deep sense of the value of the liberties intended to be secured and justified by the histories of all Governments and nations of the earth. That this amendment ought to put to silence all arguments derived from vague and general speculations in relation to the power with which Governments ought to be endowed for the preservation of those called on by the people to administer it, from the licentious tongues or pens of malicious libellers or calumniators.

But it is not on the silence of the Constitution, or the absence of delegated power to form that instrument; nor only on the amendment to that Constitution, so emphatic in its terms, that the opponents to the sedition law need rest their opposition. But, in illustration of the wisdom of its framers, understood and interpreted as we expound it, the opinion which I entertain, and avow with pride and pleasure, is, that this, and all other sedition or libel laws, having for their design and purposes the control of free and full investigation of the character and opinions of public men and public measures, without limit and without restraint, I mean from criminal prosecution, are hostile, in their very essence and principle, to liberty, and to the free and republican institutions under which we live, and which are so justly our pride and boast; for the private or individual injury, resulting from the publication of libels or malicious slanders, the incumbent of office, the representative of the people in the Congress of the United States, even their Chief Magistrate, has, by the municipal regulations, the laws of every State, his appropriate remedy, to demand and receive, in common with the lowest and meanest citizen, an equivalent for the injury he has sustained. And why is he who has been selected from amongst his fellow-citizens, to exercise, for their benefit and advantage, a little brief authority, to be hedged around with the ramparts of sovereign power, to be armed with the artillery of a criminal code, for the protection of his person or reputation, which is denied to every other citizen?

My honorable friend from Georgia has disclaimed, in pathetic strains, and my honorable friend, who sits before me, (Mr. SMITH,) has indulged in terms and anecdotes, humorous and sportive, against the slander and calumny, which flow from the licentiousness of the press. Have my honorable friends omitted to remark what is of such familiar observation in all the walks of human life, how few, if any, of the benefits of Heaven are granted us by the all-wise Disposer of Events without alloy? How liable are our greatest blessings to abuse? And that the question in the case we are now discussing is, whether the liberty of the press is not one of those political blessings inestimable in itself, the abuse of which is inseparable from its advantageous use? If gentlemen still doubt on this question, let me refer my honorable friends to the history of the late trials and prosecutions for libels in England, as well as in Ireland, for the last hundred years. What heart endowed with the common feelings of sympathy, not steeled against every soft emotion of our nature, can forbear to feel for them? Humanity herself must weep over the helpless fate of philosophers, statesmen, and patriots, the victims to the love of liberty and their country's rights, who have been offered up on the altar of their country, to the corruption, tyranny, and usurpations of power; and all under the specious pretence of punishing the licentiousness of the press; yet England boasts (how vain the boast!) that she enjoys the liberty of the press.

Believe me, Mr. Chairman, that neither the liberties of the people, nor the inestimable institutions of our free republican Government, can be preserved in their purity, while the freedom of unrestrained investigation of the character, conduct, principles, and motives of public men, or the tendency of public measures, shall be restrained and fettered by restrictions on the press; and that such investigations will never be free or useful while restrained by the perpetual terrors and actual dangers of criminal prosecutions. And I put to my honorable friends from Georgia and South Carolina, to say what legislator, jurist, or ingenious casuist, has yet been able to draw a precise line of demarcation between the liberty and licentiousness of the press, in case of political libels? In cases where party meets party in hot contention on questions of political opinions and public measures? What usurping or tyrant legislator, like the tyrant Dane, has dared to say to the political writer, investigating the opinions and motives as well as actions of the ruler of the country—thus far shalt thou go, and no farther, and here shall the proud wave of popular discontent be stayed? While therefore, Mr. Chairman, I reciprocate in the warmest terms the sentiments of indignation which my honorable friend from Georgia so forcibly and eloquently expressed against the guilt, as well as infamy, of those concerned either in the fabrication or propagation of malicious slanders—a vice, the prevalence of which is so much to be deplored, but a vice too firmly ingrafted in our frail imperfect natures—by the indulgence of which the peace and happiness of society has been so often disturbed and blasted; yet I for one must be permitted to indulge the consolatory hope, if not the fond belief, that there is in truth, integrity, and conscious worth, a charm sufficient of itself to insure the triumph of virtue; and that, armed with these, the utmost rage of malice may be defied, and that, although the excellence of such a character may, for a time, be sullied, yet, like the luminary in the heavens, which shines with light and glory on our sphere, which suffers a transient obscuration from the passing clouds, it is only permitted, that it may, when the transient vapor is passed, give fresh lustre to his beams.

But, Mr. Chairman, having detained you much longer than I intended on that branch of the discussion from which our opponents have retreated, and as the honorable gentleman from Massachusetts has declined the task for which the conspicuous part he took at the period of the enaction of this too famous law, so well qualified him, permit me to fill the chasm left by his omission in the history of the Administration at this eventful period—not from observation of the passing scene, or entirely from the documents of authentic history of the times; but in part from the contemporaneous impressions and opinions ratified and sanctioned by the public voice.

From these sources, the best which I have been enabled to procure, I feel myself authorized to infer that this sedition act was one of the last links in the chain of measures adopted and pursued by that party in whose hands the administration of the Government was then reposed, measures of a tone and character to arouse, and which had aroused strong alarms in the bosoms of the American people, for those liberties on which repeated and successive invasions had been made. These alarms, first producing expressions of discontent, had gradually increased and swelled into loud and clamorous expressions of indignation, which were echoed from one extremity of the Union to the other. It was to silence the voice of just censure, of awakened and indignant discontent—to stifle the public voice—to throw around them a rampart of defence against the assault of popular indignation. That it was the last desperate recourse of a falling party tottering on the brink of the precipice, over which this measure, intended for their preservation, as full of rashness as of danger, only served the sooner to precipitate them—and to this cause are we to ascribe the revolution of power from the hands of those who, by this measure, hoped to have secured the means of its perpetuation.

A new and extraordinary feature in this law was the short period of its duration. Other portions of your criminal code, Mr. Chairman, enacted for the prevention or punishment of offences, are, as it seems they should always be, calculated for all times and all circumstances.

But this is one among the few which have met my observation, which was for the short and limited duration of two years and a half, and by its limitation was to expire with the term of service of the then President of the United States. On that day, by a happy change, Mr. Jefferson by the voice of his country, was called to preside over its destinies. The commencement of this new and happy era furnished an illustrious proof to an admiring world of the futility and folly of sedition and libel laws. The inaugural speech of this enlightened statesman asserted the true and genuine principles of liberty, and of our free republican institutions; and established the dominion of integrity, truth, and honor, over the demons of error, falsehood, and malice. It claimed no exemption of rulers, magistrates, and representatives; their motives, designs, or measures, from the rigid strictures, from the free and unrestrained investigations of the press.

He demanded no libel or sedition act to shield the purity of his motives, the integrity of his character, from the assaults of a virulent and implacable, though fallen party. But, armed with the conscious integrity of his own heart, with this immortal ægis, stronger than adamant or brass, this illustrious philosopher and enlightened statesman reared his head above the stormy clouds of faction, intrigue, and passion; and the envenomed shafts of calumny fell harmless at his feet.

But our opponents, Mr. Chairman, not choosing to encounter this question by arguments in support either of the constitutionality or expediency of the sedition act; not willing to encounter the general sentiments of reprobation with which this obnoxious measure is now held and viewed in these United States; and entertaining, as I fondly trust my honorable friends from Georgia and South Carolina do, the same opinions with myself in relation thereto; they have taken shelter behind the bench of judges; contending that the Constitution is a government of checks and balances; that, by this theory, the judiciary of the United States is the efficient check on the usur-

pation of Congress, in the enaction of laws, not warranted by the Constitution; and that, when this department has interposed the sanction in the exposition or execution of a law, that no other department of our Government have a right to interfere. And that, as the law in question, during its existence, was enforced by the judicial power and is now expired, that Congress have no Constitutional right to interfere. These doctrines are beautiful in theory, and the arguments deduced therefrom are plausible and ingenious. They are such as caught my youthful mind as sterling political orthodoxy, but which recent events in the history of our country have taught me to receive with caution and distrust; as subject to many limitations; and as entirely inapplicable to the questions we are now called upon to decide.

But, before I proceed to their refutation, permit me, Mr. Chairman to premise that there is no honorable gentleman on this floor who can entertain a higher reverence for the judicial character than myself, believing as I do, that there is no station in the social body requiring for the discharge of its arduous duties more exalted qualities of mind and heart; and, next to the ministers of our holy religion, they have my esteem and veneration—sentiments which I have cherished during an intercourse of more than twenty years, during which, my professional pursuits have produced an almost daily intercourse with gentlemen who have filled the bench with honor and integrity. But, entertaining these sentiments, as I sincerely do, I cannot forget that judges are at best but men, partaking, in common with us all, the frailties, passions, and imperfections, incident to our nature. That, like us, they are what nature, education, habit, and particular modes of life, have made them. I must be permitted to express my own opinion with much humility indeed, that the judiciary of the United States is not the only depository of the Constitution of the United States, and of the rights and liberties of its citizens; the only expositors in the last resort of the Constitution and laws of the different States as regards the delicate and important questions which have occurred, and will again occur, from the conflicting claims of national and State sovereignties. Much as these conflicts are to be deprecated, they must occur, and whenever they do occur, believe me, Mr. Chairman, I speak it in no spirit of evil augury or melancholy foreboding, but from my limited observations on men and events which have passed before me, or are to be found recorded on the page of history, you will find the opinions of your judiciary arrayed on the side of that power from which they have derived their honors and emoluments, and so of our State judiciaries too. It is human nature, which in spite of the utmost efforts of the virtuous and the wise, will bend the human mind, unconscious of the bias, to the dominion of her imperious sway.

But, admitting the truth of this doctrine of the Constitutional power, as well as of the efficiency of the judicial power to check the usurpations of the Congress of the United States, in its utmost latitude, it is entirely inapplicable to the present case. What is the complaint of the petitioner before you? What the argument of the advocates of the proposition on your table? Is it that the judicial power interposed a check improperly; that, without Constitutional authority it interposed its power to shield the citizen, to protect the liberties of the country from legislative usurpation? No, sir; directly the reverse. As far as complaint or imputation is directed towards the judges, it rests upon the charge, not that they did, but that they did not, interfere to arrest the career of legislative usurpation in the enaction of unconstitutional laws. It is, Mr. Chairman, when the firm, virtuous, and upright judge, strong in the integrity of his heart and the dignity of the station assigned him by his country, who, when the tempest of frenzied and infuriated party spirit rages round our happy land, like the tall and majestic oak, rears his head and hears the storm of angry passions beat in vain against its side; and not the supple, obliged, and obliging friend of a party from whom he derives his undeserved honors, like the gentle ozier plant, nods and bends his head at every gale that blows, that this salutary judicial check is to be ascribed.

What, then, is the state of fact, in relation to the application of this salutary judicial check, in the trial of Matthew Lyon? Why simply this. That one of the five judges who formed the bench of the Supreme Court of the United States, without the aid, and probably without a previous consultation with his associate judges, presided at this trial in the circuit of Vermont. That an indictment on the sedition act against Matthew Lyon, was framed by the attorney for the district; on which the culprit was arraigned; to which he pleaded not guilty; upon which a jury, impannelled by a marshal holding his office at the pleasure of the President of the United States, returned their verdict of "guilty" against the prisoner; on which the judge presiding pronounced his sentence, condemning the prisoner to an imprisonment of four months; the payment of a fine of one thousand dollars, and to be imprisoned until the fine was paid. Now, I put it distinctly to my honorable friend from Georgia, from this brief narrative of the trial, to inform the Senate in what part of the transactions attending this trial does he find the materials of which to erect the defences by which the opponents to the proposition on your table are to shelter and protect themselves from the investigation in which we have challenged them to enter. The constitutionality of the sedition law. Are they to be found in any check interposed by the judiciary, to the execution of what we pronounce an unconstitutional act?

Has there been any decision by the highest judicial power of the United States, the Supreme Court of the nation? Was the constitutionality of the law in question raised, discussed, or decided on, by the judge who presided at the trial? Or was it even a subject of deliberation in the judge's mind? To all these interrogatories, as far as we are informed by evidence, either recorded or traditional, we must answer in the negative. On

what, then, I ask emphatically, is the argument predicated, that this law, having received the judicial sanction, that Congress are thereby precluded from a solemn decision on the question?

If, indeed, Mr. Chairman, after having invested your judges with their ermine, (spotless, if you please,) with their silk or satin gowns, you could place in their hands the magician's wand, with the powers of necromantic change, then, indeed, might its potent touch convert the sedition act, before unconstitutional, and a violation of the sacred charter of our rights, into a Constitutional law, free from blemish and from stain. But, until some such magic power is conferred on, or to be assigned to, judges, it is, I must confess, beyond the reach of my comprehension to perceive how the simple facts attending the indictment and trial of Matthew Lyon can confer on this act the character of Constitutional, which it never had before.

But there is another view of the subject, Mr. Chairman, which is, if possible, more conclusive than that which has been just pointed out to the consideration of the Senate, to show the entire inefficiency of the supposed sanction of the Federal judiciary, to confer on this act, otherwise unconstitutional, the attributes of a Constitutional law. My honorable friends from Georgia and South Carolina, as members, and honorable and distinguished members of a profession, whose study as well as daily occupation are, or have been, the municipal laws, and who must be familiar with the principles of that law which concern the jurisdiction of the courts appointed for its administration, must concede at once what it seems impossible to deny, that if the sedition law had never been enacted, that the Federal courts would have had no power or jurisdiction in the case of Matthew Lyon, to have received an indictment, caused an arraignment of the prisoner, a trial and conviction to be had, followed by a sentence of condemnation, all under the sedition act, on which the indictment is framed. If, then, this law is admitted by our opponents to be unconstitutional, as, by retreating from the discussion of that question, they are bound to do, what is the conclusion? Irresistible as fate, from this admission, that the sedition act being unconstitutional, was, for that cause, void in its inception, and that, being a perfect nullity, it could confer no power or jurisdiction on the courts of the United States to take cognizance of the case. And that the whole of the proceedings of the circuit court for Vermont, in relation to the arraignment, indictment, trial, and condemnation, of the prisoner, were, in the technical language of the law, *coram non judice*, and therefore void, and that, consequently, the trial of Matthew Lyon, though accompanied with the usual ceremonies, and clothed with all the solemn forms of law, was, in truth, but a solemn farce, not only without the solemn sanctions of the law, but in positive violation of the inhibitions of the Magna Charta of our liberties—the Constitution of the United States.

But it is contended by our opponents on this occasion, that the act in question having long since expired by its own limitation, that Congress is not authorized by the Constitution of the United States to restore to those from whom were exacted fines, exacted under judicial decisions of the courts of the United States while the act remained in force.

This argument seems to be susceptible of an easy and conclusive answer. If Congress possess the power to repeal an unconstitutional act of their predecessors, on the ground merely that it is unwarranted by the Constitution, which is virtually a declaration that such act was never Constitutionally the law of the land, on what principle shall we deny to them the power of declaring null and void the judicial proceedings of the courts of the United States, the only warrant and commission for which proceedings is this unconstitutional law? If the Sedition act had not expired, Congress would be competent to its repeal, which would be but tantamount to a declaration of its original nullity, on account of the Constitutional inhibition of its enaction. By force of what argument, or on what principle can we refuse to Congress the power to declare the original nullity of that which is extinct by lapse of time, and of restoring to injured individuals money or rights of which they have been illegally deprived by the mistaken application and operation of the act?

Happily for this country, neither the tyranny of power, or the corruption of the Legislature, or the intemperance and fury of party spirit, have, during the short period of the existence of our liberties, yet furnished examples for the illustration of this argument. The Sedition act, the subject of this debate, is the first of the bitter fruits of the exasperated fury of party spirit, with the taste of which its authors themselves were soon sated, and from which the people turned at once with loathing and disgust. It is to repair the ravages of this short and transient evil that Congress are now called on for some small remuneration to the victims of injustice and oppression which it produced. But let us only take a glance at England, the history of which is so replete with examples full of illustration of the arguments and principles on which the resolutions on your table are predicated. Look at the numerous cases of reversals of attainders; of restoration of forfeited estates; the remissions of fines and penalties, inflicted as well by acts of Parliament as by the iniquitous and oppressive convictions and condemnations by her servile and time-serving courts of justice; reversed, remitted, and restored, by subsequent acts of Parliament, with which the records of her legislative journals, as well as the history of the times, is full; and tell me, Mr. Chairman, whether the legitimacy of this exercise of power has been ever questioned? Or whether, on the contrary, it has not received the universal sanction of the virtuous and the wise? And if a British Parliament can rescind the attainders, release the forfeitures, and remit the penalties, inflicted by the usurpations of their predecessors, by what argument, or on what principle, is the exercise of a similar power denied to the Congress of the United States? If the pretended omnipotence of the Parliament should be urged to justify these acts, may it not be replied, that the omnipotence of the Parliament who first enacted

precluded the exercise of a repealing and restoring power—the act of Parliament, or sentence of the court of justice having had their intended operation, by vesting the forfeited estates or moneys on the Crown? And does not the argument apply with accumulated force when applied to the acts of a Legislature, like the Congress of the United States, strictly limited in its powers, whose enactions, of whatever character, when transcending those limits, are admitted to be void?

In the arguments which I have endeavored to present to the Senate, in the discussion of the question under deliberation, I have not thought it necessary, Mr. Chairman, to dwell on the personal merits of the petitioner now before you, or to inquire with minuteness into the correctness of the representations made by him of the circumstances of harshness, cruelty, partiality, or injustice, which may have attended his trial and conviction; or the circumstances of aggravation with which it is alleged the sentence of the court was carried into execution. If half the circumstances detailed by the glowing eloquence of the honorable chairman of the committee by whom the resolutions are reported are true, and they have not been seriously controverted, although not susceptible of legal proof after such a lapse of time, it only adds another dark shade to the picture of usurpation and oppression which is exhibited in the history of this unhappy act, from the moment of its inception to that of its final termination; and although, with the honorable gentleman from Virginia, I will not say that Matthew Lyon has been sacrificed, or fallen a martyr, a name reserved for those who have been sacrificed in a still more glorious cause, yet, without being the eulogist of Matthew Lyon, or endeavoring to press his personal merits, or even his sufferings, into this discussion, the decision of which depends on different and higher considerations than even these, I must be permitted to say, that the whole character of these proceedings is in perfect unison with the spirit and nature of the law under color of which they were instituted, and with the temper in which it was enacted; and that the entire history of the law, and its inflictions, furnish the citizens of this free and happy country with an example replete with instruction, a full review of which, at this period of calm and quiet, when no angry passions are excited to disturb or obscure the mind in forming a cool and unimpassioned judgment on the subject, is not only demanded of us by the petitioner, but may be of lasting benefit to the whole community.

The only objection, Mr. Chairman, which has been urged by the opposers of these resolutions which remains to be answered, is, that it would be inexpedient, were it admitted that Congress possessed the power to extend the relief prayed for to the petitioner. This objection being one which results from, and is to be governed more by, sentiments and feelings, than by strict logical argument, it affords room for more diversity of opinion and action than those which have been hitherto noticed. And, in accordance with my own views and sentiments on this branch of the argument, I shall content myself with the free expression of

Supplemental Speeches.

my own opinion and rule of action, in deciding on the appeals of individuals of this nation to the Congress of the United States for the redress of injustice and oppression ; that to *do justice* is always *expedient*, and that no apprehensions of inconvenience, or speculations of future dangers, or evil consequences, to result from the application of this principle, ought to withhold its application. But there is another consideration, Mr. Chairman, which ought to apply itself with more force to the reflections of Congress than the redress of the individual wrongs of Matthew Lyon, inducing the adoption of the resolutions on your table. This consideration flows from the very circumstances of the expiration of the Sedition act by force of its own limitation, without the interposition of the active energies, or even the expression of an opinion, of any subsequent Congress, of its constitutionality or character, or the tendency of its provisions. I would therefore appeal to the Republicans of the present Congress, whether they do not owe it to themselves, to the party to which they belong, and to the principles which they profess, to place on their journals some recorded evidence of their opinion and sentiments in relation to the enactment and operations of this obnoxious measure as a monument, or seal of reprobation, to speak to all future times and future generations an interpretation of the Constitution, and of our opinions of this act, as a practical commentary on what we deem the liberty of the press. Do we not owe, sir, to the distinguished and patriotic Legislatures of the States, who interposed with the energies of freemen and with the light of truth to put down this formidable foe to freedom, and who interposed with such efficacy and success, an expression of the deliberate opinions of a Republican Congress of this measure, its spirit and tendency ? To me, the adoption of these resolutions, in this view, seems but the payment of a debt of justice and gratitude which we owe.

With a tender of my thanks to this honorable body for the attention with which they have honored me, I resume my seat.

PROCEEDINGS AND DEBATES

OF THE

HOUSE OF REPRESENTATIVES OF THE UNITED STATES,

AT THE SECOND SESSION OF THE SIXTEENTH CONGRESS, BEGUN AT THE CITY OF WASHINGTON, MONDAY, NOVEMBER 13, 1820.

MONDAY, November 13, 1820.

This being the day fixed by law for the meeting of Congress, Thomas Dougherty, the Clerk, and the following members of the House of Representatives, appeared and took their seats, viz:

From New Hampshire—Joseph Buffum, jr., Josiah Butler, Clifton Clagett, William Plumer, jr., and Nathaniel Upham.

From Massachusetts—Benjamin Adams, Samuel C Allen, Joshua Cushman, Timothy Fuller, Mark L. Hill, Jonas Kendall, Enoch Lincoln, Marcus Morton, Jeremiah Nelson, James Parker, and Henry Shaw.

From Rhode Island—Samuel Eddy, and Nathaniel Hazard.

From Connecticut—Henry W. Edwards, Samuel A. Foot, Jonathan O. Moseley, Elisha Phelps, John Russ, James Stevens, and Gideon Tomlinson.

From Vermont—Samuel C. Crafts, Rollin C. Mallary, Ezra Meech, Mark Richards, and William Strong.

From New York—Nathaniel Allen, Caleb Baker, Walter Case, Robert Clark, Jacob H. De Witt, John D. Dickinson, John Fay, William D. Ford, Ezra C. Gross, Aaron Hackley, jr., George Hall, Henry Meigs, Robert Monell, Nathaniel Pitcher, Jonathan Richmond, Henry R. Storrs, Randall S. Street, James Strong, John W. Taylor, Caleb Tompkins, Albert H. Tracy, Solomon Van Rensselaer, Peter H. Wendover, and Silas Wood.

From New Jersey—Ephraim Bateman, Joseph Bloomfield, Charles Kinsey, John Linn, and Bernard Smith.

From Pennsylvania—Henry Baldwin, William Darlington, Samuel Edwards, Thomas Forrest, Samuel Gross, Joseph Hemphill, Jacob Hibshman, Jacob Hostetter, William P. Maclay, David Marchand, Robert Moore, Samuel Moore, John Murray, Thomas Patterson, Robert Philson, Thomas J. Rogers, John Sergeant, and James M. Wallace.

From Delaware—Louis McLane.

From Maryland—Stephenson Archer, Joseph Kent, Peter Little, Samuel Ringgold, Samuel Smith, and Henry R. Warfield.

From Virginia—Mark Alexander, William S. Archer, William A. Burwell, Robert S. Garnett, James Jones, Charles F. Mercer, Hugh Nelson, Thomas Newton, John Randolph, Ballard Smith, Alexander Smyth, Thomas V. Swearingen, George Tucker, and Jared Williams.

From North Carolina—John Culpeper, Weldon N. Edwards, Thomas H. Hall, Charles Hooks, Lemuel Sawyer, Jesse Slocumb, James S. Smith, Felix Walker, and Lewis Williams.

From South Carolina—Joseph Brevard, William Lowndes, John McCreary, James Overstreet, and Starling Tucker.

From Georgia—Joel Abbot, and Thomas W. Cobb.

From Kentucky—Richard C. Anderson, jr., William Brown, Alney McLean, Thomas Metcalfe, George Robertson, and David Trimble.

From Tennessee—Newton Cannon, Francis Jones, and John Rhea.

From Ohio—Philemon Beecher, Henry Brush, John W. Campbell, and John Sloan.

From Louisiana—Thomas Butler.

From Indiana—William Hendricks.

From Illinois—Daniel P. Cook.

From Alabama—John Crowell.

The following new members also appeared, to wit:

From Massachusetts, WILLIAM EUSTIS, in the room of Edward Dowse, resigned:

From Pennsylvania, THOMAS G. McCULLOUGH, in the room of David Fullerton, resigned:

From Virginia, JOHN C. GRAY, in the room of James Johnson, resigned; EDWARD B. JACKSON, in the room of James Pindall, resigned; and THOMAS L. MOORE, in the room of George F. Strother, resigned:

From Kentucky, THOMAS MONTGOMERY, in the room of Tunstall Quarles, resigned; and FRANCIS JOHNSON, in the room of David Walker, deceased:

Who severally produced their credentials, and took their seats.

JOHN SCOTT, the Delegate from the Territory of Missouri, and JAMES WOODSON BATES, the Delegate from the Territory of Arkansas, also appeared, and took their seats.

The Clerk having announced that a quorum of the House was present, said that he had received a letter from the Hon. HENRY CLAY, late Speaker of this House, which, with the leave of the House, he read as follows:

LEXINGTON, KY., *October* 28, 1820.

SIR: I will thank you to communicate to the House of Representatives, that, owing to imperious circumstances, I shall not be able to attend upon it until after the Christmas holidays, and to respectfully ask it to allow me to resign the office of its Speaker, which I have the honor to hold, and to consider this as the act of my resignation. I beg the House also to permit me to reiterate the expression of my sincere acknowledgments and unaffected gratitude for the distinguished consideration which it has uniformly manifested for me.

I have the honor to be, with great esteem, your faithful and obedient servant,

                    H. CLAY.

THOMAS DOUGHERTY, Esq.,
   Clerk of the House of Representatives.

On motion of Mr. NEWTON, the letter was ordered to lie on the table, and to be inserted in the Journal of the House.

On motion of Mr. N., the House then proceeded to the election of a Speaker.

The Clerk declared that, as this was an election to be made from amongst members of the House, no previous nomination was necessary. No nomination, therefore, was made.

Messrs. NEWTON and MOSELEY being appointed a committee to count the ballots, reported that the votes were—For John W. Taylor 40; for William Lowndes 34; for Samuel Smith 27; for John Sergeant 18; for Hugh Nelson 10; scattering 3.

Sixty-seven votes being necessary to a choice, and no member having the requisite majority, a second ballot took place; when the votes were thus reported: For Mr. Taylor 49; for Mr. Lowndes 44; for Mr. Smith 25; for Mr. Sergeant 13; scattering 1.

No choice being yet made, the House proceeded to a further ballot, when the votes given in were as follow: For Mr. Lowndes 56; for Mr. Taylor 50; for Mr. Smith 16; for Mr. Sergeant 11; scattering 1.

No choice having been yet made, the House proceeded to ballot a fourth time, when the following result was reported: For Mr. Lowndes 61; for Mr. Taylor 60; for Mr. Smith 11; scattering 3.

No one having yet a majority of all the votes, a fifth ballot took place, which resulted as follows: For Mr. Taylor 65; for Mr. Lowndes 63; for Mr. Smith 8; scattering 2.

A motion was then made that the House do now adjourn; and the question thereon being put by the Clerk, it was decided in the negative.

The House then proceeded to ballot a sixth time; and the votes, being counted, stood thus: For Mr. Taylor 67; for Mr. Lowndes 61; for Mr. Smith 7; scattering 1.

No election having yet taken place, another motion was then made to adjourn, and the vote thereon was—for adjourning 65, against it 68.

So the House refused to adjourn, and another ballot was held, which resulted as follows: For Mr. Taylor 62; for Mr. Lowndes 57; for Mr. Smith 15; scattering 1.

No choice having yet been made, a motion was made to adjourn, and decided in the affirmative—ayes 71. And the Clerk adjourned the House to 12 o'clock to-morrow.

TUESDAY November 14.

Several other members appeared and took their seats, to wit:

From New Hampshire, ARTHUR LIVERMORE; from Massachusetts, MARTIN KINSLEY; from New Jersey, HENRY SOUTHARD; from Pennsylvania, CHRISTIAN TARR; from Maryland, RAPHAEL NEALE; from Virginia, WILLIAM LEE BALL, PHILIP P. BARBOUR, and WILLIAM McCOY; from South Carolina, ELIAS EARLE; from Tennessee, JOHN COCKE; and from Ohio, THOMAS R. ROSS.

The House then proceeded forthwith to ballot again for a Speaker of the House, in the place of Mr. CLAY, resigned. The votes having been counted, Mr. NEWTON reported, that the whole number of votes was 149; of which 75 were necessary to a choice; that the votes were: For Mr. Taylor 64; for Mr. Lowndes 54; for Mr. Smith 33; scattering 1.

No one having a majority of all the votes, the House proceeded to ballot the ninth time; when it appeared that the votes were: For Mr. Taylor 66; for Mr. Lowndes 47; for Mr. Smith 33; scattering 1.

No election having yet taken place, the House proceeded to ballot for the tenth time; and the result was declared as follows: For Mr. Taylor 64; for Mr. Smith 50; for Mr. Lowndes 25; scattering 1.

No election having yet taken place, the House proceeded to ballot for the eleventh time; when the following result was pronounced: For Mr. Taylor 61; for Mr. Smith 50; for Mr. Lowndes 31; for Mr. Sergeant 5; scattering 1.

No election having yet taken place, the House proceeded to ballot for the twelfth time; and the result was as follows: For Mr. Smith 53; for Mr. Taylor 47; for Mr. Lowndes 23; for Mr. Sergeant 19; for Mr. Tomlinson 3; scattering 3.

The thirteenth ballot resulted as follows: For Mr. Smith 48; for Mr. Taylor 32; for Mr. Sergeant 32; for Mr. Lowndes 30; scattering 3.

The fourteenth ballot resulted as follows: For Mr. Smith 42; for Mr. Lowndes 37; for Mr. Sergeant 35; for Mr. Taylor 27; scattering 3.

The fifteenth ballot resulted as follows: For Mr. Lowndes 55; for Mr. Sergeant 32; for Mr. Smith 27; for Mr. Taylor 26; scattering 6.

No one yet having a majority of the votes, a further ballot was declared necessary; when (it being half-past 3 o'clock,)

A motion was made to adjourn, and negatived.

The sixteenth ballot then took place, and was as follows: For Mr. Lowndes 68; for Mr. Taylor 30; for Mr. Sergeant 24; for Mr. Smith 23.

This ballot having been also ineffectual; another motion was made to adjourn, but without success.

The House then proceeded to the seventeenth ballot, which resulted as follows—73 necessary to a choice: For Mr. Lowndes 72; for Mr. Taylor 44; for Mr. Smith 17; for Mr. Sergeant 11.

No election being made, the House went into the eighteenth ballot, when the following result was announced—73 necessary to a choice: For

Mr. Lowndes 66 ; for Mr. Taylor 55 ; for Mr. Smith 21 ; for Mr. Sergeant 2.

No one having yet a majority of the votes, the House proceeded to the nineteenth ballot, which resulted as follows—73 necessary to a choice: For Mr. Taylor 66 ; for Mr. Lowndes 65 ; for Mr. Smith 14.

This ballot being also ineffectual ; a motion was made to adjourn, which motion prevailed, ayes 76—and, about five o'clock, the House adjourned.

WEDNESDAY, November 15.

Several other members appeared, and took their seats, to wit:

From Vermont, CHARLES RICH ; from Pennsylvania, GEORGE DENNISON ; from Maryland, THOMAS BAYLY ; from North Carolina, CHARLES FISHER ; and from South Carolina, ELDRED SIMKINS.

ELECTION OF SPEAKER.

The House, having been called to order at twelve o'clock, proceeded to ballot, the twentieth time, for a Speaker, in the place of Mr. Clay, resigned.

The votes having been counted, it appeared that the number of votes given in was 141—necessary to a choice 71. Of which there were: For Mr. Taylor 67 ; for Mr. Lowndes 65 ; for Mr. Smith 8 ; scattering 1.

No choice having been made, the House proceeded to ballot the twenty-first time ; when the result was declared as follows: Whole number of votes 147—necessary to a choice 74 ; of which there were: For Mr. Taylor 73 ; for Mr. Lowndes 42 ; for Mr. Smith 32.

No choice having yet been made, the House was about to ballot again ; when

Mr. LITTLE rose, and, remarking on the extraordinary aspect of the present proceedings of the House ; the necessity for choosing a Speaker ; the uncertainty, under present appearances, when a choice would be made ; the weariness of the House at these repeated ballotings, &c.—moved, that the House do come to a resolution, that the lowest on each ballot should be dropped at the succeeding ballot, and that any votes given for such lowest person should not be taken into account.

The CLERK of the House, after reading the resolve, expressed doubts of the power of the House to pass such a resolution, consistently with the rules established for its government.

Mr. RANDOLPH made it a point of order whether the Clerk had any right to express to the House his opinion of their powers, or to decide for them what was, or was not, in order.

The CLERK declared, that, under the rules of the House, which prescribe the mode of election by ballot, he could not receive this motion.

Some brief debate took place on the point of order, Mr. RANDOLPH protesting against what he pronounced an assumption of power on the part of the Clerk, and asserting the right of any member to propound any question to the House through

the Clerk, the Speaker's Chair being vacant, or from himself, if he thought proper.

Other gentlemen, Mr. STORRS, Mr. LITTLE, Mr. SERGEANT, Mr. MERCER, and Mr. LIVERMORE, expressed their opinions, and the following rule of the House was read:

"In all other cases of ballot than for committees, a majority of the votes given shall be necessary to an election ; and, when there shall not be such a majority on the first ballot, the ballot shall be repeated until a majority be obtained."

Mr. LITTLE, asserting his right to make the motion, yet, not desiring to prolong discussion in regard to it, waived the moving of it himself.

The House then proceeded to ballot the twenty-second time. The whole number of votes was 148—75 necessary to a choice. The votes were—For Mr. Taylor 76 ; for Mr. Lowndes 44 ; for Mr. Smith 27 ; scattering 1.

So JOHN W. TAYLOR, Esq., a Representative from the State of New York, was elected Speaker ; and, having been conducted to the Chair by Mr. NEWTON and Mr. MOSELEY, addressed the House as follows:

Gentlemen : I approach the station to which your favor invites me, greatly distrusting my ability to fulfil your just expectations. Although the duties of the Chair have become less arduous by improvements in its practice during the administration of my distinguished predecessor, I should not venture to assume their responsibilities without a firm reliance on your indulgent support. In all deliberative assemblies, the preservation of order must depend in a greater degree upon the members at large than upon any efforts of a presiding officer. The forbearance and decorum which characterized this House in its former session, at a period of peculiar excitement, afford of their continued exercise a happy anticipation. For the confidence with which you have honored me, be pleased to accept my profound acknowledgments. In my best endeavors to merit your approbation, which shall not be intermitted, I can promise nothing more than diligence, and a constant aim at impartiality. I can hope for nothing greater than that these endeavors may not prove altogether unavailing.

The new members having been sworn in—

A message was received from the Senate, informing the House that a quorum thereof was formed, and that they were ready to proceed to business.

On motion of Mr. NELSON, of Virginia, a similar message was returned to the Senate.

On motion of Mr. NELSON, also, a committee was appointed, jointly with such committee as should be appointed by the Senate, to wait upon the President of the United States, and inform him of the organization of the two Houses, and of their readiness to receive any communication he may have to make to them.

The resolutions of the Senate for appointing a Joint Committee of Enrolled Bills, and for the appointment of a Chaplain for each House, were agreed to ; and, on motion of Mr. SLOCUMB, to-morrow at twelve o'clock was assigned as the hour for proceeding to appoint a Chaplain on the part of this House.

439   HISTORY OF CONGRESS.   440

H. of R.   *Standing Committees—President's Message.*   NOVEMBER, 1820.

STANDING COMMITTEES.

On motion of Mr. LITTLE, the House proceeded to the appointment of the Standing Committees, pursuant to the rules and orders of the House: whereupon the SPEAKER appointed the following committees, viz:

Committee of Elections—Mr. Trimble, Mr. Tarr, Mr. Tucker of South Carolina, Mr. Sloan, Mr. Clark, Mr. Hooks, and Mr. Moore of Virginia.

Committee of Ways and Means—Mr. Smith of Maryland, Mr. McLane of Delaware, Mr. Burwell, Mr. Shaw, Mr. Tracy, Mr. Ross, and Mr. Jones of Tennessee.

Committee of Claims—Mr. Williams of North Carolina, Mr. Rich, Mr. McCoy, Mr. Samuel Moore, Mr. Hackley, Mr. Edwards of Connecticut, and Mr. Metcalfe.

Committee of Commerce—Mr. Newton, Mr. Tomlinson, Mr. Mallary, Mr. Nelson of Massachusetts, Mr. Hill, Mr. Wendover, and Mr. Abbot.

Committee of the Public Lands—Mr. Anderson, Mr. Hendricks, Mr. Cook, Mr. Ballard Smith, Mr. Stevens, Mr. Monell, and Mr. Brush.

Committee on the Post Office and Post Roads—Mr. Livermore, Mr. Culpeper, Mr. Russ, Mr. Tompkins, Mr. Kinsley, Mr. Johnson, and Mr. Gray.

Committee for the District of Columbia—Mr. Kent, Mr. Mercer, Mr. Neale, Mr. Swearingen, Mr. Smith of N. J., Mr. Meigs, and Mr. McCullough.

Committee on the Judiciary—Mr. Sergeant, Mr. Beecher, Mr. Robertson, Mr. Brevard, Mr. Lincoln, Mr. Tucker of Virginia, and Mr. Plumer.

Committee on Pensions and Revolutionary Claims—Mr. Rhea, Mr. McClay, Mr. Brown, Mr. Allen of Mass., Mr. Linn, Mr. Street, and Mr. Jones of Va.

Committee on Public Expenditures—Mr. Simkins, Mr. Slocumb, Mr. Rogers, Mr. Cobb, Mr. Adams, Mr. Ford, and Mr. Montgomery.

Committee on Private Land Claims—Mr. Campbell, Mr. Butler of Louisiana, Mr. Robert Moore, Mr. Eddy, Mr. Pitcher, Mr. Jackson, and Mr. Crowell.

Committee on Manufactures—Mr. Baldwin, Mr. Allen of New York, Mr. Little, Mr. McLean of Kentucky, Mr. Parker of Massachusetts, Mr. Kinsey, and Mr. Fisher.

Committee on Agriculture—Mr. Forrest, Mr. Clagett, Mr. Meech, Mr. Richmond, Mr. Ringgold, Mr. Garnett, and Mr. Earle.

Committee of Revisal and Unfinished Business—Mr. Morton, Mr. Butler of New Hampshire, and Mr. Ball.

Committee of Accounts—Mr. Smith of North Carolina, Mr. Bateman, and Mr. Upham.

The committee appointed to wait on the President of the United States reported, that they had performed that service, and received for answer that a message would be transmitted by the President immediately.

Accordingly, about three o'clock, the Message was received and read, and referred to the Committee of the Whole on the state of the Union, and five thousand copies thereof ordered to be printed for the use of the members of this House. [See Senate Proceedings, *ante* page 11, for this Message.]

THURSDAY, November 16.

Several other members appeared and took their seats, to wit:

From Massachusetts, WALTER FOLGER, Jr.; from North Carolina, HUTCHINS G. BURTON; and from Georgia, JOEL CRAWFORD and ROBERT RAYMOND REID.

Mr. SCOTT laid before the House a manuscript attested copy of the constitution formed on the 19th day of July, 1820, by the convention assembled at St. Louis, in the Territory of Missouri, for the government of the contemplated State of that name; which was referred to a select committee, and Mr. LOWNDES, Mr. SERGEANT, and Mr. SMITH, of Maryland, were appointed the said committee.

Mr. BLOOMFIELD submitted the following resolution:

Resolved, That in all cases where petitions were presented at the last session of this House, and referred to committees, but not finally acted upon, both by the committees and the House, the said petitions shall be considered as again presented and referred to the same committees, respectively, without special order to that effect. And it shall be the duty of the said committees respectively, upon application in behalf of any petitioner whose petition was presented and referred as aforesaid, to consider and report thereon, in the same manner as if it were referred to such committee by special order of the House.

The said resolution was read and ordered to lie on the table.

PRESIDENT'S MESSAGE.

The House resolved itself into a Committee of the Whole on the state of the Union, to whom had been referred the Message of the President of the United States, transmitted yesterday, Mr. NELSON, of Virginia, being called to the chair.

On motion of Mr. COBB, the following resolutions were agreed to by the Committee, reported to the House, and concurred in, viz:

1. *Resolved,* That so much of the Message of the President as relates to the subject of the late treaty between the United States and Spain; to the condition of the independent governments of South America, and all other subjects of foreign affairs, be referred to a select committee,

2. That so much of the President's message as relates to the commercial intercourse between the United States and British colonial ports, and between the United States and France, and all other subjects in relation to commerce, be referred to the Committee of Commerce.

3. That so much of the President's message as relates to fortifications and other military subjects, be referred to a select committee.

4. That so much of the President's message as relates to the navy, and the increase thereof, and to the protection of our commerce, be referred to a select committee.

5. That so much of the President's message as relates to the suppression of the slave trade, be referred to a select committee.

6. That so much of the President's message as relates to the subject of revenue, be referred to the Committee of Ways and Means.

7. That so much of the President's message as re-

lates to the sales of the public lands, and to granting relief to the purchasers thereof, be referred to the Committee on the Public Lands.

8. That so much of the President's message as relates to the civilization of and trade with the Indian tribes, be referred to a select committee.

9. That the said several select committees have leave to report by bill or otherwise.

Mr. Lowndes, Mr. Randolph, Mr. Moseley, Mr. Nelson, of Virginia, Mr. Dickinson, Mr. Reid, and Mr. Archer, of Maryland, were appointed a committee pursuant to the first resolution.

Mr. Alexander Smyth, Mr. Van Rensselaer, Mr. Cocke, Mr. Cushman, Mr. Burton, Mr. Robert Moore, and Mr. Russ, were appointed a committee pursuant to the third resolution.

Mr. Barbour, Mr. Fuller, Mr. Warfield, Mr. Case, Mr. Hall, of North Carolina, Mr. Dennison, and Mr. Crawford, were appointed a committee pursuant to the fourth resolution.

Mr. Hemphill, Mr. Mercer, Mr. Strong, of New York, Mr. Edwards, of Pennsylvania, Mr. Rogers, Mr. McCreary, and Mr. Folger were appointed a committee pursuant to the fifth resolution.

Mr. Southard, Mr. Bayly, Mr. Wallace, Mr. Walker, Mr. Williams, of Virginia, Mr. Baker, and Mr. Gross of Pennsylvania, were appointed a committee pursuant to the eighth resolution.

On motion of Mr. CROWELL, the Committee on the Public Lands were instructed to inquire into the expediency of providing by law some relief to the purchasers of the public lands in the United States previous to the 1st day of July, 1820.

Mr. FOOT moved the following resolutions, which were read and agreed to by the House, viz :

1. *Resolved,* That the subject of organizing and disciplining the militia be referred to a select committee.

2. *Resolved,* That the subject on roads and canals be referred to a select committee.

3. *Resolved,* That the subject of the public buildings be referred to a select committee.

4. *Resolved,* That the subject of Revolutionary pensions be referred to a select committee.

5. *Resolved,* That the said select committees have leave to report by bill, or otherwise.

Messrs. CANNON, GROSS, of New York, STRONG, of Vermont, PATTERSON, SAWYER, OVERSTREET, and HOSTETTER, were appointed a committee pursuant to the first resolution.

Messrs. STORRS, CRAFTS, MARCHAND, EDWARDS, of North Carolina, STREET, MONTGOMERY, and HENDRICKS, were appointed a committee pursuant to the second resolution.

Messrs. WOOD, KENDALL, ALEXANDER, HALL, of New York, MURRAY, CRAFTS, and BUFFUM, were appointed a committee pursuant to the third resolution.

Messrs. BLOOMFIELD, EDWARDS, of North Carolina, DEWITT, HIRSHMAN, HAZARD, FAY, and ALEXANDER, were appointed a committee pursuant to the fourth resolution.

The House proceeded to ballot for a Chaplain on the part of this House.

The following exhibits the result of three successive ballots :

	1st.	2d.	3d.
Rev. Mr. Allison - - -	52	50	55
Rev. Mr. Campbell - -	34	52	81
Rev. Mr. Sparks - - -	29	20	3
Rev. Mr. Post - - -	19	10	3

So the Reverend J. NICHOLSON CAMPBELL was chosen on the third trial. And the House adjourned.

FRIDAY, November 17.

Mr. BATES presented the petition of the Legislative Council and House of Representatives of the Territory of Arkansas, praying that a surveyor may be appointed for that Territory, who shall keep an office within the same.—Referred to the Committee on Public Lands.

The SPEAKER presented a petition of sundry inhabitants of the Third Congressional District of Kentucky, praying for the encouragement of domestic manufactures, by imposing higher duties on goods imported into the United States ; which petition was referred to the Committee on Manufactures.

The SPEAKER laid before the House a letter from the Governor of Pennsylvania, enclosing the certificate of the election of THOMAS G. McCULLOUGH, as a member of this House from that State, to supply the vacancy occasioned by the resignation of David Fullerton ; which was referred to the Committee on Elections.

The SPEAKER laid before the House a letter from the Commissioner of the General Land Office, transmitting copies of the reports, from No. 1 to 9 inclusive, of the land commissioners at Jackson Courthouse, and a copy of a letter which accompanied them ; which were referred to the Committee on Private Land Claims.

Mr. GROSS, of New York, offered for consideration the following resolve :

Resolved, That the Committee of Ways and Means be instructed to prepare and report to this House, as soon as may be, a list of all the expenditures, under their proper heads, authorized by the existing laws of the United States, with an opinion respecting the reduction, which, consistently with the public interest, may be made in each of them respectively.

Mr. G. said the motion related to a subject which ought, in his opinion, to receive the early and earnest consideration of the House ; but, not wishing to take the House by surprise, he should move for it to lie on the table for the present.

It was ordered to lie on the table accordingly.

Mr. FOOT submitted the following resolution :

Resolved, That the following addition be made to the standing rules and orders of the House, viz :

A committee of three members shall be appointed, whose duty it shall be to examine all bills, amendments, resolutions or motions, before they go out of the possession of the House ; and to make report that they are correctly engrossed, which report shall be entered on the Journal.

The resolution was read and laid on the table for one day.

The House adjourned to Monday.

MONDAY, November 20.

Several other members appeared and took their seats, to wit:

From Virginia, JOHN FLOYD and SEVERN E. PARKER; and from Tennessee, HENRY H. BRYAN and ROBERT ALLEN.

SOLOMON SIBLEY appeared, produced his credentials, was qualified and took his seat as a delegate from the Territory of Michigan, in the room of William W. Woodbridge, resigned.

Mr. BATES presented a petition of the Legislative Council and House of Representatives of the Territory of Arkansas, praying that the right of pre-emption may be extended to the inhabitants of that portion of said Territory lying south of the river Arkansas, in the purchase of the lands on which they have long resided and made valuable improvements.—Referred to the Committee on Public Lands.

Mr. EDDY submitted the following resolution, viz:

Resolved, That a committee be appointed to inquire into the expediency of so amending the act entitled an act allowing compensation to the members of the Senate, members of the House of Representatives of the United States, and to the delegates from the Territories, and repealing all other laws on that subject, as to reduce the compensation thereby allowed from eight to six dollars per day, and the rate of travel for every twenty miles, from eight to six dollars; and that said committee have leave to report by bill or otherwise.

The said resolution was read; and the question was taken, Will the House now proceed to consider the same? and determined in the negative—yeas 58, nays 61.

Mr. STORRS submitted the following:

Resolved, That the 18th rule of the standing rules and orders of this House be annulled.

The 18th rule is in the following words:

"Business referred to committees of the whole House shall be called for in the following order:

1. Private bills which have passed the Senate, and have been reported favorably by a committee of the House.

2. Private bills reported by committees of the House.

3. Bills and resolutions of a public nature.

4. Bills which have passed the Senate, and have been reported against by a committee of the House.

5. Reports unfavorable to petitioners."

The motion of Mr. STORRS lies on the table one day of course.

On motion of Mr. BLOOMFIELD, the House proceeded to consider the resolution submitted by him on the 16th instant, respecting the reference of petitions; and the same being again read, was modified and agreed to as follows:

Resolved, That in all cases where petitions were presented at the last session to this House, and referred to committees, but not reported upon, the said petitions shall be again considered as referred to the said committees, respectively, upon application of any member to the Clerk, without special order from the House to that effect. And it shall be the duty of the said committees, respectively, to consider and report thereon, in the same manner as if said petitions were referred by special orders of the House; but no petition shall be received or acted upon by a committee, under this order, which shall not have been endorsed in, and transmitted to the committee through, the office of the Clerk.

Mr. COCKE, of Tennessee, submitted for consideration the following resolution:

Resolved, That the Committee on the Military Establishment be instructed to inquire into the expediency of reducing the Military Peace Establishment of the United States.

And the resolution was agreed to, without debate or division.

The House proceeded to consider the resolution submitted by Mr. FOOT on the 17th instant, for the appointment of a standing committee for the examination of engrossed bills; and the same being again read, the question was taken, Will the House agree to the same? and determined in the negative.

COMPENSATION OF MEMBERS.

Mr. LINN, of New Jersey, submitted for consideration the following resolution:

Resolved, That the Committee of Ways and Means be directed to inquire into the expediency of reducing the compensation allowed to members of Congress to six dollars per day, and a proportional reduction for travelling to and from the Seat of Government; and also of reducing the pay of all the officers of Government that has been increased since the year 1809, to what it was at or before that period.

Mr. LINN made a few remarks on introducing this proposition, the import of which was, that his opinion was that Congress ought to go back to the year 1809, and restore the compensations of public officers, &c., to the condition in which they then stood. As the present proposition, however, was for inquiry merely, not requiring any expression of the opinion of the House, he hoped no objection would be made to it.

Mr. COBB, of Georgia, said a few words expressive of his opinion, that, if a reduction of expenditures, &c., was made, it ought to be more general than was proposed by this motion to be inquired into. To such a general reduction he was favorable, but was opposed to a piece-meal legislation on the subject, which must be partial, and might be unjust in its operation. This was the substance of Mr. C's. observation, though not perhaps his words. He wished the resolution to be so modified as to make it as comprehensive as in his opinion it ought to be.

Mr. SMITH, of Maryland, thought the object of this motion did not properly fall within the duties of the Committee of Ways and Means, and wished it referred to a different committee.

Mr. LINN did not wish to take the House by surprise, and consented to his motion's lying on the table, that gentlemen might have an opportunity to prepare amendments to it if they thought proper.

So the resolution was ordered to lie on the table.

AMENDMENT TO THE CONSTITUTION.

Mr. SMITH, of North Carolina, submitted for consideration a joint resolution. In doing so, he expressed his earnest hope that, as a similar resolution had passed the Senate at the last session, but not been acted upon in this House for want of time, it would have an early consideration at this session, and receive that approbation from the House which he thought it merited. The following is a copy of the resolve moved by Mr. S.

Resolved, by the Senate and House of Representatives of the United States of America in Congress assembled, two-thirds of both Houses concurring, That the following amendment to the Constitution of the United States be proposed to the Legislatures of the several States, which, when ratified by the Legislatures of three-fourths of the States, shall be valid, to all intents and purposes, as part of the said Constitution:

That, for the purpose of choosing Representatives in the Congress of the United States, each State shall, by its Legislature, be divided into a number of districts, equal to the number of Representatives to which such State may be entitled. The districts shall be formed of contiguous territory, and contain, as nearly as may be, an equal number of persons entitled by the Constitution to be represented, or of persons qualified to vote for members of the most numerous branch of the State Legislature. In each district, the persons qualified to vote shall choose one Representative.

That, for the purpose of choosing Electors of President and Vice President of the United States, the persons qualified to vote for Representatives in each district shall choose one Elector. The two additional Electors, to which each State is entitled, shall be appointed in such manner as the Legislature thereof may direct. The Electors, when convened, at the time and place prescribed by law for the purpose of voting for President and Vice President of the United States, shall have power, in case any of them shall fail to attend, to choose an Elector or Electors, in place of him or them so failing to attend. The division of States into districts, as hereby provided for, shall take place immediately after this amendment shall be adopted, and immediately after every future census and apportionment of Representatives under the same; and such districts shall not be altered until a subsequent census shall have been taken, and an apportionment of Representatives under it shall have been made.

The resolution was twice read, and referred to a Committee of the Whole on the state of the Union.

TUESDAY, November 21.

Mr. WENDOVER presented a petition of the American Society, of the city of New York, for the encouragement of domestic manufactures, praying that a duty of ten per centum be imposed on sales at auction; that the credit on duties on the importation of foreign fabrics may be abolished, and that the tariff may be so graduated as to carry into effect a complete system of protection to home industry; which was referred to the Committee on Manufactures.

Mr. McLEAN, of Kentucky, presented a memorial and petition of Matthew Lyon, praying that his petition, presented at the last session, may now be considered, and the prayer thereof granted, so that the justice to which his case may entitle him, and which has been so long withheld, may now

be granted; which was referred to a select committee; and Messrs. McLEAN, of Kentucky, FLOYD, EDWARDS, of North Carolina, PLUMER, and BEECHER, were appointed the said committee.

Mr. BATES presented a petition of the Legislative Council and House of Representatives of the Territory of Arkansas, praying that some provision may be made for the relief of the settlers on the public lands, who have been compelled to abandon their settlements made prior to the twelfth of April, 1814, under the treaty lately concluded between the United States and the Cherokee nation of Indians; which was referred to the Committee on the Public Lands.

Mr. BATES also presented another petition of the Legislative Council and House of Representatives of the Territory of Arkansas, praying that some provision may be made to coerce the attendance within their districts of individuals appointed to offices in that Territory; which was referred to the Committee on the Judiciary.

A message from the Senate informed the House that the Senate have elected the Reverend William Ryland a Chaplain to Congress on their part. And they have passed a resolution for the appointment of a joint Library Committee, who shall have the direction of the money appropriated to the purchase of books and maps, for the use of the two Houses of Congress, and have appointed a committee on their part. They have also passed a bill, entitled "An act to alter the terms of the district court in Alabama;" in which resolution and bill they ask the concurrence of this House.

Mr. ANDERSON, from the Committee on the Public Lands, made an unfavorable report on the petition of the General Assembly of the Territory of Arkansas, praying for the establishment of a surveyor's office in that Territory; which was concurred in by the House.

The resolution from the Senate for the appointment of a joint Library committee was read, and concurred in by the House; and Messrs. MALLARY, PARKER, of Virginia, and ALLEN, of Tennessee, were appointed the committee on the part of this House.

The bill from the Senate, entitled "An act to alter the terms of the district court in Alabama," was read twice, and referred to the Committee on the Judiciary.

On motion of Mr. ABBOT, the Committee on the Judiciary were instructed to inquire into the expediency of passing a law, defining under what circumstances, and by what means, private property may be taken for public use, under the emergency of war, and providing that just compensation shall be made for the same; also, of prescribing the manner in which soldiers may be quartered in any house, without the consent of the owner, in time of war.

On motion of Mr. SMITH, of Maryland, the Committee of Commerce were instructed to inquire into the expediency of admitting British vessels arriving from the Cape of Good Hope and the Mauritius, into the ports of the United States, on the same terms and conditions as if they had sailed from a port in Great Britain, so long as those ports are open to the vessels of the United States on the same terms and conditions as their own vessels.

On motion of Mr. STORRS, the House proceeded to consider the resolution, submitted by him yesterday, to annul the eighteenth rule of the standing rules and orders of this House; and the said resolution being again read, was agreed to by the House.

The said eighteenth rule, as annulled, is in the words following, viz.:

"Business referred to committees of the whole House shall be called for consideration in the following order:

1. Private bills which have passed the Senate, and have been reported favorably by a committee of the House.
2. Private bills reported by committees of the House.
3. Bills and resolutions of a public nature.
4. Bills which have passed the Senate, and have been reported against by a committee of the House.
5. Reports unfavorable to petitioners."

Mr. MALLARY submitted the following resolution for consideration:

Resolved, That the President of the United States be requested to lay before this House information respecting the progress made by the Commissioners under the Treaty of Ghent, in establishing the boundary line between the United States and the Canadas; whether any part of the boundary line is settled; whether the Commissioners of the United States and Great Britain have met during the present year; and how much money has been drawn from the Treasury for the purpose aforesaid; and how much each Commissioner, Agent, or any person on their account, has drawn; the names of each person employed by the said Commissioners and Agents, in their respective sections; the purposes for which each person was employed, the length of time employed, and the compensation each person has received for his services; a statement of all the items of account rendered by each of said Commissioners and Agents, and the particular purposes for which the moneys drawn by them have been expended; the amount of compensation each Commissioner and Agent has received since his appointment; and whether any money has been allowed to, or retained by, said Commissioners and Agents, except the sum of $4,444 44 per annum.

The resolution was agreed to *nem. con.,* and a committee was appointed to present it to the President.

WEDNESDAY, November 22.

Another member, to wit, from South Carolina, CHARLES PINCKNEY, appeared and took his seat.

Mr. KINSLEY presented a petition of sundry persons interested in commerce, inhabitants of Belfast, in the State of Maine, praying that no alteration may be made in the existing tariff of duties on foreign goods imported into the United States, injurious to the commercial interest, for the purpose of extending further protection to the manufacturing interest of the country; which was referred to the Committee on Manufactures.

Mr. SERGEANT, from the Committee on the Judiciary, to which was referred the bill from the Senate, entitled "An act to alter the terms of the district court in Alabama," reported the same without amendment, and it was ordered to be read a third time to-day; and was accordingly read a third time, and passed.

Mr. COOK, from the Committee on the Public Lands, made a report on the petition of William McIntosh, accompanied with a bill for his relief; which was read twice, and committed to a Committee of the Whole.

Mr. COOK, from the same committee, also made a report on the petition of Nicholas Jarrott, accompanied by a bill for his relief; which was read twice, and committed to a Committee of the Whole.

On motion of Mr. FULLER, it was

Resolved, That the President of the United States be requested to inform this House what naval force has been stationed for the protection of the commerce of our citizens in the West India islands, and parts adjacent, during the present year, and whether any depredations by pirates, or others, upon the property of citizens of the United States engaged in such commerce, have been reported to our Government.

Messrs. FULLER and WENDOVER were appointed a committee to present the foregoing resolution to the President of the United States.

On motion of Mr. SCOTT, the bill which originated at the last session, supplementary to the several acts for the adjusting of land claims in the State of Louisiana and Territory of Missouri, was taken up and referred to the Committee on Public Lands.

After a number of remarks from Mr. FORD, to show why favor ought to be shown in this case, the report of the Committee of Ways and Means, of the last session, unfavorable to the petition of Perley Keyes and Jason Fairbanks, was taken up, and, on motion of Mr. F., recommitted to the same committee.

Mr. LINN moved to proceed to the consideration of his motion directing the Committee of Ways and Means to inquire into the expediency of reducing the compensation of members of Congress, and of the officers of Government generally, to the rates at which they stood in 1809; but the House refused to consider the same.

Mr. FOOT, of Connecticut, remarked that several propositions had been already made, looking to a reduction in the expenditures of the Government, none of which exactly corresponded with his views; to exhibit which he offered for consideration the following resolution:

Resolved, That the Committee on Public Expenditures be instructed to prepare and report a system of retrenchment in the expenditures in the various departments of the Government, (not inconsistent with the public interest,) which will restore that rigid economy and simplicity becoming our Republican institutions, and which the present stagnation of commerce, and the embarrassments attending every branch of domestic industry, imperiously demand.

And the question being put that the House do now proceed to consider the said resolve, it was decided in the negative.

REDUCTION OF EXPENDITURES.

Mr. COBB, of Georgia, presented to the Chair the following series of propositions:

1. *Resolved,* That it is expedient that the annual expenses of the Government should be reduced; that, for the accomplishment of this object, it is further

2. *Resolved,* That such offices as are not immediately necessary for the transaction of public business, and the abolition of which would not be detrimental to the public interest, shall be abolished.

3. *Resolved,* That the salaries of all civil officers whose compensation has been increased since the year 1809 shall be reduced to what they were at that period.

4. *Resolved,* That it is expedient to reduce the Army to the number of six thousand non-commissioned officers, musicians, and privates, preserving such part of the corps of engineers, without regard to that number, as may be required by the public interest; and including such reduction of the general staff as may be required by the state of the Army when reduced as herein proposed.

5. *Resolved,* That it is expedient that the appropriations for the erection of fortifications shall be so made as to require a less sum annually, by extending the time within which they shall be completed.

6. *Resolved,* That the act making an appropriation of one million of dollars per annum for the increase of the Navy be so amended as to extend the time within which such increase shall be made, and to reduce the annual appropriation to the sum of five hundred thousand dollars.

7. *Resolved,* That it is expedient to recall from active service one-half the naval force now employed, and to place the same in ordinary.

8th Resolution refers the subjects of the preceding resolves to the proper standing and select committees, to bring in bills pursuant thereto.

The House having agreed to consider these resolutions—

Mr. COBB said, he had no intention to bring on the discussion of them at this time, having presented them by way of notice to members, that they might be prepared to discuss and decide on them when called up. He was not even himself prepared at this moment to give his views of the subjects embraced in these resolutions; nor did he know that the House ought to proceed to act on them, until it should have received, first, the annual report of the Secretary of the Treasury, and, secondly, a report from the Secretary of War, required by a resolution of the House at the last session, of a plan whereupon a reduction of the Army might be advantageously made. To place these resolves in a situation which would enable him to call them up at any time, he moved their reference to the Committee of the Whole on the state of the Union. Which motion was agreed to.

THURSDAY, November 23.

Mr. CUSHMAN presented the petition of the trustees of the Somerset Agricultural Society, in the county of Somerset and State of Maine, praying that the bill pending before Congress at the last session, establishing a new tariff of duties on goods imported into the United States, may be passed

16th CON. 2d SESS.—15

into a law, so as to extend further protection to the manufacturing interest of the country.

Mr. JONES, of Virginia, presented a memorial of the merchants and other inhabitants of the town of Petersburg, in that State, in opposition to the passage of the said bill.—Referred to the Committee on Manufactures.

Ordered, That the Committee on the Public Lands be discharged from the further consideration of the bill, supplementary to the several acts for the adjustment of land claims in the State of Louisiana, and Territory of Missouri, and that it be referred to the Committee on Private Land Claims.

On motion of Mr. BUTLER, of New Hampshire,

Resolved, That the Secretary of War be directed to report to this House the regulations which he has adopted in the administration of the act of Congress of May 1st, 1820, entitled "An act in addition to an act to provide for certain persons engaged in the land and naval service of the United States in the Revolutionary war, passed March 18, 1818." Whether any person except paupers, or such as have been partially supported by public or private charity, have been continued on the pension roll; and, if any, whether the value of their property, as returned on their schedule, in any case exceeded two hundred dollars, and how much. Whether debts, which the applicants owed, have been or are considered in the estimation of their circumstances, income, or means of subsistence; and how many are continued on the pension roll under said act.

The bill to provide for the preservation and repair of the Cumberland road having been called up, the House voted not to go into Committee thereon.

On motion of Mr. KENT, the Committee of the Whole was discharged from the consideration of the bill "to repeal part of an act to authorize the President and Managers of the Washington (Georgetown) Turnpike Company in Maryland, to extend and make their road to and from Georgetown, in the District of Columbia, through the said District, to the line thereof," and it was recommitted to the Committee on the District of Columbia.

ELIAS PARKS.

The House then resolved itself into a Committee of the Whole on the report of the Committee of Claims on the petition of Elias Parks.

[The case of Mr. Parks is substantially this: The petitioner had chartered a boat, on the morning of the attack on Oswego, (on Lake Ontario,) in May, 1813, for the purpose of transporting merchandise to a place of safety. The boat had departed from Oswego in pursuit of that object, when she was ordered back by Colonel Mitchell, who commanded the post, was taken possession of by Captain Romayne, under that order, for the use of the troops, and the goods placed on the wharf, and, with the boat, put under the charge of sentinels. Afterwards, the fort being stormed, and the town taken, the goods fell into the hands of the enemy. The petitioner prays indemnification for

451   HISTORY OF CONGRESS.   452

H. of R.   *Military Road in Maine—Public Lands.*   November, 1820.

his loss. The report of the Committee of Claims is, that his petition ought not to be granted.]

Mr. Storrs moved to reverse the report, so as to allow the petitioner the value of the goods in the boat at the time of its seizure.

This motion gave rise to considerable debate; in the course of which, the motion of Mr. Storrs was supported by Messrs. Storrs, Gross, of New York, and Stevens; and opposed by Messrs. Williams, of North Carolina, and McCoy.

The result of the debate was, that Mr. Storrs's motion was agreed to, and, the decision having been reported to the House, was then concurred in; and, on motion of Mr. Storrs, the report was recommitted to the committee who reported it, with instructions to bring in a bill pursuant to the amended report.

MILITARY ROAD IN MAINE.

Mr. Hill submitted for consideration the following resolution:

Resolved, That the Committee on Roads and Canals be instructed to inquire into the expediency of opening a military and post road from some place on the Penobscot river, in the State of Maine, to the river St. Croix.

Mr. H. in introducing this resolution, said, that Maine was a frontier State, bordering on the British Provinces, for a distance of more than five hundred miles. The distance from the Penobscot river to the British lines is not short of one hundred and twenty miles. The road, for the greatest part of the distance, is impassable for any kind of carriages. The towns of Eastport and Lubeck, with several others near the boundary line, are very fast rising into consequence. At Eastport and Lubeck there is one of the finest harbors in the United States, and it is defensible. It was of great importance, he said, that there should be a good carriage road to the extremities of Maine, whereon to transport the mail; for, in case of another war with Great Britain, which he hoped would never happen, it will be a war, not on our territories, but on the ocean and in the English provinces. Mr. H. said, he was aware that a celebrated military sovereign of Europe remarked, that "he had no idea of making roads for his enemies;" but, said Mr. H. we have no fear of an invasion in Maine by land. In the late war, there was physical, moral, and mental strength enough in Maine, if we had been masters of our own fortunes, to have driven the enemy from Castine headlong into the sea. Moreover, there are no national vessels built in Maine, although possessing a seacoast of two hundred and fifty miles, containing more than a hundred spacious harbors, having a population of three hundred thousand, owning about one-ninth of the whole tonnage of the United States, and can furnish timber and ship-builders inferior to none in America; and yet we have no dock-yards, nor patronage from the nation. We have been patriotic and dutiful children, always ready to shoulder our muskets in the defence of our country's rights. Massachusetts expended a million of dollars in the late war which has not been refunded. One-third thereof belonged to Maine. She deplores the policy of those times, in our beloved parent State, but Maine has washed her hands from that pollution; she expects justice, magnanimity, and remuneration, from the General Government, in some way or other. He hoped, therefore, the resolution would pass.

The question being taken on agreeing to said resolution, it was decided in the affirmative—52 to 41.

PUBLIC LANDS.

The House resolved itself into a Committee of the Whole on the bill to provide for paying to the State of Illinois three per cent. of the net proceeds arising from the sale of the public lands within the same.

Mr. Cobb having inquired on what grounds the merits of the bill rested—

Mr. Cook, of Illinois, briefly explained that the object of this bill was to obtain the payment to the State of Illinois of the three per cent. reserved for her use out of the moneys accruing to the Treasury of the United States for the sales of public lands in that State; the Secretary of the Treasury not feeling himself authorized to pay over the money without express authority by law. A similar law had already been passed in relation to the State of Indiana, and the passage of this bill was little more than a matter of course, it being to carry into effect a compact with the State of Illinois.

Mr. Smith, of Maryland, hesitated about voting for this bill, under the impression that it proposed to divert this fund from the purposes of making roads within the State, to a different purpose, viz: the encouragement of schools and colleges. If that were the object, he said he could not vote for it, because it would violate the compact.

Mr. Campbell, of Ohio, said he had not the least doubt of the propriety of passing the law, and he thought the gentleman from Maryland would be of the same opinion with him when the clause of the compact by which Illinois was admitted into the Union, was read. Mr. C. then read that clause, in the following words:

"3d. That five per cent. of the net proceeds of the land lying within such State, and which shall be sold by Congress from and after the first day of January, one thousand eight hundred and nineteen, after deducting all expenses incident to the same, shall be reserved for the purposes following, viz: Two-fifths to be disbursed under the direction of Congress, in making roads leading to the State, the residue to be appropriated by the Legislature of the State for the encouragement of learning, of which one-sixth part shall be exclusively bestowed on a college or university."

From this it appeared that the proposed bill was a mere legislative form for accomplishing an act already binding on the United States.

Mr. Anderson, of Kentucky, said there was no difficulty at all in this subject, well understood. In most of the ordinances for the admission of States into the Union, the stipulation is, that, of the five per cent. reserved from the proceeds of the sales of the public lands, two per cent. shall be applied to the construction of roads leading to the

States, and three per cent. shall be applied by the State itself to making roads within the State. But, in the case of Illinois, an exception was made, on the representation of her then Delegate, that the fund would not be required for roads within the State, and the Legislature was authorized to apply the three per cent. to schools and colleges instead of roads. The Secretary of the Treasury, in obedience to that caution which always governs him, declined paying over this money to the State authorities without the authority of an act of Congress; and the object of this bill was to give that authority.

Mr. SMITH, of Maryland, professing himself entirely satisfied with these explanations, withdrew his opposition; and the bill was reported to the House, and ordered to be engrossed for a third reading.

ADMISSION OF MISSOURI.

Mr. LOWNDES, from the select committee to whom was referred the constitution formed for their government by the people of Missouri, delivered in the following report:

The committee to whom has been referred the constitution of the State of Missouri respectfully report:

That they have not supposed themselves bound to inquire whether the provisions of the constitution referred to them be wise or liberal. The grave and difficult question as to the restraints which should be imposed upon the power of Missouri to form a constitution for itself was decided by the act of the last session, and the committee have had only to examine whether the provisions of the act have been complied with. In the opinion of the committee, they have been. The propositions, too, which were offered in the same act to the free acceptance or rejection of the people of Missouri, have all been accepted by them. But there remains a question too important to be overlooked.

We know that cases must often arise in which there may be a doubt whether the laws or constitution of a State do not transcend the line (sometimes the obscure line) which separates the powers of the different governments of our complex system. It appears to the committee, that, in general, it must be unwise in Congress to anticipate judicial decisions by the exposition of an equivocal phrase, and that it would be yet more objectionable, by deciding on the powers of a State just emerged from territorial dependence, that it should give the weight of its authority to an opinion which might condemn the laws and constitutions of old, as well as sovereign States. The committee are not unaware that a part of the twenty-sixth section of the third article of the constitution of Missouri, by which the Legislature has been directed to pass laws "to prevent free negroes and mulattoes from coming to, and settling in, the State," has been construed to apply to such of that class as are citizens of the United States, and that their exclusion has been deemed repugnant to the Federal Constitution. The words which are objected to are to be found in the laws of at least one of the Middle States, (Delaware,) and a careful examination of the clause might perhaps countenance the opinion that it applies to the large class of free negroes and mulattoes who cannot be considered as the citizens of any State. But, of all the articles in our constitution, there is probably not one more difficult to construe well than that which

gives to the citizens of each State the privileges and immunities of citizens of the several States; there is not one, an attention to whose spirit is more necessary to the convenient and beneficial connexion of the States; nor one of which too large a construction would more completely break down their defensive power, and lead more directly to their consolidation. This much, indeed, seems to be settled by the established constitutions of States in every section of the Union; that a State has a right to discriminate between the white and the black man, both in respect to political and civil privileges, though both be citizens of another State; to give to the one, for instance, the right of voting and of serving on juries, which it refuses to the other. How far this discrimination may be carried, is obviously a matter of nice and difficult inquiry. The committee do not propose to engage in it. They believe it best, whenever a case occurs which must necessarily involve the decision of it, that it should be remitted to judicial cognizance.

In this view (which narrows their inquiries and duties) the committee are confirmed, by a consideration of the embarrassments and disasters which a different course of proceeding might sometimes produce. When a people are authorized to form a State, and do so, the trammels of their Territorial condition fall off. They have performed the act which makes them sovereign and independent. If they pass an unconstitutional law, and we leave it, as we should that of another State, to the decision of a judicial tribunal, the illegal act is divested of its force by the operation of a system with which we are familiar. The control of the General Government is exercised in each particular case, in support of individual right, and the State retains the condition which it has just acquired, and would not easily renounce. But a decision by Congress against the constitutionality of a law passed by a State which it had authorized the establishment, could not operate directly by vacating the law; nor is it believed that it could reduce the State to the dependence of a Territory. In these circumstances, to refuse admission into the Union to such a State, is to refuse to extend over it that judicial authority which might vacate the obnoxious law, and to expose all the interests of the Government within the territory of that State, to a Legislature and a Judiciary, the only checks on which have been abandoned. On the other hand, if Congress shall determine neither to expound clauses which are obscure, nor to decide Constitutional questions which must be difficult and perplexing, equally interesting to old States, whom our construction could not, as to the new, whom it ought not to coerce, the rights and duties of Missouri will be left to the determination of the same temperate and impartial tribunal which has decided the conflicting claims, and received the confidence, of the other States.

The committee recommend the adoption of the following resolution:

This report having been read by the Clerk, the resolution therein referred to was read, as follows:

Whereas, in pursuance of an act of Congress passed on the sixth day of March, one thousand eight hundred and twenty, entitled "An act to authorize the people of the Missouri Territory to form a constitution and State government, and for the admission of such State into the Union on an equal footing with the original States, and to prohibit slavery in certain Territories," the people of said Territory did, on the nineteenth day of July, in the year one thousand eight hundred and twenty, by a convention called for the purpose, form for themselves a constitution and State government, which constitution and State government, so formed, is republican, and in conformity to the provisions of the said act:

Be it therefore resolved by the Senate and House of Representatives of the United States of America, in Congress assembled, That the State of Missouri shall be, and is hereby declared to be, one of the United States of America, and is admitted into the Union on an equal footing with the original States, in all respects whatever.

The resolution was then read a second time.

Mr. Lowndes moved to refer the resolution to a Committee of the Whole, on the state of the Union, which would put it in the power of the House to act upon it at any time it thought proper. He need not say, that there was no disposition to act upon this subject without full notice to all parties concerned; and if no other person did, he should himself, when proposing to call for the consideration of the report, give a day or two notice of his intention to do so. Whilst up, he took occasion to say, that this report, as indeed all reports of committees, must be considered as the act of a majority of the committee, and not as expressing the sentiments of every individual of the committee.

The reference was agreed to.

FRIDAY, November 24.

Two members appeared and took their seats, viz: from Maryland, Thomas Culbreth, and from Virginia, John Tyler.

Mr. Tyler presented the memorial of the merchants and other citizens of Richmond and its vicinity, against an increase of the tariff of duties on imports; a discontinuance of the credit now granted on said duties; the abolition of drawbacks of duties and other restrictions on the commerce of the United States; which was referred to the Committee on Manufactures.

Mr. Smith, of Maryland, from the Committee of Ways and Means, presented a report on the petition of Daniel Lathrop, late a postmaster at Waterbury, in New York, praying relief from the loss of a sum of money received by him for postages, the same having been wasted by a person in whose care it had been placed for the use of the General Post Office; which report was concurred in by the House.

Mr. Smith, from the same committee, presented the following report:

The Committee of Ways and Means, to whom was referred the memorial of the inhabitants of Salem, report—

That the memorialists pray Congress to exempt from duty all imported books in the learned and foreign languages, whether reprinted in this country, and all works of science, in the English language, which shall not be reprinted here within the term of one year from their original publication.

The committee submit the following resolution:

Resolved, That it is inexpedient to grant the prayer the memorialists.

The same was read, and concurred in.

Mr. Smith, from the same committee, made an unfavorable report on the petition of John Stipp; which was concurred in.

Mr. Smith, from the same committee, made an unfavorable report on the petition of Samuel Peckham, Jr., Inspector of Customs for the district of Vermont, stating that he obtained a judgment against Nathaniel Tuft for goods illegally imported, in 1812, to the amount of three thousand six hundred dollars, and that by an act of Congress said Tuft and his security were released from confinement for the debt, whereby he lost his one quarter part of the amount of said seizure, and praying that the same may be allowed to him; which report was read, and concurred in.

Mr. Sergeant, from the Committee on the Judiciary, made a report on the petition of Curtis Lewis, of Mobile, that the object of the memorial falls properly within the scope of the authority of the district court of Alabama, as regulated by an act of the present session; which report was agreed to.

Mr. Sergeant, from the same committee, reported a bill for the relief of Andrew Kennedy; which was twice read and committed.

Mr. Anderson, from the Committee on the Public Lands, reported a bill for the relief of Daniel Seward; which was read a first and second time, and committed.

The engrossed bill to provide for paying to the State of Illinois the amount of three per cent. of the net proceeds of the sales of public lands within the State of Illinois, was read a third time, passed, and ordered to be sent to the Senate for concurrence.

CLAIM OF JOHN COWAN.

The House then resolved itself into a Committee of the Whole on the report of the Committee of Claims unfavorable to the petition of John Cowan.

[Mr. Cowan prays the allowance of four hundred and sixty dollars for shoeing, at their own expense, the horses of a company of cavalry in the service of the United States, from September 28, 1814, to March 28, 1815, and of fifty-two dollars paid for forage, in consequence of the United States failing to supply the same. The committee report against the claim, as well because the allowance of forty cents per day ought to cover the expense of shoeing, as because of the informality of the evidence in support of the claim.]

Mr. Jones, of Tennessee, moved to reverse the report in this case, so as to declare that the claim ought to be allowed.

This motion gave rise to debate, being supported by Mr. Williams, of North Carolina, and Mr. Rich, of Vermont.

In the end, the motion to amend the report was negatived—55 to 41; and this being reported to the House, was there concurred in, and the original report was agreed to.

The House adjourned to Monday.

MONDAY, November 27.

Another member, to wit: from Mississippi, Christopher Rankin, appeared and took his seat.

A new member, to wit: from Massachusetts, BENJAMIN GORHAM, elected to supply the vacancy occasioned by the resignation of Jonathan Mason, also appeared, was qualified, and took his seat.

Mr. MOSELEY presented a memorial of the Chamber of Commerce of the city of New Haven in the State of Connecticut, against any alteration in the tariff of duties on imports, by way of protection and encouragement to the manufacturing interest of the country; which was referred to the Committee on Manufactures.

Mr. LOWNDES presented a similar memorial of a convention of delegates, representing the merchants and others interested in commerce, assembled in the city of Philadelphia; which was also referred to the Committee on Manufactures.

Mr. LOWNDES presented a petition of Enrico Causici, sculptor, praying to be employed to execute, in marble, a statue representing the Genius of the Constitution, a cast of which, in plaster, is now placed above the Speaker's chair, in the Hall of this House; or that he may be employed to execute a colossal statue of the General Baron de Kalb, ordered to be erected to the memory of that officer by Congress, in the year 1780; which petition was referred to the Committee on the Public Buildings.

The SPEAKER laid before the House a certificate of the election of EDWARD B. JACKSON, of Virginia; which was referred to the Committee of Elections.

On motion of Mr. CAMPBELL, the Committee on Private Land Claims were instructed to inquire into the expediency of so amending the act, entitled "An act for the relief of the legal representatives of Henry Willis," passed on the 8th day of May, 1820, so as to except from the location of the land therein mentioned, town lots and sites for towns.

Mr. SMITH, of Maryland, from the Committee of Ways and Means, to whom was recommitted a report of last session on the petition of Perley Keyes and Jason Fairbanks, reported a bill for their relief; which was twice read, and committed.

Mr. WILLIAMS, of North Carolina, from the Committee of Claims, pursuant to instructions, reported a bill for the relief of Elias Parks; which was twice read, and committed.

The House then resolved itself into a Committee of the Whole, on the report of the Committee of Claims on the petition of Joseph Janney.

[Mr. Janney, a resident in the Northern Neck, in Virginia, represents, that, during the stay of the British in the Rappahannock river, in Virginia, they destroyed, in one of their incursions, his dwelling-house, &c., which were at the time occupied by the militia; and that he believes this destruction was solely caused by the fact of the buildings having been used for military purposes. For this loss he prays compensation. The committee report against his petition.]

Mr. GARNETT, of Virginia, moved to reverse the report, so as to declare that the prayer of the petition ought to be granted.   *

On this motion a smart debate took place between Mr. GARNETT on one side, and Mr. WILLIAMS, of North Carolina, on the other; which resulted in the rejection of Mr. GARNETT's motion, by a considerable majority, and the final concurrence in the original report of the committee.

The House then resolved itself into a Committee of the Whole, on the report of the Committee of Claims unfavorable to the petition of the levy court of Calvert county, Maryland, who ask indemnification for the loss of the courthouse of that county, destroyed by fire by the British during the late war in consequence of its having been occupied for military purposes.

Mr. NEALE, of Maryland, moved to reverse the report, so as to declare that the petition is reasonable and ought to be granted; and supported his motion with much earnestness. He was seconded by Mr. SMITH, of Maryland, and opposed by Mr. WILLIAMS, the chairman of the Committee of Claims.

The motion to amend was negatived by 61 votes to 49, and the original report concurred in by the same majority.

PUBLIC BUILDINGS.

The following Message was received from the PRESIDENT OF THE UNITED STATES:

To the Speaker of the House of Representatives:

In conformity with a resolution of the Senate of the 28th of January, 1818, I communicate herewith to the House of Representatives the report of the Commissioner of the Public Buildings, required by that resolution.

              JAMES MONROE.

WASHINGTON, *Nov.* 22, 1820.

To the President of the United States:

SIR: The expenditures on account of the centre building of the Capitol, from October 1, 1819, to the 30th of September, 1820, as far as regular vouchers have been received, amount to one hundred and twenty-seven thousand three hundred and ninety-six dollars and fourteen cents. For the progress made in this building, I beg leave to refer to the report of the Architect, a copy of which, marked A, is annexed.

I have the honor to be, most respectfully, your obedient servant,

              SAMUEL LANE,
      Commissioner of Public Buildings.

              A.

WASHINGTON, *Nov.* 19, 1820.

SIR: At the close of the season for active operations, I present a statement of the proceedings for the past year, and of the progress made on the Capitol of the United States.

The alterations and improvements suggested for the Representatives' Room and Senate Chamber have been effected within the amount of the estimated expense. Considerable progress has also been made in regulating and improving the grounds: the planting of trees and shrubbery will be continued while the weather will permit.

The work on the centre of the Capitol has been urged on with as much force and despatch as the solid nature of its construction would allow. The external walls of the west projection, and the greater part of the internal walls connected with them, have been raised to the height contemplated in the estimate for the year. The roof is raised on the north flank of the centre, and that for the south flank is prepared, but has been prevented from being put on by the inclemency of the weather in October, and by an unusual sickness among the workmen. The wall of the east front is not raised as high as was expected, from an opinion that it would be more advisable that the inner walls of the great rotunda should be carried on at the same time, for the purpose of making a more equal bearing, and pressing more regularly on the foundation. The walls of the rotunda have accordingly been commenced, and give an opportunity of viewing the style and manner in which it will be finished. Although a portion of the labor has been differently bestowed from what was first contemplated, yet it is believed that it will appear that the change was judicious, and that as much progress has been made in the work as was promised or expected; that it has been done with economy; and that the expense has been kept within the estimates.

Respectfully submitted by your obedient servant,
CHARLES BULFINCH,
Architect Capitol U. S.
Samuel Lane, *Esq., Commissioner, &c.*

The Message and report having been read, were ordered to lie on the table.

PROPOSED AMENDMENT TO THE CONSTITUTION.

On motion of Mr. Smith, of North Carolina, the House then resolved itself into a Committee of the Whole on the state of the Union; and, on motion of Mr. Smith, also, proceeded to the consideration of the motion, submitted by him, proposing an amendment to the Constitution of the United States, as it concerns the election of Electors of the President and Vice President of the United States.

The resolution having been read—

Mr. Smith, declining entering into any argument in support of the proposition, on which his views had been fully expressed at the last session, said, he had called up the question at this early day, in the hope that an expression of the opinion of the House on the subject might be obtained at this session. He added a few other remarks. This House and the Senate, he said, were not, he begged gentlemen to remember, the last resort on this question. All that was asked of them was, to allow the question to be submitted to the people of the United States, as represented in the several State Legislatures, the consent of two-thirds of whom was necessary to sanction the act. If two-thirds of the people were in favor of the amendment, it ought to take place; if, on the other hand, they deemed the change inexpedient, they would say so, and the proposition would of course fall to the ground.

Mr. Overstreet, of South Carolina, moved to amend the following clause, by striking out the words therein which are printed *in italic:*

"The Electors, when convened, at the time and place prescribed by law for the purpose of voting for President and Vice President of the United States, shall *have power,* in case any of them shall fail to attend, *to* choose an Elector, or Electors, in place of him, or them, so failing to attend."

The object of Mr. O. was, that there should be a certain uniformity on this point, as well as in others embraced by the proposed amendment to the Constitution.

After a few words in reply from Mr. Smith, the question was put on Mr. Overstreet's motion, and decided in the negative.

The Committee then rose, and, without further debate, reported the resolution without amendment.

Mr. Reid, of Georgia, then moved, with a view to allow further time for reflection on the subject, to lay the resolve on the table; which motion was decided in the affirmative by a vote of 67 to 64; and the resolve was laid on the table.

Tuesday, November 28.

Another member, to wit, from New York, James Guyon, junior, appeared and took his seat.

Mr. Simkins presented a memorial of sundry inhabitants of the upper country of the State of South Carolina; also, a memorial of the inhabitants of the district of Abbeville in that State, in opposition to any increase of the present tariff of duties on imports, by way of protection to the manufacturing interest of the country; which memorials were referred to the Committee on Manufactures.

Mr. Lowndes presented a memorial of sundry inhabitants of the District of Columbia, praying for the erection of suitable buildings for a penitentiary, and the establishment of a system of penitentiary jurisprudence within the said District; which was referred to the Committee for the District of Columbia.

On motion of Mr. Cannon, the bill of the last session, to provide for clothing the militia when called into actual service, was taken up, and recommitted to a Committee of the whole House.

Mr. Campbell, from the Committee on Private Land Claims, reported a bill to amend the act for the relief of the legal representatives of Henry Willis, deceased; and

Mr. Campbell, from the same committee reported a bill for the relief of Jacob Hunsinger; which bills were severally twice read and committed.

On motion of Mr. Tyler, the Committee on Commerce were instructed to inquire into the expediency of altering the Richmond collection district, so as to make the same extend from Bermuda Hundred to the mouth of Chickahomony river, including the shores of James river, on the north, as far as mid-channel.

On motion of Mr. Strong, of New York, the Postmaster General was directed to report, as soon as may be, to this House, a list, if any, of mail contractors who are at the same time postmasters, and the compensation of such contractors and postmasters, designating the State or Territory in which they respectively reside.

Mr. Stevens submitted the following motion:
Resolved, That the Committee on Public Lands be

directed to inquire and report whether, in their opinion, the public good requires that a tract of land be surveyed and appropriated for laying a road from the north boundary line of the State of Ohio to Detroit in a place most convenient for that purpose, and also sufficient to pay for working the same; and be further directed, if in their opinion such appropriation would be of public utility, to report a bill for that purpose.

Mr. S. made a few observations to show the utility and expediency of the object contemplated by his motion; and the resolution was agreed to.

On motion of Mr. ANDERSON, the report communicated to the Senate from the Secretary of the Treasury, transmitting (pursuant to a resolution of the Senate, of 3d of April, 1820,) a statement of money annually appropriated, and paid, since the Declaration of Independence, for purchasing from the Indians, surveying, and selling, the public lands; showing, as near as may be, the quantities of land which have been purchased; the number of acres which have been surveyed; the number sold, and the number which remain unsold; the amount of sales, the amount of forfeitures, the sums paid by purchasers, and the sums due from purchasers, and from receivers in each land district—was ordered to be printed for the use of this House.

On motion of Mr. STORRS,

Resolved, That the Secretary of the Treasury Department be directed to communicate to this House the amount of moneys drawn from the Treasury of the United States, by the War and Navy Departments, respectively, from the 30th day of December, 1819, to the 13th day of November instant, designating the amount drawn under each respective appropriation, together with an account of any transfers, which may have been made at the Treasury during the last recess of Congress, from one appropriation to any other; and, also, the aggregate amount of payments made during the same period by the Treasurer of the United States, as agent of the War and Navy Departments, respectively, on warrants drawn by the said Departments on the Treasurer as such agent, designating the amount of payments made under each head of appropriation, respectively, during the same period.

On motion of Mr. COOK, the Secretary of the Treasury was directed to lay before this House a statement of the number of claims to military bounty land, for services rendered during the late war which remain unsatisfied; the aggregate amount of acres necessary to satisfy those claims; and the time when the lands will be ready to be distributed among the respective claimants.

The SPEAKER laid before the House a letter from the Comptroller of the Treasury, transmitting a list of balances on the books of the Second and Third Auditors, which have remained due more than three years prior to the 30th September, 1820; a list of such persons as have failed to render their accounts to said auditors within the year; and a list of advances made prior to the 3d March, 1809, by the War Department, and which remained to be accounted for on the books of the Third Au-

ditor; which letter and accompanying documents were ordered to lie on the table.

JACOB SHAFER.

The House, then, on motion of Mr. B. SMITH, of Virginia, went into a Committee of the Whole, on the report of the Committee of Private Land Claims, made at the last session, unfavorable to the petition of Jacob Shafer to be confirmed in his claims to certain lands.

Mr. BALLARD SMITH moved to reverse the decision of that select committee, and declare the pra er of the petitioner, to a certain extent specified, such an one as ought to be granted; which motion he supported at some length.

Mr. CAMPBELL, chairman of the select committee, opposed the motion, and maintained the justice of the report.

Mr. SMITH rejoined; and, the question being taken, the motion to amend the report was negatived.

The Committee then rose, and the report was confirmed by the House.

VACCINE INSTITUTION.

The House, on motion of Mr. KENT, next resolved itself into a Committee of the Whole, on the bill to incorporate the Managers of the National Vaccine Institution.

Considerable time was spent in the details of this bill; in amending which, Mr. FOOT and Mr. KENT took the chief part; after which, the bill was reported to the House, and the amendments agreed to; when the question was taken on ordering the bill to be engrossed and read a third time, and was decided in the affirmative—yeas 51, nays 44.

The bill for the relief of Nicholas Jarrot, also passed through a Committee of the Whole, and being reported to the House, was ordered to be engrossed for a third reading.

LOAN OF MUNITIONS.

Mr. FORREST submitted the following, to wit:

Whereas it appears, by a report of the Secretary of War, dated the 12th day of February, 1820, made in pursuance of a resolution of the House of Representatives, that large loans of powder and lead, munitions of the United States, were made to private persons by the Ordnance department:

Therefore, resolved, that a select committee be appointed to inquire and report to this House, by whom the said loans were made; and by what authority; why the same was not reclaimed at the expiration of the loan; what time the said loans were reported to the head of the department, and, if a loss should be sustained, how far, and to whom is the responsibility attached for such loss. And, further, to report the proper mode of proceeding forthwith against such delinquent or delinquents, for the recovery of the same.

Mr. LOWNDES had not the smallest objection to the proposed inquiry; on the contrary, he was willing it should have the widest possible scope that should be deemed necessary; but he suggested to the mover the impropriety of prefixing to the motion a preamble which affirmed certain facts before they were ascertained to exist. The adoption of preambles was also at variance with the practice of the House, and, he believed, inconsistent with some of the rules of the House; and, with the view of obtaining such a modification of the motion as he had suggested it should assume, he moved that it be laid on the table until to-morrow; which course was assented to by Mr. FORREST, and the resolution was laid on the table accordingly.

WEDNESDAY, November 29.

On motion of Mr. McCoy, the Committee on Private Land Claims were instructed to inquire into the expediency of providing, by law, for the location of land warrants issued to the Virginia State regiments for services during the Revolutionary war, on any of the unappropriated lands in the tract reserved in the State of Ohio for satisfying the warrants to the Virginia State line on Continental Establishment.

Mr. COOK submitted the following resolution:

Resolved, That the Committee on the Public Lands be instructed to inquire into the expediency of making some provision whereby the actual settlers on the public lands, who settled previous to the 1st of July, 1820, shall be entitled to the preference in becoming the purchasers of a specified quantity, so as to embrace their improvements, at such price as may be deemed expedient.

The resolution was read, and the question was taken, Will the House agree thereto? and determined in the negative.

The Committee of the Whole, to which is committed the bill concerning navigation, and to repeal the act concerning navigation, passed April 18th, 1818, were discharged from the consideration thereof, and it was postponed indefinitely.

The engrossed bill for the relief of Nicholas Jarrot was read the third time, and, the question being put on its passage, it was decided in the negative, and the bill rejected.

The bill authorizing the President of the United States to cause astronomical observations to be made, to ascertain the longitude of the Capitol, in the City of Washington, from some known meridian in Europe, passed through a Committee of the Whole; and, after a few remarks in support of it by Mr. FOLGER, was ordered to be engrossed for a third reading, after a division, in which 65 members, being a decided majority of those present, voted for it.

The bill to amend the several acts providing for sick and disabled seamen, and for establishing navy hospitals, coming next in order, was, on motion of Mr. SMITH, of Maryland, recommitted to the Committee of Ways and Means.

The bill for the relief of Daniel Seward (for refunding to him the purchase-money paid for land bought from the United States, which it has been decided in a court of law that the Government had no right to sell, and also the cost of defending his title to the same) passed before a Committee of the Whole, being supported by Mr. ROSS, of Ohio, and was ordered to be engrossed for a third reading.

The House then resolved itself into a Committee of the Whole, on the bill for the relief of Perley Keyes and Jason Fairbanks. [This bill proposes to authorize the Secretary of the Treasury to cancel a certain bond given by the persons above named as security for Paymaster Whittlesey, a paymaster of the militia in the service of the United States, on their giving a bond in a different form—the object being to enable them to foreclose a mortgage against the property of Whittlesey, in order to indemnify them for the payment of a balance of four or five thousand dollars due from Whittlesey to the Government.]

The object of the bill having been explained by Mr. SMITH, of Maryland, at the request of Mr. TRIMBLE it was reported to the House, and ordered, without objection, to be engrossed, and read a third time.

The bill to amend the act for the relief of the legal representatives of Henry Willis, passed through a Committee of the Whole; and, after some debate on amendments proposed to it, was ordered to be engrossed for a third reading.

The House went into a Committee of the Whole, on the bill for the relief of Elias Parks, made some progress therein, and had leave to sit again.

REGULATION OF IMPORTS.

The House resolved itself into a Committee of the Whole, on the bill "further to regulate the entry of merchandise imported into the United States from any adjacent territory," reported at the last session.

Mr. SMITH, of Maryland, explained the circumstances which had appeared to the Committee of Ways and Means to render the passage of the bill necessary—the practice of smuggling on parts of the line between the United States and Canada having increased to a degree which called for the counteracting provisions embraced by the bill, which had been prepared with great care by the Committee of Ways and Means at the last session, and was supposed to be sufficient for its object.

Mr. TRACY conceived the bill would be superfluous on the statute book, as all its essential provisions were already in force in the existing revenue laws; to show which he entered into an examination of the provisions of existing laws, compared with those in the bill before the House.

Mr. TRIMBLE was in favor of the bill, supposing it possible that it might have a tendency to prevent smuggling, and being certain that it would not have a tendency to increase it. He said, however, that the dexterity of smugglers was not very easy to be defeated or counteracted. His object, however, in rising, was to inquire whether some additional provisions were not necessary for the prevention of smuggling on the Southern frontier, the temptations to which had been of late much increased by the heavy additional tonnage duty on French vessels.

Mr. SMITH, of Maryland, said, that it was possible that, since this bill was prepared at the last session, circumstances might have made additional provisions necessary. With the view to the examination of this point, on motion of Mr. S., the Committee rose and reported progress, and the bill was recommitted to the Committee of Ways and Means.

THURSDAY, November 30.

Two other members appeared, and took their seats, to wit: from Massachusetts EZEKIEL WHITMAN, and from Georgia WILLIAM TERRILL.

On motion of Mr. CAMPBELL, the Committee on the Post Office and Post Roads were directed to inquire into the expediency of so amending the 27th section of the act, entitled "An act regulating the Post Office Establishment," passed the 30th day of April, 1810, as to require the Postmaster General, in any contract he may enter into for the conveyance of the mail, to stipulate with the person with whom such contract is to be made to carry newspapers, magazines, and pamphlets, other than those conveyed in the mail.

Mr. WALKER submitted the following resolution:

Resolved, That the Committee on Revolutionary Pensions be instructed to inquire into the expediency of providing, by law, for placing on the pension list such persons as have, or may hereafter apply for pensions under the acts of Congress of the 18th of March, 1818, and 1st of May, 1820, who may not be found on the rolls of the respective States in which they enlisted, but who, nevertheless, may be able to adduce satisfactory proof, by their own oath or other testimony, that they did serve on the Continental Establishment in the Revolutionary war.

Mr. WALKER made a number of remarks in favor, and explanatory of the object of his motion; and, the question being put on agreeing to the resolution, it was negatived.

On motion of Mr. RANKIN, the Committee on the Judiciary were instructed to inquire into the expediency of changing the time of holding the district court of Mississippi, from the first Mondays in May and December, to the first Mondays in January and July.

On motion of Mr. CASE, the Secretary of State was directed to lay before this House such information as he may possess, or can obtain, relative to the annual amount of the fees of the clerks, district attorneys, and marshals, of the respective courts of the United States, the amount of whose fees do not appear in the "register of officers in the service of the United States;" and also the annual amount of the fees of naval officers, collectors, and surveyors of the customs, of the respective ports of the United States.

On motion of Mr. PHELPS, the Postmaster General of the United States was directed to report to this House the names of those persons who were indebted to his department on the 31st day of December, 1816, and the amount then due from each person; also the names of those who, since that time have become, and were indebted to that department on the 30th day of December last, and the amount then due from each person.

Engrossed bills of the following titles, to wit: An act for the relief of Perley Keyes and Jason

Fairbanks; and an act to amend the act, entitled "An act for the relief of the legal representatives of Henry Willis," were severally read the third time, and passed.

The engrossed bill for the relief of Daniel Seward was read the third time.

Mr. BALDWIN moved to lay the bill on the table, to allow further time to examine the principle it contained, doubting whether it had any example in the practice of the Government relative to grants.

The motion was opposed by Mr. ROSS, and negatived—yeas 57, nays 63.

Considerable debate then followed, on the merits of the bill, in which it was opposed by Messrs. BALDWIN and LINN, and was supported by Messrs. ANDERSON, ROSS, and BRUSH; and which ended by laying the bill, on motion of Mr. LINN, on the table.

The engrossed resolution to authorize the President of the United States to cause the necessary observations to be made to ascertain the longitude of the Capitol of the United States, was read the third time; and, after an unsuccessful motion by Mr. COCKE to lay it on the table, the question was taken on the passage of the resolution, and carried —yeas 61, nays 45; and it was ordered to be sent to the Senate for concurrence.

The House then, on motion of Mr. STORRS, went into a Committee of the Whole on the bill for the relief of Elias Parks, which was reported to the House, and, after a few remarks by Mr. STORRS in favor, and by Mr. WILLIAMS adverse to the bill, it was ordered to be engrossed for a third reading.

Mr. ROSS, who voted yesterday against the bill for the relief of Nicholas Jarrot, moved to reconsider the same, with a view to recommit it for amendment. And the question to reconsider the vote was decided in the affirmative, by a vote of 53 to 47. The bill was then recommitted to the Committee on Public Lands.

THE TARIFF PETITIONS.

Mr. BALDWIN, from the Committee on Manufactures, to which have been referred the memorials of sundry inhabitants of Belfast, in Maine, and of the merchants and others of Richmond, in Virginia, made a report thereon; which was read, and ordered to lie on the table.

The report is as follows:

The Committee on Manufactures, to whom have been referred the petitions of sundry inhabitants of Belfast, in Maine, and the merchants and others of Richmond, in Virginia, beg leave to report:

That the general object of these petitions is to remonstrate against the passage of the bills which were reported to this House at their last session, to regulate the duties on imports and for other purposes; to regulate the payment of duties on imported merchandise; and imposing a duty on sales at auction. As neither of these bills are now depending before either House of the Legislature, but have been either expressly or virtually rejected, it would, in an ordinary case, be deemed a sufficient answer to the petitions to say that their object had been already accomplished. It might too be deemed premature in a committee of this House, to whom these subjects had been referred at the present session, and who may feel it their duty to report on some of these bills, similar in their tendency to those of the last, to make any report on the matters embraced in these petitions, until the committee had agreed on recommending something for adoption. But there seems to the committee to be, in these petitions, something of a character perfectly novel, introduced in a manner, it is believed, so totally unprecedented in the legislative history of the country, as well as inconsistent with the respect due to the representatives of the nation, that it is felt to be a duty to notice them now.

In alluding to the foregoing bills, the petitioners from Belfast assert, that a repeal of the law of debenture, the abolition of drawbacks, formed a part of the system of these bills, and depict in glowing colors the ruinous effects on the commerce of the country, which would result, though they make no direct imputation of any intention.

The Richmond memorial is more explicit, as the House will observe from the following extract : " In the next place, let us inquire into the justice and policy of the prohibitory system recommended by the advocates of internal manufactures, who may be viewed, indeed, less as the advocates of manufactures, than as the enemies to foreign commerce and navigation ; for, to what other purpose can they have introduced the bills to repeal drawbacks on exportations, and to abolish the credits given on duties, but to assail our commerce in the most vital manner, and eventually to destroy it ?"

In considering these allegations of the petition, the committee feel great regret in being compelled to say, that they are utterly unsupported by fact, and contradicted by the bills referred to, so far as they relate to the subject of drawbacks. The present system of drawbacks and debenture was, in all its parts, retained in both the bills called the Tariff and Cash Payment, and in the latter new provisions inserted, which were intended and calculated to afford new and great facilities to the re-export trade of the country. The language of both bills was clear, explicit, and, to minds disposed to examine at all, capable of no misconstruction. One bill was reported in January, the other in March last. Both were printed by the order of the House ; they excited general interest throughout the nation ; were published ; laboriously and fully discussed, and would seem, on the subject of drawbacks, as little open to any misconception as any measures ever brought before the public. How it has happened that those who are so much alive to these measures, who indulge fears that they would prove fatal to commerce, agriculture, and revenue, should have been so profoundly ignorant of their nature, is to the committee most inconceivable. Respect for the petitioners forbids the imputation of any other motive.

It is to be expected that opinions will be variant as to the operations of important measures ; friends may be too sanguine as to their good, enemies too easily alarmed about their bad effects ; there must be freedom in their discussion, both as to their tendency, the principles on which they are supported, as well as the motives of their advocates. Those who are interested have a right to speak, by petition or remonstrance to their representatives, in plain, strong, and even bold language. This right is, and ought to be, sacred in a Republic, even without the guarantee of the Constitution. Opposition, of the most decided nature,

must not only be expected, but should be wished, by the friends of such measures, as the only mode by which their propriety and expediency could be in the first instance ascertained, and by which Congress would avoid the adoption of crude and ill-advised ones. As to the policy of the bills referred to, the committee forbear as well the expression of any opinion, as an examination of the reasons urged against their adoption. Should it be deemed their duty to offer them, or any of them, to the House, the occasion will be fairly presented to test the soundness of the objections, urged in the petitions with much zeal and no little feeling. But we cannot withhold the expression of our opinion, that it derogates from the respect due to this House ; that, by abusing it, it may impair the sacred right of petition and remonstrance, to either ignorantly or wilfully misrepresent the proceedings of any branch of the Government. It prevents the fair and legitimate action of public opinion, deceives and misleads the people, by directing their attention from what is really proposed to be adopted, to phantoms which exist only in the fears and ignorance of those who raise them. It is not for the committee to impute it as intentional ; but when misrepresentation exists and spreads, its source becomes immaterial ; in its effects, it equally tends to poison and inflame the minds of the people, excites causeless alarms, and creates an unfair, ungenerous hostility, which would not exist, if the subject were candidly stated and fairly explained.

Few cases ever occur which could more clearly show the bad consequences of this perversion and misstatement of the proceedings of the National Legislature. The assertion by some, and the belief by many, that it was a part of the system recommended by the Committee on Manufactures at the last session, to abolish the right of debenture and the whole system of drawbacks, would naturally create great alarm in all the commercial parts of the nation. If true, it would justify their most active opposition : the friends of commerce might fairly say, that its destruction was a leading, if not avowed object ; the feelings of the people would be justly roused, and conveyed to the Legislature in the strong, if not indignant voice of those who, feeling themselves assailed in their most vital interest, would act in self-defence in repelling an injury. The House can well judge of the burst of public indignation which would have been called forth had those bills contained the provisions attributed, when their existence only in the fancy and groundless fears of the petitioners have justified them, in their own minds, in their petitions addressed to this House, in assailing the motives and intentions of one of your committees. Had the petitioners understood these bills, had they known that they did not abolish or restrict, but retained, extended, and offered new subjects to the present system of drawbacks : provided a new and more enlarged one, leaving it at the option of the merchant to avail himself of either ; not prohibiting, but encouraging, the exportation of foreign produce, not by adding new, but removing existing impediments ; thus, so far from destroying, aiding, and assisting this important branch of a great national interest, the committee indulge, if not the belief, at least the hope, that a tone would have been given to public feeling different from what is expressed in the spirit of these petitions. When a committee, on their responsibility to the House, recommends, when the House, on its responsibility to the nation, adopts, a system which is

469   HISTORY OF CONGRESS.   470

DECEMBER, 1820.   *Clothing the Militia.*   H. OF R.

believed to be called for by the public exigencies, it is hoped that it is not expecting too much from those who complain, that they will view them as the acts, not of an individual, but of a public body of high trust, whose motives ought not to be questioned, at least not without even the color of truth; whose conduct, motives, public and recorded acts, should not be misrepresented; that it may be held responsible for its own conduct only, not for what exists not but in the minds of those who create, then so feelingly deprecate, their imaginary grievances; and that those who avail themselves of the right of petition should use no language which is not respectful, and make no imputations which are not true. If, with the means which this House has adopted to diffuse information on all interesting subjects, the measures which it proposes will not be examined or understood by those whom they affect, or, if understood, are misrepresented, the committee can recognise no right which they can thus have to publicly, and on its own records arraign this House for what they are pleased to call schemes, projects, and State machinery; to charge a committee with being the enemies of foreign commerce, and the design to assail, in the most vital manner, and eventually to destroy, by proposing and urging the abolition of drawbacks—a charge not only not supported, but contradicted, by the bills, the progress of which, one of the petitions says, has been witnessed with much concern.

It is our duty to listen to the voice of the people; to not only adopt such measures as may promote their welfare, but to abstain from such as impair it; but they owe a duty to us, not to impute what was not proposed—not to charge us with what was not attempted, but most solemnly disclaimed and disavowed.

So far as the petitions referred to the committee relate to matters which have been, or may be, reported on by them, they will deem it a duty to bestow on them their most respectful and serious attention; but so far as these petitions impute to this House, or its committee, a scheme which was developed and nearly matured at the last session of Congress, a part of which was designed to repeal the law of debenture, abolish drawbacks, and destroy the foreign commerce of the country, the committee owe it to themselves and the House to express their strong disapprobation of conduct which they hope has been hitherto without a precedent.

They therefore recommend the adoption of the following resolution:

Resolved, That the Committee on Manufactures be discharged from the further consideration of so much of the petitions referred to them as relates to the abolition of drawbacks.

CLOTHING THE MILITIA.

The House, on motion of Mr. CANNON, resolved itself into a Committee of the Whole on the bill to provide for clothing the militia of the United States when called into actual service.

The bill was so amended, on motion of Mr. CANNON, as to require the clothing provided for the militia, to be of such color or uniform as may be prescribed by the Legislatures of the respective States.

The bill, having been otherwise slightly amended, was reported to the House; where some debate took place on the question of concurrence in the above amendment.

It was argued, by Messrs. COBB and BRUSH, that it would introduce much perplexity in the arrangements for militia service, without producing any essential benefit.

In reply, Mr. CANNON vindicated his amendment, and, in general, defended the object of the bill, which served to place the militia, in some respect, on an equality of footing with the regular troops of the army, who are clothed, as well as fed, at the expense of Government.

Mr. GROSS, of New York, concurred in Mr. CANNON's general views, but thought the amendment would be more properly introduced in a different part of the bill.

Mr. FLOYD wished the bill to lie on the table until a report, called for at the last session, was received from the War Department, of the number of militia who were in service during the late war, which would afford some data by which the expenditure that would arise from this bill could be estimated, which would probably amount to more than the National Treasury could satisfy. On this ground, and others, he thought the bill ought not to pass; but, if it did pass, it ought not to be without more satisfactory information on the subject, &c. Mr. F., therefore, moved to lay the bill on the table.

Mr. CANNON opposed this motion, fearing that the effect of it would be, by procrastination, to defeat the bill.

The question on laying the bill on the table was decided in the affirmative, by a vote of 71 to 51.

FRIDAY, December 1.

Another member, to wit: from North Carolina, WILLIAM DAVIDSON, appeared and took his seat.

Mr. BROWN presented a petition of sundry inhabitants of the State of Kentucky, purchasers of lands of the United States, stating that they have paid one or more instalments and are unable to pay the subsequent instalments as they become due, and praying for the passage of an act remitting the back interest on the several instalments prior to the time they respectively became due, and giving to the purchaser the privilege, at any time within one year after the passage of the act, of surrendering such portion of the land as he may be unable to pay for, and granting him a patent for as much land as the payments made will amount to at the purchase price, allowing the usual discounts for prompt payment; which was referred to the Committee on the Public Lands.

Mr. JONES, of Tennessee, from the select committee appointed on the petition of Daniel McDuff, made a report thereon, and, by leave of the House, accompanied such report with a bill for his relief; which was read twice, and committed to a Committee of the Whole.

On motion of Mr. EDWARDS, of Connecticut, the Committee on the Judiciary were directed to inquire into the expediency of authorizing the marshal of the district of Connecticut to make use of Newgate prison, in the State of Connecticut, for the purpose of confining and safe keeping any prisoner or prisoners who have been, or hereafter may be, sentenced to imprisonment and labor in any court of the United States within the district of Connecticut, for the violation of any act or acts of the Congress of the United States.

The engrossed bill for the relief of Elias Sparks having been put on its passage—

Mr. WILLIAMS, of North Carolina, rose in opposition to the bill, on the ground of a defect of evidence in support of the claim, contending that the evidence was not the best that the nature of the case would admit of.

A good deal of debate ensued on this bill, in which Mr. WILLIAMS of North Carolina, went into a minute examination of the claim of the petitioner. He was replied to by Mr. STORRS, at considerable length; and some remarks were added also by Mr. RICH in favor of the bill.

The question being taken on the passage of the bill, was decided in the affirmative; and the bill was sent to the Senate for concurrence.

Mr. SMITH, of North Carolina, gave notice that he should, on Monday, move the consideration of the resolution introduced by him to amend the Constitution of the United States.

Mr. LOWNDES gave notice that he should, on Wednesday next, move for the consideration of the resolution declaring the admission of the State of Missouri into the Union.

VACCINE INSTITUTION.

The engrossed bill to incorporate the Managers of the National Vaccine Institution, was read the third time; and, on the question of its passage—

Mr. LIVERMORE, of New Hampshire, moved to recommit the bill, so as to allow of its being amended in one particular, and thus obviating the only objection which he had to its passage. His object was to incorporate in the bill the words "within the District of Columbia." There was not a general agreement of opinion as to the power of Congress to establish corporations to pervade the United States; but there was no doubt of its power within the District, to which therefore he wished expressly to limit the corporate authority proposed to be conferred by this bill.

Mr. FLOYD, of Virginia said, he saw no unconstitutional feature in the bill, which he hoped, therefore, would be permitted to pass as it stood. The object of the bill was to aid in the eradication of the small pox from our country—an object which all must admit to be not only innocent but laudable. The gentleman who had been most earnest in asking from Congress the passage of this bill had devoted himself to this object with a perseverance seldom exceeded, and with desirable success. To enable those who took an interest in this matter to avail themselves of the donations of charitable persons in all parts of the United States, it was necessary that a company should be incorporated, with power to erect the necessary buildings.

Mr. KENT, of Maryland said, the gentleman from New Hampshire appeared to be under some misapprehension in relation to the bill first read. By its provisions, said Mr. K., the National Vaccine Institution is to be established here, and this provision renders unnecessary the gentleman's proposition. It will be recollected by the House that, some years past, the appointment of an agent for vaccination was authorized by law, with the privilege of franking his letters; and, although this measure gave some facility in the transmission of vaccine matter to the different parts of the country, yet it was found too limited in its effects for the accomplishment of an object fraught with such incalculable benefits to the community. Hence, the citizens of several of the adjacent States were induced to accept of a proposition made by Dr. Smith, to establish an institution here in the capital of the country, from whence should issue gratuitously the vaccine matter to such States, counties, or towns, as should subscribe a certain amount for the establishment and encouragement of this institution; by which means every class in society, the poor as well as the rich, would receive the matter free of expense. In six of the adjacent States $26,000 were subscribed on the 1st day of January last, and no doubt a considerable addition has been made during the present year to that sum. These subscriptions have been made to Dr. Smith, who is the agent for vaccination; and, in the event of his death, without the passage of some such bill as the one before you, would be lost to those who made them with such benevolent views. The bill does not propose to take from the Treasury one dollar, its only object is to withdraw from the hands of Dr. Smith the whole amount of those subscriptions, and place them under the control and direction of six discreet, judicious managers, who are named in the bill, and whose successors are to be appointed by the President of the United States. It has been under the hope of the securing the full benefit of such liberal subscriptions, that I have been induced to advocate the bill, and now ask for the concurrence of the House in its passage.

Mr. BURWELL, of Virginia, was opposed to the recommitment, on different ground from that taken by other gentlemen. He adverted to a construction which had been recently put upon the powers of Congress within the States, (in the case of the lotteries authorized by Congress,) and said that he believed that construction was too absurd to be entertained by many men of sense in this country, and he regarded it as very unfortunate that such a construction had been sanctioned by the names of any men of sense and character. Believing that Congress had not the power to make this law operative within the States, and that inserting the words proposed might, by implication, give countenance to what he considered the most dangerous and absurd construction ever given to the Constitution, he was opposed to limiting, by words in the bill, what he considered as already limited by the Constitution.

Mr. LIVERMORE said he was as friendly to the object of this bill as any gentleman within these walls, and he had no desire to impede its passage. But, he said, Congress have a power within the

District which they have not beyond it. They have here the power of exclusive legislation; beyond it, they have not that power. Within this District, he did not know that their power was any thing less than absolute. He did not know of any restraints upon it but reason and a sound discretion. It was a question whether Congress had the power to extend a corporate authority into the States; and he did not see that the remarks of gentlemen in favor of the bill had obviated the difficulty. A corporation inhabits a house not made by man; it inhabits all space—it is everywhere and nowhere. It has no body, as it is sometimes said to have no soul. For his part he wished this charter to be restricted to the District of Columbia, where almost every anomalous thing was to be found.

Mr. MERCER, of Virginia, opposed the recommitment of the bill, on the ground that such a course would have the effect to give it a quietus for the remainder of the session, especially after the notice this morning given by Mr. LOWNDES. Mr. M. said he concurred with his colleague in his view of the recent opinion of some gentlemen learned in the law, on the subject of the powers of Congress. He did not see, however, how, by by possibility, the passage of this bill could countenance that opinion. Mr. M. referred to the nature of the bill, and its unobjectionable character, as arguments in favor of its passing the House, and without recommitment.

Mr. COOK suggested a modification of the question, so as to propose a recommitment of the bill to the Committee on the District of Columbia, with instructions to report the specific amendment suggested by Mr. LIVERMORE.

Mr. LIVERMORE having assented to putting the question in this shape—

It was so put and negatived.

And the bill was passed, and sent to the Senate for concurrence.

MISSOURI EXPEDITION.

Mr. COCKE, of Tennessee, rose to present a proposition to the House. When looking into the expenditures of the last year, he said he found the account of Colonel James Johnson for transportation furnished the expedition ordered up the Missouri river. The gross amount of it, said Mr. C. is $256,818 15. Several items in this account require at least explanation. I find the sum of $333 37 per day, for forty days, charged for the detention of steamboat expedition, amounting in the whole to $13,333 33⅓. In addition to this, $200 per day, for thirty-six days, is claimed for the detention of steamboat Johnson, amounting to the sum of $7,200. The sum charged for detention alone of those two boats, for less than one month and a half, is $20,633 33⅓. He called the attention of the House, also, to some other items in this account. It appeared, he said, that three hundred officers and soldiers procured a passage, on board Colonel Johnson's boats, from Belle Fontaine to Council Bluffs, about four hundred miles, at $50 each, making the sum of $15,000 for passage alone. The sum demanded by Colonel Johnson for detention of boats and passage of three hundred men

employed on this expedition, is $35,533 33⅓. By what means the residue of the Missouri detachment found their way to Council Bluffs, said Mr. C., I am at a loss to determine, but no doubt on terms equally advantageous to the public. Knox, Haldiman & Co., contracted and furnished transportation to the Council Bluffs for the sum of $5 50 per hundred pounds. Colonel Johnson charges, for transportation to the same place, $16 25 per hundred pounds; almost three times the amount paid Knox, Haldiman & Co. for similar services. I am informed those charges have been allowed, and the account liquidated and paid. I trust the information is erroneous. Permit me to ask, was not Colonel Johnson contractor to furnish supplies as well as transportation? Why, then, the delay? Why pay a large amount for detention? This, Mr. C. said, is the expedition the President himself takes very great interest in the success of, and is willing to take great responsibility to insure it. This is the expedition that was to protect the frontier and fur trade, acquire for the United States lasting influence over the savages of Missouri, raise corn in Summer, improve navigation in Winter, and result in saving to Government, in four years, the sum of $42,485 84. The estimated cost for transportation of this favorite project, as reported to Congress at the last session, was $162,994. The sum claimed by Colonel Johnson, and he was told actually paid, is $256,818 15. To ascertain with certainty the amount actually paid for transportation and detention of boats on the Missouri expedition, and the reasons why it was paid, he offered the following resolution:

Resolved, That the Secretary of War be directed to communicate to this House what sums of money have been actually paid to Colonel James Johnson, on account of transportation furnished the expedition ordered up the Missouri river; and also what sums have been paid him for detention of steamboats or other incidental charges; whether any difference of opinion existed between the Department of War and said Colonel J. Johnson, relative to the value of transportation or other charges exhibited by him against the United States; if any differences existed, how were they adjusted; if by reference, who were the referees; what was their award, and what evidence was submitted to them, on which they formed their award.

Mr. TRIMBLE, of Kentucky, said he did not profess to know any thing on the subject of this resolve but what he was about to state. The account first preferred by Colonel James Johnson, he had understood, had been thought too high. Some discussion on that point took place between him and the Secretary of War, and he authorized his friend and brother to assent to a reference of the points in dispute to arbitrators, to be chosen, one by each party, the third by those two. Three arbitrators were accordingly chosen—gentlemen of the first standing and of the highest respectability, who passed upon the accounts. They reduced very considerably the amount claimed by Mr. Johnson, and the amount paid to him was the amount awarded in his favor by the referees. Thus much he had heard, and, as an impression adverse to him might be drawn from the gentleman's remarks, though not intended by him, Mr. T. said he had thought it proper to say thus much in behalf of Colonel Johnson, who had ever been believed to be an honest man.

Mr. Cocke said, it was far from him to question the honesty of any man whatever, in what he had said. He disclaimed any such intention. But it seemed extraordinary to him how the allowance referred to had been made without the authority of Congress. On looking into Colonel Johnson's contract, he did not find that any provision was made for allowance for the detention of steamboats. He had understood, too, that Col. James Johnson was a contractor, not only for transportation, but for supplies of provisions. If this were true, Mr. C. said, he should like to know how it did happen that the boats were detained, and whether it was in consequence of the neglect of Colonel Johnson to furnish the provisions in proper time. Not being included in the contract, application ought to have been made to this House to authorize the allowance which has been made to Colonel Johnson without its authority. Mr. C. said he should make no observations with regard to this arbitration, which was spoken of. If the matter had been referred to these exalted arbitrations, let the House know it. Why refuse the information which it was desirable to acquire in relation to it? The resolution, he said, was predicated on accounts transmitted to Congress at the last session, and he did not see why there should be any wish on the part of the gentleman from Kentucky to oppose its adoption.

Mr. Lowndes remarked, that the gentleman from Tennessee must have mistaken the gentleman from Kentucky, if he supposed there was, on his part, or on that of any other member, any objection to the object of this resolution calling for information. There could be no objection to it. But, Mr. L. said, he submitted it to the House and to the gentleman from Tennessee, whether, in calling for information on any subject, it was proper to accompany that call with animadversions on the conduct of those whose conduct could only be properly judged when the information itself was before them. Mr. L. added another remark or two of the same tone as the preceding, which were not distinctly heard by the reporter.

On motion of Mr. Rich, with the consent of Mr. Cocke, the resolution was amended so as to require an account also of the causes of the detention of the steamboats.

Mr. Trimble rose to say, that he did not intend to object to any information which might be sought for by the gentleman from Tennessee, or any other member of the House. It was not his habit to do so; and it was not his disposition to do so on the present occasion. On the contrary, he said he was sure the inquiry would meet with the approbation of even Colonel James Johnson, could his wishes be consulted. Without knowing the fact, Mr. T. said, he thought it quite likely that Colonel Johnson may have thought that he, and not the Government, had a right to complain of the manner in which his accounts were liqui-

dated. Mr. T. said he should not have opened his lips on this subject, had he not thought that the statement made by the gentleman from Tennessee might—though he was sure the gentleman could not possibly intend it—give a color to an imputation on the character of Colonel Johnson.

Mr. Cocke rejoined in a few words more, in the course of which he said he was sorry that any gentleman should suppose that he wished to cast an imputation on any man. It was not so, he said; he wished to ascertain what were the facts in the case referred to, without any personal views or motives, &c.

The question was then taken on the adoption of the resolve, and agreed to, without a dissenting voice.

MONDAY, December 4.

Another member, to wit: from Massachusetts, Nathaniel Silsbee, appeared and took his seat.

Mr. Silsbee presented a petition of the President and Directors of the United States Naval Fraternal Association, for the relief of the families of deceased officers, praying for an act of incorporation for the said association; which was referred to the Committee on Naval Affairs.

On motion of Mr. Williams, of North Carolina, the petition of the children and representatives of the late General Baron de Kalb, presented on the 10th of December, 1819, was referred to the Committee on Pensions and Revolutionary Claims.

On motion of Mr. Forrest, the House proceed to consider his motion for requiring information from the War Department respecting certain loans of gunpowder, &c.; and the same, having been modified by striking out the preamble, was agreed to.

On motion of Mr. Darlington, the Secretary of the Treasury was directed to report to this House the amount of fines certified to the Comptroller of that department, to have been imposed upon the militia of Pennsylvania, for neglect of duty, during the late war with Great Britain; the amount of said fines which has been levied and collected by the marshals of the respective districts in that State, or their deputies; and the amount thereof which has been actually paid into the Treasury of the United States; also, what proceedings, if any, have been instituted for the recovery of moneys thus collected within said districts, and not yet received at the Treasury.

Mr. Mercer submitted the following:

Resolved, That President of the United States be requested to lay before this House any correspondence that he does not deem it inexpedient to disclose, which may have existed between the Executive of the United States and the Governments of any of the maritime Powers of Europe, in relation to the African slave trade.

The question thereon, being taken without debate, was agreed to without a division; and a committee was ordered to be appointed to present the same to the President.

Mr. Eustis, of Massachusetts, after some introductory remarks, in the course of which he contrasted the old system of the Pension Establishment with that which had more recently prevailed, advantageously to the former, proposed the following resolve:

Resolved, That the Committee on Pensions and Revolutionary Claims be instructed to report a bill, providing that, from and after the 4th day of March next ensuing, no officer, soldier, seaman, marine, or other person whatsoever, shall be placed on the pension list of the United States, except by virtue of a law in which the name of the pensioner shall be inserted, together with the amount of pension to which he shall be entitled.

The resolution being read—

Mr. LOWNDES rose, not to object to the principle of the resolution, thinking it probable that the long experience of the mover would enable him to suggest valuable improvements on the present system, but to suggest, as the resolution was affirmative, and not proposing inquiry merely, that, with a view to deliberation, it should lie on the table one day.

Mr. EUSTIS assenting to this course, the resolution was, after a few words from Mr. RHEA, indicative of hostility to it, ordered to lie on the table.

MACKEREL FISHERY.

Mr. SMITH, of Maryland, from the Committee of Ways and Means, reported the following bill:

A bill for enrolling, and licensing, and granting allowances to ships or vessels to be employed in the mackerel fishery, and for the government of persons concerned therein.

Be it enacted, &c., That all acts and parts of acts now in force for the enrollment, and licensing of, and granting allowances to, ships or vessels employed in the bank and other cod fisheries, and for the government of persons concerned therein, be, and the same are hereby, extended, in all their provisions and limitations, to vessels that shall hereafter be employed, and the persons who shall hereafter be concerned in the mackerel fishery; excepting only so much of said acts as fixes the rate of allowance to vessels exclusively employed in the bank and other cod fisheries: and that, from and after the passing of this act, there shall be paid, on the last day of December annually, to the owner of every fishing boat or vessel, or his agent, by the collector of the district where such boat or vessel may belong, that shall be qualified agreeably to law for carrying on the mackerel fishery, or the cod and mackerel fishery, and that shall actually have been employed in the mackerel, or in the cod and mackerel fishery, at sea, for the term of four months at least of the fishing season next preceding, which fishing season is accounted to be from the last day of February to the last day of November in every year, on each and every ton of such boat's or vessel's burden, according to her admeasurement, as licensed or enrolled, three dollars: *Provided,* That the allowance aforesaid, on any one vessel, for one season, shall not exceed two hundred dollars.

SEC. 2. *And be it further enacted,* That when any vessel is intended to be employed exclusively in the mackerel fishery, or in the cod and mackerel fishery, the words " mackerel fishery," or the words " cod and mackerel fishery," as the case may be, shall be inserted in the license by the collector granting the

same; and that as much of the act entitled "An act laying a duty on imported salt, granting a bounty on pickled fish exported, and allowances to certain vessels employed in the fisheries," passed July 29, 1813, as grants a bounty on pickled mackerel exported, be, and the same is hereby, repealed.

The bill was twice read, and committed.

CASE OF MATTHEW LYON.

Mr. McLEAN, of Kentucky, from the committee appointed on the memorial of Matthew Lyon, made a report thereon, accompanied with a bill for his relief; which, by leave of the House, was presented, read the first and second time, and committed to a Committee of the Whole to-morrow. The report is as follows:

The petitioner states that, in violation of that provision of the Constitution of the United States of America which says " Congress shall make no law abridging the freedom of speech or of the press," Congress, in July, 1798, passed the act commonly called the sedition law; that, some time previous to the passage of this bill, there appeared in the Philadelphia Federal papers a violent attack upon his character, extracted from the Vermont Journal, charging him with many political enormities, particularly with the high crime of opposing the Executive; that he wrote a reply to this charge in Philadelphia, on the 20th of June, 1798, and on the same day put the letter, directed to the editor of the said Vermont Journal, into the post office at Philadelphia, twenty-four days before the passage of the sedition law. For the publication of this letter he was indicted in October following, in the circuit court of the United States in the Vermont district. In the same indictment, he was charged with publishing a copy of a letter from an American diplomatic character in France to a member of Congress in Philadelphia; also for aiding, assisting, and abetting in the publication of said letter.

He states said letter was written by Joel Barlow to Abraham Baldwin, then a member of Congress. He denies that he printed said letter, or aided or abetted in the printing of it; but, on the contrary, that he used his endeavors to suppress it, by destroying the copies which came into his possession. He states that, owing to the political party zeal which prevailed in the United States at that time, much unfairness was used in the trial, both by the marshal in summoning the jury, and the judge who presided, in his instructions to them, and thereby a verdict of guilty was returned against him by the jury; and upon that verdict the court sentenced him to pay a fine of $1,000, the costs of suit, be imprisoned four calendar months, and until the fine and costs were paid. He states that, by virtue of said judgment, he was arrested and confined in a dungeon, the common receptacle of thieves and murderers, fifty miles distant from the place of his trial, although there was a decent roomy jail in the county in which he lived, and in the town where the trial was had, which jail the Federal Government had the use of; that much severity was exercised towards him during his imprisonment; that he languished in the loathsome prison more than six weeks in the months of October, November, and December, in the cold climate of Vermont, without fire, before he was allowed, at his own expense, to introduce a small stove, or to put glass into the aperture which let in a small glimmer of light through the iron grate.

He states that he is poor, and asks Congress to refund to him $1,000, the fine which he has paid, the costs of suit, for one hundred and twenty-three days' pay as a member of Congress, while he was unconstitutionally detained from a seat in that body, reasonable damages for being suddenly deprived of his liberty, put to great expense, and disabled from paying that attention to his concerns which, in other circumstances, he would have been allowed to do, and such interest on those sums as public creditors are entitled to.

Your committee state that the prosecution against the said petitioner, the judgment, imprisonment, and payment of $1,000, the fine, and $60 96, the costs of suit, are proved by a copy of the record of proceedings in said cause, which is made a part of this report. The committee are of opinion that the law of Congress under which the said Matthew Lyon was prosecuted and punished was unconstitutional, and therefore he ought to have the money which has been paid by him refunded ; but, should they be mistaken as to the unconstitutionality of this law, yet they think there are peculiar circumstances of hardship attending this case which call for relief. Your committee, therefore, ask leave to report a bill.

The President of the United States to all who shall see these presents, greeting :

Know ye, that among the pleas of our circuit court of the second circuit of the United States, in the Vermont district, there is a certain record remaining, in the words following, to wit :

UNITED STATES OF AMERICA,

     Vermont District, to wit :

Pleas of the circuit court of the said United States, at their term begun and held at Rutland, within and for the said Vermont district, on Wednesday, the 3d day of October, in the year of our Lord 1798, and of the independence of the United States the twenty-third, before the honorable William Patterson, esq., one of the associate justices of the Supreme Court of the United States, and the honorable Samuel Hitchcock, esq., district judge within and for the said Vermont district, and judges of said circuit court, according to the form of the statute in such case made and provided.

United States *versus* Matthew Lyon.

Be it remembered that, at a term of the circuit court of the said United States, begun and held at Rutland, within and for the district aforesaid, on the third day of October, in the year of our Lord one thousand seven hundred and ninety-eight, and of the independence of the said United States the twenty-third, before the honorable William Patterson, esq., one of the associate justices of the Supreme Court of the said United States, and the honorable Samuel Hitchcock, esq., district judge within and for the said district of Vermont, judges of the said circuit court, according to the form of the statute in such case made and provided, the grand jurors within and for the body of said district of Vermont, to wit: Eli Cogswell, Nathan Pratt, David Osgood, Ozias Fuller, Royal Crafts, Abner Mead, Gideon Horton, Abraham Gilbert, Ebenezer Worster, John Mott, Thomas Hammond, Adgate Lothrop, John Penfield, Ebenezer Hopkins, Brewster Higly, Zadock Remington, Abijah Brownson, and Joel Culver, good and lawful freeholders of the said district, then and there empannelled, sworn, and

charged, to inquire, for the said United States, and for the body of the district aforesaid, did present, that Matthew Lyon, of Fairhaven, in the said district of Vermont, being a malicious and seditious person, and of a depraved mind and wicked and diabolical disposition, and deceitfully, wickedly, and maliciously contriving to defame the Government of the United States, and with intent and design to defame the said Government of the United States, and John Adams, the President of the United States, and to bring the said Government and President into contempt and disrepute ; and with intent and design to excite against the said Government and President the hatred of the good people of the United States, and to stir up sedition in the United States, at Windsor, in the said district of Vermont, on the 31st day of July last, did, with force and arms, wickedly, knowingly, and maliciously write, print, utter, and publish, and did then and there cause and procure to be written, printed, uttered, and published, a certain scandalous and seditious writing, or libel, in form of a letter, directed to Mr. Spooner, [meaning Alden Spooner, printer and publisher of a certain weekly newspaper, in Windsor aforesaid, commonly called Spooner's Vermont Journal,] signed by the said Matthew Lyon, and dated at Philadelphia, on the 20th day of June last ; in which said libel of and concerning the said John Adams, President of the United States, and the Executive Government of the United States, are contained, among other things, divers scurrilous, feigned, false, scandalous, seditious, and malicious matters, according to the tenor following, to wit : " As to the Executive, [meaning the said President of the United States,] when I shall see the effects of that power [meaning the executive power of the United States, vested by the Constitution of the United States in the said President] bent on the promotion of the comfort, the happiness, and accommodation of the people, [meaning the people of the United States,] that Executive [meaning the President of the United States] shall have my [meaning the said Matthew Lyon's] zealous and uniform support. But whenever I [meaning the said Matthew Lyon] shall, on the part of the Executive, [meaning the said John Adams, President of the United States,] see every consideration of public welfare swallowed up in a continual grasp for power, in an unbounded thirst for ridiculous pomp, foolish adulation, or selfish avarice ; [meaning that, on the part of the said John Adams, President of the United States, every consideration of the public welfare was swallowed up in a continual grasp for unconstitutional power, and in an unbounded thirst for ridiculous pomp, foolish adulation, and selfish avarice ;] when I [meaning the said Matthew Lyon] shall behold men of real merit daily turned out of office, for no other cause but independency of sentiment ; [meaning that men of real merit, holding offices under the laws and Constitution of the United States, were daily, by the said John Adams, as President of the United States, turned out of office for the cause of having independency of spirit ;] when I [meaning the said Matthew Lyon] shall see men of firmness, merit, years, abilities, and experience, discarded in their applications for office, for fear they possess that independence, and men of meanness preferred, for the ease with which they can take up and advocate opinions, the consequence of which they know but little of; [meaning that men of firmness, years, merit, ability, and experience, were, by the said John Adams, as President of the United States, in violation of the duties of his said office, neglected in appointments to office under the laws and Constitution of the United States, and discarded in their applications for such offices and appointments; and that men of meanness, who are unfit for the exercise of such offices, under the laws and constitution of the United States, were, by the said John Adams, as President of the United States, preferred to such offices and appointments, on account of the ease with which they took and advocated opinions, of the consequences of which they were ignorant;] when I [meaning the said Matthew Lyon] shall see the sacred name of religion employed as a State engine to make mankind hate and persecute one another, I [meaning the said Matthew Lyon] shall not be their humble advocate;" [meaning that the sacred name of religion was, by the said John Adams, in his capacity of President of the United States, employed as an engine of State to make mankind hate and persecute each other:] to the great scandal and infamy of the said John Adams in his capacity of President of the United States, and to the great scandal and infamy of the said Government of the said United States. And so the jurors aforesaid, upon their oaths aforesaid, do say that the said Matthew Lyon, at Windsor aforesaid, on the 31st day of July aforesaid, did, knowingly, wickedly, deceitfully, and maliciously, with intent and design to defame the said Government of the United States, and the said John Adams, President of the United States, and to bring the said Government and President of the United States into contempt and disrepute with the good people of the United States, and to excite against them, the said Government and President of the United States, the hatred of the good people of the United States, and with intent and design to stir up sedition within the United States against the Government thereof, write, print, utter, and publish, and cause and procure to be written, printed, uttered, and published, for the purpose aforesaid, the said false, feigned, scandalous, and malicious writing and libel aforesaid, containing, among other things, the said divers scurrilous, false, feigned, scandalous, seditious, and malicious matters aforesaid, in contempt of the good and wholesome laws of the United States, to the evil and pernicious example of others in like case offending against the statute of the United States in such case made and provided, and against the peace and dignity of the United States.

And the jurors aforesaid, upon their oaths aforesaid, do further present, that the said Matthew Lyon, being a malicious and seditious person, and of a depraved mind, and of a wicked and diabolical disposition, and also deceitfully, wickedly, and maliciously contriving to defame the Government of the said United States, and with intent and design to defame the said Government, and with intent to defame John Adams, Esquire, President of the United States, and with intent to defame the Senate of the United States, being one branch of the Congress of the United States, and to bring the said Government, President, and Senate into contempt and disrepute, and to excite against the said Government, President and Senate the hatred of the good people of the United States, and with intent and design to stir up sedition within the United States, did, at Fairhaven, in the said district of Vermont, on the 1st day of September now last past, with force and arms, wickedly, knowingly, and maliciously write, print, utter, and publish, and then and there did cause and procure to be written,

printed, uttered, and published, a certain false, feigned scandalous, and seditious writing, or libel, entitled " Copy of a letter from an American diplomatic character in France to a member of Congress in Philadelphia," in which said writing, or libel, of and concerning the said Government of the United States, and the said President and Senate of the United States, and of and concerning the speech of John Adams, Esquire, then President of the United States, and of and concerning the answer of the said Senate to the said speech, are contained, among other things, divers scurrilous, feigned, false, scandalous, seditious, and malicious matters, according to the tenor following, to wit : " The misunderstanding between the two Governments [meaning the Governments of the said United States and France] has become extremely alarming ; confidence is completely destroyed ; mistrusts, jealousy, and a disposition to a wrong attribution of motives are so apparent, as to require the utmost caution in every word and action that are to come from your Executive, [meaning the Executive Government of the United States]—I mean if your object is to avoid hostilities. Had this truth been understood with you [meaning the people of the United States] before [the] recall of Monroe, [meaning James Monroe, the late Ambassador from the United States to the Republic of France,] before the coming and second coming of Pinckney, [meaning Charles C. Pinckney, one of the late Envoys Extraordinary from the United States to the said Republic of France ;] had it guided the pens that wrote the bullying speech of your President [meaning the said speech of John Adams, then and still President of the United States, to both Houses of Congress at the opening of their session in November, 1797] and stupid answer of your Senate, [meaning the Senate of the United States, being one House of the Congress of the United States,] at the opening of Congress [meaning the Congress of the United States] in November last, [meaning at the session of the said Congress in November, in the year of our Lord 1797,] I should probably have had no occasion to address you this letter, [meaning the said writing or libel ;] but when we found him [meaning the said John Adams, President as aforesaid] borrowing the language of Edmund Burke, and telling the world that, although he should succeed in treating with the French, [meaning the Government of France,] there was no dependence to be placed on any of their engagements, [meaning the engagements of the said Government of France ;] that their religion and morality [meaning the religion and morality of the French nation] were at an end ; that they [meaning the French nation] had turned pirates and plunderers, and it would be necessary to be perpetually armed against them, [meaning the said French nation ;] though you are at peace, we [meaning the people of France] wondered that the answer of both Houses [meaning both Houses of the Congress of the United States] had not been an order to send him [meaning the said John Adams, Esquire, President of the United States] to a mad-house. Instead of this, the Senate [meaning the Senate of the United States] have echoed the speech [meaning the said speech of the said John Adams, as President of the United States] with more servility than ever George the Third [meaning the King of Great Britain] experienced from either House of Parliament," [meaning the Parliament of Great Britain ;] to the great scandal and infamy of the said Government of the said United States, and the said John Adams, President of the United States, and the said Senate of the United States, being one of the

Houses of the Congress of the United States. And so the jurors aforesaid, upon their oaths aforesaid, do say that the said Matthew Lyon, at Fairhaven aforesaid, on the 1st day of September aforesaid, did, knowingly, wickedly, deceitfully, and maliciously, with intent and design to defame the said Government of the United States, and the said John Adams, President of the United States, and the Senate, being one House of the Congress of the United States, and to bring the said Government, President, and Senate of the United States into great contempt and disrepute with the people of the United States, and to excite against them, the said Government, President, and Senate of the United States, the hatred of the good people of the said United States, and with intent to stir up sedition within the United States against the Government thereof, write, print, utter, and publish, and cause and procure to be written, printed, uttered, and published, for the purpose aforesaid, the said false, feigned, scandalous, and malicious writing and libel aforesaid, containing, among other things, the said divers scurrilous, false, feigned, scandalous, and seditious matters aforesaid, in contempt of the good and wholesome laws of the United States, to the evil and pernicious example of others in like case offending against the statute of the United States in such case made and provided, and against the peace and dignity of the said United States.

And the jurors aforesaid, upon their oaths aforesaid, do further present, that the said Matthew Lyon, being a malicious man, of a depraved mind, and of a wicked and diabolical disposition, and also deceitfully, wickedly, and maliciously contriving to defame the Government of the said United States, and with intent and design to defame the said Government, and the said John Adams, Esquire, President of the said United States, and the Senate, being one of the Houses of the Congress of the said United States, and to bring the said Government, President, and Senate of the United States into disrepute and contempt, and with intent to excite the hatred of the good people of the United States against the said Government and Senate of the said United States, and to stir up sedition within the said United States against the Government thereof, did, at Fairhaven aforesaid, on the 1st day of September aforesaid, for the purpose aforesaid, with force and arms, knowingly, wickedly, deceitfully, maliciously, and willingly assist, aid, and abet in the falsely and maliciously writing, printing, uttering, and publishing a certain false, feigned, scandalous, and seditious writing, or libel, entitled " Copy of a letter from an American diplomatic character in France to a member of Congress in Philadelphia ;" in which said writing, or libel, of and concerning the Government of the United States, and the said President and Senate of the said United States, and of and concerning the said speech of the said John Adams, as President of the United States, to both Houses of the Congress of the United States, and of and concerning the answer of the said Senate of the United States to the said speech of the said John Adams, President of the United States, in which said writing, or libel, among other things, are contained divers false, scandalous, and seditious matters, according to the tenor following, to wit : " Had this truth been understood with you [meaning the people of the United States] before the recall of Monroe, [meaning James Monroe, Ambassador from the United States to the Republic of France,] before the coming and second coming of Pinckney, [meaning Charles C. Pinckney, one of the Envoys Extraordinary from the United States to the said Republic ;] had it guided the pens that wrote the bullying speech of your President, and the stupid answer of your Senate at the opening of Congress, in November last, [meaning the speech of the said John Adams, as delivered by him to both Houses of the Congress of the United States at the opening of their session in November last, and the answer of the Senate, being one of the Houses of the said Congress, to the said speech,] I should probably have had no occasion to address you this letter," [meaning the said writing, or libel, last mentioned.] " We [meaning the people of France] wondered that the answer [meaning the answer to the said speech] of both Houses [meaning both Houses of the Congress of the United States] had not been an order to send him [meaning the said John Adams, President of the United States] to a mad-house ;" to the great scandal and infamy of the said John Adams, in his said capacity of President of the United States, to the great scandal and infamy of the said Senate, being one of the Houses of the Congress of the United States, and to the great scandal and infamy of the Government of the said United States. And so the jurors aforesaid, upon their oaths aforesaid, do say that the said Matthew Lyon, with force and arms, at Fairhaven aforesaid, in the district aforesaid, on the first day of September aforesaid, did, knowingly, willingly, wickedly, and maliciously, and with intent, and design to defame the said John Adams, President of the United States, and the said Senate, being one of the Houses of the Congress of the United States, and the said Government of the United States, and to bring the said Government, President, and Senate into contempt and disrepute with the good people of the United States, and to excite against them, the said Government, President, and Senate of the United States, the hatred of the good people of the said United States, and with intent to stir up sedition within the said United States against the Government thereof, aid, assist, and abet in the maliciously writing, uttering, and publishing, for the purposes aforesaid, the said false, feigned, scandalous, and malicious writing and libel last aforesaid, containing, among other things, the said divers scurrilous, false, feigned, scandalous, seditious, and malicious matters aforesaid, in contempt of the good and wholesome laws of the United States, to the evil and pernicious example of others in like case offending, contrary to the form, force, and effect of the statute of the United States in such case made and provided, and against the peace and dignity of the United States.

Whereupon, the marshal of the district aforesaid is commanded forthwith to apprehend the said Matthew Lyon, if to be found within his district, and him safely keep, to answer to the charges whereof he here stands indicted.

And afterwards, to wit, on the sixth day of the same October aforesaid, at Rutland aforesaid, before the court aforesaid, here cometh the said Matthew Lyon, under the custody of Jabez G. Fitch, Esq., marshal of the district aforesaid, and by the said marshal being brought, in his own proper person, to the bar of the said court here, was forthwith demanded, concerning the premises in the said indictment above specified and charged upon him, how he will acquit himself thereof ; he, the said Matthew Lyon, saith that he is not guilty thereof, and for trial puts himself upon the country ; and Charles Marsh, Esquire, attorney for the said United States within and for the district aforesaid, who prosecutes for the said United States in his behalf, doth the like.

Therefore, let a jury of good and lawful freeholders of the district aforesaid, on the eighth day of the same October aforesaid, at Rutland, in the district aforesaid, thereupon here come before the court aforesaid, by whom the truth of the matters aforesaid may be better known—who are not of kin to the said Matthew Lyon—to recognise, upon their oath, whether the said Matthew Lyon be guilty or not guilty of the charges of which he stands indicted as aforesaid; because, as well the said Charles Marsh, esquire, who prosecutes for the said United States in his behalf, as the said Matthew Lyon, have put themselves upon that jury for trial of said issue.

And afterwards, to wit, on the same eighth day of October aforesaid, at Rutland, in the district aforesaid, before the same court aforesaid, came as well the said Charles Marsh, Esquire, who prosecutes for the said United States in this behalf, as the said Matthew Lyon, in his own proper person; and the jurors of the jury aforesaid, by the said Marshal for this purpose empannelled and returned, to wit, John Ramsdel, Jabez Ward, John Hitchcock, jun., Bildad Orcutt, Andrew Leach, Daniel June, Joshua Goss, Philip Jones, Josiah Harris, Ephraim Dudley, Moses Vail, and Elisha Brown, who, being called, came, and being elected, tried, and sworn to speak the truth of and concerning the premises, upon their oaths say that the said Matthew Lyon is guilty of the charges of which he stands indicted aforesaid, in form aforesaid, as by the indictment aforesaid is supposed against him. And, upon this, it is forthwith demanded of the said Matthew Lyon, if he hath any thing further to say wherefore the said court here ought not, on the premises aforesaid, and verdict aforesaid, to proceed to judgment against him, who nothing saith. And afterwards, to wit, on the ninth day of the same October aforesaid, at Rutland, in the district aforesaid, before the court aforesaid, came the said Matthew Lyon, in his own proper person.

Whereupon, all and singular the premises being seen, and by the judges of the court here fully understood, it is considered and ordered by the court that the said Matthew Lyon be imprisoned four calendar months; that he pay a fine of one thousand dollars, and the costs of this prosecution; and that he stand committed until this sentence be complied with. Costs of prosecution taxed at sixty dollars and ninety-six cents.

Judgment entered this ninth day of October, A D. 1798.

By order of court:

CEPHAS SMITH, Jun., *Clerk.*

Mittimus issued October 9, 1798, at eight o'clock, forenoon.   CEPHAS SMITH, Jun., *Clerk.*

I hereby certify that the preceding is a true copy of the record, examined and collated this 21st day of December, A. D. 1819, by me,

JESSE GOVE, *Clerk Vt. Dist.*

DISTRICT OF VERMONT, *to wit:*

The President of the United States to the Marshal of the District of Vermont.

Whereas Matthew Lyon, of Fairhaven, in the county of Rutland, in the district of Vermont, before the circuit court of the United States, begun and held at Rutland, within and for the said district, on the third day of October, in the year of our Lord one thousand seven hundred and ninety-eight, and of the independence of the said United States the twenty-third, was convicted of writing, printing, uttering, and publishing certain false, scandalous, and seditious libels, and of aiding, abetting, and assisting therein, contrary to the form, force, and effect of the statute entitled "An act in addition to an act entitled An act for the punishment of certain crimes against the United States," and sentenced to imprisonment for the term of four calendar months, to pay a fine of one thousand dollars to the United States, and the costs of this prosecution, taxed at sixty dollars and ninety-six cents, as appears of record, whereof execution remains to be done: Therefore,

By the authority of the United States, you are hereby commanded to imprison him, the said Matthew Lyon, in either of the jails of the United States, within and for the district of Vermont, for the term of four calendar months from the date hereof; and on his (the said Matthew Lyon's) neglect or refusal to pay said fine and costs, you are to keep and detain him, the said Matthew, in imprisonment as aforesaid, until he pay the said fine and costs, with fifty cents for this writ, and the costs of commitment, together with your fees, or until he be otherwise discharged according to law. And of this writ, with your doings herein, make due return according to law, at our said court, on the first day of May next.

Witness, the honorable Oliver Ellsworth, Esquire, Chief Justice of the Supreme Court of the United States, at Rutland aforesaid, the ninth day of October, at eight o'clock, forenoon, A. D. one thousand seven hundred and ninety-eight, and of the independence of the said United States the twenty-third.

CEPHAS SMITH, Jun., *Clerk.*

DISTRICT OF VERMONT, *October* 10, 1798.

By virtue of the within writ, or warrant of commitment, I committed the body of the within-named Matthew Lyon, within the prison in the city of Vergennes, and left a true and attested copy of this writ, with my endorsement thereon, with the keeper of said prison.

Fees of commitment, fifty cents.

Attest: JABEZ G. FITCH, *Marshal.*

DISTRICT OF VERMONT,

VERGENNES, *the 9th day of February,*
8 *o'clock, A. M.,* 1799.

The within-named Matthew Lyon, having complied with the within warrant, is hereby discharged from his confinement.

Attest: S. FITCH, *Marshal's deputy.*

OHIO BOUNDARY.

On motion of Mr. ROSS, of Ohio, the House proceeded to the consideration of a resolution submitted by his colleague, Mr. BRUSH, at the last session of Congress, for inquiring into the expediency of making a survey of the northern boundary of the State of Ohio.

On this resolution there was some debate, the course of which only can be briefly stated, as follows:

Mr. McCOY wished to know whether the State of Ohio was to bear the expense of the survey; otherwise he should be opposed to it.

Mr. Ross stated the existing difficulties which make a survey necessary. The officers of the State, and those of the United States in the Territory of Michigan, both claimed jurisdiction over a considerable strip of land; the consequence of which was, that the authority of each was put at defiance there, &c.

Mr. Sibley, of Michigan, was opposed to the resolution, because he wished the House to act, in preference, upon a report on this subject, made by the Committee on Public Lands at the last session, prescribing a course which he thought correct, and to which he proposed calling the attention of the House hereafter.

Mr. Beecher and Mr. Brush both entered at some length into a defence of the claim of the State of Ohio, and in favor of the proposition before the House; contending that, in the report of the committee of the last session, the claims of Ohio had not been sufficiently regarded, &c.

On the question to agree to the proposition, as revived by Mr. Ross, it was decided in the negative. So the motion was lost.

STATE OF THE FINANCES.

The Speaker then laid before the House a letter from the Secretary of the Treasury, transmitting his annual report on the state of the Treasury; and, on motion of Mr. Storrs, three thousand copies thereof were ordered to be printed for the use of the House. The report is as follows:

Treasury Department, *December* 1, 1820.

In obedience to the direction of the "Act supplementary to the act to establish the Treasury Department," the Secretary of the Treasury respectfully submits the following report:

I. *Of the Revenue.*

The net revenue arising from imports and tonnage, internal duties, direct tax, public lands, postage, and other incidental receipts, during the year 1817, amounted to $24,365,227 34, viz:

Customs, (see statement A.)	$17,254,775 15
Internal duties	2,676,882 77
Direct tax	1,833,737 04
Public lands, exclusive of Mississippi stock	2,015,977 00
Postage and other incidental receipts	313,855 38

That which accrued from the same sources during the year 1818 amounted to $26,095,200 65, viz:

Customs, (see statement A.)	$21,828,451 48
Arrears of internal duties	947,946 33
Arrears of direct tax	263,926 01
Public lands, exclusive of Mississippi stock	2,464,527 90
Postage, dividends on bank stock, and other incidental receipts	590,348 93

And that which accrued from the same sources during the year 1819, amounted to $21,435,700 69, viz:

Customs, (see statement A.)	$17,116,702 96
Arrears of internal duties, (see statement B.)	227,444 01
Arrears of direct tax, (see statement B.)	80,850 61

Public lands, exclusive of Mississippi stock	3,274,422 78
Postage, and other incidental receipts	61,280 33
First instalment from the Bank of the United States, and dividend on the stock in that bank	$675,000 00

It is ascertained that the gross amount of duties on merchandise and tonnage which accrued during the first three quarters of the present year exceeds $13,340,000. And the sales of public lands during the first two quarters of the year, exceed $1,240,000.

The payments in the Treasury during the first three quarters of the present year are estimated to amount to - - - - - - $16,819,637 49

Viz:

Customs	$12,378,513 12	
Public Lands, exclusive of Mississippi stock	1,124,645 32	
Arrears of internal duties	104,769 20	
Arrears of direct tax		
Incidental receipts	579,749 14	
Moneys received from loans	2,545,431 47	
Repayments	86,529 24	

And the payments into the Treasury during the fourth quarter of the present year, from the same sources, are estimated at - - - - - $3,430,000 00

Making the total amount estimated to be received into the Treasury during the year 1820 - - - 20,249,637 49

Which, added to the balance in the Treasury on the 1st day of January last, amounting to - - - 2,076,607 14

Makes the aggregate amount of - 22,326,244 63

The application of this sum for the year 1820 is estimated as follows:

To the 30th of September the payments have amounted to - - $16,909,413 80

Viz:

Civil, diplomatic, and miscellaneous expenses	2,078,573 25	
Military service, including fortifications, ordnance, Indian department, revolutionary and military pensions, arming the militia, and arrearages prior to the 1st of January, 1817	6,043,068 00	
Naval service, including the permanent appropriation for the increase of the navy	2,946,762 00	
Public debt, including $1,142,879 55 for the redemption of Mississippi certificates	5,840,010 55	

During the fourth quarter it is estimated that the payments will amount to - - - - - - 8,056,000 00

Viz:

Civil, diplomatic and miscellaneous expenses - - - $450,000 00
Military service - - 1,900,000 00
Naval service - - 805,000 00
Public debt to the 1st of January, 1821 - 4,900,000 00

Making the aggregate amount of - 24,964,413 80

And leaving on the 1st of January, 1821, a balance against the Treasury estimated at - - - - $2,636,169 17

II. Of the Public Debt.

The funded debt which was contracted before the year 1812, and which was unredeemed on the 1st of October, 1819, as appears by the statement No. 1, amounted to - - $23,668,254 71
And that contracted subsequent to the 1st day of January, 1812, and unredeemed on the 1st day of October, 1819, as appears by the same statement, amounted to - - 68,060,336 29

Making the aggregate amount of - 91,728,591 00
Which sum agrees with the amount as stated in the last annual report as unredeemed on the 1st day of October, 1819, excepting the sum of $63 49, which was then short estimated, and which has since been corrected by actual settlement.
In the fourth quarter of 1819, there was added to the above sum, for Treasury notes brought into the Treasury and cancelled, the following sums, viz:
In six per cent. stock - $4,152 18
In seven per cent. stock - 10,525 00
            14,677 18

Making - - - - 91,743,268 18
From which deduct Louisiana six per ct. stock reimbursed on the 21st of October, 1819 - 2,601,871 14
And deferred stock reimbursed between the 1st October, 1819, and 1st of January, 1820 - 242,063 47
            2,943,434 61

Making the public debt which was unredeemed on the 1st day of January, 1820, as per statement No. 2, am't to - - - - 88,899,333 57
From the 1st of January to the 30th of September, inclusive, there was, by funding Treasury notes and issuing three per cent. stock, for interest on the old registered debt, added to the public debt, as appears by statement No. 3, the amount of $34,550 19
And by the loan authorised per act of May, 15, 1820 - - 2,548,431 47
            $2,579,981 66

Making - - - 91,479,315 23
From which deduct the amount of stock purchased during that period, as per statement No 3 - - - 40 34
And the estimated reimbursement of deferred stock - 253,752 78
            253,793 12

Making, on the 1st of October, 1820, as appears by statement No. 3, the sum of - - 91,225,522 11
To which add, in the fourth quarter of 1820, on account of the loan of the 15th of May of the same year - - 454,567 66

Making - - - 91,680,089 77
There will be reimbursed of the principal of the deferred stock on the 1st of January, 1821 249,444 16
Since the 30th of September last, the residue of the Louisiana stock has become redeemable, amounting to - - 2,216,408 78
            2,465,852 94

Which, if discharged before the first day of Jan'y, 1821, will leave of the public debt unredeemed on that day, as estimated - - 89,214,336 38

The Treasury notes yet in circulation are estimated, as appears by statement No. 4, at - - $37,656 00

The whole of the awards made by the commissioners appointed under the several acts of Congress for the indemnification of certain claimants of public lands, as appears by statement No. 6, [not communicated to Congress,] amounted to - - $4,282,151 12
Of which there has been received at the General Land Office - 2,439,306 31
And there was paid at the Treasury sixty-six per cent. on $1,731,635 69 - - 1,142,879 55
            3,582,187 86

Leaving outstanding on the 30th of September, 1820 - - - - $699,963 26

3. *Of the estimates of the public revenue, and expenditures for the year 1821.*

In forming an estimate of the receipts into the Treasury for the year 1821, the amount of revenue bonds outstanding on the 30th day of September last, the sum due for public land, the ability and disposition of the community to purchase, and especially the quantity and quality of the land intended to be exposed at public auction in the course of the year, present the data upon which the calculations must be made. As a portion of the duties which accrue in the fourth quarter of the present year, and in the first and second quarters of the next, form a part of the receipts into the Treasury for the latter year, the amount received will exceed or fall short of the estimate, by the difference between the duties which actually accrue in those quarters, and are payable within the year, and the amount at which they had been estimated.

The receipts into the Treasury may also considerably exceed or fall short of the sum estimated, in consequence of the issue of a greater or less amount of debentures payable during the year 1821, than had been estimated.

The degree of punctuality with which the revenue bonds are discharged, upon which the estimate is formed, must necessarily affect the amount that will be received into the Treasury.

If the accruing revenue of the present and two succeeding quarters should exceed that of the corresponding quarters of the present and last years; if the amount of the debentures which may be issued and made payable, so as to affect the receipts of the year, should be less than that of preceding years since the peace, compared with the gross amount of duties secured within those years, respectively; and if greater punctuality in the payment of the revenue bonds now outstanding should be observed than during the last-mentioned period, the receipts from the customs will exceed the estimates now presented; and they will fall short of it should all these contingencies be unfavorable, as has been the case during the present year.

The revenue bonds outstanding on the 30th of September last are estimated at $18,770,000. Of this sum $3,130,000 are in suit, of which about $1,250,000 will not be collected on account of the insolvency of the debtors; leaving the amount of bonds outstanding, upon which collections are to be made, estimated at $17,520,000. The amount of duties secured during the first, second, and third quarters of the year 1820, is estimated at $13,350,000; and that of the whole year may be estimated at $16,500,000. The amount of debentures outstanding on the 30th of September last, and payable during the year 1821, is estimated at $1,162,114 16, which is subject to be increased by the amount issued in the present quarter, and during the whole of the ensuing year, chargeable upon the revenue of that year. The average annual amount of debentures, bounties, and allowances, and expenses of collection chargeable upon the revenue, has been ascertained to be nearly equal to fifteen per cent. of the average annual amount of the duties upon imports and tonnage, which accrued from the year 1815 to the year 1819, inclusive.

If this proportion be applied to the revenue bonds outstanding on the 30th of September last; and if the receipts from the tonnage of vessels, and upon duties secured during the present and the two succeeding quarters, are assumed to be equal to any deficiency resulting from the want of punctuality in the discharge of the outstanding bonds, the receipts into the Treasury for the year 1821, from this source of revenue, may be estimated at $14,000,000.

The receipts into the Treasury from the public land, during the first three quarters of the present year, are estimated at $1,124,645 32, and those of the entire year will probably not much exceed $1,600,000.

The receipts from that source, during the year 1821, will probably not exceed those of the present year, if no incentive to greater punctuality, or inducement to make prompt payment, should be presented to the public debtor in the course of the present session of Congress.

The balances of internal duties and direct tax still outstanding are so considerable as to justify an estimate of some extent in calculating the receipts of the ensuing year, if the difficulty of enforcing payment in those States where the largest amount is due were not known to be great. Under these circumstances, the receipts from that source, for the ensuing year, are estimated at $100,000.

According to the foregoing data, the receipts into the Treasury for the ensuing year may be estimated as follows, viz:

Customs - - - - - - -	$14,000,000
Public lands, exclusive of Mississippi stock	1,600,000
Arrears of internal duties, direct tax, and incidental receipts - - - -	100,000
Third instalment from the Bank of the United States - - - - -	500,000
Bank dividends which will accrue during the year, estimated at five per cent. -	350,000
Making the aggregate amount of -	$16,550,000

The appropriations for the same period are estimated as follows, viz:

1. Civil, diplomatic, and miscellaneous	$1,769,850 04
2. Military Department, including fortifications, ordnance, Indian department, military pensions, and arrearages prior to the 1st of January, 1817 -	4,585,352 61
3. Naval Department - -	2,420,594 56
Making an aggregate of -	$8,775,790 21

But, to determine the amount of the charge upon the Treasury for the service of that year, the following additions must be made, viz:

1. Civil, diplomatic, and miscellaneous, the sum of $1,500,000; being an amount of appropriations for the present and preceding years unexpended, and which may be expended during the year 1821; and the sum of $5,477,777 76, payable on account of the interest and reimbursement of the principal of the public debt during that year.

2. The unexpended balances of appropriations for the War Department, under the different heads already enumerated, and which have been deducted from the estimates, or not included in them, (as in the case of Revolutionary pensions, because the balance of that appropriation is estimated to be equal to the expenditure on that object during the ensuing year,) amounting, together, to $2,507,267 63; the annual appropriation of $200,000 for arming the militia; and the Indian annuities, not embraced by the estimates, amounting to $152,575.

3. The annual appropriation of $1,000,000, for the gradual increase of the Navy, which will expire in

the year 1822; and an unexpended balance on the same account, which may be expended in 1821, of $1,750,000.

According to the foregoing data, the expenditure of the year 1821, and which is chargeable upon the Treasury during that year, may be estimated as follows, viz:

1. Civil, diplomatic, and miscellaneous	$3,269,850 04
2. Public debt - - - -	5,477,777 76
3. Military department, including fortifications, ordnance, Indian department, military and revolutionary pensions, arrearages prior to the 1st of January, 1817, and arming the militia, and Indian annuities - - - -	7,445,195 24
4. Navy Department, including the sum of $1,000,000 for the gradual increase of the Navy -	5,170,594 56
Making an aggregate charge upon the Treasury, for the year 1821, of -	$21,363,417 60
To which add the balance against the Treasury, on the 1st of Jan'y, 1821	2,638,169 77
Making -	24,001,586 77

Leaving a balance of $7,451,586 77 beyond the estimated means, for which provision must be made. [This balance is reduced by a subsequent estimate.]

To determine whether a deficiency to this, or any other amount, will occur in succeeding years, is extremely difficult. The data furnished by the fiscal operations of the Government since the peace, must be principally relied upon in making the calculations necessary to arrive at any general result upon this subject.

It has been ascertained that the net revenue which has accrued from imports and tonnage, from the year 1815 to 1819, inclusive, has amounted to $120,260,-052 46. If this be divided by the number of years in which it accrued, the result will be an average annual revenue of $24,052,000. But the revenue which accrued in 1815 greatly exceeded not only that of any year previous to the war, but that of any year since that epoch. It is also admitted that the quantity of produce on hand, at the close of the war, especially of cotton and tobacco, considerably exceeded the amount of the crop of those articles made during the preceding year. The ability of the community, therefore, to purchase an increased amount of foreign articles in the year 1815 exceeded, in a corresponding degree, that of subsequent years. It has also been ascertained that the importation of foreign articles during the present year has been considerably less than in any year since the peace. To form an estimate of the average annual revenue which may accrue from imports and tonnage during the next four years, that will approximate towards accuracy, it will be necessary to embrace in the calculation the revenue which accrued from the year 1814 to 1819, inclusive, amounting to $124,510,414 05, and that which shall have accrued in the year 1820, estimated at $14,000,000, making the aggregate sum of $138,510,414 05, which gives the sum of $19,787,-202 as the average annual revenue for those seven years.

Other views, derived from the fiscal operations of the Government, will be found to accord with this result. The average product of the duties upon imports and tonnage, which accrued from the year 1801 to 1807, inclusive, may be stated at $13,640,000; and that which accrued from the former period to 1813, inclusive, amounted to the annual sum of $11,570,000. The increase of population in the United States has been estimated at thirty-four per cent. in ten years; if the increase of consumption has corresponded with that of population, the revenue of the year 1820, according to the result furnished by the first seven years, would exceed $20,000,000, and would fall but little short of $17,000,000, according to the data furnished by the whole period. During the former period, the principal States of Europe were involved in wars; which not only gave to our shipping the principal part of the carrying trade, but created an unusual demand for every article of exportation, and greatly enhanced their value.

Any estimate founded upon the average revenue of those years, the duties upon imports remaining the same, would, most probably, not be realized; but as these duties were considerably increased in 1816, the objections to such an estimate are, in some degree, diminished. From the year 1808 to 1813, inclusive, the United States were engaged in a state of commercial or actual warfare. The disadvantages to which their commerce was subjected by that warfare more than counterbalanced the peculiar advantages it enjoyed in the seven years immediately preceding. An estimate for the next four years, founded upon an average of the whole term, would more probably fall short of than exceed the sum which would be received into the Treasury, notwithstanding the duties were higher during two years of that term than at present.

In the investigation of a subject of such complexity, affecting so deeply the interest of the community, every fact and circumstance connected with it ought to be considered. Since the year 1807 new interests have arisen, which claim a prominent place in this consideration. From time immemorial, household manufactures have existed in every part of the United States. The mechanical arts, (those branches of manufacture without which society, even in a very imperfect state of civilization, could not exist, (though differing in some degree from those properly denominated household, have long existed in the United States. Since the year 1807, those branches of manufacture have been greatly extended and improved. Others have been established, and a large amount of capital has been invested in manufacturing establishments, which promise to furnish, in a short time, an ample supply of cotton and woollen manufactures, and most of those of iron, glass, and various other articles of great value.

As commerce has been properly defined to be an exchange of equivalent value, it is probable that by the failure on our part to receive from foreign nations the accustomed supply of those articles which can now be produced in our domestic establishments, the articles which they have been accustomed to receive from us will lose something of the value which they would otherwise have commanded, until new channels of intercourse shall be discovered, and different articles of merchandise shall be substituted for those formerly received.

The capacity of a nation to consume foreign articles depends upon the value of its exports, and not upon its ability to furnish every article of primary or secondary necessity. The precious metals are never imported into any country when commodities which will command a profit can be obtained for importation. Giving full weight to the fact that cotton, woollen, iron, and various other articles which are now furnished by our domestic establishments, will be hereafter received from foreign nations only to a small amount, $17,000 000 of revenue may be assumed as the minimum, and $20,000,000 as the maximum, which will be annually received from imports and tonnage during the next four years. The decrease which has occurred in the last and present years furnishes no ground to distrust the correctness of the foregoing conclusion. The customs produced, in 1815, a net revenue of $35,306,022 51; in 1816, $27,484,100 36; and in 1817, $17,524,775 15. This last year was considered, at the time, as the period of greatest reaction. Accordingly, in 1818 the net revenue from the customs amounted to $21,828,-451 48.

The multiplication of banks, the state of the currency, and the high price which all exportable articles commanded until the end of 1818, strongly invited to extravagance of every kind, and particularly in the consumption of foreign merchandise. The resources of individuals had been, by these seductions, in a great degree anticipated during the first years which succeeded the peace. The sudden reduction in the value of all exportable articles which occurred about the commencement of 1819, not only prevented in a great degree further purchases, but rendered the discharge of engagements previously contracted impracticable. The pressure thus produced upon the community reacted upon the venders of every species of merchandise, whether foreign or domestic, who, without thoroughly investigating the cause of their distress, have sought for relief in measures calculated rather to aggravate than alleviate the public embarrassment.

The issue and payment of a larger amount of debentures in the present year in proportion to the exportations of the last, the increased amount of specie and diminished amount of foreign merchandise imported during the present year, and the ready sale of foreign and domestic articles now in the market, show that the importation of foreign goods is upon the eve of being regulated by the demand for them for consumption.

It has been stated that the receipts from public land during the year 1821 cannot be estimated at more than $1,600,000, unless some greater incentive to punctuality or inducement to make prompt payments should be offered by the measures which may be adopted in the course of the present session of Congress. The act of the 24th of April last, which abolished credit on all purchases of land, and reduced the minimum price from 200 to 125 cents per acre, furnishes, it is respectfully conceived, equitable ground for legislative interference in favor of purchasers under the ancient system. By that system, the price could be reduced to 164 cents per acre by prompt payment. If the act abolishing credit had fixed the minimum price at 164 cents instead of 125 cents, no equitable ground for legislative interference would exist. It is not contended that the vender of an article, under ordinary circumstances, does an injury to a purchaser by subsequently selling the same article to others at a low rate. But if he has in his possession such a quantity of the article sold as to enable him for an indefinite time to determine the price of the article, he affects the interest of every previous purchaser by such reduction, who may be

constrained, from any cause whatever, to sell that article. The extent of the national domain will, for ages, enable the Government to determine the price of unimproved land similarly situated. It is admitted that the Government has been induced to adopt this measure by the most grave considerations. The most prominent of these was the necessity of preventing the further increase of a debt, then about $22,000,000, strongly affecting the interests and feelings of a great number of citizens. If its increase was an object of deep solicitude, its diminution, by an act of grace founded upon equitable principles, will be in strict accordance with the motives in which that measure originated. Difficulties may occur in adjusting the details of such a measure, unless it be presented as a simple act of grace. Under this point of view, it should be confined in its operations to the debtors of the Government for public lands, and should affect them only to the extent of the debts which they may respectively owe.

During the excessive circulation of bank notes not convertible into specie, and to which the Government, from necessity, for some time gave currency, and the high price which every description of domestic produce commanded, large quantities of public land were sold at public auction at prices greatly beyond their real value. In many instances, the first payment which the Government has received could not be obtained by the purchaser, even if he were able to convey the land in fee-simple. The propriety of legislative interference to change the relation between debtor and creditor, for the benefit of either, may be questioned. Circumstances, however, may arise, which will influence an upright and benevolent creditor to relax his demands, and to grant relief to his debtor voluntarily, which he might resist as an act of power. Such is respectfully conceived to be the situation of the Government in relation to the purchasers of public lands, who, in a moment of infatuation, have engaged to pay for a portion of the national domain a sum greatly beyond its value, and which never will be paid.

In all cases of this kind, the forfeiture of the sum already advanced will inevitably occur, if relief to some extent be not granted.

In conformity with the foregoing views, the following propositions for the relief of the purchasers of public lands, and for the purpose of increasing the payments into the Treasury in the ensuing year, are respectfully submitted, viz:

1st. That every purchaser of public land be permitted, on or before the 30th of September next, to abandon any legal subdivision of his purchase, and that the payments made upon the part abandoned be applied to the discharge of the instalments due upon the remainder; the right to abandon in no case to involve any repayment by the Government to any purchaser. In all cases the part retained to be in the most compact form that the situation of the whole quantity purchased will permit.

2d. The difference between the former and present minimum price for cash payments being equal to $3.78 per cent. on the former, it is respectfully proposed, that on payment of the whole purchase money for any tract of land on or before the 30th day of September next, a deduction of 25 per cent. shall be made, and that any interest which may have accrued to the United States in such cases shall be remitted. An act of greater liberality, and which would still further increase the receipts into the Treasury during the next year, would be to allow a deduction of 37½ per cent. on all such payments, which is equal to the difference between 200 and 125 cents.

3d. That all sums which may be due by purchasers of public lands, who shall not avail themselves of the preceding conditions, shall be payable in ten equal annual instalments, without interest, provided that such payments shall be punctually made upon the several days in each successive year upon which the purchases were respectively made. Any failure in making such payment to revive the original terms and conditions of sale.

If these or analogous provisions should be adopted, the payments from the public land, during the year 1821, will be greatly increased ; the debt due on that account greatly diminished ; and the revenue resulting from that source acquire, in future years, a more uniform character.

If, then , be assumed that the revenue which will accrue from the customs will be equal to the mean sum between seventeen and twenty millions of dollars, the annual revenue for the four succeeding years may be estimated as follows, viz:

Customs	$18,500,000
Public lands	2,500,000
Bank dividends at six per cent.	420,000
Incidental receipts	80,000
Making an aggregate amount of	$21,500,000

But if the annual receipts from the customs shall be estimated for the next four years at the average sum of $17,000,000, the annual revenue for that period will be equal to $20,000,000.

The annual expenditure for the same period may be estimated as follows, viz :

Civil, diplomatic, and miscellaneous	$2,000,000
Public debt	5,477,000
War Department, including fortifications, ordnance, Indian department, military and revolutionary pensions, arming the militia, and arrearages prior to the 1st of January, 1817,	5,850,000
Naval Department, including $1,000,000 for the permanent increase of the navy	3,420,000
Making the aggregate amount of	$16,747,000

The balance of the Sinking Fund, after paying the interest of the funded debt, and providing for the annual reimbursement of the six per cent. deferred stock, has not, in this estimate, been considered as a charge upon the Treasury before the year 1825, as the price of the public stocks precludes the possibility of purchase within the rates prescribed by law.

This estimate is below that which is required for the year 1821, but it is believed to be less than the annual expenditure which will be required for the next four years. According to this estimate, the means will exceed the indispensable expenditure, during that period, by $3,253,000.

After the year 1823, the annual expenditure upon the navy will be diminished by $1,000,000. The expenditure of the Government after that year, including the entire appropriation for the public debt, is estimated as follows, viz :

Civil, diplomatic, and miscellaneous,	$2,000,000
Public debt,	10,000,000

Military Department, including fortifications, ordnance, Indian Department, military and Revolutionary pensions, arming the militia, and arrearages prior to the 1st of January, 1817,	5,850,000
Naval Department,	2,420,000
Making the aggregate amount of	$20,270,000

which, after the year 1824, would leave an annual deficit of $270,000.

If this sum should not be met by the annual increase of revenue, resulting from the increase of population during those and succeeding years, and the increased consumption of foreign articles resulting therefrom, it may be supplied by a corresponding reduction in those items of expenditure which depend absolutely upon the will of the Legislature, unconnected with the existing laws regulating the permanent expenditure.

It is therefore respectfully submitted, that it is inexpedient to resort, at this time, to the imposition of additional taxes upon the community. The condition of the currency in several of the States of the Union furnishes strong inducements to abstain from additional taxation at this time. The obligation of the Government to receive the notes of the Bank of the United States, without reference to the place where they are payable, has given to them their universal currency. All notes issued south and west of Washington have, in consequence of the state of exchange between those places and the commercial cities to the east of this place, centred in those cities. The bank has, consequently, found itself constrained to direct those branches to refuse to issue their notes, even upon the deposite of specie. The effect of these causes combined has been the exclusion from circulation, in all the States west and south of the seat of Government, of the notes of the Bank of the United States and its offices. In several of those States there is no sound paper circulation. To resort to internal taxation, under such circumstances, would be to require of the citizens of those States what it will be impossible for them to perform. Wherever paper circulates as money, which is not convertible into specie, it circulates to the exclusion of specie and of paper which is convertible into gold and silver coin. In all such places, the payment of direct or internal taxes in specie, or in the notes of the Bank of the United States will be impracticable. Preliminary to a resort to internal taxation of any kind, the charter of the Bank of the United States ought to be amended, so as to make the bills of all the offices of the bank, except that at the seat of Government, receivable only in the States where they are made payable, and in the States and Territories where no office is established. The effect of this modification would be to make the notes of the offices of the Bank of the United States, except the office in this District, a local currency, which will enter and continue in the local circulation of the States in which they are issued. The notes thus issued will render the local circulation of the States sound, and furnish to the citizens the means of discharging their contributions to the Government. This measure will also place the State institutions to the south and west of this city in a more eligible situation in relation to the offices of the Bank of the United States, by enabling them to adjust their accounts with these offices by the exchange of notes, instead of liquidating their balances by the payment of specie. Should it, however, be judged expe-

499   HISTORY OF CONGRESS.   500

H. of R.   *Losses, by War—Commerce of the Black Sea.*   December, 1820.

dient by the Legislature to lay additional burdens upon the people, for the purpose of meeting the existing or any probable future deficiency, it is respectfully submitted that the importation of foreign spirits be prohibited, and that a duty upon domestic spirits, equal to the amount of that now collected upon foreign spirits, and to such deficiency, be imposed on the distillation and sale of domestic spirits. In any event, a resort to loans to the extent of the deficiency of the year 1821 will be indispensable.

Of the sum of $3,000,000, authorized by the act of the 15th May last to be raised by loan, $2,000,000 have been obtained at a premium of two per cent., upon stock bearing interest at the rate of six per cent. per annum, redeemable at the will of the Government, and $1,000,000 at par, upon stock bearing interest at the rate of five per cent. per annum, redeemable at any time after the 1st day of January, 1832. There is no just reason to doubt that any sum which may be necessary to be raised by loan, can be obtained upon terms not less favorable; but, as it is probable that the surplus of the revenue, after satisfying all demands upon the Treasury authorized by existing laws, during the years 1822, 1823, and 1824, will be equal to the redemption of any debt which may be contracted in 1821, it is respectfully submitted that the President of the United States be authorized to borrow from the Bank of the United States, or from other banks or individuals, the sum which may be necessary for the service of that year, at par, and at a rate of interest not exceeding six per cent. per annum, redeemable at the will of the Government.

All which is respectfully submitted.
WM. H. CRAWFORD.

[*Note.*—For the correction of errors in the preceding report, see *post*, December 28.]

CLAIMS FOR LOSSES BY WAR.

Mr. STRONG, of New York, submitted for consideration the following resolution:

Resolved, That a committee be appointed to ascertain and report to this House the amount of individual claims upon the United States, in favor of American citizens, growing out of the last war with Great Britain, the Creek war, and the Seminole war; designating the classes of the claims, and the names of the claimants, together with the sum or sums which, in their opinion, shall be equitably and fairly due to each, so far as the same may be practicable; and, also, upon the expediency of providing for the same by issuing *scrip*, receivable in payments for the public lands, or in such other manner as the committee may deem more advisable.

Mr. ANDERSON objected to so much of this resolution as proposed to refer to a select committee what was expressly the duty of one of the standing committees, viz: an inquiry into the expediency of allowing claims. He had no objection that so much of the resolution as proposed an inquiry into the extent of these claims should go to a select committee, as proposed.

To this objection Mr. STRONG replied. He thought, where a general class of cases was proposed to be provided for, the expediency of such a provision would, very properly, fall within the duty of a special committee, rather than of the standing committee, which had already so much business before it.

Mr. SIMKINS, considering the subject of this resolution as of much importance, wished to have an opportunity of deliberating upon it, and, therefore, moved to lay it on the table for further consideration.

Mr. GROSS, of New York, in opposing the motion to lay the resolution on the table, said that it appeared to him a great change had taken place in the mode of proceeding on this subject. There was a time when claims of this sort were thought just, and promptly allowed; then came a time when they were inquired into, but relief refused—now, gentlemen would not even examine the claims—which was the only object of this proposition, &c.

Mr. ANDERSON replied that the change if any, was in the mode of bringing the claims before the House. If the gentleman from New York, or any other, would bring any claim or claims before the House, in the usual manner, he would find no objection to the examination of them. Mr. A. admitted that it was desirable to know the amount of these claims, and for that purpose was very willing that a select committee should be charged with the inquiry.

After a few more remarks, from Mr. GROSS, the motion to lay the resolution on the table was decided in the affirmative by a small majority.

COMMERCE OF THE BLACK SEA.

Mr. FULLER, of Massachusetts, offered for consideration the following resolution:

Resolved, That the Committee on Commerce be instructed to inquire into the expediency of providing by law such means as may be necessary to obtain for the citizens of the United States the navigation of the Euxine sea, and a participation of the commerce of its ports and dependencies.

Mr. F., after remarking on the expediency of affording to commerce, under present circumstances, all the facilities in the power of the Government to bestow, went on to say that our commerce with Russia, it was well known, was, at present, almost entirely carried on through the Baltic sea, which, it was equally well known, was closed against navigation for the greater part of the year by the severity of the climate. The Euxine sea, he said, afforded much greater facilities, by means of the rivers which fall into it, for carrying on the trade with Russia. But, not having any agent there, we have no means of procuring the permission to pass the straits of the Dardanelles. From the information of others, however, Mr. F. said, he had no doubt, that the requisite permission could be obtained by asking it in a proper form and manner. The free intercourse with the Euxine would, he said, be of much advantage to us in another point of view. At present, all our commerce with Turkey is carried on through Smyrna. Several ports of the Dardanelles, Mr. F. said, would be more convenient for this purpose than Smyrna. Upon the whole, he thought it quite advisable to have an inquiry made into this subject through the medium of a committee of the House.

Mr. STEVENS, of Connecticut, said, in reference to Mr. FULLER's intimation that permission to pass the straits could be obtained if asked in a proper manner, that he presumed the agent who asked it must go with something in hand, and suggested the propriety of ascertaining, before they went further, what would be the cost of this project.

Mr. RHEA suggested that the mover would, perhaps, get more directly at his object by moving at once to request the Executive to send a Minister to Turkey.

The motion of Mr. FULLER was then agreed to without a division.

TUESDAY, December 5.

A message from the Senate informed the House that they have passed a bill, entitled "An act for the relief of Ebenezer Stevens and Austin L. Sands, legal representatives of Richardson Sands, deceased, and others," in which they ask the concurrence of this House.

The SPEAKER laid before the House a report from the Secretary of War, containing the information required by the resolution of the 23d ultimo, in relation to the execution of the act of the 1st of May, 1820, amendatory of the act for the relief of certain persons engaged in the land and naval service of the United States, in the Revolutionary war; which was read, and ordered to lie on the table.

The SPEAKER also laid before the House a letter from the Secretary of the Treasury, communicating sundry statements, rendered in obedience to the resolution of this House of the 13th of May last, requiring him to lay before the House at the present session, a report of the quantity of land sold under the provisions of the act passed on the 24th of April, 1820, entitled "An act making further provision for the sale of the public lands;" as, also, the name of the purchaser; the number of acres sold to each individual, or company, or body corporate; the sum per acre for which the same was sold, distinguishing that which shall be sold at private, from that which is sold at public sale; which letter and statements were ordered to lie on the table.

The SPEAKER laid before the House a letter from the Secretary of the Treasury, transmitting, in obedience to a resolution of the House, a statement from the Commissioner of the General Land Office, of the number of claims for bounty land which remain unsatisfied, the aggregate number of acres necessary to satisfy them, and the period when they will be ready.

The SPEAKER also communicated to the House a letter from the Postmaster General, transmitting, in obedience to a resolution of this House, a list of postmasters who are also contractors for carrying mails, the amount of their compensation, &c.

Both communications, with the accompanying documents, were laid on the table, and ordered to be printed.

Mr. COOK, from the Committee on Public Lands, reported a bill, from the Senate, for the relief of Nicholas Jarrot, with sundry amendments, which were read and agreed to, and the bill ordered to a third reading.

On motion of Mr. STORRS, it was—

Resolved, That the Secretary of the Treasury Department be directed to communicate to this House the latest return made to that Department of the general statement of the Bank of the United States and its offices of discount and deposite.

On motion of Mr. SIMKINS, it was—

Resolved, That the Secretary of War be requested to lay before the House a particular statement of the expenses of the Army of the United States, from the end of the late war to the present year, including the estimates for 1821, designating the expenditures in each branch of the army for each year, with such explanations as may be necessary to render the statement clear and explicit. Also, that he lay before this House the amount of balances, if any have accrued, in each year, from the moneys appropriated for the support of the army; in what way such balances have accrued, and how they have been disposed of or appropriated.

WEST POINT ACADEMY.

Mr. CANNON moved the adoption of the following resolution:

Resolved, That the Secretary of War be directed to lay before this House, as soon as is practicable, a statement showing the aggregate amount that has been expended on the Military Academy at West Point, in the State of New York, from the establishment of the same to the present time, in the erection of buildings, barracks, repairs and materials for the same; also, the aggregate amount that has been expended in pay, subsistence, and clothing, of the teachers, officers, and cadets, that are or have been in said academy, up to the present time; also, the aggregate amount that has been expended on the quartermaster's department attached to said institution, for wood and distributing the same, forage, transportation, stationery, including articles used in the drawing department, books, mathematical instruments, printing, and all other contingencies, up to the present time; also, the number of cadets that have been educated in said academy, since the first establishment, from the District of Columbia, also the number from each State and Territory in the Union, also the number of cadets now in said academy from the District of Columbia, and from each of the States and Territories respectively; also, the number who have received an education at said academy who are in the Army and Navy of the United States, the appointment each holds, and the District, State, or Territory, they are from; and also the number of orphans, if any, of those who have fallen in the defence of their country, or died in its service, who have been educated in said academy, or are now cadets in the same, and the District, State, or Territory, each is from.

Mr. LITTLE wished to correct the resolution in one particular, in which he conceived there was a misapprehension. The mover was certainly mistaken in supposing that the teachers or cadets of the Military Academy were clothed by the Government; the cadets, Mr. L. stated, received pay, out of which they clothed themselves, and as it was not the fact that either they or the teachers of the academy were clothed by the Government, he did not wish such an idea to go abroad. He hoped, therefore, the gentleman would modify his resolution by omitting the call relative to clothing.

Mr. CANNON referred to a report of the Secretary of War, made at the last session, on the subject of the academy, to show that the Government was charged with clothing for it. An item of the report referred to, stated a disbursement of five hundred and some odd dollars for clothing furnished the establishment at West Point. If, however, the Government provided no clothing for that institution, the Secretary would report the fact to the House, so that the feature in the resolution which was objected to he conceived had better be retained. Mr. C. added a few remarks as to his motives in moving this resolution. Economy in the public disbursements was imperiously called for by the state of our finances, and, among the other national establishments, he wished to see if any retrenchment could be made in the Academy at West Point.

Mr. LITTLE replied, that there was a part of the corps of engineers employed at West Point, who were regularly enlisted, as other soldiers, and were in the same manner clothed by the Government; it was the clothing for these soldiers, no doubt, which formed the item in the report referred to. The resolution called for the expenses of clothing the teachers and cadets, and, he repeated, as no such expense existed, he wished the form of the resolution to correspond with the fact, and therefore moved that the feature he objected to should be stricken out.

Mr. SMITH, of Maryland, said, the resolution ought not to go forth in such a shape as to show ignorance of the facts on the part of the House, and, as there was certainly no such provision for the cadets as clothing, (for he presumed five hundred dollars would go very little way towards clothing two hundred and fifty cadets,) he hoped the motion of his colleague (Mr. LITTLE,) would be agreed to, and the resolution be modified.

Mr. CANNON assented to the modification proposed by Mr. LITTLE; and, thus amended, the resolution was agreed to.

AMENDMENT TO THE CONSTITUTION.

The House then, on motion of Mr. SMITH, of North Carolina, resumed the consideration of the resolution proposing an amendment to the Constitution, in relation to the election of Electors of President and Vice President of the United States and members of the House of Representatives.

Mr. REID, of Georgia, rose in opposition to the resolution, and, in a speech of near an hour, submitted his views of the impolicy of amending the Constitution in the feature contemplated, especially by substituting the mode proposed by the resolution.

Mr. SMITH, of North Carolina, replied to Mr. R.; and went into a defence, considerably at large, of the expediency of the amendment contemplated by the resolution.

Mr. BARBOUR, of Virginia, followed, and went into a general argument against the proposed amendment of the Constitution.

Mr. LOWNDES, of South Carolina, advocated the resolution, and replied, at some length, to the arguments of Messrs. REID and BARBOUR.

Mr. RHEA, of Tennessee, spoke a short time against the resolution.

The question was then taken on ordering the resolution to be engrossed and read a third time, and was decided in the affirmative, by yeas and nays. For the resolution 103, against it 59, as follows:

YEAS—Messrs. Adams, Allen of New York, Anderson, Archer of Maryland, Archer of Virginia, Baker, Ball, Bateman, Beecher, Bloomfield, Brush, Bryan, Buffum, Burton, Butler of New Hampshire, Butler of Louisiana, Campbell, Cannon, Clagett, Cobb, Cocke, Cook, Crafts, Crowell, Culbreth, Culpeper, Cushman, Davidson, Dewitt, Dickinson, Eddy, Edwards of Connecticut, Eustis, Fay, Floyd, Folger, Foot, Ford, Fuller, Gross of New York, Guyon, Hackley, Hall of New York, Hendricks, Hooks, Jackson, Johnson, Kendall, Kent, Kinsey, Kinsley, Little, Lincoln, Linn, Livermore, Lowndes, Maclay, McCullough, McLean of Kentucky, Mallary, Meigs, Mercer, Monell, Montgomery, R. Moore, T. L. Moore, Morton, Moseley, Neale, Nelson of Massachusetts, Parker of Massachusetts, Plumer, Rankin, Rich, Richards, Richmond, Robertson, Russ, Sawyer, Shaw, Silsbee, Simkins, Sloan, Smith of New Jersey, Smith of Maryland, B. Smith of Virginia, Smith of North Carolina, Stevens, Street, Strong of Vermont, Swearingen, Tomlinson, Tracy, Tucker of Virginia, Upham, Van Rensselaer, Walker, Warfield, Wendover, Whitman, Williams of Virginia, and Williams of North Carolina.

NAYS—Messrs. Abbot, Alexander, Allen of Massachusetts, Allen of Tennessee, Baldwin, Barbour, Brevard, Brown, Burwell, Case, Clark, Crawford, Darlington, Dennison, Earle, Edwards of Pennsylvania, Gross of Pennsylvania, Hall of North Carolina, Hazard, Hibshman, Hill, Hostetter, Jones of Virginia, Jones of Tennessee, Lathrop, McCoy, McCreary, Marchand, Meech, Metcalf, S. Moore, Murray, Nelson of Virginia, Newton, Overstreet, Parker of Virginia, Patterson, Phelps, Philson, Pinckney, Reed, Rhea, Rogers, Ross, Sergeant, A. Smyth of Virginia, Storrs, Strong of New York, Tarr, Terrell, Tompkins, Trimble, Tucker of South Carolina, Tyler, and Wallace.

The SPEAKER announced that the question was decided in the affirmative, and, demanding when it was the pleasure of the House to have the resolution read a third time—

Some discussion arose on the question whether, as the Constitution required that such a proposition should be supported by two-thirds of both Houses to enable it to pass, a less number than two-thirds could order the resolution to a third reading. Two-thirds of the House not having voted for the third reading of the resolution, Mr. COBB made the point of order, and Messrs. CULPEPER, LOWNDES, SMITH of Maryland, RHEA, and LIVERMORE, spoke upon it.

The SPEAKER decided that the rules and practice of the House recognised the principle that two-thirds of the votes were required on the final passage of a resolution proposing to amend the Constitution; but that any intermediate question might be carried by a majority of the House. No appeal being taken from the decision of the Speaker—

505   HISTORY OF CONGRESS.   506

DECEMBER, 1820.   *Duty on French Tonnage—Naval Discipline.*   H. OF R.

The resolution was ordered to be read a third time to-morrow.

To obtain a full vote on the passage of this resolution, which Mr. SIMKINS deemed of high importance, being no less than a proposition to amend the Constitution, he gave notice that at one o'clock to-morrow he should move a call of the House.

WEDNESDAY, December 6.

Another member, to wit: from Delaware, WILLARD HALL, appeared and took his seat.

Mr. BEECHER, from the Committee on the Judiciary, reported a bill to alter the time of holding the district court in the district of Mississippi; which was read twice, and ordered to be engrossed, and read a third time to-morrow.

On motion of Mr. CAMPBELL, the Committee on Private Land Claims were instructed to inquire into the expediency of allowing further time to the officers and soldiers of the Virginia line, on continental establishment, their heirs or assigns, entitled to bounty lands, within the tract reserved by the State of Virginia, between the Little Miami and Sciota rivers, to complete their locations.

On motion of Mr. TOMLINSON, the Committee of Commerce were instructed to inquire into the expediency of authorizing the President of the United States to require that the collector of the customs for the district of Sandusky shall reside at Portland, in the district aforesaid.

On motion of Mr. BEECHER, the Committee on the Judiciary were instructed to inquire into the expediency of revising the laws establishing the fees of the district attorney for the district of Ohio, and as respects the fees of the marshal and clerk of the circuit and district courts for the district of Ohio.

On motion of Mr. STRONG, of New York, the House proceeded to consider the resolution submitted by him on the 4th instant, respecting the claims growing out of the last war with Great Britain, the Creek war, and the Seminole war; and the question recurred, on the motion of Mr. ANDERSON, to amend the said resolution, by striking out the words following: "together with the 'sum or sums which, in their opinion, shall be 'equitable, and fairly due to each, so far as the 'same may be practicable. And, also, upon the 'expediency of providing for the payment of the 'same, by issuing scrip, receivable in payment for 'the public lands, or in such other manner as the 'committee may deem more advisable." And, being taken, it passed in the affirmative. The question was then put to agree to the resolution, as amended, and determined in the negative.

The report made on the 12th of May last, by a select committee appointed to inquire whether any, and, if any, what, further provision may be necessary to give effect to the provisions of the Treaty of Brownstown, in the Territory of Michigan, was referred to the Committee on Roads and Canals.

The bill from the Senate, entitled "An act for the relief of Ebenezer Stevens and Austin L. Sands, legal representatives of Richardson Sands, deceased, and others," was read twice, and referred to the Committee on Pensions and Revolutionary Claims.

An engrossed bill, entitled "An act for the relief of Nicholas Jarrot," was read the third time, and passed.

DUTY ON FRENCH TONNAGE.

Mr. NEWTON, from the Committee of Commerce, reported the following bill:

SEC. 1. *Be it enacted by the Senate and House of Representatives of the United States of America, in Congress assembled,* That the provisions of the act, entitled "An act to impose a new tonnage duty on French ships and vessels," passed May 15, 1820, shall not extend to, or operate upon, any French ship or vessel that shall have entered into any port within the jurisdiction of the United States prior to the 30th day of September, 1820.

SEC. 2. *And be it further enacted,* That the Secretary of the Treasury, after deducting a tonnage duty equal to that paid by every French ship or vessel which entered the ports within the jurisdiction of the United States prior to the passage and operation of the act, entitled "An act to impose a new tonnage duty on French ships and vessels," passed May 15, 1820, from the tonnage duty collected from French ships and vessels, by virtue of the above recited act, between the first day of July, 1820, and the 30th day of September following, be, and he is hereby, authorised and directed to pay and refund the remainder of such tonnage duty, free from costs and charges, to any person or persons who shall have authority to receive the same.

The bill was twice read and committed.

NAVAL DISCIPLINE.

Mr. FOOT, of Connecticut, moved the following resolution:

Resolved, That the Committee on Naval Affairs be instructed to inquire into the expediency of repealing so much of the act for the better government of the Navy of the United States, as authorizes the infliction of corporal punishment by stripes or lashes; and also to provide for the punishment of any officer or private in the Navy, who shall send or accept a challenge to fight a duel, in the same manner as is provided in the 25th and 26th articles of the first section of the act for establishing rules and articles for the government of the armies of the United States.

Mr. SMITH, of Maryland, said if he understood the resolution, it proposed a measure which would have the effect altogether to destroy the efficiency of the Navy.

Mr. FOOT replied that the resolution proposed only an inquiry, the object of which was the expediency of establishing an uniformity in the mode of governing the Army and Navy. In the act of 1812, regulating the articles of war, corporal punishment in the Army had been abolished. Whether it was expedient to establish the same rule for the government of the Navy, or not, was a matter for inquiry, which might be ascertained under this resolution.

Mr. SMITH, of Maryland, moved to lay the resolution on the table; which motion was agreed to.

507   HISTORY OF CONGRESS.   508

H. of R.   *Amendment to the Constitution—Admission of Missouri.*   December, 1820.

AMENDMENT TO THE CONSTITUTION.

The engrossed resolution proposing an amendment to the Constitution of the United States with respect to the mode of election of Representatives to Congress and Electors of President and Vice President of the United States, was read a third time.

Mr. Overstreet, desiring further time to make up his mind with regard to this question, which he considered as one of the first magnitude, on which he had not yet satisfied himself, moved to postpone the further consideration of the resolution to Monday next.

This motion, the question being put, was determined in the negative.

Mr. Anderson, after expressing his entire assent to that part of the proposition now before the House, which went to establish a uniform mode of election of Electors, intimated that he entertained some doubts as to the remaining part of it, which proposed the same rule in respect to Representatives to Congress, and on that point he desired explanation. His objection to it was, that to pass it would be legislating uselessly. By the Constitution, as it now stands, Congress have the power to declare that Representatives to Congress shall be elected in all the States by districts. If in this respect the States have not, in our opinion, done right, said Mr. A., we can, by an ordinary law, do it for them; and therefore he said he could see no reason why the fundamental charter need undergo any revision on this point. That a great object only can justify an alteration or amendment of the Constitution, was a proposition which, he said, every gentleman would assent. If no gentleman satisfied his scruples on this subject, Mr. A. said, he should move a recommitment of this resolution to a committee, with instructions to strike out that part of it to which he had taken exception.

Mr. Linn then rose and said that, for the very reason that the gentleman had given as an objection to it, he wished the postponed amendment to succeed. It was true, that Congress possessed the power to district the States, or otherwise provide the mode of elections of Representatives to Congress. But he had ever considered it a most dangerous power—a power liable to the greatest abuses. They might require every voter in the State to repair to the seat of government of the State to vote, or lose his vote entirely. With regard to the Electors, too, he had always believed it to be the true spirit and intention of the original constitution, that the people should choose the Electors. Instead of that, we now found that, in several of the States, the Legislatures choose the Electors, and the people have nothing to do with it. For these reasons, he was in favor of the resolution; and he should hope that it would receive, not only a Constitutional majority of votes, but that it would pass unanimously.

Mr. Simkins, with a view that all gentlemen might have an opportunity of giving a decisive vote on this question, and not be obliged to vote before they were fully prepared, moved that the resolution be postponed to this day week.

Mr. Eustis supported the postponement, on the ground of courtesy towards gentlemen who declared that they were not satisfied as to the vote they ought to give.

Mr. Floyd was ready to postpone this resolution on the ground now stated—the more readily as the public interest did not require its passage at this day in preference to a later day in the session. For himself, Mr. F. said he should be unwilling to give this Government any *more* power than it already possesses. He should be unwilling to make this Government more strong than it is. He had voted yesterday for the third reading of this resolution, but it was under a conviction that, in doing so, he was voting to give no more power to the General Government than it already had. When our Constitution was framed, its authors were aware that difficulties might arise in respect to the election of Representatives, and they gave the power to Congress which it now has. If it does possess the power to district the States, the Constitution cannot do more if amended as proposed; but, the advantages of putting this provision into the body of the Constitution are, that in times of difficulty, if violent parties should arise, and we cannot expect otherwise, the large States may, to effect some ambitious purpose, change their own institutions, and Congress, partaking of the same spirit, may repeal or enact laws directing the mode of election of Representatives as may best suit their purposes. But, if such a clause as is now proposed be inserted in the Constitution, such a power in this House, capable of being so dangerously employed, would be destroyed.

Mr. Smith, of North Carolina, said, the simple objects which he had in view, were, first, in regard to the election of President, to give the minority as well as the majority of the people of every State, a chance of being heard. With regard to the election of Representatives, he well knew that the Constitution gave to Congress the power of prescribing the mode, and it was to guard against that very power that he wished the amendment to prevail. He was unwilling, for one, that Congress should ever exercise that power; because they might, as had been suggested, exercise it in a despotic and dangerous manner.

The motion for postponement to Wednesday next was agreed to—85 to 47.

MISSOURI.

The House having, on motion of Mr. Lowndes, resolved itself into a Committee of the Whole on the state of the Union.

The resolution declaring the admission of the State of Missouri into the Union on an equal footing with the original States, having been read—

Mr. Lowndes rose, and delivered a speech of nearly two hours in length, of which the following is a brief sketch:

The first observations of Mr. L. were lost to the reporter, from the confusion arising from members changing their seats, &c. When Mr. L.'s observations became audible, he was speaking of the difficulty under which he should labor, in what he had to say, from being obliged to direct his observations to arguments not yet urged, and in regard to which he must depend upon what he had heard in other quarters, and upon conjecture.

In the outset, he said, he was met by an objection of a general nature, applicable to other cases as well as that now presented to the House. He could not doubt, he said, from what he had heard, that there were members of the House who considered themselves bound by the same principles which influenced them at the last session, to vote at this session against the resolution declaring the admission of Missouri into the Union. On this point, he addressed himself to the moderation and good sense of the House—of those gentlemen particularly who believed the constitution framed by Missouri to be inconsistent with the principles of our Government, to say, whether it was not inconsistent with the character of our Government, and of all Governments, that questions once decided by the legitimate authority of the country should be considered as yet open, or inconclusive? Did not such a course of reasoning lead to the conclusion that all the acts of the Government were binding only on the majority who voted for them? That all compacts are void, for example, as to the minority which refuses to sanction them? Suppose, in regard to a debt incurred in carrying on a war, a party subsequently in power were to say—*we* did not vote for the debt; *we* did not support the war; we are not bound to pay the debt. Would such an argument be entitled to respect? Take, for an example, the debt incurred in the late war with Great Britain: was it not essential to the character of the nation that that debt should be considered obligatory as well upon those who approved, as on those who disapproved, the purpose for which the debt was contracted? And were all the members of this and the other House not *equally* bound by the act of the last session respecting Missouri? Whether we ought or ought not to have given to the people of Missouri the power to form a constitution and State government, we *have* given it. Whether or not we individually wished Missouri to form a constitution, the authority to do so was given by Congress. The constitution was formed, and Congress were now asked to declare that it was so. For himself, Mr. L. went on to say, he believed that the law of the last session gave Missouri a right to form a constitution; and that, having done so, she is now a State.

If you look at the course which Congress has pursued hitherto, it will be found that, on elevating territories from the grade and dependence of a territorial government, Congress has done no more than emancipate them from its control. On doing this, said Mr. L., you have reserved nothing like an authority to remand them to their colonial condition. You have determined, in such case, by the act of allowing the territory to form a constitution, that, for certain purposes, she is an independent State. In the act of the last session, it would be found, on referring to it, there was no difference between the mode of legislation in Mis-

souri, and that which had occurred in regard to the oldest of the States admitted into the Union. Comparing that act with other acts for the admission of States, it would be found to confer the same powers and impose the same restrictions. It was impossible to distinguish, in any manner, between the power which had been given to Missouri and that which had, in like circumstances, been granted to the oldest of the new States. Mr. L. went on to quote the cases of admission of States into the Union. He referred to that of Ohio. The act for her admission was couched in the broadest terms, requiring the convention, as usual, first to determine the question whether it was expedient to form a constitution. Although the mere act for the admission of a territory into the Union does not make her a State, inasmuch as her acceptance of the offer is required, yet, at the moment that she declares that it is expedient to form a constitution—at that precise moment she acquires all the rights of a State. The people of Missouri, as of every other admitted State, at that moment acquired rights which it is not competent for the legislature of this country—which it is not competent, upon the principles which we hold sacred, for any legislature under Heaven to divest them of.

Before he proceeded further to refer to the practice of former times, Mr. L. said he would notice an argument which he had heard suggested, which was in some degree a verbal one. It is said that the words of the law in regard to the admission of Missouri are prospective; that the Constitution says that Congress may admit new States into the Union; that no authority but Congress can admit them; that Congress has not admitted Missouri into the Union; and that it is necessary she should now address Congress and obtain its consent to her coming into the Union. It is true, Mr. L. said, that the law provides that Missouri "shall" be admitted; that is, prospectively as to the date of the law. It is true, also, that new States can be admitted into the Union only by Congress. But that admission may be from the time the law passes, or on the performance of a condition, whatever that condition may be. There was nothing, Mr. L. argued, in the law of the last session, to show that the act of admission was not complete on the part of Congress when that law passed, although it did refer to a future time. That this was a just construction of the matter, he said, was obvious by a reference to former examples. In the case of Kentucky, for example, her admission into the Union was deferred, by the act of Congress authorizing it, he did not know how many months, but more than a year after the passage of the act. Nothing more was necessary, after the passage of the act for the admission of Missouri, than a lapse of time sufficient for the determination of the people to be ascertained, whether they chose to form a constitution or not.

But his strongest argument, Mr. L. said he was aware, must be derived from the course pursued by Congress in former times. He disclaimed any particular devotion to precedent; but, in a time when parties were as firmly marshalled as they were on this subject at the last session; when the true import of the Constitution was contested by nearly equal parties on this floor; when geographical lines were observable in the division of opinion, it was wise, it was becoming, to look to what had been the practice in former times, when no causes existed so likely to disturb and mislead the sober judgment. Every man ought to examine the record of those days, and rather lean to a decision consistent with them.

Referring, then, for illustration, to the case of Ohio, after she had formed a constitution and State government, although no resolution had passed declaring her admission into the Union, it became necessary to pass a law to extend over her territory the jurisdiction of the courts of the United States; and the preamble to that law recites that the people did, on a certain day, form a constitution and State government, and give a name, whereby the said State has become one of the United States—that is, by the act of forming a constitution. And such, Mr. L. said, was the principle on which the United States had always acted. But, he said, the preamble was interesting, not only because it confirmed his argument in the main, but also marked the time and circumstance which, in the opinion of Congress at that time, made a people a State, viz., the day on which a constitution is formed, and the act of forming it.

The proof afforded by other precedents, however, that a people became a State on forming a constitution under the authority of Congress, was still less equivocal than that which had been cited. In every instance, and, as far as he knew, without an attempt at resistance, whenever such a constitution has been formed by a Territory, they have not only been considered a State, but the elections which they have made under their constitution have been held to be good. If, by the act of forming a constitution, they have not become independent States, how has it happened that, without a single exception, they have elected their own governors, judges, &c., and their acts have been Constitutional and valid? Can it be said of all these cases that Congress, knowing these territorial people had usurped the powers of States, would have silently submitted to it? Their having done so was the strongest proof that every one of these States had, in the opinion of Congress, of the State governments, and of the people, the powers which they exercised.

Mr. L. said he knew there were persons who believed that the people of Missouri Territory do not become a State until, by an act posterior to the formation of their constitution, Congress declares their admission. Mr. L. said he could not admit this. It was disproved by the uniform language of precedents. The acquiescence of Congress in their elections of Senators and Representative to Congress disproved it. These elections, held previous to the submission of their constitutions to Congress, had uniformly been held valid. Who are Senators? They are deputed by the States composing the Union to represent them in Congress. If States only can vote for Senators, the uniform practice of recognising all such elections as are subsequent to the adoption of a consti-

tution, is conclusive enough that they who choose them were already in the condition of States. In the case of Kentucky, indeed, without any declaratory resolution, without any thing like a formal acknowledgment of her being a State, but by virtue of an act declaring, prospectively, that when she had formed a constitution she should be a State, she was admitted without further legislation. In the case of Indiana, there was a yet more formal and authoritative exposition of the principle for which Mr. L. contended. In the case of Indiana, the practice of a declaration of admission first occurred, which had been since followed in other cases. Properly viewed, that declaration, Mr. L. said, was only a form of notification to the other States—a proclamation by Congress to the Union, of the admission of another State into the family. That such was the light in which it was viewed on this first occasion on which it was employed, was evident from the fact, that the resolution of declaration passed on the 11th December, 1816, and the representative from the State was admitted to his seat on the 2d December, nine days preceding; so that it was evident the declaratory resolution was then regarded as a matter of form and notification merely. But there was still stronger proof, in the case of Indiana, of his position. In counting the votes for President and Vice President a few days after the above date, those of Indiana, given before the passage of the declaratory resolution, were received and counted. If a people may rightfully, and even without objection, elect a Governor, Legislature, and Judges—may elect and send to Congress Senators and Representative, and, finally, may vote for President and Vice President—upon what principle will it be said that a people, enjoying and exercising all these rights, are not a State; or that to constitute them a State, requires the further interposition of this House? He could not admit it, he repeated.

These observations, Mr. L. said, he had made with a view to show how little foundation there was for an opinion, which he had understood was not uncommon, that the act of the last session was merely a suggestion to the people of Missouri that they might form a constitution if it pleased them, and that, if that constitution met the approbation of the Congress of the United States at their next session, they should then be admitted into the Union.

Another circumstance, Mr. L. said, showed, beyond dispute, that it was not intended by this House, in passing the act of the last session, merely to give authority to the people of Missouri to propose a constitution, but that it was intended to confer on Missouri, by that act, all the rights which the oldest and proudest States of the Union are supposed to possess. When that act was under consideration, it appears by the Journal of this House that a motion was made by Mr. Taylor to amend the bill by striking out these words, "And the said State, when formed, shall be admitted into the Union upon an equal footing with the original States, in all respects whatever," and inserting, in lieu thereof, those which follow: "And if the same (that is, the constitution) shall be approved by Congress, the said Territory shall be admitted into the Union as a State, upon the same footing as the original States;" the difference being that, in the bill as it stood, (the act as it now stands,) we made her a State, and in the other we were to give her authority to form a constitution, and leave our approbation to be a condition of its final admission. A very large majority, (125 to 49,) even at that time of strong excitement and nearly equal division of opinion with respect to the restriction, voted in the negative.

The substance of Mr. L's. argument then was, he said, that, by the act authorizing the people of Missouri to form a constitution and State government, certain rights were given to them; by the former practice of the Government, he had endeavored to show that the mere circumstance of assenting to the proposition of Congress was enough to constitute the people a State, the act of declaration, now proposed to the House, being mere surplusage. Missouri had, then, a right to form a government absolutely and inalienably. If she had not now the rights of a State, let it be shown how she had lost them. It is contrary to the principles of the Constitution, contrary to the genius of our Government, that, having once given them the right of self-government, Congress can now take it from them.

Considering this question as settled, the next important question was, whether the constitution formed by the State of Missouri becomes void by the admission into it of a clause not compatible with the Constitution of the United States, admitting, for the sake of argument, that such is the fact.

Whether that particular clause of the Constitution to which exception was understood to be taken was Constitutional or not, the interest of the nation, justice to Missouri, and respect for itself, required that the House should not undertake to decide. In taking this ground, Mr. L. said he knew he should be considered by some as evading the performance of a duty which, in the present case, they supposed to be devolved on this House. On this account he should attempt to show that no duty devolved on this House to express an opinion with respect to that clause; and intimated that he could show, were it necessary, that similar provisions were contained in various acts of the United States to which exception had been taken in neither House. The clause of the Missouri constitution to which he referred was that requiring the Legislature to pass laws to prohibit the settlement of free negroes in the State, which was supposed to conflict with the provision of the Constitution of the United States which provides that "the citizens of each State shall be entitled to all the privileges and immunities of citizens in the several States." Mr. L. here went into an argument of some detail, the amount of which was, that, as to numbers, a very large majority of the free blacks in the United States were not considered citizens in their respective States; and that, in construing any general provision of a constitution, it was fair to consider it as having a general application, and not as being without exceptions. In any view there could be nothing more clear than that, if the objected provision was capable of a construction which would reconcile it with the Constitution, it ought to receive that construction. For example, in this case of Missouri, he thought it might be quite fair to say that that provision respecting free people of color must be construed liberally, as intending to exempt from its operation such of them as were citizens in other States. However this might be, he contended, as the committee had laid it down in their report, that it was a question not for this House, but for a different tribunal to determine.

But Mr. L. said there were many who object to this course—the course pursued in all other cases—who allow that the judiciary could, with more ease, certainty, uniformity, and effect, expound Constitutional law, but contend that we must decide whether the provision in question be Constitutional or not. We must express an opinion on it, however inexpedient, because it is our duty. Now, Mr. L. said he did not see that having declared that the people of Missouri should form a constitution and State government, imposed on this House the duty of construing law in this more than any other case. It might be considered rather an objection to it, inasmuch as, in doing so, they would have to expound the law themselves had made—no principle being better established than that the authority which forms the law should not construe nor apply it. The true question in this case then was, which was the best tribunal to decide the question respecting this disputed clause of the Missouri constitution. If it were asked whether this House, or the Senate, or the Judiciary of the country, were the best qualified to expound a law, there would be no difference of opinion on the question. It must, then, be a consideration of paramount duty only on the part of this House to decide upon it, which could induce it to undertake the exposition of a law in respect to the construction of which there was a doubt.

Mr. L. then examined, somewhat at large, the question, whether a judicial or legislative tribunal be the most capable to decide correctly such a question as was supposed to be presented by the particular clause in the Constitution of Missouri. He argued, from the inability of either branch of Congress to act independently on any such question, from their inability to act with uniformity, &c., that they were not the proper bodies to be charged with judicial investigations. And why, he asked, the rights of all the States being equal, should those of Missouri be subject to an adjudication different from that to which other States are subject? The rights of the old States were subject to judicial decision; and no man would pretend that, in respect to any old State, Delaware for example, her Constitution could be suspended, that her Senators and Representatives should be excluded from these Halls, on Congress thinking they had discovered something not altogether right in her constitution. It was an essential objection to the power now claimed for Congress, that, if allowed, it would be a power to be exer-

16th Con. 2d Sess.—17

cised in a new State, which none would pretend it could exercise in an old one. Upon every consideration, of which he urged several others, he was in favor of leaving the matter with the Judiciary, where, and where only, in his opinion, it properly belonged.

The principles which had influenced, from time to time, the conduct of the different branches of the Government, would lead to the same conclusion. At the time of the formation of the Federal Constitution, (to go back to that date,) it was foreseen that there might be a disposition, at some future day, in some or other of the States, to break over the barriers of the Constitution about to be formed, &c., and a provision was introduced prescribing a mode of deciding controversies of that description. If, in all other cases of Constitutional questions, it has been provided that they shall be decided by the Judiciary, the reason must apply and be conclusive why this body should not undertake to decide a Constitutional question in the case of Missouri. Justice requires that those who have the same rights shall have their rights decided by the same tribunal.

If, however, the only objection to the passage of the resolution now under consideration was, that an inference might be drawn, from the silence of Congress, that they approved the exceptionable provision in the constitution of Missouri, Mr. L. suggested that some mode might be adopted by which the objection on this point might be explained. He should himself, as an individual, with the utmost reluctance express any opinion on the subject, and he thought it would be exceedingly unwise in Congress to do so. There would be no end to such a course. There were in the constitution of Missouri, and of every State in the Union, clauses to which some might take exception, of which Mr. L. instanced the provisions respecting banks, &c., which some believed the States had no right to establish. Every consideration of prudence and propriety, in his opinion, forbade from interposing in the present instance.

Mr. L. said he did admit, however, that there might be cases in which Congress might find it to be their duty to interpose, on the moment of admission of new States into the Union. For instance, if, in relation to the term of Senators, or any other provision which, from its character, could not be brought before the Supreme Court, the new constitution were incompatible with that of the United States, it was his opinion it would be a good reason why Congress should interfere. Nor did he think this was at all inconsistent with the ground he had already taken, if for no other reason than that the judicial tribunal could decide the question now agitated, and decide it better than this House. The duty of Congress, in this respect, begins where that of the Judiciary ends.

Referring to his former remark, that gentlemen would do well to satisfy themselves that their opinions were not the effect of prejudice, by examining what was the conduct of their predecessors in more quiet times, Mr. L. said he would turn to the case of the second new State which was ad-

mitted into the Union, and the objections to whose admission were removed in the way proposed in the present case. Tennessee, without waiting for a law of Congress to authorize her, held a convention, formed a constitution, and sent it on to Congress. The objection was made in the House of Representatives, by Mr. Smith, of South Carolina, that the constitution of Tennessee was incompatible with that of the United States ; to which Mr. Baldwin replied, that, if there should be things in the constitution of Tennessee not compatible with the Constitution of the United States, " it was well known that the Constitution of the United States would be paramount—they can therefore be of no effect." He quoted this to show, that this suggestion of referring the question to another tribunal than this, was not an expedient to get over this case, but one which had prevailed in the early days of the Republic. The conflict between the constitution of Tennessee, however, and that of the United States, was much more unequivocal than in the present case, and so far the present case is more favorably presented to Congress than was that of Tennessee. In the latter case, the Legislature were required to provide some means by which the State of Tennessee should be sued in its courts, with a proviso that this advantage should be confined to citizens of that State, and not extended to those of other States. Here was a direct conflict with the Constitution of the United States, whilst that of Missouri is only constructive. Yet, in that case, the question of Constitutional law was left to those who were most likely to decide correctly, and withal competent to enforce their decision—that is, to the Supreme Judicial Tribunal. He thought it perfectly compatible with the most nice and rigid sense of duty for Congress to do the same in the case now before them.

Mr. L. said he knew an objection had been taken to leaving the Judiciary to sustain a conflict with a State, in regard to the conformity of its Constitution to that of the United States. But, surely, if in regard to all other States, it now has that authority, there can be no hardship in leaving the same power with it, in regard to new States.

Mr. L. said the views he had expressed were founded on the belief that Missouri was now, to all intents and purposes, a State. But, he said, if he did not believe, that, under the act of last session, Missouri is a State already ; if he thought she was only a State in fact and not a State in right, he should have the same opinion as he had now expressed. She has her own government, legislature, and judiciary, and exercises all the rights of a sovereign State. In this case, as in the other, he should think it expedient to pronounce on the Constitutional question ; because, should that clause be excepted from the recognition, it could be reinstated on her becoming a State, without the power of Congress to prevent it ; and the question must at last be decided by the Judiciary, the only competent tribunal.

Mr. L. here concluded his remarks, reserving for a future occasion the answers to objections which he might not have anticipated. And, on motion of Mr. SERGEANT, the Committee rose, and the House adjourned.

THURSDAY, December 7.

Two other members appeared and took their seats, to wit; from Pennsylvania, ANDREW BODEN; and from Kentucky, BENJAMIN HARDIN.

Mr. PINCKNEY presented a memorial and petition of the inhabitants of the city of Charleston, in South Carolina, in opposition to any increase of the tariff of duties on imports, by way of protection to the manufacturing interest of the country.

Mr. TUCKER, of South Carolina, presented a similar memorial from the inhabitants of the district of Newbury, in that State; which memorials were referred to the Committee on Manufactures.

Mr. SIBLEY submitted the following resolution:

Resolved, That the Committee of Claims be instructed to inquire into the expediency of allowing David Cooper eighty dollars, the estimated value of a chimney and the plank of a house, taken for the use of the United States, under an order of Captain Holder, of the seventeenth regiment of infantry, in the month of December, 1814, and applied in the erection of barracks in Fort Shelby.

The resolution was read, and the question was put to agree thereto, and determined in the negative.

An engrossed bill, entitled "An act to alter the time of holding the district court in the district of Mississippi," was read the third time, and passed.

MISSOURI.

The House then resolved itself into a Committee of the Whole, Mr. NELSON of Virginia in the chair, on the resolution declaring the admission of Missouri into the Union on an equal footing with the other States of the Union. And the question having been again stated—

Mr. SERGEANT rose. Of the speech which he delivered, occupying upwards of two hours' time, the following must be considered as a free but not a very full report.

Mr. S. began by saying that this subject had been so long and so much talked of, and written of, it was so much connected with considerations arising out of the question so much debated at the last session, that he hardly doubted every member of this Committee had for himself made up his mind on the immediate question. It was not, therefore, with any great hope of persuading others, that he now rose, but from a wish to explain the grounds of his own opinion, which was entertained with so much sincerity that he could not permit himself to doubt that the opinion of every member of the Committee was entertained with equal sincerity, and that the question would be decided, as it ought to be, on its real merits. With respect to the question hinted at by the gentleman from South Carolina, and discussed at the last session, Mr. S. said he did not agree with him that the decision of the question now before the House depended upon the decision of the question agitated at the last session. How far that question might be involved in

the present question, might be a subject for consideration; but, independently of that question, the one now presented was a very important one. However minute in itself, if it extended but to a single provision of the constitution presented by the people of Missouri, it yet involved considerations which those, who had listened to the arguments of the gentleman from South Carolina, must see, went to the whole extent of determining what power actually remained in Congress with regard to any Territory after authorizing them to form a constitution—what they have a right to insist upon, what they have a right to do and say upon the subject—in short, the question whether Congress have or have not any power at all under the Constitution of the United States, with respect to the admission of a new State into the Union, after the passage of an act authorizing the people to form a constitution.

It could not be doubted or denied, Mr. S. admitted, that there was, in looking at the admissions of States into the Union, heretofore, at least, an apparent irregularity, and much of apparent disorder. If, however, any inference were to be drawn from precedents in the case, it would be, that there never had been any precise examination of the powers of Congress in this respect—no established mode of admission—or, in other words, that there had been every variety of mode. For the sake of the future peace and harmony of the Government of the United States; for the sake of the territories hereafter applying to be admitted into the Union—for the sake of Congress alone, said Mr. S., it is incumbent on us all to examine the grounds of this question; to see what are our rights, and what theirs, and deduce, from a full consideration of these, a rule which shall be uniform as to the States hereafter to be admitted into the Union, and free from the danger of exposing us to contests such as that which appears to have arisen on the present occasion.

The power to admit a State into the Union, no one would doubt, was a very high one—a power to part with a portion of that authority which was originally vested in the old States, and which exists in the present States, and to admit to a participation in our counsels, in our power, in the control and management of every thing concerning our rights and property, a new and integral member of the Union. The question became one of graver consideration, when it was considered that it was proposed now to extend this participation to an object which was not in the contemplation of those who formed the Constitution of the United States, who had looked, in their provisions, to the territory then in possession of the United States, and probably had never calculated on the admission of States out of territory beyond the original limits of the United States. This high power was given to Congress; and, after the discussion of last session, it was needless to say, was given without limitation. The power is "to admit new States into the Union;" it is granted in the broadest and most comprehensive manner—and, it would seem to follow, as the consequence of this grant of general authority, that Congress possessed every power and authority necessary to its fair exercise. Whatever power was really given to Congress, it was their duty to exercise, and not turn it over to any other Department, confiding in it to cure the defect which Congress suffered to pass uncorrected. There was nothing in the Constitution of the United States which countenanced a different course. It is our right and our duty, said Mr. S., when a State offers herself for admission into the Union, to see that she can come into the Union under the Constitution of the United States, and in conformity with its provisions. For certainly, whatever were the terms in which the power was given to the people of Missouri to form a constitution, no one could for a single moment doubt that that power was never intended to transcend the Constitution of the United States, or to bring into the Union a State whose Constitution was not conformable to that of the United States. Such a grant would have been an exercise of authority by Congress beyond the Constitution : it would be an anomaly impossible to account for—an inconsistency with the Constitution of the United States which it would be impossible for any one to reconcile.

It would therefore seem, that when, as incident to the power of admitting States into the Union, Congress authorized a Territory to form a constitution and State government, it must follow that the constitution, so to be formed, is to be conformable to the Constitution of the United States, and that the Territory thus authorized does not in any sense become a State until she has formed such a constitution. Our power, said Mr. S., is to admit, and incidentally to authorize the formation of a constitution, with a view to admission. Have Congress the power to authorize a people to form a constitution and State government sovereign and independent of the United States? No, the power to authorize a people to form a constitution is an implied power, subordinate to the full power, which never is effectually exercised until the act of admission subsequent to the formation of a constitution.

Mr. S. said, he made these remarks in the outset, to meet at once an argument of the member from South Carolina, which was plausible, captivating, and seemed to be calculated to smooth the way, and remove every difficulty. That argument was that the State, from the moment of its formation of a constitution, became an independent and sovereign State. Where, said Mr. S., is your power in the Constitution to make such a State? Your power is to admit States into the Union, and your power to authorize the people of a Territory to form a constitution is merely subordinate and subsidiary to the main power. Can you admit a State by anticipation, as the gentleman has suggested? You transcend your authority if you do so. Mr. S. ventured to say that Congress never had done so; that they could not do so; and, in some sense or other, every member of the Committee would agree with him in this opinion. Could Congress, by anticipation, bind itself to the admission of a State, (for such was the argument yesterday pressed upon the Committee,) so as to

have no choice but to accept such a constitution as that State chose to offer? Surely not; but, according to the argument advanced by the gentleman from South Carolina, not only was the present Congress to be bound by the act of the last session, but the present Congress might, by an act passed now, bind the next Congress to the admission of a State into the Union. Was the authority given by Congress to the people to form a constitution, a compact with them that they should be admitted into the Union on any other terms than those prescribed to them? For one, Mr. S. said, he did not feel himself bound, by giving the authority to a people to form a constitution, to admit them into the Union, unless their constitution should be such as the people of the United States, through their representatives, thought fit to accept as the fundamental rule of government of the State thus to be admitted.

Mr. S. then proceeded to say, that he did not mean now to enter into the question of the last session—it had been discussed enough. He did not mean to abandon the opinion which he had then formed and expressed. It had not been formed hastily, but carefully and deliberately, and he had seen no reason to change his mind upon it. Without going into that question at all, he should proceed to the immediate question presented by the argument of the gentleman from South Carolina. This single question was, whether it is the right and duty of Congress, before admitting a State into the Union, to see that its constitution and State government be not repugnant to the Constitution of the United States. He should have hoped, he said, and he yet hoped, that the opinion would be nearly unanimous in this body, that there might be such a repugnancy between such a State constitution and the Constitution of the United States, as would not only justify Congress in interfering, but make it their imperious duty to interfere, to prevent her taking rank in the Union. Whether that was the case in the present instance, was, he said, a different question.

The preliminary inquiry was that which he had just stated. It had been said that Missouri was already an independent State; that she has formed a State government under an unlimited authority from Congress; and that she has now the same rights as the proudest and oldest States in the Union. If it be so, said Mr. S., what are we now deliberating about? Why is it, that the resolution now under consideration is proposed for our adoption? Why are this and the other House called upon to pass a legislative act which is altogether unnecessary, and which has clauses in it, if this construction be true, which are extremely objectionable? If this construction be correct, her Senators and Representative have a right to their seats on the floor of either House—to unite in the common counsels on the affairs of the Union, and to give to the votes of Missouri the same force as those of any other State. Why are they, then, said Mr. S., kept waiting at our doors, and not permitted to partake of our deliberations? Why do they wait until the fate of this resolution be known?

It was said that this resolution was nothing but

a declaration of a fact. Such a notification was not necessary for the Senators and Representative of Missouri; it was not necessary for Congress, if, the fact being known, the former had nothing to do to entitle them to a seat, but to advance to the Chair of either House and take the oath to support the Constitution of the United States. Why was it, moreover, that the constitution of Missouri had been submitted to a committee of this House? Why had a report been made by that committee, and why was this House now discussing it? And why was it that that report went into an examination of a particular clause of that constitution, and pointed out the mode in which Congress were to relieve themselves from the task of deciding on its constitutionality, by leaving it to the Judiciary? If the gentleman's doctrine were true, this is all superfluous. It is more, said Mr. S., for the resolution declares that Missouri shall be, and hereafter is declared to be, one of the United States, &c. He did not use this reference, he said, for the mere effect of verbal criticism, but for a higher purpose. When a committee, composed as that committee was, finds itself under the necessity of presenting a resolution, to be adopted by a joint vote of both Houses, declared that Missouri is thereby, not that she has been admitted into the Union, was it not as strong evidence as could be furnished, that there was something which seemed to compel those who acted on it to say, that this declaration of the fact is the virtual legislation which brings Missouri into the Union—which qualifies her for induction to the Union, and that anterior to it she was not a State, and not entitled to be? From what period, Mr. S. asked, was it that Missouri was admitted into the Union? It would be from the moment of the adoption of this resolution. Could it be said of any antecedent period? Here, Mr. S. said, he would avail himself of another concession of the gentleman from South Carolina; and, in taking to his aid a concession of his, Mr. S. said he did it with the full impression that it was the result of the conviction of his own mind, and with the benefit, therefore, of the conviction of such a mind as his. That gentleman had admitted that Congress might, if they thought proper, introduce a qualification of their assent to the admission of Missouri into the Union, which shall serve to show its dissent to a particular clause of the constitution of that State. If this resolution, then, instead of being merely formal and declaratory, was susceptible of an amendment by which Congress could exclude that interpretation of a particular clause of the State constitution which on its face it bears, would it be said that the State was a member of the Union without the adoption of that resolve? If so, where did Congress derive the authority to legislate on the interpretation of its constitution? Mr. S. further called the attention of the Committee to the terms of the preamble of this resolution, wherein it is declared that, "whereas, in pursu-'ance of an act of Congress, &c., the people of the 'said Territory did, on the 19th day of July, 1820, 'by a convention called for that purpose, form for 'themselves a constitution and State government, 'which constitution and State government, so

formed, is republican, and in conformity to the 'provisions of the said act." The reason assigned for her admission is, that she has formed a constitution in conformity to the provisions of the act of last session. How could the committee know this? By their own examination? Could Congress, then, declare this to be the case, without having examined the constitution of the new State? Certainly not. And when, in the act authorizing the formation of this constitution were found two limitations, that it should be republican, and that it should not be repugnant to the Constitution of the United States, did it not become indispensable, before passing a preamble and resolution like this, that the members of this House should be satisfied in their own minds that these requisitions have been complied with?

If, in a single article, the constitution of Missouri be repugnant to that of the United States, said Mr. S., can we seriously assert that she has formed a constitution according to the authority given to her? And, when called on to say how we can reconcile it to ourselves to sanction such a contradiction in terms, will it be sufficient to say that we have nothing to do with that question, and will leave it to the Judiciary to decide? We have nothing to do with it! exclaimed Mr. SERGEANT. Why, then, prescribe to the people of Missouri any conditions in the first instance? Why not say, we gave her a right to form a constitution; she has formed it, and, whether it be or be not repugnant to the Constitution of the United States, she is a member of the Union? The contradiction was sufficiently apparent in the fact of the introduction of this resolution: it would be seen at once, that the House was neither conforming to the Constitution of the United States, to the act of the last session, nor to any principle heretofore observed in the admission of States. Could it be said that Congress had parted with the power of looking into the constitution of Missouri, when it had expressly prescribed conditions which should be indispensable to its acceptance? The terms of the compact, if the act of the last session was to be considered a compact, between the United States and Missouri, were perfectly clear; and he took this opportunity of saying, that, if Missouri was involved in difficulty—if Congress found itself in perplexity—if the Union was disturbed on this occasion—if this House was impelled to the consideration of questions which it was painful to act upon, it was not the fault of Congress—it was not the fault of the Constitution of the United States, but it was the fault of the people of Missouri. It might be their error—an error which they would be glad to avail themselves of an opportunity to correct—for, Mr. S. said, he could not believe the people of Missouri would have wantonly introduced into their constitution a clause at variance with the Constitution of the United States, under an impression that this act of admission was a mere form. They would not wantonly have done it, for it could not be either their interest or their inclination to try the temper of the Congress of the United States—to try how far its regard to the Constitution would bear it out in the contest, or how far it would consent to surrender a portion of the rights of the whole Union to avoid a difficulty which the people of Missouri have themselves created. There was prescribed to them but one condition; to that condition they had not conformed, and they are not entitled to admission into the Union. The failure to fulfil the compact is on the part of the people of Missouri; and, said Mr. S., when we come, in a case of this sort, to the question between remanding this constitution for reconsideration, or giving up the smallest possible portion of Constitutional power, I trust that the people of every part of the Union would bear us out in saying that the Constitution shall be inviolate; and that we shall not be the first to set a precedent which, begun to-day, may be followed to-morrow, until it involves the very existence of our Government.

Would the people of Missouri, Mr. S. asked, think more highly of Congress were it to yield to them on this occasion? Would they not hereafter come into the Union with more respect for Congress, and with more respect for themselves, too—with a higher sense of the value of admission into the Union, if Congress now fairly met this question, thus giving to the people of Missouri an assurance that what was now done with respect to them should be hereafter the rule of conduct for Congress, as to others asking admission into the Union? Would it not show to them that Congress was disposed to do all in its power to preserve the blessings of this Government for them and for their posterity? What, he asked, would be the consequence of submission by Congress in the present case? Missouri will have extorted from us something; another State will extort something more; each will appeal to our fears, which may be well or ill founded; each new State will endeavor to exact from us what she thinks will make for her own interest, until at last they will not think it worth while to ask our leave to do as they choose. How much better would it be for Congress at once to take its ground, and refuse to sanction the constitution of any State which is in any respect repugnant to that of the United States!

Suppose that this constitution of Missouri, instead of being faulty in a single particular, were throughout, from beginning to end, at variance with the Constitution of the United States.—Would it be pretended, in that case, that Missouri was entitled to be admitted into the Union? Certainly not; yet the only argument in favor of her admission, with one clause of her constitution incompatible with that of the United States, went the whole length, or necessarily involved the consequence of yielding the whole; because it was founded on the ground that Congress had parted with the whole power, and had no right to pass upon the constitution; on the ground, in short, that Missouri is now admitted into the Union.

The gentleman himself, however, had, in another part of his speech, given up this, which was the essential part of his argument; for he had conceded that, if the constitution of Missouri was repugnant to the Constitution of the United States in particulars which could not be submitted to the judicial authority for decision, Congress ought to interfere. If, said Mr. S., we ought in any case to interfere, there must be a mode of interference. What is the mode, and what should be the time? When, certainly, she presents herself for admission. And, if we have then a right to inquire whether there is or is not occasion for our interference, is not the whole ground of the gentleman's argument abandoned?

Pursuing his argument, Mr. S. said he held it to be perfectly true that there could be no violation of the Constitution of the United States which would not produce injurious civil and political effects, as distinguished from individual effects over which the Judiciary have control. How many men may be injured before one man appears with a spirit to resist the injustice! What, Mr. S. asked, did the history of all Governments exhibit to us but a series of usurpations on one hand and sufferings on the other, submitted to until they became too grievous longer to be borne? Men suffer long; they suffer from necessity, from poverty, from ignorance, from the want of capacity to exert those rights which belong to them, and which it ought to be the care of a wise Government to preserve to them. Why is it that the names of men who, in all time past, have resisted oppression, have been immortalized by the historian, the painter, and the poet? Why have they been considered as entitled to peculiar honors? Because they took upon themselves the burden, and a heavy burden it is, of resisting by force the Government which had long oppressed and persecuted them and their fellow men, under the forms of law. Now, said Mr. S., if we allow bad principles to be admitted into the constitutions of States formed under our eye, or good principles to be excluded, what will be the consequence? You shift the responsibility from yourselves and leave it to individuals to fight the battle with the States. Why do our State constitutions contain declarations of rights? Why have the people been so careful thus to lay down the principles which are to guide the Government in its operations? For the purpose of preserving political and civil rights inviolate as well as individual rights, and to prevent individuals from suffering under their violation.

Coming nearer to the particular question involved in the constitution now presented by Missouri, Mr. S. said, suppose that constitution had said that no free *white* citizen of the United States should come to reside in Missouri—was there any gentleman who would say that, with such a provision in her constitution, Missouri ought to be admitted into the Union? He would not answer for others, but, for himself, he believed such a provision would produce such a shock as would occasion but one feeling throughout the country—that of resistance. This was an extreme case, he knew, (not likely to happen,) but he had put it for the purpose of illustration; and he confessed that the argument appeared to him irresistible, that a power to examine the provisions of the constitution must exist, and that a power to refuse admission, in certain cases, must necessarily result.

If Congress, having the power to reject, should yet accept the constitution of Missouri, Mr. S. contended it could not, with any propriety, be said that Congress did not approve the constitution of Missouri.

The trust of guarding the Constitution of the United States from violation, said he, in continuation, is peculiarly and emphatically ours. We are sworn to support the Constitution before we enter on the duties to which we are called under it ; and, he believed the gentleman from South Carolina himself, and every other member of this House, would go along with him in saying that their support of the Constitution ought to be active and zealous, and not a cold and penurious support. It ought to be no calculation how much they might give up of that Constitution, but a determination that even if there be doubt, that doubt should be determined in favor of the Constitution. It should be thus, said he, that by a constant, warm, and cordial support of it here, we may invigorate and quicken the respect and veneration for that instrument, which, I trust, is entertained by the whole people of the United States.

With respect to the proposition to turn over to the judiciary the decision of the question involved in this constitution, Mr. S. said, he must declare, that, with the greatest respect possible for the judiciary ; with the highest confidence in their rectitude and wisdom ; with the greatest willingness to submit to their decisions in their proper sphere ; he could not consent, on a question which was properly presented for his own decision, to say, let the question sleep till some humble individual, some poor citizen, shall come forward and claim a decision of it. He never would pass a duty by, by leaving it to some individual to do what Congress ought to have done. No, Mr. S. said, his idea of supporting the Constitution was, to give it such an active support as should convince everybody even the appearance of violation of it would not be permitted. And he begged gentlemen, before they consented to take a course different from this, that they would consider, seriously consider, what may be the effect, in a Government depending on public opinion for its support, of a disrespect of its authority exhibited on this floor.

Mr. S. then noticed the argument which Mr. Lowndes had derived from the Journal of this House of the last session, in the case of the motion of Mr. Taylor to amend the Missouri act so as to require her constitution, when formed, to be approved by Congress, &c., before she could become a State—which motion was negatived by two to one. Mr. S. admitted the fact, but argued that it proved nothing in favor of Mr. Lowndes's argument. Gentlemen had voted against it on various grounds ; some, he knew, had voted against it because they believed it superfluous, holding the opinion which he was now maintaining, that the constitution must, of course, receive the sanction of Congress before it could be of any authority, &c.

Mr. S. then referred, for illustration to the case

of Louisiana, who was required to submit her constitution to Congress, and it was submitted and approved accordingly before it went into operation. If Congress, according to the gentleman's argument, had no right to do so, this proceeding was all unconstitutional and void. And it was worthy of remark that, at the same time that constitution was required to be submitted to Congress, it was also required to be not repugnant to the Constitution of the United States. Yet Louisiana was not intended to be admitted on different terms from other States, but on the same, &c.

But, independently of the act of the last session, it had been asserted that Missouri is now a State ; that she is a State in fact. Mr. S. asked of gentlemen seriously to consider this position. From what time has she become a State ? From the moment of the passage of our act, from that of the adoption of her constitution, or from that of the organization of her government ? He did not distinctly understand from what point of time the gentleman from South Carolina dated her independence—

[Mr. Lowndes here explained what point of time he referred to. It was at the moment when, the question having been formally proposed to the people of Missouri, whether they chose to form a constitution and State government, they voted it expedient to do so, it was then that he thought arose the right in them of self-government.]

Mr. S. did not consider the point of time in this respect material. The question was, is Missouri entitled to the rights of a State until she be admitted into the Union by Congress ? In support of this opinion, he said, no reason had been assigned that was founded in the Constitution of the United States. Reasons had been assigned by the gentleman of South Carolina, which appeared to him to be founded in a convenience which amounted to a sort of necessity, but no argument had been drawn from the Constitution in support of this position. We have the power to admit a State into the Union, said Mr. S., but was it ever supposed that a State was admitted, by her own act, before we admitted her ? Could it be pretended that, when Congress authorized the people of Missouri to form a constitution, and under the circumstances of this case, they did admit them into the Union ? It might be argued, with some plausibility, that Congress had by that act engaged that, at some time, they should be admitted into the Union. If the authority given had been to erect themselves into a sovereign and independent State, Mr. S. would have been able to understand the argument that they are now a State. But, when Congress gave them authority to form a constitution to fit them for admission, to say that Congress did then admit them into the Union was an argument not intelligible ; and almost equally so was that which made her out to be a State whenever her people had formed a constitution.

The United States, with respect to her territory, stood almost in the same relation as one of the States to its territory. Virginia, for example, gave authority to the people of that part of her territory which is now Kentucky, to form a constitution. The territory called a convention, made a State government, fixed the mode of her elections, and elected her officers. Was she then a member of the Union? Yes, when Congress agreed to admit her into the Union. Was she a State before that took place? Certainly not. So with the Territories of the United States. Congress gives them authority to make a constitution, preparatory to their admission, and that being done, Congress may admit them.

If, said Mr. S. further, Representatives from a Territory which has thus formed a constitution, present themselves at the door of this House, is not the House bound to inquire whether they are the Representatives of a State? Must we not examine whether they are properly deputed, or must we admit anybody and everybody who presents himself and declares that he is the Representative of a State? We may know the fact out of doors, but it must also be known here; to ascertain it, we are obliged to examine the Constitution. Mr. S. entered into a train of reasoning to show the inconvenience which would result from each branch of the Government being left to determine for itself the independence of a State, the chance of their not concurring in their views of the subject, and the incongruity which would result from such a disagreement.

The orderly, politic, and regular course of proceeding in such a case as this, was so obvious, he said, that he was only astonished that, in any case, a different course had been pursued. In the main, he said, the construction had been that for which he contended. Whatever irregularities there might have been in other respects, with respect to the newly formed States, the full extension to a State of the benefits of its admission into the Union had never taken place until, by some act, Congress had expressly or impliedly recognised its admission.

Mr. S. then proceeded to inquire whether the practice of our Government sustained the doctrine which he had endeavored to show was inconsistent with its theory. With respect to precedents, whilst he disavowed a slavish subjection to their authority, yet he acknowledged that if they were clear and undeviating, showing an uniform practice under the Constitution to the present time, he should consider them of very high authority. He recollected, in a case at the last session, the gentleman from South Carolina had not considered them of so great weight; but Mr. S. said he agreed with that gentleman now in allowing them weight, provided they have the character of uniformity. He was mistaken if, upon examination, they did not turn out differently from what the member from South Carolina had supposed. In examining them, a precedent might be made out to warrant any course gentlemen chose, they differed so much from each other; among them might be found one for a people making a constitution without previous authority from Congress, and that too out of the territory of the United States, for which nobody would contend. Mr. S. here briefly ran over the cases of admission into the Union

commenting on each. Kentucky, Vermont, Tennessee, Ohio, and Louisiana, were admitted up to 1811, inclusive, and in every case some act of the Government had been thought necessary, precedent or subsequent, to entitle them to admission. From the year 1811, however, every State admitted (five in number, besides Maine, whose case was peculiar) had been formed by previous authority, and had come into the Union by virtue of an act or resolution expressly admitting her. Would gentlemen, then, take the single precedent of Kentucky, of Tennessee, of Vermont, with their peculiarities, and apply it to a State formed out of a new Territory purchased by the United States, or would they take the case of other States, which formed a series of precedents, each distinctly recognising the power of Congress to give previous authority to a people to form a constitution, and also the authority and right of Congress to admit them into the Union, and the necessity of such an act of admission?

With respect to elections by the inchoate States, he considered them as provisional, and made valid by the ratification of the Constitution. The Representative from Indiana taking his seat before the passage of the act for her admission, he considered an oversight. And was not the fact of the Representative from Missouri remaining absent, asserting no right as a Representative, and not being admitted as such, (and so of her Senators also,) a stronger evidence of the opinion, not only of the old States, but of the new States too, than a single precedent of irregularity, as that of Indiana?

Having shown, in his opinion, that Congress possessed the right and power to examine this question, Mr. S. proceeded to the remaining points in the discussion.

In this particular case, the mode of proceeding proposed, struck him as the most objectionable that could be devised; because it seemed to him that the report and the observations of the chairman of the committee, did admit that there was something in the Constitution formed by the people of Missouri, upon which, if the House was called upon to speak, gentlemen would be obliged to say they are of opinion it is unconstitutional; for, in the first place, the committee are willing to leave the decision on a particular clause to the Judiciary; in the next place, they think it susceptible of an interpretation not inconsistent with the Constitution of the United States; and, it is lastly suggested, that Congress may avoid the difficulty by a protest, or explanation, or interpretation of the clause, as they desire it to be understood. All this seemed to convey the impression that there was something there, which gentlemen wished to avoid voting and deciding upon.

To refer the subject to the Judiciary was one mode proposed for getting over it. To this course there were a great many objections, which doubtless had already occurred to the minds of the Committee. Among these, Mr. S. dwelt particularly on the following: that, if it be the duty of this House to pronounce on any question they had no right to shift the responsibility on the Judiciary; and that Congress cannot send the question to the

Judiciary, there being no mode prescribed in the Constitution by which they could do it.

With regard to leaving it to chance to bring it before the Judiciary, that chance might never come, &c. If the Judiciary were, indeed, the tribunal to decide the question, they ought to decide it before the House acted on it. Another great objection to the course proposed was, that it would unnecessarily throw on the Judiciary the performance of an odious duty, which he acknowledged this to be; and it seemed to him gentlemen showed too strongly, by their mode of proceeding, and their endeavors to throw it from themselves, that they felt it to be so. But this House was much better able to bear the odium of it than the Judiciary. Mr. S. said, he never would consent that the Congress of the United States should, for their own relief, burden the Judiciary with that sort of question, the decision of which makes it most obnoxious, exposes it most to that excitement which, of all departments of the Government, it was least capable of contending against. The effects of unpopular decisions in the State courts, showed what might possibly be the effect, in similar cases, on the United States Judiciary. He wished the whole strength of the Federal Judiciary might be maintained unimpaired for cases wherein the exertion of it might be necessary, which it was not in the present case. Another objection to the course proposed was, that, if the argument in its favor proved any thing, it proved too much. The more objectionable a clause of the Constitution is, the stronger is the reason against the reference of it to the Judiciary, because it would there more certainly be declared so. A full consideration of all the views which could be taken of the subject, Mr. S. said, would bring him back to the true ground, that this House ought to decide itself upon the question.

If the Judiciary had been the proper tribunal to determine this question, Mr. S. went on to argue, it was so as to all questions which could arise respecting a new constitution; and if a gross and palpable series of infractions of the Constitution of the United States were contained in a constitution formed by the people of a Territory, Congress would be justified, as much as in the present case, in referring it to the Judiciary.

It had been suggested that the present was a case which it would be difficult for Congress to decide, because the clause of the Missouri constitution was said to have offended that clause of the Constitution of the United States to which it was most difficult to give a precise interpretation. That clause, Mr. S. quoted in the following words: "The citizens of each State shall be entitled to all the privileges and immunities of citizens in the several States." Mr. S. said he should be exceedingly sorry to believe that this clause was so difficult of construction that this House could not decide whether or not it had been violated in a given case; because, in one of our standard books, (the Federalist,) one of those authorities to which we refer for light in difficult cases of construction of the Constitution, it was said, that this very clause was the "basis of the Union." Strange, indeed,

that this clause should have been considered the basis of the Union, and yet so equivocal that a construction could not be given to it.

If there was a difficulty in defining precisely the scope of the clause of the Constitution, there could be none in deciding that it does give to the citizens of each State in the Union, the humblest and lowest right enjoyed by a free man. Did any one doubt, Mr. S. asked, that this clause give to citizens of every State the free right to go into any other State, to return, or to remain there? If that was denied, then he would agree that this clause of the Constitution was all words and no meaning. Here, then, was the very point of this question. If the constitution of the State of Missouri has, either by its own positive provisions, or by enjoining it on its Legislature, excluded altogether from the State of Missouri any man who is a citizen of another State in this Union, then it is impossible to reconcile that constitution to the Constitution of the United States. It would be a defiance, which is worse than resistance, to the Constitution of the United States, if it had been intentional; but Mr. S. acquitted Missouri of any such intention.

Mr. S. declined going into the question how far a State had a right to make laws with regard to a certain class of persons referred to in the objected clause of the Missouri constitution. He briefly examined the suggestion of Mr. LOWNDES that that clause did not intend to exclude such persons as were citizens in other States. But the clause itself, Mr. S. said, made no distinction of classes, but extended equally to both classes. Missouri might make the distinction if she chose. Was it for Congress to make an exception for her which she did not choose to make for herself, and which the Legislature of Missouri might not choose to consider as any part of that clause of the Constitution? Congress had no right to interpret for them their own meaning. He then went on to show in what States free persons of color were citizens, and mentioned North Carolina, New York, and Massachusetts, among them. To make them citizens of any State it was not necessary they should have a right to vote, as Mr. S. showed by various references, that more than half the white men in some of our States did not vote, because they were not freeholders; yet no one would deny them to be citizens of those States, &c.

It was the humble simple privilege of locomotion only that was now claimed for these persons: it was a right indispensable to citizenship, and it was *all* that was asked for in the present case. If there was any way in which a citizen of one State can enjoy all the privileges and immunities of a citizen of another State, and yet not be permitted to set his foot in it, Mr. S. said he should be glad to be informed of it. With respect to the right of Missouri or of any State of the Union to regulate its own citizens, or to prescribe laws for their government, not inconsistent with the laws of the United States, Mr. S. said, no one pretended to interfere. She must regulate her own concerns, upon such policy as she thinks best, &c. On what would be her true policy, Mr. S. made a few remarks which the reporter did not hear with sufficient distinctness to report them.

Upon the whole, Mr. S. said, it was clear that, unless something was introduced, by interpretation, into the clause of the constitution of Missouri, respecting free people of color, which the framers of it have not introduced, and which it is not known that they would be willing to introduce, it is a plain and palpable infraction of the Constitution of the United States.

The plain course, then, he believed, was not to receive the constitution formed by the people of Missouri. For himself, he believed, and with him many of the members of this House believed, that it was the duty of this House to look into the Constitution, and if they found it contrary to the Constitution, that it was the duty of this House to *reject* it.

What the consequences of doing so might be, it was not for him to anticipate; but, whatever they might be, they could not be worse than the recognition of the constitution in its present shape. But why apprehend any disagreeable consequences? Might not Congress discuss a question of this sort without reference to danger? Might it not reject this constitution of Missouri, without giving her any right to unqualified independence? Or was this House to give way, right or wrong? True, Mr. S. said, Congress had been much divided in opinion on the question of the last session, and they might be on this. But, as far as gentlemen might think the consequences of such division dangerous—the consequences they dreaded were the consequences of free and fair investigation—the consequence of men doing what they believe to be right; and when men yield to fears excited by such causes, they give up the right of free discussion, the right of exercising their own judgment, the right of maintaining what, in their consciences, they think to be right. Does it follow, because there is a strong opposition to any measure, because there is great feeling and warmth on it, that therefore principle is to be abandoned? That no one would maintain. Neither was it consistent with the theory of our Government; because, at last, the will of the majority must govern. And, whatever fears might be entertained by others, Mr. S. said, he felt confident that the will of the majority would be submitted to.

With respect to what would be the condition of the Territory on the rejection of this constitution, Mr. S. said, it appeared to him it would be territorial. What provision it might be necessary to make, in respect to it he did not pretend to say, nor whether it would be necessary to make any. A case of the sort had never occurred in the history of our Government, and it would, if it occurred, deserve a careful and deliberate examination and decision. Here Mr. S. concluded his observations.

On motion of Mr. Storrs, who desired an opportunity of stating the reasons which would induce him to vote against the resolution for the admission of Missouri, the Committee rose, and the House adjourned.

Friday, December 8.

Mr. Campbell, from the Committee on Private Land Claims, reported a bill to extend the time for locating Virginia military land warrants, and returning surveys thereon to the General Land Office; which was read twice, and committed to a Committee of the Whole to-morrow.

Mr. Kent, from the Committee on the District of Columbia, reported a bill to amend the act of the last session for altering the times of holding the terms of the circuit court for the District of Columbia. [The object of this bill is to intermit the approaching December term, inasmuch as the term following is, under the new arrangement, to be held in April instead of July, as heretofore.] The bill was twice read and committed.

The Speaker laid before the House a letter from the Governor of the State of Louisiana, enclosing a certificate of the election of Josiah S. Johnston, as the representative of that State in the seventeenth Congress of the United States; which was ordered to lie on the table.

The Speaker also laid before the House a letter from the Secretary of the Treasury, transmitting sundry statements, rendered in obedience to the resolution of this House, of the 28th ultimo, respecting the amount of moneys drawn from the Treasury for the War and Navy Departments, from 30th December, 1819, to the 13th November, 1820, with the disposition thereof, and of transfers during the late recess of Congress; which were ordered to lie on the table.

Mr. Foot moved that the House do now proceed to consider the resolution submitted by him on the 6th instant, in relation to the infliction of corporal punishment, and the prohibition of the practice of duelling in the navy of the United States; and the question being taken thereon, it was determined in the negative.

MISSOURI.

The House then again resolved itself into a Committee of the Whole, on the resolution declaring the admission of Missouri into the Union on an equal footing with the original States.

Mr. Storrs, of New York, said, that the state of his health should perhaps admonish him not to address the Committee at all, on the interesting question before them. They would, however, find in this circumstance a security that he should not occupy much of their time.

I am only anxious, said Mr. S., in the vote which I shall give against the admission of Missouri into the Union as a State, to be neither misunderstood or misrepresented. The opinion which I expressed at the last session against the power of Congress to prescribe, by anticipation, to States, conditions of the nature then proposed, to be incorporated into their constitutions, places me in a situation somewhat peculiar, and entitles me to some claim of indulgence from the Committee. That opinion then formed, after much careful deliberation and anxious inquiry, I have since found no reason to change. It is not, therefore, with any view to apologize for the course which I then pursued, that I am induced to offer my sentiments at this time on the question now before us. Apology could only spring from the consciousness of error; and I have no propitiation to offer to secure the favor of any man or set of men whatever. The consciousness of rectitude is my shield against all the obloquy which has been cast upon my name, and my support under every accusation which has been laid to my charge. The Committee will pardon these observations. It has, indeed, been truly said, by one not less distinguished for his profound political attainments than his deep knowledge of the human character, that it becomes a man to speak but seldom of himself. Were I alone concerned in the subject before you, my opinion would have been expressed by a silent vote. Short as my political experience has been, (and my public services are probably near their close,) I have learned enough to know that it is an extremely difficult task for a public man to discharge his duty to his country and escape the malice or misconception of others. However plausibly it may be maintained as a matter of general political speculation, that a Representative here is bound by the will of his constituents, it is not easy to reconcile this ingenious theory with the moral sanctions imposed by our Constitution. The responsibility of the oath to support the Constitution of my country is upon me, and however highly I respect the opinion of others, the obligation to discharge it faithfully rests not upon them. To say that I am insensible to public favor, would be to deny that I am a mere man. I am more anxious, however, to deserve than to enjoy it, and my own constituents would be first to despise me, justly, were I to seek its continuance at the expense of sacrificing the first qualification which can entitle any man to their good opinion—the firm determination to discharge the trust confided to his hands, in conformity to his own sense of public duty.

Whatever our opinions may be on the subject which was here agitated at the last session, it is now to be determined whether Missouri shall be admitted to the distinguished rank of one of the sister States of our Union. Believing that the constitution which she has presented to us is repugnant, at least in one of its provisions, to the Constitution of the United States, I am constrained to express an opinion against the adoption of the resolution now under consideration. The Legislature of the proposed State are directed, "as ' soon as may be, to pass such laws as may be ne- ' cessary to prevent free negroes and mulattoes from ' coming to, and settling in, the State, under any ' pretext whatever." The authority thus conferred by the people of Missouri on their Legislature, in my judgment, infringes the security contained in the Constitution of the United States, that "the citizens of each State shall be entitled to all privileges and immunities of citizens in the several States."

The committee who reported this resolution have said, that "of all the articles in our Constitution, there is probably not one more difficult to construe well," than this. I had, indeed, supposed that, on the principle established in this article, rested the whole structure of our National Govern-

ment. It was upon considerations derived chiefly from the nature of our political system in this respect, that I had at the' last session formed the opinion against our power to insist on the restriction proposed to be inserted in the bill then before us. An attentive examination of the characteristics which peculiarly distinguish the present Government from the old Confederacy, will best illustrate the true construction and operation of this article of the Constitution.

The old Confederation was a mere league of friendship formed among the States for their mutual defence and security. It was strictly a confederacy of State sovereignties. Its powers were delegated by, and drawn from, the States in their corporate capacities, representing the sovereignty of the people of their respective jurisdictions. It was in its nature a treaty of alliance between different nations, who had recently become independent communities, and formed or adopted for themselves constitutions of civil government. The particular objects of the alliance were special and defined in the terms of the compact. These articles of union, like other treaties between sovereign Powers, were susceptible of alteration or amendment only with the unanimous consent of the States. Every power and right reserved, was reserved to the States. The people of the respective States were not as citizens amenable to its authority except as citizens of the State governments. The authority of the Confederacy operated only on the States in their political capacity; and its powers were only carried into execution through their instrumentality. Through these, as the organs of the will of the old Congress, and the agents for giving effect to its operations, it derived all its efficacy, as from them it had derived all its authority. Indeed, it might well have been doubted, if doubt could exist, if it were at all competent to the States to have established any other system of general authority. The people of the respective States could not have been subjected to a jurisdiction deriving its powers from the delegated authority of their State Legislatures. This structure of General Government, if government it might be named, was kept together during the war only by the pressure of public calamity.

At the return of peace its evils were felt, and, for all the purposes of union and defence, it was found altogether inefficient or useless. Its power was openly contemned, its operations defeated, and as all its efficacy depended on the will of the respective State Legislatures, some of whom were prepared, or had in fact resisted its authority, if the compact was not already virtually dissolved, it was rapidly hastening to annihilation, or to a state that was little more than a mockery of self-government. Being thus in its nature a mere treaty among the States, the citizens of each member of the Confederacy were considered as citizens only of their respective State governments. All their rights and immunities beyond these jurisdictions depended upon the will of any party of the Confederacy who might choose to withdraw from the alliance or set its authority at defiance. Among the evils of this system had already ap-

touched in the hands of the State Legislatures, with the single exception of the right of Congress to regulate the naturalization of foreigners or aliens. The power thus vested in Congress appears to be necessarily exclusive, and was probably intended to be so. With this diminution only of the sovereignty of the States in this respect, the original power inherent in every Government of determining the extent of the right of citizenship remains unimpaired in the States. It is worthy of remark that, while under the old Confederation, this power in the States extended to the naturalization of aliens, its exercise in some of them had produced serious complaints from the other members of the Confederacy. The adoption of aliens into our political families as citizens by the laws of one State, gave to that class of persons, by one of the articles of the Confederation, privileges of trade, and commerce, and immunities of citizenship, in the rest deemed by many to have been productive of serious inconveniences to their own citizens, and unreasonable interference with their separate interests. The power of extending the benefit of naturalization to aliens, was, therefore, in conformity with the other features of our Government, which were truly national in regard to its external relations, delegated to the General Government. With this exception only, the people of each State still retain and exercise the power of conferring upon all the various classes of persons within their respective State jurisdictions, such rights and privileges as to themselves shall appear most conducive to their interest, and most consonant to their own views of justice, equality, and good government. Whatever inconveniences may be supposed to result from the incidental operation of this power, in relation to the other States, must be attributed therefore to that principle of our Union, without which our National Government would retain as little perhaps of permanency as utility.

The description of persons disfranchised by the proposed constitution of Missouri, have been admitted to the rank of freemen in other States, and recognised as citizens. In the State of New York, for instance, they have in many cases more decisive characteristics of citizens, and enjoy greater privileges than a large class of the free white population, to whom none would deny the character of citizenship. Possessed of the qualifications for suffrage required by her State constitution, they exercise the electoral right of voting for the Executive and Senatorial departments, while a great portion of the free white population, not invested with the same qualifications, enjoy only the subordinate privilege of electing delegates to the House of Assembly, or are deprived altogether of the right of suffrage. As freemen of that State they are represented, even here, by the exercise of their electoral franchise, in virtue of their character as a portion of "the people of the several States," having the "qualifications for electors of the most numerous branch of the State Legislatures." It would be no difficult task, by referring to the constitutions and laws of many other States, to point out the same recognition of this class of persons

as free citizens; but a more decisive evidence of the soundness of this conclusion, is to be derived from the principles and practice of the National Government itself. The laws of the United States for the protection of American seamen from impressment have been construed (and without question of the correctness of such an interpretation) to extend to this class of persons. As "citizens of the United States," according to the terms of the act, they have uniformly received certificates of protection for their security against the violation of their rights. The impressment of persons of this very description, among others, contributed to our loud and just complaints against the violence of a foreign Power. In the official returns of impressed American citizens heretofore formally communicated to this House will be found many of this class. It was then justly considered that the oppression of seamen of this description, by the agents of a foreign Government involved the violation of our national sovereignty.

To establish a doctrine in relation to this class of persons who have been thus recognised by different States as free citizens, which should deprive them of the benefit of this clause of our national Constitution, would, in many cases deeply affecting their personal rights, be productive of peculiar hardship and injustice. Let us suppose that one of this class, in the State of Missouri, dying intestate, should leave the inheritance of his lands to his children, also free, but residing in Pennsylvania, and there invested with the rights of citizens. What power among us could rightfully be exerted consistently with the privileges secured by the Constitution of the United States, to deprive them of the enjoyment of such an inheritance? What principle of sovereignty reserved by our compact to the State of Missouri could thus limit the operation of the supreme right of Pennsylvania to confer upon the citizens which she had adopted or recognised these privileges?

But the exercise of such a power by the Legislature of Missouri would not only thus defeat one of the greatest blessings of the Union, but might operate as a control on the power of the General Government itself. Let us consider the effect of a measure of this sort, of the Legislature of that State, in its operation on a personal right derived from the United States. I know of no impediment to persons of this description becoming purchasers of the public lands, and deriving title to them from others. In the case, too, of the distribution of the military bounty lands, patents may issue to persons of this class. Inseparably annexed to such a grant is the right of occupation; and can we successfully maintain a doctrine which might in this way indirectly render the State laws of Missouri, if not paramount to the laws of the Union, at least effectual to defeat the rights created under them? From every view of this subject, the conclusion in my mind is inevitable, that the State of Missouri must yield up this assumption of power to the supreme control of the national Constitution. The citizens of the other States must enjoy within her jurisdiction all the rights, privileges, and immunities of citizens, sub-

peared the very defect of the security of the rights of citizens of other States, and measures adopted by some of the States had given cause for loud and just complaints of the violation of this security. The friends of our National Union were universally alarmed. It was evident to all, that, without a radical change in the structure of the system, the fairest fruits of our independence would be blasted, and that union on which depended our strength, if not even the perpetuity of civil liberty among us, might be forever dissolved. The Convention which formed our present Constitution of civil government, impressed with this conviction, discarded the principle on which the old Confederacy was framed. They retained merely that representation of the States in the new system which was necessary to the security, and which should protect the sovereignty of the States over the powers not delegated to the National Government. The great and cardinal principle of our Constitution created a National Government of the people of the United States. Its powers were derived from, and delegated by, the people, in their conventions, not as citizens of distinct sovereignties, but in their collective capacity, as citizens of one great Republic. The powers vested in the Government now operated directly on the people. Its legislature and judiciary are the legislature and judiciary of the nation. The public will no longer applies for aid to the Legislatures of the States, but extends its authority as the universal law of the nation to every citizen. The citizens of the respective States are no longer alien to each other as subjects of different sovereignties. In relation to the powers vested in the General Government we have become emphatically one people, under one National Government—allied to each other as citizens of one country—responsible to one supreme authority—controlled by the same laws—enjoying equally the blessings it dispenses, and truly brethren of the same family. Is it possible, then, that we can mistake the intention of the framers of this Constitution, or our own rights, so far as to hesitate on the true construction of that clause which secures to the citizens of each State the privileges and immunities of citizens in the several States?

But, Mr. Chairman, said Mr. S., I have already suggested that my vote of the last session was founded on considerations drawn from this view of our national system. The powers granted to the National Government are granted equally by the whole body of the people. The rights retained are retained equally by all. The Congress, acting under this uniform grant of power, acquires no control over one portion of the nation which it cannot rightfully exert over every other. Its relative sovereignty is the same over the people of Missouri as over the people of every other State in the Confederacy. An abridgment of the powers retained by one portion of the people creates, by the very exercise of such an authority, a separate and distinct frame of National Government, in regard to that community whose political rights are thus extinguished. I will not detain the Committee here by entering into an argument rather

foreign to the direct questions before us, drawn from this view of the subject under discussion. The inference which I would rather intimate than establish at this time, will perhaps more clearly suggest itself to the Committee hereafter, when I call their attention to the right reserved to each of the States in relation to its powers of determining to whom the privilege of citizenship, within their respective jurisdictions, shall extend, and the relative rights and condition of its various classes of citizens.

The foundation of this article of the Constitution is laid deep in the structure of the Government. It is capable of no construction which does not plainly denote the universality of its operation and its uniform application to individual right throughout every portion of the nation. By what tenure except this is a citizen of New York invested with the right of inheritance to lands in Ohio? By what other authority are the courts of justice thrown open in Virginia or New York to the citizens of every other State? It is the operation of this clause which reduces us to a perfect equality of rights with those around us, wheresoever we may transfer ourselves in every part of the Republic. The right of acquiring lands by purchase in other States—of devising them to our children—of enforcing private contracts, and an almost infinite variety of civil privileges, are all sustained on this obvious construction of the clause in question. To have omitted it, would, in a Government like ours, have destroyed the whole harmony of the system, and produced the most jarring and discordant confliction of privileges. Without it, the citizens of each State, except in relation to the powers specifically delegated to the Union, would have been altogether aliens and strangers to each other; without any other mutuality of privileges than those derived from their common limited National Confederacy. Instead of inheriting the estates of their ancestors in other States, the law of escheats would have transferred them to foreign sovereignty. The enforcement of private right, if not the security of personal liberty, would have depended on the will or caprice of every State Legislature. Regulations of the most unjust nature might have created and maintained the most odious and oppressive distinctions. The whole tendency of the system would have been to estrange us from each other, and probably in the course of time we should have found in the want of this equality of privileges perhaps the very source of disunion itself. If, sir, as the honorable gentleman from South Carolina (Mr. Lowndes) seemed to admit, cases might happen in which it would be the duty of Congress to reject the admission of a State into the Union for the repugnancy of its constitution to that of the General Government, can we scarcely imagine a case more deeply affecting the validity of our system, and more calculated to lead to the most dangerous encroachments on private rights and personal liberty than an impugnment of this clause of our Constitution.

The power of determining to whom the privilege of citizenship shall extend in the respective States has been vested, or rather was left untouched in the hands of the State Legislatures, with the single exception of the right of Congress to regulate the naturalization of foreigners or aliens. The power thus vested in Congress appears to be necessarily exclusive, and was probably intended to be so. With this diminution only of the sovereignty of the States in this respect, the original power inherent in every Government of determining the extent of the right of citizenship remains unimpaired in the States. It is worthy of remark that, while under the old Confederation, this power in the States extended to the naturalization of aliens, its exercise in some of them had produced serious complaints from the other members of the Confederacy. The adoption of aliens into our political families as citizens by the laws of one State, gave to that class of persons, by one of the articles of the Confederation, privileges of trade, and commerce, and immunities of citizenship, in the rest deemed by many to have been productive of serious inconveniences to their own citizens, and unreasonable interference with their separate interests. The power of extending the benefit of naturalization to aliens, was, therefore, in conformity with the other features of our Government, which were truly national in regard to its external relations, delegated to the General Government. With this exception only, the people of each State still retain and exercise the power of conferring upon all the various classes of persons within their respective State jurisdictions, such rights and privileges as to themselves shall appear most conducive to their interest, and most consonant to their own views of justice, equality, and good government. Whatever inconveniences may be supposed to result from the incidental operation of this power, in relation to the other States, must be attributed therefore to that principle of our Union, without which our National Goverhment would retain as little perhaps of permanency as utility.

The description of persons disfranchised by the proposed constitution of Missouri, have been admitted to the rank of freemen in other States, and recognised as citizens. In the State of New York, for instance, they have in many cases more decisive characteristics of citizens, and enjoy greater privileges than a large class of the free white population, to whom none would deny the character of citizenship. Possessed of the qualifications for suffrage required by her State constitution, they exercise the electoral right of voting for the Executive and Senatorial departments, while a great portion of the free white population, not invested with the same qualifications, enjoy only the subordinate privilege of electing delegates to the House of Assembly, or are deprived altogether of the right of suffrage. As freemen of that State they are represented, even here, by the exercise of their electoral franchise, in virtue of their character as a portion of " the people of the several States," having the "qualifications for electors of the most numerous branch of the State Legislatures." It would be no difficult task, by referring to the constitutions and laws of many other States, to point out the same recognition of this class of persons

as free citizens; but a more decisive evidence of the soundness of this conclusion, is to be derived from the principles and practice of the National Government itself. The laws of the United States for the protection of American seamen from impressment have been construed (and without question of the correctness of such an interpretation) to extend to this class of persons. As "citizens of the United States," according to the terms of the act, they have uniformly received certificates of protection for their security against the violation of their rights. The impressment of persons of this very description, among others, contributed to our loud and just complaints against the violence of a foreign Power. In the official returns of impressed American citizens heretofore formally communicated to this House will be found many of this class. It was then justly considered that the oppression of seamen of this description, by the agents of a foreign Government involved the violation of our national sovereignty.

To establish a doctrine in relation to this class of persons who have been thus recognised by different States as free citizens, which should deprive them of the benefit of this clause of our national Constitution, would, in many cases deeply affecting their personal rights, be productive of peculiar hardship and injustice. Let us suppose that one of this class, in the State of Missouri, dying intestate, should leave the inheritance of his lands to his children, also free, but residing in Pennsylvania, and there invested with the rights of citizens. What power among us could rightfully be exerted consistently with the privileges secured by the Constitution of the United States, to deprive them of the enjoyment of such an inheritance? What principle of sovereignty reserved by our compact to the State of Missouri could thus limit the operation of the supreme right of Pennsylvania to confer upon the citizens which she had adopted or recognised these privileges?

But the exercise of such a power by the Legislature of Missouri would not only thus defeat one of the greatest blessings of the Union, but might operate as a control on the power of the General Government itself. Let us consider the effect of a measure of this sort, of the Legislature of that State, in its operation on a personal right derived from the United States. I know of no impediment to persons of this description becoming purchasers of the public lands, and deriving title to them from others. In the case, too, of the distribution of the military bounty lands, patents may issue to persons of this class. Inseparably annexed to such a grant is the right of occupation; and can we successfully maintain a doctrine which might in this way indirectly render the State laws of Missouri, if not paramount to the laws of the Union, at least effectual to defeat the rights created under them? From every view of this subject, the conclusion in my mind is inevitable, that the State of Missouri must yield up this assumption of power to the supreme control of the national Constitution. The citizens of the other States must enjoy within her jurisdiction all the rights, privileges, and immunities of citizens, subject to no restraints or conditions not equally imposed on the citizens of Missouri herself. If the arbitrary (I mean not, despotic) distinction created in her Constitution can be maintained, she might with equal right extend it much further, and deny to all citizens of other States who had not, for instance, reached the age of forty years, or who shall be born after her admission into the Union, the right of emigration to the State.

Is Missouri, then, already an independent State, and the resolution now proposed merely declaratory of that fact? The honorable gentleman from South Carolina, (Mr. Lowndes,) if I understood him rightly, considered that when the people of Missouri, in their convention, called by virtue of the fourth section of the act of the last session, had answered the question that it was expedient to form a constitution of State government, their right of self-government as a State commenced. It was evident that this right must have been derived, if at all, from this section, and by authority conferred by the Congress, who were invested by the Constitution with the sovereignty over her. She could acquire no right to proceed to call a convention—to propound the question, or to form any constitution whatever, without our previous consent that she should exercise such powers. To determine, then, whether, by virtue of the authority given by the act, and in conformity to its provisions, (under which she has professed to act,) the power thus conferred has been executed on her part, it is first necessary to fix the fair and reasonable interpretation of the act itself. To establish this, it will not be necessary to travel out of the very section under which is supposed that this right of self-government, as an independent State, has been created. The members of the convention were by this section of the act directed at their meeting first to determine, " whe-
' ther it be or be not expedient at that time to form
' a constitution and State government for the peo-
' ple within the said Territory, &c., and, if it be
' deemed expedient, the convention shall be, and
' are, authorized to form a constitution and State
' government," &c. " *Provided*, That the same,
' whenever formed, shall be republican, and not
' repugnant to the Constitution of the United
' States." If the authority contained in this section conferred on the people of Missouri an unqualified power to form their constitution in such manner and with such provisions as they might in their own discretion choose to adopt, the authority has perhaps been executed, and they might be entitled to the benefit of the grant contained in the act. But, to my mind, no such authority was ever granted by Congress. The proviso which is annexed is, in the most liberal sense, strictly a condition, qualifying, throughout, the whole power granted in the section, and, without conformity to its spirit, no exercise of the power contemplated by the act could be valid or effectual, for any purpose, against the sovereignty of the United States. If Missouri seeks, therefore, to establish her independence as a State by virtue of the power thus conferred, she has acquired the right in violation of the very authority

under which she claims. The conformity of her constitution to that of the United States was obligatory on the convention. No power has been granted to form any constitution of civil government whatever which should not strictly accord to the National Constitution. Much less can the erection of a frame of government violating it, in one of its most essential provisions, be deemed to have been an execution of the authority granted in this section. The whole of this section must be construed together, and the qualification contained in the proviso extends its operation as well to the power of propounding the general question to the convention as to the actual formation of the proposed constitution. The question to be put to the convention was, substantially, Is it now expedient to form a constitution of State government, in conformity to the authority conferred by Congress? As this constitution is therefore repugnant to that of the United States, and to the very power under which it has professedly been made, the authority contained in the act of the last session cannot be deemed to have been executed at all. Between Missouri and the Congress, she stands on the same ground as if the convention had never met. The course of argument which has been urged against this conclusion would have equally maintained a proposition that Missouri was an independent State, had the convention, after determining that it was expedient to form a constitution, proceeded even to the creation of a monarchy. The dispensation of the condition that her government should be republican might as well, and by the same course of reasoning, been granted, as that of conformity to our National Constitution. Indeed, sir, it may well be considered that, had neither of these conditions been expressed in the act, Missouri would still have been bound to have conformed to them both.

The Congress themselves possess no power to authorize the people of the Territories to form constitutions, preparatory to their admission into the Union, which shall not conform to that of the United States. Such a power as this would defeat the very end of the Government, inasmuch as it would necessarily be a subversion of the Constitution itself. Conditions of this sort are deemed to be tacitly, and of political necessity, annexed to every authority of this kind granted by Congress. There is, in the case of Missouri, another condition, also, contained in the same proviso: that the Legislature of the State " shall never interfere with the primary disposal of the soil by the United States." Could it be reasonably or successfully maintained that a constitution containing a palpable violation of this reservation, would have been a compliance with the authority granted by this act? Nor is this all—there is one further condition: that the Legislature shall never interfere with "any regulations which Congress may find necessary for securing the title in such soil to the *bona fide* purchasers." The precise import of the regulations here intended may not be very clearly understood; but the title to the public lands could hardly be deemed to be secured by Congress in any way, so long as it was considered competent in the Legislature of Missouri to deny the right of occupation and enjoyment of them to any class of purchasers. Had the convention have failed to have provided, "by an ordinance, irrevocable without the consent of the United States," for the security of the terms stated in the proviso to the 6th section of the act, could she have claimed the benefit of the donations granted in the propositions offered to her in the same section? Certainly not; and for the reason that this proviso operates also as a condition, the performance of which is indispensable to the perfection of those grants. There is yet another condition secured, by way of proviso, in the second section of the act: that "the said State shall have concurrent jurisdiction in the river Mississippi, so far as the said river shall form" its common boundary with other States, and that it shall be "forever free, as well to the inhabitants of the said State, as to other citizens of the United States, without any tax, duty, impost, or toll therefor, imposed by the said State." Had the convention, disregarding this reservation to the citizens of the United States, expressly authorized the Legislature to impose a transit duty on the navigation of the river, would the States of Ohio, Kentucky, and Tennessee, recognise in such an infringement of their rights a compliance with the authority granted by this act? Would Missouri be recognised as an independent State, had she set at naught all these conditions, thus annexed to the power under which her convention acted? If the failure to conform to these conditions, which originate chiefly from expediency, would have deprived her, as a State government, of the privileges depending on their performance, much less can she claim the right of self-government, having failed to comply with that higher and more indispensable condition—a strict conformity to the Constitution of the United States.

But, sir, independent of any objections to the passage of this resolution, arising out of the act of the last session, I cannot reconcile it to my own sense of duty to give to it my sanction, so long as my opinion is that this clause of her constitution is repugnant to the Constitution under which I here act. Had Missouri established an hereditary Senate, or framed a government composed of King, Lords, and Commons, acting on the same principle, I should deem it no more an impugnment, except in a higher degree, of our Constitution, than in the case now before us. Missouri cannot become a party to our national compact, except on the terms of the compact itself. Any other union between us, as States, would create a political solecism in the Confederacy. It may, indeed, be true, that clauses may be found in some of the constitutions of the old States, equally repugnant to the national Constitution. I have not been able to examine them thoroughly, but, as most of these constitutions were framed previous to the adoption of the present Constitution of the Union in such States, all clauses of this sort have been virtually abrogated by the people by the adoption of our present system in the subsequent conventions called for its ratification. Had one

of the original States, however, on acceding to the Union, ratified the Constitution, with the exception of any particular article or clause, it would hardly have been contended that she should have been received into the Confederacy. For my own part, I cannot distinguish between this case and that of Missouri. In the one the State would probably have been excluded from the Union for withholding its assent to the powers granted to the National Government; in the other, the impugnment of the rights secured by the Constitution in effect abrogates one of its articles, and equally forms an exception in her assent to the same powers. The insertion of this condition into the act of the last session, is virtually an acknowledgment, on the part of the Congress, of the necessity of universally maintaining a strict conformity to the Constitution in the formation of new States.

To preserve in its original harmony the distribution of powers, under our complex system, it is not of less importance to maintain the powers of the General Government, and the privileges secured under it, than to resist its encroachments on the sovereignty of the States. The perpetuity of the whole system depends, in the chiefest degree, on the most watchful vigilance in the National Legislature on every Constitutional point. If this clause in the constitution of Missouri was clearly susceptible of an interpretation so limited in its application as not to be mistaken, I would cheerfully submit it to her own Legislature; but, to my mind, its terms are too comprehensive to enable me to arrive at such a conclusion. I have wished, indeed, that it were so, for the sake of allaying, in some measure, the excitement which has convulsed the nation. This unhappy subject seems destined, however, still to distract the national councils, and scatter discontent throughout the Union. Wherever it is met, at every step we seem to tread upon thorns.

Deeply as I regret the necessity which compels me to vote against this resolution, I do not apprehend the consequences which many imagine may be the result of our proceedings. Be they, however, what they may, I cannot, on a question affecting the Constitution, take them into my consideration. Although Missouri must, by the determination of Congress, remain a Territory still, the necessity of that coercion to any portion of the country, alluded to by the gentleman who has preceded me in this discussion, I hope is yet very far distant. Whenever the period arrives that shall render it necessary to unite the States by the arm of force, the Confederacy dissolves with the moral principle which is the foundation of our Union. It is this which pre-eminently distinguishes us from the Governments of the Old World. While in other countries Government is chiefly felt in the oppression of its citizens, and only maintained by the exertion of power in its most odious aspect, it is here known only by the blessings which it silently dispenses, and sustained by the moral sentiment of the people. Coercion may be the foundation of good government in a penitentiary or a mad-house, but, in our Republic, where military force begins there union ends. But sir, there is a fund of good sense remaining among us, and a warm attachment to our institutions pervading the hearts of our countrymen, which, when called into action, will yet heal the wounded spirits of all. The inestimable blessings of our Union are too deeply felt and valued to be lightly or rashly thrown away. The South and the North, odious as these appellations are, have found it hitherto the safety of all our rights, and will yet confidently cherish it as the sanctuary of all our liberties.

Mr. P. P. Barbour, of Virginia, took the floor. He had not expected, he said, to have engaged in the discussion to-day, and should necessarily, therefore, speak without preparation; but he promised the Committee, that, in the few remarks which he should submit, he should observe every possible degree of brevity.

The subject now under consideration, he said, was one which had become painful to the nation, and, he feared, painful to the House. But it was one to be decided, and it was his most earnest wish that the decision should be such as to avert any possible evil foreseen by any of the gentlemen who had discussed the subject.

The member from New York, (Mr. Storrs,) and the member from Pennsylvania, (Mr. Sergeant,) while they had denied to Missouri the condition of a State, would not undertake to say to the Committee what would be the condition of the people of Missouri should this resolution not pass. That question, they said, was not now before the Committee; when, however, it should be presented at some after time, and in some other shape, they would endeavor to decide it as under the circumstance should then appear to be right. But, Mr. B. said, it is a question which must, at this moment, enter into the consideration of every member of this Committee, what *is* the condition of Missouri? It is a question, the decision and consequences of which are much and intimately connected with the immediate question now submitted to the Committee.

Is Missouri a State, or is she a Territory? If she be a State, she is a sovereign and independent State, unconnected with the Confederacy, or a State deriving the rights, and subject to the obligations, which the Federal compact devolves upon every State in the Union? These are questions which must be decided in some shape, because they must be practically acted upon. Missouri is a Government; she has an Executive, a Legislature, a Judiciary—a portion of which at least have been in action. Are we, said Mr. B., prepared to recall them? Are we prepared to say to Missouri, your Legislature has no legislative powers, your Governor no executive powers? Are we prepared to say to her, you shall revert to your territorial condition, under which we are authorized to legislate for you? Is there any member of the Committee who will rise in his place and take that ground? He presumed not; and, if not, he asked, what is her condition? It is this: the people of a portion of the territory of the United States were authorized to form a constitution and State

government, and, having formed such State government, were to be received into the Union of these States on an equal footing with every other State. What is it that makes a State? Is it not the formation of a constitution—the creation of departments of government—the delineation of the manner in which the power of the people shall be exercised by their Representatives, and the distribution of that power among the agents of the people? Has this been done in Missouri? It has. The member from New York had acknowledged, that if Missouri be a State, she is a State in this Union. Mr. B. said he imagined the gentleman was driven to this conclusion: for, if Missouri be a State, and not one of the United States, in what relation does the Government of the United States stand to her? In what character does it stand as to the public lands, the navigation of her rivers, the revenue, and the various other relations of the United States to that Territory? Will it be contended, said he, that we can impose Federal obligations unless she has Federal rights? No, said Mr. B., unless she be a State of the Union, we have no control, no power over her. It might even be questioned, if she was denied to be a State of the Union, what is the extent of the claim which we have to lands within the territorial extent of that State. These, Mr. B. said, were questions which, in the view that he should take of the subject, he would not discuss further, than to say, that, by the provisions of the act of the last session, the people of Missouri were authorized to form a constitution and State government. They have done so. When they had done so, by the force of that law they were to be a State. That period has passed; and they are a State of right, and entitled to all the privileges of that condition.

What, said Mr. B., is the provision of the Constitution which has been referred to as being violated? It is, that "the citizens of each State shall be entitled to all privileges and immunities of citizens in the several States." And this provision of the Constitution was said to be contradicted by the constitution of Missouri, because a clause in the latter enjoins on the Legislature to pass such laws for the exclusion from the State of people of a certain description. To maintain this proposition, the opponents of Missouri would have to make out that the persons thus proposed to be excluded are citizens of the States. The member from Pennsylvania had yesterday told the House that he would not undertake to say what a citizen is. In that particular, Mr. B. said, in his estimation, the gentleman did not perform a duty which devolved on him. On whom, in this case, did the burden of proof devolve? We, said Mr. B., offer the constitution of a new State, formed under the authority of law. You oppose it, because you say it is incompatible with the Constitution of the United States. With what provision is it incompatible? With that which has been already stated. Did it not then belong to gentlemen who oppose the admission of Missouri to show, that those people whom she proposes to exclude are citizens, in the sense of the Constitution of the United States, before they asserted that the constitution of Missouri was irreconcilable with that of the United States?

The gentleman from Pennsylvania would not say affirmatively what makes a citizen, but he said that, to constitute a man a citizen, it was not indispensable that he should have a right of voting. To make any reasoning conclusive, Mr. B. said, we must distinctly see, in the outset, what one side admits, and what the other denies. To know this was indispensable to a correct conclusion on any disputed point. Let us then inquire, said he, who are citizens? For, in his humble opinion, that point, which the member from Pennsylvania did not choose to discuss, lay at the root of this question, and its decision was unavoidable.

I will undertake, said Mr. B., what the member from Pennsylvania would not. I will define what is meant by the term citizen—what are the qualities which constitute citizenship. He might mistake, he said, in this position; but, according to the best lights he had, it was correct; and if so, it would seem to lead to a conclusion directly contrary to that drawn by the member from Pennsylvania. The term citizen, Mr. B. said, could not with propriety be applied to any one unless under these circumstances: that he should be possessed of all at least of the civil rights, if not of the political, of every other person in the community, under like circumstances, of which he is not deprived for some cause personal to himself.

If, said he, I am correct in this definition, let us proceed to apply it to the people who are the subject of this inquiry, and see how far their condition places them within the scope of it.

This, however, was not the view of the question which he rose for the purpose of presenting. In the view which he was about to take, he should proceed upon the supposition that the constitution of Missouri was properly before the Committee for consideration, and that the true inquiry was, does this constitution contain, or not, any provision incompatible with the superior provisions of the Federal Constitution? It would be his endeavor to show that it does not. Whatever opinion he might entertain of the condition of the State, or of the powers of this House in relation to it, it did not impinge on the view that he should present, which admitted, for the opponents of Missouri, the position most favorable to them, that the constitution was now properly submitted for consideration, and for the examination of the question whether it contains any provision in conflict with the Constitution of the United States.

Before he proceeded to do this, however, he said, he would dismiss the objections which might be offered to the definition which he had taken the liberty to give. It might be said, for example, that even in Virginia one white man is entitled to a particular right, while another is not. Still, Mr. B. said, his definition applied, because all under like circumstances had like rights. Show me, in Virginia, said he, or in any other State with the laws of which I am acquainted, any white man who is deprived of the rights of other white men similarly circumstanced. *Every* white man of Virginia who has a freehold votes. Females do

not vote; but *all* females do not vote. *All* white persons in Virginia may sue and be sued; *all* are entitled to the great civil rights of personal liberty and the free possession and enjoyment of personal property. It was no objection, therefore, to the definition which Mr. B. had presented, that, in a community, there were distinctions, some having rights which others have not; because they were not in like circumstances. A young man under the age of twenty-one years cannot make a will; but *all* persons under like circumstances are subject to the same disability. A man above forty-five years of age is exempted from militia duty; but *all* above the age of forty-five are exempt. Show me an instance, said Mr. B., in any State in this Union, where, among white men, rights are enjoyed by some which are forbidden to others under like circumstances. It cannot be shown.

Is there, then, said he, pursuing the purpose of his argument, a State of this Union in which colored men have all the civil rights of any other citizen in the community to which they belong? He proceeded to examine the laws of the several States on this subject. In Virginia, a colored man—yes, even a slave, and of that class over whom it was supposed, by those unacquainted with facts, that so much tyranny was exercised—is secured against at least one undue degree of personal violence. The free man of color rises higher—to the dignity of the right to sue and to be sued, to acquire property, to make contracts. He was yet under one signal political disability—he is not allowed the right of suffrage; and under an important civil disability, not being allowed to give testimony in any suit in which a white man is a party. In North Carolina, persons of this description are indulged in the highest political privilege, the right of suffrage, and are yet deprived of the privilege of giving testimony in any case in which a white man is a party—a privilege which can only be wrested from a white man for some cause particular to himself. In Virginia, further, in regard to manumitted slaves, considering them as hostile to public peace, as the brand of discord between the whites and another class of persons, it was declared, by the law, that every manumitted slave should, within twelve months after the act of manumission, leave the State, or forfeit the rights he had acquired.

Mr. B. said he would not, as he might, go further into detail on this point: it was sufficient to say, in general, that free people of color are in all the States deprived of many of the rights of white men. Was there any State in the Union in which they were in the full enjoyment of civil rights? Mr. B. said he took some degree of interest in looking to the laws of Massachusetts in regard to this description of people, who, it had been said, enjoyed in that State an unqualified equality with the whites. But he found, on examination, it was otherwise. He found a penalty was imposed by law of fifty pounds on any minister who marries a white with a colored person, and it was declared, that any such marriages should be null and void in law—and on what grounds? Not upon the ground of crime in the parties, carrying with it disability. Was it not upon the ground of the disqualification of one of the parties to make that particular contract? How disqualified? Because of his color, certainly. The party may be of age—in the exercise of his sound senses; he may be able to make contracts in relation to property; but, in regard to marriage—in that particular in which, above all other things, we ought to pursue our own happiness, in our own way, he may not contract, but under certain circumstances, that is, with a person of color. Whom God has joined, let no man put asunder—but in old Massachusetts they do put asunder the colored person who intermarries with the white.

We find, then, said Mr. B., that in the East and North, as well as in the South and West, there are certain distinctions growing out of color. They are distinctions founded in the best good sense, in the preservation of public morality and of the dignity of our nature, and in the consideration that between the whites and the blacks there never can be an incorporation which is calculated to add to the happiness or elevate the dignity of either party. Mr. B. asked, in further illustration of the denial of civil rights, even in the Eastern States, to colored persons, whether a colored man had ever been known to sit on a jury? He was told not. This attempt to maintain a principle in theory, which was abandoned in practice, forcibly reminded him of an incident in Roman history. It was known that there was a long and severe contest in that republic between the patricians and the plebeians, in relation to a claim set up by the latter, of the right of being elected to the Consulship; and yet, after this pretension was acquiesced in, a century perhaps elapsed before any plebeian was actually elected. Was there any other State in this Union, Mr. B. asked, which had declared the free man of color to be equal in his civil and political rights to the white man? If so, he called on gentlemen to produce it.

There was a time, Mr. B. went on to say, when the man of color and the white man were not equal in any part of this country, even in theory. The population which came to this country from abroad were Europeans or the descendants of Europeans. They found the aborigines here, but, as far as they came from abroad, they were of European birth or descent. This other race, said Mr. B., got among us afterwards. I deeply regret that they did. When they came, they were slaves. He called upon gentlemen to show the words, in any of the State constitutions, which declare that a man of color, become or born free, shall be elevated to the grade of the whites. He would refer, he said, to some clauses in constitutions on which he supposed gentlemen would rely to prove this; but he would show that those clauses would not bear them out.

Do you find it, said he, in the constitution of New York or of Massachusetts, that free people of color shall vote? No; you will find that every male person or male inhabitant shall vote; and, under this clause, it is said that free persons of color have equal rights with the whites. If upon that construction, these persons are considered as citizens,

who else are not? Aliens are male persons. Were gentlemen prepared to say, that an Englishman or an Irishman, having a six months residence, and being a free citizen, should have a right to vote at all elections? He would state a case yet more impressive, deriving an argument from the condition of certain unhappy remnants of the aboriginals lingering out their wretched lives among the inhabitants of these States; there were some of those persons in Massachusetts and some in other States. Are they not free persons? Yet, do you suffer them to vote, or to sue and be sued? Do you receive them as witnesses? Are they entitled to those civil, much less those political rights, which are required to constitute them a part of the body politic? Was ever one of them a juror or a witness? Can they elect or be elected to any office? Can they hold property, except under regulations which are prescribed to them, and prescribed, too, by legislatures in which they are not represented? They cannot. What is the distinction between their case and that of the free people of color? They equally come into the definition of male persons and male inhabitants. Would any gentleman contend that Indians are citizens of every State in the Union, because they reside within any one of them? He presumed not.

It seemed to him, Mr. Barbour said, that, on a review of all the facts connected with this subject, it would be found, that free persons of color have been considered a non-descript class. In some States, they have some civil rights; in others, more. In some States they have some political rights; in others, none. It never had entered, he was persuaded, into the mind of any member of the Legislature of any State that they were citizens, under the definition which he had laid down. Had Virginia, he asked, violated the Constitution of the United States when she said that persons of color made free should depart her territory? He presumed no gentleman would contend that she had. If not, how could it be said, that she had a right to get rid of persons of that description already within her limits, and yet that she could not exclude a new torrent of that population attempted to be poured in upon her?

The member from New York had put to the Committee a number of cases, all of which Mr. B. said, if he mistook not, were susceptible of a ready answer. It would be found, indeed, that most of them were but different statements of the same proposition, and at last depend on the application of a principle. Suppose, said the gentleman, one of these persons residing in New York to acquire a right to a patent to land in Missouri; and shall he be entitled to the fee simple, and yet not entitled to occupancy of the land? The gentleman would see, Mr. B. said, that the free negro of Virginia had the same right to acquire property in Virginia as the free negro in New York could have to acquire it in Missouri; yet, being by law excluded from the State, he could not occupy it. The gentleman's argument proved, therefore, that, *quo ad* the right of purchase, the free people of color had civil rights, but not that they have *all*

549   HISTORY OF CONGRESS.   550

DECEMBER, 1820.   *Admission of Missouri.*   H. OF R.

civil rights. Could it be argued because they had one civil right, that they therefore have all? Might it not as well be argued, because a man has one political right, he therefore has all political rights?

With respect to the power of naturalization, the gentleman from New York had correctly stated that the States have a right to declare who shall be citizens thereof respectively. Ay, said Mr. B., have they so? Has not Missouri, then, the right to say who shall be entitled to citizenship within her limits? Or is she alone to be kept in a state of pupilage, and are we to say to her now, as gentlemen wished to have said to her at the last session, you shall not have all the rights enjoyed by the other States of the Union? If Missouri says that certain persons shall not be her citizens, has any other State a right to say such persons shall be your citizens, whether you will or not? Did not the right, the existence of which had been acknowledged by the gentleman from New York, involve a power of making its exercise effectual? It was idle to say that a State had a right to decide this question, and yet that other persons had a right to overrule that decision, and be its citizens whether it would or not.

Mr. B. said he knew that the powers of the States had been greatly abridged by constructions of the Constitution. He feared they would be yet more so. But he hoped it would not be here contended, that the rights of a State shall be so far abridged as that it shall not have power to protect its own safety and its own morals. If a man afflicted with a pestilent disease approached the shore of a State, there was certainly a right to keep him off. If vagabonds and fugitives from justice infest a State, they may certainly be expelled from it. What was the consequence of such a preservative power? We in the Southern States, said Mr. B., consider this description of population the most dangerous to the community that can possibly be conceived. They are just enough elevated to have some sense of liberty, and yet not the capacity to estimate or enjoy all its rights, if they had them—and being between two societies, above one and below the other, they are in the most dissatisfied state. They are themselves perpetual monuments of discontent, and firebrands to the other class of their own color. And if the time ever come when the flames of servile war enwrap this Union in a general blaze, perhaps we may have to look to them as the primary cause of such horrors. Has not a State, then, a right to get rid of them? They are not citizens in Missouri, and Missouri has as much right to say they should not be, as Massachusetts had to say that a black man shall not, within her limits, marry a white woman. Has not Missouri a right to send off beyond her limits persons of color when free? Virginia has done it, and Missouri must have the same right as Virginia. And here Mr. B. repeated his question, had Missouri a power to get rid of all the free people of color now there, and yet not the power to prevent others from going there?

He wished, he said, to put to some members of this House a case, to see how far they would go. He should suppose the persons of color in the State of Virginia, of a particular description, exceeded four hundred thousand in number. Although not willing to be dictated to by any other Government on earth, yet said Mr. B. there is, in Virginia, a sentiment, more or less prevailing among many of our people, that if a scheme of general emancipation could be devised, practicable in its character, it would be desirable that it should take place. If, in progress of time, our political society should shake its encumbered lap, and throw off this description of its property and people, should we have a right to say to them, go off, four or five thousand of you, into Pennsylvania, and settle there? What would Pennsylvania say? Would she not say, that free persons of color are, by their present experience, an intolerable nuisance to her society? If she finds such inconvenience from twenty or thirty thousand such persons, generally born free, and accustomed to the partial exercise of civil rights, what would she say to an irruption of such a host of men, who had just been relieved from the yoke of servitude, and in a more lawless condition than any other that can conceived? Yet, according to the doctrine now contended for, she must submit to it, having no power to refuse them admission into her territory. I wish gentlemen from that and other States to recollect, said Mr. B., that the time may come, when they will feel more anxiety on this subject, than I possibly can now.

Indians, free negroes, mulattoes, slaves! Tell me not, said Mr. B., that the Constitution, when it speaks of *We, the people*, means these. The argument in favor of including in the class of citizens free people of color, goes too far; it applies equally to the Indian and to the slave.

Mr. B. said he felt no difficulty, then, in coming to these conclusions: That the Constitution of the United States was framed by the States respectively, consisting of the European descendants of white men; that it had a view to the liberty and rights of white men; that, with regard to all this colored class, it was a description of people whom that Constitution did not mean to meddle with, only in the particular view in which they are expressly referred to, viz. with regard to representation. With regard to the individuals of this class, the Constitution of the United States had no reference to them or their rights, real or supposed. And why not? Because the framers of the Constitution well knew that every State in the Union, in its isolated character, was abundantly competent to the protection of the mere rights of persons and of property, where that right existed. We, the white people, wanted, not merely to exist, but we formed a Constitution to condense the will of our fellow-citizens, and to borrow the arm of a mighty people for our protection against foreign encroachments. The poor slave and the free man of color are sufficiently protected by the States. The States can give to the latter the right to sue and be sued, &c., and can protect them in every thing absolutely necessary to personal comfort and the preservation of life and property; can confer on them every thing except the great character of equality in all respects with the whites. Did we, said Mr. B., ever think it necessary to form a confederacy for the security of our property, of our lives, or of the correct administration of civil laws? No; we looked to Europe; we saw her map cut up into small squares and patches of territory—every nation hostile or rival to its neighbor, finding an enemy wherever it crossed a line. We foresaw that, among our States, too, if they remained separate and disunited sovereignties, there would be collisions of interest, on territorial and commercial questions, &c., producing animosity and wars; we entered into the federative compact to enable us to avoid a border war at home, and to resist aggression from abroad. In relation to these people of color, nothing was intended by that compact, their personal liberty and private property being abundantly secured by the laws of the several States. This was the substance of Mr. B.'s argument on this point.

With regard to precedents, Mr. B. said, he was not much in the habit of referring to them; he wished he could never hear the word in this House. But it appeared to him to be a modest request, when arguments drawn from them were continually used, to be allowed to call one to his aid. What, then, were the precedents bearing on this question? It is provided, by the Constitution of the United States, that Congress may establish an uniform rule of naturalization. Did Congress ever pass a law to naturalize people of color? On the contrary, every word of every naturalization law speaks of whites only. If, said he, we had gone abroad on such principles of knight-errantry; if we had broken down the barriers which separate the races of men, and, like the French Convention, tendered fraternity to them and all the world, we should have had a short and wild career of it, &c. Mr. B. went on to say, that stature, and other corporal qualities, had never been made the cause of distinctions in society; but color had constantly, for centuries past, been a mark of discrimination; it had been the fate of one color to be perpetually subordinate to the other.

But was this the only illustration to be drawn from the Constitution? No; there was another. Congress are invested with the power to provide for organizing, arming, and disciplining the militia. Who, said Mr. B., are the militia? The great body of every people, who are capable of military duty, subject to such regulations as the Legislature may impose. Men may be exempted, from causes particular to themselves. But the term militia includes the great body of a people contributing to the defence of their common country. Why have Congress, in their laws in execution of this provision, introduced the same words, "white men?" If colored persons are entitled to all the rights which belong to our fellow-citizens of a different complexion, how is it that, whilst every white man is authorized to bear arms, that description of men is excluded? It shows that there is something in color, more than in other circumstances, which separate the two classes.

Mr. B., in recapitulating his arguments on this head, said that he trusted he had said enough to show that free people of color were not citizens, in the same light as white persons are citizens, in the respective States. He proceeded then to make a few incidental remarks in regard to other views of this subject.

Suppose, for argument's sake, what it had been the purpose of the remarks he had already made, to deny. Give to the opponents of Missouri the aspect of this question which is the worst for its friends. Concede that one clause of the constitution of Missouri is in conflict with the Constitution of the United States. Does the nullity of one clause destroy the whole instrument? It was painful to him to appeal to professional principles in this House, but it was consistent with reason, as well as a plain and well known maxim of law, that a single vicious clause does not vitiate a whole instrument. Are we to have here, said Mr. B., in the discussion of great Federal concerns, a degree of technicality in objections to a constitution of a State which a court of law would not sustain in regard to any written instrument? Because one clause of a hundred and fifty amounts to nothing, do the remaining hundred and forty-nine also come to nothing, and all become bad? On the contrary, Mr. B. said, he had always understood that, nothing being taken from nothing, nothing remains. Mr. B. illustrated his views on this point by stating a parallel case. Congress has a clear power to lay import duties; it is just as clear that Congress has not the power to lay export duties. Suppose the chairman of the Committee of Commerce should bring in a bill, and it were possible that the bill should pass Congress, one clause of which imposed an export duty, and another an import duty. Would that clause which exceeds the powers of Congress make void the other, which is clearly within them? Perhaps, gentlemen might say, this was an extreme case. Granted, Mr. B. said. He would put another: There were certain powers of this Government which had been the bone of contention for years past, amongst which was the power to establish a bank. Suppose, in a law on any other subject, should be introduced a section exercising this power, and the Judges of the Supreme Court should think—no, they would not; he wished they would so think—that that part of the law was unconstitutional, would that make the rest of the law void? No; it would not. As much liberality at least, Mr. B. said, ought to be found in a legislative body when discussing fundamental principles of Government, as was to be found in courts of law.

The gentleman from New York said that, confessedly, a large portion of the free people of color in the United States were not citizens, and had asked for a construction of the constitution of Missouri which would embrace those who are. Now this again, Mr. B. said, was contrary to the rule of law; for, if a contract was made by two individuals, by one construction of which it was good, by another void, even a court of justice would give it that construction which would give it validity.

He stated another case, by way of illustration. No State can, according to the Constitution, without the consent of Congress, lay any duties on imports or exports. There are, then, certain duties which States may lay. Suppose a State Legislature, in laying taxes which it has a right to lay, should, contrary to the Constitution, lay an impost duty. Would a construction be given to it which, for that fault, would vitiate the whole act? Surely not. Mr. B. added some other illustrations, all tending to the same end, that, admitting (which he denied) that the clause objected to was contrary to the Constitution, it was no argument against the remainder, to which no exception had been pretended to be taken.

With regard to the question of leaving the contested and at the worst doubtful clause to be construed by the judiciary, need he argue, Mr. B. asked, that if a State constitution opposed the Constitution of the United States, it is just as void as the law of a State which comes in conflict with the same constitution? On that point, there was no doubt. It was perfectly immaterial, whether an unconstitutional provision was found in the constitution or law of a State; it was in each equally void. Do not gentlemen see, then, that they fight about a shadow? He called on them to recollect the difference of construction in regard to the powers of the State and Federal Governments. The latter possesses no power but that which is expressly given. Directly the converse of this is the rule in relation to the former. The Legislature of Missouri, whether the clause excepted to be in or out of the Constitution, possesses precisely the same power. Whenever they came to exercise it, would arise the question whether to legislate as proposed would or would not be to legislate uselessly, being contrary to the Constitution of the United States.

Suppose, Mr. B. said, this House were to declare this constitution of Missouri to be consistent with the Constitution of the United States; yet, if a free person arriving in Missouri, applied for the benefit of the act of habeas corpus, would he not, if the act under which he was seized appeared to be contrary to the Constitution of the United States, be delivered and set at liberty? Certainly he would; and the converse was true that, declaring the constitution of Missouri to be compatible with the Federal Constitution would not make it so. The Judiciary, said Mr. B., will, if the constitution be left as it is, decide this question when it comes up. What they say will be operative; what we say will not.

It was a question of extreme difficulty to decide, what powers do and what do not belong to this Government, or to the State governments. Shall we, then, said Mr. B., embarrass ourselves with the decision of questions thus difficult, and respecting which our decision, be it one way or the other, will be wholly inoperative?

Mr. B. concluded the speech, of which the preceding is an outline merely, by saying that he now came back, and closed with the proposition, that the constitution of Missouri is not inconsistent with the Federal Constitution, because, as respects the class of people there referred to, they are not citizens in the sense of the term in which it is employed in the Constitution of the United States.

When Mr. BARBOUR concluded, there seemed not to be a disposition in any person to rise.

Mr. SMYTH, of Virginia, said that he wished to present his views on the subject, but was not prepared to do so this afternoon. He therefore asked that the Committee should rise, and ask leave to sit again.

The Committee, however, refused to rise.

Mr. ARCHER, of Virginia, said, that he, too, wished to address the House on this question, but was prevented from doing so to-day by bodily indisposition.

Another motion for the Committee to rise was negatived.

At length, however, after one or two more refusals, the Committee rose and reported the resolution to the House; and, after several ineffectual attempts, a motion at length prevailed to lay it on the table.

SATURDAY, December 9.

Among the petitions presented to-day, was one by Mr. WENDOVER, from the Mercantile Society of the city of New York, praying for an imposition of a duty of ten per cent. on sales at auction; also for the establishment of an uniform system of bankruptcy; and for such a modification of the tariff of duties on imports, as is demanded by the best interests of the nation.

Mr. SMITH, of Maryland, from the Committee of Ways and Means, reported a bill, making a partial appropriation for the military service of the United States for the year 1821; which was read twice, and committed to a Committee of the Whole.

On motion of Mr. COCKE, the Secretary of War was directed to communicate to this House any information he may possess, tending to show whether the order given by Colonel King, of the fourth regiment of infantry, to shoot deserters taken in the fact, was approved by any general officer in the service of the United States, or known to, or passed over in silence by him, as stated in the defence of said Colonel King before a court-martial, sitting in the State of Alabama, in the year 1819; and, also, any information he may possess, showing that corporal punishment has been inflicted on any soldier, whereby he came to his death; and, if any, by whose order it was inflicted, and what measures have been taken relative thereto.

On motion of Mr. WHITMAN, the Committee on the Public Lands were instructed to inquire into the expediency of extending the times for issuing land warrants to soldiers of the Revolution, and for locating the same.

Mr. COOK submitted the following resolution:

Resolved, That the Committee on the Public Lands be instructed to inquire into the expediency of authorizing Benjamin Stephenson to locate four hundred and ninety-five acres of land in the State of Illinois, as a compensation for that quantity granted by the State of Virginia to George Hite, in the State of Kentucky, which, upon resurvey, was found to have been previously patented to another person, and which was transferred to the said Stephenson by the said Hite.

Upon this resolution the Speaker observed, that the more regular, and, he thought, the only correct practice was for the party asking relief, to set out his claim in a memorial or petition, addressed to the House.

After some remarks from Messrs. Culpeper and Cocke, against the practice, and Mr. Cook, in support of the resolution, it was negatived.

On motion of Mr. Rankin, the Committee on Commerce were instructed to inquire into the expediency of establishing a port of entry at the mouth of Pearl river, in the State of Mississippi.

The Speaker laid before the House a letter from the Secretary of the Treasury, transmitting the latest return made to the Treasury Department of the general state of the Bank of the United States, and its offices of discount and deposite, in pursuance of the resolution of the 5th instant; which letter and statement were ordered to lie on the table.

An engrossed bill entitled "An act to amend the act, entitled 'An act to alter the times of session of the circuit and district courts in the District of Columbia," was read the third time, and passed.

MISSOURI.

The House having resumed the consideration of the resolve declaring the admission of the State of Missouri into the Union,

Mr. A. Smyth, of Virginia, having obtained the floor, addressed the Chair. He said that the Constitution of the United States contains a clause that " the citizens of each State shall be entitled to all privileges and immunities of citizens in the several States ;" and the constitution formed for the State of Missouri contains a clause making it the duty of the Legislature of that State to pass such laws as may be necessary " to prevent free negroes and mulattoes from coming to, and settling in, that State, under any pretext whatsoever ;" and it has become a question whether the clause in the constitution of Missouri is repugnant to the Constitution of the United States. He would attempt, he said, to show that there was no such repugnance.

The Constitution of the United States provides that the citizens of each State shall be entitled to all the privileges and immunities of citizens in the several States. This can only apply to citizens who are, in their own States, entitled to all the, privileges and immunities of citizens. Can it be shown that free negroes are such citizens in any one of the States as are entitled to all the privileges and immunities of citizens? A citizen is he who is entitled to the freedom and privileges of the body politic, and has a share in its government. In Rome every citizen was enrolled in one of the thirty-five tribes, and, consequently, had the right of suffrage. When we apply the term "citizens" to the inhabitants of States, it means those who are members of the political community.

The civil law determined the condition of the son by that of the father. A man whose father was not a citizen was allowed to be a perpetual inhabitant, but not a citizen, unless citizenship was conferred on him. I consider him as a citizen of the United States who is entitled to every personal right of a civil and political nature common to the great body of the political community. The distinguishing characteristic of a citizen of the United States is the possession of those capacities which a foreigner obtains by naturalization. Those are, 1st a capacity to take a freehold ; 2d to vote at elections ; 3d to be elected, having the requisite qualifications of age, residence, and property. He who possesses these capacities is a citizen of the United States, within the meaning of the clause of the Constitution under consideration ; and he who does not possess these capacities is not. The free negro is not entitled to those civil and political rights in the United States, or in any State that adopted the Constitution. Let the State constitution be shown, which declares the free negro to be entitled to all the rights of citizenship, or the code of State laws that places him on an equality in all respects as to privileges with the white citizen.

The Revolution found the negro in America a slave. Where are the acts or constitutions which have declared him a citizen, entitled to all the privileges and immunities of citizens of the United States? They have no existence. He is everywhere inferior to the white man, as well by the laws of the States as of the United States. In the State of Massachusetts, always foremost in the work of liberty, the free negro is under considerable disabilities—one of which is, that he is not enrolled in the militia. If he comes into that State from another, he must show a certificate from the Secretary of State of his freedom, or he will be seized and deported. In Delaware free negroes convicted of larceny may be sold. If one of them comes into that State from another, he forfeits ten dollars per week for the time of his stay, and if he does not pay the penalty he is sold. In Virginia the free negro has no political, and very few civil rights. He is forbidden to come into that State, and if he does come, he is seized and removed. In Ohio he is not permitted to vote, and in North Carolina, although he is allowed the right of suffrage, yet he, and his posterity to the third generation, are refused the privilege of giving testimony in a court of justice, where a white man is a party. By the laws of the United States the negro is refused the privilege of being naturalized ; and in the code adopted for the government of this District, (which is the laws of the adjacent States,) it is provided that, on the trial of a free negro for a crime a slave may be a witness ; that a free negro may not marry a white woman ; that it is criminal to employ him, unless he has a certificate of registry ; that he may not keep or carry arms, and is punishable for lifting his hand against a white man ; and by the law incorporating the City of Washington, passed by this present Congress, a colored person is made liable to be punished by stripes for a breach of the ordinances of the city.

It is not every person who is born in a State, and born free, that becomes a member of the political community. The Indians, born in the States, continue to be aliens ; and so, I contend, do the free negroes, where the laws have not otherwise provided. A savage cannot be a member of a civilized community; he is incapable of exercising political rights; and nature seems to have made the negro a perpetual alien to the white man. Slaves are aliens. Alienage was the first foundation of slavery. Citizenship belongs to the civilized freeman. It is for Congress to provide a rule of naturalization that may admit to the rights of citizenship the civilized descendants of Indians and Africans. The States have no authority to admit citizens. When Congress have refused to naturalize any free negro, can it be tolerated that the master of a negro slave should have power to make him a citizen of the United States, entitled to all the privileges of citizens in the several States?

Who, then, are citizens of the United States? I would answer, 1st, those subjects of Great Britain who, being entitled to all the rights and privileges of British subjects, became American citizens by the Revolution; 2d, those who were declared citizens, or naturalized by the States, previous to the adoption of the Constitution of the United States; 3d, European foreigners naturalized in conformity to the law of Congress; and I would add, 4th, the children born in the country of aliens, who were of a description that might have been naturalized. Since the adoption of the Federal Constitution, no State has had a right to naturalize an alien; and, therefore, I contend that no State can make citizens of its slaves; and that, if the father is incapable of naturalization, birth will not make the son a citizen.

The mass of mankind in this country may be divided into two classes—free people and slaves; but the class of free people includes many who are not citizens. The same mass may be divided into three classes—citizens, aliens, and denizens; the latter description of persons being those who are admitted to some portion of the rights and privileges of citizens, but not to all those rights and privileges. Such of the free negroes, in our country, as are not aliens, may be denizens, but none of them, it is apprehended, are citizens within the meaning of the clause of the Constitution of the United States which is under consideration. The free negro who would claim all the privileges and immunities of a citizen in another State, must show a right to all those privileges and immunities in his own.

I shall contend, sir, that a State possesses the right of excluding from settling within its limits even the citizens of another State.

Has not every county and parish a right to exclude paupers and vagrants? May not every city and town exclude persons having infectious diseases, although they are citizens? If New York may exclude the citizens of Philadelphia when the latter city is visited with yellow fever, and if New York may do the same under the like circumstance, what gives to them this right? The right of self-preservation confers this right of exclusion. And if a town possesses this right of exclusion, founded on the right of self-preservation, does not a State possess it? May Virginia send 40,000 free negroes to settle in the State of Ohio, and has the latter

State no power to exclude them? May Massachusetts or Pennsylvania send a few thousand of their citizens into Rhode Island and Delaware, there to exercise the privilege of suffrage, and thereby bring Rhode Island under the power of Massachusetts, or Delaware under the power of Pennsylvania? Some members may recollect that, not many years since, the citizens of Baltimore, of a certain political party, resolved to direct the elections of Annapolis, by hiring a number of men to go to Annapolis, there to remain six months, to qualify them to vote at elections. Might not the councils of a State be changed by the like means, if the State has no power to exclude intruders? Sir, every State has the right of self-preservation. If it is proved that a State has the right to exclude the leper from coming and settling therein, the construction contended for on the other side, that a State can exclude no citizen of another State, is overthrown. The health laws of every city and State refute the argument.

The gentleman from Pennsylvania (Mr. SERGEANT) asked, if it would not have excited the universal indignation of the House had Missouri excluded all the citizens of the United States from her territory. It would, doubtless. But it does not prove that she has no authority to exclude some persons dangerous to her peace and happiness, that it would have excited indignation had she excluded all the citizens of the United States. Even had that extreme case happened, it would not have been a good reason for rejecting the State. In such a case, it would be the proper course to admit the State, and decide on her pretensions; to say to her, "come under the canopy of the Constitution; come under our power; and then we will decide on the extent of your rights."

I will also put an extreme case. Suppose that the leprosy—a disease certainly communicated by the touch—should appear in Philadelphia, and that 10,000 persons should be affected before proper means had been taken to stop its progress; would the corporation of Philadelphia, or the Legislature of Pennsylvania, have a right to send those lepers into Delaware; and would they have a right of "settling" there, as one of the privileges of citizens of the United States, against the will of the government of Delaware? I think it will scarcely be contended that Delaware would not have a right to oppose an intrusion so fatal to her health; and, if she would have a right to oppose it, Missouri has an equal right to oppose the intrusion of free negroes dangerous to her peace.

Usage expounds the law. The States possess the right of exclusion; for they have exercised it, and Congress has sanctioned the right. In the act of the last session for incorporating the City of Washington, power is granted to the corporation "to enforce the departure of such vagrants and 'paupers as may come into the city to reside, un-'less they give ample security, and to prescribe the 'terms on which free negroes and mulattoes may 'reside in the city." All powers not granted to the General Government are retained by the States. Have the States granted to Congress their power to exclude dangerous persons from settling within their limits? I do not find that they have granted this power to Congress.

The gentleman from Pennsylvania (Mr. Sergeant) said, that "citizens cannot enjoy the privileges and immunities of citizens in Missouri without settling there." The citizens who shall settle in Missouri will thereby become citizens of Missouri. The Constitution of the United States does not say that the citizens of one State shall have a right to become citizens of another State; but it speaks of them as continuing to be citizens of one State, yet entitled to privileges in another. A similar provision was contained in the Articles of Confederation, where it seems clear that nothing was intended but to confer privileges in passing through another State; egress and regress, the right to carry on commerce, exemption from the aliens' duty, &c.

The right of a State to close its doors against migration, is, I conceive, acknowledged by the Constitution to be in the States. [Here Mr. S. read part of section 9 of article 1.] A State possesses the right of banishing its own citizens; this has been common in ancient and modern times; and, if it may banish its own citizens, must it not have power to exclude others? The States, several of them, prescribed and banished the refugees; this banishment was sanctioned by Congress, who provided, in their naturalization laws, that those so banished should never return. The exclusion of free negroes from a white community is a politic and proper act; Congress do the same thing by their naturalization laws.

I shall contend that whatever be the just interpretation of the clause of the Constitution of the United States under consideration, it ought to be submitted for investigation and determination to the Judiciary. There are many parts of the Constitution which are addressed particularly to Congress; such are all those giving power to Congress, or to the Government of the United States, or to any department or officer thereof. There are other parts of the Constitution which are laws formed by the people, and addressed directly to the Judiciary. Those parts require no legislation by Congress; the Constitution being the supreme law. The clause under consideration is one of them; it vests no power in Congress; it calls for no legislation; it confers privileges and immunities on individuals; Congress cannot diminish or increase them; what are they the Judiciary should decide.

It might be material for Congress to inquire whether the constitution of a new State or an old State was republican or not. The Government is to guaranty to every State a republican form of government; and here, power being delegated to the Government, Congress may pass the necessary laws to carry it into effect. Should a State adopt a monarchical form of Government, I conceive Congress might pass a law repealing so much of their constitution as it was necessary to repeal, dictating a clause consistent with a republican form, which should remain in force only until the people themselves should form a republican constitution. It would not be necessary, even in that

case, to put or keep a State out of the Union. It is to States "in this Union" that the clause applies. In a case of that kind a political question would arise, to be decided on by Congress. In this case there arises a legal question fit to be decided on by the judiciary. And if the judiciary are to decide on the laws of Massachusetts, Delaware and Virginia, whether the rights of free negroes are infringed or not, why should not they decide whether the rights of the same class of people will be infringed by the laws of Missouri? If we reject Missouri as a member of the Union, for this cause, we should, to be consistent, expel Massachusetts, Delaware, and Virginia.

The clause in the constitution of Missouri is not a law in itself, as is the clause of the Constitution of the United States to which it is said to stand opposed. It directs that a law shall be passed. I venture to predict, with confidence, that no law will be passed in pursuance of this direction, by the Legislature of Missouri, that will contravene the Constitution of the United States. The members of the Legislature of Missouri will be sworn to support the Constitution of the United States; they will not be sworn to support the constitution of Missouri, and they will know that their acts contrary to the Constitution of the United States, will be void. They will, therefore, give to the constitution of their State a construction consistent with the Constitution of the United States.

To make any defect in the form of a constitution an insuperable objection to the admission into the Union of a State that it is desirable to admit, would imply a want of power in this Government to correct the error. I would, by no means consider any repugnancy in the constitution of a State as an insuperable objection to the admission of such State. We might say to a Territory: "Form a State government; if it is not republican, we will cause it to be republican; if it is repugnant, we or the judiciary will correct it." The Federal Convention expected repugnancies to be found in the Constitution of the United States, and have provided for them. It is declared in the Constitution, that "this Constitution shall be the supreme law ' of the land, and the judges in each State shall ' be bound thereby, any thing in the constitution ' of any State to the contrary notwithstanding."

Is it not better to decide some individual case upon full, calm, and deliberate investigation, before the judiciary, than to reject the resolution now before you, and thus outlaw a State? Shall we, by an ungracious and unnecessary act, produce a state of confusion, the result of which we cannot foresee? I hope not, as we do certainly know, that if there be in the constitution of Missouri a clause repugnant to the Constitution of the United States, that clause is null and void. If you had power to declare by law that any clause in the constitution of a State, repugnant to the Constitution of the United States, was void, would you not at once pass an act repealing the offensive clause in the constitution of Missouri? You would, unquestionably. Now, so far as the clause objected to is repugnant to the Constitution of the United States, the admission of Missouri will have the very same effect that your repealing act would have, had you power to pass it. If you had repealed the clause so far as it is repugnant to the Constitution of the United States, the courts would compare the Constitutions, and declare that of Missouri void, so far as it was repugnant; and, if you admit the State, the courts will, in like manner, declare the constitution of Missouri, so far as it contravenes that of the United States, to be void and of no effect. Thus admission leads you to the very end which you profess to wish to attain. It makes void the clause objected to, so far as it is contrary to the Federal Constitution.

All the constitutions of the States contained clauses repugnant to the Constitution of the United States; but the adoption thereof expunged them. Admission will have the same effect on the constitution of a new State that adoption had on those of the old. Then why not adopt the resolution before you, the effect of which will be, to expunge every repugnant clause from the constitution of Missouri?

The legislative and judicial powers of Government should be kept separate and distinct, so that the department exercising the one should not assume the duties of the other. Let us leave to the judiciary the exclusive exercise of their proper powers.

A construction should, if possible, be given to the constitution of Missouri, making it consistent with the Constitution of the United States.

If the literal construction of the constitution of Missouri was in opposition to the Constitution of the United States, yet, if we were satisfied that the convention intended the constitution which they framed to correspond with that of the United States, it should be so construed. [Here Mr. S. read several passages of law to show the rules of construction; that a thing within the letter is not within the statute, if contrary to the intention of the makers; that the word "all" admits of exceptions, &c.] The constitution of Missouri does not say *all* negroes and mulattoes shall be excluded; it does not say that negroes and mulattoes shall be excluded, being citizens of the United States. Suppose that the Legislature of Missouri should pass an act, in the very words of their constitution, that "free negroes and mulattoes shall not come to and settle in, this State, under any pretext whatever," and adds a proviso, that "this act shall not 'be construed to prevent the citizens of other States 'from being entitled to all privileges and immun-'ities of this State, as secured to them by the Con-'stitution of the United States." Would not such a law completely fulfil the intention of the constitution of Missouri, without contravening the Constitution of the United States? It would. Or should they pass a law such as that of Massachusetts, that a free negro, coming into the State, and remaining two months, may be seized and sent out of the State, unless by a certificate from the Secretary of State, he shall show that he is a citizen of the United States, it would fulfil the direction in their constitution, without contravening that of the United States.

The clause in question, of the constitution of Missouri, may have a very beneficial effect without operating contrary to the Constitution of the United States. It may operate on an extensive class of men, the emancipated blacks, and those of Africa and the West Indies, without violating, or being supposed to violate, the right of citizens of the United States. This clause makes it the duty of the Legislature of Missouri to pass a law to exclude free negroes and mulattoes; but it cannot become the duty of the Legislature, in carrying that provision of their constitution into effect, to violate the Constitution of the United States. They will construe their constitution in such a manner as to make it conform to the provisions of the Constitution of the United States. They will presume that the convention did not intend to violate the Constitution of the United States, and they will pass no law that can have such an effect.

The fair and proper construction of the constitution of Missouri will be, to carry into effect the will of the people of that State, so far as it may be carried into effect consistently with the supreme law. The Legislature will exclude whom they may lawfully exclude. Doubtless, they may exclude those whom Congress will not naturalize. They will understand the people of their State as having said to them, "You shall pass such laws as constitutionally you may, to prevent free negroes and mulattoes from settling here."

I shall contend, sir, that Missouri in now a State of this Union. The Constitution says that, "New States may be admitted into this Union." This is the grant of power which Congress may exercise by bill or resolution; in either way the President is to concur. It is not necessary that Congress should twice admit a State into the Union. Has Congress once admitted Missouri? I contend that Congress has once admitted Missouri as a State of this Union, upon the single condition precedent, of forming a State Government; that having been done, Missouri became a State of this Union.

The act of the last session declares, that the inhabitants of the Missouri Territory are "authorized to form for themselves a constitution and State government," and that "the said State, when formed, shall be admitted into the Union." The people of Missouri have formed for themselves a State government, by electing a Governor and members of the Legislature; they have thus formed "the State," and the law declared that the State, when formed, should be admitted into the Union. When was it admitted? The answer is, "when formed." It may be said the act speaks of a future admission. The time of admission was future to the time of the passage of the act of the last session, but it is now past. Congress has decided, and the people of Missouri have decided. The compact is complete. When terms are offered by one party, and not only accepted, but executed, by the other, the contract is confirmed, and it is too late for the party who offered the terms, to retract them.

Congress, then, have authorized the formation of a State, and admitted into the Union the State when formed. The State is formed, and consequently has become a member of the Union. The right of self-government is a natural inherent right of mankind. You have permitted the people of Missouri to assume the exercise of this right. The permission cannot be retracted. The right, once possessed, can never be surrendered. The moment Missouri ceased to be governed as a Territory, she became a State. The consequence of forming a State government is, to throw off the territorial government, to which the people never can return, or be subjected.

It has been said, (by Mr. Sergeant,) that "you cannot make an independent State." I agree with the gentleman. You can authorize a territory to become a State; and in so doing it becomes a member of the Union. If Congress admit a territory to form a State, it is a territory no longer; and the same instant it becomes a State it becomes a me nber of the Union; for Congress have no authority to admit a State out of the Union.

The gentleman from Pennsylvania (Mr. Sergeant) has said, that, if Missouri is a State, it is useless to pass the resolution. I admit that it is unnecessary to pass the resolution. The Senators and Representative from Missouri should have been permitted to take their seats. The resolution can be only useful to declare a fact of importance which has happened, to wit: that Missouri has become, since the last session of Congress, a State of this Union.

But is said there is a proviso in the act of the last session, that the constitution of Missouri shall be republican, and not repugnant to the Constitution of the United States. True, there is such a proviso; but I deny that this makes either a condition precedent, or a condition the violation of which would forfeit the right of Missouri to be a State. The same proviso declares that the State shall not interfere with the disposal of the soil owned by the United States, and that no tax shall be imposed on lands the property of the United States. Are these conditions precedent? They are to continue through all time. This proviso is a declaration of the law, and a caution to Missouri; but such a proviso is not a condition precedent, nor a condition on violating which Missouri will forfeit her rights. [Here Mr. S. read from Woddeson's Lectures a passage to show that where one is made a denizen, with a proviso, that he shall demean himself in a certain manner, the violation of the proviso does not forfeit his right to be a denizen; but he will be punished according to his fault.] This, said Mr. S. is a case in point. Such a proviso is no more than a warning and declaration of the law. The proviso in the act of the last session was a caution to Missouri that her constitution should be republican, and not repugnant to the Constitution of the United States.

All the new States formed of the territories of the United States have been admitted from the time of their forming State governments. Can we receive Senators and a Representative elected by a territory? If Illinois was not a State previous to the last session, when the last declaration was made respecting her admission, her Senators and Representatives have no right to seats in this body. The Senators were not elected by the Legislature of a State, or her Representatives by the people of a State. But we have admitted them, and so affirmed that they were elected by a State; therefore Illinois was a State before the last session, when the second declaration of her admission was made; and, the circumstances being the same, Missouri is now a State of this Union.

The proviso in the act of the last session that the constitution of Missouri should not be repugnant to that of the United States, is inoperative, useless, surplusage. We might as well have enacted that the stars shall not obscure the sun to-morrow as have enacted that the constitution of Missouri shall not be repugnant to that of the United States. No such repugnance can have any effect. It is, *ipso facto*, void. The Constitution of the United States has said that nothing repugnant to it in the constitution or laws of any State should stand; and why should we prescribe a rule already prescribed and declared supreme by the people?

It has been admitted that there may be cases where the constitution of a State will so contravene the Constitution of the United States that it may be proper for Congress to interfere. I also agree that such cases may arise; but those must be cases requiring legislation from Congress. Should a State provide for a different representation than is allowed her by the Constitution of the United States, it might be proper for Congress to pass a law respecting the times, places, and manner, of holding elections for Senators and Representatives in such State. In other cases, Congress might find it necessary to pass laws to carry into execution the power of the Government to guaranty to a State a republican form of government. Can any case be supposed in which it would be proper to expel a State? I cannot imagine any such case. The Constitution does not say that Congress shall guaranty to every State in the Union a constitution not repugnant to that of the United States. It says, that the Constitution shall be the supreme law of the land, and the judges in every State shall be bound thereby, any thing in the constitution of any State to the contrary notwithstanding. When we know that our Constitution is supreme, that any thing repugnant to it in the constitution and laws of Missouri is null and void, shall we proceed as if the Constitution of the United States would be endangered by the admission of Missouri? I hope not, sir.

After a new State has formed a constitution, Congress have just the same power over it, that they possess over the new constitution formed by an old State. Why should we examine, with microscopic eye, the constitutions of Illinois and Missouri, and never ask that the constitution of Connecticut should be laid before us?

The consequences which may follow the rejection of the resolution, are worthy of the consideration of statesmen, who have, or ought to have left every passion behind them at the threshold, and whose object is the peace, welfare, and happiness of the community.

We affect to fear that some hundred negroes

may lose their Constitutional right to settle as citizens in Missouri; and, under this pretence, we are about to disfranchise a State, dissolve the connexion between her and the Union, and produce difficulties, the consequences of which we cannot foresee; when we do know that no citizen of the United States can be deprived by the Legislature of Missouri of the rights to which he is entitled under the Constitution of the United States.

Sir, the States retain all power not delegated to the United States. They have not delegated power on this subject. It seems to be admitted in the Constitution that they retain it. They may admit the migration of such persons as they please until a certain time. Does it not follow that they may reject the migration of such persons as they please at all times? Let every member friendly to the rights of States beware how he sanctions an opinion, that all the barriers between the States are entirely broken down, and that the States cannot exclude persons dangerous to their health, their happiness, or their peace.

In every difficulty we should ask ourselves, what is now best to be done? Shall we send home the Senators and Representative of Missouri? What is then to follow? We ought to know what is next to be done; for the consequences ought to be maturely weighed in deciding this political question. The rejection of the representation of a State is a measure which threatens to derange the political machine. Shall Missouri be independent? Shall we bring her back to a territorial situation? Shall her laws, passed by her State Legislature, become void? It has been suggested that we may pass an act to confirm them? That I deny. We have nothing to do with the laws of the State of Missouri. Consider well the consequences of rejecting the resolution. I speak not of commotions; but I ask you to consider the effects of the doubt you will throw over the validity of their laws, and the authority of their Government; of the litigation which your decision may produce, by occasioning a belief that their acts are void. Let us adopt the resolution, which will secure every right, and preserve order and harmony.

When Mr. S. had concluded—

Mr. STRONG, of New York, said, the magnitude and importance of the subject under consideration must be his apology for claiming a small share of the attention and patience of honorable members, while he submitted the reasons for the vote he was about to give. I shall endeavor, said he, to be brief and plain in what I have to say.

The people of the Territory of Missouri were, by a law of Congress, authorized to form "a constitution and State government, provided that the same, whenever formed, should be republican, and not repugnant to the Constitution of the United States." They have formed a constitution, presented it for the approbation of Congress, and asked admission into the Union. If it violates the plain provisions of the Federal Constitution, ought it not to be disapproved, and the resolution under consideration be rejected? The constitution of Missouri contains, among other things, this remarkable clause—" It shall be the duty of the Le-

gislature to pass laws to prevent free negroes and mulattoes from coming to, and settling in, the State, under any pretext whatsoever." Here permit me to remark that the authority is express and positive, and is in restraint of personal liberty, and of the means of contesting personal rights. But are the persons here described citizens of the United States, or of a State; or of both; or of neither? If citizens, then the repugnancy is plain and palpable. But the honorable member (Mr. SMYTH, of Virginia,) on my right, who has just resumed his seat, has attempted, ingeniously, to prove, that free negroes and mulattoes are either aliens or denizens, and consequently, not citizens.

The honorable gentleman will pardon me for differing from him. I cannot assent to the proposition that this description of persons are aliens. An alien is one who owes allegiance to some Government other than that under which he lives. Allegiance to a foreign Power enters into the very essence of the term alien. To what foreign Power, or to what Government, other than that of the United States, do these persons owe allegiance? If to none—then what are they, if not citizens? But, if they are not aliens, it is insisted they are denizens. Is it so? No one can be a denizen who has not been an alien. Denization is the modification of alienage. But Congress can pass laws of naturalization only, and not of denization. It would seem to follow, therefore, that these persons cannot be denizens.

He has argued, too, at some length, to prove that a State possesses the right, not only of banishing her citizens, but excluding from her limits paupers, lepers, and persons infected with pestilential diseases; and hence inferred that each State might exclude all the citizens of the other States; and, consequently, that Missouri had a right to prohibit free negroes and mulattoes from coming to, and settling in, Missouri.

I have never understood that a State, town, or city, could prevent the admission of a pauper as such. In many of the States, and I do not know but in all of them, a pauper may be removed if likely to become a public charge; and every person, whether pauper or prince, may be prevented from gaining what the lawyers call a legal settlement. That a State may banish for crime, and guard herself against pestilence, need not be denied. The rights and privileges of peaceable, unoffending citizens, for whom we are expounding the law, do not depend upon the principles which determine the disabilities and punishment of criminals. Because a State can banish a traitor, does it follow that she can deport every or any harmless, unsuspected citizen? Because Pennsylvania may exclude from the city of Philadelphia persons infected with the leprosy or the plague, can she, therefore, exclude all the officers and troops of the Federal Government?—or any uninfected, peaceable citizen of any State or place? If not, Missouri remains undefended. She must seek some other mode of justifying the exceptionable provisions of her constitution.

It is, moreover, contended by the honorable gentleman, (Mr. SMYTH,) that Missouri became a member of this Union in fact, and in right, on the 19th of July last, the day on which the constitution was formed; and I understood him to say that, if the constitution of Missouri, now before us, had contained the provisions of a monarchical, instead of a republican form of government, Congress, by an act of legislation, could change it and make it republican. I cannot agree that Missouri is a member of this Union; or that Congress, by the silent operation of a law, could remedy the supposed evil. These shall be subjects for future consideration. But, does not the honorable gentleman in this, concede to Congress the right of making a constitution for a State, whether such State be out of, or in the Union? This is a broad concession, and yielding more than I am willing to take; whatever may be the powers of Congress in supervising the formation of State government, I have no hesitation in saying, that I think gentlemen will go with me, that when a State is in the Union, and one of the United States, her constitution and laws are beyond the inspection, or revision, or control of Congress. They must be referred for adjudication and correction to other tribunals.

The general proposition has been urged by the honorable member, (Mr. SMYTH,) that, if any clause in the constitution of Missouri be repugnant to the Constitution of the United States, which is the supreme law of the land, such clause is utterly null and void. This is true in law, not in fact. But, shall we sanction a wrong, which, until remedied, we know will produce injustice and evil? This constitution is submitted to us. For what purpose, unless it be for our approbation? If this submission and approbation are necessary, can it acquire the force and effect of a law, until Congress has approved it? But if approved and put into operation, when, by whom, and how are its repugnant provisions to be adjudged null and void? I think one must have some skill in the cultivation of chances to determine. This proposition proves too much. It proves that every law or other matter, which requires the revision and sanction of Congress to give it validity, may be passed with impunity, our oaths to the contrary notwithstanding, however flagrantly it may impugn the Constitution of the United States.

The question whether, if the resolution under consideration be rejected, Missouri will remain a sovereign independent State, or return to her territorial condition? has been so fully and ably examined, by my honorable friend, the member from Pennsylvania, (Mr. SERGEANT,) and my colleague, (Mr. STORRS,) that I shall not trespass upon your patience with any further discussion of it. And the more especially, since the honorable member from Virginia, (Mr. SMYTH,) has admitted, that Missouri cannot be a sovereign State, and independent of the United States. If she cannot, and if she be not now in full union and communion with the sister States, it seems to follow that her condition is territorial.

But it has been earnestly contended, that Missouri is now a member of this Union—one of the United States. This view of the subject has been pressed upon our attention with much feeling and eloquence, by the honorable chairman of the committee, (Mr. LOWNDES,) who reported the resolution, as well as by the honorable members (Messrs. BARBOUR and SMYTH,) from Virginia. And is Missouri a component part of the Union? Is she one of the United States? Do not the submission of her constitution to Congress, its reference to a committee of this House, the report of that committee, and the resolution we are now discussing, all admit that she is not? But if in truth she be a member of the Federal family, why is her constitution on our desks? We have no business with it. The time has gone by. Congress has no more right to approve or condemn it, than it has the constitution of Maine or Virginia.

When did Missouri become a member of this Union? It is said, from the time she formed her constitution. I shall not enter into a verbal criticism upon the language of the law which authorized her to form a constitution. A more interesting question presents itself. It is this: can Congress admit a State (to be formed from its territory) into this Union, prospectively? As for instance, suppose Congress, in the law authorizing the people of Missouri to form a constitution, had enacted that, on the 19th of July, 1820, the State of Missouri will have become a member of this Union, and from and after that day she is hereby declared to be one of the United States. The question is not so much what Congress has done, as what Congress has a right to do. The powers of Congress, although sovereign, are limited. These powers cannot be exceeded. A portion of this sovereignty may be delegated to the people of Missouri. But not unqualifiedly, as to the form and manner of its execution. Because, if unqualifiedly, they might extort the sanction of Congress to a form of government which notoriously violated the Constitution of the United States. This will be more distinctly seen by examining the necessary powers and requisites in the admission of new States, and the obligation of the nation towards them when admitted. The Federal Constitution provides, "that new States may be admitted by the Congress into this Union;" and that "the United States shall guaranty to every State in this Union a republican form of government." There must be a State formed, or to be formed. If from the territory of the United States, as was the case of Missouri, it is to be formed, and this formation can only be by the permission and authority of Congress. As Congress cannot rightfully execute a given power, so as to violate the Constitution of the United States, it would appear to follow that the same power could not be rightfully executed by any other body of men so as to conflict with the provisions of the Federal Constitution. But every State, howsoever formed, when admitted, must have a republican form of government. Is it not necessary that we should have the means of judging of this form? Yet how can we judge, in our legislative capacity, unless the instrument be submitted to us? And if submitted, it must be done before the State becomes a member of the Union. Suppose, then, that Missouri had in fact become one of the United States in July last, and that you now discovered that her constitution, instead of containing provisions for a Governor and Senators to be elected by the people, bore on its frontispiece a crown and sceptre, and contained provisions for a King and an hereditary Senate? This is a possible case. It is one of the cases provided for by the Constitution. For the United States, the faith, honor, and strength of the nation are pledged to guaranty a republican form of government. What could you do? Shake hands with royalty? This would be anti-republican. Would you remit it to the Judiciary? The Judiciary could afford no relief. What then? Legislate it right? This would be constitution-making. No, sir, your parchment would not do. Force must be applied, and the decision left to the sword. If this possible state of things may happen, although it may not disprove the power of Congress to admit a State prospectively, yet does it not utterly discountenance the policy, and go very far to deny the right of prospective admission?

In speaking of a resort to the sword, I beg to be understood as referring exclusively to the supposed case. I do not mean to intimate that serious consequences are to follow the rejection of this resolution. I have no such apprehensions. If I had, still I would preserve inviolate the Federal Constitution as my only political hope.

But the constitution of Missouri is before us, and, in my judgment, properly; for I cannot bring myself to believe that Missouri is now one of the United States. She could not be one without the assent of Congress. I cannot learn that this assent has ever been given; or, indeed, that it could have been given, consistently with the principles and safety of the Federal Constitution. Is it proper for us, then, and are we bound, to examine the constitution thus presented to us, and to determine whether it be, or be not, repugnant to the Constitution of the United States? I think this matter is cognizable by us, because we are sworn to support the Federal Constitution. What more effectual or permanent support can we give than to take care that no person, high or low, shall be deprived of a single privilege or immunity which this Constitution secures to him? If, then, the Missouri constitution, sanctioned by us, should, intermediate the time of its going into operation and the decision of the Federal courts upon it, deprive any citizen, or other person, of his Federal rights, or privileges, or immunities, would it not be in consequence of our sanction? For, without that, could it have any operation? The right to determine does not depend upon the degree of repugnancy, or upon the extent and magnitude of the injury which may be produced, but upon the question, is it repugnant, and will it injure and oppress the citizen in its operation? Some cases of palpable and flagrant repugnancy have been mentioned. I will not trouble the House with the repetition of them in this place, particularly as my honorable friend (Mr. LOWNDES) from South Carolina has, in the liberality of his mind, justly conceded that there might be cases in which it would become the duty of Congress to reject a constitu-

tion; and he supposed the case of Senators and Representatives to Congress, whose term of service should be different from that prescribed by the Constitution of the United States. This concession was necessary in the supposed case, because it would manifestly impugn the powers and privileges of the Senate and House of Representatives, and the Judiciary could afford no relief.

I am entirely opposed, sir, to remitting this matter to the Judiciary. Why send it to the Judiciary for adjudication? It may be years or ages before it reaches that tribunal. In the meantime, hundreds of American citizens may be deprived of their rights, oppressed, and persecuted. Who is to take their part? It requires money and friends to regain lost rights. Many sound objections have been urged by those who have preceded me against this inference. I shall content myself with stating one further objection. It is this: A free negro or mulatto of the District of Columbia may take and hold real estate in Missouri. This, I think, will not be denied; and, to make the case the stronger, suppose he derives the title to his land directly from the United States. Now, by the constitution of Missouri, he is not only excluded from the possession of his land, but is prevented from coming into the State and contesting his claims in the courts there, and the doors of the Federal courts are barred against him. They cannot entertain his claim and afford him relief, because he is not a citizen of a State. How is this to be answered? Or is the sufferer to be turned off remediless? And will you thus permit individual wrong to accumulate? Or will you rather prevent it, by staying the operation of the only cause which can produce it?

Are our free negroes and mulattoes citizens? This is a deeply interesting question, both as it respects them and the nation. The report of the committee seems to admit that some of them are citizens, because it says that a large class of them "cannot be considered as citizens of any State." The honorable members (Messrs. BARBOUR and SMYTH) from Virginia deny that they are citizens. But the gentleman (Mr. BARBOUR) from Virginia who first spoke, will permit me to say, that I think his definition of a citizen proves too much; for it proves that the Jews of Maryland are not citizens of Maryland, although their fathers and their ancestors have resided there since the days of Lord Baltimore. A definition may destroy a right, but never can create a right. Facts and experience in politics and morals are better than definitions. What, therefore, are some of the peculiar and distinctive characteristics of a citizen of a State? They are, the right of passing, freely and unmolested, from town to town, and place to place, within the State, and the right of residing, at pleasure, in any part of the same. That these rights belong to every one entitled to the high privilege of citizen, I think will not be denied.

But these rights are also common to all free persons, of every age and sex, within the State, except aliens, lunatics, vagabonds, and criminals; because their possession and exercise are indispensably necessary to the social relations of life, and to the preservation of the State. Indeed, vastly the greatest proportion of the citizens of a State have no other external mark 'of their citizenship. Females and minors cannot be elected to office, or vote, or sit on juries, or be subjected to taxes, as a general rule. These persons enjoy the privilege of citizenship, and the immunity of the laws of the State, to which they must demean themselves, as completely as the man who has, in addition, the qualification of a voter, or a juryman. What, then, is the meaning of that great clause in the Federal Constitution, which declares that "the citizens of each State shall be entitled to all privileges and immunities of citizens in the several States?" This has been called the basis of the Union. As I understand this clause, it does away the disability of alienism. Without it, the citizens of each State would be aliens to every other State, and could not, of right, enter another State without a passport. It confers the same common privileges and immunities upon the citizens of Maryland, for instance, in reference to the United States, as the citizens of Maryland possess in reference to that State. Hence, a citizen of Maryland may pass into and about the State of Virginia, and reside there, subjecting himself to the laws of Virginia, as he was bound to do to the laws of Maryland; because in Maryland he possessed these rights, and owed this obedience. But it does not follow, nor is it at all necessary that because he was a voter or a juryman in Maryland, he must be either the one or the other in Virginia. If this reasoning be correct, then these essential rights of citizenship are secured, and each State left in full possession of its obligation and powers to protect its peaceable citizens and defend itself against violence and crime.

From what has been said, I think it may be fairly concluded that free negroes and mulattoes are citizens, unless some positive act of disfranchisement can be shown. But I beg leave, sir, to examine this matter in another point of view. I am constrained to believe that these persons are citizens of the United States, and, as such, have a right peaceably to pass through, or reside in, any part of the United States.

The Federal Constitution, so far as I can understand it, recognises and knows but two descriptions of freemen, for the question under discussion concerns freemen only, and I shall avoid, if possible, any mention of the other class of persons. These descriptions are citizens and aliens. I shall not go into an examination of the laws or practice of ancient or modern nations to ascertain the national character of their inhabitants. Their constitutions are unlike ours, and if in ours there be any other designation of the national character of freemen than that of citizens or aliens, what is it? I have said that Congress only could naturalize aliens—that is, persons who owe allegiance to a foreign Government. But a slave has no country, and owes no allegiance, except to his master. How, then, is he an alien? If restored to his liberty, and made a freeman, what is his national character? It must be determined by the Federal Constitution, and without reference to

policy; for it respects personal liberty. Is it not that of citizen or alien? But it has been shown that he is not an alien. May we not, therefore, conclude, nay, are we not bound to conclude, that he is a citizen of the United States? Now, permit me to say that it is one of the inestimable privileges of a citizen of the United States to pass, unmolested, through the several States, and to reside where it may best suit his health and convenience. Indeed, sir, this is the essential feature in the federal character of an American citizen. If, therefore, free negroes and mulattoes are citizens of the United States, does not the constitution of Missouri conflict with the Federal Constitution, although they may not be citizens of a State? But some of them, at least, are citizens of a State.

Facts are better than theories. In many of the States they are recognised as citizens, and, among other things, are eligible to office, entitled to hold real estate, to vote, to sue and be sued. In some of the States, their fathers, with ours, fought the battles of the Revolution. Vermont was not one of the original thirteen States; she was admitted into the Union in 1791, and had then, and still has, free negroes and mulattoes, whose citizenship, by the citizens of that State, I believe, has never been doubted or denied. These are facts within the knowledge of honorable gentlemen who hear me. But I beg leave, sir, to refer to the case of Louisiana. By the third article of the treaty which ceded to the United States the territory of Louisiana, it is stipulated that "the inhabitants of the ceded territory shall be admitted, &c., to all the rights, advantages, and immunities of citizens of the United States." The term *inhabitants* is used. It is a comprehensive term; and whether it includes slaves, is not necessary for me to inquire. It clearly includes *freemen*, and consequently free negroes and mulattoes, unless excepted. And, if excepted, permit me to say it belongs to gentlemen opposed to me to show where and how they are excepted. The State of Louisiana was formed from a part of the ceded territory, and admitted into the Union; and are not the free negroes and mulattoes in that State citizens of Louisiana? They were made citizens of the United States by the treaty; and, in my judgment, they became citizens of the State when the State became a member of this Union.

As connected with the question, who is a citizen of a State? I will refer again to the Federal Constitution. It is there declared that the judicial power shall extend (among other cases) to controversies "between citizens of different States." Now, any person in the State of Maryland, who can prosecute a citizen of Virginia, under this clause, must be a citizen of Maryland; and so of every other State. Is not this a sure criterion of citizenship? Who, then, can prosecute? Is there a freeman in the nation, not an alien, and domiciled in a State, who cannot prosecute and be prosecuted in the Federal courts? If there be one, it must be owing to some legal disability. Are free negroes and mulattoes, domiciled in a State, under any disability? The Federal Constitution interposes none; and I know of no law or judicia decision which does. The fair presumption is, that they have the right to prosecute; and it devolves upon those who deny the right, to prove the disability. But, if they can prosecute in the Federal courts, under this clause in the Federal Constitution, then they are citizens of the States, and the constitution of Missouri is repugnant to the Constitution of the United States, because it acts directly upon the citizen, and does not add to, but takes away, his existing rights and privileges.

But, assuming that there are free negroes and mulattoes who are not citizens of any State, it is said by my friend (Mr. LOWNDES) from South Carolina, that the exceptionable clause in the constitution of Missouri is to be so construed as to apply to them only. The power given to the Legislature is mandatory; the language of the clause is general, and, in terms, applies to all, and may be executed upon all, free negroes and mulattoes. I cannot assent to that exposition of a power which would establish one rule in Maine and another in Missouri. No, sir, this is Constitutional law, and does not speak a language official, and a language confidential. It means what it says; and should be construed as it reads. How do you expound other similar Constitutional powers? Take the treaty-making power, for example. Will you say that you have a right to make a treaty with England, but that you have no right to make a treaty with President Boyer—with the Republic of Hayti? Take also the power to naturalize. Does it include the subjects of England and France, and exclude those of Persia and China? How, then, under a positive grant of power to prevent free negroes and mulattoes from coming into a State, will you admit some and exclude others?

I must solicit your indulgence, sir, for a few minutes more, while I examine this subject in reference to existing treaties, and the laws of Congress. These treaties and laws, if made pursuant to the Constitution of the United States, are the supreme law of the land. Does not the constitution of Missouri plainly violate the provisions and stipulations of existing treaties? I have already had occasion to refer, for another purpose, to the third article of the treaty for the cession of Louisiana to the United States. Has the time gone by when the stipulation in that article is no longer binding? How are the free negroes and mulattoes in the territory of Arkansas to be excluded from the State of Missouri? Does Missouri possess the power of disfranchising a citizen of the United States—of destroying the federal rights of an American citizen? If not, are we at liberty to sanction an instrument, the operation of which, until arrested by the tardy arm of the law, will impair and may destroy these federal rights? But this, sir, is not all. By the existing treaty between the United States and Great Britain, it is stipulated that "the inhabitants of the two countries respectively shall have liberty freely and securely *to come,* &c., and to remain and *reside in any ports* of the said territories respectively." The substance of this provision is found in the treaty between us and Sweden; and I believe in nearly all

the commercial treaties which we have made with the nations of Europe. Indeed, sir, provisions of this sort are essential to the successful operations of commerce, and to the preservation of our commercial relations. The Missouri constitution infracts this provision in the treaty, by excluding from her limits the free negroes and mulattoes of the Canadas and of the other British possessions, who may wish to go and reside in the State of Missouri for commercial purposes. It does more: the principle of it strikes at the root of the commercial relations between the several States, and between the United States and foreign nations.

Once more, and I have done. Congress has passed laws, offering bounties in land, to induce persons to enter into the Army of the United States. They have entered, done their duty, and received a title to their land; among them are many free negroes and mulattoes. Suppose they are not citizens of a State. Missouri says they shall not enjoy the bounty of their Government. Nay, more, they shall not have the humble privilege of contesting their rights in her courts of justice. Did not the Federal Government, in giving the title, pledge its faith and honor to secure the possession and the enjoyment? I humbly conceive it did; and that these, as well as the proudest American citizens, are eminently entitled to our protection, for they have endured war and peril, have wasted their strength, and shed their blood, in fighting the battles of their country.

When Mr. STRONG had concluded—

Mr. NELSON, of Virginia, moved that the resolution be recommitted to the Committee of the Whole on the state of the Union.

The question being taken thereon, it was determined in the negative—yeas 73, nays 90, as follows:

YEAS—Messrs. Abbot, Alexander, Anderson, Archer of Virginia, Baker, Baldwin, Barbour, Beecher, Bloomfield, Brevard, Brown, Brush, Bryan, Burton, Burwell, Butler of Louisiana, Cobb, Cocke, Crowell, Dickinson, Earle, Edwards of North Carolina, Fisher, Lloyd, Ford, Garnett, Gorham, Gray, Hall of North Carolina, Hill, Jackson, Johnson, Jones of Virginia, Jones of Tennessee, Lowndes, McCoy, McCreary, McLane of Delaware, McLean of Kentucky, Meigs, Mercer, Metcalf, Montgomery, T. L. Moore, Neale, Nelson of Virginia, Newton, Parker of Virginia, Pinckney, Randolph, Rankin, Reed, Rhea, Shaw, Simkins, Slocumb, Smith of New Jersey, B. Smith of Virginia, A. Smyth of Virginia, Smith of North Carolina, Southard, Storrs, Strong of Vermont, Strong of New York, Swearingen, Terrell, Tompkins, Trimble, Tyler, Walker, Warfield, Williams of Virginia, and Williams of North Carolina.

NAYS—Messrs. Adams, Allen of Massachusetts, Allen of New York, Archer of Maryland, Ball, Bateman, Boden, Buffman, Butler of New Hampshire, Campbell, Cannon, Case, Clagett, Clark, Cook, Crafts, Culpeper, Cushman, Darlington, Davidson, Dennison, Dewitt, Eddy, Edwards of Connecticut, Edwards of Pennsylvania, Eustis, Fay, Folger, Foot, Forrest, Fuller, Gross of New York, Gross of Pennsylvania, Guyon, Hall of New York, Hall of Delaware, Harden, Hazard, Hemphill, Hendricks, Hibshman, Hooks, Kendall, Kent, Kinsey, Kinsley, Lathrop,

575   HISTORY OF CONGRESS.   576

H. OF R.   _Vessels sunk for the Defence of Baltimore._   DECEMBER, 1820.

Lincoln, Linn, Livermore, McCullough, Mallary, Marchand, Meech, Monell, R. Moore, S. Moore, Morton, Moseley, Murray, Nelson of Massachusetts, Overstreet, Parker of Massachusetts, Patterson, Phelps, Philson, Plumer, Rich, Richards, Richmond, Robertson, Rogers, Ross, Russ, Sawyer, Sergeant, Silsbee, Sloan, Smith of Maryland, Stevens, Street, Tarr, Tomlinson, Tracy, Tucker of South Carolina, Upham, Van Rensselaer, Wallace, Wendover, and Whitman.

The question was then stated, shall the resolution be engrossed, and read a third time? And debate arising thereon, the House adjourned.

MONDAY, December 11.

A new member, to wit, from the State of Maine, late a part of the State of Massachusetts, JOSEPH DANE, elected to supply the vacancy occasioned by the resignation of John Holmes, appeared, was qualified, and took his seat.

JOHN A. CUTHBERT, from the State of Georgia, also appeared and took his seat.

Mr. SERGEANT, from the Committee on the Judiciary, delivered the following report:

The Committee on the Judiciary to whom was referred the memorial of the Legislative Council and House of Representatives of the Territory of Arkansas, complaining of the delay and denial of justice from the neglect and non-attendance of the judges appointed for that Territory, report—

That, if the cause of complaint still continued, it would certainly call for the interposition of this House to endeavor to remove it. But, upon inquiry at the Department of State, the committee have had the satisfaction to learn that the two judges of whom the complaint was made, have resigned, and others have been appointed to their place, who it is hoped and believed will feel a just sense of the duty that belongs to their station, and perform it accordingly. If, in this respect, there should again be a failure, it will then be necessary to consider of the propriety of some act which will not only mark it with decisive reprobation, but have a tendency to prevent its recurrence. They, therefore, offer the following resolution:

Resolved, That the committee be discharged from the further consideration of the memorial.

And the same was ordered to lie on the table.

Mr. WILLIAMS made a report on the petition of Rosalie P. Deslonde, accompanied with a bill for her relief; which was read twice, and committed to a Committee of the Whole.

On motion of Mr. BALDWIN, the Secretary of State was required to communicate to this House any information which may have been received by that department, touching any alterations in the commercial laws or regulations of any of the nations of Europe, which may have been made or adopted since the year 1817.

On motion of Mr. BUTLER, of New Hampshire, the Committee on the Post Office and Post Roads were instructed to inquire into the expediency of providing, by law, for prohibiting printers and editors of newspapers, and all other persons who are proprietors of any such printing establishment, or in any way concerned in the publication of newspapers, from being mail contractors or postmasters, and also prohibiting postmasters from being mail contractors, or being employed in the conveyance of the mail.

On motion of Mr. JACKSON, the Committee on the Judiciary were instructed to inquire into the expediency of amending the eleventh section of the act, entitled "An act for regulating processes in the courts of the United States, and providing compensations for the officers of the said courts and for jurors and witnesses," providing for the removal of suits and actions in certain cases.

Mr. WHITMAN submitted the following resolution, which was read, and ordered to lie on the table for one day:

Resolved, That the 16th rule, in relation to the "order of business of the day," be so far altered, that the Speaker, in calling for petitions, shall hereafter begin by calling for petitions from Maine.

THE DEFENCE OF BALTIMORE.

Mr. WILLIAMS, of North Carolina, from the Committee of Claims, made a report on the petition of sundry merchants of Baltimore, for compensation for vessels sunk in the harbor of that city, to prevent the approach of the British shipping in the Fall of the year 1814, accompanied with a bill for their relief; which was read twice, and committed to a Committee of the Whole. The report is as follows:

That, in the month of September, 1814, sundry vessels belonging to the memorialists were taken by public authority, and sunk at the mouth of the harbor of Baltimore, to prevent the vessels of the enemy from entering that harbor.

On the 7th March, 1815, the Secretary of War wrote to Colonel Paul Bentalou, quartermaster general at Baltimore, as follows: "As the owners of the vessels which were sunk at Baltimore will now become very importunate, and as you probably cannot raise them fast enough to meet their wishes and expectations, you may, therefore, permit individuals to raise their own vessels for a stipulated sum, or in such other manner as may, in your opinion, be compatible with the public interest, as it is my wish that you should give every facility to the raising of those vessels which may be consistent with economy and the public interest. As there no doubt will be many applications to Congress by individuals owning those vessels for compensation for damages, by injuries either to their vessels or rigging, while sunk, it would be advisable that such damages should be duly ascertained, in such manner as you may think best, at the time the vessels are respectively raised, and a report thereof made to this office."

In pursuance of these instructions, three respectable citizens of Baltimore, one an "experienced" ship-carpenter, one a ship-joiner, and the other a ship-chandler, were appointed to survey the said vessels, and appraise the damages; and, in the month of September following, a return of the amount assessed upon each vessel was made to the Secretary of War; and, in April, 1816, an appropriation was made to the amount of the several sums thus assessed, which was subsequently distributed among the claimants.

On the 7th of January, 1817, the owners of the vessels presented their memorial to Congress, claiming a further allowance, alleging that the sum previously awarded them was "not sufficient to pay one-fourth the expense of repairing," and that the appraisement

577　　　　　　　HISTORY OF CONGRESS.　　　　　　578

DECEMBER, 1820.　　　Vessels sunk for the Defence of Baltimore.　　　H. OF R.

of damages had been made without "their knowledge or concurrence." Upon this memorial there has been no decision by Congress; and, on the 15th of February last, James H. Causten, one of the memorialists, urged his claim anew upon the consideration of Congress in a separate memorial, and, to the reasons previously assigned why further compensation should be made, has subjoined a claim for a *per diem* allowance from the time his vessel was sunk till the repairs were completed, which he alleges to have been two hundred and ninety-four days. He also alleges that the vessel was in good repair when sunk; that the repairs, after it was raised, cost $3,589 03; and that irreparable injury was done by sinking, to the amount of $1,000, which, with $5 per day for demurrage, makes an aggregate of $6,059 03; and deducting therefrom $675, the amount awarded him by the appraisers, he claims a balance from the Government of $5,384 03, $384 more than his witnesses prove his vessel to have been worth before it was sunk.

Equal and exact justice may not have been done by the surveyors who appraised the damages; but it is difficult to perceive what measures could now be adopted that would be more likely to effect the object. The survey and appraisement was made by three of the citizens of Baltimore, of acknowledged skill and respectability, who appear to have commenced their labors on the 26th of March, 1815, and to have concluded them on the 15th of August of the same year; and the minuteness of their survey, (of which their records furnish proof,) together with the time their attention must have been drawn to the subject, forbid the presumption that the business of their appointment could have been lightly passed over. And were it even admitted that they could have been influenced by partial considerations, it would seem at least probable that their partialities must have inclined them to the side of their fellow-citizens rather than to that of the Government. It is believed, then, that it would be inexpedient to authorize an additional allowance for damages.

The committee are, however, of the opinion that, so far as relates to demurrage, the memorialists are entitled to relief, although, until the last session, no claim of that character appears to have been urged upon the attention of Congress. Two of the surveyors have certified (and the fact is also established by their records) that they made no allowance "for the deterioration of the vessels;" and it is equally true that none was made for the detention from their owners.

As it is impracticable to ascertain what income, if any, would have been derived from the use of the vessels antecedent to the close of the war, had they not been sunk, it is believed as substantial justice as is practicable in the case will have been done should a reasonable daily allowance be made, from the close of the war to the end of a necessary period, for repairing the injuries; and for this purpose the committee report a bill.

———

[The following documents were subsequently communicated to the House of Representatives.]

CAPITOL, February 19, 1820.

SIR: A memorial from certain merchants of Baltimore (claiming compensation for injury sustained by their vessels which had been sunk by legal authority for the preservation of that city) has been submitted to the Committee of Claims, over which you preside. I had given, prior to your last report, a verbal state-

ment to you. The report and memorial having been recommitted, it may be proper to give to your committee a detailed statement in writing.

In the year 1812 I commanded in Baltimore. The enemy appeared off the mouth of the river, and threatened the city. To prevent an attempt to pass the fort, I caused a number of vessels to be moored, head to stern, from the fort to the opposite point, prepared for sinking. The enemy did not attack during that year, and the vessels were returned to their owners. The expense of repairing the injury sustained by their exposure to the weather was paid by the city. This occurrence called my attention to the subject, and I submitted a bill (in Senate) which was signed on July 16, 1813, entitled "An act providing for the further defence of the ports and harbors of the United States," which authorised the sinking of hulks or vessels as impediments to the entrance of the ships of the enemy into the ports of the United States, and appropriated the sum of $250,000 to defray any expense that might occur in consequence.

Subsequent to the attack on Washington, I was again called into the service of the United States, as commander at Baltimore, and made a requisition on the city for vessels to be sunk; a sufficient number were delivered to Commodore Rodgers, (then acting with a body of seamen in concert with me,) and sunk under his direction.

The enemy attacked by land and water, and having completely failed in both, they evacuated the Chesapeake; and, being superseded in my command, I took my seat in the Senate. Aware of the injury the sunken vessels would sustain, I requested the Secretary of War, Colonel Monroe, to direct Commodore Barney, who had a number of seamen under his command, to cause the vessels to be raised, and an order was sent to that effect, but was not executed. The commodore alleged that his men had not been paid, and had not clothing sufficient for such work. I then requested the Secretary to direct the quartermaster general, Colonel Bentalou, to cause the vessels to be raised. The Winter had set in; few were raised; and most of the vessels remained all Winter and late in the Spring under water, and must have sustained great injury. I also recommended to the Secretary of War the propriety of appointing appraisers to value and assess the damage each vessel had sustained. That course was pursued; the ships were all raised, and delivered to their respective owners. Three respectable men were appointed by the quartermaster general as appraisers, to wit, an experienced ship-master, a ship-carpenter, and a ship-chandler; they visited each vessel, and appraised the damage or injury that was apparent.

It has been alleged that most of the owners knew not of the appraisement having been made; that the masters were not on board when made; and that the appraisers were not apprized of the real injury sustained by the destruction of the sails and rigging on board of the vessels when sunk, all which must have been completely destroyed by their long immersion. Such was the case (as I have been told) of the brig or schooner Sally, belonging to J. H. Causten. The damage sustained by that vessel was valued at $675. Nor was it possible for the appraisers, by a visit of a few hours, to ascertain the real damages that had been sustained; they could only be known by an attendance on each vessel while their repairs were making. I had two vessels sunk, and was allowed for damages sustained by the Adriana $300, which sum scarcely paid for cleaning and drying the ship. The principal injury she sustained was not discovered; she foundered at sea during her first voyage, yet she had been carefully examined. I am within the amount when I state that three times the sum allowed did not place her in the same state in which she was at the time she was sunk. My vessels were raised by the owners before the ice closed the river, and must have suffered less than others.

The vessels were kept from their owners generally from six to eight months, and I believe, some were longer under water; for which no allowance whatever was made, as appears by the certificate of the appraisers, and for which they have a fair and undoubted claim. This detention was the fault of the Government, for, with proper exertion, the vessels might all have been raised before the ice covered the river.

The detention of those vessels for so many months was a most serious injury to the claimants. The time they were detained would have enabled the owners to have made at least one voyage to Europe, and two or three to the West Indies; and there is no reason whatever, that I can conceive, to prevent the committee from reporting a bill allowing the owners a fair demurrage or per diem allowance for the time the vessels were detained. A similar allowance was made to the owners of scows used to make a floating bridge, by the act of 27th April, 1816; under which law the owners received one dollar per day for every day the scows were so employed, amounting to $2,500 for the use of twenty-four scows; whilst the owners of ships sunk are allowed only $15,188 for the great injury sustained, and for a long detention of their vessels. Can this be right or just?

Soon after Congress met, in the session of 1815 and 1816, I applied to the Secretary of War for the valuation of the damages assessed for the vessels that were sunk, and to know whether he was prepared to pay the amount to the respective owners. He put into my hand the list, (a copy of which you have,) and observed that the valuation appeared to be very low, but that he was unable to pay even that sum, the whole amount of $250,000 appropriated for that object having been applied to other items of expenditure, by order of the President. In consequence, I submitted the subject to the Senate, and an appropriation was made, on the 20th of April, 1816, to cover the valuation, in the words following, to wit: "For the payment of damages sustained by the ships and vessels sunk at the entrance of the port of Baltimore, to prevent the ships of the enemy from passing the fort and entering the harbor, $15,188 50."

You will observe that the appropriation is for damages *only;* no allowance made for detention, as appears by the certificate of the appraisers, nor was any directed to be made by the Secretary of War, as appears by a copy of his order herewith, dated the 7th of March, 1816. He only directs the appraisement of the damages actually sustained. The necessity of directing the attention of the appraisers to that object had not occurred to the Secretary. The act of 1813, however, contemplated such allowance; for it says emphatically, "that the President be authorised to hire or purchase hulks, or other means of impediment to the entrance of the ships of the enemy, to be sunk." Now, sir, the claimants demand payment for the hire of their vessels; and I believe there is no instance of wagons impressed, as those ships were, [being debarred,]

from receiving pay for their hire for the time they were detained. The claim, I repeat, is equitable; it is just; and has, I believe, been refused in no instance where vessels, horses, or wagons, have been taken and employed in public service.

I am, sir, with respect, yours, &c.
　　　　　　　　　　　　　　　　　　S. SMITH.

Hon. LEWIS WILLIAMS,
　　Chairman of Committee of Claims.

MISSOURI.

The House then resumed the consideration of the resolution declaring the admission of the State of Missouri into the Union.

Mr. ARCHER, of Virginia, said, that, having had some share in protracting the trial, to which the patience of the House was to be subjected, in the debate, he owed it the atonement of making his trespass as brief as possible. His inducement to trouble the House at all grew entirely out of the circumstances of views having been stated in support of the resolution, in which he could not concur, and to which he should be considered as assenting if the grounds of his vote were not explained. The delicate relation of the question, however, to the slaveholding States, would furnish sufficient excuse to any member, coming from that quarter of the Union, for wishing to bestow on it the fullest examination.

Mr. A. proceeded to remark that, whilst he utterly disclaimed the consequences which had been inferred from it, he was by no means prepared to contest the right of the States to admit the colored person, born within their respective limits, to the privileges of citizenship. The States had delegated, in relation to this subject, only the power of naturalization, the operation of which was known to extend only to persons born beyond the limits of the community, by whose authority it was exerted. The collateral connected power of determining the right and condition of admission to the privileges of citizenship, as respected persons born within their respective limits, could not, then, be denied to the States, or abridged in its exercise, without a construction which might equally be employed to divest every other reserved right, and to dismantle evey safeguard to be found in the Constitution. We had been told, indeed, that the exercise of this right in relation to colored persons, could not be considered as contemplated by the Constitution of the United States. Supposing it were not, the rights of the States did not depend, for their validity or exercise, on the recognition of the Federal Constitution, which, in its true character, was no more than the source of the limitations on them; nor had the advance of encroachment yet reached a construction, by which the security of these rights would not simply be impaired, but their independent existence absolutely subverted. The mode, too, of the derivation of the inference which excluded the exercise of the right in question, was as little warranted as the source of its derivation. It was derived, not from any thing in the language of the Constitution, but from the peculiarity of the circumstances of some of the parties to it, which were supposed to preclude the intention to allow such an exercise of right. This was not a case, however, in which a resort of this kind was admissible, for the ascertainment of intention. Where language was of doubtful import, this resort might be admitted with little danger, because there was a limit to the possible variety of interpretation of which language was susceptible. But where there was no doubt arising in the interpretation of language, nor any language on the subject of doubt to be interpreted, the allowance of a resort to the circumstances of parties, to an instrument for the ascertainment of its purport, would be admitting the supply, and not the explanation, of an intention. To such a principle of substitution and enlargement of the operation of instruments, there was evidently no limit short of the exhaustion of ingenuity. It was better to admit any defect whatever, in the Constitution, than a liability so indefinite, to *accretion and metamorphosis.*

The objection to the recognition of the right in question was founded in an entire misapprehension of the consequences of its exercise. It had been supposed that if the right were admitted, it would follow that colored persons, emigrating from a State in which they were allowed the privileges of citizenship, to another in which they were excluded from these privileges, would become entitled to all privileges of this character in the State to which they removed, notwithstanding the exclusion. Such an inference was founded on a view which was altogether erroneous of the operation of the first clause of the second section of the fourth article of the Constitution of the United States, assuring a reciprocity of privileges to the citizens of the several States, respectively. That clause, like every other, in that or any other instrument, must receive a construction which would not violate reason; which would not carry the operation of the clause beyond the intention which dictated it, and which would render its operation consistent, if possible, with the established rights of other parties. All these incontrovertible principles of interpretation would be violated by the construction which had been supposed. If persons removing from one State to another were to be considered as becoming entitled, under the operation of this clause of the Constitution, to all the privileges of citizens of the State to which they removed, and were not restricted to the privileges accorded to persons of the same class and description with themselves, then the anomaly would be presented of a foreign co-ordinate legislation, exerting a more efficient operation in the States than their interior legislation, and of their legislation exerting in relation to the same subject, a more efficient operation abroad than it could at home. A construction involving such consequences was absurd. Clauses were to be construed in consistency with their intention. What was the intention of this clause? The States, by the adoption of the Federal Constitution, became, to a certain extent, members of one community. It was an incident essential to the secure enjoyment of the advantages of this community, that they should be restrained from any power of inimical regula-

tion as respected the right of removal from one State and settlement in another. This was the design of the clause in question; not to inhibit to the States nor to restrain the power of regulation, as respected the conditions of the enjoyment and exercise of the privileges of citizenship, an essential, indefeasible portion of self-government; but to inhibit any power of regulation on this subject, to be directed exclusively against citizens removing from other States, any exercise of inimical discriminative regulation. The discretion was left ,unimpaired to adopt regulations affecting either the indigenous inhabitants or those removing from other States, provided these regulations were not rendered restrictive and peculiar in relation to this last description of inhabitants. Under this limitation the reserved power of the States was unsusceptible of employment to any serious or injurious counteraction of the social design of the Federal Incorporation. This construction had the advantage of reconciling the rights of the States with the clause of the Constitution in question, affording to each ample and uninterfering scope for operation. Any opposite construction led to the wildest and most unredeemed absurdities. No one could conceive it to be the design of the Constitution to communicate to persons removing from one State to another, privileges larger in number or value than they had previously enjoyed; yet, under the construction which was combatted, such persons might not only acquire an increase of privileges, the privilege of suffrage for example, but blacks from abroad might acquire privileges to which indigenous whites were not entitled. Women, in one of the States, (Jersey) were, or had formerly been, admitted to all the privileges of citizenship, that of suffrage inclusive. Under this construction, women, in States where there was a qualification on suffrage, as in Virginia, might become entitled, by migration, to privileges from which a large proportion of the indigenous white males were excluded. Constructions of this kind were no subjects for discussion. Persons, by removal from one State to another, did not, therefore, acquire any further or greater privileges than were the allotment of the indigenous inhabitants of the same class and description.

Another consequence which had been imputed to the clause of the Constitution under review, fell with that which had been examined. It had been imagined that, under the operation of this clause, colored persons, emancipated on a condition of removal from one State in which they receive their emancipation, might be returned upon the emancipating State in the character of citizens. The validity of this interference was excluded by the remarks which had been stated. It was equally excluded by other and independent considerations. The condition of emancipation alluded to, would labor, at the time of its adoption, under no defect of validity, as presenting no conflict with any provision of the Federal Constitution.

It could not, then, be brought into conflict, and rendered invalid at any posterior time, or by any act of an authority not superior to that of the party imposing it, and which was no party to the compact in which this condition was comprehended. Yet, if the inference above referred to were just, this condition, the creation of a competent authority, and the consideration of a benefit to the party accepting it, would be liable to invalidation by the posterior intervention, not of a superior, but an extraneous and merely co-ordinate authority; and be liable not simply to invalidation, but to be converted to an instrument of injury and abuse to the party who had made it the subject of stipulation. An inference of this kind had only to be represented in its true character to be disclaimed.

The endeavor had been made to show that there was nothing in the clause of the Constitution of the United States, which had been quoted, which could be construed as prohibiting the State governments from subjecting persons removing from other States to any restrictions as respected the privileges of citizenship which it was thought proper to extend to indigenous inhabitants of the same class and description. The power of the States would be found, upon further inquiry, to extend to a point beyond this—to the capacity of prohibiting the ingress of citizens of other States, provided the exclusion were for causes affecting the individual merely, and not the class: that is to say, provided the exclusion operated by what, in the technical language of the law, would be denominated *descriptionem personæ*, or for causes accidental in their access, and liable to removal. Thus, it would not be denied that a State might exclude citizens of other States, for contagious disease, by quarantine regulations; that it had competency to exclude for crimes, or to exclude paupers liable to become burdensome by regulation of police. What was the reason of the competency of exclusion in these cases? The reason had already been stated, the necessity of giving to the clause of the Federal Constitution communicating the privileges of citizenship, a construction which would reconcile its operations with the reserved essential rights of the States. There could be no danger of abuse from this construction, as long as its principle was not transcended, which required that the exclusion should be for cause affecting the individual, and not the class. Mr. A. went on to say, that perhaps a just application of the principle of exclusion, which had been now stated, might be considered as authorizing the slaveholding States to prohibit the entry and settlement among them of colored persons from other States, inasmuch as it was known that the peculiar circumstances of their population tended to communicate to the admission of persons of this description a character of mischievousness, worse than that which would attach to the admission of pauperism, and as bad as that which would attach to the admission of criminals and disease. Mr. A. said, that he did not mean, however, to push the argument to this extent. It was not necessary to his purpose to do so. Perhaps it would not be fair, as the exclusion might be said, in these circumstances, to be denounced for a cause not personal, that is to say, accidental to the excluded object; or which, indeed, was not to be considered as residing so much in the excluded object, as in a pe-

culiar condition of the community from which the object was proposed to be excluded. All that it was now designed to show was, that, notwithstanding the sweeping operation which had been attributed to the clause of the Federal Constitution, which had been adduced in the debate, the exercise, under certain circumstances, of a power of exclusion by the State governments, as respected the citizens of other States, was in perfect consistency with that operation.

If it was the wish of any of the States to have colored citizens, Mr. A. said, that he felt neither wish or authority to derogate from their right to do so. The proposition he denied was, that such citizens could be imposed on other States, who had no participation in the wish. In the lapse of time it was possible that the period might arrive, when, from the excessive multiplication of the mixed race, some of the slaveholding States might conceive themselves required, by considerations of policy, to admit this description of persons to a qualified or absolute enjoyment of the privileges of citizenship. Without pretending to express any opinion that such a period would arrive, Mr. A. could not, in the event of its occurrence, consider the competency of the State to exercise the power as a subject of question. The demarcation of color, importing a discrimination not simply of complexion, but blood, was too indefinite to be admitted as a limitation on State right. In all the slaveholding States, in a certain stage of intermixture, the legal distinction ceased. If the State right were confined in the mode supposed, there was no competency to assign the limit of this distinction.

He was not unaware, Mr. A. said, that the language he had been holding, of guarded respect for State rights, had been for some time going out of fashion. It was but too obvious to remark, that the essential defences of the States were rapidly giving way before the steady and powerful current of Federal authority. This circumstance only rendered more imperative, however, the duty of using every endeavor to sustain even the feeblest of these defences. The scope of public duty under a free constitution was peculiar. Its first object was the support of the Constitution. How was this to be effected? Not by carrying one principle victorious over every other, but by sustaining the balance between the various and conflicting principles which made up the composition of a free constitution. And how was this secondary incidental object to be effected? By enlisting on the side of the principle which, in the progress of the conflict, had been found to decline and become the weakest. It was upon a consideration of this sort, that Mr. A. thought the maintenance of the rights of the States, even in matters which bore the appearance of being immaterial and indifferent, ought to form a primary object of solicitude and effort.

The purpose of the remarks which had been submitted, was to show what Mr. A. conceived to be the just construction of the very delicate clause of the Constitution, assuming a reciprocity of the privileges of citizenship to the citizens of the several States, which had been so much referred to in the discussion. It had been seen that the recognition of the right of the States to admit colored persons to the privileges of citizenship, involved none of the abusive consequences which had been ascribed to it. The inquiry material to the present controversy next arose, whether any of the States had ever exercised the right; whether there were citizens of this description to be found in any of the States? Mr. A. thought that, upon due inquiry, it would be found there was no one of the States in which this class of persons could be fairly considered as assignable to the rank of citizens. He did not found this conclusion on any definition which had been, or, as far as appeared to him could be, given of the constituents or criteria of citizenship. He admitted that any definition which could be assumed upon this subject, must be regarded as gratuitous, and could, therefore, serve as the foundation of no conclusion. He admitted that there was no definition which would apply, under every circumstance. He thought that the only description which could be adopted, must be analogous to the definition which civilians gave of municipal law—"the rule which each State had prescribed to itself." But although there was no affirmative definition of citizenship which could be regarded as of invariable application, there was negative test which appeared to Mr. A. to be conclusive. Citizens might be admitted in various degrees to the exercise of political rights. They might even be admitted in various degrees to the enjoyment of civil rights. But those could not be considered as belonging to the rank of citizens, who, not by the mere operation of usage, but the positive enactments of law, were every where excluded from an equality with even the lowest rank of citizens, as respected the ordinary and most essential relations of domestic and social life. But this was the fact in relation to colored persons, as Mr. A. believed, in every State of the Union, without exception. Colored persons, as has been stated by his colleague, (Mr. BARBOUR,) were in no part of the Union permitted, by law, to contract with white persons that engagement, the liberty to contract which was the inseparable incident and criterion of a condition of social equality. · He alluded to the engagement of marriage. How could persons be said to belong to the same class who were every where prohibited by law from the contraction of any relation of intimacy, and from association, on the basis of social equality? It was from the influence of this consideration, and not from any concurrence in various other views which had been stated, that Mr. A. derived his conclusion that colored persons could, in no part of the Union, be assigned to the rank of citizens.

But, suppose that these persons could be assigned to this rank in some of the States of the Union. Admit that there were citizens of this description. Ought the clause of the constitution of Missouri, to which objection had been taken, to be considered as operating upon such of these persons as were citizens? Mr. A. conceived that it ought not, upon the established maxim of interpretation, which had been stated by his friend from South Carolina, (Mr. LOWNDES,) that where instruments presented

the appearance of conflict, a construction was, if possible, to be adopted, which would reconcile their operation. If there were colored persons who belonged to the class of citizens, there was, notoriously, a much larger class who did not belong to this description, on whom the clause in question might be considered as operating without the involvement of any breach of the Federal Constitution. There was a distinct peculiar reason for the adoption of this construction. The term " free negroes and mulattoes," on which the doubt in the present case arose, had acquired in the South and West an import perfectly precise, and as it might be said technical, denoting a class who were invariably excluded from the privileges of citizenship. To restrict these words in the clause of the Missouri constitution to this sense, was doing no more than was required by another established rule of the construction, confirming the words to their ordinary and received signification. There was neither force nor liability to abuse in this interpretation, because the import of the language was not enlarged so as to be made to embrace something which it did not properly comprehend, but was restricted. It was another established rule that in cases of doubt, the most mitigated construction was be adopted. " In obscuris quod minimum est querimur." But, in the present case, it also happened that the most mitigated was, at the same time, the usual and most received signification of the words to be construed. All that was asked, was, that the language should not be distorted from its customary and appropriate import, and a description applicable to, and designed for an inferior class of persons, be stretched to comprehend a higher class, in contravention of one of the most familiar maxims, that "minor non continet major." Cases analogous to the present might be easily stated from the Constitution. Mr. A. instanced the case of imports which the State were forbidden to lay unless with the consent of Congress, or for a special purpose. If Massachusetts, who was now engaged in the formation of a new constitution, were to insert a provision granting a power to her Legislature to lay imposts, would any court or reasonable man refuse to this clause a construction restricted by the competency of the State, and consistent with the prohibition of the Federal Constitution?

But let it be admitted, for the pursuit of the argument, that the controverted clause of the Missouri constitution was to be considered as inconsistent with the Federal Constitution, and void. Did it follow that the whole instrument and the act of admission of the territory into the Union, were, therefore, vacated? This being a question of the just interpretation of an instrument, must be conceded to be a juridical question, and its determination was, therefore, to be governed by juridical rules. What was this compact we had made with Missouri? It was a grant of the privilege of admission into the Union, subject to a condition of the due discharge of an authority to form a constitution of State government. Now what were the ordinary judicial rules governing the construction of the valid execution of authorities? If the discharge were inconsistent entirely and throughout, with the limitations on the authority, then the grant of it and all attending advantages were vacated. This was in effect the amount of what had been contended for by the gentleman from Pennsylvania (Mr. Sergeant) in this branch of the discussion. But, if the discharge were inconsistent only in part, it might be in some very unimportant part, with the limitations of the authority; what was the just construction then? Was the whole discharge and grant of the authority vacated, or only the offending part? Unquestionably the latter only. The discharge, so far as it was within the competency of the authority, was valid, and for so much as it transcended this limit it was void. If a rule differing from this prevailed, what would be the effect of it. Under color of the correction of injustice, injustice would be perpetuated. The attempt to exercise authority not granted would be repressed by the invasion and divestiture of that which had been granted. The reality of usurpation by one party, would be made the corrective of the mere attempt at it by another. What, too, would be the inconveniences of such a rule? If the entire discharge of an authority were to be vacated, in the occurrence of any instance of defect, who would be found to accept the exercise of authorities? Who would be found to contract engagements, to undertake subordinate functions, to assume responsibilities under those who did accept the exercise of authorities? An authority to frame a constitution, from its extreme delicacy, was liable, in a peculiar degree, to this remark. But take the subject in another view. The gentleman from Pennsylvania (Mr. Sergeant) had conceded that the insertion of the controverted clause in the Missouri constitution, was to be regarded as the effect not of any designed invasion of the Constitution of the United States, (of which neither decency nor probability admitted the supposition,) but as a mere result of error or inadvertence. Then was the forfeiture of a grant so grave and beneficial as the admission of a State into the Union, to ensue on the commission of a mere error or inadvertence? Was such a principle of forfeiture ever heard in any system of jurisprudence? There was another test which appeared to Mr. A. to be of conclusive application in relation to this branch of the question. The States already admitted into the Union were at liberty to form new constitutions. Take an example from Pennsylvania, a State which Mr. A. believed had more than once remodelled its constitution, and in which there was said to be a party favorable to a still further modification of it. Suppose Pennsylvania—such an instance of absurd and culpable fanaticism, though it could never occur in fact, might be imputed in the way of argument—suppose Pennsylvania, in new modelling her constitution, were to insert a provision, giving power to her Legislature to adopt protective regulations, in relation to persons held to service or labor in other States and escaping into that State, in contravention of the clause of the Constitution of the United States, which requires such persons instead of being protected, to be delivered up on the claim of those

entitled to their service or labor. In such an event, would Pennsylvania stand discharged from her relation to the Union; or would the whole of her new modelled constitution be vacated? If the first of these consequences would follow, it was not improbable that there was no State which had reorganized its constitution, but would be found, upon a careful inquiry, to stand discharged from its affinity to the Union. If this consequence were just, a State committing, in the re-modification of its constitution, any act of the most inadvertent violation of the Constitution of the United States, was liable to be displaced from its affinity to the Union by Congress, who, it ought to be remembered, was said to be invested with an authority to exercise judgment without control upon this subject of the contravention by a State constitution of the Constitution of the United States. But, a State was not only liable in this view of the subject to be discharged from her relation to the Union by Congress, it also followed that she would have it in her power to discharge herself, by remodelling her constitution with that design, in contravention of the known principle that the Union could only be dissolved *eo ligamine quo ligatur*, by the consent of every State, or in any event of the majority of the States, to the dissolution.

Let it be conceded, however, that only the re-modelled constitution, and not the relation of the State to the Union, was to be vacated by a provision admitting of being construed into a breach of the Federal Constitution. Was there any person to be found who would contend for this doctrine? If there were, how had it happened that, by parity of reason, the constitutions of the old thirteen States, all of which, perhaps, contained provisions inconsistent with the Constitution of the United States, had not been invalidated by the adoption of this instrument? It would be said, indeed, that there was a distinction, in this respect, between States already admitted, and those applying for admission, into the Union. Mr. A. insisted, on the contrary, that there was no adequate ground for a distinction. The condition was the same in relation to all the parties to the Union, of obligation to conformity, in their legal and constitutional regulations, to the provisions of the Constitution of the United States. The power, too, of supervisal and control on this subject, on the part of Congress, was the same, namely, that which resulted from the operation of the clause enjoining on Congress the guaranty, as respected the States, of a republican form of government. The construction, then, being excluded which rendered a constitution liable to invalidation for one inconsistent and invalid clause, Missouri was not to be rejected from the Union, although a clause of this description should be found to have crept into her constitution.

But, whatever might be the character of the disputed clause of the Missouri constitution, the inquiry remained as to the competency of Congress to pronounce any determination on the subject. The question, as relating to the construction of an instrument, was obviously one of judicial character; and where did Congress find authority, either in the general principles of free government, or the peculiar structure of our form, for the exercise of a function of this kind? The reasons which opposed such an intermixture of functions, were of peculiar application to the present case. The most obvious was the unfitness, from habits as well as number, of a legislative body for the discharge of a judicial function. The Constitution had evidently contemplated this idea in the provision respecting the guaranty of a republican form of government; the character of a government, as respected its conformity to, or departure from, a republican form, being a subject which statesmen were as well qualified to decide as judges. The expression, too, it was to be remarked, of a jurisdiction, on the part of Congress, in this case, clearly excluded its jurisdiction in any other. A farther, and unanswerable objection to the jurisdiction claimed, was to be found in the absence of all responsibility, and the operation, indeed, of positive inducement to the abusive discharge of it. The discharge was known to be liable to influence from party and sectional feelings, obedience to which was assured, not merely of exemption from blame, but of reward and favor in the source to which responsibility was due. Suppose, for example, that the constitution of Missouri had been found to embrace a restriction on slavery: was the inference either unfair or illiberal, that the lustre of this feature would have given to the instrument a countenance so prepossessing as to blunt very much the disposition and power of observation to the defects which a careful examination might have detected in it? Could a jurisdiction, indeed, which assumed an undefined discretion in one of the parties to a compact, to interpret its validity, be regarded in any other light than as an affair, not of judgment, but power? What would be the effect of the recognition of such a jurisdiction in Congress, as respected the structure of the constitutions of States hereafter to be admitted into the Union? Would not the decision of Congress come to be regarded as a mere auction, and the fabrication of these instruments be converted from a concern of grave and impartial deliberation, into a bidding for the favor of a predominating party in this body? Waiving any insinuation of charge or imputation against the purity of the present times, would it be proper, by our recognition, to establish the jurisdiction contended for in Congress, to remain a precedent and principle of mischief to times which were to come?

But what was the foundation of this claim of cognizance, on the part of Congress, over inconsistencies occurring between the provisions of a State and of the Federal Constitution? The foundation of the authority to judge of the observance by a Territory claiming a place in the Union, of the conditions of its admission, was the supposed authority of Congress to prescribe these conditions. Conceding, for a moment, the authority to prescribe conditions, the authority to interpret and decide on their observance or violation, no more followed from it than a judiciary followed in any other case from a legislative power. In the present instance the principle, if it were put, would not apply, because the condition of admission which Missouri was supposed to have violated, was prescribed, not by Congress, but by the Constitution of the United States. What though the condition had been inserted in the act of Congress of last year, that the constitution of Missouri was to contain nothing repugnant to the Constitution of the United States, was the condition of any greater validity for this insertion than it would have been without the insertion? Would not Missouri have been as strongly and as unquestionably bound to its observance? Then the whole foundation failed, which had been assigned for the jurisdiction claimed for Congress, even if the principle assumed were a sound one. But this principle could not be maintained, in point of soundness, more than in point of application. It was not true that Congress was invested with authority to impose conditions on the admission of a State into the Union. Mr. A. had no design of going into the general argument of the last session upon this subject; but there were one or two considerations which admitted of being very briefly assigned, which to his mind appeared conclusive against the existence of this authority in Congress. There was one general remark, too, to be premised, applicable to all questions of the validity of exercises of power under the Federal Constitution. This remark referred to the peculiar effect which doubt as to its validity ought to have in preventing the exercise of power under this constitution. In other constitutions, in which general powers were given, subject to particular limitations, the doubt arose on the limitation of the power, and fairly admitted of its exercise, unless the negative proposition were established. But, in the Constitution of the United States, which was admitted on all hands to be a delegation of powers, limited by enumeration; in case of doubt, the affirmative grant of the power was required to be established to authorize its exercise. If, then, the power to prescribe conditions to the admission of a State into the Union were to be considered as in any degree doubtful, there was sufficient ground for its rejection. It stood condemned, however, by a much stronger consideration—its utter inconsistence with the discriminative principle and character of a federative government. The discriminating principle of such a government was the political equality of the parties to it. The amount of power intended to be granted being specific, and being made up by equal contribution of the parties, it followed that an exact equality must subsist between these parties, as respected the amount and character of the powers which were reserved. But, if conditions might be imposed other than those contained in the original charter of compact, on new parties to be admitted, what was the security for the preservation of this equality? How could it continue for a moment? How egregious would be the folly of guarding against undue acquisitions of power at the first inception of the compact, and permitting an unlimited facility of acquisition afterwards! The objection to the political inequality of the parties was not so strong in the case of a mere confederation of States, like some of the leagues which subsisted in ancient times, as it was in the case of a compact like our own, because the design of such associations, and the scope of the exercise of the powers with which they were charged, had reference to external purposes only. But these ancient leagues were invariably regarded by historians as having received their death-blow from the moment in which parties were admitted unequal, not in federative capacities or obligations, but in power and resources. Even in physical nature bodies were found to be of no consistency or duration of which the elements were incongruous. It was by the intermixture of dissimilar elements that a quantity of frangibility was communicated to the hardest of them. Political bodies were liable in a yet higher degree to the same law of loss or diminution, as respected the coherence of their parts by impairment of their homogeneousness.

Let this view of the subject be somewhat extended, and the conclusion would be rendered yet more apparent. In our federative system, the material line of demarcation between the Federal and State jurisdiction had reference to the distinction between subjects of general and of municipal concern. The first class was considered as forming, with some exceptions, the exclusive subjects of Federal authority. But, if a power were recognised to impose conditions at discretion on new States admitted into the confederacy what was to hinder, in relation to these States, the assumption of control over any or every subject of proper municipal cognizance? If, for example, control could be assumed over the subject of the continuance or inhibition of slavery, what hindered the assumption of superintendence over every other concern connected with the interest of property—its modifications as to kind, its tenure, its modes of acquirement and distribution? The principle of the assumption would evidently authorize its extension without limit. The reason assigned for control over the subject of slavery was the deleterious character of its influence. Inheritance by a rule of primogeniture, restraints on alienation, unreasonable prolongations of periods of apprenticeship, were liable, in an equal degree, to the same remark.

If, then, sir, Congress had the power of imposing at discretion conditions on States coming into the Union, it was manifest that it had a power of assuming control and jurisdiction, in relation to these States, limited only by discretion. The federal authority, designed for little more than an external safeguard, with respect to these States became liable to be converted into the pest of ancient times, invading the chambers of their retirement, and polluting the tables of their repast. As a power involving such consequences could never be admitted the right claimed for Congress to sit in judgment on the validity of constitutions of States demanding admission into the Union, which was founded on the supposed existence of this power, fell with it. It did not belong, therefore, to the province of Congress to pronounce the invalidity of the clause of the Missouri constitution, supposing it to be unquestionably invalid.

What, then it would be asked, was the purpose of requiring the submission of the constitution to Congress, which no one denied to be essential? The answer was obvious. It was to satisfy the clause of the Constitution of the United States which rendered it incumbent upon Congress to guaranty to every State a republican form of government. The duty of supervisal was expressly devolved upon Congress as respected the political character of the constitution of a State asking admission into the Union. But this duty did not extend beyond the political character of the constitution. On the contrary, its further extension was excluded by the operation of a known rule which had already been adverted to. This distinction between defects in a constitution of a State claiming admission into the Union, which related to the form of its government, and provisions which, although contravening the Constitution of the United States, yet were not of this particular character, would be found to furnish an answer to the various cases which had been stated, in illustration of the jurisdiction of Congress, in the debate. The particular case of the irregular nomination or qualification of members of the Senate by a new State, found a particular answer in the clause of the Constitution of the United States which assigned to each House of Congress the right of judging of the election and qualification of its own members.

The proceedings which had heretofore obtained in Congress on the admission of new States had evidently had reference to the mere formality of the annunciation of the accession of the State to the Union. This was shown by the statement of precedents which had been given by the chairman of the committee. That no idea had ever been entertained of a necessity of a recognition by Congress of the validity of every part of the constitution of a State applying for admission, was proved by the fact that in cases of the formation of new constitutions by old States, in relation to which no defect of republican character could be anticipated, and no occasion existed for the annunciation of the accession of the State to the Union, the submission of the constitution to Congress had never been required; a proceeding which would be obviously indispensable in all cases, if Congress were invested with the cognizance of the validity of constitutions, which had been imputed to it.

It was not contended, it must be remembered, that there was no liability to conditions on the part of a new State about to be admitted into the Union. It was only asserted that those conditions were imposed by an authority paramount to Congress—the Constitution. It was not contended that there existed no corrective jurisdiction in the event of the violation of these conditions. It was only contended that this jurisdiction, with a particular exception, was referable to a tribunal better qualified than Congress, both by impartiality and competence—the Judiciary. If the jurisdiction belonged to the Judiciary, there were obvious and regular modes of proceeding for obtaining the effect of its decisions. If it belonged to Congress, there were none, and the want of them was evidence conclusive against the existence of the jurisdiction in Congress. The want of any regular remedy or means of enforcement, was the best evidence, in disproof of a claim of right or jurisdiction. If, in the exercise of the jurisdiction asserted for us, the constitution offered by Missouri, or any part of it, should be condemned, what was to be the effect? Missouri was to be rejected from the Union—that is to say, the mode of vindication of our authority was to consist in the discardal of it. This was the case of the foolish constable in Shakspeare, deputing authority to the watch. They are to bid any man they meet to stand. But, how if they would not stand? Then they were to let him go, and to thank God they were rid of a knave. The exercise of authority recommended to us was analogous, and, if attempted, would redound in a similar occasion of consolation. It was said, however, that Missouri might be coerced by the re-extension to her of territorial regulations. This would be a proceeding little less anomalous than the other. Whatever Missouri might be in acceptation and fiction of law, it was notorious, in point of fact, that she stood discharged from the condition of a Territory. As there was no intermediary condition for which a name could be found, the Territory must have become a State. If with our authority, then, she was a member of the Union; if without it, what was her condition? Clearly a condition of separation from the Union. The fruit, then, of our exercise of authority was the alienation and loss of the subject of our authority. This right of jurisdiction claimed for Congress was like the right of insurrection in the people, a right which operated by the dissolution of all relations between the parties to it. Mr. A. was not stating these considerations in any view of the impolicy of the course which was recommended. He stated them in disproof of the jurisdiction from which such consequences flowed. His purpose was to confront this claim of jurisdiction with its results. He admitted that if the jurisdiction really belonged to Congress, there was no competency to remit its discharge to any other tribunal than Congress. What he contended was, that its attribution to Congress subverted every established idea of the character of a legal or political jurisdiction. It was, indeed, a further argument against this extraordinary jurisdiction that it was entirely superfluous, as the objects it proposed were attainable by the more regular and milder method of the exercise of judiciary authority. What, then, was the design of the mode of proceeding recommended to us, if its professed objects were to be otherwise, and with greater facility, obtained? Upon this subject it was proper to speak out. The design was to be let in to an unconfined discretion over the question of the admission of Missouri into the Union, for the purpose of reattempting the imposition of the slavery restriction. Upon this subject Mr. A. had, at this time, but one remark to make. It related to the change which had taken place in the character of this measure since the

discussions of last year. The proposition then was to dictate a principle of civil institution to a people of whom we were neither really nor virtually the representatives. The character of the proposition at this time would be to impose the same principle against their avowed dissent, as a yoke upon their necks. If men, descended from the authors of the Revolution, could be found to propose a measure of this character, there were none boasting the same descent who could be found to yield submission to it. The reasons did not require to be adverted to; but every person knew that the measure could never be enforced. The attempt to enforce it might be effectual to the production of civil discord. It might be effectual to the production of the alienation and loss of the country. It might be effectual to the purpose of fixing the opprobrium of abortive usurpation on this House. But the direct object never could be attained. Better it was, therefore, that the rage of our fanaticism should be restricted to its proper domain, the discussions of this body, than to be let loose upon Missouri, whence its effects would be certain to recoil on those by whom it had been impelled. "Se jactet in aula Æolus," &c.

But let the preservation of the territorial character by Missouri be admitted, how perplexing was this anomalous complication of powers assumed by Congress in relation to the territories? Antecedently to the admission of a territory into the Union, an authority was claimed over it, limited only by discretion, which was but another name for a despotical authority. At the arrival of the period when admission could not, consistently with the principles of our institutions or former usage, be refused, the power was asserted of perpetuating our authority, in the form of the imposition of unchangeable conditions of political compact. The principle, too, of the imposition of these conditions, required no exclusive or essential relation between their character and the situation or character of the country and people they were to affect; but merely had reference to the gratification of visions which might be entertained here, of an abstract and speculative morality. The claim of Congressional authority over a territory, it would be supposed, must find a limit at this point. But it did not. The further power was asserted after a compact for the admission of the territory into the Union had been entered into, of a discretion on the part of Congress to judge of the validity of the execution of the compact by the territory, and, in the event of an unfavorable judgment, to remand to their former condition of vassalage the freemen by whom it was inhabited. For such a system of complicated despotism, Mr. A. said that he could find no name or description, which would adequately express its character, or truly convey his sense of detestation.

One word as to the consequences of the proceedings which might now be adopted. One gentleman had said, that no consequences of unpleasant character could be anticipated; and another, that the consequences, whatever they might be, were not to be taken into consideration. Both gentlemen were mistaken. Whatever might be the real views which would dictate the rejection of the resolution under discussion, this rejection, in the present state of the public mind, would be liable to be ascribed to the policy of re-attempting the imposition of the slavery restriction of last year. In the best event, then, the wound inflicted on the harmony of the country would be incurable. But, if the policy imputed was really to be acted on, every man must perceive that the Union was gone. Gentlemen might conceive that they were sowing the seeds of sectional influence and importance, but they would, in fact, be sowing a crop like the dragon's teeth, which would spring up in civil discord, and armed men, destined to perish in unnatural warfare, by a mutual destruction. It had been remarked the last year, that a gulf, similar to that which we read of in the early history of Rome, had been opened among us by the discussions on this subject. There was one circumstance, however, of favorable distinction. The chasm which was said to have occurred in Rome was only to be closed by the sacrifice of her most precious possession. But the chasm which had occurred in our harmony, required to heal it, only the most worthless of all sacrifices, that of our passions, or of what, in their application to human affairs, were the next most pestilent things to vile passions —our abstract and speculative notions. In what he had been saying, Mr. Archer disclaimed any intention of employing the language of menace, which would be suitable neither to his character, nor to that of the place in which he stood. His purpose was to express his sincere views of the possible consequences of the measures which Congress might adopt in relation to this important subject. The train had already been prepared by antecedent events and discussions. It now only required to be fired to produce effects which it would be equally impossible to avoid lamenting, or to repair. Mr. A. would add only a single remark. It was that, in the event of the real occurrence of the effects to which he had been alluding, their authors would stand chargeable with the greatest crime which had ever been committed against the interests of human nature, inasmuch as they would have led to the destruction of the most persuasive model of free institutions, and the overthrow of the most imposing promise of splendid destinies, which the world, in any age of it, had ever seen.

When Mr. Archer had concluded—

Mr. Hill, of Massachusetts, moved an amendment, qualifying the assent of the admission of the new State into the Union by an exception of a particular clause of the constitution. This motion, however, was withdrawn by Mr. Hill for the present, on the representation of Mr. Lowndes, that it would embarrass the main debate, by bringing on an incidental one, and would deprive him of the opportunity of replying to some objections he had not anticipated, and to others arising from a misapprehension or evasion of his first arguments in support of the resolution.

Mr. Baldwin then moved to strike out the preamble to the resolve.

Mr. Lowndes assigned briefly the reasons why, on more mature reflection, he should assent to this course, though he had at first preferred the other.

The question being taken on striking out the preamble, was decided in the affirmative—87 to 65.

Mr. Hemphill observed that the subject before the House, in its various relations, had occupied so much of the time of Congress, that it was becoming in him to make an apology for rising, and to promise, at the least, to be as brief as possible. He said he would make no exordium, but engage at once on the merits of the question.

The constitution of Missouri, as transmitted to Congress, enjoins, in the most positive manner, and makes it the unqualified duty of the Legislature to pass, as soon as may be, such laws as may be necessary to prevent free negroes and mulattoes from coming to, and settling in, the State, under any pretext whatsoever. If these free colored people are embraced in the second section of the 4th article of the Constitution of the United States, it is most clear and manifest that the constitution of Missouri is a direct infringement of the Constitution of the United States, and repugnant to it.

The section in the Constitution of the United States to which I have alluded, declares that the citizens of each State shall be entitled to all privileges and immunities of citizens in the several States. The main question, according to my conception of it, involves but this single inquiry—Are free negroes and mulattoes, or any of them, citizens of the United States? The report of the honorable committee, as I thought, admitted the fact of citizenship; and this circumstance led me from making any examination on that point, until the gentleman from Virginia, (Mr. Barbour,) yesterday assumed the broad ground of denying the rights of citizenship to any free black or mulatto man. He has endeavored to give us a definition of a citizen of this country; and although I acknowledge that gentleman's reflections on the subject were ingenious, I cannot give my assent to their accuracy. He supposes that a citizen means a person who is entitled to all the civil rights of others in like circumstances, unless deprived of some of them for personal reasons. He then proceeded to show that discriminations existed, in a variety of instances, and in different States, between the white and black people; but this definition cannot be a good one, unless he is capable of proving that, among citizens, a majority have no right to make any such discriminations. What is there to control the will of the majority when it does not come in collision with any higher power?

Discriminations are familiar to us, in the several States, both as to political and civil rights; but it never was believed that they effected a total extinguishment of citizenship. Some citizens are entitled to vote, and others are not. Some are exempted from serving in the militia, or on juries, for various reasons; and this throws an unequal burden on the rest of the community. Paupers are not allowed even to choose the place of their residence. In some cases whole professions are distinguished from others; as, for instance, when ministers of the gospel are made ineligible to office. Provisions of this character are contained in several of the State constitutions; I will, however, only read a clause or two on this subject, from the constitution of Tennessee:

"1. Whereas ministers of the gospel are, by their profession, dedicated to God and the care of souls, and ought not to be diverted from the great duties of their functions, therefore, no minister of the gospel, or priest, of any denomination whatever, shall be eligible to a seat in either House of the Legislature.

"2. No person who denies the being of a God, or a future state of rewards and punishments, shall hold any office in the civil department of this State."

The latter description of persons are citizens, although their infidelity afflicts them with a much deeper misfortune than to be distinguished from the white people, merely by the circumstance of color. Females are also citizens, but they by no means fall within the given definition, particularly in the sense in which it is intended to operate on political rights.

The gentleman has put many cases in illustration of his definition. It is unnecessary to refer to each case—I will select two only, on which I am desirous of making a few observations.

The first is on an argument deduced from a law in the State of Massachusetts which, in the opinion of the gentleman, seemed to be entitled to peculiar force, as being the offspring of a State so celebrated in espousing the cause of this race of people. It is a law by which marriages are forbidden between the white and the black people; but if this circumstance proves any thing, it proves too much, because it equally abridges the rights of both, and the argument destroys itself; for if, on that account, a black person is not a citizen, how can the white person be a citizen? And besides, it will be found, by an inspection of the law, that the penalties or fines are imposed only on the white people.

The other case stated is, that the black people are exempt from serving in the militia. But I do not consider this as a deprivation of a right: it is a privilege, and is so esteemed, when the indulgence is granted to persons advanced in age. The colored people might be compelled to form in companies by themselves, so as not to be the associates of the white soldiers, as was the case in the Revolutionary war. I have taken this brief notice of the definition by endeavoring to show its inaccuracy when applied to the complex system of our Federal Government

We shall arrive with more safety at the knowledge whether any free black people are citizens or not, by considering their acknowledged situation in a general point of view. And, at this stage of my remarks, I beg the House to recollect that, previous to the adoption of the Constitution of the United States, each State had the unquestionable right of saying who should compose its own citizens; and if, at the adoption of the Constitution of the United States, free negroes and mulattoes were citizens of any one State in the Union, the Federal Constitution gave to such citizens all the privileges and immunities of the citizens in the several States.

I have examined the constitutions of the several States, and there are but seven or eight that, in terms, exclude the colored people from voting. In these constitutions the right of suffrage is confined to white persons; but this affords a very forcible argument that it was the opinion of the members of their convention, that black people should have been included under the general term of citizens.

In the Kentucky constitution, the understanding of the convention appears plain. The words are. "Every free male citizen, (negroes, mulattoes, and Indians, excepted.")

Under the old constitution, in Maryland, this description of people voted; but the general terms were changed, by the present constitution of that State, to every free white male citizen.

In North Carolina, I understand that they still vote at elections. In Pennsylvania, there have been instances of their voting, but they are seldom. In several of the New England States they exercise this right, and did so in choosing the delegates who formed the Federal Constitution. In Massachusetts, and in the State of New York in particular, they enjoy the acknowledged and uninterrupted right of suffrage; and the constitutions of these States are both antecedent to the Constitution of the United States. The question might be very safely rested on the correctness of the opinions entertained in these two respectable States on the subject. The situation of the black people in these States was known anterior to the Revolution, and at the time of the acknowledgment of our independence; they were of course the best capable of judging, and were the only persons who had the right to judge whether these free people were embraced in the general terms of their constitutions.

When our different constitutions were formed, this class of people lived among us, not in the character of foreigners; they were connected with no other nation—this was their native country, and as dear to them as to us. Thousands of them were free born, and they composed a part of the people in the several States. They were identified with the nation, and its wealth consisted, in part, of their labor. They had fought for their country, and were righteously included in the principles of the Declaration of Independence. This was their condition when the Constitution of the United States was framed, and that high instrument does not cast the least shade of doubt upon any of their rights or privileges; but on the contrary, I may challenge gentlemen to examine it, with all the ability they are capable of, and see if it contains a single expression that deprives them of any privileges that is bestowed on others.

They have a right to pursue their own happiness, in as high a degree as any other class of people. Their situation is similar to others, in relation to the acquirement of property, and the various pursuits of industry. They are entitled to the same rights of religion and protection, and are subjected to the same punishments. They are enumerated in the census. They can be taxed, and made liable to militia duty; they are denied none of the privileges contained in the bill of rights; and, although many of these advantages are allowed to a stranger, during his temporary residence, yet, in no one instance is a free native black man treated as a foreigner.

When they enjoy all these rights, civil and religious, equally with the white people; and when they all flow from the same constitutions and laws, without any especial designation or reference to them, I have a curiosity to learn upon what principle any right can be singled out, as one of which they are to be deprived.

I appeal to the public transactions in this country, to the different constitutions, and to the laws, for the correctness of this position; that, whenever exceptions are intended to be made in regard to this class of people, that it requires express provisions for the purpose. It is said that they are not witnesses in some States; but it requires a particular law to render them incompetent to give testimony.

As citizenship has not been defined in any of the conventions, or by any of the wise assemblages of men in this country, it would be rash in me to attempt to give any thing like a confident definition; but, if being a native, and free born, and of parents belonging to no other nation or tribe, does not constitute a citizen in this country, I am at a loss to know in what manner citizenship is acquired by birth. This would be broader than necessary for the present occasion, as it would exclude the children of manumitted slaves. In England, from whence we adopt many of our customs, the sons of aliens are deemed natives; though the case is said to be different in many other countries.

When a foreigner is naturalized, he is only put in the place of a native freeman. This is the general idea of naturalization.

The word citizen, in its original sense, I believe, only meant a free person of a city; it had no application here until after our independence; and then it had to be accommodated to the customary and peculiar character of our complex system. In our political acceptation of the word, it differs in theory and origin from allegiance; that was a feudal connexion, acknowledging the distinction of superior and inferior; it was a species of slavish tenure. But citizenship is rather in the nature of a compact, expressly or tacitly made; it is a political tie, and the mutual obligations are contribution and protection.

If our free black population should be impressed in a foreign port, how could we redress the wrong if we have no political connexion with them, if they do not belong to our political family? Previous to the Revolution they were British subjects, and they were dissolved from any further connexion with that nation at the same time with the white people; and it would be exceedingly strange, if, from that moment, they ceased to be connected with any political society. Cases are familiar where they assume not only the appearance, but the reality of citizenship. If they should engage in commerce, none of the regulations, as to foreigners, would be applicable to them. Can there

exist any doubt as to their capacity of sustaining actions in the Federal courts in the character of citizens? But all our researches on this subject aim principally at one object; it is to ascertain what was the opinion of the patriots of this country, at an early day, respecting this question. This is a fountain, when reached, that cannot deceive us; and, in looking into the ancient records of this Government, we find that this very question attracted attention, and received a solemn decision. The fourth article of the Confederation reads as follows: " The better to secure and perpetuate ' mutual friendship and intercourse among the ' people of the different States in the Union, the ' free inhabitants of each of these States—paupers, ' vagabonds, and fugitives from justice excepted— ' shall be entitled to all privileges and immunities ' of free citizens in the several States." This language includes every free inhabitant, whether black or white, and clothes him with all the privileges of a citizen; and that this was the actual intention appears from the minutes taken when the Confederation was agreed to, (first volume of the laws of the United States, page 26.) When the fourth article was under consideration, the delegates from South Carolina being called, moved the following amendments in behalf of their State: 1. In article fourth, between the words free inhabitants, insert *white*—passed in the negative, ayes 2, noes 8, and one State divided. It was then moved, after the words "the several States," to insert, "according to the law of such States respectively," for the government of their own *free white* inhabitants, passed in the negative—ayes 2, noes 8, and one State divided—and in the Journals of Congress, in 1783, we are furnished with the opinion of Congress, on this subject, in terms equally clear and explicit, when it was resolved, with the exception of two States. one of which was divided, that all charges "of war and all the ' expenses that have been or shall be incurred for ' the common defence and general welfare, &c., ' shall be defrayed out of the common treasury, ' which shall be supplied by the several States, in ' proportion to the whole number of white and ' other free citizens and inhabitants of every age, ' sex, and condition," &c.

Here it is acknowledged expressly that there were other free citizens besides white citizens. If this will not convince gentlemen that free negroes and mulattoes were, from early times, considered as citizens, and composed a part of the people who chose the delegates to frame the Federal Constitution, it will be in vain for me to urge the matter any further.

I will add a few remarks on the subject of manumitted slaves. Among the Romans, as it appears from Cooper's Justinian, there were three grades; the first class of their freedmen were entitled to the privileges of Roman citizens; the other two classes were only allowed the enjoyment of inferior rights. What would be the condition of a manumitted slave, in this country, where the equal rights of man are more highly appreciated than in any other nation, I will not undertake to say.

In England, also, slight circumstances were caught at to effect the enfranchisement of persons held in villanage—such as the master bringing an action against his villain, which was construed to be the putting of him on an equal footing with himself. The idea that a free colored man, if a citizen, would be eligible to any office, however elevated, seems irreconcilable to the impressions of some gentlemen. But it will be recollected that this is an event that has never occurred in States where they are acknowledged to be citizens. The manners and practical distinctions in private life, which are observed between the white and the black people, will form a barrier, in this respect, as insurmountable as if ingrafted in the Constitution itself; and no danger need be feared that there will be any other commixture of community than we see at present. There are thousands of white people who have no better chance of being placed in office. I would not wish to see a practice prevail of putting them in situations that would create any disagreeable or unpleasant sensations; but this is no reason why they should not be allowed the practical enjoyment of such rights of citizenship as our customs and habits may approve of as suitable to their condition.

It is, however, wholly unnecessary, on this occasion, to trouble ourselves in drawing nice lines of distinction as to the propriety or power of abridging the common rights in regard to this class of people; for no one can gravely accede to the proposition, that a citizen can be denied the privilege of residing on the soil of his citizenship, when he has committed no offence; that he can be held in a state of exile without being branded with any mark of disgrace.

But, sir, as an exception to the general rule, the gentleman from Virginia, (Mr. Archer,) who has just preceded me, says that they would be a nuisance in that State, and that this gives the right of excluding them, as an object of defence. This doctrine appears to me to be vague and fancied. What is our general idea of a nuisance? Is it not a fact to be ascertained by legal investigation? One man may be guilty of a nuisance, while another of the same color may be innocent; and shall a whole description of people be condemned and deprived of valuable rights without a hearing?

The same gentleman, to show the power of a State, has instanced the case of paupers, and alleges that they can be prevented from coming into a State to reside. Paupers are clearly distinguishable from other citizens, and perhaps may form an exception; they were expressly excepted in the old Articles of Confederation; their usefulness to their country is spent, and they fall helpless on the benevolence of the society to which they belong; they have no property to go to, neither have they any election as to the place of their residence; they are as a debt on their own State, and no other State is bound to discharge it; and I should suppose that every community would contain a power to protect itself against such palpable impositions, whenever designed to be practised upon it, as much so as it would have a right to prevent persons coming from places infected with malignant diseases.

I beg leave to represent this question in another point of view, for the reflection of gentlemen who do not believe that any negroes or mulattoes are citizens.

If Congress has a power, under the Constitution, to make such a description of people citizens, the clause in the constitution of Missouri is repugnant to the exercise of such a power, and would come in immediate collision with it. State constitutions must not stand in the way of any powers lawfully exercised, or which may be lawfully exercised, by Congress. Congress having the power of establishing an uniform rule of naturalization, could make citizens of this class of people, either out of the bosom of our own country or from foreign counties. The inhabitants of Louisiana were made citizens upon a liberal construction of this power, without any uniform rule. If Congress possesses this power, it is not material whether it is exercised or not. There is no bankrupt law at present; but if there had been a clause in the constitution of Missouri that no man should be divested of his estate by virtue of any bankrupt law, under any pretext whatsoever, such a clause would certainly be unconstitutional.

The words in the constitution of Missouri extend to negroes and mulattoes, in the most extensive manner. The design evidently was to prevent them from settling in that State, at any time or on any condition, without regard to the circumstance whether they were citizens or not.

It is observed by the committee, that a careful examination of the clause might perhaps countenance the opinion that it applied to the large class of free negroes and mulattoes who are not considered as citizens of the United States; but the words are too general and positive for such a construction. They allow of no pretext whatsoever.

Suppose the constitution of Missouri had declared that the militia of that State should be commanded by its own officers, notwithstanding any pretext whatsoever, would that be construed to mean when the militia was not called into the service of the United States? Again: if a clause had said that the State of Missouri might, against every pretext, lay imposts or duties on imports or exports from that State, would Congress give it their sanction, and construe it only to mean as far as might be absolutely necessary for the executing of its revenue laws? I am persuaded that the least reflection will induce gentlemen to believe that the clause will not bear the construction which the committee seem willing to give it.

The committee go on to say, that, of all the "articles in our Constitution, there is, probably, ' not one more difficult to construe well than that ' which gives to the citizens of each State the ' privileges and immunities of citizens in the sev- ' eral States; there is not one an attention to ' whose spirit is more necessary to the convenient ' and beneficial connexions of the States; nor one ' of which too large a construction would more ' completely break down their defensive power, ' and lead more directly to their consolidation."

The doubtful apprehensions and difficulties raised concerning the construction of this clause, appear to me to be entirely imaginary; for I can perceive no part of the Constitution susceptible of a clearer understanding.

Suppose, for instance, that a foreigner should be naturalized in this District, or in a Territory; he would be a citizen of the United States, but not the peculiar citizen of any one State; still, if he should go into any State to reside, he would require no new adoption; he would be subjected only to the State qualifications, as to residence and the like, which would be equally exacted from its own citizens; he would, in fact, mingle with the citizens, and be one of them, and partake of all their privileges; and, so, if a citizen of one State should change his residence into another, he would be in a similar predicament. A citizen of one State, moreover, without removing into another, would have a right to take land by purchase or inheritance, and to part with it, at his own pleasure, according to the State laws; he would be entitled to all privileges that did not require actual residence, and could not, in any instance, be considered as a mere foreigner.

The report seems to countenance the idea, and the argument of the gentleman from South Carolina (Mr. Lowndes) enforces it, that a State may have existence antecedent to its being a member of the Union; and that, being a State, there is the same right to form a constitution as in the case of an old State; and if there should be any thing incompatible with the Constitution of the United States, it is a subject of judicial cognizance. This is correct, as it relates to an old State, for there Congress has no control over it. They are not one of the acting parties. The constitution is not to be submitted to Congress. The old State had made its compact with the Union, and if it does any thing inconsistent with that compact, it is necessarily to be corrected by the Judiciary.

I beg of the House to pay particular attention to this part of the subject. I understood the gentleman from South Carolina (Mr. Lowndes) to be of opinion that a State is created as soon as Congress grant authority to the inhabitants of a Territory to form a State government, and the inhabitants accept of the authority given, and agree among themselves to form a State government. This is supposing that Congress has parted with all its power, as to the creation of the State, and has only retained the power to say whether the State, so created, shall be admitted into the Union or not; and, if not, that it still remains a State out of the Union. If the period selected is an unfortunate one, I am willing it shall be changed to the best possible period; for I maintain the principle that Congress has no authority to give existence to a State which shall not, co-instante, be a member of the Union; a single moment cannot intervene between its complete existence as a State, and its being a member of the Union.

New States may be admitted by the Congress into the Union. This is all the power that the people have clothed Congress with. Congress has no right to create an independent and alien nation, to be composed out of the territory and inhabitants belonging to the United States. The crea-

tion of a State and its membership in the Union is to be considered as one indivisible transaction; as one connected object. If a State has complete existence, and standing alone, it must possess sovereign power. Its volition would be unbounded, and it could not be coerced into the Union against its own will. It might set the majesty of the old States at defiance. It is perfectly plain, that such a state of things could not exist under the Constitution of the United States; and this shows that it is a joint transaction; that the parties never lose sight of each other; and that nothing can be final and conclusive until there is a union of wills upon the admission of the State into the Union.

As Congress has no power to create an independent State—that which cannot be done directly, cannot be effected indirectly, by any accident or negligence on either side. The people have parted with no such power. Congress, in some shape or other, must consent to the constitution. There must be a mutuality of consent in this particular. For what other purpose is the constitution directed to be transmitted to Congress, if it is not to give Congress an opportunity to examine it, and give their opinion upon it?

The law of the last session contains a proviso, that the constitution, whenever formed, shall be republican, and not repugnant to the Constitution of the United States. In whose opinion was it to be republican, and not repugnant to the Constitution of the United States? Most unquestionably the understanding was, that it should be so in the opinion of the acting parties, and not in the opinion of any other branch of the Government. And how can Congress decide upon it until it see the constitution? It has been contended, that a State may be created prospectively; but this seems inconsistent with the nature of the transaction, and it cannot be supported, except on the principle of divesting Congress of every particle of power on the subject, after the enactment of the first law; for, if Congress has now a right of declaring whether Missouri has become a State in the Union, or not, it involves the question whether or no the law of the last session has been complied with. This mode of proceeding would want order, without producing any change in substance; and it is evident that this was not the original opinion of the committee, as the resolution reads, that Missouri shall be, and is hereby declared to be, one of the United States of America, and is admitted into the Union on an equal footing with the original States. In relation to this point the real question is, whether Congress will examine the constitution, and give an opinion upon it, either in what may be deemed a prospective point of view, or otherwise? And this is a principle which, in my opinion, Congress ought never to yield up. I think we should not be discharging the duty we owe to the people, if we merely pass a law authorizing a State to be created, and then abandon the case, and leave it to the inhabitants and others to say whether the constitution is republican, and not repugnant to the Constitution of the United States. Congress expressed their opinion in the case of Ohio, by declaring that the constitution and State government had been formed in pursuance of the act of Congress; and no State has been admitted into the Union since, without the express assent of Congress, after seeing the constitution.

If it is the duty of Congress to express an opinion, the question is, whether there has been a compliance with the law of the last session? The proviso is a condition precedent, and, until complied with, no State has been, or can be, created. This was the basis and foundation of the authority. But both the gentlemen from Virginia say, that the objectionable part may be considered as a nullity and nothing. I confess I do not understand this kind of logic. Congress put in a law a solemn provision, that the constitution, when formed, shall be republican, and not repugnant to the Constitution of the United States; but the sober meaning of this is, that it is immaterial whether it is repugnant or not. If the law has been complied with, it is very well; but, what surprises me the most is, that it is equally satisfactory whether it has been complied with or not, as the bad part may be treated as a nullity. In principle it can make no difference how many parts are repugnant, as all may be considered as nullities and nothing.

It is asked if a bad part will vitiate the whole? That depends upon the nature of the case. In some cases it will, and in others it will not. But, whenever the whole depends upon a condition, that there shall be no bad part, then it will; and that is the case in the present instance. We must agree to take the whole or none. We do not know that Missouri will consent to come into the Union, if we undertake to change her constitution. If we do not accept of the whole, we must suspend the admission until there can be a further understanding on the subject.

The report goes on to consider the constitution in the light of an unconstitutional law, and, as a case peculiarly calculated for judicial cognizance. But, in every case in which Congress acts, it must judge, in the first instance, whether its law or resolution is Constitutional or not. Can we pass the resolution before us, which, in substance, declares that the constitution of Missouri is not repugnant to the Constitution of the United States, with a kind of mental reservation, that we give no opinion on this point? Why, sir, it is the solemn duty of Congress to refrain from doing any act if they even entertain doubts as to its constitutionality. In the case of an ordinary law, the courts, out of respect to the opinion of the Legislature, will not interpose, except in a plain case.

Some go so far as even to deny this right in the courts. But, on this occasion, gentlemen seem willing to transcend every notion that has heretofore been entertained on this subject, and to surrender at once to the supremacy of the courts, by which we shall make our own escape from all responsibility. For my own part, I do not see how this case could be brought before the Supreme Court in any reasonable time; but, suppose it could, Congress could not limit the court as to their decision, or point out what should be its effect. If the court has the power, they would judge of the extent of their power; and they might decide, contrary to the private expectations of gentlemen, that the proviso contained in the law of the last session was a condition precedent, and that, until complied with, no State had, or could be brought into existence. Whenever this bad news should reach Congress, they would be very unpleasantly circumstanced; the Senators and Representative from Missouri would have to leave their seats and go home.

Could the Judiciary expunge from the Union the States created out of the Louisiana purchase, upon the principle that the whole was unconstitutional and incompatible with the original design of the compact made between the old States? This, indeed, would be a gigantic power, and, as friendly as I am disposed towards the exercise of power in the Judiciary, I should be unwilling to acknowledge it, without much greater reflection than I have as yet bestowed on the subject.

If there is any case, in which it would be indiscreet and perhaps improper, for the Judiciary to interfere over the acts of Congress, I think it would be in the case of an admission of a State into the Union. I mean as it respects the main question, whether a State has been brought into the Union or not.

I have only, in relation to this part of the subject, further to say, that here is a resolution, on which we are called upon to vote: if we believe it to be in violation of the Constitution of the United States, it is our solemn duty to reject it, regardless of the consequences. We cannot avoid giving our opinion upon it; and nothing can excuse us, if we make an unlawful breach, however slight, in the Constitution.

As to the condition of Missouri, there can be no middle station, it must be a Territory or State. There has been an ineffectual attempt to create a State, and the operation is a reversion to the old state of things—I mean in point of right; in point of fact, Missouri can make it what she pleases; but, it is most uncharitable to suppose, that she will rebel against her country, and assume the character of an independent State. I hope that gentlemen are mistaken as to the disposition of the people of Missouri. Why will they not peaceably submit to the will of the majority? How often, since the existence of our Government, have the minority been obliged to submit? What evidence have we, that the people of Missouri are less qualified to be good citizens? Is there any foundation for all this dread and apprehension, that they are disposed to give us trouble—I hope not, but that, on the contrary, it will be discovered, that they have as much anxious solicitude as the rest of their fellow-citizens, to preserve the peace and harmony of the country.

Tuesday, December 12.

Mr. Kent, from the Committee on the District of Columbia, reported a bill to repeal part of an act passed by the State of Maryland in 1784, and now in force in Georgetown, in the District of Columbia, entitled "An act for an addition to

607   HISTORY OF CONGRESS.   608

H. of R.   *Admission of Missouri.*   December, 1820.

Georgetown, in Montgomery county;" which bill was twice read and committed.

Mr. McCoy, from the Committee of Claims, made a report on the petition of William T. Nimmo, accompanied by a bill for his relief.

On motion of Mr. Allen, of Tennessee, the Secretary of the War Department was required to lay before this House such extracts from the inspection roll of the army engaged in the Seminole war, as will show whether or not the mounted men employed in that service continued to furnish, at their own expense, horses fit for duty until discharged; also, whether or not any rule was adopted, or compensation given said troops for their services, not made applicable, and given, to all other troops of the same description employed in the service of the United States.

On motion of Mr. Plumer, the Committee of Commerce were instructed to inquire into the expediency of providing, by law, that articles of export, inspected under the authority of one State, may be exported from any other State without being again inspected in the State from which they may be exported.

The House took up the proposition yesterday made by Mr. Whitman, so to amend the rules of the House as that the Speaker, in calling the States, should commence with Maine; and, after a little discussion on the part of Mr. Whitman for, and Mr. Butler, of New Hampshire, against the motion, it was negatived.

The Speaker laid before the House a letter from the Comptroller of the Treasury, transmitting from the Fourth Auditor a list of balances charged in that office, and due more than three years prior to September, 1820; also a list of persons (only five in number) who have failed to render their accounts to that office.

The Speaker also laid before the House a report of the Secretary of War, of a plan on which the Army may be reduced to six thousand men; in obedience to a resolution of this House of the 11th of May last.

The Speaker also laid before the House a report from the Secretary of the Treasury, relative to any alterations or modifications which he might deem necessary in the acts fixing the fees and emoluments of the officers of the customs, and a plan for compensating them according to their respective services; rendered in obedience to a resolution of the House of the 13th of May last.

The first named document was laid on the table, the remaining two referred to committees, and all ordered to be printed.

AMENDMENT TO RULES.

Mr. Rich submitted for consideration the following, which, proposing to alter the rules of the House, lies on the table one day of course:

"A proposition, requesting information from the President of the United States, or directing it to be furnished by the Secretary of either of the Executive Departments, or the Postmaster General, shall lie upon the table one day for consideration, unless otherwise ordered, with the unanimous consent of the House."

In offering this motion, Mr. Rich said, it would, if adopted, require that a proposition calling upon the President of the United States, or the head of a department for information, should lie one day upon the table for consideration. He said, the experience which had been afforded him in the proceedings of the House, had taught him to believe that the respect which was due the Executive officers, and which members owed to themselves, as well as a regard to economy, suggested the propriety of the amendment. He said he by no means objected to the practice abstractly, of calling for information; but he thought that, while the House was in the practice of adopting such calls with the same facility that it instructed one of its committees to inquire into the expediency of adopting the most immaterial measure incident to legislation, if it did not at some times adopt calls of the kind unadvisedly, it was, to say the least of it, extremely liable to do so, and subject the departments to great labor in cases where no adequate object could be attained by it. He said he would mention one alleged fact, of the truth of which he had no reason to doubt, although he had it only from report, viz: that six clerks had been constantly employed, from the close of the last session to the present time, in collecting the materials to enable one of the departments to answer a call made at the last session. He said he would not allege that gentlemen would not have made the call had they known the labor which would have been required to furnish the answer; but sure he was that, in such a case, they would have considered the subject at least one day.

A message from the Senate informed the House that the Senate have passed bills, and a resolution, of the following titles, to wit: An act for the relief of John Holmes, of Alabama; An act for the relief of Morgan Brown; and a resolution declaring the admission of the State of Missouri into the Union; in which bills and resolution they request the concurrence of this House.

MISSOURI.

The House again resolved itself into a Committee of the Whole, on the resolution for admitting the State of Missouri into the Union.

Mr. McLane, of Delaware, addressed the House as follows:

Mr. Speaker, in soliciting the indulgence of the House upon the present occasion, I cannot avoid expressing my sincere regret, which none can feel more deeply, that the odious Missouri question should ever have been revived. After the discussion at the last session, after the excitement it had occasioned in this House and in the nation; after the deliberate decision of the National Legislature, connected with the principle of an honorable compromise, calculated at once to allay public agitation and reconcile conflicting views, and fully and fairly executed upon one side, as far as it was practicable, it was at least to be desired that it would be the wish, as, in my humble opinion it is the duty, of every friend of his country, that this subject should have been put forever at rest; and that the people of Missouri, mingling their interests and feelings with those of the other States, should have been permitted quietly to take their station in our

National Confederacy. But it seems that all these expectations are illusory, and that the ordinary course of public business is again to be interrupted by the agitation of 'a subject, which, I fear, cannot lead to any profitable result.

I admit, with the gentleman from Pennsylvania who spoke second in this debate, (Mr. SERGEANT,) that the subject has assumed a different, though an important form; but it still appears to me to have arisen out of the old question, and that its importance is derived much more from its effects upon the national tranquillity and the interests of our white population, than that class of persons whose rights are supposed to be affected by the Missouri constitution; who, as I believe I shall be able to show, have little interest in the matter.

I can assure the House that I feel no inclination to prolong the discussion upon so unpleasant a subject beyond that which every one must feel, to prevent any misconception of his course; and the best apology, perhaps, for engaging their attention at all, is to be found in the contrariety of views by which gentlemen who think with me have been conducted to the result. I do not advert to this circumstance with the least intention of undervaluing the arguments of those who enjoy so deservedly the respect of this House and the country; but it will always happen in the first agitation of great Constitutional questions, involving the principles upon which the institutions of the Government are founded, that 'a variety of reasons may lead different minds to a similar conclusion; and when I feel it my duty to avow that, I do not rely upon all the grounds taken by other gentlemen who advocate this resolution, I desire to be understood as saying no more than that they have not the same weight with me that they appear to have had with others.

I entertain no doubt that Missouri is not, at present, a State of this Union; and I am equally clear, that it is both the right and duty of Congress to examine the constitution which has been submitted to us; and, if it be found repugnant to the principles of the Constitution of the United States, refuse to admit the State into the Union. No State can of right claim to be admitted a member unless her frame of government is conformable to the principles of the confederacy of which she seeks to be a part. This was the doctrine for which I contended when I had the honor to address the House at the last session, and I have seen no cause since to change my opinion. I have, therefore, examined the constitution of Missouri, and am satisfied that it is republican, and not repugnant to the Constitution of the United States. In the view I have taken of the subject, it appears to me to be more necessary to consider the obligations of Congress, than the actual condition of Missouri now, or what it will be if this resolution should be rejected. I am free to say, however, that, in my opinion, she is a State; for the people are in the actual exercise of State government. She is ready for admission into the Union, which could not be until the territorial disabilities had been merged in State sovereignty. We do not form a State by our act; we admit into the

16th CON. 2d SESS.—20

confederacy a State already formed by the people. Missouri would be a State if the objectionable feature were not in the constitution; she is not the less so because it is there, though it may be the means of keeping her out of the Union, and of thus producing new and very important relations with the United States. Whether Congress will possess the right or the power, should the constitution be rejected, of dissolving the State government, and of reducing the people once more to territorial subjection, is a question of fearful magnitude, upon which, though I have a very strong opinion, I feel no desire at present to make any observation.

The obligations of Congress appear to me to be equally clear. We have solemnly decided that we possess no power to impose any condition upon the people of Missouri as the price of their admission into the Union. We have so decided by rejecting an actual attempt to impose a condition, and by authorizing the people to form a State government, without any other restriction than the Constitution of the United States itself imposes. We have entered into a precise stipulation to admit the State, when formed, into the Union, upon an equal footing with the original States, in all respects whatever. Our obligation is, to execute this stipulation in good faith—regarding matters of substance rather than technicalities. We are bound to admit the State into the Union if we can do so without violating the Constitution; and it is unworthy the magnitude of the subject, to be searching for some pretext by which we may escape from our engagement.

It must be admitted on all hands, that the constitution of Missouri is republican. To deny it this character because it does not prohibit slavery, would be to pronounce the constitutions of all the original States in the Union, and that of the United States, anti-republican. Nor should it be forgotten, that, as it respects the slaves, in regard to whom the proceedings of the last session offered some admonition, its provisions are both liberal and humane; conferring upon this unhappy class of persons greater rights, and guarding them with better securities than they enjoy in any State in the Union, in which they exist.

The only objection which is taken to the constitution, is founded on that article which provides that "it shall be the duty of the Legislature, as soon as may be, to pass such laws as may be 'necessary to prevent free negroes and mulattoes 'from coming to, and settling in, this State, under 'any pretext whatsoever." It should here be remarked, that the Missouri Convention could derive no lesson upon this subject from the proceedings of the last session, which, professing only to close the territory against slaves, could not be construed into a design to open it for free negroes. In announcing this course, too, the convention have proposed merely to model their municipal policy after that of a majority of the old thirteen States, and of those subsequently admitted, dictated, as I believe by no improper temper, but rather by the danger of an influx of this class of persons from the Southern part of the continent, who alone would be likely to go there. If this policy be right in the old States, it cannot be wrong in Missouri. We cannot charge Missouri with a violation of the Constitution, without pronouncing the same judgment upon the original parties to the compact; and I shall not be readily persuaded of the unsoundness of a doctrine which has regulated the practice of the State and General governments, ever since their organization; nor will I hastily pronounce the laws of half the States in the Union unconstitutional and void.

But, I proceed to consider more particularly, the character and extent of the objectionable provision; and I beg leave to remark, first, that of itself, it is entirely inoperative. It does not infringe the rights of any person whatsoever, nor does it prohibit any free negro from emigrating to the State of Missouri. It is directory merely to the Legislature to do so, and, until they have made it by their enactment, no prohibition does, or can exist. It is not, nor can it be known, that the Legislature will ever pass such a law; if the direction be unconstitutional, they never can. If they should, the law, and not the constitution, would create the prohibition; unless the Legislature should derive the power to pass the law from this provision. But, it cannot be pretended, that this clause confers on the Legislature any new or greater power than they would possess without it. In governments not republican, the legislative is the supreme power; in those which are republican, the supreme power is in the people; and under our system, therefore, the constitutions abridge, rather than enlarge the powers of the legislative department. The provision, then, instead of conferring new power, directs the Legislature to exert a power already in them, independent of the constitution, and depending for its efficacy in no degree upon the authority of the constitution. If this clause confers no new power, so it imposes no additional obligation upon the Legislature; it directs the exercise of a legislative function, upon the supposition that the right to exercise it exists, and that it may be rightfully employed. It does not require the Legislature to pass the law, *per fas aut nefas*, right or wrong; but to do so if they can consistently with their Constitutional obligations. In referring the subject to legislative interposition, the convention could have designed nothing else, than that it should act under the same responsibilities, and with the same regard to motives of State and general policy as in other cases. They could not have made it obligatory upon the Legislature to pass the law at all events, for this would have been requiring them to violate the Constitution of the United States, which their oaths, as members of the Legislature, bound them to support. Besides, if it had been the design to enact the prohibition without regard to Constitutional restraints; or to abridge legislative discretion, the convention, themselves would have ingrafted it upon their work, and not have referred it to the Legislature. The injunctions of the convention in matters of legislative cognizance must always be subservient to the higher duties of the legislator, the first of which is to pass no law repugnant to the Constitution of the United States.

The direction in question, therefore, amounts to nothing more than that the Legislature shall originate the system, provided they shall deem it compatible with the Constitution of the United States.

If, therefore, this clause neither enlarges the power, nor increases the obligations of the Legislature of Missouri, the power of the State in relation to the General Government, and the checks and balances of the latter, are the same as they would be independent of it; and if the relation of the State to the United States, and the rights of the persons to be affected by it are the same whether the clause be in or out of the constitution, the Legislature will act, if at all, at the same peril, and under the same restraints, as though it did not exist, and it would be the law and not the constitution of Missouri which would be repugnant to the Constitution of the United States, if either could be. How then can we say, that a clause of a nature perfectly nugatory, possessing no legal force or operation, which confers no additional power, nor creates any new obligation, but directs a legislative interference subject to the higher control of the institutions of the General Government, can be unconstitutional?

If this clause do not violate the Constitution, it is not possible for Congress to anticipate the passage of an unconstitutional law, and prospectively to pronounce it void, much less can we act upon such a supposition. Suppose, for example, that this clause were not in the Constitution, but that Congress had reason to believe, that it was the intention of the Missouri Legislature to pass a similar law; could Congress require from them, as the terms of their admission into the Union, a stipulation, that no such law should ever be passed? Clearly not; for this would not only be drawing to Congress the judicial power of revising State laws, which they never can possess, but it would amount to a condition tying up the functions of the Legislature, and denying it the same powers which have been actually exerted by the other States. Sir, as it regards the municipal laws of the States, Congress must always rely upon the sound legal discretion of the State Legislature not to pass unconstitutional acts, and upon the firmness and integrity of the national judiciary, to avoid them if they should. With regard to the present States we have no other reliance, and we need no other.

And why, sir, do we fear the Legislature of Missouri more than we do of those of the other States? We have stipulated to admit these people into the Union, and, wishing to avoid our obligation, we refuse to execute it, because we are pleased to suspect that at some future time their Legislature may pass a law, which we choose to determine would be unconstitutional!

But, Mr. Speaker, suppose the clause in the Missouri constitution be considered as making it obligatory upon the Legislature to pass a law conformable to its terms, is its compatibility with the Constitution of the United States irreconcilable? The clause in the latter instrument with which it is supposed to be in conflict, provides, that " the ' citizens of each State shall be entitled to all priv-

' ileges and immunities of citizens in the several
' States." Now, on this supposition, I do not require gentlemen to refer this question to the Judiciary, for I am prepared to decide it for myself;
but, I ask them, when they attempt its interpretation here, to be guided by the same rules of construction, by which the Judiciary would decide, if
it were before them. If the State of Missouri possess any power over the subject-matter to which
the provision relates, then it is not altogether void;
it is in part at least good, and we must give it a
construction which will reconcile the powers of
the State with those of the General Government;
otherwise, we should deny to the State the power
of acting at all, lest it might transcend its proper
sphere.

It must be conceded, sir, that if there are any
free negroes and mulattoes, who are citizens of
any State, yet that the great majority of this class
of persons in the United States are citizens of no
State. As to these, by far the greatest number,
the power of Missouri is complete; their emigration to the State may be constitutionally prohibited, and, so far as it may operate upon them, the
clause is good. Missouri, then, has the undeniable
right to prevent " free negroes and mulattoes" from
acting within her State; and, in order to give any
color to the objection, gentlemen are obliged to
assert that the clause excludes all free negroes and
mulattoes, including citizens of the several States.
If Missouri had no power to prevent any free negroes from going there, the clause might be bad;
but she is admitted to possess sufficient power to
fill up the plain literal scope of the clause; and it
can never be bad, unless the Legislature exceed
even the limits of the injunction. It is fair to presume that the Legislature will do so, where they
have neither a legal nor moral obligation to urge
them forward, but have both to help them back?

It is our duty, moreover, sir, to give to the words
of the clause that sense in which they are usually
employed in all parts of the country, and by men
of all classes; and in that sense they import, _ex vi
termini_, that class of colored people who are neither slaves nor citizens. In a country where there
are slaves who can become citizens, the middle
condition of a man passing from slavery to citizenship can be no otherwise designated than by
the terms here employed, since his freedom does
not necessarily import citizenship. When we
speak of a negro slave, we mean one who owes a
lasting service to a master; when we speak of a
free negro, we refer to him who has been set free
by his master; and the appellation of citizen belongs to a higher condition and fuller rights. If
we design to discriminate between citizens of different color, we should use the terms white citizens, or black or negro citizens, which have, I confess, to my ear at least, the sound of novelty. In
common parlance, therefore, we use the term free
negro in contradistinction both to slaves and citizens, in the same way as the freedman among the
Romans denoted the middle condition between
the bondman and the Roman citizen. The convention of Missouri could not have used the terms
in any other sense, especially when it is consid-

ered that their principal design was to exclude this
class of people, of idle and dissolute habits, upon their
Southern and Eastern borders, who are confessedly not citizens, and known only as free negroes
and mulattoes, rather than those in the Northern and
Eastern States, who it cannot be supposed will be
likely ever to wander into this Western region.
But as this part of the subject has been pressed
more in detail, and with greater ability than I
could hope to employ, I will say no more in regard to it than that, while there is a sound, legal,
rational construction at hand, which reconciles the
constitution of Missouri with that of the United
States, we are bound in a fair performance of our
engagements to adopt it, rather than diligently to
hunt after some technical objection by which we
avoid the one, under the pretext of obeying the
other.

But, Mr. Speaker, these are not the principal
views which I design to submit, I confess that the
great ground upon which my opinion is formed is,
that the free negroes and mulattoes in the United
States are not that description of citizens contemplated by the Constitution of the United States
as entitled to Federal rights.

I do not mean, sir, to deny that these people
have certain rights. I admit they have many;
and these I would cherish, and, when consistent
with the safety of the white population, enlarge.
But their rights are of a local nature, dependent
upon the gratuitous favor of the municipal authority of the States, and liable to be curtailed or
enlarged by those authorities; they are limited to
the State granting them, and confer no claim to
similar privileges and immunities purely federal.
Gentlemen must not only show that a free negro
may be admitted to the enjoyment of some rights
of citizenship in a particular State, but they must
also show that he is of that description of "citizens" to whom the Constitution meant to guaranty equal rights in every State. The State authority may confer the right of citizenship within
their State upon aliens and Indians; but it was
never imagined that they would therefore be the
subjects of federal rights. Nor could the Constitution have intended to refer to any description of
persons whose privileges were matters of grace
from the local municipality. For I take it to be
clear, that no person can claim federal immunities
who cannot claim, as a matter of right, the privileges of a citizen in the State of which he is a
resident. A consideration of the nature of citizenship and the principles of the Federal Union, will
show that the free negroes in our country have no
such pretensions. An inattention to the distinction here taken has led to great misapprehension
throughout the argument. Gentlemen have seen
some few of these people voting in some one or
two of the States, and have seized upon this circumstance as conclusive evidence of citizenship,
without reflecting that, as a political right, it is
the consequence rather than the characteristic of
citizenship, and may depend upon the precarious
tenure of the local Legislature, which, if it pleased
so to order, might deprive a real citizen of the
right of voting, while at the same time it should

confer it upon an alien who could claim none of the essential rights which characterize a citizen.

I concur entirely in the definition of a citizen, as given by the honorable gentleman from Virginia on my left, (Mr. Barbour,) who has spoken with so much ability, and left I fear little for me to add. I believe that his definition will be found, in all its prominent parts, to be fully supported by the best authors upon the subject, as well as the reason of the case. I take it, sir, that a person, to be a "citizen" under one Government, must be a member of the *civil community*, and entitled as matter of right to equal advantages in that community. His rights result from his association with it, and of which nothing short of his own will or misconduct can deprive him. They are rights independent of the political power, and inalienable. They were anterior to the community, were carried into it, and their preservation formed the great object of the association. They may be modified, but cannot be destroyed, by the political power of the society. A State, for instance, may regulate the right of suffrage, and extend it to such only of its members as possess a freehold property; but it could not extend it to one freeholder and not to another; much less could it say that a citizen should not acquire a freehold; for it is the inherent right of every citizen to exert his mental and physical powers in the pursuit of happiness and for the acquisition of property, and to have his acquisitions protected. Our political system is founded upon this principle of equal rights in the members of the community, and any State regulation which should interfere with them would be unconstitutional. It follows, therefore, that those only are "citizens" who can claim these advantages as a matter of right; all others, and those whose privileges depend upon the grace or favor of the local authority, fall under the denomination of inhabitants and aliens, holding their rights at the will of the Government under which they live. Upon a subject on which so great a variety of opinion has been entertained, I pray to be indulged in referring to an authority in support of the exposition I am pursuing. It is remarked by *Vattel*, who, in this respect, follows *Grotius*, that "The 'citizens are the members of the civil society. 'Bound to this society by certain duties, and sub-'ject to its authority, they equally participate in 'its advantages. The natives are those born in 'the country of those who are citizens. In order 'to be of the country, it is necessary that a person 'be born of a father who is a citizen."

"The inhabitants, as distinguished from citi-'zens, are strangers who are permitted to settle and 'stay in the country. Bound by their residence to 'the society, they are subject to the laws of the 'State while they reside there, and they are obliged 'to defend it, because it grants them protection, 'though they do not participate in all the rights of 'citizens. They enjoy only the advantages which 'the laws or custom give them."

"The perpetual inhabitants are those who have 'received the right of perpetual residence. These 'are a kind of citizens of an inferior order, and are 'united and subject to the society without partici-'pation in all its advantages. Their children fol-'low the condition of their fathers," &c.

Of the two last of these classes, I consider the Indians and free negroes and mulattoes of the United States. The "laws and custom" nowhere give them the right of participating in all the advantages of society. Their actual advantages vary in almost every State; in some they are dealt out more liberally, in others with a sparing hand; in none are they complete. In some States they cannot be witness against the 'whites; in others they cannot be jurors; in none are they allowed to hold offices or to intermarry with the whites—a circumstance to which I shall more particularly advert hereafter. If they were citizens these disabilities could not be imposed upon them, but for some personal defect. The real truth is, sir, that they are nowhere considered as members of the civil society, but as inhabitants of the country, holding their rights at the will of the local authority.

It was competent, in the original formation of the societies which now compose this Union, to admit into the association, or to exclude from it, any description of persons whatsoever. Every one in any degree acquainted with the history of the first settlement of these States must know that the association was of white people—Europeans and their descendants. The idea of a mixture was at no time tolerated; even the aboriginal Indians were not received as a competent part of the civil or political community; but the country was settled, and the society formed, by a white population. It was essentially a white community. In its origin the black population could have formed no part of it, and throughout its progress the invincible barrier to a mixture of white and black, and the positive regulations of society, have perpetually excluded them. They could not, therefore, upon the principles of the association, and in the nature of things, be entitled to equal rights.

The American race came to the country posterior to the whites, and their original condition most unhappily was that of slaves. As such, they were clearly without the pale of the society; and it is equally clear that they never could be admitted within it afterwards, unless by some positive law, or by long usage and custom. They never have been admitted by either. In Pennsylvania, and many other States, they were expressly excluded from the benefit of the naturalization laws existing in the States, prior to the adoption of the Federal Constitution.

Where is there any positive institution providing for their incorporation into the civil community, or extending to them equal rights? Where is the State in the Union in which it is declared, by positive enactment, that free negroes shall be entitled to claim all the rights of citizens, and be entitled "equally to participate in the advantages of the civil" or political "society?" I never heard that there was one. The act of emancipation cannot have this effect, unless it should be so declared by some express statutory provision. Emancipation is the mere act of the owner; it is merely a relinquishment of his claim to the services of the negro; it gives freedom to the slave, but it is not competent for the owner, a single individual, by any act of his, to constitute him a citizen. This must be the work of the society at large. There cannot be a stronger illustration of this than that the right and form of the manumission of slaves is everywhere a matter of State regulation; under which they confer on the manumitted slaves only the rights of free negroes, not of citizens, distinguishing between the two conditions, and creating a liability on the owner to support the negro, if at any period of his life he should become unable to support himself. This would never be, if by the act of manumission the negro were admitted to the rights of a citizen, for in that case it would be the duty of the society at large to provide for his age and infirmities, and they would have no power to impose the obligation exclusively upon the owner. It is because he can neither incorporate with, nor attain to any rank in the society, whereby his means and inducements to provide for himself are diminished, that the owner is not suffered to cast him loose upon the community without becoming responsible for his maintenance. Sir, the doctrine is confirmed by the experience of all history.

The honorable gentleman from Pennsylvania (Mr. Hemphill) has referred us to *Cooper's Justinian* to prove, that among the Romans a freedman, by the act of freedom, became a Roman citizen. But the gentleman overlooked the declaration of his author, that this was the case only by the express provision of the Justinian Code, and that until that time the act of freedom conferred no such privilege. Until then the three conditions of bondman, freedman, and citizen, were distinctly marked; the second being the middle condition between the first and last, equally removed from the disabilities of the one, and the privileges of the other. The gentleman's authority, therefore, establishes the position directly against him. But, I ask, Mr. Speaker, what analogy there is between the Roman slaves and those with whom this country is unhappily afflicted? Among the Romans the bondman wore the same color with the free population, and was no otherwise distinguishable from the rest of the community than by his subjection to his master; when his shackles were loosened, he readily mixed with his fellow men like a drop added to the stream, and floated on with the mass of the community to a common destiny. But very different is the unhappy African race within the United States. Their servitude is not their only distinguishable feature; they never can mingle or assimilate with the white population, more than oil with water. The liberation of the slave from his master pushes him from the shore, on an element where he is a stranger, on which he can make but little progress. He requires to be tutored, and disciplined, and guarded, to fit him for the humble enjoyments which are afforded him. His interests are dissimilar with those of the whites; he sees them enjoying rights and advantages to which he can never attain; his road to preferment is blocked up, and he passes on his journey without any common interest with those about him. It is for this, among other reasons, sir, that the institutions of this country have never imitated the Justinian Code.

I will not stop to notice more particularly than has been done by the gentleman from Virginia, (Mr. Barbour,) the stale argument derived from the abstract doctrines announced in the Declaration of Independence, and the comprehensive expression of "We the people," prefixed to the Constitution of the United States. Broad as they appear, every one knows they were limited. They did not include the slaves, nor the Indians, because they referred only to those who were members of our civil community; and, if my position be correct, for the same reason they had no allusion to the free negroes in the country. It is impossible they could have had, when in those States in which these declarations are the fullest, free negroes were expressly excluded from the advantages of their naturalization laws.

If, then, no positive law has incorporated these people with the civil society, but on the contrary has discountenanced it, who will contend that it has ever been accomplished by the usage and custom of the country?

Usage and custom are chiefly the result of our feeling, if not our conscience, and are seldom in opposition to both. There is no instance in history of any attempt at a mixture with white and black; the natural sense and feeling of all nations have been universally averse to it, and in any country where there is found a weaker caste of people, who cannot, by any possibility, mix and assimilate in common with the stronger, their rights can never be the same. Does not the custom of our country prove it to be so? I speak now of the fact; of what is, rather than of what ought to be. Is any one prepared to say, that there is a State in the Union in which the white and the black population actually enjoy or claim equal rights? It is said, to be sure, that in one or two, the bills of rights make no discrimination; but in these, what construction have the usage and custom and laws put upon these abstract declarations? In some we have seen that they do not confer the fundamental right of being naturalized. And where can they boldly claim the enjoyment of equal rights, in defiance of the local authority? It is said, too, that in one or two States they are allowed to vote, and some have voted. But I have shown you that the right to vote is no test of citizenship; it is dependent on legislative favor, in part, and may be conferred on aliens and others, and taken away again, if it be not founded on the claim of citizenship; and therefore, if the free negroes only exercise it as a matter of grace merely, it gives them no claim to Federal immunities. What, sir, is the evidence of this right of voting? In how many instances has it been exercised? In all the political struggles to which the States have been doomed, where is the wildest partisan who has stemmed the indignant sense of the community by enlisting electors from such ranks? Sir, if it exist, it is in theory; if exerted, it is by stealth, as if apprehensive of its legitimacy; it is not commonly practised; for the usage and custom of society are against it. From what does this result, sir? From every man's own sense of the insuperable disparity which exists between white and black, as to every qualification on which the right of suffrage is founded. The white man looks at his associations, civil and political; he reflects upon the history of his municipal institutions; he surveys the relative situation of the black to the white population; he knows the unhappy condition from which the unfortunate African has emerged; and whithersoever he turns, he finds the actual condition of things marked by a line of discrimination stronger and more durable than laws of brass or iron. Founded in the natural sense of the community, it has become the common law of the land. If usage and custom have conferred equal rights, where have these people held offices, from the highest to the lowest? Where even have they been admitted with whites as members of petty incorporations? If they have never exercised, how can they claim the right by usage? And, sir, their exclusion from these is not the result of incapacity, or the humbleness of their station: for the poorest white man often fills some office of trust and profit; but it is the result of other and deeper causes.

Sir, a different and common usage and custom lie at the foundation of all our legislative provisions, in regard to these people; and the laws of the States have come in aid, and gone in advance of this usage and custom; and I beg leave to remind the gentleman from Pennsylvania, (Mr. HEMPHILL,) who attempted to found an argument upon the supposed necessity of legislative interference, that it has never been resorted to, but for the purpose of curtailing rights which did not appertain to these people as citizens, but belonged to them in common with aliens and residents merely.

All freemen have the capacity to be witnesses, jurors, and to serve in the militia; but, in most of the States, these are denied to free negroes by the municipal laws. These regulations do not make, they are founded on the previous discrimination existing in fact; they are called for by the feelings of society. Why cannot a free negro be a witness against a white man, as a foreigner or an Indian may? It is because the custom of society, having drawn a discrimination between the white and the black, disparaging to the latter, the law deems it safe and wise to deprive him of the means of gratifying feelings which such a condition might engender. Some of these disabilities, it is true, are found in some only of the States; but the most important one is found in all, rooted in the heart of the people, and enforced by the laws. In no State of the Union is intermarriage between white and black permitted. There are few men, as I hope, that would not revolt at such a union, and I know of no state of society in which such a connexion would not be indignantly reprobated; but yet, to guard against the possibility of a different feeling, the laws come in aid of and enforce the prohibition. If these people form a part of the civil society, which, in such a case, would be composed of a motley population consisting of all the variety of color, and if they are entitled to claim equal rights, by what authority can the right of forming a marriage contract be annulled? Sir, this fact proves the whole argument. It not only shows that these people are not members of the civil community, but that they can never become so, because the strong sense of the community is against it; it closes the only legitimate avenue to their amalgamation; it strengthens and sanctifies the moral feelings of society; it keeps the black man forever without its bosom, and perpetuates his discrimination. But, sir, it proves yet more; it is conclusive to show that the rights of these people, in every part of the Union, are dependent upon, and, in fact, the creatures of local jurisdiction and municipal policy. But one of the gentlemen from Pennsylvania (Mr. HEMPHILL) has been pleased to say, that if the black man cannot marry with the white, so the white man cannot marry with the black, and gravely inferred that, therefore, the whites could not be citizens! This observation might, indeed, rather afford matter for amusement, than of sober reply; but, as I deem the latter unnecessary, I will not consume time in indulging the former. The same gentleman remarks, that these people labor and are taxed, and thus contribute to the wealth of the nation; but surely the gentleman cannot suppose that these are among the rights or characteristics of citizens! they are incident to the emigrant as to the citizen, and to the aliens and civilized Indians in common with the free negroes in the United States; and, the gentleman ought to remember that while the free negro can labor and be taxed, he is denied the equal privilege of managing and holding office in common with the alien, the resident, and other inhabitants merely.

I assume the position, then, as proved, that, at the formation of the Constitution of the United States, the free negroes and mulattoes were not entitled to equal rights; they were in the nature of perpetual inhabitants, and the objects of local municipalities. This was their country, because they had no claim to any other, and their claim to residence grew out of the fact that they had been brought here by the whites, against their will, and became, on that account, entitled to protection and the other rights of perpetual inhabitants; all of which, however, are confined to the particular State of whose territory they are the inhabitants.

If such were their condition, then, it is impossible that it could have been changed since; the naturalization system of the United States being confined to whites. Now, sir, the rule is, as I have already shown, that the issue follows the condition of their fathers; and the children of the free negroes, though born in the United States, have no greater rights than those which belonged to their fathers. This is the law of nature, and applies to these people now, unless it has been altered by some positive law or by common custom. The British Constitution and the naturalization law of the United States, have, I admit, departed from this rule; but the latter is expressly confined in all its provisions to white persons; and as it was necessary to make the positive variation in regard to them, the inference would appear to be inevitable that the rule remained in force, with regard to all others. The rule of the British system never did apply, and for the plainest of reasons. That system, consisting of a train of immemorial usages, and customs, and of acts of Parliament, did not apply to their colonies, only so far as they were immediately applicable to their situation, or actually adopted by them in practice. Now, this provision of the British Constitution was wholly inapplicable to these colonies, as it respects their black population. In England it had reference only to a white population; it knew no mixture, and it never contemplated any.

But, if it could have applied, it never was adopted in practice, but expressly excluded and repudiated in all the States. There is no instance in which the laws or custom have discriminated between the free negro by emancipation, and his issue born in the United States; no instance in which the issue have enjoyed greater rights, by usage, than their progenitors; they have always been placed upon the same footing.

The same causes which begat the discrimination as to one generation, have perpetuated it, and will continue to do so in every other. I have not entered into a discussion of the right of all this, but have argued from the fact. I have set the universal usages of society against the abstract doctrine of equality, which is nowhere actually practised. But, sir, I should not shrink from the inquiry, if I deemed it necessary to be pursued. I am an advocate for some discrimination. I am an enemy to slavery; if I had the power, and could do so consistently with the safety of the white population, I would wipe it out of our history; but I never will agree to put the white and black population upon an equality, or to destroy the features of both, by the vain attempt to amalgamate one with the other! The attempt has never been, and never can be made; and I ask, sir, if we were now forming a new constitution, would any gentleman consent to place the black race upon an equal footing with the white? Sir, between these descriptions of men, reason and nature have drawn a line of discrimination which never can be effaced, till both shall be compelled to yield to the law of force.

The great question, then, Mr. Speaker, upon which I place this argument, recurs—Was it the intention of the Constitution of the United States to confer full federal rights upon this description of inhabitants? "The citizens of each State shall be entitled to all the privileges and immunities of citizens in the several States." The precise meaning of this provision is not entirely free from obscurity; and some doubts once existed whether the immunities to be enjoyed were those of the State from which the citizen removed, or of that to which he emigrated, though it seems now to be settled that the latter is the true import.

One thing, however, is clear, that it does not secure the right of only settling in a State, which is involved rather as an incident than a principal immunity in the general grant. It secures all privileges and immunities of citizens in the State, and includes the right of emigration, as necessarily incident to the enjoyment of these immunities. But, sir, it could never have designed to secure this right of emigration and settling in a State, to a class of persons who could not be entitled, after they got there, to all the immunities to which it led. It could never have designed to authorize a man to settle in a State, when the tenure and extent of his privileges depended upon the will of the municipal authority; and if I have succeeded in showing such to be the nature of the privileges enjoyed by the free negroes and mulattoes, the deduction would be inevitable. If the free negro of New York, on the allegation of citizenship by the mere exercise of partial and gratuitous rights there, can claim to go to Virginia, he would be entitled, on his arrival, to all the privileges and immunities of white citizens there, though he had previously enjoyed fewer rights than the whites in New York. Such a meaning, however, would be too preposterous to ascribe to the Constitution of the United States. It is unreasonable to conclude that the Constitution ever meant to alter the condition of the black population, or to interfere with the municipal authorities over them, so as to place all the States at the mercy of a dissolute, heterogeneous population of any one. Can it be supposed that the States would ever have entered into the Union upon the principle of allowing the free negroes in New York or Massachusetts to be placed upon an equal footing with the whites, in States whose own safety required them to deny similar privileges to their own native free negroes? Can any gentleman point out the interest which the Northern States had to require such a concession? Every thing connected with the history and formation of the Government proves that this class could not have been contemplated. The Constitution was the work of States composed of a white population, and designed to secure their interests chiefly; and to such of these who had perfect rights in one State, it guarantied the immunities in any other. It was intended to make the United States a common country for such as were full members of the particular States. At that time, too, the condition of the free blacks was known to be as I have already described it; they were known to be a distinct class everywhere, and the creatures of local and municipal policy; certainly of an inferior order, and enjoying such rights as the policy of the particular State might think proper to confer. They were everywhere considered as inhabitants merely, who had not attained to the condition of citizens, and enjoyed only partially the privileges appertaining to the former class.

The language of the old Articles of Confederation, and the variance between them and the present Constitution, offer the best illustration of these remarks. The fourth article of the former provided, that "The better to secure and perpetu-'ate mutual friendship and intercourse among the ' people of the different States, the free inhabitants ' of each of these States, paupers, vagabonds, and ' fugitives from justice excepted, shall be entitled to

' all privileges and immunities of free citizens in ' the several States." The doctrine now contended for was the precise evil experienced under the old Articles, and led to the limited phraseology in the present Constitution. This is demonstrated by every commentator upon the subject ; and Judge Tucker, in speaking of this very clause in the Articles of Confederation, says, " It seems to be a con- ' struction scarcely avoidable, and those who come ' under the denomination of ' free inhabitants' of a ' State, (although not citizens of such State,) ' were entitled in every other State to all the privi- ' leges of free citizens of the latter; that is, greater ' privileges than they may be entitled to in their ' own State. Our free negroes, for example, though ' not entitled to the right of suffrage in Virginia, ' might, by removing into another State, acquire that ' right there; and persons of the same description, ' removing from any other State into this, might ' be supposed to acquire the same right here, in ' virtue of that article, though native born negroes ' are undoubtedly incapable of it, under our con- ' stitution." To avoid this construction, the present constitution omitted the words " free inhabitants," and substituted " citizens," evidently referring to those only who were entitled to full rights in their own State.

In immediate connexion with this, is the power in Congress to pass uniform laws of naturalization. The Constitution having secured to the citizens of each State all the immunities of citizens in the several States, it became necessary to vest the exclusive power of making citizens in the General Government, in which all the States should have a voice, to avoid the very improper power in one State of making citizens in every other. This power is clearly exclusive, and the States have no longer any power to create citizens in the sense of the Constitution. They may make denizens, and extend their local rights to aliens, to Indians, or to free negroes; but these give no claim to federal rights, which belong only to full citizens. Congress have excluded this power, and by confining it exclusively to whites, they have given the clearest exposition of its latitude. The applicant for naturalization must also show a certain residence within some particular State, by which he becomes identified with it, and not, as the gentleman from Pennsylvania (Mr. Hemp- hill) has supposed, because of his residence within the United States generally. This exposition, too, was given by those who assisted in forming the Constitution, and therefore knew the scope of its provisions. It is is impossible to suppose that the power to naturalize blacks ever could have been given, for it was at once repugnant to the policy of the country, and the nature of our institutions. It could never have been intended to authorize the naturalization of a class of people who were already a burden upon the nation, and who could not, by any possibility, assimilate with our society. In the execution of the other powers vested in the General Government, Congress equally recognised the disabilities of this class of persons ; they excluded them from the militia of the States, and prohibited their employment as drivers of stages

carrying the mail. Each of these is wholly inconsistent with the rights of citizenship, especially the former, since the right of bearing arms is the highest privilege of the citizen. We have been informed, however, that black men served in the army during the late war and received bounty land. I know not how this fact may be, but be it as it may, it proves nothing in the argument. Since, if they were not citizens independent of this, their services in the army and their title to land could not make them so. Congress may sell land to aliens, but the purchase of land is not equivalent to naturalization, and would not authorize the purchaser to settle in a State in violation of its laws. The fact that protections have been issued to free negroes from the custom-houses, which has also been mentioned, is not more important. The protection is evidence rather of birth and the claim of the country granting it, than of peculiar rights of citizenship, and is designed to exempt the party from the claim of a foreign Power. It would be given to an Indian, or even to a slave who might be employed in our maritime service, and who, though not citizens within the meaning of our Constitution, would, nevertheless, be entitled to our protection whilst engaged in our service.

Recurring again to the nature of the provision in the Constitution, I beg leave to ask, if any instance can be named in which the free negroes and mulattoes have ever been permitted to claim federal rights, or in which the provision has altered or controlled the local authorities over that class of the people ? I venture to assert there is none. On the contrary, the States have ever since continued to treat them in all respects as the objects of their municipal power, wholly independent of any federal control, as they did before the Union was formed.

In Connecticut, Delaware, Maryland, Virginia, South Carolina, Georgia, Louisiana, Kentucky, Ohio, Mississippi, Indiana, Illinois, and Alabama, these people are excluded from the right of suffrage, and many civil privileges, to which, in common with aliens, they would have been entitled, but for the municipal regulations. In Pennsylvania they cannot be jurors, their abstract right of voting is illuded, and I have heard it stated that they are not permitted to be educated in public schools with the whites, and are prohibited from keeping public houses, regulations applied to the emigrant negro in common with the native.

Delaware, Maryland, Virginia, South Carolina, Georgia, Ohio, and Illinois, have each passed laws similar to that proposed to be enacted in Missouri. In Delaware, Maryland, Ohio, and Illinois, the laws have been passed since the adoption of the Constitution of the United States. The constitutions of Kentucky, Ohio, Mississippi, Indiana, Illinois, Louisiana, and Alabama, containing these discriminations incorporated in their fundamental policy, have been before Congress, and received their sanction.

In no State in the Union is there any discrimination between the native and emigrant negro. In all of these States the laws have been executed, and, in many, have passed under judicial cognizance, and in none has the right to pass them ever been questioned.

I do not refer to these examples to constitute right out of wrong, but to show the practical exposition which this clause in the Constitution has uniformly received, at all times, and under all circumstances. I ask, sir, if there can possibly be a better or sounder interpretation of the principles of our Constitution than that which has been contemporaneous with the Government, developed by its founders, and practised and acquiesced in by the whole nation from the very foundation of the Government? Sir, I hold that it would be conclusive before any tribunal who could be called upon to adjudge the case. But the doctrine now, for the first time, advocated, and by gentlemen who certainly do not understand our Constitution better than those by whom it was made, and acting under feelings of no ordinary character, denounces all this, and unsettles the established usage and laws of more than half of the States in the Union! Why does Connecticut, in her constitution, made but the other day, prohibit blacks, without distinction, from voting, if the free negroes of New York or Massachusetts may go there and claim all the immunities of citizens, of which the right of suffrage is one? Sir, I desire to be pointed to the State who will consent, upon the arrival of any number of these people from another State, to renounce a course of policy intimately connected with her safety, obliterate from her constitution the feature she most values, and place them upon an equal footing with her white population? In Delaware, we exclude them from voting, they cannot serve on juries, they cannot be witnesses against whites; we have found this policy necessary for our safety; it is rooted in the feelings of the great mass of our population, and in the nature of our institutions, civil and political, and, for one, I will never consent to relinquish it.

Have gentlemen contemplated the consequences that are to flow from the establishment of this doctrine, and are they prepared to brave them? Do they reflect upon the degraded condition in which the state of society has placed these people, and are they willing suddenly to elevate them to the enjoyment of equal civil and political rights? When following in the train of some political zealot, they may become the instruments of the worst ambition. But, sir, will these people wait for the incitement of others? Will they not claim for themselves equal political immunities, by which, however unwilling you may be to give them civil and social privileges, they will wrest them from you. Sir, if the Constitution of the Union ever meant to lead to such consequences, it contains within itself the germ of its own dissolution.

But, Mr. Speaker, one of the gentlemen from Pennsylvania (Mr. SERGEANT) disavows the doctrine in this extent; he claims, indeed, for these people only the humble privilege of setting their feet on the soil. He seems to admit, that after the free negro is in the State, he must be subject to her discriminating policy. In this admission, the gentleman surrenders the whole argument, and

betrays the poverty of his case. I have shown you, sir, that the right to emigrate is an incident, and not the principal immunity, and in seeking this privilege, humble as he denominates it, he cannot have it until he establishes his claim to all others. He only can claim to emigrate who is entitled, when he does so, to all the privileges and immunities of a citizen—to those of which the gentleman admits the State may deprive him. Think you, sir, that the Constitution gave the naked right of emigration to be fruitful only of harm? But, if the gentleman from Pennsylvania claims only this humble privilege, is he sure that they for whom he asserts it will be equally modest? Sir, the doctrine once established by the National Legislature, it will be impossible to limit its progress; and the honorable gentleman could not offer a stronger proof of the fallacy of his argument than that, when carried to its legitimate extent; nay, to the only sound basis on which it can rest, if at all, it conducts him to a precipice from which he is obliged to retreat in dismay!

But, Mr. Speaker, if this privilege of setting one's foot on the soil be the only one claimed, it is, indeed, an humble, nay, a miserable one! The privilege of going to a State to be degraded and disfranchised; to be stripped of every civil and political immunity! Who does not see that it puts it into the power of a State to convert into an injury that which was intended for a benefit? If, after these free negroes and mulattoes go to Missouri, the local authorities can render them subordinate to the whites, if they can rightfully exclude them from a participation in all civil and political immunities; and if, in doing so, she indirectly accomplishes the object of her present constitution, consults her own necessities, and imitates the example of her sister States, for what is all this struggle; for what is the Union now shaken to its centre? I ask, again, sir, if such were the privileges and immunities contemplated by the Constitution, or if such a race were ever included within its provisions? How many would go to Missouri upon such terms? How many, I ask, would go there, upon any terms, from those States in which alone it is pretended they can be citizens? And for what and for whom, then, are we contending?

Why shall we force Missouri to adopt a policy which the other States will not practice or acknowledge? Nay, why force upon her an evil which every other State is aiming to shake off? Why compel her to receive a population which cannot assimilate with her citizens; which retard the growth and prosperity of her empire; which are dangerous to her peace, and quiet, and safety, and upon which she must heap odious and continued disabilities, as the lesser evil? It is at most a contest about an abstract right, which can lead to no practical result; for, if the objectionable clause were expunged, the power of the State would remain, and might be exercised in legislative provisions, wholly beyond our control.

Is there any thing, then, sir, in this objection worth the consequences we are hazarding? To speak of nothing more, is it worth the feelings and excitement to which it is likely to give rise here, over the Union, and in Missouri? I fear no violence in Missouri, and if any should exist, I trust it would carry with it its own remedy. But, sir, I fear the weakening of public confidence more than any thing else, by the frequent jarrings and irritation to which this fatal question is likely to expose us. The confidence of the people of this country in the justice and magnanimity of the General Government, as well as in its protection, is the great rock of the Union, and with it must all the foundations of its strength be swept away. I look, also, sir, to the confidence which the people of Missouri should have in the justice of the National Government. Sir, those people must, at some time, and at no distant day, be admitted into this Union. They cannot be kept out, (for I will not yet believe that the present objection is but a pretext, and that when that is removed some new obstacle will be interposed:) and is it not important, sir, that these people should enter the Union, confiding in your justice, and without the remembrance of injury? If it be, of one thing I am certain—that such a temper will not be produced, nor will the public tranquillity be promoted by the fruitless attempt to force the recognition of technical, abstract notions against the uniform sense and practice of the whole community.

When Mr. McLANE had taken his seat—

Mr. MALLARY, of Vermont, observed, that he was conscious of his small claims to the indulgence of the House, while he presented his views on the subject which engaged its attention. He trusted, however, some excuse would be found in the interesting character of the question to be decided.

The measure proposed is calculated to effect the privileges of a part of the people of that section of the Union to which I belong, said Mr. M., and particularly of the State of which I am a Representative. I feel myself under the highest obligation to assert, feebly as it may be, the rights and privileges of those whom the institutions of other States, as well as my own, declare to be their citizens. Such as they recognise as deserving their protecting care, I hope I shall be ever ready and willing to defend.

It has been declared by some one, on the floor of this House, that Missouri was an independent State when she declared it expedient to form a constitution and government. By others it is maintained that she was a State when her convention adopted the constitution which has been presented to us for acceptance. The authority for this is found, it is said, in the first section of the law of the last session of Congress.

The first section declares, that the inhabitants of that portion of Missouri Territory, intended to be formed into a State, are authorized to form for themselves a constitution and State government; and said State, when formed, shall be admitted into the Union. Let us inquire what authority is here conveyed to the people of Missouri, and whether it has been obeyed. By this section the inhabitants of the territory may form a constitution; but they have no power to transfer this authority to others. Nor by this section are any conditions or restrictions required. Did the constitution of

Missouri contain no restriction on the sovereign powers of a State? Had its framers refused to secure to the Union its rights to the public lands? would they have found a justification in the section alluded to? Sir, do you there find that Congress demanded of the Territory of Missouri to provide, in her constitution, that the Mississippi and the navigable waters leading into the same, should be common highways, and forever free to the citizens of the United States? And did not her constitution contain such conditions, would this House hesitate a single moment to reject it? I am sure it would not find a single advocate for acceptance. But if Missouri could rely on the first section of that law, all that a sovereign State could claim under the Constitution of the United States, she would have demanded. Congress must have been silent.

Hence, sir, the necessity of recurring to the whole of the law of the last session, and ascertain what are its different provisions. The first section might be considered as a general power, modified by the subsequent requirements of the same law. The whole must be considered as operating together.

The third section declares the qualifications of the inhabitants, who may choose representatives to the convention of Missouri. Those only, whom the law designated, were allowed the right of suffrage. All of the inhabitants were not allowed that privilege. The general right was restricted.

The fourth section prescribes the power of the convention. The convention could determine the question, whether it was expedient to form a constitution. If it decided that it was expedient, the act declared that "the convention shall be, ' and hereby is, authorized to form a constitution ' and State government—provided that the same, ' whenever formed, shall be republican, and not ' repugnant to the Constitution of the United ' States."

The convention of Missouri, elected pursuant to the third article of the act referred to, proceeded, under the fourth, and adopted the constitution now on your table. Can it be pretended, with a shadow of plausibility, that the convention may accept of what conditions they please and reject such as they dislike? Shall the people of Missouri take all the privileges and advantages to themselves, and trample under foot whatever may be of value to the nation?

Thus, sir, I have endeavored to present the authority given to the people of Missouri to form a constitution. This is clearly and expressly defined. It is under the unqualified condition that whatever constitution they did form, it should be republican, and not repugnant to the Constitution of the United States. The declaration of Congress was explicit and decided to the people of Missouri, that if they chose to form such a constitution, they had the power; if they refused to comply, Congress must be absolved from every offer which had been made. If they have failed to fulfil those requirements which were demanded by the sovereign power of this Union, their acts can have no binding obligation. Their constitution is like that of any other people, formed without knowledge or consent of Congress, and entitled to no more indulgence.

It has been maintained on the floor of this House, that Missouri, at the time her convention declared it expedient to form a government, became an independent State. It seems to me, sir, that a moment's reflection will carry conviction to the mind, that this is unconditionally incorrect. I ask, what would have been the condition of Missouri, if the convention, after having decided that it was expedient to form a constitution, should have dissolved without forming one? Would it still remain a State? It may, without hesitation, be asserted, that she would not possess a single feature of a State which belongs to the Union.

Having thus seen the rights and powers conferred by Congress on Missouri; having seen that her privilege depended on the condition, among others, that her constitution should not be repugnant to that of the United States; we have now to ascertain whether her convention has violated that condition.

Is the constitution of Missouri repugnant to the Constitution of the United States?

By the twenty-sixth section of the constitution now offered for our acceptance, it is declared that " it shall be the duty of the General Assembly of ' Missouri, as soon as may be, to pass such laws, ' as may be necessary to prevent free negroes and ' mulattoes from coming to, and settling in, this ' State, under *any pretext whatsoever.*" Language, clear, precise, and energetic. It almost seems that it was feared the assembly might be disposed to relax the severity of that inexorable clause. But to prevent the possibility of disobedience, we find, not the common declaration of duty to the assembly, but a rigid admonition, not to disobey under any "*pretext whatsoever.*"

The Constitution of the United States declares that " the citizens of each State shall be entitled to all privileges and immunities of citizens in the several States."

Are negroes and mulattoes the citizens of any State. If so, it is clear, that the language which has been repeated from the constitution of Missouri, is a glaring and offending violation of the Constitution of the United States.

An honorable member from Virginia, (Mr. Archer,) has very gallantly avowed himself the champion of State rights. I consider, with him, that it should constitute a crime of the darkest hue to abandon them; but, at the same time, it is a duty of the highest order to preserve from violation those which belong to the Union. Those rights which have not been surrendered by the several States to the General Government still remain in their power. Among these, the right of a State to declare who of its own inhabitants may be its citizens still remains unimpaired. It was never given up; it has been perpetually exercised by every State, as one of its most valuable prerogatives.

We have been asked, if other States are allowed to declare who may be their citizens, shall not Missouri be indulged in the same power? She would be entitled to equal privileges, but no more. The people of that territory may make citizens of whom they please, among themselves. For one, I have little disposition to interfere. But, when they attempt to disfranchise those, who have been made the citizens of other States, it is a matter of very different import. This privilege, instead of reducing Missouri to a state " of pupilage," would elevate her to the rank of mistress of the Union. The other States must then bow in submission to her superior power. Sir, no State in the Union would presume to deprive the citizens of Missouri of their rights, nor will they with composure allow her a prerogative which they disavow for themselves.

A citizen has been defined by a member from Virginia, (Mr. Barbour,) to be a person who enjoys all the civil rights and privileges which others possess under the same circumstances, belonging to the same community, unless such rights have been forfeited by such person, by some cause existing in himself. Whether the definition is correct or not, it will, I am confident, lead to a conclusion directly the reverse to that which has been drawn by the honorable gentleman who gave it. It admits, that there are different circumstances under which the people of the Union are found. It would be morally and politically impossible that all persons in a State could be found under the same circumstances. Those will be natural or created by the civil and political institutions of society. Yet, it seems to be agreed, that when we find a person, who enjoys all the rights and privileges which others enjoy, under similar circumstances, he is a citizen.

In many, perhaps in all, of the States a distinction is made, for many purposes, between freeholders and those who are not. One may serve as a juror, the other is excluded from that privilege, or right. The freeholder in Vermont may have a certain kind of process without surety; the person who is not a freeholder is deprived of this privilege. No one, however, would presume to declare that a person who was not a freeholder could not be a citizen. Here the rule which has been mentioned would apply correctly. The person who was not a freeholder, but who possessed all the civil rights and privileges which others enjoyed, under the same circumstances, would still be a citizen. So, minority or advanced age would constitute other classes, and having equal rights with their several classes are equally citizens. If property or age are employed by the supreme power of a State to confer different rights on the white population, and yet the character of citizenship remains unchanged, why may not color be employed to distinguish another class? Color may be a circumstance which will designate a portion of population, and may be used constitutionally, as age or property. If it is so, it is a clear conclusion which will follow from the position assumed, that every colored person who is entitled to all the rights and privileges which others enjoy, under the same circumstances, must be a citizen.

A reference has been made to the laws of Massachusetts which prohibit a black man from marrying a white woman. It is said that by the operation of this law he is deprived of a civil right, which renders him unequal to others, and deprives him of citizenship. Had not this doctrine been advanced by those whose talents command respect, it would never require refutation. It may be proper to pursue this principle to its necessary conclusion. It will not be denied that the female part of society are citizens of the several States to which they belong. They have civil rights and privileges, and as citizens can demand the protection and support of Government. But the black man cannot marry a woman of a different color, therefore *he* is not a citizen, because he is deprived of a right which a white man possesses. The white woman cannot marry a man of a different color—by the same rule, which the gentleman from Virginia (Mr. BARBOUR) has laid down, *she* cannot be a citizen, because she is deprived of a right which a colored woman enjoys. The operation of the law must be reciprocal, and if one class has lost its rights as citizens, the other has also.

It is also said that the negro and mulatto are not enrolled in the militia, and compelled to perform military service. In some States, perhaps in all, they may be exempt. So are those over and under the age prescribed by the laws. Is the youth of sixteen and the man of fifty deprived of the character of citizens because others are called upon to perform more arduous duties than themselves? If this is correct, all who have been excused from these duties are most shamefully degraded. The white and black man must share one common fate.

Thus, sir, I have endeavored to prove that the position which has been assumed will lead to the inevitable conclusion, that negroes and mulattoes, who, in any State, can demand the exercise of civil rights and privileges in common with that class to which they belong, are entitled to the character of citizens.

I concur with others who have addressed the House before me, that the term citizen cannot be defined by a single expression. The rights of citizens are different in different States, and are dependent on the several constitutions and laws which have been adopted. In the same State, different persons may be confined to different rights and yet all be citizens.

I will venture to assume a position, which I am confident none will deny. Not that it will embrace all who are entitled to the rights of citizens, but will be sufficiently comprehensive for the present discussion.

A person must be considered a citizen, who, by the fundamental laws of a State, is invested with political rights. These are the rights which communicate life and give activity to a government itself. In all the States of the Union, these rights are conferred on those only who have bound themselves to the common interest and become pledged to promote the general welfare; who have been incorporated into the great family of the people, and have made one common cause in the pursuit of the great objects of human government.

It would be absurd, sir, to say, that you will allow the enjoyment of the highest prerogatives to a person while he is yet an alien and a stranger; that you will permit a man to exercise those powers on which your Government must depend, and still not be a citizen. What State in the Union permits, for instance, the right of suffrage, but to such as are its citizens? What constitution declares a person eligible to its highest honors, who is deprived of the character of a citizen? It would be fatal to the existence of any government to admit the people of other countries to control its operations, until they had been bound by some strong, indissoluble tie to the general welfare.

In the position which I have assumed, I am well supported by the assertion of the honorable gentleman from Virginia (Mr. SMYTH.) I understood him distinctly to maintain "that a citizen might be defined to be one who is entitled to political rights."

Permit me, sir, to examine whether any negro or mulatto has political rights in any State; whether there is a constitution which decrees to such person all the privileges of citizens. I should never have troubled the House with many observations on this point, had it not been so often asserted, in the most decisive language, that negroes or mulattoes, in every State in the Union, were deprived of all the essential rights of citizens. I should have supposed the most superficial examination of the constitutions of the several States would have proved, that such ideas were utterly destitute of foundation. But they have been advanced on the floor of this House, with such confidence, that I hope I shall be indulged in attempting to correct the error.

Sir, I would call the attention of the House to the constitution of Vermont. There, gentlemen will find an unequivocal declaration " that all men ' are born equally free and independent; that no ' male person, born in this country, or brought from ' over sea, ought to be holden, by law, to serve any ' person as a servant, slave, or apprentice, after he ' arrives at the age of twenty-one years; nor fe- ' male, in like manner, after she arrives at the age ' of eighteen years." It does not declare that all men except negroes and mulattoes "are born equally free and independent;" it does not declare, Mr. Speaker, that no person except negroes and mulattoes shall be holden to servitude. The language is broad and comprehensive as the race of man. And, I believe that those unfortunate beings, even where they are held in a state of the deepest degradation, are still considered as belonging to the human family.

Sir, lest this may be called an unmeaning manifesto of the rights of man, calculated for a splendid show of republicanism, but intended to confer no substantial benefits, I will again refer to that instrument. " The declaration of the political rights ' and privileges of the inhabitants of this State is ' hereby declared to be a part of the constitution of ' this Commonwealth, and ought not to be violated ' on any pretence whatsoever." Negroes and mulattoes, sir, here find protection under this firm, humane and liberal provision; to which the people of Vermont look with the proudest satisfaction, as their common safeguard.

Again, sir, it is declared "that every man of the full age of twenty-one years, having resided in this State for the space of one year next before the election of representatives, and is of a peaceable or quiet behaviour, and will take the following oath, [the oath of allegiance to the State] shall be entitled to all the privileges of a freeman of this State." This does not say, every man, except negroes and mulattoes. It embraces all of every color, whether "born in this country or brought from over sea ;" and permit me to say that the rights of a freeman confer the highest distinction that can be given to an inhabitant of that State ; they imply the perfection of all the civil and political privileges and immunities that can be enjoyed by man in the society of his fellow men. All the security which the Constitution gives to the most distinguished citizen for the protection of his life and reputation, is afforded to every freeman, whatever may be his circumstances or color. The spirit of the Constitution watches with equal eye over the rights and privileges, civil and political, of the negro and mulatto, and would chastise the least attempt to offer violation.

Here, sir, I might rest in the fullest confidence, that the position which has been assumed was fully supported. But the assertion has been so often and so emphatically made, that those people who are dreaded by the convention of Missouri are not the citizens of any State, a reference must be made to the constitutions of New Hampshire, Massachusetts, and New York. Not one withholds its political and civil rights, but confers them with indiscriminate liberality, without distinction of color. The light or shade of a countenance, which indicates an alliance with the great family of man, confers no exclusive privileges on the possessors, nor do they blot from a political charter the immunities of citizens. In those States you may see that class, who are prescribed by the constitution of Missouri, in the full enjoyment of those privileges which are the distinguishing prerogatives of freemen.

Sir, I will call the attention of gentlemen to some of the many attempts that have been made to remove the objections which may exist against the offered constitution. It is said that the objectionable clause may be construed so as to operate on none who are the citizens of a State. It is also contended that we should presume the people of Missouri would carry it into execution in a manner compatible with the Constitution of the United States. Sir, there can be nothing left to such a presumption. If the object was not to exclude citizens as well as others, why did the convention not condescend to make some exception? Not only did they use the language of imperative authority, but forbid a deviation for "any pretext whatsoever." I do not pretend to say that the framers of that constitution supposed they adopted provisions incompatible with the supreme law of the land. Such a conclusion would be a charge of deliberate violation. When they find themselves supported on the floor of this House by gentlemen distinguished for talents and a knowledge of our political institutions, can we suppose they will readily change their opinion? It will tend to confirmation, and we may presume the slave-holding policy will demand its execution with the most energetic determination.

It has been maintained in debate that this clause is not a violation of the Constitution of the United States; that the constitution of Missouri does not contain a prohibition in itself, but requires the Assembly to pass such laws as will accomplish the object desired. We are called upon to wait, and if such laws should be passed, their binding power may be tried. The force of this distinction has escaped my discernment. Can it be said, with propriety, that an act performed is illegal, and the authority by which it is done unimpeachable? Is it correct for a constitution to direct an Assembly, dependent on its power, to pass a law which, from the first moment of its existence, would be repugnant to the Constitution of the United States? You might as well command your servant to assassinate your neighbor, and have the illegality of your command depend upon its execution.

But, allowing the constitution of Missouri is not a violation of that of the United States; that the direction to the Assembly to perform what is declared to be their duty, is no offence, it would not diminish the objection. When Government have the power, it is bound to prevent an outrage on its dignity, as it is to punish one after it is committed. You may as well pull down the edifice yourself as to give the power to others.

Sir, we have been told that the several States, among other legitimate powers, may exercise such as are deemed necessary for their own defence and safety; that they may exclude from their jurisdiction those objects which are in themselves odious and pernicious. It is said, upon this principle, States have the power, and often exercise it, in the establishment of those quarantine regulations by which the citizens of other States are excluded, to prevent plague and pestilence.

If these principles be established, and are applicable to the question now to be decided by the House, consider, sir, the consequences which must inevitably follow. Every object which the people of a State may consider odious and pernicious may be excluded by their own authority. If they are uncontrolled by any rule but their own views of propriety or interest, the exercise of that authority may be unbounded as the objects of their displeasure may be numerous. It will follow, that the sovereign power of Missouri may exclude free negroes and mulattoes, because they are considered odious and pernicious. They may be considered dangerous as "plague and pestilence," and placed under eternal "quarantine." If Missouri can exercise this power against that class of citizens, she can extend it to every other. In the estimation of her people, the white citizens of the non-slaveholding States may be both pernicious and odious, and a prohibitory mandate be issued to exclude them from her soil.

Fatal, indeed, must this doctrine be to the rights of citizens. Establish the principle that every State may exclude the object which it happens to dislike, and the Constitution is annihilated. We

opinions so variant from ours. In Massachusetts, sir, there are among them those who possess all the virtues which are deemed estimable in civil and social life. They have their public teachers of religion and morality, their schools and other institutions; on anniversaries which they consider interesting to them they have their public processions; in all which they conduct themselves with order and decorum. Do we ask for them any enlargement or extension of their rights? No, sir, we ask only that, in a disposition to accommodate Missouri, their avowed rights and privileges be not taken from them.

If their number be small, and they are feebly represented, we to whom they are known are proportionably bound to protect them. But their defence is not founded on their numbers; it rests on the immutable principles of justice. If there be only one family, or a solitary individual, who has rights guarantied to him by the Constitution, whatever may be his color or complexion, it is not in the power nor can it be in the inclination of Congress to deprive him of them; and I trust, sir, that the decision on this occasion will show that we will extend good faith even to the blacks.

It has been said that an adoption on the part of Congress of the constitution of Missouri gives no additional force to the clause which we think we have shown to be unconstitutional, and that Missouri would have the right to pass the law without the injunction in her constitution; and, further, that her Legislature may or may not exercise the power given to them by her constitution; and, if she should pass an unconstitutional law, a remedy may be had by an appeal to the Judiciary.

Can language be stronger than that made use of in her constitution? "It shall be the duty of the Legislature to pass the law," &c. The Legislature, under that clause, must and will pass the law. The sanction of Congress will give additional force to its injunction, and the black citizen will then be shut out from the State. Where, then, is he to find his remedy?

That Missouri may pass such a law after her admission into the Union is conceded. Such law will not, in that case, be sanctioned by Congress. And, sir, I make a wide distinction between a law passed by a State making a part of the Union, and a provision in the constitution of a State in process of admission into the Union, and presented to Congress for approbation. The right of Congress to admit States into the Union has appeared to me to be in the nature of a sovereign power, over which no co-ordinate branch of the Government can have control; and, disguise it as we may, the admission of Missouri, with this article in her constitution, sanctions that article, and virtually at least declares it not to be repugnant to the Constitution of the United States. To those who believe it to be unconstitutional it is no satisfaction to be told that the Judiciary will correct their error. They consider it their duty to make a right decision, presuming that there will be no appeal.

Mr. Speaker, no one can address you who is more sensible than I am that this Government is the result of compromise; of a healing, heavenly, conciliating spirit, which the genius of the immortal Washington was perhaps alone capable of rallying round him; nor can any one be more sensible of the importance of cherishing these dispositions, more especially in cases where the rights of States, whether already admitted, or hereafter to be admitted into the Union, are concerned. Let us be careful that this indulgent disposition be not extended too far. Sir, this has been considered a sectional question. I must deny the position. Maine is as deeply interested in it as Missouri. In every question touching the Constitution every State in the Union has an equal, a common interest; and, let me add, however we may differ in opinion or in construction, we are bound by a common interest to extend to each other the belief that there is a common respect and an equal desire to obey its injunctions. Were this even a doubtful case, it ought to be decided in favor of common rights. Were it possible that, in the wish to accommodate Missouri, the Constitution should be made to bend in her favor, the tree is in danger, and, if a single limb be broken, Missouri is no longer safe in what would be guarantied to her. In less than twelve months the inclination may be in a different direction, and she may lose more than she would have gained.

Among the different arguments which have been made use of, I have regretted that allusions have been had to consequences which may result from a negative on the resolution under consideration. Sir, perfectly sensible of the delicate situation in which Missouri will be placed, I exclude from my own mind all considerations of this kind, from a conviction that no consequences can or will arise which ought to be compared, or put in competition, with those resulting necessarily from a violation of the compact which binds us together as a nation.

When Mr. E. had concluded—

The Committee rose, on the motion of Mr. Beecher, of Ohio, (some other gentlemen also rising to obtain the floor,) and the House adjourned.

WEDNESDAY, December 13.

Another member, to wit: from North Carolina, Thomas Settle, appeared, and took his seat.

Mr. Sergeant presented a memorial of the President and Directors of the Bank of the United States, on the part of the stockholders of the said bank, praying for an amendment in that part of the charter of said bank which provides that no director, except the president, shall be eligible for more than three years in four; that provision may be made for the punishment of such officers of the bank as may be guilty of fraud, peculation, or violation of the trust committed to them; that authority may be vested in the said president and directors, to employ persons to sign and countersign the notes of the bank; and that the bills or notes originally made payable, or which shall have become payable on demand, shall of right be received and payable only at the bank or branch of the bank, at which the same purports to be payable; which memorial was referred to a select committee, and Messrs. SERGEANT, WHITMAN, TYLER, GORHAM, and HARDIN, were appointed the said committee.

Mr. BARBOUR presented a memorial of the merchants, agriculturists, and other inhabitants of the town of Fredericksburg, and the adjacent county, in the State of Virginia, praying that the commerce of the country may not be fettered or impeded by any increase of the tariff of duties on imports, for the purpose of affording further protection to the manufacturing interest of the country.

Mr. JONES, of Virginia, presented a memorial of the merchants and other inhabitants of the town of Petersburg, in that State, in opposition to any change in the boundaries of the collection district of Petersburg.—The said memorials were referred to the Committee on Commerce.

Mr. JONES also presented a petition of the delegates of the United Agricultural Societies of Prince George, Sussex, Surry, Petersburg, Brunswick, Dinwiddie, and Isle of Wight, in the State of Virginia, praying that the tariff of duties on imports may not be increased for the purpose of affording further protection to the manufacturing interests of the country; which petition was referred to the Committee on Agriculture.

Mr. BREVARD presented sundry resolutions adopted at a numerous and respectable meeting of the inhabitants of Kershaw district, held at Camden, in the State of South Carolina, on the 4th of November last, expressive of their disapprobation of any increase of the tariff of duties on imports.

Mr. WHITMAN presented a memorial from a convention of delegates assembled from the agricultural and commercial sections of the State of Maine, in relation to the tariff proposed at the last session of Congress, and praying that no such measure may be adopted at the present session.— The said resolutions and memorial were referred to the Committee on Manufactures.

The bills from the Senate for the relief of John Holmes, of Alabama, and for the relief of Morgan Brown, were twice read and considered.

The resolution from the Senate, "declaring the admission of the State of Missouri into the Union," was read the first time, and ordered to lie on the table.

On motion of Mr. RICH, the House proceeded to consider the proposition submitted by him yesterday, to amend the standing rules and orders of the House; and the said proposition being again read, was agreed to by the House.

Mr. TRACY submitted the following resolution, which was read, and ordered to lie on the table one day for consideration, viz:

Resolved, That the Secretary of War be directed to lay before this House a list of all the lands and buildings which have been purchased by the United States for military purposes, from the 1st day of July, 1812, to the present time; the cost of each site, and of the buildings, as far as may be practicable; together with the estimated present value; also indicating those which, in the judgment of the Secretary, may be sold without injury to the public service.

OFFICES OF THE CUSTOMS.

The SPEAKER laid before the House the following letter from the Secretary of the Treasury, transmitting, in obedience to a resolution of the House of Representatives of the 15th of May, 1820, a list of the offices of the customs, which may be abolished without detriment to the public interest; which was referred to the Committee on Commerce.

TREASURY DEPARTMENT, *Dec.* 9, 1820.

SIR: In obedience to a resolution of the House of Representatives of the 15th of May, 1820, directing the Secretary of the Treasury "to report to the House, at the next session of Congress, such offices of the customs as may be properly suppressed, on account of their inutility, or from any other cause," I have the honor to report a list of offices which it is believed may be abolished without detriment to the public interest.

The information upon which this report is founded, was submitted to the Senate of the United States on the 2d day of December, 1818, with the list hereto annexed, in conformity with a resolution of that honorable House, and may be referred to No. 27 of the reports of the second session of the fifteenth Congress.

In the collection of the revenue persons are employed to weigh, measure, gauge, and mark, all merchandise imported into the United States susceptible of these different operations, the fees for which are defined by law, and form a large item in the expenses of collection.

It is ascertained that for these services there was paid during the year 1819 the sum of $116,426 71. It is also ascertained that, in one of the principal ports, these services are performed exclusively by the inspectors, who receive three dollars a day throughout the year, for their services as inspectors. The law regulating the compensation of the inspectors of the customs, authorizes the allowance of three dollars a day for the days that they are actually employed. But they cannot be considered as actually employed as inspectors every day in the year, when during the same time they are employed as weighers, measurers, gaugers, and markers, and actually receive for such services about $2,400 a year.

In several of the ports, the inspectors have voluntarily offered to perform, without compensation, such services. It is confidently believed that the inspectors employed in the several districts of the United States, at this time, are entirely competent to discharge these duties, in addition to those now required of them. The abolition of the fees for weighing, measuring, gauging, and marking, will reduce the expenses of collection at least $100,000 a year, whilst the abolition of the offices presented in the list annexed to this report will not reduce it to more than about $5,000. It is, therefore, respectfully submitted, that it is expedient to repeal so much of the second section of the act to establish the compensation of the officers employed in the collection of the duties on imports and tonnage, and for other purposes, passed March the 2d, 1799; and of all other acts which allow fees for weighing, measuring, gauging, and marking of merchandise or packages, imported into the United States, and that these services be rendered by the inspectors of the customs.

I remain, with respect, &c.

WM. H. CRAWFORD.

The Hon. J. W. TAYLOR,
Speaker House of Representatives.

CONSTITUTION OF MISSOURI.

The House then resumed the consideration of the resolution declaring the admission of the State of Missouri into the Union.

Mr. Beecher, of Ohio, delivered, at considerable length, his sentiments, in opposition to the passage of the resolution.

Mr. Cook, of Illinois, said, after the full discussion which this subject had already received, he felt much reluctance in asking the attention of the House to a single additional remark from him; and were it not for the peculiar situation in which he found himself placed, he should have been contented in giving a silent vote. He said he had fully given his constituents to understand that he should vote for the admission of Missouri. That he had given them so to understand, even previous to his re-election to a seat in the next Congress, and the result of that election had satisfied him that his vote would not be disapproved. He considered the faith of Congress pledged, by the act of the last session, to admit her, provided her constitution were made in conformity to the terms of this act, and when he had said he would vote for her admission, that declaration had always been made under the belief that such would be the case.

When Mr. C. arrived at Washington, he for the first time met the objection, which was now urged against her constitution, and perhaps under the influence of a strong anxiety for her admission, had examined the question, as he then thought, thoroughly, and for a considerable time saw no reason to change his determination. Under this conviction, produced by that examination, he had, as he hoped he always should do, fearlessly expressed his opinion in favor of her admission. He even now, notwithstanding his opinion was changed, freely declared that all his predilections were in favor of such a vote. Missouri, he said, was the near adjoining neighbor of Illinois, and notwithstanding an unhappy difference of opinion upon political subjects had created between their respective citizens a rancor and animosity, which he well knew the vote he was about to give would not in the least allay; a vote which he well knew many of his constituents would be greatly disappointed when they heard of; yet he should be glad to see her admitted and placed upon an equal footing with the State which he had the honor to represent.

Mr. C. said, it was because of his particular situation, and because there was a view of the subject which had weight with him, and which had not been taken in argument, that he ventured to beg the indulgence of the House for a single moment.

He was aware that the change his opinion had undergone, had called forth the charge of inconsistency and timidity from some, on both sides of the question. But such suggestions made no impression upon his mind. He felt shielded against the effects of all such unkind opinions and suggestions, by a consciousness of the rectitude of his own motives.

He said he considered the freedom of thought, and its fearless declaration, as the palladium of truth, and the impregnable bulwark of liberty. When reason was left free to combat error, the triumph of sound principles, he thought, could not long be doubtful.

Under the influence of these sentiments he had examined the subject for himself, and had satisfied his own mind of the incorrectness of his first opinion. And surely after the example set him by the distinguished chairman of the committee who reported this resolution, (Mr. Lowndes,) he hoped he might escape animadversion for acknowledging his error. He said that honorable gentleman had frankly and magnanimously acknowledged his error in reporting that preamble to the resolution then under discussion, which had been stricken out. An example of this kind he was by no means ashamed to imitate.

Mr. C. said, much argument had been employed on the opposite side, to prove that Missouri was now a State. In reply to which he had no hope of being able to advance stronger arguments than had already been urged, and particularly by the gentleman from Pennsylvania, (Mr. Sergeant,) and he was therefore willing to adopt them as the arguments upon which he predicated the converse of that proposition, that Missouri was not now a State, unless she were such *de facto*, and therefore entitled to none of the rights and immunities of a State of this Union.

In order to be a State of this Union, or to be entitled to become such, he considered it an indispensable prerequisite, on her part, to form a constitution in conformity to the principles of the Federal Constitution, and in conformity to the conditions presented by the act by virtue of which her constitution, upon its face, professed to have been formed.

That she had not framed such a constitution, he thought was fairly deducible from the arguments which he was about to employ. The Constitution of the United States, said he, gives to "Congress the power to dispose of, and make all needful rules and regulations respecting the territory or other property belonging to the United States." This, said Mr. C., is a general power, and in the exercise of this general power he apprehended Congress had a right to dispose of that territory to whomsoever they pleased. He said it had been admitted by gentlemen on both sides of this question, that free negroes and mulattoes were competent to hold real estate, and that they did hold it in almost, if not quite every State in the Union. They are therefore competent, he observed, under the admission of all parties, to purchase such estate from the United States. But the constitution of Missouri declares, "that it shall be the duty of 'the Legislature, as soon as may be, to pass such 'laws as may be necessary to prevent free negroes 'and mulattoes from coming to, and settling in 'that State, under any pretext whatsoever." A provision, said he, which, notwithstanding their competency to purchase, and the indisputable power of Congress to sell to them, clearly asserts a controlling power both over the rights of these individuals, and the paramount authority of Congress.

Sir, said he, every Congress is equal, and is therefore alike possessed of power to dispose of the territory of the United States, as may be thought expedient. One Congress cannot irrevocably declare that no subsequent Congress shall sell any portion of the public domain to free negroes or mulattoes; the attempt to do so, would be vain and nugatory. If Congress, then, cannot do this, can they, asked Mr. C., confer this power upon a subordinate Legislature? Surely not. It would be making the creature greater than the creator. And yet Missouri does virtually declare, by prohibiting their emigration thither, that hereafter the United States shall not sell any of the public domain within her borders to persons of that description. In doing this he thought Missouri had attempted more than Congress could do, and, he thought, had therefore violated the Federal Constitution. But, said Mr. C., there is another view of this question, which it may not be amiss to present.

The gentleman from Delaware (Mr. MCLANE) had contended that the Legislature of Missouri would have this power, even if their constitution did not expressly confer it. These people, said that gentleman, are not citizens, and may therefore be kept out. Now, if, because they are not citizens, they may be kept out, with equal reason at least may Indians, and all other aliens be also kept out. And yet, said he, we know the Government is in the constant habit of ceding to the Indians portions of the national domain, in exchange for portions of theirs. If the argument of the gentleman, therefore, proved any thing, it clearly proved too much. It is true, said Mr. C., that clause of the constitution does not give the Legislature this excluding power, in relation to Indians or aliens, but it gives a power which, if sanctioned, does by analogy sanction the doctrine of that gentleman; and, by denying the right of the Legislature to exercise this express power, we necessarily deny its right to exercise the implied.

For one, Mr. C. would be extremely glad if the State had this excluding power in relation to Indians. They are a troublesome population, and the State which he had the honor to represent might finally, for the want of such power, find herself encumbered by the settlement of Indian tribes within her borders; an event by no means desirable.

While upon this branch of the subject, Mr. C. hoped he would be pardoned for a moment's digression from the question immediately before the House. He said that the correctness of the authority which the treaty-making power had been heretofore exercising, in disposing of the territory of the United States by cession to the Indians, he thought, deserved a serious examination. He had been impressed with the idea, that the express delegation of the power to dispose of the territory of the United States to Congress, ought to exclude the idea of the existence of a similar power, and particularly by implication, in any other department of the Government. He said it was true, that the unfixed lines of, and disputed title to, any portion of territory, could only be settled by treaty;

and, in the case of war, where the cession of a portion of territory was made a *sine qua non* to the restoration of peace; this being a case of necessity, he supposed it would also be competent for the treaty-making power to make the demanded cession. But, when the indisputable title was vested in the United States, and no such necessity existed, he thought it worthy of the profoundest inquiry to determine what were the limits of the treaty-making power upon the subject.

Mr. C. said, there was another view of that clause of the Missouri constitution, under which it seemed still more obviously in violation of the Federal Constitution. Congress, he said, by virtue of the general power which it possessed to dispose of the territory of the United States, for the purpose of obtaining the military services of persons, as well of this as of every other description, had offered them a land bounty, to many of whom, and embracing free negroes and mulattoes, patents had already been issued for lands in Missouri. He said persons of this description, to his own knowledge, had purchased land in Illinois, and he had no doubt they had also in Missouri. Whether they had or not, however, did not vary the case—the principle was the same. In the soldier as well as the purchaser, therefore, he, Mr. C., begged leave to say, the Government of the United States vested a *fee simple* estate in those lands. The Government, he said, made no other description of title. This title he considered to consist of the possession, the right of possession, and the right of property; and he thought, when he asserted that the Government had guarantied all these features of the right which it vested, both to the soldier and the purchaser, that no honorable member would hazard a controversion of that assertion. Under this guarantee he considered the United States incompetent, unless for public purposes, and then only by paying a fair equivalent therefor, to deprive them of this property; and yet Missouri, a subordinate Legislature, if her constitution be allowed to operate, does virtually take it away, without paying any equivalent whatever; for, if a person be not allowed to enjoy the possession of his property, he is virtually deprived of it.

But, said he, the United States are bound both to the soldier and the purchaser to protect him in the enjoyment of his property; it constitutes, by every principle of law and reason, a part of the original contract. The Government, for this obligation, has received a full consideration, and yet Missouri, in direct violation of that provision of the Federal Constitution which forbids any State to pass any "ex post facto law, or law impairing the obligation of contracts" has virtually provided that those contracts which have been completed by the emanation of patents shall, by the ex post facto operation of her constitution, be annulled, and the force of the contract be wholly impaired; and by its prospective operation as virtually impairs the obligation of those contracts, which are yet executory for the want of patents.

Mr. C. said he had, at the last session of Congress, when discussing the question of restriction, stated that new States, when admitted into the

647   HISTORY OF CONGRESS.   648

H. OF R.   *Admission of Missouri.*   DECEMBER, 1820.

Union, could not, under his view of the subject, come in, and be upon an equal footing, in their domestic aspect, with the original States. He then attempted to prove it, by showing that a proposition was made in the Federal Convention to ingraft this provision into the Constitution: "That new States, when admitted into this Union, shall be upon an equal footing with the original States." This provision, said Mr. C., partly for the reasons which he then urged, as well as for many others equally cogent, was rejected. One other of these reasons now presented itself, and was indeed the basis upon which all others rested. It was that, the full operation of which, he had endeavored to show the Missouri constitution attempted to arrest. It was, that the Federal Government had sovereign authority over the public soil within the confines of such new States. The old States were lords of their own soil, the new are not. In the domestic aspect, therefore, the old and new States are not, nor can they be, upon an equal footing. In their federal aspect, however, he admitted their perfect equality; he meant in the enjoyment of rights exclusively federal.

Mr. C. said it would at once be seen that the force of his objection did not connect itself with the great question of citizenship, but was an objection looking to other clauses of the Constitution. That those clauses were impugned by the clause in the Missouri constitution to which he had referred, was apparent at least to his mind, and he could not therefore vote for the resolution now under consideration.

But, he said, it had been proposed to refer this question to the Judiciary. The propriety of that proposition he should not attempt to discuss.

He, however, considered it a question growing out of the exercise of a power vested exclusively in Congress—the power to admit new States; and was therefore a question which he thought Congress bound to determine. He was not over anxious to assume responsibility, but he certainly felt no disposition to shrink from that which he thought properly devolved upon him.

Mr. C. again repeated, that his feelings were in favor of admission; that both personal and political reasons combined to render it a desirable event; and were it consistent with his sense of the duty which he owed to the country and the Constitution to give such a vote upon the resolution under consideration, he was sure no member on that floor would do it with more pleasure. But, while he considered the Constitution the rock upon which our temple of liberty must stand, and having sworn to support it, he felt himself called upon to forego all such considerations, and defend it against infringement. Sir, said he, if we ever suffer our individual feelings and wishes to enter into our deliberations and discussions, so far as to govern our public conduct, those feelings and wishes, like the impereeptible rising of the tide, will finally overrun every principle of the Constitution, and we shall ultimately find ourselves floating at large upon the open sea of uncertainty, without a single landmark to guide us.

The momentary inconvenience even of the na-

tion, and much less of a small portion of it only, should not sanction the least possible violation of that instrument. The progress of despotism upon liberty, he said, was gradual, it kept pace with the loss of public morals. It would be so with encroachments upon the Constitution; they would be so gradual as hardly to be seen or felt, until it was pared down to a state of inefficiency inadequate to the purposes of its adoption; and then, and not till then, would the Government be dissolved. The line between the Federal and State Governments should be fixed, and encroachments upon either should be resisted in the bud. However anxious, therefore, he might be for the admission of Missouri, he could not, for one, consent to receive her with this clause in her constitution.

When Mr. COOK had concluded, Mr. LOWNDES, of South Carolina, addressed the Chair in substance as follows:

Mr. LOWNDES began by saying that he did not remember having ever before addressed the House twice on the same proposition. It was perhaps his duty, as chairman of the committee which had reported the resolution upon the table, to reply to the objections which had been made to their report. But he had another, though a personal, motive. The gentleman from Pennsylvania (Mr. SERGEANT) had peremptorily denied facts of which he had given the proof at the same time with the assertion; he had forgotten, and in consequence misquoted, the words of the resolution reported by the committee to which they both belonged, and from the beginning to the end of his speech had, with few exceptions, eluded every argument which he professed to answer.

The question on which they differed most essentially was that which regarded the effect and obligation of that law of the last session, by which the people of Missouri were authorized to form for themselves a constitution and State government. Mr. L. believed that under this law it was not left to our discretion to determine whether she should become a member of the Confederacy, but that upon her accepting the terms which were proposed in it, upon her engaging to fulfil the duties of a State, she had acquired its rights, and that Congress had become bound to take every measure which might be necessary for their recognition and exercise.

The gentleman from Pennsylvania had met one of the principles on which this proposition might be supposed to depend. He had denied that Congress had power to pass an act for the admission of a State, which should take effect from a future day.

The Constitution gives to Congress the power to admit States in the broadest terms. The high privileges which it is authorized to impart may commence instantly, and extend through all future time. When the convenience of a Territory required that it should become a member of the Union at a future day, what principle of the Constitution was opposed to this prospective admission? Congress may raise armies. Has any man ever suspected that this power could not be executed by giving a prospective and even a contingent authority? Congress may lay taxes. May they not be limited to take effect some time after the passage of the law? Congress may constitute inferior courts. Would such an act be void, because its operation was to commence from a future day? Void because it was not inconvenient and absurd? Run your eye along the whole list of powers which are given to the Federal Legislature, and you will find no countenance for the doctrine which would require that at the very moment when their will is pronounced, the object which they are empowered to effect, should be instantly executed. The power of making treaties, too, although given to another depository, is supposed to be pursued, although the convention with a foreign State may take effect from a future day. There is nothing plausible in the assertion which denies to Congress the power of admitting States, by an act which shall not go into operation for some time after its passage. The House would see in his subsequent observations the importance of determining whether Congress had the Constitutional right of admitting States by a prospective law. He need not say that this question of right was distinct from that of expediency.

Mr. L. conceived this to be the doctrine of the friends of the resolution, that when any people, subject to the authority of the United States, from the extent of their territory, their numbers, the habits and character of their society, seem capable of self-government, the control which Congress had reserved over their appointments and laws shall be withdrawn; they shall be authorized to form and administer their own constitution, and shall participate as an equal member of the Union, in all its privileges and powers. It is an act of emancipation. But the restraints as well as the advantages of the Federal Constitution are extended to them. What security, it is asked, do you take, that these restraints will be submitted to? We trust the people with their own constitution. We believe that Missouri, as we believe that Massachusetts and New York, will respect the obligation which the federal compact imposes, and if they shall inadvertently transgress its limitations, that they will submit to the judicial authority, which expounds and enforces alike their rights and duties. It is on this principle that we have hitherto acted in the admission of new States. It is the doctrine of the Constitution, and Mr. L. believed the only Republican doctrine. He trusted that the House would distinguish between suspicion and wisdom. The enemies of the resolution allow that the moment after the Senators and Representatives from Missouri shall have been permitted to take their seats, the constitution of Missouri may be altered, and that Congress will have no power to prevent it. What is the value of a security which lasts but for a month? If the first constitution of a new State must not contain even a doubtful provision, under penalty of disfranchisement, while succeeding forms of Government, though they may be changed annually, will be safe from examination, the consequence is plain. Every new State will frame a constitution for this review of inspection, such as shall contain no

clause to which Congress can object, and the adoption of those provisions, which are intended practically to direct the operations of the Government, will be postponed until our declaration that the State is admitted shall enable it to form a constitution without interference. Mr. L. said that the first constitution would be very short and plain; it would certainly contain no offensive feature, and hardly any feature at all; it might provide in three lines that there should be an Executive, a Legislature, a Judiciary, and that these should be elected by the people. A committee of this House would report that they could find nothing in the constitution to object to, and the gentleman from Pennsylvania would applaud their prudence in taking care not to extend the privileges of self-government to any portion of the people of this country, until they had given bond for their good behaviour.

In public or private life, he who parts with power or property, shows no wisdom in pretending still to regulate its disposition. It is prudent, as well as generous, to treat those who are about to become members of the Federal Union, with a frank and liberal confidence. Nothing can be more repugnant to the spirit of our institutions, or the practice of our Government, than a churlish and reluctant admission, which exacts security that it knows to be ineffectual, and employs the last moment of authority in proclaiming that it would willingly exert the power which it has engaged to abdicate. But he had gone a little further into this subject, (Mr. Lowndes said) than he had intended at this time. He thought that the House must admit, and as yet he contended for nothing more—that Congress has, under the Constitution, a right to admit States by a prospective law.

The gentleman from Pennsylvania (Mr. Sergeant) had said, peremptorily, that "Congress has never admitted a State by anticipation." Mr. L. observed, that when he had first spoken in support of the resolution before the Committee of the Whole, as he could not exactly know the character of the objections which would be opposed to it, he had endeavored rather to develope principles, than to apply them; and had referred to the evidence, by which material facts were established, without quoting, or even fully stating them. The gentleman from Pennsylvania had found it easy to elude his principles, and to deny his facts.

The acts by which Congress had admitted States, prospectively, were material to a just decision of the resolution, and Mr. Lowndes referred to them, with a higher view than that of proving the gentleman from Pennsylvania to be wrong. The House must bear with him while on this argument he found it necessary to quote the words of laws to which he had before referred.

The act admitting Kentucky into the Union, (*Laws of the U. S.*, vol. 2, p. 122,) in its first section, enacts and declares, that the district of Kentucky shall, upon the first day of June, 1792, be formed into a new State, &c., and its second section is in these words: "And be it further enacted and de-
' clared, that upon the aforesaid first day of June,
' 1792, the said new State, by the name and style of

651   HISTORY OF CONGRESS.   652

H. of R.   *Admission of Missouri.*   December, 1820.

' the State of Kentucky, shall be received and ad-
' mitted into the Union, as a new and entire mem-
' ber of the United States of America." The act
was passed on the 4th February, 1791. Congress
was not even in session in June, 1792. Kentucky
was admitted without any further act by Congress, in virtue of the law of 1791; and this law
of prospective admission has given her all the
rights of a State, or she has them not now.

So in respect to Vermont, a law passed on the
18th of February, 1791, enacts and declares, that,
on the 4th day of March, 1791, the State of Vermont shall be received and admitted into this
Union as a new and entire member of the United
States of America. Vermont is not now a State
unless this be an act of admission.

In these two instances of the admission of new
States, (the first which occurred under the Constitution,) the words "shall be received and admitted"
must be confessed to imply the perfect acquisition
of the rights and duties of members of the Confederacy, at the time designated in the act. They
looked to no further agency or confirmation of
Congress. The words are used as synonymous
with " shall become;" and the two States by virtue of acts which declare that " they shall be admitted" on days on which Congress did not sit, and
could not act, actually became States of the American Union on those days.

It is in defiance of these examples, that the gentleman from Pennsylvania tells us that " a State
has never been admitted by anticipation."

Mr. L. said that, before he examined the example of Ohio, he must notice an observation of
the gentleman from Pennsylvania which seemed
calculated to throw rather a ludicrous air upon any
argument which might be employed to prove that
Missouri is a State of right. If, indeed, she be a
State, what are we doing; and what are we deliberating; why pass a resolution if she be a State
without it?

To answer a merely verbal argument, it is enough
to explain the words of a proposition. Mr. L. believed that, under the law of the last session without any act upon our part, Missouri had a right to
form a State government, and to administer it; to
elect her Senators and Representative to Congress,
and that her Senators and Representative had a
right to seats in this and the other House. He
should consider these propositions, at first, without
reference to the supposed repugnance between the
constitutions of Missouri and of the United States,
or to the proviso in the fourth section of the act.
But he had not forgotten the proviso, and gentlemen might be very sure that he would not evade
its consideration.

He asked of the House that it would apply the
objections of the gentleman from Pennsylvania
to the propositions which he had stated. He would
try them only upon the last, for he was really sorry
that this style of argument should be introduced
into the public councils. It seemed, according to
this objection, that, if the Representative and Senators had a right to their seats, there was something absurd in our deliberating whether they had
the right or not. Does not the gentleman from

Pennsylvania know that the clearest rights may
be disputed and denied? Is it, then, absurd to propose that these rights shall be recognised, and their
exercise be allowed? If Missouri be a State already, it is true that we cannot proceed to make
her so; but may we not declare her to be such—
may we not treat her as such? Mr. L. said he had
not attempted to enter into the inquiry, what forms
of recognition were necessary (or whether any
were) to extend to a new State, in our courts and
elsewhere, all the privileges of its condition. If
any form of recognition be necessary for the practical enjoyment of these advantages, the State has
a right to claim that this form of recognition shall
be employed.

Among individuals those rights only may be
considered as perfect, which can be maintained in
a court of justice. Claims upon the United States,
whether political or pecuniary, are not susceptible
of this legal distinction. Against them there can
be no right more perfect than that which is founded
upon a compact proposed by them as the one party,
and formally accepted by the other.

But, Mr. L. said, he had done the gentleman
from Pennsylvania some injustice. His argument
was a little more plausible than he had represented
it to be. He construed the resolution before the
House as if it contained the words Missouri " is
hereby admitted," and then reasoned in very logical form, that, if she were admitted by the resolution, she could not have been admitted before it.

Mr. L. said, that, when he had heard this criticism, he had supposed that he should be obliged
frankly to allow that he had drawn the resolution
very carelessly, and that the gentleman from Pennsylvania, (a member of the committee which reported it,) by prudently withholding this objection
to its form, had secured every *fair* advantage in
attacking it. For once, however, he had found
himself too ready to admit an error. The resolution pronounces that Missouri is hereby—not admitted—but declared to be admitted; and the gentleman from Pennsylvania, to adapt his argument
to the fact, must convince the House that it is absurd, when a State has become one of the United
States, to declare that she is so.

After all, however, the important questions were
those which regarded not the words of the resolution, (which it was as easy to amend as to criti-
cise,) but the rights of Missouri. He thought that
these rights would be strongly illustrated by examining the admission of Ohio into the Union.

In her case, as in those of Vermont and Kentucky, the act was one of prospective admission;
to take effect, however, not at a fixed time, but
upon the occurrence of a particular contingency.
To the admission of a State, the consent of two
parties (of Congress and of the State itself) is
necessary. In the cases of Vermont and Kentucky, the consent of the State had been expressed
before the passage of the act of Congress. The
admission, therefore, by the act, was absolute,
though prospective. In the case of Ohio, and of
all the territories which have since become States,
the act of Congress has been passed before the
consent of the State, or of the people in conven-

tion, has been obtained; and the admission by the act has been not prospective only, but contingent. He would proceed to show by the conduct of Congress, and its language, upon what contingency it depended, that the State should become one of the United States.

He submitted to the House that where a form of words had been used by Congress, and these words have been the subject of legislative construction, where the same words and the same construction has been employed at successive sessions, the Congress which continues to use the same language, designs to authorize the same construction. He did not employ the authority of a subsequent Congress to determine what was meant by an earlier one; but he insisted that when Congress, at its last session, used the words of the act for authorizing the people of Ohio to form a State government, and applied them to Missouri, they intended that the new law should be interpreted as the old one had been. This was only to say of sentences as of words, that their meaning must be determined by their use.

Mr. L. read the first section of the act for the admission of Ohio into the Union, which he said was in the same words (as far as its application to a different territory permitted) with that passed at the last session, for the admission of Missouri. "Be it enacted, &c., That the inhabitants of the 'eastern division of the territory northwest of the 'river Ohio, be, and they are hereby, authorized 'to form for themselves a constitution and State 'government, and to assume such name as they 'shall deem proper; and the said State, when 'formed, shall be admitted into the Union, upon 'the same footing with the original States, in all 'respects whatever." (Laws of the U. S. 3d vol. 496.) What was the construction put upon this law? He would read it in an act of the same volume. It is found in the preamble to the act "to provide for the due execution of the laws of the United States, within the State of Ohio," vol. 3, p. 524, which recites that "the people of 'the eastern division of the territory northwest of 'the river Ohio, did, on the twenty-ninth day of 'November, one thousand eight hundred and two, 'form for themselves a constitution and State 'government, and did give to the said State the 'name of the State of Ohio, whereby the said 'State has become one of the United States."

We have then the solemn decision of Congress that Ohio, by forming its constitution, became one of the United States, without any further act by the legislative body. Congress accordingly proceeded to execute the agreement, which, having been proposed by one party, and adopted by the other, had become obligatory on both. It was with these acts on our tables that we passed the law of the last session. It was in the same words that we authorized Missouri "to form a State government." She has formed it, and thereby "has become one of the United States." Such is the language of the statute book.

The same form of words has been always since employed, in regard to the territories which have successively become States, with the exception of Louisiana, whose situation was supposed to be peculiar. The officers, judicial and executive, of the United States, have been superseded, in all of these instances, by those of the new State, and elections have been held for members of Congress, without waiting for any further act of the General Government. This, which Congress knew to have been done in every former instance, they must have intended should be done in this. But, it may be said, that occurrences in a remote territory may have passed unobserved, or that the fact of every officer of the United States being removed, and the independent government of a State being established and administered before its new constitution was submitted to examination, was rather acquiesced in than approved. Even this distinction cannot be sustained, without inconsistency, by the opponents of the resolution. They say that the constitutions of all these States have been examined and approved by Congress. Now, there is in all of them an article which fixes the period at which the operations of the new State government shall commence, and the election of members of Congress take place, and this period was in all of them earlier than the sessions of Congress which occurred after those constitutions were formed. Thus, Alabama, (for he would not fatigue the House by more remote examples) was authorized to form a State government in 1819, in the same words as Missouri was in 1820. The constitution of Alabama was formed in July, 1819, and by what is called its schedule superseded from its date all that authority over the State which the General Government had before possessed over the Territory of Alabama—directed that all criminal actions should be prosecuted in the name of the State, and provided that, on the third Monday of September, 1819, a new Governor, members of Assembly, and a Representative to Congress, should be elected. In short, it provided that, without any further act by Congress, Alabama should cease to be a Territory, and become a State. This was the construction of the act to authorize Alabama to form a State government, which her convention had given and acted on; and, if Congress had, indeed, examined her constitution, this was the construction which Congress has sanctioned. It was at the same session that they gave to Missouri the same right to form a State government which had before been given to Alabama, and in the same words. They intended then that Missouri, like Alabama, should form and administer her State government, and elect her members of Congress, without waiting for the recognition of the General Government.

That he might not be suspected of avoiding the consideration of an example which might be supposed to discountenance his views, he would advert for a moment to the case of Louisiana. In authorizing every other territory to form a State government, Congress had adopted the form and the words of the act which he had quoted in the case of Ohio. But, in respect to Louisiana, they authorized the convention to form a constitution; but provided that, if the constitution were not disapproved by Congress, she should be admitted as

HISTORY OF CONGRESS.

a State. It was doubted whether the large proportion of the inhabitants of Louisiana, born and bred under an arbitrary government, would understand or prefer that form of civil polity without which it would be unwise to make her a State. He had already expressed the opinion, that the formation of a provisional constitution, for the examination of Congress, was a nugatory and fallacious security for the future good behaviour of any people; but he had never denied that Congress had power to make the people of a territory pass through this exercise. In respect to Louisiana, they chose to exert it, and provided that "in 'case the convention should declare its assent in 'behalf of the people, to the adoption of the Con- 'stitution of the United States, and should form 'a constitution and State government," and "if 'the same should not be disapproved by Congress 'at their next session, the said State should be 'admitted into the Union upon the same footing 'with the original States." By this act Louisiana was to be admitted into the Union if her constitution was approved, and after it was approved. He freely conceded that Congress possessed the discretionary power of determining whether the State should be admitted with the constitution which she proposed for approbation—they possessed, because they had reserved it. Congress had before them, at their last session, the examples of Ohio and Louisiana. In the first example, an act had passed under which the Territory was authorized to form a constitution and State government, "whereby she became a State." In the other, the authority was substantially to propose a constitution, on the approbation of which, by Congress, she was to become a State. In choosing between these examples, Congress, at its last session, adopted the form which had been employed in respect to Ohio; and the gentleman from Pennsylvania was obliged to contend, not merely that the clause in respect to Missouri should be construed differently from an identical clause in respect to Ohio; but that it should be construed in the same way with an entirely different clause, which had been adopted for peculiar reasons in the case of Louisiana, which Congress had purposely omitted in every other case, and which they had directly rejected at the last session, when it was moved by a member from New York. Against such interpretations there could be no safety.

He had proved these two propositions, that Missouri had a right to form and administer its government, and a right to elect its members of Congress. It would seem to follow that the members whom she elected would be entitled to take their seats. The Federal Constitution gives to a State, and only to a State, the right to elect Senators and Representatives. Whatever community is proved to be a State of the Union, must have a right to elect Representatives to Congress, and it seems equally clear that the community which has a right to elect Representatives to Congress, must be a State of the Union. But the same conclusion was supported by another view.

He concurred in opinion with those gentlemen who thought that it was never intended, by Congress, to give to Missouri the power of becoming an independent community. They meant, by the act of the last session, to consolidate the empire, and not contract it. He had proved that we had authorized the establishment of a State government in Missouri, over which we had reserved no control; he supposed that it was not designed to leave the parts of the empire without connexion, even for a moment; and when the territorial condition was removed, there was but one possible connexion which could be substituted—the connexion between a State and the Confederacy.

But it may be said that if the fact of a government being administered, and members elected by the new States, under a law declaring that they should be admitted, prove that Congress intended that the government of Missouri should be administered, and her elections held without any further act by this body, the same examples show that the members elected should not be received without an act of recognition.

Mr. L. allowed that, for three years past, and only for three years, the members from new States had not proceeded to take their seats until the passage of a joint resolution declaring the admission of the States which they represented. In the case of Indiana, when such a resolution was first proposed, he had before remarked that the Representative took his seat on the second, while the resolution did not pass until the eleventh of the month. His taking his seat might, if you please, have been an act of inadvertence; but that word must have lost its meaning, if it can be applied to the conduct of the House which allowed him to keep his seat for the whole time he had mentioned, and to keep it while they were obliged to vote upon the very question, whether the State of Indiana should be declared to be admitted into the Union.

If example could prove any thing, it proved that recognition, by Congress sometimes employed, but oftener omitted, was not necessary to give to Missouri the rights of a State. Recognition, indeed, from the plain import of the word, does not give rights, but declares them. He did not doubt that the acts of the new State might be properly examined to determine whether she had accepted the terms proposed, and become a State; and the credentials of the Representative, to know whether he had become a member. Congress might, by law, or perhaps, as the gentleman from Pennsylvania proposes, by usage, require a certain form of examination; but this would ascertain and authenticate the right. It would not create it.

The gentleman from Pennsylvania had said that there was every variety in the mode of admitting States. If this were true, it would yet follow, as all of these are allowed to have been legal, and as many of the States were admitted prospectively, and without recognition, that Missouri has acquired the rights of a State in the same way. But he did not object to recognition, but proposed it; if it were necessary to the practical enjoyment of the rights of a State, the first right of Missouri was, that this recognition should be made.

The examples of admission were not, however, as various and irregular as they were represented. Under different circumstances, there were indeed different forms. When the wish of the people to constitute a State government, had been clearly and formally expressed by a convention, the act of admission has been generally absolute; sometimes, however, immediate, and sometimes prospective. When the consent of the people of the proposed State has not been already fully given and is therefore formally required, the admission is always made contingent upon that consent, and is always prospective. Every act, however, for authorizing the people of a territory to form a State government for themselves, adopts general principles, and uses words, which make a compact obligatory upon the United States, before any act of recognition by Congress, and even before the actual formation of a State constitution. He should quote the Missouri act to establish this position presently, but similar clauses were found in all the acts.

Mr. L. said that he considered himself as having proved that Congress has the right of admitting States prospectively; that this right had been legitimately exercised in the case of Vermont and Kentucky, by acts which were to take effect upon the lapse of a certain time, and in the cases of Ohio, Indiana, Illinois, Mississippi, Alabama, and Missouri, that the same right of prospective admission had been exercised, in acts which were to take effect upon a future contingency. This contingency, according to the solemn construction which he had quoted in the case of Ohio, was the formation of a constitution and State government, "whereby she became a State." But he must now inquire, whether the authority given to Missouri by the act of the last session, had not been dependent upon a condition which had defeated the grant? It became necessary, with this view, to examine the proviso in the fourth section.

He thought its import plain, but gentlemen supposed that it involved a deep legal question. The House would remember, that the first section of the act of the last session had authorized the people of Missouri to form for themselves a constitution and State government, and had enacted, that the State, when formed, should be admitted into the Union. The fourth section required that the convention of Missouri should determine whether it were expedient to form a constitution and State government. If it were determined to be expedient, the convention might either form themselves form, or provide for the election of representatives who should form a State constitution. After this provision follows the clause "provided the same shall be republican, and not repugnant to the Constitution of the United States." The opposers of the resolution insisted, that if Missouri was authorized to form no other constitution than one which should not be repugnant to that of the United States, she could derive no right from the law if such repugnance subsisted. In other words, (for it was difficult to examine the doctrines without employing the terms of law) that the formation of a constitution, which should not be repugnant to

that of the United States, was the condition precedent, upon which the right of Missouri to admission into the Union should accrue. They represent, indeed, all the rights which the act of the last session confers upon Missouri, as dependent upon the same condition.

Mr. L. said, that he had remarked, already, that the terms of that law made a part of the compact which it proposes, obligatory upon the United States, even before the formation of the State constitution.

The convention was not required to form a constitution, but first to determine whether a State government should be formed; and, if it should be determined to form one, Congress enacted that the terms of compact stated in the 6th section of the act should be proposed to the convention. If the formation of a State constitution were then left, as it might be, to a different body and different time, the compact would be perfected (it would be "obligatory upon the United States") before any State constitution existed. This compact gave rights which neither party could at pleasure withdraw; it established the relations which are usual between the General Government and the States formed out of its territories, and explicitly considered the convention as acting with the authority, and in the name of the State. A much stronger conclusion might be drawn from it, but he was satisfied to say that it proved that Missouri, under the act of the last session, had acquired very important rights before she had proceeded to consider even the first clause of her constitution.

But the words of the proviso were not susceptible of a construction which would make the conformity of her constitution the condition precedent upon which she should acquire the rights of a State. He had hoped that a friend, whose professional studies would have enabled him to do it most effectually, would have shown that the construction which even a technical lawyer would place upon the proviso could not support the objection to the resolution. To read the proviso was enough to show that it was not intended to avoid every other act of the convention, because it should exceed or mistake its powers in a single clause. Missouri was authorized to form a constitution, provided the same was republican and not repugnant to the Constitution of the United States. The clause presented, at least to the unlearned reader, no other import than this. The authority given to form a constitution must be subject to all the limitations imposed by the paramount authority of the Federal Constitution. The same limitations would have existed, though a superfluous caution had not in words expressed them. They applied to every old State as well as to this new one, and their terms neither assigned any new penalty for transgression, nor a new tribunal to ascertain and punish it.

He knew that it was often difficult to determine what was a condition precedent, but, ignorant as he was of law, he would show that the proviso contained none. That the proviso contained a condition precedent, would imply at least this proposition—that the performance of some previous act was necessary to the acquisition of the rights conferred by this section. The only right conferred in the whole section was that of forming a constitution and State government. Now, that the conformity of such a constitution, after it should be framed, should be the condition upon which the convention should be authorized to begin and form it, was a contradiction in terms which the dexterity of the whole bar would be unable to reconcile. It would be flattery to call it a sophism.

The right to form a constitution and State government, then, has been acquired, or, if gentlemen prefer the term has been vested. Has it been lost? It would be a new doctrine in this country—a strange one anywhere—that the mistake of a public body in the construction of a difficult power should not merely defeat the act which they wanted authority to perform, but should annul every other provision, though clearly within their competence, and even divest the people whom they represented of power to correct the error. We have learned, indeed, in our infancy, that governments may be abdicated and sovereigns deposed; but we have yet to learn that the people of a State may forfeit all the rights of self-government by an error of their representatives; and that the process of disfranchisement may be enforced by the Congress of the United States, and take place under the forms their constitution.

Mr. L. observed that he had as yet said nothing of the particular clause in the constitution of Missouri which all the opposers of the resolution believe to be repugnant to the Federal Constitution. "It shall be the duty of the Legis-'lature to pass such laws as may be necessary to 'prevent free negroes and mulattoes from coming 'to and settling in the State." It had been insisted that the black citizen had a right, under the Federal Constitution, to come to any State and settle there. His friends from Virginia and Delaware (Mr. BARBOUR and Mr. MCLANE) had argued, with distinguished ability, that no federal privileges had been conferred upon that degraded caste of our population, rejected as they were, in every State, from social and political privileges, either by the provisions of law or the feelings of society. If these gentlemen were right, there was certainly no repugnance between the Constitutions of the United States and Missouri; but, if they were mistaken, did the exclusion of free blacks and mulattoes apply only to that large class who can in no propriety of language be considered as the citizens of any State, or did it include the small and more favored class, whose characteristic of color would confound them with that description from which the privilege of citizenship would elevate and distinguish them? He had before submitted the suggestion that the constitution of Missouri was legitimate in nearly the whole operation which the broadest interpretation would give it, and that the authority which should expound that constitution would be bound so to limit its construction as to except from the generality of its terms the few who were protected from its application by the Constitution of the United States. If any of those gentlemen who have spoken against the resolution were called, in a judicial character, to expound the doubtful clause in the Missouri constitution, they would value their professional reputation too highly not to exclude from its operation the black citizen of the United States, if any such should appear before them. On this part of the subject, as indeed on every other which his friend before him (Mr. ARCHER) had touched, he had left no other resource but silence to opponents who would not acknowledge their error. Why had not the gentlemen who objected to the constitution of Missouri because, in imposing restraints upon the free blacks and mulattoes, it had made no exceptions in respect to citizens, explained, when they were asked to do it, the meaning of their own act of the last session, liable as it was to the same objection? He had been taught not to refer to sentences. He must quote a few from the act of the last session, to "incorporate the inhabitants of the city of Washington." "The corporation shall have full 'power and authority to restrain and prohibit the 'nightly and other disorderly meetings of slaves, 'free negroes and mulattoes, and to punish such 'free negroes and mulattoes by penalties not ex-'ceeding ten dollars for any one offence, and, in 'case of the inability of any such free negro and 'mulatto to pay any such penalty and cost there-'on, to cause him or her to be confined to labor 'for any time not exceeding six calendar months." The corporation shall also have full power and authority "to prescribe the terms and conditions upon which free negroes and mulattoes may reside in the city." There was a fair claim upon the candor of gentlemen who oppose the resolution, to say what they had meant by the act which he had quoted; what they had meant by the law on which they had voted, and for which they had voted. Did they mean that these penalties of fines and imprisonment and labor should be imposed upon the citizen if he were black? Did they mean that the corporation should prescribe the terms upon which alone the citizen who was black might reside in the metropolis of his country? There was no difference between the assumption of such a right and that of excluding the black citizens entirely. But if gentlemen would not choose to say what they meant, he would declare for himself that, in the use of general terms referring to blacks and mulattoes as a class, that portion which may be distinguished from the rest by the privilege of citizenship, never entered into his contemplation. He asked for Missouri, not the indulgence, but the justice of the House. Was it fair to require from a convention hastily collected a degree of precision and accuracy which the Congress of the United States did not employ? In a constitution which contained in a few pages the distribution of powers, and, if he might say so, the elements of future legislation, was it fair to expect a fulness of detail and an exactness of limitation, such as the men who criticised it had been unable to accomplish in an ordinary law? In short, if we had forgotten to make, in terms, the exception in favor of citizens who were black, and left their rights to the security of sound judicial construction, was not the omission as pardonable in the case of Missouri, and the security of the black citizen as good?

If the constitution of Missouri, by a fair and liberal interpretation, were not repugnant to that of the United States, there was no pretence for rejecting the resolution before the House. Even if the arguments of gentlemen from whom he differed were correct, there is no obscurity of language, no defect of provision, nothing but direct repugnance, which could justify the rejection of the constitution. He had endeavored to show that this repugnance did not exist; but, if it did, no political truth was clearer to his mind than that it should be ascertained and corrected by a judicial tribunal. In authorizing Missouri to form a constitution and State Government, Congress had proposed the terms upon which they were willing that she should become a member of the Confederacy. The consent of both parties was necessary to the compact. It imposed duties and restraints upon both. If Congress should fail to construe or fulfil well any part of its engagements with the new States, no man would be rash enough to say that all their obligations were annulled; if the new States misconstrued or violated any part of their engagements, could Congress plead that its own obligations had become void?

Gentlemen say that Missouri was enjoined by the law of the last session to frame a constitution which should not be repugnant to that of the Union: and they are right. This was the rule prescribed for her government. But the compact proposed to Missouri, provided not the rule only, but the tribunal which should expound and enforce it. Under this compact the Constitution of the United States was to be "the supreme law" of Missouri; her Legislature and judges were to be sworn to support it, and the judicial power of the United States was to decide, in the last resort, every question which should arise under the Federal Constitution. She can have no right to pass a law denying to the citizens of other States, "all the privileges and immunities" of citizens of Missouri; but she has a right to have her laws expounded by the tribunal provided by the Constitution. She has signed the article proposed by yourselves, which provides that if she pass an unconstitutional law, it shall be annulled by your courts. The very *casus fœderis* exists, and instead of carrying into effect the provisions which you yourselves proposed, you make the circumstance which was foreseen and provided for the pretext for annulling the whole compact.

We are so far from being bound, then, to determine whether the constitution of a new State is repugnant to that of the Union, that we cannot pronounce such a determination without usurping the powers of that tribunal to which we are engaged to remit it. We cannot, indeed, be bound by the terms of the Federal Constitution, to examine the statutes of a new State, if we are authorized, as he had proved we were, to admit States by a prospective law. Congress could not know what their constitutions might be at the time when such acts of admission would take effect.

The gentleman from Pennsylvania, and those who followed him, have, indeed, endeavored to show that we are bound, before we admit a State, to approve its constitution. But their whole proof, however various in their forms, resolves itself into the suggestion of cases of strong repugnance between the Federal and State constitutions. There ought to be a remedy for these. We say that there is one; that wherever a State, whether new or old, shall violate the compact which defines her rights and powers, the courts of the United States will correct the procedure, if, from the nature of the case, it can be subjected to judicial cognizance. But if it cannot, if the act of the State do not directly impugn any individual right, but affect those political principles which the people of the United States have submitted to the guardianship of the General Government, (if it should establish, according to the illustration of the gentleman from New York, Mr. Storrs, an hereditary House of Lords,) the constitution even here contains the preservative power which is to guard it from corruption. When the judges cannot interpose, Congress may, and this either with a new or an old State. "The United States guaranty to every State a republican form of government."

Gentlemen had fatigued themselves in the suggestion of possible cases, where the disorders of a State constitution might admit of no cure but from the interposition of Congress. He would not detain the House by suppositions; but if there were a thousand cases where its interposition were necessary, they would not weaken the argument that it should not be resorted to without necessity. If the Legislature of Missouri are freely elected by the people; if her judges are sworn to support the Federal Constitution, and offer no obstruction to appeals to the Supreme Court, (whenever you provide for them,) may we not say that the errors of her constitution may be safely left to judicial correction; or do we abandon this doctrine when we admit that a State which should maintain an hereditary nobility, or a standing army in time of peace, must be restrained by harsher remedies?

Mr. L. said, that nothing but the previous excitement of the country, and the character of the right which Missouri was supposed to have impaired, could, in his judgment, have induced prudent and reflecting men to undertake to examine and determine the legitimacy of State constitutions. It happened that the right in dispute was one which interested the citizens of the different States, and did not affect the relative powers of the States and the General Government.

When the question regarded rights which the citizens of one State might claim in every other, the Government of the Union seemed to be a disinterested arbitrator. But if he were to examine the conformity of State constitutions with that of the Federal Government, these were the rights which would least frequently be brought into question. In almost every instance we should be obliged to determine the extent and limit of our own powers. These were the "vexed" questions of the constitution. He had endeavored to show that we were not bound to decide them, and that we ought not to decide them. Suppose that the clause objected to in the constitution of Missouri related to the exemption of a national bank from taxation by the State, or to the power of Congress in calling out the militia. Is it not apparent that our interest in these questions disqualifies us for their decision? He was ashamed to have detained the House so long, and could not enlarge further upon the subject. But Congress was in every respect an unfit tribunal to decide upon the conformity of the Federal and State constitutions; it was a party to the compact, and interested in its construction, and, therefore, should not expound it; it consisted of two Houses which might not be able to unite in any opinion; its authority would be lost the moment that it was submitted to. The new State, which acquiesced in the decision of Congress, would be authorized, the next month, to appeal to another tribunal, and the power would last just long enough to irritate and not to coerce. He had said already that, under this system, Missouri must amend her constitution to propitiate our dignity, and re-enact it to assert her right. The examination of the constitution of Missouri had already shown the impracticability of the whole system. Among minds as active and curious as those which we might expect to find in the national councils, it might be believed that almost every article in the Federal Constitution would be exposed to different constructions, and that no form of government could well be presented by a State, (except, indeed, that form for exhibition to which he had before alluded,) which would not offer to constitutional critics a great many doubtful or repugnant clauses. He believed that the gentlemen who argued that the House was bound in conscience to examine the constitution of every new State rigidly, had examined that of Missouri but very superficially. Yet it was worth while to advert to the result of their examination. It was supposed at first, and the majority of the House perhaps still thought so, that the only clause which was repugnant to that of the United States, was the one which prohibited the admission of free negroes. In another body, however, it had been discovered that the provision of a State bank was equally unconstitutional. In our own we had heard to-day two or three other points asserted, and perhaps established by the gentleman behind him; and a friend from Ohio on his left (a zealous opponent of the resolution) was prepared to prove, that at least seven provisions in the constitution of Missouri were incompatible with that of the United States. Mr. L. was exceedingly sorry that he had not explained his views to the House; for all these arguments would prove, that if any State constitution were much examined, individuals whose objections would apply to different parts of the instrument, might form a majority for rejecting the whole. With a full examination, the best constitution would be rejected, but with the slight and partial examination which would much oftener occur, the worst provisions would be sanctioned. Mr. L. said that he had the most unaffected respect for the candor, as well as the information of the gentleman from Pennsylvania, (Mr. Hemphill,)

to one of whose views he was about to advert. But he must not lose the illustration which the argument of that gentleman had afforded, of the imperfection of any examination into a State constitution which could be expected in that House. The question was too important for fastidious delicacy.

The gentleman from Pennsylvania had contended that the expression of free negroes and mulattoes in the debated clause must be considered in its broadest sense, and include those who are citizens of some of the States. And to illustrate his view he had told the House, that, although a State has a right to maintain ships of war, it has a right to do so only in time of war, and that any provision of a State constitution for a navy, although it would be legitimate if limited to war, could not be so construed if its terms were general, but would clearly impose upon Congress the duty of rejecting it. Now it happened that the fourth article of the Missouri constitution had a provision about a navy, not limited in its terms to a period of war, and in the view of the gentleman from Pennsylvania, Congress were in conscience bound to reject it. In his view, if they did not reject, they would sanction it. Well, they made no objection to it; they had examined the constitution, and had not even noticed it. Could there be a stronger illustration of the mischief of a system which considers Congress as bound to denounce an equivocal and doubtful provision, and in the very act allows, what it considers as the plainest violation of the constitution, to pass unquestioned, if not unread? Is not the system a safer, as well as a juster, which exacts only of the new State that its obligations to the Confederacy shall be those of all the other States, which considers its constitution and ordinances as the evidence of its consent to become a State; and when we design that the rights and duties of the new and old States shall be the same, leaves them to be expounded and enforced by the same tribunal?

If we had, indeed, reserved to ourselves the power of deciding whether the constitution of Missouri were repugnant to the Federal Constitution, and the opinion of the House should be that this repugnance existed, it would become material to inquire how this judicial authority should be exercised? Should we, while exercising, in respect to a new State, the powers of the Supreme Court in respect to an old one, annul the obnoxious article? Should we, "in our brief authority," command it to be expunged? Or should we disfranchise the State, because it used words almost as carelessly as we ourselves had done in the act of the last session? But these inquiries carried him too far.

Mr. Lowndes said, that, with the strongest wish to hasten to the conclusion of his remarks, he thought himself bound to notice a doctrine, which he understood the gentleman from Pennsylvania to have avowed. The talents and character of that gentleman gave to his opinions an influence which involved no light responsibility. It was with mortification and pain, Mr. L. said, that he had understood him to express the opinion, that, under a law enacting that a new State shall be admitted, Congress, particularly if an election shall have intervened, may consider its admission as "an open question," and fulfil or disregard the law of the preceding Congress at its discretion. He had anticipated, in his former remarks, the influence of this doctrine, but not its avowal. He should be glad to know, before he proceeded further in his observations, whether he had understood the gentleman from Pennsylvania correctly. [Mr. SERGEANT explained. He was understood by Mr. L. to say, that he had expressed no opinion on the matter, but had spoken of it as a doubtful question.] Mr. L. proceeded. If the gentleman did not deny, it was hardly less extraordinary that he should doubt, whether the Government of this nation were bound by the obligations of faith and honor. But he would change the subject.

Mr. L. said he regretted that he had already consumed so much time that he could not dwell upon the view which he should hope that men of prudence and virtue would take of the condition of our country, even if they differed from him in all that he had yet said. He thought, indeed, that we were bound to admit the members from Missouri to their seats. But no one would deny that we had power to admit them. It was a comparative question, between different schemes of policy, and the country had a right to require that its Representatives should not reject one plan without weighing and adopting some alternative. Was it enough to say, with the composure of the gentleman from Pennsylvania, "it is the fault or error of Missouri?" Be it so. But it is not less our duty to guard the interests of the United States and the rights of our fellow-citizens, even in Missouri. Those who had read the law of the last session could not deny that she had acquired some rights incompatible with the dependence of a Territory. But, whatever was her condition of right, she was in fact a State, administering the government which she had formed, and enacting the laws which she preferred. Her courts were filled with judges of her own appointment; and, whatever interest of the United States might be assailed; whatever provisions of the laws or Constitution of the Union might be violated, there was now no legal method by which "an error or fault," in her judicial tribunals, could be corrected.— Should there be no appeal from their sentence? Should there be an appeal to military authority? There was now no other; and when the Representatives of the people refused to extend over Missouri the judicial authority, which would bend her laws and constitution in just submission to that of the Union, it was fair to ask them what connexion they proposed to substitute? The nation would hardly be content to learn that we satisfied ourselves with a prudent reliance upon time and chance, because "it was the fault or error of Missouri."

The gentleman from Pennsylvania has told us, that if a single citizen shall be deprived of his Constitutional right under the laws of Missouri, the fault will be upon the Congress which shall admit her. I tell the gentleman from Pennsyl-

vania, Mr. L. said, that if a citizen shall suffer in Missouri, and invoke ineffectually the laws and judicial authority of the Union, the responsibility for all that he shall suffer will be upon himself and his friends. It is he who refuses to extend the authority of our courts over the State of Missouri, and, wiser than the Constitution, he rejects the tribunal which would act peacefully and effectually in support of individual right, and prefers to it a direct coercion of the State by legislative, if not by military power. The Constitution has provided a remedy for the infractions of individual right—not a mere rule, but a court to apply and enforce it. Your injured citizens appeal to its prompt protection, and they learn with astonishment that, in your zeal to support their rights, you have suspended their only effectual remedy. As humanity to the citizen makes you deprive him of his only effectual guard, so tenderness for the Judiciary (unaffected and unmixed) induces you to withdraw from their jurisdiction a question which might involve a conflict with Missouri, and leave them only the task of deciding the same question in opposition to Carolina or Virginia.

Mr. L. repeated the opinion, that the question before the House was a comparative one—between adopting the resolution, or some other scheme of policy which gentlemen should prefer to it. Every consideration of candor and prudence required that we should know what that alternative was. Was it preferable? Was it practicable? Even since the debate had commenced, the character of the question had been greatly changed in the eye of every practical politician by the passage of the Senate's resolution. The Senate considered Missouri as a State of right. They could co-operate in no measure which would make her a territory, or treat her as such. If we refuse to pass the resolution, she must still continue to administer her government and appoint her officers; to decide in her courts every question relating to the rights and interests of the United States, within her territory, and to decide these questions without appeal. If, under these circumstances, Missouri were not rightfully a State, ought we not to make her one? It was under this view of the subject, Mr. L. said, that, in his former observations, he had brought the admission of Tennessee to the view of the House. She had formed a government for herself, not very regularly. She had elected her Governor and Assembly, and was a State in fact. Her constitution, however, besides some other articles which were objected to, contained three which were clearly repugnant to the Federal Constitution. It gave exemption from militia duty to certain classes of the community. It denied to the General Government the right to cede by treaty the free navigation of the Mississippi, and it required the Legislature to provide a method by which the State of Tennessee should be sued, excluding from this right of suing all those who were citizens of any other State. Congress knew these provisions, but it knew that the paramount authority of the Federal Constitution annulled them. Tennessee was declared to be a State; and so little was to be apprehended from a repugnance between the State and Federal Constitutions, (when Congress did not interpose in interpreting and expunging them,) that the fact of the discordance in question was probably at this time little remembered, even in Tennessee. The same consequence would follow from the passage of the resolution before the House. We should be relieved from a question which afflicts and alarms every man whose object is the public good. We should leave the construction of a doubtful provision to the only tribunal in whose determination, on such a subject, the nation will confide, and we should show a just anxiety to support the rights of the citizen, by no longer suspending his only effectual remedy.

After Mr. L. had concluded his speech—

Mr. SERGEANT rose and said, that, by the courtesy of the House, the gentleman from South Carolina, having opened the debate, had a right also to close it, and he did not mean to ask the House to depart from the usual course of proceeding, though he considered most of the arguments employed as susceptible of an easy answer. But he was not about to enter again into the discussion; he rose only to offer a few words of explanation.

He had been supposed to have misunderstood, or to have misquoted, the words of the resolution, when he had stated it to be to this effect: "And hereby is admitted," meaning to infer that the admission of Missouri was, by the resolution itself, to be by virtue of the resolution, and therefore, by the present, and not by the former legislation of Congress. He had certainly never intended, nor would he now consent, to make this a question of verbal criticism; the argument rested on much more substantial grounds. And if, in fact, the words of the resolution were, as they had been stated by the gentleman from South Carolina, that circumstance would not in the least change its character as a legislative act, and a legislative act, too, which must necessarily precede the admission of Missouri, and of course conclusively negatived the assumption (upon which the whole argument on the other side rested) that Missouri was already admitted. He had quoted the resolution from memory, according to what he believed to be the substance. But he was now satisfied that, upon every principle of construction, he was correct, and, to satisfy the House, he had called upon the Clerk to read the resolution. It is, in the material part, as follows: "Shall be, and is hereby declared to be, one of the United States of America, and is admitted." In this clause, the adverb "hereby" is connected equally with the whole of what follows. The meaning is exactly the same as if it had been "hereby is declared to be, and hereby is admitted," or, "by this is admitted;" for, "hereby," and "by this," are equivalent. But he was, perhaps, dwelling too long upon a mere verbal question, as every one at all acquainted with the phraseology of the enacting parts of laws and resolutions, would perceive at once that there was but one way of reading these words. To show, however, how entirely unprofitable the criticism upon the supposed misquotation was, he would suppose the word "hereby" to

be expunged, and the words to be simply "shall be," and "is admitted;" would not the sense be exactly the same? Would it not mean that Missouri is admitted by the resolution, and not until the resolution is adopted? Does not the necessity of any resolution at all import the same thing?

There was another point upon which he and those who acted with him were charged with error. They were supposed to be unmindful of the obligation of the contract in the law of the last session. He must say that this observation was grounded altogether upon the assumption of that which was the point in controversy, and which ought to be proved; that is to say, that the law of last session did amount to a contract. He had purposely avoided the inquiry as wholly unnecessary, because, even if the law of last session was to be considered as a contract, the people of Missouri had not complied with the terms proposed to them, and therefore could have no right to claim to be admitted; the constitution submitted did not conform to the provisions of the law of last session.

He said, he trusted he had as strong a sense of the binding nature of a contract, when once entered into, whether by the Government or an individual, as any one could have, or ought to have. But, however liberal a man might be in the construction of his own engagements, in favor of others, it was clear that, in the case of the public, implicit obedience to an obligation must necessarily be preceded by an inquiry, (which he conceived the gentleman from South Carolina had entirely passed over,) whether any obligation existed. We must examine, first, whether the law is to be deemed an ordinary act of legislation, or is in the nature of a contract. Upon this subject he had no hesitation to say, without entering further into the argument, at present, that there appeared to be strong reasons for thinking that an act authorizing a Territory to form a constitution of State government, ought to be considered as an act of ordinary legislation, and not as a contract, and that no change was made in the condition of the Territory until its constitution was submitted to Congress, and the State admitted into the Union.

He could see no reason for a different construction of the act, and there were some objections to it, in his opinion, of very great force. If it were to be deemed a contract, it would not only be binding upon the Congress who passed it, but upon any future Congress to whom the application might be made for admission, which would be an encroachment upon their authority, and the authority of the people by whom they were elected. Now, it must readily occur to every one who reflected upon the subject, (independently of the objection to binding a future Congress unnecessarily,) that, even between the passage of an act authorizing the formation of a constitution, and the time of applying for admission, circumstances might occur which would render it inexpedient to admit, and of which Congress ought to be left free then to judge; and that it would be extremely unwise and improvident to throw away the right to exercise a discretion on the subject. He could see no good purpose to be answered by it, and every consideration of policy seemed to him to forbid it. He said, however, he did not feel it necessary now to come to a decision of the question, for the reason he had already mentioned; the people of Missouri had not put themselves in a condition to claim the fulfilment of a contract, because their constitution was not conformable to the provisions of the act of last session.

He would remark, that the instance mentioned of the States formed out of the Northwest Territory presented no analogy. The Territory there was ceded to the Union by the States who claimed to be the owners of it, and was accepted by the Union, on conditions mutually agreed. Among them was one, confirmed by repeated acts of the Government, that the Territory should be formed into States; that, when they had a certain population, they should be admitted into the Union upon an equal footing with the original States; and, in the meantime, certain great principles of civil and religious liberty were agreed upon for their government, which were to be deemed fundamental, and to be the basis also of the constitutions of the States to be formed.

When an alteration of some of the terms was thought necessary, the consent of both parties was required. This was a compact with the States who made the cession, not with the inhabitants of the Territory. It bears no resemblance, therefore, to the case of a State formed out of a territory purchased by the United States, belonging in sovereignty to the United States, and held free from the obligation of any previous engagement, subject to such disposition only as the general policy might direct.

He had thought it proper to submit this brief explanation, not so much with a view to express an opinion, (which he had before purposely avoided,) as to show that the question was open, and he would detain the House no longer, as he perceived that all were desirous to come to a decision on the resolution.

When Mr. S. had concluded his remarks, the debate ended; not, however, before Mr. GROSS, of New York, had intimated his intention to move the previous question, with a view to close the debate.

The question was then taken, "Shall the resolution be engrossed, and ordered to be read a third time?" And on this question the yeas and nays were as follows:

YEAS—Messrs. Abbot, Alexander, Allen of Tennessee, Anderson, Archer of Maryland, Archer of Virginia, Baldwin, Ball, Barbour, Bayly, Bloomfield, Brevard, Brown, Bryan, Burton, Burwell, Cannon, Cobb, Cocke, Crawford, Crowell, Culbreth, Culpeper, Cuthbert, Davidson, Earle, Edwards of North Carolina, Fisher, Floyd, Garnett, Gray, Hall of North Carolina, Hardin, Hooks, Jackson, Johnson, Jones of Virginia, Jones of Tennessee, Kent, Little, Lowndes, McCoy, McCreary, McLane of Delaware, McLean of Kentucky, Meigs, Mercer, Metcalf, Montgomery, T. L. Moore, Neale, Nelson of Virginia, Newton, Overstreet, Parker of Virginia, Pinckney, Randolph, Rankin, Reed,

Rhea, Robertson, Settle, Shaw, Simkins, Smith of New Jersey, Smith of Maryland, B. Smith of Virginia, A. Smyth of Virginia, Smith of North Carolina, Swearingen, Terrell, Trimble, Tucker of Virginia, Tucker of South Carolina, Tyler, Walker, Warfield, Williams of Virginia, and Williams of North Carolina—79.

NAYS—Messrs. Adams, Allen of Massachusetts, Allen of New York, Baker, Bateman, Beecher, Boden, Brush, Buffum, Butler of New Hampshire, Campbell, Case, Clagett, Clark, Cook, Crafts, Cushman, Dane, Darlington, Dennison, Dewitt, Dickinson, Eddy, Edwards of Connecticut, Edwards of Pennsylvania, Eustis, Fay, Folger, Foot, Ford, Forrest, Fuller, Gorham, Gross of New York, Gross of Pennsylvania, Guyon, Hackley, Hall of New York, Hall of Delaware, Hemphill, Hendricks, Hibshman, Hill, Hostetter, Kendall, Kinsey, Kinsley, Lathrop, Lincoln, Linn, Livermore, Maclay, McCullough, Mallary, Marchand, Meech, Monell, R. Moore, S. Moore, Morton, Moseley, Murray, Nelson of Massachusetts, Parker of Mass., Patterson, Phelps, Philson, Plumer, Rich, Richards, Richmond, Rogers, Ross, Russ, Sergeant, Silsbee, Sloan, Southard, Stevens, Storrs, Street, Strong of Vermont, Strong of New York, Tarr, Tomlinson, Tompkins, Tracy, Upham, Van Rensselaer, Wallace, Wendover, Whitman, and Wood—93.

And the resolution for the admission of the State of Missouri into the Union was rejected.

Mr. LOWNDES then rose, and said that he did not wish to be disrespectful to a majority of the House, as declared on the vote just taken, but he now felt it to be his duty to call on them, having rejected the resolution proposed by the committee of their appointment, to devise and propose to the House the means necessary to protect the territory, the property, and all the rights of the United States in the Missouri country.

A motion being made to adjourn, was decided affirmatively, and, at a little before sunset, the House adjourned.

THURSDAY, December 14.

Mr. NEWTON, from the Committee of Commerce, reported a bill to establish the district of Pearl river; which was twice read, and committed.

Mr. SMITH, of Maryland, from the Committee of Ways and Means, to whom was recommitted the bill further to regulate the entry of merchandise into the United States from any adjacent territory, reported the same with sundry amendments, and the bill was committed to a Committee of the whole House.

On motion of Mr. TRIMBLE, the Committee on the Public Lands were instructed to inquire whether any, and what, further provision ought to be made by law to secure the safe transmission of public moneys from the several land offices to the places of deposite designated by the Secretary of the Treasury.

Mr. SOUTHARD submitted the following resolution, which was read, and laid on the table one day for consideration:

Resolved, That the President of the United States be requested to cause to be laid before this House a statement of expenditures and receipts in the Indian department; also, the nature and extent of the contracts entered into, and with whom, from the establishment of that department to the present period.

A message from the Senate informed the House that the Senate have passed a bill, entitled "An act for the relief of the officers and volunteers engaged in the late campaign against the Seminole Indians," in which they ask the concurrence of this House.

The bill was read twice, and referred to the Committee of Claims.

The bill for the relief of Daniel McDuff passed through a Committee of the Whole, and was ordered to be engrossed for a third reading.

The House then, on motion of Mr. RANDOLPH, resolved itself into a Committee of the Whole, on the bill, reported at the last session, for the relief of the family of the late Oliver H. Perry. But, it being discovered that Mr. HAZARD, of Rhode Island, one of the committee who reported the bill, was absent from the House on account of indisposition, the Committee, with the consent of Mr. RANDOLPH, rose, and obtained leave to sit again.

The bill for the relief of William McIntosh passed through a Committee of the Whole, and was by the House subsequently ordered to be engrossed for a third reading.

The bill authorizing soldiers to devise their bounty lands in certain cases, also passed through a Committee, and was ordered by the House to be engrossed for a third reading.

The report of the Committee of Claims unfavorable to the petition of John G. Bogert, was taken up in Committee of the Whole, and being reported to the House, was concurred in.

The bill for the relief of Margaret Perry passed through a Committee of the Whole, and was ordered to be engrossed for a third reading.

[These bills and report, though respecting claims of a private and personal character merely, gave rise, in the course of their investigation, to more or less debate, occupying altogether a good deal of time.]

MILITARY PUNISHMENT.

The following letter from the Secretary of War was received and read:

WAR DEPARTMENT, *Dec.* 14, 1820.

SIR: In answer to that part of the resolution of the House of Representatives of the 9th instant, requiring this Department to show whether the order given by Colonel King of the 4th infantry, for shooting deserters taken in the fact, was approved by any general officer in the service of the United States, or was known to, and passed over in silence by him, as stated in the defence of said Colonel King, I have to enclose an extract of the letter of Major General Jackson, on that subject, which was transmitted to the House of Representatives with the copy of the trial of Colonel King, and which is published in the appendix of that trial. This extract contains all the information within the knowledge of this Department on that subject.

In relation to that part of the resolution which requires any information this Department may possess, showing that corporal punishment has been inflicted on any soldier, whereby he came to his death, I have

the honor to state, that the only report of that kind, which has reached this Department, was the case of a soldier at Fort Preble, near Portland, in Maine. Major Brooks, a correct and intelligent officer commanding that post, in September last, reported that the death of a soldier, an habitual drunkard, who had been on a fatigue party, under Lieutenant Hobart, and had been confined by him, had caused much excitement among the citizens, who attributed the death of the man to the conduct of Lieutenant Hobart; that the civil authority had taken up the affair for investigation, to which Lieutenant Hobart had readily submitted himself. The report was accompanied with the enclosed certificate of the jury of inquest as to the correct conduct of Major Brooks and the other officers of the post, in relation to the transaction. It thus appearing that the affair would undergo an investigation in the district court of the United States, the Department did not think it proper to order a military investigation.

I have the honor to be, yours, &c.

J. C. CALHOUN.

To the SPEAKER, *of House of Reps.*

FRIDAY, December 15.

Among the petitions presented to-day, was one, by Mr. WENDOVER, from the New York County Agricultural Society, praying that such protection may be extended to the national industry as is demanded by the best interests of the country; which was ordered to be printed.

Mr. ANDERSON, from the Committee on Public Lands, reported a bill extending the time for issuing and locating land warrants to officers and soldiers in the Revolutionary war, which was twice read, and committed.

Mr. MALLARY, from a select committee, reported a bill for the relief of Benjamin Tyler and John Tyler, jr., of Vermont, (to renew and extend a patent for a certain invention, the term of fourteen years having expired since it was first granted;) which bill was twice read, and, on motion of Mr. LIVERMORE, who remarked that it perhaps involved a Constitutional question, as it might be contended that, after the expiration of fourteen years, the invention became, by the Constitution, vested in the public, the bill was referred to the Judiciary Committee.

The resolution offered yesterday by Mr. SOUTHARD, was taken up, and, for reasons which he stated, having been slightly modified by the mover, it was agreed to.

The engrossed bill to enable soldiers to devise their bounty lands, was read the third time.

A debate arose on the merits of this bill, occupying more than an hour, in which it was opposed by Messrs. LITTLE, SMITH of Maryland, FOOT, ANDERSON, and McCoy; and was supported by Mr. GROSS, of New York, and Mr. COCKE.

The question being taken on the passage of the bill, it was decided in the negative by a decided majority.

The engrossed bills for the relief of Margaret Perry, and for the relief of William McIntosh, were severally read the third time, passed, and ordered to be sent to the Senate for concurrence.

673   HISTORY OF CONGRESS.   674

December, 1820.   *Anti-Tariff Memorials.*   H. of R.

ANTI-TARIFF MEMORIALS.

The report made by the Committee on Manufactures, on the 30th ultimo, in relation to the anti-tariff memorials from Belfast, in Maine, and Richmond, in Virginia, being under consideration—

Mr. TYLER, of Virginia, having called up the report for consideration, said that he had taken that course under a sense of duty, and in the remarks which he should make, although he should be free and candid, yet he hoped he should violate no rule of decorum. The report was a severe denunciation against his constituents, and it became him to inquire whether they had properly subjected themselves to that denunciation or not. If, said he, they have approached this body in any other than a respectful manner, and he should be convinced of that fact, they should not find in him now an advocate, nor should he have been so lost to the respect due to himself as to have presented their memorial. In truth, he considered himself somewhat implicated in this business; for, certainly, if he had been the instrument through which an insult had been offered to this House, he should acknowledge himself to be greatly culpable. I claim, then, said he, a free inquiry into this matter. I have a right to call on the committee to point out distinctly the features in the Richmond memorial which shall be esteemed offensive. I do not mean to say that my constituents have presented themselves before you as humble suppliants—that their language is that of base menials—that they have appeared at your door covered in sackcloth, and trembling in your presence. No, sir; they have spoken as becomes freemen. They have exercised a Constitutional right in a manly manner. They have addressed you, with reasons potent and strong, against the adoption of a destructive policy. They have approached you, not as their masters, but as the servants of the people, on subjects of deep interest and high moment. The committee, in their report, have not ventured to deny to them the use of manly language in addressing this House. Unless I am grossly deceived in the character of the chairman of the committee, he would be among the last to narrow down the right of petition to a mere sycophantic appeal, couched in language humiliating and dishonorable; a language the offering of hypocrisy, and discreditable even to slaves. If, then, it be admitted to be the right of the people to speak forth their sentiments, and to speak them boldly forth, I pronounce that there is nothing in the Richmond memorial in the slightest degree offensive.

The committee have selected but one sentence from the memorial, as offensive; and, until some other be pointed out, I have a right to conclude that it, and it only, can be objected to. [Here Mr. T. read the sentence from the report.] Now, sir, said he, there is but one substantive allegation in the sentence, viz: that the advocates of manufactures may be considered more the enemies of commerce than the friends to the system which they support. He asked, in what was this offensive? It is speaking what the memorialists believe to be the truth; not that the advocates of

manufactures had declared their enmity to commerce. This is the first report, I believe, with which the committee had favored us, and, therefore its views were not made known to the nation. They left themselves to be judged of by the fruit which they produced, and I feel myself at liberty to declare in my place, that their measures can be considered in no other light than as inimical to commerce. This is not a new proposition. It was the basis of our arguments against the bills reported at the last session—we proclaimed that you were aiming a destructive blow at two of the great interests in this community, its agriculture and its trade. What did you want with high duties, but to give the home manufactures the home market; and, when the destruction of trade would follow as a necessary consequence, how, let me ask, can you take on yourselves to be offended, when you are told in plain terms of the consequences likely to flow from your measures? This language I have held to you before, and you did not esteem it offensive; I again, here in my place repeat it, and I feel assured that no one will be fastidious enough to consider it insulting.

Let me simplify the case. You and myself differ in opinion on a particular subject; you avow a disposition friendly to a certain interest, and resolve on the adoption of a course of policy, destructive, in my mind, to some other interest; shall I not be permitted to say to you in the language of friendship or remonstrance, beware lest you deceive yourself—if you adopt this policy, you will be viewed as the enemy to the interest, which, according to your declarations, you would not destroy. This is all that the sentence quoted from the Richmond memorial can be construed to mean, and in it I can see no offence. Why should gentlemen be so sensitive on this subject? Does it become the Legislature of this nation to hunt through every clause of a memorial for the purpose of culling out a sentence or a monosyllable which may contain some hidden offence? My personal knowledge of the liberality of the gentleman from Pennsylvania, creates with me inexpressible astonishment at the strictures he has indulged in on this occasion. These strictures cannot have been intended in the whole of them, for the Richmond memorial. I am authorized to say they have not arisen so much from that as from the Belfast memorial. The report itself teaches me to draw this conclusion. The committee complain of the acts of the last session being imputed to an individual, and not to the House. Now there is no imputation of this sort in the memorial which I presented, and the representation of the bills reported at the last session, "as a piece of State machinery," is to be found in the Belfast memorial. I do not feel myself bound to interfere in behalf of the inhabitants of Belfast; they are represented on this floor, and it belongs to their representative, if he thinks proper to do so, to vindicate them from the strictures of the report. But I do regret that the committee should so have connected their anathemas with the interpolation from the Richmond memorial, as to have given rise to the belief that it contained the greatest and most crying offence. I trust I have succeeded in showing that none was offered from that quarter, and that none exists.

But the committee insist that by that memorial they have been misrepresented in regard to a fact, and that the statement in the memorial that a bill was reported to repeal the drawback system is not true. I readily admit that the memorialists have fallen into error on this subject, but I utterly deny that any propriety exists in the terms used by the committee in reference to this error. The report represents this fear of a repeal of the drawback system as being a mere phantom originating " in the fears and ignorance of those who raise it." These are strong terms, and the committee ought to have been certain that they were justifiable in their use. But while they are pleased to reprobate a mistake made by others in terms of great severity, I undertake to say and to prove that they themselves have fallen into a manifest error. The fear on the subject of drawbacks is not a mere phantom existing in timidity and ignorance, but it has "a local habitation and a name," given it by the proceedings in this very hall. The propriety of repealing the drawback system has been submitted to this House for consideration. A resolution was introduced at the last session, and is imbodied in your journals, by a member from Kentucky, (Mr. Trimble,) directing an inquiry into the expediency of that measure. It is not a mere phantom then arising from ignorance, but is a reality which, considering the respectable source from which it came, was deserving of inquiry on the part of the public. That it was deserving of investigation by the people, will readily be deduced from the language of the report, for it is acknowledged that, had a bill been reported to the House proposing the repeal, it would have justly called forth an universal burst of indignation. I leave it to the committee and the gentleman from Kentucky to determine whether in truth it be a measure of such a character as to merit the indignation of the public. If the word "resolution" had been used instead of " bill" in the memorial, the sentence would have been as perfect, and the reference equally strong; and I submit to the House to decide whether a mistake in the use of a word, called for the reproaches and severe strictures which have been indulged in on this occasion. The committee will pardon me for saying that they have let go the substance and caught at the shadow. If they had attended to the object of the memorial and not its phraseology, they would have seen that its object was to defeat any measure, whether a bill or a resolution, which might be intended to repeal the drawback system. It was a legitimate object, and although the committee have abjured all intention of acting on the subject, yet I think that, without any disparagement to themselves, they might have done so in language more temperate. It is insinuated that the mistake into which the memorialists have fallen, was wilful, and with a view to misrepresentation. Now, sir, I have a right to inquire into the reasonableness of this insinuation, so far as the inhabitants of Richmond were concerned. What object was to be effected by it? Was it with the view

of obtaining signatures to the memorial? The committee must have known that such an object would have been preposterous and idle. They required no artificial aid, no phantom to unite them against the increase of duties. The South is already united on this subject, and the opposition is levelled on all hands against the proposed alteration in the tariff. There was, then, no object to be accomplished, and it is a forced and an unjustifiable inference that the mistake committed was intentionally committed. A decent respect, then, for the feelings of others should have left the committee to the use of milder language than that which they have employed.

The committee suggest that the right of petition will be brought into disrepute if the House was to sanction the language used in the memorial. I have shown to you that there is nothing offensive in the memorial which I presented; and while the committee avow themselves friendly to the right of petition, I ask, if this report is not calculated to destroy the exercise of that right? Will the people of this country condescend to approach you, if they are to subject themselves to your reproaches? Will they be so lost to themselves as to address you on subjects of great national concern, when they are liable to be scorned at as timid and ignorant? No, believe me, they will not. It does not comport with their character, nor the principles of this Government. They have a right to speak to you in the language of authority. Who are you, that you should thus elevate yourselves above them? Are you any more than their servants? If you be, sir, you have undergone a strange metamorphosis since the establishment of this Government.

I thank the House for its attention to me. I have no proposition in regard to the report now to submit. My object has been accomplished. My remarks will go forth to the nation, and, I trust, will be sufficient to relieve my constituents from any odium to which they may have been subjected; and any disposition which the House may give to the report will be satisfactory to me.

Mr. BALDWIN replied, and defended the report of the committee, in substance as follows: He referred to the language of the memorials on the subject, and the imputations on the motives of those who supported the system of protection last session, as well as to facts which these memorials falsely alleged, to show that the language of the report was justifiable; that it was strong but not rude, and might with justice have been stronger; that it said no more than that the unfounded allegations of the memorialists were untrue. Mr. B. was particularly sorry that exceptionable remarks were inserted in the Richmond memorial, inasmuch as it was the only one of all those opposed to the tariff which expressed a willingness that any thing at all should be done for manufactures, and was, therefore, characterized by a superior degree of liberality. He admitted the full right in the people to speak freely of the tendency of the measures of Congress, but not to come forward and charge the House with what was not true; that the tariff bills contained no provision for the abolition of drawbacks was obvious to every one who had read them, and therefore the petitioners had certainly asserted what was untrue. The only proposition relative to drawbacks was made in the resolutions of a gentleman from Kentucky, (Mr. TRIMBLE,) which were never called up for consideration. These unfounded reports had been in circulation a year, uncontradicted in any manner which would counteract them; and it was the object of the report to simply perform this duty, and disabuse the public on the subject, &c.

Mr. TYLER rejoined, substantially, that, to correct any error in which a portion of the people may have fallen, it was not necessary to denounce them as timid and ignorant.

Mr. KINSLEY, of Maine, offered a few remarks, intended, as the reporter understood, not hearing him distinctly, to defend the memorialists of Belfast, in Maine, from intentional misrepresentation of the views of the supporters of the new tariff. If they had supposed that the proposition to abolish drawbacks was passed at the last session, their distance from the Seat of Government, and a reliance upon incorrect channels of information, might be presumed to have caused the misapprehension; and, at any rate, the mistake, he conceived, was not worthy of this long and labored report from the Committee of Manufactures, or the severity of language which it applied to them. He could not conceive why the committee had selected from all the memorials on the subject two from such distant and almost extreme points as Richmond and Belfast for their animadversion.

Mr. TRIMBLE, of Kentucky, submitted a few observations in explanation of the resolutions which he offered at the last session relative to the cash payment of duties, and to the repeal of the duties on drawbacks. When he moved those resolutions, he was not prepared to say the drawback system ought to be abolished, though there were petitions then before the House from some parts of the country praying Congress to repeal the system. His object was inquiry only, and he brought forward the resolutions that the whole subject might be before the House. He might say, however, that such a repeal was not sustained alone by the petitions to which he referred, but it was supported by the opinion of one of the first of men and of patriots in this country or in the world, he meant Thomas Jefferson. In a letter to a friend here, which Mr. T. had perused soon after he offered his resolution, that great statesman had pointedly suggested the expediency of abolishing the whole drawback system. Mr. T. said for what he had done he should not deem it necessary to appeal to the authority of any man, and he should not, therefore, have adverted to the opinion of Mr. Jefferson, deserving as it was of respect, but that his proposition on the subject of drawbacks had been treated rather cavalierly by those who had thought proper to animadvert on it.

Mr. SWEARINGEN moved that the report and resolutions of the Committee on Manufactures be ordered to lie on the table.

Mr. BALDWIN, in reply to Mr. KINSLEY, observed that the reason why the committee had se-

lected the memorials of Richmond and Belfast was, that they only contained exceptionable and improper remarks on the friends of the tariff bills. He had no objection to laying the report on the table, as its object was merely, as he said before, to correct the misstatements which had gone abroad on the subject.

The report and resolutions were then ordered to lie on the table.

MONDAY, December 18.

A new member, to wit: from Massachusetts, AARON HOBART, elected to supply the vacancy occasioned by the resignation of Zabdiel Sampson, appeared, was qualified, and took his seat.

DEATH OF MR. HAZARD.

Mr. EDDY, of Rhode Island, rose, and briefly announced to the House the decease, on yesterday, of NATHANIEL HAZARD, Esq., a member of this House from the State of Rhode Island.

Whereupon, on motion of Mr. E., resolutions were unanimously adopted, expressive of the feelings of the House on this occasion; resolving to attend the funeral, this day, at two o'clock; appointing a committee to superintend the same; and resolving, also, as a testimony of respect for the memory of the deceased, to go into mourning, and wear a black crape round the left arm for thirty days.

Messrs. EDDY, MORTON, RUSS, SHAW, MALLARY, ARCHER of Maryland, and COCKE, were appointed a committee accordingly; and the House adjourned.

TUESDAY, December 19.

Mr. WILLIAMS, of North Carolina, from the Committee of Claims, made a report on the petition of Joseph McNeil, accompanied with a bill for his relief; which bill was read the first and second time, and committed to a Committee of the Whole to-morrow.

A Message was received from the PRESIDENT OF THE UNITED STATES as follows:

To the House of Representatives:

In compliance with a resolution of the House of Representatives of the 21st November last, requesting the President to lay before the House information relating to the progress and expenditures of the Commissioners under the fifth, sixth, and seventh articles of the Treaty of Ghent, I now transmit a report from the Secretary of State, with documents, containing all the information in the possession of that Department, requested by the resolution.

JAMES MONROE.

WASHINGTON, *Dec.* 14, 1820.

The Message was read, and, with the accompanying documents, ordered to lie on the table.

The SPEAKER laid before the House a letter from the Secretary of War, transmitting information in relation to the horses furnished by the mounted men in the war with the Seminole Indians; as also, in relation to the rules prescribed for compensating said men, not applicable to all other troops of the same description, furnished in obedience to the resolution of the 12th instant; which was read, and referred to the Committee of Claims.

On motion of Mr. FLOYD, a committee was appointed to inquire into the situation of the settlements upon the Pacific Ocean, and the expediency of occupying the Columbia river. Mr. FLOYD, Mr. METCALFE, and Mr. SWEARINGEN, were appointed the said committee.

Mr. FLOYD submitted the following resolution, which, under the rule, will lie on the table for consideration until to-morrow.

Resolved, That the Secretary of the Department of War be required to lay before this House a statement of the number and situation of the military posts in the United States at this time; together with the distribution of the army; designating the number of men, also, the number and rank of the officers at each place.

On motion of Mr. PHELPS, a committee was appointed to investigate the affairs of the Post Office Department, with power to send for persons and papers, and Messrs. PHELPS, ARCHER, of Virginia, CULPEPER, ALLEN, of New York, and HOBART, were appointed the said committee.

On motion of Mr. MONELL, the Committee on the Public Lands were instructed to inquire whether any, and, if any, what, regulations can be adopted, consistent with the interest of the Government, whereby the soldiers of the late war, who have not received their bounty lands, can be better provided for than under existing laws.

Mr. EUSTIS submitted the following joint resolution, viz:

Resolved, by the Senate and House of Representatives of the United States of America in Congress assembled, and it is hereby declared, That, on the —— day of —— next ensuing, the State of Missouri shall be admitted into the Union upon an equal footing with the original States in all respects whatsoever: *Provided,* That so much of the 26th section of the 3d article in the constitution of said State, presented to Congress at the present session, as makes it the duty of the Legislature to pass such laws as shall be necessary " to prevent free negroes and mulattoes from coming to, and settling in, this State, under any pretext whatsoever," shall, on or before that day, be expunged therefrom.

The resolution was read the first time, and ordered to lie on the table.

Mr. BALDWIN submitted the following joint resolution, viz:

Resolved, by the Senate and House of Representatives of the United States of America in Congress assembled, That the President of the Senate and Speaker of the House of Representatives shall be authorized to adjourn the respective Houses from Friday the 22d day of December, 1820, to Tuesday the 2d of January, 1821.

The resolution was read twice, and ordered to lie on the table.

Mr. TUCKER, of Virginia, submitted the following resolutions, which, under the rule, will lie on the table for consideration until to-morrow.

1. *Resolved,* That the Secretary of the Treasury be instructed to prepare, and lay before this House, a statement showing the number and tonnage of the American and British vessels which have cleared from the ports of the United States for any port in the West Indies, the Bahama Islands, and Bermuda, in the years 1816, 1817, 1818, 1819, and 1820, distinguishing, in the last year, those which have cleared before the 30th day of September, and those which have cleared since that date.

2. *Resolved,* That the Secretary of the Treasury be instructed to state to this House, as far as he has information, the number and tonnage of the French ships which have arrived, and are expected to arrive, in the course of the present year, in the river Saint Mary's, since the 1st of July last; whether their cargoes are intended for the consumption of the United States, and to be introduced within the territories of the same, in evasion of the revenue laws; and what further provision he deems necessary to be made by law for the more effectual collection of the revenue on the Southern frontier.

HALL OF THE HOUSE.

Mr. MERCER submitted for consideration the following resolution:

Resolved, That the Committee on the Public Buildings be instructed to inquire into the practicability of making such alterations in the present structure of the Hall of the House of Representatives, as shall better adapt it to the purposes of a deliberative assembly; and, if no such alteration can be effected, to ascertain whether it be practicable to provide a suitable Hall in the centre building of the Capitol.

Mr. M. briefly explained his object in offering this resolve, which, it would be observed, proposed an inquiry merely. It was, he said, utterly impossible, as every gentleman's experience must have taught him, to hear more than one half of the members who addressed the House, without changing one's seat for the purpose. For one, he declared, that, owing to this circumstance, he felt himself utterly incapable of discharging the duty imposed on him by his constituents. He had, he said, in anticipation of such a duty as he now proposed to devolve on the Committee on the Public Buildings, made it his business to examine the centre building. He had satisfied himself that the room intended for the Library, simpler in its structure than the present Hall, which was of a figure unfavorable to deliberation, would answer all the purposes of a Representative Chamber. It would be a room larger than that which often accommodates five hundred members in the British House of Commons; as large as that which has accommodated a more numerous body in Massachusetts; and larger than that which is occupied by a more numerous body than this in the State of Virginia.

The resolve for inquiry was adopted, as above stated, but not without opposing voices.

DANIEL McDUFF.

An engrossed bill entitled "An act for the relief of Daniel McDuff," was read the third time; and on the question, shall it pass? it passed in the affirmative—yeas 72, nays 70, as follows:

YEAS—Messrs. Allen of New York, Allen of Tennessee, Baldwin, Ball, Beecher, Bryan, Butler of New Hampshire, Cannon, Cocke, Crawford, Crowell, Culbreth, Cushman, Cuthbert, Darlington, Dennison, Earle, Fay, Fisher, Ford, Garnett, Gorham, Gross of New York, Gross of Pennsylvania, Guyon, Hackley, Hall of Delaware, Hendricks, Hibshman, Hill, Hostetter, Jones of Tennessee, Kendall, Kent, Kinsey, Kinsley, Little, Lincoln, Lowndes, McCreary McCullough, Mallary, Mercer, Monell, Montgomery, S. Moore, Neale, Nelson of Massachusetts, Nelson of Virginia, Overstreet, Parker of Massachusetts, Parker of Virginia, Patterson, Philson, Pinckney, Rankin, Reed, Robertson, Rogers, Sergeant, Settle, Silsbee, Simpkins, Sloan, Smith of Maryland, Storrs, Tracy, Tucker of Virginia, Tucker of South Carolina, Walker, Warfield, and Whitman.

Nays—Messrs. Abbot, Adams, Alexander, Allen of Massachusetts, Anderson, Archer of Maryland, Baker, Barbour, Bateman, Bayly, Brush, Buffum, Burwell, Case, Cobb, Crafts, Culpeper, Dane, Davidson, Dewitt, Eddy, Edwards of Connecticut, Edwards of North Carolina, Lloyd, Folger, Foot, Fuller, Gray, Hall of New York, Hall of North Carolina, Harden, Hobart, Jackson, Johnson, Jones of Virginia, Lathrop, Linn, Livermore, Maclay, McCoy, McLean of Kentucky, Marchand, Meech, Metcalf, R. Moore, T. L. Moore, Mortson, Murray, Phelps, Plumer, Rhea, Rich, Richards, Richmond, Russ, Sawyer, Shaw, A. Smyth of Virginia, Smith of North Carolina, Street, Strong of Vermont, Tarr, Tomlinson, Tompkins, Tyler, Upham, Wendover, Williams of Virginia, Williams of North Carolina, and Wood.

The Committee of the Whole, to which is committed the bill providing for the preservation and repair of the Cumberland road, were discharged from the consideration thereof; and it was recommitted to the Committee on Roads and Canals.

WEDNESDAY, December 20.

Mr. WILLIAMS, of North Carolina, from the Committee of Claims, to which was referred the bill from the Senate, entitled "An act for the relief of Morgan Brown," made a report thereon, recommending that the said bill be postponed indefinitely. The bill and report were committed to a Committee of the Whole.

Mr. WILLIAMS made a report on the petition of Lewis H. Guerlain, accompanied with a bill for his relief; which was read twice, and committed to a Committee of the Whole.

Mr. WILLIAMS also made a report on the petition of Alexander Milne, accompanied with a bill for his relief; which was read twice, and committed to a Committee of the Whole.

Mr. WILLIAMS also made a report on the petition of John Rodriguez, accompanied with a bill for his relief; which was read twice, and committed to a Committee of the Whole to-morrow.

Mr. EDWARDS, of North Carolina, from the Committee on Revolutionary Pensions, reported a bill in addition to the several acts making provision for certain persons engaged in the land and naval service of the United States during the Revolutionary war; which was twice read.

[The object of the bill is to provide for the case of persons who, owing to disability, cannot appear in open court to take the necessary oaths.]

The bill was laid on the table, for the purpose

of being printed for better examination before it should be ordered to a third reading.

On motion of Mr. BALDWIN, the House then proceeded to consider the joint resolution submitted by him yesterday, proposing a recess of both Houses of Congress from Friday, the 22d instant, to Tuesday, the 2d day of January.

Mr. RHEA having expressed his wish to hear some reasons for this proposition—but no debate thereon arising—.

The question on ordering the same to be engrossed for a third reading, was taken by yeas and nays, and decided as follows—For the engrossment 42, against it 110.

So the resolution was negatived.

The House proceeded to consider the resolutions submitted yesterday by Mr. TUCKER, of Virginia; and, the same being again read, were agreed to by the House.

Mr. ROSS submitted the following resolution, which was ordered to lie on the table one day for consideration:

Resolved, That the President of the United States be requested to cause to be laid before this House the names of all persons who have been prosecuted and convicted in the courts of the United States, under the act of Congress passed the 14th of July, 1798, entitled "An act in addition to the act, entitled 'An act for the punishment of certain crimes against the United States;'" particularly designating in what State, and before what court convicted; the amount of the fine, together with the term of imprisonment inflicted on each defendant; also, the amount of fines paid into the Treasury of the United States, and by whom; the amount of such fines as may have been collected by the officers of Government, and which have not yet been paid into the Treasury of the United States; the time when collected; also, by whom, and from whom collected.

The House proceeded to consider the resolution submitted yesterday by Mr. FLOYD; and, being again read, Mr. LATHROP moved to amend the same, by adding thereto the following words: "and whether any of the officers of the Army hold any other office under the Government, and, if so, with what salary and emoluments."

And the question being taken so to amend, it passed in the affirmative.

The said resolution, as amended, was then agreed to as follows:

Resolved, That the Secretary of the Department of War be required to lay before this House a statement of the number and situation of all the military posts in the United States at this time; together with the distribution of the Army, designating the number of men; also, the number and rank of the officers at each place; and whether any of the officers of the Army hold any other office under the Government, and, if so, with what salary and emoluments.

A message from the Senate informed the House that the Senate have passed the bill, entitled "An act for the relief of Elias Parks," with an amendment, in which they ask the concurrence of this House. The amendment was read, and concurred in by the House.

683   HISTORY OF CONGRESS.   684

H. of R.   *Ohio and Michigan Boundary—Death of Mr. Slocumb.*   DECEMBER, 1820.

OHIO AND MICHIGAN BOUNDARY.

The House then, on motion of Mr. SIBLEY, resolved itself into a Committee of the Whole, on the resolution for fixing the boundary line between Ohio and Michigan.

[This resolution declares, that the line heretofore caused to be surveyed, marked, and designated, from the southern extreme of Lake Michigan, due east, in pursuance of the provisions of the act, entitled "An act to authorize the President of the United States to ascertain and designate certain boundaries," passed May 12, 1812, so far as the same extends due east from the western boundary line of the State of Ohio, be and remain the established boundary line between the said State of Ohio and the Territory of Michigan.]

Mr. Ross, of Ohio, moved to strike out the whole of the resolution after the word "Resolved," on the ground that the line therein proposed is altogether different from that which has been established, not only by the description of boundaries contained in the Constitution of Ohio, but also in substance by the act of the Congress of the United States authorizing the formation of the constitution of that State, and by subsequent acts of Congress. In support of these positions, Mr. R. entered into an argument of some length. He contended, also, for the right of Ohio to a voice in the decision of this question, which, by this resolution, it was not proposed to allow to her.

Mr. SIBLEY, Delegate from Michigan, opposed the motion of Mr. Ross, in an argument of considerable length and detail, contending, as well for the right of Congress to settle this question as for the justice and expediency of establishing the line as now proposed.

When Mr. S. concluded, the Committee rose, and, on motion of Mr. LOWNDES, were discharged from the further consideration of the resolve, and it was referred to the Committee on the Public Lands.

THURSDAY, December 21.

DEATH OF MR. SLOCUMB.

Little business was transacted in either House of Congress to-day, both bodies having adjourned at an early hour, to make arrangements to attend the funeral of a deceased member of the House of Representatives, and, as a mark of respect, usual on such occasions.

As soon as the Journal was read in the House of Representatives, Mr. SMITH, of North Carolina, rose, and announced to the House the decease of JESSE SLOCUMB, Esq., a member from the State of North Carolina; and, on the motion of Mr. SMITH, resolutions were then unanimously adopted expressive of the feelings of the House on this occasion; resolving to attend the funeral, this day, at three o'clock—appointing a committee to superintend the same—and resolving, also, as a testimony of respect for the memory of the deceased, to go into mourning, and wear a black crape round the left arm for thirty days.

Messrs. SMITH, of North Carolina, BURTON,

FISHER, HOOKS, SETTLE, WILLIAMS, of North Carolina, and DAVIDSON, were appointed the committee of arrangements.

On motion of Mr. SMITH, also, it was resolved that the Speaker of the House acquaint the Executive of the State of North Carolina, with the vacancy occasioned in the representation from that State by the death of Mr. SLOCUMB.

FRIDAY, December 22.

Mr. NEWTON, from the Committee on Commerce, reported a bill to authorize the President of the United States to establish a port of entry in the district of Sandusky, in the State of Ohio, and for other purposes; which was read twice, and ordered to be engrossed and read a third time to-morrow.

The SPEAKER laid before the House a letter from the Secretary of War, enclosing an "organization of the army, as proposed under the resolution of the House of Representatives of the 11th of May, 1820," which is intended as a substitute for so much of table A, which accompanied his report upon the reduction of the army, as relates to the details of organization; which was read, and referred to the Committee on Military Affairs.

Mr. TRACY submitted the following resolution, which was read, and ordered to lie on the table one day for consideration:

Resolved, That the Secretary of War be directed to lay before this House a statement, showing the number of soldiers recruited for the service of the Army of the United States during the year 1820, indicating the fund out of which the expenses of said recruiting have been paid; and, if any unexpended balance of a former appropriation has been used, in what year said appropriation was made.

MILITARY LAND WARRANTS.

On motion of Mr. CAMPBELL, the House then resolved itself into a Committee of the Whole on the bill extending the time for locating Virginia military land warrants.

The blank for the term of extension was filled with two years from the 1st of January, 1821, and the time within which returns may be made was fixed at four years.

And the bill being further amended, the Committee rose and reported the same to the House; and it was ordered to be engrossed for a third reading.

The House then resolved itself into a Committee of the Whole, (Mr. DARLINGTON in the chair,) on the bill to repeal the act entitled "An act to lessen the compensation of marshals, clerks, and attorneys, in the cases therein mentioned." Considerable discussion took place on the subject of the bill among the legal gentlemen of the House, which ended in the Committee's rising and reporting progress. The Committee were then discharged from the further consideration of the bill; and it was recommitted to a select committee.

The House then, on motion, adjourned to Tuesday next.

685   HISTORY OF CONGRESS.   686

DECEMBER, 1820.   *Colonel James Johnson—Death of Mr. Burrill.*   H. OF R.

TUESDAY, December 26.

The SPEAKER laid before the House a letter from the Secretary of War, transmitting a system of field service and police, and a system of martial law for the government of the Army of the United States, submitted in obedience to a resolution of the House of Representatives of the United States of the 22d of December, 1819; which, with its enclosures, was, on motion of Mr. PLUMER, referred to the Military Committee, and ordered to be printed.

A message from the Senate informed the House that the Senate have passed the bill of this House, entitled "An act to amend an act, entitled 'An act for the relief of the legal representatives of Henry Willis," with amendments; in which they ask the concurrence of this House.

The amendments were concurred in by the House.

Mr. MONELL submitted the following resolution, which was read, and ordered to lie on the table one day for consideration:

Resolved, That the President of the United States be requested to furnish this House with an account of compensation to counsel to assist district attorneys, and judge advocates in their office, for the last eight years, and to whom such compensation has been made.

On motion of Mr. CAMPBELL, the engrossed bill, entitled "An act to extend the time for locating Virginia land warrants, and returning surveys thereon to the General Land Office," was recommitted to the Committee on Private Land Claims.

An engrossed bill, entitled "An act to authorize the President of the United States to establish a port of entry in the district of Sandusky, in the State of Ohio, and for other purposes," was read the third time, and passed.

Mr. COOK submitted the following resolution, which was read, and ordered to lie on the table one day for consideration:

Resolved, That the Secretary of War be directed to communicate to this House a statement of the number of soldiers of the late army to whom warrants have been issued for military bounty land; and, also, the whole number of soldiers, who, from the date of their enlistment, and have not received such warrants, will be entitled to receive such bounty, designating, in both cases, the number of double and single bounties.

The House proceeded to consider the resolution submitted by Mr. TRACY on the 22d instant, and the same being again read, was concurred in by the House.

COLONEL JAMES JOHNSON.

The SPEAKER laid before the House the following letter from the Secretary of War:

WAR DEPARTMENT, *Dec.* 22, 1820.

SIR: In compliance with a resolution of the House of Representatives of the 1st of December, 1820, directing that the Secretary of War communicate to that House what sums of money have been actually paid to Colonel James Johnson, on account of transportation furnished the expedition ordered up the Missouri river; and, also, what sums have been paid him for detention of steamboats, or other incidental charges, and the causes of such detention; whether any difference of opinion existed between the Department of War and the said Colonel James Johnson, relative to the value of transportation or other charges exhibited by him against the United States; and what evidence was submitted to them, on which they formed their opinion—I enclose a letter to this Department from the Quartermaster General, which, with the documents accompanying it, contains the information directed to be communicated. By reference to the report, it will appear that a difference of opinion existed between the Department and the contractor in relation to the charges of the latter; and that, according to the terms of the contract, the points of difference were referred, as was stated in the report of this Department to the House of Representatives of the 2d of February last. It was in the first instance determined to have the reference at or near to St. Louis; and General Rector, of that place, was selected with that view, on the part of the Government, and Colonel Morrison, of Lexington, Kentucky, on that of the contractor; but, on application on the part of the contractor, the place was changed to this city, under the belief that it would be a mutual accommodation, and facilitate the ultimate decision. It thus became necessary to select other persons, and Commodore Rodgers was chosen as the referee on the part of the Government, and General John Mason, of Georgetown, on that of the contractor; and, with the assent of the parties, the Attorney General of the United States was selected as the umpire. The Attorney General having declined to act, the arbitrators, in conformity to the terms of the contract, select Walter Jones, Esq., as umpire.

The statement of the amount which has been paid to the contractor, contains not only the amount paid for transportation on the Missouri, but also that on the Mississippi and the Ohio, and comprehends the sum paid to him for transportation performed both in 1819 and 1820. It may be proper to remark, that the expedition (for reasons stated in the report of the 2d of February, already referred to) not being completed in the Summer and Fall of 1819, as was expected at the time of forming the contract, the Department proposed that the rate of transportation necessary to complete the movement should be fixed, as both the contractor and the Government had acquired such a knowledge of the subject as to enable them to determine what ought to be allowed with some degree of certainty, to which the contractor assented; and the rate was fixed at eight cents per pound to the Council Bluffs.

The account of the contractor for transportation, particularly for this year, is not finally adjusted; but it is believed when it is, the account will be found to be nearly balanced.

I have the honor to be, your obedient servant,
J. C. CALHOUN.

Hon. JOHN W. TAYLOR,
     Speaker of the House of Representatives.

On motion of Mr. COCKE, the letter and its accompaniments were ordered to be referred to a select committee. Messrs. COCKE, MALLARY, OVERSTREET, and SETTLE, were appointed by the Speaker to be the committee.

DEATH OF MR. BURRILL.

The Secretary of the Senate then came in with a message, announcing the death of the Honorable JAMES BURRILL, Jr., a member of that body and

687   HISTORY OF CONGRESS.   688

H. of R.   *Public Lands—Military Peace Establishment.*   December, 1820.

that his funeral would take place from the Senate Chamber, at half past ten o'clock to-morrow.

Whereupon, on motion of Mr. Eddy, it was—

Resolved, unanimously, That this House will attend the funeral of the Honorable James Burrill, Jr., late a member of the Senate from the State of Rhode Island, to-morrow, at half past ten o'clock, A. M.; and, as a testimony of respect for the memory of the deceased, will go into mourning, and wear crape for thirty days.

The House then adjourned to Thursday next.

Thursday, December 28.

On motion of Mr. Williams, of North Carolina, the Committee on Military Affairs were instructed to inquire into the expediency of allowing to the officers of the army a salary or stated sum of money per year, instead of the pay and emoluments as now allowed by law.

The Speaker laid before the House a letter from the Secretary of the Treasury, transmitting an estimate of the appropriations necessary for the service of the year 1821; which was referred to the Committee of Ways and Means.

Mr. Rich gave notice that, on Tuesday next, in case he should be able to obtain the floor, he should submit a proposition for instructing a proper committee to inquire into the expediency of prohibiting, prospectively, the importation of distilled spirits and malt liquors, and sundry manufactured articles which come most in competition with domestic fabrics.

PUBLIC LANDS.

Mr. Anderson, from the Committee on Public Lands, reported the following bill:

Be it enacted, &c., That no lands purchased from the United States on or before the first day of July last, shall be considered as forfeited to the Government for failure in completing the payment thereon, until the 31st day of December, 1821; and that all persons indebted to the Government for lands shall be permitted, on or before the day aforesaid, to surrender to the register of the general land office of the district in which their purchase or purchases have been made, by half-quarter sections, or legal subdivisions of fractional sections, any part of the quantity which they respectively hold, and the sums which such persons may have paid on the land so surrendered shall be carried to their credit on the quantity retained; the quarter sections and fractions shall be divided for the purpose of surrendering, as by law is now directed. No interest shall be charged against any person for moneys due and unpaid on any tract surrendered as aforesaid, or on any tract retained and paid for on or before the said 31st day of December, 1821; and on complete payment being made for any tract, agreeably to the provisions of this act, a patent shall issue, as in other cases.

Sec. 2. *And be it further enacted,* That all persons indebted to the Government for lands, shall, on payment in cash of the whole purchase money, for any tract, on or before the 31st day of December, 1821, be allowed a deduction of —— per cent. on the original price at which their lands were purchased, excluding interest, and computing the moneys already paid as a part of the said purchase money.

Sec. 3. *And be it further enacted,* That all persons indebted to the Government for lands, and who shall not, on or before the 31st day of December, 1821, have made payment therefor, shall be permitted to pay the sums by them respectively due, in —— equal annual instalments, without interest, the first of which shall be payable the —— day of ——; and a failure to make payment of any of the aforesaid instalments at the time they may become due, shall deprive the person so failing of all the benefits to be derived from this section.

The bill was twice read and committed.

MILITARY PEACE ESTABLISHMENT.

Mr. Smyth, from the Military Committee, reported the following bill:

Be it enacted, &c. That, from and after the first day of May next, the Military Peace Establishment of the United States shall consist of six thousand non-commissioned officers, musicians, and privates, with a due proportion of field and company officers, according to the present organization of companies, and in such proportions of artillery and infantry as the President of the United States shall direct; and, that the corps of engineers, as at present established, be retained in service.

And be it further enacted, That the President of the United States cause to be arranged the officers, non-commissioned officers, musicians, and privates, of the several corps of troops now in service, in such manner as to form and complete the corps to be retained in service under this act, consolidating the corps of ordnance and the corps of light artillery with the corps of artillery, and the corps of riflemen with the infantry, and cause the supernumerary officers, non-commissioned officers, and privates, to be discharged from the service.

And be it further enacted, That there shall be one Brigadier General, with one Aid-de-Camp, one Assistant Adjutant General, and one Assistant Inspector General; there shall also be one Adjutant General, one Quartermaster General, and one Judge Advocate, each with the rank, pay, and emoluments, of a Colonel of Cavalry, as heretofore prescribed by law. There shall also be a Paymaster General, with a salary as heretofore fixed by law; a Commissary General of Purchases, with a salary of two thousand dollars per annum, and one Assistant Commissary General of Purchases, whose compensation shall not exceed two and a half per centum on the public moneys disbursed by him, nor the sum of fifteen hundred dollars per annum; and two Military Storekeepers, to be compensated as heretofore; one Commissary General of Subsistence, with as many assistants as the service may require; one Surgeon General with a salary of two thousand dollars per annum, and one Apothecary General, with a salary of fifteen hundred dollars per annum.

And be it further enacted, That there shall be, to each regiment of infantry, and to each battalion of artillery, one Adjutant, one Quartermaster, and one Paymaster, one Surgeon, and one Assistant Surgeon.

And be it further enacted, That the Topographical Engineers and their assistants shall be discharged from the service of the United States.

And be it further enacted, That the Judge Advocate shall keep an office in the City of Washington, and, in addition to the duties which may be assigned to him by the President of the United States, he shall keep a record of all trials by general courts martial, and report the decisions.

And be it further enacted, That all officers of the army whose continuance in service is not provided for by this act, shall be discharged from the service of the United States; and that, to each commissioned officer, who shall be deranged by virtue of this act, there shall be paid, in addition to the pay and emoluments to which he shall be entitled at the time of his discharge, three months pay.

The bill was twice read, and referred to a Committee of the Whole on the state of the Union.

Mr. F. JOHNSON, of Kentucky, gave notice, that on the 8th day of January, he should move to take up for consideration the bill, reported at the last session of Congress, to authorize the President of the United States to take possession of East and West Florida. He had been reminded of it, he said, by the bill reported this day by the Committee on Military Affairs, for the reduction of the Army.

STATE OF THE FINANCES.

The SPEAKER laid before the House letter from the Secretary of the Treasury, explanatory of his report of the first instant, upon the state of the finances; which was referred to the Committee of Ways and Means.

The report is as follows:

TREASURY DEPARTMENT, *Dec.* 21, 1820.

SIR: In conformity with the provisions of the eighth section of the act of 1st May, 1820, entitled "An act in addition to the several acts for the establishment and regulation of the Treasury, War, and Navy Departments," statements are annexed to the estimates, of the public expenditure for the year 1821, which are herewith transmitted, showing—

1. That the permanent appropriations, and those for a term of years not yet expired, amounted to $11,381,975 00

2. That, of the sums appropriated for 1820, and previous years, it is estimated that there will remain on the books of the Treasury, on the 1st of January, 1821　-　-　-　6,907,619 03

3. That there will be, on that day, in the hands of the Treasurer, as agent of the War and Navy Departments　-　-　-　-　-　927,241 29

4. That the whole amount of unexpended balances of appropriations subject to the disposition of the Executive Government during the year 1821, is estimated at　-　-　7,834,860 32

5. That, of that sum, there will be required to defray the expenses incurred in 1820, or necessary to effect the objects for which the several appropriations were made　-　3,632,659 41

6. And that there will remain unexpended, and not necessary to effect the objects for which the several appropriations were made　-　-　4,202,200 91

As it is ascertained that the sum of $4,202,200 91, with the exception of $1,860,437 57, which have been deducted from the estimates of the War Department for 1821, and which will form a part of the expenditure of that department during the year, will not be required, if that amount should be directed to be car-

ried to the account of the surplus fund, the estimates for the year 1824, and the balance against the Treasury on the first day of that year, as presented in this report, will remain to be provided for.

It may be proper to observe, that all sums which will be carried to the account of the surplus fund on the 31st day of this month, are not comprehended in any of the foregoing statements.

Inaccuracies having been discovered in the estimate of the probable expenditure of the year 1821, presented in the annual Treasury report of the 1st instant, resulting, principally, from the different manner of keeping the warrant and appropriation accounts in the Treasury, War, and Navy Departments, I avail myself of this occasion to correct those inaccuracies, and to present the amount of the deficiency which will have to be provided for during the ensuing year.

The receipts into the Treasury during the year 1820, and the amount remaining in the Treasury on the first of January of that year, were estimated in the annual report at　-　-　-　-　$22,396,244 63

The payments from the Treasury to the 30th of September last, amounted to　-　-　-　-　-　-　16,906,413 80

Which, being deducted from the aggregate amount above stated, leaves for the service of the 4th quarter　-　5,417,830 83

The payments made in the 4th quarter, and those which are required to complete the service of the year 1820, are as follows:

Civil, diplomatic, and miscellaneous, already made　-　$476,920 05
And to be made　-　-　930,293 51
　　　　　　　　　　　　　1,407,213 56

Military department, already made　-　93,688 90
And to be made　-　665,164 61
　　　　　　　　　　　　758,853 51

Naval department, already made　-　1,446,228 00
And to be made　-　1,110,000 00
　　　　　　　　　　　　2,556,228 00

Public debt, payments already made, and to be made　-　-　4,900,000 00

Making the aggregate sum of　-　-　9,622,295 07

And leaving a balance against the Treasury, on the 1st of Jan. 1821, of　-　-　-　-　-　-　$4,204,464 24

To avoid complexity, the sums estimated to be necessary to complete the service of the year 1820, or to effect the objects for which the several appropriations were made, are, in the above statement, considered a charge upon the Treasury during the fourth quarter of the year; although it is probable that a portion of those sums may not be drawn until late in the ensuing year, and possibly a small part not before the year 1825. In the annual report no sum was charged upon the fourth quarter, but what was understood would be drawn.

The estimate of the receipts into the Treasury during the year 1821, presented in the annual report of the Treasury, amounts to - - - $16,550,000 00
The estimate of the public expenditure for that year is as follows:

Civil, diplomatic, and miscellaneous - - 1,769,850 04		
Civilizing the Indians, and Indian trade - 29,200 00		
Military department, including fortifications, ordnance, Indian department, revolutionary and military pensions, arming the militia, arrears prior to the 1st Jan'ry, 1817, and the sum of $1,860,437 57, which has been deducted from the estimates, and is not included in the above balance against the Treasury - - 6,798,515 18		
Naval department, including the gradual increase of the Navy 3,428,676 81		
Public debt, being the amount of principal and interest payable in the year 1821 - 5,477,776 76		

Amounting together to - - - 17,504,018 79

Which presents an excess of expenditure beyond the receipts, of - - 954,018 79
Which, added to the balance estimated against the Treasury on the 1st January, 1821, of - - - 4,204,464 24

Leaves to be provided for the sum of 5,458,483 03
But the Secretary of the Navy has stated, in his letter of the 18th inst., herewith transmitted, that, of the appropriation of $1,000,000, for the gradual increase of the Navy, not more than $500,000 will be required in 1821; and the residue being deducted - - - - 500,000 00

Will leave a balance against the Treasury of - - - - $4,658,483 30

It will be perceived that this balance is less than that presented in the annual report of the Treasury, by $2,793,103 74; which amount consists, 1st, of the sum which, it has since been found, will not be wanted for the naval service; 2nd, of balances of appropriations, for civil list and miscellaneous objects, which, it appears upon subsequent examination, will not be required; 3d, of an excess in the estimate in the charge for the military service, resulting from the different mode of keeping the warrant and appropriation accounts in the different departments; and, 4th, of the balance in the hands of the Treasurer, on the 1st of January, 1820, as agent of the War Department, which ought to have been deducted from that charge, as it had already been drawn from the Treasury.

In determining the amount of the loan which will be necessary for the service of the year 1821, if that shall be the only mode resorted to for meeting the deficiency, it is proper to state that, of the sum now in the Treasury, there are upwards of $600,000 of special deposite, which cannot be available during the year. The time necessary to transfer the revenue collected in the Western States, and in those bordering on the Gulf of Mexico, beyond what is expended in those States, to the places where it will be expended, may be estimated upon an an average at six months. One-half of the sums collected in those States may, therefore, be considered, through the year, as in a situation not to be applicable to the demands upon the Treasury, as it will be in transitu between the places of collection and those of expenditure. If this amount be stated at $600,000, there will be, through the year, the sum of $1,200,000 which cannot be considered as available.

To insure the prompt discharge of all demands upon the Treasury, and to place the public credit beyond the reach of accident, the sum of $1,000,000 ought to remain in the Treasury. It is probable that, of the appropriations for 1821, nearly that amount will remain in the Treasury, or in the hands of the Treasurer, as agent, at the end of the year. But it is considered unsafe to trust to that contingency. It is, therefore, respectfully submitted, that provision be made for raising the sum of $7,000,000, in aid of the funds which it is estimated will be received into the Treasury during the year 1821. If that amount should be raised by loan, the interest of the debt thus created will increase the public expenditure, and render the amount proposed to be raised indispensable.

I remain, with respect, &c.
         WM. H. CRAWFORD.
The Hon. J. W. Taylor,
    Speaker House of Representatives.

TREATY OF GHENT.

On motion of Mr. Mallary, the House proceeded to the consideration of the report of the Secretary of State on the expenses attending the execution of the 5th, 6th, and 7th articles of the Treaty of Ghent, made in pursuance of a resolution of this House.

Some conversation took place as to what committee should be referred the examination of this subject. Mr. Mallary proposed a select committee, another gentleman proposed the Committee of Foreign Relations, &c.

In the course of the conversation—

Mr. Cobb said it was time some inquiry should be made into the subject, for, from this report, it appeared that the survey of the Northern boundary line, under these articles of the treaty, was likely to cost the United States a pretty round sum—having already cost the Government, as appeared by this report, *only* a hundred and ninety-five thousand dollars.

Mr. Mallary said his object was to have an investigation of the matter; to see whether the progress of the commission had been proportionate to its expenditure, &c. With that object only in view, it was not material to him what committee the subject was referred to.

Mr. Foot preferred that the subject should be referred to the Committee of Foreign Relations, with which it had an evident connexion. He further remarked that it could not be objected to its going to that committee, that they had before them at present any very important business.

The subject was finally referred to a select committee; and Messrs. MALLARY, LOWNDES, CANNON, HENDRICKS, and LINCOLN, were appointed a committee accordingly.

NOTES IN PAYMENT OF DUTIES.

Mr. LOWNDES submitted the following resolution:

Resolved, That the Committee of Ways and Means be instructed to inquire into the expediency of providing that the notes of no banks by which notes below the amount of five dollars are, or may be, issued, shall be taken in payment of duties or debts to the Government of the United States.

In introducing the resolution, Mr. L. adverted to the viciousness of the currency where notes for dollars and parts of dollars supply the place of specie, as, where such notes are issued, they always will. He spoke also of the efforts made in some of the States, and now making in Virginia, to banish those notes from circulation—efforts which were always vain, so long as such notes were issued by neighboring States, &c. No authority but Congress, he contended, was competent to correct the evil in any manner; and, the object of his resolution being for inquiry only, he did not anticipate any sound objection to its adoption.

Mr. STORRS said he had no decided objection to inquiry into this subject, but he hoped the House would reflect on the effect which the adoption of the measure suggested would have, in giving a preference to the notes of the Bank of the United States over those of all other banks. He hoped that the Committee of Ways and Means, whose information on such subjects was so extensive, would examine this question in all its bearings, and present their views of it to the House.

Mr. LOWNDES said it was hardly possible to suppose that the committee would not know, as every member of the House would see, that the effect of the adoption of such a measure must be favorable to some banks and unfavorable to others. But, Mr. L. said, there are many banks, and those among the best in the States, which do not issue notes of a less denomination than five dollars. It was for the Committee of Ways and Means to inquire whether the Government should not lend its aid to produce uniformity in this respect.

Mr. MEIGS agreed in opinion with his colleague, and was opposed even to authorizing an inquiry into this matter. When this great Bank of the United States had furnished the Union with a circulating medium of equal value in all parts of the Union, he might perhaps be inclined to give it further facilities; but, for the present, he would not, for one, consent to go further in this respect than Congress had already gone. The Secretary of the Treasury had already the power to forbid the reception of notes not in good credit, by the collectors, &c., which he had duly exercised. If a measure of the sort now proposed were to succeed, the notes of a great majority of the banks in

the United States would cease to be receivable in payment of taxes, and would be driven from circulation. He could see no other effect which could flow from the adoption of the regulation suggested in the resolve, but to give an almost exclusive circulation to the notes of the Bank of the United States, and he was therefore opposed to the resolve.

Mr. SOUTHARD spoke in favor of the resolve. He thought it was bad policy ever to have permitted the banks to issue notes of a less denomination than five dollars, and believed that such issues had a great agency in driving specie from circulation a few years ago. He was of opinion that excluding the small notes from circulation would restore specie to its former general currency.

Mr. LOWNDES spoke in reply to Mr. MEIGS, denying that the particular object of his motion was to benefit the United States Bank. Suppose no such bank were in existence, he said, and the interest of the country required that its currency should consist in part of gold and silver, and not of paper merely, would it not be well, under such circumstances, at least to inquire into the policy of prohibiting the circulation of notes of a denomination under five dollars—the effect of which measure would be to substitute specie, in part, for notes, in the circulating medium of the country? The object of the resolution was not to institute an inquiry in order to benefit the Bank of the United States; but, if it were the policy of the country to encourage the circulation of specie, which he presumed no man would doubt, he asked whether that policy ought to be disregarded, because a resort to it might incidentally benefit the Bank of the United States? If it were true that the Bank of the United States had not afforded a circulating medium of equal value, &c., that itself would be an argument not against, but in favor of this inquiry.

Mr. MEIGS resumed the floor. The great Bank of the United States, he contended, had not fulfilled the duties which it was expected to have performed. There were a hundred banks in the States, he said, about the legality of whose institution there were no doubts, whose paper was as current and in as high credit as that of the Bank of the United States, and who issued notes of a less amount than five dollars. And why should they not? Was the circulating medium of the country intended only for men who deal in tens and hundreds of dollars? The object of this resolution, he said, was plainly neither more nor less than to restrain the circulation of the notes of banks issuing notes of less than five dollars, and of course to benefit the Bank of the United States by making its notes the only current paper. He was, therefore, yet decidedly opposed to this proposition.

Mr. TRIMBLE said he should vote for the proposed inquiry, and regretted the opposition to it. The people of the United States, he said, expected that the National Government would make the inquiry, and do what appeared, on inquiry, to be within the scope of its power, to restore to this country a sound circulating medium. At a former session, a report had been made to this House, in which it had been suggested that a circulating medium might be established, to consist of small coins of convenient denominations. He presumed it was intended to take up the subject at the present session, and, if possible, to adopt some measure to carry that idea into effect. He observed, by the way, that with regard to the Bank of the United States, he was not much disposed to offer to it any advantages in addition to those which it already enjoyed. Adverting to what had fallen from other gentlemen respecting small banks and small bank notes, Mr. T. said that Congress had set the example to the States in establishing them; in this District, with a population of some thirty thousand, Congress had established twelve banks, and it had a branch of the Bank of the United States besides. Mr. T. here alluded to the miserable small notes in circulation in the District, respecting which he made a ludicrous comparison, which the reporter did not hear with sufficient distinctness to commit to paper. He hoped some measure would be adopted by Congress to effect a circulation of coins for all transactions under five dollars. It was expected from Congress. It was in the power of Congress alone to effect this object, and Congress had already too long delayed the exercise of the power.

Mr. SMITH, of Maryland, made a few remarks on the proposition before the House, the object of which he understood to be to exclude from circulation all bank notes under five dollars, with a view to introduce, in place of them, a specie currency. Such a measure, Mr. S. believed, would have the effect to prevent the general exportation of specie whenever there was a demand for it abroad, by dispersing it over the country, in such a manner that it could not readily be gathered together in large sums. Mr. S. showed, by reference to what had taken place in different parts of the country, and more recently by voluntary arrangement of the banks in Baltimore, that such would be the effect of the exclusion of small notes from circulation. Whether it was politic to do, in this respect, what would have the appearance of striking at the State banks, was another question; there could be no doubt, however, of the authority of Congress in this regard within the District of Columbia, nor of the expediency of exercising it, &c.

Mr. SILSBEE made a few observations to the same effect as those of Mr. SMITH. He was in favor of the resolution, and believed that the sooner the circulation of these small notes was stopped the better it would be for the country.

Mr. MERCER, in expressing his approbation of the resolution, said he was surprised that the gentleman from Kentucky should have reflected so pointedly on the District of Columbia; for, as the old saying is, those who live in glass houses should not throw stones. Of the banks of this District, he would only say that he believed they were in a better state than any beyond the Alleghany mountains; and, with respect to the circulation of small notes within the District, the people of the District had been the first to direct the attention of Congress to the subject; and he intimated the hope that the session would not pass without making some provision to restrain these issues of notes, particularly by the corporations of the city and towns of the District. With respect to the Bank of the United States, Mr. M. said it had nothing to do with this question. Whenever that subject should properly present itself to the House, he should take the opportunity to offer some few remarks on the impolicy of affording further advantages to that already powerful institution.

Mr. BALDWIN said he was unwilling at any time to oppose a proposition having for its object an inquiry into the expediency of any measure. But this was an exception. It was the beginning of a system of legislation which looked towards an interference with the State banks. The next step might be, to propose that no notes of State banks should be received in payments to the United States. The same principle as is found in the proposition suggested in this resolution, would equally justify that legislation which he had just mentioned. It is best to stop, said Mr. B., before we begin this course. What we have already done has led to a question of the rights of States to lay taxes; in regard to which some think the judicial decision has been too much against the States. The Secretary of the Treasury, Mr. B. said, had already a discretionary power on this subject. Why then should this House take the matter up, when the proposition submitted was at least of questionable character? He knew of no motive which could induce him ultimately to sanction the proposition; but, before he would even vote for an inquiry into it, he must have much stronger reasons in its favor than had yet been assigned.

Mr. TRIMBLE said he well recollected the proverb which the gentleman had quoted to him. The example of multiplying banks, however, was set by the Congress, and the people of Kentucky but followed it; and that example had a powerful effect. Whatever might be thought of Congress immediately around the Seat of Government, at a greater distance a very high opinion was entertained of them; and when they established the twelfth bank within this District, the people at a distance thought it a wonderfully wise measure, and the good people of Kentucky followed the example which Congress had set them. Congress, Mr. T. said, had set a pernicious example in this respect, and ought to be prompt in acknowledging their error and retracting it as far as practicable. The adoption of this resolution would be one step towards doing so.

Mr. MERCER said, if the subject had been the policy of multiplying banks, he should have thought himself unhappy in the proverb he had brought to his aid. But the question was of the absence of specie, occasioned by the circulation of small notes; and, Mr. M. said, that he believed in the State in which the gentleman from Kentucky resided there is not a specie-paying bank, whilst there is not one in operation in this District which does not pay specie. Mr. M. made some further remarks in defence and support of State banks against the Bank of the United States. He was opposed to one bank in a country, as he was to one head in a monarchy, &c., and was as much opposed as any one to subjecting the State banks to the sway of the great banking institution of the country.

Mr. BURTON said it appeared to him that the gentleman from Pennsylvania (Mr. BALDWIN) had placed this subject on its proper basis. If Congress had the power to interfere with the circulation of one dollar notes of the State banks, it certainly had the same power in regard to all the notes of State banks. Mr. B. was opposed to the resolution. The substitution of specie for small notes was a matter to be regulated by public opinion. When specie vanished some years ago, the issue of small notes was indispensable; on the other hand, when specie became plentiful in the cities, public opinion there corrected the evil. If we adopt the resolution, said Mr. B., we at once commence an attack on the State banks, and there is no knowing where it will end.

Mr. LIVERMORE said, for his part, that he considered it improper to attempt indirectly a measure which could not be directly approached. Such, he said, would be the effect of the adoption of the resolve now proposed. Every State in the Union had authority to do, by direct legislation, what it was now proposed to do indirectl . Mr. L. was, therefore, for leaving this matter wholly to the State Legislatures. In Pennsylvania a law had been passed prohibiting the circulation of notes for less than five dollars. In other States the same had been done. In New Hampshire, though attempts had been made to effect this object, the laws had been afterwards repealed. Let each State, said Mr. L., regulate this matter for itself. It was not pretended, he said, that the proposed measure was necessary in aid of the collection of the revenue. On the other hand, if it became necessary to resort to internal taxation, it would be indispensable to have small bills in circulation, without which the revenue could not be collected. Silver and gold, Mr. L. said, would forever centre in the cities; they would not remain in the remote parts of the country, and, in their absence, small bills were indispensable. He hoped, therefore, that the country banks would not be prevented from issuing them.

Mr. COBB was surprised at the nature of the objections to this resolution, which proposed to establish no principle, but merely to make an inquiry. What was the object of the resolution? It was to inquire into the expediency of a measure which, if adopted, would probably have the effect to force a general specie currency. Certainly, if it had that effect, a great benefit would result to society from its adoption; because specie is subject to no variation, and will answer all purposes in all places, which paper currency will not. He could not see that, by this measure, the United States Bank was to be benefited either one way or another; and, as to the abstract policy of the proposed measure, he did not see how a doubt could exist.

The question was then taken on agreeing to Mr. LOWNDES's resolution, and decided in the affirmative—59 votes to 40.

FRIDAY, December 29.

Another member, to wit: from the State of Ohio, SAMUEL HERRICK, appeared and took his seat.

The SPEAKER laid before the House a letter from the Secretary of the Treasury, stating that the records of the Treasury do not contain the information required by the resolution of the House of Representatives of the 20th instant, relative to the number and tonnage of American and British vessels which cleared out from the ports of the United States for the ports of the West Indies, Bahama Islands, and Bermuda, in the years 1816, 1817, 1818, 1819, and 1820; which letter was read, and ordered to lie on the table.

The SPEAKER also laid before the House two other letters from the Secretary of the Treasury, one transmitting the annual statement of the district tonnage of the United States, on the 31st of December, 1819; the other transmitting the anual statement of goods, wares, and merchandise, exported from the United States to foreign countries during the year ending on the 30th September, 1820; which were severally read and ordered to lie on the table.

APPORTIONMENT OF REPRESENTATIVES.

Mr. ANDERSON submitted for consideration the following resolution:

Resolved, That a committee be appointed to inquire into the expediency of providing by law, at the present session of Congress, for the apportionment of the representation in Congress among the several States, according to the fourth enumeration of the people of the United States.

Mr. A. made a few remarks in favor of his motion. On most subjects, he said, it was certainly desirable to have before you all the facts of the case before you legislate; on this particular subject, however, he believed Congress could legislate best without knowing the fact of the population of the States respectively. On former occasions of this sort, much difficulty had been found in legislating, from the operation of local feelings, naturally producing a desire on the part of the representatives of each State to fix on such a ratio of apportionment as should leave to it the smallest fraction of numbers. The legislating at the present session, before these numbers were known, would, it appeared to him, obviate these difficulties, as the only object of consideration would be, what ratio is of itself the most eligible? If the census of each State was waited for, he feared that the decision of Congress would be influenced by very different principles, &c. He was careless about the shape of this inquiry, but, feeling anxiety for the object of it, he hoped the resolution would be agreed to.

Mr. LOWNDES said, as the resolution proposed an inquiry merely, he certainly should not object to it. If it were possible to fix, by anticipation, the ratio of representation, he admitted it would be decidedly proper to pursue that course. But, important as the object might be, he feared it would be found wholly impracticable. Any act of this Congress fixing the ratio would, he feared, have no other effect than, as an expression of the opinion of the present Congress, it might have an influence on the next Congress. It would be an imperfect law, requiring future legislation to carry it into effect. Another act would be necessary, when the numbers of population were ascertained, to declare how many Representatives each State should be entitled to; and, he apprehended, in making that declaration, the next Congress would not be governed by any decision the present Congress might make on the subject. On this point, however, he did not mean to express a decided opinion, but he submitted, for the consideration of the committee which would be appointed, if this resolution was agreed to, whether any legislation by the present Congress would be definitive, or whether it would not in fact leave the question yet open for the decision of the Congress.

Mr. ANDERSON said that, supposing this to be, according to the suggestion of the gentleman from South Carolina, a preliminary law only, yet, being passed, it would be considered by the next Congress binding on them so as to make the actual declaration of the number of Representatives to which each State should be entitled a matter of course. The only objection to the proposed course which had ever suggested itself to his mind was, that it would leave uncertain the exact number of members of which the House of Representatives would be composed. Yet, he believed, though the number could not be exactly ascertained, it could be nearly so, and that, if Congress legislated on the subject at the present session, the total number of Representatives would be less than at present.

Mr. FULLER said he much approved the reason which had been assigned for fixing the ratio of representation at the present session; but he thought the purpose could have been better attained at the last session of Congress than at the present, because members could not by possibility have obtained any partial information which would have an influence on the decision of any one of them on the question. At the present session, said he, we are not in that situation. The States least remote can come pretty near a certainty as to the amount of their population, and some States may have an accurate knowledge of their numbers. Representatives from other States, from their situation, could not obtain similar information. If determined now, moreover, the decision would be liable to be reversed at the next session. He was, therefore, inclined to oppose the resolution.

Mr. ANDERSON said, if the population of the respective States were now really known, the fact would be a good argument against his motion. He had supposed an entire ignorance prevailed on that subject. For himself, he said, he did not know the population even of the village in which he lived, much less of the State which he represented. He did not admit that, decided now, the subject would yet be open at the next session. All the next Congress would have to do would be to pass a law conforming the number of Representatives to the principle established in the preceding law. That, he believed, might be done

without a law; but he supposed it would be most formal and proper to do it by law.

Mr. CAMPBELL said if the resolution embraced an affirmative proposition, he should say it was inexpedient to pass it. He did believe, he said, that from many of the States information might now be obtained which would influence the decision of this House as to the ratio of representation. Mr. C. also believed, if partial information could be guarded against, there would yet be as much difficulty in legislating on the subject now as at the next session, and the same opposition to a large ratio from the apprehension of its reducing the numbers of Representatives from some of the States. On the former occasions, although difficulties had occurred, the ratio had been always fixed within the proper time, and, as far as he knew, to the general satisfaction of the country. He hoped the same would be the case at the next session. Every man cannot realize his own wishes, and the majority of opinions must at last decide. Under all the circumstances, he thought it best to defer this matter to the next session, when Congress could act with the aid of all the lights that could be thrown upon it.

Mr. SMITH, of Maryland, said as this resolution proposed inquiry only, he saw no objection to it. The committee would inquire fully into the subject, and report the result of their deliberations. It would then be time enough to debate the main question, which was not presented by the question now before the House.

The question being then taken on agreeing to the resolution, it was decided in the affirmative; and Messrs. ANDERSON, LOWNDES, CAMPBELL, FULLER, and STORRS, were appointed a committee accordingly, under said resolution.

The orders of the day were called over; but many members being absent, and no disposition appearing to call up business, the House, on motion of Mr. HILL, adjourned to Tuesday.

TUESDAY, January 2, 1821.

Mr. ANDERSON, from the Committee on Public Lands, reported a bill for the relief of Clement B. Penrose and John B. C. Lucas, which was twice read and committed.

The SPEAKER laid before the House a letter from the Secretary of War, transmitting reports showing the number of soldiers recruited during the year 1820—the fund from which the expenses of recruiting have been paid, &c., prepared in obedience to a resolution of this House; which letter and report were ordered to lie on the table.

Mr. BURWELL submitted the following resolution, which was read, and ordered to lie on the table:

Resolved, That the select committee, to whom the Message of the President, transmitting an account of the expenditures of the commissioners under the fifth, sixth, and seventh articles of the Treaty of Ghent, for designating the northern boundary of the United States, was referred, be instructed to report a bill fixing the salaries of the commissioners and agents employed in that service.

On motion of Mr. HILL, the Committee of Ways and Means were instructed to inquire into the expediency of making provision by law for the compensation of persons employed in transmitting to Congress the votes for President and Vice President.

The SPEAKER laid before the House the following report from the Secretary of State:

The Secretary of State, in compliance with a resolution of the House of Representatives of the 11th instant, has the honor of reporting that a copy of the volume, containing the commercial regulations of foreign countries, which was printed under the direction of the President, conformably to a resolution of the Senate of 3d March, 1817, was transmitted to each of the Ministers and Consuls of the United States, with a request that they would examine with attention the part of the volume containing the regulations of the respective countries where they resided, and communicate to this department any supplementary information upon the same subject which might be in or come into their possession.

The communications hitherto received in answer to this request, together with some others, relating to the same subject, are herewith transmitted in obedience to the resolution of the House.

The original documents themselves are submitted, as they were received, in the belief that such parts of the information which they contain, as may be immediately desirable to the House, will be most easily collected from them; and as no satisfactory abstract or digest of them could be prepared in time to be available to the House during their present session.

JOHN QUINCY ADAMS.
DEPARTMENT OF STATE, Dec. 30, 1820.

The report was read and ordered to lie on the table.

On motion of Mr. COOK, the Committee of Ways and Means were instructed to inquire into the expediency of requiring every class of public officers, charged either with the collection or disbursement of the public money, to settle their accounts within specified periods, under the penalty of absolutely forfeiting their respective appointments.

On motion of Mr. HALL, of New York, the Committee on Commerce were directed to inquire into the expediency of erecting a lighthouse at the mouth of the Oswego river, on the shore of Lake Ontario.

Mr. SMITH, of Maryland, submitted the following resolution, which was read, and ordered to lie on the table one day for consideration:

Resolved, That the Secretary of the Treasury be directed to report to this House a statement, showing the number of tons of French vessels which have entered from any of the ports of France, and cleared outward for any such ports during the years 1816, 1817, 1818, 1819, and 1820, and the number of tons of vessels of the United States, which have entered from any of the said ports, and cleared out for the same during those years.

The following Message was received from the PRESIDENT OF THE UNITED STATES:

To the House of Representatives of the United States:

In compliance with a resolution of the House of Representatives of the 22d of November last, request-

ing the President to inform that House what naval force has been stationed for the protection of the commerce in the West India islands, and parts adjacent, during the present year; and whether any depredations, by pirates or others, upon the property of citizens of the United States, engaged in such commerce, have been reported to our Government, I now submit, for the information of the House, a report from the Secretary of the Navy, with accompanying documents, which contain all the information, in the possession of the Government, required by that resolution.

JAMES MONROE.
WASHINGTON, *Jan.* 1, 1821.

The House resolved itself into a Committee of the Whole on the report of the Secretary of War, of the 27th day of March, 1820, on the petition of Seth Weed, made some progress in the report, and had leave to sit again. Whereupon, on motion of Mr. STEVENS, the Committee of the Whole were discharged from the further consideration of the report, and the petition was again referred to the Secretary of War.

The SPEAKER laid before the House a letter from the Commissioner of the General Land Office, transmitting a copy of the report of the land commissioners at St. Helena, dated 18th November, 1820, with lists of the claims, and of the settlers; which were referred to the Committee on Private Land Claims.

Mr. STORRS, after referring to the documents to show that an agent had been employed in one of the commissions under the British Treaty, although the appropriation was withheld by Congress at the last session, in order to abolish the agency, moved the following resolution:

Resolved, That the Committee on the Expenditures in the Department of State be instructed specially to inquire whether any moneys have been disbursed through that Department, or authorized to be disbursed, on account of any salary or compensation to an agent or acting agent or any person employed in that capacity on the part of the United States, during the year 1820, under the 6th or 7th articles of the late Treaty of Peace with Great Britain; and, if any moneys have been so paid, to inquire and report to the House by authority of what law, and out of what appropriation, the same has been paid.

And, the question being taken on agreeing to the resolution, it was agreed to without opposition.

UNSETTLED BALANCES.

Mr. WARFIELD submitted for consideration the following resolution:

Resolved, That 5,000 copies of the letter from the Comptroller of the Treasury transmitting a list of balances on the books of the Second and Third Auditors of the Treasury which have remained more than three years prior to the 30th of September, 1820, a list of the names of persons who have failed to render their accounts to the said auditors within the year, and a list of advances made prior to the 3d of March, 1809, by the War Department, which remained to be accounted for on the books of the Third Auditor of the Treasury on the 30th of September, 1820, be printed for the use of the members of this House.

Mr. WARFIELD said, he considered the document

described in this resolution as among the most important which had ever been submitted to the consideration of this body. It exhibited the impositions which had been practised on the Government by persons in its employ or holding offices under it. We hear, said he, many complaints of the profuseness of the expenditure of the public money, and our fiscal concerns are in a deranged condition. He wished the people to be fully informed of the manner in which the funds of the Government had been dilapidated. This was a document which ought to be spread at large before the people. When we examine it, said Mr. W., we find under every letter of the alphabet a list of defaulters in every station, and of every rank, from that of commanding general to that of the subaltern. The people ought to know these flagitious impositions, and how money was in so many instances unaccounted for to large amounts by paymasters, quartermasters, and contractors. We are placed here as the guardians of the rights of the people, and ought not to hesitate, from the consideration of the little expense of printing it, to multiply copies of this document for their inspection.

Mr. Smith, of Maryland, remarked that this was a document of great size, and full of figures; and said Mr. S., if we print it for the people, they will understand about as little of it as we do now. The document did not, he said, afford data from which a correct opinion could be made up. We have known persons kept upon this list, said Mr. S., for twenty or thirty years as owing thousands of dollars, who, on their accounts being properly examined and balanced, did not owe a cent. The very men on the list of the present year, who appeared to owe the great amounts of which the gentleman had spoken, might not be really indebted a single cent. Mr. S. said he had considered this annual document of so little importance, that, although he filed nearly all the documents laid before Congress, he had never thought it worth while to file that. For these reasons, and for the additional reason of the expense of this printing, Mr. S. hoped the resolution would not pass.

Mr. Warfield said, that the people would not understand this document, was a supposition which was not, in his opinion, founded in fact. There was as much intelligence among the people as was to be found in their Representatives in this House. They were entirely competent to understand a document of this sort; and, if they did not examine it after it was furnished to them, the fault would be theirs, and not that of this House. As to the gentleman's not having much regarded this document, Mr. W. said, he did not consider that as a conclusive argument. Without hazarding much by the assertion, he would say that it was a document which deserved the attention of that honorable gentleman, and of every member of the House. The explanatory notes to each item were such that a pretty accurate judgment could be formed from the list; indeed, no man of common sense could fail to understand it. He did not say that this document was conclusive as to guilt on the part of the persons whose names were given, but, referring to the explanatory notes, no one could

be at a loss to comprehend, generally, what was the character of each account. The document ought to be before the people. He wished the names of those who had been thus imposing on the public to be held up to public view. The defalcation was in the general outrageous, and, where there was any modification or apology for it in particular cases, it was so stated as to leave no difficulty in comprehending it, &c.

Mr. Fuller said that the original intention of the law, under which the report in question was made, was to expose to the public odium those persons who really had the public money in their possession, for which they could not, or would not, render a just account and pay the balance; but that the lists contained not only such as merited the epithet of defaulters, but also comprehended a very great mass of individuals, whose disbursements of the funds intrusted to them had been just and legal, and against whom there was no reason to suppose any considerable balance, if any, would be found on an equitable adjustment; but, from various causes, such an adjustment could not be obtained without a departure from the rules, by which the accounting officers, were necessarily governed. In many instances the accounts were in a train of settlement, and would no doubt exhibit the most perfect fairness in the parties concerned. Thus, he said, by including all persons, whose accounts were not settled, without distinction, the weight of the odium was diminished or lost. If the gentleman from Maryland could so modify his motion as to obtain a classification of the cases reported, distinguishing those who had refused or neglected to render their accounts or to pay the balances which they respectively owed, he should readily concur in the proposition; but, in such a vast mass of cases, when only one or two of a number would probable be found culpable defaulters it was impossible to make a due discrimination, and the salutary effect and intention of the law, by which the report was required, were in a great degree frustrated. He hoped such a modification of the resolution would be made, and that the Comptroller would be required so to classify the reported cases, that the innocent might not be confounded with the guilty.

Mr. Lowndes concurred in the view which had been taken by Mr. Fuller, and wished that the resolution might lie on the table, with a view to seeing whether such a discrimination or classification of the cases might be made as to show distinctly the class of cases remaining unsettled from circumstances, separately from that of actual defalcation.

Mr. Warfield not objecting to this course, the resolution was ordered to lie on the table.

PROHIBITION OF IMPORTS.

Mr. Rich, of Vermont, rose to offer the resolutions of which he gave notice some days ago; and, in doing so, expressed himself as follows:

I rise, sir, to submit the proposition of which I gave notice a few days since; a notice, from which it will have been perceived that I propose an inquiry into the propriety of prohibiting, prospectively, the importation of sundry commodities, the product of the skill and industry of other countries, and which are at present allowed, to the prejudice of a free and vigorous employment of the skill and capital of our own citizens. Hence it will have been understood that a decision of Congress is solicited by at least *one* of its members, on the propriety of fixing upon some future period, beyond which, and in regard to the proposed articles, the American manufacturer shall enjoy the benefit of the markets of his country, uninterrupted by foreign competitors, who owe no allegiance to that country, and who will neither fight its battles nor contribute to the support of its institutions.

Sir, I submit the proposition in the most confident belief that, should the proposed measure be adopted our establishments will have reached such a state of maturity by the time the prohibitions shall have taken effect, that exorbitant prices for domestics fabrics cannot be maintained if attempted: that the merchant will find the partial loss in his hazardous foreign trade counterbalanced by an increased coasting and inland trade less hazardous: that the agriculturist will find a progressively increasing and steady demand for his products: that the manufacturer, sure of the future markets of his country, will be zealously employed in his preparations to supply them, and, for his skill and capital thus employed, will realize a reasonable and fair return : that the foreign manufacturer, deprived of our custom in his own country, will seek for it in the employment of his skill and capital in this : that a system of revenue which shall have been adapted to the change of circumstances will be more certain and productive than that which depends entirely on imports ; and that, finally, the greatest interests of the country will have been so arranged and adjusted that, whether we shall in future be met with orders in council, French decrees, embargoes, or war, neither our enterprise, prosperity, nor happiness, can be materially interrupted.

Sensible as I am that the policy of the proposed measure will be doubted by some, and unhesitatingly pronounced unwise by others, I have not obtruded myself upon the indulgence of the House without reflection, nor without the most thorough conviction on my own mind that the adoption of a measure of the character of the one proposed, would greatly promote the best interest of the country.

It having been my purpose to obtain the sense of the House upon the principle, rather than attempt the most unexceptionable details, it will certainly deserve consideration (should the main object be approved) whether the proposed prohibitions have been too far extended, or have fallen short of their proper limits. And should it be the will of Congress to adopt any measures with a view to the encouragement of domestic manufactures, and with them the general industry of the country, a consideration still more important will suggest itself, to wit : whether the encouragement shall be indirectly afforded, by a modification of the tariff, leaving the citizens to "feel their way,"

advancing with hesitancy, if at all, watching "the signs of the times" and the countervailing policy of other countries ; or whether the more direct course shall be pursued.

On this question, I may very possibly have come to an erroneous conclusion ; but, unless I am altogether mistaken, the direct course is by far the most eligible ; as it will be secure against a defeat by foreign regulations, and one the effects of which can be estimated with much the greatest certainty, and will hence prove a powerful incentive to enterprise and industry, which cannot be called into full and vigorous activity except by the influence of strong motives. But, should the indirect course be taken, neither the agriculturist, the manufacturer, the merchant, nor the financier, can calculate for the future with such certainty as will inspire the requisite confidence to insure success.

However much we may have been benefited by obtaining the manufactures of Europe in exchange for our agricultural produce, during the long succession of years, while the markets of the world have been open to them, and at prices unexampled in the annals of commerce ; and whatever advantages we may have derived from the operations and employments incident to such exchanges, I feel no hesitation in pronouncing an opinion that a period has arrived when but a single alternative is left to our choice, viz : either to retire voluntarily from a portion of our former pursuits, while our disposable means are worth preserving, and while the industry and enterprise of the country shall yet possess vigor and animation, (already very much impaired,) or be driven from them, at no remote period, by the force of necessity, with our means exhausted, and the spirits of the country depressed by a contemplation of the unfortunate contrast between our then condition and that from which we shall but recently have fallen. And, sir, when we contemplate that the happiness and prosperity of the people are undeniably the effects of a judicious and wise administration of the Government, and that by an injudicious administration directly the opposite effects will be produced ; and when we also consider that our institutions, which are the pride of freemen throughout the world, have no other support, and can have no other, than the affections of the people for whom they were ordained and established, are we not called upon to employ our best efforts to prevent such a state of despondency as may extinguish all feelings for the Government but those of cold indifference ? And is there not some danger that, should we continue to shape our measures to the maxim of "letting things alone," and that, too, while other nations are pressing upon us with their corn laws, and their other prohibitions and restrictions in one hand, and their bounties and premiums in the other, a state of public feeling may be produced which shall cause the philanthropists universally to weep for the danger to which our institutions shall be exposed ?

It is universally admitted, so far as my information extends, that, be the acts of the Government what they may, the period will some time arrive when this country will cease to look to Europe or elsewhere for its most needful manufactures; and the great difference of opinion which manifests itself, is, whether the Government should, by its measures, accelerate the arrival of that period, or whether it should not rather "let things alone," and leave to chance or the force of necessity, the accomplishment of that great national object. Were we a nation having no intercourse with the rest of the world, it would certainly be my policy to "let things alone;" and I would now do so, with regard to the internal application of the skill and industry of the citizens. But, while I would do this, I would endeavor that they should also be "let alone," by the people and Governments of other countries. Nothing appears to me more unwise, than for to imagine that the great interests of this country can be permanently promoted by a course of measures which shall have been adopted without any regard to the condition or policy of other countries. And gentlemen will permit me to inquire, how long, in their opinion, the "star-spangled banner" would waft triumphantly upon the mighty deep, should the Government "let it alone?"

I have no desire, sir, to see manufactures forced into existence by the acts of the Government or otherwise; but I desire, most sincerely, to see such measures adopted as shall gently invite our national resources to be forthcoming in the form of manufactures, to the full extent of the real wants of the country; and, consequently, sufficient to place us beyond the reach of those pressures to which, otherwise, we must always be exposed, on the occurrence of war, or other interruptions of commerce—which shall give such vigorous activity to our national enterprise and industry, as shall of itself make an American citizen proud of his country, and form the basis of new and lasting attachment to our institutions; and which, finally, will afford some protection against that kind of foreign influence which, through the magic of fashion, puts all the tailors, milliners, and mantuamakers in requisition, on the arrival of a ship from Europe or the Indies; an influence, the suppression of which, would form a new and honorable trait in our character, and diffuse a proud national feeling throughout the community.

I apprehend it will be universally conceded, that a prohibition on the import of distilled spirits and malt liquors, would greatly promote the agricultural, and subserve the general interests of the country; and that no essential interests would materially suffer, should such prohibition be made to take effect at an early period.

While, then, I would propose that a prohibition should not take effect upon manufactured articles, till time shall have been allowed to bring our establishments to a suitable degree of maturity, and enable the great interests of the country to accommodate themselves to the change, and the Government to organize its finances, I would exclude spirits and malt liquors; at the termination of a period barely sufficient to give effect to a system that should bring into the Treasury, from domestic liquors, a revenue equal at least to what is now derived from foreign. And, in the mean time, in-

stead of a general modification of the tariff, as suggested at the last session, I would propose an increase of duties upon such articles only as should be prospectively prohibited; and in regard to such, would abolish the custom-house credits, partly with a view to an augmentation of revenue, and to strengthen the invitation to our internal resources to be forthcoming, and partly to check unreasonable investments in foreign commodities, with a view to monopoly, after the prohibition shall have taken effect. And to secure a future, certain, and augmented revenue, I would levy an excise duty upon the domestic articles which should be substituted for those the importation of which shall be prohibited. The excise to take effect simultaneously with the prohibitions.

I am not insensible, sir, that, should a majority of the House concur with me in opinion that the importation of some articles may, after a given period, be prohibited, with benefit to the country; there must naturally be a great diversity of sentiment as to the articles and the times at which the prohibition in relation to each should take effect. Still I may be permitted to hope, that such diversity may not entirely defeat the proposition: that so far as gentlemen shall only doubt of the policy of the measure, (if there be any such,) they will permit the experiment to be made, if but to a very limited extent; and that, in regard to the selection of articles on which to make the experiment, a spirit of conciliation will be manifested, without which it is in vain that we attempt to legislate for the benefit of a country so extensive as that for which we have the honor to act.

Admitting the prohibitory system to be proper, under any circumstances of the country, and at any possible period of time, much, in my judgment, would be gained, if the period, although far remote, should now be rendered certain, as to some few articles at least. For, in that case, the application of the skill and capital which should incline in favor of the manufacture of such articles, might be diverted with a good degree of certainty as to the results, and an experiment would thus be made, the effect of which would be sufficiently tangible to be judged of, and of great utility in the future legislation of this country.

Sir, I have felt that it was due to the House and myself, that I should accompany the proposition with the explanations I have given of my views upon the subject; and, without consuming farther time, I will send it to the Chair, and leave it to be disposed of as the better judgment of the House shall direct.

Mr. RICH then submitted his resolutions, as follows:

Resolved, That the Committee on Manufactures be instructed to inquire into the expediency of prohibiting (except for the export trade) the importation of,

1st. All distilled spirits and malt liquors, from and after the —— day of ——, A. D. ——.

2d. All manufactures of wool, or of which wool shall constitute a component part, from and after the —— day of ——, A. D. ——.

3d. All cotton and flaxen goods, of which either cotton or flax shall constitute a component part, to wit: sheeting, shirting, counterpanes, table-cloths, stripes, checks, plaids, ginghams, chintzes, calicoes, and prints of all descriptions, hosiery and cotton yarns, twist and thread, from and after ——.

4th. All kinds of glass wares, and window glass, from and after ——.

5th. Iron in bars, rods, sheets, castings, spikes, and nails, and all manufactures of sheet iron, or of which sheet iron shall be a material of chief value, from and after ——.

6th. All manufactures of lead, copper, or tin, from and after ——.

7th. All descriptions of paper, from and after ——.

8th. All manufactures of leather, or of which leather shall constitute a component part, from and after ——.

9th. All descriptions of hats, and ready made clothing from and after ——.

Resolved, That the said committee be also instructed to inquire into the expediency of laying an excise duty upon the domestic articles which shall be substituted for those, the importation of which shall be prohibited: the excise to take effect, simultaneously, with the prohibition.

Mr. SMITH, of Maryland, suggested the propriety of laying these resolutions on the table.

Mr. LOWNDES said, as the resolutions proposed an inquiry only, he saw no objection to acting on them at once, though he did not oppose their being ordered to lie on the table. If agreeing to them were to imply any approbation of the plan which they proposed, the question would be very different and really important. It was obvious, however, that the agreement to inquire into the subject would compromit no one. In the course of his remarks, Mr. L. suggested, that the resolutions proposed to direct a committee to inquire into matters in the investigation of which that committee were probably already engaged.

Mr. RICH said, he was not unwilling that the resolutions should lie on the table for consideration. But, he said, he considered them as embracing a great principle, which sooner or later Congress must adopt, and the sooner, the better.

Mr. BALDWIN, in reference to the suggestion of Mr. LOWNDES, that probably the Committee of Manufactures might now be engaged in the investigation of this very subject of prohibitory duties, rose to say, that nothing of that sort was at present before that committee, nor did he know that it would be, unless it were specially enjoined on them to inquire into it.

After some other inconsequential observations, the resolutions were, on motion of Mr. BUTLER, of Louisiana, ordered to lie on the table.

MILITARY EXPENDITURES.

The bill making partial appropriations for the support of the Military Establishment for the year 1821, underwent some brief discussion, which was confined to one item of the proposed appropriation, that of $150,000 for the Quartermaster's department.

Mr. SMITH, of Maryland, submitted a letter from the Secretary of War explanatory of the necessity there was for this partial appropriation, to which, also, Mr. S. added a few explanatory observations.

Mr. COCKE said he wished for some information before he afforded the means of making further advances of public money. He called the attention of the House to the list of unsettled balances, amounting to somewhere about sixteen millions of dollars, which had grown out of the practice of making advances to public officers. There was already, he said, according to a late report from the Secretary of the Treasury, a considerable sum of money in the hands of the Treasurer for the use of the War Department. How was that disposed of? What had become of the immense sums which they said they had saved within the last year? We are now called upon to advance sums which, by-and-by, for any thing we know, will form additional items in the list of balances; and, until he was better informed, he should be opposed to the bill. Mr. C. assigned, as another reason against passing the bill now, that it was probable a reduction of the Army might take place during the session, which would make smaller appropriations sufficient.

Mr. SMITH, of Maryland, said, that he was as much opposed as the gentleman from Tennessee to the system of advances of money to public agents, where it could be avoided. From conversation with the Secretary of War, Mr. S. had ascertained that he also was convinced of the inconveniences of the practice, and had determined that, for the future, as few advances as possible should be made. But, for the present year, Mr. S. said, the contracts were already made, and the money must be paid: and what possible difference, Mr. S. asked, could there be between appropriating it, as now proposed, and doing it in the general appropriation bill? In regard to small contracts, payment might generally be deferred till the contract was completed; but, in regard to large contracts, every one must know that few men had capitals sufficiently large to undertake them without the aid of advances by the Government. A certain confidence must be reposed in public officers; without which they cannot discharge their duties effectually. He hoped, therefore, the gentleman would not continue to oppose the bill on this score. With respect to the reduction of the Army, Mr. S. said he had learned, on inquiry, that, in all contracts which had been made by the War Department, a proviso was inserted, that, if the quantity of provisions, &c., engaged for should not be wanted for the public service, the Government should have the right of taking one-third less than the quantity contracted. This, the gentleman would see, would obviate any difficulty which might otherwise arise in consequence of a reduction of the Army.

Mr. EUSTIS inquired whether the Committee of Ways and Means were satisfied that the whole sum ($481,000) proposed in the estimates for the Quartermaster's department would be actually necessary for that branch of the service?

Mr. SMITH, of Maryland, replied that the Committee of Ways and Means had not considered that subject, but it appeared quite probable, without much consideration, that it would be necessary. The whole sum appropriated for the same object during the past year had been expended. His honorable friend from Massachusetts had not adverted, Mr. S. presumed, to the difference between the present organization of the Quartermaster's department and that which existed some years ago. The provisions and supplies for the Army are now furnished in bulk by the Commissary General, and then taken up and distributed by the Quartermaster's department, which augments greatly the charge of that branch of the public service.

Mr. LOWNDES made a few remarks in reference to Mr. COCKE's objection to this bill. He admitted that it was not advisable, as a general practice, to make partial appropriations; but he did not see how that could be well avoided under the present practice of Congress, which was to defer the passage of the general appropriation laws until some time after the commencement of the year. The expenditures for the Quartermaster General's department, during the last year, had been settled and accounted for, as an examination of official papers would show, with an accuracy and promptitude which was indeed surprising, and could not fail to be entirely satisfactory to the gentleman from Tennessee. It was evident that the appropriation now asked for was necessary, and he trusted there would be no objection to its passage.

Mr. EUSTIS said, with respect to the amount estimated for the Quartermaster's department for the present year, he could not see how more than half of the amount asked for could be applied. The only objection to assenting to the partial appropriation now proposed for that object, was, that it might be construed into a pledge that the House meant eventually to give the whole that was asked. He had no doubt, he said, that the money, if appropriated, would be expended with the utmost economy, and that every farthing of it would be promptly and properly accounted for. His objection to the appropriation was, that, according to his present impression, in time of peace one-half of the amount proposed to be appropriated for the Quartermaster's department would be sufficient. On this subject he did not mean to express a decided opinion, but spoke according to his present view of the subject. He, therefore, protested against the vote for this appropriation being considered as a pledge to vote for the whole amount of $481,000 for the Quartermaster's department.

Mr. COBB said, that voting for this sum would by no means pledge the House as to any future vote. But connected with this was another circumstance which deserved notice. The sum appropriated for the Quartermaster's department for the last year was $450,000. It appeared, by the estimates laid on the table this morning, that the expenditures for that branch of the military service had exceeded the appropriation by $20,000, and the Secretary of War had stated, in his letter, that it was impossible to bring the expenditure within the sum appropriated. Mr. C. inquired of the chairman of the Committee of Ways and Means, if he could give any reason why it was impossible. He recollected that the House had

determined, at the last session, to bring down this item of appropriation to $450,000, in order to arrest the progress of the Yellow Stone expedition, and for no other reason that he knew of. Yet, notwithstanding that expedition had been stopped at the Council Bluffs, it appeared it had been "impossible" to bring the expenditure within the appropriations. On what account had it been impossible? Mr. C. said he should like to hear if the chairman of the Committee of Ways and Means was prepared to answer the question.

Mr. SMITH, of Maryland, said he certainly did not understand that this bill would pledge the future vote of any gentleman. When the House came to act on the general appropriation bill would be the proper time for examining the matter spoken of by the gentleman from Georgia, or any other matter respecting which gentlemen felt any difficulty or required any information. This bill did not propose any appropriation for covering deficiencies of the past year.

Mr. TRIMBLE rose to give the information which the gentleman wished. Last year so much had been deducted from the amount of appropriation for the Quartermaster's department, as was supposed would have been required by the continuation of the Yellow Stone expedition. The chairman of the Committee of Ways and Means was of opinion that $450,000 would be enough, supposing the Yellow Stone expedition to be discontinued. When the bill went to the Senate an inquiry was made of the War Department on that point; in reply to which it was stated, that four hundred and eighty thousand dollars would be wanted, though the expedition should not proceed further than it had already gone. The Senate put that amount into the bill, but the House persisted in its first determination, and therefore there had been appropriated for that branch of the service thirty thousand dollars less than was asked. The expenditure, it appeared, had exceeded the appropriation twenty thousand dollars, being less by ten thousand than had been estimated by the War Department.

Mr. SMITH confirmed the statement which Mr. TRIMBLE had just made.

Mr. STORRS remarked that, although thirty thousand dollars less than was asked had been appropriated, it appeared to be acknowledged that twenty thousand dollars beyond the amount of the appropriation, had been expended, and expressed his desire to know by what authority? Mr. S. subsequently withdrew his opposition to this bill on the ground that it did not pledge the House either in regard to the making up the deficiency or to future appropriations.

The debate subsided into a nearly general assent to the passage of the bill; and, after negativing a motion by Mr. COCKE, to postpone the subject, the bill was ordered to be engrossed for a third reading.

WEDNESDAY, January 15.

Mr. CAMPBELL, from the Committee on Private Land Claims, to which was recommitted the engrossed bill, entitled "An act to extend the time for locating Virginia military land warrants, and returning surveys thereon to the General Land Office," reported the same with an amendment, which was concurred in by the House; and the bill ordered to be re-engrossed, and read a third time to-morrow.

Mr. WILLIAMS, of North Carolina, from the Committee of Claims, made a report on the petition of Bowie and Kurtz, and others, accompanied with a bill for their relief, which was read, and committed to a Committee of the Whole.

A message from the Senate informed the House that the Senate have passed bills of the following titles, to wit: "An act for the relief of the legal representatives of Gabriel Berzat, deceased;" and, "An act for the relief of Thomas L. Ogden, and others;" in which they ask the concurrence of this House.

Mr. CANNON submitted the following resolution, which was read, and ordered to lie on the table one day for consideration:/

Resolved, That the Secretary of War be directed to lay before this House a statement of the number of cadets educated at the Military Academy that have remained in the service of the United States five years; also, the number that have received commissions, and have resigned before the expiration of five years; also, the number that have left the Military Academy without commissions, and the amount of money that has been paid to each one; also, the sums of money that have been paid to cadets who were permitted to stay at home (if any) for the time between their appointment and that of their being mustered at the academy; also, the whole number educated at the academy, who were in the service of the United States during the late war; and the number of those, thus engaged in the service, who were in any battle or battles fought during said time with the enemies of our country; also, the whole expense of maintaining officers and instructors of the academy each year, since the year 1802; the whole expense of ammunition and soldiers that have been placed at the academy, for their assistance, since its first establishment; also, how far martial law has been carried into effect there, and whether, or not, the professors and teachers are, or have been, under martial law, and whether, or not, any of the cadets have been sent from said academy, or dismissed by order of the superintendent, or any other officer, without a trial, or any specific charge being proved against them; also, how many foreigners are professors or teachers in said academy; and the number of cadets, if any, that have been admitted into the same from the families of foreigners.

Mr. MCLEAN, of Kentucky, submitted the following resolution:

Resolved, That the Committee on Military Affairs be instructed to inquire into the expediency of providing by law for Samuel G. Hopkins, late a captain in the Army of the United States, to settle his accounts with the Government upon the principles of equity.

The said resolution was read, and the question was taken to agree thereto, and determined in the negative.

On motion of Mr. BURWELL, the House proceeded to consider the resolution submitted by him

yesterday, and the same being read, was modified and agreed to by the House, as follows:

Resolved, That the select committee to whom was referred the Message of the President, transmitting an account of the expenditures under the fifth, sixth, and seventh articles of the Treaty of Ghent, for designating the northern boundary of the United States, be instructed to inquire into the expediency of fixing by law the salaries of the commissioners and agents employed in that service.

The House proceeded to consider the resolution submitted yesterday by Mr. SMITH, of Maryland, and laid on the table one day for consideration; and the same being again read, was agreed to by the House.

On motion of Mr. HENDRICKS, the Committee on the Public Lands were instructed to inquire into the expediency of allowing to the deputy surveyor of the Vincennes donation tract other and further compensation than is at present authorized by law.

The House proceeded to consider the bill in addition to the several acts making provision for certain persons engaged in the land and naval service of the United States in the Revolutionary war; and

Mr. HARDIN moved to amend it by adding to it the following sections:

SEC. 2. *And be it further enacted*, That no pensioner under the aforesaid acts shall be stricken from the rolls, who, upon giving in the schedule of his property as is therein directed, shall be worth less, after deducting his debts, than —— dollars.

SEC. 3. *And be it further enacted*, That every pensioner who has, under the act of the 1st of May, 1820, been stricken from the pension roll, shall be placed again on the pension roll, if application shall be made by him, if, upon examining his schedule, he is worth less than —— dollars.

And, debate arising thereon, the bill was again ordered to lie on the table.

On motion of Mr. BALDWIN, it was

1. *Resolved*, That the Committee of Ways and Means be instructed to inquire and to report to this House whether, in their opinion, the permanent revenue is adequate to meet the expenses of this Government.

2. *Resolved*, That the Committee of Ways and Means be instructed to inquire whether any measures may, in their opinion, be necessary to increase the revenue, and, if so, to report the measures to this House.

3. *Resolved*, That the Committee of Ways and Means be instructed to inquire into the expediency of prohibiting, or imposing additional duties on, the importation of foreign spirits, and imposing an excise on domestic distilled spirits.

4. *Resolved*, That the Committee on Commerce be instructed to inquire whether, in their opinion, any further measures are necessary to be adopted for the due enforcement of the existing revenue laws.

5. *Resolved*, That the Committee on Commerce be instructed to inquire into the expediency of making any alteration in the existing laws which relate to the verification of invoices, or to manifests of goods imported from foreign ports.

6. *Resolved*, That the Committee on Commerce be instructed to inquire into the expediency of making

any provision by law for the due enforcement of the provisions of the act, entitled "An act supplementary to an act, entitled 'An act to regulate the collection of duties on imports and tonnage, passed the second day of March, 1799.''

On motion of Mr. Cook, the House took up his motion, submitted on the 26th ultimo, calling for a statement of the land warrants issued, and yet to be issued, to soldiers of the late war, &c.— but, after some debate between Messrs. Cook and Rhea, the House refused to agree to the resolution.

On motion of Mr. Robert Moore, the Committee for the District of Columbia were instructed to inquire into the expediency of providing by law to secure mechanics and others payment for their labor and materials in erecting any house or other buildings within the District of Columbia, by giving them a lien thereon.

Mr. Warfield submitted the following motion for consideration:

Resolved, That the first Comptroller of the Treasury be directed to report to this House whether, in the statement of balances which have been due more than three years, accompanying his letter of the 27th of November last, there have been made the discriminations and suggestions required by the fourteenth section of the act to provide for the prompt settlement of public accounts passed on the 3d March, 1817.

Bills from the Senate, of the following titles, to wit: "An act for the relief of the legal representatives of Gabriel Berzat, deceased;" and, "An act for the relief of Thomas L. Ogden, and others," were severally read twice, and referred; the former to the Committee on Private Land Claims, and the latter to the Committee of Claims.

An engrossed bill, entitled "An act making a partial appropriation for the military service of the United States for the year, 1821," was read the third time, and passed.

The Speaker laid before the House a letter from the Secretary of War, transmitting a report of the number and station of all the military posts of the United States, and of the distribution of the Army; designating the number and grade of the officers, and the number of men at each post; prepared in obedience to a resolution of this House of the 20th ultimo; which was ordered to lie on the table.

REDUCTION OF EXPENDITURES.

The House having resolved itself into a Committee of the Whole on the state of the Union, took into consideration the following resolutions:

1. *Resolved,* That it is expedient that the annual expenses of the Government should be reduced; that, for the accomplishment of this object, it is further

2. *Resolved,* That all such offices as are not immediately necessary for the transaction of public business, and the abolition of which would not be detrimental to the public interests, shall be abolished.

3. *Resolved,* That the salaries of all civil officers, whose compensation has been increased since the year 1809, shall be reduced to what they were at that period.

4. *Resolved,* That it is expedient to reduce the Army to the number of six thousand non-commissioned officers, musicians, and privates, preserving such part of the corps of engineers, without regard to that number,

as may be required by the public interest; and including such reduction of the general staff as may be required by the state of the Army when reduced as herein proposed.

5. *Resolved,* That it is expedient that the appropriations for the erection of fortifications shall be so made as to require a less sum annually, by extending the time within which they shall be completed.

6. *Resolved,* That the act making an appropriation of one million of dollars per annum for the increase of the Navy be so amended as to extend the time within which such increase shall be made, and to reduce the annual appropriation to the sum of five hundred thousand dollars.

7. *Resolved,* That it is expedient to recall from active service one half of the naval force now employed, and to place the same in ordinary.

And the same having been read—

Mr. Cobb, of Georgia, rose and addressed the Chair as follows:

Mr. Chairman: The task which I have undertaken, to investigate all the subjects involved in the resolutions just read, would be a fearful one, to heads much more profound than mine. But, as I am well convinced that the Committee are not prepared to expect a display of any profound ideas from me, I deem an apology for the very imperfect views which I shall offer quite unnecessary.

Broad as the resolutions would appear, they are defective, in not embracing all the objects upon which I mean to touch in the course of my remarks. For this reason I shall take the liberty of offering one or two amendments before the investigation of them shall be closed.

I think the preference which is to be given to the form in which these resolutions have been introduced, will be obvious. They admit of the Committee's taking a full view of the state of the nation. They admit of an inquiry into the financial resources of the country, and of the sources from which revenue is derived by the existing laws; into the extent of the various establishments requiring the expenditure of the public money; the necessity and usefulness of them, and the adequacy of the revenue to their maintenance; whether they are to be supported by the imposition of additional burdens upon the people, in the shape of loans or taxes, or whether the interests and true policy of the nation would not rather point to their reduction in preference to such a resort. The importance of the question involved in such an inquiry will not be denied. Attempts at a partial view of them, and at making partial reductions in the public expenses, are always attended with the danger of doing nothing, or of running into an extreme parsimony in relation to particular objects. It is the duty of the Legislature to determine what shall be the "portion of the produce of the land and labor of the country to be placed at the disposition of Government." This must be determined by the capacity of the people to contribute this portion. When, however, it is ascertained, it is right that you should have before your eyes all the objects of expenditure, before you will be able properly to distribute it among the several objects.

By what principles the Legislature of this nation shall be governed in determining this "portion of the product of land and labor," (which is only a definition of what are called taxes,) has been a subject of great discussion and contrariety of opinion, from the institution of the Government to the present day. My opinion upon the subject can be expressed in very few words: The people of that nation are happiest whose rights are protected at the least expense, with the least danger from the instruments of protection, and where there are the fewest obstacles created, by law, to the exercise of individual industry, and the display of individual enterprise. I can scarcely conceive of controversy upon a position so reasonable and plain.

We boast that our form of Government best admits of reducing the principle I have stated into practice. I very much fear that history has yet to determine, from our conduct, whether, like the Athenians in relation to politeness, we shall show that we only know it, or, like the Lacedemonians, we practise it. That we have an idea of it I think is very evident; for no people under the sun boast more of their national simplicity, frugality, and economy, than we do, even at the very moment that an increase of the public burdens is required to defray the ordinary expenses of the year. To prove a conformity between the boast and the fact, is a task I have no disposition to undertake.

Admitting the practicability of economical principles, (which, so far from denying I shall attempt, before I conclude, to prove,) I will take the liberty to say, that in no nation can taxation be rendered more oppressive than in ours. This arises from our form of Government; from that "*imperium in imperio;*" that exercise of two distinct kinds of sovereignty by the same people, of which we are so proud. The affairs of the Confederacy are administered by one body of magistracy, under the Federal Constitution, and must be supported in its expenses. The government of each State, in whose care is confided the greatest portion of the people's rights, conducted by another body of magistracy, and must also be supported. The expenses of either government, taken separately, have nothing alarming in their amount. If added together, they are swelled to an enormous sum, and it requires but little augmentation to make them onerous indeed. Suppose the General Government should determine upon some grand and expensive political scheme, the execution of which requires an increase of revenue; for instance, a magnificent scheme of internal improvements, in favor of which a vote of this House has already been had; and that one of the States, say New York, determines on a similar scheme, as she has done, also requiring an increase of State revenue; is it not obvious that the burdens of the people of that State would be rapidly increased? I have alluded to this scheme of internal improvements only by way of exemplifying my ideas. If, however, the view is extended to all the powers which may be exercised by each sovereignty, requiring the expenditure of money, it will be seen that the adoption of but very few of these magnificent schemes will make the public burdens alarmingly oppressive, and destructive of a large share of our comforts.

The facility with which this state of things could

be produced, was most distinctly perceived by the people who authorized the formation of the Federal Constitution, and by whose authority it was put in operation. The old Federal Government asked of the States the power to impose a very small tax on commerce. The Convention which met to confer that power produced the Federal Constitution, as the result of their labors, and submitted it to the people for their ratification. In their examinations of this instrument, they could but see how injuriously the unlimited power of taxation therein conferred might be exercised.

Gentlemen can see, by turning to the various acts of ratification, how many of the States, by express declarations and limitations, attempted to guard against the abuse of the powers conferred upon the Federal Government, and to settle the principles of policy by which the agents employed in the administration of that government should be guided. These acts speak a language that cannot be misunderstood; and let it be remembered that this language is held by the people by whom the Federal Constitution was made and ratified to their servants thereafter to be appointed to execute the purposes of it. It is in these acts that we shall first discover the marks of distinction between what has since been appropriately denominated the ordinary and extraordinary sources of revenue. By the first was meant the revenue derived from commerce, to which has since been added the price of the public lands, and, by the second, internal taxes in the broadest sense of the term. Here it is that we see the makers of the Constitution declaring that "standing armies in time of peace are dangerous to liberty," and that the defence of the country shall rest upon the militia. Here, in short, we shall see asserted and dictated, in the plainest terms, all those principles of economy and rules of political conduct which I am attempting to advocate. To read the whole of these ratifications would tax the patience of the Committee more than I wish; but I pra their indulgence in reading one or two of them. The ratification of New York contains the following expressions: "That the people have a right to ' keep and bear arms; that a well regulated mili- ' tia, including the body of the people capable of ' bearing arms, is the proper, natural, and safe ' defence of a free State." "That standing armies, ' in times of peace, are dangerous to liberty, and ' ought not to be kept up, except in cases of neces- ' sity, and that at all times the military should be ' under strict subordination to the civil power." "That Congress will not lay direct taxes in this ' State, but when moneys arising from the imposts ' and excise shall be insufficient for the public ' exigencies, nor then, until Congress shall first ' have made a requisition upon the State to assess, ' levy, and pay the amount of such requisition," &c.* On this last subject the language of the ratification of North Carolina is as follows: "When ' Congress shall lay direct taxes or excises, they ' shall immediately inform the executive power of

* See Journal of the Federal Constitution, pages 427,431.

' each State," &c.* Such, sir, was the jealousy displayed by the people of the States—parties to the Constitution—in relation to the subject of internal taxes. That they intended that the General Government should rely only upon the imposts for defraying the expenses in times of peace, cannot admit a doubt. If, however, the public exigencies —if a state of war, or other extraordinary circumstance, should require it, then, and not till then, was resort to be had to other sources of revenue, so long as the necessity should continue. What was it, sir, but a departure from those principles, and some others prescribed in the same imperative manner, that caused the people, at a later period in the Government, to withdraw their confidence from their agents then in the administration of affairs, and to substitute Mr. Jefferson and his friends in their places? The mention of the name of this distinguished man leads me to call the attention of the Committee to certain opinions of his in corroboration of the ideas I have advanced; not because they are his opinions, but because they were those of the people at that period. They will also be found in the writings and speeches of the " conscript fathers," and the reports and proceedings of Congress of that day. Mr. Jefferson's opinions were then considered as the test of political orthodoxy. I am aware, sir, there has since been a considerable change in the times, and that, in this change, men have not been able to preserve a uniformity of political visage. But, if his principles were then founded in truth and political propriety, they are now equally worthy of being adopted in practice. Such is certainly my opinion of them, and, therefore, I shall not relinquish them. In his inaugural speech, among other principles advanced by him, are the following: "A well disciplined militia, our best
' reliance in peace, and for the first moments of
' war, till regulars may relieve them; the supre-
' macy of the civil over the military authority;
' economy in the public expense, that labor may
' be lightly burdened; the honest payment of our
' debts, and sacred preservation of the public faith;
' encouragement of agriculture, and of commerce,
' as its handmaid;" (the word *manufactures* is not to be found in the sentence—should it hereafter creep in, I hope it will be understood to be an interpolation,) " the diffusion of information, and
' the arraignment of all abuses at the bar of the
' public reason; freedom of religion—freedom of
' the press—and freedom of persons under the pro-
' tection of the *habeas corpus*; and trial by juries
' impartially selected."
These principles form the bright constellation which have gone before us and guided our steps through an age of revolution and reformation. The wisdom of our sages and blood of our heroes have been devoted to their attainment; they should be the creed of our political faith, the text of civic institutions, the touchstone by which to try the services of those we trust; and should we wander

from them in moments of error or of alarm, let us hasten to retrace our steps, and to regain the road which alone leads to peace, liberty, and safety. How beautiful the style—how much more beautiful the principles! It would be a speculation not entirely fruitless to compare our present political course with that of the administration just previous to the delivery of this speech, and test its correctness by the " touchstone " of these principles. Then an army in time of profound peace was deemed proper—so it is now. Then an expensive navy was to be created and supported—so it is now. Then a large debt was not considered a national curse—nor is it now. Then a latitudinous construction of the Constitution was the fashionable doctrine—so it is now, by more than one solemn vote of this House. Then a sedition law was both proper and Constitutional.* In another branch of the Legislature they have lately said it was not unconstitutional. The comparison might be urged much farther, but I will not pursue it.
In his first Message to Congress, Mr. Jefferson speaks the following language:
"War, indeed, and untoward events, may change this prospect of things, and call for expenses which the *imposts could not meet.* But, sound principles will not justify our taxing the industry of our fellow-citizens to accumulate treasure for wars to happen we know not when, and which might not, perhaps, happen, but from the temptations offered by that treasure.
" These views, however, of reducing our burdens, are formed on the expectation that a *sensible,* and at the same time a *salutary* reduction, may take place in our habitual expenditures. For this purpose those of the Civil Government, the Army, and Navy, will need revisal. When we consider that this Government is charged with the external and mutual relations only of these States; that the States themselves have the principal care of our persons, our property, and our reputation, constituting the great field of human concerns, we may well doubt whether our organization is not too complicated, too expensive; whether officers and offices have not been multiplied unnecessarily, and sometimes injuriously to the service they were meant to promote."
I beg pardon of the Committee for having detained them so long by reading these extracts. But really they are so applicable to the present situation of the nation, that they seem to be addressed to us with equal propriety as to the Congress for whom they were intended. Yes, sir, if a system of economy were not recommended to us by its evident propriety, under the most favorable circumstances, we are now driven to its adoption by the embarrassments by which we are surrounded. What is our present condition? What is the state of the nation?
We have an Army, which, with its various appendages, is more numerous than it ever was before in a time of peace.
We have a Navy, the force and expense of which have almost quadrupled in ten years.

---

* Ibid, page 444. Nearly the same language is used in the ratifications of Massachusetts, New Hampshire, Virginia, South Carolina, and Rhode Island.

* The Senate refused to refund to Mathew Lyon a fine imposed on him under the Sedition law.

We have a pension list, whose rapid growth and extended length should affright us.

We have a civil list of constantly increasing expense.

We have a national debt of $90,000,000, which, to say the least of it, is not diminishing, and the interest upon which requires more than one-fourth of the estimated receipts into the Treasury for the present year.

And, to crown the whole, for the last and the present year, the annual revenue calculated to be received, by official reports submitted to our inspection, is insufficient to support these establishments, by millions of dollars.

However coolly some may affect to view this state of things, to me it presents a subject of the most lively interest. It is, at least, sufficiently gloomy to urge us to a review of our policy, and to correct its errors, if any there are. This is a duty which the nation expects us to perform, and let us not shrink from the task.

By the reports from the Treasury Department, it will be seen that, at the last Congress, it was calculated the receipts into the Treasury for the year 1820, exclusive of loans, would be somewhere about $22,000,000. At the present session, with more certain data upon which to make the calculation, it appears that the estimate of the receipts of the year 1820 will but little exceed that sum, inclusive of the loan of $3,000,000, authorized at the last session. The appropriations then made, after very great reductions from the estimates, were about $25,000,000; so that the receipts will be less than the appropriation, by a sum of at least $2,600,000. This, however, is not the worst of the evil. If you take into consideration all the charges upon the revenue of the year 1820, inclusive of the appropriations for that year, and of the sums appropriated in 1818 and 1819, and which have not been paid, it appears that the actual balance against the Treasury is more than $4,000,000, at the end of 1820.

By the same reports it is estimated, that the receipts of the present year, (1821,) from all sources of revenue, will be $16,550,000. Of this sum, we are told that at least $1,200,000 will not be available in the course of the year, on account of $600,000 in notes upon banks that cannot be converted into current money, and on account of the time it requires to transfer a part of the revenue received in one part of the country, to another, where it is to be disbursed, and which, it is supposed, will render a further sum of $600,000 unavailable; so that the sum estimated to be received into the Treasury will really not be more than $15,350,000. By the estimates just laid on our table, it appears that the amount of money required for the current expenses of Government in 1821, is $17,519,068 22, consisting in the following items, viz :

For the public debt - - -	$5,477,776 76
The civil list, and miscellaneous expenses, &c. - - - -	1,769,850 04
The Navy, inclusive of $1,000,000 a year for its increase - -	3,428,676 81
The War Department - -	4,585,352 61

Unexpended balances, not provided for - - - - -	1,875,437 00
Permanent appropriations - -	81,975 00
	$17,519,068 22

If to this you add the interest upon the contemplated loan of $7,000,000, at 5 per cent., it will swell the sum to $17,869,068 22, exceeding the estimated available receipts by $2,519,068 22.

If to this you add the estimated balance against the Treasury, at the end of the year 1820, it will be seen that, in order to effect all objects for which appropriations have been heretofore made, and to furnish what will be required for the service of 1821, a sum but little short of $7,000,000, in addition to the available estimated receipts of the year, must be provided. It has heretofore been usual to have in the Treasury at least $1,000,000 above all charges upon it, as a contingent fund, which may be required by unforeseen circumstances. If it is conceived to be proper to preserve this fund, then the sum to be provided, above the receipts of the year, will be nearly $8,000,000.

In the Treasury documents frequent mention is made of "unexpended balances of appropriations." For instance, those of the last year, and which are deducted from the estimates of the present year. In the calculation which I have just submitted, of the expenses of the present year, I have stated these balances at $1,875,437, and said that they were to be provided for. I hope no gentleman will be deceived in relation to these "unexpended balances of former appropriations." The truth is, that their amount is not, never has been, and never will be, in the Treasury, unless Congress procure the money, and put it there. To talk, therefore, of deducting from the estimates of the year that which does not exist in fact, is absurd. If you will first borrow the amount of these unexpended balances, and place it in the Treasury, then you may deduct it from the estimates. But that will be just the same thing as taking no notice at all of them, and proceeding to provide for the whole amount of the sums estimated to be necessary for the service of the year. If you have to borrow it, it is perfectly immaterial whether you do it in the shape of money necessary for the current expenses of the year, or money necessary to make good the amount of appropriations heretofore made, but not received into the Treasury, and which, as it will not be wanting to effect the objects for which the appropriations were made, may be deducted from the estimates of the next year. The thing is in fact the same, although it may be done under two different names. The whole mystery, if any there be, is in not distinguishing between "unexpended balances of appropriations" and unexpended balances of money appropriated. In the first instance the amount may never have been received, although the appropriations were made upon the presumption that it would be. In the second, it has been received, but was not wanting for the object for which it was appropriated. Now, it will be seen, from the reports, that the balances proposed to be deducted from the estimates of the money wanted for the service of the year, are of appropriations, and not of money. By casting our eyes upon the Treasury report of the 21st December, 1820, it will be perfectly obvious that the amount of these unexpended balances has never been in the Treasury. The Secretary says:

"That, of the sums appropriated for 1820, and previous years, it is estimated there will be on the books of the Treasury," (not in the Treasury,) "on the 1st January, 1821 - - - $6,907,619 03

"That there will be on that day, in the hands of the Treasurer, as agent of the War and Navy Departments 927,241 29

"That" (consequently by the addition of these two sums) "the whole amount of unexpended balances of appropriations" (not money) "subject to the disposition of the Executive Government, during 1821, is estimated at - - - - 7,834,860 32

"That of that sum there will be required to defray the expenses incurred in 1820, or necessary to effect the objects for which the appropriations were made - - - 3,632,659 47

"And that there will remain unexpended (of appropriations) "and not necessary to effect the objects for which the several appropriations were made - - - 4,202,200 91"

In the next page the report proceeds to inform us that, of the whole "estimated receipts into the Treasury in 1820, the amount applicable to the fourth quarter of the year ending the 31st of December, 1820, will be - - - - $5,457,830 83

"That the payments made in the 4th quarter, and those which are required to complete the service of the year 1820, amount, in the aggregate, to - - - - 9,662,295 07"

Leaving a balance against the Treasury, on the 1st January, 1821, of $4,204,464 24

Now, in this sum of $9,662,295 07 is included only such part of the appropriations theretofore made as was necessary to effect the objects for which they were made, and consequently that the receipts into the Treasury will not effect the objects intended by a sum of $4,204,464 24, although it is ascertained that these objects can be effected with a sum of $4,202,200 less than was estimated for them. Had the whole amount appropriated been wanted to effect these objects, the balance against the Treasury, instead of being what it is, would have been $8,406,664 24. That I am right in this conclusion, will be evident from the explanation given by the Secretary of the Treasury. For, he says, "to avoid complexity, the sums necessary to complete the service of the year 1820, 'or to effect the objects for which the several appropriations were made, are in the above statement (which I have just referred to) considered 'a charge upon the Treasury during the fourth 'quarter of the year, although it is probable that 'a portion of these sums may not be drawn until

'late in the ensuing year, and, possibly, a small 'part not before 1822. In the annual report (that 'of 1st December, 1820) no sum was charged upon 'the fourth quarter but what was understood 'would be drawn;" thus accounting for the vast difference between the charge on the fourth quarter, as represented in the two reports. The truth is, that the payments for many objects are often not made for two years after the appropriation is passed, from a failure to settle accounts, and many other causes easy to be conceived.

Thus, then, it appears that within three years past the appropriations for the expenses of the Government have exceeded the estimated receipts into the Treasury more than $8,000,000 ; that the amount of these required to complete the objects intended has exceeded them more than $4,000,000 ; and, according to the various estimates laid before us, that the sum required for the service of the year 1821 (exclusive of the payment of any part of the principal of the public debt) will exceed the estimated receipts of that year more than $2,500,000. Who can view this state of things with indifference, unless he is prepared to impose new burdens on the hand of labor, and thus create new sources of revenue? To this, however, we must come, unless we "retrace our steps," and more especially if we adhere to the pledge which, by a statement made by a gentleman from South Carolina (Mr. Lowndes) at the last session, the Government seems to have made, with itself if not with the public creditors, and which I highly approve, to wit : that its receipts should exceed its expenses in each year, by a sum equal to the amount of the Sinking Fund, which is now $10,000,000. To release the Treasury from its present embarrassments, and to guard against their recurrence, we must now resort to one of three methods. 1st. We must impose new taxes, in some shape, to the amount required ; or, 2d. We must add to the national debt ; or, 3d. We must retrench in our expenses, by reducing our establishments to the lowest state that the public safety will possibly admit. To the first, in a time of profound peace, I am decidedly opposed. Internal taxes are sufficiently oppressive and vexatious at any time. I cannot forget, what I think is evident, that this nation ever has considered them as reserved for extraordinary occasions. To the second I am equally hostile. Mr. Jefferson has aptly called a national debt a "mortal canker." To me, there has always been something highly objectionable, if not immoral, in the idea of burdening our posterity, for the support of our extravagances. The following remarks of Mr. Jefferson are so admirable that I cannot forbear subjoining them :

"When, merely by avoiding false objects of expense, we are able, without a direct tax, without internal taxes, and without borrowing, to make large and effectual payments towards the discharge of our public debt, and the emancipation of our posterity from that mortal canker, it is an encouragement, fellow-citizens, of the highest order to proceed, as we have begun, in substituting economy for taxation, and in pursuing what is useful for a nation placed as we are, rather than what is practised by others under different circumstances. And whensoever we are destined to meet wants which shall call forth the energies of our countrymen, we have the firmest reliance on those energies, and the comfort of leaving for calls like those the extraordinary resources of loans and internal taxes. In the mean time, by payment of the principal of our debt, we are liberating annually portions of the external taxes, and forming from them a growing fund still further to lessen the necessity of recurring to extraordinary resources."—*Message of 15th December,* 1802.

My plan, therefore, is one of radical retrenchments, to the full extent, if possible, of the annual deficiency. If, however, good policy should say that these cannot be made, I will consent to unite, with such as can be, a loan of an amount necessary to answer the national wants. But the pruning knife must first be applied, and that effectually. My present impression is, and I hope I shall be able to show it, that three millions, at least, may be lopped off the annual expenses of the Government, without danger; and I now declare, that, unless such reductions are made, I will not vote for one cent of taxes or loans.

It may perhaps be urged that I have given too gloomy a picture of the condition of the finances. But let it be remembered that I have done it upon the official documents. Let it not be said that the calculation contained in these documents make matters worse than they are, and that the receipts of the present year (1821) will be greater than is estimated. Last Winter we were misled by similar suggestions, and most sincerely have we been punished for our folly in giving credit to them. Had we then made the reductions which I now propose, how much better would our situation have been. That the revenue will improve from the present sources, I have no doubt, but not in the present year. It will be seen that the data upon which the Treasury calculations have been made are given to us. Upon these data, no doubt, the estimates have been as favorable for the Treasury as they could be made. Estimates must always be attended with some degree of uncertainty; for, to make them correspond certainly with the receipts would require a degree of sagacity little short of a prophetic spirit. The receipts are sometimes above, but more frequently under the estimates. Last year, (1821,) it would seem, they were two millions less. That they will considerably increase in 1822–3–4, I believe; but I think it demonstrable that the increase will not be greater than will enable the Government, within those years, to relieve itself from the loans incurred in the last and present year, and to leave the Sinking Fund to operate upon the war debt which will then become due.

My plan, then, is, that the expenses shall be reduced three millions at least, which I think cannot be done without greatly reducing the existing establishments; that, if there should yet be a deficiency, it shall be supplied by a loan, redeemable at will. Upon what terms it can be effected, I cannot speak with certainty; but, from information I have lately received from the principal commercial cities, I am so strongly under the impression that it can be effected at five per cent. redeemable at will for a certain number of years, (say five, within which, that uncertainty concerning the investment of capital now apparent in the trading world will probably have ceased,) and afterwards at the will of the lenders, that I would be willing to incur the responsibility of effecting it on those terms.

Let us then, see, in the first place, whether the reductions proposed can be made without detriment to the public safety. In doing this, let it be remembered that we are at peace with the whole world; that the principal difficulty in our foreign relations (I allude to the Florida Treaty and our affairs with Spain) is upon the point of amicable settlement, according to the most undoubted accounts; and, therefore, that we need entertain no fears of a rupture with any foreign Power; and there is as little cause of fear from our "savage neighbors."

In looking into the civil list, I am obliged to confess that I find myself too ignorant of its details to analyze it very scrupulously. Such has been my situation, that I have never had an opportunity of examining it with attention, so as to detect its most useless and expensive parts. The first part of it which presents itself for examination is the expense of the Legislature. Upon the subject of the compensation of members of Congress, my opinions have been long known. I think now as I thought three years ago, that they are worse paid than any other public servants; that, if you wish Congress to be intelligent and independent, you must make a seat there sufficiently lucrative to place him who fills it above the reach of improper influence by more profitable stations; that the compensation should be such as to make a seat more desirable than most other offices. Since the war, the compensation of many of the officers has been increased upon the avowed and proper ground of the depreciation of the currency of the country. In my opinion the pay of Congress has never been properly proportioned to that of other public servants. Three years ago I was favorable to such proportion. Congress, however, although it determined upon increasing it, on account of the depreciation of the currency, fixed upon eight dollars a day as bearing a proper proportion to other public salaries. Well, sir, money has appreciated. Three dollars now will purchase as many or more necessaries and comforts as four would then. If depreciation of currency was a good cause for an increase of salaries, (and I admit it was,) appreciation is an equally good cause for their diminution. I shall therefore vote to diminish all that have been increased. If this should be done, can there can be any good reason why, for similar causes, we should not reduce our own compensation? I think not. Therefore, in case other salaries are reduced, I shall vote to reduce the pay of Congress. By a reduction of all salaries, and the pay of Congress, at the rate of twenty per cent. I have calculated a saving to the Treasury of fifty thousand dollars at least.

From a report laid on our tables from the Treasury Department, it would seem that by abolishing certain offices in the collection of the customs, there can be a saving of one hundred thousand dollars. In the organization of the Departments in this city, I think a considerable one could be made. There is now such a degree of complexity under the present organization that one had as well attempt to penetrate the celebrated labyrinth of the days of fable as to understand the connexion of the various offices in the several Departments with each other. We know that the difficulty of bringing to a speedy adjustment the numerous accounts of the receipts and disbursements of public money, in the late war, afforded cause for the creation of many new offices. They have now been in operation for four or five years; and it would seem to me that, if the officers have done their duty, there can be no good reason to continue them. This load of business must, or ought to have been despatched. Could not the public accounts be now managed by three auditors and one comptroller? We have an officer called a Paymaster General. Of what use is he? I have understood that, since the death of the late incumbent, (who, it would seem, died greatly in arrears,) no money is placed in his hands. For aught that I can discover, his business is merely to make out estimates of pay, and correspond with the district paymasters; and this any clerk could do, who understands the common rules of arithmetic. Nearly the same observations may be made about one or both of the commissaries. A clerk of common talents would be able to discharge their duties in examining proposals and making contracts, which at last must undergo the revision of the head of the Department. Then the Surgeon and Apothecary Generals; their duties cannot be so considerable as that one or both cannot be dispensed with. In time of peace, I should suppose each regimental surgeon would be able, if you will furnish him the money, to purchase the necessary medicines and instruments for that portion of the army whose health is intrusted to his care. At least, I think, one of them can be abolished. We have also a Postmaster General, and two assistant Postmasters General. The usefulness of the two assistants I cannot discover. What duties have they to perform that an intelligent clerk could not, and, indeed, does not now discharge? The retention of them is better calculated to destroy all responsibility than for any other purpose. Who now understands the situation of the Post Office Department? I venture to say, no one. Place the whole responsibility upon one man, and then you will be enabled to unravel all its secrets, if any there are.

Among other things, I cannot forbear to mention the host of clerks employed in the various public offices in this city. I had made, at one time, a calculation of their number and cost, but I have mislaid my memorandum. I think, however, that, giving them an average salary of twelve hundred dollars each, the sum total of their salaries is not short of three hundred thousand dollars. Whatever necessity there may have been for such a number heretofore, that necessity cannot now exist if they have done their duty; and, if they have not, they should be discharged on that account.

On the subject of miscellaneous expenditures, I can say but little. I have no doubt, however, that there could be retrenchments to some extent; the wisdom of a committee would discover wherein. On the whole, my firm impression is, that in the civil and miscellaneous list, by a new modification of the offices, by the abolition of others, and by reasonable reductions in the salaries of those retained, and by adopting all practicable means of retrenchment, there can be an annual saving of at least $230,000.

I now call the attention of the Committee to the Army. It has not escaped their attention that, at the last session of Congress, a resolution was adopted in this House in the following words, viz:

" *Resolved,* That the Secretary of War be directed to report to this House, at the commencement of the next session of Congress, a plan for the reduction of the Army to six thousand non-commissioned officers, musicians, and privates, and including such reduction of the general staff as may be required by the state of the Army as is herein proposed, and preserving such parts of the corps of engineers as, in his opinion, without regard to that number, it may be for the public interest to retain; and, also, what saving of the public revenue will be produced by such an arrangement of the Army as he may propose in conformity with this resolution."

One of the resolutions I have proposed, is to execute the principle of reduction contained in the one I have just read. The Secretary of War has submitted a plan conforming to this requisition in every thing but one, and that is, I cannot see in it any thing like "a reduction of the general staff" as the reduced state of the Army might require. It is far from my intention to examine this report in detail; I have no inclination for such a task. Differing widely, as I do, with the report, in many of its principles, I yet agree that it is the ablest, most ingenious, and, upon the whole, the best defence of a standing army in time of peace which I have seen in print since the commencement of Mr. Adams's administration to the present day. To that part of it wherein I differ with its author in principle, there is an answer prepared to my hand, by one whose profound views of national policy will be admitted by all republicans, and upon which I can more safely rely, because it has been sanctioned by the voice of the nation. It will be found in Mr. Jefferson's first Message to Congress. "A statement," says he, "has been ' formed by the Secretary at War, on mature con- ' sideration, of all the posts and stations where ' garrisons will be expedient, and of the number of ' men requisite for each garrison." (I wish we had been furnished with a similar document.) " The whole amount is considerably short of the ' present Military Establishment. For the surplus ' no particular use can be pointed out. For de- ' fence against invasion, their number is as noth- ' ing; nor is it considered needful or safe, that a ' standing army should be kept up in time of peace ' for that purpose. Uncertain as we must ever be, ' of the particular point in our circumference, ' where an enemy may choose to invade us, the ' only force which can be ready at every point and

' competent to oppose them, is the body of neigh-
' boring citizens, as formed into a militia. On
' these, collected from the parts most convenient,
' in numbers proportioned to the invading force, it
' is best to rely, not only to meet the first attack,
' but, if it threatens to be permanent, to maintain
' the defence until regulars may be engaged to re-
' lieve them. These considerations render it im-
' portant that we should, at every session, continue
' to amend the defects which from time to time
' show themselves in the laws for regulating the
' militia, until they are sufficiently perfect; nor
' should we now, or at any time, separate until we
' can say we have done every thing for the militia
' which we could do, were an enemy at our door."

An attempt to enlarge upon this extract would
hardly be pardoned by the Committee. It requires
none. To all the arguments contained in the report of the War Department, either in favor of a
standing army, or against the efficiency of the
militia for the defence of the country, I am content
to plead this extract as a set-off, and have no
doubt but that public opinion will award me judgment for a balance.

As to the extent and particular manner of reducing the Army, I shall now say but little, having
been anticipated by the bill reported by the Military Committee, many of whom I know possess so
much more knowledge upon the subject than I do,
that I willingly leave this branch of the discussion in their hands. I will simply observe, for the
purpose of making myself understood in a calculation I am about to present of the saving to be made
by the proposed reduction, that I am decidedly in
favor of reducing the officers proportionally with
the privates of the Army. I can see no utility in
an army of officers. To the idea of the Secretary
of War, that it will be proper to retain the whole
body of the officers, better to preserve a knowledge
of the science of war, I cannot subscribe. Could
you retain them for fifty years, on a peace establishment, they would be no wiser in the science of
war, at the end of that term, than they now are.

In inquiring into the present numerical force of
the Army, I find it will not do to examine the
official reports of its strength. I have made the
inquiry from the estimates of appropriations required for its support in the last year. Could I
have seen the estimates of the present year at an
earlier period, I would have made it from them. I
presume they are not essentially different. From
the estimates of 1820, I find the sum total of all
the persons for whom pay is asked, including officers, servants, and privates, of every grade and description, to be near 14,000. But let us say 13,500.
I find the amount of the appropriations estimated
for the support of these under the following heads,
viz: pay, subsistence, forage, clothing, bounties,
and premiums, medical and hospital department,
quartermaster's department, contingent expenses
of the Army, and retained bounties, if I have added
them correctly, to have been $3,380,614. Then I
have said as 10,000, the present rank and file, is to
13,500, (the whole number requiring pay,) so will
6,000 rank and file be to 8,100, the whole number
requiring pay after the reduction. Then, again,

as 13,500, the present number, is to $3,380,614, the
estimated expense, so will be 8,100, the number
after reduction, to $2,028,368, their estimated ex-
pense, which deducted from $3,380,614, will pro-
duce a saving of $1,352,264.

The sum estimated for fortifications this year is
$800,000. In saying that one-half of this sum can
be withheld, I do not wish it to be understood that
I am opposed to the erection of fortifications. I
am simply for procrastinating their erection during
the present pressure upon the Treasury. To commence without finishing them would be wrong.
But where is the necessity of hurrying their completion? Why not proceed more leisurely in the
work? Are we in danger of a war? Is there any
fear of an invasion requiring them for immediate
use? We know there is not in all human probability. Need we, then, involve ourselves in debt
to finish them? I think not. No danger can result from proceeding more slowly. Those commenced cannot fly away, and the materials are not
of a description that are likely to perish. If they
were, they would be unfit for fortifications. Should
our means increase, I shall be willing to recommence more rapid operations.

There is one expense in which I think a considerable retrenchment can be made, not included
in any specific resolution submitted by me. I allude to the Revolutionary pensions. I feel that I
am walking on ticklish ground. This is a subject as fruitful of fine speeches as any that was
ever presented before Congress. It is not my intention to move a repeal of the law, but merely
to reduce the annual amount. It will be recollected, that at the session, when the law on this
subject was passed, the currency of the country
was at a very low state of depreciation. I have
no doubt this circumstance had a principal influence in fixing the allowance to each private at
eight dollars per month. I think it can be fairly
reduced, without any charge of injustice, to five
dollars per month, with which as many necessaries and comforts can now be procured as with
eight dollars per month, when the law was passed.
An additional reason for such a reduction will be
found in this, that, in most cases, the allowance
to invalid pensioners, the wounded soldiers, is but
about five dollars per month. In some cases I
know it is higher, according to the degree of disability. The proposed reduction will make an annual saving of more than $300,000.

In the Ordnance department, I apprehend, some
saving could be made, but I know not to what
extent.

In noticing the retrenchments proposed in the
Naval Establishment, I shall not dwell long.
Here, too, I am in a great measure anticipated. I
wish it clearly to be understood that I am no enemy of the Navy. Whatever might have been my
opinion when the building of the Navy was commenced, I now think there would be extreme folly
in building ships of war to sell them, or let them
rot. As we have them, let us take care of them.
I do not oppose its gradual increase; but I think
we are increasing faster than necessary. We have
now no use for it. Let us increase, but more

slowly. Instead of applying $1,000,000 annually, let us apply only $500,000, and extend the term within which all the intended increase shall be made. The Treasury will be relieved; there is no fear that the materials collected will be lost, and the public service does not require expedition in the work. I am happy to learn that the Naval Committee agree with me on this subject, and I see that the Secretary of the Navy and Commissioners of the Navy Board, with a candor and magnanimity that do them honor, have expressed themselves not unfavorable to the measure.

From the estimates, I see it is proposed to keep in service, during the present year, about 3,000 able seamen, ordinary seamen, and boys. It is worthy of remark that, in this country, Congress have no other check upon the number of seamen to be employed than what may be exercised in withholding the appropriations. In England, I believe the number is always settled by a solemn vote of Parliament. We limit by law the number of soldiers, but not of seamen. I do not perceive the necessity of keeping in service a number so large. Our vessels of war are to be found in the Mediterranean sea, on the coast of Africa, in the Indian seas, in the Pacific ocean, in the West Indies—scattered almost over the world, under the plea of protecting commerce and suppressing the slave trade. I apprehend the expense of their maintenance is nearly equal to the commerce protected. By this time the Algerines must be sufficiently intimidated, and all the pirates and slave-traders are either captured or driven off the ocean, so that we might safely reduce the naval force now in active service one-half for two or three years, within which, it is hardly probable they would renew their depredations. It is to be hoped we shall then be in a better financial condition. I propose this as a mere temporary measure, to be continued only until the Treasury is better filled. My calculation is, that, by so doing, a further present annual saving can be made of $500,000. The estimated expense of the Navy for the year 1821, (exclusive of the $1,000,000 per annum, and the expenses of the Marine corps) is $2,207,740.

Should the Committee think the proposed plan worthy of adoption, I have calculated that the sum total of reductions will be $3,230,000, or, in round numbers, let us say $3,000,000,* in the annual expenses of Government. Let it not be supposed that I think this saving can be made in the year 1821. I think no such thing. Time will elapse before we can pass the laws, and more,

---

* To wit, in round numbers:

In the civil and miscellaneous list	-	$230,000
The expenses of the Army	-	1,300,000
Fortifications and ordnance	-	400,000
Revolutionary pensions	-	300,000
The appropriation for increase of Navy	-	500,000
Expenses of the Navy	-	500,000
		$3,230,000

In some of these items the saving would be probably more, in others less.

---

before the arrangements can be made to carry them into execution; advances may be made to the soldiers, seamen, and officers, discharged, and the very changes in the establishment will create some expense; so that, probably the saving for this year will not be greater than $1,000,000 or $1,500,000. But, in 1822 and 1823, it will be fully equal to the sum proposed, if no change takes place in our foreign affairs, which is believed. But, whatever saving is made in this year will lessen the proposed loan to the amount of the saving.

My object, in conclusion of my remarks, is, to show what will be the result insured by the proposed reductions until the year 1825. As I have said, I cannot believe the receipts in the Treasury in 1821 will exceed the estimate of the Secretary of the Treasury. The average receipts for the next four years he calculates at $20,000,000. I wish it may be so. I shall make considerable allowances, so as to be upon more certain grounds to accomplish the objects I have in view, (beyond the introduction of greater economy in the expenses of Government,) which are, to pay off the debt incurred in the expenses of the last and present year, before the war debt becomes due, so as to leave the Sinking Fund unencumbered, to operate with its full force upon that debt. I therefore have proceeded upon the calculation, that the receipts into the Treasury in the year 1821, inclusive of a loan of $6,000,000, (all that is necessary,) will amount to $21,350,000. That the expenses of that year, reduced only $1,000,000, (when probably it will be $1,500,000, if the whole of the retrenchments are adopted,) will be about $21,000,000, leaving a balance in favor of the Treasury. That, in 1822, the receipts of available funds will be $17,000,000, being (exclusive of loans) $2,650,000 more than in 1821.

That, in 1823, they will be $19,000,000, and in 1824, they will be $21,000,000; that, with these funds, after making reductions to the amount of $3,000,000 per annum upon their estimated amount of this year, we cannot do more than pay the expenses of Government, the interest upon the old debt, and redeem the money borrowed in the last and the present year, by the end of the year 1824, (at which time the war debt becomes due,) and yet leave in the Treasury such an unappropriated amount as ought always to be there; that, if you do not reduce at all after the end of this year, you may, to be sure, bear the expenses of Government, but your debt will then be increased to more than $96,000,000. It would seem to me that such results must compel us to adopt some measures similar to those I have proposed.

The calculations whence these conclusions are drawn are subjoined:

The expenses of the year 1821 will be as follows:

Balance against the Treasury, on the 1st of January, 1821, as stated in the Treasury report of the 21st of December, 1820	$4,204,464 24
For the principal and interest of public debt	5,477,776 76
Other current expenses of the Government, consisting of the following items, viz:	

Civil and miscellaneous $1,769,850 04
Navy, including the
$1,000,000 for its
gradual increase - 3,426,676 81
War Department - 4,565,352 61
Unexpended balances,
to be provided for - 1,875,437 00
Interest on $6,000,000,
to be borrowed at 5
per cent. - 300,000 00
     ————————
     12,341,271 46
Deduct amount sup-
posed to be saved in
1821, by proposed
retrenchments - 1,000,000 00
     ———————— 11,341,291 46

Total expenses in 1821 - - $21,023,582 46
Which may be paid by—
1. Amount of estimated available receipts in 1821 - - $15,350,000
2. Loan of - - - 6,000,000
     ———————— 21,350,000 00

Balance in Treasury on 1st of January, 1822 - - - - $326,468 00

In the year 1822, it is supposed that the available receipts, (being $2,650,000 more than in 1821,) will
be - - - - $17,000,000 00
The charge upon the Treasury is supposed to consist of the following items, viz :
Principal payable, and
interest on public
debt - - - $5,447,776 76
Current expenses of
the year, reduced
$3,000,000 upon the
estimates of 1821 - 9,341,291 00*
     ————————
     14,819,067 76
For the reimbursement
of the debt of 1820
and 1821 - . - 1,000,000 00
     ———————— 15,819,067 76

Balance in Treasury, on 1st of January, 1823 - - - - 1,180,935 23

In 1823, the available receipts and balance in Treasury, on the 1st of January, 1823, may be stated
at - - - - - $19,000,000 00
The expenses of the
year will be as above,
for old debt and in-
terest, and current
expenses - - $14,819,067 00
Amount of debt of
1820 and 1821, re-
imbursed - - 3,000,000 00
     ———————— 17,819,067 00

Balance in Treasury, on 1st of January, 1824 - - - - $1,180,933 00

* Permanent appropriations are included in this sum, to the
amount of $362,000.

In the year 1824 the available receipts may be stated
at - - - - - $21,000,000 00
The expenses of the
year, as above - 14,819,067 00
Reimbursed, the bal-
ance of debt of 1820
and 1821 - - 4,000,000 00
     ———————— 18,819,067 00

Balance in Treasury on 1st of January, 1825, at which time the war
debt becomes due - - - $2,180,933 00

NOTE. It is believed always to have been the practice of the
Government to have in the Treasury an unappropriated sum of
about $1,000,000. This sum, in the above calculations, is not
more than provided at the end of each year, until the 1st of January, 1825 ; nor would it have then been exceeded, if the whole of
the loans of 1820 were reimbursable ; but one million is not payable until 1832.
The national debt on the 1st of January, 1821 - $89,214,128 98
Add loan in 1821 - - - - - 7,000,000 00
     ————————
     $96,214,128 98

THURSDAY, January 4.

Mr. LOWNDES submitted the following resolutions :

Resolved, That the Secretary of the Treasury be instructed to report to this House a statement of the
money in the Treasury on the 1st of January, 1821, together with a statement of the money in the hands of
the Treasurer, as agent for the War and Navy Departments, on that day.

Resolved, That the Secretary of the Navy be instructed to report to this House the balance of each
distinct appropriation for the Navy remaining in the
Treasury, or in the hands of the Treasurer, as agent
for the Navy Department, on the 1st January, 1821,
with an estimate of the amount of each of those balances which will not be required to defray expenses
actually incurred before that day.

Which, being read, and the rule requiring them
to lie on the table one day being unanimously dispensed with, they were agreed to by the House.

On motion of Mr. LOWNDES, the Committee of
Ways and Means were instructed to inquire into
the expediency of amending the laws which direct
the manner in which money shall be drawn from
the Treasury for the expenditures of the War or
Navy Departments, or ordered for the use of those
Departments.

Mr. SMITH, of Maryland, from the Committee
of Ways and Means, who were instructed to inquire into the expediency of making provision by
law for compensating persons employed in transmitting the votes for President and Vice President
of the United States, reported a resolution, declaring that it is inexpedient to increase the allowance
authorized by the existing laws ; which, being
read, was concurred in by the House.

The SPEAKER laid before the House the following letter from the Secretary of State :

The Secretary of State, conformably to the direction
of the House of Representatives, expressed in their resolution of 30th November last, has the honor of submitting a copy of a report made to the President of the
United States, on the second of May last, containing

all the information in the possession of this Department, relative to the annual amount of the fees of the Clerks, District Attorneys, and Marshals, of the respective Courts of the United States, the amount of whose fees does not appear in the Register of Officers in the service of the United States. He submits, also, copies of a letter from the Secretary of the Treasury and of a report of the Comptroller of the Treasury, with a return of the statements required by the resolution of the House, with reference to the naval officers, collectors, and surveyors, of the customs.

JOHN QUINCY ADAMS.

DEPARTMENT OF STATE, *Jan.* 3, 1821.

The report was read, and, together with the documents, ordered to lie on the table.

The engrossed bill to extend the time for the location and return of location of Virginia military land warrants, was read a third time, passed, and sent to the Senate for concurrence.

The bill for the relief of Daniel Seward was taken up, on motion of Mr. Ross, and ordered to be engrossed for a third reading.

MILITARY ACADEMY.

On motion of Mr. CANNON, the House proceeded to the consideration of the resolution, yesterday submitted by him, calling for certain information relative to the Military Academy.

The adoption of this resolution was opposed by Mr. SIMKINS, as calculated to give needless trouble to the public officers, as requiring information already heretofore given to Congress, and which, if it were received, would not be made use of, &c.

Mr. CANNON declared that he at least considered the information important, as preliminary to a motion which he intended to make, in some shape or other, during the present session, with respect to the Military Academy, &c.

Mr. LITTLE was opposed to acting on the resolution, believing that the required information was already before Congress, or would come before them under resolutions already adopted at the present session, &c.

After some further conversation between Messrs. CANNON, SIMKINS, and FOOT, the resolution was ordered to lie on the table.

MISSOURI.

Mr. ARCHER, of Virginia, read from his seat the following resolution :

Resolved, That the Committee on the Judiciary be instructed to inquire whether there be at this time existing, and in force, in Missouri, any legal tribunals or tribunal, derived from the authority of the United States, invested with competent jurisdiction and powers for the examination and determination of cases of controversy which have arisen, or may arise therein, under the Constitution, laws, or treaties of the United States, or controversies to which the United States are or may become a party ; and, if there be no such tribunals or tribunal, then to report to this House the provisions and measures which, in their opinion, may be necessary to be adopted by Congress, for causing the authority of the Government and laws of the United States to be respected, and for assuring protection to the property and other rights of the United States, and of their citizens, within Missouri.

Before forwarding the motion to the Chair, Mr. A. stated the motives which induced him to offer it. Whatever might be the situation of Missouri, with respect to this Government, the propriety remained the same of instituting the inquiry he proposed, and of adopting the resolution. He must be candid enough to state, however, that to him it appeared that Missouri stood entirely disconnected from any legal or political relation with this Government. With our own hands, said Mr. A., we have cut all the moorings which attached her to it, and she floats entirely liberated and at large. She stood formerly in the relation of a Territory to the United States ; she had proposed to assume the new relation of a State of the Union. This House had refused her permission to do so, and, Mr. A. said, she stands discharged from all relation to the Union. It was vain to tell him that Missouri was a Territory. Such an assertion was disproved by the fact, known to every one, that she had discarded every attribute of that character. The concession which Congress made to Missouri at the last session, Mr. A. said, consisted of two parts : the permission to depart from the existing relations of a Territory, and the permission to assume, under certain conditions, the relations of a member of the Confederacy. She must have departed from the relation of a Territory before she could have availed herself of the second part of the concession to her. What is it that Congress can admit into the Union ? Not a Territory, but a State. Missouri was therefore obliged to cease to be a Territory before she could be in a condition to claim admission into the Union ; and she became a State. Not only, then, in point of fact, but in legal acceptation, Missouri is no longer a Territory.

Mr. A. said he was not intimating, nor would he be understood as intimating, that the people of Missouri wished to be permanently disconnected from the Union. He was assured she was attached to the Union by feelings generated by her descent from it, and by a true reverence for the principles of its institutions. Nor did he say that she had shown any disposition to throw off the yoke of allegiance to the Union ; it was this House which had itself cut loose the harness, and thrown away the reins. Mr. A. went on to say, that, if Congress could act at all at present with reference to Missouri, such was now her condition, that it could not act by law, but must act by force. The authority of the Union might hang over her, but there was no legal modes by which it could be exercised. All its ordinary and regular conductors were broken off. With regard to Missouri, Mr. A. said the citizens of the United States had individual rights, which it was the duty of Congress to secure. Many of them, for example, had received donations of land in that Territory, in requital of their services, of their blood, and of the glory they had acquired for their country. Congress were bound, by the most sacred of all obligations, to insure protection to those rights. The question, therefore, which he wished to present to the consideration of gentlemen was this : Where are the tribunals and methods by

HISTORY OF CONGRESS.

which these and other rights can be protected—where the channels by which the authority of the Government can be enforced? No man could say that there existed such tribunals, or channels, for the enforcement of our authority. My proposition, said Mr. A., is not presented because of any peculiar situation of Missouri, but because of the ambiguity of it—because no man can say what it is. Suppose, he said, that he was right in his opinion of the condition of Missouri, every one would say that an inquiry ought to be instituted with the view to establish some bonds of relation between Missouri and this Government. But, suppose that he were mistaken on this point, the inquiry would yet be proper, in order to remove the doubts which he and others entertained. In every view in which he considered the subject, he thought the inquiry ought to take place. He did not propose that this inquiry should be committed to himself, or to those who agreed with him in opinion, but he proposed to refer it to a standing committee of the House, which might reasonably be supposed to be an impartial tribunal, and at the head of which (Mr. SERGEANT) was one of the most prominent of those who differed from him in opinion on this topic.

Mr. A. said he was far from supposing that there would be any opposition to this proposition; but, if there were, he would say to the opponents of it, that they had taken upon themselves to direct the course of our legislation on this subject, and, if they had not foundered, they had at least brought us into the neighborhood of shoals and breakers. If gentlemen who constitute the late majority of this House were to refuse to agree to the proposed inquiry, he would then say, what he was now very far from saying, that they were afraid to pursue the principle of their own vote in its operation, and to stand confronted with the results.

The resolution having been read from the Chair—

Mr. SERGEANT suggested that the resolution was one of such a description as ought not to be acted upon without affording an opportunity to every member of the House to vote upon it. He therefore moved that it lie on the table.

Mr. COBB said it was a very unusual course to move to lay on the table a resolve proposing inquiry merely. It would seem almost a matter of course to agree to such a resolution moved by any gentleman. When the committee should report would be the time for deciding any principle involved in this proposition.

Mr. SERGEANT said, if this were a simple proposition for inquiry, in the ordinary shape of such propositions, there would be no force in the remark of the gentleman from Georgia. But, Mr. S. said, he thought it perfectly plain and obvious that this resolution assumed, as the ground work of it, certain opinions in regard to Missouri, about which the sentiments of the members of this House had already been more or less expressed. It was taken for granted, no doubt, by the mover, and his proposition assumed it as a fact, that, in consequence of something which has happened, a change

has been produced in the position of Missouri in regard to the Union, which renders it necessary that there should be new legislation in regard to it; and it of course took for granted what had been a source of litigation certainly, and what a large portion of this House will not accede to. If a question existed whether the relation of Missouri to the Union be thus changed, it was a question which ought to be discussed and decided in this House, before a committee was charged with it in any shape. The inquiry whether the relation of Missouri to the Union be in reality changed, must precede the adoption of a resolution such as this is, which assumes that a new code of laws is necessary for its government. He thought this House ought not at once, without notice, to go into the discussion of the question whether Missouri has or has not changed her condition. So strongly impressed was he with this opinion, that he had moved to lay the resolution on the table; and, if the discussion were pressed at this time, he should certainly vote against the resolution.

Mr. LOWNDES said he had hoped the resolution would have appeared to the House to be such a one as did not involve any of the questions which had been suggested. As, however, time was desired, he hoped the gentleman from Virginia would consent to its lying on the table until to-morrow. But assuredly, Mr. L. said, it did not involve any such question as had been supposed. It proposes an inquiry into the matter of fact, whether there now exists a tribunal in Missouri adequate to particular objects. It proceeds on the supposition that every party in the House is desirous to know the actual relation which Missouri bears to the Union—to decide whether it be necessary to legislate or not to legislate on the subject; not only to ascertain what is the relation between Missouri and the Union, but what it may be proper to do, if any thing, in consequence of the fact thus to be ascertained. Whilst, however, Mr. L. said, he believed that resolutions of inquiry ought in general to be assented to without objection, and whilst he believed this to be of that character merely, yet if, from the terms of the resolution, it should appear to any member, and most of all it appeared to a member of the committee to whom it was proposed to assign the consideration of the subject, that it involved an important principle, he admitted it would be proper to give time for the consideration of it.

Mr. GROSS, of New York, said, that though he presumed he entertained, with respect to the answer which ought to be given to this resolution, the same opinion as the gentleman at the head of the Judiciary Committee, he was ready to act upon it without delay. If he believed that it took any thing for granted, particularly if he believed that it took for granted that there was no legal tribunal by which such questions could be settled, he should certainly vote for laying it on the table, and finally against the resolution. But, as he was of a different opinion, he should vote for the resolution, and against laying it on the table. It would be well recollected, he said, that during the discussion of the subject at the present session, the position had been taken that Missouri was a State, and that, though admitted into the Union, she was an independent State. This position was taken by a gentleman whose weight of character and talents gave a color to whatever he should advance. For his part, Mr. G. said, when the question on the admission of Missouri was before the House, he had made up his mind on the subject of this resolution. He hoped that, if the resolution passed, the true answer would be given, and he was therefore in favor of the resolution.

Mr. FLOYD said, it was a very unusual thing for the House to hesitate in respect to motions for inquiry. He was glad to find that the gentleman from New York thought so clearly on the subject. As this was an important subject, he wished to record his opinion on the postponement, and therefore required that the question should be decided by yeas and nays.

The yeas and nays having been ordered—

Mr. ARCHER, of Virginia, said, if the wish of the gentleman from Pennsylvania for delay were pressed, though it was so unusual a course, he should be bound, by considerations of courtesy, to accede to the motion now before the House. He was rather disposed, however, to take the same view of this matter as had been taken by the gentleman from New York, that every one, before he gave a vote against the admission of Missouri, must have foreseen the necessity for a resolution and inquiry of this sort. Every member of the majority of the House must have known that the question must have come upon him in some shape or other, and must therefore have been prepared for it. With regard to the character of this proposition it was not novel. If the facts should be ascertained as the gentleman from New York supposed, there would be no occasion for any expression of the opinion of the Judiciary Committee as to what ought to be done, &c.

Mr. FULLER made a few remarks to the effect that he did not consider it of much importance whether the resolution passed to-day or to-morrow; that he had examined it, and had no great objection to it; but, only to save the needless trouble of calling the yeas and nays, he hoped the gentleman from Virginia would withdraw his objection to laying it on the table.

Mr. ARCHER said he had already done so, if the gentleman from Pennsylvania pressed it, though such a course was not usual, nor in his opinion necessary in this case.

Mr. SERGEANT said that the gentlemen from South Carolina and Virginia had concurred in considering this resolution as proposing an inquiry into a matter of fact. Mr. S. said, if he understood this resolution at all, it proposed an inquiry, not into a matter of fact, but a matter of law, and that matter of law involving a point on which there was known to be more or less difference of opinion in this House. The question, whether there now exists a tribunal in Missouri, was not a question of fact, but it was a question of law. It was not a question whether tribunals heretofore have existed, but whether they do now exist. There was an objection to referring to a commit-

tee an inquiry into a matter of law, which is not to be tested by evidence, &c., but must depend upon opinion, which every member in his place would form as well as a committee, whose report on such a subject would only leave the question where it stood before. With respect to what is to be done in relation to Missouri, it must be perfectly obvious that this cannot be ascertained until the sense of the House is ascertained on the previous question; and the clear course would be to ascertain the sense of the House, and then send the matter to a committee to report such bills as should be calculated to give effect to it. He did not know that, on further examination, the resolution might be liable to the objection he now felt to it; but he wished time to decide that point.

Mr. STORRS wished the resolution to lie on the table, for this reason—that he wished gentlemen to have time to obtain the necessary information to enable them to act on the subject. He had himself no information whatever which went to show that Missouri was not in the same situation now that she had been for the few years past, except that her convention had met, and agreed upon a form for her future government. He did not say, that he had not heard, out of doors, that she had elected a Governor, Legislature, &c. But he did not wish to proceed to the consideration of this resolution until the information was given to him officially, on which he was to act. A resolution addressed to the Executive, who is charged with the execution of the laws of the United States, would, he supposed, elicit the necessary information. For aught we know officially, said Mr. S., the officers of the United States in that Territory may be at this moment in the full discharge of all their functions. He could not consent to assume it as a fact, that the authority of the United States in Missouri was in full operation. He could not assume it as a fact, that the President has failed in his duty of appointing a Governor and other officers, in pursuance of the laws. By entertaining this inquiry, said Mr. S., the House would assume, in some degree, the duties of the Executive, and bring us in collision with that department. For his part, he said, he could not consent that this House should thus take upon itself the responsibility which belonged to another department of the Government. Whenever the authority of the United States in Missouri was set at defiance, or whenever, from any cause whatever, the authority of the United States in that Territory should be at an end, he presumed Congress would receive from the Executive department information of it. Until such information was received, he could not agree to consider the subject. When it did come, he reserved to himself to decide what course ought to be taken. But the proper course for gentlemen at the present time appeared to him to be, to call on the Executive to inform the House whether the laws of the United States were at present duly executed in Missouri, &c. If the President should say, in reply, that the laws are not executed, and our authority not in existence, it would then be time enough to refer the subject to a committee.

Mr. CAMPBELL said the time might come, during the present session, when he should not have the smallest objection to this resolution ; but, he must be allowed to state, that he did not think the present was the proper time. It was well understood, that there were several projects on foot for the admission of Missouri into the Union. When all these failed, he said, he should be as ready as any gentleman to assent to this resolution. If gentlemen were prepared to say that no further efforts would be made to accomplish that object, he was ready to vote for the resolution now. But, he said, in every quarter of the country, it is anticipated that the discussion will be revived on the resolution from the Senate : in the paper from Richmond received to-day, there were two or three letters from Washington to that effect. The understanding was, he believed, that perhaps next week the resolution on the table of the Clerk might be called up, and decided on. If every effort should fail for the admission of Missouri, it would be proper to adopt such a resolution as this, but, in his opinion, not till then.

Mr. FOOT rose to show, by example, that the motion to lay this resolution on the table was not unprecedented. He agreed fully in opinion with the gentleman from Ohio, that the resolution ought to be laid on the table, and should not agree to take it up again until the resolution from the Senate should have been finally acted on.

Mr. LOWNDES said, a very little reflection would satisfy any one that it was not necessary to postpone this resolution until the other question referred to should be decided. He submitted to the House the consideration, that the report of the committee under this resolution might have considerable influence on the question to be decided on the proposition from the Senate. It appeared to him, he had no hesitation in saying, that no man could vote on the various propositions which had been alluded to, unless his mind was made up on the topics presented by the resolution now before the House. Whilst up, Mr. L. adverted to what had fallen from his friend from New York, who opposed the resolution because we know nothing officially of any change in the actual condition of Missouri. If we knew nothing on that subject, said Mr. L., it would be reason enough for inquiry that there is out-of-door conversation on the subject. We must not act on such information, but was it ever before heard that we must not inquire into any matter because it has been spoken of out-of-doors only ? The practice of every day was different. But, if official information was necessary, the House had that information. It had information, from the constitution presented by Missouri, that, at a certain time, the authority of the United States was to determine, and that of a new State to commence. He did not here speak of the question of right in regard to the people of Missouri, but of the question of fact. It was true that there was a question of fact presented by this resolution, but it was also true that there was a question of law, and nothing was more usual than, in regard to questions of law, to refer them to the committee of this House consisting of legal men, constituted

to consider such questions, being the committee to which it was proposed to refer this resolution.

Mr. STORRS explained, that he had reserved the question of the expediency of an inquiry into this matter. His objection to acting on the subject now was, that it appeared to him the proper course would be, first to call on the Executive.

Mr. ARCHER said, he acceded to the proposed postponement, only because, as the mover of the resolution, he felt bound to do so. If not thus obliged, he should have voted against postponement. The objections of the gentleman to the resolution, he said, were not consistent—one gentleman opposed it because it proposed an inquiry into facts; another because it proposed an inquiry into a matter of law. Both objections could not be sound. He believed, he said, in conclusion, that the responses to this resolution would be very easy indeed ; and he must be allowed to indulge the remark, that, in the reluctance of gentlemen to act on the subject, he found a confirmation of his belief that the answer could be easily given.

The question on laying the resolution on the table was decided in the affirmative, by yeas and nays, 91 votes to 58, as follows :

YEAS—Messrs. Adams, Alexander, Anderson, Archer of Virginia, Baker, Bateman, Beecher, Boden, Brush, Buffum, Butler of New Hampshire, Campbell, Clagett, Clark, Cushman, Cuthbert, Dane, Dennison, Dickinson, Eddy, Edwards of Connecticut, Eustis, Fay, Folger, Foot, Forrest, Fuller, Gorham, Gross of Pennsylvania, Guyon, Hall of New York, Hall of Delaware, Hardin, Hendricks, Herrick, Hill, Hobart, Hostetter, Kendall, Kinsley, Lathrop, Lincoln, Lowndes, Maclay, McCullough, McLane of Delaware, Mallary, Marchand, Meech, Meigs, Monell, R. Moore, S. Moore, Morton, Moseley, Murray, Nelson of Massachusetts, Parker of Massachusetts, Patterson, Phelps, Phileon, Plumer, Randolph, Rich, Richards, Richmond, Robertson, Rogers, Ross, Russ, Sawyer, Sergeant, Settle, Silsbee, Sloan, A. Smyth of Virginia, Southard, Stevens, Storrs, Street, Strong of Vermont, Strong of New York, Tomlinson, Tracy, Upham, Van Rensselaer, Wallace, Wendover, Whitman, and Wood—91.

NAYS—Messrs. Abbot, Allen of Tennessee, Archer of Maryland, Baldwin, Barbour, Bayly, Bloomfield, Brevard, Brown, Bryan, Burton, Burwell, Butler of Louisiana, Cannon, Cobb, Cocke, Cook, Crafts, Crawford, Crowell, Culpeper, Earle, Edwards of North Carolina, Fisher, Floyd, Gray, Gross of New York, Jackson, Johnson, Jones of Virginia, Jones of Tennessee, Kinsey, Little, McCoy, McCreary, McLean of Kentucky, Metcalf, Montgomery, T. L. Moore, Neale, Nelson of Virginia, Overstreet, Parker of Virginia, Rankin, Reed, Rhea, Simkins, Smith of New Jersey, Smith of Maryland, Swearingen, Terrell, Trimble, Tucker of Virginia, Walker, Warfield, Williams of Virginia, and Williams of North Carolina—58.

REDUCTION OF EXPENDITURES.

The House then again resolved itself into a Committee of the Whole, on the state of the Union; and the consideration of Mr. COBB's resolutions for reducing the expenditures of the Government was resumed.

Mr. SMITH, of Maryland, delivered a speech in

reply to Mr. Cobb's speech of yesterday, generally in opposition to the resolutions.

Mr. Eustis followed, in reply to a part of Mr. Smith's remarks; and, at 4 o'clock, the Committee rose, and the House adjourned.

FRIDAY, January 5.

Mr. Rhea, from the Committee on Revolutionary Pensions, reported a bill for the relief of John Crute, which was twice read and committed.

Mr. Livermore, from the Committee on the General Post Office, made an unfavorable report on the petition of Erastus Granger; Mr. Tracy moved to reverse the report; when, on motion, the report was ordered to be laid on the table.

Mr. Smith, of Maryland, from the Committee of Ways and Means, reported a bill for the relief of J. Ottramare, which was twice read and committed.

Mr. Barbour, from the Committee of Naval Affairs, reported a bill to amend the act for the gradual increase of the Navy. [Repealing the first section and reducing the appropriation for that object of that law, from one million of dollars, annually to five hundred thousand dollars, for six years.] The bill was twice read and committed.

Mr. Williams, of North Carolina, submitted the following resolutions, which were read, and ordered to lie on the table one day for consideration:

1. *Resolved,* That the Secretary of War be directed to inform this House what amount of appropriation will be necessary to complete existing contracts for the erection of fortifications.

2. *Resolved,* That the Secretary of the Navy be directed to inform this House what sums of money will be requisite to complete existing contracts, made in pursuance of the act for the gradual increase of the Navy.

On motion of Mr. Fuller, the Message from the President of the United States, received the 2d instant, communicating information in relation to the protection afforded to the commerce of the United States in the West Indies, &c., was referred to the Committee on Naval Affairs.

Two Messages were received from the PRESIDENT OF THE UNITED STATES.

The first of the said Messages was read, and is as follows:

To the House of Representatives:

I communicate to the House of Representatives a report from the Secretary of State, which, with the papers accompanying it, contain all the information in the possession of the Executive, requested by a resolution of the House of the 4th December last, on the subject of the African slave trade.

JAMES MONROE.

WASHINGTON, *Jan.* 4, 1821.

The Message and documents were referred to the Committee on the subject of the African slave trade.

The other of the said Messages was read, and is as follows:

To the House of Representatives:

In compliance with a resolution of the House of Representatives of 15th of December last, requesting the President of the United States to cause to be laid before that House a statement of expenditures and receipts in the Indian Department; also, the nature and extent of the contracts entered into, and with whom, from the 2d of March, 1811, to the present period, I now transmit a letter from the Secretary of War, with a report of the Superintendent of Indian Trade, which contain the information desired.

JAMES MONROE.

WASHINGTON, *Jan.* 4, 1821.

The Message and documents were ordered to lie on the table.

REDUCTION OF EXPENDITURES.

The House then again resolved itself into a Committee of the Whole, on the state of the Union; and the consideration of Mr Cobb's resolutions was resumed.

Mr. Smyth, of Virginia, said, the resolutions under consideration covered much ground on which he should not enter. He would leave what related to the revenues of the country to the honorable chairman of the Committee on Finance, (Mr. Smith, of Maryland.) He was satisfied to hear that honorable member affirm that the receipts of the year 1821 would exceed the expenditures of the year. I would not, said Mr. S., destroy or cripple any of the institutions of the country for the purpose of paying off immediately the national debt. If we should borrow at a lower rate of interest a part of the sum which we pay off, we are diminishing the debt and its interest, and doing well. I will put a case to the honorable member from Georgia, (Mr. Cobb.) Suppose that he owed $100,000 to the bank at Savannah, and had determined with himself to pay it off in ten annual instalments: would he, if his cotton crop failed a year or two, break up his establishments, and allow his plantations to go to ruin, that he might pay the amount of his contemplated annual instalment, or would he not renew his notes, and wait for more favorable seasons before he paid off his debt? He would, doubtless.

The proposition made by the honorable member from Georgia, for retrenchment of the expenditures of Government has my approbation, and I will go with him in making every reasonable retrenchment. The principles laid down by Mr. Jefferson in his addresses to Congress, and quoted by the honorable member from Georgia, are worthy of universal approbation. Those principles constitute a republican text, to which the legislator should often refer. But, although a people may have too much law, too much public force, too many offices, too much of the machinery of Government, it by no means follows, that therefore they should have none. The question to be considered is, how much is essential, or how much is useful?

Mr. Jefferson furnished a practical commentary on his own principles, relative to the expediency of having an army in time of peace. In the year 1802, when the policy of retrenching the expenditures of the Government was carried to the greatest extremity, he retained in service an army of

3,300 men, and in the year 1808, after he had tried for some time his system of Government, he increased the Military Establishment to 10,000 men, at a time when there was no war, and when, owing to his extremely pacific temper, there was little probability of a war. It appears, therefore, to have been the mature opinion of Mr. Jefferson, that a nation should, in time of peace, be prepared for war, by having in service, previous to its commencement, a respectable military force.

The honorable Speaker of this House having thought proper to assign to me the situation of chairman of the Military Committee, it has become my duty to offer my opinion as to so much of the resolutions before you as affects the Army. A great question has arisen in this debate highly interesting to this nation. It is this: Can the people of the United States most safely trust their defence in time of war to the militia, or can that defence be more safely confided to regular troops? One having popularity in view might well shrink from the investigation of this question. The duty which I owe to the nation and to the House shall be performed without any regard to the consequences, as they may relate to myself. I will examine this question with the best lights I have been able to obtain, and without favor.

The militia are a portion of the people; and we should remember that the regular troops are also a portion of the people. We are apt to view the latter as if they were strangers. It is the difference of organization that constitutes the difference between the militia and regular troops in the service of the United States; both are composed of citizens; and the same man may alternately serve in both. In the militia, when in service, you have a force composed of men drawn by compulsion into the service, for six months only, and serving under officers appointed by the States, called into service for the same time. In the regular troops you have men who have willingly entered the service for five years; serving under officers appointed by the Government of the United States. The question is, can we, the people, best confide in that portion of ourselves which constitute a militia, as heretofore organized, or in that portion of ourselves which may constitute a regular army, as heretofore organized?

I will contend, and I expect to prove, that the militia, as organized, do not deserve the confidence of the nation for the purpose of carrying on war; that militia are the most expensive force that the nation can employ; that to keep a militia army in the field is most distressing to the people; that the laws for that purpose operate most unequally and unjustly; that the regular troops of the American army have deserved the confidence of the nation, for the purposes of carrying on war; and that the nation ought therefore to have an adequate army of regular troops in time of war.

The first position that I am to maintain is, that the militia, as organized, do not deserve the confidence of the nation, as a means of carrying on war. Let me not be misunderstood. I speak of the militia as now and heretofore organized. It is not to be denied, that an organization might be given to the militia that would produce from them an army of regular troops; but no such organization is likely to be given to the militia. What are the qualities which entitle troops to the confidence of a nation in time of war? I answer—subordination, patience, and fidelity in service; steadiness and firmness in action. Do the militia of the United States, when called into service, possess these qualities? This is a delicate question. I will not take upon myself to answer the question. History shall answer. I will first examine the conduct of the militia during the war of the Revolution; and, secondly, their conduct in the last war; and I will only notice their conduct when serving under commanders of high military reputation.

Judge Marshall, in his Life of Washington, has taught important lessons on this subject. Yet, it would seem as if the members of Congress, during the last war, had forgotten the events of the war of the Revolution. In speaking of the defects in the structure of the American army, the historian says:

"Militia were not merely depended on as auxiliaries, and as covering the country from the sudden irruptions of small parties, for which purposes they ought certainly to be competent, and with a view to which they will always be important; but they were also relied on as constituting the main body and strength of the army. Their absolute incapacity to maintain this station in the military arrangements of any country engaged in war with an enemy of nearly equal strength, employing a permanent force, at all times capable of being used to its utmost extent, was demonstrated to the conviction of scepticism itself; and under the weight of this conviction, every exertion was made by Congress, though almost too late, to remedy the very extensive mischief which this fatal error had already produced."

But, said Mr. S., it is to the letters of General Washington himself that we are to look for evidence, to enable us to determine whether militia are subordinate, patient, and faithful in service. In September, 1776, he says: "The militia, instead of calling forth their utmost efforts to a ' brave and manly opposition, in order to repair ' our losses, are dismayed, intractable, and impa- ' tient to return. Great numbers of them have ' gone off—in some instances almost by whole ' regiments, by half ones, and by companies, at a ' time." And, in speaking of the militia of Connecticut, who were considered as inferior to none, he says: "The impulse for going home was so ' irresistible, it answered no purpose to oppose it. ' Though I would not discharge, I have been ' obliged to acquiesce; and it affords one more ' melancholy proof how delusive such dependen- ' cies are."

Deeply impressed with the subject, and foreseeing ruin from a reliance on militia, he says, "If ' I was called to declare, upon oath, whether the ' militia have been most serviceable or hurtful, ' upon the whole, I should subscribe to the latter;" and he adds, in the same letter, "no man who re- ' gards order, regularity, and economy, or who has ' any regard for his honor, character, or peace of 'mind, will risk them upon this issue." Again he says, "I plainly foresee an intervention of time 'between the old and new army, which must be 'filled up with militia, if to be had; with whom 'no man who has any regard for his reputation 'can undertake to be answerable for consequences." Here, said Mr. S., we have the oath of Washington that militia are pernicious. I say, his oath; for his offer to swear is the same to me as if he had done so. Here we discover that, of all the untoward events that happened to him, nothing so distressed him, nothing so preyed upon his mind, as the employment of militia, whom he considered as endangering his honor and the independence of the country.

Such having been the character of the militia in the war of the Revolution, let us inquire if it has undergone any material change. Let us see if they were subordinate, patient, and faithful, in service, during the last war. I will refer you to a historical work, "the Life of General Jackson," for a development of the conduct and character of the militia of Tennessee, a State whose militia is perhaps entitled to the post of honor among the several States. The historian, when relating events which happened in the country of the Creeks, says, "at length revolt began to show it- 'self openly. The officers and soldiers of the mi- 'litia, collecting in their tents, and talking over 'their grievances, determined to abandon their 'camp. In the morning, when they were to carry 'their intentions into execution, he (Jackson) 'drew up the volunteers in front of them, with 'positive commands to prevent their progress, and 'compel them to return to their former position in 'camp. The next day, however, presented a sin- 'gular scene. The volunteers, who, the day be- 'fore, had been the instruments for compelling the 'militia to return to their duty, seeing the destruc- 'tion of those hopes on which they had lately 'built, in turn began to mutiny themselves." The writer says all must have felt a consciousness "that the privations of which they complained 'were far less grievous than they had represented 'them; by no means sufficient to justify revolt, 'and not greater than a patriot might be expected 'to bear without a murmur." Such were the difficulties with which General Jackson had to struggle, that scarce was one mutiny quelled until another appears. The historian tells us, "on his '(Jackson's) arrival, he found a much more exten- 'sive mutiny than that which had just been 'quelled. Almost the whole brigade had put it- 'self in an attitude to move forcibly off." No sooner have we read the account of this evidence of a want of subordination, than we are presented with another. "At length, on the evening of the '9th, General Hall hastened to the tent of Gen- 'eral Jackson, with information that his whole 'brigade was in a state of mutiny." Soon after, the historian informs us of the disaffection of General Coffee's brigade. "They had proceeded as 'far as Ditto's Ferry, when the greater part of 'them, refusing to cross the river, returned in a 'tumultuous manner, committing, on the route, 'innumerable irregularities, which there was no

'force sufficient to restrain." Of these men, General Jackson, in an official order, says, "that they 'are returning home, not only like deserters, but 'in the real genuine character of such, is, indeed, 'a lamentable truth." The historian closes this relation by telling us that, "thus, in a tumultuous 'manner, they broke up, and, committing innu- 'merable extravagancies, regardless alike of law 'and decency, continued their route to their re- 'spective homes."

It appears, said Mr. S., that the character of the militia in the last war, was not materially changed from what it had been during the war of the Revolution. It is not possible to add to this evidence so as to make it more conclusive in proving that the militia are not subordinate, patient, faithful, and persevering, when in service; therefore, they are not to be relied on by the American people, for the purpose of carrying on war.

I find, in a late newspaper, this paragraph: "The session of the supreme court at Utica closed 'on Saturday last. Among the important causes 'argued before them, was one involving the va- 'lidity of the proceedings of the court martial un- 'der General Stediford, organized for the purpose 'of trying those militiamen who 'declined, neg- 'lected, or refused,' to go into the service of the 'United States during the latter part of the last 'war, in obedience to the orders of the Governor 'of this State, issued in conformity to the requi- 'sitions of the President of the United States. 'The fines imposed by that body are supposed to 'exceed $100,000, and the number of delinquents 'amounted to upwards of nine thousand." Would it be proper, said Mr. S., after this, to place our reliance on militia, when we find them refuse, in such numbers, in one of the most patriotic States, when legally called, to enter the service of the United States? And, until they join your service, you have not, by the existing laws, any command over them. The effect of efforts to raise an army of militia is to produce a multitude of fines; in collecting which, the courts shall be engaged some years after the war is ended. On such a system of defence it would be folly to place our reliance.

I will next inquire of history whether militia are firm and steady in action. We will return to the war of the Revolution, and to the battle of Camden, where Gates commanded about four thousand men, opposed to about two thousand of the enemy. Better troops than the American regulars who fought in that action never appeared in any field. But there, the historian tells us, "the intimidated mili- tia *threw down their arms* and fled from the field with the utmost precipitation;" (and these were Virginia militia too.) "Except one regiment 'commanded by Colonel Dixon, an old continen- 'tal officer, which was posted nearest the conti- 'nental troops, the whole North Carolina division 'followed the shameful example. Dixon's regi- 'ment maintained its ground for great part of the 'action. Other parts of the same brigade, which 'was commanded by Gregory, made a show of 'fighting, and the whole paused for an instant; 'but the terror of their brethren was soon commu-

' nicated to them, and they, also, *threw away their* ' *arms*, and sought safety in flight. Very few of ' the militia of North Carolina or Virginia dis- ' charged a single musket, and a still smaller num- ' ber brought one off the field."

Thus, said Mr. S., in consequence of the mis-conduct of the militia, of their utter want of firm-ness in action, our regular troops were cut to pieces, the enemy with a force greatly inferior in point of numbers triumphed, the Carolinas were lost, the independence of the country brought into jeopardy; and the declaration of Washington again fully justified; that no man, who has any regard for his honor, character, or peace of mind, should risk them on militia.

I will bring you next to the battle of Guilford, where we had more than four thousand men, op-posed to less than two thousand of the enemy; and as we had more than one thousand six hundred regular troops, the entire defeat of the enemy must have been the result, had the militia performed their duty in a tolerable manner. The historian having given us the order of battle, says "the ' British troops advanced to the charge with the ' cool determined courage which *discipline* inspires. ' Notwithstanding the great advantages of their ' position, and the security afforded by the cover of ' a thick wood, strong fence, and a second line in ' their rear, the North Carolina militia *fled with the* ' *utmost precipitation.* At the distance of one hun- ' dred and forty yards their fire commenced on an ' enemy advancing through an open field. Many ' of them did not once discharge their loaded ' muskets; and except the small part of one of the ' battalions in Eaton's brigade, none gave more ' than a second fire. The exertions of their gene- ' rals and field officers were entirely unavailing. ' *Terrified at the sight of the enemy*, they fled in every ' direction. Many of them *threw away their arms ;* ' and dispersing themselves through the woods, ' made the best of their way to their respective ' homes. The few who kept their ground gave ' way, *of course*, on the first fire that was made ' upon them."

Thus, said Mr. S., as the misconduct of the mi-litia of Virginia gave the enemy possession of the Carolinas, so the misconduct of the militia of North Carolina, and their equal want of firmness in action, gave the enemy a victory where he should have met with an entire defeat; and this led to the invasion of Virginia. Another confirmation of the declaration of General Washington, that, " To place any dependence upon militia, is assur-edly resting upon a broken staff."

Let us inquire if the militia in the late war ex-hibited a greater degree of firmness and steadiness in action, than they did in the war of the Revolu-tion. I have seen an opinion ascribed to a distin-guished friend of the United States, to whom they owe the debt of perpetual gratitude, which incul-cates an error that I am laboring to remove. The Marquis La Fayette, to whom I allude, says "the ' battle which closed this war, that of New Or- ' leans, is one of the curious phenomena of military ' history, and one of the best arguments in favor ' of the employment of militia to resist the attacks

' of regular troops." Let the Marquis think so. Let all Europe think so; it is well: but let us not be deceived; it would be a fatal deception. The victory of New Orleans was owing to the great ability of the American General, the advantages of his position, and the incapacity of his oppo-nent, who neglected to advance until it was too late. But, General Jackson did not command militia alone; and he probably would have failed, had he commanded militia only. It appears, by documents which I hold in my hand, that, in ad-dition to a little more then four thousand militia, General Jackson had under his command nine hundred and three United States' troops, of whom fifty-two were officers, and he was aided by seven hundred and four seamen and marines, of whom sixteen were commissioned officers. General Jack-son deserves immortal renown ; nor does it detract from the praise justly due to him, that of the force who fought at New Orleans, one thousand six hundred were trained men, commanded by skilful officers.

To assist you in deciding whether the militia in the last war were firm and steady in danger, I will first offer you the testimony of General Cass. In a letter written in January, 1814, from Williams-ville, near Buffalo, he says : " The circumstances ' attending the destruction of Buffalo, you will ' have heard before this reaches you ; but the force ' of the enemy has been greatly magnified. From ' the most careful examination, I am satisfied, that ' not more than six hundred and fifty men, of reg- ' ulars, militia, and Indians, landed at Black Rock. ' To oppose these we had from two thousand five ' hundred to three thousand militia ; all except a ' very few of them behaved in the most cowardly ' manner. They fled without discharging a mus- ' ket." I will next offer the testimony of General Brown, given from Sackett's Harbor, in June, 1813, and containing an account of his first battle. He says, " our strength at this point was now five ' hundred men, all anxious for battle, as far as ' profession would go. My orders were that the ' troops should lie close, and reserve their fire till ' the enemy had approached so near that every ' shot might hit its object. It is however, impos- ' sible to execute such orders with raw troops, un- ' accustomed to subordination. My orders were ' in this case disobeyed. The whole line fired, ' and not without effect ; but in the moment when ' I was contemplating this, to my utter astonish- ' ment, they rose and fled. It was during this last ' movement that the regulars under Colonel Backus ' first engaged the enemy ; nor was it long before ' they defeated him. The result of the action, so ' glorious to the officers and soldiers of the regular ' army, has already been communicated in my let- ' ter of the 29th." It does not, said Mr. S., ap-pear from history that the conduct of the militia in the last war was different in action from what it was in the war of the Revolution The general testimony of history is, that militia are not to be relied on to oppose regular troops in the field. They have generally fled from regular troops at the first fire. They thus fled at Camden, at Guilford Courthouse, at Sackett's Harbor, at Buffalo, and at Bladensburg. This Capitol burned by incendiaries, will be a monument, as long as it stands, to prove that militia are an unsafe dependence for defence. Militia to oppose regular troops require either the advantage of a rampart, or that they shall be highly irritated. General Washington remarks that, "when men are irritated and the passions inflamed, they fly hastily and cheerfully to arms." At Bunker's Hill and at New Orleans, the militia had a rampart. At Saratoga, and the immediately preceding actions, the minds of the militia were highly inflamed by the cruel and impolitic proceedings of the enemy.

The honorable member from Massachusetts has informed us of a contest seen and reported to him by General Brown, wherein a militia regiment attacked a regiment of regular troops in open space, and put them to flight. I have inquired of the honorable member where this happened, and he says the place was not named to him. As this is a subject on which I have conversed with that distinguished officer, I was somewhat surprised at the information; and apprehend the honorable member must have been mistaken in what he supposed General Brown said to him. In a written paper which I hold in my hand, given to me by General Brown, he says, "It is believed that undisciplined men never did achieve a victory, when opposed by regulars in open space, or by field engagement." This is directly at variance with the information which the honorable member from Massachusetts supposes he received from General Brown.

I will proceed to show that militia are the most expensive defence that a nation can employ. Here, again, I will offer the testimony of the historian of the life of Washington. He says, "The immense loss of arms resulting inevitably from their being placed in the hands of troops who were soon to return home, and who could not be subjected to discipline while in camp, was a very serious mischief." He tells us, "They carried off arms and blankets, which had been unavoidably delivered to them to be used while in camp, and thus wasted in advance the supplies collected for the use of the army, now recruiting for the ensuing campaign." The testimony of General Washington himself is still more full, clear, and conclusive. He says, "Certain I am that it would be cheaper to keep fifty thousand or one hundred men in constant pay than to depend on half the number, and supply the other half occasionally by militia. Again he says, "The saving in the articles of stores, provisions, and a thousand other things, by having nothing to do with militia, unless in cases of extraordinary exigency, would amply support a large army, which, well officered, would be daily improving, instead of continuing a destructive, expensive, and disorderly mob. I am clear in opinion, that, if forty thousand men had been kept in constant pay since the first commencement of hostilities, and the militia had been excused during that period, the continent would have saved money." Equally remarkable, said Mr. S., for profusion and waste was the conduct of the militia during the late war. The writer

of the Life of General Jackson, speaking of a brigade of militia, says, "They committed the wildest extravagancies, profusely wasting the public grain, which with much difficulty and labor had been collected there for the purpose of the campaign, and indulging in every species of excess."

I hold in my hand a still more satisfactory piece of evidence of the monstrous expense attending the employment of militia by the United States. It is an abstract, showing, in part, the number of militia who, during the last war, were in the service of the United States, and paid separately. Can you guess, sir, within an hundred of the number of militia generals employed? The number was one hundred and seventy-four. Yes, sir, you had one hundred and seventy-four militia generals in service in the last war; and an aggregate of four hundred and ten thousand men.(a) The pay of these militia, including the subsistence and forage of officers, amounted to more than twelve million six hundred thousand dollars, exclusive of the subsistence of the men, the quartermasters' supplies, the transportation, ordnance stores, medical stores, and other expenses, which must have amounted to an enormous sum.*

I have said, that to keep a militia army in the field is most distressing to the people. To prove this, I will recur one moment to the Life of Washington. The writer says, "The frequent demands made on the militia were extremely harassing and distressing to the great body of the people. In those States most exposed to these calls, serious apprehensions were entertained for the agriculture of the country." Again he says, "The burden of calling militia from their domestic avocations at every threat of invasion, and of watching the different stations of the enemy with men whose principal pursuit was the cultivation of the soil, began to be so intolerable, that the people cast about for other expedients to relieve themselves from its weight." He adds, "The inconvenience of relying on militia only for security against even sudden invasion, was so strongly felt that the States generally resolved to raise particular corps of regular troops for individual defence." We know that, in the last war, the same cause produced the like effect, and that Virginia determined to raise a regular army of ten thousand men for the defence of the State. The distressing consequences of frequent calls on the militia are also noticed by General Washington, who says, "The militia, who have been harassed and tired by repeated calls upon them, (and farming and manufactures in a manner suspended,) would, upon any pressing emergency, have run with alacrity to arms; whereas the cry now is, they may be as well ruined in one way as another."

It should be recollected, said Mr. S., that the militia are drawn into service by a conscription. You take the unwilling man, you force the father from his family, the stripling from his widowed mother. You produce much private distress, besides injuring agriculture and manufactures. How

---

* See statement of General Jesup.

many of the youth of Virginia died ingloriously at Norfolk, who were constrained into the service against their will, and never saw an enemy! A regular force, raised by bounties, is composed of willing men—of those least attached to, and least important to society. If we must offer human sacrifices to the Moloch of war, let them be willing sacrifices.

I have said, that keeping up the militia army for the purpose of carrying on war, operates unequally and unjustly on the people. Such an army will be kept up by those States which are near to the seat of war, while those at a distance will be wholly exempted from this distressing service. Thus, in the last war, the militia of New York, Tennessee, and some other States, were called on to make immense sacrifices for the common cause, while those of South Carolina, New Jersey, New Hampshire, and other States, were almost entirely exempted. Not only is the tax on human life made very unequal, but the bounties paid for substitutes amount to an oppressive tax, paid in particular districts, and by particular individuals in those districts. Many persons during the last war paid $300 each, as bounties to keep up the militia army, while thousands of the wealthy paid nothing, and rendered no service. The militia laws have operated unjustly in the same districts. In some cases you have gone half through the militia rolls; one-half have performed tours of duty, or paid $300 each for substitutes, the other half have not done any duty, or paid any thing.

Militia service operates as a capitation tax—the most unjust of all taxes. If an army is raised by bounties, those bounties are paid by the Treasury, and raised by just principles of taxation on the whole wealth of the community.

You should also consider the effect which the bounties given by militiamen for substitutes had on your recruiting service. When you were inclined to make a great exertion to get a regular army in the last war, you gave a bounty of $124 for five years service; but you at the same time continued your calls on the militia, who offered a bounty of $300 for six months service. How could you expect your recruiting service to succeed when you produced such a competition? Let it be observed, too, that if a militia army of fifty thousand men is raised by a bounty of $300 to each man, then fifteen millions of dollars are paid in bounties for six months service; when you would get a regular army of the same number at $100 each, or five millions for five years service; and these five millions will be paid from the Treasury, and raised by an equal tax on the United States, while the fifteen millions given for six months service of militia substitutes will have been paid by particular individuals in particular districts.

I proceed to show that the regular troops of the American Army deserve the confidence of the American people, for the purpose of carrying on war. I have noticed their conduct in the war of the Revolution, at Camden and at Guilford; but it is to the battles of the late war that I will refer, to show that the same men, who in the militia are, as General Washington has observed, "timid, and

ready to fly from their own shadows," become in the regular service the best soldiers in the world. In the paper which I received from General Brown, from which I have already read an extract, he states, the American Army at Chippewa, on the 5th July, 1814, was composed of 2,500 regulars, of whom 1,200 were in the action, and of 500 irregulars, who were in the action; he states General Rial's command on the same day as composed of regular 3,350, of whom 1,800 were in action, and of 300 irregulars, who were in the action; thus it appears that 1,700 Americans defeated 2,100 British troops, and of the Americans only 1,200 were regulars. We know that the battle was won by them.* He states the American Army at Bridgewater as composed of 2,850 regulars and 350 volunteers, and that of General Drummond as composed of 3,950 regulars, and 1,000 Indians and militia; thus it appears that 3,200 American troops did defeat 4,950 British troops. He states the American Army at Fort Erie, on the 25th August, at 2,500, and that of General Drummond, all regulars, at 3,550; thus it appears that 2,500 American troops did repulse and defeat 3,550 British troops. He states the American Army, on the 17th September, as composed of 1,300 regular troops, and 1,000 volunteers, and that of General Drummond as composed of 4,157; thus it appears that 2,300 American troops defeated nearly double their number of the enemy.

Courage is confidence. The very same man who in the militia has no courage, and flies at the first shot, because he has no confidence in himself, his comrades, or his officers, becomes a hero in the regular service, because discipline inspires him with confidence in himself, in his companions, and in those by whom he is commanded. Discipline is the principle of victories. Without it you cannot have an armed force on which the nation can rely. You cannot have a militia effective for the purposes of war, without subjecting them to discipline and subordination; and this you cannot do without taking up too much of the time, and taking away too much of the liberties of the people.

This is an old question, whether veterans or undisciplined men are to be preferred for making war? History answers this question uniformly in favor of veterans, from the time of the first wars on record to the present day. We should make war with regular troops; and, with a view to be prepared to raise immediately a considerable army, I would keep in time of peace a regular force to occupy our military posts, and I would provide an immense quantity of the materials for war. I would have in service a number of supernumerary company officers, with a view to increase the Army, when necessary, with facility. I should not have been willing to discharge a single soldier of the present establishment, had not the Secretary of War reported a plan for reduction, in which he seems to acquiesce in the expediency of discharging a part of the soldiers now in service. With regard to the general officers and the staff, I ap-

* Scott's brigade.

prehend there may be a partial reduction without injury to the service.

The great object of a militia is to have an armed people, ready to repel every invasion of their liberties. The militia belong essentially to the States. It could not have been the intention of those who formed the Constitution that Congress should make war with the militia, or they would have given to the General Government power to appoint the officers, and to train the militia; which powers are retained by the States, who thus retain the control of the militia. The States may authorize an annual election of militia officers; and how can you confide in a force which is placed essentially beyond your control?

Sir, it is with the most powerful nations of the world that we are most likely to have collisions. We should avail ourselves of the advantages resulting from fortifications and from military skill, as our physical force is inferior to that of the nations who may become our enemies. We cannot be in too much haste to finish our fortifications It would be better to pay interest on the sum they will cost than to leave our maritime frontier unprotected. If you would maintain your authority in your seaports, you must have cannon and soldiers there. We should secure peace by presenting an iron front to our foes. When we have expended more than one hundred millions of money, and fifty thousand lives, to maintain our rights by war, shall we refuse to expend a few millions annually to preserve those rights in peace?

Before you destroy the Army, you ought to pass an efficient militia law. A bill was drawn and reported, four years ago, which would have given you a militia system much more efficient than you have at present. It proposed to call out the officers for the war, and the privates for two years. Such an army might have acquired discipline, and become respectable; but you did not pass the bill. Will you now enact such a law? I apprehend you will not. And, surely, before you destroy one system of defence you should provide another.

Sir, I would not break down any of the necessary institutions of the Government. It is not necessary to do so. It is singular that the Government should be charged in this House with prodigality and oppression, when no taxes whatever are imposed on the people; and the only complaint made by them is, that the duties imposed are not high enough.

(a) General officers	-	-	-	-	174
General staff	-	-	-	-	235
Field officers	-	-	-	-	1,867
Regimental staff	-	-	-	-	3,083
Non-commissioned staff	-	-	-	1,750
Captains	-	-	-	-	6,510
Subalterns	-	-	-	-	15,385
Non-commissioned officers	-	-	-	48,237
Musicians	-	-	-	-	6,651
Privates	-	-	-	-	326,011

	Total	-	-	-	382,649
	Aggregate	-	-	-	410,603

Pay, $12,618,967 38.

It will be understood that the foregoing statement embraces only the pay of the militia, and the pay, subsistence, and forage of officers, so far as the calls exhibited the same. The subsistence of the militia; the Quartermaster's supplies; the transportation, ordnance stores, and all other expenses incident to their service, form no part of the estimate.

(b) *Memorandum by General Jesup, Quartermaster General.*

In time of peace, when the Army is mostly stationary, and its expenditures rigidly economised, the proportion its pay bears to its other expenses of every description, is estimated as sixty-five is to one hundred and ninty-five, or as one to three. But in time of war, with the same rigid economy, its expenses, from the multiplied movements, and unavoidable waste and expenditures may, without erring much, be estimated as one is to five, so is the pay to the other expenses. This ratio is applicable to the expenses of the regular Army, and, though the militia expenses would not embrace the item of clothing which is included in estimating the ratio above, yet it is believed, from their superior skill in waste and destruction of arms and property generally, that their pay would stand to their other expenses as one is to six. Hence, when the pay amounts to $12,600,000, their other expenses would be $75,600,000.

Mr. EUSTIS followed, in reply to parts of Mr. SMYTH's speech. When he concluded, the Committee rose.

SATURDAY, January 6.

DEATH OF MR. LINN.

Mr. SOUTHARD announced the death of JOHN LINN, one of the members of this House, from the State of New Jersey. Whereupon,

Resolved, unanimously, That a committee be appointed to take order for superintending the funeral of John Linn, deceased, late a representative from the State of New Jersey.

Messrs. SOUTHARD, BATEMAN, BLOOMFIELD, KINSEY, SMITH, of New Jersey, CULPEPER, and MARCHAND, were appointed the said committee.

Resolved, unanimously, That the members of this House will testify their respect for the memory of John Linn, late one of their body, by wearing crape on the left arm for one month.

Resolved, unanimously, That the members of this House will attend the funeral of the late John Linn this day at three o'clock.

Resolved, unanimously, That a message be sent to the Senate to notify them of the death of John Linn, late a member of this House, and that his funeral will take place this day at three o'clock, from the Hall of the House of Representatives.

And then the House adjourned.

MONDAY, January 8.

A new member, to wit, from the State of Pennsylvania, DANIEL UDREE, elected to supply the vacancy occasioned by the resignation of Joseph Hiester, appeared, was qualified, and took his seat.

Mr. CANNON, from the Committee upon the subject of the Militia, reported a bill to provide an uniform system of organization for the militia of the different States and Territories; and for instructing the officers of the same at the expense of the United States; which was twice read, and committed to a Committee of the Whole.

Mr. GROSS, of New York, submitted the following resolution, which was ordered to lie on the table one day for consideration:

Resolved, That the President of the United States be requested to inform this House (if, in his opinion, proper) whether any, and, if any, what, regulations, since the first of January, 1816, have been had with the Six Nations of Indians, or any portion of them; who the commissioners or agents were; the objects of the negotiations; the expenses of the same; the compensation of each commissioner, secretary, and agent, and to whom the moneys were paid.

On motion of Mr. STRONG, of New York,

Resolved, That the Committee on the District of Columbia be instructed to inquire into, and report to this House, the number of lotteries which have been instituted in said District, by virtue of an act to incorporate the inhabitants of the city of Washington, and to repeal all acts heretofore passed for that purpose, passed the 15th of May, 1820; the purposes for which the moneys are to be raised; the amount of each scheme, and the total nominal value of the tickets offered for sale; the rate of deduction proposed to be made from the prizes, and the gross amount of the proceeds of said lotteries, which will come into the hands of the managers; and, also, whether the condition of the said act of incorporation has been complied with, so far as it respects the authority to raise money by lotteries.

Mr. TRIMBLE submitted the following resolution, which was ordered to lie on the table one day for consideration:

Resolved, That the Secretary of the Treasury be instructed to inform this House when, and why, the agency of the Treasurer of the United States for the War and Navy Departments was first established, and whether the same may not be discontinued without detriment to the public service.

The bill from the Senate entitled "An act for the relief of Robert Purdy," was read, and referred to the Committee on Military Affairs.

The resolutions moved by Mr. WILLIAMS, of North Carolina, calling for information of the amount of money necessary to complete the contracts which have been made for the increase of the navy and for building fortifications, were taken up and agreed to.

REDUCTION OF EXPENDITURES.

Mr. COBB having moved again to go into Committee of the Whole on the state of the Union—

A short debate arose which resulted in a motion by Mr. BEECHER to discharge the Committee of the Whole on the state of the Union from the further consideration of the resolutions introduced by Mr. COBB.

In this debate Messrs. ANDERSON, ARCHER, COBB, LOWNDES, SIMKINS, BEECHER, HARDING, FLOYD, SERGEANT, and BALDWIN, took part.

The question discussed was, simply, whether the subject of a general reduction of the expenses of the Government, with reference to expediency and to the state of the finances, could be more practically and efficiently considered by continuing to debate the declaratory propositions of Mr. COBB, or the bills which have been, and probably will hereafter be, introduced, for the reduction of the expenditures of various branches of the public service.

The debate terminated in agreeing to Mr. BEECHER's motion, by a vote of 82 to 49; and the resolutions, being then before the House, were ordered to lie on the table.

A message from the Senate informed the House that the Senate have passed a bill, entitled "An act for the relief of Robert Purdy;" and they have also passed a bill of this House entitled "An act for the relief of Perley Keys and Jason Fairbanks," with an amendment; in which bill and amendment they ask the concurrence of this House.

The said amendment was read, and concurred in by the House.

REDUCTION OF THE ARMY.

The House, then, on motion of Mr. WILLIAMS, resolved itself into a Committee of the Whole, on the state of the Union. And,

On motion of Mr. BEECHER, the Committee proceeded to consider the bill reported by the Military Committee, for reducing the Military Peace Establishment. The first section having been read—

Mr. SIMKINS rose, and spoke substantially as follows:

Mr. Chairman, the same arguments apply to this particular bill which have been used on the general retrenching resolutions offered by the gentleman from Georgia, (Mr. COBB;) for, however diverse the resolutions may have been in their nature, every one must have seen that the army was mainly in view, and has occupied, principally, the attention of every member who has spoken upon them.

Mr. Chairman, when the present Chief Magistrate came into the administration of the Executive Department of the Union, it was shortly after the late war, in which he acted a most firm, conspicuous, and useful part; and when himself, with the whole nation, had a strong and full view of the commencement, dangers, and events, of that war. It was seen by the President and all enlightened men, (and the impression was too strong to be disregarded,) that the few fortifications for the defence of our whole coast which were then erected were either half finished, in a state of dilapidation, or nearly deserted; that the army had no efficient staff, or arrangement given to it by Congress, and could have, of course, but little organization or efficiency; and, to complete the picture, Congress had failed to pass laws for the "common defence" of the country, so as to make the militia what they always ought to be, more particularly in the absence of an efficient standing army. On the contrary, the state of this main body of defence was, in general, deranged, disorganized, and relaxed.

The war commenced; and, during its two first

years, such events did take place as was to be expected from the defenceless state of the country—events, many of which were mortifying and disgraceful beyond measure to every man who had a heart to feel for his country! Your treasure speedily exhausted, your Union interrupted, your moral character and energy fast wasting away, and your country bleeding at every pore!

I have had occasion heretofore to bring those scenes to the view of Congress on this same subject. From the strong current which now seems to be running through this House against the army, there never was such need to present the picture, in strong and vivid colors, as at this time.

In a state of glorious and perfect peace, and with a knowledge of the past, what was the imperious duty of the Chief Magistrate and of the Congress? Can any man who has sagacity to see, or a heart to love his country, doubt about what ought to have been the policy which should have been adopted? The President did distinctly see the necessity of protecting the great outlets on your whole coasts, by fortifications, which should be as lasting as your hills—of an army, which, from its staff, organization, and number, should man your forts and protect your immense frontiers during peace—should defend you efficiently during the first onsets of war, and be the means of infusing discipline and power into much larger bodies of regulars or militia, which would be promptly added. This sound and practical course, so wise in itself, and so loudly and universally called for by the whole nation, has been most happily begun, and has progressed with a pace so steady and energetic that at this time not a single doubt remains of its completion, if persisted in, or of its inestimable importance when completed. The great and exposed points of your coast have been surveyed with the accuracy and skill of engineers inferior perhaps to none in the world, and fortifications already erected thereon, or in a state of rapid advancement. Your army, too, has received an organization in its arrangement, an economy in its management, and an efficiency in its effect, approaching to that perfection which alone the highest energies of the human mind can expect to give it.

But, has this policy, of putting the country in "an armor and an attitude of defence," for the purposes of war, and the greater purposes of preserving peace, been sanctioned by the people? I answer, emphatically, yes, from one end of the continent to the other. We have not heard even a whisper against it. On the contrary, the highest recommendations of the course, and, what may fairly be considered as conclusive of the question is, the almost unanimous re-election, at this very time, of that Chief Magistrate who has lent the whole force of his distinguished talents and high moral character to the constant progress and completion of this policy. Yet there is, some how or other, a spirit in this body, (and in this body alone, it appears to me to exist,) which, in its loud cry for economy and retrenchment, says, stop your fortifications, diminish the progress of your navy, lessen all your salaries, dismiss your staff,

and cut down (or destroy, for destruction will be the consequence of such a measure,) your little army to the command of a single Brigadier General; and these gentlemen bottom themselves upon what they represent an exhausted state of our Treasury and resources. This is an attack upon the whole course and spirit of the present Administration; upon the most clear policy of the country, as sanctioned by the people; and so well aware was the President, at the opening of the present session, that the state of the Treasury might be the ground-work of delaying or pulling down our defensive institutions, that he gave a general, but a candid and fair view of our fiscal concerns, which were by no means in a situation as discouraging as had been supposed.

I acknowledge that a report of the Treasury Department, subsequently made, represents us for 1821, as $7,000,000 worse than nothing; but a mistake or over estimate, of the same Department, has already been acknowledged to the amount of $2,700,000, and when the resolutions submitted by my honorable friend and colleague from South Carolina, (Mr. LOWNDES,) calling for an account of the balances in the Treasury, on the 1st of January, 1821, are answered, we shall see another error or over estimate (if I am not greatly mistaken) of from one and a half to $2,500,000, so that the deficiency to be borrowed for 1821, instead of being $7,000,000, will be little more than $2,000,000; and if the Louisiana stock, to the amount of $2,000,000, shall not be paid this year, the deficiency will not be, perhaps, more than six or $800,000! For the three next years, it is admitted, on all hands, that our deficiency will be very little, if any, taking the estimates as they are now made, and our disbursements as they now stand.

Sir, it is well known that the exhausted state of the Treasury, and a cry about improper disbursements and great extravagance, are fruitful themes of declamation for those who wish to render themselves acceptable, by efforts to save the people's money. The cry of extravagance, retrenchment, and economy, is easily raised, for words cost nothing; but show me the real practical economist; the man who, in the departments of your Government, really saves your money, at the same time that he advances your best interests, and I will pronounce him a person worthy of the highest confidence. I wish not to see him who talks a great deal, but him who acts, and can show you the fruits of his actings.

We have been repeatedly called back to the pure economical times of Mr. Jefferson's administration. Let us for a moment examine it, and candor will constrain us to confess that this Administration, so far as it regarded the army and some other defensive measures, was founded on a reaction of what were conceived to be the high-handed measures of Mr. Adams's administration, and went too far on the other side, and leaving the army too small, disorganized, and inefficient. This was the greatest error into which the then President fell; and this is the precise error into which all your proposed measures of retrenchment directly lead.

Sir, I suppose no one claims an entire exemption from error. Of Mr. Jefferson's administration it is a fact that some acts have since been found by experience, and so acknowledged by the people, to have been impolitic. I refer to the Army and Navy.*

The number of men retained on the peace establishment by Mr. Jefferson, at the beginning of his administration, was 3,300. Now, small as this number was, it was certainly but little smaller at that period of our history than our ten thousand is at this time; considering the acquisition of Louisiana, and the consequent immense extension of our frontier, the necessary increase of our military posts from twenty-seven to about eighty, the vast augmentation of our fortifications to be manned, the rapid increase of our resources, and the almost doubled number of our population. But, sir, Mr, Jefferson gave us the best commentary on his own administration, in this respect, that we could possibly have wished for.

The army was increased in the year 1808, by Mr. Jefferson himself, to ten thousand men, precisely our present number, and the main reason why it remained comparatively weak and inefficient, till the beginning of the war, was because there never was any thing like a proper staff to arrange, discipline, and organize it. It had nearly sunk by its own weight, for the want of such a staff and such officers as your present bill, at one sweep, strikes from your army. The cardinal error then committed, we are now, in the short space of a few years, about to slide into. The very pit then dug for us, utterly regardless of the past, we are now with a blind fatality about to plunge into! It may be said that the army was then increased because there was a prospect of war. Sir, a wise nation will always adopt the obvious policy of preparing for war in time of peace; not merely to meet its dangers, but to preserve peace.

Mr. Chairman, it has been with utter astonishment that I have seen how clearly the horrors of the late war have been erased from the minds of gentlemen. The present retrenching course of policy, vindicated so strongly by the honorable member from Massachusetts, (Mr. EUSTIS,) the other day, would seem to indicate, that he and others, were out of existence at that time! Was not our treasure then given to the winds—squan-

dered on idle, afflicting, and unavailing efforts? Was it not a murderous waste of the blood of our fellow citizens, our families, our brothers? Have gentlemen calculated how many millions might have been saved by judicious fortifications, an efficient army, and passable roads? I sincerely believe, enough to maintain our little army a quarter of a century. Do gentlemen pretend to calculate the responsibility, the awful responsibility, they should feel for lives lost, by reason of this want of preparation! I tremble for the country when I see gentlemen ready to plunge us into the same dread abyss! We may calculate the loss of dollars and cents, but who can calculate, by what criterion can you calculate the value of union, the waste of our moral character and energies, and the sacrifice of our best blood?

It has been said, that the people demand retrenchment, and a reduction of the army. Sir, the people always demand economy and retrenchment, whenever and wheresoever their money shall be wasted or misapplied. Fidelity and accountability in the application of your funds, are indissolubly connected with the prosperity of your country, and the duration of your liberties. In this view, the vigilance of members cannot be too great; but I expressly deny that the people have demanded or even resolved upon the reduction of the army. There is not the slightest evidence to prove the truth of such an assertion. When the people require of this body a law to be passed, they instantly express their desire. Have you, then, seen a single petition for the reduction, although the attempt has been made here for two or three succeeding sessions, without success? On the contrary, (and it is fair to collect the public opinion in this way, in the absence of other evidence,) have you not seen by almost every newspaper, from all parts of the continent, and of all political parties, that the reduction of the army is disapproved, as rash and dangerous.

It is said, however, that the militia are our main defence; and that he who is an enemy to the militia is an enemy to his country. To what, sir, could such an observation refer? Who, in this land of freedom, can be an enemy to the militia? Can there be a man in the nation so base as not to wish to give it organization, discipline, and energy? An enemy to the militia! If any man is so, then he is an enemy to his father, his brothers, his sons, for they compose the militia.

Is it not strange that members should continually contend for the militia as our great defence, when they have always failed to pass laws to promote their discipline and strength? Is not this the more strange, when we know that in most of our States they are weak, deranged, and inefficient from this very cause? It is made the duty of Congress, by the charter which we have all sworn to support, to provide for the "common defence" of the country; we fail to pass laws to make the militia this common defence, and yet we diminish, impair, and destroy all other modes of defence.

It is admitted, from the very nature of things, that, in the progress of a war, men drawn from the great body of the people, must furnish the

---

* Justice requires me to state, that I was not a cold, but an ardent admirer of Mr. Jefferson's general course. I approved of that great act, the acquisition of Louisiana, and the spirit of economy and philanthropy of that great and distinguished lover of mankind; his pure love of country, and opposition to all foreign influence among us. I still am of the same opinion. I will, however, not be driven from an independent course, by mere names, to which gentlemen choose to attach odium. I will not fail to confess an error, if I believe it such, although it spring from Mr. Jefferson; nor would I scout a wise measure merely because it sprung from Mr. Adams. I say thus much, because I have been misunderstood on this point.

main defence of the country. This must be so, because I admit it to be inconsistent with the nature of our institutions, to maintain large standing armies. But is it not clear, and was it not proved by the chairman of the Military Committee, (Mr. Smyth, of Virginia,) that, to be powerful and efficient, the militia must be trained and disciplined? All history, from the earliest ages down, all experience, the experience of both our own wars, and even common sense itself, prove that men without discipline can never successfully resist a well trained army. This gentleman (Mr. S.) proved, with the utmost precision and clearness, that the militia were more inefficient, more expensive, and the calling them out, (which was but another name for conscription, for they go against their will,) more unjust, partial, and oppressive, than regulars, who enlist of their own accord. I will not do him the injustice to occupy ground which he occupied before me, with so much greater ability; but I make the appeal to every man's sense, whether, when your divines, your lawyers, and even your tradesmen, require some years of education and practice to fit them for their duties, your officers and soldiers, who have the tenfold arduous duty of defending their country, at the risk of their lives, could be expected to do so successfully, without a week's, or a month's, or a year's education and discipline? In the ruder ages, when science was unknown, all who met in war might be upon something like equality; but in the present improved state of military science, which can, in its higher grades, not be acquired without years of study and discipline, he would justly be esteemed a madman who would lead raw militia in an open field, against a disciplined army! What wise country would rest its fate on such an issue? Turn your attention to Europe, and behold, for many of the first years of Bonaparte's wars, how even regular armies, opposed to him, were cut up, vanquished, and destroyed, by superior military skill? They never could compete with him, till, in a succession of years, he himself taught them the higher arts of war.

The gentleman from Massachusetts points to Baltimore and New Orleans, as places at which the great strength of the militia was evinced. Did not the gentleman remember Castine, Washington City, and other places, where their failure stained their country with a disgrace which must long remain matter of the deepest mortification to every American? At New Orleans, they were, in part, regulars, and trained militia, (which is the same thing,) besides, General Jackson was judicious enough to throw up ramparts to protect his men. The same reasons, in part, insured the victory of Baltimore; and yet no man can doubt but there were hundreds of as brave, noble spirited men at the capture of this place, as were at New Orleans or Baltimore; but, being raw and undisciplined, they partook of a panic, which, becoming general, dispersed rapidly the whole force.

Mr. Chairman, I have said that I disliked a great noise about economy. The practice of rigid economy is a course which would give us greater

pleasure than talking about it. Will the members of this Committee have the goodness to look at the official report of the Secretary of War, and they will find that in 1818, the army proper, cost the nation $3,748,445, and consisted of 7,916 officers and men.

In 1819, $3,351,363; and consisted of 8,941 men.

In 1820, $2,616,516; and consisted of 10,281 officers and privates.

And in 1821, but $2,590,136 as asked for its support, and it contains ——, a larger proportion than has filled the ranks, perhaps, since the war.

From this statement it appears that, by the introduction of the Commissariat Department, and a most rigid system of economy, there is saved to the country, in three years, upwards of $1,158,308 in the army, properly so called.

This system of economy, and rapid diminution of expenses, with a staff, too, much larger than formerly, and by which the War Department has been loudly accused of wasting the public money, might be traced, in detail, into various branches or departments of the army; but I have only time to turn your attention to the medical department, as a fair sample of the rest.

The appropriation for that department, for three years in succession, viz: for 1809, 1810, and 1811, $145,600 total, when at that time the average of the army was only 5,581 men.

In 1819, 1820, and 1821, the whole appropriation will be $132,500, when the aggregate of the army is about 10,037.

By this statement it will be seen, that, although you have added considerably to the number of the medical officers, yet that department does not cost half the money it once did.

When then it is considered, (for the facts cannot be too often or too strongly presented,) what an immense sum in money, and how many lives, might be saved by a disciplined army and a well regulated staff, at the beginning of a war; and when to these you add the immense saving exhibited above, in the annual disbursements, and that your regular soldiery, besides their daily discipline, are constantly engaged in erecting fortifications, or in embellishing and improving your whole frontier, by making roads, or are engaged in the cultivation of the earth near your military posts, thereby saving something for their families and themselves from that ruinous idleness and dissipation which almost constantly attend camps—I say, when these incontrovertible facts are considered, we, who oppose the present bill, must be viewed, in the eyes of all mankind, as the true economists. We are not the "penny wise and pound foolish." We are not among those embracing the niggardly policy which would refuse to disburse one million to day, to save ten, twenty, or fifty millions to-morrow. The people, I again repeat, wish not the reduction of your army. Experience enables us to decide that they will ever bear taxes to support what is of importance to their interests; for, in the late war, when it dragged on so heavily for the want of funds, the people of the South, I well know, anticipated Congress in a system of taxation. They were anxious to pay their money freely, as the means of rendering the war vigorous and decisive.

The gentleman from Massachusetts, (Mr. E.,) has said, it would be the highest injustice to suppose that those officers who have covered themselves with such imperishable glory, would wish to continue in service a single hour after their services ceased to be required. Sir, their services are required. Their talents, their experience, their moral energies, and military skill, are required, to preserve and give reputation and life to your army. They are conscious that their country—the great body of the people, do require their services, or it is certain they would not remain in commission.

The same gentleman also said that, should the time ever arrive when the influence of military chiefs should find its way into the House, so far as to command a single vote, then it might command many more, and the law should be levelled against it.

Sir, I have never heard of such an influence, and I am glad the gentleman does not declare it now to exist, because not a shadow of evidence could be produced to support such an assertion. The gentleman could not, and he did not, intend to insinuate it. The unassuming conduct of the officers of the army generally vindicate them against any interference in this House, or in any other legislative body.

There is, on the contrary, such a jealousy of the army, (an unfounded jealousy,) as to keep many of the officers at a greater distance, perhaps, than citizens, alike interested in all matters of legislation, should keep. There is the same prejudice against the army that exists in Europe against standing armies, without the shadow of foundation for it. There the slavery entailed on the people by the dreadful curse of large standing armies, and the intolerable burden of taxes to support them, create a natural and a well founded prejudice. Here our army is so small, scattered over such an immense expanse of territory, stationed at so many different posts, and so identified with the great body of our citizens, that the idea is chimerical and ridiculous in the last degree. It is matter of astonishment that so many, even in this enlightened body, should seem ready to give it currency.

Gentlemen speak of waste, extravagance, and idleness. Let them point it out—let them name the officer, and show the extravagance. It is their solemn duty to do so, if they can. If they do not, what will the world say? If they do, let your law strike at the root of the evil, and I will join in it.

If I understood the gentleman (Mr. EUSTIS) correctly, he did say, that fortifications had been reared at particular points to gratify a particular man or set of men. [Here Mr. EUSTIS rose, and said, he had been misunderstood; that he had only said that fortifications had been made at exposed points, where they could not be defended.]

Mr. S. expressed his pleasure that the gentleman disavowed saying what he had understood him to say. The fortifications have been placed (continued Mr. S.) at those points only which were directed by a survey, made with great labor, by

engineers, one of whom was a foreigner, but perhaps as able in his department as any man in the world. The others were able men, all of whom agreed, and have deposited a report and survey of our coast in the proper department, which I am told would do honor to any men, in any age.

But, says the gentleman, our coast cannot be fortified. From its great extent, it is impracticable. I admit that you cannot fortify every little inlet making into every village; but we can fortify, and pretty effectually fortify, certain great and exposed points, which are the vital arteries leading into the great body of our country. I mean at Boston, New York, the Chesapeake, which leads into all the principal towns of the Middle States, Charleston, Mobile, and New Orleans.

It is triumphantly declared, let us get rid of General A. or General B. if not wanted. Sir, your generals are not made in a day. Their talents and renown give strength and reputation to your army. It will be easy to cut off, or in the language of the bill to "dismiss" from the service Jackson, Brown, Scott, Gaines, and others, but with them you greatly prostrate the strength of your little army. Do you, can you hope, that they will serve in the inferior offices you now create, and on the petty theatre you now prescribe?

No, sir, they will not. Can you supply their places? Let the American people answer. It is a light, and it would almost seem a triumphant task to dismiss them now; but remember you thereby destroy the efficiency of your Peace Establishment. A brigadier general's command for such a number of posts, such a population, and such a continent as this, appears to me a burlesque on warlike preparation.

The very names of those generals, whose services it seems now to be so proper to dispense with, would give a union, a firmness, and a moral power to your army in the hour of trial, which would be beyond calculation. Their talents and experience on some great emergency would be worth millions.

And are we sure that this day of trial, this hour of emergency, is never to arrive, or to arrive at some distant day when we may be ready for it? Deceive not yourselves.

Look at the unsettled state of France; the revolution not over, perhaps, in Spain; Germany ready for a change of Government; the great autocrat of Europe, the Emperor of all the Russias, having his eye on the dominions of the Ottoman Porte, and extending onward still further to the vast possessions of the British in the East Indies; revolution in Naples, other revolutions going on in South America; and the agitated state even of England; I say look at all these, and see also our commerce and connexions, ramified and extended into every sea, and with every nation, and who can be hardy enough to pronounce that this commerce will not be cut up, and these pacific connexions not be disturbed! Who is bold enough to say how early or how late it may be, before we may be driven to protect our rights, and to defend our soil? Has the nature of our free institutions ceased to make this Government and these people objects of jealousy and hate to the Holy Alliance; to all the crowned heads of Europe? Sir, the hour of peril will come, and when that shall arrive, overwhelming as the current for retrenchment and cutting down may now be in this House, then will every man here agree with me in wishing that they had sought the preservation of our little army, navy, fortifications, and other defensive institutions, and had given them their greatest practicable strength and efficiency.

At this period of profound peace, and when gentlemen suppose that war will never come, we do disagree most pointedly. The first cannon that shall be fired by an enemy, will be the signal for universal regret, that we had not preserved a more imposing attitude. At such a period as that, and even now I would not give the consolation I shall feel for the vote I am to give against this bill, small as may be the minority in which I may stand, for any other consolation I could derive from my public life. Prostrate, or even weaken your army and navy, and you invite aggression; your enemies will pour upon you with the ferocity of lions, and the strength of Hercules.

Sir, I reiterate again and again, that I am for the practice of true economy, and for making every officer accountable even to the last cent; but I deprecate the present wavering policy of cutting down army, navy, and diminishing almost every salary. I deprecate the policy of unsettling every thing; of rendering all those institutions, which should be held most permanent and sacred, cheap, inefficient and worthless, by the rash and versatile course of this body, to which the people look for wisdom and protection. The very foundation on which the pillars of our Federal fabric is raised is "the common defence and general welfare." Shall we subvert the spirit of the Government by our present course?

Shall we make our officers, of all kinds, poor and dependant? Our own body is changeable enough already; but shall we render it still more so, by a reduction of pay? Shall we send members of Congress here to seek Executive offices and patronage, rather than pursue a wise independent course, calculated to benefit the country?

Mr. Chairman, I have already proved, by a few general suggestions, that there is no such necessity for all this, as was supposed to exist. The situation of the Treasury, which gives the greatest spring to a cry for retrenchment, is not so startling, not so alarming, as was at first represented by the head of that department. Moderation, wisdom, and consistency, cry, forbear. Let us not, by our acts, hastily and rashly attack and prostrate the whole policy of former Congresses and of the present Chief Magistrate, which has been to place every part of this rising nation in such an attitude of defence, as is required, not only by the Constitution, but by the loud and solemn warnings of fatal experience. If we break into these institutions of defence, we do vitally assail that wise policy upon which the future fame of the present Executive must rest.

When Mr. S. had concluded—

Mr. WILLIAMS said that he concurred with the gentleman from South Carolina, (Mr. SIMKINS,) who had just taken his seat, in one sentiment, which was, that the bill now under consideration depends for its support on the exhausted condition of the Treasury. But, although this was at any time a very sufficient reason, he would yet remind the gentleman from South Carolina, that it was not with him (Mr. W.) the only reason. He had other, and he might add still higher motives for supporting the bill, as had been evinced by his conduct on many previous occasions. When there was no deficiency in the Treasury; when there was in fact a surplus of some millions he had been in favor of reducing the Army on account of the essential propriety, or natural adaptation of such a measure to the principle of our Government. Passing, however, for the present this part of the subject, he would subscribe fully to the opinion of the gentleman from Massachusetts, (Mr. EUSTIS,) that we cannot go on with our establishments as they now exist. To the gentleman from Massachusetts, Mr. W. said, he would seize that opportunity of offering the tribute of his sincere thanks for the very instructive, impressive, and eloquent speech which he delivered the other day on the subject of retrenchment and economy. That gentleman's age indicated the wisdom and the history of his past life, the experience with which he could claim to speak and to be heard in this House; and on no occasion, said Mr. W., was he ever more gratified than he was when attending to the sentiments expressed by the gentleman from Massachusetts; with him, Mr. W. thought the time had arrived when we must resume the practice of economy; when we must return to that path of frugality and prudence from which we had most unwisely departed, or persist in a career of extravagance, profusion, and prodigality, as hostile to the nature of our political institutions, as it is repugnant to the individual prosperity and happiness of our fellow-citizens.

Mr. W. said, if he could hesitate between these alternatives he should deem himself unfit to occupy a seat on this floor. Not that he would condemn any gentleman who entertains a different opinion. "*Tot capitum, totidem millia studiorum,*" is a maxim, the truth of which is every day displayed in the proceedings of this House. I know well that gentlemen will honestly differ in opinion, not only on this subject, but on every other which may be agitated. But it appears to me that this difference would not be so great, so glaring, so irreconcileable, if we all built our systems of reasoning on a proper basis; if we all started from the same point. Some reason from the Government to the people; while others reason from the people to the Government: some appear to think that the good, or, in other words, that the power and amplitude of the Government should alone be consulted, regardless of the effects which any particular measure might have on the people; but others assert that we should, in the first place, look to the circumstances and condition of the people; that their ease, comfort, and happiness, should be the scope, the end, the object of all our laws. It is thus we are made to arrive at different conclusions. For his own part, Mr. W. said, he would look to the people as the proper basis for all our acts; he would examine the consequences, immediate and remote, likely to result to them from the adoption of every measure which might be proposed. Those who start from any other premises must, in my judgment, always arrive at false conclusions. For, sir, who are the people of this country? The very Constitution tells you that they are supreme; that they are the sovereign authority; that all power emanates from them. The President, in his message to Congress at the commencement of the present session, observed, "that this Government is founded by, administered for, and supported by the people." Whatever, then, promotes the happiness of the people must conduce, in an equal degree, to benefit the Government, since it was to promote that happiness that the Government was founded. On the other hand, whatever injures, afflicts, or distresses the people, must, in the same degree, injure, afflict, or distress the Government, since it was to prevent that injury, affliction, and distress, that the Government was formed. And here, Mr. Chairman, suffer me to correct a very erroneous idea, frequently propagated abroad, and which, much to my surprise, has been reiterated within these walls by the member from South Carolina, (Mr. SIMKINS.)

When an attempt is made to retrench expenditures, we hear loud cries raised against those who think proper to advocate the measure. It is said that we who favor retrenchment "are opposing Government," &c. Now, sir, this idea is full of error; it is false. I do not mean by this to charge the gentleman from South Carolina with falsehood; but I mean to say, and I will say, that he does not rightly judge our motives. No doubt, sir, the gentleman has more intimate acquaintance with some portion of Executive views than I have. But, if this attempt to economise in our expenditures, and to relieve the burdens of the community, should be regarded as an attack on the Executive Government, or any of its branches, I for one will say, that I cannot help it; that it is my duty to pursue what appears to me most conducive to the public good, without reference to any such extraneous considerations.

Suppose, for example, half of the present Army would answer every purpose which this nation could desire. I ask, if an attempt to reduce it would be acting against the people, or, if you please, against the Government? Not at all; but, on the contrary, it would be promoting the just ends of Government to reduce the Army, because, by that reduction, our expenditures would be lessened, and the happiness of the people would be proportionably advanced. There are, indeed, a set of officers, of sinecure placemen, of political grasshoppers, warmed and animated into existence by the sunshine of the Treasury; sustained and supported, not by General Atkinson's turnip patches at Council Bluffs, but by the streams of nourishment which flow from the Treasury, who will, when any attempt is made to reduce expenditures, cry out—"The Government is in danger;

the necessary establishments of the country are about to be broken in upon," &c. But, sir, all this is nothing more than false alarm. It is true, you may take from such persons the salaries they do not earn, and which consequently they do not deserve; but you leave in the pockets of the people the money which is thus saved. And I ask again, whether the interest of the people, or of Government, does not require that officers that do nothing, or next to nothing, should be disbanded? I should think it does. But yet these characters swell into factitious importance, and exclaim, when you are about to disband them, that "you are opposing Government." They seem to think that they are the Government; that their individual benefit should alone be considered. But, sir, I think the people at large are the Government, and that their good ought to be promoted, without reference to any particular persons whatsoever.

There are, said Mr. W., two courses of policy: one is a course of economy; the other a course of extravagance. The first employs few officers; gives moderate but sufficient salaries, and conducts the whole machinery of Government with the least possible expense. The effect of this is, that every man in the community is either taxed very lightly, or not all. He has of course all the benefits and the richest blessings the social state can afford. He has protection to his person and property; he has an abundance of materials for food and raiment, and is never subjected to the severities of cold and hunger. On the other hand, an extravagant course of policy leads to very different results. There many useless officers, with exorbitant salaries, are employed, and the machinery of Government cannot be carried on without large disbursements of public money. The consequence is, that the expenditures surpass the receipts, and the people must be heavily taxed. Of course every man in the community finds himself distressed for money. His means of subsistence become scanty; he is compelled, perhaps, to lie down supperless at night, and to rise in the morning with no better hopes for the ensuing day. Such, sir, are the two courses of policy which this Government may pursue, and which, at different times, it has pursued. Under Mr. Jefferson's Administration economy was the order of the day; but, under another Administration, great extravagance obtained.

The gentleman from South Carolina had said that the American people had renounced their preference for economy, as pursued in 1802, and had now attached themselves to the policy pursued by Mr. Adams. Mr. W. said he would beg leave to differ from the gentleman, and would willingly submit to the decision of the people the point at issue between himself and the member from South Carolina. He was confident the people would decide that, under Mr. Jefferson's Administration, they were as free as air; that little or nothing of the profits of their labor was taken from them by taxation; that the hand of Government was not felt to be upon them, only in the protection it afforded them; that swarms of revenue officers, of domiciliary visitors, of merciless tax gatherers, were banished from their presence; that every man had wherewith to be clothed and fed, and wherewith to be happy. This was exactly that administration of the Government which the people want; it was such an administration as every one must wish to see in a Government founded by, administered for, and supported by, the people. To what other Administration, let me ask the member from South Carolina, can or ought the people to be attached?

If, by the course of policy pursued, you conflict with the interest of the citizen, or mar his happiness, is it not unreasonable to suppose he will be attached to that policy? How can any one of common sense admire the policy which tends to strip his body or starve his stomach? As "this Government is founded by, administered for, and supported by, the people," it will be most strong when the people are most attached to it; and the people will be most attached to it when least oppressed by it; in other words, when they are required to contribute, by taxation, as little as possible of their hard earnings to support Government.

We hear much about national glory. The gentleman from Maryland (Mr. SMITH) has dwelt eloquently on this topic. No one has a greater right than he has to speak on such subjects, because he has participated largely in those scenes which have tended to illustrate and dignify the name of his country. Although I bow with deference to whatever that gentleman may be pleased to say, yet, on this occasion, I must differ from him, not because I admire national glory less, but because I love national happiness more. Of what avail is it to talk about the splendid victories of a Decatur, if, in order to obtain those victories, the people had been obliged, by taxation, to give up so much of their own property as would compel them to go supperless to bed? Indeed, sir, they would be in an ill condition to relish those victories with an empty stomach. But feed them, clothe them, make them, in these respects, contented and happy, which Government can do by the means it employs, or the measures it adopts, and then, with all imaginable zest, they can enter into and realise those fine elevated feelings, inspired by a recollection of our great achievements by sea and land. We have also been referred, said Mr. W., to the glory of other countries, particularly to that of England. No example could be held up to his view which he would imitate with greater caution than that of England. She had paid too dearly for her glory, for her distinction among the nations of the world. To prove this, it would be necessary to advert only to what her people themselves had said; and he would now do so, by asking the attention of the House while he read an extract from the Review of Seybert's Statistical Annals of the United States. The extract is as follows:

"We can inform Jonathan what are the inevitable consequences of being too fond of glory. Taxes upon every article which enters into the mouth, or covers the back, or is placed under the foot—taxes upon every thing which it is pleasant to see, hear, feel, smell, or taste—taxes upon warmth, light, and locomotion—taxes on every thing on earth, and the waters under the earth—on every thing that comes from abroad, or is grown at home—taxes on the raw material—taxes on every fresh value that is added to it by the industry of man—taxes on the sauce which pampers man's appetite, and the drug that restores him to health—on the ermine which decorates the judge, and the rope which hangs the criminal—on the poor man's salt, and the rich man's spice—on the brass nails of the coffin, and the ribands of the bride—at bed or board, couchant or levant, we must pay. The school-boy whips his taxed top—the beardless youth manages his taxed horse with a taxed bridle, on a taxed road; and the dying Englishman, pouring his medicine, which has paid 7 per cent., into a spoon which has paid 15 per cent., flings himself back upon his chintz bed which has paid 22 per cent.—making his will on an eight-pound stamp, and expires in the arms of an apothecary who has paid a license of a hundred pounds for the privilege of putting him to death. His whole property is then immediately taxed from 2 to 10 per cent. Besides the probate, large fees are demanded for burying him in the chancel; his virtues are handed down to posterity on taxed marble; and he is then gathered to his fathers, to be taxed no more. In addition to all this, the habit of dealing with large sums will make the Government avaricious and profuse; and the system itself will infallibly generate the base vermin of spies and informers, and a still more pestilent race of political tools and retainers of the meanest and most odious description; while the prodigious patronage, which the collecting of this splendid revenue will throw into the hands of Government, will invest it with so vast an influence, and hold out such means and temptations to corruption, as all the virtue and public spirit even of Republicans will be unable to resist."

This, sir, is what the English themselves say as to the effects of that excessive, that blind but eager pursuit of national glory, in which they have been engaged. Surely, then, it is not a fit example for our imitation. On the contrary, I say, let our glory consist in the happiness of our people; let our freedom from such oppressions as those under which the people of England now labor, be our boast. It is then we shall have obtained true glory; it is then we shall have accomplished the great object for which our Government was instituted.

Thus much Mr. W. thought it was necessary to say on the subject of the bill generally, and in reply to the remarks which had fallen from gentlemen. He would not, however, be understood to say, that the extravagant course of policy pursued in Mr. Adams's administration was carried to all those pernicious consequences he had pointed out. He said only, but he said it boldly, that, unless the good sense of the American people had arrested the course, changed the policy, and diverted the tendency of that Administration, we should now be as much oppressed, *cæteris paribus*, as the people of England. As the voice of the nation could not then, so he hoped it would not now be resisted; and that we should again resume those wholesome habits of economy from which we had departed. He would, therefore, proceed

773   HISTORY OF CONGRESS.   774

January, 1821.   *Reduction of the Army.*   H. of R.

immediately to the consideration of the bill which embraced the principle for which he contended.

Propositions of this kind, it would be recollected, said Mr. W., had been before Congress for several years, but as yet they have been unsuccessful. He rejoiced, however, in the belief he had, that now the subject would be thoroughly investigated; that it would receive that full and free examination which its importance, both intrinsic and relative, may demand. For, sir, the amount of a military force and the manner of its support are, in every country, questions of the first importance. But, with us, they deserve infinite consideration, because, in proportion as our Government differs from all others, will these questions be found to rise in magnitude, claiming the attention and vigilance of the American people. So important did Congress believe them to be, at the last session, that a resolution was passed, calling upon the Secretary of War to make a report on the subject at the present session. The report, sir, has been received, and what is its aspect? According to my judgment, it is a practical renunciation of the principles upon which our Government is founded, as well as of the principles inculcated at an early period, by that class of politicians to whom the Secretary has heretofore professed to belong. To prove this, the attention of the House is respectfully solicited, while I read some passages from the report. Page 3, the Secretary says—"It will 'be readily admitted that the organization of the 'Army ought to have reference to the objects for 'which it is maintained, and ought to be such as 'may be best calculated to effect such objects; as 'it must be obvious, on the slightest reflection, 'that, on considerations connected herewith, ought 'to depend not only its numbers, but also the 'principles on which it ought to be formed."

Again, in the same page, he says, "The objects 'for which a standing army in peace ought to be 'maintained, may be comprised under two classes: 'those which, though they have reference to a 'state of war, yet are more immediately connect-'ed with its duties in peace; and those which re-'late immediately and solely to war. Under the 'first class may be enumerated, as the leading ob-'jects, the garrisoning the forts along our Atlan-'tic frontier, in order to preserve them, and to 'cause the sovereignty of the United States to be 'respected, and the occupying of certain com-'manding posts in our inland frontier to keep in 'check our savage neighbors, and to protect our 'newly formed and feeble settlements in that 'quarter. These are, doubtless, important objects, 'but are by no means so essential as those which 'relate immediately and solely to a state of war; 'and, though not to be neglected wholly, ought 'not to have any decided influence in the organi-'zation of our Peace Establishment."

From the foregoing, it appears, said Mr. W., to be the opinion of the Secretary, that the duties to be performed by an army in time of peace, ought not to have "any decided influence in the organization of the Peace Establishment." This sentiment, with others which would be noticed hereafter, he deemed a palpable abandonment of the principles of the Government. Whatever he might have previously thought, there was no longer room to entertain a doubt of the fact, since the speeches of the gentleman from Virginia, (Mr. Smyth,) and the gentleman from South Carolina, (Mr. Simkins.) The first of these gentlemen, from his official station in this House, as Chairman of the Committee on Military Affairs, must be supposed to be intimately acquainted with the views and sentiments entertained by the head of the War Department. Whether the latter gentleman has had access to the same source of information was for the House to determine.

Both gentlemen, pursuing what I had believed was the opinion of the Secretary, have discarded the militia as a means of defence for this country. The gentleman from Virginia, in particular, entered into a series of reasoning founded upon what he was pleased to call historical facts, to prove that the militia force was not worthy to be relied on. Mr. W. said he also would rely on history to prove not only that the militia were to be depended on, but that they were the only sort of force to which this Government could safely trust. It was not, indeed, history, in the simple acceptation of the term, such as the member from Virginia had produced, but it was of a higher and more authoritative character. It was not history, written by one individual, containing only the opinions of that individual, and that opinion, too, fraught with all the prejudices of him who expressed it, but it was constitutional history, pronounced by the patriots and sages of the country assembled for the all-important purpose of creating and establishing Governments for the several States in this wide-spread Republic. Examine this history from the earliest periods to the present moment—from the constitution of Massachusetts down to the constitution of Missouri, and the same great fundamental truths are seen to pervade the whole; they are these: "That standing armies are dangerous to liberty, and ought not to be allowed; that a well-regulated militia are the only sure and certain defence of a free people." Gentlemen on the other side may give what force and effect they please to their history, but we will rely on constitutional history, which is more solemn, and entitled to infinitely greater weight than any authority they can possibly produce. From it, I hope we shall be able to point out the dangers we are likely to incur or should labor to avoid.

In reply to the gentlemen espousing the opposite side in this debate, Mr. W. said, he would endeavor to show, in the language and spirit of that constitutional history to which he had referred, first, that standing armies are dangerous to liberty, and ought not to be allowed; second, "that the militia are the only sure and certain defence of a free people;" that the Army of this country is unnecessarily large at present, and should therefore be reduced.

A government, like an individual person, has certain principles or laws impressed on it at its creation, which are natural to it in every stage of its existence, and from which it can never depart, but at the risk of consequences always hazardous, if not utterly destructive. Nature dictates to man, in his individual capacity, the love of truth and justice, and if he ever disregards the impulse of that sentiment he will incur certain evil. In like manner, whatever appears to be the natural dictate of a government, should be carefully discerned and scrupulously obeyed; for, if not, the body politic will become disorganized, and rendered the subject of every dangerous infection. It would not do for a monarchy to practise upon the principles of a republican government, nor, on the other hand, for a republic to practise upon the principles of monarchy. These two governments are opposites in the various systems of polity, and should go on in the separate spheres in which they have been destined to move. It would be as rational to expect the repeated occurrence of strange anomalies in nature, as to suppose that a republic could occasionally ·dart into the sphere of monarchy and still preserve its blessings in all their pristine excellence. If, therefore, in the course or revolutions of republican government, it is ever found to be erratic; if it is seen to deviate from those laws impressed on it by the mighty hand of the people who created it; if it courts conjunction with, or solicits indulgence in the costly, the expensive trappings and appendages of monarchy, then I pronounce the time has arrived for arresting its progress and reforming its example.

Of all the principles connatural with the people of these United States, impressed upon them at their political creation, none appears more important, or announced with more solemnity than this —"that standing armies are dangerous to the liberties of a free people, and ought not to be allowed." This truth is distinctly written in constitutions formed contemporaneously with the birth day of our independence, as well as in those ordained and established at different periods. But it is particularly the saying of our ancestors—of the fathers of the freedom and independence of their country. Throughout their works you find the same cautious concern, the same jealous solicitude about the fatal effects resulting from an overgrown, a redundant, and an inactive army in time of peace. Let me ask if their imaginations were distempered; if they were alarmed at an airy phantom; or whether they did not speak the language of sobernees and truth, teaching their posterity how to avoid dangers, certain, real, and extremely formidable? The latter conclusion must be adopted, and we should receive these Constitutional provisions, the arguments of gentlemen to the contrary notwithstanding, as so many credenda in the articles of our political faith.

Yes, sir, the champions of our independence and our rights knew well that the laws and rules of an army were, in fact, the laws and rules of absolute despotism; that an army was dangerous to our civil and political institutions, not only on account of its physical force, but also on account of its moral effects, its contaminating influence over our principles, feelings, and habits. In England, the country, from which in order to be separated America lavished so prodigiously of her blood and treasure, martial law is considered so much at variance

with the small portion of liberty she enjoys, that it is called "in reality not a law, but something indulged rather than allowed as a law." If an army and its rules be thus dangerous to British liberty, how much more so are they to the liberty of American citizens? As citizens we boast of our equality; but in vain do you look for it in the army. Here are all those distinctions of rank— all that slavish submission to the will of a superior which are to be seen in the most absolute governments. If an inferior officer or soldier strikes his superior, the punishment of death is inflicted as the necessary, the only adequate atonement. Monstrous indeed is the punishment for so trivial an offence! The Grand Sultan of Turkey, who vaingloriously styles himself the "Shadow of God—a God on earth—brother to the sun and moon—disposer of all earthly crowns," could not support his imaginary greatness with more tremendous exactions, with more awful penalties. As citizens we also boast of our liberty; but, as soldiers, a long ascent of ranks and grades rises before us; the command of each is a law, and to disobey is to forfeit our lives. I know well, said Mr. W., the excuse which is generally offered for the continuance of these inexorable rules. It was commonly said they are founded upon necessity, but he hoped he should be able to show how dangerous it was to suffer any system founded upon such necessity to exist in a great or unreasonable degree.

That the military life will corrupt the feelings and habits of those who were engaged in it was, Mr. W. thought, also evident. Suppose two characters, A and B, have acted in the army for ten years—A in the capacity of an officer, B in that of a soldier; that, after their term of service had expired, they both return to the walks of civil life. Now, I ask whether these two characters will associate together upon the terms of their original footing of equality as citizens, or whether they will not be more likely, from their feelings and habits, to preserve that distinctive condition of officer and soldier in which they had been recently placed on the Military Establishment. My word for it, the latter condition will obtain. For no matter how well disposed, how zealously devoted to the cause of liberty and equality, a person might have been before he had become the subject of military discipline, yet, after being inured to it for a while, he will be attached to it; he will forget the blessings which attend the condition of a citizen, or, being himself deprived of those blessings, he will be envious that no others should be permitted to enjoy them. Hence it is that standing armies have always been dangerous to liberty throughout the world. In despotic governments, it is true, there is no difference between the condition of a common subject and that of a soldier; both are equally doomed to the scourge of tyranny, in which perhaps both may delight; nothing is to be gained by a change, which perhaps they are unable to contrive or accomplish. But, in our free country, persons habituated to military life become, as officers, on the one hand, domineering and intolerant, and, as soldiers, on the other, servile and dependent.

In short, sir, our army is subject to the same sort

of discipline as the other armies of the world; but is our Government like other Governments? Look to the Sultan of Turkey, the late despot of France, or to the King of England, and you will find nearly the same system in use for the discipline of their armies. Compare it with our system, and there appears no very great or considerable discrepancy. But between their governments and our own you behold an immense difference. If, then, their systems of military discipline are adapted to the nature of their governments, and calculated to support them, our system, being like theirs, cannot be adapted to the nature of our Government, or calculated for its support. As widely, therefore, as the governments of the old world differ from our own, so widely do the rules and discipline of our army differ from the nature of our Government.

I hope, said Mr. W., not to be misunderstood. It is not my purpose to contend that we ought to dispense with the whole Military Establishment, because the system of rules adopted for its government are at variance with the nature of our civil and political institutions. My object has been to show, that all armies are governed upon principles similarly, if not equally, despotic; that, as this is the case, we should be careful how we introduce that system of things into the United States, because our Government, being a Republic of the most liberal kind, will not be able to consociate (if I may use the expression) with that system. It is impossible for two opposite natures to exist in the same being, and I would as soon expect the military despotism of Bonaparte could exist in identity with our Government; that it could flourish at the same time, and be maintained over the same people, as to suppose our own Government could exist under the influence of a very extended Military Establishment, in time of peace. The Army and the Government would inherit different natures, and perpetual warfare must ensue, till the spirit of one had subdued that of the other. In such a contest the civil would fall prostrate before the military power. The constitutions of our governments, the precepts and sayings of our forefathers; the evidence of all mankind, as transmitted to us through the records of history; in short, the very nature of the thing itself, will not permit us to entertain a doubt on this subject.

From this view, it is evident that if the Army is necessary, it is a kind of *necessary evil,* and it should be the object of the American people to have as little of it as possible. The question for us to decide, at all times, should be, "with how much of this evil can we dispense?" not "with what quantity of it can we be able to subsist?" The rule should be to keep in service as few men as possible, not as many as possible. A patient, laboring with sickness and threatened with death, willingly takes the most disgusting potions of medicine, but by no means does he calculate that these are to become articles for his daily subsistence. It may sometimes be proper for the United States to keep in service forty, fifty, or a hundred thousand troops, but it does not follow from this, that it will always be requisite to have an army of the same size. The Military Establishment

ought to be regulated by the necessities of the country. In cases of danger, it may be greater; but at other times, when peace reigns throughout our borders, when not the least aspect of war is to be seen, it should be reduced to the lowest possible standard, regarding it always as an evil necessary to be used occasionally, but to be employed with care, and to be watched with vigilance.

Believing the House will be disposed to concur in the sentiments which have been advanced, I shall proceed immediately to inquire what reduction it would be proper to make in the present Military Establishment, reserving any other remarks I may have to offer in relation to the danger of armies, and the propriety of relying on the militia, for future occasions, as they may arise in the course of my observations.

Whatever difference of opinion may have heretofore existed, as to the number of men, yet all have seemed to think, that the number of officers in the Army was unnecessarily great. The Secretary of War, however, has invariably adhered to this branch of the Army with wonderful tenacity. That he should have done so, in the report made at the present session, is, to me, a matter of perfect surprise. He knew well the condition of the Treasury; he knew there would be a deficiency of several millions; he also knew that the officers materially contributed to the expense of supporting the Army, and, yet, after all this information, he gravely recommends that the officers should be retained. I should have supposed that a very different course would have been pursued; that he would have recommended the retention of a proportion of more men and fewer officers than exists in the present organization of the Army. For, in the report made by the Secretary in 1818, he says, page 5, "it is obvious that, as the officers are 'much more expensive in proportion to their num- 'bers than the soldiers, that the pay of the Army, 'in relation to its aggregate numbers, will be in- 'creased or diminished with the increase or dimin- 'ution of the former." It is, then, I say, a matter of surprise, that the Secretary should have recommended the retention of all the officers, when he knew that economy was the object contemplated in the proposed reduction of the Army, and when, from his own statement, the officers were much more expensive, in proportion to their numbers, than the soldiers.

From the same report of 1818, it appears that if the Army were full, there would be, according to the present organization, about four men to each officer, non-commissioned officer, and musician. This disproportion has always been a great objection to the Military Establishment. The people saw, and the Secretary of War himself has said, that the expense of the Army was greatly owing to the number of officers. In this state of things a resolution was passed at the last session, requiring that a report from the Head of the War Department should be made at the present session, containing a plan for the reduction of the Army. Well, sir, the report comes in, and what is proposed? Why, that the organization of the Army shall be a little changed; but it is not proposed to reduce the number of officers. Not only so, but the objections to the proposed organization are much greater than to the present; for, by that which is proposed, there will be something more than two men for each officer, non-commissioned officer, and musician. Yes, sir, it is a fact which no one scarcely could have believed, that this enormous disproportion is recommended to us for our approbation.

I will venture to say, there is not an army in the world, not even in Governments the most profuse and prodigal, where the disproportion of officers to men is so great as it is with us at this time; and, yet, by the plan of the Secretary, this disproportion is to be greatly increased. Military characters say, the staff in particular is now large enough for fifty, some say a hundred thousand men. But yet, we are told, we must not reduce it, when it is admitted, or determined by the resolution of last session, that we shall reduce the number of men nearly one-half. If the staff officers under the old organization have had not much to do; if, on account of their numbers, they have been permitted to idle away their time, how much more will this be the case under the proposed organization!

In 1818, the Secretary reported to us that the staff of the Army, under the existing organization, amounted only to 96. I then objected to the correctness of the statement; I mentioned that the number was upwards of 200, and called upon any gentleman who might see the thing differently to correct me, if I was wrong, or give such explanations as might satisfy the House. To prove now that I was then correct, I beg leave to call the attention of the House to some tabular and other documents contained in the two reports of the Secretary. Document B, of the late or new report, professes to be the same as document A, of the report submitted in 1818; but, yet, the former is quite at variance with the latter in some of its details. In the organization, as proposed in the new report, it is not intimated by the Secretary that the number of the staff will be increased beyond that set forth in the report made in 1818. But the number of the Staff, in the organization proposed in the new report, amounts to 228, and, of the organization reported in 1818, only to 96. Whence, sir, is this difference? Could the Secretary have thought to impose on Congress? I hope not. But, if he did, I trust he will be mistaken. I must, however, say that both these reports have appeared to me more like speeches addressed to the army, than communications made to this House.

I will now proceed to notice more particularly the staff recommended by the Secretary. There are two Major Generals, four Aids de Camp, four Brigadier Generals, four Aids de Camp, one Judge Advocate, six Topographical Engineers, four Assistant Topographical Engineers, one Adjutant and Inspector General, two Adjutant Generals, four Assistant Adjutant Generals, two Inspector Generals, four Assistant Inspector Generals, ten Regimental Adjutants, eight Battalion Adjutants, making, in this department, a total of 56; in the

Quartermaster's department there are 37; Paymaster's department 20; Purchasing department 4; Subsistence department 1, with as many Assistants as the service may require; Medical department 75; Engineer Corps 23; Military Academy, 12 Professors and Masters; making an aggregate of 228, exclusive of Cadets; but, if they be added, of 478. At the head of this prodigious staff stand the two Major Generals. No one but the Secretary, or some other person zealously and determinately devoted to the army, could have thought of retaining the Major Generals. The Secretary says, page 8 of the report:

" It is proposed to retain the two Major and four Brigadier Generals. Although it is not probable there will be concentrated, in time of peace, at any point, a force equal to the command of a single Major, or even a Brigadier General, yet, it is conceived important to the service that they should be retained; as two regiments, with a proper proportion of artillery and light troops, constitute, in our service, one brigade, and two brigades a division, the command of a Major General, the number of regiments and battalions under the proposed organization, thus giving a command equal to that of two Major, and four Brigadier Generals."

Here, sir, the Secretary admits that there will be concentrated at no one point a number of men equal to the command of a single Major, nor even a Brigadier General. He would indeed have been equally correct if he had said that the whole Army, under the plan proposed, would, if assembled at one point, scarcely be equal to the command of one Major General and two Brigadiers. But, yet, he recommends the retention of two Major and four Brigadier Generals, thus advising us to keep in service double the number of general officers which, according to this part of his reasoning, he proves to be necessary. I ask if we shall be gravely told this; if we shall assume it as a rule of our conduct, and keep in service the whole of these general officers, when it cannot be denied that there are not men for their command. The most that the Secretary could have done, under such circumstances, would have been to show that there were men for the officers to command, and then to recommend that they should be retained. But he seeks further justification by saying that the number of regiments and battalions give a command for all the generals.

This, sir, is a deception in argument easily exposed and entitled to no weight. For, why did he not show, not that the number of regiments and battalions, but that the number of men in those regiments and battalions, would justify the course proposed? You may call a Captain's company a regiment, and thus give to a Brigadier General the command which ought to belong to two Captains, or to a Major General the command which ought to belong to four Captains. In this way, sir, we might have the greatest plenty of general officers; nay, in such abundance as to satisfy the Secretary of War himself, whose appetition for officers of this rank seems quite inordinate. For my own part, I am unwilling to keep in service, at any time, general officers, when there are not men for their command. But, when there is a deficiency of several millions in the Treasury; when the country is oppressed with debt, I would dispense with officers even if they had men to command; because, by so doing, we get clear of a great expense, whereas, if only the men are discharged from service, and the officers retained, we get clear of a very inconsiderable expense.

Of what use, let it be asked, are the two Major Generals? The Secretary says, page 8 of the report, "But a more weighty and, in my opinion, 'decisive reason why they should be retained, may 'be found in the principle already stated, that the 'organization of the Peace Establishment ought to 'be such as to induce persons of talent and respect-'ability to enter and continue in the military ser-'vice." Now, said Mr. W., the argument presented in so much of the report as I have just read, is perfectly illusory. Do the Colonels remain in service because they are satisfied with their condition as Colonels, or from a hope of becoming Brigadier Generals? Do the Brigadiers remain in service because they are satisfied with their condition as Brigadiers, or from a hope that they will become Major Generals? I take it, sir, that the officers, from the highest to the lowest, remain in service because they are satisfied with their present condition, and not from any hope of getting to be Major Generals. It is with them a money-making business, perhaps more profitable than any in which they could engage, and this is the reason they remain in the Army, as I shall hereafter show. Besides this, the argument is defective in another point of view. It is said that, even with the office of Major General, many resignations take place. Assuming, then, the opinion of the Secretary as the fact, in this case, to wit, that the rank and compensation now given to the Generals are not sufficient to prevent resignations, what does it prove? It proves this: that you have not yet done enough; that you must even go further, and institute the office of Lieutenant General, attaching to it the highest honors and emoluments. For, we are told it is necessary to prevent resignations in the Army, and that high offices will have the desired effect. But we are told, again, that the offices of two Major and four Brigadier Generals, already established by law, will not prevent resignations. It follows, then, as a necessary consequence, from the Secretary's own reasoning, that we must create the office of Lieutenant General, in order to prevent resignations. This course of argument proves quite too much.

But I differ from him altogether on the subject of the resignation of officers of the Army. It is to be ascribed to very different causes. Perhaps the most influential cause has been, the belief officers have had that the Army would be reduced; and, rather than wait for this event, they have anticipated it by handing in their resignations; at the same time they have solicited the best civil offices which were to be had; not because they preferred those civil offices, but because they thought them the only alternative. But let it once be understood that the Army is not to be reduced, and my word for it you will hear no more of these voluntary resignations. This would be the case, whether or not you have the office of Major or Brigadier General. If there were no higher rank than a Colonel, then all officers subordinate to that rank would hold on to their commissions just as they do at present. It is not the office so much as the highest office, which is the object of emulous pursuit amongst men. If the rank of Colonel or Brigadier General were the highest office known to our laws, then there would be all that aspiration to attain it; there would be all that complacency and self-satisfaction in having attained it, which are to be observed in the conduct of those who (according to the Secretary's views) may now be in pursuit of the office of Major General. Did the officers of Mr. Jefferson's Peace Establishment think themselves deficient in rank? Not at all. There was then no Major General. But the officers, knowing they filled the highest military stations in the country, were satisfied, and consequently remained in service. Therefore, the reasoning of the Secretary on this head either proves nothing, or it proves too much, which is worse than nothing.

This plan, said Mr. W., of retaining men in service by the hope of receiving the greater rank, pay, and emoluments, attached to the office of Major General, is radically wrong. It costs too much. It is paying too dear for the whistle. We have two Major Generals, with two great divisions—the Northern and Southern. The headquarters are at Brownville, in the North, and at Nashville, in the South. This arrangement was evidently made for the convenience and accommodation of those officers, not for the good of the service; on the contrary, it introduces complexity and confusion into our system of military affairs. We all recollect the strife between the War Department and the Major General of the South, relative to certain rules of etiquette to be observed in the transmission of orders. As matters now stand, an order must travel all the way to Nashville, and then back to Washington, before it can reach an officer stationed at the Marine barracks, not distant more than a mile from this Capitol; that is, an order must travel twelve or fifteen hundred miles before it comes to the officer who is the subject of it, and who has always been distant about one mile from the Department from whence the order issued. The same regulation, I understand, exists in regard to the Northern division; and, if it is thus necessary that orders should pass through the Major Generals, why not direct their headquarters to be at more favorable positions—at Washington and Baltimore for example. Then there could be no delay in the progress of orders to inferior officers, because the Major Generals, through whom we understand they must pass, would be stationed immediately on the lines of direct communication. But, no, this would not do; these officers must be accommodated; and, for their especial benefit, they have been permitted to reside at home; to live on their own farms, and to mind their own business, receiving from the Government, at the same time, as nearly as I can estimate, about seven thousand dollars a year. Some calculate that the amount received is considerably greater, as much perhaps as eight or ten thousand dollars a year. Sir, I think it, if not an abuse, at least a very great grievance, that these officers, while they reside at home, should have received the whole pay and emoluments attached to their office. The allowance for forage, fuel, four servants, seven horses, three rooms and a kitchen, I have believed, was intended for actual service; for a state of war, and not for a state of profound peace to the country and domestic retirement to the officer. When they go abroad, it is said all these paraphernalia accompany them. Forage, fuel, four servants, seven horses, three rooms and a kitchen, and 1,250 pounds of baggage, all adhere to and march on with the Generals! Indeed, sir, they must have great strength to draw after them such a ponderous and heterogeneous load of items. No Eastern Satrap could move with greater pomp.

As to preserving and perpetuating a knowledge of the military science, by keeping these Generals in service, the plan, I say, is utterly fallacious. Their situation at home precludes the possibility of learning any thing new, and almost of retaining what they do know. The knowledge to be preserved, or information to be acquired by them, while they reside on their own farms, will qualify them much better for the cornfield than the field of battle, and no doubt they study the operations of the former much more than of the latter. It is true, they come on sometimes to the Seat of Government, but for what purpose nobody knows, unless it be to drill Congress or attend the parties.

Another reason assigned by the Secretary for retaining the Generals is, that it will operate upon the army like the "high prizes in a lottery;" that men of talents will thereby be induced to enter and continue in the service. Of all the figures of speech with which our language abounds, I think this "metaphor" the most unfortunate which could possibly have been selected. For there are two things so little comparable to each other as a lottery and a regular gradation by which officers are advanced in the army. The high prizes in a lottery are distributed, not according to any rule whatever, but entirely by chance, by accident, by the most capricious turns of fortune. Not so in relation to the advancement of officers in the army: there you have certain fixed rules, a perfect scale of gradation, according to which every one must be promoted. Does not every inferior officer know that all his superiors must be promoted in preference to himself? Surely, he does. Then it follows that this inducement proposed by the Secretary operates, not as a lottery, hereafter to be drawn, and in which no one knows how the prizes will be distributed, but rather as a lottery which has already been drawn, and in which the fate of every adventurer is fixed and determined. Many of the remarks which have been made respecting the Major Generals are also applicable to the Brigadiers. I cannot, for my life, determine what use the Secretary intends to make of the four officers of this rank he proposes to keep in service; that is, as I understand it, in the pay of Government. These officers are allowed forage, fuel, three servants, five horses, two rooms and a kitchen. But the Secretary tells us there will not be concentrated at any one point a force equal to the command of a single Brigadier; and why be at the expense of keeping four of them? I call upon gentlemen to tell us what they are to do. It has been suggested that we ought to retain three Brigadiers: one to be stationed here, another in the North, and a third in the South. But, cannot one Colonel in the North, and another in the South, answer the same purpose? Our desire for general officers seems truly inextinguishable. When going abroad, these Brigadiers must also assume the style of Satraps, and draw after them a great load of items: nay, more, I have understood from good authority, that between three and four thousand dollars have been allowed to one Brigadier, as a sort of extra pay (I suppose) for fatigue duty performed in travelling over Europe—or, perhaps the allowance was made out of the fund appropriated for foreign intercourse. But I never heard of any treaties being negotiated by that gentleman, or that he was in any respect to be considered the diplomatic agent of the United States.

By dispensing with the two Major Generals and three Brigadiers, we also get clear of seven Aids-de-Camp.

Next comes the office of Adjutant and Inspector General. This is a pretty decent snug commission, to be held by a clerk in the Department. His duties are entirely those of a clerk, and why is it that he has the rank, pay, and emoluments, of a Brigadier General? I can perceive no reason, unless it be for the purpose of illustrating the Military Establishment. But the better way is to graduate and pay men according to the service they render. If they act as clerks, let them be ranked and paid as such. If I am correctly informed, many officers of the army complain of this anomaly in our Military Establishment. It is said the present incumbent would probably not know how to march a corporal's guard, and yet his rank, pay, and emoluments, advance him quite beyond officers who have seen active, efficient service. Permit me here to say that I have nothing personal against that officer. When I have had occasion to correspond with him, he has answered me promptly. Sometimes I find a little difficulty in reading his communications.

Instead of two Adjutants and four Assistant Adjutant Generals, the whole business of this branch of the army may be transacted by one Adjutant General and one assistant. Thus, we may dispense with one Adjutant General, and three assistants, and thereby save to the nation their pay and emoluments.

Two Inspector Generals and four Assistant Inspectors are also too many for our service. When this subject was considered in the session of 1818–19, I mentioned that the Inspectors, if my information was correct, were young men and not qualified to perform their duties; but, if qualified, they have nevertheless failed to perform their duty, and that a regiment in the northern division had been reviewed only once by an Inspector, since the introduction of this part of the staff, which was three years previous to that time. In reply to this, a gentleman from New York, (Mr. STORRS,) whom I now see in his place, mentioned a fact which no doubt he learned from the Inspector General of the Northern division, who was then in this city. The fact was this, "that the officer in question had himself, the Summer preceding, visited every post, examined every musket, and performed every duty which appertained to his office in that·division." Now, sir, if the Inspector General performed all these duties in the Northern division, why is it that he has two assistants? I take it for granted, that the Inspector General of the Southern division can likewise perform all the duties of his office; and why is it that he also has two assistants? Here you have six officers to perform duties to which only two are fully competent. Indeed, sir, I must say, that our whole Military Establishment seems to have been built up more from a regard to the men who were to fill offices, than to the service it was expected these men would render.

The bill provides for as many regimental and battalion adjutants as will be necessary, under the proposed plan of reduction. If gentlemen think otherwise, I should be glad they would point out any deficiency.

The Quartermaster's department is next in order, as reported by the Secretary. He proposes to retain in it thirty-seven officers. I admit, said Mr. W., that if there is any one branch of the Army more ably and faithfully conducted than all others, it is this; and would be willing to let the rank of the officers remain, but would reduce their number. My friend, the gentleman from Virginia, (Mr. FLOYD,) submitted a resolution the other day, calling upon the Secretary of War for a statement of the rank, number, and distribution of the Army at each post. This statement has been made accordingly, but has not yet been printed, so as to be laid on our table. I must, then, rely, on the information previously possessed, from which it will be seen that, in 1818, two assistant deputy quartermaster generals were in General Jesup's office at this place. At Detroit there were also two, while the whole duties of the sixth regiment, stationed at Plattsburg, were performed by one quartermaster. At Boston, there were two; at New York, two; at West Point, there was a quartermaster, where, also, a lieutenant of engineers received the pay of quartermaster, whether he performed the duties or not. These facts are mentioned to show that the number of officers in this department was unnecessarily great in 1818. As their duties have not increased, but rather decreased since that time, the number of these officers may be proportionably lessened. Instead of sixteen assistant deputy quartermaster generals, I would have only eight; and, instead of eighteen regimental and battalion quartermasters, I would reduce them to the number of regiments and battalions proposed in the bill. This would be my plan. But if it should not meet the views of my friends, I will concede whatever preference I might have, and will vote for the bill, because retrenchment is with me a paramount object.

The medical department requires, I should think, considerable excision. The Secretary proposes to retain seventy-five doctors. If good, they are more than necessary. If bad, they are enough to kill a nation. In 1818, he reported to us there were seventy-three posts. I shall show, hereafter, that it is not necessary to garrison more than one-half, at any rate, not more than two-thirds of the number of posts stated to us. But yet, it is proposed to keep seventy-five doctors, a number more than equal to the whole number of posts. This seems to me very strange, because, if I was correctly informed, the surgeon at Albany, in 1818, performed little or no duty; the surgeon at Watertown practised among the people at large, professing, at the same time, to belong to an arsenal which was not finished, and in which there was no garrison. The surgeon at Boston was stationed there ostensibly for the purpose of inspecting recruits, but as soon as recruits were made, they were sent to the garrison in the harbor, where there were two surgeons. The surgeon at New York was similarly situated. If a like examination could have been had at that time of the position of the surgeons in the Southern division, no doubt they would have been found to be engaged with equal profit to themselves, if not to the Army. The apothecaries I would entirely discharge. How can they, at New York or Philadelphia, tell the medicines necessary to be purchased for the troops who may be sick at Charleston or New Orleans? Would it not be much better to let the surgeon at any particular post purchase such medicines as may be wanted for the sick at that post. Besides, I have been credibly informed, by a gentleman from Tennessee, who is not now, but was then a member, that the apothecaries were very deficient in performing their duties. He mentioned one striking fact as coming within his observation. It was this, that an apothecary stationed at Baltimore had purchased orange peel to send all the way to New Orleans. Now, sir, every body ought to know that oranges grow in the greatest abundance at New Orleans; and that, of all articles of medicine, this was the least wanted at that place. It would, then, seem scarcely possible that any apothecary, however unskilful or injudicious he might be, could think of running Government to the greater cost of the article at Baltimore, and expense of transporting it to New Orleans, where, in the first instance, it could have been had for nothing. If this be the way in which they discharge their other duties, the sooner we get clear of them the better.

The subject of the Engineer Corps, in connexion with the Military Academy, Mr. W. said, he would leave to his friend, the gentleman from Tennessee, (Mr. CANNON,) who would treat it with much more justice than he should be able to do, by any remarks he might offer.

He had now, he said, taken a cursory review of the staff proposed to be retained. The officers of the line also, in his judgment, appeared too numerous. The Secretary says, page 9, "No posi-' tion connected with the organization of the peace ' establishment is susceptible of being more rigidly ' proved than that the proportion of its officers to

' the rank and file, ought to be greater than in a
' war establishment." But what these rigid proofs
are, or what should be the exact proportion of officers to the rank and file, he has not vouchsafed
to tell us. Most of those with whom I have conversed have believed that the duties of an army
were more multiplied and laborious in war than in
peace, and therefore, that a greater number of
officers would be required for the former condition.
The Secretary, however, says, " It results imme-
' diately from a position, the truth of which can-
' not be fairly doubted, that the leading object of a
' regular army in time of peace, ought to be, to
' enable the country to meet, with honor and safety,
' particularly at the commencement of war, the
' dangers incident to that state." On no previous
occasion have I ever before heard it announced
that we should retain in peace officers for a war
establishment. It appears to me more rank doctrine than was maintained in Mr. Adams's administration. What, sir, would have been said if he
had advocated such opinions—opinions as hostile
to the principles of the Government as to the principles of that class of politicians to whom the
Secretary has heretofore professed to belong. For,
sir, it is a principle inherent in the very nature of
the Government, and which, I had believed was
almost universally admitted, that a well regulated militia is the only sure and certain defence
of this country. But the Secretary, in effect, disclaims this doctrine; he holds out the idea that
the militia are not to be relied on, and therefore,
you must keep on the peace establishment officers
to command your armies in a state of war. I protest against this doctrine with my whole strength;
I disclaim it, as anti-republican, as useless, as dangerous, as extravagant.

It is anti-republican, because it is forbidden by
the nature and spirit of our Government. It is
dangerous, because it cannot be denied that the
officers are the persons who originate and carry
into effect designs fraught with mischief and ruin
to the country in which they live. The disposition of mankind is such that, if not employed in
doing good, they will be employed in doing evil.
Officers, in peace, having nothing to do, and in
the habit of commanding those about them, begin
at length to feel impatient under the restraints of
Government, and have, in every instance, been
the first to meditate the overthrow of liberty. Did
Cæsar pass the Rubicon when fighting the enemies of Rome, or after they were subdued, and he
had nothing else to do but to make a conquest of
the liberties, of his own country? Let us attend
to our own history. At what time were written
the letters of Newburgh? Examine the conduct
of all armies, and you will find, I think, that officers are most dangerous in peace. It is then they
have leisure to meditate, and opportunity to execute, such plans as the more wicked and designing
among them may wish to accomplish.

Again—it is of no use to keep officers in service
when they can render no service; this is the solecism, the contradiction in terms, to which the
advocates of the proposed organization must necessarily be driven. They say it is right to retain

the officers, but when called upon to point out the
service these officers are to perform, they are at a
loss for an answer. Some reason, however, is attempted to be given by saying that, although the
officers may not now be of any immediate use, yet
they will hereafter be useful when the country is
engaged in war. The Secretary says we shall
certainly be involved in war, and that no one, unless he has the " imagination of a poet," can think
otherwise. Now, sir, I readily admit that the Secretary has not the imagination of a poet; and,
further, if a sort of tautology and alliteration; if
a kind of synonymous repetition are any defects in
style, that he has as slender pretension to prose.
But, in whatever character he is to be considered,
whether of poetry, prose, politics, or prophecy, he
has gone equally wide from the mark. He has
not, indeed, told us the nation from whom we are
to expect war—only an obscure hint is given, a
kind of passing allusion is thrown out that we
may have war with Spain. But the late news
from that quarter, although not official, yet entitled to credit, fully explodes this idea. Without
this news I would as soon apprehend invasion from
the inhabitants of the moon as to suppose Spain
would ever attempt to make incursions into our
territory. But it may be supposed we are shortly
to have war with England. This will turn out
like the apprehension of hostilities with Spain. The
points in controversy between us and England are
so far removed as to render war with that Power
a very improbable event. I ask, whether any man
of common sense can seriously apprehend it in
any short time? But if it comes it will be confined to the ocean. No one in the possession and
exercise of his right mind can suppose Great Britain will ever attempt to wage war effectually
against the United States by land. We may be
temporarily invaded at different points along our
maritime frontier, but whoever thought we should
keep a regular army to meet that contingency!
The militia were always intended to be used and
thought competent for this service. Indeed, the
framers of the Constitution provided expressly for
this particular case when they gave to the General
Government power to call out the militia to repel
invasion. But the Secretary says, page 4, "the
' organization of the army ought to be such as to
' enable the Government, at the commencement of
' hostilities, to obtain a regular force adequate to
' the emergencies of the country, properly organ-
' ized and prepared for actual service." If, sir, the
militia are not to be called out at the commencement of hostilities, if they are not to be relied on
to repel invasion, when, I pray you, are they to
render any service? Certainly not after the war
shall have progressed for some time, because then,
every one admits, Government will have provided
an adequate force of regular troops. It follows,
then, according to this plan of the Secretary, that
the militia in no instance and at no time are to
render any service. If they are to be thus entirely
superseded, let us at once know the fact. Let us not
hereafter, as we have done heretofore, appropriate
hundreds of thousands of dollars to arm them;
to prepare to repel invasion; to qualify them to

sustain that rank in the country which the Constitution assigns to them, and which the policy of our institutions requires them to hold.

We speak only of a war in which the United States are invaded and act on the defensive, because, in an aggressive war begun by ourselves, we can select our own time, and cannot therefore be taken by surprise. Well, then, I say no one ever had the madness to suppose that we should keep a sufficient regular force to meet the first emergency. Can you, sir, can any other one tell me the number of troops necessary for that purpose? The Secretary says that, should a just precaution growing out of our foreign relations render it necessary, we may, on the basis proposed, augment the Peace Establishment 11,558; and pending hostilities, by adding a few more officers, we may have an aggregate of 19,035. Now, sir, what could this army do in a state of war? The whole of them might be required to defend, for example, the town of Boston, as being the only kind of force, in the language of the Secretary, "able to meet the first shocks of hostilities with unyielding firmness." But, before our troops could have marched fifty miles on the seacoast, the enemy might invade New York, and here again you would want another army of 19,035. In this way regular troops could be had to meet the enemy, the militia must be called out to defend New York. In this way an enemy could invade your whole maritime frontier, from Passammaquoddy to New Orleans, and at every point except one, as in the example of Boston, above supposed, you must rely on the militia for defence. How idle, then, is it for us to talk about keeping a regular force able to meet the first attacks of an invading enemy. It would require perhaps half a million of troops; and the accumulation of debt, the pressure of taxation consequent upon such a measure, would produce greater prostration of our energies, would affect more vitally the prosperity and happiness of our fellow-citizens, than any thing else which could be designed.

Our distance from Europe, said Mr. W., will always allow us one, two, or perhaps three years previous notice, and we can never be invaded without having sufficient time to prepare for the emergency. In Europe powerful nations border upon each other; nothing but a river, a road, or an imaginary line, separates them. Hence it is necessary they should always be ready, because they know not at what moment they may be attacked. But, with us, the state of things is very different, and yet gentlemen discuss this question according to principles of policy derived from Europe, and not by such as are adapted to the situation and circumstances of our own country.

As to war with the Indian tribes it is not necessary to retain a single portion of the regular army for that purpose. Throughout our whole history the militia have been the force to encounter Indian hostilities. Even in the Seminole war, where you had to fight three or four hundred half starved, half naked and miserable Indians, the regular army did no good. The militia of Tennessee and Kentucky were called out to meet the enemy wherever

he was met. There is however, no prospect of collision with the Indians, unless it grows out of the expedition ordered up to Council Bluffs, on Missouri river. But, this we can prevent when we please, by withdrawing the troops, who ought never to have been sent upon so wild and chimerical a project.

The gentlemen from Virginia and South Carolina, (Mr. SMYTH, and Mr. SIMKINS,) have said, that the Peace Establishment of 1802, amounting to 3,323, was excessively economical; that it was found to be too small, and afterwards, in 1808, was augmented to 9,996. In saying this, they must have forgotten what was mentioned by the gentleman from Maryland (Mr. SMITH.) He was in Congress at that time, and told us, in his speech the other day, that in 1802 some were for reducing the army much lower, while others wished to retain a force considerably greater; that, finally, a middle course was pursued, and 3,323 was determined on as a proper Peace Establishment. Those gentlemen then were mistaken in saying that it was "excessively economical," or that it was subsequently augmented, because it was found to be too small. This increase was a measure preparatory for war, and in support of this assertion I can offer those gentlemen authority they will be very much inclined to respect. It is the report of the Secretary of War, made in 1818. In page 4 he says: "It is obvious that the establishment of 1808, compared with the then wealth and population of 'the country, the number and extent of military 'posts is larger, in proportion, than the present; 'but the unsettled state of our relations with 'France and England, at that time, renders the 'comparison not entirely just. Passing then that 'of 1808, let us compare the establishment of 1802 'with the present." Here, sir, is evidence which those gentlemen must believe, that our unsettled relations with France and England, caused the augmentation of the army in 1803. I hope then we shall not again be told that it was increased because it had been reduced too low in 1802, for such is not the fact.

Another position assumed by the gentleman from South Carolina, is, that 12,656 is not a greater army now than 3,323 was in 1802, because of the increase, since that time, of our population, of the number of posts, and of the line of frontier. Mr. W. said he knew the Secretary had urged these same arguments in 1818, and he had hoped he should not hear them again, because it appeared to him the report then made was composed of materials entirely too frangible to be relied on as authority in this House. But, as the member from South Carolina had brought it forward, he hoped to be pardoned while he briefly noticed each argument, in the order stated.

First. The Secretary says, (and in this he is followed by the member from South Carolina,) that, because our population is double what it was in 1802, an army of 12,656 is not now greater than 3,323 was in 1802. This is about as conclusive as if any one should undertake to prove that three and three make twelve; for a double population could require only a double army; and as, in 1802, we had an army of 3,323, so we ought now to have only 6,646. But instead of this, it is said we must have 12,656, which, to me at least, is a *non sequitur* in argument.

Second. It was reported to us in 1818, that we then had seventy-three posts, but in 1802 there were only twenty-seven. On the supposition that it was necessary to garrison each post, it would follow, not that you could employ the present establishment of 12,656, but only about 8,000, a little more than the aggregate proposed to be retained in the bill. But I deny that the posts necessary to be garrisoned amount to seventy-three. The Secretary himself told us, in answer to certain inquiries respecting the Yellow Stone expedition, that Indian hostilities had essentially terminated in the southwest, and therefore the troops had been ordered on service up the Missouri. If the troops could be spared, I should think the posts might also be spared. A gentleman who resides in the northwest told me the whole of that line of posts might be demolished. He said the people there did not want them. Admitting, however, that it is necessary to keep some posts both in the northwest and southwest, it still follows that you cannot show a greater number than about fifty, and consequently that you cannot, on the data assumed by the Secretary, find any use for an army larger than that proposed in the bill.

Third. The Secretary says, the line of frontier is greater than it was in 1802, in the proportion of seventy-three to twenty-seven. He has given both the line of frontier and the number of posts for the year 1818; but for 1802, only the number of posts. To enable us to determine fairly, he should have given the frontier at both periods. But, from the materials furnished, scanty as they are, we shall be led to conclude that the frontier has not increased in the proportion stated. Chesapeake Bay, for example, had the same indentations and sinuosities of coast. There were also the same distances from point to point, and the same meanders of rivers at both periods. It is said we have acquired Louisiana since that time. But every one knows the geographical and military frontiers are not always commensurate with each other, or extended precisely in the same degree. The Secretary calculated the acquisition of Florida would not extend our frontier more than about one hundred and twenty miles from point to point, while all agree that our geographical limits would be considerably increased. Indeed, the possession of Louisiana may be said, in several respects, to contract the military frontier. When Spain held it, the Indians were under her control, and were liable to be excited against us at any moment; but now there is no danger from that source. At any rate, then, the necessity for military defence has not increased in the manner stated by the Secretary, and repeated by the member from South Carolina.

The increase of public property, Mr. W. admitted, involved the necessity, correspondingly increased, for a greater number of men to take care of that property. How or in what proportion public property has increased we have not been told. But, taking for the basis of calculation the number of guns and the number of men, reported to us as being at New York in 1818, (and certainly there is not a more important post,) we find that, on the whole seacoast, there could not be employed more than about 1,100. But there were stationed at that time, on the whole coast, 2,408 men, which is more than double the requisite number. The navy is intended to defend our shores. As it increases, I should suppose the army might be diminished. It is now three times as large as it was in 1802, and therefore three times as competent for our defence. But yet gentlemen demand for the seacoast an army much larger than when we had little or no naval strength. They seem to think the army ought to be increased in a direct ratio with the increase of the navy. On the contrary, I think it may be lessened as the navy is increased.

In 1802, when there was no danger of Indian war in that quarter, there were between 500 and 600 men only on the whole northwestern frontier; but in 1818, after the danger had quite subsided, we had between 1,500 and 1,600. It is the first time I have known the rule of inverse proportion applied to the defence of the country; that is, when the danger was greater, a less force was deemed sufficient; but, since the danger has become less, it is now thought expedient to have a greater force. In short, sir, if we view the whole subject with reference to the danger which may threaten us, (and this is certainly the correct criterion,) we can find no use at this time for an army as large as it was in 1802. The great, perhaps the only, object of an army, in time of peace, is to preserve the public works, to keep the guns from rust, and the fortifications from decay. I hold in my hand, sir, a list of the fortifications, and the number of men necessary to be stationed in each. From it it appears that about 4,500 are amply sufficient for the whole frontier, both maritime and inland. I have seen another statement, showing that about 3,150 would answer. If these statements are incorrect, I would thank gentlemen to point out the inaccuracy. But, taking either, we find there is not the least reason for keeping the present establishment of 12,656.

Why, then, shall it not be reduced to 6,000 men, as proposed in the bill? The gentleman from Virginia (Mr. Smyth) had assigned one reason in opposition to the bill, which Mr. W. said, was particularly surprising. He said, militia endangered the liberties of their country, and, to prove it, mentioned that they lost the battle at Camden, in the Revolution! But can we not prove, by exactly the same kind of argument, that regular troops, when defeated, have endangered the liberties of their country, precisely in the same manner? Examine the history of the wars which have desolated Europe for the last twenty-five years, and you will find abundant evidence of this fact. Who endangered France at the battle of Waterloo? The regular troops of France, who were defeated on that occasion. Was not the Austrian army defeated by Bonaparte at Wagram? Yes, and if my memory serves me, the Archduke Charles ordered his troops to be decimated for their cowardice in that engagement. These were regular soldiers, in whom the member from Virginia so much delights. If he had exerted his talents and industry to find evidence against regular armies, as he did against the militia, he would have been able to produce a much darker catalogue against the former than the latter. Militia, like other troops, are subject to the fortunes of war. They may be defeated; they may not in every instance act with becoming bravery; but the same objections apply to every other description of force. If militia are defeated, and thereby endanger their country, it is a misfortune from which I have shown you regular troops are not exempt. But regular troops, after they have vanquished the public enemy, turn round and subdue their own country, which is an act of great criminality. In a comparison between them, the one may be called unfortunate, while the other is highly criminal. The gentleman from South Carolina says, no danger is to be apprehended from our Army. But I ask him whether he has heard of no instances in which the civil authority has been violated by our Army, harmless as he supposes it to be? If he has not, I shall not put myself to the trouble of pointing them out to him. I will merely remark, however, that an army is dangerous, on account of its moral as well as physical force; that a Government may be destroyed by the gradual prostration of its principles, as well as by a sudden overthrow; that every nation is disposed to admit the danger of all other armies, except its own, which is commonly supposed too good even to think of any mischief; that from this delusion a nation does not often awake till it is too late to profit by the recovery of their senses.

It has been said that this measure for reducing the Army is an attack upon the fame of the Administration. No doubt, said Mr. W., the member from South Carolina has more precise information on this subject than I have. Although one or more members of the Executive department may view it in the light mentioned by the gentleman, yet I shall not believe that it is so regarded by all of them, or by the President himself. But, if it was, shall we, for that reason, be diverted from a measure we believe to be right? Or shall we, before we are at liberty to mature our judgments upon a given proposition, be required to run off to the Executive, to ascertain what is thought of it in that quarter? Sir, I hope not. The Executive knows that this House, in connexion with the Senate, make a constituent part of the Government, and certainly will not attempt to circumscribe the right we have to think and act for ourselves. Let me be convinced that a measure is right, and I shall act upon my own responsibility, without reference to any opinion which may be entertained by the Executive. Take, for exemple, the case before us. The country is groaning under a weight of debt and pecuniary embarrassment. There is a deficiency in the Treasury of several millions, which the gentleman from South Carolina thinks not at all alarming, although he cannot deny that we are obliged to borrow money. The people are threatened with taxes, and call aloud for help. Now, I ask, if we, their immediate representatives, shall not afford them relief, for fear it may conflict with some views of the Executive or his Cabinet? The system of economy, of which the bill before us is a part, is the best means of relief which can be adopted, and I for one will support it. Gentlemen have offered no arguments against it, which would not have applied, with equal propriety, against the reduction of the Revolutionary army, or the army at the close of the late war. The Army was made for the country, not the country for the Army. No matter how distinguished the individuals who compose it; yet, if the country does not require their service, they ought to return to private life. Thus acted the army of the Revolution. Washington, when it was no longer necessary he should use it, voluntarily surrendered his sword into the hands of Congress, from whom he received it. For this last, but greatest act, historians have ascribed to him more enviable fame, more true glory, more godlike virtue, than for every other act of his illustrious life. Is the Army now any better than it was then? Heaven forbid we should think so! Let us then follow the example of past, but wholesome times. Let us adopt this bill, and afford the people that relief from debt, from the prospect of taxation, which they have so just a right to expect.

Mr. GORHAM presented a memorial of the merchants and others of Boston, in the State of Massachusetts, against any increase of the tariff of duties on imports by way of protection to the manufacturing interests of the country; which memorial was referred to the Committee on Manufactures.

Mr. SERGEANT, from the Committee on the Judiciary, reported a bill providing compensation for marshals, clerks, and attorneys in the courts of the United States, and to repeal parts of former acts; which was read twice, and committed to a Committee of the Whole.

Mr CAMPBELL, from the Committee on Private Land Claims, reported a bill for the relief of Peggy Mellen; which was read twice, and committed to a Committee of the Whole.

Mr. STORRS, from the Committee on Roads and Canals, who were directed, by a resolution on the 23d of November last, to inquire into the expediency of opening a military and post road from some place on the Penobscot river, in the State of Maine, to the river St. Croix, made a report thereon, adverse to the opening said road; which was read, and ordered to lie on the table.

Mr. STORRS, from the same committee, to whom was recommitted the bill to provide for the preservation and repair of the Cumberland road, reported the same with amendment; which was read, and, together with the bill, committed to a Committee of the Whole to-morrow.

The SPEAKER laid before the House a letter from the Secretary of War, transmitting statements showing the amount of expenditures at the Mili-

795   HISTORY OF CONGRESS.   796

H. of R.   *Arrears of Pay, &c.—General de Kalb.*   JANUARY, 1821.

tary Academy from the establishment thereof, in the erection of buildings and repairs; also the aggregate amount of expenses, up to the present time, for the pay and emoluments of teachers, officers, and cadets, and the number of cadets educated at said academy, &c., rendered in obedience to a resolution of the 5th ultimo; which letter and accompanying documents were ordered to lie on the table.

The SPEAKER also laid before the House another letter from the Secretary of War, accompanied with a statement, showing the expenditures of the moneys appropriated for the contingent expenses of the Military Establishment for the year 1820.

Ordered, That the report of the select committee, "appointed to inquire if any, and if any, what, farther provision may be necessary to give effect to the provisions of the treaty made at Brownstown, in the Territory of Michigan," made on the 12th of May last, be referred to the Committee on Roads and Canals.

Mr. SMITH, of Maryland, from the Committee of Ways and Means, reported a bill for the relief of William Smith; which was read twice, and committed to a Committee of the Whole.

ARREARS OF PAY, &c.—GENERAL DE KALB.

Mr. RHEA, from the Committee on Pensions and Revolutionary Claims, to whom was referred, on the 4th of December, 1820, the petition of Elie, Baron of Kalb, knight of the royal order of military merit, and Maria Anna Carolina, of Kalb, widow Geymuller, made the following report, which was read and laid on the table:

That on the 10th of December, 1819, the petition of the said petitioners was referred to the Committee on Pensions and Revolutionary Claims; that on the 7th of February following that committee made report thereon.

This petition being again referred to the Committee on Pensions and Revolutionary Claims, the committee have had recourse to the Treasury Department for information relating to the accounts of the Baron de Kalb, and, by a report from that Department, it appears that "the only information on the subject of his accounts during the Revolutionary war is to be found in one of the legers of the late office of commissioner of army accounts, preserved from the fire which destroyed the public buildings; a copy of his accounts is extracted therefrom and enclosed. There does not appear, as far as the evidence in this office affords information, that any final settlement was made of the accounts of the Baron de Kalb; and at this period, when the records have so generally been destroyed, it would be impracticable to make one with accuracy."

By the account alluded to, it appears that there is a balance standing to the debit of the Baron de Kalb amounting to $234,100 70-90.

The committee further report that the petitioners appear to claim the payment of any arrears of pay which may be due to their late father. On this subject the committee observe that the large balance appearing on the books of the Treasury, and standing debited in the account of the late Baron de Kalb, goes to preclude the expectation of any arrears of pay being due to the Baron de Kalb.

The petitioners appear to claim five years' pay as being due to their late father, the Baron de Kalb. On this subject the committee observe that, on the 15th of May, 1778, Congress unanimously resolved "that all military officers commissioned by Congress, who now are, or hereafter may be, in the service of the United States, and shall continue therein during the war, and not hold any office of profit under these States, or any of them, shall, after the conclusion of the war, be entitled to receive, annually, for the term of seven years, if they live so long, one-half of the present pay of such officers; provided that no general officer of the cavalry, artillery, or infantry, shall be entitled to receive more than one-half part of the pay of a colonel of such corps, respectively: and provided that this resolution shall not extend to any officer in the service of the United States, unless he shall have taken the oath of allegiance to, and shall actually reside within, some one of the United States." The resolution alluded to appears to be expressly intended for those officers only who, being in the service of the United States, did actually reside within some one of the United States, and did continue in the service of the United States during the war; and to the exclusion of all other officers who, although being in the service of the United States, did not actually reside within some one of the United States, or who did not continue in the service of the United States during the war. The Baron de Kalb, in the resolution of Congress of the 14th of October, 1780, is stated to be a brigadier in the armies of France. The family of the Baron de Kalb is believed to have resided, and continued to reside, in France; hence it is inferred that France was the place of his residence, and therefore that he is included within the proviso of that resolution. The resolution of Congress of the 15th of May, 1778, contains not any provision for the widows or orphans of officers who had died, or thereafter might die, in the service of the United States. On the 16th of August, 1780, the Baron de Kalb, major general in the service of the United States, in the action near Camden, in South Carolina, leading on troops of the Maryland and Delaware lines against superior numbers, and gloriously contending on behalf of the rights of mankind, was mortally wounded, and died on the 19th of that month. On the 24th of August, 1780, Congress resolved "that the resolution of the 15th of May, 1778, granting half-pay for seven years to the officers who should continue in service to the end of the war, be extended to the widows of those officers who have died, or shall hereafter die, in the service, to commence from the time of such officers' death, and continue for the term of seven years; or, if there be no widow, or in case of her death or intermarriage, the said half pay be given to the orphan children of the officer dying as aforesaid, if he shall have left any; and that it be recommended to the Legislatures of the respective States to which such officers belong to make provision for paying the same on account of the United States."

That resolution of the 24th of August, 1780, is explanatory of the resolution of 15th of May, 1778, and manifesting that that resolution was limited and confined to officers who did actually reside in some one of the United States, and not otherwise, and recommending to the several States, respectively, to make provision accordingly for the widows and orphans of officers who did reside within some one of the United States, respectively. On these resolutions of Congress it does not appear that the heirs of the Baron de Kalb can bottom any claim for five years' full pay as mentioned in their petition. By a resolution of Congress of the 21st of October, 1780, half-pay for life was granted to officers in the service of the United States, alluded to in that resolution: that resolution does not include the case of the heirs of the Baron de Kalb. On the 26th of January, 1784, Congress resolved "that half-pay cannot be allowed to any officer, or to any class or denomination of officers, to whom it has not been heretofore expressly promised." The resolutions of Congress of the 21st of October, 1780, of the 22d of March, 1783, and of the 8th of March, 1785, allowing half-pay for life, or commutation thereof for five years' full pay, do not include this case of the petitioners. Their claim for five years' pay does not appear to be included in or provided for by any act or resolution of Congress.

This committee do further report that evidence has not been adduced to prove that any arrears of pay are due to the Baron de Kalb, and that therefore his heirs, the petitioners, have not any just claim against the United States for any arrears of pay said to be due to their late father, the Baron de Kalb; that the claim of the heirs of the Baron de Kalb to the full pay of five years on account of the services of the Baron to the United States is not bottomed on any act or resolution of Congress, and is therefore inadmissible, and ought not to be allowed. By the report from the Department of the Treasury alluded to, it appears that, on reference to the register of officers of the Revolutionary army returned as entitled to land, the name of the Baron de Kalb is entitled to land, for which application is to be made to the Department of War.

This committee, after consideration of this case of the petitioners, and taking into view the circumstances attending it, are of opinion that it does not appear that any arrears of pay are due to the late Baron de Kalb, as intimated by the petitioners in their petition; that it does not appear that the petitioners, heirs of the Baron de Kalb, have any just claim against the United States for five years' pay in consequence of services by him performed to the United States; and therefore submit the following resolution:

Resolved, That the prayer of the petitioners, so far as relates to their claim of any arrears of pay supposed to be due to their late father, the Baron de Kalb, and so far as relates to their claim of pay for five years in consequence of services of their late father, the Baron de Kalb, to the United States, be not granted; and that the petitioners have leave to withdraw so much of their said petition as relates to their claim for land as heirs of the Baron de Kalb, so that they may apply to the Department of War for the same.

MISSOURI.

Mr. ARCHER, of Virginia, moved that the House do now proceed to consider the resolution submitted by him on the 4th instant, in relation to the judicial condition of the Territory of Missouri.

On the question being taken, Will the House now consider the said resolution? it was determined in the negative—yeas 66, nays 78, as follows:

YEAS—Messrs. Abbot, Alexander, Allen of Tennessee, Anderson, Archer of Maryland, Archer of Virginia, Ball, Barbour, Brevard, Brown, Bryan, Burton, Burwell, Butler of Louisiana, Cannon, Cobb, Cocke, Cook, Crawford, Crowell, Culpeper, Cuthbert, Davidson, Earle, Edwards of North Carolina, Fisher, Floyd, Garnett, Gray, Gross of New York, Hooks, Jackson, Johnson, Jones of Virginia, Jones of Tennessee, Kinsey, Little, Lowndes, McCoy, McCreary, McLane of Delaware, McLean of Kentucky, Meigs, Metcalf, T. L. Moore, Neale, Nelson of Virginia, Parker of Virginia, Pinckney, Rankin, Reed, Rhea, Robertson, Settle, Simkins, Smith of New Jersey, Smith of Maryland, A. Smyth of Virginia, Swearingen, Terrell, Trimble, Tucker of Virginia, Walker, Warfield, Williams of Virginia, and Williams of North Carolina—66.

NAYS—Messrs. Adams, Allen of Massachusetts, Allen of New York, Baldwin, Bateman, Beecher, Boden, Brush, Buffum, Campbell, Clagett, Clark, Crafts, Cushman, Dane, Darlington, Dennison, Dickinson, Eddy, Edwards of Connecticut, Edwards of Pennsylvania, Fay, Folger, Foot, Forrest, Fuller, Gorham, Gross of Pennsylvania, Hall of New York, Hardin, Hemphill, Hendricks, Herrick, Hibshman, Hill, Hostetter, Kinsley, Lathrop, Lincoln, Maclay, McCullough, Mallary, Marchand, Monell, R. Moore, S. Moore, Morton, Moseley, Murray, Nelson of Massachusetts, Parker of Mass., Patterson, Philson, Plumer, Rich, Richards, Richmond, Rogers, Ross, Russ, Sergeant, Silsbee, Sloan, Southard, Stevens, Storrs, Street, Strong of Vermont, Strong of New York, Tomlinson, Tracy, Udree, Upham, Van Rensselaer, Wallace, Wendover, Whitman, and Wood—78.

The House proceeded to consider the resolution submitted yesterday by Mr. TRIMBLE; and, the same being again read, was agreed to.

REDUCTION OF THE ARMY.

The House then again resolved itself into a Committee of the Whole, (Mr. WHITMAN in the chair,) on the bill to reduce the Military Peace Establishment of the United States.

Mr. WILLIAMS, in an address of about two hours, concluded the speech which he yesterday commenced, in favor of a reduction of the Army; which speech is given entire in preceding pages.

Mr. A. SMYTH, of Virginia, then rose, and moved the following as an amendment to (substitute for) the bill under consideration:

Be it enacted, &c., That, from and after the first day of May next, the Military Peace Establishment of the United States shall consist of six thousand non-commissioned officers, musicians, and privates, in such proportions of artillery, light artillery, infantry, and riflemen, as the President of the United States shall direct.

And be it further enacted, That the corps of artillery shall consist of one colonel commandant, four lieutenant colonels, four majors, forty captains, eighty lieutenants, and eighty second lieutenants, divided into four battalions, each to consist of ten companies.

And be it further enacted, That the regiment of light artillery shall consist of one colonel, one lieutenant colonel, one major, ten captains, ten lieutenants, ten second lieutenants, divided into two battalions, each to consist of five companies.

And be it further enacted, That the regiment of riflemen shall consist of one colonel, one lieutenant colonel, one major, ten captains, ten lieutenants, ten second lieutenants, divided into two battalions, each of five companies.

And be it further enacted, That the corps of infantry shall consist of eight colonels, eight lieutenant colonels, eight majors, eighty captains, eighty first lieutenants, eighty second lieutenants, divided into eight regiments, each to consist of ten companies.

And be it further enacted, That there shall be retained in service three brigadier generals, each of whom shall be allowed an aid-de-camp, to be taken from the subalterns of the line.

And be it further enacted, That there shall be a department of order and inspection, to consist of one adjutant and inspector general, who shall have the pay, rank, and emoluments of a colonel of cavalry, as heretofore established, and of three assistant adjutants and inspectors general.

And be it further enacted, That the Quartermaster's Department shall consist of a quartermaster general, with the rank, pay, and emoluments of a brigadier general, two deputy quartermasters general, and sixteen assistant deputy quartermasters general. The paymaster's department shall consist of one paymaster general, and nineteen paymasters. The purchasing department shall consist of a commissary general of purchases, with a salary of two thousand dollars per annum; and one assistant commissary general of purchases, whose compensation shall not exceed two and a half per centum on the public moneys disbursed by him, nor the sum of fifteen hundred dollars per annum, and two military storekeepers. The Subsistence Department shall consist of a commissary general with as many assistants as the service may require, to be taken from the subalterns of the line. The Medical Department shall consist of one surgeon general, one apothecary general, twenty-five surgeons, and forty-four assistant surgeons, the latter to have the pay and emoluments heretofore allowed to surgeons' mates.

And be it further enacted, That the corps of engineers shall be retained in service, and shall consist of one colonel, one assistant engineer, one lieutenant colonel, two majors, six captains, six lieutenants, and six second lieutenants; that one-half of the officers of the corps of ordnance, and one-half of the topographical engineers and their assistants, shall be retained in service.

And be it further enacted, That there shall be appointed a judge advocate general, who shall have the pay, rank, and emoluments of a colonel of infantry, who shall keep an office in the city of Washington; and, in addition to the duties which may be assigned to him by the President of the United States, he shall keep a record of all trials by general courts martial, and report the decisions, an abridgement of which shall be published from time to time, as the President shall direct.

And be it further enacted, That all officers of the Army, whose continuance in service is not provided for by this act, shall be discharged from the service of the United States; and that, to each commissioned officer who shall be discharged by virtue of this act, there shall be paid, in addition to the pay and emoluments to which he shall be entitled at the time of his discharge, three months' pay.

On motion of Mr. CUTHBERT, the Committee then rose.

———

WEDNESDAY, January 10.

Mr. ANDERSON, from the Committee on the Public Lands, made a report on the petition of James McFarland, Hampton Pankey, and William Frizell, accompanied with a bill for the relief of the said James McFarland; which was read twice, and referred to a Committee of the Whole.

Mr. WILLIAMS, of North Carolina, from the Committee of Claims, made a report on the petition of Pierre Denis De La Rondé, accompanied with a bill for his relief; which was read twice, and committed.

Mr. WILLIAMS, from the same committee, to which was referred the bill from the Senate, entitled "An act for the relief of the officers and volunteers engaged in the late campaign against the Seminole Indians," made a report thereon, recommending that the said bill be postponed indefinitely; and the bill and report were committed to a Committee of the Whole.

Mr. STORRS, from the Committee on Roads and Canals, reported a bill for the promotion of internal improvements in the United States; which was read twice, and committed to a Committee of the Whole to-morrow. The bill is as follows:

Be it enacted, &c., That the President of the United States be, and he is hereby, authorized to convey to any State or States which shall provide by law for the laying out and completion of any canal or canals within such State or States, such part of the public lands of the United States which shall be occupied by the route of any such canal or canals, and the necessary towing paths, ditches, aqueducts, locks, culverts, feeders, dams, waste weirs, or other works connected therewith: *Provided,* That the plan or plans of every such canal, and the works connected therewith, with its route, and an estimate and survey of such lands through which the same shall pass, shall, before the construction of the same through such lands shall be commenced, be laid before the President of the United States for his approbation, and no conveyance of any such lands shall be made until such proposed canal or canals be entirely completed and navigable for boats.

The SPEAKER laid before the House the following communications, viz:

A letter from the Secretary of State, transmitting a list of American seamen registered in the several ports of the United States for the three first quarters of the year 1820; which was ordered to lie on the table.

A letter from the Secretary of the Treasury, transmitting a report of the register of the land office for the district of Edwardsville, upon the claims exhibited under the act of the 15th of May, 1820, for the relief of the inhabitants of the village of Peoria, in the State of Illinois; which letter and report were referred to the Committee on the Public Lands.

A letter from the Secretary of the Navy, accompanied with the annual statements in relation to the Navy pension fund; which was ordered to lie on the table.

A letter from the Secretary of the Treasury, transmitting a statement of the amount of drawback on merchandise exported from the United States during the years 1817, 1818, and 1819, compared with the amount of duties which accrued on the same respectively; which was read, and ordered to lie on the table.

A letter from the Secretary of the Navy, transmitting a statement of the expenditure and application of the moneys drawn from the Treasury on account of the Navy, for the year ending on the

30th September, 1820, and of the unexpended balances of former appropriations remaining in the Treasury on the 1st October, 1820; which letter and statement were ordered to lie on the table.

On motion of Mr. SOUTHARD, the Speaker of this House was requested to inform the Executive of the State of New Jersey of the death of JOHN LINN, late one of the Representatives from said State.

On motion of Mr. COBB, the Committee on Naval Affairs were instructed to inquire into the expediency of making an appropriation for making an experiment of a machine (a model whereof is now in the office of the Commissioners of the Navy Board) for raising ships of war from the water, and placing them under cover, for repair or protection.

On motion of Mr. MEIGS, the House proceeded to the consideration of the report of the Committee of Claims, on the petition of Thomas Staniford, late a paymaster in the Army of the United States, praying equitable allowance for certain payments, the vouchers for which were lost by fire in New York; which report recommends that the prayer of the petitioner be rejected. The reading of the papers was going on, when, on motion of Mr. WILLIAMS, of North Carolina, the report was referred to a Committee of the Whole.

A message from the Senate informed the House that the Senate have passed a bill, entitled "An act to incorporate the Columbian College in the District of Columbia;" in which they ask the concurrence of this House.

On motion of Mr. GROSS, of New York, the House proceeded to the consideration of the resolution submitted by him a few days ago, the object of which is to request information from the President whether any negotiations have been made by commissioners of the United States with the Six Nations of Indians in the State of New York, &c.

Some conversation took place on the subject of this motion, between Messrs. STORRS and GROSS.

The former of these gentlemen considered the inquiry as unnecessary; the facts being, as he was informed, that the United States had no land in that State to which the Indian title was unextinguished; that, however, certain individuals had claims on such lands, under pre-emption rights granted by the State of Massachusetts; that, to extinguish the Indian title, the Executive had been requested to authorize commissioners to treat with the Indians—a request which could not reasonably be refused, and the expenses of those commissioners, and all other expenses attending the transaction, had been paid by the individuals claiming the land, &c.

To this Mr. GROSS replied, that if the gentleman had a knowledge of all the circumstances of this transaction, and there was no possibility of his being mistaken, why then, indeed, there would be no occasion for the passage of the resolution. But, as certainty with regard to the facts was the object of this resolution, the answer to which he presumed would furnish it in an official manner, he hoped it would be agreed to.

16th CON. 2d SESS.—26

The resolve was agreed to without a division, though not without dissentient voices.

MISSOURI.

Mr. ARCHER, of Virginia, then moved that the House proceed to the consideration of the resolution moved by him, directing the Judiciary Committee to report certain facts with regard to the present condition of Missouri, and their opinion of what legislative measures may be necessary in regard thereto.

And the question being taken by yeas and nays, on proceeding to the consideration thereof, it was decided in the negative—yeas 65, nays 85, as follows:

YEAS—Messrs. Alexander, Allen of Tennessee, Anderson, Archer of Maryland, Archer of Virginia, Ball, Barbour, Bayly, Bloomfield, Brevard, Brown, Bryan, Burton, Burwell, Butler of Louisiana, Cannon, Cobb, Cocke, Cook, Culpeper, Cuthbert, Davidson, Earle, Edwards of N. Carolina, Fisher, Floyd, Gray, Gross of N. York, Hall of N. Carolina, Hooks, Jackson, Johnson, Jones of Va., Jones of Tenn., Kinsey, Little, Lowndes, McCoy, McCreary, McLane of Delaware, McLean of Kentucky, Mercer, Metcalf, T. L. Moore, Neale, Nelson of Virginia, Parker of Virginia, Pinckney, Reed, Rhea, Robertson, Settle, Shaw, Simkins, Smith of New Jersey, A. Smith of Maryland, A. Smyth of Virginia, Smith of North Carolina, Swearingen, Terrell, Trimble, Tucker of Virginia, Walker, Williams of Virginia, and Williams of North Carolina.

NAYS—Messrs. Abbot, Adams, Allen of Massachusetts, Allen of New York, Baldwin, Bateman, Beecher, Boden, Brush, Buffum, Butler of New Hampshire, Campbell, Clagett, Clark, Crafts, Cushman, Dane, Darlington, Dennison, Dickinson, Eddy, Edwards of Connecticut, Edwards of Pennsylvania, Eustis, Fay, Folger, Foot, Fuller, Gorham, Gross of Pennsylvania, Guyon, Hall of New York, Hall of Delaware, Hardin, Hemphill, Hendricks, Herrick, Hill, Hobart, Hostetter, Kendall, Kinsley, Lathrop, Lincoln, Livermore, Maclay, McCullough, Mallary, Marchand, Monell, R. Moore, S. Moore, Morton, Moseley, Murray, Parker of Massachusetts, Patterson, Philson, Pitcher, Plumer, Rankin, Rich, Richards, Richmond, Rogers, Ross, Russ, Sawyer, Sergeant, Silsbee, Sloan, Southard, Stevens, Storrs, Street, Strong of Vermont, Strong of New York, Tomlinson, Tracy, Udree, Van Rensselaer, Wallace, Wendover, Whitman, and Wood.

REDUCTION OF THE ARMY.

The House then having again resolved itself into a Committee of the Whole on the bill for reducing the Military Peace Establishment—

Mr. CUTHBERT, of Georgia, spoke as follows:

Mr. Chairman, one of the greatest faults of our Government, the best that has ever been framed by the wisdom of man, is its tendency to pursue an unsteady and changeable policy. The causes which produce this defect, at the same time form one of the strong defences of our liberty; and while enjoying the advantage which springs from them, we should guard against the danger to which they expose us. The constant succession of different men to fill the chief offices of Government, especially the incessant changes of this assembly, which springs every two years immediately from the bosom of the people, preserves us from the danger of a long continuance of unwise or corrupt measures; but the same changes subject us too much to the influence of momentary causes. There is reason to apprehend, that, forgetful of the past, and blind to the future, we shall limit our view to the circumstances of the present year. Believing that the anxiety now manifested for the reduction of the Army, has been excited by this contracted view, and that it is not justified either by the experience of the past, or the probabilities of the future, I am opposed to the passage of the bill on the table. In deciding upon it, the answer to two questions should govern us: Is the Military Establishment proposed in this bill, sufficiently large for the wants of our country? If not, are the resources of our country, not for one or for two years, but for a series of years, its average resources, adequate to the support of a larger establishment than that proposed in this bill? I believe that the Army might, with propriety, suffer some partial reduction; I see no need of retaining as many general officers as we now have; and it probably has excrescences elsewhere which might be lopped off without injury to the country; but the proposed reduction I think dangerous, and not required by the state of our finances.

Differing in my opinions from the gentleman from North Carolina, (Mr. WILLIAMS,) I shall be constrained to take some liberties with his remarks which I hope he will pardon, as I shall do it with no unfriendly feeling. He is much offended at the late report of the Secretary of War, submitted in compliance with a resolution of this House. It is not my part at present to defend that report; and you will recollect that the Secretary does not think that the Army ought to be reduced; and that, in his report he only recommends that organization which he deems proper for a peace establishment of six thousand men. However, I will express my opinion, that the gentleman from North Carolina has not refuted the argument of the Secretary. What is that argument? That your Military Peace Establishment should be so organized as to form a preparation for a state of wa.. This principle is denied, in words by the gentleman from North Carolina, but it is admitted by his reasonings and conclusions, as I shall attempt to show in the course of my remarks.

In the progress of this discussion, our Government has been accused of an extravagant and wasteful expenditure of public money. I think this charge entirely unjust; and it is impossible that it can be intended by any gentleman to be applied to the present Secretary of the War Department. Under his control, that Department has been administered with a responsibility, an economy, a wisdom, which challenge a comparison with its administration at any former period.

The gentleman from North Carolina has drawn the picture of a wise and virtuous Government, under which the people are protected in their rights and enjoy the fruit of their industry. He has drawn, in like manner, the picture of an extravagant, rapacious, and oppressive Government, under whose tyranny the rights of the people are contemned, and by whose excessive burdens they are reduced to extreme want and misery. Does he design this for a portrait of our Government? Of a Government which sits so lightly on the people, which imposes not one tax, and which leaves to every citizen the entire control of his labor, and the free enjoyment of its profits? You cannot trace the likeness in a single feature: it is a perfect contrast. If he did not design it as a portrait of our Government, why did he insinuate its resemblance, and use this insinuation as an argument for the proposed reduction of our expenditures? Is he willing that his remarks should cross the Atlantic, and be quoted in foreign countries, as conveying a correct description of the character of our Government?

The gentleman from North Carolina says, that the maintenance of a standing army during peace is contrary to the spirit of the Constitution; and, to support his position, he quotes the naked, abstract proposition, that "standing armies are dangerous to liberty," not from the Constitution, but from certain declarations of rights. The framers of the Constitution felt the force of this truth, and they knew, with equal certainty, that standing armies are sometimes necessary for the defence of liberty.

To prohibit the use of this formidable but necessary instrument, would have been madness in them; and to guard against its abuse, they employed, not abstract propositions, but positive enactments. Of this character is that clause of the Constitution which prohibits the raising of armies without the consent of this House, the immediate representatives of the people, and the guardians of their liberty: and that clause which requires that bills, appropriating money, without which an army cannot be maintained, must originate in the same popular branch of the Legislature; and that clause which, distrusting the discretion even of the representatives of the people, forbids that any appropriation for that purpose shall be for more than two years. Then, maintenance of a standing army, within proper limits, is opposed neither by the letter nor the spirit of the Constitution; and is consistent with the practical exposition given to it by that gentleman himself.

He fears that the subordination necessary in an army will be dangerous to liberty; he dreads the contagious example of a soldier returning to the walks of civil life, with habits of degrading subjection to authority. And does he really dread the influence of a few individuals, for the most part ignorant and obscure, over a population of twelve or fourteen millions, spread over vast regions? You may mingle with large societies; you may pass over extensive sections of country, and not see one man who has belonged to the regular army; and does he really believe that a cause, thus trivial and limited, will be found sufficient to undermine the love of liberty, so firmly fixed in the American character?

He has expressed his fear of the physical strength of the army. Will he, on reflection, believe that an army of ten thousand men can enslave the American people? Will he say that he believes this possible? Truly the fears of that gentleman are entirely visionary; it is idle to combat them. As if conscious that the arguments which have been employed, are not sufficient to justify the proposed reduction of the army, the gentlemen who urge it have endeavored to sustain their policy by the authority of Mr. Jefferson's name. If the reputation of this enlightened and virtuous statesman, so dear to the American people, shall be injured, the fault will be attributable to the imprudence of those men who drag in his name to support a system of measures which cannot be sustained by their own merits. Has the Congress of the United States withdrawn itself from the guidance of reason, and surrendered its rights to the empire of authority? We ask not what name sanctions, but what reason justifies any measure which is proposed? If we believe it to be wise and salutary, we adopt it without caring by whom it is recommended. If we believe it to be inexpedient or improper, the authority of no name, however high, is sufficient to remove our objections to it. Then, why introduce into our discussions a name which is not needed in aid of a wise, and which cannot justify an unwise, policy? While censuring such a course of argument, I also deny that they have the authority of Mr. Jefferson for the reduction of the army, which is now under consideration. Will any one venture to say, that after a lapse of twenty years, during which the resources of our country have greatly increased, and during which it has acquired much experience, both in peace and in war, the mind of that great man alone remaining stationary, he would, under so great a change of circumstances, now pursue, in all respects, the same policy which he observed in 1801? Is any one authorized to say, that Mr. Jefferson entertains the same opinion of the administration of Mr. Monroe, which he entertained of the administration of his own predecessor? that it is wasteful, extravagant, and inclining to monarchy? that it everywhere needs retrenchment and reform? No sir; even that authority fails them on which they have sought to lean.

The supporters of this bill think that we shall not be engaged in war for many years, and that it is unnecessary to prepare for an event which is not expected. If those gentlemen could give us an assurance that we shall not be drawn into war in less than ten or fifteen years, their policy might be safe. But, with Spanish provinces on our southwest, with English provinces on our north, with Russia erecting strong military works on our northwest, with our commerce floating on every sea, they know that we are in constant danger of collisions, which may terminate in war. Most of our military preparations look to a state of war with England; and the present internal condition of that country should not lull us into security. It is well known that the people of Great Britain participate with their Government, in their hatred of the American Republic, and is it not possible that a dexterous ministry, availing themselves of this national feeling, may attempt, by the excitements of an American war, to divert those passions which now threaten them with destruction? Or, may not that country be revolutionized? And,

under a more popular and virtuous government, impelled by all the energies of a free people, would it not be more formidable than at any former period?

War is not certain; it may be improbable; but even folly may shun dangers which openly menace it, and it is the part of prudence to guard against those dangers which are more remote and less obvious. A wise statesman, prepared for every contingency, will not carry his plans of economy so far as to leave his country exposed to the hazards of an unequal contest, to the losses of treasure, of honor, and of men, which she must suffer if drawn into a war for which she is unprovided. To a certain extent, the advocates of the bill agree to this proposition; they all acknowledge that we ought to have garrisons of regular soldiers in our fortresses. During the last war, when the fleets of the enemy occupied our harbors, and threatened our wealthy cities, when, for the want of adequate fortifications, we were constrained to call to their defence great numbers of militia, exposing them to the fatal ravages of a sickly climate, to which they were not inured, every one felt the necessity of erecting strong fortresses in situations proper for the defence of these harbors and cities. With universal approbation, this plan was adopted; many of these works are now completed, and others are in progress. If we have fortresses, it is necessary to garrison them with men who know how to defend them. Nations about to engage in hostilities are not restrained by a punctilious sense of justice. Should we, omitting this precaution, have a dispute with a nation disposed to engage in war with us, it might determine to anticipate us, to strike the first blow, to seize our empty fortresses. Remember the attack on Copenhagen! What would then be the fate of our cities? I do not think that our fortresses should have full garrisons during peace; I would keep in them only a sufficient number of disciplined soldiers to defend them against a sudden attack. When the occasion requires, you may reinforce them with militia, who, mingling with the regulars, would be able to make an efficient defence. In like manner, a part of our force must be employed to guard our Indian frontier, and prevent the hostilities of our savage neighbors. In this employment of our troops, the advocates of the bill agree with us. But I go one step further; and, in doing so, I draw on myself the terrible denunciation of the gentleman from North Carolina. We need a body of men who will serve as a depository of military science, and from whom correct discipline may be rapidly infused into a new army. Our troops in garrison cannot perform this service; because, if they are needed in the fortresses during peace, they cannot be withdrawn from them while we are engaged in war. For this purpose, we shall need a distinct force, in addition to the six thousand men who, almost all agree, should be retained in our fortresses. This part of our system is denounced as anti-republican by the gentleman from North Carolina. Why? Because our army would thus, during peace, be employed, as a preparation for a state of war. I ask him, for what purpose does he acknowledge that our garrisons should be retained, unless as a preparation for a state of war? For what other purpose does he consent to retain any portion of the standing army? He is caught in his own denunciation. It comprehends the great man to whose authority he appealed; for he, too, recommended a standing army.

In declaring that those who advocate this system, renounce republican principles, he seems not to have reflected that, under arbitrary government, the Army may be employed during peace for other purposes, to support unjust authority, to enforce oppression, decrees to extort ruinous taxes; and that, in a free Government, the only legitimate use of an army during peace is, to prepare for a state of war. I would retort on him the charge of renouncing republican principles, did I believe that he had understood the character of his own doctrines.

But, it is said, that in future wars, our battles must be fought on the ocean, and that we ought to avoid a contest on the land. Will this be left to our choice? We should most diligently prepare a strong naval force for the defence of our shores and our commerce. But, in a war with England, she will not leave her Canadian provinces without defence, to become an easy conquest to us. She will send an army to Canada. If we are unprepared to encounter this army, will she courteously keep it on her own territory? Will she not prefer making our territory the seat of hostilities, and inflicting on our citizens the calamities of war? This was her policy in the last, and this will be her policy in any future war. If we are not prepared to encounter her army on the Canadian frontier, we shall feel its attacks in the bosom of our country. But, the advocates of this bill believe that the militia may be relied on to fight our battles, and defend our country on the land. Far be it from me to speak contemptuously of the militia; they are the people of our country, our fellow-citizens, and our brethren. I believe that they have an intelligence, a courage, a spirit of enterprise, a sense of honor, and love of country, which, with proper experience and instruction, would make them the best soldiers in the world. But they want this instruction and experience; and all history teaches us that troops wanting these, cannot succeed against disciplined soldiers. Sometimes, from the superior talents of their officers, or the superiority of their numbers, and sometimes from that heroic courage which liberty inspires, they may obtain brilliant victories. But far, very far more frequently they suffer disgrace and defeat when opposed to regulars. I know that some gentlemen in this House presume to censure us for holding such language; but is it not true? And is the fault ours that it is true? And is it wise to close our eyes against the truth? The experience of the past teaches us this painful lesson, and a little reflection would convince us that it always must be so. Suppose that our General, commanding undisciplined soldiers, such as a very large proportion of our militia always have been, and I fear always will be during the first two or three campaigns of a war, is opposed to a General

commanding an army of regulars. In our camp all is imperfect, all is to be learnt. The mind of the General is occupied by all the cares of camppolice. There is frequent neglect of the regulations and habits, which are necessary to prevent waste, to preserve the health of the army, to guard it against surprise. In the hostile camp, that military police, so essential to the welfare of the army, is already established, the mind of the General is left at liberty to revolve and prepare his plans of march and of battle; his army is always ready for attack or defence. Is it wise to send our armies to the contest under such disadvantages? Suppose the armies arrayed in the field of battle. The enemy, in manœuvring, exposes a weak point, on which our General determines to make a decisive attack; he orders a column to be formed on a certain point with instructions to advance. His orders are slowly and imperfectly obeyed; the movements of his soldiers are confused and tumultuous; half an hour is occupied in forming a column, which should have been formed in half that time. The enemy perceives the manœuvre, has time to reinforce his weak point, and the precious opportunity of victory is lost by the want of discipline in our army. From the very nature of things the General of our undisciplined troops, whether militia, or new untrained levies, can but seldom gain a victory. And they are as illy prepared to defend themselves.

Suppose the hostile army to make an unexpected movement on our flank. To oppose him, it is necessary rapidly to form a new line. For this purpose our General issues orders. The enemy approaches with a steady line, and on our part all is confusion and tumult. Our soldiers, wanting discipline, here crowd together, and embarrass each other; there they leave an open space for the enemy to penetrate. An army thus assailed will abandon the field; or, if it resists, it must be slaughtered. In the early campaigns of a war we cannot prudently rely on the militia, and it is inhuman to lead them to a contest in which such decisive advantages are found on the side of the enemy. But it is said that, in peace, our regulars cannot learn the art of war, and that at the commencement of hostilities they will not be better prepared for the field than our militia. The gentlemen who expressed this opinion seem not to have remembered that there are two branches of tactics, entirely distinct. The one comprehends those principles which should guide a General in choosing the route of his march, in forming the plans of his campaigns and his battles. The camp of a Peace Establishment furnishes no peculiar advantages for the acquisition of this branch of military science—exhibits no field for its exercise and application. I believe that, retaining only one General on our Peace Establishment, we should be as well prepared for war as with our present complement. The other branch of tactics includes the knowledge and practice of those regulations which form the police of an army, and insure its order and subordination, its health and its vigilance, and of those evolutions which pre-

809   HISTORY OF CONGRESS.   810

JANUARY, 1821.   *Reduction of the Army.*   H. OF R.

pare it for every movement on the field, and make it a perfect machine in the hands of the General. This part of military science is as easily acquired and perfected in peace as in war. In this our small army, retained in peace, should be perfect. The principles which I advocate do not require the maintenance, in peace, of an army sufficiently large for a state of war; they demand only a few thousand men in addition to the troops necessary for our garrisons. Then, sir, when we are engaged in war, as at some future time we certainly shall be, when we are compelled to raise a larger army, by mingling our veterans with our new levies, we may engage in an equal contest with older armies. In every subdivision, in every section of the new army, we may place some disciplined soldiers, whose instructions, and example, and guidance, will rapidly perfect its discipline, infusing into it subordination and vigilance in camp, with skill and steadiness in the field. But, by passing the bill under consideration, we shall deprive our country of this resource; by pursuing this rash policy, we will force her, when engaged in war, to rely on undisciplined troops; we will decide that, in the first campaigns, she shall be inferior in military skill; we will expose her to the hazard of the incalculable losses of treasure, of territory, of honor, and of life, which are the consequences of this inferiority. Such is the economy of this bill!

The friends of this bill say, that the deficiency in our revenue imposes on us the necessity of retrenchment, whether that retrenchment be in itself salutary or pernicious. And is this youthful nation already sinking under the decrepitude of old age? Are her resources so exhausted that she can no longer maintain those establishments which are necessary to her welfare? I think that when some documents, expected from the Treasury Department, are received, and the subject shall have been fully examined, it will appear that the deficiency for the present year is but small; and calculations from both sides of the House agree, that, in one or two years, the revenue arising from imposts will be adequate to the maintenance of our establishments on their present scale. But grant, for a moment, that these expectations should be disappointed, have we no other resource? Those gentlemen shrink from the policy of imposing taxes. Why? Out of tenderness for the people? Because they will not take the money of the people? I ask them whose is the money derived from imposts which they are so willing to receive? Is it not drawn from the people? And is it their principle to take the money of the people, in order to defray the expenses of the Government, as long as they can keep the operation concealed from their constituents? They gladly receive, and freely spend, fifteen, eighteen, twenty-five millions annually, when it can be drained from the people by imposts. This is ample proof that their reluctance to impose taxes arises not from any peculiar tenderness for the people. I do not believe that they intend to deceive, but their conduct bears that aspect. I would pursue a more open and candid course. I would say to our fellow-citizens, "we

' will pursue the most rigid economy that is con-
' sistent with the public welfare; we will impose
' on you no unnecessary burdens, but the institu-
' tions of our Government cannot with safety be
' impaired. The revenue derived from customs,
' by which principally the Government is sup-
' ported, is furnished by you; but our commerce
' now languishes, our revenue is diminished; it is
' necessary that you should supply its deficiency,
' in order to maintain those establishments which
' are essential to the prosperity of our country."
The people would be gratified by our confidence; their patriotism would be roused by our call; for they are ever ready to maintain their Government, when not misled by timid politicians, or designing candidates for office. To deny this, would be to dishonor them, to believe them devoid of patriotism, lost to honor, the miserable slaves of a blind and sordid avarice.

I repeat it—should our customs be permanently inadequate to the support of the Government, I would make an appeal to the patriotism of the people; and that appeal would be heard. But there is no such permanent deficiency; apply the calculations of all parties to a series of years, and, without any change of system, we shall find our average annual revenue sufficient to maintain all of the establishments of the Government on their present scale, and to progress with the gradual extinction of the public debt.

Then, sir, in our finances there is no such failure as would impose on us the necessity of lopping off a portion of the army, which we cannot safely spare. Prudence admonishes us to keep garrisons in our fortresses, and to preserve an additional corps to be the depository of military science, and to serve as instructors, and examples, and guides, to our militia and new levies, in any future war. For these purposes a peace establishment of 6,000 men is not sufficient.

Mr. FISHER, of North Carolina, addressed the House as follows:

Mr. Chairman, the gentlemen who have preceded me in this debate have taken a wide survey of the subject, discussing it as well in detail as on general principles. Should I be led by their example into the same latitude of remark, I can, nevertheless, promise that I will not harass the Committee with a very long speech. The question for reducing the present Military Establishment is not a new one, but not the less important on that account. My worthy colleague, (Mr. WILLIAMS,) has, on several occasions, brought this subject before Congress, and, heretofore, always without success. The army, some how or other, has grown up under his opposition, and flourished under his speeches; but I hope a season has now come more favorable to its reduction.

The first argument that I shall urge for reducing this establishment will be drawn from the present state of the finances of the country. Sir, we have reached that period in our history, when the ordinary revenues of the country are insufficient to meet the ordinary expenditures of the Government. This must arise either from imperfection in the system providing the revenue, or from defects in the system expending it. Be it chargeable to either, it equally merits serious inquiry and speedy correction. I pretend not to be deeply learned in the science of finance; but it does not require much sagacity to discover that the finances of this Government are in a declining and dilapidated condition; and that there are only three alternatives set before us, by which to supply the deficiency in the Treasury. 1st. By loans; 2d. By imposing taxes; and, 3d. By retrenchment and economy. The question is, to which of these alternatives shall we resort? Shall we go on as we have begun, with the borrowing system, making loans after loans, as long as we can obtain them? For one, I think not. The readiness with which capitalists lend their surplus funds to the Government is no inducement why we should borrow them. Sir, the facility of obtaining money on credit is one of the most unfortunate and seductive temptations that can be held out either to individuals or to Governments. If any proof of this position is required, we need only look to the history of this country for the past four or five years. What man of extravagant habits will forego his gratifications, and give over his projects, when he can obtain money on credit merely by asking for it? What set of office-holders will willingly give up their snug berths when they can retain them by borrowing money at five per cent.? But, as the individual who is always borrowing will soon come to bankruptcy and ruin, so the Government that draws its revenues from loans must sooner or later reach the period of taxation and oppression. Loans are but temporary expedients, and should never be resorted to but in cases of extreme emergency, and then only in anticipation of the ordinary revenues of the country. Is this our case? Is there, at this time, any such emergencies pressing upon us? Certainly not. In times of profound peace we resort to loans, and for what purpose? To meet the ordinary, the regular and every day expenses of the Government.

Sir, to what will all this lead? It will lead to a large national debt, and then, as an inevitable consequence, to oppressive taxes. Do gentlemen consider the operation of these loans? That every loan only increases the necessity for another, at least in the ratio of the preceding loan? As an example: for the last year we authorized a loan of three millions of dollars: we are told that a loan of seven millions must be made for this year; and, for aught I can see in our affairs, a loan of five millions at least will be required for each of the remaining years of the present Administration—making in all twenty-five millions. That much for principal; but at the end of that time, it will be found that the debt contracted during the five last years of the present Administration, will be within a fraction of thirty millions. Again: at the last session we directed a loan of three millions of dollars; but, from the Secretary's report, it appears that only two millions five hundred and fortyfive thousand four hundred and thirty-one dollars have been received into the Treasury; so that we are actually paying interest on three millions, when only about two millions and a half

and a fraction has been received to the use of Government. I only mention this, to show how profitable loans are, even on the favorable terms of five per cent.

Sir, as well might you expect to quench thirst in dropsy, by drinking, as to restore your finances to a sound state by loans: every draught only increases the want of another. There is no end to this borrowing system; it is like the clue of Ariadne, the further you pursue it, the deeper it involves you in the inextricable labyrinth. We have the awful example of England before us, and we ought to profit by that example. What is it but the great national debt that presses down to misery and wretchedness the people of that country? A debt, the bare interest of which swallows up the greater portion of the revenues of that Government: a debt, for the payment of the interest of which, the people are taxed literally from the crowns of their head to the soles of their feet. And, sir, let me here remark, that the national debt of England, as is indeed the debts of all the other States of Europe, were incurred principally by the *military establishments* of these States, first, from keeping up, in times of peace, standing armies unnecessarily large, and, next, from the wars carried on with those armies. It is not hazarding much, to say, that at least two-thirds of the revenue of every Government in Europe is consumed by the army, or by persons connected either directly or indirectly with the military.

We see, then, the consequence of loans. They only put off the evil day, which, when it does come, we will feel only the heavier, by the previous procrastination. But, sir, the honorable Chairman of the Committee of Ways and Means, in his speech the other day, tells us not to be alarmed; that the condition of our finances is not so bad as we fancy; and, he kindly consoled us by promising better times. I always listen with great pleasure to the speeches of that gentleman, for he always speaks good sense; he always gives us facts and reason; but, however much I may value the information he imparts, I cannot think that his calculations are always infallible. Sir, I distinctly recollect that the gentleman at the last session promised us better times; and I leave it to members to say, if his predictions have been verified. But, sir, that gentleman is not the only person that has been deceived in his hopes and mistaken in his calculations. Even the Secretary of the Treasury himself has now and then fallen into an error. Sir, not a year since the present incumbent came into office, have his estimates of the revenue come within two millions of the mark; sometimes exceeding, and sometimes falling short by that amount.

In his annual report for 1818, he says that the revenue of that year may be considered as the "average amount which will be annually received;" this amount was about twenty-six millions; but, we find that the revenue of the very next year, (1819,) fell short of that estimate by about two millions of dollars—that the revenue for 1820 fell short by a still larger sum. Even, sir, in ordinary calculations, we find that mistakes may sometimes be made. The Secretary, in his report of fourth

December last, informs us that the deficit for the present year will be about seven millions and nearly a half of dollars; but, in his supplemental report of the 20th of the same month, he says that the deficiency is only about four millions six hundred and fifty-eight thousand dollars: thus making a difference between the two reports of two millions seven hundred and ninety-three thousand dollars. But, a worthy gentleman from South Carolina (Mr. SIMKINS) gives us to understand that there are a few more errors still behind: and a gentleman from Pennsylvania has dropped a hint more consoling than all the rest. He tells us it will be found that the deficit of the past year is only about six hundred thousand dollars. Which of these ingenious financiers will prove right it is rather difficult to say: but, from the Secretary's report, one thing is plain, viz: that our finances are in a declining state, while the expenditures of the Government remain stationary. Take the years 1819, 1820, and 1821, and there is a falling off of about four millions annually.

Sir, I make these remarks not in disparagement of any gentleman, but merely to show how little reliance ought to be placed upon calculations of the revenue of years yet to come. Our revenue is principally drawn from commerce—our commerce depends upon the state of the world, and who can say what that will be a short time hence? No, sir, there is no dependence to be placed on these calculations for better times: if we sit here waiting for better times we may wait until ruin tumbles about our heads. But, gentlemen may say, if you will not wait for the flowing of the waters, and in the mean time supply our wants by loans, what will you do? Will you resort to the next alternative and lay taxes? Sir, this question of taxation is a very trying one; it comes home to the feelings of gentlemen. Now, although I do not claim to possess more independence than other gentlemen, yet I am bold to say, that if there is no other alternative, I would prefer a gentle system of taxation to this everlasting, still beginning, and never ending business of making loans upon loans until the resources of the country will be absorbed in the payment of bare interest: but, there is another alternative, and until that is tried and found wanting, I for one will not consent to impose taxes. This alternative consists in the reduction of useless establishments, in retrenchments of unnecessary expenditures, and, in a word, in bringing the expenses of the Government within the means of the country. Sir, in making these remarks, I would not be understood as casting the smallest censure on any department of the Executive: the burden of censure must fall upon us and our predecessors. We pass the laws requiring these expenditures, and the Executive only carries into operation what we authorize. The natural tendency of all Governments is to run into extravagance. That our Government runs powerfully in this direction cannot be denied; and that the late war, by requiring many extraordinary exertions, accelerated this tendency, is equally evident; but, the exigencies requiring these efforts have ceased to exist, and the expenses incident thereto should also cease. I do

not hesitate to say that at the close of the late war it was right to fix the Peace Establishment upon the present organization. It was right on two considerations; first, because our situation with the Indians was extremely precarious; secondly, our relations with Spain were then unsettled. But, our Indian wars are now over, and we are at peace with every tribe: our relations with Spain are now settled, and we have Florida by the ratification of the treaty. The chief causes for fixing the army on its present basis being removed, I must think that it may with safety be reduced to six thousand men.

Sir, in the course of the debate, several gentlemen have made allusions to Mr. Jefferson's Administration. I will briefly refer to the same period of our history. Let it here be remembered that the second President of the United States, together with his political friends, were ejected from power for certain obnoxious measures; and let it be further remembered that one of those measures was the keeping up a standing army in time of peace. The newspapers of the day were filled with essays against the army; the Legislatures of the States remonstrated and instructed their members to urge its reduction. And, sir, how large was the army that created all this alarm? Only 5,000 men; only half as large as the present Peace Establishment, and yet the people of that day thought it too large; even Mr. Jefferson entertained the same opinion, for, in his first Message to Congress, he tells them that he has supplied all the garrisons with men, and that there is a surplus left for which the Government has no use; and accordingly we see the army cut down from 5,000 to about 3,300 men, thus saving to the nation annually the sum of $522,000. Yes, sir, the Peace Establishment of that day consisted only of 3,300 men, and only cost about one million of dollars annually. Now, sir, contrast that with the present army, consisting of 10,000 men. Two Major Generals, four Brigadier Generals, with aids, Colonels, Lieutenant Colonels, Majors, and inferior officers in the greatest abundance, costing annually more than three millions of dollars.

Let me ask, what wonderful changes have taken place in our affairs, to justify this great increase of the Peace Establishment? The gentleman from South Carolina (Mr. SIMKINS) tells us, indeed, that our frontiers have considerably enlarged in their extent, and that the number of our posts have multiplied. This is all true, and I will answer the gentleman by simply asking him, have our frontiers enlarged in the proportion of ten to three, and have our posts increased in the same ratio? Surely not. We are at peace with the savages, with the world; and if it is said we shall have Florida to occupy, I will answer that Mr. Jefferson, with his three thousand men, took possession of, and occupied, Louisiana, a country of many times the extent, and a thousand times the value, of Florida, and that, too, where there was much greater disaffection than will be found in Florida. Then, sir, I come to this conclusion: if 3,300 men were sufficient for the purposes of the country in 1803, surely double that number will answer for the present times. By fixing the Peace Establishment at six thousand men, we save to the nation more than one million of dollars annually, and send to the plough four thousand citizens. But I have other, and, to my mind, even weightier reasons than those of economy, in favor of reducing the present large standing army of the country.

Sir, in the early days of our Government, (and I believe the time will come when those days will be celebrated by historians, and sung by poets, as the golden age of this Republic,) in those days it was held that standing armies were dangerous in times of peace; not dangerous, as some gentlemen would suppose us to mean, from their physical force. No, sir; we are not so timid as to fear that the country has any thing to apprehend from the swords and bayonets of the army, were it even much larger than it is; but dangerous from their moral and political tendency to corruption. My colleague, who has gone before me in this debate, has so fully shown the immoral tendency of standing armies, that I shall not dwell long upon this part of the argument.

Sir, the military establishment, in all Governments, and, above all, in our Government, is essentially different from the civil establishment. The army is a body of men separated and removed from the great mass of the people. They are governed by different laws and upon different principles. Blind obedience to the will of their officers is their only principle. On the part of the soldier, this begets a spirit of servility; on the part of the officer, a spirit of overbearing tyranny—both equally averse to the theory and practice of our Government. In this point of view, standing armies are great evils in our country, and, like all other evils, we should have as little of them as possible. The absolute necessity of the case should be the rule by which to regulate the size of the army; if we can garrison our posts with 6,000 men, why have more than that number? I say, *garrison* our posts; for the idea of defending the country with a standing army is preposterous. The Constitution never contemplated such a defence, nor did it ever enter into the heads of our political forefathers. The militia is the legitimate, the Constitutional defence of the country. Sir, I was shocked to hear the gentleman from Virginia (Mr. SMYTH) deliver the sentiments he did upon this subject. If ever his notions of the militia become the prevailing ones of this people, good bye to your Republican institutions—they are gone forever. But his argument is entirely fallacious. In speaking of the militia, he has taken them, as they were, at the beginning of the Revolutionary war, and all the extracts that he read from the letters of WASHINGTON and others, describe the militia as they then were—without order or previous discipline. This is unjust, sir. We should consider what the militia are capable of being made, and not what they were before we existed as a nation—before we became an independent people. This is the light in which WASHINGTON viewed the militia when he said, " The ' militia may be trained to a degree of energy equal

' to every military exigency of the United States;" and Jefferson says: " A well disciplined militia is ' our best reliance in peace, and for the first mo- ' ments in war, till regulars may relieve them."

But, sir, the arguments of the gentleman from Virginia have been so fully refuted by the venerable member from Massachusetts, (Mr. EUSTIS,) that I shall add nothing further upon that, but proceed to another part of the question.

Sir, standing armies have a political tendency subversive of the principles of our Government. I lay this down as a proposition—in the proportion in which a Government keeps up a large military establishment, in that proportion will the Government neglect the militia of the country. This is a proposition which the history of all free Governments that ever existed fully proves. Let but a Government, let but the people, once place their reliance on standing armies for defence and protection, and the militia, as a natural, as a certain consequence, will fall into neglect, and sink into disrepute. It is plain that, when nothing is expected from them, they will expect to do nothing. Their ability is distrusted, their enterprise is gone. Yes, sir, standing armies weaken the military spirit of a nation. If any illustration of this principle is required, it can be furnished from English history. It was in the reign of the Second James that a standing army was first established in that country. This monarch, under various pretences, formed a standing army of four thousand five hundred men. This was the nucleus of the English standing army; it soon grew larger, and we now see what it is; and, mark it! at the very time at which we date the origin of standing armies in England, at that very time we may also date the decline of the militia; and, sir, it is a striking circumstance, that the very same arguments used by James and his Ministry, to justify their armed force in time of peace, are now urged by gentlemen on this floor in defence of the present establishment, namely, that the militia are inefficient, and that no reliance can be placed upon them. This, then, being the practical tendency of standing armies, I ask, if it is proper, in times of peace, to keep up a single company more than the absolute necessity of the country demands?

But, sir, I have another objection against the present size of the Peace Establishment. We should never enlarge the army beyond what necessity strictly requires, for the reason that it increases the patronage of the Government; it extends the influence of the Executive branch. The patronage of this Government, I admit, is small, compared to that of other Governments, but yet its increase is alarming. Look at the progress of patronage in this Government for the past twelve years; turn over your laws, and examine them, and it will be found that not a year has gone by, not a Congress has passed over, but the powers of the Executive have been enlarged. Indeed, it would seem that all the powers of the States are passing into the hands of Congress, and many of the powers of Congress into the hands of the Executive. The army adds to this patronage. The

President is Commander-in-Chief of the Army; he virtually has the appointment of all the officers; he, at pleasure, has the power of removing them. He and the head of the War Department are the only persons seen by the army; Congress is never seen, until first felt by some law.

Patronage is power. See what it does in Great Britain; what a mighty machine in the hands of that Government! And, whenever corruption dims the glory of our institutions, it will enter in at the door of patronage. If, then, we value our republican privileges, guard against the increase of Executive patronage.

Again: I will advance another objection against large military establishments. To keep up a large army necessarily requires to have at the head of the army great military chieftains. Now, these chieftains, commanding the army, may at times have the power to involve the country in difficulties and war. The chiefs of armies are generally men of great influence and popularity in the Government, and it may so happen that they themselves may not only violate the Constitution and laws of the country, but, by their influence, bring the Government to support and protect them in this violation. History furnishes examples to support this view. I think gentlemen will remember what happened a year or two since, when our army, led perhaps by the military science so much talked of, entered into a neighboring province, not only without orders, but plainly contrary to orders, and, what is worse than all, contrary to the Constitution of the country. I need not recall to the minds of gentlemen the excitement produced on the occasion, not only in this House, but in many parts of the country.

There are other cases in point, but I shall only adduce one more in support of the proposition; and for this one I am indebted to the annals of England—a country from which we draw so many of our good and bad examples. Sir, those anywise conversant with English history will remember the long wars that were waged by that nation against the Continent during the reign of Queen Anne. It is now known that these wars might have been terminated long before they were, but for the intrigues of the Commander-in-Chief of the British forces. Peace would at once have deprived him of his emoluments, and cut short his career of glory. He determined, therefore, to continue the war, though the treasures and blood of his country might flow in torrents. This commander, sir, was the great Duke of Marlborough. But this is not all. The chiefs of the army are always apt to take a part in the civil disputes of the country; and let it be remembered that the soldiery always take the side espoused by their commanders. Sir, how many civil disputes have been decided by the army? In England, we see Cromwell, with a force not three times as large as our present army, drive the Parliament out of doors, overturn the Constitution, and set himself quietly on the throne. We see Gustavus, of Sweden, with a less army than ours, subvert the Constitution, and establish a new order of things. And, sir, how long is it since a handful of guards

in Russia murdered their King, and made Catharine their Empress? In short, look to the seat of an ancient Republic, the master State of the world, and say, from Cæsar down, how many Emperors were made, how many destroyed, by the prætorian bands—the standing army of Rome? All this shows what may be expected of standing armies, what they have done, and always will do.

I will now briefly consider some of the arguments advanced in favor of keeping up the present establishment.

First, it is said to be necessary to preserve the present Army for the purpose of keeping alive the military science of the country. This is a favorite argument of gentlemen, and, I fear, we, who doubt its great force, subject ourselves to the imputation of ignorance and illiberality. Be that as it may, I rejoice that we do not live under a military government, and that it is not our interest to have a great deal of this military science. The best method, in my humble judgment, to preserve this science, is to diffuse it among the militia. Organize them; look to their discipline; put arms in their hands, and let them see that the country relies on them for defence. Do this, sir, and when the voice of the country calls, it will be heard. When military spirits are wanting, they will arise—they will spring from every corner of the country. Sir, I would ask, whence came your best Generals in the late war?—your *Jackson* and your *Brown?* They were not educated in a standing army; they issued from the walks of civil life; and, it is worthy of remark, that the first laurels that crowned their brows were won with the bayonets of the militia.

Sir, the Secretary of War has laid before us a very able defence of the present establishment. He certainly has placed the subject in its strongest lights. But, it appears to me, before we yield to the full extent of his reasoning, we must admit two hypotheses—first, that war is not distant; and, secondly, that when it does come, it will come upon us suddenly. Now I apprehend that neither of these suppositions should be taken for granted. We see no immediate prospect of war; our political horizon is without a speck; the only little cloud that appeared in it, has been swept away by the ratification of the treaty. And, in the next place, whenever war does come, it will not come upon the nation suddenly. In other Governments, where the war-making power is lodged in the hands of kings and ministers, war may be declared unexpectedly to the country; but here there must first be a sufficient cause of war; negotiation must fail; the whole nation must see and feel the necessity of war; and surely in this time a wise Government and prudent Congress will have sufficient time to make ample preparations. There are two things that this Government will never do, until impelled to them by the public sense: to declare war, and to impose taxes.

Sir, I have always thought, that one of the best features in our Government is its unfitness for war; this very unfitness for belligerent operations will save the country from many wars and preserve much blood and treasure. It cannot be denied that a nation, combining the political facilities of war, is much easier propelled to that state than one not calculated to carry on wars. It is with Governments as it is with individuals—give them power, and they will soon find pretences for the exercise of that power. Frederick of Prussia has furnished us an illustration in point; he candidly avows that one of his leading inducements for declaring war against Maria Theresa, was the martial appearance of his fine army—for, said he, "I had a mind to play upon the instrument which I found in such excellent tune." This King has written another sentiment, that should be well remembered by every member of this House; which should be inscribed in glaring letters over the doors of the War Office, "Great armies render governments enterprising, but they make the people slaves."

But, as an argument to preserve the present Army, gentlemen have attributed all the disasters of the late war to the reduction of the Peace Establishment in 1802. This is a view of the subject to which I will not consent. I deny that the reduction of the army in 1802 was the cause of these disasters. There are plainer causes, some of which I will name. First, a want of correct knowledge of the resources of the enemy, and of the difficulties of the enterprise against Canada. The Congress declaring the war, if we judge from their speeches, thought the capture of Canada would be a mere frolic; that a few regiments of militia would take it in six weeks; in fact, so misinformed were they of the dispositions of the Canadians, and the resources of the enemy there, as to make disappointment and discomfiture inevitable.

A second cause of these disasters, was owing to treachery, or something very like it, in the commander that moved the first army towards Canada. This failure set the current of fortune against us, and at once gave confidence to the enemy, and cause of accusation to the opposition among ourselves.

But, sir, the great cause of the disasters of the late war was the want of union among ourselves; in our councils, in the nation. A formidable minority in the country doubted the justice and propriety of the war; and they used every means to shackle the powers and energies of the Government, and to prevent its prosecution. No war or great enterprise can ever be successfully conducted by this Government when the nation is divided among themselves. Disunion paralyzes all our energies. To prove that this was the fruitful source of the disasters of the late war, we have only to look to the theatre where they occurred. In the South, where there was no difference of opinion among the people as to the propriety of the war, our failures were few. From the woods of Talladega to the battle of New Orleans success and victory crowned our arms. But come here, in the very focus of discord; go to the North, where treason stalked abroad, and you see defeat and disgrace rise up before you at every turn.

And, sir, another cause of our failures was the treason of our citizens on the frontier, who gave every aid and comfort to the enemy, as well as speedy information of all our movements. Among these may be placed the blue-light traitors. And, let me not forget another class, who by their conduct shackled our efforts and gave hopes to the enemy. I mean, sir, that class of politicians who, about the close of the war, concentrated in the Hartford Convention; a set of men that should never be forgotten; on whom should fall the lasting imprecations of posterity; on whom should rest "the curses of hate, and hisses of scorn" of all who love their country. These, sir, are the causes of the disasters of the late war, and not as gentlemen would suppose the reduction of the Army in 1802, or its bad organization in 1808.

Again, the gentleman from South Carolina has called in, as an argument, the examples and situation of Europe; that our Army is nothing compared to the establishments of the Governments of Europe. Sir, I deny that the examples of Europe, in this particular, should have any influence upon us; because there is no similarity in our situation and that of any Government in Europe.

The Governments of Europe keep up large standing armies for two purposes. First, to keep down their own subjects. What but a standing army prevents the people of England from reforming the abuses of their Government? What but a standing army keeps Louis XVIII on the throne of France? All the legitimates are supported on their thrones but by the bayonets of their armies. But this is not the case in our blessed land. Our rulers hold their seats by the free suffrages of the people, and no army is necessary to keep down the people.

In the second place, the Governments of Europe keep up large standing armies to repel foreign invasion. Every kingdom in Europe has powerful neighbors, separated only by a river, a hill, or an ideal line. They have reason to look at each other with distrust and suspicion, and wisdom and past experience warns them always to be ready. Take for example the kingdom of Prussia, with the immense front of Russia pressing on one side of her frontier, France looking over on another, and the German empire on a third, her natural attitude is that of defence, and her only defence is a standing army. She must keep up a strong military force because her neighbors do so. The same may be said of all the other Governments of Europe, for in reality that continent presents rather the appearances of war than of peace. This is not our case; we have no fears of sudden invasion. If we pursue the true American policy, keeping clear of all foreign entanglements, we will require no standing armies to defend us from invasion. But the gentleman from South Carolina says we know not how soon our foreign commerce may be cut up. Admit, for the sake of argument, that it is cut up to-morrow, and I should like to learn from him how he proposes to defend our foreign commerce with a standing army. Our commerce is on the ocean, and if any enemy strikes at it on that element, how will you reach him on the mountain wave? Surely not with the Army, but with our glorious little Navy. And here, by the way, permit me to observe, that the Navy is our proper and only efficient defence against attacks from abroad; and I, for one, will not consent to touch even a cockboat of the Navy, if, by doing so, we weaken the force of that defence. Sir, while your soldiers are demoralizing in camp, the tars of the Navy are exercised on the rough bosom of the ocean, and purified by the winds of Heaven.

Mr. Chairman, I have already detained you longer than I could have wished, but, before I sit down, I must express my dissent from some of the remarks of my coadjutor and colleague, (Mr. WILLIAMS.) Although I do not entirely agree with the results of the report of the Secretary of War, yet I cannot by any means think of that report as lightly, and with the same feelings, as does my colleague. On the contrary, it seems to me that his strictures were very illy bestowed. The report, in my humble opinion, is not only highly creditable to the distinguished gentlemen that produced it, but it is the ablest defence of the present establishment that I have seen, or expect to hear in this House. As for the lameness of any figures of speech used by the Secretary to illustrate his reasoning, I profess no skill in that way, nor do I think that this floor is a proper place for exhibitions in the art of hypercriticism. Notwithstanding I cannot agree with the opinion of the Secretary, as regards the proper organization of the Peace Establishment, I am impelled by feelings of justice to say, that his course, on this occasion, as in the whole of his political career, so far as I am capable of judging, has been that of the fearless politician and the enlightened statesman. How does the case stand? We called upon him for a report upon the subject of reducing the Army, and he has frankly given us his best lights and ablest views. Because we differ from him in opinion, would it be just in him to accuse us of motives other than those for the public good? Because he differs from us, what right have we to suspect his motives to be less pure than our own? Sir, it is uncharitable. He cannot possibly have any selfish views; the reduction of the Army can neither take from his scanty emoluments or lessen his honors. He can have no other feelings on the occasion than those of a public man. I then, sir, extremely regret that my worthy colleague should have betrayed so much feeling in the course of his speech. I regret it on two accounts: First, because it lessens the merits of the speech itself, in other respects very able; and, secondly, it gives to the world, always too censorious, some grounds to attribute his conduct, on this occasion, to other motives than those for the public good.

However we may differ from one another, or from the Executive, on any occasions, surely courtesy, if nothing else, should make us assign to them motives as pure and as disinterested as our own.

When Mr. FISHER concluded—

Mr. SMITH, of Maryland, made some explanatory remarks, and Mr. BALDWIN spoke at large against the bill.

The Committee rose, and the House adjourned.

THURSDAY, January 11.

Mr. LOWNDES presented three memorials of the Senate and House of Representatives of Missouri; one praying that the purchasers of public lands may be permitted to apply the payments already made to such of their entries as the said payments will cover at two dollars per acre, relinquishing the residue of the land to the United States; another, praying that persons entitled to the right of preemption, in the purchase of public lands, may be permitted to make payments for said lands within the times heretofore prescribed by law, or prompt payment, at the option of the person holding such pre-emption right; the other praying that the right of pre-emption, in the purchase of public lands, may be extended to certain settlers therein prescribed; which memorials were referred to the Committee on Public Lands.

On motion of Mr. WHITMAN, a committee was appointed to inquire into the expediency of reviving and continuing in force, for a limited time, so much of an act, the provisions of which partially expired on the 1st day of November, 1819, entitled "An act regulating the currency within the United States, of the gold coins of Great Britain, France, Portugal, and Spain, and the crowns of France, and five franc pieces," as relates to the gold coins of these countries; and Mr. WAITMAN, Mr. SILSBEE, Mr. STREET, Mr. ROGERS, and Mr. LOWNDES, were appointed the said committee.

Mr. TRACY submitted the following resolution, which was read, and ordered to lie on the table one day for consideration:

Resolved, That the Secretary of War be directed to transmit to this House a statement, showing the amount and value of goods (estimated at cost) on hand, by the last return, at the different Indian trading houses, and at the depot in Georgetown, designating the amount at each place.

Mr. COBB submitted for consideration the following resolution:

Resolved, That the Committee on Naval Affairs be instructed to inquire into the expediency of limiting by law the number of able seamen, ordinary seamen, and boys, to be annually employed in the service of the United States; and also into the expediency of reducing the number now in actual service.

Resolved, That the Committee on Revolutionary Pensions be instructed to inquire into the expediency of reducing the pensions now allowed under the acts of Congress, to certain persons in the land and naval service of the United States, on continental establishment, during the Revolutionary war: [so that hereafter the pension allowed to each officer shall be twelve dollars per month, and to the privates five dollars per month.]

The first of these resolutions was agreed to without a division.

The second met with great objection; in consequence of which Mr. COBB modified it so as to make the inquiry general, by erasing the words in brackets.

On the resolution thus modified, there were ayes 53, noes 59. So the resolution was not agreed to.

Mr. ARCHER, of Virginia, rose and said that, as,

823   **HISTORY OF CONGRESS.**   824

H. of R.   *Reduction of the Army.*   JANUARY, 1821.

by the notice given yesterday,* by a gentleman from Massachusetts, the condition was realized upon which alone, according to his former declaration, he should refrain from calling up his motion, he should not repeat that call until after Monday next, the day named by the gentleman from Massachusetts for calling up his resolution.

Mr. JACKSON submitted for consideration the following resolution :

Resolved, That the Committee on the Post Office and Post Roads be instructed to inquire into the expediency of authorizing contractors for transporting the United States' mail to frank way-letters addressed to their mail carriers.

The question being taken on agreeing thereto, without remark, it was decided in the negative without a division.

REDUCTION OF THE ARMY.

The House having again resolved itself into a Committee of the Whole on the state of the Union, the consideration of the bill for the reduction of the Military Peace Establishment was resumed.

Mr. CANNON said, the subject under discussion was one of great importance, as it involved in its consideration, either directly or indirectly, the policy and principles of our Government, which, he supposed it would be granted on all sides, was formed by the people for their own safety and benefit; therefore, it never could have been intended by those engaged in its original formation, to elevate too high those officers who were or might be at any time engaged in its administration, its armies, or any where else; nor did he believe it was intended to depress the people who bear all its burdens too low; and while he thought a sufficient compensation ought at all times to be allowed those we retain in our employment, we should at the same time be guarded against paying them too high. Either of the extremes should be avoided. In this, as in other cases of a similar nature, there is a medium which it is proper we should observe.

This Government, we must recollect, does not yet belong to those engaged in its administration, or those employed in its army, or any where else; nor ought it to be administered for their exclusive benefit, but with a view to the general good of the community at large. When administered with that view it had been, and he had no doubt ever would continue to be considered a great blessing, by all who enjoy its benefits. Yet should a change take place, and it should be administered with different views, to gratify the thirst for power or ambition of those to whom power is given, it may assume a very different character in the estimation of the world.

He said it would be found, by reference to the Constitution, that to the different departments of Government it has given certain powers, and to

this body certain powers also, which, if properly exercised, would at all times be found to be amply sufficient to control the great measures of policy of this nation; and this power he believed, it was the duty of the House of Representatives independently to exercise. But the question now is, how are we to do this? He agreed with the gentlemen who opposed 'the reduction of the Army, that, while acting under this power, amongst other things it is the duty of Congress to prepare for war ; also, that this preparation should be made during a state of peace. But he differed with them as regards the manner in which we are to make this important and necessary preparation. They contend that we must prepare for war by keeping up a large regular army during a state of peace. I contend that we should prepare for war by arming, organizing, and diffusing military science among the great body of the people—the militia.

To which of these kinds of force, then, shall we turn our attention for safety and protection when war comes? For it will be conceded on all sides that we are now enjoying a state of profound peace, without the least prospect of war from any quarter whatever. Yet, in one way or the other, we must be prepared for war. Between the two modes of preparation that have been alluded to, it seemed to him no one with a knowledge of the principles and nature of our Government could hesitate. Our attention has been drawn, with great force and ingenuity, to the regular Army, by the Secretary of War, whose report contains a very able argument on this important question, which he would presently notice more fully. It had, however, fell very far short of convincing him that our main reliance for defence, in time of war, should be on a regular army in preference to the militia. This was a doctrine in which he could not be made to believe. He, however, here took occasion to say, that no financial difficulties or deficiency in the revenues of the country had, in the language of the gentleman from Georgia, (Mr. COBB,) "forced" him into the opinions he now entertained on this subject; they were opinions he had always entertained, and had indicated them to the House on more than one occasion since the termination of the late war. The question was not, not had it ever been with him, how large a regular army can we support during peace? The true question, he thought, was, what is the smallest number of a regular army that can be made to answer the purposes of the country in a state of peace? for we all know that any army that can be maintained in peace will not answer our purposes in time of war. He thought, then, that a number sufficient to take care of the public arms and munitions of war, when deposited in as few forts as was practicable, and convenient for distribution in the event of war taking place, was the proper number to be retained in service in peace, and he had no doubt but that duty might be performed by a much smaller number than that proposed by the bill under discussion. He thought we had, in some degree, been led into an error by the prosperity of the Treasury immediately after the late war. We have not had a proper regard

* This reference is to a notice, yesterday given by Mr. EUSTIS, that on Monday next he should move for the consideration of his resolution for the admission of Missouri into the Union, conditionally that she expunge from her constitution the clause concerning free people of color.

(in fixing the Military Establishments of our country, consisting of our Army, Navy, and military fortifications) to such times as we now experience; he believed we ought to endeavor to guard against fluctuations in public opinion, in regard to those establishments. This, he thought, could be done to a considerable extent, by limiting those expenditures in the same way as though the money appropriated was taken directly from the people by taxes.

Had this been done heretofore it would have prevented us from running into many useless expenditures. The whole expenses of Government, especially during peace, should be regulated by the principle he had just laid down; then we should not be making so many changes in our policy; for, as long as the people retain their attachment to the Government, they will willingly contribute as much as is really and indispensably necessary for its support either during a state of peace or war. It has been contended that we must not reduce the Army because the situation of the officers disbanded would be worse than at present; but, he said, it must be remembered that the Government has the right to call into its service the whole population of the country should it become necessary; it also had the right to dismiss from service whenever it was thought that their services could be dispensed with; this was done with privates, and he could see no reason why it should not be done also with officers. Whether their condition will be made better or worse by their being dismissed from service, he thought was not a proper inquiry; for his part, he said, he would suppose, until the contrary should appear, that those who had received so much of the favor of the Government as to be made officers, and retained so long on the Peace Establishment, possessed as much patriotism as the common people of the country, who had never murmured at being disbanded from your service, but rejoiced that the situation of the country was such as to require their services no longer; and such, he thought, must be the feelings of the patriotic officer of the regular army, on being dismissed from service; he would, like the honest and patriotic citizen, rejoice that the condition of his country was such as to enable the Government to dispense with his services; though, should there be found some to complain, yet we should look to the great interest of the country in preference to the few, or, indeed, the many, that are officers, or holding appointments. In the view he had here taken of the subject of reducing the Army, he begged leave to state that his opinions were not influenced by any feelings or motives of personal dislike, or personal favor, or partiality, toward any individual holding a commission in it; or any individual in any way employed in the administration of our Government. Such feelings and such motives he might claim the right to indulge in private life; but he denied himself the right to indulge or be influenced by them in public life. He was unconscious of the influence of any such feelings on any part of his course in public; and he hoped he always should remain so while acting, not only as the representative of a part of the people of the

State he had the honor to reside in, but as the representative, also, of the whole people of the United States. He trusted his opinions had, at all times, and on all subjects, whether correct or incorrect, been influenced by higher and better motives; for he, at least, endeavored to look while acting as a statesman to the happiness and prosperity of his country; and, while he did not profess to have less sensibility in regard to reflections that were made on his public conduct than other men; yet, neither the humorous play of newspaper scribblers or editors, their satire, nor the severest censure that can be vented by their spleen, ever has, and, he hoped, never would, prevent him from the attempt, at least, to discharge what he might believe to be his duty, on this floor or elsewhere.

He said, the gentleman from Georgia (Mr. Cuthbert) had called our attention to the report of the Secretary of War; and says, the arguments contained in it have not been met or answered by the gentleman from North Carolina, (Mr. Williams,) that the Secretary looks to a state of war, while the gentleman from North Carolina looked to a state of peace; and the gentleman from Maryland, (Mr. Smith,) has told us that this report contains sound political principles. [The gentleman from Maryland explained.] He assured the gentleman from Maryland, he felt no wish to misunderstand him, and he was glad now to find the gentleman and himself did not differ so widely as he had supposed However, he said, he thought it necessary to examine some of the doctrines contained in the report. The Secretary of War has told us that, "however remote our situation from the great ' Powers of the world, and however pacific our ' policy, we are, notwithstanding, liable to be in- ' volved in war; and to resist, with success, its ca- ' lamities and dangers, a standing army in peace, in ' the present improved state of the military science, ' is an indispensable preparation. The opposite ' opinion cannot be adopted without putting to haz- ' ard the independence and safety of the country." Now, sir, said Mr. C., I would be as far from doing any thing that would put to hazard the independence of my country as the Secretary of War, or as any other individual in the community, but, that a standing army is indispensably necessary for the safety of the country, I cannot agree. At the same time I am willing to retain as much of this army, in time of peace, as is necessary to occupy as many of our forts or garrisons as may be necessary to take care of our public arms and munitions of war. But I would not look to this army to preserve the independence of our country; for this, sir, I shall look to the great body of the people, the militia. I consider this to be the only safe reliance for the preserving of our liberties. Again, the Secretary of War, speaking of the organization of the army, &c., has told us, "it is thus only that we can be ' in a condition to meet the first shocks of hostilities ' with unyielding firmness, and to press on an enemy ' while our resources are yet unexhausted." He thought the experience of the late war had proved that a regular army could not be so fully relied on in the first outset of a war; for, in the commencement of the last war this kind of force had

by the notice given yesterday,* by a gentleman from Massachusetts, the condition was realized upon which alone, according to his former declaration, he should refrain from calling up his motion, he should not repeat that call until after Monday next, the day named by the gentleman from Massachusetts for calling up his resolution.

Mr. JACKSON submitted for consideration the following resolution :

Resolved, That the Committee on the Post Office and Post Roads be instructed to inquire into the expediency of authorizing contractors for transporting the United States' mail to frank way-letters addressed to their mail carriers.

The question being taken on agreeing thereto, without remark, it was decided in the negative without a division.

REDUCTION OF THE ARMY.

The House having again resolved itself into a Committee of the Whole on the state of the Union, the consideration of the bill for the reduction of the Military Peace Establishment was resumed.

Mr. CANNON said, the subject under discussion was one of great importance, as it involved in its consideration, either directly or indirectly, the policy and principles of our Government, which, he supposed it would be granted on all sides, was formed by the people for their own safety and benefit ; therefore, it never could have been intended by those engaged in its original formation, to elevate too high those officers who were or might be at any time engaged in its administration, its armies, or any where else ; nor did he believe it was intended to depress the people who bear all its burdens too low ; and while he thought a sufficient compensation ought at all times to be allowed those we retain in our employment, we should at the same time be guarded against paying them too high. Either of the extremes should be avoided. In this, as in other cases of a similar nature, there is a medium which it is proper we should observe.

This Government, we must recollect, does not yet belong to those engaged in its administration, or those employed in its army, or any where else ; nor ought it to be administered for their exclusive benefit, but with a view to the general good of the community at large. When administered with that view it had been, and he had no doubt ever would continue to be considered a great blessing, by all who enjoy its benefits. Yet should a change take place, and it should be administered with different views, to gratify the thirst for power or ambition of those to whom power is given, it may assume a very different character in the estimation of the world.

He said it would be found, by reference to the Constitution, that, to the different departments of Government it has given certain powers, and to

* This reference is to a notice, yesterday given by Mr. EUSTIS, that on Monday next he should move for the consideration of his resolution for the admission of Missouri into the Union, conditionally that she expunge from her constitution the clause concerning free people of color.

this body certain powers also, which, if properly exercised, would at all times be found to be amply sufficient to control the great measures of policy of this nation ; and this power he believed, it was the duty of the House of Representatives independently to exercise. But the question now is, how are we to do this ? He agreed with the gentlemen who opposed 'the reduction of the Army, that, while acting under this power, amongst other things it is the duty of Congress to prepare for war ; also, that this preparation should be made during a state of peace. But he differed with them as regards the manner in which we are to make this important and necessary preparation. They contend that we must prepare for war by keeping up a large regular army during a state of peace. I contend that we should prepare for war by arming, organizing, and diffusing military science among the great body of the people—the militia.

To which of these kinds of force, then, shall we turn our attention for safety and protection when war comes? For it will be conceded on all sides that we are now enjoying a state of profound peace, without the least prospect of war from any quarter whatever. Yet, in one way or the other, we must be prepared for war. Between the two modes of preparation that have been alluded to, it seemed to him no one with a knowledge of the principles and nature of our Government could hesitate. Our attention has been drawn, with great force and ingenuity, to the regular Army, by the Secretary of War, whose report contains a very able argument on this important question, which he would presently notice more fully. It had, however, fell very far short of convincing him that our main reliance for defence, in time of war, should be on a regular army in preference to the militia. This was a doctrine in which he could not be made to believe. He, however, here took occasion to say, that no financial difficulties or deficiency in the revenues of the country had, in the language of the gentleman from Georgia, (Mr. COBB,) "forced" him into the opinions he now entertained on this subject ; they were opinions he had always entertained, and had indicated them to the House on more than one occasion since the termination of the late war. The question was not, nor had it ever been with him, how large a regular army can we support during peace ? The true question, he thought, was, what is the smallest number of a regular army that can be made to answer the purposes of the country in a state of peace? for we all know that any army that can be maintained in peace will not answer our purposes in time of war. He thought, then, that a number sufficient to take care of the public arms and munitions of war, when deposited in as few forts as was practicable, and convenient for distribution in the event of war taking place, was the proper number to be retained in service in peace, and he had no doubt but that duty might be performed by a much smaller number than that proposed by the bill under discussion. He thought we had, in some degree, been led into an error by the prosperity of the Treasury immediately after the late war. We have not had a proper regard (in fixing the Military Establishments of our country, consisting of our Army, Navy, and military fortifications) to such times as we now experience; he believed we ought to endeavor to guard against fluctuations in public opinion, in regard to those establishments. This, he thought, could be done to a considerable extent, by limiting those expenditures in the same way as though the money appropriated was taken directly from the people by taxes.

Had this been done heretofore it would have prevented us from running into many useless expenditures. The whole expenses of Government, especially during peace, should be regulated by the principle he had just laid down; then we should not be making so many changes in our policy; for, as long as the people retain their attachment to the Government, they will willingly contribute as much as is really and indispensably necessary for its support either during a state of peace or war. It has been contended that we must not reduce the Army because the situation of the officers disbanded would be worse than at present; but, he said, it must be remembered that the Government has the right to call into its service the whole population of the country should it become necessary; it also had the right to dismiss from service whenever it was thought that their services could be dispensed with; this was done with privates, and he could see no reason why it should not be done also with officers. Whether their condition will be made better or worse by their being dismissed from service, he thought was not a proper inquiry; for his part, he said, he would suppose, until the contrary should appear, that those who had received so much of the favor of the Government as to be made officers, and retained so long on the Peace Establishment, possessed as much patriotism as the common people of the country, who had never murmured at being disbanded from your service, but rejoiced that the situation of the country was such as to require their services no longer; and such, he thought, must be the feelings of the patriotic officer of the regular army, on being dismissed from service; he would, like the honest and patriotic citizen, rejoice that the condition of his country was such as to enable the Government to dispense with his services; though, should there be found some to complain, yet we should look to the great interest of the country in preference to the few, or, indeed, the many, that are officers, or holding appointments. In the view he had here taken of the subject of reducing the Army, he begged leave to state that his opinions were not influenced by any feelings or motives of personal dislike, or personal favor, or partiality, toward any individual holding a commission in it; or any individual in any way employed in the administration of our Government. Such feelings and such motives he might claim the right to indulge in private life; but he denied himself the right to indulge or be influenced by them in public life. He was unconscious of the influence of any such feelings on any part of his course in public; and he hoped he always should remain so while acting, not only as the representative of a part of the people of the State he had the honor to reside in, but as the representative, also, of the whole people of the United States. He trusted his opinions had, at all times, and on all subjects, whether correct or incorrect, been influenced by higher and better motives; for he, at least, endeavored to look while acting as a statesman to the happiness and prosperity of his country; and, while he did not profess to have less sensibility in regard to reflections that were made on his public conduct than other men; yet, neither the humorous play of newspaper scribblers or editors, their satire, nor the severest censure that can be vented by their spleen, ever has, and, he hoped, never would, prevent him from the attempt, at least, to discharge what he might believe to be his duty, on this floor or elsewhere.

He said, the gentleman from Georgia (Mr. CUTHBERT) had called our attention to the report of the Secretary of War; and says, the arguments contained in it have not been met or answered by the gentleman from North Carolina, (Mr. WILLIAMS,) that the Secretary looks to a state of war, while the gentleman from North Carolina looked to a state of peace; and the gentleman from Maryland, (Mr. SMITH,) has told us that this report contains sound political principles. [The gentleman from Maryland explained.] He assured the gentleman from Maryland, he felt no wish to misunderstand him, and he was glad now to find the gentleman and himself did not differ so widely as he had supposed However, he said, he thought it necessary to examine some of the doctrines contained in the report. The Secretary of War has told us that, "however remote our situation from the great 'Powers of the world, and however pacific our 'policy, we are, notwithstanding, liable to be in- 'volved in war; and to resist, with success, its ca- 'lamities and dangers, a standing army in peace, in 'the present improved state of the military science, 'is an indispensable preparation. The opposite 'opinion cannot be adopted without putting to haz- 'ard the independence and safety of the country." Now, sir, said Mr. C., I would be as far from doing any thing that would put to hazard the independence of my country as the Secretary of War, or as any other individual in the community, but, that a standing army is indispensably necessary for the safety of the country, I cannot agree. At the same time I am willing to retain as much of this army, in time of peace, as is necessary to occupy as many of our forts or garrisons as may be necessary to take care of our public arms and munitions of war. But I would not look to this army to preserve the independence of our country; for this, sir, I shall look to the great body of the people, the militia. I consider this to be the only safe reliance for the preserving of our liberties. Again, the Secretary of War, speaking of the organization of the army, &c., has told us, " it is thus only that we can be 'in a condition to meet the first shocks of hostilities 'with unyielding firmness, and to press on an enemy 'while our resources are yet unexhausted." He thought the experience of the late war had proved that a regular army could not be so fully relied on in the first outset of a war; for, in the commencement of the last war this kind of force had been relied on to no good purpose. We were not successful until the citizens of the country were called into action. We are also told, from the same source, that, "to give to the officers of the 'army the necessary skill and acquirements, the 'Military Academy is an invaluable part of our 'establishment; but that alone will be inadequate." The conclusion of this sentence I have no doubt is correct. It will be inadequate to fill your army with military science. I am, however, opposed to maintaining this Military Academy at public expense, because it is repugnant to every principle of equality, and fixes a system of favoritism contrary to the principle of a free Government. He should not, however, discuss the merits of this institution now, as he intended to say more about it at some future time. Again, we are told by the Secretary of War, that "the number of resignations has been 'very great, of which, many are among the most 'valuable officers. Should the number of Gene-'rals be reduced, the motive for entering or con-'tinuing in service must also be greatly reduced : 'for, like the high prizes in a lottery, though they can 'be obtained by a few only, yet they operate on all 'those who adventure." Here it seems to be rather admitted that it is not patriotism that retains these officers in your service, but rather the hope and prospect of future promotion. Again, we are told, that "no Government can, in the present improved 'state of military science, neglect with impunity 'to instruct a sufficient number of its citizens in 'a science indispensable to its independence and 'safety." It seems, said Mr. C., from the whole of this report, that our attention is directed to the regular army for the safety of our independence and the protection of our liberties. He said, for his own part, he could not hold with such doctrine, let it come from whatever quarter it might ; but when such doctrines were urged upon the House from such a source, and with so much force and ability, he confessed he almost felt alarmed for the liberties of his country. We must not make the regular Army our principal reliance. Our Army and Navy, with all our extensive fortifications, cannot be relied on.

It is the great body of the American people, the militia, you must and ought to rely on, and it is to them you should extend this military science that is recommended by the Secretary of War; it is to them we must look in the hour of danger, and it is to them we should now turn our attention, in time of peace, to relieve them from unnecessary burdens, and teach them this necessary science of war; for, so long as the Government shall lean on any regular army that may be kept in peace, for safety and protection in war, they will be leaning on a broken staff. The strength of our nation, as I have said on a former occasion, and will repeat again, is in the great body of the people, and their attachment to the Government; and he had no doubt it would be found that, in the same proportion that our attention is drawn to the improvement of a regular army, as a means of defence, in the same proportion will the militia and their improvement be neglected.

Mr. C. said he was glad to find that the gentle-man from Maryland (Mr. SMITH) was now willing to dispense with the recruiting service, though he much regretted that that gentleman had not consented to put a stop to this useless expenditure of public money sooner. During the last session he had endeavored to put a stop to the business of recruiting. It would be recollected by the House he had made a motion to strike out of the appropriation bill the $21,000 that were appropriated for that purpose, and he had no doubt, if he had been supported by the gentleman from Maryland, he would have succeeded in preventing not only the expenditure of this amount of $21,000, but a much larger amount, which he found had been expended in that way. He believed an amount of more than $60,000 had been expended, during the last year, in the recruiting service. This whole amount would have been saved, provided the House had refused any appropriation.

The gentleman from Maryland, he said, had told us that he is in favor of economy, so far as we can go without endangering the public safety. For his part, he said, he could hardly see how the public safety could be endangered by economy, though he thought it might be endangered by a useless and extravagant expenditure of the public money. The same gentleman had also drawn our attention again to the Military Academy, from which he seems to think great benefits will result to us. He says it is there that military science *is* taught and diffused throughout the army, and, also, to the militia. As respects the army, he said, it was possible it might derive some benefit *from* this institution ; but, as respected the militia, he believed very little science was diffused amongst them from this Academy. If a plan was proposed, he said, to teach military science to the militia, he would give it his support; but an institution like the Military Academy, on which we are expending every year large sums of money to give an education to a favorite few, privileged and selected young men of wealthy families, he could not support. What are we doing by this institution but creating a privileged order, who are to take commands in your armies, to the exclusion of all others, no matter what their merits may be? Sir, said he, it is an aristocracy of the rankest order, and he called on the gentleman from Maryland, and all others who are the advocates of this institution, to show wherein it is not so. He said he was not opposed to military science, or any other useful science, but he was opposed to teaching a few favorites at the expense of the people of the United States. Nor did he believe this institution added much to the general science of the country. Indeed, he believed none was gained by it, for he had no doubt those that were receiving educations there were, with very few exceptions, the sons of men able to educate them at other institutions, and would do so if deprived of this institution, in which it not only costs them nothing, but gives them a large bounty to receive it. They are paid sixteen dollars per month, and allowed two rations per day, which makes it nearly equal to thirty dollars per month, which you are paying out of the Treasury of the United States

829   **HISTORY OF CONGRESS.**   830

JANUARY, 1821.   *Reduction of the Army.*   H. OF R.

to the boys of rich men, who may happen to be favorites of the Executive or Secretary of War. Is it not better, he asked, is it not more just, is it not more consistent with the principles of this Government, that this money should be appropriated to the instruction of your militia officers, and thereby diffuse this military science among the people generally, instead of confining it to a few peculiar favorites in this way? He thought none who could feel exempt from partiality could hesitate to say it was.

The gentleman from Virginia, (Mr. SMYTH,) in the course of the argument he had made against the reduction of the army, has said that the worst that can happen, in the event we do not reduce the army, is, that "we cannot discharge as much of the public debt as we otherwise could." Now, sir, said Mr. C., although I view a public debt as one of the greatest evils in any country, and although I believe it is the true policy of this country to pay off this public debt, and get rid of it, in these times of peace, in the shortest possible time, yet I believe there are other consequences that may result from a failure to reduce the army still worse, and more to be deprecated. He meant the establishment of the doctrines which had been urged with so much zeal (by the gentleman from Pennsylvania, Mr. BALDWIN, the gentleman from South Carolina, Mr. SIMKINS, and the gentleman from Georgia, Mr. CUTHBERT, as well as the gentleman from Virginia,) in favor of a regular army as the principal reliance of this country in time of war. He said he regretted to have seen these doctrines gaining ground in this country for years past. They have inched along, a little at a time, to avoid being noticed, until they have arrived, as it were, at the line which the gentlemen he had alluded to seem to have overleaped, and think themselves safely landed on the other side. In this way the same doctrines have been imposed on the people of other countries, and in other Governments; but he hoped the people of the United States had too much regard for their liberties to intrust their defence to any regular army. The gentleman from Virginia (Mr. SMYTH) thinks an important question is stirred, and one which he thought had long since been settled, "that militia would not answer the purposes of war." I admit this is an important question; but I will not admit that it has yet been settled in the way that it has been supposed to be settled by the gentleman from Virginia, and he hoped the time was far distant when it should be settled in that way. Indeed, he hoped that decision never would be made, and, if made in this House, never would be sanctioned by the people of this country. The gentleman had asked us, if we can intrust the defence of the country to the militia? I answer him in the affirmative. I know no other defence that can safely be relied on in this Government; they are our great bulwark of safety in time of war, in the hour of danger. They have proved themselves, on all occasions, to be the safest and surest reliance for the defence of our Constitution, and the liberties that are enjoyed under it. The gentleman from Virginia has said the regulars are "wil-

ling, disciplined men, and the militia unwilling and undisciplined men." This he would presently notice. He had also said, " the militia, during the Revolutionary war, had endangered the liberties of the country;" but that part of the gentleman's argument he would not notice, for he considered it fully and ably answered by the gentleman from Massachusetts, (Mr. EUSTIS.) Although the gentleman from Virginia had been pleased to say he had as much or more confidence in the militia of the State of Tennessee, as that of any other State, yet his remarks had reflected rather severely on the character of a large part of the people of that State. To this he felt it to be his duty to make a reply. The gentleman had referred to the book he held in his hand as authority to show the "re-'volt of the militia of Tennessee and volunteers ' of Coffee's brigade, returning as deserters, com-' mitting depredations in the country through which ' they passed, and discouraging others from enter-' ing the service."

Mr. C. said he begged leave distinctly to state to that gentleman, and to the House, that the book referred to (the Life of General Jackson) was not good authority on this subject with him; he was himself in the service at that time, and under General Coffee, as were also two of his colleagues, and he thought he had some knowledge of what took place during the time referred to by the gentleman from Virginia. He said he knew all the facts were not recorded in the book. It gave a very partial history of that part of the Creek war. It was true, he said, that difficulties had occurred during the first campaign of this war, between the commanding General and some of the different corps; but at least some of the difficulties were produced by the conduct of the commanding General himself, by attempting to force them to serve longer than the period for which they had engaged. This attempt, he said, was resisted by the volunteers, who demanded to be discharged at the expiration of the period for which they had engaged, which discharge was refused them, and threats made to them of being published as having disgracefully left the service, in order to force them to continue longer; and the result was what might always be expected from freemen acting under such circumstances. They resisted the despotic power attempted to be exercised over them, and did leave the service without the consent or discharge of the commanding General, who, under that state of feeling produced by being disappointed in the attempt to force them beyond the period they had engaged to serve, had the document published which had been read by the gentleman from Virginia, (in one of the newspapers of Nashville, perhaps the *Whig*.) But, Mr. C. said, he had himself (as the commanding officer of the regiment of volunteer mounted riflemen which was a part of General Coffee's brigade) felt it to be his duty to reply to the publication alluded to, so far as it related to the regiment he had commanded, and had, in the same newspaper, contradicted and refuted the aspersions that were thus attempted to be thrown on what he considered to be a meritorious, patriotic, and highly respectable class of the people of Tennessee. To which publication no reply was ever made in any public paper whatever, as he knew of or believed.

He said, this part of the volunteers of Tennessee were not ordered into service by the Governor of the State, General Jackson, or anybody else; they had precipitated themselves into the service on the spur of an occasion, on hearing of the horrid massacre at Fort Mims; and had furnished and equipped themselves, marched into the Indian country, and after destroying one of the enemy's towns, formed a junction with the army under the command of General Jackson. When these troops, who had thus entered the service with an express stipulation to serve not exceeding three months, were organized into a regiment, and fought in the first battle at Tallasachee, under the command of General Coffee, where a most decisive victory was obtained over the enemy; an event which he had no doubt had great influence on the whole army, and tended as much towards the elevation of Tennessee towards military fame as any other that had taken place during the whole war. They had again fought in the second battle of Talledega, where the conflict was equally severe, of much longer duration, and the victory equally decisive; in which, it is known by those who shared the dangers of that day, they acted a most conspicuous part. Although it does not appear in this history, which has been referred to, and although he did not hold it as good authority, he would read from it a part of the letters of General Jackson written in relation to those two battles. [Which he read.] He thought it was fair to meet the gentleman from Virginia with the same kind of authority he had used.

In the letters he had just read, General Jackson had spoken in high terms of the conduct of these volunteers, who he afterwards reflected on so unjustly. They had encountered hardships, difficulties, and dangers, that are unpleasant to think of, and he would not attempt a relation of them. They had rendered services to their country, which you have some reason to believe are duly appreciated by those persons who are best acquainted with them. He regretted that the remarks and references of the gentleman from Virginia (Mr. SMYTH) had made it his duty to say thus much in defence of this meritorious and respectable part of his fellow-citizens.

He said he would next proceed to notice the remarks of the gentleman from Virginia respecting the militia generally during the late war. The gentleman thinks he has shown, from high authority, that no reliance whatever can be placed on them. But, Mr. C. said, he thought he could show, from equally as high authority, that the utmost reliance could be placed in them when engaged in the defence of the country, and that they were equally as much entitled to the confidence of the nation as regular troops were, if not more so. In order to show this, he would call the attention of the Committee to the conduct of the militia in the defence of Fort Erie, by referring

to General Gaines's official despatch, dated Fort Erie, August, 1814. He says:

"Brigadier General Porter, commanding the New York and Pennsylvania volunteers, manifested a degree of vigilance and judgment in his preparatory arrangements, as well as military skill and courage in action, which proves him to be worthy the confidence of his country and the brave volunteers who fought under him. Of the volunteers, Captains Boughton and Harding, with their detachments, posted on the right, and attached to the line commanded by Captain E. Foster of the veteran 9th infantry, handsomely contributed to the repulse of the left column of the enemy under Colonel Scott."

Here, said Mr. C., we have the best authority that the militia of New York and Pennsylvania do not deserve the character which has been given to this species of force by the gentleman from Virginia. But let us see what has been said of them on other occasions. I will next see how they acted in the defence of Fort Meigs. In the official despatch of General Harrison, dated at Lower Sandusky, May 13, 1813, he says:

"That American regulars, although they were raw recruits, and such men as compose the Pittsburg, Pennsylvania, and Petersburg, Virginia, volunteers, should behave well, is not to be wondered at; but, that a company of militia should maintain its ground against four times its numbers, as did Captain Sebre's, of Kentucky, is truly astonishing. These brave fellows were at length, however, entirely surrounded by Indians, and would have been entirely cut off, but for the gallantry of Lieutenant Gwynne of the 19th regiment, who, with part of Captain Elliott's company, charged the enemy and released the Kentuckians."

Here, said Mr. C., we have evidence again from the highest authority, testifying to the gallantry and good conduct of these "unwilling and undisciplined" militia, who the gentleman from Virginia thinks cannot be trusted. But I will not stop here; I will call the gentleman's attention to another official despatch from the same officer, dated Camp Meigs, the 9th of May, 1813, where, in speaking of the defence of Fort Meigs again, he says:

"The two actions on this side the river on the 5th, were infinitely more important and more honorable to our arms than I had at first conceived. In the sortie made upon the left flank, Captain Waring's company of the 19th regiment, a detachment of twelve months' volunteers under Major Alexander, and three companies of Kentucky militia under Colonel Boswell, defeated at least double the number of Indians and British militia."

And again, in General Harrison's general order, dated at Fort Meigs, 9th of May, 1812, he says:

"Majors Ball of the dragoons, Lodwick, and Major Ritzer of the Ohio militia, and Major Johnson, of the Kentucky militia, rendered the most important services. To each of the above gentlemen, as well as to each captain, subaltern, non-commissioned officer and private of their respective commands, the General gives his thanks and expresses his warmest approbation. To Colonel Boswell and Major Fletcher, for their gallantry and good conduct in leading them in the charge made on the enemy, and to Captains Dudley, Simmon, and Metcalf, the subalterns, non-commissioned officers, and privates, for the distinguished valor with which they defeated the enemy. The General has in the order of the 6th instant expressed his sense of the conduct of the regular troops and volunteers which were engaged in the sorties on the left flank, but he omitted to mention Captain Sebre's company of Kentucky militia, whose gallantry was not surpassed by that of any of the companies which fought by their side. The Pittsburg Blues, led by Lieutenant McGee, in the illness of their gallant Captain, sustained the reputation which they had acquired at Messissancoy. The Petersburg volunteers and Lieutenant Drum's detachment discovered equal intrepidity."

Again, in the same, he says:

"It rarely occurs that a General has to complain of the excessive ardor of his men, yet such appears always to be the case, whenever the Kentucky militia are engaged ; it is indeed the source of all their misfortunes ; they appear to think that valor alone can accomplish any thing. The General is led to make this remark, from the conduct of Captain Dudley's company, of the —— regiment, as he has understood that that gallant officer was obliged to turn his espontoon against his own company, to oblige them to desist from the further pursuit of the enemy, in compliance with an order from the General."

Mr. C. said, this was further evidence of the good conduct, valor, and intrepidity, of the militia, he thought, sufficient to contradict the assertion of the gentleman from Virginia, that they were "unwilling, undisciplined, and no dependence ought to be placed in them." He thought the conduct of the militia generally, during the late war, had entitled them to the respect and confidence of the country, and had by no means deserved the very severe reflections of that gentleman. That they had sometimes had to encounter misfortunes, was true, but even under those unpleasant circumstances, it would be found they have borne them with a patience and fortitude becoming a patriot, and one who feels the strongest attachment to the principles of our free Government; as evidence of this, he would refer to the composure and good order of the Kentucky militia, after Winchester's defeat, on their return home. The historian says:

"These men are of the first respectability and intelligence, the flower of Kentucky, and they reflect the highest honor on the State from which they come and on their country. The easy gracefulness of manner, the manly independence of sentiment, the ardent love of country which they have displayed under all the reverses of fortune, entitle them to the first place in the hearts of their countrymen. Notwithstanding the unparalleled fatigues they have undergone in a dreary wilderness, the dangers to which they have been exposed, and the numerous privations they have suffered, still their noble spirits are unbroken, not a murmur has escaped their lips, no imbecile apprehensions are entertained by them for the safety of their brethren in arms, but their honest hearts spring forward with elastic hope, that their wrongs will be avenged, and that the day of retribution is at hand."

These are nothing but the common feelings and sentiments of a freeman and a patriot, and he would say a militiaman too, while under the re-

verses and misfortunes of defeat. Dangers are met by them willingly, and misfortune borne with composure, while thus engaged in the defence of their own rights and their own liberties. He said he could not leave this part of the subject without reminding the Committee of the very important services that had been rendered by the militia of the State of Kentucky, in the battle of the Thames, when led by the patriotic Shelby and the gallant Johnson. They obtained a victory of not much less importance than any other gained during the whole war. Here, again, he begged the gentleman from Virginia to recollect that the militia had put the most veteran regular forces of our enemy to flight. Six hundred and nine regulars were made prisoners in this battle; also, two colonels, four majors, and seventeen officers of the line, with twelve pieces of cannon and six thousand stand of arms. We have had another demonstration of the efficiency of the militia, of what freemen will do when their rights and liberties are assailed. Indeed, their conduct, during the late war, has shed an imperishable glory on the military character of our nation.

He would next call the attention of the Committee to the services rendered by the militia, in the defence of Baltimore, on the approach of the enemy. The historian tells us, here they were met by General Stricker, with his entire Baltimore brigade; except that he had only one company of the regiment of artillery. Again, he says, the men took deliberate aim, and the carnage was great; the invincibles dodging to the ground and crawling in a bending posture to avoid the militia, the men they were taught so much to despise. Again, he says, Major General Ross, who did not care if it rained militia, the incendiary of the Capitol, paid the forfeit of that act by his death. He was killed in the early part of th.· action, and there is reason to believe that two or three other officers high in command met the same fate. And, again, we are told by the same historian, that "never was the mortification of an invader 'more complete than that of our enemy. Beaten 'by militia and defeated by the fort, he went away 'in the worst possible humor, and a total loss that 'may amount to not less than eight hundred. 'men.' "

He would also beg leave to refer the Committee to the official despatch of his friend from Maryland, (Mr. SMITH,) who, much to his honor, had. acted so conspicuous a part in the affairs of that day, in order to show that the militia of the East have also done their duty, and have been an efficient force when it became necessary to defend the country. In the official despatch of General Smith to the Secretary of War, dated Headquarters, Baltimore, September 19, 1814, he says:

"General Stricker gallantly maintained his ground against a great superiority of numbers during the space of an hour and twenty minutes, when the regiment on his left (the 51st) giving way, he was under the necessity of retiring to the ground in his rear, where he had stationed one regiment as a reserve. He here formed his brigade; but the enemy not thinking it advisable to pursue, he, in compliance with previous arrangements, fell back, and took post on the left of my intrenchments and half a mile in advance of them. In this affair the citizen soldiers of Baltimore (with the exception of the 51st regiment) have maintained the reputation they so deservedly acquired at Bladensburg, and their brave and skilful leader has confirmed the confidence which we had all so justly placed in him. I take the liberty of referring you to his letter for the more particular mention of the individuals, who, new to warfare, have shown the coolness and valor of veterans, and who, by their conduct on this occasion, have given their country and their city an assurance of what may be expected from them when their services are again required. I cannot dismiss the subject without expressing the heartfelt satisfaction I experience in thus bearing testimony to the courage and good conduct of my fellow-townsmen."

Mr. C. said, the authority here given was the highest that could be given, and would not be doubted by any, from which it appears that the militia of Baltimore and Maryland were competent to their own defence against a regular force, and proves, beyond doubt, that militia are not that "unwilling and undisciplined" kind of force that the gentleman from Virginia seems to suppose. He said he had intended to call the attention of the Committee to a number of other official statements, all going to place, not only the militia of Baltimore city and Maryland on high ground, but also the militia of Pennsylvania and Virginia equally so. But he found, by doing so, he should consume too much of the time of the Committee, and he thought he had already produced sufficient evidence to vindicate the character of the militia of the East and North against what he considered the unjust reproaches of the gentleman from Virginia. He would next inquire how far the gentleman's description of the character of the militia would apply to the people of the West and South, and see whether they were there dragged into the service, "unwilling and undisciplined." What, he said, was the history of that country during this trying period? Why, sir, we are told by the historian (3d vol. Niles's Weekly Register, page 300) that a requisition on the State of Tennessee for her quota of troops had been made from the War Department for the protection and defence of the Southern frontier. The distance of the point to which they could be led, even under the destructive doctrines preached, (of not going out of the limits of the United States' territory,) was not less than 1,500 miles by water, and eight or nine hundred by land, through a wilderness, great part of which was only inhabited by wild beasts and savages. The day appointed for rendezvous was the 10th of December, at Nashville. The State of Tennessee is divided into East and West, the latter of which thirty-one years ago received the first impression of a white man's foot, is now represented by one Representative in Congress, and was called upon to furnish 1,500 men for its part of the quota. On the day appointed, although severely cold, and during a heavy fall of snow, the troops began to arrive, and, before 5 o'clock in the evening, 1,800 men had filed through Nashville, and pitched their tents in its vicinity.

Five companies more, who had not arrived, sent despatches to the commanding officer, apologizing for their absence, as they were on their march and would be there as soon as possible. The troops already arrived, with these five companies, are volunteers, and furnish five hundred more than those called for. So sudden was the impulse that public feeling had marched far beyond the requisite comforts of such an army. Inasmuch that there was not more than one blanket for three men, although the country was bound in icy chains of snowy winter. Such is the fruit of patriotism in the infant section of that infant State. While the efforts of faction on the Atlantic board are directed to the destruction of their liberties, those hardy sons of the West are bereaving themselves of the comforts of domestic life, to sustain a part of the highest value given by God to man, and recovered from tyranny by the toil and suffering of a glorious ancestry.

This shows with what alacrity the people of the West had entered the service of their country, not to repel any invasion about to be made near their own homes, but to repel the threatened invasion of a distant point of the Union. A number far beyond what was required of the militia, had voluntarily assembled, in the severest and most inclement season of the year. Did this, he asked, seem like being dragged into the service "unwillingly?" No, he said: it was the natural impulse given by a good government, in favor of its protection and defence, whenever its invasion is threatened. It is the liberty and safety the people enjoy under our free Government, that inspires those feelings of patriotic devotion we have so often and so eminently seen displayed by the people during the late war; and it is those feelings of devotion to the cause of liberty and free government, that nerves the arm of the patriot citizen soldier, the militiaman, which makes him superior to the mercenary slave, in the hour of battle. This, he said, had been demonstrated on more than one occasion during the late war. In support of this, he begged leave, in pursuance of the example set him by the gentleman from Virginia, to refer to General Jackson's letter dated, Camp, below New Orleans, 26th December 1814, in which he says: "The attack ' was made on the night of the 23d, since then ' both armies have remained near the battle ground ' making preparations for something more decisive. ' The enemy's force exceeds ours by double, and ' their loss was proportionally greater."

In his official despatch, dated the 27th December in the morning, he says, "My force at this ' time consists of parts of the 7th and 44th regi- ' ments, not exceeding six hundred, together with ' the city militia, part of General Coffee's brigade ' of mounted gunmen, and the detached militia from ' the western division of Tennessee, under the ' command of Major General Carroll."

In another part of the same despatch, speaking of the enemy's force, he says, "His forces, amount- ' ing at that time on land to about three thousand, ' extended half a mile on that river, and in the ' rear nearly to the wood."

In another part of the same despatch, he says,

"General Coffee's men, with their usual impetu-
' osity, rushed on the enemy's right, and entered
' their camp, while our right advanced with equal
' ardor. There can be but little doubt that we
' should have succeeded on that occasion, with our
' inferior force, in destroying or capturing the en-
' emy, had not a thick fog which arose about 8
' o'clock, occasioned some confusion among the
' different corps. Fearing the consequence, under
' this circumstance, of the further prosecution of a
' night attack with troops then acting together for
' the first time, I contented myself with lying on
' the field that night."

Again, he says, " in this affair the whole of the
' corps under my command deserve the greatest
' credit. The best compliment I can pa to Gen-
' eral Coffee and his brigade, is, to say they behaved
' as they have always done while under my com-
' mand." Again, sir, he remarks, that " Savery's
' volunteers manifested the greatest bravery, and
' the company of city riflemen, having penetrated
' into the midst of the enemy's camp, were sur-
' rounded, and fought their way out with the great-
' est heroism, bringing with them a number of
' prisoners."

He said that this also proved the practicability
of defending the country by militia. On this occasion the volunteer militia of Tennessee, under
the command of General Coffee, on the ever memorable night of the 23d, had attacked a British
regular force of more than double their number,
and defeated them, without the assistance of a regular force, and perhaps thereby the safety of the
city of New Orleans was preserved. Here again
was displayed an intrepidity, on the part of these
citizen soldiers of our country, which is not often
to be found recorded in the pages of history. This
gallant band were influenced by feelings of attachment for their country, that do not often animate
with the same zeal a regular army, and never are
found to exist under the old oppressive governments of the world.

Mr. C. said he had intended to call the attention
of the Committee to the official statements of all
the differents battles in which the militia had been
engaged, while defending New Orleans, but he
knew he would be trespassing too much on their
patience, though it would be found by referring to
them, as well as to the general order of the commanding General, after the different contests were
over, that on all the different corps of militia that
had been engaged, with one single exception, the
highest praise is bestowed. They had, he believed,
during the whole of the contest, proved themselves
to be equal to regulars, if not superior. The gentleman from Virginia, had referred to authorities
in support of the position he had taken against the
reduction of the army, and also in support of the
ground he had taken against the militia ; and he
thought it was proper in opposing the arguments
and doctrines which had been advanced by that
gentleman, to produce authorities also. This he
had done in order to rescue the people of his country, the militia, from the unjust reproaches that
were attempted to be heaped upon them. The
principal part of the authorities he had relied on

were official statements of the officers of the regular army, who, it was not to be supposed, could be
influenced by partiality for the militia in the smallest degree. However, he said, if the militia were
indeed that "unwilling and undisciplined" kind
of force that they were said to be by the gentleman from Virginia, and a reliance on them would
" endanger the liberties of his country," he should
also be in favor of a regular army, or some other
means of defence for the country. But he trusted
he had shown, or rather that the militia themselves
had shown, that they were fully competent to the
defence of the country during a state of war, even
in the present unimproved state of their organization and discipline ; to improve which the General
Government has never, as yet, expended a single
dollar. If in this situation they have shown themselves to be competent, how much more so would
they be by having even one half the amount expended to teach them military science, that has
been expended on the regular army since the late
war !

Mr. C. said, however invidious it was to make
comparisons between the militia force of the country and the regular army, he would beg leave to
call the attention of the Committee a few moments
to one or two authorities, in order to show that the
regular army had sometimes been unfortunate,
during the late war, as well as the militia. It
seems that the highest expectations had not been
realized by that kind of force, in defence of this
place, as we are informed by a part of the history
of that day. Speaking of the defence of the District of Columbia, the Common Council of Alexandria says : " The forts erected for the defence
' of the District, having been blown up by our
' own men, (United States' regular troops,) and
' abandoned, without resistance, the town of Alex-
' andria was left without the means of defence."
He did not mean to say they had acted incorrectly
in this case or any other, for he did not pretend to
know whether they had or not. But he hoped the
gentleman from Virginia would allow him, however, to refer to his own proclamation for authority
against the regular army, dated 12th November,
1812, and addressed to the men of New York.
He says:

" For many years you have seen your country oppressed with numerous wrongs. Your Government,
although above all others devoted to peace, has been
forced to draw the sword, and rely for redress of injuries on the valor of the American people. That
valor has been conspicuous, but the nation has been
unfortunate in the election of some of those who have
directed it. One army has been disgracefully surrendered and lost. Another has been sacrificed by a
precipitate attempt to pass over at the strongest point
of the enemy's lines, with most incompetent means.
The cause of these miscarriages is apparent. The
commanders were popular men, destitute alike of theory and experience in the art of war. In a few days
the troops under my command will plant the American standard in Canada. They are men accustomed
to obedience, silence, and steadiness. They will con-
quer or they will die."

Mr. C. said he had only called the attention of

the Committee to this proclamation, for the purpose of showing that the gentleman from Virginia himself had not at all times, and particularly at that time, entertained this high opinion of regular forces; for here he had made the severest reflections against them, and he thought the authority of the gentleman himself was entitled to great consideration. There were other circumstances which took place in the early part of the late war, that would go very far to show that the main reliance of this country ought never to be placed on a regular army; but he would not longer consume the time of the Committee by referring to them.

The gentleman from Virginia had told us that there were 1,600 regulars engaged in the defence of New Orleans. [Mr. SMYTH here explained by saying, including the naval force.] Mr. C. said the official letter of the commanding officer, which he had previously read, had said the regulars consisted of a part of two regiments, not exceeding in the whole six hundred; however, this did not include the naval force, nor would the admission of a larger regular force make the argument more favorable on his side; for although the gentleman from Virginia had said that if it had not been for the regular force employed there, the victory would not have been achieved, yet, said Mr. C., it unfortunately happens for him that facts are directly against him; for it will be recollected by all who are acquainted with the history and events of the great battle of the 8th of January, that the regulars gave way in the contest, and the part of the line intrusted to their defence was taken possession of by the British forces. They were reinforced by the militia of New Orleans, and the bastions retaken after considerable loss on the part of the enemy at that point. Here it will be seen that the battle, so far as the regular forces were concerned, was lost; while the militia of Tennessee and Kentucky, who defended the other part of the line, encountered a superior force with firmness, not a single man of them was known to give way; therefore, instead of any argument being drawn from this great event in favor of the position of the gentleman from Virginia, it is directly against him. Indeed, if the whole of the events of the late war were taken into view, he believed it would be found that the militia forces that had been called into action had been equally as efficient as the regular forces were. Mr. C. said he had not taken the ground, nor did he intend to say, that the militia were a more efficient force in proportion to numbers than regulars. It was enough for him to show they were as much so; he admitted militia had sometimes been unfortunate, and so had regular troops; they had sometimes wanted bravery and firmness, and so had regulars; at other times the militia had distinguished themselves for their gallant exploits, and so had the regular army. But it must be admitted on all sides, that the defence and preservation of the liberties of the people of this country cannot be entirely intrusted to a regular army, of any size whatever. Then why not, he asked, withdraw from it a part of the public expenditure, and apply it to the discipline of the great body of the

people, the militia, on whom at last you are obliged to depend in time of war? The gentleman from Pennsylvania, (Mr. BALDWIN,) who opposed the reduction of the army with so much zeal, has called on us, who advocate this measure, to go more minutely into detail, and show all the different posts and places where there are too many men. Sir, I shall not do this; it is the business of those who wish to retain these men in service, to show in what way they can employ them beneficially to the Government. This they have not done, nor did he believe it was in their power to show even the number proposed by the bill under discussion, could be usefully and beneficially employed during a state of peace; and until this was shown, he should take it for granted that it was not in the power of the opponents of the bill to do so.

Mr. C. said he himself believed that a much smaller number than was proposed by the bill would be sufficient to take care of the public arms and munitions of war during a state of peace; and he did not think it indispensably necessary that more should be retained than would answer this purpose, for it was all the service they could render during a state of peace; and when war comes the people must fight their own battles. He could not agree to the doctrine of the gentlemen from Pennsylvania and Virginia, and others who oppose this bill, that a freeman shall depend upon a slave to protect him in the enjoyment of his liberties. This was the doctrine of despots and tyrants. He well knew that in the same proportion that the reliance of the Government of the United States increased in favor of a standing army, as a means of defence in time of war, so in the same proportion would the improvement of the militia be neglected, until they would ultimately be lost sight of altogether. Such, he thought, was now, and had been, the tendency of the Government for many years past. That there was an increasing predilection in favor of this doctrine of standing armies in time of peace, he thought, must be obvious to the most common observer—a doctrine repugnant to the very principle of liberty, and contrary to his most sober judgment; a doctrine which he hoped would now be stopped in its progress, for he feared if it survived the present conflict, it would be in vain hereafter to attempt to resist, and if it prevails will be fatal to the boasted liberty and happiness of the people.

If any thing further should be required to prove that a standing army was not calculated to answer the purposes of this Government, it would be found in the history of what was called the Seminole war. It would be recollected, when this petty war took place, we had a regular standing army of ten thousand at least, but according to the calculation of some gentlemen, an army of twelve or thirteen thousand; and with this army of ten thousand, you could not subdue two or three hundred deluded savages and runaway negroes, who had collected in the wilds of the South, without calling on the militia of the States of Georgia and Tennessee to assist you. This would always be the case with any regular force so widely dispersed. You never can with facility concentrate them at any one point; therefore must always rely on the inhabitants of the most adjacent States to repel invasions. He did not entertain fears that the liberties of the people of this country were about to be subverted immediately by this army of ten or twelve thousand, though, if such doctrines as had been advanced were indulged, we should soon come to that period. The influence of the present military establishment on this body had been seen on almost every subject that had any relation to the army. It had been known to have an influence in the councils of every nation in existence during a state of peace; and that influence was always found to be in proportion to the magnitude of the army. He said, Spain, Italy, and other European countries, had recently given a lesson on the subject of what changes regular standing armies can make in Governments.

Mr. C. said he believed the history of nations furnished us abundant proof, that, as a nation advances in the habit of keeping up standing armies in time of peace, in the same degree are the principles of free government abandoned, until liberty and equality are no longer known to exist; therefore, he felt it to be his duty to guard against the encroachment of such doctrines, however gradually they may be made. He said he had always believed the people were competent to the formation of their own government, and also to the defence of it after it was formed. But let us consider for a moment what this doctrine in favor of standing armies and the reproaches against the militia are calculated to lead us to. Why, sir, they say the free people of the United States are not competent to their own defence. This is the doctrine which has been contended for; and if it obtains the sanction of this House, it is to be considered as settled. They then will have gained the first step towards the great object, and that, too, by far the most important; for they can go but one step further, and that is, to settle the doctrine that the people of the United States are not competent to self-government. The one is just as reasonable as the other; and, let me tell you, sir, that when this first step is gained, the other will shortly follow. He said he hoped such doctrines as these would never prevail in any department of the Government, and, if it should, that they would never meet the sanction of this House, nor the people; and then, indeed, would vanish the last vestige of human liberty.

He said he had not gone through the whole of the arguments he had intended to offer to the Committee; but he had consumed much more time than he had intended; he would therefore decline any further remarks at that time on the subject.

FRIDAY, January 12.

AMENDMENT OF THE JOURNAL.

The first entry in the Journal of yesterday was read, in the following words:

"Mr. Lowndes presented three memorials of the Senate and House of Representatives of Missouri—

one praying that the purchasers of public lands may be permitted to apply the payments already made to such of their entries as the said payments will cover, at two dollars per acre, relinquishing the residue of the land to the United States—another praying that persons entitled to the right of pre-emption in the purchase of public lands, may be permitted to make payment for said lands within the times heretofore prescribed by law, or prompt payment, at the option of the persons holding such pre-emption right—the other, praying that the right of pre-emption in the purchase of public lands may be extended to certain settlers therein described; which memorials were referred to the Committee on the Public Lands."

Mr. ROBERTSON, conceiving that Missouri had, in this entry, been styled a territory, objected to her being so styled; but, on examination, finding it was not so, waived a motion he was about to have made to amend it.

Mr. COBB, however, adverting to the terms of the memorial, said, that it appeared to be from the Senate and House of Representatives of "the State of" Missouri, though not so stated in the Journal. Mr. C. moved to amend the Journal in this particular, by inserting the words "the State of," before the word "Missouri."

When the reporter entered the Hall, Mr. BARBOUR was up, arguing in favor of an amendment, which would make the Journal conform to the fact, which, he contended, it did not as it now stood.

Mr. ANDERSON expressed his opinion that the Journal, as it stood, expressed truly the fact of a memorial being presented from Missouri. Though it might have been more distinctly stated, yet the omission of the words proposed to be inserted did not take from Missouri the character of a State, it being a frequent mode of expression in regard to other States, to speak of them without the prefix of "the State of." Mr. A. also suggested a wish that his friends should not press the objection they had set up, by way of obtaining a decision of the Missouri question, on a motion to amend the Journal.

Mr. ROBERTSON made some remarks in favor of the motion. The memorials, he said, professed to be from the Legislature of the State of Missouri. If Missouri had not been considered as a State, of course the memorials in that shape would not have been received. Having been received as memorials from the State, why should not the fact be correctly stated on the Journal?

Mr. McLANE, of Delaware, was in favor of the proposed amendment, on the general ground that, if it took place, the Journal would correspond more precisely with the fact, than in its present shape.

Mr. WARFIELD said, that a decision in favor of the proposed amendment would not express the sense of the House, either in one way or the other. Conceiving that the entry on the Journal, as it now stood, was an entry of that description which would explain sufficiently what was the nature of the memorial, he was opposed to the amendment.

Mr. SMITH, of Maryland, proposed, in order to obviate the difficulty, to insert in the Journal the words "purporting to be," a memorial from the

Senate and House of Representatives of the State of Missouri, &c.

Mr. COOK was opposed to the proposed amendment. If made, he said, it would decide no principle. If Missouri was not a State, calling her so would not make her so. It would be an equally appropriate amendment to style her the Republic of Missouri, as her Convention had styled her in the preamble to the constitution which had been formed for her government, &c.

Mr. COBB, in reply to a wish which had been expressed, that he would withdraw his motion, said, that he could not consent to do it. He wished the Journal to conform, as it ought, to the fact. Three memorials had been presented from a body, organized under a constitution of government, formed by virtue of a law of Congress authorizing the people of Missouri to form a State government. In that shape having been presented, in that and in no other shape could the memorials have been received; and the Journal ought to state the fact as it occurred.

Mr. BALDWIN was sorry, he said, that any discussion should have arisen as to the description of any paper presented to the House in the shape of a memorial. It had been the uniform practice, in making up the Journal, to give to memorialists the name which they themselves assumed. By way of illustration, he referred to the memorial presented at the present session from persons styling themselves the National Institution for the protection of domestic industry, from the delegates of Agricultural Societies, from the delegates from various interests at Philadelphia, &c., all of which, without investigating the merits of the pretensions of the respective memorialists, had been announced in the Journal in their own language. We pay that respect to petitioners, said Mr. B., that we designate them as they choose to designate themselves. The annunciation on the Journal of their designations, was, properly, a mere recital of what they chose to call themselves. If the principle were now to be introduced, that every person or association of persons were to be held to prove that they really are what they profess to be, it would involve the House in endless difficulties. He was therefore in favor of the amendment proposed by Mr. COBB.

Mr. RANDOLPH, after a preliminary remark or two, not distinctly heard from the pressing of members round him, said, that he rose to introduce a precedent applicable to this occasion, which, he trusted, would be received with all the respect due to so high and transcendental authority. The conduct, said he, which this Government has to this instant pursued towards the State of Missouri, is sanctioned by the conduct which was pursued towards these States when colonies, by His Britannic Majesty and his faithful Lords and Commons in Parliament assembled. What was their language after our independence was declared? What was their conduct which led to the long and bloody war which terminated in the acknowledgment of our independence? The very language which we are holding, and the very conduct we are pursuing towards Missouri. The parallel, said Mr. R., runs on all fours. In our extreme tenderness for the rights and privileges of the colored citizens, we have already brought into jeopardy the rights and privileges of our white fellow-citizens as well as of those colored ones who are the objects of our solicitude. Mr. R. said he had intended to abstain, as he had until now abstained, from taking any part or lot in this affair. But when he saw the Congress of the United States pursuing a course of conduct in servile imitation of the British Parliament, he could no longer refrain. He would stake his salvation, he said, dear to him as that was, that, if the constitution of Missouri had contained an inhibition of slavery, the House would never have heard of the objection now raised to it; and, were he to engage in the discussion of it, he would take that ground. However that might be, he said, it was a more important matter that the Journals of this House should contain the truth. An honorable member behind him had uttered the sentiment, the other day, that it was proper that petitions to this House should contain the truth. It was of infinitely more importance, Mr. R. said, that the Journal should contain the truth; and he pronounced that the Journal for yesterday, in its present mutilated, mangled, and garbled state, did not speak the truth. It holds out that, said he, which we know to be false. And is it a mere matter of form that we should send out to the people, as the record of our proceedings, a paper which contains, on the face of it, a palpable and atrocious falsehood?

Mr. LITTLE called for the reading of the memorial; it was read in part, when Mr. L. expressed himself satisfied, and said he was sorry the Chair had departed from the uniform practice and regular rule in recording the proceedings of the House.

Mr. RHEA was in favor of the proposed amendment. It was the duty of the House, he thought, to see that facts were correctly stated on the Journal. This House had, in its public acts, styled Missouri a State; and why should she not be so called on the Journal? He read the caption of one of the memorials to show that it purported to be from the Senate and House of Representatives of the State of Missouri, in General Assembly, &c. The Journal, he said, ought to describe the memorial as it really was.

The question on Mr. COBB's motion was then taken, by yeas and nays, as follows:

YEAS—Messrs. Abbot, Alexander, Allen of Tennessee, Archer of Maryland, Archer of Virginia, Baldwin, Ball, Barbour, Bayly, Bloomfield, Brevard, Brown, Brush, Bryan, Burton, Burwell, Butler of Louisiana, Cannon, Cobb, Cocke, Crawford, Crowell, Culpeper, Cuthbert, Edwards of North Carolina, Eustis, Fisher, Floyd, Foot, Garnett, Gorham, Hackley, Hall of North Carolina, Hardin, Hill, Hooks, Jackson, Johnson, Jones of Virginia, Jones of Tennessee, Little, Livermore, Lowndes, McCoy, McCreary, McLane of Delaware, McLean of Kentucky, Meigs, Mercer, Metcalf, T. L. Moore, Neale, Nelson of Virginia, Newton, Parker of Virginia, Pinckney, Randolph, Rankin, Rhea, Robertson, Sawyer, Settle, Shaw, Simkins, Sloan, Smith of New Jersey, Smith of Maryland, A. Smyth of Virginia, Smith of North Carolina, Stevens, Terrell, Trimble, Tucker of Virginia, Walker, Williams of Virginia, and Williams of North Carolina—76.

Nays—Messrs. Adams, Allen of Massachusetts, Allen of New York, Anderson, Beecher, Boden, Buffum, Butler of New Hampshire, Campbell, Clagett, Clark, Cook, Crafts, Cushman, Dane, Darlington, Dennison, Dickinson, Eddy, Edwards of Connecticut, Fay, Fuller, Gross of New York, Gross of Pennsylvania, Guyon, Hall of New York, Hall of Delaware, Hemphill, Hendricks, Herrick, Hibshman, Hobart, Hostetter, Kendall, Kinsley, Lathrop, Lincoln, Maclay, McCullough, Mallary, Marchand, Monell, R. Moore, S. Moore, Morton, Moseley, Murray, Nelson of Massachusetts, Parker of Massachusetts, Patterson, Philson, Pitcher, Plumer, Rich, Richards, Richmond, Rogers, Ross, Russ, Sergeant, Silsbee, Southard, Storrs, Street, Strong of Vermont, Strong of New York, Tomlinson, Tracy, Udree, Upham, Van Rensselaer, Wallace, Warfield, Wendover, Whitman, and Wood—76.

The yeas and nays being equal in number, the Speaker declared his vote with the nays. So Mr. Cobb's motion was rejected.

On this result being declared—

Mr. Parker, of Virginia, rose. The vote which had just been taken, he said, was, with a few exceptions, of that geographical character which had marked the whole proceedings in regard to Missouri. For his own part, he said, he did not at first consider this question as involving any matter of principle; but, being a new member, he had referred to the Journal, and he found that, in all cases of memorials from States, they had been stated to be from States; and that the same uniformity of practice prevailed as to memorials from Territorial legislatures. He saw no reason why a deviation from this uniformity of practice should have occurred in this particular instance of Missouri, and not in any other. There was, he said, something in it—he did not say what it was—but he was for consistency, at all events, in the records of the Congress of the Union. He was for the records of this House speaking, in the words of the law, the truth, the whole truth, and nothing but the truth. Under this impression, as the House had refused to acknowledge Missouri to be a State, and as she must be a Territory if she be not a State, he moved to insert in the Journal, before the word "Missouri," the words "the Territory of."

Mr. Brush objected to this amendment, for reasons which he assigned at length. He was of opinion that Missouri was constitutionally and politically a State, and not a Territory. But, as it was the custom of this Government to give to its Territories a first and second grade of government, preparatory to their assuming the rank of a State of the Union, he did not see why it could not give to them a third, fourth, or fifth grade of government. He considered Missouri to be in a grade between territorial dependence and the condition of a member of the Union; which idea he illustrated by reference to the situation of the State of Vermont, before she adopted the Federal Constitution.

Mr. Edwards, of North Carolina, apprehended that this proposition would operate as a trap question, producing embarrassment without benefit, and expressed his hope that the mover would withdraw it.

Mr. Livermore made a few remarks to this effect; that the House ought to regard the substance and not the shadow; that the name was of no importance to the actual condition of Missouri. When the question should present itself in a proper form, he was ready to decide it; but it could not be affected, either in one way or the other, by the appellation which should be given to Missouri on the Journal of this House.

Mr. Mercer was gratified that this motion had been made. As this was the commencement of our intercourse with the people of Missouri he was desirous that every step of it should be marked. Mr. M. made some further remarks, in the course of which he expressed his regret that the course of the remarks of the gentleman from Illinois, (Mr. Cook,) had been, in his view, disrespectful to Missouri.

Mr. Cook disclaimed any intention to speak disrespectfully of the people of Missouri, whom, on the contrary, he said, he held in high respect; and he sincerely hoped that Missouri would be admitted into the Union, and soon.

Mr. Butler, of Louisiana, said, that, on inspecting the Journal, it appeared that the original entry in it corresponded with the caption of the memorial, in which the word *State* is employed. As the Journal now reads, moreover, in the part speaking of the public lands, the words "within the said State" had been erased in two instances, to avoid the word *State*, which made the whole entry absurd, inasmuch as the memorial is made to apply not to purchasers of land "within the said State," which words were erased, but to purchasers of land throughout the United States. Mr. B. said he would therefore ask whether the Clerk had undertaken to make these alterations.

The Speaker then stated from the chair, that it was the practice that the Journal should be written by the Clerk. The rules of the House made it the duty of the Speaker to "examine and correct the Journal before it is read." If, being so examined and corrected by the Speaker, it should not, in the opinion of any member, be correct, it was competent for any member to move to amend it, and for the House, should such be its pleasure, to direct it to be amended. In the present instance, the presiding officer had thought proper so to correct the Journal, as that it should not be taken either to affirm or deny that Missouri was a State, that being a question on which the House was greatly divided in opinion.

Mr. Trimble requested the Clerk to state the date of the petition, in order to show that the petition was not posterior to the decision of this House against declaring the admission of Missouri into the Union, and that therefore Missouri had not assumed a name which had been denied to her by Congress. Mr. T. expressed his satisfaction that Mr. Cook had explained his meaning; having believed, until he had made it, that his observations in regard to Missouri had been ironically intended. Mr. T. did not by any means consider the present motion as a trap, but as a serious proposition, which gentlemen would not find it easy to dispose of. There were members of this House who believed that Missouri was yet a territory. Mr. T. said he was not one of them; but those who did believe so would of course vote for the resolution. He was obliged, he said, to the gentleman from Virginia for having suggested what he had done in regard to the parallel between the proceedings of the British Parliament during our Revolution and those of the present Congress. He did remember himself many instances in which the petitions of the people of these States were refused to be received in Parliament because the petitioners did not correctly describe themselves. He remembered the letter of Washington was refused to be received because it purported to come from *General* Washington. Had not the people of Missouri a right to baptize themselves by such name as they chose? Mr. T. said he regretted that the Chair should have thought itself under the necessity of altering the Journal. The subject, in itself not very important, had been made so by the alteration of the Journal, which alteration it seemed had been made by the Speaker. It appeared to betray an unreasonable jealousy on this subject, to say the least of it. He begged the Speaker's pardon, he said—he did not mean to say that he felt this jealousy; but, in the course which he had taken, there was an overweening caution—an appearance of a jealousy which ought not to have been betrayed towards this people. Mr. T. said he trusted gentlemen would not feel much difficulty in voting on this question. We find, he said, that the question just taken, small as it was, has drawn a line across the United States. Let the Journal stand as it ought to do. Do not tell the people of Missouri, We are so jealous of you, we are fearful of your thrusting yourself into the Union, and partaking at the sacred board and drinking of the cup of wine. Do not say to them, We are so apprehensive you will come to the communion table by the name which you give yourselves, that we will give you no name. Mr. T. said he should vote against the proposed amendment, because, in his opinion, Missouri was a State, and not a Territory. Those who held the other opinion must be compelled to vote in favor of this proposition, or acknowledge that their ground was untenable.

Mr. EDWARDS, of North Carolina, said, in regard to this motion, he did not, when up before, mean to insinuate that the gentleman from Virginia (Mr. PARKER) had meant to set a trap for others. He might have laid a snare without designing it. For himself, Mr. E. said, he believed Missouri was a State. He feared that the motion of the gentleman might be adopted, and that the misnomer would be entered on the Journal. For no other reason had he wished the motion to be withdrawn. He should vote against the motion with pleasure, because he believed Missouri had lost her territorial character and could not be otherwise than a State.

Mr. PARKER said he was placed in a difficult situation, by the application to him to withdraw his motion. Other friends were opposed to his withdrawing it. He had concluded to persist in it. It was not intended as a trap for any one. Had it been so intended, he did not know but that he might have found illustrious examples. It was not a question of mere form. The state of the vote just taken proved that it was not. The question in fact, as voted upon, had been, is Missouri a State or a Territory? If she was a Territory, as she had been voted not to be a State, why reject this proposition so to designate her? I say, said he, she is a State; and were I a citizen of that State I would never, at your suggestion, strike out that clause in the constitution to which objection has been made. If I found it convenient to myself to do so, I would; but I would not do it on your recommendation, even for the important boon of being admitted in the Union. I would rather be trodden down by the armies from the North and East, and, if you could get them, from the South, than yield this point; and I avow it in the face of the world. If ever on earth a people has been maltreated it is this people. There seemed, Mr. P. said, to be a suppression of something on that journal; because the very words which had been stricken out of it were to be found in the caption of the memorials. Why are they suppressed? For the purpose, evidently, of implying the other way. He was not for this mode of dealing; he was for having the facts stated in plain English, that all might understand them. Mr. P. said he wanted to hear no more of precedents here—he had heard more than enough of them; but if a matter was to stand for precedent, even as to the form of the Journal, he wished it should be a precedent either one way or other, and not a mere equivocation.

Mr. ROSS said, he was aware that the House had involved itself in some difficulty by the reception of the petitions in the form in which they were presented, as being from a State. They ought not to have been received in that form. Missouri, Mr. R. said, was either a Territory or a State. If she be a State, she is a State known to the Constitution of the United States. She is not one of the old original thirteen States. Has she ever been received into the Federal family as a State? She has not. Does she assume the character of a State without being so received? Does she tell you, we were once a Territory, but we have thrown off our territorial character, and assumed that of a State without your authority? If this doctrine is to be tolerated, said Mr. R., away with your forms of territorial government at once. Let your Territories at once assume the character of States. If Missouri be a State, she must be a lawful State. By what law is she made a State? It was sound orthodoxy in politics, that there cannot be a State within the territorial limits of the United States, without the authority of the Congress of the United States. Missouri was not a State by that authority, and he was perfectly ready to vote and declare his opinion that Missouri is now a Territory.

Mr. RHEA referred to the act of the last session

of Congress, to show that Congress had authorized the people of Missouri to form a State government, and assume such name as they might think proper. They had assumed a name accordingly, and Mr. R. said it could not be taken from them except by law. This House, then, had given them the name, which was now refused to them on the Journal. Nay, at this very session a joint committee of the House, appointed to consider the subject, had reported a resolution, declaring the admission of the State of Missouri into the Union. With respect to the Journal, Mr. R. said, the Speaker had a power over it analogous to that which a court has over the presentment of a jury—a power to alter it in manner or form, but not in substance. Mr. R. here required the Clerk to read the Journal, as it was before it was altered by the Speaker this morning.

The SPEAKER pronounced that it was not in order to read any Journal, as the Journal of the House, but that which had been corrected by its presiding officer.

After a few further remarks, to the same effect as the preceding, Mr. RHEA took his seat.

Mr. PLUMER said he had voted against the motion to insert the word "State," and he should vote against this, because he considered it not advisable or proper to decide incidentally a main question, and one which was much contested. To avoid affording precedents, for precedents had been already quoted from the Journal, he thought it proper to leave the Journal in its present shape, neither affirming nor denying any thing. He should, therefore, vote against the amendment now under consideration, as he had against that first proposed.

Mr. LOWNDES rose, in consequence of a suggestion from Mr. ROSS, to say, that when he yesterday presented these memorials, he distinctly stated, in audible words, that they were from the State of Missouri. He did not mean to enter into this question; but, he said, in the anxiety to escape one difficulty, the object of one of the memorials, at least, was presented on the Journal differently from what that object was. It was necessary that the object of each petition should be stated on the Journal of the day on which it was presented. By the erasure of the words "within the State" twice, where it ought to have occurred on the Journal, the objects of the memorialists were perverted. But he did not mean to enter into the discussion, having only risen to state the fact which occurred yesterday.

Mr. ARCHER, of Virginia, said, the House had decided one-half of the question respecting Missouri. They had decided what she is not, and must now say what she is. He put the question to gentlemen of the majority, whether they could, after their former votes, hazard the assertion that Missouri is not a Territory, which they must do by voting against this amendment? If they did not now declare her a Territory, the course they had hitherto pursued stood condemned by their own votes, because every man knows that Missouri is either a Territory or a State. He hoped, he said, that gentlemen would not shrink from the

consequences of their own vote. He called upon them to stand to it. If they refused to do so, he should consider their refusal, as he did their refusal the other day to consider the resolution offered by him, as a proof that they were not willing to meet the consequences of the votes which they had given. He appealed to the pride of gentlemen to meet this question. One word more—who are the memorialists? In what light must we consider them? In the character which they profess—in that which they assume. Can you, said Mr. A., receive a paper which these people present to you, and fashion it according to your conceptions, and not according to theirs? Must you not pursue the course, if you do not receive it as offered, of rejecting it altogether, as suggested by the gentleman from Ohio? His honorable colleague had said that the conduct of this House towards Missouri equalled the tyrannous proceedings of the British Parliament towards this country. Mr. A. said, it not only equalled, but went beyond it. If, said he, you can change the character of the memorialists, I should like to know whether you cannot likewise alter their prayer, and make it unlike the prayer they intended? And would any man say that this House could receive a petition from any quarter, and make it what it was not intended to be?

Mr. ANDERSON said his friends, he apprehended, would, in the course they were now pursuing, find themselves in the situation in which men are very apt to be when they act under the influence of passion rather than of reason—in the wrong. It is always wrong to fight where you cannot but sustain defeat. It is always wrong for a minority to irritate a majority; and this motion could have no other effect but to irritate. It is the essence of determination that it prove something. But the vote on this motion would prove nothing. Nothing would be gained by it, and nothing would be lost. How can that be substance, which, whether lost or won, means nothing? No ingenuity could make of it any thing but a matter of words.

As to the subject of the main question, not now presented, no man could feel more anxiety than he; no man's mind was more excited, by day and by night, on that subject. By conciliation, said he, we may succeed in ultimately procuring what I consider a correct decision on it; by exasperation we are sure to fail. I deny, said he, that the vote which has just been taken proves that Missouri is not a State. It proved nothing else but that, in the opinion of those who voted against the amendment, the description in the Journal is sufficient and intelligible. Mr. A. deprecated all attempts to exasperate the majority as injudicious and impolitic; it was not by such a course that the object of the friends of Missouri could be attained.

Mr. BARBOUR assured the gentleman from Kentucky, that, as far as he had any thing to do with this subject, he was not acting under the influence of exasperation, but of an earnest wish to do what was right. If gentlemen were not disposed to express any opinion on this subject, the proper course would be to propose an indefinite postponement. But, if a direct vote were taken on the proposed amendment, no reason satisfactory to him could be assigned for voting against it, except that Missouri is not in fact a "Territory." Gentlemen called it by different names; but, call it by what name they would, a memorial had been presented from two organized branches of what he called the Legislature of the State of Missouri. For what purpose? Did the Representatives of the people of that State mean to intrude into the councils of the nation in regard to all the public lands within our almost illimitable bounds? Certainly not; and yet, by the erasure of the words "within the said State," their memorial was made to bear that construction. This observation Mr. B. made to show that this was not a mere dispute about words. With regard to the question before the House, he thought it one of considerable importance. If nothing had been done to the Journal; if it had followed the recital of the memorial, there would have been some plausibility in the remark that it was unimportant. But, by the alterations which had been made, a new description had been given to the memorial; and the decision of the House had the effect of expressing a determination to get rid of the description which the memorialists gave to themselves and to their memorial, &c. With regard to the precedent, Mr. B. said, if the Journal were permitted to stand in its present shape, it would afford a much stronger precedent than many which are introduced to influence the decisions of this House. In conclusion, Mr. B. made some remark, which caused the Speaker to repeat his decision, that "there is no Journal but that which is before the House as corrected by the presiding officer, and read by the Clerk."

Mr. Cobb said, as he was desirous to hear the Journal read as originally written, he must appeal from the decision of the Chair on this point.

The question on the appeal having been stated from the Chair—

Mr. Lowndes expressed his regret that his friend from Georgia had made this appeal, and his hope that it would not be pressed to a question. If it were determined that the Journal should be read as first written, the principle would apply to the whole detail of composing the Journal, and thence to the minutest particulars of it, which would show that the Journal, as presented to the House in form, was the only Journal of which the House properly had cognizance, &c.

Mr. Cobb withdrew his appeal.

Mr. Mercer was called up by what had fallen from Mr. Anderson. In the course which he had taken, Mr. M. said, the last sentiment of his heart was disrespect to the majority of the House. It was awful anxiety, and not passion, which he felt on this subject. Much less did he wish to draw the House into a discussion whether Missouri is a State or not, on a motion to amend the Journal. Mr. M. said he was sorry that any question had arisen involving the Chair; he thought, with the Speaker, that what had passed *out* of the House in regard to this Journal ought not to be known *in it*, and that the corrected form of the Journal only ought to be considered as be-

fore the House. He deprecated any thing like irritation as much as any one. Nothing but a sentiment of mutual forbearance, of good-will to each other, of high respect and confidence, could lead the House to correct decisions on so difficult a subject as the main question respecting Missouri. That was, he said, a subject of great importance. If Missouri was not a State, all her present proceedings were contrary to law. If it were so, and under her laws a man was convicted of a crime, and punished with death, it was murder! Every sentence of a court was void, and every verdict of a jury. Every act of her Legislature, superseding the regular course of the laws of the United States, was treason! He implored of gentlemen to pause before they finally pronounced a decision which would be crowned with such terrible results.

Mr. Warfield said he should of course vote against this motion, on the same grounds as he had voted against the preceding one, viz: that the alleged and proposed alteration of the Journal was neither important nor material; that the alteration objected to had been made by the competent authority, and that there was nothing in it which required the interposition of this House; that, if it could be made to touch the main question with regard to the actual relation of Missouri to the Union, that was a question which it would not be proper to decide in the manner in which this question had been submitted to the House.

Mr. Archer, of Maryland, said he should not have risen, were it not that he was one of those who believed that Missouri is now a Territory of the United States, and yet should vote against the proposition. His object was that the Journal should conform to the fact. In his opinion, it does so at present. It was in vain to tell the House that this was a matter of importance. It was a mere dispute between tweedle-dum and tweedle-dee. It was impossible, by any mode of argument, to make that important which is of no importance. By voting on the motion, as had been well observed, the House would decide nothing. With all deference and respect to gentlemen, it appeared to him that this course of proceeding was idle. In my estimation, said he, Missouri is a Territory of the Union, and will so remain until she is Constitutionally admitted into the Union. He would not present his whole view of this question. It was enough to say, that Congress has no power in regard to States, but the power to admit new States into the Union. Have we said that Missouri is admitted into the Union? No. She is not then a State of this Union. Is she independent? I say not; because, first, she is not in rebellion against the General Government; she has not set our authority at defiance; and, because, secondly, Congress could not make her an independent State, inasmuch as the power of Congress is to admit new States into the Union, and not to make States of any other description.

The question being then taken on the motion to insert the words "the Territory of" befor the word "Missouri," in the clause of the Journ first above recited, it was decided by yeas and *nve* The yeas were Messrs. Mallary, Ross, St of Vermont, and UPHAM. All the other votes, 150 in number, were in the negative.

So the motion was rejected.

Mr. BARBOUR then moved to amend the entry in the Journals by inserting, after the words "public lands," the words "in the late Territory of Missouri."

Mr. ROSS moved to amend the amendment by striking out of it the word "late."

Mr. BARBOUR showed that this motion presented precisely the same question just decided in the negative by a vote of 150 to 4. His object was merely to give a correct recital of the memorial. Suppose it were a memorial from the late Bank of the United States, and it were proposed to strike out the word "late," the House would see how essentially the fact would be varied by such an alteration, &c.

Mr. STORRS, on inspecting the Journal and memorial, expressed his impression that the entry, as it stood, was not incompatible with the contents of the memorial.

Mr. WARFIELD considered this again as a mere matter of form, and thought it perfectly immaterial whether it was inserted or not, as he thought of the first proposition. As, however, the House appeared to be in no manner relieved from difficulty by the decisions already made, he moved, in order to get rid at once of any difficulty on the subject, to reconsider the vote on the first motion, which was, to insert the words "the State of," before Missouri.

The question on reconsideration having been stated—

Mr. BROWN spoke in expression of his satisfaction at the question being again presented, and in support of the principle, that, where there was an attempt to violate personal or political rights, resistance was a duty, not to be departed from for any views of conciliation.

Mr. ROSS expressed his astonishment at this motion for reconsideration, and, without accusing any one of inconsistency, said he should consider himself extremely inconsistent had he voted against the motion at first, and then moved to reconsider it.

Mr. ROBERTSON expressed his pleasure that there was again a prospect that the Journal would be made to conform to the fact, which he argued to show that it did not at present.

Mr. FOOT said that the last vote showed that the insertion of these words would decide nothing, and need therefore not be objected to, inasmuch as only four members of the House had voted Missouri to be a Territory, though so many were known to believe her to be a Territory.

Mr. WARFIELD defended himself from the insinuation of inconsistency. He considered it the right of every man to change and to retract his opinions on conviction. With regard to his legislative proceedings, he said he held himself amenable to those who did him the honor of giving him a seat here, and he held himself responsible no where else. He assigned reasons why he had made his motion, arising from the maze of perplexing questions in which, by disagreeing to the

first motion, the House seemed to be getting deeper and deeper involved.

The question on Mr. WARFIELD's motion for reconsideration of the first vote was then decided by yeas and nays, as follows:

YEAS—Messrs. Alexander, Allen of Tennessee, Archer of Maryland, Archer of Virginia, Baldwin, Ball, Barbour, Bayly, Bloomfield, Brevard, Brown, Brush, Bryan, Burton, Burwell, Cobb, Cocke, Crawford, Crowell, Culbreth, Culpeper, Cuthbert, Earle, Edwards of North Carolina, Eustis, Fisher, Floyd, Foot, Garnett, Gray, Hall of North Carolina, Hardin, Hill, Hooks, Jackson, Johnson, Jones of Virginia, Jones of Tennessee, Little, Lowndes, McCoy, McCreary, McLane of Delaware, McLean of Kentucky, Meigs, Mercer, Metcalf, T. L. Moore, Neale, Nelson of Virginia, Newton, Parker of Virginia, Pinckney, Randolph, Rankin, Reed, Rhea, Robertson, Settle, Shaw, Simkins, Smith of Maryland, A. Smyth of Virginia, Stevens, Terrell, Trimble, Tucker of Virginia, Walker, Warfield, Williams of Virginia, and Williams of North Carolina—71.

NAYS—Messrs. Adams, Allen of Massachusetts, Allen of New York, Anderson, Baker, Beecher, Boden, Buffum, Butler of New Hampshire, Butler of Louisiana, Campbell, Clagett, Clark, Cook, Crafts, Cushman, Dane, Darlington, Dennison, Dickinson, Eddy, Edwards of Connecticut, Fay, Folger, Fuller, Gorham, Gross of New York, Gross of Pennsylvania, Guyon, Hackley, Hall of New York, Hall of Delaware, Hemphill, Hendricks, Herrick, Hibshman, Hobart, Hostetter, Kendall, Kinsley, Lathrop, Lincoln, Maclay, McCullough, Mallary, Marchand, Monell, R. Moore, S. Moore, Morton, Moseley, Murray, Nelson of Massachusetts, Parker of Massachusetts, Patterson, Philson, Plumer, Rich, Richards, Rogers, Ross, Russ, Sergeant, Silsbee, Sloan, Storrs, Street, Strong of New York, Tarr, Tomlinson, Tracy, Udree, Upham, Van Rensselaer, Wendover, Whitman, and Wood—77.

So the House refused to reconsider the first vote of to-day.

Mr. BARBOUR, who had withdrawn his motion, to make way for that of Mr. WARFIELD, now renewed it, as stated above; and

Mr. ROSS renewed his motion to amend it, by striking out the word "late." The House, he said, had just solemnly decided, the second time, that the memorials were not from the *State* of Missouri—yet this amendment proposed to describe it as being from the late Territory, &c., meaning from the State of Missouri.

Mr. BARBOUR asked of the gentleman whether the House had not, with equal solemnity, and by a vote of 150 to 4, decided that Missouri is not a Territory; and whether his amendment, if it succeeded, would not be in the teeth of that decision?

The question was then taken on Mr. ROSS's motion, and negatived by a large majority.

Mr. STORRS moved to amend Mr. BARBOUR's amendment, so as to read, "in the United States," instead of "in the late Territory of Missouri."

Mr. RANDOLPH in rising said, that the errors of the wisest men are not the least. The House had just refused to strike out the word "late" from the amendment under consideration, and had of course decided that it should be retained; so that, if the amendment of the gentleman from New York prevailed, it would read, "in the late United States!" How was it competent for the gentleman from New York to move, as a substitute for the amendment of his colleague, a recital not according to the words of the petition, but such as he wished the words of the petition had been? If the recital was to correspond with the fact, the House should reinstate the words of the memorial, the erasure of which had led to all this—he would not say what; but, if he were anywhere else, he would say—shuffling and cutting.

Mr. NELSON, of Virginia, made a point of order, whether the motion of Mr. STORRS was not a substitute for that of Mr. BARBOUR, and therefore out of order.

The SPEAKER decided that the word "late," though the House had refused to strike it out by itself, might be stricken out in connexion with other words, as now proposed. He also decided that the motion of Mr. STORRS, to strike out a part, but not the whole, of Mr. BARBOUR's amendment, was not a substitute so as to bring it within the rule; illustrating it by a reference to the common practice of moving to strike out the whole of a bill, except the enacting clause, in order to introduce a bill in a different form. He, therefore, pronounced Mr. STORRS's motion to be in order.

The question was then taken on Mr. STORRS's motion, and decided in the negative.

During the past and following proceedings, various ineffectual attempts were made to procure an adjournment.

Mr. COOK moved, in order to get rid of this question altogether, to postpone indefinitely the further consideration of this subject.

Mr. JOHNSON, of Kentucky, in a speech of some length, protested against the postponement. The Journals, he said, were distorted, and not made up as they ought to be, because the word Missouri occurred in them. What is Missouri? said he; is it a river? Is it a tribe of Indians? Why should we shrink from reciting her proper title on the Journal, when we find she has presented us a constitution of State government? Will we suffer it to be said, that sectional feelings have operated to prevent us from correcting our Journals so as to make them what they ought to be? If this question was not connected with Missouri, would there be any hesitation in making the proposed amendment? Mr. J. went on to say, that he trusted the House would go on and vote, that the Journals should declare the truth. I wish, said he, the Journal to show why we are opposed to correcting the Journals, and who we are that oppose it, and not to give these questions the go-by, as now proposed.

Mr. BRUSH demanded, whether it was in order to move to postpone indefinitely a motion to amend the Journal.

The SPEAKER decided that it is in order. There were, he said, certain forms of questions prescribed by the Rules of the House, and their relative rank assigned them. It was not for the Chair, but for the House, to judge of the propriety of those questions, when proposed. Being proposed, it became his duty to propound them to the House.

Mr. NELSON, of Virginia, objected to this decision; and demanded whether, as a proposition to amend could not be postponed without postponing the main question, which, in the present case, was the Journal, it was in order thus to postpone the Journal?

Mr. EUSTIS suggested for consideration whether every difficulty could not be avoided by directing the whole of the memorials from Missouri to be inserted on the Journal, instead of a description of them.

The SPEAKER decided that the motion to postpone a question to amend the Journal *is* in order. The Journal, he said, is a subject on which no question is to be put, until a question is made by a proposition to amend it. A motion to postpone that question, therefore, it being the only question, was evidently in order.

Mr. COOK disclaimed any intention to evade the question. He had made the motion to postpone, in order to get rid of irritating and unnecessary debate. As he had failed in this object, he withdrew the motion for postponement.

The question recurring on Mr. BARBOUR's motion to amend the Journal—

Mr. ANDERSON called for the reading of the memorial, to show that the amendment was not necessary, and might be dispensed with.

Mr. CULBRETH said he had been accidentally absent, this morning, on the vote to insert the word *State* as applied to Missouri, and he wished he could have an opportunity to record his vote on that principle. At first he had thought that the present question would afford him that opportunity; but, during the discussion, he had examined the Journal and the memorial, and he was convinced that the amendment, if agreed to, would make the prayer of the memorial what it is not. He should therefore vote against it.

The question was taken on agreeing to Mr. BARBOUR's motion to insert "the late Territory of" before the word "Missouri," and decided in the negative—yeas 61, nays 79, as follows:

YEAS—Messrs. Abbot, Alexander, Anderson, Archer of Virginia, Baldwin, Ball, Barbour, Bayly, Bloomfield, Brevard, Brown, Brush, Bryan, Burton, Burwell, Butler of Louisiana, Cobb, Cocke, Crawford, Crowell, Cuthbert, Earle, Edwards of North Carolina, Fisher, Floyd, Garnett, Gray, Hall of North Carolina, Hooks, Jackson, Johnson, Jones of Virginia, Jones of Tennessee, Little, Lowndes, McCoy, McLane of Delaware, McLean of Kentucky, Meigs, Mercer, Metcalf, T. L. Moore, Neale, Nelson of Virginia, Newton, Parker of Virginia, Pinckney, Randolph, Rankin, Reid, Rhea, Robertson, Settle, Simkins, Smith of Maryland, Terrell, Trimble, Tucker of Virginia, Walker, Williams of Virginia, and Williams of North Carolina.

NAYS—Messrs. Adams, Allen of Massachusetts, Allen of New York, Archer of Maryland, Baker, Beecher, Boden, Buffum, Butler of New Hampshire, Campbell, Clark, Cook, Crafts, Culbreth, Culpeper, Cushman, Dane, Darlington, Dennison, Dickinson, Eddy, Edwards of Connecticut, Eustis, Fay, Folger, Foot, Fuller, Gorham, Gross of New York, Gross of Pennsylvania, Guyon, Hall of New York, Hardin, Hemphill, Hendricks, Herrick, Hill, Hobart, Hos-

857   **HISTORY OF CONGRESS.**   858

JANUARY, 1821.   *Reduction of Expenditures.*   H. OF R.

tetter, Kendall, Kinsley, Lathrop, Lincoln, Maclay, McCreary, McCullough, Mallary, Marchand, Monell, R. Moore, S. Moore, Morton, Moseley, Murray, Nelson of Massachusetts, Parker of Massachusetts, Patterson, Philson, Plumer, Rich, Richards, Rogers, Ross, Russ, Sergeant, Silsbee, Sloan, Storrs, Street, Strong of Vermont, Strong of New York, Tomlinson, Tracy, Udree, Upham, Van Rensselaer, Wendover, Whitman, and Wood.

So the motion was rejected.

As soon as this decision was pronounced, several persons addressing the Chair at once, a motion to adjourn obtained the preference.

Before the question was put, a member inquired whether an adjournment now would preclude any amendment of the Journal of yesterday on to-morrow?

The SPEAKER decided that it would, unless a motion to amend it were the unfinished business at the time of adjournment on this day.

The question on the motion to adjourn being decided affirmatively, here ended the controversy respecting the Journal.

A message from the Senate informed the House that the Senate have passed the bill, entitled "An act making a partial appropriation for the military service of the United States for the year 1821," with an amendment, in which they ask the concurrence of this House.

SATURDAY, January 13.

Mr. WILLIAMS, of North Carolina, from the Committee of Claims, to which was referred the bill from the Senate, entitled "An act for the relief of John Holmes, of Alabama," reported the same without amendment; and the bill was committed to a Committee of the Whole on Monday next.

Mr. WILLIAMS, of North Carolina, from the same committee, made a report on the petition of Francis B. Languille, accompanied with a bill for his relief; which bill was read twice and committed to the Committee of the whole House to which is committed the bill for the relief of John Rodriguez.

Mr. ANDERSON, from the Committee on the Public Lands, made a report on the petition of Matthew Dockery, accompanied with a bill for his relief; which bill was read twice and committed.

Mr. MERCER, from the Committee for the District of Columbia, to which was referred the bill from the Senate, entitled "An act to incorporate the Columbian College, in the District of Columbia," reported the same without amendment, and the bill was ordered to a third reading.

Mr. BUTLER, of Louisiana, from the Committee on Private Land Claims, to which was referred the bill from the Senate, entitled "An act for the relief of the legal representatives of Gabriel Berzat, deceased," reported the same with amendments; which were read, and, together with the bill, committed to a Committee of the Whole.

On motion of Mr. HENDRICKS, the Committee on the Judiciary were instructed to inquire into the expediency of providing by law for the decision of cases arising within States in which there is no circuit court, and where the district Judge, from any cause, may decline to adjudicate.

The SPEAKER laid before the House a report from the Secretary of the Treasury, respecting the number of French vessels which have arrived, and are expected to arrive in the present year, in the river St. Mary's, since the first of July last, and whether their cargoes are intended to be illicitly introduced into the United States, &c., made in obedience to a resolution of the House of the 20th ultimo; which report was read, and referred to the Committee on Commerce.

The amendment proposed by the Senate to the bill, entitled "An act making a partial appropriation for the military service of the United States for the year 1821," was read, and concurred in by the House.

On motion of Mr. STREET, the Committee on Pensions and Revolutionary Claims were instructed to inquire into the expediency of continuing in force the act, entitled "An act to provide for persons who were disabled by known wounds received in the Revolutionary war," and the several acts amending and extending the same, which acts will expire on the 15th day of May next.

The House proceeded to consider the resolution submitted by Mr. TRACY on the 11th instant, and, the same being again read, was agreed to.

REDUCTION OF EXPENDITURES.

Mr. ROBERTSON, of Kentucky, after a few remarks on the propriety of the inquiry which he was about to propose, submitted the following resolution for consideration:

Resolved, That the Committee of Ways and Means be instructed to inquire whether any, and, if any, what, offices in the civil department of Government may be abolished without prejudice to the public interest; and also whether any of the salaries or compensations now allowed by law to the officers and other persons employed in the said civil department, and, if any, what, and to what extent, may be, consistently with justice and sound policy, reduced.

Mr. CULBRETH, after observing that it had been his intention to offer a similar motion himself, if no other gentleman had done so, moved to amend the resolution so as to refer the inquiry to a special committee instead of the Committee of Ways and Means, deeming the latter committee not competent, consistently with a due attention to its numerous ordinary duties, to bestow on this subject the necessary attention.

This motion to amend the resolution, brought on a discussion of more than an hour's continuance, on the question whether it was better to refer the inquiry to the Committee of Ways and Means, a select committee, or to the committees severally appointed on the expenditures of the different departments, (which last course was suggested by Mr. SMYTH, of Virginia.) Messrs. CULBRETH, ROBERTSON, SMITH, of Maryland, STORRS, SMYTH, of Virginia, FOOT, GROSS, of New York, TRIMBLE, and LOWNDES, joined in the debate, which referred principally to the duties of different committees of the House, their nature, &c., and the possibility of discharging fully and properly the duty proposed by this resolution. After two unsuccessful motions to lay the resolution on the table, the debate ended by adopting Mr. CULBRETH's amendment. Being thus amended,

The resolution was agreed to; and Messrs. CULBRETH, ROBERTSON, FOOT, STORRS, HEMPHILL, TRIMBLE, and ALLEN, of New York, were appointed the committee.

JOURNAL OF THE HOUSE.

Mr. REID, of Georgia, rose and addressed the Chair as follows:

Mr. Speaker: The resolutions which I hold in my hand were prepared yesterday, and should have been then submitted, but for the anxiety of the House to adjourn, and the lateness of the hour. They are now presented, not with any view to promote or prolong excitement, because I believe excitement to be unfavorable to correct legislation; nor do I intend any remark which I may offer to be disrespectful to the officer chosen to preside over the deliberations of this House. Self-respect, if there were no other reason, would not permit me to pursue such a course; but I desire to mark, by an expression of the opinion of the House, an event which, were I more conversant with legislative proceedings, I would say, is the most extraordinary of its kind to be found in parliamentary annals.

The Constitution of the United States requires both Houses of Congress to keep a Journal of their proceedings, and, for the purpose of giving effect to this provision, the usage of the House and the acts of government have made it the duty of the Clerk to keep a correct account of the daily proceedings, while, by the rules of the House, it is made the duty of the Speaker to "examine and correct the Journal" of the Clerk. But, that no error may escape unnoticed, and that the history of our transactions may be entirely faithful, the Journal of the preceding day is read daily, in the face of the House. Is this a mere ceremony, a form, which, adopted without object, may be suspended without injury? It appears to me to be altogether of substance, because both the Speaker and the Clerk are mere agents in the compilation of the Journal, and, consequently, the House is entitled to the supervision of their conduct. Every member, having sworn to support the Constitution, which requires the House to keep a Journal of its proceedings, is deeply interested—as much so as the obligation of an oath can make him—in the proper performance of the duties, which, in this respect, devolve upon the Clerk and the Speaker. If then an error be produced, whether by the negligence of the Clerk or the supposed corrections of the Speaker, the House surely possesses the power to apply the corrective by amending the Journal—restoring it to its original shape, or in such other manner as its wisdom may devise.

What shall be done upon the present occasion will best be known by a resort to the facts as they exist. They are these: a member presents, in his place, a memorial from the Senate and House of Representatives of the State of Missouri; he announces, as is his duty, the purport and the character of the petition; the document is received by the House, referred to one of its committees, and the Clerk, as he is bound to do, minutes the transaction among the occurrences of the day. The Speaker, when he comes to perform his duty, erases the words "State of," and, when the corrected Journal is presented to the House, it recites, that the member presented the memorial of Missouri. Now, the question is—has the Speaker performed his duty, under the rule of the House, or has he acted without the pale of the authority which that rule conveys to him? If the erasure be within the rule, there is an end of the matter, and I am trespassing unnecessarily upon your patience, and doing injustice to the Speaker. But, if the Speaker has altered without correcting your Journal, his act is void, because it is beyond his authority, and is itself an error, which demands the correction of the House. Did the Speaker, when he applied his pen to the Journal, describe the fact as it had taken place more truly than it had been described by the Clerk? No, sir. The Clerk stated what had happened exactly as it did happen. Now, the rule is—the Speaker shall "examine and correct" the Journal. The power to correct implies the existence of error. There was no error, not even the slightest mistake. The Speaker had, then, no duty to perform, and any other journal than that in which the Clerk had truly recorded the proceedings of the House is not the true, but a spurious journal. The act of the Speaker was gratuitous and without warrant.

But it may be said, as I think it was yesterday, that the Speaker is to be justified, because he had stated the actual fact. That is to say, he has refused to designate Missouri as a State, because she is not a State. I know that there are varying opinions; that some gentlemen consider Missouri a State; others, *quasi* a State; others, a Territory; while there are some some who do not clearly express what their opinions are. With this subject, I have at present no concern. Sufficient for the day is the evil thereof. The question is not, whether the true quality of Missouri should appear upon the Journals; but whether it shall appear as represented in her memorial, in the announcement of the member presenting that memorial, and in the act of the House receiving it. If an individual, arrogating a title to which he has no claim, present his petition to the House, and it be determined to listen to his plaint, no one will contend that the Clerk or the Speaker, in making up or correcting the Journal, has a right to inquire into the legitimacy of the dignity assumed. It is not their duty to ingraft the fact upon the Journal, contrary to the representation of the petitioner, and the determination of the House to hear him in the character he has chosen to adopt; but it is their duty to detail events as they actually occurred, although these may involve falsehoods, and misrepresentations.

Sir, if Missouri had presented herself in borrowed feathers, it was the duty of this House, by plucking them from her, to have exposed her in the nakedness of her deformity. If she assumed a rank incompatible with your dignity, or a tone and a style too lofty, you should at once have taught her language more humble, and admonished her, that she was not yet fitted to occupy the station to which she aspired. But, did you do this? No, sir. Whatever may be the matter or the manner of her memorial, you received it. That it was received, was noted by the proper officer, under your order; and you referred it for investigation to a committee. Now, these are solemn measures adopted by the House, and, I ask, have they been rescinded by the same authority? No; not by the alteration of your Journal; an alteration not governed by any known rule prescribed by this body. Is it come to this? Shall the officers of this House frame the Journals of the House according to any vague notions of propriety which they may entertain? If, indeed, they have this power, they may mould and alter, and garble, and destroy, until your diary shall wear the semblance of romance, rather than of history. If we yield them such a power, we are apostates from the true faith; we are no longer the representatives of freemen; we are ourselves slaves, and, what is worse, willing slaves.

It may certainly happen that the House, from inadvertence, or some other cause, may be led into mistake, and may order that to be recorded which should not of right have a place. It may then be the duty of the Speaker to point out the impropriety, leaving it to be corrected at the will of the House. He cannot go further; he cannot alter the solemn acts of the House, upon the presumption that they were irregularly or unadvisedly done.

. I have heard it suggested that this is a little matter; which does not deserve our consideration. If it be so, why were words so harmless and unimportant stricken from the Journal? Their very insignificance should have protected them; the more especially as they corresponded with the fact as it transpired. But it is not a good reason against resisting any innovation, to say that it is so slight nothing is to be feared from it. A delegated authority should be jealously watched, or it will rapidly extend itself beyond its prescribed boundaries. We are told in Arabian story that a mist, rising from the bosom of the ocean, which the gentlest breeze might have dissipated, took to itself consistency and form, and became a monstrous and a fearful giant. It is thus with the encroachments of power—at first scarcely perceived, at last not to be opposed. Constant attrition will waste even the rock of ages!

Before I sit down, I would controvert a doctrine which has received the sanction of high authority. It is, that the House has no authority to ask the reading of the original draught of the Journal, because none other can be read than that corrected by the Speaker. Sir, it may be shown—I think it has been shown—that the House is the ultimate judge of the correctness of its own Journal, and it has a right to inquire, whether the Speaker has corrected it, as he has the power to do, or altered it without authority. How, then, is the House to exercise this right, if you withhold the data upon which its decision must be founded? Shall members inquire among themselves for the facts, with a view to the correction of mistakes or faults? One will answer, he was absent; another, he was engaged; a third, he was inattentive.

Apply to the Clerk, and he will say his duties are so numerous, and so many the subjects he is forced to record, that, if he must shut his eyes to the Journal, he can give you no account of the matter; but, if you will allow him to read from the Journal itself, he can divest it of interlineations and erasures, and tell you how it originally stood. It is only by a comparison of the Journal, after it has received the correction of the Speaker, with what it was in the hands of the Clerk, that you can be prepared to decide upon the propriety or impropriety of their corrections. Suppose a mischievous or malignant individual were, covertly, to find access to your records, and should vitiate them by blots and scrawls. When you sought to restore them to their true shape, would you not call upon the Clerk to decipher to you their original reading? The case is perfectly parallel, if an officer of the House have so altered the Journal that it no longer retains its true form.

I have considered it a duty to say thus much, by way of preface to the resolutions I offer. I will only add, if the Speaker has done that which he ought not to have done, it comports with the dignity of the House to assert its own rights. Let us ever cling to truth and justice, and resist even their slightest violation with the utmost pertinacity.

Mr. R. then handed the following resolutions to the Chair:

Resolved, That it is the duty of the Speaker, under the rules of the House, to examine and correct the Journals of the House.

Resolved, That the House possesses the right to inquire into and decide upon the propriety of any correction which may be made by the Speaker.

Resolved, That the erasures made by the Speaker in the Journal of the 11th January are *alterations,* and not *corrections,* inasmuch as the Journal, in its original form, corresponds with the fact intended to be described, viz: that a petition from the Senate and House of Representatives of the State of Missouri was presented by a member from South Carolina.

The SPEAKER having propounded the question, Will the House now proceed to consider these resolutions? it was decided as follows:

YEAS—Messrs. Abbot, Alexander, Archer of Virginia, Barbour, Bayly, Brown, Brush, Bryan, Burton, Burwell, Butler of Louisiana, Cannon, Cobb, Crawford, Crowell, Culbreth, Davidson, Earle, Edwards of North Carolina, Fisher, Floyd, Garnett, Gray, Hall of North Carolina, Johnson, Little, McCoy, McLean of Kentucky, Meigs, Metcalf, T. L. Moore, Neale, Nelson of Virginia, Newton, Parker of Virginia, Rankin, Reid, Rhea, Simkins, Smith, of New Jersey, Terrell, Trimble, Tyler, Walker, Warfield, Williams of Virginia, and Williams of North Carolina—47.

NAYS—Messrs. Adams, Allen of New York, Allen of Tennessee, Anderson, Archer of Maryland, Baldwin, Ball, Beecher, Boden, Brevard, Buffum, Butler of New Hampshire, Campbell, Clagett, Clark, Cocke,

Cook, Crafts, Culpeper, Cushman, Cuthbert, Dane, Darlington, Dennison, Dickinson, Eddy, Edwards of Connecticut, Eustis, Fay, Folger, Foot, Forrest, Fuller, Gorham, Gross of New York, Gross of Pennsylvania, Guyon, Hackley, Hall of New York, Hardin, Hendricks, Herrick, Hibshman, Hill, Hobart, Hooks, Hostetter, Jackson, Kinsley, Lincoln, Livermore, Lowndes, Maclay, McCreary, McCullough, McLane, of Delaware, Mallary, Marchand, Mercer, Monell, S. Moore, Morton, Murray, Nelson of Massachusetts, Parker of Massachusetts, Patterson, Philson, Plumer, Rich, Richards, Richmond, Robertson, Rogers, Ross, Russ, Sergeant, Shaw, Silsbee, Sloan, Smith of Maryland, A. Smyth of Virginia, Smith of North Carolina, Southard, Stevens, Storrs, Street, Strong of Vermont. Strong of New York, Tomlinson, Tracy, Tucker of Virginia, Udree, Wallace, Wendover, Whitman, and Wood—96.

So the House refused now to consider the resolutions.

MONDAY, January 15.

On the Journal of Saturday being read—

Mr. REID, stated that, in speaking of the petition from the Legislature of Missouri, he meant to have styled it a memorial and not a petition, moved that the Journal be amended by substituting, in the third resolution moved by him, the word "memorial" for the word "petition." And the question thereon being taken, it was decided in the negative without a division.

Mr. WILLIAMS, from the Committee of Claims, made a report on the petition of John Thomas, a Major General of the militia of Kentucky, accompanied by a bill for his relief; which was read twice, and committed to a Committee of the Whole.

Mr. WILLIAMS also made a report on the case of Henry Cain, accompanied by a bill for his relief; which was read twice, and committed to a Committee of the Whole.

Mr. SMITH, of Maryland, from the Committee of Ways and Means, reported a bill giving further time for the redemption of lands sold for taxes under the act of August 2, 1813, entitled "An act to lay and collect a direct tax within the United States;" which was read twice, and committed to a Committee of the Whole.

Mr. SMITH, from the same committee, reported a bill authorizing the Secretary of the Treasury to transfer certain balances of appropriations to the surplus fund; which was read twice, and committed to a Committee of the Whole to-morrow.

Mr. BALDWIN, from the Committee on Manufactures, reported a bill to regulate the duties on imports and for other purposes, accompanied by a detailed report on the subject. The bill having been twice read, Mr. BALDWIN moved to refer it to a Committee of the Whole on the state of the Union. Mr. SMITH, of Maryland, opposed this course, as giving it a preference over ordinary business. Mr. BALDWIN replied, that the same direction had been given, at this session, to several bills, that for the reduction of the army, &c., not more important than this. The motion of Mr. BALDWIN prevailed, by a vote of 65 to 61. The

ordinary number of copies of the bill and report were ordered to be printed for the use of the House.

Mr. BEECHER moved to print three thousand copies of the report. On this motion there were some remarks made. The printing of an extra number was opposed by Messrs. CULBRETH, WILLIAMS, of North Carolina, FOOT, and TYLER, on the ground that the subject had been so much discussed for two or three years past, that the report, however able, could hardly be expected to shed much additional light on the subject; that the distribution of these documents, among the people, must always be partial and limited, though the number were larger than proposed; that the expense of the printing proposed would be greater than the benefit to accrue from it. To this Mr. BEECHER opposed the importance of the subject, the great interest the people felt in it, and the propriety of making generally known the views of the committee of this House on the subject. The motion of Mr. BEECHER was, in the end, negatived by a vote of 73 to 61.

Mr. BALDWIN, from the same committee, to whom have also been referred, during the present session, sundry petitions and memorials in relation to the imposition of duties on sales at auction, reported a bill laying duties on sales of merchandise at auction; which was read twice, and committed to a Committee of the Whole on the state of the Union.

Mr. CAMPBELL, from the Committee on Private Land Claims, made a report on the petition of James Brady, accompanied by a bill for his relief; which was read twice, and committed to the Committee of the Whole to which is committed the bill extending the time for issuing and locating military land warrants to officers and soldiers of the Revolutionary army.

Mr. RUSS submitted the following resolution, which was read, and ordered to lie on the table one day for consideration:

Resolved, That the Secretary of the Treasury be directed to lay before this House a statement of the precise amount of special deposites to the credit of the Treasury of the United States, which is referred to in his supplementary report of the 28th ultimo, as not being available the current year; stating particularly of what such deposites consist; if, of depreciated bank paper, the bank or banks which issued the same, with the amount by each, and the present current specie value thereof, and the year or years, respectively, when the same was received.

On motion of Mr. EUSTIS, the House proceeded to the consideration of the resolution r omitted by him, for the conditional admission of Missouri into the Union; and, on his motion, :, order that it might not interrupt the discussion of the Army bill, it was referred to a Committee of the Whole on the state of the Union.

On motion of Mr. LOWNDES, the House then took up the resolve from the Senate, for the admission of Missouri into the Union; and it was read a second time, and referred to a Committee of the Whole on the state of the Union.

The bill from the Senate " to incorporate the

Columbia College of the District of Columbia," was about to be read a third time, when

Mr. CAMPBELL objected to this bill taking a course different from the ordinary practice in regard to bills, which was, to refer them to a Committee of the Whole for discussion.

Mr. MERCER earnestly pressed the bill to a decision without commitment, and expressed great satisfaction in having it in his power to vote on a bill of this description, having for its object the encouragement of learning, &c., in the District.

After considerable conversation on the subject between Messrs. MERCER, STORRS, and CAMPBELL—

The bill was ordered to lie on the table, and to be printed for the use of members.

A Message was received from the President of the United States, transmitting certain documents in relation to correspondence with foreign Governments on the subject of the slave trade, accidentally omitted to be transmitted from the Department of State, when the documents were sent which have been already published.

The documents now sent are the following :

Extracts of a letter from Mr. Rush to the Secretary of State, dated 19th November, 1819.

Lord Castlereagh to Mr. Rush, 11th of November, 1819.

Address from House of Commons, 7th July, 1819, to the Prince Regent.

Same, House of Lords, 9th do.   do.   do.

Mr. Rush to Lord Castlereagh, 16th of November, 1819.

The Message was read, and referred to the committee having that subject under consideration.

REDUCTION OF THE ARMY.

The House then again resolved itself into a Committee of the Whole on the state of the Union, and resumed the consideration of the bill to reduce the Military Peace Establishment.

Mr. SIMKINS's motion to strike out the first section of the bill being yet under consideration—

Mr. WALKER, of North Carolina, said, at the commencement of the debate he had no intention of taking any part in the discussion on this question; it was his choice, and he would have been content to have given a silent vote; but the course it had taken, and the manner in which it had been agitated, had given it additional importance, and, like all other subjects of a national character, had a tendency to excite the interest and feelings of members, and diffuse its influence throughout the nation, and, as iron sharpens iron, he felt a participation of public feeling, as it passed along, and the few remarks he had to make, although they might not shed much light or have much influence, he felt himself bound to offer.

Sir, by the provisions of this bill we are about to embark in the important business of retrenchment, and he fondly hoped that the Representatives of the people, on this proposition, would prove themselves the guardians of their interest; and, although he was disposed to believe there were favorable symptoms, an impulse of public feeling in

16th CON. 2d SESS.—28

this House, to correspond with the principle in reducing our national expenditures within the provisions of our revenue, yet, in the progress of this inquiry, our prospects are not so promising as could be wished or expected ; as the diversity of opinions which appears to be entertained, relative to the measures that should be adopted, seems to be the only impediment in our way, the greatest obstacle which can prevent us from arriving at the object we all wish to accomplish. If there is an inherent weakness, an inefficiency in republics, it must be in a division of their councils, in the want of unanimity in their national policy. From the views taken on this question, it is clearly discovered that our opinions are various. Different directions of policy are pointed out to arrive at the principle. Some gentlemen have strong objections to a reduction of the Army, as if it would leave our country defenceless, without physical strength, and liable to be assailed from every quarter. Others are zealously devoted to the establishment of the Navy. It must stand unimpaired, not to be touched by unskilful hands. Not one ship or vessel ought to be diminished or spared from the service. Our flag must float on the ocean, not a sail to be taken down. A favorite system seems to prevail with all. We cannot unite in measures to effect a change of so much importance, in which our country is so deeply interested. It is incumbent and indispensably necessary, that some concessions of policy be made—some relinquishment of political opinion on all sides. What is legislation but the surrender of private sentiment for public good ? It is peculiarly necessary that, in this redeeming principle, we make some sacrifice—must part with our Delilahs, or we shall not be able to return to the narrow path of economy from which we have deviated. For, unless this course be adopted, all our efforts will be unavailing.

Sir, there are three alternatives presented to our view, which must be the result of our deliberation, and one of them we must adopt, to rescue our country from the present state of embarrassment. To borrow money, to tax our citizens, or retrench ; to borrow money in the sunshine of peace and tranquillity, when the desert blossoms as the rose, no foreign wars to encounter, no enemy to contend with, is at variance, and almost irreconcilable with wise and economical legislation. To tax our citizens at such a time, and under auspices so favorable, is a measure that would present an odious and frightful prospect, the people would not bear with it, nor with us in pursuing such a policy. They would hold us accountable for our legislative conduct—our responsibility is pledged. They have confided to us their best interest, and we must return and submit to the tribunal of public opinion.

Sir, we believe to retrench is practicable, and within the reach of the present inquiry. The exhausted state of our Treasury points out the necessity of a radical change in the system of our finances, to provide for the national exigencies without oppressing our citizens, and demands our unremitting endeavors to remedy the evil. But, sir, on this principle I have no prepossessions to gratify, no personalities in view, no anxious solicitude for any department in preference to another. Let the denunciation be equal and general. If justice is to be the standard by which we are to exercise our judgment in correcting the excesses of Government, let it be administered with equal hands. If your Army is too large, and exceeds the proper number necessary for the Peace Establishment, reduce it to such proportion as may be adequate to the present day. If your Navy be too extensive or expensive, lessen it, leaving only so many vessels as are necessary for our maritime protection. If there are any or many supernumerary officers created for the purpose of emolument, abolish them; take a skirt from every garment, in order to attempt the principle of reduction. We have made our first approach towards the Army, as the most formidable branch of our expenditures, consisting of ten thousand men, a number considered at the end of the war barely sufficient to guard our posts, and protect the nation from danger.

The present bill proposes a reduction of that army to six thousand; and from the view I have taken, I am bound to believe it will safely admit of that reduction without danger or inconvenience to Government. In the remarks I am about to make in favor of reducing the Army, I trust I shall not be misunderstood as to calculate I entertain any hostile propensities or unfriendly feelings towards the Military Department. No, sir; I am one of the last men who would attempt to prostrate its honors, or put down military science. I know the sufferings and privations of military men; I venerate the character of a soldier, in the exercise of his profession; in the performance of his duty in defence of his country; but, Mr. Chairman, I have a most high and unqualified respect for the militiaman, the citizen, and the soldier, employed in the humble occupations of domestic life, cultivating his farm, and reaping the fruits of the soil, contributing in his place both to the support and defence of his country; nor do I entertain any fearful apprehensions of the danger of military power from military men, or from any army that could be raised or concentrated in this nation; the people, in their aggregate capacity, having the supreme power wisely placed in their hands, are feelingly alive to all their interests, and will ever, with a watchful and vigilant eye, hold a jealous control over their liberties, and will not suffer any excess in the different establishments of Government. Nor do I believe it has ever entered into the speculative view of any of the commanders of our armies, since the commencement of our Government, to attempt such an innovation on the liberties of the people. Such an enterprise would be as romantic and disastrous as Don Quixotte buffeting his wind-mill. I believe we have always had the purest military on earth, with the solitary exception of one general officer of the Revolutionary war whose name is too disgraceful and too well known to mention in this place. A Cæsar, a Scylla, a Kouli Khan, could have no place here. Tyrants could not long breathe in our Republican atmosphere; but, Mr. Chairman, as much as I venerate and esteem the well disciplined soldiery of my country, it must

be confessed they are only the minute-hand to government, auxiliaries called to our assistance and defence in time of war and invasion. It is then, and not till then, they are wanting and really necessary; and could my vision penetrate so far as to discriminate and discern the exact number necessary to be retained in service, was it six, ten, or twenty thousand, that number should have my support, were I convinced they were required for the safety and protection of the nation. But, from what has been presented to our view in the peaceful and tranquil situation of our country, it must be believed that six thousand men are competent to all the purposes of the present Peace Establishment, and the best guess we can make. Gentlemen opposed to the reduction of the Army, advocate the doctrine of maintaining a strong military force in order to be prepared for the event of war. This would be going beyond the bounds of Constitutional prescription, which declares that standing armies ought not to be kept up in time of peace, and would only be preparing to be prepared for such a crisis. Should war come as it has come, your regulars will commence hostilities, and begin the conflict.

But, as it has been in the old war of the Revolution and in the late war, the militia will have to end the contest, and give the last blow. Sir, the militia is our stronghold and sure pledge; they are recognised as such by all the States: and upon the faith and reliance of the yeomanry of our country, our Government was founded, as our support in peace and defence in war; and experience has assured us that our confidence has not been misplaced. It has been said, in very emphatical language, that the militia will not stand the fire of the cannon, or the point of the bayonet; be it so—in some instances,

> He that in battle runs away,
> Will live to fight another day.

But, to where do they retreat? not to the enemy, but to their homes—to the bosom of their country, there to renew their courage, and to recruit their strength, and return to the conflict with renewed vigor and enthusiasm. The art of war is a science that must be learned, as well as a mechanic his trade, or a lawyer or a physician his profession. Sir, towards the latter period of the Revolutionary war, in the Southern section of the Union, the courage and patriotism of the militia were almost unparalleled and proverbial. It was said of them as of the ancient Parthians who defeated the Roman legions, that when advancing to the attack they were invincible and not to be resisted; and when they retreated, in their flight were not to be overtaken. Sir, the valor and heroism of the militia, both in the old and new war, is covered and attested by a cloud of witnesses; and had I not heard an odium cast on the courage and patriotism of that class of our citizens, my voice should not have been heard on this occasion, nor should I have taken any part in this debate. But, sir, it is with no small sensations of gratitude that I find myself at this time placed in a situation so as to become the humble advocate of the militia of my country, whose valor, courage, and skill, in military science, has been witnessed throughout the continent. To sanction the position, I am under no necessity of recourse to history or far-fetched testimony. The facts are within my reach and personal recollection. At a late period in the Revolutionary war, when times were gloomy, and desperation stared us in the face, and was thought by some all was lost, at the memorable battle of King's Mountain, where Major Ferguson, a celebrated British officer, with a force of veterans detached from Cornwallis's army, having penetrated to the mountains to the extreme parts on the frontiers of North Carolina; and on his return, as he believed from a triumph over the rebels, was pursued by the militia of North Carolina, South Carolina, and Tennessee, commanded by Colonels Campbell, Shelby, and Sevier, officers whose memory will be perpetuated, and live in their country while their country lives; and overtaken at King's Mountain, South Carolina, was beaten, defeated, and totally routed; none escaped to carry the news; and let it be ever remembered that no one officer who commanded, not one soldier who was engaged in the action and obtained the victory, were of the regular army, but all militia.

And, at the celebrated battle of the Cowpens, South Carolina, which terminated so favorable and triumphant, and shed such lustre on the American arms, where Colonel Tarlton, with his legion of cavalry, and the flower of the British army, advanced up the country flushed with the assurance of victory, was met by the militia commanded by Generals Pickens and McDowell, with a few regulars under the command of General Morgan, and was there totally defeated, routed, and dispersed; and so decisive was the victory, that the number of prisoners exceeded the number of the army who guarded them after the battle. Such was the bravery of the militia in the old war, which is conclusive evidence, that when they become acquainted with the art of war, and brought into action, they are the best soldiers in the world.

The battle of the Hanging Rock was also gained by the militia. It is beyond the bounds of my inquiry to relate the many skirmishes and engagements wherein the militia were always victorious to the South. But, Mr. Chairman, I must differ in opinion from the relation given by some gentlemen, as it relates to the battle of Camden, where General Gates was met, surprised, and defeated by the British. It has been said that the militia fled and deserted from the battle, and was the cause of the defeat. Sir, they fled when they were beaten, with the other troops; but it must be remembered that General Gates brought to the South an army of the best disciplined troops in the United States, with able officers, was met and surprised by the British army, commanded by Lord Cornwallis, near Camden, South Carolina, where neither the shame nor disgrace of that defeat should or ought to be attached to the militia or regulars, but to the lack of vigilance in the commanding officer, in suffering himself to be surprised in so critical a moment. Let history or report relate what it may, I am authorized to say

this is a correct statement of facts relative to the action, from officers of high standing, and from the general impression made on the public mind of the people in the South. I do not pretend to affirm it by my own testimony, for I was neither in the battle nor in the race.

Sir, in the Revolutionary war, when our rights were invaded, our liberties assailed, and our country in jeopardy, the militia were the only and the best defence on which we could rely. Although unaccustomed to the art of war, they wanted not courage to defend their rights; no monitor but one; no mercenary views to prompt or induce them. Inspired by the love of liberty and hopes of independence, with the rifle in one hand and their country in the other, they marched to the field of battle, without money and without price, determined to die or be free. But, Mr. Chairman, those days of heroism appear to have passed away and descended with our ancestors to the tomb. In the present period of modern refinement, in this polite age, when the morning star of peace and prosperity has risen in our hemisphere, which gladdens every scene and cheers every heart, we are seized with an epidemic; the fever of national importance, and national and individual wealth and precedence, prevails throughout the continent. It is caught from breast to breast; few escape the contagion. This prevailing principle is fully verified in the late war. When the necessity occurred to enlist men to fill the ranks of the army, for the defence of the nation, we were compelled to give large premiums; give much, and promise more, to raise a regular force sufficient for the purposes of the war.

The purse and the sword then were together; nay, sir, more; the purse must go before the sword, and whet it for the day of battle.

But, sir, I must not be misunderstood in these remarks, so as to suppose I intend to give any unfriendly insinuations, or cast a shade, or the least imputation, on the army of the late war and the present day. We owe them gratitude for their valor and services; but I must be permitted to bring into view, and discover, the unparalleled difference between them and their fathers of the Revolution, who, with empty pockets, suffering the extremes of every climate, the privation of every comfort, conflicting with all the horrors of war, by their valor and courage obtained the liberty we now enjoy. While the late army and them of the present day, receives a full compensation and good reward from Government for their military services. The prevailing passion for national and individual wealth, manifests the principle in strong colors, in the various moneyed institutions disseminated throughout the United States, in the banking system, until it appears that some of them are almost suffocated by their own excess. This stimulus, this same overwhelming principle, has had a sensible operation on the measures of the Government, and has led us into the same temptation. A few years past, from the prosperous state of our commerce and products of the agricultural interest, we were rich, and increased in wealth; had a flowing Treasury and flowing hearts; made large appropriations; turned none empty away, and even created means to exhaust our finances: but now, sir, our condition is in a measure reversed, and we begin to feel the effects of our own indiscretion. It is high time to retrace our steps, and return to that happy medium of administration between the extremes of parsimony on the one hand, and profusion on the other; and the bill on your table is one of those effective measures, calculated to accomplish that object.

Mr. W. said he was not gratified with all he heard from gentlemen on the same side with himself. His friend and colleague (Mr. WILLIAMS) had taken an able and comprehensive view of the subject, and had brought conviction to his mind that a reduction of the army was not only practical, but compatible with the safety and interest of the nation; but, sir, his strictures on the report of the Secretary of War are calculated to make an unfavorable impression on the public mind relative to the official conduct of that officer. The Secretary of War partakes of the fallibility of human nature, and, as a man, was liable to involuntary error; but, Mr. W. said, he could not bring his mind to such unfavorable conclusions, respecting the report alluded to, as that to which the mind of his colleague had come; on the contrary, he had thought himself justified in saying that the Secretary of War was considered an intelligent and vigilant officer, and had administered the duties of his department with diligence and ability. He would state one fact in support of this opinion. The land lying in the chartered boundary of North Carolina was acquired, he believed, chiefly by the exertions made by the Secretary of War in the late treaty held with the Cherokee nation. Whatever difficulty was involved in the negotiation—and he (Mr. W.) knew there was much difficulty —the Secretary succeeded in obtaining the purchase, without any specific charge on that State. Mr. W. said, it had not been his course to pass encomiums on men in office; but he thought it decorous, and, in common justice, felt it his duty to offer these remarks on a transaction that came within his own knowledge, of which he was occasionally made acquainted, and in which he took a deep interest, in behalf of that section of the State he represented.

And had his other friend and colleague (Mr. FISHER) been so fortunate as to have passed by, and not given a resurrection to the Seminole war, a subject long since approved and laid to rest, and inscribed in the annals of fame, recorded in your Journals, wherein he stated that the commanding officer of that expedition had exceeded his authority, acted contrary to orders, and violated the Constitution; had the gentleman, where he came to that point, turned aside some other way, or on the one side or the other evaded these remarks, his speech would have been highly acceptable and conclusive in his favor, and saved his friend from being compelled to make this reluctant reply. Sir, the three preceding Administrations have been brought into view, and argued with ability; gentlemen have given them as vouchers for the political ground which they have taken; some in favor, and some against standing armies in time of peace. I admit, sir, that every respect is due to the wisdom and policy of those who have gone before us; but, sir, it is the happy privilege of our Government for every generation to legislate for themselves. The lapse of time always brings with it a revolution of politics; and that which was proper and consistent with the interests of the nation twenty or thirty years past, may not be applicable to us in the present period; and, therefore, it is necessary we should look out for ourselves, and pursue such measures of policy as we believe to be best adapted and most suitable for us in our situation, and at the present day.

Although, Mr. Chairman, the situation of our finances is not so favorable as could be wished, and our agricultural interest greatly depressed, our commerce measurably diminished, our resources of national wealth impeded, and, for want of a due proportion of circulating medium, the individual interest of many of our citizens much embarrassed; yet, amidst all these unfavorable appearances, our country presents a pleasing prospect of better times: the blessings of peace are yet ours, we have none to contend with, none to provide for but our own households; and, could we arrive at the true policy of governing ourselves with temperance and moderation, that course would lead us to individual happiness and national prosperity, unparalleled by any other nation on earth. Our resources are great; we have the means, and the duty devolves on us to make the application. And, sir, the bill on your table contains one of the leading features of that policy. I therefore feel bound to give it my support.

When Mr. W. had concluded,

Mr. SERGEANT took the floor in favor of the motion. When he concluded, the House adjourned.

TUESDAY, January 16.

Another member, to wit: from Kentucky, HENRY CLAY, appeared, and took his seat.

The SPEAKER laid before the House a letter from the Secretary of the Navy, enclosing a report of the Commissioners of the Navy, containing information as to the sums of money requisite to complete existing contracts, entered into in pursuance of the act for the gradual increase of the Navy, made in obedience to the resolution of this House of the 9th instant; which letter and report were ordered to lie on the table.

On motion of Mr. RUSS, the House proceeded to consider the resolution submitted by him yesterday, and, the same being again read, was agreed to.

The SPEAKER laid before the House a letter from the Secretary of the Navy, transmitting a statement, showing the balance of each distinct appropriation for the Navy remaining in the Treasury, and in the hands of the Treasurer, as agent for the Navy Department, on the 1st of January, 1821, and other information required by the resolution of the 4th instant; which letter and statement were referred to the Committee of Ways and Means.

REDUCTION OF THE ARMY.

The House then again resolved itself into a Committee of the Whole on the bill for the reduction of the Army of the United States; the motion of Mr. SIMKINS to strike out the first section yet depending—

Mr. TRIMBLE, of Kentucky, said, that he was in favor of reducing the Army to six thousand rank and file. He knew that there were some well-founded objections to the bill as reported by the Military Committee; but these would be removed by amendments, in case the motion to strike out the first section should not prevail. He hoped that those who were opposed to reduction would not urge objections to the details of the bill, and, to be candid, he thought they had no right to do so, because, by the rules of the House, the friends of the bill had a right to make it as perfect as possible, by amendments, before a motion to strike out the first section could be offered; and, as this privilege on their part had been waived to allow the present motion, the courtesy of Parliamentary concession would be violated if the bill should be assailed in its details. He wished it to be distinctly understood that he should, on his part, confine the discussion to the principles involved in the measure, and to the necessity and expediency of reduction.

Some of the friends of reduction had allowed their zeal to carry them from the main question into a comparative view of the militia and the regular Army; while others, alarmed at the arbitrary propensities of military power, had rambled over the pages of history, ancient and modern, in search of examples to prove that standing armies are dangerous to civil liberty. He did not wish to impugn the reasoning of his friends, but he was fearful that their arguments had more of theory, and less of substantial fact, than was proper on a subject of this kind. Perhaps, in fairness, the friends of the present Peace Establishment ought to show that the public service requires an Army of ten thousand, but they had very adroitly thrown the *onus probandi* upon the friends of reduction, and then challenged them to go into the details of the service, and designate the places where troops are uselessly employed, and show that six thousand is sufficient. Two or three members have pressed the attack in that quarter, supposing it, no doubt, to be the weakest part of our line of defence. The gentleman from Pennsylvania (Mr. SERGEANT) broke ground, and opened his battery upon that point, and it was but just to say that he had occupied the best position which the field afforded. Another gentleman, from the same State, (Mr. BALDWIN,) called for facts as triumphantly as if the victory was gained, and he had only come in to claim a portion of the spoils of argument. Mr. T. said he would meet the call; he would engage to dig up some *ore*, if the gentleman would promise to manufacture it into ploughshares and spindles. The gentleman himself had stated some facts which might be useful, if properly applied. He had stated that one of the Major Generals was at his farm in New York, attending to the concerns of agriculture; and another near Nashville in Tennessee, equally well employed. And this was stated to prove that the militia of the Union, being about eight hundred thousand, are not likely to be destroyed by those two officers of the regular Army. And so it does prove it; and what of it? But it proves another thing: that the operations of the Army were going on without the personal attendance or assistance of those two Generals; and that, consequently, they could be disbanded without much detriment to the public service. The same gentleman insisted that the disbursements of the Government were controlled by a liberal economy, and, to prove this, he drew a contrast between the expenditures of the nation and some city corporations. Baltimore, he said, expended annually about one hundred and thirty thousand dollars upon the local service of that city. This, Mr. T. said, was quite probable. He had been in that city more than once, and had some knowledge of the public works and public spirit of the place. Its citizens, said he, are a generous, liberal, open-handed, high-minded people; they have some splendid monuments, surpassing in magnitude every thing of the kind in the Republic. One is the Washington Monument, proudly ascending one hundred and forty feet above the plane of its horizon, erected, by a grateful people, to immortalize the glory of the "Father of his Country." Another is in progress to perpetuate the fame of those who fell in defence of the city; in defence of their wives, and families, and sacred homes. It is a monument of generous sympathy and noble feeling, consecrated by orphans' sobs and widows' tears. And another yet, of vast dimensions, the base of which is upwards, and the cone pointing downward, piercing the earth—the plan is yet on paper. No part of the Union can show a parallel, and centuries may elapse before one of equal magnitude and like materials will be seen. A gentleman asks me for its name. Here it is—*Bankruptcy*—to the amount of millions.

The gentleman from South Carolina (Mr. SIMKINS) had informed the Committee that the Executive departments were opposed to reduction, especially the War Department, and contended that we ought not to act hastily in disbanding the present Army against their better judgment and more deliberate opinion. Mr. T. thought it would be as well to leave their opinions out of the argument. For his part, he was not hostile to any of them—State, Treasury, War, or Navy. He had no grievances to complain of, no disfavors to resent. He would support any of them when he believed them right, and he would follow his own opinion when it tells him they are wrong. In doing this, he had no fears of giving umbrage to any one; and, if he did, what of it? Must he pine himself to death, and be buried at the public charge, or "fork his fingers in their faces hale and hearty," and try to be, what every member of a legislative body ought to be—free and independent? The same gentleman (Mr. SIMKINS) had asserted that there were no petitions against the army, and insisted that Congress ought not to reduce it, unless the people should petition for reduction and retrenchment. Mr. T. would tell his friend, that when the people send petitions for reduction of expenses, they usually turn out old members, and send new ones in their places. That was the way in 1798. He would tell his friend another thing: the people had already walked forth into the field of expenditure; they had found the Army a barren fig tree, and had said, "Cut it down, why cumbereth it the vineyard of the Treasury?" But the husbandmen of the Army, those who expect to gather its fruits, implore you to spare it yet another year. They promise to dig about, and water it, and if next year it bring not forth fruit of utility, then, say they, ye may lay the axe to the root and hew it down. In his opinion the day of retrenchment had come. No one ventures to advocate loans after this year, and we must retrench expenses, or find new means of raising revenue. The present condition of the country forbids the adoption of any system of taxation, and the existing state of the Treasury, and the barren prospect before it, would enforce a rigid system of economy.

He did not intend, however, to rest the argument for reduction upon the want of means in the Treasury. If the principles he intended to rely upon should be found correct, and fairly applicable to the subject, a deficit of five thousand or five millions would not change the conclusion which would follow. To be better understood, he would state that there are three questions involved in the inquiry before the Committee:

1st. Is the present Army necessary for the peace service of the country?

2d. Is the Treasury able to support it?

3d. Will its reduction lessen the strength of the nation—diminish its capacity to meet the emergencies of future wars?

The argument in favor of reduction would be conclusive, if it could be shown that a force of six thousand is adequate to the peace service of the Republic, and that the money saved by reduction could be more usefully employed. He had the temerity to believe that he should be able to show this in the view he would take of the three questions just propounded. But, said he, the gentleman from Pennsylvania (Mr. SERGEANT) says, that a part of the peace service consists in preparing for war; that standing armies have been established by all Governments; that they make a part of the police of nations; and that we invite aggression when we weaken that arm of our national defence. Yes, sir, said Mr. T., and an iron-handed system of arbitrary power, supported by those armies, makes a part also of the police of nations; and the occlusion of the body of the people from the rights of self-government makes another part of the police of nations; and public debts, to a fearful amount, created in supporting these armies, make another part of the police of nations; and vast loans, made for the purpose of marching these armies to the field of battle, where they can slay and be slain, makes another part of the police of nations; and ponderous systems of taxation make another part of the police of nations—until

all Europe is stoop-shouldered under the tremendous pressure of these onerous systems of police. And what has Europe gained by these sacrifices? He would not insult misery and wretchedness by asking if she is prosperous or happy? He would only ask, if she had purchased peace and tranquillity? Will any statesman have the hardihood to assert, with the history of the last two centuries before him, that the augmentation of the armies of Europe has promoted forbearance and good fellowship among the sovereigns, or forestalled aggression, or diminished the number of their desolating wars? And why should the people of this continent make haste to naturalize the false maxims and mad policy of Europe, and follow her along the road to ruin? We are warned, said he, by the agonies she has suffered, and is now suffering, and is destined to suffer, to eschew her systems of military police.

Is the present Army necessary for the peace service of the country? What are its peace duties? To garrison our posts and fortifications, and control and overawe the Indians. What quantum of force is necessary for these purposes? Gentlemen opposed to us talk about the Peace Establishment of 1802 and 1808, but carefully omit the comparison between the peace service of that period and the peace service of the present. From 1802 to 1808, the Peace Establishment was fixed at three thousand rank and file, and that Army performed the service which we are now told requires ten thousand. The contrast stares gentlemen in the face like sunshine, and, to escape the painful conclusion, they tell us that the peace service has greatly increased. They say—

1st. That our population is nearly doubled.

2d. That we have nearly doubled our posts and forts.

3d. That our frontiers are greatly extended.

Let us examine these facts, and see how far they justify the argument. If the gentlemen from South Carolina and Pennsylvania (Messrs. SIMKINS and SERGEANT) mean to say, that an increase of population implies an increase of facility in filling the ranks, agreed. If they mean that it implies an increase of means to support an army, he would frankly admit it. But if they intend to affirm that an increase of population enlarges the peace service of the Army, or makes it necessary to augment the Army in time of peace, he must boldly deny it. Do they mean to say that faction and discontent increases with population, and calls for an augmentation of military force to quell its bold audacity? Such a sentiment is not to be endured. Can the census of any nation be the standard of its Peace Establishment? The argument, he said, was surely used as a make-weight; it came across his pride and feeling, and he would not trust himself to speak further of it. It would refute itself.

The posts and forts are increased in number; and, in the same proportion, he admitted it was necessary to have more troops than we had at 1802 and 1808. At 1803 and 1804 we had 34, and at 1808 we occupied 47 posts and fortifications. At this time we occupy 54, or at most 69. The returns laid upon our tables show 124 posts, 54 of which have garrisons of not less than ten rank and file; fifteen others of them have one, and three, and five, and eight, officers and men at them; just enough to lock the gates, and the rest, 53 in number, are abandoned as useless. In fact some of them had no existence, and he could not perceive why they were reported. We offer an army of 6,000; and it is clear that this army, when properly distributed among the posts and forts now occupied, would give each a force superior to the average of that which they had from 1802 to 1808. Separately considered, therefore, the argument upon posts and forts was against the opposers of reduction. But as it was his intention to meet the argument fairly, in all its force, he would proceed to inquire into the alleged enlargement of our frontiers, and would treat the subject as if the arguments of populations, and forts, and posts, was consolidated with the other. Are our frontiers extended since 1802, so as to require an additional force for the peace service? To avoid all complexity of ideas on the subject, he said he would divide the frontiers of the Union into four parts.

1st. Our maritime frontier, extending along the seaboard, from Eastport, in Maine, to the mouth of St. Mary's, in Georgia.

2d. Our left flank, resting upon Nova Scotia, and the Canadas, and extending from Eastport, in Maine, to Fort Mackinac.

3d. Our right flank, resting upon the Floridas, the Gulf of Mexico, and the Spanish provinces; and,

4th. Our rear, or Western settlements, along the valley of the Mississippi, and which are protected by a cordon of posts from Fort Mackinac, head of Lake Huron, to Fort Smith, in the Arkansas.

Two or three general remarks, he said, would shorten the argument. He was proceeding upon the tacit admission that the front and flanks of the Union require a force at this time, double that which was distributed upon the same lines from 1802 to 1808. But this was conceding more than he was bound to grant. It is admitted that the forts and fortifications have been doubled on the front and flanks since 1804. And, as the natural defences are the same now as then, it follows that the artificial strength of those lines has been doubled; and, therefore, he could assert, without fear of denial, that the same military force, distributed upon those lines, would make them stronger now than they were at 1802 and 1808. Would this be contradicted? Do fortifications weaken the country? If so, why construct them? Do they not increase its strength? Does not every fort increase the strength of its line of defence? Will you not double the strength of a given line (all other things being equal) by doubling the number of forts upon that line? Surely you do. And it follows of course that, as you increase the defensive strength of a line, by erecting fortresses, you may diminish its military force. Now, therefore, as the bill proposes an army double that of 1802, and, as it is certain that the front and flanks of the country will receive their due proportion of the six thousand, it is fair to contend that the military, as well as the permanent artificial strength

of the front and flanks, will be double that of 1802 and 1808. How, then, stands the argument, in reference to our maritime front? It was as far from Eastport, in Maine, to St. Mary's, in 1802 and 1808, as it is at this day, and the same harbors and estuaries along the coast to be defended. There is, therefore, no extension of territory upon our seaboard. But its natural defences are the same, and its fortifications are doubled, and the bill proposes to give it double the number of troops to garrison those fortresses. And will it still be said, that a reduction of the army to six thousand, will reduce the strength of our maritime front to below the standard of 1802 and 1808. Would it not be fair to say, at once, that we shall leave the seaboard twice as strong as it was at that period? These remarks, he said, were equally applicable to the peace service of our left flank, beginning at Eastport, in Maine, and extending along our boundary line westward, to the St. Lawrence and the lakes, and up the lakes to Detroit, and from thence to Mackinac; and also to our right flank, beginning at St. Mary's, in Georgia, and extending westward and southwest as far as Fort Smith, on the Arkansas. There is no extension upon either of those lines since 1802 and 1808; nor is there any demand for additional troops, save that which is created by the erection of forts; to garrison which, a fair proportion of the six thousand is fully adequate. Where, then, said he, is this vast extension of territory, which makes an increase of the army necessary? On the west, say gentlemen, the defensive line of our rear has been extended. Let us refer to facts. The Committee would recollect that he left them at Mackinac on the left flank, and at Fort Smith on the right. The space between those two points is our military rear. On the 20th of November, 1803, the province of Louisiana was surrendered, at New Orleans, to the United States, under the Treaty of St. Ildefonso. The fort of St. Louis, and the intermediate posts, were transferred on the 10th of March following. At and before this acquisition, we had a cordon of posts from Mackinac to Fort Adams, on the Mississippi six miles above the Spanish line. But, to make the contrast free from all color of inequality, he would omit Fort Adams, and stop at the old Spanish post of Arkansas. To avoid mistake he would enumerate the posts upon the cordon, and give the strength of each at several periods. They were as follow:

	Aggregate force.		
	1802.	1808.	1809.
1. Fort Mackinac - -	125	104	90
2. Chicago, i. e. Fort Dearborn -		66	77
3. Fort Wayne - -	64	76	53
4. Post St. Vincennes - -	75		14
5. Belle Fontaine, Mississippi		89	51
6. Kaskaskias, same river -	78		
7. Fort Massac - - -	71	84	32
8. Fort Pickering, Chick'w Bluffs	78		
9. Post Arkansas, Arkansas river		17	
Total - -	491	436	318

The total, as here given, is not exactly correct, because there were some changes in the posts; as, for instance, the troops were withdrawn from Fort Pickering after the acquisition of Louisiana, and the garrison at Kaskaskias was discontinued, and the troops sent to Fort Osage, in the Missouri Territory. But it is positively true, he said, that the aggregate force on that frontier did not exceed five hundred rank and file at any time between 1802 and 1811. And this force, during that period, maintained the posts, overawed the Indians, protected the frontier, and were found to be adequate to the peace service in that quarter. At present we have the following cordon of posts; the force at each of which, is taken from the last returns, viz:

1. Fort Mackinac, head of Lake Huron -	115
2. Fort Howard, Green Bay, mouth of Fox river - - - - - - - -	524
3. Chicago, Fort Dearborn, Lake Erie - -	134
4. St. Peter's, mouth of river St. Peter's, Cantonment Leavenworth - - - -	354
5. Fort Crawford, Prairie du Chien, mouth of Wisconsin - - - - - -	101
6. Fort Armstrong, Rock Island, Mississippi -	80
7. Council Bluffs, 720 miles up the Missouri -	851
8. Fort Smith, —— miles up the Arkansas -	76
Total - -	2,235

Formerly the cordon terminated at the Chickasaw Bluffs, and then again at Post Arkansas, after its surrender to us, but at this time both of these posts are discontinued, and Fort Smith established in lieu of them.

Now, said Mr. T., contrast this and that, and then tell us what has become of the argument of extension. In the former period, you had one post more than at present; and although you have changed the location of forts and posts, as the frontier settlements advanced, yet the line from Fort Mackinac to Post Arkansas, was as long, or nearly so, as the line from Mackinac to Fort Smith, on the Arkansas. You have only thrown out the centre of the line; and in this alone consists the prodigious elongation of which we hear so much. But the frontier settlements are stronger now than they were in 1803–6–9—have better rifles, and more of them, and are in every respect better able to defend themselves. Are the Indians more numerous, or more warlike, or more hostile now than they were then? The fact is well known, that the number of warriors are greatly diminished since 1802. Some of the tribes are almost extinct; others are our avowed friends or allies, or quasi subjects. Their proud spirit has been quailed. Their warlike habits and intrepidity of character are on the wane. In short, the tribes immediately upon our border, are less warlike and more drunken and worthless, than at any former period. Besides, our control over them has been extended quite as much as our posts. The British traders are entirely excluded from some of the tribes, and their influence is everywhere diminished, and constantly diminishing; and what is of more consequence, the Indians must, for the future, look to us for supplies, especially arms and munitions of war, which would always be withheld the moment they manifested indications of hostility; and then, in addition to the military force on that frontier, we have an army of traders, and factors, and military agents, all of whom assist in smoking the pipe of peace.

Hence, it appears, that we have quadrupled our force on that line of frontier, although the actual demand there for troops has not increased; has, in fact, greatly diminished since 1802. And thus it is manifest, that the argument of extension is a mere exaggeration, a phantom of the forest, which vanishes the moment you break up the margin of the Union into lines, and apply the standard of 1802–6–8, to the present peace service of the country. Will the reduction of the Army make it necessar to withdraw a part of this force from the West? In this he was unwilling to control the Departments. But, it was his decided opinion, that at this time the Army was unequally and improperly distributed. New York, for instance, has a force of one thousand seven hundred, with one Major General and one Brigadier; and Kentucky has a force of one officer and servant. It was true, that Kentucky had rifles enough to defend it; but surely the great State of New York ought not to be degraded by treating it as a conquered country, to be held only by a strong force in garrison. If the battalions or regiments are kept entire for the purpose of drill and manœuvre, let them be sent to the West, where subsistence is cheap. New York has a force of one thousand seven hundred, and the whole Western frontier only two thousand three hundred and sixty-three. He would not complain of these things, but he would say, after reducing the Army to six thousand, a reinforcement could be sent to the West equal to the whole force with which that frontier had been protected, from 1802 up to 1809.

It was possible, he said, that he might be incorrect in some of the facts he had stated. The Army report, as printed, had only been laid on the tables yesterday, and from the hasty glance he had given it, he could not assure the House that he was exactly correct in all the details he had given, but he would confidently assert, that he was substantially correct in all the leading facts. And if so, it was now his turn, he said, to call upon gentlemen for information. He demanded of them to show that the state of our relations, interior or exterior, foreign or domestic, requires at this time a stronger military force upon the flanks of our country, or on our rear, or maritime front, than we had there from 1802 to 1808. The gentleman from South Carolina, (Mr. SIMKINS,) aided by the gentleman from Pennsylvania, (Mr. SERGEANT,) had given a catalogue of reasons. They say we shall presently occupy Florida; have they forgotten that the Army of 1802, occupied the great province of Louisiana in 1803–4, without any increase of force? Must we retain the forts along the present line, and establish new posts in Florida, to defend it against ourselves? Or may we not do as we did in 1803–4, break up the useless posts on that flank and order the troops down into Florida, as we then did into Louisiana? Again, they say we must keep up the Army to defend Florida, and garrison its posts and forts, and overawe the Indians. But, if a part of the Army of three thousand defended Louisiana and garrisoned its forts, and overawed the Indians, surely a due proportion of six thousand can perform that service in Florida. How many troops do you want there? Three hundred at St. Augustine, two hundred at Pensacola, fifty at St. Marks, and one hundred at the mouth of the Appalachicola, to aid the gunboats in seizing those who attempt to smuggle negroes or goods into that part of the Union. Does the acquisition of Florida make that frontier stronger or weaker than it was before? If stronger, why do you want more troops there now, than we had there in 1803–4–8? If weaker, why did we make the treaty? Is it really true that we shall weaken the Union by this arrondissement of our territory? Must we entail upon ourselves and upon posterity an increase of the Army, with all its concomitant expenses, for the purpose of occupying a country which, being acquired, makes us weaker than we were without it? Are we to pay $5,000,000 for an encumbrance? Must we pay that sum for Florida, and surrender a great fine dukedom beyond the Sabine, to make ourselves more defenceless than we were before? Where are the friends of the treaty? Let them stand forth and defend it. Bad as it was, and hostile to it as he always had been, he would still do justice to all sides. He was ready to admit, he was prepared to prove, that the Floridas would add greatly to the strength of our Southern frontier; and for that very reason, said he, we want no increase of the Army to defend it.

But, again; they say our dispute with Spain is not yet settled. He would ask, if we had no dispute with Spain in 1802? Was not the right of deposite withheld? Had they forgotten that Federal gentlemen on this floor called loudly for war, and demanded that the nation should prepare for hostilities? But the Army was not increased, the affair with Spain blew over, and the Peace Establishment was reduced, and fixed at three thousand.

Again; we must look, it is said, to our foreign relations. Do we not see, say they, that the materials for revolution are prepared throughout Europe, and that dreadful convulsions may be apprehended? And what then? Only this—Europe will be fully employed at home, and will find no leisure to wage war in our hemisphere. Spain is named. What can she do? Can she find means to assail us at a moment when she cannot reduce the weakest of her revolted colonies? But, she must finish her self-renovation; her undivided attention is employed in her domestic concerns; in the re-establishment of order and the constitutional system; and in creating ways and means to pay the public debt. From that Power we have nothing to fear; Mexico is our hostage with her. Have a little patience, said he, until the allied sovereigns can persuade Ferdinand that he is strong enough to reclaim the ancient prerogatives of the Crown, and re-establish arbitrary power, and you will cease to speak of her as an argument against reduction. Austria—and what of her? The van-

guard of free government approaches her dominions; to repel it, she is preparing a crusade upon the kingdom of Naples. Free principles have entered her territories, and missionaries of the new political Testament—a work published in Europe, under the title Constitution—representative government, and equal rights. Russia—the enlightened head of that empire can feed ambition nearer home; Europe and Asia spread their feasts before him, and bid him come and sate his appetite for glory. France—we got an army up for her in '98; let us remember the consequences, and grow wiser. England—when had we less to fear from her? The Throne has exhausted its power in a wrangle with the Queen. The nobility are scandalized by the trial of the Queen. Public opinion has put the Crown in Coventry; the quiverings of commotion are felt from the centre to the extremities of the Kingdom. Disaffection rages; the cloud of discontent rolls on, increasing as it goes, and gathering electric fires by the attritions of resistance; where it will burst none know; but burst it will, upon the lordly palace or lowly cottage.

Last, and least of all, comes the argument of manufactures. You were told by the member from Pennsylvania (Mr. SERGEANT) that if you turn four thousand laborers loose upon the country, you will discourage manufactures. He suggested this, as worthy of attention, but would not urge it. Perhaps, said Mr. T., it may have some weight among the friends of manufactures, and if so, he would suggest a set-off, for those who oppose the tariff. Congress will refuse loans after this year. If the revenue fails, you must reduce the army or levy direct taxes, or impose an excise, or increase the tariff; but the moment you come to these dilemmas, the friends of manufactures will vote to raise the tariff, while those who oppose it, will divide upon a system of excise and direct taxation; and the tariff will be carried. Those, therefore, who wish to avoid the painful operation of increasing the tariff, will recollect that they can only do so by seasonable reductions and rigid economy. He was surprised, he said, to hear the army spoken of as the basis of national prosperity. He had always supposed that productive labor and economy was that basis, and that armies were great consumers, and not producers, hanging like mill-stones upon the spindles of productive labor, and taking a heavy toll for grinding. He would not trouble them further, he said, upon this branch of the subject. Every view which he had been able to give it, in the gross or in detail, brought him to the conclusion that the peace service of the country did not require an army of ten thousand. In his opinion, six thousand was fully adequate to that service.

The ability of the Treasury to support the army had been maintained by some and denied by others. He would not volunteer his services as umpire between them.

One gentleman gave a flattering account of the prospect before us, and asserted that we had paid off the national debt too fast. Another had dissected the Treasury report, and found balances enough to bring both ends of the year together. It would be cruel to dissipate these consoling delusions. Another thought the army so essential to the service of the country, that he was willing on the part of his constituents to sustain it by loans. Another agreed that the army was indispensably necessary, and insisted that taxes should be levied to supply the Treasury with means: and thus their arguments are made to terminate in loans and taxes. Mr. T. was tempted to engage in the fiscal discussion, but he would forego it until the loan bill should come up. One thing was agreed on all sides—that the hand of pressure lies heavy on the country, and he for one would not increase the weight; he would reduce it if possible; and to make sure work of it, he would search diligently for the causes. And what, said he, are the causes of this pressure, and these fiscal embarrassments? Is it want of means or want of economy in their application? Is any thing withheld from us which fertility of soil and manual labor can procure? Has Heaven pronounced a malediction against the Republic? Has the earth become sterile? Has hungry famine and pale pestilence swept away the people, and desolated the country? No, sir. Everywhere the eye is filled with abundance, and the heart made glad with the richness of the harvest. Plenty has spread her ample means in prodigal profusion. But we have no market. The surplus of our labor perishes upon our hands. We cease to purchase foreign labor, because our labor is not taken in exchange. We import less than formerly. The revenue from customs sinks apace, and while all things are falling to a common level, the Government mounts upwards to its maximum of expenditure. Our fault is this: We live beyond our income. Our schemes are too magnificent. We must season our disbursements with economy. Our friend (Mr. SERGEANT) says that this pressure arises from two permanent causes. The loss of the carrying trade, and the fall in the price of our produce in foreign markets, both of which events, he says, are owing to the peace in Europe. But, if this is the result of peace, will it not last as long as peace continues? Most surely; and yet our friend made it appear that a reaction was about to begin, which would relieve the Treasury and the country from all embarrassment. He made a comparison between nations and individuals; the contrast was rather unfortunate. He said that a private citizen, who borrows a sum and pays a debt with it, is nothing poorer than he was; and just so with a nation. Yes, said Mr. T., such people take loans to keep themselves afloat, hoping as we do for better times, and praying for it quite as ardently. They count upon reaction as we do, predicting every year that it will begin the next; ever consoling themselves with brighter prospects, until bankruptcy and ruin ends the delusive scene, and leaves them in a dungeon with nothing but despair to comfort misery. Such, also, is the fate of nations when they live on loans, and feast on capitals instead of income. And such, if we hold on our course in these hard times, may be the end and termination of our Treasury. It is a maxim,

asserted by Mr. Hamilton, that a nation's wants are always equal to its means; and, if so, to live upon loans is treason against posterity. The means of every nation has its limits, and you have found those limits when you take loans to pay the current service of the year. He who seeks to organize the army upon a basis which requires more money than the country can afford, is the deadliest of enemies to the army and the nation. But, said he, let us waive the fiscal argument. Let us agree that the Treasury is full-handed; and with that admission proceed to discuss the third proposition, viz: Will the reduction of the army lessen the strength of the nation; diminish its capacity to meet the emergencies of future wars?

We are told that we have jealous neighbors, and that a reduction of the army will invite aggression. We are reminded of the maxim, "that peace is the time to prepare for war." But there is another maxim equally true and equally well known to military men: that the basis of preparation varies in every nation; nay, that it varies at different times in the same nation. Shall the war be offensive or defensive? If the latter, then you must know the force of the Powers who are likely to assail you; the kind and quantity of strength with which they may annoy you, and whether by land or water, or by both. Then you must carefully examine the natural barriers of your country, its positions, and defences, their relative influence upon each other, their action and reaction; and then, and not till then, are you prepared to make estimates for the kind and quantity of artificial means to complete your system of defence. Then you may begin to construct a basis for our army. But we must always remember that a proper basis for our peace establishment will not be found in books, or in Europe; we must search for it upon the profile of our country; in the customs, and habits, and occupations, of our people; in the genius of our Government, and in the resources of the nation. At this time, happy for us, we have no prospects of war with any Power, and all that prudence can ask—all that the most vigilant caution can require is, that the nation shall augment its strength by all the means within its reach. But there is at present no specific object claiming the application of military means: general preparation is all that we can make, because the object is general and specific. We are called upon to congregate the materials of national defence, and stand prepared for war. A statesman, before he begins the work, would ask himself what is the best preparation? The answer is obvious: that preparation which will make the nation strongest, and give the greatest facility to its active powers. And what constitutes the strength of a nation? Its moral energy, its purse, and its sword. Mind is power, the purse is power, and the sword is power. But what are their relative values? In a Republic moral energy has the first rank, the purse next, and the sword last: in a despotism the sword ranks first, but the primary object of a free people is, to foster and preserve its moral energy and its purse. This is its best and most efficient preparation. We have lectures upon military skill and experience, as if that was the only means of defence, as if it was the only needful preparation. But we must recollect that the sum total of means is composed of various items of which the military arm is only one, and that one of a secondary grade. Moral energy is national defence, and therefore we should create it and preserve it. Money is national defence, and therefore we should preserve the purse. Public credit is national defence, and therefore let us pay up the debt, and clear the Treasury decks for action. Roads and canals are national defence; they give facility to military operations, and peace is the proper period to construct them. Productive labor is national defence; encourage that and you are preparing for hostilities. Economy is preparation for defence. How long do nations prosper? Just so long as industry and frugality are in advance of idleness and prodigality. The nation that increases and preserves its purse will be more powerful than the nation that exhausts its means in "creating and perpetuating military skill." It is a maxim among statesmen that the purse is more available than the sword, and is most dreaded by rival nations. Marshal Saxe considers it the sinews of war, and so the great Turenne. Was it the purse of England, or the sword of the allies, that congregated all Europe into one military body, and precipitated the whole mass upon disloyal and disunited France? Let us bethink ourselves, said Mr. T., lest, in our haste for preparation, we omit that which should be first done—lest our mistaken zeal may expose us to defeat, by leaving too much space between the columns of defence. Like his opposers, he was in favor of preparing for war in time of peace, but he differed from them in the mode. Suppose, said he, that every other preparation was completed, and that Congress was now called on to finish the system by forming a nucleus for the military arm. A question would arise, what basis of preparation will embody the greatest quantity of military strength? How shall the raw material of the country be manufactured into its maximum of "military power?" By reducing the army we save one million of dollars; but suppose we resolve to expend that sum in military preparation. That mode of disbursement should be preferred which will secure the largest quantum of military skill and experience. Shall we expend the money upon the militia or the standing army? In compliment to the militia, they were called the "great bulwark of liberty;" but they had been totally neglected, as unsafe and useless in the hour of danger. Mr. T. held a different opinion, and he would suggest a mode by which they could be made as effective as the standing army, or nearly so.

If, said he, we form a class of from twenty-one to twenty-eight years of age, we shall have about two hundred and fifty thousand militia. The proportion of officers and non-commissioned officers for that body of militia would be about forty thousand, or perhaps less, (but that is not material,) and making in the aggregate a force of two hundred and ninety thousand. The officers would of course be distributed among the States upon the ratio of their militia, or upon any equitable ratio. Let the Government cause this body of militia to be instructed in the military science. Several modes may be adopted. For example: Let the General Government establish arsenals in the several States, and deposite a proper quantity of arms at each. Let cantonments or camps of instruction and discipline be formed at places convenient to those arsenals. Let the officers and non-commissioned officers of each State, belonging to the class of militia just mentioned, be ordered to these camps, and be kept in service one month in each year. Let them be armed and equipped at the arsenals, and let the most skilful officers of your army be ordered to the camps to conduct the drills and manœuvres. The cadets who have returned from West Point, after passing through the several classes of the Military Academy, could also assist at these drills, and thus become practically useful to the country. This process would form excellent officers, and, as they would be ordered to command in rotation, each would have an opportunity of displaying his military genius, and the War Department could possess itself of the names of the most promising military men in each State. At the expiration of the month, this army of officers would return home, and proceed to instruct their respective companies and regiments, until the next annual camp, and so on from year to year. So much, said he, for the mode of instruction, and now a word or two upon the application of the money. By reducing the army to 6,000 you save one million of dollars, which sum, divided equally among the forty thousand officers and non-commissioned officers, would pay them $25 per month each. You could distribute the pay in equal or unequal portions, as should be thought best; but, as this should not be made a money-making business, that principle of distribution should be adopted which would create least jealousy, and give most satisfaction. He could easily make out details, but it was sufficient for his present purpose to show that one million of dollars would keep forty thousand in the field for one month. He knew very well that the sum mentioned could be made to call out 60,000 upon the same plan, but he had selected 40,000, because that number would officer a body of 250,000 militia, which would be as large a force as this nation would want for centuries. It was easy, however, to change the calculation; as, for instance, if you wish to make the officers more efficient, you can, with the same sum, keep 20,000 at the camps of instruction for two months in each year; or, if you wish to save money, half that sum will keep 20,000 at the camps one month, and this number would officer a class of 125,000 militia. The present average price of the ration is ten cents, and upon that basis every member could amuse himself by making calculations, and exercise his liberality by making the pay six, eight, ten, or twenty dollars per month—always keeping this in view, that he is forming a system to instruct officers, who are to instruct the men, and that the system should be as effective as possible, at the smallest possible expense.

Here, said Mr. T., are two modes of preparing for war in time of peace; each is to cost the same sum, and the choice must be determined by superior efficiency. A brief contrast will show which has the "vantage ground." The Secretary of War tells us, "that the great object of a military peace establishment is to create and perpetuate military skill and experience." These are his own words, and what are the facts? We offer you an army of six thousand, and you ask ten. This additional 4,000 will cost the Treasury one million of dollars, and this is your nucleus of military science; this is your dispensatory of superior skill; this is your repository of the art of war. In lieu of this, we propose to disburse the same sum in establishing camps or schools of instruction and discipline for the officers of 250,000 militia, who are to instruct that body of militia from year to year. And can any man hesitate between these two modes of "creating and perpetuating military skill and experience?" Will any one doubt that the latter is the better preparation for the emergencies of future wars? He that gives preference to the first must labor under strange delusions. For himself, he had no doubt that, upon experiment, the system suggested would be found most useful to the Republic. He was sure it was more in unison with national policy and national feeling, and the true spirit of the Constitution. The sound judgment of the country would one day decide between the modes, and to them it must be left. But he would implore the friends of freedom and free government to reflect before they abandon the military, as unworthy of their fostering care; as unfit to defend the body of the nation; as unsafe repositories of the art of war. Who are the militia? The great body of the nation. And is the body of the nation unfit to bear arms and defend itself? Are the people their own worst enemies? May they not be trusted with their own protection? We betray their cause if we sap the confidence of the nation in this arm of its defence. The Constitution requires us to prepare a "well regulated militia" for our service; and yet we leave the militia a disorganized mass, untrained, undrilled, undisciplined, and then denounce them as useless to the country. We waste annually upon the army and other objects sums of money that would give the militia an effective organization, and then stigmatize them as unfit for service. What have we done for the standing army? Every thing. What for the militia? Nothing. How long will the people tolerate this negligence? It is a question to be settled, how far sound policy allows us to preterit, from year to year, the adoption of an effective militia system?

Mr. T. would have been glad if the opposers of reduction had contented themselves with eulogiums upon standing armies. He had to regret that they thought it necessary to disparage and defame the militia. They came with books prepared for action. With sword in hand they made the assault, and cut and hacked as furiously as if they had orders to give no quarter. We were told again and again by the gentleman from Virginia, (Mr. SMYTH,) and by others on his side, that the

militia could not be relied upon in time of danger; that they wanted firmness, and were unfit for national defence. A catalogue of instances had been g ven to show how shamefully they had fled when faced by regular troops; but they had forgot how often regular troops had been beaten by militia, and how often, when opposed to them, old veterans had turned recreant in the battle fray.

He feared that those who complained most of the militia were least able to command them. In his judgment, some of the arguments advanced were political heresies. When the second amendment to the Constitution was adopted, "a well regulated militia was considered necessary to the security of a free State." And who, said he, caused that article to be inserted? The schoolmen and tyros of the day, who had collected their knowledge of men and Governments from European authors, as ignorant of the subject as themselves? No, sir. It was a great political truth, promulgated by the sages of the Revolution, by men who understood the human passions, and knew how to close the avenues to arbitrary power; men of disinterested public virtue; who had fought and bled for freedom, and had been taught the science of free government in the schools of experience; men who knew that liberty is held upon condition of perpetual vigilance, and only secure when guarded by the body of the people, well armed and disciplined. As statesmen, said he, we should ponder well before we expunge from our liturgy the doctrines of '76 and '89. There are moral ligaments between freedom and the use of arms; cords of sympathy and union between liberty and a well organized militia, which should not be rashly cut or broken by the hand of folly. Liberty is gone when the military art is taught and practised only in the standing army. Deracinate the use of arms, and the people become timid and pusillanimous. Abandon the Republic to the protection of standing armies, and a prostration of political virtue will ensue, that must terminate in the spasms of despotic power. There was a period, he said, in the history of nations, which he fondly hoped our country would never know; that period in which the body of the people neglect the use of arms; that fatal period in which the nation, enfeebled by luxury, and overcome by lassitude, surrenders its protection and defence to standing armies and mercenary troops. Select an example where you please, of ancient or of modern date; take any nation that has figured on the theatre of time; look steadily into its history; search for the causes of its rise and progress—its decline and fall; mark the summit of its highest elevation, the point of its decline; seat yourself upon that eminence, while you survey the boundless ruin and gloomy desolation around you; inquire for the moral character of the generation that lies buried where you sit, and in that generation you will find that the use of arms was neglected; that the people had surrendered their protection and defence to standing armies and mercenary troops. Before that period, when every citizen bore arms, and flew, when called upon, to the ramparts of his country, you will find the nation marching upon its destiny with a steady eye and fearless front: after it, when the people had surrendered their protection and defence to standing armies and mercenary troops, you will find the nation falling, to rise no more.

The first, is the doric age of economy and strength; heroic virtues and love of liberty, vigorous measures and glorious achievements; national renown, and general prosperity. The second, is the corinthian period of luxury and refinement, and indolence and ease; voluptuousness and effeminacy; venality and corruption; cowardice, treachery, baseness and depravity, and all the catalogue of wayward vices, passions, and propensities. With such a people, liberty is not an effulgent body, fixed and located to the nation; it is a comet, blazing for a moment, or a meteor, gleaming across the horizon of their night, flashing and sparkling for an instant, and vanishing for ever. Sir, said he, it is a great political truth, attested by all experience, that a well regulated militia is necessary to the security of a free State. It is madness to deny it. If it be not true, then all history is false, and he that has not learnt it from the chronicles of nations, has read history to little purpose. When did a national militia erect a despotism? When, and where, have standing armies established free government and equal rights? It is the stratagem of tyrants to let the people neglect the art of war, and persuade them to abandon the use of arms, and thus make the protection of standing armies *necessary.

Mr. T. was prepared to urge some general remarks, which he would suppress, rather than forfeit the indulgence of the Committee. He had attempted to show, that an army of six thousand is adequate to the peace service of the country. He had waived the fiscal argument, and admitted, hypothetically, that the Treasury could sustain the expenditure required by the present Peace Establishment, and upon that supposition had contended, that a reduction of the army would not diminish the strength of the nation. He had made it appear, he hoped, that the money saved by reduction could be more usefully and effectively applied in various modes of preparation for hostilities. Among these modes, that of regulating, drilling, and training the militia, was suggested as the best preparation for future wars, and a better and safer repository of the military science. He had, while upon the fiscal subject, expressed a doubt of the ability of the Treasury to meet the future disbursements of the Government, unless aided by an excise, or a system of direct taxation; and in referring to the state of the country, had avowed his belief, that frugality had become an imperative duty; to which he would only add, as his fixed opinion, that at all times, and under every possible relation, in which events may place it, the nation that is first in the practice of economy, will be foremost in the march of power and true glory.

When Mr. TRIMBLE had concluded—

Mr. WOOD advocated generally, but briefly, a reduction of the Army.

Mr. COCKE spoke at considerable length in support of reduction, and of the bill under consideration.

Mr. BRUSH opposed, decidedly, a diminution of the present number of the Army; and

Mr. STEVENS advocated a reduction generally, without declaring a preference of any particular plan.

The speech of Mr. S. terminated the debate on the main question; but

Mr. LOWNDES having, as well from what had fallen from others, as from his own inability to vote on the subject understandingly until the Committee of Ways and Means had made their report, and exhibited to the House the true state of the national finances—suggested the propriety of postponing this bill until that committee should make their report.

A desultory conversation followed this suggestion, embracing various points, but chiefly touching the best mode of proceeding with the consideration of the subject—in which Messrs. BALDWIN, SIMKINS, FOOT, WILLIAMS of North Carolina, McLEAN, SERGEANT, COBB, FLOYD, CAMPBELL, and BARBOUR took part. Finally, a little before sunset, the question was put on Mr. SIMKINS's motion to strike out the first section of the bill, (to destroy it,) and was decided in the negative, by a large majority, only four or five rising in favor of the motion; and the Committee rose, and reported progress.

WEDNESDAY, January 17.

Mr. STREET, from the Committee on Pensions and Revolutionary Claims, to which was referred the bill from the Senate, entitled "An act for the relief of Ebenezer Stevens and Austin L. Sands, legal representatives of Richardson Sands, deceased, and others," reported the same without amendment, and the bill was committed to a Committee of the Whole.

Mr. WILLIAMS, from the Committee of Claims, made a report on the petition of Bartholomew Duverge, accompanied by a bill for his relief; which was read twice, and committed to the Committee of the Whole to which is committed the bill for the relief of Lewis H. Guerlain.

Mr. ANDERSON, from the Committee on the Public Lands, made a report on the petition of Benjamin Freeland, accompanied by a bill for his relief; which was read twice, and committed.

Mr. ANDERSON, from the same committee, to whom was referred the case of the deputy surveyor of the "Vincennes tract," made a report thereon, accompanied by a bill for the relief of Robert Buntin; which was read twice, and committed to the Committee of the Whole to which is committed the bill making provision for the payment of debts due the United States from purchasers of public lands.

Mr. BARBOUR laid before the House a letter from the Secretary of the Navy, addressed to the Chairman of the Naval Committee, stating that no change is necessary or expedient in the organization of the marine corps; and communicating a report of the Navy Commissioners upon the subject of rations; the number of officers necessarily wanting for actual service in 1821; upon the propriety of reducing the number of pursers, and dispensing with the service of sundry superintendents, storekeepers, &c., at the several navy yards ; the average cost per annum of the various sized vessels of the Navy while cruising and in ordinary ; which letter and report were ordered to lie on the table.

On motion of Mr. SIBLEY, the Committee on the Judiciary were instructed to inquire into the expediency of establishing a district court of the United States in and for the Territory of Michigan.

On motion of Mr. SIBLEY, the Committee on Military Affairs were instructed to inquire whether any, and, if any, what, amendments are necessary to be made to the act, entitled "An act relating to the ransom of American captives of the late war," passed the first day of March, 1817, in order to give effect to the provisions thereof.

On motion of Mr. TOMLINSON, the Committee on Commerce were instructed to inquire into the expediency of repealing the act passed April 26, 1816, by which was allowed an additional compensation of fifty per cent. to the compensations of certain officers of the customs, therein named.

The SPEAKER laid before the House a letter from the Secretary of War, transmitting a statement of the whole number of militia in service during the late war with Great Britain, showing the periods of their service, their pay, and from what States and Territories drawn; prepared in obedience to a resolution of this House of the 15th of April, 1820; which letter and statement were referred to the committee on the subject of the militia.

On motion of Mr. WARFIELD, the House proceeded to the consideration of a resolution moved by him, calling on the First Comptroller of the Treasury for certain information in respect to discriminations in the list of balances due to the Government; and, after a few remarks between Messrs. SMITH and WARFIELD, it was agreed to.

REDUCTION OF THE ARMY.

The House then again resolved itself into a Committee of the Whole, and the consideration of the bill for the reduction of the Military Peace Establishment was resumed.

Mr. SMYTH, of Virginia, moved to strike out the first section of the bill, with a view to the insertion of the substitute moved by him some days ago.

Mr. COBB having requested from the mover an explanation of the considerations which had led to this motion—

Mr. SMYTH explained at length his views of the relative merits of the two systems embraced by the bill and proposed substitute.

Mr. EUSTIS followed, in reply to a part of Mr. SMYTH's observations, and giving his views of the proper organization of the Army.

Mr. COCKE next spoke in opposition to the details of the proposed substitute.

Mr. FLOYD, of Virginia, rose and said, that he had listened with great attention to the arguments which his honorable colleague (Mr. SMYTH) had delivered in support of the amendment he had offered to the bill now under consideration, but he had not been persuaded to accept it; and he had no hesitation in saying, he preferred the bill reported by the Committee on Military Affairs, who, after the most mature deliberation, had offered this to the House as the result of their labors; and if, said he, there was any dissenting voice besides that of his honorable colleague, he was not apprized of the fact, and desired to be corrected if he was in an error. There can be little doubt that the mover of this amendment, who is chairman of that committee, proposed his system of reduction to his committee previous to the report of the bill; but finding no support from them, has now offered it as an amendment. I am, said he, unwilling to make any change in a measure, the result of much labor and patient inv .tigation of the ablest military gentlemen in the House; and, sir, I cannot but recur to the recommendation made to the House at the last session, by a member who has lately taken his seat, when the bill, reported by the member from Pennsylvania, I mean the honorable chairman of the Committee on Manufactures, (Mr. BALDWIN,) was under discussion, that we ought not to dot an *i* or cross a *t*—the advice is good now. For a year or two we could not find the right time to begin the work of retrenchment ; this, we are told, was not the proper object to begin with, or not the place; we have, in this way, been Talleyranded in every instance, in every attempt; and, for my own part, I do not choose, upon a subject of this importance to the nation, to be Talleyranded any more. Now is the time, and this the proper object. The national debt last year was increased three millions of dollars by a loan; and this year the Secretary of the Treasury tells us, the impoverished state of your finances will require a loan of seven millions more. This is the issue: you must either retrench your expenditures, or tax the people. To tax I will not consent; nor can it be any thing short of prodigality, that, during two years of profound peace, you increase the national debt the enormous sum of ten millions of dollars, when we ought to be paying it off. I know that the honorable gentleman from Pennsylvania (Mr. SERGEANT) has labored hard to persuade us so large a loan was not necessary, but even he tells us we must have a loan—we must borrow.

I am not a little surprised, on every question, to find gentlemen ready with examples, drawn from the history of Europe, to induce us to adopt their measures; for my own part I cannot see the parallel, and believe the wisest policy is to suit our own views to our own country. There is no similarity in our situations. When you talk of war and military preparations, the policy of Europe, her standing armies, her posts and fortifications, are continually presented to us. In what do we resemble them? Take Germany, for example. She has a foreign Power on every side; armies, fortifications, and all the paraphernalia of military array must be kept up; as, upon the recurrence of hostilities, she is liable to the sudden inroads of all these Powers. How will this apply to us? What neighbor have we? Canada, it might be answered. That country, from the nature of things, can never make war upon us; a country we could grasp any day, but so miserable, if I were to judge from the brilliant military plans of the late war, we would not have. The only parallel, then, which I can see, is in our inordinate desire to become suddenly a "great people." Yet, sir, I confess we have good cause to suspect there is something very attracting on the other side of the water, as our citizens are so very fond of going there; but always come back worse than they go, except they know all about etiquette.

Mr. Chairman, I did not believe I should ever have been brought so low as to approve any of the institutions of that country; but when I heard a distinguished member last night speak of the European system of permitting their officers to retire upon half-pay, I could not otherwise than think that plan would be a greater relief to the people of this country than the mode now pursued.

Sir, I would certainly prefer their retiring upon half-pay, rather than maintain, according to this plan proposed by the Secretary of War, such an host of officers upon full pay; then, indeed, we would save to our bankrupt Treasury the one-half of this expense. Surely half-pay would retain the science of the Army, which some gentlemen talk so much about; and, in the meantime, they could add, by useful labor, something to the general good.

If the habits of soldiers have unfitted them for business, as has been said, let them learn and add to their half-pay by useful employments. I believe, however, the science of the Army seems to consist in transmitting an order through the scientific channel; for instance, when an order is issued from the Department of War, at an officer at Fort Washington, twelve miles below this city, it must go to Nashville, in Tennessee, and scientifically come back within twelve miles of the department, to its place of destination! And so, I suppose, one would go to Brownsville, in New York, and then return to Baltimore, to preserve the science of the Army. But I will say nothing about this little matter, as I do not scientifically understand it, though you know, Mr. Chairman, how it went with the Department of War—very glad to get off on any terms.

We are told that peace is the time to prepare for war, and gentlemen have said that this bill will tear down the defence of the country, and overturn the wise regulations of the Administration, and many such fine things. I know that peace is the time to prepare for war. But does that preparation consist in a few men more, or a few less? Where is the visionary who can think ten thousand a warlike preparation for this country? Notwithstanding all that has been said to deride the militia, you must at last depend upon them—an army of even twenty or thirty thousand could not guard your maritime frontier. Suppose, sir, an enemy, Great Britain, for example—I take her because I think there is a great willingness in some people to take her for example—was to arrive upon your coast with a force of forty or

fifty thousand men, and threaten Boston, would the whole of your thirty thousand be sufficient to defend it? And, after putting the whole country in commotion, sail down the coast and threaten New York—what then? Your Army cannot follow them in time to render any service; you must call out the militia. When he has run you to all the expense of preparation, he changes his position, and threatens the Chesapeake Bay with an immediate invasion. Here, again, you have to rely upon the militia. Thus, every point on our whole coast is threatened with invasion. Charleston next, or Savannah, and New Orleans. And, if the enemy, during the late war, did not take advantage of your fruitless attempts to procure a regular army, it was the result of his ignorance: while his ignorance did not not secure you—the degraded militia secured you. No, sir; that is not the preparation for war. Choose your positions well upon the coast, fortify them strongly, place in them a sufficient body of troops to keep them in repair, and, in time of war, place enough of men in them to maintain and defend them. These ought to be the points from which the intermediate country should be defended; that the space between would suffer greatly, none can doubt. But did any man ever expect a country to be at war and not suffer? What kind of talk is that which insists on "driving insidious foes from our shores," and not suffering our "soil to be polluted by a foreign footstep?" Do not gentlemen know that, in war, a country has no limits but those marked by the edge of the sword? And could this country, under any circumstances, maintain an army equal at all points to an invading foe? If he has fifty thousand men on board his ships, I hold the entire expense to have been encountered; and it costs no more on the coast at Boston than it did at Liverpool. If, then, you would oppose an invading enemy of that force with success, you should have, at each of those points, at least sixty thousand men, as it is utterly impossible for the forces at Boston to follow his ships round to New Orleans. What, then, is the consequence? That your coast would require three hundred and sixty thousand troops. Let us take things as they are. This bill will keep us enough of the military to preserve our fortifications, which is all we want. In war, it would be necessary to have a regular army to promote the success of some particular design. But, at last, the militia of the country is the great reliance, as we are compelled to know, from the document this morning laid upon our tables, which shows the militia force called into the service of the country during the late war, to have amounted to three hundred and twenty-six thousand; while that of the regular army amounted to perhaps thirty-five thousand.

I am a little surprised to see how things cut about in these times; and not less surprised to find a letter of Mr. Monroe, written at the close of the late war, when Secretary of War, make its appearance in the newspapers just at the very nick of time, while this bill was before the House. How it got there is more than I can tell; for what purpose I know not; but it does appear to me to be one of those little obliquities which now and then we see in this our day. Will not every gentleman at once see that the letter, when written, contemplated a state of things which then existed totally different from that which now exists? We had just then finished a war with a powerful nation; then, too, Lord Castlereagh had just said, in his place, in the British Parliament, that if Bonaparte had been victorious at the battle of Waterloo, he could not have succeeded, as Europe had at that time one million two hundred thousand bayonets marching against him. And, sir, do we not recollect that two distinguished members of this House, whom I now see on the other side of the way, here declared, in their places, that they did not believe the peace with England to be a lasting one; that it was a mere interval of hostilities, and a war of severer conflict would soon recommence. These were the circumstances of the times when the letter recommended an army of twenty thousand men, and Congress fixed upon ten thousand as the proper number, though the House of Representatives, even then, thought six thousand the proper amount of force. But will any man think, if the condition of the world then required ten thousand, that six is not now enough, as we believe our peace a lasting one, and there is less likelihood of collision now than there has ever been since the adoption of the Constitution? While all Europe is at peace, tired and exhausted; nay, almost the whole world reposing in a dead peace, unknown to history, I believe, from the days of Moses until the present time, with the exception of the Augustan reign; and now we have another.

The Secretary of War has here given us a report upon the subject of organizing the Army, which is to consist of officers, and says, "no posi-' tion connected with the organization of the Peace ' Establishment is susceptible of being more rigidly ' proved than that the proportion of its officers to ' the rank and file ought to be greater than in a ' War Establishment." Sir, if this be true, mankind has for ages been in error and darkness, and Great Britain been to us doubly unjust. During the late war she falsely charged us with putting a double proportion of officers on board our ships, that if one should be killed there should be another ready to take his place. And when the frigate Chesapeake was taken, in her battle with the Shannon, we always have believed it was because the gallant Lawrence and most of his officers had been killed. How wrong we have been! But the Secretary had not then informed us more officers were necessary in time of peace than in time of war.

We are told of our increasing population; and some gentleman think a corresponding increase of the Army necessary. This doctrine would lead to frightful consequences. We have a certain frontier to defend, and, as I have always said, certain positions on that frontier ought to be fortified; and then, whether our population shall be great or small, or increase to any extent, these posts will be adequate to their protection. We have now ten millions of inhabitants, and, accord-

ing to the narrowest calculations, it doubles itself every twenty-five years. What a fearful army this, in a few years, would require, were it to double with our population! And what an increased number of posts and fortified places it would require to accommodate them!

Now, Mr. Chairman, we come to the military posts, and this document which I hold in my hand is that which, under a call of this House, the Secretary of the Department of War has sent to us; and, from the examination which I have been enabled to give it, I am compelled to say, that either the Secretary must believe Congress wholly ignorant of the defences of this country, or he himself must be destitute of the necessary information which a man in his office ought to possess. If, sir, we take all the places marked upon this list, including the places where our Generals reside, we find it spun out to the wonderful length of an hundred and twenty-six! I wish clearly to be understood; and, if I am in an error in supposing that a military post where the Generals are stationed, I will thank any gentleman in this House to correct me before I proceed any farther.

I believe, sir, from a reference to the report of the Secretary of the Department of War, in the year 1818, already reverted to by my friend from North Carolina, (Mr. WILLIAMS,) it will be found we then had seventy-three military posts; and now, in two years, by some strange occurrence, unknown to the country, they have of late wonderfully increased, until, indeed, they number us one hundred and twenty-six.

I have heretofore believed, in common with the rest of the citizens of this country, who did not understand the science of the army, that a military post was a place so fortified and provided with men, cannon, and defences, as to be, upon any occasion, of some advantage to the military operations of the country. But this report shows us to have been in an egregious error, as there are here many military posts where there is neither forts, magazines, cannons, arms, or men, or any single thing, except the ground where an army happened to encamp for a few days, during the late war. Sir, I will examine this wonderful list of military posts. I will, however, say nothing about those to the North, as I am not acquainted yet with that part of the country; but some of them, you will perceive, like persons wanting office, carry their labels on their foreheads, on which you may read, "I want," at every turn.

Here you see, occupying a conspicuous position, is Fort Mims. How this fort has been revived, I know not; but I had believed there was not a boy in the whole nation who had not heard of its destruction; and many fine speeches, said a gentleman on the left the other day, have been made about the blood and tomahawk, the relentless savage, which spared neither age or sex, and the bones of unfortunate victims, left to blanch upon the dreary plains; to the end, I suppose, we might not forget the poor Indians, whilst all, with a sentimental delicacy for the honor of civilization, choose to forget the scenes at Hampton as soon as possible. But this fort, I suppose, possessed the properties of the phœnix, and has risen from its ashes in all its military array. Next to this we find Fort Stoddart. How this came here is equally strange, as, Mr. Chairman, I believe for the last ten years there has not been any thing in this fort, without it is an alligator, that sometimes chooses that as a place of retirement, to bask undisturbed in the sun. Fort St. Stephens is on the list, and shows how amply we have been disposed to provide for the safety of the government of the State of Alabama, as that place has been, until lately, the metropolis of the State. This partiality for that State ought to create some jealousy among us to the South; but, as it is among ourselves, we will forgive the predilection. Next in order is Fort Claiborne, which is now, as my friend from Alabama will testify, a beautiful little town, containing about two or three thousand inhabitants. After passing this town to the next military post, we find it to be Fort Strother, which we are told is on the Coosa river, at the junction of the Etawha; and here we find, in the establishment of this fort, that valuable corps we hear so much about, called the topographical engineers, displayed a skill and accuracy equal alone to this report, as there is no stream at all entering the Coosa river at that fort. But there we find the Secretary's local prejudices in full growth, which I must confess I had rather seen otherwise, as Fort Strother is one of the most flourishing cotton plantations in all the South. Fort Williams, it is true, is on the Indian land; but, whilst it stands on one side of the Coosa, the other is in the highest state of cultivation, covered with the finest cotton plantations in the country. Look here! About twelve miles above St. Louis is a military post, called Fort St. Charles, a beautiful little town, containing a thousand inhabitants. But, Mr. Chairman, here are some military posts which startle us with their warlike preparations. This is Belle Fontaine, on the Missouri, defended by three men! and Fort Osage, at the confluence of the Osage and Missouri rivers, as ably defended by one man! There too is Fort Edwards, in Illinois—in what part of the State I cannot learn; but it does appear that it is not quite so well defended as Fort Osage. It appears too that the mouth of Licking, in the State of Kentucky, on the opposite bank of the Ohio river from the city of Cincinnati, is a military post, defended by the imposing force of one man!

Sir, if this report had not come in so opportunely, we should have gone home without knowing that the city of New Orleans, Natchez, St. Louis, the town of Nashville, in Tennessee, and Brownsville, in New York, were all important military posts. But, here we have a new scene. As if they did not grow up fast enough by ones, we get them by twos. Here, sir, is Fort Plaquemine and Fort St. Philip, two names for the same spot, as my friend from Louisiana (Mr. BUTLER) assures me. Next in order are Fort Bowyer and Fort Mobile Point, which prove to be the precise same place. Then come Fort Toulouse and Fort Jackson, not less extraordinary than the others. The history of Fort Toulouse, if I am not greatly mistaken, is

16th CON. 2d SESS.—29

this; that, when the extravagant pretensions of England produced the war of 1755, when she was opposed by France and Spain, a chain of military posts was attempted by France, to be established from Canada to the Gulf, to confine the British within their own territory, and this Fort Toulouse was one of them. But, after the peace of 1763, that military post remained a retreat only for wildcats and foxes, until the late war; when, at the close of the Creek campaign, the army cut away the trees which had grown up in the meantime, and removed some old iron cannon which lay in their way, with their trunnions broken off, and built Fort Jackson upon the selfsame spot; and yet the Secretary gives us Fort Toulouse and Fort Jackson as two military posts.

I must confess, sir, this reminds me very forcibly of an anecdote I once heard of an Irishman, who said, he liked to live in America very well, but he believed he would have remained in his own country, where he had every convenience, and as fine a farm as any in Ireland; but there was a little encumbrance upon it, which made it rather disagreeable, which was, that another man's land lay right on the top of it.

Mr. Chairman, I am indeed astonished how it is possible for the head of a department to have been so imperfectly informed as to the real state of what are here reported to us as military posts; and how they can be mentioned both in debate and in official documents as existing posts, where a portion of our force may be required, and used indeed as a pretext to palliate the retention of this present useless force, is not less astonishing. If, sir, you reject from this report all the arsenals, the houses of the generals, the camps and cantonments, where troops chanced to stay for a few weeks during the late war; and all the forts, where there are neither soldiers, guns, nor fortifications; and all those in cotton fields, as well as those the long time den of wild beasts; you will find this list of one hundred and twenty-six, dwindled down to fifty-eight; and, I do not hesitate to say, the true military aspect of this country will never require that number; and, when another subject comes before the House, I think I shall be able to show that not more than perhaps thirty are in any event necessary.

I cannot divine how it is the gentleman from South Carolina undertakes to brand the supporters of this measure as aiming a blow, through it, at the Executive. Does he know the Executive to be hostile to the measure now under debate? He tells us, too, the President's glory is in the magnitude of the fortifications of the country. For my own part, I think myself a better friend to him than to believe he would place his glory upon any other basis than the administration of the laws for the prosperity of the country and the welfare of the people.

It is difficult for me to see the necessity for this army, organized as it is. We have two Major Generals and four Brigadiers in service, whilst we have not as many men at any one place as would constitute a captain's guard; but I suppose it must be necessary to us, as we must be a "great people." These officers receive near seven thousand dollars a year, for no other service than living comfortably at home, and transmitting the orders of the Department of War; as it seems the Secretary of that department has no choice left him but compliance. This sum is enormous; yet I will not say it is an abuse, as it is drawn through the medium of the law; though, whilst their pay is two thousand four hundred dollars a year, their allowance for servants, houses, quarters, kitchens, fire-wood, and other little matters, swells it to that sum. The life though, of some of them, is not a dull monotony, in "these piping times of peace," as we might suppose; as we are informed a visit is made each Winter to this imperial city, by some means or other, moving in the style of an Eastern satrap, says my friend from North Carolina, with all the pomp of military indulgence, having twelve hundred pounds of baggage, three rooms, and a kitchen in the train, come to Washington by an order from the Department of War, and obtain transportation for it all; should, however, the journey have been commenced without an order, one is kindly furnished when the city is entered; such would be the beneficent disposition of a well drilled department.

These things, when we had a Treasury overflowing with money, would have been wrong; but now, when the Treasury is unable to pay, it is little else than an abuse of the trust reposed in us by the people, who expect from us a faithful account of our conduct. When the welfare of the country shall require taxes, I will vote them. But to borrow millions every year, thereby increasing the national debt in time of peace instead of paying it off—to tax the country, already embarrassed with difficulties of their own, to support this prodigal system, is what I cannot do. A prudent man will limit his expenditures to the amount of his income, and that which is right in an individual, cannot be wrong in a nation.

We have heard much of the services of our officers, their high expectations, and generous sacrifices of personal prospects; all this may be true, and, as an individual, I am always proud to honor the meritorious officer. But, can it be possible for an individual as brave, as patriotic, and disinterested as they are represented to be, should desire to remain one moment in the army, after they know their country did not stand in need of their services? Would they not rather feel dishonored by the belief that pecuniary compensation was all they sought? Let us do the country justice, Mr. Chairman, and when the services of these officers are wanting, let us require them and pay them; when they achieve deeds of valor, let us reward them; when they display heroic patriotism and devotion to the country, let us give them our distinguished consideration. This, sir, is the highest reward any man can receive from a free people.

The officer who would wish to remain in service one minute longer than his country desired him, or wanted his services, is unworthy of its confidence or commission. Why are we told of irritated feelings or animosity of individuals? If these exist, then instantly disband the army; it has already existed too long for the good of the country. The danger of a standing army is not that there is any fear of their overthrowing the Constitution at one blow; but the tainted feelings they engender, and the influence it acquires upon public opinion. I hope the day has not arrived when we fear to disband an army, even though its number should be ten or fifty thousand; if we do, then liberty has fled, we have nothing left us but the shadow. Let us beware in time, and keep pure the national feeling from the influence of this dangerous doctrine of "you can't do enough," and you are "bound to fulfil expectations yourselves have created." Against this, and the impatient desire to cram into every office military men, to the exclusion of citizens of better pretensions, I must protest. It is ruinous and unjust.

Sir, at a future day, when our population will have increased, and we involved in some future war, necessity or favor will compel us to create major generals, lieutenant generals, generals, and field marshals; when the doctrine of the science of the Army will apply then as now; and to guard against future evil as much as we can, we ought to give an example now of that moderate and disinterested justice to disbanded armies, which future ages ought to pursue.

We ought to remember a lesson already given in the exhibition of feeling in a publication addressed to the nation by the disbanded officers of the late war. It is only necessary to advert to it, the memory of every gentleman in the House will recall it to their recollection; a more severe, acrimonious, bitter, biting, rancorous piece, I yet have never seen. It is in this way inroads are made upon the national feeling, and whenever the representatives of the people shall fail to consult any interest but that of their country, there is an end to the Constitution. Control them now; when you cannot, you are slaves. Gradual approach is the march of tyranny. Can any man believe there was much to surprise the people of Rome when a certain Emperor created his horse priest and consul? Could this have been done in the purer days of Rome? No, sir, they had been accustomed to see small changes and innovations, until, from one step to another, they arrived at this last degree of degradation; themselves impotent and despised, doubtless beheld this spectacle without wonder or astonishment.

Much has been said of the inutility of the militia. They have been contemned and despised to enhance the claim and usefulness of a standing Army. We are told, too, that this Army is necessary for the protection of our Western frontier, which is feeble and defenceless. Mr. Chairman, I will not speak on that subject. I cannot trust my feelings; but, sir, this I may say, that I know well the kind of protection given to the West by your standing armies. No man has suffered more than myself by the wars of the country, though I was too young to have any personal concern in them; then it was the brave and dauntless frontier man protected himself, and often your Army—for all was war; then, sir, every individual could aim the unerring rifle, and often their wives and daughters could use them with skill and effect; and whilst tilling their fields of corn, each would in turn remain on guard; then, too, battles were fought, where deeds of valor were displayed, which would have rivalled the boast of any age or country; nor did they expect rewards in office, favor, swords, or medals, for the enemies they killed or did not kill.

But I will not, as I have not spoken of these things. My friend from Kentucky, who I see before me, (Mr. HARDIN,) is better acquainted with these occurrences than I am, or any gentleman in the House, may picture them to you. He is more capable than I am, and can do the subject more justice. Let him speak, and you will learn whether your militia ought to be so despised.

I will not trouble you further. Under any view which I can take of this matter, I cannot see any good cause why the Army should not be reduced. Let it be fixed upon the most economical basis, and we yet may avoid loans and taxes in time of peace, which will some day ruin this country. Let us often recur to the pure original feelings and opinions which we once had, and then perhaps we may preserve the Republic from the inevitable fate which the gradual change of original principle must bring upon it. Let us recur to the maxims of 1801, and all will be well; if not, expect prodigality and ruin.

Mr. TRIMBLE followed Mr. FLOYD in opposition to so indiscriminate a reduction of the Staff of the Army as was desired by some gentlemen.

The question was then taken on Mr. SMYTH's motion, and decided in the negative.

Mr. HARDIN then, after some general remarks in favor of his object, moved to amend the bill by adding thereto a new section, to abolish any commutation for subsistence of the officers, forage, servants and servants' hire, and subsistence and clothing, transportation, and any other incidental charges whatever, and to allow in lieu thereof —— per cent. on the amount of pay now allowed the officers respectively.

Before deciding on this motion, the Committee rose, and the House adjourned at 4 o'clock.

THURSDAY, January 18.

The SPEAKER laid before the House a letter from Peter Stephen Chazotte, of Philadelphia, enclosing a printed pamphlet, entitled "Facts and Observations on the Culture of Vines, Olives, Capers, Almonds, &c., in the Southern States, and of Coffee, Cocoa, and Cochineal, in East Florida."—Referred to the Committee on Agriculture.

Mr. SERGEANT presented a petition of Edward Barry, a sailing-master in the Navy of the United States, praying compensation for his household furniture, destroyed in the navy yard, in the city of Washington, on the 24th of August, 1814; which petition was referred to the Committee on Naval Affairs.

The Committee on the Public Lands were discharged from the consideration of the memorial of the Senate and House of Representatives of Missouri, praying that relief may be extended to certain purchasers of public lands, referred to that committee on the 11th instant; and that the said memorial be referred to the Committee of the Whole to which is committed the bill regulating the payment of debts due from purchasers of public lands.

Mr. SMITH, of Maryland, from the Committee of Ways and Means, reported a bill authorizing Benjamin H. Rand to import a certain piece of plate free of duty; which was read twice, and committed.

On motion of Mr. STORRS, the Committee on the Judiciary were instructed to inquire into the expediency of altering the times of holding the terms of the district court of the United States for the northern district of the State of New York.

Mr. SILSBEE submitted the following resolution, which was read, and ordered to lie on the table one day for consideration:

Resolved, That the Secretary of the Treasury be required to lay before this House a statement of the number of inspectors, and of weighers, gaugers, and measurers, employed in each port of the United States, and of the amount of pay received by each of those officers for each of the last five years; and, also, a statement of the names of persons who have been employed as agents for building or supplying lighthouses, revenue cutters, or marine hospitals, in the several districts of the United States, with the amount of compensation which has been paid to each of them, for these services, within the last five years.

On motion of Mr. SILSBEE, the Committee of Commerce were instructed to inquire into the expediency of allowing imported goods, on which the duty has been paid or secured, to be transported coastwise, from the district into which they were imported, to one or more other districts, without losing the benefit of debenture when exported from the United States, within the time prescribed by law.

REDUCTION OF THE ARMY.

The House again resolved itself into a Committee of the Whole on the state of the Union, and took up the bill to reduce the Army to six thousand men—Mr. HARDIN's amendment offered yesterday being still under consideration.

Mr. HARDIN having since yesterday ascertained, in conversation, that the Military Committee had now a proposition before them, similar to that which he had offered by way of amendment to this bill, said he would leave the subject to them at present. He therefore withdrew his amendment.

The Committee then proceeded with the consideration of the details of the bill.

Mr. SMITH, of Maryland, moved an amendment, going to retain one-half of the topographical engineers, and followed his motion by a number of remarks on the valuable services this corps had rendered; the destitute condition of the Government and the military service of topographical information, at the commencement of the late war; the disasters which had ensued therefrom, instances of which he detailed; the mass of useful and essential information which they had given, and were daily acquiring, by their surveys, for the public use, &c.

Mr. COCKE opposed the motion, and spoke to show that the information wanted in some of the instances referred to by Mr. S., might have been acquired by any of the citizens in the vicinity of the scene of operations, &c. He was further opposed to any material amendments, as they might tend to defeat the bill; it was a course deprecated and avoided at the last session by the friends of the tariff bill, and he wished to show the House that the friends of this bill could not be outflanked, and that, though militia had been so much decried, he wished it to be seen that, on this occasion, there was something like discipline in their ranks, and that they would not be decoyed from their object by amendments.

Mr. SMITH said he really had never heard so broad a declaration as this in the House—that the friends of reduction were to rally round a bill, good or bad, right or wrong. He avowed himself a friend of the bill, so far as regarded a reduction of the Army; but he desired to make the organization as perfect as possible.

Mr. MERCER entered into a detail of many of the duties devolved on the topographical corps, for civil as well as military purposes, to show the great value of their talents and services to the nation. He adverted to the small number (ten or twelve) of which this corps even now consisted, and the little expense they were to the country. He referred, particularly, to many instances in which their talents and services had been of the utmost importance to the national defence, and many in which, had they been employed, they would have prevented defeat and disgrace to the arms of the Republic. Mr. M. concluded his remarks by moving to amend his amendment so as to retain the *whole* instead of *half* of the corps of topographical engineers. Believing, however, that the provision retaining the corps of engineers would be construed to retain the topographical corps connected therewith, he hoped this motion would be withdrawn, that it might be made when another part of the bill should be reached.

The motion was withdrawn by Mr. SMITH.

Mr. FORD moved to strike out the provision for retaining a surgeon general, considering him to have little or nothing to do, and that his duties might be discharged by the apothecary general.

This motion was opposed by Mr. STORRS, and was supported by the mover; but who, subsequently, withdrew his amendment, to obtain further information on the subject.

Mr. SMITH, of Maryland, moved so to amend the bill as to give to the Quartermaster General (as at present) the rank, pay, and emoluments of a brigadier general, instead of reducing his rank, pay, &c., to that of a colonel of cavalry, as proposed by the bill.

The question on this amendment was decided in the negative—ayes 50, noes 58.

Mr. MERCER moved to strike out the fifth section of the bill, which abolishes the topographical engineers and their assistants—wishing, as he before stated, to retain in service the whole of that corps, and further advocated his object.

Mr. HARDIN spoke at some length against the amendment, and to show that the information collected by this corps and embodied in maps was not of such importance to military movements; the whole face of the country, in its water courses, roads, bridges, &c., constantly changing, rendered the maps made now useless in future wars, &c. He might not be averse to retaining a part of the topographical corps; but deeming this bill the result of much military knowledge and experience in the committee which pronounced this corps unnecessary, he was not prepared to act in opposition to the plan which they recommended, &c.

Mr. MERCER replied to Mr. H. If the argument of Mr. COCKE, that the bill was not to be touched, lest it should be endangered, and that of Mr. HARDIN, that all amendment was precluded by an implicit confidence in the views of a committee, were to prevail in this House, he could have nothing more to do with this bill, or indeed with any other. He proceeded to reply in detail to the objections of Mr. H. to the corps in question, and to show the necessity of retaining them.

Mr. HARDIN rejoined at considerable length.

Mr. MALLARY referred to the duties of the different branches of the engineers, as laid down in the rules and regulations of the War Department, to show that the duties of the topographical corps were called for only in a state of war, and that they would consequently not be requisite in a Peace Establishment; objecting particularly to retaining the number now in service, which equalled the whole number in service during the late war.

Mr. MERCER went into a further exposition of his views in defence of the topographical corps, and in reply to Mr. HARDIN.

The question being taken on Mr. MERCER's amendment, it was decided in the negative, without a count.

Mr. SMITH, of Maryland, then renewed his motion to retain one-half of the topographical engineers.

Mr. BRUSH spoke in reply to Mr. MALLARY, in regard to the relative duties of engineers and topographical engineers, to show that his conclusions were not accurate, and to show the great utility of the duties of the latter corps as well as the former; and to retain at least a part of the topographical corps, even at the expense of part of the engineers themselves; that to have a perfect system, a part of each corps ought to be retained, and not any one sacrificed entirely.

Mr. SMITH's amendment was also negatived—ayes 43.

Mr. CANNON moved to amend the 7th section, so as to make the same allowance of three months extra pay to the disbanded non-commissioned officers, musicians, and privates, as is provided for disbanded officers.

After some little discussion, this motion was lost without a division.

Mr. BALDWIN moved to amend the bill so as to allow a salary of three thousand, instead of two thousand dollars, to the Commissary General of

Purchases, and followed his motion with some remarks against reducing, (as the bill proposed,) the salary of an officer whose duties were so important and had been so ably and faithfully discharged as they had been by the officer now in service.

Mr. EUSTIS added his opinion that the sum of $3,000 was not more than an adequate salary for this officer. He as fully deserved this sum, from the nature of his duties, and the fidelity of their execution, as any laborer was worth a dollar a day.

Mr. COOKE argued, from the duties incident to this office, which he detailed to the Committee, that the sum of $2,000 a year was an adequate compensation; considering it also probable that this officer was engaged in other business of his own, &c.

Mr. SERGEANT supported the motion, from a conviction of its justice, derived from a personal knowledge of the entire and exclusive devotion of the present Commissary General of Purchases to the discharge of his duties.

Mr. SMITH, of Maryland, said $3,000 was the sum originally given to this officer and argued that if a reduction of it should drive the present officer, now fully experienced in his duties, from the service, it would probably be extremely detrimental to the service; he disbursed perhaps a million of dollars annually, and $3,000 was a very low commission on the amount of the disbursement; his duties were also multifarious and laborious; and his salary ought to be such as not to drive him to other means of support, if not from service; indeed if he were to engage in any private business, he ought not to be retained in the public service.

Mr. WILLIAMS, of North Carolina, was averse to arguing thus *ad hominem*. The salary of this officer was no more than $3,000 during the war, when his duties were much greater, and Mr. W. thought the diminished duties of a Peace Establishment made a corresponding reduction of salary equitable and proper.

Mr. RICH was opposed to reducing the salary of any particular officer—he was willing to go into the subject of a general reduction of salaries; but, until then, would not consent to single out a particular case. He was, therefore, in favor of the amendment.

Mr. FOOT hoped, then, that this subject would be laid by for the present, and the subject of salaries taken up, in which case he trusted that if the Commissary General of Purchases would not be the only one reduced.

Mr. SMITH, of Maryland, remarked, in reply to Mr. WILLIAMS, that this salary was fixed at $3,000 long before the late war; and during that war he had many deputies to assist him.

The amendment proposing to make the salary $3,000 was rejected without a division.

Mr. FULLER moved to amend the bill by adding a provision for one Adjutant and Inspector General in addition to the Assistant Adjutant and Assistant Inspector General.

This motion, after some discussion, was negatived without a division.

Mr. STORRS moved to change the provision of one Assistant Inspector General, to a provision for one Inspector General; and supported his motion by referring to the important, essential, and valuable duties of this branch of the service.

After some debate, this motion was also negatived, without a division.

Mr. ARCHER, of Virginia, moved an amendment, the effect of which, in substance, was to prevent the consolidation of the corps of ordnance with that of the artillery, and to preserve the corps of ordnance distinct and separate, as at present.

This amendment was briefly discussed, without any strong objections being urged against it, and it was agreed to—ayes 64, noes 37.

On motion of Mr. ARCHER, of Virginia, the bill was further amended by substituting the word *discharged* for the word *deranged*, as applied to those to be disbanded under the bill.

Mr. TRIMBLE moved to amend the bill by adding thereto the following section:

Be it further enacted, That hereafter, of the pay allowed by law to each enlisted soldier there shall be retained —— dollars and —— cents per month, until the term of enlistment shall expire, or until legally discharged; at which time the retained sums shall be paid to each soldier personally, without regard to any transfer or assignment, and without being subject to any lien arising upon any contract or engagement made after the date of enlistment; and, in the event of death in service, the sums so retained shall be paid only to the widow of the deceased, or to his heirs at law, or their guardian, under the same rules and regulations now established in similar cases.

Mr. T. wondered that such a provision had not been before incorporated in the system. The desertions were very numerous, and it was proper that part of the soldiers' pay should be retained to operate against desertion and as a penalty for it. The practice in the Roman army, he remarked, was excellent. The books of the regiment always accompanied the colors of the regiment—if the colors were lost, the books were lost too, and the State thereby gained all the retained pay; but the consequence was, that the colors were seldom lost.

The amendment was opposed by Mr. COCKE, and Mr. WILLIAMS of North Carolina, on the ground that such a provision would be reported in a different bill, in which it would be more appropriate.

The amendment was negatived.

The Committee of the Whole then rose, and reported the bill and amendments to the House; and the amendments of the Committee were successively adopted, without variation, except as related to the ordnance corps, which, on motion of Mr. COBB, was so modified as to consist of one colonel, one lieutenant colonel, one major, six captains, six first, six second, and six third lieutenants.

Mr. BALDWIN, Mr. STORRS, and Mr. FULLER, renewed, without success, the motions which they had respectively made in Committee to amend the bill.

Mr. COBB renewed, and spoke in support of the motion, unsuccessfully made in Committee by

Mr. SMITH of Maryland, to give the Quartermaster General the rank, pay, and emoluments of a Brigadier General, in lieu of those of Colonel of Cavalry.

The motion was opposed by Mr. FLOYD, on principle, and was supported by Mr. SMITH of Virginia, also on principle.

The motion was negatived.

Mr. LATHROP moved to deprive the Adjutant General, the Quartermaster General, and Judge Advocate, of the proposed rank, but to leave them the pay and emoluments of a Colonel of Cavalry; which motion was negatived without a division.

Mr. ANDERSON, after some remarks in opposition to the plan of reduction proposed by the present bill, and in explanation of his views of a different organization, moved that the House come to the following resolution:

Resolved, That the bill be recommitted to the Committee on Military Affairs, with instructions to report a bill placing the present Military Establishment of the United States under the command of one Major General, and two Brigadiers General, and containing other provisions necessary for making the staff of the Army conform to this arrangement.

The motion was negatived without debate, ayes 26; and the House adjourned.

FRIDAY, January 19.

Mr. ANDERSON, from the Committee on the Public Lands, reported a bill authorizing the President of the United States to remove the land office in the district of Lawrence county, in the Territory of Arkansas; which was read twice, and ordered to be engrossed, and read a third time on Friday next.

Mr. SERGEANT, from the Committee on the Judiciary, reported a bill to alter the times of holding the district court in the northern district of New York; which was read twice, and ordered to be engrossed, and read a third time on Wednesday next.

Mr. WILLIAMS, of North Carolina, from the Committee of Claims, reported a bill authorizing the settlement of the accounts of the late Le Roy Opie; which was read twice, and committed to the Committee of the whole House to which is committed the report made at the last session on the petition of Hoel Lawrence.

Mr. MERCER, from the Committee for the District of Columbia, reported a bill authorizing the establishment of a penitentiary within the District of Columbia; which was read twice, and committed to a Committee of the Whole.

The following Message was received from the PRESIDENT OF THE UNITED STATES:

To the House of Representatives:

In compliance with a resolution of the House of Representatives, requesting the President to inform the House (if in his opinion proper) whether any, and, if any, what negotiations, since the first of January, 1816, have been had with the Six Nations of Indians, or any portion of them; who the commissioners or agents were; the objects of the negotiation; the expenses of the same; the compensation of each commissioner, secretary, or agent, and to whom the moneys were paid; I now transmit a report from the Secretary of War, communicating the information desired.

JAMES MONROE.

WASHINGTON, *January* 18, 1821.

The Message was read, and ordered to lie on the table.

The SPEAKER laid before the House a letter from the Secretary of War, transmitting a statement of the amount of merchandise on hand at the different Indian trading-houses, and in the hands of the superintendent of the Indian trade, at cost; rendered in obedience to a resolution of this House of the 13th instant; which letter and statement were ordered to lie on the table.

Mr. MALLARY, after some remarks, going to show that there was reason to believe there were several officers of the Army, employed in certain of the public offices, to whom compensation was paid for their clerical services, in addition to their pay as officers, and with the view of obtaining precise information on this subject, submitted the following resolution:

Resolved, That the Committee on Military Affairs be instructed to inquire whether any officers of the Army of the United States are employed as clerks or in any other capacity, in any of the Departments, or in the office of the Surgeon General or Apothecary General, and whether such officers, if any, have received any other compensation than their pay as officers; if so, what are their names, and what extra compensation have they received.

Mr. LITTLE moved to amend the resolution so as to make it a direct call on the Secretary of War for the information; which motion, after some conversation between three or four gentlemen, was negatived, and the resolution was agreed to.

Mr. RANDOLPH gave notice that he should on Monday next call for the consideration of the bill making provision for the family of the late Commodore Perry.

On motion of Mr. GORHAM, the Committee of Commerce were directed to inquire into the expediency of placing such a number of buoys on the Nantucket shoals, in the Vineyard sound, on the coast of Massachusetts, as may be necessary to render the navigation the more secure.

REVENUE OFFICERS.

The following resolution submitted yesterday by Mr. SILSBEE was taken up for consideration:

Resolved, That the Secretary of the Treasury be requested to lay before this House a statement of the number of inspectors and weighers, gangers and measurers, employed in each port of the United States, and of the amount of pay received by each of those officers for each of the last five years; and also a statement of the names of persons who have been employed as agents for building or supplying lighthouses, revenue cutters, or marine hospitals, to the several districts of the United States, with the amount of compensation which has been paid to each of them for their services within the last five years.

Mr. TOMLINSON wished the call somewhat ex-

909   **HISTORY OF CONGRESS.**   910

JANUARY, 1821.   *Hall of the House—Revolutionary Pensions.*   H. OF R.

tended, so as to obtain information on a subject in which there were considerable abuses practised, some particulars of which he referred to. He moved therefore to add the following to the resolution:

"Designating the persons who during the said period were paid as inspectors, and who at the same time performed the duties and received the fees of weighers, gaugers, and measurers, and the amount paid to such persons respectively, for services rendered in each of the capacities aforesaid."

This amendment was accepted by Mr. SILSBEE, and thus modified, the resolution was agreed to.

HALL OF THE HOUSE.

Mr. WOOD, from the Committee on Public Buildings, in the House of Representatives, to whom was referred the resolution of this House of the 19th of December, 1820, instructing them " to inquire into the practicability of making such ' alterations in the present structure of the Hall of ' the House of Representatives, as shall better ' adapt it to the purposes of a deliberative assem- ' bly ; and, if no such alteration can be effected, ' to ascertain whether it be practicable to provide ' a suitable hall in the centre building of the Cap- ' itol," delivered the following report:

That, in obedience to the above-recited resolution, they have examined the practicability of making any alterations in the Hall of the House of Representatives, that would render it more convenient for the transaction of public business, with all the attention in their power.

They have, also, submitted the different plans for this purpose that have occurred in the course of their inquiries, or that have been suggested to them, to the examination of the architect of the public buildings, who has furnished them with his opinion of the alteration most likely to produce the desired effect in the Hall of the House of Representatives, accompanied with a drawing exhibiting the form and construction of such alteration, and an estimate of the expense of its construction.

From the result of their own inquiries, as well as the examination of the public architect, the committee have reason to believe, that a level glass ceiling, at the foot of the dome, resting on the stone entablature over the columns, would, in a great measure, prevent the evils that are now experienced from the expansion of the voice and the reverberation of the sound ; and is, on every account, the most eligible alteration for this purpose of which the room is susceptible, compatible with the preservation of the proportions of the Hall and the use of the gallery, and least injurious to the beauty of its appearance.

But, although the committee have no doubt that the alteration suggested may be so constructed as to be perfectly secure, and might contribute to improve the facility of speaking and hearing in the Hall of the House of Representatives, yet they think it questionable whether the alteration is absolutely necessary, and whether the disadvantages incident to it would not counterbalance the benefits to be derived from it.

Independently of the objection arising from the expense, in the present state of the Treasury, it is objectionable on other accounts : it would lessen the circulation of the air in the room, and render it soon-

er liable to become impure ; would obstruct the view of the dome, and impair the beauty of the Hall.

Experience proves that the members speak with more ease, and hear more readily, at the present session, than they did during the last. The difference, it is believed, is in a great measure to be ascribed to the drying of the walls, and there can be but little doubt but that further improvement may be expected from the same cause.

The centre building of the Capitol does not furnish a suitable Hall for the members of the House of Representatives. The only room that would admit them is the one destined for the Library of Congress, and that, in the opinion of the committee, is not calculated for their convenient accommodation, or the admission of spectators.

The committee are induced to believe that, by carpeting the gallery, to prevent the noise which arises from moving from one place to another, and by strict order in the House, business may now be done with tolerable facility, and a few years' experience will ascertain the full effect of the drying of the walls.

The committee are, therefore, of opinion, that provision should be made for carpeting the gallery ; and, that any further alteration in the Hall should await the result of further experience. They submit the following resolution, viz :

Resolved, That a sum of money be added to the appropriations for the public buildings, for the present year, for the purpose of carpeting the gallery of the House of Representatives.

The report was read, and committed.

REVOLUTIONARY PENSIONERS.

The House, then, on the motion of Mr. BARBOUR, proceeded to consider the "bill in addition to the several acts making provision for certain persons engaged in the land and naval service of the United States in the Revolutionary war."

This bill was discussed, in Committee of the Whole, on the 3d instant, and, having been reported to the House, Mr. HARDIN moved to amend the bill by adding thereto the following sections:

SEC. 2. *And be it further enacted,* That no pensioner under the aforesaid acts shall be stricken from the rolls, who, upon giving in the schedule of his property as is therein directed, shall be worth less, after deducting his debts, than —— dollars.

SEC. 3. *And be it further enacted,* That every pensioner who has, under the act of the 1st of May, 1820, been stricken from the pension roll, shall be placed again on the pension roll, if application shall be made by him, if, upon examining his schedule, he is worth less than —— dollars.

The question was on the adoption of this amendment ; and on this question, as well as on the bill itself, incidentally, much debate again took place— Messrs. HARDIN and GROSS, of New York, advocating the amendment, and Messrs. BARBOUR, ROBERTSON, TOMLINSON, and BROWN, opposing it. The debate had continued some time, when, On motion of Mr. BARBOUR, (who in calling it up had no idea of interfering materially in the progress of the other business before the House,) the bill and amendment were again laid on the table.

REDUCTION OF THE ARMY.

The House resumed the consideration of the bill to reduce the Military Peace Establishment of the United States.

Mr. STORRS submitted to the House a number of remarks to show the inexpediency of abolishing the existing provisions for the inspection of the army, and of the substitute proposed by the bill for one assistant inspector, and concluded his remarks with a motion to strike out the clause providing "an assistant inspector general," with a view of moving afterwards to insert a provision for one inspector general.

The amendment was opposed by Messrs. WILLIAMS of North Carolina, FOOT, and COCKE; and was supported by Messrs. STORRS, GROSS of New York, ROBERTSON, SMITH of Maryland, and MERCER. The debate continued until near 4 o'clock; when,

The question being taken on the proposed amendment, it was decided in the affirmative—yeas 75, nays 71.

Mr. STORRS then moved to insert a provision for "one inspector general;" and the motion was agreed to without debate—yeas 76, nays 69.

Mr. FORD moved to amend the bill by striking out the provision for one apothecary general, conceiving that the duties belonging to that office might be well discharged by the surgeon general, and the office dispensed with, to show which he offered several remarks.

The amendment was opposed by Mr. FLOYD, and was negatived by a large majority.

Mr. MERCER moved to strike out the fifth section of the bill, which abolishes the topographical corps; which motion was negatived without a division.

On motion of Mr. NELSON, of Virginia, who asked for the opponents of the bill an opportunity to present their views on the subject, the House adjourned.

SATURDAY, January 20.

Mr. JOHNSON laid before the House certain resolutions of the General Assembly of the State of Kentucky, instructing their Senators and requesting their Representatives in Congress "to use their exertions to procure the passage of a law, permitting the purchasers of public lands at private sale to apply the instalments already paid to the payment in full for such portion of their purchases as such instalments may be adequate to pay for at the price of two dollars per acre, and to relinquish the balance of their purchases to the United States," and requesting them to present the same to the Senate and House of Representatives; which resolutions were read, and committed to the Committee of the Whole to which is committed the bill regulating the payment of debts due from the purchasers of public lands.

Mr. RHEA, from the Committee on Pensions and Revolutionary Claims, reported a bill concerning invalid pensioners; which was read twice, and committed to a Committee of the Whole on Monday next.

On motion of Mr. WHITMAN, the committee on the subject of reviving, for a limited time, the currency of foreign gold coins in the United States, were instructed to inquire into the expediency of continuing also, for a further limited time, the currency of French crowns and five franc pieces; and, also, into the expediency of increasing the relative value of the gold which may hereafter be coined at the Mint of the United States.

The SPEAKER laid before the House a letter from the Secretary of the Treasury, transmitting a statement showing the tonnage of vessels of the United States which entered from, and cleared for, ports in France, together with the tonnage of French vessels which entered the ports of the United States from the same, during the years 1816, 1817, 1818, and 1819, prepared in obedience to the resolution of the House of the 3d instant; which letter and statement were referred to the Committee of Commerce.

REDUCTION OF THE ARMY.

The House then again proceeded to the consideration of the bill for reducing the Military Peace Establishment.

Mr. FULLER delivered at large the reasons, general as well as of detail, which induced him to oppose the passage of this bill in its present shape.

Mr. TOMLINSON, of Connecticut, addressed the Chair as follows:

Mr. Speaker: The bill now before the House has been so ably, and, I may add, so eloquently discussed by honorable gentlemen who have preceded me, and that discussion has been protracted to such an extent, that, for prolonging it, I am conscious an apology may be expected. Anxious, as the House evidently is, to take the final question on this bill, I very reluctantly occupy any portion of its time. But the objections to the bill under consideration, which have been offered by the gentleman from Massachusetts, (Mr. FULLER,) who has just resumed his seat, deserve a reply, and have determined me to put the patience of the House to a further trial. Knowing, however, that the honorable gentleman from South Carolina, (Mr. LOWNDES,) wishes on this day to present to the House his views in relation to the financial condition of the country, I shall not enter as fully into the various considerations connected with this question, as, under different circumstances, I should feel disposed to do.

My honorable friend from Massachusetts alleges that the bill under consideration ought not to pass, because by its provisions the corps of topographical engineers, in his opinion a necessary part of a Peace Establishment, will not be retained in the service of the country.

Not being a military man, and making no pretensions to practical military science, I have, for the purpose of acting understandingly on this subject, adverted to "the military laws, and rules, and regulations for the army," which a friend near me has put into my hand. In this book the duties of the topographical engineers, and also those required of the engineers, are particularly detailed, and it will be distinctly seen that those duties do not essentially differ in time of peace. By this military code, which has been compiled under the direction of the Department of War, for the government of the army, the topographical engineers are required to make such surveys, and exhibit such delineations of these, as the commanding General shall direct, and make plans of all military positions which the army may occupy, and of their respective vicinities, indicating the various roads, rivers, creeks, ravines, hills, woods, and villages, to be found therein.

From the same authority I learn that the duties assigned to "the corps of engineers, comprise the ' direction of fortifications, military reconnoiter- ' ings, embracing surveys and examinations of the ' country, and surveys of sites that may be desig- ' nated for defence, with maps and plans of the ' same. These reconnoiterings, surveys, maps, and ' plans, will be made, from time to time, by such ' engineers as may be assigned to those duties."

Now, sir, will the honorable member from Massachusetts, or any other member who may be disposed to retain the topographical engineers, as a distinct department, designate the exclusive duties of that corps? They seem not to differ even in name from those required to be performed by the corps of engineers. Are any duties assigned to the former corps which may not be properly and efficiently discharged by the other? Surveys, maps, and plans, are to be made by each, with the same objects, and for the same purposes, and under precisely the same regulations.

Will it be pretended that the corps of engineers are not adequate to the performance of these duties? If so, dismiss them from the public service. But their skill and ability will not be questioned. They are men of experience, and practical military science. Are they not, then, sufficiently numerous? This corps now consists of one colonel, one assistant engineer, one lieutenant colonel, two majors, six captains, six lieutenants, and six second lieutenants, besides non-commissioned officers and privates. Surely the addition of the topographical engineers, drawing a considerable amount of compensation, cannot be necessary, nor even expedient, in time of peace.

It ought not, however, to be concealed that, in a time of war, certain duties are assigned to the topographical engineers, which, by the existing regulations, are not required of the engineers. These are, "to accompany all reconnoitering par- ' ties sent out to obtain intelligence of the enemy, ' or of his positions, &c.; to make sketches of their ' route, accompanied by written notices of every ' thing worthy of observation thereon; to keep a ' journal of every day's movement when the Army ' is in march, noticing the varieties of ground, of ' buildings, of culture, and distances, and state of ' the roads between given points, throughout the ' march of the day; and, lastly, to exhibit the rel- ' ative positions of contending armies on fields of ' battle, and the positions made, whether for at- ' tack or defence." But these duties seem to me more properly to belong to the staff of the acting Commander-in-Chief of the Army, and some of

them might be performed even by his private confidential secretary, with more utility to the service than by a distinct corps. Indeed, during the Revolutionary war, these duties were often performed by the Commander-in-Chief in person. Besides, should the country unfortunately be again involved in a war, those duties may be easily transferred to the corps of engineers, who, I trust, will be found to possess sufficient military science to keep a journal of the movements of the Army. I trust it will not be seriously contended, that a distinct and separate corps must be preserved and paid, for the purpose of performing services so inconsiderable.

But, sir, it is further objected, that the bill now before the House proposes to abolish the office of adjutant and inspector general. Whatever may be the importance of such a "department," it has not the authority of long experience to sustain it. I had supposed that the duties of an adjutant general and an inspector general were entirely dissimilar, and could not well be discharged by the same person.

The adjutant general is the officer through whom all orders from the Department of War are communicated to the Army, and from whom "reports ' of services performed, and returns intended to ' exhibit the strength of the corps, are transmitted ' to the same department. To this officer is com- ' mitted the direction of the military correspond- ' ence."

The inspector general is required to be with the Army. It is his duty to inspect the troops; "to ' ascertain the exact state of their arms, equip- ' ments, and clothing, and of every other circum- ' stance tending to show the actual condition of ' the troops so inspected," and may be said to exercise a general superintendence over "the police of the army." On this officer depends the discipline of the army.

The bill under consideration contains a provision that there shall be an adjutant general and an inspector general attached to the Army. Why, then, continue the office of adjutant and inspector general with his clerks? Why not suffer the adjutant general and the inspector general to communicate with the War Department? What need of this intermediate department? Sir, it is worse than useless; it is a mere excrescence; its continuance would materially affect the symmetry of the establishment proposed by the present bill, and in my judgment it ought to cease.

But the gentleman from Massachusetts has thought proper to bring to the consideration of the House the character and qualifications of the officer who now holds the station of adjutant and inspector general, and to say that, if he were not "actually engaged on the lines during the late war, it was because his repeated requests to be so employed were denied." Sir, with the character of that officer, or any other in the Army, I have nothing to do on the present occasion. The officers and men of our Army, during the late war, distinguished themselves by their valor, and both deserved and received the almost unqualified applause of a grateful country. But I will not detract from the glory which they acquired in that eventful and victorious contest, by admitting, for a moment, that they were influenced by any but the most honorable considerations. I trust they joined the Army to defend, not to become a burden to their country.

The gentleman from Massachusetts will not claim that they were mercenaries. If their patriotism impelled them to the field, can it be supposed that, disregarding the example of their predecessors of the Revolution, they will reluctantly quit the profession of arms, and resume the pursuits of private life, when their country no longer needs their services? A contrary supposition would, in my judgment, tarnish the glory which they have so bravely won. Sir, the man who wishes to hold a sinecure in this Government is unworthy of its confidence.

But, sir, I do protest against this mode of legislating. I will not suffer myself, in forming an opinion upon this question, to inquire how it may affect particular individuals—who may be retained and who discharged? The sole inquiry I feel disposed to make is, what does the good of this nation require? Having ascertained that the demands of individual friendship must yield to that consideration which, in legislating, is paramount to all others, the interest of my country.

If the considerations which have been suggested by the gentleman from Massachusetts were to govern, you could never disband an army. The force found necessary in war, must be retained in peace. But on the termination of the late war, with the flattering prospect which then cheered the country as to its accruing revenue, the Army was reduced to ten thousand men. The nation could not, or would not retain in service a larger number. The revenue was deemed inadequate to the maintenance of a greater force, and the discharge of the other necessary expenditures of the nation.

The question now to be settled is, whether this Army shall be further reduced to six thousand men? It is a question as to the maximum of military force which this nation ought to maintain in time of peace. In deciding it there is an obvious propriety, not to say necessity, of adverting to the state of the finances of the country; it being an axiom in this Government, which I hope never to see controverted, that our permanent expenditures are not to exceed our permanent revenue. The examination which I have been able to give this subject, has resulted in the settled conclusion that neither the present condition of this country, nor that which may be reasonably anticipated, for years to come, will be found adequate to the maintenance of our present Military Establishment, and the discharge of the other authorized and necessary expenses of the nation. This being granted, will any gentleman venture to pronounce the proposed reduction of our military force inexpedient?

What, then, sir, is the amount of the revenue which may be expected to accrue during the year 1821, and what will be the condition of the Treasury at the termination of the current year, if all the present objects of expenditure be continued? I choose to confine this examination to the revenue which may be expected to accrue during the present year, believing that it will afford a fair sample of that which may accrue in subsequent years.

In drawing the attention of the House to this interesting, and, I may add, intricate and difficult subject, I do not propose to examine the various calculations which honorable members have already submitted to your consideration, no two of which produce the same result; all admitting, however, that, at the close of the year 1821, the balance against the Treasury will amount to several millions. Indeed, no gentleman seems disposed to pronounce, with much confidence, what is now the situation of the Treasury, much less what it will be at the close of the current year.

Laying aside all the calculations of honorable gentlemen in relation to this subject, I resort for information to the report of the Secretary of the Treasury, exhibiting the state of the finances. This is the official statement on which alone this House will venture to act. I shall, therefore, discard all the ingenious, and probably fallacious calculations of gentlemen, and consider the expenditures of the current year as correctly exhibited in the official document to which I have referred, taking the balance which will be against the Treasury on the 1st January, 1822, as estimated in the supplementary report from that department, as accurately stated upon the hypothesis, that the receipts into the Treasury will equal the estimate by that department. In that report we are informed that the estimated balance against the Treasury on the 1st of January, 1822, will be $5,158,483. But if from this sum there be deducted $500,000 of the sum heretofore appropriated for the gradual increase of the Navy, which sum will not be wanted during the year 1821, the actual balance against the Treasury on that day will be $4,658,483. With respect to this there can be no doubt; the report distinctly so states. But it will not be forgotten that this balance will depend entirely upon the actual receipts into the Treasury during the present year, and must, of necessity, fluctuate with those receipts.

The official report from the Treasury estimates the receipts into the Treasury for the year 1821, at - - - - - - $16,550,000

This sum is estimated to accrue from customs - - - - - $14,000,000
Public lands, exclusive of Mississippi stock - - - - - - 1,600,000
Arrears of internal duties and direct tax, and incidental receipts - - 100,000
Third instalment from the Bank of the United States - - - 500,000
And from bank dividends, which may accrue during the year, estimated at five per cent. - - 350,000

Making the aggregate of - $16,500,000

Now, sir, it is obvious, that, if the receipts shall fall short of this estimate, the estimated balance against the Treasury will be proportionably increased. Although that diminution may not be

917   HISTORY OF CONGRESS.   918

January, 1821.   *Reduction of the Army.*   H. of R.

felt to its full extent in the current year, yet it will materially affect the revenue which may become available in the two first quarters of the year 1822. Hence the importance of inquiring what amount of revenue may be expected to arise from customs during the present year? For the sake of brevity, I confine this inquiry to a single year. The subject is liable to so many contingencies, that no one will hazard a precise calculation upon it. But from the reflection which I have been able to bestow on this subject, I have formed the conclusion that the official estimate is much too high.

What, sir, is the situation of your commerce, from which this part of your revenue is to accrue? The prospect is appalling, but you must look at it. With the West India islands, that trade which in former times was so lucrative to the merchants engaged in it, and contributed so largely to the revenue, is very greatly diminished. The reduced price of the produce of this country in those islands, and the high duties on the return cargo, combined with the existing regulations, or rather restrictions, of a portion of that trade, forbid the hope that the revenue arising from this source during the current year, will equal that of former years of peace.

The importations from the East Indies, it is believed, will decline. Already the coarse cottons of India, which have contributed largely to the revenue in former times, have given place to the manufactures of our own country, under the influence of our existing tariff; and it may be reasonably apprehended that our trade to that quarter of the world will be still further diminished by causes which I will not detain the House to detail.

If we turn our attention to the other side of the Atlantic, we shall discern nothing to justify the opinion that our commerce has there experienced its greatest depression. With France, our trade is suspended, I had almost said annihilated, by the countervailing system to which each nation has deemed it proper to resort. The tonnage duty surcharged upon American vessels arriving in French ports, by the ordinance of July last, has instantly effected that which the commercial regulations of France have for years tended gradually to produce, the entire exclusion of American vessels from French ports.

The discriminating duty imposed by the act of the last session of Congress, on French vessels arriving in the ports of the United States, equal to the charges then collected from American vessels in French ports, with the declared intention to procure that just reciprocity in the commercial regulations of the two countries, which the United States offer to all nations, and desire to make the basis of their commercial intercourse, has diverted French ships from our ports. We have been officially informed by the Secretary of the Treasury, that already several French vessels are hovering upon our Southern border, with large cargoes, for no other conceivable purpose but to smuggle those cargoes into the United States. We have it from the same authority, that more are expected shortly to arrive in the same quarter. The design is apparent. It will probably be de-

feated by the vigilance of the Treasury Department; but it is most evident that the revenue which will accrue during the present year, from French commerce, must be very inconsiderable.

With Great Britain and the continental nations of the north of Europe our trade is still open, and placed upon a fair and reciprocal basis. But it is much circumscribed by the present condition of those Powers. At peace with each other, and with us, it is evidently not only the interest but the determination of those Powers to resuscitate their own commerce, and to direct it in the natural channel, in which it flowed previous to its diversion to our shores, which commenced in 1790, and continued with partial interruptions to 1812. During that period we enjoyed the carrying trade, so immensely profitable to us, and under the influence of which this country increased in wealth and population, with a rapidity unprecedented. But the causes which made us the carriers of Europe have ceased, and with them has ceased this source of profit.

But it has been said that, notwithstanding we have lost the carrying trade, we shall continue to import for our own consumption the manufactures and produce of other countries, and thus the revenue will be sustained. Sir, be not deceived. This expectation will not be realized. This country will not import foreign goods to an extent equal to former years. Our exports will not enable us to do it. The value of our exports having been diminished by the production of the same articles in other countries, it seems to me a necessary, an inevitable consequence, that our imports will be equally diminished. That our imports will be restrained by our exports is clear, unless the people of this country shall become so infatuated as to consent to contract a debt to foreign nations for articles which may be produced by their own industry. While the enormous debt which was contracted by the excessive importations of former years is still unpaid and producing widespread embarrassment, it is to be hoped that even common prudence will restrain us from enlarging that debt. Should the individual embarrassments, to which our extravagance, as a people, has subjected us, result in the successful cultivation of our own resources, our condition may be ameliorated. But, to continue our imports by contracting new debts abroad, or at our own banks, would be madness. And, sir, I must confess I am not much dissatisfied to find that we have not the firmness to resist the progress of extravagance in this country. The time is not far distant when stern necessity will bring us back to the simplicity of former days, and compel us to rely upon our own energies.

But, sir, the honorable gentleman from Pennsylvania, (Mr. Sergeant,) who sits near me, and with whom I usually take pleasure in acting, has told us that the two last have been "bad years," and that "we may hope for better times." But that gentleman has failed to show us any ground to justify this hope. He tells us that commerce is indeed depressed; that it languishes; that our exports are diminished; but that we may expect a

" reaction." Trust not, sir, to a reaction. Under given circumstances, it is true, action and reaction are equal; but let it be remembered that where there is no resistance there will be no reaction. Your commerce has gradually declined since the general peace in Europe; and what is there, I ask, to prevent its further depression? Will "re-action" give you the carrying trade, which has afforded a clear profit of 30,000,000 annually? Will it bring your productions into competition with those of the same character in the countries where they are raised with less expense? Will it prevent the efforts of foreign nations to supply their own wants from their own resources?

I come then to the conclusion that the revenue which will accrue from the customs, during the year 1821, will not equal the estimate of the Treasury. And, sir, in my judgment there is no good reason to expect that it will exceed $13,000,000.

Besides we have been informed by the Secretary of the Treasury that of the bonds outstanding, on the 30th of September, 1820, $3,130,000 are in suit; of which about $1,250,000, will not be collected on account of the insolvency of the debtors. Now what guarantee have we, that from the same cause an equal amount will not be lost during the current year? Is it not now as difficult for the collectors of the customs to ascertain the solvency of those who may be entitled to a credit for duties, as it was during the year ending on the 30th of September last? If then the losses " on account of the insolvency of the debtors," during the current year, be estimated at only one-half of that of the last year, a further deduction of $625,000, must be made from this portion of our revenue; giving an unavailable amount of $12,375,000.

The revenue which is estimated to arise from the " public land exclusive of Mississippi stock," which, in the report heretofore referred to, is stated at $1,600,000 next presents itself for our consideration. This sum it is expected will be received from persons who are now indebted for lands heretofore purchased; and from the sales to be made under the law of Congress passed at the last session, providing " that credit shall not be allowed, for the purchase money on the sale of any of the public lands." On this subject my information is limited, not being particularly acquainted with that section of the Union from which this portion of the revenue is to be drawn; but certain facts have been communicated to this House which seem to justify the conclusion that the available amount of receipts from this source will fall considerably below that at which they have been estimated. Although the amount due for the public land is enormous, exceeding $20,000,000, yet the debtors tell you they cannot pay it. Your table has been loaded with memorials, not only from individuals, but from the Legislatures of several States, praying that further time may be allowed for the payment of the loan. If, sir, the people of the West cannot pay the debt already contracted for the public lands, can it be supposed that any considerable quantity will be sold for cash? Unless some measures shall be adopted to relieve those who are indebted for public lands, there is, in my apprehension, no good reason to believe that the receipts into the Treasury from this source during the year 1821, will exceed $1,000,000.

If then it be admitted that " the bank dividends which may accrue during the year" will amount to the sum of $350,000, which is by no means certain, it may be estimated that the revenue accruing in the year 1821 will not exceed $14,325,000. If this calculation be correct, and no diminution of the public expenditures take place, the balance against the Treasury, on the 1st day of January, 1822, will exceed that which has been estimated at the Treasury, and will probably not be much less than $7,000,000.

Now, sir, I readily admit that this calculation depends upon contingent events, the effect of which it is impossible to determine, and which may occasion a very great fluctuation in our receipts. But we are made officially certain, by the report of the Secretary of the Treasury, that provision must " be made for raising the sum of $7,000,000, in aid of the funds which it is estimated will be received into the Treasury during the year 1821."

With this appalling financial prospect before us, I anxiously ask, what is to be done? And I trust the people of this country will, with not less anxiety, respond the inquiry.

Sir, you must either boldly meet the crisis and supply this deficiency, which, for aught I can see, must be as great in future years, by resorting to a permanent system of internal and direct taxation, or to perpetual loans; or, by a judicious and thorough retrenchment, you must bring your expenditures within your income.

Will you, I ask, impose a land tax, in time of profound peace?

Should you, the people cannot pay it. The produce of the farmer is depressed to a price unexampled since the formation of this Government. The distress of the country is universal. If I have been correctly informed—and I have my information from sources entitled to the highest credit—there are farmers in this country, who have heretofore lived in affluence, that cannot command ten dollars in cash, while many of them are deeply in debt, and are compelled to witness the sacrifice of the earnings of " better times," to satisfy debts which they have contracted at the banks in those times. This, I admit, is an unpleasant picture, but it is no fiction. I wish it were.

But, sir, you will not impose internal taxes. The voice of the nation is opposed to this course, and you must and will listen to it.

Will you, then, resort to loans! Sir, I hope the long exploded doctrine, that " a national debt is a national blessing," is not now to be revived. I, for one, cannot consent to transmit that inheritance which was achieved by the wisdom and valor of our predecessors to posterity encumbered with the expense of our improvidence. I have hoped to see the day when this nation shall, by a steady and persevering course of economy, and a rigid application of its means to useful ends, present the solitary and cheering spectacle of a nation free of debt. Although the public debt is now $90,000,000 more than it was when the operations of this Government commenced, I will not yet relinquish this hope.

But, should Congress now resort to loans in preference to relieving the Treasury by a general retrenchment of our expenditures, I should indeed despair.

It is said that a loan may be taken on terms favorable to the Government. I admit it. There is no difficulty in procuring the money. You need but authorize a loan, and foreign capital will fill it. The rate of interest which is here given will draw capital from abroad. But, be it remembered, that, by the use of a foreign capital, the nation becomes in a measure tributary to foreigners. The principal must ultimately be refunded, and the interest paid quarterly. Already, sir, as we have been told by an official report from the Treasury, above $25,000,000 of our national debt is due to foreigners, the annual interest of which, at six per cent., is one million five hundred thousand dollars. Shall we, sir, increase this monstrous tribute by additional loans? If you value your independence, your liberty; nay, your existence as a nation, I warn you to abstain. Profit by the examples of other nations who are sinking under the weight of their augmented debts. Practise upon the maxim, that money is power; pay your national debt; and with a full Treasury, you will be prepared for any emergency.

There is then, sir, but one course left, and that is, to adopt a judicious and prudent, but thorough system of retrenchment. This nation must pursue that course which every wise and considerate man, who had maintained a splendid establishment, would adopt on finding his income diminished, to which many individuals in this nation have already given their practical sanction; it must reduce those establishments which are not absolutely necessary. Sir, would a wise and prudent individual, who had been accustomed to a coach and four, on finding his income inadequate to his expenditures, borrow money to meet those expenditures? No, sir, he would take off a pair, and then another, and dispose of his coach, and take a gig, and even travel on horseback, if necessary, in order to conform his establishment to his income. He would put an end to every expenditure which should not be indispensably necessary, notwithstanding it might contribute to his convenience. Splendor would be laid aside, and plain simplicity take its place. The legitimate and necessary effect of a contrary course would be individual ruin. And can a nation, pursuing that course which would ruin an individual, expect to escape national destruction?

In my judgment nothing but a thorough and persevering system of economy and retrenchment will preserve the useful institutions of this nation. Unless some of our superfluous establishments be curtailed, and the Treasury thereby relieved, there is great danger that we may be ultimately compelled to prostrate those which are of vital importance, and that here a "reaction" will produce an unfortunate effect. But it has been asked, where will you begin this work of retrenchment? By the bill on your table our attention is directly drawn to the Army. This bill proposes to reduce your Army from ten to six thousand men, retaining the number of officers requisite to command that force. And can gentlemen point me to a more fit object of retrenchment in time of peace? It has indeed been urged, that this force will not be adequate to meet the emergency of an unexpected war. This I will not deny, if we are to rely solely upon an army to repel invasion; nor would 50,000 men be adequate to that object, unaided by any other force. But I do deny that it is, or ever has been, the policy of this nation to maintain a large standing army in time of peace.

The Constitution of the United States gives to Congress the power "to provide for organizing, arming, and disciplining the militia." For what purpose? "To repel invasions." Sir, the militia are the Constitutional defence of this country in time of peace, and in the onset of war, until regulars can be raised. In the language of the first President of the United States, they are "the army of the Constitution." The framers of that instrument, deeply impressed as they were with a sense of the manifold evils arising from a large standing army, manifestly intended that the militia should be looked to as the legitimate and principal defence of this nation upon the land.

This great principle of our Government, as to national defence, has received the repeated sanction of Washington. In his speech delivered to Congress at the opening of the session in December, 1793, after adverting to the necessity of procuring supplies of arms and military stores, leaving nothing to the uncertainty of procuring a warlike apparatus in the moment of public danger, he says, with a force peculiar to himself, "Nor can such arrangements, with such objects, 'be exposed to the censure or jealousy of the 'warmest friends of republican government.— 'They are incapable of abuse in the hands of the 'militia, who ought to possess a pride in being the 'depository of the force of the Republic, and may 'be trained to a degree of energy equal to every 'military exigency of the United States." This, let it be remembered, is the language of the founder of American liberty and independence. Sir, when I have such authority for my opinions, I pronounce them, fearless of contradiction. I rest upon a basis which is not easily shaken.

Shall I hereafter be told that the militia are not to be relied upon to defend the country? Sir, who are the militia against whom so much has been said, and who have been pronounced so inefficient? They are the freemen of this country with arms in their hands; they are a band of citizen soldiers, 800,000 strong. And will not they defend the country which contains all they hold dear? Will they "refuse" to defend their firesides, their wives, their children, and the Government of their choice? Sir, they will present a front of steel to an invading foe; a protection, in my judgment, much to be preferred to the "iron front" of a standing army, so highly appreciated by the honorable gentleman from Virginia, (Mr. A. SMYTH.)

This country will probably be attacked by a

foreign Power, on its maritime frontier, and on the Lakes which divide the United States from the British possessions bordering on those Lakes. Will it be pretended that an Army such as that which we now have is, or that one vastly larger will be, adequate to the defence of our immensely extended frontier?

Sir, the natural, the cheapest, and the most effectual defence of the maritime frontier of this country, as well that bordering upon the Atlantic ocean, as the Lakes, is the Navy. Experience has fully demonstrated the truth of this proposition. With a few ships-of-the-line, and a proper proportion of frigates, moving, as they can so easily do, as the position of an invading enemy may be changed, and combining the aid of the militia of that portion of the country immediately threatened with an invasion, an attack may, at all times, be successfully repelled. The character acquired by the Navy of this country, during the late war, is a safe pledge of what may be expected from it on any future emergency. The results of the battles of Erie and Champlain decisively determine its utility on those inland seas. With a knowledge of these results, no one, it is presumed, will doubt the expediency of employing this species of force for the protection of that frontier. Let, then, the wealth of the nation be directed to the augmentation of its naval force to an extent which will afford that protection which is, or ought to be, the object of all military preparations.

I admit that a limited military force upon the land may be usefully employed, in time of peace, in overawing the Indian tribes upon our inland frontier, in the performance of garrison duty, and in protect ng and taking care of the public stores and arms; but for all these purposes, in my apprehension, the force to be retained by the present bill is entirely incompetent. It will constitute the nucleus of an army, to which at any time, a force may be added, to meet the exigencies of war.

But, sir, the present situation of the world, and of our foreign relations, does not justify the expectation that we shall be involved in war for a long period to come. The nations of Europe are reposing in the arms of peace, and although certain movements are there taking place, of deep import to themselves, yet there is no reason to apprehend that this nation will be materially affected by them.

If we may place reliance upon the accounts from Spain, the long protracted diplomatic war, in which we have been engaged with the Spanish Government, has been amicably and satisfactorily terminated. There is no danger that it will be followed by a war of bayonets.

From France we have nothing to apprehend. With that Power we are not likely to come in collision. The commercial dispute which has unhappily arisen between the two countries, in consequence of what may be deemed their municipal regulations, has, it is true, occasioned a suspension of a direct commercial intercourse, to the mutual injury of both; but there is good reason to believe that this matter is susceptible of such friendly explanations as will restore the good understanding which has heretofore existed between the two countries.

But the honorable gentleman from Georgia (Mr. Cuthbert) admonished the House that Russia might assail us, she having evinced a disposition to occupy the mouth of the Columbia river, and that we may find it necessary to resist such an unwarrantable encroachment upon our territory by an armed force. Sir, the gentleman may dismiss his fears. Russia has in view objects of greater magnitude. Her attention is directed to another quarter. The occupation of the unsettled territory at the mouth of the Columbia river comes not within the scope of her policy. She looks with a far more longing eye to the Dardanelles. Besides, Russia has uniformly manifested the most friendly disposition towards the United States, and it is evidently for the mutual interest of the two countries to cultivate that good understanding which has so long subsisted between them.

With England your relations appear to be permanently peaceful. England will cautiously avoid a war with the United States. She has too recently and too severely felt the effects of such a war. You have taught her a lesson which she will not soon forget. The lapse of half a century will not obliterate from her recollection the demonstrations of your force, which she was made to feel during your late contest, so eventful in its progress, and in its termination so honorable to this nation. She may indulge a jealousy of the rising power of this nation, but, profiting by experience, she will not strengthen that power by calling it into action.

If, then, sir, no speck of war be discernible in all your political horizon, will gentlemen contend that the safety of the country demands a standing army of ten thousand men? If such an army be now necessary, will the time, can it, ever arrive when it will be less so? Should Congress now decide to reject the bill under consideration and to retain the army as at present organized, it may be considered as finally settled that this country will maintain a standing army of ten thousand men as a permanent peace establishment.

Sir, it is my fixed opinion that the ordinary revenue of the United States will not enable them to maintain such an army, with their other establishments; that the safety of the country does not demand it. and that the proposed reduction of the army is consistent with sound policy.

Sir, I will detain the House a single moment to notice an observation which has been reiterated here, and perhaps elewhere, that those who support the bill under consideration, are opposing "the whole course and spirit of the present Administration." Sir, this assertion, so far as it repects me, is unwarrantable. The Administration possesses my confidence and that of the State which I have the honor in part to represent. On this point the late election speaks a language which cannot be misunderstood, and to the force of which I cannot add.

It has, too, been often repeated, and I deem it my duty to reply to the remark, that the bill before

925   HISTORY OF CONGRESS.   926

JANUARY, 1821.   *Reduction of the Army.*   H. OF R.

the House is in hostility to the recommendation of the Secretary of the Department of War, and that its adoption may be considered disrespectful to that valuable officer. Sir, I repel the charge, and I improve this occasion to say, that I entertain the highest respect for the distinguished gentleman who presides over the War Department. The energy and rigid economy of the system which he has introduced into that Department has greatly diminished the expense of supporting the army. The able manner in which he has discharged the arduous and responsible duties of his station, entitle him to the confidence of this nation.

But great as is my respect for that gentleman, I will not consent to make even his opinions the rule of my own conduct. I act here upon my own responsibility, and shall be directed by the dictates of my own judgment. Being convinced that the passage of the bill now before the House will advance the best interests of the nation, I shall give to it my cordial support.

When Mr. T. had concluded—

Mr. BURTON, of North Carolina, spoke as follows:

Mr. Chairman: In rising to address you, I disclaim all intention to throw censure upon any person connected with the Executive branch of the Government; motives of that kind shall never influence my conduct, while I have the honor to occupy a seat on this floor. Indeed, I should not trouble the House at all upon the subject but for the circumstance that I belong to the committee that reported this bill. This committee has frequently been called upon for explanations; and, as one of its members, I feel it my duty briefly to state some of the reasons that influence my vote upon the question.

I shall not attempt to follow the gentlemen who have preceded me in this debate, through all their various statements and calculations, particularly on the subject of the Treasurer's report. I am not sufficiently skilled in the finances of the country to throw much light on the subject; for even those gentlemen who have, for years, turned their attention that way, are far from agreeing in their results. It is enough for my purpose to know that the Treasury is empty; that we must either lay taxes, borrow money, or curtail our expenditures. As to the first, for many reasons, which it is not necessary now to examine, the people at this time are not in a situation to pay taxes. As to the second, it is believed, by many judicious persons, that the borrowing of money is only postponing the evil which in the end will come; and that it will lay the foundation of a large public debt which may ultimately prove extremely oppressive to the citizens of this country.

The third alternative—retrenchment—appears to meet the approbation of a large majority of this House; but, sir, when we come to point out the particular items, what is the result? If you attempt to reduce our own pay, we are met at the threshold, and told that members of Congress are worse paid than any other persons in the Government. If you look to the heads of departments and their numerous clerks, why, it is with the greatest difficulty, and most rigid economy, that they can support themselves and families with their present salaries. As to the pension list, gratitude and justice forbid that we should take from the old soldier his miserable pittance. As to the Navy, the pride of our country, and which has heaped upon us imperishable fame, touch but a plank and we shall become the prey of some foreign Power; and, sir, to continue the catalogue, when we come to the Army, and are about to dismiss so much of it as we can do without, we are accused of prostrating essential establishments, and are told that, when we get to war, some fifteen or twenty years hence, perhaps with the inhabitants of the moon, that we cannot again expect to obtain the services of these men. So that, after going the rounds, we find ourselves precisely where we started; and we shall not even have it in our power, on returning home, to say to our constituents, as was pleasantly remarked by an honorable gentleman from Kentucky (Mr. CLAY) at the last session—we have saved two hundred dollars of the public money, after spending thousands in debate.

The rules that apply to the conduct of an individual, are certainly, in some measure, applicable to Governments; and, to borrow a comparison used by the gentleman from Connecticut, (Mr. TOMLINSON,) it is very easy for a man, after riding on horseback, or in a gig, to persuade himself that a carriage would be more comfortable; and, next, that four horses would make it run much easier; immediately the two foremost horses become an indispensable part of the establishment. In this manner, sir, individuals and Governments go on adding *ad infinitum* to their establishments, believing that every part is essential. Sir, if there is any thing proven by history it is this, that Governments, as well as individuals, may commit errors; and, whenever convinced of that fact, to retrace their steps is, to my mind, the highest evidence of wisdom and magnanimity—to persist in error, from the fear of being charged with vacillating in their conduct, and changeable in their plans, is the reverse.

To attempt to prove that standing armies are dangerous to liberty, in time of peace, would be as unnecessary as to attempt to prove that the sun has done shining; but, I do not believe that any danger is to be apprehended from the present number of our Army, nor even were it much larger than it is; and this is an argument, to my mind, in favor of reducing the Army. If fifty thousand men, connected with the community by all the ties of relationship, can produce no impression upon it, is it not fair to presume that these people can defend themselves against any foe that might be sent against them from abroad? Was not this fully exemplified in our Revolutionary war? Great Britain sent her armies here, chose her own points of attack; we were then in our infancy, and yet, notwithstanding all these advantages on her side, we established our independence. Does not this show that it is the moral sense of the people on which we must rely for defence? and that any army, larger than what is necessary to take care

923   **HISTORY OF CONGRESS.**   924

H. OF R.   *Reduction of the Army.*   JANUARY, 1821.

of our public property is totally useless, unless employed in foreign conquest? and I do not believe that there is an individual in this House, or in the nation, that would vote a single dollar for purposes of that kind. Further to illustrate my idea, let us recur to the history of France. Republican France was able to withstand the Powers of Europe, because the people were defending what they believed to be their rights. A few years after, when France had added greatly to her territory, and her military fame had reached its highest point—when her armies were commanded by as able generals as the world ever produced—when every citizen was a well trained soldier, and even her drill sergeants were capable of commanding armies—we see her Emperor dethroned and sent into banishment, and another individual, who, to say the least, did not meet with the approbation of the nation, seated on the throne.

Are we certain that it is the true policy of this Government to encourage this military spirit to any great extent? Even now, we find that it is with much difficulty that we restrain our citizens from overrunning the territory of our neighbors. Notwithstanding that we have express laws, prohibiting our citizens from taking up arms against any nation with whom we are at peace, yet we have seen Toledo, Robinson, and others, assemble troops and march them into the Spanish provinces; and at this very time, a General Long, with his adventurers, are in Texas, in despite of all law.

If, sir, we turn to the history of England, we will find, that the standing army of that country had but a small beginning, and that after each successive war, some speck of another war was discovered in the horizon, or some other phantom of the brain was conjured up, by which a considerable addition was made to the Peace Establishment; it went on, like a ball of snow, accumulating at each revolution, until at length it has become so ponderous as now literally it threatens to crush to death the honest yeomanry of the country.

The whelp of the tigress is an inoffensive animal; but, as it grows in size and strength, it becomes mischievous and dangerous. Should we keep up our present Army, may it not, a few years hence, be found that active employment is the best way to improve in the military science? And, may this not prove a temptation to foreign conquest? To use a plain comparison, would any farmer of common sense ever think, of giving a considerable part of his income to a set of idle fellows to watch his grounds, lest, peradventure, some twenty years hence, rogues might break in and plunder his property? Surely not. Such a man would meet with derision. But, we are told, we must keep up the present Army to preserve military science, for, if we dismiss those now in service, they will not again return, should they be wanted. Sir, for the same reason, we should always keep in their places all civil officers; for I believe the science of Government is as important and as difficult to learn as the art of war. Yet, we see when one civil officer is turned out, there is no want of a successor. Even for a seat

in this House, where the term is only two years, there is no scarcity of candidates; and, in the Senate, I have never heard any complaint on that score. As for the office of Chief Magistrate, which is only four years, I believe we are likely to have a plentiful crop of candidates at the next election.

So far as my observation goes, the good people of this country are at no loss for characters to fill any appointment, and, should we be so unfortunate as not to obtain the services of these gentlemen when required, I hope there will be no difficulty in supplying their places. Sir, the two most distinguished generals in the late war, (Generals Brown and Jackson,) were not educated in the standing army. A letter, written some years ago, by the presen[t] Chief Magistrate, was published in the papers a few days ago. This letter recommends fixing the Peace Establishment at twenty thousand men, but Congress at that time held a different opinion, and fixed it at ten thousand. I think that too large for our present finances. To do justice to the writer of that letter, we should advert to the circumstances under which it was written—the unsettled state of Europe, and the probability that she might soon again be involved in war.

Mr. Chairman, I took my seat on this floor with the strongest predilection and attachment to the Army. I had not the pleasure of a particular acquaintance with many of the officers, but for the few that were known to me, I entertained the highest regard. I viewed the Army as a band of brave and patriotic men, devoted to the service of their country; who, in the hour of her danger, had overlooked all personal considerations, and manfully came forward in her defence. Under such feelings I could deny the soldier nothing, and I hope, from the vote I am about to give, that it will not be considered that I have lost any of my respect for the distinguished individuals that compose our Army. But, from my short experience in this House, I have discovered that personal feelings and wishes are very unsafe guides when legislating for the nation. It is a maxim as old as our system of jurisprudence, that individual convenience must give way to the public good; and, however much I may regret the hard fate of those who may lose their offices by this bill, yet no feelings of this kind can have the smallest influence on my mind in determining this question. I believe that the best interest of the country, at this time, calls for a reduction of the Army, and for that reason alone I shall vote for the passage of the bill.

Mr. BROWN then moved to amend the original third section, by striking out that portion of it which, as previously amended, reads thus: "one ' Brigadier General, with one Aid-de Camp, one ' Inspector General, one Assistant Adjutant Gen- ' eral," and in lieu thereof to insert "three Briga- ' dier Generals, with one Aid-de-Camp, one Assist- ' ant Adjutant General, and one Assistant Inspec- ' tor General;" which, upon the request of Mr. SMITH, of Maryland, Mr. BROWN modified to read as follows: "three Brigadiers Generals, one of

‘ whom shall reside at Washington, and perform
‘ the duties heretofore confided to the Adjutant
‘ and Inspector General, together with the duties
‘ of Inspector General of the army, with one Aid-
‘ de-Camp, one Assistant Adjutant General, and
‘ one Assistant Inspector General to each.”

Mr. BROWN said he had waited to this late period with an expectation and hope that some other person would have proposed the amendment which he should offer; none having done so, he felt it his duty to submit it, although he could not flatter himself from the temper of the House that it would succeed. He said that an honorable gentleman, Mr. COCKE, of Tennessee, with whom he had acted on the principal provision of this bill, had suggested the necessity of discipline among its friends; for one he should protest against discip'ine in civil, for the same reason that he should applau,d it in military service; by doing so, the object sought was most likely to be attained. He hoped that gentlemen who took upon themselves the labor of argument would not suppose that those who chose to be silent, surrendered the right to reflect and decide upon measures; and that they were ready to obey rules of discipline. Should such an impression prevail, the number of speakers would greatly increase, and, he could say, much to the detriment of the public service.

Mr. B. said he was favorable to the reduction of the army to the number proposed by the bill, of six thousand, because he believed that number sufficient for all the legitimate duties of soldiers in this country, in a time of such profound peace, and not because he believed the Government unable to support them. He would not use an argument here, predicated upon a fact, at the bare suggestion of which an American in passing through Europe would feel himself highly insulted: I mean the incapacity of the American nation to support such establishments and officers, as were deemed necessary for their prosperity and safety; he would not permit himself to be driven into argument to support a proposition so plain as was the negative of this. He should predicate his legislation on this and other measures of the Government, on the ample capacity of his country to support all necessary establishments and officers. Mr. B. said that he thought too much stress had been laid on the deranged state of our finances; for one he thought their distressed condition should induce the Government to pursue the course of a prudent individual; to look into her expenditures, and to curtail wherever it was not incompatible with her safety and prosperity; and if there required it, he would be willing to increase the army beyond its present size; he feared not the resources of the country.

Mr. B. desired that gentlemen, in reply, having maps before them on which our line of posts and extent of frontier were exhibited, would point out the places and posts at which a greater force could be beneficially used, and not confine themselves to the proof of our capacity to pay them. He yielded them that ground. He said, that, although friendly to a reduction of the army to six thousand men, he was in favor of a liberal and efficient organiza-

16th CON. 2d SESS.—30

tion, and had voted for many of the amendments proposed. From a belief that three general officers, instead of one, would produce a higher state of subordination and discipline, a surer protection of the fortifications and public property, and this number being also indicated by the geographical situation of the United States, and the rank and file of the army, he would beg leave to offer the proposed amendment.

The amendment was then rejected without a division.

Mr. LOWNDES then took the floor against the bill generally, but spoke more particularly on the considerations growing out of the condition of the finances of the country. He spoke at considerable length.

Mr. BARBOUR then signified a wish to make some remarks on this bill, but would not press them if the House desired to take the question this afternoon; when, a motion to adjourn was made; and the House adjourned.

MONDAY, January 22.

Mr. RHEA, from the Committee on Pensions and Revolutionary Claims, reported a bill to continue in force an act, entitled “An act to provide for persons who were disabled by known wounds received in the Revolutionary war,” and for other purposes; which was read twice, amended, and ordered to be engrossed, and read a third time tomorrow.

Mr. ANDERSON, from the Committee on the Public Lands, reported a bill giving the right of pre-emption in the purchase of lands to certain settlers in the Territory of Arkansas; which was read twice, and committed to a Committee of the Whole.

The SPEAKER laid before the House a letter from WILLARD HALL, containing a notification of his having resigned his seat in this House, as one of the Representatives from the State of Delaware.

The SPEAKER also laid before the House a letter from the Secretary of the Governor and Council of the State of Maryland, accompanied with two copies of the Laws of Maryland, lately compiled by Chancellor Kilty, and Messrs. Harris and Watkins, presented by the General Assembly of that State to the Congress of the United States.

TREASURY REPORT.

The SPEAKER laid before the House the following report:

TREASURY DEPARTMENT, *Jan.* 19, 1821.

SIR: In obedience to a resolution of the House of Representatives, of the fourth instant, instructing the Secretary of the Treasury to report to the House “a statement of the money in the Treasury on the first of January, 1821, together with a statement of the money in the hands of the Treasurer, as agent for the War and Navy Departments, on that day,” I have the honor to state, that there was in the Treasury on that day the sum of $1,076,261 18, and in the hands of the Treasurer, as agent for the War and Navy Departments, the sum of $1,050,378 25, viz: For the War Department, $151,373 29, and for the Navy Department, $799,004 96.

Of the sum of $1,076,271 18, in the Treasury on the first of January, 1821, $500,000 were paid by the Bank of the United States, on the 30th of December, 1820, but which were payable on the first day of January thereafter, and were estimated in the receipts into the Treasury for 1821. If this sum is deducted, the amount in the Treasury on that day will be $576,271 18. If it is considered a part of the receipts of 1820, the estimated receipts for 1821 will be diminished by that amount. With this explanation, it will not be material whether it is placed to the credit of the one or the other year; the general result of the two years will be the same.

The receipts of the fourth quarter, with the exception of payments made at Mobile and New Orleans, in the two last weeks of December, 1820, and in the whole month at most of the land offices, are ascertained to be $4,045,585 99. In the annual report, the receipts of the fourth quarter were estimated at $3,430,000; the actual receipts, therefore, exceed these that were estimated by $615,585 99, and by $115,585 99, if the payment made by the bank on the 30th of December be deducted from the receipts of 1820.

If the sum of $615,585 99 be added to the sum of $5,417,830 83, which was stated in my letter of the 21st of December, 1820, to be the aggregate means for the fourth quarter of that year, the amount at the disposition of the Treasury, in that quarter, will be augmented to $6,033,416 82.

It is ascertained that the payments from the Treasury, during that quarter, have amounted to $4,957,145 24, which, being deducted from the estimated means of that quarter, will leave in the Treasury, as already stated, on the 1st day of January, 1821, the sum of $1,076,271 18. But if the $500,000, paid by the bank, be deducted from the receipts of 1820, the balance on the 1st day of January, 1821, will be, as has already been stated, $576,271 18.

The demands upon the Treasury during the year 1820, in order to complete the service of that year and to effect the objects for which the several appropriations were made, and which are not included in the foregoing sum of $4,957,145 24, which amounts to $4,707,987 96, viz:

Civil, diplomatic, and miscellaneous, (being the difference between the sum of $1,407,213 56, estimated to be paid in the fourth quarter, and the sum actually paid,) - - - - - - $855,905 20
Public debt - - - - - 2,076,918 15
War Department - - - - 665,164 61
Navy Department - - - - 1,110,000 00

Which leaves an excess of demand beyond the money in the Treasury of $3,631,716 78, and of $4,131,716 78, if the payment made by the bank be deducted from the payments into the Treasury in the year 1820.

It may be proper to observe, that, if the sum of $2,076,918 15, of the Louisiana stock, has not been pressed for payment, it has been the result of forbearance on the part of the holders of that stock, and of confidence in the faith of the nation, that such forbearance will not operate to their injury. The other demands upon the Treasury, which were estimated as a charge upon it in the fourth quarter of the year 1820, and which are not embraced in the estimates of the expenditure for 1821, and which constitute a part of the deficit above stated, will, it is presumed, be demanded of the Treasury.

It will be perceived that the sums in the hands of the Treasurer, as agent of the War and Navy Department, exceed the estimate of them, annexed to the estimates of the service of the year 1821. These moneys are drawn from the agent, as the demands upon the respective departments are presented, or requisitions from the disbursing officers of those departments are received. The amount drawn from the agent depends, therefore, upon contingencies over which the heads of those departments have no control, and may exceed or fall short of any estimate made by them for any definite period of time.

It may be proper, also, to state, that, in contemplation of law, money is not considered to be in the Treasury until a warrant is issued by the Secretary and receipted by the Treasurer, for the sums paid by the receiving officers into the bank; but, for the practical purposes of the Treasury, all sums paid into bank to the credit of the Treasurer are considered by him to be in the Treasury. Generally, the warrants covering the money received on account of the Government are issued quarterly for all sums received during the quarter. These warrants are usually issued about two months after the expiration of the quarter, as the payments made into the banks which are the depositories of the public money are not ascertained sooner.

The statements which accompany this letter are explanatory of the views which it presents, or afford information connected with them, which it is presumed may be useful.

I remain, with respect, &c.,
WM. H. CRAWFORD.
Hon. JOHN TAYLOR,
    Speaker of the House of Representatives.

The report was read, and, with the documents, referred to the Committee of Ways and Means.

REDUCTION OF THE ARMY.

The House resumed the consideration of the bill to reduce the Military Peace Establishment of the United States.

Mr. McCULLOUGH moved further to amend the third section of the bill (as recited on the Journal of the 18th instant) by expunging from the fifth and sixth lines thereof the words following, viz: "each with the rank, pay, and emoluments of a colonel of cavalry, as heretofore prescribed by law;" and also, from the eighth and ninth lines thereof, the words "with a salary of two thousand dollars per annum;" and also, after the word "purchases" in the tenth line, the following words: "whose compensation shall not exceed two and a half per centum on the public moneys disbursed by him, nor the sum of fifteen hundred dollars per annum; and also, from the thirteenth and fourteenth lines, the words "to be compensated as heretofore;" also, after the words "surgeon general," in the sixteenth line, the words "with a salary of two thousand dollars per annum;" and also, after the words "apothecary general," in the seventeenth line, the words "with a salary of fifteen hundred dollars per annum;" and to add to the section the following words, viz: "the said several officers to hold the rank, pay, and emoluments which now are, or hereafter may be, prescribed by law."

After considerable debate, in which Messrs. McCULLOUGH, RICH, McLEAN, BURTON, FLOYD, BRUSH, and MERCER, took part, the motion of Mr. McCULLOUGH was negatived, first on the question of inserting, and then on striking out the existing compensations.

Mr. BRUSH then moved to strike out the word "general," after "Quartermaster," so that there should be a Quartermaster without the addition of "general," the rank of general being proposed to be taken from the office.—Negatived.

Mr. EUSTIS moved an amendment, the object of which was to place the deputy commissaries and quartermasters on the footing on which they will be found to stand in the amended bill, instead of that in which they stood in the original bill.

This motion was agreed to 51 to 47.

The question having been then stated on ordering the bill, as amended, to be engrossed for a third reading—

Mr. BARBOUR and Mr. MERCER addressed the House, each at great length; the first in favor of the bill, the latter against it.

The question was then taken on ordering the bill to be engrossed for a third reading, and decided as follows:

YEAS—Messrs. Abbot, Adams, Alexander, Allen of Massachusetts, Allen of New York, Allen of Tennessee, Baker, Ball, Barbour, Bayly, Beecher, Brown, Bryan, Buffum, Burton, Butler of New Hampshire, Campbell, Cannon, Clay, Cobb, Cocke, Crafts, Crawford, Culpeper, Cushman, Dane, Dennison, Earle, Eddy, Edwards of Connecticut, Edwards of North Carolina, Eustis, Fay, Fisher, Floyd, Foot, Garnett, Gray, Gross of New York, Gross of Pennsylvania, Guyon, Hall of New York, Hall of North Carolina, Hardin, Hendricks, Herrick, Hibshman, Hill, Hobart, Hooks, Hostetter, Jackson, Johnson, Jones of Virginia, Kendall, Kinsey, Kinsley, Lathrop, Lincoln, Livermore, Maclay, McCoy, McCreary, McCullough, Mallary, Marchand, Meigs, Metcalf, Monell, Montgomery, R. Moore, T. L. Moore, Morton, Moseley, Murray, Neale, Nelson of Massachusetts, Patterson, Philson, Plumer, Randolph, Rankin, Rhea, Rich, Richards, Richmond, Ross, Russ, Sawyer, Shaw, Silsbee, Sloan, Southard, Stevens, Tarr, Terrell, Tomlinson, Tracy, Trimble, Tucker of Virginia, Tucker of South Carolina, Tyler, Upham, Van Rensselaer, Walker, Warfield, Williams of Virginia, Williams of North Carolina and Wood—109.

NAYS—Messrs. Anderson, Archer of Maryland, Baldwin, Bloomfield, Brevard, Brush, Butler of Louisiana, Cass, Clark, Cook, Crowell, Cuthbert, Darlington, Davidson, Dickinson, Ford, Fuller, Gorham, Hemphill, Jones of Tennessee, Little, Lowndes, McLane of Delaware, McLean of Kentucky, Mercer, S. Moore, Nelson of Virginia, Newton, Parker of Massachusetts, Parker of Virginia, Pinckney, Ringgold, Robertson, Rogers, Sergeant, Simkins, Smith of New Jersey, Smith of Maryland, A. Smyth of Virginia, Smith of North Carolina, Storrs, Street, Strong of New York, Udree, Wallace, Wendover, and Whitman—47.

So the bill was ordered to be engrossed and read a third time to-morrow, in the following shape, as amended:

Be it enacted by the Senate and House of Representatives of the United States of America, in Congress assembled, That, from and after the first day of May next, the Military Peace Establishment of the United States shall consist of six thousand non-commissioned officers, musicians, and privates, with a due proportion of field and company officers, according to the present organization of companies, and in such pro-

portions of artillery and infantry as the President of the United States shall direct; and that the corps of engineers, as at present established, be retained in service.

SEC. 2. *And be it further enacted,* That the corps of ordnance shall be retained in service, and shall hereafter consist of one colonel, one lieutenant colonel, one major, six captains, six first lieutenants, six second lieutenants, and six third lieutenants.

SEC. 3. *And be it further enacted,* That the President of the United States cause to be arranged the officers, non-commissioned officers, musicians, and privates, of the several corps of troops now in service, in such manner as to form and complete the corps to be retained in service under this act, attaching the corps of light artillery to the corps of artillery, and the corps of riflemen to the infantry, and cause the supernumerary officers, non-commissioned officers, and privates, to be discharged from the service.

SEC. 4. *And be it further enacted,* That there shall be one brigadier general, with one aid de camp, one inspector general, and one assistant adjutant general; there shall also be one adjutant general, one quartermaster general, with as many assistant deputy quartermasters as the service may require, to be taken from the subalterns of the line, who shall perform all the duties which may be required of them in the quartermaster's department, and in the department of the commissary general of subsistence, and who shall receive, as a compensation for their services, fifteen dollars per month in addition to their monthly pay; and one judge advocate, each with the rank, pay, and emoluments, of a colonel of cavalry, as heretofore prescribed by law; there shall also be a paymaster general, with a salary as heretofore fixed by law, commissary general of purchases, with a salary of two thousand dollars per annum, and one assistant commissary general of purchases, whose compensation shall not exceed two and a half per centum on the public moneys disbursed by him, nor the sum of fifteen hundred dollars per annum; and two military storekeepers, to be compensated as heretofore; one commissary general of subsistence, one surgeon general, with a salary of two thousand dollars per annum, and one apothecary general, with a salary of fifteen hundred dollars per annum.

SEC. 5. *And be it further enacted,* That there shall be to each regiment of infantry, and to each battalion of artillery, one adjutant, one quartermaster, and one paymaster, one surgeon, and one assistant surgeon.

SEC. 6. *And be it further enacted,* That the topographical engineers, and their assistants, shall be discharged from the service of the United States.

SEC. 7. *And be it further enacted,* That the judge advocate shall keep an office in the city of Washington, and, in addition to the duties which may be assigned to him by the President of the United States, he shall keep a record of all trials by general courts-martial, and report the decisions.

SEC. 8. *And be it further enacted,* That all officers of the army, whose continuance in service is not provided for by this act, shall be discharged from the service of the United States, and that to each commissioned officer, who shall be discharged by virtue of this act, there shall be paid, in addition to the pay and emoluments to which he will be entitled at the time of his discharge, three months' pay.

The above bill having been disposed of:—

Mr. RANDOLPH, agreeably to notice, then moved

that the House do now proceed to the consideration of the bill for the relief of the family of Oliver Hazard Perry, and to provide for the education of his children.

To this course, by the rules of the House, an unanimous vote was necessary, it not being in the ordinary routine of the business of the House. The motion was objected to, and therefore failed of course.

Subsequently, however, on motion, the orders of the day preceding that bill were postponed, which gives it priority in the order of business for to-morrow.

TUESDAY, January 23.

Mr. NEWTON, from the Committee of Commerce, reported a bill for the relief of Alexander Elmslie and Samuel Clarkson, merchants of Philadelphia; which was twice read, and committed.

Mr. COOK submitted the following resolution:

Resolved, That the Committee of Elections be instructed to inquire whether any, and if any, what, alterations are necessary to be made in the law, entitled "An act relative to the election of President and Vice President of the United States, and declaring the officer who shall act as President in case of vacancies in the offices both of President and Vice President;" and also whether it be expedient to increase the compensation of any of the persons appointed to transmit the votes of the Electors of President and Vice President at the late election.

The said resolution was read, and ordered to lie on the table.

Mr. STORRS submitted the following resolution; which was read, and ordered to lie on the table one day for consideration:

Resolved, That the Secretary of the Treasury be directed to report to this House a statement of the moneys now in the Treasury, or collected at any place, which are applicable to the redemption of the stock created by the act providing for the indemnification of certain claimants of public lands in the Mississippi Territory, passed March 31, 1814.

On motion of Mr. CROWELL, the Committee on the Public Lands were instructed to inquire into the expediency of granting to the State of Alabama all the unsold islands in the Tennessee river, the proceeds of which shall be applied to the improvement of the navigation of said river.

Mr. SMITH, of Maryland, submitted the following joint resolution:

Resolved, by the Senate and House of Representatives of the United States of America in Congress assembled, That the recruiting service for the Army be suspended for and during the present year, and until the end of the next session of Congress.

The said resolution was read twice, and ordered to be engrossed, and read a third time to-morrow.

An engrossed bill, entitled "An act to continue in force an act, entitled 'An act to provide for persons who were disabled by known wounds received in the Revolutionary war, and for other purposes;'" was read the third time, and passed.

Mr. SMITH, of North Carolina, gave notice that he should, on Thursday next, move to proceed to the consideration of the motion to amend the Constitution of the United States, so as to establish an uniform mode of election of Electors of President and Vice President of the United States.

The SPEAKER laid before the House a letter from the Secretary of the Treasury, transmitting two statements of goods, wares, and merchandise, imported in American and foreign vessels; together with an aggregate view of both from the 1st October, 1818, to the 30th September, 1819, rendered in obedience to a resolution of the House of Representatives of 29th May, 1798.

The letter was read, and, with the documents, ordered to lie on the table.

Mr. MERCER, from the Committee on the District of Columbia, submitted the following report:

The Committee on the District of Columbia, to whom was referred a resolution of the House of Representatives instructing them " to inquire into the expediency of providing, by law, to secure to mechanics and others payment for their labor and materials, in erecting any house or other building within the District of Columbia, by giving them a lien thereon," have had the same under consideration, and respectfully report: That, under the existing laws of the United States, within the District of Columbia, a security, analogous to that contemplated by the resolution, may be provided by special contract, in every case wherein any house or building is about to be erected, against any loss which any mechanic or merchant, contributing labor or materials towards the erection thereof, might sustain from the failure of the proprietor to pay voluntarily therefor. Whether for this, or any other reason, existing in the institutions or state of society of the District of Columbia, no complaint to Congress, by petition or otherwise, has ever been made by any of the inhabitants of the District, of any defect of their present laws in relation to the object for which the resolution of the House of Representatives suggests a provision. The committee, therefore, recommend to the House of Representatives the adoption of the following resolution:

Resolved, That it is inexpedient to make, by law, the provision suggested by the aforesaid resolution.

The report was read, and agreed to.

REDUCTION OF THE ARMY.

The engrossed bill for the reduction of the Military Peace Establishment, was read a third time.

Mr. SIMKINS rose, and spoke against the passage of the bill, and in reply to the gentlemen who had supported it.

Mr. FLOYD made a few explanatory remarks.

Mr. SMITH, of Maryland, assigned the reasons why he should vote against this bill, though not opposed to a proper reduction of the Military Establishment.

Mr. EUSTIS replied to Mr. SMITH, and defended the bill in regard to some of its details.

Mr. NELSON, of Virginia, opposed the bill in toto, in its objects and in its details, as contrary to the public interest.

Mr. RICH briefly assigned the reasons why he should vote for the bill.

Mr. CLAY stated the reasons why he thought the interest of the country called for the passage of the bill.

The question on the passage of the bill was then

taken by yeas and nays, and decided in the affirmative—109 to 48, as follows:

YEAS—Messrs. Abbot, Adams, Alexander, Allen of Massachusetts, Allen of New York, Allen of Tennessee, Archer of Virginia, Baker, Ball, Barbour, Bayly, Beecher, Brown, Bryan, Buffum, Burton, Burwell, Butler of New Hampshire, Campbell, Clagett, Clay, Cobb, Cocke, Crafts, Crawford, Culpeper, Cushman, Dane, Dennison, Earle, Eddy, Edwards of Connecticut, Edwards of North Carolina, Eustis, Fay, Fisher, Floyd, Foot, Gray, Gross of New York, Gross of Pennsylvania, Guyon, Hackley, Hall of New York, Hall of North Carolina, Hardin, Hendricks, Herrick, Hibshman, Hill, Hobart, Hooks, Hostetter, Jackson, Johnson, Jones of Va., Kinsey, Kinsley, Lathrop, Lincoln, Livermore, Maclay, McCoy, McCreary, McCullough, Mallary, Marchand, Meigs, Metcalf, Monell, Montgomery, R. Moore, T. L. Moore, Morton, Moseley, Murray, Neale, Nelson of Massachusetts, Patterson, Philson, Pitcher, Plumer, Randolph, Rankin, Rhea, Rich, Richards, Richmond, Ross, Russ, Shaw, Silsbee, Sloan, Southard, Stevens, Tarr, Terrell, Tomlinson, Tracy, Trimble, Tucker of Virginia, Tucker of South Carolina, Tyler, Upham, Van Rensselaer, Warfield, Williams of Virginia, and Wood—109.

NAYS—Messrs. Anderson, Archer of Maryland, Baldwin, Bloomfield, Brevard, Brush, Butler of Louisiana, Case, Clark, Cook, Crowell, Cuthbert, Darlington, Davidson, Dickinson, Ford, Fuller, Gorham, Hemphill, Jones of Tennessee, Little, Lowndes, McLane of Delaware, McLean of Kentucky, Mercer, S. Moore, Nelson of Virginia, Newton, Parker of Massachusetts, Parker of Virginia, Pinckney, Reed, Ringgold, Robertson, Rogers, Sergeant, Simkins, Smith of New Jersey, Smith of Maryland, A. Smyth of Virginia, Smith of North Carolina, Storrs, Street, Strong of New York, Udree, Wallace, Wendover, and Whitman—48.

COMMODORE PERRY'S FAMILY.

The House then resolved itself into a Committee of the Whole, Mr. FOOT in the chair, on the bill reported at the last session of Congress, for the relief of the family of the late Oliver Hazard Perry, and to provide for the education of his children at the public expense.

The bill having been read through—

On motion of Mr. RANDOLPH, who declined occupying the time of the House by speaking on the subject, the blanks in the bill were filled, so as to make the proposed allowance to be $330 per annum for the mother of the late Commodore Perry, $400 for his widow, (during life, or until intermarriage,) and $150 for each of the children, until they arrive at twenty-one years of age. The whole amount proposed to be annually appropriated being $1,330, the estimated amount of half the pay which Commodore Perry, whilst living, would have enjoyed whilst on separate command.

Mr. HARDIN moved to strike out all the bill except the enacting clause, and insert, in lieu thereof, a provision, allowing to the family of Commodore Perry half-pay for the term of five years, being, Mr. H. said, the amount which they would have received had Commodore Perry fallen in battle.

On this motion there arose a short debate.

The motion of Mr. HARDIN was negatived, on a division, by apparently a large majority.

The Committee then rose, and reported the bill. The House having concurred in filling the blanks as reported from the Committee—

Mr. HARDIN renewed the motion he had made in Committee of the Whole, and demanded the yeas and nays on it.

The yeas and nays being taken, there were, for the amendment 62, against it 82, as follows:

YEAS—Messrs. Abbot, Anderson, Baker, Ball, Barbour, Beecher, Campbell, Cannon, Case, Clagett, Cobb, Culpeper, Cushman, Dennison, Earle, Edwards of Connecticut, Edwards of North Carolina, Fay, Fisher, Floyd, Foot, Ford, Forrest, Gray, Gross of New York, Guyon, Hall of New York, Hardin, Hendricks, Herrick, Hibshman, Hooks, Hostetter, Jackson, Lincoln, Maclay, McCoy, McCreary, Marchand, Metcalf, Monell, R. Moore, T. L. Moore, Murray, Newton, Patterson, Philson, Rankin, Rich, Richards, Richmond, Rogers, Ross, Russ, Sloan, A. Smyth of Virginia, Stevens, Tarr, Tucker of South Carolina, Tyler, Wendover, and Wood.

NAYS—Messrs. Allen of Massachusetts, Allen of Tennessee, Archer of Maryland, Archer of Virginia, Baldwin, Bayly, Bloomfield, Brevard, Brown, Brush, Bryan, Buffum, Burton, Butler of Louisiana, Clark, Clay, Cook, Crafts, Crawford, Crowell, Cuthbert, Dane, Darlington, Davidson, Dickinson, Eddy, Eustis, Fuller, Gorham, Gross of Pennsylvania, Hackley, Hall of North Carolina, Hemphill, Hill, Hobart, Johnson, Jones of Virginia, Jones of Tennessee, Kinsey, Lathrop, Livermore, Lowndes, McCullough, McLane of Delaware, McLean of Kentucky, Mallary, Meigs, Mercer, Montgomery, S. Moore, Morton, Moseley, Neale, Nelson of Massachusetts, Nelson of Virginia, Parker of Massachusetts, Parker of Virginia, Pinckney, Plumer, Randolph, Reed, Rhea, Ringgold, Robertson, Sawyer, Sergeant, Shaw, Silsbee, Simkins, Smith of Maryland, Storrs, Terrell, Tomlinson, Tracy, Trimble, Tucker of Virginia, Udree, Van Rensselaer, Wallace, Warfield, Whitman, and Williams of Virginia.

So it was not agreed to.

Mr. CLAY, though decidedly in favor of the object of the bill, objected to that part of it proposing an allowance of $330 per annum, during life, to the mother of the deceased; and, on his motion, that part was stricken out.

Mr. RANDOLPH moved a reconsideration of the allowance of $400 per annum to the widow of Commodore Perry, with a view to make it $730, by adding to it the $330 just stricken out; so that the amount to the family should be the same, though the distribution would be different.

The motion of Mr. R. was negatived, by a vote of 69 to 52.

On the question for ordering the bill to be engrossed for a third reading, the yeas and nays being demanded by Mr. BRUSH, there were, for the bill 76, against it 62, as follows:

YEAS—Messrs. Allen of Massachusetts, Archer of Maryland, Archer of Virginia, Baldwin, Bayly, Bloomfield, Brevard, Brown, Brush, Bryan, Butler of New Hampshire, Butler of Louisiana, Clark, Clay, Cocke, Crawford, Crowell, Cushman, Cuthbert, Dane, Darlington, Davidson, Dickinson, Eddy, Eustis, Forrest, Fuller, Gorham, Gross of Pennsylvania, Hemphill, Hill,

Hobart, Jones of Virginia, Jones of Tennessee, Kinsey, Lathrop, Lowndes, Maclay, McCullough, McLane of Delaware, McLean of Kentucky, Mallary, Meigs, Mercer, Montgomery, S. Moore, Moseley, Neale, Nelson of Massachusetts, Nelson of Virginia, Newton, Parker of Mass., Pinckney, Randolph, Reed, Ringgold, Robertson, Russ, Sergeant, Shaw, Silsbee, Simkins, Smith of Maryland, Storrs, Street, Terrell, Tomlinson, Trimble, Tucker of Virginia, Udree, Upham, Van Rensselaer, Wallace, Warfield, Whitman, and Williams of Virginia.

NAYS—Messrs. Alexander, Anderson, Baker, Ball, Barbour, Beecher, Burton, Campbell, Cannon, Case, Clagett, Crafts, Culpeper, Dennison, Earle, Edwards of Connecticut, Edwards of North Carolina, Fay, Fisher, Floyd, Foot, Garnett, Gray, Gross of New York, Guyon, Hall of New York, Hardin, Hendricks, Herrick, Hibshman, Hooks, Hostetter, Jackson, Johnson, Lincoln, Livermore, McCoy, McCreary, Marchand, Metcalf, R. Moore, T. L. Moore, Morton, Murray, Parker of Virginia, Patterson, Philson, Plumer, Rhea, Rich, Richards, Richmond, Rogers, Ross, Sawyer, Sloan, Stevens, Tarr, Tucker of South Carolina, Tyler, Wendover, and Wood.

So the bill was ordered to be engrossed, and read a third time to-morrow.

Mr. EUSTIS gave notice that he should, on to-morrow, call for the consideration of the resolution submitted by him, proposing the conditional admission of Missouri into the Union.

WEDNESDAY, January 24.

At the usual hour of meeting, but few members being present, when the Speaker took the Chair, Mr. BRUSH moved that there be a call of the House. [The object of a call, as it is technically termed, is to place on the Journal the names of the members present, whence may be inferred the names of the absentees.] After some conversation on this motion, in the course of which it was suggested that the quantity of business before the committees required them to sit sometimes beyond the hour of meeting, and it would be harsh to record them, whilst thus engaged, as absentees, &c. Mr. BRUSH consented to withdraw his motion.

Mr. SAMUEL MOORE, from the Committee of Claims, made a report on the petition of James May, of Detroit, accompanied with a bill for the relief of the said James May and the legal representatives of William Macomb; which bill was read twice, and committed to a Committee of the Whole.

Mr. COOK, from the Committee on the Public Lands, made a report on the memorial of the Legislature of the State of Illinois, respecting the title to the land upon which their seat of government is located, accompanied with a bill confirming the location of the seat of government of the State of Illinois, and for other purposes; which bill was read twice, and ordered to lie on the table.

Mr. VAN RENSSELAER, from the Committee on Military Affairs, reported a bill supplementary to "An act relating to the ransom of American captives of the late war;" which was read twice, and committed to a Committee of the Whole.

Mr. FULLER, from the Committee on Naval Affairs, reported a bill to incorporate the United States Naval Fraternal Association for the relief of the families of deceased officers; which was read twice, and committed to the Committee of the whole House to which is committed the bill for the relief of sundry citizens of Baltimore.

On motion of Mr. RHEA,

Resolved, That the Committee on Pensions and Revolutionary Claims be instructed to inquire into the expediency of suspending, for a limited time, so much of an act, entitled "An act making further provision for the support of public credit, and for the redemption of the public debt," passed the 3d of March, 1795; and so much of the act, entitled "An act respecting loan office and final settlement certificates, indents of interest, and the unfunded and registered debt, credited on the books of the Treasury," passed the 12th day of June, 1798, as bars from settlement or allowance, certificates, commonly called loan office and final settlement certificates, and indents of interest.

On motion of Mr. STORRS, the House proceeded to consider the resolution submitted by him yesterday, and the same being again read, was agreed to.

An engrossed bill, entitled "An act to alter the times of holding the district court in the northern district of New York," was read the third time, and passed.

The SPEAKER laid before the House a letter from the Governor of the State of Pennsylvania, enclosing an authentic return of the election of DANIEL UDREE, as a Representative of that State in this House, to serve in the room of Joseph Hiester, resigned; which was referred to the Committee of Elections.

An engrossed resolution to suspend the recruiting service for a limited time, was read the third time, and passed.

The following bills passed through Committees of the Whole, in succession, viz: The bill for the relief of Jacob Hunsinger; the bill extending the time for issuing and locating land warrants to officers and soldiers of the Revolutionary war; the bill to regulate the location of land warrants, and the issuing of patents in certain cases; the bill for the relief of James Brady; the bill for the relief of Joseph McNiel; the bill for the relief of Alexander Milne; the bill for the relief of Lewis H. Guerlain; the bill for the relief of John Rodriguez; the bill for the relief of Francis B. Languille; the bill for the relief of Bartholomew Duverge. And the said bills were all ordered to be engrossed and read a third time to-morrow.

The engrossed bill for the relief of the family of the late Oliver Hazard Perry, and for the education of his children at the public charge, was read a third time.

Mr. BEECHER moved to recommit the bill to a Committee of the Whole, but subsequently varied his motion so far as to move its recommitment to the Committee on Naval Affairs, with a view to incorporate the amendment yesterday proposed by Mr. HARDIN, or, failing in that, to reinstate the allowance of three hundred and thirty dollars to the mother of Commodore Perry, which was yesterday stricken out.

941   HISTORY OF CONGRESS.   942

JANUARY, 1821.   *Fugitive Slaves—Fine Arts—Missouri.*   H. OF R.

After a short debate, the motion for recommitment was negatived.

The bill was then passed, 73 to 63, and sent to the Senate for concurrence.

FUGITIVE SLAVES.

Among the papers offered during the presentation of memorials to-day, was the following, presented by Mr. BROWN, of Kentucky:

Whereas it is represented to the present General Assembly that many negroes and persons of color, the property of citizens of this Commonwealth, have escaped from their lawful owners into the province of Canada, and are there protected from recapture by the subjects of His Majesty the King of Great Britain, residing in said province of Canada: And whereas the practice of concealing and countenancing slaves that thus escape from their lawful owners, tends greatly to the injury of the people of this State, and, if persevered in, may lead to unhappy consequences between the subjects of his said Majesty's Government and the citizens of the United States:

Resolved, therefore, That it is the opinion and desire of the present General Assembly, that the Government of the United States invite the attention of the British Government to this subject, and, if practicable, procure arrangements to be made, on the part of that Government, for the restoration of such fugitive slaves as shall have heretofore escaped, or may hereafter escape, from their lawful owners, (being citizens of the United States,) into any of his said Majesty's North American dominions. And the Governor is requested to transmit to the Executive of the United States, and to each of the Senators and Representatives in Congress from this State, copies of the foregoing resolution.

The SPEAKER stated that, according to the rules of the House, this resolution could not be received, not being "addressed to the House;" though the subject might readily be brought before the House in a different form. Upon which, Mr. B. withdrew the resolution, with the intention of presenting the subject to the House in a different shape.

ENCOURAGEMENT OF THE FINE ARTS.

Mr. WOOD, from the Committee on the Public Buildings, to whom was referred the petition of Julia Plantou, of the city of Philadelphia, made the following report, which was ordered to lie on the table:

That the petitioner states that, having from early life an ardent attachment to the art of painting, she was encouraged by the approbation of intelligent gentlemen, on whose judgment she relied, to cultivate her talents for this branch of the fine arts; that, for this purpose, she visited Europe to inspect the works of the great masters of the art, in order to improve her taste and talents, and to render them worthy of the consideration of her enlightened countrymen; that, while there, she spared no pains in her improvement, under the direction of the first artists of the age.

Anxious that her own country should reap the fruits of her improvement, and desirous to commemorate some of its distinguished events, she selected as the most interesting subject of her pencil the concluding scene of the late war, and has, with great labor and assiduity, accomplished an emblematical representation of the Treaty of Ghent, which she now offers to the acceptance of Congress, and prays for such remuneration for her performance as the design and execution may, in their estimation, be worth.

The committee are not insensible of the importance of the fine arts in the scale of social improvement, or of the claim those who cultivate them have upon the public munificence; they derive much pleasure from contemplating the progress of improvements in the United States, and are happy to perceive the cultivation of the arts that contribute to the embellishment of society, as well as such as are essential to its well-being.

It must be admitted that the fine arts not only serve to amuse and please as the evanescent exertions of rare and extraordinary genius, but they elevate the mind, purify the moral feelings, create a relish for pure and refined pleasures, and diffuse a taste for kindred arts and improvements; they serve to commemorate important eras in the history of nations, to preserve the memory of distinguished citizens, and to inspire succeeding ages with an emulation of their virtues; they, in effect, connect the past with the present, and thus invigorate public spirit, keep alive a sense of national honor, and contribute to promote the national glory.

The committee cannot behold without the most pleasing emotions a female fellow-citizen, prompted by the ardor of genius, abandoning all the pleasurable amusements of her sex, and braving the dangers of the ocean in search of the aid and instruction in foreign regions which her native soil did not afford; and would most cheerfully recommend her productions to the patronage of Congress did they conceive it compatible with the powers of Congress to afford it, or consistent with the duty they owe their country.

Such a course is, indeed, not without precedent, but the committee are not able to perceive by what article of the Constitution it can be sustained.

A government without restriction doubtless possesses powers commensurate with every public improvement that can contribute to the welfare or glory of a nation; but the Government of the United States is restricted to the objects enumerated in the Constitution, and the committee cannot discover that the encouragement of the fine arts is among the number.

Independently of this difficulty, the committee conceive that the pressure of the times and the exhausted state of the Treasury imperiously require that the public buildings should be completed before any further appropriation is made for their embellishment.

The committee, therefore, recommend the following resolution:

Resolved, That the prayer of the petitioner ought not to be granted.

MISSOURI.

The House then, on motion of Mr. EUSTIS, resolved itself into a Committee of the Whole, and proceeded to the consideration of the following resolution:

Resolved, by the Senate and House of Representatives of the United States of America in Congress assembled, and it is hereby declared, That, the —— day of —— next ensuing, the State of Missouri shall be admitted into the Union upon an equal footing with the original States, in all respects whatsoever: *Provided,* That so much of the 26th section of the 3d article of the constitution of said State, presented to

Congress at the present session, as makes it the duty of the Legislature to pass such laws as shall be necessary "to prevent free negroes and mulattoes from coming to and settling in this State, under any pretext whatsoever," shall, on or before that day, have been expunged therefrom.

The resolution having been read—

Mr. Eustis stated the objects he had in view in moving this resolution to be, to remove the only objection which he had to the admission of Missouri into the Union ; to give facility and despatch to the admission of the State into the Union, and thereby to preclude the possibility of this question ever again coming before Congress. These were his only motives, and he had, in moving the resolution, acted without consulting with any one else. Foreseeing a difficulty in prescribing the mode in which the amendment might be made, he had left that a question for separate consideration, in order to obtain a decision on the principle of the resolution. Having introduced the resolution with a sense of duty, should it not meet with the approbation of the House, he should be entirely satisfied with having, in proposing it, performed what he believed to be his duty.

On motion of Mr. Eustis the blanks in the resolution were filled with the first of October next.

Mr. Foot moved to postpone the resolution, in order to take up that from the Senate, under the impression that doing so would facilitate a final decision on the subject.

Mr. Lowndes suggested that in all probability nothing would be gained by this course, as the same question now before the House might, and probably would be, brought up by a motion to amend the resolve in the Senate.

The motion to postpone was negatived.

No debate arising—

The Chairman put the question to agree to the resolution, and it was negatived by a large majority.

The Committee then rose and reported their decision to the House.

The Speaker put the question on agreeing to the amendments made in Committee, (by filling the blanks in the resolution.)

It being objected that the report of the Committee had been to *reject* the resolution—

The Speaker decided that no committee, whether select or of the Whole House, has the power of rejecting any bill or resolution referred to it. Bills and resolutions are referred to committees to be discussed and amended or not, and not to be agreed to or rejected in form, though sometimes virtually rejected by striking out their vital parts.*

. * " If it be a paper *referred to them,* (a committee, whether select or of the whole,) they proceed to put questions of amendment, if proposed, but no final questions on the whole ; because all parts of the paper, having been adopted by the House, stand of course, unless altered or struck out by a vote. Even if they are opposed to the whole paper, and think it cannot be made good by amendments, they *cannot reject it,* but must report it back to the House without amendments, and there make their opposition."
         [*Jefferson's Manual.*

The decision was objected to by Mr. Randolph, Mr. Barbour, and Mr. Cobb, but justified by Mr. Sergeant, and in part at least by Mr. Lowndes. In the end, however, no appeal was taken from the decision of the Chair.

The House having agreed to the amendments made in Committee of the Whole—

The question was then taken, Shall the resolution be engrossed, and read a third time ? and determined in the negative—yeas 6, nays 146, as follows :

Yeas—Messrs. Baldwin, Eustis, Hill, Little, Smith of Maryland, and Stevens.

Nays—Messrs. Abbot, Adams, Alexander, Allen of Massachusetts, Allen of New York, Allen of Tennessee, Anderson, Archer of Maryland, Archer of Virginia, Baker, Ball, Barbour, Bayly, Beecher, Bloomfield, Boden, Brevard, Brown, Brush, Buffum, Burton, Burwell, Butler of New Hampshire, Butler of Louisiana, Campbell, Cannon, Case, Clagett, Clark, Clay, Cobb, Cocke, Cook, Crafts, Crawford, Crowell, Culpeper, Cushman, Cuthbert, Dane, Darlington, Davidson, Dennison, Dickinson, Earle, Eddy, Edwards of Connecticut, Edwards of North Carolina, Fay, Fisher, Foot, Ford, Forrest, Fuller, Gorham, Gray, Gross of New York, Gross of Pennsylvania, Grosvenor, Hackley, Hall of New York, Hall of North Ca., , Hardin, Hemphill, Hendricks, Herbart, Hooks, Hostetter, Jackson, Johnson, Jones of Virginia, Kinsey, Kinsley, Lathrop, Lincoln, Lowndes, Maclay, McCoy, McCreary, McCullough, McLane of Delaware, McLean of Kentucky, Mallary, Marchand, Meigs, Metcalf, Montgomery, R. Moore, S. Moore, T. L. Moore, Morton, Moseley, Murray, Neale, Nelson of Massachusetts, Nelson of Virginia, Newton, Parker of Massachusetts, Parker of Virginia, Patterson, Philson, Pinckney, Pitcher, Plumer, Randolph, Rankin, Reid, Rhea, Rich, Richards, Richmond, Ringgold, Robertson, Rogers, Ross, Russ, Sawyer, Sergeant, Shaw, Silsbee, Simkins, Sloan, Smith of New Jersey, Smith of North Carolina, Southard, Storrs, Street, Strong of New York, Tarr, Terrell, Tomlinson, Tompkins, Tracy, Trimble, Tucker of Virginia, Tucker of South Carolina, Tyler, Udree, Upham, Van Rensselaer, Walker, Warfield, Wendover, Whitman, Williams of Virginia, and Wood.

So the resolution was rejected.

After a pause—

Mr. Clay rose, and gave notice, that, if no other gentleman made any motion on the subject, he should on the day after to-morrow move to go into Committee of the Whole on the state of the Union, to take into consideration the resolution from the Senate on the subject of Missouri.

THURSDAY, January 25.

Mr. Anderson, from the Committee on Public Lands, made a report on the memorial of the General Assembly of Missouri, respecting preemption rights, referred to them on the 11th instant ; which was read, and the resolution therein submitted was concurred in by the House as follows :

Resolved, That the prayer of the memorialists ought not to be granted.

Mr. Smith, of Maryland, from the Committee of Ways and Means, to which was recommitted

945　　　　　　　　HISTORY OF CONGRESS.　　　　　　946

JANUARY, 1821.　　　　　Occupation of the Columbia River.　　　　　H. OF R.

the bill to authorize the Secretary of the Treasury to transfer certain balances of appropriations to the surplus fund, reported the same with an amendment ; which was read, and, together with the bill, ordered to lie on the table.

Engrossed bills of the following titles, to wit: "An act for the relief of Jacob Hunsinger ;" "An act for extending the time of issuing and locating military land warrants to officers and soldiers of the Revolutionary army ;" "An act for the relief of Joseph McNeil ;" "An act for the relief of Alexander Milne ;" "An act for the relief of Lewis H. Guerlain ;" "An act for the relief of John Rodriguez ;" "An act to regulate the location of land warrants, and issuing patents in certain cases ;" An act for the relief of Frances B. Languille ;" "An act for the relief of James Brady ;" and "An act for the relief of Bartholomew Duverge ;" were severally read a third time, and passed.

OCCUPATION OF THE COLUMBIA RIVER.

Mr. FLOYD, from the committee appointed on the 19th ultimo to inquire into the situation of the settlements on the Pacific Ocean, and into the expedi――― of occupying the Columbia river, made a detailed report, accompanied with a bill to authorize the occupation of the Columbia river, and to regulate the intercourse with the Indian tribes within the United States and territories thereof; which bill, by leave of the House, was reported, read twice, and committed to a Committee of the Whole to-morrow. The report is as follows :

The committee to whom was referred the resolution of the 19th of December, 1820, to inquire into the situation of the settlement upon the Pacific ocean, and the expediency of occupying the Columbia river, report: That they have carefully examined the subject referred to them, and, from every consideration which they have been able to bestow upon it, believe, from the usage of all nations, previous and subsequent to the discovery of America, the title of the United States to a very large portion of the coast of the Pacific ocean to be well founded; nor have they been able to ascertain that any other Government than Spain has made claim to any part of it, from Cape Horn to the sixtieth degree of north latitude.

When this continent was first made known to Europe, by the bold and enterprising genius of Christopher Columbus, it seemed for a long time conceded that the Spanish monarchy, which alone could be prevailed upon to listen to his plans and propositions, was most entitled to the benefits resulting from the successful issue of his undertaking. Though Ferdinand and Isabella, who, at that time, filled the throne of that country, did not rest their title upon the tacit consent of other nations, or even upon their armies or fleet, which was, at that period, formidable, and well provided ; but, instructed by the example of the Portuguese, who had obtained a grant for all countries east of the Azores, from pole to pole, they obtained a similar grant from the Roman Pontiff of all the territories they wished to occupy west of the same point, as the superstition of the times conferred on him a right of dominion over all the kingdoms of the earth. Thus, in virtue of his power, as the vicar and representative of Jesus Christ, did Alexander VI., in 1493, grant to the Crown of Spain, in full right, all the countries inhabited by infidels, which they had or should discover.

Enormous as the power was, which the Popes then exercised, it was recognised and submitted to by the monarchs of that day, and considered as having vested in Spain a title which they deemed completely valid, and authorized her to extend her discoveries and establish her dominion over a great portion of the new world. The Spanish Crown, as well as individuals, the subjects of that Power, continued to fit out ships for voyages of discovery, and, in the space of a few years, had visited various parts of the coast of America, from the Gulf of Mexico, to many degrees south of the equinoctial line, taking possession, according to the custom of that day, in the name of the Spanish King. Nor was their zeal for discovery confined to the Atlantic shore alone ; parties, under daring and enterprising leaders, penetrated far into the interior of the continent, and even to the shores of the Pacific ocean, wresting by violence the rich Empires of Peru and Mexico from the peaceful and legitimate sovereigns who reigned over them, and annexed them to the Crown of Spain, by the triple title of conquest, discovery, and the grant of the Pope.

So well satisfied do the rest of Europe seem to have been of the rights of Spain, derived from such high authority, that they permitted her to progress unmolested in her career of discovery and conquest for many years, until she had acquired the undisputed possession of most of the Atlantic coast of South America, and the whole shore of the Pacific, as high as the northern extremity of California, as they affirmed, after they came in possession of Louisiana, to a point far to the northward of that.

Though discoveries were frequently made of countries among the most beautiful and fertile, where nature seemed to invite the industry of man to the enjoyment of luxuriant abundance, yet none seemed to arrest the attention of either Government or people, but those which contained the precious metals ; this morbid thirst for gold may be the cause why no settlements were made north of California, as no metal of that description is believed to be found in that region.

About this time it became the interest of the British Crown to think differently on the subject of religion from the See of Rome, and, separating entirely from it, assumed the right of annexing to their Crown all the territories discovered by their subjects, and of bestowing them by charter upon individuals. To this end, grants were issued by Elisabeth in the year 1578 and 1584, the one to Sir Humphrey Gilbert, the other to Sir Walter Raleigh, which were limited to a certain number of leagues, but those issued in 1606, 1608 and 1611, by James I., in the charters for Virginia, were declared to embrace the whole extent of country from thirty-four to forty-five degrees of north latitude, extending from sea to sea, always excepting the territories of any Christian Prince or people.

It is believed that when these charters were granted by the Monarchs of England, they were not well apprized of the extent of country they were giving away, but from their reservations, in regard to the title of Christian Princes or people, they were apprized of the title of Spain upon the western ocean, though not informed of its extent ; as it is evident from the words Christian and infidel often occurring, both in the charters of the Monarchs and the bulls of the Pope, the legitimate sovereigns, as well as people of this country, in that day, were considered as possessing no rights. With whatever care they avoided collisions with each other respecting territory which might produce a war with a Power equally skilled in the military art with themselves, they were not scrupulous in dispossessing the natives of both Americas of their country, all of whom were as brave, as generous, and magnanimous as themselves, and some of whom as far advanced in civilisation and the arts of peace, though not professing to be Christians, or skilled in war.

The opinion of Europe undergoing another change upon the subject of discoveries in unknown regions, they were now reduced to a more definite and reasonable extent, consequently, in a few years, a third mode of obtaining territory came to be admitted by all as the basis on which they could safely rely for a just decision of their claims, should difficulties present themselves; and one which, to a moderate extent, gave to all nations the benefit of their own labors. By this rule, too, all the territory thus acquired was vested in the State rather than the Crown, which Spanish jurisprudence, under the authority of the Pope, seemed to consider.

Hence, the Power which discovered a country was entitled to the whole extent of soil watered by the springs of the principal river or water course passing through it, provided there was settlement made, or possession taken, with the usual formalities, in the name and on the behalf of the Government to whom the individual owed allegiance. Though the tacit consent of all seemed to yield the sovereignty from sea to sea, where no settlement or express possession was had of an intermediate country; and such right was held good to the whole extent, but not wholly confirmed until another settlement was made at a distinct point upon the same territory beyond the water of the first, or so distant as not manifestly to encroach upon the establishments of the coast; other Powers, though, might avail themselves of the failure of the first to occupy another principal stream, or distant point, and become thereby vested with a full right of sovereignty. This seems to have been the condition of America until the close of the war of 1812; since which time all treaties have yielded to the different Powers, in full right, all they claimed, either by settlement, or from the failure of others to occupy the principal streams when they might do so. There is now no longer territory to be obtained by settlement or discovery; and if there should be any difficulty, it will be where the different limits of the different Powers shall be fixed.

Impressed with a belief, that, under this mode, valuable possessions might be added to the French monarchy, it is presumed Sieurs Joliet and Marquette penetrated the unknown wilderness from Canada, and discovered the Mississippi so long ago as the year 1673, and explored it down to the Arkansas. Perhaps, encouraged by their success, a few years after, Hennepin visited those regions, and pursued that river to its mouth. His representations, with other considerations, two years after, induced M. de la Salle and M. Tonti to descend that river with a considerable force to the Gulf of Mexico, and they are believed to have built the fort during that trip, the bricks and other remains of which are now to be seen on the first high ground on the west side of the Mississippi, below the mouth of the White river.

After this period, in 1685, M. de la Salle, being on his return from France, landed on the west side of the Rio Colorado, in the bay of St. Bernard, and planted a considerable colony there, taking possession, in due and solemn form, in the name of the French King. Such were the discoveries which gave to France the country called Louisiana, from the Rio Grande del Norte, being the next great river to the west of that settlement, along the mountains of Mexico and Spain west, as the western limits, and California as the eastern boundary. That France, and all other nations interested in its boundary, considered it in the same light, is ascertained in various ways, to the conviction of the most incredulous.

In consequence of these settlements and discoveries of the French, Louis XIV. granted, by letters patent, in the year 1712, to Anthony Crozat, the exclusive commerce of that country, and defines its boundary, declaring that it comprehends all lands, coasts, and islands, situated in the Gulf of Mexico, between Carolina on the east, and Old and New Mexico on the west. The French title to these boundaries is further established by the Chevalier de Champigny, who lived in the country, and declares Louisiana to extend to the Rio Grande del Norte, and the mountains of Mexico. This appears to be the opinion of other writers, who, it is presumed, had the most intimate knowledge of the subject, and among them we find that intelligent statesman, the Count de Vergennes, in a work entitled an Historical and Political Memoir of Louisiana, where he says, it is bounded by Florida on the east, and by Mexico on the west. The same extent is assigned to it by Don Antonio de Alcedo, an officer of high rank in the service of Spain, entitled "Diccionario Geografico Historico de las Indias Occidentales ó America." Don Thomas Lopes, geographer to the King of Spain, in a map published in 1762, is of the same opinion, which is supported by the opinion of De Lisle, of the Royal Academy of Paris, in the year 1782.

Upon the testimony of so many respectable writers, many of whom were in the employment of both France and Spain, not to mention the authority of Du Prats, it is believed the United States may with safety rely, they having, by the Treaty of Paris of 1803, become possessed of the French title. If, however, there exists any obscurity in the boundary of that province, Spain, with whom it is supposed the title conflicts, has no right to claim any benefit arising from it, as all the writers and geographers above referred to agree in fixing Mexico, New Spain, the Rio Grande del Norte, and the mountains of Mexico, as the true boundary anterior to the treaty of 1763. If she, then, by treaty, obtained from France that country, with these limits, as asserted by France, and different ones not being stipulated for by her, she cannot now, with any shadow of justice, propose others. Moreover, Spain, by the Treaty of St. Ildefonso, retroceded this same country to France, with the same extent of boundary it had when originally in her possession, thereby confirming to France, without doubt, all she originally claimed, particularly, as no notice is there taken of the invalidity of the original French title to the full extent of their claim; at all events, it is believed, if there was difficulty in regard to it, during this last transfer would have been the time to adjust it; or, by the law of nations, it is thought, as well as candor and good faith, she has not, or ought not, to be permitted to insist upon other boundaries. That law, in one place, declares, that "if the party making them (meaning grants or cessions) fails to express himself clearly and plainly, it is the worse for him; he cannot be allowed to introduce, subsequently, restrictions which he has not expressed."

It is proper, before this part of the subject is passed over, to remark, that, from the examination of the best records of the times, from the discovery of America until the year 1763, the bull of the Pope rather gave a title to the country, the coast of which had been examined by the Spaniards, than confirmed, beyond the participation of other nations, the hemisphere west of the Azores; but, where an extensive coast had been discovered by them, and no settlement attempted previous to 1763, that coast, and its extended interior, has been considered the property of the nation so discovering it; or discovering the interior, the unoccupied coasts becomes a part.

Great Britain, as was her interest, maintained for a long time the old notion of a right to grant by charter all the countries from sea to sea, where it did not interfere with the territory of any Christian Prince or people; and her obstinate adherence to that system is considered as largely contributing to the production of the war of 1755, when she was opposed by France and Spain, as granting away almost all Mexico and the French possessions, both claiming much of the intermediate country, and the coast of the Pacific. Great Britain, at the close of that war, abandoned her pretensions, and gave manifestations of her sincerity, by revoking the first charter granted to Georgia, and in the second, in 1764, limited it to the Mississippi, and agreed, in 1763, to limit her whole territory to that river in the west.

Where territory has been acquired, as already shown, upon any coast, and the same coast is actually settled, or occupied by another Power, at such a distance as not manifestly to encroach upon the first, the point equidistant from either is considered as the utmost limits of each. This principle, it is believed, was fixed and settled by all the most important treaties which have engaged the Powers of Europe in affairs appertaining, in any way, to possessions in this country, and, it is believed, was acted upon and sanctioned, not only by the treaty of 1763, but, in some measure, by that of Utrecht, in 1713.

Spain, by virtue of her original discovery, and actual settlement in Mexico, together with her title to Louisiana, claimed the Pacific coast of North America, as high up as the sixtieth degree of north latitude; and, to enforce her claim, in the year 1789, sent a ship of war up the coast to capture or drive from those waters several English vessels fitted out in the East Indies by English merchants, upon their own authority, and at their own risk, to trade with the natives in that quarter. This service was performed by Martinez, of His Catholic Majesty's navy; and, in the year 1790, became the subject of a message from the British King to his Parliament. Although much debate ensued, and some resentment was expressed towards Spain for her treatment of the British subjects who were made prisoners, yet no claim was alleged on the part of England to territory there. Great Britain, in the course of that transaction, seems to have recognised the claim of Spain, and was willing to treat for the enjoyment of privileges on that coast, which she obtained, and was, by stipulations, invested with a further right to fish even as low down as the Gulf of California.

The Spanish monarch, being in possession of the French title, regardless of that which the United States had obtained, according to the mode last adopted, felt great confidence in his negotiations with the British Government, in the year 1790. But the territory, the title to which gave that confidence, has since, by the Treaty of Paris, come into the possession of the United States, and it is believed the Treaty of St Ildefonso confirmed to France the full extent of boundary originally claimed, Spain taking no notice of the original error, if any existed.

Under this view of the case, the United States, being possessed of the title of France, and, by a just application of the law of nations, that of Spain too, if she ever had any, leaves them the undisputed sovereignty of that coast, from the sixtieth degree of north latitude down to thirty-six, which is believed to be the situation of the mountains of Mexico, alluded to in all the authors and charts before referred to. If, however, there should remain a doubt, that doubt is relieved by a reference to the subordinate principle recognised by the Treaties of Utrecht and Paris, in 1763. When we know that all the formalities deemed necessary in the possession of a newly discovered country have been complied with on the part of the United States; that, in the year 1785–'6, an establishment was made at the mouth of the Columbia river, by Mr. Hendricks, the full and entire benefit of whose courage, enterprise, and success, results to this Union; and that at a later day, in 1805, Messrs. Lewis and Clark, in executing the desires of this Government, again visited the Columbia and the Western ocean, twelve miles from which they built Fort Clotsop, yet to be seen—these establishments made by the United States, not so near the settlements of California as manifestly to encroach upon them, entitle them to the whole country north of Columbia river. And, in applying the principle known to govern in such cases, the point equidistant from the Spanish actual settlements and the mouth of that river is the true point at which a line drawn separating the two countries should commence. The actual settlements of Spain are believed to have been, at that time, upon the Colorado of California, in latitude 32° north; but, even supposing the point to be the extreme south of the claim of the United States, which is believed to be 36°, then the line of separation would fall at 41°. And, if any doubt arose as to the claim of the United States to the full extent of the Spanish title, to the north of Fort Clotsop, so high as 60 degrees of latitude, there could remain no doubt as far as the equidistant point, which would be at the completion of the 53d degree of latitude, leaving us twelve degrees of coast on that ocean.

From every information that can be obtained, worthy to be relied upon, our coast on the Pacific, for years past, has been the theatre of much individual enterprise, stimulated by the rich returns of numerous whale ships, and the great profit of the fur trade, together with the flattering accounts of Messrs. Lewis and Clark, relative to the resources of the interior, though no regular trade or well organised system of commerce existed until the year 1810, in the course of which year a vessel was fitted out in the city of New York, well supplied with provisions and seed of every description necessary in a permanent occupation of the coast, which they contemplated. This little colony consisted of an hundred and twenty men when it arrived in the Columbia; and after ascertaining its soundings, they removed some miles above Fort Clotsop, and built the town of Astoria, where a portion of them cultivated the soil, whilst the others engaged in the fur trade with the natives. The soil was found to be rich, and well adapted to the culture of all the useful vegetables found in any part of the United States; as turnips, potatoes, onions, rye, wheat, melons of various kinds, cucumbers, and every species of pease. In the course of a year or two, it was believed their interest would be promoted by cultivating and securing the friendship and confidence of the tribes inhabiting the waters of that great river; to which end, the town of Astoria was maintained by about thirty men, whilst the rest established themselves at five other points, to become fixed stations, to raise their own vegetables, trade with the natives, and receive supplies of merchandise from the general depot of Astoria, and to return to it the fruits of their labor. One of these subordinate establishments appears to have been at the mouth of Lewis's river; one at Lantou; a third on the Columbia, six hundred miles from the ocean, at the confluence of the Wantana river; a fourth on the east fork of Lewis's river; and the fifth on the Multnomah. Thus situated, this enterprising little colony succeeded well in all their undertakings, nor met with but one misfortune, which seemed to partake largely of that kind which had, for a long time, so certainly and so unseen, been inflicted upon our Western inhabitants; this was the loss of the Tonquin, a vessel they had taken from New York, whilst trading down the coast, where, in time past, she had been, in common with the ships of some European Powers, enjoying the friendship and confidence of the natives. This confidence had by some means been destroyed, and, whilst they induced many of the ship's company to go on shore, many of their own number went on board the ship, and suddenly attacking the crew, the whole were destroyed, as well as the vessel. This, though a great affliction to the survivors on the Columbia, did not dishearten them, as other vessels were expected soon to arrive, and, with these expectations, they continued their trade, which, becoming profitable, they were the less inclined to abandon. But the operations of the war of 1812, which took place between the United States and Great Britain, were destined to mar their prosperity. That Government, it appears, despatched a vessel of war called the Raccoon, to destroy or possess Astoria, which, by the assistance of the Indians, influenced by the Northwest and Hudson's Bay Companies of fur traders, they were easily enabled to do; and have, from that period to the present time, continued to reside at it, as well as on the river above, though a messenger or agent was sent by the authority of the United States to receive, and did receive, that post from them, at the close of the late war.

From every reflection which the committee have been able to bestow upon the facts connected with this subject, they are inclined to believe the Columbia, in a commercial point of view, a position of the utmost importance; the fisheries on that coast, its open sea, and its position in regard to China, which offers the best market for the vast quantities of furs taken in those regions, and our increasing trade throughout that ocean, seems to demand immediate attention.

The fur of every country which has produced it, has been ever esteemed one of its most valuable commodities, and has long held a rank among the most profitable articles of commerce; it was much sought for even in the days of Tatila, a Visigoth, who reigned in Italy about the year 522, at which time they drew their supplies from the Suethons, who inhabited that part of Europe called Sweden. The Welch set a high value on them as early as the time of Howel Dda, in 940, and, from its being first an article of dress, used only by the poorer class of the community, it by gradually extending itself came to be one of luxury of the highest value, in which kings and princes vied with each other in their costly magnificence and display; their clothes were not only fashioned of them, but even their tents were lined with the finest varieties. Such was the display of the Cham of Tartary, when he was visited in his tent by Marco Polo, about the year 1252. It had become so much in use, and so high in price, that Edward III., in the year 1337, deemed it expedient to prohibit its use to any but those who could afford to spend an hundred pounds a year, without detriment to their property. At that day, having exhausted those parts of Europe which had supplied them, the price increasing with a growing demand, they were obliged to seek them elsewhere, and procured their supplies from the north of Asia. This, for a long time, poured into the adjoining parts of Europe, immense sums, as it was in that direction they were brought to market. This trade, so valuable to that part of the world, had no competition, nor were other sources of supply even known until Francis I. of France, in the year 1514, sent Jacques Curtis, of St. Maloes, to make discoveries in this country. That gentleman entered the St. Lawrence, and exchanged his merchandise for fur, which was the commencement of a feeble trade, that was continued until the year 1608, when Samuel Champlain went some distance up that river, and laid the foundation of the town of Quebec, as a trading establishment, and commenced a system which, however, did not greatly flourish until about the year 1649. But very soon after that country came into the possession of England, this trade was cherished and greatly increased, and the dominion of the Hudson's Bay enabled her not only to supply Russia itself, and all Europe, but even to send it to Turkey, and round the Cape of Good Hope, to distant China. That trade which had destroyed all competition, and, in the hands of well regulated companies, was capable of enriching an empire, had yielded a part of its profits to the skill and industry of individuals upon our western shore; that skill and that industry has withered, not for the want of fostering care, but justice and protection.

The fur trade of Canada has long been conducted by well organized companies; and, although they encounter infinite difficulties, yet the great profit of their business enables them to overcome them, and to divide a considerable per centage. All those articles intended as supplies for the Indians are shipped at Montreal and carried far into the interior, through lakes, and rivers, and difficult streams, until they arrive even in the vicinity of the Rocky Mountains. The increasing wealth derived from this source, induced a large increase of capital, and corresponding exertions to obtain a more extensive knowledge of the rivers and lakes through which their merchandise was to be carried, and a more extensive acquaintance with the natives, among whom they were eventually to be disposed of for furs, the produce of the labor of the savage. With views of this kind, small parties have been despatched, at different times, from the year 1774 until the year 1793, to examine the rivers of the West. At the period last mentioned, one of those parties, under the direction of Alexander McKenzie, penetrated even to the Western ocean, thereby greatly adding to their stock of useful knowledge in that branch of commerce, which they have not failed duly to appreciate. Notwithstanding the great difficulties which the British furriers encounter, from the embarrassment of their commerce by their different systems of exclusive privilege, these companies find it a source of vast profit, far exceeding any thing known in the United States; this, too, when the merchandise is so much advanced in price, from the distance and the numerous obstructions. The enhanced value of the articles, and their difficulties in transporting them, may be fully understood, when it is known the tract of transport is equal to three or four thousand miles, through more than sixty lakes, some of them very considerable in extent, and numerous rivers, and the means of transportation are bark canoes. Furthermore, these waters are interrupted in at least an hundred places, by falls and rapids, along which the trader has to carry his merchandise on his back, and over an hundred and thirty carrying places, from twenty or thirty yards in extent to thirteen miles, where both canoe and cargo have to be conveyed by the same means.

These are some of the obstructions which the Northwest Company encounter; yet their exports from Quebec alone are valued at more than a million of dollars annually, without reference to those brought to the United States, and shipped from New York and Philadelphia direct to China, rather than incur the cost and delay in procuring them a passage to London, and thence to India, in the ships of the East India Company. Indeed, it appears that many of the goods of that company, destined for this trade, particularly on the coast of the Pacific, are shipped to Boston, and immediately reshipped in American vessels, for the benefit of drawback. These vessels are sometimes employed to make a voyage for them from the mouth of Columbia to Canton. To illustrate more fully the increasing value of this trade, it is only necessary to observe, that from Quebec, in 1803, there were exported the skins of six hundred and fifty thousand seven hundred and twenty-nine quadrupeds, ninety-three thousand seven hundred and seventy-eight of which were the beaver. Since that time they have extended their trade beyond the Rocky Mountains, and have, as has already been observed, established themselves at the mouth of the Columbia. The amount of their export from that port cannot be ascertained, but it is thought to be of great value. The Hudson's Bay Company is believed to be considerable, and, from a state of former depression, is fast becoming the rival of the other, but for several years past have withdrawn their traders from the west side of the Rocky Mountains; they have fewer difficulties to overcome in arriving at the highest point of navigation than the Northwest Company. Their route is through the Hudson's Bay, the Nelson river, to Lake Winnipeg; thence, by passing other lakes, they ascend the Red river to their establishment, which is within ninety miles of the Missouri river, at a point called the Mandan villages. This river takes its rise in the Rocky Mountains, in about the forty-third degree of latitude, and observes a course north and northeast towards Hudson's Bay, until it arrives at the Mandan villages, a distance of nearly twelve hundred miles, when it turns short to the south, without any apparent cause, and joins the Mississippi: the water running to the Hudson's Bay at that point, approaching within one mile, and no hill or high ground to separate them, of any magnitude. Yet, notwithstanding the many advantages which the

Hudson's Bay Company possessed over the Northwest Company, the Earl of Selkirk, the patron of the former, and a man of uncommon enterprise, was exceedingly desirous to obtain the privilege of supplying his establishments upon the Red river, by ascending the Mississippi to the St. Peter's; thence, to its source in Stone Lake; then, by a short portage, through open woods and a level country, to his stations; or, taking the route by the Missouri to the Mandan villages, thence by a portage of ninety miles, to his place of destination. The exports of this company, for a short time past, have been very little less than those of the Northwest Company.

The committee, from carefully examining all the facts connected with the subject referred to them, are well persuaded that the situation of the United States is such as to enable it to possess all the benefits derived from this trade, which, in the hands of others, amounts to millions; many of whose trading establishments east of the Rocky Mountains are within the acknowledged limits of this Republic, as fixed by the Convention of London of the 20th of October, 1818; and, it is believed, that no Power, with the exception of Spain, has any just claim to territory west of them, or on the Pacific. The dependence for subsistence of many of those establishments, is upon the buffalo beef hunted by the Assiniboin Indians, who inhabit the country between the river of that name and the Missouri; their hunting ground is far within our boundary. To succeed in procuring to the people of the United States all the wealth flowing from this source, it is only necessary to occupy with a small trading guard the most northeastern point upon the Missouri river, and confine the foreigners to their own territory; at the same time occupying, with a similar guard, the mouth of Columbia. The great profit derived from this trade by the Canadian companies, when we know the distance and obstructions in their rivers, and in the various streams they ascend in carrying it on, the advance of price consequent upon it becomes rather a matter of amazement than otherwise, and inclines us to examine our own rivers with a view to the same object. Instead, however, of those formidable obstructions, we find a smooth and deep river running through a boundless extent of the most fertile soil on this continent, containing within its limits all those valuable furs which have greatly enriched others; a certain, safe, and easy navigation, with a portage of only two hundred miles, uniting it with another river, equally smooth, deep, and certain, running to the great Western ocean. Thus are these two great oceans separated by a single portage of two hundred miles! The practicability of a speedy, safe, and easy communication with the Pacific, is no longer a matter of doubt or conjecture: from information not to be doubted, the Rocky Mountains at this time, in several places, are so smooth and open that the labor of ten men for twenty days would enable a wagon with its usual freight to pass with great facility from the navigable water of the Missouri to that of the Columbia; the actual distance from river to river several hundred miles from their source, that is, from the great Falls of Missouri to the fork of Clark's river, is one hundred and forty-nine miles; the distance, therefore, of two hundred miles is to good navigation on the Columbia, which is the only river of any magnitude upon that whole coast, north of the Colorada of California, though there are several good harbors, secure and safe for vessels of any size.

The region of country from the ocean to the head of tide water, which is about two hundred miles, is heavily timbered, with a great variety of wood well calculated for ship building, and every species of cabinet or carpenter's work; though there is a heavily timbered country thence for two hundred miles further, yet it is of a lesser growth, and quality not so durable; at that point commences the plain country, when the soil becomes more thin, and almost without wood, until it arrives at the table lands below the mountain. Though the soil of this region is not so good as in any other part of this great valley, yet it produces grass of the finest quality, and is emphatically called the region favorable to the production of the horse; this noble animal, so far surpassing all others in usefulness, courage, and swiftness, is here produced in greater perfection than even in Andalusia or Virginia. But, independent of all the wealth which may be derived from the fur trade of that river and the Missouri, the security too which the peace of this country would find in the influence which the American traders would obtain over the native, is the increasing commerce in the Western ocean. There is no employment so well calculated to make good seamen as the whale fisheries, which are known to be more profitable on this coast than any other; at the same time the oil is far preferable to that taken on any other coast, being clear and transparent as rock water. While so many of our citizens are industriously engaged in the various branches of trade in those seas, more valuable to this country, it is believed, than any other; while all nations who have claims upon that coast, and some who have none, are anxious to occupy some position upon it, even at a vast expense, to enable them to participate in its benefits, we have neglected to extend to it any portion of our care, though it appears, from the best information, that there is at this time eight millions of property owned by citizens of this Republic in the Pacific ocean.

Russia, whose dominions on the Asiatic coast, occupy nearly the same position upon that side, which ours do on this, has long been well informed of the great and increasing value of that commerce; and while she has been nowhere visible, not even to the powers of Europe, only as she has of late taken part in a few memorable enterprises, she has been felt everywhere. No labor, care, or expense, is avoided, to make tributary the four quarters of the globe; forts, magazines, towns, cities, and trade, seem to arise on that coast as if by magic; with an army of a million of men, she sits not only in proud security as it regards Europe, and menaces the Turk, the Persian, the Japanese, and Chinese, but even the King of Spain's dominions in North America are equally easy of access, and equally exposed to her fearful weight of power. Her watchfulness is ever in advance in discerning the most practicable avenues to profitable commerce. In the midst of all her busy arrangements she has not neglected the opportunity of possessing herself of two important stations on the American shore of the Pacific—the one at a place called New Archangel, in about 59 degrees of north latitude, the other at Bodiga Bay, in latitude 38 degrees, 34 minutes. At the former of these military positions, for the protection of her commerce it is presumed, she has incurred much expense, and built a fort of great strength, situated upon one of the best harbors on the coast, standing upon a point of land projecting into the little bay, giving something of the appearance of

a conical island in the centre of it; this fort is well supplied at all times with provisions and military stores, mounting a hundred and twenty cannon, carrying balls from eighteen to twenty-four pounds weight. That at Bodiga is well constructed and supplied with cannon, and has a good harbor; at this point they have ammunition and merchandise in abundance, and find the Indian trade at this post as well as New Archangel very considerable; besides the fine condition of this fort and its defences, they have many field pieces, some of brass, of the finest construction, in good order and well mounted.

All these supplies have been conveyed to those places through immense oceans, round Cape Horn, which would have appalled any but Russian policy and perseverance.

The light articles destined for this trade are transported from St. Petersburgh in sledges, which will perform in three months that which would require two Summers of water-conveyance to effect; their communications are open to Kamtschatka, to Fort St. Peter and St. Paul, by Okhotsk, in the Pacific, where they have the finest harbor in the world; the distance is estimated at ten thousand miles. The nation which can encounter such journeys as these, often through seas of ice, and storms of snow so terrible as to obscure an object beyond the distance of a few paces, to prosecute any branch of commerce, must be well and fully informed of its value. That the objects she has in view may not, by any event, be taken from her grasp, after encountering such vast difficulties, she has found it expedient to occupy one of the Sandwich Islands, which not only enables her effectually to maintain her positions, but to command the whole northern part of the Pacific ocean. These islands, lying just within the tropics, in the direct course from the lower coast of North America to Canton, are well supplied not only with all the fruits of that climate, but with every vegetable and animal known in this country.

It is worthy of remark, that among other advantages which the Russian position on the opposite coast possesses, is, that a voyage from Kamtschatka to Japan can be made in an open boat, as it is a continued chain of islands from the Okhotsk sea until it arrives at its place of destination.

Your committee are well persuaded that, by a little care and small expense, the citizens of this Republic might reap all the benefits of this trade, not only profitable now, but from every view of the subject there is a strong probability that it will increase for many years.

Were an establishment made at the mouth of Columbia, which should be allowed to take with them their women and children, there can be no doubt of success, as so many year's experience of the English fur companies have amply shown this mode has the most powerful effect in separating the minds of the men from pursuits which often in frontier countries lead to strife, as it gives them a local interest and feeling, and makes them even more vigilant and prudent in the discharge of all their duties. It is believed that population could be easily acquired from China, by which the arts of peace would at once acquire strength and influence, and make visible to the aborigines the manner in which their wants could be supplied. The coast of the Pacific is, in its climate, more mild than any part of the continent in the same parallel, and many vegetables on that shore grow in great abundance in the native forest, which are likewise natives of China.

It is known that when the Spanish Government, in 1789, sent their ships of war up the coast to capture the British vessels which were intruding, they found seventy Chinese, whom the English had procured to emigrate, that they might be employed in the mechanic arts; and, though the people of that country evince no disposition to emigrate to the territory of adjoining princes, it is believed they would willingly, nay, gladly, embrace the opportunity of a home in America, where they have no prejudices, no fears, no restraint in opinion, labor, or religion.

The committee cannot doubt that an establishment made on the Pacific would essentially benefit the natives, whilst it would give this country the advantage of all its own treasures, which otherwise must be lost forever or rather never enjoyed; and, from all that can be ascertained relative to its present and increasing value, of more profit to this country than the mines of Potosi.

From the best information which can be had, it appears that the Indian trade on the Missouri, below the Mandan villages, is worth about $120,000, and that on the Mississippi is valued at $250,000, making the sum of $370,000 annually. They have reflected upon this trade, and that prosecuted by the whalers on that coast, and are irresistibly drawn to the conclusion, that they are the most valuable to this nation, and demand its care and attention in a high degree. This trade, unlike any other, originates its own capital, and may fairly be said to bring into the United States $370,000 every year, where not one dollar previously existed, and adds that much to the wealth of the community as decidedly as though it had been fished from the bottom of the rivers in gold and silver, as it is in the market of China, or any other market, capable of purchasing as much; and if, with that amount in furs, a vessel should sail from the mouth of the Columbia to Canton, which is a voyage of from fifty to seventy days, she would return with that in exchange which would sell for perhaps double that amount, thereby contributing to the comfort, enjoyment, and accommodation of the community, $740,000, which is the result not of a profitable voyage but a creative trade.

It is believed that a shipment of tobacco, flour, or cotton, bears no comparison, in point of profit, with this, as they are properly the rough manufactures of the country, and the result of considerable capital, and the cargo brought back in return for them, in European or other fabrics, is only an increased value they receive by being exported and returned to us in that shape. Hence, the exportation of $370,000 worth of tobacco or cotton, should it return to us $740,000 in European silk and cloth, is still the original cargo of tobacco or cotton, as nothing but these have been paid for them; but, in the first instance, he who manufactures either the tobacco, flour, or cotton, is compelled to take into consideration the capital employed, and then the balance is his gain; but in the fur trade and the whale sheries, there is in the one little capital, in the other none.

Under the strongest belief that by a new organization of the system of Indian trade, comprehending a settlement on the Columbia river, great benefits would result to the citizens of the Republic, whilst the aborigines would be better protected and provided for by instructing them in agriculture and the minor branches of the mechanic arts, the committee ask leave to report a bill.

The bill is as follows:

Be it enacted, &c., That the President of the United States be, and he is hereby, authorized and required, to occupy that portion of the territory of the United States on the waters of the Columbia river, and to extinguish the Indian title to a district of country not exceeding —— miles square, on the borders of said river, in the region of tide water; and that —— acres of land be allowed to each actual settler, being the head of a family, and to each unmarried man, between the age of eighteen and forty-five years, who shall establish himself in said district, and cultivate ground therein within —— years after the Indian title shall be extinguished thereto.

SEC. 2. *And be it further enacted,* That the President shall prescribe regulations for the government of said district, and the administration of justice therein, and appoint the necessary officers for carrying the same into effect.

SEC. 3. *And be it further enacted,* That the President be authorized to open a port of entry, as soon as he shall deem it expedient, within the said district, and to appoint custom-house officers for the regulation of the same; from and after which time the revenue laws of the United States shall be extended over said district, and be of full force therein.

SEC. 4. *And be it further enacted,* That the President be authorized and required to appoint agents for the Indian tribes on the waters of the Columbia, and to fix the salaries of the agents so appointed, not exceeding the salary now allowed to the agent to the Indians on the Upper Missouri; and that from and after such appointment, all the laws of the United States for regulating intercourse with the Indian tribes, shall be deemed and held to be in full force throughout the territories inhabited by the said tribes.

SEC. 5. *And be it further enacted,* That there shall be a Superintendent of Indian Affairs, who shall reside at St. Louis; and all the Indian agents to the different tribes on the waters of the Upper Mississippi, the Lakes Michigan, Erie, and Superior, and the waters of Missouri, Arkansas, Red River, and Columbia, shall be under his control and direction, and shall correspond with him, and through him, to the Department of War. The said Superintendent shall be authorized and required to grant all licenses to Indian traders, and shall have over them a general superintendence; that each trader shall make a full and accurate report to him of the state and condition of the Indians with whom they trade, at least once a month; and the Superintendent shall forward the same, digested in a general report, to the Department of War, once in three months, or oftener if thereto required.

SEC. 6. *And be it further enacted,* That so much of every act which establishes a superintendency of Indian affairs at Washington city, and so much of every act which establishes factories among the Indian tribes, be, and the same is hereby, repealed.

SEC. 7. *And be it further enacted,* That the property in the hands of the Superintendent of Indian Affairs at Washington city, and the respective factors in the service of the United States, be sold, and the proceeds accounted for in such manner as the Secretary of the Department of War may direct.

SEC. 8. *And be it further enacted,* That licenses shall not be granted to trade with any of the Indian tribes, to any but citizens of the United States, of approved moral character, and of ability to embark at least —— dollars annually in the trade; and every trader obtaining a license so to trade, shall have a fixed habitation; to which end he may lease from the tribe where such habitation is fixed, a tract of land not exceeding —— miles square, and for a term not exceeding —— years, nor shall it be within —— miles of a similar location previously made, and shall have leave to trade within the limits of their respective licenses; and each trader shall set up a blacksmith shop, and shall supply the Indians with such working tools as they may be willing to purchase; and are hereby required to cultivate at their establishments the different kinds of grain and fruit, which the climate and soil will produce, and shall rear the domestic animals in common use; and shall furnish seed and stock animals to such Indians as may wish to buy them, and shall induce them to cultivate the soil and rear the domestic animals. Nor shall any trader be permitted to sell to any of the Indian tribes ardent spirits of any kind, under the penalty of —— dollars for every such offence, and shall ever after be debarred the privilege of trading with any Indian tribe. Each trader shall pay —— dollars annually for his license, but it shall be granted during good behaviour upon his giving bond with sufficient security, which shall be judged of by the superintendent, and may by him be required to give additional security in proportion to his additional capital employed every two years, the license to be annulled for breach of conditions, which shall be determined by the verdict of a jury.

Sec. 9. *And be it further enacted,* That the money paid to the superintendent annually for licenses by the Indian traders, shall be by him appropriated to the purchase of any kind of seed or domestic animals, for such Indians as may want to cultivate such seed, or rear such animals; but if, at the end of the year, there should be money remaining in his hands accruing from this fund, he shall make payment of it into the Treasury of the United States, where it shall be kept as a distinct fund, to be applied to the building of mills in such place and manner among the different tribes as the President may direct; and it is hereby made the duty of the agent who has the care of the affairs of that tribe where such mill is built, to superintend the building of the same, and to transmit an accurate account of his disbursements to the superintendent, and by him to the Department of War.

Sec. 10. *And be it further enacted,* That it shall be the duty of every Indian agent to report to the Superintendent of Indian Affairs upon the state and condition of the Indians, and the conduct of the traders, within their respective agencies, at least once a month, and oftener if thereto required; the said reports to be made in the form prescribed by the Secretary of the Department of War, and upon all such points as may be indicated by the said department; and the superintendent shall forward the same, digested into a general report, to the Department of War, at least once in three months, and as much oftener as may be required.

Sec. 11. *And be it further enacted,* That all Indian agents, not under the direction of the superintendent as herein directed, shall be authorized to issue licenses to traders within the limits of the Indian territory under their authority, and shall correspond directly with the Department of War.

Sec. 12. *And be it further enacted,* That the sum of —— dollars is hereby appropriated to carry into effect the provisions of this act, to be paid out of any money in the Treasury not otherwise appropriated.

AMENDMENT TO THE CONSTITUTION.

On motion of Mr. SMITH, of North Carolina, the House proceeded to the consideration of the resolution proposing an amendment to the Constitution of the United States, so as to establish an uniform mode of electing, by districts, Electors of President and Vice President of the United States, and Representatives in Congress.

And the question having been stated on the passage of said resolution, this being its final reading in this House—

Mr. GROSS said, that he had voted for a similar resolution at the last session of Congress, without, as he confessed, having examined the subject in the most attentive manner; but subsequent consideration had confirmed his original impression. He was of opinion that the permanent interests of the United States demanded the adoption of the proposed amendment. A variety of objections, he said, had been taken to the resolution during a former discussion. The gentleman from Georgia (Mr. REID) warned us against rashly altering the provisions of the Constitution; while the gentleman from Virginia (Mr. BARBOUR) entered into an arithmetical calculation to show that the amendment would lessen the power and influence of the larger States. Other gentlemen thought they foresaw still greater evils. All their arguments were directed to the same point, and were of three kinds: those drawn from considerations of the sacred character of the instrument, and the danger of rash amendments; those addressed to the pride and jealousy of States; and, lastly, those which result from an inquiry into the present practices of the different States, in choosing their Electors, and their general tendency and effect. The first class of arguments, he said, were certainly worthy of respectful consideration. No one, perhaps, had a right to object to those of the second; but he would venture to say that those of the third alone involved the real merits of the question.

If, said Mr. G., we admit that it be ever lawful or proper to examine the Constitution, with a view to its amendment, when, he would ask, has there ever been a time, or when are we to expect the arrival of a period, better adapted to our purpose than the present? In some States the fire of discord is rekindled, but the nation is comparatively tranquil. Party spirit is now, for the most part, local in its nature, and local in its effects. Where is the party, or where is the citizen, who does not desire the union and prosperity of these States? He confidently believed they were not to be found. He presumed that no one doubted that the framers of the Constitution were both patriotic and enlightened; yet they have thought proper to prescribe a mode of amendment in the instrument itself. Would they have done this had they designed to conceal it from public view, and to permit none but the initiated, none but priests and Levites, to approach? They knew, he said, indeed, that rash amendments might be productive of evil, and had accordingly provided ample means of precaution. The House cannot alter the Constitution; Congress itself cannot do it. It can only propose and recommend amendments to the States. With these preventives against precipitate movements, the representatives of the people, as well as the people themselves, instead of being warned to depart, should be invited to approach and examine the instrument, with the same honesty of intention which actuated its framers, and, if it be found defective, boldly to advise its amendment.

It was, he said, a doctrine long, too long, established in some countries, that every thing relating to the Government was too sacred for the view of the people; a doctrine which, he hoped, would never flourish on this side the Atlantic. Priests and politicians united their tender cares for the welfare of the human race, and accordingly the Bible was prohibited by the one, and the book of laws by the other. He highly appreciated the motives of the gentleman from Georgia, (Mr. REID) but his remarks on this part of the subject reminded him of the habitual answer given by the ministry of a certain country to every application for reform. The national reputation abroad, he said, was, by them, made an excuse for the oppression of the people, and the excellency of the abstract principles of the Constitution for the corrupt practices of the Government.

I am, said Mr. G., as zealous for the preservation of State rights, and will oppose any infringement of them with as much zeal, as the gentleman from Virginia. He would not consent to any measure which would impair their independence as recognised by the principles of the Constitution. That gentleman has shown that, should the proposed amendment be adopted, it may happen that the votes of the small State of Delaware will neutralize those of Virginia or New York. He has even demonstrated that, should the Electors of New York give a majority of but one vote for a particular candidate, those of Delaware might give a majority of four to the other, and thus secure his election. Sir, all this may happen, and where would be the harm if it should? Is it proper that one vote in any State should overbalance and overpower four votes in another? What matters it, whether the Electors of this or that State be divided or in the minority, so long as the majority of the people of the United States prevail? Sir, said Mr. G. I have the honor of being one of the Representatives from a State which has been called, sometimes seriously, sometimes, perhaps, laughingly, but I trust always truly, a great State. The intrinsic excellence of her soil, and her internal as well as external advantages, must ever preserve her a great State in point of population. But, of what advantage will this kind of greatness be to her, should jealousies be excited, should discord prevail, and should the Union be dissolved? He trusted that it was a proposition which would not be controverted on that floor, that the greatness of every State depended on the preservation and harmony of the Union. Why, then, he asked, should we, under the pretence of preserving State rights, seek an unnatural advantage, the exercise of which can only serve to cherish faction, foment discord within, excite jealousy without, and jeopardize the

best interests of the country? It is enough that the Constitution guaranties to us the advantage of a superiority of numbers, by giving us a proportionate superiority of votes. It is a miserable ambition, he hoped it might not prove a fatal one, that seeks the temporary disfranchisement of a great minority of our fellow-citizens, for the purpose of showing our power to a smaller member of the Confederacy. Do gentlemen fear that party concert cannot be preserved, if Electors of President and Vice President be chosen by districts? The members of the House were thus chosen, in all the larger States, during periods of the greatest excitement, and the Journal will show that the Administration never lacked support.

It has been thought proper, said Mr. G., to point out the possible inconveniences of the proposed method of choosing Electors of President and Vice President. He did not consider argument of this kind very conclusive, because all human institutions and plans are, from their origin, in a greater or less degree defective. We were, he said, to search for and adopt the least objectionable one. The present system is liable to the same inconvenience as the one proposed; for, although New York should give all its votes for one candidate, Pennsylvania or Virginia might give theirs to another, and thus enable Delaware and Rhode Island to turn the election. So far the two modes present the same objections. The present system, however, furnishes others of a still weightier character. Let us suppose, after the manner of the gentleman from Virginia, that the votes of the several States were so distributed that one-half of the votes of the State of New York, if given to a particular candidate, would secure his election. Suppose that candidate to be favored by Virginia, and, further, that it should so happen, as it certainly may happen, that all the votes of the State should be given to his opponent. Let us suppose, moreover, that the Legislature which appointed these Electors was chosen several months before, at a time of public excitement, and that, in fact, they did not express the sentiment of the people, and that, had the Electors been chosen by districts, a majority of them might have given a different vote. What would gentlemen say to such a state of things? Mr. G. thought that, under such circumstances, they would gladly have exchanged the insignificant State right of altering, from year to year, the mode of choosing Electors, for the permanent benefit of enabling the voice of the people to be heard.

I am ready to acknowledge, said Mr. G., that uniformity and permanency in the mode of appointing Electors is of more consequence than the mode itself. If gentlemen choose to have them elected by a general ticket, let it be so. It was the present variety of modes, adopted by the different States, and the power of change to suit the times, against which he objected. Some States appoint their Electors by districts, some by general ticket, and some by their Legislatures. Virginia, at first, adopted the former mode, but changed it afterwards to that of a general ticket, in order to throw her whole weight into the scale at a particular election. Other States may make changes in this particular as well as Virginia, and for a similar purpose. What will be the result? The objects of party may be attained. A particular candidate may succeed by a particular manœuvre; but the effect of such practices cannot fail to be injurious, if not fatal, to the liberties of the people. Aristocrats and monarchists have never been able to combat successfully the principles upon which our Government rests: but they have asserted that such a Government cannot long exist. Their predictions have hitherto been verified by the event. The safety of a republic does not essentially depend upon the particular form of its government, or upon particular laws; for what are forms and what are laws to a degenerate people, without force to maintain them? It does not depend on an armed force, for republics will not, and ought not, to endure the rigorous police nor the pensioned spies which infest a community under a monarchical form of government. On the contrary, our security consists in the intelligence and virtue of the people, and in the favorable opinion which they entertain of the purity of our institutions, in practice as well as in principle. When the Constitution ceases to be revered by them, it will no longer be worth preserving. It is, then, of the greatest importance that the election of a citizen to fill the high and responsible office of President of the United States, should be the effect of the free, unbiassed, and unbought will of the people.

It may happen that a single State, by changing its mode of appointing Electors, will give a turn to the election. If it happen once, it may happen again. Will the people bear with this? They surely will not. If they are compelled to submit, they will lose all confidence, not in the Government only, but also in the efficacy of the Constitution. Is such the end for which our ancestors resisted the usurpations of Great Britain? And is such to be the practical result of our boasted freedom? Shall we not be content with the legitimate superiority which a numerous population gives us; but must we also adhere to a system by which a great State may accidentally acquire an unjust and odious advantage, and by which she may also be made to suffer with her sister States? The object does not justify the risk, and, the sooner it is abandoned, the better it will be for the country.

Mr. G. said that alarm had been expressed at the increasing influence of the General Government. He was glad, he said, that these expressions proceeded from the quarter they did. The General Government possessed patronage; and this patronage, properly exercised, might prove salutary, by cementing the bonds of our Union. Its abuse was, indeed, to be dreaded. In his opinion, the amendment proposed would, instead of increasing the influence of the Executive, curtail it in a salutary manner. How was the National Government to influence the elections in the different States? Its officers may, indeed, exert themselves, and even make an improper use of their official influence to promote the views of a party; but, against this, separately considered, we had the security of that mass of patriotism and intelligence which pervades the community. No, sir, said Mr. G., it is not at the polls of election that this kind of influence is most to be dreaded. A whole community is not to be bribed. Can we say as much, he asked, of a Legislature, consisting perhaps of no more than one hundred and fifty men, and governed by a caucus composed of little more than one-half its numbers? It was here, he said, that foreign and sinister views had full scope; and it was here that the violence of party brought forth its fruits in perfection. If, said Mr. G., there be a member of this House who feels himself inclined to oppose the proposed amendment in order to secure the supremacy of a party, let him reflect that the same weapons which he now makes use of for the harmless purpose of defeating an opponent, may, by some future party, be turned against the liberties of the country.

In conclusion, Mr. G. said that he felt bound to support the amendment, as well on the broad principles of justice, as to secure the Constitutional independence of the States and the preservation of the Union.

Mr. ROSS, of Ohio, assigned at length the reasons which influenced him to oppose this resolution; first, because, in one part of it, respecting Representatives, it was wholly unnecessary, and in the other part, respecting Electors, inexpedient.

Mr. STRONG, of New York, next spoke, in opposition to the resolution, on the grounds generally taken in opposition to it, and with the additional reasons that the proposed amendment goes to affect the powers of the people, and should therefore be approached with more hesitation than if it related to any of the powers of the Government, and should not be touched at all unless under an indispensable necessity.

Mr. BREVARD said, that he had intended on this occasion, as on others, to have refrained from taking any part in the debate, as he had generally found, that what occurred to him, as necessary or proper to be said, was as well or better said by others. But, as it was his misfortune not to agree with some of his friends and colleagues, and other members of the House, for whose opinions he entertained great respect and deference, he thought it due to them and himself to assign some of the reasons which influenced his conduct. In doing so, he said he would be as concise and as little tedious as possible; for, said he, I am desirous of avoiding what I conceive to be a great evil here, namely, a profusion and waste of words; involving what is much to be regretted—a loss of precious time, and an useless expenditure of public money. For time is money, and the economy of time is important.

Mr. B. said, he had ever held in the highest estimation, in reverence, that instrument which it was then proposed to alter, for the purpose, as it was said, of amending it. He had always believed that it was our highest political interest, and therefore a duty incumbent upon us, to cherish a veneration for this instrument, and inculcate it in others. He therefore regarded as a species of sacrilege every attempt to change or alter any of its features on any pretence whatever.

He was not ignorant, he said, that the Constitution contained a provision for its own amendment; that, in virtue of this provision, it had been altered; and that the alteration then proposed was in conformity to this provision. But, he said, he was not entirely satisfied that every innovation and change which had been made was an improvement which would be sanctioned by time and experience.

This Constitution, he said, was formed at a most propitious period, and under circumstances peculiarly fortunate. Those who formed it brought to the work more of pure unmixed patriotism, and less of human passion, prejudice, and interest, than had ever happened, or would, perhaps, ever happen again on any occasion of equal importance.

We owe it, said he, to the virtue and the wisdom of those enlightened patriots to believe that what they did was not done without consideration; and, also, to those able men, who afterwards severely examined and finally approved it, to believe that it is as perfect as human wisdom and skill can make it. In his judgment then, he said, it would be unwise and unsafe to abridge, enlarge, or otherwise change any of its provisions, without the most evident and urgent necessity, and without the clearest and most perfect conviction of the utility and safety of the measure.

It is not, he said, for every cause, productive of possible evil, which the speculative mind of man may discover, and would guard against by anticipation, that this invaluable charter is to undergo a change at the will or the caprice of the Legislature.

He did think it important that this charter ought to be held in high and dear respect by the people of the United States; not as imperfect, uncertain, and mutable—but as perfect—clear as light—and as stable as the hill of this Capitol.

He was not, he said, for removing one barrier of the Constitution, and replacing it by another, on any pretext, however plausible it might appear at first view; and he would not incline to do so till he could clearly discern and appreciate the consequences of such a change. With the lights he then had, Mr. B. said, he could not clearly see that the alteration proposed might not produce, eventually, full as much harm as good.

There was, perhaps, he said, evil to be apprehended in either view of the subject. On which side the evil was most likely to preponderate, was, to his mind, at least problematical. He was, therefore, for preserving the Constitution inviolate, until there should be a necessity more pressing than any that, to him, was then perceptible, for amending it.

It is better, said he, to bear those ills we have, than to fly to others that we know not of. It will be time enough when some serious evil is felt, or seen to approach so near as to be distinctly observed, and to threaten our peace and safety, to prepare the necessary defence against it.

The nature and magnitude of the evil, said Mr. B. will then more clearly suggest the appropriate safeguard.

The Legislature of each State, Mr. B. said, now has the power of prescribing the times, the places, and the manner of holding elections for Senators and Representatives; but Congress may make any alteration as to the times, and the manner, but not as to the places of election. In the election of President, the Legislature of each State is empowered to direct the manner of appointing Electors. An opinion, said he, is entertained by some, that the power vested in the Legislature of each State, of directing the manner of appointing Electors, does not imply the power of appointment by the Legislature itself, in exclusion of popular election. He would not, he said, on this point (as he did not think it necessary) deliver any opinion. His friend from New York, (Mr. STRONG,) who sat near him, had argued it with ability and success. The power and the duty, Mr. B. said, of expounding the Constitution in relation to that point belonged to the Legislature of each State, when required to act in obedience to its provisions; and he did not doubt they would act with proper deliberation and caution.

Mr. B. said, it is a principle which lies as the foundation of all our institutions, political and civil, that the will of the majority shall govern. When, said he, we advert to the nature and character of the Federal compact, and take into consideration that it was formed by the people of the several States, composing separate and distinct communities—that the ends for which it was contrived were the defence and safety of each and every of these distinct communities, as well as the defence and safety of them all, and the maintenance of the Confederacy—we will be induced rather to incline in favor of preserving the power, which the several States now have, of regulating the subject under consideration, than of depriving them of it, and vesting it in the Congress. Occasions may render it necessary for the States to exercise it, and the time has been when, in some of the States, it had been considered of the utmost importance to the public welfare to exercise it by providing against division, and insuring unanimity in the choice of Chief Magistrate of the Union. Mr. B. said, he was by no means clear that this power ought not to rest where it now resides, although it might, possibly, sometimes be abused. Every thing of human invention, however excellent, however admirable and beneficial, is liable to abuse. An argument derived from the possible abuse of a power, was not a sufficient argument against its legitimate exercise. He said he would not go into detail—that had been done by others better qualified for the task. He could, he said, add little by way of illustration to what had been already advanced.

Mr. RANDOLPH, of Virginia, expressed the grounds of his hostility to this resolution, which he considered as proposing a pernicious innovation on the Constitution, under the influence of fanciful and theoretical notions, under circumstances of the House and of the country not favorable to a correct decision.

Mr. STORRS, of New York, opposed the resolution on principle, and on the ground of the impolicy of lightly invading the present provisions of the Constitution.

Mr. SMITH, of Maryland, defended the resolution, on the ground of the necessity of some change in the Constitution, (he did not pronounce this the only change which could be made, or the best, though he inclined to think it the best,) to guard against the effects of intrigue on elections.

Mr. WHITMAN, of Massachusetts, strongly supported the resolution on its known merits, and on the ground that the amendment which it proposes to the Constitution involves no innovation, but to restore to that instrument a feature in regard to Electors, which it originally possessed, which had been taken from it by construction. The delivery of Mr. W.'s speech occupied nearly an hour.

Mr. WOOD, of New York, spoke decidedly in support of the resolution, as calculated to restore to the people the exercise of the sovereign power, of which they had in practice been divested, contrary to what ought to have been the construction of the Constitution.

The question on the passage of the resolution was then taken, and decided as follows:

YEAS—Messrs. Adams, Allen of New York, Archer of Maryland, Baker, Ball, Bayly, Beecher, Bloomfield, Brown, Brush, Burton, Butler of New Hampshire, Butler of Louisiana, Campbell, Cannon, Clagett, Clay, Cobb, Cocke, Cook, Crafts, Crowell, Culpeper, Cushman, Cuthbert, Dane, Davidson, Eddy, Edwards of Connecticut, Edwards of North Carolina, Fay, Fisher, Floyd, Foot, Ford, Gross of New York, Hall of New York, Hall of North Carolina, Hendricks, Herrick, Hobart, Hooks, Jackson, Johnson, Kinsey, Kinsley, Little, Lincoln, Livermore, Lowndes, Maclay, McCullough, McLane, of Delaware, McLean of Kentucky, Mercer, Metcalf, Monell, R. Moore, T. L. Moore, Morton, Moseley, Neale, Nelson of Massachusetts, Parker of Massachusetts, Pitcher, Plumer, Rankin, Rich, Richards, Richmond, Ringgold, Robertson, Russ, Sawyer, Silsbee, Simkins, Sloan, Smith of New Jersey, Smith of Maryland, Smith of North Carolina, Stevens, Street, Tomlinson, Tracy, Tucker of Virginia, Upham, Walker, Warfield, Wendover, Whitman, Williams of Virginia, and Wood—92.

NAYS—Messrs. Abbot, Alexander, Allen of Massachusetts, Allen of Tennessee, Baldwin, Barbour, Brevard, Burwell, Case, Clark, Crawford, Darlington, Dennison, Dickinson, Earle, Edwards of Pennsylvania, Forrest, Garnett, Gray, Gross of Pennsylvania, Guyon, Hardin, Hibshman, Hill, Hostetter, Jones of Virginia, Lathrop, McCoy, McCreary, Marchand, Meigs, S. Moore, Murray, Nelson of Virginia, Newton, Parker of Virginia, Patterson, Philson, Randolph, Reid, Rhea, Rogers, Ross, Sergeant, A. Smyth of Virginia, Southard, Storrs, Strong of New York, Tarr, Terrell, Tucker of South Carolina, Tyler, Udree, and Wallace—54.

Two-thirds of the members present not having voted in its favor, the resolution was of course declared to be *rejected.*

FRIDAY, January 26.

Mr. GORHAM presented a petition of sundry inhabitants of the State of Massachusetts, praying that measures may be adopted by the Government of the United States, in concert with the Governments of other civilized and Christian nations, to abolish the practice of privateering, or capturing and condemning private property in time of war; which petition was referred to the Committee of Commerce.

Mr. SMITH, of Maryland, from the Committee of Ways and Means, reported a bill making appropriations for the support of Government for the year 1821; which was read twice, and committed to a Committee of the Whole.

Mr. RICH, from the Committee of Claims, made a report on the petition of Samuel T. Anderson, accompanied by a bill for his relief; which was read twice, and committed to a Committee of the Whole to-morrow.

Mr. ANDERSON, from the Committee on the Public Lands, reported a bill to establish an additional land office in the Territory of Michigan; which was read twice, and committed to a Committee of the Whole.

Mr. BRUSH, from the same committee, reported a bill granting certain islands in the Tennessee river to the State of Alabama; which was read twice, and committed to a Committee of the Whole.

Mr. SERGEANT, from the Committee on the Judiciary, reported a bill to amend the act, entitled "An act for regulating process in the courts of the United States;" which was read twice, and ordered to lie on the table. The bill is as follows:

Be it enacted, &c., That in all suits and actions in any district court of the United States, in which it shall appear that the judge of such court is any ways concerned in interest, or has been of counsel for either party, or is so related to, or connected with, either party, as to render it improper for him, in his opinion, to sit on the trial of such suit or action, it shall be the duty of such judge, on application of either party, to cause the fact to be entered on the records of the court, and also an order that an authenticated copy thereof, with all the proceedings in such suit or action, shall be forthwith certified to the next circuit court of the district; and if there be no circuit in such district, to the next circuit court of the State, and if there be no circuit court in such State, to the most convenient circuit court in an adjacent State; which circuit court shall, upon such record being filed with the clerk thereof, take cognizance thereof in the like manner as if such suit or action had been originally commenced in that court, and shall proceed to hear and determine the same accordingly. And the jurisdiction of such circuit court shall extend to all such cases so removed as were cognizable in the district court from which the same was removed.

The SPEAKER laid before the House a report from the Secretary of the Treasury, made in obedience to a resolution of this House of t.1e 9th instant, requiring him to state "when and why the agency of the Treasurer of the United States for the War and Navy Departments was first established, and whether the same may not be discontinued without any detriment to the public service;" which report was read, and referred to the Committee on Expenditures in the Treasury Department.

969   HISTORY OF CONGRESS.   970

JANUARY, 1821.   *Lotteries in the District of Columbia.*   H. OF R.

An engrossed bill, entitled "An act authorizing the President of the United States to remove the land office in the district of Lawrence county, in the Territory of Arkansas," was read the third time, and passed.

A message from the Senate informed the House that the Senate have passed bills of the following titles, to wit: "An act for the relief of John Coffee;" "An act explanatory of an act for the relief of James Leander Cathcart," passed May 15th, in the year 1820; and "An act for the relief of Nicholas Perkins;" in which bills they ask the concurrence of this House.

The House resolved itself into a Committee of the whole House on the bill from the Senate, entitled "An act for the relief of Morgan Brown;" and, after some time spent therein, the Committee rose, and had leave to sit again.

The House resolved itself into a Committee of the Whole on the report of the Committee of Claims on the petition of Charles Townsend and Jonas Williams; and, after some time spent therein, Mr. SPEAKER resumed the chair, and Mr. HILL reported the resolution submitted in the said report, with an amendment, to wit: strike out the word *not* before the word *allowed*, so as to make the resolution read, "*Resolved*, That the claim of Charles Townsend and Jonas Williams, of Buffalo, in the State of New York, ought to be allowed."

And on the question to concur with the Committee of the Whole in the said amendment, it was determined in the negative.

The resolution submitted in the said report was then concurred in by the House as follows:

Resolved, That the claim of Charles Townsend and Jonas Williams, of Buffalo, in the State of New York, ought not to be allowed.

The House resolved itself into a Committee of the Whole on the bill to establish the district of Pearl river; which was reported without amendment, and ordered to be engrossed, and read a third time to-morrow.

The House resolved itself into a Committee of the Whole on the bill to regulate the entry of merchandise imported into the United States from any adjacent territory. The bill was reported without amendment, and ordered to be engrossed, and read a third time to-morrow.

The House resolved itself into a Committee of the Whole on the bill for the relief of John Webster; which was reported without amendment, and ordered to be engrossed, and read a third time to-morrow.

The House resolved itself into a Committee of the Whole on the bill for the relief of sundry citizens of Baltimore; which was read and concurred in by the House, and the bill was ordered to be engrossed, and read a third time to-morrow.

Bills from the Senate of the following titles, to wit: "An act for the relief of John Coffee;" "An act explanatory of the act for the relief of James Leander Cathcart," passed May 15th, in the year 1820; and "An act for the relief of Jacob Perkins;" were severally read the first time.

A message from the Senate informed the House that the Senate have passed a bill, entitled "An act for the relief of Nathan Ford," in which they ask the concurrence of this House.

DISTRICT LOTTERIES.

Mr. MERCER, from the Committee for the District of Columbia, who were instructed, on the 8th instant, to make certain inquiries respecting the lotteries authorized by the act of the 15th of May, 1820, entitled "An act to incorporate the inhabitants of the City of Washington, and to repeal all acts heretofore passed for that purpose," made a report; which was read, and referred to the Committee on the Judiciary. The report is as follows:

The Committee on the District of Columbia, to whom was referred a resolution of the House of Representatives, instructing them to "inquire into and report to the House the number of lotteries which have been instituted in the District, by virtue of an act which passed the 15th of May 1820, 'to incorporate the inhabitants of the City of Washington, and to repeal all acts heretofore passed for that purpose;' the objects for which the moneys are to be raised; the amount of each scheme, and the total nominal value of the tickets offered for sale; the rate of reduction proposed to be made from the prizes; and the gross amount of the proceeds of the said lotteries, which will come into the hands of the managers; and, also, whether the condition of the said act of incorporation has been complied with, so far as it respects the authority to raise money by lotteries;" have, accordingly, had the said resolution under consideration, and respectfully report:

That, under the act of incorporation referred to in the said resolution, one lottery only has been authorized by the Corporation of the City of Washington; but the committee presuming it to have been the purpose of the resolution of the House of Representatives to ascertain how the power to raise money by lottery has been hitherto exerted by the Corporation, have extended their inquiry to the lotteries authorized by an amendment of the former charter of the Corporation.

The terms of that amendment which, as far back as the 6th of May, 1812, vested in the City Corporation the power of raising money by lottery, are, in substantial import, the same with those of the renewed charter, except that in the latter the duration of this power is limited to ten years. In both, it is subjected to the control of the President of the United States; and every resolution adopted by the Corporation, in pursuance of this power, has been subsequently approved by the President.

The first resolution of the Boards of Aldermen and Common Council of the City, in which its legislative power is vested by its charter, authorised the raising of ten thousand dollars by lottery, "for building, establishing, and endowing two public school-houses on the Lancasterian system," and received the approbation of Mr. Madison on the 23d of November, 1812.

Seven other resolutions, each giving power to raise by lottery a like amount, have emanated from the same authority since the above period; one of these resolutions having been approved in every subsequent year, except the year 1818, and the last on the 31st of October, 1820.

The three resolutions next following the first, add to the objects of public utility sought to be provided for by that resolution—a penitentiary and a city hall.

971   HISTORY OF CONGRESS.   972

H. of R.   *Lotteries in the District of Columbia.*   January, 1821.

In pursuance of these resolutions, the managers, in whom the Corporation vested the power of carrying their purpose into effect, have contracted, at different periods, for the drawing of five lotteries, or classes of a lottery. The first of these authorized the sale of tickets to the amount of one hundred and fifty thousand dollars; and for this the Corporation was, by the contract of the managers with the lottery agent, to receive ten thousand dollars; but the managers have stated to the committee that, owing to a misunderstanding between themselves and the agent for that class, they have, as yet, received no part of that sum.

From the second and third classes, authorizing the sale of a number of tickets of the value of $300,000, the managers have realized $20,000, being $10,000 for each class.

From the fourth class, which is now drawing, and the tickets of which amount in gross value to $210,000, the managers will have received in course of the ensuing month $6,666 67; and from the fifth class, the tickets of which are computed at $400,000, they expect to realize the further sum of $13,333 33, being in all $40,000, from the authority granted by the resolutions of eight years.

Copies of the schemes of these lotteries have been submitted to the committee by the Mayor of the city of Washington, through whom the preceding facts have been collected. In all of them the rate of reduction from the prizes is fifteen per centum.

The committee having reported all the facts called for by the resolution of the House of Representatives, are required to pronounce an opinion on the question, "whether the condition of the act of corporation of the city of Washington has been complied with, so far as it respects the authority to raise money by lotteries."

As this question is likely to be involved in a judicial inquiry, now pending in one or more of the courts of the United States, the committee hope to be excused by the House for forbearing to express any opinion on it. They have annexed to this report the original correspondence through which the preceding facts have been collected; together with a copy of one of the contracts between the managers, appointed by the city corporation, and the contractor for drawing one of the lotteries authorised by a resolution of the corporation; and such extracts from the old and new charters of the city of Washington as may serve to illustrate the nature and extent of the authority vested in the corporation to raise money by lottery; in relation to all which they respectfully submit the following resolution to the House of Representatives:

Resolved, That it is inexpedient for the House of Representatives to express any opinion on the question, whether the condition of the act of incorporation of the city of Washington has been complied with by the corporation, so far as regards the authority to raise money by lottery.

Washington, Mayor's Office,
January 16, 1821.

Sir: Your note of the 12th instant has been received, enclosing a resolution passed by the House of Representatives of the United States on the subject of the city lotteries. I am now collecting the information you may require, and the moment it is obtained I shall transmit or wait on you with the same.

I have, &c.   S. N. SMALLWOOD.
Hon. Charles F. Mercer,

Washington, Mayor's Office,
January 16, 1821.

Sir: In compliance with your note of the 12th instant, submitting to me a resolution of the House of Representatives of the 8th instant, relative to the city lotteries heretofore authorized by Congress, I transmit letters, with other documents, from the register of this city and the president of the board of managers of said lotteries, which contain the information desired. As to the purposes for which the moneys are to be raised, I reply, that a penitentiary, two Lancasterian school-houses, and a city hall, are to be built out of those funds. The latter has been commenced on a magnificent scale, and is progressing with great rapidity, and, if not impeded by the acts and proceedings of the different States, as it respects our lotteries, we shall, in a few years, accomplish these desirable objects, and thereby improve and embellish the metropolis of the Union to a considerable extent, which, in a national point of view, is the property of the nation; therefore, it is reasonable to conclude, for reasons obvious to us all, that it would be the pride and interest of every man in the country to aid the inhabitants of this city in beautifying and adorning the metropolis of their Union. I beg you will excuse this small digression from the subject of your call.

I have the honor to be, sir, &c.
     SAMUEL N. SMALLWOOD.
Hon. Charles F. Mercer,
     Chairman District Committee.

Washington, Register's Office,
January 15, 1821.

Sir: In compliance with your request, I herewith transmit to you a copy of the first resolution of the corporation authorising the raising of $10,000 by lottery; and an abstract of all the succeeding resolutions. First resolution:

Resolved by the Board of Aldermen and Board of Common Council of the City of Washington, That it is expedient to raise, by lottery, the sum of ten thousand dollars (clear of expenses) for the following object, to the accomplishment of which the ordinary funds of the city are inadequate, viz:

For building, establishing, and endowing two public school-houses on the Lancasterian system, (one in the eastern, and one in the western section of the city,) the sum of ten thousand dollars.

Resolved, That the Mayor be, and he is hereby, requested to present the foregoing resolution to the President of the United States, and respectfully solicit his approbation thereto.

Approved, November 23, 1812.
     JAMES MADISON.

Second resolution, authorizing the raising of ten thousand dollars for a penitentiary.
Approved, August 3, 1814.
     JAMES MADISON.

Third resolution, authorizing the raising of ten thousand dollars for a town-house or city hall.
Approved, May 10, 1815.
     JAMES MADISON.

Fourth resolution, authorizing the raising of ten thousand dollars for two public school-houses, a penitentiary, and a city hall.
Approved, April 20, 1816.
     JAMES MADISON.

973   HISTORY OF CONGRESS.   974

JANUARY, 1821.   *Lotteries in the District of Columbia.*   H. OF R.

Fifth resolution, authorizing the raising of ten thousand dollars for same.—Approved, April 5, 1817.
           JAMES MONROE.

Sixth resolution, authorizing the raising of ten thousand dollars for same.—Approved, Oct. 19, 1818.
           JAMES MONROE.

Seventh resolution, authorizing the raising of ten thousand dollars for same.—Approved, Oct. 29, 1819.
           JAMES MONROE.

Eighth resolution, authorizing the raising of ten thousand dollars for same.—Approved, Oct. 31, 1820.
           JAMES MONROE.

I am, respectfully, your obedient servant,
           WILLIAM HEWITT,

ROGER C. WEIGHTMAN, Esq.

Extracts from the old and new charters of the City of Washington, illustrative of its power to raise money by lottery.

That the said corporation shall have full power and authority to authorise, with the approbation of the President of the United States, the drawing of lotteries for the erection of bridges, and effecting any important improvements in the city which the ordinary revenue thereof will not accomplish, for the term of ten years: *Provided*, That the amount so authorized to be raised in each year shall not exceed the sum of ten thousand dollars, clear of expenses.

The said corporation shall also have power and authority to provide for the establishment and superintendence of public schools, and to endow the same; to establish and erect hospitals or pest-houses, watch and work-houses, houses of correction, penitentiary, and other public buildings, and to pass all laws which shall be deemed necessary and proper for carrying into execution the powers vested by this act in the said corporation or its officers. [Pamphlet copy, page 87 of the acts of the 1st session, 16th Congress.]

By an act to amend the charter of the city of Washington, which passed May 6, 1812, the corporation was vested with full power to authorize the drawing of lotteries, for effecting any important improvement in the city which the ordinary funds or revenue thereof will not accomplish: *Provided*, That the amount to be raised in each year shall not exceed the sum of ten thousand dollars: *And provided, also,* That the object for which the money is intended to be raised shall be first submitted to the President of the United States, and shall be approved of by him; and to pass all laws which shall be deemed necessary and proper for carrying into execution the foregoing powers; and all other powers vested in the corporation or any of its officers, either by this act or any former one. [Vol. 11, Laws of the United States, page 153.]

WASHINGTON, *January* 14, 1821.

SIR: I have this moment received your communication of this morning, enclosing a resolution of the House of Representatives, and a letter of the Chairman of the Committee on the District of Columbia, on the subject of the lotteries authorized by the charter of this city, and, by direction of the board of managers of the lotteries, have the honor to state that the corporation has, by authority of the late and present charter, authorized, up to this period, the raising by lottery of $80,000, for the erection of two Lancasterian school-houses, a penitentiary, and a city hall, as will more fully appear by the enclosed letter from the register of the city.

That the board of managers have, by authority of the resolutions of the corporation, contracted for five classes of lotteries; that the first class amounted, in gross, to $150,000, for which the managers were to receive $10,000, but that, owing to a misunderstanding between them and the contractor for that class, they have not, as yet, received a cent; that, from the second and third classes, amounting in gross to $300,000 each, the managers have realized $20,000, being $10,000 for each scheme; that, from the fourth class, now drawing, amounting in gross to $210,000, the managers have received, and will receive in the course of the month of February ensuing, $6,666 67; that, from the fifth class, amounting in gross to $400,000, the managers expect to realize $13,333 83; that 15 per cent. has been the uniform deduction from all prizes, as will appear by the enclosed schemes.

I am, sir, very respectfully, &c.

           R. C. WEIGHTMAN,
           President of the Managers.

SAMUEL N. SMALLWOOD, Esq., *Mayor.*

Scheme of first class national lottery.

1 prize of	$30,000	- is -	$30,000
1	do	20,000	- -	20,000
2	do	10,000	- are -	20,000
3	do	5,000	- -	15,000
5	do	1,000	- -	5,000
6	do	500	- -	3,000
20	do	100	- -	2,000
100	do	50	- -	5,000
2,000	do	25	- -	50,000

2,138 prizes. $150,000
3,862 blanks.

6,000 tickets at $25 is $150,000.
Subject to a deduction of 15 per cent.

Scheme of third class national lottery.

1 prize of	$50,000	- is -	$50,000
1	do	25,000	- -	25,000
1	do	10,000	- -	10,000
4	do	5,000	- are -	20,000
70	do	1,000	- -	70,000
50	do	100	- -	5,000
10,000	do	12	- -	120,000

10,127 prizes. $300,000
19,873 blanks.

30,000 tickets at $10 is $300,000.
Subject to a deduction of 15 per cent.

Scheme of fourth class national lottery.

1 prize of	$35,000	- is -	$35,000
1	do	10,000	- -	10,000
3	do	5,000	- are -	15,000
40	do	1,000	- -	40,000
10	do	500	- -,	5,000
50	do	100	- -	5,000
10,000	do	10	- -	100,000

10,105 prizes. $210,000
19,895 blanks.

30,000 tickets at $7 is $210,000.
Subject to a deduction of 15 per cent.

Contract for the fifth class of a lottery.

Memorandum of an agreement made this 7th day of October, 1820, between Roger C. Weightman, president of the board of managers of the lotteries authorized by a law of the corporation of the City of Washington, entitled "An act authorizing a lottery or lotteries in the City of Washington, for the purposes therein mentioned," by and with the advice and consent of a majority of the said managers, of the one part, and David Gillespie, of the city of New York, of the other part, viz:

The said Roger C. Weightman, as president, hath agreed to sell to the said David Gillespie the right and privilege of a lottery, for the purpose of raising $13,-393 33, clear of expenses, as authorized in and by the said act of the corporation of Washington, he conforming, in all respects, to the provisions and true intent and meaning of the said act; that the said David Gillespie shall not publish the scheme of the said lottery until the same shall be submitted to and approved by the said managers, or a majority of them, nor until he shall execute and deliver a bond to the said managers, with sufficient security, in the penal sum of $20,000, to be approved of by the said managers, or a majority of them, conditioned for the true and faithful discharge of his duty in selling the tickets, the payment of the prizes, and for conducting the said lottery fairly and honestly, according to the true intent and meaning of this agreement, and of the said law of the corporation of Washington; that the said David Gillespie is to be at the entire expense of the said lottery, and shall, before the commencement of the drawing thereof, pay to the president of the said board of managers the sum of $13,333 33, being the full consideration for the said lottery to the said managers; that the said managers, or a committee of them, or such other person or persons as they may appoint, shall have the privilege at all times of examining into the state of the said lottery, which shall be drawn in the City of Washington, in the presence of at least three of the said managers, and shall be concluded within one year from the commencement of the drawing, and the prizes paid within the time limited in the said act of the corporation; that the scheme of the said lottery shall not exceed, in the gross amount, the sum of $400,000.

And it is the understanding of the parties that the said David Gillespie shall have the refusal of the lotteries for raising the balance of the money authorized by the said act of the corporation of Washington, paying at the rate of $3,333 33 for every $100,000 of the gross amount.

In witness whereof, the said parties have hereto subscribed their names, the day and year first above written.

DAVID GILLESPIE,
R. C. WEIGHTMAN,
President.

BALANCES OF APPROPRIATIONS.

The House proceeded to consider the bill authorizing the Secretary of the Treasury to transfer certain balances of appropriations to the surplus fund; and the amendment reported thereto yesterday by the Committee of Ways and Means was read, and agreed to, as follows:

SEC. 2. *And be it further enacted,* That, in the settlement of the accounts of the Navy Department for services or supplies accruing prior to the first day of July, eighteen hundred and seventeen, the expenditures shall be charged to arrearages; and that the unexpended balances of any appropriations made for the naval service prior to that time may be applied to the payment of such expenditures without regard to the particular object for which such appropriations were made.

Mr. MEIGS moved further to amend the bill by striking out these words: " Of the moneys appropriated for the payment of the interest, and redemption of the principal of the public debt, one million five hundred and ninety thousand seven hundred and forty-five dollars and seventy cents ;" so as to exempt this sum from being carried to the surplus fund.

And, the question being taken so to amend, it was determined in the negative. And the bill was ordered to be engrossed and read a third time to-morrow.

The House adjourned to Monday.

MONDAY, January 29.

Mr. WENDOVER presented a memorial of the Chamber of Commerce of the city of New York, remonstrating against a proclamation of the Supreme Director of the Republic of Chili, dated the 20th of August last, declaring in a state of rigorous blockade all the ports and anchorages of South America, from Iquiqui to Guayaquil inclusive, embracing a range of coast more extensive than the whole Atlantic frontier of the United States, and praying that the naval forces of the United States, in the Pacific ocean, may be so augmented as to afford efficient protection to the commerce of the United States in that sea; which memorial was referred to the Committee on Foreign Affairs.

Mr. RHEA reported a bill to authorize the payment of certain certificates ; which was read twice, and committed to the Committee of the Whole, to which is committed the bill for the relief of John Crute.

Mr. WHITMAN, from the committee appointed on the 11th instant, reported a bill to continue in force an act, entitled "An act regulating the currency within the United States of the gold coins of Great Britain, France, Portugal, and Spain," passed on the 29th day of April, 1816, so far as the same relates to the crowns and five franc pieces of France ; which was read twice, and committed to a Committee of the Whole.

The SPEAKER laid before the House a letter from the Secretary of the Treasury, in reply to a resolution of the House of the 11th instant, respecting the inspectors, weighers, gaugers, and measurers, employed in the custom-houses of the United States within the last five years, and accompanied with a statement of the names of the persons employed as agents for building and supplying lighthouses, revenue cutters, and marine hospitals, for the last five years, with the moneys paid to each ; which letter and statement were referred to the Committee of Commerce.

Mr. FLOYD submitted the following resolution, which was read, and ordered to lie on the table one day for consideration:

Resolved, That the Secretary of the Department of War be required to inform this House how many factors, or trading-houses, are now established in the United States, and territories thereof; the date of the establishment of each; the points at which they are located; the number of persons attached to each; the number of troops, if any, and other military protection allowed to each; likewise a detailed statement of the business done at each house for ten years last past, showing the amount of goods sent to each station annually; the expense of transportation there; the amount sold, and the receipts at each house, distinguishing between cash and peltries, and the expense of transporting them to Washington City; the price at which peltries have been sold at Georgetown, in the District of Columbia; the expense of keeping up each trading-house, distinguishing between the salary of the factors and their assistants; the contingencies and the military protection; with a list of the Indians civilized and converted to the Christian faith by the operation of the factory system, from its establishment in 1796, up to this day; together with a statement of the entire amount of money drawn from the Treasury on account of the factory system, from its commencement until this time.

On motion of Mr. WILLIAMS, of North Carolina, the Committee on Military Affairs were instructed to inquire whether there be any tracts or parcels of land belonging to the United States, and now or heretofore used as sites for forts, garrisons, or camps, and which are no longer necessary for such purposes, and may be sold without injury to the public service.

The bill from the Senate, entitled "An act for the relief of Nathan Ford," was read twice, and referred to the Committee of Claims.

Bills from the Senate of the following titles, to wit: "An act for the relief of Nicholas Perkins;" "An act explanatory of an act for the relief of James Leander Cathcart," passed May the 15th, in the year 1820; and "An act for the relief of John Coffee;" were severally read the second time, and referred, the first to the Committee on Private Land Claims, the second to the Committee of Claims, and the third to the Committee on the Public Lands.

Engrossed bills of the following titles, to wit: "An act to establish the district of Pearl river;" "An act for the relief of John Webster;" and "An act to regulate the entry of merchandise imported into the United States from any adjacent territory;" were severally read the third time, and passed.

Mr. BARBOUR, from the Committee on Naval Affairs, reported a bill authorizing a machine to be built for hauling up ships; which was read twice, and committed to the Committee of the Whole on the state of the Union.

An engrossed bill, authorizing the Secretary of the Treasury to transfer certain balances of appropriations to the surplus fund, was read the third time; and, being on its passage, on motion of Mr. LOWNDES, it was recommitted to the Committee of Ways and Means.

An act for the relief of sundry persons in Baltimore (for the detention of the ships sunk during the late war for defence) was read a third time.

Mr. WILLIAMS, of North Carolina, moved to recommit the bill to the Committee of Claims, on the ground that it proposed to go too far in allowing for the whole time the vessels remained sunk, instead of such a time as might have been necessary to raise and repair them.

On request of Mr. SMITH, of Maryland, the motion was so varied by Mr. WILLIAMS as to embrace a reference to a Committee of the Whole, instead of the Committee of Claims, and was then agreed to.

SEAMEN—UNITED STATES NAVY.

Mr. BARBOUR, from the Committee on Naval Affairs, who were instructed, on the 11th instant, to inquire into the expediency of limiting by law the number of seamen, ordinary seamen, and boys, to be annually employed in the service of the United States, and also into the expediency of reducing the number now actually in service, made a report thereon; which was read, and committed to the Committee of the whole House on the state of the Union. The report is as follows:

That, by an act of Congress, approved the third of March, 1801, a Naval Peace Establishment was fixed by law, providing the number of ships which should be kept in constant service, in time of peace, and that the residue should be laid up in ordinary, with a sailing-master, certain petty officers, seamen, and marines, attached to each vessel thus laid up; authorizing the President to officer and man the vessels to be retained in actual service, as he might direct, limiting him, however, to two-thirds of the then present complement of seamen and ordinary seamen, (by which the committee understand the two-thirds of the then full crews of the ships retained,) limiting the number of captains, lieutenants, and midshipmen, to be retained in the navy service in time of peace, and authorizing the President to discharge all the other officers in the navy service of the United States. That, by another act of Congress, approved April 21st, 1806, the President was authorized to keep in actual service, in time of peace, as many of the frigates and other armed vessels of the United States, as, in his judgment, the nature of the service might require, and to cause the residue to be laid up in ordinary in convenient ports; and the President was authorized to officer and man the public armed vessels in actual service in time of peace as he might direct; but the act just referred to limited the number of captains, masters commandant, lieutenants, and midshipmen; it limited, too, the number of able seamen, ordinary seamen, and boys, to nine hundred and twenty-five, and authorized the President to appoint, for the vessels in actual service, as many officers of the grades therein mentioned as might, in his opinion, be necessary and proper. That, by another act, approved March third, 1807, the President was authorized, in addition to the then present Naval Peace Establishment, to employ a number of able seamen, ordinary seamen, and boys, not exceeding five hundred, should the exigency of the public service require it. That, by another act, approved January 31st, 1809, it was provided that, in addition to the frigates then employed in actual service, there should be fitted out, officered, and manned, four other frigates by name; and that the President might equip, man, and employ, in actual service, as many of the public armed vessels, then laid up in ordinary, and gunboats, as, in his judgment, the public service might require ; and, for the purpose of carrying the provisions of the said act into effect, the President was authorized, in addition to the number of petty officers, able seamen, ordinary seamen, and boys, then authorized by law, to appoint, and cause to be employed, three hundred midshipmen, three thousand six hundred able seamen, ordinary seamen, and boys, to be engaged to serve for a period not exceeding two years, but subject to be sooner discharged. That, by another act, passed June 28th, 1809, the President was authorized, in the event of a favorable change in the foreign relations of the country, to cause to be discharged from actual service, and laid up in ordinary, such of the frigates and public armed vessels as, in his judgment, a due regard to the public security and interest would permit. That, by another act of Congress, passed March 30th, 1812, the President was authorized to cause to be immediately repaired, equipped, and put into actual service, three frigates by name ; and it was provided, that the officers and seamen of the navy might be increased so far as was necessary to officer, man, and equip the vessels so to be put into service. That, by another act of Congress, passed January 2, 1813, it was provided, that the President should cause to be built, equipped, and employed, four ships, to rate not less than seventy-four guns, and six to rate forty-four guns each ; and the number of commissioned and warrant officers, petty officers, able seamen, ordinary seamen, and boys, to be employed on board each of the said ships of seventy-four guns, was fixed by the act ; the crew, so far as it consisted of seamen and boys, was limited to two hundred able seamen, and three hundred ordinary seamen and boys. That, by another act, passed March 3d, 1813, the President was authorized to have built, manned, equipped, and commissioned, for service, six sloops of war, and, also, to have built or procured, as many sloops, to be employed on the lakes, as the public service might require ; and, by the second section of the last mentioned act, the President was authorized to appoint such officers, and to employ such number of seamen, as might be necessary for such vessels as were authorized by law to be put in commission, any law to the contrary notwithstanding.

The committee have thought it proper to give to the House a brief view of the progress of legislation in relation to this subject, and they believe the foregoing sketch substantially to present it. Upon a reference to the various acts of Congress before referred to, it will be found that, both in the years 1801 and 1806, there was a Naval Peace Establishment fixed by law, limiting not only the number of seamen and boys, but of officers also. It will be found, too, as your committee believe, by reference to dates compared with the history of the country, and indeed to the language of some of the acts of Congress themselves, that the subsequent provisions, in relation to the Naval Establishment of the United States, had reference directly to what either then was or probably soon would be, the relation of the country to foreign Governments ; in short, that they looked directly to a state either of actual or probable war.

Your committee understand the resolution referred to them to relate to the number of seamen and boys necessary to be employed in time of peace, and whether that shall be fixed by law. In the present state of things the only limitation upon the number of seamen is to be found in the appropriation bill, which, in effect, annually limits the number to be employed by the amount of the appropriation annually made for that object. Your committee believe, that the proper office of the appropriation bill, is, as far as practicable, to provide means for objects authorized by existing laws ; there are indeed, cases which, on account of the contingent or uncertain character of the expenditure, constitute exceptions to this rule ; but, in general, the rule is considered as a sound one.

Your committee would further remark that, in investigating this subject, they have extended their inquiries beyond the mere scope of the resolution, into the propriety of fixing a Naval Peace Establishment, embracing as well the number of officers as ships to be kept in the service of the United States in time of peace ; and they beg leave shortly to submit some of their reasons for thinking that there should be a Peace Establishment in the Navy as well as the Army. Although, by the Constitution of the United States, the President is commander-in-chief of the Army and Navy, yet it belongs to Congress to "raise and support" the one, and "to provide and maintain" the other ; the power to provide and maintain implies that of determining the quantum ; a question, the decision of which ought not to be left, in the opinion of your committee, to the Executive Department, and yet, in practice, it is in effect left to Executive decision ; for, as has been before remarked, there being no permanent law in force limiting the number of officers, ships, or men, to be kept in service, the only limitation is in the amount of appropriation ; and your committee believe that in practice the amount of the estimates has generally been appropriated, without any discussion in Congress as to the necessity of them. Whatever confidence we may have in the Executive, it seems not to be right, in principle, to leave to its discretion, in effect, the decision of a question which belongs to the Legislature.

Your committee believe that in Great Britain, though the number of seamen is not fixed by a permanent law, yet it is settled by the annual vote of Parliament. If there were probable danger of war, or difficulty in our foreign relations, it might not be expedient to fix the number of seamen by a permanent law, but, in the present circumstances of the country, it seems to your committee it may be done. It will be remembered it is a Peace Establishment which is contemplated ; when war shall come, or even upon its probable approach, both the Army and Navy will doubtless be placed upon a footing suited to the then altered state of the country.

Your committee would further remark, that an additional reason with them for inclining to a Peace Establishment is to fix the number of officers who, they believe, in many grades, are too numerous, and yet for all whom, unless their number shall be reduced by law, an appropriation must be made.

Your committee are aware that this is a difficult and delicate subject ; the officers of the Navy in the recent war not only distinguished themselves, but, by breaking the charm of invincibility belonging to the British Navy, contributed much both to our glory and our solid strength as a nation. The committee are also aware that many of them have devoted some of their best years to their profession ; yet, if the interest of the country requires a reduction, painful as the duty is, it is one which ought to be performed. In relation to the number of ships to be retained in service, the reasons which would prove the propriety of fixing the number of seamen, would apply with full force to them; indeed, it is another state of the same question, in substance, since, if the number of seamen be fixed, no more vessels will be employed than they can man; and the fixing a certain maximum of seamen is considered a more judicious course than to fix the number of ships, inasmuch as the President will then be left at liberty to use such classes of vessels as may, in his opinion, be best adapted to the nature of the service; the aggregate of the guns, however, being limited by the number of men allowed to man them.

Your committee have said, that they consider the officers of many of the grades as too numerous; they will now proceed to state the grounds of their opinion. They have not for a moment entertained the idea of paring down the officers of the Navy to any thing like a mere sufficiency to officer the ships to be actually retained in service in time of peace; it is obviously impossible, upon this subject, to select any given number, and show that it is precisely the right one; some reasonable rule must be adopted.

Your committee have acted upon the principle that, whilst, on the one hand, the mere number of officers necessary for the vessels in actual service is not sufficient, with a view to the future progress and prosperity of the Navy, on the other, it would be entirely out of the question to employ, in time of peace, as many as would officer our whole Navy, built and to be built, in time of war. They have, therefore, selected what they consider a medium between these extremes; it appears, by the Naval Register of 1821, that the total number of guns of our ships, which are built, equipped, and launched, (which description includes the three line-of-battle ships Ohio, North Carolina, and Delaware, which are believed not to be equipped,) amounts to seven hundred and ninety-seven, of all classes of vessels, gunboats included.

Your committee have thought that, if we retained in service in time of peace a sufficient number of commissioned and warrant officers to officer all those upon the War Establishment, it would afford a liberal Peace Establishment. Bringing the number of officers to this standard, the committee find that there are various ranks in which the present number considerably exceeds that which would be required by the rule just stated; they will descend to particulars in a few grades, in which the excess is relatively most considerable; thus, upon this scale, there is an excess of fifteen post captains; of twenty masters commandant; of seventy lieutenants; of twenty-seven surgeons; of more than forty sailing-masters. There are, perhaps, two or three grades in which an allowance of a few more than even this scale would produce, might be judicious; amongst them, probably, might be placed the midshipmen, who may be considered as constituting the nursery of the future commanders of our ships; this, however, would only vary the result in an inconsiderable degree. The committee forbear to go into further detail upon this subject, because, if the House should adopt the principle, the detail could be presented in a bill.

As to the seamen, if it should be decided to fix the number by law, the resolution then directs the committee to inquire into the expediency of reducing the number now in actual service. Upon this subject the committee would remark, that it will be seen, by adverting to a letter from the Navy Department, under date of the 11th December, 1820, amongst the printed documents, that the whole force of the vessels of war in the actual service of the United States amounts to about three hundred and thirty-five guns, distributed as is mentioned in the same letter. Your committee incline to the opinion, that the following diminution of that force may be made without injury to the public service, viz: instead of corvettes and a sloop on the coast of Africa, whose object is the suppression of piracy and the slave trade, three of the schooners authorized by the act of the last session would be sufficient, making a deduction of 34 guns; instead of a 36 gun frigate in the Indian Seas, the corvette Cyane of 28 would be sufficient, making a deduction of eight. If to these deductions be added the force of the Macedonian and Ontario, of which the one is returning after being replaced by the Constellation, and the other is proceeding to take the place of the Peacock, amounting together to 54 guns, the whole force which would remain after these deductions from that now in service, would be 239 guns; but suppose an additional number of 36 guns to be included for any contingent service, such, for example, as the replacing of a vessel returning from a cruise, then the whole force which, according to the views before presented, would be necessary, would be 275 guns: to man this force upon a War Establishment, if the committee have not erred in calculation, would require 856 able seamen, 802 ordinary seamen, and 195 boys; to this add, according to a document of the last session, for the ships in ordinary, navy yards, and navy stations, 287 able seamen, 314 ordinary seamen, and 67 boys; and the aggregate is of able seamen 1,143, of ordinary seamen 1,116, and of boys 262; total of able seamen, ordinary seamen, and boys, 2,521. The estimate from the Navy Department for the service of the year 1821, embraces 1,332 able seamen, 1,307 ordinary seamen, and 293 boys; making an aggregate of 2,932; from which it would seem that, if the force suggested by the committee be retained in service, there might be a reduction of about 411, viz: 187 able seamen, 191 ordinary seamen, and 31 boys.

Upon the whole view of the subject, the committee beg leave to recommend to the House the following resolution:

Resolved, That a Naval Peace Establishment ought to be fixed by law.

MISSOURI.

On motion of Mr. CLAY, the House resolved itself into a Committee of the Whole on the state of the Union; and the resolution from the Senate, for admitting Missouri into the Union, with a *caveat* against the provision, if there be any, which conflicts with the Constitution of the United States, was taken up.

Mr. RANDOLPH moved to strike out the proviso (or *caveat*) from the resolution, but waived his motion for the present, to accommodate Mr. CLAY, who wished to address the Committee on the whole subject.

Mr. CLAY then delivered his sentiments at large on the present state of this question. He was in favor of the resolution from the Senate, and should vote for the resolution, even though more emphatically restricted against any supposed repugnance of one of its provisions to a provision of the Constitution of the United States, the existence of which however, he did not by any means admit.

When Mr. CLAY had concluded—

Mr. RANDOLPH renewed his motion to strike

983   HISTORY OF CONGRESS.   984

H. of R.   *Proceedings.*   JANUARY, 1821.

out the proviso, and spoke for about fifteen minutes in support of it.

Mr. LOWNDES deprecated the motion, as going to present to the House the naked question which it had already decided in the negative, and as preventing a decision upon the proposition as it now stands.

Mr. BARBOUR assigned the reasons why he should vote against the motion; himself regarding the proviso as useless and unnecessary, but willing to retain it to gratify gentlemen who were of a different opinion.

Mr. SERGEANT inquired whether it would be in order, this proviso being stricken out, to move to introduce a different one.

The CHAIRMAN decided that it would.

The question was then taken on striking out the proviso, and decided in the negative, 82 to 54. So the proviso was retained.

Mr. STEVENS assigned the reasons why he should vote against the resolution.

Mr. FOOT moved to amend the resolution by adding to it another proviso, that it be taken as a fundamental condition on which said State is admitted into the Union, that so much of the constitution as requires the Legislature to pass laws to prevent the migration of the free people of color thither, shall be expunged from the constitution of the State within two years from this time, in the mode prescribed for amending the constitution. [This would admit Missouri into the Union forthwith, on the condition stated.]

Mr. FOOT observed, that he could not consent that the question be taken on this resolution, with a certain prospect of its rejection, without making one effort for an amicable settlement of this distracting question. I have, therefore, said he, risen for the purpose of offering an amendment to the resolution—not with the vain hope that this particular amendment will be adopted, but with a sincere desire (if I know my own heart) to afford to gentlemen an opportunity of proposing such modifications of the amendment as will unite the votes of a majority of this Committee, who appear to be desirous of admitting Missouri into the Union upon terms which will not compromit principle.

It is due from me, and the Committee will expect, a candid and plain statement of my views of the effect which will be produced by its adoption. The majority of this House have already decided that the constitution of Missouri does not contain a provision which, in their opinion, is repugnant to the Constitution of the United States. It has not been proposed by any gentleman to revive the question of restriction, so much agitated at the last session; and it may be presumed no such intention exists. This amendment proposes the admission of Missouri into the Union upon a certain conditions. The act for the admission of Louisiana into the Union, furnishes a precedent for the course now proposed. The condition proposes that Missouri shall expunge the offensive article from her constitution, in the manner provided by her constitution for its amendment, and give sufficient time for the amendment, without the trouble and expense of calling a convention for the purpose.

Mr. BALDWIN having expressed his intention to vote for this proposition—

Mr. CLAY moved to amend the amendment by adding words to this effect : " so far as the same ' (the clause of the Missouri constitution) tends to ' deprive citizens of each State of the privileges ' and immunities of citizens of the several States." This motion, however, he subsequently withdrew.

It being suggested, that other gentlemen had amendments which they wished to propose, and that it would be well to have them all presented to-day, so as to be examined and compared—

Mr. SERGEANT rose, as it might be supposed, from the question he had put, that he had an amendment to offer, to say that he had not; that he should vote for every amendment which should bring the resolution nearer to what he wished, but with a clear determination, for which he would hereafter assign his reasons, to vote against the resolution, however amended.

Soon after this, the Committee rose, without coming to any decision; and the House adjourned.

TUESDAY, January 30.

Mr. SMITH, of Maryland, from the Committee of Ways and Means, reported a bill to authorize the collectors of the customs to pay debentures issued on the exportation of loaf sugar, and spirits distilled from molasses; which was read twice, and committed to a Committee of the Whole.

Mr. MERCER, from the Committee on the District of Columbia, to which was recommitted the bill reported on the 6th of May last, to repeal, in part, "An act to authorize the President and Managers of the Washington Turnpike Road Company of the State of Maryland to extend and make their turnpike road to, or from Georgetown, in the District of Columbia, through the said District to the line thereof;" made a report thereon, recommending that the said bill be rejected, which report was read.

Whereupon, the question was taken, Shall the said bill be engrossed, and read a third time? and determined in the negative. And so the bill was rejected.

Mr. ANDERSON, from the Committee on the Public Lands, to whom was referred, on the 4th instant, the petition of the Mayor and Aldermen of the city of Mobile, reported a bill granting certain lots to the said Mayor and Aldermen; which was read twice, and committed to a Committee of the Whole.

Mr. NEWTON, from the Committee on Commerce, reported a bill to authorize the President of the United States to designate a place for a port of entry in the district of Miami, Michigan Territory; which was twice read.

Mr. SLOAN moved to refer the bill to a Committee of the whole House to-morrow; which being rejected, it was ordered to lie on the table.

Mr. WOOD, from the Committee on the Public Buildings, made a detailed report upon the subject of the appropriations and expenditures upon the said buildings during the last year, accompanied with a bill making further appropriations for the same; which bill was twice read, and committed to a Committee of the Whole.

A message from the Senate informed the House that the Senate have passed bills of the following titles, to wit; "An act for the relief of the representatives of Patience Gordon, widow, deceased;" an act supplementary to an act passed the 11th of May, 1820, entitled "An act to provide for the publication of the laws of the United States, and for other purposes;" in which they ask the concurrence of this House.

On motion of Mr. FLOYD, the House proceeded to consider the resolution, yesterday submitted by him, calling for certain information in regard to the Indian Trading Establishments, &c.

After some remarks from Mr. McLEAN, of Kentucky, and Mr. SOUTHARD, in opposition to this resolution, on the ground that some of the information would be impracticable to obtain, and that, of what was practicable, the material part was already before the House; and some observations from Mr. FLOYD, sustaining his motion, on the ground of the necessity of full and accurate information to correct legislation on the subject of our relations with the Indian tribes—

The question was taken on agreeing to the resolution of Mr. FLOYD, and decided in the negative—63 votes to 55.

On motion of Mr. SLOAN, the Committee on the Public Lands were instructed to inquire into the expediency of granting to the Connecticut reserve, in the State of Ohio, so much of the lands belonging to the United States in said State, for the use of schools, as may, with the grants heretofore made, be equal to that allowed to other parts of said State.

Mr. HERRICK submitted for consideration the following resolution, which was read, and ordered to lie on the table one day:

Resolved, That the President of the United States be requested to cause to be reported to this House, whether any, and, if any, what, progress has been made by the commissioners appointed under the act of last session, for the purpose of surveying, marking, and locating a road from Wheeling, in Virginia, to the left bank of the Mississippi river, through the States of Ohio, Indiana, and Illinois.

Bills from the Senate of the following titles, to wit: "An act for the relief of the representatives of Patience Gordon, widow, deceased;" and "An act supplementary to an act passed on the 11th of May, 1820, entitled 'An act to provide for the publication of the laws of the United States, and for other purposes;" were severally read the first time.

The bill for the relief of Rosalie P. Deslonde; the bill for the relief of William T. Nimmo; the bill for the relief of Denis P. De La Ronde, passed through a Committee of the Whole, and were ordered to be engrossed for a third reading.

The SPEAKER laid before the House a report from the Comptroller of the Treasury, in obedience to the resolution instructing him to report whether, in the statement of balances which have been due more than three years, which accompanied his letter of the 27th of November last, there have been made the discriminations and suggestions required by the fourteenth section of the act to provide for the prompt settlement of public accounts; which report was ordered to lie on the table.

The SPEAKER also laid before the House a letter from the Secretary of the Treasury, transmitting a statement of the funds applicable to the payment of the stock created by the act for the indemnification of certain claimants of public lands in the Mississippi Territory, passed the 31st March, 1814; which letter and statement were referred to the Committee of Ways and Means.

MISSOURI.

The House having then again resolved itself into a Committee of the Whole on the state of the Union, the resolution from the Senate, for the admission of Missouri into the Union, was resumed—the motion of Mr. FOOT being under consideration; which motion is to strike out the proviso to the Senate's resolution, and in lieu thereof to insert the following:

Provided, That it shall be taken as a fundamental condition, upon which the said State is incorporated in the Union, that so much of the 26th section of the 3d article of the constitution which has been submitted to Congress, as declares it shall be the duty of the General Assembly "to prevent free negroes and mulattoes from coming to, or settling in, this State, under any pretext whatsoever," shall be expunged, within two years from the passage of this resolution, by the General Assembly of Missouri, in the manner prescribed for amending said constitution.

Mr. BUTLER, of New Hampshire, spoke as follows:

I do not rise, Mr. Chairman, said Mr. B., to revive the discussion of the question of restriction, as it has been called, which was very elaborately argued and determined at the last session, nor for the purpose of provoking further debate upon the several questions, relative to the admission of Missouri into the Union, which have been thoroughly investigated during the present session. I am aware, sir, that the patience of the House, and I fear the patience of the people we represent, is much fatigued, if not exhausted, by the numerous editions of the same arguments which have been delivered upon the subject now under consideration. But, sir, as the subject comes from the Senate in a new shape, and as I seldom trouble the House on any occasion, I shall be permitted briefly to assign the reasons which will govern my vote on this question before the Committee.

Sir, the resolution under consideration, if possible, is more exceptionable than that which was reported by a committee of the House, and rejected. Those who doubted whether any provision in the constitution of Missouri contravened the Federal Constitution, might support the former resolution, but cannot, I apprehend, agree to the resolution from the Senate now before the Committee; because it admits and avoids the very point or matter in controversy. Sir, if you pass this resolution, you proclaim to the world a disregard of the sacred obligations imposed by the Constitution of your country. The language of the resolution implies your right to examine and judge of the constitution of Missouri, and, also, that it is, or at least may be, repugnant to the Constitution of the United States, and waives the solemn obligation of supporting that sacred instrument.

Sir, if we must receive Missouri into the Union, under her present form of government, I hope we shall not, by the admission, convict ourselves of a breach of the Constitution, and fix the mark of the beast upon our foreheads. The guilt of sinning against the Constitution of our country is not concealed by the magical proviso in the resolution, nor does it obviate in any degree the objection, or remedy the evil of which you complain. By this mode of procedure, if the constitution of Missouri had been throughout repugnant to the Constitution of the Union, or, as the gentleman from Connecticut (Mr. Stevens) said, a perfect monarchy, you might admit Missouri into the Union, protesting against the form of her government, or so much as might be supposed anti-republican in its features. Sir, I protest against this mode of legislating, by exclusions of conclusions, as it has been called by some learned doctors in politics, whereby the rights of citizens may be sacrificed, and the Constitution of the Union suspended.

The gentleman from Kentucky (Mr. Clay) said, admitting the clause of the constitution of Missouri, respecting free negroes and mulattoes, to be incompatible with the Constitution of the United States, it could not be an objection to her admission into the Union; because the legistors of Missouri would be bound by an oath to support the Federal Constitution, which would be paramount to the oath to support their State constitution, and of course would never make any enactment pursuant to that clause. Besides, he said, if they did enact any law in pursuance of that clause in their constitution, it would be declared void by the courts of the United States. But, sir, though I admired the eloquence, the candor, and love of country, which that honorable gentleman exhibited in this discussion, I was not convinced by his argument.

The members of this House, as well as the legislators of Missouri, are under a sacred obligation to support the Constitution of the United States; and the act of Congress authorizing Missouri to form a constitution provides, in order to her admission into the Union, that her constitution shall be republican, and not repugnant to the Constitution of the United States. But, without this provision in the act, it is as much the duty of Congress to examine her form of government, and determine whether it is compatible with the Constitution of the Federal Government, as it is to consider the same question on the passage of any law. Congress is the proper tribunal to decide this question, and cannot absolve itself from this sacred obligation by leaving it to the courts of the United States. But, if it were in our power, I would not turn this question over to the Judiciary sooner than I would pass a law without inquiring whether it was within the Constitutional powers of Congress, and trust wholly to the courts. Sir, would you admit a new State under a constitution giving its

legislature power to regulate commerce with foreign nations, to raise armies and declare war, and trust to the judicial authority of the United States to vacate the laws which might grow out of such powers, and to keep the administration of such State government within the pale of your Federal Constitution?

If the judiciary could remedy all the evils which may grow out of the constitution of Missouri, I am not disposed to neglect my duty, and disregard the rights which are guarantied even to the black man. The rights of the colored citizens, and it has been demonstrated by my friend from Massachusetts (Mr. Eustis) that there are many such in the Northern States, are as sacred as those of the white citizens.

The gentleman from Kentucky, (Mr. Clay,) said, that a limitation or restriction upon the power of the Legislature of Missouri might be imposed, by adding to the resolution under consideration a provision, that no law should be enacted under the clause in question, to affect the rights of citizens of other States. But, sir, that gentleman must be aware that such a provision, though it be made a fundamental consideration of the admission, can have no force or effect against her will. No act of Congress can qualify or make void any article of her constitution after or at the time of her admission. Such a provision is no more than a naked proposition, which Missouri will be at liberty to accept or reject, and without her assent would be inoperative and futile.

Sir, though I am sincerely desirous to terminate the discussion, and settle the question at the present session, I cannot adopt such a provision, and trust to Missouri to expunge the offensive clause in her constitution.

The gentleman from Virginia (Mr. Barbour) said he was in favor of the proviso of the resolution from the Senate, though it was not only unnecessary but unmeaning. He was willing, if I understood him, to encumber the resolve of admission with as much surplusage, as gentlemen could hang upon it, if it would afford any relief to any scrupulous mind.

Sir, I cannot doubt that the clause in the constitution of Missouri, which requires the Legislature to pass laws to prevent free negroes and mulattoes from going to and settling in that State, is wholly incompatible with the Constitution of the United States, which gives the citizens of each State all the privileges and immunities of citizens of the several States, notwithstanding the construction given to that article by the gentleman from Kentucky, (Mr. Clay.) Had not that honorable gentleman represented this article in the Constitution of the United States as equivocal and uncertain, I should have supposed it beyond the art of logic or subtlety of metaphysics to mislead any one who read it, or to pervert its very obvious signification.

Sir, I consider this article one of the most important provisions in the Federal Constitution, and believe that no principle could be adopted by any of the State governments, which would more certainly defeat the great objects of the Confederation than that to which I have referred in the constitution of Missouri. The right, which every citizen of every State has of emigrating to and becoming a citizen of another State, is the bond of social intercourse and harmony among the several States. Without this privilege, each State would become a distinct nation of people, of peculiar habits, of separate interests, and singular character. Not only the laws, but the passions of the people of each State would soon be in martial array against one another. Without this right, of what avail is the power of Congress to regulate commerce among the several States and with the Indian tribes? In short, sir, without this right, trivial as it may seem to some gentlemen, how long would this boundless empire exist as a republic?

I will not trespass longer on the patience of the Committee, because I most ardently with that we may speedily terminate the present discussion. As I prefer the amendment proposed by the gentleman from Connecticut, to the resolution in its present form, I shall vote for it, reserving the privilege of voting against the resolution finally, if it should be thus amended. But, sir, if none of the amendments which have been suggested should succeed, I shall offer, if I have an opportunity, an amendment, which I hold in my hand, to come in after the word "that," following the enacting clause in the resolution, by striking out the residue of the resolution, and is in these words, viz:

"Whereas so much of the constitution formed by the people of Missouri, by virtue of an act of Congress passed March, 1820, as requires the Legislature thereof to pass such laws as may be necessary to prevent free negroes and mulattoes from coming to and settling in this State, under any pretext whatever, is repugnant to the Constitution of the United States, the people of Missouri be, and they hereby are, authorized to form a new constitution, or to alter the constitution which they have already formed, in such way and manner as they shall judge most proper, and submit the same to Congress, for their consideration, for the purpose of being admitted into the Union."

I am willing, sir, to admit Missouri into the Union when her constitution shall be conformed to the Constitution of the United States, and I cannot perceive any serious inconvenience which can arise to her by a delay until another session of Congress. It is the fault of the people of Missouri that their constitution was not made in conformity to the Constitution of the United States, and I shall, without any fear of the consequences which the gentleman from Kentucky seems to apprehend, vote against any proposition for the admission of that Territory as a member of the Union at the present session.

Some conversation passed between Mr. LOWNDES and Mr. FOOT, as to the mode of proceeding.

Mr. FOOT observed he was very glad the gentleman from South Carolina had disclaimed any intention of applying his remarks to him. He appealed to that gentleman, or any member of this House, to point out a single instance in which any proposition made by him was designed or calculated, either to embarrass any subject or involve

the House in difficulty, as suggested by the gentleman. He had uniformly opposed any attempt to effect an object by indirect legislation or by stratagem. He considered that the correct course in legislation was to meet every subject in an open, fair, and direct way, and he would never shrink from responsibility; and assured the gentleman his object in proposing the amendment to the resolution, in preference to making it a distinct proposition, was, that he considered this the most regular course which could be adopted, and, in his opinion, most likely to effect the object which seemed to be wished by a great majority of the House.

With these impressions he could not consent to withdraw the proposed amendment, nor for a moment abandon the hope that on this, as a basis, the propositions of gentlemen might, by affording an opportunity for a free interchange of opinions, eventuate in the adoption of some amendment to the resolution by a large majority of this House, by which Missouri might, during the present session, be admitted into the Union; and, as the difference between the two sides of the question seemed not insurmountable, since gentlemen had distinctly disclaimed any intention to revive the question of restriction, he could not but cherish the hope that confidence and harmony would soon be restored in the national councils and through the Union.

Mr. STORRS, after a few introductory remarks, moved an amendment to Mr. FOOT's amendment, which was, to strike out all of the latter, after the word "Union," in the third line, and in lieu thereof to insert the following:

And to be of perpetual obligation on the said State, (in faith whereof this resolution is passed by Congress,) that no law shall ever be enacted by the said State impairing or contravening the rights, privileges, or immunities, secured to citizens of other States, by the Constitution of the United States: *And provided, further,* That the Legislature acting under the constitution already adopted in Missouri as a State, shall, as a convention, (for which purpose the consent of Congress is hereby granted,) declare their assent by a public act to the said condition before the next session of Congress, and transmit to Congress an attested copy of such act, by the first day of the said session.

Mr. FLOYD, of Virginia, said, he rose for the purpose of protesting against these proceedings, and opposing his voice to the assumption of enormous powers by this House; powers so great that the oldest statesmen, a few little years ago, would have trembled to assert. You have made deep inroads into the Constitution, and if you now assume the power to legislate over a new State, I know not how soon you will exercise it over others; and I, as a Representative from an old State, can never consent to such usurpations.

I know there is a North and South side to this question; but gentlemen are mistaken if they imagine our anxiety to admit Missouri so great, that we are willing to trample all the rights of the States under foot to effectuate that object. Have not members from the North as much interest in admitting Missouri as we have? Have they not as much to hope from the continuance of this Union as we have? And ought they not to be as solicitous on all these points as ourselves? I have seen, with infinite pain, the different attitudes in which gentlemen have placed this subject, who seem not to believe that any limitations exist upon the powers of this National Government, as it is called, and no pause is seen in their exertions to give it the power of such, and law, history, and England, continually recurred to for confirmation. I wish it were possible for gentlemen of the present day to expunge from their memory the progress of European liberty and institutions, and take our own, unconnected as we find them. Then we would find a number of States, or separate, independent, and distinct nations, confederated for common safety and mutual protection, taught wisdom by the eternal feuds of Spain, England, France, and Germany, now consolidated into large empires. These States, before the Confederation, could make war or peace, raise armies, or build a navy; coin money, pass bankrupt laws, naturalize foreigners, or regulate commerce. Why can they not do it now? Informed by Europe, they knew jealousies would arise, and constant strife render armies in every nation necessary to their defence, which would endanger their liberties at home.

These States, then, in their sovereign and independent characters, were willing to enter into a compact, by which the power of making war and peace, and regulating commerce, possessed alike by all, should be transferred to a Congress of the States, to be exercised with uniformity, for their mutual benefit; thus avoiding the evils of superannuated and enslaved Europe. These two were the only powers ever intended to be granted by the States. All other powers conferred by the compact are necessary to carry these two into execution. But could it ever have been imagined by these independent nations, that they were granting any power but that which was necessary to act upon foreigners—in war, to defend the whole—in peace, to regulate the commerce of the whole?

The States have been satisfied that while they enjoyed the proud feeling of managing their own affairs in their own nation, by means of their assemblies, which ought to be the highest and most honorable stations known in this country, their agents here were superintending the military defences of them all, and regulating their commerce. Little could they have imagined that their agents would have erected this Congress of the States into a great National Government, and exercise, exclusively, all the power granted by the compact, but, also, by construction, exercise all that which was reserved to the States, and now even attempt to expunge a clause from their constitution.

The voice of the States has been raised against this assumption of power, and this abuse of the trust reposed in Congress, by the passage of a sedition act, and a bank. They have been told that "the subject would admit of a doubt." The next effort has been to construct roads and canals, and boldly plunge into the heart of the States. Complaint was answered by, "the subject would admit of a doubt." Then, if discontents manifest themselves, we are told that things called Kings or Emperors, beyond seas, (where some of our citizens are very fond of going, and always come back worse than they go, save that they learn all about etiquette,) will believe Republics cannot last long, or that men cannot govern themselves; and this is reason for submission.

The States have borne all these wrongs, and are not content. The great political necromancers abroad are persuading them that the power of this body is competent to prescribe conditions even to a State, and that she ought not to be permitted to admit such persons as she might choose should be taken into her territory, "let the consequences be what they may." Now, indeed, it is asserted that she does not possess the power to prohibit the entry of any who choose to go there. I must frankly own, sir, with this view of the subject, I am at a great loss to know what has become of the States. They once existed; they once had rights. Now, indeed, they have Legislatures, which, if this doctrine continue without the bayonet, will leave us the idea of something visible, but not tangible, and even that, I presume, will, in a short time, like the white lady of Avenel, vanish into moonshine.

Having prescribed conditions at the last session, says one gentleman, upon which Missouri should come into this Union, have we not, therefore, the power of looking into her constitution? This terrific power is derived, says he, from the simple expression in the Constitution of the United States which says, "New States may be admitted by Congress into this Union." The same gentleman has said, if we send Missouri back to form another constitution, when she comes here again she will have more respect for us. This will admit of no reply. That gentleman, as well as one from New York, thought the offensive clause in the constitution of Missouri would be abrogated by the Constitution of the United States, which was paramount; yet the one thought we ought to act upon it, because we had it before us; the other, to relieve the judges from an odious duty.

Sir, this is both kind and generous; but, for my own part, I have seen so many odious things since I have been in Congress that I am well inclined to permit the judges their share of this.

That gentleman asked, who it was but the poor, the friendless, and the ignorant, that suffered by this injustice and oppression? And why is it that men have been immortalized for opposing governments, but because they took upon themselves the burden of defending these miserable beings, too ignorant to do themselves justice? I had thought, sir, the champions of liberty, who have been venerated for their deeds, were those who established or affirmed the great principles of liberty, without reference to an individual. In this instance, however, I think it seems like going into a foreign land, and I am inclined to believe it is a good maxim to let every people pursue their own happiness in their own way. If we have power to admit a State, (for surely we can admit none else,) we may reject an application for admission. What then is the fact? That a State applied for admission into this Union, and was rejected. Is she not then a foreign State; or, at all events, a State not in this Union?

In vain, sir, is it to feel for the Constitution of the United States, when gentlemen, even in their arguments, admit it to be paramount to all State laws and constitutions. Has it not already destroyed some of the clauses in different constitutions of the States—North Carolina and Virginia, for example, which existed long before this was formed? And may it not do the same for Missouri? I, sir, will vote for any thing declaratory of the powers of Congress, which gentlemen's tender consciences may suggest; but, voting for expunging a clause in the constitution of a State, I will not agree. This would, in my opinion, be overthrowing, at one blow, the settled principles of this country, and I hope there is not yet a gentleman who would seek immortality by that road. Would any attempt to cause a State to allow greater privileges to their free negroes and mulattoes than the same States allow their own? By what rule is it a free negro of New York has more rights in Missouri than the native free negro of Missouri has, or that the same negro has even in New York? Do gentlemen think Missouri will tamely submit to be the subject of legislation, and have an article of her constitution expunged by Congress? If she will, I have mistaken the stuff of which she is composed, and, when convinced of that fact, I would think her unworthy of a place in this Union, and would adopt the opinion of some gentlemen in this House, that this republic ought not to extend beyond the Mississippi.

Who is there that ever believed negroes and mulattoes were ever parties to the compact? Who is there that believes they ever had any rights but such as the indulgence of the States permitted? Could not the States now seize their persons, and make them slaves? None will doubt. But, says one gentleman, they could buy land, and ought they not to be permitted to live upon it? Could not an Indian, or even a slave, buy land, and will not the same argument apply? I cannot believe, for a moment, that any reliance is placed upon such arguments as these. If gentlemen choose this course to free the judiciary from so odious a task, or because it is convenient being now before us, let me say, that it is usurping the powers of the judiciary, and overthrowing whole States.

I hear of immortality. There is a strange something in that word, which operates alike on all, from the plain Quaker to the proud laurel planted upon the rock of St. Helena. What is immortality? A word, a sound— it is no more! Who now enjoys Cæsar's fame and immortality? Is it Cæsar or the scavenger of Rome? Sir, it is anybody's, 'tis nobody's—'tis your's, 'tis mine, 'tis every one's—it is but a word.

But, sir, is there not another kind of immortality, or, as I would think, word, in the world? *Catiline!* I do not say this to alarm the feelings of any one here. I hope there are none such; but,

should ills and evils come upon this country, when they could be so easily avoided, I know not what qualifying term the future historian of this country will give to that word. Let us not be deceived. There is great danger in any measure which might, even by possibility, overthrow the peace of a community. Let us be solicitous to enjoy the distinguished respect of those about us, whilst alive, for the dead are all equally provided with plenty of immortality.

We are told it is proper to reject the applications of this State; and, if other steps are to be taken, it is time enough afterwards to consider them. This is the proper period to determine what should be done. Will you have another republic west of the Mississippi, or will you compel Missouri to return to her territorial condition? The one course is calculated to embody ideas of evils not less great, though more gradual in their approach; the other, all the horrors of revolution. Tell us, then, the course to be pursued. Surely, no gentleman is willing to take a step without distinctly seeing the consequences which are to flow from it, and be ready to meet them. Can the mind of any man picture to itself a community of Americans, born to liberty, with the rich inheritance and blessings of this Constitution, with an organized government, and arms in their hands, brought so low as to crouch to the injustice of a body possessing no power but to "admit them into this Union." Reject them if you will—let them remain a foreign Power, as they would be, if rejected. And let those who opposed the purchase of Louisiana now reflect, and draw consolation from the reflection, if they can, that their persevering hostility has at length divided this Union. Sir, I, for one, must deprecate the consequences; but it is time we know the worst; and no time better than the present. If the doctrine held by a member last session, that "the Constitution of the United States did not sanction slavery, but only forebore to meddle with it," is the ultimate end of these proceedings, we cannot too soon know it. Though I have great doubt whether all the enjoyment of pomp and place, in this imperial city, could compensate for the gnawing recollections that it had produced the ruin of the country—this is immortality!

Mr. COBB assigned the reasons why he could vote for neither of the amendments.

Mr. ROSS stated the reasons of his opposition to the resolution from the Senate in any shape it was likely to assume.

Mr. HARDIN, in an earnest desire to see the question settled, was willing to agree to both the amendments.

Mr. RHEA, after making some remarks, moved the Committee should rise, with a view to demanding the previous question, which would preclude all debate and amendment, and present to the House a naked and direct question on the resolution from the Senate.

Mr. CLAY earnestly opposed this course, as going to close the door on the spirit of accommodation.

The motion for the Committee to rise was negatived by a large majority.

Mr. CLAY, then, after an earnest appeal to all parts of the House to bring to the future discussion of this subject minds prepared to harmonize, and forever settle this distracting question to mutual satisfaction, and expressing his desire more fully to examine Mr. STORRS's proposition, to see whether he could bring his mind to assent to it, as he wished to do, moved that the Committee now rise, in order to have the several propositions for amendment printed.

This motion was agreed to.

Mr. CLAY then gave notice he should again call up the subject to-morrow.

Mr. LOWNDES wished it deferred until Friday next, to give more time.

Mr. CLAY said he would compromise with his friend for Thursday. He did not like the idea of taking up this question on Friday.

Mr. COBB said that he proposed, at a future day, to offer the following amendment, which he now read, to follow the word " Union:"

" That the Legislature of the State of Missouri shall pass no law impairing the privileges and immunities secured to the citizens of each State, under the first clause of the second section of the fourth article of the Constitution of the United States."

This amendment was ordered to be printed, as well as the others.

WEDNESDAY, January 31.

Mr. MACLAY, from the Committee on Pensions and Revolutionary Claims, reported a bill for the relief of the legal representatives of John Guthry, deceased; which was read twice, and committed to a Committee of the Whole.

Mr. WILLIAMS, of North Carolina, from the Committee of Claims, made a report on the petition of Solomon Prevost, accompanied with a bill for his relief; which was read twice and committed to a Committee of the Whole.

Mr. WILLIAMS, from the same committee, also made a report on the petition of Noel Destrehan, legal representative of Edward McCarty, deceased, accompanied with a bill for the relief of the heirs of the said McCarty; which was read twice and committed to the Committee of the Whole last appointed.

Mr. WILLIAMS also reported a bill explanatory of an act, entitled "An act authorizing the settlement of the accounts between the United States and Richard O'Brien, late American Consul at Algiers;" which was read twice and committed to the Committee of the Whole to which is committed the bill from the Senate for the relief of Robert Purdy.

Mr. CAMPBELL, from the Committee on Private Land Claims, made a report on the petition of Jesse Powel, accompanied with a bill for his relief; which was read twice and committed to a Committee of the Whole.

Mr. TRACY laid upon the table a paper in the shape of a bill "providing for the indemnity of certain citizens of the United States for losses sustained by the destruction or loss of property during the late wars with Great Britain and with the Seminole Indians;" and, on his motion, it was ordered to be printed, with a view hereafter to call for its consideration.

The following Message was received from the PRESIDENT OF THE UNITED STATES:

To the House of Representatives :

I transmit to Congress a report from the Secretary of the Treasury submitting copies of the instructions given to the commissioners appointed under the act of the 15th of May, 1820, authorizing the location of a road from Wheeling, in the State of Virginia, to a point on the left bank of the Mississippi river, between St. Louis and the mouth of the Illinois river, and copies of the report made by the said commissioners to the Treasury Department, of the progress they have made in the execution of the duties prescribed by the said act, together with maps of the country through which the location is to be made.

                   JAMES MONROE.

WASHINGTON, *January* 31, 1821.

The Message was read, and referred to the Committee on Roads and Canals. Whereupon, Mr. HERRICK withdrew the resolution submitted by him yesterday.

Mr. S. MOORE submitted the following, which he wished to propose as an amendment to the resolution respecting Missouri:

" Strike out the proviso attached to the resolution from the Senate, and in lieu thereof insert the following, viz:

" *Provided,* That the following conditions, be taken as fundamental conditions and terms upon which the said State is incorporated into the Union, viz: That the fourth clause of the twenty-sixth section of the third article of the constitution, submitted by the people of Missouri to the consideration of Congress, shall, as soon as the provisions of said constitution will admit, be expunged, or so amended that it shall not be applicable to citizens of any State in this Union. And that, until so expunged or amended, no law, passed in conformity thereto, shall be construed to extend to any citizen of either State in this Union.

This amendment was ordered to be printed.

On motion of Mr. FISHER, the Committee on the Judiciary were directed to inquire into the expediency of authorizing by law the executors of John B. Mebane, late a deputy collector of internal duties and direct taxes in North Carolina, to collect whatever arrearages may yet be due him from individuals, and for which he has accounted with the principal collector.

The House proceeded to consider the bill confirming the location of the seat of government of the State of Illinois, and for other purposes. Whereupon, the bill was ordered to be engrossed, and read a third time to-morrow.

The Committee of the Whole, to which is committed the bill for the relief of sundry citizens of Baltimore, were discharged, and the bill was committed to the Committee of the Whole to which is committed the report of the Committee of Claims on the petition of Eli Hart.

Bills from the Senate of the following titles, to wit: "An act for the relief of the representatives

997   HISTORY OF CONGRESS.   998

JANUARY, 1821.   *Columbian College.*   H. OF R.

of Patience Gordon, widow, deceased;" and "An act supplementary to an act passed on the 11th May, 1820, entitled 'An act to provide for the publication of the laws of the United States, and for other purposes;" were severally read the second time, and referred, the first to the Committee on Pensions and Revolutionary Claims, and the second to the Committee on the Judiciary.

COLUMBIAN COLLEGE.

The House, on motion of Mr. MERCER, proceeded to the consideration of the bill to incorporate the Columbian College, in the District of Columbia.

Mr. STORRS stated a number of objections which he had to the bill, as it now stood, and particularly dwelt on its having originated with a religious society, and that clause of it which proposes to give to this corporation a general capacity to hold lands, from which might be inferred a capacity to hold them in any State in the Union; concluding by suggesting certain alterations which he proposed to make in the constitution of the College, should the bill pass, though opposed himself to the passage of the bill in any shape. Mr. S. moved to recommit the bill to the Committee on the District of Columbia, with instructions:

1st. To reduce the number of trustees for the said institution to twenty-one.

2d. That the Secretaries of the Treasury, War, Navy, and State Departments, the Attorney General of the United States, and the Judges of the Circuit Court of the District of Columbia for the time being, shall be respectively ex officio trustees of the said institution.

3d. The vacancies in the said Board of Trustees shall be filled by the same body.

4th. That a visitorial power over the said institution shall be vested in a joint committee, to be appointed by the Senate and House of Representatives.

5th. To fill up the Board of Trustees to the number of twenty-one.

Mr. MERCER opposed the recommitment, as inevitably leading to a rejection of the bill; particularly as coming from a gentleman who had declared that he should vote against the bill in any shape. Mr. M. protested against this bill being rejected on the ground of hostility to the establishment of any literary institution in this District, which the gentleman from New York had so broadly avowed. He went into a general view of the subject, vindicating the bill, and asserting the right of the people of this District to expect from Congress, their sole legislators, that they would at least be allowed to educate their children within the District if they chose, and that they should, therefore, be enabled to secure and properly administer the funds they might establish for that purpose, &c.

There then arose, on this subject, a debate which occupied the whole of the remainder of the day's sitting, which was desultory in its nature and comprehensive in its objects, embracing the general powers of Congress to confer power by granting acts of incorporation, as well as the merits of this particular bill, and even the Missouri question, somehow or other, wedged its way into the debate.

Messrs. SERGEANT, MEIGS, CULPEPER, and CUTHBERT, sided with Mr. MERCER, in opposition to the amendment, and Mr. STORRS replied.

The motion of Mr. STORRS was negatived.

Mr. BALDWIN, to obviate the objection which existed to the bill, on the ground of its supposed comprehensiveness, moved to amend it by adding thereto the following:

And, provided, also, that nothing in this act contained shall be so construed as to authorize said College to purchase or hold any real estate out of the District of Columbia, without the consent of the Legislature of the State within which such real estate shall be situated.

The bill being on its third reading, an unanimous consent only could make the amendment; and, objection being made, it fell of course.

Mr. CAMPBELL moved to recommit the bill to the Committee on the District of Columbia, with instructions to make the above amendment to the bill.

Here ensued a further debate, in which Messrs. CLAY, BALDWIN, BARBOUR, MERCER, TUCKER, WARFIELD, and BRUSH, took part.

The amendment was objected to both by friends and adversaries of the bill; by its friends, as being unnecessary—by its enemies, on the ground that its insertion would leave an implication that, without its insertion, the College would have had the power proposed to be denied.

The opinion recently given by celebrated counsel on the operation of lotteries authorized by Congress became the subject of incidental remark. The greatest respect was professed for the counsel in the case, but not much for their opinion. The matter, however, was not so much argued as alluded to.

The motion of Mr. CAMPBELL was negatived, 71 votes to 60.

The bill was then read the third time, and the question was taken on its passage, by yeas and nays, and decided: For the bill 79, against it 60, as follows:

YEAS—Messrs. Abbot, Allen of New York, Anderson, Archer of Maryland, Baker, Bateman, Bayly, Beecher, Brevard, Brown, Brush, Burton, Butler of Louisiana, Clay, Cobb, Cook, Crawford, Culpeper, Cushman, Cuthbert, Dane, Darlington, Davidson, Eddy, Edwards of Connecticut, Eustis, Floyd, Foot, Garnett, Gross of New York, Guyon, Hackley, Hendricks, Hill, Hobart, Jackson, Johnson, Jones of Virginia, Jones of Tennessee, Kent, Kinsey, Kinsley, Lincoln, Lowndes, Maclay, McCreary, McCullough, McLane of Delaware, Meigs, Mercer, Monell, Morton, Moseley, Neale, Nelson of Massachusetts, Nelson of Virginia, Newton, Pitcher, Plumer, Reid, Robertson, Russ, Sawyer, Sergeant, Silsbee, Simkins, Smith of New Jersey, Southard, Street, Strong of Vermont, Terrell, Tomlinson, Tompkins, Tucker of Virginia, Upham, Walker, Warfield, Wendover, and Williams of Virginia.

NAYS—Messrs. Alexander, Allen of Massachusetts, Allen of Tennessee, Baldwin, Ball, Barbour, Boden, Bryan, Buffum, Butler of New Hampshire, Campbell, Cannon, Clagett, Clark, Cocke, Crafts, Dennison, Edwards of North Carolina, Fay, Ford, Forrest, Gray, Hall of New York, Hall of North Carolina, Hardin,

Herrick, Hibshman, Hooks, Hostetter, Lathrop, Little, McCoy, McLean of Kentucky, Marchand, Metcalf, R. Moore, S. Moore, Murray, Parker of Massachusetts, Parker of Virginia, Patterson, Philson, Randolph, Rankin, Rhea, Richards, Rogers, Ross, Shaw, Sloan, Smith of North Carolina, Stevens, Storrs, Tarr, Tracy, Tucker of South Carolina, Tyler, Udree, Williams of North Carolina, and Wood.

So the bill was passed.

An engrossed bill, entitled "An act for the relief of William T. Nimmo," was read the third time; and the question stated, Shall it pass? Whereupon the House adjourned.

THURSDAY, February 1.

Mr. LIVERMORE, from the Committee on the Post Office and Post Roads, reported a bill to alter and establish certain post roads; which was read twice, and committed to a Committee of the Whole.

Mr. SERGEANT, from the Committee on the Judiciary, reported a bill authorizing the Secretary of State to issue a patent to Thomas Oxley; which was read twice, and ordered to lie on the table.

Mr. MONELL, from the Committee on the Public Lands, who were instructed, on the 19th of December last, to inquire whether any, and, if any, what, regulations can be adopted, consistent with the interest of the Government, whereby the soldiers of the late war who have not received their bounty lands can be better provided for than under existing laws, made a report, accompanied with a bill further to regulate the issuing of patents of military bounty lands; which was read twice, and referred to the Committee of the Whole to which is committed the bill regulating the payment of debts due from the purchasers of the public lands.

The SPEAKER laid before the House a letter from the Secretary of War, transmitting a list of all the lands and buildings which have been purchased by the United States for military purposes, from the first day of July, 1800, to the present time, the cost of each site, and the buildings, as far as practicable, together with remarks on the estimated present value of the same, &c., prepared in obedience to a resolution of the 14th ultimo; which letter and list were ordered to lie on the table.

The SPEAKER also laid before the House a letter from Ethan A. Brown, Governor of the State of Ohio, transmitting a report of the joint committee of both Houses of the General Assembly, on the subject of the proceedings of the Bank of the United States against certain officers of the government of that State, in the circuit court of the United States; which was ordered to lie on the table.

Mr. McLANE offered the following paper, as an amendment which, when the subject came up, he proposed to move to the resolution for the admission of Missouri into the Union:

Provided, That nothing in the constitution of the said State of Missouri shall be construed to authorize or make it obligatory on the Legislature to pass any law denying to the citizens of each State any of the privileges and immunities of citizens in the several States: *And provided, further,* That no law of the said State shall be construed to deny to the citizens of each State any of the privileges and immunities of citizens in the several States.

And the same was referred to the Committee of the whole House on the state of the Union, and ordered to be printed.

A message from the Senate informed the House that the Senate have passed a bill entitled "An act concerning Thomas Shields and others," in which bill they ask the concurrence of this House. The bill was read twice, and referred to the Committee on Naval Affairs.

Mr. BALDWIN laid before the House sundry documents in relation to the trade of the United States with the empire of China; the state of sundry manufacturing establishments within the United States, and other papers, illustrative of the principles contained in the report of the Committee on Manufactures, which was accompanied by the bill to regulate the duties on imports, and for other purposes; which documents were ordered to lie on the table.

On motion of Mr. RANKIN, the Committee of Ways and Means were instructed to inquire into the expediency of changing an appropriation made by an act of Congress of the 27th of March, 1818, for the purpose of "repairing and keeping in repair that part of the road leading from Columbia, in the State of Tennessee, by the Choctaw Agency, to Madisonville, in the State of Louisiana, which lies between the southern boundary line of Tennessee, and the Indian boundary line in the State of Mississippi," so as to apply so much thereof, as, under the direction of the Secretary of War, may be found necessary to open a road from a point on the United States military road at or near Columbus, in the State of Mississippi, through the Choctaw nation of Indians, to Turner Brashears's stand on the old road leading from Natchez to Nashville.

Mr. STORRS submitted the following order, which was read, and ordered to lie on the table until to-morrow:

Ordered, That, during the remainder of the present session of Congress, business referred to Committees of the whole House shall be called for consideration in the following order:

1. Private bills which have passed the Senate, and have been reported favorably by a committee of the House.

2. Private bills reported by committees of the House.

3. Bills and resolutions of a public nature.

4. Bills which have passed the Senate, and have been reported against by a committee of the House.

5. Reports unfavorable to petitioners.

The engrossed bill for the relief of Rosalie P. Deslonde; the engrossed bill for the relief of Pierre Denis de la Ronde; the engrossed bill confirming the location of the permanent seat of government of the State of Illinois, and for other purposes, were severally read a third time, passed, and sent to the Senate for concurrence.

WILLIAM T. NIMMO.

The engrossed bill for the relief of William T. Nimmo, was read a third time; and, on the question of its passage—

Mr. NEWTON spoke in support of the bill. From what he said in favor of it, the bill proposes to indemnify Mr. Nimmo for the building, on the bay shore below Norfolk, usually known by the name of the Pleasure House, which was burnt by the enemy during the late war, on the ground, as alleged by the petitioner, and contended by Mr. N., that the building was occupied as a military post.

Mr. FLOYD having called on Mr. MERCER, who was performing military duty at Norfolk about that time, for information on the subject—

Mr. MERCER stated the facts within his knowledge upon the subject, which were, that the building had been occupied as barracks or lodgings for a vidette, the outguard of the Army, and was destroyed, as was universally admitted at the time, from mere wantonness, or on the pretence of retaliation. Mr. M. drew a distinction between military posts and fortified places, destroyed in legitimate warfare, and mere barracks or houses occupied as such, destroyed wantonly, or on the plea of retaliation. Mr. M. was opposed to indemnifying the losers in any of the whole class of cases of the latter description, including those on the Niagara frontier, &c. He paid a high compliment to the personal character and merit of the claimant in this case, and expressed his satisfaction that such a case had presented itself, that he might vote upon it on principle, to show what his opinion was on this subject, where his feelings would lead him to vote differently if he could.

Some further debate took place on this subject, in which Messrs. MCCOY, METCALF, MERCER, NEWTON, and RICH, engaged.

The question being taken on the bill, it was rejected, by a vote of 78 to 50.

MISSOURI.

On motion of Mr. CLAY, the House then again resolved itself into a Committee of the Whole, on the resolution from the Senate, declaring the admission of the State of Missouri into the Union, and the amendments proposed thereto.

The whole day was spent in animated debate, and interesting proceedings.

The amendment moved by Mr. FOOT was, to strike out the proviso of the resolution from the Senate, and, in lieu thereof, to insert the following:

"*Provided*, That it shall be taken as a fundamental condition, upon which the said State is incorporated in the Union, that so much of the twenty-sixth section of the third article of the constitution which has been submitted to Congress, as declares it shall be the duty of the General Assembly ' to prevent free negroes and mulattoes from coming to, and settling in, this State, under any pretext whatsoever,' shall be expunged within two years from the passage of this resolution, by the General Assembly of Missouri, in the manner prescribed for amending said Constitution."

Mr. STORRS had moved to amend the amendment, by striking out the whole of it, after the word "Union," in the third line, and inserting the following:

"And to be of perpetual obligation on the said State, (in faith whereof this resolution is passed by Congress,) that no law shall ever be enacted by the said State, impairing or contravening the rights, privileges, or immunities, secured to citizens of other States by the Constitution of the United States: *And provided further*, That the Legislature acting under the constitution already adopted in Missouri as a State, shall, as a convention, (for which purpose the consent of Congress is hereby granted,) declare their assent, by a public act, to the said condition, before the next session of Congress; and transmit to Congress an attested copy of such act by the first day of the said session."

After much debate, the motion of Mr. STORRS was negatived—80 votes to 61.

Mr. HACKLEY then moved to strike out all Mr. FOOT's amendment, after the word "Union," and insert, in lieu thereof, the following:

"And to be of perpetual obligation on the said State, (in faith whereof this resolution is passed by Congress,) that no law shall ever be enacted by the said State, to prevent such free negroes or mulattoes from entering into, and settling in, said State, as may be citizens of any of the States of the Union: *And provided, further*, That the Legislature, acting under the constitution already adopted in Missouri as a State, shall, as a convention, (for which purpose the consent of Congress is hereby granted,) declare their assent, by a public act, to the said condition, before the next session of Congress; and transmit to Congress an attested copy of such act by the first day of the said session."

After debate, the motion of Mr. HACKLEY was negatived—70 to 66.

Mr. COBB then moved the amendment previously suggested by him, viz: to strike out so much of Mr. FOOT's amendment as follows the word "Union," and insert, in lieu thereof, the following:

"That the Legislature of the State of Missouri shall pass no law impairing the privileges and immunities secured to the citizen of each State, under the first clause of the second section of the fourth article of the Constitution of the United States."

After debate, this motion was negatived—74 votes to 66.

The question was then taken on Mr. FOOT's motion to amend as above, and decided in the negative by a large majority.

Mr. MCLANE then moved his amendment, as stated; and then, after having previously several times refused to rise, a motion to that effect prevailed, and the House adjourned.

FRIDAY, February 2.

Mr. NEWTON, from the Committee on Commerce, reported a bill to repeal an act passed the 26th of April, 1816, increasing the compensations of inspectors, measurers, weighers, and gaugers; which was read twice, and committed to a Committee of the Whole.

Mr. FORREST, from the Committee on Agriculture, made a report on the memorial of the United

Agricultural Society of Virginia; which was committed to the Committee of the whole House on the state of the Union.

Mr. WARFIELD submitted for consideration the following resolution, which was read and ordered to lie on the table one day:

Resolved, That the Secretary of the Navy be directed to furnish this House with a statement of the annual expense of the Marine Corps at the city of Washington; the manner in which the said corps are employed; the annual amount paid to each officer, distinguishing their pay from their perquisites and emoluments; also, the duties required to be performed by each officer attached to said corps.

Mr. RICH rose to say, that, in consequence of the great length of time which has been taken up in discussing the proposed reduction of the Army, and other subjects, and the limited period of the present session, he had come to the conclusion not to ask for the further consideration at the present session, of the resolution which he had submitted, some time ago, proposing the prohibition of the importation of certain articles of foreign growth or manufacture. He hoped, he said, that he might be indulged in the further remark, that, being fully satisfied, that, should the condition of the country remain unchanged, its resources must gradually melt away and disappear, he should, if here at the next session of Congress, at an early day call the attention of the House again to this subject; and, should he not be here, if he had any influence with his successor, it should certainly be employed to induce him to move for the consideration of the subject.

IMPRISONMENT FOR DEBT.

Mr. NELSON, of Virginia, submitted for consideration the following resolution:

Resolved, That a select committee be appointed to inquire into the expediency of abolishing imprisonment for debt, in all cases of process issuing from the courts of the United States, and that they have leave to report by bill or otherwise.

The resolution having been read—

Mr. NELSON said, as the resolution proposed an inquiry only, it would be unnecessary for him to enter into an argument to show the propriety of its adoption. The distress which pervaded the country, he said, was known to every one, and its situation demanded relief, as far as it was in the power of this House to afford it. It had already too long been a stain on the statute books of the country, that men were liable to be imprisoned, not for crime, but for their misfortune. He hoped it would not be suffered to continue so longer.

Mr. WOOD inquired whether it was proposed to include the courts of the United States within this District.

Mr. CAMPBELL expressed his hope that the proposed inquiry by a committee would be made. He had long formed the opinion, on much reflection, that, as far as Congress had power in this respect, it ought to be exercised in the abolition of imprisonment for debt.

Mr. NELSON said the resolution, as to its object, spoke for itself. If Congress had any power over the subject in the States, he would have made his motion universal. But, as far as we have power, said he, I would exercise it, as well in regard to the courts of this District as to the other courts established by the authority of the United States.

The motion of Mr. NELSON was agreed to, and a committee of five ordered to be appointed accordingly; and Mr. NELSON, of Virginia, Mr. STORRS, Mr. HEMPHILL, Mr. ROSS, and Mr. EDWARDS, of Connecticut, were appointed the said committee.

REPORT ON GOLD COIN.

Mr. WHITMAN, from the select committee, appointed to inquire into the expediency of altering the relative value of the gold hereafter to be coined at the Mint of the United States, made a report thereon, accompanied by a bill. The report and bill are as follows:

The committee who were directed to inquire into the expediency of increasing the relative value of gold hereafter to be coined at the Mint, have attended to that subject, and beg leave respectfully to report that they are of opinion the value of American gold, compared with silver, ought to be somewhat higher than by law at present established. On inquiry, they find that gold coins, both foreign and of the United States, have, in a great measure, disappeared; and, from the best calculation that can be made, there is reason to apprehend they will be wholly banished from circulation, and it ought not to be a matter of surprise, under our present regulations, that this should be the case.

There remains no longer any doubt that the gold coins of the United States are, by our laws, rated at a value lower than in almost any other country, in comparison with that of silver. This occasions the gold to be constantly selected, when it can be obtained, in preference to silver, whenever required for remittance from this to foreign countries; and, at the same time, prevents those who have occasion to remit to the United States from doing it in gold. Hence there is a continual and steady drain of that metal from this country, without any correspondent return, which must continue while there remains any of it among us. The importations of it will be confined to small quantities, and from countries from which nothing better can be obtained.

There have been coined at the Mint of the United States nearly six millions of dollars in gold. It is doubtful whether any considerable portion of it can, at this time, be found within the United States. It is ascertained, in one of our principal commercial cities, quite in the vicinity of the Mint, that the gold coin in an office of discount and deposite of the Bank of the United States there located, in November, 1819, amounted to $165,000, and the silver coin to $118,000. That, since that time, the silver coin has increased to $700,000, while the gold coin has diminished to the sum of $1,200, one hundred only of which is American. And it is stated that the vaults of the State banks in the same city, having a capital in the aggregate, as is believed, of nearly eight millions, exhibit a similar result. It is scarcely to be doubted, that, on examination in the other commercial cities, similar additional proof would be furnished.

It now becomes a question of serious import, to be decided by the nation, whether a gold currency be at all desirable, or whether it should wholly give place to silver? By some a silver currency is deemed the most

1005   **HISTORY OF CONGRESS.**   1006

FEBRUARY, 1821.   *Admission of Missouri.*   H. OF R.

eligible. They contend that our circulating metallic currency should be ponderous, and inconvenient of transmission; that it would, in such case, remain in the country and stationary.

On the other hand, it is believed, by your committee, that a more portable currency may be, on many accounts, and, in many instances, must be, much more convenient, and in some cases absolutely necessary. It cannot be denied, that the lighter and smaller the currency, in proportion to its value, the greater will be the accommodation in the negotiations between the great extremes of the Union. In proportion to this facility the price of exchange will be lessened; commercial transactions would thus be carried on at an enhanced profit to all concerned. Moreover, in time of war, it will never fail to become requisite to make use of specie in payments and remittances; and these will be demanded, almost exclusively, at the extreme borders and frontiers of the Union. In such case gold furnishes a medium which will not only be light and convenient, but which can be transmitted with secrecy, thereby avoiding the risks incident to war and commotion. Those who carry their recollections back to the incidents of the late war, cannot fail of being forcibly impressed with this idea.

Our empire is widely extended, and becoming more so; and, at the same time, sparsely settled. The transmission of large sums, especially in time of war, if in ponderous silver, must be extremely inconvenient, and oftentimes attended with great danger. It would seem, therefore, that, as currency, the gold coin has, in this country, manifest advantages over that of silver.

But there is another particular not unworthy of consideration. We have before stated that the gold coins are worth, in foreign countries, more, in comparison with silver, than in our own. The average of this increased value is believed to exceed six-tenths of a dollar in every fifteen dollars. In Spain and Portugal, three half eagles are worth sixteen dollars; in Cuba, seventeen; in the West Indies, generally, sixteen; in England, fifteen and one-fifth; in Holland, fifteen; and in France, fifteen and a half. These calculations may not be precisely as stated, but are believed to be nearly accurate.

In the United States, before the establishment of the present Government, it has heretofore been ascertained by a committee of Congress, that, by custom, the value of gold has been considered as equivalent to about fifteen and six-tenths of its weight in silver. This, without doubt, arose from finding this to be the average of the different values affixed to the gold in different foreign countries.

Why it was thought proper, on establishing the Mint of the United States, to reduce this value to fifteen for one, it is not now material to inquire. It is sufficient to know, from unhappy experience, that its tendency is to rid us of a gold currency, and leave us nothing but silver.

The merchants, if they have occasion to import specie, and cannot obtain silver, are compelled to import gold, at a loss of from two to ten per cent. If they have a remittance to make, they will, if possible, exchange silver for gold, as, thereby, they will gain from two to ten per cent., according to the value of gold in the country to which the remittance is to be made.

An occurrence, strikingly illustrative upon this point, is stated in an elaborate report of a former committee, on the subject of the currency, to which your committee would beg leave to refer, as affording much useful information on this subject generally. The Bank of the United States entered into a contract with Messrs. Baring & Co., of London, for the supply of two millions of dollars in specie, in equal parts, as near as might be practicable, of gold and silver, at the American standard. The amount was, accordingly, furnished; but not a dollar of it in gold; although gold is the currency of Great Britain, and silver is admissible there, as a tender, in but very small sums.

It will, of course, be objected, that if we should now render gold four per cent. better, we shall, thereby, put into the hands of its present holders a clear net gain to that amount, provided they hold it with an intent to use it in this country. But it is not perceived how this will injure the public or individuals. And it will not be regretted by the benevolent that individuals should be benefitted if no one be injured. If, however, individual wealth be a public blessing, all will be benefitted. At any rate, this is an incident utterly unavoidable, to a certain extent, in this case. It must be submitted to; as, otherwise, a positive national evil, of great magnitude, as your committee deem it, must be encountered.

It will, moreover, be objected, that speculators will take advantage of the unwary, and, ere they will have been apprized of the increased value of their gold, will have purchased it of them at the former rate. This, however, your committee believe, will, in a great measure, be counteracted by a provision in the bill, accompanying this report, that the coin at its increased value shall not be a legal tender, until the first of July next. In this way, those who would buy it with a view to speculation would sustain a loss of interest amounting to nearly or quite as much as would otherwise be gained by the purchase.

If it be expedient to adopt the measure in contemplation, the present is the moment when it can and ought to be done. The longer we continue under the present regulation the worse will be our condition and the greater the injury we shall have sustained.

Your committee, therefore, in conformity to the foregoing sentiments, ask leave to report a bill.

The bill is as follows:

Be it enacted, &c., That the eagles hereafter to be coined at the Mint of the United States shall contain two hundred and thirty-seven grains and ninety-eight hundredths of a grain of pure, or two hundred and fifty-nine grains and sixty-one hundredths of a grain of standard gold; and the half eagles and quarter eagles the same proportion of fine or standard gold; and the said eagles, half eagles, and quarter eagles, so to be coined, being of the weight aforesaid, shall, from and after the first day of July next, pass, and be a legal tender in the payment of all debts and demands whatsoever, at the rate of ten dollars for each eagle, and in that proportion for half and quarter eagles; and, when of less than the weight aforesaid, being of the standard fineness, in proportion to their weight.

The bill was twice read and committed.

MISSOURI.

The House again resolved itself into a Committee of the Whole, on the Senate's resolution for the admission of Missouri.

The following amendment, proposed on yesterday by Mr. McLANE, of Delaware, being under consideration, viz: to strike out the proviso to the resolution as follows:

Provided, That nothing herein contained shall be so construed as to give the assent of Congress to any provision in the Constitution of Missouri, (if any such there be,) which contravenes that clause of the Constitution of the United States, which declares that the citizens of each State shall be entitled to all the privileges and immunities of citizens in the several States.

And, in lieu thereof, insert the following:

Provided, That nothing in the constitution of the said State of Missouri shall be construed to authorize or make it obligatory on the Legislature to pass any law denying to the citizens of each State any of the privileges and immunities of citizens of the several States: *And provided, further,* That no law of the said State shall be construed to deny to the citizens of each State any of the privileges and immunities of citizens of the several States.

A long debate took place, not so much on this particular amendment as on the whole subject of the evils of slavery, the rights of the South, the balance of power, the nature of the obligations and benefits of the Union, &c.

Mr. CAMPBELL rose and said, he was not ignorant of the anxiety of gentlemen on all sides of the House, to have the question now under discussion determined. Notwithstanding he felt this anxiety in common with others, he hoped a disposition to cultivate patience a little longer would be indulged, particularly when a member, not in the habit of obtruding, wished to be heard.

Mr. C. said, the gentleman from Delaware, (Mr. McLANE,) who presented the amendment now under consideration, had evinced so much candor, and so often repeated his invitations to those disagreeing with him on the main question, to meet him in the spirit of amity on his proposition to amend, that he would offer his reasons why he could not. What, Mr. C. asked, is the object of the amendment? If he understood its import, it is intended, at least indirectly, to alter the constitution of Missouri. If not to expunge the exceptionable clause, certainly to give it, or any act passed in conformity thereto, such an interpretation as the convention never intended. Whence does Congress derive this immensity of power? Or on what occasion has the employment of it been indicated? This doctrine is very different from that for which the gentleman at the last session so ably contended. At that time it was alleged we had no right to intermeddle with the constitution of a State about to apply for admission into the Union. If Congress be competent to interfere in any way with one clause of the constitution of Missouri, an interference with another, and indeed with every other, would be equally admissible. Mr. C. said, he considered the amendment a perfect cypher, and so would it, if adopted, be deemed by the people of Missouri. To any such modification their consent would be indispensable. And how was this to be obtained? Mr. C. said, he knew of no way but through another convention, and he defied gentlemen to point out any other legitimate mode. Mr. C. said, Missouri is unrepresented here; and if she were, who could believe

her representation vested with power to enter into any compact binding on her, relative to her constitution?

The gentleman who had just resumed his seat, (Mr. ALEXANDER,) has importuned his opponents to vote for the amendment, and terminate this unbecoming strife. Mr. C. said, he admired the disposition of the gentleman, and so far as it respected himself he would gratify him in his wishes, were it possible, without a dereliction of what he believed to be duty. That he might now be distinctly understood, he declared his unwillingness to vote for any amendment which could be offered, and which would result in the admission of Missouri at this time. This unwillingness he expected to continue, unless arguments were offered sufficient to produce a change. He would go further, and candidly acknowledge he was unable to imagine a proposition for which he could vote, that would be in accordance with the desires of his Southern friends.

Mr. C. said, it had been remarked by many of the friends of Missouri, and by none with greater energy than by a distinguished member from Kentucky, (Mr. CLAY,) that if the constitution of Missouri be incompatible with the Federal Constitution, it is so far void, and the legitimate tribunal for the decision of the question is the Judiciary. This is a position, he said, to the correctness of which he could not in conscience subscribe. It was so repugnant to his views that he must reject it as most dangerous in practice. By an act of the last session we authorized the people of Missouri to form a constitution, which, among other conditions, was required to be in conformity to the Constitution of the United States. A constitution has been framed and submitted to us for inspection—inspection for what purpose? Certainly that we might decide upon its provisions, which, if not repugnant to the rule prescribed, she would be entitled in good faith to admission—if repugnant, she must suffer rejection, with however much pain accompanied. To come to a decision in this manner, Mr. C. said, he conceived it to be the duty of Congress; a duty, from the performance of which, he could assure gentlemen he felt no disposition to shrink by remitting it to the Judiciary. Is not the question fairly before us, and how can we evade a direct and unequivocal answer, regardless of consequences? Should Missouri be admitted, and that part of her constitution to which objection is made be brought to bear upon the rights of an individual, he believed the court ought to and would interfere. This he had always understood was peculiarly the province of the judicial department, where the constitutionality of an act was called in question. It was a power which he hoped would always be prudently exercised.

Mr. C. said, he was willing, if it were thought necessary, to vote for another act or resolution to enable the people of Missouri to call a convention to form a new constitution, or to alter the present one in such a way as to obviate objections. Or if she chose to do this without the assistance of Congress, he for one would not be disposed to take advantage of the circumstance.

Mr. C. said, as he now had the opportunity, he would declare, he had yesterday listened to the gentleman from Pennsylvania (Mr. SERGEANT) with impatience. That gentleman had assigned sundry reasons why the subject should be postponed until the commencement of the next Congress, when it could be settled more to the satisfaction of the nation. He thought the question was fully understood, as well as the bearings it would probably have upon our national character; and he for one was prepared to decide the naked proposition of admission or rejection. The gentleman has alluded to a strife for power, and if he understood him, he meant a power which was to be acquired by a new party. Such considerations, Mr. C. said, should have no influence on him in pronouncing judgment on a Constitutional question. What, he would ask, could the new party, which it is supposed is now springing up, profit him, or the State which he assists to represent? Should it increase and attain full stature, could the Northwest expect favors which are now denied?

The gentleman from Pennsylvania (Mr. S.) has, at least, intimated a wish to see the old question of restriction revived. With him, Mr. C. said, he could not accord in opinion on this subject. He should regret to see a question reagitated which had, in some degree, become odious. His opinion might be different, could he discover that any practical benefit might result. Whatever the success of such an effort might be in this House, he felt confident that gentlemen could predict, with certainty, its fate elsewhere. Every one must know that the Senate would give it a veto. And why, he would inquire, should we engage again in so unprofitable a consumption of time? Duty did not appear to require it; neither did he believe that it was the wish of the nation, particularly when the session was so near its close. Mr. C. said he would not assert that he would never vote for the restriction. Circumstances, at some future period, might indicate the propriety of considering such a provision; but he was sure that period would not arrive until a great change had taken place in the other House.

[*Additional remarks of Mr. Campbell, in reply to Mr. Nelson, of Virginia.*]

Mr. CAMPBELL rose and said, the observations which he had some time ago submitted, had drawn upon him the reprehension of the gentleman from Virginia, (Mr. NELSON,) and, in his estimation, made it his duty again to ask the indulgence of the Committee. This he did with reluctance, but he felt no disposition that an attack should be made upon him from any quarter unrepelled.

Mr. C. said the gentleman had, in a very forcible manner, charged him with evincing such a temper towards Missouri as did Great Britain towards her colonies; those colonies which contended for and effected their emancipation from bondage. Mr. C. said this allegation was not well founded. He was perfectly willing that Missouri should be represented, as much so as the

gentleman himself, whenever she exhibited to us a constitution which he could, under the sanctions of the oath which he had taken on becoming a member of this House, pronounce to be compatible with the Constitution of the United States.

Mr. C. said, when he alluded to the circumstance of Missouri being unrepresented here, he was endeavoring to combat the doctrine of the gentleman from Kentucky, (Mr. CLAY,) who contended that, if she were admitted on some such condition as he suggested, she was bound absolutely, from the moment of her admission, for its performance, and he meant no reproach upon her or her friends.

The gentleman (Mr. N.) has told us, said Mr. C., what may properly be considered the laws of the land. He has declared that all resolutions and acts of Congress, made in conformity to the Constitution, could not be otherwise than obligatory; for such they were declared to be by the Constitution itself. This, said Mr. C., is true; but he would ask the gentleman, whether, if this amendment were changed into the restrictive principle, and adopted, it would be considered by him as coercive on Missouri? [Mr. NELSON explained, and denied the analogy of the cases.] Mr. CAMPBELL said, but was utterly at a loss to comprehend the want of analogy. The adoption of either would, if gentlemen were correct, be the same thing in effect. One would be adding a provision not now in the instrument, the other expunging one already in it. Mr. C. said he would assert that the amendment must be either efficient or inefficient; if efficient, it is intended so far to change the constitution of Missouri as to annihilate the objectionable clause, or to render any act passed in obedience thereto altogether inoperative and harmless; if inefficient, in whatever garb it may be dressed, or with whatever plausibility urged, he could not give it his support. His own sentiment was, that this amendment, or any similar one, would be as ineffectual in the construction of the constitution of Missouri as our naked opinion, or the celebrated one given in the lottery case.

The gentleman (Mr. NELSON) has expressed his astonishment at the course pursued by the representation from Ohio, inasmuch as their own constitution and laws embrace the very principle which they are so determined on denying to Missouri. Mr. C. said, he would admit that the constitution of Ohio denied to persons of color the right of suffrage. With this provision he was satisfied, and he doubted not the ability of the convention to sanction it, as well as to define the qualifications of an Elector. With the correspondent clauses of the constitution of Missouri, Mr. C. said he found no fault, and he thought on this account he ought not to be exposed to censure. He said he would also admit that a law had been passed, many years since, in Ohio, the object of which was to restrain the migration of free persons of color to that State. This act, he understood, had been decided to be unconstitutional, and he never heard that its provisions had, in one instance, been enforced. The constitution of Ohio forbids any person convicted of an offence being sent out of the State as a punishment. Hence, Mr. C. said, the courts have decided that an immigrant black, who had failed to comply with the act adverted to, could not be removed. If the regulations of Ohio on this subject had been such as the gentleman supposed, Mr. C. said he doubted not the settlement of a colony of two hundred and seventy black emigrants from Virginia, in his district, would have been prevented. These could not have been considered citizens of any State, and they formed a population whose vicinity was dreaded by the surrounding country.

The gentleman from Virginia (Mr. NELSON) has expressed his regret at the disappearance of the old political distinctions, as others are generated in this unpleasant contest, much more ruinous to the Republic, as they are to be marked by geographical lines. Mr. C. said, if this were to be the case, it would likewise be to him a source of grief. It would be, he confessed, a calamity long to be deplored; but, in forming an opinion on a grave Constitutional question, under the solemnities of an oath, he considered a departure from honesty as still more calamitous. He thought that the violation of the charter to which every member of this great federal family owes obedience, was one of the most terrible disasters that could betide this country, particularly when that violation takes place in Congress. The gentleman's expectation of a strife for power in the East may be realized; but whatever motives might be ascribed to members from that quarter, he was strongly inclined to be charitable, and to believe them to be such as had been professed. True, Mr. C. said, if this irksome contest were long continued, some demagogue, under the garb of patriotism, may avail himself of the turmoil, and establish himself in power, which it will not be easy to demolish. However, considerations of this kind were but secondary, and could not authorize the desertion of evident duty.

The gentleman has expressed, in the strongest terms, his apprehension that the principles advanced by the friends of restriction are to produce most fearful consequences in the South; that the scenes of St. Domingo, with all their horrors, are there to be exhibited. Mr. C. said he hoped the day which would give birth to these distresses was remote, if it were ever to be, and that nothing which had been uttered within these walls would accelerate its arrival. He, for one, had no inclination to disturb the relation subsisting between master and slave, or to render the condition of the latter more intolerable, by augmenting his impatience of bondage. As a human being, the black man had rights, but an attempt, on his part, to assert them, would be an addition to his misfortune. To the helots of this country he was willing the recitation of the songs of Alcman and Terpander should be strictly forbidden.

Mr. C. said, whatever fault the gentleman might find with his notions of freedom and slavery, he would inform that gentleman he was principally indebted to Virginia for them. They are such as have been advanced and defended by Jefferson, Tucker, and the authors of the memorable ordinance of 1787.

Mr. RHEA said, the third section of the fourth article of the Constitution of the United States provides that "new States may be admitted by the Congress into the Union." This provision evidently intends that such new State is formed, and does exist, not formally only, but in fact, completely organized, and in full operation, as a sovereignty, acting in pursuance of a constitution ordained by the people of such new State. Such a State is Missouri, erected under the authority of an act of Congress, entitled "An act to authorize ' the people of the Missouri Territory to form a ' constitution and State government, and for the ' admission of such State into the Union, on an ' equal footing with the original States, and to ' prohibit slavery in certain Territories." It may here be noticed, to prevent misconstruction, that the words " and to prohibit slavery in certain Territories," do not refer to the State of Missouri, but to the Territory particularly adverted to in the eighth section of that act, passed on the 6th March, 1820. The seventh section of that act provides, " that in case a constitution and State government ' shall be formed for the people of the said Terri- ' tory of Missouri, the said convention, or repre- ' sentatives, as soon thereafter as may be, shall ' cause a true and attested copy of such constitu- ' tion, or frame of government, as shall be formed ' or provided, to be transmitted to Congress." In pursuance of that act of Congress, a convention of the people of Missouri did make a constitution and frame of State government; and thereupon that frame of government was put in force, so far that the same has been completely organized, and in full operation. And " the said convention, or representatives," have, in pursuance of the said act of Congress, caused a true and attested copy of the said constitution, or frame of State government, to be transmitted to Congress, and it has been received.

The State of Missouri is denied admission into this Union, by reason of objections to that constitution, particularly because that constitution provides, in the 26th section of the third article, that " it shall be their duty, (to wit, the General As- ' sembly,) as soon as may be, to pass such laws as ' may be necessary, first, to prevent free negroes ' and mulattoes from coming to, and settling in, ' this State, under any pretext whatsoever." And, for this, the opposition say, that the State of Missouri ought not to be admitted into this Union. Mr. R. said that the opposition to admitting the State of Missouri might see in that constitution a humane and noble principle inserted, to wit: that, by that constitution, it is made the duty of the General Assembly of that State "to oblige the ' owners of slaves to treat them with humanity, ' and to abstain from all injuries to them, extend- ' ing to life or limb."

An attempt is made to bring the Constitution of the United States to bear against the admission of the State of Missouri into this Union. On this point, it is right to examine what are the objections which that Constitution expressly declares shall be taken against the admission of a new State into this Union. The Constitutional objections are expressly declared in the 3d section of the 4th article of the Constitution of the United States, and enumerated as follows, namely ; "but ' no new State shall be formed or erected within ' the jurisdiction of any other State; nor any ' State be formed by the junction of two or more ' States, or parts of States, without the consent of ' the Legislatures of the States concerned, as well ' as of the Congress." If there be any other objections expressly declared in the Constitution of the United States against the admission of a new State into this Union, let them be referred to.

The Constitution of the United States, in the 4th section of the 4th article, declares, that " the United States shall guaranty to every State in the Union a republican form of government." Against whom is this guarantee provided ? Is the guarantee against the State so guarantied ? And, if not, who is the guarantee against ? Is the guarantee against a foreign or internal innovation ? Is it against individual ambition, attempting the overthrow of the rights of man ? In the illustration of that which is intended by the guarantee alluded to, it may be observed that a republican form or frame of government is that in which the people are sovereign, and have the right of self-government, and act accordingly, in legislation, to preserve their sovereignty and safety. On this principle all the States in this Union have acted, and continue to act, as sovereignties. The constitution of Missouri provides for that self-government, sovereignty, and safety, of the people who made and ordained it. The Constitution of the United States guaranties to the State of Missouri that republican right of self-government and sovereignty; and hence it is that the State of Missouri is an equal in this Union, and not a subordinate—subordination is inferiority. Do the gentlemen in opposition desire to put the State of Missouri under the control or dictation of the other States of this Union ? If they do, the State of Missouri will demand the Constitutional guarantee.

The constitution of the State of Missouri is under examination in this House, composed of the representatives of the sovereign people of these United States ; and, said Mr. R., we are examining whether the constitution of the State of Missouri is republican : that is, this House of Representatives are examining whether the people of Missouri are qualified to decide on their own business, and to know what will operate for their good ; and, being of opinion that the State of Missouri is not a proper judge of its own sovereign attributes, this House will provide better for them. If this principle, said Mr. R., shall be insisted on, then let Congress at once command all the States of this Union severally to submit their respective constitutions, or frames of government, to the Congress of the United States for examination. I do not believe, said Mr. R., that the States will submit to such command—for one good reason, viz : that Congress has not any such power. In the sixth article of the Constitution of the United States it is declared that " this Constitution, and

' the laws of the United States which shall be made ' in pursuance thereof; and all treaties made, or ' which shall be made, under the authority of the ' United States, shall be the supreme law of the ' land, and the judges in every State shall be bound ' thereby, any thing in the constitution or laws of ' any State to the contrary notwithstanding." Here, then, said Mr. R., is the great Constitutional principle eminently presiding over and controlling the constitutions and laws of the States respectively ; and the judges shall be bound thereby. Hence is inferred, that, if any collision, real or imaginary, shall be pretended to be or exist between the Constitution or laws of the United States and the constitution or laws of any State of this Union, that the judges shall be bound by the Constitution and laws of the United States. And hence also is inferred, that, if there be in the constitution of the State of Missouri any thing contravening the Constitution of the United States, it is *nudum vagum*—void and of no effect, to all intents and purposes. But the rendition of such judgment will be by the Supreme Court of the United States, and not by Congress, who have power to enact laws, but will not be a tribunal to decide thereon, or on the constitutionality of the constitution or law of any State of this Union.

The second clause of the third section of the third article of the Constitution of the United States provides, that " the Congress shall have ' power to dispose of and make all needful rules ' and regulations respecting the territory or other ' property belonging to the United States ; and ' nothing in this Constitution shall be so construed ' as to prejudice any claims of the United States, ' or of any particular State."

It is manifest that the power given by this clause of that section of the Constitution acts only on the territory or other property of the United States, in any State or Territory, and never can, by any construction, be made to act or operate on any thing but the territory or other property of the United States. The people of the State of Missouri are not the property of the United States ; on them, therefore, that clause of that section cannot operate in that point of view, nor in any other, so far as relates to property referred to in that clause of that section. The State of Missouri, however, is very much interested in the last sentence of that clause of that section, which declares, "and nothing in this Constitution shall be so construed as to prejudice any claims of the United States, or of any particular State." This clause contains a Constitutional guarantee against a violation of any claims of the United States, or of any particular State, or of any State right. The State of Missouri has, in pursuance of the act of Congress alluded to, certain rights : the fifth section of that act provides, "that until the ' next general census shall be taken, the said State ' (Missouri) shall be entitled to one Representative ' in the House of Representatives of the United ' States." The people of Missouri, in virtue of said act, have formed a constitution, or frame of State government ; they have agreed to the first second, third, fourth, and fifth provisions or conditions of the sixth section of that act; and having so done, the State of Missouri has claims against the United States. One of these claims is expressly mentioned in the fifth section of that act, which provides that, until the next general census shall be taken, the said State shall be entitled to one Representative in the House of Representatives of the United States. The Representative from the State of Missouri has attended since the beginning of the session of Congress, and is not yet admitted to his seat in this House. Are not the claims of the State of Missouri prejudiced thereby? But the State of Missouri has a claim of a higher nature; that is, a claim to be admitted into this Union as a sovereign State, on an equal footing with the original States.

Mr. CUSHMAN, of Maine, spoke as follows:

Mr. Chairman: Not being habituated to parliamentary debate, and possessing a set of nerves easily disconcerted, I but seldom lift my voice for or against any thing. But, on this occasion, I have strong inducements to depart from my usual silence. Besides the right which I have, in common with others, of expressing my opinions, I now have reasons peculiar to myself. A man suspected of high crimes and misdemeanors—the high crime of a patriotic ambition—the misdemeanor of endeavoring to preserve the Union entire, by preserving the balance of its parts, may surely claim the right to be heard in his own defence.

I shall not, with intention, wound the sensibility of any one. But avoiding all "bitter words," which stir up strife," I shall aim at that blandness of expression which may be adapted to the subject.

An honorable gentleman from Kentucky, (Mr. HARDIN,) with his characteristic wit and pleasantry, has insinuated that he has at length found out the secret of our boasted humanity, and learned, from a letter, which he was pleased to call celebrated, that it resolves itself into a love of power, or a policy to restore the sceptre to Judah. I have read, sir, with some attention, most of the letters which have been circulated in the public prints. But in no one of them can I perceive a sentiment like that alluded to above. In one[*] of these letters, the writer seems to be of the opinion that this Union is virtually dissolved; in another[†] there is an intimation that the next President is to make his entrance into this city, to be inaugurated in a style somewhat novel. The novelty of the scene, I presume, will attract much notice; and, being this in season announced, will bring together a vast concourse of people from all parts of our country. In a third,[‡] there is an allusion to an event which might arise from the question now agitated. But the change of power insinuated was not mentioned as a cause, or motive, or object of the present contest, but a probable result. The honorable gentleman is assured that the writer had no such design as has been imputed to him. His solicitudes were not, lest the sceptre

[*] Mr. Jones's, of Tennessee.
[†] Mr. Barton's, of Missouri.
[‡] Mr. Cushman's, of Maine.

should depart from Judah, but lest Judah should be crushed under a weight of power, to be derived from, what some have supposed to be the seed of Cain, and others the descendants of Ham. He believes it to be in the order of nature, that the sceptre should depart from the North. From time immemorial, the march of empire has been westward. Even some of the celestial bodies, apparently, move in that direction. The sun, the most luminous of them, brightens in the east, moves over the globe diffusing blessings, and at length appears in the west in full glory. Thus it may be with the American Empire. It arose in the East, with a mild radiance—it has shone from the South in majestic lustre—and it will probably be seen in the West, in all the splendor and beneficence of its beams. Such glory awaits the West; which nothing is so likely to prevent as the dark cloud which hovers round its horizon. Should this be driven back by a strong gale of patriotism, all there would be peace, serenity, and joy.

It is true, Mr. Chairman, that I am opposed to slavery in every form. And I contend against its extension on what I conceive to be the purest principles of humanity. It appears to me to be fraught with the most deleterious evils. It cannot but have an effect, in some instances, injurious to the finer feelings of the heart. I know, Mr. Chairman, that there are high-minded gentlemen, who not only seem to deny to the African the capability of becoming a citizen in this country, but also are inclined to refuse him a place on the roll of human beings. I shall attempt no learned analysis to prove that a negro is a man. I shall not contend that he is possessed of an organized human body, to which there is superadded a rational soul. The definition of man, by an ancient philosopher, is sufficient for my purpose—*Animal bipes implume.* If this definition be correct, it will follow that a negro is a man. He is certainly an animal with two legs; and though he may have something resembling wool, he is also without feathers—which corresponds to the definition given. And, if a man, he is "endowed with certain inalienable rights;" for, in the first article of the political creed of our country, it is declared to be a "self-evident truth that all men are created equal." But, however this may be, it will be agreed that an African is endowed with a degree of sensibility—that he is susceptible of pleasure and pain—that many of the race are capable of strong sensations of gratitude and love. If so, these feelings, by their condition even in this country, must be injured to a degree at which humanity cannot but recoil. Who, unmoved, could behold the anguish of conjugal attachment, the yearnings of parental affection, the pathetic cries and tears of filial tenderness, which cannot but be felt and expressed, when husband and wife, parent and child, brother and sister, are forcibly separated from each other, and transferred, like beasts of burden, or as insensible property, from owner to owner! Sir, could I even reflect with indifference on such scenes of agony and human woe, I should be ashamed to claim kindred with the human race; and even blush to call God my Heavenly Father.

Slavery, sir, in our country, admits of no apology but stern imperious necessity. There is no color of excuse by extending to increase the evil.

But, though I contend against the spread of slavery, on humane principles, yet I never insinuated that these were my only motives. I have also strong reasons of policy. It is not, in my opinion, wise or safe to spread over a new country a population which, instead of adding, must impair its physical strength. A slave is neither a soldier, nor a seaman, nor an artisan, except of the lowest kind. Many of them are but menial servants, who do not reproduce the food which they consume. The earth, in general, is not so well cultivated by slaves, nor made to exhibit those scenes of fertility and beauty which are to be seen where the owners are the cultivators of the soil. Nor can a section of country, where the population consists but in part of slaves, furnish such numbers, for common defence, as can be spared in a free State, where every able-bodied man is a soldier. It is known that in all our wars, some of the slaves are too much inclined to go over to the enemy. This, to be sure, is wrong—but it is in a degree natural. For, according to Mr. Jefferson, if a slave has any country, it is not that in which he is holden in bondage. Allured by the hope held out by an insidious foe, they are ready to engage in some work of mischief or blood. Hence, in times of danger or invasions, a country so circumstanced, instead of furnishing its fair proportion of soldiers to oppose a public enemy, might retain somewhat of its physical strength at home for purposes of safety—to suppress domestic insurrection—to protect their wives and children, their altars and their firesides. It would be peculiarly impolitic to place our frontiers—those inlets of an invading foe—in such jeopardy.

The territories of the United States, the common property of the nation, are to become constituent parts of our Republic. Every portion of the Union, therefore, must feel a deep interest, that the population of the States, which are to be formed out of these territories, especially if the West is destined to be the seat of the empire, should consist, not of slaves, who might endanger the public safety, but of citizens—enlightened, virtuous, enterprising citizens—able to contribute to the ornament and defence of our common country.

Honorable gentlemen need not peruse private letters to learn secrets. At proper times, and on suitable occasions, I shall be willing to avow my sentiments. Strong in my cause, and strengthened by the powerful auxiliaries of right, of reason, of justice, of humanity, and feeling, what is there to be feared? It is manly, it is noble, to take the open field, and to acquaint the adversary with the whole grounds of the controversy. It appears to be as ungenerous as it is useless, to display doubtful colors, or to maintain the conflict under masked batteries. For myself I have no hesitancy in saying, that it is in part, according to my view, on one side as well as the other, a contest for power. The States where slavery is proscribed cannot, consistently with their own interest, yield the point in dispute. By yielding, they part with the inheritance received from their fathers—a portion of their relative importance in this Union. As to the binding force of the celebrated compromise, I shall hold my opinion in reserve. But, considered as a bargain, it appears to me, on the part of the North and East, to be far from a wise one. It scarcely has a parallel in all history, except in the improvidence of an oriental huntsman, who, in very remote times, as we are informed, "parted with his birthright for a mess of pottage, or a morsel of meat." By the accession of new States on the South or West, with the privilege of holding slaves by the power thus derived, the scale of empire is there more than on the poise. Every State added, with the like privilege, increases the weight in the preponderating scale.

It is, sir, in the nature of man, especially of irresponsible bodies of men, and all triumphant majorities are irresponsible when fortified by power, to be forgetful of right. Those but seldom obtain justice, who are not in a situation to cause its claims to be respected. The soundest maxims of policy require that no section of our country should gain such an enormous ascendency as to give the law to the rest. It would, in time, crush the other under its feet. To guard against such an abuse, there should be preserved a balance of power—yes, sir, a balance of power. At the repetition of the phrase gentlemen seem to take the alarm. As if struck with a panic, they almost lose the balance of their minds, to say nothing of the harmony of their good feelings. The balance of power! exclaim gentlemen, in astonishment—as if they saw in it an ill omen, portentous of direful events—some dreadful calamity impending over our Republic. What do you mean, say they, by the balance of power? I mean, sir, in the nation, something like that equilibrium preserved in the natural world by the operation of the centripetal and the centrifugal forces of nature—the action of the one, and the reaction of the other. As on this equilibrium depends the order and harmony of the natural system, so on a balance of power resembling this depends the safety of our confederated Republic. But if gentlemen are displeased with this illustration, I will attempt another—I mean, sir, something in our Federal system, resembling the barriers which prevent the ocean from overflowing the land—fixed by the Almighty, when he said to its turbulent waters, "Hitherto thou hast come, but thou shalt proceed no further—and here shall thy proud waves be staid." This balance of power has been highly useful in other countries. When it has been entirely broken down the consequence has been fatal to nations, as it has lately been seen in the convulsions of Europe. But fortunate, sir, for the world, by the magnanimous policy of the Emperor Alexander, this balance has been restored, and nations, as the result, are beating their swords into ploughshares, and spears into pruning-hooks, and seem to be inclined to learn war no more! I believe, sir, that a balance of power would not be without some salutary effect in this nation. It might restrain the intemperance of inordinate ambition in individuals, and

1019 .HISTORY OF CONGRESS. 1020

H. of R. Admission of Missouri. February, 1821.

check the proud assumptions of aspiring States. But, sir, to return from this seeming digression into which I have been led by the observations which have been made in the course of the debate, I have further to say, that the Northern and Eastern portions of this Union, for the purpose of preserving it entire, at the adoption of the Federal Constitution, submitted to an evil for which they could provide no speedy remedy. Our country was then bounded by the Mississippi, and little was to be apprehended, as the condition of the States was at that period, from an overgrown power, derived from a slave population. But could it have been foreseen that a territory west of that river, larger than the old thirteen United States, would have been added to our country, out of which new States, almost to infinity, were to be formed, with the privilege of holding slaves, I am persuaded that neither Massachusetts, nor any part of New England, and perhaps none of the now free States then extant, would have consented, on such terms, to have come into this Union.

There was, sir, in the North, at the adoption of the Federal Constitution, much sensibility on the score of slavery. This was only quieted by the belief then entertained, that, "though slavery was not smitten by an apoplexy, yet it had received a mortal wound, and would die of a consumption."

It is, sir, deeply to be regretted, that slavery has taken such deep root in our country that it cannot be soon extirpated. The correction of the evil, if it can be corrected, must be left to time and the wonder-working power of Heaven. Nothing can be farther from the free States than the design to meddle with the subject of slavery where it exists by Constitutional compact. But, to consent to its extension, is revolting to all the principles of liberty in which they have been educated. By opening a new market for this species of property the demand and the price will be increased, and additional encouragement given to continue this execrable "traffic in human blood."

Gentlemen expatiate on the hardships and humiliations endured by Missouri. I sympathize, sir, with the people of Missouri, and the more readily, because, having experienced similar misfortunes, I know how to feel for the disappointed. But what are the griefs and mortifications of Missouri, compared to those, of a like nature, endured by Maine for a series of years? Long and laborious were her struggles for independence, and for the right of self-government; and, though she lost no blood, she exhausted much treasure. Her progress was that of a ship, making its way against winds and tides, and a strong current; and when, by the ardor and perseverance of the crew she had surmounted these obstacles, and with full sail and joyful acclamation was entering the port, she was driven from the Federal wharf, and refused anchorage in the harbor of the Union.

This treatment was not for any alleged fault— for no repugnance, real or pretended, of her constitution to that of the United States. It was as painful as unexpected, and the more distressing to a generous sensibility, as it was not done by an enemy. It was the act of our friends—the friends with whom we had, in a common cause, lately fought and bled; with whom we had mingled our sorrows and our joys; the patriots and statesmen with whom we had taken wholesome counsel, and in whose company we had moved to the temple of liberty, and on its altar inscribed our civic vows. Notwithstanding the wounds which Maine received by the predicament in which her delegation was placed—wounds which, upon recollection, almost bleed afresh—the ardor of her loyalty is not abated; her affection for the National Government is not alienated. Her attachment to the Union is vigorous and strong. Her wealth and resources, such as they be, are ready to replenish your Treasury; her physical strength is at your disposal; her blood will generously flow in a righteous cause; and her brave and spirited militia, at the call of the Government, will promptly rally round the standard of the nation, either to "repel invasion, to suppress insurrection, or to execute the laws of the Union." I am persuaded, sir, that Missouri, less aggrieved, and with less cause of complaint, will not yield to the suggestions of passion, but profit by an example which, in circumstances somewhat similar, I am proud to propose to her imitation. Resentment for unintentional wrongs, though real, and inconsiderate modes of redress, do not savor of manly wisdom or patriotic virtue. To attribute such a temper and conduct to the people of Missouri, would be doing them the greatest injustice. Under the delay of their hopes and prospects, they will feel like patriots, and act like men, intelligent, dispassionate men. As I have this opinion of the good sense and patriotism of Missouri, if left to herself, I cannot be alarmed at consequences so often menaced. I believe that the evils predicted will have no existence but in fervid imaginations.

I have the honor, sir, to think, with the honorable gentleman from Pennsylvania, (Mr SERGEANT,) whose opinions, from his high standing in this House, and in the nation, are entitled to respect, that if the admission of Missouri into this Union should be a short time delayed, no essential injury or inconvenience would accrue, either to her or to the United States. She has already an organized government in operation, competent to all local purposes. The benefits of this she can quietly enjoy, as did Vermont her government, till all obstacles were removed to her becoming a member of this confederacy of States. Time and reflection, which produce great revolutions in human affairs, not unfrequently produce some changes in the minds of men. The people of Missouri will not deem themselves spurned at, or frowned upon, by the conduct of this House. No audacity is imputed to her; no censure is implied in withholding from her the object so ardently sought. On her part, it is candidly considered mere inadvertency; on ours, it is the result of principle, of the soundest maxims of policy, and of an adherence to the paramount laws of the land. For myself, sir, I wish to Missouri every species of prosperity and glory; and when she shall present herself with a constitution republican in spirit, as well as in name, I shall most joyfully hail her entrance into this Union.

From the sensations which I cherish, I cannot possibly believe that the delay which I have suggested, in order to give time for voluntary amendments in the constitution of Missouri, would lay a foundation for hatreds and ill-will, or cause those heart-burnings or alienations of affection among the members of this community, which some have so precipitately announced. After the feelings of the moment, engendered by the ardor of debate, shall have subsided, and sober reflection ensued, we shall respect each other the more for the adherence to principle, the firmness of character, the rectitude of intention, and ardor for the common weal, which, in the discharge of duty, may have been indicated or displayed. Upon the same principle that a brave man will respect courage in an enemy, sound patriots and able statesmen, with clear heads and good hearts, will habitually cherish a mutual regard, and reciprocate acts of civility. Local interests and discrepancies of views may occasion, at times, a coolness and reserve. But a congeniality of soul, a sympathy of affections, and a largeness of mind, will fix, among such characters, as has been seen among the sages and heroes of the Revolution, a lasting bond of friendship. At least, I may venture to affirm, that no such character, because not personally or sectionally gratified, will attempt to embroil this Union, nor sacrifice to his own resentments the peace, prosperity, and glory, of our beloved country.

Indulge me, sir, with a few observations concerning myself, which are forced upon me by allusions and insinuations which it is impossible for me not to understand. So unconscious am I of an intention to sow the seeds of discord, to foment divisions, or to "enfeeble the ties by which the several parts of our country are linked together," that I do not believe any thing I have said or written could be construed to have this tendency, unless seen by distempered optics, and through a medium which distorts the natural import. The whole history, sir, of my life, private, professional, and political, could it be known, would evince an ardent attachment to the Union, and a devotedness to the National Government. During times of alarm and danger, I supported the policy of the South. I supported this policy, because I believed it connected with the honor and interest of the nation. There is, sir, in the Library of Congress, the most ample proof of the exalted opinions which I entertained of Mr. Jefferson, and of my approbation of his administration—even at a period when some who now, *vivified* by *Southern rays*, are endeavoring to render me suspected, by means as *indecorous* as they are unjustifiable, held no *undistinguished* rank among the most virulent of his calumniators. For the North, I claim no superiority. To the South, I cheerfully attribute a fair portion of the talent, the wisdom, the patriotism, the virtue, the refinement, and, if you please, the good, the noble, and the elevated feelings of the nation. Am I an enemy to the South, because I

cannot yield up every thing? May I not be permitted to retain some spice of mental independence? As a Northern man, may I not be allowed to indulge, without offence, my sensibilities and predilections, and to be alive to the interest of that section of the country with which I am more immediately connected, where are my affinities, my hopes, and enjoyments? Are these the crimes which have called forth such severe animadversions, for which I am virtually arraigned before the bar of public opinion? I glory in such crimes. If my neighbor, whom I highly esteem, informs me that I am to receive his will for my law, as the condition of his kind offices, I shall promptly give him to understand, that, as highly as I prize the amenities of life, on such terms I cannot accept his friendship. Would a wise man suffer his eyes to be plucked out, or a strong man his arms to be cut off, for the sake of living in peace with his assuming neighbor, who had neither the discretion nor politeness to conceal the feelings nourished in his heart? I repeat, sir, that the policy of checks and balances which I advocate is not alarming to this Union. This Union cannot be in danger by the strictest adherence to the principles on which it was founded, the inalienable rights with which all mankind are endowed by their Creator, "among which are life, liberty, and the pursuit of happiness." This basis of our republican system is a balance of power, and must be supported by a reciprocity of interests. As long as it shall remain on this stable foundation, and be thus supported, the winds may blow, the rains may descend, and the floods may come, but it will fall not, for it is founded and supported on a rock.

I cannot close, sir, without expressing my hope, that, as the Union is safe, the harmony of its parts will continue; that Missouri will weigh well the consequences of her own actions; that she will listen to the advice of her more dispassionate and less interested friends; that she will take counsel from wisdom, and not from passion; that, in fine, she will study and pursue her own interest and honor, as connected with the peace, prosperity, and glory of the United States.

Mr. TYLER said that he had, during the present session, maintained a profound silence on the interesting topic which had so long engaged the attention of the House and nation; that nothing but the exposé which had been made to the House by the gentleman from Pennsylvania, (Mr. SERGEANT,) could have induced him now to present himself to the notice of the House upon a subject so hackneyed. The remarks made by that gentleman were of a character so novel and alarming that it would not become him to pass them by unnoticed. The gentleman (Mr. SERGEANT) had talked about the balance of power. What is it that the gentleman means by this language? Had he well weighed it before he gave it utterance? To his mind the gentleman had conjured up a fearful fiend. He had told us that no danger was to be apprehended from keeping alive this question. He had cried "peace, peace," when he had presented himself as fighting under the banners of a fiend from which Mr. T. turned with fear and dismay. Look on the page of history, and tell me (said Mr. T.) what has been the most fruitful cause of war, of rapine, and of death? Has it been any other than this struggle for the balance of power? Desolation has, in all ages, marked its existence, and hecatombs of slaughtered victims have been raised to appease its fury. Sir, said he, it is a monster that feasts on the bodies of mangled carcasses, and swills on human blood. And has it come to this, that we are now to enter into this struggle for power? And against whom do gentlemen propose to carry on this war? Against brethren—members of the same common family. It might be natural to wish to elevate ourselves to a superiority of power in reference to foreign nations; but it is unnatural, to say the least of it, for one section of a common country to entertain a wish of the sort in reference to the rest. Equality is all that can be asked for, and that equality is secured to each State of this Union by the Constitution of the land. But what is the character of the power sought now to be obtained by the gentleman and his associates? Do they want to secure to the non-slaveholding States a preponderance in the National Legislature? We have been told correctly by the gentleman from New York, (Mr. STORRS,) that they already have the preponderance of twenty odd votes. This, then, it is obvious, cannot be the power, for the acquisition of which they are ready to undertake this crusade against the South and West. I, said Mr. T. follow but the inference which the member from New York (Mr. STORRS) has drawn, when I express the hypothesis, that it must be a power of a different character which gentlemen are in pursuit of. It may be their purpose to elevate to high stations some particular favorites. Some may be prompted by the "patriotic ambition" of the gentleman from Maine, (Mr. CUSHMAN,) an ambition which may be sorely disappointed by the settlement of this question at the present session. I will not ascribe any such motive to the gentleman from Pennsylvania. I have heretofore admired him for his talents, and I will not permit myself to indulge too hastily an unfavorable impression towards him.

But what can a majority of this House hope to gain by this unhallowed struggle? It is a game at which only a few can win, and all that will remain to the majority of the actors in this drama will be the slave-like privilege of worshipping at the feet of an idol. And has it come to this, that, instead of looking to the advancement of our country's happiness, we shall now use our efforts to advance the political views of an individual? I should be willing to sacrifice myself on the altar of my country, for the common good. I idolize the institutions of this highly favored land; but I never will consent to become the idolater of any man on earth. I know but of one rule to govern me in selecting men for office, and it is found in the wisdom, intelligence, and virtue of the candidate. Whether he be born in Massachusetts or Virginia, is a consideration unworthy of being taken into the estimate. If, then, there be a man in this House or nation, governed by motives of a

different character, in the name of virtue and patriotism, I demand that he shall abjure them.

The gentleman, (Mr. SERGEANT,) as another reason for postponing this question to the next session of Congress, urged the propriety of submitting it to the people, and intimated that they might be dissatisfied with a decision now. No man, said Mr. T., holds in higher reverence the wishes of the people than I do. The wishes of my constituents on any subject other than a constitutional question, would be my law. But they have elected us to act for them, and on this subject they leave us uninstructed. While it would but answer the end of our agency here to bow to their will, when properly expressed, it would be worse than degrading for us to hesitate about acting, lest we might incur their displeasure. In such a case as this, what would be the weight of their displeasure? Our country is agitated from one end of it to the other; a state of things exists calculated to fill the mind of the patriot with awful forebodings of the future; a breach has been made in the affections of this people for each other, which every day serves but to enlarge. Is there a man who hears me, who would not be willing, like another Curtius, to devote himself to destruction to heal this breach? Would you prefer the ephemeral popularity of the hour to the renown which lasts for ages? Our lineage would give the lie to such a slander. No, sir; let us not delay to settle this question, and forever. The gentleman tells us the majority alone will make a sacrifice by voting for any proposition of compromise. What is the fact? The South contends that Missouri should be instantly admitted into the Union; the North cannot agree to this, because it descries something in the constitution repugnant to the Constitution of the United States. The answer to this objection has been repeated over and over again. If such, in truth, be the fact, let her come into the Union, and the Constitution of the United States will vindicate its own supremacy. Your objection, however, still remains unshaken, and you propose that she shall be admitted, upon the condition that her Legislature shall pass no law violatory of the Constitution of the Union. We meet you on this half-way ground, and close in with your proposition. Now, sir, where is the sacrifice of principle on either side? You guard the Constitution from infraction, and we have no hesitancy in uniting with you in this good work. If, then, gentlemen are sincere in the objection which they raise, that objection may readily be removed, and I will still entertain the hope that this session will not terminate without the final adjustment of this odious subject.

The question being taken on agreeing to the proposed amendment, the Chairman pronounced the division to be in the affirmative—yeas 75, nays 73.

The Committee then rose, and reported the amendment to the House; and the question being put on agreeing to the amendment reported by the Committee of the Whole, the vote was as follows:

YEAS—Messrs. Abbot, Alexander, Allen of Tennessee, Anderson, Archer of Maryland, Archer of Virginia, Baldwin, Ball, Barbour, Bayly, Bloomfield, Brevard, Brown, Bryan, Burton, Butler of Louisiana, Cannon, Clay, Cobb, Cocke, Crawford, Crowell, Culpeper, Cuthbert, Davidson, Earle, Eddy, Edwards of North Carolina, Fisher, Floyd, Garnett, Gray, Hall of North Carolina, Hardin, Hill, Hooks, Jackson, Johnson, Jones of Virginia, Jones of Tennessee, Kent, Little, Lowndes, McCoy, McCreary, McLane of Delaware, McLean of Kentucky, Meigs, Mercer, Metcalf, Montgomery, Neale, Nelson of Virginia, Newton, Parker of Virginia, Pinckney, Rankin, Read, Rhea, Ringgold, Robertson, Sawyer, Shaw, Simkins, Sloan, Smith of New Jersey, Smith of Maryland, A. Smyth of Virginia, Smith of North Carolina, Swearingen, Terrell, Trimble, Tucker of Virginia, Tucker of South Carolina, Tyler, Walker, Warfield, Williams of Virginia, and Williams of North Carolina—79.

NAYS—Messrs. Adams, Allen of Massachusetts, Allen of New York, Baker, Bateman, Beecher, Boden, Brush, Buffum, Butler of New Hampshire, Campbell, Case, Clagett, Clark, Cook, Crafts, Cushman, Dane, Darlington, Dennison, Dickinson, Edwards of Connecticut, Edwards of Pennsylvania, Eustis, Fay, Folger, Foot, Ford, Forrest, Fuller, Gorham, Gross of New York, Gross of Pennsylvania, Guyon, Hackley, Hall of New York, Hemphill, Hendricks, Herrick, Hibshman, Hobart, Hostetter, Kendall, Kinsey, Kinsley, Lathrop, Lincoln, Livermore, Maclay, McCullough, Mallary, Marchand, Monell, R. Moore, S. Moore, Morton, Moseley, Murray, Nelson of Massachusetts, Parker of Massachusetts, Patterson, Philson, Pitcher, Plumer, Randolph, Rich, Richards, Richmond, Rogers, Ross, Russ, Sergeant, Silsbee, Stevens, Storrs, Street, Strong of Vermont, Strong of New York, Tarr, Tomlinson, Tompkins, Tracy, Udree, Upham, Van Rensselaer, Wallace, Whitman, and Wood—88.

So the amendment was rejected.

The resolution from the Senate being then again read, in the words following, to wit:

Resolved by the Senate and House of Representatives of the United States of America, in Congress assembled, That the State of Missouri shall be, and is hereby declared, one of the United States of America, and is admitted into the Union on an equal footing with the original States, in all respects whatever: *Provided,* That nothing herein contained shall be so construed as to give the assent of Congress to any provision in the constitution of Missouri (if any such there be) which contravenes that clause of the Constitution of the United States which declares that the citizens of each State shall be entitled to all the privileges and immunities of citizens in the several States.

Mr. STORRS moved to amend the same as follows, viz: Strike out from the word "declared" the balance of the resolution, and insert, in lieu thereof, the following:

"To be admitted into the Union as one of the United States, on an equal footing with the original States, on the first day of the next session of Congress: *Provided,* That it shall be taken as a fundamental condition upon which the said State shall be incorporated into the Union, and to be of perpetual obligation on the said State, (in faith whereof, this resolution is passed by Congress,) that no law shall ever be enacted by the said State, which shall impair or contravene the rights, privileges, or immunities, secured by the Constitution of the United States to any persons who now are, or

hereafter may be, citizens of other States, or to prevent such persons from removing to, and settling in, said State: *And, provided further,* That the Legislature, acting under the constitution already adopted in Missouri as a State, shall, as a convention, (for which purpose the consent of Congress is hereby granted) declare their assent by a public act to the said condition, before the next session of Congress, and transmit to Congress an attested copy of such act by the first day of the next session of Congress."

Mr. CLAY moved to amend the motion by striking out the words "on the first day of the next session," where they first occur; and the motion was agreed to—78 votes to 71.

Mr. FLOYD moved to amend the amendment so as to make it read "citizens of the United States," instead of "citizens of other States." This motion was negatived by 79 votes to 70.

Mr. ROBERTSON moved to amend the proposed amendment by striking out of it the words "or to prevent such persons from moving to and settling in said State." This motion was negatived by 79 votes to 70.

Mr. BARBOUR then moved to amend the said amendment by striking out the following words, viz: "That no law shall ever be enacted by the 'said State which shall impair or contravene the 'rights, privileges, and immunities, secured by the 'Constitution of the United States to any persons 'who now are, or hereafter may be, citizens of the 'other States," and, in lieu thereof, inserting "that 'no law which may be passed by the said State 'shall be so construed as to impair or contravene 'the rights, privileges, or immunities, secured to 'citizens of the other States by the Constitution 'of the United States."

On the question being taken so to amend the amendment, it was determined in the negative.

Mr. CUTHBERT having called for a division of the question on Mr. STORRS's amendment, so as to take it first on agreeing to the following words:

"To be admitted into the Union as one of the United States, on an equal footing with the original States, on the first day of the next session of Congress: *Provided,* That it shall be taken as a fundamental condition upon which the said State shall be incorporated into the Union, and to be of perpetual obligation on the said State, (in faith whereof this resolution is passed by Congress,) that no law shall ever be enacted by the said State which shall impair or contravene the rights, privileges, or immunities, secured by the Constitution of the United States to any persons who now are, or hereafter may be, citizens of other States"—

The question was so taken accordingly, and decided by yeas and nays as follows:

YEAS—Messrs. Abbot, Alexander, Allen of Tennessee, Anderson, Archer, of Maryland, Archer of Virginia, Baldwin, Barbour, Bayly, Bloomfield, Brevard, Brown, Bryan, Burton, Butler of Louisiana, Cannon, Clay, Cobb, Cocke, Crawford, Crowell, Culbreth, Culpeper, Cuthbert, Davidson, Earle, Fisher, Gray, Hall of North Carolina, Hardin, Hill, Hooks, Jackson, Johnson, Jones of Tennessee, Jones of Virginia, Kent, Little, Lowndes, McCoy, McCreary, McLane of Delaware, McLean of Kentucky, Meigs, Mercer, Metcalf, Montgomery, Neale, Nelson of Virginia, Newton, Pinckney, Rankin, Reid, Rhea, Ringgold, Robertson, Sawyer, Shaw, Simkins, Smith of New Jersey, Smith of Maryland, A. Smyth of Virginia, Smith of North Carolina, Stevens, Swearingen, Terrell, Tompkins, Trimble, Tucker of Virginia, Tucker of South Carolina, Tyler, Walker, Warfield, Williams of Virginia, and Williams of North Carolina.—75

NAYS—Messrs. Adams, Allen of Massachusetts, Allen of New York, Baker, Ball, Bateman, Beecher, Boden, Brush, Buffum, Butler of New Hampshire, Campbell, Case, Clagett, Clark. Cook, Crafts, Cushman, Dane, Darlington, Dennison, Dickinson, Eddy, Edwards of Connecticut, Edwards of Pennsylvania, Edwards of North Carolina, Eustis, Fay, Floyd, Folger, Foot, Ford, Forrest, Fuller, Garnett, Gorham, Gross of New York, Gross of Pennsylvania, Guyon, Hackley, Hall of New York, Hemphill, Hendricks, Herrick, Hibshman, Hobart, Hostetter, Kendall, Kinsey, Kinsley, Lathrop, Lincoln, Livermore, Maclay, McCullough, Mallary, Marchand, Monell, R. Moore S. Moore, Morton, Moseley, Murray, Nelson of Massachusetts, Parker of Massachusetts, Parker of Virginia, Patterson, Philson, Pitcher, Plumer, Randolph, Rich, Richards, Rogers, Ross, Russ, Sergeant, Silsbee, Sloan, Storrs, Street, Strong of Vermont, Strong of New York, Tarr, Tomlinson, Tracy, Udree, Upham, Van Rensselaer, Wallace, Whitman, and Wood—92.

So the first part of the amendment was rejected, and the remainder fell to the ground of course.

Mr. S. MOORE then moved to amend the resolution of the Senate by striking out the proviso thereto annexed, and inserting in lieu thereof the following:

Provided, That the following conditions be taken as fundamental conditions and terms upon which the said State is incorporated into the Union, namely : that the fourth clause of the twenty-sixth section of the third article of the constitution submitted by the people of Missouri to the consideration of Congress, shall, as soon as the provisions of said constitution will admit, be expunged, or so amended that it shall not be applicable to citizens of any State in this Union ; and that, until expunged or so amended, no law passed in conformity thereto shall be construed to extend to any citizen of either State in this Union.

This motion was negatived—ayes 56.

Mr. CLAY, then, seeing that all effort at amendment had failed, and anxious to make a last effort to settle this distracting question, moved to refer the Senate's resolution to a committee of thirteen members.

This motion was agreed to, and the following gentlemen were appointed a committee accordingly :

Messrs. Clay, of Ky.,	Messrs. Archer, of Va.,
Eustis of Mass.,	Hackley of N. Y.,
Smith of Md.,	S. Moore, of Pa.,
Sergeant, of Pa.,	Cobb, of Ga.,
Lowndes, of S. C.	Tomlinson, of Con.,
Ford, of N. Y.,	Butler, of N. H.,
and Campbell, of Ohio.	

SATURDAY, February 3.

Mr. SERGEANT, from the Committee on the Judiciary, reported a bill for the relief of the legal representatives of John H. Mebane, deceased ; which was twice read and committed.

Mr. SERGEANT also made the following report :

The Committee on the Judiciary, to whom was referred the report of the Committee for the District of Columbia, upon the subject of lotteries, make the following report :

That they concur in the opinion expressed by the Committee for the District of Columbia, that it is not necessary or expedient for Congress now to interfere ; they therefore offer the following resolution :

Resolved, That the committee be discharged from the further consideration of the subject.

The report was concurred in by the House.

Mr. SERGEANT, from the same committee, to which was also referred a bill from the Senate, entitled "An act supplementary to an act passed on the 11th day of May, 1820, entitled 'An act to provide for the publication of the laws of the United States, and for other purposes," reported the same without amendment, and it was committed to a Committee of the Whole.

Mr. MALLARY, from the committee to whom was referred the Message of the President of the United States respecting the progress and expenditures of the Commissioners under the fifth, sixth, and seventh articles of the Treaty of Ghent, made a report, accompanied by a bill to establish the salaries of the Commissioners and agents appointed under the Treaty of Ghent ; which bill was read twice, and committed to a Committee of the Whole.

The Committee on Foreign Affairs were discharged from the consideration of the memorial of the Chamber of Commerce of New York, respecting the exposed state of the commerce of the United States in the Pacific Ocean, and it was referred to the Secretary of State.

The SPEAKER laid before the House a letter from the Postmaster General, transmitting a list of the names of those persons who were indebted to his department on the 31st December, 1816, and the amount then due from each person; also, the names of those, who, since that time, have become, and were indebted to the said department on the 30th day of September last, and the amount then due from each person ; prepared and rendered in obedience to a resolution of this House of the 30th of November last ; which letter and lists were referred to the committee appointed on the 19th of December, to inquire into the concerns of the General Post Office.

The Committee of the Whole to which is committed the bill to incorporate the United States Naval Fraternal Association for the relief of the families of deceased officers, were discharged, and the said bill was committed to the Committee of the whole House, to which is committed the bill to authorize the inhabitants of the District of Columbia to form a frame of government.

Mr. McLANE submitted the following resolution, which of course lies on the table :

Resolved, That the Secretary of the Treasury be directed to communicate to this House a statement of the bounties and allowances paid to fishing vessels each year, from the commencement of the Government to the present time.

OHIO AND THE UNITED STATES BANK.

Mr. Ross, after some remarks in favor of the propriety of the course which he was about to propose, founded on the importance of the subject to the particular State and to the Union, moved that the communication from the Governor of Ohio, received a few days ago, and the report of a committee of the Legislature relative to the controversy between that State and the Bank of the United States, be printed for the use of the members of this House.

Mr. TRIMBLE rose only to ask information from the Chair. He had no information of any case in which a paper of this description had been ordered to be printed. The object of printing a paper was to enable members to understand subjects pending before the House, and by it referred to committees, who would in due time report thereon. This subject was one upon which the House was not called upon to act in the usual course of legislation. He wished to know from the Chair, whether any case had occurred in which the House had ordered a paper to be printed, when it was distinctly understood that no legislative proceeding was in contemplation? and whether it was usual to print any paper, referring to the concerns of a corporation, and not the public interests? If there was any precedent, he would vote for printing the document, but if not, he would vote against it.

Mr. McCoy also opposed it, because the document was already ordered to be printed by the Senate, by which each member of this House would be furnished with a copy of it, and it was, therefore, unnecessary to incur the expense of having it printed again for this House.

The motion to print was supported by Mr. SLOAN, for the reason that the document was of great importance so far as regarded the question of State rights; and though he was aware that no legislative act would grow out of it here, it related to a controversy which had been much misrepresented, and was much misunderstood; and he hoped, in justice to the State, it would be permitted to be printed, that misconstruction might be as far as practicable corrected.

Mr. BALDWIN adverted to the resolutions of the Legislature of Pennsylvania, relative to the Bank of the United States, which had been referred to a committee of this House, at the last session, and were now before it; the document from Ohio was calculated to elucidate that subject, and therefore was a proper one to be printed for the information of members on the matter before them.

The motion to print the papers, was agreed to—ayes 63, noes 37.

Mr. SMITH, of Maryland, moved to go into Committee on the general appropriation bill, but temporarily withdrew his motion, at the request of Mr. CLAY.

SOUTH AMERICAN STATES.

Mr. CLAY then rose to make a motion. It would be recollected, he said, by the House, that, by a majority very decisive, a resolution was adopted at the last session, declaring it expedient to make an appropriation, by law, for a mission to such of the Governments of South America as had established their independence. It remained for the House to carry that resolution into effect; and he thought that it was a solemn duty of this House to give complete effect to its own decision. He rose, therefore, to move that the resolution adopted at the last session be referred to the same Committee of the whole House to which was referred the bill making appropriations for the support of Government, that it might come up for consideration, in a regular manner, and a clause be inserted in that bill to accomplish the object of the resolution. Mr. C. made this motion to prevent the imputation of taking the House by surprise. Conceiving it proper to act in the spirit of that resolution, he now proposed the preliminary step.

The motion was agreed to without a division, though not without dissenting voices.

APPROPRIATION BILLS.

The House then, on motion of Mr. SMITH, resolved itself into a Committee of the Whole, and proceeded to the consideration of the several appropriation bills referred to it.

The first bill taken up was the bill making appropriations for the public buildings, (according to the recommendations contained in the report of a select committee on that subject.) A good deal of discussion took place on some of the items of the bill, particularly that which proposed $7,000 for covering the President's house with copper. This, however, as well as the other appropriations proposed by the select committee, was eventually agreed to; and the committee proceeded to the consideration of the bill making appropriations for the support of Government for the year 1820.

On opening the first item of this bill, the Missouri question was discovered lurking in it!

Mr. SMITH, of Maryland, having moved to fill the first blank in the bill with $314,866, to defray the expense and compensation to the Senate and House of Representatives, their officers, and attendants—

Mr. COBB moved to fill the blank with a smaller sum, presuming that the sum moved by Mr. SMITH was founded on estimates including the Delegate from Missouri. As there was no such Delegate recognised on the floor of the House, the appropriation ought to be diminished accordingly.

A good deal of desultory debate followed on this proposition, the leading features only of which are sketched below.

Mr. BUTLER, of Louisiana, inquired of the chairman of the Committee of Ways and Means, whether the sum which he had proposed was intended to cover the pay for the Senators from Missouri.

Mr. SMITH said, the sum was proposed in conformity with the estimate of the Secretary of the Treasury, and was not predicated on any additional expenditure, as the State of Missouri had not been admitted. But at any rate the sum would be sufficient, because there was always, from the absence, the sickness at home, or the death of members, a considerable surplus left.

Mr. McLean said, the gentleman from Missouri did not present himself as the Delegate, but as the Representative from that State. Mr. McL. went on to remark, that this question about Missouri met them at every step, and in every shape; and it really would be better to postpone this bill, and, indeed, all other important bills, until that embarrassing question could be settled. With that view he moved that the Committee now rise, and report progress.

Mr. Tyler coincided in opinion with Mr. McLean, and hoped the motion would prevail, especially as the public interest could not suffer from a little delay in passing the bill.

Mr. Baldwin hoped the Committee would not rise. The clause in question did not go into items at all, and it could not, therefore, well give rise to the question concerning Missouri, which had been started by the gentleman from Georgia.

The motion for the Committee to rise was negatived—ayes 31.

Mr. Trimble spoke, to show that Mr. Cobb would gain nothing, if he should even carry his motion to reduce the appropriation. The appropriation was made as though Missouri was a State; if she were not admitted into the Union as such, she must be abandoned altogether, or must be legislated for as a Territory, and that question would with more propriety come up in another part of the bill, making provision for the Territories. He thought it not necessary, therefore, to impede the bill by pressing this motion.

Mr. Cobb observed, in substance, that the sum proposed by the chairman of the Committee of Ways and Means was either too large or too small. If intended to provide for Missouri as a State it was too small, as it did not provide for the Senators; and if otherwise, it was too large. He did not wish to bring up at all the question concerning the present character or condition of Missouri, but he did not think it right to appropriate for a Delegate unless for the Senators also.

Mr. Lowndes remarked, that whether they took the larger or the smaller sum was immaterial, as either would be sufficient for the object in any event; there being always a balance of the appropriation left from this branch of the expenditure. The adoption, therefore, of either sum proposed, could involve no question relative to Missouri.

Mr. McCullough did not conceive that the appropriation involved the Missouri question at all. They made appropriations for the Senate and House of Representatives generally, without undertaking to say who were Senators and members. Such as were so would come forward and receive their pay, and no others. This appropriation was intended for the current year; if Missouri should be admitted, her members in both Houses would be paid of course; if not, the money would remain in the Treasury.

Mr. Trimble said, the gentleman had told the Committee how the members were to be paid if that State should be admitted; but suppose Missouri should not be admitted, Mr. T. asked, how her Senators and members were to draw their pay then?

Mr. McCullough was understood to say, in reply, that if the State were not admitted her Senators could not be paid under this appropriation; and that it would require a special vote of Congress to authorize them to draw pay.

Mr. Livermore, by way of obviating all difficulty, moved an amendment, containing a separate appropriation of the necessary sum for the Senators and member from Missouri.

This motion was agreed to—yeas 50, nays 44.

The Committee then proceeded with the bill; on many of the items of which, as usual, there was a good deal of debate, particularly in regard to the salaries of different officers in the Executive departments at the seat of Government; but no motion was made but the following:

Mr. Johnson, of Kentucky, objected to the appropriation for the salary of the First Comptroller of the Treasury, ($3,500,) which he thought entirely too high, considering the nature of his duties; he protested against abandoning the fortifications, and other useful establishments, for the sake of economy, and yet maintain such extravagance in the salaries of the civil officers. Mr. J. moved to reduce the appropriation to $2,500.

The motion was opposed by Messrs. Cobb, Robertson, and others, on the ground that the appropriation was authorized by law, and that if this, or any other salary was too high, the proper mode was to reduce it by law, and not by refusing an appropriation, so long as the expenditure was legally authorized.

Mr. Johnson finally withdrew his motion; and the Committee spent some time longer on the bill, and made considerable progress in filling up the items of appropriation. Before the bill was got through, however, the Committee was left nearly without a quorum, and the usual hour of adjournment having arrived, the Committee rose, and reported progress.

Monday, February 5.

Mr. Williams, from the Committee of Claims, to which was referred the bill from the Senate, entitled "An act for the relief of Nathan Ford," made a report thereon, recommending that the said bill be postponed indefinitely; which report was read, and, together with the bill, ordered to lie on the table.

On motion of Mr. Hooks, the House proceeded to the consideration of the resolution submitted by him some days ago, calling for certain information respecting the Marine corps, and agreed thereto.

The House then took up the report of the Committee of the Whole, on the bill making certain appropriations for the Public Buildings; and, though not without considerable objections to some of the items, the report of the Committee of the Whole was concurred in, and the bill was ordered to be engrossed for a third reading.

GENERAL APPROPRIATION BILL.

The House then again resolved into a Committee of the Whole, on the General Appropriation Bill for the current year.

The discussion of the bill, or rather of particular items of it, occupied the whole day.

A motion was made by Mr. COOKE, to strike out the clause proposing an appropriation for the clerk to the Attorney General. On this motion there took place a debate, which ended in a rejection of the motion.

On the question to fill the blank reported by the committee, ($1 000,) it was decided in the negative. The blank was then filled with $800.

The appropriation of $1,000 for the salary of the reporter of the Supreme Court, was objected to by Mr. HARDIN, but was agreed to.

In the course of proceeding to agree to the several items of appropriation, as moved by the chairman of the Committee of Ways and Means, it appeared, from the statement of Mr. SMITH, of Maryland, that it was expected that our Minister to France might return within the present year, and, therefore, an appropriation was asked for an outfit for a Minister to France. It also appeared that, for the present, it was not contemplated to send a Minister to replace Mr. Graham, our late Minister to Rio Janeiro, but that the United States were to be represented there by a Chargé des Affaires.

In the course of the debate a motion was made, by Mr. TARR, to amend the bill, by inserting the following item:

"For the erection of a bridge over the Monongahela river, where the Cumberland road crosses the same, the unexpended balance of the money heretofore appropriated for completing the Cumberland road."

This motion gave rise to much debate; in the course of which it appeared that there remains, of the money appropriated for the completion of the Cumberland road, an unexpended balance of seventy thousand dollars. It is supposed that the proposed bridge will cost $40,000. The Secretary of the Treasury had not thought it proper to cause the bridge to be erected, without express authority from Congress.

The gentlemen who engaged in the debate were, Messrs. BALDWIN, ROSS, SMITH, of Maryland, HARDIN, TARR, McCOY, MERCER, ROBERTSON, COBB, BRUSH, McLANE, SERGEANT, BROWN, CLAY, BEECHER, and RHEA.

Mr. McCULLOUGH moved to amend this amendment by adding the following: "and for repairing the road from Chambersburg to Pittsburg —— dollars."

This motion was negatived.

Mr. ARCHER then, to obviate some difficulties which gentlemen had stated, moved to amend the amendment, by adding to it a clause to the following effect: "*Provided*, That the unexpended balance shall be sufficient to complete the bridge."

Mr. TARR accepted this amendment as part of his motion.

After further debate the amendment, as amended, was finally negatived, by 65 votes to 60.

Mr. RANKIN moved to amend the bill, by inserting the following clause:

"For opening, under the direction of the Secretary at War, a road from a point near Columbus, on the United States military road, to a point near Turner Brashears' stand, on the old road leading from Natchez to Nashville, five thousand dollars of an unexpended balance of an appropriation made by an act of Congress of the 27th of March, 1818, for the purpose "of repairing and keeping in repair so much of the road leading from Columbia, in the State of Tennessee, to Madisonville, in the State of Louisiana, as lies within the Indian country."

The amendment was agreed to.

On motion of Mr. SILSBEE, aided by Mr. LINCOLN, the House agreed to increase the appropriation for the contingent expenses of Congress one thousand dollars, for the purpose of erecting a monument over the grave of the late Vice President Gerry, who died and was buried in Washington City, during his term of service.

At a late hour the Committee rose, and obtained leave to sit again, on motion of Mr. CLAY, who was prepared to move an amendment, respecting a mission to South America, but thought the hour too late, and the House too thin.

TUESDAY, February 6.

The SPEAKER presented a petition of sundry mechanics and others, concerned in building in the City of Washington, praying for the passage of an act giving mechanics, and persons furnishing materials for buildings, a lien on the property on which such house may be built, to secure the payment of their respective accounts; which petition was referred to the Committee for the District of Columbia.

Mr. NEWTON, from the Committee of Commerce, reported a bill for the relief of William Bartlett and John Stearns, and others; which was read twice, and committed to a Committee of the Whole.

Mr. ANDERSON, from the Committee on the Public Lands, to which was referred the bill from the Senate, entitled "An act for the relief of John Coffee," reported the same without amendment, and it was committed to a Committee of the Whole.

On motion of Mr. CANNON, the Committee on Military Affairs were instructed to inquire whether or not the Military Academy, under the existing laws and regulations, is consistent with the principles and policy of the Constitution and Government of the United States; also, to inquire into the expediency of repealing or altering the laws in relation to said Academy, and reducing the expenditures of the public money on the same.

On motion of Mr. WILLIAMS, of North Carolina, the Committee of Ways and Means was instructed to inquire into the expediency of prohibiting, by law, any clerk, or other officer of the departments, from entering, either directly or indirectly, into any contract with the Government of the United States.

An engrossed bill, entitled "An act making appropriations for the public buildings," was read a third time, and passed.

A message from the Senate informed the House that the Senate have passed bills of the following titles, to wit: "An act for the relief of Samuel

Tucker, late a Captain in the Navy of the United States;" and "An act authorizing the sale of certain grounds belonging to the United States in the City of Washington;" in which bills they ask the concurrence of this House.

THE REVENUE.

Mr. SMITH, of Maryland, from the Committee of Ways and Means, who were instructed by three resolutions adopted by this House on the 3d ultimo, to inquire and report "whether, in their opinion, the permanent revenue is adequate to the expenses of Government; whether any measures are necessary to increase the revenue; and, if so, to report those measures; and into the expediency of prohibiting or imposing additional duties on the importation of foreign spirits, and imposing an excise on domestic distilled spirits," made a report thereon; which was read, and ordered to lie on the table; and that 3,000 copies thereof be printed for the use of the members of Congress. The report is as follows:

That they have had these important subjects under their consideration, and have obtained from the several departments all the information which the officers at their head could furnish; yet, such are the difficulties that present themselves, that they enter into the discussion and the statements necessary to elucidate the subject with great diffidence. They may differ in opinion with gentlemen for whose talents they have the highest respect, and in whose integrity they have unbounded confidence; the subject is one, however, on which the best friends may fairly differ in opinion.

Is the permanent revenue adequate to the expenses of the Government?

The revenue is mainly bottomed on the duties arising on the importations of foreign goods; it is, therefore, dependent on fortuitous circumstances, which cannot easily be foreseen, and which may tend to its increase or decrease; there are some, however, which can, in a degree, be appreciated. The tariff of 1816 was expected to operate a loss to the revenue, by giving what was considered at the time sufficient encouragement to the manufactures of the country. A variety of causes, arising out of excessive and ruinous importations, and the time required for diverting one channel of commerce or supplies into another, has, until lately, prevented the effect from being materially felt. The operation of that tariff is now beginning to be known, and the effect on the revenue is believed to be considerable, and, to its extent is, however, not completely developed. Its operation on a few of the principal articles may afford some idea of the increase of our manufactures, and the consequent decrease of the revenue resulting from the duties on the importation of such articles.

The tariff of 1816 increased the duty on brown sugar about 20 per cent., and gave a protecting duty to that article of 3 cents per pound. No material decrease has, as yet, resulted to the revenue therefrom. The tariff was enacted during the existence of the excise on domestic distilled spirits, and an additional duty was imposed for the protection of the domestic article. The excise on imported spirits was repealed; the duty was continued; and the duty on foreign spirits exceeds, at this time, the whole value of the domestic; the average duty on the imported being 43 cents per gallon, when the value in the market of the

domestic does not exceed 33 cents the gallon. This has tended, it is believed, to decrease the consumption of foreign spirits, and, of course, the amount of the revenue. In 1818, the net revenue from imported spirits, after deducting the debentures, amounted to $2,646,186, and in 1819 to $1,959,125.

The tariff of 1816 raised the duties on cotton and woollen cloths from 12½ per cent., the duty imposed prior to the late war, to 25 per cent., and it valued all cotton cloths under a cost of 25 cents the square yard (although some cost as low as 6 cents) as if they had actually cost 25 cents, and charged the duty thereon accordingly. The result has been, that cotton goods imported from India, under a cost of 25 cents the square yard, pay a duty exceeding 60 per cent. on the average cost of those heretofore imported from that country, and above 40 per cent. on the average cost of similar goods when imported from Europe. The operation has had a salutary effect on our infant manufactures of cotton, which begins to be understood by the manufacturers. The importations from India of such cottons as are under a cost of 25 cents the square yard have almost ceased for consumption, and those from Europe have decreased, it is believed, to a considerable extent. The coarse cottons of our domestic manufactures have entered, it is believed, into the consumption of the nation, nearly equal to the wants of the people. The increase of our woollen manufactures has afforded a considerable quantity of woollen cloths for consumption, but we have no information on which to form a decided opinion as to its extent. Other important articles of domestic manufacture are silently entering into competition with those heretofore imported from foreign nations. These circumstances, added to the distresses of the people, and to the price of our exports, being such as in a great degree to affect the means of paying for imports, make it extremely difficult to form a correct estimate of the revenue which may arise hereafter from duties on imports, estimated on that which had been received in former years.

With these views, which the committee have deemed it proper to submit, they proceed to answer the first resolution.

They are of opinion "that the revenue which will be received in the present year will be adequate to the expenses of the Government;" and, should no change take place, the revenue will, in their opinion, during the years 1822, 1823, and 1824, be not only equal to the expenses of Government, but afford such a surplus, applicable to the payment of the loan of the last year, and any that may be authorised for this year, as will, before the first day of January, 1825, fully repay the amount borrowed. The House will remember that, as the appropriation bills have not passed, the real or true expenses of Government cannot be correctly stated. The committee are compelled, therefore, to bottom their statement on the estimated expenses, as submitted to Congress, which will, it is confidently believed, be reduced at least one and a half million of dollars.

It is now reduced to a certainty that the actual receipts from the customs into the Treasury, during the year 1820, has been $15,005,328, which amount, it is humbly conceived, may be safely relied on as the receipts for the present year. The committee are of opinion that the receipts of 1821 (from that source) will exceed that amount. They form that opinion from the following circumstances, to wit: the bonds for duties in the Treasury amounted, on the first day of October, 1820, to nearly the same sum as those in the Treasury on the 1st of October, 1819; that from those of 1819 an extraordinary deduction was made by the more common amount of debentures issued on the reshipment of goods during that year; that a similar amount of drawbacks, it is believed, will not occur during the present year, and, of course, that the revenue from imports will be greater in 1821 than that of 1820; and, in this opinion, they are confirmed by the following view of the customs for the present year:

Bonds in the Treasury on the first day of October, 1820 - - - - - $18,770,000

From which must be deducted—

Bonds irrecoverable -	$1,250,000	
Bonds in suit, which may not be received during the present year - - -	750,000	
Bonds paid in fourth quarter of 1820 - - - -	2,626,815	
Debentures actually issued, prior to the 1st October, on those bonds - - -	1,163,000	
Debentures which may be issued on the same, estimated at - - - -	637,000	
		6,426,815

Estimated net proceeds from those bonds -		12,343,185
Add thereto the amounts of receipts into the Treasury from bonds taken during the last quarter of the year 1820, and taken, or to be taken, during the two succeeding quarters of 1821, which, bottomed on the receipts into the Treasury for actual receipts from bonds taken during the fourth quarter of 1819, and the first and second quarters of 1820, are estimated to give, for the present year, the sum of - - - -		4,437,205
		$16,780,390

The committee have submitted the preceding view of the customs for 1821 for the consideration of the House, but would not be willing to pledge themselves for the result. The items they believe to be correct; and the present appearance of our commerce, becoming less unfavorable, warrants them in the belief that the revenue from customs for 1821 will not be less than sixteen millions of dollars. They, however, deem it more safe to assume the receipts of the present on that of the preceding year, and therefore submit the following statement:

Estimated receipts for 1821.

Customs received in the first, second, and third quarters of 1820, (see Secretary's report,)	$12,378,513	
Customs received in the fourth quarter -	2,626,815	
A statement from the Treasury to your committee, assumed as the receipt for 1821 - - - -	15,005,328	
Land, agreeably to the report of the Secretary of the Treasury - - -	1,600,000	
Internal taxes, by same - - -	100,000	
Bank dividend, by same - - -	350,000	
Post Office and incidental receipts may be estimated at - - - -	100,000	
	17,155,328	

Estimated expenditures. (See Treasury report of December 4, 1820.)

Civil - - - -	$1,769,850	
Civilizing Indians - -	29,200	
Military Department - -	6,798,515	
Naval Department - -	2,928,676	
Public debt, principal and interest, for 1821 - -	5,477,776	
		17,004,017

Excess of receipts over payments - -		$151,311

The preceding statements show that there will be an excess of receipts over the expenditures, even if the whole amount estimated for by the different Departments should be granted and expended. But it is known that the amount is estimated on the presumption that all the expenditures authorized by law will be required. This, however, in time of profound peace, has seldom been the case. The reform in the army, and reduction from the estimates of the several Departments, will amount at least to one and a half million of dollars, and thus confirm the opinion expressed by the committee, "that the revenue for 1821 will be fully adequate to the expenses of Government for that year."

The committee submit their views for the succeeding years of 1822, 1823, and 1824, to prove the opinion that the revenue will be fully equal to the payment of the expenses of Government during those years. In addition to the statement given of the receipts from customs for the year 1821, and with the view of further elucidating the subject, they submit the following statement of the receipts derived from the customs, land, &c., for the years 1817, 1818, 1819, and 1820; three of those years are known to be the minimum years, the fourth not uncommonly productive.

In 1817 the customs produced net -	$17,524,778
In 1818 the customs produced net -	21,828,431
In 1819 the customs produced net -	17,116,702
In 1820 the customs produced net -	15,005,328
	$71,475,239

$71,475,239, averaged on four years, gives for one year - - - -	$17,868,809

Although your committee think it probable that the average receipts from the customs, during those four years, will be realized for the years 1822, 1823, and 1824, yet, under the uncertainty arising from the view already given, they consider it more safe to assume a less amount, and therefore submit the following statement of receipts and expenditures as one which they have full confidence may be relied upon for 1822, 1823, and 1824.

Receipts.

Customs - - - -	$17,000,000	
Land, (per report of Secretary,) -	2,500,000	
Bank dividends - - -	420,000	
Postage and incidental - -	200,000	
	$20,120,000	

Expenditures for those years.

Civil, miscellaneous, and diplomatic - - -	$1,750,000	
Civilizing Indians - -	29,000	
		$1,779,000

Military Department, to wit:

Arming militia - - -	$200,000
Indian annuities - - -	152,000
Revolutionary pensions -	1,200,000
Invalid pensions - - -	300,000
Fortifications - - - -	400,000
Indian Department - -	170,000
National armories - - -	360,000
Cannon, shot, and shells	50,000
Arsenals - - - -	30,000
Army proper, (including the ordnance service and the Military Academy at West Point,) estimated, agreeably to the bill which has passed the House, at its utmost amount, to cost - - - 2,000,000	

	4,862,000
Naval, including $500,000 per annum, for the gradual increase of the Navy, amounting, agreeably to the estimate for 1821, to - - - -	2,928,676
Public debt, (see report,) - - -	5,477,000
	$15,046,676

leaving a surplus of $5,673,324 per annum, from which will be deducted the interest on any loan that may be authorised during the present year.

The preceding view will show that the committee, in answer to the second question, to wit: " Whether any measures are necessary to increase the revenue ?" are of opinion that the revenue is amply adequate to the expenses of the Government, and, of course, that no measure for its increase is necessary.

To the third resolution, to wit: " Is it expedient to prohibit or impose additional duties on the importation of foreign spirits, and to impose an excise on domestic spirits ?" the committee answer, that the revenue from imported spirits amounted in 1818 to $2,646,496, and in the year 1819 to the sum of $1,959,125; and it is believed that that of the year 1820 will not amount to the sum received in 1819. But the committee are of opinion that the imposition of an excise, at this time of extreme distress, would be unwise, and is not demanded by the condition of the Treasury; and that, if imposed, it would be difficult to collect; and, if collected, it would, in some parts of the Union, be in paper little available to the Treasury. They therefore submit their opinion against any immediate imposition of an excise on domestic spirits, or of any new duty on, or prohibition of, the importation of foreign spirits.

The committee have thus far confined themselves to the answering of the three resolutions referred to them, they have, however, deemed it not improper, whilst on the subject, to submit their views of the financial state of the Treasury.

The demands on the Treasury, necessary to complete the payments for the year 1820, are—

For civil, diplomatic, and miscellaneous	$855,905 00
Public debt - - - -	2,076,913 15
Mississippi stock - - -	571,827 57
Navy Department, (report of the 21st December,) - - - -	1,110,000 00
War Department, agreeably to a letter from the Secretary, dated 31st of January, to the Committee of Ways and Means - -	$692,285 75

From which must be deducted, agreeably to the same letter, the amount of money in the hands of the Treasurer, as agent for that Department, on the 1st day of January, the sum of - 251,565 30

               $440,720 45

	5,055,366 17

From which is to be deducted—

Amount of money in the Treasury on the 1st day of January $1,076,271 18
Less the notes of insolvent banks, which will not be available during the present year - - - 600,000 00

Leaving available funds in the Treasury, on the 1st of January - - 476,271 18

Balance against the Treasury, on the 1st day of the present year - - $4,579,094 99

The committee believe the above statement to be accurate, and that the balance against the Treasury on the first day of the present year amounted to the sum of $4,579,094 99; that balance will, it is believed by your committee, be reduced by retrenchment in expenditures, as already stated, to an amount not less than one and a half million, which will reduce the actual deficit to be provided for to the sum of three millions seventy-nine thousand ninety-four dollars and ninety-nine cents; say three millions seventy-nine thousand and ninety-four dollars and ninety-nine cents. But if the estimate of the Secretary of the Treasury should prove correct, to wit: That the customs of 1821 will produce only fourteen millions, then the two years will show the following result:

Deficit, as above, on the 1st January $4,579,094 99
Excess of expenses over receipts in the year 1821, estimated on the demands made by the several Departments, conformably with the existing laws - 854,017 00

          $5,433,111 99

From which deduct amount of expected retrenchment - - - - - 1,500,000 00

          $3,933,111 99

The item of $854,017 will be found in the difference of $1,005,328 between the Secretary's estimates of the receipts from customs in the year 1821, and that of your committee; from which must be deducted the excess of receipts over expenditures of $151,311, in the view they have taken above of the receipts and expenditures of 1821, which will leave the item of $854,017.

In this last view, bottomed on the estimate of the Secretary of the Treasury for the receipts in the present year, there appears to be an actual deficit in the two years of 1820 and 1821 of $5,433,111 99, from which the committee believe that there may be deducted for retrenchment $1,500,000, which will leave the sum of $3,933,111 99 to be provided for.

The committee have deemed it proper to give to the House these two views of the subject. If the estimates of the Secretary of $14,000,000 from the customs should prove correct, the amount to be provided for will be, as already stated, $3,933,111 99.

If that of your committee should appear to the House as one to be relied upon, then the amount to be provided for will be $3,079,094 99. The committee ask leave to observe that a more accurate view of the actual amount to be provided for will be taken by your committee, if the appropriation bills shall pass in time to afford the opportunity.

The House have been correctly informed by the Secretary of the Treasury, that it requires time to transfer the money received in the Western States and in Louisiana, to the Treasury, for which the Secretary asks the aid of $800,000; that difficulty will, in the opinion of your committee, be surmounted by the amount of appropriations which will remain unclaimed at the expiration of the present year. The unclaimed demands of appropriations at the expiration of each year have, on an average of years, amounted to about three millions of dollars; but, as the appropriations for the present year will be of a kind that will be called for to a greater proportionate amount than those of former years, it would be unsafe to calculate on a larger amount than that which would afford the time necessary to draw the funds from the States mentioned; but to that amount, say six hundred thousand dollars, and to meet unforeseen demands on the Treasury, the committee are of opinion that the appropriations unexpended at the end of the present year will be amply adequate, and therefore they do not recommend any provision therefor.

The House will duly appreciate the difficulties under which the committee have acted, and will pardon unintentional errors, if any. The committee will only add, that they have used every exertion in their power to arrive at a correct view of the important subjects submitted to their consideration. All which they respectfully submit.

REDUCTION OF SALARIES.

Mr. CULBRETH, from the committee appointed on the 13th ultimo, to inquire if any, and what, salaries in the civil department may be reduced, consistently with the public interest, reported a bill to reduce the salaries, and fix a maximum of the compensation of certain officers and other persons employed in the civil department of the Government; which was read twice, and committed to the Committee of the whole House on the state of the Union. The bill is as follows:

Be it enacted, &c., That, in lieu of the salaries now allowed by law to the following officers, and other persons, employed in the civil department of the Government, there shall be paid to them, quarterly, the following annual salaries, respectively, and no more; that is to say, to the Secretary of State, five thousand dollars; to the Secretary of the Treasury, five thousand dollars; to the Secretary of War, five thousand dollars; to the Secretary of the Navy, five thousand dollars; to the Attorney General, three thousand dollars; to the Postmaster General, three thousand five hundred dollars; to the Assistant Postmaster General, and additional Assistant Postmaster General, each two thousand dollars; to the Commissioners of the

Navy Board, each three thousand dollars; to the Naval Constructors, each two thousand dollars; to the First Comptroller of the Treasury, three thousand dollars; o the Librarian, one thousand dollars; to the Commissioner of the Public Buildings, one thousand five hundred dollars; to the Superintendent of the Patent Office, one thousand dollars; to the clerk of the Attorney General, five hundred dollars; to the clerk of the Commissioner of the Public Buildings, five hundred dollars; and to the clerk of the Superintendent of the Patent Office, five hundred dollars.

SEC. 2. *And be it further enacted,* That the salaries of each of the officers and clerks of the Senate and House of Representatives, and of each and every other officer, clerk, or other person, employed in any of the public offices, at the Seat of Government, not herein particularly designated, shall be reduced twenty per centum from the respective amounts now allowed by law.

SEC. 3. *And be it further enacted,* That, whenever the annual salaries and other compensation or emoluments, now allowed by law to each or any of the following officers, after deducting therefrom the necessary expenditures incident to their respective offices, shall exceed the following sums: that is to say, to the Collectors of the Customs, four thousand dollars; to the Naval Officers, three thousand dollars; to the Surveyors of the Customs, two thousand five hundred dollars; to the Registers of the Land Offices, two thousand five hundred dollars; to the Receivers of Public Moneys at the several Land Offices, two thousand five hundred dollars—the several surplusses shall be accounted for, and paid by them, respectively, to the Treasury of the United States: *Provided, always,* That nothing herein contained shall be construed to extend to fines, forfeitures, and penalties, under the revenue laws of the United States.

SEC. 4. *And be it further enacted,* That the salaries of Military and Naval Storekeepers shall be limited not to exceed six hundred dollars each.

SEC. 5. *And be it further enacted,* That the operation of this act shall commence and take effect from and after the fourth day of March next, and that so much of any and every act, heretofore passed upon the subject, as is inconsistent with, or repugnant to the provisions herein contained, be, and the same is hereby, repealed, from and after that date.

SOUTH AMERICAN STATES.

The House then again resolved itself into a Committee of the Whole, and resumed the consideration of the General Appropriation bill.

Mr. CLAY moved the amendment, which he a few days ago intimated it to be his intention to propose to the bill, and was as follows:

"For an outfit and one year's salary to such Minister as the President, by and with the advice and consent of the Senate, may send to any Government of South America, which has established and is maintaining its independency on Spain, a sum not exceeding $18,000."

Mr. CLAY followed his motion with a speech of more than an hour's length in its support.

Mr. LOWNDES submitted briefly the reasons why he conceived the adoption of the proposition at this time inexpedient, and the mode of obtaining the object improper.

[The following is the substance of the remarks

made by Mr. ROBERTSON, of Kentucky, on the 6th and 9th of February, on the motion to appropriate eighteen thousand dollars for an outfit and salary for a Minister to South America.]-

I regret (said Mr. ROBERTSON) the necessity which impels me to a participation in this discussion. While my feelings strongly incline me to silence, my judgment commands me, in self-justification, to obtrude on your patience a brief explanation of the reasons which influence my vote. If I could support the motion, I would be content with a silent affirmative; but, feeling it my duty to oppose it, it is proper, and perhaps necessary, that I should vindicate myself, lest some persons, recollecting the vote which I gave last Winter on the South American resolution, and, not understanding the intent and import of that vote, and the operation of that which I am now required to give, might charge me with inconsistency—with dereliction of principle, or the influence of motives inconsistent with the character which, if I have earned, I am unwilling to lose.

Whatever my conduct on the subject might (if unexplained) indicate, to those who do not understand the real character of the resolution of last session, and the tendency of this motion, or who will not analzye them, I flatter myself that all who will take the pains to comprehend them fully, will see in it consistency instead of inconsistency—constancy to principle, instead of any aberration from it, and a just attention to my own constitutional rights and duties, instead of an encroachment, either wanton or inadvertent, on those of a co-ordinate department of the Government.

However paradoxical it may appear to a superficial observer, yet, I feel a strong confidence that a thorough knowledge of the design and effects of the two propositions will, while it approves the vote which I gave on the resolution, maintain the propriety of that which I shall give on this motion, and show, not only that both will be excusable, but right, and that the latter is required by a regard as well to consistency as propriety.

I have not changed any opinion which I entertained last Winter, in relation to this subject, nor am I less animated now by the feelings and wishes which I then cherished. But I think that the resolution then, and the motion now, are radically different.

The motives which recommended the adoption of the former, cannot be connected with the latter; indeed they will not justify it. They do not even exist. All the ends which the resolution was designed to produce, have been accomplished. If this motion be intended for the same purposes, it is unnecessary; if, for others, they are ascertained to be either impracticable or unconstitutional in their operation. Wherefore, I believe that, while the resolution was justified by the ends it was intended to answer, this motion is indefensible by the same consideration, or by any argument of expediency or constitutionality. This I expect to show. The one was auxiliary, the other will be supererogatory or coercive.

I do not mean to say that such is the object of the motion, but that such must and will be its op-

eration and construction. And this is confirmed, not only by the nature of the proposition, but by some traits of the eloquent speech just concluded by my colleague (Mr. CLAY) in support of his motion. The only feature which I shall now take notice of, is his declaration, that "the resolution of last session was an expression of public sentiment which no monarch in Europe would ever have dared to disregard."

This indicates that he is surprised that the resolution did not induce the President to recognise the Patriots, and that he intends, by this motion, (if adopted,) to urge him still more persuasively to do what he is unwilling to do. This would be a reasonable inference from the remark. Yet I hope such a construction was not intended; because it argues a spirit of dictation and unconstitutional coercion; and I am sure that such a sentiment was not only not expressed last Winter, but was disavowed; and I am equally sure that, if it had not been disavowed, the resolution could not have been adopted. The tone of the speech made at the last session, in favor of the resolution, by its mover, was materially different from that which characterizes the one which he first made to-day in support of his motion. Then, he announced his object only to be an abstract expression of our sympathies with the Patriots, for their encouragement, and of our will for relief to the Executive : and he positively disavowed any wish that it should be construed into dictation or even a recommendation to the President. Now he seems to consider it as an enunciation of public sentiment which the President was bound to obey; and, consequently, that its reiteration now may be coercive. Although this discrepancy will tend to show the reasons of my vote last session and now, yet I regret that it has occurred ; because the design which it might indicate, in my colleague, is inconsistent with the elevation of character which so pre-eminently distinguishes him, and the candor and disinterestedness which have so signally marked his political career. I wish not to be misunderstood. I do not intend to intimate that he has any other object than what he has announced. I am not willing to suspect him for any other. But others, less friendly to him, when they observe the tone of his speech, delivered to-day, and its discordancy with that of last Winter, and examine the character and effect of his motion, might apprehend that the motives which stimulate his efforts are not such as become him, or ought to be encouraged.

Before I state my objections to the proposed appropriation, and the circumstances which distinguish it from the resolution adopted last Winter, I must notice the speech to-day, for another purpose. It intimated that the vote on this motion will be a test of the feelings of this House towards the Patriots, and of its opinions on the subject of their recognition. This might have been one of the effects of the resolution—but this motion cannot draw the line between the friends of the Patriots and their enemies ; because, however friendly we may be to the success of the Patriots, we cannot do them any service by the adoption of the motion. Whatever we may think about their recognition, we cannot recognise by any vote we can give: and because this motion will be opposed on grounds which have no connexion with our feelings or opinions in regard to the South American struggle. Besides, in regard to myself, I must say that I feel as much solicitude for the independence of Spanish America now as I ever did; and I have given some evidence of the deep interest I have felt on that subject. While I am not an enthusiast or madman on that interesting subject, I have no doubt that I feel as sincere and patriotic an anxiety about the ultimate results of the great struggle in South America as any prudent or rational man does or ought to feel, in this House or this nation. It is, indeed, as it has been so feelingly denominated by its distinguished advocate, (Mr. CLAY,) "a great, a glorious cause." It is a cause interesting to all mankind, and peculiarly so to the votaries of freedom: a cause on the issue of which are staked the dearest rights of the civilized community. In such a cause the people of this country are not, cannot be indifferent. No, sir; they feel a deep and lively interest in every incident of its progress. No one is more gratified than I am with the intelligence of the splendid conquest of Lima by Cochrane, just announced with such inspiring eloquence by my colleague. I hope that it may be true, and that the principles of enlightened liberty may march onward and triumphantly in the South, until they shall have extirpated every remnant of royalty, superstition, and despotic hierarchy, and until the whole population of Spanish America shall not only achieve their independence, but establish civil institutions, habits, and manners, adapted to secure to themselves and their posterity the full fruition of all the blessings of free government and free religion. This is a consummation most devoutly to be desired by all philanthropists of the world, whatever may be the various speculations about the capacity of the South American Spaniards to sustain free and liberal institutions until they shall have become more enlightened in the principles of civil and religious liberty; and I pray that it may soon be effected, and that the day may not be distant when the whole South American population may be seen worshipping as freemen, in the temple of freedom, and bowing as Christians at the altar of a Christian God. No man, in his sober senses, feels more anxiety for such a result than I do—not only on account of its beneficent effects on the people of the South, but also on account of the magic impulsion it would give to the people's cause, in "the great moral battle" in which the present generation are engaged, by encouraging, and inspiring, and invigorating the friends of human rights throughout the world.

But, whatever may be my feelings, my wishes, or my prayers, in so good and so great a cause, I do not consider myself permitted, by considerations of duty or prudence, to express them in this appropriation bill. I can see no desirable or Constitutional purpose to be effected by the success of the motion; and I think I can see a mischievous tendency in it.

If we could, by such an effort, achieve the in-

dependence of Spanish America, or even render it any essential service, without transcending our authority, or endangering our own safety, I would be one of the last men in this House to refuse or withhold my approbation and most cordial support. I would act with as much decision and alacrity as would become so good a purpose. But, if those who advocate the motion think that its success will contribute to accomplish, or even facilitate, the enfranchisement of South America, or that it is prudent, or safe, or Constitutional, for us to adopt it for that purpose, or any other which it can effect, I think they will find, on a careful examination of the whole subject, that they are mistaken, and that the only tendency of the measure (if it have any) will be to distract our own councils, or embarrass and coerce a co-ordinate department of the Government.

If the ends designed to be effected by the vote of last session, be the only ones which the motion to appropriate is intended to accomplish, there can be no necessity to adopt it. I see nothing to be gained by it. The avowed purposes of Congressional interposition have been accomplished. The opinions and feelings which prompted me to vote for the resolution of last session, and which I still cherish, do not require me to vote for this motion; and, when I look at the inevitable tendency of the motion, if adopted, (and if it shall have any effect at all,) I feel sure that it is inconsistent with the opinions, and motives, and purposes, avowed last session. I then went as far as I thought I had a right to go, and as far as I intended to go; I cannot be lured or forced any farther.

I acted last Winter under the influence of the motives and for the purposes then avowed by the advocates of the resolution; and, if any others had been avowed, especially such as I fear will be imputed to this motion, I would not, I could not, have supported the resolution. I cannot with certainty say what were the motives of all those who constituted the majority on that resolution, but I hazard nothing in speaking of those which, and which alone, were avowed, and those which were disavowed; which avowals and disavowals I then thought, and still believe, influenced, if not all, at least a majority of those with whom I then co-operated. And I believe I will be supported by the recollection of those who were here at the last session, when I say that those avowals and disavowals indicated a policy and a purpose which did not recommend any ulterior measure on our part, and which will not justify it now. I shall, therefore, advert to the declarations of last session, and to the character and effects of the appropriation proposed, for the purpose of showing not only that the course I am about to pursue is consistent and defensible, but that it is the only one which can be in consonance with the motives and purposes which were announced at the last session, and under the influence of which I then acted, and shall still act.

The Executive is, by the Constitution, vested with the exclusive power to nominate and to receive foreign Ministers. It will not be denied that, in the exercise of this highly responsible power, he should be free and independent, and that, so far as he is the depository of power, he, and he alone, should exert it; and that he, and he alone, is responsible for the manner in which it is exerted. No one department of the Government should embarrass, dictate to, or control any other, in the exercise of its Constitutional rights and duties. This is the theory of the Constitution, and a due and uniform adherence to its maxims is necessary to the preservation of the Constitution itself. Whenever any department is under the influence of any other, either openly or covertly exercised, the checks and balances of the Constitution are destroyed, and there is danger of a virtual metamorphosis of the Government, by a concentration of powers which are distributed in such a manner as to prevent such a tendency, if exercised honestly and independently by their Constitutional depositories.

In the exercise of the power to nominate Ministers, therefore, the President should not be instructed or awed by the House of Representatives. This view will show that the resolution of last session could not have been intended to have any coercive or dictatorial operation or construction. But this idea is fortified by the avowals and disavowals made by its mover and others who advocated it. It was adopted in the spirit of confidence in the Executive, and of co-operation with him, and acquiescence in whatever course he might, in the exercise of his own discretion and more informed judgment, think it most expedient to pursue, and not in a tone of dictation, or for the purpose of changing his opinion, or relaxing his resolution. It was not intended even to whisper advice, otherwise those who voted for it would have transcended their authority, because this House is not, and ought not to be, the adviser of the Executive. Doubts were said to exist whether the President was not deterred from sending a Minister to Spanish America, by an apprehension that public sentiment would not sustain him, and that this House would refuse an appropriation. It was also urged that the President had not the right to recognise the independence of a new Government without the assent of this House as well as of the Senate; and this is my own opinion. For the purpose, then, of giving him a pledge that public opinion would be with him, and that we would give him the money, provided he, with all the information he possessed, should think it expedient to send a Minister, and for the purpose of giving our assent to recognition, as far as we were or might be concerned in it, and not to command, or even recommend it, the resolution was introduced and adopted. It was intended only to strengthen, embolden, and disembarrass the President, by an assurance of our support, and not to censure or persuade. As far as the subject of recognition was affected, these, I affirm, without fear of contradiction, were the objects, and only objects, of the resolution. At least, they were the only ones that influenced me, and the only ones that were avowed, and I assert that all others were positively disavowed. I would have opposed the resolution if I had suspected that it was intended to have, or could have, either in construction or operation, any other effect on the Executive than a simple declaration that we were willing to appropriate money, and to support and co-operate with him, if he, acting alone on his own opinion and his own responsibility, should think fit to send a Minister to Spanish America, and that we gave our assent to recognition, leaving him free to discharge his power, in relation to it, in his own way, and according to his own wishes and opinion. And I venture to say, that, if any other design had not been disavowed, the resolution would have been rejected.

All that I intended, and all that I believe the majority intended, by the vote of last session, so far as the subject of recognition was concerned, was to say to the Executive: "We do not know 'what you are willing to do towards the Patriots; 'we do not even pretend to know or to say what 'you ought to do; but, lest you may be embar-'rassed by doubts as to public opinion, we inform 'you, that we will be content if you, with all the 'information you have, determine to recognise their 'independent existence; and, so far as we may 'have a right to participate with you in the exer-'cise of this high power, we give our assent to 'any act you may do, having confidence that any 'decision made by your discretion and wisdom, 'will be a correct one; but we do not wish you to 'understand that we advise you to any particular 'course. You must act on your own information 'and responsibility; we will furnish you with the 'means."

Sir, this was the language used in debate, and this was the language of those who adopted the resolution. Further than this I did not intend to go—further I could not go.

It was declared, that such an assurance to the Executive was one object of the resolution, and that another, and the only other, was to give encouragement to the Patriots, by giving them some testimony of our good feelings and wishes towards them. It was said, that such an expression of our disposition in their favor would have a great "moral effect" in their struggle, and would animate and invigorate them. So far as I could produce such a result by any abstract vote, without entangling ourselves in the contest, I was glad to have an opportunity to do it; and with that view, in addition to those I have mentioned, I voted for the resolution with pleasure and alacrity.

I was willing, as far as such a resolution would operate on the spirits of the Patriots, to inspire them with confidence, and stimulate them to new and more vigorous and persevering efforts. But I did not intend to pledge the United States to recognise their independence, or give them any aid; nor did I intend to make any appropriation after the adoption of the resolution, unless it should be called for by the President; and, although the resolution itself might authorize a different inference, the avowals that were made, and the nature of the objects to be obtained by its adoption, will abundantly show, that no more was intended by it than I have stated. The form was immaterial, so that the ends could be accomplished, and this was frequently mentioned in argument. Perhaps the form was liable to as few exceptions as any other which could have been devised. It only meant to give support to the Executive, and encouragement to the Patriots; we had no right or motive to do more. I trust that I have now shown satisfactorily the character and intent of the resolution; and, in doing so, I flatter myself that I have also justified the support which I gave it, by exhibiting the avowed objects of its adoption, all of which were constitutionally attainable, and right and proper, because within our power, and well intended.

But the reasons which would justify, and even render necessary, that vote, do not apply to the motion now under consideration, and cannot warrant, but do forbid, its adoption; because, by the resolution, all the ends have been achieved which were intended, and the adoption of this motion cannot be necessary to effect the same results, but must (if it have any practical operation) produce such as were never designed before, and such as we have no right to attempt. I repeat, that the objects of the resolution were, first, to animate the Patriots by an abstract proposition of our wishes for their success; and, second, to inform the President of our willingness to support him, as far as we had the power, in any measure which he, in his own opinion, might think it most expedient to adopt towards the Patriots, and to give our assent to recognition, as far as it might be supposed that we had a right to act. And here I beg leave to say, that this latter consideration had great influence on my vote. I did think, and still do, that the Executive should never recognise the independence of any new Government without the assent of this House. It would not be permissible for me here to make an argument to prove the correctness of this opinion. I will only observe, that it is in accordance with that expressed by my colleague, (Mr. CLAY,) and is fortified by one of the ablest arguments of one of the most enlightened statesmen who ever adorned this country. I will inquire, whether this doctrine was not urged as a reason why it was our duty to pass the resolution? Was it not said, that the Executive could not, would not, act without having our assent? I will now appeal to the author of the resolution, and of the motion now before us, to say, whether any other motives for the adoption of his resolution were avowed than those I have mentioned, and whether all others were not disavowed? I know he would answer affirmatively. These then are the reasons which rendered proper the vote of last session; and I declare that, if we had never yet passed a resolution on South American affairs, I would now vote for one with the same motives which induced me to vote for it last session. But having, by the adoption of that resolution, done all that was necessary, I see no motive to do any thing more, and think I see unanswerable objections to an attempt to go farther than we have gone. By going further we have no desirable or legitimate end to attain, and that is always a good objection to any species of legislation. But this is not my only objection.

And here may be seen the ground on which I feel bound to oppose the appropriation. If, instead of the resolution of last session, the motion had been made which is now offered, or if, immediately after the adoption of that resolution, we had been asked to make the appropriation, I should, for the reasons which induce me to vote for the resolution, have given such a measure my entire assent and most cheerful support; because then it could not be known what would be the President's determination on the subject of the mission, and it was immaterial, as was alleged in debate, whether the appropriation preceded the nomination of a Minister, or the nomination the appropriation. But the time which has interlapsed since the adoption of the resolution has given us indubitable evidence of the course of policy which the President is resolved to pursue. The motives, therefore, which recommended the resolution do not exist, and I can see no object to be attained by the appropriation, unless it be intended, by being used as the echo of public sentiment, to drive the President from the course of policy which he deems most expedient, and has determined to observe. If we could reasonably doubt whether the Executive has resolved not to send a Minister to South America, or whether he understood the resolution of last session, or whether he requires an appropriation before he can make up his mind, then we should have some pretext for making the appropriation. But is there a member on this floor who has the remotest doubt on this subject? Can any man tell me that he is not convinced that the President does not intend to nominate a Minister to the South; or that he has any hope that he intends to do so on the event of an appropriation; or that he would have done it heretofore if an appropriation had been made; or that he wants any further expression of public sentiment than that which he has received on that subject? No, sir; we have the strongest reasons to impress the conviction that he neither expects nor wishes an appropriation; that he needs no further information or assistance from us; and that if we had made an appropriation last Winter no Minister would have been sent. Did we not, by the resolution which was adopted, tell him that we would assent to recognition? Did he want more, if he had been disposed to send a Minister? Is it usual to vote an appropriation for a mission before it is called for? Why, then, did he not send a Minister? There is but one answer; it is, because he did not think it wise and prudent to do so. He has called for an appropriation for an outfit for a Minister to France to succeed Mr. Gallatin. Why has he not called for one for a Minister to South America? It is, because he intends to send a Minister to France, and has determined not to send one to South America. Having, then, given the Executive all the information and assistance which were necessary to exempt him from doubt or embarrassment, as far as we are concerned, and knowing, as we do, that he has, after having carefully considered our resolution and weighed all the arguments for and against a mission to the South, resolved against it, I would ask, what is the object of this motion? Is it to inform the Patriots of public feeling in this country? We have done it; and it is not necessary or dignified to repeat it every Winter. Is it to give assurance of our support to the Executive? We have done it. Is it to recognise the independence of any of the South American provinces? As far as we have any power on that subject, we have exercised it. All these ends have been effected by the resolution of last session.

Then, for what purpose make the appropriation? I hope there is no illegitimate object. But, whatever the object be, it is either unnecessary or unauthorized. It is unnecessary, if it be no other than that for which the resolution was adopted. If it be for any other, I repeat that it is not only unconstitutional, but inconsistent with the ends of that resolution. For, whatever may be the purposes intended by the motion, it can have either no effect, or a coercive one. And if this latter be either the design or the tendency of the motion, even those who are most anxious to have the Patriots acknowledged, cannot, if they revere their own Constitution, and understand its theory and principles, be willing that such an end should be produced by such means. The Constitution has distributed the sovereign power among three departments; and made each independent. On this distribution of power, and independence of its depositories, depend the preservation of the Constitution, and the conservation of all the rights which it was made to guard. And the moment one department can successfully encroach on and control, directly or indirectly, either of the others, the equilibrium of the Constitution is destroyed, and its theory changed. However flattering it may be to our pride, that the Judiciary should decide, and the Executive act, in all cases confided to their discretion, exactly as we wish, or as we would do if we had the power, yet, if this conformity be produced, not by their own uncontrolled judgments, but by a wish to gratify us, or a fear of offending us, they are not the Ministers of the Constitution, but the humble instruments of our own will. It is just as improper that we should control the Executive as that he should control us. We should all confine ourselves strictly to our sphere, and submit cheerfully to the conduct of each, as long as it is within the scope of the Constitution. I do not fear that the President will be alarmed by this motion, if it be adopted, into an abandonment of the policy which the suggestions of his own judgment have recommended to him. If he should be, he is unworthy of the high trust confided to him. But its tendency, without any adequate object, will be to annoy and embarrass him; and the example will be deleterious, because it may, in worse times, serve as a precedent to sanction similar measures, intended for sinister purposes, (for which this is not,) and crowned with fatal success. We should never countenance any measure, however good its motives, which may have such a pernicious tendency. I am unwilling to believe that any one here will vote for this motion in the hope that it will embarrass, coerce, or reproach the President. But I think that all will acknowledge, that, if it should not have this effect, it can have

none all. It might, indeed, have the effect of rendering the President obnoxious to popular resentment, by showing our importunity and his pertinacity, and by implying distrust in him, and reproach for the course which he pursues. And it may have the further effect of inducing a belief that we think he has wantonly disregarded the voice of public sentiment, and have determined to goad him with it until he shall be forced to obey it. No statesman can desire such consequences. Why, then, when we know that the President does not intend to send a Minister, are we required to make an appropriation? And this he has told us, by his conduct, as unequivocally as the plainest language could speak. For reasons satisfactory to himself, he has, on his own responsibility, after deliberating on our resolution, and consulting the lights he possesses, and carefully, and no doubt anxiously, weighing the whole matter, come to this determination. And, however some gentleman may regret this determination, we cannot control it; we should not attempt it. We have discharged our duty to the Patriots and the President; we have done all we could rightfully do; we agreed to make an appropriation, if he would take it; he will not use it. What more can we, should we do? If we could force the President to recognition, what will the country gain by it? And what may it not lose?

I would dictate to, I would coerce the Executive, or any other man or men, however exalted, as promptly as any other individual would, if I had the right to do it, and could thereby achieve any desirable end. But I cannot vote for a proposition which can produce no practical good, and may do mischief by its operation, its construction, or its example.

I have another objection to this motion: It is, that it will force the President, when the bill shall be presented to him for his signature, either to reject the whole appropriation, or, by his signature, give his assent to this appropriation for a Minister. And, in the latter event, he might be supposed to be bound to send a Minister, because he had approved an appropriation for that purpose. Sir, we act on our own responsibility; let the President act on his. I am not willing (if I had the power) to take it from him, or to impose any more on him than the Constitution imposes. Let him, with the exception of Constitutional restraint, and that of his own conscience and judgment, be as free as air. It is our interest as well as his that he should be. Let us attend carefully to our own duties, and enjoy our own pr v leges, and permit him to enjoy his rights and discharge his duties in his own way, without interference, dictation, or annoyance. This policy is safe to all. Any other is dangerous. If we repeatedly press this subject on the Executive, the inference will be that we do it to coerce him.

I have thus crudely endeavored to show my objections to this motion, and the consistency of my conduct. My opinions may be wrong, yet they are my opinions, and may justify or condemn my course. But I submit it to the candor of those who hear me to say, whether the vote I gave at the last session, and that which I shall now give, are not in perfect consonance, and whether any other course would not be incongruous? Is it consistent with the vote of last session to make this appropriation? We gave the vote last Winter for the information and support of the President, and would not have adopted it for any other or stronger purpose. We know now that he needs no further appropriation, if we make it. How can we consistently, then, with the objects of the vote of last session, adopt this amendment?

Sir, the appeal which has been just made to us by my colleague, (Mr. CLAY,) is as sensibly felt by me as by any other member of this House; and no one would promote his personal interests, or gratify his feelings, where it could be done consistently with public duty, sooner than I would. I know he will acknowledge the sincerity of this declaration. He is not without proofs of it. But whatever may be my inclinations, personal considerations must give way when they carry me to the boundaries of my power, and encroach on the confines of principle. I voted with my colleague last Winter, for the reasons which I have mentioned with increased pleasure, because I was aiding him in that which was to him a splendid triumph, and one which was achieved without sacrifice of principle. I knew that he would soon leave us, (which I regret,) and I was anxious that he should retire with honor and applause; and, in regard to that retirement, (which I hope will only be temporary,) I thought it but due to his distinguished services that his country should say to him, as Jove did to Hector—

"Yet live, I give thee one illustrious day,
One blaze of glory, 'ere thou fad'st away."

Sir, the vote of last Winter, by giving success to his exertions for the Patriots, did crown him with laurels. I would not wither them, or pluck one leaf from the bright wreath. I wish they may flourish and be forever green. But I cannot water them by the vote I am about to give. I am sorry the motion is made. I hoped that the subject was buried last Winter, and that it should not be resuscitated. To carry the motion can confer no additional honor on the mover; to lose it, may diminish the glory of the triumph he has won. If he would be content with an abstract expression of our feelings towards the Patriots, although it is unnecessary and superfluous, (having done this before,) I would vote for it, because it will speak only what I feel in common with my constituents, and will not be liable to the principal objections which I have to the proposition which he has made. And why would not such a resolution satisfy all his wishes? Why annoy the Executive, session after session, with our opinion and advice, when we know that he does not desire them, and will not conform to them? And why do this, too, when every legitimate or desirable object has been already achieved, and can be again effected, if desired, as far as the Patriots are to be benefitted, in the manner which I have just suggested?

I have been charged with fastidiousness and metaphysical distinctions. I will only say, that

the reasons of my vote belong to my judgment and conscience. My feelings towards the Executive can never induce me to give a vote which my judgment disapproves. It will be well if all others are in the same situation. No personal considerations influence me. I hope I stand on higher and prouder ground—on ground consecrated by principles and not men. I do not court Executive smiles—I do not fear Executive frowns. I have nothing to gain by the one—nothing to lose by the other. And on this subject I need only refer to my course in this House for four years. When I believe the Executive wrong I oppose him; when right, I defend him: and while I would never oppose a measure which my judgment should approve merely because the Executive might be opposed to it, I would never advocate one which my judgment should not approve, merely to annoy or embarrass him.

I have not said any thing about the policy of recognition, because I rose only to vindicate my own vote, without intending or expecting to influence those of other members; and because the whole decision of that subject belongs to another department, from whose judgment, right or wrong, there is no appeal. And this shows the inefficacy of our argument on that point. I am, therefore, surprised to hear arguments intended to prove that it is right to recognise, and appeals made to our feelings to enlist us in the cause of recognition. If we intend to do no more than our duty, these arguments and appeals are unnecessary; for we know that we cannot recognise more than we have already done. All must now be done by the President.

But while on this subject I beg leave to say, that I have no reason to believe that the cautious course which the Executive has observed towards the Patriots has been unwise. He understands the whole subject, and I have no doubt the motives and reasons which have directed him are good and disinterested. And I must say, too, that I have no reason to believe that the people are dissatisfied. It is true, that they feel a deep solicitude for the success of the Patriots, but it does not follow that they condemn their Government for not entangling itself with their destinies. Having already, through their proper organs, expressed their feelings, they are content to leave the decision to the discretion and judgment of that department to which they have confided all the power that now remains to be exerted; and with whatever decision it shall make, I believe they will be satisfied. For myself I can say that, having discharged my duty, I am willing that the President should freely discharge his. With whatever he shall do I shall be content. I do not wish to control his conduct—I am unwilling to be responsible for it.

But, before I sit down, I declare that, if the President should determine to send a Minister to any of the Patriot Governments of South America, no man will be more gratified than I shall be; not only because such an event might animate the Patriots, and facilitate and confirm their triumphs, but because, after the prudent, cautious policy of the Executive heretofore, it would be the strongest and most satisfactory evidence of their capacity, moral and physical, to maintain their independence, and to preserve and enjoy its rights and its blessings.

When Mr. R. had taken his seat—

Mr. FLOYD, of Virginia, advocated, decidedly and earnestly, an immediate and unqualified recognition of South American independence.

Mr. STEVENS, of Connecticut, followed on the same side, and spoke at some length in support of the amendment.

Mr. TRIMBLE, of Kentucky, also advocated, at some length, the adoption of the proposition.

Mr. CULPEPER, of North Carolina, stated succinctly why he should vote for the amendment.

Mr. CLAY again occupied the floor some time in reply to Mr. LOWNDES, and in a zealous support of the proposition.

Mr. RHEA, of Tennessee, briefly offered the reasons which influenced him to oppose the proposition.

The question was then taken on adopting the proposed amendment, and decided in the negative. For the amendment, 73; against it, 77.

The Committee then rose and reported the bill and the amendments made thereto to the House.

Mr. CULBRETH moved to lay this bill on the table, before the amendments were acted on, with the view of first acting on the bill reported by him to-day to reduce the salaries of the officers and clerks in the civil department of Government; but, before this motion was decided, the House adjourned.

WEDNESDAY, February 7.

A new member, to wit: from North Carolina, WILLIAM S. BLACKLEDGE, elected to supply the vacancy occasioned by the death of Jesse Slocumb, appeared, produced his credentials, was qualified, and took his seat.

Mr. FORREST, from the committee appointed on the 4th of December last, to inquire respecting certain loans of lead and gunpowder by the ordnance department to certain individuals, made a report thereon, giving the view which the committee entertain of the transaction, but not recommending any interposition on the part of this House; and the report was ordered to lie on the table.

The SPEAKER laid before the House a report of the Commissioners of the Sinking Fund, detailing their operations subsequent to their report dated the 5th of February last; which was read, and ordered to lie on the table.

The bill from the Senate for the relief of Commodore Tucker, and the bill authorizing the sale of certain grounds belonging to the United States in the city of Washington, were twice read, and committed.

Mr. ROBERTSON submitted for consideration the following resolution:

Resolved, That the Committee on Military Affairs be instructed to inquire into the expediency of establishing at some eligible place on the Western waters a military academy.

And the question being taken on agreeing thereto, without debate, it was decided in the negative.

The House then resolved itself into a Committee of the Whole, on the bill to authorize the collectors of customs to pay debentures on loaf sugar, and spirits distilled from molasses, exported. The committee having filled the blanks therein—

The bill was reported to the House, and was ordered to be engrossed for a third reading.

The House, on motion of Mr. STORRS, went into Committee of the Whole on the report of the Committee of Claims unfavorable to the petition of Alvin Bronson, (who, having a boat in the public service on Lake Ontario, during the late war, which was sunk by the commanding officer to save the boat and its cargo of munitions from capture by the enemy, but was captured notwithstanding, now prays compensation for the said boat.)

Mr. STORRS opposed the report very zealously, and concluded a long speech against it by moving to reverse the report and instruct the committee to prepare a bill for the relief of the petitioner.

Messrs. McCOY, EDWARDS of Connecticut, and METCALF, argued at some length to sustain the report, and to show that the petitioner was not entitled to relief either under the claims law of 1816, or any other rule, as the boat would inevitably have been captured, if it had not been taken into the service of the United States.

Mr. STORRS rejoined at great length, but his motion was ultimately negatived; and the House concurred in the report of the Committee of Claims.

The House then, on motion of Mr. ANDERSON, went into Committee, and took up the bill for the relief of Robert Buntin, which it considered, and agreed to report.

The Committee then took up the bill further to regulate the issuing of patents for soldiers' bounty lands.

The discussion of this bill occupied the House until 4 o'clock; in which Messrs. MONELL, COOK, HARDIN, McCOY, FULLER, and RHEA engaged, and in the course of which Mr. McCOY, to destroy the bill, moved to strike out its first section. Before this motion was decided, the Committee rose, and reported their proceedings to the House; when it obtained leave to sit again on the last bill, and that for the relief of Robert Buntin was ordered to be engrossed for a third reading.

PAY OF ARMY OFFICERS.

Mr. COCKE, from the Committee on Military Affairs, reported the following bill:

Be it enacted, &c., That, from and after the first day of May next, there shall be paid to the officers of the Army the following salaries, in lieu of their present pay and emoluments, to wit:

To a Brigadier General three thousand dollars per annum; to the Paymaster-General, two thousand four hundred dollars; to the Adjutant General, two thousand dollars; to the Inspector General, two thousand dollars; to the Assistant Adjutant General, one thousand six hundred dollars; to the Assistant Inspector

General, one thousand six hundred dollars; to the Quartermaster General, three thousand dollars; to a Deputy Quartermaster General, one thousand six hundred dollars; to the Judge Advocate, two thousand dollars; to the Commissary General of Subsistence, two thousand dollars; to the Commissary General of Purchases, two thousand dollars; to the Assistant Commissary General of Purchases, one thousand dollars; to a Colonel, one thousand dollars; to a Lieutenant Colonel, one thousand six hundred dollars; to a Major, one thousand five hundred dollars; to a Captain, nine hundred and fifty dollars; to a First Lieutenant, eight hundred dollars; to a Second Lieutenant, seven hundred dollars; to a Third Lieutenant, seven hundred and fifty dollars.

SEC. 2. *And be it further enacted,* That when subalterns are employed in the Staff of the Army, they shall receive, in addition to their pay in the line, at the rate of one hundred and eighty dollars per annum for the time they are so employed.

SEC. 3. *And be it further enacted,* That there be paid to the Surgeon General, two thousand dollars; to the Apothecary General, one thousand five hundred dollars; to a Regimental Surgeon, one thousand two hundred dollars; and to an Assistant Surgeon, nine hundred dollars.

SEC. 4. *And be it further enacted,* That there be paid to the Professor of Natural and Experimental Philosophy, one thousand dollars, and to his Assistant, seven hundred dollars per annum; to the Professor of Mathematics, one thousand dollars; to his Assistant, seven hundred dollars; to the Professor of the art of Engineering, one thousand dollars; to his Assistant, seven hundred dollars; to the Chaplain and Professor of Geography, History, and Ethics, one thousand dollars; to the Teacher of the French Language, seven hundred dollars; to the Teacher of Drawing, seven hundred dollars; to the Master of the Sword, five hundred dollars; to a Cadet, one hundred and forty-four dollars, per annum, and two rations per day.

SEC. 5. *And be it further enacted,* That there shall be retained in service twelve military storekeepers, each with a salary of seven hundred and fifty dollars.

SEC. 6. *And be it further enacted,* That when any officer of the Army is ordered from one post to another, he shall be allowed and paid twelve and a half cents per mile for travelling, in lieu of transportation.

SEC. 7. *And be it further enacted,* That when an officer chooses to draw rations or forage in kind, there shall be deducted for the same, from his compensation, a sum equal to the contract price of such rations or forage.

The bill was twice read, and committed.

GENERAL APPROPRIATION BILL.

The House proceeded to the consideration of the general appropriation bill, and the amendments made thereto by the Committee of the Whole—the motion being still pending which was made by Mr. CULBRETH on yesterday, to lay the bill on the table, with the view of taking up the bill to reduce the salaries in the Civil Departments of the Government.

The motion to lay the appropriation bill on the table was opposed by Messrs. SMITH of Maryland, and STORRS, and was advocated, for the purpose proposed, by Mr. COCKE. The motion was negatived, without a division.

The discussion was renewed and continued some time on some of the items which had been the subject of debate in the Committee—particularly the appropriation for opening a road from the United States' military road in the Mississippi Territory, to the old road leading from Natchez to Nashville, which was defended by Mr. RANKIN, at some length, and in the discussion of which Messrs. STORRS, BUTLER of Louisiana, McLEAN of Kentucky, and RHEA, engaged. In the end, this appropriation was negatived. The amendments having all been disposed of—

The bill was, on motion of Mr. SMITH of Maryland, laid on the table, with the view of affording Mr. CLAY an opportunity of renewing, in the House, the motion unsuccessfully made by him in Committee of the Whole, on Tuesday; that gentleman being now absent on the committee appointed on the Missouri subject—which committee obtained leave yesterday to hold its sittings during the sessions of the House.

In the course of the day, Mr. BARBOUR gave notice that he should on to-morrow move to go into Committee of the Whole on the subjects relative to the Navy.

Mr. BALDWIN gave notice that he should on Monday next move to go into a Committee of the Whole on the tariff and auction duties' bills; and the House adjourned.

THURSDAY, February 8.

The SPEAKER laid before the House a report from the Secretary of the Treasury, on the petition of James Morrison; which was read and ordered to lie on the table.

Mr. BUTLER, of Louisiana, submitted for consideration the following resolution, which was read and ordered to lie on the table one day:

Resolved, That the Secretary of War be directed to report to this House the progress which has been made by the Board of Engineers in determining the sites, and plans of the fortifications of the coast of the United States; the sites which may have been selected; the estimate of the expense in completing the several works; the number of troops necessary to garrison them in peace, and in war; the progress made in erecting the fortifications; the advantages resulting from the system when completed, particularly in reducing the expense of defending the Atlantic frontier.

Engrossed bills of the following titles, to wit: "An act for the relief of Robert Buntin;" and "An act to authorize the collectors of customs to pay debentures issued on the exportation of loaf sugar, and spirits distilled from molasses;" were severally read the third time and passed.

A message from the Senate informed the House that the Senate have passed a resolution for the appointment of a joint committee, to ascertain and report a mode of examining the votes for President and Vice President of the United States, and of notifying the persons elected of their election; in which they ask the concurrence of this House.

The resolution was read and concurred in by the House. Mr. CLAY, Mr. SERGEANT, and Mr.

VAN RENNSELAER, were appointed the committee on the part of this House.

THE NAVY.

The House, on motion of Mr. BARBOUR, resolved itself into a Committee of the Whole on the report of the Committee on Naval Affairs, which concludes by recommending to the House the adoption of the following resolution :

Resolved, That a Naval Peace Establishment ought to be fixed by law.

Mr. BARBOUR, chairman of the Committee on Naval Affairs, rose, and in a speech of considerable length, submitted his reasons in favor of fixing, by law, a Peace Establishment for the Navy, and for making the reductions therein which are suggested in the report.

Mr. FULLER, of Massachusetts, replied to Mr. BARBOUR, in a speech of three quarters of an hour, of which the following is only a brief sketch. He said that the Peace Establishment of the Army, as far as it was practicable, was fixed by the annual appropriation; but that there was a wide difference between the circumstances which rendered a Peace Establishment proper for the Army, and those which apply to the Navy. That the Army, in time of peace, had little occupation, except in maintaining the several frontier posts, and sometimes to check a predatory irruption of savages. On the other hand, said he, the Navy may be considered, in some degree, as engaged in perpetual active service, as arduous and indispensable as actual war. On the coast of Africa, in the Pacific ocean, and often on the Mediterranean, this service was little different from war itself. The Naval Establishment, fixed during Mr. Jefferson's Administration, had been found very inconvenient, and had been gradually abandoned. On the return of peace, when the Army was placed on a Peace Establishment, it was considered unwise to limit the Navy, either as to ships, officers, or seamen, except by the actual appropriation. By this system, when any emergency called for an additional force, during the Summer, or before the session of Congress, the Executive could, forthwith, despatch such as he deemed necessary, without convening the Legislature. But what could require, at this moment, such an establishment, Mr. F. said, he was unable to comprehend. Did any one doubt the prudence of the Executive, and his disposition to reduce the expenses of the Navy, and all others, as much as possible? Let gentlemen advert to a document of the last session, by which it appeared that the number of seamen in service at that time was 4,354, whereas the number for the present year is only 2,932, a reduction of about one-third. Surely, said Mr. F., such a sudden reduction ought to satisfy the gentleman from Virginia of the disposition to retrench. But the report proposes a further reduction to about 2,500. Now, Mr. F. continued, this would be extremely pernicious to our commerce in several quarters of the world, and no less so to our naval reputation. Instead of sending only schooners of 12 guns each on the coast of Africa, which are liable to be overpowered by a combination of slave ships, which are often of considerable force, it is proper to send, at least sometimes, even larger vessels than we have hitherto employed.

In the West Indies, Mr. F. said, especially in the Windward islands, our commerce, during the past year, from May to November, was almost defenceless. The depredations committed in the neighborhood of St. Thomas had been such as greatly to diminish and discourage almost the only profitable commerce with the Spanish Main adjacent to those islands, it being well known that St. Thomas was a free port, and consequently a convenient depot and general rendezvous for our merchantmen. We have official documents to confirm this statement, and from merchants resident there with whom he had conversed. He was assured that much greater annoyance had been suffered, and that many lives had been sacrificed by those merciless pirates. In the Pacific, Mr. F. said, besides our whale fisheries, we have had a valuable trade; and, although a gentleman from Kentucky (Mr. CLAY) had lately styled the merchants engaged in that commerce "a few adventurers from Boston," he would assure the Committee that they were honorable adventurers, engaged in a lawful traffic, and their laudable exertions, while they were gradually reviving the capital, and increasing the resources of their country, were restoring the revenue and the credit of the Government. He was sorry, Mr. F. added, to hear such men stigmatized as "adventurers," because they complained of the paper blockade of Lord Cochrane, as the outrage of an unprincipled freebooter. Except Callao, the port of Lima, the Chilian fleet had never attempted actually to blockade a single port ; and he was sorry that any gentleman should treat a remonstrance against such a measure with disrespect. The presence of a respectable force in the Pacific would prevent Lord Cochrane, and those with whom he acted, from daring to invade our rights, whether in capturing-ships, or enticing or kidnapping our seamen. It was not intended, nor was there any danger of involving us in a war with these Patriots, so much the object of regard. Our officers were limited by their instructions, and no one doubted their faithful and discreet observance.

With regard to reducing the officers of our Navy, Mr. F. said, we could not do it without a dereliction of the great system which we had commenced in 1816, of the "gradual increase of the Navy." If the Committee were prepared for this, it might be in their view consistent to dismiss the officers; but the nation, Mr. F. said, he was convinced, would raise its voice against such an abandonment. It would dishonor us in the eyes of the civilized world, and afford a precious triumph to our enemies. By comparing the complement furnished by the Navy Department for the ships now in service, it appears that when the seventy-fours and frigates provided for by law are finished, a greater number of officers will be required to bring them into service than are now in commission. It was easier, Mr. F. said, and would require a shorter time, to build ships than to train officers fit to command them. The officers of the Navy who had reached the higher grades had, without exception, been in service from their earliest youth, and, without such actual experience, and passing through all the grades, they could not be qualified to command. This, though in some measure true of officers in the Army, was far more so in the Navy; and, indeed, he believed, scarcely an exception existed in the last war. In the highest grade known in our Navy, the pay was hardly equal to the salaries of chief clerks in the departments; and, after having spent their lives in the service of their country, it is proposed, by this report, to dismiss them without ceremony or regard. He could not agree to the justice of this, and he was confident it would be as destructive to the naval force as it would be disgraceful; for what a father, after seeing such a termination of the labors and of the glorious career of one-half our officers, in a few short years after their wounds are healed, will permit his sons to engage in such a service? It would be madness. When war shall come hereafter, and war must come, however we may deprecate its horrors, our country will too late repent this act of ill-timed, of wasteful retrenchment. Mr. F. concluded by saying, that the measures proposed by the report and resolution were peculiarly inexpedient towards the close of the session, when the other public business would leave little time to arrange the details of any bill which could be introduced with the view proposed by the majority of the Naval Committee.

Mr. SILSBEE, of Massachusetts, spoke much at large in reply to Mr. BARBOUR, and in opposition to the report of the committtee, and a reduction of the Navy.

Mr. BARBOUR replied at some length, and Mr. FULLER rejoined.

Mr. MEIGS, of New York, stated succinctly the reasons which would induce him to vote against the report.

Mr. LOWNDES admitted the propriety of fixing by law the Naval Peace Establishment, but being decidedly opposed to any reduction of the establishment as at present constituted, in support of which opinion he briefly gave his reasons, he moved to add to the resolution the following proviso:

Provided, That the number of commissioned officers to be authorized, shall not be less than that of those who are now commissioned in the naval service.

This amendment was agreed to, ayes 76, noes 54; and

The Committee then rose and reported the resolution to the House, as amended.

Mr. BARBOUR, after stating his objections to the amendment, suggested that, in its present shape, it would prevent a reduction of the number of surgeons, who were commissioned officers, and might restrict the committee in the bill to be reported, to an extent, perhaps, not intended by the mover.

Considerable debate followed, as well on the main object of the report as on the amendment, in which Messrs. BARBOUR, EUSTIS, MERCER,

SILSBEE, and LOWNDES participated, more or less; Mr. MERCER entering a good deal into the whole ground of controversy, in arguing against the report.

To accommodate the views of other gentlemen, Mr. LOWNDES moved so to modify his amendment as to read: "Provided, the number of captains, lieutenants, and midshipmen, shall not be less," &c.

On the suggestion of Mr. SILSBEE, masters commandant were included in the modification.

Mr. TRIMBLE said, that he had voted in Committee of the whole House for the amendment of the gentleman from South Carolina, (Mr. LOWNDES,) for mitigating the proposed reduction; but, from the remarks just made by the chairman of the special committee who had reported the resolution, he was fearful that the committee would be so much restricted by the amendment, that it would not be able to give the Peace Establishment the most efficient organization which might be adopted.

He did not intend to attempt a discussion of the subject, and would only ask leave to express his opinion, which was decidedly against reducing the Navy. His reflections had conducted him to the conclusion, that, for the future, nations would wage war for maritime supremacy; that the theatre of contest would be the ocean, and not the land; and that the dominion of the seas would be the primary object of the commercial world. Upon this element, said he, we come in contact with all the commercial and maritime Powers, but with none so often as Great Britain. Contest with her could not be avoided. She was too jealous of us as a rival to be easy. There were some things in her land and naval service which he could not approve, but, taken in the aggregate, she was the most potent maritime Power that had ever existed; and, what was not less important, she had, with all her faults, a mass of intellectual power that would give activity and impulse to her maritime means. In a word, he said, it was our destiny to stand in conflict with the most powerful, the most heroic, and perhaps, with all her failings, the most magnanimous maritime Power the world had ever known; and for that reason, if he had no other, he would oppose any reduction of the Navy. On the contrary, he wished to see it placed upon the most efficient footing. If the amendment restricts the committee in that respect, he would rather see it modified. The chairman of the committee intimates that it will not, and Mr. T. was satisfied.

After some further debate on the part of Messrs. SMITH of Maryland, BARBOUR, SILSBEE, WILLIAMS of North Carolina, COBB, and FLOYD, the modification of the proviso was agreed to.

Mr. MERCER moved to add *seamen* also to it; but the motion was negatived.

The question was then put on the proviso, as amended, as follows:

Resolved, That the number of captains, masters commandant, lieutenants, and midshipmen, shall not be less than that of those who are now commissioned in the naval service.

And it was agreed to, by yeas and nays, by the following vote:

YEAS—Messrs. Allen of Massachusetts, Anderson, Archer of Maryland, Archer of Virginia, Baldwin, Ball, Bayly, Beecher, Blackledge, Brevard, Brown, Brush, Buffum, Butler of New Hampshire, Butler of Louisiana, Clagett, Clark, Cook, Crawford, Crowell, Cushman, Cuthbert, Dane, Darlington, Davidson, Dennison, Dickinson, Eddy, Edwards of Connecticut, Edwards of Pennsylvania, Fay, Folger, Fuller, Gorham, Gross of New York, Guyon, Hemphill, Hill, Hobart, Hooks, Jones of Tennessee, Kent, Lathrop, Livermore, Lowndes, McCullough, McLane of Delaware, Mallary, Meigs, Mercer, Monell, S. Moore, T. L. Moore, Morton, Neale, Nelson of Massachusetts, Nelson of Virginia, Newton, Parker of Virginia, Pinckney, Pitcher, Plumer, Reid, Rich, Ringgold, Robertson, Rogers, Sergeant, Smith of New Jersey, Smith of Maryland, Smith of North Carolina, Southard, Storrs, Street, Strong of New York, Tomlinson, Tompkins, Trimble, Tucker of Virginia, Tyler, Udree, Upham, Van Rensselaer, Wendover, Whitman, Williams of Virginia, and Wood—87.

NAYS—Messrs. Abbot, Alexander, Allen of New York, Allen of Tennessee, Baker, Barbour, Bateman, Boden, Bryan, Burton, Campbell, Cannon, Case, Cobb, Crafts, Culbreth, Culpeper, Edwards of North Carolina, Eustis, Floyd, Foot, Forrest, Gray, Gross of Pennsylvania, Hall of New York, Hall of North Carolina, Hardin, Hendricks, Herrick, Hibshman, Hostetter, Johnson, Kinsey, Lincoln, Maclay, McCoy, McCreary, McLean of Kentucky, Marchand, Metcalf, R. Moore, Murray, Parker of Massachusetts, Patterson, Philson, Rankin, Rhea, Richards, Richmond, Ross, Russ, Sawyer, Shaw, Sloan, Stevens, Strong of Vermont, Tarr, Terrell, Tracy, Tucker of South Carolina, Walker, Warfield, and Williams of North Carolina—63.

Mr. COBB then moved to subjoin to the resolution the following order:

Ordered, That the foregoing resolution be recommitted to the Committee on Naval Affairs, with instructions to report a bill conformably thereto, and to reduce the number of seamen, ordinary seamen and boys, to the number of 2,521.

Mr. LOWNDES moved to strike out of this proposition all which follows the word *thereto,* in the third line.

A debate ensued on these questions, and continued some time; when

Mr. BRUSH, of Ohio, moved that the entire subject, the report, resolution, and amendments, be indefinitely postponed; but before the question was taken, a motion to adjourn prevailed.

FRIDAY, February 9.

The House proceeded to the consideration of the resolution yesterday submitted by Mr. BUTLER, of Louisiana, calling for information respecting fortifications, and agreed thereto.

Mr. CULBRETH gave notice that he should, on Tuesday next, move for the consideration of the bill reported by him for reducing the salaries of the several officers of the Government.

The House then resumed the consideration of the unfinished business of yesterday, (relating to the Navy;) but it was ordered to lie on the table, the House being considered too thin, from the absence of committees, &c., to act definitively on the subject.

The bill to amend and establish certain post roads, then passed through a Committee of the Whole, where it received many amendments, and, being reported to the House, was ordered to be engrossed for a third reading.

THE SLAVE TRADE.

Mr. HEMPHILL, from the committee on so much of the Message of the President of the United States as relates to the Slave Trade, made a report, which, with the documents accompanying it, was ordered to be printed. The report is as follows:

The committee to which is referred so much of the President's Message as relates to the slave trade, and to which are referred the two Messages of the President, transmitting, in pursuance of the resolution of the House of Representatives of the 4th of December, a report of the Secretary of State, and enclosed documents, relating to the negotiation for the suppression of the slave trade, report:

That the committee have deemed it advisable, previous to entering into a consideration of the proposed co-operation to exterminate the slave trade, to make a summary review of the Constitution and laws of the United States relating to this subject. It will disclose the earnestness and zeal with which this nation has been actuated, and the laudable ambition that has animated their councils to take a lead in the reformation of a disgraceful practice, and one which is productive of so much human misery; it will, by displaying the constant anxiety of this nation to suppress the African slave trade, afford ample testimony that she will be the last to persevere in measures wisely digested to effectuate this great and most desirable object, whenever such measures can be adopted in consistence with the leading principles of her local institutions.

In consequence of the existence of slavery in many of the States, when British colonies, the habits and means of carrying on industry could not be suddenly changed; and the Constitution of the United States yielded to the provision that the migration or importation of such persons as any of the States now existing shall think proper to admit shall not be prohibited by the Congress prior to the year 1808.

But, long antecedent to this period, Congress legislated on the subject wherever its power extended, and endeavored, by a system of rigorous penalties, to suppress this unnatural trade.

The act of Congress of the 22d of March, 1794, contains provisions that no citizen or citizens of the United States, or foreigner, or any other person, coming into or residing within the same, shall, for himself or any other person whatsoever, either as master, factor, or owner, build, fit, equip, load, or otherwise prepare any ship or vessel, within any port or place of the United States, nor shall cause any ship or vessel to sail from any port or place within the same, for the purpose of carrying on any trade or traffic in slaves to any foreign country; or for the purpose of procuring from any foreign kingdom, place, or country, the inhabitants of such kingdom, place, or country, to be transported to any foreign country, port, or place, whatever, to be sold or disposed of as slaves, under the penalty of the forfeiture of any such vessel, and of the payment of large sums of money by the persons offending against the directions of the act.

By an act of the 3d of April, 1798, in relation to the Mississippi Territory, to which the Constitutional provision did not extend, the introduction of slaves, under severe penalties, was forbidden, and every slave imported contrary to the act was to be entitled to freedom.

By an act of the 10th of May, 1800, the citizens or residents of this country were prohibited from holding any right or property in vessels employed in transporting slaves from one foreign country to another, on pain of forfeiting their right of property, and also double the value of that right in money, and double the value of their interest in the slaves; nor were they allowed to serve on board of vessels of the United States employed in the transportation of slaves from one country to another, under the punishment of fines and imprisonment; nor were they permitted to serve on board of foreign ships employed in the slave trade. By this act, also, the commissioned vessels of the United States were authorized to seize vessels and crews employed contrary to the act.

By an act of the 28th of February, 1803, masters of vessels were not allowed to bring into any port (where the laws of the State prohibited the importation) any negro, mulatto, or other person of color, not being a native, a citizen, or registered seaman of the United States, under the pain of heavy penalties; and no vessel, having on board persons of the above description, was to be admitted to an entry; and if any such person should be landed from on board of any vessel, the same was to be forfeited.

By an act of the 2d March, 1807, the importation of slaves into any port of the United States was to be prohibited after the 1st of January, 1808, the time prescribed by the Constitutional provision. This act contains many severe provisions against any interference or participation in the slave trade, such as heavy fines, long imprisonments, and the forfeitures of vessels; the President was also authorized to employ armed vessels to cruise on any part of the coast where he might judge attempts would be made to violate the act, and to instruct the commanders of armed vessels to seize and bring in vessels found on the high seas contravening the provisions of the law.

By an act of the 20th of April, 1818, the laws in prohibition of the slave trade were further improved; this act is characterized with a peculiarity of legislative precaution, especially in the eighth section, which throws the labor of proof upon the defendant, that the colored persons brought into the United States by him had not been brought in contrary to the laws.

By an act of the 3d of March, 1819, the power is continued in the President to employ the armed ships of the United States, to seize and bring into port any vessel engaged in the slave trade by citizens or residents of the United States; and such vessels, together with the goods and effects on board, are to be forfeited and sold, and the proceeds to be distributed in like manner as provided by law for the distribution of prizes taken from an enemy; and the officers and crew are to undergo the punishments inflicted by previous acts. The President, by this act, is authorized to make such regulations and arrangements as he may deem expedient, for the safekeeping, support, and removal beyond the limits of the United States, of all such negroes, mulattoes, or persons of color, as may have been brought within its jurisdiction, and to ap-

point a proper person or persons residing on the coast of Africa, as agent or agents for receiving the negroes, mulattoes, or persons of color, delivered from on board of vessels seized in the prosecution of the slave trade.

And, in addition to all the aforesaid laws, the present Congress, on the 15th of May, 1820, believing that the then existing provisions would not be sufficiently available, enacted, that if any citizen of the United States, being of the crew or ship's company of any foreign ship or vessel, engaged in the slave trade, or any person whatever, being of the crew or ship's company of any ship or vessel, owned in the whole or in part, or navigated for or in behalf of any citizen or citizens of the United States, shall land from any such ship or vessel, and on any foreign shore seize any negro or mulatto, not held to service or labor by the laws of either of the States or Territories of the United States, with intent to make such negro or mulatto a slave, or shall decoy or forcibly bring, or carry, or shall receive, such negro or mulatto on board any such ship or vessel, with intent as aforesaid, such citizen or person shall be adjudged a pirate, and on conviction shall suffer death.

The immoral and pernicious practice of the slave trade has attracted much public attention in Europe within the last few years; and in a Congress at Vienna, on the 8th of February, 1815, five of the principal Powers made a solemn engagement, in the face of mankind, that this traffic should be made to cease; in pursuance of which, these Powers have enacted municipal laws to suppress the trade. Spain, although not a party to the original engagement, did, soon after, in her treaty with England, stipulate for the immediate abolition of the Spanish slave trade to the north of the equator, and for its final and universal abolition on the 30th of May, 1820.

Portugal likewise, in her treaty in 1817, stipulated that the Portuguese slave trade on the coast of Africa should entirely cease to the northward of the equator, and engaged that it should be unlawful for her subjects to purchase or trade in slaves except to the southward of the line. The precise period at which the entire abolition is to take place in Portugal does not appear to be finally fixed; but the Portuguese Ambassador, in the presence of the Congress of Vienna, declared that Portugal, faithful to her principles, would not refuse to adopt the term of eight years, which term will expire in the year 1823.

At this time, among the European States, there is not a flag which can legally cover this inhuman traffic to the north of the line; nevertheless, experience has proved the inefficacy of the various and rigorous laws which have been made in Europe and in this country; it being a lamentable fact that the disgraceful practice is even now carried on to a surprising extent. During the last year, Captain Trenchard, the commander of the United States sloop of war the Cyane, found that part of the coast of Africa which he visited lined with vessels, engaged, as it is presumed, in this forbidden traffic; of these he examined many; and five, which appeared to be fitted out on American account, he sent into the jurisdiction of the United States, for adjudication. Each of them, it is believed, has been condemned, and the commanders of two of them have been sentenced to the punishment prescribed by the laws of the United States.

The testimony recently published, with the opinion of the presiding judge of the United States court of the southern district of the State of New York, in the case of the schooner Plattsburg, lays open a scene of the grossest fraud that could be practised to deceive the officers of Government, and conceal the unlawful transaction.

The extension of the trade for the last twenty-five or thirty years must, in a degree, be conjectural, but the best information that can be obtained on the subject furnishes good foundation to believe, that during that period the number of slaves withdrawn from western Africa amounts to upwards of a million and a half; the annual average would be a mean somewhere between fifty and eighty thousand.

The trade appears to be lucrative in proportion to its heinousness; and, as it is generally inhibited, the unfeeling slave dealers, in order to elude the laws, increase its horrors; the innocent Africans, who are mercilessly forced from their native homes in irons, are crowded in vessels and situations which are not adapted for the transportation of human beings; and this cruelty is frequently succeeded, during the voyage of their destination, with dreadful mortality. Further information on this subject will appear in a letter from the Secretary of the Navy, enclosing two other letters, marked 1 and 2, and also by the extract of a letter from an officer of the Cyane, dated April 10, 1820, which are annexed to this report. While the slave trade exists, there can be no prospect of civilization in Africa.

However well disposed the European Powers may be to effect a practical abolition of the trade, it seems generally acknowledged that, for the attainment of this object, it is necessary to agree upon some concerted plan of co-operation; but, unhappily, no arrangement has as yet obtained universal consent.

England has recently engaged in treaties with Spain, Portugal, and the Netherlands, in which the mutual right of visitation and search is exchanged. This right is of a special and limited character, as well in relation to the number and description of vessels, as to space; and, to avoid possible inconveniences, no suspicious circumstances are to warrant the detention of a vessel; this right is restricted to the simple fact of slaves being on board.

These treaties contemplate the establishment of mixed courts, formed of an equal number of individuals of the two contracting nations, the one to reside in a possession belonging to his Britannic Majesty, the other within the territory of the other respective Power. When a vessel is visited and detained, it is to be taken to the nearest court, and, if condemned, the vessel is to be declared a lawful prize, as well as the cargo, and are to be sold for the profit of the two nations; the slaves are to receive a certificate of emancipation, and to be delivered over to the Government on whose territory the court is which passes sentence, to be employed as servants or free laborers. Each of the Governments binds itself to guaranty the liberty of such portion of these individuals as may be respectively assigned to it. Particular provisions are made for remuneration, in case vessels are not condemned after trial, and special instructions are stipulated to be furnished to commanders of vessels possessing the qualified right of visitation and search.

These Powers entertain the opinion, that nothing short of the concession of a qualified right of visitation and search can practically suppress the slave trade. An association of armed ships is contemplated, to form a species of naval police, to be stationed principally in the African seas, where the commanders of the ships will be enabled to co-operate in harmony and concert.

The United States have been earnestly invited by the principal Secretary of State for Foreign Affairs of the British Government to join in the same or similar arrangements; and this invitation has been sanctioned and enforced by an unanimous vote of the House of Lords and Commons, in a manner that precludes all doubts as to the sincerity and benevolence of their designs.

In answer to this invitation, the President of the United States has expressed his regret that the stipulations in the treaties communicated are of a character to which the peculiar situation and institutions of the United States do not permit them to accede.

The objections made are contained in an extract of a letter from the Secretary of State, under date of the 2d of November, 1818, in which it is observed that, " in examining the provisions of the treaties communicated by Lord Castlereagh, all the essential articles appear to be of a character not adaptable to the institutions or to the circumstances of the United States. The powers agreed to be reciprocally given to the officers of the ships of war of either party, to enter, search, capture, and carry into port for adjudication, the merchant vessels of the other, however qualified and restricted, is most essentially connected with the institution, by each treaty, of two mixed courts, one of which to reside in the external or colonial possession of each of the two parties, respectively. This part of the system is indispensable to give it that character of reciprocity, without which the right granted to the armed ships of one nation, to search the merchant vessels of another, would be rather a mark of vassalage than of independence. But to this part of the system, the United States, having no colonies, either on the coast of Africa or in the West Indies, cannot give effect. That, by the Constitution of the United States, it is provided that the judicial power of the United States shall be vested in the Supreme Court, and in such inferior courts as the Congress may, from time to time, ordain and establish. It provides that the judges of these courts shall hold their offices during good behavior; and that they shall be removable by impeachment, on conviction of crimes and misdemeanors. There may be doubts whether the power of the Government of the United States is competent to institute a court for carrying into execution their penal statutes beyond the territories of the United States— a court consisting partly of foreign judges, not amenable to impeachment for corruption, and deciding upon statutes of the United States without appeal.

" That the disposal of the negroes found on board of the slave-trading vessels, which might be condemned by the sentence of these mixed courts, cannot be carried into effect by the United States; for, if the slaves of vessels condemned by the mixed courts should be delivered over to the Government of the United States as free men, they could not, but by their own consent, be employed as servants or free laborers. The condition of the blacks being, in this Union, regulated by the municipal laws of the separate States, the Government of the United States can neither guaranty their liberty in the States where they could only be received as slaves, nor control them in the States where they would be recognised as free. That the admission of a right, in the officers of foreign ships of war, to enter and search the vessels of the United States in time of peace, under any circumstances whatever, would meet with universal repugnance in the public opinion of this country; that there would be no prospect of a ratification, by advice and consent of the Senate, to any stipulation of that nature ; that the search by foreign officers, even in time of war, is so obnoxious to the feelings and recollections of this country, that nothing could reconcile them to the extension of it, however qualified or restricted, to a time of peace ; and that it would be viewed in a still more aggravated light if, as in the Treaty with the Netherlands, connected with a formal admission that even vessels under convoy of ships of war of their own nation should be liable to search by the ships of war of another."

The committee will observe, in the first instance, that a mutual right of search appears to be indispensable to the great object of abolition; for, while flags remain as a cover for this traffic, against the right of search by any vessels except of the same nation, the chance of detection will be much less than it would be if the right of search was extended to vessels of other Powers; and as soon as any one nation should cease to be vigilant in the discovery of infractions practised on its own code, the slave dealers would avail themselves of a system of obtaining fraudulent papers, and concealing the real ownership under the cover of such flags, which would be carried on with such address as to render it easy for the citizens or subjects of one State to evade their own municipal laws; but, if a concerted system existed, and a qualified right of mutual search was granted, the apprehension of these piratical offenders would be reduced to a much greater certainty ; and the very knowledge of the existence of an active and vigorous system of co-operation would divert many from this traffic, as the unlawful trade would become too hazardous for profitable speculation.

In relation to any inconveniences that might result from such an arrangement, the commerce of the United States is so limited on the African coast that it could not be much affected by it ; and, as it regards economy, the expense of stationing a few vessels on that coast would not be much greater than to maintain them at any other place.

The committee have briefly noticed the practical results of a reciprocal right of search, as it bears on the slave trade; but the objection as to the propriety of ceding this right remains. It is with deference that the committee undertake to make any remarks upon it. They bear in recollection the opinions entertained in this country, on the practice of searching neutral vessels in time of war ; but they cannot perceive that the right under discussion is, in principle, allied in any degree to the general question of search; it can involve no commitment, nor is it susceptible of any unfavorable inference on that subject; and, even if there were any affinity between the cases, the necessity of a special agreement would be inconsistent with the idea of existing rights. The proposal itself, in the manner made, is a total abandonment, on the part of England, of any claim to visit and search vessels in a time of peace, and this question has been unequivocally decided in the negative in her admiralty courts.

Although it is not among the objections that the desired arrangement would give color to a claim or right of search in time of peace, yet, lest the case in this respect may be prejudiced in the minds of any, the committee will observe that the right of search, in time of peace, is one that is not claimed by any Power as a part of the law of nations; no nation pretends that it can exercise the right of visitation and search upon the common and unappropriated parts of the sea, except upon the belligerent claim. A recent decision

in the British admiralty court, in the case of the French slave ship Le Louis, is clear and decisive on this point. The case is annexed to this report.

In regard, then, to the reciprocal right wished to be ceded, it is reduced to the simple inquiry whether, in practice, it will be beneficial to the two contracting nations. Its exercise, so far as it relates to the detention of vessels, as it is confined to the fact of slaves being actually on board, precludes almost the possibility of accident or much inconvenience.

In relation also to the disposal of the vessels and slaves detained, an arrangement perhaps could be effected so as to deliver them up to the vessels of the nation to which the detained vessel should belong. Under such an understanding, the vessels and slaves delivered to the jurisdiction of the United States might be disposed of in conformity with the provisions of our own act of the 3d of March, 1819; and an arrangement of this kind would be free from any of the other objections.

An exchange of the right of search, limited in duration, or to continue at pleasure, for the sake of experiment, might, it is anxiously hoped, be so restricted to vessels and seas, and with such civil and harmonious stipulations, as not to be unacceptable.

The feelings of this country on the general question of search have often been roused to a degree of excitement that evince their unchangeable character ; but the American people will readily see the distinction between the cases ; the one, on its exercise to the extent claimed, will ever produce irritation, and excite a patriotic spirit of resistance ; the other is amicable and charitable ; the justness and nobleness of the undertaking are worthy of the combined concern of Christian nations.

The detestable crime of kidnapping the unoffending inhabitants of one country, and chaining them to slavery in another, is marked with all the atrociousness of piracy; and, as such, it is stigmatized, and punishable by our own laws.

To efface this reproachful stain from the character of civilized mankind, would be the proudest triumph that could be achieved in the cause of humanity. On this subject, the United States, having led the way, owe it to themselves to give their influence and cordial co-operation to any measure that will accomplish the great and good purpose ; but this happy result, experience has demonstrated, cannot be realised by any system, except a concession by the maritime Powers, to each other's ships of war, of a qualified right of search. If this object was generally attained, it is confidently believed that the active exertions of even a few nations would be sufficient entirely to suppress the slave trade.

The slave dealers could be successfully assailed on the coast upon which the trade originates, as they must necessarily consume more time in the collection and embarcation of their cargoes than in the subsequent distribution in the markets for which they are destined. This renders that coast the most advantageous position for their apprehension; and, besides, the African coast frequented by the slave ships is indented with so few commodious or accessible harbors, that, notwithstanding its great extent, it could be guarded by the vigilance of a small number of cruisers. But, if the slave ships are permitted to escape from the African coast, and to be dispersed to different parts of the world, their capture would be rendered uncertain and hopeless.

1071   HISTORY OF CONGRESS.   1072

H. of R.   *Appropriation Bill—Minister to South America.*   FEBRUARY, 1821.

The committee, after much reflection, offer the following resolution:

Resolved by the Senate and House of Representatives of the United States of America, in Congress assembled, That the President of the United States be requested to enter into such arrangements as he may deem suitable and proper, with one or more of the maritime Powers of Europe, for the effectual abolition of the African slave trade.

GENERAL APPROPRIATION BILL.

The House then resumed the consideration of the annual appropriation bill for the support of the civil list.

Mr. TARR moved further to amend the bill, by adding to the end of the first section thereof the following item, viz: "For the erection of a bridge 'over the Monongahela river, where the Cumber-'land road crosses the same, the unexpended bal-'ance of the amount heretofore appropriated for 'completing the Cumberland road; provided such 'unexpended balance shall, in the opinion of the 'Secretary of the Treasury, be sufficient to com-'plete that object." And the question being taken thereon, it was determined in the negative.

Mr. CLAY submitted the same proposition which he made in Committee of the Whole, the other day, viz: to amend the bill by inserting therein the following clause:

"For an outfit and one year's salary to such Minister as the President, by and with the advice and consent of the Senate, may send to any Government of South America, which has established, and is maintaining its independency on Spain, a sum not exceeding eighteen thousand dollars."

On this motion a debate arose.

Mr. CLAY spoke at some length in further support of his proposition on the grounds formerly and frequently taken in support of it.

Mr. ROBERTSON replied to some of Mr. CLAY's remarks, and vindicated the ground which he had taken on a former day in opposition to legislating on a subject not properly within the scope of its duty, supposing this appropriation to be considered as an instruction or advice from this House to the Executive.

Mr. WOOD delivered his sentiments in opposition to the motion of Mr. CLAY, at considerable length, on the ground that the adoption of it would be inexpedient, as well as travelling out of the proper sphere of this department of the Government. Mr. W. fully approved of the course which the Executive had hitherto pursued in regard to South America.

Mr. RHEA also opposed the proposition, as contemplating an irregular and unusual proceeding.

Mr. TUCKER, of Virginia, delivered his sentiments in favor of the proposition, regarding it as an expression by this House of what was the known feeling of the country towards the South Americans, called for by the existing state of things.

Mr. SOUTHARD followed on the same side of the question, speaking earnestly in favor of the motion of Mr. CLAY.

Mr. REID, of Georgia, spoke as follows:

Mr. Speaker, it can scarcely be necessary to declare in this place my deep solicitude for the success of the Patriots of South America. That man must, indeed, possess a cold heart, who, witnessing the blessings so profusely flowing from our own free institutions, can look unmoved upon the struggle of a brave people for their liberties—a people who have been so long the victims of civil and religious despotism!

Sir, I think, with the member from Kentucky, that the contest is no longer doubtful; and that if the overtures of the parent country produced no immediate conciliatory result, a renewed warfare must at last end in the annihilation of the power of Old Spain over her colonies. It cannot be otherwise. When once liberal principles obtain in society, the power to prevent their extension, or to check their growth, must be infinitely greater than that which can be brought to operate upon South America. But, much as my best wishes are devoted to this holy cause, sanguine as are my hopes of its success, I yet think that there are reasons to influence the House to the rejection of the amendment now proposed. If there were no other reason to be urged against it, it seems to me to be a good objection that the amendment, if adopted, will be partial in its effect. We are given to understand that there are several distinct Republics in South America—Buenos Ayres, Chili, Colombia; and to these may shortly be added, Peru, if recent intelligence is to be trusted. Have not, then, all of these equal claims upon your sympathies? Why depute a Minister to the one in exclusion of the rest? Would it not be more just, by asking an ample appropriation, to give to all that encouragement, which the cause of all, so bravely defended and so gallantly pursued, would seem to demand? If you really desire to conciliate these infant Republics, to show them that you are alive to their wrongs and their calamities, why do you not address yourself to each and every of them? Why make a distinction unfounded in reason, niggardly in itself, and invidious in its effect? It may be answered, that it will be time enough to provide representatives of this nation for these Governments, when affairs have settled into certainty, and when it shall be shown into how many separate States South America is to be divided. If this be the reply, it may be directed very forcibly against the proposition now before you. It is, in truth, not proper that we should send an ambassador to a country, whose Government has been hastily built up under the sword of the oppressor, and may, in the versatility of revolutionary fortunes, fall beneath its power! Let us wait until a nation be completely formed and organized, before we exercise towards her that comity which belongs to the intercourse of nations. Let me not be misunderstood. I would not be considered to vary from the convictions which I have just avowed. I do not mean at one moment to say that it is my fixed belief that the Patriots will succeed, and then to indicate a contrary opinion. But who can calculate with certainty upon the events of futurity? Who can say that the armistice concluded between Morillo and Bolivar, under circumstances so soothing to humanity, will be followed by an acknowl-

1073 HISTORY OF CONGRESS. 1074

FEBRUARY, 1821. *Appropriation Bill—Minister to South America.* H. OF R.

edgment of the independence of the Patriots? Is it altogether certain that Spain will withdraw her armies and her dominion, and quietly give up that which she has valued as the brightest, certainly the richest jewel of her crown? Have we not learned from experience—from her profuse expenditure of treasure—from her reckless waste of human blood—that nothing but necessity can compel her to relinquish the contest? Her interest, her pride, her habitual control, all incite her to perseverance! Besides Spain, under the auspices of the constitution of the Cortes, has offered to her colonies a participation in the Government, and a relief from some of the most odious of the evils against which they have been contending. It is, indeed, probable that these terms will be rejected, with an emotion nearly allied to disdain, but this, too, is only conjecture. The provinces desolated by a ruinous war, and thirsting for peace, may lend a favorable ear to propositions which, although not unexceptionable, promise to the weary and exhausted a repose, temporary, perhaps, but agreeable and invigorating. Sir, whatever events may ensue, if you adopt the amendment now under consideration, you are in danger of producing embarrassment to the Government. If the war in South America continue, you acknowledge the independence of a State yet struggling for its liberty. If Spain succeed in reconciling her provinces, you will present to the world a singular spectacle. You will have deputed an ambassador to the mother country, and another to her colonies.

Sir, the President of the United States possesses the power, with the consent of the Senate, to appoint ambassadors. From his elevated station, he has certainly a better view of the relations of this with other nations, than we possibly can have. Why, then, with limited means of information, do we desire to dictate to that department, which, from its nature and situation, is so much better informed? There is surely no necessity for an interference upon our part. The age, integrity, and experience of your President, the unquestioned ability of those gentlemen to whom he may at all times apply for advice and assistance, the acknowledged wisdom of the Senate demand your confidence. The Executive has doubtless deeply reflected upon this subject. It feels as the people feel, and if it has heretofore forborne to gratify the wishes of the member from Kentucky, it is because it has been restrained by prudential considerations, and not by an apathy towards the future destinies of South America. But it is insisted that the President has acted unwisely, and it becomes proper to coerce him to recognise the independence of some one of the Patriot Governments by making this appropriation. Do you not perceive how powerless and nugatory is such legislation? You resolved, at the last session, that it was expedient to send a Minister to South America, and what was the result? Why, no Minister has yet been appointed. You now appropriate money, and what is to be the consequence? It will be this: although the President, as a faithful public servant, must give due consideration to your enactment, yet, if he think the measure it proposes

unwise, he will, as he is bound to do, entirely disregard it, and the money appropriated will remain idle and unexhausted in your Treasury, at the moment, too, when you are borrowing millions! I deny not that we may fall upon evil times, when it may become necessary, from the corruption or partiality of the Chief Magistrate and the Senate, that this House should interpose. But this is a case merely possible, and most assuredly not now existing. But if it were—if the Executive had actually declined to send an ambassador to any Government, where our best interests required he should be sent, I ask, could you counteract such a policy by a mere appropriation? Believe me, it would be *brutum fulmen*, hard, indeed, but inoperative! No; the course, I think, would be to withhold your appropriations for all Ministers, until the Executive should perceive the necessity of pursuing the path of duty. Such a course would produce the desired effect, but it would be harsh and uncourteous, and only to be justified by the necessity to be found in an extreme case.

We have been told, that it is due to the dignity of this House to carry into effect the measure of the last session. I had thought that the dignity of a nation, like that of an individual, depended more upon achievement than loud boasts or pompous promises. Let your appropriation be passed. The President still refuses to appoint an ambassador; and I ask you, where is your dignity then? You have wrestled with the Executive, but you have gained nothing by the contest; on the contrary, you suffer defeat, and the dignified attitude you would assume belongs to him who has obtained the victory!

This House is called upon to be consistent with itself, and to receive the proposed amendment, because it passed the resolution of the last session. It appears to me that the resolution of the last session obtained the votes of a majority on a ground entirely distinct from that taken in support of the present proposition. It was then said, "pass the resolution, it will give vigor to the cause of the Patriots; it will restore their confidence, revive their drooping spirits, advance their interests!" The House listened to the inspiring invocation; it was passed, and I have yet to learn that it was productive of any of the happy consequences which were foretold. Was it received with joy, with bonfires, and illuminations? Did it strike terror to the Royal army, or lead the Patriots to victory? If these were its effects, they have to this moment been to me a secret. Now, however, the object is varied. It is no longer to assist and encourage the Patriots by an expression of pu lic opinion, but to coerce the Executive openly to recognise, as a permanent and established Government, some one of the South American Republics. If, indeed, the supporters of the resolution of the last session intended to pursue their project to this point, why did they not follow up that resolution by a proposition like that now submitted? Was it because they were hopeless of success? If so, the principle upon which their resolution passed must of necessity be different from that upon which they would support the appropriation; because,

1075　　　　　　HISTORY OF CONGRESS.　　　　　　1076

H. OF R.　　　　　　*Appropriation Bill—Minister to South America.*　　　　　　FEBRUARY, 1821.

if they were the same, the majority sustaining the resolution would likewise have supported an appropriation. If they could have succeeded, and did not make the effort, did they act wisely in postponing a measure which they have so much at heart, and which, they say, is so intimately connected with the dignity of this House and this nation?

It is said, that our respect for Spain should not deter us from adopting the amendment, because Spain, regenerated as she is, has levelled a severe blow at our commerce. If this be so, we shall make it the subject of negotiation. We shall fairly develope the causes of complaint, and require the proper redress; but I hope we shall not, for the purpose of avenging an injury, no matter how serious it may be, recognise the independence of the colonies. Such a policy would justly be considered by the world as wanting in that candor and magnanimity for which this nation has been singularly remarkable; and the provinces themselves would be but little obliged to you for a patronage extended at the latest hour, not by your good will and devotion to liberty, but by feelings of resentment towards Old Spain. If your commercial difficulties with Spain be really great, and it be important to remove them, so far from operating to the adoption of a measure which must be offensive to her, they should teach us greater circumspection, and we should take care to remove, rather than increase, the obstacles impeding the way to negotiation.

As an inducement to adopt the amendment, a resort has been had to the perfidy of Spain since, and the long diplomacy preceding the first ratification of the Florida treaty. Sir, I am perfectly aware of the violation of a pledged faith, of which Spain has been guilty, and I admire the intrepidity and integrity of the American envoy, who poured the language of truth into the ear of a corrupt Government; but I cannot perceive why, if Spain has forgotten that justice which belongs to a virtuous nation, we should, on that account, hasten to acknowledge the independence of her colonies. It would be to shield your imprudence under the cover of her wickedness. No, sir. The time was when you might have repaired the injury you had sustained by using the remedy within your reach. That day has passed by, and the nation by whom you were wronged is now voluntarily upon the point of doing you justice. The treaty has been ratified, and Florida—which gentlemen have been pleased to describe as a howling desert, a collection of morasses, but which, I am credibly informed, is possessed of the most delightful climate, and contains some of the finest lands in the world—Florida will soon pass into your possession. We have demanded, and we shall receive, ample retribution for the injuries of which we complained, and if we are a generous people, we will consign to forgetfulness at once our discontents and their provocations.

But, it seems, it is highly necessary to us to preserve the affection of the Patriots. Sir, I am little skilled in the conduct of nations, but I have been taught to believe, that we are to expect nothing from the affection of any nation. It is to self-interest that we must address ourselves, and not to disinterested friendship, which scarcely has existence among men, even in the smallest societies, where early association and long habit would be most likely to cherish it. Rely upon it, it was this selfish feeling which gave to us our European allies, during the Revolutionary war, and not the admiration of our efforts, or the love of our institutions. It is true, the sympathy of the American people enlists itself in behalf of the suffering colonies; but, when we deliberate upon the conduct of the nation, we must ask, not whether we shall pursue the feelings of the people, but if it be our interest to pursue them? I speak not of sordid interest, but of the honor, reputation, and happiness of the nation.

We have listened to a story as horrible as a hideous barbarity and a collection of obscene circumstances could make it. It is not the first time I have heard such a narrative. Atrocities have been related which leave far behind them the bloodiest incidents of the most frantic period of the French revolution. Some of these doubtless have their foundation in fact, but may they not derive a deeper coloring from that love of the marvellous and terrible which is inseparable from our nature? If we remember that this has been a contest of extermination on both sides, unregulated by the laws of civilized warfare, can we believe that to the royalists alone belongs the guilt of cold-blooded murder, and more cruel butcheries? Or, would it not be fair to admit, that the same circumstances have produced the like excesses in both parties? In this point of view, then, there can be no reason why you should extend favor to the one at the expense of the other. But, unless my friend from Kentucky (Mr. TRIMBLE) shall insist that his authority is indisputable, I cannot implicitly give credence to the anecdote he has told. And why? Because I, in common with that gentleman, have a high respect for the character and talents of the patriot chieftain Bolivar. When the late armistice was concluded, those who had long been foes met as friends; in the moment of conviviality all sorrows and enmities were forgotten, and Morillo was clasped in the warm embrace of Bolivar! Sir, who is Bolivar? Ask the gentlemen who urge this appropriation, and they will tell you, he is the emancipator of an empire; a hero to whom history furnishes no resemblance, but in the magnanimity and virtues of our own Washington! And do we find this wisest, bravest, best of men, courting corruption to his arms; greeting a fiend in human form with the emotions of friendship?

Sir, the scene I have just described either places the character of Morillo in a more favorable point of view, or obscures, in some measure, the reputation of Bolivar. I am not the apologist of the Spanish General; I like his character little, and his cause less; but we are taught that it is proper to rescue even the worst men from unmerited obloquy. Admit, however, all that has been said to be true, is this the argument by which it is made manifest that we ought to recognise the independence of South America ? Sir, it may move your pity, or rouse your abhorrence, but it cannot reach the judgment.

Finally, Mr. Speaker, it appears to me inexpedient to make the appropriation proposed, because Spain and her colonies are at this moment endeavoring to put an end to their long, and barbarous, and bloody warfare. Why then should we interpose between the negotiating parties, and decree that for them which they are, of themselves, considering ? It would be an act of supererogation in our Government to interfere at such a crisis.

For these reasons I am constrained to vote against the proposition of the gentleman from Kentucky.

Mr. LOWNDES made the closing speech, in further objections to the motion.

The question was then taken on Mr. CLAY's motion, by yeas and nays, as follows:

YEAS—Messrs. Allen of New York, Allen of Tennessee, Anderson, Archer of Virginia, Baker, Ball, Baternan, Beecher, Blackledge, Boden, Brown, Bryan, Butler of Louisiana, Campbell, Cannon, Case, Clark, Clay, Cocke, Cook, Crawford, Crowell, Culbreth, Culpeper, Cuthbert, Darlington, Davidson, Earle, Fisher, Floyd, Ford, Gross of New York, Gross of Pennsylvania, Hackley, Hall of N. York, Hendricks, Herrick, Hibshman, Hooks, Hostetter, Johnson, Jones of Tennessee, Kinsey, Kinsley, Lincoln, McCreary, McLean of Kentucky, Mallary, Marchand, Meech, Metcalf, Monell, R. Moore, S. Moore, T. L. Moore, Murray, Parker of Massachusetts, Patterson, Philson, Pitcher, Richmond, Rogers, Ross, Shaw, Sloan, Southard, Stevens, Storrs, Tarr, Tracy, Trimble, Tucker of Virginia, Udree, Upham, Van Rensselaer, Walker, Wallace, and Williams of Virginia—79.

NAYS—Messrs. Abbot, Adams, Alexander, Allen of Massachusetts, Archer of Maryland, Barbour, Bayly, Brevard, Brush, Buffum, Burton, Butler of N. Hampshire, Clagett, Cobb, Crafts, Cushman, Dane, Dennison, Dickinson, Edwards of Connecticut, Edwards of Pennsylvania, Edwards of North Carolina, Eustis, Fay, Folger, Foot, Forrest, Fuller, Gorham, Gray, Guyon, Hall of North Carolina, Hardin, Hemphill, Hill, Hobart, Jones of Virginia, Kendall, Kent, Lathrop, Livermore, Lowndes, Maclay, McCoy, McCullough, McLane of Delaware, Meigs, Mercer, Montgomery, Morton, Neale, Nelson of Massachusetts, Nelson of Virginia, Newton, Parker of Virginia, Pinckney, Plumer, Rankin, Reid, Rhea, Rich, Richards, Ringgold, Robertson, Russ, Sawyer, Sergeant, Silsbee, Simkins, Smith of New Jersey, Smith of Maryland, Smith of North Carolina, Street, Strong of Vermont, Strong of New York, Swearingen, Terrell, Tomlinson, Tompkins, Tucker of South Carolina, Tyler, Warfield, Wendover, Whitman, Williams of North Carolina, and Wood—86.

So the motion was rejected.

Mr. BEECHER then moved to amend the bill by inserting a provision appropriating the sum of twenty thousand dollars for the repair of the Cumberland Road, being a part of the unexpended balance of appropriations for completing that road.

The motion was negatived ; and the bill was then ordered to be engrossed for a third reading.

On motion, the House then adjourned until tomorrow.

SATURDAY, February 10.

Mr. RHEA, from the Committee on Pensions and Revolutionary Claims, to which was referred the bill from the Senate, entitled "An act for the relief of the representatives of Patience Gordon, widow, deceased," made a report thereon, recommending that the said bill be rejected ; which was read, and, together with the bill, was ordered to lie on the table.

On motion of Mr. HARDIN, the Committee of Ways and Means were instructed to inquire into the expediency of exempting from the custom-house duties all such articles which are now by law subject to duty, as may have been, or may hereafter be, imported for the express use of the Roman Catholic cathedral and college erected and established at Bardstown, in Kentucky.

Mr. CANNON moved that the Committee of the whole House, to which is committed the bill to provide an uniform system of organization for the militia of the different States and Territories, and for instructing the officers of the same at the expense of the United States, be discharged, and that the said bill be committed to the Committee of the whole House on the state of the Union. And, the question being taken thereon, it was determined in the negative.

Engrossed bills of the following titles, to wit :

"An act making appropriations for the support of Government for the year 1821 ;" and

"An act to alter and establish certain post roads ;"

Were severally read the third time, passed, and sent to the Senate.

MISSOURI.

Mr. BUTLER, of New Hampshire, submitted the following joint resolution:

Resolved, by the Senate and House of Representatives of the United States of America in Congress assembled, That the people of Missouri be, and they are hereby, authorized to form a new constitution, or to alter the constitution which they have already formed and presented to Congress, in such way and manner as they may judge most proper, and submit the same to Congress, for the purpose of being admitted into the Union on an equal footing with the original States.

Mr. TOMLINSON said, the proposition of the gentleman from New Hampshire was certainly entitled to the deliberate consideration of the House, and, for the purpose of affording gentlemen an opportunity to examine the proposition, Mr. T. moved that it be laid upon the table and printed.

The motion was agreed to.

Mr. CLAY, from the select committee, to whom the subject was referred, delivered in the following report and amendment:

The select committee to whom was referred the resolution from the Senate declaring the admission of the State of Missouri into the Union, have, according to order, had the same under consideration, and beg leave to submit to the House the following report :

That they have entered upon the discharge of the duty assigned them by the House, with the most anxious desire to arrive at a conclusion which would give general satisfaction; that, in the prosecution of this purpose, it seemed to them to be useful to ascertain, in the first place, by a full and frank comparison of opinions among themselves, whether any, and what, conditions ought to be prescribed to the admission of Missouri into the Union; that, on making this comparison, the opinion appeared to be nearly unanimous in the committee, that no other conditions ought now to be required than those which were specified in the act of the last session of Congress, providing for the admission of Missouri into the Union; and that, considering all the circumstances attending that act, the settlement which it made of the question of restriction ought not to be disturbed; that this opinion limited their subsequent inquiry to the consideration of the single question, whether the constitution which Missouri has formed for herself contained any thing in it which furnished a valid objection to her incorporation in the Union? And, on that question, they thought that there was no other provision in that constitution to which Congress could of right take exception, but that which makes it the duty of the Legislature of Missouri to pass laws to prevent free negroes and mulattoes from going to and settling in the said State. In regard to that clause, the same diversity of opinion existed among the members of the committee which had been previously manifested in the House—one portion believing it liable to an interpretation repugnant to the Constitution of the United States, and the other thinking it not exposed to that objection, or that, if it were, the exceptionable interpretation was superseded by the paramount authority of the Federal Constitution.

With these conflicting opinions, the committee thought it best that, without either side abandoning its opinion, an endeavor should be made to frame an amendment to the Senate's resolution, which, compromitting neither, should contain an adequate security against the violation of the privileges and immunities of citizens of other States in Missouri; and, a majority of the committee thinking that such security could not be sufficiently afforded without some previous act to be done by the Legislature of Missouri, the amendment was finally agreed upon, which they now beg leave to report.

According to this amendment, Missouri is to be admitted into the Union upon the fundamental condition, that she shall never pass any laws preventing any description of persons from going to and settling in the said State, who now are, or hereafter may become, citizens of any of the States in this Union; and, upon the Legislature of the said State signifying its assent to that condition, by a solemn public act, which is to be communicated to the President of the United States, he is to proclaim the fact, and thereupon the admission of the said State into the Union is to be complete, without any further or other proceeding on the part of Congress. To prevent, however, this amendment from being considered as impairing any right which may appertain to Missouri, in common with other States, to exclude from her jurisdiction persons under peculiar circumstances, (such as paupers, vagabonds, &c.,) a further proviso is added, declaring that nothing in the said amendment is to be construed to take from Missouri, when admitted into the Union, the exercise of any right or power which the original States may constitutionally exert.

The modification which the committee thus respect-

fully recommend of the Senate's resolution, is the result of a spirit of concord, under the guidance of which they have anxiously sought, without the sacrifice of principle on either side, to reconcile the variant opinions among them. There cannot be a doubt but that Missouri, solicitous as she must be, to participate in all the high advantages of our excellent Union, will eagerly seize the opportunity of testifying her attachment to the Federal Constitution, by giving the solemn pledge which she is asked to make, to respect the privileges and immunities which it secures to citizens of other States—a pledge become necessary, in the opinion of a large and respectable portion of the House, by the terms which she has employed in a clause of her constitution. Nor will there be a doubt of the sincerity or efficacy of such a pledge. On the other hand, if, by postponing, for a short period, her admission into the Union—a circumstance every day less and less important, in consequence of the lapse of the time allotted to this session, those who thought her invested with a perfect right to be admitted, without delay, are not fully gratified, they will be consoled by the reflection that the amendment requires only the performance of a precise and simple act, which cannot be mistaken by the highly responsible officer to whom the judgment of its execution is confided; and the whole House must be gratified with any proper disposition of the subject, which will henceforth free the public deliberations from the agitation and disturbance to which it is but too likely always to give rise. And your committee believe that all must ardently unite in wishing an amicable termination of a question which, if it be longer kept open, cannot fail to produce, and possibly to perpetuate, prejudices and animosities among a people to whom the conservation of their moral ties should be even dearer, if possible, than that of their political bond. Sharing, as the committee do, largely in this sentiment, they respectfully submit to the House the amendment which they propose, in the hope that it will be received and considered in the same spirit in which it has been devised.

Strike out all after the word "be" in the third line of the Senate's resolution, and insert

"Admitted into this Union on an equal footing with the original States, in all respects whatever, upon the fundamental condition, that the said State shall never pass any law preventing any description of persons from coming to and settling in the said State, who now are or hereafter may become citizens of any of the States of this Union: *And provided, also,* That the Legislature of the said State, by a solemn public act, shall declare the assent of the said State to the said fundamental condition, and shall transmit to the President of the United States, on or before the fourth Monday of November next, an authentic copy of the said act; upon the receipt whereof, the President, by proclamation, shall announce the fact; whereupon, and without any further proceeding on the part of Congress, the admission of the said State into this Union shall be considered as complete: *And provided further,* That nothing herein contained shall be construed to take from the said State of Missouri, when admitted into this Union, the exercise of any right or power which can now be constitutionally exercised by any of the original States."

The resolution, with the report, was, on motion of Mr. CLAY, ordered to lie on the table; and Mr. CLAY gave notice that he should call for its consideration on Monday.

SOUTH AMERICAN PROVINCES.

Mr. CLAY rose, and submitted for consideration the following resolution:

Resolved, That the House of Representatives participates with the people of the United States in the deep interest which they feel for the success of the Spanish provinces of South America which are struggling to establish their liberty and independence; and that it will give its Constitutional support to the President of the United States, whenever he may deem it expedient to recognise the sovereignty and independence of any of the said provinces.

In offering this resolution, Mr. C. said, he was influenced by the general solicitude which he felt on this subject, and by the conviction that there was a majority of the House in favor of an expression of a sentiment favorable to the cause of the people of the Spanish provinces. The vote of yesterday, to the contrary, was influenced, in a great degree, it was evident, by considerations of form. He had framed this resolution so as, he hoped, to be unexceptionable in that respect; and, though it did not go as far as he wished to go, it went to a certain extent in giving the countenance of this House to the exertions of the people of the South. Mr. C. said, as the subject was well understood, and he wished not to consume the time of the House, he should not debate the proposition, unless he should be obliged to do so by debate against it.

Mr. REID moved that the resolution lie on the table, for consideration, as well because of the general importance of any proposition on this subject, and the propriety of acting on it with deliberation, as because the gentleman who was at the head of the Committee of Foreign Affairs (Mr. LOWNDES) was this day absent.

Mr. CLAY stated, that he had informed his friend at the head of the Committee of Foreign Affairs, who was absent from a temporary indisposition, that he intended to submit such a proposition as this to-day; and received for answer that he did not care about being present at the discussion, and did not wish to be sent for.

Mr. SMITH, of Maryland, made a few remarks, to show that the House ought to act with caution and deliberation on a proposition of this sort, which, for aught they knew, might compromit the peace of the country.

The question on the motion to lay the resolution on the table, resulted thus: For it laying on the table 71; against it 72.

So the motion was lost; and the question was stated on agreeing to the resolution.

Here arose a debate, which occupied the whole day.

Mr. WOOD first spoke in opposition to the motion; because it proposed to make needless professions, and was not therefore consistent with self-respect; because, if it had any object, it was an encroachment on the power of the Executive, and might produce a collision between the two departments of Government, which was much to be deprecated.

Mr. FLOYD referred to an early message of President Washington to Congress, to show that, at that time, the previous consent of Congress was thought necessary to the institution of foreign missions; thence, and from other considerations, arguing that this resolution, so far from interfering with the Executive prerogative was a fair exercise of the undoubted rights of this House. Mr. F. also supported the proposition on the ground of expediency, and as going to counteract the policy of the Holy Alliance by organizing a different policy on this side of the water, &c.

Mr. ARCHER required a division of the question, so as to take it first on the first member of the resolution. And the question was accordingly stated on agreeing thereto in the following words:

Resolved, That the House of Representatives participates with the people of the United States in the deep interest which they feel for the success of the Spanish provinces of South America which are struggling to establish their liberty and independence.

Mr. ROBERTSON deprecated the passage of the whole resolution as supererogatory, if not of injurious tendency. If it was intended only to apprize the Executive that this House would support him, that had been done by the vote of last session; if it was to express the sentiment of this House in regard to the subject, that too had been done by the vote of last session; and a repetition of such declarations could serve only to show a doubt of our own constancy. If, however, it was intended to goad the Executive into a departure from its hitherto wise policy on this subject, he was decidedly opposed to it, &c. Mr. R. concluded by saying, that as the proposition was divided, he should, though he deemed such a declaration wholly superfluous and unnecessary, vote in favor of the first clause of the resolution, and against the second.

Mr. WOOD then moved that the whole subject be indefinitely postponed.

Mr. MONTGOMERY assigned the reasons why he should vote for the indefinite postponement, and, should that not prevail, against both branches of the resolution. He was opposed to the first part of it, as asserting what he did not know to be the fact, and what he did not believe to be the fact as regarded his immediate constituents—that the people take a deep interest in a matter wholly foreign to them. The second part of the resolution he wholly disapproved. He believed it to be the true policy of this country to stand aloof from this conflict, as the Powers of Europe, more deeply interested, had done. Were we to engage in it, it was difficult to predict how it would end, &c. Mr. M. suggested, however, that the motion had an object something deeper than an expression of the opinion of this House, and that it might be intended to goad the President into a course of policy which his judgment did not approve, and which the nation did not wish for.

Mr. TYLER assigned the grounds on which, though he had voted against all the other propositions of the gentleman from Kentucky, he should vote for this. The first part of it, he said, asked him only to speak the sentiments of his constituents; and, knowing well their feelings on this subject, he could not hesitate to vote in the affirmative upon it. The second part of the resolution only proposed to declare, that the President of the United States enjoys so much the confidence of this House, that, whenever he should think proper to recognise the independence of any of the Southern provinces, it will support him in it. To this, Mr. T. had no objection. In voting for the whole proposition, he should only express the sentiment of his heart, a deep sympathy for a people struggling for liberty, &c.

Mr. WALKER expressed his sentiments decidedly in favor of the whole resolution. The subject, he said, was near his heart; and he would not hesitate to throw our weight into the scale of liberty. He enumerated several considerations which influenced him to this course, among which were the general duty of individuals and of societies to sympathize with and do good to one another; the similarity of the struggle of these provinces with Spain to that of our Revolution; the similarity, too, of their forms of government, &c. He was not afraid of trusting the President and had no fear of committing him, by passing this resolution.

Mr. MERCER assigned the reasons why he was in favor of this resolution, and against the postponement. He disclaimed any want of confidence in the Executive: nor did the resolution go upon any such ground, but on the contrary its very terms excluded such a conclusion. He considered it as differing widely in principle from the proposition to make an appropriation for sending a Minister or Ministers to South America. Adverting to the supposed power of the President to recognise the independence of a Government by receiving a Minister as well as by sending one, in which recognition the Senate would have no voice, it became this House, he said, to share a part of the responsibility which the Executive would incur by such a recognition. He doubted, himself, whether the President could recognise the independence of a foreign Power, by receiving a Minister, without the consent of this House. By this resolution, without prescribing any thing to the President, that difficulty would be removed. With regard to his constituents, Mr. M. expressed in strong terms his conviction of the deep feeling which they entertained favorable to the South Americans. Though approving of the course of the President in regard to the colonies hitherto, more than he did of his course to the mother country, (alluding to the occupation of Florida during the Seminole war,) he should yet cheerfully vote for the whole resolution.

Mr. CLAGETT stated the reasons why, though approving of the sentiments in the resolution, he could not vote for it. He considered the question to be the same in substance as that to which he yesterday gave a negative vote. So far as the provinces were engaged against the Spanish Government, they had his best wishes and sincere sympathy; but, he suggested, that, according to the best accounts we have, their struggle is more amongst themselves, and, so far, was one in which we could feel no sympathy. He expressed his surprise at the comparisons which had been so of-

ten made between the case of these province that of our Revolution, between which the r blance was at least remote. Believing that power of recognition was confided to ano branch of the Government, both competent a disposed to exercise it when proper, and for ot reasons which he assigned, he was opposed to t resolution.

Mr. COBB assigned the considerations which duced him to doubt the propriety of passing t resolution, though entertaining a feeling of d sympathy with the Southern provinces. He had said, almost a similar feeling in regard to the p ple of old Spain, now regenerated and comp tively free. The relative situation of Spain a her colonies, he argued, was now essentially d ferent from what it was two or three years a They were then struggling against a relentl tyranny; but there was now at least a probabil (referring to the pacification between Morillo a Bolivar, and to other indications) that old Sp would voluntarily do justice to the colonies. M C. thought therefore it was not true policy at th time for this country to do any act on this subjec however inclined. For this consideration, an because he believed the Executive felt on this sub ject in the same manner as this House and th nation, and as he had indeed expressly said in hi message, he saw no occasion for passing this reso lution. It would be time enough to act, he argued when the course of old Spain was clearly marked out. If, however, the direct vote on the resolution was forced upon the House, he should vote for the first part, but against the second, believing that sound policy was opposed to it.

Mr. BALDWIN opposed the resolution, not from any hostility to its avowed object, but because it proposed to refer to the President an act which, in his opinion, it was not for him, but for the three branches of the Government collectively, to perform. If any thing was done on this subject, he wished it to be done by all the branches of the Government.

Mr. MACLAY opposed the resolution, although. were he to suffer his feelings to govern him, he should be in favor of it. The subject, he said. had been long before the Executive, and much deliberated upon. Before such a resolution as th: was passed, Mr. M. argued, that gentleman ought to be possessed of full information on the subject— of all the information which the Executive possesses, and by which its course has been influenced, that they might judge whether that Department had or had not performed its duty. Believing that it had done so, and would hereafter do so, he was against the resolution.

Mr. STEVENS defended the Constitutional right of this House to express its opinion on any topic of public interest. So far from interfering with the Executive authority, he regarded such expressions of opinion as facilitating the exercise of that authority, this being a Government of opinion, and as it must be desirable to the Executive to know what public opinion is, &c. With regard to this measure being a goad to the Executive, Mr. S. suggested that there was no reason to aprehend that the Executive of this day was to be alarmed or driven from his course by any such measure. He was in favor of the resolve as an expression of the opinion of this House, on a point which he had no hesitation in expressing his individual opinion.

Mr. BROWN said, that he did not rise to enter into a lengthy argument, nor would he have arisen at all had there not appeared a difference of opinion between two of his colleagues, (Mr. CLAY and Mr. MONTGOMERY,) upon a point in which the character of his immediate constituents and the State at large, seemed to him much concerned. He meant no less than a diversity of opinion as to the sensibility of Kentucky to the cause of liberty, in which the patriots of South America were engaged, and to the protracted suffering of that oppressed people. His colleague, the honorable mover of this resolution, (Mr. CLAY,) believed that the people of Kentucky took a deep interest in the struggle of the patriots of South America. His colleague (Mr. MONTGOMERY) did not know that his constituents felt such an interest. Mr. B. said, that he was free to declare it as his belief that the people of Kentucky did feel a lively and strong interest for the success of the Patriot cause; and that he was led to this conclusion whether he judged from the expressions of those with whom it had been his pleasure to mingle, the rumor of the country at large, from the entertainments given in honor of his colleague (Mr. CLAY,) at which sincere thanks had been expressed for his disinterested ardor and fervid eloquence, in support of the cause of the Patriots; or whether he judged from the almost universal expression of the wish of the people for the success of the Patriots, at each successive anniversary of our independence, when, in the social and festive circle, the feelings of the heart have been most free and undisguised. He said, finally, to trouble the House no further upon this point, that, whatever might be the feelings of the constituents of his honorable colleague, (Mr. MONTGOMERY,) he would unhesitatingly pledge himself to the House, that the people of that portion of the State which he had the honor to represent did take a warm and deep interest in the cause of South American liberty.

Mr. B. said that, while up, he would take occasion to say, that no member upon that floor entertained more favorable sentiments of the patriotism and wisdom of our venerable Chief Magistrate than he did; a patriotism established by a long life of devotion to his country, in high and responsible stations. He would, on all occasions, refrain from invading the prerogatives of every co-ordinate branch of the Government, or from wantonly or lightly injuring the feelings of any of her officers; the first would be unwise, the last cruel. But, while he entertained these sentiments, he must be permitted to say, that he had felt, on more occasions than one, this House somewhat humiliated, by the display of an inflamed sensibility for the feelings and prerogatives of the Executive Department. For one, he was disposed to act, when impelled by a sense of duty, without so much regard to these considerations. He begged

leave to suggest, for the consideration of gentlemen who claimed to be the exclusive friends of the Executive, whether the course which they pursued was not calculated to defeat the object which they had in view, by authorizing an opinion that their approbation was a blind one; or that they feared his measures would not bear scrutiny? He hoped and believed that the President would not disappoint the favorable expectations of his country. Mr. B. said, that each branch of the Government, must, or ought to act upon the information which each severally possessed, and not upon that which, by possibility, might be possessed by another.

He knew not what information was possessed by the President beyond his own; he admitted it to be his right, and often his duty, (and he should not contend that he had violated either on this occasion,) to retain within his own department the information which he collected; and while he most willingly admitted that the President might be free from blame, judging by the facts before him, the President would have the liberality not to censure Congress, should they arrive at a different conclusion from the facts within their knowledge, and not those known to him, and of which they were ignorant. Mr. B. said, that he would frankly declare, that, from the information which he had, (by some reading and inquiry obtained,) but which he would not consume the time of the House to communicate,) he had believed this Government too cold and tardy in its advance towards a recognition of the Patriot Governments of South America; but, whether right or wrong, he entertained no doubt that the President had, with the most anxious wishes for his country's good, pursued the course of policy which he had done. He believed this an occasion on which it comported with the dignity and character of the American Congress to express their own sentiments, as well as those which they believed actuated their constituents; and, after having borne this evidence, he had great confidence that the President, giving that consideration to this proceeding which it merited, and reviewing the whole circumstances, would decide wisely and satisfactorily. And should the adoption of the resolution, in which is contained a pledge of support, have the effect of encouraging and strengthening the confidence of the President in the policy of treating the revolutionary governments of South America with more kindness than heretofore, he, for one, should not deplore the result. But, Mr. B. said, I have felt myself still more humiliated when any department of the Government, and more particularly the members of this House, have esteemed it necessary to predicate our movements, essentially, upon the smiles or frowns of foreign Governments.

Several gentlemen have alluded to the disasters which might arise from giving offence to the crowned heads across the Atlantic. I would not, sir, disregard the interests, opinions, or even the feelings of foreign nations; but, giving a due weight to these considerations, the American Government should decide upon its true interest and policy, and having done so, proceed with a firm and steady pace, fearless of the consequences of displeasure from abroad. Mr. B. said, that gentlemen who opposed the resolution had not been altogether consistent; most of those who have favored us with their views, have bottomed their opposition upon the ground that it is the exclusive duty of the President to decide upon the policy of foreign missions, and were fearful that this measure might be construed into a censure, or an attempt at coercion upon him. A gentleman from Pennsylvania (Mr. BALDWIN) did not fear an encroachment upon the feelings or prerogative of the President, being of opinion that Congress, and not the Executive, ought to decide upon the policy of recognising the Patriots; and that Congress seemed by this resolution to recede from a discharge of their duty, and to be willing, tamely, to cast it upon the President. While another equally distinguished member from the same State (Mr. SERGEANT) concurred in the conclusion that the resolution ought to be rejected, but upon grounds altogether different from, and repugnant to, those of his colleague. These are some of the inconsistencies into which gentlemen had been driven by a precipitate opposition to a resolution so manifestly plain and unexceptionable. Mr. B. said that he believed the Executive branch of the Government possessed of the Constitutional power of performing those acts which would amount to a recognising; that he would not now detain the House with the arguments upon which he rested his opinion; that he would say, with the utmost sincerity, that he was equally opposed to censure or coercion; but that he did wish the Executive to be fully and officially informed of the feelings of this House and of the nation; as well as of their confidence in his wisdom and their determination to support him. And this course had become doubly necessary, since a doubt had been expressed upon this floor, as to the feelings of the nation. The resolution amounted to no more, without the most palpable distortion, than an expression of good will towards the South American provinces; and a determination, from our confidence in the President, to support him. The opposition was, to him, wholly unaccountable. Mr. B. said, sir, acting upon such information as I possess, I shall do my duty as dictated by the feelings of my heart, and the operations of my judgment, though the sensibility of the President should be offended, or though, about which I care still less, Kings or Emperors should think us uncourteous. I am sure they will think us fair, frank, and generous. I will not shrink from my portion of responsibility, and let the President take his.

Mr. SMITH, of Maryland, stated several objections to the resolution, among which were the following: That it attributed to the President a power (that of recognition) too important to be exercised by any authority less than the three branches of the Government; that it proposed to make this House, incompatibly with the Constitution, the adviser of the President, thus taking from him a part at least of his Constitutional responsibility; that it would afford a bad precedent, which, in future times, may be used, through the influence of the President, in this House; that it proposes that this House should compromit its successors in office, which it could not do, and which it was therefore improper to attempt, &c.

Mr. COOK opposed this resolution, though he had yesterday voted in favor of Mr. CLAY's proposition, because it proposed an empty declaration, after refusing an efficient act. So far from believing that such a resolution as this would aid the cause of the South American Patriots, he believed it would inspire them with contempt for the course of this House. It was saying, in connexion, with yesterday's vote, we wish you well, very well, but not as much well as eighteen thousand dollars.

Mr. CLAY then delivered a speech of half an hour's length in support of his motion. He opposed to one another the objections to the resolution, to show that they would not stand together, and therefore denied their claim to respect taken separately. He quoted the precedent of the resolution of Congress to support the President in any consequences which might follow the dismission of the British Minister, Mr. Jackson, some years ago, and alluded to other precedents of expressions of opinion by this House. He ridiculed and reasoned against the argument that this resolution would hurt the feelings of the Executive, or encroach on his authority. It was, on the contrary, he contended, assuming only a fair responsibility on the part of this House, and adding strength to the Executive. He referred to the vote of last session, and the counter vote of yesterday, which appeared to him imperiously to require the passage of this resolution. He protested against the argument of the gentleman from Georgia, drawn from the situation of Old Spain, as absolutely founded on the idea that the colonies ought to repass under the yoke of Spain. The argument which denied the power of one Congress to bind its successors, would, he contended, equally apply to the most important acts of legislation, such as declarations of war, &c. As to the sentiments of the people on this subject, Mr. C. said that was a matter of fact which each gentleman must determine for himself, and vote accordingly. For his own part, he had no doubt what were the sentiments of his constituents on this subject; and, repeating a sentiment thrown out by Mr. MERCER, he said, if they did not entertain such sentiments, so help him God he would not represent them. If the matter of fact was certain, he could see no reason against avowing it. With respect to the mode of recognition of foreign Powers, Mr. C. reviewed the various opinions which had been expressed at different times, as well as to-day, on this subject. He concluded that both Congress and the Executive had this power, but that the most regular, ordinary, and usual course was by the Executive; and it was, therefore, proper to assure him of the support of this House, &c. There was a peculiar propriety, Mr. C. contended, in this House moving in this business, being the immediate representatives of the people, and the cause of South America being that of the people, as being the cause of human liberty, &c. Mr. C. concluded by saying, if this proposition did not satisfy gentlemen, it was impossible for him to conceive in what shape a proposition on this subject could be placed, so as that they could vote for it.

Mr. SMITH, of Maryland, then rose, and took a wider view of the question than he had done before, going into the general argument which recommends great caution in the recognition of the independence of a country embroiled in civil war. He again denied the right, attributed to the President by the resolution, to make such recognition without the assent of Congress. He expatiated on the magnitude of such a power, the exercise of which would, if any thing could, plunge the nation into a war; for illustration of which he referred to the war between France and England, caused solely by the recognition, by the former, of our independence. All history, he said, spoke the same language. If the Hartford Convention, during the late war, had realized the view of some of its projectors, how, he asked, should we have acted in regard to any neutral nation which had recognised the independence of the States represented in that Convention? Mr. S. strongly protested against the resolution, as inexpedient in every view, and asserting for the Executive a power which it did not possess.

Mr. KINSEY made a glowing appeal to the feelings of the House in favor of liberty, and to its sympathies for those contending for it. The sentiment of the country, he argued, could not be doubted, and it ought to be expressed. If war should come, said he, in consequence of the expression of our opinion, let it come. He trusted no man would shrink from the expression of his honest opinion from any such apprehension as that. In reply to the question *cui bono*—what good was to come of this? Mr. K. drew a vivid picture of the scenes of our Revolution, and of the vivifying effect of the news of the recognition of our independence by France. Was it no good, he asked, that we should be instrumental in elevating so large a portion of the human race to the same rank as we enjoy, and to a participation of the blessings of freedom and liberty? Mr. K. said he had confidence that this question would carry. It *must* carry; and it would meet with the decided approbation of the people of this country.

Mr. SERGEANT delivered his objections to the resolution, though believing that, if the question were taken on the first part of it only, there would be but little or no objection to it. His objections were, in general terms, that it expresses an individual opinion, and professes to give a pledge which must be utterly inefficacious; that it is not a legislative act, and is not to lead to a legislative act; that it contains a declaration by which neither this House, the President, nor the Senate, would be bound; that it would involve the House in difficulties on Constitutional ground; that, if Congress wish a recognition, having the power equally with the Executive, they should effectuate their wish by a legislative act; that, if the opinion of this House was to be expressed, even that should not be done without due inquiry and examination of facts, none of which had been placed before

the House in any thing like an official shape; that the House ought to take care not to lose sight, in acts of kindness and expressions of good will to other Powers, of the duty which it owed to this nation—to the interests of the people whom they represent; that general and vague oral information was not a sufficient ground for Congress to act upon; that, if official information was before the House requiring it to act, its act should be something plainer than this, and presenting on its face a direct proposition; that its not doing so, caused it to be more lightly considered and voted upon that it ought to be; that, however independent of the Executive, as an individual, this House might be, yet, with respect to the Executive as a branch of this Government, it was important that this House should not disturb the harmony of the different departments of Government, as adjusted by the Constitution itself, and that it should not rush from its sphere, and jostle the others in their course.

Mr. BRUSH assigned his reasons for voting for the resolution. His reason was, that the Executive would look at both votes of this House, that of yesterday, and that of to-day. The vote of yesterday approved his conduct in 'not sending a Minister; this resolution did the same, assuring him of the continued and consistent support of this House—and on that ground alone he should vote for it.

Mr. REID assigned the reasons why he should vote against the second part of the resolution, should it not be postponed, because, to pass it would be without object, because, in principle and spirit, it was a repetition of the vote of last session, and, therefore, unnecessary, the vote of last year not being rendered nugatory by the vote of yesterday, but perfectly reconcilable with it; that the resolution, if it proposes to bind not only this House, but its successors, makes a pledge which it may be impossible to redeem; that it pledges, moreover, a support to an unknown act—to an act which may or may not be unwise or pernicious to the public interest; that such a pledge was an acknowledgment of Executive infallibility which it did not become the House to sanction. With regard to the first part of the resolution, Mr. R. said, he should vote for it, if presented to him, believing it to correspond 'fully with the feelings and wishes of his constituents.

Mr. ROBERTSON concluded the debate by some remarks in favor of the indefinite postponement of the resolution, on the ground that, to act on the subject, would be an useless consumption of time, and, having already once expressed the same sentiment, (at the last session,) would be an undignified proceeding. With respect to the bearing of this resolution, in one way or another, in regard to the Executive, Mr. R. remarked that it somehow or other had happened that, during the four years he had been in Congress, he had never yet voted with the Executive on any administration question, unless the Army question was considered one. In this course he had not been influenced by any disposition to embarrass the Executive, but his personal opinion of what was right. But, he added, whilst he would never vote for any proposition to gratify the Executive, he would never give his vote for any proposition calculated to embarrass and perplex him in the discharge of his proper functions.

The question on indefinite postponement was then taken, and decided in the negative.

Mr. FOOT, in order to get rid of a subject on which he considered the time of the House to be unprofitably occupied, moved to lay the resolution on the table.—Negatived by a considerable majority.

Mr. WOOD moved to amend the resolution by adding thereto a proviso to the following effect: "*Provided*, That this resolution shall not be construed to interfere with the independent exercise of the treaty-making power."

This motion was negatived.

The question on agreeing to the first clause of the resolution was then taken by yeas and nays, and decided in the affirmative—yeas 134, nays 12, as follows:

YEAS—Messrs. Abbot, Adams, Alexander, Allen of New York, Allen of Tennessee, Anderson, Archer of Maryland, Archer of Virginia, Baker, Baldwin, Ball, Barbour, Bateman, Bayly, Beecher, Blackledge, Boden, Brevard, Brown, Brush, Bryan, Burton, Butler of New Hampshire, Butler of Louisiana, Campbell, Cannon, Case, Clagett, Clark, Clay, Cobb, Cocke, Cook, Crawford, Culbreth, Culpeper, Cushman, Cuthbert, Dane, Darlington, Davidson, Dennison, Dewitt, Dickinson, Earle, Eddy, Edwards of Connecticut, Eustis, Fisher, Floyd, Ford, Fuller, Gray, Gross of New York, Gross of Pennsylvania, Guyon, Hackley, Hall of New York, Hall of N. Carolina, Hardin, Hemphill, Hendricks, Herrick, Hibshman, Hill, Hobart, Hooks, Hostetter, Johnson, Jones of Virginia, Jones of Tennessee, Kendall, Kinsey, Kinsley, Lincoln, Maclay, McCoy, McCreary, McLean of Kentucky, Mallary, Marchand, Meech, Meigs, Mercer, Metcalf, Monell, R. Moore, S. Moore, T. L. Moore, Morton, Murray, Neale, Newton, Parker of Massachusetts, Patterson, Philson, Pitcher, Plumer, Rankin, Reid, Rhea, Rich, Richmond, Robertson, Rogers, Ross, Russ, Shaw, Simkins, Sloan, Smith of New Jersey, Smith of Maryland, Smith of North Carolina, Southard, Stevens, Storrs, Swearingen, Tarr, Tomlinson, Trimble, Tucker of Virginia, Tucker of South Carolina, Tyler, Udree, Upham, Van Rensselaer, Walker, Wallace, Warfield, Wendover, Williams of Virginia, Williams of North Carolina, and Wood.

NAYS—Messrs. Allen of Massachusetts, Buffum, Crafts, Edwards of North Carolina, Fay, Folger, Foot, Livermore, Montgomery, Nelson of Virginia, Richards, and Strong of Vermont.

So this clause was agreed to.

Mr. MACLAY then moved to amend the second member of the said resolution by prefixing thereto the following: "That it approves of the course heretofore pursued by the President of the United States with regard to the said provinces." And, the question being taken thereon, it was determined in the negative without debate.

The question was then taken to agree to the second member of the said resolution, to wit: from the word *and*, after the word *independence*, to the end thereof, and passed in the affirmative—yeas 87, nays 68, as follows:

YEAS—Messrs. Abbot, Allen, of New York, Allen of Tennessee, Anderson, Archer of Virginia, Baker, Ball, Bateman, Bayly, Beecher, Blackledge, Boden, Brown, Brush, Bryan, Butler of New Hampshire, Butler of La., Campbell, Cannon, Case, Clark, Clay, Cocke, Culbreth, Culpeper, Cuthbert, Darlington, Davidson, Dewitt, Earle, Fisher, Floyd, Ford, Gross of New York, Gross of Pennsylvania, Hackley, Hall of New York, Hendricks, Herrick, Hibshman, Hooks, Hostetter, Johnson, Jones of Tennessee, Kinsey, Kinsley, Lincoln, McCreary, McLean of Kentucky, Mallary, Marchand, Meech, Mercer, Metcalf, Monell. R. Moore, S. Moore, T. L. Moore, Murray, Neale, Parker of Mass., Patterson, Philson, Pitcher, Richmond, Rogers, Ross, Shaw, Sloan, Southard, Stevens, Storrs, Swearingen, Tarr, Tracy, Trimble, Tucker of Va., Tucker of South Carolina, Tyler, Udree, Upham, Van Rensselaer, Walker, Wallace, Warfield, Williams of Virginia, and Williams of North Carolina.

NAYS—Messrs. Adams, Alexander, Allen of Massachusetts, Archer of Maryland, Baldwin, Barbour, Brevard, Buffum, Burton, Clagett, Cobb, Cook, Crafts, Cushman, Dane, Dennison, Dickinson, Eddy, Edwards of Connecticut, Edwards of Pennsylvania, Edwards of North Carolina, Eustis, Fay, Folger, Foot, Forrest, Fuller, Gorham, Gray, Guyon, Hall of North Carolina, Hardin, Hemphill, Hill, Hobart, Jones of Virginia, Kendall, Kent, Lathrop, Livermore, Maclay, McCoy, Meigs, Montgomery, Morton, Nelson of Massachusetts, Nelson of Virginia, Newton, Plumer, Rankin, Reed, Rhea, Rich, Richards, Robertson, Russ, Sergeant, Silsbee, Simkins, Smith of New Jersey, Smith of Maryland, Smith of North Carolina, Street, Strong of Vermont, Strong of New York, Tomlinson, Wendover, and Wood.

So that clause was agreed to.

The question was then taken on agreeing to the proposition, as a whole, and carried in the affirmative; and a committee of two members was ordered to be appointed to lay the same before the President.

MONDAY, February 12.

Mr. NEWTON, from the Committee on Commerce, reported a bill further to establish the compensation of the officers employed in the collection of duties on imports and tonnage, and for other purposes; which was read twice and committed to the Committee of the Whole.

Mr. WILLIAMS, of North Carolina, from the Committee of Claims, to which was referred the bill from the Senate, entitled "An act for the relief of Thomas L. Ogden and others," reported the same with amendments; which were read, and, together with the bill, committed to a Committee of the Whole to-morrow.

The SPEAKER laid before the House a letter from the Secretary of the Navy, transmitting papers containing the information required by the resolution adopted on the 5th instant in relation to the Marine Corps; which letter and papers were referred to the Committee on Naval Affairs.

On motion of Mr. CLAY, the Committee on the Judiciary were instructed to inquire whether any, and, if any, what, provision by law is necessary to secure the due execution of process issuing from the courts of the United States.

[From a few explanatory remarks of Mr. CLAY, in offering this resolution, it appeared that his object was to inquire whether any provision was necessary to authorize a Judge of the United States to provide for the contingency of a State's refusing to the United States the use of its jails—a law to that effect having actually been passed by the Legislature of one of the States, (Ohio,) with a view to process of a certain description.]

On motion of Mr. ROBERT MOORE, the Committee on Commerce were instructed to inquire into the expediency of providing by law for the removal of the obstructions in the entrance of Erie harbor, in the State of Pennsylvania.

Mr. MOORE accompanied the above resolution with an attested copy of a resolution adopted by the Senate and House of Representatives of the State of Pennsylvania, approved by the Governor on the 1st of February instant, "requesting their Senators and Representatives in Congress to use their exertions in procuring the passage of a law providing for the removal of the obstructions in the entrance of the said harbor; and pledging that Commonwealth to co-operate with the United States in the accomplishment of that object;" which resolution, together with the memorial of sundry inhabitants of the borough of Erie, in the said State, heretofore presented on the 29th of December, 1817, was referred to the Committee of Commerce.

The House then, on motion of Mr. STORRS, proceeded to the consideration of the resolution submitted by him a few days ago, with regard to the order of business in the House; and the same was, after some conversation, agreed to, in the following words:

Ordered, That, during the remainder of the present session of Congress business referred to Committees of the whole House shall be called for consideration in the following order:

1. Private bills which have passed the Senate, and have been reported upon favorably by a committee of the House.
2. Private bills reported by committees of the House.
3. Bills and resolutions of a public nature.
4. Bills which have passed the Senate and have been reported against by a committee of the House.
5. Reports unfavorable to petitioners.

A message from the Senate informed the House that the Senate have passed a bill, entitled "An act for the relief of purchasers of public lands prior to the 1st July, 1820," in which they ask the concurrence of this House.

MISSOURI.

The House then, on motion of Mr. CLAY, proceeded to consider the report of the committee appointed on the Missouri subject. On motion of Mr. C. it was referred to the Committee of the Whole on the state of the Union. And, also on motion of Mr. C., the House forthwith resolved itself into a Committee of the Whole, to take the subject up.

The amendment proposed by the committee having been read from the Chair—

Mr. CLAY gave a detailed account of the proceedings in the committee, of the difficulty which interposed, and of the considerations which led to the recommendation of this amendment. This statement of course corresponded with that contained in the report of the committee. Mr. C. then went on to obviate some objections to the report which had been made by the friends of Missouri, as well as by those opposed to her admission into the Union. Although those in favor of her admission into the Union could not succeed entirely in their particular views, Mr. C. was of opinion that they had, as regarded the report of the committee, nothing to complain of. At the same time, this report was calculated to obviate the objections of those who had opposed the admission of Missouri on the ground of the objection to her constitution, which had been avowed. Thus consulting the opinions of both sides of the House, in that spirit of compromise which is occasionally necessary to ceive the countenance of the House. Mr. C. concluded by earnestly invoking the spirit of harmony and kindred feeling to preside over the deliberations of the House on the subject.

Mr. MALLARY moved to amend the amendment proposed by the committee, by striking out all of it, after the words "respects," and, in lieu thereof, inserting the following:

"Whenever the people of said State, by a convention appointed according to the manner provided by the act to authorize the people of Missouri to form a constitution and State government, and for the admission of such State into the Union on an equal footing with the original States, and to prohibit slavery in certain territories, approved March 6, 1820, adopt a constitution conformably to the provisions of said act, and shall in addition to said provisions, further provide, in and by said constitution, that neither slavery nor involuntary servitude shall ever be allowed in said State of Missouri, unless inflicted as a punishment for crimes committed against the laws of said State, whereof the party accused shall be duly convicted. Provided that the civil condition of those persons who now are held to service in Missouri shall not be affected by the last provision.

This motion was negatived by a considerable majority.

Mr. TOMLINSON addressed the Chair, as follows:

Mr. Chairman: Having had the honor to be one of the committee which reported the resolution now under consideration, and dissenting to that report, I am aware that it is a duty incumbent on me briefly to state the grounds of such dissent. The state of my health will prevent me from occupying any considerable portion of your time. I have indulged the hope that some honorable member of the select committee, coinciding with me in the opinions which I have deliberately formed, upon the proposition now under consideration, would favor this committee with his views in relation to it; but as no gentleman has thought proper to do so, I am compelled, on this occasion, in justice to myself, to deviate from the course which I have hitherto pursued respecting the discussion of the question which has so long agitated the National Councils, and to state the objections to this resolution which have presented themselves to my mind, and which will induce me to vote against it. I know not how they may be viewed by other gentlemen, but with me they are conclusive.

By the act, passed at the last session of Congress, the inhabitants of the Territory of Missouri, included within boundaries therein designated, were authorized to form for themselves a constitution and State government, for the purpose of being admitted into the Union. This act provided that such constitution, whenever formed, should not be " repugnant to the Constitution of the United States." The inhabitants of the Territory of Missouri, under the authority of the act to which I have referred, have formed a constitution, and have presented the same to Congress. For what purpose? That Congress may perform a mere ministerial act, and admit that people into this Union as a matter of course? No, sir; Congress have a higher duty to perform. It is the duty of Congress to determine whether that constitution be republican and not repugnant to the Constitution of the United States.

On examining this constitution it is found to contain, under the title of " the legislative power," a provision that it shall be the duty of " the Gen-
' eral Assembly as soon as may be, to pass such
' laws as may be necessary to prevent free negroes
' and mulattoes from coming to, and settling in, this
' State, under any pretext whatsoever." This provision is deemed incompatible with, and directly repugnant to, the Constitution of the United States, which provides that " the citizens of each State shall be entitled to all the privileges and immunities of citizens in the several States." Sir, I have not been an inattentive observer of what has passed, on this subject, so deeply affecting the feelings of Congress and the nation, and I do not recollect that, either in this House or in the Senate, (if it be not out of order to refer to the proceedings of that honorable body,) any other objection has been urged, during the present session, against the admission of Missouri into this Union. This House, after an elaborate discussion, has solemnly determined that this objection is well founded, and has rejected the resolution for the admission of Missouri into this Union, reported by the committee to which her constitution was referred. This expression of the opinion of this House, repeated in a variety of forms, renders it unnecessary, and, I may add, improper, for me again to agitate this question. A majority of this House have determined that the constitution of Missouri does deprive citizens of some of the States of the privileges and immunities of citizens in that State. I shall, therefore, ·take it for granted, (which, indeed, the appointment and report of the committee, now under consideration, evidently do,) that the constitution of Missouri is repugnant to that of the United States, and subversive of the fundamental principles of this Confederacy. In my judgment, the Constitution of the United States does not contain a provision more important than that which is infringed by the constitution of Missouri. Admit the principle, sir, that a State may restrain the citizens in the several States from

coming to, and residing within it, and this Confederacy is at an end. Believing, therefore, that the General Assembly of Missouri are required, as soon as may be, to pass laws, which will deprive persons who are citizens of the several States, of all privileges and immunities of citizens in the proposed State of Missouri, I have been compelled to refuse her admission into this Union. She has no right to such an admission. Missouri has not complied with the provisions of your act. She disregards the distinguishing feature of our Constitution. On taking my seat in this House, I solemnly engaged to support the Constitution of the United States. Entertaining the opinion which I have avowed, can I admit Missouri into this Confederacy, with a constitution containing a provision directly repugnant to that which I have sworn to support? To admit Missouri with such a provision, I must approve it; I must give to it my sanction. Sir, the Constitution of the United States is the charter of our liberties, and must be preserved inviolate. I stand upon its verge, and no encroachment shall be made upon it with my consent. When a new member presents herself to be admitted into this Union, let her bow to the Constitution; let her submit to its paramount authority. If she be not prepared to do this, she is unworthy of this high privilege; she does not deserve the destiny she seeks.

But it has been said by the honorable gentleman from Kentucky, (Mr. CLAY,) that, if the constitution of Missouri be repugnant to that of the United States, the section thus repugnant is annulled by the paramount authority of the latter. Sir, it seems to me, that this argument proves too much.

Is it not equally true that any law of Congress violating the Constitution of the United States is void, and will be so pronounced by the judiciary? But will the honorable gentleman contend that Congress are, therefore, at liberty to pass such a law? Are Congress absolved from all inquiry as to the constitutionality of a proposed measure, because such a measure, if adopted, would be annulled by the paramount authority of the Constitution? Sir, the proposit on of the honorable gentleman, if carried to its illegitimate extent, will bring him to this result. The argument of the honorable gentleman, like all his arguments, is ingenious, but it certainly is not solid. This Government never has been, and never ought to be, administered upon this principle. Adopt it, and Congress is no longer restrained by the Constitution, but may be considered afloat upon the ocean of unlimited power.

But, sir, my sense of duty will not allow me, knowingly, to pass an unconstitutional act, in the expectation that the judiciary will declare it inoperative. No, Mr. Chairman, it is the duty of Congress to meet every Constitutional question, and deliberately to determine it. The powers of Congress are limited to the Constitution, and it is bound not to transcend those powers. The Constitution of Missouri is before Congress, and you are bound to pronounce upon it. Congress is bound to decide whether the constitution of Mis-

1097   HISTORY OF CONGRESS.   1098

FEBRUARY, 1821.   *Admission of Missouri.*   H. OF R.

souri be, or be not, repugnant to the Constitution of the United States. There is no escape from it, except by the prostration of those great principles on which this Confederacy depends. The performance of our duty here can, under no circumstances, be transferred to another branch of this Government. Besides, sir, if we neglect our duty, how do we know that the judiciary will not follow our example?

Entertaining the settled opinion that the clause in the constitution of Missouri, which has been so often adverted to, is entirely incompatible with the Constitution of the United States, I can never consent to her admission into this Union, until she shall have expunged that clause from her constitution. The resolution before this committee does not propose that this shall ever be done. By this resolution Missouri is to be admitted into this Union, retaining the objectionable feature in her constitution with a qualification of the section in question, to say the least, of very doubtful import. It does not propose to do that which I deem indispensable; it does not propose to expunge the unconstitutional section.

But, sir, the manner in which this restriction upon the constitution of Missouri is to be effected, is altogether unjustifiable. The Legislature of Missouri, now acting under her constitution and by its authority, are required to stipulate, as a fundamental condition of the admission of that State into the Union, that neither they, nor any subsequent Legislature in that State, will pass certain laws, which the constitution by which they will be organized, under which they will act, and which they will have sworn to support, makes it their duty to pass. Sir, this is a most extraordinary requirement. It is humbling to Missouri. It substantially requires the members of her Legislature perpetually to disregard their oaths.

Mr. Chairman, I contend that the Legislature of Missouri have no power to make the stipulation required by this resolution. What does the resolution provide? That Missouri shall be "ad-'mitted into this Union on an equal footing with 'the original States in all respects whatever, upon 'the fundamental condition that the said State 'shall never pass any law preventing any descrip-'tion of persons from moving to, and settling in, 'the said State, who now are, or hereafter may 'become, citizens of any of the States in this 'Union;" requiring at the same time "that the 'Legislature of the said State, by a solemn public 'act, shall declare the assent of the said State to 'the said fundamental condition." The Legislature of Missouri will be required by the authority of Congress to stipulate, by a solemn public act, that the Legislature of said State shall never pass a law which their constitution makes it their duty to pass. Not only the power of the present Legislature is to be restrained by this solemn public act, but it is to be of perpetual obligation. The principle contained in this resolution is, that the Legislature of Missouri may not only control the powers of subsequent Legislatures, but even restrain the power of the people themselves, and may forever part with the power of legislating on

a given subject. Indeed, it is nothing less than admitting the existence of a power to abrogate, by a legislative act, the constitution of a State. This, sir, is a dangerous power. The States of this Union might easily, and would most certainly, be prostrated by the exercise of such a power.

But, sir, from what source does the Legislature of Missouri derive the power to make the stipulation which this resolution demands? That body acts under the constitution of Missouri, which defines their powers, and surely no power will be found in it to pass the act in question. On the contrary, the constitution absolutely requires them to do that which you call upon them to refrain from doing forever. If there were no such provision, it cannot be successfully claimed that power like that to be exercised by the Legislature of Missouri, under this resolution, resides in any legislative body, however free from constitutional restraints.

But, Mr. Chairman, the constitution formed by the people of Missouri provides a special mode in which it shall be altered or amended. Now is it in the power of her Legislature to stipulate that it shall be altered in another mode? Surely not. If then the section in question could not be expunged from the constitution of Missouri by an act of her Legislature, can it be rendered inoperative by such an act? Can the Legislature of Missouri stipulate that, although standing in her constitution, it shall be considered as annulled? Were I to admit this, it seems to me I must admit that the same Legislature may annul any other part of the constitution, and finally the constitution itself. Thus, the delegated power would be rendered paramount to the power which created it. Sir, I had supposed that the acts of the agent must be controlled by the authority of the principal, and could never transcend it. But, will it be contended that the people of Missouri, when they elected their present Legislature, intended that they should exercise, or be invested with, this gigantic power? I think not. They have, then, no shadow of authority to pass the solemn public act in question; and should they think proper to pass such an act, it must be pronounced a perfect nullity, and might, and probably would, be disregarded by their successors.

If then the Legislature of Missouri have no such power, which is to my mind extremely clear, can Congress delegate to that body a power to alter the constitution of that State? If Congress possess the power to authorize the Legislature of Missouri to alter or amend the constitution, they can authorize any other body of men to do it. Her Senators and Representative here may be thus authorized; nay, Congress may frame a constitution for that people. Sir, this resolution involves an assumption of power on the part of Congress utterly unjustifiable, and entirely unprecedented. Congress may, it is true, require of a State, on its admission into this Union, certain conditions, but those conditions must be approved and accepted by the people, either in their primary assemblies, or by their delegates especially elected, and assembled in convention for that purpose.

It has, however, been said by the honorable gentleman from New York, (Mr. FORD,) who last addressed the Committee, that it would be "impossible to congregate a set of rascals in Missouri, 'who would disregard an act passed under the 'circumstances which would attend the passage of 'this act." I believe this to be the language of the honorable gentleman. Sir, I am far from imputing to the people of that Territory any thing improper. They undoubtedly would be influenced by motives the most honorable and correct; but what do you call upon them to do? You require of them to disregard the Constitution which they will have sworn to support; to lay aside their oaths, and to impose upon themselves and their successors a perpetual disability. It seems to me that such a proposition is not much calculated to strengthen their principles of integrity. If they be that high-minded people which they have been represented to be, will they not treat this proposition with indignity? Will they not reject a proposition, the adoption of which would seem to involve a dereliction of public duty? But should the Legislature of Missouri, already elected under the constitution recently adopted by that people, submit to this "fundamental condition," and by "a solemn act declare the assent of the said State" thereto, and should a subsequent Legislature, acting under the same constitution, and feeling the obligation of an oath to support that constitution, disregard this "fundamental condition," would they deserve the imputation to which the honorable gentleman from New York is disposed to consider them liable? Would they be bound in good faith to fulfil a pledge which their predecessors had no right to make? As honest men, which would control their acts, the unauthorized pledge of their predecessors, or the constitution of the State? But it has been said that, having been admitted into this Union with this condition, a spirit of magnanimity would impel them to the fulfilment of this stipulation; but that magnanimity which has for its basis a neglect of a public duty is an unsafe dependence.

Sir, if Congress are to depend upon the magnanimity of the people of Missouri, why not admit them into the Union at this time, and without condition? Why not say to them, you are indeed a magnanimous and high-minded people, and we are willing to trust to your good faith; you have, it is true, a provision in your constitution which is repugnant to the Constitution of the United States, but we are willing to trust to your good sense and liberality, and friendly disposition, and high regard for the institutions of this nation, to expunge the objectionable section. Such a measure would at least possess the merit of consistency. But, by the resolution before the Committee, you propose to require of them to make a positive stipulation, to be of perpetual obligation, and then trust to the magnanimity of that people to perform it. Sir, I will not for a moment insinuate that it will be possible to "congregate" in Missouri a Legislature composed of any but the most upright and honorable men; but I will say that, by violating an unconstitutional stipulation of their predecessors, they would not forfeit this character. Sir, the act required of Missouri is a mere legislative act, and a subsequent Legislature may at all times repeal it. It may be called "a solemn public act;" but words will not change its character; disguise it as you will, it is nothing more than an act of the Legislature of Missouri, repealable at their pleasure.

But, Mr. Chairman, this resolution provides that the Legislature of Missouri "shall transmit to the 'President of the United States, on or before the 'fourth Monday in November next, an authentic 'copy of the said act; upon the receipt whereof 'the President, by proclamation, shall announce 'the fact, whereupon, and without any further pro- 'ceedings on the part of Congress, the admission 'of the said State into this Union shall be consid- 'ered as complete." To this provision, sir, I cannot assent. You propose to admit a new State into this Union, as a member of this confederacy, upon a "fundamental condition," and to authorize the President to "announce the fact," that she has complied with this condition.

Sir, I entertain the highest respect for the enlightened statesman who presides over this nation, and have the most entire confidence that the duties of his station will be faithfully and satisfactorily discharged, but I cannot consent to transfer to him a power which belongs to Congress alone. What is the President to do? He is to announce, by proclamation, that Missouri has complied with the fundamental condition required by Congress; that a solemn public act has been passed by the Legislature of Missouri, of the character prescribed by this resolution. This, sir, may be a very delicate and difficult question; it certainly is a grave question, as it affects the rights and privileges of a considerable portion of the citizens of this Confederacy. The power to admit new States into this Union is by the Constitution given to Congress; that instrument provides that "new States may be admitted by the Congress into this Union." Now, sir, can Congress part with this power, and provide that "new States may be admitted into this Union by the President?" But does not this resolution propose thus to transfer this high power? Missouri is not admitted into this Union absolutely, but prospectively, upon a "fundamental condition." If this condition be not acceded to, she is not a member of this Confederacy. Who is to decide this question? The President. By whom will she be admitted, then? By the President. Sir, it is the Constitutional duty of Congress to determine whether Missouri have or have not complied with this condition. Missouri has a right to call upon Congress to decide it; the nation may claim the same right; and the Constitution has intrusted Congress with the exercise of this power; and, in my judgment, Congress cannot properly delegate it to the Executive.

The act of the last session of Congress admitted Missouri into the Union, provided, among other provisions, that the constitution which she might form should not be repugnant to the Constitution of the United States; and we have been occupied during the greater part of this session in discussing the question whether there be any such repugnancy. Now a question of similar import, and of not less importance, and, as it may be of not less difficulty, is to be referred to the decision of the Executive. Why was not this expedient thought of at the last session? If it be now proper, it was equally so then. The whole course of proceedings in relation to this subject, at this session, has been upon the ground that some act of Congress is necessary to complete the admission of this new State. Missouri is not now a State in this Union, and can never become so without the consent of Congress.

If, then, it be admitted that a further act of legislation is necessary to complete the admission of Missouri; that Congress must decide whether any provision in her constitution be incompatible with that of the United States, and that this incompatibility, if found to exist, must be removed by her before she can be admitted, is it proper to authorize the Executive to declare by a proclamation that this condition has received the assent of Missouri, and thus to render her admission complete? Sir, this momentous question ought to be determined by Congress, upon a view of the constitution of Missouri, and all the circumstances attending it, at the time of her admission.

The admission of a new State has been termed an act of sovereignty, and has been confided by the Constitution of the United States to Congress. Will you, then, transfer to the President a power which rightfully and constitutionally belongs to the next Congress? You have rejected the constitution of Missouri for reasons which are satisfactory to a majority of this Committee. You have done your duty. Let those who may follow perform that which shall devolve on them.

But, why are gentlemen unwilling to bring this question before the next Congress? Are they unwilling to trust that body? Sir, I feel entirely confident that the next Congress will do its duty, in regard to this and every other subject which may be brought before it. They come directly from the people of this nation, and will speak the sentiments of the nation; and on that account may be safely intrusted with the exercise of this power.

I have, sir, thus briefly stated the reasons which will compel me to vote against the resolution before the Committee.

Sir, I feel as great anxiety to see this "distracting question" settled as the honorable gentleman from Kentucky, (Mr. CLAY,) but it must be settled upon Constitutional principles. There is danger that any other mode of settling this question, instead of allaying, will increase the excitement which it has occasioned throughout this nation. Sir, there are two parties to this great controversy, and any settlement which should prostrate the rights of either ought to be reprobated. Great as is my anxiety to see this matter put to rest, to effect it I will neither renounce my principles nor surrender the privileges of any portion of the citizens of this empire. If a settlement of this grave question take place, the good, and, I may add, the peace of this nation demands that it be satisfactory

to all its parts. A "compromise," sir, which shall bring Missouri into this Union, may, indeed, put an end to this dispute here; but, let me tell gentlemen, that if, in a settlement of this momentous question, the feelings of a large portion of this community shall be disregarded, the peace of the nation may not be restored.

To insure such a desirable and happy result, it must be settled upon a fair, and just, and Constitutional basis. To such a settlement, and to no other, will I assent.

After a long debate, protracted to a late hour, the question was taken in Committee of the Whole on the amendment to the Senate's resolution, as proposed on Saturday by the select committee of this House, and was decided in the negative—73 to 64.

The Committee rose and reported their decision to the House; and, the question being on concurring in that decision—

Mr. STORRS moved to postpone the whole subject indefinitely.

Mr. BROWN, of Kentucky, rose, and said that he must ask pardon of the House for having risen at so late an hour, and after so much anxiety had been evinced to take the vote; that he had not designed to address the House at this advanced period of the debate, although, having prepared himself upon the merits, he would have been glad to have found an opportunity, without contending for the floor with those better qualified to do it justice, before the subject had been literally exhausted; and that he would not 'now incidentally have said a word, but that the gentleman from Pennsylvania, near to him, who had just resumed his seat, (Mr. SERGEANT,) had, with a dexterity better adapted to the bar of a court than to the Hall of the House of Representatives, ingeniously, though unjustly, endeavored to cast from himself and the majority on the Missouri question, the odium of an argument, derived from its influence upon the balance of power in the United States.

Mr. B. said that his resentment at the offered injury would not admit of his remaining passive while the majority voted down the rights of Missouri, and then attempted to relieve themselves from responsibility, by endeavoring calmly and cunningly to throw the censure of so unworthy an argument used by them upon an injured minority, who he had reason to fear had so deeply suffered by the influence of the argument itself. Mr. B. said that, upon arriving at the seat of Government, and finding this question assuming an importance, and producing effects so little expected by him, he was led to expect that all was not right; that there was something artificial about it; and had, therefore, at an early period, set himself at work to investigate it to the bottom, and to develope, if possible, the real as well as ostensible considerations which had swollen it to such an alarming magnitude; and he begged it should be recollected that motives were not the less operative or dangerous for not being avowed. Mr. B. said that he had carefully reviewed the proceedings of the fifteenth Congress, in which this bitter subject was opened, as well as the speeches delivered by the advocates of the restriction, marking well the feelings and prejudices displayed, the suggestions made, and the principles avowed. He had pursued them with great attention and anxiety, and he believed, without arrogating too much to himself, that he could give the gentleman from Pennsylvania, (Mr. Sergeant,) who had just resumed his seat, the House, and the nation, a correct history of this argument, or suggestion, amounting to the same thing, of the influence of the Missouri question on the balance of power in the United States. The origin, progress, and effect, of the contest for the balance of power in Europe would be recollected: he would only say that its course had been marked with blood!

In reading two speeches delivered by an eminent and venerable member, (Mr. King,) then and now of the Senate, from New York, every word of which had been well weighed, he found some remarks truly ominous. Mr. B. said, he wished it understood that he should not pretend to detail every thing which that gentleman had said upon the same subject, to whose speeches he might take the liberty of referring; that it was not necessary to the fair attainment of the purpose which he had with candor assured the House he had in view; but all might rest satisfied that he labored under no mistake in the quotations which he should make; for, having been seriously impressed by them, he had made memoranda, considering them justly alarming, and looking askance from the motives which should influence Congress. The venerable gentleman, than whom none knew better, (having been a member of the Convention which formed the Constitution,) says that, but for this clause, the Union never would have been formed; this clause, in reference to the computation of slaves, in fixing the ratio of representation, "that the effect of this concession had 'been obvious, in the preponderance which it had 'given to the slaveholding States over the other 'States; nevertheless, it was an ancient settle-'ment; and faith and honor stood pledged not to 'disturb it. But the extension of this dispropor-'tionate power to the new States would be un-'just and odious." Here is the argument from the preponderance—the disproportionate power—almost in terms from the balance of power—surely so in substance; and which he confirms from experience; and the odium which he was pleased to say should follow the extension of it to the new States, and among them to Missouri, proves how strongly, not to say violently, this venerable gentleman felt on the subject of restriction. Another gentleman, (Mr. Tallmadge,) from the same State, who had, in the fifteenth Congress, supported the restriction with ability and warmth, was betrayed into a similar view. In speaking of Missouri, he said, "that portion of country has 'no claim to such an unequal representation, un-'just in its results upon the other States."

Here again you perceive the *grudging* at *Constitutional*, which is called *unequal*, representation, in its effects upon the other States, to wit, the non-slaveholding States. This gentleman also displayed his determination and violence, by exclaim-

ing "that his purpose was fixed, and that if dissolution of the Union and civil war come, let it come!" These were some of the allusions made in the Fifteenth Congress, to the effect of the Missouri question upon the balance of power; and they, too, by the majority on this floor, who, or some of whom, deny the influence of the consideration, as well as the use of the argument.

Mr. B. said, Mr. Speaker, I will now proceed to refer to some instances in which the same argument was renewed at the last session. I had become, sir, so fearful, nay almost sure, that this consideration had more to do than it should have, with the Missouri question, that, whenever the argument was recurred to, it made a strong impression upon my mind, in consequence of which, I am now the better enabled to refer to the remarks of some gentlemen upon that point. An honorable gentleman from New Hampshire, (Mr. Plumer,) who aimed to asperse Kentucky with having, some thirty years ago, menaced disunion, had said: "Feeling the weight of this slave represen-'tation, is it strange that the free States, believing 'they possess authority under the Constitution, 'should wish to prevent its existence in States 'hereafter to be admitted?" This gentleman utters the habitual wailing of the malcontents and restrictionists at Constitutional representation, which they are pleased to designate slave representation, accompanied by his belief in its influence on the balance of power. Another gentleman, then from Massachusetts, now in his seat from Maine—the same who presented his constituents, and, by accident, the people of the United States, with a Christmas-gift, (which, and such like, may prove their curse,) after the most mature consideration, I say mature, because the gentleman first wrote and then read his speech to the House—this gentleman avowed dangerous and inflammatory doctrines, and, among other things, said, in reference to the slaveholding States, "for emoluments and power you give us commercial restrictions," &c. Here the benign gentleman seemed to sigh for power, to avenge supposed wrongs.

The gentleman from Pennsylvania, (Mr. Sergeant,) not many days past assigned as a reason, among others, to show the importance of the question, and why it should be left for the decision of a future Congress, mentioned the influence which it might have upon the balance of power; for this he was immediately rebuked, and he seemed to stand corrected. This evening, the gentleman, in an effort to relieve himself from so reproachful a consideration, charged the minority with having first used it, and particularly charged my colleague (Mr. Clay) with having made some allusion to it at the last session, which my colleague has denied, and which I will venture to say no one else recollects. The idea of calculations of power influencing the House in their deliberations on the Missouri question, (views so inexorable to the demands of justice and reason,) always excited alarm in my mind; and, from a reference to it, at the last session, by a very able and influential member, as was the honorable gentleman from Pennsylvania, (Mr. Sergeant,) who now disclaims it,

I am enabled to settle the point in dispute between him and my colleague, by calling to their minds the facts as they transpired, and of which I have the most vivid recollection.

My colleague, (Mr. CLAY,) in the spirit of conciliation, which has characterized his every word and action from the beginning to the end of this contest, in one of his speeches of the last session appealed to the great and republican State of Pennsylvania, who had been regarded the key-stone of the federal arch, magnanimously to interfere and settle, as she might do, this contest, so big with the fate of the Union; the gentleman from Pennsylvania, (Mr. SERGEANT,) whilst replying, observed in substance, if not in words, and as I then thought, and still think, very impressively and significantly, that, true it was, Pennsylvania had been regarded as the key-stone of the federal arch, but if Congress went on to admit new States into the Union, he did not know how long she would continue so; manifestly indicating his jealousy of the growing importance of the West, and the loss of the attitude of Pennsylvania as the key-stone of the federal arch; or, in other words, by a manner and in terms too plain to be misunderstood, the influence of the Missouri question upon the balance of power. Thus, said Mr. B., it is plain to demonstration, as it is true in point of fact, that the majority, meaning to be understood several influential members of the majority, were the first to avow, and to continue exclusively to avow, this consideration; and that, not my colleague, (Mr. CLAY,) but the gentleman himself, at the last session, and at this, has consistently, though I cannot say wisely, presented the same view. And that which induced me to rise, without reflection, under every disadvantage of a House worn down with tedious sessions from day to day, at a late hour, when their impatience had been so fully evinced, was the indignation which I felt at the attempt made by the gentleman who had just resumed his seat, being himself the offender, to throw the blame and odium of the use and influence of this argument upon my colleague and the injured minority.

Mr. BROWN said, that, having redeemed his pledge, and thus long imposed himself upon the attention of the House, although he was capable of developing still further this history of the balance of power, he felt great reluctance at proceeding further—[those around him requested that he should go on.] Mr. B. resuming his argument said, Mr. Speaker, I profess to be well read in the proceedings and mysteries of a certain convention, which was organized in the East, at the gloomiest period of our late struggle with Great Britain; in which three of the New England States were represented by members, chosen by their State Legislatures, and the remaining ones had, the largest of them, two, and the smallest, one, chosen by districts. A convention which, considering its time, and purpose, and organization, and proceedings, entitled it to the emphatic appellation of the gunpowder plot of the United States; and which, like its prototype in Great Britain, upwards of two centuries ago, would, seemingly,

without providential interposition, have carried with it a wide-spread destruction. The glorious victory of New Orleans, and the consummation of the Treaty of Ghent, the first won in three days from its adjournment, and the last made public soon after, gave the people of these States time to reflect and inform themselves; the consequence of which was, that, by their judgment, the projectors of that dark scheme were consigned to merited infamy. Mr. B. said, that he wished it constantly borne in mind, that he drew a plain and just line of discrimination betwixt the good people of the New England States and the projectors and members of this convention; the first were for a time deluded, the last understood their own purpose full well, and for a season deluded the people. That the people might for a time be deceived; but, having no adequate motive to err, they would ultimately decide right. Before it proceeded to business the Hartford Convention drew up rules for its government, the first was, " that the meeting should on each day open with prayer;" and permit me to tell you that several distinguished clergymen of New England swarmed around them as bees around their hive; and that this is not the first instance in which the lovely mantle of religion has been used to cover ambition and depravity. The second rule was, " that the most inviolable secrecy should be observed." Thus, God's name was impiously called upon, and invoked, to prosper an infernal work, which was carried on in mysterious darkness. Now, said Mr. B., let us consider the subjects upon which this convention deliberated, taking care to remember that the fell and treasonable speeches which none heard but themselves, and that God, whose attention and aid they first of all implored, never have, and probable never will come to light; all that we can judge from is their journal and report, drawn up with the greatest caution, and arrayed in the most acceptable garb for meeting the public eye; still, through the fissures which they have not been able to close, you plainly discern the fires that burnt within. In their report, they state, that they first proceeded to deliberate on dangers which " menace immediate pressure," meaning thereby the acts which the Government had recently passed, and the course pursued by the administration in relation to raising men and money; the organization, disposition, and pay of the militia, &c.; these I consider of minor importance. They next proceeded to what I conceive the great purpose of the convention, which was to attain, in their own language " future security," and were, therefore " of more remote and general discussion." They further say, in their report, that " events may prove that the ' causes of our calamities are deep and permanent; ' and that whenever it shall appear that their causes ' are radical and permanent, a separation by equita- ' ble arrangement will be preferable," &c. What did the convention consider the causes that were radical and permanent? Out of their own mouths they shall be condemned. Let their two first reso-lutions proposing amendments to the Constitution of the United States, and the reasons assigned in support of them, speak. The first resolution is in the following words: "Representatives and direct 'taxes shall be apportioned among the several 'States which may be included within this Union, 'according to their respective numbers, of free per-'sons, including those bound to service for a term 'of years, and excluding Indians not taxed, and 'all other persons," &c. Thus, as you will per-ceive, excluding the enumeration of three-fifths of the slave population, as now authorized by the Constitution of the United States. The reasons assigned in the report are, "that it had proved 'unjust and unequal in its operation. Its ten-'dency, in future, adverse to that harmony and 'mutual confidence, which are more conducive 'to the happiness and prosperity of every confed-'erated State, than a mere preponderance of 'power (the prolific source of jealousies and con-'troversy) can be to any of them."

The second resolution proposed to amend the Constitution by providing that "no new State 'should be admitted into the Union by Congress, 'in virtue of the power granted by the Constitu-'tion, without the concurrence of two-thirds of 'both Houses." Prohibiting, as you will observe, a majority, as authorized at present, from exercis-ing the power of admitting new States. The reasons assigned are in the following words: "By 'the admission of these States the balance of 'power has been materially affected, and unless 'the practice be modified, must ultimately be de-'stroyed. The Southern States will first avail 'themselves of their new confederates to govern 'the East, and finally the Western States, mul-'tiplied in number, and augmented in population, 'will control the interests of the whole."

Mr. Speaker, said Mr. B., I know the decorum and respect due to myself and to the House, and I will not designedly violate either; I impugn the motives of no member; and if, in the views which I have felt it my duty to take, gentlemen find them-selves unpleasantly associated, I shall not consider myself in the least blameable, while my references to the arguments of the one, and to the proceed-ings and report of the other, are true, and often literally correct. The gentleman from Maine, (Mr. Cushman,) to whom I have had occasion already to refer, in a confidential letter to some of his con-stituents, says, "that the signs of the times do not 'augur perpetuity, or uninterrupted succession to 'the Southern dynasty. The spirit engendered 'will not fail to produce the same effects on the 'affairs of the nation—may place power in other 'hands. Not on the indiscriminate offerings of 'peace, but on the balance of power, depends the 'safety of our Republic." And, in a speech de-livered by the same gentleman a few days ago, these sentiments are reiterated and justified. Sir, said Mr. B., candor compels me to say, from these comparisons, that there appears to be an identity of objects and views between the friends of re-striction and the members of the celebrated con-vention of which I have spoken. The members of the convention grudged the Constitutional rep-resentation of slaves, denouncing it unjust and unequal in its operation; and so do gentlemen in

the speeches to which I have referred. The con-vention complained of the admission of new States into the Union from the West, as calculated ma-terially to affect, and ultimately to destroy, the balance of power; so have gentlemen indicated in their speeches, and particularly the gentleman from Pennsylvania, (Mr. Sergeant,) has feared that the admission of new States would change the federal arch in such manner as to deprive Penn-sylvania of the honor of continuing, longer, to be the key stone, and has considered the Missouri contest important in its effects upon the balance of power. The only radical diversity, visible to my optics, is, that the convention proposed to effect their objects by the amendments to the Constitu-tion of the United States; while Congress, more discerning and bold, are endeavoring to effect them, not by the legitimate operation of amend-ments, but by stretching the Constitution to these purposes. Mr. B. said that the Hartford Conven-tion was not so much execrated because it made attempts, otherwise than according to the Consti-tution of the United States, but because the object which they had in view was to weaken and burst the bands of the Union; and the means they used were the best, of all others, calculated to attain the proposed end. Those who originated and com-posed the convention have the same object in view, to wit, disunion, but I will say that they employ the same materials; and I refer gentlemen to the con-vulsed state of Congress, and the agitation of the nation, to attest whether they are not, at least, driven on to the same alarming result.

Mr. B. said, that before forming the Constitu-tion of the United States, the several States held their prejudices, their habits, their interest, and their slaves; that they were sovereign and inde-pendent, having the exclusive government of their slaves, and might have continued so; and, he could venture to say, would have continued so rather than have yielded the power to the General Gov-ernment; that they had become members of the Confederation upon the well understood, and equally well defined, condition of having the sub-ject left to their own exclusive control—the Con-stitution of the United States taking no further notice of it than to require other States to deliver up persons held to service, viz: slaves, who might escape from their owners into the limits of such other States; and that now to attempt a disregard of the terms and stipulations of the compact of Confederation was unjust and unwise, and would never be submitted to by the slaveholding States.

Mr. B. said, that, painful as it was to him to continue his encroachment upon the House, he would, while on the floor, take a very rapid view of the proceedings of Congress in relation to Mis-souri, and the obstacles which she has had, and now has, to encounter. During the 15th Con-gress, Missouri set up her claim to a law authorizing her to form a constitution and State government; something having been done at the first, at the second session of that Congress, after some angry discussions, parts of which have been referred to, the House of Representatives passed the law, but imposed a restriction against slavery, by a very small majority; the Senate would not agree to the restriction; the bill of course fell, and Missouri was still further deprived of the right of State government, which all agreed she was entitled to. At the commencement of the last, being the first session of the sixteenth Congress, the mover of the restriction (the present Speaker, Mr. TAYLOR,) moved and obtained the appointment of a special committee for the avowed purpose of compromising and settling, if possible, this subject; the committee for some time labored to effect the object of their appointment, but their efforts proving unsuccessful, upon their application, they were discharged. The members differed not from principle, all agreeing that, if the divided lines could be settled, a compromise ought to be made. Gentlemen, after having thus proceeded upon a concession of the correctness and policy of the doctrine of compromise, which was also the connecting and redeeming principle in the Convention that formed the Constitution, should not, afterwards, have uttered aught against the mode of adjustment. This laudable effort to settle the controversy by compromise having failed, the House of Representatives took up the bill for the admission of Missouri into the Union, and, after discussing it the greatest part of the session, passed it, with an imposition of the restriction, and reported it to the Senate. The Senate had, at the same time, a bill before them for the admission of Maine into this Union, from the extreme northeastern limits of the United States, as Missouri was from the southwestern. There were fierce jealousies prevailing, and a strong impression that, under the guise of humanity and religion, there was carried on a struggle for power.

The subject-matter of the bills being the same, connected with the jealousies each felt at the advancement of the other towards admission, the Senate determined to unite them, and did unite them, that they might proceed *pari passu,* and enter the threshold together. And as Maine was left without restriction, that condition, imposed upon Missouri by the House of Representatives, was taken off. And Mr. Speaker, Mr. B. said, permit me here to repeat, what I have always believed, and often said, that for this prudent caution and even-handed justice, the Senate have not received the applause to which it so justly entitled them. The bill for the admission of Maine and Missouri, thus amended, passed the Senate, and was reported to the House of Representatives; there it was disagreed to; the Senate insisted, the House rejected; whereupon a committee of conference was appointed, who, preserving the spirit of the mover of the restriction himself, compromised the whole matter—the friends of Missouri to the West agreeing that Maine should be admitted from the East, and agreed further to submit the whole territory west of Missouri to a restriction against the admission of slaves; in consideration whereof, the friends of Maine in the East agreed to admit Missouri from the West without restriction. Maine was immediately admitted, and it should be recollected that such was the momentous crisis with her, that, according to the act of Massachusetts, giving her assent for Maine to become an independent State, a limitation was fixed, which would have expired in a few days, and it thereafter became doubtful whether Massachusetts would ever again have yielded her consent. The restriction was also imposed in pursuance of the compromise upon the territory, and the law passed authorizing Missouri to form a constitution and State government, stipulating that she should be admitted into the Union upon the footing of the original States. Sir, said Mr. B., I believed then, as I believe now, that the attempt to interfere with the internal and State government of Missouri, by dictating to her on the subject of slaves, was a sheer act of usurpation in the Congress of the United States, and was indirectly struggling to avert what was thought would be the effect upon the balance of power, by the Constitutional admission of Missouri into the Union as a slaveholding State. Nevertheless, perceiving that such violent elements were in operation, and that great heat and sectional animosity would grow out of a perpetuation of the unhappy contest, I sir, agreed to the compromise, and accordingly voted for it in all its parts; while, at the same time, I must do myself the justice to say, I felt humbled at a necessity, the result of what I deemed force, to yield up the interest of my constituents, and the slaveholding States in general, in this immense territory, secure from encroachment, a right which I believed guarantied to them by the Constitution of the United States, by the treaty with France, whereby this territory was acquired, by the eternal principles of justice and sound policy.

But I was glad to be done, as I supposed I was, with this unhappy subject forever. Sir, Mr. B. said, Missouri, under the faith of the law of Congress for that purpose, called a convention, formed her constitution, laid down her territorial government, organized a State government, and put it into operation, and sent forward her Representative and Senators, with her constitution, at the commencement of the present session, who presented it to Congress. And, sir, the same gentlemen, with a little variation, who contended for the restriction last session, gave an objection to her constitution, and to her admission, on account of the single clause which requires her Legislature to pass laws to prevent free negroes and mulattoes from removing to, and settling in, that State; which clause they contend to be repugnant to that clause of the Constitution of the United States which secures to the citizens of each State "all the privileges and immunities of citizens in the several States."

Sir, we have denied that free negroes and mulattoes are citizens of the United States, in the sense designed by the Constitution; but that, even if repugnant, the clause therefore became null and void, and ought not to operate to the rejection of the constitution, otherwise acceptable. But this principle of the paramount efficacy of the Constitution of the United States to all other constitutions and laws, (one better settled, if possible, than any other,) is overlooked, and its efficacy, though not denied, not admitted. Gentlemen have retreated to an inaccessible fortress—their belief that it violates the Constitution of the United States, and their determination not to violate their consciences.

We have evidenced our sincere desire to terminate this protracted and unhappy struggle, by proposing and arguing amendments to the ordinary resolution for immediate admission, explanatory of this objectionable clause, and providing that it shall not operate so as to violate the Constitution of the United States. Gentlemen then say, that Missouri might still be incorrigible enough to disobey the proviso of the resolution. To obviate this scruple, we have proposed that she shall, by solemn covenant, agree that no construction shall be given, or law passed, violating the Constitution of the United States. The ingenuity of the human mind in finding arguments to justify the pursuit of inclination, surpasses conception. We are now answered by doubts as to the power to make the compact as proposed, which would remove the alleged difficulty; and apprehensions are still expressed that Missouri might not, in good faith, conform to it.

Mr. Speaker, said Mr. B., is it not visible that there is no satisfying the consciences, or evading the ingenuity of gentlemen, and that, like the honorable gentleman from Pennsylvania, (Mr. Sergeant,) they are, at all events, determined to transmit this *tranquillizing* subject to the next Congress; and for no other reason, that I can comprehend, so strong as that given by the honorable gentleman from Maine, (Mr. Cushman,) who has deliberately and wilfully, not in an open speech, delivered on this floor, but in a private letter to a friend, which has been accidentally brought to light, given it as his opinion, "that the safety of the Republic depended upon the balance of power, and not on indiscriminate offerings of peace." And "that a premature compromise might forever blast the hopes of a patriotic ambition."

Mr. B. said, a gentleman from Virginia (Mr. Archer) had correctly compared their situation in this contest to that of litigants in an inferior court, from which there could be an appeal; the appeal here was directly to the people. Sir, said Mr. B., this is a tribunal on which I have the greatest reliance; upon the virtue and intelligence, and therefore upon the safety, of the people, I have the most unshaken confidence, and whenever the people of the United States can be brought to think upon, investigate, and decide, this unexampled contest, they will cause their will to be done. I admonish gentlemen to recollect, that arguments felt, but not expressed, will be inoperative; that none but substantial ones will be there received; and I will hazard my judgment upon it, that arguments not sufficiently sound and pure to be resorted to upon this floor, dare not be urged before the people.

Sir, said he, Missouri ought not, and will not, under the existing circumstances, lay down her State government, and resume the territorial garb; and, without professing unusual discernment, he could foresee a period at which, if not sooner, the people of the United States would make a solemn pause, and carefully explore the untrodden path which they would be invited to tread. Sir, said he, that period will be when the Congress shall, to enforce their policy, call upon them for men and money, to be used in waging a war of father against son, and of brother against brother. Then, said Mr. B., I will venture to say, that the gentleman's qualms, and scepticism, and technicality, will be disregarded, along with any considerations which may have been felt, though not avowed, and the people will decide with justice and wisdom, and will select servants to enforce their decisions who dare not disregard their interest or disobey their voice.

Sir, the coincidence which I have shown between the objects and reasoning of a construction so justly execrated, and the suspicions, not to say more, which may so naturally be excited against the alternate views of the majority, should cause them at least to ponder and weigh well their own arguments, that they may become satisfied themselves, as well as prepared to satisfy others, that their grounds and reasons for refusing Missouri admission into the Union are solid.

Sir, said Mr. B., it has been hinted, that Missouri had probably inserted this clause in her constitution to try the temper of Congress. Can this be believed for a moment? She had no motive to do so, but had every one, except the suggestion of folly itself, to avoid a conflict, and to conciliate her favor. Is a further evidence wanting? I beg leave to refer gentlemen to the mild, patient, and pacific conduct of her delegates, and of the people of Missouri themselves, under their most unparalleled ordeal. Still . further: Read her constitution throughout, and you will lay it down, entirely satisfied, that no other constitution in the United States so well secures, not only the lives and limbs, but the health and comfort, of slaves. Had Missouri desired to taunt Congress, she had ample opportunity to have done so without the slightest imputation of infringing upon the Constitution of the United States, by withholding many of their humane provisions, and inserting others of greater severity. So far, indeed, from there being any thing calculated to raise a suspicion that the convention of Missouri felt resentment at Congress for the embarrassment which she had thrown in her way, that they seem cautiously to have sought a gratification of her prejudices and principles.

But, sir, said Mr. B., I will recur to one other objection which has been urged against the adoption of the qualified resolutions for the admission of Missouri into the Union, and I shall have done. I have felt more than surprised—I have felt astonished, that any distrust should have been expressed of the good faith of Missouri in complying with any requisition of Congress, or in fulfilling any compact into which she might enter, upon her admission into the Union. Mr. B. inquired, who were the people of Missouri? Sir, said he, they are principally citizens from the surrounding slaveholding States; they are flesh of our flesh, and had carried with them the same high ideas of honor which those societies possessed from which they had emigrated, and were equally discerning of their rights, and would be equally firm and zealous in their support. But have gentlemen reflected that Missouri offered as her sureties all the slaveholding States? That their faith stood pledged for a faithful compliance? And, when the tranquillity of the Union seemed, in some degree, affected by the arrangement, could not the faith of these States, and their attachment to the Union, and to the non-slaveholding States, be confided in? Have not those States who propose the arrangement for Missouri, evinced the highest sensibility at any encroachment upon the tranquillity, the rights, or the integrity of the Union, and particularly those of their Eastern brethren whom they have fostered and protected in peace, and have supported and vindicated by a war? Least of all, have our Western non-slaveholding States, members from which (Mr. Ross and Mr. CAMPBELL) have some distrust of faithful compliance, any ground to question the estimation in which we hold their good will, their rights, and their safety? Sir, said he, when their houses, their wives, and their little ones, were menaced, during the late war, by the fierce savages and their cruel allies, (impelled by no sinister motives or legal obligations,) have the gentlemen so soon forgotten, that we hastened to their extensive frontier, stood to their right and left; encircled them around, and drained our dearest veins to secure them from fire and massacre? And that the bleaching bones of our favorite sons, now lying thickly strewed upon their borders, attest the sincerity of our attachment, and the reliance to be placed upon our firmness, our honor, and our faith?

When Mr. BROWN had concluded—

The motion of Mr. STORRS to postpone indefinitely was decided about sunset, by yeas and nays—for the motion 42, against it 127, as follows:

YEAS—Messrs. Adams, Allen of Massachusetts, Allen of New York, Baker, Buffum, Case, Clagett, Dennison, Edwards of Connecticut, Edwards of Pennsylvania, Eustis, Fay, Folger, Forrest, Gorham, Hemphill, Herrick, Kendall, Kinsley, Maclay, Marchand, Monell, S. Moore, Murray, Nelson of Massachusetts, Patterson, Rich, Richards, Richmond, Rogers, Ross, Russ, Sergeant, Silsbee, Storrs, Street, Strong of Vermont, Strong of New York, Tracy, Van Rensselaer, and Wallace.

NAYS—Messrs. Abbot, Alexander, Allen of Tennessee, Anderson, Archer of Maryland, Archer of Virginia, Baldwin, Ball, Barbour, Bateman, Bayly, Beecher, Blackledge, Bloomfield, Boden, Brevard, Brown, Brush, Bryan, Burton, Butler of New Hampshire, Butler of Louisiana, Campbell, Cannon, Clark, Clay, Cobb, Cocke, Cook, Crafts, Crawford, Crowell, Culbreth, Culpeper, Cushman, Cuthbert, Dane, Darlington, Davidson, Dickinson, Earle, Eddy, Edwards of North Carolina, Fisher, Floyd, Foot, Ford, Fuller, Garnett, Gray, Gross of New York, Gross of Pennsylvania, Guyon, Hackley, Hall of New York, Hall of North Carolina, Hardin, Hendricks, Hibshman,

Hill, Hobart, Hooks, Jackson, Johnson, Jones of Virginia, Jones of Tennessee, Kent, Kinsey, Lathrop, Lincoln, Little, Livermore, McCoy, McCreary, McCullough, McLean of Kentucky, Mallary, Meech, Meigs, Mercer, Metcalf, Montgomery, R. Moore, T. L. Moore, Morton, Moseley, Neale, Nelson of Virginia, Newton, Parker of Massachusetts, Parker of Virginia, Philson, Pinckney, Pitcher, Plumer, Randolph, Rankin, Reid, Rhea, Ringgold, Robertson, Sawyer, Shaw, Simkins, Sloan, Smith of New Jersey, Smith of Maryland, A. Smyth of Virginia, Smith of North Carolina, Stevens, Swearingen, Tarr, Terrell, Tomlinson, Tompkins, Trimble, Tucker of Virginia, Tucker of South Carolina, Tyler, Udree, Upham, Walker, Warfield, Wendover, Williams of Virginia, Williams of North Carolina, and Wood.

So it was rejected.

Mr. MALLARY then renewed the motion which he had unsuccessfully made in Committee of the Whole, as before stated; and the question thereon was decided by yeas and nays, thus: For the amendment 61, against it 107, as follows:

YEAS—Messrs. Adams, Allen of Massachusetts, Allen of New York, Baker, Boden, Buffum, Case, Crafts, Cushman, Dennison, Dickinson, Edwards of Connecticut, Edwards of Pennsylvania, Fay, Folger, Forrest, Fuller, Gorham, Hall of New York, Hemphill, Hendricks, Herrick, Hibshman, Kendall, Kinsley, Lathrop, Livermore, Maclay, McCullough, Mallary, Marchand, Meech, Monell, R. Moore, Morton, Moseley, Murray, Nelson of Massachusetts, Parker of Massachusetts, Patterson, Philson, Pitcher, Plumer, Rich, Richards, Richmond, Ross, Russ, Sergeant, Silsbee, Sloan, Street, Strong of Vermont, Strong of New York, Tarr, Tracy, Upham, Van Rensselaer, Wendover, Whitman, and Wood—61.

NAYS—Messrs. Abbot, Alexander, Allen of Tennessee, Anderson, Archer of Maryland, Archer of Virginia, Baldwin, Ball, Barbour, Bateman, Bayly, Beecher, Blackledge, Bloomfield, Brevard, Brown, Brush, Bryan, Butler of New Hampshire, Butler of Louisiana, Campbell, Cannon, Clagett, Clark, Clay, Cobb, Cocke, Cook, Crawford, Crowell, Culbreth, Culpeper, Cuthbert, Dane, Darlington, Davidson, Earle, Eddy, Edwards of N. Carolina, Eustis, Fisher, Floyd, Foot, Ford, Garnett, Gray, Gross of New York, Gross of Pennsylvania, Guyon, Hackley, Hall of North Carolina, Hardin, Hill, Hobart, Hooks, Jackson, Johnson, Jones of Virginia, Jones of Tennessee, Kent, Kinsey, Lincoln, Little, McCoy, McCreary, McLane of Delaware, McLean of Kentucky, Meigs, Mercer, Metcalf, Montgomery, S. Moore, T. L. Moore, Neale, Nelson of Virginia, Newton, Parker of Virginia, Pinckney, Randolph, Rankin, Reid, Rhea, Ringgold, Robertson, Rogers, Sawyer, Shaw, Simkins, Smith of New Jersey, Smith of Maryland, A. Smyth of Virginia, Smith of North Carolina, Stevens, Storrs, Swearingen, Terrell, Tomlinson, Tompkins, Trimble, Tucker of Virginia, Tucker of South Carolina, Tyler, Udree, Walker, Warfield, Williams of Virginia, and Williams of North Carolina—107.

The question was then taken on agreeing with the Committee of the Whole in its disagreement to the report of the select committee, and the decision was as follows: For concurring 83, against it 86.

YEAS—Messrs. Adams, Allen of Massachusetts, Allen of New York, Baker, Beecher, Boden, Buffum,

Burton, Butler of New Hampshire, Campbell, Case, Clagett, Cook, Cushman, Dane, Darlington, Dennison, Dickinson, Edwards of Connecticut, Edwards of Pennsylvania, Edwards of North Carolina, Eustis, Fay, Folger, Foot, Forrest, Fuller, Garnett, Gorham, Gross of New York, Gross of Pennsylvania, Hall of New York, Hemphill, Hendricks, Herrick, Hibshman, Hobart, Kendall, Kinsey, Kinsley, Lathrop, Lincoln, Livermore, Maclay, McCullough, Mallary, Marchand, Meech, Monell, R. Moore, S. Moore, Morton, Moseley, Murray, Nelson of Massachusetts, Parker, of Massachusetts, Parker of Virginia, Patterson, Philson, Pitcher, Plumer, Randolph, Richards, Richmond, Rogers, Ross, Russ, Sergeant, Silsbee, Sloan, Street, Strong of Vermont, Strong of New York, Tarr, Terrell, Tomlinson, Tracy, Udree, Upham, Van Rensselaer, Wendover, Whitman, and Wood.

NAYS—Messrs. Abbot, Alexander, Allen of Tennessee, Anderson, Archer of Maryland, Archer of Virginia, Baldwin, Ball, Barbour, Bateman, Bayly, Blackledge, Bloomfield, Brevard, Brown, Brush, Bryan, Butler of Louisiana, Cannon, Clark, Clay, Cobb, Cocke, Crafts, Crawford, Crowell, Culbreth, Culpeper, Cuthbert, Davidson, Earle, Eddy, Fisher, Floyd, Ford, Gray, Guyon, Hackley, Hall of North Carolina, Hardin, Hill, Hooks, Jackson, Johnson, Jones of Virginia, Jones of Tennessee, Kent, Little, McCoy, McCreary, McLane of Delaware, McLean of Kentucky, Meigs, Mercer, Metcalf, Montgomery, T. L. Moore, Neale, Nelson of Virginia, Newton, Pinckney, Rankin, Reed, Rhea, Rich, Ringgold, Robertson, Sawyer, Shaw, Simkins, Smith of New Jersey, Smith of Maryland, A. Smyth of Virginia, Smith of North Carolina, Stevens, Storrs, Swearingen, Tompkins, Trimble, Tucker of Virginia, Tucker of South Carolina, Tyler, Walker, Warfield, Williams of Virginia, and Williams of N. Carolina.

So the House refused to concur, and the amendment reported by the select committee was agreed to.

The resolution, as thus amended, is in the following words:

Resolved, &c., That the State of Missouri shall be admitted into the Union on an equal footing with the original States, in all respects whatever, upon the fundamental condition, that the said State shall never pass any law preventing any description of persons from coming to and settling in the said State, who are now, or hereafter may become, citizens of any of the States of this Union : *And provided, also,* That the Legislature of the said State, by a solemn public act, shall declare the assent of the said State to the said fundamental condition, and shall transmit to the President of the United States, on or before the fourth Monday of November next, an authentic copy of the said act; upon the receipt whereof the President, by proclamation, shall announce the fact : whereupon, and without any further proceeding on the part of Congress, the admission of the said State into this Union shall be considered as complete : *And provided further,* That nothing herein contained shall be construed to take from the said State of Missouri, when admitted into this Union, the exercise of any right or power which can now be constitutionally exercised by any of the original States.

The question being then stated on ordering the resolution to be read a third time—

The names of the members were called over.

The Clerk, having come to the end of the list, was about to pronounce the result; when

Mr. KENT, whose delicate state of health scarcely enables him to attend the House, and who was not in the House when his name was called, requested leave to record his name.

Mr. JACKSON, under the same circumstances, except that he was within the walls of the House when his name was called, though not within the bar, made the same request.

The SPEAKER offered to receive their votes, if there was a unanimous consent to his receiving them; the rule of the House peremptorily requiring that no member should vote on any question unless he was within the bar of the House when his name was called.

Objection was made to their voting.

It was evident, from the sensation which filled the House, that the vote was a close one, though its result had not been announced.

Mr. CLAY, finding that the objection to these gentlemen would not be withdrawn, moved to suspend the rule of the House which forbids a change of the rule without one day's notice, in order to suspend or repeal the rule which forbids these gentlemen from voting. After awhile, however, he withdrew his motion, relying on the magnanimity of some member of the majority to move for a reconsideration of the question.

The result of the vote was then proclaimed, as follows : For the third reading 80, against it 83.

YEAS—Messrs. Abbot, Alexander, Anderson, Archer of Maryland, Archer of Virginia, Baldwin, Ball, Barbour, Bateman, Bayly, Blackledge, Bloomfield, Brevard, Brown, Bryan, Butler of Louisiana, Cannon, Clark, Clay, Cobb, Cocke, Crawford, Crowell, Culbreth, Culpeper, Cuthbert, Davidson, Earle, Eddy, Fisher, Floyd, Garnett, Gray, Guyon, Hackley, Hall of N. Carolina, Hardin, Hill, Hooks, Johnson, Jones of N. Carolina, Little, McCoy, McCreary, McLane of Delaware, McLean of Kentucky, Meigs, Mercer, Metcalf, Montgomery, T. L. Moore, Neale, Nelson of Virginia, Newton, Pinckney, Rankin, Read, Rhea, Ringgold, Robertson, Sawyer, Shaw, Simkins, Smith of New Jersey, Smith of Maryland, A. Smyth of Virginia, Smith of North Carolina, Stevens, Storrs, Swearingen, Tompkins, Trimble, Tucker of Virginia, Tucker of South Carolina, Tyler, Walker, Warfield, Williams of Virginia, and Williams of North Carolina.

NAYS—Messrs. Adams, Allen of Massachusetts, Allen of New York, Baker, Beecher, Boden, Brush, Buffum, Butler of New Hampshire, Campbell, Case, Clagett, Cook, Crafts, Cushman, Dane, Darlington, Dennison, Dickinson, Edwards of Connecticut, Edwards of Pennsylvania, Edwards of North Carolina, Eustis, Fay, Folger, Foot, Forrest, Fuller, Gorham, Gross of New York, Gross of Pennsylvania, Hall of New York, Hemphill, Hendricks, Herrick, Hibshman, Hobart, Kendall, Kinsey, Kinsley, Lathrop, Lincoln, Livermore, Maclay, McCullough, Mallary, Marchand, Meech, Monell, R. Moore, Morton, Moseley, Murray, Nelson of Massachusetts, Parker of Massachusetts, Patterson, Philson, Pitcher, Plumer, Randolph, Rich, Richards, Richmond, Rogers, Ross, Russ, Sergeant, Silsbee, Sloan, Street, Strong of Vermont, Strong of New York, Tarr, Terrell, Tomlinson, Tracy, Udree, Upham, Van Rensselaer, Wendover, Whitman, and Wood.

So the whole resolution, amendment and all, was rejected.

Mr. LIVERMORE, who had objected to the above contested votes, then gave notice that he should, at 12 o'clock to-morrow, move for a reconsideration of this question, that every member might have an opportunity of voting on it. And then the House adjourned.

TUESDAY, February 13.

The Journal of yesterday having been read—

Mr. LIVERMORE, with the view of affording to members who were absent yesterday an opportunity of voting on the resolution from the Senate, rose to carry that purpose into effect; and, to obtain his object, moved to amend the Journal of yesterday's proceedings, by striking therefrom the order "that the Clerk should acquaint the Senate with the decision of this House on yesterday;" that, by withholding that Message, he might be enabled to move the reconsideration of the decision, when the time should arrive at which such a motion would be in order.

Mr. CLAY seconded the motion, and took the occasion to make a few remarks explanatory of an incident which occurred at the last session, on a question of reconsidering the final vote of the House on the Missouri bill, and to vindicate the then Speaker of the House from a presumed interference on that occasion, and to show that the Clerk did no more than his duty required him to do, in carrying the bill to the Senate without waiting the motion for reconsideration.

The motion to amend the Journal, as proposed, was agreed to without a division.

Mr. SMITH, from the Committee of Ways and Means, to whom was referred the petition of James Crawford and others, reported a bill for the relief of certain persons who have paid duties on certain goods imported into Castine; which was twice read, and committed.

Mr. ANDERSON, from the Committee on Public Lands, reported a bill giving the right of pre-emption in the purchase of public lands to certain settlers in that part of the Territory of Arkansas ceded to the Cherokee Indians; which was twice read and committed.

The bill from the Senate, entitled "An act for the relief of purchasers of public lands prior to the 1st July, 1820," was read twice, and referred to the Committee on Public Lands.

Mr. COCKE, from the Committee on Military Affairs, who were instructed to inquire whether any officers of the Army of the United States are employed as clerks, or in any other capacity, in any of the departments, or in the office of the Surgeon General or Apothecary General, and whether such officers, if any, have received any other compensation than their pay as officers, what are their names, and what extra compensation they have received, made a report concluding with the following resolution:

Resolved, That no officer or other person, employed by the Government of the United States, ought, under any circumstances or pretext whatever, to be allowed and paid any other or greater compensation than is authorized by law; and that the practice which has heretofore prevailed to make extra compensation in certain cases, without such authority, is incorrect, and ought to be abandoned.

The report was read and ordered to lie on the table.

On motion of Mr. GARNETT, the Committee on the Public Buildings were instructed to inquire into the practicability of more effectually ventilating the Hall of the House of Representatives, and to report such plan as may appear to them best calculated to effect the object, as speedily as possible.

MISSOURI.

Mr. LIVERMORE moved to reconsider the vote of yesterday, by which the resolution from the Senate, as amended, for the admission of Missouri, was rejected.

Mr. TRACY, that the attendance of the members might be as general as possible, moved a call of the House, (Mr. LIVERMORE having waived his motion for the present, to give an opportunity for this motion.)

The motion for a call of the House was negatived—yeas 51 nays 73.

The question was then stated on the reconsideration of the vote of yesterda .

Mr. EDWARDS, of North ṛCarolina, gave the reasons why he should vote for the reconsideration, from motives of comity to other members, and yet should again vote, as he did yesterday, against the resolution, should it be reconsidered.

Mr. GARNETT said, feeling, as he did, disposed to vote against the motion for reconsideration, and as his vote would be apparently inconsistent with that he had yesterday given for the engrossment of the resolution, it was a duty he owed to himself to state the reasons which influenced him. When he first came to the House yesterday, he had read the amendment, and his impressions were against it. He had therefore voted against its adoption. His attention, however, having been subsequently attracted to the *proviso,* he had, without sufficiently examining the previous part of the resolution, believed that its effect was to do away and render nugatory all its provisions; and, under this idea, and in the spirit of conciliation, he had voted for engrossing the resolution as it had been amended. Subsequent and serious reflection had, however, induced him to think that he was mistaken as to the effect of the proviso, and that his first impressions were correct. It was perhaps true, that it was calculated to do away any inequality that might be produced by the conditions of the resolution, between the rights of Missouri, and those of the other States, "when admitted;" but it was an attempt to impose on her a condition previously to her admission, which we had no right to require her to perform. How was it possible that we who think that Missouri is, to all intents and purposes, now a State, and that she is only kept out of the Union by violence and injustice, can believe that we can impose on her any condition precedent to her admission; and that a condition, too, which requires her to relinquish a right which she can now exercise in common with every other State in this Union. It requires her to say that she will not pass any law preventing any description of persons who now are, or may hereafter become, citizens of any State, from coming to and settling in Missouri. Now, we all believe that she has the power to prevent a certain description of persons from coming in and settling in the State; and I am disposed to go still further, and to say, that she has the right to exclude any description of persons—even the white citizens of another State; for, if a State does not possess this right, this obviously absurd consequence follows—that a State could not banish a citizen upon any pretext whatever, for treason, or for the most infamous crimes; for he would have nothing to do but to become a citizen of another State, when he might return and reside in the State from which he was banished, in spite of its laws. But, however this might be, we all agree that Missouri has a right to exclude some description of persons, even though citizens of another State; and, agreeing in this, we cannot impose any precedent condition to her admission requiring her to abandon this right. It was useless to say that the solemn public act by which the resolution requires her to relinquish this right, is null. If it was so, it would not justify our supporting it. If you analyze the doctrine in its extremest possible result, the least that we concede by the resolution is, that Congress can impose conditions on a State which are null, but cannot impose any which are efficient and operative. But, if we admit this doctrine, it will not be easy always to discriminate between conditions that are null and those that are operative; and if we concede the right of Congress to impose conditions at all, precedent to the admission of a State, whether void or otherwise, we deprive ourselves of the argument against their constitutionality, in any future attempt that may be made to impose such conditions on Missouri or any other State. If, hereafter, restriction itself should be attempted on Missouri or Arkansas, or any other State, we should be bound, if the opposite party could fairly make out their case, on the ground of expediency, to vote for it; for we would voluntarialy have relinquished the argument founded on its unconstitutionality. Mr. G. said he could see no difference between requiring a convention of Missouri to expunge from her constitution a certain provision, and requiring her Legislature to pass a law nullifying, as far as it could do, that very provision. That provision renders it obligatory on the Legislature to pass a law preventing a certain description of persons from coming to and settling in the State, and the resolution of Congress requires her Legislature to pass a law in direct violation of this positive injunction, declaring that any decription of persons, who may be citizens of another State, may come in ; or, in other words, shall not be prevented from coming in and settling. At any rate, this requisition on the part of Congress, which demands that the Legislature of Missouri should pass a law directly in the teeth of their own constitution, before she should be admitted, could not

be considered otherwise than degrading to Missouri. These ideas had been thrown out, Mr. G. observed, as exhibiting his own views of the subject. In consequence of his indisposition yesterday, he had been frequently obliged to leave the House, to escape its oppressive atmosphere, and had therefore not been able to give that attention to the arguments of gentlemen who supported the resolution which he desired. His mind was, however, open to conviction ; and, if the difficulties he had stated could be overcome, so as to permit him, without a violation of the Constitution, to vote for the resolution, he should rejoice at it ; for, if there ever was an occasion when it was desirable to make all concessions, compatible with principle, it was the present.

Mr. RANDOLPH made a few remarks, by way of protestation against the proposed reconsideration. The battle, he said, had been fairly fought, and fairly won—or lost, as gentlemen should please to consider it. He considered the proposed reconsideration to be, under the circumstances, contrary to parliamentary usage, and as tending to prostrate the great Constitutional barriers which surround the powers of this House. Mr. R. concluded by vouching his life for it that this question might be settled without recourse to reconsideration.

Mr. CLAY replied, regretting the unfortunate situation in which he was placed, having to meet objections of an opposite nature, and from quarters of the House whence he had no right to expect them. Though gentlemen might not be in favor of the resolution as amended, they ought yet to vote for reconsideration, that the door might be kept open for a different amendment if a different one should be thought necessary. He threw himself on the frankness and courtesy of the House, to allow the members who were absent on yesterday an opportunity of recording their votes.

Mr. FLOYD intimated his intention to vote for the reconsideration, but stated that more important questions than this had been lost during his observation, by the absence of members from their seats. Conceiving that a remedy ought to be provided for this evil, he stated his intention of moving, at some time during the session, an amendment to the rules of the House so as to require, that, on each call of the yeas and nays, the names of absentees should be entered on the Journals, designating the States which they respectively represent.

After some further conversation, of an incidental nature—

The question of reconsideration was taken, and decided by yeas and nays : For the reconsideration 101, and against it 66, as follows :

YEAS—Messrs. Abbot, Alexander, Allen of Massachusetts, Allen of Tennessee, Anderson, Archer of Maryland, Archer of Virginia, Baldwin, Ball, Bateman, Bayly, Beecher, Blackledge, Bloomfield, Brevard, Brown, Brush, Bryan, Burton, Butler of Louisiana, Campbell, Cannon, Clark, Clay, Cobb, Cocke, Cook, Crawford, Crowell, Culbreth, Culpeper, Cushman, Cuthbert, Davidson, Dewitt, Dickinson, Earle, Eddy, Edwards of North Carolina, Eustis, Floyd, Foot, Ford, Fuller, Gray, Gross of New York, Guyon, Hackley,

Hall of New York, Hall of North Carolina, Hardin, Hill, Hooks, Jackson, Johnson, Jones of Virginia, Jones of Tennessee, Kent, Kinsey, Little, Livermore, McCoy, McCreary, McCullough, McLean of Kentucky, Meigs, Mercer, Metcalf, Montgomery, S. Moore, T. L. Moore, Neale, Nelson of Virginia, Newton, Parker of Virginia, Pinckney, Rankin, Reid, Rhea, Ringgold, Robertson, Sawyer, Shaw, Simkins, Sloan, Smith of New Jersey, Smith of Maryland, Smith of North Carolina, Stevens, Storrs, Swearingen, Tompkins, Trimble, Tucker of Virginia, Tucker of South Carolina, Tyler, Walker, Warfield, Williams of Virginia, Williams of North Carolina, and Wood—101.

NAYS—Messrs. Adams, Allen of New York, Baker, Boden, Buffum, Butler of New Hampshire, Case, Clagett, Crafts, Dane, Darlington, Dennison, Edwards of Connecticut, Edwards of Pennsylvania, Fay, Folger, Forrest, Gorham, Gross of Pennsylvania, Hemphill, Hendricks, Herrick, Hibshman, Hobart, Hostetter, Kendall, Kinsley, Lathrop, Lincoln, Maclay, Mallary, Marchand, Meech, Monell, R. Moore, Morton, Moseley, Murray, Nelson of Massachusetts, Parker of Massachusetts, Patterson, Phelps, Philson, Pitcher, Plumer, Randolph, Rich, Richards, Richmond, Rogers, Ross, Russ, Sergeant, Silsbee, Street, Strong of Vermont, Strong of New York, Tarr, Tomlinson, Tracy, Udree, Upham, Van Rensselaer, Wallace, Wendover, and Whitman—66.

So the House determined to reconsider the vote of yesterday rejecting the resolution from the Senate in its amended shape.

The question then again presented itself in this form: Shall the amendment be engrossed, and, with the resolution, read a third time?

Mr. HACKLEY, of New York, assigned, at considerable length, the reasons which had induced him, as a member of the select committee, and on the subsequent vote in the House, to give his suffrage in favor of the amendment reported by the select committee.

Mr. FULLER delivered to the House the grounds on which he was opposed to this resolution, not believing that the condition annexed to the admission of Missouri obviates the objection to that clause of her constitution which is supposed to conflict with the Constitution of the United States.

Mr. EDWARDS, of North Carolina, said, feeling it his painful duty, upon the present occasion, to differ from those with whom it had been his pleasure to act upon almost every proposition concerning Missouri, he trusted he need offer no apology for the part he should take in consuming the valuable time of the House. He would not, he said, detain the House long; he knew it was impatient for the question, and would endeavor to state, as succinctly as possible, the reasons which determined the course he was about to take. Whatever, Mr. E. said, might be his views upon this resolution, to whatever conclusion he may have come, he could but distrust his own judgment when opposed by the opinion of the select committee who reported it to the House. With some of the members of that committee, he said, he was well acquainted; he had the fullest confidence in their abilities, and regretted he could not go along with them. His great anxiety to put to rest this distracting subject was manifest from his course

hitherto; and no gentleman could, for a moment, believe he would hesitate to vote for any proposition to admit Missouri which his judgment approved.

He had bestowed the fullest consideration upon this resolution, and could not bring himself to support it. What, sir, is the first member of it? It is declared to be a fundamental condition upon which Missouri is to be admitted into the Union, that she "shall never pass any law preventing any ' description of persons from coming to, and set- ' tling in, the said State, who now are, or hereafter ' may become, citizens of any of the States of this ' Union." Did it, he asked, recite in so many words the clause in the Constitution of the United States, which declares "the citizens of each State ' shall be entitled to all the privileges and immu- ' nities of citizens in the several States?" No, sir. It in truth contained our own construction of that clause; it set forth our own opinion, to a certain extent, of the obligation it imposed, and we demand of Missouri submission to that opinion as a *sine qua non* of her admission. And are gentlemen prepared to maintain this doctrine? Would they tell him that Congress possess the power to cut down and restrict the State sovereignties by legislative construction of the Federal Constitution; and that, too, of a clause intended merely to restrain the legislative discretion of the States themselves? Establish this doctrine, and to what will it lead? What will be the powers of this Government, and where the limit to them? I ask, said Mr. E., do gentlemen mean to say, that whatever may be our construction of the Federal Constitution; whatever rights we may think we ourselves possess, we can demand of a State who asks admission into the Union to stipulate, she will adopt the one and not violate the other? If so, what is to prevent us from saying to Missouri, to Michigan, to Arkansas, or any other Territory who may hereafter apply to become a member of the Union, "we have a right to promote the inter- ' nal improvement of the country by a system of ' roads and canals, when, how, and where we ' please, and we demand of you, as a condition of ' admission, a stipulation that you will pass no law ' interfering with the exercise of this right, or, in- ' deed, of any other right which we may imagine ' we possess?" And why not? We may say then, as now, it is consistent with our interpretation of the Constitution, and we impose no new obligation. Sir, I will never consent to establish such a principle by my vote. The powers of this Government are mighty enough; their march is onwards; and I wish they may not sooner or later entirely absorb the powers of the States. He knew he should be told that his objections to the first proviso were obviated by the last, which asserts that Missouri, when admitted, shall have all the powers of the original States. But he could not so view it; whether our construction of the Federal Constitution, in this particular, be right or wrong, the principle still remained. He objected to the exercise of a right by Congress to decide for the States the extent of their political powers.

This resolution must receive such a construction

as will give effect to every member of it, as will reconcile all its parts. And was he to understand gentlemen to say that Missouri, thus restricted, will have all the powers of the original States; or that the original States had the same powers, and no more than she had? Gentlemen are mistaken when they say the import of the terms "privileges and immunities" is remitted to judicial cognizance; we have ourselves, in some degree, given their meaning. The resolution uses the words "any description of persons," and declares them entitled to go to, and settle in, Missouri, if they be citizens of any of the States. It does not say of the United States. What privileges and immunities are secured to the citizens of the United States by the clause in question, the Legislatures of the States must decide, subject to revision by the judiciary; and how far the States are restrained, in this respect, there is much difference of opinion even in this House. Let Missouri, then, enjoy the rights her sister States possess; let her be at liberty, as they are, to expound the Constitution of the United States according to her sense of her own obligations of duty and of conscience.

But, Mr. E. said, if the objections which he had already examined did not exist, he could not accept the resolution with the second proviso; which makes it the duty of the Legislature of Missouri, by a solemn public act, to give its assent to the condition contained in the first, and make it a fundamental part of her political system. He asked gentlemen who had examined the constitution of Missouri, if they were serious in imposing this task upon the Legislature? Would they demand of the Legislature to pass an act which they shall declare upon its face to be fundamental and irrevocable? Sir, they will understand too well their powers; they will be able to find in the Constitution which gave them birth, and under which they will convene to deliberate for the public weal, no authority to bind subsequent Legislatures, and to give to their enactments any higher dignity than that of mere laws; they will not be so ignorant as to think they possess the plenary powers of a convention, and will not presume, in their character of legislators, in open violation of their duties as such, and of their constitution, to which all their measures must conform, to pass a law which they shall declare to be more permanent and unalterable than even the constitution itself. High-minded and honorable men will not sport thus with their reputation and their oaths. Let us forbear then to make this demand. If we mean not to admit her at this session, let us not throw at her new taunts, but leave her to herself for the present. Have the friends of Missouri considered the situation in which they will be placed, if she refuse to comply with the terms now offered? And he had no expectation she would comply, because she could not. She comes here next Winter—asks you to receive her into the family of States—to permit her to submit to your authority, and to participate in your councils. Will her friends then say, she has treated them with contumacy? Will gentlemen, on all sides, say, we have offered you terms, and you would not accede to them—you have spurned them—and thus drive her again from our doors? Deny to her again that which by the law of the last session she is entitled to, and which we are pledged to grant her? We should at least be cautious in interposing new obstacles. But he much feared we should, by our own proceedings, heap objection upon objection, until we bring Missouri to our feet; if, indeed, she can be brought there. I do hope, said Mr. E., we shall leave her to pursue that course which may seem to herself best; that her friends, at least, will not be the means of throwing new difficulties in the way of her admission into the Union.

He regretted much the resolution passed by the Senate had been rejected by the House; he had prevailed upon himself, with great difficulty, to vote for it; it was his ultimatum; nothing but a spirit of conciliation could have carried him so far; but conciliation itself appeared now to be exhausted; he could not tell what more gentlemen on the other side could have reasonably required. It expressed, by the strongest implication, that doubts existed as to the compatibility of the much disputed clause in the Missouri constitution with the Constitution of the United States; and declared, if it were incompatible, the assent of Congress was not given to it. He had hoped this was enough to satisfy gentlemen.

He was fully sensible of the high responsibility of his duty upon the present occasion, but, as great as it was, he should consider himself an unworthy member of this body if he were to shrink from it. However much he respected the opinions of others, he should fearlessly obey the dictates of his own judgment; he could not be alarmed by consequences; he could say, let them come. If it should be his misfortune to incur the frowns of others, he should have the consolation to know he had the approbation of his own conscience. It is often our lot, both in private and public life, to be called upon to discharge duties painful to our feelings; but, he hoped, he should never want resolution to sustain him in such a trial.

Sir, said Mr. E., I will not detain you longer. I am sorry I was obliged to have addressed you at all. I have hastily presented you my views, and trust they will sufficiently account for, and vindicate, my course in separating from my friends upon this trying question.

Mr. RANDOLPH stated some of the grounds on which he was opposed to this resolution. He considered it as proposing a sacrifice of the rights not only of Missouri, but collaterally of all the States of the Union, to mistaken notions of expediency; and entered into an argument to support that position. He declared himself to be opposed to the annexation of any condition to the act of admission of Missouri.

Mr. STORRS followed, in an argument in support of the resolution, and the sufficiency of its provisions to obviate the objection which he had entertained to the naked resolution for admission, when that question was presented at an earlier period of the session. He earnestly deprecated the disposition which appeared to prevail with some gentlemen, to leave Missouri in a state of disconnection from, and independence on, the Government, proposing to do nothing with her now, and promising to do nothing more hereafter, &c.

Mr. CLARK, of New York, spoke as follows:

Mr. Speaker, I do not rise with the hope that any thing that I can say will materially alter the vote that will finally be given on this question; and I would have contented myself with giving a silent vote on it, were it not that my motives may be possibly called into question by designing persons. I rise, therefore, in vindication of the course which I have marked out for myself, and which I shall consider it my duty to pursue.

During the last session of Congress, when the question of restricting slavery in that State was discussed, I supported it, in every instance, by my vote. Congress, however, decided against those who thought and acted with me on the question. How that decision obtained I will not now inquire. It is sufficient for me that the opponents of restriction were not indebted to me for their success, either by my absence or by a change of my vote. But, however that decision was obtained, I considered it binding on Congress. By it Congress solemnly pledged itself to Missouri that, if she would present a constitution, in other respects republican, and not repugnant to the Constitution of the United States, she should be admitted into this Union. I considered myself bound by this pledge. I have no alternative left. I cannot for a moment consent, as a member of this House, to observe a Punic faith even to Missouri. I know it is objected that Missouri has not fulfilled her part of the compact; that her constitution, in one of its provisions, is repugnant to that of the United States. I agree that it is. But we have no evidence that this repugnant clause was inserted with intent to violate any of the provisions of the Federal Constitution; and we certainly are warranted in judging charitably of her intentions, when we reflect that several of the States have enacted laws of the same tendency, and equally repugnant to the Constitution of the United States. It is a common judicial maxim, equally applicable to States and individuals, that every one is presumed innocent until proven guilty. Adopting this maxim, we cannot yet pronounce sentence against Missouri. If gentlemen will prove to me, by reasonable argument, that we are not bound by the law of last session, and that we still have the right, consistent with good faith, to revive the question of the restriction of slavery in Missouri, and that there is any, even the most distant hope of bringing it to a successful termination, I will go with them; for I wish it distinctly understood, that I am not excited to my present course by any sympathy for Missouri; I feel none: nor am I prompted by fear. The menaces of gentlemen have no influence on my mind.

But, sir, while I disclaim any sympathy for Missouri, I confess to you I feel a strong sympathy for my country; for the people whose interests are suffering, and some of them sacrificed by the continued agitation of this unhappy question. Yes, sir, your agricultural, your manufacturing, and

your commercial interests, are all in a suffering state, and all anxiously looking to you for protection and support. I ask every member of this House whether, in each of their districts, they have not observed a general prevalence of unparalleled suffering and distress? And yet those great, those vitally important interests, confided to your care by your Constitution, you have abandoned and neglected. Your agriculturists no longer find a market for their surplus produce, but trusted that Congress would at least attempt to create one. Your manufacturers, who were induced by you to vest their capitals in manufacturing establishments, are overwhelmed by foreign competition, and many of them ruined by confiding in you, and very many more verging on bankruptcy. Your commerce also languishing, and many who were engaged in its pursuits ruined, and many more on ruin's brink. Yet you have not as yet devised, or even attempted to devise, any plan for their relief. Your enterprising citizens who have penetrated your Western domain, and who have given you all their money in part payment for a home, and, calculating upon past events, thought they could pay you the balance which is your due, by the produce of the lands which they have purchased from you, have been disappointed, and at least partly through your neglect. Shortly after the close of the late war, you passed an act promising compensation to those whose property was lost or destroyed in your service or by your means. It is a well known fact, that many of this class have spent the wreck of their fortunes in dancing attendance upon you, without being able to obtain a decision upon their applications. To these people a delay of justice is injustice.

Sir, your table is, at this time, groaning under a load of petitions from a distressed community, who have, with unparalleled patience and perseverance, supplicated from you that justice which, in many instances, you had no right (although you had the power) to delay or withhold.

And why is it thus? Why is it, I ask you, that this Congress have now been in session nearly nine months, and the universal distress of the country staring them in the face, and not one decisive act passed for their relief? Why is it that, although you have had abundant evidence, both at the last session and this, that your revenue was materially diminished, and your Treasury empty, that you have not taken one step toward augmenting your revenue or replenishing your Treasury, but by loans? Sir, we can make but one answer: we had to spend the best half of last session discussing the propriety and impropriety of imposing a restriction of slavery on Missouri, and we have spent the best half of this session discussing the merits and demerits of her constitution. Both discussions have been alike pleasant and profitable; but there appears to be this difference: Congress brought the question of restriction to a termination, such as it was; but this question they seem determined shall live and die with them. Die with them did I say? No; it is so pleasant and so profitable a subject, we are determined it shall survive us; we seem inclined to bequeath it as a valuable legacy to the next Congress; and if they husband it as well as we have done, it may, for ought we know, last for many years; and I think we have convincing proof that, while it does live, it will live to the exclusion of all other important business; for, besides the time it engrosses, it excites the passions and prejudices, and sours the minds of gentlemen so, that they are totally disqualified for acting in concert for the public good.

Sir, these are the reasons which have induced me to support, with my vote, the resolution from the Senate, as amended by the Committee. I wish this controversy ended; it is incumbent on this Congress to terminate it. The people of the United States, as well as of Missouri, expect it, and I think we are bound in duty not to disappoint their just expectations.

Sir, upon the supposition that this proposition is rejected, I would solemnly ask gentlemen what will suit them? Will you admit Missouri unconditionally? No. Will you admit her with the condition annexed by the Senate? No. Will you admit her by that resolution, as amended by your Committee? No. Sir, I will not detain this House by enumerating all the various propositions which have been made for her admission, and all of which have shared the same fate. Well, will you revive the subject of the restriction of slavery, and make that a *sine qua non* of her admission? No. You have declared, by a large majority, that you will not. Then, seeing you cannot agree to admit her upon any terms which have been proposed, will you postpone the consideration of the subject indefinitely, and let us attend to some other of our duties? No.

Sir, the course pursued by this House, on this subject, is (to say the least of it) most extraordinary. You will neither dismiss it nor decide on it, but you cling to this firebrand of discord with the utmost pertinacity, without intimating what your ultimate object is. Is it with a hope that others will do for you what you wish done, but dare not do? Is it with a hope that you will tire out some of the Northern members, so that they will unite with the South, upon some plan of admission which will pass, and to which, at the same time, you will have the pleasure to give your negative; and, by this means, evade the odium which you think will attach to an act which you wish accomplished? Sir, this course of policy may serve for a time, but it will not always last. I will never advise a man to be engaged in an act in which I could not consider myself justified in co-operating. I cannot consent, as a member of this House, to act the part of a waterman, looking one way and rowing another.

Mr. Speaker, I am well aware of the sentiments of my constituents, and how feelingly alive they are to any act that would either practically or theoretically compromit any of the rights even of the meanest of their citizens. There is no man in this House who entertains a higher veneration and respect for the opinions and wishes of his constituents than I do. But, in acting on this question, I have a high and important duty to perform to my country and to my own conscience; and if

I should be so unhappy as to incur their disapprobation by the vote I am about to give, I shall at least enjoy the consolation of carrying with me into that retirement to which their displeasure would consign me, a full and perfect conviction of having acted according to the dictates of my own conscience, with the sole intention of promoting the peace, prosperity, and happiness of our common country.

Mr. Simkins spoke as follows:

Mr. Speaker, in rising, principally to ask for the ayes and noes on this now apparently desperate resolution, my bosom swells with emotions to which my tongue can give no utterance. I feel myself authorized to warn gentlemen, in the most solemn manner, that the nation is heart-sick of this question; and I do believe, if it were left to the people, Missouri would be declared to be admitted almost by acclamation. The inhabitants even of the North and East abhor the existence of a subject which has been so pressed upon Congress as not only to occasion great expense and loss of time, but to agitate the nation from Maine to Georgia; and although it may not be strictly parliamentary to speak of information coming in any other than an official shape, yet I venture to assert, upon that on which I place the most implicit reliance, that, in many sections of the New England States, there is a vast majority in favor of unconditional admission! Shall I, then, on a matter of such moment, of such national importance, that almost every day it exists adds to the bad feelings, jealousies, and spirit of disunion, so destructive to our peace, stop to argue the lawyerlike and attenuated argument of the gentleman from Connecticut, (Mr. Tomlinson,) as to the power of the Legislature of Missouri to give its assent to the proposition submitted by the Committee; a proposition most ably and zealously vindicated by the gentlemen from Kentucky and from New York, (Messrs. Clay, Ford, and Hackley.) Sir, this is no time to consider technical arguments and sceptical objections; it is the time to insure the harmony of the country by a settlement of this ominous and ill-boding question.

Sir, in my opinion, Missouri is already a State of this Union, and was so the moment she formed a constitution, appointed her judges, and elected her members to the Senate and to this House. She had then performed those acts upon which she was to be prospectively admitted; and she then became a State of this Union; and the only difficulty is, that you refuse now to declare her admitted. You deny to her an unquestionable, and a vested right. But, sir, I will not attempt to go over ground so ably occupied by my friend and colleague, (Mr. Lowndes,) I content myself by moving for the ayes and noes, that the nation may see who still oppose the admission of this State. Gentlemen may consider that they now stand on popular and strong grounds. The next election will, I believe, show that they are playing a hazardous game; that they stand on "slippery places."

Mr. Ross, of Ohio, spoke at some length, and with much earnestness of manner, in opposition to the resolution, on the ground that its provisions were inefficient in themselves; or, being otherwise, were of a most pernicious tendency. He considered it an expedient to avoid a responsibility which gentlemen were afraid to meet. He reprobated the change of sentiment which some gentlemen had evinced, and intimated that, if honest in their first opinion, they had acted dishonestly, or under the influence of improper motives in voting differently now, &c.

Mr. LITTLE, of Maryland was about to speak in reply to Mr. ROSS, and in vindication of his course on this question—

When an explanation took place between Mr. CLAY and Mr. ROSS, which induced Mr. L. to waive his remarks.

Mr. BALDWIN, of Pennsylvania, next spoke earnestly in support of this resolution, and in reply to those who had spoken against it. He invoked those, whom the resolution, as it now stood, did not please, to say explicitly what would please them, it having been decided by a large majority that the restriction of last session was out of the question.

Mr. SMITH, of Maryland, spoke briefly upon one point of the resolution which had been particularly objected to.

Mr. PINCKNEY, of South Carolina, spoke as follows:

Mr. Speaker, there are many reasons which make it incumbent on me not to suffer this question, which I consider the final one on the acceptance or rejection of the constitution of Missouri, and her admission into the Union, to pass without presenting my views on the subject to the House. These reasons are, the importance of the question itself, the great interest the State I represent, in part, has in it, and, not among the least, the frequent calls made upon me in this House, and references in the other, as to the true meaning of the second section of the fourth article of the Constitution of the United States, which it appears, from the Journal of the General Convention that formed the Constitution, I first proposed in that body.

We are now arrived at the most awful period which has hitherto occurred on this delicate and distressing subject. On the decision of the question before you is to depend whether we are to rise in harmony with each other, having made the necessary provision for the admission of Missouri on an equal footing with the other States, or to reject her constitution, and leave her, erected as she completely is, by our own authority, into a State, unowned and unadmitted into our Union, of which, under the fostering care of Government, she soon bids fair to become a most valuable member.

Mr. Jefferson says, in a letter to a friend, which has been published, at least this sentence of it: "The Missouri question is the most portentous 'one that ever threatened our Union. In the 'gloomiest moments of the Revolutionary war, I 'never had any apprehension equal to that I feel 'from this source." I agree perfectly with him, and join those gentlemen in opinion who consider this, beyond all comparison, the second question in point of importance, which has been agitated among us since our revolt from the parent State. The first was the memorable declaration which confirmed the Union, and gave birth to the independence of our country. This is the only one which may, in its consequences, lead to the dissolution of that very Union, and prove the death-blow of all the political happiness and national importance once so rationally to be expected from it. I feel myself authorized to express this fear by the fact, that the gentlemen in opposition have now thrown off the veil, and expressly declare their intention is to leave, if possible, this question to the next Congress; to leave to them, unfettered by any act of ours, the power to decide how far the true interest of the Union may then make it necessary to produce anew, and struggle for the imposition of the restriction on slavery in Missouri, which has, during the three last sessions, shaken the Union to its very foundations. They openly avow that they do not consider themselves bound by the compact of the last year, confining that restriction to the territory north of 36 degrees, 30 minutes, but aver, if they have strength enough to do so, their intention to leave the next Congress free to decide it as they please.

In considering the subject, I shall endeavor to prove to you that Missouri, in complying with the act of Congress of the last session, has submitted to you the very best republican constitution I have ever seen; one not only superior to that of the other States, but even to the boasted one of the United States; and that if she has, without the least intention to violate it, inserted the article respecting the prohibition of free negroes and mulattoes, she may fairly be considered as not only having done it under the sanction of Congress, but I may almost be justified in saying under their recommendation.

In examining the constitution of Missouri it will be found, that while it has carefully avoided all those defects which time and experience have discovered in the constitution of the other States, it has wisely ingrafted all their excellencies, and made addition of others heretofore omitted or not thought of. The first branch of her Legislature is, contrary to all the others, except South Carolina and Tennessee, elected for two years, thereby avoiding the almost continual irritation and intrigue incident to annual elections, while sufficiently short to continue the Representative as connected with his constituents, as he ought to be. The Senate are elected for a longer term, and with a proper rotation, so as to unite firmness, stability, and system, with a due degree of dependence and responsibility. Their Executive is elected for four years, possesses the same revisionary power as the President of the United States does, and has exactly that permanence, nomination to office, and patronage, which an Executive ought to have, to give weight and respectability to his office, and no more.

Her judiciary are wisely appointed, and are completely independent in the tenure of their office and salaries, all the provisions it has made for the government of their militia, and the distribution of knowledge among the rising generation of their country, do honor to the talents that formed the constitution, while those which provide for the humane treatment of slaves by their masters, and their trial by jury, and punishment in the same manner as the whites, and make the murder, or dismemberment of a slave, punishable as if committed on a free white person, are honorable and liberal improvements on the policy which has hitherto governed other States in these respects; the declaration of rights annexed to their constitution recognises and establishes all the great and indispensable principles of free government; in short, in every thing except with respect to those provisions which are held to interfere with its claim to admission into the Union, Missouri must appear to every impartial man to have done herself credit by her constitution, of which the essential ingredient of general suffrage, or in other words, equal political rights, is the basis.

I have said no other State constitution is comparable to it, and to prove this, for brevity sake, let us shortly examine the constitution of Massachusetts, New York, Pennsylvania, Maryland, and Virginia, and we shall, as republican systems, find them far inferior indeed to Missouri; and as the question is on the acceptance of her constitution, and admission into the Union, this examination becomes peculiarly proper.

In Massachusetts we have seen, for years, the odious establishment of a religious test; the anti-republican one of a pecuniary qualification for voters; the shifting, vacillating policy of an annual House of Representatives, and a feeble Executive, checked and bound down by a council, without whose assent he can do nothing.

In New York the same improper establishment of a pecuniary qualification exists, and the many evils arising from an annual House of Representatives in this State, are most amazingly and grievously increased by the election of their Council of Appointments being annually made by the Legislature; and as in this State parties are nearly equally balanced, the inconvenience, confusion, and injury, arising to the public by this annual struggle, are inconceivable. The Council of Appointment to all the offices of the State, consist of four members, chosen by the Legislature from each great division of the State, who, with the Governor, who has no right to nominate, and is only there as a member of the council, on an equal footing with the rest, appoint all the officers of the government; as this power, therefore, depends upon who are elected members of the Legislature, there arises an almost never-ceasing struggle for superiority; for the elections are for so short a time, that scarcely one is ended before the plans to carry the next, and all the intrigues incident to them, begin, and the moment the party who were out succeed, that moment they sweep, as with a deluge, every office in the State, except the judges, that has a salary or is worth holding. Who of us belonging to other States can witness the complete and general removal of every officer in their government, of honor and profit, that has within these few weeks taken place, without rejoicing that in our own State we are at least exempt from the effect of so

wavering and fickle a system. In every view in which such a council presents itself to our consideration, it is highly wrong and injurious; for where it happens, as lately, the Governor and Council are at variance, and all the appointments are made contrary to his wish, it not only embarrasses and unnerves his administration, but reduces him almost to a cypher; while, on the other hand, when they are of his party, or with him, and appoint as he wishes, in case of improper choices they operate as a cloak to him.

In Pennsylvania we find the same evils arising from the annual choice of their House of Representatives, which I have depicted in the other States, but there is in this so remarkable a departure from those democratic principles which ought to prevail in the constitution of every State of the Union, that it is astonishing how their republicans, boasting as they do of their principles, love of liberty and equality, and so feelingly alive, as they appear to be, to the rights of their black brethren, should have so long remained quiet under or still be content with. It is the enormous power granted to their Executive, of appointing all the officers, including judges of the Commonwealth, without the least restriction, and just as his own unchecked will, or the influence of his partisans may please; a power before unheard of, or unexercised in any part of the Union, and one so degrading to persons calling themselves the citizens of a free republic, that it is astonishing none can be found among them sufficiently alive, not only to the true interests, but to the honor of their State, to wish in this respect to assimilate their Executive to that of the others.

In Maryland, a State, perhaps, as equally torn by the near division of parties as any other, to the error and inconvenience of an annual House of Representatives and feeble Executive, either checked or cloaked by a council, as his opponents or partisans may prevail in it, is superadded the singular provision of an aristocratic Senate, elected for five years, by electors chosen by the people, consequently all of the party that may happen accidentally to prevail among the electors.

In this Senate no rotation is established, and of course, nothing like dependence or responsibility; and if, as has frequently happened, the parties change in the House of Delegates, and their opponents prevail there, a scene of perpetual hostility between the two branches is exhibited, adverse to the harmony which is always so essential to good government; besides, there is annexed so large a pecuniary qualification, as is sufficient to render a considerable majority of their citizens ineligible to it; in this State also are the great evils of a *viva voce* choice of their Representatives, and a religious test; which last, according to the republican opinions now generally prevailing among us, may be considered as almost amounting to barbarism.

In Virginia the same defect prevails of annual elections of her House of Representatives and Executive, whose powers are small, and are administered under the same check or cloak as from party it may happen of a council, as in Maryland, where, like her too, all elections are to be *viva voce*, and none are to vote but freeholders, thereby excluding a very great proportion of her citizens who have much better pretensions to the exercise of this right than the holder of a few barren acres of land can have. Surely, the man who is obliged to defend the liberties and government of a country, and who, although without that small landed property which may entitle him to vote, may still be bound by the ties of birth and of a family to his country, ought not to be deprived of this important right. We should remember that, as all the rest of the civilized world are monarchies, in case of necessity we must depend essentially on ourselves; that it is our true policy, therefore, to unite every citizen and inhabitant to defend the country of their birth or adoption, by all the proper encouragements in our power; that none is so powerful as that of giving them the right to vote for the persons who are to make laws for them; that to deny them this is to establish invidious distinctions, and to make them believe your Government pays more respect to property than to privileges, and that you attach more weight to the man who has a few barren acres of land, and is perhaps unable to render you the least personal service, than to him who has been, or may be obliged to risk his health and person for a whole campaign in the field, and who possibly may be a native too.

To the limiting the right to vote to freeholders, and to the giving of votes at elections *viva voce*, so many solid objections instantly arise, that it is astonishing a State like Virginia, which, from her Revolutionary merits, certainly has a better claim to the title of "cradle of the Revolution," than any other, could so long have retained them. If a constitution intends, in conferring the right to vote, to give the elector the opportunity to vote for those he pleases, surely no other mode than that of ballot can give it him. The fear of giving offence to those he does not wish to displease, and particularly relations, friends, and acquaintances, frequently induces the giving a vote which, by ballot, would have been given to one more worthy. Voting by ballot is certainly the only method to remove all restraint, and leaves the voter perfectly at liberty to follow the dictates of his own conscience and judgment.

To avoid being prolix on this subject, I shall not go into an examination of any other of the State constitutions, most of which, however, with the exception of the religious test, and viva voce vote, have the same defects.

In examining the constitution of Missouri, you find it free from all these defects; and, as the great question now before us is the acceptance of her constitution and admission into the Union, I wish, as far as I am able, to show to the people of this country its excellence and superiority, as a republican one, over those of the important States I have mentioned, and, indeed, of all the others, that they may be enabled to judge whether it can be possible so excellent a system can be rejected for the trifling reason that it inadvertently contains a provision prohibiting the settlement of free negroes and mulattoes among them, or whether it is not infinitely more probable that other reasons of a

much more serious nature, and pregnant with the most disastrous events to the future union and peace of these States, are at the bottom of this unexpected and inexcusable opposition. My reason for being of this opinion is, that if this was not the case the course of their proceeding on this subject would have been most probably as follows: There would have been, as there must inevitably have been, a unanimous approbation of every part of the system except this prohibitory clause, and this would have been considered, as it certainly is, nothing more than a strong recommendation from the convention that formed the constitution to the future Legislature, which might or might not comply with it, after giving it a much more full and deliberate examination than it was in the power of the convention to do, as, in their opinion, was most consistent with the Constitution of the United States or the interest of their own State. If the convention had not determined to leave it wholly to the discretion of the Legislature, why did they not, in express terms, declare that no free mulattoes or negroes should ever be allowed to enter into Missouri, and make it a part of the constitution? It was easy to have framed a short article on the subject, and not to have made the intervention of the Legislature necessary; besides, what shows that the Legislature are of this opinion is, that, as far as we know, they have hitherto passed no such law, and, if they should not, where is there a penalty annexed to their not doing so, or where is the power to compel them? But I now proceed to state, in my opinion, the article is not an unconstitutional one; and that, even if it was, it might be considered, in some degree, as sanctioned virtually, or tacitly recommended by Congress.

I say it is not, in my judgment, unconstitutional, for the following reasons, in which I mean briefly to answer to the call that has been made upon me: It appears by the Journal of the Convention that formed the Constitution of the United States, that I was the only member of that body that ever submitted the plan of a constitution completely drawn in articles and sections; and this having been done at a very early stage of their proceedings, the article on which now so much stress is laid, and on the meaning of which the whole of this question is made to turn, and which is in these words: "the citizens of each State shall be entitled to all privileges and immunities in every State," having been made by me, it is supposed I must know, or perfectly recollect, what I meant by it. In answer, I say, that, at the time I drew that constitution, I perfectly knew that there did not then exist such a thing in the Union as a black or colored citizen, nor could I then have conceived it possible such a thing could ever have existed in it; nor, notwithstanding all that is said on the subject, do I now believe one does exist in it; and, in order to prove this, the only true question for consideration is, what is a citizen of the United States? And I now answer, as we consider one in the State to which I belong.

In South Carolina we consider all white persons born in the same, or adopted according to law, to be citizens, and entitled, as such, to all the privileges of a citizen, where not disabled by something personal to themselves. Their privileges vary according to their sex and situation. Females are wholly excluded from a right to vote, or to office, and are confined to their proper sphere; but all males born in the State, or in the United States, after a certain residence in that State, or adopted according to law, are equal, except clergymen, who, on account of their office, are excluded from the Legislature. At the age of eighteen they are all enrolled into the militia, and serve as the defenders of their country. At twenty-one they are, from our general suffrage law, qualified to vote, to serve on juries, and to be eligible to the Legislature, and all offices except two, which require greater age. They have a right to sue, and are liable to be sued; to take a freehold, and hold property. They are all entitled to the trial by jury, and intermarry at any age.

This, and this alone, is called a citizen there; and nothing less than this can, in my opinion, constitute a citizen of the United States. Now let us compare this *white* citizen of the South with the *black* or colored man, such as he is in the Eastern or Northern States; and then let it be seen whether, for the protection of the comparatively few rights of such a being as he is—of a person so situated, so unlike a citizen, and so almost wholly without his privileges—gentlemen can be serious in refusing the admission of Missouri, and risking the consequences.

At the close of the war all the States had slaves; the Northern and Eastern to a considerable amount, and the Southern to a much more numerous one. The former, extremely anxious to get rid of them, passed laws for the gradual abolition of slavery, and, by their ill-treatment, by the contempt they exhibited for them, and the marked line of distinction drawn between them and the whites, I am told, in the Eastern States, they have almost driven the whole of them away—many to the West Indies, and more to the Southern States; so that in the six Eastern States, I am informed, not more, at present, than a few thousand remain.

And here let me ask, how have they effected this? Why, as I have just said, by treating them, on every occasion, with the most marked contempt—by never employing them when whites can be procured, thus reducing them to great penury and distress—by refusing to trust them with the defence of the country, or enrolling them in their militia—by denying them the right to serve on juries, or in their courts to give credit to their oaths in suits where whites are concerned—by preventing their marrying, under heavy penalties, with the whites—and by even refusing to them the right of remaining more than two months in their State, under penalty of whipping; thus showing that, so far from wishing to treat or consider them as citizens, they view the mixture of their blood, and any connexion with them, as a disgrace to the whites. The only solitary privilege which it seems is granted them, is, on pressing occasions, where votes are wanted, these degraded beings are frequently, in a most improper state, dragged to the polls, with tickets in their hands which they cannot read, and compelled, by men under whose influence they are obliged to act, to disgrace, in the most shameful manner, the highest privilege our Republic boasts, and which, I will venture to say, is in no other country equally degraded, as by a view of their condition, and the manner the blacks are treated in Europe will presently be shown. And, perhaps, this is the proper place to remark, that it was impossible for Missouri to have held any other opinions on this subject than those she did, when, in addition to all this, she well knew Congress had never, by their laws, naturalized any but whites, or admitted any other to be enrolled into the militia, or had, by any act, in the most remote degree, acknowledged or considered a black or colored man as a citizen.

I find it difficult to say what opinion ought to be attached to the perseverance which the majority of this House have exhibited for three successive sessions, on this occasion, in struggling to establish the points for which they have contended, and in which they have shown so little attention, or have had so little respect for the feelings of their brethren of the Southern and Western States. It must have arisen either from a wish to dissolve the Union, and separate themselves from the slaveholding States, or from a total want of knowledge of the distinction which has, from time immemorial, existed in the civilized world, between the black and white race, and the strong and immovable line which has separated, and will forever continue to separate, them in the Southern and Western States of this Union.

There can be no question what the opinion of Europe is as to the black race; for there the line of distinction is as strongly drawn as it is between the whites and them in the Southern and Western States. Nor is this peculiar to the moderns; the same opinion was entertained by the ancients of the then civilized world as exists at present.

In speaking of the situation of the interior of Africa, where the black race were first found, it is natural to turn our attention to what it has been from the earliest ages we are acquainted with. In doing so we find that, of all the quarters of the globe, this is the only one which remains completely unaltered from the creation until the present moment. The African man is still as savage as ever—he is as unchanged as the lion or tiger which roams in the same forests with himself.

It may be asked, Why this unchanged situation while always in the neighborhood, and within the reach of all the most civilized part of the then known world? Why should every part yield to the extension of learning and the arts, while the Africans still continued the barbarous and cannibal race they were from the beginning? The reason is plain from the only data given us to judge from. They certainly must have been created with less intellectual powers than the whites, and were most probably intended to serve them, and be the instruments of their cultivation. A strong reason in favor of this opinion of their inferiority to the whites is, there never having been one of the race, notwithstanding all the pains taken with them, that has attained any thing like what may be termed mediocrity in learning; and, for this and other reasons, some of the most able philosophers in both continents, among whom may be named Mr. Hume and Mr. Jefferson, have invariably expressed the same sentiments.

Such, too, has unquestionably been the opinion of all the most enlightened nations of Europe; or else, when England, and Spain, and France, and Holland had, by the discovery of America, acquired colonies there, why did they instantly send their ships to Africa, to stock them with slaves, and to no other place? Why not send to Asia, or take the native Indians in their neighborhood, and employ them? The reason was, that they found no other part of the human race so inferior in intellect to the whites as the Africans, or none which it can be so fairly presumed were created for the purpose of serving them.

Let us now view the conduct of England. It is true, in the case of Somerset, her courts determined no human being could be held in slavery in England, but there they stopped. You never have heard of any of the colored race being admitted to the rights of British subjects so far as to vote at their elections, to serve on juries, to be admitted to swear in their courts; to be enrolled in their militia; or to be eligible to Parliament; or to hold any office of honor or profit under their Government.

In their colonies they keep them in abject slavery, perhaps more so than exists in any part of the world, not even excepting the Portuguese or Spanish colonies.

In the dominions of France in Europe they carry the exclusion of the blacks further than in any European nation; for, by an ordinance of France, issued long ago by one of their monarchs, and still in force, they are forbid to enter, and all persons are forbid to bring them, under severe penalties, into France; stating in the ordinance, among the principal reasons which induced it, the determination of the French Government to prevent any intermixture between the white and black blood. It is not a little singular that, in the discussion which took place last session, on the restriction, the able Senator whose recent death is so justly deplored as a public loss, should have used exactly the same reasons in support of it.

We are, sir, very fond of imitating the Romans in every thing we can, without inquiring how far, from the very different nature of our Government, it was strictly appropriate. We have, in imitation of them, made the most ferocious of all the birds of prey our national standard, and named the edifice in which we are now legislating, the Capitol. Why not follow them in their opinions respecting the African race? Rome was well acquainted with them. She had carried her victorious eagles to Carthage, and afterwards to Alexandria; they were well acquainted with the interior of Africa, whose inhabitants were essentially different from those of Carthage and Egypt in color, and infinitely their inferiors in intellect. They were, as they are now, cannibals and barbarians. So far from any of them, or their de-

scendants, ever having been considered as citizens by the Romans, it does not appear they even condescended to make them their slaves; for, like the Greeks, all the slaves among the Romans were white. It is therefore probable that, like the French in Europe, they disdained to mix the Roman blood with them. How different must have been their opinions and feelings from those of our Northern and Eastern brethren, who now not only consent to receive and cherish them themselves, but wish to throw in upon Missouri and all the Southern and Western States, in the shape of citizens, the very race which Rome refused to receive and use as slaves!

But, sir, it will be impossible for them to succeed. The distinction which has existed from the earliest ages, in Europe and in America, from its discovery and settlement, down to the present moment, can never be removed. Instead of diminishing, the very discussion of this question will increase its strength, as is now daily proved by the laws which have just passed, and others of a similar character now under discussion in the Southern States, and which never would have been passed but for this attempt; and so much more dangerous and alarming than that of the last session; it has come most unexpectedly on them.

They, in common with the people of all the States, supposed that the question had been put at rest forever—they viewed the compromise as binding in honor on every part of the Union—they had the good sense to know that, in a Government so extensive as this, and differing in its climate and productions, and consequently in its interests, that every thing must be done by compromise—that the Constitution of the United States itself was the work of compromise, and in nothing so remarkably and of such importance as on the very subject of slavery, in not only consenting the Southern States should have a representation for their slaves, but going the very extraordinary length further in allowing them, if they pleased, to keep the African trade open for twenty years—and that this Constitution of compromise was formed by a body of men, at least as well informed and disinterested, and as much the lovers of freedom and humanity, as may probably ever again be assembled in this country; while therefore the Constitutional compromise is, as it had always been, strictly adhered to, they can see no reason why on the same subject the compromise of the last session should not be—they fear that the mere admission of a few free negroes and mulattoes cannot be the true cause of all these exertions, and of all this perseverance on the part of the majority of this House, but that something of greater importance is intended, by the astonishing anxiety now shown to keep the question open to the next session.

If this was not the case I should have supposed a train of reasoning something like the following ought to have weight with the House. The constitution of Missouri, now under examination, is formed truly republican, and indeed excellent in all its provisions, except the one objected to—in defence of this it is asserted that it is no violation of the Constitution of the United States, because no free negro or mulatto in any of the States, in the circumstances in which he is at present, can be considered as a citizen.

That, except in the solitary right to vote in a few Northern States, he is destitute of every other qualification, and that until they, either by an alteration of their constitution or laws, admit him to a full participation of all the political rights of their white citizens, neither the Supreme Court or any other could consider him as such—that Missouri having no idea of the existence of such a thing as a black or colored citizen of the United States, and knowing that all the Southern and Western States had for many years passed laws to the same effect, which laws are well known to Congress, being at this moment in their library and within the walls of the Capitol, and which were never before objected to by them or their courts, they were no doubt warranted in supposing they had the same right. I repeat here what I asserted before, as I think it an argument of great weight, that the silence of Congress on the antecdent laws of the Southern and Western States, on this very subject, might indeed be fairly considered as a sanction to the proceeding, or, might we not go further and say, this silence of Congress ought to be considered as full proof that they knew the imminent danger there was in the Southern and Western States admitting such persons, and, therefore, on every occasion where they were passed cheerfully acquiesced in them, and to go a little further, might not this acquiescence, under the operation of the maxim long received among jurists, and agreed to, " *Qui non prohibet, quando prohibere potest, jubet,* be viewed as at least a kind of tacit or implied recommendation ?

As to the idea which has been frequently thrown out in this debate, that Missouri knew it was repugnant to the Constitution, and notwithstanding did it, as it were, to defy Congress, it is the most unfounded one imaginable. On the contrary, it appears by her constitution she has done every thing with respect to slaves she consistently could to recommend it to Congress; she certainly has done every thing she could, with propriety, to better their situation, and to display a very kind and humane disposition towards them; they are carefully guarded from bodily injury; a fair trial is secured to them, and, from the provisions respecting equality of punishment, no unusual severity can ever be exercised towards them.

Nor is it to be supposed if they had had the most remote idea that the article objected to would have been considered as offensive or repugnant to the Constitution of the United States, they would have inserted it; for what purpose could they wish to irritate a Government from which they had every thing to expect, whose protecting arm was necessary to their growth and happiness, and whose refusal to accept their constitution and admit them into the Union must involve them in difficulties of the most inconvenient if not serious nature? No, sir, the idea of its being repugnant to the Constitution could never have been conceived by them, much less could they have sup-

posed it should have been considered as a defiance of your authority. They certainly had no such ideas, and if every other part of their constitution is in complete accordance with your act—if all the rest of it is strictly republican, and in conformity with the Constitution of the United States, even supposing, which I do not admit, that this article or recommendation, or call it what you please, might be thought to clash with it, will you suffer a single clause or article to give a character to the whole, and while you confess, which no man can deny, that all the rest is excellent, that this single article shall suspend your admission of her into the Union, and leave you exposed to the difficulties such a state of things must produce?

If the present Congress should refuse to admit Missouri, a very serious question arises as to the situation she is to be in : Whether she is to be considered as a State, although not in the Union, or is to return to the Territorial state? In my judgment there can be no doubt that Missouri is now a State; she has thrown off every thing like a Territorial government; she has formed her constitution ; elected her Legislature and Executive ; chosen her judges, and appointed all the other officers of her government and members of Congress, and has now a State government completely in operation. Whether admitted or not into the Union, she is irrevocably a State, and it is for those who still refuse her admission to take the consequences upon themselves.

As to the idea of passing an act to direct and authorize the President to cause her to be restored to the Territorial state, you are to remember such an act will require the assent of both the Senate and President, neither could, in all probability, be obtained, and I confidently hope very few, even of the members of this House, could be brought to vote for such a measure; and to rise, leaving things as they are, and without even making provision for the security of the public property, I mean of the United States, in Missouri, could only be less impolitic or culpable than to do so without admitting her.

There are some other points I intended to have remarked on, but they have been fully stated and argued upon by other gentlemen. I shall only add a few observations on the propriety and necessity of a compromising spirit in Congress on all questions connected with the subject of slavery, let them arise from any source. In the compromise of the last session great joy was certainly diffused through the Union by the overwhelming majority with which that compromise was carried; it was viewed as .forever putting all differences on the subject at rest; before the compromise it was seen that the same unhappy contests might again arise when Arkansas and Florida should become sufficiently numerous to be admitted; but after the compromise no man entertained any fears on it; they viewed, as forever settled, the only question which might produce a dissolution of the Union, as it was the only one on which ambitious and artful men might play, not only upon the bigotry and fanaticism, but the honest feelings and prejudices of their unsuspecting countrymen, and turn them to their own parricidal views; they, I mean that valuable and honorable part of our community, who, having no ambitious views of their own, wish only to see their country flourish and be happy, and be sufficiently strong to protect her rights against the invasions of foreigners, thought they saw in that compromise the demolition of every hope of those who wished to fan the flame of discord, to create new parties, and to give to them dangerous directions and irritating names, and may Heaven grant they may not be mistaken in their calculations or disappointed in their wishes.

Surely, sir, if ever there was a nation which required, in the conduct of her national concerns, a compromising spirit, it is this: and may I not add, if ever there was a time when it required it more than at any other, this is the time. There are at this period stronger reasons than there were the last year when I adverted to them in discussing the law then depending to allow Missouri to form a State government. I then entreated the House to recollect that we were the only Republic of any force or consequence in the world, that, from the combination of all the despots of the greatest Powers in Europe, to maintain their monarchical systems in their present state, and what they had done respecting France, there was no doubt it would give them great pleasure to remove what they must consider as the most dangerous evil and example to monarchy in the world—to destroy the ark, in which alone, amidst all the deluges of despotism, the seeds and principles of freedom have been, and are still safely, preserved. That the distance, and our force united at present, with the immense expense attending such an attempt, were the only obstacles—that if we were to divide on this or on any other question, and from friends become enemies, particularly such as they would suppose might be turned against each other, there could be no doubt they would attack us, if not with the intention of dividing parts of our territory among themselves, at least with the view to oblige us to change our Government into monarchy. However remote such a danger may appear, let us recollect the wonderful changes we have seen in the last twenty years. View the same spirit, and with nearly the same means that overturned France again at work, and determined to put down, if able, every thing like the attempt in Italy, to change their Government. When the war once again begins there, who knows the extent to which it will spread? And should the allied sovereigns be successful, who can tell to what length the enthusiasm, or perhaps to call it by a more proper name, the fanaticism of despotism, may carry them?

Be assured, sir, if ever there was a time when our true interests called upon us to exhibit to the world proofs of the most complete harmony and indissoluble union, this is it. In addition to the one already mentioned there is another cause, and of more immediate pressure, which requires us to strengthen, as far as possible, the bond of union, and suffer no minor consideration to weaken it— it is the depressed state of our commerce, and, of course, our revenue. It is not necessary for me to take up your time in stating the distressed situation of our commerce everywhere, and particularly in the Northern and Eastern States. Our tables are loaded with petitions and memorials from all parts of them, representing the distress they are reduced to, and, although recommending wrong remedies, all going to prove the fact of the general distress, and which it appears at present extremely difficult for Congress to remove or even to alleviate. The distress of the Northern States is very much owing to the fall in the price of flour, so low as to make its export from them impossible. This arises from a larger quantity of land being now cultivated in Europe than before, and the great improvement in their agriculture. Indeed, it is stated that one of the principal causes of the distress which prevails in Europe among the agricultural interests is the excess of production, and the want of a vent for it. To the Northern and Middle States the fall of their principal staple must be a serious evil, as there is little hope of its ever reviving, and, such is the rigor of their climate, it will be difficult for them to find a substitute. They, therefore, must become more dependent now than ever on the Southern and Western States, as well for the employment of their shipping as by the furnishing them with exports; for almost the whole employment their shipping now receives is from them, and almost all their trade is by the import and re-export of the Southern and Western products.

To prove this, let us examine the Secretary of the Treasury's report of exports of native products, made only six weeks ago to this House, and you will find the exports of the States are as follows in domestic produce:

South Carolina, $8,690,000, being the largest in domestic produce; Louisiana, including all the Western States as the whole comes to New Orleans, $7,240,000; Georgia, $6,520,000; Maryland, $4,681,000; Virginia, $4,540,000.

The other Southern States are under one million each. But the aggregate of the whole Southern and Western States exports of domestic produce is upwards of $34,000,000, while those of the whole Northern and Eastern States is not more than $17,000,000, of which, however surprising, you will find Pennsylvania has less than $3,000,000, and Massachusetts less than $4,000,000. New York, it is true, has $8,000,000; but, upon examination, it will be found that New York, like Pennsylvania and Massachusetts, is indebted to the Southern and Western States for more than two-thirds of her exports of native products, which she brings to New York in her vessels and re-exports as her own. This is most unquestionable; for if, as it appears by the Secretary of the Treasury's report, the whole export of wheat and flour for all the United States is but five and a half millions of dollars, of which Virginia and Maryland must, no doubt, have one-half, or nearly so—then to Pennsylvania, Jersey, and New York, there are left no more than three millions of the flour and wheat export to divide between them. The fisheries of the Eastern States amount to about two millions, and the fur trade, such provisions as are the product of animals, and various smaller items, compose the remainder of the seventeen millions, the amount of the whole of the Northern exports. And, if it could be correctly ascertained what proportion of it is in the products of those States, it would be found to be very small. But it is not comparatively the great value of the Southern and Western exports, which is of the highest importance to the Northern States. It is the very bulky nature of the commodities; for no products can be more bulky than cotton, rice, tobacco, sugar, and lumber, and none require for the amount in value a larger quantity of shipping to export them; and, if it was not for these and the employment they give to the Northern and Eastern shipping in the present state of peace and commerce, where all nations that can are striving to be their own carriers, what, in the name of Heaven, would our Northern brethren do with their vessels, or what use could they make of them?

In this state of things it is almost superfluous to ask if it is not of much greater consequence to the Northern and Eastern States to preserve an union from which they derive such very important benefits, than to risk it to give to a few free negroes and mulattoes the right to settle in Missouri contrary to the declared unanimous wish of the people of that State? But, it may be here asked, what is the desire, and to what extent do the Northern and Eastern States wish to go in requiring concessions from the Southern and Western? Has it not always been the policy of Congress to favor American commerce and American tonnage at the expense of foreigners? Have they not made such discriminations between imports of foreign produce in foreign vessels and the same species in American bottoms as to give the latter great advantages? Have they not, by heavy tonnage duties, secured to the shipping of the Eastern and Middle States the almost entire coasting trade? Have they not lately passed an act to counteract the colonial policy of the British Government as regards their West India islands? And were at the last session did they not impose a retaliatory duty on French vessels for the exclusive benefit of the shipping interest? In addition to all this, have they not imposed on every species of foreign merchandise, with very few exceptions, such heavy duties as are, in the opinion and by the confession of the ablest, most experienced, and skilful of our manufacturers, fully sufficient to give them all the·advantages they have a right to expect? So far, therefore, as the commerce, shipping interest, and manufactures of the United States are concerned, surely every candid and impartial man must confess Congress have given them every support they ought to wish, and that in doing this the Southern States, in the most generous and fraternal manner, have always assisted. Nor have they been at all behind the Northern and Eastern in giving still further encouragement to the increase and employ of their seamen, by, upon all occasions, strenuously supporting, as far as our friends will permit, the augmentation of that great bulwark, and pride of our nation, the Navy.

If, to the necessity arising from our general situation for a compromising spirit, it can be shown that the enemies to the extension of slavery in the new States have, in the act of last session, obtained a great advantage, and that the Southern and Western members have yielded much for the sake of compromise, the opposition to the admission of Missouri must appear still more extraordinary when coming from the Northern and Eastern members. It is asserted, by those who have made the best calculations upon the subject, that, by the boundary, as fixed by the treaty with Spain of 1819, the number of square miles within the slave district, including Missouri and Louisiana, may be estimated at not exceeding 180,000, while the area of the district north of thirty-six degrees thirty minutes, excluding Missouri, may be calculated at 1,500,000 square miles; so that not more than two slaves may exist south of the line, while there is room for twenty excluding slavery north of it.

It would, I am sure, be unnecessary for me now to go again into the arguments which I used so much at length the last year, to prove that the origin of the attempt to restrict slavery in the new States was very different from that of the love of liberty, humanity, or religion; these had nothing to do with it. It is the love of power, and the never-ceasing wish to regain the honors and offices of the Government, which they know can never be done but by increasing the number of the non-slaveholding States. This once done, we shall soon see a system established which, if it did not even go the length gradually to mould our republican institutions into forms much less democratic than the present, would at any rate soon make the interest of the South subservient on all occasions to the North, by protecting duties, and that whole train of policy, the mischievous effects of which I so fully explained the last year, and to which the people of the South, while they continue to know their own interest, must ever be opposed; and, indeed, their opposition has been hitherto the only obstacle to their success.

These, sir, are the sentiments which my duty to the Union of these States, to my constituents, and to myself, have made it incumbent on me to express on this momentous question. Our ancestors, with those gone, and a few, very few, of our Revolutionary heroes and statesmen still left, by the noblest effort which ever adorned the page of history, have erected such a monument to rational liberty as the world has never before seen. It has enlightened, and still continues to irradiate, not only the polished nations of Europe, but late movements, even in the most remote countries of it, give us reason to believe there is no part of it on which some share of this light has not been shed; that, however it may be smothered by force for a time, it can never be wholly extinguished; that the improvements in favor of the rights of the people already made in some of the ancient despotisms, and which are acquiring greater stability every day, must in time, and perhaps very soon, extend to others. And shall we, when our example has already done so much for the benefit of mankind—for it is from it that all these ameliorations have sprung—shall we, with parricidal hands, destroy the work for which its illustrious founders have received the thanks and gratitude of every friend of freedom throughout the globe, and draw down deservedly upon ourselves, not only their contempt, but imprecations? In a word, shall we destroy that Union on which not alone depend our own existence, as a free, a powerful, or a happy people, but the only example left to prove to succeeding generations what real patriotism, firmness, and prudence, might realize in the cause of liberty and self-government? I hope, I pray not.

Mr. FORD, of New York, next spoke in vindication of his course on this subject, and in warm reply to Mr. Ross's remarks casting blame on those whose course had been the same as that of Mr. FORD.

Mr. CLAY concluded the main debate, by a speech of about an hour's length, in which he alternately reasoned, remonstrated, and entreated with the House to settle forever this agitating question, by passing the resolution before it.

Mr. FOOT said, he felt himself called upon, by the remarks which had fallen from the gentleman from Ohio, who had made an allusion to him, as if addressed to him by name, with a direct charge of inconsistency, to rise in his own defence, and to repel the charge; and he trusted the Committee would excuse him for trespassing on their patience.

Sir, said Mr. F., I would inform that gentleman that my course, during the whole discussion of this subject, during the last as well as the present session, has been regulated by one uniform principle, viz : a sacred regard to the Constitution of the United States. This has been my pole star. Believing, as I did, that the Constitution did not warrant the imposition of the restriction, I voted against it.

With the same regard to my oath, to support that Constitution, I voted against the resolution for the unconditional admission of Missouri, at the present session, because her constitution contains an article which, in my opinion, is repugnant to the Constitution of the United States, and does not comply with the conditions proposed by the act of last session.

And, sir, I must say, I can never vote for her admission on any other condition than that Congress require that this offensive article be expunged. Self respect, and a due regard to our laws, require it. And I demand of that gentleman to show the inconsistency.

Look at your act of last session authorizing the people of Missouri to form a constitution and State government, and for her admission into the Union. What condition did you impose ? "That her constitution, when so formed, shall be republican, and not repugnant to the Constitution of the United States."

What does the amendment propose ? That, as a condition upon which she is admitted into the Union, Congress now require that she comply with the condition imposed by the act of last session, and expunge the article which a majority of this House have declared, by their vote, is repugnant to the Constitution of the United States. Do you deprive her of any right ? No! Does Missouri claim the right to violate the Constitution of the United States? If she claims this right, I shall never vote for her admission. But, sir, she makes no such claim. I believe she had no intention, by the insertion of that clause, to infringe the Constitution, or affect the rights of any citizen of any State.

In common with all our brethren of the South, as has been declared on this floor, she did not suppose that people of color were considered as citizens in any State of this Union ; and I have no doubt she will cheerfully amend her constitution, by expunging the offensive clause. For myself, I am perfectly willing to trust to the honor and magnanimity of our brethren of Missouri to amend their constitution in the manner proposed by my amendment, and to vote for the resolution with this proviso.

The question was then taken on ordering the resolution to be engrossed for a third reading, and decided in the negative—yeas 82, nays 88, as follows :

YEAS—Messrs. Abbot, Alexander, Allen of Tennessee, Anderson, Archer of Maryland, Archer of Virginia, Baldwin, Ball, Barbour, Bateman, Bayly, Blackledge, Bloomfield, Brevard, Brown, Bryan, Butler of Louisiana, Cannon, Clark, Clay, Cobb, Cocke, Crawford, Crowell, Culbreth, Culpeper, Cuthbert, Davidson, Earle, Eddy, Floyd, Ford, Gray, Guyon, Hackley, Hall of North Carolina, Hardin, Hill, Hooks, Jackson, Johnson, Jones of Virginia, Jones of Tennessee, Kent, Little, McCoy, McCreary, McLane of Delaware, McLean of Kentucky, Meigs, Mercer, Metcalf, Montgomery, T. L. Moore, Neale, Nelson of Virginia, Newton, Pinckney, Rankin, Reid, Rhea, Ringgold, Robertson, Sawyer, Shaw, Simkins, Smith of New Jersey, Smith of Maryland, A. Smyth of Virginia, Smith of North Carolina, Stevens, Storrs, Swearingen, Tompkins, Trimble, Tucker of Virginia, Tucker of South Carolina, Tyler, Walker, Warfield, Williams of Virginia, and Williams of North Carolina.

NAYS—Messrs. Adams, Allen of Massachusetts, Allen of New York, Baker, Beecher, Boden, Brush, Buffum, Burton, Butler of New Hampshire, Campbell, Case, Clagett, Cook, Crafts, Cushman, Dane, Darlington, Dennison, Dewitt, Dickinson, Edwards of Connecticut, Edwards of Pennsylvania, Edwards of North Carolina, Eustis, Fay, Folger, Foot, Forrest, Fuller, Garnett, Gorham, Gross of New York, Gross of Pennsylvania, Hall of New York, Hemphill, Hendricks, Herrick, Hibshman, Hobart, Hostetter, Kendall, Kinsey, Kinsley, Lathrop, Lincoln, Livermore, Maclay, McCullough, Mallary, Marchand, Meech, Monell, R. Moore, S. Moore, Morton, Moseley, Murray, Nelson, of Massachusetts, Parker of Massachusetts, Patterson, Phelps, Philson, Pitcher, Plumer, Randolph, Rich, Richards, Richmond, Rogers, Ross, Russ, Sergeant, Silsbee, Sloan, Street, Strong of Vermont, Strong of New York, Tarr, Tomlinson, Tracy, Udree, Upham, Van Rensselaer, Wallace, Wendover, Whitman, and Wood.

So the resolution was rejected.

1147   HISTORY OF CONGRESS.   1148

H. of R.   *The Election of President and Vice President.*   FEBRUARY, 1821.

WEDNESDAY, Februrary 4.

Mr. LIVERMORE, from the Committee on the Post Office and Post Roads, reported a bill in addition to the act regulating the Post Office Establishment; which was read twice, and ordered to lie on the table.

[This bill contains provisions, to reduce the compensation to postmasters to three per cent. on any excess of receipt of postage over three thousand six hundred dollars per quarter; to repeal the extra allowance of one thousand dollars per annum to the postmaster at Washington City; to prohibit any postmaster, or editor or printer of a newspaper, from contracting for the transportation of the mail; to require bonds from persons stipulating for the carriage of newspapers other than in the mail, that they shall carry all papers delivered to them and on equal terms; to compel postmasters to reside in the city, town, village, or place in which their offices are established, and to limit their privilege of franking, to letters, newspapers, and packets, directed to and from their respective offices.]

A message from the Senate informed the House that the Senate have appointed Mr. BARBOUR a teller, on their part, agreeably to the resolutions of the 13th instant, in relation to the mode of examining the votes for President and Vice President of the United States.

ELECTION OF PRESIDENT AND VICE PRESIDENT.

Mr. CLAY, from the joint committee, to whom the subject had been referred, reported the following resolution:

Resolved, That the two Houses shall assemble in the Chamber of the House of Representatives, on Wednesday, the 14th February, 1821, and the President of the Senate, seated on the right of the Speaker of the House, shall be the presiding officer of the Senate, and the Speaker shall be the presiding officer of the House; that two persons be appointed tellers on the part of the House, to make a list of the votes as they shall be declared; that the result shall be delivered to the President of the Senate, who shall announce the state of the vote, and the persons elected, to the two Houses assembled as aforesaid, which shall be deemed a declaration of the persons elected President and Vice President of the United States, and, together with a list of the votes, be entered on the Journals of the two Houses.

Resolved, That, if any objection be made to the votes of Missouri, and the counting or omitting to count which shall not essentially change the result of the election; in that case they shall be reported by the President of the Senate in the following manner: Were the votes of Missouri to be counted, the result would be, for A. B. for President of the United States, —— votes; if not counted, for A. B. as President of the United States, —— votes; but in either event A. B. is elected President of the United States; and in the same manner for Vice President.

Mr. CLAY offered some remarks explanatory of the considerations which governed the committee in recommending the resolutions which had been reported. As convenience rendered it necessary for the Senate to meet this House here, in its own Hall, it was due to that body, by courtesy and propriety, that the President should be invited to preside, he being the officer designated by the Constitution to perform a certain duty appertaining to the occasion which called the two Houses together. As to the second resolution, the state of the votes for President and Vice President was well known, though unofficially, and, as the votes of Missouri could not affect the result, it was considered by the committee, to obviate the unpleasant difficulty which would otherwise arise in the joint meeting, better to provide for the case in the manner proposed. This course was deemed by the committee the most expedient, under all the circumstances, and he hoped the House would adopt it, the more especially as the Senate had already concurred in it.

The question was taken on the first resolution, and agreed to without a division, though several nays were heard.

The question being stated on the second resolution—

Mr. RANDOLPH said he could not consent to this special verdict, as it had been called, in the case of Missouri. He could not recognise in this House or the other House, singly, or conjointly, the power to decide on the votes of any State.* Suppose, he said, you strike out Missouri and insert South Carolina, which also has a provision in its constitution repugnant to the Constitution of the United States; or Virginia, or Massachusetts, which had a test, he believed, in its constitution; was there any less power to decide on their votes, than on those of Missouri? He maintained that the Electoral College was as independent of Congress, as Congress of them; and we have no right, said he, to judge of their proceedings. Mr. R. said, he would rather see an interregnum, or see no votes counted at all, than to see a principle adopted which went to the very foundation on which the Presidental office rested. Suppose a case, in which some gentleman of one House or the other should choose to turn up his nose at the vote of some State, and say that if it be so and so, such a person is elected; and if so and so, what-you-call-em is elected—did not everybody see the absurdity of such a proposition? Mr. R. added other remarks illustrative of his opinion of the course proposed by the resolution—deeming it not only erroneous, but erroneous in a matter of vital importance—in the ascertainment of the person who had been elected by the people Chief Magistrate of this nation—the most important officer under the Constitution—the monarch—for, whoever, in any country, commands the army and navy, and collects and distributes the revenue, is a king, call him what you will. The time of this House was precious, and he would not consume it, by saying all he thought and felt on the subject.

Mr. TRIMBLE was far from desiring to consume the time of the House, or to embarrass the House, but he could not give his consent to this resolution. If any thing was due to State rights, this resolution ought not to be adopted; as it would, however immaterial in the present case, be cited hereafter as a precedent; and precedents were becoming important things in the public transac-

1149   HISTORY OF CONGRESS.   1150

FEBRUARY, 1821.   *The Election of President and Vice President.*   H. OF R.

tions. The House might set an example by this vote, as ruinous in its consequences, as any decision which could be made. It was about to declare, not what was the true vote for President of the United States, but to state it hypothetically. Mr. T. argued at some length against such a course. Suppose some member in joint meeting should ask the President of the Senate how many votes were given—he must answer in the words of the resolution, and therefore would not state the fact, according to the law. It was the duty of the two Houses to enunciate the true state of the vote for President and Vice President, and the proposed annunciation would not be the fact. He concluded by saying that he would rather that the votes of Missouri were left out altogether, than adopt the course proposed.

Mr. RANDOLPH observed that the gentleman was under some mistake on one point. The Constitution of the United States provides, not that the person having a majority of votes should be President, but a majority of the votes of the Electors appointed. Now, he desired to know whether the Electors of Missouri were appointed or not.

Mr. FLOYD said he was aware that the question to agree to the resolution was tantamount to a motion to reject, but he would prefer the latter shape for the question, to show more strongly his opinion of it—it would suit his feelings towards it better. We have been going on for several years, said he, accumulating power until scarcely any is left but in Congress. If they had any power over the votes of Missouri at all, he said, it was when her votes were first received; but no such power existed. The votes of Indiana, at the last election for President, were counted when precisely in the same situation as those of Missouri now. He protested against this assumption of authority on the part of Congress, and wished to show his disapprobation of the resolution in the strongest manner.

Mr. CLAY said the Constitution required of the two Houses to assemble and perform the highest duty that could devolve on a public body—to ascertain who had been elected by the people to administer their national concerns. In a case of votes coming forward which could not be counted, the Constitution was silent; but, fortunately, the end in that case carried with it the means. The two Houses were called on to enumerate the votes for President and Vice President; of course they were called on to decide what are votes. It being obvious that a difficulty would arise in the joint meeting, concerning the votes of Missouri, some gentlemen thinking they ought to be counted, and others dissenting from that opinion, the committee thought it best to prevent all difficulty by waiving the question in the manner proposed, knowing that it could not affect the result of the election. As to the condition of Missouri, he himself thought her a State, with a perfect moral right to be admitted into the Union, but kept out for the want of a ceremonious act which was deemed by others necessary to entitle her to admission. Though, in his opinion, a State in fact, yet not being so in form, her votes could not be

counted according to form. He was aware that the question of her admission might come up and be decided in this very shape; for if Congress allowed her to vote for President and Vice President, and counted her votes, it would be a full admission of the State into the Union; but the committee thought, as there were other and more usual modes of admitting the State into the Union, it was better not to bring up the question in the discharge of this solemn and indispensable duty, but to allow that ceremony to proceed, if possible, without difficulty or embarrassment.

Mr. RHEA said the Constitution had in it neither waiving or elasticity, and it would not bend to circumstances of expediency. The Constitution had declared the duty of Congress in ascertaining the votes for President—it was not competent for them to mend the Constitution, nor to decide such a question as this proposed, and he was opposed to the resolution.

Mr. TRIMBLE said the very reason urged for this resolution, was that which constrained him to oppose it; and proceeded further to argue that it would be better to exclude the votes entirely than set such an example.

Mr. CULBRETH said he could hardly say whether he was most gratified at being relieved, by the gentleman from Virginia, (Mr. RANDOLPH,) from being the first to make objection to the proposed resolution, or grieved that he could not have the support of the gentleman from Kentucky, with whom it had given him great pleasure usually to act. The people of Missouri were, by the act of the last session of Congress authorized to form a constitution and State government; and, in the first article of that constitution. it is declared that the said State, when formed, "shall be admitted into the Union upon an equal footing with the original States, in all respects whatever." Believing that the people of Missouri, having formed a constitution and State government, in compliance with the act of last session, in all its provisions and conditions, and considering that she is, in fact, a State, and of right, if not in fact, (and he inclined to believe she was in fact,) a member of the Union, and that she is kept out of the enjoyment of her rights by a sheer act of power—he spoke this in reference to the act, and not to the actors—that simple justice required her admission to the enjoyment of her rights. Mr. C. said he found, on examination of the constitution of Missouri, that all officers, civil and military, are required, before entering upon the duties of their respective offices, to take an oath to support the Constitution of the United States, as well as of that State. It is declared (I use the word *declared* emphatically) by the constitution of the said State to be the duty of the General Assembly, as soon as may be, to pass such laws as may be necessary "to prevent free negroes and mulattoes from coming to and settling in said State, under any pretext whatsoever." This last clause is supposed by some to be repugnant to the Constitution of the United States. It is believed that a fair construction of the clause referred to, taken in connexion with the oath which the individual members of the General As-

1151　　　　　　　HISTORY OF CONGRESS.　　　　　　1152

H. of R.　　　　　The Election of President and Vice President.　　　　　FEBRUARY, 1821.

sembly are required to take, does not warrant such a conclusion. In the spirit of candor, I ask gentlemen, said Mr. C., who entertain this opinion, what is the actual duty of the General Assembly of Missouri, resulting from the oath which they are required to take and the declaratory clause above referred to? I appeal to them as statesmen, as politicians, as common lawyers, nay, as gentlemen of common sense, whether a fair and liberal construction—whether the obvious and only fair construction that can be given to the clause objected to, will not reconcile it with the Constitution of the United States? Will it not be the duty of the General Assembly of Missouri, acting under their oath to support the Constitution of the United States, to pass no law which shall violate that oath or be repugnant to that Constitution? To use the language of the gentleman from Ohio, (Mr. Ross,) on yesterday, can it be believed that they will commit perjury by the passage of such a law? [Here the Speaker reminded Mr. C. that the hour for counting the votes had arrived, and intimated the propriety of his remarks being brought to a conclusion.] Mr. C. respectfully answered that he knew of no hour appointed for any purpose in relation to the business of the House; that, under the suggestion of the honorable Speaker, as well as from a sense of propriety, he should bring his remarks to a conclusion as speedily as possible, consistent with a distinct expression of his views upon the subject before the House. It seems to me, Mr. Speaker, said Mr. C., that if gentlemen could divest themselves of all prejudices—if they were not insensibly influenced by feelings and considerations not necessarily excited by the provision in question, that they would have no difficulty in reconciling the seeming conflict between the Constitution of the United States and the so often referred to clause in the constitution of Missouri. The General Assembly of Missouri will undoubtedly feel themselves bound to perform the duty enjoined upon them by the constitution of that State, limited by the paramount authority of the Constitution of the United States, conformably to the oath which they are required to take. If they were to attempt to extend the provisions of any law beyond this limit their act would be, so far, not only void, but, if knowingly committed, the members would be guilty of perjury. I have no more to add.

Mr. TRACY was compelled, he said, to vote against the resolution, but for reasons very different from those of Mr. CULBRETH. He was opposed to the resolution because Missouri was neither a State in the Union nor one out of the Union; but was in fact a Territory. He could not, therefore, consent that her votes should be counted at all—considering them entirely foreign to the election of President and Vice President of the United States.

Mr. CLAY said he would merely observe, that the difficulty is before us; that we must decide it when the two Houses meet, or avoid it by some previous arrangement. The Committee being morally certain that the question would arise on the votes, in joint meeting, thought it best, as he had before stated, to give it the go-by in this way. Suppose this resolution not adopted, the President of the Senate will proceed to open and count the votes; and would the House allow that officer, singly and alone, thus, virtually, to decide the question of the legality of the votes? If not, how then were they to proceed? Was it to be settled by the decision of the two Houses conjointly, or of the two Houses separately? One House would say the votes ought to be counted, the other that they ought not; and then the votes would be lost altogether. Would the gentleman from New York prefer that it be decided in the joint meeting? In that case he would find himself in a much leaner majority than on the question yesterday. In fact, Mr. C. said there was no mode pointed out in the Constitution of settling litigated questions arising in the discharge of this duty; it was a *casus omissus;* and he thought it would be proper, either by some act of derivative legislation, or by an amendment of the Constitution itself, to supply the defect.

Mr. LIVERMORE made a few remarks in favor of the resolution.

Mr. RHEA made a few remarks in opposition to the resolution. The ground he took was this: that it was not in the power of this House, or of both Houses, by resolution, to remedy a defect in the Constitution.

The question on agreeing to the resolution was then decided in the affirmative—yeas 90, nays 67, as follows:

YEAS—Messrs. Abbot, Alexander, Allen of Massachusetts, Allen of New York, Anderson, Archer, of Maryland, Baker, Bateman, Beecher, Campbell, Cannon, Clagett, Clark, Clay, Cook, Cushman, Dane, Darlington, Davidson, Dennison, Dickinson, Eddy, Edwards of Connecticut, Eustis, Fay, Folger, Foot, Ford, Fuller, Gorham, Gross of New York, Gross of Pennsylvania, Hackley, Hall of New York, Hemphill, Hendricks, Herrick, Hill, Hobart, Hostetter, Kendall, Kent, Kinsey, Kinsley, Lathrop, Little, Livermore, Maclay, McCoy, McCreary, McCullough, McLean of Kentucky, Mallary, Marchand, Meech, Meigs, Monell, Montgomery, R. Moore, S. Moore, T. L. Moore, Moseley, Murray, Neale, Nelson of Massachusetts, Parker of Massachusetts, Patterson, Philson, Pitcher, Plumer, Rogers, Russ, Sawyer, Sergeant, Silsbee, Sloan, Stevens, Storrs, Street, Strong of Vermont, Strong of New York, Tomlinson, Udree, Upham, Van Rensselaer, Walker, Wallace, Wendover, Whitman, and Wood—90.

NAYS—Messrs. Adams, Allen of Tennessee, Archer of Virginia, Baldwin, Bell, Barbour, Bayly, Blackledge, Bloomfield, Boden, Brevard, Brown, Brush, Bryan, Buffum, Butler of Louisiana, Case, Cobb, Cocke, Crafts, Crawford, Crowell, Culbreth, Culpeper, Cuthbert, Earle, Edwards of Pennsylvania, Edwards of North Carolina, Floyd, Forrest, Gray, Hall of North Carolina, Hooks, Johnson, Jones of Virginia, Jones of Tennessee, Lincoln, Mercer, Metcalf, Morton, Nelson of Virginia, Newton, Parker of Virginia, Pinckney, Randolph, Reid, Rhea, Richards, Richmond, Ringgold, Robertson, Ross, Shaw, Simkins, Smith of New Jersey, Smith of Maryland, A. Smyth of Virginia, Smith of North Carolina, Swearingen, Terrell, Tracy, Trimble, Tucker of Virginia, Tucker of South Ca-

1153   HISTORY OF CONGRESS.   1154

FEBRUARY, 1821.   *The Election of President and Vice President.*   H. OF R.

rolina, Tyler, Williams of Virginia, and Williams of North Carolina.—67.

So the second resolution was agreed to.

On motion of Mr. CLAY, it was then ordered, that a message be sent to the Senate, informing that body, that this House, on its part, concurs in the report of the joint committee, and is now prepared to proceed, with the Senate, in the performance of its Constitutional duty.

[Messrs. CLAY, SERGEANT, and VAN RENSSELAER, were the committee on the part of the House of Representatives, to act with the committee of the Senate, in considering the proper mode of proceeding in regard to counting out the Electoral votes.]

Mr. EDWARDS, of North Carolina, gave notice he should, on to-morrow at twelve o'clock, offer for the consideration of the House a resolution declaring the admission of the State of Missouri into the Union, containing in all respects the same provisions as were contained in the resolution from the Senate, which was rejected in this House.

On motion of Mr. CLAY, and by general consent, it was determined that the members of this House should receive the Senate, on their entrance into the House, standing and uncovered. In the same manner it was determined that a sufficient number of the seats on the right hand of the Chair, should be set apart for the Senators.

Mr. CLAY moved that a committee of two members be appointed to receive the Senate, and conduct the President of the Senate to the chair, and the members to the seats assigned to them.

Mr. NELSON, of Virginia, declared his opposition to this course. It had been usual for the Speaker of the House to receive the President of the Senate, and invite him to a seat beside him; and he saw no reason, at this time, for the proposed innovation.

Mr. CLAY said it was true it never had been done before; but, having, whilst he had the honor to preside over this House, witnessed the embarrassments occasioned by the want of such a regulation, he now thought it would be proper to adopt it.

The motion of Mr. CLAY was then agreed to without a division, though not without negative votes.

Mr. NELSON remarked, in an under tone, that he wished he had required the yeas and nays upon it.

Mr. CLAY and Mr. HILL, were appointed a committee accordingly.

Soon after, the Senate came into the Hall, preceded by its President, and attended by its Secretary and Sergeant-at-Arms; and the President was conducted to the Speaker's chair, the Speaker occupying a chair at his left hand.

The PRESIDENT of the Senate then delivered the votes of the States, in the following order, to the committee for counting the votes, (Mr. BARBOUR of the Senate, and Messrs. SMITH of Maryland, and SERGEANT of this House)—and the official authentications, &c., were each of them twice read in an audible tone, and the votes recorded by the Secretary of the Senate and by the Clerk of the House of Representatives, as follows:

16th CON. 2d SESS.—37

STATES.	For President. James Monroe.	For Vice President. D. D. Tompkins.
New Hampshire - -	7	7
Massachusetts - -	15	7
Rhode Island - -	4	4
Connecticut - -	9	9
Vermont - - -	8	8
New York - - -	29	29
New Jersey - -	8	8
Pennsylvania - -	24	24
Delaware - - -	4	
Maryland - - -	11	10
Virginia - -	25	25
North Carolina - -	15	15
South Carolina - -	11	11
Georgia - - -	8	8
Kentucky - -	12	12
Tennessee - -	7	7
Ohio - - -	8	8
Louisiana - - -	3	3
Mississippi - - -	2	2
Indiana - - -	3	3
Illinois - - -	3	3
Alabama - - -	3	3
Maine - - -	9	9

The scattering votes were as follows: For President, in New Hampshire, there was for John Quincy Adams, one vote. For Vice President, there was, in New Hampshire, for Richard Rush, one vote; in Massachusetts, for Richard Stockton, eight votes; in Delaware, for Daniel Rodney, four votes; in Maryland, for Robert Goodloe Harper, one vote.

The process of this ceremony was very tedious, from the length of the verifications, proclamations, &c., and the House did not arrive at this stage of it till after four o'clock.

When the votes of the Electors for Missouri were announced, by the PRESIDENT of the Senate, and handed to the tellers—

Mr. LIVERMORE, of New Hampshire, rose, and said: Mr. President and Mr. Speaker, I object to receiving any votes for President and Vice President from Missouri, because Missouri is not a State of this Union.

A motion was then made by a member of the Senate, that the Senate do now withdraw to its Chamber; and, the question having been put, was decided in the affirmative; and the Senate retired.

The House being called to order—

Mr. FLOYD, of Virginia, then rose and submitted the following resolution:

Resolved, That Missouri is one of the States of this Union, and her votes for President and Vice President of the United States ought to be received and counted.

Mr. F. said, he believed, that gentlemen must now begin to see the precipice to which the decisions of this House in respect to Missouri had brought them. He was, as every member must be, tired of the debate on this subject; but he thought that no one could discharge his duty as he ought without investigating the merits of the

1155   HISTORY OF CONGRESS.   1156

H. of R.   *The Election of President and Vice President.*   FEBRUARY, 1821.

question which he had now proposed. He thought it proper, also, that the yeas and nays should be recorded on every question connected with this subject. That the votes of States, whose admission into the Union had not been declared previous to the votes being given in, had heretofore been received for President and Vice President, he believed the gentleman from New Hampshire would not deny. If such a course had been right heretofore, he did not see why an objection should now be made. If innovations on established usage were to be justified by their novelty, then indeed all disquisitions on the subject were vain. But the time was, when members from new States were admitted to their seats in this House, without the previous passage of a declaratory resolution. That there was a law on the statute book that any Territory having a population of sixty thousand souls might form a constitution and State government and be admitted into the Union, no one would deny. Whenever we turn our eyes, said Mr. F., and observe the progress of the Government, until the present time, the States have been admitted upon this principle, until in the present case; and in this case, at the last session, a compromise, as it was thought and called, was entered into. Mr. F. hesitated to express in terms all he thought on this subject; but he would say, if he had voted for that law at the last session; and opposed now those principles which would naturally grow out of it, he should have said to himself, when he had done so, that he had done in his life one act which he thought dishonorable. Let us now, said he, have the question fairly at issue. Let us know whether Missouri be a State in the Union or not. If not, let us send her an Ambassador, and treat for her admission into the Union. Sir, we cannot take another step, without hurling this Government into the gulf of destruction. For one, I say, I have gone as far as I can go in the way of compromise—and if there is to be a compromise beyond that point, it must be at the edge of the sword.

Mr. ARCHER, of Maryland said, that entertaining the same sentiments as the gentleman from Virginia with respect to the refusal to admit Missouri into the Union, he yet felt himself bound to move, as he now did, to postpone the further consideration of this resolution indefinitely. He was opposed to this House undertaking to proceed in any manner as to the legality of the Electoral votes. He could recognise no power in the House of Representatives on this subject separate from the Senate. The expressions in the Constitution, in regard to the counting of the votes of Electors, &c., he considered as imperative. All questions arising out of it, according to his construction, must be settled in joint meeting of the two Houses. He could not agree that this House had a right to determine whether any vote should be received or rejected. What are the words of the Constitution? "The President of the Senate shall, in 'the presence of the Senate and House of Repre- 'sentatives, open all the certificates, and the votes 'shall then be counted." Does it not follow, asked Mr. R., that the votes must be counted in

the presence of the two Houses? For what purpose do they assemble together, unless it be to determine on the legality of the votes? If not for this purpose, the joint meeting is for form and show, and nothing else. We must, in my apprehension, determine the question in joint meeting, and in no other way. Entertaining this opinion, he said, he should vote for the indefinite postponement of any proposition, the object of which is to determine, in this House, the legality or illegality of any Electoral vote. At the last election of President, an objection was made, by the gentleman who now presides, to receiving the votes of Indiana, because they were given in before the passage of the act declaring her admission into the Union. On that occasion, as now, the Senate retired. I thought then, as now, said Mr. A., that they had no right to retire until the question was settled. On that occasion, the House determined to postpone indefinitely the objection. The motives which induced that determination were doubtless various; it was my opinion, then, that it was improper to entertain the objection in the House, and I think the same of the present proposition.

Mr. RANDOLPH said, it was not without reluctance that he offered himself to the attention of the House at this time; but he submitted to the very worthy gentleman from Maryland who had just taken his seat, whether the object which he had in view could, according to his own views of propriety, be effectuated by the course which he had recommended to this House. It was no part of his nature, Mr. R. said, nor of his purpose, to inflate to a greater magnitude this exaggerated question of the admission of Missouri into the Union. But the question had now assumed that aspect which, had it depended on him, it should have taken at an earlier period of the session. It was, he said, not only congenial with the principles and practices of our free Government, but unless he was deceived with the practice of that country from which we had adopted, and wisely adopted, our manly institutions, that on any occasion when any person presents himself to a representative body with credentials of title to a seat, he shall take his seat, and perform the functions of a member, until a prior and a better claim shall not only be preferred, but established. It was seen that, but the day before yesterday, the Committee of Elections of this House came forward with a report, stating that the qualifications and returns of certain members were perfect who have been acting and legislating, and on whose votes the laws of the land have depended for the last three or four months. Just so it ought to have been with regard to the Representative from the State of Missouri. She had now, said Mr. R., presented herself, for the first time, in a visible and tangible shape. She comes into this House, not *in forma pauperis*, but claiming to be one of the co-sovereignties of this confederated Government, and presents to you her vote, by receiving or rejecting which the election of your Chief Magistrate will be lawful or unlawful. He did not mean by the vote of Missouri, but by the votes of all the States.

1157   HISTORY OF CONGRESS.   1158

February, 1821.   *The Election of President and Vice President.*   H. of R.

Now comes the question, whether we will not merely repel her, but repel her with scorn and contumely. *Cui bono?* And, he might add, *quo warranto?* He should like to hear, he said, from the gentleman from New Hampshire, (Mr. Livermore,) where this House gets its authority—he should like to hear some of the learned, or unlearned, sages of the law, with which this House, as well as all our legislative bodies, abounds, show their authority for refusing to receive the votes from Missouri. Mr. R. said, he went back to the first principles. The Electoral Colleges, he said, are as independent of this House, as this House is of them. They had as good a right to pronounce on their qualifications, as this House has of those of its members. Your office, said, he, in regard to the electoral votes, is merely ministerial. It is to count the votes, and you undertake to reject votes. To what will this lead? Do you ever expect to see the time when there shall be in the Presidential chair a creature so poor, so imbecile, not only not worthy of being at the head of the nation, but not worthy of being at the head of a petty corporation—do you ever expect to see in that office an animal so poor, as not to have in this House retainers enough to enable him to reject the vote of any State which, being counted, might prevent his continuance, and their continuance, and that of their friends, in office? He spoke not of the present incumbent—he was not so wanting in common decency and decorum as to do so—he spoke in reference not only to what is past, but to that which is prospective, and which every man, who looks the least into futurity, must know will happen, and, in all probability, will very shortly happen. He undertook to say that if this House should, by a vote of indefinite postponement—for the form was immaterial—or in any other way, and it would be observed, for the first instance in the person of Missouri, of this much injured, long insulted and trampled-upon member of this confederacy, was this example to be set—if, said he, you do, for the first time, now receive the votes of a State, it will be created into a precedent, and that in the life-time of some of those who now hear me, for the manufacture of Presidents by this House. The wisest men may make constitutions, on paper, as they please.

What, Mr. R. asked, was the theory of this Constitution? It is, that this House, except upon a certain contingency, has nothing at all to do with the appointment of President and Vice President of the United States, and when it does act, must act by States, and by States only can it act on this subject, unless it transcend the limits of the Constitution. What, he asked, was to be the practice of the Constitution, as now proposed? That an informal meeting of this and the other House is to usurp the initiative, the nominative power, with regard to the two first officers of the Government; that they are to wrest from the people of the United States their indefeasible right of telling us whom they wish to exercise the functions of the Government, in despite and contempt of their decision. Is there to be no limit to the power of Congress—no mound or barrier

to stay their usurpation? Why were the electoral bodies established? The Constitution has wisely provided that they shall assemble, each by itself, and not in one great assembly. By this means, assuredly, that system of intrigue which was matured into a science, or rather into an art here, was guarded against. But, Mr. R. ventured to say, that the electoral college of this much-despised Missouri, acting conformably to law, and to the genius and nature of our institutions, if it were composed of but one man, was as independent of this House as this House was of it. If, however, said he, *per fas aut nefas,* the point is to be carried; if the tocsin is to be sounded; if the troops are to be rallied, and Missouri is to be expelled with scorn from our august presence—how august, Mr. Speaker, I leave it for you to decide—there are those who will be willing to take her to their arms. And, in point of mere expediency, he would ask of gentlemen—he put the suggestion in that shape, because he believed they were inaccessible to other considerations—in point of expediency, he asked them, what were they now doing but riveting those ties by which Missouri would, he trusted, forever be bound to that section of the country by which, with whatever reason, her rights have been supported on this floor? I do look with a sentiment I cannot express, said Mr. R.—I look with a sentiment of pity—and that has been said to be nearly allied to love, as I know it to be allied to a very different emotion—I look with pity on those who believe that, by their feeble efforts in this House, governed by forms and technicalities—your Sergeant-at-Arms and committees of attendance, and mummeries such as belong to other countries where I have never travelled, and trust in God I never shall—they can stop the growth of the rising Empire in the West. Let gentlemen lay a resolution on the table, let it be engrossed in a fair hand, and do you, Mr. Speaker, sign it, that the waves of the Mississippi shall not seek the ocean, and then send your Sergeant-at-Arms to carry it into execution, and see whether you can enforce it with all the force, physical or moral, under your control. Mr. R. concluded by expressing his hope that the gentleman from Maryland would withdraw his motion for indefinite postponement.

Mr. Archer, of Virginia, said he believed it was pretty well ascertained that he was willing to go as great lengths as any man in this House to support the rights of Missouri. He regretted that, even in this skirmish, he was obliged to separate himself from those with whom he had acted with so much pleasure and with so much zeal. But he could not maintain, what he should do by voting for this resolution, that Missouri is now a State of this Union. Was it contended that Congress has not a right to require the submission of the constitution of a new State to its consideration before she becomes a member of the Union? If so, would any man contend that Congress had not a right to pass, in some shape or other, upon the constitution of any new State? Was there any one of his colleagues who would say, that there was no possible case in which he might not be

1159   HISTORY OF CONGRESS.   1160

H. OF R.   *The Election of President and Vice President.*   FEBRUARY, 1821.

induced to reject the constitution of Missouri? Suppose the constitution she has offered had been notoriously aristocratical, was there any man among them who would not have given his vote for the exclusion of Missouri from the confederacy? We presume not. If he were to give his vote for this resolution, Mr. A. said, he should contradict all the language he had hitherto held in respect to Missouri; for, if she was a State without the consent of Congress, she had no right to complain of oppression by the refusal of Congress to recognise her.

Mr. A. said, he should continue to reprobate the odious and foul combination by which Missouri is kept out of the Union; but should he give a vote for this resolution, he should feel himself precluded from doing so. If, indeed, the case were presented, whether the member from Missouri should be admitted to a seat on this floor, he should give a vote affirmatively; for it would be tantamount to an admission of the State of Missouri into the Union. But, were he to vote for this proposition, he should vote for an evident solecism; it would be saying that, though it has been decided that Missouri shall not be admitted into the Union, yet she shall exercise the highest functions of a member of the Confederacy. Mr. A. said he could not hold that language, or present himself in that character. Opposed in general to postponements, he should vote against the proposed postponement, in order to meet the question directly. He had no notion, he added, of the doctrine which he had heard for the first time to-day, that you may have a problematical or hypothetical election of a President and Vice President. Suppose the result of the election depended on the votes of Missouri, and the same course was to be pursued which was now indicated; the President of the Senate would have to announce that, in one event, we had a President, whilst in another we had not, and the Government would be left without a head, and a dissolution of the Union would be the possible immediate consequence. He was a little surprised, he said, at one ground which had been taken on this occasion: that the House had no power to pass any judgment on any return. He had always thought that, wherever was lodged the power to receive a return, there also was the power to pass a judgment on the validity of that return. Suppose any territory, not within the limits of the United States at the time, Florida, for example, to send votes here for Electors; was there no authority by which these votes could be rejected? Suppose a State, entitled to 27 votes, should send 37 votes, would any gentleman contend that there was no power in this House to judge of the proper number? Could there ever be a pure election—could it ever be ascertained who was elected, in the event of the establishment of a doctrine of that sort? Mr. A. concluded, by declaring his readiness to adopt any measure to bring Missouri, now trampled down by power, into the Union, but he could not vote for this resolution.

Mr. CLAY next obtained the floor, but gave way to allow Mr. RANDOLPH to make an explanation.

Mr. RANDOLPH said, it was highly probable that

the few remarks which he had made might give rise to misapprehensions in the minds of other gentlemen, as they had done in the mind of his colleague. He, therefore, wished to explain. His position, he said, was misunderstood. It had been said, and pertinently said, that Missouri might be admitted into the Union in more ways than one. His position, then, was, that this is the first instance in which Missouri has knocked at the door and demanded her rights. It is now for us, said Mr. R., by permitting her to come in, or rather by refraining from extruding her from this Hall, to determine whether she shall now be one of our Commonwealth, or, as the fashion is to call it, of our Empire. Mr. R. said he had no doubt that Congress might drive Missouri into the wilderness, like another son of Hagar. If we do, said he, we drive her at our own peril. If either of the worthy Senators and Representative from Missouri, whose long forbearance had excited surprise in no man's breast more than in that of Mr. R.— he did not mean to blame them for pursuing the counsel of cooler heads than his—had presented themselves here, would you (addressing the Speaker) have felt yourself bound to exclude them from the communion with more than papal power; not only from the cup of wine, but from the bread of life itself? Let me tell my friend before me, (Mr. ARCHER,) we have not the power which he seems to think we possess; and if this be a *casus omissus* in the Constitution, I want to know where we acquire the power to supply the defect. You may keep Missouri out of the Union by violence, but here the issue is joined. She comes forward in the person of her Presidential and Vice Presidential Electors, instead of that of her Representative; and she was thus presented in a shape as unquestionable as that of New York, Pennsylvania, Massachusetts, or the proudest and oldest State in the Union. She comes forward by her attorneys —her Electors. Will you deny them admittance? Will you thrust her Electors, and hers only, from this Hall? Mr. R. said his friend had not given to this subject the sort of consideration which he knew him to be capable of giving it. I made no objection, said Mr. R., to the votes of New Hampshire, Maine, or Vermont: I have had as good a right to object to the votes of New Hampshire, as the gentleman from New Hampshire has to object to the votes of Missouri. Who made thou, Cain, thy brother's keeper? Who put Missouri into custody of the honorable gentleman from New Hampshire? The Electors of Missouri are as much *homines probi et legales* as the Electors of New Hampshire. This, Mr. R. said, was no skirmish, as it had been called. This was the battle when Greek meets Greek; it was a conflict not to be decided between the phalanx and the legion, whether the impenetrability of the one or the activity of the other shall prevail. Let us buckle on our armor, said Mr. R.; let us put aside all this flummery, these metaphysical distinctions, these legal technicalities, these special pleadings, this dry minuteness, this unprofitable drawing of distinctions without difference; let us say now, as we have said on another occasion, we will assert, maintain,

1161   HISTORY OF CONGRESS.   1162

February, 1821.   *The Election of President and Vice President.*   H. of R.

and vindicate our rights, or put to every hazard what you pretend to hold in such high estimation.

Mr. R. said he recollected perfectly well, in the celebrated election of Thomas Jefferson and Aaron Burr—they live, said he, illustrious examples of the merits of their respective partisans—what were we then told? Why, that we must withdraw our opposition, or there would be no election; that a dissolution of the Union impended; that volcanoes began to play; that earthquakes yawned beneath us; and, recollect, sir, we had a President in the chair who had a majority in this House, small as it was. He treated the idea of giving way with derision and scorn. We said we will not give way, and you must take the consequences. We appealed, said Mr. R., to the good sense of the nation; and I do now appeal to this nation, said he, whether this pretended sympathy for the rights of free negroes and mulattoes is to supersede the rights of the free white citizens, of ten times their whole number. They gave way, sir, said Mr. R.; the sheep is the most timid and helpless of all animals; it retreats before any attack is offered to it. The President of the United States, said Mr. R., possesses great powers and highly responsible functions, and should be looked up to with veneration and deference, because he is the Chief Magistrate of a people, legally appointed by their suffrages. But a President of the United States, appointed by the exclusion of the votes of those who are the same flesh and blood as ourselves—for the people of Missouri are not natives of Missouri, with the exception of a few French and still fewer Spaniards—is no more the Chief Magistrate of this country than that thing—that pageant, which the majorities of the two Houses proposed to set up just twenty years ago—a President made by law— no, by the form and color of law, against the principles of the Constitution, and in violation of the rights of the freemen of this country. Sir, said Mr. R., I would not give a button for him. On his personal account, and for his personal qualities, I might treat him with respect as an individual, but as Chief Magistrate of this country, he would be more odious to my judgment than one of the house of Stuart attempting to seat himself on the throne of England, in defiance of the laws of succession and of the opinion of the people. We have, I am afraid, so long basked in the impure atmosphere, not of this House, but of this Court, that—

Mr. CLAY here claimed the floor, which he had yielded to the gentleman only for the purpose of making an explanation.

Mr. RANDOLPH took his seat, saying that he would give way to the honorable gentleman in every thing but one.

Mr. CLAY said he really saw no difficulty in this business; and, before he sat down, should make a motion, with a view to put an end to this discussion. The House and Senate have, by a joint act, this day agreed, that, in the event of an objection being made to the vote of Missouri, her vote should be counted hypothetically; that the whole number should be announced, including the vote of Missouri, and that the number should also be stated as it would be, the vote of Missouri being excluded; and, the result not varying, that it should be declared that, in either case, the person having the largest number of votes was duly elected. The motive which operated on the joint committee in recommending this course, and on the two Houses in adopting it, was to avoid the very difficulty into which the House was about to precipitate itself. It was an effort to provide, by previous arrangement, for the very contingency which has arisen. The moment the objection was made, in that instant the rule adopted this morning took effect. Mr. C. said it therefore appeared to him, with very great deference to the course of the presiding officer of the Senate, that he ought to have gone on, and, after the votes had been summed up, to have made the annunciation as proposed in the joint resolution adopted this morning.

The two Houses ought not, in the opinion of Mr. C., to have separated until they had consummated what had been stipulated for. He was now not willing to take up any proposition on this subject or any other, however unwilling he might have been to meet it at any other time. He was opposed to do so, because to do so is a violation of good faith between the two Houses, as pledged by the arrangement of this morning. He had not a doubt, he said, that Missouri might be admitted into the Union in a variety of ways, and very possibly, on proper examination, the mode now proposed might be one of them, by the two Houses, jointly or separately, giving her the exercise of a right which, as a State, would belong to her. The House, however, as well as the Senate, had virtually determined to get round that question to-day, and to put an end to any controversy which might arise in respect to it, in the manner contemplated by the second resolution passed this morning. Mr. C. therefore moved that the subject now under consideration be laid on the table, in order to resume the business which had been interrupted by the retirement of the Senate.

Mr. STORRS demanded the reading of the first resolution which passed this House, as compared with that which passed the Senate.

[Here took place an explanation of a variation which had taken place in the form of the resolve. As it came from the Senate the President of the Senate was to preside over the joint meeting. As reported by the committee on the part of this House the President of the Senate was to preside over the Senate, and the Speaker was to preside over the House of Representatives. This alteration was made, because it was known that the House of Representatives would not have agreed to the other course, and a collision might have arisen between the two Houses. It may be added, that the Senate were not aware, when they came into the Hall, of the change of the arrangement, but supposed it to stand, as they had voted it. Their retirement from the Chamber arose from the President of the Senate having learned these facts after he was seated in his place in the Hall. He would otherwise, it is supposed, have gone on to proclaim the result, immediately after Mr. LIVERMORE's objection, as prescribed in the resolution.]

1163 HISTORY OF CONGRESS. 1164

H. of R.   *The Election of President and Vice President:*   FEBRUARY, 1821.

Some conversation took place between Messrs. SMITH of Maryland, CLAY, RANDOLPH, NELSON of Virginia, FOOT, and COBB, as to the state in which matters would be, on the Senate's return. Some of the gentlemen contended that, on the Senate's return, matters would stand just as they did before, and the same difficulty as had already presented itself would again arise. Others contended, and the majority appeared to be with them, that, on the return of the Senate, the President would go on to declare the result, as directed in the second joint resolution of this morning.

Mr. LIVERMORE, in the course of these desultory remarks, took an opportunity to vindicate his conduct in offering the objection to the votes of Missouri. It was a duty necessary to be performed by somebody; having no wish to be forward in the business, he had endeavored to persuade several gentlemen to present it—but, they declining to do so, it had become his duty to do it, and in his opinion he had done it at the proper moment.*

The question was taken on Mr. CLAY's motion to lay Mr. FLOYD's resolution on the table, and decided in the affirmative, ayes 103. And then, on motion of Mr. Clay, it was ordered, that a message be sent to the Senate to inform that body that the House is now ready to receive the Senate in the Chamber of the House of Representatives, for the purpose of continuing the enumeration of the votes of the Electors for President and Vice President, according to the joint resolutions agreed upon between the two houses; and that the Clerk go with the said message.

The Clerk accordingly went with the said message; and be being returned—

The Senate again appeared, and took seats in the House as before.

* FEBRUARY 17, 1821.

Messrs. Gales & Seaton :

In your report of the transactions in the House of Representatives on the 14th instant, you observe that "Mr. Livermore took an opportunity to vindicate his conduct in offering his objections to the votes from Missouri." But you omit the only circumstance which rendered any observations on his part necessary; for certainly the objection was in substance proper, and every member of Congress had a right to make it. The truth is, Mr. Smith, of Maryland, in the course of debate, said to this effect: that the abrupt departure of the Senate, and all the difficulty which ensued, ought to be imputed to the gentleman from New Hampshire, Mr. L., who made his objection *too soon; instead of waiting, as he should have done, till after the Missouri votes were counted.* In answer to this charge, Mr. L. made a few remarks, which you have not reported, but which probably convinced even Mr. Smith that the objection to counting the votes from Missouri was interposed at the proper moment.

A. D.

[Our correspondent is perfectly right. Mr. Livermore did not certainly vindicate the course he had taken, until it had been impugned by others. We were so cramped for room in our report, that we were obliged to generalize the incidental remarks, and, in doing so, perhaps a wrong impression may have been given to Mr. L.'s observations.]—*Editors National Intelligencer.*

The President of the Senate, in the presence of both Houses, proceeded to open the certificate of the Electors of the State of Missouri, which he delivered to the tellers, by whom it was read, and who registered the same.

And the votes of all the States having been thus counted, registered, and the lists thereof compared, they were delivered to the President of the Senate, by whom they were read, as already printed.

The President of the Senate then, in pursuance of the resolution adopted by the two Houses, proceeded to announce the state of the votes to the two Houses of Congress, in joint meeting assembled, as follows :

" Were the votes of Missouri to be counted, the result would be—For JAMES MONROE, of Virginia, for President of the United States, 231 votes : if not counted, for JAMES MONROE, of Virginia, 228 votes :—For DANIEL D. TOMPKINS, of New York, for Vice President of the United States, 218 votes : if not counted, for DANIEL D. TOMPKINS, of New York, for Vice President of the United States, 215 votes. But in either event, JAMES MONROE, of Virginia, has a majority of the votes of the whole number of Electors for President, and DANIEL D. TOMPKINS, of New York, has a majority of the votes of the whole number of Electors for Vice President of the United States."

The President of the Senate had proceeded thus far, or nearly thus far, in the proclamation, when Mr. FLOYD, of Virginia, addressed the Chair, and inquired whether the votes of Missouri were or were not counted.

Cries of Order! Order! were so loud as to drown Mr. FLOYD's voice.

[The President of the Senate had hesitated in the proclamation, on Mr. FLOYD addressing the Chair.]

Mr. RANDOLPH rose, and was addressing the Chair, when loud cries of Order! Order! resounded from many voices.

The SPEAKER pronounced Mr. RANDOLPH to be out of order, and invited him to take his seat.

Mr. BRUSH demanded that Mr. RANDOLPH should be allowed to proceed, and declared his determination to sustain his right to do so. Mr. B. was also loudly called to order.

Mr. FLOYD demanded of the Chair whether he was considered in order or not.

The SPEAKER determined that he was not in order at this time, the only business being at that present time that prescribed by the rule of this morning.

There was considerable murmuring at this decision ; but order was restored ; when the President of the Senate concluded his annunciation as follows :

" I therefore declare that JAMES MONROE, of Virginia, is duly elected President of the United States, for four years, to commence on the fourth day of March, 1821 ; and that DANIEL D. TOMPKINS, of New York, is duly elected Vice President of the United States, for the like term of four years, to commence on the said fourth day of March, 1821."

As the President concluded—

Mr. RANDOLPH addressed the Chair ; but was required to take his seat.

On motion by a member of the Senate, the Senate retired from the hall.

After they retired, and the House being called to order—

Mr. RANDOLPH, who had still retained the floor, was heard addressing the Chair. He spoke for some time, without being distinctly heard, owing to the confusion in the hall. He had, he said, seen every election of President of the United States, except that of the present Chief Magistrate, and he had never before heard any other form of proclamation than that such was the *whole* number of votes given in; that such a person, A or B, had so many, and was therefore elected President or Vice President of the United States. On this occasion no such annunciation had been made, and the presiding officer might just as well have said that James Claxton or Thomas Dunn was elected President of the United States. Were gentlemen to be put down by clamor and by force here for getting up to assert, not only their rights, but the rights of the whole people of the United States? Sir, said he, your election is vitiated; you have flinched from the question; you have attempted to evade the decision of that which was essential to the determination of who is and who is not elected Chief Magistrate of the United States. Mr. R. concluded his remarks by moving resolutions declaring the election to be illegal, &c. They were as follows:

1. *Resolved*, That the electoral votes of the State of Missouri have this day been counted, and do constitute a part of the majority of two hundred and thirty-one votes given for President, and of two hundred and eighteen votes given for Vice President.

2. *Resolved*, That the whole number of Electors appointed, and of votes given for President and Vice President, has not been announced by the presiding officer of the Senate and House of Representatives, agreeably to the provision of the Constitution of the United States, and that therefore the proceeding has been irregular and illegal.

Whilst Mr. R. was reducing his motion to writing, several gentlemen claimed the floor.

The SPEAKER determined that Mr. LATHROP was entitled to it; and Mr. L. moved to adjourn.

Mr. FLOYD claimed the right of the floor, as rising first, and demanded to be heard.

The SPEAKER affirmed Mr. LATHROP's right.

Mr. FLOYD was about appealing from the decision of the Chair, but did not.

Mr. RINGGOLD having demanded the yeas and nays on the question of adjournment, the question was taken accordingly, as follows:

YEAS—Messrs. Adams, Allen of Massachusetts, Allen of New York, Anderson, Baker, Bateman, Beecher, Boden, Buffum, Cannon, Case, Clagett, Clark, Clay, Cook, Crafts, Culpeper, Cushman, Cuthbert, Dane, Darlington, Dennison, Eddy, Edwards of Connecticut, Edwards of Pennsylvania, Fay, Folger, Foot, Forrest, Fuller, Gorham, Gross of New York, Gross of Pennsylvania, Guyon, Hackley, Hall of New York, Hardin, Hemphill, Hendricks, Herrick, Hibshman, Hill, Hobart, Hooks, Hostetter, Kendall, Kinsey, Kinsley, Lathrop, Lincoln, Livermore, Maclay, McCoy, McCullough, Mallary, Marchand, Meech, Meigs, Monell, R. Moore, S. Moore, Morton, Moseley, Murray,

Nelson of Massachusetts, Parker of Massachusetts, Patterson, Phelps, Philson, Pitcher, Plumer, Rankin, Richards, Richmond, Robertson, Rogers, Ross, Russ, Sergeant, Silsbee, Sloan, Stevens, Street, Strong of Vermont, Strong of New York, Tomlinson, Tompkins, Tracy, Udree, Upham, Van Rensselaer, Wallace, Wendover, Whitman, and Wood—95.

NAYS—Messrs. Alexander, Allen of Tennessee, Archer of Maryland, Archer of Virginia, Baldwin, Barbour, Bayly, Bloomfield, Brevard, Brown, Brush, Bryan, Campbell, Cobb, Cocke, Crawford, Culbreth, Davidson, Earle, Edwards of North Carolina, Floyd, Garnett, Gray, Hall of North Carolina, Jackson, Johnson, Jones of Virginia, Little, McCreary, McLean of Kentucky, Mercer, Metcalf, T. L. Moore, Neale, Nelson of Virginia, Newton, Pinckney, Randolph, Reid, Rhea, Ringgold, Shaw, Simkins, Swearingen, Trimble, Tucker of Virginia, Tucker of South Carolina, Tyler, Williams of Virginia, and Williams of North Carolina—50.

THURSDAY, February 15.

Mr. NEWTON, from the Committee on Commerce, reported a bill to abolish certain ports of entry; to establish ports of delivery, and for other purposes; which was read twice, and committed.

Mr. SMITH, of Maryland, from the Committee of Ways and Means, reported a bill making appropriations for the naval service of the United States for the year 1821; which was read twice, and committed to a Committee of the whole House to-morrow.

Mr. ANDERSON, from the Committee on the Public Lands, to which was referred the bill from the Senate, entitled "An act for the relief of the purchasers of public lands prior to the first day of July, 1820," reported the same without amendment; and it was committed to the Committee of the Whole, to which is committed the bill regulating the payment of debts due from the purchasers of public lands.

Mr. EDWARDS, of North Carolina, waived for the present his intention to make a motion on the Missouri subject, according to his notice of yesterday, partly because he had little hope of success in the motion, and partly because it was probable some motion might be made more palatable to the House.

Mr. CLARK, of New York, submitted the following motion, accompanying it with some remarks in support of it:

Resolved by the Senate and House of Representatives of the United States of America, in Congress assembled, That Missouri shall be admitted into this Union on an equal footing with the original States, in all respects whatsoever, on the first Monday in December next: *Provided*, That, previous to the said first Monday in December next, Missouri shall have expunged from her constitution the following clause, to wit: "It shall be the duty of the Legislature, as soon as may be, to pass laws to prevent free negroes and mulattoes from coming to or settling in this State, under any pretext whatever." And that on said day, certified copies of said constitution, so amended, shall be delivered to the President of the Senate and Speaker of the House of Representatives of the United States.

On the question to proceed to the consideration of this resolution, it was decided in the affirmative, by a vote of 60 to 46.

Mr. CLARK, not desiring the resolution to be acted on to-day, moved to lay it on the table; and the motion was agreed to—ayes 73.

The SPEAKER laid before the House a letter from Colonel Decius Wadsworth, of the Ordnance department, explanatory of the circumstances attending the loans of powder, lead, &c., belonging to the United States, to private individuals, and which have been made the subject of inquiry in this House, as, also, containing a defence of his conduct in those transactions; which was read, and ordered to lie on the table.

The SPEAKER also laid before the House the following letter from the Secretary of War:

DEPARTMENT OF WAR, *Feb.* 12, 1821.

SIR: In compliance with a resolution of the House of Representatives of the 9th instant, directing "that the Secretary of War report to that House the progress which has been made by the Board of Engineers in determining the sites and places of fortifications of the coast of the United States; the sites which may have been selected; the estimates of the expense in completing the several works; the number of troops necessary to garrison them in peace and in war; the progress made in erecting the fortifications; the advantages resulting from the system, when completed, particularly in reducing the expense of defending the Atlantic frontier," I have the honor to enclose a report of the Board of Engineers, marked A, and a report of the Engineer department, marked B, which give the information required by the resolution.

It may be proper to observe, that the projected fortifications have been distributed into three classes, according to their relative importance, and that it is determined to erect those of the 1st class previous to the commencement of the 2d and 3d classes, with the exception of the works at Mobile Point and Dauphine Island. These works were commenced in preference to those projected at Bayou Bienvenue and Fort St. Philip; for, although the latter are placed in the first class, it was not, however, deemed proper to commence with them, as they were much less extensive than the two former, and could be completed in a short time, should the state of our relations with other Powers render it necessary.

The contractors for the works at Regolets were, by the arrangements with them, to have erected those contemplated at Chef Monteur, but so many impediments have been encountered that it has been necessary for them to confine their operations wholly to the former.

I have the honor to be, &c.
　　　　　　　　　　J. C. CALHOUN.
Hon. J. W. TAYLOR,
　Speaker House of Representatives.

The letter and accompanying documents were ordered to lie on the table.

The SPEAKER then announced the unfinished business of yesterday, being Mr. RANDOLPH's resolutions respecting the legality of the Electoral votes. And on the question, will the House now proceed to the consideration of these resolutions? it was decided in the negative, by a majority of about 30 votes.

BOUNTY TO FISHING VESSELS.

The House then, on motion of Mr. McLEAN, proceeded to the consideration of the resolution submitted by him some time ago, viz:

Resolved, That the Secretary of the Treasury be directed to communicate to this House a statement of the bounties and allowances paid to fishing vessels each year, from the commencement of the Government to the present time.

Mr. NELSON, of Massachusetts, moved to amend the same by adding thereto the following:

"And of the quantity of salt imported annually, and not re-exported with benefit of drawback; also the amount of duty annually collected on the same during the period aforesaid."

This motion to amend was negatived by a small majority.

Mr. NELSON, of Massachusetts, then moved to amend Mr. McLEAN's motion by adding thereto the following:

"And of the quantity of salt annually imported into each State and not re-exported with benefit of drawback; also, the amount of duty annually collected on the same in each State during the time aforesaid."

This amendment was agreed to; and the resolution, as amended, was then adopted, as follows:

Resolved, That the Secretary of the Treasury be directed to communicate to this House a statement of the bounties and allowances paid to fishing vessels in each year, from the commencement of the Government to the present time; and of the quantity of salt annually imported into each State, and not re-exported with benefit of drawback; also, the amount of duty annually collected on the same, in each State, during the time aforesaid.

THE SLAVE TRADE.

Mr. MEIGS, of New York, rose for the purpose of calling the attention of the House to certain resolutions which he had the honor of submitting to its consideration at the last session of Congress. These resolutions related to the subject of slavery. He had, he said, somewhat modified the resolutions offered at the last session, and would now read them to the House before he proceeded further to explain his views in relation thereto. He was aware that, on the first mention of this subject, unpleasant feelings might be excited in one part of the House, but he trusted, on examination of the proposed plan, it would appear less objectionable than was believed; and he ardently hoped, indeed, that ultimately it might be found the means of closing forever, by one of the most glorious acts of legislation that ever proceeded from any legislative body, the growing controversy between the North and South, acknowledged on all hands to be of a most serious and alarming nature. [Mr. M. read his resolutions, as below.] When, he said, it was considered that, in the certain increase of our population, doubling in twenty-five years, we should see, in half a century, not less than forty millions of people in the United States, of which perhaps twenty would be inhabitants of the vast countries beyond the Mississippi, we cannot fail to admit that the five hundred millions of acres, contemplated to be devoted as a fund for the emancipation of slaves, will have had a value more than competent to the redemption and colonization of all such of our slave population as it shall be found expedient or desirable to part with. Let me endeavor, said he, to show in a few words the practical operation of this fund. Suppose the lands, intended to constitute this fund, to be surveyed into the usual sections and quarter sections, and numbered; that the alternate numbered portions be sold for certificates of the value of slaves; that the intermediate portions be disposed of only for cash; that the certificates of value of slaves be furnished in the following manner: whenever the owner of slaves is willing to part with them, let him make application to the district judge of the district, who, with the marshal of the district, shall, together with the owner and some discreet person appointed on his part, ascertain the value of the slaves proposed to be emancipated; that, when such valuation is made, it shall be at the option of the owner finally to accede to it; that, on his consent, the district judge shall deliver to him a certificate of such valuation, which shall be receivable only in payment for the alternate sections of which I have spoken. Then, will it not be apparent, that, if such alternate sections are purchased with such certificates, the intermediate portions will acquire a value which will command sufficient sums of money to defray the expenses of colonization? Will not this operation proceed *pari passu?* Mr. M. said he had witnessed, with constant anxiety, the progress of the great controversy which now agitates us, and had, from the beginning of his career, as a member of this House, determined, if it should become necessary, to devote himself a sacrifice for the great object, if possible, of keeping the two great parties in peace. I do not know, said he, whether I have made such a sacrifice. It is probable I have, by the well known course which I have pursued upon this subject. But, sir, if indeed I have lost the confidence of those whom I represent, I will, before I leave my present station, at least make one effort for the purpose of uniting the parties by the only measure which appears to me to be calculated to unite them; one, too, in which both may participate, and in which they will, as I repeat, perform one of the most noble acts of legislation; one which I would not exchange for all the laws on our statute book from 1789 to this day. I have even indulged what may be considered an extremely romantic opinion, that the original race of Las Casas, of preventing the destruction of the Indian race by supplying their place with the hardy natives of Africa, may yet terminate in restoring to Africa, from the pressure of the great necessity which we feel on the subject, her long estranged children, with the first principles of the Christian religion and of education, so that Africa, long benighted, may assume a respectable rank among the people of the world. Mr. M. then submitted the following resolution:

Whereas slavery in the United States is an evil acknowledged to be of great and increasing magnitude, and which merits the greatest efforts of this nation to remedy; therefore,

Resolved, That a committee be appointed to inquire into the expediency of devoting five hundred millions acres of public lands next west of the Mississippi as a fund for the purpose of, in the first place, employing a naval force, competent to the annihilation of the slave trade. Secondly, the gradual emancipation of slaves, by a voluntary exchange of the lands for them; and, lastly, colonizing such emancipated slaves in such way as may be conducive to their happiness in their original country, Africa: *Provided*, That no such exchange of lands for slaves shall ever be suffered or allowed, except upon the perfectly ascertained consent of such slaves, to be colonized in Africa: *And provided also*, That, wherever such exchanges are, or shall be made, no separation of husband and wife, or parent and child, shall be permitted contrary to their well ascertained consent.

The question on proceeding to consider the resolution was decided in the affirmative—63 to 50 votes.

Mr. FLOYD said, he did not much approve of this plan himself, but, if it was to be adopted, he wished to make it as perfect as he could. He therefore moved, as an amendment, to come in immediately before the proviso, the following: "or 'distributed in equal proportions among the Con-'gressional districts of the different States, begin-'ning with the State of Maine, and so in regular 'order southward."

Mr. CLARK, of New York, moved to lay the resolution on the table.

Mr. MEIGS expressed his regret that the gentleman should have thought proper to offer this amendment, which had the air of treating his proposition with contempt. There was reason why a different treatment should have been extended to him; and he had hopes that the gentleman, to oblige him, would withdraw his proposed amendment.

Mr. FLOYD said, that the gentleman from New York was one of the last whom he should have thought of treating disrespectfully. To oblige him, he would withdraw his amendment. At the same time he thought it a good one, and that some such must necessarily be a part of any plan of the kind.

The question on laying the resolution on the table was decided in the affirmative—66 to 55.

PAY OF ARMY OFFICERS.

On the motion of Mr. COCKE, the House resolved itself into a Committee of the Whole on the bill to equalize the pay of officers of the Army.

Mr. COCKE explained to the House, much in detail, the amount of emoluments now received by the officers of the Army, &c.

The consideration of this bill, and the questions on filling the blanks with the various sums proposed, involving a discussion of the amount of compensation proper for the different grades, positively and relatively, occupied the Committee until the usual hour of adjournment.

Mr. FOOT, of Connecticut, remarked, that he had hoped some member of the committee which reported the bill would have given the answer to the gentleman from Louisiana (Mr. BUTLER) who moved to strike out the first section, with the avowed design of destroying the bill, and had expressed his full belief that no saving of money would be effected by its passage; and had also demanded of any member to point out a single instance in which even a cent would be saved by the passage of the bill. But, said Mr. F., as the gentleman who reported the bill is not in his seat, I beg leave to call the attention of the gentleman, who has made the appeal to any member, to one good effect which will result from the passage of this bill; and I presume the gentleman will be satisfied that a very considerable reduction in the expenditures in the Treasury Department will be made by its passage.

The gentleman, on a moment's reflection, must see that the saving will not be confined to the emoluments of the officers of the regular army. For the precise amount in this particular, I will refer him to the committee, who will undoubtedly be both able and willing to give the gentleman full information. But, sir, it requires no proof to convince any one, who will for one moment turn his attention to the list of clerks in the Treasury Department, whose whole employment is to examine the accounts for rations, forage, officers' quarters, fuel, servants' hire, clothing for servants, transportation of baggage, &c.; that the labors of these clerks will not be required, and, of course, their further services may well be dispensed with, if the bill shall pass; and, let me inform the gentleman, that more than one half of the present emoluments of the officers arises from the allowances for rations, forage, &c.; and, under the present system, employs the labor of at least one-fifth of the whole number of clerks, who are engaged in the settlement of the accounts of the officers.

In reply to the gentleman from Pennsylvania, (Mr. Sergeant,) I need only call his attention to the remaining sections of the bill, to furnish a complete and satisfactory answer to all his arguments in favor of striking out the first section. If the gentleman will consent to leave the first section in the bill, he may rest assured the remaining sections will obviate every objection which he has raised against the first section, and against the bill itself.

My friend from Pennsylvania (Mr. Baldwin) has challenged one good and substantial reason why salaries which have been established by law should be altered. Sir, I will endeavor to give him at least one good and substantial reason, and one which I think will satisfy him. If the salary of any officer, although it may have been fixed by law, is found inadequate to the support of the officer, or so low that a competent officer will not accept the office, I presume he would agree with me that it ought to be increased. But, sir, I have one reason to offer in favor of the reduction of the present salaries of the officers of the Government— they have within a few years been greatly increased. The Legislatures of almost every State in this Union have reduced the salaries of their own officers; this is an expression of the voice of the people, which cannot be misunderstood. I ask the gentleman to look at the proceedings of the Legislature of Pennsylvania! the voice of the

people has been fully expressed, and it must, and will be respected.

But, sir, I have other reasons for voting against the proposition to strike out the first section of this bill. Equal justice is not done to the officers under the present system. Officers of the same rank, and performing the same duties, do not receive equal compensation for the same services. The monthly pay of your officers, which is fixed by law, forms but a small part of the emoluments; other charges and allowances depend upon the statements of the officers themselves, and it is by no means certain that the most honest receive the greatest emoluments.

It is important that the compensation be fixed and known to prevent imposition and frauds. The returns, which have been made to this House during the present session, of the amount of compensation to different officers, vary very much in amount. By recurring to the printed documents, it appears that the estimated compensation to a Major General varies, or rather vibrates, from five to seven thousand dollars, while the amount of pay fixed by law is but two thousand dollars per month, making $2,400 per annum.

Sir, the people have a right to know the amount which they pay for services. This House surely ought to know it. Pass this bill; give to each a fixed salary, and you will know the precise amount. But, under the present system, I do not hesitate to say, no member of this House does know, or can know the amount which has been, or will be, paid to the officers of your army.

The Committee on Military Affairs are certainly entitled to the thanks of this House, and of the nation, for their patient and laborious investigation. And it will not be claimed that the bill does not provide liberal salaries for most of the officers in the army; but, sir, I beg leave to inquire for some reason why the salary of the Professor of Natural and Experimental Philosophy, who is the President of the Military Academy at West Point, should not be entitled to the same salary as officers in the army of the same rank? By your laws, his rank is that of a Lieutenant Colonel; and, while the bill fixes the salary of Lieutenant Colonels at $1,600 per annum, the salary which is proposed by this bill is only $1,000.

One of the members of the committee had stated that the salaries of the professors in that institution have been regulated by those of other literary institutions. But, sir, I cannot be satisfied with the salary of $1,000 for the gentleman who presides over that institution, holding the rank which the law gives him, while officers of the same grade in the army receive $1,600; and I hope the House will not concur with the Committee in filling the blank with $1,000, but will allow to this officer a salary of 1,500, according to his rank.

No gentleman will contend that his services are less arduous, or less useful, or that less talents are indispensably necessary to fill this office, than of a Lieutenant Colonel in the army. Besides, gentlemen ought to recollect that this officer was selected, by Mr. Jefferson, (then President,) on account of his superior qualifications, at the time of the first institution of this school of military science, as the first President of the Academy; and, in addition to this, that he left an office with a salary of $2,000 per annum, at the particular and urgent solicitation of that enlightened statesman. And I appeal to the Committee, whether it would be just and reasonable to make the reduction of the salary of this officer, as proposed by the bill? Can the gentleman point out a single instance in which the president of a literary institution does not receive a greater salary than the other instructors? If you refer to your laws, you there find the other professors holding the rank of Majors, and of course receiving a less salary than this officer, who holds the rank of Lieutenant Colonel. I presume it is not designed to degrade this officer from his present rank, and I hope the House will be disposed not to reduce his pay below his rank.

Having got through the bill, the Committee rose, and reported it to the House with amendments; and the House adjourned.

Friday, February 16.

In calling over the States for the reception of petitions, when petitions were called for from Tennessee—

Mr. Jones, of Tennessee, rose and said that, from the commencement of the session, he had discovered that the presiding officer of the House had, in his call for petitions from the House, uniformly called for petitions from "the delegate from Missouri;" when, in his opinion, there was no such personage in this House, and therefore moved a discontinuance of such call.

Mr. Speaker declared such motion out of order at this time, and Mr. Jones reluctantly gave way, apparently with an intention to renew the proposition when it should be in order.

Mr. Newton, from the Committee on Commerce, reported a bill to authorize the building of lighthouses on Cross and Pond Islands, in the harbor of Boothbay, and at the mouth of Oswego river, and placing buoys on the Shoals of Nantucket and Vineyard Sound, near the harbor of Wickford, and on the Altamaha river, and for other purposes; which was read twice, and committed to the Committee of the whole House to which is committed the bill making appropriations for the naval service of the United States for the year 1821.

Mr. Campbell, from the Committee on Private Land Claims, made a report on the petition of the legal representatives of Colonel John Girault, deceased, accompanied with a bill for their relief; which bill was read twice, and committed to a Committee of the Whole.

A Message, received yesterday from the President of the United States, was read, transmitting to the House the following letter from the Director of the Mint:

Mint of the United States,
January 1, 1821.

Sir: I have now the honor of laying before you a report of the operations of the Mint for the last year. From the statement of the Treasurer, herewith

transmitted, it will appear that, during this period, there have been struck at the Mint—

In gold coins, 263,806 pieces, amounting to $1,319,030 00.

In silver coins, 1,821,153 pieces, amounting to $501,680 70.

And in copper coins, 4,407,550 pieces, amounting to $44,075 50.

Making, in the whole, six millions four hundred and ninety-two thousand five hundred and nine pieces; amounting to $1,864,786 25.

The above coinage of gold and silver has, in fact, been the work of no more than nine months; for, from the deficiency of deposites, the actual coinage did not commence till the beginning of April, and was even afterwards frequently interrupted, from the same cause. The press employed in the copper coinage did not continue in operation more than six months, as the quantity of copper coins had accumulated far beyond the public demand.

From the above statement, with other well ascertained data, it may, I presume, be confidently affirmed, that the Mint, in its present improved state, will be found fully adequate to all the purposes for which it was originally established.

I have the honor to be, &c.

R. PATTERSON.

James Monroe, *President of the U. S.*

The Message was ordered to lie on the table.

PAY OF ARMY OFFICERS.

The House proceeded to consider the amendments reported from the Committee of the Whole to the bill to fix and equalize the pay of the officers of the Army of the United States; and the said amendments being read, were in part concurred in, and in part disagreed to by the House.

Mr. Cannon moved further to amend the bill, by striking out these words, being the latter clause of the 4th section: "to a cadet, one hundred and forty-four dollars per annum, and two rations per day." And, also, to insert in the bill a new section, as the fifth, to wit:

Sec. 5. *And be it further enacted,* That all laws or parts of laws, allowing pay and rations to the cadets of the Military Academy, be, and the same are hereby, repealed, from and after the 1st day of May next, and that from and after the period aforesaid the cadets are released from any obligation they may be under to remain at said Academy, or in the service of the United States.

And the question being taken to agree to the said amendment, it was determined in the negative—yeas 27, nays 116, as follows:

Yeas—Messrs. Adams, Allen of Tennessee, Baker, Ball, Blackledge, Bryan, Cannon, Cocke, Earle, Gray, Gross of New York, Hooks, Hostetter, Johnson, Kendall, McCreary, Metcalf, Patterson, Philson, Rhea, Ross, Sawyer, Strong of Vermont, Tarr, Tucker of South Carolina, Walker, and Wallace.

Nays—Messrs. Abbot, Allen of Massachusetts, Allen of New York, Anderson, Archer of Maryland, Archer of Virginia, Baldwin, Barbour, Bateman, Bayly, Beecher, Bloomfield, Boden, Brevard, Brush, Buffum, Butler of Louisiana, Campbell, Case, Clagett, Clark, Cobb, Cook, Crafts, Crawford, Crowell, Culbreth, Culpeper, Cushman, Cuthbert, Dane, Darlington, Davidson, Dennison, Dewitt, Dickinson, Edwards of Connecticut, Edwards of Pennsylvania, Edwards of North Carolina, Fay, Floyd, Foot, Ford, Fuller, Garnett, Gorham, Gross of New York. Guyon, Hackley, Hall of New York, Hall of North Carolina, Hemphill, Herrick, Hibshman, Hill, Jackson, Jones of Virginia, Kinsey, Kinsley, Lathrop, Lincoln, Little, Livermore, Maclay, McCoy, McCullough, McLean of Kentucky, Mallary, Marchand, Meigs, Montgomery, R. Moore, S. Moore, T. L. Moore, Morton, Murray, Neale, Nelson of Massachusetts, Nelson of Virginia, Newton, Parker, of Massachusetts, Parker of Virginia, Phelps, Pinckney, Pitcher, Plumer, Rankin, Rich, Richards, Richmond, Ringgold, Robertson, Rogers, Russ, Sergeant, Shaw, Silsbee, Simkins, Sloan, Smith of New Jersey, Smith of North Carolina, Stevens, Street, Strong of New York, Swearingen, Tomlinson, Tracy, Tyler, Udree, Van Rensselaer, Warfield, Wendover, Williams of Virginia, Williams of North Carolina, and Wood.

Mr. Foot moved further to amend the bill by adding to the 4th section thereof the following proviso:

Provided, That no appointment of cadets in said Academy shall be made until the number shall be reduced to one hundred: and from and after that period the number of cadets in the Military Academy at West Point shall not exceed one hundred: *And provided further,* That each cadet shall be liable to serve in the Army, at least five years, unless dismissed the service for misconduct.

And the question being taken to agree to the said proviso, it was determined in the negative.

Mr. Williams, of North Carolina, moved to amend the bill by inserting therein the following section, as the fifth:

Sec. 5. *And be it further enacted,* That the number of cadets in the Military Academy shall not, after the first day of May next, exceed one hundred; and that the supernumerary cadets shall be discharged from service, in such manner as the Secretary of War shall determine.

And the question being taken thereon, it was also determined in the negative.

Mr. Cannon then moved to amend the bill by inserting therein the following section, as the fifth, viz:

Sec. 5. *And be it further enacted,* That no cadet now in said institution, or hereafter admitted, shall be entitled to the pay and rations allowed by law, unless it shall be made appear, to the satisfaction of the Secretary of War, that the parents of the cadet are unable to pay for his support while there.

And the question being taken thereon, it was also determined in the negative.

The bill being further amended, Mr. Cannon moved to amend the fourth section thereof by striking out the word *two,* contained in the twelfth line of that section, and, in lieu thereof, inserting the word *one,* so as to reduce the cadets to one ration per day each; which motion being negatived—

Mr. Johnson said he would propose to strike out that part of the bill which related to the salaries of the officers of the army. His reasons for doing so he would state in as concise a manner as he could. He said he had voted for the reduction of the army with a view to retrenchment and economy, and that, from a view to the same principles, he was induced to make the present motion. Two objects only, he said, had been suggested for the introduction of this bill: one was to prevent impositions upon the Government, in the commutation of rations, quarters, forage, &c., the other was to save the expense of some twelve or fifteen or more clerks that were engaged in keeping these commutation accounts; that he did not conceive that that part of the bill was calculated to produce any saving to the Government, but would, in his opinion, tend to increase rather than diminish the expense. That he had been led to believe that some system of the kind proposed was necessary to prevent future abuses, and would cut off much expense to the Government; that he had therefore been favorable to any plan which would effect a beneficial change. That since the subject had been agitated, he had examined into it, and had endeavored to understand it: that his investigations and reflections had induced him to believe that the provisions of this bill would produce a very different result from what the movers of it intended: that the accounts for the commutations of rations, quarters, forage, &c., had been furnished by the War Department, item by item, which every member of the House had seen: that he had examined them, and found no such contemplated impositions. He said that whatever may have happened in former times, he felt well satisfied that, from the clear manner in which these accounts were now kept, and from the strict accountability which was diffused throughout the whole of that department, impositions of that kind could now rarely happen without detection, and detection would produce discharge from office: that as to the saving of clerks, that part of the subject was left where it was before; for by this bill, said he, you will allow transportation extra, and you will also allow the officers to have rations at the contract price, to be deducted from their wages: so that here are the same sort of accounts still to be kept, for the purpose of deduction instead of addition, which neither adds to nor diminishes the labor; so that the second object proposed *to be* attained, the saving of the expense of clerks, is also defeated.

There is, said he, another objection to the proposed change, that, however well it might look on paper, or sound in theory, it would operate most unequally and unjustly among officers of the same grade. For, example, said he, the pay of a colonel is 900 dollars per annum; his rations, if commuted for money, would amount to 438 dollars, making a total of 1,338 dollars for pay and rations. This bill proposes to give each colonel $1,800 per year, in lieu of the present pay and rations, &c., except transportation, which is still allowed.

This addition of near five hundred dollars was, he presumed, intended in lieu of forage, quarters, &c. Great portion of our army, said he, are quartered on the frontier, where quarters are furnished by the Government, and forage and fuel by the soldiers, and does not now cost the Government a cent. Is there any reason, then, for this additional pay to them? certainly not. The same grade of officers stationed in the interior and seaport towns, have necessarily to purchase their forage, fuel, &c., and the additional sum proposed may not be more than will meet what they may necessarily expend on those articles. The same argument will apply to, and the same results, said he, are applicable to, every other grade of officers in the army. The same rule is fixed for all.

Mr. J. said, for his part, he could see neither justice to the officers nor saving to the Government from the plan proposed by the sections he wished stricken out. Besides, you propose to pay each officer the same, whether he is on furlough or in actual service. By the present regulations of the War Department, no officer on furlough is entitled to either forage, fuel, transportation, or quarters. Nor does he receive them either in kind or in money, nor as many rations. Yet you give all by this bill, in service or on furlough.

Mr. JOHNSON said, that the gentleman who had reported this bill, (Mr. COCKE,) he understood to say, that the additional allowances made to the different officers was barely sufficient for the perquisites thus commuted. If, he said, it was barely sufficient for the officers on the outposts, they are not, then, sufficient for those stationed in the interior and at seaports. But, if sufficient for those in the interior and seaports, where every thing is to be purchased at the dearest rate, it is then more than sufficient for those stationed at the outposts, where these things are purchased by the soldiers and the Government without charge, and therefore operates unequally and unjustly upon the officers of the Army, and against the Government. He said he believed the old way the best, to pay for so much as is necessary, and where necessary, and not pay for it, whether necessary or not. He further said, that no officer now was allowed for forage, fuel, nor any thing else, unless necessary; and was actually used; for such, he repeated, was the accuracy and strictness with which that department was now administered, that no improper or unnecessary charge was now allowed or paid, and, if attempted, would not escape the animadversion of the head of the department.

Mr. J. said he had another objection to this part of the bill: that it was a novel attempt to convert the military into a civil department. The history of no country furnished an instance of the kind; that gentlemen would acknowledge—it would not answer for a state of war. So far as he had understood, there was no complaint as to the salaries of the officers. He believed the pay to officers was the same now as in the Revolution. But if the pay of the officers is too high, he would go with gentlemen to reduce the wages, to reduce the rations, to reduce the forage, the quarters, and every other perquisite. He could not view the present proposition as effecting any reduction; and from every view he had been able to give the subject, he saw no purpose to be answered by that part of the bill, unless it were to increase expense, to produce inequality in the pay of officers of the same grade, and to convert the military into a civil establishment. He was the advocate of economy,

but not that sort of economy proposed by this bill; an economy enhancing expenditure, and destroying the system it proposed to regulate.

Mr. J. said, that the residue of the bill he was in favor of, because it tended to lessen the expense of the Military Academy, which was in fact stationary, and a civil establishment, intended to produce materials only for war, not to move in war itself; and in relation to which no difficulty existed in commuting all perquisites.

Mr. J. said, in conclusion, that, from every consideration he had given the subject, he was of opinion that the present plan of payment, under the present arrangement and management of the department, was to be greatly preferred, in its economy to the Government, in its equality and justice to the officers, and as more consistent with the nature of military operations, to the one proposed by the part of the bill he then moved to strike out.

On motion of Mr. NELSON, of Virginia, the bill was then ordered to lie on the table.

DEATH OF WILLIAM A. BURWELL.

Mr. NELSON, of Virginia, then announced the death of WILLIAM A. BURWELL, a member of this House from that State: Whereupon,

Resolved, unanimously, That a committee be appointed to take order for superintending the funeral of WILLIAM A. BURWELL, deceased, late a Representative from the State of Virginia.

Mr. NELSON, Mr. RANDOLPH, Mr. NEWTON, Mr. McCoy, Mr. BARBOUR, Mr. TYLER, and Mr. ALEXANDER SMYTH, were appointed the said committee.

Resolved, unanimously, That the members of this House will testify their respect for the memory of William A. Burwell, late one of their body, by wearing crape on the left arm for the remainder of the session.

Resolved, unanimously, That the members will attend the funeral of the late William A. Burwell, to-morrow at 10 o'clock.

Ordered, That a message be sent to the Senate to notify them of the death of WILLIAM A. BURWELL, late a member of this House, and that his funeral will take place to-morrow, at 10 o'clock, A. M.

Mr. NELSON informed the House that it was the wish of the deceased to be interred in the city of Baltimore, and the attendance of the members on the funeral would not be required beyond the lines of the city.

And the House adjourned to 10 o'clock to-morrow morning.

SATURDAY, February 17.

The House met, and, together with the Senate, attended the funeral of the late WILLIAM A. BURWELL, in the manner recommended by the Committee of Arrangements appointed for that purpose; and, having returned to their Chamber, on motion—

The House adjourned to Monday.

MONDAY, February 19.

The SPEAKER laid before the House a letter from the Governor of Pennsylvania, enclosing the returns of the election of persons to represent that State in this House during the Seventeenth Congress; which letter and returns were ordered to lie on the table.

The SPEAKER also laid before the House a letter from the Secretary of the Treasury, transmitting a statement of the precise amount of the special deposites to the credit of the Treasury of the United States, rendered in obedience to a resolution of this House of the 16th of January last; which letter and statement were ordered to lie on the table.

Mr. SMITH, of Maryland, from the Committee of Ways and Means, reported a bill to prevent abuses in public contracts; which was read twice and ordered to lie on the table. It is as follows:

Be it enacted, &c., That, from and after the passage of this act, no clerk in any department, or other person holding an office under the Government of the United States, shall, directly or indirectly, himself, or by any other person in trust for him or for his use or benefit, or on his account, undertake, execute, hold, or enjoy, in the whole or in part, any contract or agreement hereafter to be made or entered into with any officer of the United States, on their behalf, or with any person authorized to make contracts on the part of the United States; and if any clerk or person holding an office under the Government of the United States, directly or indirectly, himself or by any other person in trust for him, or for his use or benefit, or on his account, enter into, accept of, or agree for, undertake, or execute, any such contract or agreement, on the whole or in part, every such clerk or officer so offending shall, for every like offence, upon conviction thereof before any court of the United States, or of the territories thereof, having cognizance of such offence, be adjudged guilty of a misdemeanor, and shall be fined one thousand dollars, and also be deemed incapable of holding any appointment or office under the Government of the United States; and every such contract or agreement, as aforesaid, shall moreover be absolutely void and of no effect: Provided, nevertheless, That in all cases where any sum or sums of money shall have been advanced on the part of the United States, in consideration of any such contract or agreement, the same shall be forthwith repaid; and, in case of delay or refusal to pay the same, when demanded by the proper officer of the department under whose authority such contract or agreement shall have been made or entered into, every such person so delaying or refusing, together with his surety or sureties, shall be forthwith prosecuted at law for the recovery of any such sum or sums of money advanced as aforesaid.

Mr. BALDWIN submitted to the House an amendment which he intends to propose to the bill to regulate the duties on imports and for other purposes, when the same shall come under the consideration of the House; which amendment was ordered to lie on the table.

Mr. CLAY, from the committee appointed to present to the President of the United States the resolution adopted by this House on the 10th instant, in relation to the contest now carrying on between Spain and her South American colonies, reported—

That the committee had according to order presented the resolution to the President; that the President assured the committee that, in common with the people of the United States and the House of Representatives, he felt great interest in the success of the provinces of Spanish America which are struggling to establish their freedom and independence; and that he would take the resolution into deliberate consideration, with the most perfect respect for the distinguished body from which it had emanated.

On motion of Mr. CLAY, the Committee of Claims were instructed to inquire into the expediency of making provision by law for the reimbursement to the Planters' Bank of New Orleans, of certain advances made by it upon pay rolls of the Army.

Mr. CLAY accompanied the above resolution with sundry documents in support of the claim of the said bank; which were referred to the Committee of Claims.

PAY OF ARMY OFFICERS.

The House resumed the consideration of the bill to fix and equalize the pay of the officers in the Army of the United States; when—

Mr. CASE moved further to amend the said bill, by striking out the fourth section thereof, and inserting the following sections in its stead, viz:

SEC. 4. *And be it further enacted,* That there be paid to the Superintendent of the Military Academy, one thousand eight hundred dollars per annum; to the professor of natural and experimental philosophy, one thousand six hundred dollars; to his assistant, nine hundred and fifty dollars; to the professor of mathematics, one thousand six hundred dollars; to his assistant, nine hundred and fifty dollars; to the professor of engineering and military tactics, one thousand six hundred dollars; to his assistant, nine hundred and fifty dollars; to the chaplain and professor of geography, history, and ethics, one thousand six hundred dollars; to the teacher of the French language, nine hundred and fifty dollars; to the teacher of drawing, nine hundred and fifty dollars; to the master of the sword, five hundred dollars; to each cadet, one hundred and forty-four dollars and two rations; Provided, always, That whenever the place of residence of a cadet shall be at a greater distance than one hundred miles from said Academy, he shall be allowed at the rate of twelve cents and a half per mile for his travelling expenses in going to, and returning from, said Academy; first deducting from the distance travelled one hundred miles, and allowing for no more than once going and returning.

SEC. 5. *And be it further enacted,* That no more cadets shall be admitted in said Academy until the number shall be reduced by the annual graduation to one hundred and ninety, and that after that period no greater number of cadets shall be educated at the same time in said Academy.

SEC. 6. *And be it further enacted,* That in selecting the cadets for said Academy, one shall be taken from each Congressional district, one from the District of Columbia and one from each territory, provided that application be made to the Secretary of War from the respective districts before the time for filling the vacancies has arrived; and in case there should be no application from any one or more districts, it shall be lawful for the Secretary of War to select a cadet or cadets from the other districts from which applications for admission in said Academy have been made, until the whole number of cadets shall amount to one hundred and ninety.

SEC. 7. *And be it further enacted,* That other persons than cadets, of a suitable age, (not exceeding in number one hundred,) who may be desirous of being instructed in said Academy, shall be permitted so to be, on making application to the Secretary of War for that purpose: *Provided,* That they conform in all things to the rules and regulations of said institution, and submit to the discipline of said Academy, in all respects as if they were cadets, and support themselves at their own expense during the term of their education.

SEC. 8. *And be it further enacted,* That the superintendent and each of the professors of said Academy shall be permitted to reside, during the time he shall be employed as aforesaid, in said Academy, in such one of the public buildings as the Secretary of War may designate, rent free.

Mr. CANNON moved to amend this amendment by striking out the *rations,* with the view of adding in lieu of them a certain sum to the annual allowance in money.

This motion was negatived; and the amendment of Mr. CASE, being supported by himself and opposed by Mr. COCKE, the question was taken on agreeing thereto, and decided in the negative.

Mr. F. JOHNSON, of Kentucky, proposed the amendment to the bill indicated by him on Friday last, to strike out the whole of the bill except that part which relates to the Military Academy.

This motion was negatived without debate.

Mr. CANNON, expressing his regret at having failed in his several motions to amend this bill, said he would make one other effort. He, therefore moved the amendment the part relating to the pay of the cadets, so as to allow them ninety-six dollars per annum instead of one hundred and forty-four dollars, as proposed by the bill.

Mr. CANNON said, he would not have brought this subject before the House by an amendment to the bill now under consideration, only for the circumstance that it could not be brought up in any other way during the present session. The committee to whom it had been referred had not yet made a report, and, when made, would not probably be in time to be finally acted on; and, in addition to this, the bill before the House contains provisions regulating the pay of the teachers, professors, and cadets, of this Academy; therefore, he thought this the most proper time, and the only opportunity that would be afforded, to try the sense of the House, which he wished to see expressed on the subject. He said, the amendment he had offered did not contemplate the discontinuance of this Academy, but, if adopted by the House, would lessen the public expenditure on it very much. The Academy, and the teachers and professors employed in it, would still be supported out of the Treasury of the United States, but the cadets would not receive the enormous pay and emoluments they had done heretofore. He thought the amendment he had offered went far enough, and, indeed, farther than he would go, was it entirely left to him, for he would not give one dollar out of the Treasury of the United States for its support,

or that of any other institution conducted on the same principles. He had always thought that the principles of equality were amongst the best principles maintained in our Government. Equal liberty, equal rights, and equal privileges, should always be maintained to the utmost extent by the Congress of the United States; and when peculiar favor is shown, or peculiar privileges and emoluments granted, it ought to be done only on the ground of peculiar merit. But, sir, I ask this House to reflect and consider what we are doing by maintaining this establishment, and paying to the sons of rich men the amount of $372 per year, besides some other emoluments. This is the amount that has been heretofore allowed, in pay and rations, to 250 boys or young men that may have this peculiar favor bestowed on them by the President of the United States or Secretary of War, which amounts to nothing more or less than giving to these Departments of the Government not less than one hundred thousand dollars, (the amount expended on this institution heretofore, including the pay of teachers, professors, &c.,) to be distributed among their peculiar favorites, or their sons, or relatives. I am unwilling to continue this kind of patronage to the President of the United States and the Secretary of War, or to give it to any other person; and this is not all, sir: these cadets are generally the sons of your heads of Departments, members of Congress, Governors of States, officers of the Army and Navy, and other public characters; men of wealth and influence, on whom you are not only so lavishly bestowing the people's money, but are doing what is worse, if possible; you afterwards give commissions in your Army and Navy in preference to, and to the utter exclusion of, every other person in the United States, who is not so fortunate as to be made one of this privileged order, but who has been educated at the expense of his parents or the sweat of his own brow. No matter what their merits may be; no matter how much military science, or however well qualified, they are all excluded from being officers, to give place to these favorites; and if they enter your service at all, it must be as private soldiers, to be "hewers of wood and drawers of water," for these highly favored few. Is this, I ask you, sir, consistent with the plain principles of a Republican Government? I say it is not. Let your offices be left free and open to all who may wish to obtain them by fair and honorable competition, on the ground of superior merit alone. I object to the patronage that is afforded by this institution. I also object to this mode of bestowing favor where there is no merit; and teaching, at the public expense, persons, not only for the purpose of giving them commissions in the Army, but also leading them on to be your rulers and governors in the end. The circumstance of giving these cadets a preference to the commissions in the Army, he said, was calculated to put down all spirit of emulation to acquire military science in all the other literary institutions in the United States, as well as amongst the militia officers.

What encouragement, he asked, could any young man have, to acquire military science, who is not made one of this "privileged order?" Or what inducements are held out to the officers of the militia to improve in military science, so long as these highly favored cadets are to hold of right all the commissions of your Army? You keep out all others to give places to them. But, sir, withdraw your support from this aristocratic institution, and abandon this system of keeping up a privileged order in our country, and military science will, I have no doubt, soon become a part of the instruction at other academies and colleges in the United States. He said, if he was correctly informed, there was an institution now in existence in the State of Vermont, (he alluded to the school under the direction of Captain Partridge,) where every branch of military science was taught to the same perfection that it was at West Point, and he had no doubt that it would be sufficient to furnish the Army with plenty of officers, could they have a preference given them, without the expenditure of the public money to qualify them. I am in favor, said he, of military science, when taught on any general plan that will diffuse it among the great mass of the people, and I am opposed to this kind of science being confined to a few, as is the case, in regard to the course heretofore pursued. He denied the right of the House of Representatives to appropriate the people's money to any such partial purposes. I will admit, said he, that benefits are derived from this institution to all those who obtain so much of the favor of the Executive as to get their sons not only educated at the public expense, but receive large sums of money besides, as a bounty.

This benefit, I have no doubt, is generally bestowed on the rich ; the poor never have nor never will obtain much of it ; and he did not know that it added much to the science of the country in general ; for those persons who had their sons educated at this academy, at the public expense, were generally able to give them an education at their own expense, and would do so if deprived of this privilege, which enabled them only to save the expense they would otherwise incur, and lay up something besides out of the pay given the cadets. This institution was first set on foot, said Mr. C., in the year 1802, when only ten cadets were allowed to be kept there; and this continued to be the whole number until the year 1812, (about the time the declaration of war took place,) when the number of the cadets was increased to two hundred and fifty, the present number allowed by law, with the pay of sixteen dollars per month, and two rations each; some other emoluments have been allowed, he believed, besides. Thus it has crept along, in the shade of executive and legislative patronage, about eighteen years, without any inquiries having been made respecting the amount of public money expended on it, or the people of the United States knowing much about the policy or principles it is calculated to promote. He believed he could venture to say that the people knew very little about this Military Academy; nor had they generally enjoyed much of its benefits, notwithstanding the vast amount of their money that has been expended to keep it up. He had

no doubt but that the heads of the departments of the Government, the members of Congress, and their particular friends, had enjoyed a very large share of the benefits resulting from this mode of expending the public money. Establish a few more institutions of the same character, and what is the consequence? Why, sir, it must be to take the Government out of the hands of the people. And, if it is so important that you should educate officers for your regular Army at public expense, it is equally as important to educate persons at public expense to fill all the other departments of the Government; and, by the same rule, when you establish those institutions, you must exclude all who are not admitted to be educated there from a participation, or even a chance of obtaining those offices. Sir, I have said, on a former occasion, it was an aristocracy; and I repeat it to be one, of the rankest order, not only that ever existed in this Government, but that ever existed in any known Government on the face of the earth. I have repeatedly challenged the supporters of this institution to meet me on this point, and show its Republican features; but they have not as yet undertaken it, nor is it in their power to controvert the facts I have stated to the House.

Gentlemen misunderstand me when they suppose that I am opposed to the encouragement of military science. If they will only take the trouble to examine the provisions of a bill I have reported to the House, (by the direction of the committee on the subject of militia,) they will find I am in favor of diffusing military science throughout the whole United States, not only to extend it to every State and Territory, but equally to every brigade, regiment, and even to every captain's company. They will there see a plan proposed annually to teach and instruct 60,000 (being the whole number of the militia officers of the United States, of every grade) in all the duties necessary for a state of war; and that, too, on principles of republicanism, on principles consistent with, and congenial to, the free principles of our own Government. This was, he said, a great system, for it was calculated to diffuse military science throughout the whole United States, and to extend it equally to every militia officer. This system has been objected to, in conversation and out of doors, because it will cost too much; but if the House should, in the course of the session, indulge him so far as to take up the bill he had referred to, he would show, by arithmetical calculation, that this system to extend military science to the whole militia of the United States would cost less than $500,000 annually, a sum not much greater than was required to maintain, in the regular service, one regiment, and only five times the amount expended at this Military Academy ; the sum he had stated he could show would be sufficient to encamp the whole militia officers of the United States one week, for instruction, in each year, and pay them their full pay, as though they were in service, also provide them with rations. His course was to retrench the expenses of this Military Academy, in order to enable us better to adopt the system he had alluded to.

But, Mr. Speaker, if we keep up a Military Academy at the public expense, for whose benefit should it be maintained? I say, sir, it ought to be for the benefit of the orphan of him who has fallen in defence of his country; but they have not enjoyed the benefit of this institution, nor ever can, until you change your laws on the subject. I hold the doctrine that there is an obligation on the part of the Government to support the widow and orphan of those who have fallen in its defence, until they are able to protect and support themselves; but what have you done for them? Why, sir, you have turned them off at the age of five years; they are driven from the door of your bounty, to starve or be supported and protected by their friends, or the society of their neighborhoods, to give place to these favorites—this privileged order, composed of the sons of the wealthy, who never fought in your defence. This is what we are doing; and I beg gentlemen to reflect, and look at the course they are pursuing. I am indeed glad that the orphans of those whose blood has been shed in defence of our liberty have been taken notice of by Congress; but let us see what it is we have done for the family of a poor soldier whose life has been sacrificed on the altar of our liberties, and has left in our charge a wife and nine helpless children. We have, it is true, allowed them half pay for five years, amounting, in the whole period, to $240: this is all you have done to support this whole family, of ten times in number, for five years, while you give a much larger sum to support the son of a rich man, who never shouldered a gun in the defence of his country, one year, as a cadet at this Military Academy. You have given each of the orphans I have alluded to only forty cents per month for support, while you give a cadet thirty-one dollars per month in pay and rations for his support.

You have given your orphans only four dollars and eighty cents each year.

And have given your cadets three hundred and seventy-two dollars each year.

You have given your orphans only twenty-four dollars each, in the whole five years.

And have given your cadets one thousand eight hundred and sixty dollars each in the same period, in pay and rations, besides other emoluments that are not taken into view in the above estimate.

Mr. Speaker, I ask you, and I ask every member of this House, if this looks as if we had been governed either by the principle of justice or equality. No, sir, we have abandoned them long since, and pay no regard to them whatever, for the purpose of creating and supporting this odious aristocracy. I have found great difficulty in even obtaining an inquiry respecting it, and I fear it will be still more difficult to put it down. I fear the anticipations of a very respectable and intelligent correspondent of mine will be realized, who, after speaking of the course I have heretofore pursued, and am now pursuing, in regard to this institution, in terms of approbation has said, " he feared all my exertions would be unavailing, because it gives patronage to all the members of Congress." Yes, sir, it is too true: it does give patronage to

16th Con. 2d Sess.—38

the members of this House and of the Senate, as well as the Executive and heads of Departments, for it is them, and their particular friends, who enjoy the whole benefits of this vast expenditure of the public money; nor do I believe they will unite with me in reducing the expenditure of the public money on it until forced to do so by their constituents, who will remain silent on this subject just so long as they are kept in ignorance. This has been the case heretofore, I have no doubt; but the people generally have known little or nothing about the principles on which it was conducted, nor the effect it is calculated to produce in our Government. But, sir, so far as it is in my power to give the people of the United States information, they shall have it, on this subject as well as on all others. It is their right to know the purposes to which you appropriate their money; and they ought to know and understand truly the principles on which we legislate. I deny that any public benefit whatever is derived from this Military Academy. Your Army would be as well filled with officers without it as it was with it—perhaps better—and with an equal portion of military science. Put down this aristocracy, this way of monopolizing the offices in the Army, and leave them free and accessible to all, on the ground of merit alone, and you will always find a sufficient number who will qualify themselves in order to obtain them. But, so long as you keep up this system of giving such bounty without regard to merit—this system of a kind of hereditary succession to offices from which all others are excluded, you suppress and discourage every possible motive in others to obtain the qualifications requisite to fill those offices. Such a course is calculated in the end to sap the very foundation of our liberties, and will not, I have no hesitation in saying, be supported by the people in any part of the United States, when they fairly examine and properly understand the effects that it is calculated to produce in our Government.

Mr. Warfield replied to Mr. Cannon, and the question being taken on Mr. Cannon's motion, it was decided in the negative, 70 to 31.

The bill was then ordered to be engrossed for a third reading, without a division.

PUBLIC LAND DEBT.

On motion of Mr. Crowell the several orders of the day were postponed, in order to take up the bill from the Senate for the relief of certain purchasers of public lands; and the House resolved itself into a Committee of the Whole on the said bill.

Some time was spent in Committee of the Whole on the bill, in the course of which Mr. Crowell made some remarks in favor of the bill, Mr. McCoy, and Mr. Allen, of Tennessee, against it, and Mr. Wood, rather in doubt on the subject than in opposition to the bill. Mr. Campbell, Mr. Anderson, Mr. Hendricks, and Mr. Cook, suggested and supported the propriety of the Committee's rising and obtaining leave to sit again, it being obvious that the House had prematurely entered on the subject, and were not prepared to act upon it. [There were barely a hundred members in the House, many being absent, attending the argument on the great question this day argued in the Supreme Court.]

Mr. ALLEN, of Tennessee, observed, that he was in favor of the motion made by his honorable friend from Virginia, to strike out the second section of the bill before the Committee, and would be glad to see the first section go with it, being opposed to the principle entire.

Sir, said he, before I can agree to part with as much of the public revenue as is contemplated to be thrown away by this bill, I must be better satisfied that the objects upon whom it is to be bestowed deserve it. If the people learn that debts can be paid with petitions and fair stories, you will soon have your table crowded. The next application will be from those who have completed their payments, asking Congress to refund as much as will place them on an equality with those now to be relieved. Numbers have already forfeited, and thought themselves well out of a bad bargain at that; but, have they not a fair claim on having returned to them all that was paid, if you cancel the contract and prevent such an occurrence with others. Sir, if we begin the work either with a view of doing justice, or an act of beneficence, there is no point at which we can stop without greater cause of complaint. At this time the Government is under no obligation or promise, directly or indirectly, to meddle at all in this matter; but, advance one step in changing the contracts of these people, and, by a legislative interference, alter the relation between debtor and creditor, and you will have to go the whole length; nothing short of the land, in their own way, and at their own price, will suit them. We are told there is not money in the country to pay this enormous debt, and to attempt exacting it is requiring from the people who owe it impossibilities. Not so, Mr. Chairman. Let them alone, and the existing laws will set the matter right; in five years, the Government will either have the money or the land; and the situation of him who has had the worst of it—if you please, forfeited his claim to the land on which he has paid something—still his situation is preferable to that of all others who went in debt for property when every thing run high, and, as it were, was at a bubble price, which bursted round him before pay day came. The purchaser of public land under existing laws is relieved from debt by forfeiting a bad bargain, losing only one-fourth, or the sum paid in advance, often in that way advantageously getting out of a bad bargain. But, between individuals, the last farthing must be paid, whatever may have been the loss upon the purchase; and in every part of the country you may find men that have purchased property that would not now sell for half the sum given for it. No relinquishment for them; no cancelling the contract, or compounding with creditors, as long as there is any thing found to make the money out of, although the money for which the debt was raised will not satisfy one-tenth part thereof under an execution. What has that class of debtors done to prevent their sharing in this benevolent act of

grace? Have they no part in the common stock about to be distributed? We have the same right to relieve the one as the other; the difference is only between giving money out of the Treasury and permitting that to be withheld which ought to be there. I know of no class of men who have less claim upon the paternal indulgence or gracious favor of the Government than most of the purchasers of public land—I mean that portion most clamorous for relief, and the most to be benefited by this bill. They associated themselves in companies, with all the money the banks (with whom they were mostly connected) could lend, and at the auction sales put down all competition from actual settlers; the prudent man's home was bought over his head, at a price he could not give for it. It is now in the hands of one of these speculators, who has other lands adjoining. Will you pass a law that permits him to keep it by a relinquishment of other bad bargains, thus avoiding the payment of a price which deterred the occupant from buying? Certainly nothing is more unjust.

Such is the effect intended to be produced by the first section of this bill, going to make the Government insure a profit to him who bids highest, and a party with him, in fact, in a fraud practised on others by a show of price never intended to be paid. Could any scheme be invented more effectually to suit the purpose of those who were determined to have the choice that they have had, and, after selecting and buying all they wanted, and effectually trying the market, and finding what could be made out of the speculation, we must play to their hand, and secure to them all that is profitable, and relieve them from that which is not. I don't know who would not buy lands under these circumstances.

Sir, I am aware that these remarks do not apply to all the purchasers of public land, and that many actual settlers will find great difficulty in making payment; but they never would have thought of coming here with such a demand as this bill embraces had they not been encouraged by that knowing class which depends on management to get relieved, and out of the toils they had intended for others. I do not believe that many of the actual settlers on tracts purchased alone for cultivation are going to forfeit their lands, notwithstanding all we have heard said. They have carefully laid up every dollar that they have been able to lay their hands on since the purchase; the sum lacking they can procure at a trifling sacrifice, which they are content to make. The land forfeited will be by the speculator, whose only dependence was on making sales to meet the purchase money. If he has been disappointed, has he any right to call on the whole community to bear his loss? No; no more than they would have had to share his profit, had his expectations been realized. Let us not direct all our sympathy to one particular class of traders; others are looking on. The sufferers in the late war remember how coldly many of them have been treated here, who in their favor could plead that their loss grew out of acts of the Government over which they had

1189   HISTORY OF CONGRESS.   1190

FEBRUARY, 1821.   *Reduction of Salaries—Pay of Army Officers.*   H. OF R.

no control. What will they say at this display of beneficence towards those who only have themselves to blame?

If sympathy and feeling are permitted to guide us in legislating for the Union, have the purchasers of the public land any right to the exclusive exercise of it? I think not; and, in making this demand, their friends have inconsiderately defeated an object, that might have been attained, by going too far, and asking too much; for, whatever might have been my course towards them in times of peculiar difficulty like the present, had their application been confined to an extension of time only, I have no hesitation in saying that what they now claim is unreasonable, and has put me on my guard against doing any thing that encourages demands that must lead to a total abolition of the whole debt. Before we begin this gracious act, would it not be well to inquire whose money it is we are bestowing away, and think of an old maxim, which teaches us to be just before we are generous?

On motion of Mr. ANDERSON the Committee rose, reported progress, and obtained leave to sit again.

REDUCTION OF SALARIES.

On motion of Mr. CULBRETH, the House resolved itself into a Committee of the Whole on the state of the Union to take into consideration the bill for a general reduction of the salaries of the officers of the Government.

The bill having been read—

Mr. CULBRETH stated that the Committee had been influenced by different considerations in agreeing to the report; but that, for himself, he had been influenced by the single consideration whether the salaries in the several cases embraced by the bill are or are not at present more than sufficient. Where he thought them no more than sufficient he had voted against their reduction, and for their reduction where he thought them otherwise.

The Committee then proceeded with the consideration of the details of the bill.

On motion of Mr. KINSEY, after a considerable debate on the merits of the Patent Office, its duties, &c., that part of the bill which proposes to reduce the salary of the Clerk of the Patent Office to five hundred dollars per annum, was stricken out.

On motion of Mr. LIVERMORE, the part of the bill which proposes to reduce the salary of the Superintendent of the Patent Office to one thousand dollars, was also stricken out.

A motion, by Mr. SERGEANT, was under consideration for excluding the Librarian's compensation from the proposed reduction; when the Committee rose and reported progress.

Mr. LIVERMORE moved to discharge the Committee of the Whole from the further consideration of the bill, and to lay it on the table; but the motion was negatived, 63 to 48.

TUESDAY, February 20.

Mr. KENT presented a memorial of Joseph Pearson, Thomas Law, and Daniel Carroll of Dud-

dington, proprietors of a large amount of real property in the City of Washington, complaining of the conduct of the corporate authorities in the said city, and of the exorbitant amount of taxes levied and collected by them, and praying that further provisions may be enacted by Congress upon the subject of the imposition and collection of taxes in said city; which petition was referred to the Committee for the District of Columbia.

Mr. NEWTON, from the Committee of Commerce, reported a bill for the relief of Nathaniel Carver, and others; which was twice read, and committed.

Mr. SMITH, of Maryland, from the Committee of Ways and Means, reported a bill further to amend the several acts relative to the Treasury, War, and Navy Departments; which was twice read, and committed. [This bill proposes to abolish the agency of the Treasurer for the War and Navy Departments.]

Mr. FORREST presented a letter addressed to him by Lieutenant Colonel George Bomford, accompanied with sundry documents, in relation to the loans of gunpowder and other munitions of war, from the public magazines, to private individuals; which were ordered to lie on the table.

Mr. FULLER, from the Committee on Naval Affairs, reported the bill from the Senate for the relief of Samuel Tucker, late a captain in the Navy of the United States, with an amendment.

Mr. METCALF moved to refer the bill to a Committee of the Whole.

Mr. COBB moved that the bill be postponed indefinitely, which motion was negatived, by yeas and nays—79 to 66.

The amendment to the bill having been agreed to, the question was taken on ordering the bill to a third reading, as amended, and decided in the negative, by a majority of one vote. So the bill was rejected.

A message from the Senate informed the House that the Senate have passed a bill, entitled "An act to establish an uniform system of bankruptcy throughout the United States," in which they ask the concurrence of this House.

The bill was read twice, and referred to the Committee on the Judiciary.

PAY OF ARMY OFFICERS.

An engrossed bill, entitled "An act to fix and equalize the pay of the officers of the Army of the United States," was read the third time; and on the question, Shall the said bill pass? it passed in the affirmative—yeas 106, nays 39, as follows:

YEAS—Messrs. Adams, Alexander, Allen of Tennessee, Anderson, Archer of Maryland, Archer of Virginia, Baker, Ball, Barbour, Bateman, Bayly, Beecher, Boden, Bryan, Buffum, Campbell, Cannon, Cobb, Cocke, Crafts, Culbreth, Culpeper, Cushman, Cuthbert, Dane, Dennison, Earle, Eddy, Edwards of N. Carolina, Fay, Fisher, Floyd, Foot, Forrest, Fuller, Garnett, Gray, Gross of New York, Gross of Pennsylvania, Guyon, Hall of New York, Hall of North Carolina, Hardin, Hendricks, Herrick, Hibshman, Hill, Hobart, Hooks, Hostetter, Jackson, Jones of Virginia, Kinsley, Lathrop, Lincoln, Maclay, McCoy, McCreary, McLean of Kentucky, Mallary, Marchand, Meigs,

Metcalf, Monell, Montgomery, R. Moore, T. L. Moore, Morton, Moseley, Murray, Nelson of Massachusetts, Nelson of Virginia, Parker of Massachusetts, Patterson, Phelps, Philson, Plumer, Rhea, Rich, Richards, Richmond, Robertson, Rogers, Ross, Russ, Shaw, Silsbee, Sloan, Southard, Stevens, Strong of Vermont, Tarr, Terrell, Tomlinson, Tracy, Tucker of Virginia, Tucker of South Carolina, Tyler, Upham, Van Rensselaer, Walker, Wendover, Williams of Virginia, Williams of North Carolina, and Wood.

Nays—Messrs. Abbot, Allen of New York, Baldwin, Brush, Butler of Louisiana, Case, Clark, Cook, Crowell, Darlington, Davidson, Dewitt, Dickinson, Folger, Ford, Hackley, Johnson, Jones of Tennessee, Kent, Little, Livermore, Mercer, S. Moore, Neale, Newton, Parker of Virginia, Pinckney, Pitcher, Reid, Ringgold, Sergeant, Simkins, Smith of New Jersey, Smith of Maryland, A. Smyth of Virginia, Street, Swearingen, Udree, and Wallace.

REDUCTION OF SALARIES.

The Committee of the Whole on the state of the Union were discharged from the further consideration of the bill to reduce the salaries and fix the maximum of the compensation of certain officers and other persons employed in the Civil Department of the Government.

Mr. Crowell then moved that the bill lie on the table; which being negatived.

The House then proceeded to consider the bill: when, Mr. Silsbee moved to amend the same by adding five hundred dollars per annum to the salary of each of the Commissioners of the Navy Board; which motion was negatived,

Mr. Wood moved to strike out of the first section of the bill these words: to the Commissioner of the Public Buildings, one thousand five hundred dollars. Agreed to.

Mr. Robertson moved to insert, after the word dollars, in the 22d line of the first section of the printed bill these words: "To the Secretary of the Senate, three thousand dollars; to the Clerk of the House of Representatives, three thousand dollars." Negatived.

Mr. Silsbee moved so to amend that part of the first section of the bill which relates to the salaries of the Naval Constructors, to read thus: "To the first Naval Constructor, two thousand three hundred dollars, and to each of the other Naval Constructors, two thousand dollars; which being negatived,

Mr. Sergeant moved to strike out from the first section of the bill these words: "To the Librarian, one thousand dollars;" which motion was also negatived.

Mr. Cocke moved to amend the first section of the bill by adding five hundred dollars to the salary of the First Comptroller of the Treasury. Negatived.

Mr. Nelson, of Virginia, then moved to amend the bill by inserting after the word *designated*, in the fifth line of the second section of the printed bill these words: *whose compensation exceeds eight hundred dollars per annum ;* so as to confine the reduction of twenty per cent., therein provided, to such salaries as exceed eight hundred dollars per annum.

Mr. Warfield moved to amend the amendment by striking out eight hundred dollars, and inserting one thousand two hundred dollars; which motion was negatived.

Mr. Nelson then modified his amendment, which was agreed to as follows: "Provided, nev-' ertheless, that no salary now established by law ' at or under eight hundred dollars per annum ' shall be reduced: And provided, further, that no ' salary now established by law at a sum above ' eight hundred dollars per annum shall be reduced ' below that sum."

The bill was then further amended: when

Mr. Campbell moved further to amend the same by inserting the following sections, to come in after the first sections thereof, viz:

Sec. 2. *And be it further enacted,* That at every session of Congress, and every meeting of the Senate in the recess of Congress, each Senator shall be entitled to receive six dollars for every day he shall attend the Senate, and shall also be allowed six dollars for every twenty miles of the estimated distance by the most usual road from his place of residence to the seat of Congress; at the commencement and end of every such session and meeting; and in case any member of the Senate shall be detained by sickness on his journey to or from such session or meeting, or after his arrival shall be unable to attend the Senate, he shall be entitled to the same daily allowance; and the President of the Senate *pro tempore,* when the Vice President shall be absent, or when his office shall be vacant, shall, during the period of his services, receive, in addition to his compensation as a member of the Senate, six dollars for every day he shall attend the Senate: *Provided,* That no Senator shall be allowed a sum exceeding the rate of six dollars a day from the end of one such session or meeting, to the time of his taking a seat in another.

Sec. 3. *And be it further enacted,* That at every session of Congress, each representative and delegate shall be entitled to receive six dollars for every day he shall attend the House of Representatives, and shall also be allowed six dollars for every twenty miles of the estimated distance by the most usual road from his place of residence to the seat of Congress, at the commencement and end of every such session; and in case any representative or delegate shall be detained by sickness on his journey to or from the session of Congress, or after his arrival shall be unable to attend the House of Representatives, he shall be entitled to the same daily allowance; and the Speaker of the House of Representatives shall be entitled to receive, in addition to his compensation as a representative, six dollars for every day he shall attend the House: *Provided, always,* That no representative or delegate shall be allowed a sum exceeding the rate of six dollars a day from the end of one session to the time of his taking his seat in another.

Sec. 4. *And be it further enacted,* That the said compensation which shall be due to the members of the Senate shall be certified by the President thereof; and that which shall be due to the representatives and delegates shall be certified by the Speaker, and the same shall be passed as public accounts, and paid out of the public Treasury.

The said amendment was read; when

The House adjourned.

WEDNESDAY, February 21.

A message from the Senate informed the House that the Senate have passed a bill, entitled " An act to amend an act, entitled 'An act to incorporate the subscribers to the Bank of the United States ;" and a resolution proposing the appointment of a joint committee to wait upon the President of the United States, and inform him of his re-election to that office, and have appointed a committee on their part; in which bill and resolution they ask the concurrence of this House.

On motion of Mr. CLAY, the report of the Secretary of the Treasury, made on the 8th instant, in the case of James Morrison, concerning his advances to Colonel Buford, together with the additional documents presented by him on the 19th instant, was recommitted to the Secretary of the Treasury, with instructions to report thereon to the House of Representatives at the next session of Congress.

The SPEAKER laid before the House a letter from the Secretary of the Treasury, communicating the information required by the resolution of the 15th instant, on the subject of bounties and allowances paid to fishing vessels, and the quantity of salt imported, and not re-exported with benefit of drawback, and amount of duties thereon ; which letter and statement were read, and ordered to lie on the table.

The bill from the Senate, amendatory of the charter of the Bank of the United States, was twice read and committed.

Mr. SERGEANT, from the Judiciary Committee, to whom was referred the bill from the Senate, to establish an uniform system of bankruptcy throughout the United States, reported the same without amendment ; and, on motion of Mr. SERGEANT, the bill was ordered to lie on the table, with a view to being called up thereafter.

Mr. SERGEANT, from the same committee, reported the following resolution :

Resolved, by the Senate and House of Representatives of the United States of America in Congress assembled, That where any State or States, having complied with the recommendation of Congress in the resolution of the 23d of September, 1789, shall have withdrawn, or shall hereafter withdraw, either in whole or in part, the use of their jails for prisoners committed under the authority of the United States, the marshal in such State or States, under the direction of the judge of the district, shall be, and hereby is authorized and required, to hire a convenient place to serve as a temporary jail, and to make the necessary provision, until provision shall be made by law for that purpose, and the said marshal be allowed his reasonable expenses incurred for the above purposes, to be paid out of the Treasury of the United States.

The resolution having been briefly explained by Mr. SERGEANT, to have become necessary by the recent proceedings of the State of Ohio, was ordered to be engrossed for a third reading without a division.

Mr. CLAY rose to give notice to the House, that he should on to-morrow make a motion, the ultimate object of which was the declaration of the admission of the State of Missouri into the Union.

Mr. WOOD, from the Committee on the Public Buildings, who were instructed to inquire into the practicability of more effectually ventilating the Hall of the House of Representatives, made a report thereon ; which was read, and the resolution therein submitted concurred in by the House, as follows :

Resolved, That the Commissioner and the Architect of the Public Buildings be instructed to take measures more effectually to ventilate the Hall of the House of Representatives by the next session of Congress, either by tubes communicating with apertures in the body of the Hall, or in such other way as may, on further inquiry, be deemed more advisable.

On motion of Mr. STORRS, a committee was appointed, jointly with such committee as may be appointed by the Senate, to inquire and report what subjects before the two Houses are proper to be acted on during the present session of Congress ; and Messrs. STORRS, SERGEANT, and BARBOUR, were appointed the committee on the part of this House.

A message from the Senate informed the House that the Senate have passed a bill, entitled "An act further to establish the compensation of the officers employed in the collection of duties on imports and tonnage, and for other purposes ;" in which they ask the concurrence of this House.

The resolution from the Senate for the appointment of a joint committee to wait on the President of the United States, and notify him of his re-election to the office of President of the United States, was read, and agreed to by the House; and Messrs. SMITH, of Maryland, and EUSTIS, were appointed of the committee on the part of this House.

CAPTAIN TUCKER.

On motion of Mr. ALLEN, of Massachusetts, the House agreed to reconsider the vote, whereby the bill granting a pension to Commodore Samuel Tucker was yesterday rejected.

The bill was amended, so as to reduce the proposed annuity to the rate of $20 per month ; and, the question being put on ordering the bill, so amended, to be read a third time, it was decided by yeas and nays: For the third reading 70, against it 70, as follows:

YEAS—Messrs. Adams, Allen of Massachusetts, Allen of New York, Baldwin, Bateman, Bayly, Beecher, Brush Campbell, Case, Clark, Clay, Crowell, Culpeper, Cushman, Dane, Darlington, Dennison, Edwards of Pennsylvania, Eustis, Fay, Folger, Ford, Forrest, Fuller, Gorham, Guyon, Hackley, Hemphill, Hendricks, Herrick, Hill, Hobart, Kendall, Kinsley, Kinsey, Lathrop, Lincoln, Maclay, McCreary, McCullough, Mallary, Meech, Meigs, Mercer, Monell, S. Moore, Moseley, Murray, Neale, Nelson of Virginia, Newton, Parker of Massachusetts, Pinckney, Pitcher, Reid, Rogers, Russ, Silsbee, Simkins, Sloan, Smith of New Jersey, Street, Strong of Vermont, Swearingen, Tucker of Virginia, Udree, Walker, Wallace, and Whitman.

NAYS—Messrs. Alexander, Allen of Tennessee, Anderson, Archer of Maryland, Archer of Virginia, Baker, Ball, Barbour, Blackledge, Boden, Bryan, Buffum, Cannon, Clagett, Cobb, Cocke, Crafts, Culbreth, Cuthbert, Dewitt, Earle, Eddy, Edwards of North Carolina, Floyd, Foot, Garnett, Gray, Gross of Pennsylvania, Hall of New York, Hall of North Carolina, Hardin, Hooks, Hostetter, Jackson, Johnson, Kent, Livermore, McCoy, McLean of Kentucky, Marchand, Metcalf, R. Moore, Parker of Virginia, Patterson, Phelps, Philson, Plumer, Rhea, Richards, Richmond, Robertson, Ross, Shaw, A. Smyth of Virginia, Smith of North Carolina, Southard, Stevens, Storrs, Tarr, Terrell, Tomlinson, Tompkins, Tracy, Tucker of South Carolina, Tyler, Wendover, Williams of Virginia, Williams of North Carolina, and Wood.

The votes being equal, the Speaker voted in the affirmative. So the bill was passed, and ordered to be read a third time to-morrow.

MISSOURI.

Mr. Brown, of Kentucky, submitted for consideration the following resolution:

Resolved, That the Committee on the Judiciary be directed to inquire into the expediency of repealing the 8th section of the act of Congress, approved March 6, 1820, entitled "An act to authorize the people of the Missouri Territory to form a constitution and State government, and for the admission of such State into the Union, on an equal footing with the original States, and to prohibit slavery in certain Territories;" said 8th section imposing a prohibition and restriction upon the introduction of slaves in all that territory ceded by France to the United States, under the name of Louisiana, which lies north of 36 degrees 30 minutes north latitude, not included in the State contemplated by that act.

On submitting the resolution, Mr. Brown addressed the Chair as follows:

Mr. Speaker: I rise, with unfeigned reluctance, to present to the consideration of this honorable body the resolution which I hold in my hand, with a concise statement of the views upon which it is founded. Nothing short, sir, of an imperative sense of duty would have influenced me, at this late day of the session, to have consumed one moment of that time which has become so important to the interest of this nation. I have been imboldened to ask your attention, and that of the honorable body over which you preside, from a reflection that a few days more will close my Congressional labors, probably forever, and that, up to this period, I have been sparing of your time, and do not expect again, while I remain on the floor, to ask your indulgence.

Mr. Speaker, while taking leave of those with whom it has been my honor to be associated in the councils of the nation, I feel a pleasure which I cannot suppress, at the recollection that there has prevailed between myself and them entire personal respect, and as much harmony and friendship as has been at all possible, considering the embarrassing and distracting subject which has haunted us, by day and by night, from the beginning to the end of each session; and I can say, with an approving conscience, that I have not malice or ill will against any. Sir, while indulging this pleasing train of reflection, an unpleasant occurrence of the last session intrudes itself upon my mind; and I cannot fail to do what I consider an act of justice towards an honorable and venerable member from New Hampshire, (Mr. Livermore,) the only person towards whom I have been betrayed into an illiberal expression. Designing to be ever prompt in the protection of my own feelings, I hope I shall always be inclined, when convinced of having unwarrantably assailed the feelings of another, to make reparation. The occasion has passed by; the honorable member and myself are, and have been during this session, upon good terms; but the injury, if it deserve the appellation, was a public one, from this seat; and before I leave it, I will use it to do as ample justice. During the fermentation of the last session, under the influence of excitement from this miserable subject, in some remarks made by me to the House, I attributed to the gentleman what I then believed an attempt, with an unworthy view, to operate upon the minds of members. During the present session I have had an opportunity, and have used it, to become better acquainted with that honorable gentleman, and I have found him an useful, fair, and liberal member, and an agreeable associate; and, had further evidence been wanting, a late occasion has afforded it. After the resolution for the admission of Missouri into the Union had been rejected by about three votes, it was believed by his friends that, if several members who were accidentally out of their seats had voted, Missouri would have been admitted. This gentleman, although opposed to them on the resolution, to afford an opportunity of a fair and full trial of strength, moved and obtained a reconsideration; and, although the result did not justify our expectations, I accord most heartily to the gentleman the reward of my humble applause for his magnanimity; and I am now free to say, that I did him injustice in the imputation of the last session.

Having closed, Mr. Speaker, my affairs with the House, I now proceed to prepare for a settlement of the account with my conscience and my constituents. Sir, this is the more necessary when I assure you that I came here upon their feelings of good will and indulgence, more than upon an exercise of their judgments; and that, having thought it prudent to decline a re-election, they still bore evidence of a continuation of their kindness, by uttering some expressions of regret. I feel grateful for their favors, and my highest ambition, on leaving the disturbed theatre from which I retire, is to maintain their good opinions and wishes. I made them no vain promises of doing, or attempting to do, much; but I did promise to be faithful and zealous in watching over and preserving their best interests, as far as my humble qualifications should enable me to do. Owing, sir, to that credulity incident to sincerity and inexperience, I feel myself constrained to acknowledge my co-operation in so managing the subject of Missouri and restriction, as to have inflicted upon their interest an extensive injury. My object is to regain for them, by following up the purpose of this resolution, a part of what has been lost by mismanagement; but, should I fail in this, I shall gain the consolation of having done my duty. The object of this resolution I never should have favored; so far from it, that I should have felt myself dishonored by giving it support or encouragement, had not faith been broken by the other party to the compact, and Missouri been rejected. This having been done, I feel myself at liberty—nay, more, I feel it my imperative duty—to offer this resolution. I will state that, at the solicitation of a friend from Pennsylvania, (Mr. BALDWIN,) I have been already induced, for a short time, to delay the introduction of the resolution, upon the ground that the majority would probably originate some measure by which Missouri would be admitted before Congress adjourned, and that it might, by some, be construed into a menace. Having no such design, feeling a high confidence in the good will and judgment of my friend, and wishing not to disoblige him, I have yielded to him in making some delay. If, sir, I have any trait in my character more prominent, and in which I feel more pride than others, it is that of sincerity. I happily feel a contempt for one who endeavors to beget impressions, and raise expectations, without an intention of supporting and realizing them. I have but little charity for the man who falls below his boasted feats and purposes. I acknowledge that I can see no good ground for an expectation that any thing further can now be done. The few remaining days of the session are fast whiling away, and I contemplate leaving here before its close. The minority, sir, have urged peace and good will, and have acknowledged and cringed, until I feel myself driven to the wall, and my feelings outraged. There is a point beyond which importunity deserves reproach; and gentlemen should recollect that there is danger even in pressing humility, itself, too far. She might at length raise her lowly head, and bring dismay upon her oppressors. Should the majority relent, and admit Missouri into the Union, I shall be satisfied; otherwise, (and should I not be upon this floor when this resolution can be taken up,) I wish it brought before Congress, and gentlemen will do me the favor to recollect such of my views as they may think deserving consideration; and also further recollect, that I have laid by the tone of supplication, and demand its adoption as due to faith, to honor, and to right.

Mr. Speaker, knowing no wish incompatible with the perpetuity, the happiness, and tranquillity of the Union, I have, upon every subject brought before Congress, consulted the good of the whole, without regard to the class of individuals or section of country from which it proceeded; whether merchants, manufacturers, or farmers: from the North, or from the South: from Maine, in the East, or Missouri, in the West, has been the same thing to me; I have not permitted myself to inquire who they were, or where from; and, for the few days that I shall yet remain with you, I will pursue the same wide and liberal policy; and that, too, whether called to act upon navigation acts, for the benefit of commerce; tariff laws, for the benefit of agriculture and manufactures; bankrupt bills, called for by our merchants of the East; or relief land laws, loudly required by our Western friends of Ohio, Indiana, and Illinois. And, sir, I

will take this as the last occasion which I shall have, to say, that, had I remained in Congress, I would have pursued the same policy until every impartial man in the nation should have said, nay, until the marble columns themselves, that stand in stately pride around us, should have acknowledged that my feelings and desires of good will were not reciprocated; and that sectional feelings and views had usurped the habitation of those which warmed into life and usefulness our happy Constitution. And after becoming thus satisfied, that kind offices, persuasive arguments, and solid reasoning, were appealed to in vain, I frankly acknowledge that I know of no course left more likely to avoid greater evils, than a mild, but unvarying system of retaliation; under the operation of which, different classes and sections of the United States might become convinced, from appeals to their interest, that mutual kindness and a reciprocal spirit of concession ought to influence our councils: begetting a due and tender respect to the interest, the principles, the wishes, and even the prejudices of all classes and portions of our great national family.

Before I advance to the investigation of the merits of the resolution, I owe it to my colleague, (Mr. CLAY,) who is also my friend and messmate, to explain why, having communicated to several others my design of proposing this resolution, I have carefully avoided mentioning the subject to him, though in daily habits of intimacy, and although I have no friend, living, whose approbation I more highly prize. My mind has been made up, after much reflection, upon the purpose of this resolution, so soon as it should be decided that Missouri was not to be admitted into the Union; that decision has already taken place, and there is not, apparent to me, any reasonable ground for expecting its reversal here. My colleague, (Mr. CLAY,) who has labored arduously and zealously to settle this question, and tranquillize the Union, is not willing yet to despair; he indulges the hope that something may still be done. Had I communicated my design to him, I thought it likely that he might advise the withholding it, yet longer; and admonished and determined against further delay, by a recollection of the early close of my privilege on this floor, and the still earlier day at which circumstances required me to leave it, I have thought it better to proceed, without the possible approbation of my colleague, than against his probable advice.

But, Mr. Speaker, there is a peculiar aptness between the subject which I propose for your consideration and the remnant of the session; let it be recollected, that two sessions have been wasted away in the fruitless discussion of propositions relating to Missouri; all parts of the United States and all classes of your citizens have suffered and groaned, without that legislative aid which was required by their wants, and called for by their petitions; while you have denied them your attention, and even withheld from them your sympathy. Sir, there exists a further objection to this untimely effort to despatch the important business of the nation; nearly an equal half of this House, from the South and West, feel themselves and their constituents deeply aggrieved; they cannot bend and confine their attention, at this late hour, to new and important subjects, called for by those who have, with apparent unconcern, set at naught their rights, their interest, and their feelings; and, if stoical enough to do so, they should recollect the frailty of humanity, and avoid temptation. Sir, with me, (I cannot dissemble,) the salt of legislation has lost its savor. The subject I propose is one rendered just and necessary by the result of the legislation of almost the whole preceding part of this Congress: I mean your refusal to admit Missouri into the Union. I do not believe the few remaining days of the session can be better employed than in adapting the laws and measures of this Government to the extraordinary crisis, at which we have at length arrived.

Mr. Speaker, you will perceive that the same act of Congress which contains the clause authorizing the people of Missouri to form a constitution and State government, contains also the clause which I now propose to repeal. The history of that act is better known in this Hall, than it is out of it; and as it has become important that it should be fully understood by the nation, although I referred to it on a former occasion, while addressing the House, it seems so necessary to a clear comprehension of my proposition, that I must entreat your patience, while I again make a statement of the facts. I appreciate the indulgence shown me, and will be as concise and rapid as possible.

I now, sir, proceed to make the statement upon which my resolution is predicated, and I invite the correction of gentlemen who may believe me in any degree incorrect. Upon the motion of the present honorable Speaker of this House, who was also the mover of the restriction, a committee was raised early in the last session, upon the subject of the contemplated restriction on Missouri, for the avowed purpose of compromising and allaying a subject which even then, in the cradle, gave indications of its being an infant Hercules: and I will do the honorable Speaker the justice to say, that I do not believe he would have proposed a mode or suggested a principle by which this affair should be settled, that he did not believe consistent with the dictates of morality and reason. The committee thus raised did not disagree upon principles, but upon lines of longitude and latitude. All were willing for a compromise, but the position of the lines presented insuperable difficulties, and the committee, on their application, was discharged. The bill preparatory to the admission of Missouri passed the House of Representatives with a restriction, and was reported to the Senate; the Senate had a bill before them for the admission of Maine into the Union: Maine was on the extreme eastern, Missouri on the extreme western limb of the United States. Maine was called for by the non-slaveholding States of the North and East; Missouri, by the slaveholding States of the South and West; the East was jealous of the growth and power of the West, which excited alarm and jealousy in the West: Maine in the east was to be admitted without restrictions; Missouri in the west claimed the same exemption from the intrusion of the

General Government: to calm these jealousies, allay these fears, and at the same time to do equal justice to the East and West, the Senate determined that Maine and Missouri should, by the same act, and at the same instant, pass the threshold into the Union; and that each should enter, equally unfettered by restriction. This was just and wise, and did honor to the calm and well-balanced minds of that venerable body. The bill from the House of Representatives preparatory to the admission of Missouri, being thus amended by the Senate, was reported to the House; the House disagreed; the Senate insisted; the House rejected; a committee of conference was appointed to settle, if possible, these differences between the two branches of Congress and the friends of Maine and Missouri. The joint committee, after much anxious deliberation, came to a settlement, satisfactory to a large majority of Congress, and to a much larger proportion of this nation; the friends of Missouri having agreed that Maine, unfettered, should be admitted forthwith into the Union; and having reluctantly consented to the imposition of a restriction upon the territory west of Missouri. Those who opposed Missouri agreed to withdraw their opposition, and to consent to her admission without restriction. When I speak of the parties agreeing to propositions, I do not intend to be understood that every person agreed, but a sufficient number to constitute a majority, and to carry their arrangement through Congress. The terms of the compromise being thus well understood and agreed upon, the bill for the admission of Maine into the Union immediately passed; and this bill also passed authorizing Missouri to form a constitution and State government without restriction, and containing upon its face a stipulation that she should be admitted into the Union upon the footing of the original States; which bill also imposed the restriction upon the territory, which restriction I now contend should be repealed. Missouri assembled her convention, and formed her constitution, laid down, according to the practice of other States, the territorial government, and put into full operation her State government: she chose her Representative and Senators, who, under the faith of this law, presented her constitution, and asked admittance into the Union. They have been unjustly and unkindly rejected; and the attempt has been renewed to impose upon her the odious restriction, bought off at the last session; and, what would seem almost incredible, none can have been more zealous to produce her rejection than the Representatives, with a single exception, from this very State of Maine, who could not have been upon this floor at this time, or probably in all after time, but for the compromise; for Massachusetts, whose consent was indispensable to the emancipation of Maine, had cautiously given it with a limitation, which would have run out in a day or two after the compromise and her admission; and it was represented here to be very doubtful whether Massachusetts would ever afterwards have again yielded her consent. To the honor of Maine, her Senators (Holmes and Chandler) and one of her Representatives

(Shaw*) have preserved good faith, and have contended and voted for the admission of Missouri, and the fulfilment of the terms of compromise, with such modification of her constitution as obviated the objectionable feature.

Now, Mr. Speaker, upon the principles of eternal justice which govern the intercourse and contracts of individuals, and the negotiation and compacts of communities, states, and nations, I demand of Congress, not for myself, but for one half of the United States, the repeal of this restriction upon the territory west and north of Missouri. The consideration promised for this restriction has not been paid; the plighted faith of Congress for the admission of Missouri has been violated; then take off, at least, the restriction. Give us Missouri without restriction, or place us in the same situation, by taking it off of the territory, in which we were when you entered into the covenant, and gave us the solemn pledge of a law to do so. Sir, the course of the majority can be justified by no principle of reason or sound policy, but must rest, for its support, upon the antiquated doctrines of schoolmen and casuists, of pious fraud; the end sanctifying the means; of doing evil that good may come of it; which, though they have received the reprobation of true moralists, may find a place in the new code of ethics, likely to grow out of these times. Are we to hear it contended, that the furtherance of humanity and religion will justify making the Southern and Western people dupes to your promises and their credulity? Will you sir, (do not misunderstand me, Mr. Speaker, I do not mean you personally, but the House over which you preside,) contend, that the restriction is right and just, and that, unimportant how obtained, it ought to be maintained and continued?

Sir, if this principle were correct, the conclusion does not follow; I deny your premises, and will proceed to show that the restriction, which I seek to repeal, is unjust—unjust, because this immense territory, this fair portion of America, over which the honorable Speaker has said he contemplated with pleasure the numerous States that would hereafter unfurl their banners; this spacious territory was procured by the wisdom, the policy, and the money, of all the States within this Union; each contributed their due proportion of the fifteen, nay, all things considered, nearer twenty millions of dollars towards its purchase; it is, therefore, the common of the United States, into which all should equally have the privilege to enter, to roam, and to sit down. But will it be said that, notwithstanding the restriction against the introduction of slaves, all may now do so? I grant you they may. But we should view and speak of things practically. Will they do so? Sir, I will take occasion to say, that if I have any capacity, capable of being rendered of the smallest use to my country, it results from the humble faculty of viewing things in their practical operation. When you recollect their prejudices and habits,

* When this question was again revived, and Missouri admitted, Mr. Hill, of Maine, voted for her admission.

and that slaves constitute the principal fortunes in many of the slaveholding States, will you not grant that the prohibition of slavery in this territory is virtually and practically the exclusion from it of those and their posterity, who have contributed so largely and most largely to its acquisition? Sir, we have jointly toiled and paid to acquire it, but our Eastern friends and their new Western allies now contend, and are likely to obtain, the exclusive enjoyment.

Mr. Speaker, when this Confederation was formed, the characters and rights of the people in the slaveholding States were known, respected, acknowledged, and secured; and now, upon any supposed principle of policy, without their deliberate consent, to destroy or abridge them, deserves the appellation of (what I consider it in fact) an usurpation. I trust I have shown the restriction to be unjust. Sir, the idea of a restriction upon the introduction of slaves into Missouri, or the territory being better for the slaves, seems at length exploded, abandoned, and given up, upon this floor, as untenable. Indeed, it should never have been urged. The permission asked by Missouri, which you have denied, and that now urged by me for the territory, for the liberty to decide for themselves upon the policy of introducing slaves, did not, nor does it now, contemplate an augmentation of one to the number of slaves; not one human being is asked to be reduced to the condition of a slave, who is not so already. So far, sir, is it from being better for slaves with whom you so strongly sympathize, to impose the restriction, that it is manifestly worse for them; impose the restriction, and slaves are thereby kept crowded together in the South; you chain them to their sterile and burning fields, and to their present owners, many of whom have great numbers, and are thereby rendered the less able to provide for them abundantly, and the less disposed to treat them with humanity and indulgence; but give up your unmeaning contest about restriction, and permit slaves to be taken into those extensive and fertile regions of the West, you will thereby disperse them; increase the numbers of owners, and you decrease the number of slaves held by each; the effect of which, and that clear to the view of every practical man, must be to secure more abundant provision and humane treatment, and further to increase the prospects for manumission by masters, and gradual abolition by the State governments. But, sir, I have said, that withholding the restriction increases the prospect for manumissions, because universal experience proves that correct notions of the rights of man and the principles and feelings of humanity are gaining ground, and in proportion as you increase in any section of country the white population over that of the black, you remove the pressure from the growth of those principles and feelings, and increase the quantum of sentiment in favor of the blacks. This encourages, persuades, and excites to manumissions; and has led, and would always lead, to gradual but ultimate abolition. Sir, I am free to declare it as my opinion, the result of some reflection, that if you were to abandon the contest, and permit slaves to break up from crowded plantations, and scatter over our vast Western world, whilst a portion would be relieved from Southern servitude, and, as some would have it, want, and would have brighter prospects opened to their view, the condition of the residue would, from the operation of the same principles, become greatly ameliorated. So far from the principles favorable to African slavery being on the growth, as has been inconsiderately asserted, they are rapidly on the wane, as is attested by the policy of all civilized nations, in relation to the African slave trade; and, beyond all others, by the feelings and policy of the people of the United States, in regard to it. From these considerations, and some others, which I will not detain you by presenting, I have, sir, contemplated, with no unpleasant sensations, the extension of these principles and the dispersion of the blacks, until a portion of the present slaveholding States, and all those which might be hereafter admitted into the Union, would find it consistent with their feelings and not incompatible with their interest, to pass laws for their gradual emancipation. Their numbers being reduced comparatively low, this might then be done without danger, serious apprehensions, or great inconvenience—the chief obstacles, everywhere, to such laws at this time. But, Mr. Speaker, driven from the ground of the restriction being better for the unfortunate blacks, whose condition, gentlemen profess, impelled by feelings of humanity, they are desirous to improve; they now contend that it is, at all events, better for the whites. This position, not as disinterested and magnanimous as the former, remains also to be proven. Sir, I have been forcibly struck at the want of correct information in Legislatures of the non-slaveholding States, upon the subject of slavery, and particularly the extent of the present contest, as evidenced by their proceedings and resolutions, and have also made the same remark, on gentlemen of great information, occupying high stations and possessing undoubted integrity. I do not, therefore, esteem it at all remarkable that the mass of the population in those States should labor under gross misapprehensions.

The honorable Speaker, who, I am quite sure, would represent no fact otherwise than as he believed it, proceeding, in one of his speeches, upon a mistaken view of the state of society in the slaveholding States, asks the question, Who but slaveholders were elected to the State Legislatures, &c.? And he appealed to us to say whether the selection of a laboring man, however well educated, would not be considered an extraordinary event? I answer, sir, without the fear of contradiction from the Representatives of those States, and in the face of their people, that, when a candidate presents himself for office, it never entered into the mind of folly itself to inquire, by way of ascertaining his qualifications, whether he held slaves? I have reflected, and could, would it not be an unprofitable consumption of your time, enumerate very many of my acquaintances and friends, not being slaveholders, who have been preferred to office, and, like others, elected to the

Legislature; and, I further state, with the most sincere conviction of its truth, that if the possession of slaves, more than the possession of money, or other property, elevates a man in the estimation of society, I have remained to this hour altogether ignorant of such an effect. Sir, a venerable and distinguished Senator from New York, (Mr. KING,) said, when speaking of the slaveholding States, that in them "manual labor dishonored the hands of freemen." And the same sentiment has been re-echoed in this House. I deny the proposition to be true; and can and now will proceed to show that this is not one of the evils of African slavery; but, that its existence in a society elevates the poor and laboring white man, and that its non-existence invites and leads to his depression and dishonor. Sir, where slavery is tolerated, slaves perform, for others, the servile and menial duties of the stable, the kitchen, and the house—I say they perform for others, because no one would expose himself so much as to contend that a man was dishonored by catching his own horse, or a female by doing her own house labor; the whites engage in the dignified and honorable labor of agriculture and the mechanic arts; and in these, respectable men and their sons, slaveholders and non-slaveholders, indiscriminately join; and, if I have not to learn all that I have seen and known, a man is respected among us in the degree that he is industrious, honest, and honorable; and is degraded and dishonored, as he is vagrant, lazy, and unprincipled. Men ought to be, and are, graduated in society by the principles which I have mentioned. When, sir, in the State which I have, in part, the honor to represent, a man in the higher walks of life meets his poor, but honest neighbor, he salutes him, and treats him with the attention which belongs to merit; if he comes to his house, he is met at the door, and cordially taken by the hand, invited to a seat in the hospitable circle, and constitutes a welcome guest at his smoking board. But what is the picture in the non-slaveholding States? I speak the language of experience and truth. The wealthy employ, I do not say culpably, the poor and miserable whites in all the round of servile duties from the stable to the kitchen; they ride before and behind their carriages, and stand often trembling in the presence of their august employers, in practice and truth their masters; they act as their cooks, their shoe-blacks, and their scullions. The wide chasm between their stations and pursuits forbids intercourse at all, much less a cordial one. Thus the miserable, poor, and laboring white man is degraded and dishonored in the non-slaveholding States; whilst in those of the opposite character, he is saved and redeemed by the intervention of blacks. Since the days of Adam to the present time, men have occupied the various stations of high and low, rich and poor, dignified and servile; and the practical difference betwixt the slaveholding, and the non-slaveholding States upon this subject is, that the former has degraded their black, and the latter their white brethren, to those servile duties. Mr. Speaker, I hope it may be understood, that I have not made these remarks in a spirit of reproach; and do hope that I shall be pardoned for having examined this false doctrine, of labor dishonoring the hands of a freeman, a little at large, when it is recollected that by far the greatest portion of those generous freemen, by whose votes I have been elevated to a seat in this hall, do not own slaves; it is my duty, no, sir, it is my privilege and pleasure, to defend their honor as well as their rights; and I do, with indignation, repel the insinuation, though from high authority, that they are dishonored by labor; sir, I repel it for myself, for I too find pleasure and advantage in labor, and cannot, patiently, listen to such an imputation. Sir, I will use this last occasion to impress upon our brethren of the non-slaveholding States the extreme indelicacy, censoriousness, and impolicy of raising our latches and attempting to disturb the sacredness of domestic relations and quiet; and will say to them " Why beholdest thou the mote that is in thy brother's eye, but considerest not the beam that is in thine own eye?"

We never have, and never will submit to have our natural and Constitutional rights revised and qualified by them; we deny their authority to catechise us, and to fulminate their denunciations against our principles of morality, religion, or honor. I will not, sir, engage in the inviduous task of comparing, much less in attempting to elevate ourselves above our brethren of the East; if I can show that we occupy the level with them I shall be satisfied. There is one fact of which I entreat gentlemen to be assured, that in the States beyond the mountains, so far as I have been enabled to collect from observation and inquiry, there exists as much, not to say more practical morality, religion, and honor, as can be found in the land of steady habits. Sir, while the Congress of the United States keeps within its proper limits, which will be without the pale of State authority, confining its operations to Federal and not State duties, as they have failed to do, in the attempt to impose a restriction upon Missouri; while it magnanimously, disregarding local feeling, listens to the rights, wants, nay wishes, of every class and section of the Union, kindly affording relief where practicable; and where not, as kindly rejecting, taking care to proceed upon strong and satisfactory, not nice and technical reasoning; while Congress will proceed thus, it will answer the designs of its authors, and gain for itself the love of the people and the admiration of the world.

Mr. Speaker, I feel so deeply impressed with its importance that I must be allowed to say, that above all things, the bitter subject of African slavery is one which can never be touched with impunity by the General Government. The Convention that formed the Constitution found it so; a celebrated Convention to the East found it so; and so have Congress and the nation fully ascertained. The Convention was constrained to leave it as they found it, save that to effect the very object of confining it to the condition in which found; the citizens of other States are required, on the escape of slaves to such other States, upon the application of their owners, to deliver them up for the purpose of being taken whence they came. Congress should not meddle, and will never be permitted to meddle, nor will other States, further than to pass laws for securing, on an escape, their custody for their owners. Such, sir, are the mischievous and alarming consequences incident to the interference of the General Government with this subject, which, if once permitted, might be followed by another and another measure of encroachment, all exciting and eliciting in slaves themselves and in those who might engage in the crusade, as well as in their owners, the most deeprooted prejudices and violent passions of the human heart. I say that such are the consequences attendant upon this assumption of power by the General Government, that every parent should impress upon the susceptible mind of his child its great danger, and the necessity of carefully avoiding it; and much more should those in the slaveholding States enjoin upon theirs the necessity of constant vigilance; and upon the first discovery of an attempt at encroachment, of raising the alarm, and never ceasing resistance, until every Constitutional effort should be exhausted. Sir, I wish it understood that I am no friend to African slavery, not for many of the reasons usually assigned, but because it is a violation of the rights of man, as derived from his God, and I will pledge myself to go as far as most men for its amelioration or abolition. But I owe higher obligations to the white population of the United States, particularly to those who have sent me here; to my friends and family, than those which I feel, or ought to feel for the black. Mr. Speaker, it should never be forgotten that, according to the laws of the slaveholding States, slaves are property, and protected by the Constitution of the United States; which Constitution vests the General Government with no power to touch the subject; that the condition and treatment is better understood, and exclusively understood, by those States themselves, and that, whatever ought or can be done for this unfortunate class of people, should be left to the States respectively in which they are situated.

But, sir, I have been strongly reminded of the necessity of this resolution by a recollection of the manner in which an honest post-rider, and no slaveholder, in my neighborhood, reprimanded and put me to silence, on my return home last Spring: for the people in the Western country not owning slaves, hold their heads, and take upon themselves to inquire about public business, and into the conduct of those whom they elevate to office. This honest man asked me what important measures we had passed during the session. I proceeded to enumerate all, which you know were but few, and apologized for not doing more, from the great length of time which had been employed on the Missouri question. Sir, said he, that ought not to have taken so wise a body as Congress half an hour to decide it; for I satisfied my mind upon it in less time. I endeavored to evade the severity of the stroke, by remarking that it was an important question, and the arguments on both sides had been lengthy and able. He promptly replied that he could not see what ground there was for argument upon so plain a question as the right of

Congress to dictate to Missouri about having or not having negroes; a matter which concerned her, and which other States had decided for themselves. I was heartily tired of the Missouri question, and made another attempt to divert him, by remarking that we had this consolation, that, at the next session, the public business could be attended to, having finally compromised and settled the disagreeable contest, by allowing a restriction on the Territory; and there, said he, you suffered yourselves to be yankied, by giving up the restriction on the Territory, for a right to which Missouri was entitled without it. Such is the force of sound, impartial, unsophisticated sense, that it carried conviction to the bystanders; they laughed to hear the post-rider gain so fair a triumph, and I could not deny him a victory. Now, sir, I have anticipated with some concern, that I should meet this plain, common-sense man again; and, if so, I have imagined that he would say, sir, I thought you told me that the Missouri question had been finally settled, and that you would, at the next session, be able to do the people's business. I would answer: true, I did, but the friends of restriction found fault with the constitution of Missouri, because free blacks and mulattoes were forbidden to go there; and they were said to be citizens of the United States, and therefore privileged. He will be almost certain to say, because he has a knack of putting things in a strong point— and what! are blacks and mulattoes citizens of the United States! and have they, therefore, a right to be members of Congress or President of the United States? But, I shall repeat that this was the opinion—right or wrong I leave you to decide—of a majority of the House of Representatives, and, therefore, they were dissatisfied. He will then likely inquire, is not the Constitution of the United States above all other laws? for, I assure you that it is a principle well known to our constables and magistrates, who sometimes decide a law to be repugnant to the Constitution, and therefore void. I must repeat it to have been the opinion of a majority, that they could not trust to the Constitution of the United States to weigh against the constitution of Missouri. The inquiry will then be made, whether, as the first section of the law which provides for the admission of Missouri had been violated, the last section of the same law, which imposed the restriction, as the consideration of the admission of Missouri, had not been repealed? I wish, sir, to be prepared to tell this honest man and others, for great is the solicitude, and numerous will be the inquiries, that the restriction has been repealed; or, at least, to have the poor consolation of being enabled to say, that I performed my duty, by endeavoring to have it repealed. And I beg that my dilemma may not be disregarded; for, if the restriction should not be repealed, he will surely repeat the charge before made, and with greater reason, that we had suffered ourselves to be thoroughly yankied. For, if this resolution be not adopted, you will have the advantage both in land and negroes.

Mr. Speaker, I feel myself constrained to com-municate my sensations on a late occasion, although I had designed, until this moment, to confine them within my own breast. I verily believe, sir, that if members would, upon this floor, use more ingenuousness, not only in disclosing their views, but in temperately exposing their feelings, our discussions would be much simplified and curtailed. We should then know where to direct arguments, or whether it were worth while to use them at all. But, sir, to proceed: After the late vote by which Missouri was refused admittance into the Union, while descending the hill westwardly from this Capitol, with my face turned towards ill-fated Missouri, my home, and my friends, strongly and deeply feeling the unkind blow given to her rights and those of one-half the Union, I felt such maddening sensations as I only recollect to have experienced on a few former occasions: One, sir, on the occlusion of the port of New Orleans by Spain; when distress and ruin threatened our land! Another, when the President's proclamation arrived in the West, containing an annunciation that the sovereignty and flag of the United States had been violated and insulted in our own waters, by the attack of the British ship Leopard of 50 guns, upon the United States frigate Chesapeake of 38; and the third, when, at the commencement of the late war, owing to the weakness or treachery of General Hull, or both, Detroit and the Northern army were surrendered, and the whole northwestern frontier of Ohio, Indiana, and Illinois, threatened with blood and desolation. Upon all these occasions, my voice was heard endeavoring to explain our wrongs and dangers, and to inspire my fellow-men with just feelings of resentment; nor did I decline offering the aid of my feeble arm.

Mr. Speaker, I beg that I may not be misunderstood; these were my involuntary emotions, but they have subsided and become calm. I know my rights and my duty as an American citizen; and I am incapable of thinking of any force except that which is moral and Constitutional. But, sir, though I retire from this magnificent hall to my humble fireside and my fields, the injuries of Missouri shall not be forgotten or concealed; they will continue to be uppermost upon my mind, on my lying down and rising up, on my going out and coming in. Mr. Speaker, it surely becomes the councils of this nation to inquire with care and anxiety into the course likely to be pursued by Missouri. I, sir, will use this occasion to say to their Representatives and Senators, and, through them to the people of Missouri, what I have not communicated to those gentlemen, personally, that, as they have come forward and offered her constitution, or, to use the language of court etiquette, have called and left their card, which has not been returned, but rejected, and have also offered to pay a personal visit, but have had the door shut in their face, and refused admittance, that they now, although mortified and humiliated, should return quietly to their growing State, and there remain, with an elevated mien and inflexible purpose, until the future agents of this Government shall forward to them an invitation to attend her councils in this Chamber. Will Missouri lay down the full and proud dress of *State government*, and again cover herself with the lowly dishabille of a *Territory?* Sir, I know the character of the population of Missouri, and have the pleasure of a personal acquaintance with many of her respectable and influential citizens; they are enterprising, intelligent, and bold; they have an ardent and invincible attachment to liberty; while they reverence legitimate government and laws. And, sir, from my knowledge of this people, I will venture to say, with great confidence, that you might as soon expect, by your mandate, to roll back the onward floods of her majestic Missouri from the ocean! You, sir, may desolate their fields, and raze their habitations, but you cannot bend their necks to your unconstitutional yoke.

Mr. Speaker, I do not design to use, I will not use, the language of menace. I speak, however, fearless, and without disguise. Sir, he knows but little of the character of the Southern and Western delegation and States, who, while Missouri's wrongs remain unredressed, can look for happy and calm legislation on this floor. While our young sister Missouri, for imputed wrongs, not her own, but ours, remains bowed down and covered with distress; while she remains shut out from this Hall pale and sorrowful, and exposed to the most wasteful elements, your sentinels may cry peace, peace, all's well!—but, I tell you, deceive not yourselves, there is no peace!

Mr. Speaker, I have detained you longer than I designed to have done; my remarks have been warm and desultory, but I beg you to believe, that I have honestly and frankly laid open the feelings and sentiments of my heart, and have advanced no principle, not matured by reflection. Permit me, sir, to return to you, and the members of this House, my kindest thanks for the patience and attention with which you have heard my valedictory and uninteresting discourse. And, with the most fervent sincerity of heart, I implore, for the tranquillity and future grandeur of our common country, the blessing and protection of that God who has guided us, triumphant, through the perils of two wars; that God, who binds the winds of heaven in his hand, and calms the troubled seas.

Mr. B. having concluded—

The preliminary question was put—"Will the House now proceed to consider this resolution?" It was decided in the negative—seventy-nine votes to 43. So the resolution lies on the table.

REDUCTION OF SALARIES, &c.

The House resumed the consideration of the unfinished business of yesterday, which was the bill to reduce (on an average by twenty per cent.) the salaries of the officers of the Government, with the amendment proposed by Mr. CAMPBELL, the object of which was to reduce the pay of the members from eight dollars to six dollars per diem.

Mr. SIMKINS, of South Carolina, said he could not refrain from expressing his warm and decided approbation of the sentiments delivered by the two gentlemen from Kentucky, (Messrs. ANDERSON and ROBERTSON.) In doing this the House can-

not but see how utterly mistaken the gentleman from Ohio is when he attempts to justify his motion by saying that, for six dollars a day, the ablest men can be got to serve in Congress, and that they will be sufficiently permanent. Every step this debate progresses, and almost every member that rises to address you, contradict the gentleman's position, and show that scarcely a man can be got to serve here for any considerable length of time. Many are induced to come from a spirit of patriotism, some from the eclat of being for a while members of Congress, some from one motive, and some from another; but experience, the best of all tests, has invariably proved (in a very few instances excepted) that, by the time such members learn the routine of business—yes, at the very time when they become fitted to render real service to their country—they are literally driven from Congress by the poverty of the salary at eight dollars a day. What then are we to think of a proposition that goes to lessen even this allowance? Sir, I, with the gentleman from Kentucky, from Maryland, and, indeed, almost every gentleman who has spoken, can speak disinterestedly on this question. A few days will also number me among those who were so kind as to send me here, free from all Congressional interests and duties; and I venture to assert for the Southern States, and I think I might for the Middle States, that no man with a family can, at the present pay, hold a seat here for any length of time, unless he would madly and unnaturally sacrifice his domestic comforts and private interests—unless, indeed, he would sacrifice his family. Sir, do you not see that even every two years there is a change of a third, and sometimes a half of this body? What does this show but that professional men and others so sacrifice their interests by seats here that they are driven to abandon them? And hence, this House is doomed to an instability and a fluctuation so ruinous as to unsettle and sacrifice every thing dear to the country. In truth, almost every class of the community are denied to come here, except two—those who are very rich, and those who are seeking other and more profitable places through Executive patronage and otherwise. If the present order of things exists, the endeavor to preserve this body pure and independent will be fruitless and vain. In vain will it be that the Constitution, for the wisest purposes, has declared the three main branches of the Government separate and independent. Lower your present pay, (already too low,) and this independence and purity will exist only in name.

Sir, the importance of this subject swells as we progress. I should not have risen but from a consideration of its being of the last importance. I forbear to press a view indelibly stamped with interest, though not with novelty.

The gentleman from Ohio (Mr. CAMPBELL) says that, whilst diminishing the salaries of the military and civil officers, the majority would be inconsistent not to embrace their own; that they ought first to have begun with themselves. With the consistency of the majority in this matter I rejoice to have had nothing to do—no sin to answer for. Let gentlemen look to their own consistency. They have made their own choices. I not only opposed the change in the method of paying your military officers, as a retrocession instead of an advance in military science, as novel, unequal, and unprecedented, but I have opposed the diminution of pay and salaries, both civil and military, for various reasons, but particularly because this is not the proper time to settle them. Some salaries, I admit, upon the change of times, may be a little too high; but is it not clear that we ought not to unsettle and render fluctuating every salary, at a time when the state and circumstances of the nation are evidently unsettled? Look at the state of our importations and of our currency. They are at their lowest point of depression; perhaps may have already risen a little from the lowest point. Is it not evident that the importations will increase; that bank stock is rising, because our banks will discount more liberally, and throw into circulation a great deal more money? Is it not seen from these premises, that no man can now tell what would be an adequate salary for any number of years; that what may be ample pay this year, will be too little the next, and still more inadequate the next after; that, by legislating at this moment, we not only act with too much precipitation, but are actually legislating in the dark? I know these arguments, which were urged by me on the bill reducing the salaries of military officers, two or three days ago, had no weight. They were not even answered, because every thing then was carried by a dead, determined, unyielding majority. On our own pay I trust they will have more weight.

But the gentleman from Ohio says, we must legislate according to our circumstances. Sir, this is the very reason, urged in part before, but which permit me to repeat, why we should not now legislate at all. How do we know under what circumstances the next Congress may meet? Here we are at the very heel, not merely of the session, but of the Congress, legislating, not for ourselves, with a due and becoming delicacy, but legislating, hastily and officiously, for the next Congress. The gentleman should have begun earlier. He should have begun as soon as it was ascertained by the annual Treasury report of the last session, that loans or taxes would be necessary.

Sir, with the first gentleman who addressed you, from Kentucky, (Mr. ANDERSON,) I regret extremely that this subject was now touched, because, as has been well urged, it is one of extreme delicacy, and the investigation of which has hardly failed to agitate the continent from one end to the other. This is not all; for nothing is so well calculated to create distrust towards us, and so to humble this body in the eyes of the people.

Mr. FOOT observed, that he had determined not to take any part in the discussion of the merits of this bill; but, since the chairman of the committee had only stated his own views of the subject, and the reasons which had influenced himself—and in addition to this had also stated, that he was prevented by ill health from attending with the committee during their investigation of the subject referred to them, and had assigned this as the reason for not answering the questions which had been proposed by several gentlemen respecting the principles which had governed the committee—he felt himself bound, by considerations of respect to the House, as well as to individual members, and in justice to the committee to state frankly his own views, and also the reasons which had induced the committee to present this bill to the consideration of the House, so far at least as he was able to understand and to express their sentiments on the subject.

Sir, the committee have investigated, with considerable labor and attention, the several subjects referred to them; and the bill now under consideration is the result of their examination, so far as respects the amount of the compensation to the officers and others embraced in the resolution. They have endeavored to equalize and apportion the compensation to the services performed, with a due regard to the talents and qualifications necessary for the faithful discharge of the duties assigned to them. They have been guided in some measure by the amount of salaries, which the officers and others received previous to the year 1815, since which period most of the salaries have been increased.

The committee believed that if the compensation was not reduced below the amount fixed by law, previous to 1816, it could not be claimed that the salaries contemplated by the present bill would be insufficient, considering the present appreciation of the value of money; and they do not hesitate to say that salary officers, even with the reduction proposed by the present bill, would suffer less than any other portion of the community; for, if the same salaries furnished an adequate support in 1815, they certainly would be amply sufficient at the present time.

It will not be denied that the present state of the finances of the country, and our future prospects of revenue, demand a very considerable reduction of the present salaries of the officers in the civil, as well as in every other department of the Government, in addition to other practicable retrenchments, in order to bring our expenditures within our means, and prevent the necessity of resorting to loans or direct taxation to meet the expenditure of Government in profound peace.

The committee have endeavored to discharge faithfully the duties assigned to them; they feel no personal solicitude for the fate of this bill, but in common with those who consider retrenchment in our expenses necessary for the welfare of the country. But, sir, they do feel a deep solicitude, that some measures may be adopted by which the Government may, by a reasonable retrenchment, prevent the entire destruction of our most valuable institutions, which will be the inevitable consequence of our increasing expenses and our diminished resources.

Sir, my attention has been drawn to this subject from the first commencement of the last session, in consequence of the enormous increase of the appropriations for the Treasury, War, and Navy Departments. It will be recollected that a resolu tion was introduced by me at the last session for instructing the Committee of Ways and Means to inquire into the expediency of repealing the act of April, 1818, increasing the number, as well as the compensation of the clerks in the several Departments, but which, with every other effort in favor of retrenchment during the session, failed.

I consider the extraordinary and unprecedented increase of expense in the various Departments of our Government, after the conclusion of the war, a growing evil, wholly inconsistent with that republican simplicity which formerly characterized our Government, and which, in my opinion, is essential to its very existence.

Sir, we have been too much in the habit of apeing the manners, luxuries, and extravagance of the Old World; we have taken the monarchial governments of Europe as a pattern for the administration of our plain republican system; and we have been following, with rapid strides, in the path which has led to the destruction of all the ancient republics, and unless our progress is soon arrested, the same inevitable doom awaits our own.

The investigation of this subject has convinced my mind that a radical reform has become necessary; and, to use the phrase which a gentleman at the last session applied to the revenue system on the tariff bill, there is something rotten in the system.

The gentleman from New Jersey (Mr. KINSEY) has my warmest acknowledgements, for the motion which he has made to amend the bill by erasing the clerk of the superintendent of the Patent Office, with the explanation made by him; and confirmed by the honorable chairman of the Committee of Ways and Means, who has informed the House that the superintendent and clerk of the Patent Office are officers unknown to our laws. They have relieved me from the necessity of appealing to the laws to prove the fact. By your laws the Patent Office is a branch of the State Department, and has always been kept by a clerk of that Department until the act of 1818, and until 1808 is not even found in your appropriation bills. But what is its present condition? It has lately grown into a department with all the paraphernalia of office, a superintendent, with his clerk and messenger, created by your appropriation bills. Yes, sir, messenger! another creature of appropriation bills, which have become of late a very convenient mode of creating offices, and increasing the number of officers without the usual formalities of ordinary laws.

It is only necessary to call the attention of the House to the consideration of the subject, to convince every member of the impropriety of this mode of legislating men into place. Look at your appropriation bills! What is their language? "For paying an assistant to the Chief Clerk and messengers" not authorized by existing laws, &c., "and for extra clerks" ―― dollars.

Sir, this mode of, (I had almost said of smuggling) officers into place by appropriation bills, has become a most fertile source of abuse and of extravagant expenditure. Instead of creating those offices by special laws, when a thorough examina-

tion could be had, it has, I believe, often been found convenient after an appropriation bill has been under consideration for several days, and its details fully examined, to add a few more clerks by way of amendment, because it is said their services are found to be indispensable, and the motion prevails, because the bill must be passed, or the wheels of Government must stop.

The gentleman from Maryland has rather intimated than openly declared that the pay of the clerks has not been increased since the year 1815. Sir, in answer to this, I beg leave to call the attention of the House to the printed documents on our tables, and to an examination of the gentleman's own appropriation bills, within the last five years. A document has been laid before us which purports to be "summary of compensations for executive departments in the years 1790, 1795, 1800, 1808, 1816, 1820," which shows a most enormous increase of the expenditures in those Departments even since the close of the late war.

I beg leave to call the attention of gentlemen particularly to this document, the authenticity and accuracy of which will not be questioned; and I would only ask the gentleman from Maryland to reconcile his remarks with this official statement.

We find, by turning to this document, the expenditure in the several Departments, at the different periods, to be as follows:

In 1790	-	-	-	$41,868 73
1795	-	-	-	71,997 06
1800	-	-	-	125,581 32
1808	-	-	-	142,352 83
1816	-	-	-	274,442 47
1820	-	-	-	353,097 60

Sir, this document speaks a language which cannot be misunderstood. It needs no comment.

Will the people of the United States consent to pay taxes, or borrow money to support this expensive, not to say extravagant, system? For one, I can say, my vote will not be given either for loans or taxes, in a time of profound peace, to support this rapidly increasing expenditure―nor on any conditions, until I can see some favorable prospect of a thorough reform and general retrenchment in the expenditures of the Government.

Mr. CAMPBELL withdrew his amendment, and, in lieu thereof, proposed the following, to come in after the enacting clause of the second section, viz: "That the compensation now allowed to the members of the Senate, and members and delegates of the House of Representatives, and to the President of the Senate, *pro tempore*, and Speaker of the House of Representatives, shall be reduced twenty-five per cent., and"

Which being read, and the question stated thereon, Mr. ANDERSON moved that the bill be postponed indefinitely; and, the question being taken thereon, it was determined in the negative―yeas 49, nays 107, as follows:

YEAS―Messrs. Abbot, Alexander, Allen of Massachusetts, Anderson, Baldwin, Bayly, Brevard, Brush, Butler of Louisiana, Clay, Crafts, Crowell, Cushman, Cuthbert, Dickinson, Edwards of Pennsylvania, Fisher, Folger, Ford, Fuller, Gorham, Hackley, Jones of Tennessee, Kinsley, Lathrop, Little, McCullough, McLean of Kentucky, Meech, Montgomery, S. Moore, Moseley, Neale, Newton, Parker of Virginia, Pinckney, Rankin, Reid, Ringgold, Robertson, Sergeant, Simkins, Smith of New Jersey, Smith of Maryland, Smith of North Carolina, Street, Trimble, Upham, and Wallace.

NAYS—Messrs. Adams, Allen of New York, Archer of Maryland, Archer of Virginia, Baker, Ball, Barbour, Bateman, Beecher, Boden, Bryan, Buffum, Butler of New Hampshire, Campbell, Cannon, Case, Clagett, Cobb, Cocke, Culbreth, Culpeper, Dane, Darlington, Davidson, Dennison, Dewitt, Earle, Eddy, Edwards of N. Carolina, Fay, Floyd, Foot, Forrest, Garnett, Gray, Gross of New York, Gross of Pennsylvania, Guyon, Hall of New York, Hall of North Carolina, Hardin, Hemphill, Hendricks, Herrick, Hibshman, Hill, Hobart, Hooks, Hostetter, Jackson, Johnson, Jones of Virginia, Kent, Kinsey, Lincoln, Livermore, Maclay, McCoy, McCreary, Mallary, Marchand, Meigs, Mercer, Metcalf, Monell, R. Moore, T. L. Moore, Morton, Murray, Nelson of Massachusetts, Nelson of Virginia, Parker of Massachusetts, Patterson, Phelps, Philson, Pitcher, Plumer, Randolph, Rhea, Rich, Richards, Richmond, Rogers, Ross, Russ, Sawyer, Shaw, Sloan, A. Smyth of Virginia, Southard, Stevens, Strong of Vermont, Strong of New York, Swearingen, Tarr, Tomlinson, Tompkins, Tracy, Tucker of South Carolina, Tyler, Udree, Walker, Warfield, Wendover, Williams of Virginia, Williams of North Carolina, and Wood.

The question then recurred on the amendment moved by Mr. CAMPBELL; when,

Mr. ARCHER moved to substitute, in lieu of that amendment, the following: "That an act of Congress, passed on the 22d day of January, 1818, entitled 'An act allowing compensation to the members of the Senate, members of the House of Representatives of the United States, and to the delegates from Territories, and repealing all the laws on that subject,' shall, from and after the third day of March next, be repealed."

And the question being taken thereon, it was determined in the negative.

The question then again recurred on Mr. CAMPBELL's amendment.

Mr. RHEA moved to amend the same, by inserting, after the words "per cent.," these words: "from and after the first day of August, 1820."

Mr. CLAY, with the expressed intention of putting the bill and amendment to sleep, as one which would be productive of nothing but a useless consumption of time, moved to lay the bill on the table; and the motion was agreed to—84 to 62.

So the bill was laid on the table.

THURSDAY, February 22.

The bill from the Senate, entitled "An act further to establish the compensation of the officers employed in the collection of duties on imports and tonnage, and for other purposes," was read twice, and referred to the Committee on Commerce.

An engrossed resolution providing for jails, in certain cases, for the safe custody of persons committed under the authority of the United States, was read the third time, and passed.

On motion of Mr. COCKE,

Resolved, That this House will, at 12 o'clock on Monday next, proceed to ballot for a printer to execute its work during the next Congress, according to the provisions of the "resolution directing the manner in which the printing of Congress shall be executed, fixing the prices thereof, and providing for the appointment of a printer, or printers," passed on the 3d day of March, 1819.

Mr. CROWELL moved that the several orders of the day which precede the bill from the Senate, entitled "An act for the relief of purchasers of public lands prior to the 1st of July, 1820," be postponed, for the purpose of taking the said bill into consideration.

And the question being taken thereon, it was decided in the negative.

On motion of Mr. SMITH, of Maryland, the orders of the day which precede the bill making appropriations for the naval service of the United States, were postponed until to-morrow.

The SPEAKER laid before the House a letter from the Secretary of State, transmitting a report on the subject of weights and measures, prepared in obedience to a resolution of the House of Representatives of the 14th December, 1819; which letter and report were ordered to lie upon the table.

The following Message was received from the PRESIDENT OF THE UNITED STATES:

To the Senate and House of
    Representatives of the United States:

The Treaty of Amity, Settlement, and Limits, between the United States and Spain, signed on the 22d of February, 1819, having been ratified by the contracting parties, and the ratifications having been exchanged, it is herewith communicated to Congress, that such legislative measures may be taken as they shall judge proper, for carrying the same into execution.

                JAMES MONROE.

WASHINGTON, *February* 22, 1821.

The Message was read, and, together with the Treaty, referred to the Committee on Foreign Affairs.

NAVAL APPROPRIATIONS.

The House resolved itself into a Committee of the Whole, on the bill making appropriations for the support of the Navy of the United States, for the year 1821; and on the bill to authorize the building of lighthouses on Cross and Pond Islands, in the harbor of Boothbay, and at the mouth of Oswego river; and placing buoys on the Shoals of Nantucket and Vineyard Sound, near the harbor of Wickford, and on the Altamaha river, and for other purposes; and, after some time spent therein, Mr. SPEAKER resumed the chair, and Mr. FOOT reported the former of the said bills with amendments, and the latter without amendment.

The House proceeded to consider the amendments aforesaid; when

Mr. RANDOLPH moved that the bill with the amendments lie on the table; which being rejected, the said amendments were concurred in, and the bills were ordered to be engrossed, and severally read a third time to-morrow.

CASE OF COMMODORE TUCKER.

The bill from the Senate, for the relief of Commodore Samuel Tucker, as amended in this House, so as to reduce the annuity to $30 per month, was read a third time. There was a good deal of debate on the bill. The gentlemen who spoke on the subject were:

For the bill—Messrs. MONTGOMERY, FULLER, and PINCKNEY.

Against the bill—Messrs. METCALF, COBB, HARDIN, LITTLE, and TUCKER, of Virginia.

The bill was supported on the ground of the great merit of Commodore Tucker as a warrior of the Revolution, and his present reduced circumstances. The objections were twofold: 1st, on the score of hostility to pensions in general, on any other principle than that of wounds or disability incurred in service; and, secondly, to paying out of a fund (the Navy Pension Fund) created since the adoption of the Constitution—a pension for Revolutionary services. To the first objection it was replied, that this case was very similar in principle to that of General Stark, and to other cases in which pensions had been granted for services, and not for disability; and to the second, that the act creating the Navy Pension Fund contained a provision that the surplus thereof should be applied to objects of this description, and that there was no reason for discriminating between our naval heroes, whether they served before or after the passage of this act; being in the one case or the other entitled to stand on the same footing.

These were the general grounds of argument, *pro* and *con.*

Mr. METCALF spoke as follows:

I do not rise, said he, in opposition to the passage of the bill now under consideration, because I have less of the good feelings of sympathy and of kindness for our distinguished Commodores, for officers and soldiers, than the worthy gentlemen who have so zealously advocated the measure. The bill will be partial in its operation—in principle unjust. Commodore Tucker, too wealthy to avail himself of the provisions of the general pension law, seeks to obtain a pension from the Government, by the passage of an act for his special and exclusive benefit. I will not call into question the merits of the application; but I believe the claims of many others, of equal merit, have been very righteously rejected. If we had an inexhaustible fund, a pile of jingling dollars as high as a mountain, to which we could resort for the purpose of obtaining the means by which to make a display of our generosity, I would go as far as any other man in dealing out the bounty of my country to Commodores, to officers, and soldiers. But in this, as in every case of a similar character, I consider it the duty of Congress to look at both sides of the question, and not altogether at the one side; that we should decide between the citizen and the soldier on principles of stern and undeviating justice.

It does seem to me, that we should not suffer our feelings in behalf of those upon whom the public treasury appears to have such powerful attractions, to mislead our judgment; or, rather, that

we should not entirely forget to feel for that class of our fellow-citizens from whose pockets the cash is to be drawn, by which we are to manifest our liberality.

Reward the officers and soldiers of your country, I beseech you—amply reward them: give pensions to those who are entitled to pensions, and never withhold your bounty from those who have sustained injuries and wounds, and have shed their blood in the service and battles of their country; withhold justice from none. But do not sacrifice your industrious and productive citizens, whose lot it is to drudge and toil for the support of the whole, upon the altar of a misapplied generosity. When I reflect on the past and the present, said Mr. M., it fills me with the most afflicting and melancholy forebodings for the future. We have but little to fear from our enemies, much from our friends. In discharging the obligation of gratitude to public functionaries and military men, both liberty and property will in the end be required. Tell me not of precedents; a righteous cause requires no such propping, but relies for success upon its own intrinsic merits. If the Government has before done wrong, will you plead it in justification of another wrong which you wish to impose on your citizens? If the treasure of this people has, at any former period, been wasted with the hand of profusion and extravagance, until they have been imperceptibly conducted to the very brink of ruin, will you plead the precedent which met the sanction of an inconsiderate and an evil hour, for precipitating them from the precipice?

Shall we not retreat while it is in our power to do so, and when we have such fair warning of the dangers that lie immediately before us? Shall we go on to justify one wrong with another, until we oppress, with excessive burdens, the great mass of our fellow-citizens, and make them bow down, dispirited and despairing, beneath a load of intolerable taxation?

With these feelings and sentiments, I will only add, that I do enter the most solemn protest against the passage of the bill before us.

The yeas and nays on the final passage of the bill were as follows:

YEAS—Messrs. Adams, Allen of Massachusetts, Allen, of New York, Baldwin, Bateman, Bayly, Beecher, Bloomfield, Brush, Butler of Louisiana, Campbell, Case, Clark, Clay, Crawford, Crowell, Cushman, Dane, Darlington, Denison, Dickinson, Edwards of Pennsylvania, Eustis, Fay, Folger, Ford, Forrest, Fuller, Gorham, Gross of New York, Hackley, Hemphill, Hendricks, Herrick, Hill, Hobart, Jones of Tennessee, Kinsey, Kinsley, Lathrop, Lincoln, Maclay, McCreary, McCullough, Mallary, Meech, Meigs, Mercer, Monell, Montgomery, S. Moore, Morton, Moseley, Murray, Neale, Nelson of Virginia, Newton, Parker of Massachusetts, Pinckney, Pitcher, Reid, Ringgold, Rogers, Russ, Sergeant, Silsbee, Simkins, Sloan, Smith of Maryland, Street, Strong of Vermont, Strong of New York, Udree, Van Rensselaer, Walker, Wallace, and Whitman—77.

NAYS—Messrs. Abbot, Alexander, Allen of Tennessee, Anderson, Archer of Maryland, Archer of Virginia, Baker, Ball, Barbour, Blackledge, Boden, Brevard, Brown, Bryan, Buffum, Cannon, Clagett,

Cobb, Cocke, Crafts, Cuthbert, Davidson, Dewitt, Earle, Eddy, Edwards of North Carolina, Floyd, Foot, Garnett, Gray, Gross of Pennsylvania, Hall of New York, Hardin, Hibshman, Hooks, Hostetter, Jackson, Johnson, Jones of Virginia, Kent, Little, Livermore, McCoy, McLean of Kentucky, Marchand, Metcalf, R. Moore, T. L. Moore, Parker of Virginia, Patterson, Plumer, Randolph, Rhea, Rich, Richards, Robertson, Ross, Shaw, A. Smyth of Virginia, Smith of North Carolina, Southard, Stevens, Swearingen, Terrell, Tomlinson, Tracy, Trimble, Tucker of Virginia, Tucker of South Carolina, Tyler, Upham, Wendover, Williams of Virginia, Williams of North Carolina, and Wood—75.

MISSOURI.

Mr. CLAY then rose to make his expected motion respecting Missouri, which was in the following shape:

Resolved, That a committee be appointed, on the part of this House, jointly with such committee as may be appointed on the part of the Senate, to consider and report to the Senate and to the House, respectively, whether it be expedient or not to make provision for the admission of Missouri into the Union on the same footing as the original States, and for the due execution of the laws of the United States, within Missouri; and, if not, whether any other, and what provision, adapted to her actual condition, ought to be made by law.

On this motion there took place a debate of about one hour's length.

Mr. FLOYD moved to amend the same by striking out these words, viz: "and if not, whether any other and what provision adapted to her actual condition ought to be made by law."

And the question being taken so to amend, it was determined in the negative.

The question was then taken to agree to the resolution, and passed in the affirmative, yeas 101, nays 55, as follows:

YEAS—Messrs. Abbot, Allen of Tennessee, Anderson, Archer of Maryland, Archer of Virginia, Baker, Baldwin, Ball, Bateman, Beecher, Blackledge, Bloomfield, Brevard, Brown, Brush, Bryan, Campbell, Cannon, Clark, Clay, Cobb, Cocke, Crafts, Crowell, Culpeper, Cushman, Cuthbert, Dane, Darlington, Davidson, Dickinson, Earle, Eddy, Eustis, Fisher, Folger, Ford, Fuller, Gross of New York, Gross of Pennsylvania, Guyon, Hackley, Hardin, Hendricks, Hill, Hobart, Hooks, Jackson, Jones of Tennessee, Kent, Kinsey, Little, Livermore, McCoy, McCreary, McLean of Kentucky, Mallary, Meech, Meigs, Mercer, Metcalf, Montgomery, R. Moore, S. Moore, T. L. Moore, Morton, Murray, Neale, Newton, Parker of Virginia, Pinckney, Pitcher, Plumer, Rankin, Reid, Rhea, Ringgold, Robertson, Rogers, Ross, Simkins, Sloan, Smith of New Jersey, Smith of Maryland, A. Smyth of Virginia, Smith of North Carolina, Southard, Stevens, Storrs, Strong of New York, Swearingen, Terrell, Tucker of Virginia, Tucker of South Carolina, Tyler, Udree, Upham, Walker, Wendover, and Williams of North Carolina.

NAYS—Messrs. Adams, Alexander, Allen of Massachusetts, Allen of New York, Bayly, Boden, Buffum, Butler of Louisiana, Case, Clagett, Crawford, Denison, Edwards of Pennsylvania, Edwards of North Carolina, Fay, Floyd, Foot, Forrest, Garnett, Gorham,

Gray, Hall of New York, Hemphill, Herrick, Hibshman, Hostetter, Johnson, Jones of Virginia, Kendall, Kinsley, Lathrop, Lincoln, Maclay, McCullough, Marchand, Monell, Moseley, Nelson of Massachusetts, Nelson of Virginia, Parker of Virginia, Patterson, Randolph, Rich, Richards, Russ, Sergeant, Shaw, Silsbee, Street, Strong of Vermont, Tomlinson, Van Rensselaer, Wallace, Williams of Virginia, and Wood.

On motion of Mr. CLAY, it was ordered that the said committee consist of twenty-three members; and that they be elected by ballot, pursuant to the rules and orders of the House.

Mr. RANDOLPH then moved that one member of the said committee be chosen from each State; which being negatived,

Mr. CLAY moved that the House do now proceed to the said election.

Mr. ALLEN, of Massachusetts, moved that the House proceed to the election to-morrow at 12 o'clock.

Mr. TRACY moved that the House proceed to the election on Monday next, at 12 o'clock.

This latter motion being rejected, the question was taken on the motion to proceed to the election to-morrow at 12 o'clock, and passed in the affirmative.

FRIDAY, February 23.

Mr. KENT, from the Committee for the District of Columbia, to which was referred the bill from the Senate, entitled "An act authorizing the sale of certain grounds belonging to the United States in the city of Washington," reported the same with an amendment; which was read, and the bill and amendment were committed to a Committee of the Whole.

Mr. KENT, from the same committee, also reported a bill to regulate the fees of the register of wills in the several counties within the District of Columbia; which was read twice, and committed to a Committee of the Whole.

Engrossed bills of the following titles, to wit:

An act making appropriations for the support of the Navy of the United States, for the year 1821; and an act to authorize the building of lighthouses on Cross and Pond Islands, in the harbor of Boothbay, and at the mouth of Oswego river, and placing buoys on the Shoals of Nantucket and Vineyard Sound, near the harbor of Wickford, and on the Altamaha river, and for other purposes; were severally read the third time, and passed.

The House proceeded to consider the bill authorizing the Secretary of State to issue a patent to Thomas Oxley; and the same being read—

Mr. LITTLE moved that it be committed to a Committee of the Whole to-morrow; which being negatived—

Mr. MALLARY moved to amend the same, by adding thereto the following, viz:

Provided, That the said Thomas Oxley shall take no advantage of this act after the time limited by the laws of the United States for the naturalization of foreigners, unless he becomes a citizen of the United States.

And the question being taken thereon, it was also determined in the negative, and the bill was ordered to be engrossed, and read a third time.

The SPEAKER laid before the House a letter from the Commissioner of the General Land Office, transmitting the reports numbered 10 and 11 of the land offices at Jackson Courthouse, in Louisiana, on claims for land; which were referred to the Committee on the Public Lands.

On motion of Mr. SOUTHARD, the Committee of the Whole was discharged from the further consideration of the bill to continue in force the act for regulating trade and intercourse with the Indian tribes; and, a motion of Mr. TRACY to lay the bill on the table having been negatived, the bill was ordered to be engrossed for a third reading.

PUBLIC LAND DEBT.

The House then, on motion of Mr. CROWELL, again resolved itself into a Committee of the Whole on the bill for the relief of purchasers of the public lands prior to the 1st of July, 1820.

Mr. McCOY had moved to strike out so much of the bill as permits a conditional surrender to the United States of the land purchased; so much as dispenses with interest on the money due for lands; and so much as makes a deduction, in certain cases, of twenty-five and thirty-seven and a half per cent. from the amount of the debt.

This motion gave rise to a wide debate on the merits of the bill, in the course of which the principle of the bill was supported and opposed by the following gentlemen: For the bill—Messrs. ANDERSON, BRUSH, HENDRICKS, JONES, and CLAY. Against the bill—Messrs. HARDIN, CULPEPER, ALLEN of Tennessee, and McCOY.

Mr. ALLEN, of Tennessee, said: The argument so much relied upon by the friends of the bill, that the Government is the creditor, and ought not to exercise that rigor in exacting compliance with contracts ruinous to her debtors that individuals would, because it is the common stock of all, as well as that urged on account of the depreciation of certain bank paper that will not pay the holder's debts without a discount equal to the reduction contemplated in the second section of the bill, would apply with force if the whole community were debtors of this description, and to be provided for in this bill; but, when not one in a thousand has purchased public land, and all are laboring under the difficulty so feelingly described, can it be right to apply the remedy to a few and leave others to struggle through as they can?

I hope I shall never be found hindmost in binding up the wounds inflicted by misfortune upon any of the sons of Adam. But, sir, the wretched and the poor presented to us here in such lively figures, have no part or lot in this matter; it is not the poor that buy land in any country.

Can any man make me believe that a farmer, owning a plantation on which he has resided three or four years without rent, is to be broken up and ruined by the payment of eighty dollars a year, the sum required to complete his title to a tract of a hundred and sixty acres of fertile land, under the law as it now stands? Such purchasers, I repeat it, can and will pay, and the greater part of them have done so already.

The provisions of this bill give such purchasers the liberty of paying annually fifty dollars, without interest, for eight years. If punctually paid it is not half the rent the poor have to pay for a home in any country; and if in default, you give them the chance of eight years more without paying anything. This is going further than they could ask. But, in getting at the class of purchasers for whom this bill is intended, it is necessary to attend to the poor, as, on other occasions, sometimes it is done to suit the views of the rich; they are the class whose interest is consulted in this bill; they have contrived to get all the land that is worth any thing in their possession; and a careful examination of the first section of the bill will convince any disinterested man that the object is to get the whole eventually for nothing.

If it is to be given away, I want a distribution more equal. The most deserving get none; men who risked their lives disputing the title of the aborigines, and marched over the dead bodies of your enemies to gain this land, get not one foot of it, but that which has been refused by these avaricious landmongers.

Independent of all the injustice that must follow this gratuity, among the land debtors, I view the precedent as a dangerous one in relation to the collection of revenue—I think I see another class of debtors ready to put in for their share.

The whole dependence of this Government is on revenue derived from imports that is now owing by merchants who have experienced greater losses than any class of men in the community. They are too useful and meritorious to be left beggars, after we finish the good work in the West. And, sir, the cordial support given this bill, by a certain section of the country, puts me on my guard, not being accustomed to see any extraordinary display of sympathy for the people of the West, except for those who we all know hold no land. I do not know that self-interest would influence any one in a solicitude for the passage of this bill. I am a stranger to all management in legislation. I belong to no party; I know of none; and far be it from me to impeach the motives of any. It is enough for me to judge for myself—in doing so, on this occasion, I believe sound policy and impartial justice requires from me a vote to strike out the first and second sections of this bill, and as much more as will defeat its passage.

The question being taken on Mr. McCOY's motion, it was negatived by a large majority.

Mr. ANDERSON moved to strike out that clause of the bill which proposes to allow an absolute reduction of thirty-three per cent. on the amount due by the debtors, and so to amend the bill as to confine the discount to those who should make prompt payment of the whole sum due.

This proposition brought on a long debate, in which Messrs. BEECHER, JONES, COOK, HARDIN, SERGEANT, ANDERSON, and CLAY, joined.

The amendment was finally negatived—yeas 55, nays 62.

1223   HISTORY OF CONGRESS.   1224

H. OF R.   *Missouri Committee—Imprisonment for Debt.*   FEBRUARY, 1821.

Mr. TUCKER, of Virginia, moved to add the following proviso to the first section of the bill:

Provided, also, That where any purchaser has purchased at the same time two or more quarter sections, he shall not be permitted to relinquish less than a quarter section.

This amendment was also negatived.

Mr. HARDIN then, for reasons which he stated, moved the following additional proviso to the third section of the bill:

And provided further, That the discount allowed in this bill shall not be made where the debtor shall fail to pay any of the said several instalments, as the same shall become due and payable.

This amendment, after some debate, was also rejected.

The Committee then rose and reported the bill to the House without amendment.

An unsuccessful motion was made to lay the bill on the table, with the view (it being late) of receiving the report of the tellers relative to the appointment of the committee on the subject of Missouri, (in examining the ballots for which the tellers had been employed nearly four hours.)

Mr. HARDIN then renewed the motion he made in Committee to amend the bill; when, a motion to that effect prevailing, the bill and proposed amendment were laid on the table.

MISSOURI COMMITTEE.

Mr. ARCHER, of Virginia, then reported that the tellers appointed to examine the ballots given for a committee of 23 members on the Missouri subject, according to the resolution of yesterday, had performed that duty—the result of which ballot he delivered in.

It appeared that 157 members had been voted for, but that the following 17 gentlemen only had a majority of the ballots given, and were elected, viz:

Messrs. Clay, of Ken.	Messrs. Eddy, of R. I.
Cobb, of Geo.	Ford, of N. Y.
Hill, of Maine.	Culbreth, of Md.
Barbour, of Va.	Hackley, of N. Y.
Storrs, of N. Y.	S. Moore, of Pa.
Cocke, of Tenn.	Stevens, of Con.
Rankin, of Miss.	Rogers, of Pa.
Archer, of Va.	Southard, of N. J.
Brown, of Ky.	

Seventeen only being elected, there remained six members yet to be appointed.

Mr. CLAY moved, as the operation of balloting again to-morrow would be tedious and create delay, that the House agree, by general consent, to select the remaining six members from those having received the next highest number of votes.

It was also suggested that the Speaker appoint the remaining six; and the Speaker having intimated to the House that if the duty devolved on him, he should, from a sense of propriety, make the appointment from the names standing next highest to those elected on the list, the latter course was concurred in by the House, Mr. CLAY having withdrawn his motion in favor of that course.

It appeared then that the five following gentlemen are also elected on the committee, being the next highest on the list:

Messrs. Darlington, of Pa.	Messrs. Gross, of N. Y.
Pitcher, of N. Y.	Livermore, of N. H.
Sloan, of Ohio.	

After these, Messrs. RANDOLPH and BALDWIN were next highest on the list, and having an equal number of votes, it remains for the Speaker to designate the gentleman who shall make the twenty-third member of the committee.

The House then adjourned.

SATURDAY, February 24.

Messrs. RANDOLPH, BALDWIN, and SMITH, of North Carolina, were appointed, in addition to those already named, to be of the joint committee on the Missouri subject; the first of these to fill up the number of the committee, and the two last to supply the vacancies occasioned by the resignation of Mr. LIVERMORE, and Mr. GROSS, of New York, who were excused from serving on the committee.

Mr. SERGEANT presented a memorial of Richard W. Meade, a citizen of the United States, and formerly, a merchant residing in Cadiz, in Spain, setting forth the nature and extent of his demands against the Government of that country, and praying that in such act or acts as may be passed for carrying into effect the stipulations contained in the treaty concluded and signed between the United States and Spain, on the 22d of February, 1819, and ratified, and the ratifications exchanged on the 22d instant, provision may be made for paying, without deduction, his claims which have been liquidated and acknowledged by the Government of that country, amounting to $491,153 33, according to the obligations of good faith contracted by the United States to Spain, under the express stipulations of the treaty aforesaid; which memorial was referred to the Committee on Foreign Affairs.

Mr. SMITH, of Maryland, from the Committee of Ways and Means, reported a bill making appropriations for the support of the Military Establishment for the current year; which was read twice, and committed.

Mr. CUTHBERT gave notice that he would, on Monday next, move the House for leave to bring in a bill to provide for sick seamen in the port of Savannah, in the State of Georgia.

The engrossed bill authorizing the Secretary of State to issue a patent to Thomas Oxley, was read a third time, passed, and sent to the Senate for concurrence.

IMPRISONMENT FOR DEBT.

Mr. NELSON, of Virginia, from the committee appointed on the 2d instant to inquire into the expediency of abolishing imprisonment for debt on process issuing from the courts of the United States, made a report, accompanied with a bill for that purpose; which bill was read twice, and committed to a Committee of the Whole. The report and bill are as follows:

The committee to whom was referred a resolution directing them to inquire into the expediency of abolishing imprisonment for debt on process issuing from the courts of the United States, report:

That the practice of imprisoning the body of a debtor, though sanctioned by very ancient usage, seems to have had its origin in an age of barbarism, and can only be considered an amelioration of that system by which the person of the debtor was subjected to be sold. Were it not wholly repugnant to every principle of free government, and incompatible with every sentiment of generous humanity, the exposure to sale of the debtor might seem more tolerable than his subjection to imprisonment. Policy and individual interest appear to combine to justify the servitude of the debtor, in preference to his seclusion from society, and his confinement in a dreary dungeon. By the former system, the profits of the labor of the debtor, brought into the common stock, would contribute to augment the wealth of the nation, and might eventually reimburse to the creditor the amount of his demand. It would certainly avoid those expenses which are annually incurred by subsisting so many unprofitable prisoners, without occupation, confined in the jails of the country. The unfortunate debtor, himself, might at least be blessed with the enjoyment of air and of light, and the occasional society of family and friends, from which, by the latter, he is oft-times most cruelly secluded, and closely immured within the walls of a prison; yet, who is there in this liberal age, and in this country, where the blessings of freedom are so extensively diffused, who would not recoil with horror and disgust from a proposition to expose to sale and servitude a fellow-citizen, whose misfortunes might subject him to the griping pressure of a hard creditor? And yet how few are there among the fortunate and successful, and even among those whom the benign precepts of our religion have taught "to melt at others' woe," who will be roused from apathy and indifference, when they daily learn that our jails are crowded with groups of these victims of misfortune; and who do not bury, in the oblivious round of frivolity and pleasure, even the momentary sensibilities which such a picture may produce? Nor are the rulers of this happy land free from the reproach which such a stain upon our code of laws cannot fail to imprint. Year after year has elapsed, and misery upon misery has been heaped upon these victims, and yet the hand of mercy is withheld. This crying indifference to the miseries of the wretched; this cold insensibility to the distress and suffering of our fellow-creatures, has too long stained the annals of our country, and blurred with the imputation of incongruity our boast of independence, liberty, and happiness, when contrasted with our practice of imprisonment for misfortune, not for crime. Rescued from this thraldom, the ingenious and the active, restored to a condition for energy and enterprise, may happily find means for accumulation, to the advantage of their creditors, and the subsistence in comfort for their families and themselves. Nor will it fail to add one other and important item to the long catalogue of blessings which spring from the fruitful source of happiness, founded in the liberal principles of free and equal government. Whilst, in other Governments, regulated by no such principles of equity and justice, imprisonment at the will of the despot may be enforced; whilst subject may prey upon subject, through the instrumentality of law and the extinction of his liberty; here let it be our boast that none can be deprived of his liberty but by the judgment of the law, upon conviction of crime; that none can be

imprisoned by his fellow-citizen for his poverty or misfortune; here let the possessions and the effects of the debtor be made subject to his debts, but spare his person at least for the solace and the comfort of his beggared and impoverished family.

In some of the States of this Union laws exist whereby the unfortunate may be relieved from this confinement. It is an example worthy of imitation by this Government. This singular phenomenon is presented, that a man imprisoned under one jurisdiction, in the same country, may, by one code of laws, be liberated from confinement, whilst another, confined in the same prison, under another jurisdiction, is denied this privilege, and must continue in hopeless and irremediable occlusion. To rescue the character of this Government from such a stigma, is the object of the committee. Aware that great delicacy and difficulty are to be encountered in devising such a system as would conduce to the complete attainment of this desirable object, and at the same time combine with it the most ample security to the rights of individuals, your committee might be deterred from making the attempt, were they not encouraged by the benevolence of the object, and strengthened by the persuasion that any errors which may spring from the novelty of the trial, may in future be corrected by the experience which will be readily acquired in the progress of the experiment.

Believing that the remedy heretofore extended to the creditor, whereby he has been enabled to use this coercion for the recovery of his debts, is completely within the control of the National Legislature to alter and modify as in their discretion shall seem wise, and, whilst they endeavor to exempt the person of the debtor, they supply the most unrestrained control over his goods and effects, they have no scruple to recommend the interference of Congress. Nor have your committee been unmindful of one of the happy consequences which may result from this innovation, in the limitation of that unbounded credit which has so extensively prevailed, to the great injury, and even ruin, of many honest, but imprudent debtors. The diminution of this system, so fascinating and seductive to many, may prove a real blessing to those who so often disregard the strongest dictates of prudence and discretion.

Upon the whole, whilst your committee attempt to shield the unfortunate debtor from cruel and useless oppression, they propose, in the most ample and unrestrained manner, to subject all his property to the rights and interests of the creditor.

They therefore beg leave to report the following bill:

Be it enacted, &c., That, from and after the passing of this act, imprisonment for debt on process issuing from the courts of the United States be, and the same is hereby, abolished; and, for the further enabling creditors to recover their just debts, *Be it enacted*, That the lands, tenements, goods, chattels, rights, and credits, of every debtor, shall be subject to be seized and taken, on execution, to satisfy any judgment, attachment, decree, or award of execution, rendered in any of the courts aforesaid. And the Supreme Court of the United States is hereby authorized and required to prescribe the necessary forms of all such process and executions, to be used in the courts aforesaid, as may be required to enable creditors to recover their just debts in every case whatever.

SEC. 2. *And be it further enacted*, That this act

shall not be construed to repeal any of the laws now existing which enable creditors to sue for and recover their debts, (except so far as relates to abolishing imprisonment for debt,) but shall be construed in aid of, and for the furtherance of, the prompt recovery of all just debts and demands whatever.

A message from the Senate informed the House that the Senate have passed the bill, entitled "An act to reduce and fix the Military Peace Establishment of the United States," with an amendment, in which they ask the concurrence of this House. The amendment was read, and referred to the Committee on Military Affairs.

TRADE WITH THE INDIANS.

The engrossed bill to continue in force the bill to establish trading-houses with the Indian tribes was read a third time.

A motion was made by Mr. RANKIN, to recommit the bill to the Committee on Indian Affairs, with instructions to report a bill for winding up the present establishments on the first day of September next.

On this motion there took place a debate, in which Messrs. SOUTHARD and WALKER opposed the motion, and Messrs. STORRS, TRACY, and FLOYD, supported it. The grounds on which the motion was opposed were, of course, the utility of this establishment; its value as a means of civilizing, and, at the same time, protecting the Indians, and the necessity of its present continuance, for the purpose of protecting the public property employed in it. The grounds taken on the other side, were, that the system was no longer recommended by the considerations which induced its first establishment; that it did not contribute to civilize the Indians, but rather to keep them in the hunter state, by holding out inducements to them to preserve furs; and that abuses were practised at the public trading establishments, by exacting profits not authorized by law, and not accounted for to the Government.

The motion to recommit, as above, was decided in the affirmative by a majority of fifty votes.

DUTY ON SALES AT AUCTION.

On motion of Mr. BALDWIN, the House resolved itself into a Committee of the Whole on the state of the Union, to take into consideration the bill laying a duty on sales of merchandise at auction.

Out of this bill grew a debate, which lasted the whole day.

Mr. SMITH, of Maryland, moved to strike out the proposed duty of two per cent. in order to insert a duty of one per cent.

This motion was supported by Messrs. SMITH, of Maryland, SILSBEE, and GORHAM, and opposed by Messrs. BALDWIN, SERGEANT, MEIGS, FOOT.

Mr. NELSON, of Virginia, being hostile to the whole bill, moved to strike out the first section; and then the Committee rose, and the House adjourned.

MONDAY, February 26.

Mr. NEWTON, from the Committee on Commerce, to which was referred the bill from the Senate, entitled "An act further to establish the compensation of the officers employed in the collection of duties on imports and tonnage, and for other purposes," reported the same with sundry amendments; which were read, and, together with the bill, committed to a Committee of the Whole.

Mr. SMITH, of Maryland, from the Committee of Ways and Means, reported a bill to authorize the President of the United States to borrow a sum, not exceeding $4,500,000; which was read twice, and committed to the Committee of the Whole on the state of the Union.

A Message was received from the President of the United States, transmitting an annual return of the militia of the United States, prepared by the Adjutant and Inspector General, conformably to the militia laws on that subject; which was ordered to lie on the table.

A message from the Senate informed the House that the Senate have passed bills of the following titles, to wit: "An act to continue in force for a further time the act, entitled 'An act for establishing trading-houses with the Indian tribes;'" "An act confirming the title of the Marquis de Maison Rouge;" and "An act to extend the charters of certain banks in the District of Columbia;" in which bills they ask the concurrence of this House.

MISSOURI.

Mr. CLAY, from the joint committee appointed on the Missouri subject, reported the following resolution:

Resolved, by the Senate and House of Representatives of the United States of America in Congress assembled, That Missouri shall be admitted into this Union on an equal footing with the original States in all respects whatever, upon the fundamental condition, that the fourth clause of the twenty-sixth section of the third article of the constitution submitted on the part of said State to Congress shall never be construed to authorize the passage of any law, and that no law shall be passed in conformity thereto, by which any citizen of either of the States in this Union shall be excluded from the enjoyment of any of the privileges and immunities to which such citizen is entitled under the Constitution of the United States: *Provided,* That the Legislature of the said State, by a solemn public act, shall declare the assent of the said State to the said fundamental condition, and shall transmit to the President of the United States, on or before the fourth Monday in November next, an authentic copy of the said act; upon the receipt whereof the President, by proclamation, shall announce the fact: whereupon, and without any further proceeding on the part of Congress, the admission of the said State into this Union shall be considered as complete.

The said resolution was twice read, and ordered to lie on the table, on motion of Mr. CLAY, with the avowed intention of calling for its consideration in the course of this day.

PUBLIC LANDS.

The House then proceeded to the consideration of the bill for the relief of certain purchasers of public lands.

Mr. FOOT moved to recommit the bill to the Committee on Public Lands, with instructions to report a bill to amend the third section of the act of the 24th of April, 1820, entitled "An act making further provision for the sale of public lands," so as to fix the price at which the public lands shall be offered for sale at one dollar and sixty-four cents per acre; and also to provide for suspending, for a limited time, the sale or forfeiture of lands, for failure in completing the payment thereon.

This motion was opposed by Mr. ANDERSON, supported by Mr. FOOT, and negatived by no large majority.

Mr. WOOD moved to amend the bill, so as to strike out that part which classifies the land debtors, deferring their payments for eight, six, or four years, &c.

After a few remarks from one or two gentlemen, for and against this motion, it was decided in the negative without a division.

Mr. ROBERTSON then, after some introductory remarks, moved to amend the bill—his object being avowed to be to exclude mere speculators from the benefit of its provisions—so as to confine the right of relinquishment to "as much thereof ' (of the land) as shall then be paid for, and no ' more nor less: *Provided*, That all persons who ' reside on or have improved, before the passage ' of this act, any section, half section, or quarter ' section, upon which the whole purchase-money ' has not been paid, shall have the privilege of re-' linquishing any legal division or subdivisions ' thereof."

This motion was earnestly opposed by Mr. HENDRICKS, and as zealously supported by Mr. ROBERTSON; and was finally negatived by a small majority.

Some other amendment was made to the bill, which the reporter did not distinctly understand.

Mr. METCALF, of Kentucky, rose and said, the times had truly been such, especially in the Western country, as to involve almost indiscriminately the rich and the poor, the prudent and the imprudent. That almost all classes were suffering, and he was fearful those difficulties, embarrassments, and sufferings, were increasing. He rejoiced to see such a disposition prevailing to pass an act of general amnesty and relief to those individuals who had been beguiled into error by the injudicious and impolitic movements of the Government, and hoped it might be done without detriment to the public interest. If so, it was kind and parental in the Government to shield a portion of its citizens from inevitable ruin. He was delighted with the sentiments which had just been expressed by his friend from New York, (Mr. WOOD,) who sat near him. He concurred most heartily in opinion with that gentleman "that it was better to *settle* than to *sell* the public lands." To people this vast region of country with innumerable happy human beings, ought to be the first and primary object of every statesman and politician, whose own happiness is so nearly connected with the happiness of his fellow men as to form a material part of it. The revenue to be derived from the sale of those lands was a matter of but secondary consideration. His reflections had long since conducted him to such a conclusion.

Mr. M. said he was also delighted with the sentiments which were yesterday expressed by both the advocates and opposers of this bill. All parties professed to be in favor of relieving the poor man and the actual settler. The only objection urged against the bill, was made upon the ground that the relief was too liberal to extensive purchasers, and to those whom gentlemen were pleased to denominate speculators. The relief of the poor man and the actual settler, was professedly the principal object of the advocates of the bill, but they insist upon the impracticability of distinguishing, or of drawing a line of demarcation between the various classes of purchasers.

Entertaining no doubt, said Mr. M., of the sincerity of gentlemen on both sides of the question, I cannot but feel a lively hope that the proposed amendment will meet with the approbation of all parties. All of us roundly assert our readiness to relieve from oppression the suffering poor; and none but the poor can be relieved by the amendment. That class of citizens which it embraced were generally stigmatized with the name of squatters; and it was said they had located themselves on the public lands in violation of the law. What law? A law, if any such there be, both unnatural and unjust. They were moved by the paramount law of necessity—by the strong and irresistible impulse of nature. They were destitute of the means with which to purchase in the interior or elsewhere. They had families to provide for—they moved to the wilderness; surmounted all the obstacles to which the first settlers are subjected; paved the way, he hoped, to the future way and residence of a numerous and happy population. In doing so they had thrown themselves upon the mercy of the Government; and who can be more entitled to legislative protection? All those, Mr. Speaker, said Mr. M., who live in the same age with you and me, are no doubt deeply interested in a fair and proper disposition of the public land. And future generations are probably more interested than the present.

The soil, the territory which we are about to dispose of, may be considered in the light of a goodly inheritance—a rich legacy bequeathed to us by our common parent, who is all kindness, for the use and benefit of those who wish to cultivate it. And I am persuaded that the happiness and prosperity for centuries to come, will, to some extent at least, depend on the wisdom and justice of those to whom the power of disposing of this vast tract of country is delegated.

Then will it not be well that we should endeavor to base our measures on principles of equity and justice? And that we should suffer no part of the soil to be diverted from its legitimate purposes to that of speculation or monopoly.

History informs us that when the German and Scythian nations conquered and took possession of a portion of the Roman empire, a few great military chieftains usurped themselves the whole of the lands. Add to this the laws of primogeniture, and of entailments that succeeded, and who that does not close his eyes against the light can be at a loss to discern the causes that enabled the few to bind in chains not to be broken countless millions of their fellow sojourners here, and to make them bow in base and degrading submission for a succession of ages—for many centuries—to their arbitrary and despotic rule. Will not the same causes produce the same effects? And what is the difference, whether your landed domain, this joint inheritance of all, shall be seized upon by military force, by unjust laws, or by the magic power of cash in hand?

But, perhaps, I may be told that we have no laws of primogeniture—no entailments; that landed estate is alienable, and even subject to the payment of debts; and, therefore, that there is no danger of creating a feudal aristocracy; and at all events, that the time is very remote. But, it does seem to me to be a solemn duty we owe to ourselves and to posterity, in the first place, not to deliver over all the rich and valuable portions of this great national domain, so as to exclude from a just participation all those who are without money, lest those to whom it is given, should, in time, discover the art of securing it to themselves in large quantities, to the great injury of the multitude who may live in a future day and generation.

What is this territory, this soil, but a vast capital in the hands of the nation? And a capital that ought not to remain inactive as long as there is a solitary individual laborer who wishes to cultivate it unemployed. Is it not by the application of labor to capital that a nation contributes to the comfort, and happiness, and wealth of its citizens, and, consequently, to its own greatness and grandeur? Then shall we withhold a small portion of this vast capital of which we possess so much from the use and benefit of those who wish to apply their labor to it; who have already made some improvements which you are about to wrest from them by the strong arm of power; who are extremely poor, and who, if they are thus driven out from beneath their only shelter, have no other resource beneath the sun from which they can expect to procure the means of comfortable living and of raising a family? And shall it be said that the acts of a great, a magnanimous, and free people are more oppressive, and less humane, than were the acts of His Catholic Majesty touching this matter? We all know that, to the man with a family, he gave without price four hundred arpens, and fifty additional arpens for each child, on condition that he would settle upon, cultivate, and improve it. To the single man, who had been four years a resident, who was industrious, and under a good moral character, he gave two hundred arpens on the same conditions. But, if he could obtain a certificate from a meritorious old farmer, stating that he was willing to give him his daughter in marriage; in that case, he was entitled to his two hundred arpens as soon as the marriage contract was consummated, though he had not been so long a resident. Admirable policy! and well calculated to prevent a fearful and dangerous increase of old bachelors in the land. I am aware, Mr. Speaker, said Mr. M., that I am surrounded even on this floor by a number, I will not say of old, that would be an uncourteous ex-

pression, but I will say of honorable bachelors—bachelors who have become so from choice, and not from compulsion. But, from my knowledge of these my worthy and respectable friends, of their generosity, of the nobleness of their feelings, and of their gallantry, too, I am warranted in saying that they would be among the very last who would interpose the slightest barrier to matrimony, or make bachelors from compulsion. I, therefore, confidently calculate on their assistance in removing every obstacle of the kind alluded to out of the way of our young but poor fellow-citizens.

This policy of the Spanish Government, in my estimation, sprung from the soundest suggestions of wisdom; and the voice of humanity too, was consulted in its adoption.

Now, let us look at the condition of a vast population in the Unon, and, though we shall find much cause for gratulating and rejoicing, we shall also find that much remains to be done, for thousands and tens of thousands of our fellow-citizens. If I am not mistaken, it has lately been said on this floor that at least one-half of the free white citizens of one of the old States were deprived of the inestimable right of suffrage because they were not possessed of the landed, or some other property qualification.

Other old States have adopted similar provisions; and with their State regulations, however repugnant to my feelings, I have nothing to do. I only mention it incidentally in adverting to the condition of our common country. It will be admitted, I presume, that, in all the old States, and, in some of the new, there is a vast proportion of the citizens who own no land, who are destitute of house and home; who cannot find employment in manufacturing establishments, or otherwise, by which to procure the means of comfortable living and of raising a family.

What is the language of an aged patriot and statesman, (who was once President of the United States,) in the late Convention of Massachusetts? It is that "more than half of the citizens of that State have no property." Mark this language well—"more than *half have no property*." Here, then, are objects upon whom their representatives might legitimately exercise all their benevolence.

But, sir, let the Government beware of a policy so oppressive, lest in the end we endanger if not subvert the liberties of the country. Is there no danger in a loose, disjointed, floating population, whose interests are utterly disregarded? With all the deference and all the respect so justly due to gentlemen with whom it is my lot to differ in opinion on this subject, I must say that I would not dispose of the public land with an eye solely to the immediate revenue derivable from it; but, I would guard most cautiously against either speculation or monopoly.

With all his superior intelligence and his knowledge, man is, perhaps, less consistent with himself than any other animal. He is blessed with certain powers to do good; and, notwithstanding the narrow and contracted limits within which these powers are circumscribed, yet if he would give a proper direction to his energies, if he would exert them on objects within his sphere of action, as would seem to be the duty of a rational being, his virtues, his benevolence, and his philanthropy, would be seen, and felt, and acknowledged with feelings of gratitude by his fellow men. But he overlooks the real and substantial good which he has in his power to render with certainty and effect, and in search of remote and visionary objects he travels on in trackless mazes,

> " Led on by Fancy's meteor ray,
>   By passion driven."

Though the poet's other couplet, I fear,

> " But yet the light that leads astray
>   Is light from Heaven,"

is wholly inapplicable to such an individual. He seems to have some unsubstantial and unattainable object always in view. He is tickled with the idea of an Abolition Society, well pleased with a Colonization Society, (in which I wish him success with all my heart,) and he thinks he has discharged his duty to his Maker by promoting the views and giving an impulse to missionary societies. Yes ; to missionary societies—objects laudable enough in themselves. The restless mind must have employment ; and by the evening's fireside the Christian, the philosopher, and the philanthropist, may indulge in these pleasing but abstract and speculative views and theories—and a pleasant dream that night is the fruit of their labors, and, I fear, their only reward.

Shall the practical statesman, too, when he is contributing, with his purse and his influence, to the extension of his religion among the heathen—while he is commiserating the condition of the unfortunate and devoted African, and magnifying his merits by making them the constant theme of his conversation, the seasoning and chief ingredient to his eloquence, the unceasing burden of his song ; and that, too, without even pretending that he has made the slightest discovery of the means by which his condition is to be ameliorated—while his bosom is burning with the most ardent desire for the success of the South American Patriots in their generous struggle for self-government ;—shall he, too, I say—the practical statesman, with all these seemingly generous and noble feelings, spurning dull reality, neglecting to be serviceable where it is in his power to be so, overlooking those immediately around him, who ought to be the first objects of his care and his solicitude—raise himself on the pinions of fancy, penetrate the clouds, and from thence attempt to direct his idle gaze to the remotest corners of the habitable globe, in search of a Hindoo, a Brahmin, a Tartar, a Hottentot, or of some such object, upon whom to bestow his benevolence! If he does this thing, sir, will he not in the end be apt to share the fate of an ambitious one of old, who was cast down from a very desirable height for his arrogance and his presumption? Or, at least, like the dove from the ark, (the innocence of its nature excepted,) may he not expect to return at last among his brethren, without having found whereupon to rest the sole of his foot ?

Now, in the disposal of the public lands, he has it in his power to render certain, substantial, and lasting services to thousands and tens of thousands of the sons and daughters of men—" bone of his bone, and flesh of his flesh," his neighbors—I mean, his white neighbors, his relations, children of the Republic, individuals who would rejoice to have a home upon those lands, where they might cultivate the soil in peace, and raise, for the benefit of their country, a virtuous, a laborious, agricultural, and republican family. I confess, sir, said Mr. M., that, if I could have my way, instead of pushing off these poor individuals from the small quantity of public lands they now occupy—instead of turning them out to the buffetings of the pitiless storm, and violently wresting from them their little cabins and other improvements, I would consider that we already had land enough in the market, and I would invite a stream of population from the old States. Many Eastern boys and girls among them, who, though poor at first, and "owning no property," would, in time, like so many lofty pines or sturdy oaks, with roots shot deep beneath the ground, defy the howling storm—defy the rude assault of their country's foes. Yes! I would plant the young couple, whose whole estate consisted in nothing more than a horse, a cow, a bed, and gun—perhaps not so much as that—but who had health and strength to labor, while their hearts were warm, and cheeks still glowing with the blood of youth, far from the haughty landlord's frown, where they might rear their lovely offspring, and learn them how, in the paths of virtue, of innocence, of patriotism, and of independence, too, to walk with souls erect, acknowledging no superior, save Him alone who made us all—who made this land for the use of those who might wish to cultivate it ; and of which they can only be deprived by the mistaken policy or injustice of their fellow-men.

Mr. Metcalf then moved to amend the bill, by adding thereto the following as a new section :

" *Be it further enacted,* That every person, or the representatives of every person, who, prior to the passage of this act, did actually inhabit or cultivate a tract of unappropriated land belonging to the United States, shall be entitled to a preference in becoming the purchaser of one quarter section, including his or their settlement, at the minimum price of the Government. And the fact of such settlement being established in conformity to existing laws, before the Register and Receiver in either of the land districts of the United States, before the day upon which the same is exposed to public sale, the said sale shall be suspended for the term of —— years : *Provided, however,* That every person who it shall appear is the owner of any other land shall be excluded from the benefit of this act."

And the question being taken thereon, it was decided in the negative by a large majority.

The bill was then further amended, on the motion of Mr. Tucker, of Virginia.

Mr. McCoy moved to amend the bill by striking out the whole of the bill, after the enacting clause, and inserting the following in lieu thereof :

" That the operation of all acts providing for the sale of the lands of the United States be, and the same is hereby, suspended until the 30th day of April, 1822,

1235   **HISTORY OF CONGRESS.**   1236

H. of R.   *Admission of Missouri.*   FEBRUARY, 1821.

in favor of purchasers of public lands, at any of the land offices of the United States, for any instalment or instalments, remaining unpaid, or which may fall due, previous to the day aforesaid."

The question being taken on this motion, it was negatived—68 to 40.

Mr. CANNON moved to amend the bill so as to allow to those who purchased lands at a rate less than three dollars per acre the same discount as is allowed to purchasers above that rate, and to reduce that discount from thirty-three and a third per cent. to twenty-five per cent.

This amendment was supported by Mr. CANNON, and spoken upon by Mr. HENDRICKS and Mr. HARDIN, and was agreed to—69 to 53.

Mr. ANDERSON then moved to amend the bill, (since the system of the Senate had been broken in upon) so as to strike out all that proposes an absolute reduction of 25 per cent. on the amount due by each purchaser of public land, his object being to substitute for it an allowance of discount for prompt payment.

This motion was opposed by Mr. CLAY, and supported by Messrs. ANDERSON, FULLER, and COBB. The vote thereon was as follows:

YEAS—Messrs. Abbot, Alexander, Allen of Massachusetts, Allen of Tennessee, Anderson, Archer, of Maryland, Ball, Barbour, Bateman, Bloomfield, Bryan, Buffum, Case, Cobb, Cocke, Culbreth, Culpeper, Cuthbert, Davidson, Denison, Dewitt, Dickinson, Eddy, Edwards of North Carolina, Fisher, Floyd, Folger, Foot, Gray, Guyon, Hall of New York, Hardin, Hibshman, Hill, Hooks, Hostetter, Little, Livermore, Maclay, McCoy, McCreary, McLean of Kentucky, Mercer, Metcalf, Monell, Montgomery, S. Moore, T. L. Moore, Morton, Murray, Neale, Nelson of Massachusetts, Parker of Massachusetts, Parker of Virginia, Phelps, Philson, Pinckney, Plumer, Rankin, Reid, Richards, Robertson, Rogers, Russ, Settle, Silsbee, Simkins, Southard, Stevens, Storrs, Terrell, Tomlinson, Tracy, Trimble, Tucker of Virginia, Tucker of South Carolina, Udree, Walker, Warfield, Wendover, Williams of Virginia, Williams of North Carolina, and Wood—83.

NAYS—Messrs. Adams, Allen of New York, Baker, Baldwin, Bayly, Beecher, Blackledge, Boden, Brush, Butler of Louisiana, Campbell, Cannon, Clark. Clay, Cook, Crowell, Cushman, Dane, Darlington, Edwards of Con., Edwards of Penn., Eustis, Fay, Ford, Fuller, Gorham, Gross of N. York, Gross of Penn., Hackley, Hemphill, Hendricks, Herrick, Hobart, Jackson, Johnson, Jones of Virginia, Jones of Tennessee, Kendall, Kinsey, Lathrop, Lincoln, McCullough, Mallary, Marchand, Meech, R. Moore, Moseley, Nelson of Virginia, Newton, Patterson, Pitcher, Rhea, Rich, Richmond, Ringgold, Ross, Sergeant, Shaw, Sloan, Smith of New Jersey, Smith of Maryland, A. Smyth of Virginia, Smith of North Carolina, Street, Strong of Vermont, Strong of New York, Swearingen, Tarr, Tyler, and Van Rensselaer—70.

So the motion of Mr. ANDERSON was agreed to.

On motion of Mr. TUCKER, of Virginia, the House then agreed to reconsider the amendment, adopted on Friday last, on the motion of Mr. HARDIN; and Mr. H. then withdrew the same.

Mr. ANDERSON then moved to amend the bill, by adding thereto a provision contemplating the

allowance of a considerable deduction (37½ per cent.) for prompt payment of the money due.

This motion was opposed by Mr. CLAY, as going to favor moneyed men only, who have no occasion for indulgence from the Government. He concluded, by moving that the bill and amendment lie on the table, with a view of taking up the Missouri resolution, which, he hoped, there was a general wish to see acted upon this day.

The motion was agreed to.

MISSOURI.

The House then took up the resolution, as above reported by the joint committee on the Missouri subject.

Mr. CLAY briefly explained the views of the committee, and the considerations which induced them to report the resolution. He considered this resolution as being the same in effect as that which had been previously reported by the former committee of thirteen members; and stated that the committee on the part of the Senate was unanimous, and that on the part of this House nearly so, in favor of this resolution.

Mr. ADAMS, of Massachusetts. delivered his objections to the resolution, on the ground of the defect of power in the Congress of the United States to authorize or require the Legislature of a State, once admitted into the Union, to do the act proposed by this resolution to be demanded of the Legislature of Missouri. *

---

* *To the Editors of the National Intelligencer:*

GENTLEMEN: In your paper of Tuesday last, stating the proceedings of the House of Representatives, on the resolution for the admission of Missouri into the Union, is the following erroneous paragraph : "Mr. Adams, of Massachusetts, delivered his objections to the resolution, on the ground of the defect of power in the Congress of the United States to authorize or require the Legislature of a State, once admitted into the Union, to do the act proposed by this resolution to be demanded of the Legislature of Missouri."

I did not object to the resolution on the ground in this paragraph mentioned. But, on that occasion, I did say that Congress had no power to authorize those who are called the Legislature of Missouri, to declare the assent of said State to the fundamental condition contained in said resolution; neither had the people of Missouri given their said Legislature authority to give any such assent; their constitution, by which they are to be governed, directly forbids it; therefore, if this Legislature should give their assent to this fundamental condition, it would not be binding on the people of Missouri. If Missouri is to be admitted on this fundamental condition, under the power of Congress, why have this assent transmitted to the President? Let Congress empower the gentlemen Missouri has sent here as Senators and Representative, by their solemn public act, to declare the assent of the said State to the said fundamental condition ; and let them transmit this to Congress, and have the whole business settled at once. This would be equally as binding upon the people of Missouri as the other.

I also said that Congress, at the last session, passed an act authorizing the people of Missouri to call a convention, form a constitution, and be admitted into the Union upon certain conditions; one of which was,

Mr. BROWN, of Kentucky, replied to the arguments of Mr. ADAMS, and defended the resolution from the objections set up against it. He earnestly invited the House to support the resolution, and thus to end the distracting and painful controversy respecting Missouri.

Mr. ADAMS spoke in explanation.

Mr. ALLEN, of Massachusetts, next obtained the floor, and delivered his sentiments with much earnestness, and pretty much at large, in opposition to the resolution, on the ground as well of its terms, as of hostility to the toleration of slavery in any shape, or under any pretence, by the legislation of Congress.

[During the progress of this speech, Mr. ALLEN was called to order by Mr. TRIMBLE, because discussing not the question before the House, but a question decided at the last session. The SPEAKER, however, overruled this objection.]

Mr. ALLEN concluded, by moving to amend the resolution by striking out the word "citizen," wherever it occurs in the resolution, as above printed, and to insert in lieu thereof, "free negro or mulatto."

---

that her constitution should not be repugnant to the Constitution of the United States. The people of Missouri did call a convention, and this convention did virtually declare that Missouri would *not* come into the Union upon the conditions proposed by Congress in said act. But they formed a constitution which the Senate and this House, by their votes, have declared to be repugnant to the Constitution of the United States. Missouri, not accepting the terms of admission set forth in the act of the last session, that act, so far as relates to Missouri is at an end, and Missouri is just where she began; and, if she desires to come into the Union, she must begin anew, unless Congress will admit her into the Union with a constitution repugnant to the Constitution of the United States. These constitutions, so far as they are repugnant to each other, cannot both stand; one of them must give way. In forming this compact for the admission of Missouri into the Union, the Congress of the United States is one party and Missouri the other, and in this particular case their powers are equal. Missouri has as good a right to say upon what terms she will become a member of the Union, as for Congress to say upon what terms she shall be received. When one party proposes terms, and the other accepts them, there is a union and binding on both parties. Missouri, in her constitution, has said upon what terms she will become a member of the Union; if she be admitted, Congress must admit her on these terms, and no other.

Should Congress admit Missouri into the Union upon a fundamental condition, which has not been agreed to by the people of Missouri, but is in direct opposition to what they, in their constitution, have declared are the terms upon which they would come into the Union, and should enforce this condition, Congress would usurp a power over Missouri, it not having been given by the Constitution of the United States.

These are some of the remarks I made on that occasion, and I will trouble you with these only, which tend to place the said paragraph in its true light.

      Your very humble servant,

    MARCH 1.   BENJAMIN ADAMS.

Mr. R. MOORE, of Pennsylvania, then required the previous question, believing that this subject had been so long debated, as to require that it be decided, in one way or another, without further consumption of the time of the House.

Ninety-five members having risen to second this motion, and the yeas and nays having been required thereon by Mr. RANDOLPH—

The question was stated in the following form: "Shall the main question be now put?" and was decided—for the previous question 109, against it 50, as follows:

YEAS—Messrs. Abbot, Alexander, Allen of New York, Allen of Tennessee, Archer of Maryland, Baker, Baldwin, Ball, Barbour, Bateman, Bayly, Beecher, Blackledge, Bloomfield, Boden, Brevard, Brown, Brush, Bryan, Buffum, Campbell, Cannon, Case, Clagett, Clark, Clay, Cocke, Crawford, Crowell, Cushman, Cuthbert, Darlington, Davidson, Dewitt, Eddy, Fisher, Foot, Forrest, Fuller, Gross of New York, Guyon, Hackley Hardin, Hendricks, Herrick, Hibshman, Hill, Hobart, Hooks, Hostetter, Jones of Tennessee, Kinsey, Kinsley, Lincoln, Little, Maclay, McCoy, McCreary, McCullough, McLean of Kentucky, Marchand, Meech, Meigs, Metcalf, Monell, Montgomery, R. Moore, S. Moore, T. L. Moore, Murray, Newton, Overstreet, Parker of Massachusetts, Patterson, Phelps, Philson, Pinckney, Pitcher, Rankin, Reid, Rhea, Rich, Richmond, Ringgold, Robertson, Rogers, Ross, Settle, Shaw, Simkins, Sloan, Smith of New Jersey, Smith of Maryland, A. Smyth of Virginia, Smith of North Carolina, Southard, Stevens, Storrs, Tarr, Trimble, Tucker of South Carolina, Tyler, Udree, Upham, Van Rensselaer, Walker, Wallace, and Williams of North Carolina.

NAYS—Messrs. Adams, Allen of Massachusetts, Anderson, Archer of Virginia, Butler of New Hampshire, Butler of Louisiana, Cobb, Cook, Culbreth, Dane, Dickinson, Edwards of Connecticut, Edwards of Pennsylvania, Edwards of North Carolina, Eustis, Fay, Floyd, Gorham, Gray, Gross of Pennsylvania, Hall of New York, Hemphill, Jackson, Johnson, Kendall, Lathrop, Livermore, Mallary, Morton, Moseley, Neale, Nelson of Massachusetts, Nelson of Va., Plumer, Randolph, Richards, Russ, Sergeant, Silsbee, Street, Strong of Vermont, Swearingen, Tomlinson, Tracy, Tucker of Virginia, Warfield, Wendover, Whitman, Williams of Virginia, and Wood.

The main question was then put, to wit: *Shall the resolution be engrossed and read a third time?* and passed in the affirmative—yeas 86, nays 82, as follows:

YEAS—Messrs. Abbot, Alexander, Allen of Tennessee, Anderson, Archer of Maryland, Archer of Virginia, Baldwin, Ball, Barbour, Bateman, Bayly, Blackledge, Bloomfield, Brevard, Brown, Bryan, Butler of Louisiana, Cannon, Clark, Clay, Cobb, Cocke, Crawford, Crowell, Culbreth, Culpeper, Cuthbert, Davidson, Eddy, Edwards of North Carolina, Fisher, Floyd, Ford, Gray, Guyon, Hackley, Hardin, Hill, Hooks, Jackson, Johnson, Jones of Virginia, Jones of Tennessee, Little, McCoy, McCreary, McLean of Kentucky, Meigs, Mercer, Metcalf, Montgomery, S. Moore, T. L. Moore, Neale, Nelson of Virginia, Newton, Overstreet, Pinckney, Rankin, Reid, Rhea, Ringgold, Robertson, Rogers, Sawyer, Settle, Shaw, Simkins, Smith of New Jersey, Smith of Maryland, A. Smyth of Virginia, Smith of North Carolina, Southard, Stevens, Storrs,

1239   **HISTORY OF CONGRESS.**   1240

H. of R.   *Proceedings.*   February, 1821.

Swearingen, Terrell, Trimble, Tucker of Virginia, Tucker of South Carolina, Tyler, Udree, Walker, Warfield, Williams of Virginia, and Williams of North Carolina.

Nays—Messrs. Adams, Allen of Massachusetts, Allen of New York, Baker, Beecher, Boden, Brush, Buffum, Butler of New Hampshire, Campbell, Case, Clagett, Cook, Cushman, Dane, Darlington, Denison, Dewitt, Dickinson, Edwards of Connecticut, Edwards of Pennsylvania, Eustis, Fay, Folger, Foot, Forrest, Fuller, Garnett, Gorham, Gross of New York, Gross of Pa., Hall of New York, Hemphill, Hendricks, Herrick, Hibshman, Hobart, Hostetter, Kendall, Kinsey, Kinsley, Lathrop, Lincoln, Livermore, Maclay, McCullough, Mallary, Marchand, Meech, Monell, R. Moore, Morton, Moseley, Murray, Nelson of Massachusetts, Parker of Massachusetts, Patterson, Phelps, Philson, Pitcher, Plumer, Randolph, Rich, Richards, Richmond, Ross, Russ, Sergeant, Silsbee, Sloan, Street, Strong of Vermont, Strong of New York, Tarr, Tomlinson, Tracy, Upham, Van Rensselaer, Wallace, Wendover, Whitman, and Wood.

The resolution was then ordered to be read a third time this day, but not without considerable opposition.

The resolution was accordingly read a third time, and put on its passage.

Mr. Randolph, in a speech of some twenty minutes, delivered the reasons why he should not vote for the resolution.

The final question was then taken on the resolution, and decided in the affirmative, as follows:

Yeas—Messrs. Abbot, Alexander, Allen of Tennessee, Anderson, Archer of Maryland, Archer of Virginia, Baldwin, Ball, Barbour, Bateman, Bayly, Blackledge, Bloomfield, Brevard, Brown, Bryan, Butler of Louisiana, Cannon, Clark, Clay, Cobb, Cocke, Crawford, Crowell, Culbreth, Culpeper, Cuthbert, Davidson, Eddy, Edwards of North Carolina, Fisher, Floyd, Ford, Gray, Guyon, Hackley, Hall of N. Carolina, Hardin, Hill, Hooks, Jackson, Johnson, Jones of Virginia, Jones of Tennessee, Little, McCoy, McCreary, McLean of Kentucky, Meigs, Mercer, Metcalf, Montgomery, S. Moore, T. L. Moore, Neale, Nelson of Virginia, Newton, Overstreet, Pinckney, Rankin, Reid, Rhea, Ringgold, Robertson, Rogers, Sawyer, Settle, Shaw, Simkins, Smith of New Jersey, Smith of Maryland, A. Smyth of Virginia, Smith of North Carolina, Southard, Stevens, Storrs, Swearingen, Terrell, Trimble, Tucker of Virginia, Tucker of South Carolina, Tyler, Udree, Walker, Warfield, Williams of Virginia, and Williams of North Carolina—87.

Nays—Messrs. Adams, Allen of Massachusetts, Allen of New York, Baker, Beecher, Boden, Brush, Buffum, Butler of New Hampshire, Campbell, Case, Clagett, Cook, Cushman, Dane, Darlington, Denison, Dewitt, Dickinson, Edwards of Connecticut, Edwards of Pennsylvania, Eustis, Fay, Folger, Foot, Forrest, Fuller, Gorham, Gross of New York, Gross of Pennsylvania, Hall of New York, Hemphill, Hendricks, Herrick, Hibshman, Hobart, Hostetter, Kendall Kinsey, Kinsley, Lathrop, Lincoln, Livermore, Maclay, McCullough, Mallary, Marchand, Meech, Monell, R. Moore, Morton, Moseley, Murray, Nelson of Massachusetts, Parker of Massachusetts, Patterson, Phelps, Philson, Pitcher, Plumer, Randolph, Rich, Richards, Richmond, Ross, Russ, Sergeant, Silsbee, Sloan, Street, Strong of Vermont, Strong of New York, Tarr, Tom-

linson, Tracy, Upham, Van Rensselaer, Wallace, Wendover, Whitman, and Wood—81.

So the resolution was passed, and ordered to be sent to the Senate for concurrence.

Mr. Clay moved that the House do now resume the consideration of the bill from the Senate, entitled "An act for the relief of the purchasers of public lands, prior to the 1st day of July, 1820;" and, the question being stated thereon, the House adjourned.

Tuesday, February 27.

Mr. Culbreth presented a printed copy of a report made to the Senate of the State of Maryland on the 30th of January, 1821, and assented to by that body, and by the House of Delegates on the 13th instant, relative to appropriations of public land for the purposes of education; to which is attached resolutions expressive of the opinion of the General Assembly of Maryland, "that each of the United States has an equal right to participate in the benefit of the public lands, the common property of the Union." That the States in whose favor Congress have not made appropriations of land for the purposes of education, are entitled to such appropriations as will correspond, in a just proportion, with those heretofore made in favor of other States; and that their Senators and Representatives in the Congress of the United States be requested to lay the said report and resolutions before their respective Houses, and use their endeavors to procure the passage of an act to carry into effect the just principles therein set forth; which report and resolutions were ordered to lie on the table.

Mr. Kent presented a petition of the President and Directors of the Mechanics' Bank of Alexandria, praying that the said bank may be included within the provisions of the bill which has passed the Senate, and is now pending before this House, to renew the charters of certain banks in the District of Columbia; which petition was referred to the Committee for the District of Columbia.

Mr. Williams, of North Carolina, from the Committee of Claims, made a report on the petition of Alexander Roddy, accompanied by a bill for his relief; which bill was read twice, and committed.

Mr. Smith, of Maryland, from the joint committee appointed to wait on the President of the United States, and to inform him of his re-election, reported that the committee had performed that duty, and were informed by the President that he would attend in the Hall of the House of Representatives on Monday next, at 12 o'clock, to take the oath of office prescribed in the Constitution of the United States.

Mr. Storrs, from the joint committee appointed to report what subjects before the two Houses are proper to be acted upon during the present session, made a report; which was ordered to lie on the table.

Mr. Nelson, of Virginia, from the Committee on Foreign Affairs, reported a bill for carrying into execution the treaty between the United State and Spain, concluded at Washington, the 22d of February, 1819; which was read twice, and committed to a Committee of the Whole on the state of the Union.

A message from the Senate informed the House that the Senate have passed bills of the following titles, to wit: "An act to authorize the appointment of certain Indian agents;" "An act to authorize the President of the United States to ascertain and designate certain boundaries;" "An act to establish the district of Blakeley;" and "An act providing for the adjudication and payment of claims arising under the Treaty of Amity, Settlement, and Limits, between the United States and His Catholic Majesty;" in which bills they ask the concurrence of this House.

Bills from the Senate of the following titles, to wit: "An act to continue in force, for a further time, the act entitled 'An act for establishing trading-houses with the Indian tribes;" "An act to authorize the appointment of certain Indian agents;" "An act confirming the title of the Marquis de Maison Rouge;" "An act to extend the charters of certain banks in the District of Columbia;" "An act to authorize the President of the United States to ascertain and designate certain boundaries;" "An act to establish the district of Blakeley;" and "An act providing for the adjudication and payment of claims arising under the Treaty of Amity, Settlement, and Limits, between the United States and His Catholic Majesty;" were severally read the first and second time, and referred; the first and second to the Committee on Indian Affairs; the third to the Committee on Private Land Claims; the fourth to the Committee for the District of Columbia; the fifth to the Committee on the Public Lands; the sixth to the Committee of Commerce; and the seventh to the Committee on Foreign Affairs.

On motion of Mr. SMITH, of Maryland, the bill further to amend the several acts relative to the Treasury, War, and Navy Departments, was taken up, and ordered to be engrossed for a third reading.

On motion of Mr. CANNON, the bill for the relief of Robert Purdy was passed through a Committee of the Whole; when

Mr. COBB moved to postpone the bill indefinitely. This motion gave rise to debate, in which Messrs. COBB, MOORE, CANNON, ROSS, McCoy, RHEA, COCKE, METCALF, CULPEPER, BALDWIN, and WILLIAMS, of North Carolina, took part. [From the debate, it appears that this bill proposes to indemnify Colonel Purdy from a judgment obtained against him by an individual, who was the keeper of a disorderly house on the skirts of an encampment of the army, which house, in order to preserve the discipline of the army, Colonel P. had caused to be destroyed.]

The vote being taken on the question of indefinite postponement, was decided in the affirmative, 57 to 47. So the bill was rejected.

Mr. WILLIAMS, of North Carolina, with a view to acting on the great mass of private bills before the House, moved that the House now have a recess of two hours, with a view to acting on business of that description on meeting again. This motion was negatived, 49 to 46.

MILITARY PEACE ESTABLISHMENT.

Mr. A. SMYTH, from the Committee on Military Affairs, to which had been referred the amendments of the Senate to the bill to reduce the Military Peace Establishment, reported the same with sundry amendments thereto—one of which was a section adopting for the government of the army and militia, when in service, the system of Regulations for the Army, compiled by Major General Scott—the other amendments were of a minor character.

The amendments reported by the Military Committee were severally agreed to.

Mr. COCKE moved to strike out of the Senate's amendments the provision for "one Major General, with two Aids-de-Camp;" which motion was supported by Messrs. COOKE, FOOT, COBB, HARDIN, LITTLE, MALLARY, and R. MOORE, on principle and expediency; and it was opposed by Messrs. BARBOUR, STORRS, CLAY, and NELSON, of Virginia, on the ground that as the Senate had made the amendment, they would probably adhere to it; that if disagreed to by this House, it might put the whole bill in jeopardy; that much would still have been done in the way of retrenchment even if this provision passed, and it would be better not to endanger the bill by rejecting this provision. Mr. KINSEY opposed the motion on principle, deeming a Major General necessary to make the proposed system perfect and fully efficient. After an ineffectual call, by Mr. NELSON, of Virginia, for the previous question—the debate having continued some time—

The question was taken on striking out the provision for the Major General, and was negatived, by yeas and noes. For striking out, 73; against it 79, as follows:

YEAS—Messrs. Abbot, Adams, Alexander, Allen of Massachusetts, Allen of Tennessee, Archer of Maryland, Archer of Virginia, Ball, Bateman, Bayly, Blackledge, Boden, Buffum, Butler of New Hampshire, Campbell, Cannon, Clagett, Cobb, Cocke, Crawford, Culpeper, Cuthbert, Eddy, Edwards of North Carolina, Fay, Fisher, Foot, Forrest, Gray, Gross of Pennsylvania, Guyon, Hardin, Hendricks, Herrick, Hibshman, Hill, Hostetter, Jackson, Jones of Virginia, Kendall, Kent, Kinsley, Lathrop, Little, Livermore, McCoy, McCreary, Mallary, Marchand, Meech, Metcalf, R. Moore, Murray, Neale, Patterson, Phelps, Plumer, Rankin, Rhea, Richards, Shaw, Stevens, Strong of Vermont, Tarr, Terrell, Tomlinson, Tompkins, Tucker of South Carolina, Tyler, Upham, Walker, Williams of Virginia, and Williams of North Carolina—73.

NAYS—Messrs. Allen of New York, Anderson, Baker, Baldwin, Barbour, Beecher, Bloomfield, Brevard, Brown, Brush, Butler of Louisiana, Case, Clark, Clay, Cook, Crowell, Culbreth, Cushman, Dane, Darlington, Davidson, Dewitt, Dickinson, Edwards of Connecticut, Edwards of Pennsylvania, Folger, Ford, Fuller, Gorman, Gross of New York, Hackley, Hall of New York, Hemphill, Hooks, Johnson, Jones of Tennessee, Kinsey, Maclay, McCullough, McLean of Kentucky, Meigs, Mercer, Montgomery, S. Moore, Morton, Moseley, Nelson of Massachusetts, Newton,

1243   HISTORY OF CONGRESS.   1244

H. of R.   *The Public Lands—Duties on French Vessels.*   FEBRUARY, 1821.

Parker of Massachusetts, Pinckney, Pitcher, Reid, Ringgold, Robertson, Rogers, Ross, Russ, Sergeant, Settle, Silsbee, Simkins, Sloan, Smith of New Jersey, Smith of Maryland, A. Smyth of Virginia, Smith of North Carolina, Southard, Storrs, Street, Strong of New York, Tracy, Trimble, Tucker of Virginia, Udree, Van Rensselaer, Wallace, Wendover, Whitman, and Wood—79.

Mr. Cobb moved further to amend the said amendment by striking out the word *two* wherever it occurs in the eighth line of the second section, and inserting in each place the word *one;* so that there should be *one* first lieutenant, and *one* second lieutenant, to each company of artillery, instead of two first and two second lieutenants.—Negatived.

Mr. Smith, of Maryland, moved to strike out the provision "for one Judge Advocate, with a salary of two thousand dollars;" and the motion was agreed to without a division.

Mr. Cannon then moved so to amend the amendments of the Senate, as, instead of *four* regiments of artillery and *seven* regiments of infantry, to reduce the number of regiments to *two* of artillery and *four* of infantry; and to make the companies consist of eighty-four, instead of forty-two men. After some remarks by Mr. C. in support of his amendments,

The motion was negatived without a division.

The amendments of the Senate, as amended by this House, were then agreed to; and ordered to be returned to the Senate for concurrence in the amendments of this House thereto.

THE RELIEF BILL—PUBLIC LANDS.

The House then resumed the consideration of the bill for the relief of the purchasers of the public lands—the following section proposed to be added to the bill, by Mr. Anderson, being still under consideration, viz:

Sec. 4. *And be it further enacted,* That in all cases where complete payment of the whole sum due, or which may become due, for any tract of land purchased from the United States as aforesaid, shall be made on or before the —— day of ——, a deduction at the rate of thirty-seven and a half per centum shall be allowed on the sum so remaining.

Mr. Crowell moved to fill the blank in the amendment with the 30th of September, 1823; which was negatived—yeas 9.

The blank was then, on motion of Mr. McLean, filled with the 30th of September, 1822.

Mr. McCoy made an unsuccessful motion to strike out thirty-seven and a half, and insert twenty-five per cent.

These questions, as well as the merits of the amendment, were largely discussed by Messrs. Anderson, Clay, Hardin, McCoy, Cook, and McLean.

The amendment offered by Mr. Anderson was finally adopted by yeas and nays—yeas 72, nays 62, as follows:

Yeas—Messrs. Abbot, Alexander, Allen of Massachusetts, Allen of New York, Baker, Baldwin, Ball, Beecher, Boden, Brown, Brush, Butler of Louisiana, Campbell, Cannon, Clark, Clay, Cobb, Cook, Craw-ford, Crowell, Cushman, Cuthbert, Darlington, Denison, Earle, Fay, Fisher, Garnett, Gorham, Hackley, Hardin, Hendricks, Herrick, Hill, Hostetter, Jackson, Johnson, Jones of Virginia, Kent, Kinsey, Kinsley, Lathrop, Livermore, McCullough, McLean of Kentucky, Mallary, Marchand, Meigs, Mercer, Metcalf, Montgomery, S. Moore, T. L. Moore, Moseley, Patterson, Pitcher, Plumer, Rankin, Reed, Rhea, Rogers, Ross, Settle, Sloan, Smith of New Jersey, A. Smyth of Virginia, Street, Strong of New York, Tarr, Tyler, Van Rensselaer, and Wallace—72.

Nays—Messrs. Adams, Allen of Tennessee, Anderson, Archer of Maryland, Archer of Virginia, Barbour, Bateman, Bayly, Bloomfield, Brevard, Buffum, Butler of New Hampshire, Case, Clagett, Culbreth, Dane, Dewitt, Dickinson, Eddy, Edwards of Connecticut, Edwards of North Carolina, Floyd, Folger, Foot, Ford, Gray, Gross of New York, Guyon, Hall of New York, Jones of Tennessee, Kendall, Maclay, McCoy, McCreary, Meech, Morton, Murray, Neale, Newton, Parker of Massachusetts, Phelps, Philson, Rich, Richards, Ringgold, Robertson, Russ, Simkins, Smith of Maryland, Stevens, Swearingen, Terrell, Tompkins, Tracy, Tucker of Virginia, Tucker of South Carolina, Udree, Upham, Wendover, Williams of Virginia, Williams of North Carolina, Wood—62.

The amendments were then ordered to be engrossed, and the bill be read a third time to-morrow.

DUTIES ON FRENCH VESSELS.

On motion of Mr. Newton, the House proceeded to the consideration of the bill to exempt French ships from certain duties.

Mr. N. explained the object of the bill. By the original act, time enough had not been allowed to give notice to French vessels of the passage of the act; in consequence of which, a few vessels had found their way into our ports, and the extraordinary duty had thus been levied in cases not intended by the act. This bill was to provide for a remission of the amount of extra duty in such cases.

Mr. Baldwin said that he thought the original law wrong; but if right at the last session, it could not be wrong now. Why not let the experiment go on and be fairly tried? He wished that the course of the Government should be uniform; that it should be either one way or the other. If the law be right in itself, said he, let it stand. If not, let it be repealed at once.

Mr. Mallary said there was nothing whatever in this bill which went to defeat the legitimate effect of the act of last session, but rather to make that act what it was intended to be, an act with fair notice to the parties. Mr. M. further explained the cases to which the act applied, and expressed his hope that the bill would be passed.

Mr. Clay expressed the same sentiments. If a partial and rigorous construction had been given to the act of last session, the effects of it ought to be remedied. He was the more disposed to this course, since it was understood that an arrangement was in negotiation between the two Governments, which would produce a reciprocal revocation of the extra duties by both Governments. France, Mr. C. said, is our natural friend, and he should be glad that Congress would, by the passage of this bill, add another motive to a conclusion of the arrangement which is necessary to a good understanding between the two Governments.

The Committee then rose and reported the bill, which was ordered to be engrossed for a third reading, and was subsequently read a third time and passed, without a division.

Mr. BALDWIN then moved that the House do resolve itself into a Committee of the Whole, to take into consideration the bill laying a duty on sales at auction. This motion was negatived.

INCREASE OF THE NAVY.

The House then, on motion of Mr. BARBOUR, of Virginia, resolved itself into a Committee of the Whole, on the bill to amend the act for the gradual increase of the Navy, so as to reduce the annual appropriation therefor from one million to half a million of dollars per annum, and extend the term of appropriation from three to six years.

Mr. BARBOUR indicated his intention to propose an amendment to the bill, the object of which was to limit the reduced appropriation to three years ; his object being to have the ships contemplated to be built, so far completed as regarded the frames of them, as to be in a state to be secured and covered in by houses built over them. Mr. B. explained at large his views of this subject, the leading feature of which was, that however advisable it might be to build more ships, it was not necessary at present to put them afloat. He therefore moved that the Committee rise, with a view to moving that the bill lie on the table, giving notice that at 12 o'clock to-morrow he should call it up, with a view to moving the amendment which he had indicated.

Mr. FULLER rose merely to say, that when the amendment should be before the House, he should endeavor to show why, in his opinion, the bill should not be adopted at this session at least.

The Committee then rose, and, on motion of Mr. BARBOUR, the bill was laid on the table.

WEDNESDAY, February 28.

Mr. ARCHER, of Maryland, from the Committee on Expenditures, in the Navy Department, made a report upon the subject of the expenditures in that Department; which was laid on the table.

Mr. ARCHER, from the same committee, also reported a bill providing for the pay and reorganization of the Marine Corps; which was read twice, and committed to a Committee of the Whole.

Mr. NEWTON, from the Committee on Commerce, to which was referred the bill from the Senate, entitled "An act to establish the district of Blakeley;" reported the same without amendment, and it was committed to a Committee of the Whole to-day.

A message from the Senate informed the House that the Senate have passed bills of this House entitled "An act for the relief of James Brady ;" "An act for the relief of Nicholas Jarrott," with amendments ; and they have also passed bills of the following titles, viz : "An act authorizing the payment of a sum of money to John Gooding and James Williams ;" "An act for the relief of General Robert Swartwout ;" "An act to authorize the clerk of the district court of the United States for the district of Louisiana to appoint a deputy to aid him in the discharge of the duties of his office;" "An act for the relief of J. L. B. Macarty ;" and "An act for the passage to the credit of Nathaniel Allen of certain moneys by him disbursed in the public service ;" in which amendments, and five last mentioned bills, they ask the concurrence of this House.

The amendment proposed by the Senate to the bill entitled "An act for the relief of James Brady," was concurred in by the House.

The amendments proposed by the Senate to the bill entitled "An act for the relief of Nicholas Jarrott," were also concurred in by the House.

Bills from the Senate of the following titles, to wit : "An act authorizing the payment of a sum of money to John Gooding and James Williams;" "An act for the relief of General Robert Swartwout ;" "An act for the relief of J. L. B. Macarty ;" "An act for passing to the credit of Nathaniel Allen certain moneys by him disbursed in the public service ;" and "An act to authorize the clerk of the district court of the United States for the district of Louisiana to appoint a deputy to aid him in the discharge of the duties of his office;" were severally read twice, and referred, the first to the Committee of Ways and Means ; the second, third, and fourth, to the Committee of Claims ; and the fifth to the Committee on the Judiciary.

The bill from the Senate, entitled "An act to extend the charters of certain Banks in the District of Columbia," was read the third time and passed—Yeas 74, nays 34.

An engrossed bill entitled "An act further to amend the several acts relative to the Treasury, War, and Navy Departments," was read the third time, and passed.

Mr. ANDERSON, from the Committee on Public Lands, reported without amendment the bill to authorize the President of the United States to ascertain and designate certain boundaries. Mr. SIBLEY moved to refer the bill to a Committee of the Whole, in order that he might have a proper opportunity of stating his objections to it.

Mr. HENDRICKS opposed the motion on the ground of its tendency to defeat the bill. But the motion prevailed, and the bill was referred to a Committee of the Whole.

Mr. RICH, from the Committee of Claims, reported without amendment the bill from the Senate to amend the bill for the relief of James L. Cathcart ; which was referred to a Committee of the Whole.

On motion of Mr. BLOOMFIELD, the Committee on Revolutionary Pensions were discharged from the consideration of all the subjects which have been referred to them, and not yet reported on.

Mr. FULLER, from the Committee on Naval Affairs, reported without amendment the act concerning Thomas Shields and others; and it was referred to a Committee of the Whole.

WAYS AND MEANS.

Mr. Smith, of Maryland, from the Committee of Ways and Means, made a detailed report upon the state of the finances; which was read, and ordered to lie on the table. The report is as follows:

The Committee of Ways and Means, to whom was referred so much of the President's Message, at the commencement of the session, as relates to the finances, respectfully submit to the following report:

The total net receipts of the Treasury, during the year 1820, amounted to - - - $20,969,001

State of the Treasury, public revenue, and appropriations, for the service of the year 1821.

1. The State of the Treasury.

The amount of available money in the Treasury on the 1st day of January, agreeably to report of the committee, dated the 6th February, was believed to be - - - - - $476,271 18

From which must be deducted amount of deposites in the Bank of Vincennes, which it cannot pay - - 214,808 00

Leaving available funds in the Treasury, on 1st day of January, the sum of 261,463 18

2. The revenue for 1821.

Customs, as estimated by the Committee of Ways and Means, in their report of Feb. 6th $15,005,328
Lands, estimated by the committee - 800,000
Internal taxes, agreeably to the report of the Secretary of the Treasury 100,000
Bank dividend, by the same - 350,000
Post office receipts from debts of banks, and other incidental receipts - - 100,000

Estimated amount of means available for the service of the year 1821 - $16,355,328

3. Amount of the several appropriations for 1821.

1. Permanent appropriations, viz:
Principal and interest of public debt - - - - $5,477,776
Gradual increase of the navy 500,000
Arming the militia - - 200,000
Indian annuities - - - 152,000
Indian trading houses - - 19,000
Civilization of Indians - - 10,000
         6,358,776

2. Temporary, agreeably to the several appropriations made for the service of the present year.
For the service of the navy - $2,209,093
For the military - - 4,936,451
Civil Department - - 1,517,352
Public Buildings - - 90,445
Private claims, estimated at - 200,000
Treaty of Ghent, presumed - 45,000
Spanish Treaty, supposed - 100,000
         9,098,341

         15,457,117

Leaving an excess of receipts, over the expenses authorized by law, of - - $898,211

4. State of the Finances.

Actual balance against the Treasury, on the 1st day of January; see report of the Committee of Ways and Means - $4,579,094
To which must be added amount due by the Vincennes bank, and which will not be available for the service of the present year; see Secretary's letter of the 12th instant - - - - 214,808

Actual deficit to be provided for - 4,793,902
To supply that deficit there may be applied the surplus of the estimated receipts, in 1821, over the expenditures authorized by the several acts of appropriation passed during the present session, which is presumed by the preceding view, to amount to the sum of - - 898,211
And the available funds in the Treasury on the 1st day of January - - - - 261,463
         1,159,674

Leaving an actual deficit to be provided for by loan, of - - - - 3,634,228
But if the estimate of the Secretary of the the Treasury should prove correct, to wit: that the customs will yield only fourteen millions, then there must be added (the difference between his estimate and that of the committee) the sum of - - - - - 1,005,328
         $4,639,556

The committee, under all these circumstances of difficulty and doubt, submit a bill authorizing a loan for four millions five hundred thousand dollars.

The House will perceive a difference between the present report and that of the 6th of February, arising out of the expenditures being bottomed in the one as estimates, and the other as the actual sums appropriated for the service of the present year; and in the estimate of receipts for the land during the year 1821, the committee have, in their present report, assumed only one-half the amount of their former, which was taken from the estimate of the Treasury. The committee do not pretend to much personal knowledge on the subject, but, from conversation with well informed gentlemen from the West and South, and a correspondence with the Secretary of the Treasury, they were induced to believe it would be unsafe to rely on a larger sum than eight hundred thousand dollars to be received for land during the present year. The House will also perceive a difference in the available fund arising from the default of the Bank of Vincennes.

Retrenchments in the public expenditures.

The deductions made from the estimates of the several departments for 1820, amounted to the sum of - - - - - $2,130,000
Those for 1821, amounted to - - 2,317,155
         4,447,155

Civil - - - - - 116,508
Military - - - - - 1,481,064

Naval, including five hundred thousand dollars from gradual increase - - -	719,563

Total amount of retrenchments in the annual public expenditures during the sixteenth Congress - - - - - $4,447,155

It will be perceived, by the preceding view, that the expenditures for the present year are less than fifteen and a half millions. The committee are of opinion that those of the next year will not exceed fifteen millions, for, during that year, the whole effect of the reduction of the Army will be felt; that reduction has reduced the expense of the present year $561,000, and will reduce that of the next, nearly $1,000,000. The Revolutionary pensioners will cost in future $200,000 less than the sum appropriated for the present year. In fine, the committee are of opinion that the receipts will, (if no unforeseen change should happen,) greatly exceed the annual expenditures.

All which the committee respectfully submit.

PUBLIC LANDS.

The bill from the Senate, entitled "An act for the relief of purchasers of public lands prior to the first July, 1820," was read the third time as amended; and on the question, shall it pass? It was passed in the affirmative—yeas 97, nays 40, as follows:

YEAS—Messrs. Abbot, Adams, Alexander, Allen of Massachusetts, Allen of New York, Anderson, Baker, Baldwin, Ball, Beecher, Bloomfield, Brown Brush, Butler of Louisiana, Campbell, Cannon, Clark, Clay, Cobb, Cook, Crawford, Crowell, Culbreth, Cushman, Cuthbert, Darlington, Dewitt, Dickinson, Edwards of Connecticut, Edwards of Pennsylvania, Eustis, Fay, Folger, Ford, Fuller, Gorham, Gross of New York, Hackley, Hardin, Hemphill, Hendricks, Herrick, Hill, Hooks, Jackson, Johnson, Jones of Virginia, Kendall, Kent, Kinsey, Kinsley, Lathrop, Maclay, McCullough, McLean of Kentucky, Mallary, Marchand, Meigs, Mercer, Metcalf, Monell, Montgomery, R. Moore, S. Moore, T. L. Moore, Moseley, Murray, Neale, Nelson of Massachusetts, Nelson of Virginia, Patterson, Pinckney, Plumer, Rankin, Rhea, Rich, Ringgold, Robertson, Rogers, Ross, Sergeant, Settle, Silsbee, Simkins, Sloan, Smith of New Jersey, Smith of Maryland, Street, Strong of New York, Swearingen, Tarr, Tucker of Virginia, Tyler, Udree, Van Rensselaer, Walker, and Wood.

NAYS—Messrs. Allen of Tennessee, Archer of Maryland, Archer of Virginia, Bateman, Blackledge, Bryan, Buffum, Butler of New Hampshire, Case, Clagett, Cocke, Culpeper, Denison, Eddy, Edwards of North Carolina, Floyd, Foot, Gray, Guyon, Hall of New York, Hibshman, Lincoln, Little, Livermore, McCoy, McCreary, Morton, Newton, Parker of Massachusetts, Phelps, Philson, Richards, Russ, Stevens, Tomlinson, Tucker of South Carolina, Upham, Wendover, Williams of Virginia, and Williams of North Carolina.

The bill was ordered to be sent to the Senate for concurrence in the amendments.

DISTRICT BANKS.

Mr. KENT, from the Committee on the District of Columbia, reported, without amendment, the

bill from the Senate for continuing the charters of certain banks in the District of Columbia.

[This bill provides for the continuation of the charters of the Bank of the Metropolis, the Bank of Washington, the Patriotic Bank in the City of Washington; the Union Bank, the Farmers' and Mechanics' Bank, the Bank of Columbia, in Georgetown; the Bank of Alexandria, and the Farmers' Bank, in Alexandria, until the year 1836. It authorizes the consolidation of the Union Bank of Alexandria with the Bank of Potomac, and extends the charter of the said united bank to the same term as the others. The Central Bank is allowed to proceed forthwith to liquidate and close all the concerns of the corporation, and for that purpose its corporate authority is continued for five years.]

Mr. COCKE moved to lay the bill on the table, but afterwards withdrew the motion; which was renewed by Mr. COBB, opposed by Mr. HARDIN, and Mr. MERCER, and negatived by a large majority.

Mr. COCKE moved to amend the bill so as to extend the charters to 1826, instead of 1836, being five years instead of fifteen.

This motion gave rise to a short debate.

The motion was supported by Mr. COCKE and Mr. COBB, and opposed by Mr. HARDIN, Mr. MERCER, and Mr. NELSON, of Virginia—and was negatived—yeas 68, nays 47.

Mr. EDWARDS moved that the bill be recommitted to the Committee on the District of Columbia, with instructions so to amend it as to authorize any stockholder, if he thinks proper, to withdraw himself from any of the said companies, and to receive such funds as he may have therein. Negatived—yeas 30.

The bill was then ordered to be read a third time this day, and was subsequently read a third time and passed.

INDIAN TRADE.

Mr. SOUTHARD, from the Committee on Indian Affairs, reported, pursuant to instruction, an amendment to the Indian trade bill, to the following effect:

" That the Secretary of War shall cause to be disposed of at public sale all the property, now belonging to the United States, employed in the Indian trade, and the proceeds thereof to be paid into the public Treasury; and that, from the first day of November next, the offices of superintendent of Indian trade and of factors, &c. shall cease and determine."

This amendment was agreed to; and the question being on ordering the bill to be engrossed for a third reading—

Mr. SOUTHARD caused to be read by the Clerk three or four articles of different treaties between the United States and Indian tribes, wherein the Government had expressly stipulated to maintain trading houses, and then asked how, after these solemn pledges, Congress could abolish the whole system?

Mr. McLEAN, of Kentucky, said he had voted for the amendment, not being aware of these provisions of treaties. He wished that vote to be re-

1251　　　　　　HISTORY OF CONGRESS.　　　　　1252

H. of R.　　　　　　　　General Post Office.　　　　　FEBRUARY, 1821.

considered, that a bill might be passed to continue the system in existence for one year, to give an opportunity to the next Congress to revise it.

Mr. WILLIAMS, of Virginia, stated, that the readiest course would be, to reject this bill, and take up the bill from the Senate, containing the very provision which the gentleman had suggested.

After some conversation between Messrs. RANKIN, FLOYD, SOUTHARD, and SIMKINS, the bill was, on motion of Mr. RANKIN, ordered to lie on the table—in the course of which—

Mr. FLOYD said, incidentally, that the Choctaws had fairly retorted on the United States their own policy, and got possession, by treaty, of about one-third of the whole of the population of the Territory of Arkansas. The bill was ordered to lie on the table.

GENERAL POST OFFICE.

Mr. PHELPS, from the select committee, delivered in the following report:

The select committee to whom was referred the investigation of the affairs of the Post Office Department, according to order have had the same under examination, and beg leave to submit to the House the following report, in part : That, immediately after their appointment, they commenced a performance of their duties, and believed it would be in their power to effect an extensive investigation. They began an inquiry into several important subjects, which the state of health of several members of the committee compelled them to abandon. They have recently devoted their attention entirely to such inquiries as offered a fair prospect of termination during the present session of Congress.

When it is recollected that the transactions of this Department embrace a period of many years, and extend to almost every part of our country, it will be obvious that obstacles would occur in the investigation of them, which could be surmounted only by an expensive and protracted inquiry.

The committee never entertained a belief, that, during the present session of Congress, they should be able to review, in a manner satisfactory to themselves, or the House, the quarterly receipts and expenditures of this department. This service the law requires of the accounting officers of the Government, when the proper vouchers are exhibited by the Postmaster General, and which, by law, he is bound to render quarterly.

The following subjects have been investigated by the committee :

1. The expenditure of public money by the department, for transporting the mail from Washington City to Fredericksburg, in the years 1814, 1815, and 1816.

2. Whether duplicates of all contracts made by this department, and all proposals respecting them, have been lodged with the Comptroller of the Treasury or not.

3. Whether the Postmaster General has, once in three months, rendered to the Secretary of the Treasury a quarterly account of all receipts and expenditures of the department or not.

4. Whether the Postmaster General has paid into the Treasury of the United States the balance due from him, as the law requires, or not.

5. Whether the public money was not loaned to Benjamin Tallmadge and John G. Jackson.

6. Whether the Postmaster General, in his annual reports to Congress of the contracts made by his department, has reported them conformably with law, or not.

7. Whether he has annually reported to Congress all contracts made by his department, or not.

The evidence, in relation to these several subjects of inquiry, consists of the original applications to transport the mail from Washington City to Fredericksburg, during the years, 1814, 1815, and 1816, a copy from the original list of bids, as furnished by the Postmaster General, and official documents.

The evidence, in connexion with the several heads, is referred to numerically.

In reference to the first head of inquiry, the committee find that, in the month of September, 1813, a contract was made by the Department with four persons, believed to be entirely responsible, for transporting the mail from Washington City to Fredericksburg, during the years 1814, 1815, and 1816, for the sum of $3,300 per annum, amounting in the whole to the sum of $9,900: a part of which contract was afterwards transferred to another person. No farther contract embracing the same route and period, has been discovered in the list of the contracts ; duplicates of which have been returned to the Comptroller of the Treasury, or been furnished to the committee by the Post Office Department ; but, it appears that a sum considerably larger than that stipulated by the above contract has been paid for the service in question, on behalf of the United States. The reason assigned for this additional expenditure by the Postmaster General, is, the occurrence of a change in the mode of transporting the mail, alleged to have been rendered necessary by the war, and to have been adopted in obedience to the direction of a superior authority. The sum paid under this variation of arrangement, for the three years above mentioned, appears from the returns of the Treasury to have been $31,551 52, of which amount $16,150 81, were paid for the year 1816. These entries are alleged by the Postmaster General to furnish an erroneous exhibit of the real expenditure, resulting from the manner of making up the returns to the Treasury, in which various sums paid to the same person, though for different services, are comprehended in the same entry. Thus, from the account in detail on the books of the Post Office Department, the whole sum paid for the transportation of the mail from Washington to Fredericksburg, for the year 1816, appears to be $8,915 45, instead of $16,150 81, as shown by the returns to the Treasury. The committee have no time or opportunity to obtain testimony in relation to the facts connected with the subject. They submit the documentary evidence they have collected, numbered from one to eleven, the letter of the Postmaster General to the committee ; and two extracts marked A and B from the books of the Post Office Department, verified by the Chief Clerk of that Department.

In relation to the second head of inquiry, the committee find the duplicates of all contracts, and proposals respecting them, have not been lodged with the Comptroller, as is required by law.—Documents No. 12 and 13, and letter of the Postmaster General.

In relation to the third head of inquiry, it appears that the Postmaster General has not rendered his accounts to the Treasury Department for settlement, to a later period than the 31st day of March, 1819.—Reference to documents No. 14 and 15, and the explanation on the subject offered by the letter of the Postmaster General.

In relation to the fourth head of inquiry, it appears that the balance due from the Post Office Department to the Department of the Treasury, amounted, on the 1st day of January, 1819, to the sum of $653,491 99, which includes all money then on hand, and debts due to the Post Office Department; the amount of which the committee have no documents to ascertain.—Reference to documents Nos. 16, 17, and letter of the Postmaster General, accompanying his report of debtors to his Department.

In reference to the fifth head of inquiry, no evidence has been obtained by the committee. It will be found embraced, however, by the explanation contained in the letter of the Postmaster General, which, on this point, was satisfactory to the committee.

In relation to the sixth head of inquiry, the committee, by adverting to several annual reports of contracts, made to Congress by the Postmaster General, find that the dates and duration of those contracts are not reported, which the law, in express terms, requires. As these reports are to be found in the Clerk's office, and the committee considered it to be unnecessary to swell their report with them.

In relation to the seventh head of inquiry, the committee find that the Postmaster General has not made a report to Congress of the contracts made by his Department in the year 1818, until after the commencement of the present investigation. See document No. 18, and letter of the Postmaster General to the committee.

The committee have contented themselves with submitting the above brief statement of the objects to which their inquiries have been directed, together with the connected evidence and explanations for the information of the House, without suggesting any resolution or act for its adoption.

The report was, with the documents accompanying the same, referred to a Committee of the Whole, and ordered to be printed.

The following letter accompanied the report of the committee of the House on the subject of the Post Office transactions:

GENERAL POST OFFICE DEPARTMENT,
February 20, 1821.

To the Honorable the Committee of the House of Representatives, appointed to investigate the concerns of the General Post Office Department.

GENTLEMEN: Agreeably to an understanding with the committee at my interview on Friday last, I shall now proceed to give such information and explanations, in relation to the several points proposed by the committee, as I trust will prove entirely satisfactory. I was gratified to learn, explicitly, from the committee, at that interview, that the cases exhibited were not regarded as charges which had appeared in evidence against the Department, or on which any testimony had been taken; but that some were facts drawn from the official documents that required an explanation to satisfy the committee of the correctness of the proceedings of the Department, and that others were rumors, in relation to which the committee desired the statement of facts.

1st. The first point is, "that the public money has been improperly expended by the Post Office Department, for transporting the mail from Washington to Fredericksburg, in the years 1814, 1815, and 1816."

A plain and simple narrative of the facts in relation to that case, it is presumed, will fully justify the course which was taken. But, before entering upon the subject, it may not be improper to remind the committee, that most of these proceedings were anterior to my official duties as Postmaster General, which commenced in April, 1814.

It appears that a contract was made by my predecessor, with a company of gentlemen, in October, 1813, to transport the mail between Washington and Fredericksburg, for the years 1814, 1815, and 1816, with a distinct understanding that the letter mail was to be carried through by express, on horseback, during the Winter, while the roads on that route are so bad as to render it impossible for stages to move with any degree of rapidity; and that the mail containing newspapers and pamphlets, which was too heavy to be carried on horseback, should be subject to the more tardy movement of the stages, which occupied nearly two days.

It appears that, in November, 1813, after the above contract had been made, but before the performance under it commenced, the President and Secretaries of departments thought it advisable, in consequence of the general anxiety which the war excited, to obtain the earliest possible intelligence, that the whole mail, newspapers as well as letters, should be carried through by the express. This arrangement, which required much more than double the expense of carrying it agreeably to the plan at first contemplated, entirely vitiated the original contract. It could not be carried with sufficient rapidity in stages, and it was too heavy to be carried on horseback. It became necessary, therefore, to transport it in curricles—an expensive mode, but the only one practicable. After several unsuccessful attempts to have it satisfactorily performed at a low price in curricles, the department appears to have employed an experienced agent, who purchased horses and carriages, and carried that part of it between Alexandria and Dumfries, on account of the department; that being the worst part of the road, and on which no contractor would perform. An extra price was given to those who carried it on the other parts of the route, in consequence of the extra expense.

In this situation I found it when I came into the department in April, 1814. It remained thus until the commencement of 1815, when, finding it troublesome and expensive to transport the mail through an agent of the department, the property employed on the route was sold at a fair valuation to Colonel Tayloe, and a new contract entered into with him, upon terms considerably lower than what it cost the department while transported by its agent. It has since been advertised, and no other person has proposed to carry it at a lower rate than what was then given.

The rumors of which the honorable committee have spoken, were propagated in 1816, by certain malcontents, who were then clerks in this office; when, at my own request, a committee of the House of Representatives was appointed to investigate the fiscal concerns of this department. That committee, one of whom, the honorable Timothy Pickering, had been Postmaster General, and was perfectly acquainted with the nature of all the operations of the department, entered fully into this case; and I would respectfully refer the honorable committee to the report then made on this point, which is contained in the following sentence:

"The facts stated in this charge, viz: ('that a contract for carrying the mail from Washington to Fredericksburg, had been superseded by order of the Postmaster General, before it expired, and about double the amount given for the same service,') are admitted to be correct, and the letter of the Postmaster General, (No. 19,) contains a satisfactory explanation of the reasons for altering the terms of the contract; whether too much was eventually given for the service, under the changes required by the Postmaster General, is a subject not in the power of the committee to decide; nor would they be justified in presuming any misconduct in a transaction which appears to have been so fairly conducted."

2d. The second point is, " that duplicates of all contracts made by the department, and proposals respecting them, have not been lodged with the Comptroller of the Treasury."

To this I reply, that, since my time, they have always been regularly lodged in the office of the Comptroller, before the accounts and payments relating to them have come before him for examination, so that the spirit and design of the law have been strictly complied with. The letter of the law enjoins what is found impracticable, on account of circumstances which the committee will readily perceive. The number of contracts made at one time is usually between three and four hundred; many of which are with persons at extreme parts of the Union. These contracts are prepared 'at the department, and sent to them to be executed; and it often happens, from some misconception on the part of the contractor, or some explanation desired by him, or, sometimes, from his declining to comply with the conditions, that several communications pass between him and the department before he returns the contract, which prolongs the time considerably beyond the period specified in the law for lodging them with the Comptroller. They might, indeed, be sent to him, one by one, as they are received, but that would not be a literal compliance with the law; and the depositing them together, filed alphabetically, is found much more convenient to the department, while it furnishes superior facilities to the Comptroller, for reference. This subject was regarded of so little importance by my predecessor, that, during the thirteen years of his administration, he made but two lodgments of the duplicate contracts and proposals in the office of the Comptroller. All that were omitted by him, I have sent there, and all that have since been made, up to 1818. The remainder require only the formality of removing from one building to another, which will be done, as all others have been, before the accounts growing out of them shall come before the Comptroller.

3d. The third point is, " that the Postmaster General has not rendered, once in three months, to the Secretary of the Treasury a quarterly account of all receipts and expenditures."

To this I reply, that the law which requires the Postmaster General to render his accounts once in three months, has ever been understood simply to require these accounts to be presented in regular periods of three months each, agreeably to the common rule of the Treasury transactions, and not that they shall be rendered at the close of each quarter, for the three months immediately preceding, for this would be requiring an impossibility. There are 4,669 post offices in the United States, the accounts from which, after the close of a quarter, are all to be forwarded to the General Post Office. When received here, they are examined and registered in quarterly accounts current, from which they are posted into legers. After this, these accounts current are copied in the proper form for the Treasury. Besides these, there are upwards of a thousand mail routes, on which the mails are transported, at the average rate of 27,559 miles a day, during every season of the year. The payments made to the contractors after the close of a quarter, by remittances to every part of the Union; the obtaining receipts for these payments, to accompany the accounts to the Treasury, as vouchers, necessarily occupy a considerable length of time. As only one person at a time can be employed upon the same book, and as the labor of preparing the accounts, first for the Department, and then for the Treasury, must be performed after the necessary documents have come to hand; it must be obvious that they cannot be rendered at the Treasury till long after the expiration of the term to which they relate. It appears, from the documents of the office, that none of my predecessors, from the commencement of the Government, ever rendered their accounts sooner after the transaction occurred, than I have done, though the extension of the Department has increased in a tenfold ratio. In addition to the above, it may be proper to inform the Committee that this part of the business was far in arrears at the commencement of my official duties. When I came into the Department, in April, 1814, the accounts had been rendered to the Treasury only to the 30th June, 1809, being nearly five years behind. By unceasing and laborious exertions, all those arrearages have been brought up, and the whole accounts have been rendered to the Treasury, up to the 1st July, 1819, making a period of ten years, prepared and rendered since April, 1814. Others are in a state of forwardness, and will be rendered long before those which are already in the Treasury Department can be gone through and adjusted there.

4th. The fourth point is, "the Postmaster General has not paid into the Treasury of the United States the balance due from him."

From conversation with the committee I learned that this conclusion was drawn from the balance which appears against this Department, on the books of the Treasury. That balance exhibits not the amount of moneys collected by the department, but it embraces all balances due to the department from postmasters. The General Post Office Department is held accountable to the Treasury Department for the whole amount of postages throughout the United States; and almost the whole of the Auditor's balance remains due to this office, as will appear from the list furnished the House on the 23d of January, and for an explanation of which I would refer the committee to my letter accompanying the same. The balances have been promptly paid over as they have been collected, reserving only a sufficiency to meet such current expenses and contingencies as are daily arising; a practice sanctioned by the example of all my predecessors, and demonstrated by experience to be necessary to the successful operations of the department. I find that the whole amount paid over to the Treasury by this department, from the organization of the Government, in March, 1789, to March, 1814, a period of twenty-five years, is $702,386 40, making an average of $28,095 53 a year. Since I came into the department, from March, 1814, to March, 1820, a period of six years, the different payments to the Treasury amount to $379,411 76, making an average of $63,-235 29 a year, more than double the average for the former period. But, owing to the increased length of the mail routes, principally through new and very thinly populated regions of the country, added to the general pressure which is felt, it is very doubtful whether it will be possible, for a considerable time, in future, to collect more than will be required to pay for the transportation of the mails, or even sufficient for that purpose.

5th. The fifth point is, "That he had loaned the public money to John G. Jackson and Benjamin Tallmadge."

At my interview with the committee, they informed me that no evidence of these transactions was before them, but rumor had repeated the circumstance, and a statement of facts was desired in relation thereto. This rumor appears to be a re-echo of what was brought before the committee of 1816, which committee had this subject before them: and after a thorough investigation of the facts, embraced it in the third article of their report, to which I would also respectfully refer the committee. The transactions were anterior to my time, and I can only inform the committee of what appears to have been their nature.

I find that, as early as 1806, those gentlemen, being members of Congress, frequently made collections for their constituents, principally from offices of the Government, and that it was common for them, through the Assistant Postmaster General, to remit such collections by drafts from this department, in lieu of which he received either moneys or drafts upon places where he had occasion to make remittances to pay contractors; and as, in some instances, the drafts thus exchanged did not exactly correspond in amount, he kept a memorandum of the difference; which, for the purpose of keeping more regularly, he transferred to the books of the office, the former in 1809, the latter in 1812. When I came into office, I found these accounts still open, and that the balances had been always very inconsiderable, sometimes in favor of the individuals, and sometimes in favor of the department. One of the accounts was finally closed in 1814, the other in 1816; since which time no account has been kept with any individuals who were not connected with the department. It was suggested also by the committee, that rumor informed them these exchanges were made at a time when a depreciation had taken place in the currency which was received. In answer to this, I will assure the committee, that only one payment was ever made to General Jackson after the banks had stopped specie payment, and that was made in the depreciated notes of this District; and that only one payment was ever made to Colonel Tallmadge after I came into the department, and that was made at New York, when all the banks were paying specie, and (the very reverse of a loan) it was in payment of a balance which was found due to him to close his account.

6th. The sixth point is, "That in his report to Congress of contracts made by his department, he has not reported them conformably with law."

On this point I will only remark that, as the object of the last section of the law referred to, appeared to be to show to Congress whether any of the members of either House were contractors; in making the reports which is required, this point was principally kept in view; and, as all contracts entered into by this department have been publicly advertised, with their dates and duration, in preparing the statements required by the law, there appears to have been an inadvertent omission of the date and duration of the contract, a circumstance in no degree surprising amidst the great mass of business to be performed; and an omission in no degree affecting the object of the report. In all other respects it is believed both the letter and the spirit of the law have been strictly adhered to in such reports.

7th. The seventh point is, "That he has not annually reported to Congress the contracts made by his department."

To this I reply, that the contracts made by this department have always been reported annually to Congress, except one instance, in which, owing to an accidental omission of one of the clerks, the report was not made at the time required, but the omission was subsequently discovered, and the report sent to the House.

In addition to the foregoing points, the committee asked an explanation of a difference which appears between the Fifth Auditor's statement of the post office accounts, and the account of receipts and disbursements furnished by this department.

In relation to this, the committee will observe, that the Auditor's report states the "gross amount of postages" in the United States, for a given time. From this " gross amount" is deducted the whole amount of postmasters' commissions, and contingent expenses of their respective offices. The remainder constitutes the amount of balances arising in favor of the department for that time. The report furnished from this office exhibits, not the amount of postages, but the amount of payments actually made by postmasters and received by the department. The difference, therefore, must always be considerable; and if it should so happen, that the whole amount of balances arising in favor of the department within a given time, should be paid over to this office within that time, yet, the difference between the gross amount of postages and the actual receipts by the department, would be equal to the whole amount of postmasters' commissions and contingent expenses of their offices.

I have the honor to be, with respect, your obedient servant,   R. J. MEIGS, Jr.

Prefixed to this letter, was the following note, by the committee:

To one remark, contained in the first paragraph of this defence, the committee would advert. It is that in which it is observed, that he "was gratified to learn, explicitly, from the committee, at that interview, that the cases exhibited were not regarded as charges which had appeared in evidence against the department, or on which any testimony had been taken,"- &c. This remark is not correct.

FEBRUARY 24, 1821.

Mr. BALDWIN moved that the House resolve itself into a Committee of the Whole on the bill concerning sales at auction; but the motion was negatived—ayes 53, noes 62.

SYSTEM OF BANKRUPTCY.

Mr. SERGEANT moved that the House proceed, to the consideration of the bill from the Senate to establish an uniform system of bankruptcy; on which motion Mr. EDWARDS, of North Carolina, demanded the yeas and nays.

The question was accordingly taken by yeas and nays, and decided in the affirmative—ayes 78, noes 58; and the bill was taken up.

Mr. EDWARDS, of North Carolina, then moved to commit the bill to a Committee of the Whole; which motion was opposed by Mr. SERGEANT, as a course that would be fatal to the bill, from the delay it would produce, and was also unnecessary.

Mr. HARDIN advocated the motion to commit, being friendly to the principle of the system, but wanted to examine its details.

Mr. CLAY said to commit the bill would place it at the foot of the docket of business, and that course would be tantamount to a rejection of the bill. If gentlemen were sincere in a desire to examine it in Committee, he would propose a compromise, and that was to agree by general consent to go into Committee of the Whole on the bill forthwith; and added some remarks on the imperious necessity which existed for taking up the subject and deciding on it at the present session, as well as on the circumstances of the country which required its passage.

Mr. COBB declared himself heartily sick of all compromises, and spoke to show the necessity of acting on this subject with due deliberation. He was in favor of commitment, and could not take the system on the simple prescription of Mr. SERGEANT, or consent to act on the faith of any gentleman in the perfection of the details of the bill.

Mr. CULPEPER made a few remarks in favor of the course proposed by Mr. CLAY.

Mr. SERGEANT referred to the great length of time this subject had been before Congress; the frequency with which it had been discussed at former sessions, and the necessary general understanding which must exist of it. It had been printed at an early period of this session, as well as the last, and had been long before the members; it had been matured with great care and labor in the Senate, and he did not think it would require so much time to act on it as was apprehended.

Mr. STEVENS, of Connecticut, said the House was called on to work by faith; and he would as soon act by faith as works, if those works were not their own. The Senate had matured the bill to their liking, but it was proper the House should examine it for itself; for which there was not time, he argued, compatible with a due regard to other indispensable subjects.

The question being taken on committing the bill, it was negatived—ayes 49, noes 63.

Mr. McLEAN, of Kentucky, avowed his hostility to the bill; and to ascertain whether there was a majority in favor of the principle of the bill, without which it would be extremely impolitic to consume the precious time of the session in discussing its details, moved, for the purpose of trying the question and saving time, to postpone the bill indefinitely.

On this motion a debate commenced on the merits of the bill, as well as on the expediency of now acting on it. The debate had continued some time, and several gentlemen yet indicating a wish to speak—

Mr. McLEAN withdrew his motion; his object having been, in making it, merely to save time.

Mr. RHEA renewed the motion to postpone the bill indefinitely.

Messrs. WOOD, ROBERTSON, TOMLINSON, SERGEANT, and LITTLE, submitted briefly their reasons for being in favor of the bill, and for advocating its consideration and decision.

Messrs. CANNON, RHEA, TUCKER, of Virginia, and WILLIAMS, of North Carolina, offered their reasons against taking up the bill; for which they contended there was not time enough left, without neglecting every other subject, of which there were several of more consequence to the country. Mr. TUCKER, of Virginia, offered also some remarks against the bill itself.

Messrs. MEIGS and BRUSH submitted some arguments in favor of the bill, of its importance, and of proceeding to act on it.

Mr. F. JOHNSON said he thought this course would be to refuse to the petitioners, for some measure of the kind, who were both creditors and debtors, a just hearing of their complaints; he pointed out the general objects of the creditors and debtors who had petitioned for the measure, the importance of the subject, and the consideration which was due to it, and said that, although he should vote against the indefinite postponement, he should nevertheless vote against the bill in its present shape, and probably in any shape it might assume; but it was due, upon that, as well as upon all important occasions, particularly where the people had petitioned, that the friends of a measure should have a full and fair opportunity of making it as perfect as possible, and of then presenting the merits for consideration. Such a course, he said, was the liberal and proper one, and best calculated to effect a just and satisfactory result, &c.

Messrs. COBB and CANNON maintained the other side of the question, and were averse to consuming the time of the session in the further consideration of the bill.

Mr. CLAY advocated the bill very earnestly, in a speech of some length.

Mr. STEVENS reiterated and enforced anew the opinions he had expressed against the consideration of the bill.

Messrs. STORRS and WARFIELD supported the justice and policy of the measure, and the imperative necessity of acting on it at the present session.

Mr. TRIMBLE, of Kentucky, offered briefly his reasons for being opposed in principle to a system of bankruptcy.

Mr. SERGEANT replied at some length, to obviate the objections which Mr. TRIMBLE and others had adduced against the bill.

Mr. NELSON, of Virginia, spoke with great earnestness in favor of the indefinite postponement of the bill, on the ground of its demerits.

Mr. JONES, of Tennessee, then moved to adjourn. The motion was negatived.

Mr. COBB then delivered the reasons why he was most decidedly opposed to the passage of the bill in any shape.

Mr. TUCKER, of Virginia, then moved to adjourn—negatived, 60 to 54.

Mr. NELSON, of Virginia, then moved to lay the bill on the table; which motion was negatived.

Mr. BALL then moved to adjourn; and the question thereon was decided by yeas and nays, as follows: For adjournment 59, against it 77.

So the motion was rejected.

Mr. CLAY made a few remarks in favor of deciding to-night the question of indefinite postponement, and then adjourning to discuss the subject in detail on the morrow.

Mr. RHEA next spoke against the bill; and concluded by moving to adjourn.—Negatived, 71 to 48.

Mr. JONES, of Tennessee, then addressed the House at some length in favor of indefinite postponement.

Some rather confused proceedings then took place; when

Mr. JONES, of Tennessee, moved to lay the bill on the table, and required the yeas and nays upon the motion; but a sufficient number did not rise to second the call.

The House then divided on the motion; when there were, for laying the bill on the table, 55; against it, 73.

So the motion was negatived.

Mr. BRYAN then moved to adjourn, and required the yeas and nays on the motion; and the question on adjournment was decided by yeas and nays as follows: For the adjournment, 62; against it, 73.

So the motion was negatived.

Mr. HOOKS then moved to lay the bill on the table, and required the yeas and nays on the motion.

Mr. ARCHER, of Virginia, invited those who, with him, were opposed to the bill, to withdraw their opposition to taking the question of indefinite postponement, in order to oppose the bill directly, on the morrow, when, if gentlemen desired it, the motion for indefinite postponement could be renewed.

Mr. HOOKS declined withdrawing the motion, and the question on laying the bill on the table was decided in the negative, 70 votes to 51.

Mr. CULPEPER entered his protest against the precipitation with which the main question was urged on the House, as being contrary to usage and unparliamentary.

The question was then taken on the indefinite postponement of the bill, and decided as follows:

YEAS—Messrs. Abbot, Alexander, Allen of Tennessee, Archer of Virginia, Baldwin, Ball, Blackledge, Bryan, Buffum, Campbell, Cannon, Clagett, Cobb, Cocke, Crawford, Culbreth, Culpeper, Davidson, Edwards of North Carolina, Floyd, Garnett, Gray, Hardin, Hibshman, Hooks, Hostetter, Jackson, Jones of Virginia, Jones of Tennessee, Kinsey, Lincoln, McCoy, McCreary, Metcalf, R. Moore, T. L. Moore, Morton, Murray, Neale, Nelson of Virginia, Newton, Parker, of Massachusetts, Patterson, Phelps, Philson, Plumer, Rankin, Reid, Rhea, Richards, Ringgold, Ross, Stevens, Swearingen, Tucker of Va., Tucker of South Carolina, Williams of Virginia, and Williams of North Carolina—58.

NAYS—Messrs. Adams, Allen of Mass., Allen of N. Y., Archer of Md., Beecher, Bloomfield, Brevard, Brush, Case, Clark, Clay, Cook, Crowell, Cushman, Cuthbert,

Dane, Darlington, Denison, Eddy, Edwards of Connecticut, Edwards of Pennsylvania, Eustis, Fay, Folger, Foot, Forrest, Fuller, Gorham, Gross of New York, Guyon, Hackley, Hall of New York, Hemphill, Herrick, Hill, Hobart, Johnson, Kendall, Kent, Kinsley, Lathrop, Little, Livermore, Maclay, McCullough, Mallary, Marchand, Meigs, Mercer, Monell, Montgomery, S. Moore, Moseley, Nelson of Massachusetts, Pitcher, Rich, Robertson, Rogers, Russ, Sergeant, Silsbee, Simkins, Sloan, Smith of Maryland, Storrs, Street, Strong of New York, Tomlinson, Upham, Van Rensselaer, Warfield, Whitman, and Wood—73.

The question then recurred that the bill be ordered to a third reading. When the House adjourned.

THURSDAY, March 1.

Mr. HENDRICKS, from the Committee on the Public Lands, to which was referred, on the 2d of January last, the memorial of the Legislature of the State of Indiana, made a report thereon, accompanied with a bill authorizing the taxing of certain lands within the new States; which bill was read the first time, and ordered to lie on the table.

A Message was received from the President of the United States, transmitting to Congress certain extracts, and a copy of letters received by the Secretary of State from the Marshal of the United States, for the eastern district of Virginia, in relation to the execution of the act of the 14th of March, 1820, to provide for taking the fourth census; which were referred to the Committee on the Judiciary.

Mr. SMITH, of Maryland, from the Committee of Ways and Means, to which was referred the bill from the Senate, entitled "An act authorizing the payment of a sum of money to John Gooding and James Williams, reported the same without amendment, and it was committed to a Committee of the Whole to-day.

On motion of Mr. NELSON, of Virginia, the Committee of Accounts were authorized and directed to make the same allowance for extra services to each person serving this House, as was granted at the end of the last session; and that there be allowed to the two assistant messengers, David Pancoast and Charles Cooper, the sum of fifty dollars each, for extra services.

Mr. LITTLE submitted for consideration the following resolution, which was ordered to lie on the table till to-morrow:

Resolved, That the President of the United States be requested to lay before this House, at the next session of Congress, a system of revenue that shall meet all the expenses of Government without the aid of loans, and suggest such reductions, which, in his opinion, are least prejudicial to the public interest, as will bring the expenditures within the actual receipts of the Treasury.

The House proceeded to consider the report of the Committee on Roads and Canals, and the report of the Committee on the Judiciary, made during the present session on the petition of John

Good; and the said reports being read, it was ordered that the petition of John Good be referred to the Secretary of the Treasury, with instructions to report thereon to this House at the next session of Congress.

Mr. Rich, from the Committee of Claims, to whom was referred the bill from the Senate "for passing to the credit of Nathaniel Allen certain moneys by him disbursed in the public service," reported the same without amendment, and it was ordered to be read a third time, and was accordingly read a third time, and passed.

Mr. R. also, in the same manner, reported the bill for the relief of J. L. B. McCarty, which was referred to the Committee of the Whole.

Mr. Southard, from the Committee on Indian Affairs, to whom was referred the Senate's bill for continuing in force the act establishing trading houses with the Indian tribes, reported the same without amendment; and, after some consideration, the bill was then ordered to lie on the table.

Mr. S. also reported, without amendment, the bill for appointing certain Indian agents; and the bill was referred to a Committee of the Whole.

On motion of Mr. Smyth, the Military Committee was discharged from the further consideration of the various subjects on which it had not reported.

Mr. Butler, of Louisiana, from the Committee on Private Land Claims, to whom had been referred the bill from the Senate confirming the title of the Marquis de Maison Rouge to a tract of thirty square leagues of land in Louisiana, reported the same without amendment; and the bill was committed to a Committee of the whole House. [We are requested to state that this bill was examined deliberately in the Committee on Private Land Claims, and that the committee was unanimous, as many as were present, in favor of the bill.—*Editors N. I.*]

Mr. Floyd moved to print three thousand additional copies of the report of the Committee of Ways and Means on the Finances. It was short, he said, and the nation ought to have all the information they could have on the subject. This motion was opposed by Mr. Foot, on the ground that it would be an unnecessary expenditure, and it was negatived.

Mr. Livermore, for the reason that the report of the Secretary of State on Weights and Measures, &c. was highly interesting, and would be a valuable addition to the stock of science of the country, moved that five hundred additional copies thereof be ordered to be printed for the use of this House. The motion was agreed to—69 to 30.

A message from the Senate informed the House that the Senate have passed the bill of the House, entitled "An act further to regulate the entry of merchandise imported into the United States from any adjacent territory; with amendments. And they have passed bills of the following titles, viz: "An act to extend the time for unlading vessels arriving from foreign ports in certain cases;" "An act to authorize the reconveyance of a tract of land to the city of New York;" "An act to establish a new land office in the State of Mississippi,

and for the better regulation of certain land districts in the States of Alabama and Mississippi ;" and "An act to extend the term of Samuel Parker's patents for his improvement in currying and finishing leather of all kinds ;" in which amendments and bills they ask the concurrence of this House.

The amendments proposed by the Senate to the bill, entitled "An act further to regulate the entry of merchandise imported into the United States from any adjacent territory," were read and concurred in by the House.

The bill from the Senate, entitled "An act to extend the time for unlading vessels arriving from foreign ports, in certain cases," was read twice, and ordered to be read a third time to-day. It was accordingly read the third time and passed.

Mr. Sergeant, from the Committee on the Judiciary, reported a bill authorizing the Secretary of the Treasury of the United States to sell and convey a certain tract of land in Northumberland county, in the State of Virginia; which was read twice, and ordered to be read a third time.

The Speaker laid before the House a letter from the Secretary of the Treasury, transmitting a statement of the number and tonnage of British and American vessels cleared from ports of the United States for Bermuda, the Bahamas, and the British West India Islands, during the years 1816, 1817, 1818, 1819, and 1820, rendered in obedience to a resolution of the House of the 20th of December, 1820; which was ordered to lie on the table.

The bill from the Senate, entitled "An act to authorize the reconveyance of a tract of land in the city of New York," was read twice, and ordered to be read a third time to-morrow.

The bill from the Senate, entitled "An act to establish a new land office in the State of Mississippi, and for the better regulation of certain land districts in the States of Alabama and Mississippi," was read twice, and ordered to lie on the table.

The bill from the Senate, entitled "An act to extend the term of Samuel Parker's patents for his improvement in currying and finishing leather of all kinds," was also read twice, and referred to the Committee on the Judiciary.

A message from the Senate informed the House that the Senate have passed bills of this House of the following titles, to wit: "An act to release French ships and vessels entering the ports of the United States prior to the 30th September, 1820, from the operation of the act, entitled 'An act to impose a new tonnage duty on ships and vessels, and for other purposes ;" and "An act making appropriations for the support of Government for the year 1821 ;" with an amendment to each. They have also passed bills of the following titles, to wit: "An act for the relief of William Whitehead and others ;" "An act to amend the act, entitled 'An act to provide for taking the fourth census or enumeration of the inhabitants of the United States, and for other purposes ;" and "An act to authorize the President of the United States to take possession of East and West Florida, and establish a temporary government therein ;" in which amendments and bills they ask the concurrence of this House.

YELLOW STONE EXPEDITION.

Mr. COCKE, from the committee to whom was referred an inquiry into the nature of the contracts of Colonel James Johnson for transportation of supplies, &c., up the Missouri, and especially into the merits of the arbitration of his accounts with the Government, made a report thereon, being a particular examination of the subject, and expressing opinions rather against the allowances made. The report is as follows:

That a contract was entered into on the 2d of December, 1818, between the United States and Colonel James Johnson, of Kentucky, by which Colonel Johnson stipulated to furnish two steamboats, calculated to navigate the Mississippi and its waters, and place them subject to the orders of Government, by the first of March, 1819; and further agreed, in case he should be required, that he would, in a reasonable time, furnish one other or more steamboats, all of which were designed for the transportation of provisions, ordnance, and other military stores, to an expedition destined for the Mandan villages, or the Yellow Stone river; to this agreement the committee invite the attention of the House. It appears, by said agreement, that the rate of transportation was not definitively settled and ascertained, but, in case of disagreement as to the rate of compensation, it was to be fixed and determined by arbitrators indifferently chosen; a disagreement, as might have been expected, did arise, and referees were chosen. From the evidence submitted to them, it appears that the two steamboats were not placed subject to the orders of Government until some time in May following, and that on the arrival of the first boat at Belle Fontaine, the place from which the expedition was to have sailed, the Bank of St. Louis sued out an attachment against the property of Colonel Johnson, and delivered the writ to the proper officer to execute. It appears that he was not only inclined to prevent, but determined to resist with force, and called on the commanding officer at that station for a corporal's guard and arms, to enable him to oppose its execution with success; this, the committee are informed, was promptly refused. Colonel Johnson, on discovering this determination, came to anchor on the east side of the Mississippi, within the State of Illinois. The committee have thought proper to advert to those facts, believing that in some degree they contributed to the delay of the expedition, but are far from believing this the only cause. To illustrate more fully the views of the committee, and to enable the House to judge how far justice has been done the Government, they think it incumbent on them to state that Colonel Johnson was the sole contractor to this expedition, and bound to transport the military stores and ordnance from Pittsburg, in the State of Pennsylvania, to Belle Fontaine, on the Missouri, and also, the contractor to furnish the necessary provisions. The committee discover, from the documents referred to them, that, owing to the failure on the part of Colonel Johnson to deliver the stores and munitions of war, it would have been impracticable for the expedition to have moved before the ——— of June, at which time the Jefferson steamboat reached Belle Fontaine, on board of which were the stores before mentioned, together with the clothing for the soldiers employed on the Yellow Stone expedition. The committee think it due to Colonel Johnson to state that this delay was occasioned by the breaking of the piston head of this boat, and not from wanton neglect. It is, however, a strong reason, in the opin-

ion of the committee, why the United States should not pay Colonel Johnson for detention of his boats, when there was no failure on their part. It appears that a sufficient quantity of provisions had not reached the garrison at Belle Fontaine, even on the arrival of the steamboat Jefferson; that the subsistence for this expedition was partly on board another of Colonel Johnson's boats, called the Calhoun, and from the feebleness of her machinery she was unable to resist the current of the Mississippi, and never reached the garrison on the Missouri, where the troops were to embark; thus creating a deficiency of provisions which was not remedied by Colonel Johnson until about the 28th of June, and not until Colonel Atkinson, the commanding officer, called on him to complete the number of rations required, and assured him, if he did not, that the agent of the United States would be ordered to purchase, and he, Colonel Johnson, charged with them. For a more minute detail on this part of the subject, the committee refer to the evidence submitted to the arbitrators, which they have thought proper to lay before the House, together with the arguments of counsel, on the investigation before the referees. The committee will be content with a cursory examination, and notice only a few prominent facts. The clause in the argument of the 2d of December, 1818, and on which the claim of Colonel Johnson, of indemnity, for detention of his boats, is founded, provides " that if, in the arrangements and operations of Government, the said steamboats should be detained in their destination from the want of concentration of the articles to be transported or otherwise, and not imputable to the negligence of Colonel Johnson, the Quartermaster General obliged himself, on the part of the Government, to make from time to time advances, which are reasonable, on account of his transportation." The advance of money, by this provision in the contract, the committee believe, was esteemed by Colonel Johnson not only convenient, but of great importance, and a sufficient indemnity for all expenses incident to the detention; to justify this opinion they refer to an obligation executed by Colonel Johnson, of equal date with the agreement, of which the above is an extract. This obligation expresses the intention and views of the parties, and recites the previous agreement; an extract of which is submitted. "And whereas, by the terms of the said contract or agreement, the said Thomas S. Jesup hath engaged to make advances of money from time to time to the said James Johnson, on account of transportation, &c., Now, therefore, for the faithful performance of the several conditions and obligations contained in the said contract or agreement, on the part of the said James Johnson, and for the repayment and final adjustment of all and singular such advances as may be made to him by virtue of this contract," &c. From this it is evident that neither party contemplated more than a liberal advance of money, if perchance there should be any detention of the expedition; and it would have been proper in Colonel Johnson to require advances, in proportion to the time, but they cannot believe his claim is just as exhibited; if in this, however, they are mistaken, they must say, no operations of the Government caused the detention of Colonel Johnson's boats, while up the Missouri, and for which pretended claim the sum of $41,275 13 cents was awarded him. They find, from the evidence submitted to the referees, that the boats were detained solely in consequence of their inability to complete their voyage. The Jefferson was too feeble in machinery to stem the current, but for a short distance, when she was compelled to halt, and her cargo was chiefly transported by the boats of the United States. The Expedition and Johnson steamboats also failed, and that neither reached the Council Bluffs that season.

The committee are unable to discover even an apology for this allowance of $41,275 13, and are satisfied no principle of justice will sanction it; they cannot admit for a moment the idea, that when an accident happens to Colonel Johnson's boats, and over which the Government had no control, it is proper to make the United States responsible for detention, whilst the delay is indispensable to repair damages. The committee can perceive no rule of equity that will support this award; every award must be reasonable, and it is contrary to the duty of an arbitrator to do any thing that would be unjust between the parties. They also award Colonel Johnson the further sum of $5,875 39, including, they say, nothing but the actual expenses, wear and tear, and loss of time, throwing out all allowance for risk, which they supposed compensated in the freight for the detention of two boats before the expedition moved from Belle Fontaine, and for the detention of three of Colonel Johnson's boats, after they were damaged, unladened, and unable to proceed further; they say, after making due allowance for the actual expenses, the loss of time and employment, the wear and tear, and the risk of wintering in so exposed a situation, they award the further sum of $41,275 13; thus the United States has paid Colonel Johnson $47,249 51, for the detention of his boats, under the notion that, in the operations and arrangements of Government, the articles to be transported were not concentrated. The committee feel it their duty to state, that it appears, for the transportation actually furnished by Government, there has been paid Colonel Johnson, in obedience to the award, the sum of $14,969 28, for the transportation of articles not conveyed by him, or at his expense; and also the sum of $13,700 for the passage of troops in his boats to the Council Bluffs, when, in fact, the said boats never reached there, and were compelled to halt as before stated; the payment of those sums, under all the circumstances, in the opinion of the committee, cannot be sanctioned, and are not supportable, consistent with equity and justice. They feel constrained to remark, that the charge for detention of those boats up the Missouri, and for which there is awarded the sum of $41,275 13, did not make an item in the account of Colonel Johnson, when first exhibited, and must have been conceived after Congress refused an appropriation further to prosecute the expedition up the Missouri. The committee have attentively examined the account of Colonel Johnson as regards the claim for transportation of military stores and provisions; by his contract of the 2d of December, 1818, he agreed to receive a reasonable compensation for his services, and use of boats employed in transportation, and fixes as the basis the ordinary rates of transportation for such allowance. The committee can see no good reason why the sum of sixteen and one-fourth cents per pound should be paid Colonel Johnson for all articles conveyed by keel-boat navigation, when it is evident that the ordinary rate of transportation by this mode of conveyance did not exceed five and a half cents per pound; and in fact this was the sum paid by the United States to others performing at the same time similar services. In order that the House might have all the means of judging of the

merits of this transaction between the Government and Colonel Johnson, and to enable the nation fully to understand how far economy has been consulted, a comparison between the prices now allowed, and those given by the arbitrators to Colonel Johnson, was considered somewhat important. The committee called on the Quartermaster General for information on this point; the answer is, that Colonel Johnson became a bidder to transport military stores, &c., to the Council Bluffs, during the year 1821, at the rate of three and three-fourth cents per pound, as has been observed. The arbitrators allowed Colonel Johnson for similar services performed in 1819 sixteen and one-quarter cents per pound. It further appears, that, among fourteen or fifteen bidders for transportation to that post for the year 1821, but one required over four cents per pound, and he less than five cents per pound: what are the causes for such a change of prices the committee are unable to conjecture. That the present scarcity of money may make some difference is admitted; but the navigation of the Missouri river is the same; the same means of transportation existed which are now used. A reduction in price from sixteen and one-fourth cents to three and three-fourth cents, about one-fifth of the price heretofore given, affords some ground, at least, for the opinion, that what once was alleged to be prudent and economical, now appears to be profuse and extravagant.

If the committee are correct in their construction of the contract between the United States and Colonel Johnson, and their views relative to the advances from time to time being esteemed by Colonel Johnson equivalent to any delay that might happen by the operations of the Government, they have no hesitation in saying the advances have not only been liberal, but profuse, and, in one instance, not guarded by such security as will, in all probability, secure the Government against the loss of a sum of more than $50,000. The only security taken for this advance, as the committee believe, is a mortgage on Colonel Johnson's steamboats, which appear to have been broken, feeble, and subject to constant decay. The committee find that, after giving Colonel Johnson credit for every allowance awarded, there is still due from him to the United States the sum of $76,372 65, and which the arbitrators did not award he should pay, although justly due. From a full view of this subject the committee think the award ought to be set aside, and, to this end, recommend the following resolution:

Resolved, That the Attorney General of the United States be directed to use all legal means in his power to set aside the award made between the United States and Colonel James Johnson; and, also, use the legal means to recover, for the United States, whatever may be due from said Colonel James Johnson.

On motion of Mr. COCKE, the report was laid on the table. He then moved to print the report, which, from its length, was not read through. To this motion Mr. BROWN and Mr. F. JOHNSON, of Kentucky, objected, on the ground that it would be unjust to the parties concerned to publish the report without the documents. They animadverted, too, on the lateness of the hour at which the report had been made, which would prevent a due investigation. To this Mr. COCKE replied, that the committee had used due diligence, and had made a report as soon as they could, consistently with the duty reposed in them. He did not ob-

1269   HISTORY OF CONGRESS.   1270

MARCH, 1821.   *Bankrupt Bill—Military Appropriation Bill.*   H. OF R.

ject to the printing of the documents if the gentlemen wished it ; but must insist on the publication of the report. Mr. CANNON also supported the motion for printing ; which was agreed to, so as to include the printing of the whole of the documents as well as the report.

BANKRUPT BILL.

The unfinished business of yesterday, being the bill to establish a uniform system of bankruptcy, being announced as the business of the day—

Mr. CLARK moved to lay the bill on the table. On this motion the yeas and nays having been required by Mr. SERGEANT, were—for laying on the table 62, against laying it on the table 65, as follows :

YEAS—Messrs. Abbot, Alexander, Archer of Virginia, Baker, Baldwin, Ball, Barbour, Blackledge, Boden, Buffum, Butler of Louisiana, Campbell, Cannon, Clark, Cobb, Cocke, Culbreth, Culpeper, Davidson, Dickinson, Edwards of North Carolina, Fisher, Floyd, Garnett, Gray, Hooks, Hostetter, Jackson, Jones of Ten., Kinsey, Lincoln, McCoy, McCreary, McLean of Kentucky, Metcalf, R. Moore, T. L. Moore, Morton, Murray, Neale, Nelson of Virginia, Newton, Parker of Massachusetts, Patterson, Phelps, Philson, Plumer, Rankin, Reid, Rhea, Ross, Settle, Smyth of Virginia, Stevens, Swearingen, Terrell, Tucker of Virginia, Tucker of South Carolina, Wallace, Wendover, Williams of Virginia, and Williams of North Carolina.

NAYS—Messrs. Adams, Allen of Mass., Bloomfield, Brevard, Brush, Case, Cook, Cushman, Dane, Darlington, Denison, Dewitt, Eddy, Edwards of Connecticut, Edwards of Pennsylvania, Eustis, Fay, Folger, Foot, Ford, Forrest, Gorham, Gross of New York, Guyon, Hall of New York, Hemphill, Hendricks, Hill, Hobart, Johnson, Kendall, Kinsley, Lathrop, Little, Livermore, Maclay, Mallary, Marchand, Meigs, Mercer, Monell, S. Moore, Moseley, Nelson of Massachusetts, Pitcher, Rich, Rogers, Sawyer, Sergeant, Silsbee, Sloan, Smith of New Jersey, Smith of Maryland, Southard, Storrs, Street, Strong of New York, Tracy, Udree, Upham, Van Rensselaer, Warfield, Whitman, and Wood.

So the motion was negatived, by three votes. On this vote it appears nearly sixty of the whole number of members were absent from the House.

The SPEAKER then commenced the reading of the bill by sections ; and the first section having been read—

Mr. HOOKS moved to strike it out ; in other words, to reject the bill.

Mr. A. SMYTH rose, and, in support of this motion, delivered a speech of three hours in length, covering the whole ground of opposition to the bill.

Mr. STORRS followed in a speech of about half an hour, in support of the bill.

Mr. SAWYER, of North Carolina, delivered his sentiments in favor of the bill.

Mr. COBB then moved to lay the bill on the table ; which motion was decided, by yeas and nays, in the affirmative, as follows :

YEAS—Messrs. Abbot, Alexander, Allen of Ten., Archer of Virginia, Baldwin, Ball, Bateman, Blackledge, Boden, Brevard, Bryan, Buffum, Butler of N. Hampshire, Campbell, Cannon, Clagett, Clark, Cobb, Cocke,

Crawford, Culbreth, Culpeper, Earle, Edwards of N. Carolina, Floyd, Ford, Garnett, Gray, Hardin, Herrick, Hibshman, Hooks, Hostetter, Jackson, Johnson, Jones of Virginia, Jones of Tennessee, Kinsey, Lincoln, McCoy, McCreary, McLean of Kentucky, R. Moore, T. L. Moore, Morton, Neale, Nelson of Virginia, Newton, Parker of Mass., Patterson, Phelps, Philson, Rankin, Reid, Rhea, Richards, Settle, Smyth of Virginia, Stevens, Swearingen, Tucker of Virginia, Tucker of South Carolina, Wallace, Williams of Virginia, and Williams of North Carolina.

NAYS—Messrs. Allen of Massachusetts, Allen of N. York, Archer of Maryland, Bayly, Beecher, Bloomfield, Brush, Case, Cushman, Dane, Darlington, Denison, Eddy, Edwards of Connecticut, Edwards of Pennsylvania, Eustis, Fay, Folger, Forrest, Fuller, Gorham, Gross of New York, Guyon, Hall of New York, Hill, Hobart, Kendall, Livermore, Maclay, Marchand, Meigs, Mercer, Monell, Montgomery, S. Moore, Nelson of Massachusetts, Pitcher, Rich, Rogers, Russ, Sawyer, Sergeant, Silsbee, Simkins, Sloan, Smith of New Jersey, Smith of Maryland, Storrs, Street, Strong of New York, Tomlinson, Tompkins, Tracy, Udree, Van Rensselaer, Wendover, Whitman, and Wood.

So the bill was ordered to lie on the table.

MILITARY APPROPRIATION BILL.

The House then resolved itself into a Committee of the Whole, on the bill making appropriations for the Military Establishment for the year 1821.

Considerable debate took place on the item of appropriation for fortifications. Mr. SMITH of Maryland moved, by instruction of the Committee of Ways and Means, to fill the blank for that object with $172,000. Mr. NEWTON moved to fill the blank with $300,000.

After a debate of more than three hours—

The question was taken on Mr. NEWTON'S motion, and there were—for the motion 21, against it 63. A quorum not having voted—

The Committee rose and reported the fact. The SPEAKER, having counted the House, announced that there was not a quorum present ; and, the House adjourned, after a session of nearly ten hours.

———

FRIDAY, March 2.

Mr. NELSON, of Virginia, from the Committee on Foreign Affairs, to which was referred the bill from the Senate, entitled "An act for the adjudication and payment of claims under the Treaty of Amity, Settlement, and Limits, between the United States and His Catholic Majesty," reported the same without amendment, and it was committed to the Committee of the Whole on the state of the Union.

Mr. SERGEANT, from the Committee on the Judiciary, to which was referred the bill from the Senate, entitled "An act to extend the term of Samuel Parker's patents for his improvement in currying and finishing leather of all kinds," reported the same without amendment, and the bill was ordered to be read a third time to-morrow.

Mr. FORREST, from the Committee on Agriculture, made a report on the petition of P. S. Chazotte, stating in substance that it is too late to act upon it at the present session; which was ordered to lie on the table.

The bill from the Senate to authorize the Clerk of the United States' court for the Louisiana district to appoint a deputy, was ordered to be read a third time; and was accordingly read a third time, and passed.

The Committee of Ways and Means; the Committee on Private Land Claims; and the Committee on the Post Office and Post Roads; were severally discharged from the consideration of all petitions, and other matters to them, respectively, referred at the present session, upon which they have not reported to the House.

On motion of Mr. SMITH, of Maryland, the Clerk was directed to pay, out of the funds of the House, to the assistant in his office, from the period at which he was last paid by order of the House, to the end of the present session, and at the lowest rate of compensation allowed to clerks employed in his office.

The amendment proposed by the Senate to the bill, entitled "An act making appropriations for the support of Government for the year 1821, was read, and concurred in by the House.

A message from the Senate informed the House that the Senate have passed bills of this House of the following titles, viz: "An act making appropriations for the public buildings;" and "An act to alter and establish certain post roads;" with amendments. They have also passed bills of the following titles, viz: "An act supplemental to an act, entitled 'An act to authorize the appointment of commissioners to lay out the road therein mentioned;'" "An act to provide for the due execution of the laws of the United States within the State of Missouri;" "An act to amend the act, entitled 'An act supplementary to an act, entitled 'An act to regulate the collection of duties on imports and tonnage,' passed the 2d of March, 1799;'" and "An act to revive and continue in force 'An act fixing the compensations of the Secretary of the Senate, and Clerk of the House of Representatives, of the clerks employed in their offices, and the Librarian;' approved the 18th of April, 1818;" in which amendments and bills they ask the concurrence of this House.

The amendments proposed by the Senate to the bill, entitled "An act making appropriations for the public buildings," were read, and concurred in.

The bill from the Senate, entitled "An act to amend the act, entitled 'An act supplementary to an act, entitled 'An act to regulate the collection of duties on imports and tonnage," passed the 2d day of March, 1799, was read twice and referred to the Committee of Ways and Means.

The amendment of the Senate to the bill to amend the act of last session laying an extra tonnage duty, was taken up. [This amendment gives a power to the President of the United States to suspend the operation of the act of the last session, on a satisfactory arrangement being made, during the recess, by the President.]

Mr. NELSON, of Virginia, moved to amend the amendment by striking out the word "dominions," where it occurs (as applicable to the United States,) and inserting "territories," the former being an expression unusual in our laws. Mr. NEWTON said he should not quarrel about words. The motion was rejected, though not by a large majority—but a different amendment, having the same effect, was made.

The amendment of the Senate was then agreed to, without opposition.

The bill from the Senate for giving further time for taking the third census was read twice, and afterwards read a third time and passed.

The bill from the Senate for authorizing the reconveyance of a tract of land to the State of New York, gave rise to considerable opposition, and was supported by Mr. MEIGS, Mr. WOOD, and others. Mr. WARFIELD moved to postpone it indefinitely. But a motion of Mr. COCKE, to lay the bill on the table, was agreed to.

The bill for the relief of William Whitehead was twice read, and referred to a Committee of the Whole.

The bill from the Senate, concerning the road now laying out from Wheeling to the Mississippi, was read and ordered to a second reading.

Mr. COBB, from a hostility to the further prosecution of this road, moved to reject the bill.

This motion was opposed by Mr. CLAY, and supported by Mr. HARDIN. On motion of Mr. BRUSH, the bill was then ordered to lie on the table—yeas 69, nays 49.

The bill from the Senate to provide for the due execution of the laws of the United States within the State of Missouri, was read the first and second time. The bill was referred to a Committee of the Whole.

The bill from the Senate to revive and continue in force the act fixing the compensation of the Secretary of the Senate and the Clerk of the House of Representatives, of the clerks in said offices, and of the librarian, was twice read, ordered to be read a third time, and finally read a third time and passed.

The bill from the Senate to provide for the occupation of Florida and for the establishment of a temporary government therein, was twice read and referred to the Committee of the Whole on the state of the Union.

The engrossed bill authorizing the Secretary of the Treasury to dispose of a tract of land in Northumberland, late the property of Presley Thornton, was read a third time and passed.

The amendments of the Senate to the annual post road bill were taken up and agreed to.

A message from the Senate informed the House that the Senate have passed "An act authorizing the President of the United States to establish a port of entry in the district of Sandusky, in the State of Ohio, and for other purposes;" "An act making appropriations for the support of the Navy of the United States for the year 1821;" and "An act to authorize the building of lighthouses on Cross and Pond islands, in the harbor of Boothbay, and at the mouth of Oswego river; and placing buoys on the shoals of Nantucket and Vineyard Sound, near the harbor of Wickford, and on the Altamaha river, and for other purposes,"

1273   HISTORY OF CONGRESS.   1274

MARCH, 1821.   *Revenue and Expenditures—Military Appropriation Bill.*   H. OF R.

with amendments; in which amendments they ask the concurrence of this House.

Ordered, That the bill making appropriations for the Military Establishment of the United States for the year 1821, be committed to the Committee of the Whole on the state of the Union.

The SPEAKER laid before the House a letter from the Secretary of the Treasury, transmitting a statement of the payments to inspectors, weighers, gaugers, measurers, and markers, employed by the collectors of the customs in the years 1816, 1817, 1818, 1819, and 1820, so far as the returns have been received; which letter and statement were ordered to lie on the table.

PENSION LAW.

Mr. MALLARY, after adverting to a late decision of the Attorney General under the pension law, offered the following joint resolution for consideration:

Resolved, by the Senate and House of Representatives of the United States of America in Congress assembled, That the Secretary of War be, and he hereby is, authorized to restore to the pension list any person who may have been, or shall be, stricken from the pension list, on the evidence of such person's schedule, agreeably to the act of the 1st of May, 1820, in addition to the pension law of 1818, whenever the Secretary of War shall be satisfied, by other or additional evidence, that such person is in such reduced circumstances as to come within the provisions of the aforesaid acts.

The House having agreed to consider this resolution, and the resolution being put on its second reading, was objected to by Mr. McLEAN; and the question then, according to the rule of the House, was on the rejection of the resolution.

Mr. WILLIAMS, of North Carolina, on the ground that there would not be time to act on the resolution at the present session, moved to lay it on the table; which motion was carried, 53 to 47.

REVENUE AND EXPENDITURES.

The House then proceeded to the consideration of the following resolution, which was yesterday submitted by Mr. LITTLE:

Resolved, That the President of the United States be requested to lay before this House, at the next session of Congress, a system of revenue that shall meet all the expenses of the Government, without the aid of loans, and suggest such reductions, which, in his opinion, are least prejudicial to the public interest, as will bring the expenditures within the actual receipts of the Treasury.

Mr. COBB moved to strike out that part of the resolution which relates to a system of revenue; but, after a few observations from Mr. LITTLE against it, the motion was negatived—ayes 39.

Mr. TUCKER, of Virginia, said that he should vote against the resolution. The House, he said, was getting too much into a habit of devolving its proper business on the Heads of Departments. The subject of this resolution was properly within the scope of the duties of the House, and he hoped the House would not transfer it elsewhere.

Mr. COBB said, that experience sufficiently proved that there was no great disposition on the part of

the executive officers to retrench expenditures, and that every thing of that sort that is done is forced upon them by Congress. The better opinion, too, now appeared to be, that the present revenue would be found sufficient, if a proper economy was infused into the expenditure of it. If this resolution were to pass, the House might rely upon it, that the suggestions received would be, in substance, that no retrenchment can be made in the public expenditures, consistent with the public interest.

Mr. FOOT expressed himself decidedly in opposition to the resolution. He was not for this House giving bond for the performance of its duty, nor requiring of other public officers to do so.

Mr. COCKE objected to the resolution, because it was calling on the President to do what he is already constitutionally bound to do, that is, to give such information as he may deem expedient, &c. This House ought not to touch the subject in this manner, having their own duty to discharge.

Mr. EUSTIS was opposed to the resolution, because it calls on the Executive to do what is peculiarly the duty of this House.

Mr. F. JOHNSON, of Kentucky, said he thought it would be as well not to act on the resolution at all. He therefore moved to lay it on the table, and the motion was agreed to.

MILITARY APPROPRIATION BILL.

The House then again resolved itself into a Committee of the Whole on the state of the Union, on the military appropriation bill.

[The Committee of the Whole, to which was referred the bill making appropriations for the military service of the United States for the year 1821, having risen last night for the want of a quorum, and reported the fact to the House, a question arose this morning whether the bill was in Committee or in the House.

The SPEAKER decided that the bill was in the House, and that the Committee, having risen for defect of a quorum, could make no other report than to inform the House of the fact; whereby the Committee was dissolved.[*] Whereupon, on motion of Mr. SMITH, of Maryland, the bill was committed to a Committee of the Whole on the state of the Union, and the House proceeded, in that Committee.]

And the question again presenting itself on the amount to be appropriated for fortifications for the current year; and the question being on filling the blank, as proposed by Mr. NEWTON, with three hundred thousand dollars, the debate, which occupied so much time last night, was resumed; and the largest amount proposed was warmly supported by Mr. NEWTON, Mr. BUTLER, of Louisiana, and Mr. F. JOHNSON, of Kentucky, and was opposed

---

[*] See Jefferson's Manual, page 40. "This quorum (that of the Committee of the Whole,) is the same as that of the House, and if a defect happens, the Chairman, on a motion and question, rises, the Speaker resumes the chair, and the Chairman can make no other report than to inform the House of the cause of their dissolution." 2 *Hats.* 125.

1275   HISTORY OF CONGRESS.   1276

H. of R.   *Military Appropriation Bill.*   MARCH, 1821.

by the Chairman of the Committee of Ways and Means. The largest amount was at length negatived, and the amount of $170,000, as proposed by Mr. SMITH, of Maryland, was agreed to.

Mr. F. JOHNSON, of Kentucky, said, that he understood one object of the gentleman from Virginia, in making the motion he had, was to enable the Secretary of War to carry on and complete the fortifications at Mobile bay, which he esteemed essential to the best interests of the Western country; that he had, upon all occasions, from principle, manifested an aversion to a profuse and unnecessary expenditure of public money; that he could not consider the subject embraced by the motion as of that character; that, upon the present occasion, he should have remained silent, had not so strong a disposition been manifested yesterday and to day, by the Committee, to abandon those fortifications, notwithstanding the expenditures already made there. He considered the fortification of Mobile bay as important, and necessary to the security of the outlet of the Mississippi; and upon every thing which tended to weaken or strengthen the security of the free commerce of that great river, he could but feel a deep interest. The present bill proposes to appropriate $172,000 for carrying on fortifications at Fort Delaware, Fort Washington, Fort Monroe, Fort Calhoun, and the Rigoletts; but not one cent for Mobile bay. Such seems to be the policy which the Committee of Ways and Means, who reported the bill, would dictate.

Under this view of the subject, Mr. J. said he would ask the patience of the Committee to bear with him till he should make a few remarks. He said he should not inquire now into the policy of fortifications; the necessity of them had long since been demonstrated, and the system had been pursued, until almost every other part of the Union was secured, and he could see no good reason for abandoning those at Mobile. Why, he would ask, was every other part of the nation to be secured by fortifications, except the Gulf of Mexico? For his part, he conceived that the Executive and the Secretary of War, in attending to that quarter, had done nothing more than their duty, and shown a just regard to the interest of the West; and he should, he conceived, do nothing more than justice to the Secretary of War to say that he was the first officer of the Government, who, by efficient measures, had paid that just regard due to the great and vital interest of the Western States. Until his time, he would inquire, what had been done there, while fortifications were rising in almost every other direction? The fortifications at Dauphin Island were progressing more rapidly than that at Mobile Point. Both are going on; but they are to be abandoned—and why? It was said by some gentlemen that the contracts have not been complied with, and they apprehend one of the contractors would fail. Was that, he said, any reason, were it so, for abandoning the work? But it was not the fact; for the time in which the works were to be completed had not arrived: the failure had not yet taken place, and may not; and if the contemplated failure does happen, he said

he was informed, from undoubted authority, that the undertaker had given the most ample security for his performance. But if, he said, we refuse to make appropriations to fulfil the engagements of the Government, the breach may be somewhere else than on the part of the undertaker; and there was no danger, while there was a prospect of failure, that any money that shall be appropriated would go into the hands of the contractor.

It is said, moreover, by some gentlemen, that money has been appropriated, year after year, for fortifications, and they don't know how it has been expended. The reason why gentlemen don't know, said Mr. J., is because they have not taken the trouble to inquire and inform themselves. Not a dollar, he presumed, had been expended upon these fortifications, but what a particular and detailed account of it might be seen; and because gentlemen will not inform themselves, they don't know, and make that another argument against completing those fortifications. No, Mr. Chairman, he said, we ought to inform ourselves upon all these points, and as to the necessity and utility of every proposed fortification; and not, by anticipated failures in contracts, and the want of knowledge, which a little labor might supply, to seek an apology for abandoning important and necessary measures.

Again, said Mr. J., gentlemen seem to deny the necessity and utility of fortifying Mobile bay, and the Committee of Ways and Means had refused to report any thing for that purpose; but the honorable chairman of the committee had been good enough to admit the necessity of protecting that bay by fortification, but protests most roundly that he would as soon built a fort on the Alleghany mountain, as on Dauphin island, for the protection of that bay, and says, Mobile Point is the only place where there ought to be a fortification, and there he admits it is necessary. And if that point was necessary to be fortified, why leave it out of the bill? The honorable gentleman tells us he was willing himself to have included Mobile Point, but the rest of the committee opposed it. But, to fortify Dauphin island, it is alleged it is altogether unnecessary; and why? Because gentlemen say that the channel into the bay by Dauphin island affords only nine or ten feet water, and therefore no vessel of war of any size can pass it into, the bay, and the only channel they can pass is by Mobile Point. It is true the channel by Dauphin island is not more than nine or ten feet, and that large vessels of war cannot pass through it; but it is also true that between this island and Pelican island, which lies to the South, there is a most excellent and safe anchorage for large ships, which would be commanded by a fort on Dauphin island, and the conclusions which are drawn from the facts stated by gentlemen, that it is unnecessary to fortify on Dauphin island, by no means follow, when its peculiar and important position is ascertained. For his own part, said Mr. J., he was disposed to hearken to what the corps of engineers had reported upon the subject, at whose head was General Bernard, a most distinguished and able engineer, who had surveyed, actually surveyed, Mobile bay and our coast on the Gulf of Mexico; had actually sounded the passes by Mobile Point and Dauphin island, and all about them, and had ascertained the condition and position of Point Mobile and Dauphin island, and their importance, as well in regard to Mobile bay itself, as in relation to the adjacent coasts and country, and the Gulf of Mexico generally; and that they had, in his opinion, taken a just and proper view of the subject in all its bearings. They tell us, continued Mr. J., first, what is evident to every reflecting man, that, from the peculiar circumstances under which that country labors, (Louisiana and Alabama,) in its population, its Indian neighbors, its natural position, and its connexions, that it becomes all important (beside the regard to the safety of Mobile bay) to protect all the indirect, as well as the direct, approaches to New Orleans; to fortify every harbor on our side the Gulf, which might be important to an enemy, on account of the excellencies of its anchorage, or as a safe place of arms to operate from against any part of the frontier. To these propositions, he said, we must all assent, as this plan, if carried into execution, would "compel an enemy to carry these frontier works or fortified harbors, as a preliminary to any military designs against the country;" and, if an invasion should be attempted, without carrying such works, the enemy would have to resort to insecure anchorage grounds near the sea islands, and of effecting landings in boats on some intermediate points on the seashore, unprotected by their ships of war—an enterprise too hazardous to be attempted without subjecting them to the worst results. It would seem, said Mr. J., then only necessary to ascertain whether Mobile bay be a point of importance; whether it can be defended, and how it can be defended. In the first place, then, said he, Mobile bay is the principal harbor which belonged to the United States, in the Gulf of Mexico, previous to the late cession of the Floridas, and it has not diminished in its importance by that event. It is a large and spacious harbor, sufficient to contain a fleet of any size or magnitude, that could pass the bar at its mouth, of seventeen or eighteen feet water. He said, independent of the necessity of its defence for the protection of Alabama, and the commercial depots of Blakeley and Mobile, it was important that it should not fall into the hands of an enemy, because it would afford him a safe anchorage and secure harbor for transports, a secure place of arms to operate from on the inhabitants of Tombigbee and Alabama, and to create a diversion in a direct or indirect attack on Orleans, and to harass the whole frontier, and menace and annoy Pensacola.

The engineers concur in opinion that Mobile bay can only be defended from Mobile Point and Dauphin island; that the distance between these two points exceeds three miles; that there are only two channels in that place offering any facilities to vessels of magnitude attempting to enter the bay; that the east or main channel approaches Mobile Point, and the west channel, admitting of nine or ten feet water, within eleven or twelve hundred yards of Dauphin island. The space between these two channels, from actual sounding, is found to be a sand bank, admitting of irregular soundings of three, four, five, and six feet water, and changeable by every gale of wind agitating the ocean; that there is no communication between the channels, and no one position, it is expressly stated, can be selected to command both; that the east or main channel can be defended from Mobile Point alone, and the west from Dauphin island. The occupancy of one of these points alone cannot, therefore, insure the object for which fortifications at that place would be necessary, and hence it is found necessary to command both of these points, or to abandon the defence of Mobile bay. And are Congress prepared to abandon the defence of Mobile bay? Surely gentlemen from the West are not, nor should he suppose the nation was. It was, he thought, obvious that the defence of Mobile bay was essential to the security of New Orleans in another point of view; that it was so to secure the communication between New Orleans and Mobile bay, by Lake Ponchartrain and the lesser lakes, comprised between the main land and the chain of islands bounded by Cat island to the west, and Dauphin island to the east.

Another specific object, he said, to be obtained in fortifying Dauphin island, was to command the western channel, to prevent vessels from penetrating into the bay, which might be constructed for that purpose, to carry ten or twelve guns, and to draw only eight or nine feet of water, who would be capable of annoying the whole adjacent country, and conveying transports for interior operations—and is it of no importance to check these sort of operations? But, another object, not less important to be attained by the fortification there, was to deprive an enemy of the excellent anchorage between Pelican island and Dauphin island, which would be completely commanded by its guns, and secure it to the Navy of the United States. Leave Dauphin island unfortified, he said, and you leave it and the anchorage between that and Pelican island subject to the possession of an enemy, and what would be the consequence? It would afford him a secure place of arms, a safe anchorage, a rallying point, from which he might sally forth, and return at pleasure, from incursions against New Orleans or any other part of the frontier, and certain it was it would afford great facility for blockading the bay and penetrating the western channel, and even of annoying Pensacola. Sir, said Mr. J., let me but state what the justly celebrated engineer General Bernard has reported in relation to this point and Pensacola: He says, "if, 'in consequence of the acquisition of the Floridas, 'Pensacola becomes a naval depot and a harbor of 'rendezvous (for the American Navy,) Mobile bay 'would be a most favorable place of arms for an 'enemy to operate from thence upon the naval 'establishment at Pensacola;" and this, he said, was no guess work of General Bernard's; it was from examination and observations made upon the ground, and his judgment in these matters no one will question. So that we find that, instead of the acquisition of Pensacola making it unnecessary to fortify Mobile bay, as has seemed to be thought by some, the acquisition of Pensacola, and the establishment of a naval depot there, forms an additional reason for continuing the fortifications at Mobile bay.

There was another reason, Mr. J. said, which should induce us now to be more attentive to the security of Mobile bay; that, by the same treaty by which we had acquired Pensacola, we had surrendered the Texas country, and thereby deprived ourselves of all protection to New Orleans and the mouth of the Mississippi from the harbors and shores to the west of it. And surely, said he, we are not prepared to leave the east, subject to the insult and encroachment of an enemy. It was hazarding too much; it was leaving New Orleans and the Gulf of Mexico substantially without defence, and in a situation too precarious and uncertain for its great importance to the Western country. He said it was unnecessary for him to say any thing as to the importance of New Orleans and the permanent security of the free outlet of the Mississippi; that it was a subject upon which every intelligent man in the nation was well informed, and he could but be surprised to see gentlemen from the West opposing the measure.

It is true, he said, that the country is in a depressed state; that our revenue does not promise us an excess in the Treasury; but it is equally true that, for years, $800,000 has annually been appropriated for fortifications; that all our seashores and harbors, except those on the Gulf of Mexico, are nearly secured; and now the committee has reported $172,000 principally for the completion of those objects, and an additional hundred is asked by the motion of the gentleman from Virginia, principally to favor the completion of the defence of Mobile bay and New Orleans, and it is objected to. If gentlemen, he said, would abandon other fortifications, there would be some apology for abandoning these; but as fortifications are to go on, and have gone on, he said, he could see no reason or justice in denying an equal participation to the people of the West, in the benefits to be derived from fortifications. Some gentlemen, he said, could vote without scruple for the appropriation of upwards of $100,000, in these hard times, to cover in the centre building of the Capitol; but to vote the same sum for the protection of the commerce of the West, and the security of the people bordering on the coast of the Gulf, they would not do that—the times are too hard, the work is unnecessary. But times are not too hard to build an addition to a Capitol that is not necessary, but for show and splendor.

Sir, said he, it would seem, from the arguments of some gentlemen, that the Executive and War Departments alone were interested in these great works of defence; for they seem to imply that these works are to be carried on merely to gratify the desires of the Executive and Secretary of War. What interest have they in the defences of the country more than we ought to have, or more than any other friend to the nation has? They can have no other interest than the security against invasion of this country, which is dear to all, and the protection of its commerce. The greater the anxiety they shall manifest to the permanent peace and security of the country, the greater praise is due them; the greater confidence will they derive; it is a faithful discharge of the great trust reposed in them. It is a laudable desire to defend our common country, the blessings and protection of which we all in common enjoy. He said he should not, that he knew of, himself have proposed any thing toward fortifications this session, more than was indispensable for the preservation of those erected and erecting; but he did not like to see the cup pass by without sharing a little of its contents. And, after again urging the propriety and necessity of continuing those fortifications, and speaking of the great waste of public money heretofore expended upon fortifications injudiciously situated, before the nation had employed competent engineers to survey the seaports and harbors, and to fix on the proper places of defence, he concluded by declaring himself in favor of the amendment proposed.

Mr. BUTLER, of Louisiana, then moved to amend the bill, by inserting an appropriation of $40,000 specially for Mobile Point.

On trying this question, as on several others during the day's sitting, there was not a quorum present. But, a quorum being at length assembled, the vote was 58 to 35 against it.

A motion was also made, with no better success, to make a special appropriation for fortifications at Dauphin Island.

A great deal of other debate took place on various amendments proposed to the bill, the consideration of which occupied the House, in Committee of the Whole, until a late hour.

Among the amendments proposed to the bill, was an appropriation of $40,000 to pay arrears of the cost of the erection of an arsenal at Augusta, in Georgia. This was opposed by Mr. MALLARY and Mr. CULPEPER, on the ground that the expenditure was unauthorized by law; and was supported by Mr. REID, Mr. CUTHBERT, and Mr. SIMKINS, on the ground that individuals ought not to suffer from their having complied with contracts which they had made with the Government. Mr. FLOYD also spoke on the subject. The amendment was agreed to—yeas 48, nays 45.

Mr. SIMKINS was understood to say that he should not have raised his voice on this subject, had it not been for the extraordinary turn of the debate; but, feeling onl the interest which all American citizens should feel, he should have left this appropriation bill to share the fate destined for most measures by the spirit and temper predominant in this House. But, sir, said he, as distrust and allegations of fraud against public officers and public contractors are not only the order of this debate, but the order of the day, he could not sit still and hear those charges made, without repelling them in the most pointed and unequivocal manner. Sir, he continued, on what grounds, and on what evidence, are these charges made? They are supported by not a single vestige of truth. What head of department has refused to furnish the most ample information? Had the

House called, in a single instance, on the head of that department charged with the disbursement of the intended appropriation, and has he refused fully and amply to answer such call? Let an instance be pointed out. But contractors are charged with fraud and wilful dishonesty in the performance of their contracts. No charges are easier made; but, sir, the merest reptile that crawls on the earth should be shielded from criminal imputation till evidence can be produced for such charge. This House presents now, as it has for some time back presented, the extraordinary spectacle of a tribunal for criminal accusations; and still more extraordinary is it that these accusations are made upon public rumor, hearsay, and out-of-door accusation, and, when proof is demanded, (which he now demanded,) nothing tangible exists!

Sir, every avenue and subject of legislation here seem to be bottomed on suspicion and distrust. In this spirit the gentleman from Vermont, (Mr. MALLARY,) and from North Carolina, (Mr. WILLIAMS,) say that no account has been given of the money appropriated for fortifications. Have they asked information on this point? And, if they have, let them show when and where it has been refused? Sir, your public officers must have your confidence to a certain extent, otherwise the Government stops; but, if any member will or can show that all matters of contract, in every part of this vast continent, cannot be fully shown and faithfully accounted for by the Secretary of War, then he would join in the present unjust cry of accusation. To cast a prejudice, however, against the granting the appropriation in this instance, it is said that a gentleman, (not here to defend himself,) a clerk in the War Department, was interested in a contract to build the fortification at the Rip Raps. He was, he said, one of a committee, at the last session, for the investigation of these very contracts, (together with the gentleman from Tennessee, Mr. COCKE, and one from New York, Mr. STORRS, which last took notes on the examination at length, and who he was sorry not to see in his place;) he should state the facts, as far as he could remember them. Sir, it appeared that this gentleman was once interested in the contract; but he did not become so till nine months after the contract was entered into, and at the very time when the contract was thought to be a bad one; for stone of a particular kind, much nearer the fortification, was refused or rejected, and the undertaker had to get it at perhaps twice the distance. Immediately, however, after the rising of the last session, this gentleman, (the chief clerk,) supposing that he would be subjected to further accusation, as he had already been to flagrant misrepresentation, entirely discharged himself, by consent of all parties, from this famous contract.

The gentleman from New York (Mr. TRACY, of the "Ways and Means,") has said that the fort at Mobile Point was disproportioned in size to the good to be produced by it. Sir, said he, it is admitted that, shallow as the water is at that point, it is deep enough for vessels of eighteen feet; and, although these are not of the largest size, yet the number may be multiplied; and, so far from two

little towns only to be protected, as stated by the member from Georgia, (Mr. COBB,) this river waters, and these forts would protect, the immensely rich country up the Alabama, and is nearly connected with the lake leading to that most important point—New Orleans. These forts, with the important ones on the Chesapeake, are pronounced by gentlemen to be worthless, and that their progress ought to be instantly stopped. After the surveys, most diligently and skilfully made, by some of the first engineers in the world, acquiring their professions by years of the most diligent and profound study, who have disinterestedly fixed the sites of these forts, he would as soon go into the Supreme Court, without ever having studied law, and pronounce a legal opinion, as to pronounce in this House, without any professional skill, that these fortifications are worthless.

The gentleman from New York (Mr. TRACY) says he conceives the estimates of money for the Rip Raps are not at all to be relied on, because a very large sum (perhaps upwards of $400,000 out of an estimate of near a million) was given, or contracted to be given, for stone alone. Sir, this is by no means wonderful, when it is considered that the whole of the fortification, from the depth of the water, is to be raised by stone; that, in fact, stone is the principal, and almost the only, material of the work.

But prospective contracts, as they are called, are improper, and ought not to be entered into. Sir, said he, a resolution of this kind would destroy your public works, or cause you to pay more than double the price for their erection. Contracts are not to be prospective! And pray, sir, said he, will gentlemen have the goodness to point out what other contracts can be entered into? Will they show how the public works are to be executed?

Sir, said he, I rose unexpectedly, under an imperious sense of duty, and to demand evidence of that general and hateful distrust, jealousy, and spirit of crimination, which are urged to fill our minds with prejudice, unfit us for dispassionate legislation, and which seem intended to sap the foundations of our national defence. He deemed the Navy, from the very nature and situation of the country, our most indispensable defensive institution. Fortifications and the Army come next. May the efforts which seem to be making, not merely to lessen, but to destroy them, be arrested.

The Committee rose, and reported the amendments which had been made to the bill. The question on concurrence in the appropriation for completing the arsenal at Augusta was decided by yeas and nays—yeas 66, nays 48, as follows:

YEAS—Messrs. Alexander, Allen of Massachusetts, Allen of New York, Archer of Maryland, Baker, Baldwin, Barbour, Blackledge, Bloomfield, Brush, Bryan, Campbell, Clark, Cobb, Cook, Crowell, Cushman, Cuthbert, Dane, Eddy, Edwards of Connecticut, Edwards of Pennsylvania, Edwards of North Carolina, Floyd, Folger, Ford, Fuller, Gorham, Gross of New York, Hackley, Hemphill, Johnson, Kent, Kinsey, Little, McLean of Kentucky, Meigs, Montgomery, S. Moore, Moseley, Neale, Nelson of Virginia, Newton, Parker of Massachusetts, Pitcher, Plumer, Rankin, Reid, Rhea, Rich, Robertson, Rogers, Sawyer, Settle. Silsbee, Simkins, Smith of New Jersey, Smith of Maryland, A. Smyth of Virginia, Street, Strong of New York, Swearingen, Terrell, Tucker of South Carolina, Udree, and Walker—66.

NAYS—Messrs. Adams, Allen of Tennessee, Ball, Bateman, Boden, Buffum, Case, Cocke, Culbreth, Denison, Earle, Fay, Foot, Forrest, Gray, Guyon, Hall of New York, Hardin, Hibshman, Hobart, Hooks, Hostetter, Jackson, Jones of Virginia, Jones of Tennessee, Lathrop, Lincoln, Maclay, McCoy, Mc-Creary, Mallary, Metcalf, R. Moore, T. L. Moore, Murray, Patterson, Philson, Richards, Richmond, Ross, Russ, Sloan, Stevens, Strong of Vermont, Tracy, Tucker of Virginia, Williams of Virginia, and Williams of North Carolina—48.

So the amendment was concurred in.

Mr. BUTLER, of Louisiana, renewed the motion which he had made for the specific appropriation of $40,000 for fortifications at Mobile Point, and $40,000 for the fortification at Dauphin Island. On suggestion of Mr. F. JOHNSON, of Virginia, Mr. B. modified his motion so as to make it $30,000 for each point. The question having been divided, on the motion of Mr. SMITH, of Maryland, the question was first taken on the appropriation for Mobile Point, and decided in the affirmative—yeas 68, nays 43, as follows:

YEAS—Messrs. Abbot, Alexander, Allen of Mass. Anderson, Archer of Md., Archer of Va., Baldwin, Ball, Barbour, Blackledge, Bloomfield,, Brush, Bryan, Butler of Louisiana, Cannon, Case, Clark, Cook, Crowell, Cushman, Cuthbert, Dane, Denison, Eddy, Edwards of North Carolina, Eustis, Fay, Ford, Fuller, Gorham, Gray, Hackley, Hobart, Jackson, Johnson, Jones of Virginia, Kent, Kinsey, Little, McLean of Kentucky, Meigs, R. Moore, S. Moore, Murray, Neale, Nelson of Virginia, Newton, Parker of Massachusetts, Pitcher, Rankin, Reid, Rhea, Rich, Robertson, Rogers, Sawyer, Silsbee, Simkins, Smith of New Jersey, Smith of Maryland, A. Smyth of Virginia, Stevens, Swearingen, Tucker of Virginia, Udree, Walker, Wendover, and Wood.

NAYS—Messrs. Adams, Allen of Tennessee, Bateman, Beecher, Buffum, Cocke, Crawford, Edwards of Connecticut, Edwards of Pennsylvania, Floyd, Foot, Forrest, Gross of New York, Guyon, Hall of New York, Hardin, Hendricks, Hooks, Hostetter, Jones of Tennessee, Lathrop, Lincoln, Maclay, McCoy, Mc-Creary, Mallary, Metcalf, Monell, T. L. Moore, Moseley, Patterson, Plumer, Richards, Richmond, Ross, Russ, Sloan, Strong of Vermont, Tomlinson, Tracy, Tucker of South Carolina, Williams of Virginia, and Williams of North Carolina.

So this clause of the amendment was agreed to. The question was then taken on the remaining clause of Mr. BUTLER's motion, and decided in the negative—yeas 31, nays 85, as follows:

YEAS—Messrs. Abbot, Anderson, Archer of Maryland, Archer of Virginia, Baldwin, Ball, Bloomfield, Brevard, Brush, Butler of Louisiana, Crawford Crowell, Cushman, Cuthbert, Edwards of North Carolina, Jackson, Johnson, Little, McLean of Kentucky, Montgomery, Nelson of Virginia, Newton, Pitcher, Reid, Robertson, Sawyer, Sergeant, Simkins, Smith of New Jersey, Swearingen, and Tucker of Virginia.

NAYS—Messrs. Adams, Allen of Massachusetts,

Allen of New York, Allen of Tennessee, Barbour, Bateman, Beecher, Blackledge, Bryan, Buffum, Cannon, Case, Clark, Cobb, Cocke, Cook, Culpeper, Dane, Denison, Eddy, Edwards of Connecticut, Edwards of Pennsylvania, Fay, Floyd, Folger, Foot, Ford, Forrest, Fuller, Gorham, Gray, Gross of New York, Guyon, Hackley, Hall of New York, Hardin, Hemphill, Hill, Hobart, Hooks, Hostetter, Jones of Virginia, Jones of Tennessee, Kendall, Kent, Lathrop, Lincoln, Livermore, Maclay, McCoy, McCreary, Mallary, Meigs. Monell, S. Moore, T. L. Moore, Moseley, Murray, Neale, Parker of Massachusetts, Patterson, Philson, Plumer, Rich, Richards, Richmond, Rogers, Ross, Russ, Sloan, Smith of Maryland, A. Smyth of Virginia, Stevens, Street, Strong of Vermont, Tomlinson, Tracy, Tucker of South Carolina, Udree, Walker, Wendover, Whitman, Williams of Virginia, Williams of North Carolina, and Wood.

So this clause of the amendment was rejected. The bill was then ordered to be engrossed and read a third time.

SATURDAY, March 3.

Mr. SMITH, from the Committee of Ways and Means, to whom was referred the Senate's bill to amend the act, entitled "An act supplementary to 'An act entitled an act to regulate the collection of duties on imports and tonnage,' passed the second day of March, one thousand seven hundred and ninety-nine," reported the same without amendment; and the question being on ordering it to be read a third time—Mr. BALDWIN, regarding it as conflicting with the salutary provisions of the appraisement law, expressed his hope that it would not pass. Mr. SILSBEE supported the bill at some length, as being important to the importing merchants. Mr. BALDWIN replied, and stated that the lateness of the session would prevent the obtaining proper information on the subject; one fact, however, he knew from the best authority, viz: that an association had been formed in England to throw goods into this country at an under valuation, and that their names had been communicated to the Treasury, and by the Treasury to the custom-house officers. Mr. B. concluded by moving that the bill lie on the table; which motion was agreed to.

The Committee on the Public Lands, the Committee of Claims, and the Committee on Naval Affairs, were discharged from the further consideration of all petitions and other matters to them respectively referred at the present session, upon which they have not reported to the House.

The Committee on Foreign Affairs were discharged from the further consideration of the petition of Richard W. Meade, and it was laid on the table.

Mr. SWEARINGEN, from the select committee, to which was referred the petition of Catharine Wager, and others, made a report thereon, accompanied with a bill for the relief of the widow and children of John Wager, junior, deceased; which was read twice, and ordered to lie on the table.

A message from the Senate informed the House that the Senate have passed the bill of this House, entitled "An act for the relief of Robert Buntin," with amendments; in which they ask the concurrence of this House.

The amendments were read, and concurred in by the House.

The amendments proposed by the Senate to the bill entitled, "An act to authorize the building of lighthouses on Cross and Pond Islands, in the harbor of Boothbay, and at the mouth of Oswego river, and placing buoys on the shoals of Nantucket and Vineyard sound, near the harbor of Wickford, and on the Altamaha river, and for other purposes," were read, and committed to a Committee of the Whole to-day.

The House then resolved itself into a Committee of the Whole on the said amendments; and, after some time spent therein, the Committee rose and reported its agreement to the said amendments, which were concurred in by the House, together with that proposed to the title thereof.

The SPEAKER laid before the House the following communication, viz:

To the Speaker of the House of Representatives:

SIR: We have the pleasure of informing you, that, in the case of Anderson *vs.* Dunn (with the defence of which we had the honor to be charged on behalf of the House of Representatives,) the Supreme Court has fully affirmed the power of the House, *sui juris,* to vindicate its own privileges against every attack of violence or fraud, necessarily tending to control the freedom, or taint the purity of legislative deliberation.

The interest so justly manifested by the House, in the issue of this important question, has induced us to communicate, without delay, the determination of the court, in order that it may be known to the House before its approaching separation.

We have the honor to be, with the highest respect, sir, your obedient servants,

WM. WIRT,
W. JONES.

WASHINGTON, *March* 2, 1821.

The said letter was read, and ordered to lie on the table.

Mr. STORRS, from the Committee on Expenditures in the Department of State, delivered in the following report:

The Committee on Expenditures in the Department of State, report—

That they have attended to the duties imposed on them by order of the House, as far as the business of the House would possibly permit, since the committee was appointed, and that they find the accounts and expenditures of the said Department to be correct.

That they have also, conformably to the order of the House, inquired into the facts relating to the employment of an agent on behalf of the United States, under the 6th and 7th articles of the Treaty of Ghent, and find that Mr. Joseph Delafield was employed during the past year, as a secretary, for the performance of the duties which would have been required of an agent, under the said articles. They find, however, that the employment of Mr. Delafield, or some person in that capacity, was indispensable to the interests of the United States; that the compensation allowed to Mr. Delafield was much less than the salary of an agent; and that the allowance of such compensation is not, in their opinion, improper or unreasonable. The committee respectfully refer the House, for the

particular facts relating thereto, to the Message from the Executive Department on that subject.

The report was ordered to lie on the table.

The amendments proposed by the Senate to the bill, entitled "An act making appropriations for the support of the Navy of the United States for the year 1821," were read, and committed to a Committee of the Whole to-day.

The House then resolved itself into a Committee of the Whole on the said amendments; and, after some time spent therein, the Committee reported their agreement to the amendments, which were concurred in by the House.

The amendments proposed by the Senate to the bill, entitled "An act to authorize the President of the United States to establish a port of entry in the district of Sandusky, in the State of Ohio," were read, and concurred in by the House.

An engrossed bill, entitled "An act making appropriations for the military service of the United States for the year 1821," was read the third time, and passed.

The bill from the Senate, entitled "An act to extend the term of Samuel Parker's patents for his improvement in currying and finishing leather of all kinds," was read the third time, and passed.

The Committee of the Whole, to which is committed the bill to establish an additional land office in the Territory of Michigan, were discharged from the consideration of the same, and it was ordered to be engrossed, and read a third time to-day.

A Message was received from the PRESIDENT OF THE UNITED STATES, which was read, and is as follows:

To the Congress of the United States:

I communicate to the two Houses of Congress copies of a treaty this day ratified on the part of the United States, concluded and signed at the Indian Springs, on the 8th of January last, with the Creek nation of Indians, in order to such legislative measures as may be necessary for giving effect to it.

JAMES MONROE.

WASHINGTON, *March* 2, 1821.

The Message was ordered to lie on the table.

A message from the Senate informed the House that the Senate have passed the bill, entitled "An act to regulate the location of land warrants, and the issuing of patents in certain cases," with amendments; in which they ask the concurrence of this House.

The amendments proposed by the Senate to the bill, entitled "An act to regulate the location of warrants, and the issuing of patents in certain cases," were read, and concurred in by the House.

THE NAVY.

The House proceeded to consider the bill to amend the act, entitled "An act for the gradual increase of the Navy of the United States:"

The second section whereof is in the words following, viz:

SEC. 2. *And be it further enacted,* That, instead of the appropriation therein contained, there shall be and is hereby appropriated the sum of five hundred thousand dollars per annum for six years, from the year 1821, inclusive, to be applied to carry into effect the purposes of the said act.

Mr. BARBOUR moved to amend the said second section by striking out the word *six*, and inserting in lieu thereof the word *three ;* to strike out the words " to be applied to carry into effect the purposes of the said act," and to add to the section the following words, viz:

" To be applied to the purchase of the remaining materials necessary for the construction of the ships authorized by the said act, and to their construction, so far as to frame, plank, bolt, and stay them, and their preservation, by the erection of houses over them; and any balance thereof which may remain after the completion of these objects to be applied to the equipment of said vessels *?*"

And the question being taken thereon, it was determined in the negative—-yeas 66, nays 67, as follows:

YEAS—Messrs. Abbot, Adams, Alexander, Allen of Tennessee, Barbour, Blackledge, Boden, Brevard, Bryan, Cannon, Cobb, Cocke, Culpeper, Earle, Edwards of North Carolina, Floyd, Foot, Ford, Forrest, Garnett, Gray, Guyon, Hall of New York, Hardin, Herrick, Hibshman, Hooks, Hostetter, Jackson, Johnson, Jones of Tennessee, Kendall, Kinsey, Maclay, McCoy, McCreary, McLean of Kentucky, R. Moore, T. L. Moore, Murray, Nelson of Virginia, Patterson, Philson, Rhea, Rich, Richards, Richmond, Rogers, Ross, Russ, Sawyer, Settle, Sloan, Southard, Stevens, Strong of Vermont, Swearingen, Tracy, Tucker of South Carolina, Udree, Upham, Walker, Wallace, Warfield, Williams of Virginia, and Williams of North Carolina.

NAYS—Messrs. Allen of Massachusetts, Allen of New York, Anderson, Archer of Virginia, Baker, Baldwin, Ball, Bayly, Bloomfield, Brush, Buffum, Butler of Louisiana, Campbell, Case, Clark, Cook, Culbreth, Cushman, Cuthbert, Dane, Darlington, Dewitt, Dickinson, Eddy, Edwards of Connecticut, Edwards of Pennsylvania, Eustis, Fay, Folger, Fuller, Gorham, Gross of New York, Hackley, Hendricks, Hill, Kent, Lathrop, Lincoln, Little, Mallary, Meigs, Mercer, Montgomery, S. Moore, Moseley, Nelson of Massachusetts, Newton, Pinckney, Pitcher, Plumer, Rankin, Reid, Robertson, Sergeant, Silsbee, Smith of New Jersey, Smith of Maryland, Storrs, Street, Strong of New York, Tomlinson, Tompkins, Tucker of Virginia, Wendover, Whitman, and Wood.

Ordered, That the said bill be engrossed, and read a third time to-day.

BANKRUPT BILL.

A motion was made by Mr. SERGEANT that the House do now proceed to consider the bill from the Senate, entitled "An act to establish an uniform system of bankruptcy throughout the United States."

And the question being taken thereon, it was determined in the negative—yeas 58, nays 70, as follows:

YEAS—Messrs. Allen of Massachusetts, Allen of New York, Bayly, Bloomfield, Brush, Case, Crowell, Cushman, Darlington, Dewitt, Eddy, Edwards of Connecticut, Edwards of Pennsylvania, Fay, Folger, Foot, Forrest, Gorham, Gross of New York, Guyon,

Hackley, Hall of New York, Hemphill, Hendricks, Hill, Hobart, Kendall, Lathrop, Little, Meigs, Mercer, Montgomery, S. Moore, Moseley, Nelson of Massachusetts, Pitcher, Rich, Richmond, Robertson, Rogers, Russ, Sawyer, Sergeant, Silsbee, Sloan, Smith of New Jersey, Smith of Maryland, Storrs, Street, Strong of New York, Tomlinson, Tompkins, Tracy, Udree, Upham, Warfield, Whitman, and Wood.

NAYS—Messrs. Abbot, Adams, Alexander, Allen of Tennessee, Archer of Virginia, Baker, Baldwin, Ball, Barbour, Blackledge, Boden, Brevard, Bryan, Buffum, Butler of Louisiana, Campbell, Cannon, Clark, Cobb, Cocke, Crawford, Culbreth, Dane, Davidson, Dickinson, Earle, Edwards of North Carolina, Floyd, Ford, Gray, Hardin, Herrick, Hibshman, Hooks, Hostetter, Jackson, Johnson, Jones of Virginia, Jones of Tennessee, Kent, Kinsey, Lincoln, Maclay, McCoy, McCreary, McLean of Kentucky, Metcalf, R. Moore, Murray, Nelson of Virginia, Newton, Patterson, Philson, Plumer, Rankin, Rhea, Richards, Ross, Settle, Simkins, Stevens, Swearingen, Terrell, Tucker of Virginia, Tucker of South Carolina, Walker, Wallace, Wendover, Williams of Virginia, and Williams of North Carolina.

THE GENERAL POST OFFICE.

Mr. PHELPS, from the committee appointed on the 19th of December to investigate the concerns of the Post Office Department, made a further report; which was read, and ordered to lie on the table. It is as follows:

The select committee appointed to investigate the affairs of the Post Office Department, beg leave further to report, in part; that the abstract of payments for transporting the mail from Washington city to Fredericksburg, and the Postmaster General's explanation of it, cannot be understood but in connexion with three mail contracts, and abstracts of the payments of them. These contracts are, one with Hazlewood Farish for the transportation of the mail, in the years 1814, 1815, and 1816, from Fredericksburg to Charlottesville; one with Woolfolk, Smock, & Co., for transportation of the mail, in the same years, from Charlottesville to Richmond; and the other with William C. Garner for transportation of the mail, in the same years, from Charlottesville to Staunton. The committee obtained copies of those mail contracts, and also of the abstracts of payments rendered by this Department to the Comptroller of the Treasury, for explanatory evidence. But, as these documents contain important facts, they are not reported as explanatory evidence only, but to show the expenditure of public money for transporting the mails upon these routes.

The committee find that the contract price for carrying the mail from Washington city to Fredericksburg, in the years 1814, 1815, and 1816, was -   9,900 00
From Fredericksburg to Charlottesville, in same years -   7,200 00
From Fredericksburg to Richmond, for the same years -   10,500 00
From Charlottesville to Staunton, for the same years -   3,000 00

     $30,600 00

The committee find that there was paid for transporting the mail, in the years 1814, 1815, and 1816, upon these four routes, the following amount :

To Williams, Farish, Crawford, Davis, and

Tayloe - - - - - -	31,551 52
Woolfolk, & Co. - - - -	22,779 49
Hazlewood Parish - - - -	14,811 59
Wm. G. Garner - - - -	7,289 00
	$76,431 60

The committee find that the Post Office Department has paid for transporting the mail upon these four routes, $45,821 60 more than the mail contractors were entitled, by their contracts, to receive.

[On the subject of the above Report, the following note was addressed to the Printers to Congress by the Postmaster General:]

GENERAL POST OFFICE, *March* 15, 1821.

MESSRS. GALES & SEATON: I was informed by a portion of the committee of investigation that the annexed document was to have formed a part of their report. Presuming that some mistake had caused the omission, I addressed a note to the Clerk of the House of Representatives upon the subject, a copy of whose reply is annexed. I likewise addressed a note to the printers of Congress upon the same subject, whose reply is likewise annexed. I shall write to the chairman, requesting him to cause it to be restored to the proper files. I deem it due to justice to give the whole publication in your paper, and I will thank you to publish it without delay.

With great respect, your obedient servant,
R. J. MEIGS, JR.

CLERK'S OFFICE, HOUSE OF REPS.,
March 6, 1821.

SIR: Yours of this morning is before me; in answer to which I have the honor to state that the report by Mr. PHELPS, on Saturday evening, was received and ordered to lie on the table, (the reading having been dispensed with,) and the report and accompanying papers ordered to be printed. I never opened the papers, and therefore can only say that, if the letter alluded to formed part of the documents, it will be found with the report, which is yet in the hands of Messrs. Gales & Seaton, as printers to the House of Representatives of the United States.

I have the honor to be, very respectfully, your humble servant,
THO. DOUGHERTY, *Clerk.*

Hon. R. J. MEIGS, *Postmaster General.*

WASHINGTON, *March* 6, 1821.

There was no letter from the Postmaster General accompanying the second report of the committee of investigation, as delivered at the office of the Clerk of the House of Representatives to the undersigned.
GALES & SEATON.

GENERAL POST OFFICE, *March* 3, 1821.

SIR: It was stated to the committee, in my previous verbal communications, that, owing to the state of war and other circumstances, the contracts for carrying the mail between Richmond and New York, and some others, were partially vacated by my predecessor in 1813, and new agreements were entered into, making adequate compensation for the service.

It seemed to be considered in my conversation with the committee that the route from Washington to Fredericksburg was, on account of the increased pay to Colonel Tayloe, the strongest case, and that was taken as a sample for investigation. My remarks in relation to that route apply in extenso to all the others, with the exception of an additional trip per week between Fredericksburg and Charlottesville, and between Charlottesville and Staunton. I am now advised that another portion of these routes has been started in the aggregate payments for carrying the mail on the routes from this to Fredericksburg, already discussed and reported on, with that of four or five other routes, and that those are contrasted with the aggregate of the payments, that might have been made in several years, if the contracts had not been vacated. But it has already been shown that the carriage of the mail, according to the contracts, was not then satisfactory to the public; and it is difficult to perceive the utility of contrasting an operation which answers its object with one which has become useless. The accumulation of the amount of expenditure on many routes, for several years, serves to make a great sum, but by no means shows its disproportion to its real worth.

But it seems we must at this late hour recur to first principles; and the chairman has asked if I had a right to alter contracts. The Postmaster General has by law the power of causing the public mails to be transported in such manner as he shall deem expedient and most promotive of the public interest. The law declares "that he shall provide for the carriage of 'the mail on all post roads that are or may be estab-'lished by law, and as often as he, having regard to 'the productiveness thereof, and other circumstances, 'may think proper." And, in the schedule of the contracts, provision is made for any alteration which the Postmaster General shall direct.

In a country like this, where new villages, towns, counties, and even States, are continually rising, the post office arrangements cannot be permanent, but must vary with the exigency of the times. It was under this authority, and the then existing circumstances of the nation, that my predecessor made the alteration, which produced the enlargement of expenditure.

When I afterwards came into the superintendency of the department, I did not deem it decorous or expedient to annul the arrangement of my predecessor, supported as he was, in that arrangement, by the highest authorities of the nation. But if I had, it would not have been practicable on this route, even after the return of peace, for, as I had stated in my communication to the former committee of investigation, a steamboat had been established between this place and Fredericksburg.

The price of conveying the mail by contract was predicated on its being carried in stages, to be supported by passengers. This price was altogether below the expense of carrying it in curricles. The establishment of the steamboat took away the passengers, and of course a support for the stages. They have not run since, excepting for a short time in the winter, when they cannot carry the mail. The establishment of the steamboat applied with like injury to the stages running between Fredericksburg and Richmond; for the steamboat ran to suit its own convenience, and not so as to throw its passengers into a line of stages that could carry the mail; and no alteration could be made in the arrangement of the mail to suit that object without producing an inconvenience to the large cities from which most of the revenue of the establishment was derived. But, if the contracts had not been vacated in the beginning, no material advantage could have been derived from it, for the proprietors could not have sustained the expense without certain loss, if not ruin; and new contracts would have been as high, and probably much higher. If the committee had cause to believe the compensation paid to the contractors too high, the contractors were at hand and could have been summoned to show their actual expenditures. They could have given them all the minutiæ in that respect, necessary to the formation of a proper estimate.

The subject has been in the hands of the committee upwards of three months. The chairman has indeed been out of health a short time; but there has been most ample time for a full investigation when the chairman was in health.

There has not been time, since your communication of the amount paid for carrying the mail on sundry routes has been handed me, to make a proper comparison and statement of particulars. But I find it embraces payments and credits for services in 1813, for carrying the mail between Richmond and Charlottesville; for express mails to the President, and for expresses sent with the President's despatches in relation to the conclusion of peace; but the whole amount has not yet been ascertained. In concluding my remarks, you will permit me very respectfully to add, that, in investigating the concerns of the General Post Office the office itself would seem to be the proper theatre for operation. There the books, papers, officers, and clerks, are all at hand, to show what may be desired, and to elucidate what might appear to be doubtful. These the condensed statements rendered to the Treasury can neither show nor elucidate. And here, although I have had the pleasure to see all the other members of the committee, I have not had that of seeing yourself, the chairman, at whose instance the investigation was instituted. I am sensible that a practical economy is everywhere due to the principles of this Government; and, though a decided friend to official responsibility, I may be permitted to observe, that the chief of a Department has every motive, of loyalty to his nation, of honor, and of justice to his own moral and legal obligation, and of respect to his own reputation, to avoid an unnecessary and prodigal disbursement of public moneys. If a contrary presumption is to prevail, the rule of law is reversed, and a system of political ethics is to be introduced founded on palpable error and injustice.

I have the honor to be, very respectfully, your obedient servant,

         R. J. MEIGS, Jr.

Hon. E. PHELPS, *Chairman, &c.*

ELECTION OF PRINTER.

Mr. COCKE submitted the following resolution, viz:

Resolved, That this House will forthwith proceed to ballot for a printer to execute its work during the next Congress, according to the provisions of the resolution "directing the manner in which the printing of Con- ' gress shall be executed; fixing the prices thereof, and ' providing for the appointment of a printer or printers," passed on the 3d day of March, 1819.

The SPEAKER put the previous question of consideration on this motion, and it was determined in the affirmative. Mr. Sergeant moved to lay it on the table; which was negatived. The resolution was then agreed to. The SPEAKER then laid before the House letters from E. De Krafft, Elliot & Irvine, Davis & Force, and Gales & Seaton, offering themselves as candidates for this employment; the first named offering to do the work for 25 per cent. less than the prices established by the act of March 3, 1819, and the second named offering to do it for 25½ per cent. less. An attempt was then made by Mr. ALLEN, of Massachusetts, and Mr. WOOD, of New York, to suspend or dispense with the election; but the motion for that purpose was pronounced out of order, the House having determined to proceed forthwith to the election. The House then balloted accordingly, and the tellers (Mr. GROSS, Mr. BEECHER, and Mr. COBB) reported that the votes were—

For Gales & Seaton	- - -	87
Elliot & Irvine	- - -	31
Davis & Force	- - -	9
E. De Krafft	- - -	6

and that Gales & Seaton were of course elected.

In the Senate, the election took place on the same day, on the motion of Mr. BARBOUR. The votes in that body were—

For Gales & Seaton	- - -	23
Scattering	- - -	3

The House proceeded to consider the bill to amend an act, entitled "An act for regulating process in the courts of the United States;" whereupon, it was ordered to be engrossed, and read a third time to-day.

The House then adjourned until five o'clock, P. M.

Five o'clock, P. M.

Engrossed bills of the following titles, to wit: " An act to amend the act, entitled 'An act for the gradual increase of the Navy of the United States;" and "An act to amend an act, entitled 'An act for regulating process in the courts of the United States:'" were severally read the third time, and passed.

An engrossed bill, entitled "An act to establish an additional Land Office in the Territory of Michigan," was read the third time; when

Mr. ROSS moved that it lie on the table; which motion being negatived, the question was taken, Shall the bill pass? and passed in the affirmative.

The House again resolved itself into a Committee of the Whole on the state of the Union; and, after some time spent therein, the Speaker resumed the chair, and Mr. LATHROP reported that the Committee had again had the state of the Union under consideration, and directed him to report the bill thereto committed on the 27th February ultimo, for carrying into execution the treaty between the United States and Spain, concluded at Washington the 22d of February, 1819, with several amendments; which were read, and concurred in by the House.

The bill was then further amended; and

A motion was made by Mr. ALLEN, of Massachusetts, further to amend the same by inserting after the word Territories, where it first occurs in the second section, these words: "not incompatible with the Constitution and laws of the United States;" so that the civil, military, and judicial powers exercised by the Spanish authorities within the territories of East and West Florida, and which are established by the said bill for the government of said territories until otherwise provided, shall "not be incompatible with the Constitution and laws of the United States."

And the question being taken to agree to this amendment, it was determined in the negative. The bill was then ordered to be engrossed, and read a third time to-day.

The House again resolved itself into a Committee of the Whole on the state of the Union; and, after some time spent therein, the Speaker resumed the chair, and Mr. COBB reported that the Committee had again had the state of the Union under consideration, and directed him to report the bill thereto committed on the 26th of February ultimo, to authorize the President of the United States to borrow a sum not exceeding four millions five hundred thousand dollars, without amendment.

Ordered, That the said bill be engrossed, and read a third time to-day.

Engrossed bills of the following titles, viz:
"An act for carrying into execution the treaty between the United States and Spain, concluded at Washington, the 22d of February, 1819;" and "An act to authorize the President of the United States to borrow a sum not exceeding four million five hundred thousand dollars," were severally read a third time, and passed.

A motion was made by Mr. EDWARDS, of North Carolina, that the several orders of the day which precede the bill from the Senate, entitled "An act to provide for the due execution of the laws of the United States within the State of Missouri," be postponed for the purpose of taking that bill into consideration. This motion was negatived by the House.

Ordered, That the Committee of the whole House, to which is committed the bill to continue in force an act, entitled "An act regulating the currency within the United States of the gold coins of Great Britain, France, Portugal, and Spain," passed the 29th day of April, 1816, so far as the same relates to the crowns and five-franc pieces of France, be discharged from the consideration thereof, and that the said bill be engrossed, and read a third time to-day.

The House proceeded to consider the bill from the Senate, entitled "An act for the relief of General Robert Swartwout." Whereupon, it was ordered that the bill be committed to a committee of the whole House to-day.

The House then resolved itself into a Committee of the Whole on the said bill; which was reported without amendment, read the third time, and passed.

The House resolved itself into a Committee of the Whole on the bill from the Senate, entitled "An act for the relief of Thomas Shields and others;" which was reported without amendment, read the third time, and passed.

An engrossed bill, entitled "An act to continue in force an act entitled 'An act regulating the currency within the United States of the gold coins of Great Britain, France, Portugal, and Spain,'" passed the 29th day of April, 1816, so far as the same relates to the crowns and five-franc pieces of France," was read the third time, and passed.

The House resolved itself into a Committee of the Whole on the bill to establish the salaries of the commissioners and agents appointed under the Treaty of Ghent. The bill was reported with sundry amendments, which were concurred in by the House; and the bill was ordered to be engrossed, and read a third time to-day.

A message from the Senate informed the House that the Senate have elected Gales & Seaton printers, on their part, in pursuance of the resolution of Congress of the 3d of March, 1819. They have passed the bill, entitled "An act making appropriations for the military service of the United States for the year 1821," with an amendment, in which they ask the concurrence of this House.

The amendments proposed by the Senate to the bill "making appropriations for the military service of the United States for the year 1821," were read, and committed to a Committee of the whole House to-day.

The House then resolved itself into a Committee of the Whole on the said amendments; and, after some time spent therein, the Committee reported their disagreement to the same. The question was then taken to concur with the Committee of the Whole in their disagreement to the said amendments, and passed in the affirmative.

A message from the Senate informed the House that the Senate have passed a bill of this House of the following title, viz: "An act to continue in force an act entitled 'An act regulating the currency within the United States of the gold coins of Great Britain, France, Portugal, and Spain,'" passed on the 29th day of April, 1816, so far as the same relates to the crowns and five-franc pieces of France," with an amendment, in which they ask the concurrence of this House.

Another message from the Senate informed the House that the Senate have passed a bill of this House of the following title, viz: "An act to authorize the President of the United States to borrow a sum not exceeding four millions five hundred thousand dollars," with amendments, in which they ask the concurrence of this House.

An engrossed bill, entitled "An act establishing the salaries of the commissioners and agents appointed under the Treaty of Ghent," was read the third time, and passed.

THANKS TO THE SPEAKER.

Mr. CLAY rose, and addressed the House to the following effect:

I rise to submit a motion, which, if it should conciliate the general concurrence of this House, I shall be extremely glad. The present session was commenced under very unpleasant auspices. In the appointment of a presiding officer of the House, the first manifestation was made of that unfortunate division of opinion which has been the peculiar characteristic of the session. The storm has happily subsided, and we have the great satisfaction to behold the ship of our Confederacy unimpaired by its rage; her hull, her rigging, and her patriotic crew completely fit for a long and glorious voyage, under the star-spangled banner which proudly floats aloft.

The moral of that agitating drama, of which for more than two years past our country has been the theatre, is that, whilst our Federal Union is admirably fitted to accomplish all the national purposes for which it was intended, there are delicate subjects, exclusively appertaining to the several States, which cannot be touched but by them, without the greatest hazard to the public tranquillity. They resemble those secluded apartments in our respective domicils, which are dedicated to family privacy, into which our nearest and best neighbors should not enter. Let us terminate the session by making that officer the depository of our entire reconciliation, whose election first elicited our divisions, and whose situation has been extremely arduous and difficult. For my part, I have great pleasure in testifying to the assiduity, impartiality, ability, and promptitude, with which he has administered the duties of the Chair since I was able to take my seat. I move the following resolution:

Resolved, That the thanks of this House be given to the honorable JOHN W. TAYLOR, for the assiduity, promptitude, and ability, with which he has administered the duties of the Chair.

Mr. NELSON, of Virginia, (who was temporarily in the Chair,) having stated the question—

Mr. RHEA said he hoped this resolution would obtain an unanimous vote. He had been long a member of this House, and he had never seen the duties of the Chair discharged more satisfactorily than by the present Speaker.

Mr. HARDIN said, that it was with great satisfaction he should vote for this resolution, because it met his entire approbation. To be candid, the Speaker had, in the discharge of the duties of the Chair, far outgone his expectations; and he would vote him the thanks proposed with a great deal of pleasure.

The question was then taken on agreeing to the resolution, and decided in the affirmative, one negative voice only being heard.

A message from the Senate informed the House that the Senate insist on their amendments to the bill, entitled "An act making appropriations for the support of the military service of the United States for the year 1821," except the latter part of the last of the said amendments, from which latter they recede.

MILITARY APPROPRIATIONS.

The House proceeded to consider the message from the Senate informing this House that they insist on certain of their amendments to the bill, entitled "An act making appropriations for the military service of the United States for the year 1821." Whereupon, it was, on motion of Mr. HARDIN, resolved that this House doth insist on their disagreement to the amendments aforesaid.

[The following is the substance of Mr. SIMKINS's remarks on the motion to insist on the disagreement of the House to the Senate's amendments of the military appropriation bill.]

I hope, Mr. Speaker, that neither the extraordinary zeal of the member from Kentucky (Mr. HARDIN) or of the member from Maryland (Mr. SMITH) against the amendments to this bill, made by the Senate, will prevent the House giving them that most serious and deliberate consideration to which they are entitled. Sir, it has been somewhat fashionable, in this House, not only to distrust a co-ordinate branch of the Government, but to reject their acts, with a haste and an impatience bordering on contempt. I do not think that a body so grave and dignified has deserved such treatment. On the contrary, it must be admitted, by all impartial men, that for two years past its wisdom and firmness have rescued this nation from the most disastrous measures. Dislike as we may the opposition of this branch of our Legislature to certain favorite doctrines and favorite measures impetuously urged upon us by the majority of this House, yet we shall be compelled to respect it, as a barrier to great evils, and as a body to which the people look with anxious and increasing solicitude.

The member from Kentucky (Mr. HARDIN) says, that every thing wears the appearance of bustle and activity of preparation, as if we were about to be involved in war. Nothing, sir, can be further from the fact. The Senate amend our bill by adding a comparatively small sum, say about $200,000, for carrying on the most indispensable fortifications of our country, placed with the most perfect skill, and after accurate and skilful surveys on our exposed points; a sum altogether but little more than one half of what has been appropriated for a series of years; and the gentleman calls this a great preparation for war. Sir, so far from preparing for those perilous exigencies which must arise, we are retrograding into a state of apathy most alarming to every American who can extend his views beyond the present moment. We assume to ourselves a wisdom which brands with the imputation of folly and extravagance every session of Congress since the late war. Eight hundred thousand dollars annually has been most deliberately resolved upon as the sum necessary for these important works for several years, and now you reduce it down to $300,000, without a solitary reason to justify you. I say without a shadow of reason; for who will say that these works are less important with an exhausted Treasury than they were with a full one? You last year appropriated $800,000, and allow the Secretary of War to make contracts for this year, in some degree, at least, proportioned to a similar appropriation. After he has made the contracts, and pledged the faith of the nation, you desert him, by offering a small sum which will not cover them, and but little more than preserve the works and materials. You break the faith of the nation, ruin public contractors, and send them petitioning at your heels, for years, for damages sustained by your conduct; and which you will be compelled in the end to

1297   HISTORY OF CONGRESS.   1298

MARCH, 1821.   *Closing Business.*   H. OF R.

pay. This is not all. You so prostrate the United States' credit that nobody will work for you without double price. Besides this, you impede, and finally will endanger, the important defences of the country. Fortifications placed at proper points, and well built, have been determined, by the universal consent of all ages and nations, to be of infinite moment; and yet it is found out by the talent and wisdom of this Congress, and of this Congress alone, that they are of little importance, and have been pronounced by some gentlemen to be absolutely worthless! This Congress may be the wisest of any, but its policy is diametrically opposed to the policy of every session since the war. Indeed, we have heard some gentlemen pinning their whole faith on the Committee of Ways and Means, and have given a decided preference to the sweeping judgment of this committee, not a member of which will pretend even to have become scientifically acquainted with the subject of engineering, against the opinions of all your officers, and particularly against some of the first engineers that ever adorned the scientific annals of any country on earth!

The chairman of that committee has boldly taken upon himself the responsibility of condemning the fort on Dauphin Island as utterly useless. I will not detain the House further on this point than to say, that it has been demonstrated by the gentlemen from Louisiana and Kentucky (Messrs. BUTLER and JOHNSON) that this fort will effectually command the waters of a spacious and deep harbor, which a naval enemy would instantly possess, and, with it, seize Dauphin Island, which would give them a secure and perfect foot-hold, from which they would not only destroy our trade up the bay, but annoy the whole adjacent country, stop the communication to New Orleans by the lake, and materially injure Pensacola. This is no dream; the facts are palpable to every man who has actually examined the country, and yet such men are flatly contradicted by members here, not distinguished for military science, and who have never for a moment placed their eyes on the spot!

The gentleman from Kentucky (Mr. HARDIN) says the best means of defence is to make the people easy and happy, by lightening their burdens. Sir, we have never imposed any burdens; and, from the temper of this House, can it be supposed that any ever will be imposed? In truth, it seems that every institution would be prostrated, destroyed, and sunk, sooner than tax the people; although they would never hesitate to pay taxes indispensable to the due and vigorous and proper support of the Government. Taxes present no such frightful and hideous monster to the people as they are represented here. They are, to be sure, the constant, never ceasing bugbear presented to our view, whenever an army, navy, or fortifications, are to be preserved and perfected. It seems to be no crime to make the people pay taxes indirectly, by way of impost; whilst it is horrible, and unpardonable, past endurance, to ask these same people to pay taxes directly levied upon them. It is laudable, if you can cheat them into the payment, but past forgiveness, if you openly tell them to

pay! It is, however, matter of joy that our essential preparations may be preserved for many years to come, and perfected without the imposition of a single additional tax of any kind, notwithstanding the eternal noise made about taxes.

Sir, a single hour will put an end to my existence as a member of this body; but I cannot take my leave without expressing my most unfeigned sorrow at the ruinous fluctuating policy now pursued by the representatives of the people. I hope (and the hope is indeed faint) that we shall agree to the amendments made by the Senate.

CLOSING BUSINESS.

The House proceeded to consider the amendments proposed by the Senate to the bill, entitled "An act to authorize the President of the United States to borrow a sum not exceeding four millions five hundred thousand dollars;" and the same being read twice, were disagreed to.

That portion of the said bill to which the third amendment proposed by the Senate applies, reads thus, viz: "reimbursable at the will of the Government, and at the will of the creditor, at any time after the first day of January, 1835."

The third amendment of the Senate proposes to strike out the words, *and at the will of the creditor.*

Mr. BARBOUR moved to amend the said third amendment so as to make the aforesaid clause in the bill read thus: "reimbursable at the will of the Government at any time before the first day of January, 1835; and at the will either of the Government or the creditor, at any time after that period."

And the question being taken to agree to this amendment, it was determined in the negative; and the said amendment was then concurred in by the House.

The amendment proposed by the Senate to the bill, entitled "An act to continue in force an act, entitled 'An act regulating the currency within the United States of the gold coins of Great Britain, France, Portugal, and Spain,' passed on the 29th day of April, 1816, so far as the same relates to the crowns and five-franc pieces of France," was read and concurred in by the House.

A motion was made by Mr. CANNON, that the several orders of the day which precede the bill from the Senate, entitled "An act for the relief of the officers and volunteers engaged in the late campaign against the Seminole Indians" be postponed, for the purpose of taking that bill into consideration.

And the question being taken thereon, it was determined in the negative.

Mr. SERGEANT moved that the several orders of the day which precede the bill authorizing Benjamin H. Rand to import a certain piece of plate free of duty, be postponed, for the purpose of taking that bill into consideration. This motion was rejected by the House.

Mr. NELSON, of Virginia, moved that the several orders of the day, which precede the bill to abolish imprisonment for debt, be postponed, for the purpose of taking the bill into consideration. This motion was rejected by the House.

A Message was received from the PRESIDENT OF THE UNITED STATES, as follows:

To the House of Representatives of the United States:

The treaty concluded between the United States and the Kickapoo tribe of Indians, on the 30th of July, 1820, having been ratified, by and with the advice and consent of the Senate, I now lay a copy of the said treaty before the House of Representatives, in order to such legislative provisions being made as may be necessary to carry into effect the stipulations therein contained, on the part of the United States.

JAMES MONROE.

WASHINGTON, *March* 3, 1821.

The Message was ordered to lie on the table.

The House proceeded to consider the bill from the Senate, entitled "An act to continue in force for a further time the act, entitled 'An act for establishing trading houses with the Indian tribes."

A motion was made by Mr. STORRS to amend the said bill, by striking out *June,* and inserting *February,* so as to limit the continuance of the said act to the 1st day of February, 182–, instead of the 1st day of June, 182–, as provided for in the said bill.

The question being taken to agree to this amendment, it was determined in the negative.

The bill was then read a third time, and passed.

The Committee of the whole House, to which is committed the bill authorizing the settlement of the accounts of the late Le Roy Opie, were discharged from the consideration thereof, and the bill was ordered to be engrossed, and read a third time to-day.

Mr. FULLER moved that the several orders of the day, which precede the bill to incorporate the United States Naval Association, for the relief of the families of deceased officers, be postponed for the purpose of taking that bill into consideration. This motion was rejected by the House.

Mr. RHEA moved that the several orders of the day, which precede the bill concerning invalid pensioners, be postponed, for the purpose of taking that bill into consideration. This motion was rejected by the House.

Mr. SAMUEL MOORE moved that the several orders of the day, which precede the bill from the Senate, entitled "An act explanatory of the act for the relief of James Leander Cathcart," passed May 15, 1820, be postponed for the purpose of taking that bill into consideration. This motion was rejected by the House.

Mr. CULPEPER moved that the several orders of the day, which precede the bill from the Senate, entitled "An act for the relief of Ebenezer Stevens, and Austin L. Sands, legal representatives of Richardson Sands, deceased, and others," be postponed, for the purpose of taking that bill into consideration. This motion was rejected by the House.

Mr. SMITH, of Maryland, moved that the several orders of the day, which precede the bill from the Senate, entitled "An act for the relief of William Whitehead and others," be postponed, for the purpose of taking that bill into consideration. This motion was rejected by the House.

A motion was made by Mr. CANNON, that the Committee of the Whole, to which is committed the bill from the Senate, entitled "An act for the relief of the officers and volunteers engaged in the late campaign against the Seminole Indians," be discharged from the consideration thereof.

And the question being taken thereon, it was determined in the negative.

An engrossed bill, entitled "An act authorizing the settlement of the accounts of the late Le Roy Opie," was read the third time, and passed.

A motion was made by Mr. JOHNSON that the Committee of the Whole to which is committed the bill from the Senate, entitled "An act to provide for the due execution of the laws of the United States within the State of Missouri," be discharged from the consideration thereof.

And the question being taken thereon, it was determined in the negative.

Mr. COBB then moved that the several orders of the day which precede the said bill be postponed, for the purpose of taking the same into consideration. This motion was also negatived by the House.

A message from the Senate informed the House that the Senate insist on their amendments disagreed to by the House to the bill, entitled "An act authorizing the President of the United States to borrow a sum not exceeding four millions five hundred thousand dollars," and ask a conference upon the subject-matter of the disagreeing votes of the two Houses on the said amendments; to which conference they have appointed managers on their part. The Senate *further insist* on their amendments to the bill, entitled "An act making appropriations for the military service of the United States for the year 1821," and ask a conference upon the subject-matter of the disagreeing votes of the two Houses on the said amendments; to which conference they have appointed managers on their part.

The House proceeded to consider the message from the Senate informing this House that they insist on their amendments, disagreed to by this House to the bill, entitled "An act to authorize the President of the United States to borrow a sum not exceeding four millions five hundred thousand dollars;" whereupon,

Resolved, That this House do recede from their disagreement to the said amendments.

The House proceeded to consider the message from the Senate asking a conference upon the subject of the disagreeing votes of the two Houses on the amendments proposed by the Senate to the bill, entitled "An act making appropriations for the military service of the United States for the year 1821:" whereupon

Resolved, That this House doth agree to the conference asked by the Senate upon the subject of the amendments depending to the said bill, and that managers be appointed to attend the same on their part.

Mr. HARDIN, Mr. TRACY, and Mr. COBB, were appointed managers in pursuance of the foregoing resolution.

Mr. WOOD moved that the several orders of the day which precede the bill from the Senate, entitled "An act for the relief of Ebenezer Stevens, and Austin L. Sands, legal representatives of Richardson Sands, deceased, and others," be postponed, for the purpose of taking that bill into consideration. This motion was again rejected by the House.

Mr. CANNON moved that the several orders of the day which precede the bill from the Senate, entitled "An act for the relief of the officers and volunteers engaged in the late campaign against the Seminole Indians," be postponed, for the purpose of taking that bill into consideration. This motion was again rejected by the House.

Mr. BEECHER moved that the bill from the Senate, entitled "An act supplemental to an act, entitled 'An act to authorize the appointment of commissioners to lay out the road therein mentioned," be now read the second time; and the question being taken thereon, it was determined in the negative.

Ordered, That the Committee of the Whole on the state of the Union be discharged from the further consideration of the bills from the Senate, entitled "An act providing for the adjudication and payment of claims arising under the Treaty of Amity, Settlement, and Limits, between the United States and His Catholic Majesty;" and "An act to authorize the President of the United States to take possession of East and West Florida, and establish a temporary government therein ;" and that the said bills lie on the table.

A motion was made, by Mr. RHEA, that the several orders of the day which precede the bill from the Senate, entitled "An act for the relief of the officers and volunteers engaged in the late campaign against the Seminole Indians," be postponed, for the purpose of taking that bill into consideration. This motion was again rejected by the House.

Mr. HARDIN, from the managers appointed on the part of this House to attend a conference with the managers appointed on the part of the Senate, upon the subject of the disagreeing votes of the two Houses on the amendments depending to the bill, entitled "An act making appropriations for the military service of the United States for the year 1821," reported, that they had met the managers on the part of the Senate, and conferred freely upon the subjects committed to them; that they had agreed to recommend to the House of Representatives to recede from their disagreement to the residue of the fourth amendment of the Senate, containing an appropriation for carrying into effect the treaty concluded on the 30th of July last, between the United States and the Kickapoo tribe of Indians; and that they could come to no agreement whatever upon the subject of the other amendments depending to the said bill.

Mr. HARDIN then moved that this House adhere to their disagreement to the said amendments, with the exception of the residue of the fourth. Pending the question on this motion, a message was received from the Senate informing the House that the Senate recede from all their amendments to the bill, entitled "An act making appropriations for the military service of the United States for the year 1821."

A message from the Senate informed the House that the Senate have passed a resolution for the appointment of a joint committee to wait upon the President of the United States, and inform him that the two Houses of Congress are about to adjourn, if he has no further communications to make to them, and have appointed a committee on their part.

The resolution was read, and concurred in by the House; and Mr. SMITH, of Maryland, and Mr. CUSHMAN, were appointed of the said committee, on the part of this House.

THE SPEAKER'S ADDRESS.

Mr. TAYLOR, the Speaker, rose and addressed the House, as follows :

Gentlemen of the House of Representatives :

Deeply penetrated with a sense of the kindness and liberality, which, in terms, and from a source the most flattering, have dictated the recent expression of your approbation, I shall ever esteem it the highest reward of my public services. If the duties of the Chair have been discharged in any degree to your satisfaction, it is attributable chiefly to those feelings of generosity which have covered my numerous errors, and which have rendered to purity of motive the deference due to superior merit. My inexperience has been compensated by your prudent counsels, and by a dignified deportment, which has seldom required the interposition of a presiding officer.

Entertaining, gentlemen, for every member of this House no other sentiment than respect and friendship; endeared to many by recollections of united deliberation and effort, in a period of great national embarrassment ; and grateful to all for the magnanimous support which constantly has been afforded me, I shall never cease to rejoice in your individual welfare.

Carry with you, gentlemen, to the bosom of your families and friends my best wishes for your prosperity, and, under the protecting care of a benign Providence, may each of you enjoy the continued confidence of the wise and good, and largely contribute to perpetuate the union and glory of our common country.

Mr. SMITH, of Maryland, from the joint committee appointed to wait on the President of the United States, and inform him that the two Houses of Congress are about to adjourn if he has no further communications to make to them, reported that the committee had waited upon the President of the United States, and was informed by him that he had no further communications to make to Congress at the present session.

A message from the Senate informed the House that the Senate, having completed the Legislative business before them, are now ready to adjourn.

A message was then sent to the Senate, by the Clerk to inform them that the House is also ready to adjourn.

The Clerk having gone with the said message, and being returned, the Speaker adjourned the House *sine die.*

A Message was received from the PRESIDENT OF THE UNITED STATES, as follows:

To the House of Representatives of the United States:

The treaty concluded between the United States and the Kickapoo tribe of Indians, on the 30th of July, 1820, having been ratified, by and with the advice and consent of the Senate, I now lay a copy of the said treaty before the House of Representatives, in order to such legislative provisions being made as may be necessary to carry into effect the stipulations therein contained, on the part of the United States.

JAMES MONROE.

WASHINGTON, *March* 3, 1821.

The Message was ordered to lie on the table.

The House proceeded to consider the bill from the Senate, entitled "An act to continue in force for a further time the act, entitled 'An act for establishing trading houses with the Indian tribes."

A motion was made by Mr. STORRS to amend the said bill, by striking out *June*, and inserting *February*, so as to limit the continuance of the said act to the 1st day of February, 182—, instead of the 1st day of June, 182—, as provided for in the said bill.

The question being taken to agree to this amendment, it was determined in the negative.

The bill was then read a third time, and passed.

The Committee of the whole House, to which is committed the bill authorizing the settlement of the accounts of the late Le Roy Opie, were discharged from the consideration thereof, and the bill was ordered to be engrossed, and read a third time to-day.

Mr. FULLER moved that the several orders of the day, which precede the bill to incorporate the United States Naval Association, for the relief of the families of deceased officers, be postponed for the purpose of taking that bill into consideration. This motion was rejected by the House.

Mr. RHEA moved that the several orders of the day, which precede the bill concerning invalid pensioners, be postponed, for the purpose of taking that bill into consideration. This motion was rejected by the House.

Mr. SAMUEL MOORE moved that the several orders of the day, which precede the bill from the Senate, entitled "An act explanatory of the act for the relief of James Leander Cathcart," passed May 15, 1820, be postponed for the purpose of taking that bill into consideration. This motion was rejected by the House.

Mr. CULPEPER moved that the several orders of the day, which precede the bill from the Senate, entitled "An act for the relief of Ebenezer Stevens, and Austin L. Sands, legal representatives of Richardson Sands, deceased, and others," be postponed, for the purpose of taking that bill into consideration. This motion was rejected by the House.

Mr. SMITH, of Maryland, moved that the several orders of the day, which precede the bill from the Senate, entitled "An act for the relief of William Whitehead and others," be postponed, for the purpose of taking that bill into consideration. This motion was rejected by the House.

A motion was made by Mr. CANNON, that the Committee of the Whole, to which is committed the bill from the Senate, entitled "An act for the relief of the officers and volunteers engaged in the late campaign against the Seminole Indians," be discharged from the consideration thereof.

And the question being taken thereon, it was determined in the negative.

An engrossed bill, entitled "An act authorizing the settlement of the accounts of the late Le Roy Opie," was read the third time, and passed.

A motion was made by Mr. JOHNSON that the Committee of the Whole to which is committed the bill from the Senate, entitled "An act to provide for the due execution of the laws of the United States within the State of Missouri," be discharged from the consideration thereof.

And the question being taken thereon, it was determined in the negative.

Mr. COBB then moved that the several orders of the day which precede the said bill be postponed, for the purpose of taking the same into consideration. This motion was also negatived by the House.

A message from the Senate informed the House that the Senate insist on their amendments disagreed to by the House to the bill, entitled "An act authorizing the President of the United States to borrow a sum not exceeding four millions five hundred thousand dollars," and ask a conference upon the subject-matter of the disagreeing votes of the two Houses on the said amendments; to which conference they have appointed managers on their part. The Senate *further insist* on their amendments to the bill, entitled "An act making appropriations for the military service of the United States for the year 1821," and ask a conference upon the subject-matter of the disagreeing votes of the two Houses on the said amendments; to which conference they have appointed managers on their part.

The House proceeded to consider the message from the Senate informing this House that they insist on their amendments, disagreed to by this House to the bill, entitled "An act to authorize the President of the United States to borrow a sum not exceeding four millions five hundred thousand dollars;" whereupon,

Resolved, That this House do recede from their disagreement to the said amendments.

The House proceeded to consider the message from the Senate asking a conference upon the subject of the disagreeing votes of the two Houses on the amendments proposed by the Senate to the bill, entitled "An act making appropriations for the military service of the United States for the year 1821:" whereupon

Resolved, That this House doth agree to the conference asked by the Senate upon the subject of the amendments depending to the said bill, and that managers be appointed to attend the same on their part.

Mr. HARDIN, Mr. TRACY, and Mr. COBB, were appointed managers in pursuance of the foregoing resolution.

Mr. WOOD moved that the several orders of the day which precede the bill from the Senate, entitled "An act for the relief of Ebenezer Stevens, and Austin L. Sands, legal representatives of Richardson Sands, deceased, and others," be postponed, for the purpose of taking that bill into consideration. This motion was again rejected by the House.

Mr. CANNON moved that the several orders of the day which precede the bill from the Senate, entitled "An act for the relief of the officers and volunteers engaged in the late campaign against the Seminole Indians," be postponed, for the purpose of taking that bill into consideration. This motion was again rejected by the House.

Mr. BEECHER moved that the bill from the Senate, entitled "An act supplemental to an act, entitled 'An act to authorize the appointment of commissioners to lay out the road therein mentioned,'" be now read the second time; and the question being taken thereon, it was determined in the negative.

Ordered, That the Committee of the Whole on the state of the Union be discharged from the further consideration of the bills from the Senate, entitled "An act providing for the adjudication and payment of claims arising under the Treaty of Amity, Settlement, and Limits, between the United States and His Catholic Majesty ;" and "An act to authorize the President of the United States to take possession of East and West Florida, and establish a temporary government therein ;" and that the said bills lie on the table.

A motion was made, by Mr. RHEA, that the several orders of the day which precede the bill from the Senate, entitled "An act for the relief of the officers and volunteers engaged in the late campaign against the Seminole Indians," be postponed, for the purpose of taking that bill into consideration. This motion was again rejected by the House.

Mr. HARDIN, from the managers appointed on the part of this House to attend a conference with the managers appointed on the part of the Senate, upon the subject of the disagreeing votes of the two Houses on the amendments proposed to the bill, entitled "An act making appropriations for the military service of the United States for the year 1821," reported, that they had met the managers on the part of the Senate, and conferred freely upon the subjects committed to them ; that they had agreed to recommend to the House of Representatives to recede from their disagreement to the residue of the fourth amendment of the Senate, containing an appropriation for carrying into effect the treaty concluded on the 30th of July last, between the United States and the Kickapoo tribe of Indians ; and that they could come to no agreement whatever upon the subject of the other amendments depending to the said bill.

Mr. HARDIN then moved that this House adhere to their disagreement to the said amendments, with the exception of the residue of the fourth. Pending the question on this motion, a message was received from the Senate informing the House that the Senate recede from all their amendments to the bill, entitled "An act making appropriations for the military service of the United States for the year 1821."

A message from the Senate informed the House that the Senate have passed a resolution for the appointment of a joint committee to wait upon the President of the United States, and inform him that the two Houses of Congress are about to adjourn, if he has no further communications to make to them, and have appointed a committee on their part.

The resolution was read, and concurred in by the House ; and Mr. SMITH, of Maryland, and Mr. CUSHMAN, were appointed of the said committee, on the part of this House.

THE SPEAKER'S ADDRESS.

Mr. TAYLOR, the Speaker, rose and addressed the House, as follows :

Gentlemen of the House of Representatives :

Deeply penetrated with a sense of the kindness and liberality, which, in terms, and from a source the most flattering, have dictated the recent expression of your approbation, I shall ever esteem it the highest reward of my public services. If the duties of the Chair have been discharged in any degree to your satisfaction, it is attributable chiefly to those feelings of generosity which have covered my numerous errors, and which have rendered to purity of motive the deference due to superior merit. My inexperience has been compensated by your prudent counsels, and by a dignified deportment, which has seldom required the interposition of a presiding officer.

Entertaining, gentlemen, for every member of this House no other sentiment than respect and friendship ; endeared to many by recollections of united deliberation and effort, in a period of great national embarrassment ; and grateful to all for the magnanimous support which constantly has been afforded me, I shall never cease to rejoice in your individual welfare.

Carry with you, gentlemen, to the bosom of your families and friends my best wishes for your prosperity, and, under the protecting care of a benign Providence, may each of you enjoy the continued confidence of the wise and good, and largely contribute to perpetuate the union and glory of our common country.

Mr. SMITH, of Maryland, from the joint committee appointed to wait on the President of the United States, and inform him that the two Houses of Congress are about to adjourn if he has no further communications to make to them, reported that the committee had waited upon the President of the United States, and was informed by him that he had no further communications to make to Congress at the present session.

A message from the Senate informed the House that the Senate, having completed the Legislative business before them, are now ready to adjourn.

A message was then sent to the Senate, by the Clerk to inform them that the House is also ready to adjourn.

The Clerk having gone with the said message, and being returned, the Speaker adjourned the House *sine die.*

INAUGURATION OF THE PRESIDENT.

[From the National Intelligencer, of Tuesday, March 6, 1821.]

The inauguration of the President of the United States, whose second term of service commenced yesterday, took place according to previous arrangement. The oath of office having been administered to the President, by Chief Justice Marshall, he delivered the speech which will be found annexed.

The day proved very unfavorable for the attendance of spectators, there having fallen during the preceding night a good deal of snow and rain; notwithstanding which, an immense crowd thronged the doors of the Capitol. The number of persons who obtained admission within the walls of the Representatives' chamber (gallery of course included) could not have been less than two thousand.

There was not much form about this ceremony, which, in truth, requires no form but the forms of decency and decorum; but the scene was not the less impressive. The President was placed on the platform in front of the Speaker's Chair; the Chief Justice stood by his side during the delivery of the speech. The Associate Judges, the President of the Senate, the Speaker of the House of Representatives, the Heads of Departments, and many of our distinguished Military and Naval Officers, were near him. Assigned to their proper places were the members of the various Foreign Legations. The seats in the interior were principally occupied by a numerous collection of ladies; and all around, above, and below, were countless numbers of the people, of whom, without discrimination, as many were admitted, after the ladies and privileged persons were seated, as the room could accommodate. On the entrance and exit of the President, the music of the Marine Band enlivened the scene, which was altogether characterized by simple grandeur and splendid simplicity.

It is well, considering the great crowd which filled the avenues to the door of the Representatives' chamber, and pressed onwards for admittance, that no accident occurred to mar the enjoyment of those who had the pleasure to witness this truly Republican ceremony.

INAUGURAL SPEECH.

Yesterday, at 12 o'clock, on taking the oath to support the Constitution of the United States, the following speech was delivered by JAMES MONROE, President of the United States:

FELLOW-CITIZENS: I shall not attempt to describe the grateful emotions which the new and very distinguished proof of the confidence of my fellow-citizens, evinced by my re-election to this high trust, has excited in my bosom. The approbation which it announces of my conduct, in the preceding term, affords me a consolation which I shall profoundly feel through life. The general accord with which it has been expressed, adds to the great and never-ceasing obligations which it imposes. To merit the continuance of this good opinion, and to carry it with me into my retirement, as the solace of advancing years, will be the object of my most zealous and unceasing efforts.

Having no pretension to the high and commanding claims of my predecessors, whose names are so much more conspicuously identified with our Revolution, and who contributed so pre-eminently to promote its success, I consider myself rather as the instrument than the cause of the union which has prevailed in the late election. In surmounting, in favor of my humble pretensions, the difficulties which so often produce division in like occurrences, it is obvious that other powerful causes, indicating the great strength and stability of our Union, have essentially contributed to draw you together. That these powerful causes exist, and that they are permanent, is my fixed opinion; that they may produce a like accord in all questions, touching, however remotely, the liberty, prosperity, and happiness of our country, will always be the object of my most fervent prayers to the Supreme Author of all good.

In a Government which is founded by the people, who possess exclusively the sovereignty, it seems proper that the person who may be placed by their suffrages in this high trust, should declare, on commencing its duties, the principles on which he intends to conduct the Administration. If the person, thus elected, has served the preceding term, an opportunity is afforded him to review its principal occurrences, and to give such further explanation respecting them as, in his judgment, may be useful to his constituents. The events of one year have influence on those of another; and, in like manner, of a preceding on the succeeding Administration. The movements of a great nation are connected in all their parts. If errors have been committed, they ought to be corrected; if the policy is sound, it ought to be supported. It is by a thorough knowledge of the whole subject that our fellow-citizens are enabled to judge correctly of the past, and to give a proper direction to the future.

Just before the commencement of the last term, the United States had concluded a war with a very powerful nation, on conditions equal and honorable to both parties. The events of that war are too recent, and too deeply impressed on the memory of all, to require a development from me. Our commerce had been, in a great measure, driven from the sea; our Atlantic and inland frontiers were invaded in almost every part; the waste of life along our coast, and on some parts of our inland frontiers, to the defence of which our gallant and patriotic citizens were called, was immense;

in addition to which, not less than one hundred and twenty millions of dollars were added at its end to the public debt.

As soon as the war had terminated, the nation, admonished by its events, resolved to place itself in a situation which should be better calculated to prevent the recurrence of a like evil, and, in case it should recur, to mitigate its calamities. With this view, after reducing our land force to the basis of a peace establishment, which has been further modified since, provision was made for the construction of fortifications at proper points, through the whole extent of our coast, and such an augmentation of our naval force, as should be well adapted to both purposes. The laws, making this provision, were passed in 1815 and 1816, and it has been, since, the constant effort of the Executive to carry them into effect.

The advantage of these fortifications, and of an augmented naval force, in the extent contemplated, in point of economy, has been fully illustrated, by a report of the Board of Engineers and Naval Commissioners, lately communicated to Congress, by which it appears, that in an invasion by twenty thousand men, with a correspondent naval force, in a campaign of six months only, the whole expense of the construction of the works would be defrayed by the difference in the sum necessary to maintain the force which would be adequate to our defence with the aid of those works, and that which would be incurred without them. The reason of this difference is obvious. If fortifications are judiciously placed on our great inlets, as distant from our cities as circumstances will permit, they will form the only points of attack, and the enemy will be detained there by a small regular force, a sufficient time to enable our militia to collect, and repair to that on which the attack is made. A force adequate to the enemy, collected at that single point, with suitable preparation for such others as might be menaced, is all that would be requisite. But, if there were no fortifications, then the enemy might go where he pleased, and, changing his position, and sailing from place to place, our force must be called out and spread in vast numbers along the whole coast, and on both sides of every bay and river, as high up in each as it might be navigable for ships of war. By these fortifications, supported by our navy, to which they would afford like support, we should present to other Powers an armed front from St. Croix to the Sabine, which would protect, in the event of war, our whole coast and interior from invasion; and even in the wars of other Powers, in which we were neutral, they would be found eminently useful, as, by keeping their public ships at a distance from our cities, peace and order in them would be preserved, and the Government be protected from insult.

It need scarcely be remarked, that these measures have not been resorted to in a spirit of hostility to other Powers. Such a disposition does not exist towards any Power. Peace and good will have been, and will hereafter be, cultivated with all, and by the most faithful regard to justice. They have been dictated by a love of peace, of economy, and an earnest desire to save the lives of our fellow-citizens from that destruction, and our country from that devastation, which are inseparable from war, when it finds us unprepared for it. It is believed, and experience has shown, that such a preparation is the best expedient that can be resorted to, to prevent war. I add with much pleasure, that considerable progress has already

been made in these measures of defence, and that they will be completed in a few years, considering the great extent and importance of the object, if the plan be zealously and steadily persevered in.

The conduct of the Government, in what relates to foreign Powers, is always an object of the highest importance to the nation. Its agriculture, commerce, manufactures, fisheries, revenue; in short, its peace, may all be affected by it. Attention is, therefore, due to this subject.

At the period adverted to, the Powers of Europe, after having been engaged in long and destructive wars with each other, had concluded a peace, which happily still exists. Our peace with the Power with whom we had been engaged, had also been concluded. The war between Spain and the colonies in South America, which had commenced many years before, was then the only conflict that remained unsettled. This being a contest between different parts of the same community, in which other Powers had not interfered, was not affected by their accommodations.

This contest was considered, at an early stage, by my predecessor, a civil war, in which the parties were entitled to equal rights in our ports. This decision, the first made by any Power, being formed on great consideration of the comparative strength and resources of the parties, the length of time, and successful opposition made by the colonies, and of all other circumstances on which it ought to depend, was in strict accord with the law of nations. Congress has invariably acted on this principle, having made no change in our relations with either party. Our attitude has, therefore, been that of neutrality between them, which has been maintained by the Government with the strictest impartiality. No aid has been afforded to either, nor has any privilege been enjoyed by the one, which has not been equally open to the other party; and every exertion has been made in its power, to enforce the execution of the laws prohibiting illegal equipments, with equal rigor against both.

By this equality between the parties, their public vessels have been received in our ports on the same footing; they have enjoyed an equal right to purchase and export arms, munitions of war, and every other supply—the exportation of all articles whatever being permitted under laws which were passed long before the commencement of the contest; our citizens have traded equally with both, and their commerce with each has been alike protected by the Government.

Respecting the attitude which it may be proper for the United States to maintain hereafter between the parties, I have no hesitation in stating it as my opinion, that the neutrality heretofore observed should still be adhered to. From the change in the Government of Spain, and the negotiation now depending, invited by the Cortes and accepted by the colonies, it may be presumed that their differences will be settled on the terms proposed by the colonies. Should the war be continued, the United States, regarding its occurrences, will always have it in their power to adopt such measures respecting it as their honor and interest may require.

Shortly after the general peace, a band of adventurers took advantage of this conflict, and of the facility which it afforded, to establish a system of buccaneering in the neighboring seas, to the great annoyance of the commerce of the United States, and, as was represented, of that of other Powers. Of this spirit, and of its injurious bearing on the United

States, strong proofs were afforded by the establishment at Amelia Island, and the purposes to which it was made instrumental by this band in 1817, and by the occurrences which took place in other parts of Florida, in 1818, the details of which, in both instances, are too well known to require to be now recited. I am satisfied had a less decisive course been adopted that the worst consequences would have resulted from it. We have seen that these checks, decisive as they were, were not sufficient to crush that piratical spirit. Many culprits brought within our limits have been condemned to suffer death, the punishment due to that atrocious crime. The decisions of upright and enlightened tribunals fall equally on all, whose crimes subject them, by a fair interpretation of the law, to its censure. It belongs to the Executive not to suffer the executions, under these decisions, to transcend the great purpose for which punishment is necessary. The full benefit of example being secured, policy, as well as humanity, equally forbids that they should be carried further. I have acted on this principle, pardoning those who appear to have been led astray by ignorance of the criminality of the acts they had committed, and suffering the law to take effect on those only in whose favor no extenuating circumstances could be urged.

Great confidence is entertained that the treaty with Spain, which has been ratified by both the parties, and the ratifications whereof have been exchanged, has placed the relations of the two countries on a basis of permanent friendship. The provision made by it for such of our citizens as have claims on Spain, of the character described, will, it is presumed, be very satisfactory to them; and the boundary which is established between the territories of the parties, westward of the Mississippi, heretofore in dispute, has, it is thought, been settled on conditions just and advantageous to both. But, to the acquisition of Florida too much importance cannot be attached. It secures to the United States a territory important in itself, and whose importance is much increased by its bearing on many of the highest interests of the Union. It opens to several of the neighboring States a free passage to the ocean, through the provinces ceded, by several rivers, having their sources high up within their limits. It secures us against all future annoyance from powerful Indian tribes. It gives us several excellent harbors in the Gulf of Mexico for ships of war of the largest size. It covers, by its position in the Gulf, the Mississippi and other great waters within our extended limits, and thereby enables the United States to afford complete protection to the vast and very valuable productions of our whole Western country, which find a market through those streams.

By a treaty with the British Government, bearing date on the twentieth of October, one thousand eight hundred and eighteen, the convention regulating the commerce between the United States and Great Britain, concluded on the third of July, one thousand eight hundred and fifteen, which was about expiring, was revived and continued for the term of ten years from the time of its expiration. By that treaty, also, the differences which had arisen under the Treaty of Ghent, respecting the right claimed by the United States for their citizens, to take and cure fish on the coast of His Britannic Majesty's dominions in America, with other differences on important interests, were adjusted, to the satisfaction of both parties. No agreement has yet been entered into respecting the commerce between the United States and the British dominions in the West Indies, and on this continent. The restraints imposed on that commerce by Great Britain, and reciprocated by the United States, on a principle of defence, continue still in force.

The negotiation with France for the regulation of the commercial relations between the two countries, which, in the course of last Summer, had been commenced at Paris, has since been transferred to this city, and will be pursued, on the part of the United States, in the spirit of conciliation, and with an earnest desire that it may terminate in an arrangement satisfactory to both parties.

Our relations with the Barbary Powers are preserved in the same state, and by the same means, that were employed when I came into this office. As early as 1801 it was found necessary to send a squadron into the Mediterranean for the protection of our commerce, and no period has intervened, a short term excepted, when it was thought advisable to withdraw it. The great interest which the United States have in the Pacific, in commerce and in the fisheries, have also made it necessary to maintain a naval force there. In disposing of this force, in both instances, the most effectual measures in our power have been taken, without interfering with its other duties, for the suppression of the slave trade, and of piracy, in the neighboring seas.

The situation of the United States, in regard to their resources, the extent of their revenue, and the facility with which it is raised, affords a most gratifying spectacle. The payment of nearly sixty-seven millions of dollars of the public debt, with the great progress made in measures of defence, and in other improvements of various kinds, since the late w r, are conclusive proofs of this extraordinary prosperity, especially when it is recollected that these expenditures have been defrayed, without a burden on the people, the direct tax and excise having been repealed soon after the conclusion of the late war, and the revenue applied to these great objects having been raised in a manner not to be felt. Our great resources, therefore, remain untouched, for any purpose which may affect the vital interests of the nation. For all such purposes they are inexhaustible. They are more especially to be found in the virtue, patriotism, and intelligence, of our fellow-citizens, and in the devotion with which they would yield up, by any just measure of taxation, all their property, in support of the rights and honor of their country.

Under the present depression of prices, affecting all the productions of the country, and every branch of industry, proceeding from causes explained on a former occasion, the revenue has considerably diminished; the effect of which has been to compel Congress either to abandon these great measures of defence, or to resort to loans or internal taxes to supply the deficiency. On the presumption that this depression, and the deficiency in the revenue arising from it, would be temporary, loans were authorized for the demands of the last and present year. Anxious to relieve my fellow-citizens in 1817, from every burden which could be dispensed with, and the state of the Treasury permitting it, I recommended the repeal of the internal taxes, knowing that such relief was then peculiarly necessary, in consequence of the great exertions made in the late war. I made that recommendation under a pledge that, should the public exigencies require a recurrence to them at any time while I remained in this trust, I would, with equal prompti- tude, perform the duty which would then be alike in- cumbent on me. By the experiment now making it will be seen, by the next session of Congress, whether the revenue shall have been so augmented as to be adequate to all these necessary purposes. Should the deficiency still continue, and especially should it be probable that it would be permanent, the course to be pursued appears to me to be obvious. I am satisfied that, under certain circumstances, loans may be re- sorted to with great advantage. I am equally well satisfied, as a general rule, that the demands of the current year, especially in time of peace, should be provided for by the revenue of that year. I have never dreaded, nor have I ever shunned, in any situation in which I have been placed, making appeals to the vir- tue and patriotism of my fellow-citizens, well knowing that they could never be made in vain, especially in times of great emergency, or for purposes of high national importance. Independently of the exigency of the case, many considerations of great weight urge a policy having in view a provision of revenue to meet, to a certain extent, the demands of the nation, with- out relying altogether on the precarious resource of foreign commerce. I am satisfied that internal duties and excises, with corresponding imposts on foreign articles of the same kind, would, without imposing any serious burdens on the people, enhance the price of produce promote our manufactures, and augment the revenue, at the same time that they made it more secure and permanent.

The care of the Indian tribes within our limits has long been an essential part of our system, but, unfor- tunately, it has not been executed in a manner to ac- complish all the objects intended by it. We have treated them as independent nations without their having any substantial pretension to that rank. The distinction has flattered their pride, retarded their im- provement, and, in many instances, paved the way to their destruction. The progress of our settlements westward, supported as they are by a dense popula- tion, has constantly driven them back, with almost the total sacrifice of the lands which they have been com- pelled to abandon. They have claims on the mag- nanimity, and, I may add, on the justice of this nation, which we must all feel. We should become their real benefactors, we should perform the office of their Great Father, the endearing title which they emphatically give to the Chief Magistrate of our Union. Their sovereignty over vast territories should cease, in lieu of which the right of soil should be secured to each indi- vidual, and his posterity, in competent portions, and for the territory thus ceded by each tribe some reason- able equivalent should be granted, to be vested in per- manent funds for the support of civil government over them, and for the education of their children, for their instruction in the arts of husbandry, and to provide sustenance for them until they could provide it for themselves. My earnest hope is, that Congress will digest some plan, founded on these principles, with such improvements as their wisdom may suggest, and carry it into effect as soon as it may be practicable.

Europe is again unsettled, and the prospect of war increasing. Should the flame light up in any quarter, how far it may extend it is impossible to foresee. It is our peculiar felicity to be altogether unconnected with the causes which produce this menacing aspect elsewhere. With every Power we are in perfect amity, and it is our interest to remain so, if it be practicable

on just conditions. I see no reasonable cause to ap- prehend variance with any Power, unless it proceed from a violation of our maritime rights. In these con- tests, should they occur, and to whatever extent they may be carried, we shall be neutral; but as a neutral Power we have rights which it is our duty to main- tain. For light injuries it will be incumbent on us to seek redress in a spirit of amity, in full confidence that, injuring none, none would knowingly injure us. For more imminent dangers we should be prepared, and it should always be recollected that such prepara- tion, adapted to the circumstances, and sanctioned by the judgment and wishes of our constituents, cannot fail to have a good effect, in averting dangers of every kind. We should recollect also that the season of peace is best adapted to these preparations.

If we turn our attention, fellow-citizens, more im- mediately to the internal concerns of our country, and more especially to those on which its future welfare depends, we have every reason to anticipate the hap- piest results. It is now rather more than forty-four years since we declared our independence, and thirty- seven since it was acknowledged. The talents and virtues which were displayed in that great struggle were a sure presage of all that has since followed. A people who were able to surmount in their infant state such great perils, would be more competent as they rose into manhood to repel any which they might meet in their progress. Their physical strength would be more adequate to foreign danger, and the practice of self-government, aided by the light of experience, could not fail to produce an effect equally salutary on all those questions connected with the internal organi- zation. These favorable anticipations have been real- ized. In our whole system, National and State, we have shunned all the defects which unceasingly preyed on the vitals and destroyed the ancient republics. In them there were distinct orders, a nobility and a peo- ple, or the people governed in one assembly. Thus, in the one instance there was a perpetual conflict between the orders in society for the ascendancy, in which the victory of either terminated in the overthrow of the Government and the ruin of the State. In the other, in which the people governed in a body, and whose dominions seldom exceeded the dimensions of a county in one of our States, a tumultuous and disorderly movement permitted only a transitory existence. In this great nation there is but one order, that of the people, whose power, by a peculiarly happy improve- ment of the representative principle, is transferred from them without impairing in the slightest degree their sovereignty, to bodies of their own creation, and to persons elected by themselves, in the full extent ne- cessary for all the purposes of free, enlightened, and efficient government. The whole system is elective, the complete sovereignty being in the people, and every officer in every department deriving his authority from and being responsible to them for his conduct.

Our career has corresponded with this great outline. Perfection in our organization could not have been expected in the outset, either in the National or State Governments, or in tracing the line between their respective powers. But no serious conflict has arisen, nor any contest but such as are managed by argu- ment, and by a fair appeal to the good sense of the people; and many of the defects which experience had clearly demonstrated, in both Governments, have been remedied. By steadily pursuing this course, in this spirit, there is every reason to believe that our

Inauguration of the President.

system will soon attain the highest degree of perfection of which human institutions are capable, and that the movement, in all its branches, will exhibit such a degree of order and harmony, as to command the admiration and respect of the civilized world.

Our physical attainments have not been less eminent. Twenty-five years ago the river Mississippi was shut up, and our Western brethren had no outlet for their commerce. What has been the progress since that time? The river has not only become the property of the United States from its source to the ocean, with all its tributary streams, (with the exception of the upper part of the Red river only,) but Louisiana, with a fair and liberal boundary on the western side, and the Floridas on the eastern, have been ceded to us. The United States now enjoy the complete and uninterrupted sovereignty over the whole territory from St. Croix to the Sabine. New States, settled from among ourselves in this, and in other parts, have been admitted into our Union, in equal participation in the national sovereignty with the original States. Our population has augmented in an astonishing degree, and extended in every direction. We now,

fellow-citizens, comprise within our limits the dimensions and faculties of a great Power, under a Government possessing all the energies of any Government ever known to the old world, with an utter incapacity to oppress the people.

Entering, with these views, the office which I have just solemnly sworn to execute with fidelity, and to the utmost of my ability, I derive great satisfaction from a knowledge that I shall be assisted in the several departments by the very enlightened and upright citizens from whom I have received so much aid in the preceding term. With full confidence in the continuance of that candor, and generous indulgence, from my fellow-citizens at large, which I have heretofore experienced, and, with a firm reliance on the protection of Almighty God, I shall forthwith commence the duties of the high trust to which you have called me.

DANIEL D. TOMPKINS took the Constitutional oath on entering his second term of service in the office of Vice President of the United States, at his own residence, on Saturday, the third instant.

APPENDIX

TO THE HISTORY OF THE SIXTEENTH CONGRESS.

[SECOND SESSION.]

COMPRISING THE MOST IMPORTANT DOCUMENTS ORIGINATING DURING THAT CON-
GRESS, AND THE PUBLIC ACTS PASSED BY IT.

SUPPRESSION OF THE SLAVE TRADE.

[Communicated to the House, January 5, 1821.]

I communicate to the House of Representatives a report from the Secretary of State, which, with the papers accompanying it, contains all the information in possession of the Executive, requested by a resolution of the House of the 4th of December, on the subject of the African slave trade.

JAMES MONROE.

WASHINGTON, Jan. 4, 1821.

DEPARTMENT OF STATE, Jan. 4, 1821.

The Secretary of State, to whom has been referred the resolution of the House of Representatives, of the 4th ultimo, requesting the communication to that House of any correspondence that the President does not deem it inexpedient to disclose, which may have existed between the Executive of the United States and the Government of any of the maritime Powers of Europe, in relation to the African slave trade, has the honor of submitting copies of the papers requested by the resolution. With the exception of a note from the late Spanish Minister, Onis, communicating a copy of the treaty between Spain and Great Britain on this subject, the only Government of Europe with whom there has been such correspondence is that of Great Britain; and these papers contain all that has passed between them, on the subject, in writing. Since the arrival of Mr. Canning, various informal conferences between him and the Secretary of State have been held, in which the proposals on the part of Great Britain have been fully discussed, without effecting a removal of the objections upon which the President had, in the first instance, found himself under the necessity of declining them. They have not yet terminated, nor have any written communications passed on the subject, with the exception of the note from Mr. Canning and the answer to it, herewith submitted, both of a date subsequent to that of the resolution of the House.

JOHN QUINCY ADAMS.

16th CON. 2d SESS.—42

Don Louis de Onis to the Secretary of State.

WASHINGTON, May 14, 1818.

SIR: The introduction of negro slaves into America was one of the earliest measures adopted by the august ancestors of the King my master, for the improvement and prosperity of those vast dominions, very shortly after their discovery. The total inaptitude of the Indians to various useful, but painful labors, the result of their ignorance of all the conveniences of life, and the imperfect progress in civil society, made it necessary to have recourse to strong and active laborers for breaking up and cultivating the earth. With the double view of stimulating them to active exertion, and of promoting the population of those countries, a measure was resorted to by Spain, which, although repugnant to her feelings, is not to be considered as having originated the system of slavery, but as having materially alleviated the evils of that which already existed, in consequence of a barbarous practice of the Africans, upon saving the lives of a considerable portion of the captives in war; whom they formerly put to death. By the introduction of this system, the negroes, far from suffering additional evils, or being subjected, while in a state of slavery, to a more painful life than when possessed of freedom in their own country, obtained the inestimable advantage of the knowledge of the true God, and of all the benefits attendant on civilization.

The benevolent feelings of the sovereigns of Spain did not, however, at any time permit their subjects to carry on this trade, but by special license; and in the years 1789, 1798, and on the 22d of April, 1804, certain limited periods were fixed for the importation of slaves. Although the last term had not expired when His Majesty our lord Don Ferdinand the Seventh was restored to the throne, of which a perfidious usurper had attempted to deprive him. His Majesty, on resuming the reins of Government, soon perceived that those remote countries had become a prey to civil feuds, and, in reflecting on the most effectual means of restoring order, and affording them all the encouragement of which they are susceptible,

His Majesty discovered that the numbers of the native and free negroes had prodigiously increased under the mild regimen of the Government, and the humane treatment of the Spanish slave owners; that the white population had also greatly increased; that the climate is not so noxious to them as it was before the lands were cleared; and, finally, that the advantages resulting to the inhabitants of Africa, in being transported to cultivated countries, are no longer so decided and exclusive, since England and the United States have engaged in the noble undertaking of civilizing them in their native country.

All these considerations combining with the desire entertained by His Majesty of co-operating with the Powers of Europe, in putting an end to this traffic, which, if indefinitely continued, might involve them all in the most serious evils, have determined His Majesty to conclude a treaty with the King of the United Kingdom of Great Britain and Ireland, by which the abolition of the slave trade is stipulated and agreed on, under certain regulations, and I have received his commands to deliver to the President a copy of the same, His Majesty feeling confident that a measure so completely in harmony with the sentiments of this Government, and of all the inhabitants of this Republic, cannot fail to be agreeable to him.

In the discharge of this satisfactory duty, I now transmit you the aforesaid copy of the treaty, which I request you will be pleased to lay before the President, and I have the honor to renew the assurances of my distinguished respect.

God preserve you many years.

LUIS DE ONIS.

Extract of a letter from Mr. Rush to the Secretary of State, dated Feb. 18, 1818.

" You will probably have perceived, by the proceedings in the House of Commons, that treaties have been formed between this Government and both Spain and Portugal, securing, as far as may be done by treaty, the final abolition, after a specified time, not very remote, of the slave trade. Thus, is a last hand to be put to the work of America, whose legislators led the way, with Europe against them, in this transcendant moral reform. But it is a triumph which as little the Courts as the public of Europe seem willing in any shape to acknowledge. The palm is claimed by others. America is even placed in fault. In his speech on the Spanish treaty, delivered in the House of Commons on the 8th instant, Lord Castlereagh observed, that it was in vain for Britain alone to shut the door of her colonies against the slave trade; for that, unless there was a concert of exclusion, the other islands of the West Indies, ' and the southern *provinces* of the United States,' would become the asylum and depot of it.' I gladly caught the opportunity of this accidental meeting [with Lord Castlereagh] to say what could not have been otherwise than acceptable to the zeal for abolition. I stated the nature of our laws. I said, I felt sure that he would hear from me with pleasure, that it was upwards of nine years since

the traffic had been abolished throughout the Union; and that so far had our acts of Congress carried the prohibition, that to import even a single slave into any of the States, had, during the same period, been denounced as an offence, and subjected to unusually rigorous penalties of fine and imprisonment. His Lordship admitted the prohibitions, but intimated fears lest we could not enforce them, alluding to the recent state of things at Amelia. In the end, he invited me to look into all their conventions with other Powers upon this subject, with a view to future conversation, adding that he was well disposed himself to a proper concert of action between our two Governments for the more effectual extirpation of the traffic.

"I shall look into the conventions accordingly, and wait the renewal of the topic. Whether policy would dictate any concert, is a point upon which, not being instructed, I will not presume to give any opinion. But I hope I do not misjudge in thinking that, for the present, I am merely bound to listen to, without seeking any further conversation. I will take care punctually to communicate, for the President's information, whatever may be said to me, in like manner as my duty devolves it upon me to transmit this first sentiment, so cursorily thrown out by Lord Castlereagh. It will be understood, that, in adverting to our municipal prohibitions, I intended no advance to the point of national co-operation. It was barely for the sake of an incidental and gratuitous vindication, after public remark, which, to say no more, was susceptible of unjust interpretation. On his allusion to Amelia Island, I reminded him that it was the very anxiety to prevent the illicit introduction of slaves that had formed a ruling motive with the President for breaking up, with the public force itself, the establishment at that place."

Extract of a letter from Mr. Rush to the Secretary of State.

APRIL 15, 1818.

"He (Lord Castlereagh) next spoke of the slave trade. The Government of Great Britain felt, he said, an increasing desire that the Government of the United States should lend itself to the measures of regulation going forward in Europe for its complete extirpation. These measures mean, in effect, a reciprocal submission to the right of search. He explained by saying, that only to a limited number of the armed vessels of each of the maritime States would a power to search be deputed, while the exercise of it would be strictly forbidden to all others. It was contemplated, he continued, to form, out of an association of these armed vessels, a species of naval police, to be stationed chiefly in the African seas, and from whose harmonious and co-operating efforts the best results were anticipated. He added, that no peculiar structure, or previous appearances in the vessel searched, no presence of irons, or other presumptions of criminal intention; nothing but the actual finding of slaves on board was ever to authorize a seizure or detention. He said that they had lately pressed France upon the subject, and that there was no doubt of her eventual agreement. The recent vote, in both her Chambers, on the broad principle of abolition, he regarded as a full pledge of her ulterior steps.

"I replied, that I was sure that the President would listen, with an ear the most liberal, to whatever distinct proposals were made, more especially as the United States had been long awake, as well to the moral guilt as to the political and social evils of the traffic, and had, as was known, aimed against it the denunciations of their own laws. The distinct propositions, his Lordship gave me reason to think, would be made known before long, through Mr. Bagot."

Extract of a letter from Mr. Rush to Mr. Adams, dated London, June 24, 1818.

"In two former despatches I have mentioned what Lord Castlereagh has said to me relative to the slave trade. In my interview with him on the eleventh of this month, he spoke of it in a manner more formal and definitive."

"He first alluded to the late treaties concluded between Great Britain and several of the Powers of Europe upon this subject. Entering into conversation upon their particular nature and provisions, he said, that the period had arrived when it was the wish of the British Government to invite the Government of the United States to join in the measures which Europe was so generally adopting, for the more perfect abolition of this traffic; and that it was now his design to submit, through me, proposals to this effect. It will be perceived by my despatch, No. 14, [April 15, 1818,] that, at that period, it had been contemplated to make them through the channel of the English mission at Washington. What may have led to a change in this respect, his Lordship did not state, nor did I deem it material to inquire.

"It had occurred to him, he said, to make the proposals by sending me, accompanied by an official note, entire copies of all the treaties in question. They would best unfold the grounds and principles upon which a concert of action had already been settled by the States that were parties to them, and it was his intention to ask the accession of the United States upon grounds and principles that were similar. He added, that he would willingly receive my suggestions as to any other course that might strike me as better adapted to the object. I replied, that none appeared to me more eligible, and that whenever he would enclose me the treaties, I would lose no time in transmitting them, for the consideration of the President."

"It naturally occurred to me, during our conversation, that the detached and distant situation of the United States, if not other causes, might call for a modification in some parts of these instruments, admitting that the broad principle of concert met approbation. His Lordship upon this point was full in assurances, that the British Government would be happy to listen to whatever modifications the Government of the United States might think fit to propose. Its anxious and

only desire, he said, was, to see a convention formed that would prove free from all objection, and be conducive to the single and grand object to which both sides looked. He ended by expressing the belief which was felt, that the maritime co-operation of the United States would usefully contribute to the advancement of this great work of humanity."

"Nothing further passed necessary to the full understanding of the overture, beyond what the documents themselves and his Lordship's note, are calculated to afford. To these I have, therefore, the honor to refer, as disclosing, in the most authentic and detailed manner, the whole views of the British Government upon this interesting subject."

Lord Castlereagh to Mr. Rush.

FOREIGN OFFICE, June 20, 1818.

SIR: The distinguished share which the Government of the United States has, from the earliest period, borne in advancing the cause of abolition, makes the British Government desirous of submitting to their favorable consideration whatever may appear to them calculated to bring about the final accomplishment of this great work of humanity.

The laudable anxiety with which you personally interest yourself in whatever is passing upon this important subject, will have led you to perceive that, with the exception of the Crown of Portugal, all European States have now either actually prohibited the traffic in slaves to their subjects, or fixed an early period for its cessation, whilst Portugal has also renounced it to the north of the equator. From May, 1820, there will not be a flag which *can legally* cover this detested traffic to the north of the line, and there is reason to hope that the Portugese may also, ere long, be prepared to abandon it to the south of the equator; but, so long as some effectual concert is not established amongst the principal maritime Powers, for preventing their respective flags from being made a covert for an illicit trade, there is too much reason to fear (whatever be the state of the law upon this subject) that the evil will continue to exist, and, in proportion as it assumes a contraband form, that it will be carried on under the most aggravating circumstances of cruelty and desolation.

It is from a deep conviction of this truth, founded upon experience, that the British Government, in all its negotiations upon this subject, has endeavored to combine a system of alliance for the suppression of this most abusive practice, with the engagements which it has succeeded in lately contracting with the Government of Spain and Portugal for the total or partial abolition of the slave trade. I have now the honor to enclose to you copies of the treaties which have been happily concluded with those Powers, together with the acts which have recently passed the Legislature, for carrying the same into execution.

I have also the satisfaction to transmit to you a copy of a treaty which has been recently concluded with the King of the Netherlands, for the like purpose, though at too late a period in the session to admit of its provisions receiving the sanction of Parliament. I am induced the more particularly to call your attention to this convention, as it contains provisions which are calculated to limit, in some respects, the power mutually conceded by the former treaties, in a manner which, without essentially weakening their force, renders them more acceptable to the contracting parties.

The intimate knowledge which you possess of this whole subject renders it unnecessary for me, in requesting you to bring those documents to the observation of your Government, to accompany them with any more detailed explanation. What I have earnestly to beg of you is, to bring them under the serious consideration of the President, intimating to him the strong wish of the British Government that the exertions of the two States may be combined upon a somewhat similar principle, in order to put down this great moral disobedience, wherever it may be committed, to the laws of both countries. I am confident this cannot effectually be done, except by mutually conceding to each other's ships of war a qualified right of search, with a power of detaining the vessels of either State, with slaves *actually on board.*

You will perceive in these conventions a studious, and, I trust, a successful attempt, to narrow and limit this power within the due bounds, and to guard it against perversion. If the American Government is disposed to enter into a similar concert, and can suggest any further regulations, the better to obviate abuse, this Government will be most ready to listen to any suggestion of this nature, their only object being to contribute, by every effort in their power, to put an end to this disgraceful traffic.

I have the honor to be, with great truth, sir, your most obedient humble servant,

CASTLEREAGH.

Mr. Rush to Lord Castlereagh.

LONDON, *June* 23, 1818.

MY LORD: I have been honored with your Lordship's note of the twentieth of this month, enclosing copies of treaties recently concluded between this Government and the Government of Portugal, Spain, and the Netherlands, respectively, in relation to the slave trade, and designed to draw the attention of the Government of the United States to this subject, with a view to its co-operation upon principles similar to those held out in these treaties, in measures that may tend to the more complete and universal abolition of the traffic.

The United States, from an early day of their history, have regarded with deep and uniform abhorrence the existence of a traffic attended by such complications of misery and guilt. Its trancendant evils roused, throughout all ranks, a corresponding zeal for their extirpation. One step followed another until humanity triumphed, and against its continuance, under any shape, by its own citizens, the most absolute prohibitions of their code have, for a period of more than ten years, been rigorously, and, it is hoped, beneficially

levelled. Your Lordship will pardon me this allusion to the earnest efforts of the United States to put down the traffic within their own limits, falling in, as it merely does, with the tribute which you have been pleased to pay to their early exertions in helping to dry up this prolific source of human woe.

Whether any causes may throw obstacles in the way of their uniting in that concert of external measures, in which Europe generally, and this nation in particular, are now so happily engaged, the more effectually to banish from the world this great enormity, I dare not, in the total absence of all instructions, presume to intimate, much less have I any opinion of my own to offer upon a subject so full of delicacy and interest. But it is still left to me to say, that I shall perform a duty peculiarly gratifying in transmitting, by the earliest opportunities, copies of your Lordship's note, with the documents which accompanied it, to my Government, and I sufficiently know the permanent sensibility which pervades all its councils upon this subject, to promise that the overture, which the former embraces, will receive, from the President, the full and anxious consideration due to its importance, and, above all, to the enlarged philanthropy on the part of this Government, by which it has been dictated.

I have the honor to be, with the highest consideration, your Lordship's obedient faithful servant,

RICHARD RUSH.

Extract of a letter from the Secretary of State to Messrs. Gallatin and Rush, dated Department of State, November 2, 1818.

"SLAVE TRADE.

"The President desires that you would make known to the British Government, his sensibility to the friendly spirit of confidence with which the treaties lately contracted by Great Britain with Spain, Portugal, and the Netherlands, and the legislative measures of Parliament, founded upon them, have been communicated to this Government, and the invitation to the United States to join in the same or similar arrangements has been given. He wishes you also to give the strongest assurances that the solicitude of the United States for the accomplishment of the common object, the total and final abolition of that odious traffic, continues with all the earnestness which has so long and so steadily distinguished the course of their policy in relation to it. As an evidence of this earnestness, he requests you to communicate to them a copy of the act of Congress of the last session, in addition to the act of 1807, to prohibit the importation of slaves into the United States, (Acts of the last session, chapter 86, page 81,) and to declare the readiness of this Government, within their Constitutional powers, to adopt any further measures, which experience may prove to be necessary, for the purpose of attaining so desirable an end.

"But you will observe that, in examining the provisions of the treaties communicated by Lord Castlereagh, all their essential articles appear to be of a character not adapted to the institutions or to the circumstances of the United States.

"The power agreed to be reciprocally given to the officers of the ships of war of either party to enter, search, capture, and carry into port for adjudication, the merchant vessels of the other, however qualified and restricted, is most essentially connected with the institution by each treaty of two mixed courts, one of which to reside in the external or colonial possessions of each of the two parties, respectively. This part of the system is indispensable to give it that character of reciprocity, without which, the right granted to the armed ships of one nation to search the merchant vessels of another, would be rather a mark of vassalage than of independence. But, to this part of the system, the United States, having no colonies, either on the coast of Africa or in the West Indies, cannot give effect.

"You will add that, by the Constitution of the United States, it is provided, the judicial power of the United States shall be vested in a Supreme Court, and in such inferior courts as the Congress may, from time to time, ordain and establish. It provides that the judges of these courts shall hold their offices during good behaviour; and that they shall be removable by impeachment and conviction of crimes or misdemeanors. There may be some doubt whether the power of the Government of the United States is competent to institute a court for the carrying into execution their penal statutes, beyond the territories of the United States, a court consisting partly of foreign judges, not amenable to impeachment for corruption, and deciding upon statutes of the United States without appeal.

"That the disposal of the negroes, found on board the slave-trading vessels, which might be condemned by the sentence of these mixed courts, cannot be carried into effect by the United States; for, if the slaves of a vessel condemned by the mixed court should be delivered over to the Government of the United States as freemen, they could not, but by their own consent, be employed as servants or free laborers. The condition of the blacks being, in this Union, regulated by the municipal laws of the separate States, the Government of the United States can neither guaranty their liberty in the States where they could only be received as slaves, nor control them in the States where they would be recognised as free.

"That the admission of a right in the officers of foreign ships of war to enter and search the vessels of the United States, in time of peace, under any circumstances whatever, would meet with universal repugnance in the public opinion of this country; that there would be no prospect of a ratification, by advice and consent of the Senate, to any stipulation of that nature; that the search by foreign officers, even in time of war, is so obnoxious to the feelings and recollections of this country, that nothing could reconcile them to the extension of it, however qualified or restricted, to a time of peace; and that it would be viewed in a still more aggravated light if, as in the treaty with the Netherlands, connected with a formal admis-

sion that even vessels under convoy of ships of war of their own nation, should be liable to search by the ships of war of another.

"You will therefore express the regret of the President that the stipulations in the treaty communicated by Lord Castlereagh, are of a character to which the peculiar situation and institutions of the United States do not permit them to accede. The Constitutional objection may be the more readily understood by the British Cabinet, if they are reminded that it was an obstacle proceeding from the same principle which prevented Great Britain from becoming, formally, a party to the Holy Alliance. Neither can they be at a loss to perceive the embarrassment under which we should be placed by receiving cargoes of African negroes, and be bound at once to guaranty their liberty, and to employ them as servants. Whether they will be as ready to enter into our feelings with regard to the search by foreign navy lieutenants, of vessels under convoy of our own navy commanders, is perhaps of no material importance. The other reasons are presumed to be amply sufficient to convince them that the motives for declining this overture, are compatible with an earnest wish that the measures concerted by these treaties may prove successful in extirpating that root of numberless evils, the traffic in human blood, and with the determination to co-operate to the utmost extent of our powers, in this great vindication of the sacred rights of humanity."

Copy of a letter from Mr. Rush to Lord Castlereagh, dated

LONDON, *December* 21, 1818.

The undersigned, Envoy Extraordinary and Minister Plenipotentiary from the United States, has the honor to present his compliments to Lord Castlereagh.

In the note of the twenty-third of June, which the undersigned had the honor to address to his Lordship, in answer to his Lordship's communication of the twentieth of the same month, relative to the slave trade, the undersigned had great pleasure in giving the assurance that he would transmit a copy of that communication to his Government, together with the documents which accompanied it, being copies of treaties entered into on the part of Great Britain, with Spain, Portugal, and the Netherlands, for the more complete abolition of the odious traffic in slaves. He accordingly lost no time in fulfilling that duty, and has now the honor to inform his Lordship of the instructions with which he has been furnished by his Government in reply.

He has been distinctly commanded, in the first place, to make known the sensibility of the President to the friendly spirit of confidence in which these treaties, and the legislative measures of Parliament founded upon them, have been communicated to the United States, and to the invitation which has been given that they would join in the same or similar arrangements, the more effectually to accomplish the beneficent object to which they look. He is further commanded to give the strongest assurances that the solicitude of the United States for the universal extirpation of this traffic continues with all the earnestness which so long and steadily distinguished the course of their policy in relation to it. Of their general prohibitory law of 1807, it is unnecessary that the undersigned should speak, his Lordship being already apprized of its provisions; among which the authority to employ the national force, as auxiliary to its execution, will not have escaped attention. But he has it in charge to make known, as a new pledge of their unremitting and active desire in the cause of abolition, that, so lately as the month of April last, another act of Congress was passed, by which, not only are the citizens and vessels of the United States interdicted from carrying on, or being in any way engaged in, the trade, but in which, also, the best precautions that legislative enactments can devise, or their penalties enforce, are raised up against the introduction into their territories of slaves from abroad, under whatever pretext attempted, and especially from dominions which lie more immediately in their neighborhood. A copy of this act is herewith enclosed for the more particular information of his Lordship. That peculiarity in the eighth section which throws upon a defendant the labor of proof as the condition of acquittal, the undersigned persuades himself will be regarded as signally manifesting an anxiety to suppress the hateful offence, departing as it does from the analogy of criminal jurisprudence which so generally requires the independent and positive establishment of guilt as the first step in every public prosecution. To measures of such a character, thus early adopted and sedulously pursued, the undersigned is further commanded to say, that the Government of the United States, acting within the pale of its Constitutional powers, will always be ready to superadd any others that experience may prove to be necessary for attaining the desirable end in view.

But, on examining the provisions of the treaties, which your Lordship honored the undersigned by communicating, it has appeared to the President that their essential articles are of a character not adapted to the circumstances or to the institutions of the United States.

The powers agreed to be given to the ships of war of either party to search, capture, and carry into port for adjudication, the merchant vessels of the other, however qualified, is connected with the establishment, by each treaty, of two mixed courts; one of which is to have its seat in the colonial possessions of the parties respectively. The institution of such tribunals is necessarily regarded as fundamental to the whole arrangement, whilst their peculiar structure is doubtless intended, and would seem to be indispensable, towards imparting to it a just reciprocity. But to this part of the system, the United States, having no colonies upon the coast of Africa, in the West Indies, or elsewhere, cannot give effect.

Moreover, the powers of government in the United States, whilst they can only be exercised within the grants, are also subject to the restrictions of the Federal Constitution. By the latter instru-

ment, all judicial power is to be vested in a Supreme Court, and in such other inferior courts as Congress may from time to time ordain and establish. It further provides, that the judges of these courts shall hold their offices during good behaviour, and be removable on impeachment and conviction of crimes and misdemeanors. There are serious doubts whether, obeying the spirit of these injunctions, the Government of the United States would be competent to appear as party to the institution of a court for carrying into execution their penal statutes in places out of their own territory—a court consisting partly of foreign judges not liable to impeachment under the authority of the United States, and deciding upon their statutes without appeal.

Again : Obstacles would exist towards giving validity to the disposal of the negroes found on board the slave-trading vessels, condemned by the sentence of the mixed courts. If they should be delivered over to the Government of the United States as freemen, they could not, but by their own consent, be employed as servants or free laborers. The condition of negroes and other people of color in the United States being regulated by the municipal laws of the separate States, the Government of the former could neither guaranty their liberty in the States, where they could only be received as slaves, nor control them in the States where they would be recognised as free. The provisions of the fifth section of the act of Congress, which the undersigned has the honor to enclose, will be seen to point to this obstacle, and may be taken as still further explanatory of its nature.

These are some of the principal reasons which arrest the assent of the President to the very frank and friendly overture contained in your Lordship's communication. Having their foundation in Constitutional impediments, the Government of His Britannic Majesty will know how to appreciate their force. It will be seen how compatible they are with the most earnest wishes on the part of the United States that the measures concerted by these treaties may bring about the total downfall of the traffic in human blood; and with their determination to co-operate, to the utmost extent of their Constitutional power, towards this great consummation so imperiously due at the hands of all nations to the past wrongs and sufferings of Africa.

The undersigned prays Lord Castlereagh to accept the assurances of his distinguished consideration.

RICHARD RUSH.

Mr. Rush to the Secretary of State—Extract.

LONDON, *March* 5, 1819.

"Lord Castlereagh sent me, a few days ago, the enclosed printed parliamentary document. It will be found to comprise a variety of interesting papers relating to the slave trade, exhibiting all that has lately been done by the Powers of Europe upon the subject, and the actual and precise footing upon which it now stands. Its receipt was the first notice that I had in any shape of the fact of the publication, or of there being any intention to publish my notes to this Government of the 23d of June and 21st of December. It will be seen, from one of the papers, how unequivocal and animated has been the refusal of France to allow her vessels to be boarded and searched at sea for slaves. Now, there is nothing more evident, as may be collected from my despatch of the 15th of last April, than that this is a result which, at that period, Lord Castlereagh did not anticipate. Nevertheless, it would seem, from a passage in his Lordship's letter to Lord Bathurst, from Paris, dated the 10th of December, the last paper in the collection, and written subsequently to all the conferences and declarations at Aix la Chapelle, that he still indulges a sanguine expectation that 'the French Government may be brought, at no distant period, to unite their naval exertions with those of the other allied Powers, for the suppression of the trade.' Some of the evidence furnished by the African Society, in London, and from Sierra Leone, as to the extent in which the trade continues to be unlawfully carried on, may probably command attention in the United States.

"What communications may, at any former periods, have been made to the Government of the United States, by the Government of France, Russia, or Prussia, through any channel, either in Europe or at Washington, of their intentions in regard to this naval combination for putting down the traffic, I am not informed. It is impossible to refrain from remarking, that, to me, they remained utterly unknown, until I saw them recorded in these pages of a document given to the world by England."

Extract of a letter from Mr. Rush to the Secretary of State, dated London, November 10, 1819.

"On the 7th of this month I received a note from Lord Castlereagh, requesting that I would call upon him at his house on the 9th. I waited upon him at the time appointed.

"His object, he stated, was to say to me, that the Government of Great Britain had lost none of its anxiety to see produced among nations, more universal and effective co-operation than had yet been witnessed, for the total abolition of the slave trade. It was still carried on, he observed, to an extent that was afflicting. In some respects, as the evidence collected by the African Institution and from other sources would show, the voyages were marked by more than all their original outrages upon humanity. It was the intention of the Prince Regent again to invite the United States to negotiate upon the subject, in the hope, notwithstanding what had heretofore passed, that some practicable mode might still be adopted by which they could consent to become party to the association for finally extirpating the traffic. That I was aware of the addresses which had been presented to his Royal Highness by both Houses of Parliament, at the close of the last session, for the renewal of negotiations with the Governments both of the United States and France, to effectuate this

most desirable end. That it was his Lordship's design to enclose to me, at an early day, copies of these addresses, as a foundation upon which to build in the new endeavor which this Government was now prepared to make. In doing so, his object, however, merely would be, that of bespeaking my interposition towards making known to the President the measures contemplated; since it was intended that all further negotiation should be carried on at Washington. This he thought indispensable after the past failure, as it could not be supposed that I was prepared with any new authority or instructions to resume it upon this side of the water. That the new Minister, Mr. Canning, who, his Lordship now informed me, was to sail as early in the Spring as practicable, would accordingly have the whole subject in charge, and be prepared to enter upon it on his arrival, under ardent hopes for an auspicious termination of his labors. I replied that I would, in the same spirit as before, make known the communication to my Government. I adverted again to the obstacles which the Constitution of the United States interposed to the project; and also to the peculiar and extreme caution with which the momentous question of search mingled with it would be looked at throughout every part of the country. I said that these reasons superadded themselves to that derived from the failure of the attempt already made here to give great propriety, as it struck me, to a change of the scene of negotiation. That if any thing could be done, it could be done only, or at all events be done best, at Washington. That the President, I was sure, continued to possess all his original sensibility to the importance of the subject, and would entertain any proposals, differently modified, that were submitted, with the same anxious dispositions as ever, for a favorable result to their objects.

"The conversation went off by reference on my part to the Holy League. I remarked that, as the Government of Great Britain had declared, that the principles of that league had its entire approbation, although it had not formally become a party to it, so the United States, acting within their Constitutional limits, had long and earnestly striven, and would, it might be confidently affirmed, though restrained from going hand in hand with Europe, always continue their efforts in the same beneficent spirit, for putting down totally the slave trade. It is well known that the Earl of Liverpool, not longer ago than last February, described, in the House of Peers, the character of this league, as well as the insurmountable impediment which held back this country from signing it. He distinctly declared that, as the signatures were all in the autograph of the respective sovereigns, England, in point of form, could never accede to it; for it was not consistent with her constitution that the Prince Regent should himself sign such an instrument, without the intervention of a responsible Minister. Upon my reminding Lord Castlereagh of this declaration, which I was the more ready to do so since it was your wish that the illustration should be brought into view, he candidly admitted that we too doubtless had our Constitutional embarrassments; but he nevertheless hoped that such, and all others, might, by proper modifications of the plan, be overcome."

Mr. Canning to the Secretary of State.
WASHINGTON, *Dec.* 20, 1819.

The undersigned, His Britannic Majesty's Envoy Extraordinary and Minister Plenipotentiary, took an early opportunity, after his arrival in the City of Washington, to inform Mr. Adams that, in pursuance of Lord Castlereagh's note, dated the 11th November, 1819, communicating to Mr. Rush an address of both Houses of Parliament, relating to the African slave trade, he was instructed to bring that important question again under the consideration of the American Government, in the hope of being found practicable so to combine the preventive measures of the two countries as materially to accelerate the total extinction of an evil, which both have long united in condemning and opposing.

Mr. Adams will find no difficulty in recollecting the several conversations which have passed between him and the undersigned on this subject; he will remember that the last of those conversations, which took place towards the close of October, was terminated with an assurance on his part, that the proposals of the English Government would be taken into full deliberation as soon after the meeting of Congress as the state of public business would allow, with a sincere disposition to remove any impediments which appeared at first sight to stand in the way of their acceptance.

An interval of considerable length having elapsed since that period, the undersigned is persuaded that Mr. Adams will shortly be at liberty to communicate the definitive sentiments of his Government on a subject which is of too deep and too general an importance not to engage the attention and benevolent feelings of the United States.

In this persuasion, the undersigned conceives it unnecessary, on the present occasion, to go over the various grounds which formed the matter of his late conversations with Mr. Adams.

Notwithstanding all that has been done on both sides of the Atlantic for the suppression of the African slave trade, it is notorious that an illicit commerce, attended with aggravated sufferings to its unhappy victims, is still carried on; and it is generally acknowledged that a combined system of maritime police can alone afford the means of putting it down with effect.

That concurrence of principle in the condemnation and prohibition of the slave trade, which has so honorably distinguished the Parliament of Great Britain and the Congress of the United States, seems naturally and unavoidably to lead to a concert of measures between the two Governments, the moment that such co-operation is recognised as necessary for the accomplishment of their mutual purpose. It cannot be anticipated that either of the parties, discouraged by such difficulties as are inseparable from all human transactions of any magnitude, will be contented to acquiesce in the continuance of a practice so flagrantly immoral; especially at the present favorable period, when the slave trade is completely abolished to the north of the equator, and countenanced by Portugal alone to the south of that line.

Mr. Adams is fully acquainted with the particular measures recommended by His Majesty's Ministers as best calculated, in their opinion, to attain the object which both parties have in view; but he need not be reminded that the English Government is too sincere in the pursuit of that common object, to press the adoption of its own proposals, however satisfactory in themselves, to the exclusion of any suggestions equally conducive to the same end, and more agreeable to the institutions or prevailing opinion of other nations.

The undersigned embraces this opportunity to offer Mr. Adams the assurance of his high consideration.

STRATFORD CANNING.

The Secretary of State to Mr. Canning.
DEPARTMENT OF STATE,
Washington, Dec. 30, 1820.

SIR: I have had the honor of receiving your note of the 20th instant, in reply to which, I am directed by the President of the United States to inform you that, conformably to the assurances given you in the conversation to which you refer, the proposals made by your Government to the United States, inviting their accession to the arrangements contained in certain treaties with Spain, Portugal, and the Netherlands, to which Great Britain is the reciprocal contracting party, have again been taken into the most serious deliberation of the President, with an anxious desire of contributing, to the utmost extent of the powers within the competency of this Government, and by means compatible with its duties to the rights of its own citizens, and with the principles of its national independence, to the effectual and final suppression of the African slave trade.

At an earlier period of the communications between the two Governments upon this subject, the President, in manifesting his sensibility to the amicable spirit of confidence with which the measures, concerted between Great Britain and some of her European allies, had been made known to the United States, and to the free and candid offer of admitting the United States to a participation in these measures, had instructed the Minister of the United States residing near your Government to represent the difficulties, resulting as well from certain principles of international law, of the deepest and most painful interest to these United States, as from limitations of authority prescribed by the people of the United States to the legislative and executive depositaries of the national power, which placed him under the necessity of declining the proposal. It had been stated that a compact, giving the power to the naval officers of one nation to search the merchant vessels of another for offenders and offences against the laws of the latter,

Execution of the Treaty of Ghent.

backed by a further power to seize and carry into a foreign port, and there subject to the decision of a tribunal composed of at least one-half foreigners, irresponsible to the supreme corrective tribunal of this Union, and not amenable to the control of impeachment for official misdemeanor, was an investment of power over the persons, property, and reputation, of the citizens of this country, not only unwarranted by any delegation of sovereign power to the National Government, but so adverse to the elementary prnc ples and indispensable securities of individual rights, interwoven in all the political institutions of this country, that not even the most unqualified approbation of the ends to which this organization of authority was adapted, nor the most sincere and earnest wish to concur in every suitable expedient for their accomplishment, could reconcile it to the sentiments or the principles, of which, in the estimation of the people and Government of the United States, no consideration whatsoever could justify the transgression.

In the several conferences which, since your arrival here, I have had the honor of holding with you, and in which this subject has been fully and freely discussed between us, the incompetency of the power of this Government to become a party to the institution of tribunals organized like those stipulated in the conventions above noticed, and the incompatibility of such tribunals with the essential character of the Constitutional rights guarantied to every citizen of the Union, has been shown by direct references to the fundamental principles of our Government, in which the supreme, unlimited, sovereign power is considered as inherent in the whole body of its people, while its delegations are limited and restricted by the terms of the instruments sanctioned by them, under which the powers of legislation, judgment, and execution, are administered; and by special indications of the articles in the Constitution of the United States, which expressly prohibit their constituted authorities from erecting any judicial courts, by the forms of process belonging to which American citizens should be called to answer for any penal offence, without the intervention of a grand jury to accuse, and of a jury of trial to decide upon the charge.

But, while regretting that the character of the organized means of co-operation for the suppression of the African slave trade, proposed by Great Britain, did not admit of our concurrence in the adoption of them, the President has been far from the disposition to reject or discountenance the general proposition of concerted co-operation with Great Britain to the accomplishment of the common end—the suppression of the trade. For this purpose, armed cruisers of the United States have been for some time kept stationed on the coast which is the scene of this odious traffic—a measure which it is in the contemplation of this Government to continue without intermission. As there are armed British vessels, charged with the same duty, constantly kept cruising on the same coast, I am directed by the President to propose that instructions, to be concerted between the two Governments, with a view to mutual assistance, should

be given to the commanders of the vessels respectively assigned to that service; that they may be ordered, whenever the occasion may render it convenient, to cruise in company together, to communicate mutually to each other all information obtained by the one, and which may be useful to the execution of the duties of the other, and to give each other every assistance which may be compatible with the performance of their own service and adapted to the end which is the common aim of both parties.

These measures, congenial to the spirit which has so long and so steadily marked the policy of the United States, in the vindication of the rights of humanity, will, it is hoped, prove effectual to the purposes for which this co-operation is desired by your Government, and to which this Union will continue to direct its most strenuous and persevering exertions.

I pray you, sir, to accept the assurance of my distinguished consideration.

JOHN QUINCY ADAMS.

Rt. Hon. STRATFORD CANNING,
Envoy Extraordinary, &c.

EXECUTION OF THE TREATY OF GHENT.

—

[Reported to the House, February 3, 1821.]

The select committee, to whom was referred the Message of the President of the United States respecting the progress and expenditures of the commissioners under the fifth, sixth, and seventh articles of the Treaty of Ghent, respectfully submit the following report:

The fifth article of the Treaty of Ghent provides for ascertaining the boundary from the source of the St. Croix to the northwest corner of Nova Scotia, and also from that corner, westwardly, between the United States and Canada, until the line strikes the Iroquois, now called the St Lawrence, in latitude forty-five degrees north.

Mr. Van Ness is the commissioner of the United States for this section of the boundary line.

The sixth article of the Treaty of Ghent provides for ascertaining the boundary line, westwardly, from the above mentioned point on the St. Lawrence, through Lakes Ontario, Erie, and Huron, and their water communications to Lake Superior.

Mr. Porter, of New York, is the commissioner on the part of the United States assigned to this section.

By the seventh article of that treaty, it is stipulated that when the commissioners appointed under the sixth article shall have performed the duties required by that article, then they are authorized to determine the boundary line from the water communication between Lakes Huron and Superior to the northwest corner of the Lake of the Woods; the whole boundary to be established agreeably to the provisions of the treaty of 1783.

Mr. Porter will, of course, become the American commissioner; when he shall have finished the duties required by the sixth article of the Treaty of Ghent.

By their resolution of the 21st of November last, the House requested the President of the United States to lay before them information respecting the progress made by the commissioners in establishing the boundary above mentioned, and the expenses already incurred. With his message of the 14th December last, the President transmitted a report of the Secretary of State, containing all the information in the possession of that Department requested by that resolution.

So far as relates to the boundary from the head of the St. Croix to the St. Lawrence, it seems that no information had been afforded to the Government at the date of the President's Message. Mr. Van Ness, in his letter of the 25th of November last, observes, "with respect to the progress which has been made by the commission, I understand the agent has already given to the Government all the information which it would be in my power to communicate." He also mentions that "the commissioners under the fifth article of the treaty have held two sessions the present year;" but there is no disclosure of past exertions or future prospects in the discharge of the duties assigned to him.

Since that time, the committee have been furnished with a communication from Mr. Van Ness, (marked No. 18 in the manuscript documents attending this report,) dated January 6, 1821, in which he observes that the next meeting is to be held on the 14th May, and that the commissioners intend at that meeting to continue in session until they have decided upon all questions submitted to them by the treaty. To this letter the committee would call the attention of the House, as containing much information of the progress which the commissioners under the fifth article have made. No satisfactory reason, however, is assigned why earlier information has not been given to the Government. The committee have not seen any occasion for secrecy on the part of the commissioners. They were appointed to ascertain certain facts which were supposed to exist. A disclosure of their proceedings would neither change the position of the northwest corner of Nova Scotia, nor alter the forty-fifth degree of north latitude.

The information of the progress of the commissioners under the sixth article of the Treaty of Ghent is found in the letters of Mr. Delafield, dated October 13th and November 1st, and in one from Mr. Porter, of December 2d, 1820, which are among the printed documents. These gentlemen express a belief that the surveys under the last mentioned article will be completed during the next season. But it appears that no part of the boundary is finally settled. Whether it will be done next season, must depend on the termination of the surveys and the agreement of the commissioners. Any event which should prevent the agent or commissioner on either side from attending to his duties would probably delay a decision for another year; and should the calculations of the American commissioner and agent prove correct, they will

have devoted about six years to the performance of this part of their duty.

After this they will be ready to turn their attention to the boundary from the water communication between Huron and Superior to the northwest corner of the Lake of the Woods, according to the seventh article of the treaty.

It is observed in the letter of Mr. Porter, above referred to, that "the seventh article of the treaty relates to a country which is comparatively of little importance, and a system of operations is proposed to be adopted for designating the boundary, which will greatly reduce both the time and expense of its execution." What this system of operations may be is not disclosed. It is presumed, however, to be such a system as will not endanger the rights of the nation, while it is a subject of regret that it had not been sooner applied.

From an examination of the printed documents, it appears that the sum of $194,137 63 has been drawn from the Treasury on account of the two commissions under the treaty which have been mentioned.

Mr. Van Ness, as commissioner under
the fifth article, has received - -	$82,444 00
Mr. Bradley, as agent - - -	16,655 10
	$99,099 10

Of this sum, $25,676 13 has been expended by the agent, and the accounts adjusted by the American and British commissioners; but the statements afforded are in such general terms that explanation is required to determine how far they could be approved by this Government. The remainder of the sum drawn under the fifth article remains without evidence of its disbursement, except what may be retained for the commissioner's salary.

Mr. Porter, the commissioner under the sixth and seventh articles of the treaty, has drawn from the Treasury $65,315 95. No part has been accounted for. He has transmitted statements of expenditures to the amount of $47,263 09, exclusive of his salary. He informs the Secretary of State that "the vouchers will be transmitted to Washington on the closing of the sixth article."

Mr. Hawkins, the late agent under
the sixth and seventh articles, has drawn from the Treasury - -	$28,891 80
Received from Mr. Parker - -	1,815 95
Amounting to the sum of -	30,707 75
Statements of expenditures, which yet are not adjusted, are furnished, including salary while employed, amounting to - - -	18,548 97
Balance against Mr. Hawkins	$12,158 78

It has not been explained to the committee why the persons employed under the treaty have not accounted for the moneys which have been drawn from the Treasury. The nation is as deeply interested in the proper application of its funds expended under a treaty as under any other law. It is important, also, that the Government should have a knowledge of past expenditures, that it may properly provide for future wants.

Agreeably to the resolution of the House of January 3, the committee have considered the expediency of fixing, by law, the salaries of the commissioners and agents under the Treaty of Ghent.

In order to come to a conclusion on the subject of that resolution, recurrence must be had to the provisions of that treaty. By the eighth article it is stipulated " that the said commissioners shall, respectively, be paid in such manner as shall be agreed between the contracting parties, such agreement being to be settled at the time of the exchange of the ratifications of this treaty ; and all other expenses attending the said commission shall be defrayed equally by the two parties. It is clear that the treaty does not fix the amount of compensation which those officers are to receive. It declares that the commissioners shall be paid in such manner as shall be agreed upon by the contracting parties. The contracting parties must be understood to be the Governments of the United States and Great Britain. If this opinion of the committee be correct, it would seem to require an exercise of the same power, on the part of this Government at least, to agree upon the manner in which the commissioners should be paid, as was required to form the treaty itself.

The committee requested the Secretary of State to inform them whether any agreement had been made between the two Governments at the time of the ratification of the treaty, or since, as to the salaries of the commissioners, and whether any communication had taken place between the two Governments on the subject of that or any other expense attending the commission.

The answer to these and other inquiries, deemed material by the committee, is contained in the manuscript documents attending this report. No. 8, to which the committee would call the attention of this House, is a paper signed by Mr. Baker, containing the evidence of an exchange of the ratifications of the treaty. This paper contains the following expressions, viz : "At the same time Mr. Monroe (acting Secretary of State) expressed the willingness of the Government of the United States to arrange the payment of the commissioners to be appointed in pursuance of the treaty on the same principles as was observed in carrying into execution the treaty of 1794 between the same Powers, that is, the expense to be equally borne by the two Governments ; to which arrangement the undersigned consented."

This is the only document relating to this subject which the committee have received. It appears, therefore, to the committee, that the two contracting parties have not settled the salaries nor amount of compensation which the commissioners or agents shall receive for their respective services.

It would seem, therefore, that each Government was at liberty to make such allowance to those of its own officers as should be equitable and just.

By the letter of the Secretary of State (No. 1 of the manuscript documents) the House will be fully informed what compensation has been allowed heretofore by the Executive Government to the commissioners and agents. That letter contains a full explanation of the principles by which the Executive has been governed in regulating such compensation.

Congress having made general appropriations for carrying into execution the provisions of the Treaty of Ghent, without designating the amount for any particular service, the expenditure was left, in a great measure, to the discretion of the Executive. Such salaries were then authorized as had been allowed under the treaty of 1794 for similar services, which had received the approbation of Congress. But, as this Government is under no obligation, by any provisions of the treaty, to allow any definite compensation to those officers, they cannot derive their present salaries from any higher authority than a law of Congress. It is considered by the committee that Congress has the same power to increase or diminish any future allowances in this as in ordinary cases, where salaries are regulated by its laws.

The salaries of the commissioners under the treaty of 1794 were a subject of negotiation. The arrangements then made are referred to, as has been noticed, as principles for the execution of the Treaty of Ghent in this particular point, after having received the sanction of Congress.

Mr. Van Ness, in his letter of the 25th November, (contained among the printed papers,) observes that the British commissioners receive £1,200 sterling ; and he considers it is in accordance with the treaty that the American commissioners should receive the same salary, as they are the joint officers of the two Governments.

The committee consider the opinion of Lord Grenville is correct, as expressed in No. 3 of the manuscript papers. He observed to our Minister, when in the discussion of this point, that " the clause in the treaty of 1794 did not imply that the payment of all the commissioners should be the same." It is considered that equality of salaries in this case is no more necessary than that American and British Ministers should receive an equal compensation. The same may be said of the agents. This is the opinion of one of the American commissioners, Mr. Porter. In his letter of December 2d, (among the printed documents,) with great propriety he observes, in relation to the compensation of Mr. Delafield, the acting agent under the sixth and seventh articles of the treaty, that " I believe the board of which I am a member has heretofore considered that neither considerations of justice nor national etiquette required that the compensation of the two agents should be the same."

It is observed in the statements of expenditures exhibited by Mr. Porter and Mr. Hawkins that charges are made for personal expenses, exclusive of their salaries. By recurring to the laws which have been mentioned by the Secretary of State, and considered by him as the basis of present allowances, it is provided that the compensation of commissioners who shall serve in the United States shall not exceed the rate of $4,444 per annum. It would seem as just that the judges of the Supreme Court, or the officers of the Departments of Government, should charge their personal expenses while discharging their respective duties, as that this privilege should be allowed to commissioners and agents.

Nos. 9 and 15 of the manuscript documents contain the sentiments of the Executive respecting the expense and dilatory progress of the several commissions. No. 11 expresses the feeling of the British Government on the same subject. It is believed that these papers speak the language of this nation, while they afford satisfactory evidence that the Executive has exerted all the power he possesses in urging forward a prompt and faithful execution of the treaty.

The committee, however, are of opinion that, had particular instructions, as far as practicable, been issued to the commissioners and agents respecting the proper objects and amount of expenditure, and required a frequent adjustment of their accounts, their proceedings would have been rendered less expensive.

It is considered that the salaries now allowed are far greater, in proportion to the services performed, than those which are usually given to any officers of Government; that they are subject to the authority and control of Congress, and ought to be reduced.

It is also considered that the commissioners and agents should be required to render an account for the public moneys they may have received without delay; and while they were allowed, as a salary, the sum of $4,444, it should be in full of all personal expenses.

For these purposes the committee ask leave to report a bill.

Mr. Van Ness to the Secretary of State. (No. 18.)

BURLINGTON, *January* 6, 1821.

SIR: Having just received a copy of the Message of the President of the United States to the House of Representatives, on the subject of the boundary lines to be settled under the Treaty of Ghent, and finding nothing in it that relates to the progress made by the commission under the fifth article of the treaty, I feel it my duty to trouble you with a further communication.

In the letter which I had the honor to address to you from New York on the 25th November last, I said nothing on that point, because, as I stated therein, I understood the agent had already given to the Government all the information which it would be in my power communicate. That such was the fact, and that you had been pleased to express yourself entirely satisfied with the course pursued by the officers appointed on the part of the United States, as also had the President, was stated to me by the agent in November last, after a visit made to Washington for the express purpose of giving information and making explanations in relation to the proceedings of the commission.

I had, therefore, no reason to doubt that the President was in possession of sufficient information to state to the House of Representatives the progress which had been made in the execution of the fifth article of the treaty. But, it now appearing that the President could not have so considered it, I hasten to inform you that all the surveys and explorations relating to the northwest angle of Nova Scotia, as designated in the treaty of 1783, and to the northwesternmost head of Connecticut river, which are essential to the discussion and decision of those two contested and important points, and the observations on the parallel of latitude between Connecticut river and the Iroquois river, which are necessary to a determination of that line, have been completed.

The obstacles to be encountered in making these surveys have been great and numerous. The whole extent of country from the source of the river St. Croix, north to the river St. Lawrence, and between that line and the head of Connecticut river, is one vast and entire wilderness, inhabited by no human being, except a few savages, and, in one spot, a few Frenchmen. The services performed have been extremely arduous, and the difficulty and expense of transportation, and of subsisting the persons engaged in the work, have necessarily been very considerable.

That a knowledge of the different ranges of high lands, and of the sources and destination of the principal streams of water in the tract of country alluded to, derived from actual and proper observations and surveys, is indispensable to a just execution of the fifth article of the treaty, will not, I think, be questioned; particularly as the claims of the respective parties are much at variance, and in view of a poss l t that the case may be ultimately referred to a foreign Power.

All the reports and plans of the last season's work will soon be completed and delivered to the agents, so as to enable them to be prepared to submit their arguments to the board at its next meeting on the 14th day of May next—a period as early as it is practicable for the agent of His Britannic Majesty to come from St. John's, in New Brunswick, the place of his residence, to New York, the place of meeting. The commissioners intend at that meeting to continue in session until they shall have decided upon all questions submitted to them by the treaty. If they agree, there will only remain some running and marking of lines at a very diminished expense. But, if they should differ in their opinions, they will make separate reports, and the commission will be at an end in that way.

As to the contingent expenses, it may be remarked that they have thus far been enhanced in consequence of the performance of two distinct services at the same time—the surveys to the eastward of Connecticut river, and the astronomical operations on the parallel of latitude. But by this there will, in the end, be a saving, as, in hastening the completion of the whole business, the salary offices will the sooner expire.

I cannot close this letter without an expression of my confidence that it will not escape the observation of any person that, in a case like this, many things may not be fully understood and approved by those not immediately acquainted with all the proceedings of the commission, which, if the indi-

Spain—Ratification of the Treaty of 1819.

viduals concerned were on the spot, might be susceptible of explanations perfectly satisfactory, but which cannot be anticipated by those individuals.

I rely upon your kindness, sir, to transmit to the honorable the House of Representatives of the United States a copy of this communication as soon after its receipt as shall be convenient.

I have, &c.   C. P. VAN NESS.

The Hon. JOHN Q. ADAMS,
        Secretary of State.

SPAIN—TREATY OF 1819.

—

[Communicated to the Senate, February 14, 1821.]
WASHINGTON, *February* 13, 1821.

To the Senate of the United States :

The ratification by the Spanish Government of the Treaty of Amity, Settlement, and Limits, between the United States and Spain, signed on the 22d of February, 1819, and on the 24th of that month ratified on the part of the United States, has been received by the Envoy Extraordinary and Minister Plenipotentiary of that Power at this place, who has given notice that he is ready to exchange the ratifications.

By the sixteenth article of that treaty, it was stipulated that the ratifications should be exchanged within six months from the day of its signature ; which time having elapsed before the ratification of Spain was given, a copy and translation thereof are now transmitted to the Senate for their advice and consent, to receive it in exchange for the ratification of the United States, heretofore executed.

The treaty was submitted to the consideration of the Cortes of that kingdom before its ratification, which was finally given with their assent and sanction. The correspondence between the Spanish Minister of Foreign Affairs and the Minister of the United States at Madrid, on that occasion, is also herewith communicated to the Senate ;* together with a memorandum by the Secretary of State of his conference with the Spanish Envoy here, yesterday, when that Minister gave notice of readiness to exchange the ratifications.

The return of the original papers now transmitted, to avoid the delay necessary to the making of copies, is requested.   J. MONROE.

General instructions to Mr. Forsyth, Minister Plenipotentiary to Spain.

DEPARTMENT OF STATE,
        Washington, March 8, 1819.

SIR : The Treaty of Amity, Settlement, and Limits between the United States and Spain, con-

---

* These papers having been returned to the Department, the correspondence relating to this transaction, inserted in this compilation, has been collected from the communications made to Congress on the 7th December, 1819, March 9th, 14th, and 27th, 1820, May 9th and 12th, 1820, and February 2d, 1824.

---

cluded on the 22d ultimo, and ratified on the part of the United States, having provided for the adjustment of all important subjects of difference between the two nations, the first object of your mission will be to obtain the ratification of the Spanish Government, and receive it in exchange for ours, the authentic instrument of which is committed to your charge. The United States ship Hornet, Captain Read, is in readiness at Boston, and orders have been despatched, under which you will take passage in her for Cadiz. It is desirable that you should embark without delay. On your arrival in Spain, the Hornet will remain at Cadiz, subject to your orders, until the exchange of the ratifications can be effected ; and if, as is anticipated, no obstacle should intervene to delay that transaction, you will, upon receiving the Spanish ratified copy, immediately forward it to Captain Read, with directions to bring it immediately to the United States. As the ulterior destination of the Hornet will be the Gulf of Mexico, the port to which it will be advisable for him to come will be New York.

On exchanging the ratifications, certificates of the fact will be mutually executed and delivered by you and the Spanish Minister with whom you will make the exchange. Copies of that which passed in both languages on the exchange of the ratifications of the convention of the 11th of August, 1802, are now furnished you, and will serve as forms to be used in the performance of this ceremony. On this occasion, as upon all others upon which you may have occasion to execute any document, joint or reciprocal, with a foreign Minister of State, you will be careful to preserve the right of the United States to the *alternative* of being first named, and your own right, as their representative, to sign first in the papers executed ; while, in the counterparts, the other contracting party will be named first, and the foreign Minister will first sign and seal. A rigid adherence to this practice has become necessary, because it is strictly adhered to by all the European sovereigns in their compacts with one another ; and because the United States having heretofore sometimes forborne to claim this conventional indication of equal dignity, some appearance of a disposition to allege the precedent against them, as affecting their right to it, was manifested by the British Plenipotentiaries on executing the convention of 3d July, 1815, and by Mr. De Onis at the drawing up and signing of this treaty. The scruple was, however, in both cases abandoned, and the right of the United States to the alternative was conceded. It is not expected that it will hereafter be questioned, and you will consider it as a standing instruction to abide by it in the execution of any instrument of compact which, as a public Minister of the United States, you may be called to sign.

After the exchange of the ratifications, your attention will be directed to the object of carrying the provisions of the treaty into effect. The orders for the evacuation by the Spanish officers and troops of the places occupied by them in the Floridas will no doubt be immediately issued ; and, as the transports and escort for conveying them to the Havana are to be furnished by the United States, it is hoped you will obtain copies of the orders, and transmit them here with the ratification of the treaty. You will think it advisable to keep the Spanish Government reminded of the necessity to include, in the orders for the delivery of possession, that of all the archives and documents relating to the dominion and sovereignty. The appointment of a commissioner and surveyor for running the line of the western boundary must also be kept in remembrance, and notice given to us as soon as possible after their appointment. You will collect from the archives of the legation at Madrid all the documents relating to the claims of citizens of the United States upon the Spanish Government, which have been deposited there, and which come within the description of claims to be exhibited to the commissioners under the eleventh article of the treaty. You will send all these documents, together with the ratified treaty, to this department, retaining descriptive lists of them, and, if necessary, copies of such papers for which no equivalent substitute could be produced in case of their being lost. Should you have reason to believe that any documents, which you should be able to specify, were in possession of the Spanish Government, tending to elucidate any of these claims, you will endeavor to obtain them. The treaty provides that they shall be furnished at the demand of the commissioners; but, as much time may be saved if they can be sent here to be ready when the commission will be organized and commence the exercise of its functions, you will, should the occasion present itself, use your endeavors to that effect.

JOHN QUINCY ADAMS.

To John Forsyth.

Certificate of exchange of ratifications, referred to in the preceding instructions.

We, John Quincy Adams, Secretary of State of the United States of America, and Don Luis de Onis Gonzales Lopes y Vara, lord of the towns of Rayaces, Macadina, and Lagartera, Member of different Academies and Societies, both national and foreign, perpetual Regidor of the Corporation of the city of Salamanca, Knight Grand Cross of the Royal American Order of Isabella the Catholic, decorated with the Lys of La Vendée, Knight-pensioner of the royal and distinguished Spanish Order of Charles III., Member of the Supreme Assembly of the said Royal Order, of the Council of His Catholic Majesty, his Secretary, with exercise of decrees, and his Envoy Extraordinary and Minister Plenipotentiary near the United States of America, certify that the ratifications of the convention between the said United States of America and his said Majesty, concluded on the 11th day of August, 1802, accompanied with all suitable solemnities, and after due comparison each with the other, and with the original examples of the convention, have been exchanged by us this day.

In witness whereof we have signed this act in triplicates, and have sealed the same with our respective seals, at the City of Washington, this 21st day of December, 1818.

JOHN Q. ADAMS, [L. S.]
LUIS DE ONIS. [L. S.]

The Secretary of State to Don Luis de Onis.

DEPARTMENT OF STATE,
Washington, March 10, 1819.

SIR: By the eighth article of the Treaty of Amity, Settlement, and Limits, signed by us on the 22d of last month, all grants of lands in the Floridas, made by His Catholic Majesty, or his legitimate authorities in those provinces, subsequent to the 24th of January, 1818, are declared to be null and void. This date, as you will recollect, was agreed to on the part of the United States, with a full and clear understanding between us that it included the grants alleged to have been made in the course of the preceding winter by the King to the Duke of Alagon, the Count of Punon Rostro, and Mr. Vargas. As these grants, however, are known to the Government of the United States only from rumor, without the knowledge of their dates, it is proper that, on exchanging the ratifications, your Government should know that, whatever be the date of those grants may have been, it was fully understood by us that they are all annulled by the treaty, as much as if they had been specifically named, and that they will be so held by the United States. To avoid any possible misconception, your answer to this statement is requested; and the exchange of the ratifications will be made, under the explicit declaration and understanding that all the above mentioned grants, and all others derived from them, are null and void.

I pray you to accept the assurances of my distinguished consideration.

JOHN QUINCY ADAMS.

Don Luis de Onis, *Envoy, &c.*

Don Luis de Onis to the Secretary of State.

WASHINGTON, *March* 10, 1819.

SIR: I have received the note you were pleased to address to me of this day's date, in which you state that, by the eighth article of the treaty signed by us on the 22d of last month, it was agreed, on the part of the United States, that all grants of land in the Floridas, made by His Catholic Majesty, or his legitimate authorities, subsequent to the 24th of January, 1818, are declared to be null and void, with a full understanding that it included the grants alleged to have been made in the course of the preceding Winter, by the King, to the Duke of Alagon, the Count of Punon Rostro, and Mr. Vargas; and that, therefore, you request of me a declaration that, whatever the date of those grants may have been, it was fully understood by us that they are annulled by the treaty, as much as if they had been specifically named.

With the frankness and good faith which have uniformly actuated my conduct, and which distinguish the character of the Spanish nation, I have to declare to you, sir, that, when I proposed the revocation of all the grants made subsequent to the date above mentioned, it was with the full belief that it comprehended those made to the Duke of Alagon, as well as any others which had been stipulated at that period.

But, at the same time that I offer you this frank, simple, and ingenuous declaration, I have to express to you that, if my conception had been different, or if it had appeared to me that any of those grants were prior to the date above mentioned, I would have insisted upon their recognition, as the honor of the King, my master, and the unquestionable rights of his sovereignty of his possessions, and the disposal of them, obviously required.

I will hasten to transmit to my Government due information of the whole; and, impressed as I am with the conviction of His Majesty's most earnest desire to meet the wishes of the President, I persuade myself that he will, with pleasure, participate in that sentiment, by admitting the explicit declaration which you have requested of me. In the meantime, I beg you will favor me with your answer to the explanations I requested yesterday, in relation to the late act of Congress concerning piracy.

Be pleased to accept the assurance of my distinguished consideration. God preserve you many years.

LUIS DE ONIS.

The Secretary of State to Mr. Forsyth.

DEPARTMENT OF STATE,
Washington, March 10, 1819.

SIR: By the eighth article of the Treaty of Amity, Settlement, and Limits, between the United States and Spain, signed on the 22d of last month, all the grants of lands made by His Catholic Majesty, or by his lawful authorities, since the 24th of January, 1818, in the territories ceded by His Catholic Majesty to the United States, in the Floridas, are declared and agreed to be null and void. This date was proposed by Mr. Onis, and acceded to on the part of the United States, with a full and clear understanding, on both sides, that the grants made, or alleged to have been made, in the course of the preceding Winter, to the Duke of Alagon, the Count of Punon Rostro, and Mr. Vargas, were among those agreed and declared to be null and void. Copies of the grants to the Count of Punon Rostro and to Mr. Vargas, in the form of orders to the Governor General of the island of Cuba and to the Governor of the Floridas, had been transmitted to this department by Mr. Erving; the first of which bears date the 6th of February, and the second the 11th of March, 1818; but no copy has been received of that to the Duke of Alagon. As, however, the authenticity of these documents might be denied, and the grants have never been made public, it is proper that the possibility of any future question, with regard to those grants, should be guarded against; for which purpose, the form of a declaration is enclosed, which it will be proper for you to deliver, on exchanging the ratifications of the treaty, to the Spanish Minister with whom you will make the

exchange. The fact of the mutual understanding, that those grants were annulled by the treaty, is fully and explicitly admitted by Mr. Onis, in his answer, dated this day, to a note from me on this subject; copies of which, with a translation of his answer, are herewith enclosed. It is not anticipated that any objection will be made to receiving the declaration; if, however, there should be, you will, nevertheless, exchange the ratifications; it being sufficient to give the notice and the proof of the understanding, on both sides, of the operation of the article, and of the effect which will be given to it on the part of the United States.

I am, with much respect, &c.
JOHN QUINCY ADAMS.
JOHN FORSYTH, *Minister to Spain.*

Form of the declaration referred to in the preceding letter.

The undersigned, Minister Plenipotentiary from the United States of America at the Court of His Catholic Majesty, is commanded by the President of the United States to explain and declare, upon the exchange of the ratifications of the Treaty of Amity, Settlement, and Limits, between the United States and His Catholic Majesty, signed by the respective Plenipotentiaries at Washington, on the 22d day of February last, that, in agreeing upon the 24th day of January, 1818, as the date subsequent to which all grants of land made by His Catholic Majesty, or by his legitimate authorities in the Floridas, were declared to be null and void, it was with a full and clear understanding between the Plenipotentiaries of both the high contracting parties, that, among the grants thus declared null and void, were all those made, or alleged to have been made, in the course of the preceding Winter, by His Catholic Majesty, to the Duke of Alagon, the Count of Punon Rostro, and Mr. Vargas, and all others derived from them; and the ratifications of the treaty are exchanged under the explicit declaration and understanding that all the said grants are null and void, and will be so held by the United States.

MADRID, ——— —, 1819.

The Secretary of State to the Minister of France.

WASHINGTON, *March* 17, 1819.

SIR: By the eighth article of the treaty lately concluded between the United States and Spain, all grants of land made by the King of Spain, or by his legitimate authorities in Florida, before the 24th of January, 1818, are confirmed, on certain conditions; all those made after that date are declared null and void.

Since the conclusion of the treaty, a rumor has been circulated that certain grants made by the King of Spain, in the course of the preceding Winter, to the Duke of Alagon, the Count of Punon Rostro, and Mr. Vargas, were made on the 23d of January, 1818. Mr. Forsyth has therefore been instructed, on exchange of the ratifications of the treaty, to declare that it was fully and explicitly understood on both sides, at its signature, that all those grants, and all others derived from them, were, by the treaty, included among those declared to be absolutely null and void. Mr. De Onis himself, in answer to a note from me, has readily declared that such was his understanding. From the friendly part taken by you, in concert with Mr. De Onis, in this negotiation, you were apprized of all the circumstances attending it; and I have to request that you would have the goodness to state your impressions on the subject, particularly in relation to the absolute nullity of those grants, and, as far as you think proper, the facts in connexion with this transaction which you have mentioned to me in conversation.

I pray you, sir, to accept the assurance of my distinguished consideration.

JOHN QUINCY ADAMS.

Mr. Hyde de Neuville, *Envoy, &c.*

The Minister of France to the Secretary of State.

LEGATION OF FRANCE IN THE U. S.,
Washington, March 18, 1819.

SIR: I was very sure, and you were of the same opinion, that, to destroy the rumor which had been spread, it would suffice to inform the Minister of Spain of it. The loyalty which characterizes him did not permit the smallest uneasiness on the subject. After the declaration of Mr. Onis, mine can be of no importance; however, as you desire (in case the mistake of date should be real) that the fact resulting from the treaty should be well established, and by all those persons who took part, directly or indirectly, in the transaction, I have the honor, sir, to declare to you, in the most formal manner, that it has been understood—always understood, by you, by the Minister of Spain, and, I will add, by myself—that the three great grants of land made to the Duke of Alagon, to the Count of Punon Rostro, and to Mr. Vargas, were of the number of those annulled.

The date of 24th January was proposed and accepted in the complete persuasion, on one part and the other, that these three great grants were subsequent to it.

I will add, sir, because it is the exact and pure truth, having been charged by Mr. Onis, during his illness, to discuss with you several articles of the treaty, particularly the eighth article, you consented to the drawing up of this article more in conformity with the desire of the Spanish Minister, only on the admission, as a fact beyond doubt, that the three principal grants were and remained null, and as not having taken place. Mr. Onis has not ceased thus to understand it. He has explained himself upon it frankly and loyally, as well since as before the treaty. The mistake of date, if it exists, can, then, give birth to no difficulty whatever at Madrid. The good faith of Mr. Onis, and that of his Government, are guarantees too strong to render any other explanations necessary. Between Governments, as between individuals, the same laws of honor and probity govern transactions. The convention exists only by the convention; therefore, sir, in this case the simple statement of the fact will be sufficient to rectify the mistake.

In answering, sir, immediately the letter which you did me the honor to write to me, I embrace with much pleasure this new opportunity to assure you of the high consideration with which I have the honor to be, &c.

G. HYDE DE NEUVILLE.

Hon. Mr. ADAMS,
Secretary of State.

Observations on the eighth article of the treaty of the 22d February, 1819, *between the United States and Spain, submitted to Mr. De Neuville July* 14, 1819.

It will be recollected by Mr. De Neuville that, on the 15th of February last, Mr. De Onis being confined to his house by indisposition, Mr. De Neuville, at his request, had a conversation with Mr. Adams, in which were discussed the projet of a treaty which had been delivered on the 9th of February by Mr. De Onis to Mr. Adams, and the counter-projet sent by Mr. Adams to Mr. De Onis on the 13th of the same month.

The ninth article of the projet of Mr. Onis was in these words:

"All the grants of land made by His Catholic Majesty, or by his legitimate authorities, in the aforesaid territories of the two Floridas, and others which His Majesty cedes to the United States, shall be confirmed and acknowledged as valid, excepting those grants which have been made after the 24th January of last year, the date that the first proposals were made for the cession of those provinces, which shall be held null in consideration of the grantees not having complied with the conditions of the cession."

The eighth article of the counter-projet sent by Mr. Adams was as follows:

"All grants of land made by or in the name of His Catholic Majesty, in the aforesaid territories, after the 24th January, 1818, shall be held null, the conditions of the said grants not having been performed by the grantees. All grants made before that date by His Majesty, or by his legitimate authorities, the conditions of which shall have been performed by the grantees according to the tenor of the respective grants, and none other, shall be confirmed and acknowledged as valid."

Mr. De Neuville's particular attention is requested to the difference between the two projected articles, because it will recall particularly to his remembrance the point upon which the discussion concerning this article turned. By turning to the written memorandum drawn up by Mr. De Neuville himself of this discussion, he will perceive he has noted that Mr. De Onis insisted "that this article could not be varied from what is contained in the Chevalier's projet, as the object of the last clause therein was merely to save the honor and dignity of the sovereignty of His Catholic Majesty."

It was then observed by Mr. Adams that the honor and dignity of His Catholic Majesty would be saved by recognising the grants prior to the 24th of January as "valid to the same extent as they were binding on His Catholic Majesty," and he agreed to accept the article as drawn by Mr. Onis, with this explanation; (see Mr. De Neuville's memorandum.) It was on this occasion that Mr. De Neuville observed that, if the grants prior to January 24, 1818, were confirmed only to the same extent that they were binding on the King of Spain, there were many *bona fide* grantees, of long standing, in actual possession of their grants, and having actually made partial settlements upon them, but who have been prevented, by the extraordinary circumstances in which Spain had been situated, and the revolutions in Europe, from fulfilling all the conditions of the grants; that it would be very harsh to leave these persons liable to a forfeiture, which might, indeed, in rigor be exacted from them, but which very certainly never would be if they had remained under the Spanish dominion. It will be well remembered by Mr. De Neuville how earnestly he insisted upon this equitable suggestion, and how strongly he disclaimed for Mr. Onis every wish or intention to cover, by a provision for each person, any fraudulent grants. And it was then observed by Mr. De Neuville that the date assumed, of 24th January, 1818, was not sufficient for guarding against fraudulent grants, because they might be easily antedated. It was with reference to these suggestions of Mr. De Neuville, afterwards again strenuously urged by Mr. De Onis, that the article was finally modified as it now stands in the treaty, declaring all grants subsequent to 24th January, 1818, absolutely null, and those of a prior date valid to the same extent only that they would have been binding upon the King; but allowing to *bona fide* grantees, in actual possession, and having commenced settlements, but who had been prevented, by the late circumstances of the Spanish nation and the revolutions in Europe, from fulfilling all the conditions of their grants, time to complete them. It is needless to observe that, as these incidents do not apply to either of the grants to Alagon, Punon Rostro, or Vargas, neither of those grants is confirmed by the tenor of the article as it stands; and that it is perfectly immaterial in that respect whether they were dated before or after the 24th January, 1818, it being admitted on all sides that these grants were not binding upon the King conformably to the Spanish laws. The terms of the article accord precisely with the intentions of all the parties to the negotiation and the signature of the treaty. If the dates of the grants are subsequent to 24th January, 1818, they are annulled by the date; if prior to that date, they are null, because not included among the prior grants confirmed.

Mr. Forsyth to the Marquis of Casa Yrujo.

MADRID, *May* 18, 1819.

SIR: The treaty concluded on the 22d of February, 1819, at Washington, by Mr. Adams on the part of the Government of the United States, and the Chevalier de Onis on the part of His Catholic Majesty, has been intrusted to me by the President of the United States, duly ratified; and I am prepared to exchange the ratifications of this instru-

16th CON. 2d SESS.—43

ment at any moment it may suit the convenience of your Excellency. From the nature of the engagement, it is desirable that the earliest exchange should be made; and this would be particularly convenient, as an opportunity is afforded of sending this important document to my Government by the American ship of war Hornet, now in the harbor of Cadiz, and destined in a few days to the United States.

I seize with avidity every opportunity to present to your Excellency, whom may God preserve, the assurances of my distinguished consideration.

JOHN FORSYTH.
The MARQUIS OF CASA YRUJO.

Mr. Forsyth to the Marquis of Casa Yrujo.

MADRID, *June* 4, 1819.

SIR: On the 18th of May last I addressed to your Excellency an official note to inform you "that I was ready to exchange the ratifications of the convention, &c., concluded at Washington by Mr. Adams and the Chevalier de Onis, on the 22d February, 1819; that it was desirable, from the nature of that instrument, that an immediate exchange of ratifications should be made, the more especially so as I had an opportunity of sending it, when ratified by the King, to the United States, by the American sloop of war Hornet, then and now lying in the harbor of Cadiz." The time at which it will be necessary for that vessel (by the return of which the American Government expects to receive the treaty ratified by His Majesty) to sail for the United States has so nearly arrived, that it is my indispensable duty to call your Excellency's attention again to the subject of that note. It would be painful for me to see this vessel depart without the treaty. The Government of the United States had a just and well founded expectation that no unreasonable delay would take place, and therefore looked to the return of this vessel for the instrument, executed with due formalities. Her arrival without it will not fail to make the most unfavorable impressions. To obviate such an effect is beyond my power, as I can perceive no adequate motive to prevent His Majesty's Government from acting on this subject prior to her departure from Spain. Your Excellency will not deem me unnecessarily importunate or unreasonable when I ask an immediate attention to this business, and express my conviction that an answer will be given to this and to my note of the 18th of May, already alluded to, on the earliest day that the convenience of His Majesty's Government will permit.

I renew to your Excellency, whom may God preserve, the assurances of my distinguished respect and consideration.

JOHN FORSYTH.

Don Manuel Gonzales Salmon to Mr. Forsyth.

PALACE, *June* 19, 1819.

SIR: The King, my august master, has informed himself of the contents of your two notes of the 18th of May last and 4th instant, in both of which

Spain—Ratification of the Treaty of 1819.

you state that you are ready to exchange the ratifications of the treaty concluded at Washington, on the 22d of February last, by Don Luis de Onis and Mr. Adams, and that, from the nature of that treaty, and the favorable opportunity of transmitting it to the United States, by the Hornet sloop of war, you are desirous that the said exchange may be made as expeditiously as may be.

I have also submitted to His Majesty the purport of your verbal communications to me on this subject, and I again brought to his view your observations thereon in the two several conferences I have had the honor to hold with you.

His Majesty has, in consequence, commanded me to inform you, in reply, that, on reflecting on the great importance and interest of the treaty in question, he is under the indispensable necessity of examining it with the greatest caution and deliberation before he proceeds to ratify it.

This being all I am enabled to communicate to you on this point, for the present, I avail myself, with pleasure, of the renewed occasion it affords me to offer you my respects, and I pray God to preserve you many years.

M. GONZALES SALMON.

Mr. Forsyth to Don Manuel Gonzales Salmon.

MADRID, *June* 21, 1819.

SIR: The determination of His Catholic Majesty to delay the exchange of ratifications of the treaty signed on the 22d February, at Washington, by Mr. Adams and the Chevalier de Onis, as communicated by your Excellency's note of the 19th instant, in reply to my notes of the 18th May and the 4th of the current month, fills me with regret. As the subject-matter of that treaty has been for years before the two Governments, both of whom have no doubt long since discussed and deliberately determined upon what they would respectively claim and yield, I took it for granted no motive for delay could exist. Your excellency's note, whilst it states to me the fact that a longer delay is contemplated, does not enlighten me as to the cause. The measure is, no doubt, important and interesting to His Majesty's kingdom, but no new light can have broken in upon the subject since the instructions were given to the Chevalier de Onis, upon which the treaty is founded, on the part of Spain—no change of the circumstances of the parties to it had occurred—no new causes of difficulty or complaint are known to exist. Although the words of the treaty allow six months to elapse before the instrument is annulled, if the exchange of ratifications is not previously made, I must represent to your excellency that every hour's delay is at variance with the spirit of the instrument. The stipulated time was, to guard against accidents, extended to the longest period which, under any circumstances, could be required to effect the change. Had the distance of our respective Governments permitted, the time fixed would not have been extended beyond a single day. If the Government of the United States had not gratuitously offered the exchange here, His Majesty would have been compelled ere this

to have transmitted the treaty ratified on the part of Spain to America, or have lost the benefit of the convention. You will recollect that no place is fixed at which the exchange is to be made. It is to the confidence of the American Government in the good disposition of Spain that the King, your master, is indebted for the opportunity thus to delay acting upon the subject. The ill consequences which will ensue from this postponement, and the impression likely to be made by it, can be easily foreseen. Your excellency may correctly estimate the conjectures to which it will give birth in the United States from what is passing here. You, perhaps, are yet to learn that the delay of the last month has given rise, at the seat of His Majesty's Government, among his own subjects, to the most monstrous and absurd suppositions. Among the subjects of Spain, those who best know the integrity of the King, and the purity of his councils, it is asserted that an act required by the policy of this Government, essential to the interests of this kingdom, and demanded by the honor of the King, will not be performed. Yes, sir; the King is calumniated in his very capital by a most unjust surmise that there will be a refusal to do that which the reputation of Spain requires—that which Spain dare not refuse to do. Your excellency will not understand this as threatening His Majesty's Government with the consequences which might ensue from the resentment of the United States, if it were possible for Spain to act in this business with bad faith. Threats are used by conscious weakness, not by conscious strength. I know too well the abundant resources, the expanding power, the youthful vigor of my country, to degrade her character by using language unworthy of it; if not by my respect for Spain, I should be prevented by the fear of the deserved resentment of my own country; I should not be easily forgiven for condescending to say how she would punish an act of perfidy. It is by her acts, and not by the railings of her ministers, that she will be known to those who violate the faith pledged to her. But there is this, which a just Government will more cautiously avoid than even the well-founded resentment of a powerful nation: the degradation of conscious baseness. No wise King will dare to do an act which would deprive him of the respect of all nations, sully the reputation of his kingdom in the eyes of the civilized world, and deprive his people of the strongest incentive to virtuous exertions, under every dispensation of Heaven—the confidence in the integrity of their Government. If, even in Spain, unjust surmises and unfounded mistrusts are entertained, your Excellency, recollecting the lately-subsided irritations of long-continued disputes with the Government of His Majesty, will not be surprised that, in the United States, the same cause should produce, not suspicions, but firm convictions of the intention of this Government to disappoint the expectations reposed in its good faith. I know full well that in two months the act of the exchange of ratifications will prove that these harsh convictions have been hastily and incorrectly formed; but the impression of them may remain, and the motive for the delayed exchange may be misunderstood. I have used every effort to avert it, but in vain. If my apprehensions should not be realized, I shall heartily rejoice.

It only remains for me to say, in this last note that I shall address to your Excellency on this subject that whenever His Majesty directs you to exchange the ratification of the treaty of 22d of February, 1819, I am prepared, at any period before the 22d of August, on the part of my Government, to perform that ceremony.

I renew to your Excellency, whom may God preserve, the full assurance of my perfect respect.

JOHN FORSYTH.

Don Manuel Gonzalez Salmon to Mr. Forsyth.

MADRID, *August* 10, 1819.

SIR: I duly received the note you were pleased to address to me, dated the 21st of June last, in answer to that which I had the honor to write to you on the 19th of the same month, being my reply to your notes of the 8th of May and 4th of June, requesting the speedy ratification and exchange of the treaty lately concluded at Washington, on the 22d of February of the present year, between His Majesty the King, my master, and your Government.

In my said reply, I confined myself to stating to you that His Majesty, having taken that important subject into his most serious consideration, had found it indispensably necessary to examine the treaty with the utmost caution and reflection before he proceeded to ratify it.

In your answer you express your surprise at the delay attending a transaction which, having been already thoroughly discussed, could require no renewed examination of its final and definitive decision; and the more so, as the circumstances which led to it had experienced no change with either party. You proceed to develop, at length, the injurious effect that, in your opinion, must be produced by the delay of the Spanish Government in concluding this affair, and also of the disagreeable consequences that you foresee must result from that delay; and you conclude by stating that, whenever His Catholic Majesty shall please to authorize me to exchange the ratifications of the treaty of 22d February, 1819, you are ready to execute that act on behalf of your Government at any time prior to the date of the 22d of August.

It would have been desirable if you had confined yourself, in your said note, to expressing your surprise and that of your Government at the delay on the part of Spain in terminating, by her ratification, an affair which, according to the intention of both, was to be considered as concluded, and to earnestly requesting the exchange of the same, by which the wishes of your Government, and one of the principal objects of your arrival at this Court, would be accomplished.

Thus, it is to be supposed that you would have only conformed to the instructions which you will probably receive from your Government; and, therefore, other expressions and phrases you have used in your note cannot fail to appear very extraordinary, which your ardent zeal for the interests of your nation has doubtless prompted you to employ, but in which you have been carried farther than really could have been wished.

The expressions and phrases alluded to, which I refrain from otherwise specifying, are, to say the least, entirely superfluous, and consequently foreign to the subject in question; they have, therefore, surprised the more, as in no possible case can they be applicable to the Spanish Government or to its agents. Convinced of the rectitude and justice of its rights, and of those ever prescribed by the bounds of moderation, it never has, in its communications, permitted itself to go to such extremes as would justify the proceeding now adverted to.

There would be much to remark upon a style so unusual in diplomatic communications, and still less conformable to the sentiments of mutual friendship and harmony which should exist between the two Governments of Spain and the United States of America, as well as of those which, as its representative, you are in a situation to express; but I shall abstain from any particular detail or comment upon your expressions, and confine myself merely to declare to you, as I have already done, the extreme surprise produced by that part of the contents of your note.

I am at the same time authorized by the King, my master, to inform you that, having deliberately weighed the important subject which forms the principal object of your communication, he is of opinion that a final decision cannot be taken thereupon without previously entering into several explanations with the Government of the United States, to some of which your Government has given rise.

His Majesty has therefore been pleased to charge with his full confidence a person possessing all the qualifications necessary for bringing this interesting trust to a happy conclusion, who will forthwith make known to the United States His Majesty's intentions on this point, in order that, all obstacles being removed on the one side and cleared up on the other, all the doubts which have arisen may be done away, and a full and satisfactory accomplishment given to the earnest desire which has animated the King, my master, on this subject, which certainly has uniformly been to see the friendship and good understanding subsisting between both Governments established on the most solid basis, and secured against future chances of interruption.

His Catholic Majesty persuades himself that the Government of the United States, in accordance with these principles and sentiments, far from refusing to admit these new explanations, will cheerfully receive them as a proof of the good faith and frankness of the conduct of Spain; and that they will accede to her views, by promoting also on their part the speedy conclusion of an affair productive of the mutual advantage of both Powers.

I offer, &c.

MANUEL G. SALMON.

JOHN FORSYTH,
    Minister, &c.

Spain—Ratification of the Treaty of 1819.

Mr. Forsyth to Senor Don Manuel Gonzales Salmon, Secretary of State, &c.

MADRID, *August* 12, 1818.

SIR: I received this morning your official note of the 10th instant. Some of the expressions of the note which I had the honor to present to His Majesty's Government on the 21st of June last appear to have given offence. As you have not specified the particular phrases or expressions which are considered censurable, I can only say that it was far either from my wish or intention to treat His Majesty's Government with disrespect, or to use terms calculated to interrupt the harmony and good understanding which ought to exist between it and the United States. I came here instructed by the President, and animated by the warmest wishes to strengthen, not to weaken, the almost broken bands of amity by which the two nations are still united. I can but regret that, in my zeal to promote this great object, I have used language capable of being misunderstood. You will consider that this regret does not spring from a conviction that the construction put upon my note is just. So far from admitting this, I must insist that there is nothing contained in it which, if rightly interpreted, could be deemed objectionable; and I cannot but indulge the belief that the language has been held offensive, not from its genuine and original import, but from some fatality in its application. As to the remarks you have been pleased to make, that these unusual expressions were idle, (*ociosos*,) not pertinent to the business in question, and not common in diplomatic communications, they are not sufficiently important to merit a distinct reply. The first two it is not the province of His Majesty's Government to reprove; to my own Government I look for approbation or censure. There is no doubt that the pertinency of the matters referred to will not escape its penetration. Should I be convicted of the offence of departing from the ordinary diplomatic style, I shall find abundant consolation in the consciousness of having expressed just sentiments in simple terms. The course pursued by the Government of His Catholic Majesty, and intended to be persisted in, as indicated by your note, is much more likely to disturb the harmony of the two nations than the intemperate zeal of the representatives or agents of either. On the 22d of February, the convention was signed at Washington, by Mr. Adams and the Chevalier de Onis. In April, a copy of it was received in Spain from the messenger sent by the Spanish Minister from America. It is not necessary to remind you that the satisfaction of this Government in the termination of this important business was marked by the distribution of honors in the gift of the Crown to persons very remotely connected with the transaction. What has produced the very surprising change in the opinions then entertained on this subject, is for you, sir, to explain, if you think proper, but is what I cannot imagine. On the 18th of May, immediately after my introduction to His Majesty, the note of that date was delivered. It was therein stated that the treaty ratified by the United States

was in Madrid, and an immediate exchange of ratifications was asked, that this important document might be sent to my Government by a vessel of war bound in a short time from Cadiz to America: to this no reply was given. Under the expectation entertained from several conversations with the Marquis de Casa Yrujo, the substance of which has been verbally stated to you, the vessel was detained in the port of Cadiz until the 2d of July. In this interval the only communication received on this important subject was your note of the 19th June, the purport of which was, that His Majesty found it necessary to proceed with the deliberation and slowness demanded by its importance, to consider the subject of the treaty. On the 12th day of August, His Majesty's Government gives notice, by your note of the 10th, of its determination—to ratify? no, sir, to send a person to Washington, possessing the confidence of the King, and having the necessary qualifications to terminate happily this affair. Can it have escaped the observation of this Government that this affair must terminate in ten days? While a failure to resolve finishes the business in a few days, this Government thinks that a definitive resolution cannot be taken without first entering into various explanations with the United States, to some of which the Government of the said States has given occasion. *What* circumstance in the history of this affair *sustains the* assurances that His Majesty finds himself animated by the most vehement desires to preserve a good understanding with, and the friendship of, the United States? Is it the disappointment of the rational anticipation, indulged in America, that the treaty ratified by Spain would be carried there in the ship of war Hornet? The determination to send a messenger to the United States for explanations, at this period, when his voyage, as it regards the convention, must be useless; and the only hope which can be entertained from it is, that a new negotiation may be commenced—a circumstance of especial weight, when it is recollected that this messenger might have been sent to Washington, the desired explanations might have been asked, and given there prior to the 22d of August, if the King, your master, had desired promptly on this course. Or is it in the inexplicable and studious avoidance of the natural order of proceeding in a case of this kind—an application to the Minister of the United States near the Court of His Majesty for these necessary explanations, when they might have been, possibly, long since given, and still may be given before the period arrives when the convention of the 22d of February ceases to be obligatory upon the parties to it? You will forgive me, sir, if I perceive in none of these circumstances indications of those vehement desires by which His Majesty's Government is animated, to establish, on a solid basis, a good understanding with the United States, to which, in the usual style of diplomatic communications, you refer. Since, however, I am bound and most willing to believe their existence, although the conduct of Spain has a tendency to force a different conviction upon the mind, allow me to suggest the only mode in which they can now be fully manifested and gratified; with that frankness and openness so honorable to all nations, and by which the Castilian character has been distinguished, disclose the difficulties that appear to interpose themselves to prevent the immediate conclusion of this affair. I am fully instructed by the Government of my country upon the only point on which it can have given a motive for explanations; and while I cannot imagine what others are wished for, I persuade myself that I am so well possessed of its wishes and intentions as to be able to give full satisfaction to His Majesty upon any part of the treaty, the elucidation of which may be desired.

I renew to you, sir, the assurances of my distinguished consideration.

JOHN FORSYTH.

The Secretary of State to Mr. John Forsyth.

DEPARTMENT OF STATE,
Washington, August 18, 1819.

SIR: Captain Read, of the Hornet, has delivered to me your despatches of the 10th, 17th, and 22d of June, which have been submitted to the consideration of the President.

However extraordinary the conduct of the Spanish Government, in relation to the treaty signed on the 22d of February last, has been, the President is unwilling to abandon the hope that, within the period of six months allowed for the exchange of the ratifications, a sense of justice, and of decent regard for the public faith of the King and nation, solemnly pledged by the treaty, will prevail over the individual intrigues and lurking influence which prompted the delay that has taken place. Should this expectation, however, be disappointed, and should the treaty remain unratified by Spain at the time when you shall receive this despatch, you will immediately make an official communication to the Minister of Foreign Affairs, stating that the ratification of Spain, with the explicit understanding, on her part, that the alleged grants to the Duke of Alagon, Count of Punon Rostro, and Mr. Vargas, and all others which may have been made under the same circumstances, are, by the eighth article of the treaty, null and void, and will be so held by the United States, will be accepted as valid; and that you are authorized to receive the Spanish ratification in exchange for that of the United States, though after the lapse of the stipulated six months, provided the exchange shall be immediate, and in such time that you can despatch the ratified treaty by the messenger who will be the bearer of this in season to arrive here before the meeting of Congress, on the first Monday in December; that, if the ratified treaty should not arrive here at that time, a full communication will be made by the President to Congress of all the transactions relating to the treaty, and such measures will be adopted by that body as they shall think required by the exigency of the case; that, whatever their determination may be, the Spanish Government will be responsible to the United States for all damages and expenses which may arise from the delay or refusal of Spain to ratify, and from the

measures to which the United States may resort to give efficacy to their rights; and that, for the indemnities to which they will be justly entitled for this violation of faith by Spain, the United States will look to the territory west of the Sabine river.

The only reason assigned by the Minister of State *ad interim*, Salmon, for the postponement of the Spanish ratification was, the determination of the King, founded upon the great importance of the treaty, to act upon it with full deliberation. This may have been sufficient to justify delay within the period stipulated by the treaty, but, after the expiration of that period, can no longer be alleged. Delay beyond that period will be a breach of faith; for the treaty, in all its parts, from the moment of its signature by Mr. Onis, and the ratification of the United States, was as binding upon the honor and good faith of the Spanish King and nation as it would be after the ratification. It is scarcely supposable that Spain will contest this position, or that it should be necessary to present it to her view in the following terms of the full power of Mr. Onis, the original of which, signed by the King of Spain, was delivered to me before the signature of the treaty. The words of His Catholic Majesty are, after authorizing Mr. Onis to treat, negotiate, and conclude a treaty, whereby past differences may be adjusted, and a firm and lasting peace established between the two Governments: "Obliging ourselves, as we do hereby oblige ourselves and promise, on the faith and word of a King, to approve, ratify, and fulfil, and to cause to be inviolably observed and fulfilled, whatsoever may be stipulated and signed by you; to which intent and purpose, I grant you all authority and full power, in the most ample form, thereby as of right required."[*] If language so explicit and unqualified were, in regard to its import, susceptible of any doubt, founded on the usage which requires the ratification of the sovereign for the full consummation of a treaty, there is nothing dubious or uncertain in the extent of obligation resting upon him, by the signature of his Minister, vested with such a full power. The following passages from Vattel and Martens are decisive authorities upon the principle:

"Sovereigns treat together by the agency of their attorneys or mandatories, clothed with sufficient powers; they are commonly called plenipotentiaries. All the rules of the law of nature, concerning things performed by commission, are here applicable. The rights of the agent are defined by the authority given him. From this he must not depart; but whatever he promises within the terms of his commission, and according to the extent of his powers, is binding upon his constituent."

"At this time, to avoid all danger and diffi-

---

[*] "Obligandonos y prometemos, en fe y palabra de Rey, que aprobaremos, ratificaremos, cumpliremos, y haremos observar y cumplir inviolablemente quanto por vos fuere estipulado y firmado; para lo qual os concedo todas las facultades y plenos poderes en la forma mas amplia que de derecho se requieren."

culty, princes reserve to themselves the right of ratifying that which has been concluded by their minister in their name. The full power is merely a commission, *cum libera*. If this commission were to have its full effect, it should be given with the utmost circumspection; but, as princes can be constrained to fulfil their obligations only by force of arms, the custom has arisen of relying upon their treaties only after they have sanctioned and ratified them. Whatever the minister has concluded remaining ineffectual until the ratification of the prince, there is less danger of giving him a full power. But to refuse, with honor, to ratify that which has been concluded in virtue of a full power, the sovereign must have strong and solid reasons for it, and, particularly, he must show that his Minister transcended his instructions."—*Vattel, book 2, chapter 12, § 156.*

"Every thing that has been stipulated by an agent, in conformity to his full powers, ought to become obligatory for the State, from the moment of signing, without even waiting for the ratification. However, not to expose a State to the errors of a single person, it is now become a general maxim that public conventions do not become obligatory till ratified. The motive of this custom clearly proves that the ratification can never be refused with justice, except when he who is charged with the negotiation, keeping within compass with respect to his public full powers, has gone beyond his secret instructions, and consequently has rendered himself liable to punishment, or when the other party refuses to ratify."—*Martens's Summary, book 2, chapter 1, sec. 3.*

The obligation of the King of Spain, therefore, in honor and in justice, to ratify the treaty signed by his Minister, is as perfect and unqualified as his royal promise in the full power; and it gives to the United States the right, equally perfect, to compel the performance of that promise.

Should it be suggested that the United States themselves have, on more than one occasion, withheld or annexed conditions to the ratification of treaties signed by their Plenipotentiaries in Europe, it will readily occur to you that, by the nature of our Constitution, the full powers of our Ministers never are or can be unlimited; that whatever they conclude must be, and by the other contracting party is always known and understood to be, subject to the deliberation and determination of the Senate, to whose consideration it must be submitted before its ratification; that our full powers never contain the solemn promise of the nation to ratify whatever the Minister shall conclude, but reserve, expressly, not only the usual right of ratification, but the Constitutional privilege of the Senate, to give or withhold their assent to the ratification; without which assent, by a majority of two-thirds of the members present at the vote taken after consideration of the treaty, the President has no authority to ratify. In withholding or refusing the ratification, therefore, no promise or engagement of the State is violated. But neither the same reason nor the same principle applies to the King of Spain, who possesses the sole, entire, and exclusive power of ratifying treaties

made by his Ministers, and who, therefore, by the promise, on the faith and word of a King, to ratify whatever his Minister shall sign, commits his own honor and that of his nation to the fulfilment of his promise. This distinction is well known and clearly recognised by the law of nations.[*]

The Spanish Government cannot allege either that Mr. Onis transcended his secret instructions, or that the ratification of the United States has been refused, or that any unfair advantage was taken on the part of the United States in the negotiation, or that Spain was not fully aware beforehand of the full extent of the engagements contracted by Mr. Onis. It is too well known, and they will not dare to deny it, that Mr. Onis's last instructions authorized him to concede much more than he did; that those instructions had been prepared by Mr. Pizarro; that, after the appointment of the Marquis de Casa Yrujo to the ministry, they were by him submitted to the King's council, and, with their full sanction, were transmitted to Mr. Onis; that, both in relation to the grants of lands in Florida, and to the Western boundary, the terms which he obtained were far within the limits of his instructions; that it was known to and understood by him that the grants to Alagon, Punon Rostro, and Vargas, were annulled by the treaty; that, so fully was this his understanding, that, in his despatches to his Government, he pointed out to them means of indemnifying those grantees for their disappointment from other lands. The Government of the United States, indeed, considered the moderation and generosity of the terms to which they had acceded as a pledge that they would be received with pride and joy by the Spanish Government; and so, it will not be denied, they were in the first instance received by the King of Spain and his Cabinet. If, afterwards, from the unexpected extent of sacrifices which the United States made, for the purposes of conciliation and of sincere amity, Spain has drawn the inference that this temper may be trifled with and abused, it is proper, and will be just, that she should be effectually undeceived.

Should the ratification be withheld, it is to be presumed that some other reason than the importance of the treaty will ultimately be assigned by Spain for withholding it. What that will be, can at present only be conjectured. If the grants to the Duke of Alagon and Count Punon Rostro should be assigned as forming the objection, you will explicitly declare that the United States have no compromise to make, and will listen to none on that subject. The insinuation of the Marquis of Casa

Yrujo that those grants, by the letter of the eighth article, would be confirmed if dated before the 24th of January, 1818, was totally unfounded. Mr. Onis knows that the whole of the eighth article was finally drawn up as it stands, with the express intention, declared by me, and agreed to by him, to exclude them from confirmation, whatever might be their dates. Mr. Onis, on the first projet of a treaty, delivered on the 9th of February, had drawn the article in such terms as to confirm all grants made before the 24th of January, 1818. If the article had even been accepted by us in those terms, it could only by an unworthy deception be pretended that it covered the grants of Alagon and Punon Rostro, because it had been explicitly agreed, on both sides, that they should be annulled, and because Mr. Onis, who always spoke of them as fraudulent grants, of which he was ashamed for his country, has repeatedly declared to me that he signed the treaty without knowing their dates, but fully believing them to be subsequent to the 24th of January. If, then, the confirmation of the grants prior to that date had been, as it was first proposed by Mr. Onis, positive and unqualified, and if the grants had been completely made before that date, there might be some pretence that they were covered by the letter of the article, though by a mistake common to both parties, of which a just and honorable Government would disdain to take any other advantage than that of manifesting its good faith by its cheerfulness and promptitude in rectifying the error, and fulfilling the intention instead of the letter of the engagement. But the article was not accepted in this form. In the counter-projet, delivered by me on the 13th of February, the grants prior to the 24th of January, 1818, the conditions of which should have been performed by the grantees, and none other, were declared to be confirmed. At the time that the counter-projet was received by Mr. Onis, he was confined to his house by indisposition; at his request, the communications between him and me were made by the friendly interposition of the French Minister, M. Hyde de Neuville. Mr. Onis insisted on the article concerning the grants as drawn up by him, not for the purpose of covering these grants, for he professed an earnest desire that they should be annulled, for the vindication of his own character from the aspersion which had been circulated here, that he had a personal interest in them; but he had drawn the article in these terms merely to save the honor of the King. It was then observed that the honor of the King could be saved by declaring the grants prior to the 24th January, 1818, binding to the same extent as they would have been upon the Spanish Government if the cession to the United States had not been made. It was known and admitted that neither of those grants would, in that case, have been valid, because the conditions, by the laws of the Indies, indispensable to their validity, neither had been, nor could be, fulfilled by the grantees; and their non-performance had been formally assigned by Mr. Onis, in his letter to me of November 16, 1818, as his reason for agreeing to their being annulled. But

he observed that there were grants of old standing, made *bona fide* to persons in actual possession of the lands, and having made improvements and settlements upon them, but who, by the late revolutions in Europe, and the convulsed state of Spain, had been prevented from completing all the conditions of their grants; that it would be but equitable to allow them time from the date of the treaty to fulfil them. To this a ready assent was given, and the article was thus agreed to—limiting to such grants alone the confirmation prior to the 24th of January, 1818.

Minutes of the discussion upon this article were drawn up in writing, at the time, by Mr. De Neuville, copies of which were furnished both to Mr. Onis and to me prior to the signature, and recognised by us both to be correct. An abstract from them of all that relates to this article, together with the draught of the article as first proposed by Mr. Onis, of that in our counter-projet, and of the article as finally agreed to, is herewith enclosed. They will show that the confirmation of the grants to Alagon, Punon Rostro, and Vargas, is as effectually excluded by the limitations in the first part of the article, if their date is prior to the 24th of January, 1818, as by the date itself if made subsequent to that time. They were not excluded by name for two reasons: First, conformably to the desire of Mr. Onis to save the honor of the King. You will see this distinctly noted in the minutes of Mr. De Neuville. Secondly, because, from the despatches of Mr. Erving, it was supposed there were other grants of the same kind, and made under similar circumstances. To have named them might have left room for a presumptive inference in favor of others. The determination was to exclude them all.

No reliance was placed upon the exclusion by the date, because the grants having been secretly made, and without the usual formalities, the copies of them received by Mr. Erving might be unauthentic; because no copy of the grant to Alagon had been received; and because, if fraud was to be guarded against, it was well known that antedating was one of its most familiar and favorite expedients. When, shortly after the signature of the treaty, a rumor was circulated here that the date of the grants was one day prior to the 24th of January, 1818, and that this last date had been assumed with the intention, at least on the part of Mr. Onis, that they should be confirmed, without admitting the suspicion that he had attempted a deception for which the language of decency has no name, it was yet thought advisable that no shadow of a pretence should by any possibility be raised after the ratification of the treaty, by Spain or the grantees, that those grants were confirmed, or that either party of the compact had understood that they would be by the article as it stood. You were therefore instructed, on exchanging the ratifications, to deliver a declaration of this construction, which it had been the avowed intention of both parties at the signature that the eighth article should bear in relation to the grants in question, and the only one which the United States should ever admit. Mr. Onis, by his answer to my note of the 10th March, unequivocally recognised that such had been his understanding of the import of the article when he signed it. He added, indeed, that, if he had known that the grants were of a prior date, he should have insisted upon their being confirmed. But, without remarking that his ignorance of their dates could have no possible effect to render valid that which he had agreed and understood to be null and void, it had escaped his recollection that, in his note to me of the 16th November, 1818, he had agreed that these grants should all be annulled, because their conditions had not been fulfilled by the grantees. The President of the United States is yet willing to accept of the ratification of that treaty by Spain. It settles important interests; it secures pacific and harmonious relations with Spain ; it provides indemnities to many of our citizens for injuries which Spain acknowledges they have suffered from her; and it gives us Florida, a land useless and expensive to Spain, though, chiefly by its position, valuable to us. But, for all these advantages, we know that we have given in the same treaty ample and generous equivalent to Spain, and she will find herself much deceived if, in the hope of making hereafter a better bargain, she now disdains them. To possess Florida, with the full and fair consent of Spain, is undoubtedly an object of interest to the American Government; but an object of infinitely deeper and dearer interest to them is to observe towards Spain, and all other nations, a just and candid and single-hearted course of conduct, free from fraud, artifice, or disguise; and that which they observe, they demand in return. They will neither themselves practise, nor from others submit to, a disingenuous, double-dealing system of treachery, paltering with its own engagements, and spreading snares for the generous confidence of good faith.

You will, therefore, on no consideration, exchange the ratifications without delivering the declaration prescribed by your instructions when you took charge of the treaty; and you will not fail, if the ratification be withheld, to address an earnest remonstrance to the Spanish Government against the grants themselves, and the circumstances under which they were issued.

The proposal of Mr. Onis's letter to this department, of the 31st October, 1818, was as follows : " That the late grants made by His Majesty in the Floridas, since the 24th of January last, the date of my first note announcing His Majesty's willingness to cede them to the United States, (the said grants having been made with a view to promote population, cultivation, and industry, and not with that of alienating them,) shall be declared null and void, in consideration of the grantees not having complied with the essential conditions of the cessions, as has been the fact." And in his letter of the 10th March, referring to this proposal, he says: "With the frankness and good faith which have uniformly actuated my conduct, and which distinguish the character of the Spanish nation, I have to declare to you, sir, that when I proposed the revocation of all the grants made subsequently to the date above mentioned, it

was with the full belief that it comprehended those made to the Duke of Alagon, as well as any others which had been stipulated at that period." Here, then, is the express declaration of the Spanish negotiator of that treaty: 1st. That the grants in question were all, in his full belief when he made the proposal, included among those positively annulled by the date; 2d. That these grants had been made by the King, with a view of promoting population, cultivation, and industry, and not with that of alienating the territory; and 3d. That the grants were all null and void, because the grantees had not complied with the essential conditions of the grants.

Now, what shall be said after these plain and positive declarations, when Spain advances, as the only ground of pretence, that these grants were confirmed by the treaty; that they were dated before the 24th of January, 1818, indeed, but after the instructions by which Mr. Onis was authorized to make his proposal of that date for the cession of the Floridas had been despatched to him from Madrid? What becomes of his positive assurance that these grants were made for the population and improvement of the territory, and not with a view of alienation? And what was the meaning of Spain in stipulating that an acknowledged debt of indemnities from her to citizens of the United States, at least to the amount of $5,000,000, should be paid from the proceeds of public lands in Florida, when she now comes and says that even while her Minister was signing this compact on her part, his Sovereign, by a secret and irregular alienation of the lands, had made its accomplishment impossible? In whatever other light it is to be considered, it is an injury to the United States, for which they are entitled to demand and obtain satisfaction. When the Government of a nation degrades itself by flagrant and notorious perfidy, those who are constrained to entertain political relations of neighborhood with them are justified by the law of nature, and it is their duty to themselves, in subsequent transactions with such a State, to take pledges of security for the performance of its engagements more effectual than confidence in its good faith. Such pledges are amply within the reach of the United States in their intercourse hereafter with Spain; nor is it to be presumed that those who are intrusted with the maintenance of the rights and interests of this nation will overlook or neglect the duty which may be devolved upon them of taking them.

This despatch will be delivered to you by Captain Read, of the Hornet. If the ultimate decision of the Spanish Government upon the treaty should be still pending on his arrival at Madrid, you will demand it immediately, giving notice that a delay of more than one week after your communication will be taken as a refusal. At the expiration of that time, or sooner if the decision be made known sooner to you, you will despatch Captain Read, that his return to this place may, with all confidence, be expected by the 20th of November. Should the ratifications be exchanged, your leave of absence, contemplated when you left this country, may be used at your discretion; but, if not, the President thinks it best that you should remain at Madrid, to await the contingency of events upon the meeting of Congress.

I am, very respectfully, &c.,
JOHN QUINCY ADAMS.
JOHN FORSYTH, Esq., *Minister, &c.*

Don Manuel Gonzales Salmon to Mr. Forsyth.

PALACE, *August* 19, 1819.

SIR: I have received the note you were pleased to address to me of the 12th instant, in answer to that which I had the honor to write to you on the 10th, announcing the decision which the King, my master, had judged proper to adopt in relation to the treaty concluded at Washington between the Government of Spain and the United States. In that note you begin by endeavoring to justify the meaning of the expressions contained in yours of the 21st June, which, however, appear not the less extraordinary and surprising, as I have already intimated to you. But, on this head, I refer to what I have had the honor to express to you in my said note, by which the question will be considered as put at rest, and that on no account will it be agreeable to revive it.

I therefore proceed at once to reply to the leading object of your note; and I flatter myself that my answer will convince you, on the one hand, that the Government of His Catholic Majesty could not observe a course different from that which it has taken on this occasion; and, on the other hand, that the determination of His Majesty to adopt that course is founded upon his earnest wish, as I have already stated to you, to establish the amicable relations of both our Governments upon a secure and permanent basis.

It is a fact of general notoriety, and must, therefore, be well known to you, that, as soon as the treaty concluded between His Catholic Majesty and the Government of the United States was received here, and its stipulations become known, this important subject was taken into the most serious consideration by the King, my master, as well to examine its provisions minutely as to investigate the consequences to which it might give rise in relation to your Government. From that time this important business has almost exclusively occupied the attention of the Spanish Cabinet; and it was not until after it had received the most mature deliberation that His Catholic Majesty resolved that no final decision could be taken upon it, without previously entering into various explanations and *eclaircissemens* with the Government of the United States of America.

Any other determination which might have been taken previous to this step would have been, to say the least, precipitate, and exposed to the inconveniences which it is wished to avoid; and especially not to leave the relations of good understanding re-established between both nations liable to interpretations, but to place them on solid and stable principles, as permanent as the sincere and perfect friendship and harmony which it is

desired to establish between the two Governments.

The explanations and *eclaircissemens* desired by His Majesty before a definitive resolution could be taken by him on the affair in question, are not of a nature to be obtained by the means of a messenger despatched to the United States, and the answer to which could arrive here before the 22d of the present month; and still less by reason of the retreat of the Minister Plenipotentiary of His Catholic Majesty, who, having made the treaty, and being thoroughly possessed of the whole course of the negotiation, was best qualified to demand the explanations desired. Besides, it having been the uniform wish of His Catholic Majesty to proceed with all possible care and circumspection in an affair of such moment, and having thus investigated it, as I have before stated to you, this circumstance could not have given occasion for the despatch of the messenger as intimated by you.

Nor could the explanations alluded to be entered into here under existing circumstances, on account of the want of time in the short space proposed by you. His Majesty has, therefore, resolved to appoint a confidential person to proceed to the Government of the United States for the purpose of obtaining them; thereby giving a new proof of his deference for the American Government, by his desire to be thoroughly informed of every thing which has passed in relation to the treaty.

It is true that, when this determination which the King, my master, has been pleased to take in relation to this affair will come to the knowledge of your Government, the epoch of the 22d August will have elapsed; but this circumstance need prove no obstacle to the obtaining the requisite explanations and *eclaircissemens* on the treaty, as it is to be supposed that the American Government would readily have afforded them at an earlier period if the circumstances before pointed out had not prevented their being required immediately.

The communication which I had the honor to make to you on the 10th instant, and which could not have been made sooner, has been realized in due time; and certainly the Government of the United States cannot fail to receive it favorably, if their desires, in conformity with those of His Catholic Majesty, are directed to the auspicious object of seeing the differences which existed between both Governments at once terminated, and their amicable relations consolidated upon a firm and permanent basis.

This being the sole object proposed by His Catholic Majesty, he has judged that, in order to attain it, there was no mode more fit and suitable than to investigate and explain before he gave his sanction to an agreement which is to serve as a basis of the future relations between the two Powers, whatever doubts and elucidations it might have given rise to. He has, therefore, determined to despatch to the seat of the American Government a person charged with stating to it frankly and candidly the wishes of the King, my master, which he flatters himself will be fully accomplished if he is met by similar dispositions, which it appears must be the case if your Government cherish the same sentiments by which His Majesty is animated.

In consequence of what I have herein stated, I trust that you will agree with me that the Government of the King, my master, has proceeded in this affair with all prudence and circumspection; that it has not been possible for it to take a decision upon it until it had previously instituted a full investigation, without being exposed to the hazards of a precipitate determination; and, finally, that the resolution of His Catholic Majesty, far from being liable to an unfavorable interpretation, is the most conducive to promote the principle connected with this affair, and the most likely to regulate in a satisfactory manner, while it, at the same time, reconciles the interests of both nations.

In this persuasion, I cannot but flatter myself that your communications to your Government will accord with this sentiment, and that they will tend to remove any doubtful interpretation that it might give to the determination adopted by His Catholic Majesty, and which I have already had the honor to communicate to you.

I avail myself with pleasure of this renewed occasion to offer you the assurances of my high and particular consideration. God preserve you many years.

M. GONZALES SALMON.

Mr. Forsyth to Don Manuel G. Salmon.

MADRID, *August* 21, 1819.

The undersigned, Minister Plenipotentiary of the United States near His Catholic Majesty, perceives with regret, but without surprise, from Sr. Don Manuel Gonzales Salmon's note of the 19th instant, that the determination made by the Government of Spain not to ratify the convention of the 22d February, signed at Washington by Mr. Adams and the Chevalier de Onis, will not be changed. The undersigned will not waste his own time, nor encroach upon that of His Majesty's Government, by any observations on the said note, but will proceed to discharge the only duty which, on this subject, remains for him to perform. He has the honor formally to announce that, after the 22d day of the present month, as the ratifications of the convention of the 22d February will not have been exchanged, all the claims and pretensions of the United States, which, with the spirit of moderation, the love of peace, and the delusive expectation that all causes of difference and dispute with Spain would be thereby adjusted and settled, they consented to modify or waive, will stand in the same situation as if that convention had never been made; that the United States will hold themselves free to press and enforce them in any and every mode consistent with honor that their interest may require. On the extraordinary steps taken by His Majesty's Government in this affair, the undersigned will not remark, lest he should forget that respect which is due to the Government near which, as the representative of another, he is sent to reside. Of the rumors that prevailed on this subject before the decision of

His Majesty's Government was known, (a decision he could not anticipate,) the Minister of the United States expressed himself in terms sufficiently strong. As the recent determination has proved that there was but too much truth in what he believed to be unfounded reports and gross calumnies, the undersigned must leave it to His Majesty's Government, upon whom that obligation rests, to show upon what grounds that determination is reconcilable to honor and good faith. The undersigned laments that, while communicating to his own country this unexpected result, it is not in his power to unfold the train of reasoning by which His Majesty's Government has been deluded into a belief that the course taken could be followed without serious injury to the reputation of Spain. The United States, after waiting more than twenty years, with a patience and forbearance unexampled, the operations of reason and justice upon the councils of Spain, will see with astonishment this new instance of her apparent disregard to both. The Minister of the United States, when transmitting his correspondence with His Majesty's Government to his own country, will not omit to state the assurances verbally given to him of His Catholic Majesty's earnest desire to cultivate the good-will of the United States—unfruitful professions, that cannot but produce all the effect they deserve, and all that could be rationally expected from them.

The undersigned renews to Sr. Don Manuel Gonzales Salmon the assurances of his perfect consideration and respect.

JOHN FORSYTH.

Sr. Don M. GONZALEZ SALMON, &c.

Extracts of a letter from Mr. Forsyth (marked private) to Mr. Adams, dated

MADRID, *August* 22, 1819.

The duplicates of my despatches by the Hornet not having been forwarded before this, I deem it unnecessary to send you the extract of that part of my private journal, a copy of which was transmitted with my former letters. To the information contained in my official letter of this day's date, I have little to add of much importance. The most interesting fact I am able to communicate is, that the affair of the grants is not the sole or the principal difficulty with this Government. After receiving Mr. Salmon's note of the 10th instant, and ascertaining from Duke Laval that this Government expected me to insist on the King's agreeing to receive Mr. Onis's declaration, or to make one of his own, I gave information to the Duke, with the expectation and belief that he would communicate to the Government, and to the parties interested, that this was a mistake. I had no instructions to insist upon either. We expected the King might offer it; but if he did not, the treaty was already ratified by the United States, and the act could not be recalled. To produce a good effect, I said, also, that the mistake about the grants must be corrected, if the business should be (what was altogether improbable) settled amicably in the United States. The only hope of the grantees was, to have the exchange of ratifications made here. Relying upon the correctness of the information received here of the date of Punon Rostro's and Alagon's grant, and the opinion that the cedula was the first valid act of the concession, and, of course, the date of the grant must be the date of the cedula, I intimated to Mr. Salmon that the difficulty in regard to the donations could be obviated here. His reply was, that there were other points upon which the King wished explanations. What these are, I have collected from other sources. The first and great object in view is to procure an assurance that we will not recognise Buenos Ayres, &c. The extreme pertinacity and anxiety on this subject has its origin in the disclosure made by Great Britain of the conversations between Mr. Rush and Lord Castlereagh on the contemplated reception of a Consul General, to reside officially in the United States, from the provinces of La Plata. This disclosure has done us no good. Sir Henry Wellesley, to whom, on his stating that he was endeavoring to promote our objects here, I remarked that I considered much of the difficulty of our affair was imputable to this cause, gave a very plausible answer; of its truth I am sceptical. He said the object was to show to Spain the absolute necessity of a settlement of our differences with her. Whatever was the motive, the effect has not been happy. The instructions to Onis were given before this disclosure was made; it was not useful in producing those instructions; and it is equally clear, from the conduct of Spain, that it has not had the effect of inducing her to ratify what her Minister, under these instructions, promised in her name. Sir Henry Wellesley has at all times held very reasonable language, and friendly, in relation to this affair; and, since the above conversation, he has certainly taken some pains to promote our wishes. He tells me that he sent a message by a confidential agent to the Duke of Infantado, who had urged the argument that Great Britain ought not to be irritated by the cession of Florida to us; that he was entirely mistaken in supposing Great Britain adverse to the ratification of the convention, and that he had directions from the British Ministry to press the ratification. He told Salmon that Spain would hazard much by refusing it, and that the objects he had in view could be better accomplished by ratifying immediately. After the determination of this Government was known, (and it was known immediately,) he conversed with me, and wished me to believe that it was all imputable to the dispute about the grants. I said this could not be, as the Government must know that the King, having it in his power to accept or reject Onis's declaration, he could throw upon us the burden of refusing the exchange of ratifications. He then asked if the affair of the grants could be got over here. For the reasons stated in the first part of this letter for my disclosures to Laval and Salmon, and believing myself justified by my instructions after the receipt of the letter of the 10th of August, I replied I was confident they could be. He proposed to me to permit him to engage Tatischeff, the Russian Minister,

whose influence and means of communicating with the Government are said to be superior to all the rest of the *corps diplomatique*, to have this suggestion communicated to the King. To this I consented; but as I thought it would be better, if Tatischeff did any thing, to procure his good offices by an immediate application, I apprized him of this conversation. He was very friendly in his expressions, personally believed the ratification necessary and proper for Spain, and certainly the policy of Europe required it to be done. Sir Henry and Tatischeff had a similar conversation, and the suggestion was made. The next time I saw the Russian Minister, he said, If you can give assurances that there will be no recognition of the South American Governments, the treaty will be ratified. I replied, if that is the case, there will be no ratification. I had previously furnished Duke Laval with a memorandum on this topic, which, after keeping twenty-four hours, and, I have no doubt, showing it to Lozano Torres, who is supreme here, he returned it to me. The substance of it was, that the system of the Government was an impartial neutrality; it had been adhered to when we had, in our differences with Spain, the most powerful inducements to abandon it; that, when these differences were settled, there could be no inducement to change it. If Spain desired us to remain stationary in the dispute with her colonies, the first step to secure her object was to ratify our treaty, then to consult our wishes, and so to shape her policy as to inspire a sentiment of good-will powerful enough to counteract the prepossessions naturally entertained for the people of South America by the people of the United States. This was the rational mode, and, in fact, the only mode of reaching her point. To refuse our treaty, and ask, as a condition of it, that we would not recognise, was the certain way to disappoint their wishes. The Government would not consider such a proposition. This memorandum I showed to Tatischeff. He said, what it contained was true and just, but there was no reasoning with ignorance and presumption. I did not hold any of these conversations until after the note of the 10th was received; and I was careful to express the desire that these gentlemen should do what was done, not with a view to our interest, but to prevent Spain from injuring herself, and endangering what is termed the pacific policy of Europe. On the whole, I am impressed with a belief that they will propose to exchange ratifications in Washington, with the insertion of a promise not to recognise the Patriot Governments, and to preserve the grants. The latter will be a dernier resort, given up as the price of the first. Without this, or something equivalent, we may do ourselves justice; they will not.

Mr. Forsyth to the Duke of San Fernando.

MADRID, *October* 2, 1819.

SIR: The Government of the United States, having been prepared to expect the possibility of a failure on the part of Spain to ratify the convention of the 22d of February last, by the extraordinary delay to decide upon this subject, and the determination of the King further to postpone that decision, as communicated in the note of Mr. Salmon to me of the 19th of June; have instructed me, should the final decision on it by the King not be made prior to this time, to inform the Government of His Catholic Majesty that, although the six months stipulated in the treaty, within which the ratifications were to be exchanged, have expired, the ratification of Spain, made with the explicit understanding that the large grants of land in Florida to the Duke of Alagon, the Count of Punon Rostro, and Mr. Vargas, and all others made under similar circumstances, are, by the eighth article of that convention, null and void, and will be so held by the United States, will be accepted as valid; and I am authorized to receive the Spanish ratification for that of the United States, provided this exchange shall be immediate. This exchange must take place soon enough to enable me to send the ratified treaty to the United States by Captain Read, of the sloop of war Hornet, of the Navy of the United States, who will remain in Madrid ten days to carry to the President the final determination of Spain on this subject. Having received from your Excellency's predecessors in office no explanation of the particular causes of the delay that has taken place, it is in my power only to explain the reasons which induce the Government of the United States to insist upon an explicit understanding of the force and obligation of the eighth article of the treaty prior to the exchange of ratifications—an understanding which will be fully shown by a declaration I am instructed to present at the time of the exchange, should it ever take place, a copy of which is enclosed. It was rumored in the United States, and, since my residence in Madrid, I have been informed, that the large grantees declare that their grants are valid under the eighth article. It has been asserted, with the strongest appearances of truth, that the determination of the Government of the United States to hold them void, as expressed in the letter of Mr. Adams, the Secretary of State, to Mr. Onis, of the 10th of March, 1819, has been one of the chief causes of the extraordinary delay to decide upon the ratification of the instrument in Spain. It is necessary to the honor and the interest of the United States, whose conduct to Spain and to all nations is governed by frankness and justice, free from fraud, artifice, and disguise, which they will never practise, nor from others submit to a disingenuous, double-dealing system of treachery, paltering with its own engagements, and spreading snares for the generous confidence of good faith, to place this subject beyond the reach of difficulty or doubt. Without knowing, therefore, the dates of the respective grants alluded to, and supposing it barely possible that there is a foundation for a pretension of the grantees under the eighth article, the Government directs me to present the declaration in question, not less essential to its own interest than to the honor of the King of Spain, since His Majesty would be subjected to the most unworthy imputations if, under the circumstances, a claim should be made by his subjects, or those holding under them, founded upon the alleged validity of these grants.

To suppose that your Excellency is not in possession of all the facts in relation to this subject, would be a reflection on the zeal and fidelity of the representative of Spain in the United States, which I would be unwilling to cast upon any officer of His Majesty's Government. I do not, therefore, send you copies of those documents, which show explicitly that, prior and subsequent to the signature of the treaty, it was expressly understood by the negotiators of that instrument that the eighth article, written by the Spanish Minister himself, excluded these grants. In fact, when the lands of Florida were ceded, with an express stipulation that the claims of the citizens of the United States upon Spain were to be paid out of the proceeds of the sale of them, to suppose that the Spanish Government had disposed of the whole or the greater part of them in gifts to its subjects, and will insist upon the validity of those gifts, is to suppose it capable of an act of notorious and deliberate perfidy. The Government of my country considered that the treaty became, from the moment of its signature by the Chevalier de Onis, and the ratification of the United States, as binding upon the honor and good *faith of the* Spanish King and nation as it would be *after the* ratification. Although I do not understand that this position is, or will be, contested by Spain, it may not be useless to show its strength fully to the view of your Excellency. The words of His Catholic Majesty, in the full power given to Mr. Onis, the original of which was delivered to the American Government before the signature of the treaty, are, after authorizing Mr. Onis to treat, negotiate, and conclude a treaty, whereby past differences may be adjusted, and a firm and lasting peace established between the two Governments: "Obligandonos y prometemos, en fe y palabra de Rey, que aprobaremos, ratificaremos, cumpliremos, y haremos observar y cumplir inviolablemente quanto por vos fuere estipulado y firmado; para lo qual os concedo todas las facultades y plenos poderes en la forma mas amplia que de derecho se requieren." If the usage of nations, which requires the ratification of the sovereign for the full confirmation of a treaty, could create any doubt of the import of language so unqualified and explicit, there is nothing dubious or uncertain in the extent of the obligation resting upon him by the signature of his Minister, vested with such full powers. Upon this principle, the following quotations from Vattel and Martens are decisive authorities: "Sovereigns treat together by the agency of their attorneys or their mandatories, clothed with sufficient powers; they are commonly called Plenipotentiaries. All the rules of the law of nature, concerning things performed by commission, are here applicable. The rights of the agent are defined by the authority given to him. From this he must not depart; but whatever he promises within the terms of his commission, and according to the extent of his powers, is binding upon his constituent." "At this time, to avoid all dan-

Spain—Ratification of the Treaty of 1819.

ger and difficulty, Princes reserve to themselves the right of ratifying that which has been concluded by their Ministers in their name. The full power is merely a commission, *cum libera.* If this commission were to have its full effect, it should be given with the utmost circumspection; but, as Princes can be constrained to fulfil their obligations only by force of arms, the custom has arisen of relying upon their treaties only after they have sanctioned and ratified them. Whatever the Minister has concluded remaining ineffectual until the ratification of the Prince, there is less danger in giving him a full power. But to refuse, with honor, to ratify that which has been concluded in virtue of a full power, the sovereign must have strong and solid reasons for it, and, particularly, he must show that his Minister transcended his instructions."—*Vattel, book* 2, *chap.* 12, § 156.

"Every thing that has been stipulated by an agent, in conformity to his full powers, ought to become obligatory for the State from the moment of signing, without ever waiting for the ratification. However, not to expose a State to the errors of a single person, it is now become a general maxim that public conventions do not become obligatory until ratified. The motive of this custom clearly proves that the ratification can never be refused with justice, except when he who is charged with the negotiation, keeping within the extent of his public full powers, has gone beyond his secret instructions, and consequently rendered himself liable to punishment, or when the other party refuses to ratify."—*Martens's Summary, book* 2, *chap.* 3. But why should quotations be made to prove a principle so familiar to every man in public or private life, that what is promised in his name, by his authority, and according to his directions, is as binding in honor and conscience as if he had pledged himself in person? The obligation of the King of Spain, therefore, in honor and in justice, to ratify the treaty signed by his Minister, is as perfect and unqualified as his royal promise in the full power, and it gives to the United States the right, equally perfect, to compel the performance of that promise. It is well known to my Government that the Spanish Government cannot allege that its Minister transcended his secret instructions, or that the ratification of the United States has been refused, or that any unfair advantage was taken by the United States in the negotiation, or that Spain was not well aware beforehand of the full extent of the engagements contracted by Mr. Onis. It is too well known to be denied that the last instructions of Mr. Onis authorized him to concede much more than he did. The Government of the United States, indeed, considered the generosity and moderation of the terms to which they had acceded as a pledge that they would be received, as in the first instance they were received, by His Catholic Majesty and his royal council with pride and joy. If, from the unexpected extent of the sacrifices the United States made for the purposes of conciliation, the conclusion has been drawn that their conciliatory temper may be trifled with and abused, it *is* just and proper that Spain should be effectually unde-

ceived. I am, therefore, instructed further to inform your Excellency that, if the ratified copy of the treaty should not arrive in the United States before the first day on which the Congress of the United States meets, the President will lay before that body all the transactions relating to the treaty, and such measures will be adopted by the competent authority as the exigency of the case may require. Whatever may be determined upon, Spain will be responsible to the United States for all damages and expenses which may arise from the delay to ratify, and from the measures to which the United States may resort to give efficacy to their rights, and that, for the indemnities to which they will be justly entitled by this violation of faith by Spain, the United States will look to the territory west of their present western boundary on the Gulf of Mexico.

To this proposal, made in the spirit of moderation, of generous forbearance, and with the earnest desire of sincere amity with Spain, I am instructed to require an immediate, explicit, and unequivocal reply. Should this reply not be made before the 10th of the current month, I give formal notice to your Excellency that the proposal will be considered as rejected, and the proper communication will be made to the President of the United States.

I renew to your Excellency, whom may God preserve, the assurances of my distinguished consideration.   JOHN FORSYTH.

  DUKE OF SAN FERNANDO AND QUIROGA.

Duke of San Fernando and Quiroga to Mr. Forsyth.

               PALACE, *October* 8, 1819.

SIR: Having had the honor to lay before the King, my master, the contents of the note which you addressed to me on the 2d instant, His Majesty, whose justice and impartiality are so universally known, having examined the principal points embraced therein, has commanded me to answer you as follows:

The official communications addressed to you by Don Manuel Gonzales Salmon might exempt me, it would seem, from all further discussion of the subject in question; inasmuch as His Majesty, actuated as well by the claims of his honor and duty as by a uniform spirit of justice and conciliation towards the United States, and pursuing the example of his august predecessors, who, at an early period, and to promote the very establishment of the American Government, gave such abundant proofs of similar dispositions, had determined, upon mature reflection and deliberation, to send a Minister to that Government, who, after requiring and giving the necessary explanations, might terminate this affair; and as neither the actual state of the question, nor what you have been pleased to communicate to me, presents any motive for changing a resolution so deliberate and so just, and which the honor of His Majesty also forbids, there appears to be a still more urgent motive to confirm it.

With this answer I might leave you completely satisfied; but I especially take leave, with the permission of the King, my lord, to reply to some of the points treated of in your note with the brevity and precision which characterize me; and because you state that you have not yet received an explanation of the delay in ratifying the treaty, and attribute it to the difficulties arising out of its eighth article. You will permit me to remark to you that this delay does not manifest that want of good faith, or the artifice which is indirectly insinuated; it is rather the declaration now demanded by you, and previously announced by your Government, after having signed and ratified the treaty—a declaration which, by annulling one of its most clear, express, and conclusive articles, seemed much more likely to give room for a similar charge in opposition to yours.

If your Government, as you are pleased to state to me, really believed that the treaty, from the moment it was signed, became equally obligatory on Spain as it was on the United States, under whose immediate inspection it was formed, signed, and ratified, you will permit me to remark that, whether we consider that point, or weigh the authority of authors cited by you in support of your opinion, the deductions from them, and the weight of many others I now forbear to adduce, as it might seem to offend your illustration, militate against you. But even fancying them for a moment, without ever admitting them, the very authorities which you deem conclusive in relation to a treaty signed but not ratified, are opposed to you, or require still more forcibly that an agreement concluded, signed, and solemnly ratified, as the present one has been by your Government, should be subjected to a due investigation. And if, notwithstanding this, declarations are required at the moment of its solemn conclusion, and before its ratification by the other party, which totally annul one of its most clear, precise, and conclusive articles, without the sanction of a secret agreement authorizing the same, how should it appear strange that His Majesty, while yet unfettered by its stipulations, might and should demand explanations rendered necessary by so unlooked-for a proceeding? In the transaction of settlements or agreements between nation and nation, the solemn act which consummates them, namely, the ratification, would become wholly illusory, if the principles which it is now in vain attempted to establish were to be admitted. I again repeat, that the very authorities cited by you literally declare, as I have already remarked, that the sovereign, for strong and solid reasons, or if his Minister has exceeded his instructions, may refuse his ratification, [*Vattel, lib.* 2, *cap.* 12,] and that public treaties are not obligatory until ratified.—[*Martens, lib.* 2, *cap.* 3. *See note.*]

No less erroneous, and even unprecedented, is the judgment or consequence you draw from the instructions which you suppose to have been given to His Majesty's Minister for the conclusion of this treaty. Truly it would be the first time that a diplomatic communication, professing to be thoroughly and minutely acquainted with these instructions, should cite them as being perfectly well known. The respect due to the King's negotiators will not for a moment allow me to be-

lieve they have failed in their obligations, by violating secrecy; nor will the high consideration I entertain for your Government permit me to think it capable of having employed the oblique and vicious means that such information must imply. It is, therefore, wholly impossible for me to admit your assertion on this point.

But, dismissing so unpleasant a discussion, and desiring to express to you anew the spirit of conciliation and friendship which prompts the King, my master, to put an end to these differences, as I declared to you in the beginning of this note, I am enabled to assure you that it is a subject of great regret to His Majesty that such weighty considerations should have hitherto obliged him to defer the ratification of the treaty concluded by his Minister to the Federal Government. These considerations, already stated by Don Manuel Gonzales Salmon on communicating to you His Majesty's determination, acquire additional force when we find that intelligence has been received, through the medium of general information, newspapers, and correspondence, that an expedition directed against the province of Texas has been tolerated or protected, and other acts committed within the limited but unexpired term assigned for the ratification, which, as you will be duly informed, have justly called for the remonstrances of His Majesty's Chargé d'Affaires to your Government. Notwithstanding His Majesty has uniformly evinced a desire to maintain a perfect union and amity with the American Government, yet, to render these stable and permanent between two nations who, under favor of a state of amity, are endeavoring to settle their differences, it is necessary they should be based upon reciprocal utility and confidence. In the indulgence of these noble and generous sentiments, His Majesty confidently looks to the attainment of this desirable result. This was the object of the treaty—an object unfortunately not attained, notwithstanding the enormous sacrifices which the King, my master, condescended to make. In these feelings and dispositions His Majesty still perseveres, by adopting a measure judged indispensable—that of sending to the Government of the United States, as will promptly be done, a person possessing his entire confidence, and who, by smoothing the obstacles or removing the difficulties which have hitherto opposed the accomplishment of his beneficent intentions, may fully convince the Federal Government of the frankness and loyalty, as well as of the honor and dignity, which it is His Majesty's desire to maintain in his relations of amity and union with that Government.

Whereupon, I renew to you my sincere respects, and I pray God to preserve you many years.

SAN FERNANDO Y QUIROGA.

To the MINISTER *of the United States.*

Extract of a letter of Mr. Forsyth to the Secretary of State, dated

MADRID, *October* 10, 1819.

Captain Read reached Cadiz on the 17th instant. The condition of that dreadfully afflicted

Spain—Ratification of the Treaty of 1819.

place, and the neighboring towns, obliged him, after remaining some hours in the bay, to go to Gibraltar. From Gibraltar he made his way, with some difficulty, to Santa Cruz, one hundred miles from Madrid. From Santa Cruz, I received information that he was stopped there. I applied immediately to the Secretary of State for permission for him to pursue his journey. I directed Mr. Brent, who went to see the Duke of San Fernando, to say that if the permission to Captain Read could not be given, I must request a passport for myself to ride that far to confer with him. While in a very uneasy state of suspense, Captain Read arrived, and delivered me your letter of the 18th August, with duplicate of your No. 6, with the documents. Two or three hours after he reached Madrid, I was informed by the Secretary of State that he must perform at Santa Cruz a quarantine of eight or ten days. The correspondence between us will show in what manner the Captain was enabled to continue his journey; copies are enclosed, marked Nos. 6, 7, 8. On the night of the 3d, I had, preparatory to the offer to exchange the ratifications according to my instructions, a long conversation with the Duke of San Fernando. I did not discover in this interview any reasonable prospect of the immediate acceptance of the treaty. The Duke professed to be anxious to preserve a good understanding with the United States—that the King wished explanations, &c. On my asking him what would be the conduct of Spain? would the treaty be ratified if these explanations were not satisfactory? he replied, that was a point upon which his royal master had not expressed his pleasure. In the course of the conversation, he expressed the hope that my note would be couched in respectful terms; that, if it was not, I must not be surprised if it was returned to me. I told him that the note was prepared by, and according to the instructions of my Government, and, if returned to me, I should not consider the offence as personal, but as offered to the United States.

To avoid the very disagreeable consequence which must ensue, I suggested that if he found any thing harsh in the note, I would change it, if it could be done without altering its meaning or impairing its strength; but that no term could be touched which was essential to convey, substantially, what the note contained. After a very long interview, not at all satisfactory, except that it proved the good dispositions and politeness of the Secretary of State, I delivered my official note, copy marked No. 9,* with the proposal in Spanish, marked P, that the Minister might be immediately master of what was asked and expected of the King. The answer of the Minister was delivered this afternoon. The copy of it is marked No. 10. The Spanish Government will persist in the plan of sending a Minister to ask explanations at Washington. The note of the Duke of San Fernando confirms the information already given of the points on which these explanations will be asked.

---

* Communicated to Congress with the message of 7th December, 1819.

I cannot venture to conjecture what will be the conduct of this Government, should it not receive what it wishes to procure from us. In the mean time, although it is said that General Vives is named to go to Washington, it is not certain. To-morrow I shall ask for copies of the grants to Alagon, Punon Rostro, and Vargas, preparatory to the remonstrance I am directed to make, and to my reply to the note of the Duke. I hope to send you copies of the grants, and of my reply; but shall not detain Captain Read if they are not ready before he is prepared for his journey. He will leave this on Tuesday morning for Malaga, to which place the Hornet must go from Gibraltar, to take him on board, all travelling from Spain being interdicted by the governors of that fortress.

JOHN FORSYTH.

No. 6.

Mr. Forsyth to the Duke of San Fernando and Quiroga.

MADRID, *September* 30, 1819.

SIR: Captain Read, commanding the sloop of war Hornet, of the Navy of the United States, bearing despatches to me from the American Government, has been stopped on his way from Gibraltar to this place. I have the honor to apply to your Excellency for an order to the proper authority to permit him to pursue his journey. Captain Read arrived at Gibraltar on the 20th instant, his crew in good health, from the port of New York. Although the quarantine regulations at Gibraltar are at this time particularly severe, his vessel was immediately admitted to *pratique.* At St. Roque the captain received assurances from the director of posts that he would meet no difficulty in proceeding to this city. The Hornet was anchored for a few hours in the bay of Cadiz. The enclosed correspondence between the American Consul and the *junta de sanidad* will show that she had no communication with any vessel in the harbor during her short stay in the bay. Under these circumstances, I trust the order for which this application is made will be immediately given.

I seize every occasion to renew to your Excellency the assurances of my very distinguished respect.

JOHN FORSYTH.

No. 7.

The Duke of San Fernando and Quiroga to Mr. Forsyth.

PALACE, *September* 30, 1819.

SIR: Having received information from the supreme board of health, in consequence of your note of this day's date relating to the detention of Captain Read at Santa Cruz, conformably with the opinion given by the aforesaid board, and founded upon the laws enacted for the preservation of health, it is my duty to inform you that the said captain and his crew are respectively subjected to a quarantine of eight or ten days, with the requisite purification of all effects susceptible of contagion; and that, if it be your determination to go and confer with him, you may proceed to do so, on subjecting yourself to the same conditions.

I hope, therefore, that you will inform me of your

intentions on this point, that I may transmit the necessary orders by to-morrow's mail.

I reiterate the assurances of my high consideration, and I pray God to preserve you many years.

SAN FERNANDO Y QUIROGA.

To the MINISTER *of the United States.*

No. 8.

Mr. Forsyth to the Duke of San Fernando and Quiroga, First Minister of State, &c.

MADRID.

SIR : Captain Read, of the Navy of the United States, with despatches from my Government, whose detention at Santa Cruz caused me to address your Excellency on the 30th September, arrived in Madrid a few hours before I had the honor to receive a reply. A short time after he was stopped at Santa Cruz he learned that the order of the junta de sanidad was directed only to the director of the posts, and prohibited only travelling with post-horses from Andalusia. As he came from Gibraltar with regular passports, there was nothing to prevent him from pursuing his journey in the private or hired conveyance in which he prosecuted it to this place. In performing his own duty, he had neither inclination nor intention to violate any of the ordinances of any of the authorities of the kingdom, nor, as far as he was informed, did he infringe upon the established regulations. I should not have thought it necessary to mention his arrival, except incidentally, had not the answer of your Excellency to my official note, in his behalf, been written under the expectation that he would be detained in quarantine eight or ten days, and had it not given also the very extraordinary intimation that I should be subjected to a similar restriction if I went to confer with him at the place to which he was restricted.

I renew to your Excellency the assurances of my high consideration.

JOHN FORSYTH.

P.

Proposal (in Spanish) transmitted by Mr. Forsyth to the Duke of San Fernando and Quiroga, in his note dated October 10, 1819.

Although the six months stipulated for the exchange of the ratifications of the treaty concluded between the Government of the United States and Spain, at Washington, on the 22d of February last, have expired, I am authorized by the President to make known to His Catholic Majesty that the ratification by Spain will be received as valid on the precise and express condition that the grants of land in the Floridas, made to the Duke of Alagon, the Count of Punon Rostro, and Mr. Vargas, and, in like manner, any others which shall have been made under similar circumstances, shall, in conformity with the eighth article of the said convention or treaty, be null and void, and shall never be admitted by the United States. The force and effect of the said article shall be shown by a declaration to be presented on the exchange of the ratifications by the American Minister,

unless His Catholic Majesty should prefer the declaration to be made by the Spanish Government. I am authorized to make the exchange immediately when this is done. .It is essentially necessary that the exchange be made in season, so as to enable me to transmit the ratified treaty to the United States by Captain Read, of the national sloop of war Hornet, who will remain ten days at Madrid for the purpose of being the bearer to the President of the final decision of His Catholic Majesty on this important concern.

Extract of a letter from Mr. Forsyth to the Secretary of State, dated

MADRID, *October* 10, 1819.

The arrival of the Hornet produced a great deal of anxiety here. As soon as it was known that Captain Read was in Madrid, the Duke Laval paid me a visit to learn for what she was sent back. Anxious to apprize the Government as early as possible what we required of it, I told him what I should immediately propose, and gave him permission to communicate it to the Secretary of State if he thought proper. Before my official letter was copied, Duke Laval paid me another visit. He had seen the Secretary of State, and had promised to engage me to have a conversation with the Secretary before my note was sent in ; seeing no objection to this, I kept back my note, to be delivered at our interview, which took place the ensuing night. I was led to believe that the Government might be induced to agree to the proposal I was directed to make, but was apprehensive that the manner of presenting it would form an insurmountable obstacle. With this view, I prepared the Spanish note sent with my despatch of to-day, intending to say to the Duke of San Fernando, if the proposal was accepted, that that might be considered the official note, and the other would be received again from his hands. Finding no just grounds in his conversation to believe the proposal would be acceded to, I determined to present it, as I did, as an unofficial paper for the convenience of the Minister of State. The subsequent observation that my note would be returned, if not respectfully written, satisfied me that this determination was more than judicious. This suggestion was made with as much delicacy as it could be made, and seemed to arise from the apprehension that their dignity would compel them to a step it was very obvious they would have taken with great reluctance. Indeed, when the Duke informed me that the courtesy of nations did not permit one Power to prescribe to another the time within which a thing required must be granted or refused, I began to imagine that, according to their ideas of respectful treatment, the return of the note was certain. Had it been returned, I should have had the honor of making this communication to you in person. The present Secretary of State is sincerely disposed to preserve good terms with us. The influence of the grantees is still predominant, and will, I apprehend, continue until something stronger than words is used to bring our disputes to an end. Onis has been in Madrid since the last of August,

Spain—Ratification of the Treaty of 1819.

a private man; it is understood that the King does not impute blame to him, yet he has never been consulted in any of the several councils that have been called on the subject. The present Minister has had some informal conversation with him, but he has given neither explanation nor advice to the Government, because he has not been asked for either.

It will surprise you to be informed that there are persons about this Court who want a war with the United States. There are very many individuals who have licenses to fit out privateers; these are looking with eagerness to the chance of enriching themselves at our expense. As to the effect upon their country, that is another affair, about which they are indifferent. The maxim is almost universal here—if I am enriched, it is of no consequence how much the country is distressed.

Extracts of a letter from the Secretary of State to Mr. Forsyth, dated

MADRID, *October* 28, 1819.

"By return of the Hornet, which sailed from Malaga on the 20th, you have been informed that I applied, on the 10th instant, to the Spanish Government for copies of the large grants to Alagon, Punon Rostro, and Vargas. Receiving no answer to this application before Captain Read left Madrid, I addressed a second note on the 15th. On the 16th, I received from the Duke of San Fernando the refusal to furnish them. The whole correspondence on this subject is enclosed, marked Nos. 1, 2, 3, and 4. This refusal was as unexpected to me as it no doubt will be to you." "The best information I could procure of these donations was immediately obtained." "You will perceive that, in the remonstrance made, (according to your instructions received by the Hornet,) a copy of which is enclosed, marked No. 5, I have not made any distinction between the three grants, but examined the questions between the two Governments as if they stood on the same footing. If my idea is correct, that the royal order conveys no title, they are alike, the cedulas of the three being subsequent to the 24th January, 1818; and, as it regards the conduct of the United States, the stipulation was perfect for the exclusion of all. In addition to this, as the Spanish Government has not explained itself fully, I was not bound to know that they made any distinction between them. It may, for aught that appears, insist that Vargas's grant is valid, either from the date being different from what I suppose it to be, or on some other ground. As to the conduct of Spain, the difference of the dates of the grants, and the accidental difference of a day between the date fixed by the treaty and that of the donation of Vargas, cannot affect the conclusion drawn; while the peculiar nature of the last donation is important to show the character of the whole transaction. By the extract of your letter to Mr. Onis of the 31st October, 1818, it appears that some remonstrances were made by Mr. Erving to Mr. Pizarro about the time these donations were made. No trace of these remonstrances [is] to be found in this legation, except a letter, marked *private*, from Mr. Pizarro, of the 19th July, in which he requests Mr. Erving not to give himself any uneasiness on the subject of these donations.

"I have already, in my No. 7, informed you that there is no copy here of Mr. Erving's correspondence with the Department of State. Not knowing the extent of his communications on that subject, I am not aware that any benefit could have been derived from them. I am told here that the proceedings in these donations were suspended for some time; that Alagon, Punon Rostro, and Vargas, were required to give up, and did surrender, their grants to the Crown; and that Punon Rostro was preparing, if he did not actually make a memorial to the King, for certain commercial privileges, as a remuneration for his loss. This information, although it came from such a quarter that I could place perfect reliance on its correctness, did not come to me in such a shape that I could use it in addressing the Spanish Government. The Court has been so fully occupied with the marriage of the King, and the distribution of the *gracias* usually bestowed on these occasions, that our affair seems to be forgotten. General Vives, who is still said to be destined for the United States as Minister Plenipotentiary, has not yet arrived in Madrid. He had a command within the limits of the country, between which and the capital intercourse was prohibited on account of the yellow fever; and it is said that he is performing quarantine, preparatory to coming to this place. I use the impersonal, for no part of the information respecting Vives, his appointment or movements, comes to me, directly or indirectly, from this Government.

"A report has been industriously circulated here that some arrangement had been made by Spain and Britain, in consequence of the probability of a war between Spain and the United States. So much was said about it, that, without giving any credit to it, I deemed it prudent to inquire into its truth. My first application was made to Sir Henry Wellesley, to whom I spoke of it jestingly, as a proof of the extravagance and folly of the suppositions and surmises of the Puerta del Sol; (the place where the news of the day is discussed by Spanish politicians.) He spoke of it in the same strain; but our conversation concluded by a most solemn assurance given, on his honor, that there was not the slightest foundation for such a report; that the only arrangement lately made with Spain related to the terms of an old contract for permission to the British Government to purchase specie in Spanish America."

No. 1.

MADRID, *October* 10, 1819.

John Forsyth, Minister Plenipotentiary of the United States, presents his respects to the Duke of San Fernando and Quiroga, Secretary of State and Despatch, and requests that authenticated copies of the grants to the Duke of Alagon, Count Punon Rostro, and Mr. Vargas, should be sent to him as early as the convenience of the Department of State will permit

John Forsyth, American Minister, offers to the Duke of San Fernando, the assurances of his respectful consideration.

No. 2.

Mr. Forsyth to the Duke of San Fernando and Quiroga.

MADRID, *October* 15, 1819.

The Minister Plenipotentiary of the United States presents his compliments to the Duke of San Fernando and Quiroga, and had the honor to request of his Excellency, on the 10th instant, copies of the grants made to the Duke of Alagon, to the Count of Punon Rostro, and to Mr. Vargas, which it is very important for him to have.

The Minister trusts that these copies will be furnished as expeditiously as possible, and renews the assurance of his distinguished respect.

No. 3.

The Duke of San Fernando and Quiroga to Mr. Forsyth.

PALACE, *October* 15, 1819.

The Duke of San Fernando and Quiroga presents his compliments to Mr. John Forsyth, Minister Plenipotentiary of the United State of America, and has the honor to inform him that, having made known to the King, his lord, the wish of Mr. Forsyth to obtain authentic copies of the grants of land made to the Duke of Alagon, the Count of Punon Rostro, and Mr. Vargas, His Majesty has declared that it is not possible for him to comply with this wish without being wanting in what is due to his dignity; as he conceives that his word, alone, in the matter of the grants, is, in addition to their publicity, the most authentic certificate that can or ought to be given.

The Duke renews to the Minister Plenipotentiary his wish to be entirely devoted to him, and that God may long preserve his life.

No. 4.

Mr. Forsyth to the Duke of San Fernando and Quiroga.

MADRID, *October* 16, 1819.

John Forsyth, the Minister Plenipotentiary of the United States of North America, presents his respects to the Duke of San Fernando and Quiroga, and acknowledges the receipt of his note of the 15th October.

The American Minister considers the refusal to furnish the copies of the grants of the Duke of Alagon, Count Punon Rostro, and Mr. Vargas, for which he applied, as singular as the reason that is assigned for it. These donations having unfortunately produced new differences between the United States and Spain, he believed that he had a right to expect copies of them whenever an application was made to procure them. He is not aware that the royal word has been given in this business, and would now request where it is to be found, if he was confident it could be done without offending the royal dignity—a dignity so refined and etherial as to be above the comprehension of an American Minister. His Excellency the Secretary of State and Despatch has said, individually, and by permission of the King, that the dec-

laration intended to be presented by the American Minister, if the exchange of the ratification of the convention of the 22d of February took place contradicted the eighth article of that instrument From this assertion an inference was to be drawn that the above-mentioned grants, or some of them. were of a date prior to the 24th January, 1818, the day named in that article of the treaty. Without failing in the respect due to the Secretary of State. and which the American Minister desires at all times to exhibit, it was important for him to ascertain whether *all* or a *part* of these grants were considered valid by Spain; whether made *prior to. at the time of,* or *subsequent* to the authority given to Mr. Onis to offer a cession of Florida to the United States; whether *the whole,* or only a part, and, if a *part,* what part of the lands in that territory was included in them—information necessary to the formation of a correct judgment of the character of this transaction. His Excellency the Duke of San Fernando and Quiroga must be sensible that copies of these grants can be obtained only from the persons owning them, or from the archives of the Indies, and that the Minister of the United States, having no right to believe that the owners would submit the original papers to his inspection. or suffer copies to be taken of them, had no resource but an application to the Government.

Not having procured the desired information from the most authentic source, he will be under the necessity of seeking it wherever it can be found; and if, in presenting this subject hereafter to His Majesty's Government, any error should be communicated, the Duke of San Fernando and Quiroga will not forget the application made for correct information, and the refusal to give it.

John Forsyth, the American Minister, reiterates to his Excellency the Duke of San Fernando and Quiroga the assurances of his profound consideration.

No. 5.

Mr. Forsyth to the Duke of San Fernando and Quiroga.

MADRID, *October* 18, 1819.

SIR : I have had the honor to receive your Excellency's answer of the 8th instant to my official note of the 2d.

It is not with a vain hope of producing any effect upon the opinions of this Government that I refer again to this subject; a determination being deliberately made, and comporting, as your Excellency says, with the honor of the King, it will no doubt be adhered to. Time and experience are the correctors of the errors of States and Kingdoms; and the hour comes when the wisdom or imprudence of this determination will be sufficiently apparent.

Having communicated to my Government the correspondence between us, the business is at rest; but I avail myself of the opportunity offered by the performance of another duty to make some observations called for by your Excellency's note. That His Majesty should recur to the example of his predecessor in considering the subject of the convention, is perfectly natural; since, to the friendship existing between the United States and his ancestor, His Majesty is indebted for the possession of that territory of Florida proposed to be ceded by it ; but the King is deceived and misled when he believes that the United States or any other Power can see in the recent or previous conduct of his Government the spirit of conciliation and good-will. The stubborn integrity of reason rejects all the professions that are contradicted by the actions of Princes and States. Knowing his intentions, your Excellency's royal master may consider the opinions already formed as harsh and injurious ; but it is the unfortunate peculiarity of this negotiation that every thing done and left undone by Spain serves to justify them. I will not recapitulate what has been previously urged, but content myself with reminding your Excellency that two months have elapsed since I was informed by Mr. Salmon that explanations would be asked at Washington ; I am still to learn to whom this duty is to be intrusted. Judging from this delay, I might, did I consider it important, ask your Excellency, Will the person in whom the King confides see the United States in the beginning or towards the end of the ensuing year ?

Your Excellency has misconceived the purport of what has been urged in regard to the obligation imposed by the signature of his Minister to the treaty on the King. You suppose it to be directed to the obligation to execute the treaty ; it was directed to the obligation to ratify it. Nothing is more clear than the obligation imposed in this case by justice and honor. What is extraordinary in your Excellency's answer is, the supposition that the United States are bound by the treaty, while Spain is at liberty, and according to circumstances, to bind herself or not. The United States were bound until the 22d of August last ; beyond that period the question of the treaty is as open to my Government as that of your Excellency's royal master. The offer made to accept the ratification of Spain as valid since that period was altogether gratuitous, and sprung from motives, it would appear, not duly appreciated or understood. It is true the Government of the United States has an alternative to choose : the treaty may be considered as binding on both the parties to it, and an attempt made to compel a performance ; or a resort may be had to the original claims, and an exertion made to enforce them.

Your Excellency supposes it impossible that the assertion that Mr. Onis did not exceed his secret instructions can be made good. If the production of a copy of those instructions were necessary to show the correctness of such an assertion, certainly it could not be shown ; but there is a species of moral demonstration of the terms of secret instructions which is sufficiently strong to satisfy the judgments of men, without the necessity of calling in question the integrity of negotiators or the purity of Governments. Abundant materials for the demonstration of this assertion exist, and will be used whenever it shall be necessary. To the number of these your Excellency has furnished an additional one, of conclusive force, by resting your observation *not* upon *the fact* that the secret

instructions *were violated*, but upon the *impossibility* of *producing proof that they were not.*

Your Excellency errs in supposing me acquainted with the reclamations made by His Majesty's Chargé d'Affaires in America, or with the incursions into the territory of Texas—incursions neither protected nor tolerated by my Government ; and, if they have been made, were secretly prepared and executed before it was practicable for it to interfere. As they could have no possible connexion with the question of ratification, they have not been communicated to me by the Government of the United States. Neither of these, however, can justify the delay that has taken place, since the power of His Majesty to require, and the inclination and ability of the United States to make, reparation for any injuries done to Spain would not have been affected by the ratification of the treaty. It may not, however, be useless to suggest to His Majesty's Government that the failure to ratify by Spain has deprived her of the right to expect reparation for any incursion into Texas, as a large portion of what is termed the province of Texas is within the limit claimed by the United States—a claim yet existing, since the convention of the 22d of February is not ratified by Spain, whose best title to the said territory was contained in that instrument.

Your Excellency is not happy in supposing there is any justification for the delay to ratify, and the determination to ask explanations, in the example of my Government in relation to the eighth article of the treaty. The United States have not asked, nor do they ask, any explanation of the article in question. They understand it to impose a certain obligation entered into according to the intention of the parties. They were informed that their intention was not fairly or fully expressed, and, as justice and good faith required, they gave notice to the Spanish Government of their resolution to execute the article according to its spirit and intention. The address to Mr. Onis was to procure, in the simplest form, the evidence to show what that intention was. Your Excellency will pardon me for saying that I am shocked at the assertion now made, that the declaration intended to be presented at the exchange of ratifications annuls the said article, as it obliges me to conclude that the grants to the Duke of Alagon, the Count of Punon Rostro, and Mr. Vargas, are, in the opinion of this Government, of a date prior to the 24th of January, 1818, the date named in that article of the treaty ; and that the Government of Spain believes itself authorized to insist that they would be valid under it. This disclosure compels me, from the duty I owe to my country, and in obedience to the instructions I have received, earnestly to remonstrate against the conduct of Spain in relation to these grants—a conduct towards the United States injurious, unjust, and deceptious, and which cannot fail, when made known, to excite the resentment of all nations who prize honorable dealing and love good faith.

The history of these donations, and of the stipulation in regard to them, will show that the determination of the United States to consider them void under the treaty was justifiable, proper, and necessary to the honest fulfilment of the engagement into which they had entered ; and that a denial of this position would fix upon the Spanish Government a charge of an attempt to commit a deception, for which the language of decorum has no appropriate name. The possession of Florida has long been an object of interest to the United States—a land useless and expensive to His Catholic Majesty, and chiefly valuable by its position to them. Ever since the restoration of His Majesty to the throne of Spain, the question of the cession of that territory has been agitated. In the Summer or Autumn of 1817, after the determination to negotiate all matters in dispute at Washington, it is to be presumed authority was given to Mr. Onis to offer the Floridas for an equivalent to the United States. In July, 1817, Mr. Pizarro informed Mr. Erving that the instructions for Mr. Onis were preparing. Comparing the date of the offer of cession made by that Minister, of the 24th January, 1818, with the time necessary for transmitting the instructions under which it was made, the conclusion is, that, prior to November, 1817, the authority was given to Mr. Onis to offer Florida to the United States, according to the instructions preparing by Mr. Pizarro at the date of his communication to Mr. Erving, of the 27th July, 1817. (See No. 1.) In November following, the prospect of a cession to the United States having made property in that territory valuable, petitions were presented to His Majesty for grants of land in Florida by the Duke of Alagon and Count Punon Rostro. In December, 1817, the King decided, by royal orders, that these petitions should be allowed ; in February, 1818, the royal letters patent were issued to the petitioners in the Council of Indies.

The donation to Duke Alagon included all the uncultivated land in East Florida, not previously ceded, between the margins of the rivers St. John and St. Lucia, to their entrances into the sea, and the coast of the Gulf of Florida and the adjacent islands, the mouth of the river Hijuelos from the twenty-sixth degree of latitude, following its left bank to its source ; thence, by a line drawn to the Lake of Macao ; thence, by the way of the river St. John, to the Lake Valdes ; thence, by a line, cutting the extreme north of that lake, as far as the source of that river, and by the coast of the sea, with all adjacent islands, to the mouth of the river Hijuelos.

To the Count Punon Rostro was granted all the uncultivated lands not before ceded, in East Florida, which are situated between the Rio Perdido, to the west of the Gulf of Mexico, and the rivers Amasuca and St. John, from Popa to its mouth, and the southern boundary line of the United States and the Gulf of Mexico, with all the uninhabited islands near the coast.

About the close of 1817, or beginning of 1818, Mr. Vargas petitioned for lands in Florida. On the 25th January, 1818, a royal order allowed his petition ; and the cedula is of the date of the 9th April, 1818.

The donation to Mr. Vargas was,

1st. All uncultivated and not before ceded lands between the bay of Mobile, the river Perdido, the boundary line of the United States and the Gulf of Mexico.

2d. All the lands lying south of Alagon's grant, from the mouth of Hijuelos, on the Gulf of Mexico, and the mouth of St. Lucia, on the Gulf of Florida, to Tancha point, or Cape Florida, with all the islands, &c.

3d. All lands in West Florida to which Spain was entitled, and all lands in dispute with the United States.

While these extraordinary and enormous donations were making in Spain, Florida had been offered to the United States, and the terms of cession were in the course of adjustment. After great labor and delay, the negotiation terminated by the convention of 1819. To provide an indemnity for the claims of American citizens upon Spain, some of which were acknowledged in 1804 to be just, although the treaty providing for their adjustment and payment, made in that year, had been but just ratified by Spain, was one of the causes of the cession of Florida in full property to the United States, who engaged to pay their own citizens out of the vacant lands in that territory, but it was previously necessary to ascertain that the fund provided was sufficient for that purpose. Mr. Onis insisted, in his note of the 24th October, 1818, that all grants made prior to that date should be held valid. The answer of the Secretary of State, of the 31st October, is, that the United States cannot renounce their claims upon Spain, and those of their citizens, and at the same time recognise all grants as valid. He says to Mr. Onis, "Notice had been given by the Minister of the United States in Spain to your Government, that all the grants of land lately alleged to have been made by your Government within those territories must be cancelled, unless your Government should provide some other adequate fund from which the claims above referred to, of the United States and their citizens, may be satisfied."

On the 16th of November, Mr. Onis proposes that the late grants, made since the date of this note offering a cession, should be declared null and void, in consideration of the grantees not having complied with the essential conditions of the cession, as had been the fact. The late grants, as was explicitly understood by both the negotiators, and can only be so understood, referred to the large grants of land to Alagon, Punon Rostro, and Vargas, respecting which notice had been given by Mr. Erving to Mr. Pizarro. To remove all possible doubt, Mr. Onis states to have been the inducement to the grants the same causes which are stated in the royal orders respecting them—a desire to promote population, cultivation, and industry—causes assigned for no other modern donations. It being perfectly understood by the parties that these grants were to be annulled by the convention, all that remained was to reduce the intention of the parties to a formal article. Mr. Onis, who had expressly agreed to exclude them, whatever might be their dates, in the first projet of the treaty delivered on the 9th February, had drawn the article in such terms as to confirm all grants made before January 24, 1818. The article was not accepted in that form. In the counter-project of the Secretary of State, Mr. Adams, on the 13th February, the grants prior to the 24th January, 1818, the conditions of which should have been performed by the grantees, and none others, were declared to be confirmed. Mr. Onis was at this time confined to his house by indisposition, and, by his request, the communications between the negotiators were made through the friendly interposition of Mr. Hyde de Neuville; Mr. Onis insisted upon the article as drawn up by him, not for the purpose of covering these grants, but merely to save the honor of the King. As it was obvious that the honor of the King would not be affected by declaring the grants made prior to January, 1818, binding to the same extent as they would have been on Spain if a cession had not taken place, Mr. Onis yielded to a modification proposed by the Secretary of State to that effect, but at the same time observed that these were grants of old dates, made *bona fide* to persons in actual possession of the lands, and who had improvements and settlements on them, but who, by the revolutions in Europe, and the convulsed state of Spain, had been prevented from completing all the conditions of their grants; that it would be equitable to allow them time from the date of the treaty to fulfil them. This was readily assented to, and the article, as presented by Mr. Onis, was thus modified: "do exclude, absolutely, all grants made subsequent to the 24th January, 1818."

2d. To confirm all grants prior to that period, to the same extent that they would have been valid had the territory ceded remained under the dominion of His Majesty.

3d. To allow all whose titles were imperfect, and who had been prevented, by the recent circumstances of the Spanish empire, and the revolutions in Europe, from fulfilling the condition of their grants, a limited time to complete them. When, after the signature of the treaty, a rumor prevailed that the grants to Alagon, Punon Rostro, and Vargas, were valid under the treaty, being dated but a short time before the 24th of January, 1818, and that this date was assumed with the intention that they should be confirmed; without admitting the suspicion of any unfair dealing in the conduct of the negotiator of Spain, that no pretence should, by any possibility, be raised after the ratification of the treaty that these grants were confirmed, or that either party to the compact had understood that they would be confirmed, I was instructed to deliver, on the exchange of ratifications, the declaration of the construction it was the avowed intention of both parties at the signature that the eighth article should bear in relation to the grants in question, and the only one the United States would ever admit. In a correspondence of March, 1819, between Mr. Adams and Mr. Onis, the Spanish Minister unequivocally admits that such had been his understanding of the article when he signed it —a fact fully confirmed by the declaration of Mr. Hyde de Neuville.

Such, sir, is the history of these grants, and the

negotiation in relation to them. It would not be difficult to prove that the declaration of the American Government (a copy of which I had the honor to transmit to your Excellency, as it is in strict conformity with the intention of the parties) is also in unison with the very letter of the compact. Without entering into a minute discussion of the difference in the force and obligation of the royal order, made prior, and the royal cedula, made subsequent, to the 24th January, 1818, I may venture to assert that no title was vested in the several grantees until the royal cedula given in the Council of Indies. Even if I should err in this position, of the solidity of which I have the most perfect conviction, these grants would not be valid under the treaty, as the conditions of them have not been complied with; nor could the grantees claim the benefit of the stipulation to give time to the old claimants to perfect their titles, since they could not pretend that they were prevented from fulfilling the essential conditions of their donations by the recent circumstances of the Spanish monarchy, or by the late revolutions in Europe. The declaration presented by me to your Excellency might have been safely withheld, had not the Government of the United States determined not to be embarrassed by any pretended claims under these grants, either on the part of Spain, her subjects, or the persons holding under them. The course pursued has been justifiable as it relates to Spain, proper as regards the character of the American Government, and necessary to the honest discharge of the obligation of the convention, by which it bound itself to pay to its own citizens, out of the fund of the Florida lands, their claims upon Spain, to the amount of five millions of dollars.

Having thus vindicated the character of the United States, by showing that they have made no attempt to alter, in any degree, the obligations of the convention, it remains for me to establish the position laid down in regard to Spain. With infinite reluctance I approach the execution of this painful but not difficult task. The convictions of its truth arise so forcibly out of the circumstances of this transaction, as already detailed, that a bare reference to particular portions of them will be sufficient for my purpose. I must call your Excellency's attention to the period at which these donations were made; the departure from the ordinary regulations of the Spanish Government in the quantity of land given away to the grantees; the reasons assigned for making the donations; to the conduct of the Spanish Minister in the United States in arranging the eighth article of the convention; and to the malignant influence these donations seem to have had in preventing the ratification of that convention. The idea of making these grants was not entertained until Spain had determined to cede the Floridas to the United States. Authority was given to offer a cession of that country; between the grants and the execution of that authority the resolution is formed, and partially carried into effect, to render the thing to be ceded, as far as it was in the power of Spain to render it so, worthless. It may be suggested that the sovereignty of the territory was all that the

Spanish Government proposed to cede; and that this was, of itself, sufficiently important to the United States to render unnecessary any attention to the property in the soil. The force of such a suggestion is destroyed by the fact that Spain proposed to provide for the payment of the claims of the United States, and of their citizens upon her, out of the vacant lands of the territory to be ceded. What was the meaning of this proposal, and the stipulation made in consequence of it, when, by secret and irregular donations of all the vacant lands, His Catholic Majesty had rendered its fulfilment impossible; and this, too, while the Spanish Minister was in the very act of discussing it? Was it made in mockery, to add insult to the injuries of which the American Government had so long complained, and satisfaction for which they had generously forborne to take? By reference to the archives of the Indies, your Excellency will find that the donations to the Duke of Alagon, Count Punon Rostro, and Mr. Vargas, include all the vacant land, not only in that part of the Floridas possessed by Spain, but also that possessed by the United States under the cession of Louisiana from France. I make this reference from a belief that the description of the different grants herein contained is nearly if not entirely correct.

The colonial regulations of Spain, made for Louisiana and Florida, expressly forbid the alienation of more than a named or small portion of land to the same person. This, it is true, is a restriction upon the governors and authorities of those territories, and was not obligatory upon the King; but it shows the general policy of the Government widely departed from, in the donations to two favorite officers of the Crown and a Spanish subject, between whom, in a sweeping transfer, a few millions of acres were liberally granted by the King; and what, sir, were the reasons assigned for these liberal gifts? "For the increase of population in the territory of Florida;" "for the fulfilment of His Majesty's beneficent wishes in favor of the agriculture and commerce of his said possessions, which were very much in want of a population adequate to the fertility of the land and the defence of the coast." At the moment of determining to pass away the territory to the dominion of a foreign Power, the anxiety is discovered to render it populous, to foster its agriculture and commerce, to furnish an adequate defence for its coasts. That individuals, who sought the acquisition of wealth at the expense of the moral character of their country, should attempt to conceal the real, the selfish motive of their application for g fts, under the pretence of being actuated by a desire of promoting the interest of the State, is not surprising, since the history of the world affords so many unhappy examples of it; but it is both wonderful and lamentable that Governments should be deluded to adopt such hollow pretences, and assign them as the motives of their conduct. In the present case, how are these reasons of State reconcileable with the proposed cession of the territory? Either Spain offered a cession, intending never to make it, or these were not the real inducements to these donations.

A territory which had been almost abandoned for years by the Government of Spain, alternately used by the British troops, the Indians, and the blacks, for the annoyance of the United States, which had been left to be preyed upon by every adventurer who could command a pilot boat and a musket, becomes, at the moment it is to be ceded away, an object of parental solicitude—a solicitude discovered by giving monopolies of its lands to three persons, who affected the intention to cultivate and improve them; an intention established by the notorious fact of these lands having been frequently offered for sale by the claimants in Spain and in the United States. It is somewhat singular that the Spanish Minister in the United States, who, in the whole of the negotiation, professed the most perfect readiness to stipulate that they should be given up, should yet be ignorant of the dates of these donations, and should have arranged an article in respect to grants so as to leave room for a pretence that the large donations were valid. How happened it that he was thus ignorant—he, upon whose knowledge of these instruments the United States relied—and they could rely upon no other? How did it occur that, in the short space of twelve days after the signature of the treaty, the information was given to satisfy him that he might have been mistaken in the belief with regard to their dates? I reject the supposition that all this was diplomatic finesse, intended to secure the large donations to the claimants of them, but refer to this circumstance to prove still more clearly how injuriously Spain has acted to the United States in this business. The allegation that the American Government ought not to have relied upon information derived from the Minister with whom they were negotiating will never be urged by Spain. The American Government could not procure authentic information from any other source; and if a mistake had been made from a reliance upon that which was procured, a just and honorable Government would disdain to take any other advantage of it than that of manifesting its good faith, by its cheerfulness and promptitude in correcting the error; fulfilling the intention, instead of the letter of its engagement. In fine, sir, the injustice of this transaction has been perfected by the influence these donations appear to have had in preventing the ratification of the convention of 22d February, 1819; a convention which settled important interests; secured the pacific and harmonious relations between the United States and Spain; provided indemnities for injuries that Spain acknowledged American citizens had suffered from her; removed all causes of future dispute and difficulty, and laid deep and broad the foundation of a permanent good understanding between the two Powers. Such, sir, has been the conduct of Spain. She offered a cession, and endeavored to render it worthless; she proposed indemnities, and attempted to destroy the fund out of which they were to be made. To do this, she abandoned her ancient territorial policy, and assigned reasons for her conduct which could not have regulated it. Her negotiator acted as if he knew of facts of which he subsequently professed himself to have been ignorant, and, in consequence, made an arrangement which laid the foundation of new embarrassments between this Government and that of the United States; and, because the United States frankly avow their resolution to do what they engaged to do, I am told that their example justifies Spain in an indefinite delay of a determination to accept or reject that arrangement. In whatever light this transaction is viewed, grievous injury has been done to the United States, for which they have a right to demand and obtain satisfaction. Having thus experienced its necessity and propriety, your Excellency must not be surprised if the United States, in future, take pledges of security for the performance of any engagements they may enter into with Spain more effectual than confidence in her good faith.

I renew to your Excellency, whom may God preserve, the assurance of my most distinguished consideration.

JOHN FORSYTH.

Duke of San Fernando and Quiroga.

No. 1.

Extract of a letter from Mr. Pizarro to Mr. Erving, dated

MADRID, *July* 27, 1817.

And no time shall be lost in preparing the instructions of which Don Luis Noeli will be the bearer to the Minister Onis, it being His Majesty's intention that no step or measure shall be omitted which may promote the settlement upon terms consistent with the welfare of his subjects and the honor of his crown.

Extract of a letter from Mr. Forsyth to the Secretary of State.

MADRID, *November* 16, 1819.

Since my official letter, by way of Gibraltar, numbered 9, nothing important in relation to our affairs has occurred here. General Vives has not yet found his way to Madrid.

It is now said Vives will go by the way of England. The expedition of Cadiz is again the subject of interest with Spain. It is contemplated to send it out in February, and the force is to be 15,000 men.

Extract of a letter from Mr. Forsyth to the Secretary of State.

MADRID, *November* 27, 1819.

Late in the evening of the 16th of the present month, after my letter to you of that date had been sent to the post office, I was very much surprised to receive from the Duke of San Fernando the remonstrance addressed to him on the 18th of October last. The causes assigned for this step you will find in the copy of the Duke's note of the 12th November, marked No. 1. After mature deliberation, it appeared to me that the only course which I could pursue was to insist upon the reception of the remonstrance, and, if that was refused, to leave Madrid; believing that, in doing

this, I should only anticipate the wishes of the President. It is possible that this determination will gratify the wishes of this Government, whose good-will has been lost to me ever since the delivery of my official note of the 21st of June to Mr. Salmon. The truth of this supposition will be ascertained by the effect of my note of the 20th; a copy of which, marked No. 2, is enclosed. If they wish me to remain, they will either receive the remonstrance, or give me such assurances with respect to the grants as will justify me in withholding it altogether. I shall give you the earliest possible information of what is done. At all events, I shall not quit Madrid until the 1st of January, and will, if I am obliged to leave it, remain in France until the beginning of March, with the hope of hearing before that period what direction Congress will give to our affairs with Spain. General Vives was in Madrid at the date of my last letter. I did not hear of his arrival until the 17th, although he arrived on the 15th. I have been told that his appointment has been made known to him officially, and that he has, with great reluctance, accepted it. From the Government of Spain I know nothing about him, either formally or informally.

No. 1.

The Duke of San Fernando and Quiroga to Mr. Forsyth.

PALACE, *November* 12, 1819.

SIR: I have perused with due attention your note of the 18th ultimo; and although I wished, on reflecting on the friendly sentiments entertained by the King, my master, for your Government, and on those which, on my part, I have for it and for yourself personally, to have found them reciprocated in your note, since I had every reason to be persuaded, from what had passed in our conference on the 3d of the same month, that they really existed, I have, notwithstanding, to regret that my expectations have unfortunately been disappointed. So far, indeed, is your note from exhibiting those feelings, that it gives me extreme concern only to discover in it ideas which seem wholly incompatible with the principles professed by your Government, and expressed in terms (since I am compelled to say so) equally unprecedented, and repugnant to the delicacy and attention which are peculiar to, and are invariably observed in all diplomatic communications. I should have failed in the very high consideration I owe, to the American Government, in the due respect I entertain for you, and especially in my duty as the principal secretary of His Majesty the King, my lord, by communicating to him the contents of a note which attacks the honor of His Majesty, without tending in the least to elucidate the subject in question. Upon it the King will, in a direct course, demand of and give to the Federal Government the requisite explanations, as I have already had the honor more than once to inform you. It is, therefore, with the greatest concern that it becomes my indispensable duty to return to you such a note, with the assurance that I will, with as great pleasure, promptitude, and eagerness, submit to His Majesty such communications as you may address to me which are conceived in fit and becoming terms, as I am wholly averse to laying before him those which cannot fail to prove offensive to his exalted character and sovereign dignity.

In repeating to you the keen regrets I feel on this occasion, I have to renew the assurance of my perfect readiness to receive from you such communications as you may be pleased to make to me, and as are conformable to the received usage and custom of European diplomacy. God preserve you many years.

SAN FERNANDO Y QUIROGA.
To the MINISTER *of the U. S.*

No. 2.

Mr. Forsyth to the Duke of San Fernando and Quiroga.
MADRID, *November* 20, 1819.

SIR: Your Excellency's note of the 12th was delivered to me on the 16th. The official remonstrance of the 18th October, which your Excellency has felt yourself reluctantly compelled to return to me, was prepared and sent by the instructions of the Government of the United States. It must be obvious to your Excellency that, if representations to His Catholic Majesty which I am directed to make are not received, my further residence near His Majesty's Court would be worse than useless to my country. I should have preferred that your Excellency would either have pointed out precisely what you deemed inadmissible, and requested an alteration, or have desired me to recall the remonstrance, for the purpose, if possible, of putting it in terms more acceptable. I need not, after our conversation of the 3d ult., assure your Excellency that I should have done every thing consistent with the obligations of duty to meet your wishes. No doubt it occurred to the enlightened understanding of your Excellency that, from the nature of the subject, but few sacrifices could be made to diplomatic courtesy.

I regret that the censure bestowed upon the remonstrance had not been made with more precision. As your Excellency has remarked upon it in very general terms, I am compelled to follow the example. The objections are that the remonstrance does not contain the friendly sentiments which ought to animate the United States towards Spain, as such sentiments animate His Catholic Majesty towards the United States; that it contains ideas which are not, and cannot be, analogous to the principles which ought to govern the United States, and terms disused and foreign to the delicacy and attention always so much observed, and so peculiar to diplomatic communications; that you cannot place it before His Majesty, because it attacks the honor of the King without serving as any illustration of the matter discussed in it, which His Majesty will know how to ask and give directly to the Federal Government. Objections, in terms so general, might with safety be made to any embarrassing official document on an important subject of dispute. Upon which of these does your Excellency rely to justify the return of the remonstrance? To secure the reception of an

official note, is it necessary that the sentiments of it should be friendly? that the ideas it contains should, in the opinion of the organ of the Government to whom it is addressed, be analogous to the principles which ought to govern the Power from whom it is sent? that the terms of it should be well chosen, courteous, and delicate, according to the usages of diplomacy? or even that it should not attack the character of the Government? Your Excellency's candor, enlightened by the history of the intercourse of nations, must admit that few diplomatic notes would be received, if these were prerequisites. The sentiments, ideas, and terms of diplomatic, like all other correspondence, change according to the situation and determination of the parties, and the nature of the subject of it. The correspondence is courtly and delicate while the parties can rely upon the good dispositions of each other. Sometimes, indeed, the language of courtesy is continued to conceal intentions of deadly hostility—to blind an adversary to preparations which are making for his destruction. This dishonorable artifice has become, by frequent use, too well known to deceive. But in every controversy which terminates in a serious misunderstanding, a period arrives when delicacy and attention give place to plainness and truth. All that can be required is, that the *head of the* Government shall not be treated with personal disrespect. In many instances the subject-matter is of a character so peculiar that it cannot be touched without calling in question the honor of the Government whose conduct is examined. In reclamations made for the violation of treaties, for outrages upon the rights of humanity, for fraudulent designs, so soon as the Government refuses to give the reparation required, the charge of bad faith, of inhumanity, or fraud, is fixed upon it, if not by direct assertion, by necessary implication.

Every remonstrance supposes some wrong committed, and, of necessity, questions the conduct of the Government which has given occasion to it. There is this difference between remonstrances made before and after the Government itself declares its approbation of the act complained of. The first are made with a professed belief that the act will be disavowed, and reparation will be made; the last cannot contain such a courteous admission. Strange, indeed, would it be if nations should suffer injury from fraud, injustice, or violence, and should be restrained from the expression of their sentiments, by the danger of sinning against the high character and dignity of the offending Power. I claim the right, as the representative of my country, of placing any remonstrance I may deem necessary to the interest and honor of the United States, before the King, your Excellency's royal master, that is not couched in terms personally disrespectful to the sovereign of Spain; and even were I capable of forgetting the obligations of personal respect to the King himself, I should question your Excellency's right to refuse to receive the representations I should make. If your Excellency proposes to be governed by the usages of European diplomacy, the usual course in such case would be, either to direct the minister who forgets the respect due to the person of the sovereign near whom he resides to withdraw, or to request his recall from the Government he represents.

But to come to a more particular examination of the several causes of complaint against the note of the 18th October, 1819. "It does not contain the friendly sentiments which should animate the United States to Spain." Allow me to refer your Excellency to all the official correspondence of the United States with foreign nations: you will find that we do not deal in professions; we know they are worthless, and, therefore, leave all nations with whom we have intercourse to judge of our dispositions by our conduct. What meaning your Excellency proposes to convey when you state that my note contains ideas which are not, and cannot be, analogous to the principles which ought to govern the United States, I do not comprehend. Whether your Excellency refers to the principles of morality, of national law, or of municipal policy, I trust and believe there is nothing in it which is not consistent with the purest morality, and justified by the soundest maxims of national law. If your Excellency refers to the principles of municipal policy, I must be allowed to say that your Excellency's judgment has deceived you upon a subject on which it was not competent for you to decide. Your Excellency may hope that the principles that are not consonant with those contained here do not govern the United States; but when your Excellency proceeds to say what should or should not govern my country, your Excellency volunteers an opinion on a subject upon which we do not admit of foreign interference. We know full well that our principles, not of morality, or of national law, (for on those points it is to be hoped there is but little difference of opinion in all quarters of the world,) but of government, could scarcely be approved by a politician of Spain. With all my respect for your Excellency, and knowledge of your excellent character, I cannot suppose you sufficiently well acquainted with the principles of free government to decide correctly upon this subject, since it is a species of knowledge not fashionable in Spain, or particularly calculated to render the possessor of it useful in the high departments of His Majesty's Government.

But the terms of my note are unusual, and not consistent with delicacy, &c. Let me entreat your Excellency to re-examine the offending paper. I venture to say that there are no unusual terms in it, or terms inconsistent with the most scrupulous delicacy. It is true that the subject is one of the most unpleasant nature. The facts, and the reasoning upon them, go to fix a serious charge upon the Government of Spain. If the facts are undisputed, and no unfair conclusions are drawn from them, your Excellency must be satisfied that the fault lies not upon its author, or upon those by whose command it was prepared, but upon those who made it necessary—upon those whose misconduct or evil counsel has made it necessary

for a foreign Government to make such representations to the King. That it is necessary for the United States to remonstrate on this subject, I will not attempt to demonstrate. That question has been decided by them, and your Excellency appears to be satisfied of its propriety, when you suggest that the King will know how to ask and give an illustration of this matter directly to the Federal Government. The Federal Government, however, prefers to have this illustration indirectly through its Minister at the Court of Spain; the more especially as it appears there is but little prospect of its being speedily afforded in the direct mode. I think more than a month has elapsed since your Excellency spoke of the intention of sending a Minister to the United States, not then appointed. I have yet to learn from your Excellency if that appointment has been made. To this representation I will add that, if my official note of the 18th October contains any thing personally offensive to His Majesty, it was not inserted with such a design. I desire to treat the sovereign of Spain with every possible respect and decorum. The intentions of the head of this Government I always suppose to be correct; the King may be deceived by false representations, misled by evil counsel, while his own intentions are pure and honorable. This the decorum of diplomacy always takes for granted; and if I have violated this rule, as soon as I am made sensible of it, I will hasten to correct the error. Your Excellency thinks that I ought to have remained satisfied with the conversation of the 3d of October, on the subject of the difference between our two Governments. I appeal confidently to your Excellency duly to estimate the value of the assurances received from you. They did not differ from those previously received from your Excellency's predecessor in office. They were, indeed, given more sparingly, and with greater caution. With every portion of your Excellency's deportment I had reason to be satisfied; but on the important matter of our interview I had but too much cause to apprehend what subsequently occurred—a new refusal on the part of His Majesty's Government to do what we think justice and honor require. If reliance is to be placed on the information given by the public journals, (and your Excellency has quoted them as authority, even since that interview,) an instructive commentary has been furnished upon the designs of Spain. On the 18th of July last, in consequence of orders for preparation, which must have issued simultaneously with Mr. Salmon's note to me of the 19th June, a portion of the force collected at Cadiz was hurried off under General Cagigal. The conjecture entertained was, that it was intended to strengthen the royal forces in some portion of the dominions of Spain to revolt against the authority of the King. It appears by recent notices that a moiety of this expedition has been sent to Florida. This fact, in addition to the numerous circumstances already brought to the view of this Government in my previous correspondence, will certainly be considered sufficiently marked to excuse, if not justify, a little incredulity.

As the business of the remonstrance is likely to produce very unpleasant consequences, I propose, out of a prudent but possibly useless caution, to direct the note of the 18th to be carefully translated by the person attached to this legation. It will then be sent to your Excellency for re-examination, unless I should previously receive some formal assurances on the subject of the grants which have occasioned it, which will justify me in withholding it altogether—an occurrence which would afford me the liveliest sensations of pleasure.

If, on the re-examination of the document, your Excellency's determination should remain the same, you will do your duty, and I shall do mine.

May God preserve your Excellency many years. I renew the assurances of my most distinguished consideration.

JOHN FORSYTH.

Duke of San Fernando and Quiroga.

The Secretary of State to Mr. Lowndes.

Department of State,
Washington, Dec. 16, 1819.

Sir: With reference to the question proposed by the committee, "whether the Executive considers the Florida treaty as a subsisting one, valid according to national law, and giving the same perfect rights, and imposing the same perfect obligations, as if it had been ratified, I have the honor to state that the President considers the treaty of 22d February last as obligatory on the honor and good faith of Spain, not as a perfect treaty, (ratification being an essential to that,) but as a compact which Spain was bound to ratify; as an adjustment of the differences between the two nations, which the King of Spain, by his full power to his Minister, had solemnly promised to approve, ratify, and fulfil. This adjustment is assumed as the measure of what the United States had a right to obtain from Spain, from the signature of the treaty. The principle may be illustrated by reference to rules of municipal law relative to transactions between individuals. The difference between the treaty unratified and ratified may be likened to the difference between a covenant to convey lands and the deed of conveyance itself. Upon a breach of the covenant to convey, courts of equity decree that the party who has broken his covenant shall convey, and, further, shall make good to the other party all damages which he has sustained by the breach of contract.

As there is no court of chancery between nations, their differences can be settled only by agreement or by force. The resort to force is justifiable only when justice cannot be obtained by negotiation; and the resort to force is limited to the attainment of justice. The wrong received marks the boundaries of the right to be obtained.

The King of Spain was bound to ratify the treaty; bound by the principles of the law of nations applicable to the case; and further bound by the solemn promise in the full power. He refusing to perform this promise and obligation, the United States have a perfect right to do what a court of chancery would do in a transaction of a similar character between individuals—namely, to compel the performance of the engagement as far as compulsion can accomplish it, and to indemnify themselves for all the damages and charges incident to the necessity of using compulsion. They cannot compel the King of Spain to sign the act of ratification, and, therefore, cannot make the instrument a perfect treaty; but they can, and are justifiable in so doing, take that which the treaty, if perfect, would have bound Spain to deliver up to them; and they are further entitled to indemnity for all the expenses and damages which they may sustain by consequence of the refusal of Spain to ratify. The refusal to ratify gives them the same right to do justice to themselves as the refusal to fulfil would have given them if Spain had ratified, and then ordered the Governor of Florida not to deliver over the province.

By considering the treaty as the term beyond which the United States will not look back in their controversial relations with Spain, they not only will manifest a continued respect for the sanctity of their own engagements, but they avoid the inconvenience of re-entering upon a field of mutual complaint and crimination so extensive that it would be scarcely possible to decide where or when negotiation should cease, or at what point force should be stayed for satisfied right; and by resorting to force only so far as the treaty had acknowledged their right, they offer an inducement to Spain to complete the transaction on her part, without proceeding to general hostility. But Spain must be responsible to the United States for every wrong done by her after the signature of the treaty by her Minister; and the refusal to ratify his act is the first wrong for which they are entitled to redress.

JOHN QUINCY ADAMS.

William Lowndes, Esq.,
　　Chairman Committee Foreign Relations.

The Secretary of State to Mr. Lowndes.

Department of State, *Dec.* 21, 1819.

Sir: In answer to the questions contained in your letter of the 10th instant, I have the honor to state for the information of the committee—

1st. That information has been received by the Government of the United States, though not through a direct channel, nor in authentic form, that another motive besides those alleged in the letter of the Duke of San Fernando to Mr. Forsyth did operate upon the Spanish Cabinet to induce the withholding of the ratification of the treaty—namely, the apprehension that the ratification would be immediately followed by the recognition by the United States of the independence of one or more of the South American provinces. It has been suggested that, probably, the most important of the explanations which the Minister to be sent by Spain will be instructed to ask, will consist of an explicit declaration of the intentions of this Government in that respect. There is reason, also, to believe that the impunity with which privateers fitted out, manned, and officered, in one or more of our ports, have committed hos-

Spain—Ratification of the Treaty of 1819.

tilities upon the Spanish commerce, will be alleged among the reasons for delay, and perhaps some pledge may be required of the effectual execution against these practices of laws which appear to exist in the statute book.

It may be proper to remark that, during the negotiation of the Florida Treaty, repeated and very earnest efforts were made, both by Mr. Pizarro at Madrid, and by Mr. Onis here, to obtain from the Government of the United States either a positive stipulation or a tacit promise that the United States would not recognise any of the South American revolutionary Governments; and that the Spanish negotiators were distinctly and explicitly informed that this Government would not assent to any such engagement, either express or implied.

2d. By all the information which has been obtained of the respective views of the French and Russian Governments in relation to the course which it was by them thought probable would be pursued by the United States, it is apparent that they strongly apprehend the immediate forcible occupation of Florida by the United States, on the non-ratification by Spain of the treaty within the stipulated time. France and Russia both have most earnestly dissuaded us from that course, not by any regular official communication, but by informal friendly advice, deprecating immediate hostility, on account of its tendency to kindle a general war, which they fear would be the consequence of a war between the United States and Spain. It was alleged that, in the present state of our controversy with Spain, the opinion of all Europe on the point at issue was in our favor, and against her; that, by exercising patience a little longer, by waiting at least to hear the Minister who was announced as coming to give and receive explanations, we could not fail of obtaining, ultimately, without resort to force, the right to which it was admitted we were entitled; but that precipitate measures of violence might not only provoke Spain to war, but would change the state of the question between us, would exhibit us to the world as the aggressors, and would indispose against us those now the most decided in our favor.

It is not expected that, in the event of a war with Spain, any European Power will openly take a part in it against the United States; but there is no doubt that the principal reliance of Spain will be upon the employment of privateers in France and England as well as in the East and West India seas and upon our own coast, under the Spanish flag, but manned from all nations, including citizens of our own, expatriated into Spanish subjects for the purpose.

3d. The enclosed copies of letters from Mr. Fromentin contain the most particular information possessed by the Executive with regard to the subjects mentioned in your third inquiry. In the month of September, a corps of three thousand men arrived at the Havana from Spain, one-third of whom are said to have already fallen victims to the diseases of that climate. By advices from the Havana as recent as the 4th of this month, we

are assured that no part of this force is intended to be, in any event, employed in Florida.

4th. A communication from the Secretary of War, also herewith enclosed, contains the information requested by the committee upon this inquiry.

5th. At the time when Captain Read left Madrid, (13th October,) Mr. Forsyth had no positive information even of the appointment of the person who is to come out as the Minister. Indirectly we have been assured that he might be expected to arrive here in the course of the present month.

I am, with great respect, sir, your obedient serv't,
                              JOHN QUINCY ADAMS.

WILLIAM LOWNDES, Esq., *Chairman, &c.*

Extract of a letter from Mr. Forsyth to the Secretary of State, dated

                    MADRID, *January* 3, 1820.

A few days after the date of my last, numbered 10, I had a visit from the Count Bulgary, the Russian Chargé d'Affaires. He came to see me in consequence of a conversation he had just had with the Duke of San Fernando respecting my official letter of the 18th of October, and the subsequent correspondence in relation to it. He stated to me that the Duke regretted the necessity of sending back the letter, but that it was so harsh in its terms he could not place it before the King. To this were added a great many assurances of personal kindness and good-will, not necessary to be repeated. I replied that it was very mortifying to me to be obliged to send the letter in the first instance, and not less so to insist on its being received; that the Duke had put it out of my power to act otherwise than I had done; but that there was no difficulty in avoiding the unpleasant consequences likely to ensue. The Duke had nothing to do but to give me such assurances in regard to the grants as would render it superfluous for me to say any thing about them. His answer was at once curious and dissatisfactory; he said that the Duke could not give me any assurances, such was the predominating influence of the grantees with the King. He was sincerely disposed to settle all the differences with the United States, and hoped in a short time to have power to effect it; had authorized Count Bulgary to say to the Russian Government that General Vives was going immediately to the United States, and would have competent powers; and that every thing would be amicably arranged. I made the Russian Chargé d'Affaires sensible that one part of this statement contradicted the other. General Vives could not receive powers competent to the purpose of amicable settlement, if the Secretary of State's despatch was unable, from the influence of the grantees, to say any thing about the large donations. This was a subject upon which the American Government would listen to no terms, friendly arrangement was out of the question, and General Vives's visit to the United States useless, unless the Spanish Government was prepared to abandon their pretensions in favor of the grantees. On the subject of the mission of General Vives, I

Spain—Ratification of the Treaty of 1819.

desired the Count to remind the Duke that I knew nothing of it. The general and loose declaration made months before, that the King would authorize some person to ask explanations at Washington, was all that the Spanish Government had chosen to communicate to me. The Count assured me of the personal anxiety of the Minister to arrange every thing satisfactorily between the two countries; that his hopes were strong of being able to effect it; that this business of the returned note was embarrassing, and that, if I went away in consequence of its not being received, what he believed to be the wish of the United States and of his Government, and almost all other Powers, might be frustrated. Matters were in a bad state at present, and this would make them worse. To this I answered, in general terms, that matters must become worse before they become better; that the Government of the United States had every disposition to be friendly with Spain, and had evinced it in a variety of modes; for myself, I had personally every wish to be the instrument of promoting good-will between the two nations. He said this Government had a different impression. I was very sorry for it; unfortunately, the conduct of the Spanish Government had compelled me to speak with a plainness and openness which was disagreeable, as they were not accustomed to it. In the course of a long conversation, it occurred to me that this dispute about the note might be useful, as I found the Spanish Government anxious to avoid receiving it, and, contrary to my expectations, desirous that I should remain here. I believed it practicable to accelerate their movements in our affairs without yielding the point in dispute. With this belief, I stated to Count Bulgary that, if the Duke of San Fernando would officially say to me at once that General Vives was going immediately to the United States, with ample authority to arrange the business of the convention, and that it was the particular wish of His Majesty's Government that the letter of the 18th should be withheld, and that all matters relating to the convention should be discussed in Washington, notwithstanding I had positive instructions to remonstrate on the subject of the grants, and the conduct of Spain in relation to them, I would take the responsibility of retaining the obnoxious paper in my hands until compelled by events to deliver it, or until I should receive further advices from the President. The Duke must understand that this was done with a perfect understanding that I insisted upon the right of returning the paper, and should exercise that right whenever I deemed it necessary The Count left me with the expectation of making this arrangement. A few days afterwards we had another interview; he told me that the Duke would write to tell me of the appointment of General Vives, and of the intention of sending him immediately to Washington; that he would have full powers, &c., but that the Duke thought he could not advert particularly to the remonstrance, or the correspondence in relation to it, without commenting upon it, and this he desired to avoid. I answered, that I could not tell how I should act until I saw the Duke's note. If I found in it a

sufficient justification for retaining the remonstrance, I would do so, and would look at it with a view to find that justification. The Duke knew, from me, that I was instructed to remonstrate earnestly on the subject of the grants, and might judge, from my manner of performing that duty, of the sentiments of the American Government. A week elapsed after this last conversation without my hearing from the Secretary of State. I called on the Russian Chargé d'Affaires to say that I was surprised at this delay, and that I should certainly return the remonstrance if I did not hear from the Duke in a few days. He saw the Secretary of State in consequence of this visit, who assured him that his personal indisposition had prevented him from sending me the intended note. On the 18th of December I received the Duke's note, a copy of which is enclosed, marked No. 1; you will see that it is not what I had reason to expect. He does not request a suspension of any correspondence, or say that it is the wish of the Spanish Government that every thing should be left to the negotiation of General Vives. He merely states that, in his view, to continue discussion here would be superfluous, and likely to embarrass the direct negotiation. Perhaps, considering their peculiar mode of doing business, I had no right to calculate upon any thing more; nevertheless, I am not at all satisfied with it; and had I consulted my own inclinations only, I should immediately have sent back the note of the 18th of October, with the translation. What has occasioned me to delay and deliberate, and still keeps me uncertain how to act, is the apprehension that my judgment of what is proper might be involuntarily influenced by my own wishes. I need not conceal from you that my situation here is unpleasant, and that I find no sufficient consolation for my personal mortification in the consciousness of being useful to the United States, feeling, as I do, that I am almost, if not altogether, useless. The very awkward state of my private affairs in Georgia, in consequence of my unlooked-for detention here, increases my anxiety to leave Spain. What I fear (and I hope it is not an unworthy apprehension) is, that these circumstances may unconsciously induce me to believe that the more energetic course is the best. What I have at last resolved upon is, to delay my answer until I see the President's Message. It will then be sent before General Vives leaves Europe. He is still in Madrid; goes in a coach and *colleras* to Bayonne, a journey of twelve or fifteen days; thence to Paris; from Paris to England; and from England to the United States. His rapid journey to Washington will probably be finished in May. My answer will be regulated by the advices I hope soon to receive from Washington. I shall certainly not go further, in any event, than to say that I shall retain the letter of the 18th of October for a short time, under the hope that His Majesty will render it unnecessary to make any remonstrance on the subject of it.

                      JOHN FORSYTH.

John Q. Adams,
      Secretary of State.

No. 1.

The Duke of San Fernando and Quiroga to Mr. Forsyth.

PALACE, *December* 16, 1819.

SIR: In consequence of the decision of the King, my master, and in conformity with the communications which my predecessor and I have had the honor to make to you, the moment has arrived when the person of whom His Majesty had made choice is about to proceed to America, for the purpose of asking of your Government the explanations which His Majesty has judged to be indispensable, previous to the ratification by His Majesty of the treaty concluded and signed by Don Luis de Onis.

The Plenipotentiary appointed is the Mariscal-del-Campo Don Francisco Dionisio Vives, a distinguished person, in whom the King, my master, has the fullest confidence, and to whom he has given the most ample powers to settle all the difficulties he so earnestly wishes to see removed, and succeeded by the establishment, on a solid basis, of that harmony between Spain and the United States to which their mutual interests so strongly invite them.

As Don Francisco D. Vives will set out immediately on his journey, and proceed expeditiously, I consider the measure now communicated to you, and which you will be pleased to make known to your Government, as dispensing with any further discussion here of the points which form the object of the above-named gentleman's present mission; as a continuance of it would only tend to embarrass the course of the direct negotiation about to be established.

I renew to you, sir, the assurances of my distinguished respect, and I pray God to preserve you many years.

SAN FERNANDO Y QUIROGA.

To the MINISTER *of the United States.*

Extract of a despatch from Count Nesselrode to Mr. Poletica, Minister of His Imperial Majesty the Emperor of Russia in the United States, dated

NOVEMBER 27, [*December* 9,] 1819.

You have doubtless been able to obtain information how far the President's last instructions to Mr. Forsyth were positive. The Emperor will not now take it upon him to justify Spain; but he charges you to plead with the Government at Washington the cause of peace and concord. That Government is too enlightened to take hasty steps, and its rights appear to be too solid not to be weakened by a violent course of proceeding; and, on the other hand, such is the character of the considerations which command the ratification by Spain of the arrangement relative to the Floridas, that it is to be hoped she will at length yield to the force of evidence. The United States will then have added to the reputation of an able that of a moderate policy, and will gather with security the fruits of their wisdom.

His Imperial Majesty therefore wishes that, if there be yet time, you would engage the Government at Washington to give to the Spanish Ministry a proof of patience which its circumstances might, indeed, seem to suggest. Nevertheless, the Emperor does not interpose in this discussion. He makes, above all, no pretension to exercise an influence in the councils of a foreign Power. He merely expresses a wish dictated by his concern for the general welfare, and worthy of the generous good faith which characterizes the Government of the United States.

To the House of Representatives of the U. S.:

WASHINGTON, *May* 9, 1820.

I communicate to Congress a correspondence which has taken place between the Secretary of State and the Envoy Extraordinary and Minister Plenipotentiary of His Catholic Majesty, since the message of the 27th March last, respecting the treaty which was concluded between the United States and Spain on the 22d February, 1819.

After the failure of His Majesty for so long a time to ratify the treaty, it was expected that this Minister would have brought with him the ratification, or that he would have been authorized to give an order for the delivery of the territory ceded by it to the United States. It appears, however, that the treaty is still unratified, and that the Minister has no authority to surrender the territory. The object of his mission has been to make complaints, and to demand explanations, respecting an imputed system of hostility, on the part of citizens of the United States, against the subjects and dominions of Spain, and an unfriendly policy in their Government, and to obtain new stipulations against these alleged injuries, as the condition on which the treaty should be ratified.

Unexpected as such complaints and such a demand were, under existing circumstances, it was thought proper, without compromitting the Government as to the course to be pursued, to meet them promptly, and to give the explanations that were desired on every subject with the utmost candor. The result has proved, what was sufficiently well known before, that the charge of a systematic hostility being adopted and pursued by citizens of the United States against the dominions and subjects of Spain is utterly destitute of foundation; and that their Government, in all its branches, has maintained with the utmost rigor that neutrality in the civil war between Spain and the colonies which they were the first to declare. No force has been collected, nor incursions made, from within the United States, against the dominions of Spain; nor have any naval equipments been permitted in favor of either party against the other. Their citizens have been warned of the obligations incident to the neutral condition of their country; the public officers have been instructed to see that the laws were faithfully executed, and severe examples have been made of some who violated them.

In regard to the stipulation proposed as the condition of the ratification of the treaty, that the United States shall abandon the right to recognise the revolutionary colonies in South America, or to form other relations with them, when, in

Spain—Ratification of the Treaty of 1819.

their judgment, it may be just and expedient so to do, it is manifestly so repugnant to the honor and even to the independence of the United States that it has been impossible to discuss it. In making this proposal, it is perceived that His Catholic Majesty has entirely misconceived the principles on which this Government has acted in being a party to a negotiation so long protracted for claims so well-founded and reasonable, as he likewise has the sacrifices which the United States have made, comparatively with Spain, in the treaty, to which it is proposed to annex so extraordinary and improper a condition.

Had the Minister of Spain offered an unqualified pledge that the treaty should be ratified by his sovereign on being made acquainted with the explanations which had been given by this Government, there would have been a strong motive for accepting and submitting it to the Senate for their advice and consent, rather than to resort to other measures for redress, however justifiable and proper. But he gives no such pledge; on the contrary, he declares explicitly that the refusal of this Government to relinquish the right of judging and acting for itself hereafter, according to circumstances, in regard to the Spanish colonies—a right common to all nations—has rendered it impossible for him, under his instructions, to make such engagement. He thinks that his sovereign will be induced by his communications to ratify the treaty; but still he leaves him free either to adopt that measure or to decline it. He admits that the other objections are essentially removed, and will not in themselves prevent the ratification, provided the difficulty on the third point is surmounted. The result therefore is, that the treaty is declared to have no obligation whatever; that its ratification is made to depend, not on the considerations which led to its adoption, and the conditions which it contains, but on a new article, unconnected with it, respecting which a new negotiation must be opened of indefinite duration and doubtful issue.

Under this view of the subject, the course to be pursued would appear to be direct and obvious, if the affairs of Spain had remained in the state in which they were when this Minister sailed. But it is known that an important change has since taken place in the Government of that country, which cannot fail to be sensibly felt in its intercourse with other nations. The Minister of Spain has essentially declared his inability to act, in consequence of that change. With him, however, under his present powers, nothing could be done. The attitude of the United States must now be assumed, on full consideration of what is due to their rights, their interest, and honor, without regard to the powers or incidents of the late mission. We may, at pleasure, occupy the territory which was intended and provided by the late treaty as an indemnity for losses so long since sustained by our citizens; but still nothing could be settled definitively without a treaty between the two nations. Is this the time to make the pressure? If the United States were governed by views of ambition and aggrandizement, many strong reasons

might be given in its favor. But they have no objects of that kind to accomplish; none which are not founded in justice, and which can be injured by forbearance. Great hope is entertained that this change will promote the happiness of the Spanish nation. The good order, moderation, and humanity which have characterized the movement are the best guarantees of its success. The United States would not be justified in their own estimation should they take any step to disturb its harmony. When the Spanish Government is completely organized, on the principles of this change, as it is expected it soon will be, there is just ground to presume that our differences with Spain will be speedily and satisfactorily settled.

With these remarks, I submit it to the wisdom of Congress whether it will not still be advisable to postpone any decision on this subject until the next session.

JAMES MONROE.

Recall of Mr. Onis.

Don Ferdinand the Seventh, King, by the grace of God, of Castile, Leon, and Arragon, of the Two Sicilies, Jerusalem, Navarre, Granada, Toledo, Valencia, Galicia, Majorca, Seville, Sardinia, Cordova, Corsica, Murcia, Jaen, the Algarves, Algesiras, Gibraltar, the Canary islands; of the two Indies, and of the islands of the ocean sea; Archduke of Austria; Duke of Burgundy, of Brabant, and Milan; Count of Hapsburg, Flanders, Tyrol, and Barcelona; Lord of Biscay and Molina: To my great and good friends the United States of America:

Great and Good Friends: It having been represented to us by Don Luis de Onis, our Envoy Extraordinary and Minister Plenipotentiary to you, that he is desirous to return to Europe, for the recovery of his health, we have thought fit to grant him the necessary permission for that purpose. We have, therefore, authorized him to take his leave of you, and have charged him, in so doing, to assure you of our constant friendship and desire to maintain and strengthen the ties of amity now happily subsisting between us. On his faithful execution of these our commands, we rely with confidence, as we do that you will receive with satisfaction these renewed assurances.

We conclude by commending you to God; and we pray that he would have you in his safe and holy keeping. Your good friend,

FERDINAND.
J. J. M. DE RUIZ DEVALOS.

A true copy:

SAN FERNANDO Y QUIROGA.

Madrid, ——, 1819.

Don Luis de Onis to the Secretary of State.

Madrid, *January* 27, 1820.

Sir: Having received from my sovereign an appointment to other duties, and being thereby deprived of the satisfaction of presenting to the President the letters of re-credence of the King, my master, I am under the necessity of transmitting them to you, with my request that you would be pleased to lay them before his Excellency the President, to whom you will also make it known that His Majesty, on deciding to terminate my mission to your Government, has commanded me to express to it the assurance of his unalterable desire to maintain the strict friendship now happily subsisting between both Powers.

In fulfilling these orders of my sovereign, permit me, sir, also to express to you the deep sense I entertain of the personal attentions with which I was honored by the President, by yourself in particular, and by the citizens of the Union in general; and to add the assurance that it will ever be to me a subject of the most grateful reflection, if, in the discharge of my duties, and in the execution of the orders of my Government, whose object it always has been to establish the most perfect harmony between the two countries, I shall have been so fortunate as to have acquired the esteem of the President, together with yours.

I pray you, sir, to receive the further assurance of my distinguished sentiments, and my wish that God may preserve you many years.

LUIS DE ONIS.

Credential letter delivered by General Vives to the President of the United States

Don Ferdinand the Seventh, King, by the grace of God, of Castile, Leon, and Arragon, of the Two Sicilies, Jerusalem, Navarre, Granada, Toledo, Valencia, Galicia, Majorca, Seville, Sardinia, Cordova, Corsica, Murcia, Jaen, the Algarves, Algesiras, Gibraltar, the Canary islands; of the two Indies, and of the islands of the ocean sea; Archduke of Austria; Duke of Burgundy, of Brabant, and Milan; Count of Hapsburg, Flanders, Tyrol, and Barcelona; Lord of Biscay and of Molina: To my great and good friends the United States of America:

Great and Good Friends: Being animated by the most sincere desire to maintain the friendship and good understanding happily subsisting between both countries, and it being necessary, to that end, that another person, possessing our entire confidence, should forthwith be deputed to you as a successor to our late Envoy and Minister Plenipotentiary, Don Luis de Onis, to whom we have granted leave to return to Europe for the reestablishment of his health, we have thought fit to confer the said appointment on Don Francisco Dionisio Vives, a Major General of our Armies, Knight of the third class of the Royal and Military Order of Saint Ferdinand, and a member of the Supreme Council of the said order; Knight of the Royal and Military Order of St. Hermenegildo; twice honored by decrees of thanks for patriotic services; decorated with the North Star and crosses of honor for distinguished conduct and valor at the battles of Albuera, Sorauren, Lugo, Tamanes, and Medina del Campo, also at the surrender of Villa Franca to the army of the left; he uniting the requisite qualifications for the discharge of the said trust:

We therefore hope that, on his presenting to

you this our letter of credence, you will grant him a kind and favorable reception, giving all faith and credit to what he shall say to you on our behalf. Done at Madrid, this 15th day of December, 1819.

FERDINAND.

J. J. M. DE RUIZ DEVALOS.

A true copy:

SAN FERNANDO Y QUIROGA.

Extract of a letter from Mr. Forsyth (marked private) to Mr. Adams, dated

January 28, 1820.

General Vives left this place on the 25th for Paris, on his way to Washington. He went post to France, and I am informed is directed to remain as short a time as possible in Paris. He goes to England to embark for the United States. The alteration in his mode of travelling, and the directions he has received not to delay, give me some hope that he will arrive in America time enough to prevent the necessity of doing that without the consent of Spain which the American Government prefers to do with her consent.

I send this by the way of Gibraltar, that the earliest notice may be had of General Vives's movements. In the course of the coming week I shall write officially, and enclose a copy of my answer to the Duke of San Fernando's last note, written to inform me of General Vives's appointment.

[Referred to in Mr. Forsyth's despatch of January, 28.]

Mr. Forsyth to the Duke of San Fernando and Quiroga, First Minister of State, dated

Madrid, *January* 27, 1820.

Sir: I have had the honor to receive your Excellency's official of the 16th December, giving me notice of the appointment of the Mariscal-del-Campo Don Francisco Dionisio Vives as Minister Plenipotentiary of the United States. According to the request of your Excellency, I communicated, by the first convenient opportunity that occurred, a copy of your note to the American Government.

The appointment of the Minister Plenipotentiary has been so long delayed, his departure so much procrastinated, his route to the United States is so circuitous, and his movements are so deliberate, that I very much apprehend he will find, on his arrival, the determination, before now taken by the American Government, executed. His Catholic Majesty may be assured by your Excellency that, should this be the case, the American Government will nevertheless, governed by that temper of conciliation which has at all times marked its policy, give any explanations which may, in the spirit of amity, be asked in the name of the King.

Your Excellency views it as superfluous to continue discussions here of the points of the transaction with which His Majesty's Minister goes charged, and as likely to embarrass the course of the direct negotiation. As to the future, I have to inform your Excellency that I have no directions to discuss any of those points; and certainly

I have received here very slender encouragement voluntarily to encounter them. My duty, in regard to the convention, was terminated when I had the honor to send you the remonstrance of the 18th of October, which has given rise to an unpleasant question between us. From circumstances well known to your Excellency, I understand that the observations quoted have reference also to that question. With this understanding, I give you the strongest proof in my power of my anxious desire to promote harmony between the two nations, by taking upon myself the responsibility of having so long withheld the return of the remonstrance, and in determining still longer to retain it in my hands. I do this with the confident expectation that the justice of His Catholic Majesty has, in the powers given to General Vives, rendered a further recurrence to that unhappy affair altogether unnecessary. While I give to your Excellency this proof of my wishes to conciliate, I must repeat that I hold it as unquestionably my right to have that paper, or any other I may deem it necessary to send, laid before your Excellency's royal master for his perusal and consideration; holding myself responsible to my own Government only for the language in which it may be expressed, or the sentiments it may contain.

I renew to your Excellency the assurances of my profound consideration.

JOHN FORSYTH.
The DUKE OF SAN FERNANDO Y QUIROGA.

Mr. Gallatin to the Secretary of State.

PARIS, *February* 15, 1820.

SIR: General Vives, the new Minister of Spain to the United States, arrived at Paris on the 11th instant, and left it on the 14th for London, with the intention to embark at Liverpool in the New York packet which will sail on the 1st day of March.

Mr. Pasquier, after having seen him, invited me to an interview on the 12th, and said that he was in hopes that the differences might still be adjusted. General Vives had told him that the principal points with Spain were, that the honor of the Crown should be saved (*mis à couvert*) in the business of the grants, and to receive satisfactory evidence of our intention to preserve a fair neutrality in the colonial war. Mr. Pasquier had observed to him that it would be a matter of deep regret that private interest should prevent the conclusion of such an important arrangement; and that, when it was clear that there had been at least a misunderstanding on the subject, the King's dignity could not be injured by a resumption of the grants, or by an exchange for other lands. He seemed to think that this would be arranged, and asked me what I thought we could do respecting the other point. I answered that the fullest reliance might be placed on the fairness of our neutrality, and that I was really at a loss to know what could be added to the measures the United States had already adopted to enforce it. Mr. Pasquier gave me to understand that, if there was any defect, however trifling, in our laws, and that

was amended, it would probably be sufficient to satisfy the pride of Spain, as there now appeared a real desire to ratify, provided it could be done without betraying a glaring inconsistency. He had expressed to General Vives his opinion of the impropriety of asking from the United States any promise not to recognise the independence of the insurgent colonies, and had told him that on that subject Spain could only rely on the moral effect which a solemn treaty, accommodating all her differences with the United States, would have on their future proceedings.

I expressed my hope that the explanation which General Vives was instructed to give on the subject of the grants, and to ask on that of our neutrality, might be such as to remove all the existing difficulties. But it was most important that he should arrive in the United States before the adjournment of Congress, and that he should be the bearer of the King's ratification of the treaty, so that, if every thing was arranged, those ratifications might be at once exchanged at Washington. If that was not done, the President would have no more security that the King would ratify General Vives's than Mr. Onis's acts: and it was impossible to suppose that he would run the risk of a second disappointment. This observation forcibly struck Mr. Pasquier, who said that he would make further inquiries on that point.

I saw, the same evening, the Spanish Ambassador at this Court, and, in the course of a short conversation, he suggested that the grants in dispute might be set aside, the grantees not having fulfilled certain conditions or formalities; and, after acknowledging that General Vives was not the bearer of the King's ratification, he hinted that he was authorized to give the United States satisfactory security that Spain would fulfil her engagements.

On the 13th I dined at the Minister of Foreign Affairs' with General Vives, who repeated to me in substance what he had said to Mr. Pasquier. I told him that the President would judge of the explanations he had to give on the subject of the grants; that he might rely on the determination of the United States to preserve their neutrality, and not less on the manner in which the laws for enforcing it were executed, than on the tenor of those laws, which, I observed, were, and had always been, more full and efficient than those of either England or France on the same subject; that I could not say whether the question of recognising the independence of the insurgent colonies would be agitated during the present session of Congress, but that, if it was, the decision would probably have taken place before his arrival.

I then repeated what I had said to Mr. Pasquier respecting the importance of his being authorized to exchange the ratifications of the treaty. He answered that, although he was not, he could, in case of an arrangement, give satisfactory security to the United States, and that it would consist in consenting that they should take immediate possession of Florida, without waiting for the ratification of the treaty.

General Vives repeated, in the course of the

Spain—Ratification of the Treaty of 1819.

evening, the same thing to Mr. Pasquier, with whom I had afterwards a short conversation on the subject. He seemed extremely astonished that the Spanish Government should have adopted that course rather than to authorize their Minister to exchange at once the ratifications. Since, however, the measure they proposed coincided with the views of the President as stated in his Message, and would, at all events, prevent a rupture, we both agreed that no time should be lost in communicating to you General Vives's declarations.

I have the honor to be, &c.
ALBERT GALLATIN.

Extract of a letter from Mr. Forsyth, Minister Plenipotentiary of the United States in Spain, to Mr. Adams, Secretary of State, dated

MADRID, February 15, 1820.

By the return of Lieutenant Weaver who came to this place yesterday, with a letter from Captain Stewart, I have a convenient opportunity of sending, enclosed, a copy of my last note to the Duke of San Fernando, (No. 1,) dated the day after General Vives left Madrid. It was written in conformity to what I believe, from the Message at the opening of Congress, to be the wishes of the President. If in this I should unhappily be mistaken, the affair stands in such a state that I can at any moment correct the error. Having informed this Government that I only detain the remonstrance, I can at any moment present it if directed so to do, or if I shall be satisfied that the King has not given such authority to General Vives as will render unnecessary a recurrence to this disgraceful business.

Extract of a letter from Mr. Forsyth to Mr. Adams.

MARCH 30, 1820.

Soon after the change of Government was officially made known to me, I determined to see the Duke of San Fernando respecting our affairs, to learn if the powers given to Vives were such that no bad effect would be produced by the recent events upon the relations of Spain with the United States, and to endeavor to procure, in this season of generous feelings, the release of the Americans in confinement. Waiting a few days for the first bustle to be over, the Duke was removed from office, and a further delay unexpectedly occurred. As the new secretary was not expected for some time, on the 27th I asked, by a written note, for an interview with Mr. Jabat, who had charge of the office; it was appointed for the 29th. I saw him at the time fixed, and had a very long conversation with him. I stated the objects I had in view; he answered with great frankness. The substance of what I learned from him is, that General Vives did not carry the treaty ratified by the United States; that the King, having taken the oath to observe the constitution, could not now ratify; that instructions had been just prepared for General Vives to apprize him of the change that had taken place, and of the want of power in the King to act further in the business; the whole

matter would be laid before the Cortes, and the Minister had no doubt it would be arranged to the mutual satisfaction of the two Governments, as the Cortes would probably be composed of the most liberal and enlightened men of the nation—men who had the disposition, the ability, and the courage to give and to act upon good counsel. He spoke of the resemblance of the institutions of the two nations, and of his anxious wish to see them on the best terms. Of the American prisoners he professed a desire to do what would be agreeable to us, and would bring the subject before the King. For this object it was agreed upon between us that I should address him an official note; a copy of it (marked No. 6) is enclosed. It was prepared immediately after the interview, and sent on the 30th. Mr. Jabat asked me, in turn, what would be the determination of our Government in this new state of things. I replied that I was exceedingly disappointed to learn that General Vives had not the ratified treaty to exchange in the United States; that I apprehended his going without it would produce a very bad effect; and that I had no doubt there would be an immediate occupation of Florida, as recommended by the President to Congress; that we had always the strongest desire to be friendly with Spain—a desire which recent circumstances would increase. I was perfectly aware that the King had no power to ratify, and trusted, with him, that every thing would be arranged satisfactorily when the Cortes assembled. In the meantime, I hoped that no unpropitious effect on the dispositions of this Government would be produced by the measures we should have been reluctantly compelled to take. I expressed the greatest satisfaction at the prospect of a favorable answer to the application in favor of the confined Americans, and assured him it would be considered as a conclusive proof, on the part of Spain, of a desire to do us justice and kindness in all things. The revolution will produce the best effects for us, if a judgment is to be formed from the language of the people in office and of those out of office. The Government of the United States is considered, with reason, more friendly to them than any other. The European Governments, without exception, see, in the change which has been produced here, a dangerous example to their people, and speculate with dread upon its probable effect. I had supposed that the influence of Great Britain would be very great under the new order of things; at present, there is a very wholesome jealousy and prejudice against that Government existing among the people, and carefully cherished by the ruling men. It is to be traced, in part, to the conduct of the English on the return of the King from his captivity; they were supposed to have had some agency in preventing at that time the King's acceptance of the constitution. The language used here is, there are but two free nations—the Spaniards and the people of the United States; the English were free, but have been recently enslaved by their Ministry and Parliament. I hope that, before General Vives receives and communicates to the President the change in the Government, Florida will be occupied by us, or at least that

Congress will have passed a law in such terms as to render it obligatory upon the President to take it. Delaying to take it until the news is received of the establishment of a free Government and liberal institutions here, might be injurious; at present, every body here expects it will be seized, and the event will have no bad effect unless it can, by misrepresentation, be made to appear the consequence of the recent events in Spain. It is important that Florida should be in our possession when the Cortes deliberate on the treaty. The defect of granted authority in that body to cede territory was not adverted to by Mr. Jabat, and has probably escaped notice. The general assertion, that the sovereignty resides essentially in the nation, which is represented by the Cortes, would no doubt be considered sufficient when the territory was held by us; it might admit of dispute if it was not. You will perceive that two deputies from Cuba and the Floridas are to be in the Cortes. Before July I hope to receive from you particular and special instructions on this and all other subjects connected with our interests. During the Cortes would be the most favorable time for a commercial arrangement, if one is to be made here; and I indulge the belief that, should, as is probable, the business of Florida be amicably arranged, an advantageous commercial treaty may be formed. I look with anxiety for directions from you, formed upon the determination Congress may have made.

General Don Francisco Dionisio Vives to the Secretary of State.

WASHINGTON, *April* 14, 1820.

SIR: In conformity with the orders of my Government, which were communicated to Mr. Forsyth on the 16th of December last by His Excellency the Duke of San Fernando and Quiroga, and with the earnest desire of the King, my master, to see a speedy adjustment of the existing difficulties which obstruct the establishment, on a permanent basis, of the good understanding so obviously required by the interests of both Powers, I have the honor to address you, and frankly to state to you that my august Sovereign, after a mature and deliberate examination, in full council, of the treaty of 22d February of the last year, saw, with great regret, that, in its tenor, it was very far from embracing all the measures indispensably requisite to that degree of stability which, from his sense of justice, he was anxious to see established in the settlement of the existing differences between the two nations.

The system of hostility which appears to be pursued in so many parts of the Union against the Spanish dominions, as well as against the property of all their inhabitants, is so public and notorious, that, to enter into detail would only serve to increase the causes of dissatisfaction. I may be allowed, however, to remark that they have been justly denounced to the public of the United States even by some of their own fellow-citizens.

Such a state of things, therefore, in which individuals may be considered as being at war while their Governments are at peace with each other, is diametrically opposed to the mutual and sincere friendship and to the good understanding which it was the object of the treaty (though the attempt has failed) to establish, and of the immense sacrifices consented to by His Majesty to promote.

These alone were motives of sufficient weight imperiously to dictate the propriety of suspending the ratification of the treaty, even although the American envoy had not at first announced, in the name of his Government, and subsequently required of that of Spain a declaration which tended directly to annul one of its most clear, precise, and conclusive articles, even after the signature and ratification of the treaty.

The King, my master, influenced by considerations so powerful as to carry with them the fullest evidence, has therefore judged it necessary and indispensable, in the exercise of his duties as a sovereign, to request certain explanations of your Government; and he has, in consequence, given me his commands to propose to it the following points, in the discussion and final arrangement of which it seems proper that the relative state of the two nations should be taken into full consideration:

That the United States, taking into due consideration the scandalous system of piracy established in and carried on from several of their ports, will adopt measures, satisfactory and effectual, to repress the barbarous excesses and unexampled depredations daily committed upon Spain, her possessions, and properties, so as to satisfy what is due to international rights, and is equally claimed by the honor of the American people.

That, in order to put a total stop to any future armaments, and to prevent all aid whatsoever being afforded from any part of the Union, which may be intended to be directed against and employed in the invasion of His Catholic Majesty's possessions in North America, the United States will agree to offer a pledge (*a dar una seguridad*) that their integrity shall be respected.

And, finally, that they will form no relations with the pretended Governments of the revolted provinces of Spain situate beyond sea, and will conform to the course of proceeding adopted, in this respect, by other Powers in amity with Spain.

In submitting to you these just and natural demands, I have received the orders of the King, my master, to make known to the President that they would have been regularly communicated to the Minister Plenipotentiary of the United States at Madrid, if, in the excess of his zeal, he had not, at an early period, been induced to express himself in terms disrespectful to the dignity of His Majesty; and I am, at the same time, commanded to give the assurance that, in alluding to an incident of so unpleasant a nature, it is not intended to make the conduct of Mr. Forsyth a subject of complaint, but merely to make your Government fully acquainted with the motives of my august Sovereign in adopting the resolution as already stated.

I flatter myself that the President, on an attentive examination of the contents of this note, entirely dictated by sentiments of justice, will see a decisive evidence of the sincere desire of the King, my master, to attain with promptitude the definitive settlement of a transaction no less important in itself than it is essential to the mutual interests of the two countries.

I eagerly avail myself of this occasion to assure you of my perfect respect and highest consideration. I pray that God may long preserve you.

FRANCISCO D. VIVES.

The Secretary of State to General Don Francisco Dionisio Vives, Envoy Extraordinary and Minister Plenipotentiary from Spain.

DEPARTMENT OF STATE,
Washington, April 18, 1820.

SIR : Before replying to the letter which I have had the honor of receiving from you, dated the 14th instant, I am directed by the President of the United States to request a copy of your full powers, and to be informed whether you are the bearer of the ratification by His Catholic Majesty of the treaty signed on the 22d of February, 1819, by Don Luis de Onis; and are ready, in the event of suitable explanations being given upon the points mentioned in your letter, to exchange the same for the ratification on the part of the United States, if the Senate should advise and consent that such exchange of ratifications should now be accepted.

Please to accept the assurance of my distinguished consideration.

JOHN QUINCY ADAMS.

General Don Francisco Dionisio Vives to the Secretary of State.

WASHINGTON, *April* 19, 1820.

SIR : In answer to your note of yesterday's date, and in compliance with the request stated in its first point, I have the honor to enclose a copy of my full powers.

I have at the same time to inform you that I am not the bearer of the ratification of the treaty of the 22d of February, 1819, signed by Don Luis de Onis; nor does it seem agreeable to the natural course of things, and to established usage, that a treaty should be ratified previous to a removal of the obstacles which have expressly caused the suspension of its ratification; but I am enabled to assure you that I am fully authorized to offer a solemn promise, in the name of the King, my master, that, if the result of the proposals presented in my first note be satisfactory, the ratification of the treaty will be attended with no further delay than the time indispensably necessary for the arrival at Madrid of one of the gentlemen attached to my legation, who has accompanied me for that especial purpose.

I renew to you, sir, the assurance of my distinguished consideration, and I pray God long to preserve you.

FRANCISCO D. VIVES.

JOHN QUINCY ADAMS,
Secretary of State.

Full power of General Vives.

Don FERDINAND THE SEVENTH, King, by the grace of God, of Castile, Leon, and Arragon, of the Two Sicilies, Jerusalem, Navarre, Granada, Toledo, Valencia, Galicia, Majorca, Seville, Sardinia, Cordova, Corsica, Murcia, Jaen, the Algarves, Gibraltar, the Canary islands, of both Indies, and of the isles of the ocean ; Archduke of Austria ; Duke of Burgundy, Brabant, and Milan; Count of Hapsburg, Flanders, Tyrol, and Barcelona; Lord of Biscay and of Molina, &c.

The state of peace, amity, and good understanding, now happily subsisting between us and the United States of North America, being favorable to the mutual and amicable adjustment and settlement of all existing differences between the two Governments; and it being expedient to that end to authorize a person having our confidence, and possessed of the requisite information, experience, and political knowledge for so important a trust, which qualities uniting in you, Don Francisco Dionisio Vives, a Major General in our service, a Knight of the Royal and Military Order of San Fernando, and member of the Supreme Council of the said Order, a Knight of the Royal and Military Order of San Hermenegildo, twice honored by decrees of thanks for public services, decorated with the Order of the North Star and crosses of honor for distinguished conduct and valor at the battles of Albuera, Sorauren, Lugo, Tamanes, and Medina del Campo, the surrender of Villa Franca del Vierzo, in the operations of the army of the left at the sieges of Pampeluna and Bayonne, and our Envoy Extraordinary and Minister Plenipotentiary to the abovenamed States:

We have authorized, and by these presents we do authorize you, granting you full power, in the most ample form, to meet and confer with such person or persons as may be duly authorized by the Government of the United States, and with him or them to settle, conclude, and sign whatsoever you may judge necessary to the best arrangement of all points depending between the two Governments; promising, as we do hereby promise upon the faith and word of a King, to approve, ratify, and fulfil such articles or agreements as you may conclude and sign.

In testimony whereof, I have commanded the present to be issued, signed by us, sealed with our privy seal, and countersigned by the undersigned, our principal Secretary of State and of Universal Despatch. Given at Madrid, the 15th of December, 1819.

I, THE KING.

J. J. M. DE RUIZ DEVALOS.

The Secretary of State to General Don Francisco Dionisio Vives.

DEPARTMENT OF STATE,
Washington, April 21, 1820.

SIR : I am directed by the President of the United States to express to you the surprise and concern with which he has learned that you are not

Spain—Ratification of the Treaty of 1819.

the bearer of the ratification by His Catholic Majesty of the treaty signed on the 22d February, 1819, by Don Luis de Onis, by virtue of a full power equally comprehensive with that which you have now produced—a full power, by which His Catholic Majesty promised, "on the faith and word of a King, to approve, ratify, and fulfil whatsoever might be stipulated and signed by him."

By the universal usage of nations, nothing can release a sovereign from the obligation of a promise thus made, except the proof that his Minister, so empowered, has been faithless to his trust, by transcending his instructions.

Your sovereign has not proved, nor even alleged, that Mr. Onis had transcended his instructions; on the contrary, with the credential letter which you have delivered, the President has learned that he has been relieved from the mission to the United States only to receive a new proof of the continued confidence of His Catholic Majesty, in the appointment to another mission of equal dignity and importance.

On the faith of this promise of the King, the treaty was signed and ratified on the part of the United States; and contained a stipulation that it should also be ratified by His Catholic Majesty, so that the ratifications should, within six months from the date of its signature, be exchanged.

In withholding this promised ratification beyond the stipulated period, His Catholic Majesty made known to the President that he should forthwith despatch a person possessing entirely his confidence to ask certain explanations which were deemed by him necessary previous to the performance of his promise to execute the ratification.

The Minister of the United States at Madrid was enabled, and offered, to give all the explanations which could justly be required in relation to the treaty. Your Government declined even to make known to him their character; and they are now, after the lapse of more than a year, first officially disclosed by you.

I am directed by the President to inform you that explanations which ought to be satisfactory to your Government will readily be given upon all the points mentioned in your letter of the 14th instant; but that he considers none of them, in the present state of the relations between the two countries, as points for discussion. It is indispensable that, before entering into any new negotiation between the United States and Spain, that relating to the treaty already signed should be closed. If, upon receiving the explanations which your Government has asked, and which I am prepared to give, you are authorized to issue orders to the Spanish officers commanding in Florida to deliver up to those of the United States who may be authorized to receive it, immediate possession of the province, conformably to the stipulations of the treaty, the President, if such shall be the advice and consent of the Senate, will wait, with such possession given, for the ratification of His Catholic Majesty; till your messenger shall have time to proceed to Madrid; but, if you have no such authority, the President considers it would

be at once an unprofitable waste of time, and a course incompatible with the dignity of this nation, to give explanations which are to lead to no satisfactory result, and to resume a negotiation the conclusion of which can no longer be deferred.

Be pleased to accept the assurances of my distinguished consideration.

                                   JOHN QUINCY ADAMS.

General Don Francisco Dionisio Vives to the Secretary of State.

                                   WASHINGTON, *April* 24, 1820.

SIR : In acknowledging the receipt of your note of the 21st instant, I have the honor to remark, in the first place, that you appear to have misconceived a material part of my letter of the 14th, by reproducing arguments which have been already sufficiently refuted by my Government. You will, therefore, excuse me from reviving them here, in so far as they relate to the question whether a Sovereign is or is not bound to ratify what may have been signed by his negotiator, it being well known that various instances may be cited of cases in which the ratification of a treaty has been justly suspended, without alleging, as the motive for so doing, that the negotiator had transcended his powers or instructions. There may, unquestionably, be other reasons sufficiently valid to exonerate him from the obligation of ratifying, supposing that to have been the case.

It is evident that the scandalous proceedings of a number of American citizens, the decisions of several of the courts of the Union, and the criminal expedition set on foot within it for the invasion of His Majesty's possessions in North America, at the very period when the ratification was still pending, were diametrically opposite to the most sacred principles of amity, and to the nature and essence of the treaty itself. These hostile proceedings were, notwithstanding, tolerated by the Federal Government, and thus the evil was daily aggravated; so that the belief generally prevailed throughout Europe that the ratification of the treaty by Spain, and the acknowledgment of the independence of her rebellious transatlantic colonies by the United States, would be simultaneous acts. The pretensions advanced by Mr. Forsyth, in relation to the eighth article, were also evidently calculated to render that treaty illusory. It is, therefore, not possible to assign reasons more powerful, or more completely justificatory of the sovereign resolution of the King, my master, to suspend his ratification of that instrument.

In my first note, I also hinted at the offensive terms employed by the American Minister at Madrid, from the very outset; which you notice no further than by taking up the second point, upon which the one which I now have the honor to contest essentially turns. Although His Majesty might certainly have kept aloof from a deportment so void of moderation, and so derogatory to his dignity, it is obvious that any discussions commenced with the Minister so situated were only likely to produce unprofitable results—his correspondence tending more powerfully to dis-nite than to reconcile the contracting part es. It was, indeed, a subject of great regret that the incident just referred to, the distance of Spain from the New World, which, from the obstructions to correspondence, produced unavoidable delay in receiving correct information of the events passing here, and which to His Majesty appeared incredible, and, in fine, his wish to avoid whatever had the appearance of an unfounded complaint and an unpleasant difference between the two Governments, should have retarded my arrival, and the happy conclusion of the transaction now pending.

I have further to state to you, that I am not authorized by His Majesty to give the necessary orders to the Spanish authorities in the Floridas to deliver up those possessions to the United States; nor was this to be presumed, since, if it appeared contrary to the natural order of things and to established usage that the treaty should be ratified previous to receiving the explanations which necessitated its suspension, it would consequently seem the more so that it should receive its due accomplishment before it was finally ratified.

It is with equal surprise and concern that I observe, in the conclusion of your note, that you intimate the intention to decline any discussion of my proposals previous to the possession of the Floridas, since it appears to me that such discussions could not be long, in the event of your Government being ready to accede to them; (in which case I repeat that I am authorized solemnly to promise, in the name of His Majesty, that the ratification of the treaty shall be no longer delayed;) nor that the delay unavoidably produced by that particular cause, in the occupation of the territories in question, could be considered as derogatory to the dignity of the United States; and the more so as, until then, His Catholic Majesty would not be in the full possession of his rights.

I flatter myself that, on a consideration of the contents of this note, you will favor me with an answer more agreeable to my wishes.

In the mean time I reiterate the assurance of my distinguished consideration and respect, praying God to preserve you many years.

FRANCISCO D. VIVES.

Extract of a letter from Mr. Thomas L. L. Brent, acting as Chargé d'Affaires at Madrid, containing the substance of a conversation between him and Mr. Jabat, 27th April, 1820, *to Mr. Adams.*

He [Mr. Jabat] then adverted to the bill reported by the Committee of Foreign Relations to the House of Representatives, for the occupation of Florida, asked me if I had received instructions to give any explanations on the subject. He intimated that, if we did not extend our views farther than its occupation, every effort would be made to preserve amicable relations with the United States—every sacrifice, consistent with a due self-respect; but that the United States ought not to expect Spain would go any farther. Now that this had become a representative Government, they would be under the necessity of examining, with more scrupulous attention than ever, every act of theirs which could, in any degree, compromit the just pride and dignity of the nation. I told Mr. Jabat I had no instructions on the subject; I only knew, I said, from the public papers, that such a bill was before Congress, and, consequently, did not feel authorized to give any explanations; that, as soon as I received, I would make them known to him. I begged him to tranquillize himself; I said I hoped, with such dispositions as were manifested by the new Government, and the corresponding sentiments of mine, that every thing would finally be amicably arranged, and that matters might be so managed as that the steps which the United States may have thought it necessary to take for the assertion of their rights might be made reconcileable with the pride of his Government—steps which they will have been compelled to resort to, from the conduct of the former administration of his Government, and the measures of the old system. It may be proper to notice that this Minister was evidently under an apprehension that the United States might not limit themselves to the occupation of the territory of Florida alone. In the course of the conversation, Mr. Jabat said that, as there would be opposition, blood might be spilt in the occupation of Florida; and the idea of it seemed to give him great pain. Mr. Jabat's manner during the whole of this interview was mild and friendly, and mine corresponded to his.

The Secretary of State to General Don Francisco Dionisio Vives, Envoy Extraordinary and Minister Plenipotentiary from Spain.

DEPARTMENT OF STATE,
Washington, May 3, 1820.

SIR: The explanations upon the points mentioned in your letter of the 14th ultimo, which I had the honor of giving you at large in the conference between us on Saturday last, and the frankness of the assurances which I had the pleasure of receiving from you, of your conviction that they would prove satisfactory to your Government, will relieve me from the necessity of recurring to circumstances which might tend to irritating discussions. In the confident expectation that, upon the arrival of your messenger at Madrid, His Catholic Majesty will give his immediate ratification to the treaty of the 22d February, 1819, I readily forbear all reference to the delays which have hitherto retarded that event, and all disquisition upon the perfect right which the United States have had to that ratification.

I am now instructed to repeat the assurance which has already been given you, that the representations which appear to have been made to your Government of a system of hostility, in various parts of this Union, against the Spanish dominions and the property of Spanish subjects, of decisions marked with such hostility by any of the courts of the United States, and of the toleration in any case of it by this Government, are unfounded. In the existing unfortunate civil war between Spain and the South American provinces, the United States have constantly avowed, and faithfully maintained, an impartial neutrality.

No violation of that neutrality by any citizen of the United States has ever received sanction or countenance from this Government. Whenever the laws previously enacted for the preservation of neutrality have been found, by experience, in any manner defective, they have been strengthened by new provisions and severe penalties. Spanish property, illegally captured, has been constantly restored by the decisions of the tribunals of the United States; nor has the *life itself* been spared of individuals guilty of piracy committed upon Spanish property on the high seas.

Should the treaty be ratified by Spain, and the ratification be accepted, by and with the advice and consent of the Senate, the boundary line recognised by it will be respected by the United States, and due care will be taken to prevent any transgression of it. No new law or engagement will be necessary for that purpose. The existing laws are adequate to the suppression of such disorders, and they will be, as they have been, faithfully carried into effect. The miserable disorderly movement of a number of (not exceeding seventy) lawless individual stragglers, who never assembled within the jurisdiction of the United States, into a territory to which His Catholic Majesty has no acknowledged right other than the yet unratified treaty, was so far from receiving countenance or support from the Government of the United States, that every measure necessary for its suppression was promptly taken under their authority; and, from the misrepresentations which have been made of this very insignificant transaction to the Spanish Government, there is reason to believe that the pretended expedition itself, as well as the gross exaggerations which have been used to swell its importance, proceed from the same sources, equally unfriendly to the United States and to Spain.

As a necessary consequence of the neutrality between Spain and the South American provinces, the United States can contract no engagement not to form any relations with those provinces. This has explicitly and repeatedly been avowed and made known to your Government, both at Madrid and at this place. The demand was resisted both in conference and written correspondence between Mr. Erving and Mr. Pizarro. Mr. Onis had long and constantly been informed that a persistance in it would put an end to the possible conclusion of any treaty whatever. Your sovereign will perceive that, as such an engagement cannot be contracted by the United States, consistently with their obligations of neutrality, it cannot be justly required of them; nor have any of the European nations ever bound themselves to Spain by such an engagement.

With regard to your *proposals*, it is proper to observe that His Catholic Majesty, in announcing his purpose of asking *explanations* of the United States, gave no intimation of an intention to require new articles to the treaty. You are aware that the United States cannot, consistently with what is due to themselves, stipulate new engagements as the price of obtaining the ratification of the old. The declaration which Mr. Forsyth was

instructed to deliver at the exchange of the ratifications of the treaty, with regard to the eighth article, was not intended to annul, or in the slightest degree to alter or impair, the stipulations of that article; its only object was to guard your Government, and all persons who might have had an interest in any of the annulled grants, against the possible expectation or pretence that those grants would be made valid by the treaty. All grants subsequent to the 24th January, 1818, were declared to be positively null and void; and Mr. Onis always declared that he signed the treaty, fully believing that the grants to the Duke of Alagon, Count Punon Rostro, and Mr. Vargas, were subsequent to that date. But he had, in his letter to me of 16th November, 1818, declared that those grants were null and void, because the essential conditions of the grants had not been fulfilled by the grantees. It was distinctly understood by us both that no grant, of whatever date, should be made valid by the treaty, which would not have been valid by the laws of Spain and the Indies, if the treaty had not been made. It was therefore stipulated that grants prior to the 24th January, 1818, should be confirmed only " to the same extent that the same grants would be valid if the territories had remained under the dominion of His Catholic Majesty." This, of course, *excluded* the three grants above mentioned, which Mr. *Onis* had declared invalid for want of the fulfilment of their essential conditions—a fact which is now explicitly admitted by you. A single exception to the principle that the treaty should give no confirmation to any imperfect title was admitted; which exception was, that owners in possession of lands, who, by reason of the recent circumstances of the Spanish nation, and the revolutions in Europe, had been prevented from fulfilling all the conditions of their grants, should complete them within the terms limited in the same from the date of the treaty. This had obviously no reference to the above-mentioned grants, the grantees of which were not in possession of the lands, who had fulfilled none of their conditions, and who had not been prevented from fulfilling any of them by the circumstances of Spain or the revolutions of Europe. The article was drawn up by me, and, before assenting to it, Mr. Onis inquired what was understood by me as the import of the terms " shall complete them." I told him that, in connexion with the terms " all the conditions," they necessarily implied that the indulgence would be limited to grantees who had performed some of the conditions, and who had commenced settlements, which it would allow them to complete. These were precisely the cases for which Mr. Onis had urged the equity of making a provision, and he agreed to the article, fully understanding that it would be applicable only to them. When, after the signature of the treaty, there appeared to be some reason for supposing that Mr. Onis had been mistaken in believing that the grants to the Duke of Alagon, Count Punon Rostro, and Mr. Vargas, were subsequent to the 24th of January, 1818, candor required that Spain and the grantees should never have a shadow of ground to expect or allege

Spain—Ratification of the Treaty of 1819.

that this circumstance was at all material in relation to the bearing of the treaty upon those grants. Mr. Onis had not been mistaken in declaring that they were invalid, because their conditions were not fulfilled. He had not been mistaken in agreeing to the principle that no grant invalid as to Spain should, by the treaty, be made valid against the United States. He had not been mistaken in the knowledge that those grantees had neither commenced settlements, nor been prevented from completing them by the circumstances of Spain or the revolutions in Europe. The declaration which Mr. Forsyth was instructed to deliver was merely to caution all whom it might concern not to infer, from an unimportant mistake of Mr. Onis as to the date of the grants, other important mistakes which he had not made, and which the United States would not permit to be made by any one. It was not, therefore, to annul or to alter, but to fulfil the eighth article as it stands, that the declaration was to be delivered; and it is for the same purpose that this explanation is now given. It was with much satisfaction, therefore, that I learned from you the determination of your Government to assent to the total nullity of the abovementioned grants.

As I flatter myself that these explanations will remove every obstacle to the ratification of the treaty by His Catholic Majesty, it is much to be regretted that you have not that ratification to exchange, nor the power to give a pledge which would be equivalent to the ratification. The six months within which the exchange of the ratifications were stipulated by the treaty having elapsed, by the principles of our Constitution the question whether it shall now be accepted must be laid before the Senate for their advice and consent. To give a last and signal proof of the earnest wish of this Government to bring to a conclusion these long-standing and unhappy differences with Spain, the President will so far receive that solemn promise of immediate ratification, upon the arrival of your messenger at Madrid, which, in your note of the 19th ultimo, you declare yourself authorized, in the name of your sovereign, to give, as to submit it to the Senate of the United States whether they will advise and consent to accept it for the ratification of the United States heretofore given.

But it is proper to apprize you that, if this offer be not accepted, the United States, besides being entitled to resume all the rights, claims, and pretensions which they had renounced by the treaty, can no longer consent to relinquish their claims of indemnity, and those of their citizens, from Spain, for all the injuries which they have suffered, and are suffering, by the delay of His Catholic Majesty to ratify the treaty. The amount of claims of the citizens of the United States, which existed at the time when the treaty was signed, far exceeded that which the United States consented to accept as indemnity. Their right of territory was, and yet is, to the Rio del Norte. I am instructed to declare that, if any further delay to the ratification by His Catholic Majesty of the treaty should occur, the United States could not hereafter. accept either of $5,000,000 for the indemnities due to their citizens by Spain, nor of the Sabine for the boundary between the United States and the Spanish territories.

Please to accept the renewed assurance of my distinguished consideration.

JOHN QUINCY ADAMS.

General Don Francisco Dionisio Vives to the Secretary of State.

WASHINGTON, *May* 5, 1820.

SIR: In answer to your note of the 3d instant, and in pursuance of what I expressed to you in both our late conferences, I have to state to you that I am satisfied upon the first point of the proposals contained in my note of the 14th ultimo, and am persuaded that, if the existing laws enacted for the suppression of piracy should prove inadequate, more effectual measures will be adopted by your Government for the attainment of that important object.

I also admit as satisfactory the answer given to the second point, but I cannot assent to your assertion that the laws of this country have always been competent to the prevention of the excesses complained of, it being quite notorious that the expedition alluded to has not been the only one set on foot for the invasion of His Majesty's dominions; and it is, therefore, not surprising that the King, my Lord, should give credit to the information received in relation to that expedition, or that he should now require of your Government a pledge that the integrity of the Spanish possessions in North America shall be respected.

I mentioned to you, in conference, and I now repeat it, that the answer to the third point was not such as I could, agreeably to the nature of my instructions, accept as being satisfactory; and that, although His Majesty might not have required of any of the European Governments the declaration which he has required of yours, yet that ought not to be considered as unreasonable, it being well known to the King, my master, that those Governments, so far from being disposed to wish to recognise the insurgent Governments of the Spanish colonies, had declined the invitation intimated to them some time past by yours, to acknowledge the pretended Republic of Buenos Ayres. I notwithstanding renew to you the assurance that I will submit to His Majesty the verbal discussion we have had upon this point, and accompany it with such additional arguments as will, in my judgment, probably determine His Majesty to declare himself to be satisfied therewith.

In the event of the King's receiving as satisfactory the answer of your Government to the third point of my proposals, the abrogation of the grants will be attended with no difficulty; nor has that ever been the chief motive for suspending the ratification of the treaty; for the thorough comprehension of which I waive at present any reply to the remarks which you are pleased to offer on that topic. I cannot, however, refrain from stating to you that, in discussing with you the validity or the nullity of the grants above mentioned, I merely

Spain—Ratification of the Treaty of 1819.

said that, "in my private opinion, they are null and void, through the inability of the grantees to comply with the terms of the law."

It is to me a matter of great regret that I have it not in my power to repeat the solemn promise that His Majesty will ratify the treaty; inasmuch as I cannot, agreeably to my instructions, accept as satisfactory the answer given to the third point of my proposals. I am, however, persuaded that His Majesty, upon consideration of the representation which I shall have the honor to lay before him, and of the reasons assigned by your Government for withholding its assent to the third point, will consider himself as satisfied, and ratify the treaty.

I further conceive it my duty to state to you that, at the time when I communicated to your Government the substance of my present answer, I mentioned, speaking of my individual capacity, that, although I had no official information of it, yet I consider as authentic the current intelligence of an important change said to have taken place in the Government of Spain; and that this circumstance alone would impose on me the obligation of giving no greater latitude to my promise previous to my receiving new instructions.

I therefore hope that your Government, upon consideration of what I have now submitted to you, and of the contents of my former notes, will agree to wait the final decision of the King, my master, upon the only point still pending, and the adjustment of which is not within my competency; so that the past differences may be satisfactorily terminated, and the treaty receive its final accomplishment; thereby securing and perpetuating a perfect harmony and good understanding between the two Governments.

Be pleased to accept the assurances of my distinguished consideration. I pray God to preserve you many years.

FRANCISCO D. VIVES.

The Secretary of State to General ' Vives.

DEPARTMENT OF STATE, *Washington, May* 6, 1820.

Sir: In the letter which I have had the honor of receiving from you, dated yesterday, you observe that you renew the assurance that you will submit to His Majesty the verbal discussion we have had on the third point, concerning which you were instructed to ask for explanations. I have to request of you to state specifically the representation which you propose to make to His Majesty of what passed between us in conference on this subject.

I pray you to accept the renewed assurance of my distinguished consideration.

JOHN QUINCY ADAMS.

General Don Francisco Dionisio Vives to the Secretary of State.

WASHINGTON, *May* 7, 1820.

Sir: I have received the note you were pleased to address to me of yesterday's date, and, in answer

thereto, I have to state that the verbal discussion between us upon the third point of my proposals is comprised in your note of the 3d, and in my reply of the 5th instant; and that, consequently, the statement of it which I shall transmit for His Majesty's information will be in strict accordance with the tenor of the said notes.

I renew to you the assurance of my high esteem, and I pray God to preserve you many years.

FRANCISCO D. VIVES.

The Secretary of State to General Don Francisco Dionisio Vives, Envoy Extraordinary and Minister Plenipotentiary of Spain.

DEPARTMENT OF STATE, *Washington, May* 8, 1820.

Sir: In the letter which I had the honor of writing to you on the 3d instant, it was observed that all reference would readily be waived to the delays which have retarded the ratification by His Catholic Majesty of the treaty of the 22d February, 1819, and all disquisition upon the perfect right of the United States to that ratification, in the confident expectation that it would be immediately given upon the arrival of your messenger at Madrid, and subject to your compliance with the proposal offered you in the same note, as the last proof which the President could give of his reliance upon the termination of the differences between the United States and Spain by the ratification of the treaty.

This proposal was, that, upon the explanations given you on all the points noticed in your instructions, and with which you had admitted yourself to be personally satisfied, you should give the solemn promise, in the name of your sovereign, which, by your note of the 19th ultimo, you had declared yourself authorized to pledge, that the ratification should be given immediately upon the arrival of your messenger at Madrid: which promise the President consented so far to receive as to submit the question for the advice and consent of the Senate of the United States, whether the ratification of Spain should, under these circumstances, be accepted in exchange for that of the United States heretofore given. But the President has, with great regret, perceived by your note of the 15th instant that you decline giving even that unconditional promise, upon two allegations; one, that, although the explanations given you on one of the points mentioned in your note of the 14th ultimo are satisfactory to yourself, and you hope and believe will prove so to your sovereign, they still were not such as you were authorized by your instructions to accept; and the other, that you are informed a great change has recently occurred in the Government of Spain, which circumstance alone would prevent you from giving a further latitude to your promise previous to your receiving new instructions.

It becomes, therefore, indispensably necessary to show the absolute obligation by which His Catholic Majesty was bound to ratify the treaty within the term stipulated by one of its articles, that the reasons alleged for his withholding the ratifica-

Spain—Ratification of the Treaty of 1819.

tion are altogether insufficient for the justification of that measure, and that the United States have suffered by it the violation of a perfect right, for which they are justly entitled to indemnity and satisfaction—a right further corroborated by the consideration that the refusal of ratification necessarily included the non-fulfilment of another compact between the parties which had been ratified—the convention of August, 1802.

While regretting the necessity of producing this proof, I willingly repeat the expression of my satisfaction at being relieved from that of enlarging upon other topics of an unpleasant character. I shall allude to none of those upon which you have admitted the explanations given to be satisfactory, considering them as no longer subjects of discussion between us or our Governments. I shall with pleasure forbear noticing any remarks in your notes concerning me, which might otherwise require animadversion.

With the view of confining this letter to the only point upon which further observation is necessary, it will be proper to state the present aspect of the relations between the contracting parties.

The treaty of the 22d February, 1819, was signed after a succession of negotiations of nearly twenty years' duration, in which all the causes of difference between the two nations had been thoroughly discussed, and with a final admission on the part of Spain that there were existing just claims on her Government, at least to the amount of five millions of dollars, due to citizens of the United States, and for the payment of which provision was made by the treaty. It was signed by a Minister who had been several years residing in the United States in constant and unremitted exertions to maintain the interests and pretensions of Spain involved in the negotiation—signed after producing a full power, by which, in terms as solemn and as sacred as the hand of a sovereign can subscribe, His Catholic Majesty had promised to approve, ratify, and fulfil whatever should be stipulated and signed by him.

You will permit me to repeat that, by every principle of natural right, and by the universal assent of civilized nations, nothing can release the honor of a sovereign from the obligation of a promise thus unqualified, without the proof that his Minister has signed stipulations unwarranted by his instructions. The express authority of two of the most eminent writers upon national law to this point were cited in Mr. Forsyth's letter of 2d October, 1818, to the Duke of San Fernando. The words of Vattel are: "But to refuse with honor to ratify that which has been concluded in virtue of a full power, the sovereign must have strong and solid reasons for it ; and, particularly, he must show that his Minister transcended his instructions" * The words of Martens are: "Every thing that has been stipulated by an agent, in

conformity to his full powers, ought to become obligatory on the State from the moment of signing, without ever waiting for the ratification. However, not to expose a State to the errors of a single person, it is now become a general maxim that public conventions do not become obligatory until ratified. The motive of this custom clearly proves that the ratification can never be refused with justice, except when he who is charged with the negotiation, keeping within the extent of his public full powers, has gone beyond his secret instructions, and consequently rendered himself liable to punishment, or when the other party refuses to ratify."*

In your letter of the 24th ultimo, you observe that these positions have already been refuted by your Government, which makes it necessary to inquire, as I with great reluctance do, how they have been refuted.

The Duke of San Fernando, in his reply to this letter of Mr. Forsyth, says, maintains, and repeats, "that the very authorities cited by Mr. Forsyth literally declare that the sovereign, for strong and solid reasons, *or* if his Minister has exceeded his instructions, may refuse his ratification ; (*Vattel, book 2, chap. 12*,) and that public treaties are not obligatory until ratified."—*Martens, book 2, chap. 3. See note.* In these citations the Duke of San Fernando has substituted for the connective term *and*, in Vattel, which makes the proof of instructions transcended indispensable to justify the refusal of ratification, the disjunctive term *or*, which presents it as an alternative, and unnecessary on the contingency of other existing and solid reasons. Vattel says the sovereign must have strong and solid reasons, and particularly must show that the Minister transcended his instructions. Vattel not only makes the breach of instructions indispensable, but puts upon the sovereign the obligation of proving it. The Duke of San Fernando cites Vattel not only as admitting that other reasons, without a breach of instructions, may justify a refusal of ratification, but that the mere fact of such a breach would also justify the refusal, without requiring that the sovereign alleging should prove it.

Is this refutation?

The only observation that I shall permit myself to make upon it is, to mark how conclusive the authority of the passage in Vattel must have been to the mind of him who thus transformed it to the purpose for which he was contending. The cita-

* "Mais pour refuser avec honneur de ratifier ce qui a été conclu en vertu d'un plein-pouvoir, il faut que le souverain en ait de fortes et solides raisons, et qu'il fasse voir, en particulier, que son ministre s'est écarté de ses instructions.—*Liv.* 2, *ch.* 12, § 156.

* "Ce qui a été stipulé par un subalterne en conformité de son plein-pouvoir devient à la rigueur obligatoire pour la nation du moment même de la signature sans que la ratification soit nécessaire. Cependant, pour ne pas abandonner le sort des états aux erreurs d'un seul, il a été introduit par un usage généralement reconnu que les conventions publiques ne deviennent obligatoires que lorsqu'elles ont été ratifiées. Le motif de cet usage indique assez qu'on ne peut y provoquer avec justice, que lorsque celui qui est chargé des affaires de l'état, en se tenant dans les bornes de son plein-pouvoir publique, a franchi celle, de son instruction secrette, et que, par conséquent, il s'est rendu punissable."—*Liv.* 2, *ch.* 3, § 31.

Spain—Ratification of the Treaty of 1819.

tion from Martens receives the same treatment. The Duke of San Fernando takes by itself a part of a sentence—"that public treaties are not obligatory until ratified." He omits the preceding sentence, by which Martens asserts that a treaty signed in conformity to full powers is in rigor obligatory from the moment of signature, without waiting for the ratification. He omits the part of the sentence cited, which ascribes the necessity of a ratification to a usage founded upon the danger of exposing a State to the errors of its Minister. He omits the following sentence, which explicitly asserts that this usage can never be resorted to in justification of a refusal to ratify, unless when the Minister has exceeded his secret instructions; and thus, with this half of a sentence, stripped of all its qualifying context, the Duke brings Martens to assert that which he most explicitly denies.

Is this refutation?

While upon this subject, permit me to refer you to another passage of Vattel, which I the more readily cite, because, independent of its weight as authority, it places this obligation of sovereigns upon its immoveable foundation of eternal justice in the law of nature. "It is shown by the law of nature that he who has made a promise to any one has conferred upon him a true right to require the thing promised; and that, consequently, not to keep a perfect promise is to violate the right of another, and is as manifest an injustice as that of depriving a person of his property. All the tranquillity, the happiness, and security of the human race rest on justice, on the obligation of paying a regard to the rights of others. The respect of others for our rights of domain and property constitutes the security of our actual possessions. The faith of promises is our security for the things that cannot be delivered or executed on the spot. There would be no more security, no longer any commerce between mankind, did they not believe themselves obliged to preserve their faith and keep their word. This obligation is then as necessary as it is natural and indubitable between nations that live together in a state of nature, and acknowledge no superior upon earth, to maintain order and peace in their society. Nations and their conductors ought, then, to keep their promises and their treaties inviolable. This great truth, though too often neglected in practice, is generally acknowledged by all nations."[*]

[*] "On démontre en droit naturel, que celui qui promet à quelqu'un a lui conféré un véritable droit d'exiger la chose promise; et que, par conséquent, ne point garder une promesse parfaite, c'est violer le droit d'autrui, c'est une injustice aussi manifeste que celle de dépouiller quelqu'un de son bien. Toute la tranquillité, le bonheur, et la sûreté du genre humain reposent sur la justice, sur l'obligation de respecter les droits d'autrui. Le respect des autres pour nos droits de domaine et de propriété fait la sûreté de nos possessions actuelles; la foi des promesses est notre garant pour les choses qui ne peuvent être livrées ou exécutées sur-le-champ. Plus de sûreté, plus de commerce, entre les hommes, s'ils ne se croient point obligés de garder la foi, de tenir leur parole. Cette obligation est, donc, aussi nécessaire qu'elle est naturelle et indubitable entre les nations qui vivent ensemble dans l'état de nature, et qui ne connaissent point de supérieur sur la terre, pour maintenir l'ordre et la paix dans leur société. Les nations et leurs conducteurs doivent, donc, garder inviolablement leurs promesses et leurs traités. Cette grande vérité, quoique trop souvent negligée dans la pratique, est généralement reconnue de toutes les nations."—*Liv.* 2, *ch.* 12, § 163.

The melancholy allusion to the frequent practical neglect of this unquestionable principle would afford a sufficient reply to your assertion that the ratification of treaties has often been refused, though signed by Ministers with unqualified full powers, and without breach of their instructions. No case can be cited by you in which such a refusal has been justly given; and the fact of refusal, separate from the justice of the case, amounts to no more than the assertion that sovereigns have often violated their engagements and their duties; the obligation of His Catholic Majesty to ratify the treaty signed by Mr. Onis is therefore complete.

The sixteenth and last article of this treaty is in the following words: "The present treaty *shall be ratified,* in due form, by the contracting parties, and the ratifications shall be exchanged in six months from this time, *or sooner if possible.*" On the faith of His Catholic Majesty's promise, the treaty was, immediately after its signature, ratified on the part of the United States, and, on the 18th of May following, Mr. Forsyth, by an official note, informed the Marquis of Casa Yrujo, then Minister of Foreign Affairs at Madrid, that the treaty, duly ratified by the United States, had been intrusted to him by the President, and that he was prepared to exchange it for the ratification of Spain. He added that, from the nature of the engagement, it was desirable that the earliest exchange should be made, and that the American ship of war Hornet was waiting in the harbor of Cadiz, destined in a few days to the United States, and affording an opportunity peculiarly convenient of transmitting the ratified treaty to the United States.

No answer having been returned to this note, on the 4th of June Mr. Forsyth addressed to the same Minister a second, urging, in the most respectful terms, the necessity of the departure of the Hornet, the just expectation of the United States that the ratified treaty would be transmitted by that vessel, and the disappointment which could not fail to ensue should she return without it.

After fifteen days of further delay, on the 19th of June, Mr. Forsyth was informed by a note from Mr. Salmon, successor to the Marquis of Casa Yrujo, that "His Majesty, on reflecting on the great importance and interest of the treaty in question was under the indispensable necessity of examining it with the greatest caution and deliberation before he proceeded to ratify it, and this was all he was enabled to communicate to Mr. Forsyth on that point."

Thus, after the lapse of more than a month from the time of Mr. Forsyth's first note, and of more than two months from the time when your Government had received the treaty, with knowledge that it had been ratified by the United States, the ratification of a treaty which His Catholic Majesty had solemnly promised, so that it might be exchanged within six months from the date of its signature, *or sooner if possible*, was withheld merely to give time to His Catholic Majesty to *examine* it; and this treaty was the result of a twenty years' negotiation, in which every article and subject contained in it had been debated and sifted to the utmost satiety between the parties, both at Washington and Madrid—a treaty in which the stipulations by the Spanish Minister had been sanctioned by successive references of every point to his own Government, and were, by the formal admission of your own note, fully within the compass of his instructions.

If, under the feeling of such a procedure on the part of the Spanish Government, the Minister of the United States appealed to the just rights of his country in expressions suited more to the sense of its wrongs than to the courtesies of European diplomacy, nothing had till then occurred which could have restrained your Government from asking of him any explanation which could be necessary for fixing its determination upon the ratification. No explanation was asked of him.

Nearly two months afterwards, on the 10th of August, Mr. Forsyth was informed that the King would not come to a final decision upon the ratification without previously entering into several explanations with the Government of the United States, to some of which that Government had given rise, and that His Majesty had charged a person possessed of his full confidence, who would forthwith make known to the United States His Majesty's intentions. Mr. Forsyth offered himself to give every explanation which could be justly required; but your Government declined receiving them from him, assigning to him the shortness of the time—a reason altogether different from that which you now allege, of the disrespectful character of his communications.

From the 10th of August till the 14th of last month, a period of more than eight months, passed over, during which no information was given by your Government of the nature of the explanations which would be required. The Government of the United States, by a forbearance perhaps unexampled in human history, has patiently waited for your arrival, always ready to give, in candor and sincerity, every explanation that could with any propriety be demanded. What, then, must have been the sentiments of the President upon finding, by your note of the 14th ultimo, that, instead of explanations, His Catholic Majesty has instructed you to demand the negotiation of another treaty, and to call upon the United States for stipulations derogatory to their honor, and incompatible with their duties as an independent nation? What must be the feelings of this nation to learn that, when called upon to state whether you were the bearer of His Catholic Majesty's ratification of the treaty to be exchanged upon the explanations demanded being given, you explicitly answered that you were *not?* And, when required to say whether you are authorized,

as a substitute for the ratification, to give the pledge of immediate possession of the territory from which the acknowledged just claims of the citizens of the United States were stipulated to be indemnified, you still answer that you are not; but refer us back to a solemn promise of the King, already pledged before in the full power to your predecessor, and to a ratification as soon as possible, already stipulated in vain by the treaty which he, in full conformity to his instructions, had signed?

The ratification of that treaty can now no longer be accepted by this Government without the concurrence of a Constitutional majority of the Senate of the United States, to whom it must be again referred. Yet even this promise you were, by my letter of the 3d instant, informed that, rather than abandon the last hope of obtaining the fulfilment of His Catholic Majesty's promise already given, the President would, so far as was constitutionally within his power, yet accept.

The assurances which you had given me, in the first personal conference between us, of your own entire satisfaction with the explanations given you upon all the points on which you had been instructed to ask them, would naturally have led to the expectation that the promise which you was authorized to give would, at least, not be withheld. From your letter of the 5th instant, however, it appears that no discretion has been left you to pledge even His Majesty's promise of ratification in the event of your being yourself satisfied with the explanations upon *all* the points desired; that the only promise you can give is *conditional*, and the condition a point upon which your Government, when they prescribed, could not but know it was *impossible* that the United States should comply—a condition incompatible with their independence, their neutrality, their justice, and their honor.

It was also a condition which His Catholic Majesty had not the shadow of a *right* to prescribe. The treaty had been signed by Mr. Onis with a full knowledge that no such engagement as that contemplated by it would ever be acceded to by the American Government, and after long and unwearied efforts to obtain it. The differences between the United States and Spain had no connexion with the war between Spain and South America. The object of the treaty was to settle the boundaries, and adjust and provide for the claims between your nation and ours; and Spain, at no time, could have a right to require that any stipulation concerning the contest between her and her colonies should be connected with it. As His Catholic Majesty could not justly require it during the negotiation of that treaty, still less could it afford a justification for withholding his promised ratification after it was concluded.

The proposal which, at a pr or period, had been made by the Government of the United States to some of the principal Powers of Europe, for a recognition, in concert, of the independence of Buenos Ayres, was founded, as I have observed to you, upon an opinion then and still entertained that this recognition must, and would at no very remote period, be made by Spain herself ; that the joint acknowledgment by several of the principal Powers of the world at the same time might probably induce Spain the sooner to accede to to that necessity, in which she must ultimately acquiesce, and would thereby hasten an event propitious to her own interests by terminating a struggle in which she is wasting her strength and resources without a possibility of success—an event ardently to be desired by every friend of humanity afflicted by the continual horrors of a war, cruel and sanguinary almost beyond example; an event not only desirable to the unhappy people who are suffering the complicated distresses and calamities of this war, but to all the nations having relations of amity and of commerce with them. This proposal, founded upon such motives, far from giving to Spain the right to claim of the United States an engagement not to recognise the South American Governments, ought to have been considered by Spain as proof at once of the moderation and discretion of the United States ; as evidence of their disposition to discard all selfish or exclusive views in the adoption of a measure which they deemed wise and just in itself, but most likely to prove efficacious by a common adoption of it, in a spirit entirely pacific, in concert with other nations, rather than by a precipitate resort to it on the part of the United States alone.

The conditional promise, therefore, now offered by you, instead of the positive one which you had declared yourself authorized to give, cannot be accepted by the President; and I am constrained to observe that he can consider the procedure of your Government, in thus providing you with powers and instructions utterly inefficient for the *conclusion* of the negotiation with which you are charged, in no other light than as proceeding from a determination on its part still to protract and baffle its final successful issue. Under these circumstances, he deems it his duty to submit the correspondence which has passed between us, since your arrival, to the consideration of the Congress of the United States, to whom it will belong to decide how far the United States can yet, consistently with their duties to themselves, and the rights of their citizens, authorize the further delay requested in your note of the 5th instant.

In the conclusion of that note you have remarked, alluding to a great change which appears to have taken place since your departure from Madrid in the Government of Spain, that this circumstance alone would impose on you the obligation of giving no greater latitude to your promise previous to your receiving new instructions. If I have understood you right, your intention is to remark that this circumstance alone would restrain you, in any event, from giving, without new instructions, the unconditional promise of ratification, which, in a former note, you had declared yourself authorized, in the name of your Sovereign, to give. This seems to be equivalent to a declaration that you consider your powers themselves, in the extent to which they were intrusted to you, as suspended by the events to which you thus refer. If I am mistaken in taking this as

your meaning, will you have the goodness to inform me how far you do consider your powers affected by the present state of your information from Spain ?

Please to accept the assurance of my distinguished consideration.

JOHN Q. ADAMS.

General Vives to the Secretary of State.

WASHINGTON, *May* 9, 1820.

SIR: In answer to your note of yesterday's date I have, in the first place, to give you the explanation requested of me, of the import of my last proposal; and, in so doing, to repeat, in other words, that I am authorized solemnly to promise to the Government the ratification of the treaty by His Majesty only in case the third point of my proposals be satisfied; but as the answer given to this point has not been such as I could, agreeably to my instructions, receive as satisfactory, I can by no means commit myself by giving a greater extension to my promise than that expressed in my note.

My object in intimating to you that, although I knew nothing officially, yet I considered as authentic the information circulating of an important change in the Government of Spain—a circumstance which would, of itself, *effectually* prevent me from giving greater latitude to my promise—was, to apprize your Government that as, by the adoption of the constitution of 1812 in Spain, the powers of the King would be limited, it would no longer depend on His Majesty alone to fulfil my solemn promise, admitting that my instructions had empowered me to give such a promise; so that my sole motive for offering a remark upon that topic was to strengthen the grounds on which my proposal was founded, and, further, to enable your Government so to appreciate as no longer to decline assenting to it.

I shall, on this occasion, waive all reply to the arguments again advanced by you, an extenso, upon the question of His Majesty's obligation to ratify the treaty, and confine myself to a single remark, namely, that all the authorities cited by you lay down the peace and happiness of mankind in general, and of States and their respective people in particular, as a fundamental principle. And having, in my first note, shown the notoriously hostile disposition prevailing throughout the Union towards the interests of the Spanish monarchy, it necessarily follows that, when the objects of treaties are not obtained, the ratification of that of 22d February, 1819, would, in like manner, become illusory; and, therefore, that His Majesty's motives for suspending it were founded upon a competent view of evident facts.

I shall also leave it to the general sense of the reflecting part of mankind to decide whether the reasoning you rely on, in stating the motives of the American Government for proposing to other Powers to acknowledge the revolted provinces of Spanish America, and in exhibiting them as favorable, not only to suffering humanity, but to the interests of Spain herself, be not, in the highest degree, specious; for, if such maxims were to be adopted, nations could no longer count upon the integrity of their possessions, or upon the maintenance of that mutual amity and good understanding which it is equally their duty and their interest to cultivate in their relations with each other.

I have the honor to offer you anew the assurances of my distinguished consideration, and I pray God long to preserve you.

FRANCISCO D. VIVES.

General Don Francisco Dionisio Vives to the Secretary of State.

WASHINGTON, *May* 10, 1820.

SIR: In conformity with the orders I have this moment received from my Government, I have the honor to inform you that His Catholic Majesty hath sworn to the political constitution of the Spanish monarchy as sanctioned by the extraordinary Cortes in 1812, and to enclose a printed copy of His Majesty's manifest to the nation, for the purpose of giving the President a just view of the noble and generous sentiments which actuate the august mind of the King.

Please to accept the renewed assurances of my perfect consideration, and my wish that God may preserve you many years.

FRANCISCO D. VIVES.

(From the National Press.)

GAZETTE EXTRAORDINARY OF MADRID,
Sunday, March 12, 1820.

Proclamation of the King to the Nation.

SPANIARDS: When, by your heroic efforts, you succeeded in terminating a captivity in which I was detained by the most unheard-of perfidy, every thing I saw and was informed of, on my entering into my native land, conspired to persuade me that the nation wished to see revived its ancient form of government; and this persuasion must have decided me to conform myself with the general wish of a magnanimous people, who, vanquisher of a foreign enemy, feared the still more dreadful evils of intestine divisions.

I was, however, well aware that the rapid progress of civilization in Europe; the universal diffusion of knowledge, even among the lower classes; the more frequent intercourse with the different parts of the globe; and the wonderful events of the present era, have given rise to ideas and desires unknown to our forefathers, which imperiously demand the most energetic measures in the Government. I also knew well that it was indispensable that the political institutions should agree with such principles, thereby to obtain that harmony between the people and the laws on which the stability and peace of society so much depend.

But, while I was maturely planning, with the solicitude of my paternal heart, the changes to be effected in our fundamental administration, more suitable to the national character and to the present state of the different provinces of the Spanish monarchy, and also more analogous to an enlight-

ened nation, you have let me know your wishes for the re-establishment of the constitution proclaimed at Cadiz, in the year 1812, amidst the bustle of arms, and while, to the astonishment of the world, you were fighting for the liberty of your country. I have listened to your desires, and, as a loving father, I have condescended to grant what my children thought most conducive to their happiness. I have sworn to that constitution for which you longed, and I will always be its firmest supporter. I have already taken the most effectual measures for the immediate convocation of the Cortes. In them, and united to your representatives, I will make it my glory to concur in the great work of national prosperity.

Spaniards! Your glory is my only ambition. The desire of my heart is to see you all united and happy around my throne. Trust, then, to your King, who addresses you with that sincere effusion of his soul which the circumstances in which you are, and a sense of the high duty imposed upon him by Providence, inspire him with. Your happiness will henceforth depend, in a great measure, upon yourselves. Do not suffer yourselves to be seduced by the deceitful appearances of a chimerical happiness, which often prevents the attaining of real bliss. Allow not your passions to be exalted, as they are wont to make enemies of those who ought always to live as brothers, and be as unanimous in their wishes as they are in the possession of one religion, the speaking of one language, and the conforming to the same manners and customs. Repel the perfidious insinuations so artfully disguised by your enemies. Let us conform ourselves strictly to the constitution, as I myself will be the first to do; and let us show to Europe a pattern of wisdom, order, and perfect moderation, in a crisis which, in other nations, has been accompanied by scenes of bloodshed and havoc. Let us make the Spanish name admired and respected, at the same time that we establish forever our happiness and our glory.

FERDINAND.

AT THE PALACE, MADRID, *March* 10, 1820.

General Don Francisco Dionisio Vives to the Secretary of State.

WASHINGTON, *May* 11, 1820.

SIR: Among the documents transmitted with the President's Message to both Houses of Congress, and published in this day's National Intelligencer, I have seen with surprise the letter of Mr. Gallatin, stating that I positively told him that "I could, in case of an arrangement, give satisfactory security to the United States, and that it would consist in consenting that they should take immediate possession of Florida without waiting for the ratification of the treaty." Although I have with all frankness proved, in my correspondence with you, that I had no such authority, and that it will not, under any view which may be taken, appear presumable that I made so doubtful, so useless, and inconsiderate a disclosure, I request, however, that you will be pleased to communicate this to the President, in order that, by

Spain—Ratification of the Treaty of 1819.

giving publicity to this document, it may be understood that I made no such proposal, either to Mr. Gallatin or to Baron Pasquier. I renew, &c.

FRANCISCO D. VIVES.

[The following report on the same subject was made to the House of Representatives, March 9, 1820.]

The committee, to whom has been referred so much of the President's Message at the commencement of the session as relates to foreign affairs, respectfully report:

That their attention was directed, immediately upon their appointment, to the state of the relations of the United States with Spain, and that their delay in making a report on them must be attributed to their wish "to afford an opportunity for such friendly communications during the present, session of Congress" as the Government of Spain had authorized us to expect. They thought it better that Congress should postpone its determination until events might enable it to make that determination definitive, than that it should pass a contingent act for authorizing measures which it was not proposed immediately to execute; that it should found its determination upon relations ascertained to exist, than upon a calculation of events which might be expected to occur during its sitting.

But more than a year has passed since the signature of the treaty by which it was proposed to terminate the long differences between the United States and Spain; more than six months since the appointment of a new Minister from Spain, who was "forthwith" to make known to the United States the intentions of his Government; and we have advanced so far in the session as to make it necessary to propose, without further delay, any measure on which it is expected that Congress shall act before its adjournment.

The committee will not attempt to add any thing to the exposition of the rights of the United States and the obligations of Spain which is contained in the correspondence between the two Governments. We can hardly expect from continued negotiation the redress which has been claimed for twenty years, and promised for eighteen; which has been a second time promised, and a second time withheld. In such a negotiation, the signature of a treaty seems to be a mere incident, and not its term.

For the spoliations which have been committed upon the property of our citizens, for the invasion of our soil, for the weakness or partiality which has made a Spanish territory the place of rendezvous and encampment of an enemy, and which has, still more lately, permitted the Indian inhabitants of that territory (whom Spain was bound by treaty to restrain) to engage in savage hostilities against us—for all these acts of war, a people less attached to peace would seek redress only by war. To capture and confiscate the ships and property of the wrong-doer would be admitted to be a policy of mildness and forbearance. But, by such reprisals, the Government that does the wrong suffers less than the unoffending subject. It seems

a more just reprisal to occupy th· *woodnet which* has been made an instrument of jury, which has been designated by Spain herself as the fund for our indemnity, and whose occupation by the United States will stop the accumulation of those claims for compensation and redress which the misgovernment of that neglected colony continually produces. The committee submit to the House a bill to authorize the President of the United States to take possession of East and West Florida, and establish a temporary Government therein.

There appears too much reason to believe, from the mistake of the Spanish negotiator as to the dates of the Spanish grants which it was intended to annul if the projected treaty had been ratified, that the Crown lands in Florida may be insufficient to provide the expected indemnity for our losses. But these may be applied, as far as they will go, to the compensation of our citizens; and for the excess of our claim, Spain, by whose act the domain of Florida has been rendered inadequate, must expect us to look westward. Perhaps, when our attention is thus forced to a direction more interesting to Spain, her Government may at last admit that it is as much her interest as ours that the just claims of the United States should be provided for by friendly convention, and we may hope that the next treaty between the two nations may be executed as well as signed.

Extract of a letter from Mr. Forsyth to Mr. Adams, (No. 18,) dated

MAY 20, 1820.

By the Gibraltar mail of the —— instant, I received the duplicate of your No. 11. You will herewith receive copies of Mr. Jabat's letter, giving notice of the birth and title of the son of the Infante Don Francisco de Paula, and my answer. On the 12th I paid the Minister a visit at the Office of State, and, as I expected, he inquired if I had any recent advices from America. I stated to him very frankly that I had received nothing but the permission from our Government to return to the United States, which, from a belief that it would be most agreeable to the President, I should not use until after the celebration of the Cortes. He professed to be much gratified by this determination, which he thought was calculated to promote that good understanding between our respective Governments, to secure which was the object of our mutual wishes. From this, the conversation naturally turned to the unofficial notices from the United States, and particularly to the report of the committee on the affairs of Florida. He did not appear to apprehend that we should do more than occupy the territory; but he expressed a great deal of dread lest there should be blood shed in effecting that object, and carrying into effect the act proposed by the committee.

As I had been told (as stated in my No. 17) that some uneasiness was felt on the first point, I thought it prudent to show him that, with the dispositions now entertained in Spain, there was no reason that we should be disposed to go beyond the limits of the treaty of February, 1819. He would recollect that the only motives we could have were to procure satisfaction for the injury sustained by the delay of Spain to ratify the treaty, and compensation for any deficiency in the fund for the payment of our citizens occasioned by the mistake of Mr. Onis about the date of the large grants. On the first, I was sure a reasonable explanation would be deemed sufficient; on the second, there could be no difficulty, as the abandonment of all pretension in favor of the grantees was more necessary to the character of Spain than it was important to the interests of the United States.

I did not suppose there was much ground for the fears he seemed to entertain of a formidable resistance to the occupation of Florida; nevertheless, as he was seriously apprehensive, I suggested that the President would no doubt employ a force so powerful that resistance would be hopeless, and I presumed the good sense of the Spanish authorities would prevent them from making a useless sacrifice of the lives of the soldiers committed to their care. It was obvious, from the conversation of Mr. Jabat, that the seizure of the territory was anticipated, and that the only fear really entertained was, that the mode of occupation would impose an obligation on the present rulers to make a noise about it. The interview terminated by a renewal of the assurances formerly given, of the desire of the Government to establish a permanent friendship with us, and with the hope, reciprocally expressed, that nothing might occur to render it difficult. On the 15th, I received a note from Mr. Jabat, (copy enclosed,) inviting me to see him the next day at eleven. I saw him at the hour appointed, and his first question was, "Have you any thing from Washington?" To my reply in the negative, he said, "Then I shall have the pleasure of giving you very recent advices from that place." He showed me a despatch from Mr. Serna, of the 28th of March, enclosing copies of the President's Message to the House of Representatives of the 27th, and of the documents accompanying it. Mr. Jabat was highly gratified; said nothing could have occurred more favorable to the future amity of the two nations; that he had shown these papers to the King, who was pleased both with the measure proposed, and the reasons offered for it by the President. Mr. Jabat did not omit to suggest, what I knew perfectly well, that the accomplishment of the expectations of the President, would have to be imputed to the recent revolution in Spain. He explained to me what I did not understand in our previous conversation, the foundation of his fears of a formidable resistance in Florida. It seems the ports of the territory had been reinforced in Cuba, and the Governor General of that island had given official notice of it to the Secretary of State. Joining with the Spanish secretary in his expressions of satisfaction, I suggested the hope that General Vives would not arrive until after the adjournment of Congress, as it was impossible to foresee what might be the effect produced by his arrival without competent power to meet the just expectations

of the American Government. I did not fear any ill consequences if news of the revolution in Spain could reach Washington before a determination was taken. I was confident that, irritating as this authority might be, the President would be disposed to give to the King of the Spains proofs of the moderation and good will which had distinguished the conduct of the United States to the King of Spain. Taking the time at which Congress has usually adjourned as the criterion, I suppose that General Vives would scarcely see Washington before the adjournment of the legislative body. I have since learned from our newspapers that Congress would have continued in session until the beginning of this month, and that General Vives reached New York on the 5th of April. I now hope that Mr. Hackley, who carried my despatches of the 9th March, and who left the Straits of Gibraltar about the 27th March, will be in the United States within a short time after the arrival of the Spanish Minister. In the present state of things, nothing could be more auspicious than the proposed delay of acting against Florida, although the President will have perceived from your first communications with General Vives, that, but for recent events, we should have given another proof of useless forbearance, if the utility of forbearance was to be estimated by the good effect it would have produced on the Government of Spain. Mr. Jabat proposed to me to see the King at the circle that day—a ceremony I have not thought it necessary to observe since the postponement of the ratification of the treaty. Always, however, replying politely to the notes sent on particular occasions, and once calling at the palace when the King was ill, I had resolved to renew these visits of ceremony immediately after the liberation of the Americans, prisoners in Spain, and therefore the more readily acceded to this proposal. I attended the circle with the diplomatic body, and was received, as I had been taught to expect, perfectly well, and as if there had been no interruption in my visits to it.

Extract of a letter from the same to the same, (No. 19.)
JULY 13, 1820.

A few days after the arrival of the Minister of State, (Perez de Castro,) I called at his office to see him on our affairs. I stated that the time for the meeting of the Cortes was near at hand, and that I was desirous to know what was proposed by this Government to be done. He declared himself to be unable to converse on the subject of the negotiation with the United States. He was not master of the correspondence, and that his numerous and pressing engagements had rendered it impossible for him as yet to become so. He was examining, and hoped to speak advisedly on it in a short time. I gave him a translation of the remonstrance of the 18th of October, to apprize him of the state of the dispute in relation to the eighth article of the treaty, not officially, but as a document for his own examination, telling him that I did not conceive it necessary, from the disposition manifested since the revolution, to make an official representation on this subject. He received it very willingly. He had seen, as he stated, in the foreign newspapers, that it was asserted by the American Government that the treaty was obligatory upon Spain, although not ratified: this position he could not consider as founded either in the opinion of the best authorities, or in the usages of nation. I explained to him that we considered the treaty as obligatory in justice and in honor as if ratified by Spain. As no satisfactory reason had been, or, as we believed, could be given for the refusal to ratify, there could be no question as to our right to resort to any measure we deemed proper to obtain satisfaction. The least we could do was to execute the treaty; and when we gave to Spain all the advantages she could derive from it, we should take from her all just cause even to complain of the course pursued. He spoke a good deal at large of the charge of bad faith which was urged against Spain, and said she had no motive of avarice or ambition to gratify in her negotiation with us; and if her policy required her to procrastinate, this was no reason to charge her with ill faith. To all this I answered that the systematic procrastination, although at all times vexatious, had never been urged as a proof of bad faith; it was the noncompliance with engagements actually made by persons duly authorized and empowered by this Government; that, if the avarice or ambition of the Government was not known in the negotiation, that of individuals who had possessed influence in Spain was but too visible. I saw him again after ten days. He had run over the whole correspondence; talked of the treaty of 1802; the proposals of Mr. Pinckney; the guaranty of the Spanish American dominions, as an inducement to cede Florida; in short, of all that had passed prior to the convention of 1819; of the losses Spain had sustained, and of our gains. I listened patiently to all he had to advance; when he had finished, I replied that we had gained nothing from Spain; if her arrangement with another Power was matter of regret, it was not our fault; what we had obtained was purchased and paid for; that I had no instructions from the President since August, 1819, and, therefore, could not speak certainly of what might be the wish of my Government; but that it appeared to me it would be better for Spain, at the present juncture, not to look beyond the treaty of 1819, but to consider what obligations were imposed upon her by it, and by her as yet unexplained refusal to ratify it. He did not seem unwilling to adopt this idea, and entered into a short examination of the conduct of the United States in the dispute between the colonies and Spain; the expeditions fitted out by Miranda, Mina, &c.; of the patriot privateers, &c. I replied that we had done all Spain had a right to expect from us; that, determining to be neutral between the contending parties, we had taken every means necessary to preserve that neutrality. If the laws of the United States had been sometimes violated with impunity, it was what had occurred, and would occur, in all nations, by the escape of persons who had committed offences; that all recla-

mations founded upon them by causes of complaint were removed by the convention, &c. Previous to this conversation, I had seen in the English newspapers the President's Message to Congress of the 9th April, headed by a sort of abstract of your correspondence with General Vives, in which it was stated that this Government had not asked explanations of me relative to the treaty because of my intemperate conduct. I remarked to the Minister that this was not the fact. Explanations were not asked of me, because, anticipating what would be required, I had given the Ministry to understand that, upon the subject of the dispute with the colonies, I had no explanations to give, and that it was informally made known to me, before the 22d of August, that I could have the convention if I was authorized to promise that the Government of the United States would not recognise the independence of any of the Patriot Governments. He said he had read the note I had given him, and those previously written, and that there were expressions stronger than he had ever met with in diplomatic correspondence, but he supposed they were written when I was a little warm. I questioned whether he had ever met with a similar case in the history of diplomacy, and that I was not a little warm, but indignant at seeing the character of a great nation, and its peace, and that of my own country, put in jeopardy for the sake and by the intrigues of selfish individuals. As the Minister had not seen the message, I promised to procure and send it to him. He was not prepared to say what course would be recommended to the Cortes, upon whom every thing depended. I pressed upon him the necessity of doing what was done promptly. He was satisfied of the importance of doing so, and promised to let me know the determination of the Ministry as soon as it was made. At parting, he referred to the assistance received from Spain during our revolutionary war, which he said we ought not to forget. The reply was, we never forget when you permit us to remember it. I met the Secretary of State at dinner on the same day at the English ambassador's. He told me had received that morning, from General Vives, despatches, the President's Message, and the correspondence sent with it to Congress. He had not yet had time to read them attentively, but appeared to be pleased with what he had seen in glancing over the papers. On the 4th of July Mr. De Castro dined at my house, and brought with him a copy of the message and correspondence, which he left with me, to be returned, as he had but the one copy. On the 6th the Cortes was installed, Espiga chosen president, a priest, but one of the most liberal; and Quiroga vice president. I was in the tribune prepared for the diplomatic corps during the votation, and went from it to the office of Mr. De Castro, to restore to him the documents he had loaned me. He was just going to the King, and had but a few moments to converse with me. In these few, he said he thought the President did not look beyond the ratification of the convention, the grants being set aside, and there could be no difficulty about them. It was his opinion that this should be done.

Spain—Ratification of the Treaty of 1819.

I do not say, he continued, it will be done; that depends on another body; but it is my opinion that it will be. What say you, he asked—will this be satisfactory? I reminded him that I had no instructions—hoped to receive them. I could give him only an opinion in turn. Judging from the correspondence and message, I saw no sufficient reason to change the opinion already given to Mr. Jabat, that the ratification of the treaty, accompanied by satisfaction for the injury caused by the delay, would be accepted by the United States. I was present at the session of the Cortes on the 9th. The oath required by the constitution was taken by the King in due form, and an address made to him by the president. The King said a few words in reply, and then read his speech. Copies furnished by the Department of State are enclosed, as also copies of the answer of the Cortes, prepared by a select committee appointed for that purpose. The answer to that part of the King's speech which refers to the dispute with the United States is marked by the introduction of a very emphatic word. The King says: "Although a complication of various circumstances has not permitted as yet the adjustment of those differences, (with the United States and Portugal,) I hope that the justice and moderation of the principles which direct our diplomatic operations will produce a result decorous to the nation, and agreeable to the pacific system, &c. &c. of Europe." The answer is: "The Cortes only regret that there exist differences with the United States and His Most Faithful Majesty; but the principles of moderation that will direct now our diplomatic negotiations give hope to the Cortes that they will conclude in terms which, being a termination decorous to the nation, may not interrupt the pacific system, &c. &c. of Europe."

On the 11th the Minister of State read his report to the Cortes, and gave them an account of the state of the dispute with the United States. I was not present. A very imperfect account of it is published in the newspapers. I hope to procure it to send with this despatch, as also a very interesting report of the Minister of the Government of the Peninsula, Augustin Arguelles.

Extract of a letter from the same to the same, (marked private) dated

JULY 30, 1820.

On the 22d I wrote to Mr. De Castro, to say to him that the President would accept the treaty of 1819, subject to the advice and consent of the Senate, if immediately ratified by Spain. Had the Secretary of State been in Madrid, after what has occurred in our conversation, I should only have stated to him, verbally, what I had been instructed to say; but, as the time of his stay at Sacedon was uncertain, I thought it better to write than to ask an interview at that place, as the latter might be imputed to an anxiety on the subject which I was instructed not to discover. His answer is of the 25th, and is perfectly satisfactory. He has the commands of the King " to bring the business of the negotiation immediately

16th Con. 2d Sess.—46

before the Cortes, and is using all exertion to do so." Mr. Jabat called on me on the 27th, to say that, in consequence of this correspondence, the King would shorten his stay at Sacedon, would come to Madrid on the 10th of August, and that the negotiation would be, by the 12th, before the Cortes. There is, therefore, every reason to hope that all will be finished by the 20th. As so little time is to elapse before I shall have it in my power to say what has been done, I write hastily, intending, immediately after the determination of the Cortes, to forward copies of the correspondence, and a more formal statement of what has occurred and may occur.

Extract of a letter from the same to the same, (marked private,) dated

AUGUST 27, 1820.

My hopes of seeing the business of the Florida treaty definitively arranged by the 20th of this month have been disappointed. The King did not come from Sacedon until the 12th. I was taught to expect an immediate movement in our affairs, but it was not made. Early last week I had an accidental interview with one of the Ministers, (Mr. Jabat,) who told me the necessary papers were prepared, and would be before the Cortes during the week. Yesterday morning, as nothing had been done, I called at the office of Mr. De Castro, to know what was the motive for delaying to present the subject to the Cortes. Mr. De Castro imputed it entirely to the press of important matters at home. He had just sent to ask the Cortes to designate the day and hour when he could lay before them, in the name of the King, the business of the treaty for the cession of Florida. Before I left the office, the Secretary of State was informed that the Cortes would receive him immediately. At one o'clock yesterday, the Cortes had a secret session, and no doubt the proper communication was made. I still refrain, therefore, from sending you copies of the previous correspondence with this Government, believing that within a few days I shall be able to give you the result of the deliberations of the National Cortes.

With the expectation of giving you, in a very short time, the final resolution of this Government on the affairs of the treaty, I am, dear sir, respectfully, your most obedient servant.

Extract of a letter from Mr. Forsyth to Mr. Adams, (marked private,) dated

SEPTEMBER 21, 1820.

Apprehensive that the decision of the Cortes on the business of Florida will not be made in time to enable me to give you notice of it before the meeting of Congress, I have thought it prudent to forward to you my despatch of this day's date. You will see the grounds I had for believing that a speedy decision would be made, and that the decision would be what was desired by the President. Although the delay is apparently without motive, I have no reason to doubt that the decision, when made, will be what we have a right

Spain—Ratification of the Treaty of 1819.

to expect. I saw Martinez de la Rosa, appointed to the political commission in place of Count Toreno, who was elécted president of the Cortes three days since; he told me the Secretary of State had pressed them to make an early determination, and that the report of the commission would be soon prepared; he acknowledged, at the same time, that he did not know the state of the business. Mr. De Castro on Tuesday expressed the greatest anxiety to have the affair arranged before the meeting of Congress, and had directed General Vives to give you every assurance of the wish of the Government to satisfy us. It is true that the change in the head of the political commission accounts for a portion of this delay, and that the Cortes have been occupied by the consideration of questions apparently more pressing, as they related to the affairs of the peninsula, and were connected with the public tranquillity; still, however, there has been ample time for the adjustment of this business.

Mr. Onis has published a memoir on the negotiation between the United States and Spain, with a statistical notice of our country—a work that does little credit to his penetration or candor. He accuses us of ambition and avarice, and yet endeavors to show that the treaty of cession of Florida ought to be considered as a treaty of exchange of Florida for Texas, a country more extensive, fertile, and valuable. I send you an extract from that part of the work which relates to the correspondence on the subject of the grants after the treaty was signed. In another part of the work he imputes the refusal to ratify prior to August, 1819, to a belief that England would make use of the cession of Florida to us as a pretext to seize the island of Cuba, and to a belief that we would occupy the territory by force, and by this means secure the donations to Alagon, Punon Rostro, and Vargas.

Extract of a letter from the same to the same, (No. 20,) dated

SEPTEMBER 21, 1820.

In a postscript, dated July 20, to my despatch of No. 19, I had the honor to acknowledge your No. 12, of the 25th of May. On the 21st I wrote to Mr. De Castro, who was at Sacedon with the King, a note, (copy marked No. 1.) His answer, (copy marked No. 2,) dated the 25th, was received on the 26th July. On the 27th I had a visit from Mr. Jabat, who called by the desire of Mr. De Castro. Mr. Jabat informed me that the King would shorten his stay at Sacedon; would be in Madrid on the 10th of August; that all the documents relating to the treaty of cession, and the late correspondence, would be presented by the 12th to the Cortes, and he hoped all would be despatched before the 20th. For the reasons explained in my private letter of the 27th August, the necessary communication was not made to the Cortes until the 26th. The subject was referred to the political commission, who have not yet given to the Cortes the result of their examination of it. Mr. De Castro has uniformly assured

me of his anxiety to have an immediate decision. He solicited a speedy decision when he presented the papers to the Cortes. Although I look daily for further information of the movements of that body, I am without the means to know certainly when they will be made.

No. 1.

Mr. Forsyth to Don Evaristo Perez de Castro, Secretary of the Despatch of State, &c.

MADRID, *July* 21, 1820.

SIR: In the several conversations I have had with your Excellency on the relations of our respective Governments, arising from the convention of 1819, I have expressed my conviction that, notwithstanding what has occurred, a prompt ratification of that instrument by Spain, accompanied by satisfaction for the injuries sustained by the United States in consequence of its being heretofore withheld, would be accepted by my Government. I have now the instructions of the President, and am authorized to assure you that the immediate ratification by Spain of the convention of February, 1819, will be accepted by the President, subject to the advice and consent of the Senate of the United States.

Relying implicitly upon the assurances received of the desire of this Government to terminate at once, and in the most amicable manner, the dispute with the United States, I with pleasure avoid the unpleasant task of remarking upon the disagreeable occurrences connected with this subject, since my residence near the person of His Catholic Majesty, or upon the surprise and disappointment felt in the United States on the discovery of the object of the mission of General Vives, and the limited power granted to him. Your Excellency is already apprized that the Government of my country has been induced to delay acting decisively against Spain by the extraordinary change in the constitution of this monarchy—a revolution without example in the history of the world—the admiration of the present, as it will be of every future age. The expectation that all differences between Spain and the United States would be speedily and satisfactorily adjusted as soon as this Government was completely organized on the principles of the change which had taken place, was the cause of this delay. The moment has arrived which will see this expectation realized or disappointed. His Catholic Majesty now sees in his capital the representatives of the people. The Cortes are in the full and tranquil exercise of the high and important duties confided to them by the constitution of the Spanish monarchy. I refrain from indulging the free expression of my congratulation to the King and to the nation at the interesting events of which I have been the witness. Were I to use the only language I am accustomed to use, that which truly expresses my sentiments, my motives might be misunderstood, or I should be accused of substituting the effusions of enthusiasm for the offerings of diplomatic respect. I content myself, therefore, with the simple expression of my satisfaction at the situation in

APPENDIX.

Spain—Ratification of the Treaty of 1819.

which this Government finds itself, as it affords the opportunity of bringing to its close the long-protracted negotiation with my own country. The attention of the Cortes has been already called to this subject, and they have been informed by His Majesty that their intervention will be, under the present system, necessary to its final settlement. This intervention cannot be too prompt, considering either the effect to be produced on the future relations between the two countries, or the time which has elapsed, not only since the signature of the convention, but since the expiration of the period at which the ratifications of it were, by express stipulation, to have been exchanged. The only questions presented for decision are of a character that demand but little consideration. The principles which must regulate this decision are so well known as scarcely to admit a difference of opinion respecting them.

What are the obligations imposed upon Spain by the signature of the treaty, and the subsequent failure to ratify it? The obligation to ratify is the inevitable result of the formation of a treaty, and can only be avoided by showing (what, in this case, has never been asserted) that the negotiator who signed it stipulated, in the name of his Government, what he was not authorized to stipulate. Upon the principles universally recognised by the law of nations, it is beyond dispute that the faith of the nation, once pledged by its monarch, having competent power, no change in the internal government can release it. The promise of the King once given to a foreign Government, no subsequent engagement with his own subjects, or with other nations, can impair its strength. If these principles are true, the obligations consequent upon the failure to ratify are unquestionable. The first of these is the prompt ratification of the instrument; the second, an explanation of the causes justifying the postponement, to this time, of the ratification, or an atonement for the injuries resulting from it. In urging an immediate decision, I am specially instructed to add, that it is not the intention of the President to avail himself of the incidents of this negotiation, and of the principles of the laws of nations applicable to them, to fasten a hard and unequal bargain upon Spain. He has always considered, and still views, the treaty as highly advantageous to Spain, and would not now desire its ratification if, in the just and reasonable estimation of Spain herself, it could be viewed in any other light.

The causes which have heretofore delayed this ratification here present themselves for examination; but, for the reason already indicated, and from a desire to avoid all unpleasant and useless recollections, I shall not dwell upon them; it is enough that, however satisfactory they may have been made to appear to His Catholic Majesty, they do not justify, in the eyes of the United States, the course that has been pursued. But even these causes, so far as the judgment of His Majesty's Minister in the United States can be relied upon, no longer present obstacles to the immediate and final decision of this affair. But, while the Government of the United States is far

from considering the delay which has taken place as justifiable, I am not instructed by the President to insist upon, or even to ask, satisfaction for the injuries occasioned by it. That this satisfaction has not been claimed by the United States, is to be imputed not to any doubt of their right to demand, or of the obligation of Spain to afford it, but has sprung from the desire to manifest more clearly the principles of forbearance and moderation that have governed their march in this negotiation.

That it is not asked now arises from sentiments towards the Spanish nation, no one more truly than your Excellency can understand and appreciate.

What follows will, I trust, be found to be altogether unnecessary; nevertheless, it is incumbent upon me to say to your Excellency that, if the determination of Spain to ratify the convention of February, 1819, is not immediate, the claim to further satisfaction will be no longer waived; that, upon any future adjustment, the United States will insist upon an indemnity; that an additional provision will be indispensable for the existing claims of their citizens upon the Spanish Government; and that the right of the United States to the western boundary of the Rio del Norte will be reasserted, and never again relinquished.

I renew to your Excellency, whom may God preserve, the assurances of my perfect respect.

JOHN FORSYTH.

Don Evaristo Perez de Castro, &c.

No. 2.

Don Evaristo Perez de Castro to Mr. Forsyth.

Sacedon, *July* 25, 1820.

Sir: I have lost no time in laying before the King, my august master, the contents of your Excellency's note of the 21st instant. His Majesty has received with the greatest interest and satisfaction the information contained in the communication which you were pleased to make to me concerning the instructions which you had received from your Government, and which are conformable to what has been communicated by the Minister of Spain at Washington. You may be firmly persuaded that the desires of this cabinet to see a prompt termination of the business left pending by the non-ratification of the treaty of February, 1819, on the part of the King, are as lively and sincere as its will is decided; and it is full of hope that the decision of this subject will be satisfactory for both States, and apt to found upon unalterable bases the friendship which His Majesty is desirous of preserving with the United States.

It being indispensable to hear the Cortes of the kingdom, before the King, my master, can take the final step which the President desires, and with which his Majesty flatters himself to see the present dispute happily terminated, he has been pleased to command me to put this business in a state of being presented to the National Congress so speedily as that it may experience no more de-

Spain—Ratification of the Treaty of 1819.

lay than may be absolutely indispensable to accomplish it. I have received this order with singular pleasure, as being so agreeable to my personal sentiments, and overcoming, by dint of activity, every impediment which might oppose the desired ready despatch of this important subject, through my recent entrance into this ministry, and the imperious necessity of my informing myself of its former and present state. I have the honor to assure you that I hasten, and, if I may be allowed the expression, count the moments, to present myself before the Cortes with this business; it being my solicitude to give every activity to its resolution, and not to delay an instant the desired conclusion of the whole. In the meantime, His Majesty has seen with satisfaction the sentiments which animate the President of the United States, (an estimable proof that he has confidence in those of the King, my august master, and in the punctuality and good faith of the nation, happily regenerated by the new institutions,) which cannot fail to designate in the acts of the Government that firm and loyal march of which the noble Spanish character and the wisdom of their representatives are the guarantees.

I avail myself of this occasion to reiterate to you the demonstrations of my great consideration; and I pray God to preserve you many years.

Your most obedient servant,

E. PEREZ DE CASTRO.

Mr. Forsyth to Mr. Adams, (marked private.)

OCTOBER 5, 1820.

DEAR SIR: Three days since, the political commission made a report to the Cortes, and this day, in secret session, that body advised the King to cede the Floridas to the United States. They have also declared null and void the cessions of land to Alagon, &c., although the treaty of February, 1819, should not be ratified. I presume I shall receive from the Minister of State early information of the King's ratification of the treaty.

I am, dear sir, sincerely and respectfully, your obedient servant,

JOHN FORSYTH.

JOHN QUINCY ADAMS, *Secretary of State.*

Mr. Forsyth to Mr. Adams, (No. 21,) *dated*

MADRID, *October* 11, 1820.

SIR: On the 5th I had the honor to inform you that the Cortes had authorized the King to cede the Floridas to the United States, according to the convention of February 22, 1819. On the 6th I received from Mr. De Castro an official notice of the determination of the Cortes, and a request to be informed of the wishes of the American Government in regard to the eighth article, as I supposed with a view to have the ratification of the King in such terms as to prevent the necessity of any thing but the mere delivery of the treaty at Washington, where the ratifications are to be exchanged. A copy of his note is enclosed, marked No. 1. I replied on the 7th; a copy of my answer is marked No 2. This answer I carried with

me to the palace, it being Court day. In the Secretary of State's office I received a message from Mr. De Castro, who was confined to his bed at home, requesting me to visit him. I went immediately, and carried with me my answer to his note. As he reads English with difficulty, he opened, but did not read it. His object appeared to be to ascertain if I was authorized to make any stipulations about the eighth article of the treaty, or if there was a probability of obtaining any stipulations in Washington favorable to Spanish claimants for injuries suffered from the United States. He said the Cortes had given the King authority to execute the treaty, and to set aside the grants of Alagon and Punon Rostro; that of Vargas was out of the question, being subsequent to the 24th of January, 1818. He spoke of the cession of Vargas as a fund for the payment of American claims on Spain; said the treaty was clearly in favor of Alagon and Punon Rostro. The 24th of January was not assumed as an arbitrary date, but fixed upon on principle by Mr. Onis, who, in his letter to Mr. Adams of the 10th of March, stated, after acknowledging he believed them to be posterior to the 24th January, that he would have insisted on their being admitted as valid had he known them to be anterior. Mr. De Castro had no desire to procure any thing for such people as Alagon and Punon Rostro, but thought it equitable that the United States should set apart a portion of this fund, increased by Spain's abandoning the literal import of the treaty, for the benefit of Spanish subjects. To all this I answered what was contained in my letter—I had no authority to make any stipulations. So far as regarded the Government of the United States, the question was considered as settled. I begged him not to think of asking any thing at Washington; it could not be granted; might do injury; could not produce any good result. I reminded him that the offer made in October, 1819, to the Duke of San Fernando and Quiroga, the admission of the American declaration against the grant, was a condition upon which alone the ratification of the treaty by Spain could be admitted; and also of the declaration of General Vives, that, upon the subject of the grants, he was satisfied with the explanations given to and received from Mr. Adams, at Washington; and that these donations were never insurmountable obstacles to the ratification of the treaty on the part of Spain. He replied that this admission was on the supposition that the other explanations would be satisfactory. Satisfaction not having been received on the last and most important, the others might again be brought into view. He talked of the guarantee offered by Mr. Pinckney; of there being no provision in the treaty for Spanish claimants, as there was in that of 1802; and how desirable it would be if something could be procured for them on the adjustment of this difficulty in the convention—an adjustment in which Spain gave up what was clearly secured to some of her subjects. I remarked to him that the offer made by the instructions of the President in July last was made on the admission of General Vives that there would be no demur respecting the grants.

Spain—Ratification of the Treaty of 1819.

If these were brought again into question, my Government was not bound by the offer then made. He said it appeared somewhat unequitable and hard to insist upon the alteration or modification of the treaty without any equivalent. To this I answered, that all he had urged might have been plausible if urged before August 22, 1819; but, after the delays which had occurred, and the incidents of the negotiation, we thought we exercised a degree of unexampled moderation in agreeing to take the ratification on the terms originally agreed upon and understood between the two negotiators. We had some conversation on the mode of ratification by the King, to obviate all difficulty at Washington. I stated to him that this, of course, was a matter in which we would do whatever was agreeable to the Spanish Government. The American declaration of the force of the eighth article might be received by Spain; a declaration might be made by the King, declaring the sense in which His Majesty understood it; or a joint declaration might be made. He proposed seeing me again on the following day at twelve, in company with a confidential person, at the office, if he was able to go out, or in his room, if he was not; to which I consented. At parting, I pointed out to him, in the published documents relating to the treaty, which I carried for the purpose, the declaration I was directed to present by my first instructions; the instructions relating to it; the subsequent instructions modified, which came to me by the Hornet; and my offer to the Duke of San Fernando and Quiroga, made in conformity with them. He said he would examine the papers, sketch something to show me in our next interview, would despatch every thing with the greatest possible expedition, and send off a messenger to Washington.

On the 8th I saw him again at his house, at twelve; he had with him the elder Heredia; the conversation was a repetition of that of yesterday. The only new idea expressed was, that it was important to the new Government to gain credit by procuring some advantage in arranging the business of the treaty, and a suggestion that Mr. Onis would not have made the treaty in any terms but those in which the eighth article is expressed. To the first I replied that the new Government would deserve and receive all praise for saving the country from the consequences of the impolitic steps of the old, and preserve the honor of the nation by abandoning pretensions which injured its character; to the last, that this suggestion was altogether at variance with the declaration of Mr. Pizarro, Mr. Onis's expressed willingness to give up the donations, and with the remark made to me by Mr. Casa Yrujo, "that he regretted that the grants had not been executed by name." Heredia urged, in the conversation, that the United States had, in the treaty, admitted it to be necessary to the King's honor that the grants prior to the 24th of January, 1818, should be preserved. This conclusion I positively denied. In allowing Mr. Onis to shape the eighth article, we did not become parties to the correctness or propriety of his opinions; on the contrary, in our opinion, the honor of the King was concerned to make void all donations made subsequent to the date of his full power to his negotiator to cede the Floridas. The conversation concluded by a formal request from Mr. De Castro to know what my impressions were on this point, and whether they could calculate on my good offices with my Government to procure some advantage to Spain, in consideration of its desire to gratify us in this business, and of the similarity of the institutions of the two Governments. I gave him my thoughts without reserve: "that the ground which must be taken was altogether untenable; that it would injure, could not benefit, the Spanish Government; that the United States would receive any intimations on this point with surprise and regret. As for myself, with the strongest desire to do every thing to gratify this Government, I could not say any thing to my own in favor of pretensions I believed to be altogether unreasonable." Mr. De Castro said that, in presenting the subject, it would be done in such a way as to prevent any bad effect: turning to Heredia, he remarked that it must be attempted at Washington. He concluded by saying that he should pass to me a note, imbodying what had been urged in our conversation, which he hoped I would answer in the shortest convenient time, as he was anxious to send off a messenger to the United States. This I promised, stating to him, at the same time, the necessity of despatching his messenger at the earliest hour possible, as Congress would be in session before he could possibly arrive.

On recollection, I find I have omitted a remark made by both Heredia and de Castro, that, according to my first instructions, as contained in the printed documents, I was authorized to exchange the ratifications without insisting upon the declaration of the import of the eighth article being received; that this exchange would have secured to the claimants the large grants, which they might have recovered in the courts of the United States. To this I answered, that such were my instructions, but they were founded upon the belief that the notice given to the Spanish Government, through Mr. Onis, rendered the declaration unimportant; that, certainly, if the treaty had been ratified by Spain, the question of the grants would have become a judicial in place of a political one. But supposing, what I could not admit, that the tribunals of the United States could have decided in favor of the claimants: this decision would have been the foundation of a demand on Spain for an equivalent or satisfaction. This conversation endured two hours. In this, as well as in that of the 7th, I am unable to give any thing but the substance, without regarding the order of what was said. My impressions are, that, after making all exertions to obtain some advantage, and failing, they will proceed on the business as they ought to have done without having made any exertion. What is most unpleasant is, to perceive that the opinions of Mr. Onis, as expressed in his book, have weight with this Government, and that what is done is rather a sacrifice to policy than founded on a conviction of the justice and equity of our demands, or on a proper sense of our moderation and forbearance.

Late at night on the 9th I received Mr. De Castro's letter of that day's date, the copy of which is marked No. 3, to which I replied on the day succeeding; the copy of the answer is marked No. 4. This reference to the affair of the grants is disagreeable, and will be altogether unexpected. After what has occurred, I cannot suppose the Spanish ministry can hope to succeed in procuring any thing more at our hands; perhaps the sole object is to enhance the value of the ratification on their part. I am endeavoring to procure accurate information of all that occurred in the Cortes. My private letter of the 5th is almost a literal translation of a note from one of the deputies; and I have been since informed that the Cortes would not hear a petition from Punon Rostro in relation to his claim, considering the whole affair at an end by their previous decision on the treaty.

Shortly after the publication of Mr. Onis's book, I conceived that some of its statements were so injurious to us as to require examination, and proposed to publish a review of it, to be distributed among the members of the Cortes. The affair of the treaty came so soon under the consideration of that body after I had procured a copy of the book, that it was impossible to do more than to make a few hasty remarks upon it, and to have distributed five or six copies of a translation of them among the principal members. A copy of this translation is sent to you, marked No. 5. No. 6 is the copy of an original paper received from ——, an extract from which, in cipher, was forwarded to you some time ago.

The Cortes have resolved, according to the constitutional provision, to continue their session until November.

AT NIGHT.

At 5, this afternoon, I received Mr. De Castro's letter of this day's date, which I answered immediately. The copies of the letter and answer are marked Nos. 7 and 8.

This last letter confirms the conjecture I have made that the object is to enhance the value of what will be called the concession of Spain to the American construction of the eighth article of the treaty. I regret extremely that any thing has been said by the Ministers of this Government on this topic, as it will have the effect of weakening, in some degree, the confidence, not so much in the uprightness of their intentions as in the frankness of their mode of proceeding. No doubt something will be said by General Vives on this point, or, at least, he will formally communicate the letter of Mr. De Castro of the 9th. I shall send triplicates of this communication—one by Bordeaux, one by Gibraltar, and one by the Spanish courier who carries the ratified treaty to the Spanish Minister at Washington.

As soon as he is fairly out of Madrid, I shall think of using the permission of the President to return to the United States; before I leave this, however, I shall have occasion to write to you again. I am, sir, very respectfully,

JOHN FORSYTH.

No. 1.

Mr. De Castro, Minister of Foreign Despatch, to Mr. Forsyth, Minister Plenipotentiary of the United States of America.

MADRID, *October* 6, 1820.

SIR: I have the honor to acquaint your Excellency that the Cortes of the nation, in secret session, have authorized His Majesty's Government to ratify the cession of the territory situated east of the Mississippi, which is known by the name of East and West Florida, to the United States, and that, consequently, there is no inconvenience in proceeding, on the part of the King, to the ratification of the treaty concluded at Washington on the 22d day of February, 1819.

His Majesty would have immediately proceeded to command the ratification of the treaty to be extended, had it not been for the interference of the circumstance that your Excellency's Government, after confirming and ratifying, on its part, the said instrument, as the Plenipotentiaries duly authorized by the high contracting parties had extended it, manifested its desire to have some explanations or modifications in the text of the eighth article, which relates to the property of certain unoccupied and royal lands in both Floridas. This incident, or proposal of modification, made by the Government of the United States, which has contributed, in a great part, to the delay and difficulties which have occurred, might have rendered improper, at that time, and an event little agreeable to the American Government, a ratification extended in the usual form, which, relapsing upon the said instrument with all and each of its clauses and articles, would, consequently, embrace those of the eighth article, referred to in the form in which it had been conceived. This being the case, and His Majesty being desirous, conformably to the intention of the Cortes, that the ratification of the treaty should terminate at once all the differences which have for so many years existed between the two Governments whose interest in a reciprocal good understanding has been increased by the nature of their political institutions, has thought it necessary that, for extending the ratification, an explanation should precede, limited and circumscribed to the point of the modifications which your Excellency' Government requires to be in the text of the eighth article, since all the other articles present no difficulty, nor need any further explanation in order to be ratified, on the part of His Majesty, according to their literal tenor. Your Excellency's Government has indicated a desire of having a modification in the context of the said article; and as, for determining what ought to be and what is agreeable to the interest of both countries, it may be necessary to proceed by common consent, I am desirous of knowing if your Excellency is authorized to point out the modification and explanation, as I also am by His Majesty for the same purpose. If your Excellency be so, we might, in a very few days, have this point settled in a manner reciprocally satisfactory; and, in case of your not being so, I could desire at least that we had a conference for the purpose of agreeing

Spain—Ratification of the Treaty of 1819.

on the means by which this only obstacle may be removed, which might present itself to the exchange of the ratifications in Washington, if it should be remitted by His Majesty, extended in the usual form, embracing all and each of the clauses of the sixteen articles of the treaty confirmed at Washington on the 22d of February of the past year, 1819.

I therefore renew to your Excellency the assurances of my distinguished esteem, and pray God that you may live many years.

I am your Excellency's most obedient, faithful servant,

E. PEREZ DE CASTRO.

To the MINISTER *of the United States.*

No. 2.

Mr. Forsyth to Mr. De Castro, dated

MADRID, *October* 7, 1820.

SIR: I had the honor to receive yesterday your Excellency's official, announcing to me that the Cortes had authorized the Government of His Majesty to ratify the cession of the Floridas to the United States. In reply to the inquiry contained in it, I must refer your Excellency to my letter of the 21st of July, in which I stated, by the instructions of the President, that, under the Constitution of the United States, it would be necessary that the advice and consent of the Senate should again be given, before the exchange of ratifications of the treaty of the 22d February, 1819, could take place, inasmuch as the six months within which it should have been made had expired. I am not, therefore, authorized to do more than has already been done. Perfectly possessed, however, of the opinions and wishes of my Government in relation to the eighth article of the treaty, I can give your Excellency all the information that can be desired to prevent the possibility of any difficulty in the exchange of ratifications at Washington. In my official communication of the 2d of October, 1819, to the Duke of San Fernando and Quiroga, accompanied by the copy of a declaration to be delivered on the exchange of ratifications, should it be made, your Excellency will probably find all that it may be important to know. If these should not be sufficient, it will give me pleasure to confer with your Excellency at any hour it may be convenient for you to appoint. In expressing to your Excellency the very great satisfaction I have received from the near prospect of a most friendly termination of the disputes which have so long unhappily agitated our respective Governments, I must take leave to add that the United States have never desired to change or modify any part of the treaty of 1819; their sole object has been, and still is, to have it ratified upon the well-known terms, and according to the acknowledged intentions of the respective negotiators of it.

I renew your Excellency, to whom may God preserve, the assurances of my most respectful consideration.

JOHN FORSYTH.

Don E. PEREZ DE CASTRO, &c.

No. 3.

Mr. De Castro, Minister of Foreign Despatch, to Mr. Forsyth, Minister Plenipotentiary of the United States of America, dated at

MADRID, *October* 9, 1820.

SIR: On the 6th current I had the honor to communicate to your Excellency that the Cortes had authorized His Majesty's Government to cede the Floridas to the United States; and that, in consequence of that act, no other obstacle presented itself against proceeding, on the part of the King, to the ratification of the treaty confirmed at Washington the 22d February, 1819, except that which arose from the modification or explanation of the eighth article of the same treaty, solicited by the American Government after the confirmation, and even the ratification, on its part, of the said agreement; adding that, if your Excellency were authorized, we could proceed to make the desired explanation, with regard to the object of said eighth article, in terms agreeable to the interests of both countries; that we could terminate this business very soon; and that, by all means, I was desirous of a conference between us, in order to the removal of this only obstacle which could oppose the exchange of the ratifications in Washington. Your Excellency has had the goodness to reply to me, dated the 7th, complimenting me on the proximity of an order that went to terminate the differences that existed for so long a time between the two Governments, but manifesting to me at the same time that, in consequence of the period fixed for the ratification of the treaty by that instrument having been overrun, it ought again to be presented to the Senate of the United States, agreeably to the Constitution; by which circumstance your Excellency had not the power to act in the negotiation further than you had done, although, being perfectly instructed in the intentions of your Government upon the said article of the treaty, you could furnish me with the necessary dates in regard to them in the conference which we might have, and which we actually had on that day.

Both yesterday and before, I had the honor to point out to your Excellency the difficulties which opposed the explanation or modification demanded by the American Government of the context of the eighth article, since, according to the literal and very explicit tenor of it, every donation or grant of lands in the Floridas made by authority of His Majesty, prior to the 24th January, 1818, was declared valid or firm, at the same time that every grant made after the said 24th of January was annulled. It appeared at the same time, that the determining of that date was not a casual occurrence, unpremeditated, and directed solely to mark one day or epoch; since then nothing could have been more obvious and natural than to have designated the 1st day of the same month of January, 1818, which was the beginning of the year; and it was distinctly considered that the intention of the Plenipotentiaries was to establish a principle legal and justly expressed in the text of the same article, in continuance from the date, which it was to give for a foundation—that His Majesty's

Plenipotentiary on that day solemnly offered the cession of the Floridas to the United States, in order to denote that it was then, and not before, when His Majesty, by said offer, tied up his hands from making innovations in those territories, and when, by the same offer, the indisputable right, which, without that, enabled him to dispose of the absolute property of any lands belonging to his Crown, was suspended. The tenor of this article was already not only admitted and confirmed by the Plenipotentiaries, but was also ratified by the American Government, jointly, with all the other articles which the treaty embraced, when the Secretary of State, Mr. Adams, thought fit to ask of Mr. Onis an explanation about the grants of land made by His Majesty at the end of the year 1817, the validity of which appeared to have been recognised by the letter of the treaty, they being anterior to the 24th January, 1818, and upon which both Plenipotentiaries were supposed to have proceeded with a certain equivocation of the fact, having believed them posterior to the epoch mentioned. Mr. Onis, notwithstanding that all his functions and powers upon the subject had expired with the conclusion and confirmation of the treaty, did not refuse to give a firm proof of the good faith of his Government, and of his own, by frankly confessing that in fact he had understood that the grants of land referred to were posterior to the 24th January, 1818, but added at the same time a circumstance worthy of notice, and perfectly conformable to the tenor of the eighth article ; and it was that, as the fixing of that epoch had been founded upon the principle that the 24th January, and not before, was the day on which, by means of the solemn offer of the Floridas, the indisputable power which His Majesty before had of disposing of those lands remained suspended, if he had known that all or any of said grants were anterior to the 24th January, he would have insisted upon the acknowledgment of such as were so, and would not have consented to their being annulled. Taking the first part of this declaration of Mr. Onis as a foundation, and feigning ignorance of the second, the American Government solicited, by means of your Excellency at this Court, that, to the ratification of the treaty on the part of His Majesty, an explanation should be added, which was fundamentally a real revocation of the literal context of the eighth article. The scrupulous good faith of His Majesty's Government restrained it from entering upon a question about what wrong the equivocation, or, to speak more properly, the want of exact knowledge of a fact, authentic, solemn, and of more than a year's notoriety and publicity in a supreme council and chancery of the nation, could do to one who had the means, and, in a certain degree, the necessity of being informed of it with evidence. But two essential points did not cease to call the attention of His Majesty: 1st. That if any equivocation could have happened about the date of the grants, in order to their being a pure deed, it never could have been, nor was it, in the recognition of the principle which served as a basis, and was the real foundation of the eighth article—that is, that the Spanish Government did not consider itself bound,

nor did the American Government consider it bound, in the use of its right as absolute lord of the lands of Florida, unless by means of the offer made on the 24th January, 1818, and only from that epoch ; that an essential equivocation could have been in this date, it was necessary to prove that it was not that of the said solemn offer, since that was the module or symbol to which all the dates of the grants ought to be adjusted, and with which they ought to be compared, in order to decide upon their validity or nullity, and not to pretend, as had been pretended, to accommodate it to the others, by altering that date inversely. 2d. That if the American Government availed itself of, and founded its desires of an explanation upon, the former part of Mr. Onis's declaration, which in any way favored it, neither could it in honor and good faith reject the second part of that declaration, to constitute the whole one self-same act and a single document. If Mr. Onis confessed the equivocation about the date of the grants, he also confessed that he would not have, for his part, subscribed to annul that which had taken place anterior to the 24th January. What will be inferred, then, in reality and sound logic, from that declaration, taken conjointly ? Will it be an accident which had expressed the real, or at least the intentional, connivance of both the Plenipotentiaries concerning the annulling of the grants referred to, which were anterior to the 24th January, as the American Government pretends ? An interpretation like this is diametrically opposite not only to the second part of the declaration of Mr. Onis, but even to the legal principle established in the same eighth article. All that can be inferred, at most, was, and is, that the error into which both parties had run about the substance of the eighth article had rendered it null, invalid, and baseless ; and that it was necessary to remodel it, and agree upon something to the point by a new mutual agreement, and not by the way of a declaration or explanation, which its context did not admit.

The question accidentally presented in this humble view would not have been offered, nor given an opportunity for the many difficulties which have occurred. The grants made to Don Pedro de Vargas could have been immediately separated, and, as being posterior to the 24th of January, 1818, might have been declared the property of the United States, according to the letter and spirit of the article; and, with regard to the other two, anterior to the said day, upon which grants the equivocation had relapsed, the liberal medium might have been adopted, which is generally used in doubtful cases, by yielding to each one a part of his claims, in compliance with a good understanding. But as this was not solicited by your Excellency, and if the text of the eighth article, whose letter, and the principle which supported it, favored Spain, might yet receive an interpretation diametrically opposite to the said letter, being founded for that purpose on a declaration of Mr. Onis, the second part of which evidently resisted a similar interpretation, difficulties seemed easily to arise from hence, which, with more or less foundation, might be

Spain—Ratification of the Treaty of 1819.

likewise converted into suspicions concerning the stability of the other articles of the treaty, on seeing the readiness with which doubts had arisen also concerning one, the literal tenor of which seemed less ambiguous. This disposition of the thoughts brought to recollection the offer of a guarantee of the Spanish possessions in North America, made by his Excellency Mr. Pinckney, on the 7th of February, 1802, in the name of the United States, in case the Spanish Government would consent to cede the Floridas to the United States for a sum to be stipulated—a guarantee which was not asked by the Government of Spain, and yet offered in the name of the United States, but to which my Government gave so much importance, that, if his offer had been renewed, it would have ceded in compensation any right over the grants of land which remained by the eighth article of the treaty. From these principles flowed, no doubt, the new mission of General Vives to the United States, and all the other incidents of which your Excellency is informed.

The changes which happened a little afterwards in the Government of Spain, and the reunion of the national representation, have been the cause that the Government of His Majesty, complying with the provision of the constitution of the State, should offer to the consideration of the Cortes all that has occurred in this long and complicated negotiation, for the purpose of obtaining their consent, as well as that the dismemberment of the Spanish territory in America might be discussed. It must have been a sensible grief to the representatives of the nation, in the first steps of their august functions, to be obliged to authorize a dismemberment of the territory; they have been solely guided by the consideration that this sacrifice may be conducive to cement upon a solid basis the relations of friendship and harmony between Spain and the United States, by avoiding the causes of future discords, and establishing a fixed and permanent dividing line which shall prevent all ambiguity and indecision for the future. Besides the reciprocal interests which ought always to unite the Governments of both countries, the great analogy which now actually exists between their political institutions, after the change that has occurred in those of Spain, appears to have given greater weight to that interest, and to have increased the importance of a good understanding. These, at least, are the dispositions which have produced the resolution I have mentioned of the representatives of the Spanish nation: may they be answered with similar and reciprocal dispositions on the part of the Government and people of the United States for the well-being of both nations! But at the same time that the Cortes and His Majesty's Government have rendered easy even the most serious difficulty which the subject could present, they could not but direct their attention to the reflections made known to your Excellency, which have been expressed above, on the explanation which the American Government desired to give to the eighth article, diametrically opposite to its literal tenor, and to the principle or rule which is established in the same article. The Spanish Government does not pretend that it may not be firm and be executed as it is printed; its delicacy does not permit it to pretend ignorance of the equivocation committed, which the declaration of Mr. Onis lays open sufficiently in its first part; but this equivocation does not destroy the principle which serves as the basis for the formation of the article to which the second part of the declaration of the same Mr. Onis is evidently referred. It cannot be agreeable to the honor and the good faith of the American Government to take advantage of that part of the declaration of the said Minister, or of any act or instrument which it may find useful, in order to tie it down and quote it in its favor, and to pretend not to understand that which does not favor it in the same instrument. No impartial person, who examines the eighth article, and the declarations of Mr. Adams and Mr. Onis, will see in the whole of it any thing else but that, by the involuntary error which has intervened, there has not been a real contract or agreement upon the point of the waste lands; and that, if there is any thing existing in the article, it is the rule or principle of leaving untouched what the King did when his hands were not bound by means of the offer of the 24th of January, 1818.

In this case, then, it appears that harmony, the desire of peace, the honor of both Governments, and the necessity of repairing an equivocation that had passed their Plenipotentiaries, dictate that middle path which is proper in doubtful cases and questions of this nature. The grants made to Don Pedro de Vargas may remain immediately in favor of the United States, because, inasmuch as they are posterior to the 24th January, 1818, they are excluded by the letter and by the spirit of the eighth article; and those, respectively, to Alagon and Punon Rostro, which, as anterior to the 24th of January, 1818, constitute the real point of the doubt, may be divided by equal parts, or by the mode which may be agreed upon by the Spanish and American Governments. His Majesty, agreeably to the intentions of the Cortes, is desirous of being able to make a better exchange of property by applying one part of this fund to the redress and indemnification of the Spaniards injured, and comprehended in the agreement of 1802, whose indemnification was at the charge of the American Government, even whilst the treaty was not ratified, and whose lot was entirely unattended to by the Plenipotentiaries of 1819. The American Government and Congress, so jealous of the interests of their fellow-citizens, can do no less than applaud these correct intentions of the King and the representatives of the Spanish people towards their own people. On the other hand, it would appear very indecorous that the Cortes, in the commencement of their august functions, should not only have to authorize the dismemberment of the territory, but also to assent that a doubtful act, which was in favor of Spain, (the letter of the article, and the foundation on which it is supported,) should be explained in a sense diametrically opposite to its tenor, and that upon the basis of a declaration of the Spanish Minister truncated and disregarded in its second part.

If the means hinted had not been thought admissible, there still remained another equally conformable to the spirit and to the letter of the treaty. All the waste lands of the Floridas, including the three grants of Vargas, Alagon, and Punon Rostro, may be valued according to the prices of lands of their class in the bordering territories of the United States; the amount of $5,000,000 may be deducted from their value, in which the same treaty adjusts, and with which the American Government obliges itself to satisfy, the amount of the claims; and the surplus may be declared to belong to Spain, because it can liquidate the indemnifications of its subjects, for which the United States are responsible by the agreement of 1802, which continues in force whilst the treaty is not ratified. It may be objected that the claims exceed the sum agreed upon; but it ought also to be considered that, even to this day, an examination or liquidation of such claims has not taken place; and that, if the agreement of 1802, and the mixed tribunal established by it, had been carried into effect, perhaps the claims admitted and approved of by the mixed Spanish and American tribunal might not have amounted to the said sum, especially if the fifth commissioner, chosen by lot, had been of the nation which was bound to pay them; so that, on the whole, $5,000,000 being the sum which the treaty fixes, and there having been even to this day no examination or liquidation of individual claims, this sum, and no other, is that which legally represents the amount of said indemnifications.

Such have been the reflections and observations which I have had the honor of making to your Excellency in our two conferences, by order of His Majesty, conformably to the intentions of the Cortes. By these, and by all besides, which I had the honor to point out by word, your Excellency will have come to the knowledge of His Majesty's resolution to terminate entirely the subjects pending by means of a prompt exchange of the ratifications of the treaty. I have been very sensible that your Excellency has not been authorized to agree to the explanation which the eighth article requires, but I am assured, by the candor, good faith, and spirit of conciliation, which animate your Excellency, that you will present to your Government the observations referred to, in regard to the only point upon which an explanation is desired by both parties—that, at the time of General Vives's presenting the ratification of the treaty on the part of His Majesty's Government, which it is about to send, an explanation may be presented and submitted of the sense of the eighth article, in the terms of equity and reciprocal satisfaction which I have hinted, or others equivalent, such as the good faith and the honor of both Governments dictate. The King and the representatives of the Spanish nation see, in this honorable and impartial explanation, the beginning of a new order of political relations, which, by tightening the bonds of friendship between both nations, present the most sure guarantee to their union and prosperity in future.

I renew to your Excellency the assurances of my most exalted and distinguished consideration, and pray God that your Excellency may live many years. Your obedient, humble servant,

E. PEREZ DE CASTRO.

No. 4.

Mr. Forsyth to Mr. De Castro.

MADRID, *October* 10, 1820.

SIR: I had the honor, last night, to receive your Excellency's official of the 9th. From our two conversations, previously held, and from your letter imbodying the substance of what was suggested and urged in those conversations, I learned, with concern, that I had mistaken the object and intention of the note of the 6th instant. I supposed it intended merely to enable your Excellency to determine on the most convenient mode for the ratification of the convention of February, 1819, by His Catholic Majesty, to prevent any discussion or delay preceding the exchange of the ratifications at Washington. It was with unfeigned surprise and great regret that I discovered that the object was to bring again into view what is considered by the Government of the United States as no longer a subject of discussion with that of His Majesty. In the verbal communications I have made in our two conversations, my intention was solely to prevent, if possible, any further attempts to discuss this matter, satisfied that no advantage could be derived from a reference to a topic of such an unpleasant character. As I have had the misfortune not to produce this desired effect, I do not think myself authorized to enter into any further investigation of the subject. I shall communicate to my Government the notes received from His Majesty; and such replies will be given to General Vives as the case may require. But I cannot take leave of the subject, without stating, explicitly, that the official communication made to your Excellency on the 31st July was framed and bottomed upon the admission of General Vives, that he was satisfied with the explanations given at Washington on the subject of the eighth article of the treaty, and that it was the determination of his Government to assent to the total nullity of the large grants. If this admission was unauthorized, the offer of the President I had the honor to communicate to His Majesty, through your Excellency, is not obligatory upon the United States; the whole ground of dispute is open for re-examination; and the original claims and pretensions of my Government will be reasserted and maintained.

Although beyond my duty, I cannot forbear to remark to your Excellency that a great error is committed in supposing the construction put on the eighth article by the United States is founded altogether upon the declaration given by Mr. Onis after the signature of the treaty. This construction is taken from the instrument itself, explained and elucidated, as all instruments must be, by the intention of the parties, and the nature of the subject-matter of it. Mr. Onis's letter of the 10th October is no further of importance than as a simple evidence to all nations, and to His Catholic Majesty, of the act and intention of his Minister to annul the large grants, and the express recognition by him of the correctness of the assertion of the American negotiator, that the phrases supposed to be equivocal were admitted only upon the condition that the annulment of those grants was not affected by the use of these favorite phrases. The qualifying addition to Mr. Onis's frank declaration of what he believed and understood, amounts to nothing more than an assertion that the treaty would not have been agreed to without a recognition of such of the large grants as were of a date prior to the 24th January, 1818—an assertion altogether at variance with the declarations of Mr. Pizarro to Mr. Erving, that these donations would not be obstacles to the treaty, contradicted by Mr. Onis's perfect readiness to annul them, and by the reasons he assigned for it, "that the essential conditions of them had not been complied with," and altogether irreconcilable to a remark made to me in person by the Marquis of Casa Yrujo when Minister of State *ad interim,* "that he regretted the large grants had not been particularly named in the treaty, and their annulment expressly stipulated."

From an anxious desire to see buried in oblivion all recollections unfavorable to the perfect harmony between Spain and the United States, in closing this note, I would entreat His Majesty's Government to re-examine this whole subject before it is again pressed; to reflect that all that has occurred has arisen from a reliance on the information and good faith of the Minister, and confidence in the purity of the Government of Spain. The Duke of San Fernando stated that the American Government wished to change the eighth article by a declaration, a copy of which I had enclosed to him. Your Excellency now tells me the wish of the American Government is diametrically opposed to the literal text of the treaty, inasmuch as Alagon and Punon Rostro's grants are of a date prior to the date fixed in the eighth article. The Duke of San Fernando refused, as inconsistent with the honor of the King, to order me copies of those donations! What would your Excellency think, were I to say to you, "Sir, I do not know that your assertion is true; show me the documents!" If the Duke of San Fernando and Quiroga thought his general assertion that the declaration changed the treaty was so full that further information could not be asked without reflecting upon His Majesty's honor, what would be the reply to a doubt of the correctness of your Excellency's unqualified, deliberate, and explicit assertion? Yet, in relying upon the information and the word of Mr. Onis, the United States had the same reason to confide, as they now have, in the assertion made by your Excellency, unless it should be supposed that there is a difference in the degree of confidence due to the representative of Spain at home and abroad. I feel, however, that I am treading upon the yet warm ashes of a previous unprofitable controversy, and exceeding the limits to which, at the outset, I proposed to confine myself.

I hasten, therefore, to assure your Excellency that the United States wish nothing but what they believe to be just and equitable; what is equally honorable to Spain and to the United States; nothing inconsistent with the decorum and glory of His Catholic Majesty, or with the duties and obligations of the Cortes, by whose advice and authority the treaty of February, 1819, is to be ratified.

I renew to your Excellency, whom may God preserve many years, the assurance of my perfect respect.

JOHN FORSYTH.

Don E. Perez de Castro, &c.

No. 7.

Mr. De Castro, Minister of Foreign Despatch, to Mr. Forsyth, Minister Plenipotentiary of the United States of America at Madrid.

PALACE, *October* 11, 1820.

SIR: I have received your Excellency's note of yesterday's date, in which you seem to agree with mine of the 9th. In said note I proposed to myself to recapitulate, and send to you all the essentials of the controversies which we had on the two antecedent days, not with the view, which your Excellency appears to have apprehended, of commencing new discussions incompatible with the desire which animates His Majesty of seeing all the points which have been the object of the treaty speedily terminated, but with that of agreeing here with your Excellency upon the proper terms of extending the explanation or declaration of the eighth article in a mode satisfactory, and such as that the exchange of the ratifications might not experience any obstacle or inconvenience at Washington.

On a view, therefore, of what your Excellency had the goodness to express in the said conferences, and of what you manifested in your said note of yesterday, I confine myself to secure that which was contended for in the ratification on the part of this Government; which will be sent back to the United States, in terms which will be no doubt satisfactory to the American Government, and which avoid the discussions which your Excellency seems to fear, to ascertain that neither the tenor of our conferences, nor that of my said note, is intended for this object, which inspires your fear.

If your Excellency should please, in order to forward despatches to your Government, to avail yourself of the opportunity of a courier, who must be despatched as soon as possible, with the ratifications and packets for General Vives, you may begin to prepare them immediately; in expectation of which, I shall again give you information some hours before the departure of the courier.

I renew to your Excellency the assurances of my high consideration, and pray God that you may live many years.

I am your obedient and humble servant,

E. PEREZ DE CASTRO.

No. 8.

Mr. Forsyth to Mr. De Castro.

MADRID, *October* 11, 1820.

SIR: I have received, with great satisfaction, your Excellency's note of this day's date. If I have misapprehended the object in our conferences, and the tenor of the note of the 9th, your Excellency must do me the justice to impute it to my imperfect knowledge of the Spanish language, and to my anxiety to comply with your Excellency's request to give an immediate answer to the note.

I shall with pleasure use the occasion you have offered to me of sending despatches to my Government by the Spanish courier. A messenger will go from this legation to the United States the close of the present week. Should your Excellency have any thing to send to General Vives, it will gratify me to forward it by this opportunity.

I renew to your Excellency, whom may God preserve many years, the assurance of my most distinguished consideration.

JOHN FORSYTH.

Don PEREZ DE CASTRO.

Mr. Forsyth to Mr. Adams, (marked private.)

MADRID, *October* 12, 1825.

DEAR SIR: I have this moment learned that the Cortez, in authorizing, by an almost unanimous vote, the ratification of the treaty, and annulling the donations, at the same time recommended to the Ministers to endeavor to procure some advantages to the nation on account of the difficulty about the eighth article. With this recommendation the Ministers must comply, even although they may be satisfied the effort will be useless. The attempt once made, and failing, the affair will proceed to its proper conclusion without further trouble. I am, dear sir, very sincerely, your obedient servant,

JOHN FORSYTH.

Hon. J. Q. ADAMS, *Washington.*

Mr. Forsyth to Mr. Adams, (marked private,) dated

MADRID, *October* 15, 1820.

DEAR SIR: In great haste I send you a rough copy of a note from Mr. De Castro to Count Bulgary, of this day's date. I believe the Count Bulgary has enclosed in the accompanying letter to Mr. Poletica a copy of the same paper.

I had on the 14th a short conversation with the Spanish Minister, which served to confirm the opinion expressed in my private letter of the 12th instant.

I am, dear sir, respectfully, your obedient serv't,

JOHN FORSYTH.

Hon. J. Q. ADAMS, *Sec'ry of State.*

The Spanish Minister to the Chargé d'Affaires of Russia.

MADRID, *October* 15, 1820.

SIR: His Majesty's Government having given information to the Cortes of the nation concerning the existing differences with the United States of America, resulting from the treaty entered into between Spain and that Power on the 22d of February, 1819, and not ratified by the King, in order that the legislative power might authorize His Majesty to cede the two Floridas, as is stipulated in one of the articles of said treaty, and grant power to proceed, consequently, to the ratification of it, which His Majesty has thought fit to do, and the Cortes having resolved to give to the Government the authority required, carries into effect the ratification.

His Catholic Majesty, to whom are evident the good offices of His Majesty the Emperor of all the Russias at several stages of the negotiation with the American Government, proving his august and friendly solicitude in favor of Spain, discharges the grateful task of communicating to the Cabinet of his Imperial Majesty the flattering state in which this affair is, and the resolution of His Majesty to ratify the treaty mentioned, which will produce the re-establishing of that perfect harmony between Spain and the United States which it is of so great importance to both Powers to maintain without the least shadow of discord.

With this motive the King rejoices to repeat to his august friend the Emperor of all the Russias the esteem and gratitude with which, on all occasions, he has seen His Imperial Majesty take the most distinguished interest in the prosperity of His Majesty, and that of his people, &c.

[Signed by the Spanish Minister, and *addressed* to the Chargé d'Affaires of Russia.]

Extract of a letter (No. 22) from Mr. Forsyth to Mr. Adams.

MADRID, *October* 24, 1820.

The delay of the departure of the Spanish messenger enables me to give you copies of my correspondence with Mr. De Castro subsequent to the decision of the Cortes on the cession of Florida, in regard to the execution of the convention of February 22, 1819. No. 1 is a copy of my note calling the attention of the Spanish Minister to the provisions of the first and seventh articles of the treaty. I saw Mr. De Castro on Saturday; he had received my letter; the propriety of issuing the order suggested in my note had not escaped him, and he would send, as I requested, a copy of it as soon as it was made. To-day I received his answer, with a copy of the order to which it refers. Copies are marked Nos. 2 and 3.

No. 1.

Mr. Forsyth to Mr. De Castro.

MADRID, *October* 17, 1820.

SIR: By the seventh article of the convention of the 22d February, 1819, the ratification of which is preparing on the part of His Catholic Majesty to be sent to General Vives, at Washington, it is stipulated that the officers and troops of His Majesty shall evacuate the Floridas within six months after the exchange of ratifications, or sooner if possible, and shall give possession of them to the officers or commissioners of the United States who may be properly authorized to receive them. Calculating on a speedy exchange of ratifications, I would suggest, if it has not already occurred to

Spain—Ratification of the Treaty of 1819.

your Excellency, that it would be extremely convenient if the order of His Majesty for the evacuation and delivery of the territory, as also the archives and documents relating to the sovereignty and property of the same, should go to General Vives with the ratified treaty, to be forwarded to the proper authority on the exchange of ratifications, as by these means the United States would have timely notice to prepare the escort and transports to carry the officers and troops of His Majesty and their equipage to the Havana, in conformity with the obligation of the said article. I should be pleased to be enabled, by the politeness of your Excellency, to furnish to my Government a copy of this order, if His Majesty's Government should send it to General Vives.

I seize with avidity every occasion to offer to your Excellency, whom may God preserve, the assurance of my distinguished respect.

JOHN FORSYTH.

No. 2.

The Minister of Spain to Mr. Forsyth.

PALACE, *October* 24, 1820.

SIR: I have received your esteemed note of the 17th current, in which you say that you have taken the liberty of suggesting to me, in case it should not have already occurred to His Majesty's Government, it would be extremely convenient if the order of His Majesty for the evacuation and delivery of the Floridas, and of the archives and documents relating to the sovereignty and property of those provinces, should go to General Vives with the ratification of the treaty; that it should be sent, at the same time, to the proper authorities, in order to be transmitted after the exchange of the ratifications; and that it would be very agreeable to your Excellency to have it in your power to send a copy of said order to your Government, if His Majesty should transmit it to General Vives, and should find no inconvenience in granting it.

The idea had occurred to His Majesty's Government, as it could not fail to do, of transmitting to General Vives the proper order for the delivery of the Floridas, and whatever else is stipulated in the seventh article of the treaty of the 22d February, 1819, in order to be forwarded to the proper authorities, after the exchange of the ratifications. Estimating, as it deserves, your Excellency's suggestion, produced, no doubt, from a desire of connecting more closely the relations of amity and good understanding between Spain and the United States, by removing every obstacle or distant incident which might retard so desirable an object, and cheerfully acceding to the desire which your Excellency has manifested to me of obtaining a copy of the order which may be sent to the proper authority for carrying into effect the seventh article of the treaty, I have the honor of enclosing to you a copy of that which is addressed to the Captain General of the island of Cuba, through the medium of General Vives, in order that he may make use of it immediately after the exchange of the ratifications has been certified.

In all to-morrow an extraordinary courier will go to convey the despatches of the Government to His Majesty's Minister in the United States; and I have the satisfaction of giving your Excellency this advice beforehand, that you may, if you please, forward any packets to your Government by this opportunity; in which case, I hope you will have the kindness to send me them by two in the afternoon, of to-morrow, the 25th current.

I renew to your Excellency the assurances of my distinguished consideration, and pray God that you may live many years.

Your most humble and obedient servant,

EVARISTO DE CASTRO.

No. 3.

Translation of the royal order of the King of Spain to the Captain General and Governor of the island of Cuba and of the Floridas.

OCTOBER 24, 1820.

Ferdinand the Seventh, by the grace of God, and by the Constitution of the Spanish monarchy, King of the Spains, to you, the Captain General and Governor of the island of Cuba and of the Floridas:

Know you that, by a treaty concluded in the City of Washington on the twenty-second of February of the last year, one thousand eight hundred and nineteen, by plenipotentiaries duly authorized for the purpose of arranging the differences which have existed between the Government of Spain and that of the United States of America, and the limits of their respective territories, there was stipulated, on the part of Spain, the cession to the United States of all the country situated east of the Mississippi, known by the name of East and West Florida; the adjacent islands dependent upon the two Floridas being comprehended in said cession; together with all public lots and squares, vacant lands, public edifices, fortifications, barracks, and other buildings which are not private property, with the archives and documents which relate directly to the property and sovereignty of said provinces; it being provided at the same time that the inhabitants of the territories so ceded shall be secured in the free exercise of their religion without any restriction; and that all those who may desire to remove to the Spanish dominions shall be permitted to sell or export their effects at any time whatever, in order that they may better effect their purpose without being subject, in either case, to duties; and those who prefer remaining in the Floridas shall be admitted, as soon as possible, to the enjoyment of all the rights of citizens of the United States; it being added, by another article of the same treaty, that the Spanish officers and troops shall evacuate the said territories ceded to the United States six months after the exchange of the ratifications of the same treaty, or sooner if possible, and shall give possession of them to the officers or commissioners of the United States duly authorized to receive them; and that the United States shall provide the transports and escort necessary to convey the Spanish officers and troops and their baggage to the Havana.

And I, having considered and examined the tenor of the articles of the treaty, after having obtained the consent and authority of the General Cortes of the nation with respect to the said cession, have thought proper to approve and ratify the treaty referred to, the ratification of which must be exchanged at Washington with that which was formed by the President of the United States with the advice and consent of the Senate of the same; after which exchange, the said treaty will begin to be obligatory on both Governments and their respective citizens; therefore I command you, and ordain, that, after the information, which shall be seasonably given you by my Minister Plenipotentiary and Envoy Extraordinary at Washington, of the ratifications having been exchanged, you proceed, on your part, to make the proper dispositions, in order that, at the end of six months, counting from the date of the exchange of the ratifications, or sooner if possible, the Spanish officers and troops may evacuate the territories of both Floridas, and that possession of them be given to the officers or commissioners of the United States duly authorized to receive them, in the understanding that the United States shall provide the transports and escort necessary to convey the Spanish officers and troops and their baggage to the Havana. You shall arrange, in proper time, the delivery of the islands adjacent and dependent upon the Floridas, and the public lots and squares, vacant lands, public edifices, fortifications, barracks, and other buildings which are not private property, as also the archives and documents which relate directly to the property and sovereignty of the same two provinces, by placing them at the disposal of the commissioners or officers of the United States duly authorized to receive them; and all the other papers and the effects which belong to the nation, and which have not been comprehended and mentioned in the express clauses of the cession, you shall have conveyed and transported to another part of the Spanish possessions which may be most convenient for the public service. As, also, you shall take care that, previous to the delivery, it may be made known by edicts to all the present inhabitants of the Floridas that they have power to remove to the Spanish territories and dominions, the sale or exportation of their effects being permitted to them by the United States at any time whatever, without being subject to duties; and also the advantages stipulated in favor of those who shall prefer to remain in the Floridas, to whom I have wished to give this last proof of the protection and affection which they have always experienced under the Spanish Government. Of the delivery which you may make, or be made by your delegation, in the form which has been expressed, you shall make, or cause to be made, a corresponding receipt, duly authenticated, for your discharge; and, in order that you may proceed with entire knowledge in the execution of this commission, there shall be likewise sent to you, by my Minister Plenipotentiary at Washington, an authentic copy of the treaty referred to of the twenty-second of February, one thousand eight hundred and nineteen, with the insertion of the ratifications of both parties, and of the certificate relative to the exchange of the same; of which documents, and of this my royal order, you shall send a copy, in authentic form, to the Governors of both the Floridas, and to the person or persons who may have, in your name, the accomplishing of the delivery, if it has not been made by yourself.

All which you shall well and completely execute in the form which I have prescribed to you, agreeably to the public service, advising me of your having executed it through my underwritten Secretary of Despatch of State.

Given at Madrid, the 24th of October, 1820.

Mr. Adams to General Vives.

DEPARTMENT OF STATE,
Washington, February 28, 1821.

SIR: I have submitted to the consideration of the President of the United States the observations which, in conformity to the instructions of your Government, were verbally made by you in the conference which I had the honor of holding with you, when you notified me of your readiness to exchange the ratifications of the treaty of 22d February, 1819, between the United States and Spain.

With regard to the omission on the part of the Spanish negotiator of the treaty to insist upon some provision of indemnity in behalf of Spanish claimants, to whom a pledge of such indemnity had been stipulated by the previously ratified convention of 1802—an omission stated by you to have been peculiarly dissatisfactory to the Cortes—I am directed to observe that, as in all other cases of the adjustment of differences between nations, this treaty must be considered as a compact of mutual concessions, in which each party abandoned to the other some of its pretensions. These concessions on the part of the United States were great; nor could it be expected by the Spanish nation that they would be obtained without equivalent. Probably the Spanish negotiator considered the claims of Spanish subjects embraced by that convention so small in amount as scarcely to be worthy of inflexible adherence to them; he certainly considered the whole treaty as highly advantageous to Spain—a sentiment in which the Government of the United States always entirely participated, and still concurs.

This also furnishes the reply which most readily presents itself to the proposition which you have also been instructed to make, that some compensation should be allowed by the United States for the benefit of the grantees of lands recognised by the treaty to have been null and void. While appreciating in all its force the sense of justice by which, after the maturest deliberation and the fullest examination, the Cortes have declared that those grants were so, as at the signature of the treaty they had been clearly, explicitly, and unequivocally understood to be by both the Plenipotentiaries who signed it, the President deems it unnecessary to press the remark which must naturally present itself, that, to grantees whose titles were in fact null and void, and by all parties to

Suppression of the Slave Trade.

the negotiation were known to be null and void, no indemnity can be due, because no injury was done.

Nor can it be admitted that this is one of the cases of misunderstanding from which the grantees could be entitled to the benefit of a doubtful construction. The construction of the article was in nowise doubtful; for any construction which would have admitted the validity of the grants would have rendered impossible the fulfilment of other most important stipulations of the treaty.

The discussion of this subject, having already been a subject of correspondence between the Minister of Foreign Affairs of your Government and Mr. Forsyth, could now be continued to no profitable purpose. I take much more satisfaction in assuring you of the pleasure with which the President has accepted the ratification of the treaty, as an earnest of that cordial harmony which it is among his most ardent desires to cultivate between the United States and Spain. This disposition he cherishes the hope will be further promoted by the community of principle upon which the liberal institutions of both nations are founded, and by the justice, moderation, and love of order which they combine with the love and the enjoyment of freedom.

I pray you, sir, to accept the assurance of my distinguished consideration.

JOHN QUINCY ADAMS.

Don FRANCISCO D. VIVES, Envoy, &c.

[The following resolution was thereupon adopted by the Senate of the United States.]

IN SENATE OF THE UNITED STATES,
February 19, 1821.

Resolved, (two-thirds of the Senators present concurring therein,) That the Senate, having examined the Treaty of Amity, Settlement, and Limits, between the United States of America and His Catholic Majesty, made and concluded on the 22d day of February, 1819, and seen and considered the ratification thereof made by his said Catholic Majesty on the 24th day of October, 1820, do consent to and advise the President to ratify the same.

SUPPRESSION OF THE SLAVE TRADE.

[Communicated to the House of Representatives, January 15, 1821.]

To the House of Representatives.:

I transmit to the House of Representatives a report from the Secretary of State, with the enclosed documents, relating to the negotiation for the suppression of the slave trade, which should have accompanied a Message on the subject, communicated to the House some time since, but which were accidentally omitted.

JAMES MONROE.

WASHINGTON, *January* 12, 1821.

DEPARTMENT OF STATE, *Jan.* 11, 1821.
The Secretary of State has the honor of submitting to the President a copy of a despatch from the Minister of the United States at London, enclosing documents relating to the negotiation for the suppression of the slave trade, which should have been transmitted with those accompanying the Message of the President to the House of Representatives, of the 4th instant, but which were accidentally omitted.

JOHN QUINCY ADAMS.

Extracts of a letter from Mr. Rush to the Secretary of State, dated
LONDON, *November* 19, 1819.

"I received, on the 14th instant, a note from Lord Castlereagh, dated the 11th, on the subject of the slave trade. The addresses from the House of Commons and House of Lords, to the Prince Regent, came with it. As the whole purport of this communication has been detailed beforehand, in my last despatch, I am not aware that any further explanations from me are now requisite.

"The distinct testimony which is borne in both these addresses, to the United States having been the first in point of time, among the nations of the world to abolish the trade, will be perceived with satisfaction. It is, so far as I know, the first occasion upon which the acknowledgment has been made, in any official or authentic manner, by any State in Europe.

"It appeared to me prudent to frame an answer of entire conciliation to Lord Castlereagh's note; and I hope that the spirit which it breathes may meet the President's approbation. It bears date on the 16th, and is among the enclosures transmitted herewith."

Lord Castlereagh to Mr. Rush.

FOREIGN OFFICE, *Nov.* 11, 1819.
The undersigned, His Majesty's principal Secretary of State for Foreign Affairs, has the honor to transmit to Mr. Rush, by command of the Prince Regent, copies of addresses which were presented by both Houses of Parliament, at the close of the last session, to His Royal Highness, which His Royal Highness has to request Mr. Rush will lay before the President, with an intimation that it is the Prince Regent's earnest desire to enter, without delay, into discussion with the Government of the United States upon the important subject to which those addresses refer, and in the successful accomplishment of which the common feelings and reputation of both States are equally and deeply involved.

It has occurred to the Prince Regent's Government, that the difficulties which have hitherto operated to prevent a common system of concert and prevention, as directed against the illicit slave trade, between the two Governments, can be most satisfactorily examined by selecting Washington for the seat of deliberation. Under this impression, the undersigned has delayed to transmit to Mr. Rush the addresses in question, till he could ac-

Suppression of the Slave Trade.

company them with some proposition to be conveyed to the Government of the United States for giving practical effect to the views of Parliament.

The undersigned having lately had the honor of acquainting Mr. Rush that Mr. Stratford Canning had been selected by the Prince Regent to replace Mr. Bagot, as his Envoy and Minister Plenipotentiary in America, and as that gentleman will proceed to his mission early in the Spring, the undersigned has to request Mr. Rush will invite his Government, on the part of the Prince Regent, to enter, as soon as may be after Mr. Canning's arrival, upon the proposed discussions.

Upon a subject so deeply interesting to humanity, the Government of the United States can never require any other impulse than that of its moral principles to awaken it to exertion; but, whatever of aid good offices can contribute to smooth the way for an amicable and advantageous proceeding on such a matter, the undersigned is convinced will be supplied by Mr. Rush's zeal and enlightened attachment to the success of the great cause which this inquiry involves; and in this view the communication is specially recommended to his personal support and protection.

The undersigned avails himself of this opportunity to renew to Mr. Rush the assurances of his distinguished consideration.

CASTLEREAGH.

MERCURIE, 7 *die Julie,* 1819.

"*Resolved,* That an humble address be presented to his Royal Highness the Prince Regent, to assure his Royal Highness that we acknowledge, with becoming thankfulness, the zealous and persevering efforts which, in conformity with former addresses of this House, his Royal Highness has made for accomplishing the total annihilation of the African slave trade by all the foreign Powers whose subjects have hitherto been engaged in it.

"That we also congratulate his Royal Highness on the success with which his efforts have been already attended; that guilty traffic having been declared, by the concurrent voice of all the great Powers of Europe, assembled in Congress, to be repugnant to all the principles of humanity and of universal morality.

"That, consequently, on this declaration, all the States whose subjects were formerly concerned in this criminal traffic, have since prohibited it; the greater part absolutely and entirely, some for a time, particularly on that part of the coast of Africa only which is to the north of the line Of the two States which still tolerate the traffic, one will soon cease to be thus distinguished—the period which Spain has solemnly fixed for the total abolition of the trade being near at hand. One Power alone has hitherto forborne to specify any period when the traffic shall be absolutely abandoned.

"That the United States of America were honorably distinguished as the first which pronounced the condemnation of this guilty traffic; and that they have since successively passed various laws for carrying their prohibition into effect; that, nevertheless, we cannot but hear, with feelings of deep regret, that, notwithstanding the strong condemnation of the crime by all the great Powers of Europe, and by the United States of America, there is reason to fear that the measures which have been hitherto adopted for actually suppressing these crimes, are not yet adequate to their purpose.

"That we never, however, can admit the persuasion, that so great and generous a people as that of France, which has condemned this guilty commerce in the strongest terms, will be less earnest than ourselves to wipe away so foul a blot on the character of a Christian people.

"That we are, if possible, still less willing to admit such a supposition in the instance of the United States; a people derived originally from the same common stock with ourselves, and favored, like ourselves, in a degree hitherto perhaps unequalled in the history of the world, with the enjoyment of religious and civil liberty, and all their attendant blessings.

"That the consciousness that the Government of this country was originally instrumental in leading the Americans into this criminal course, must naturally prompt us to call on them the more importunately to join us in endeavoring to put an end to the evils of which it is productive.

"That we also conceive that the establishment of some concert and co-operation in the measures to be taken by the different Powers, for the execution of their common purpose, may, in various respects, be of great practical utility, and that, under the impression of this persuasion, several of the European States have already entered into conventional arrangements for seizing vessels engaged in the criminal traffic, and for bringing to punishment those who shall still be guilty of these nefarious practices.

"That we therefore supplicate his Royal Highness to renew his beneficent endeavors, more especially with the Governments of France and of the United States of America, for the effectual attainment of an object which we all profess equally to have in view, and we cannot but indulge the confident hope that these efforts may yet, ere long, produce their desired effect; may insure the practical enforcement of principles universally acknowledged to be undeniably just and true; and may obtain for the long afflicted people of Africa the actual termination of their wrongs and miseries; and may destroy forever that fatal barrier which, by obstructing the ordinary course of civilization and social improvement, has so long kept a large portion of the globe in darkness and barbarism, and rendered its connexion with the civilized and Christian nations of the earth a fruitful source only of wretchedness and desolation.

"*Ordered,* That the said address be presented to His Royal Highness the Prince Regent, by such members of the House as are of His Majesty's most honorable Privy Council.

"G. DYSON."

"*U. D. Dom. Com.*"

[An address, precisely similar, was voted about the same time, and presented in due course, by the House of Lords.]

Spain—Richard W. Meade.

Mr. Rush to Lord Castlereagh.

LONDON, *November* 16, 1818.

The undersigned, Envoy Extraordinary and Minister Plenipotentiary from the United States, has the honor to present his compliments to Lord Castlereagh, and to acknowledge the receipt of his note of the 11th of this month.

The copies of the addresses to His Royal Highness, the Prince Regent, from both Houses of Parliament, at the close of the last session, respecting the slave trade, which, by command of His Royal Highness, came enclosed in his Lordship's note, with a request that they might be laid before the President, the undersigned will lose no time in transmitting to the Secretary of State with that view. The intimation of its being the earnest desire of the Prince Regent to enter, without delay, into discussions with the United States, upon the important subject to which these addresses refer, and in the successful accomplishment of which the two nations have a common interest, will, the undersigned is persuaded, be met by his Government in the same spirit of elevated benevolence which has given birth to the desire in the mind of His Royal Highness.

The undersigned cannot avoid expressing his acquiescence in the opinion that the difficulties which have hitherto operated to prevent a system of concert against the illicit slave trade between the two Governments, are most likely to be satisfactorily examined by selecting Washington as the seat of deliberation. If, happily, they are of a nature to be removed, it is by such a transfer of the scene of a new endeavor that the best hopes may be formed; and it is hence, with a peculiar satisfaction that the undersigned learns that Mr. Canning, when proceeding on his mission to the United States, will carry with him such full instructions upon the whole subject as may prepare him for entering upon the interesting duty of giving effect to the views of Parliament. The undersigned will not fail to make known this intention to his Government, by the earliest opportunity that he can command.

Upon a subject so universally interesting to humanity, Lord Castlereagh has justly inferred that the Government of the United States can never require any other incentive than that of its own moral impulse to awaken it to exertion. But, if, upon the present occasion, it needed any other, the undersigned must be permitted to say that it would be abundantly found in the friendly and enlarged spirit of this renewed overture from the Government of the Prince Regent, and in the liberal justice rendered to the early and steadfast efforts of the United States in the cause of abolition, by the Addresses in question, from both Houses of the Parliament of this realm. Following up their uniform policy in this great cause, never tired of adopting new expedients of prohibition, where new evasions have pointed to their necessity, the undersigned feels happy in being able to state, feeling sure that the information cannot be otherwise than acceptable to the unwearied and useful zeal of his Lordship in the same cause, that,

16th Con. 2d Sess.—47

besides the law of April, 1818, of which the undersigned had the honor to speak in his note of the 21st of December of that year, a subsequent act of Congress, of date so recent as last March, has raised up additional means for the extirpation of the baleful traffic. By this act the President is specially authorized to employ armed vessels of the United States to cruise upon the coast of Africa; and other new provisions are introduced for intercepting and punishing such delinquent citizens as may be found forgetful of the denunciations of their Government, no less than of their own moral duties, abandoning themselves to the enormity of this transgression. It is well known that the sentiments of the President are in full and active harmony with those of Congress, in the beneficent desire of putting a stop to this deep rooted and afflicting evil. With such pledges before the world, the undersigned cannot err in confidently anticipating that the fresh proposal of the Government of His Royal Highness will be promptly taken up at Washington, under the deepest convictions of their importance, and with every anxious desire for a favorable result that can be made compatible with the Constitution and other essential interests of the Republic.

The undersigned is happy to embrace this occasion of renewing to Lord Castlereagh the assurances of his distinguished consideration.

RICHARD RUSH.

SPAIN—RICHARD W. MEADE.

[Communicated to the Senate, February 14, 1821.]

WASHINGTON, *Feb.* 13, 1821.

To the Senate of the United States:

I transmit herewith to the Senate a copy of a memorial received from Richard W. Meade, together with a report of the Secretary of State concerning it.

JAMES MONROE.

DEPARTMENT OF STATE,
February 13, 1821.

The Secretary of State, to whom has been referred the letter and memorial to the President of R. W. Meade, has the honor of reporting his opinion:

That, from the nature of the claim, now first announced by Mr. Meade in the letter, it will be proper that it should be communicated to the Senate, when the ratification by Spain of the treaty signed on the 22d of February, 1819, shall be submitted to that body for their advice and consent to receive it in exchange for the ratification of the United States heretofore given.

With regard to the material facts alleged by Mr. Meade in support of his claim to a distinct and separate engagement, involved in the treaty on the part of the United States, to pay the whole of his liquidated demand upon Spain, he has been misinformed. Neither his nor any other individual claim was ever mentioned between the negotiators of the treaty; no proposal was consequently ever made by Mr. Onis that it should be inserted by name. It was known that Mr. Meade had a large unliquidated claim on the Spanish Government, and he had been informed, according to his request, that it would be considered by the Government of the United States in common with others at the negotiation of the treaty; but of the amount or validity of the claim this Government had no knowledge sufficient to warrant any special engagement to assume it, had such a proposal been made; and by Mr. Meade's own statement, it was not liquidated until nearly a year after the signature of the treaty, and then without the privity of this Government, and not in the manner prescribed by the treaty for all claims provided for in it.

The argument of Mr. Meade's memorial, drawn from the law of nations as in his opinion applicable to the case, and founded upon a statement of facts, the most essential of which are unfounded, may be left to the sound judgment of the Senate. The distinction drawn in the memorial between the claims of a citizen of one country upon the Government of another, arising from contract or from wrong, is undoubtedly so far just, that the claimant by contract cannot resort to the interposition of his own Government to obtain from the other satisfaction for his claim to the same extent as the claimant from wrong. The Government of the claimant by contract can interpose in his behalf only by its good offices, and cannot, as the memorial states, press to the extent of reprisals for the satisfaction of the claim. It has no right to interpose at all, without the solicitation of the claimant himself, who, having stated his interest upon his own confidence in the Government with which he contracts, may properly abide by the result of that confidence, without calling upon his country to make itself a party to his demand. But if he does appeal to his own Government for that adventitious aid to which other contractors with the same party, and on the same security, cannot resort, he thereby voluntarily makes his claim a subject of negotiation and of those compromises in which all national adjustments of individual claims must and do always consist. It is unnecessary to pursue this position into the detail of argument by which it is susceptible of illustration. No special provision for the individual claim of Mr. Meade, no express renunciation of it, was ever made or contemplated by the treaty; nor was any mention made of it by General Vives in delivering to me the ratification of his sovereign.

By the statement of the memorial itself, it was questionable to the Cortes and to the Spanish Minister of Finance whether it was included in the renunciations of the ninth article or not. If it was, Mr. Meade will be entitled to the indemnities stipulated by the treaty, and in the forms provided by the same instrument; if it was not, his resort is, as it originally was, exclusively to the Spanish Government; and the Cortes, in recognising his claim, have given directions for its payment.

JOHN QUINCY ADAMS.

MEMORIAL.

WASHINGTON, *February* 8, 1821.

SIR: Since the recent intelligence from Spain has reduced it nearly to a certainty that the treaty concluded at Washington on the 22d February, 1819, has been ratified by the Government of Spain, and that it is speedily to be offered for the ratification of this Government, it becomes highly expedient that all the collateral and implied as well as the direct and explicit obligations which such ratification may carry with it should be fully understood and distinctly recognised before any definitive and irrevocable determination be taken in the business. My most vital interests are so deeply involved in the interpretations with which the terms of the treaty may be understood and accepted, and may, moreover, enter so essentially into the motives which might dictate the ratification or rejection of it, in the whole or in part, that I owe it as a duty equally to myself and to the Government to make a preliminary and frank declaration of the nature and extent of the indemnities which the ratification of the treaty may give me a right to claim from the United States. The validity of such a claim was, without doubt, prospectively contemplated and admitted by the functionaries directly concerned in the negotiation, if, as I have every reason to conclude was the fact, it formed the groundwork of any one of the treaty stipulations; nor do I apprehend that the tedious procrastinations and vexatious shifts which have since been interposed by the late administrators of public affairs in Spain have at all impaired the force of the original considerations and impressions by which our own Government was actuated. But the more definite and authentic shape which subsequent events have given to my claim, and the further development of the views of the Spanish Government respecting it, would alone have justified the propriety of this preliminary explanation, even if the full execution of the treaty did not mainly depend upon the collective wisdom and discretion of Congress, to whom the involved consequences of its stipulations are not supposed to be so distinctly enunciated as to the original negotiators. I shall submit it, with the most entire deference and respect, to your own judgment and discretion to devise the most proper and effectual mode, when the occasion shall arise, of communicating to the Senate an official notification of this claim, and also of recommending to Congress, among the measures necessary to carry the treaty into practical effect, a distinct provi⸱⸱ the complete and immediate satisfaction ⸱ ⸱ claim; so that its distinct recognition as o⸱ ⸱⸱ the treaty stipulations may be concomitant w⸱⸱⸱ the treaty through its several stages of final ratification and complete execution. The advantages resulting from this mode of clearing away all ambiguities, and obviating future misunderstandings, are evident, besides saving me from expensive solicitations and ruinous delays.

In conformity to these views, I shall proceed, without further apology, to lay before your summary exposition of my claim (as it has⸱⸱⸱ ⸱ ⸱⸱

Spain—Richard W. Meade.

recognised and admitted) upon the Spanish Government, and of the process by which the Government of the United States may become identified with that of Spain in the obligation to satisfy that claim immediately upon the exchange of ratifications.

As soon as I was released, through the humane and decided interposition of my country, from the prison to which I had been consigned by the unparalleled injustice and perfidy of some of the ministers and agents of the restored Government which superseded the illustrious Cortes, by whose wisdom and heroic constancy Spain had been saved from a foreign yoke, I lost no time in preferring the most urgent solicitations for the settlement of my claims, to an immense amount, upon the Spanish Government. These claims were due on account of extensive supplies of provisions and advances of money, at a time when the nation was in the most trying and doubtful crisis of its fate; to the timely assistance of which supplies and advances, it has been distinctly and gratefully acknowledged by the great body of patriotic Spaniards, both in public and private life, that the nation was mainly indebted for the ultimate achievement of its independence. Notwithstanding the counteractions thrown in my way from the same corrupt sources of selfish intrigue by which my most iniquitous imprisonment had been planned and prolonged, so manifest and so cogent was the equity of my claims, and so powerful the appeal to the gratitude of the nation, that the Government could not avoid giving serious attention to the case. It was notorious enough how unprepared they were to meet my demands, and, indeed, that the conscious embarrassment of the Government on that head was one of the mainsprings of action put in motion by the intriguers, who were permitted, for so long a time, to evade the pressing instances of Mr. Erving and my friends for my release, and even to nullify the effect of royal orders ostensibly commanding it. Very soon, however, after my release, they turned their attention to the Crown lands in Florida as a resource for discharging the debt; and, accordingly, it was insinuated to me that I might receive payment by means of an equivalent in those lands. But I knew that the Government of the United States had long contemplated a cession of the Floridas as the ultimate satisfaction and indemnity for the insults and injuries which our flag and commerce had sustained through the instrumentality, active or passive, of Spain. I therefore felt myself not only bound by   neral obligations of a good citizen, but es-
G.   y moved by the strongest sense of gratitude
1   e disinterested and magnanimous interference
.. .ay country in my behalf, to avoid every step which might possibly traverse even the ulterior and contingent views and projects of the Government in its diplomatic relations with Spain; and, accordingly, without stopping to inquire whether the r getiation had assumed such a shape as to give . `United States any right, either absolute or incl ate, to insist upon specific indemnity in the Floridas, I addressed a letter to Mr. Adams, da...ur.. ``h of June, 1818, (eight months before
16tl.

the signature of the treaty,) in which I stated the proposition, expressly with a view to ascertain whether my acceptance of it would be agreeable to this Government. As soon as the answer of Mr. Adams, dated 18th September, 1818, informed me that this Government apprehended ill consequences from admitting the precedent of the grant in question pending the negotiation, as it might open a door for other grants, tending materially to diminish the value of the desired cession, I abandoned all thoughts of accepting payment in that mode, and applied myself exclusively to the direct means of obtaining satisfaction. Having experienced, throughout the whole affair, the greatest inconvenience from the dilatory proceedings of the Spanish Government, I presented, in the month of December, 1818, a memorial to the King, backed by an official letter from Mr. Erving, urging the appointment of two or three persons in the entire confidence of the King to audit and settle my claims. My petition was finally granted, and a junta or commission, consisting of four counsellors, was accordingly appointed by a royal order. The report of that junta, on the 20th September, 1819, after a laborious and minute investigation of six or seven months' duration, and a critical examination into all the merits of the case, specifically admitted and passed my claim, to an amount less than I had all along stated, both directly to this Government and to Mr. Erving. The report of the junta, in frank and explicit terms, acknowledges and enforces the most cogent motives for the speedy satisfaction of the debt by the Spanish Government—motives avowedly derived, not only from the faith of the most solemn contracts, but from the national gratitude for the signal and meritorious services I had performed in the execution of those contracts. That report or award has been approved, ratified, and adopted, in all its terms, by the Spanish Government, and sanctioned by all the highest solemnities that can be invoked to bind the faith of the State.

The delay of the report to so late a period as September, 1819, was, in a great measure, occasioned by the multiplicity of contracts to be examined, and of departments from which information was to be sought. After the report had been sent in, it was returned, with various suggestions and observations from the Minister of Finance to the junta, who, after considering the suggestions of the Minister, on the 15th November, 1819, confirmed their first report, reasserting and enforcing all the reasons upon which it was founded, and even declaring that the sum awarded was less than what, in justice and equity, the Government ought to pay me. Still the Minister of Finance thought it necessary to consult, in succession, the Treasurer General of the kingdom and the Comptroller General of Accounts; and their decision concurring with that of the junta, the King finally ratified the award. A formal certificate was made out and delivered to me, signed by all the members of the junta, and approved by the Minister of Finance, by order and acting in the name of the King; and the royal seal is affixed thereto—solemnities observed only in cases of high commissions, and in affairs of the utmost importance. This certificate, (which, together with another royal order, was transmitted to me in May, 1820, by Mr. Arguelles, the new Minister of Finance,) imports the clearest and most unequivocal acknowledgment that the Spanish Government.is indebted to me in the sum of $491,153 33, and directs that the same shall be paid out of the funds of the Royal Finance Department, with interest.

The embarrassments of the new revolution, which ensued in the interval between the definitive award of the junta and its final ratification by the King, delayed and impeded the full measure of justice which I had every reason to expect from the more enlightened and just Government of the Cortes, which that revolution has now restored to Spain. I nevertheless pressed for a settlement with all the diligence that the magnitude of the claim and my necessities justified and required; and, as soon as its definitive and official recognition, in the form of the certificate just mentioned, was communicated to me by the Minister of Finance, I petitioned the Cortes to order its immediate payment, and to designate the mode of payment. I could obtain no definitive resolution from the Cortes till the 5th October last, the day they decided in favor of ratifying the treaty for the cession of the Floridas to the United States; upon which occasion they ordered that my memorial should be united with the papers relative to the treaty, and submitted to the King, in order to have it ascertained whether the American Government had consented to the introduction of my individual claim into the negotiations on the treaty; and, if so, that the American Government had distinctly assumed upon itself the payment of my claim, and had wholly exonerated Spain from it; but, if it should be found that my case had not been taken into view by the negotiators, and was not distinctly understood as embraced in the treaty stipulations, they, in that case, decreed the immediate payment of the debt by the Spanish Government. Upon this reference from the Cortes, the Spanish Minister of State pronounced an unequivocal opinion that the debt had been distinctly and specifically assumed by the United States, in exoneration of Spain, or would be so upon the exchange of ratifications; consequently, I was referred to the eventual ratification of the treaty for the ultimate satisfaction of my claim. The opinion of the Minister was founded (as I was informed from high authority) upon facts said to have been notorious to the negotiators of the treaty, and verified, as it was said, by the official communications of Mr. Onis to the Spanish Government, to wit, that my claim had been introduced by name into the discussions between Mr. Adams and Mr. Onis, who finally agreed, in their *verbal conferences,* that it should be assumed and paid by the United States; that Mr. Onis proposed the insertion of my name, and a specific stipulation to that effect in the treaty, but that Mr. Adams thought it unnecessary to do so, though he agreed to the insertion of a clause intended to comprehend my case without naming it, and to exonerate Spain from the debt, with the understanding, nevertheless, that it was

to be specifically assumed and paid by the United States. The clause alluded to as the one intended to embrace my claim is the *fifth* of the renunciations declared on the part of the United States in the ninth article of the treaty.

From an examination of the three documents—the protocol of the treaty as delivered by Mr. Onis, the counter-projet of Mr. Adams, and the treaty as it was actually concluded and signed, so much is certain and evident, that the protocol contains a clause nearly equivalent to the one in question, which is entirely omitted in the counter-projet; and so it becomes highly probable that it was inserted in the treaty in consequence of some new arrangement or substantive understanding, discussed and adjusted in the latter stages of the negotiation. What were the nature and extent of such arrangement or understanding, and of the preliminary discussions which led to it, and whether Mr. Onis had made an accurate report of them in his alleged communications to his own Government, are matters of which you, sir, must have far more authentic and certain information than any I can pretend to offer. If the fifth renunciation on the part of the United States were, in fact, designed to extend beyond such claims as arose out of injuries and aggressions in which the nation, in its sovereign capacity, was immediately concerned, and for which it might, conformably to the law and usage of nations, have claimed restitution and indemnity under the peril of reprisals; and if, in truth, it were intended to reach and comprehend claims arising out of civil contracts—in other words, *bona fide* debts due from the Spanish Government to private citizens of the United States—then it is perfectly clear that the sweeping terms of the stipulation are broad enough to embrace my identical claim; and it is equally clear and certain that it was the identical claim (if not the sole and only one of the kind) intended to be so embraced. It may, therefore, be conceded that the Spanish Government, so far, was warranted in concluding that they were to be as effectually exonerated and discharged from their debt to me as if it had been mentioned by name in the treaty; and their corollary, that the United States would then be bound to pay and satisfy that debt without defalcation or delay, was surely a very natural one, and as surely founded in the soundest principles as well of the moral as of the conventional law.

I have, however, positively denied and formally protested against one of the postulates assumed by the Spanish Government, which is, that any stipulation of the United States could be competent, *per se,* to cancel the debt, and exonerate Spain from her original and inherent obligation, in any other way than by actually paying the debt to me. Not that I have ever been in the least averse from accepting the United States for my debtor in lieu of Spain; on the contrary, if the undertaking of the United States were co-extensive in point of legal and moral obligation with that of Spain, so that the existing pecuniary debt of the one, with all its concomitant duties, becomes identically the debt of the other, I should then most willingly accede to the proposed transposition of the indebted party. But it is precisely on this point that the most alarming ambiguity exists; for, if this particular debt be embraced by the terms of the fifth renunciation on the part of the United States, and was so intended by the negotiators, then there is no distinct and substantive provision for the payment of it, unless the official report, alleged to have been made by Mr. Onis, of a verbal arrangement and understanding on the subject between him and Mr. Adams, and not fully expressed on the face of the treaty, should be distinctly and formally recognised by this Government. The terms of the treaty, taken simply and strictly, without being interpreted by any such supplemental arrangement or understanding, clearly import that all the claims embraced by all the five renunciations on the part of the United States are to be thrown into one heterogeneous mass, and placed on the same level, and subject to the same rule of compensation; whereas nothing could be more unjust and injurious than such an operation in regard to my claim; because nothing can be more dissimilar in their nature, in their origin, and in all their circumstances, and nothing more unequal in the cogency of the legal and moral obligations out of which they arise, than my claim, and the mass of others with which it is apparently confounded.

The broad distinction, in all their moral and political consequences and relations, between a mere debt voluntarily contracted by a State in the ordinary transactions of business with a private person, whether citizen or foreigner, and a claim for unascertained damages on account of injuries to private property, involved and bound up in national injuries, is manifest and universally admitted. Depredations upon the commerce, aggressions upon the flag, either of the military or commercial marine of a nation, equally with invasions of its territory, are always considered and treated as direct aggressions upon the sovereignty of the nation, and equally to be resented and repelled as acts of hostility, if a reasonable satisfaction be not made. All forcible and violent seizures, at sea or upon land, of the persons or property of private citizens, partake of the same character of hostility, and, according to the various degrees of the offence, may give just cause for reprisals. When the State is injured or insulted in the persons of its citizens, if the aggression be manifestly and flagrantly unjust, the State is bound by its correlative duties to its citizens, whilst it avenges its own wrongs, or, by peaceable means, vindicates the violated rights of its sovereignty, to demand just reparation for the injuries inflicted on its citizens. In all these cases, however, the compensations for the private injuries, equally with the satisfactions for the public wrongs, must necessarily be fair subjects of compromise and mutual accommodation. The offended State is not bound, nor has it any right, to set up its own judgment as paramount and infallible, and to insist upon the *summum jus*, according to that judgment; otherwise, disputes and wars would be interminable. These compromises between States, both of the public wrongs and of the private injuries involved in them, are of necessity, and agreeable to the universal usage of civilized nations; but that a mere failure in contract, on the part of one State towards a private citizen of another, should be treated as a violation of the high rights of sovereignty, so as either to justify reprisals, or to give occasion for any of those compromises or mutual concessions usually incident to a treaty of pacification, would be an assumption as absolutely destitute of any countenance from precedent as from any of the analogies of public law.

From the following comparison of my actual condition, as an acknowledged creditor of Spain, having a present and perfect right to demand instant payment, with that to which I should be reduced as a deferred claimant of a precarious dividend under the eleventh article of the treaty, there will appear abundant cause for my anxiety, and for my having protested to the Spanish Government, as I now do to this, against the competency of the treaty, either to operate the release, without providing for the payment of the debt, or to annex to its transposition such interpolations upon the terms of the original obligation as the letter of the said eleventh article would seem to imply.

I have shown what procrastinations, what long, wearisome, and expensive solicitations and investigations I have had to wade through; and what sacrifices of my time, my means, and my comforts, I have had to endure, in order to have my claim definitively and conclusively adjusted, ascertained, and settled, by the only party connected with me in the contract, or responsible to me under it, by a party in all respects competent to take upon himself the most perfect obligation. After I have surmounted every difficulty, and have at last conclusively fixed upon this party a consummate obligation to pay me an ascertained sum of money, instanter; upon what terms and for what equivalents am I called upon to renounce or to transpose this perfect right? Why, if the ostensible stipulations of the treaty, as defined in the eleventh article, are to be strictly taken as the only rule for determining the equivalents, then what is now an ascertained debt, standing upon the basis of a consummate obligation, is reduced to a mere outstanding claim, open to fresh and reiterated contestations from unknown parties, from intermeddling strangers without privity or interest in the original contract, or any motive for engaging in the controversy but an eager emulation for the apportionment of the very inadequate sum set apart for the satisfaction of all the claims. It is to be re-examined and adjudicated over again by a new commission, which may not, and probably will not, be closed in less than a period of three years, commencing from some undefined point of time hereafter, viz: the meeting of the commissioners in Washington; and which, if it decide, as possibly it may, to investigate over again the merits and details of my claim, will have to invoke documentary evidence from the bureaus of a foreign country peculiarly tenacious of its archives. Now, suppose the claim, as it stands adjudicated by the

Spanish authorities, to be affirmed by the American commissioners; then, instead of a present right to demand payment of the whole sum, without defalcation or delay, from a party abundantly solvent and of presumed good faith—a party not yet declared bankrupt, either in character or circumstances—I am to wait for a contingent quota or dividend out of the gross sum set apart for the satisfaction, *pro rata*, of the entire mass of claims; and even that quota cannot be ascertained and declared until the whole of the claims are finally adjudicated, within the aforesaid period of three years. Lastly, this tedious process being accomplished, and the commission *functus officio ;* all the claims being definitively adjusted, and the respective quotas ascertained and declared; even then, the mode and the time of payment are left at the absolute discretion of Congress, viz: first, immediately at the Treasury; or, secondly, in six per cent. stock, payable out of the proceeds from the sales of public lands in the ceded territory; or, lastly, in such other manner as Congress may prescribe by law.

I beg leave to advert, very cursorily, to the principles of public law and of natural justice upon which I have founded my protest against the assumed power so to dispose of my rights of property, if, indeed, contrary to my best hopes and expectations, any such power was ever to be exerted in the case.

All debts, both public and private, are universally held, among civilized nations, as a species of property more sacred and inviolable than any other. This principle seems to have been peculiarly acceptable to the moral sense of the people of the United States. The constitution, whilst it leaves to the several States the discretionary rights of sovereignty over the ordinary property of their citizens, expressly prohibits them from making any thing but gold and silver coin a tender in payment of debts, and from passing any law impairing the obligation of contracts—a clause which, in its established construction and practical effect, has been held to annul all State laws professing, under any pretext, to discharge debtors from the obligation of their debts. By the treaty of 1794 with England, all debts, both public and private, are to be held absolutely inviolate in case of war between the two nations, while every other species of property is left exposed to belligerent confiscation and reprisals. That clause of the treaty is further remarkable for its clear and emphatic enunciation of the abstract principles of national morality and good faith upon which the stipulation is founded. Since the benign and prevailing influence of these principles has been able to relax the iron grasp of war, I cannot doubt their sovereign efficacy in that temperate state of the body politic when its passions or necessities claim no prescriptive charter to consecrate force and vengeance on the altars of justice and mercy. With respect to private property in general, the power of the sovereign to cede or dispose of it without the consent of the owner has been held to result from the various modifications of that high prerogative of majesty supposed to be vested in absolute princes, and by some jurists and writers on public law styled the *eminent domain ;* by virtue of which, in its pure, unmodified state, all property is theoretically supposed to be enjoyed by the citizens under the tacit condition of being resumed by the sovereign when the necessities or the safety of the State shall require it. It is agreed, however, by all the most approved expounders of the laws of nature and nations, that this right of ceding private property, in virtue of the eminent domain, is restrained within certain rules, founded in natural justice, which cannot be transgressed by any State that is civilized and governed by laws, no matter how absolute the form of government in other respects. In the first place, it is lawful only upon occasions of the highest State necessity and for the public safety; and, in that case, full compensation must be made to the owner; for which purpose, if the ordinary revenue of the State be inadequate, the deficiency must be made up by contributions from all the citizens. The power to cancel debts, under any circumstances, is treated as one of the most questionable and pernicious results of the eminent domain, and, of course, cannot be justified by any inferior necessity than what is requisite to give validity to cessions of other property. It is no ordinary conjuncture, no inducement of mere expediency or convenience, no bargaining or compromising for the settlement of disputed limits or of indemnities for injuries; it is nothing, in short, but an imperious political necessity and an indispensable regard to the common safety that can justify even an absolute prince in bartering away, by a treaty of cession, the private property of the citizen, and then only upon the condition of making full compensation. Indeed, no treaty can well be brought within these rules but a treaty of peace for the conclusion of some destructive war menacing extreme danger to the State, and for the termination of which cessions of private property had, in some way, become necessary. If, by the common consent of mankind, an absolute monarch cannot transgress these wholesome regulations of the eminent domain without the stigma of a lawless violator of public faith, far less admissible would be the supposition that the Government of the United States could ever have aimed at any more unlimited prerogative. Indeed, so little do the assumed privileges of this eminent domain accord with the theory of our Government, and the known and defined origin and limits of its powers, as to have raised no inconsiderable doubt of the expediency of that amendment to the Constitution which forbids the taking of private property for public use without just compensation, apprehending that it was calculated to extend, by implication, rather than to limit the specific powers of the General Government; since, without the aid of such implication, the power to take private property for public use, upon any terms, might not have been inferred. However that be, it is certain that the practice of the Government has strictly and invariably conformed (unless this treaty shall so be interpreted and executed as to establish a solitary exception) to that great principle of universal ethics and public law so distinctly recognised and imperatively enjoined by the Constitution ; for, upon all the occasions when the prerogative of taking private property for public use has been exerted, (and it has been exerted only in cases of the highest necessity, and for the public safety,) full compensation has invariably been made to the citizen. Witness the numerous instances of the last war—a war of invasion and devastation—in which it became necessary, occasionally, to take military occupation of private houses, which caused their destruction ; or to burn bridges, and otherwise use or destroy private property, for the advancement of military operations: in every case the proprietor has been compensated to the full value of the property lost.*

I need not institute any comparison between that sort of necessity contemplated by the great expounders of public law, when they undertake to define the rightful limits of the eminent domain, and that necessity created by the motives of profit or convenience, which operated in the present instance ; nor any inquiry into the authority of the Government of the United States, by mere dint of power, to release a claim under the circumstances of mine, namely, a debt due from a foreign State, upon a contract not made within the jurisdiction nor under the legal sanctions of the United States, of which they had no privity or control but what may have resulted from the mere circumstance of the creditor's being a citizen, sojourning and carrying on trade in foreign parts. All that can be required to make out my case is this brief and simple state of it: my property, to the value of near half a million, is taken to pay for the Floridas. Then, upon any principle of public law, or of a constitutional bill of rights, what is there to cast the shadow of a doubt over my claim to be compensated and reimbursed that instant the cession of the Floridas is consummated?

The history of the negotiation, through all the stages of its progress, whereof any monuments are extant, infers an intent entirely conformable to the legal and moral obligations (such as I have endeavored to expound them) of the high contracting parties. Upon the great question of adjusting the equivalents for the long desired, anxiously expected, and all-important cession of the Floridas, it has already been shown how material a term in the calculations of the parties, and how much discussed, was that of exonerating Spain from her debt to me: being first demanded by Mr. Onis, as appears by his proctocol ; at first refused by Mr. Adams, as appears by his counter-project ; still insisted on by Mr. Onis; at length conceded by Mr. Adams; and, accordingly, the fifth renunciation, framed purposely to embrace that specific object, was admitted in the treaty. There is one other circumstance, however, of itself, conclusive to expound the genuine intent of the parties at that stage of the transaction. It is this : in the counterprojet of Mr. Adams, the gross sum of $5,000,000

is designated for the aggregate satisfaction of all the claims proposed to be renounced by that instrument ; which, be it remembered, did not include mine, or any of the like description ; yet, after the fifth renunciation (including my claim, and every other of the like description, and enhancing by so much the price of the cession, comes to be inserted) nothing more is appropriated by the treaty for private indemnities than the same identical $5,000,000. Thus the sum of compensation remains precisely the same ; whilst the sum of claims to be compensated is so materially increased, by the addition of this entirely new description of claims to the list of renunciations. This fact alone imperatively demands the hypothesis of an implicit understanding between the parties that the satisfaction of my claim was to be substantively provided for, apart from the others renounced by the treaty ; otherwise, we have a paradox equally perplexing to the casuist, the arithmetician, and the jurist ; namely, that the price to be received by the vender may be increased *ad infinitum*, without adding any thing to the price to be paid by the vendee.

If the report said to have been made by Mr. Onis to his Government, corroborated as it is by so many circumstances, should encounter no emphatic contradiction from any quarter which we are bound to consider as more authentic, it must be taken as a concession that the debt was to be fully and absolutely assumed by the United States : and so the case becomes clear and intelligible, and the whole proceeding fair and just. Nothing then remains but to clear it from all ambiguity, by distinct recognitions in the act of ratification, and in the appropriations for carrying the treaty into effect.

But, suppose it turn out that no verbal or implicit arrangement or understanding, supplemental to the letter of the treaty, can be admitted ; still there is no essential difference in the right of the case; for it is clear the debt is embraced by the sweeping terms of the fifth renunciation, and was intended to be so : then the United States have stipulated absolutely to cancel the debt and exonerate Spain, and must, at all events, perform that stipulation. How is it to be performed ? Why, there is but one just and rightful way, which is, simply, to pay the debt. It signifies nothing to say the treaty designates the mode and the extent in which the debt shall be compensated, and binds the United States to nothing more ; because, I answer conclusively, first, the act is yet *in fieri ;* and the precise question is, how shall it be consummated ? Whether in conformity, or in direct opposition to principles consecrated by public law, by the Constitution, and by the faith of nations ; and, secondly, when consummated, it is *res inter alias acta ;* it concludes the high contracting parties as to all that it stipulates for the benefit of either; but as to any stipulation volunteered for or against him who was neither party nor privy, and whose particular claim was not necessarily involved or committed in the negotiation, it concludes not him ; he is perfectly free to accept it, if it be for his benefit, or to renounce it, if it be otherwise. I maintain that Spain cannot be exonerated ; the debt cannot be cancelled until it

* For the rule of indemnity to individuals for losses by war, vide Grot. De Jure Bel. et Pa. 3, 20, § 8; Puf. 8, 6, §7 ; Vat. 3, 15, § 232.

Spain—Richard W. Meade.

is paid, either by Spain herself, or by some guarantee for her. Until then, it subsists, *de jure*, in as full force after as before the ratification of the treaty ; and unless it be distinctly pronounced by the terms of the ratification that the United States are to be made the guarantee, I shall not cease to urge Spain for payment, by all the sacred and inviolable ties of national faith and honor, and to avail myself of all the legal remedies that her tribunals are competent to entertain. Then, would not a clear right result to Spain to come upon the United States for indemnity, under the stipulation which obliges them to cancel the debt and exonerate Spain ? That stipulation is not made to depend upon the condition of my accepting this or that equivalent, but is absolute; and if the United States cannot have the debt cancelled, and Spain exonerated, in the way most agreeable to themselves, it is their business to devise an adequate mode; but, at all events, their duty to exonerate Spain. So long as the obligation, legal or moral, of Spain, is permitted to continue in force, though there be no adequate remedy for coercing her to payment, still, if one *scintilla juris* be left unextinguished, she cannot be said to be exonerated in any sense of the term ; her appeal to the yet untarnished faith of the United States could not be resisted. Thus, the United States, by taking the direct course of paying the debt to me, do nothing more than strictly fulfil a clear and unconditional stipulation with Spain. In no other way can it be fulfilled; and no better can be desired. The only alternative is an arbitrary invasion of private right, and a very ambiguous implication of the faith of treaties.

I would also submit, with great deference, that the circumstances of this transaction have given me a strong claim to the equitable consideration of the Government. In the purchase of the Floridas, my property has been freely used, and every advantage has been derived from it, just as if it had been committed to the negotiation by the most valid assignment. Now, whether the stipulation to cancel the debt and exonerate Spain be effectual or not, yet, in fact, that stipulation has supplied to Spain an apology, a pretext, and a color of right, to deny or evade the payment of a debt, otherwise acknowledged under circumstances of such persuasive and cogent equity as to have made the prompt payment of it necessary and inevitable. I need not remark how notorious it is that, with sovereigns, who are amenable only to the *ultima ratio*, an apology, a pretext, or a color of right, is too often equivalent to a legal defence or plea in bar in disputes between private persons amenable to the ordinary process of law. I can truly say that, under my present circumstances, with all my means and resources absorbed and bound up in this large debt, the delay is little less than the denial of justice.

In every possible view that can be taken of the case, as regards the question either of strict right or of equitable discretion, I humbly submit whether it be not obviously just and expedient for the Senate to annex to the ratification of the treaty, by way of rider, a distinct recognition of my claim,

so that it may be specifically provided for amongst the appropriations necessary to carry the treaty into effect. But if, for any reason, it be decided that the debt shall not be assumed by the United States, then I think there is one act of justice I may boldly presume to ask, without fear or hesitation ; and that is, to have the fifth renunciation distinctly excepted from the ratification, and expunged from the treaty, or, at least, to have my claim excepted from it by name. I shall then be left free to prosecute it where it is unquestionably due, unembarrassed with the imposing renunciation of my country. I have the most assured confidence that Spain, when her moral sense and good faith are no longer perplexed by the salvo of that renunciation, cannot resist one moment my instances for an immediate liquidation of the debt. In all events, it is my clear and decided election to abide the issue of an appeal to the moral sense and good faith of that nation, rather than the chances of that contingent and long-deferred indemnity provided for the other claims, into whose company mine has been introduced by the treaty, though introduced as casual acquaintances merely, and not, I hope, with any view to force them into a loathed and unnatural union.

For the freedom, and probably the superfluous elaboration, with which I have thus claimed your attention to the facts and the *principles upon* which my rights are asserted, I have no apology but my deep interest in the consequences of the public act about to become the subject of executive and legislative deliberation. Indeed, if an individual interest were at stake, of far less import than the fruits of a life of honest enterprise and active exertion, in the preservation of which the inestimable blessings of personal independence and the comfortable existence of a large family are involved, I should do injustice equally to the spirit of our institutions and the character of the Government, if I thought it necessary to deprecate censure or offence for a respectful and well-founded remonstrance against the effect of any public act, consummate or intended, upon my private rights. The implicit confidence, so absolutely due to the Government collectively, would be most unjustly withheld, sir, from any department of it under your exclusive administration. I therefore repose myself with an unlimited trust in the habitual equity of your mind, when I defer to your judgment and discretion that disposition of this memorial which may give me the benefit of the facts and reasons it advances, wherever the authority resides to administer the proper remedy.

With the profoundest sentiments of respect, I remain your much obliged and grateful fellow-citizen,

RICHARD W. MEADE.

To the PRESIDENT OF THE U. STATES.

NOTES.

" Every thing in the political society ought to tend to the good of the community ; and if even the citizen's person is subject to this rule, his fortune cannot be excepted. The State cannot subsist, or constantly administer public affairs in the most advantageous manner, if it has not the power of disposing, on occasion, of all kinds of goods subject to its authority. It may even be presumed that, when the nation takes possession of a country, the property of certain things is only allowed to individuals, with this reserve. The right which belonged to the society, or to the sovereign, of disposing, in case of necessity, and for the public safety, of all the wealth contained in the State, is called the "eminent domain." It is evident that this right is, in certain cases, necessary to him who governs; and, consequently, is a part of the empire, or sovereign power, and ought to be placed in the number of the prerogatives of majesty. When, therefore, the people submit the empire to any one, they at the same time yield to him the eminent domain—at least, if it is not expressly reserved. Every Prince who is truly a sovereign is invested with this right, in the same manner that his authority is limited in other respects.

"If the nation disposes of the public property, in virtue of his eminent domain, the alienation is valid, &c.

"When he disposes, in like manner, in a case of necessity, of the possessions of a community, or of an individual, the alienation will be valid for the same reason. But justice demands that this community, or this individual, be recompensed out of the public money; and, if the treasury is not able to pay it, all the citizens are obliged to contribute to it," &c.—*Vat. b.* 1, *ch.* 20, *sec.* 244.

"The necessity of making a peace authorizes the sovereign to dispose of things even belonging to private persons; and the eminent domain gives him this right. In some degree, by virtue of the power which he has over all his subjects, he may dispose of their persons. But these cessions being made for the common advantage, the State is to indemnify the citizens who are sufferers by them."—*Vat. b.* 4, *ch.* 2, *sec.* 12.

"The promises, the conventions, all the private contracts of the sovereign, are naturally subject to the same rules as those of private persons. If there arise any difficulty, it is equally conformable to prudence, to the delicacy of a sentiment that ought to be particularly conspicuous in a sovereign, and to the love of justice, to cause it to be decided by the tribunals of the State. This is the practice of all the States that are civilized and governed by laws."

The author next treats of the conventions and contracts made by the sovereign, in his quality of sovereign, and in the name of the State, with private persons, either subjects or foreigners, and of the manner of deciding controversies arising from such contracts; and he then proceeds as follows:

"Authors add that the sovereign may cancel these contracts if he finds they are contrary to the public welfare. He may doubtless do it, though not from any reason taken from the particular nature of these contracts, but either from the same reason that renders even a public treaty invalid when it is fatal to the State and contrary to the public safety, or in virtue of the eminent domain, which gives the sovereign a right to dispose of the property of the citizens with a view to the common safety. We speak here of an absolute sovereign."

"The conductor of the nation may have his private affairs, and his particular debts; these kinds of debts he is obliged to pay out of his own private fortune. What he borrows for the service of the State, the debts contracted in the administration of public affairs, are

contracts of strict right, obligatory upon the State and the whole nation. Nothing can dispense with the discharging of these debts. As soon as they have been contracted by a lawful power, the right of the creditor is not to be shaken," &c.—*Vat. b.* 2, *ch.* 14, *sec.* 213, 214, 216.

For a further development and various illustrations of the doctrine, vide Grot. De Ju. Bel. et Pa. 1, 1, sec. 6. ·Id. 2, 14, sec. 7. Id. 3, 8, sec. 4, (3.) Id. 3, 20, sects. 7, 8, 16. Puf. 8, 3, sec. 23, n. (11.) Id. 5, sec. 7. Id. 6, sects. 19, 20. Id. 8, sec. 3. Id. 10, · sec. 7. Id. 12, sec. 2. Hub. De Ju. Civ. 1, 3, 6, 44. Bynk. Q. J. P. 2, 15, p. 290. Turnbull's Heinec. 2, 8, sects. 116–170. Burl. 3, 5, sects. 25–29.

REMONSTRANCE AGAINST AN INCREASE OF DUTIES ON IMPORTS.

—

[Communicated to the Senate, Nov. 21, 1820.]

At a meeting of the citizens of Petersburg, Va., convened at the court-house, Friday, 17th November, 1820, to receive the report of the committee appointed to prepare a memorial to Congress in opposition to the tariff bill, Thomas Wallace, Mayor, was appointed chairman, and John F. May, secretary.

The committee presented the following memorial, which was read and unanimously agreed to.

Resolved. That one copy be transmitted to James Barbour and James Pleasants, Senators from this State, and one to Doctor James Jones, the Representative from this district in the Congress of the United States.

The memorial of the merchants and other inhabitants of Petersburg, Va., respectfully showeth:

That your memorialists are deeply impressed with the ruinous tendency of the restrictive system of commerce advocated by an association styling themselves the friends of national industry, and fully convinced that the tariff bill, presented at their suggestion, during the last session of Congress, and intended to be again brought forward at the present session, if passed, will prove highly detrimental to the commercial and agricultural interests of the nation and to our revenue, already reduced to comparative insignificance by the operation of the same system, whilst no advantages can be expected to result from the bill, in any degree counterbalancing the inevitable evils of the measure.

We believe that the prosperity and independence of nations, as of individuals, are essentially connected with an unrestricted state of commerce, securing to each the liberty of selling in the dearest market the produce of his industry, and buying in the cheapest such articles as his necessities demand.

National prosperity and national independence we consider as nothing but the aggregate of individual prosperity and independence. If individuals, restricted to a particular market for the sale of their produce and purchase of necessaries, would feel their prosperity and independence abridged, we cannot conceive how nations, where

Remonstrance against an increase of Duties on Imports.

every individual is restricted on the same points, should believe their independence and prosperity promoted by those very restrictions.

The idea of forcing a people to manufacture among themselves articles which they can purchase abroad at a much lower price than they can produce them at home, we conceive to be equally repugnant to justice, to policy, and to the principles of our Constitution. Such a scheme can be carried into effect only by taxing the many for the emolument of the few; by forcing multitudes from the occupations to which they have been bred, and in which they have thriven, to expend their labor and risk their capitals in projects where they have neither knowledge nor experience to guide them. The powers necessary to execute such measures we consider as too despotic to have been delegated by the American people to their Government, and such as we cannot suspect our representatives of wishing to assume, by the instrumentality of inference or construction.

The doctrine inculcated by the friends of the prohibitory system, that a nation, to accumulate wealth by commerce, must import less than it exports, is certainly erroneous. Capital exchanged for a more valuable consideration is not lost; that the importer gains, we must presume, since he desires the exchange; that the consumer gains, there can be no doubt, so long as he can procure necessaries at less expense from the importing merchant than from the home manufacturer. A few great capitalists only are disappointed. On the whole, it appears to us that the product of our exports cannot in any way be so profitably invested as in the form of imports.

The advantages of a free trade are fully demonstrated in the commercial history of the nations of Europe, from the unexampled prosperity of the Hanse Towns, under the influence of an unrestricted system of commerce, to the commercial ruin of Great Britain, under the most complete prohibitory system that has ever been devised.

In the history of this latter nation, we learn, too, that manufactures cannot be always forced; for, with all her industry, perseverance, and ingenuity, there are certain manufactures she has not been able to force to sufficient perfection to support themselves. We learn, also, that those branches of commerce, fisheries, &c., with which her Legislature has interfered the most, have generally been unproductive, and that nearly in the proportion of the fostering care extended to them; and we learn a still more instructive lesson, that a nation may become so deeply involved in the protective system, as to be unable to extricate herself, though aware of the ruin to which it leads.

The obvious tendency of this system is to destroy foreign commerce, by prohibiting our merchants from importing the products of other countries in return for the exports of ours; thus provoking them to retaliate on us as they have already done on Great Britain, by refusing to receive our produce except on such terms as we cannot afford to export it. With the destruction of foreign commerce, we expect not only the ruin of those immediately engaged in imports and exports, in the carrying trade, ship building, &c., but of almost every individual directly or indirectly concerned in commercial affairs. Nor can the fate of the agricultural interest be long protracted under the operation of such a system. Loaded with heavy internal taxes, imposed to supply the defect of the revenue formerly drawn from foreign commerce; compelled to pay double or treble prices for every necessary they purchase; excluded from a market for the produce of their own labor, the landholders must sink into poverty and insignificance, Our seamen, for want of employment at home, must emigrate to commercial countries, or resort to smuggling and piracy for support; our navy rot in our docks; our fisheries and coasting trade be left to the mercy of every invader.

How incapable a nation without foreign commerce is of protecting her coasting trade, China, the most populous country under the sun, taxed or plundered by every piratical islander on her coast, affords an impressive example.

Those who expect a home market from the establishment of manufactures can neither have calculated how many manufacturers one agriculturist can feed, nor how immense an addition to the products of our soil and the number of its cultivators half a century of unrestricted agricultural enterprise will make, by clearing the rich and extensive forests of our back country, now lying useless.

The evils of the prohibitory system are obvious, universal, and highly oppressive; its advantages limited to a few great capitalists; the ostensible reason for its introduction wholly unfounded, for our manufactures are already most amply protected; an average duty of about twenty-five per cent. on imports already exists in their favor. Freight, insurance, double commission, storage, and sundry other charges incident to shipping and transporting foreign manufactures to this country, operate as a further bounty of at least fifteen per cent. The British artisan, the most formidable rival in every market, is taxed to the amount of one-third of the whole produce of his labor; this, too, operates as a bounty of thirty-three and a third per cent. in favor of the American competitor. If we add to this the increased value of money in this country, we may confidently assert that the advantages in favor of the American manufacturer amount to upwards of one hundred per cent.

When we find that the protective system, carried to this enormous extent, instead of producing a commensurate energy on the part of our manufacturers, has produced only louder cries for still more inordinate concessions, it is time for us to pause and consider whether the revenue wasted on this unthrifty scheme could not have been expended on something more productive.

With this view of the subject, your memorialists respectfully solicit your honorable Houses, that, instead of embracing the ruinous system recommended in the tariff bill presented at your last session, you may adopt such measures as your wisdom may suggest for disembarrassing our trade from all restraints incompatible with the increase of our revenue, and the promotion of commercial and agricultural enterprise.

THOS. WALLACE, *Chairman.*

J. F. MAY, *Secretary.*

MEMORIAL FROM MAINE.

To the honorable the Senate and the honorable the House of Representatives of the United States of America in Congress assembled :

The memorial of the delegates from the commercial and agricultural sections of the State of Maine, met in convention at Portland, in behalf of the great interests of this portion of the Union, beg leave respectfully to make known to your honorable body their views and sentiments in relation to the propositions made at the last session of Congress, and which, it is understood, will be renewed at the approaching session, in relation to the national revenue.

Maine is more deeply interested, in proportion to its population, in the commercial prosperity of the Union, than any other of the States. Its tonnage has been proportionally greater, and its facilities for navigation, its rivers, bays, and harbors, its opportunities for carrying on the fisheries, its immense forests of exportable lumber and ship timber, are unequalled. A vast portion of the population are devoted and habituated to commerce, to navigation, and the fisheries. Maine is, at the same time, calculated to become an agricultural State, and will be the first grazing country in America.

Under these circumstances, your memorialists cannot but feel the deepest solicitude for the prosperity of the commerce of the country. They believe, at the same time, that the vital interests of the Union depend upon it. The Federal Government was ushered into existence with almost a single eye to it. The revenue is, and must be, essentially connected with it. It has, heretofore, been believed that experience afforded the best school. In politics it has been pre-eminently so; can it be said to have failed us in regard to the commerce of the United States?

If we turn our eye to the period anterior to the commencement of the Federal Government, and compare the situation of this country with that of any period since, the contrast is immense. By what other means than imposts, growing out of a judicious regulation of commerce, could we have collected, in the short space of thirty years, three hundred and fifty millions of revenue, with but little, or indeed, comparatively, with no distress to the people, and in a manner scarcely felt or perceived by them? What distress, perplexity, and vexation, would have attended the collection of such a sum by direct taxation?

We have had some little experience of the effects of this mode of raising a revenue. It is what the people in a free Government will not endure, if not unavoidable.

Your memorialists conceive that the present is not the time for a great and embarrassing change in relation to commerce. Those connected with it have for years been struggling against a series of untoward events, such as it could hardly be believed could be withstood. The restrictive system fell upon them with great force.

The war succeeded, and very nearly accomplished that portion of their ruin which had not before been effected. At the conclusion of peace, crippled as they were, their only alternative was to attempt to regain their hold upon commerce, in competition with a state of things as novel as it was embarrassing. They found all the world also at peace, and ready and determined, in a commercial warfare, to dispute every inch of ground. In this contest the commercial men of this country have been ever since engaged. It is impossible the wisdom of Congress should not have discerned the arduousness of this struggle. And it will not escape observation, at the same time, that, in the five years which it has progressed, more than one hundred millions of dollars of revenue have been derived from commerce alone. Your memorialists are fully aware that the community, generally, have felt the effects of the distress and embarrassment to which the mercantile class has been subjected. Whatever affects commerce will affect the community.

But the disease is necessarily the most acute and raging in the part where it first commences. Other parts of the system will, however, ultimately feel it in a greater or less degree. Commerce is the great pillar in the temple of national prosperity; that being demolished, the superstructure will follow.

Even the present rate of duties upon importation is embarrassing to commerce and injurious to the revenue. It was the result of a state of things which had been induced by the restrictive system and the war. During that period manufactures had experienced a premature and unnatural growth. At the conclusion of the war the Government was compelled to protect them by the imposition of duties, well known at the time to be injurious to the revenue, and adding to the already appalling prospects of the merchant. The duties in many instances were so great as to amount to an exclusion of the article. This was the case particularly with coarse India cottons, an article of which the poorer classes made great use; and the imposition is, in effect, a tax upon them for the benefit of the manufacturer of coarse cottons. The tax or duty on these articles amounts to an average of one hundred per cent., thereby doubling the price of the article to the poor, to enable the manufacturer here to sell at a similar rate.

There are duties imposed on other articles to an exorbitant amount, which have tended to depress the commerce, the revenue, and the agriculture of the country. An enormous duty has been imposed upon spirits of all kinds and upon wines, under the idea that they were luxuries, and with a vain hope, as is believed, of discouraging intemperance. Under the idea of their being luxuries, they should be taxed to the utmost they would bear, without discouraging importation. But the idea of taxing, and thereby checking the disposition to intemperance, will always prove fallacious, so

Remonstrance against an increase of Duties on Imports.

long as we allow ardent spirits to be manufactured among ourselves without any check whatever. If the duties on the rum of the West Indies, the brandy of France, and the wines of Portugal and Spain, and the islands appurtenant, had been predicated upon the single principle of raising a revenue, a vast commerce would have been open to the people of this country, which the exorbitant duty now imposed has in a manner cut up by the roots. Formerly, when the duties were less, the grain, which is now manufactured into whiskey, was exported to those countries; and for it the farmer then availed himself of a great price in cash, or the necessaries of life. Now, he converts it into whiskey; too great a portion of which he himself is tempted to consume, to the destruction of his health and the ruin of his morals: and thus the benevolent intentions of the Legislature have been wholly frustrated, and a regulation which they intended as a blessing has proved a curse. It has now got to be fashionable in some parts of the Union to say that the production of whiskey must be encouraged, and for that purpose that all other ardent spirits must be excluded, in order that agriculture may be promoted! How much better it would be to remove from the farmer all temptation to the consumption of ardent spirits, and to furnish him with a better as well as a more salutary vent for his grain!

Your memorialists have not been led to these remarks by any thing like hostility to the manufacturing interests. They are, on the contrary, decidedly in favor of all reasonable encouragement to promote, uphold, and cherish every thing of that kind.

But your memorialists had never dreamed it would ever be considered necessary or proper that all other interests should be made to yield as secondary and tributary to that alone. They are sure this was not the original design of the framers of the Constitution. In that instrument we find nothing about manufactures.

They, however, have pressed into their service an elaborate essay of the celebrated Alexander Hamilton on this subject. They have adopted his principles, but disregard their application. He insisted on the encouragement of manufactures so far as might be consistent with a due regard to commerce and the collection of revenue. The duties now are nearly treble what they were when he wrote, and, on an average, higher by one hundred per cent. than he, in the height of his zeal for manufactures, ever recommended.

In the case of iron, the duty on which was not half what it now is, he recommended a diminution, under an idea that it was almost a raw material, necessary in every kind of mechanism; and the same with regard to molasses, which we could ourselves distil. At the time he wrote it was necessary to urge, with great vehemence, upon the attention of Congress, this subject of encouraging manufactures, in order to have it attended to so far as might be compatible with the other great interests of the community. But he could not have foreseen this abuse and perversion of his reasoning. He never could have imagined that the time would come when it would be deemed good policy to make the people pay from thirty to one hundred per cent. more for goods to the manufacturer than they might otherwise be bought for of the importing merchant.

Your memorialists believe the duties now imposed on foreign manufactures to be fully adequate to any reasonable demand on the part of the American manufacturer. All the cotton and woollen manufactories which have been providently established and well managed are perfectly satisfied with the present rate of duties. From these we hear no complaint; and they are considerably numerous in the Northern and Eastern States. All such as were established without judgment, without capital, and without the aid of any skill whatever, have, of course, mouldered into ruin. Such it cannot comport with the wisdom or policy of Government to attempt to revive and uphold.

Your memorialists believe that the excitement in favor of manufacturers has had its origin rather in the improvidence and rash enterprise of some of our fellow-citizens than in any well-grounded cause of complaint. It may be that between 1812 and 1815 a state of things existed which induced individuals, in great numbers even, to plunge inconsiderately into extravagant and wild schemes in relation to manufactures. But it does not follow that the Government is, at all hazards, bound to uphold, protect, and save them from ruin. Every step which the Government might take, under such a supposed obligation, would but increase the evil, and create still new obligations predicated upon a similar unfortunate state of things. The final result would be a state and condition like that of Great Britain.

There, unfortunately, such solicitations in times past have been yielded to; and the nation now stands committed, at whatever cost, to stand by and uphold establishments which it would now gladly shake off. A glaring instance of the folly and stupidity of such engagements was but lately witnessed in that country. The merchants there petitioned for a greater freedom of trade, and complained, among other things, of being obliged to import timber from North America, stating that it could be imported from Norway at half the cost that it could from America. The ship-owners who were engaged in the importation from America preferred a counter petition, stating that since the Government had confined the importations to timber from America, they had been at immense expense in preparing ships to bring the vast quantities from America necessary for the supply of the kingdom; that if the trade of Norway in that article should be opened, no timber could be imported from America; and that one-half of their ships and equipments must be laid aside, as the other half would be adequate to bring the requisite amount from Norway; it being practicable to make two voyages to Norway in the time that would be requisite to perform one to America.

Thus it appeared that a vast quantity of shipping, and sailors in proportion, must be thrown out of employment, and ruined, if the British Government should not continue to compel its subjects to buy timber at twice what it would cost elsewhere.

And this is the case with an infinity of other establishments in that country. By the improvident interference of Government, establishments have been reared up and fostered, which they must uphold at every hazard, the faith of Government in this particular having been virtually pledged so to do. There is not a circumstance more alarming to your memorialists than that the manufacturers in this country are continually holding up the conduct of the British Government in this particular as affording the most perfect model for our imitation.

They are delighted with British exclusions, premiums, drawbacks, high and prohibitory duties, and the whole train of extravagant schemes, to retain the power of manufacturing exclusively for themselves, and, if possible, for the world besides.

The situation of this country is in nowise similar to that of Great Britain. We have no surplus population that cannot be retained but by such means. We have vacant territory without limit, and almost without price, inviting cultivation. There, they must manufacture or emigrate. And, notwithstanding the utmost of their exertions to find employment for their laboring poor, every seventh individual is a pauper, and dependent on charity. In this country, as yet, it is not even every hundredth individual that is a subject of charity; and many centuries may elapse before the proportion will be greater, if this manufacturing mania can be kept within bounds.

Your memorialists lament those strides on the part of manufacturers for another and more important reason. Steadiness in governmental regulations affecting the industry of the people is highly essential. There is at present a perfect acquiescence in all parts of the Union in relation to what has been done to favor manufactures, although it bears hard upon the revenue and upon commerce.

The effect of an extraordinary action is to produce reaction. If the manufacturers should now succeed, the consequence will be a deficit in the revenue. A direct tax must ensue; irritation will be produced; and, by the time the manufacturers shall have got their great establishments in operation, a new tariff will be enacted with a view to revenue solely. When the tariff was settled in 1816, the manufacturers were duly represented. The then Secretary of the Treasury was from the city of Philadelphia, and partook, it is believed, of all the feelings of the people upon this subject. At any rate, he recommended the tariff at that time with an express view to manufactures; and his recommendations, so far as they affected manufactures, in every instance, it is understood, except in relation to iron, were implicitly adopted. At that time the manufacturers, excepting those of iron, were perfectly satisfied; and in 1818, at the instance of the manufacturers, the duty on iron was increased from nine to fifteen dollars per ton. They, at the same time, requested that the duty of 25 per cent. on cotton and woollen goods, which had been limited to five

years, might be made perpetual. In this, also, they were gratified. Your memorialists expected to have heard no more from the manufacturers about further protecting duties. But the stride they are now contemplating is, to your memorialists, truly astonishing. Nothing now will satisfy them short of twenty-five dollars per ton upon iron, an article necessary in every piece of mechanism; thirty-five per cent. upon printed books, by way, it may be presumed, of discouraging science; ten cents per gallon on molasses, to protect the distillers of whiskey; thirty-three and a third per cent. upon cotton and woollen goods, and so upon other manufactured articles in proportion; and, to crown all, cash payment, without credit, for duties!

Should the wisdom of your honorable body deem it expedient and proper to yield to solicitations so unreasonable, the commerce of the country must be considered as at an end, and all concerned in it as devoted to inevitable ruin. The long established habits of the country must be subverted, and a shock will be felt in the community such as will arouse from their slumbers the mass of the people, and awaken them in time, but perhaps too late, to a sense of their true interests.

Your memorialists have thus, with the characteristic frankness of fellow-citizens, intimated some of their views and feelings on this all-important subject. Their destinies are in the power of the National Government, on whose wisdom and justice they trust they can rely. It is for Congress to determine whether the great interests of the nation, on which depend its power, its glory, and its resources, shall be sacrificed to the cupidity of a handful of improvident and speculating manufacturers.

Signed by order and in behalf of the convention.

ARTHUR McLELLAN,
Chairman.

HENRY CLARKE, *Sec'ry.*
PORTLAND, *October* 19, 1820.

INCREASE OF DUTIES ON IMPORTS.

[Communicated to the Senate, November 27, 1820.]

The memorial of a convention of delegates representing the merchants and others interested in commerce, assembled at Philadelphia, to the Congress of the United States:

Although much has already been addressed to your honorable body on the subject of the new tariff, yet, unless it could be said to be entirely exhausted, its pre-eminent importance may well claim still further attention from all who are interested, and may be allowed to constitute a valid excuse for those who venture once more to appear before you in the character of petitioners against its adoption.

Among the great diversity of subjects which, from time to time, have occupied our National Legislature, not one, it is believed, within the whole scope of their proceedings, has ever been

Remonstrance against an increase of Duties on Imports.

agitated which involves a greater variety of interests, fiscal, moral, and political; which strikes more deeply at the very foundation of all true and enlightened policy; and which, according as it shall be ultimately settled, will be productive of more lasting, more beneficial, or more pernicious consequences. In short, this nation, through its highest public functionaries, is called upon to determine whether we will plunge still deeper into all those measures of prohibition and restrictions upon trade; of duties, premiums, and bounties; of stimulants to rear exclusive interests at the national expense, which have contributed more than any other causes to bring the greatest commercial and manufacturing empire that the world ever saw to the very verge of destruction; or, by taking warning in time, and pursuing a different course, achieve for ourselves a far higher degree of national prosperity than any people, of whom there is any record, have ever before attained. Let it not be said that we are too much inclined to magnify, beyond their just dimensions, the various objects involved in this inquiry; still less let it be said that the injuries or benefits which must necessarily result from the adoption or the rejection of the proposed tariff will not be fully equal, in process of time, to any thing which we have ventured to imagine. If the observation of Doctor Smith has been thought just, that heavy taxes upon necessaries become "a curse equal to the barrenness of the soil and the inclemency of the heavens," let it not be thought extravagant in us to assert that the additional duties required of you, of operating continually upon almost all the purchases of every member in the community, although a small and insignificant sum, comparatively speaking, in each individual purchase, would amount, in a few years, to a sufficient number of millions almost entirely to alter the existing relations of society, by forcing capital out of those channels in which it is naturally inclined to flow, and alluring it into others, where, but for this legislative process, it never, perhaps, would have gone. Can this be consonant either to policy or justice? Can such a power be found, either in the constitutions or codes of any free Government upon earth, as would authorize the Legislature of such Government to say to any of the great classes into which society naturally divides itself, "thus far shalt thou go and no farther" in thy fair and honest endeavors to better thy condition? And yet, in what does such a power differ in effect from that by the operation of which any one of these classes may be fostered, cherished, and elevated at the expense of the rest, until the others, who are forced into this most unnatural state, are so ground down as to be compelled to abandon the trade, profession, or calling of their choice? Once admit that Congress may use the power of taxing imports *ad libitum*, for any other purpose than that of revenue, and you give them, in reality, the power to say to the citizens of these United States—you must devote yourselves to agriculture, commerce, or manufactures, not as you may happen to be inclined, but according to our sovereign will and pleasure. Let it never be forgotten that the question now about to

be determined is not so much what may be beneficial to manufacturers, as whether Government has a right to benefit them to the manifest injury both of the agricultural and commercial classes; whether the Constitutional provision against taxing exports can be rendered in a great measure nugatory, by diminishing, at pleasure, the value of our exportable commodities, through the instrumentality of a tax upon imports; and, finally, whether the direction and employment of individual capital are matters to be regulated and controlled by individual choice, or by the will of the National Legislature.

If it be asked who are the rightful judges in regard to the expediency and justice of the proposed tariff, it is surely fair to answer, that the payers, who constitute a very large majority of the whole nation, are certainly more competent to decide than the expectant receivers; when the only inquiry is, how much of the money of the former shall be paid to the latter, and to what extent it shall be taken, not only without their consent, but in opposition both to their entreaties and remonstrances. This is the plain unvarnished state of the case; and, let sophists and casuists disguise it as they may, still, whenever it is contemplated, unadorned by the embellishments of geographical parties, and divested of the exaggerations of exclusive interests, it will be seen as a case where, on the one hand, a certain portion only of manufacturers (for very many of them are opposed to it) are importuning the Government to compel all the commercial and agricultural classes to buy their manufactures at enhanced prices or to go without; whilst, on the other hand, the sons of commerce and agriculture, almost to a man, are begging that they may not be exposed to any such exaction. It is not a boon or treasure, already in possession of the Government, of which each party is praying to have the exclusive enjoyment—for that would be a mere contest of cupidity, wherein both would be alike selfish and culpable; but it is a plain undisguised effort, on the part of certain manufacturers, either to coax or alarm our rulers into the ruinous project of coercing the farmers, planters, artisans, and merchants, into giving a much larger portion of their substance than they at present do to these manufacturers; whilst, on the part of agriculture and commerce, it is an arduous struggle to hold fast only what is already theirs, and not to be forced to part with it contrary to their inclinations. Are we, therefore, enemies to the manufacturers? Are we, consequently, (as has often been said,) selfish, unnatural, antisocial, grovelling, and ignorant, alike deaf to the voice of humanity and to the calls of patriotism? God forbid! But if we have incurred these degrading censures simply for praying that your honorable body will not put it in the power of the manufacturers to make us pay more for all which we must necessarily purchase of them than we do at present, we must still submit to be denounced.

But lest the mere pecuniary loss in our purchases alone, which we should incur from the proposed addition to the duties upon foreign commodities, should be considered the principal cause of our solicitude, we beg leave to suggest a few other considerations of far deeper interest, and of still more comprehensive character, that appear to us to forbid the adoption of the proposed measure. If it be a fixed principle that we are to rely for our revenue chiefly upon a system of duties upon imports, can any thing be more obviously necessary and proper than that such system should be both uniform and permanent? Can a single instance be cited, from the annals of any nation upon earth, where an augmentation of duties, already high, has been found to augment the national income? On the contrary, are there not many to be found wherein a diminution of duty has been immediately followed by an increase of revenue? We beg leave to quote only a few, and we will take them from the history of that country whose commercial regulations and restrictions some of our political economists have so earnestly importuned you to imitate. "Previous to 1744, the East India Company's sales of teas amounted to no more than about six hundred thousand pounds weight, annually, producing a revenue of about £140,000. In the early part of 1745 an act was passed by which the tea duties were greatly reduced; and in 1746 the sales amounted to nearly two millions of pounds weight, and the revenue to £228,000. But this unanswerable demonstration of the superior advantages resulting to the revenue itself from low duties, was unable to restrain the rapacity of the Treasury. In 1748 the duties were again increased, and fluctuated between that epoch and 1784 from 64 to 119 per cent. In the last-mentioned year, however, the Government, having in vain tried every other means to prevent the smuggling and adulteration of tea, reduced the duty from 119 to 12½ per cent.; and the revenue, instead of falling off in the proportion of one to ten, owing to the increased consumption only declined in the proportion of one to three. In 1787 the duty on wine and spirits was lowered 50 per cent., but the revenue, notwithstanding, was considerably augmented. The average annual produce of the tax on coffee, for the three years previous to 1808, amounted to £166,000. In the course of that year the duty was reduced from two shillings to seven-pence the hundred weight; and the average annual produce of the reduced duty for the next three years, instead of being diminished, rose to £195,000."

These few remarkable facts serve, incontestably, to prove, more than whole libraries of theoretical reasoning could do, that the financier who calculates upon raising revenue by duties upon imports must, unavoidably, be content to make them moderate, or to lose his object. They also force upon our minds this important question: Whether the deficit which occurred in our revenue last year, and the still greater one which threatens us for the present year, are not both attributable, at least in part, to the very high rates of many of our existing duties?

If the design of the proposed tariff be to force into being certain manufactures which had no previous existence here, or to foster, at the national expense, such as have been found, after sufficient

trial, incapable of being otherwise supported, the hope of revenue from this source must be abandoned; for it is a physical impossibility that the two projects can be consummated together. If manufactures are to be forced, the Treasury coffers must remain empty, for any thing that the tariff can bring into them; on the contrary, if the duties upon imports are to augment the revenue, the manufacturing interest must be content to rely upon her own energies, without calling on Government to make crutches for her of both agriculture and commerce, to support that body which, in the mania of speculation, has been dieted and swelled into an unnatural growth, too unwieldy for her own natural limbs to sustain.

Let us take another view of the subject. If it has become a settled point in our policy that no justifiable means are to be neglected to render this nation a great naval Power, (as essential to the Union as protective of the great and only outlet for all the agricultural products of the immense regions of the West,) it is well worthy of inquiry whether it possibly can be effected by multiplying discouragements to foreign commerce. Can our hardy, magnanimous, and dauntless seamen, whose pursuits have heretofore exposed them to the perils of every ocean, to the vicissitudes of every clime, and inured them to that constant regimen and discipline so well calculated to fit them for all the purposes of nautical life—can such men, with any advantage to our rising navy, be converted into a set of skulking, profligate smugglers, or of sailors confined solely to the coasting trade? Yet, that such must be the inevitable result of either destroying, or much further injuring our foreign commerce, is a consummation which appears to us as unavoidable as that death must follow the destruction of all our vital functions. Commerce is to the body politic what the circulation of the blood is to the body natural; to check either materially, is to produce disease; and to augment such check, in any degree, is to destroy the healthful existence of both. Again: is it possible that we shall add much either to the moral or physical power of this nation by interposing legislative aids to accelerate the natural increase of that class of citizens, who, from the very nature of most of their occupations, must necessarily be brought up in a way which (to say the least of it) is surely not the most favorable either to health, to morals, or to bodily or intellectual vigor? Can it be within the scope of any rational anticipation that our manufacturers, one and all, can ever be made successful competitors to those of Sheffield, Birmingham, and Manchester, who, by means of the very system of which some of us are so exceedingly emulous, are forced to labor from fourteen to seventeen hours in the twenty-four, and to live almost exclusively on vegetable diet, in order to earn a miserable pittance of wages, scarcely sufficient to keep body and soul together? Can any the most sanguine projector calculate on realizing any such successful rivalry, except at an expense of taxation, of national happiness, and legislative oppression, such as the citizens of the United States will never willingly incur?

Remonstrance against an increase of Duties on Imports.

In whatever way we view this subject, (and we have endeavored to bestow on it all the consideration which its great importance so justly merits,) we cannot avoid anticipating, from the success of the tariff project, irreparable injury, not only to agriculture and commerce, but to many of the mechanical trades immediately connected with and dependent upon these two great sources of the wealth and physical power of this nation. Agriculture, already bereft of half her ability to pay taxes by a combination of circumstances, among which our protecting duty system holds a prominent station, is now called upon to pay a still further tax of some ten, twenty, or thirty per cent. upon almost all her necessary purchases—at a time, too, when the existing duties have been more than doubled in value to those who receive the benefit of them, by the appreciation of money, and the depreciation of domestic provisions of every kind; a depreciation, moreover, so continued and portentous, as to threaten to terminate even the culture of several of those products which heretofore have most contributed both to our emolument and to our comforts. What is to be the consequence? Why, a rapid and appalling retrogradation throughout the community, compelling us not only to relinquish most of those embellishments of civilized life which polish and adorn the social structure, but also to bid adieu to all fond hopes which solace the parent and animate the patriot, in regard to the progress of education, the improvement of morals, and the general diffusion of national happiness. Commerce, curtailed in all her branches by the same sinister combination of events, is required still further to furl her sails, or to spread them only to the breezes of our bays, our rivers, and our seaboard; or, if not deterred by the numerous difficulties which present themselves to her customary pursuits, she still essays to spread her canvass over the bosom of those distant seas, from navigating which she has heretofore hoped to derive a fair and honorable reward for her toils, she is told that a large portion of her now scanty profits must go to foster a new interest in our community, which it has been found upon trial cannot be gotten up without levying still heavier contributions both on agriculture and commerce. The numerous artisans, too, whose reliance for comfortable support has hitherto been placed upon the prosperity of agricultural and commercial occupations, must now be transferred to some other less precarious dependence, or their present employments exchanged for hopeless inaction. And what is the inestimable boon held out to us as a compensation for all these privations? Why, truly, an adequate home market for all our domestic products! That this idea is altogether fallacious, we trust can be made manifest by a very few remarks. The manufacturing establishments which, it is said, will grow out of the tariff, are to be peopled from the population already within the country, or to be supplied by foreign importations. If in the first mode, then it is obvious that, unless we suppose the intended recruits can live in their present scattered condition without food altogether, they will not, when imbodied, con-

sume so much more additional provision as to compensate for the great diminution of exports which the new tariff must necessarily occasion. It is only, then, by the importation of that class of foreigners, (the least desirable part, in general, of foreign population,) that the number of manufacturing consumers, and consequently the quantum of consumption, can be materially augmented. This is unquestionably true as to provisions. But, it will be said, our raw materials will then find so much more extensive a market than they have at present, as amply to remunerate us for all additional costs. If it were true that we had no home market at all for our agricultural products, it might become a question with some whether it would not be worth while to incur a considerable national expense with a view to create one, provided it was probable that the domestic sale for our surplus produce would then be so much greater than the foreign sale extinguished by this creation as to reimburse those at whose cost it was made for all additional expenses. But this happens not to be a fact. Your honorable body cannot be ignorant that our home market for the product of the soil, especially for cotton, is even now on the increase; that a large portion of our manufacturers claim no further protection, ask no additional duties; that the stockholders of one of the most considerable and flourishing manufactories in the United States, (we mean that of Waltham, in Massachusetts,) at this time divide twelve per cent. on their capital; and that most others of any standing are known to be in a sufficiently flourishing condition to ask no aid from Government. The question, then, is simply reduced to this; shall we impose additional duties upon almost every article of foreign importation, either to gratify the sanguine expectations of those who wish to make trial of such manufactories as do not exist here at present, or to enable those who have failed, no matter from what cause, in manufacturing experiments already made in various parts of our country, to renew them at the expense of more than three-fourths of the nation? Relying as we do upon the wisdom and patriotism of our Legislature, we cannot for a moment believe that, from the freest Government upon earth, we are to expect a system of policy so repugnant to every principle of reason and justice as would be that which your honorable body has been so importunately urged to adopt. And we confidently trust that the men to whose intelligence and virtue the American people have intrusted the preservation of their dearest rights and interests are as deeply impressed as any of their constituents themselves can possibly be with the truth and importance of the following cardinal maxims in legislation:

That, if the principles both of justice and policy forbid the majority of a nation to impose any tax on the minority alone, *a fortiori* they inhibit the imposition of any tax to be levied upon the former for the sole benefit of the latter. That, where revenue is to be derived from impost on foreign commodities, universal experience has demonstrated that moderate duties contribute much more than high ones towards the attainment of this object.

Remonstrance against an increase of Duties on Imports.

That, where such duties are imposed to foster the particular interest of any class who pay no part thereof, those duties must necessarily come out of the pockets of all other classes in the community, and are in direct violation of the fundamental maxim "not to tax the many for the benefit of the few."

That the practice of frequently changing those revenue laws which operate as taxes upon agriculture and commerce have a much more pernicious effect upon both, but especially on the last, than permanent taxes of the highest kind, compatible with the permanent existence of those two great sources of national wealth and power.

That for Government, by legislation, to add to those casualties and uncertainties which naturally affect the profits of labor, is to infringe on the natural right which every man has to pursue any trade, profession, or calling that he pleases, and is to administer oppression instead of justice.

That, by the exercise of such a power, Governments may not only force individual capital into any channel which they please, but may either create or suppress, *ad libitum*, any particular class among the various ones into which communities are usually divided.

That the reciprocal wants of agriculture, commerce, and manufactures, with their relative capacities of supply, are sure guarantees of mutual good and friendly offices, when left to exert their respective energies in their own way; but that the interference of Governments with their private concerns rarely fails to produce a jarring of interest, and consequent hostilities both of feelings and conduct.

That the natural diversities of soils and climates, and the artificial varieties of manners, habits, and customs, are far better regulators of supply and demand than the wisest legislators can possibly contrive.

That a due proportion of heat, moisture, and the pabulum of plants, will not more certainly produce a vigorous and healthful growth in the vegetable kingdom, than will the natural inclination of mankind to improve their condition produce it in the political world, if left to exert itself entirely free from all legislative restraints but such as peace, order, justice, and good morals require.

And that it may be laid down as a maxim admitting of no exception, that national industry is invigorated by free trade, and depressed by every thing opposed to it. All which is, &c.

WILLIAM BAYARD,
President of the Convention.

JOHN VAUGHAN, *Secretary.*

PHILADELPHIA, *November* 4, 1820.

INCREASE OF DUTIES ON IMPORTS.

[Communicated to the Senate, December 8, 1820.

To the honorable the President and members of the Senate of the United States of America:

The citizens of Charleston have seen, with deep regret, the efforts which were made at the last

16th CON. 2d SESS.—48

session of Congress to impose a high rate of duties on all manufactured articles imported into the United States—efforts made for the express and avowed purpose of creating, encouraging, and supporting, in this country, great manufacturing establishments; of modifying and curtailing extensively our mercantile intercourse with foreign nations; and of forcing from their present employments much of the labor and capital of our fellow-citizens.

As there is much cause to apprehend that this measure will again be presented to the consideration of Congress, your memorialists beg leave to state the reasons which have led them to view this measure as one unfavorable to the general interests of the United States; as one likely to prove partial in its operations, injurious in its effects, uncertain in its results; as one which departs equally from the spirit of our constitution and the best established principles of national economy. It is a position almost too self-evident for controversy, that, in every free or well-regulated Government, labor and capital should be permitted to seek and to find their own employment. To the sagacity of individuals this trust may be safely committed. A Government can never regulate to advantage, the employment of capital; because success in the pursuit of wealth, in every department of life, depends on local circumstances, or minute details, on personal exertions, which cannot be regulated, on causes that escape those general views which alone a Government can take of the transactions of its citizens. It is sufficient that a Government takes care that the employment of each individual shall inflict on others or on the community at large no injury, and that each shall receive equal and uniform protection; all interference beyond this is useless or pernicious. It is equally obvious that those employments of capital which are most profitable to the individual must, on a general scale, prove the most advantageous to the State. National is but the aggregate of individual wealth; whenever, therefore, capital is diverted from one employment, in which it makes a certain profit, to another, in which a smaller profit only can be obtained, the difference between these employments of capital is exactly, to the extent of that difference, an actual loss to the community. Now, whenever individuals are induced to engage in the less profitable employment by assurances of national indemnity; whenever the rest of the community are compelled to make good the losses which, by these enterprises, may be sustained, the results are not only injurious, but unjust; because, while the nation, as the whole, becomes a loser by these idle projects, the many are obliged to surrender a portion of their fair and well-earned profits to enable the few to amuse themselves unnecessarily with unprofitable speculations. But if, from the state of society, or from local circumstances, this measure should be partial in its operation; if this forced employment of capital should be confined to a particular portion of country, the injustice becomes doubly great; because it then not merely causes a transfer of property among the individuals of each particular division of territory, without affecting the general wealth of those divisions, but some entire districts are absolutely impoverished, while others are exclusively enriched.

Under all these aspects, the new tariff presented to Congress at its last session merits our disapprobation. Its avowed object is, by imposing heavy duties on the importation of foreign manufactures, to grant high bounties to all of the capital which shall be employed in manufactures in the United States; and by shackling, at the same time, and curtailing our commerce, to force, by these united measures, to the loom and the workshop much of the labor and capital which are now employed in agriculture and commerce. This is unnecessary or unwise. If labor and capital employed in manufactures will produce as much profit as in agriculture or commerce, it is unnecessary; because the cupidity and intelligence of individuals, when unrestrained in their pursuits, will soon turn them into this channel. If they will not produce as much profit, it is unwise; because labor and capital will, by these means, be forced into an unprofitable employment. Every laborer employed in unproductive occupations must become, directly or indirectly, a burden on the community. He will either become a pauper, to be supported directly by the charity of his fellow-citizens, or he must be supported indirectly, by their consenting to pay more for the products of his labor than would purchase the same products from other quarters. It is to this point that the premature establishment of manufactures will lead; and the effort now made to impose heavy duties or prohibitions on foreign manufactures is only to disguise, in this shape, the bounties we must pay to the laborers engaged in the domestic fabrication. We are aware that the employment of capital is not always determined by its absolute profit. Other circumstances have, and deserve to have, much influence on the pursuits of men. It has heretofore been said that the price of labor and provisions in this country was so high as to render the establishment of manufactures impracticable; that bounties were indispensable to give them life, and even a temporary existence. This was virtually to abandon the question, and to acknowledge that labor in other pursuits obtained a profit which could not be afforded to it in this. But a new aspect is now given to this discussion. The price of provisions, which, for many years continued unusually high, has now fallen to a level preternaturally low; labor must fall in proportion; and when these preliminary advantages are obtained, why should systems of restriction be still wanting? Why should public exertions be required to force labor into this channel? There can be but one reply, which is, that to the establishment of manufactures our state of society is still unpropitious. The surface of our vast territory is still insufficiently supplied with laborers; our forests are still uncleared; and much of our most fertile soil is still untrodden. Man—even the poor man—will not seclude himself within the walls of a manufactory while he can possibly find a maintenance in the more cheerful walks of agricultural industry. The life of the husbandman is one of

comparative enjoyment. In his path are health, and temperance, and peace, with a mind exercised and improved, and a proud spirit of independence encouraged and preserved. He looks for his subsistence not to one man, nor to a few; wherever there is earth, and air, and a soil to be cultivated, he may find employment. But the monotonous and melancholy toils of the manufacturer, confined for days and years to one spot and one unchanging occupation, contract the mind, debilitate the constitution, and render him more dependent than the laborer in any other occupation. One country in Europe bears, in this point of view, a strong resemblance to our own. Russia possesses an almost unlimited extent of fertile territory, thinly inhabited, and still offering to the husbandman unstinted occupation. In Russia, for the last forty years, (perhaps for a century past,) provisions and labor have been cheaper than in any other country in Europe; yet, in Russia, manufactures have made no permanent progress. Like ourselves, the inhabitants manufacture a few articles to which their circumstances are peculiarly favorable. During the existence of what was termed the continental system, efforts were made in that country to diffuse manufactures extensively; and the necessity is now imposed on the Government of embarrassing its commerce, in order to afford some protection to the establishments which have been prematurely called into existence. But the Russians are not, and will not soon become, a manufacturing nation. The same causes appear to have produced with them, and with us, similar effects. The peasantry, even when unthralled by their system of vassalage, can still find subsistence by tilling the soil; and the ineffaceable love of nature, only to be overpowered in the human mind by a stern necessity, leads them to prefer the coarse and scanty enjoyments of the rustic laborer to the more dependent, though more flattering, occupation of the manufacturer. Surely the moral influence of such feelings and opinions ought not to be disregarded, nor can their political effects be overlooked in an enlightened Government. When an overflowing population shall naturally give rise to extensive manufactures, we will then rejoice in their establishment, as a means of varying the application of capital, and of giving employment to suffering industry; we will share with them equally our rights, our privileges, and our immunities: but we perceive no motive for producing artificially such a state of society. The experience of Europe teaches us that the population of great manufacturing cities is very ignorant, very immoral, very poor, and very dependent; and yet, from the facility with which, from their numbers, the workmen can combine, from their misery, and from the fluctuating nature and results of the pursuits in which they are engaged, they become the most disorderly and discontented citizens in the whole community. For such a population shall we voluntarily exchange the tillers of our soil? Shall we drive, almost with violence, our citizens from the ploughshare and the scythe? And if, upon this subject, we require additional cautions, let us remember how much more stable has been the power and prosperity of agricultural nations than of those founded on any other basis.

Every duty on imported commodities operates as a tax on the consumer. When these taxes are imposed only to supply the necessary wants of the Government, they are cheerfully paid; when imposed to enrich individuals, we should surely consider well on what grounds the claims of such individuals are advanced; we should inquire carefully what reciprocal benefit the public will receive. It is the interest of every member of the community to purchase the articles he may wish, or be obliged to consume, at the lowest possible price. This increases the value of his exchangeable commodities, and increases, of course, his enjoyments. Whenever this privilege is abridged, it becomes him to inquire whether, as an individual, or as a member of the community, he receives an equivalent advantage. The great plea for taxation advanced in this case is, that domestic manufactures will make us independent of foreign nations. This is certainly important in itself; but, when advanced as a ground for forcing artificially the production of every thing we want, the plea is every way fallacious. Physical independence consists in possessing those articles absolutely necessary for our existence. These we have long since enjoyed. Few nations are, from the bounty of Providence, more independent than the United States. Beyond this, the independence of the savage consists in his exemption from all wants; the independence of the civilized man, in his power of supplying and gratifying the wants of social life. Wealth to him, in this view, is independence; and wealth consists in the quantity of consumable articles he can obtain for the surplus labor or produce he may have to exchange; and this, in a great measure, depends on the liberty he possesses of exchanging those articles under the fewest restraints, and consequently, to the greatest advantage. Whatever curtails this power lessens his wealth; whatever diminishes his wealth abridges his independence. If, under a new system, the surplus labor of an individual will procure for him but one-half of the articles of consumption which he has hitherto been accustomed to receive for the same labor, what compensation will it be to him to know that this diminished supply was produced in his own country, or even on his own farm? But if this argument is really valid, it will extend much farther than its present advocates mean to apply it. If it is necessary that a nation, to be independent, should raise within itself every article it has occasion to consume, it will be much more important to raise those of general consumption than those which may merely gratify the wants of luxury and fashion. If, therefore, we are by bounties to fill our Northern cities with manufactories to furnish articles with which we could well dispense—if this is necessary to our independence, equally so will it be to cover our pine barrens with hot-houses, to raise the sugar and coffee, the tea and pepper, and the other productions of tropical climates; to give high rewards for the manufacture of wine, and oil, and salt, and many other articles, which are daily required in our domestic consumption.

Sufficient bounties will furnish us with a domestic supply of those articles, all of which are now in common use; and some, from our habits, articles almost of necessity. And when one portion of our countrymen call for bounties to create manufactures to which our state of society is unfavorable, let them act uniformly, and at the same time grant bounties to raise those articles to which our climate is unpropitious. The attempt will be equally practicable, and equally wise. In truth, if this plea is of any avail; if this absolute local independence is of real importance, it applies as strongly to sectional as to national divisions. If it is desirable that a nation should produce within itself all the articles necessary for its consumption, it is equally desirable that each division of that nation, each province or State, each district, each plantation, each farm, each individual, should equally possess this power. If every nation is dependent that is obliged to purchase the production or manufactures of other climates or countries, every individual must be in the same degree dependent who has to purchase the products of the labor of other men. There is no distinction in the argument; there is no pause until we arrive at that state where each individual shall produce for himself every article which he may wish to consume, and must consent to want every article which he cannot raise or fabricate. This will carry us back to that condition in which the semi-barbarous people of Europe existed during the pressure of the feudal system; when almost all intercourse between individuals and nations was interdicted; when nothing was interchanged but injuries, nothing remembered but oppression and wrong. How much more simple and more wise is it for each nation to raise or manufacture those articles which are most congenial to its soil and to the habit of the people, and exchange its superfluous productions for the productions of other climates and other conditions of society; to perpetuate, if possible, amicable relations with all countries, by the firmest of all ties—reciprocal advantages; remembering always that, in proportion as this interchange is free and unrestricted, will be the mutual benefit it will confer! We acknowledge that most foreign Governments still impose great restrictions on national intercourse; that they have made great exertions and immense sacrifices to produce at home manufactures of all descriptions; great efforts to secure this species of independence; and it is really from the experience of foreign nations that we are inclined to suspect the wisdom of their practice. We have seen them impose upon themselves a population which they are obliged to support; entangle themselves in a system from which, even when their ablest statesmen deplore its effects, they cannot, without a revolution, be extricated. The very magnitude of the evil prevents a remedy. The amount of capital and the number of people engaged in an unprofitable employment may render it cruel, if not impracticable, to withdraw from it the countenance and support by which it was first encouraged. And the influence which so strong an interest, and one so easily combined, can exert over any Government, should make us in this country very cautious how we render that a claim which, at first, may be regarded as a favor. It is, in the present instance, to the extraordinary combination of interests and of exertions among a class of citizens whose pursuits are very distinct, and whose title or pretensions to support are widely different—it is to this demand for indiscriminate encouragement, that we particularly object; it is from this combined effort to force our Government from its position, that we view with apprehension and alarm the application of the united body of manufacturers, even when advancing new, and, as we think, unreasonable claims. What administration would ever have the power or the resolution to withdraw from them hereafter any privileges which may have once been improvidently granted. Neither should it be forgotten how hostile to the general spirit of our Constitution is every system of restriction, of monopoly, of particular privileges. It has been our boast and our highest advantage that we have been able to commence an experimental Government, liberated from fall those encumbrances and embarrassments which time and circumstance, and prejudice and ignorance, have imposed on the old Governments of Europe—encumbrances which, even in an enlightened age, they cannot remove; that we have been able to bring to the test of experience the theories and speculations of the statesman and the philosopher; that we have been able to exemplify, most particularly, the advantages of unlimited freedom in the pursuits and opinions of men. Our own career has been one of unexampled prosperity; our own experience forms one of the most instructive records of history. Most unwise shall we be, if, forsaking our own doctrines, and untaught by our own lessons, we shall abandon the simple but sublime principles by which we have hitherto been guided, to adopt the temporary, fluctuating, disjointed expedients of European practice.

We regret when we are compelled to advert to local or sectional advantages, or to view our own interests as distinct from those of any other portion of our fellow-citizens; but the circumstances which have lately been forced upon our attention oblige us to view this question in relation to our own immediate interests. The Southern States are not, and cannot for a long series of years become, a manufacturing nation. We have not a population equal to the cultivation of our soil; and the insalubrity of our climate forbids the hope that this deficiency will soon, if ever, be supplied by a population of white laborers. We raise, and must continue to raise provisions, articles of the first necessity for man in every climate, and raw materials for the use and consumption of manufacturing nations. It is, therefore, peculiarly our interests that our interchange with the world should be free; that the markets for the consumption of our produce should be extended as widely as the habitations of man. It is equally our interest that the articles we are compelled to consume should be procured on the most advantageous terms. We are among the last people who should wish to restrict the freedom of commerce, or, by limiting

on our part national intercourse, induce other nations to impose countervailing restrictions upon us. Let us not flatter ourselves that the statesmen of Europe will permit a system of restrictions to be partial in its operations. It is a matter almost of delicacy to touch this part of the subject; but it is idle to shut our eyes to our danger. Let us, then, examine the possible (we may say probable) effects of this system on the great staple of our country. Our cotton is now admitted into Great Britain on terms as liberal as the cotton of any foreign nation. It can be carried to her ports in our own vessels. In fact, this trade is now chiefly carried on in the vessels of the United States; and by this means some of our most important manufactures (those connected with ship building) are encouraged, and the security and reputation of our country are increased by the seamen it nurtures and protects. To this trade Great Britain consents, because to her the general commerce of the United States is highly important, and because our consumption of her manufactures offers an equivalent for the advantages we now enjoy. But let us once declare that this trade in future shall be beneficial only to ourselves; that we will take nothing from her, while we wish her still to continue the great consumer of our produce; and we may soon feel the error of such calculations. If, for instance, we should prohibit in this country the introduction of the manufactures of Great Britain, or impose on them duties amounting to a prohibition, have we no reason to apprehend that she may, on her part, prohibit totally the introduction into her ports of our cotton, our rice, and our tobacco, and turn to other quarters for the supply she may require? Brazil and the East Indies can even now furnish her with these articles in sufficient abundance, and, independent of the advantages she would derive from her general intercourse with these countries, the transportation of these very commodities would be exclusively in her own vessels, and her ship owners and her seamen would equally profit by this direction of her commerce. The new Governments, too, arising in South America, possess an immense extent of territory adapted to the production of cotton, and tobacco, and flour, and rice. All of them must at first become agricultural nations, and for a long time they will have to exchange the rude productions of their soil for the manufactures of other countries. On all sides we shall meet competitors in the consuming markets, ready to avail themselves of our errors and profit by our mistakes; ready to occupy any position which we may abandon, or from which we may be driven. Nor can we doubt of this result. Have we ever found the statesmen of the civilized world insensible to the interests of their respective nations? Have we ever found them deficient in sagacity to perceive, or in promptness to meet, the hostile combinations of foreign commerce? The interchange of nations, like the intercourse of individuals, can only be maintained by mutual and reciprocal advantages; and the experience of the world appears clearly to demonstrate that the more free is that intercourse, the more unfettered the commerce and capital of any nation, the more will the pursuits of that nation become extensive and diversified, and exempt from the fluctuation and ruin which finally must attend every system established on a forced employment of capital. Against these evils the prospect is held out to us of a domestic market for the consumption of our raw materials. This prospect is certainly delusive. In the United States we could only calculate to manufacture for the supply of our own wants, and this would not consume one-half—perhaps not one-third—part of the cotton we now raise, without adverting to the other staples of the country, or without bringing into view the rapidly increasing production of our Western States. Surely we cannot expect to become exporters of manufactures when we are obliged to call for enormous duties to protect them against competition even in our own markets, and when it is acknowledged that the removal of these duties will at any moment prostrate the whole system in remediless ruin. And for this insufficient and insecure market we are called upon to invite and provoke the commercial hostility of the whole civilized world, and to expose ourselves to the risk of having our productions driven from every country where the Government may think that reciprocal advantages should form the basis of every encouraged or even tolerated commerce. The Southern States will derive no immediate advantage from this measure, even if it should prove successful; but they are urged to promote it with the hope of creating a market for their productions, which may protect them from the evils they may feel on the possible failure of all foreign markets. And for this remote and contingent benefit, for this possible supply of a possible want, they are to endure many privations, to submit to many impositions, and to jeopardize the most important and valuable interests of our country. Of the importance of our foreign commerce—of its influence on the revenue, or even on the protection of our country, it is idle to expatiate. But one view, connected intimately with the question before us, we wish to notice. Foreign commerce draws wealth from abroad, and those engaged in it may prosper, without in any degree injuring the prosperity of other portions of the community. It is, in fact, the great principle of life which gives activity and energy to all of the operations of productive industry. It ranges over the world to discover the markets in which each particular commodity can most advantageously be exchanged; and the very transportation of these commodities becomes a source of great profit, and furnishes at the same time an arm of defence, which no nation should, without very serious consideration, perm t to decay.

It is easily seen and acknowledged that, by this system, our foreign commerce will be deranged and materially diminished; but no one has undertaken to predict the extent of the injury. Indeed, the combinations of commerce are rarely seen or understood even by those most deeply engaged in its operations. The exchanges that appear the most simple are sometimes the result, sometimes only a term, in a series of exchanges that have been made, or are yet to be completed in the most

distant regions of the globe. The commerce that is carried on with one country is frequently dependent for its success on a commerce carried on through different channels, and under a different aspect, with some remote and unconnected nation. When we touch such a system rudely, we know not what portion may perish from our rashness or our ignorance. Surely, at a moment like the present, when the commerce of the whole world is embarrassed and debilitated, it would be most unwise to add to the inevitable evils of the hour. Let us rather foster that portion which remains; extend, by every possible means, its enterprises; and give new vigor to its exertions. Every interest and occupation in our country has suffered within the last two years by the rapid decrease of the circulating currency of the world, and by the fall in the price of labor and of produce, which has resulted in part from this diminished circulation, and in part from the steady continuance of peace among the civilized nations of the globe. But of the great interests of our country, no one can doubt that the mercantile has suffered most; and if bounties could be afforded to any one class of our citizens, the claims of the merchant for past losses and present embarrassments would be the strongest. Yet on this class we now wish to impose new burdens, and render more precarious the still hazardous ocean of commercial enterprise. Nor can we possibly overlook, on this occasion, that class of our citizens to whom this nation is virtually indebted for so much of its wealth and so much of its renown; nor think, without emotion, of discarding from our employment and driving into foreign service the seamen who, through so many years of discouragement, continued faithful to their country; who, in the hour of peril, have always been the foremost to rally around her banners; who, in war, have encircled her with glory, and in peace, still patient, still laborious, have quietly returned to an arduous, an unceasing, and a dangerous occupation. With such a race we wish not to part. Another evil of great magnitude presses on our attention. A duty of thirty, fifty, and one hundred per cent. is called for on all articles of foreign manufacture. This is virtually to admit that the productions of the foreign artisan can be sold in our markets at one-half or two-thirds of the price for which they can be manufactured at home. Will not the prospect, therefore, of immense profits lead to the illicit introduction of foreign manufactures—to the creation on our frontiers of an organized system of smuggling? This will be the more to be apprehended when these impositions are opposed to the general interests and wishes of the community. Public opinion will no longer, as at present, guard from violation the revenue laws of the country. Now, they are considered merely as the means of providing for the necessary support of our Government; as operating fairly, mildly, and equally on all classes of our citizens, and as preventing the imposition of more direct and more vexatious burdens. Yet, even now, intelligent men doubt whether the tariff is not in many instances unwisely high, and whether the temptations held out to smuggling

Remonstrance against an increase of Duties on Imports.

are not greater than a prudent Government ought to offer. Under a higher tariff, the duties will be considered as partial, and for the exclusive benefit of a small portion of the nation. They will be transgressed; the revenue of the country will be injured; and the Government will be compelled to increase the severity of our penal laws, and to add enormously to the expense of guarding those laws against violation. This is not all. It is candidly admitted that this system, if adopted, will so derange and circumscribe our commerce that we shall no longer look to our custom-houses for the support of our Government. We must, as a constituent part of this plan, adopt a regular and permanent system of direct taxation. After having paid bounties innumerable for the support of manufactures, we must pay taxes to make good that revenue which those very bounties have tended to diminish. We shall have to divert to our daily support the resources which will be wanted, and should be reserved, for the hour of danger; and we shall incur unnecessarily the risk of alienating from the Government the affections of the people. We have yet to add the probability (perhaps, the certainty) that, after all, this great effort will be altogether useless. If these manufactures can only exist by excluding from our markets the productions of foreign workshops, what power moral or physical that we possess can secure the exclusion? If Bonaparte, while enforcing his continental system by the most arbitrary and sanguinary decrees, and by the efficient power of a great military despotism, could not close the continent of Europe against British manufactures; if Great Britain, with her insular situation and her multitude of ships, cannot prevent her coast from becoming a great mart and theatre of smugglers, how can we hope, with our mild laws, to prevent intrusion on every point of our extended and unprotected shores? How can we guard the long line of our Northern and Northeastern frontier, even from the mid-day trespasser? Our revenue will be destroyed, our legal and honorable commerce curtailed, and the morals of our citizens vitiated by the temptations and frauds of a contraband traffic; while the manufacturers themselves may be overwhelmed by the reaction of their own system; for there can be little doubt that our country would be inundated by foreign manufactures, liberated even from the impositions, and those not light ones, which they are now compelled to pay. And, surely, when we examine the present claims advanced by the manufacturers, we should be tempted to suppose that the much which has been already granted had on all sides passed into oblivion. The tariff which now exists, and which was imposed, in most cases, for the particular benefit and under the direction of the manufacturers, is probably as high as the circumstances of the country will bear. We have, already, perhaps, transgressed in their favor the limits which principle would concede. Our manufacturers are not only placed by the side of the agriculturists; they are, as far as Government bounties can operate, advanced and preferred. When has the agricultural interest called for bounties to

enable it to continue a culture which has been found unprofitable? Yet this may become necessary. In Great Britain it has already occurred. The corn laws of that country now act as a bounty on agriculture. They are a necessary supplement to the manufacturing system. The Government has been compelled to adopt them, to place the farmer on a footing with the manufacturer, to whom so many bounties had previously been granted. One evil has naturally produced another. Every interest in that country now rests on an unnatural foundation, and requires artificial support; in consequence, every thing is precarious—every thing unstable. The elements of convulsion are on all sides prepared, and nothing but the power of a military Government prevents the explosion.

The only stable employments of capital, those only which can be free from incessant fluctuation, are those which arise spontaneously from the situation of a country or the state of its society. The manufactures that can only flourish during war or under impolitic restrictions—those that wither at the approach of peace or of an unshackled commerce, merit not our encouragement. Those that require no bounty will dread no competition; and the capital and labor which are employed in them may be considered as permanently vested. If we begin once to give bounties—and the duties now proposed are but bounties in an indirect shape—let us make the system uniform and equal. Let us give bounties on the exportation of cotton and tobacco, on the exportation of rice and flour; let us give bounties on the labor that brings these commodities to our markets, and on the vessels that transport them abroad; let us, in short, give bounties to every production of domestic industry. If, from the magnitude of this effort, we recoil as from a thing impossible, we must then demand why this system should be partially adopted—why one-twentieth part of our citizens should be enriched by bounties drawn from the labor of all the remaining classes of society?

To manufactures we have no hostility; we wish to see them rise, flourish, and attain a vigorous and permanent maturity; but we wish them *to* advance gradually, as our wants, our means, and the state of our society, shall be adapted to their establishment. We think it unwise, by precipitate measures, to force manufactures into a premature being, and then impose upon ourselves the necessity of supporting them through a precarious, a diseased, and, after all, a temporary existence. To the establishment, at any cost, of manufactures, which, like the munitions of war, are necessary for our national security, we have never objected; but to an organized system for the general creation of manufactures upon speculative principles, we pointedly object. It is at the threshold we must yet pause; the steps we now take we may not be able to retrace; the pledges we now give to our citizens we may not be able to recall. When thousands, perhaps millions, of dollars shall have been invested in manufactures, with the assurance of public support and protection, we know not how, with justice, this system could be abandoned, and the property vested under such assurance be

Remonstrance against an increase of Duties on Imports.

devoted to irretrievable destruction. Even if the evils attendant upon these efforts should prove in every respect pernicious, and should press sorely on every other branch of national industry, we must go on. It is impossible to point out the limits at which this system will rest. The tariff which was adopted with the approbation of the manufacturers in 1816 is now found insufficient; the tariff proposed in 1820, if it should be adopted, after having induced the investiture of additional millions of money, may be found equally unavailing. And when more capital, and a much greater proportion of our population, shall be engaged in manufactures, the influence of the wealthy and the claims and the necessities of the needy, whom we ourselves have seduced into these occupations, may force the Government, even reluctantly, and with a consciousness of its errors, into more disastrous measures—to the imposition of still higher duties, to restrictions, to prohibitions, to the necessity of lining our coasts with armed vessels and our shores with revenue officers, to the necessity of injuring the best interests of our country, and debasing the character and moral principles of a large portion of our citizens.

To manufacturers, we repeat, we have no hostility. We wish them to share in the general prosperity of our country, and repose and flourish under its liberal protection. But we perceive in them no features which would entitle them to partial favors or peculiar privileges. Against a system, therefore, designed to elevate one interest in society to an undue influence and importance; against a system intended to benefit one description of citizens at the expense of every other class; against a system calculated to aggrandize and enrich some States to the injury of others; against a system, under every aspect, partial, unequal, and unjust, we most solemnly protest.

STEPHEN ELLIOTT,
*Chairman of the meeting of
the citizens of Charleston.*

James Jervey, *Secretary.*

INCREASE OF DUTIES ON IMPORTS.

—

[Communicated to the Senate, December 18, 1820.]

*To the Senate and House of Representatives of the
United States in Congress assembled:*

The petition of the delegates of the United Agricultural Societies of Prince George, Sussex, Surry, Petersburg, Brunswick, Dinwiddie, and Isle of Wight, respectfully showeth: Your petitioners, a portion of the independent agriculturists of Virginia, again present ourselves to your honorable Houses, respectfully soliciting your attention to the present state of the tariff duties, and your protection against the wild speculations and ruinous schemes of an association denominating themselves the friends of national industry.

We should not again have obtruded our opinions, still less our arguments, on the wisdom and experience of our representatives, but from a conviction that the decision of this question is of vital importance; that, by the establishment of that system of exclusion developed in the tariff bill presented at your last session, the commercial and agricultural prosperity of the nation would be completely prostrated; the whole frame of our Constitution strained to accommodate this monstrous anomaly in a free Government; and, as a necessary consequence, nothing left of our boasted freedom and anticipated greatness but an empty name.

Though we do not believe that all who support this measure are aware of its consequences, yet we cannot conceal from ourselves, nor would we from our fellow-citizens, that the authors of this project contemplate nothing less than a radical change in our political institutions.

We cannot persuade ourselves that the fabricators of so formidable a machine should not have calculated both its powers and tendencies, and adjusted both to the views of its projectors. That their views are not directed solely or principally to the protection of manufactures, we are convinced, by the single fact that our manufactures are already more than sufficiently protected.

The present tariff duties operate as a bounty of at least twenty-five per cent. in their favor. Freight, insurance, commissions, and the various other expenses of information, cannot be estimated at less than fifteen per cent. The British manufacturer, the most formidable rival in this and every other market, is taxed by his own Government to the amount of one-third of the whole produce of his industry; which also operates in favor of our manufacturers, adding thirty-three and one-third per cent. to the former amount. The extraordinary rise in the value of money in this country must also be taken into account, as it operates as a bounty in favor of our manufacturers—the increased value here enabling them to procure necessaries as well as labor for a smaller sum; while the comparatively low value of money in Europe, compelling the foreign competitor to keep up the price of his goods, enables the American to keep up his prices also, nearly to the former standard.

The aggregate of these bounties will be found considerably upwards of one hundred per cent. in favor of our manufacturers. With these facts before us, we cannot be persuaded that the protection of manufacturers is the real object of the new tariff bill. But, to come at the true design of its authors, we have only to investigate the obvious tendency of the measure. The means will generally discover the end.

The first operation of the prohibitory system will be ruinous to those immediately engaged in foreign commerce, with whom almost every individual, directly concerned in any branch of trade, will be more or less involved. Other nations will retaliate, by excluding our products, as we have excluded theirs. The carrying trade, of which the superiority of our vessels would, under different circumstances, always insure us a valuable portion, must cease. Ship building, after being brought to astonishing perfection, and daily becoming a more lucrative business, will be forgotten; our vessels rot in our harbors; and our seamen emigrate, or resort to piracy or smuggling, for want of honest employment. Our coasting trade and fisheries will soon be at the mercy of our enemies; for neither can be long protected by a nation without foreign commerce.

The mercantile and agricultural interests are so intimately connected, that the ruin of the farmer must follow that of the merchant in no distant succession. The diminution of revenue derived from imports and sale of public lands must be made up by heavy internal taxes—the principal weight falling, as usual, on the agriculturist; the price of almost every article he is obliged to purchase will be increased at the pleasure of the pampered monopolist, who, competition being removed, will be limited in his demands only by the measure of his own cupidity—of the latitude of which we have had a fair opportunity of judging during the late war. The quantity of produce must be reduced to the limits of home consumption, as we can no longer calculate on a market for the usual surplus among nations whose goods we refuse to take in exchange; without exchange of goods, commerce cannot exist; the value of lands, buildings, and stock, will rapidly depreciate; and the owners, once the pride and strength of their country, sink into poverty and insignificance.

While our independent yeomanry are to be thus humbled, while their proud spirits are in training for the yoke, another party, less attached to the soil, and completely dependent on the bounty of Government, is to be raised to opulence and power, to be invested with exclusive privileges, more especially in taxing their fellow-citizens at discretion; and this, as we are told, for the sake of national independence. it is more easy to see how zealously such men would support even the most obnoxious and unprincipled measures of a Government on whose breath their wealth and consequence depend, than how national independence can be promoted by the oppression of a vast majority of the people for the benefit of a small minority.

National independence has always appeared to us something very different from the oppression of the people and the creation of privileged orders. That this is the end to which the prohibitory system inevitably leads, we have no doubt; that such is the favorite object of its authors, charity may still hesitate to pronounce.

The history of any branch of the forced manufactures of Great Britain exhibits a seri... pressions so extensive in their range, so ... revolting in their operation, as would, w... deter any friend ... ity or justice from ... the experiment ...

been unproductive; while millions have been ... to the nation by excluding the silks of France ... Italy, and, in return, having their manufac... excluded by those nations.

The abortive attempts repeatedly made, the union of Great Britain and Ireland, to ... lish the woollen manufacture in the latter co... are worthy of consideration, as immense both of English and Irish capital, have been in the undertaking; and we cannot but that the establishment of the same man in England has been effected at a price people would consent to pay.

These facts would induce us to suspect only certain results of the system in which about to involve ourselves are enormous and gross violation of principle.

To obviate all these difficulties, we are that, by the establishment of manufactures, a market will be obtained for the whole of our duce. As this argument has been so often and confidently reiterated, it will be necessary to ascertain its value.

If we already supply the whole people of America with as much corn, wheat, and tobacco as they can consume and export, besides a large surplus. by what operation of the new tariff bill is this surplus to be disposed of? We cannot presume that the appetites and capacities of our people will be so much increased by the operation of ... or the gin as to work such a miracle.

The only solution this difficulty admits of is the one given by the advocates of the prohibitory system, to wit: that it may be made the interest of the farmer and planter to embark their capital in manufacturing establishments; that, by thus diminishing the number of cultivators, and consequently of produce, we may get rid of our surplus by not raising it. Now, we really consider this as one of the most impudent proposals ever made by the most unblushing empiric to a reflecting people. The agriculturists of the United States (an immense majority of the nation) are called on not only to abandon every prospect of clearing the millions of acres of rich land in their back country, but also to abandon a part of that already in cultivation; to consent to have it made their interest to engage in manufactures, by the joint operation of exclusion from market, increased taxes, and manufacturing impositions. In plain English, the hardy, independent sons of our forests and our fields are called on to consent to be starved into weavers and button-makers. But, be it remembered, that, before this conviction of their interest has reached them, few will be found disposed to purchase lands and stock no longer valuable... any, it will be for a ... not sufficient, ... bly, to pay their debts ...

... these people would ... ration of the earth ... all are idlers who ... of course, be fi... in deserts, th... these precious... the daught... industry...

Remonstrance against an increase of Duties on Imports.

purity of mind; and their sons, temperance, soberness, and chastity, as practised in the best institutions of Leeds and Manchester.

That the despotic power of driving any class of citizens from the employments of their own choice, and forcing them into others, profitable or unprofitable, congenial or uncongenial, has been delegated to the Federal Government, we can no more believe, than that the authority to divide our people (like the Hindoos) into castes has been conveyed under the form of powers to regulate trade.

After demonstrating the ruinous tendency of the prohibitory system, with respect to the agriculture, commerce, and revenue of these States, and its entire inconsistency with the spirit of our free institutions, it is scarcely necessary to dwell on more remote consequences, amongst which may be anticipated a regularly organized system of smuggling, introducing in its train fraud, perjury, the exercise of lawless force, swarms of tide-waiters and sycophants, increased Government expenses, and an immense executive patronage.

We cannot restrain the expression of our surprise that a system, the impolicy of which has been long since demonstrated by the ablest political writers of Europe, and confirmed by the experience of the greatest commercial nations of the world, should, at this day, cost a moment's discussion in America. England confesses the ruin in which she has been involved by the pursuit of this system, and her inability to extricate herself. The commerce of Holland has been completely paralyzed by the protection afforded by their King to the manufactures of his Belgian subjects.

The idea of enriching a country by confining its whole wealth within its own limits is a mere chimera. The only use of wealth that we can conceive is, to enable its possessors to procure the necessaries and comforts of life; and, if we can procure these in greater abundance by sending a part of our wealth abroad, we increase our happiness in the same proportion, and, in effect, increase our wealth also.

So far from wishing to realize the vision of supplying all our wants by the labor and ingenuity of our own citizens, and thus being enabled to insulate ourselves from the rest of mankind, we would consider such a consummation the heaviest misfortune that could befall us.

That freedom and science can be kept alive amongst a people only by an extensive intercourse with the rest of the world, a glance at the condition of nations, ancient and modern, clearly establishes. In the whole range of history, we find those nations only enlightened, powerful, and free, who have cultivated an extensive foreign intercourse; while those whose jealous policy insulated them from the other nations of the earth have been ignorant and slavish in proportion to the degree of seclusion they have practised. Of this l tter description, the Chinese, Persians, and ' urks, (and, indeed, the whole of the eastern onarchies,) afford most deplorable specimens.

Considering the whole system of bounties, monies, and protecting duties, as tending, in all its bearings, to interrupt the prosperity, deteriorate the morals, and subvert the liberties of our citizens, we respectfully and earnestly solicit your honorable Houses to protect us from those evils, by disembarrassing every species of industry from all artificial impediments and restraints, as far as may be consistent with the production of the necessary revenue, and leaving them to the surest of all protection—their own utility, and the interest of those engaged in them.

RICHARD FIELD,
President Delegation, pro tem.
EDMUND RUFFIN, *Secretary.*

[Communicated to the Senate, December 22, 1820.]

CLARKSVILLE, MECKLENBURG CO., VA.
December 7, 1820.

To the Congress of the United States: The memorial of the Roanoke Agricultural Society:

Your memorialists beg leave to represent, that the section of country in which they reside has hitherto been marked for its quiet acquiescence in the will of the constituted authorities, and a becoming obedience to their dictates. Removed at a considerable distance from the sphere of political action, they have hitherto been contented to remain silent (though not uninterested) observers of public measures. The majority of the people consisting of independent husbandmen, they are willing that the affairs of Government should be left to the guidance of those to whom they have been intrusted, so long as a due regard of their rights and interests is observed. Believing that the course of public measures hitherto has, in general, been conducive to the public weal, their voice has not on any former occasion been obtruded on the ear of your honorable body. But their silence has not proceeded from a disregard or an ignorance of those rights and interests. They would consider themselves unworthy of the high political enjoyments to which they have been so long accustomed, could they contemplate with apathy the invasion of the one or a wilful neglect of the other.

The tariff bill introduced at the last session of Congress, and which, it is apprehended, may again be introduced at the present, could not fail to agitate the feelings and excite the alarm of your memorialists. In that measure they perceive a blow aimed at their welfare, which the voice of self-defence calls on them to endeavor to avert. It is deemed unnecessary to enter into details for the purpose of exposing to your honorable body the *impolicy* and *injustice* of attempting to encourage manufactures by legislative interposition. The good sense of every reflecting mind, the wisdom of statesmen, and universal experience, bear decisive testimony against such interposition.

The peculiar circumstances of each country must point to the pursuits of its inhabitants. In one like ours, reaching to every clime, and embracing every soil, with a population thinly scattered over it, agriculture is the occupation to which its inhabitants naturally look. They possess suffi-

Remonstrance against an increase of Duties on Imports.

men emigrate, or resort to piracy or smuggling, for want of honest employment. Our coasting trade and fisheries will soon be at the mercy of our enemies; for neither can be long protected by a nation without foreign commerce.

The mercantile and agricultural interests are so intimately connected, that the ruin of the farmer must follow that of the merchant in no distant succession. The diminution of revenue derived from imports and sale of public lands must be made up by heavy internal taxes—the principal weight falling, as usual, on the agriculturist; the price of almost every article he is obliged to purchase will be increased at the pleasure of the pampered monopolist, who, competition being removed, will be limited in his demands only by the measure of his own cupidity—of the latitude of which we have had a fair opportunity of judging during the late war. The quantity of produce must be reduced to the limits of home consumption, as we can no longer calculate on a market for the usual surplus among nations whose goods we refuse to take in exchange; without exchange of goods, commerce cannot exist; the value of lands, buildings, and stock, will rapidly depreciate; and the owners, once the pride and strength of their country, sink into poverty and insignificance.

While our independent yeomanry are to be thus humbled, while their proud spirits are in training for the yoke, another party, less attached to the soil, and completely dependent on the bounty of Government, is to be raised to opulence and power, to be invested with exclusive privileges, more especially that of taxing their fellow-citizens at discretion; and this, as we are told, for the sake of national independence. It is more easy to see how zealously such men would support even the most obnoxious and unprincipled measures of a Government on whose breath their wealth and consequence depend, than how national independence can be promoted by the oppression of a vast majority of the people for the benefit of a small minority.

National independence has always appeared to us something very different from the oppression of the people and the creation of privileged orders. That this is the end to which the prohibitory system inevitably leads, we have no doubt; that such is the favorite object of its authors, charity may still hesitate to pronounce.

The history of any branch of the forced manufactures of Great Britain exhibits a series of oppressions so extensive in their range, so gross and revolting in their operation, as would, we believe, deter any friend of liberty or justice from repeating the experiment. We collect, also, from the same source, the uncertain issue of attempting to force manufactures; for, with all the characteristic ingenuity, patience, and industry of her artisans, backed by powers such as a free people can never delegate to their Government, or permit them to assume, we find that there are some manufactures which Great Britain has not been able to force. We note the silk manufacture, which, from the revocation of the edict of Nantz to this day, has

been unproductive; while millions have been lost to the nation by excluding the silks of France and Italy, and, in return, having their manufactures excluded by those nations.

The abortive attempts repeatedly made, since the union of Great Britain and Ireland, to establish the woollen manufacture in the latter country, are worthy of consideration, as immense sums, both of English and Irish capital, have been sunk in the undertaking; and we cannot but observe that the establishment of the same manufacture in England has been effected at a price no free people would consent to pay.

These facts would induce us to suspect that the only certain results of the system in which we are about to involve ourselves are enormous expense and gross violation of principle.

To obviate all these difficulties, we are assured that, by the establishment of manufactures, a home market will be obtained for the whole of our produce. As this argument has been so often and so confidently reiterated, it will be necessary to ascertain its value.

If we already supply the whole people of America with as much corn, wheat, and tobacco as they can consume and export, besides a large surplus, by what operation of the new tariff bill is this surplus to be disposed of? We cannot presume that the appetites and capacities of our people will be so much increased by the operation of the shuttle or the gin as to work such a miracle.

The only solution this difficulty admits of is the one given by the advocates of the prohibitory system, to wit: that it may be made the interest of the farmer and planter to embark their capitals in manufacturing establishments; that, by thus diminishing the number of cultivators, and consequently of produce, we may get rid of our surplus by not raising it. Now, we really consider this as one of the most impudent proposals ever made by the most unblushing empiric to a reflecting people. The agriculturists of the United States (an immense majority of the nation) are called on not only to abandon every prospect of clearing the millions of acres of rich land in their back country, but also to abandon a part of that already in cultivation; to consent to have it made their interest to engage in manufactures, by the joint operation of exclusion from market, increased taxes, and manufacturing impositions. In plain English, the hardy, independent sons of our forests and our fields are called on to consent to be starved into weavers and button-makers. But, be it remembered, that, before this conviction of their interest has reached them, few will be found disposed to purchase lands and stock, no longer valuable; if any, it will be for a pittance, not sufficient, probably, to pay their debts.

These people would really persuade us that the cultivation of the earth is no species of industry; that all are idlers who neither weave nor spin, and may, of course, be fairly prosec ed; their fields turned into deserts, that factories may be established, (those precious seminaries of spotless virtue,) where the daughters of our ruined farmers may learn industry, simplicity of manners, and purity of mind; and their sons, temperance, soberness, and chastity, as practised in the best institutions of Leeds and Manchester.

That the despotic power of driving any class of citizens from the employments of their own choice, and forcing them into others, profitable or unprofitable, congenial or uncongenial, has been delegated to the Federal Government, we can no more believe, than that the authority to divide our people (like the Hindoos) into castes has been conveyed under the form of powers to regulate trade.

After demonstrating the ruinous tendency of the prohibitory system, with respect to the agriculture, commerce, and revenue of these States, and its entire inconsistency with the spirit of our free institutions, it is scarcely necessary to dwell on more remote consequences, amongst which may be anticipated a regularly organized system of smuggling, introducing in its train fraud, perjury, the exercise of lawless force, swarms of tide-waiters and sycophants, increased Government expenses, and an immense executive patronage.

We cannot restrain the expression of our surprise that a system, the impolicy of which has been long since demonstrated by the ablest political writers of Europe, and confirmed by the experience of the greatest commercial nations of the world, should, at this day, cost a moment's discussion in America. England confesses the ruin in which she has been involved by the pursuit of this system, and her inability to extricate herself. The commerce of Holland has been completely paralyzed by the protection afforded by their King to the manufactures of his Belgian subjects.

The idea of enriching a country by confining its whole wealth within its own limits is a mere chimera. The only use of wealth that we can conceive is, to enable its possessors to procure the necessaries and comforts of life; and, if we can procure these in greater abundance by sending a part of our wealth abroad, we increase our happiness in the same proportion, and, in effect, increase our wealth also.

So far from wishing to realize the vision of supplying all our wants by the labor and ingenuity of our own citizens, and thus being enabled to insulate ourselves from the rest of mankind, we would consider such a consummation the heaviest misfortune that could befall us.

That freedom and science can be kept alive amongst a people only by an extensive intercourse with the rest of the world, a glance at the condition of nations, ancient and modern, clearly establishes. In the whole range of history, we find those nations only enlightened, powerful, and free, who have cultivated an extensive foreign intercourse; while those whose jealous policy insulated them from the other nations of the earth have been ignorant and slavish in proportion to the degree of seclusion they have practised. Of this latter description, the Chinese, Persians, and Turks, (and, indeed, the whole of the eastern monarchies,) afford most deplorable specimens.

Considering the whole system of bounties, monopolies, and protecting duties, as tending, in all its

bearings, to interrupt the prosperity, deteriorate the morals, and subvert the liberties of our citizens, we respectfully and earnestly solicit your honorable Houses to protect us from those evils, by disembarrassing every species of industry from all artificial impediments and restraints, as far as may be consistent with the production of the necessary revenue, and leaving them to the surest of all protection—their own utility, and the interest of those engaged in them.

RICHARD FIELD,
President Delegation, pro tem.
EDMUND RUFFIN, *Secretary.*

[Communicated to the Senate, December 22, 1820.]

CLARKSVILLE, MECKLENBURG CO., VA.
December 7, 1820.

To the Congress of the United States: The memorial of the Roanoke Agricultural Society:

Your memorialists beg leave to represent, that the section of country in which they reside has hitherto been marked for its quiet acquiescence in the will of the constituted authorities, and a becoming obedience to their dictates. Removed at a considerable distance from the sphere of political action, they have hitherto been contented to remain silent (though not uninterested) observers of public measures. The majority of people consisting of independent husbandmen, they are willing that the affairs of Government should be left to the guidance of those to whom they have been intrusted, so long as a due regard of their rights and interests is observed. Believing that the course of public measures hitherto has, in general, been conducive to the public weal, their voice has not on any former occasion been obtruded on the ear of your honorable body. But their silence has not proceeded from a disregard or an ignorance of those rights and interests. They would consider themselves unworthy of the high political enjoyments to which they have been so long accustomed, could they contemplate with apathy the invasion of the one or a wilful neglect of the other.

The tariff bill introduced at the last session of Congress, and which, it is apprehended, may again be introduced at the present, could not fail to agitate the feelings and excite the alarm of your memorialists. In that measure they perceive a blow aimed at their welfare, which the voice of self-defence calls on them to endeavor to avert. It is deemed unnecessary to enter into details for the purpose of exposing to your honorable body the *impolicy* and *injustice* of attempting to encourage manufactures by legislative interposition. The good sense of every reflecting mind, the wisdom of statesmen, and universal experience, bear decisive testimony against such interposition.

The peculiar circumstances of each country must point to the pursuits of its inhabitants. In one like ours, reaching to every clime, and embracing every soil, with a population thinly scattered over it, agriculture is the occupation to which its inhabitants naturally look. They possess suffi-

Duty on Sales at Auction.

cient intelligence to perceive the path of their interest, without having it pointed out to them by their law-makers; and so soon as it shall become their interest to betake themselves from one occupation to another, they will do so without legislative compulsion; and, until they lead the way, it will be worse than folly to force them.

It is an axiom in political economy, that when a nation can import cheaper than she can manufacture, she should not pretend to set up workshops of her own, but should rely on those of her neighbors; for nothing can be clearer than that if the same labor devoted to raising produce and exporting it for exchange will procure more in the way of manufactures than if employed in manufacturing, the fruits of the national industry will be diminished by manufacturing. Such is precisely the situation of this country. None are so ignorant as not to know that we import better and cheaper than we can manufacture ourselves. Indeed, the simple fact of the requisition of prohibitory duties speaks more than a volume on the subject. If our own manufactures were of equal quality with and cheaper than those imported, they would have nothing to fear from foreign competition; but it is because they are inferior and dearer that their sickly tone is heard praying for protection.

Your memorialists would beg leave to direct your attention to what has been said of our *protecting duties* by European politicians of great celebrity. The Edinburgh reviewers, speaking of our manufacturing interest, remark: "Had the Americans acted wisely, they would have left this new interest to defend its own resources; but, in humble imitation of the wisdom of their ancestors, they immediately set about fostering and dandling the ricketty bantling; and, to save it from the effect of foreign competition, increased the duty on imported cotton and woollen goods from 12½ to 25 per cent. This increase of duty, (or, which is the same thing, this addition of 12½ per cent. to the price of all the cotton and woollen cloths made use of by the American people,) not having been found sufficient to protect those rash and imprudent speculators who had engaged in a branch of industry which, they must have been certain, could only exist by means of a monopoly, Congress have favorably entertained a proposal for making so large an addition to the present duties as will go far to render them prohibitory. Now, we feel perfectly assured that nothing but the example of Great Britain could ever have induced the American Legislature to listen for a moment to so *monstrous* a proposal. The boundless extent of fertile and unappropriated land in that country must, for ages to come, render the raising of raw produce the most profitable species of industry in which her citizens can possibly engage; and any attempt to encourage the premature growth of manufactures, by forcing the investment of a very large proportion of the capital of the country in a less productive employment, must occasion a proportional diminution of the power to accumulate stock, and of the wealth and riches of the country."

Deeply impressed with the truth of these remarks, your memorialists are compelled to ascribe to feelings of favoritism alone the officious care which has been manifested of this "new interest." For the purpose of forcing and pampering a puny and comparatively insignificant manufacturing interest, agriculture is attempted to be grievously taxed, our revenue diminished, and commerce, in a great measure, destroyed. Thus raised, it will be like the production of a hot-bed forced out of season; its curiosity may surprise, but it can never ripen into any degree of usefulness.

But there are other considerations, connected with our political institutions and situation, which may be suggested. No condition is so well calculated to inspire feelings of freedom and independence as that of the agriculturist who cultivates his own soil; none so fitted to debase and to degrade as that of the hireling manufacturer, who depends for his sustenance on the scanty wages afforded him by his wealthy employer. To keep alive those feelings is deemed indispensable to the preservation of our republican frame of government. Every measure, then, which has a tendency to increase the number of the latter, and decrease that of the former description of population, weakens the pillars by which that frame of government is supported. To your wisdom *it is* left to determine whether, in the hour *of* impending peril, we should look for defence to the sweepings of our manufactures or to the yeomanry of our country.

Again: identity of feeling and interest is the cement of our Union. Without it, the component parts of our confederacy must hang too loosely together to withstand the jars to which it must be exposed. That identity would be destroyed by a rigid system of prohibitory duties. In the nature of man, it cannot be expected that the agricultural and commercial portions of the Union could experience any other feeling than that of the bitterest hatred towards the manufacturing interest, by whom they would be burdened to the utmost of their power to bear; they would cease to feel as members of one great family.

We have no favors to ask at the hands of Government. All we require is, to be left to ourselves, and to our own resources. As we desire not to interfere with others, we hope and trust not to be interfered with.

We therefore respectfully pray that no augmentation of duties may take place which will have any other object than an increase of revenue.

THOMAS M. NELSON,
President.

Charles L. Wingfield, *Secretary.*

DUTY ON SALES AT AUCTION.

[Communicated to the Senate, January, 4, 1821.]

To the honorable the Senate and House of Representatives of the United States in Congress assembled:

The memorial of the subscribers, auctioneers of the city of New York, respectfully showeth: That

Duty on Sales at Auction.

your memorialists are engaged in an extensive business, whose general influence upon other branches of trade has of late become a subject of much controversy. Your honorable bodies were, at your last session, petitioned, by those who consider the interests of commerce as unfavorably affected by the great extent of auction sales, to adopt such restrictive measures as would tend to limit or suppress them. On the failure of the effort at that time, no means were left unattempted by which the discordant interests of the different classes of the community might be united in furtherance of this enterprise; and the application is now renewed, supported by more powerful influence, and urged with greater zeal.

Your memorialists respectfully disclaim the intention of urging their unimportant interests upon the attention of your honorable bodies. Their remonstrance is grounded upon principles distinct from any motives of private consideration, which, they are aware, would have but little influence on your decision. Their object in addressing you is to give such practical information as will lead to a just estimate of the nature of their business, and correct the misconceptions that may have prejudiced the inquiry.

The result of your deliberations on this important subject will materially affect the whole course of trade. A system which has gradually grown into importance; which has been improved, matured, and, they might almost say, perfected; which necessity originated, and acknowledged advantages have continued and enlarged, will be established as a safe and salutary medium of sale, or suppressed as a dangerous and pernicious agency. Your memorialists cheerfully submit their interests to the decision of your honorable bodies on the merits of this question, and would humbly suggest whether a subject at this moment should not be approached with respect and delicacy; whether it does not merit the most careful deliberation; and whether the argument and evidence that involve the interests of the whole should not outweigh the clamors of a few.

Your memorialists respectfully request the indulgent attention of your honorable bodies to a brief exposition of the general nature of their business, and of their manner of conducting it; and to the correctness of their representations they pledge their individual and collective respectability. Your honorable bodies will perceive, from this detail of their general practice, that there is nothing to warrant the charges of fraud and deception which have been urged against sales at auction, and that, in yielding to popular impressions derived from the objectionable mode of conducting the business which formerly prevailed, the opponents of the trade must have overlooked its actual importance and respectability. Were evidence necessary to disprove these calumnies, it would be found in the unlimited confidence reposed in your memorialists; and the slightest investigation would have corrected a position at variance with the very nature of the business.

Your memorialists, in the statement offered to your honorable bodies, have confined themselves to that branch of the trade which has been repre-sented as productive of the most extensive injury—that is, the public sale of imported dry goods. Other commodities of every kind are sold under similar regulations; it would be obtrusive on your patience to particularize each.

Sales of dry goods are made at auction by the package or by the piece; and this is the only important distinction to be observed in all the varieties of the trade. Package sales, being more important in amount, and more attractive, by the assortments of merchandise they combine, excite most interest, and are attended with greatest competition. When the sale is of magnitude, it is generally advertised in the principal commercial cities, with an enumeration of the articles to be sold. Printed catalogues are prepared, specifying the term of credit, with the other conditions of sale, and detailing the contents of each package, the number of pieces, the varieties of quality, by number or otherwise, and the lengths; all of which are guarantied to the purchasers. The widths are also in some instances specified, but always with a reservation expressed in the conditions of the sale, on the printed catalogues, or published by verbal explanation, that there is on that point no warranty, except that the goods not exhibited shall correspond in this as well as in every other respect with the samples shown. This exception is made to the general guarantee to the purchaser, as well to protect the seller from arbitrary and unreasonable claims as to establish the general rule that no description of width can be depended upon with as much security as the evidence of actual observation; it being well understood that British cotton goods are universally invoiced at more than their actual width, whether they are of the finest or most inferior quality, put up for public or private sale. The misrepresentation has become sanctioned by universal practice, and is innocent because notorious. It is no more supposed that goods invoiced as six-fourths of a yard, and measuring but a yard, will produce more in consequence of the exaggeration, than that the United States' duty will be calculated by the custom-house on the invoice width rather than upon the actual measurement.

The packages are arranged in lots corresponding with their numbers on the catalogue, and are exhibited sometimes two entire days before the sale, sometimes but one; the length of the exhibition being regulated by the magnitude of the sale. When the goods are prepared for inspection, the purchasers are invited by public notice in the papers to examine them. Where it is necessary for an advantageous examination, whole packages are opened and displayed; where it can be made with more convenience from samples, one or more pieces of each quality are exhibited; and where there are many packages exactly corresponding, one only is shown.

Pattern cards are exhibited displaying the assortment of colors, &c. The purchaser receives every information and facility that can contribute to his convenience and protect him from mistake. The goods are arranged with so much attention to the accommodation of the purchasers, that three or

Duty on Sales at Auction.

four hundred packages may be examined with care and accuracy in one day.

On the day of sale the purchasers assemble, each prepared with a catalogue marked with his estimate of the value of the articles wanted; a practice that not only guards the buyer against any disadvantageous excitement which competition naturally produces, and refers him to the deliberate opinion formed upon careful examination before the sale, but also promotes a general knowledge of merchandise in every variety, and creates a useful register of the fluctuations of the market, as these catalogues are generally preserved, with notes in the margin of the prices at which every article has been sold. At the commencement of the sale the conditions are recapitulated by the auctioneer, among which is a provision that no allowance will be made for damage or deficiency after the goods have left the city, (a regulation at once equitable and necessary,) as otherwise there would be no protection for the auctioneer in the settlement of his accounts, or for the seller against the fraudulent claims of strangers. This being, however, at all times a declared condition, the publicity of the rule insures the prompt examination of the goods. All merchandise sold at public auction is warranted by the auctioneer to be perfect in the manufacture, free from damage and imperfection, of the quantity specified, and of fair merchantable character, as regards the description of width and size. For this the auctioneer is held liable, as well as for every delusion calculated to deceive the senses or betray the judgment. The auctioneer is not only legally and by common practice is responsible for the correctness of his merchandise, but it is deemed a point of honor and of common justice to expose every art by which the interests of the purchaser would be sacrificed; and it is no uncommon thing for the buyer to acquire the first information of fraud from the auctioneer himself. The security to the purchaser is, however, necessarily subject to limitation; and public notice is always given that claims of all kinds must be made within a specified period. Immediate redress is obtained for deficiencies and damages reported within that time. The deficiencies, being properly certified, are promptly allowed: the damages are settled by return of the goods, or by the appraisement of disinterested persons appointed by the auctioneer and the purchaser. The period established for the required report of claims is a matter of convention between the auctioneer and the buyers at the sale; it being, however, understood that errors of all kinds which arise from the neglect or inaccuracy of the seller or his agent will at any time be corrected.

The nature of this business, by which sales are effected and accounts closed with so much despatch, absolutely requires that the stipulations specified should be rigidly enforced; and those regulations cannot be deemed disadvantageous by which care, punctuality, and promptitude are promoted.

Your memorialists have entered into a more particular detail of this part of their system, because the frauds of British agents and others are alleged as the prominent objection against auction sales.

Practical evidence is not wanting that imposition is most effectually guarded against by the very means which it is said encourage and promote it. The average amount of deduction made from package sales of British dry goods, for claims of every nature, will not equal the one-sixteenth of one per cent.; and it is rarely that any other causes of complaint occur than an accidental deficiency or an unavoidable damage. Claims based upon the suspicion or the discovery of fraud are so unusual, and would tend so much to the discredit of the proprietor of the goods, that many, if not all of your memorialists, would esteem it sufficient grounds to decline the transaction of further business with the person attempting the deceit. Your honorable bodies will perceive, from this simple statement, how groundless is the charge against auction sales of encouraging deception, that the evil which is made the basis of all the objection against them is but imaginary.

Your memorialists have detailed every part of their practice in the management of package sales which can be of any importance in establishing a correct understanding of the nature of their business. Rice sales are conducted on the same general principles, but differ in many particulars. Package sales are resorted to when entire cargoes are to be sold, or where the quantity of goods is too great to be disposed of in detail. Large assortments of merchandise are daily offered at the piece sales, where packages are opened, and the goods sold in small or large lots, as may most tend to the interest of the seller and the convenience of the purchaser. These sales are regular and systematic, being held by each auctioneer of extensive business on two or more specified days in each week, and are principally depended upon by the retailers as well as the larger dealers for their uniform supplies; they are held under the same implied regulations which govern sales by the package. Every article is opened and exhibited on shelves on the morning of the sale; a sample piece of every package, as it is offered by the auctioneer, is displayed upon a counter for examination, and several others distributed among the company in the original folds; the rest of the package, if of similar quality, is sold in order; but the same process takes place whenever any difference in value exists, or where the accommodation of the purchasers makes it necessary. Ample time is given during the sale to examine accurately every article as it is offered; and the purchaser, in every respect, is secured against error and imposition, by an open and unlimited display of the merchandise, and by the public proclamation of every circumstance known to the auctioneer which may tend to enhance or depreciate its value. Where concealment has been used by the proprietor of the goods, it is necessarily detected in their free exposure to inspection. Articles imported of a specific length, which are sold by the piece, are guarantied of the usual length. By these means the purchaser has the double advantage of being allowed in the first instance to examine minutely, and of afterwards being relieved, if he has been unwarily deceived. It is a general regulation, that claims for deductions must be made the day after the sale; but they are generally allowed if notice is given before the settlement. These precautions operate only upon obvious damage, or upon deficiencies which are evident, or might with ease have been ascertained: they are intended to guard against the neglect of the purchaser, not to protect the frauds of the seller. In cases where it can be satisfactorily proved that goods have been put up with intent to deceive, no exertion is wanting on the part of the auctioneer to remedy any injury sustained in consequence.

A credit of three, four, or six months, is usually given on sales by the piece, where the amount purchased exceeds $100, and approved security is always required by the auctioneer. Legal interest is allowed for cash payment; and men of limited means, by a combination of their purchases, secure the credit which is at all times convenient, and frequently necessary—their united responsibility being admitted for amounts for which either individual would not be accepted. When it is considered that these transactions take place daily, and that the supplies so obtained are essential to the support of numerous inferior establishments, the importance and value of the accommodation will be evident.

Your memorialists respectfully represent that the system of public sales, in theory combining advantages and facilities which establish its utility in extensive markets, is attended in practice with that despatch, accuracy, and convenience, which alone have extended its operations and confirmed its necessity. It has long been the honorable distinction of our commercial transactions, that frauds on the revenue are scarcely known; it cannot be doubted that auction sales have had an influence in establishing this character for mercantile purity, inasmuch as they encourage so strict and impartial an examination of all imported merchandise; that if imposition should elude the vigilance of custom-house officers, it cannot escape the industrious observation of a trading community, which is ever watchful to detect fraud, and prompt in proclaiming it. Let not, then, auction sales be charged with the encouragement of a species of iniquity which does not in truth exist, and which it is at least presumable they have had an influence in suppressing.

As the public revenue is guarded from injury by the intervention of auction sales, so also do the purchaser and consumer obtain, through this impartial medium, undoubted assurance of the security of their transactions. No artful mode of exhibition can be used to ensnare the inexperienced; the examination of goods is deliberate and cautious; and it is fully in the power of the buyer to protect himself against the possibility of error. He deals not, as in private contract, with one whose interest it is to deceive; his bargain is made with an unbiassed agent, whose interest it is to expose deception; and in all cases of injury he looks for redress from a disinterested source.

Goods of inferior quality, of cheap and temporary dye, of specious appearance, and slight fabric, may be collected and exhibited as evidences of deception encouraged by auction sales.

Your memorialists respectfully represent that the evidence submitted by them to your honorable bodies must, if admitted as correct, be conclusive that merchandise exhibited for public sale cannot be estimated otherwise than at its actual value; or, if its apparent value be heightened by artificial means, that the responsibility of the auctioneer is pledged for the exposure of the artifice. What is it, then, that encourages the introduction into our market of articles of worthless fabric? Undoubtedly it must be their currency with the consumer, who has no immediate and direct dealings with the auctioneer, but obtains them from the jobber, who, himself perfectly aware of their intrinsic value, promotes their importation, by being the principal agent in their distribution. Your memorialists do not, by any means, intend to repel this charge by the imputation of unworthy motives to any other class of men; they are of opinion that goods of inferior fabric are necessary for the consumption of the country, and that the prices at which they are sold universally correspond with their value. The dressing, the glazing, and decorations employed in the preparation of inferior British manufactures for this and other markets are so notorious that they do not deceive the most inexperienced. These are not new inventions; nor have the humbler classes of the community but lately learned to clothe themselves in articles of cheap but showy fabric. The custom, however, is falling into disuse, and a taste for more simple and substantial merchandise begins to prevail. As far as regards the employment of fraud in the sale of goods through the medium of auctions, it presents itself so rarely to the observation of your memorialists that they cannot but doubt its prevalence, and would rather, from their experience, esteem it a matter of congratulation that the country merchant can come into the market in the confidence of ascertained good faith and fairness, than believe there can be reason to call either in question.

Your memorialists respectfully represent that the periodical exposure of large and general assortments of merchandise at public sale must have a tendency to promote the convenience of those who resort to the great commercial marts for their supplies, while it benefits the importer by the consequent increase of competition. If distant purchasers are attracted by public notice to large and valuable sales, where they may carefully examine the assortments that are offered, effect their purchases, and accomplish all their business in so short a period; if the holders of goods may, with so much despatch and certainty, complete the sale of whole invoices, at the current market prices, with full protection against all risk, and secure the advantages of prompt remittances, accommodations and benefits must result, that would at least counterbalance many evils, if, indeed, the existence of any had been proved. When new plans or principles are suggested, encouraged, and established; when men of different interests and views coincide in their adoption; when, after

Duty on Sales at Auction.

long and successful experiment, they are confirmed and become universal, it is a common and reasonable inference that their popularity is the result of admitted utility. On what other reasoning can it be explained, that, with a powerful interest in opposition, auctions have become, in most of our commercial cities, so considerable a medium of sale, that both classes of the mercantile community, the buyers and sellers, have united in supporting them? There can be no doubt that when public convenience no longer requires their interference, they will naturally and rapidly decline, without legislative interposition.

To those whose operations are conducted on an humble scale, the amount of whose purchases must necessarily be regulated by their daily sales, the suppression of auctions would be a fatal and distressing blow. This numerous class is dependent on public sales for their regular assortments; their responsibility, though not adequate to purchases of magnitude, is yet sufficient, by mutual union and support, for their small but frequent obligations; having an established credit, they are assisted in the advantageous employment of their capital, while their intercourse with the auctioneer gives him that constant information which is his best security, and insures the prudence of their engagements. In common with the country merchant, they owe to auctions the advantage of procuring their supplies without the necessity of intermediate profits, which are evidently a tax upon the consumer; they buy their goods at auction, and the fifteen or twenty per cent. which would have formed the profits of an intervening class is saved to that part of the population by whom the difference would be most sensibly felt. The country merchants go into the market on the best terms; the labor and difficulty of their purchases are reduced; they select from the daily assortments their necessary and regular supply, in quantities to suit their convenience. The price of commodities is equalized between the city and country consumer, and reduced to both; and the country gains in the saving of the time, the industry, and resources of her most valuable citizens. But it is not only in their immediate advantages that auctions are a public benefit; the influence of the great body of strangers, invited by their facilities, is profitably felt in every department of useful industry, and imparts activity and animation to every branch of trade.

If, then, the population of the country is through auctions, supplied with comforts and necessaries at the cheapest rate; if a saving be effected in the most valuable resources of the nation, of what moment is it that a wealthy and influential class of men, who are provoked to hostility by the loss of a productive business, denounce auctions as a public calamity, and influence others to unite with them?

Your memorialists respectfully represent that it is to the influence of auction sales that our domestic manufactures owe their introduction to general notice and that encouragement and aid which has, in some measure, overcome the prejudices that opposed their advancement; that the valuable products of native industry, which public opinion discouraged and condemned, were forced into use and estimation. To the manufacturer, the aid of the auction business, as a medium of sale, is almost indispensable. A law of our State has been obtained for their encouragement, by which the sale of domestic goods has been exempted from duty; and the great disproportion in amount between the public and private sales of our home manufactures sufficiently disproves the supposition that auctions operate to their disadvantage. Those manufacturing establishments whose operations are sustained by great resources may, perhaps, view with indifference the decision of this question; but to those of humbler means, whose business is almost exclusively transacted through the agency of auctioneers, it is of vast importance.

The small resources that would be quickly exhausted in limited enterprise are, by the aid of auctions, continued in active circulation. The distress consequent upon the failure of employment, during the tedious disposal of the merchandise and collection of the proceeds, is prevented by the promptitude of the sale and payments. The manufacturer is aided by the judgment and experience of his agent, which render his presence and attendance unnecessary; so that his goods are sold, the raw materials purchased, or his funds remitted, while there is no interruption to his industry; and the time and labor are saved which would be consumed by making sales of his merchandise in detail.

It is objected against auction sales that they have produced a revolution in the commerce of the country, and originated the difficulties which it is said now oppress it. Your memorialists would respectfully urge that the decline of business may be attributed to more probable and evident causes than the extension of auction sales, which has, in fact, resulted from the same circumstances that produced the decline in our commercial prosperity, and has tended greatly to relieve the general distress. It is to the extravagant introduction of foreign fabrics after the late war, when profitable sales allured to importations far exceeding the ordinary consumption; to the fall in the cost of goods abroad, when our merchants were overburdened with a heavy stock; to the injudicious extension of business at a period of hazard and uncertainty; to the loss of several important and profitable branches of trade, which employed our ships and seamen, and enriched our merchants and our country, but of which the universal restoration of peace throughout Europe deprived us; to the extensive scale on which the precarious experiment of domestic manufactures was commenced; and to the embarrassments of a disordered exchange, that commercial distress is to be referred; and practical men are aware that the interference of auction sales alone could have prevented a more extensive ruin, by their forced distribution of goods throughout the country, at a rate which relieved our importers, though at an admitted sacrifice. Such were the causes which produced the gradual decline of our commercial prosperity, and created that reaction in our mercantile situation from whose shock we are but now recovering. But on what grounds can it be urged that the present character of our trade is ruinous? The day of commercial disaster has passed away with the extravagant enterprise that produced it; and commerce, reviving, asks but freedom from restraint and liberty of action. A safe and advantageous internal trade employs the capital and industry of one part of the mercantile community; while our foreign intercourse, established upon secure and beneficial principles, invites the enterprise of the other. The mass of old goods, the surplus of former excessive importations, has been disposed of, and a field opened for a lucrative trade. Commercial credit and confidence are established; and though our own produce but scantily rewards the labor of the husbandman, (an evil certainly not attributable to auction sales,) yet foreign manufactures and produce generally have fallen proportionably, while the improvement of our domestic exchanges denotes a composed and settled state of things.

Our importers have, during the last season, enjoyed a trade that has well rewarded their enterprise. Our market has been enlivened by strangers from every quarter of the Union, and presented a scene of activity and successful industry that sufficiently relieves auctions from the charge of having effected a ruinous change in the character of our trade.

Your memorialists are represented as holding an important and dangerous monopoly. On the contrary, it is their influence in destroying the power of monopolizing that renders them of public service. They are a barrier to that inordinate warmth of speculation which is in direct opposition to the principles of a secure and moderate trade. They prevent the involvement of capital in the attempt to engross scarce and desirable articles, and those ruinous combinations of extensive dealers which frequently distress a whole community.

From these considerations, your memorialists respectfully remonstrate against the imposition of legislative restrictions upon a business whose advantages have been carefully thrown into the shade, while none but groundless objections have been urged against it. Public sales, in their general character, are no longer the resort of the necessitous, who are compelled to the sacrifice of property by the pressure of distress. Buyer and seller now meet on neutral ground for their mutual advantage; auctions are employed as the most secure and convenient medium for the sale and purchase of merchandise at the current market rate; and any addition to the present charges, however trifling, so far from being a productive source of public revenue, would force the business into another channel, introduce the practice of selling inconsiderable samples at auction, by which the prices of large parcels at private sale would be regulated, encourage frauds on the revenue, and operate directly as a tax upon the yeomanry of the country.

All which is respectfully submitted, &c.

FRANKLIN & MINTURN,
And others.

BANK OF THE UNITED STATES.
—
[Communicated to the Senate, January 12, 1821.]

To the honorable the Speaker and Members of the House of Representatives of the United States:

The memorial of the President and Directors of the Bank of the United States, on the part of the stockholders of the said bank, respectfully showeth:

That the institution of which they are managers is laboring under several grievances, not only injurious to the bank, but, as they respectfully conceive, to the nation also, which call for legislative relief. Some of these arise from the original omission of appropriate legal enactments; others, from certain provisions of the charter not suited to the condition and circumstances of the bank; and one, of a very important character, from a regulation concerning the fiscal receipts of the Government of the Union. For the remedy of these evils, the stockholders of the Bank of the United States can only look to Congress. Under the pledge of its sacred faith, and by its authority, the institution was established; and their natural refuge is, therefore, to the National Legislature for that relief and protection which the citizen has a right to claim of his Government. Of that body they know they can obtain nothing forbidden by the sound policy of the State; and could their interest dictate a request inconsistent with that policy, they would forbear to make it; but it is under a conviction of the justness and correctness of their requests, that, as citizens, and as a portion of those whose prosperity constitutes the public good, they respectfully ask the attention of Congress to the grievances under which they labor. They ask relief only if it be found to be consistent with the public welfare; and if it be, they will, they are convinced, not ask in vain; while they feel satisfied that they will be able to show to your honorable body not only that their claims are consistent with it, but that they are eminently calculated to advance and promote it.

Your petitioners are aware that strong prejudices have existed against the Bank of the United States, and certainly there has been abundant cause for more than prejudice against some of the acts which have marked the progress of the institution. But these acts have been offences not against the public or the Government, (except as it is a stockholder,) but against the innocent and undesigning stockholders, on whose behalf your petitioners now ask protection and relief. Offences of inferior turpitude and of inferior public injury, under almost all Governments, have been restrained by severe punishments. By the charter granted by the Congress of the Confederation to the Bank of North America, it was proposed to make some of these offences felony, and they were accordingly made felony by the several acts of the Legislature of Pennsylvania. But though, in the progressive experience of this institution, one example of infidelity, peculation, and fraud, has produced another, and that another and another, and though it has been defrauded of millions of dollars, it is yet entirely without the preventive protection of effective and appropriate penal laws. Will it be believed, too, that these acts, so injurious to the bank—that these losses, so afflictive to the innocent and suffering stockholders, have excited against the institution the prejudices which your petitioners now so anxiously deprecate? Yet it is a truth, that those are the sole causes of which your petitioners have any knowledge. For they cannot believe that it is considered a crime (at least not in the eyes of that Legislature from whom they purchased their privileges) for the stockholders to have associated together and to have placed their property under the protection of the most solemnly considered act that has marked the existence of the Government—an act, the validity of which all political denominations of men in the country, (at long intervals of time, giving ample room for reflection and investigation,) and all departments of the Government, have repeatedly and solemnly considered and confirmed. The usefulness of the bank to the Government and to the country, its purifying effect upon and sustaining aid of the currency, its support of the public credit, and its general benign influence on the interests of every solvent man and every solvent institution in the country, if not readily acknowledged, your petitioners believe can be satisfactorily shown. But, more effectually to dissipate the public prejudices, if any remain, your petitioners entreat your honorable body to inquire who now are the persons really interested in this much injured institution? They will be found to be, with few exceptions, original subscribers, who have continued to hold their stock, alike ignorant and innocent of the frauds to which their interests were a prey; or they are unfortunate purchasers, who, deceived by the false appearances which the affairs of the institution exhibited, gave an advance of from twenty to fifty per cent. on their purchases. Among those now interested are all the classes of human helplessness; and among the funds involved in the fate of the institution are those of charity and religion to no inconsiderable amount. Of these facts your petitioners are ready to give satisfactory proof to your honorable body, and crave to be permitted to do so, if it shall be doubted or deemed material.

Under these circumstances, your petitioners will proceed succinctly to state the particular objects on which they respectfully request relief and protection of Congress.

First. The charter provides that no director, except the president, shall be eligible for more than three years in four. This provision has, in practice, been found to deny to the bank the services of those men who are best qualified to administer its affairs with safety and profit to the institution. It is a provision not contained, your petitioners believe, in the charter of any other respectable banking institution. It was not contained in the charter of the former Bank of the United States; and it would seem that the provision of the charter which forbids the re-election of more than three-fourths of the directors in office, at the time of an annual election, (to which your petitioners

have no objection,) is calculated to effect all the ends of the embarrassing provision from which your petitioners now crave relief.

Second. At present there is no authority under the laws of Congress to punish any fraud, peculation, or violation of trust, committed by any of the officers of the bank or its offices; and on this point the State laws are also supposed to be deficient. Nor is there any adequate civil remedy for the bank against its faithless agents, who may the hour before their dismissal from office, while the investigations necessary to their removal indicate to them that result, take the property of the bank from its vaults and withhold it, spend it, and, if they please, give it in payment to their other creditors, in exclusion of the bank from which it has been thus purloined.

Third. Under the charter it has been doubted whether the bank has power to authorize the issuing of notes not signed by the president and countersigned by the cashier. The labor and the time necessary to sign notes for the bank and all its branches are much greater than either of those officers can bestow upon that object; and hence the bank has been unable to put in circulation a sufficient amount of notes of the smaller denominations, which the public most want, and which are best calculated to serve the interest of the bank. If authority were given to the board from time to time to appoint one or more persons to sign notes of the smaller denominations at the parent bank, under the superintendence and direction of the board and its principal officers, there would be no public risk, and it would afford all the aid which your petitioners desire on that point.

Fourth. Under the fourteenth section of the act incorporating the bank, the bills or notes of the bank originally made payable, or which shall have become payable on demand, are made receivable in all payments to the United States, unless otherwise directed by act of Congress. Under this regulation, the power of the bank to make its capital available, either for its own profit or the public good, is greatly abridged. The sphere of its circulation is limited to those places where it is least wanted, and made to exclude those where it would be eminently useful, while the whole currency of vast sections of the country is thereby frequently greatly embarrassed.

Your petitioners forbear to enter at this time into a further exposition of the grounds of their application for relief on these points; but respectfully hope and request that your honorable body will so dispose of the subject as to give them an opportunity of manifesting the justice, as it regards the bank, and the policy as it regards the public, of the relief and protection which they respectfully claim.

On behalf of the board of directors.

                L. CHEVES, *President.*
Attest: THOS. WILSON, *Cashier.*

DOCUMENTS ACCOMPANYING THE MEMORIAL.

The Committee of the Bank of the United States beg leave respectfully to represent to the committees of Congress, to whom the memorial of the bank has been referred, that the directors of the bank were forbidden, by the nature of the instrument, from developing in their memorial, at length and in detail, the particulars of the grievances under which the establishment labors, or the reasons which, in their opinion, authorize and recommend the measures of relief which they seek. To supply this deficiency, the committee now desire respectfully to bring before the committees of Congress some of those details and reasons, which they will do as briefly as the nature of the subject will permit. They will notice the several points in the order in which they are stated in the memorial.

I. *The ineligibility of directors who have served three years in succession.*

On this point, the committee beg leave to consider, 1st, The evil; 2d. The relief desired; 3d, The possible objections to that relief.

1. The memorial states, very truly, that the most competent and safe men cannot generally be induced to accept seats at the respective boards of the bank and its offices. The directors of such an institution ought to be, if possible, of undoubted credit, great experience, and extensive business. Neither integrity nor abstract talent, nor both, are enough. They ought, at least a considerable portion of them, to be men extensively engaged in business, and well acquainted with men of business. Such men not only are better qualified to govern the affairs of the bank, but give to it their own business, which is valuable, not merely on account of its extent, but also on account of its character, and attract to it numerous customers like themselves; and thus secure to it, in the aggregate, business to a greater extent, and of a better character, than men of a different description can do. Not to obtain the services of such men, is to fail in managing the institution to the best advantage, and to limit its usefulness and its benefits, both public and private. But, under the existing provisions of the charter, such men decline, too generally, the station of directors of the bank and its branches, when they can (as they always can) obtain seats at the boards of respectable local banks, from which they will not be periodically removed. The reasons of their preference are obvious. It is desirable with such men always to have seats at the boards of respectable banks; and to remove them periodically, is to suspend periodically the advantage which they seek. But, besides the motive of interest or convenience which may govern them, they have a much greater objection to the necessary removal required by the charter of the Bank of the United States, founded on the unpleasant feelings which it excites. The bank may succeed in a first appointment, but at the end of one year it displaces one-fourth. This offends those who see themselves removed, without admitting or believing that the preference which excludes them is just, and places them in a light of inferiority, which mortifies their pride, and often provokes their resentment; nor are these feelings assuaged or subdued by exhibiting to them

the original charter, which renders it necessary. This, however, it is admitted, must be borne to meet the demands of a prudent jealousy. But the evil increases almost in geometrical proportion, as the process of exclusion annually occurs, until, at the quadrennial appointments, it ends in a state of things absolutely incompatible with the good management of the bank; for as many of the best directors who were first appointed will be retained as the law permits, and, on the fourth appointment, the whole of them will be excluded; leaving but one-fourth of the preceding board, and those who compose that small portion will have had but one year's experience. Undoubtedly the bank has succeeded, in many instances, in procuring the services of fit men, under all these difficulties; but it has been the result of good fortune, and in opposition to causes which almost necessitate a contrary effect; and it is hoped the National Legislature, in its wisdom, will not see fit to leave such great national and private interests to the sport of chance.

The committee find it quite impossible fully to express the magnitude of the practical evil, which can only be understood and felt by marking attentively the operation and progress of it. In their humble opinion, the change desired is altogether indispensable to a prosperous and safe management of the bank.

2. The relief desired is simply that length of service, which may be considered as expressive of extraordinary usefulness and capacity, shall not create ineligibility. The request does not embrace the Government directors, nor any change in the provision which excludes a numerical proportion (one-fourth) of the board of the year preceding each appointment; guards which, the committee cannot doubt, will fully carry into effect the policy and object of the Legislature on this point.

3. It is not denied, the committee believe, that the change desired is calculated to promote the interest of the stockholders. But it is alleged that banks generally, and particularly this bank, are to be viewed in the double aspect of instruments of private advantage and national good, and that it ought to be shown that the tendency of the change is not likely to be injurious in the latter view. The committee do not hesitate to admit the justice of the remarks; but they entreat that it may be considered whether both ends are not attainable by the same means, and whether the means proposed are not the most fit to accomplish both. The desire of the stockholders is to have the institution managed by the most honest and most capable men that can be procured. If this end be attained, the national object will undoubtedly be attained. That commendable jealousy which has been before alluded to may cease to be wise if carried too far. If carried so far as to exclude the most fit men from the management of the bank and its branches, it will undoubtedly be carried too far. It may put the affairs of the institution into the hands of designing and unprincipled men; and against their arts the provision of ineligibility from length of service will be a security feebler than a cobweb. If, then, the committees of Con-

gress shall be satisfied that the provision which renders the best men ineligible periodically is not calculated to keep the management in the hands of men of the highest integrity and capacity, it will follow that, to meet the public object, the change ought to be adopted. And as a matter of fact and experience, in the past management of the bank and its offices, it has failed to do so.

II. *The punishment of frauds upon the bank by its officers.*

On the policy and propriety of punishing, by penal enactments, frauds and peculation committed on the bank by its officers, the committee deem it unnecessary to enlarge.

III. *On the substitution of agents instead of the president and cashier to sign the notes of the bank of the lower denominations.*

On this point also the committee deem it unnecessary to dwell at much length. The request now made is unlike that which was some time since made to Congress and refused. That was to delegate the authority required to the officers of the branches as well as those of the bank. The present is merely to authorize other persons than the president and cashier, who shall be, however, equally responsible agents, to act under the immediate eye of the mother bank, and only to a limited extent. It has been suggested that the authority which is desired might diminish the securities against counterfeiting. This would be true if the officers designated were to be temporary or numerous; but the objection will be entirely removed if they be not more numerous, and be as permanent in their appointments as the officers who now discharge the same duties. All this the bank, with a view to its own interest and security, would order, should it not be prescribed by law, which, however, may be done. That the authority desired may not be misunderstood, the committee will remark, (though it is probably unnecessary,) that it is not desired that the bank shall be allowed to issue notes of lower denominations than those now authorized by the charter, nor is it desired that the substituted agents shall be allowed to sign notes of a higher denomination than twenty dollars. Indeed, the power may be limited to those of the denomination of ten dollars and under. Or, if it shall be deemed any additional security, or a preferable plan, to abolish entirely the authority of the president and cashier on this point, and require all the notes of the bank and its offices to be signed by the substituted agents, there can be no objection to it on the part of the bank. Under these guards, it will surely appear that there can be no objection of public policy to this request of the bank. But the grant of it is required by the public interest as well as the convenience of the bank. It will scarcely be questioned that the extension of the circulation of the notes of the Bank of the United States of the lower denominations would be a public benefit. This, however, cannot be effected, if it be required that the president and cashier shall sign each note. The duties of each of these officers, in relation to the mother bank alone, in-

cluding the transfer department of the bank and the loan office, and a complicated voluminous daily correspondence, are greater than are assigned to any like officers in the United States; but when to these are added a minute and vigilant superintendence of the business, accounts, and general management of seventeen offices, the aggregate constitutes a mass of labor that can leave no time for signing notes.

IV. *Circulation of the notes of the Bank of the United States.*

No subject connected with the currency can be of more importance than the circulation of the notes of the Bank of the United States. They may be made infinitely useful in purifying, sustaining, and increasing the sound currency of the Union. But they are but partially so at present; and it it not in the power of the bank, so long as they are receivable by the Government at all points where they may be tendered, instead of being received only where they may be payable, to make them co-extensively useful with the Union. Thus, for example, the notes of the Western and Southern offices are receivable in Philadelphia, New York, Boston, &c., in payment of all debts to the Government. The bank is not bound to pay to the Government except where its notes are payable, though they may be received elsewhere; but it is bound to transfer the funds of the Government from place to place, and could only gain a little time, perhaps with inconvenience to the Government, by refusing to pay where they may be received. It has, accordingly, always (except for a moment, when the safety of the bank rendered it necessary to ask the time to which it is entitled,) paid where the notes were received, without reference to the places where they were payable. The result is very embarrassing to the bank, and frequently very distressing to the community. There are some facts which it will be proper to state, before we present a more detailed view of the evil.

The exchanges between the West and the Atlantic are always against the former, which is a large debtor habitually to the latter. The exchanges between the North and the South run for one portion of the year against the latter, and for another in its favor. When the exchanges are unfavorable to the South and West, the notes of the Southern and Western branches all pass to the North, as a substitute for exchange. They are equal to cash, or very nearly so, in all the principal cities north of the Potomac. They are so, because they are receivable in payment of the duties to the Government, the portion of which payable to the north of the Potomac in any quarter of the fiscal year of 1819 was, taking that year as an example, nearly as much as the whole circulation of the Bank of the United States at the same time, and, of course, kept up a steady demand for the notes of the Southern and Western branches. The union of this demand with the course of exchanges draws the whole of the notes of the Western offices to the Atlantic, and, at particular seasons of the year, the greater part of the notes of the Southern

Bank of the United States.

offices to the North. The revenue collected to the South being comparatively small, there can never be any material reflux of their notes, because they will be absorbed by the Northern demand before the exchanges turn; and the balance of payments being always against the West, there is never any towards that quarter. We will now proceed to enumerate some of the evils resulting from the receipt of the notes of the bank and its branches, in this manner, and under these circumstances.

1st. It greatly deranges and distresses the money market, both of the places where the notes are received and where they are payable. The Bank at Philadelphia, and the offices at New York and Boston, did not receive less than between five and six millions of the notes of the offices South and West of them in the short period of fourteen months, exclusive of the notes of the office at Washington. These points were obliged to pay the Government the amount of these notes, and in vain sought for speedy reimbursements from the offices where they were payable. The state of the exchanges, which caused this flux of their notes, created an inability to reimburse the offices which had received them until the exchanges turned. The offices receiving them, were, of necessity, obliged to curtail their business suddenly, to provide the means of paying them. Accordingly, the curtailments at Philadelphia, New York, and Boston, within the same period, amounted to upwards of four and a half millions of dollars, and exhausted almost the whole of the capital placed at these points. The capital of New York and Boston united was, at some periods, less than nothing. What distress and embarrassment must have been caused by these circumstances will easily be conceived by those who have reflected on the nature and effects of the sudden withdrawal of a large portion of the active capital of a trading community.

The evil suffered in the community where the notes were thus received and paid was not all. The offices whose notes were thus received and paid were necessarily called upon to provide the means of reimbursement, and curtailments to a corresponding amount were ordered in them, and like distress and embarrassment produced in the communities where they were located. Double the amount of the notes thus circulated was, in this way, withdrawn from use to provide for their payment. The aggregate curtailments in the fourteen months before alluded to (from 1st September, 1818, to 1st November, 1819) were upwards of ten and a half millions of dollars; and, it is confidently believed, it would not have been necessary to reduce the discounts of the bank a single cent but for this cause. When these reductions commenced, the discounts were very moderate for the capital of the bank. They did not amount to $42,000,000.

Nor is the extent of the distress and embarrassment measured by the immediate effects of the reduction of the discounts of the bank and its branches. These reductions, in their operation, throw back upon the State banks a portion of their circulation, and reduce their deposites; and they also are obliged to curtail their business, and add to the general mass of distress.

The uncertain liability of the bank and its branches, (as each is, in a certain degree, liable to pay the notes of all the rest,) and the perpetual alteration of the capital of each, by paying the notes of the others, and having its notes paid by them, put it beyond the power of calculation to determine the extent of business which can be safely done, and leave the bank to vacillate between the hazards of rashness and the fruitless results of a torpid prudence. To-day a branch shall have a million of capital, and in three months it may be without a cent.

2d. It diminishes and deranges the currency of the whole country. The bank was under the necessity, to protect itself from danger, and to avoid charging itself to an unlimited amount with the cost of adverse exchanges, to forbid the offices with which the exchanges were unfavorable to issue their notes. It, however, issued its own notes; and the offices against which the exchanges did not run issued their notes without any limit but that of the demand; yet the circulation of the bank was, by this cause, greatly decreased. Thus, for example, in the short space of five months (from the 1st April, 1819, to the 30th August, 1819) it was reduced from $6,045,428 to $3,838,386.

This, however, does not show the entire extent of the abstraction from the currency which this cause produces. Let it be supposed that the circulation of the bank is four millions of dollars and that one-half of it has been issued by offices to the South and West, and is in use for the purposes of being remitted to the North and East. It is thereby as much taken out of the currency as if it were destroyed; and it leaves only two millions of currency furnished by the bank. But the bank will, probably, have four millions of specie in its vaults; and it cannot safely have less, under these peculiar circumstances: this sum, also, is withdrawn from circulation. Thus, the bank, not by its fault, but by the necessity which is imposed upon it, has withdrawn four millions of specie from the currency, and has given a substitute, in its notes, only to the amount of two millions. In this view, the currency has been diminished two millions. But even this is not the worst view of it. Let us suppose that the notes of the bank and its branches could not be converted into bills of exchange, (and there is no doubt, it is presumed, that, with its high credit, it could easily do what many local banks have accomplished,) it could circulate two dollars of its bills for every dollar it should have in its vaults. Then it is supposed to have four millions of dollars in its vaults, and could circulate eight millions of its notes, which would be equal to gold and silver. It then would have added four millions to the currency, while, at present, it diminishes it to the amount of two millions: making a practical difference of no less than six millions in the sound currency of the country. The view may even be extended, because the Bank of the United States could, had its capital not been deranged by this very cause, have given a greater addition of the currency with the greatest ease and safety, if a demand had existed for it, by increasing its specie. No evil can be greater than a decreasing currency. In the words of a great man, "poverty, and beggary, and sloth," follow in its train.

But this evil of a decreasing currency will not occur as a rare calamity once, perhaps, in a century; but will be renewed with every flux and reflux of the exchanges between the different portions of the country, as long as the bills of the Bank of the United States are thus receivable by the Government.

3d. It makes the necessary public burdens, in some instances, doubly oppressive. In all the States south of Virginia, and in nearly, if not all, the Western States, the Government of the United States does not expend half the revenue it collects; the surplus must be remitted to other points, where it is necessarily to be expended. This draws so much of the capital of those States from them, and adds it to the capital of another—New York, for example. This is not a subject of complaint, though it is certainly an evil. But when the revenue of New York is collected in the notes of the offices of the South and West, perhaps to an equal amount, and drawn from the necessary currency of these portions of the country, the evil produced by the remittance of the surplus revenue becomes intolerable, because the means of making it have been taken away. The capital of these States is fettered by the necessary curtailments of their banks; their currency is diminished, and that state of things which is called a scarcity of money is produced; exchange rises, and, when the revenue is to be remitted, the means of doing it no longer exist. .

These are the principal disadvantages arising from the receipt by the Government of the notes of the bank and its offices where they are not payable. There are many others, some of which are scarcely inferior in importance. Among them, none, perhaps, are more worthy of notice than the disadvantages suffered in those very particulars in which it is supposed the present practice is beneficial to the Government and the country.

The following are the advantages which have been supposed to result from the existing regulation:

1st. It is supposed that the notes form, as at present received, a currency coextensive in its sphere with the limits of the Union.

2d. That they form a substitute for exchange, free of the usual expense.

3d. That they form a sound currency, especially calculated for the payment of debts to the Government.

1st. The notes of the bank and its officers certainly do possess, as at present received, a credit coextensive with the limits of the Union, but they are by no means invariably of their nominal value at all times and places. From the middle of December to the middle of March or April the notes of the bank and the Northern offices will generally be at a discount in the South. And there

will be many other instances of their being under their nominal value. They are, however, always only a commodity where they are not payable, and their price will depend on the quantity in market and the demand for them; the demand for them will depend on the amount of revenue payable in the place where they are held compared with the quantity in the market. They will serve no purpose of a general currency against the current of exchange; nor will they ever, under any circumstances, serve the purpose of a currency, in a correct sense, where they are not payable. They will be at par, bear a premium, or be below par, according to circumstances. Even on the spot where they are issued they will frequently bear a premium, unless they are freely issued. In Ohio, for example, they are said to have commanded fifty per cent. premium in the current money of the State. But the overruling difficulty will be that the bank, in its own defence, will not issue its notes where they are to be used as a substitute for exchange; and it is only when they can be thus advantageously used that they are supposed to serve the purpose of general currency. But this will be more properly considered under the next head.

For one object of a general currency, (the only one for which such a currency is either desirable or practicable,) the Bank of the United States has furnished the most admirable expedient that has ever existed in any country—we mean a currency for the use of travellers. By making its five dollar bills payable at all its branches, there is no spot in the twenty-two States of the Union at which they will not be preferable to gold and silver; and there will be few places where they will not be instantly convertible into these metals. More in this way need not be done than to multiply them, which the bank will no doubt do to the extent of the demand, if the receipt of its other notes by the Government, at all points, be not allowed to continue embarrassments which may lessen or destroy its ability to do so.

2d. They do serve the purpose of exchange, and, if they can be drawn directly from the bank or its offices, they will of course be free of the usual expense of exchange. But this very rarely happens. The person who uses them as exchange has generally to pay to some low or cunning dealer in money a premium higher than a just premium on exchange in its accustomed form. And though there was, until the last twenty months, no restraint on the issue of notes by the offices, the bank, unless it choose wantonly to waste the capital of the stockholders, cannot, and will not in future, suffer its notes, under an adverse state of exchange, to be issued at one office, to create a demand at another, where money is from five to ten per cent. more valuable. This is no part of the duty of the bank, and its burdens are sufficiently great without adding to them. The bank will, with a view to its own just interests, furnish exchange, whenever and wherever it may have the ability to do so, at fair and reasonable rates.

Exchange, like all other mercantile transactions, but in a more especial degree, depends for its fair operation on an unembarrassed money market, on a well-adjusted currency, and on a state of established confidence. We have seen that the receipt by the Government of the notes of the bank and its branches where they are not payable has a powerful effect in distressing the money market, diminishing the currency, and impairing the pecuniary ability of the States from whence they are drawn to be used as a substitute for exchange; and we must therefore infer that it is a most unhappy means of supplying or facilitating exchanges. But why should the bank furnish exchange free of expense? Is not the premium of exchange as justly chargeable on the operations of commerce as any other charge? Why make the bank pay the price of exchange on the funds with which a cargo may be purchased in South Carolina or Georgia, and not the freight? Why should a desire exist—how can a desire justly exist—to throw this charge on the stockholders of the Bank of the United States, rather than on any other portion of the people? They are certainly, in a very peculiar degree, entitled to the protection of the General Government. With it the bank originated. It was in the confidence of its strength, of its faith, and of its wisdom, that the present holders subscribed for or bought the stock they hold. There was, unfortunately, gross and unprincipled gambling in the stock, but not by those who hold it. Few of them would probably have become interested in the institution, had it not been for the high degree of confidence they placed in the management of an establishment which was under the immediate eye and protection of the Government. The present holders are either original subscribers, innocent of the frauds and speculations which have been so justly the subject of reprobation; or they are injured persons, who have given twenty, thirty, forty, and fifty per cent. advance for the stock. If this fact be doubted, let it be inquired into.

If the stock list be regarded, it will be seen that large portions of the stock are held by all the classes of human helplessness—by the aged and infirm, by the widow and the infant, and by charitable and religious institutions. Are they fit subjects to be charged with the burdens of commerce, and with the equalizing of the exchanges? The people of the United States, generally, are direct owners of one-fifth part of this stock. Is there any reason why they should bear one-fifth of this particular charge on commerce? Is this charge to be imposed on the bank, on the ground of enormous profits? That, unfortunately, cannot be pretended. The present stockholders have been heavy losers, and have had their capital diminished; while the bank has paid large pecuniary considerations, for its privileges, and has rendered invaluable services to the Government. On what ground, then, it is respectfully asked, can a desire exist to heap so unreasonable a burden on this institution? But these pages are not intended to supplicate an exemption from any obligation that can be legally imposed, though it be harsh or distressing, if it have any foundation in public policy. If it have any foundation in public policy, disregard that fostering protection of the Govern-

ment, which the citizens ought to be taught to expect, and which attracted, no doubt, the honest portion of the stockholders to a bank which was national, in which the Government was a partner, and in the management of which it largely participates through its directors. Spare not the fund of charity, the sacred deposite of the church, the bread of the hungry, or the pittance of the wretched. Let these hallowed funds be made to bear exclusively the burden of paying the expense of a common mercantile operation, if they can be made to serve the end; but, before this sacrifice be made, (which surely cannot be made without some compunctious visitations,) let us dispassionately inquire, can they be made to serve the purpose intended?

We have said, that if a local circulation were allowed to the bank, it would furnish exchange on fairer terms, and at a lower rate, than is now paid for its notes; that its own interest would limit it to fair and moderate premiums; and that these would be enforced by an unembarrassed money market, a well adjusted currency, and an established confidence. All this we conceive to be demonstrable. Some, however, think differently, and suppose that private competition would be unavailing against the Bank of the United States, and that it might demand exorbitant premiums; but, perceiving the evils of driving the bank out of the exchange market, and of the derangements of the money and currency, which we have pointed out, they agree that, if a maximum of exchange were established, the notes of the bank should cease to be receivable, as at present. The first answer to this suggestion is, that it is absolutely impracticable. What would be the maximum of exchange, if the peace of the country were to become doubtful, and under a great variety of other circumstances, which may be easily imagined? It is useless to multiply examples; the point is too clear to require discussion: forty and fifty per cent. have been paid in the current medium in some parts of the Western States for the notes of the branches of the Bank of the United States. If the notes of the branches had been made a local currency from their first establishment, the business of the bank would have been under control, and would, no doubt, have been so regulated as to have judiciously distributed the capital of the bank. Under such circumstances, for example, there is no doubt it would have been the interest of the bank to have sold exchange in the Western States, on the Atlantic, at a light premium, and to have received its payment by another operation of exchange on New Orleans, where the products of the Western States find their market. The premium of exchange, whatever it may at any time be, will be fixed by uncontrollable causes, which are perfectly just, and almost perfectly accurate. It must inevitably be as equitably and correctly fixed as the price of wheat, cotton, tobacco, rice, or any other commodity. It is an utter misconception of the principles of exchange to suppose that the Bank of the United States, with any capital, or any means, for terms of any material duration, could exact an unreasonable premium, if the currency be sound. If that be unsound, there is no basis for fair dealing, and it is idle to project remedies against unfair practices. The discerning will easily perceive, and the candid will readily admit, that the bank is more likely to suffer than gain in such a state of things; but if the currency be sound, the rates of exchange can never be excessive, because they can never materially, and for any considerable length of time, exceed the expense, risk, and loss of interest incurred by the transportation of specie. The person desirous of purchasing exchange will either have the specie in his hands, or will receive it on demand from some bank whose notes he holds. Who, then, will be guilty of the folly of giving much more than the expense of transportation, &c.? There will be competition, too, wherever there is gain, which will be carried on as far, and continued as long, as it continues to be gainful. It is true that exchanges between some of the States have, for a considerable time past, been very high. But wherever it was high, the currency was in a greater or less degree unsound; the banks were curtailing, and the currency decreasing. These causes could produce no other result. Had these causes not existed, the premiums of exchange would not have been high. In some places, though the banks pretended to pay specie for their notes, they evaded it in effect. Let specie be paid promptly and bona fide to-morrow in places where exchange is high, and the premiums of exchange will immediately fall to rates founded on the charges and risk of transporting specie, and a trifle, perhaps, beyond their aggregate. That this is an inevitable result, it is believed, has never been denied. In England, it was denied that the adverse state of exchanges which that country suffered while its notes were inconvertible depended on the suspension of cash payments; but it was never denied that, if the currency could at any time be converted into the precious metals, the rates would be governed by the cost of transportation, &c. Let the currency be sound, and the premiums of exchange must be precisely just. To attempt to equalize exchange, or to place the charge of it on any other operations than those which shall cause a demand for it, will be as impracticable as it will be unjust.

3d. The next ground on which the receipt of the notes of the Bank of the United States, at all points, is considered politic, is, that they form a sound currency, in which the revenue may be collected. Any discrimination between the currency in which the demands of the Government may be collected, and the general currency of the country, is founded on a very limited view of the subject. The Government should never wish to collect its revenue in a better currency than that which its policy provides, and its laws ordain, for the purposes of the citizen. It is a distinction which can never be made with justice. The object of the Government should always be to establish a sound currency for the general use of society, in the advantages of which the revenue should only incidentally participate. If the Government does not insure a sound currency to its citizens, it can have no right

to demand of them a sound currency. They can only pay in such currency as they are enabled to procure. The sole inquiry, then, ought to be, whether the state of the currency is benefited or injured by the present regulation. This inquiry we have sufficiently attended to already. But we will go further, and show that the advantage supposed to be gained in the collection of the revenue is not gained; that it is, on the contrary, defeated by the very regulation which is supposed to afford it. Where the notes of the Bank of the United States will circulate as a currency, they are thrown out in abundance, and, in common with other good currency, are used in payment of the revenue. But where this is the case, there is no bad currency, and they yield no great immediate and local advantage that is not afforded by other notes. They, no doubt, keep the others in the sound state in which they are found, and that is probably what was really expected when it was supposed they would enable the Government to collect its revenue in a sound currency: that construction would be most consistent with good sense and sound policy. But if the object was that they should furnish a currency in which the revenue might be collected where there was no other good currency, certainly that object is frustrated by the present regulation. In the Western States, for example, the currency is unsound, and the regulation ought to have a tendency to keep the notes of the Bank of the United States there, that the revenue might be collected in them. But the tendency of it is directly the contrary; it is to remove them to a returnless distance from the place where they are wanted.

There is a mistake on this subject, in relation to the local banks, which it may be fit to notice. It is apprehended by some, that, by rendering the circulation of the offices of the Bank of the United States in a certain degree local, it would diminish and embarrass the circulation of the local banks. If this were true it would hardly be a sufficient reason to contravene an act of national policy, laying the claims of the Bank of the United States, merely in its corporate capacity, entirely out of the question; but the effect would be directly contrary where the regulation proposed would be at all operative. To the north of the Potomac it would have no operation at all, or none worth consideration; there, the bills of the Bank of the United States now remain, in common with the notes of the local banks, in a local circulation, without inconvenience to these banks, and with all the benefits which were expected from the establishment of the bank to the community. In the South and West, the change proposed, far from being injurious to the local banks, would be greatly beneficial. It is no doubt true, that, could they be permitted to furnish the whole circulation, and have that undisturbed by the receipts and remittances of the revenue, they would be gainers by the exclusion of the notes of the Bank of the United States; but both these advantages they cannot enjoy. If the revenue be collected exclusively in their notes, because the Bank of the United States shall be unable to issue any, they must pay the whole to that bank, as the pub-

Bank of the United States.

lic receiver, in specie; or it must remain their creditor, and pay the Government the amount without receiving it. There is no alternative. Not being thrown back again into circulation, the masses of their notes, thus withdrawn in the heavy collections of the Government, will not only diminish the aggregate of the general circulation, to the great injury of the country, but will, from destroying its equilibrium, and perverting the operation of its principles, actually reduce the circulation of those banks below the probable amount which they would enjoy in a joint and equally protected participation in the privilege with the Bank of the United States. This embarrassment has been felt by many of the local banks to the South, which have complained that the branches of the Bank of the United States did not issue their notes to relieve them from it; not perceiving that, had they done so, these notes would immediately have been converted into instruments of exchange, and, instead of relieving them, would have increased the evil, by adding to the embarrassments of the moneyed concerns of the community.

It is not true, as has been frequently but falsely alleged, that the Bank of the United States has any hostility to the local banks; and this committee is ready to demonstrate to the committees of Congress, if particular instances shall be stated, so as to render the subject susceptible of proof, that this is a calumny without the most slender foundation; and, on the contrary, they are ready to show signal instances in which it has fostered and sustained the local institutions. The Bank of the United States has always acted under the impression that its own prosperity was inseparably connected with the general prosperity of the country. It is needless, therefore, to say that the change proposed is not intended (while it is very obvious it will have a contrary effect) to lessen the advantages of the local institutions. Its object is to use its privileges with fair and reasonable advantage, in a manner which will not impair, but advance the public good. The regulation of which it complains is practically equivalent to an absolute prohibition to issue any notes in the Western States, and to a like prohibition to issue them to the South of the Potomac, during six months in the year, while the collection of the revenue, the convenience of all classes of the people in these quarters of the Union, and the restoration and perpetuation of a sound currency, all require them to be issued largely and diffused widely.

The remedy for all these evils is to make the notes receivable by the Government only where they are payable. To this general rule, without materially impeding the attainment of the object, there may be some exceptions. Indeed, these exceptions may even advance the general object, while they will serve other important purposes. The following may be safely allowed:

1. Let the notes of the parent bank be received everywhere.

2. Let the notes of the office at Washington be received everywhere.

3. Let all the notes of the bank and its offices be received in the States and Territories where the bank has no establishment.

4. Let the five-dollar bills of the bank and all the offices be received everywhere.

These exceptions ought to satisfy the advocates of the present regulation, because they will much more effectually than the general rule carry their views into effect, while they will produce few or none of the evils resulting from that regulation. The privilege given to the notes of the office at Washington alone will be, in itself, a much greater advantage to the Government and its agents than all the conceivable advantages (the evils aside) of the present regulation. It will render unnecessary a direct and sudden draught of the Government funds from the places where they may have been collected, to Washington, where they will be wanted: and it will save the bank the trouble and expense, and the bank and Government the odium of the transfer. The exception of five-dollar notes will confirm and enforce the existing regulation of the bank which directs the receipt and payment of notes of this denomination, as well of the bank as of the offices, at all the establishments of the bank. The proposed change rests entirely with the Government. It affects no part of the charter. The existing rule is a regulation entirely under the control of Congress. Let it, therefore, be remembered, that if the proposed change be made, and it be found not to be useful and salutary, it may be repealed at the next, or any other session of Congress; it will confer no right upon the bank. Is it not, then, manifest that great evils exist from the present regulation? Is there any concomitant advantage, except that enjoyed by the lowest class of money-dealers? Is there any possible danger that can result from a change by way of experiment? May we not hope, then, that the experiment may be made?

Finally, the committee beg leave to remark that it is not true, as has been represented, that the bank is asking new privileges of Congress. Is it a new privilege which would remove a restraint whose operation denies to the institution the services of safe and competent managers? Is it a new privilege which would punish great crimes with adequate punishments? Is it a new privilege which would merely substitute one class of agents in the place of another for the discharge of a duty consisting entirely of manual labor? In fine, is it a new privilege to the bank for the Government not to receive its notes in a manner productive of great public evil, because it will combine a benefit to the bank with the public good? Are they not mere modifications of existing privileges, or the exclusive exercise by Government of its own right, for the public advantage?

The statement annexed, marked A, will show the evil and embarrassing effects of the existing regulation, when the notes of the offices to the South and West were freely issued, on the distribution of the capital of the bank. It will appear from it, that, at the date of that statement, notwithstanding great exertions had been made to place and keep capital at Boston, the effect not only failed, but that the office at that place had

Bank of the United States.

less than no capital by $372,000—that is to say, that the bank was indebted to it that sum; and that the office established in the great commercial city of New York had no more than $245,000 of the immense capital of the bank.

The statement annexed marked B will show the immense amount of the branch notes which have been redeemed where they were not payable.

Accompanying this communication the committee of Congress will also receive a list of the stockholders* of the bank on the 1st October, 1820, which will enable them to see who are now the stockholders; from which it will, it is believed, appear that they have been justly characterized by the memorial.

A.

* *Distribution of the capital of the Bank of the United States, May 28, 1819.*

Portsmouth	- - - -	$117,678 70
Providence	- - - -	335,208 54
Middletown	- - - -	255,985 11
New York	- - - -	245,287 81
Baltimore	- - - -	5,646,395 28
Washington	- - - -	555,737 97
Richmond	- - - -	1,760,502 88
Norfolk	- - - -	861,764 16
Fayetteville	- - - -	677,963 81
Charleston	- - - -	1,935,042 35
Savannah	- - - -	1,420,543 45

New Orleans	- - - -	1,664,596 47
Lexington	- - - -	1,502,388 44
Cincinnati	- - - -	2,400,987 30
Louisville	- - - -	1,129,009 00
Chilicothe	- - - -	649,858 83
Pittsburg	- - - -	769,031 36
Philadelphia	-	$13,418,742 96

Deduct this sum, due to the Boston office 372,825 79

—————————13,045,917 17

34,973,828 63

This statement of the capital at Philadelphia is merely nominal, if considered as a capital for the proper operations of banking, as in the above sum are embraced all the property and debts due the institution, including therein the five per cent. stock which the Government subscribed, debts due by State banks, &c.

It is proper to add, that, since the date of this statement, the necessary restraint put upon the issues of the notes of the offices to the South, at seasons when the exchanges are unfavorable to them, and upon those of the West, at all seasons, the exchanges being always unfavorable to them, has enabled the bank, by great efforts and great vigilance, to place and keep adequate capitals at all points.

B.

The following sums, in branch notes, received at the Bank of the United States, have been disposed of as follows:

Offices.	Returned to offices.	Notes of offices destroyed.	Notes of offices on hand.	Total redeemed at parent bank.
Portsmouth - - - - -	25,310	100	2,775	28,185
Boston -	32,575	142,655	3,215	178,445
Providence - - - - -	21,640	570	1,780	23,990
Middletown	42,920	920	10,385	54,225
New York -	373,490	812,330	29,240	1,215,060
Baltimore -	2,111,405	214,540	1,730	2,327,675
Washington -	3,467,370	28,375	54,885	3,550,630
Norfolk -	451,550	13,520	18,725	483,795
Richmond -	922,439	9,610	16,120	948,169
Fayetteville -	301,308	259,980	7,190	568,478
Charleston -	611,799	128,580	12,850	753,229
Savannah -	969,055	479,440	11,730	1,460,225
New Orleans -	430,115	195,010	30,040	645,165
Louisville -	27,550	222,210	94,340	344,100
Lexington -	170,280	379,500	84,800	634,580
Cincinnati -	198,000	492,540	119,010	809,550
Chilicothe -	26,000	227,360	33,850	287,210
Pittsburg -	248,750	290,790	41,410	580,950
	$10,421,556	$3,898,030	$574,075	$14,893,661

* The list is omitted.

To the foregoing amount of　-　$14,893,661 00
there ought to be added the following amount of post notes issued by the parent bank, and destroyed, because they were used in the Southern and Western States in lieu of branch notes　-　-　-　-　　5,528,981 96

Amount redeemed　-　-　$20,422,642 96

The sum thus redeemed is exclusive of considerable sums in branch notes, received at offices other than those which issued them, and which were not returned through the parent bank, but directly from the offices which redeemed them to the offices which had issued them.

JAMES HOUSTON,
Assistant Cashier.

Bank U. S., *Dec.* 7, 1820.

PROTECTION TO MANUFACTURES.

[Communicated to the House, January 15, 1821.]

Mr. Baldwin, from the Committee on Manufactures, to whom had been referred the various memorials praying for and remonstrating against an increase of the duties on imports, respectfully reported:

That they have directed their best attention to the subjects submitted to them by the House, and feel it their duty to state their views fully and freely, so that it may be enabled to act with promptitude. It is certainly time that the propriety of extending protection to the objects now claiming it should be finally settled; the nation expects, and their interest demands it.

It is not a matter of very great consolation to the committee to know that, at the end of thirty years of its operation, this Government find its debt increased $20,000,000, and its revenue inadequate to its expenditure; the national domain impaired, and $20,000,000 of its proceeds expended; $35,000,000 drawn from the people by internal taxation, $341,000,000 by impost, yet the public Treasury dependent on loans; in profound peace, and without any national calamity, the country embarrassed with debts, and real estate under rapid depreciation; the markets of agriculture, the pursuits of manufactures, diminished and declining; commerce struggling, not to retain the carrying the produce of other countries, but our own. There is no national interest which is in a healthful, thriving condition; the nation at large is not so; the operations of the Government and individuals alike labor under difficulties which are felt by all, and for which some remedy must be discovered. It is not a common occurrence in the history of nations, that in peace the people should call on the Government to relieve their distresses; the Government reciprocate the call, by asking the people to relieve theirs; the resources of both exhausted; both marching to poverty or wealth (as

opinions may vary) in the same road, on the same principles; their expenses exceeding their receipts; unable to discover, or unwilling to develop, new sources of wealth or industry; pursuing theories too far, or not far enough; too much or too little guided by the opinion of foreign authors and reviewers or domestic statesmen, (as each mind may fancy;) unmindful of the policy which has secured the great interests of other nations, or unable to devise a better for ours; too unwise to profit by the lessons of experience; too wise to need them, or unable to agree as to their dictates—we are certainly not at that point of public or private prosperity which can be a source of satisfaction. Others "rejoice at the beams of peace" which bring their attendant blessings; but, if the people of this country may judge of the five next by the five last years, war will be peace to them. Five years of peace on the continent of Europe have nearly repaired the ravages of twenty-five years of war; four years of peace in this authorized the official declaration "that but few examples have occurred of distress so general and severe as that which has been exhibited in the United States."

For the first twenty-two years we enjoyed all the advantages of peace at home and war abroad; we prospered amidst the distresses of others. But it ought not to be said of a Republic that its institutions are calculated only for a state of foreign convulsion; that it can flourish only when others suffer. Our history justifies the observation that our prosperity is in a ratio inverse to that of Europe; when it is in a state of convulsion, we rise to greatness in proportion to its throes; its repose causes a revulsion which shakes all our interests to their foundation. If it be really true that we have adapted our systems to a state of war in Europe, that they are inconsistent with the relations which flow from general peace, it behooves us to pause, and ask if this is a prudent basis for legislation? if it is not a bold and a dangerous experiment to make all our calculations on a state of things which no longer exists, and was forced and unnatural? We are too apt to think the events of our own times common ones. We become familiarized to them by their continuance, and cease to appreciate their magnitude. History has never presented to our contemplation such a succession of great events as in the last thirty years. Future generations will wonder at them, and wish they had occurred in their days. We, under whose observation they have passed, bestow less of our attention to their nature, and are not sufficiently convinced that, in proportion to their importance, their recurrence is less probable. When the fancy or pride of the historian shall have swelled them beyond truth, those which we now contemplate with so much admiration will lose their interest. An imported head of antiquity, which may have been on the shoulders of Pompey, excites more curiosity than the heads of greater men whom we have all seen: future ages will look more to that of Washington. It is not for curiosity alone we look to other ages and other countries; we eagerly search the records of ancient Republics for the rules of government and the lessons of experience;

Protection to Manufactures.

we could better profit by the examination of our own; posterity will look to this for example. Other nations have followed and now profit by our political institutions, but all shun and avoid our internal policy, our principles of economy, and national interest, because our experience has proved their fallacy; our moral influence still operates everywhere but at home; we alone are unjust to ourselves, unwilling to profit by our own practice. The present Cortes of Spain, at the moment of assimilating their religious and political establishments to ours, evince, by their corn laws, tariff, and commercial regulations, that our history has been instructive to them; when it shall prove so to ourselves, it will not be thought unsafe or unwise to build our systems of revenue on domestic and not foreign industry, on the foundation of our own laws, internal production and internal employment. As to stability, it is the difference between the waves and the land; as to certainty, between the return of the seasons and the fluctuations of foreign regulations; as to the means of consumption, between the steady demand for the surplus of labor and production, and the one which varies with every importation. History does not furnish another instance of a nation relying on the importation of goods as the main and almost exclusive source of revenue. It has now become more like the daring throw of desperation than the settled result of financial knowledge, or the deliber-

ate deductions of reason. In every other nation, agriculture, manufactures, and commerce, have been deemed intimately connected, each necessary to the growth and wealth of each other, all essential ingredients of national happiness; in ours, there is said to be an hostility deep, inveterate, and incurable. To every individual among us, it is the first lesson of economy to earn more than is expended, to sell more than is bought, to export more than import; yet this is said to be bad policy for a nation. It has been deemed sound policy to bottom the public resources on the consumption of the people, and that the articles of that consumption should be furnished from abroad. Thirty years of experience has tested the wisdom of our measures; they may suit a state of war, but are ruinous to us in peace. It is verily believed that the last five years of European peace have taken from the resources of the people more than was acquired in twenty-two years of European war; that, if the debts of the country were deducted from the value of the property, the nation is poorer than in 1790. If this be thought a bold assertion, the committee beg that its correctness may be decided, not by general exclamation, but by practical observation and calculation. Our population has increased nearly three-fold: have our exports increased in proportion? The following *statement* may not be without instruction:

Exports for the years 1790 and 1820.

Exports.		For 1790.	For 1820.	Increase.	Decrease.
Pot and pearl ashes	- - tons	6,280	8,625	2,345	
Beef - - - -	- barrels	62,371	53,891	–	8,480
Flour - - -	- barrels	619,681	1,177,036	557,355	
Fish, dried - - -	- quintals	383,237	321,419	–	61,818
Fish, pickled - - -	- barrels	57,424	87,916	20,492	
Flaxseed - - -	- bushels	409,444	220,914	–	188,530
Indian corn - - -	- bushels	1,713,241	533,741	–	1,179,500
Pork - - -	- barrels	26,635	44,091	17,450	
Rice - - -	- tierces	73,329	71,663	–	1,666
Tobacco - - -	- hogsheads	101,272	83,940	–	17,332
Tar - - -	- barrels	51,044	38,176	–	12,868
Pitch - - -	- barrels	3,818	3,798	–	20
Turpentine - - -	- barrels	58,107	75,749	17,642	
Wheat - - -	- bushels	1,018,339	22,137	–	997,202

It would be descending to minuteness to pursue the comparison to all the items of our exports; the general result would not differ from this specimen. In cotton, there has been not only a prodigious increase, but as it were a new creation; the value of this article exported is to the amount of all our domestic exports as twenty-two to fifty-one. It exceeds all the other agricultural productions of the country, but can be raised only in the southern sections; to them and the nation at large it is of infinite interest; it relieves the general gloom; but to sixteen States it affords no profits, except by carrying and consumption; it furnishes no foreign market for other productions.

If the amount of exports be a test of national wealth, if agriculture be an interest worthy of national attention, this presents a serious picture of our progress; it ought to be well examined by every farmer who cannot raise cotton. So far as the exportation of domestic produce is the support of commerce, so far the picture applies, and the merchant must seriously examine it. So far as the ability to consume productions imported from foreign countries depends on the quantity of ours exported, the financier must look to the prospects of the revenue; and in its effects on all the interests of the nation, the statesman has much for contemplation. When he has compared the imports with the exports, he can well account for the following official view of our situation:

" The currency of the United States has in three years been reduced from \$110,000,000 to \$45,000,000. This reduction exceeds fifty-nine per cent. of the whole circulation of 1815." "All intelligent writers upon currency agree that where it is decreasing in amount, poverty and misery must prevail. The correctness of the opinion is too manifest to require proof; the united voice of the nation attests its accuracy. As there is no recorded example in the history of nations of a reduction of the currency so rapid and so extensive, so but few examples have occurred of distress so general and so severe as that which has been exhibited in the United States."—[*Treasury Report on the Currency, p.* 496.]

Without inquiring whether the state of the currency is a cause or an effect, it is enough to know and feel the melancholy truths thus avowed. Why are these things so? The sea, the forest, the earth, yield their abundance; the labor of man is rewarded; pestilence, famine, or war, commit no ravages; no calamity has visited the people; peace smiles on us; plenty blesses the land. Whence, then, this burst of universal distress? In former ages, seven years of plenty would feed seven years of famine. Plenty was a blessing, not a curse; it seems reversed in the present. Our last five years have been well favored and fat fleshed, our corn been rank and good, but our individual and national resources are " withered, thin, and blasted with the east wind;" "our full corn has become blasted, our fat kine poor and very ill favored and lean fleshed, such as we never saw before in all the land." When the bounties of Providence fail to prove beneficent in their effects, man must be perverse or Government unjust. Past the thirtieth year of our existence in the present form, approaching the fiftieth of independence, and, counting from that of its recognition, we have had fewer months of war than years of peace, yet abundance cannot relieve our wants; the market for the one, the supply of the other, are neither within the control of the people, or directed by the Government. A Government, too, of the people's choice, bound to reward filial attachment by national protection, it was not instituted—it is not supported—to suffer all the interests of the nation to be writhing under foreign policy, and, while imploring relief, to be sunk under the appalling answer of "regulate yourselves."

When Government calls on the people for revenue, they will answer " let us alone." If legislation will neither lead to wealth nor relieve from distress, it must not legislate the people out of wealth or into poverty. When plenty is attended with the effects of famine, when superfluity will not avert wants, and peace to us produces all the miseries of war to others, there must be some deep and radical error; it must be most powerful in its operation, and be inherently fixed in a system which thus involves a whole nation in general distress. History affords no example of a people impoverished while in the full fruition of health, peace, and plenty; it has fallen to the lot of ours

to furnish a new item to its records. Elsewhere, an overflowing treasury indicates national prosperity; with us, the two years of the greatest revenue have been selected as the epoch which consummated our embarrassments. There are sources of taxation which will supply the public wants from the people's surplus; those sources are traced in every country but this. Our system of revenue is founded on the markets and consumption of the country, and both are dependent on foreign power and interest. Success may justify the bold experiment at a time when moral and political principles have been deranged by a great revolution; but when pursued in a time of settled order and general repose, it savors not of wisdom or justice. It failed even in the age of wonders; it would be a new one, indeed, if it succeeded now.

It cannot be unwise or unprofitable to search for the causes which have brought the country to its present condition. The evils, being neither local nor partial, can be of no ordinary kind; their origin cannot be in the people. It could not be their intention to blast the interests of agriculture, manufactures, and commerce, for they are their own; to exhaust their public treasury, for that must tend to their oppression; it could not be in their power, if their Government was wise enough to discover the tendency, and strong enough to control their operations; and if it has not wisdom to discover or strength to direct the true interests of the nation, it cannot be such a one as its founders intended to secure to their posterity. It is a poor compliment to their wisdom as well as ours, a poor recommendation to republican forms and principles, if this Legislature cannot " provide for the common defence and promote the general welfare ;" we trust it will be never said that it shall not by its efforts deserve success. If the fault is not in the people, it must be in the Government, either foreign or domestic; if foreign systems have produced these lamentable consequences, it cannot be necessary to enforce the necessity of their counteraction; if a domestic system, or the want of one, has led us to our present state, its abolition, or the adoption of a new one, is a solemn duty due to our constituents. If the majority in our councils should think that a change of policy may be dangerous, it must mean domestic; their patriotism would forbid the imputation of their being unwilling to relieve the country from the operation of foreign policy, if that should be the cause of our grievous condition. If it is not foreign, it must be domestic; and they ought to be well assured that their course is consistent with reason and sanctioned by experience. If it be true that our present legislation is calculated on a state of war in Europe, that it has then but partially succeeded, and wholly failed in peace, would seem but the natural connexion between cause and effect. The change of all the relations on which a system is built must affect the system itself; it is in vain to expect a uniformity in its operations when all the moving principles are reversed. We build our revenue on consumption, yet expect it to be permanent while consumption is in a consumption; we found the people prospered when exportation gave a market for their surplus, and look for a continuance of prosperity when the sources of it are stopped. The expenses of this Government increase with the population of the country; yet, while expenditure is on the advance revenue is on the decline. Ours is the last Government in the whole community of nations which is willing that the markets for the production, the establishments for fabrication, should be in a foreign country, under the influence of foreign Powers; we give efficient protection only to the means of distributing our wants. We seem not to follow the experience of ages, but to be making a daring effort to persevere in the assertion of principles exploded by all national practice; yet, in their application to one great and important branch of national industry, we have discovered and corrected our error (if error it may be called) before any practical injury was sustained. During five-and-twenty years we adhered to our discriminating duties on tonnage; they probably aided our commerce during the French revolution; but it was foreseen they would injure it when the occupations displaced by that event should have obtained their accustomed employment, when the interest of nations would suffer them to pursue their policy; and only fourteen days elapsed from the promulgation of our treaty of peace before we repealed our whole system of discriminating duties as to the ships of all nations who would repeal theirs. We offered reciprocity to all the world; but where reciprocity was refused, the discrimination remained; it still remains, and this Congress adheres to the same rigid course which is pursued towards American shipping. The committee deem it not improper to recommend the lesson of its own experience; it is but for this Congress to apply its own principles to another co-ordinate and equally important branch of national industry. Laws founded on war will not suit a state of peace in this more than any other. Let there be no system of restriction, but one of reciprocity—of liberal interchange; as one of the great family of nations, let our laws keep pace with theirs in liberality; let them even make the first friendly offer.

The act of March, 1815, is our own definition of free trade. It declares that reciprocity of duties is the true principle by which to ascertain whether a system is restrictive or free. This act has met with the approbation of the whole country. So far as the reciprocity has been obtained, it has aided our commerce; and all we ask of others is the adoption of this principle. But, though we repeal our laws, it is only conditional—"such repeal to take effect in favor of any foreign nation, whenever the President of the United States shall be satisfied that the discriminating or countervailing duties of such foreign nation, so far as they operate to the disadvantage of the United States, have been abolished." Reciprocal duties are within the spirit of this law; its policy is wise and sound; its application to the interest of agriculture and manufactures, it is believed, would relieve their distresses. That the exclusion of the productions of our soil operates to the disadvantage of the United States cannot be denied. Reciprocal duties on theirs is our practical commentary on the text. It is, then, most respectfully submitted to the House that it, at least, deserves the trial whether the same rule ought not to be applied with equal force to the raising, the making, as well as to the carrying of our articles of consumption. Year succeeds year; our troubles increase. For the five years of the new state of things, no changes have been made in our laws in relation to any concern but commerce; each year finds them worse. At the last session the attempt to effect a change was called premature; and it seems that even now the convenient season has not arrived. The measures then and now proposed are said to be ruinous to the great concerns of the country. No better or other plan is proposed for their relief, when all admit the evil; some must offer a remedy; those who object to the plans of others should present some of their own, or prove that none is necessary. If the country labors under distress, the cause should be discovered as well as the remedy. If it is not to be found in the declension of our agriculture and manufactures, then where is it? If their revival will not effect the cure, then what will? The people of this country expect that something will be done; and as the measures must originate in this House, it assigns the various subjects of consideration to the appropriate committees. No measure has yet been proposed by the Committee of Ways and Means to provide relief to the treasury, or by those on agriculture and commerce to relieve those interests. It has thus devolved on the Committee on Manufactures, not to act in concert with the other committees of this House in devising the measures which may afford, by their harmonious co-operation, equal relief to all the suffering interests of the country, but, unaided, as it were, on a forlorn hope, to look for the means of assistance to the interests peculiarly confided to their care. The committee do not shrink from the arduous duties. In their discharge they find great relief in the conviction, which results from their investigations, that there is no great interest of this nation distinct from another; that there exists among them a most intimate union, connexion, and dependence; that, in our happier days, they were as little divided as they are now in those of their despondency. If all now flourished but one, it might well be doubted if it would be proper to risk their safety, by attempting a change. But the committee think there can be no danger in moulding our system into such shape as is necessary to meet the changes in its foundation; to apply the same principles, which have been approved of by every Congress since the peace, to all the sources of national industry. We think them the heads of tributary streams which form the great river of public prosperity. We know of no dividing ridge which prevents their union. All history, past and present; all experience, foreign and domestic; the opinion of the statesman in council, and the farmer in the field; the coincidence of national laws and national toasts, connect agriculture, manufactures, and commerce. We are not aware that this union is forbidden, or ought to be dissolved by sound legislation. Believing it exists, and is indispensable to national happiness, we beg leave to present a bill, which is the offspring of our judgment, guided by no attachment to one interest at the expense of another, by no hostility to any system, except such as "operate to the disadvantage of the United States."

If common defence requires a revenue to provide the means, that revenue should be as certain as the expenditure, permanent as the wants it is designed to meet, built on the consumption, supporting and supported by the industry of the country. If the means of consumption depend on the facilities of exchange, a market must be secured to agriculture; provisions and raw materials must have a permanent and steady demand; manufactures must exist somewhere to furnish and secure this demand, and the supply of the articles for use which commerce must distribute. Then another question occurs: Where should these means exist and be in operation? In our own country, in the hands of our own citizens, under the control of our own Government: these appear to us the essence of independence. The materials for building and equipping our ships, clothing and arming our soldiers and sailors, consuming the surplus, and supplying the wants of the people, are items in the general system of common defence and general welfare. It is time to know whether this country can or ought to command them. The effects of foreign command have been tried; it is but a common mode of coming at truth to try the domestic.

National interest and national pride have already been put to a severe test; it is yet grating to national feeling to find the benefits of our laws accruing not to our own citizens, but to a people who have no attachment to our institutions, whose interest is adverse to ours. The raising of raw materials, and their conversion into manufactures, have, in all other countries, been deemed a source of general wealth; the placing the raiser, the manufacturer, and the consumer as near to each other as possible, has been in every trial found to be the advantage of all. The supply of the want of manual by the labor of machinery is a practical remedy for a sparse population, all tending to increase the certainty and facility of exchange, which promote alike all the branches of national industry. The country is not known where commerce has not grown with manufactures, and agriculture been nourished by both. In this we have not paid as much attention to internal as external industry, yet it cannot be less important. We have built our revenue on importations, but have been indifferent about securing the means of purchasing imported articles; our custom-house credits are a bounty to the importer, yet it seems of no concern whether that importer is a resident or an alien, whether the profits of importation are scattered within the country, through the thousand channels of domestic expenditure, or sent abroad to produce the same good effects to others. If the wealth or poverty of a nation can be ascertained from its abundant or diminished currency, it becomes most interesting to know what gives it amount and activity; it must be industry, employment, and the resulting profits, of which currency is more the effect than the cause. The flood of importations has lessened their employment and the sources of gain; currency is deprived of its occupation; the pursuits of active industry, profitably employed, require some common medium to pass from hand to hand, to go the rounds of society and continue active till demand for it ceases. In its course through the great circle, the same sum may pay twenty times its amount of debts, be the foundation of twenty new contracts, furnish a market for twenty different products or employments. It thus performs, in its twenty operations, the same duties that twenty times the same would, if confined to one. As a means of paying for imports, its movement is in a straight line to the merchant as an article of remittance; it is only on its arrival in a foreign country that it travels the rounds of employment. In the interior, the dollar which reaches the store does not come back to the farmer, mechanic, or laborer; expended in a manufactory, it returns again for provisions, materials, and labor, current; while it can find employment affording and receiving it, it passes through every occupation; from the store it has but one. It is the difference between circulation and remittance, furnishing employment at home or abroad. Profits being the life of currency, currency being the criterion of general prosperity, the committee will not further examine whether it is better for the nation that those profits should accrue from domestic sources and to the residents of our country.

The estimate of the Treasury Department is, that, in three years, the currency of the country was diminished $65,000,000, counting from 1815; that this diminution has produced unexampled distress and misery. How has it produced this state of things? If the currency has been thus reduced, it has been from the want of employment. There is, perhaps, more specie in the United States, than at any former period, but it is not currency while it is unemployed; when it does not pass from hand to hand, it is no more currency than an equal value of silver or gold in ingots, or the boxes or vaults of the bank which contain it. Bank notes are currency when they are current and in circulation, but while they are in the bank are no more currency than if they had not been signed. The diminution of the currency is, therefore, not owing to its extinction, but to the want of use and employment. There is now but the one duty for it to perform—remittance. There is no want of capital to enliven the pursuits of agriculture, to push manufactures into operation, or to give activity to commerce. But there is no employment; the materials of currency are abundant, but no occupation to set them in motion; $65,000,000 has been withdrawn from circulation, because there has ceased to be any cause to produce action. Coin, or bank notes, or both, are currency when current and in action; they cease to be so when there is no use for them. In 1815, the production, fabrication, and distribution of the country,

Protection to Manufactures.

kept $110,000,000 of currency in active operation; the business of the nation, required it. Now it is reduced to $45,000,000, for this plain reason—the business of the country requires no more. Business had decreased 59 per cent.; embarrassment and distress have increased in the same ratio. The history of those three disastrous years will tell us the kind of business which has so decreased as to bring about such consequences. It is not the business of importation of foreign goods, for it was never so great; if they add to a nation's wealth, riches have indeed flowed over the land without stint. It is not the business of remittance; so far as that is an employment for currency, it still continues in full activity, requiring not only money, but bank stock, public stock, book debts, notes, bonds, judgments, and bankruptcies, to pay the balance against us. It is that rectilinear current which makes the merchant only the conduit to the great foreign reservoir. Unless, then, it shall be first made to appear that the state of our foreign trade is such that the balance-sheet is in favor of our merchants, that the foreign manufacturers and exporters are the debtors and not creditors of our merchants, until they send out more than they bring home, foreign importations call for more currency. If, however, on this important subject of the balance of trade, we should labor under an error, it can easily be corrected by the exhibition which every importer has it in his power to make, which would add to his credit at home and abroad, which would remove deep and dangerous delusions, quiet the public fears, and end discussions which will never cease without some practical test. It becomes here indispensable to settle it. If the balance of trade is against us, and more remittance is required, then there is one employment for currency left, and the reduction is not for the want of importations to keep it active; if, on the other hand, there are no remittances due, no employment for the currency, the falling off in importations may, in such case, be put down as one leading cause of the decrease of currency and growth of public misery. It solves at once the great question: What is that employment of currency which adds to and secures general wealth, and guards against poverty—imports or exports, foreign or domestic manufactures? It is the subject on which volumes have been and will be written, public opinion and the national councils divided, and on the correctness of the decision of which all the public and private interests of this nation depend. Authors, reviewers, essayists, statesmen, and printers, can never convince each other by any thing depending on reasoning. But there is one book that contains the convincing and conclusive argument which none can resist—the importer's leger. If the excess of exports over imports is the measure of a profitable trade, the merchant's leger will show it, being the only person concerned in the trade; if he pays for the goods imported, his and the country's profits are the same. Now, this book shows whether the excess of imports or of exports is the profit. If he has paid for all imports, and has a balance of goods on hand, or of money due him, the trade is profitable. To settle at once

this great controversy, to take a bond of fate, to exhibit such a case as will prevent a recurrence of another attempt to induce Congress to pass a law which shall never destroy agriculture, commerce revenue, and all the interests of the nation, let the importers of foreign goods proudly exhibit their balances on the credit side, if they exist; they must increase their credit, and will convince Congress that importations add to national and individual wealth. The committee would withdraw their recommendation of manufactures when one small item of information should be communicated. For what purpose are stocks sent to Europe? why are foreign collectors seen in our commercial cities? property sold by foreign plaintiffs and assignees and, probably, not an instance of an importer's insolvency without foreign creditors in the schedule? If the balance is favorable, why is not opposition silenced where it is so easily done? When it is not done, the fair inference is that it cannot be done. It may, then, be taken for conceded that there is yet employment for currency in remittances, and that this has not been the source of its useful or profitable occupation.

This at once solves the great mystery, and settles the great question; it points to that use and circulation which makes the amount and activity of currency the test of general prosper ty—*internal*, not external. It accounts for the ieagerness of foreign nations, foreign artisans, merchants abroad, and foreign agents among us, to monopolize that circulation from hand to hand, through the whole round of internal commerce, which gives its vigor and profits; for the willingness of all of them to leave to us the miserable and ruinous circulation of currency for remittance to them. Foreign writers and foreign statesmen may well inculcate on ours the doctrine that the excess of imports over exports is the rate of profit; their doctrines are like the profits, sound and solid to the nation that reaps the benefit. Whether it is the one which pays, or the one which receives; the one which holds the coin, or the one which hears it jingle; the one whose currency flows in a torrent-like stream beyond its jurisdiction, never to return, or the one whose currency becomes a steady, gentle current, meandering through every occupation within the great circle of national industry, giving use and value to every production, floating it to every market, the state of the currency and of the nation furnishes convincing proofs. It is then no longer left to · conjecture the reasons why this country flourished in war, and has become depressed in peace; why the people could then pay the Government twelve millions of internal taxes a year from sources that would not now furnish one. They had a currency; it was active, it reached every man. Manufactures flourished every where within the sphere of their operations; all the agriculture of the country flourished with them; it was depressed only in those parts of the Union beyond their influence. Profits remained where they were acquired; they were impelled out through the arteries, and returned through the veins; each occupation, being healthy and active, aided another; their united efforts were felt

Protection to Manufactures.

by the nation. Currency was confined in its course and variety only by the general mass and complication of the mutual wants of our whole population. And where manufactures are yet flourishing, the same effects are yet felt; the sphere of their action bounds the circle of circulation. Beyond that circle there is scarely a currency left, except in the cotton-growing States; there it continues, because foreign policy and the interest of foreigners will not suffer its exclusion from a market. But to all the grain-raising States, those abounding in raw materials for manufactures, and population, fuel, and machinery to conduct them, the prospect is gloomy indeed. The fertile soil of the interior and the West produces measureless products; roads, canals, and noble rivers, afford infinite means of distribution; but there is no market, no employment. Foreign systems, with unresisted, unchecked sway, have attained the command of our consumption, deny the use of our products, monopolize the profits of converting rough materials into manufactures, and would have acquired the profits of their distribution had this Government "let it alone." Foreign agriculture supplies the materials, foreign industry the labor which produces to the American people their clothing, their utensils, and means of defence against foreign aggression. American materials have no value; American labor has not employment; and the American Government has adopted no system of counteraction, no measure of resisting or defensive policy. If ever a people were groaning under a restrictive system, one of bounties, premiums, privileges, and monopolies, which denies the operation of every one principle of free trade, which coerces occupation and paralyzes industry, which prohibits a foreign market to our productions, and forces every thing foreign on ours, thus depriving us of both, it is the people of whom we are the representatives, who have honored us with their confidence, and confided their interests to our patriotism. If this system was the offspring of our legislation, error of judgment might be an apology for its commencement, and a disposition to make no sudden changes for its continuance; that the moving motive for its enactment was the good of this nation; a conviction that it was the best mode of drawing, in fair exchange, the resources of others, retaining our own. But when we admit this is a foreign system, enacted by foreign Governments for the benefit of their subjects, not of our citizens—as the means by which to draw our wealth to them, and not to throw theirs to us, we have a serious account to render to a suffering people. Commerce has been rescued from the grasp of foreign usurpation by legislation—so far, at least, as granting all that has been asked. Agriculture and manufactures are struggling, unaided, under a weighty pressure; we all unite in wishing them well; many bestow their blessings, rejoice in their good prospects, feel and acknowledge their importance, glad they are doing so well, and hope they will do better. The commercial codes of Europe are, at the people's expense, laid on our tables; there is not a production of our country at which some of them are not directed; not a branch or source of

national industry which they do not attempt to destroy; this is the pressure, this causes the struggle which, in every district, some of us witness; to let them alone is to leave them in a foreign grasp. Why bestow our blessings or ever breathe a wish for the success of our industry, if it is not a national contest? If it be the nation's and the people's cause, why will not the Government that has an eye to pity stretch forth its arm to save? In no small portion of the nation, oceans, roads, canals, and rivers afford little else than the means of importing and distributing foreign productions; the land, of little other use but a resting-place on which to consume them. Thus have "our soil and our seas" already been usurped from those to whose use they were designed, and to whose use it is our duty to secure them. The consummation of foreign has left no good foundation for the fear of domestic usurpation. We have told the people that reciprocal duties are no restriction—do not impair free trade. We have proclaimed it to the world that reciprocity is the basis of our legislation; that discrimination shall continue while reciprocity is refused. We have given a pledge to the nation; its principles embrace all its interests; it can be redeemed only by general and equal protection. A people struggling on the ruins of all their interests have a right to ask, nay, to demand, much of their Government; to review its past and revise its present systems; to seriously examine whether they are built on the experience of other nations and other times, on tried, established, and practical principles, and justified by our own; whether their success does not depend on the reversal of every rule of individual economy when applied to national, in dissolving the chain which connects causes and effects; whether any thing less than a total change in all the laws of trade, the principles of intercourse, the relations of society, (we might almost say the order of nature,) can make a nation wise by the means which must make its component parts poor, when all its interests have declined, and its Treasury become emptied; whether they shall be left to regulate themselves, or something done to revive and replenish. Providence has been bounteous in furnishing all the means; have we done our best in using them to secure private and public happiness? This question must be answered to the people. If any one will propose a measure in his opinion better calculated to " provide for the common defence, and promote the general welfare," he ought not to withhold it. If he has none, we most respectfully ask the House to give its sanction to the one the committee believe lays the foundation of efficient relief, and contains no principle injurious to any item of national industry.

The committee deem it unworthy of themselves to repel any suggestions of hostility to the revenue or agriculture of the country. Did it depend on their own feelings, they would deem it equally so as to commerce, if it would not be thought to indicate too much indifference to the language of the memorials submitted to their consideration. Some avowal is due to public opinion, which has, in some measure, countenanced the belief that

Protection to Manufactures.

commerce and manufactures are rival, if not hostile interests. We publicly disclaim such belief, and avow the conviction that there is a union in their true interests, and ought to be a harmony in their movements; that they are allies and friends by nature; members of the same great society; twin children of agriculture, looking to it as its source, aiding and extending it by friendly co-operation. But commerce, as the child of agriculture, the sister of manufactures, is exporting, not importing; by reversing her employment, she becomes a stranger, expatriated from her own country, naturalized in some other. Imports of articles congenial to our soil are the bane of agriculture; the employment of foreign industry on fabrics to which our own is competent, is death to manufactures; and both exhaust the national resources. No interest has felt it more severely than commerce; and convinced, by the evidence of experience, she has, in our records, entered a verdict that importation is the small, exportation the great source of her prosperity. This Congress has rendered its judgment on the verdict,* and this committee will not arrogate the power or express a wish to reverse the decision. It fully accords with our convictions of national interest and public defence. If the foreign export commerce requires further protection, by resisting foreign restriction; if it can be assisted by opening new sources, or removing obstructions from existing ones, we pledge ourselves, that though commerce may find in this House friends who can better discern, and, possessing more of their confidence, will be more enabled to co-operate with those engaged in its pursuits, none will more zealously lend their assistance than the Committee on Manufactures.

By those who will read, it shall not be said that we have not listened to and examined their remonstrances; it was our duty to well weigh their many objections, to yield to them, or attempt their refutation; in doing so, it has been not with the expectation that we could produce conviction. We are not vain enough to think that the settled opinions of those who have not formed them for their own sole guidance, but to give an impulse to others, will be changed by any efforts of ours; they are more directed to minds as yet open, as well to justify ourselves as to lead others to inquiry; to elicit information; to draw out the lights of experience, and appreciate the principles of political economy, as their application may best suit the interests of the country. In the conscientious discharge of our duty, we are conscious that some portion of the nation has viewed our conduct with suspicion and distrust, perhaps with a hostile feeling. Though we know that the hand of friendship, when offered by us, will be spurned, it shall never be raised for aggression; the first law of nature authorizes it for defence.

Having no predilection for foreign importations, whether of goods or opinions, we have thought it a duty to recommend the adoption of principles which have received the approbation of our best statesmen; on which this Government commenced its operations; which, when pursued, have produced prosperity; when abandoned, have left us in adversity. Disregarding theory, we have endeavored to discover facts; less anxious to be consistent with political logic than practical results; less desirous to force facts to conform to reasoning, than to apply reasoning to facts. Believing that the difficulty in the ascertainment of the true and sound principles of legislation is not in their mystery, but simplicity; in not being above, but adapted to common understandings, we have investigated the matters submitted to us under the conviction "that error hath proceeded from too great a reverence and a kind of adoration of the mind and understanding of man, by means whereof men have withdrawn themselves too much from the contemplation of nature, and the observations of experience, and have tumbled up and down in their own reason and conceits. Men sought truth in their own little worlds, and not in the great and common world; for they disdain to spell, and so, by degrees, to read in the volume of God's works; and, contrariwise, by continual meditation and agitation of wit, do urge, and, as it were, invocate their own spirits to divine and give oracles unto them, whereby they are deservedly deluded." The useful discoveries in science have been more owing to accident than the researches of philosophers. "Logic doth not pretend to invent sciences, and, therefore, we see that they who discourse of the originals and inventions of things refer them to chance, not art. You will rather believe that Prometheus first struck the flints and marvelled at the spark, than that when he first struck the flints he expected the sparks." The needle points to the pole, philosophers cannot tell why; they knew there was electricity and lightning, but could neither discover their nature nor disarm the latter of its terrors; a kite, the schoolboy's plaything, taught it to Franklin. The mind that searches to be enlightened, and would avoid benightment, will find, "the truth is, they be not the highest instances that give the securest information, as may be well expressed in the tale so common of the philosopher, that, while he gazed upwards to the stars, fell into the water; for, if he had looked down, he might have seen the stars (and kept out of the water) in the water; but, looking aloft, he could not see the water in the stars. So it cometh often to pass, that mean and small things discover great better than great can discover small; and for that cause we inquire into the nature of a commonwealth, first, in a family and the simple congregations of man and wife, parent and child, master and servant, which are in every cottage. Even so, likewise, the nature of this great city of the world, and the policy thereof, must be first sought in mean concordances and low portions." Tracing, therefore, the true principles of political economy to the conduct and the interest of the individuals who compose the nation, we feel abundantly satisfied that we cannot err in their adoption.

We are obliged to trespass on the patience of the House, but hope they will not deem it a waste

---

* Navigation acts.

of time to notice the prominent objections which have been urged.

Protecting duties are unconstitutional.

One objection has been made which, if valid, will preclude all inquiry into the policy or necessity of the proposed measures; it is, that, by the Constitution, there is no power given to Congress to impose any tax or duty for any other than purposes of revenue. This objection has not been raised to meet a case of fancy, or one which might possibly exist; but was urged in debate during the last session, and has been renewed in various memorials presented at this, in opposition to the bill which passed this House. Being, therefore, applied to a definite measure, its validity can be examined without ranging through a variety of supposable or possible cases, or being compelled to examine whether a power which was intended to be practical—the great one on which the existence of the Government depended—might be extended to an arbitrary or illimitable extent.

The power " to regulate commerce with foreign nations, and among the several States, and with the Indian tribes," is unlimited in its extent, confined to no particular objects or purposes, and may fairly be said to be commensurate with all the objects of commercial regulation, except those embraced in the fifth clause of the ninth section of the first article of the Constitution. The power to lay and collect taxes, duties, imposts, and excises, has no other limitation, except that they shall be uniform, and capitation or other direct taxes shall be laid in proportion to the census. If there are any of the powers which are confided to the General Government by general comprehensive terms, which require no latitude of construction, which were intended and ought to be supreme, they are the regulation of commerce and the imposition of taxes. To derogate from these powers; to interpolate uses, purposes, and objects, beyond which Congress should not pass; to impose constructive limitations where the Constitution has given the unlimited power to act, would be as subversive of its principles and the security of the Government as to assume powers by construction where the Constitution was silent, and the States had made no delegation. The uniform practice of this Government, the acquiescence by the States, would seem to leave no doubt as to the legitimate power of Congress, in the regulation of commerce, to prohibit exports by an embargo, or imports by non-intercourse laws, making the prohibition general or partial, according to the objects to be effected. Foreign vessels are excluded from the coasting trade; the ports of the United States are closed against all British vessels from the British American colonies or islands; and no foreign goods can be imported from those places, even in American vessels, unless the produce of those islands or colonies whence imported. It is unknown to the committee if the States have complained of any of these acts as usurpations, or the mercantile portion of the country have denied either the power to pass or the policy of adopting those which relate to the coasting trade or navi-

gation. The latter operate both on navigation, produce, and manufactures, and exclude all articles. If they are Constitutional, it would seem that the admission or exclusion of foreign articles was a matter in the discretion of Congress, to be exercised according to their opinion of the interest of the nation. Whether this exclusion shall be direct and absolute, or be virtually so by the imposition of high duties on tonnage or produce, will probably not be thought a Constitutional question; they are but modes of effecting a given object; both are expressly given by the Constitution.

In the imposition of duties, it was the early policy of our Government to discriminate between foreign and American tonnage, as well as goods imported in foreign and American vessels; light-money was imposed only on foreign. If it should be questioned whether the object was revenue or protection to our shipping by those laws, this doubt would probably not apply to the act of last session imposing a duty of eighteen dollars a ton on French shipping. This act was called for by petition from our mercantile cities, and recommended by the Executive; its avowed object was to countervail a duty on produce. If the passage of countervailing or retaliatory laws is Constitutional, the committee can perceive in the Constitution no selection of objects on which alone they may operate. Shipping, produce, and manufactures, seem alike within our reach; either might be selected, as it might present to France reasons of greater or less weight for relaxing her system. If a high duty on the importation of her manufactures would be the most efficient and judicious measure to induce her to repeal her duty on our raw materials, our power to adopt it would seem undoubted. If the object of such duty should be the protection of cotton planters or cotton manufacturers, would it not be as legitimate as the protection of the cotton carriers? Whether it shall be extended to all, or must be confined to the one class concerned in this great national staple, is, we think, less a question of power than expediency and justice. In every act of Congress imposing duties on imports an addition of ten per cent. to the rate of duty is imposed on goods imported in foreign vessels. This discrimination is coeval with the Government; the power to make it, cannot, at all events, now be questioned; yet none of the laws declare the object for which it was made, but leave it to be inferred as a matter of policy. If the Supreme Court should infer it was for revenue, or the encouragement of navigation, and declare the law valid, it is believed they would not declare it void if they could discern the encouragement of manufactures. If the act of last session, in order to counteract the French duty on cotton imported in American ships, had, instead of adding eighteen hundred per cent. to the duty on French tonnage, added it to French cotton goods, silks, wines, brandies, or other goods; if, to coerce England to repeal her Orders in Council, and France her decrees, instead of embargo and non-intercourse, our laws had prohibited the import of their manufactures, or imposed additional duties which would have excluded them;

if, to counteract the operation of their corn laws, which directly exclude our provisions—their system of impost, which virtually excludes our wool, hemp, and flax—their system of bounties and drawbacks, which frustrates the policy of our impost, so far as it tends to the aid of our manufactures—their navigation acts, so far as their object is to exclude us from the colonial trade, Congress should think it most effectual to aim their measures more at the manufactures of England than her navigation, it could not be well contended that the Constitution forbade it; for the object might be the exclusive protection of the shipping and commercial interest. Though the component members and each branch of the Government might concur in the law, there might be much diversity in the motives and objects which brought it about. The motives which would influence the members of this House might be the protection of manufactures; of the Senate, commerce; of the President, agriculture; and those objects be publicly avowed. In such a case, the Supreme Court, which must decide on the constitutionality of this law, would find it no easy task to extract the governing principle. Their difficulties would be increased, if the Secretary of the Treasury should have recommended it as a revenue bill, either by imposing high duties to increase the impost, or a prohibition of the foreign to rear up the domestic manufacture, as the subject of an excise. If revenue is the only legitimate object of taxation, prohibition, or the regulation of commerce, the validity of such a measure would depend on the opinion of the Secretary, for the three branches of Government would, unless supported by him, have passed it for unconstitutional purposes. He has recommended that, if any measure of revenue be adopted at the present session, it be the exclusion of foreign and an excise on domestic spirits; if Congress should adopt it, it will be hard to decide whether it will most benefit the farmer who raises the grain, the distiller who manufactures it, the merchant who transports the whiskey, or the Treasury which receives the duty. The court, in deciding on the validity of such a law, must do it by certain settled principles of construction, and not their opinion of the exclusive or relative legitimacy of either object; for they, like other men, may lean more to one great national interest than another.

The whole course of our legislation for thirty years affords the highest evidence of the power of this Government to protect navigation and commerce; almost every session has presented practical proof of the conviction of Congress that it is expedient to do it. No one has been hardy enough to deny the power or the policy of encouraging agriculture. But it would seem that manufactures, which in all other countries are cherished as the most valuable offspring of human industry, have become with us a spurious progeny, born with a Constitutional malediction, stern and irrevocable; they must forever be doomed to struggle under legal disabilities, so incurable as to interpose a perpetual barrier to their protection, although all the branches of Government should be convinced that their depression involves the whole country in one common calamity, which would be averted by their prosperity; that it is a lawful object in a system of revenue or commercial retaliation, to reach every other source of the wealth and power of a foreign nation except her manufactures; that it is a duty we owe to the people of this country, to extend the national guardianship over all their other interests, but to thrust this beyond the pale of the Constitution and laws. If such is the imperious injunction of the Constitution, the committee have not so understood it; what policy or expediency may require is one thing, what the Constitution prohibits is another. That instrument designates no national interests in preference to another; excludes none, but throws all alike on the discretion of Congress: legitimate objects of national protection, if in its opinion called for by the public good. This principle gives validity to the laws giving our shipping the monopoly of the coasting trade. Bounties on fisheries, drawback of duties on foreign goods exported, tonnage on French ships, prohibiting intercourse with the British colonies, discriminating duties on tonnage and merchandise, are all Constitutional acts growing out of the plenary power to regulate commerce.

It may be proper to ask of those who urge this objection to protecting duties to point out the rate of duty when revenue ceases, and protection begins to become the ruling object; to define the line which shall limit the Constitutional powers of Congress, as well as to afford the means of ascertaining the object of a law, and the interest it is designed to protect. The duty on rum is at least eighty per cent. ad valorem. Is this a revenue, or a protecting duty? The duty on coarse cottons is about the same; that on teas is one hundred: on spices, about the same; on nails, sixty; gunpowder, forty; linen, fifteen. It is deemed useless to inquire whether the object in imposing these rates of duties can be so definitely ascertained as to afford any rule on which to limit our Constitutional power. The duty on teas can have no other than revenue for its object; the power to impose that tax has never been questioned, for the Constitution affixes no limitation to the extent or amount of a tax or duty; it only excludes one, and proposes the apportionment of others. The committee can therefore entertain no doubt that Congress may, in their sound discretion, impose such duties on foreign merchandise as shall advance the great interest of the nation. In expressing this opinion, they fall far short of the judicial exposition of the Constitutional powers of any Government which is empowered to impose a tax, and acts on legitimate objects. Had they gone so far as to say, "It is admitted that the power of taxing the people and their property is essential to the very existence of Government, and may be legitimately exercised on the objects to which it is applicable, to the utmost extent to which the Government may choose to carry it; the only security against the abuse of this power is found in the structure of the Government itself. In imposing a tax, the Legislature acts upon its constituents; this, in general, is a sufficient security against enormous and oppressive taxation. That the power to tax involves the power to destroy, is a proposition not to be denied;" the committee would but echo the solemn opinion of the supreme judicial tribunal of the Union.

Manufactures are injurious to morals, and produce pauperism.

That manufactures tend to destroy the morals of those engaged in them, is an objection which, it is believed, has not arisen from the experience of their effects among us. Neither the personal knowledge of the committee, nor the information of those who have formed an opinion from their own observation, would justify the belief that this pursuit or occupation is more prejudicial to morality than any other; no reason can be discovered why it should be, and there are certainly some why it should be otherwise. If idleness is the parent of vice, employment must be the mother of virtue; poverty can be no apology for crime, where subsistence can be obtained by industry. Manufacturing establishments open sources of labor, and give employment to those who are able to earn support in no other manner; affording materials which are beyond their means to procure, and requiring labor which can be performed by children and others incapable of the fatigues of more active and laborious occupations. It may be thought invidious to draw a comparison between the relative morality of those engaged in the various pursuits of life, and an objection ought not to have been made to any which would compel it, without strong evidence of its being justified by facts; but it has been urged by the opponents of manufactures, and the advocates of other interests, with an apparent seriousness which seems to force it upon the committee to say, that, whatever may be said of manufacturing towns, the morality of seaports is not proverbial. On whichever side the balance may be, it ought not be forgotten that this is not pressed as an objection against commerce or its protection. If all large towns contain the haunts of vice, which are beyond the power of the magistracy to extirpate, it may not be so much attributable to the pursuits which attract a crowded population as to other causes of a general application. It is not so important to inquire what are the effects in other countries as in ours; there may be local causes, or some growing either out of the peculiar nature of foreign institutions, or the want of similar ones to ours, which may combine to produce different effects. It would not, in other cases, be deemed fair reasoning, that the opponents of manufactures should disclaim the experience and practice of other nations, as affording any evidence of its being our policy to encourage them, and yet press upon their friends an objection, which, though it may be supported by observation abroad, is certainly contradicted by experience at home. But the tendency of manufacturing establishments in other countries to promote immorality may well be questioned; for an eminent author on the police of England has proved, from official documents, that, in proportion to the population, a greater number of crimes are committed in the agricultural and commercial than in the manufacturing districts of that kingdom. If experience, therefore, is to be adopted as the test of the soundness of this objection, it will fail to support it; and it would seem to be capable of as little support by any reasons which could be drawn from the nature of the employment, the entire and constant superintendence which is necessary to the management, or the objects which draw together a dense population.

The manufactory at Waltham is said to employ two hundred and sixty persons, equal to the population of a village containing fifty families. This establishment, then, affords a fair criterion by which to test this objection; it is probably the largest in the Union. The committee are convinced that it would be doing great injustice to the proprietors and manager to indulge for a moment the belief that any of its operations have given rise to, or even color for, any imputations as to its immoral tendency; and, having no reason for thinking that other less extensive manufactories have given greater cause for this objection, we cannot refrain the expression of our belief that it has arisen from other reasons than its practical application to our establishments.

Connected with this, and equally, in our opinion, ill-founded, is the allegation that manufactures tend to increase the number of paupers. The example of England is urged with much earnestness as evidence of the fact; but we are unable to account for the increase of paupers by the increase of the means of employment. If new and additional objects of occupation are presented; if women, children, and old men, can be employed in a manufactory, and employed nowhere else, it must decrease the number of those ,who cannot earn the means of subsistence. It is not the excess, but the want of employment, that makes those paupers who are not diseased, disabled, or infirm; and if the immense extent to which the manufacturing establishments of England are carried is not sufficient to prevent the extension of pauperism, it would serve to afford evidence that they had progressed, not too far, but not far enough. There must be the requisite number for the pursuits of commerce, the labors of agriculture and manufactures, leaving a surplus of laborers unemployed. The poor taxes are large in amount, and oppressive on all classes of the community; it can be the interest of none to add to their burdens, but of all to furnish occupation to those whose labor would pay for their food. The laws of no country impose a tax for the maintenance of those who are able, and can find by their industry the means of support. It is therefore impossible that manufactures, which increase the employment of laborers, can add to the number of paupers. The existence of both to a great extent only proves that there may be a population so dense that the enterprise of individuals, aided by the steady policy and unceasing exertions of the Government, may not furnish such employment as will procure the necessaries of life.

In England, it may be an objection that the use of labor-saving machinery diminishes the want of manual labor. If labor by machinery supersedes labor by hands, and thus increases the burdens' of the community for the support of the poor, it affords a striking illustration of the immense advantages of a policy which makes it a matter of calculation and choice to submit to the imposition of enormous poor rates. If mere manual labor would suffice for the fabrication of articles to meet the supply of the domestic and foreign market, and at prices which would exclude competition, the number of paupers might be more limited; but, if machinery is necessary to increase the quantity and diminish the price, to effect these objects, pauperism is the lesser evil, being more than balanced by the individual and national profits, by which foreign nations are indirectly compelled to pay, not only the poor, but all other taxes.

But the application of the objection to this country cannot be perceived. It is a common objection to the establishment of manufactures here, that our population is not sufficient. If this be true, it affords the strongest argument in favor of the adoption of machinery, which supplies the want of population, enabling the few to do the work of many. If the poor of our country have ever had employment sufficient for their support, it is not known that a solitary fact can be produced which shows that it has been taken away by the operation of manufactures. It is a fact easy to be decided, by the observation in our large towns, whether the increase of poor taxes has been in the same ratio as manufactures. The result will probably show that the proportion is less in manufacturing towns and in the neighborhood of large establishments than elsewhere. If the objection was indeed a valid one, it would prove more than those who urge it would wish for; it would be conclusive evidence that the population of the country had attained to such a height as not only to justify the erection of extensive establishments, but that there was a surplus of labor beyond the means of its employment. If agriculture or commerce would furnish it, there could be but few paupers; if it requires the aid of manufactures, and all are insufficient, then they must be increased till they meet all the demands for labor. Until it can be made to appear that the population of towns decreases with the extension of their manufactures, and that experience demonstrates that there is a proportionate increase of poor rates, the comparison is again forced on us, and the national character of the objection may be fairly tested by estimating the relative amount of poor taxes in large commercial and other places. If the objection should prove to be well founded, it would only apply to those branches where the greatest portion of the labor is performed by machinery, as cotton and woollen; but it could not, by possibility, extend to those whose operations are almost exclusively manual, as glass, paper, cutlery, shoes, clothing, &c. The necessary consequence of the advancement of those manufactures must be the increase of industry, and the decrease of pauperism. As the objection can therefore only embrace, in its fullest latitude, but a few items, it is deemed unimportant; as to those, it is believed to be without foundation. The Waltham factory employing two hundred and sixty persons, it remains to be proved that its machinery deprives that number of an employment they would otherwise have from other sources.

No further protection is necessary.

If this objection is founded in fact; if it be, indeed, true that manufacturers need no further protection; that the national objects which call for their encouragement are already accomplished, the committee would deem it a truly happy consummation for the country. If this is understood to be alleged by the friends of a general and equal protection of national industry, as well as those opposed to it, it would seem that further aid would produce no benefit to the one, or injury to the other class. If the present duties have excluded foreign articles, and secured our markets to our own citizens, it cannot be perceived how higher duties can have a good or bad operation. They must have none; and thus all the interest that the proposed measures have excited, of hope on one side and fear on the other, is, that additional duties might diminish the importation of articles already excluded. If the objection is understood as coming exclusively from those opposed to the general policy of protecting duties, it presents the great question only in another form; but if it has its origin with those interested in any particular branch of manufactures which may be now so protected as to command our market, we are bound to believe that it is intended to apply to their own appropriate branch only. It would be too serious an imputation upon their patriotism and sense of common justice to charge them with assuming to their own establishment a national character which could belong to no other, and a disposition to withhold from others a small portion of the legislative guardianship which has been so liberally imparted to them. It would be at once boldly and avowedly aiming at a monopoly, and asking Congress to be partial in their measures. It would confirm the objection, which is pressed with much zeal as well as warmth in the various memorials, that protecting duties tend to create a privileged order of great capitalists, supported at the expense of the nation. It would effectuate the objects of those who wish to impress the nation and the Government with the belief that the encouragement of manufactures is for individual emolument, and not national interest. It would sanction the principle that the powers of this Government are only to be exercised in favor of enormous money capitals, leaving humble industry to struggle, unaided, against foreign competition and domestic indifference; that the employment of machinery, and not of manual labor, was worthy of encouragement; that one item of clothing alone was so supremely important to the nation, that all others must be overlooked. We ought to hesitate long before we give way to a conviction that manufacturers would expose themselves to these reflections. If their opponents could wish the advocates of equal protection to descend from the high ground of national principles to private speculation; to contend for principles unjust and partial in their practical effects; and to present themselves before the National Legislature in a contest for the exclusive protection of capitalists, or of one branch of industry to the destruction of others, no means would more readily suggest themselves than to associate, as an ally, the proprietor of some overgrown establishment, already protected by a duty of 100 per cent., to aid them by the declaration that "we want no further protection." Though the effects might be somewhat lessened by a suspicion that others than those interested alone in manufacturing interests may have furnished a part, at least, of the enormous capital, and thus be concerned in the monopoly of one article by manufacturing, and of all others by importation; yet it would, in some degree, tend to support an objection which, when fully examined, will afford a very strong reason for giving the protection called for.

Viewing it, as the committee hope they may truly do, as one of the numerous arguments against a general system, they proceed to an examination of its application to the present tariff. It would be tedious to take each item in detail; one is selected, on which is imposed the highest ad valorem duty—coarse cottons. The nominal rate of duty on this article is 25 per cent.; the real, according to an estimate of high mercantile authority, 83. The beneficial effects of this duty to the consumer of the article are well known and universally admitted, and have been fully explained by the committee. Since the experiment has been fully and successfully tried as to one important item, why not extend it to others? Why should the duties on coarse cottons be 83 per cent.; on linens, worsteds, stockings, silk, and iron, 15—a difference of 68 per cent.? If the effects have been so salutary on coarse, why not, by an increased rate of duty, bring the finer fabrics within the operation of the same wholesome principle? Why leave glass at a rate of duty which does not equal the foreign bounty? Why make the nominal duty on cotton efficient for 83, and leave the nominal duty on paper of 30 per cent. efficient only for 15; or, at the most, for 20 per cent.? When other manufactures are placed on the same footing as cotton; when protecting duties are imposed by a principle of equality, and graduated by some settled rule; when it shall exceed the ordinary and average amount of a mere duty for revenue, and an opportunity be offered for a fair experiment of its general tendency, then may be the time to urge that, if the experiment is successful, the article wants no further protection; if it fails, that there is something of a peculiar character attached to it, which, as to any given article, prevents that connexion between causes and effects which exists as to others. The complete success as to one article is the best evidence of the good policy of extending the same rule to others; affording, at the same time, strong practical proof that, when carried to the proper extent, legislative protection to manufactures results in the reduction of the price to the consumer.

When this is the effect, the protection is to the people, not to the manufacturer; the saving of the price is the "economy to the consumer;" he is protected by not being compelled to purchase the foreign article of an inferior quality, and at a higher price. The reduction of the present duty on cotton goods would, by destroying the domestic competition, bring the article to the same price it bore before such competition existed. From the great reduction in the price, it is evident that there must have been a great profit arising to the foreign manufacturer, or the importer, which was paid by the consumer. The article must come to him at the old price, in order to make the same profit accrue to the domestic manufacturer; if it come at a less, then the real and efficient protection is to those who buy it; they are protected from paying the higher price. The true application of this word *protection* will tend to unite opinion on this most interesting question; if it means protection to the people, to the mass of the nation, by reducing the price of the article used, and increasing the means of payment, there could be no national objection to it; as little could there be, if protection was understood to be the guarding the people against the operation of foreign laws and systems of government, associations and combinations of individuals, which tend to enhance the price, and to depreciate the means of payment. It could not then be said that no further protection was necessary, until the protection was complete; till it extended to all items where it was required. The committee wish it to be distinctly understood, that this is their definition of *protection*, and, when it is used by them, it means protection to the consumer. They disclaim that definition or application which makes it consist in protecting the manufacturer against the interest and sound policy of this country—of protecting him in speculation or monopoly, at the expense of the people, or any national interest. We recognise in the manufacturers no claims to exclusive or any other protection than what is due to others; we view them as other classes, as men engaged in other occupations and pursuits in life, entitled to protection as instruments for promoting national and general prosperity; as men by whose agency the public good and the general welfare will be advanced. If they can effect this object, and with profit to themselves, it is to us a subject of congratulation, and will become one of pride, if the measures we have devised have tended to produce it. But, if it only adds to their individual emolument, we renounce it as an object which is equally repugnant with our intentions and feelings. Believing, as we do, that "economy to the consumer" is best secured by the domestic supply of our demands, domestic manufactures are the only efficient means; as such, we think them entitled to national protection. The same principle applies to commerce and agriculture; they are but the varied means of supplying our demands, and, like manufactures, are the component parts of the great system which is necessary, to secure the great object of all sound policy—"economy to the consumer."

The three great occupations in society are, agriculture to produce, manufactures to fabricate, commerce to distribute, the articles of consumption. The first and the third are admitted by all to be of infinite importance, worthy of all protection; both have received it. Sound policy has never suggested a doubt that the production and distibution should be domestic. The country, with one united voice, has declared, and yet declares, that "economy to the consumer" consists in not being dependent on foreign soil to produce, or foreign shipping to carry, the supplies of our wants. Yet it is much divided on the policy of dependence on foreign labor and foreign machinery for fabrication. This is not deemed the least important item; without it, production is useless, and, except food, no materials would exist for distribution. The manufacturers, to meet our demands, must exist somewhere; shall they be in a foreign country, or our own? is the great question. To decide this, it would seem to be sufficient to apply to this item the same reasons which have led to the unanimous conclusion in relation to the other two; or to show, by any cogent reasoning, and from clear experience, that it is safer, sounder policy, more conducive to "economy to the consumer," to place the command of that item in the hands of foreigners than our own citizens. Domestic agriculture has the command of our production; domestic shipping of our distribution; why not domestic manufactures of our fabrication? If experience has not justified the remark that the protection of agriculture and commerce has been a tax on the consumer, neither has it as to manufactures; hitherto every result has been economy to the consumer. This Government did not say to commerce "You want no further protection," until it had attained a monopoly of the coasting trade, and nearly so of the foreign. It does not now make the remark because a few merchants, with large capitals, and by successful enterprise, can continue their operations; the old, continues, and new protection is added; enough is not given till the object shall be accomplished. The object a national one—the command of our distribution—is it unreasonable that, so far as fabrication is a national object, it should be protected to consummation? It is not to draw invidious distinctions, but to show their impropriety, that it is deemed proper to observe, that, if the protection afforded to commerce has enabled those engaged in its pursuits to acquire princely fortunes; or, if they have been the consequence of their enterprise and intelligence, it has been deemed evidence of the general prosperity. The acquisitions of commerce have not been charged as "fleecing" the rest of the community; "merchants have not been designated as an organized corps, distinct from the rest of the nation, aiming at exclusive privileges at the general expense." Theirs has not been represented as an interest which, of necessity, draws a line between their emolument and the public good. If foreign nations want our produce, they will come here for it; if we want their manufactures, they will bring them to us. It is not, therefore, from necessity, but a conviction of general economy, that has led to our settled policy of giving such protection to our shipping interest as will enable it to do what is indispensable for our wants. Merchants are not considered as men who do not

feel a common regard for the general welfare—so divided from the rest of the nation, that their interest is necessarily in opposition to all others.

They are not called an organized corps when they unite in petition to us to save them and their interest from foreign policy; they are not repulsed by the charge of exclusive interest, privileged orders, bounties, premiums, and monopolies. If those charges were applied to them, proof would be required of their truth; it would be illiberal to make them, unless it was clear and convincing. When they are applied to manufacturers and their petitions, common justice would dictate the same rule; that when they ask for protection against the same foreign policy, the same laws which bear with the same force on commerce and manufactures, charity should be so far extended as to admit that, however mistaken their opinion, they craved no object adverse to the interest of the country, but made it the basis of their requests. Though they may be less capable of judging than others, they may not be more selfish. Experience may be assumed to be the safest guide; it does not justify the objection that more enormous wealth has been accumulated by manufactures than agriculture or commerce, or that what has been acquired has been more at the expense of the nation. The chain of mutual interests which connects society does not separate manufactures from the common mass. The ties of mutual dependence and support, which form a nation into a family, which lead all to consider themselves as parts of a great whole, are not of necessity dissolved by their pursuits or their interest; they are of no distinct caste, and most of them are engaged in other pursuits. Manufacturing capital is made up by the acquisitions from other sources; the labor is supplied by the want of other employment; and it is believed that in this, as in all others, there is an intimate connexion with national interests. The greatest manufacturing establishments are in or near our commercial cities. Who are their proprietors? Whence is derived their capital, labor, and how far their success or decline has a correspondent bearing on the value of property or produce, the poor, the industrious, the farmer, the mechanic, and the mass of population—how far they present an interest distinct from, or connected with, those who compose the circle of society, can well be ascertained by those who represent the districts which contain them. The records of this House afford no bad criterion. The protection of manufactures, as an important item of national industry, is not asked for by manufacturers alone; a reference to the petitions will show that their numbers are few; all classes have united. It cannot, therefore, be in public opinion, or in practice, that we can discover the evidence of their being a class excluded from common feeling and general interest. So far as the opinion of petitioners is entitled to any weight, those who have called for an auction duty have given one entitled to no small respect—they require it for the protection of commerce, manufactures, and agriculture. A reference to those petitions, to the various occupations of those who have signed them, will not fall short of

Protection to Manufactures.

conclusive proof that, in practice as well as in principle, there is such a connexion between the three great branches of national industry—production, fabrication, and distribution—as all to require protection, and to be capable of receiving it by the same act of legislation. But though we cannot but think that the union of all classes of citizens in favor of the protection of these three greatest interests is strong evidence that there is no discordance between them, it must not be understood as implying that no such discordance does exist, because the measure required for the protection of one is called for only by those engaged in its appropriate and peculiar pursuits. Those through whose direct interest a national injury is inflicted feel it the soonest, and must be the first to complain; the inquiry should be, not who complain, but is the injury sustained ? must it be redressed ? and by what means ? If protection is required, it should be to the extent of the injury; and, if no further protection is wanted, it must be because the injury has been redressed, the cause which produced become inoperative, and a sufficient guard supplied to prevent its recurrence. What has been done, is not an inquiry dictated by national feeling, but the good or bad effects it has produced; what ought yet to be done can then easily be ascertained—it is by selecting the legitimate objects of protection, and making that protection effectual. If economy to the consumer and defence to the nation are already secured, it cannot be necessary, and may be unwise, to proceed further; the situation of the country affords the best means of deciding. Protection is not asked against our own Government, or the interest of our own citizens, but against foreign. Freedom of trade and occupations consists in the perfect liberty of pursuit, without any legislative partiality or preference; to be governed entirely by mutual or general interest. That freedom is destroyed by foreign as well as domestic legislation and interference. If there was neither, there would be nothing to protect against; industry would be left free to select its application; a pressure which bears upon it with a given weight, must be balanced with an equivalent protection before it can become free. That there is this foreign pressure is admitted; its extent cannot be estimated, for it is made up by a complex and intricate system of policy, that varies in its application to different objects. Being more versed in that of England than other countries, it is selected as an illustration; and, being bound by our convention with her to impose on her products no higher duties than on those of other nations, they must be uniform; but as our greater portion of manufactures is imported thence, our duties should rather be imposed with a reference to the pressure of the system which bears on the greater, and not on the lesser portion of our importations.

A bounty or an excise drawback is a direct pressure to the nominal amount; it is the difference in the price of the article to the British or the American consumer. The English Government makes it dearer to their own people than ours by the amount of the drawback and bounty; a barrel of

beer drank in England costs three dollars more than if exported to France and drank there, (deducting charges of exportation and freight.) When a code gives a direct bounty, the effect can be measured; but the indirect drawbacks and bounties have a more serious effect. Taking the amount of taxation in England to be at any rate, say thirty per cent. of the income of all the property and all the products of the kingdom, and it is so apportioned as to leave those products and occupations untaxed which are for the supply of articles for a foreign market, and a double amount on such as must be consumed at home; for example, if, instead of an excise of thirty per cent. on cotton, woollen, linen, iron, glass, hardware, crockery, none is imposed on these manufactures, and sixty per cent. is imposed on spirits, malt liquors, paper, &c., the sum of taxation is the same. Thirty per cent. is paid in the aggregate, and should be added to the cost of manufacturing. On the article which pays none, this thirty per cent. is a bounty, and the effects to us are the same; it is an exemption from taxation, a real drawback. When, then, a comparison is made between the expenses of manufacturing here and there, the average rate of taxation must be allowed for, not its particular apportionment. Does, then, this system operate as a pressure on our industry, or to its aid ? If the effects of bounties, drawbacks, or exemptions, were to add to the resources of this nation, and diminish those of England, it is difficult to assign the reason for its continuance. We risk much by acting on the belief that the Government of that nation does not understand its interest; a simple calculation will settle the question. Take any given article of manufacture; compare it with the value of the raw material required to make it; the difference of the price is made up of the labor bestowed upon it and the subsistence of the laborers. Iron ore will not pay freight; it has then no value, unless in a country where iron is made; a ton of bar iron, worth one hundred dollars, derives all its value from labor and subsistence; it gives a new market for so much of industry and the products of agriculture; and as much as this market is worth to the nation, so much is every ton of iron worth in clear profits when it can be exported, and those profits drawn from another country. Such a bounty is then given, as, being less than the profits accruing by the making of iron, will make its export a profit. It is not credible that a bounty greater than the general profits accruing would be given by any Government not mad. The nation, then, who buys the iron pays the profit, and not the nation that, by paying the bounty, secures the profit. If clay, and sand, and ore, can be turned into money by such means as bounties, drawbacks, exemptions, as will still leave a profit, it is easy to see that the profits accrue to those whose otherwise worthless products become valuable, and not to those whose products remain by these means forever worthless.

If the profits derived by the various interests in England were not more than a penny-halfpenny a yard on coarse linen, or twenty-five shillings a hundred on glass, the Government would not pay that bounty; if a profit remains, it is paid by those who buy their linen and glass. If, by means of those bounties, &c., they draw these profits to themselves from us, and leave our ores, sand, clay, of no use; deprive the farmer of the market for subsistence to the laborer, who shall otherwise be employed in manufactures, then it becomes the duty of our Government, by a resisting defensive system, to protect our raw materials, labor, and provisions, to give to our citizens the profits of converting them into articles of use. That duty is of the most inoperative kind, if all the occupations of the country are now unprofitable. The farmer raises more than he can sell; he has no inducement to raise more; the country can derive no benefit from increasing a surplus now unproductive. There is labor enough in the country for all the profitable pursuits of agriculture, and to manufacture all the articles for our consumption; all the raw materials are in abundance, or may be made so. Protection shall end, then, only after securing employment from all.

That the increase of duties will lead to smuggling.

This is an object depending so much on opinion, that it is difficult either to support or rebuke it by facts. If its existence to any great extent was known, the records of our custom-houses and courts would afford official evidence; but, unlike other crimes, the extent of this can only be ascertained by detection; it may prevail to a very considerable degree, yet the evidence of it be beyond the means of procurement. While, therefore, it cannot be reasonable to ask for the most definite proof from those who urge it, it may not be too much to expect that the objection would be supported by strong reasoning and probable inferences. The suggestion ought not to be listened to with too much readiness, as it imparts a severe reflection on the character of our countrymen, and holds out the Government as unable to enforce the payment of a duty imposed for revenue or policy. Judging from the uniform practice of Congress, it seems that the fear of smuggling has not deterred them from increasing the duties for the aid of the revenue. When additional sums have been required, additional duties have been imposed, and always, it is believed, with the desired effect. At the commencement of the late war, the duties on imports were doubled, certainly not with a view to the protection of manufactures, when the war precluded foreign competition, and the law was limited to one year after the conclusion of the peace,* but solely for revenue. The war duties continued until the 1st of July, 1816, a period of near eighteen months after the peace; they were, on an average, much higher than those proposed in the bill of last session, and afforded a fair criterion by which to judge of the tendency of high duties to increase smuggling.

The committee have not perceived, in any of the memorials which dwell on this objection, the period which elapsed from the conclusion of the peace and the commencement of the present tariff, selected as one which exhibited evidence of the increase of smuggling. These memorials are from gentlemen of great mercantile experience, guided by their own and the observation of others; if they have not been led to select this period in our financial history as the era of smuggling, it is a fair inference that, in their opinion, none has existed. That inference is much strengthened when we find them unwilling or unable to point out in our tariff an article the revenue on which has been diminished by the increase of duty, but compelled to resort to the example of a foreign Government, to overlook the experience of our own, in order to procure proof of their suggestion. In selecting the articles of tea and coffee as those which were dangerous to tax high, it was most prudent for them to refer to the British tariff and not to ours;* as the one may support, but the other directly contradicts their supposition. The selection of a foreign precedent is at best presumptive evidence that no domestic one would confirm their position. Until that presumption is rebutted, and evidence adduced more satisfactory to the mind than the uniform and successful practice of the Government, the official documents from the Treasury, and the inferences which irresistibly follow known facts, the committee must think this objection founded more in conjecture than fact.

The annexed statement will very clearly show that the amount of importations and revenue is not in an inverse ratio to the rate of duty. An inspection of the existing tariff conclusively shows that the highest duties are those imposed for revenue merely, with some few exceptions; the difference between those imposed on teas, spices, wines, and spirits, and on manufactured articles generally, is very great: on mace it is one dollar a pound, on bar iron seven mills and a half; on teas averaged thirty-two and three-tenths cents per pound, equal to one hundred per cent. ad valorem; on linen and worsteds fifteen per cent.; on manufactures, the same duty is imposed on the coarse and bulky as the fine, on articles of necessity as luxury; blankets and silks at fifteen. Smuggling would never have entered into the minds of the Legislature, in such an apportionment of impost; mace is easier smuggled than bar iron, teas than blankets; yet on these high-taxed articles the fear of smuggling does not seem to dwell; it rests only on manufactures. So far as protecting duties have been raised to the height of revenue ones, it seems to have justified no such fears. Coarse cottons are at eighty-three; it is admitted that this article is nearly, if not quite, excluded; it is, of course, not smuggled. It may then be fairly inferred that the duty on other manufactures, equally bulky and not more valuable, might, with equal safety, be advanced to this extent; if less bulky and more costly, to fall proportionally short of amount could not be an unsafe standard; or, if this is thought too high, the average duties of 1815 and the first half of 1816 cannot be objected to. Assuming either as the basis, and comparing them

*Afterwards extended to 30th June, 1816.

* Memorial of a convention of delegates in Philadelphia.

with the bill of last session, the committee entertain a confident conviction that it would be entirely unaffected by this objection. It is, indeed, incredible that a duty of twenty-five per cent. on crates, glass, iron, linen, hardware, cutlery, &c., could furnish inducements to smuggling, which are not even alleged to exist as to articles of more value and charged with a higher rate of duty. Such belief could not, in the minds of those who entertain the fear, amount to conviction, since they have not selected an item from our tariff, or appealed to a fact in the history of this country. Again, it may be remarked that, when the experience of other countries is not supported by ours, it is not sound reasoning to urge the propriety of basing our legislation on a state of things which does not exist here. It is well known that, in proportion to the amount of imports, there is more smuggling on our Northern and Southern frontiers than on the seacoast ; the rate of duty being the same, it must be owing to other causes. Separated from the dominions of foreign Powers by narrow seas, rivers, or territorial lines, facilities are afforded to the illicit introduction of merchandise which are not within the reach of those who must cross an ocean in a large and valuable vessel ; whose arrival, destination, and departure, are notorious, and announced in numberless papers, and watched by revenue cutters. The vigilance of our officers, aided by all the efforts of individuals, is wholly incompetent to watch an immense frontier, most of it a wilderness. He would surely be an unwise statesman who, because there were found examples of smuggling there, would change a fiscal or political system to meet such cases, which will exist, not only while there are high duties, but while there are any. The same obvious reasons will apply to England, or any other European nation ; and these may be the causes which have led to the selection of an example from abroad. There, smuggling is not carried on in sea vessels which are entered at the custom-houses, but in boats which pass in the night. The Isle of Man was a principal scene for illicit trade ; since its sovereignty has been purchased by the Crown, it has ceased. The contiguity to foreign nations affording means of unlawful communication, is the principal source of this danger. It is not carried on by merchant vessels fit to navigate the ocean, and cannot prevail to a great extent here. It cannot be the meaning of the memorialists, that the merchants of our country would engage in, or countenance, this illicit and immoral traffic ; no others would have the means of doing it, especially when doubly watched by a class of men who have paid the duties on their own importations, and do not want intelligence to discern their interests, or vigilance to guard against all attacks, open or covert.

A tax on the many a bounty to the few.

Of the numerous objections which are urged against the proposed measure, there is none which carries with it more plausibility, till examined, or would be more conclusive, if true. The committee most freely admit, that, if a general system

for the protection of manufactures is necessarily a permanent tax on the community for the mere benefit of those engaged in them, it must be radically wrong, and partially so, as the same effect follows the encouragement of particular branches. Disclaiming the word bounties as wholly inapplicable to any part of the bill, they are willing to test it by the principles laid down by its active and intelligent opponents. " There is, however, an argument in favor of encouraging particular employments by bounties and taxes, which merits a different consideration. It has been justly urged that there may be occupations peculiarly adapted to our situation and character, and which, if once established, might be carried on better here than elsewhere, so as to afford their productions at a cheaper rate than is now paid for them ; and yet habit and indolence, and the natural attachment of men to the pursuits in which they have been educated, and the immediate expense of commencing the business, and the want of that skill which only time and experience can give, and a doubt how soon or how certainly the profit may be realized, may deter individuals from engaging in those occupations, and induce them to persist in others less profitable to themselves and the public ; and that if these difficulties can be overcome by a present tax, which will be more than compensated by the reduction of prices hereafter, it is good policy and economy to impose it. On this principle, encouragement has alwas been given by our Government to particular pursuits, and it should always be given to the full extent that this principle will warrant. By its adoption, the whole subject is made a mere question of economy—of economy to consumers, who are all the people ; and it becomes our duty to study not how to make manufactures dear, but how to make them, on the whole, cheap and abundant. The best, and perhaps the only mode of doing it, is to promote competition at the lowest prices."[*]

A general acquiescence in these sentiments would leave for our consideration only the question of their application. In ascertaining the most effectual means of promoting national industry, it is truly gratifying to find both sides starting on the same principles ; this gives them a stability which saves the trouble of examining their soundness. It would be indeed useless ; for who will deny that "economy to the consumer" should be the guiding maxim for individuals and legislators ? The meaning of the term cannot be understood. Economy, whether individual or political, is probably not a very complicated science, when studied not by theory and speculative reasoning, but the book of practical life and experience. Principles, to be correct, must be drawn from practical observation more than reasoning ; if to be applied to theory, they may be drawn from the same source ; but, if intended for universal practice, they should flow from the lessons of experience. Practical economy to the consumer teaches him to procure what he wants at the cheapest rate, and that mode is cheapest by which he can buy

----
[*] Report of the Boston Committee.

with the least labor and expense. The price of an article is not its nominal rate in dollars, but in the quantity of a given article which will procure it. Assuming any sum as the standard price of any article, the great question for the consumer is, how to obtain it on the best terms; how to exchange his own surplus productions for those he needs, to most advantage; to select the object on which he may employ his own industry so as to realize the greatest production. If the mere transfer of the same labor from one object to another will enable him to attain his ends, it is his interest to do it. If, for the reasons stated in the above extract, and the powerful ones which result from the policy of foreign Governments, such transfer becomes useless or impracticable, the interference of a Government which would remove these difficulties is not coercive on its own citizens, but becomes auxiliary to their wishes and interest. If a foreign Government allow an enormous bounty on a manufacture, the raw material of which is excluded by law, or duty, or the difficulties and expense of its transportation, and thus break down all domestic competition in the supply of an article of which every consumer would furnish the rough material, it would not be an arbitrary measure if Government should create the competition, transfer the manufactory to its own jurisdiction, and thus give the consumer an option of paying for it with the produce he could easiest raise and most conveniently spare. A farmer, in devising the means of clothing his family, will at once inquire into the most economical means of doing it. He has on hand a surplus of grain, wool, flax. The stores in his neighborhood groan with imported goods from England. But the merchant cannot export grain, flax, or wool. England excludes them; she has enough of her own; and as we purchase our buttons, woollens, and linens, from her, there is no resource but to purchase on credit. If a manufactory were within his reach, he could exchange the material for the manufacture; this affords him the only means of exchange or sale. If there were no manufactories, and Government would build them up by imposing duties on foreign fabrics, such duties would not be a tax on the farmer, but an efficient bounty, by giving a value to his otherwise useless products. It will scarcely be contended by those who so loudly protest against a forced transfer of occupations, that the farmer may turn spinner, weaver, bleacher, dyer, fuller, &c. His occupation is the extraction of the produce of the earth, and he has a right to ask of the Government that they adopt such a system as shall make it most valuable.

Competition is the security of the consumer against imposition in what he buys, and of a market for what he has to spare. If the articles of consumption are supplied by importation, the competition is confined to three classes—the foreign manufacturer and exporter and the American importer; theirs is a struggle for the sale of the manufacture, which can only diminish the price; but as the provisions and the raw materials raised by the mass of consumers are prohibited, there can be no competition for their purchase. But to the farmer this reduction of price produces no benefit. Price is composed of two items—the rate of the thing sold, and the rate of the thing received in payment. Economy to the consumer is the low rate of one, the high of the other. The competition for provisions and wool being now entirely domestic, the price is necessarily limited to home consumption, and cannot be affected by the price of foreign importations, but only by a diminution of the quantity. If the price of the finest British broadcloth was reduced to eight dollars a yard, it would, at the present price of wheat, cost the farmer sixteen bushels a yard—of wool, sixteen pounds; if the cloth should rise to sixteen dollars a yard, wheat would not rise to one a bushel, and wool to one dollar a pound, unless the domestic demand increased in the same proportion: this would be impossible, unless accompanied with a proportionate increase of domestic manufactures. If all our supply was by imports, their price could have no bearing on the price of domestic articles, which would not be received in exchange. Can it be doubted that the system which insures this exchange is true economy? If our woollens are made at home, the price of the fabric will be governed by the price of materials; the rates are immaterial; one pays for the other; competition will regulate them by a just standard. The tax on the importation becomes a mutual benefit; it operates not to force the farmer from his occupation, but to secure him the choice of products, by rearing up new establishments, to furnish him with a market for his raw materials, say of wool, flax, and hemp. By abstaining from the imposition of such duties on the foreign as would open our markets to the domestic products of those articles, the farmer is, in effect, forced from his occupation, and prevented from raising them. Foreign bounties produce the precise effect which is so much dreaded from our laws; foreign restrictive systems virtually compel our farmers to confine their labor not to what they can produce with the greatest ease and profit, but what suits their Government to receive, thus effectually preventing the consumer from consulting his economy, he is obliged to look to foreign laws to know what productions he shall raise to supply his family with food and raiment, utensils and furniture.

That system of dealing among the members of the same community is the best which produces such exchanges of the wants of the one may be supplied by the surplus of the other. If our habits of intercourse with other nations have kept off the adoption of the system of exchange among ourselves, and those nations will not agree to its adoption; if, in consequence, we look round this country, and find that the aggregate means to supply the wants of all are most abundant if properly distributed, yet there is general distress, because the surplus of one article cannot supply the deficiency of another, it cannot be an unwise or an oppressive regulation of Government which would at least remove foreign restraints and interference, so as to leave our citizens in the uninterrupted selection of their pursuits and modes of employment. It cannot be sound policy to suffer them to remain under

APPENDIX.

this external coercion, and influenced by the fear of a restrictive system, adopted by a paternal Government of our own choice, yet submit to one imposed on us by one between whom and this people there can be no common tie. To guard the consumer against the maker and seller of an article, competition is most effectual. If it be safe to have it confined to foreign and mercantile, it may be equally so to have it domestic and manufacturing. Those who prefer the former will protest against protecting duties; the second will advocate them; and others so apportion them as to enable both to come into the market on equal terms. If the commerce of the world was free, a low rate of duty would suffice; while it is restricted, there must be as much tax as will counterbalance foreign interference, and afford the opportunity of exchange. Whether the rate of duties, so low as to leave the supply of our consumption at the command of one class, so high as to throw it into the hands of another, or the medium between revenue and prohibition ascending to the one or descending to the other point, as the economy and interest of the consumer may require, can better be settled by experience than reasoning, it is believed that acknowledged facts leave no room to doubt. The duty on coarse cottons being prohibitory, the supply is now entirely domestic; the quality is better than the imported, and the price to the consumer reduced more than forty per cent. The protecting duty is, then, no tax on the many—no bounty to the few. But the additional forty per cent., allowing nothing for the quality, was a direct tax on the whole community for the benefit of the importer. The amount of this tax paid and bounty will appear from a statement furnished from a report which dwells much on this objection to manufacturers.* "From the most accurate information, founded chiefly on official documents, it appears that, from the year 1800 to the year 1812, both inclusive, the duties received on the importation of the coarse cottons of India amounted to more than $3,936,000." During the first four years of this period the duties were twelve and a half per cent.; the last eight, the Mediterranean fund added made them fifteen, averaging about seven dollars of goods to one of duty, equal to - - - $27,552,000
The same number of yards of the
   same goods of American manufacture would cost forty per cent.
   less, equal to - - - - 11,020,800

Leaving the price of the domestic at $16,531,200

Thus the imported article costing $27,552,000, the domestic $16,531,200, the difference, $11,020,800, has been paid by the people; deducting duties, $3,936,000, leaves $7,084,800, paid by the consumer to the merchant, more than would have purchased the same quantity from the manufacturers —a tax of $545,000 a year. This presents a practical illustration of the objection now under consideration—the tax on the many, the bounty to the few. But the few were not manufacturers; the

* Boston Report.

premium was not paid to them. If such have been the salutary effects of the high duty on cottons, it ought to be a most instructive lesson, and induce us to extend the same protection to other articles of clothing.

This is not a solitary instance in the experience of the country; the same effect has been produced by high duties on nails, gunpowder, and every high taxed article of manufactures; and it is believed that there is no instance of the increase of the price of any article the high duties on which have secured our market to our own manufacturers. Had there been any, it would probably not have escaped the attention of those who so zealously oppose the increase of duties. In tracing the progress of manufactures in other countries, it is universally true that the nation which has the materials, and manufactures for itself, can undersell others; and hence, our best and greatest statesmen have laid it down as a maxim, that domestic competition will always tend to the reduction of the price—a maxim not only consistent with reason, but supported by fact and experience. It is not, therefore, without some surprise, that it should be so generally alleged, by the opponents of protecting duties, that they are a tax on the many to enrich the few. It may comport with the theory of foreign writers on political economy, but the allegation has not grown from experience here, or elsewhere, but is contradicted by uniform and admitted facts. Manufactures are not the work of yesterday; their tendency is not for the first time to be now ascertained; enough has been seen and witnessed in the past, to afford a guide for the future; and if there is safety in any path, it is that which has been lighted by the practice and experience of years in this country, and almost centuries in others. It is indeed, not easily conceived that duties short of prohibitory can easily operate as a bounty to the manufacturer; if the price of the article advances with the duty, it still leaves the same profit to the importer. Duties are no burden to him; he obtains a credit equal to what he allows, and the amount of the duty is an addition to his capital. The manufacturer can derive no benefit from a duty, unless it checks or excludes the foreign importation; while imported goods meet him in the market, the price is indifferent to him; be it high or low, it excludes him from the competition, while the importer can have a profit. The duty begins only to operate in favor of the manufacturer when the quantity of the foreign production comes to be diminished; if it remains the same, it adds only to the amount of revenue. The ad valorem duty of thirty per cent. on paper and cut glass is no bounty to the owners of paper mills and glass works, while foreigners supply us; if it excluded paper and glass, and the proprietors exacted from the consumers, so that the market price of paper and glass would advance to the same amount, importations would be resumed and continued until the prices were reduced below competition. High prices would create and tempt it; the interest, therefore, of manufacturers would impel them not to expose their establishments to continual fluctuations, by the ebbs and flows of imports. An absolute prohibition might

Protection to Manufactures.

enable them to exact from the community; time will ascertain the point at which the rate of duties might amount to it; but it is difficult to conceive that mere rates of duties, which do not exceed those imposed on articles taxed purely for revenue, can prove dangerous or injurious to the consumer; and, with such duties, no other mode can be discerned by which the domestic market can be secured but low prices. The reverse of the proposition is undoubtedly true; low duties could not take the market from domestic goods, unless the imported were cheaper. On what other reason to account for the exclusion of coarse cottons, the committee are unable to imagine. If the eighty per cent. duty was a bounty to the manufacturer, it must be by adding that amount to the price of his cloth; the foreign, if of the same quality, would command the same price. Reason and experience alike assign the true cause—the diminution of price. There may be a period between the imposition of a new duty and the domestic supply of our market that may be one of high prices; but "if these difficulties can be overcome by a present tax, which will be more than compensated by the reduction of prices hereafter, it is good policy and economy to impose it." True legislation is not ephemeral; it looks beyond the present to the future, laying the foundations of national policy commensurate with all the great interests of the country; it will build up a system, not of temporary, but permanent protection; it will not be retarded or withheld, from a fear that a monopoly of either domestic manufacturing or domestic navigation will tax the many, give a bounty to the few, or raise up a privileged order, dangerous to the liberties, or injurious to the welfare of the people.

A restrictive system.

It is said that this country is about adopting a restrictive system, when others are desirous of abandoning it, and their best statesmen are convinced of its bad policy. When terms are used as weapons, it may be useful to inquire into their meaning and application; the same measures may acquire a good or bad character, as they may be called parts of a system of revenue or restriction. Impost, as a means of taxing the consumption of the country for the support of Government, and prohibition, for the purpose of creating and maturing the subjects of an excise, are fiscal measures, acknowledgedly proper to meet the exigencies of the nation. The Secretary of the Treasury has recommended that if any revenue law be passed for the aid of our finances, it be one of the latter description—a prohibition of foreign, an excise on domestic spirits. No complaints have been heard against the proposition, and perhaps none would be heard if it had embraced iron, glass, paper, cottons, or woollens. Though the direct tendency would be to give the monopoly of the home market to the domestic manufacturer, yet, emanating from the Treasury, the same fearful consequences are not anticipated as if it could be traced to a different source, and its leading motive the promotion of other objects. The resources of

the Treasury have failed; it is of no importance to the people whether there is a prohibition of foreign, and an excise on domestic manufactures, for the purpose of filling the Treasury, and, by consequence, sustaining manufactures; or, for the purpose of fostering manufactures, and, by consequence, filling the Treasury; both objects are accomplished; which is direct and which consequential is immaterial for any other purpose than giving a name to the measure—fiscal in the one case, restrictive in the other. This consideration must not leave our minds when we review the systems of other Governments. At first view, they seem illiberal, and dictated by a jealous spirit of rivalship and monopoly; but, taking England as an example, and asking ourselves by what other means she could, from a small population, extract as large a revenue as would keep in operation the immense machinery of her mighty empire, we must admire it as a masterly effort of human policy. With less than double our number, she meets an expenditure of £50,000,000 by the receipts of her treasury. Her corn laws, her revenue and commercial systems, tend to the same great object. The former is the basis of the land and income tax; the latter of excise and customs. It is not so much from a system of hostility to others, but of self-defence to herself. This is evinced by her warehousing system, displaying a liberality worthy of our imitation. It is scarcely credible that her statesmen are willing to abandon those systems which have been maturing for ages, for others yet unknown and untried. The source of her revenue is now dependent, not on the fluctuations of imports, but the income, the property, as well as the consumption of the country; though each source may be extended to its maximum, none can be abandoned; and it may not be very uncharitable to believe the contrary opinions which many have expressed may be intended for exportation, with the benefit of drawback and custom bounty.

The example of other nations furnishes no exceptions to these remarks. The code of France, adopted at a late date, furnishes no evidence of a disposition to an abandonment of the same policy. She persists in the discrimination of the duty on produce imported in French and foreign ships, and, in a spirit of defiance, gives a bounty on South American cotton. Spain, at the moment of throwing off a despotic, and assuming a representative Government, has passed a corn law, and prohibited the importation of soap into her colonies. It would be a severe reflection by one Congress on another to charge the spirit which led to the adoption of these measures as flowing from jealousy and illiberality, and not a conviction of national interest. It would be a severe and serious reflection on ourselves, who, in the navigation acts of last session, extended to prohibition and non-intercourse the principle of what, when applied to manufactures, is called the restrictive system, but the character of which, in our opinion, does not depend on its application. Whether these measures are considered as commencing a new, or only following up the old system of discrimination adopted at an early period of our Government, whether retaliatory, aggressive, or defensive, does not depend on the selection of objects for its operation. The shipping, produce, or manufactures of foreign nations are their assailable interests. We choose the one which will best insure our objects of coercion. Those laws embraced all the objects, yet they passed one branch of Congress with unanimity, and the other without discussion. It is thought unnecessary to press on the same Congress the unfairness of opposing or condemning the same principle, merely because of its application to different national interests. With France, the contest was, whose shipping should carry to her our cotton, rice, and tobacco, and bring back to us her manufactures, wines and spirits; with England, who should take to her colonies our timber, provisions, and live stock, and bring to us their various productions. If the mere carrying back and forth was worthy of a contest of legislation, and justified prohibition, non-importation, aud non-intercourse, it was because it gave a value to the materials for ship building, labor in the construction, and employment to seamen in their navigation—objects, it is admitted, imperiously calling for a national movement to coerce their completion. But, though truly national, these objects embrace but a small portion of our population ; extend to but a comparatively limited extent of territory ; the benefits resulting are not alike extended to the mass of the nation. The number of carriers, compared to the consumers, is insignificant. To the latter it is infinitely more important that a market should be found for their provisions, the raw materials for manufactures. They cannot feel that it is not a wise policy in this nation to induce others to receive such articles as it is the interest of ours to export, but only that our ships may carry such as their policy may admit. The interest of the contest to a majority of the people, if their productions are excluded, at all events, is small ; it makes no difference in the price. As little does it concern them who carries foreign manufactures to our market ; it does not vary the demand for grain or materials. A single ship may bring a cargo worth more than the annual labor of a thousand men, yet not affording an item for exchange. To whom that ship belongs, is not the all-important question ; where built, or how navigated ; but what additional value its contents afford to the productions of our soil, the fruits of our labor. A few ships would suffice for the importation of the manufactures we consume, forming a small item in our navigation. The transportation of our surplus and now useless produce would present one far greater.

The carrying of all our exports and imports would not furnish a market for one-fourth of the materials, or employment to one-fourth of the labor, required to make the articles of our consumption. Yet it would seem that, while the policy of protecting, and even forcing, the one interest has been coeval with this Government, sanctioned by general acquiescence, continued to the present session, and persistance in it recommended, the same policy, as applicable to other greater and more general interests, is reprobated as destructive

to the prosperity of the nation. It is well known that, if success attend our attempts to effect a reciprocity of duties and regulations as to the ships and their cargoes, whether of our own or other nations, it will give to ours nearly a monopoly of transportation, and prevent competition. While this reciprocity is refused, we enforce a restrictive system, because France and England refuse admission to our shipping on equal terms. Equal justice would require that we apply the same system to their manufactures, while our provisions and raw materials are excluded. The expectation that either will give up one provision in their code is as reasonable as that they would abandon another. If they would cling the longest to any, and give it up the last, it might be their navigation. There can be no difference in principle between aiming at the repeal of their corn laws or their navigation acts. We ought not to be governed in our choice by the particular interest it might most affect, but the greatest national good it would produce. In adopting this as the criterion, it may deserve the inquiry whether, if the only great interest, or the only favored one of England, was manufacturing, it would be thought unwise or unjust in our national councils to endeavor to build up our own, either in retaliation or self-defence. If it would, then strong reasons indeed must exist for the constant, strenuous, and almost unanimous efforts to rear up and cherish our navigation. The measure so much complained of proposed no prohibition, bounty, or premium ; the highest rates of duties on manufactured goods did not amount to the existing one on cotton ; articles which interfered with our most important manufactures were classed lower than the most important items of consumption, and merely for revenue. It asked for no prohibition of intercourse to counteract foreign bounties, duties, or restrictions ; it excluded no article of produce or manufacture, unless by its tendency to promote domestic competition, which, by affording a market for the raw material, enabled, and, by improving the quality and reducing the price, induced, the consumer to prefer the domestic to the foreign. Yet it has been, is, and will be, called a restrictive measure, illiberal in its design, ruinous in its tendency, oppressive in its operation, partial and unjust in its very nature and original conception ; as an attempt to wrest the soil and the seas from those to whose use God had given them ; "a measure which would doom the merchants to poverty, prohibiting their ordinary and honorable pursuits, presenting a horrid picture of prospective misery ;" "striking deeply at the foundations of all true and enlightened policy ;" "plunging deeper into measures of prohibition, restrictions on trade, premiums, bounties, and stimulants to rear exclusive interest at the national expense ;" "an undisguised effort to coax or alarm our rulers into the ruinous project of coercing the farmers, planters, artisans, and merchants ; to make crutches of agriculture and commerce, to support a body which, in the mania of speculation, has been dieted and swelled into an unnatural growth, too unwieldy for her limbs to sustain ;" "to convert our seamen into skulking, profligate smug-

Protection to Manufactures.

glers, at an expense of taxation, national happiness, and legislative oppression;" " the vote of this House viewed with astonishment and concern; the reasons for it, a repetition of trite and exploded doctrines;" a "triumph of passion and interest over reason and justice;" "political quackery, which proposes to legislate a nation into wealth and prosperity;" "a call for a most onerous tax, with no view to national defence, (for this is not pretended by its candid admirers,) but merely to take some millions of dollars annually from the pockets of the agriculturists and merchants, to give as a bounty to manufacturers."

This is the character given to this measure; these are the motives ascribed for its passage, in the memorials addressed to us; if with justice, then there is much of our past and some of our present policy to condemn in relation to other subjects and other interests. Measures purely restrictive, and strictly prohibitory, have been prayed for by those who now so oppose this; with what consistency or regard to general interest, alike, opinions may vary. When they apply strong language, like the foregoing, to this proposed bill, to those who advocated and the body which passed it, they must have forgotten that the war duties were higher than those now so much deprecated; that they continued for eighteen months after the peace, and did not produce the fearful, dreadful consequences predicted from this. Those duties being imposed for revenue, and not followed by such effects, if those now proposed will produce them, it must follow that, not the provisions or enactments of a law, but the motives and objects of those who bring it forward, give it its character and control its operation; that prohibition and excise, if recommended from the Treasury, may be salutary; if asked for by farmers and distillers, ruinous and oppressive. Had the French tonnage duty, the non-importation and non-intercourse with the British islands and colonies been petitioned for by manufacturers, those measures must have injured and destroyed; as merchants prayed for them, they have benefited and saved commerce. Had the bounty on Brazil cotton followed the passage of the tariff, it would have been a curse; as it is consequent on the navigation acts, planters will view it as a blessing. Ought it not rather to be viewed as a solemn warning, a lesson of instruction, to teach us that, if we expect by our legislation to change the policy of other nations, it is safer to select new points of attack than to persist in one which has already more seriously endangered our remaining staple export than could have been foreseen? Is the allowance of this bounty a practical illustration of the explosion of all restrictions on trade, the adoption of liberal principles and free trade?

It cannot well be considered as a part of a system of restriction, that, in providing for the public expenditure, an excise on any articles of consumption should be adopted. In selecting for taxation objects which will bear it, they must be those which are permanent, not fluctuating. It may be necessary to create some, and to give stability to others. If the exclusion of foreign competition

is necessary to effect this, it becomes a measure of revenue and not restriction—of internal, not external policy; affording no just ground of complaint to foreigners, as they have no right to judge of our domestic legislation. To our own citizens it becomes a measure of restriction or benefit, according to its operation. In the present state of foreign markets, the exclusion of foreign spirits would open a domestic market for our grain, which in vain seeks one abroad. It cannot be called illiberal in us, but called for by self-defence. We may have as little cause to complain of their exclusion, as it results from a calculation of interest; our excise on domestic spirits becomes a mere matter of revenue, to supply the impost on imported spirits. Thus there may be mutual prohibitions, dictated by national interests, and yet consistent with the principles of free trade. In apportioning our imposts, for the united purposes of supplying the Treasury, giving a value to our productions, and employment to the labor of the nation, it well cannot, and ought not, to be called a system of restriction, unless, in its operation on foreign nations, or our own people, it extends beyond those objects, to individual or general oppression. If, in its details, the proposed bill contains features of this description, they are certainly objectionable, and the committee would be unwilling they should be retained; but, as they are unable to perceive them, as none of the memorialists have pointed them out, but confined their objections to general allegations, we must be allowed to believe that none of its provisions extend beyond the dictates of sound policy, and are undeserving of the strong epithets which have been so liberally applied to them.

Destroy revenue.

It is a very common objection that this bill will destroy the revenue, and make a resort to direct taxation inevitable. If this was an evil which would never befall the country under the present system, and would be a consequence of a new one, there might be much weight in the suggestion. But it must be recollected, that if we have not hitherto, and do not now, resort to direct and internal taxation, it is not because our revenue is sufficient to meet our expenditure; the aid of loans is indispensable. Internal taxation is now avoided only by borrowing, not because our other means are abundant; these loans are not in anticipation of the receipt of taxes already imposed, or merely temporary until an efficient system shall come into active operation, but made on the general credit of the nation, without any definite and certain provision for their repayment. If it can be called one, then our present system is not impost, but impost and loans; every change in the tariff, let the effects be as they may, can only change the proportions of the two items. Admitting it may become loans and impost by the new, it is not certain that it may not by the old. If it is not unwise or unsound policy to resort to the general credit of the nation in time of profound peace, no possible bad consequences can follow the adoption of the proposed plan. It is only the difference between the people paying as they go, and paying interest; for the people must pay in the end. Loans are not revenue, and are to the nation what a judgment and mortgage are to an individual, binding the person, personal property, and soil. If loans are ever to be paid, and interest is not to be a perpetual tax on the country, we have already as much debt to redeem as the present generation is able to pay; the burden must be removed by us, or left as a legacy to posterity. If loans are injudicious, then other means must be resorted to to supply the deficiency in the Treasury; those means are, an increase of the impost and tonnage duties, or internal and direct taxes. If the former is the most eligible mode, then the bill of last session becomes necessary for revenue, and is free from the objection now urged; if it fails in this object, it must be because the present tariff is as high as the country can bear; in other words, because impost cannot be made efficient. If this is already so certain and clear that it is useless to even try the experiment, another mode becomes indispensable, and must be adopted immediately. What is that other mode? Direct taxes, excise, &c. It is conceived hardly necessary to examine into the expediency or justice of assessing on the real estate of the people a sum sufficient to meet the deficit of the Treasury, as it is believed to be within the personal knowledge of every member of this House that the farmers and landholders are unable to pay a tax on their lands. The depression of agricultural produce, the depreciation in the price of real property which is universal, the state of the currency, the want of a circulating medium, and the means of procuring it, forbid the hope that this would be an available mode. In the present embarrassment which pervades the whole country, it would be unjust and oppressive; the people have not the means or the ability; an attempt to coerce them would throw the Government into unnecessary expense, or enable them and speculators to purchase the fee simple of our soil. In this situation of the country, the committee would express their decided opinion that the imposition of this tax would produce evils of the most serious and alarming nature, and be equally repugnant to the wishes of the Legislature and the interest of the nation.

In looking around for other objects of direct taxation, none could be discovered which could materially relieve the public embarrassments. Excise seems to be the only expedient. Excise is, as well as impost, a tax on the consumption of the country; one operates on the imported, the other on the domestic article; the difference is in name, not substance; it is in both a duty laid—an assessment made on the value, weight, dimensions, or quantity of an article imported from abroad, or made at home. The term excise is with some an odious one, implying compulsion to pay it; while impost is said to be a voluntary tax; but it is surely as easy to abstain from the use of domestic spirits, and thus avoid the payment of an excise, as from the use of foreign spirits, and thus avoid an impost. Those who will use spirits must pay one or the other; and if the amount of the as-

sessment on both is the same, it makes the same addition to the price, and, in either case, operates with as much compulsion. An impost on woollen or cotton goods to those who choose to wear them is an addition to the price—a tax; if they wear them, they must pay it; an excise is no more compulsory, and ought to be no more odious or unpopular. There is great magic in names and words. Finance and revenue are said to be sciences; darkness conceals their principles; political and mental research is necessary to understand them; there is this veil which conceals them from common and simple observation, which can only be raised by those initiated in their mysteries. Hence has arisen the delusion which presents commerce as the principal source of revenue. This illusion would be effectually dissipated, if a few plain practical considerations were bestowed upon it; but it continues, not because it is so difficult, but so easy to remove it. There are no truths, either in science or common life, so difficult to inculcate and enforce observance as plain and simple ones; when they are applied to the great operations of Government they are doubted, because it is a common belief that great machinery can only be put and kept in motion by great principles, above common comprehension; hence they are not examined. From the want of this examination has arisen the common accepted opinion that excise is an oppressive, impost a mild mode of taxation. Had it changed, and applied the word impost to domestic articles, excise and external taxation to foreign, the popularity of the two modes of taxation would have been transposed; for their operation on the people is the same. A moment's reflection will bring about the conviction, that a dollar impost, or a dollar excise, on a yard of cloth, which is in both cases added to the price, is of no further importance to the one who buys it than in paying it in the one case to the man who imports it, and in the other to the man who makes it. To the Government it is the same, as the same amount is received into the Treasury; whether derived from the one source or the other, it is alike revenue. This revenue is in neither case paid by commerce or manufactures; the tax is on the article, not on the carrier or the maker. Commerce is the means by which the foreign article manufactures the means by which the domestic article is furnished to the consumer or purchaser, who pays the tax; when he buys the goods, he pays the revenue. If the articles could not be sold, none would be imported by the merchant, or made by the manufacturer; the Government would receive no revenue.

Impost being a tax on consumption and not on commerce, consumption and not commerce furnishes the revenue: so of excise; it is consumption, not manufactures. Both the merchant and manufacturer make the tax an article of merchandise, by adding it to the cost, and apportioning the profit on their aggregate expenditure. The consumer will purchase from the one or the other, as he can best and easiest pay, or most profitably exchange. The present state of the country offers a decided preference. The merchant cannot purchase or receive in exchange the provisions or raw materials of the farmer; their importation is prohibited in the country whence he imports his goods. But the manufacturer wants provisions for his laborers, and materials for his establishment; he can purchase or exchange. When grain can be exchanged for spirits, it pays the tax to the Government and the price to the distiller; it is, therefore, an easier and cheaper mode of discharging the portion of the burdens of Government, which every man must pay, than by being compelled to turn his grain into money at any price which a bad market would afford. If, therefore, the operation of the proposed tariff would be to substitute excise for impost, as the principal source of revenue, it would be a most salutary effect to the mass of consumers, who would thus be enabled to pay in kind, and by exchange, what they must, by the other mode, pay in money. To accomplish this, there must be subjects for the operation of an excise; while foreign productions supply the consumption of the country, there will be no domestic ones on which to impose an excise; or, if an impost should create such a consumption as would divide the market, an excise on the domestic article would render the impost on the foreign no discrimination, and enable it to supersede the domestic in the market. The domestic market must be secured to the domestic production; then it can pay an excise, and render the revenues of the Government permanent and certain as the consumption of the country. A sudden change in systems of taxation creates revulsions injurious to established interests; it should be so gradual as to give time to the business of the country to direct its operations in conformity to the new measures. This is best done by such revision of the tariff as will make the most from items for revenue, and to enable those of manufacture to progress to such a state as to meet the demand. If the proposed tariff has not this tendency, it is not because the most assiduous exertions of the committee have not been directed to those objects.

The important inquiry now presents itself, will such a change be injurious to the revenue, or is it necessary for its preservation and increase?

The official documents before us present the alarming facts, that, besides the absorption of the balance of the sinking fund, the deficits of the last and present year amount to nearly $10,000,000; that the revenue from the customs for the "last three years has rapidly decreased, and those of the last are less than any preceding one since the peace." As the consumption of the country is the source of the customs, it is thus rendered certain that it does not keep pace, but diminishes, with the increase of the population of the country; one principal reason must have occurred to the personal observation of every member of this House in his district—the means of purchasing imported articles have become, and are becoming, lessened. A hope is, indeed, left us, that we may anticipate more from the future than we have realized from the past and present; but we are left without any certainty of the means by which the future consumption of the foreign goods may be increased

beyond the present, or any assurance that it will not be less. In trusting to estimates and conjectures, and by basing our legislation on them as facts and certainties, we make ourselves responsible for their correctness, if they prove delusive; and yet we shall, by implicitly confiding in them, have persisted in a system injurious, and retarded the adoption of one beneficial to the national revenue, interest and credit. The responsibility may be unpleasant, for we shall have avoided the course to which facts, experience, and perhaps policy, pointed, and followed that to which we had been allured by expectation and hope. If the resources of the country, if the means of purchasing the materials which can be exchanged, have become diminished, it is not by any calamity of a general nature at home, or any unexpected events abroad. Many think it has resulted from trusting to external, and not to internal sources of revenue, from not securing our market to our own productions; if they are mistaken in the reasons, they are not in the fact. The revenue has been insufficient, and is yet so. Will it not then become prudent to adopt our measures on the belief that it will continue so under the operation of existing measures, and in the existing state of things? There is at least, safety in this course; no change is even conjectured till 1822, and then may not be very sudden, or to an amount greater than will be required to redeem the public credit. In 1825 $18,000,000 of public debt becomes due, and it is not probable that the revenues of the intermediate period will more than meet the expenditure, the loans of the last and present years, and that installment of the public debt. There is no danger that too much money will flow from the present system of revenue to the Treasury; but there is much danger that there will not be enough to meet the demands. A prudent, safe, and sound policy would then seem to dictate the propriety of providing for a contingency, which, if not certain, is highly probable; and not trust implicitly to one which is barely possible, and which must take effect, or the whole country present one general distress, heightened by the loss of national credit, the destruction of public confidence, and justly ascribable to our want of foresight, possibly to the pride of opinion.

It may happen to the best administered Governments that their settled course of policy may be defeated by unexpected, untoward events. Our fiscal embarrassments cannot be traced to such a source; if they could, then temporary expedients would become justifiable, till a settled order of things were restored. But, if the calculations which have led ours to adopt imposts as the almost exclusive source of revenue have been that a general war in Europe would secure such a price to our produce as to furnish the means of an indefinite consumption of foreign goods; if our reasons for now adopting no other system arise from the expectation that another great convulsion will happen, it will have presented a bold experiment, which nothing but success could justify. It is building the support of the Government not on the resources of the nation, but the fluctuating policy of foreign Powers, which will not be conformed to meet the demands of our treasury, or the interest of this people. The experiment was made on a forced and unnatural state of things; settled order has now returned; and we must increase the present, afford new means for the consumption of foreign goods, or base our revenue on the domestic. The latter is no new or untried measure; it has succeeded, by developing and retaining the resources of the country, enabling them to supply the deficiencies of the Treasury.

A reduction of the existing duties has been suggested as a mode of increasing the revenue. It is not perceived how this consequence would follow; though the price of the articles consumed would be lessened, the quantity consumed must increase in a ratio greater than the price decreased, or it could not produce a greater revenue. It could not add to the means of the consumer to purchase the greater quantity; it would open no new market for the exchange of the products of his labor or soil. And, if it is dangerous to now raise the duties to a rate preparatory for an excise, by creating too sudden a revulsion, it would be still more so if the point of depression should be made still lower, and it shall hereafter be found necessary to resort to the proposed bill. One thing must not be forgotten—admitting that the increase on the tariff will impair the revenue, it will only be in consequence of the substitution of the domestic for the foreign supply for consumption; if, from both sources, the aggregate amount of consumption remains the same, it only requires the substitution of an excise to produce to the Government the same revenue with the same exaction from the people. The only possible inconvenience must arise from the refusal of the Legislature to impose the excise, or the people to pay it. The objection, therefore, should not come from either of these sources, that the revenue will be destroyed. They must make impost efficient, or try new sources; if they will cling alone to this, let them make the most of it; not, when its incompetency is publicly and officially acknowledged, object to any alteration extending or reducing it; if it has failed in its present shape, to give it another; if the modification the committee recommend is wrong, to offer one which will be right. When the expenses of a Government exceed its income, there is a responsibility somewhere; expenses must be reduced, or income raised. If all the expenses are necessary, then it is as necessary to make provision to meet them, unless the inconvenience to the people in providing the means to meet such expenses is greater than the good which is derived from the objects to which the money is applied; in that case they become secondary, and must be dispensed with. If all our present expenditure is required for the common defence and general welfare of the nation, the common defence and general welfare become secondary objects, unless they justify the means of defraying it, and must be sacrificed by the refusal or neglect to do it.

If the expense is neither to be brought within the income, nor the income raised to the expense, it must be bad policy in one aspect or the other.

16th Con. 2d Sess.—51

If the retention of the army, navy, and civil list is connected with the system of common defence, the means of their support is the essential part of the same system; the friends of the one cannot be the enemies to the other; if the means are not worth providing for, the establishments are not worth their cost. Important as are our army, navy, and the other machinery of the nation, there is yet one item more important, more to be cherished, as the great means of public defence, the vital principle which infuses life and imparts vigor to all others—public credit. Armies, navies, and civil lists, cannot create or preserve that; it is the effect of wise policy, prudent councils, and sound legislation. Credit can create the other instruments for defence; it is the moving, the inspiring cause, which gives efficient impulse to national movements; the extent of its creative preserving powers is bounded only by the emergencies of the nation, but it should be guarded with a watchful eye; our only resource in time of war, it should not be exhausted in time of peace; with it, all the great defences of the country are broken down. If in peace it be prudent to provide for war; if this be the maxim which convinces us of the policy of retaining an army and building a navy to defend the country, the same policy will dictate the ruinous consequences of destroying the only efficient source of their support If our calculations are founded on the belief that war is a calamity too distant to be guarded against, then there can exist no stronger reasons for providing force than for retaining credit. Credit is a fund on which this nation may largely draw, but it is a fund not yet untouched; if it accepts the bill now drawn upon it for $7,000,000, it will have advanced nearly 100,000,000. The war drafts will soon arrive at maturity, and no provision is made for their redemption. Credit rests on confidence; it will have but slender support if we commence another war with this heavy load. The means of payment will soon be called for; the public lands are probably pledged already for their full value; and the customs are inadequate to the ordinary expenses. No permanent fund for the payment of the interest; no source to which we can look for the redemption of the principal of the public debt—these will be sufficient clogs on loans which may be required in times of danger and trouble; they ought not to be increased by additional ones in ordinary and peaceful times. It is far from the wish of the committee to draw a cloud over the bright scenes of the late war; but it cannot derogate from the glory they imparted to the country to remind the House of the instructive lessons it afforded. We commenced it with a national debt of $45,000,000; the country less embarrassed than at present. With what difficulty, at what sacrifices, loans were obtained, it is unnecessary to examine; to sustain public credit unimpaired ceased to be an exertion; any efforts made were to prevent its extinction. The known fruitlessness of the attempt forbade the Government to even ask the nominal value for the evidences of public debt; the first great inquiry was, if they could be sold at all; the last at what depreciation. Happier results cannot be expected, if

Protection to Manufactures.

with diminished resources and more than doubled debt, we commence another war without a permanent source of revenue. Public credit does not fall in the mere ratio of the increase of the public debt; its decline will become more rapid as the means of sustaining it are neglected or denied; lenders will look to the security for the punctual payment of the interest, and the eventual payment of the principal; the value of that security will depend not on general, indefinite, though positive assurances, but the permanent efficient measures which will insure the redemption of our plighted faith. As the amount of the debt is in a greater or less proportion to our efficient resources; as our foreign relations may present a more or less pacific aspect; as our domestic policy may more or less tend to impair our institutions, to strengthen or weaken the common bond which alone makes us great; as the history of our past legislation shall give confidence to the existing, or justify the demand for new pledges for the future, so will the solidity of this great national defence be secured or impaired. Entertaining these views, deeply impressed with their intimate connexion with the general welfare, it will not be expected that the committee will further pursue the inquiry whether it is wise or safe to supply the deficit by loans; that they can hesitate in believing that it should be a resort only after the failure of all other means; and that the time when old sources of revenue fail is the proper period for laying the foundations of new. It can only be found in some species of taxation; that it is not in the present tariff is admitted; that it could not be in a reduced one, is certain; it must be in an increased one, excise, or direct taxes. If an increased tariff will afford the remedy, it removes the revenue objection, and presents conclusive arguments for its adoption; if it fails of this effect, and excise shall become indispensable, the measure is still necessary to so far reduce foreign imports as to give the market to the home products, to enable them to become commensurate with the demands of the country, to supply its consumption, and be thus reared up as the effective subjects of excise, by a gradual and not a sudden and radical operation. Viewed thus, it may be defended and justified as a mere measure of revenue, and ought to lose none of its importance or value because it combines the protection of national resources and industry; tending to retain within this country its currency and profits; giving to this, and not to another nation, the benefits of the circulation of the one and the expenditure of the other.

Ruin commerce.

When a measure is recommended for adoption, which contains not only general provisions, but a variety of details, which are alleged to bear with peculiar and intentional oppression upon a highly respectable and useful portion of the nation; when their memorials on our table attribute the tendency and the design of that measure to be the destruction of a great national interest which affords them the means of employment and support, it should be deemed incumbent on those who make to sup-

port these charges. When it had ceased to be th act or project of individuals, by its adoption by th representatives of the people, it ought then at lea to be thought to have emanated from a convictio of public duty; if the result of errors, that the were those of judgment; motives and intentio might have been spared. However little it ma have been deserved by others, charity should hav extended to the representatives of five of the greate commercial cities in the Union, some of whom assisted in devising, and all of whom concurre in the passage of the measure, the want of a desig to destroy the interest confided to them. If th motives ascribed are discernible in any feature o the bill with such clearness as authorizes the im putation, it is the least favor that can be grante to those who disclaim and do not feel conscious o having indulged a feeling of hostility to any in terest, and at least profess the desire to promot the general good, that such particular feature should be designated; it may serve as a friendly admonition by which to avoid future errors; a willingness to retract them might follow from the conviction of their existence, and reputation be restored by repentance.

The committee thus publicly declare, that if the proposed tariff had, in their opinion, partaken of the character imputed to it, it would not have received their sanction; this House certainly would withhold theirs. Those on whom these direful evils have been impending possess both intelligence and industry to trace their sources in the particular parts of the bill; it ought to have been expected from their candor that, when they knew of their existence and inevitable consequences, which ar so deeply deplored and so feelingly portrayed, they would not have confined themselves to genera remarks. It was not enough to complain that agriculture, commerce, and revenue would k destroyed; how it would have been done should have been explained. High duties have been tried on various articles; their practical operation cannot be unknown; the benefits of experience should have been imparted to us. General objections can be made by any one not versed in the operations of commerce or finance; but to ascertain whether they are founded in fact, an apply to a definite proposition, can best be de cided by the observation and practical knowledge of men whose pursuits lead and peculiarly qualif them to judge of the effects of legislation on the occupations and interests. On this subject, most than perhaps any other, the fairest opportunity o judging has been presented. This bill is not bot tomed on any new policy; the encouragement o manufactures is no uncommon subject of discus sion. We have a right, nay, may be bound, t presume that the tariff which would authorize such strong objections, and must produce such fearful consequences, has been well and thorough examined; that when it has assumed such impor tance as to call the notice of conventions from States, of committees, and delegates, selected fo their intelligence, to represent the great interest about to be prostrated, and by their exertions "di fuse such information as may tend to make it consequences rightly and generally understood," to urge to an enlightened Legislature reasons which should withdraw their sanctions from a measure which one branch had adopted, they would be drawn from the bill, apply to its provisions, and be the most forcible which could be selected ; it is a fair inference that those which have not been deemed important have been omitted, and that the objectionable character is to be tested by those which have been pressed.

Those which relate to commerce are the following general ones: "Its avowed object is to direct and control the occupations of men, by granting special privileges to those engaged in particular pursuits." The committee are not aware by whom such avowal was made; they have searched the bill in vain for the evidence of it, and cannot see it in its provision, still less do they recognise the existence of the object in their own minds.

" This tariff would impose on' certain foreign manufactures duties professedly and effectually prohibitory ; and the question involved in its adoption is not whether the consumer of those goods shall pay a higher price for them, but whether he shall be prevented from purchasing them at all." Conjecture must be allowed a wide range before it could alight upon the tariff intended for this remark. It is not the one which the committee had the honor of presenting to the House; that contained no prohibition. The highest ad valorem duty was forty per cent., and few, if any, specific ones were higher; that tariff prohibited no one from purchasing if he would pay the price. If the certain manufactures prohibited, and the goods which were forbidden to be purchased, had been particularly designated, it would have furnished a clue for our researches; without that aid, our labors would be useless. "A system of restriction so unequal, so repugnant to all sound theory." In its application to commerce, this term is believed to have received no definite construction by its common acceptation among merchants; in extracting it from our laws, it may be found rather more applicable to tonnage duties, professedly, effectually, and practically prohibitory; to the occlusion of our ports to shipping or produce of a certain national or local description; to non-importation, non-intercourse, than to impost for revenue or the protection of national interests. Until either commercial or legal usage shall have embraced those objects in the definition, we cannot think that they necessarily constitute a restrictive system. The committee forbear from noticing another objection to this bill in its bearing on commerce, [drawbacks;] like the others noticed, its want of application is a sufficient answer.

"We cannot afford to export our productions to other countries, unless we will take what they give us in return."

It is with much pleasure that the committee have an opportunity of examining one objection which may have some connexion with the general principles of the bill. It is among its first objects to check the importation of foreign goods to an extent that will give some protection to our products. If the natural effect of this will be to injure our foreign market more than to benefit the domestic, it becomes a duty to so modify and vary it as to impose less duties on such foreign products as insure a demand for ours; but when this object can be accomplished without disturbing other parts of the system of the bill which are essential for our national purposes, it becomes no less a duty to retain those than to expunge the others. No particular provision, no item, has been designated, except food and materials for manufactures. The application of this objection thus specified to the proposed bill will, we think, furnish a satisfactory answer. Our importation of manufactures is from Europe and the East Indies. To the latter, it is believed, we export no provisions. Their importation is absolutely prohibited by England, France, and Spain ; and it is not known that any considerable quantity is required by other European nations. The European and India markets, then, cannot be rendered worse for our food, unless there can be some measure more rigid than exclusion. Our only market is in the colonies and islands of those Powers, from which we import but few, if any, articles of manufacture; the duties on their produce are necessary for revenue. And it is here proper to remark, that, though there is a great falling off in the ad valorem duties, the amount of revenue from specific duties has diminished in a very trifling extent. The duties on colonial produce from the East and West Indies are among the highest in our present tariff; that they will bear it, is evidenced from the amount of their consumption, and the almost uniform revenue produced ; that they will bear the proposed addition cannot well be doubted ; and, if necessary for revenue, we cannot suppose that any class of the community, especially the mercantile, would object. High duties on produce which we must consume are paid by ourselves, and not by those from whom we purchase; it cannot, therefore, induce them to refuse to receive our produce in exchange. At all events, the objection, if allowed its whole force, can only apply to the increased duties on West India produce, not to those on the manufactures of Europe or India. If the state of the Treasury would justify it, the committee might yield to the modification without impairing the general system of the bill. It would afford much gratification if those who press the objection would at the same time express their willingness to withdraw it from those parts of the new tariff to which the reason is wholly inapplicable. The committee would, in such event, be happy to meet this spirit of concession and mutual conciliation, and carry it to any general and detailed provision of the bill, (although they might well doubt whether an objection was founded in fact or in reason, and that it might be contradicted by both,) to which any specific objection has been made, and is applicable by fair mercantile or legal construction, provided the remaining parts might be adopted by general concurrence. This would smooth a course of legislation, and save the country the agitation which has been caused by almost classing the nation into parties on this subject, by general questions of comparative interests, by exciting fears

Protection to Manufactures.

and magnifying dangers which cannot grow out of any measure proposed for adoption, if examined, discussed, and modified in a spirit of generous and national feeling.

When one portion of the nation asks a great deal from its representatives, and are convinced that it is all reasonable and required for the general welfare; when one house of Congress, in their sound, and, we must be allowed to say, sober discretion, and not from the "ardor of the moment," have felt it a public duty to grant them a part, it certainly affords some presumption in favor of its policy. If another portion of the community objects to the whole, to any interference at all, they should give the best of reasons, which will extend to all; when none exist or are offered affecting parts, that those parts should be retained they cannot complain who are allowed the benefit of all their suggestions, founded on intelligible and tangible grounds. Where the public opinion is at all divided, each should, in deference and respect to even the erroneous opinions of others, yield a part; each acts from the purest impressions; each feels itself right; but both are wrong: if one decides on the principles and motives of the other, and each is believed. It will be the work of time to bring about the happy event when all will think, that, though one party may ask too much, it is entitled to something; when the other party objects to all, they may be unreasonable in some things. But the memorials before us afford at least one pleasing indication of the hope that this time may arrive. One of them,* in a spirit of candor and liberality highly worthy of praise and imitation in these times of general agitation, admits that the encouragement of the "manufacture of such articles as are the production of our own soil, for the purpose of turning our industry to the best account, and of procuring the means of defence," avowing themselves the "friends of internal manufactures as a means of fostering national industry, and, therefore, avowing that they ought to be fostered as far as they can be without injury to other branches of industry, would most gladly suggest any thing which might conduce to that end, without being highly injurious to the revenue, destructive to the interests of commerce, and oppressive on the great body of the people." The committee would deem it unworthy of themselves to withhold their entire assent to these principles— to ask their measure to be tested by any other. If they could be presumptuous enough to ask this House to violate them, the effort would recoil on themselves. May we not, then, justly expect and hope that the attempts of others may be equally unavailing? We ask not that they should react, only that they may not be operative or effectual. Applying, then, this criterion to this bill, it has been seen that it can have no unfavorable effect on the exportation of provisions. Raw materials are the remaining item of objections. The principal articles of manufacture on which the additional duties were imposed are, iron, glass, hemp and cordage, paper, linen, silks, woollens, cottons.

* From Richmond.

The raw materials of iron and glass will no bear the expense of transportation; commerce ca give them no value abroad. We have an infini abundance; it can only be made valuable by manufacturing at home; of hemp and flax we hav none to export, and are obliged to import to me the limited demand of our present manufactures both are subject, when dressed, to an almost prohibitory duty in England; flax £9 0s. 8d., sa $40 per cwt.; hemp £4, say $18 per cwt.; in th stem, undressed, both are too bulky for exporta tion. Cordage we import; it is subject in En land to a duty of $4 per cwt. Of rags, the raw material of paper, we import large quantities, and it is believed export none, as the country does no afford our papermakers a sufficient supply. Rag in the present and proposed tariffs, are duty fre So far, then, as applies to the material, commer gains by the manufacture of this article. The same remark applies to raw silk; we have now for exportation; there is a duty on the importation of 15 per cent. ad valorem in the present tariff; the new one makes it duty free.

Wool is subject to a duty of six-pence sterling per pound in England, say twelve cents; it excludes all coarse kinds. Wool is probably less an article of export now than of import; there is no supply beyond the demand; immense numbers of sheep have been killed, because there was no market for their fleeces. The new tariff would not, therefore, deprive commerce of this material for export.

Cotton.—Commerce has no other interest in this article than as a carrier; but, whether in this capacity, or as the guardian of agriculture, she protests against the increase of duty on goods, it surel cannot extend to the coarse fabrics of India— Commerce, as a great national interest, is of infinite importance as the means of encouraging the first of manufactures—ship building, affording a nursery by the employment of seamen, providing for the naval defence of the nation, and for efficient attack. These furnish strong motives for its encouragement; for protection from foreign as well as domestic assailments. Commerce not that selfish, sordid interest, which looks only to the profit of the individuals concerned in its pursuits, alive only to the means by which the can draw from the consumer the greatest difference between the price which an article costs and tha which can be received for it. It raises its view general and national objects, and watches its peculiar interests only as component items in th great work of public prosperity. In the applica tion of these observations to the coarse cottons of India, it will be at once evident that the objection in the various memorials were not, and could no have been, intended to embrace this item. (It is indeed, referred to in one, but must have been wit an exclusive aspect to revenue.) India cottons are not made from American wool, or paid for b American produce. No ships are built, no seame employed to carry our productions to the Britis East Indies. Our exports in 1819 were $24,914 in 1820, $5,700. The exclusion of their cottons cannot, then, affect agriculture which raises, or commerce that carries, either the materials or other produce which pays for the manufacture; and thus one important item in the new tariff remains clear of these objections. As to the increased duties on European cottons of eight per cent., it should be considered that, since the present tariff was adopted, France by her new tariff has imposed a duty equal to about twenty per cent. ad valorem on cotton wool, and England about eight or ten. The reasons ought, therefore, to be of the strongest kind, which would show the injurious effect of a corresponding duty on their manufactures. It must be extremely difficult to prove that an addition of thirty-three per cent. on the present duty could produce worse effects on commerce than the addition of one hundred has already produced. Though till 1812 the permanent duties on cotton goods were twelve and a half per cent. ad valorem, and since that time they have been twenty-five, this duplication has not been injurious to commerce. It is a fact, almost too familiar to be stated, that we have not since exported less cotton than before; American shipping has not carried a less proportion; England has not purchased less. If the additional duty on cotton goods so far promotes the growth of our manufactures as materially to diminish the foreign, it would in the same proportion increase the domestic demand; the only difference it could make to commerce would be in the transportation of cotton from the place of growth to the nearer or more distant place of manufacture; a difference too trifling to at all endanger, or materially injure, the commercial interest.

There is one definite and specific objection which deserves serious consideration. It is said the enormous tax proposed on hemp and iron would strike a severe blow at our freedom and independence; " that the imposition of new and heavy burdens on our shipping would tend to give the British the monopoly of our trade, and to make them our sole carriers." If this duty is of that character, and will produce such effect, it ought to be abandoned. The following calculation will show the operation of this tax.

The additional duty on iron is ten dollars a ton; if four tons are required for every one hundred tons of shipping, the difference would be forty cents on a ton.

The additional duty on hemp is twenty dollars a ton; if four and a half tons of cordage are required for every one hundred tons of shipping, the difference would be ―――― on a ton.

We are not left to conjecture to know what has been and will be the practical effect on ship-building by the increase of duties on these articles. In 1810 and 1811, the duty on iron was seventeen and a half per cent. ad valorem; on hemp, one dollar per cwt. New vessels built in 1810, 127,575 tons; in 1811, 146,691. In 1812, the duty on iron was raised to thirty-two and a half per cent ad valorem, and hemp to two dollars per cwt. The period of the war can furnish no criterion. In 1815, new vessels built, 154,624 tons; in 1816, 131,667. In the last part of the last year iron was nine dollars the ton, and hemp thirty. In 1817, new vessels built, ―――― tons; in 1818, 82,421; in July of that year, iron was raised to fifteen dollars a ton; in 1819, new vessels, 79,819 tons.

The original duties on iron were five per cent. ad valorem; on hemp, sixty cents per cwt.; in the increase from those rates to thirty-two and a half on one, and two dollars on the other, it will not be asserted that there was a corresponding decrease in ship building; and the above data conclusively show that the proposed rate would not have that effect. So slight an addition to the expense would not destroy the competition between ours and foreign shipping—it does not hang by so slender a thread. In noticing this objection, it will be perceived that the full weight of it has been allowed for; but the committee must not be understood as admitting for any other than the purpose of illustration that the increase of duty would be a permanent increase of price. The negative of that proposition is proved by the history of all the items in our tariff, when the domestic has superseded the foreign supply, and fair scope afforded for domestic competition.

The House will excuse the committee in remarking that it is a source of grat felicitation to them to find that, after the most thorough examination and critical review which has been had on this bill, and perhaps not with the most preconceived disposition to approve, the most objectionable items, those which have alone been thought deserving of specification, should so little justify the severe animadversions which have been so liberally bestowed. It is a most pleasing proof that where there is a disposition there is also the power of shaping the legislation of the country that the interest of one class can be essentially promoted without injury to another.

If, in the various memorials on this subject, there should be found any thing like general allegations of the ruin of commerce, the impoverishment of merchants, the destruction of navigation, and foreign monopoly, it must not be expected that much time will be thrown away in meeting suggestions which can as easily be made, and urged with feeling and eloquence on public measures which are beneficial to commerce, as those which are injurious. Our own history teaches us that the merits of a system cannot be fairly tested by the plaudits or remonstrances of the interest on which it appropriately bears, though it might be fairly inferred that none could better judge of the tendency of a measure than those whom it most affects; who, having often asked, and uniformly obtained, legislative aid, could duly appreciate its policy; yet, when we refer to the discriminating duties on tonnage, we are compelled to doubt the correctness of the inference. This system was adopted in 1790, to aid the commerce of this country; the consequences are well known. In 1802, during the temporary peace in Europe, the British Government was desirous that all countervailing duties on British American tonnage should be mutually abolished. When it was ascertained that this Government was disposed to accede to the measure, the table of this House was loaded with remonstrances against it. A reference to the records will show whether the same fearful and dreadful

APPENDIX.

Protection to Manufactures.

evils were not then predicted and deprecated; whether the commerce of the country was not then alleged to be in the most imminent danger; and the progress of the measure effectually defeated by the strong and simultaneous·movements of the whole mercantile community. The new tariff did not excite more alarm and fear; a comparison of the memorials will decide. In the next peace which followed, (1815) our Government acceded to the principle; its effects on our commerce have been most salutary. Now, this Congress, receiving its impulse from public policy has been urged by mercantile memorials, praying for measures to ·coerce France in relation to the trade with her and England to her colonies, to adopt the system so much dreaded in 1802, so beneficial in 1815, so much pressed in 1818 and 1819, and so unattainable in 1820. It may not be thought disrespectful to observe· that, if the measures of last session could be recalled, there would be some doubt of their adoption at this; that those who asked for them are now convinced that the interest most to be served has been but little, if any, advanced; and that, if national feeling did not forbid the retrogression, national interest would sanction it.

With such an example before us, may it not, without being illiberal, be prudent to doubt whether memorials are the safest guides to sound policy; whether those who should be best enabled to judge may not sometimes be too much drawn from reasoning and calculation, from experience to the indulgence of feeling and groundless alarm; whether the vacillation which we discern in the retrospect may not be renewed in the prospective; and whether, like the repeal of the discriminating system of tonnage, it may not be the fate of the new tariff, after being decried as baleful in principle, and destructive in its practice, to be yet hailed as auspicious? To properly estimate its bearings on commerce, the causes of the rise and decline of that interest must be traced; that it has not been from the export of our own productions, or the importations of manufactures, the official history of its progress conclusively shows that it has not ebbed and flowed with the price or quantity of domestic exports or foreign imports. But the exportation of foreign produce, the carrying trade, the war in Europe, left us without competition; peace has overwhelmed us with it. While the war continued all nations profited by our commerce; since the other has returned they can profit by their own. Two items of colonial produce required in their transportation more tonnage and seamen than all the imported manufactures consumed in the United States. Of sugar there was exported, in 1806, 145,630,000 pounds; in 1807, 143,119,000; of coffee, in 1806, 47,000,000; in 1807, 24,122,000 pounds; in 1819, of sugar, 11,-267,000 pounds; of coffee, 8,570,000; in 1820, sugar, 31,388,000; coffee, 11,656,000. In 1806, of our two great domestic staples the following quantities were exported: cotton, 35,657,000 pounds; flour, 156,544,000; in 1819, cotton, 87,996,000; flour, 150,000,000; in 1806, aggregate of sugar and coffee, 192,630,000; cotton and flour, 192,-

201,000; in 1819, sugar and coffee, 19,842,000; cotton and flour, 237,996,000; aggregate of both in 1806, 384,831,000; in 1819, 257,838,000—a falling off in the foreign exports of 126,993,000; an increase of domestic of 55,366,000. The state of commerce in the two years will show the kind of employment which is necessary for its support. It is not for the committee to pursue this subject into detail; but it would have been very instructive if some calculations had been made to show how far the commerce of the country depended on the mere importation of foreign manufactures. how many tons of shipping are employed, and how many seamen, in bringing the whole supply of cottons, woollens, silks, iron, hardware, crates, glass, paper, hemp, and other articles of consumption, which are made from raw materials which are or may be produced from our soil; whether the transportation from one part of the country to another of materials to supply our manufactories, and of manufactures back to the raiser of the materials, and the export of manufactures, might not employ as much shipping and as many seamen as the importation alone of foreign supply. Except of cotton, foreign manufactures afford freight but in the return voyage; requiring none of our materials, or compelled to use those of their own country, they afford no outward freight. *During peace in Europe the fate of our foreign commerce is fixed.* We have in vain, and shall in vain, continue to endeavor to force for our shipping the colonial trade. Foreign nations must, and will, protect their own, with a resolution proportioned to their estimate of its national importance. It is with as much reluctance that they will abandon the interest of their navigation as we of ours. In the contest it is believed that we have suffered much, and may suffer more; and the most sanguine dare not even predict success. Commerce must, like other interests, yield to foreign competition, backed by an unyielding policy of legislation, which, having built on its commerce an immense system of revenue, is bound in self-defence to reciprocate the support it receives. If foreign nations would permit the consumption of our provisions and materials, and the carrying of them in our own shipping, it might afford some indication of the restoration of our commerce. The new corn law of Spain, the exclusion of our soap, the French bounty on South American cotton, tell us emphatically that this is not the era of that extent of liberal principles which, because it may be morally right, will restore us a monopoly that we once enjoyed, not from their good will, but necessities. Now they will submit to privations and positive losses, by forcing the importation of an article on which we now mainly depend; and this not to counteract a restrictive system on our part, but to continue one on theirs. If the pursuits of the committee in private life have not enabled them to draw, in relation to commerce, just deductions from either reasoning or facts, they feel confident that they cannot err in passing their opinion on the conduct of this Government, called for by the petitions, and sanctioned by the approbation, of the mercantile community, and adopted, not in the darkness of former years, but in the light of the last.

Our present commercial and legislative contest with France and England is to secure to our commerce the export, not the import trade of our country. Those nations do not deny to our shipping the exportation of their manufactures, or produce, on equal terms with their own. That, as a source of commerce, is unrestrained; their duties are not on exports, or on vessels arriving in ballast. It would be a strange policy to discourage or embarrass the exportation of surplus productions, and a truly unaccountable contest, if it was merely or mainly whose navigation should take them to market. A market must be the first great object; the mode of reaching it secondary. Our object is not the exclusion of French manufactures; we impose no additional duty on them by the late law; its operation is to prohibit their introduction in French ships. We submit to the loss of carrying them in our own. Being willing to abandon this branch of commerce, it is deemed conclusive evidence of the general conviction that its importance is secondary. The worst effect of the new tariff could produce no more fearful results; for it must be equal, with American commerce, whether no manufactures are imported, or none in American ships. Merchants willingly embrace the latter alternative to effectuate the greater object, the one which is the foundation, the sustenance of commerce—exportation, not importation. In thus estimating their relative importance, it is a great relief to be furnished with a practical acknowledged standard; no longer left to search for one by conjecture or mere reasoning. This enables us to speak with certainty that this bill, in its worst aspect, bears only on the unimportant operations of commerce. Whether it will injure it at all or not remains to be examined. It must be remembered that there is an internal as well as external commerce: one we now and can forever monopolize; the other is subject to continual competition: one is as permanent as our Government; the other as much swelled to an unnatural size by war as it is emaciated in peace, forever fluctuating with foreign policy, which we cannot control: one limited in its extent by foreign wants, looking only to countries which, having perhaps arrived at their maximum of population and resources, can furnish no new market or increased demand;* the other drawn to a mighty empire, with a population of various habits and pursuits, embracing all the varieties of the temperate climates, fitted to the supply of all our wants; fertile in resources as yet not tried or developed; in itself a continent,

destined to open new, and capable of furnishing boundless employment to industry and enterprise. As the best portion of foreign commerce has passed into other hands; as it is now irreclaimable, and can never be certain and uniform, it would be a reasonable hope that there would be a common effort to increase and enlarge the sphere of domestic. It has been as yet untried. It is not prudent to so far decide on the consequences of the attempt as to pronounce it not deserving the experiment. If the same zeal was displayed in discovering new as in retention of old subjects of commerce, and the effort failed, experience would guide us to the wisest measures. While there is a refusal to appeal to this unerring standard, and we are determined to trust only to preconceived opinions, (the result of habit, and possibly prejudice,) we can never avail ourselves of the example of others, and will afford none for ourselves. In other countries, of limited extent, internal commerce has not been deemed unimportant; it has not been found unproductive of employment, of wealth, or injurious to national interests. Ours is a union of confederated nations; if the intercourse between them is commerce, it may, from its great distance, the variety of its products, and articles of exchange, be called foreign commerce. The extent of water communication between the remoter parts is equal to the space which separates us from Europe and the West Indies. As a material for commerce, there can be discerned no difference between the sugar of Louisiana and of Cuba; the lead of Missouri or of England. Nature has not denied to the immense region watered by the Mississippi, the Ohio, and the Lakes, the means of ship building, or the supply of cargoes. Man refuses them a market, because he looks only abroad. If one portion of our country can furnish articles for the supply of another; if the vehicles of transportation, the employment of men, and the distance, are the same, foreign can present no preference over domestic commerce, as a national interest. It cannot be that habit, or the laws of nature, have infused into commerce such a spirit that it can only exist by foreign action; its solid interest is not in the ephemeral magnitude of its operations, but their certainty and uniformity. It has suffered more from fluctuation than want of employment. While it acts abroad its movements are among rivals and enemies, not protected by the paternal guardianship, but checked and thwarted by the jealousy and hostility of the Government under whose influence it must, and against whose policy it may operate. In seeking domestic sources its course is among friends, divided only by mutual interests; between nations united by the common bond of feeling and power, and under the protection of a Government which, supported by the affections, aims, in return, to provide for the good of all. If considerations growing out of these reflections do not carry conviction, may they not awaken attention and lead to inquiry, so far as to justify one fair experiment? If it should appear that a partial trial has been made, and with success; if there are any of our towns whose trade and tonnage have remained unimpaired by

---

* The amount of our exports of domestic productions in 1790, before the European wars, affords some specific and satisfactory rule by which to test the foreign demand in peace. The prospects for commerce, agriculture, and revenue, can, by this comparison, be safely estimated. Those who are willing to trust all to hope should, at least, be called on to show that there are now any markets for our produce which were not open to us in 1790, and that the demand has or will increase.

Protection to Manufactures.

the general pressure, where the growth of domestic has exceeded the decline of foreign commerce, it cannot be uninstructive to search for the causes, or unwise to profit by the example.

As the importation of foreign manufactures might become lessened, it cannot be doubted that the increased internal communication would balance the loss to commerce; it would be more in raw materials, which are not now exported, and, being more bulky than the manufacture, would require more tonnage in their transportation. When the value and weight of the manufactures we import from Europe and the East Indies are compared with our articles of export, it will be apparent that a small amount of tonnage is required for the carrying of goods in a finished state; and that there must be more domestic commerce in collecting the materials and distributing, than there is now of foreign in merely importing the manufacture.

It is not believed to be a rule growing out of the course of trade, or inferrible from experience, that the foreign demand for any of our products depends on what we receive in return. Such a rule would necessarily limit commerce to exchange, and none would be carried on where there was only the payment of money by one party, the purchase of goods by the other; there could be no balances of trade. There is no friendship in trade; demand is limited by wants and the means of payment; exchange is the most desired; but when that fails money and credit will be given. The official statements of our commerce with the East Indies and other countries abundantly prove that we do not refuse to purchase manufactures from those who will not purchase our articles. Though our means of importing from England are diminished in consequence of her corn laws, duties, and prohibitions, there does not seem to be the less inclination to purchase her manufactures. Though we are her best customers, no part of her system is relaxed in our favor. She takes from us only what is for her interest, and necessary for her wants. France does not exclude our cotton, or we her manufactures. Intercourse among nations must be regulated by interest, not feeling; those we deal with take from us what they want, while we supply them on the best terms; their laws do not bend because we receive payment in their products. We do not deal only with those who buy from us, nor is that a rule by which we apportion duties on imports. The duties on Madeira wine, and silks from China, strikingly illustrate this principle. The official tables, the history of our commerce, and all its experience, concur in the proof that the refusal by one nation to receive what it does not want will not prevent another from furnishing what it does, while it possesses means. It must, therefore, be made apparent, that our refusal to import will deprive the two nations, with whom we principally deal, of the means of purchasing from us; that it must not only turn the balance of trade with England in our favor, but to such an extent that she could not pay it, before the objection can have any weight. If this would be the effect of the new tariff, it

might not be a very effectual mode of defeating it by urging such objections on this Legislature. The usage of all trade proves that what is wanted will be bought while it can be procured by exchange, money, or credit; the seller will not receive what he cannot use or sell; the buyer, in such case, and not the seller, must submit to terms. He cannot force his produce into market against the laws of the place or the interest of the seller.

It has been thought the fairest mode to meet these objections to the full extent to which they have been urged, and not limit our views to their application to the bill the committee have felt it their duty to report. Its provisions do not tend to destroy the importation of all manufactures; it only progresses towards a system which, if judicious and healthful to the country, can be built upon, and made the foundation of others; it is not that rapid stride which can shake any interest to its destruction; if it is wrong, it will cause no sudden convulsion in retracing its errors. It falls as far short of the expectation of one part of the country, as it exceeds the wishes of another; it is the duty of both to yield a part, and becomes ours to listen to both. The committee are aware that the subject submitted to them has excited much sensibility; that their views have been, and will be, misunderstood, is to be expected; when their acts excite, professions will not allay opposition and alarm; it would have better suited their feelings had it been referred to them in terms of less censure and reproach, but it cannot affect their consciousness of having faithfully discharged a public duty; can never prevent them from imparting to one great national interest such degree of protection as comports with the general welfare; and will never lead them to devise injury to another which is intimately connected with the wealth and glory of our common country. We will not stop here, and content ourselves with the mere disclaiming hostility to commerce. If we understand what it is, if we are not radically mistaken in ascribing its former prosperity to exportation, and its present depression to the want of it, there cannot be an interest which more imperiously calls for legislation and national support. Such an interest is not local, or confined to those engaged in its pursuits; it pervades the whole country, and reaches every occupation; it carries our produce and manufactures to every accessible market; it creates and secures employment for all our industry, and, in the import and export of foreign articles, earns the freight of our shipping, the wages of our seamen, and acquires a profit to the employer, which is drawn from others to us. If this is foreign commerce, it is no less a favorite with us than manufactures; if they can be separated, we will not say it may not be more so—the extent of the market it would furnish might be the criterion. If our existing laws impose any restrictions on it, none would more willingly aid in their removal; it should be as free as air, and not be burdened even for revenue. If it has passed, or is passing, into the hands of foreigners, we would be happy to have within our cognizance the means of averting the evil; equally so in de-

Protection to Manufactures.

vising the best mode of enlarging and extending the sphere of its operations, under the control of our own citizens.

Destroy agriculture.

There can be no measure of sound policy which impairs the interests or checks the pursuits of agriculture; the committee, therefore, do not inquire into the expediency or justice of sacrificing agriculture to manufactures; they will confine themselves to the question, whether this bill, or the system for which it lays the foundation, tends to aid the latter at the expense of the former. Agreeing in this principle with its opponents, the solution of the question depends more on fact than reasoning.

It contains no direct tax, duty, or assessment on the products or occupations of agriculture; it touches nothing of domestic origin; to this there must be general assent. If it imposes a duty on articles other than manufactures, it is solely for revenue, which all admit is wanted, and which the opponents of the bill say is raised by impost from the farmer with less inconvenience than any other mode. If the additional revenue thus raised, to supply a deficit occasioned by its decrease on articles of manufacture, does not increase the aggregate amount of revenue, then are no new burdens imposed on the community; it is only a new apportionment, which becomes more or less grievous as articles of manufactures are more or less, in comparison with others, necessaries of life. He who consumes imported articles pays a tax; there is none on domestic: if, by its substitution for foreign, there is a loss of revenue, which is added to the duty on some other, it is a gain or a loss, as he consumes the one or the other article. The poor farmer, who has substituted rye for coffee, would be a gainer by an increased tax on that, and a reduced one on iron and clothing; to the one who preferred coffee, the amount of tax would be the same. Admitting that, by the mass of the nation, the consumption of coffee would be the same with a higher as the lower duty, and the reduced price on iron and clothing enable them, with the same means, to pay the advanced price on this, then, in a national point of view, the only question would be, whether it bears hardest on those best or least able to bear it. This would depend on a comparison of the articles affected—which were necessaries and which luxuries. In classing them generally, they are dye-woods, dye-stuffs, drugs, clothing, furniture, utensils and instruments of occupation, on the one hand; groceries on the other. In applying this discrimination to the two classes, and the items of each, it will not be found that the rates of duty are peculiarly onerous to the poor or the cultivator of the soil. Where it may be though to exist, allowance must be made for the small bulk or weight when compared with the value of the article as a temptation to smuggling. It is conceived, therefore, that the relative rates of duties afford no color for the imputation of hostility to agriculture.

But the great objection to the bill—the one which is pressed in all the memorials as the foundation of all the opposition—is, that the increase of the duty is, of course, an increase of the price to the consumer. This is admitted to be true as to those articles the sole supply of which is by importation, but no further. Even here the increased price accrues to the public Treasury; it cannot go to the manufacturer till he brings his products to market and sale. Before he can profit by the rise, he must check the foreign competition by acquiring a part of the supply or custom. He cannot do this by exacting a higher price, unless the quality of his goods is proportionately better; he must sell as cheap, and furnish articles of as good a quality, or he cannot begin his operations; they can be continued by no other means. If he puts down foreign competition, and monopolizes the market, it must be by making better or selling cheaper, and by such an amount as will equal the freight and importer's profit; for importations will continue while the article will yield either. If the market should be divided between the foreign and domestic supply, it would keep both at the same price, and, while this continued, operate as a tax to the consumer; it would be temporary or not, as the country would afford the means of furnishing a sufficient amount for the demand: if it would, and the price afford a profit to the maker, the competition must cease, by reducing it so as to exclude the foreign; if the country could not produce enough, the policy of imposing more than a revenue duty might well be questioned. But true "economy to the consumer" would be a permanent reduction by a mere temporary increase of the price. There can, then, be but one class of manufactures a high duty on which can tend to the benefit of the manufacturer at the expense of the consumer—those of which a competent supply cannot be furnished from our own resources. If such are discernible in the proposed measure, it ought not to be an object to retain them for the mere emolument of the manufacturer. The great articles of consumption are such as can be supplied from our own soil, and by the employment of our own labor and machinery. It is a fact, which cannot be too often repeated, which has been verified by every experiment, confirmed on every trial, that, when the domestic market has been secured to the domestic manufacturer, domestic competition has reduced the price to the consumer. Every family in the country which consumes coarse cotton goods is now deriving a direct and positive advantage from the highest duty on any manufactured article in the present tariff; it is of a better quality and at a cheaper rate than the article was before imported. No theory, no argument, can reason away this fact; it carries conviction to the understanding; the price, the quality, is practical economy, political as well as personal; a saving to the nation and the individual. It is not a solitary item in our experience; nails, gunpowder, umbrellas, cotton and wool cards, present the same results. The purchaser finds these articles at a reduced price, without asking the cause. He may be an active, a conscientious opponent to the encouragement of domestic manufactures; may have heard the charge

Protection to Manufactures.

of there being a "tax on the many, a bounty to the few," repeated so often, that it becomes impressed on his belief, while, at the same moment, he is deriving a pecuniary gain from their success, after they have attained the height of their efforts, the command of the consumption. Thousands are reaping the profits of a competition among manufacturers to acquire employment by a cheap and good supply, while they are laboring under the imputation of conspiring to oppress; as to many items, of which they cannot furnish a full supply, they are enabled to check foreign exaction, and, without duly appreciating it, the country is deriving great benefit from their enterprise.

There would seem to be no reasons for apprehending different results from the further extension of the same principles which have hitherto produced these general effects; if there are the same materials and skill which can be applied to the finer fabrics, there can be no more danger in their exclusion than the coarse. Cotton, as an item of clothing, is as much a necessary of life, and gunpowder of defence, as any other; daily and profitable experience teaches us that we are secured from imposition by leaving the supply of these articles in the hands of our countrymen; there may be as much safety in giving them that of woollens and iron.

The experiment has never yet failed, and those who wish it tried on new objects believe it never will. Those who doubt or fear its success should at least be willing that new subjects should be brought to the test of the principle. Without some act of legislation the country must be forever divided in opinion, and her councils agitated by petitions praying for, and remonstrances protesting against, a measure. If it was the introduction of a new feature into our code, it might well be left to the deductions of reasoning; being but the application of an old and original one, coeval with our first act of fiscal legislation, the lights of experience come fairly to its aid. When facts are admitted, and reasons may exist in favor of a proposition, the opposition to it ought not to rest on reasoning and assertion only; some one fact or instance should be required to do away the conviction which has been caused by many. Admitting that, on this great question of the encouragement of manufactures, the arguments tending to prove that there will be a consequent reduction of price are balanced by those which are offered to show that they will be increased, and the mind thus left in doubt, and it cannot be expected that any further admission can be made; admitting that a uniform series of experiments had been successfully tried for thirty years, and all resulted in the decrease of the price of the article, protected by an increased or high duty, it would be strange to contend that this should not turn the scale. In the numerous memorials on this subject, our researches have not enabled us to discover one case mentioned which has supported the objection; we have been furnished with none from any other source of information, and must, therefore, believe there is none. On other subjects, it is conceded that experience affords the safest guides; no good reason appears

why we should exclude it from the investigation of this: when it shall sanction this objection, its full weight ought to be allowed; until this is given to it, while it contradicts it, we cannot yield to its force. It may not be considered unfair to make a reciprocal application of this rule: if the uniform consequence of giving the domestic manufacturer the command of our market, by the imposition of high duties on foreign products, had been to increase the price to the consumer, and he, grown rich by a tax on the country, would be thought to present himself before Congress with poor claims to furnish him with the means of increasing the tax, under the name of protection to him, it would be a conclusive answer—experience is against you. May not the same answer be given to this objection? It is supported by nothing but itself. Hitherto, the profit of the manufacturer has been a saving to the nation; no reasons have been given why it may not be so for the future; it is time enough to give way to the objection when there shall be the same weight of facts to support that there exist to remove it. Let the cupidity of manufacturers be what it may, it can never be gratified when there is no prohibition; foreign supplies must be an effectual security to the consumer, if domestic competition is not; it has never *failed*; for when a people, so eagle-eyed as ours, are at liberty to select the occupation of their labor, capital, and skill, discern that inordinate or unusual profits accrue to any particular manufacture, the same self-interest which looks to its own gratification will direct their application to the same object, and thus reduce the profits to what is a reasonable compensation. The danger of prohibition is thus averted. If there is reasonable ground to apprehend that this competition may not be an effectual check, prohibition may be avoided, unless required as the foundation of an excise. Where the object is merely protection, a high duty will suffice; the increase of price can never be beyond the duty; according to its rate, it might support an excise on the article protected. It is confidently thought that, even allowing to this objection its possible application, the proposed addition of duties does not throw the consumer into the power of the manufacturer. Very far short of prohibition, the bill does not come in the way of an argument which would appear to apply, if it all, to a system not to be found in any duty proposed. There must have been some misapprehension on this subject; the measure so much deprecated is one which it is said will destroy alike revenue, commerce, agricultural and mechanical labors; the objection cannot be good as to all, and, in part at least, must defeat itself. The average rates of the ad valorem duties are about twenty-eight per cent.; now, if this destroys commerce, by withdrawing materials for carrying, and revenue, by stopping importations, the evil must stop here, and cannot reach the farmer. If the price rises in proportion to the duty, the merchant can still afford to import; the Government will still receive tax. It can only be by a fall in the price that commerce and revenue suffer; it must bring the article cheaper to the consumer; if smuggled, it must reduce

Protection to Manufactures.

the price, as it then comes to him duty free; by all these operations the farmer gains. That an argument intended for a prohibition must be fallacious as to a moderate or (if it must be called so) a high duty, is evident from these and other reflections, which will occur to every mind, unless the mode of paying the manufacturer is more oppressive than the merchant.

This is an important inquiry. The mode, the means of payment, constitutes the real price of an article purchased. If a bushel of wheat will buy a yard of linen, it may be supposed an equivalent exchange, and each article worth, say one dollar; it remains equal while the merchant will take wheat at one dollar; when he receives it at fifty cents, either linen has risen, or wheat has fallen, one-half—of no consequence which; it requires two bushels of wheat to purchase one yard of linen. A few years since it was the reverse; one bushel of wheat would buy two yards of linen. Comparing the prices of the two periods with the means of payment, linen has become increased four-fold, as it takes now as much wheat to buy one yard as it did formerly to buy four; linen is therefore four times as dear. Cloth sold five years ago at twelve dollars per yard; six bushels of wheat or six pounds of fine wool would pay for it; now it requires twenty-four bushels of the one, and twenty-four pounds of the other. To keep up the uniformity of price, and bring these articles as cheap to the farmer, linen should be reduced to twenty-five cents and superfine cloth to three dollars a yard. The farmer being able to buy cheapest when he can pay the easiest, he must ask who will give him the greatest quantity of what he wants for the smallest quantity of what he can spare.

The foreign manufacturer of linen and woollen is prevented from purchasing flour, flax, or wool; the importing merchant cannot pay in those articles, and cannot receive them from the farmer in payment for the goods. If the farmer buys them, they afford no additional demand for his produce; he, at all events, cannot be benefited by the foreign manufacturer, or domestic importer or retailer, because neither afford him a good or bad market; they give him none at all; nothing can be received but his money. To whom must he look for that? Evidently to other sources; to some other foreign or domestic market. He then becomes indebted to those other sources for his means of paying for these foreign manufactures, not to the manufacturers or to the sellers of them. These remarks will apply to all other articles for which the farmer cannot pay in produce. When foreign manufacturers, from compulsion or interest, will not take the provisions or raw materials from the consumer, the latter can claim no benefit from them. If he must in some other way obtain the money to pay for them, he can be in no worse situation if he buys them from the domestic than the foreign maker, so far, at least, as respects the means of paying him in products which he either will not or cannot receive. The full force of this remark will apply to the great bulk of foreign manufactures of every nation, and the agricultural productions of the Northern and Middle States. It is as

correct in reasoning as it is true in fact, that the latter will not pay for the former. The gross produce of farms will not now purchase clothing, groceries, and utensils necessary for supporting the families of the farmer, raising the produce of the farms, and carrying it to market. Their surplusses of one article, or various articles, will not enable them to supply the deficiency of another; one thing will not enable them to buy another; one will not pay for another; his own products are useless; those of others are beyond his reach. The obvious remedy, then, is to enable him to sell what he can spare, to buy what he wants. If foreign artisans will not give him broadcloth for wool, linen for flax, or either for flour, and the domestic artisan will, then one great object is accomplished; he has a market; he can exchange; one article will buy another at some rate of exchange; what that rate may be, will depend on mutual wants and mutual interest. The farmer is no longer compelled to seek a money market; he has one for exchange; his product becomes as necessary to supply the wants of the manufacturer as theirs to him, and each has a custom for his surplus. The great chain which forms the circle of society is composed of separate links, each link a distinct occupation—we may suppose a hundred. Take one hundred men, each pursuing a different calling, and separated from others; each deals with the other; one's surplus meets his neighbor's wants; the price is indifferent; relatively, it must be equal; one buys and pays for another, each having ninety-nine customers is secured in employment, and a market for the fruits of his industry; it is permanent, and cannot fluctuate by any foreign action. This circle is independent, perfectly secured from imposition; for as each must have the products of the others, he cannot add to the price of his, without paying more for that which he must purchase; the price of one article must regulate the value of another. If, in this state of things, it should be found out that a foreign supply of the same articles, which are thus furnished from these one hundred different occupations, could be procured from the merchant at one-half the nominal rate of that which had been fixed on by common consent, and each should decide on purchasing the imported article, then each must lose his ninety-nine customers. The merchant will not exchange, but requires money. Where is it to be procured? None can sell his products at half their value, because all have lost their market. There can be no exchange, and no means of raising money to purchase. It becomes an easy question to decide which is "economy to the consumer," which is cheapest.

This comparison may illustrate the operations of society; they are all governed and controlled by mutual dependence and support—all tending to enhance individual and promote public prosperity; they are the same. The nation differs from the village only in extent, both being composed of individuals, and must partake of the qualities and character of its component parts; their interest must be national. In testing these principles by practical operation, in taking the

Protection to Manufactures.

above comparison to the actual pursuits of life, it will be found that the facility of exchange is the great ingredient in the prosperity of agriculture; the contraction of our wants, the extension of the means of supplying them, depend on the activity of this principle. In tracing its effects on the cultivators of the soil, there has resulted a general assent to this position; that the farmer who has the greatest means of exchange is the most prosperous, the less dependent on others, the more free to direct his labor to the most profitable production; the more he manufactures in his own family, the better security for a good and against a bad market. In accounting for the different appearance of two adjoining farms, their comparative state of cultivation, improvement, repair, and production, as well as the relative appearance of comfort and enjoyment, it is no bad criterion to examine the clothing of the owners and their families; their domestic or foreign origin will explain the appearance of the farms. But there is one rule which is unerring—the merchant's leger; the balance on the debtor or credit side is the true touchstone of agricultural prosperity; why not of national? No instance can probably be adduced of a farmer being injured by manufacturing for the use of his family; of the value of his produce or land being depressed by the establishment of manufactures in his neighborhood, or raised by their destruction; of the increase of the wealth, prosperity, or business of a town in an increased ratio to its industry; of national power, resources, and independence being endangered or impaired by the command of its own consumption and means of defence.

Manufactures increase the objects and facilitate the means of exchange. To individuals they afford a nearer and more accessible market, not liable to interruption by war or foreign policy. Roads, rivers, canals, oceans, are but highways to market, the conduits to exchange, the paths by which we send away what we can spare, and bring back what we want. The shorter, the less dangerous the path; the less the expense of travelling, the quicker the return; the more certain the exchange, the better for the producer and the consumer; the more direct the exchange, the smaller the number of intermediate agents who are employed between the two classes, and who must all have their profits, the greater is the amount received to both on the article exchanged. The raiser of flax wants the manufacture, the maker of linen wants the raw material. If they reside near each other, the farmer takes his flax to the manufactory, and brings home his linen; no third person being employed, each receives the full value of his article; the farmer receives the full amount of whatever the flax is worth to the manufacturer; he the full value of what the linen is worth to the farmer. If the manufactory is in a foreign country, the farmer exchanges his flax with the domestic retailer, he remits it to the importer, he to the foreign exporter, he to the manufacturer, who receives it with all the intermediate charges and profits taken from its value to him. He sends back the linen, through the hands of the exporter,

to the importer; he to the retailer; and it comes to the farmer with all their deductions. He then receives as much less linen in exchange for his flax as is equal to the expense of sending his flax to the manufactory and bringing back the linen in exchange. He and the manufacturer are both taxed to the amount of the charges and profits of the double transportation, which would be saved to both if the exchange was made on the spot. The nearer, then, that they can be made to approach each other, the better for both. It increases the means and lessens the expenses of exchange. If it would produce this effect when the raw material will purchase the manufacture at any price, it would be of much greater advantage when it will not be received at all. How, then, a linen manufacture can injure the farmer, cannot be perceived; or what more injury could result from his contiguity to those of woollen, paper, iron, glass, or earthenware. They must bring his provisions, materials, ores, minerals, fuel, and a vast variety of small items from his farm which cannot be exported, and are of no value when confined to a distant market, to a domestic one, which will afford him all he wants in exchange. Such have been the effects in all parts of this country. Wherever there is an opportunity of making the experiment, it would seem impossible to be *otherwise;* whether it is the mill which grinds his wheat, or the mill which spins his flax, wool, hemp, or cotton, it is the same thing to him as to the quantity of the manufacture he can receive for his raw material. Each is equally affected by the distance and expenses of transportation, which lessen their value.

The manufactories of France and England, united, do not furnish a market for one pound of flour, wool, flax, or hemp. The manufactories in Oneida county, New York, consume annually, it is said, $110,000 of agricultural productions, which are excluded from use by those who sell us manufactures to the amount of more than forty millions a year; and the few manufactories in the United States consume more of our breadstuffs than the continent of Europe and the East Indies; for the farmers of this country must know that the market for their produce is not in the countries whence they import their manufactures. It has been the policy of the Government to tax at a high rate the produce of our good customers, and the produce of our bad ones at a low rate; and, strange as it may seem, this policy has never been deemed injurious to agriculture. When a high duty is imposed on the good customers of our agriculturists, there is no complaint from them, or those who are so alive to their interest. The island of Madeira consumed, the last year, of our produce $233,928, British East Indies $5,740. The duty on Madeira wine is one dollar per gallon, on fine muslins from Calcutta twenty-five per cent. These cases are selected for illustration. The statistical tables of our commerce with other countries all tend to give the same practical answer to a different opinion, and to show its entire futility.

The course of trade and all experience prove, beyond a doubt, that the market for our produce

Protection to Manufactures.

does not depend on what we receive in return, and that the market afforded for their manufactures by our policy yields us no equivalent. If the committee are mistaken in this deduction from facts, some reason must be given for the state of our trade with foreign nations. We believe there can be no mystery in its operations, and that ordinary minds can comprehend them. Until better evidence than Treasury documents and general experience be offered, the mind can come to no other conclusions than these:

That foreign nations are governed by their interest and policy in permitting the importation of our produce, excluding or taxing it.

That they will buy what they do want, and will not buy what they do not want.

That their laws form a system of general policy from which they will neither be driven nor persuaded by any means which our Government has yet attempted. If, therefore, it is sound policy to look alone to a foreign market for our agricultural productions, (and one must be found by legislation,) there is but one mode left—aim at their manufactures. Our market cannot be worse than it is; therefore we lose nothing; it may become better. It is not possible that the establishment of manufactures among us can deprive us of the European demand of what we now export, which is neither breadstuff nor raw materials; they exclude these from choice, and take others from necessity. Thus far, then, the farmer is safe. But fears are entertained that the remaining exports may be excluded if we impose additional duties on imported manufactures. Cotton being now our grand staple, it must be important to ascertain the effects on this.

It will be at once evident that, as to the quantity consumed, it is the same whether worked up at home or abroad; if the amount exported becomes lessened by the amount required to make as much cloth as will supply our market, the same amount is retained at home. The cotton planter, then, cannot lose by this effect. Will it affect the price of what is used in our manufactories? As the purchase must precede the manufacture; as there would be a competition in the first instance between two sets of purchasers and consumers, the foreign and domestic; as it must end in the ascendancy of the one or the other, the gainer must pay as much for the raw material as the loser. If he is overbid, he could not procure the raw material while another will give a better price; he cannot continue his ascendancy if he refuses the terms the other offers. As the raw material is indispensable, the raiser of it must profit in every possible event; as the market of the manufactured article can only be secured by the one who commands the material, his interest must, of necessity, be an effectual protection to the planter. Will the price of what is exported be diminished? If this country can produce a quantity sufficient for both the foreign and domestic demand, and no more, then it must be wanted somewhere, and all that is wanted will be bought at a fair price; if less is produced than might be wanted, the price must rise; if more, it must fall. But, on this subject, time is thrown

away on conjecture. It is well known that this country can produce more cotton than will meet all demands; that the foreign market is completely gorged, and the prices rapidly declining. In the foreign market we have much competition; it is not extending with our means of supply, but contracting; the reasons for creating and extending a domestic one would, to the interest of the planter, seem imperious. Will foreign nations change their policy, and impose additional burdens on the importation of our cotton? This affords room for conjecture. There are no arguments so difficult to answer as general ones, which cannot be located, which will not be specified, and, from their nature, have their origin not in fact, but fancy; their want of weight in every other analogous case will not prevent their being pressed in a new one. If those who urge them will agree that their validity shall be tested by any known rule, resulting from our legislative or commercial experience, there would be some means of ending the discussion. It is hoped that the light which practice has shed on the other subjects of legislation may not be lost on this. If facts tend to one conclusion, it must be taken to be the just one, unless reason absolutely rejects it.

If England wants our cotton, she will take it, and, in proportion to the extent of that want, will receive it on terms more or less favorable; taking it while it is her interest, and no longer. So far as our supply of her market depends on the ordinary rules of trade, it has been considered, and has no bearing on the present view of the subject. The question is, whether her Government will depart from interest to considerations of policy, and adopt a retaliatory measure. She has not done it in consequence of our exclusion of the coarse cottons from her East India colonies; she did not do it when we, in 1812, doubled the duties on all cotton and woollen goods—her two favorite manufactures; we cannot perceive why she should do it if the proposed increase be made. Her corn laws do not relax or extend in rigor according to the ebbs and flows in our tariff. The imposition of our war duties did not occasion the exclusion of our raw materials; their abolition did not give them a better market. The flourishing state of our manufactures in 1815 and 1816 did not produce any new measure of retaliation or policy; their depression since has not brought about the repeal of any old one. Our free intercourse with her colonies did not affect her navigation acts; our non-intercourse now does not make them more rigid. The immense amount of her manufactures which we purchase, failing to produce any feeling of peculiar friendship beyond her interest, it is hard to believe that the diminution of the amount will create a spirit of hostility adverse to her interest. Fully convinced that her future course of policy will be guided by the principles of the past, and seeing in that no indications of the course apprehended, we do not think there can be any reasonable fears. Unwilling to pursue this investigation into detail, we close it by remarking, that thus far the cotton planter has benefited by high duties on cotton; the East Indies has afforded him no mar-

Protection to Manufactures.

ket; the exclusion of the fabrics of that country has certainly opened a new market, and as certainly it has not impaired the European, for that is glutted. If the exclusion should be extended to all India cottons and nankeens, this new market would be increased, and probably to a greater extent than the interest of any European nation would permit it to diminish theirs. As an agricultural objection, therefore, it seems entitled to less weight from the raiser of cotton than any other; for though the East Indies afford a very bad and small market for other productions, they still take some; but of cotton they do not, and never will, take any.

If it be impracticable to legislate a nation into wealth, and impolitic to attempt it, it does not follow that it may not be preserved from poverty; if neither object is attainable, it is not perceived that Government can be of any use to the people; if its operations can tend neither to preserve nor increase the fruits of their labor, we are at a loss to know the legitimate objects of legislation. To what object ought all national machinery to tend, but the common defence and general welfare of the people? If this does not consist in increasing their resources, as well as preventing their extinction, we must pursue this subject no further till better informed.

The encouragement of manufactures is called coercion—a forcing from one occupation to another. Like the other objections, the best answer seems to this is, its want of application in fact. During the late war, manufactures flourished; farmers were not then forced from their occupations. The planter of the South was not prevented from raising cotton; he had no foreign market, but he had a domestic one. But he felt the practical difference between a market at home and one abroad; the land transportation from the place of production to the place of manufacture, and back again, taught him how much of the value of the raw material, to him, was diminished by the intermediate expenses. Had their manufactories been at home, had the same persons who then established them at the North commenced and completed them to the South, it would have been called no forcing of occupation, no tax on agriculture. One pound of cotton will now pay for one yard of cotton cloth; when it shall appear that, before the establishment of our cotton manufactories, or since their decline, a pound of cotton has produced more to the raiser, it will be time to answer any additional objections of this kind. Generally speaking, as there were no manufactories in the Southern States, their existence in the Northern and Middle could not have forced them from their occupation, unless the current of emigration from the South to the North should have been the fact from which this objection has been raised. In Kentucky there were manufactories to a great extent; the farmers in their neighborhood, and those who represent them, can say whether they are now more prosperous; whether they have now a greater freedom in the selection of their pursuits, or profit in following them. If the same question were put to the farmers in the Northern and Middle States; if any member of this House, who represents them, were asked if he could point out an instance of even an individual farmer who was against his will forced to abandon his soil, and go to a manufactory for employment, the force of this objection can be tested by the application of theory to practice.

It may be asserted with truth, that, wherever the principle has been fairly tried, it has been found that the interest of the farmer and manufacturer has been completely identified; one rises and falls with the other. This is verified not only by personal observation, but attested in the most impressive manner by the petitions presented to the present Congress. Last year thousands of farmers asked you for protection to manufactures; they were from States in all of which their practical effects had been seen and felt for years. With all the efforts used to excite opposition and alarm during the present year, it is a remarkable fact, that, in the whole scope of country from Maryland to New Hampshire, a solitary petition, memorial, or remonstrance of farmers, has not been offered in opposition to the proposed tariff. Those which have been presented are from parts of the country where manufactures never were in operation, and where no correct opinion could be formed of their effects. So far, then, as respects farmers, this is the result; when their opinion has been founded in fact, it is favorable to manufactures; when from theory only, it is unfavorable. There are memorials, it is true, from another class, who, in the name and for the protection of the farmers, decry the ruinous effects of this measure on agriculture. It is not yet known that farmers have not discernment to know, and spirit to complain of their grievances; they have shown it, and asked for a measure like this. When as numerous petitions from them (not from others in their name) shall ask for its rejection, then, petitions being balanced, the question may be settled by general principles of policy.

The war duties forced no man from his employment, but gave him security in its pursuit, opened new sources, gave the means of selecting the most profitable, most suited to inclination, habit, and capacity. The war built up establishments which were rapidly developing the resources and employing all the industry of the nation. The peace, and the repeal of the war duties, prostrated those establishments, and forced the mechanic, the artisan, from an occupation to which he was led by education, habit, and interest, and in which he felt his best security to be the policy of the Government coinciding with the general interest of the people. If complaints of forcing from profitable to ruinous occupations are just from any one class, they must come from those who are practically and virtually forced by the policy of the Government to abandon their trade and occupation. Give a mechanic appropriate employment, he acquires wealth for himself, and adds to the interest of others; drive him to the soil for support, he makes a bad farmer: he may raise enough to feed, but cannot clothe his family. If any of us have seen the instances in actual life of mechanics forced, from the want of employment, to turn farmers, and been enabled to compare their relative situations in both occupations, we can duly estimate the consequences.

If farmers can be considered as a distinct class of society, and their interest separated from the rest of the nation, it is very certain that it cannot be promoted by increasing the number of those who engage in its pursuits; it increases the competition, and diminishes the profits of the productions. To the nation, it is not so important that their pursuits should be productive of amount as value, extensive as profitable. The great object is to afford a market, and give a value to what is raised. We abound in provisions and raw materials; more is now produced than can be consumed or sold; to increase the quantity is only a loss to the raiser; it can give no new value to what he now has, or what he may acquire; it can give him no profit. To the Government it can give no revenue, for it does not increase his means of consuming articles of foreign production; and from no other source of taxation does it leave a surplus that can be spared from the wants of the farmer to the calls of the Treasury. Who, then, can be interested in the mere increase of agricultural products, which want a market abroad and value at home? The definition and application to agriculture of the terms *coercion, restriction,* and *forcing of occupations,* is now practically understood by all those who will look to the state of the country. Where there is no prohibition, duty, or taxes on imports or exports, shipping or tonnage—occupations, trade, and commerce are free. Whether these clogs are imposed by our own or a foreign Government, is immaterial; so far as they extend, they prevent the people from the perfect freedom of choice of occupation, employment, and production; and that freedom can only be restored by the removal of these clogs. Whether the character of the proposed bill has been fairly judged of, will become apparent. The clogs on our agricultural products are not on their export; there is perfect freedom in raising and shipping them, but the corn laws of England, France, and Spain, prevent their consumption; when they reach their shores, free trade ends. The worst effect of domestic coercion would be to prevent their production or exportation; foreign coercion becomes as effectual when it accomplishes the same object, by rendering production and exportation unavailing; the privilege of raising is a useless one, when there is a prohibition to sell or to use. It cannot be less grating to national feeling that it is the act of a foreign Government. The duty of forty cents a pound on our dressed flax is no less a prohibition to our farmer to raise any more than suffices for his wants than if a positive law forbade it; the bounty on linen is as effectual a check on the making of it here as a domestic excise. The operation of a foreign system, which excludes our productions and forces theirs on us, is the practical restraint on agriculture, the essence of a system of restriction under which the whole country now labors; which, when imposed by a foreign Government, seems to be more admired than dreaded by those who, speaking in the name, assume the protection of farmers. Every farm in this nation will produce flax, yet we do not export a pound; foreign Governments refuse it a market. We do not make our own linen; they give a bounty on theirs, to prevent us from making it. They thus, by legislation, force us from the market, acquire its command; the farmer is prevented from raising flax, and, forced to another product, he tries wool, hemp, breadstuffs; they are also excluded; he is not left free to sell to the people of England, or they to buy what they want. He is virtually bound to raise only what their Government will permit him to dispose of; his freedom of occupation is gone; it is controlled by a foreign Power; directed by their policy, he is driven to the pursuit which best meets their views, and most promotes the interests of its subjects. The coercion rests not here; it not only forces ours out, but thrusts their productions in, and the domestic market is thus taken from the farmer. When national policy and individual association combine to prevent our manufacturers from affording the home market to the farmer, and succeed in the object, coercion becomes complete. How far the Middle and Western States are now from suffering under the full scope of a foreign restrictive policy, the condition of the farmers will best testify. If the North is saved, it is by manufactures; if the South is yet free, it is because the great manufacturing nations find it their interest, and not against their policy, to permit the consumption of their staples. It would, perhaps, not be a useless inquiry to ask whether their demand and price are increasing? The state of the country fully justifies this remark: foreign policy has forced from employment our agriculture, manufactures, and commerce; each interest is low, each complaining; with the infinite capacity to produce, fabricate, and distribute, the power has become useless, without the means of using it; our industry has become paralyzed by the employment of foreign, which has been forced on us by a persevering, unyielding course of legislation by other nations. Now, when our citizens ask of their own representatives to counteract foreign laws, systems, and combinations, and, if not to retaliate, at least to compel them to restore to us a freedom they have taken away or destroyed—the freedom of production and exchange—that, if the monopoly of our market is to be given by legislation, it shall be such as flows from a conviction of its tendency to promote our interest, and, enacted by our representatives, not such as it may please a foreign legislator or monarch to prescribe to us; how far the increased duties proposed will tend to more or less balance the foreign coercion which now bears grievously on all the country; how far it is defensive or offensive; how far it accords with or contradicts the policy which this Government has adopted in relation to other interests, the House must determine.

There is no portion of the community more injuriously affected by changes in the policy of a country than the farmers; none have suffered more seriously by the repeal of the duties imposed during the war; none felt more practically the

Protection to Manufactures.

dependence on a foreign market for their means of exchange. While they were at his door, the price of goods did not affect him; produce and goods rose together; the same quantity of one would still buy the same amount of the other. Now the scene is changed; goods remain at the old prices, but it takes three or four times the quantity of produce to purchase the same amount. It is often mentioned, as a symptom of better times, "goods are looking up." This may be, by some, deemed an indication of returning prosperity; but, however it may be to others, to the farmer it is ominous of despair; his produce is looking down. When goods look one way, and grain another, the farmer must look to some new mode of turning his grain into something which will produce him his necessaries. While every change depresses domestic, and swells the price of foreign products, he feels coercion, and what it is to be forced, not from his occupation, but from all the comforts it once produced him. Till goods fall as much as grain, or grain rises to the price of goods, the farmer pays two or three hundred per cent. more for them, though they may be quoted at the old nominal rates. He who, in other times, could pay for his iron by produce, or the use of his teams when their labor was not required on his farm, can now estimate the difference between buying at the forge or at the store. When iron was at a duty of $32\frac{1}{2}$ per cent. personal observation did not cause the objection that it forced the farmer from his occupation, or made it less profitable; when, by the existing tariff, it was reduced from 30 per cent. to $9 per ton, it neither gave new employment nor increased profits to agriculture. In extending the observation to all other articles of which our country furnishes the raw material, or which, when made at home, could be paid for in provisions, it is thought to be fully justified by the melancholy experience of the last four years. It has pointed out to the farmer in what true economy consists; it has taught him what is cheap and what is dear; the difference between having his market at his door, or transferred to a foreign country. The books of the merchants, the dockets of justices and courts, tell a story that all can understand. It was not so when manufactures flourished; it cannot continue so when they revive. The farmer will be the first to profit by the change; his is the first interest that should excite our attention; though we may not legislate him into wealth, we may save him from the danger which hangs over him. While we refuse to counteract the coercion of foreign legislation, we do not make his occupation free by removing foreign restraints on his markets, or give him an equivalent by securing him a new one. It is said, this new market cannot be afforded; that the farmer now feeds all our population, and can feed no more in any event. If this remark were true to its full extent, it could only apply to provisions. The production of raw materials, which have now no value; the extraction of ores and minerals from the earth, which now will not pay the expense; the supply of fuel, which is now useless; the increased demand for potash and dye-stuffs,

for the various small items of the prod[e] farm, which, though not necessaries, are c[?] and may add very importantly to the [?] market, as the same population has greate[r] of payment—all tend to enlarge his mean[s] change, his sources of occupation. T[he] necessaries of life are few in number and[?] value; their production is not the most p[r?] employment of agriculture; it is, perha[ps] most expensive. The garden, the orcha[rd] dairy and poultry yard, the sty and the st[?] matters of no little importance; they affor[d] profit and require less labor than the gra[?] The market for their production depends [on] the mere amount of population, but the m[?] that population to extend their purchases [?] necessaries to comforts and luxuries. Th[e] ply of these is the farmer's profit; the rai[se] them employs the labor and attention of [?] dren, (who are of no use in a field,) by [?] pations in which are combined health, ple[?] economy, and industry. If foreign bounti[es] duties were removed or counteracted, the [?] ture of flax, hemp, and wool, would be no less [?] orable or useful pursuits of agriculture than gr[?] and there is one raw material for the cultu[re] which this country is well adapted, in wh[?] only required the attention of children to en[?] insects to labor for the emolument of the fa[?] raw silk. These are all new sources of w[?] by the establishment of manufactures, thoug[h] population is the same. There is another[?] mechanics, who are, for want of employment [?] compelled to procure a scanty subsistence by [?] cultivation of the soil, without means to purcha[se] or stock, or knowledge to cultivate a farm; w[?] add nothing to their own or the wealth of societ[y] who have nothing to spare for the support of G[?] ernment; forming no part of the solid yeoman[ry] of the country, who, identified with its soil [?] strength, may be truly called "the salt of [?] earth;" but a miserable tenantry or mere occ[u?] pants, who, having been forced by foreign poli[cy] from the occupations for which they are fitted, [?] now only waiting for some act of this Gove[rn?] ment which will enable them to resume them[?] the number of these is not small, and each one[?] these and their families will become new custo[m?] ers to the farmers. Foreign artisans must not[?] overlooked: foreign capital will flow to us in[?] small current; foreign owners and foreign ar[ti?] sans, who are now waiting to see in our legis[la?] tion some assurance of permanent policy. Th[ey?] are a valuable, useful class of citizens abroad, a[nd] so far as our observation extends, we should [?] them injustice in withholding the expression of o[ur?] opinion that they are distinguished for their pub[lic?] spirit, their good conduct, and devotion to the tr[ue?] interests of their adopted country.

There is one other aid to agriculture whi[ch] must be admitted to be a natural consequence [of?] the establishment of domestic manufactures. [?] Whatever the market of the farmer may be, [it?] will be permanent; co-extensive with the con[?] sumption of the country, it will expand with it[?] increase. He will know to what objects to appl[y?]

his labor and skill; the demand will be steady; he can vary his culture to meet the varying wants of society; he will look alone to his own Government, to his own Representatives, for the rules of policy which may have a bearing on his occupations; which can be affected only by those who are united alike with him in their devotion to the common interest of their own common country; whose pursuits will intermingle with his, forming the common mass of national industry, from which no just Government can withhold its protection.

With the notice of one other objection the committee will close their remarks, with not less relief to themselves than to the House.

If manufactures will produce these effects, why are they not established? If the foreign article can be undersold, why is it not done without the aid of legislation? We answer, because the effects of foreign legislation cannot be removed by individual exertion or enterprise. Whatever may be done here by our citizens to acquire the command of our consumption is equalled by foreign individuals to retain it; each feel the advantages, know the profits, and make equal exertions. The superior numbers and greater wealth of foreign capitalists are, of themselves, formidable obstacles; but, when backed by the policy and wealth of a nation, by their laws and systems, the competition becomes unequal. To restore the balance, make the competition a fair one between individuals, the weight of one Government must be taken from the one scale, or balanced by the same weight of another Government in the other. We might here ask, if this would insure the desired protection, why withhold it?

When business has for years taken an established course, it is no easy matter to divert it. The progress of our manufactures was slow till the late war. The consequent diminution of imports, and the duplication of the permanent duties, gave them a powerful impulse; they were rapidly advancing to meet the full demands of consumers. The revulsion caused by the present modification of the tariff has been in force ever since. If it has been beneficial to the country, then let it continue; but if injurious, let it be stopped; legislation caused, and alone can cure it. The war duties were not imposed for the protection of manufactures, and repealed when the object was found unattainable or prejudical. They were imposed for the revenue—the object was effected; they protected manufactures—the country prospered; an excise was built on manufactures—the support was mutual. The Government wanted revenue, and obtained it; it now wants it, and, the same means in their power; why, then, not resort to them—if for no other, at least the same reasons as before? It ought not to make revenue the less acceptable because it encourages domestic industry.

If the enterprise and capital of individuals were competent to the object, it must be the work of time; before it arrives, the public resources will require new means of supply; it then becomes the duty of Congress to hasten the time, and this for its own protection and support. But, if it should

be true that, in the present state of the world, no new manufactory can be successfully established without legislative aid, (that it is true, is proved by the experience of all manufacturing nations, confirmed by our own, and it has by one of our greatest statesmen been declared to be a maxim of universal application,) the fact once established, it would be in other subjects deemed superfluous to assign the reasons, (for the want of reason cannot do away facts;) but it being required on this subject that no proposition can be made out from fact and experience alone, it is better to meet than evade the requisition. A most obvious reason occurs at once, that a new manufacture can only attain success by excluding an old one, which is in possession of the market; without the aid of a law on either side, or the competition of any capital, except of the individuals who are struggling for the market, the one who can make it the interest of the consumer to purchase from him must prevail, if the capital of both is equal; if it is unequal, the greatest will eventually prevail. The competition is not for the momentary, but the permanent command of the market; the losses, during the temporary contest, will be refunded by the future profits when the market is secured. Who then can hold out the longest becomes the question. This is at once settled, when a Government bounty comes in aid of the one set. An excise drawback, or a custom bounty, is a contribution from the public funds in aid of individual enterprise to acquire or retain the supply of a foreign market; it is not merely an addition to the capital of the individual, but a gratuitous donation to him. Competition must cease between them, unless one individual has funds equal not only to the other, but to his Government likewise. Hence, no new establishment, which diverts employment from an old one, can, under such circumstances, succeed. It will be an ungenerous objection to say that our Government is not bound to furnish capital to manufacturers; that is not asked or expected. But, it is understood that, in answering the objection now under consideration, it is taken for granted that manufactures, once established, are of advantage to the country at large; and that the question is, whether Government should interfere to aid them in their infancy, or whether such interference is necessary? If this question be answered yes, then it is to be hoped that it will not be contended that it is generous or just to withhold that interference on account of the capital of the persons concerned; that moderate capital, skill, industry, and enterprise, must be suffered to sink under the foreign action brought to bear upon it; nothing be thought worthy of legislative aid but immense capitals, which require less in proportion to their amount. While on this subject, it would be proper to remark, that, before this objection should have any influence on us, some standard should be fixed, some sum named by law, which should be deemed as bringing the proprietors within the policy of protection. Manufacturers would then know that if they invested to that amount, they could compete with the foreigner. It is not so important what sum should be named,

Protection to Manufactures.

as that some should be fixed upon; it is believed that a Republican Legislature would not require an amount beyond the means of their constituents to procure. If it was more consistent with theirs, and the principles and practice of the Government, to graduate the protection in the ratio of the wealth of those who asked it, that would be more just than to refuse it wholly to the middling class. If the nation at large will be benefited by protection to manufacturers, it is no answer to say their capital is not sufficient. We must say what is sufficient; till that is done, the answer will not be accepted, for it affords no rule, no security; it means any thing, nothing; it becomes mockery. If manufactures are a national interest, and justify protection, there cannot be a better rule, more equal and fair, than to require, as a preliminary to protection, the investment of the same amount of capital as by our uniform legislation for thirty years has been required of another co-ordinate interest—commerce. Equal justice to all makes it our duty to make the comparison; it is done with no unfriendly or invidious feeling, but merely to remind the House that want of capital has never excluded the merchant from the pale of protection; if he had enough to commence his operations, those operations have been protected from foreign aggression. It is believed that the capital invested in manufactures has been equal to the investments in commercial pursuits, in proportion to the amount of business done, and, including the credits at the custom-house, that commerce has been conducted more on credit than manufactures.

A linen or glass manufactory is about to be established in our country; there is capital to erect the buildings, purchase the machinery, and stock to commence; the proprietors meet at once competition from the following sources: foreign manufacturers, foreign exporters, American importers, American retailers, and a foreign Government. The American manufacturer stands alone; he asks for a fair chance, fair play. Willing to take a contest against equal force, but unable to contend against numbers, wealth, and power, he calls on his Government to equalize the competition; to make it individual; to impose on the importation a duty equal to the premium which the foreign exporter receives from his Government, for the express purpose of breaking down the competition. A custom bounty, or excise drawback, is not to give the command of the home consumption; that is done by prohibition and duty; it is to prevent us from using our raw materials; to compel us to use theirs; to employ their labor, and give a value to their industry. The American manufacturer is the only person who can obstruct their policy; if he can be broken down, the American people must depend on England for a market as well as for the articles of their consumption. It would not be unreasonable to call on this Government to give them duties beyond the bounty. If the duty is twenty-five, and the bounty twenty-five, there is no protection except of a negative kind; the bounty received from one Government equals the duty imposed by the other; yet even this meets

with objections; it is called a restrictive system. In the case of glass, the oppression on our manufacturer is still greater; the custom bounty, or excise drawback, is equal to twenty-eight cents a pound; yet the proposed import duty of ten cents a pound has not—except in one memorial, (Richmond) to the liberal principles of which the committee must again give their approbation—been excepted from the general and heavy charges made against the new tariff. Unless manufactures are to be proscribed; if those engaged in their pursuits, and to whose benefit they tend, are to be thus abandoned; if the unequal, and (in part) unnatural, anti-national pressure under which they labor is to be increased by a foreign Government, and ours stands neutral—it may be asked, for what Government is instituted? Where are the benefits imparted? The farmer has the raw material, the artisan the capital and skill; but they cannot use it. If on the faith of a revenue system the capital is invested, the labor of years is lost by a reduction of duties below the amount of foreign bounties and drawbacks. It is not the manufacturers alone who suffer; they alone, it must be remembered, are the class of men who can ever interpose between the importer and consumer; put them down, the agriculture of the country is completely dependent on foreign Powers. Such is our present situation; the people of this nation cannot believe it is their interest to remain so; they support the Government, and ask protection. The committee think it their duty not to withhold it, and to afford it to such extent as will give a fair opportunity of bringing into active and useful operation all the resources of the country; to give a market and a value to all the products of our soil; to counteract foreign legislation, so far as it bears on the industry of our own people, by directing its pursuits and occupations to subserve the policy and interest of other nations.

If it should be remarked that the proposed bill falls short of the principles on which it is founded, it must not be alleged as evidence of a want of confidence in their correctness, but of the deference which is felt and paid to the opinions of those who differ from us in their views, equally conscientious with ourselves; it was due to all the members of this House to convince them that our convictions are so decided and deliberate that we would be content for the present to lay a proper foundation, leaving it to experience to direct what should be built upon it; if insecure, the more easily removed; if the substantial basis of national industry, the easier to finish the structure.

[The tabular statements accompanying the report, being of great volume, are necessarily omitted.]

DOCUMENTS ACCOMPANYING THE REPORT.

To the honorable the Senate and House of Representatives of the United States:

The memorial of the Chamber of Commerce of the city of New York respectfully shows: That your memorialists view with much alarm the renewal of an attempt to repeal the acts making dis-

Protection to Manufactures.

crimination between American and foreign duties on imports and tonnage, and pray leave to submit to the consideration of Congress the following objections: *First.* It will diminish the revenue to an amount which, taking past years as the guide, would not be less than $450,000 per annum. *Secondly.* It will essentially injure the commerce of the United States, as its effects will be, by opening the market for freight to the lowest bidder, to shift the carrying trade from the hands of our own merchants into those of foreigners. This, your memorialists believe, will appear from the following considerations: *First.* Foreigners build their vessels much cheaper than we do. From actual calculation, it is found that a vessel built of European oak, and equal to those built of live oak, (which, besides, is nearly exhausted,) costs, when equipped for sea, at the rate of $36¼ per ton ; and, if built in Finland, of their fir, of which they have abundance, equal in duration to our common oak, and fitted for sea in the same manner, she will cost at the rate of $19 per ton ; while the American vessel, built of our common oak, and not so well equipped, will cost at the rate of from $40 to $45 per ton ; but built of live oak and cedar, she will cost at the rate of from $50 to $55 per ton.

Secondly. The materials composing equipment, such as iron, hemp, sailcloth, &c., are all cheaper abroad than they are here, and the price of labor for working them is supposed to be fifty per cent. less there than in the United States.

Thirdly. Foreigners navigate cheaper, seamen's wages are lower, and many of their crews consist of apprentices without wages. The apprentice act of Great Britain renders it incumbent on every owner or master of a vessel to take with him a certain number of apprentices; and this they find so advantageous that they frequently double or treble that number, more especially vessels from the North of England. Every merchant engaged in commerce knows that the Hollanders, Hamburghers, Danes, Swedes, &c. man their vessels with a still greater proportion of apprentices; and in the cheapness of their living, clothing, &c. they have a very material advantage over the vessels of the United States.

Thus it appears that foreigners can build cheaper, equip cheaper, and sail their vessels cheaper, than we can; and it may be added, that Europeans are generally satisfied with a less gain than the American merchant can afford to receive.

Lastly. Although it has been said that for us to meet the advance on the part of Great Britain, and to repeal our countervailing acts, would place the two nations on an equal footing, yet your memorialists conceive that, while Great Britain retains her present navigation act, this would be very wide of the truth. We, on our part, should thus permit Great Britain to bring hither not only goods the growth or manufacture of that country, but of all others ; while, on her part, by the navigation act we have just referred to, we shall be expressly confined to the carriage of goods the growth or manufacture of the United States. To this may be added, that British vessels would then bring a cargo from their own country to this, take a freight here to their colonies where our vessels are not admitted, and from thence a third freight home : making thus three freights in one voyage. The value of the importation cargoes is so much greater than the value of our exportation dutiable cargoes, that the extra duties paid by the foreigner are in many cases equal, and in some cases more than equal to the whole freight; so that the acts which are now proposed to be abolished operate nearly as a prohibition to the foreigner, and leave us, in a measure, without competitors in our own markets. After all that has been said, it hardly needs to be added, that if our ports are thrown open to foreign on the same terms with our own vessels, as by this repeal is contemplated, (for it is in vain to attempt to confine the measure to the British,) they will crowd our wharves, underbid our freight, monopolize the markets, and leave American vessels idly to rot in our docks. Your memorialists have therefore no hesitation in declaring that, in their opinion, this measure will be a fatal blow to the American carrying trade. It would be easy to show, in detail, that this would, in its consequences, prove extremely injurious to the agricultural and the mechanical classes of our citizens; a few general observations only will be indulged.

First. As to the agricultural. Although, generally speaking, freight is paid by the consumer, and therefore it may be said it is immaterial to the farmer how high or low it may be, yet this is not the case when the demand ceases or slackens; it then falls back on the husbandman. But to transfer our carrying trade to foreigners will be to lessen very much the chance of the demand.

The active enterprise of the American merchant is constantly looking abroad to every part of the world for a market ; and if it is any where to be found, or if there is only a reasonable presumption that it may be found, the farmer meets with a ready vent for his produce. Perhaps the calculations of the merchant may be disappointed, and he even ruined ; yet the misfortune reaches not the farmer ; he has the same benefit of a good market: but should the American vessels once disappear, he must then be entirely at the mercy of chance adventures for a market; and when the demand is not very great, the price of the freight will be deducted from the article itself. All this must necessarily tend essentially to lessen the value of the farmer's produce.

Secondly, As to the mechanical. That numerous class of mechanics who are connected with shipbuilding, the carpenter, the blacksmith, the sailmaker, the ropemaker, &c., &c., will of course be deprived of employment ; their labor will be neither wanted nor paid for.

To conclude: our ships being thus banished from our shores, we shall no longer furnish a nursery for our seamen, but that valuable class of citizens will be driven to seek for their bread in other countries ; and in any future European wars which may happen, and which are constantly liable to happen, we shall find ourselves without seamen or ships, to avail ourselves of that neutral position which reflection and experience equally warrant

Protection to Manufactures.

us in calculating upon as one of the blessings allied to our remote and secure situation.

On the whole, your memorialists cannot refrain from expressing the belief with which they are strongly impressed, that to repeal the discriminating laws, which have operated so happily to increase our navigation and commerce, would be a measure highly prejudicial to various and important interests in the community, detrimental to the revenue of the country, and, in a national point of view, extremely impolitic. They therefore pray that the repeal may not take place.

JOHN MURRAY.

J. W. LAWRENCE, *Secretary.*

NEW YORK, *January* 15, 1803.

Importations of goods from Europe paying ad valorem duties.

		Per cent.
1816.	In American vessels - $83,676,283 ==	83.67
	In foreign vessels - 8,706,122 ==	8.7
1817.	In American vessels - 30,350,835 ==	30.35
	In foreign vessels - 5,750,856 ==	5.75
1818.	In American vessels - 49,719,785 ==	49.71
	In foreign vessels - 5,324,243 ==	5.32

Importations from France.

1816.	In American vessels - 8,816,147 ==	8.8
	In foreign vessels - 383,433 ==	.3
1817.	In American vessels - 3,493,176 ==	3.4
	In foreign vessels - 488,072 ==	.4
1818.	In American vessels - 6,668,600 ==	6.6
	In foreign vessels - 688,195 ==	.6

To the Senate and House of Representatives of the United States of America in Congress assembled: The memorial of the Chamber of Commerce of the city of New York respectfully showeth:

That your memorialists have witnessed, with feelings of deep concern, the consequences resulting to the shipping interest of the United States from the discriminating duties established in France on the staple products of this country.

At the period of their imposition, and for a considerable time subsequent to the late war in Europe, the trade carried on by French vessels with the United States was chiefly confined to New Orleans and other Southern ports, whose productions constitute the principal exports from this country to France, whilst their interest in shipping is very limited; so that the effects of the enormous discriminating duties payable on the importations into France of cotton and tobacco, in transferring to French vessels the carrying to that country, were not immediately perceived or felt by the ship owners or merchants in this quarter of the Union. But the severe losses sustained by those who employed our vessels in that trade have since led to an investigation of their causes, and created a universal feeling of the injury and injustice to which our flag is subjected.

In giving to this subject the attention which its importance demands, your memorialists find that the foreign tonnage duty and light money payable in the United States are very nearly equal to the foreign tonnage duty and port charges in France, and may therefore be considered as regulated upon the principle of a just and fair reciprocity; whilst the discriminating duties imposed on the importation of merchandise operate on the shipping interests of the two countries in a manner altogether disproportionate and unequal.

The foreign or discriminating duties paid by American vessels importing the following articles into France, are: 1¼ cent per pound (French weight) on cotton; 1½ cent per pound on tobacco; 55 cents per 100 pounds on potashes; which extra duties exceed the whole freight now paid for the transportation of those articles from the United States, whether in French or in American bottoms.

The present rates of freight, in French vessels, are about 1¼ cent per pound for cotton; ¾ cent per pound for tobacco; ½ cent per pound for potashes; and, in American vessels, about one-third below these rates; making the difference of duty by a French vessel exceed the gross amount of freight by an American vessel at least one-third.

To form an estimate of the practical result of these regulations, it will be assumed that a vessel of 300 register tons burden will carry 560,000 pounds weight of tobacco; the difference of duty on which, at 1½ cent per lb. would be - $6,300

Which is equivalent to twenty-one dollars per register ton.

Or, in a vessel of the same description, carrying 280,000 pounds weight of cotton, and 220,000 pounds of potashes, the difference of duty, estimated at 1½ cent on the cotton, is - - - - - 4,200

And that on the potashes, at 55 cents per 100lb., is - - - - - - - 1,210

Would be, together - - - - $5,410

Which is equivalent to eighteen dollars per register ton.

The discriminating duties chargeable on the three articles above enumerated, which constitute the bulk of our exports to France, form an aggregate much greater than the foreign duty of ten per cent. payable in the United States would amount to, if calculated on the whole importations from France. And the experience of the last two years confirms, (what, indeed, is sufficiently obvious from the preceding statement,) that a perseverance in the present regulations of our intercourse with France must operate to exclude American vessels from all participation in the carrying trade connected with it.

Your memorialists, in earnestly soliciting that the attention of your honorable body may be engaged in devising some remedy for an evil so serious and alarming, beg leave to suggest their conviction of the utter inefficacy of any system of countervailing discriminating duties to be levied on the importations into the United States of French merchandise, inasmuch as the articles which would be the necessary objects of such duties bear no proportion in their bulk, and in the price of their transportation, to those which form our exports to France. And the course of the colonial trade, moreover, enables French vessels to avoid the inconveniences of performing the voyage across the Atlantic in ballast, by taking a freight from the ports of France to those of her colonies, and then turning their course advantageously to our ports, either in ballast, or with colonial produce; whilst our vessels, generally, return direct from France in ballast, or only with inconsiderable ladings.

To exhibit in its proper light the importance of the subject under consideration, it will be necessary not only to advert to the actual amount of tonnage employed in the transportation of our produce to France compared with the aggregate tonnage employed in foreign trade generally, but also to take into view their future relative proportions when our trade to France shall have received all the extension of which it is susceptible, by the progressive increase in the cultivation of our Southern products, and when our shipping shall have experienced the reduction it is to suffer by the effects of the further development of the actual state of our foreign commerce.

It would be superfluous to enter into details to show how extensively, and almost entirely, all the sources of that commerce are cut off. It is a lamentable fact, that more than half the number of vessels lately arrived in this from foreign ports are dismantled, from the absolute absence of any advantageous object of commercial pursuit. And this state of commerce seems the natural and necessary result of the new order of things which has prevailed since the pacification of Europe. Every restraint that lately shackled the navigation of the principal maritime nations of Europe has been removed, whilst the general trade and navigation of those States are, at the same time, regulated with a studious regard to the interests of their own subjects. So that the United States have not only ceased to be the carriers for Europe but are deprived of the means of entering into a fair competition in the transportation to foreign countries of the principal products of their own soil.

It would seem obvious that, during the continuance of a state of peace in Europe, the great elements of our commerce in that quarter of the globe will be confined to the exchange of our products for such articles of foreign production as may be required for home consumption.

The quantity of American cotton, tobacco, potashes, and other staples, now consumed in France, cannot be correctly stated by your memorialists, but they presume it to be equal to a fourth of the whole quantity exported to Europe.

The aggregate tonnage employed last year in the direct trade from the United States to France is estimated at fifty thousand tons; in addition to which, an indirect trade of considerable extent has been carried on by the circuitous channel of England. (The saving on the duties, by reshipping our cotton and tobacco thence to France, in French vessels, instead of shipping them direct from the United States, in American vessels, being more than equivalent to the extra freight and charges attending the additional voyage.)

If we limit our views of this carrying trade to the employment of fifty thousand tons of shipping, the freight out and home, calculating twenty dollars per ton, amounts to one million of dollars; which sum, if gained by vessels, might justly be considered as so much capital added annually to the stock of national wealth.

However small the net profit may be to the ship owners on this amount of freight, the disbursements for the equipment, and the wages for the navigation of the vessels, would be left at home; and, together with the employment it would require of so large a body of seamen, would materially conduce to create and maintain the elements necessary to advance our commercial and naval interests.

The act of Congress offering to foreign nations the means of a free intercourse with this country, on terms of perfect reciprocity, has not, as is believed by your memorialists, been found as beneficial in its operation as was justly to have been expected.

Those nations whose acceptance of the invitation it held forth might subserve the views and interests of the United States are found to remain passive; while Holland, Sweden, Prussia, and the Hanseatic Towns, adopting the principle of reciprocity, secure to themselves an important exemption in our ports, without affording any privilege in theirs not before enjoyed by the United States, and, in fact, gratuitously granted to every other nation.

Until lately, we found some advantages in our commercial relations with the possessions of the King of the Netherlands, by participating in the trade to the colony of Java; but now heavy discriminating duties are laid to confine all the advantages of that trade to Dutch vessels. Your memorialists do not notice this circumstance as requiring the application of any remedies within the purview of this memorial, but to show the progressive extension on the part of the European Powers of a system of absolute colonial monopoly, and to evince the necessity of devising means to counteract the growth of that system, by some vigorous effort on the part of our Government.

Louisiana was acquired by the United States in her colonial state, and the monopoly of her extended and growing trade would be more valuable than that of any two colonies whatever. And the Floridas, if they pass from their present abandoned and miserable condition to be integral parts of the Union, cannot fail, by the quickening influence of our free institutions, to open vast resources of trade, and may add to the list of our present exports even the articles of sugar and coffee, hitherto deemed exclusively colonial.

The liberal policy of the United States, in opening to all nations a free trade to the vast marts of their colonial acquisitions ought, it would seem, to entitle them to some corresponding privileges from those nations, at least, who participate largely in the benefits of that trade. But no such reciprocation has been experienced; nor, as the result of gratuitous concession, is it to be expected:

In reference to the oppressive discriminating du-

Protection to Manufactures.

ties on the importation of American products into France, which it is the principal object of the present memorial to bring under the notice of Government, your memorialists take leave most respectfully to suggest, that they can devise no expedient more likely to produce a favorable change in the present system of the French Government, nor better calculated to enable the citizens of the United States successfully to resist it, if persevered in, than the imposition of a heavy tonnage duty; and, at the same time, no measure appears to your memorialists so consistent with the general policy of the United States.

Referring to the statement already made, exhibiting the effects of the discriminating duties in France on cotton, tobacco, and potashes, considered as a tonnage duty on American vessels, your memorialists leave to the superior wisdom of Congress to determine, on a full consideration of all the circumstances connected with the case, what tonnage duty should now be imposed, so as to make this a fair and effective countervailing measure.

Your memorialists, considering, moreover, that some new provision is necessary in order to render beneficially operative the act of Congress which offers to foreign nations the means of commercial intercourse upon the principle of reciprocity, respectfully suggest that this duty should be made to apply to all nations which shall not adopt that principle.

A general regulation of this nature, whilst it would violate neither the letter nor spirit of our treaties with France, appears to be equally expedient in reference to other nations. Spain, for instance, besides imposing, as is believed, discriminating duties on the articles of our exports imported into the mother country, exacts most excessive extra duties on provisions imported by American vessels into her colonies. Among others, that on the article of flour amounts in Cuba to $3 37½ per barrel. The regulations of trade in the ports of the Spanish colonies are such as not to place the intercourse with them under any of the restrictions contained in the navigation act; and thus, whilst this trade remains open to both nations, the discriminating duties imposed in those colonies must operate to transfer it altogether to Spanish vessels, as soon as their flag can navigate securely.

Your memorialists are persuaded that a measure like the one proposed could produce no injurious effects upon the agricultural and commercial interests of the United States, by abridging in foreign markets the sale of their produce. The prohibitory regulations of different Governments prove that the want of our provisions is the only security we now enjoy for their admission into foreign ports; and wherever this want exists they will continue to be received, direct, or by intermediate ports.

The principal articles exported to France are so essential to the supply of the manufactories that they cannot be dispensed with; so that, if a system of commercial regulations could be supposed to exist, operating to prevent a direct exportation of those articles to that country, its whole supplies of cotton and tobacco must be derived through the circuitous channel of England, (as has been partially practised for the last two years,) or through some of the neighboring ports of the continent; and, in either case, we should at least partake in the advantages of their transportation across the Atlantic.

The right of the citizens of the United States to participate, on equal terms, in the advantages to be derived from their commercial intercourse with foreign nations, appears to your memorialists to be indisputable. And they appeal with confidence to Congress for such interference on their behalf as the public policy may justify. Although it may be questionable, in a case like the present, whether it would comport with the dignity of the nation to offer any considerations to foreign Powers in order to obtain a just reciprocity of commercial benefits, yet your memorialists take leave to suggest the expediency of holding out to France some further encouragements to the consumption in the United States of French wines and silk manufactures. Encouragements of this nature, if not required as an inducement to France to place the regulations of her trade with this country on a more equal and just footing, may possibly be used to obtain some relaxation to her colonial restrictions, and induce the repeal of the late order directed to the national tobacco manufactory in France, which restricts the employment of the foreign growth of that article to the proportion of one-sixth part for five-sixth parts of domestic growth.

It is true, in reference to the article of wines, (the duty on which is now sufficiently reduced,) the United States could, in the way of inducement to France, only assure to her the continuance of that reduction. But, in regard to silk manufactures, the imposition of additional duties on the same articles imported from China might be adopted as a measure of reciprocal advantage.

It would certainly be of great importance to France to check the immense importations from China of silk goods in imitation of French fabrics. And, considering the heavy drains of specie from the United States, which are caused by the prosecution of the trade to China, it would at least be equally advantageous to us to receive the same articles from countries where they can be obtained in exchange for our own products.

Your memorialists are anxious to maintain the national prosperity, and would discredit the unreasonable clamor of desponding and embarrassed traders; but the foreign commerce of this country, at the present period, is so rapidly declining, and its shipping interest so particularly depressed, that they feel themselves constrained to declare their firm conviction, that both must dwindle into comparative insignificance, unless the measures of foreign Governments, operating to deprive this country of an equitable participation in the benefits of its commercial intercourse with them, shall be promptly met and counteracted.

Under a deep impression that the prosperity of the nation is intimately connected with the prosperity of its commerce, and that the rising hopes of its future naval power are essentially dependent on the maintenance of its navigation, your memorialists have thought it a duty they owe to the community to submit these considerations to the wisdom of Congress; humbly praying that they will afford such relief in the premises as the nature of the case may require.

WM. BAYARD, *President.*
JOHN PINTARD, *Secretary.*

Questions addressed by the Committee on Manufactures to the Mercantile Society of New York, with their answers.

THE NEW TARIFF BILL.

You will recollect that the tenth section was stricken out, and the ninth so modified as to be unobjectionable.

Question 1st. State the items on which you think so high a duty was proposed as would lead to smuggling.

Answer. Smuggling cannot be carried to any extent except on our frontiers, and, generally speaking, there would be but little difference then, whether the duty was 15 or 40 per cent. Those who are most conversant with our revenue laws, know that the difficulties attending smuggling from on shipboard are so great that the gain would not justify the risk. European and Indian ships and cargoes are so valuable that, supposing character in no way affected, the owners would never jeopardize them for the sake of clandestinely introducing a small part; to thus introduce any considerable part would be impracticable, without the connivance of the officers of the customs. Under the duties of 1815 and 1816, the whole amount smuggled from on shipboard in our commercial towns did not probably amount to a twentieth of one per cent. on the cargoes imported. Watches, jewelry, laces, and sewing silks, are the principal articles that are and would continue to be smuggled, because their bulk is so trifling that they are imported by passengers and others, and not entered on the manifest; therefore the vigilance of the officers cannot, in all cases, prevent their being landed without paying the duties. As such goods so introduced must almost necessarily be sold by auction, any saving in the duty might be met by an equivalent auction duty.

Question 2d. Enumerate those which you think would amount to a prohibition.

Answer. Article 5th will amount to a prohibition of all kinds of paper, except colored and stained paper and paper hangings; all kinds of hats, except Leghorn straw. It will probably ultimately amount to a prohibition of prunello and silk shoes, flint, cut, and window glass, slates, and tiles for building, common corks, salted fish, and inferior kinds of gunpowder.

Question 3d. Generally, would the rates of duty proposed diminish or increase the revenue? in other words, would the increased duties equal the diminished importation? If you think it would, state the items specifically.

Answer. The proposed tariff, if adopted, would, in our opinion, diminish the revenue. The articles enumerated in the answer to the 16th question

are all now recollected that will bear an increase of duty without injury to the revenue.

Question 4th. Are there any general provisions in this bill that would have an injurious effect on the revenue or on commerce? If so, specify them. This does not refer to the rate of duties.

Answer. In the 5th article of the tariff bill, "allowances or discounts" ought to be stricken out, as they throw insurmountable difficulties in the way of many descriptions of goods.

Question 5th. What is the cost of a British ship of, say 300 tons; what of an American of the same force and burden; and, generally, the difference in the price of shipping by the ton in each country, completely equipped?

Answer. A British ship of 300 tons, equipped for sea, will cost $24,000, or $80 per ton; an American ship, of the same quality, will cost $18,000, or $60 per ton.

Question 6th. The quantity of iron and cordage to the 100 tons of shipping?

Answer. It will require four tons of iron, 1,500 pounds of copper bolts, 4½ tons of cordage, and 20 bolts of duck, to the 100 tons.

Question 7th. Would the proposed increase of duty on iron, hemp, and cordage, have the effect of inducing the merchants to build their vessels abroad, or of giving foreign a preference over our own shipping?

Answer. As to American merchants building vessels in foreign countries, it is out of the question; for, by our navigation laws, American papers could not be obtained for them. Foreign vessels would not have a preference in our ports over American built vessels, unless at a reduction in freight of 25 per cent., or advantages equivalent, at the port of destination, as is now the case with French and other foreign vessels taking cargoes for France.

Question 8th. State the price of the following articles in 1811, or any other year or years before the war, which will present a fair average of their price in the years of a flourishing commerce: coarse cottons, umbrellas, nails, gunpowder, playing cards, carriages, cabinet wares, wafers, hats, &c., boots and shoes, and any other manufactured articles which were formerly imported, but are now in a great measure, if not wholly, made in the United States; the present prices of the same articles; the relative quality of the imported and domestic articles.

Answer. Common coarse cottons, such as are manufactured in the United States, may be fairly stated to be 50 per cent. lower than in 1811, and are much superior to the piece goods of similar description from Calcutta.

Cabinet wares are greatly superior, and full 25 per cent. lower.

Gunpowder, 25 to 50 per cent. lower.

Umbrellas, 33⅓ per cent. lower.

Carriages, 50 per cent. lower.

Hats, 25 per cent. lower.

Boots and shoes, 20 per cent. lower.

Silver ware is now made in this country as cheap as in London, and is 12½ per cent. lower than in 1811.

Protection to Manufactures.

Question 9th. Where the domestic has superseded the foreign supply of our market, state the general effect it has produced as to price and quality, and whether it has resulted in the benefit or injury of the consumer.

Answer. As far as our own information has given us an opportunity of judging, the consumer is supplied with a better article for the same price; it is particularly so with coarse cottons, hats, boots and shoes, cabinet wares, carriages, fancy chairs, looking-glass and picture frames, silver plate, andirons, brass head shovels and tongs, grates for burning coals, gold leaf, woollen sattinets, cut nails, fancy mock tortoise shell and fine ivory combs, rifle guns, cut tacks and brads, and tin wares.

Question 10th, Taking the article of cotton as an example, and supposing coarse cotton goods are excluded, have the effects been injurious to commerce? Is there as much tonnage, and are there as many seamen, employed in the transportation of the raw material and the manufactured article coastwise, as there would be in the importation of the foreign manufacture and the exportation of as much cotton as would make the goods we import from Europe? If more or less, state the difference.

Answer. The exportation of the raw material to Europe, and the importation of the article when manufactured, would give employment to a greater number of seamen, and more tons of shipping, than the transportation of the same raw materials and manufactured articles coastwise. So far as relates to a prohibition of India cottons, (manufactured,) our commerce has no doubt been benefited, because it could only be employed in bringing an article manufactured from a raw material of foreign growth; whereas, the raw material of which the substitute is made, as well as the manufactured article, are both transported coastwise, and give employment to more shipping, and a greater number of seamen, than the importation of India manufactured cottons could possibly do. It would take five cargoes of unmanufactured cotton to make one of manufactured goods.

Question 11th. Take a given number of tons of shipping, say 100,000, in the East India trade; what would be the number of seamen employed; what number would be employed in the European trade, the same number of tons; same in the West Indian; the same in the coasting trade?

Answer. Take 100,000 tons of shipping in the East India trade, the number of seamen employed would be one man to twenty tons, equal to 5,000 men; the same number of tons in the European trade, one man to twenty-three tons, equal to 4,347; in the West India trade, same number of tons, one man to twenty tons, equal to 5,000; in the coasting trade, same number of tons, one man to fifteen tons, equal to 6,666 men.

Question 12th. Does the consumption of cotton in the American manufactories diminish the price of what is exported to Europe; in other words, are or can the fruits of cotton manufactories be injurious to those who raise this article?

Answer. The consumption of cotton at home increases the price to the growers. The demand in this market for home consumption is generally considered to keep the price from one to two cents per pound higher than it would otherwise be.

Question 13th. Generally speaking, do you think there would be as much employment for our shipping and seamen in the transportation of raw materials and manufactures coastwise as in their exportation and importation? This must be understood as applying generally to our articles of consumption.

Answer. The kind of foreign trade here named employs more tonnage, and probably more seamen, than the coasting trade would, in exchanging the same amount of articles.

Question 14th. Except cotton, how much tonnage is employed in the transportation to other countries of the raw material of the manufactures which we import?

Answer. We know of no raw material, of any magnitude, excepting cotton, the production of this country, which is exported, and returned in a manufactured state.

Question 15th. State your opinion of the probable operation of this bill on commerce; if injurious, point out, specifically, the objections. Would it decrease our tonnage or number of seamen? Would it diminish the price of any of our articles of export? If so, state of what. Is the price of these articles, and their demand abroad, regulated by the wants of other nations, or by the amount of manufactures we receive in exchange? State not only your opinion, but experience, and the information of others that is to be relied upon, if no general revision of the tariff should be proposed.

Answer. We think, generally, it will not be prejudicial to commerce; it would not diminish the value of any article of domestic produce exported; the price of our articles abroad, and the demand for them, is regulated by the wants of other nations, and not by what we in return receive for them.

Question 16th. State the articles on which an additional duty might be laid for the purposes of revenue, without injury to commerce, and the amount of such additional duty.

Answer. The following articles may be raised from their present rate of duty to that annexed to each article, for the purpose of revenue, and would not diminish the importation or consumption:

Linen goods to 25 per cent.

Silk goods manufactured in China and other places beyond the Cape of Good Hope, 35 per cent.

Silk goods from France and other places, except beyond the Cape of Good Hope, 25 per cent.

All staple and fancy hardwares under 25 per cent. to be raised 25 per cent.

China and earthen wares, 35 per cent.

Ale and porter, in bottles or casks, 25 cents per gallon.

Almonds, 4 cents per pound.

Cassia, from China, 10 cents per pound.

Cocoa, 3 cents per pound.

Coffee, 6 cents per pound.

Cotton, 6 cents per pound.

Protection to Manufactures.

Hemp, $2 per cwt.
Iron, in pigs, 75 cents per cwt.
Iron castings, $1 50 per cwt.
Sewing silks and twists, of silk and worsted, $1 50 per pound.
Nutmegs, 75 cents per pound.
Cigars, $5 per thousand.
Linseed oil, 25 cents per gallon.
Blankets, 25 per cent.
Bombazetts and stuff goods, 25 per cent.
Worsted and cotton hosiery, 25 per cent.
Buttons of all kinds, and moulds, 25 per cent.
Lace goods, 15 per cent.
Clocks and time-pieces, 35 per cent.

Question 17th. Have you any reason to believe, that from the 1st March, 1815, to the 1st July, 1816, there was more smuggling than at any former or subsequent period? If so, state them specifically.

Answer. It is not believed that smuggling of any consequence is carried on now, or was at any other period since the restrictive measures, and then the places were mostly confined to the eastern lines, and along the river St. Lawrence. From the 1st March, 1815, to 1st July, 1816, goods commanded a ready and profitable sale; therefore the inducement was less. The evils of the auction system can here be introduced with much propriety, as through that channel almost all the smuggled goods introduced during the restrictive measures were scattered. It was well understood at that time that the amount which was introduced and sold at auctions was for account of the smugglers; the facility to spread the goods prevents in a great degree the possibility of detection; the auctioneer is not bound to ascertain how the parties came by the property, whether stolen or otherwise.

Question 18th. State your opinion of the propriety of the following regulations: appraisers to examine each package imported; surveyor of the port to examine each package exported for drawback; whenever a manifest is required by the existing law to be verified before the American Consul at the place of exportation, all goods to be entered in a manifest of the place of export, (same as in the coasting trade,) to be verified before the American Consul, if any; if none, before the collector, or other officer having the superintendence of the customs.

Answer. Collectors should be instructed to designate particularly the packages to be sent to the public store from each invoice, for examination. It would be well if it were the surveyor's duty to examine every package exported for drawback.

Question 19th. What is the value of a full cargo of woollen and cotton goods assorted for our market; of silks and linens from Europe; of silks and nankeens from China; of cotton and muslin shawls from Calcutta; of glassware and crates from Europe?

Answer. This question can only be answered by application to the Secretary of the Treasury, or applying at the custom-house.

Question 20th. What number of vessels are employed in the direct trade with England (say American vessels) from the port of New York, and the usual number of seamen in each?

Answer. We refer you to the Secretary of the Treasury; we are unable to answer it.

CASH PAYMENT BILL.

Question 1st. Should there be any reduction of the present credits?

Answer. Yes.

Question 2d. If any, state what. Examine the bill of last session. There are three parts to this bill.

1. The abolition of credits on deposite, for six months, on some articles, and diminishing them on others.

2. New system of drawbacks.

3. The deposite, till payment of duties.

Point out the alterations under each item.

Question 3d. What, in your opinion, will be the effect of such a system as is proposed by this bill on the general commerce of this country?

Question 4th. How will it affect the commerce in the hands of the American merchant?

Answer to 2d, 3d, and 4th questions. A reduction of credits on goods to three and six months, with increased caution in taking the bonds at the custom-house, would have on the general interests of the country a beneficial effect; we believe that it would be productive of much benefit to the Treasury, and likewise to the mercantile concerns of the country, and not injurious to the interests of any class of citizens, not even excepting those who are the immediate objects of the munificence of Government. The reduction of credits would tend greatly to discourage importations on foreign account, and give the command of the American markets to our own citizens, and it would also tend greatly to check speculations.

Question 5th. Can any auction bill be efficient with the present credits? What is, in your opinion, the difference between the expenses of an American merchant resident in New York, who sells $100,000 a year, and a foreign consignor who ships them to an agent in New York, say an auctioneer?

Answer. A duty of ten per cent. on sales at auction would be efficient, without any alteration in credits; but should an alteration be made by reducing the credits, the effect of that act, without the duty on auction sales, would be offering a premium or bounty on the capital of the auctioneer, and thereby add to the existing evil. After carefully estimating the difference in the expenses attending the sale of $100,000 made by an auctioneer for account of a foreign consignor, and the same amount sold by an American merchant at private sale, our opinion is, that the foreign consignor has the advantage over the American merchant from 7½ to 10 per cent.

Question 6th. What is the average difference in the quality of *consigned* and *order* goods? What difference in measurement?

Answer. The difference in quality of goods consigned or ordered for auction, and those ordered by the regular merchant of character, taking the difference of quality and measurement into estimation, a less sum than 7½ to 10 per cent. cannot be named; it is often much more than that.

Question 7th. If you think the bill of last session goes too far, what would you say to the old credits of the year 1790?

West Indies, four months.
Madeira wine, twelve months.
Teas from China, twelve months.
All other, six months.

Answer. As it respects the payment in cash for the greater part of the duties, there exists a great variety of opinions; many are for cash payments, many for reducing the credits, and many for their remaining as they now are. Our opinion is, that cash payments would be inexpedient, as an entire new system in drawbacks and collection of the duties must be adopted, which would create great difficulty, and would be extremely embarrassing to the merchant. By shortening the credits, the present system of collecting might be continued, and the effect would be that Government would lose nothing compared with what they have lost by the long credits now given. It would have the further effect of reducing the general and pernicious system of long credits among merchants, which all practical commercial men admit to be necessary, to place business upon a sure and solid basis.

We see no propriety in making a distinction in credits on goods from different countries. Why should the merchant engaged in the East India trade, who is the overgrown capitalist, have the extended credit of twelve months on his duties, the amount of which on one cargo furnishes nearly a sufficient capital for completing another voyage, before his bonds are payable? His goods imported are generally of the most ready sale, and considered almost a circulating medium; his sales are through the auctioneer, for cash or approved paper, which he anticipates without any difficulty. Madeira wines are mostly imported by our wealthy merchants.

We therefore recommend that the credits on duties be reduced to three and six months from every quarter of the world.

Question 8th. Would a diminution of credits tend to throw too great a proportion of our foreign commerce into the hands of capitalists? Discriminate under the following heads the kind of trade which is carried on by men of small and large capital:

Importations from the East Indies; importations from Europe; importations from the West Indies.

State the average value of a cargo from Canton, of silks, teas, nankeens, china, &c.; from Calcutta, of piece goods, &c.; from East Indies, of mauds of pepper, spices, sugar, coffee, &c.; from West Indies, of rum, sugar, coffee, molasses, pimento, and fruit; from Spanish main, of wood, dye-stuffs, hides, &c.; from Europe, an average cargo from England, from France, from the Straits and Levant, and from other parts of the continent of Europe.

Of the above cargoes, which sell at the shortest credit?

Which branch of the above trade would be most affected by prompt payment of duties?

Which have afforded the greatest and most certain profits?

Which is carried on most by credit in proportion to the amount of importation—European, East or West Indian?

By *credit* is meant not only purchases abroad on credit, but loans or other credit at home.

Answer. In the present state of commerce, and the abundance of money in almost every seaport town of consequence in the country, we believe that the effect of shortening the credit on duties would by no means tend to give large capitalists an extraordinary advantage over those of smaller capital, or more than they now enjoy; and the reason is very obvious: security must be given for the payment of the duties, and upon the same security, the money might with equal facility be realized from the banks or individuals. Those engaged in the East India and China trade are generally considered the greatest capitalists. They would be most affected by shortening the credit on duties, because their credits for duties are longer than on importations from any other part of the globe, and the duties bear a greater proportion to the actual cost of the goods than from any other quarter.

Importations from Europe, especially what little has been done of late on American account, is not confined to large capitalists, and those from the West Indies are mostly on consignment for foreign account; the productions from the latter are sold on the shortest credit.

The other inquiries can only be answered from official documents and records of the custom-house.

AUCTION BILL.

Question 1st. What alterations would be proper in the auction bill, as reported last Winter? Examine them in detail.

Answer. An alteration would be proper requiring auctioneers to pay the same duty on all the private sales as on the public sales which they may effect, as they are now by law compelled to do in the State of New York.

Question 2d. Would you recommend the same duty on domestic as on foreign articles of manufacture?

Answer. It is deemed of great importance that the duty should be the same on domestic as on foreign articles.

Question 3d. Should there be a discrimination in the duty on manufactured goods, and on what are generally called groceries, as sugar, tea, coffee, spirits, wine, and drugs?

Answer. There should be no difference between the duty on groceries and other goods sold at auction.

Question 4th. Amount of auction sales at New York?

Answer. The proportion of goods sold by auction in 1820 was greater than in any previous year. The amount of those sales, owing to the low prices of goods, may be less than in some previous years; it cannot be ascertained till the annual return of the Comptroller of the State is made, in February.

Objections to an increase of Duties.

Question 5th. Importations on foreign account, for 1820, compared with those on American?

Answer. From information and inquiries, which are deemed satisfactory, from two-thirds to three-fourths of the whole quantity of goods imported in 1820 from Europe and the West Indies were imported on foreign account. From England, Scotland, and Ireland, there were imported of dry goods 23,606 packages—

Which were on domestic account -	-	4,932
On foreign account - - -	-	18,674
Total - - - -	-	23,606

OBJECTIONS TO AN INCREASE OF DUTIES ON IMPORTS.

[Communicated to the House, February 2, 1821.]

Mr. FORREST, from the Committee on Agriculture, to whom was referred the memorial of the delegates of the United Agricultural Societies of Prince George, Sussex, Surry, Petersburg, Brunswick, Dinwiddie, and Isle of Wight, having had the same under consideration, made the following report:

The committee consider it a duty which they owe to the object of their institution, to the importance of the subjects referred to in the memorial, to the character of the memorialists themselves, and to the threatened interests of agriculture, to present a full, candid, and impartial statement of the views which they entertain of the policy of increasing the duties established by the present tariff.

Believing, as they do, that the agriculturists, as the most numerous portion of the community, are more deeply interested than any other class in the decision of this question, and that they must necessarily continue to be so for many ages to come, they conceive that no apology will be required if they enter somewhat at length into the investigation of those principles which the policy involves. Nor will such a course be deemed incompatible with the object for which the committee was originally created, which they suppose was not so much to devise and propose plans for the positive encouragement of agriculture, as, by a vigilant exercise of their functions, to guard its political interests from encroachment.

The committee regard the question presented by the proposed tariff as one of the most important that has ever been offered to the consideration of Congress. Important, however, as this question is, when considered in reference to the change which any further restrictions on trade must produce in our foreign relations, it is yet more important when viewed in reference to those which it would effect in the subsisting relations of the several classes of the community; for, even if the favorite though impracticable and useless object of the friends of the restrictive system could be realized—that of raising the prices of all commodities, al-

though it would then no longer be a question as to the degree of intercourse we should maintain with other countries, but there would be no intercourse at all—for commerce never goes in quest of dear commodities—and the sources of wealth, intelligence, and improvement, derivable from an intercourse with the rest of the world, would be entirely destroyed; yet this evil, great as it is, would be inconsiderable in comparison with those which the system would produce on our domestic prosperity and happiness; in other words, its financial would be less injurious than its political consequences.

There are obviously two leading points of view in which this, as well as other restrictive systems, may be considered—its effect to increase or diminish the national wealth, and its tendency to promote independence and happiness. These views, though necessarily, in some degree, blended with each other, are, in many important particulars, distinct. But, before the committee enter into an examination of the system, they will notice briefly some of the arguments which have been employed to recommend it, which they believe have only an incidental and collateral connexion with the subject, but which have been so much relied on by the advocates of the system that they cannot with propriety be overlooked.

Among the most prominent of these is the argument derived from the productive power of manufacturing in comparison with agricultural and commercial industry, and the inducements which the quick returns of the home trade, the relative increase of population in Europe and America, the local advantages we possess, in having at our command all the chief materials for manufacturing, the obstacles which the restrictions other nations oppose to an intercourse with them, and many other propitious circumstances, hold out to the capitalist to embark in manufactures. It will not now be attempted to claim any pre-eminence for agriculture and commerce over manufactures, or for one kind of trade over another. The latest and most judicious speculations on this subject tend to show that if there be any difference at all, it is much less than has been imagined; but it will merely be observed that all those arguments which go to show the favorable circumstances under which manufactures may be commenced, and the disadvantages under which they must be procured from abroad, so far from being auxiliary to the system, tend directly to impeach it; for the question is, not the desirableness of manufactures, but the expediency and legality of the means of promoting them; whether, in order to establish them, we must not part with something still more desirable. Now, all those arguments which go to prove that we can do without the aid of the law, are arguments against the interference of law. If the times and circumstances have a natural tendency to promote the objects desired, why should we seek to obtain them prematurely, and by oppressive means? Such arguments are undoubtedly proper when employed to persuade the capitalist voluntarily to engage in manufactures; but they are absolutely preposterous when used to induce the

Government to assist him, by taxing the rest of the community.

Another argument has been founded on the necessity or propriety of giving relief to those manufacturers who were induced, by the state of things growing out of the late war and the measures that preceded it, to vest their capital in manufactures, and who, it is alleged, have suffered since the return of peace for want of sufficient protection. This claim is not considered as well founded, because it is derived from the asseverations of the manufacturers themselves that those persons were generally compelled, in consequence of their heavy losses, to sell out their establishments, at a considerable sacrifice, so that their present proprietors must now hold them under extremely advantageous circumstances, and the proposed relief would not reach its intended objects. But, independently of this, the principle itself is too capacious to be admissible. It amounts to this: the Government is bound to indemnify its citizens for all losses that can be remotely connected with its necessary acts, though they have been produced chiefly by their own voluntary agency. Such a principle would furnish just as good a claim for relief to the farmer and merchant as to the manufacturer. The diminished price of agricultural produce during the war would be as good a reason for relieving the agriculturist, as the diminished price of manufactured produce on the return of peace would be for relieving the manufacturer. Even, therefore, if it could be made to appear that an improvident spirit of speculation had no share in producing the distress of the manufacturers, that the other classes of the community did not equally participate in them, and that relief would reach the true sufferers, it would be inexpedient to grant it, to say nothing at this time of the right of the Government thus to relieve one class by taking the means from another.

An argument which is not deemed by the committee as material in the investigation of this question, but which has been perhaps more universally relied on than almost any other, is this: that it is admitted that the system of free trade would be the best, provided other nations would pursue it; but it is said, if they will not buy of us, so neither should we buy of them, but should meet regulation by regulation, restriction by restriction. It is difficult to say whether this argument is addressed to our interest or to our honor, or whether it is addressed to either; for it is neither proposed, by the adoption of the restrictive system; on our part, to compel foreign nations to abandon it, nor is it proposed to retaliate their injuries, with a view of punishing them for their alleged offence. Indeed, so far from its being contemplated by the manufacturers to coerce other nations to relinquish their restrictions, it can scarcely be doubted that such an event would occasion great regret, because it would take away one of the principal arguments on which they have relied for the adoption of their policy, whilst other considerations which recommend it to them would remain. But in whatever the advice "not to buy of foreigners unless they will buy of us" may have originated, it is evidently worse than useless. How is it pos-

sible that we should buy of them unless they buy of us? The very word "buy," implies that something is given in exchange for that which is received; and what is giving in exchange but "buying?" That foreigners do not admit our products on the same terms that we admit theirs, does not render it less true, that in our intercourse with them there is a complete exchange of equivalents. Undoubtedly the foreign system is injurious to us, and it is certainly not less so to themselves. Every retaliatory measure on either side injures both, unless it has the effect of making the other party recede, and even then the injury suffered by the retaliating party is not necessarily counterbalanced by the good received; but to adopt restrictions with any other view than to force other nations to abandon them, is a course for which no apology can be offered. As long as capital continues to be employed in the foreign trade, it can only be because it is more profitably employed than it could be if it were withdrawn. It would be very unwise, because a portion of our capital is not so advantageously employed as it might be under possible circumstances, to make it less so than it is; because we cannot make things better, to make them worse. Besides, the refusal of foreigners to receive our raw produce is to the injury of the agriculturist, not of the manufacturer. The object of the system, therefore, should be to redress the grievances of the former, not those of the latter. But the agriculturist declares that he does not ask the assistance of the Government; that all he requires is to be let alone; and that it is absolutely unjust to make an actual grievance the pretext for imposing on him additional burdens. There appears to be less excuse for this system on the score of honor than on that of interest; yet the appeal to honor is one of the favorite topics of the friends of restriction. National honor is too often made to usurp the empire of reason and justice, and to decide controversies where it has no jurisdiction; and on no occasion have its just prerogatives been more prostituted and abused than when it has been made to extend over the province of trade and commerce, which, though they should always be guided by individual honor, and indeed can only be sustained by a strict adherence to its principles, renounce all other authority but that of interest in questions of their extent or direction. When the honor of the nation is really involved, the agriculturists will be among the last to abandon it. National, like individual honor, is not averse to interest, but is identified with it. National, like individual honor, is reputation, and reputation is power; it is safety in peace and strength in war. But when the honor of an individual or a nation is assailed, it is by the violation of some indisputable right which authorizes the assailed party to demand redress, and if it is not rendered to punish the assailant. But can it be pretended that any indisputable right of this nation would be violated by the refusal of foreigners to receive our surplus produce? Is it not the undoubted right of every nation to adopt whatever municipal regulations it believes necessary for its own internal administration? As well might it

Objections to an increase of Duties.

be said that an individual would compromise his honor by agreeing to purchase an article of his neighbor, because this neighbor refused to receive that which he produced in return, but required him first to commute it into money. Honor has nothing to do with this matter; it is regulated, as it ought to be, solely by convenience. But it must be again repeated that it is incorrect, in point of fact, to say that foreigners do not purchase of us to the same extent that we purchase of them, because it is impossible. "There can be no buying without an equal selling." If we have had occasionally to pay them a balance in money, it is no more than they have often had to do to us; and if it always happened that we had to pay some nations a balance in money, it would not alter the case; for, before we can purchase the products of any nation with money, we must previously have purchased that money of other nations with our products. Our most invaluable trade with the East Indies is entirely carried on with money.

Another argument has been founded on the encouragement which it is alleged has been given by Congress to agriculture and commerce, and which, it is urged, affords an equitable claim for encouragement to manufactures. It will hardly be asserted that agriculture and commerce have received greater aids from Government than manufactures. With respect to agriculture, it is not admitted that Government has rendered it any service whatever; and it is moreover believed that it cannot render it any service, unless it be to remove the restrictions which oppress it. With regard to commerce, it is alleged that it has been encouraged in two ways—by a navy, and by a system of commercial regulations. It is apprehended that the true and legitimate purpose of a navy is the national defence; but if the navy can be considered, in any degree, as intended to protect commerce, it is evidently intended to protect it, not against competition, but against violence; and there can be no doubt that the navy, and the army too, would be employed to protect manufactures, if they were assailed by violence. Even in this point of view, it is not believed to be the true policy of this nation to create an immense overgrown navy for the protection of our commerce in distant seas, but to confine it to such limits, when it shall be deemed to have attained them, as is compatible with the national defence. Whether those regulations and acts were intended to encourage the commerce and navigation of the country involve a departure from the maxims of letting things alone, and of not taxing one class for the support of another, the committee are not called on now to decide; but, passing over the argument for the navigation laws, that they were intended to be subservient to national defence, by creating a nursery for our seamen, and regarding them purely as commercial regulations, the encouragement they are designed to afford to commerce and navigation differs, both in nature and degree, from that which has been already given, and which it is proposed still further to extend to manufactures. A nation adopting a restrictive system, with a view of coercing another nation to abandon it, is very differ-

ent from its adopting it as a permanent part of its policy, under the delusive idea of promoting national wealth and independence. It proposes only to forego present for the sake of future and greater advantages. Undoubtedly, even in this case, it should be certain that the means selected will insure success; that success will pay for the sacrifices made to obtain it; and that it can be obtained in no better way. How far the navigation laws will fulfil these conditions, time will fully decide.

It has also been urged, that when a nation has peculiar advantages for particular manufactures, and is ripe for them in every respect but that of skill, the Government should afford such protection as will procure that skill. The propriety of the proposed tariff does not depend on the truth of this position; for, in the production of many of the articles on which it is proposed to increase the duties, we already equal other nations in skill, and, in others, the duties are more than sufficient to obtain it. But, it is asked, where is the propriety of the distinction which would make the nation pay for a deficiency in skill more than in any thing else? The only ground on which any one would think of justifying the policy which would make either an individual or a nation the purchaser of this skill, or of any other requisite, would be, that the temporary loss occasioned by the purchase would be repaid when it was completely acquired. But does this prove that the nation should be the purchaser? Is it not more consistent with justice that the capitalist, who is to derive the benefit of the acquisition, should make the sacrifices necessary to obtain it? If his capital is insufficient, the nation might as well be expected to supply that, as to supply the skill it employs.

The foregoing are some of the principal arguments which have been resorted to in support of the manufacturing system, and which the committee think have little to do with the real merits of the question. It is not a complete enumeration of all of that description, and it is hoped that no excuse is necessary for not attempting to achieve such an enumeration. They therefore approach, with satisfaction, what they consider as the true question involved in the proposed alteration of the tariff; namely, will the national wealth be augmented or diminished; and, if it will be diminished, are there any advantages which will compensate for the sacrifice? And they will undertake to show, not only that the necessary effect of such an alteration is to diminish, both immediately and ultimately, the national wealth, but that, so far from there being any compensatory circumstances, it is even more objectionable in other points of view than as a question of loss or gain; and that the distribution of the wealth of the nation which it will effect will be more injurious than the diminution.

The committee have endeavored to divest the subject of all extraneous considerations, with a view of giving to their arguments a greater degree of precision; and they conceive that, if the positions they have assumed can be clearly established, by a fair deduction from the most indisputable principles, they will save themselves the necessity

Objections to an increase of Duties.

of replying in detail to a multiplicity of irrelevant arguments which have been employed in defence of the restrictive system.

The first view of the subject, that which relates to the national wealth, presents a question strictly of political economy. The second, that connected with our independence and happiness, is partly a question of political economy, and partly one of general policy. The committee will not, at the expense of precision and force, encumber their arguments with numerous statistical facts and arithmetical calculations. Such calculations often have a tendency to mislead instead of to instruct; and the facts which are best established have, after all, to be explained by the application of general principles. It is pre-eminently the case in the controversy between the manufacturers and their opponents, that the *data* which they have respectively relied on for the support of their opinions have always been considered, by the opposite party, either as proving nothing, or as proving directly the reverse of what was intended. This can only be accounted for by the supposition, that the general principles of one or the other party, which they apply to the explanation of these *data*, are erroneous. It will be attempted to show that the principles on which the restrictive system is opposed are not liable to this charge; and that the soundest and most incontrovertible maxims of political economy—maxims derived from the impartial observation of facts, from accurate analysis, and from long and diversified experience—warrant this opposition in its greatest extent. They are aware that those who appeal to general principles render themselves liable to the charge of theory, by those who lay claim to exclusive practical knowledge; and, as there has been a good deal of unmeaning declamation against the opponents of the manufacturing system on this common-place, they will very briefly examine its justice. Theory is not the opposite of experience, for it may be strictly deduced from experience. It is nothing more than a system of general rules, founded on the observation of particular facts, or it is such a system founded on hypothesis. In the one case it is true—in the other it is generally false. But this character of truth or falsehood is not peculiar to theory; it belongs equally to practice. Practice may be true or false; that is, it may be sound or unsound, good or bad; but all good practice must be founded on true theory. It is not enough, then, to say that an opinion or a system is a theory; it must be proved that it is a false theory; that it is not the rigorous result of an attentive examination of facts. And, in attempting to prove it, it will not suffice to oppose to it a single repugnant fact or doubtful experiment, or even many such facts and experiments, without showing in what respects they are incompatible with the theory—where the error lies—in what its falsehood consists. The committee must, however, be permitted to observe, that the charge of theory comes with but little propriety from the manufacturers. Their notions of a home market, balance of trade, national industry, and their doctrines generally, involve theories which are not only not

founded in facts, or even plausible hypothesis, but are in direct opposition to all experience. But to come at once to the subject.

The first position that it will be attempted to prove is, that the necessary effect of an increase of duties is to diminish, both immediately and ultimately, the amount of national wealth. The loss, however, of the nation, the loss of those who pay the duties, and the gain of those who receive them, do not always correspond, but vary with particular circumstances. In what manner this loss and gain are distributed in society will be best illustrated by an example. If, for instance, a community of four persons were engaged in an occupation which enabled them to realize six per cent. on equal capitals, and three of them were to give the fourth one per cent., or one-third of one per cent. each, to enable him to carry on an employment in which, unassisted, he could only make five per cent., it is evident that the loss of the contributors would be one per cent., and that it would be exactly the loss of the community, whilst the gain of the receiver would be nothing; and unless that part of his profits which he received from the others was as productively employed as it was by them, he might be a loser, and thus still further augment the loss of the community. But this is a case that would not be apt to occur. The fourth individual must have something more than *six* per cent., which he already made, to induce him to abandon his old occupation, and pursue a new one—say seven per cent. In this case, the others would have to pay his two-thirds of one per cent. each. It is obvious, now, that the loss of the contributors would be two per cent., that the gain of the receiver would be one per cent., and that *it* would correspond with the loss of the community, which would also be one per cent., or the difference between the productive value of his old and new employment. If this bounty were given to induce an individual to continue an occupation in which he was already engaged, then, although the contributor would lose all he paid, and the receiver would gain it, the community would lose nothing, as there would only be a transfer of wealth from one to another. This, however, would not be the case with a manufacture thus continued by a bounty. There would be an immediate loss, occasioned by the increased cost of consumption; nor would it be possible to make one employment so much more profitable than another, without its attracting capital from that other; and this would be the source of innumerable other losses, hereafter to be noticed. In the case that has been stated, it is clear that the loss of the contributors is exactly what they pay; the gain of the receiver is their loss, less the difference between the productive value of his old and new employment, and the loss of the community is precisely this difference. In manufactures, such would be the operation of a duty that was prohibitory; a duty that was merely protective would permit a portion of the commodities consumed to be bought of foreigners, and thus a part of it would go into the treasury. This would not vary the proportion of the loss and gain of the contributors and receivers, but would, in some degree, increase the loss of the community, as composed of both, as this portion of the duty would be less productively employed by the Government than it would have been had it remained in the hands of either of the parties. This does not prove that prohibitory are better than protecting duties. There are other consequences which make duties injurious in proportion to their amount. All these observations may be applied (*mutatis mutandis*) to the consumers, the manufacturers, and the nation, under the protecting-duty system. Two descriptions of persons would derive the benefit; a few who continue their old employment, and a great many who engage in new ones. In both cases, the loss of the consumer is what he pays, and is unredeemed by any circumstances whatever. In the first case, the loss of the nation arises from the increased cost of consumption; in the second, it arises from this cause, and the diminished productive value of the new employments of society. In the first case, the gain of the manufacturer is the loss of the consumer, less the increased cost of his own consumption; in the second, it is this loss diminished by the same cause, and the diminished productive value of his labor. But, besides these direct losses, there are others indirect and collateral, which are, however, not less inevitable; losses which affect the consumers, and, in some degree, ultimately reach the manufacturers themselves.

Whenever one employment becomes more profitable than another, capital will desert the less for the more profitable. Every such change, however, is attended with the loss, generally, of the whole of the fixed, and a portion of the circulating, capital of the deserted occupation. But it is easy to perceive that a duty on a single article may occasion the loss of several such capitals. If, for example, by a duty on foreign boots and shoes, we prevent a certain quantity from being brought into the country, we immediately destroy the market for the commodities which were given in exchange for them; and if this is a manufactured article, we then destroy the market for the agricultural product, which constitutes its basis; so that the loss falls ultimately on agriculture. Now, if the agriculturists who are thus thrown out of employment become boot and shoemakers, there would be the loss of only one capital; but if, as is more probable, they should apply themselves to some other branch of agricultural industry, as being more analogous to their recent occupation, and, for the same reason, the additional boots and shoes required were made by labor and capital taken from the saddle and harness business, there would be the loss of two capitals. It is not difficult to perceive that the loss might be extended to a greater number. Perhaps it may be said that this loss would be repaired by the superior profits of the new employment; but this would not be the case. The new employments, except those which were the objects of the bounty, would be less profitable than the old ones. If they were equally so, there would still be the loss of the whole of the fixed capital, which would be entirely sunk. The committee have already noticed that cause of loss

which arises from a diminution of skill, and the other facilities of production. This great and inevitable source of loss is embraced in what has been said of the diminished productive powers of the new employments of the community. They have also noticed that source of loss which arises from the unproductive employment of that portion of the duty which is paid into the treasury, and which, if it remained in the hands of individuals, would be devoted to reproduction, and augment the national wealth. As, however, we must have revenue, this loss is only to be objected to when duties are excessive. But there is another source of loss in the constant tendency of the system to diminish production, and, of course, accumulation. The increased cost of consumption, however, which is one of the means by which this effect is produced, will affect chiefly the laboring classes and the raisers of raw produce. Every thing on which the wages of labor are expended, except the products of agriculture, will rise in price; but labor itself cannot rise, and may fall, for the demand for labor created by the new employments will be more than supplied by that thrown out of the old ones; and thus the comforts of the laborer, who will have to purchase dearer articles with smaller means, will be materially impaired. It is thought, too, that the value of money must be proportionally higher in a country which pursues this system; and this is another circumstance which must injuriously affect the wages of labor. In the infancy of manufactures, too, the coarser kinds being first produced, the tax is chiefly borne by the poor who consume them. This evil is increased, too, by the manner in which the duties are adjusted on the finer and coarser manufactures; for, in the present, as well as in the proposed tariff, the duties are much higher on the latter than on the former. On coarse and on fine cottons, for example, there is a difference of not less than twenty-three or twenty-five per cent. in favor of the latter; on common glass tumblers, and on cut glass tumblers and decanters, a difference of from 27 to 39 per cent. in favor of the cut glass. The duty on molasses and on brown sugar, if the proposed tariff is adopted, will be about 100 per cent. on the cost; on salt 120 per cent., and on many other articles, consumed chiefly by the poor, the duties will be oppressively heavy. It has been estimated, by a very intelligent writer, that the duties which would be paid under this new tariff, by the great body of the people, would not average less than 75 per cent. on articles of necessity; whilst the duties on articles of luxury, used by the rich, would not amount to more than 30 per cent. To tax the poor for the benefit of the poor would be bad enough; but to tax them for the benefit of the rich is intolerable. This oppressive operation of the system on the poorer and laboring class is one of its least pleasing effects, and, when we consider their relative number to the capitalists, it is one of the most alarming; for, independently of its political consequences, nothing can be more unfavorable to accumulation than inequality of wealth. There is always proportionally less of the income of the wealthy devoted to reproduction, because there is more of it expended on factitious wants; on those luxuries which have, besides the pernicious effect of producing imitation on the part of the poor, and of bringing in their train the extravagant expenditure of the Government, which, it is well known, when it once begins, never stops.

Diminished consumption must necessarily diminish production; but it is diminished in another way, and that is by the decreased price of agricultural produce. This effect of the system is inevitable; yet, strange to tell, the increased price of agricultural produce has been one of those delusive promises made use of to recommend it; and, still stranger to tell, one that a great many have believed in. The home market has been talked of, and its mysterious virtues have been highly extolled, though no one has shown the fashion of operating of this wonder-working agent. The following considerations, it is believed, will show how completely fallacious are the expectations of any benefit from such a source. If the price of commodities is regulated by the relations of supply and demand, (and their market price undoubtedly is,) then, provided the number of consumers in the country remain the same after the adoption of the system as before, inasmuch as we shall be deprived of the foreign market to the same extent that we cease to purchase, (for foreigners cannot buy of us unless we buy of them,) the relation of the supply to the demand must be increased; consequently, there can be no rise of price, but there must be a fall. But we are told that foreigners are to be attracted hither by this system. Although it can scarcely be imagined, in any event, that as many would be attracted hither as we supply abroad, let us admit that this might be the case; then the relation of supply and demand would be unaltered, and consequently prices cannot rise, but must remain stationary. The only conceivable mode by which the relation of supply and demand could be altered, would be by a portion of the persons who were employed in agriculture leaving it to engage in manufactures. It might readily be conceded that, if the same quantity of manufactures could be consumed in the country after the adoption of the system as was consumed before, as, from diminished skill, a greater number of hands would be required to produce them, the consumers of agricultural produce would be multiplied; but we have already seen that this could not be the case, because the cost of consumption would be vastly increased, and the means diminished. But the committee deny, distinctly, that any such change in the relation of supply and demand could be produced by an increase of duties; or, if it could, that those duties could have the effect to raise the price of one kind of agricultural produce but at the expense of another, or to raise the price of any kind permanently at all. Suppose, for instance, a duty is laid on the raw cotton of other countries; it is evident that, if it has the effect to diminish the quantity imported, it must destroy the market for the commodities with which it was purchased. Let us admit that its immediate effect would be

to enhance the price of raw and of manufactured cotton, (and if it would, it must be enhanced to all its consumers; to the manufacturer himself, so far as he is a consumer, and even to the planter, who is, however, made to pay back on the fabric what the manufacturer advanced on the raw article, the market price of commodities is increased by increased demand or diminished supply; their natural price can only be increased in consequence of its becoming necessary to bestow on them an additional quantity of labor. Now, it is evident that, in a country where lands of the first quality are not all in cultivation, the additional quantity required to satisfy the demand would be produced almost immediately, and that the price could not be permanently increased; and, if it were increased, it must be observed, that it would be at the expense of that agricultural product which has been displaced. It would be produced, too, without the necessity of resorting to poorer lands, so that the cost of production remaining the same, there would be no increase of its natural price. Indeed, is it not obvious that, if labor is made to leave agriculture for manufactures, the poorest lands will be deserted first, and that the cost of production, therefore, instead of being increased, would be lessened? This, perhaps, might be an advantage, provided the labor and capital taken from agriculture were, independently of the bounties they receive, as productively employed as they were before; but this, it has already been shown, would not be the case. Even if the products of that labor and capital, in consequence of the bounties paid on them, and the increased cost of consumption, had a greater exchangeable value, it is not the exchangeable value of the products of a country which constitutes its wealth, but their quantity and utility. But, even if it were admitted that poorer lands would have to be resorted to in order to produce the additional supply, it is maintained that, with respect to those commodities that go abroad in the great marts of the world, and there come into competition with similar commodities of other countries, it is not the cost of production here, but in that country where they are produced with the greatest quantity of labor, that regulates their natural price. It will no doubt be said, if such is the effect of competition to reduce the price of agricultural products, why will it not reduce the price of manufactured produce? For this obvious reason: that the field of production is limited in the one, and is unlimited in the other; that the cost of production cannot be increased in the one, and may be vastly increased in the other. As the expectation that domestic manufactures will be reduced, by competition, to an equality of price with foreign manufactures, has been held out to allay our apprehensions of this system, it may not be improper to examine on what it is founded. It is denied that competition can produce a permanent diminution of price. It may undoubtedly reduce the market price for a time, but it cannot reduce the natural price; and the former cannot permanently remain below the latter. Competition may produce a glut in the market, and thus bring prices so low

APPENDIX.

Objections to an increase of Duties.

as not to repay the expense of production; but it is evident that this state of things must be temporary; there must be some profit, or the business cannot be carried on. It is the increased facility in producing an article which alone can diminish the price. Domestic will never be sold lower than foreign manufactures until we equal foreigners in skill, and in all those circumstances which enter into the cost of production. When we equal them in these respects, (as we probably will after a long series of years,) we may, indeed, then undersell them, by the difference in the cost of transportation. But what shall we gain by this? It will not even pay for the destruction of the capital employed in the transportation; never will it compensate for that waste of income and of capital, and the other incalculable losses which will ensue from the system. The whole of this reasoning will doubtless be controverted by the declaration of the fact that cotton goods are now lower in this country than they were before the present tariff was adopted. Here, as in many instances, we agree in the fact, but differ in the principles by which it must be explained. The manufacturers ascribe it to competition; their opponents ascribe it to the fall in the price of the raw material and of labor, to greater facility in production, and to the general stagnation of trade; and this reasoning is corroborated by the fact that the fall in this article has been general all over the world. Still, the ratio of the fall in this country and in England being about the same, and the duty nearly or quite prohibitory, English cottons can not be imported. If the duty was taken off, or even considerably diminished, we should undoubtedly see that coarse cottons would be still lower than they are at this time. As to the assertion that the price of raw cotton in this country is kept up one or two cents higher in consequence of the competition of the American with the English manufacturers, it is totally gratuitous. It is utterly useless to talk of underselling foreigners until we can produce the article at less cost; the thing is impossible. Nor is it desirable that we should ever undersell foreign manufacturers; for, in order to do so, we must not only equal them in skill, machinery, ingenuity, industry, &c., but we must equal them in human degradation and wretchedness. We must drive our laborers from the fields, from the beauties and bounties of nature, to those dismal and demoralizing abodes, where they sink into hopeless stupidity and penury, or where want goads ingenuity to reluctant exertion for a scanty subsistence, and where the health and morals frequently become victims to hard and untimely labor, and the imperious laws of poverty and hunger.

Another source of loss is in the tendency of this system to drive commercial capital abroad, and this it will much more probably do than attract manufacturing capital hither, as well from the superior facility of its removal, as from the distrust which the system is calculated to produce in the equity of the Government and stability of its policy; to which, perhaps, may be added the inducements afforded by the vast fields of industry which

the enlightened policy of other nations will probably, at no very distant period, open to commercial enterprise. It is believed that the prevalence of sound principles of political economy, and the light of returning reason, have produced a disposition in all the commercial nations of the world to restore the system of free trade, and that they are only prevented from returning to it at once by the consideration that the sudden abandonment of a system so interwoven with all the interests of society must necessarily be productive of great immediate mischief; a consideration which should teach us the propriety of serious deliberation before we adopt it—the more particularly so, as the expediency of making it permanent is made to depend on the contingency of other nations continuing it. A still more alarming effect of this system will be to drive population and capital from one State to another. The poorer agriculturists of the Atlantic States will be compelled, by the increased cost of consumption, and the diminished price of produce, to go the West in search of more fertile lands; whilst capitalists will go to those States where manufactures are best established and most flourish. And shall we submit to this unlawful effect of this system without calling in question the policy which produces it? The committee are disposed to do more—to call in question the authority and power of the General Government to enforce a system which can thus aggrandize one State and ruin another.

A still further source of loss is in the effect of this system to drive capital from one kind of manufactures to another. The manufactures that languish will be deserted for those that flourish, or they must be continually bolstered up by new protection. Indeed, even the manufactures that are best established must be sustained in this way, if, as is very possible, by the invention of new machinery, or by any other means which will diminish the cost of production, foreigners can come again into the market, and, in spite of the duties, undersell the American manufacturer. This is one of the most vexatious effects of the system. It will never be done with, but new exactions will be perpetually made.

It has been contended that the arguments which go to show the impropriety of extending manufactures are merely theoretical, and that they are refuted by experience. It is said that England has pursued the restrictive system; that England is wealthy and prosperous; and, therefore, that the tendency of the system is to promote wealth and prosperity. The committee cannot, however, help thinking that it is rather an unfortunate specimen of practical reasoning, when an effect is gratuitously assigned to a cause without any attempt to show their connexion, and where many other causes are operating better calculated to produce the effect. England is wealthy and powerful; but she is not prosperous in consequence of this system, but in spite of it. She is wealthy and powerful in consequence of the indomitable energies of her genius, her enterprise, and her comparatively free institutions. The English system is not the result of foresight, as has been im-

Objections to an increase of Duties.

agined; and if it were, it is pretty well understood by what kind of foresight the affairs of nations are generally governed. It is the result of compromise between the avarice of individuals and the needy ambition of the Government. The privileged orders of that country have always been enabled to make successful encroachments on the rights of the people, by bribing the cupidity of the Government with a share of the spoil. This is the kind of foresight which has produced the British system—that system which is now held up for our admiration and imitation. But experience, as well as theory, contradicts the conclusions in favor of restriction. The success of the Dutch policy refutes the idea that restrictions have produced the grandeur of Britain. The following judicious remarks, extracted from an excellent treatise on this subject, show the prosperity which flows from an opposite policy:

"Notwithstanding the immense losses which the Dutch nation sustained for upwards of twenty years, by British captures, French exactions, and the almost entire prostration of commerce, yet their trade, and with it their national importance, appear to have become equal, or nearly equal, to what they were before the war of 1793. Their capital city, Amsterdam, has again become the chief mart of Europe. If the policy of any of the European nations is proper to be imitated by the United States, why is not the example of the United Provinces, as regards their fiscal concerns, as worthy of imitation as that of England? At least, seeing that in Holland her citizens have, for the most part, been left to themselves in the direction of their industry, ought we not to pause before we decide that an opposite system will promote and extend the prosperity of our citizens? How little the Dutch commercial policy has been directed by the protecting system may appear by the low duties on the following articles, most of which come in competition with their own produce and manufactures, viz:

Arms, fire - - -	10 per cent.
Baskets - - -	15 per cent.
Butter - - -	one-half cent per lb.
Books, bound - -	5 per cent.
unbound	3 per cent.
Bristles and brushes -	10 per cent.
Blankets - - -	10 per cent.
Cheese, foreign - -	80 cents per 100 lbs.
Cordage - - -	2 dols. per 100 lbs.
Carriages, new - -	10 per cent.
Clocks - - -	10 per cent.
Copper manufactures	10 per cent.
Candles, tallow -	2½ cents per pound.
Clothes, ready made -	10 per cent.
Cotton - - -	16 cents per 100 lbs.
Cotton manufactures	13 flor. per 100 lbs.
about - -	2 to 3 cents per yd.
Cloths, woollen, and other manufactures, wool and worsted - -	8 per cent.
Linens, unbleached -	2 per cent.
bleached	4 per cent.
Sail cloth - -	2 per cent.

Sugar, raw or clayed -	12 cents per 100 lbs.
refined - - -	4 cents per lb.
Sealing wax - - -	10 per cent.
Spirits pay no duty, but an excise, which for common proof (probably our 3d proof) is - - -	28 cents per gal.
Spirits, highest proof -	42 cents per gal.
Wine of all kinds - -	16 cents per gal.
Tobacco, manufact'd snuffs, &c. - - - -	8 per cent.
Toys, turnery, manufactures of wood and leather, necklaces, lookingglasses, trunks, snuff, and tobacco boxes, fans, with a great variety of similar articles - - -	6 per cent.

Foreign vessels.

Teas, Bohea and Congou	$3 20 per 100 lbs.
Other - - -	6 40 per 100 lbs.

Dutch vessels.

Teas, Bohea and Congou	$1 00 per 100 lbs.
Other - - -	2 00 per 100 lbs.

"This extract is from the tariff of Dutch duties for the year 1816, every article of which, with very few exceptions, is rated about in proportion to those quoted above. Most of them, as is well known, are manufactured or produced in Holland, especially butter and cheese, of which the amount of exports, some years since, was, to the best of my recollection, about three millions sterling. Their sugar refineries are only protected by a duty of four cents a pound, yet Ricardo affirms that in his time, (about forty years since,) there were one hundred refineries, which manufactured one hundred thousand hogsheads of sugar. Tobacco is very extensively manufactured in Holland. Gin, as every one knows, is one of their great staples. This wise nation seems to have thought that goodness of quality and cheapness of price were surer foundations for national industry to rest on than protecting duties."

The invariable tendency of low duties to increase consumption, and, of course, production, is another argument from experience. Both in England and France this effect has frequently been observed at various epochs of their history. The following statement, extracted from a British journal, will suffice to place this subject in a strong point of view: "In 1744 the East India Company's sales of teas amounted to about six hundred thousand pounds annually, producing a revenue of about £140,000 sterling. Early in 1745 the tea duties were greatly reduced, and in 1746 the sales amounted to two million pounds, and the revenue to £228,000. In 1748, however, the duties were again increased, and fluctuated between that epoch and 1784 from 64 to 119 per cent. In the last mentioned year, however, the Government, having in vain tried every other means to prevent the smuggling and adulteration of tea, reduced the duty from 119 to 12½ per cent.; and the revenue, instead of falling off in the propor-

Objections to an increase of Duties.

tion of one to ten, owing to the increased consumption only declined in proportion of one to three." Similar experiments, with regard to wine and coffee, give the same results. The reason is obvious: every diminution of a duty on an article brings it within the range of consumption of some who could not afford to consume it before, while every increase has a contrary effect. To adjust the duties, generally, so as to produce the greatest possible revenue, is a matter which requires great skill and experience. Although we have made no such decisive experiments as the British, (for the effect of the imposition and repeal of the double duties, owing to the period when they operated, proves nothing,) there is still reason to believe that the operation of the present duties, on many articles, has been to diminish consumption and revenue. It is difficult to make the proper allowances for the effect of the rapid increase of population in this country; but the fact that revenue has not increased in the same ratio with the duties and population is considered as decisive proof that the duties on many important articles must be too high. Indeed it is generally admitted, by the most intelligent and practical men, that they are so.

Now, the general principles from which the committee have reasoned are either true or false. If they are false, it will be easy to show wherein the fallacy lies. If they are true, it will be necessary to show that there is something peculiar in the situation of the United States which makes an exception to their general operation. If there is nothing peculiar in our situation, then these principles must stand immovable. The most extraordinary argument that has been used to justify the system is the great and universal distresses of the country. But in this there is nothing peculiar; it is almost universal. But even if it were true that we are the only people in this state of distress, it would remain to be proved that this system furnishes the remedy for the disease. So far from this being the case, it is believed to be one of its causes. Undoubtedly, a great proportion of our distress may be ascribed to the cessation of those convulsions in Europe, which, throwing a vast deal of the trade of the world into our hands, enabled us to reach an extraordinary pitch of prosperity in a short time. But it should not, therefore, be supposed that there have been no internal causes of this distress. To say nothing of the contributions levied on the nation, by funding and banking, the restrictions which preceded the war, the war itself, though a just and necessary measure, and the subsequent prosecution of the restrictive system, had a share in producing the general distress. The revenue from the imposts gives us some idea of the tax which the system imposes on us; but we cannot form an adequate idea of it, unless we could ascertain the quantity of domestic manufactures consumed in the country, and the average of the duties paid on them. There are no means by which this can be ascertained with precision, but we may form a rough estimate of it from a few items. Supposing there are forty or fifty millions of yards of domestic cottons consumed in the United States annually, the consumers may be supposed to pay on them at least $2,000,000. As much more is probably paid on woollens, (and it is probably not an exaggeration to say that the tax paid on domestic articles, which goes to the manufacturers, is fully equal to one-half of the average duties on imports;) this is the direct loss; to which must be added the indirect and collateral losses that it has been attempted to be shown result from the system. When we superadd this to the other causes that have been indicated, can our distresses any longer present a mystery? And is it not more natural to ascribe them to these obvious, undeniable, and constantly operating causes, than to look for those causes in futurity? Is it not reversing the usual order of things to attempt to explain a past or existing effect, by imputing it to what has not been done, instead of what has been done? Is it not contrary to reason to tell us that the remedy for evils which have arisen from taxation is further taxation? It is much more rational to remedy the evil by removing the cause. This we can certainly do, partially, if not wholly. We can remove some, if not all of the causes. We can gradually get rid of all those burdens which have had so great a share in producing the present calamitous state of things. This is all that we can do; the rest must be left to time. If it be true that the duties on importations have diminished consumption, they must have had the same effect on production; and their diminution would increase both. In the present depressed price of all the great staples of agriculture, what can be so likely to relieve the agriculturist as to open a market for his produce? And what will be so apt to do this as to increase the demand for them, by diminishing the prices of the commodities that are exchanged for them? It is said that nations now produce these staple of agriculture themselves, and would not take them from us. To a certain extent they do; and this has been occasioned partly by our own policy, as in the instance of the island of Madeira, which, in consequence of our excluding her wines by heavy duties, procures the corn she once bought of us from other countries. But how is it that nations now make their own breadstuffs? In England, for example, they have resorted to their fourth and fifth rates of land. Now, would not any circumstance which would increase the demand for those articles which they produced with greater facility than corn be an inducement to withdraw capital from the raising of the latter to apply it to the former? This reasoning will apply to every country. Open a market for their products; they will then make that which they make at least cost, and purchase with it, of other countries, what they can only make at a greater cost. If it be said that a relaxation on the part of one nation will not, perhaps, produce a correspondent relaxation on the part of another, it will still be beneficial, unless by continuing restriction you can coerce other nations to abandon it—the only pretext, as has been already said, under which the countervailing policy can claim even plausibility. As long as the absurd doctrine prevails that it is the interest of a nation to countervail

Objections to an increase of Duties.

every restriction of another nation, there never can be a relaxation, or a return to the free system ; the warfare of nations will be interminable. The truth is, if restriction on the part of one country injures another, to retaliate makes it worse, unless it drives the other from its policy. The most probable way of producing an abandonment of the restrictive system by other nations is to tempt them by relaxation ; if it does not produce reciprocity, it at least benefits both, as retaliation injures both. It is evident that there has been a great change in public opinion throughout the whole civilized world, in favor of freedom of commerce; and, though Governments are always the last to abandon antiquated errors, sentiments favorable to free trade have been avowed even by them, and they have not been altogether unaccompanied by acts. It is not to be expected that countries like England, which have pursued the restrictive system so long, could get rid of it but very gradually. She has, however, shown some wish to do this, by the abandonment of some of her restrictions on her trade with Sweden and Norway ; and it is understood that both France and herself have, even before our navigation acts, manifested a willingness to put our trade with them on a more favorable footing. In Spain, the Cortes have (unwisely, indeed,) imitated England in their corn law and other restrictive measures ; but, in general, their regulations are more favorable to trade than they were under the old Government. The monopolies on tobacco, salt, quicksilver, lead, powder, sulphur, &c., have been abolished ; the first allowed to be imported, and the others exported at moderate duties. Prior to the revolution, the importation of tobacco was prohibited ; the King had the monopoly, and sold it at three dollars and seventy cents per pound. By the new tariff, after March next it will be charged with a duty of only thirty-five maravedis, about eight and a quarter cents per pound, which will enable the people of Spain to procure it very cheap, and thus occasion a large demand for it. They have abolished the Cinco Gremios and Philippine companies, on the ground that their privileges were incompatible with free government, and have, with some modifications, re-established the tariff of 1816, which was the first evidence of liberal policy that Spain ever gave.

But if we cannot, consistently with our interests, begin the system of relaxation, let us at all events refrain from further restrictions, which may tempt all other nations to retaliate, as they are now doing in the British province of New Brunswick, under the pretext of our navigation act, and thus place ourselves and the world at a still greater distance from each other, and from the restoration of commercial freedom.

The committee are of opinion that, so far from there being any thing peculiar in the situation of the United States, which renders the general principles they have advanced inapplicable, there are peculiar circumstances which make them apply with more force than to the nations of Europe. It will be recollected that, in a former part of their observations, it was attempted to be proved

that, in a country where lands of the first quality are still out of cultivation, and are abundant, a system of duties cannot raise the price of one agricultural product but at the expense of another, and cannot raise the price of any kind permanently at all. But this is not the case in such a country as England. Where the field of production is limited, supply cannot keep pace with demand. In England, therefore, the agriculturists may obtain some compensation for the taxes they have to pay the manufacturers, and, in turn, receive taxes from them. But, in this country, the sole benefit is on one side; the agriculturist has no compensation ; it is out of the power of the Legislature to do any thing for him, but to refrain from oppressing him.

Again: Europe is more dependent on us than we are on her; because we furnish her with necessaries, and she furnishes us with luxuries ; because her means of producing those necessaries which she possesses will be daily diminished, and her dependence on this country will be increased, unless we force her to find out another to furnish her with food, and take off her surplus population. In the next place, we are not yet so deeply involved in the restrictive policy as to prevent us from getting rid of it without mischief, as we shall be if we go a few steps further. There are many other peculiar circumstances which forbid our resort to the British policy, but the most important belong to the other branch of the subject proposed to be discussed.

The committee regard the principles they have appealed to as irrefragable. They are not to be refuted by the charge of theory, by the cry that we are supporting foreigners, or by the doctrines of the home market and the balance of trade. What is this balance of trade? Certainly it is not a very creditable mode of gaining ; but is it not evident that, if we cannot pay for what we buy, it is clear gain ; and that, if our citizens wish to buy again on these terms, it is unnecessary for the Government to interfere, as foreigners will refuse to sell ? If we can pay for what we buy, it is all well and good ; if we can pay only at a sacrifice, then we will cease to trade. The whole of this fallacy proceeds from that fatal error in political economy, that the commodity called money is regulated by different laws from all other commodities; or from that no less fatal error, which springs, perhaps, from the first, that a nation must sell more than it buys in order to become rich. Now, the very reverse of this is true; for, although in one sense commerce is an exchange of equivalents, what each party receives must be worth more than what it parts with, or neither is benefited. A nation buying more than it sells is supposed to be the same with its spending more than it makes; but the cases are not alike. What it sells is surplus, and what it buys is surplus; surely it cannot be a matter of regret when the latter is worth more than the former, and when there is an excess to devote to reproduction. It could hardly have been imagined that, in the nineteenth century, in a country whose Government is bottomed on the principle that the people are capable of seeing their

Objections to an increase of Duties.

own interests, it could have been thought necessary for the Legislature to interfere, to prevent the merchants of the country from buying more than they ought to buy. What reason there was for this interposition is shown by the subjoined facts. In 1818, the exportation of cotton goods from Great Britain to the United States amounted to £2,432,301; in 1819, it amounted only to £1,109,138; being a falling off of £1,323,163. The exports of glass, earthenware, hardware, cutlery, in 1818, were £971,285; in 1819, only £546,741. The amount of woollen goods, in 1818, was £3,160,406; in 1819, it dwindled down to £1,703,024. In all the great leading branches of manufactures there was a falling off in the exports to the United States of a full half in the amount, as compared with the year before, and of above £3,500,000 as compared with the average of exports during the last three years.

A case has been proposed as a very strong one, which is this: Suppose that all the various employments of capital are on the lowest level which will continue them. In this state of things one class is entirely thrown out of employment by foreign competition. They must either be protected or must be ruined; and this, it is said, is the actual condition of the United States. It is divided into two classes, one of which has no employment, and the other barely enough. Without stopping to inquire whether it be possible for such a case to exist, it will merely be observed, that if it did it would be improper to give the required protection. If the one class has barely such profits as will continue them in employment, they have nothing to spare. If they have any thing to spare, it is proof that their employment is not so full as to preclude new capital, which is contrary to the supposition. The one can only be raised up by the other being put down. Nor is the case different whether the classes which have employment make small or great profits. That which is employed can only be employed at their expense. In both cases it is unjust; in the latter unnecessary, as great profits will furnish the employment required.

It is not believed that any circumstances exist which will justify the United States in adopting the proposed system. No writer of any reputation ever contended that such a system was compatible with the greatest extension of the national wealth. Even Mr. Hamilton, its great advocate, admitted that if the system of perfect liberty and free trade were the prevailing system of nations, they might attain a greater pitch of wealth and prosperity. It has been attempted to be shown that this limitation to his proposition is founded in a fallacious view of the subject. To propose to increase the wealth of the nation by increasing its taxes is enough to revolt the understandings of ordinary men; yet it seems that a mode of doing this has been discovered, and that the whole mystery lies in calling that which was before called tax—tariff. In the opinion of the committee it is the worst kind of tax, carried to the extent that is proposed; and it would be much better to raise a sum of money by direct taxes at once, and distribute it in bounties among the manufacturers. We should

then escape at least some of the oppressive effects of the system.

The chief recommendation of this system has been supposed to be its tendency to promote domestic independence and happiness. This leads the committee to the second view which they proposed to take of the subject. This is a view which belongs not merely to the political economist, but also to the statesman. The political economist concerns himself only with the manner in which wealth is produced, distributed, and consumed, with a view to its augmentation. The statesman regards this also, but he sometimes sees the necessity of sacrificing a portion of the national wealth in order to attain objects still more desirable; and no objects would appear better to justify such a sacrifice than the promotion of national independence, happiness, and security. It will be attempted to show that the system will be more objectionable in this point of view than in any other.

The observations the committee have already made on the effect of the system to diminish the national wealth serve to establish this position. If such really is the consequence, this alone is an unanswerable argument against the supposed effect of the system to render us independent of foreign Powers. If this general position be correct, it is useless to enter into any details to prove that the revenue must be diminished; for whatever diminishes that on which the revenue acts—the general wealth—must diminish the revenue itself, or else increase the burden of taxation. Even if we could preserve entire the capital of the country, and employ the same number of hands, as they would be less productively employed, there would be less net revenue, less of that great agent which has been said to be the first, second, and third requisite in war. Now, it is not the gross amount of its capital, but its net revenue, which a nation employs to defend itself. If men and ships could be multiplied by a magic wand, you could not add one soldier to your Army, or one vessel to your Navy, without an addition to your net revenue. If the income of the nation is destroyed, we must still have revenue; and how shall we get it but by taxing capital? Indeed, where will be our boasted advantages over other nations with regard to taxation, if the proposed tariff be adopted? If we add twenty-five per cent. to the duties, and then have to raise the same amount of revenue by direct taxes, or by an excise on manufactures, (and in the latter case we should have to pay the duties twice,) we at once add one hundred and fifty per cent. to our taxes—that is, every man who before paid a dollar will now have to pay two dollars and fifty cents; and, if we take into consideration the increased value of money, more, if estimated by the price of corn, than a hundred and fifty per cent., every man who before paid a dollar will have to pay six dollars and twenty-five cents. It would appear that the appreciation of money ought to affect all articles equally; but, in point of fact, it is known, that whilst grain has fallen more than one hundred and fifty per cent., and the other staples of agriculture

Objections to an increase of Duties.

considerably, the fall in manufactured products is comparatively small, so that it is quite immaterial whether it is from the appreciation of money, or from external and domestic causes, the ability of the agriculturist to pay taxes will be diminished by the tariff fully in the proportion stated, and the argument against imposing them is not the less strong. Is it possible that they can submit to this intolerable load of taxation without making every lawful attempt to oppose it? Is it possible for them to believe for a moment that this increase of taxation is the remedy for their distresses?

It is not designed by the committee to claim any preference for agriculture and commerce over manufactures. They mutually depend on each other; their interests are not adverse; and, if not equally productive, they are all equally necessary to society. But, whilst the political economist might regard it as a matter of indifference in what proportion the three great classes are distributed in society, the statesman and patriot could scarcely hesitate to wish that the agricultural class should greatly predominate. The agricultural state is more favorable than any other to the improvement of the physical and moral powers of man. Whilst an agricultural nation will be as powerful as others, it will be more virtuous and happy. It is in this state that the body is invigorated by healthful exercises; that the mind is ennobled by the freedom and independence of rural life; and that man feels the true dignity of his nature. Who would think of comparing the brave, hardy, and independent yeoman of this, or any country, to the miserable, half-starved, rickety population of an English cotton factory? Who would compare the hardy mountaineer who pursues the deer, or slays the buffalo, their equal in swiftness and in strength, to the poor, decrepit, emaciated creature who has been all his life engaged in the same dull, stupifying routine of drawing out a ten yard thread, or manufacturing the eighteenth part of a pin? Yet it has been attempted to be proved that there is more vice among the agriculturists than among the manufacturers, because Colquhoun, a writer who is the partisan of the latter, has asserted that more crimes are committed in some of the agricultural than in some of the manufacturing districts of England; whilst the just answer to the argument implied in this statement has been overlooked, that, where it has happened at all, it has been owing to the laborers, from want of employment, being thrown back from the manufacturing towns, which have converted them from healthy and well disposed children to weakly and depraved adults, on the county from which they originally came.

But if we are agricultural, we must also be commercial; and commerce, it is said, produces more wars than it pays for. If this be true at all, it can only be true of commerce pursued under the dark influence of the restrictive system. Commerce, free and unfettered, so far from being the cause of wars, would be the source of wealth, power, and prosperity, and a bond which would bind in peace and harmony the universal society of nations. And it is not an unreasonable expectation that this is the kind of commerce that will be pursued, whenever nations are governed by enlightened rulers, or rather when they assume the right of governing themselves. The whole civilized world is now essentially commercial. From the period that commerce first emancipated the nations of Europe from feudal vassalage, its march has been steady, progressive, and rapid. It has been the great agent by which the treasures of the earth and the collected wisdom of mankind have been spread throughout the world, and the source of the prosperity and grandeur of empires. To attempt to impede its progress is to disregard the spirit of the times and the admonitions of experience. It is as useless as to oppose the march of the human mind towards freedom, knowledge, and happiness, or to contend against the irreversible decrees of nature. Nations have become acquainted with each other, and with the advantages which they may derive from liberal intercourse; and laws are not strong enough to keep them asunder. They can only vex and disturb their intercourse; they cannot prevent it. It is the interest of every nation to pursue commerce, but peculiarly so of the United States and of every free Government. *It is equally* important to us, whether we consider it as the basis of our Navy, or as the grand instrument for the extension of science, social feelings, and freedom throughout the world.

To pursue the subject: If we give to manufactures all the activity which they must derive from the agricultural and commercial classes being taxed to support them, we must, in time, become exporters of manufactures. When this takes place, will we not be exposed to all and greater inconveniences than we now are, from the refusal of foreigners to receive our raw produce? Which, indeed, would be most apt to suffer from vicissitudes in the affairs of the country—a nation engaged in producing the first necessaries of life, or one engaged in producing luxuries, or only a secondary sort of necessaries?—one employed in producing commodities subject to the caprices of taste and fashion, or one employed in producing those which are essential to human existence?—one pursuing occupations which can be changed with facility, or one pursuing those which can be changed only with great difficulty and loss? What, it is asked, would have been the situation of England—where would have been her independence—if Napoleon had succeeded in carrying into effect his continental system? And now, since this system has been partially adopted by the continental nations of Europe, and by ourselves, is not this destruction of the markets for her manufactures, next to taxation, the principal cause of the distresses of that nation?

It is urged that a nation should have in time of war the necessaries which will enable it to carry on a war; and so it should; but the proposed tariff goes infinitely beyond this point. It is believed that the manufactures of all the necessaries of war are now perfectly established in this country. Coarse clothing, and arms, and ammunition, are not considered as requiring further support. The inquiry now making, in connexion with the

Objections to an increase of Duties.

census, will prove that we have almost every necessary in great abundance. It must be recollected, too, that in a future war, unless by our policy we destroy the Navy, our commerce will not be so entirely kept down, even if that war be with England. Our Navy is now strong enough to prevent the coast from being blockaded, and we shall be enabled to maintain an intercourse with the nations with whom we are not at war. But, it is asked, even if we could not get some of the necessaries we required, does any one seriously believe that the result of any war would be affected by such privations? and if they only affect some of its details, delay a march, or even increase the general mass of suffering, what is this compared with the wide-spread and endless calamities that this system would give rise to? Should our policy be adapted to peace or to war—to the rule or the exception? Undoubtedly, in time of peace we should prepare for war; but let us not make this preparation at so great an expense that its exhausting operation will incapacitate instead of fit us for war.

The demoralizing effects of this system, its tendency to impair the principles of honor and honesty in society, and to give rise to fraud, to smuggling, and to all the low artifices and depravity which are inseparable from all arbitrary legislation, and thus to force upon us a sanguinary code of revenue laws, utterly incompatible with the free and humane principles of our Government, are too obvious, and have been too fully exposed, to require further comment from the committee.

If these are the disastrous effect of this system, what will be thought of those which our free institutions themselves must experience from this unwarrantable interference of the General Government with the rights of private property? An interference which may render nugatory the whole frame of civil polity which the States have adopted for the preservation of their institutions and the promotion of their happiness, and which may, ultimately, break down and destroy the very barriers which secure their rights and sovereignty. The blessings of a free Government are so great, and the evils of an arbitrary one so grievous, that we cannot be too careful to preserve the one when we have it, or to avoid the other. It would therefore appear, that whenever a new measure is proposed, the first inquiry of every citizen of a republic should be, what will be its effects on our institutions? Yet, as obvious as is the truth of this observation, it is somewhat remarkable, that in all that has been so ingeniously written and spoken on the subject of banking, and funding, and manufacturing, they have scarcely ever been considered in their effects on our institutions, but merely in reference to their financial and pecuniary operations. Our legislators and writers have, for the most part, viewed these subjects as political arithmeticians rather than as statesmen.

If the view that has been taken of the manufacturing system be correct, it must not only diminish the amount of national wealth, but must distribute it very unequally. This is by far the worst effect of the two. It taxes one class for the support of another, and, what is worse, taxes the poor for the sake of the rich. It thus produces that inequality which is the bane of republics; for it is, in fact, the influence of the few, or, in other words, aristocracy.

Now, though no just Government will interfere, by sumptuary laws, to restrain the acquisition of wealth, and thereby prevent inequality, so neither will any just Government, by fostering particular interests at the expense of others, promote inequality. This is the opposite and the worst extreme of sumptuary laws. Nor is the inequality which is produced by the interference of the law by any means as harmless as that which results from different dispositions and different capacities in human beings. Whilst the one may act as a salutary stimulus to industry, and its worst consequences are continually neutralized by the alienation and division of property, the other, by creating distrust in the Government, produces despair and depresses industry; and the dread of retributive justice, which always accompanies wealth unjustly acquired, so far from giving rise to division of property, inevitably leads to concentration and primogeniture, to legal safeguards, corporations, charters, monopolies, and privileged orders. The fear that the law which has given may also take away, produces the necessity of usurping the law-making power. An alliance between the privileged classes is the inevitable consequence; hence a new accumulation of powers, new pretexts, and new means of oppressing the people. The Government must be rewarded for its protection by an increase of power, patronage, salaries, taxes, and a diminution of responsibility. The various departments of the Government will no longer move in their appointed spheres, but usurp each other's authority. The State sovereignties will be merged in the General Government, and the legislative authority in the Executive. Such is the natural consequence of creating separate interests by law; such is the effect of that inequality which is produced by the interference of the law with individual wealth; such the process by which free Governments are metamorphosed into aristocracies. It is remarkable, that, although the fundamental maxim of our Government is that the people are capable of self-government, our Legislatures often practically deny it. They place too much reliance on the efficacy of technical rules and artificial restraints. Legislators consider themselves as the rulers, not the agents of the people; as their guardians, not their attorneys. The disregard of that fundamental maxim, that there is an inherent disposition in man to improve his condition, and sagacity to perceive the means, is believed to be the source of innumerable errors in legislation, and particularly of that which dictates the usurpation of the right to direct individual wealth.

It is not to be wondered at that the advocates for the supremacy of the General Government should defend a policy which is calculated to aggrandize it, by creating a new class of dependants; but it is greatly to be wondered at that the friends of State rights should ever have defended it; it can only be because they have not fully perceived its certain consequence. It is believed that no candid mind can fail to perceive that the effect of the manufacturing and its kindred systems will be to transfer a great portion of the wealth of the agriculturists to the other classes. If wealth is thus transferred, so are the means of education, of knowledge, and, consequently, of power. This is a subject which demands the serious attention of every agriculturist in the Union. The evil is augmented, too, by the heavy duty on books, which bears with peculiar hardship on the agriculturist, who does not enjoy, as the merchant, the manufacturer, and the mechanic, the advantage of the public libraries of the cities. The material with which they cultivate the earth, and that with which they cultivate the mind, are alike under the interdiction of this system.

The great influence which the manufacturers, scattered as they will be over the whole face of the country, must acquire, will leave the agriculturists little hope that if they once assent to their system it will ever be revoked. Among the means by which their influence in the Government must be increased, the facility which they must derive from our popular modes of election, of directing the suffrages of the persons they employ, is not the least worthy of consideration. This apprehension is not diminished by the consideration that their dependants, as we are told, will consist principally of foreigners. As much as we respect that class of people, and as willing as we always are to afford them an asylum in our free and happy land, it is not believed that our legislation could derive much improvement from the counsels of the cotton weavers of Manchester and the blacksmiths of Birmingham. They have imbibed their political notions under a Government too dissimilar to ours to be useful citizens in the capacity of legislators.

The committee have already adverted to the effect of the system to drive population and capital from one State to another, and to aggrandize the General Government at the expense of the States. Now, it must occur to every impartial mind, that, if there be any force at all in these observations, the right of the General Government to adopt such a system must be more than questionable. Passing over those Constitutional objections which admit of being urged with great force, that Congress cannot lay taxes but for the purpose of revenue, and that this system is equally incompatible with that part of the Constitution which prescribes uniformity of imposts, and with that which forbids taxes on exportation, they will appeal only to that sacred spirit of justice which we all equally venerate, and the authority of which we equally acknowledge; and they ask, in the name of that justice, whether it is possible to believe that the Congress of the United States can, without violating every principle on which our republican system is founded, tax one class of the community for the support of another? whether they can debar a man the use of the faculties he has derived from nature? compel him to abandon an occupation to which he has devoted his life, and which he understands, and to pursue another which he does not understand? whether it can take away the fruits of one man's industry, earned by the sweat of his brow, and bestow them on another who has not earned them? No Legislature, much less a limited one, has any such right. Those who become parties to Government cannot be supposed to agree to any other exactions than such as are necessary to defray its just expenses, and to preserve public order and morals. Even, therefore, if it could be made to appear that the effect of the system would be to augment the whole wealth of the nation, this object could not justify a Legislature in taxing particular classes, without their consent, for the benefit of the whole. The object of government is to secure men in the exercise of their faculties, not to restrain or direct them; to secure them in the full and free enjoyment and control of their property, and not to distribute and regulate it by its own arbitrary will. It never could have entered into the contemplation of the States, when they agreed to the Constitution, that the General Government had a right, by its legislation, to change their mutual relations towards each other; to enrich one, and impoverish another; to strengthen one, and weaken another; and to impair, and perhaps ultimately destroy, the wealth, freedom, and happiness of them all. Let it not be thought that this is the language of hyperbole. The committee speak of the natural tendency of the system. No one knows how far, in conjunction with its kindred systems, it may stop short of these consequences; no one knows how far it may go beyond them. Our only safety is in arresting it now, when almost every circumstance is unfavorable to its adoption. There never was a time when there was less apology for it. The adoption of it by the continental nations of Europe will enable us to obtain some benefit by abstaining from it—will diminish the advantages of our manufacturing, and increase those of our tilling the earth. The unparalleled distresses of the country, of which agriculture experiences by far the heaviest portion; the increased facility of manufacturing, without artificial aid, from the fall in the price of labor and materials—every circumstance opposes this policy, and recommends a contrary one.

The people of these States, like the three great occupations that employ them, are united by the strongest ties of reciprocal interest. They feel a just pride in the inheritance bequeathed to them by their ancestors, their common freedom and glory; and they equally appreciate the blessings which they derive from that union, which is the result of their mutual exertions, and which it is mutually their interest to preserve. But these blessings must be seriously impaired without the cultivation of good will, and the undeviating exercise of justice towards each other. It is by this means only that the temple of our Union can be cemented and consolidated, and that we can preserve it from the fate which the dissoluble fabrics of other Governments have shared. The committee believe that nothing can have a greater tendency to diminish our confidence in the Government of the Union, and to impair our affec-

The Sinking Fund.

tion for it, than all those measures which distribute its advantages partially and unequally. They believe that such will pre-eminently be the effect of the manufacturing system as proposed by the tariff bill that has been reported, and they fear that this is only the commencement of the system; not that they attribute any unfriendly designs or impure motives to its friends, but that the same reasoning which has begun the policy will dictate its continuance; and that the unsuccessful issue of every effort will be an argument, not for abandoning it, but for making a new attempt.

The committee are fully aware of the great importance of certainty and stability in the regulations of trade, and of the tendency of constant fluctuations to impair that confidence which is necessary to the activity and success of commercial operations; but it is desirable that agriculture should experience at least some of the benefits of those changes which our present system seems destined to undergo. Believing, however, as the committee do, that the proper object of a system of duties is revenue, they regard the revision of the tariff as being strictly the province of the Committee of Ways and Means. With these impressions, and representing, as they do, only one of the great interests of the community, they forbear to propose any positive measures which might seriously and extensively affect them all. They have freely expressed their own sentiments on the important subject referred to them, and they believe those of the great majority of the agriculturists throughout the country. In conformity with these sentiments, they offer the following resolution:

Resolved, That the increase of the duties proposed in the bill entitled "A bill to regulate the duties on imports, and for other purposes," reported by the Committee on Manufactures, is incompatible with the interests of agriculture and of the community generally, and ought not to be adopted.

SINKING FUND.

[Communicated to the Senate, February 7, 1821.]

The Commissioners of the Sinking Fund respectfully report to Congress:

That the measures which have been authorized by the board, subsequently to the last report of the 5th of February, 1820, so far as the same have been completed, are fully detailed in the report of the Secretary of the Treasury to this board, dated the 5th day of the present month, and in the statements therein referred to, which are herewith transmitted, and prayed to be received as a part of this report.

JOHN GAILLARD,
President of the Senate pro tem.
JOHN QUINCY ADAMS,
Secretary of State.
WM. H. CRAWFORD,
Secretary of the Treasury.
WASHINGTON, *Feb.* 6, 1821.

TREASURY DEPARTMENT, *Feb.* 5, 1821.

The Secretary of the Treasury respectfully reports to the Commissioners of the Sinking Fund:

That the sum disbursed from the Treasury, during the year 1819, on account of the principal and interest of the public debt, as per the last annual report was - - - $7,721,020 96		
From which deduct the amount of repayment in that year - - 17,199 09		
		$7,703,821 87
Which, with a sum arising from damages and interest on two protested bills of exchange, repaid in 1819, which in that year had been purchased and remitted to Europe, for payment of interest on Louisiana stock - -		(a) 2,631 78
Together with this sum, being the difference between the principal of stock purchased during the year 1819 and the money paid for the same - -		47,608 49
And a further sum, being gain on remittances to Europe in 1819, as appears by statement D, annexed to the last annual report - - -		1,322 87
Amounting, together, to - -		$7,755,385 01

Have been accounted for in the following manner, viz:

There was applied for the payment of a sum short provided on account of the public debt, due prior to the 1st January, 1819, as per statement B, annexed to the last annual report - -		$128,427 69
The application during the year 1819 towards the payment of the principal and interest of the public debt, as ascertained by accounts rendered to this Department, amounted, as appears by the annexed statement A, to the sum of -		$7,656,873 16
In the reimbursement of the principal of the deferred stock	485,863 45	
In the purchase of the domestic debt, (cost $664,356 62,) -	711,957 55	
In the redemption of the Louisiana stock	1,215,449 73	
In the payment of the principal of Treasury notes - -	80,000 00	
In the payment of certain parts of the domestic debt -	64 32	
	2,493,335 05	
On account of the interest and charges	5,163,538 11	
	7,656,873 16	

(a) Amount of repayment by J. M. Ehrick, including interest and damages - - -		$15,520 66
Cost of two bills purchased by him in 1818, £2,900 sterling, at par - -		12,888 88
		$2,631 78

Ohio—Bank of the United States.

Of this sum there was short provided, consisting of unclaimed dividends on the public debt, not applied for by the proprietors, as per the annexed statement B   -   -   -   29,915 84
                                                                                    7,626,957 32
                                                                                    —————————
                                                                                    $7,755,385 01

That, during the year 1820, the following disbursements were made out of the Treasury on account of the principal and interest of the public debt:

On account of the interest on the domestic debt and reimbursement of the principal of the deferred stock   -   -   -   -   - $5,474,378 88
On account of the principal and interest of Treasury notes   -   -   -   105,444 57
On account of the redemption of the Louisiana stock   -   -   -   1,785,662 04
On account of the interest on the same   -   -   -   188,133 87
On account of the redemption of the domestic debt   -   -   -   1,718 77
On account of certain parts of the domestic debt   -   -   -   -   124 08
On account of the Mississippi stock   1,150,468 32

Making, together, as will appear by the annexed statement C, the sum of   -   -   -   -   - $8,705,930 53

Which disbursements were made from the appropriation of $10,000,000, for the year 1820, agreeably to the act of the 3d March, 1817, to the amount of   -   -   - $8,628,514 28
And from repayment into the Treasury, on account of moneys heretofore advanced for the interest and reimbursement of the public debt and Treasury notes, as per the annexed statement E,   -   -   -   77,416 25
                                                                                    —————————
                                                                                    $8,705,930 53

and will be accounted for in the next annual report, in conformity to accounts which shall then have been rendered to this Department.

In the mean time, the manner in which the said sum has been applied is estimated as follows:

There is estimated to have been applied to the payment of the deficiency at the end of 1819, as per statement B   -   -   -   - $29,915 84
Also, in the reimbursement of the deferred stock   -   - $503,196 94
Also, in the payment of the principal Treasury notes   -   -   -   100,000 00
Also, towards the redemption of the Louisiana stock   -   -   1,785,662 04
Also, in the purchase of stock and payment of certain parts of the domestic debt   -   -   -   180 83
Also, in the payment of the Mississippi stock   1,150,468 32

Also, in the payment of the interest on the funded debt and Treasury notes   -   -   5,024,737 57
And for replacing funds heretofore advanced for the payment of converted 6 per cent. stock, which in 1819 had been repaid into the Treasury   -   -   1,678 43
                                                                                    —————————
                                                                                    8,565,964 13

In the next annual statement, the repayments in 1820 will be exhibited as a deduction from the total amount of warrants issued for the public debt for that year, to the amount of   -   -   77,416 25
And there is estimated as remaining unapplied in the hands of the agents in Europe, and in protested bills, on the 1st of January, 1821, per estimate G   114,439 79
                                                                                    —————————
                                                                                    8,757,830 17

From which deduct this sum short provided on account of unclaimed dividends, payable but not demanded at the Treasury   -   -   81,815 48
                                                                                    —————————
                                                                                    8,676,014 69
                                                                                    —————————
                                                                                    $8,705,930 53

A statement marked H is annexed, which exhibits the balance of the annual appropriation of $10,000,000 unexpended on the 1st January, 1821.

And statement marked I, of the funded debt of the United States on the 1st January, 1821.

All of which is respectfully submitted.

WM. H. CRAWFORD.

RIGHT OF A STATE TO TAX A BRANCH OF THE UNITED STATES BANK.

[Communicated to the Senate, February 1, 1821]

COLUMBUS, *January* 22, 1821.

SIR: I have the honor to transmit to you the enclosed report and resolutions on the subject of certain proceedings of the Bank of the United States, and to request that you will lay the same before the Senate, over which you preside.

With great respect, I am, sir, your obedient servant,

ETHAN A. BROWN.

To the PRESIDENT *of the Senate, U. S.*

Report of the Joint Committee of both Houses of the General Assembly of the State of Ohio on the communication of the Auditor of State upon the subject of the proceedings of the Bank of the United States against the officers of State in the United States circuit court.

From the papers submitted to the committee, it appears that, in the month of September, 1819, the Bank of the United States exhibited a bill in chancery before the circuit court of the United States, then sitting at Chilicothe, against Ralph Osborn, auditor of the State of Ohio, and obtained in that court an order of injunction against him, prohibiting him, as auditor, from performing the duties enjoined upon him by the "Act to levy and collect a tax from all banks and individuals, and companies and associations of individuals, that may transact banking business in this State without being authorized to do so by the laws thereof."

It further appears that the auditor, not being satisfied, before the time appointed by law for him to act, that an injunction had been ordered, issued his warrant in conformity to the law under which the tax imposed by law was collected and paid into the State treasury.

It further appears that the circuit court of the United States, at their last term, adjudged that this act of official duty was a contempt of court; for committing which, they awarded a writ of attachment against the auditor, returnable to January term next.

It appears, also, that, at the September term last, upon the application of the Bank of the United States, an order was made allowing them to file an amended and supplemental bill making Samuel Sullivan, the Treasurer of State, a defendant, "as present treasurer of Ohio, and in his private and individual character;" and also making Hiram Mirick Curry, late treasurer, and John L. Harper, the officer that collected the tax, defendants; upon the filing of which amended and supplementary bill, a further order of injunction was made, prohibiting the Treasurer of State from negotiating, delivering over, or in any manner parting with or disposing of the money collected for tax, and paid into the State treasury according to law. And it further appears that, besides these proceedings, an action of trespass, at the suit of the Bank of the United States, was commenced, and made returnable to the last September term of the same circuit court, against Ralph Osborn, John L. Harper, Thomas Orr, James McCollister, John C. Wright, and Charles Hammond, in which the plaintiffs have filed a declaration charging, among other things, the taking and carrying away the same sum of money in the proceedings in chancery specified, under color and pretence of the law of Ohio.

Whatever attempt may be made to characterize this proceeding as a controversy between individuals, it is evident that its practical effect is to make the State a defendant before the circuit court of the United States. In every thing but the name, the State is the actual defendant. No other interest but that of the State is involved. In every stage of the inquiry, the rights, interests, and powers of the State only are presented for adjudication. The final process must operate directly upon the State, and, if effectual, must derange totally the official accounts both in the Auditor's and Treasurer's departments; for, if there be a specific decree, as prayed for in the supplemental bill, a specific execution may be sent into the State treasury to carry that decree specifically into effect.

Nor is it only in its practical effect that the real character of this proceeding is to be perceived. It is distinctly avowed in the body of the bill, both by naming the General Assembly of Ohio as the offending party, and by calling on the court to restrain the Auditor of State from performing official acts in his official character; and, in fact, it would seem, from the foundation upon which the injunction was allowed, both on the first and second applications, that the court must have regarded it as, substantially, a proceeding against the State.

All judicial proceedings are founded upon facts established judicially. The transactions of individuals are verified by testimony judicially taken; but the proceedings of States and Governments are regarded as of public notoriety, to be received upon the evidence of general history. When an individual applies for an injunction against another individual, his application is never regarded unless the matter alleged in his petition be established by his own affidavit, or that of others. The court never restrain an individual in the exercise of his supposed rights, upon the naked suggestion of another. The law of Virginia, of Kentucky, and of Ohio, alike requires that, before any injunction shall be granted, the judge or court granting it shall be satisfied, by affidavit at the foot of the bill, or by other means, that the allegations in the bill are true. The practice of the federal court and federal judges in Ohio has been to require proof. No injunction has been granted upon mere suggestion until that against Ralph Osborn, Auditor of State. No other injunction has been granted upon mere suggestion but that against Samuel Sullivan, Treasurer of State. Both these injunctions were granted instantly, upon application by bill alone, without any proof being offered or required that one single allegation contained in the bill was true. This departure from the common course of proceeding can be accounted for and vindicated but upon one ground—that the party substantially a defendant was a sovereign State, all of whose proceedings were matters of public notoriety, of which the court was informed without proof in the ordinary mode.

By the original provisions of the Constitution of the United States, the federal judic ar were empowered to take cognizance of controversies between a State and citizens of another State; but by the same instrument this jurisdiction was vested exclusively in the Supreme Court. A State never could be held to answer or be made amenable before a circuit court of the United States. By the eleventh amendment to the Constitution, this power to call a State to answer before the Supreme Court, at the suit of a citizen, was wholly taken from the federal judiciary. It is perfectly clear that, before this amendment to the Constitution was made, the circuit court of the United States could not have entertained jurisdiction of a suit in equity, enjoining the State officers from executing the State laws, in a case of the direct action of the State sovereignty, like that for the collection of taxes. The principal, and not the ministerial agent is always the proper defendant in such a suit. That principal being directly and personally amenable in the Supreme Court, his case could not be drawn to a tribunal that had no jurisdiction over the principal, by instituting a suit against the agent alone. The State, before the amendment, could be sued in equity before the Supreme Court of the United States, and could, in a proper case, be there enjoined. In that court only could a State be prohibited from carrying her laws into operation. For that very reason her officer could not be enjoined in a circuit court. It would be to subject the interest and rights of the State to the decision of a tribunal that had no jurisdiction to decide them, and where the State could not be admitted a defendant to defend them. It is, therefore, a strange doctrine to maintain that an amendment to the Constitution, expressly forbidding the judges so to construe the Constitution as to call States before the supreme courts as defendants, at the suit of individuals, is to operate as vesting the circuit courts with powers to do that indirectly which they never had any direct power to do. The amendment was intended to protect the States from a direct responsibility, upon process before the Supreme Court, the only tribunal before which they were then liable to be called to answer. By the construction now attempted, this amendment is made to vest the circuit court with a jurisdiction equally effective against the State, though indirect in its form of proceeding. It effects nothing but the degradation and humiliation of the States. Instead of the distinction of being called to defend its rights before the highest judicial tribunal of the nation, the State is reduced to the level of the most ordinary citizen, and made answerable in an inferior tribunal. Instead of enjoying the privilege of managing directly its own interests, and absolutely controlling its own defence, the State must submit to the consequence of blending its interests with the timidity or treachery of others, and must be concluded in a decision made by a case which it is in the power of others to manage as they please. The committee are persuaded that such was not the object of the amendment, and that such is not the correct construction of the Constitution.

It is asserted that this is an individual proceeding against the persons named as defendants; that although the State cannot be sued, yet persons remain responsible, and may be made subject to every proper process. It has heretofore been deemed a sound maxim in ethics, that whatever could not be lawfully done directly, could not be justly effected by indirect means. If this maxim be regarded, (as the State never could be directly proceeded against in the circuit court without a violation of the Constitution,) every indirect mode of proceeding ought to be considered inadmissible; but, in fact, and

substantially, this is not a proceeding against individuals.

A court of chancery proceeds against the person and against the subject: in technical language, *in personam* and *in rem*. The proceeding in this case is not against Ralph Osborn and Samuel Sullivan for any matter in which they have an individual or personal concern; it is only in the performance of official duties that the process of the court interferes to control them. It was not for himself, or upon his individual account, that Ralph Osborn issued his warrant to collect a tax from the Bank of the United States; it was for the State, and in his character as auditor, that he acted: it is not in the transaction of individual business, or upon his own contracts, that Samuel Sullivan is forbidden to dispose of, or part with, particular funds. He is inhibited from paying away money received by him as treasurer, held by him as such, and for the disbursement of which he is officially responsible to the State.

A State, in the abstract, is an intangible entity, like a corporation; in substance, it is a community of individuals; it can only act by individual agents, and its power of action is completely destroyed when these agents are restrained from acting. It is solemn trifling to admit that a State cannot be sued in the circuit court, and, at the same time, insist that every agent that the State employs may be controlled and restrained from performing his official functions by the same circuit court.

The Auditor of State is a ministerial agent in the executive department of the Government; it is his duty to superintend the collection of the revenue; he acts directly for the whole people upon each; in every one of his official acts he exercises a portion of the sovereign power; and when he is restrained from acting officially, it is the sovereign power of the State that is restrained.

Injunctions to stay proceedings in the courts of law are founded upon a different principle; they act upon the party and not upon the court, and call in question the conduct of the party, not the justice or integrity of the judges. The people, too frequently called the Government, never intend that one individual shall use their power to do injustice to another. Courts of chancery are instituted, not to control the courts of law, but to control individuals who may have obtained unconscionable advantages in the law courts. The proceedings of the chancery court is the act of the people; but it does not operate upon the people themselves in and through the courts of law; it only withdraws the subject from the judgment of the people in their law court, to their judgment in their court of chancery, upon the principle that adequate justice cannot be administered elsewhere.

This injunction operates through the auditor upon the whole people of the State. He is their agent; his acts are their acts; he proceeds under their direction, and for their sole benefit. They are responsible for his errors, and are bound to protect him from unjust responsibility.

If the injunction was intended, and did in fact operate upon Ralph Osborn alone, his resignation or removal from office would render it unavailing.

His successor in office would be at liberty to act notwithstanding the injunction. But that this was not the intention, and is understood not to be the effect of this injunction, is placed beyond all doubt. The bill prayed not only that Ralph Osborn, Auditor of State, but that all others whom it concerned, should be enjoined, and so the order of injunction was made. The court have judicially declared that this order did not extend to Ralph Osborn and his agent alone, but to all who might act upon the subject. By resigning his office after notice of an application for the injunction, Ralph Osborn would have ceased to have any concern in the subject of it. Yet we are distinctly given to understand that his successor in office was enjoined, as well as every other agent or officer whom the law might appoint, to perform any duty connected with the collection prohibited. This fact alone would seem decisive that the proceeding is not personal against Ralph Osborn, but is direct against the Auditor of State.

It is charged in the supplemental bill that the money collected was delivered to Hiram Mirick Currey to keep upon deposite, and by him delivered to Samuel Sullivan to keep in like manner; it is also charged that at the time of receiving the money Currey was treasurer of the State of Ohio, and at the time of delivering it to Sullivan he was the successor of Currey; and the bill prays that Currey as late treasurer, and Sullivan as present treasurer, and also in their individual capacities, may be made defendants; the bill also prays that Sullivan may be enjoined from disposing of the specific moneys received by him upon account of the tax. This injunction, too, is granted upon the suggestions contained in the bill, without any evidence that the money was paid to Sullivan as alleged.

This proceeding is not merely personal against the treasurer, it is direct against the subject; and that subject is money in the State treasury received by the treasurer as revenue of the State, receipted for as such, and as such carried into his official accounts. But this is not a proceeding against the State, because the complainants allege that the "nature and character of the whole transaction forbid the supposition that the money was received by the defendants in the capacity of treasurer." Thus the court are called to determine the whole transaction to be illegal, and then to invest themselves with jurisdiction to reach the specific funds, by shutting their eyes to the real facts of the case, and supposing a state of things that never did exist.

When a State was liable to be sued before the Supreme Court, the process issued against the State, and the court directed a service to be made upon the Governor for the time being. If the proceedings in the present case are correct, it is now sufficient to issue process against the person who may happen to be treasurer, and name him both as treasurer and as an individual, and, upon such process, at the mere suggestion of a complainant, prohibit him from using, for the benefit of the State, any moneys paid to him officially whch it may be alleged were collected illegally.

In due season a decree may be passed for the specific restitution of the money thus claimed, and this decree will bind the treasurer that may be in office when it is pronounced, and subject him to the responsibilities of a defendant. If he refuse to pay the money, the court may attach him for a contempt; if he does pay it without a legislative appropriation, he is liable upon his bond, and subject to impeachment. Such might have been the consequence of a judgment against a State in the Supreme Court; and it was, no doubt, an apprehension of such a result that induced the amendment to the Constitution forbidding the Federal courts to call a State before them as a defendant at the suit of an individual.

It is evident that the principle of the proceeding secures to the Federal tribunals every power supposed to be taken from them by the amendment. If the Auditor of State can be enjoined from acting officially; if the treasurer can be decreed to pay back money received as revenue, upon the doctrine that the court consider them wrongdoers, there is no case of the exercise of State power that may not be completely controlled. The Legislature levy a tax; the Federal court are called upon, and, upon motion, adjudge it to be contrary to the Constitution of the United States; they regard the collector as a wrongdoer, and enjoin him from collecting it; the tax is collected and paid into the State treasury; the Federal court are applied to; they pronounce the tax unconstitutional; the collection a trespass; the State treasurer a baillee for the claimant, and decree a restitution of the amount. The Legislature of the State enact a law for the punishment of crimes; an individual is convicted under its provisions, and imprisoned in the penitentiary; he complains that the law under which he is convicted is repugnant to the Constitution of the United States; he calls upon the Federal court for redress; the court decide the law to be unconstitutional, the conviction illegal, the keeper of the penitentiary a trespasser, and order the prisoner to be discharged. In such a proceeding they keep the State entirely out of view, and regard it as a mere personal matter; they shut their eyes to the real state of facts, and assert "that the nature and character of the whole transaction forbid the supposition" that the State could have had any agency or concern in the imprisonment. In this manner the States may be placed at the foot of the Federal Judiciary, as well in its administration of its criminal justice as in its fiscal concerns.

In granting an injunction against the Auditor of State, in the first instance, and in awarding an attachment against him for disobedience to that injunction, the federal circuit court In Ohio have unequivocally asserted a jurisdiction over the State and its officers in the collection of revenue. The circumstances under which the attachment was ordered admonish us that the jurisdiction thus asserted will be without reluctance enforced. The auditor will be fined or imprisoned, or both, for executing his official duty; and the State must either acquiesce in the correctness of the proceeding, and avert the consequence, by retracing their steps, or, regarding it as an encroachment upon their just authority, must prepare to take such a stand against it as the Constitution and a just regard to their rights may warrant.

The committee conceive that the proceeding in this case, by bill in chancery and injunction against the auditor and treasurer, is, to every substantial purpose, a process against the State. The auditor and treasurer are defendants in name and in form only, and can only be made and regarded as defendants to evade the provisions of the Constitution. From the view they have taken of the subject, the conclusion seems inevitable, that the Federal court have asserted a jurisdiction which a just construction of the Constitution does not warrant; and the committee conceive, that to acquiesce in such an encroachment upon the privileges and authority of the State, without an effort to defend them, would be an act of treachery to the State itself, and to all the States that compose the American Union.

The committee are aware of the doctrine, that the Federal courts are exclusively vested with jurisdiction to declare, in the last resort, the true interpretation of the Constitution of the United States. To this doctrine, in the latitude contended for, they never can give their assent.

Every court of justice, where they have jurisdiction over the parties to the suit and the subject of controversy, are, of necessity, invested with power to decide every question upon which the rights of the parties depend; and their decision is conclusive, unless a superior court be invested with jurisdiction to review it. On this subject the powers of the Federal and State judiciary are precisely the same. These powers are not founded upon any express Constitutional provision, but result from the very nature of written constitutions and judicial duty.   •

Among other things, the Constitution of the United States declares that "no State shall pass any bill of attainder, *ex post facto* law, or law impairing the obligation of contracts." A defendant, prosecuted for a crime before a State court, may insist that the law upon which he is accused is *ex post facto*. If the State court decide in his favor it is conclusive, because there is no law authorizing the Federal court to review it. If the decision be against him, it is, for the same reason, conclusive. No person can be criminally prosecuted before the Federal courts for the violation of a State law. No appeal or writ of error from the decision of a State court, in a State prosecution, lies to the Federal court. The interpretation of that provision of the Constitution of the United States, which declares that ' no State shall pass an *ex post facto* law is now exclusively vested in the State courts. Nor can the Federal courts ever be vested, under the Constitution, as it now stands, with effective jurisdiction to interpret and enforce this provision. They cannot be empowered to take the administration of criminal justice from before the State courts, in the incipient stages of a prosecution; and a writ of error after judgment would clearly be a suit at law, in which the State must be defendant,

and would come directly within the terms of the amendment.

In this case, then, the Federal courts cannot now pronounce an effective judicial decision. They cannot possess themselves of jurisdiction over the parties upon whom any decision they might make could operate. Yet individuals may contrive some feigned action, or make some feigned issue, and present to the Federal court for decision a case, calling upon them, and thus empowering them to decide that, upon a particular state of facts, the operation of a State law would be *ex post facto*, within the meaning of the provision of the Constitution of the United States. A decision thus obtained would be entitled to respect as the opinion of eminent men, but never could be regarded as a judicial declaration of the law of the land.

By an express provision of the Constitution of the United States, a provision introduced purposely to effect that object, the States, in any controversies they may have with individuals, are placed beyond the jurisdiction of the Federal courts. It would seem incontrovertible that the amendatory article placed the States and the United States in a relation to each other different from that in which they stood under the original Constitution—different in this: that, in all cases where the States could not be called to answer in the Federal courts, these courts ceased to be a Constitutional tribunal to investigate and determine their power and authority under the Constitution of the United States. The duty of the courts to declare the law terminated with their authority to execute it.

The committee conceive that such is the true, and such is the settled construction of the Constitution; settled by an authority paramount to all others, and from which there can be no appeal—the authority of the people themselves.

So early as the year 1798, the States and the people were called to declare their opinions upon the question involving the relative rights and powers of the Government of the United States and of the Governments of the separate States. In the month of November of that year, the State of Kentucky resolved :

"That the several States comprising the United States of America are not united on the principle of unlimited submission to their General Government ; but that, by compact, under the style and title of a Constitution for the United States, and amendments thereto, they constituted a General Government for special purposes, delegated to that Government certain definite powers, reserving to each State itself the residuary mass of right to their own self-government ; and that, whensoever the General Government assumes undelegated powers, its acts are unauthoritative, void, and of no force ; that to this compact each State acceded as a State, and is an integral party, its co-States forming, as to itself, the other party ; that the Government created by this compact was not made the exclusive or final judge of the extent of the powers delegated to itself, since that would have made its discretion, and not the Constitution, the measure of its power ; but that, as in all other cases of compact among parties having no common judge, each party has an equal right to judge for itself, as well of infractions as of the mode and measure of redress."

In the month of December of the same year, (1798,) the Legislature of Virginia resolved:

"That this Assembly doth explicitly and peremptorily declare that it views the powers of the Federal Government as resulting from the compact to which the States are parties, as limited by the plain sense and intention of the instrument constituting that compact, as no further valid than they are authorized by the grants enumerated in that compact; and that, in case of deliberate, palpable, and dangerous exercise of other powers not granted by the said compact, the States who are parties thereto have the right, and are in duty bound, to interpose for arresting the progress of the evil, and for maintaining within their respective limits, the authorities, rights, and liberties appertaining to them."

It cannot be forgotten that these resolves, and others connected with them, were occasioned by the acts of Congress commonly called the alien and sedition laws, and by certain decisions in the Federal circuit courts, recognising the obligatory force of the common law, as applicable to the federal jurisprudence.

The resolutions of Virginia were submitted to the Legislatures of the different States; Delaware, Rhode Island, Massachusetts, the Senate of New York, Connecticut, New Hampshire, and Vermont returned answers to them, strongly reprobating their principle, and all but Delaware and Connecticut asserting that the Federal Judiciary were exclusively the expositors of the Federal Constitution. In the Virginia Legislature, these answers were submitted to a committee, of which Mr. Madison was chairman, and in January, 1800, this committee made a report, which has ever since been considered the true text-book of republican principles.

In that report, the claim that the Federal Judiciary are the exclusive expositors of the Federal Constitution is taken up and examined. The committee say:

"But it is objected that the judicial authority is to be regarded as the sole expositor of the Constitution, in the last resort; and it may be asked for what reason the declaration by the General Assembly, supposing it to be theoretically true, could be required at the present day, and in so solemn a manner?

"On this objection it might be observed, first, that there may be instances of usurped power, which the forms of the Constitution would never draw within the control of the judicial department; secondly, that if the decision of the judiciary be raised above the authority of the sovereign parties to the Constitution, the decisions of the other departments, not carried by the forms of the Constitution before the judiciary, must, be equally authoritative and final with the decisions of that department; but the proper answer to the objection is, that the resolution of the General Assembly relates to those great and extraordinary cases in which all the forms of the Constitution may prove ineffectual against infractions dangerous to the essential rights of the parties to it. The resolution supposes that dangerous powers not delegated may not only be usurped and executed by the other departments, but that the judicial departments also may exercise or sanction dangerous powers beyond the grant of the Constitution; and, consequently, that the ultimate right of the parties to the Constitution, to judge whether the compact has been dangerously violated, must extend to violations by one delegated authority as well as by another, by the judiciary as well as by the executive or legislative."

"However true, therefore, it may be, that the judicial department is, in all questions submitted to it by the forms of the Constitution, to decide in the last resort, this resort must necessarily be deemed the last in relation to the authorities of the other departments of the Government; not in relation to the rights of the parties to the Constitutional compact, from which the judicial as well as the other departments hold their delegated trusts. On any other hypothesis, the delegation of judicial power would annul the authority delegating it; and the concurrence of this department with the others in usurped powers might subvert forever, and beyond the possible reach of any rightful remedy, the very Constitution which all were instituted to preserve."

The resolutions of Kentucky and Virginia, and of Massachusetts, Rhode Island, the Senate of New York, New Hampshire, and Vermont, in reply, and the answer to these replies by the Legislature of Virginia, were a direct and Constitutional appeal to the States and to the people upon the great question at issue. The appeal was decided by the Presidential and other elections of 1800. The States and the people recognised and affirmed the doctrines of Kentucky and Virginia, by effecting a total change in the administration of the Federal Government. In the pardon of Callender, convicted under the Sedition law, and in the remittance of his fine, the new administration unequivocally recognised the decision and the authority of the States and of the people. Thus has the question, whether the Federal courts are the sole expositors of the Constitution of the United States in the last resort, or whether the States, "as in all other cases of compact among parties having no common judge," have an equal right to interpret that Constitution for themselves, where their sovereign rights are involved, been decided against the pretension of the Federal judges, by the people themselves, the true source of all legitimate powers.

In the opinion of the committee, the high authority of this precedent, as well as the clear right of the case, imposes a duty upon the State, from which it cannot shrink without dishonor. So long as one single Constitutional effort can be made to save them, the State ought not to surrender its rights to the encroaching pretensions of the circuit court.

But justice should ever be held sacred. Pride and resentment are alike poor apologies for perseverance in error. If it were admitted that the proceedings of the Federal court against the State, through its officers, are not warranted by the Constitution, still, if the State has commenced in error, it should abandon the controversy. Before, therefore, we determine upon the course we ought to pursue, it is necessary to review and examine the ground upon which we stand.

The Bank of the United States established an office of discount and deposite at Cincinnati, in this State, which commenced banking in the Spring of the year 1817. The Legislature met in December following, and upon the 13th day of December a resolution was proposed in the House of Representatives, and adopted, appointing a committee to inquire into the expediency of taxing such branches as were or might be established within this State. The committee reported against the expediency of levying such a tax, but the House of Representatives reversed their report by a majority of 37 to 22. A substitute for their report was then offered, asserting the right of the State to levy such a tax, and the expediency of doing it at that time. The Constitutional right of the State to levy such a tax was carried by 48 to 12, and the expediency of proceeding to levy the tax by 33 to 27. A bill assessing a tax was reported to the House, and passed to be engrossed for a third reading and final passage, and, upon the third reading, was postponed to the second Monday of December, 1818.

After this solemn assertion of the right to tax, and when a bill for that purpose was pending before the House of Representatives, the bank proceeded to organize a second office of discount and deposite at Chilicothe, in this State, which commenced banking in the Spring of the year 1818. In January, 1819, the Legislature enacted the law levying the tax, and postponed its execution until the September following, that the bank might have abundant time so to arrange their business as not to come within the provisions of the taxing law.

At the period of adopting these measures, the constitutional right of the State to levy the tax was doubted by none but those interested in the bank, or those who expected to derive pecuniary advantages for themselves or their friends by the location of branches. It seemed impossible that a rational, disinterested, and independent mind could doubt. During the existence of the old Bank of the United States, the State of Georgia had asserted this right of taxation, and actually collected the tax. The bank brought a suit to recover back the money in the federal circuit court of Georgia. This suit was brought before the Supreme Court, upon a question not directly involving the power of taxation. The Supreme Court decided the point before them in favor of the bank, upon such grounds that the suit was abandoned, and the tax submitted to. When the charter of the present bank was enacted, it was known that the States claimed, and had practically asserted, the power of taxing it; yet no exemption from the operation of the power is stipulated by Congress. The natural inference from

the silence of the charter upon this point w̄ ꝛuld seem to be, that the power of the States was recognised, and that Congress were not disposed to interfere with it.

The Constitution of the United States had distinctly expressed in what cases the taxing power of the States should be restrained. No maxim of legal construction is better settled, and more universally acknowledged, than that express limitations of power, either in constitutions or in statutes, are distinct admissions that the power exists, and may be exercised in every other case than those expressly limited. With a knowledge of these facts and doctrines in their minds, that a confidence in the power of the State to levy this tax should be almost universal, is what every intelligent man would expect.

But, after the law was enacted that levied the tax, and before the time of its taking effect, the Supreme Court of the United States, in the case of Maryland and McCulloch, decided that the States were debarred, by the Constitution of the United States, from assessing or levying any such tax. And upon the promulgation of this decision it is maintained that it became the duty of the State and its officers to acquiesce, and treat the act of the Legislature as a dead letter. The committee have considered this position, and are not satisfied that it is a correct one.

It has been already shown that, since the eleventh amendment to the Constitution, the separate States, as parties to the compact of Union, are not subject to the jurisdiction of the Federal courts upon questions involving their power and authority as sovereign States. Not being subject to the jurisdiction, no State can be concluded by the opinions of these tribunals. But these are questions in respect to which there is no common judge, and, therefore, the State has a right to judge for itself. If, by the management of a party, and through the inadvertence or connivance of a State, a case be made, presenting to the Supreme Court of the United States for decision important and interesting questions of State power and State authority, upon no just principle ought the States to be concluded by any decision had upon such a case. The committee are clearly of opinion that such is the true character of the case passed upon the world by the title of McCulloch *vs.* Maryland.

It was once remarked, by a most profound politician, that words are things ; and the observation is most unquestionably a correct one. This case, dignified with the important and high-sounding title of "McCulloch *vs.* the State of Maryland," when looked into, is found to be an ordinary *qui tam* action of debt, brought by a common informer, of the name of John James ; and it is, throughout, an agreed case, made expressly for the purpose of obtaining the opinion of the Supreme Court of the United States upon the question whether the States could constitutionally levy a tax upon the Bank of the United States. This agreed case was manufactured in the Summer of the year 1818, and passed through the county court of Baltimore county and the court of appeals of the State of Maryland in the same season, so as to be got upon the docket of the Supreme Court of the United States for adjudication at their February term, 1819. It is only by the management and concurrence of the parties that causes can be thus expeditiously brought to a final hearing in the Supreme Court.

It must be remembered that, through the extravagant and fraudulent speculations of those intrusted with conducting the concerns of the bank, it stood, at the close of the year 1818, upon the very brink of destruction. At this critical juncture of its affairs, it was a manœuvre of consummate policy to draw from the Supreme Court of the United States a decision that the institution itself was constitutionally created, and that it was exempt from the taxing power of the States. This decision served to prop its sinking credit; and if it inflicted a dangerous wound upon the authority of the States, both with the bank and with John James, this might be but a minor consideration. It is truly an alarming circumstance if it be in the power of an aspiring corporation and an unknown and obscure individual thus to elicit opinions compromitting the vital interests of the States that compose the American Union.

It is not, however, either in theory or in practice, the necessary consequence of a decision of the Supreme Court, that all who claim rights of the same nature with those decided by the court are required to acquiesce. There are cases in which the decisions of that tribunal have been followed by no effective consequence.

In the case of Marbury vs. Madison, the Supreme Court of the United States decided that William Marbury was entitled to his commission as a justice of the peace for the District of Columbia; that the withholding of this commission by President Jefferson was violative of the legal vested right of Mr. Marbury. Notwithstanding this decision, Mr. Marbury never did obtain his commission; the person appointed in his place continued to act; his acts were admitted to be valid; and President Jefferson retained his standing in the estimation of the American people. The decision of the Supreme Court proved to be totally impotent and unavailing.

So in in the case of Fletcher vs. Peck, the Supreme Court decided that the Yazoo purchasers from the State of Georgia were entitled to the lands. But the decision availed them nothing, unless as a make-weight in effecting a compromise.

These two cases are evidence that, in great questions of political rights and political powers, a decision of the Supreme Court of the United States is not conclusive of the rights decided by it. If the United States stand justified in withholding a commission when the court adjudged it to be the party's right; if the United States might, without reprehension, retain possession of the Yazoo lands after the Supreme Court decided that they were the property of the purchasers from Georgia, surely the State of Ohio ought not to be condemned because she did not abandon her solemn legislative acts as a dead letter upon the promulgation of an opinion of that tribunal.

This opinion is now before us, and the committee conceive that it is the duty of this General Assembly calmly to examine the principles and reasoning upon which it is founded. Much deference is due to the respectable individuals by whom it was formed, and more to the high station they occupy in the Government. Although their opinion is not admitted to have the force of absolute authority, yet a course of proceeding pronounced by such eminent statesmen and lawyers to be unconstitutional, ought not to be lightly and unadvisedly adopted.

It is not perceived that the power of the State to tax the officers of the Bank of the United States established within their jurisdiction is necessarily connected with the question whether Congress have, or have not, the Constitutional power to create a corporation. This power may safely be admitted, if, at the time of making this admission, we clearly comprehend the principles upon which the corporation is to be instituted.

"A corporation," says Chief Justice Marshall, in the case of Dartmouth College, "is an artificial being; invisible, intangible, and existing only in contemplation of law. Being the mere creature of law, it possesses only those properties which the charter of its creation confers upon it, either expressly, or as incidental to its very existence.— These are such as are supposed best calculated to effect the objects for which it was created. Among the most important are immortality, and, if the expression may be allowed, individuality—properties by which a perpetual succession of many persons are considered as the same, and may act as a single individual. They enable a corporation to manage its own affairs, and to hold property without the perplexing intricacies, the hazardous and endless necessity of perpetual conveyances for the purpose of transmitting it from hand to hand. It is chiefly for the purpose of clothing bodies of men, in succession, with these qualities and capacities, that corporations are invented and are in use. By these means a perpetual succession of individuals are capable of acting for the promotion of the particular object, like one immortal being. But this being does not share in the civil government of the country, unless that be the purpose for which it was created. Its immortality no more confers on it political power, or a political character, than immortality would confer such power or character upon a natural person. It is no more a State instrument than a natural person exercising the same powers would be."

To this definition of a corporation, the committee see no reason to object; and when the true character of a private banking company is correctly understood, there seems to be no cogent reason why it may not be incorporated by Congress upon the principles here defined.

Banking, where the capital is owned by an association of individuals, is a private trade, carried on by the individuals constituting the company for their own profit. A mercantile company trade in produce and merchandise; a banking company trade in money, promissory notes, and bills of exchange. Both may carry on their trade without a charter of incorporation; the trade of both may be regulated by the law of the State in which they are located; and a charter of incorporation may be conferred upon either, without changing the character of their business, or clothing them with any portion of political power.

It is competent for the Government of the United States to make contracts with an association of individuals as well as with a single person. The Secretary of the Treasury may be authorized to employ an unincorporated banking company to take charge of, and transmit from place to place, the public revenue. For the performance of this service he may stipulate a compensation, but he cannot be authorized to barter a privilege inconsistent with the laws of the State where the company is located, by way of compensation for services to be performed. If such banking association be prohibited by the laws of the State, a contract with the General Government cannot suspend the operation of those laws. If such banking association be subject to State taxation, they cannot be exempted from their responsibility by a contract with the United States. But a capacity to transact its associate concerns in a legal and artificial name; a capacity to exist by perpetual succession, notwithstanding the natural death of the individuals; a capacity to sue, and a liability to be sued, without abatement, by the death of any one of the parties; an exemption from personal responsibility for the company debts, and conferring a separate character upon the company funds, so as to preserve them distinct from the individual property of the members of the company, are not privileges incompatible with State laws. And if investing a private company with these privileges may conduce to the public convenience and the public safety, in making contracts to receive and transmit the public moneys, conceding that Congress are empowered, under the Constitution, to confer these privileges, as a consideration for the performance of the services agreed upon, and for the purposes of public good, cannot possibly compromit the safety of the States. If their charter of incorporation confer upon the Bank of the United States no other privileges than are here enumerated, it is manifest that, in every other respect, their property and business stand upon the same footing with that of other individuals.

It was in this light that a charter incorporating a bank was contemplated by the first founders of the Bank of the United States. The power of establishing themselves where they pleased, without respect to the State authority, was not claimed by the old bank, nor did they arrogate to themselves any federal character, or any privilege which did not appertain to them as individual citizens. No new or extended privileges are conferred by its charter upon the present institution. It is created a private corporation of trade, " as much so as if the franchises were invested in a single person." But it has received its chartered privileges from the Government of the United States, and therefore it is that it is exempt from State taxation.

If the committee have been able to understand the opinion of the Supreme Court, this consequence is deduced from the five following propositions:

1. The Government of the Union, though limited in its powers, is supreme within its sphere of action.

2. It is the very essence of supremacy to remove all obstacles to its action within its own sphere, and so to modify every power vested in subordinate governments as to exempt its own operations from their influence.

3. A power to create implies a power to preserve.

4. A power to destroy, if wielded by a different hand, is hostile to and incompatible with, these powers to create and to preserve.

5. Where this repugnancy exists, that authority which is supreme must control, not yield to, that over which it is supreme.

These propositions are plausible and imposing, but, when carefully examined, and applied to the subject under consideration, it is conceived that no one of them can be sustained to the extent here laid down.

At the threshold of the inquiry, we demand what is meant by the assertion that " the Government of the Union is supreme within its sphere of action ?" If this observation is applied to a subject where no question of conflicting power arises, its truth may be safely admitted; and the proposition is equally applicable to the States. In the same sense, each State is equally " supreme within its sphere of action." In regulating our foreign trade, the Government of the Union is supreme; and in establishing the modes of conveyance, and the canons of descent, each State is equally supreme. But this proves nothing upon either side, when the relative powers and authorities of the General and State Governments are drawn into discussion.

The power to establish lighthouses, beacons, buoys, and public piers, is within the sphere of action of the Government of the Union; but, in practice, this power has never been considered supreme. It has always been exercised with the assent of the States, and with cessions of territory made by them.

The Cumberland road was laid out and constructed by the Government of the Union; consequently, the power to do it is considered within their sphere of action. Yet this power was not claimed as supreme; it was only exercised with the assent and approbation of the States through which the road was made.

Murder is an offence against all government, yet the Government of the United States cannot punish murder unless it be committed in the Army or Navy, upon the high seas, or within their forts and arsenals, or other places where they exercise exclusive jurisdiction. Except in the cases specified, the murder of an officer of the United States cannot be distinguished from an ordinary homicide. A judge of the federal courts, a marshal, a collector of the revenue, a postmaster, a member of either House of Congress, the President or Vice President, may be murdered, and, if the respective States refuse to interpose their authority to punish the perpetrator, he must escape with impunity. This Government, though supreme within its sphere of action, cannot protect the lives of its public functionaries by the punishment of those who may assail them. It can assert no jurisdiction, unless violence be offered to them in their official characters, and in the performance of official duties.

It may be answered to this that the punishment of murder is not within their sphere of action. True. But how futile is it to talk of a Government being supreme, which is not invested with the most common and ordinary mode of preserving its existence. It is supreme over individuals in cases entirely subject to Federal cognizance. But is it supreme over the States? It cannot coerce them either to elect Senators in Congress, or Electors of President and Vice President. A combination between one-half of the States, comprising one-third of the people only, possesses the power of disorganizing the Federal Government, in all its majesty of supremacy, without a single act of violence. It is expressly inhibited by the Constitution, from which this supremacy is derived, from calling the States as defendants before its courts. It cannot save from punishment one single citizen whom the State authorities have condemned. It is neither supreme to save, nor to punish. In what, then, does this supremacy consist, in which the separate States are not also supreme? In one thing only, and that is, the exercise by the Federal courts of appellate jurisdiction in cases, and between parties, made subjects to their jurisdiction by the Constitution. But the States, as parties, are not subject to their jurisdiction, but are expressly exempt from it; and, therefore, over the States and upon questions involving the extent of their powers and authority, the Government of the Union is not supreme. It cannot, according to the hypothesis of the second proposition, remove all obstacles to its action, and so modify the powers of the State governments as to exempt its own operations from their influence.

Is this second proposition sustainable upon any acknowledged principle of Constitutional law? It is certainly a doctrine of portentous import when connected, as it necessarily must be, with the proposition that precedes it: it claims, as an attribute of the Government of the Union, a power to *modify* every power vested in the State governments, so as to remove all obstacles to its own action, and exempt its own operations from their influence.

According to this doctrine, the States are not co-parties to the compact of Union, as asserted in 1798, by the States of Kentucky and Virginia, and established in 1800 by the American people. The rights, powers, and authorities of the States are not immutably established by Constitutional provisions; but are subject to modification, in order to give scope for the action of the Government of the Union.

The two propositions stand in a perfectly natural and logical connexion, though not thus arranged in the opinion: "The Government of the Union, though limited in its powers, is supreme within its sphere of action."

"It is of the very essence of supremacy to *remove* all obstacles to its action within its own sphere, and so to *modify* every power vested in *subordinate* governments as to exempt its own operations from their influence."

Therefore, we may very properly add the consequent—it is competent for the Government of the Union to remove all obstacles to its action, by so modifying the powers of the State governments as to exempt its own operations from their influence. If the postulates be admitted, this consequent is inevitable.

This result will hardly be contended for in explicit terms; it asserts a supremacy nowhere recognised in the Constitution. The powers retained by the States cannot be modified by the Government of the Union. To modify is to change, or give a new shape to, the power modified; and if the Government of the Union can give a new character to the powers reserved by the States, for the purpose of removing obstacles to their own power of action, there must soon be an end to the State governments. The Government of the Union asserts an exclusive authority in itself to determine its own sphere of action. On this point it is as supreme as upon any other. So soon as it has resolved that the exercise of any power appertains to it, that power assumes the character of supremacy, and removes by modification—puts down before its march—every power previously supposed to be vested in the States that may present any obstacle to its action. Thus, the Government of the Union may, and undoubtedly will, progressively draw all the powers of government into the vortex of its own authority. Against these doctrines the committee conceive that it is the duty of the States to enter their most solemn protest.

The committee do not admit that supremacy is an attribute either of the Government of the Union or of the State governments. Supremacy is an attribute of the people, and an attribute of the laws. In relation to the Governments the people are supreme, and the laws supreme over individuals. Government is but the medium through which the supreme power acts: the Government of the Union is the medium through which the American people act upon particular subjects that concern their interest and their welfare; the governments of the States are the medium through which the same people act upon other subjects, equally interesting and important to them. These two mediums of action are only brought into collision by the usurpations of one or the other. Neither is invested with power to render its encroachments permanent, by a modification of the powers of the other. While moving within its proper limits, neither can present an obstacle to the action of the other: both must proceed harmoniously. In respect to each other, neither is supreme, neither subordinate. The Government of the Union and the governments of the separate States are alike the property and the agencies of the whole American people. This principle is the base and bond of the American Union.

The third proposition is, "that a power to create implies a power to preserve."

As applicable to the Government of the Union

and the incorporation of the Bank of the United States, this proposition, in the broad sense of its expression, is considered totally inadmissible.

The committee have already attempted to demonstrate that the Bank of the United States is a mere private corporation of trade. Their charter confers upon them neither political character nor political power; it gives them corporate capacity, nothing more. The provision that the bank may establish branches in the States and Territories, when fairly construed, can only be regarded as giving corporate capacity to do so; and this is the only provision of the charter that, by any colorable interpretation, can be understood to vest them with a semblance of political power.

The legal faculty and capacity conferred by the charter, if constitutionally created, are preserved in existence by the very law that originates them. They become private vested rights, and are preserved by the same universal law that protects individual contracts.

But the trade and business of the bank, and the franchises conferred to aid in carrying them on, are separate and distinct matters. To lend money and drive a trade in bills of exchange and gold and silver bullion are not corporate franchises. These trades exist independent of the charter, and may be pursued by individuals without an act of incorporation. It is not the business itself, but the particular method of conducting it, that is created by the act of Congress incorporating the Bank of the United States.

Natural persons are clothed with an original, inherent capacity to make contracts, and to acquire property. In a corporation this capacity is artificial. In other respects, natural persons, and corporations of legal persons, stand upon the same principles. The power of making contracts, enjoyed by individuals, is subject to the regulations of law; the property acquired by individuals is liable to taxation for the support of those laws that originate and protect it. Private corporations of trade, upon every maxim of justice and common sense, are subjected to the same regulations and exactions.

The employments, professions, business, and trade of natural persons may be taxed as such; and laws for this purpose are not considered as violative of individual rights, or as incompatible with the existence and preservation of trade, business, and employments. No just principle is perceived upon which these laws should receive a different interpretation in their application to the trade and business of a private corporation.

According to the definition of a corporation heretofore given, the corporate franchises of the Bank of the United States invest the stockholders with immortality and individuality; with a capacity to act like one immortal being, to perpetuate their existence, to manage their own affairs, to hold property, and transmit it from hand to hand as a natural person could. These franchises are conferred by the Government of the Union to enable the company to conduct the business of lending money, and the trade in bills of exchange and gold and silver bullion, with convenience and security;

but the business and trade to be conducted are not corporate franchises, and are not created by the act of Congress. A tax assessed upon the business of the company does not touch their corporate franchises, however it may affect their convenience or their profit. This power to preserve, as asserted by the court, and applied to the subject before them, is not asserted for maintaining and preserving the corporate franchises of the bank, but for the purpose of giving to these corporate franchises action and employment everywhere, independent of State laws, and beyond the control of State legislation. When fairly traced to its consequences, the doctrine asserted amounts to this: that a corporation created by the Government of the Union is clothed with supreme authority to conduct its business, without respect to the existing laws of the States, and free from any apprehension of those that may be enacted.

A most serious objection to this doctrine is, that it asserts the power to preserve, not as pertaining to the Government of the Union, to be employed or not, at the discretion of Congress, but as incidental to the charter, and to be secured to the company by the judicial power alone.

The committee conceive that the power to create a corporation, and the power to preserve it by special privileges and exemptions, are powers of the same class and description; both are legislative powers, to be conferred or withheld at the discretion of the Legislature; and where a charter of incorporation stipulates no special privileges and exemptions, none can be supposed to exist. "Being the mere creature of law, it possesses only those properties conferred upon it, either expressly, or as incidental to its very existence."

Had Congress intended to exempt the bank from the taxing power of the State as the means of preserving its existence, a provision for that purpose should have been introduced into the charter. The power to make this provision would have been examined before the charter was created, and the intention of Congress would have been manifested. The people and the States would have been apprized of the pretensions of the bank before it got foothold among them, and before it had established a moneyed influence to support itself. Every privilege claimed by the company, when inserted in the charter, has received the sanction of the legislative authority, and is open to the examination of all. But to invest them with unknown and latent privileges to any extent that the Supreme Court may deem convenient, to preserve, not only their corporate franchises, but the most beneficial use of them, is undoubtedly a new doctrine as applied to corporations, and as dangerous as it is novel.

This company have claimed that the States cannot tax their corporate operations, or the profits arising from them; and the Supreme Court have sustained their claim as a privilege necessary to preserve their existence. By their charter, they are authorized to employ officers, clerks, and *servants*. Should the company claim to send slaves into Ohio, and employ them in their branches as *servants*, the committee would conceive the claim as well founded, and as likely to be sustained, as the exemption from taxation. It stands upon the same principle. If the States may control the company in the employment of servants, they may embarrass its operations, and impede a free and unrestrained exercise and enjoyment of their corporate faculties. By the laws of Ohio, a promise to pay the debt of another is not obligatory unless made in writing; but the charter of the company is silent as to the mode of binding parties that contract with them: they may claim that this law of contracts applies to individuals only, and cannot touch them without narrowing the beneficial use of the faculty conferred upon them by Congress. Who shall say that this claim may not be sustained? In short, who can undertake, with any prospect of success, to enumerate the privileges and exemptions to which, upon this doctrine, the bank are entitled?

It is important to glance at the train of implications with which this doctrine is connected. The power to create the bank implies the power to preserve it. The power to create is itself derived by implication. It is found among the subsidiary powers as incident to the choice of means for the administration of the Government. This implied power to create is made the foundation for further implication; it implies the power to preserve: and again, of necessity, the power to preserve implies a choice in selecting the means of preservation; and upon the doctrine of the court, all these powers are supreme, to the operations of which the constitutions and laws of the States can oppose no obstacle. It is certainly difficult to see the point where these implications terminate, or to name the power which they leave to the States unimpaired.

The Government of the Union have no authority, by the express provisions of the Constitution, to interfere with the law of contracts. They have found authority to institute a bank, or, in other words, to create a private corporation of trade; and with the power to create, they have possessed themselves of power to preserve, not the corporation they have created, but the business in which the corporation have engaged. This business extends over the whole region of contract, either direct, in negotiating loans of money, and purchasing and selling bills of exchange and gold and silver bullion, or indirect, in receiving and disposing of merchandise and real estate, pledged or mortgaged for debts previously contracted. From the aid of this corporation the States may withdraw their law of conveyances; or, as applied to their dealings, the States may introduce provisions regulating contracts, which the corporation may deem obstructions to the enjoyment of their corporate trade. From this doctrine, that the power to create implies the power to preserve, Congress may derive a power to frame a new law of contracts, and devise a new system of conveyances, suitable to the beneficial enjoyment of the trade of this corporation; and this new system, in the supremacy of its action, may disregard both fundamental laws and established maxims of jurisprudence.

The Government of the Union was not insti-

tuted to protect individual rights or to redress individual wrongs; but this power to preserve the trade, business, and property, of a corporation created by themselves, invests them with the power to frame a code of criminal law for the punishment of those who violate the property of the bank, and thus draw into the federal courts the ordinary administration of criminal justice. This is already attempted in the provision for punishing those who counterfeit the notes of the bank, and, upon the doctrine asserted, may be extended to cases of larceny, burglary, or robbery, upon their corporate property. No doctrine has ever yet been advanced that draws to the Government of the Union such a host of powers—none that contains such a potency for "rending into shreds" the authority of the States.

Those who claim for the Government of the Union the power of creating corporations hold that "one may be created in relation to the collection of the taxes, or to the trade with foreign countries, or between the States, or with the Indian tribes; because it is the province of the General Government to regulate those objects, and because it is incident to a general sovereign or legislative power to regulate a thing to employ all the means which relate to its regulation to the best advantage." The power to create all these corporations, upon the principle asserted, implies the power to preserve them; and the power to preserve implies a power in the Government of the Union to bargain with companies for monopolies of trade and exemptions from taxation; to place such companies above the power of the States, as means employed by themselves, which they have a right to use to the best advantage.

In the discussion of this subject an extraordinary and the most miraculous efficacy is given to the terms "employment of means;" and it is worthy of remark, that no effort is made to explain their true import, or the sense in which they are used. We are told that the collection of taxes, and the safe-keeping and transmission of money from place to place, are an end or object of Government, and that the bank is a convenient means of obtaining this end. But it is not the charter or corporate franchise that is used or employed for this purpose; it is the individuals that compose the company, as an aggregate body, that are thus used; and the corporate franchise bestowed upon them by the Government is conferred to enable them to transact their own business, and perform this service for the Government with greater security and convenience. At this moment the Government of the Union employs the Franklin Bank of Columbus to receive and pay out the public moneys; and, while thus employed, this bank is used as a means of Government; but, being thus used, is not supposed to invest it with any privilege peculiar to the public functionaries.

The Government and all its machinery and officers are but the means of the people for attaining the great ends declared in the preamble to the Constitution. Every person employed under the Constitution, from the President of the United States to the post-boy that carries the mail, partakes of this character of means. The law that the President is bound to see faithfully executed, and the horse that the post-boy rides, are alike, in a certain sense, means of the Government; but, in respect to privileges and exemptions, no man ever supposed them to stand upon the same footing. Those who hold offices directly under the Government may be regarded as principal means; those who are employed by contract, as incidental or subsidiary. The first class compose, as it were, a part of the Government direct, are intrusted with the exercise of some portion of political power, and are clothed with privileges and exemptions attached to their official stations. Those engaged by contract to perform services have no official character, and consequently cannot claim the exemptions attached to public office. Thus, a deputy postmaster is an officer under the Government, invested with privileges, and subject to disabilities attached to his office; but a contractor to carry the mail has no such character; yet both are means used by Government, under the Constitutional authority "to establish post offices and post roads."

The Bank of the United States is not a mean of the Government of the Union in the same sense with the Mint and the Post Office, but in the same sense with contractors to supply public stores, or to carry the mail. The director, assayer, chief coiner, engraver, treasurer, melter, and refiner, of the Mint, are public officers; so are the Postmaster General and deputy postmasters.— They cannot hold their offices and seats in Congress at the same time; they are appointed to and take an oath of office. But the workmen employed in the Mint, like contractors to carry the mail, and the drivers and riders they employ, are not public officers; nevertheless, they are necessary means in the employment of the Government. The stockholders in the Bank of the United States and the president and directors of that institution are not public officers. Even the directors appointed by the Government are destitute of public character. They are eligible to seats in Congress, which is conclusive evidence upon this point; and it is a monstrous doctrine to maintain that corporations created by the Government of the Union, in point of privilege and exemption, are principal means of Government, not to be distinguished from the officers of the Mint and the Post Office, while all the members and officers of such corporations are eligible to seats both in the Congress of the Union and the Legislatures of the several States. By this doctrine, the great principle of separating the departments of Government is completely broken down. Collectors of revenue, officers of the customs, Indian agents, and receivers of public moneys, under the Government of of the Union, may become legislators and judges in their own case, both in the General and State Governments. This consequence alone would seem sufficient to expose the unsoundness of the doctrine asserted.

It is singular that, in the very elaborate opinion which the committee have been engaged in examining, no definition should be given of the true character of the bank, but that, like the terms "employment of means," it should be left to doubtful and various interpretations. It is a public institution, or a private corporation of trade. If the former, with the privileges of office, the corporators must be subject to the disabilities of office. If the latter, like any other individual or bank employed by the Government of the Union, its trade and business must be regulated by State laws, and subject to State exactions. In support of their position that it is a private corporation of trade, the committee can adduce a judicial opinion delivered in the Supreme Court itself : "For instance, (says Mr. Justice Story,) a bank, created by the Government for its own uses, whose stock is exclusively owned by the Government, is, in the strictest sense, a public corporation. So is a hospital, created and endowed by the Government for general charity. But a bank whose stock is owned by private persons is a private corporation, although it is erected by the Government, and its objects and operations partake of a public nature. The same doctrine may be affirmed of insurance, canal, bridge, and turnpike companies. In all these cases, the uses may, in a certain sense, be called public, but the corporations are private; as much so, indeed, as if the franchise were vested in a single person."

We have seen that, by the employment of natural persons or State banks to perform those services stipulated to be performed by the Bank of the United States, they become, to a certain extent, means employed by the Government, and yet have never been regarded as public officers, privileged from the operation of State laws. May we not, therefore, paraphrase the language of the Chief Justice, and ask "If, then, a natural person or State bank employed by the Government of the Union to receive, keep, and pay out public moneys, would not become a public officer, or be considered as a member of the civil government, how is it that this artificial being, created by law for the purpose of being employed by the same Government for the same purposes, should become a part of the civil government of the country ? Is it because its existence, its capacities, its powers, are given by law ? Because the Government has given it the power to take and to hold property, in a particular form, and for particular purposes, has the Government a consequent right (as over all members of the civil government it must have) substantially to change that form, or to vary the purposes to which the property is to be applied ? This principle has never been asserted or recognised, and is supported by no authority."

Thus reasoned the judges of the Supreme Court upon the 2d of February, 1819. The case of McCulloch *vs.* Maryland had not then been argued or decided. And the doctrine that the Government, by chartering a private corporation of trade, placed the association upon the same foundation with the Mint and the Post Office, had then never been recognised in a court of law, and was "supported by no authority." If the public character of the Bank of the United States stands upon other foundation than that expressly negatived in these quotations, the committee have been unable to discover it: it is not explained or developed in the opinion that places them on a level with the Mint and the Post Office, and gives to their trade in bills of exchange and gold and silver bullion the same character as to the process of the federal courts.

When the committee deny that "a power to create implies a power to preserve," they are to be understood as denying the application of this principle only to the case of creating corporations. A power to create a public office necessarily implies a power to preserve that office; but a power to bestow a corporate franchise to carry on a private trade is totally different from creating a public office. A distinction between the corporate franchise, and the business to be conducted under it, must be always borne in mind; the power that creates a corporate franchise for private purposes not only can preserve such franchise, but cannot new model or impair it; its corporate character and existence are as secure as the existence and personal rights of a natural person; but its trade and business, like the employments of natural persons, remain subject to regulation by the local authorities where it seeks to locate them. Thus a power in the States to tax, or even to prohibit a trade in bills of exchange and gold and silver bullion, is not a power to destroy the corporate franchises of the Bank of the United States. These corporate franchises remain, notwithstanding the exercise of this power, just as the existence and rights of an individual remain, though his business is taxed, or he is forbidden to engage in certain employments. The Government of the Union has conferred upon the bank certain capacities for engaging in trade, but it has not and cannot confer an absolute right and power to drive this trade in contempt of State laws. It is made capable, but not sovereign; its capacity must be examined, not with a single eye to the supremacy of the power that created it, but with a whole view of what that power could confer, and what it has conferred.

If the committee have succeeded in showing that the power which created the Bank of the United States is not supreme, in the sense of the first two propositions, but is limited in its powers and means of preserving the bank, so as to render the third proposition untenable, the fourth and fifth propositions, which are founded upon, and consequences derived from, the other three, must necessarily be given up. As applied to the question under discussion, however, it has been shown that a power to tax their trade is not a power to destroy the corporation. It is not perceived how a power to diminish the profits of labor and capital, by exacting a portion of their proceeds for the support of Government, can be construed into a power to destroy human life and annihilate capital. The power of taxing the bank is denied, because it might be so used as to prevent the corporation from driving a profitable trade; and this is deemed a power to destroy the charter, which did not originate the trade, but merely created a facility for conducting it. But what is most singular is this: that, after arriving at this conclusion, an admission is made that at once demolishes the whole doctrine upon which it is founded.

It is conceded that each State may tax the stock owned by its citizens in this bank. Then it is not a public institution, exempt from State taxation, upon the great principle that the States cannot tax the offices, institutions, and operations of the Government of the Union. It is not that the States have no power to tax the bank; but that this power exists only over its capital, and does not extend to its operations. What, then, becomes of all the labored doctrines of the opinion? The Government of the Union, though supreme within its sphere of action, removing all obstacles, and so modifying all powers vested in subordinate Governments as to exempt its own operations from their influence, cannot, after all, preserve what it can create. Those who advance this pretension are compelled to admit, that, upon their own principles, a power to destroy may be wielded by the State Governments.

In its utmost extent, a State tax upon the operations of the bank can produce no other injury than a suspension of its business. By ceasing to trade, a tax upon business can always be avoided. Not so a tax upon capital. Should the States of Pennsylvania, New York, and Massachusetts combine to tax the stock in the Bank of the United States owned by their citizens, to an amount that must consume the annual profits and encroach upon the capital advanced, the destruction of the bank must be inevitable; for this tax upon capital may be exacted, whether it be productive or not. The power of the States to tax the business of the bank is denied upon the broad ground that the power to levy such a tax is tantamount to a power to destroy the bank, and is incompatible with a power in the Government of the Union to create it. Yet this power to tax the capital, though incontestably of greater potency to destroy the institution, is admitted to exist. Between the point decided and the point conceded there is a palpable contradiction, to which sound argument and just conclusions are never subject.

Another very absurd consequence results from the decision and admission, when connected together as they are in the opinion under consideration. A State tax upon the stock or actual capital invested by its citizens in the bank cannot reach or affect the stock owned by foreigners or by the other States; but a tax upon the business operates alike upon all the stockholders. Should Massachusetts tax the stock of her citizens, stock in the bank must be worth less in Massachusetts than elsewhere. Should all the States tax the stock owned by their citizens, stock held by foreigners must be most valuable. Should one State tax the stock so as to exhaust the capital, the citizens of that State must sell out to citizens of other States or to foreigners. Should all the States assess such a tax, the whole stock must be transferred to foreigners, or the bank annihilated. One consequence, therefore, of this admission, may be to throw the institution into the hands of foreigners, when our

Government will exhibit the strange spectacle of a company of foreign bankers regarded as a national institution, and, as such, protected by the Constitution of the Union from any of the burdens to which citizens are subject.

It may be said that this admission was unwarily made, and, upon further consideration, would be retracted as inconsistent with what had been previously decided. But the committee conceive that this explanation is quite unsatisfactory. It has been already stated that the Constitution does, in express terms, declare what subjects shall be exempt from the taxing power of the States. It was felt that indirectly to exempt other subjects was unwarrantable, upon all established principles of interpreting laws and constitutions. This argument was pressed; and, to escape its force, the admission was made, so that evidently it is part of the decision, and, as such, sweeps away the grand pillar upon which the whole decision rested.

If the committee have taken a correct view of the subject, it would seem manifest that, in denying to the States a power to tax private corporations of trade incorporated by the Government of the Union, where no doubt exists of the power to create the incorporation, it becomes necessary to maintain many doctrines of very doubtful character and dangerous tendency; while conceding to them this power involves nothing either doubtful or dangerous. It strips such corporations of all pretensions to be regarded as instruments of Government, in the same sense as the Mint and the Post Office; but it preserves untouched their corporate franchises, and concedes to them every right and privilege which a natural person is entitled to claim. It presents no obstruction to the legitimate action of the Government of the Union, but places it, in the establishment of private corporations of trade, upon the same foundation as in erecting lighthouses and constructing roads.

It is in nothing derogatory to this corporation called the Bank of the United States, nor to the Government of the Union that created it, to place its trade upon the same footing with that of a private citizen employed by the Government. The contractor to transport the mail must use horses and carriages; without them, he cannot comply with his contract. They are means or instruments employed by Government, but they are subject to State taxation, as other property of the same description. This has been a universal practice, and has never been deemed any obstruction to the action of the Government of the Union. The States cannot tax the transportation of the mail without obstructing the action of the Government; but were an association incorporated to transport the mail all over the Union, with capacity to trade in live stock and agricultural products, there can be no doubt but that their private trade and property would be subject to State taxation.

The committee have not deemed it necessary to examine any argument founded upon a supposed abuse of power by the States. As, between States, every argument of this sort is inadmissible, because it may be urged with equal force against

the exercise of any power by either, and concludes to the destruction of all authority. There can be no doubt but the States will at all times be ready to encourage, rather than repress, the introduction and employment of capital within their dominion, where it may probably be of any general advantage. Of this the State authorities are much more competent judges than capitalists, or their agents, at a distance can be. It must always be unwise to force a capital into a country against the sense of those who administer the Government. That the Bank has sustained great losses by sending branches into this State, is now notorious; that their trade and loans have been highly injurious to all the best interests of the State, cannot be disputed. This loss on the one hand, and injury on the other, would have been avoided, had the Bank consulted the authorities of the State instead of holding counsel with money-jobbers and speculators.

The committee have carefully examined the subject; and, without pretending to present it in all the views of which it is susceptible, have urged only those which appear to them most prominent. The result of their deliberations is, that the Bank of the United States is, in their opinion, a mere private corporation of trade, and, as such, its trade and business must be subject to the taxing power of the State.

In considering what course the committee should recommend as proper to be adopted at this time, one point of difficulty has presented itself. It is urged by many that the tax levied and collected is enormous in amount, and, therefore, unequal and unjust. It is readily admitted that this allegation is not entirely unfounded, and all must agree that it does not comport with the character of a State to afford any color to accuse her of injustice. Even in the assertion of a right, it is highly derogatory for a State to act oppressively; and all injustice is oppression. It cannot be doubted but that the tax was levied as a penalty, and that it was not supposed the Bank would venture to incur it. It was an act of temerity in them to do so; and although in this view the tax was justly, and, in the opinion of the committee, legally collected, yet, under all the circumstances of the case, the committee conceive that the State ought to be satisfied with effecting the objects for which the law was enacted.

At this time the Bank can have little object in continuing its branches, except to maintain the point of right, which may not be definitively settled by the controversy. The State, having refused to use the money collected, has no interest but that of character and an assertion of the right. If an accommodation can be effected without prejudice to the rights upon either side, it would seem to be desirable to all parties. With this view, as well as with a view to remove all improper impressions, the committee recommend that a proposition of compromise be made by law, making provision that, upon the Bank discontinuing the suits now prosecuted against the public officers, and giving assurance that the branches shall be withdrawn, and only an agency left to settle

Ohio—Bank of the United States.

its business and collect its debts, the amount collected for tax shall be paid, without interest.

But the committee conceive that the General Assembly ought not to stop here. The reputation of the State has been assailed throughout the United States; and the nature of the controversy, and her true course of conduct, have alike been very much misunderstood. It behooves the General Assembly, even if a compromise be effected, to take measures for vindicating the character of the State, and also for awakening the attention of the separate States to the consequences that may result from the doctrines of the federal courts upon the questions that have arisen. And, besides, as it is possible that the proposition of compromise may not be accepted, it is the duty of the General Assembly to take ulterior measures for asserting and maintaining the rights of the State by all Constitutional means within their power.

In general, partial legislation is objectionable; but this is no ordinary case, and may therefore call for and warrant extraordinary measures. Since the exemptions claimed by the bank are sustained upon the proposition that the power that created it must have the power to preserve it, there would seem to be a strict propriety in putting the creating power to the exercise of this preserving power, and thus ascertaining distinctly whether the executive and legislative departments of the Government of the Union will recognise, sustain, and enforce the doctrine of the judicial department.

For this purpose the committee recommend that provision be made by law forbidding the keepers of our jails from receiving into their custody any person committed at the suit of the Bank of the United States, or for any injury done to them; prohibiting our judicial officers from taking acknowledgments of conveyances, where the bank is a party, or when made for their use, and our recorders from receiving or recording such conveyances; forbidding our courts, justices of the peace, judges, and grand juries, from taking any cognizance of any wrong alleged to have been committed upon any species of property owned by the bank, or upon any of its corporate rights or privileges; and prohibiting our notaries public from protesting any notes or bills held by the bank or their agents, or made payable to them.

The adoption of these measures will leave the bank exclusively to the protection of the Federal Government, and its Constitutional power to preserve it in the sense maintained by the Supreme Court may thus be fairly, peaceably, and constitutionally tested. Congress must be called on to provide a criminal code to punish wrongs committed upon it, and to devise a system of conveyances to enable it to receive and transmit estates; and, being thus called on to act, the National Legislature must be drawn to the serious consideration of a subject which the committee believe demands much more attention than it has excited. The measures proposed are peaceable and Constitutional; conceived in no spirit of hostility to the Government of the Union, but intended to bring fairly before the nation great and important questions, which

must one day be discussed, and which may now be very safely investigated.

The committee conclude by recommending the adoption of the following resolutions:

Resolved by the General Assembly of the State of Ohio, That in respect to the powers of the Governments of the several States that compose the American Union, and the powers of the Federal Government, this General Assembly do recognise and approve the doctrines asserted by the Legislatures of Kentucky and Virginia in their resolutions of November and December, 1798, and January, 1800, and do consider that their principles have been recognised and adopted by a majority of the American people.

Resolved, further, That this General Assembly do protest against the doctrines of the Federal circuit court sitting in this State, avowed and maintained in their proceedings against the officers of State upon account of their official acts, as being in direct violation of the eleventh amendment to the Constitution of the United States.

Resolved, further, That this General Assembly do assert, and will maintain, by all legal and Constitutional means, the right of the States to tax private business and property of any private corporation of trade, incorporated by the Congress of the United States, and located to transact its corporate business within any State.

Resolved, further, That the Bank of the United States is a private corporation of trade, the capital and business of which may be legally taxed in any State where they may be found.

Resolved, further, That this General Assembly do protest against the doctrine that the political rights of the separate States that compose the American Union, and their powers as sovereign States, may be settled and determined in the Supreme Court of the United States, so as to conclude and bind them in cases contrived between individuals, and where they are, no one of them, parties direct.

Resolved, further, That the Governor transmit to the Governors of the several States a copy of the foregoing report and resolutions, to be laid before their respective Legislatures, with a request from this General Assembly that the Legislature of each State may express their opinion upon the matters therein contained.

Resolved, further, That the Governor transmit a copy of the foregoing report and resolutions to the President of the United States, and to the President of the Senate and Speaker of the House of Representatives of the United States, to be laid before their respective Houses, that the principles upon which this State has, and does proceed, may be fairly and distinctly understood.

HOUSE OF REPRESENTATIVES, *Dec.* 28, 1820.

The foregoing report approved, and resolutions adopted.—Attest: WM. DOHERTY,
Clerk House of Rep's.

IN SENATE, *January* 3, 1821.

Report and resolutions concurred in.
Attest: RICHARD COLLINS,
Clerk of the Senate.

MILITARY PEACE ESTABLISHMENT.

—

[Communicated to the House, December 12, 1820.]

WAR DEPARTMENT, *Dec.* 12, 1820.

SIR: In obedience to a resolution of the House of Representatives, of the 11th of May last, "directing that the Secretary of War report to this House, at the commencement of the next session, a plan for the reduction of the Army to six thousand non-commissioned officers, musicians, and privates, and preserving such parts of the corps of engineers, as in his opinion, without regard to that number, it may be for the public interest to retain; and also what saving of the public revenue will be produced by such arrangement of the Army as he may propose in conformity with this resolution," I have the honor to make the following report:

I deem it proper, before a plan is presented in detail for reducing the Army, as proposed in the resolution, to state briefly the general principles on which it is conceived our Military Peace Establishment ought to be organized. It will be readily admitted, that the organization of the Army ought to have reference to the objects for which it is maintained, and ought to be such as may be best calculated to effect such objects; as it must be obvious, on the slightest reflection, that on considerations connected therewith ought to depend, not only its numbers, but also the principles on which it ought to be formed.

The necessity of a standing army in peace is not believed to be involved in the subject under consideration, as the resolution presupposes the propriety of maintaining one; and, in fact, its necessity is so apparent, that even those least friendly to the Army have never attempted to abolish it, or even to reduce it, since the late war, much below the number proposed in the resolution. The objects for which a standing army in peace ought to be maintained, may be comprised under two classes: those which, though they have reference to a state of war, yet are more immediately connected with its duties in peace, and those which relate immediately and solely to war. Under the first class may be enumerated, as the leading objects, the garrisoning of the forts along our Atlantic frontier, in order to preserve them, and to cause the sovereignty of the United States to be respected in their immediate neighborhood, and the occupying of certain commanding posts on our inland frontier, to keep in check our savage neighbors, and to protect our newly formed and feeble settlements in that quarter. These are, doubtless, important objects, but are by no means so essential as those which relate immediately and solely to a state of war; and though not to be neglected wholly, ought not to have any decided influence in the organization of our Peace Establishment. Without, therefore, making any farther remark on this point of the inquiry, I will proceed to consider the other class, on which, as it comprises the great and leading inducements to maintain in this country a regular army in peace, the prominent features of its organization ought to depend.

However remote our situation from the great

Powers of the world, and however pacific our policy, we are, notwithstanding, liable to be involved in war; and, to resist with success its calamities and dangers, a standing army in peace, in the present improved state of the military science, is an indispensable preparation. The opposite opinion cannot be adopted, without putting to hazard the independence and safety of the country. I am aware that the militia is considered, and in many respects justly, as the great national force; but, to render them effective, every experienced officer must acknowledge that they require the aid of regular troops. Supported by a suitable corps of trained artillerists, and by a small but well disciplined body of infantry, they may be safely relied on to garrison our forts, and to act in the field as light troops. In these services their zeal, courage, and habit of using fire-arms, would be of great importance, and would have their full effect. To rely on them beyond this—to suppose our militia capable of meeting in the open field the regular troops of Europe—would be to resist the most obvious truth, and the whole of our experience as a nation. War is an art, to obtain perfection in which much time and experience, particularly for the officers, are necessary. It is true, that men of great military genius occasionally appear, who, though without experience, may, when an army is already organized and disciplined, lead it to victory; yet I know of no instance, under circumstances nearly equal, in which the greatest talents have been able, with irregular and undisciplined troops, to meet with success those that were regularly trained. Genius, without much experience, may command, but it cannot go much further. It cannot at once organize and discipline an army, and give it that military tone and habit which only, in the midst of imminent danger, can enable it to perform the most complex evolutions with precision and promptitude. Those qualities which essentially distinguish an army from an assemblage of untrained individuals, can only be acquired by the instruction of experienced officers. If they, particularly the company and regimental officers, are inexperienced, the Army must remain undisciplined; in which case the genius, and even the experience of the commander, will be of little avail. The great and leading objects, then, of a Military Establishment in peace, ought to be to create and perpetuate military skill and experience; so that at all times the country may have at its command a body of officers sufficiently numerous, and well instructed in every branch of duty, both of the line and staff; and the organization of the Army ought to be such as to enable the Government, at the commencement of hostilities, to obtain a regular force, adequate to the emergencies of the country, properly organized and prepared for actual service. It is thus only that we can be in the condition to meet the first shocks of hostilities with unyielding firmness, and to press on an enemy while our resources are yet unexhausted. But if, on the other hand, disregarding the sound dictates of reason and experience, we should in peace neglect our Military Establishment, we must, with a powerful and skilful enemy, be exposed to the most distressing calamities. Not all the zeal, courage, and patriotism of our militia, unsupported by regularly trained and disciplined troops, can avert them. Without such troops, the two or three first campaigns would be worse than lost. The honor of our arms would be tarnished, and the resources of the country uselessly lavished; for, in proportion to the want of efficiency, and a proper organization must, in actual service, be our military expenditures. When taught by sad experience, we would be compelled to make redoubled efforts with exhausted means, to regain those very advantages which were lost for the want of experience and skill. In addition to the immense expenditure which would then be necessary, exceeding manifold what would have been sufficient to put our Peace Establishment on a respectable footing, a crisis would be thus brought on of a most dangerous character If our liberty should ever be endangered by the military power gaining the ascendency, it will be from the necessity of making those mighty and irregular efforts to retrieve our affairs, after a series of disasters, caused by the want of adequate military knowledge; just as, in our physical system, a state of the most dangerous excitement and paroxysm follows that of the greatest debility and prostration. To avoid these dangerous consequences, and to prepare the country to meet a state of war, particularly at its commencement, with honor and safety, much must depend on the organization of our Military Peace Establishment; and I have, accordingly, in the plan about to be proposed for the reduction of the Army, directed my attention mainly to that point, believing it to be of the greatest importance.

To give such an organization, the leading principle in its formation ought to be, that, at the commencement of hostilities, there should be nothing either to new-model or to create. The only difference, consequently, between the peace and the war formation of the Army, ought to be in the increased magnitude of the latter; and the only change, in passing from the former to the latter, should consist in giving to it the augmentation which will then be necessary.

It is thus, and thus only, the dangerous transition from peace to war may be made without confusion or disorder; and the weakness and danger, which otherwise would be inevitable, be avoided. Two consequences result from this principle: First, the organization of the staff in a Peace Establishment ought to be such that every branch of it should be completely formed, with such extension as the number of troops and posts occupied may render necessary; and, secondly, that the organization of the line ought, as far as practicable, to be such that, in passing from the peace to the war formation, the force may be sufficiently augmented, without adding new regiments or battalions; thus raising the war on the basis of the Peace Establishment, instead of creating a new army to be added to the old, as at the commencement of the late war. The next principle to be observed is, the organization ought to be such as to induce, in time of peace, citizens of

adequate talents and respectability of character to enter and remain in the military service of the country, so that the Government may have officers at its command, who, to the requisite experience, would add the public confidence. The correctness of this principle can scarcely be doubted, for, surely, if it is worth having an army at all, it is worth having it well commanded.

These are the general principles upon which I propose to form the organization of the Army, as proposed to be reduced under the resolution. By reference to tables A and B, which contain the proposed and present organizations, it will be seen that the principal difference between them is in the reduction of the rank and file. The present organization of the staff, with its branches, is retained, with slight alterations. The principal changes in it are, in that of the Commissary General of Purchases, and the Judge Advocates, by which it is intended that they should conform more exactly to the principles on which the other branches are now formed. It is believed that the true principle of its organization is, that every distinct branch of the staff should terminate in a chief, to be stationed, at least in peace, near the Seat of Government, and to be made responsible for its condition. It is thus that the Government may at all time obtain correct knowledge of the condition of the Army in every particular, and be enabled to introduce method, order, and economy, in its disbursements. It is, at present, with slight exceptions, thus organized, and the beneficial effects of it have already been strikingly exemplified by experience. Since the passage of the act of the 14th of April, 1818, which gave the present organization to the staff, the expense of the Army has been greatly reduced, while, at the same time, the various articles supplied have been improved in quality, and the punctuality with which they have been issued; and while the movements of the Army have, at least for the present, been rendered more expensive by occupying the distant frontier posts at the mouth of the St. Peter's and at the Council Bluffs. By a statement from the Adjutant and Inspector General, and the books of the Second Auditor, marked C, containing the Army disbursements from 1818 to 1820 inclusive, it appears that the expense of the Army in 1818, the year in which the present organization commenced, amounted to three millions seven hundred and forty-eight thousand four hundred and forty-five dollars and one cent, while the amount of warrants issued for current disbursements to the first of November this year, has amounted only to two millions six hundred and sixteen thousand five hundred and twenty-six dollars and eleven cents, and the disbursements of the whole year will, probably, not exceed two millions seven hundred thousand dollars. In the year 1818, the aggregate average number of the Military Establishment, including the cadets, amounted to eight thousand one hundred and ninety-nine, and that of this year to nine thousand six hundred and eleven. It is admitted that, during the same period, a considerable reduction has taken place in many of the articles which

Military Peace Establishment.

constitute the supplies of the Army, the effect of which has been to reduce its expense; but, on examination, it will appear that the diminution on this account is much less than what on the first impression might be supposed. Many of the more considerable items, which constitute the expenses of the Army, are fixed by law, and do not fluctuate with the change of prices, such as the pay of the officers and men, the subsistence of the former, and the allowance to them for servants, forage, transportation of baggage, &c. All of the items estimated for, by the Paymaster General, excepting clothing for servants, which is of small amount, partake of this character; to which, if we add those in the Quartermaster General's estimates, which, although the price of some of them have in the period under consideration been reduced, yet that has been at least balanced in the increased expenditure of that department for the last two years, by the extension and increased number of the military posts; it will result, that the reduction in the expense of the Army by the diminution of prices is substantially confined to the clothing, medical, and subsistence departments. Some pains have been taken to ascertain this diminution, in the various articles supplied by them, and it has resulted in the belief, that the average of these supplied by the clothing and medical departments were, in the year 1818, about seven per cent. higher than in this, and in the subsistence about forty per cent. With these data, it is ascertained, that the expense of the Army this year, had no diminution in price since 1818 taken place, would have amounted, deducting for the difference of the average number of the two years, and allowing for the expenditure of the Seminole war in 1818, to about two millions seven hundred and ninety-one thousand, and thirty-eight dollars and fifty-five cents. This sum, deducted from three millions seven hundred and forty-eight thousand four hundred and forty-five dollars and one cent, the expense of the Army in 1818, gives for the actual saving, after allowing for the diminution of prices, the sum of nine hundred and fifty-seven thousand three hundred and fifty-six dollars and forty-six cents, (see table D,) which has been effected through the organization of the present staff, by enabling the department to superintend, in its minute details, as well the various disbursements of the Army, as the measures taken to prevent the waste of public property. The amount of saving may appear to be very great, but it is confidently believed, that it cannot be materially reduced by any just mode of calculation of which the subject is susceptible.

As great as this result is, it is only in war that the benefits of a proper organization of the staff can be fully realized. With a complete organization, and experienced officers, trained in time of peace to an exact and punctual discharge of their duty, the saving in war (not to insist on an increased energy and success in our military movements) would be of incalculable advantage to the country. The number of deputies and assistants in each branch ought to be regulated by the exigency of the service, and this must obviously depend much more on the number of posts than on the number of troops; and as no material change can, consistently with the public interest, be made as to the posts, under the proposed reduction, little diminution can be made in the number of subordinate officers belonging to the staff.

It is also proposed to retain the two major and four brigadier generals. Although it is not probable that there will be concentrated, in time of peace, at any one point, a force equal to the command of a single major, or even a brigadier general, yet it is conceived that it is important to the service that they should be retained. As two regiments, with a proper proportion of artillery and light troops, constitute, in our service, one brigade, and two brigades a division, the command of a major general, the number of regiments and battalions, under the proposed organization, thus gives a command equal to that of two major and four brigadier generals. But a more weighty and, in my opinion, decisive reason, why they should be retained, may be found in the principle already stated, that the organization of the Peace Establishment ought to be such as to induce persons of talent and respectability to enter and continue in the military service. To give to the officer of the Army the necessary skill and equivalents, the Military Academy is an invaluable part of our Establishment; but that alone will be inadequate. For this purpose, respectability of rank and compensation must be given to the officers of the Army. Every prudent individual, in selecting his course of life, must be governed, making some allowance for natural disposition, essentially by the rewards which attend the various pursuits open to him. Under our free institutions, every one is left free to make his selection; and most of the pursuits of life, followed with industry and skill, lead to opulence and respectability. The profession of arms, in the well established state of things which exists among us, has no reward but what is attached to it by law; and if that should be inferior to other professions, it would be idle to suppose individuals, possessed of the necessary talents and character, would be induced to enter it. A mere sense of duty ought not, and cannot, be safely relied on. It supposes that individuals would be actuated by a stronger sense of duty towards the Government than the latter towards them.

If we may judge from experience, it would seem that the Army, even with these important commands, which, from their rank and compensation, must operate strongly on those who have a military inclination, does not present inducements to remain in it, stronger than, nor even as strong as, those of most of the other respectable pursuits of life.

The number of resignations has been very great, of which many are among the most valuable officers. Should the number of generals be reduced, the motive for entering or continuing in service must also be greatly reduced; for, like the high prizes in a lottery, though they can be obtained by a few only, yet they operate on all those who adventure; so those important stations which they occupy are, with those the best qualified to serve their country, the principal motive to enter or remain in the Army. To retain them is, in fact, the cheapest mode of commanding such talents; for, to pursue the metaphor, if the high prizes were distributed among all of the tickets, there would be but few adventurers; so, if the compensation attached to the general officers were distributed proportionably among the other officers, the inducement which the Army now holds out for a military profession, to individuals of suitable character, would be almost wholly lost. If the generals were reduced to one major and two brigadiers, the saving would not exceed $14,432 annually, which, distributed among the officers in proportion to their pay, would give to a lieutenant but $25 59 additional pay, and to a captain $30 87 annually, a sum too inconsiderable to have much effect.

I will proceed next to make a few remarks on that portion of the organization which proposes to reduce the rank and file, without a correspondent reduction of the battalions and regiments. By a reference to statement A, it will be seen that it is proposed to add the rifle regiment to those of the infantry, and unite the ordnance and light and heavy artillery, into one corps of artillery, which, when thus blended, to form nine regiments of infantry, and five battalions of artillery, from the latter of which the corps of ordnance is to be taken, to consist of one colonel, one lieutenant colonel, two majors, seven captains, and as many lieutenants as the President may judge necessary. This organization will require all the officers of the line of the present Army to be retained.

No position connected with the organization of the Peace Establishment is susceptible of being more rigidly proved, than that the proportion of its officers to the rank and file ought to be greater than in a War Establishment. It results immediately from a position, the truth of which cannot be fairly doubted, and which I have attempted to illustrate in the preliminary remarks, that the leading object of a regular army in time of peace ought to be, to enable the country to meet, with honor and safety, particularly at the commencement of war, the dangers incident to that state; to effect this object, as far as practicable, the peace organization ought, as has been shown, to be such, that, in passing to a state of war, there should be nothing either to new-model or to create; and that the difference between that and the war organization ought to be simply in the greater magnitude of the latter. The application of this principle has governed in that portion of the formation of the proposed Military Establishment now under consideration. The companies, both of the artillery and infantry, are proposed to be reduced to their minimum peace formation, the former to consist of sixty-four privates and non-commissioned officers, and the latter of thirty-seven, which will give to the aggregate of both corps, thus formed, six thousand three hundred and sixteen non-commissioned officers, musicians, and privates. Without adding a single officer, or a single company, they may be augmented, should

a just precaution, growing out of foreign relations, render it necessary, to eleven thousand five hundred fifty-eight; and, pending hostilities, by adding two hundred and eighty-eight officers, the two corps, on the maximum of the war formation, may be raised to the respectable force of four thousand five hundred and forty-five of the artillery, and fourteen thousand four hundred and ninety of the infantry, making in the aggregate nineteen thousand and thirty-six officers, non-commissioned officers, and privates. The war organization, thus raised on the basis of the Peace Establishment, will bring into effective operation the whole of the experience and skill of the latter, which, with attention, would, in a short period, be communicated to the new recruits, and the officers recently appointed, so as to constitute a well disciplined force. Should the organization of full companies, on the contrary, be adopted for the Peace Establishment, this process could be carried to a very limited extent. Six thousand men so organized can be augmented on the full War Establishment only to nine thousand one hundred and fifteen by doubling the battalions. Any additional force, beyond that, must be obtained by adding new regiments and battalions, with all the disadvantages of inexperience in the officers and men, without the means of immediate instruction. This was the fatal error at the commencement of the late war, which cost the country so much treasure and blood. The Peace Establishment which preceded it was very imperfectly organized and did not admit of the necessary augmentation; nor did the Government avail itself of even its limited capacity in that respect. The forces raised were organized into new corps, in which, consequently, every branch of military duty was to be learned by the officers as well as men. But, with all these disadvantages, the experience and discipline of the old establishment was of immense use, and has not been duly appreciated. The officers belonging to it gradually diffused their military knowledge through the Army, and contributed much to the brilliant results of the campaign of 1814. For the truth of this assertion, I might with confidence appeal to those officers who then acquired so much glory for themselves and their country.

Another reason remains to be urged, why, in the peace establishment, the number of officers ought to be great compared with the actual force. At the commencement of war an adequate number of experienced officers is of greater importance than that of disciplined troops, even were it possible to have the latter without the former; for it is not difficult to form in a short time well disciplined troops by experienced officers, but the reverse is impossible. The qualifications of the officers are essentially superior to those of the soldiers, and are more difficult to be acquired. The progress of military science has not added much to the difficulty of performing the duty of the soldier, or of training him, but it has greatly to that of the officer. No Government can, in the present improved state of military science, neglect with impunity to instruct a sufficient number of its citizens in a science indispensable to its independence and safety, and to perfect which instruction, it is necessary that some portion of them (the number to be regulated by the resources of the country and its relation with other Governments) should make arms their profession.

I have thus presented an organization which I deem the most effective, and which, in the future exigencies of the country, may be of the utmost importance. A different one, requiring for the present an expenditure something less than that proposed, might, in some respects, be more agreeable at this moment; but, believing that nothing in our situation or in our relation with other Powers, however pacific at this time, can give a certain assurance of uninterrupted peace, a state which may exist in the imagination of the poet, but which no nation has yet had the good fortune to enjoy, I have deemed it my duty to present that organization which will most effectually protect the country against the calamities and dangers of any future contest in which it may be our misfortune to be involved.

Economy is certainly a very high political virtue, intimately connected with the power and the public virtue of the community. In military operations, which, under the best management, are so extensive, it is of the utmost importance; but, by no propriety of language can that arrangement be called economical, which, in order that our Military Establishment in peace should be rather less expensive, would, regardless of the purposes for which it ought to be maintained, render it unfit to meet the dangers incident to a state of war.

With a single observation, which was omitted in its proper place, I will conclude my remarks. The plan proposed for the reduction of the Army gives six thousand three hundred and sixteen non-commissioned officers, musicians, and privates, instead of six thousand, the number fixed in the resolution. It was found difficult to form an organization on proper principles, which would give that precise number, and, as the difference was not deemed very material, I have ventured to deviate to that extent from the terms of the resolution.

I have the honor to be, &c.,
         J. C. CALHOUN.

Hon. JOHN W. TAYLOR,
    Speaker of the House of Representatives.

REPORT ON FORTIFICATIONS.

[Communicated to the House, February 15, 1821.]
DEPARTMENT OF WAR,
         February 12, 1821.

SIR: In compliance with a resolution of the House of Representatives of the 9th instant, directing "that the Secretary of War report to that House the progress which has been made by the Board of Engineers, in determining the sites and plans of fortifications of the coast of the United States; the sites which may have been selected;

the estimates of the expense in completing the several works; the number of troops necessary to garrison them in peace and in war; the progress made in erecting the fortifications; the advantage resulting from the system when completed, particularly in reducing the expense of defending the Atlantic frontier," I have the honor to enclose a report of the Board of Engineers, marked A, and a report of the Engineer Department, marked B, which give the information required by the resolution.

It may be proper to observe that the projected fortifications have been distributed into three classes, according to their relative importance, and that it is determined to erect those of the first class, previous to the commencement of the second and third classes, with the exception of the work at Mobile Point and Dauphin Island. These works were commenced in preference to those projected at Bayou Bienvenue, and Fort St. Philip, for, although the latter are placed in the first class, it was not however deemed proper to commence with them, as they were much less extensive than the two former, and could be completed in a short time, should the state of our relations with other Powers render it necessary.

The contractors for the works at the Rigolets were, by the arrangements with them, to have erected those contemplated at Chef Menteur, but so many impediments have been encountered, that it has been necessary for them to confine their operations wholly to the former.

I have the honor to be your obedient servant,
         J. C. CALHOUN.

Hon. JOHN W. TAYLOR,
    Speaker of the House of Representatives.

CITY OF WASHINGTON,
         February 7, 1821.

SIR: The following summary of the operations of the Board of Engineers, called for by your order, is respectfully submitted:

The commission charged with reconnoitering the frontiers of the United States has completed the three most important sections of the maritime boundaries, viz: The coast of the Gulf of Mexico, the coast between Cape Hatteras and Cape Cod and the coast between Cape Cod and the River St. Croix. The coast between Cape Hatteras and Cape Fear has likewise been surveyed; and the only section which remains to be examined, to complete the reconnoissance of the coast, is South Carolina and Georgia.

The reports presented in 1818, 1819, 1820, and 1821, to the Hon. Secretaries of the War and Navy Departments, were accompanied by every necessary plan, table, &c., and embrace every naval and military consideration, both as to the attack, and as to the defence of the frontier, as to fixing the sites for the great naval depots, and as to protecting, by the general system of defence, the general system of internal navigation. We must refer to the details of these reports to show the importance of establishing a complete system for the protection of the frontiers, and the necesity of building this system upon principles harmonizing with the modern system of warfare. It will be seen that most of the existing forts only defend single points, and satisfy only a few essential conditions; and that they have not been planned with a view to the defence of the frontiers, considered as one great and combined system, whose several parts should be connected and should mutually support each other. The navy yards (excepting that of Charlestown near Boston) have all been improperly placed; the conveniences for the erection of the necessary establishments having alone been taken into consideration, while all other requisites for points so important, such as security against attack by sea or land, facility of receiving all kinds of building materials in time of war as well as in time of peace, vicinity to a place of rendezvous, have been overlooked.

A defensive system for the frontiers of the United States is therefore yet to be created; its bases are, first, a navy; second, fortifications; third, interior communication by land and water; and, fourth, a regular army and well organized militia; these means must all be combined so as to form a complete system.

The navy must, in the first place, be provided with proper establishments for construction and repair, harbors of rendezvous, stations, and ports of refuge. It is only by taking into view the general character, as well as the details, of the whole frontier, that we can fix on the most advantageous points for receiving these naval depots, harbors of rendezvous, stations, and ports of refuge.

On these considerations, Burwell's bay, in James river, and Charlestown, near Boston, have been especially recommended by the commission, as the most proper sites for the great naval arsenals of the South and of the North. Hampton Roads and Boston Roads as the chief rendezvous, and Narraganset bay as an indispensable accessary to Boston Roads. (See reports of 1819 and 1820.)

It is also from an attentive consideration of the whole maritime frontier, of the interior, and of the coastwise navigation, that Mobile bay on the Gulf of Mexico, St. Mary's in the Chesapeake, the Delaware, New York bay, Buzzard's bay, New London, Marblehead, Portsmouth, Portland, the mouths of the Kennebeck and Penobscot, and Mount Desert bay, have been fixed upon as stations and ports of refuge, as necessary and essential to our merchant vessels as to our navy.

Smithville and Beaufort, North Carolina; Annapolis and Baltimore, Maryland; New Haven, Connecticut; Salem, in Massachusetts; and Wiscasset, in Maine, have likewise been examined with attention, with a view to secure them from attack by sea or land. (See reports of 1819, 1820, and 1821.)

St. Mary's river and Savannah, in Georgia; Beaufort, Charleston, and Georgetown, in South Carolina, will be examined and surveyed in the course of this year.

After determining the general and connected system of naval depots, harbors of rendezvous, stations, and ports of refuge, the commission, in the next place, traced the scheme of fortifications

necessary to protect this system, and at the same time to guard the whole frontier against invasion. The forts projected by the commission for this purpose satisfy one or more of the following conditions:

1. To close important harbors to an enemy and secure them to the navy of the country.

2. To deprive an enemy of strong positions, where, protected by his naval superiority, he might fix permanent quarters in our territory, maintain himself during the war, and keep the whole frontier in perpetual alarm.

3. To cover our great cities against attack.

4. To prevent as much as possible the great avenues of interior navigation from being blockaded by a naval force at their entrance into the ocean.

5. To cover the coastwise and interior navigation, and to give to our navy the means necessary for protecting this navigation.

6. To cover the great naval establishments.

A rapid review of the works which have been projected by the commission, will exhibit, with sufficient distinctness, the advantages which must result from their construction.

In Louisiana, the forts projected at the Turn of Plaquemines, at the Bayou Bienvenue, at the Chef Menteur, at the Rigolets, form altogether a system of defence, not only covering New Orleans, but preventing an enemy from taking and holding his position at the northern point of the Delta of the Mississippi, where, presenting a small front, easily fortified in a few days, and impossible to turn, he might defy all the forces of the West. Supposing even that he were expelled from it, he might, in his retreat, pillage and burn all the habitations, and carry off the slaves from both sides of the river for a length of one hundred and fifty miles. This whole projected system of works will cost a little more than $1,000,000; a sum small indeed to avert such calamities, and which bears no sort of proportion to the effects which it will produce. The fortifications projected at the mouth of Mobile bay, prevent as far as practicable its blockade, secure the communication of the Tombigbee and Alabama with the ocean, as well as that which is proposed to connect these rivers with the Tennessee; protect also the communication between Mobile bay and Lake Pontchartrain by the interior channel, lying between the main and the chain of islands bounded by Cat island to the west, and Dauphin island to the east, and deprive an enemy of a station whence he might act either against New Orleans, or the establishments which the United States may form hereafter in Pensacola. At present, Fort Boyer, at Mobile Point, which could not hold out three days against a regular attack, and Fort St. Philip, which is much too small and weak to defend the Mississippi, are the only protection to Louisiana.

The forts which will be projected at St. Mary's river and Savannah, in Georgia; Beaufort, Charleston, and Georgetown, in South Carolina, will have for object to secure the communication between the sea and the interior, to prevent the blockade of the rivers and harbors of these States, to secure

APPENDIX.

Report on Fortifications.

naval stations, necessary in guarding the coasting trade, and to cover the great commercial cities against attack by land or sea.

The forts of Smithville and Beaufort, North Carolina, will have for object to close the only two important issues by which the interior of that State communicates with the ocean; they defend the access to the interior navigation, which, sooner or later, will be opened between the Chesapeake and Cape Fear river, and which, by means of canals, will secure in time of war the arrival of naval approvisionnements at the maritime depot of Burwell's bay, while in time of peace it will give to the commerce of the country in general, and of North Carolina in particular, great facilities for avoiding the dangerous and difficult navigation of Albemarle and Pamlico Sounds.

In the Chesapeake the projected works at the entrance of Hampton Roads, have for object to close this road against an enemy, and to secure it to the United States; to secure the interior navigation between the Chesapeake and the more southern States; to make sure of a naval place of arms, where the Navy of the United States may protect the Chesapeake, and the coasting trade; to cover the public docks, &c. at Norfolk, and those which may be established in James river; and to prevent an enemy from making a permanent establishment at Norfolk.

While on this subject we will observe, that an enemy might land in Lynnhaven Bay, and, in one day's march, reach the narrow position which lies to the east of Suffolk: bounded on one side, by the Dismal Swamp, and, on the other, by Bennett's creek, near the mouth of the Nansemond, this position cannot be turned, and may easily be fortified. An enemy might there defy all the forces of Virginia and North Carolina. Secure of a retreat as long as his fleet occupied Hampton Road, he would compel the United States to make the greatest possible sacrifices, both in men and money, before he could be driven out. But, if Hampton Road is fortified, he will only be able to anchor in the open road of Lynnhaven Bay: his march thence upon Suffolk may be turned by our forces crossing at Hampton Road, and he will, therefore, find it impossible to take permanent quarters in the country. The expense at which these results will be obtained, is $1,800,000; a trifling sum if compared with the magnitude of the advantages which will be procured, and the evils which will be averted.

At Baltimore the forts projected at Hawkins' Point, and on the shoal of Soeller's Point, cover the harbor; and the last mentioned work will force an enemy to land, if he intends attacking the town, at a greater distance from it, and will thus prevent him from turning the defensive position which our forces might take against him. The batteries of St. Mary's secure a good station to the vessels of war charged with guarding the Chesapeake; protect an anchorage accessible by vessels of the largest class; and, as do also the batteries at Annapolis, offer a safe asylum to merchant vessels which might find it impossible to reach Baltimore. St. Mary's is not at all defended, and Fort McHenry at Baltimore has no influence

whatever over an attack by land, and cannot even secure the city and harbor from bombardment.

In the Delaware, the fort on the Pea Patch Island, and the one on the Delaware shore opposite, defend the water passage as far below Philadelphia as localities will permit; they force an enemy to land forty miles below the city to attack it by land, and thus afford time for the arrival of succors; they secure to the forces of the country successive defensible positions, where part may delay an enemy, while part file upon his flank, or cross the river in his rear, and cut him off from his fleet. At present, Fort Mifflin, seven miles below the city, is the only obstacle an enemy would encounter: he might, therefore, land very near the city, and attack it within a few hours of his landing. The two projected forts will also have the advantage of covering the canal destined to connect the Chesapeake with the Delaware, if the junction of the canal be, as in all probability it must be, to the north of the Pea Patch.

The projected works on the waters of the Hudson and East rivers have for object to cover the city of New York against an attack by land or sea; to protect its numerous shipping; to prevent, as much as possible, the blockade of that immense river, which will soon have added to the wealth of its own shores the productions of the boundless regions on the northern and western lakes; and to cover the interior navigation which is projected to connect the waters of the Delaware with those of the bay of New York, by a canal from the Rariton. The forts projected at the Narrows, and at the pass of Throgg's Neck on the East river, while they defend the entrances into the bay, force the enemy to land in the Sound at a great distance from the city, and place Brooklyn Height at the bottom of an interior curve of the frontier of which these works occupy the extremities, in rear of an enemy moving upon Brooklyn, and afford time, by their resistance, for the militia to assemble and march to the relief of the city; thus greatly diminishing the chances of success to the enterprise. The expense of these works will be about $1,800,000.

As to the forts projected for the East Bank and Middle Ground, they will complete the defence of the city, by depriving an enemy of the place in Gravesend Bay, the only spot on the south shore of Long Island where he can safely land to march on Brooklyn. They will also deprive him of the possibility of establishing himself on Staten Island; and thus reduce the points of attack to one in the Sound. Besides thus strengthening the defences of the city, they will prevent an enemy from anchoring in the outer harbor to blockade the Hudson, alarm the country, and intercept the interior communication by the Rariton.

The harbor of New York, in its present state, is scarcely at all defended against a sea attack, and the city is not at all defended against an attack by land. An invading enemy might reach the city within two or three days, either by the Sound or harbor, and, after accomplishing his object would find his retreat secure.

The batteries projected for New Haven protect that city against depredations, and secure a port of refuge in the Sound to merchant vessels escaping from privateers. The existing batteries are too small to offer any resistance.

The forts at New London will secure to the largest vessels safe and excellent anchorage at all seasons: as the Thames never freezes, they protect a good station, whence our navy can, at all times, keep good watch over the coasting merchant vessels, and, especially, over the navigation of Long Island Sound.

The projected defences on Narraganset Bay will deprive an enemy of the possibility of occupying that excellent roadstead, and secure it to the United States. The possession of this bay will be to us of inestimable advantage. It is the only one on the coast which vessels can enter with a N. W. wind, and, as the same winds serve for entering both New York and Boston harbors, (N. N. W. to S. S. W. round by the east) while Narraganset Bay is accessible with all winds, from N. W. to E. round by the W.; it follows, that, on this part of the coast, vessels may be certain of making a harbor with every wind of the compass, except the four points from N. W. to N. N. W. Narraganset Bay and Hampton Roads are also the only harbors from Cape Hatteras to Cape Cod, which are proper for naval rendezvous. This bay is besides a most important station for protecting the transit of vessels from the Vineyard into Long Island Sound.

If Narraganset Bay was left in its existing state, as to defence, an enemy would seize it without difficulty, and, by the aid of his naval supremacy, form an establishment in Rhode Island for the war. For this purpose it would be sufficient for him to occupy the position of Tiverton heights, opposite Howland's Ferry, which is of narrow front, easy to secure, and impossible to turn. He might then defy all the forces of the Eastern States; drive the United States to vast expense of blood and treasure; and while his troops would thus put in alarm and motion all the population of the East, feigned expeditions against New York, by Long Island Sound, would equally alarm that State and the neighboring ones; and, if he merely contented himself with menacing the coast, it is difficult to calculate the expenses into which he would drive the Government. The advantages which the United States will derive from the occupation of this bay, and those of which this occupation will deprive an enemy, seem to us of infinitely more importance than the sum of $1,600,000, which will be required to close and fortify it completely.

The forts projected to cover Boston will have for object to defend the channel at its junction with the ocean, to cover Nantasket road against an attack by sea, to render any attempt against the naval depot and arsenal at Charlestown and the city of Boston impracticable, and to secure and facilitate the sailing out and in of the fleets of the United States.

The works projected for Plymouth, Provincetown, and Marblehead, will deprive an enemy who might attempt to blockade Boston of important anchorages; and, whilst the occupation of these

points will render a blockade of that port almost impossible, it will secure, at the same time, a refuge to our own vessels which may be prevented by contrary winds from entering Boston harbor. These works will also deprive an enemy of landing points whence he might march upon Boston and Charlestown, and thus secure these important positions against an attack by land.

The works projected at Salem protect that city and its commerce from the depredation of a hostile naval force, and deprive the land forces of an enemy of a landing place whence the whole country might be alarmed, and the naval depot of Charlestown be menaced.

The forts projected at Portsmouth and Portland secure to the Union these ports, important both to the commercial and naval interests of the country; they protect the sailing in and out of the ships destined to guard the coasting trade. The defence of these harbors by proper forts will enable the Government to form, under their cover, victualling and repairing establishments, and thus convert these harbors into ports of refuge for the navy.

The works projected at the mouths of the Kennebeck, Sheepscut, and Penobscot, will secure the entrance of these rivers, protect the navy stationed on the coast to guard the coasting trade, and afford asylums to our privateers and merchant vessels when chased, and safe points whence the privateers can keep watch upon, and act against, the commerce of an enemy.

The forts to be erected for the defence of Mount Desert Bay will deprive an enemy of an important station whence he might menace and paralyze all the navigation of the coast of the State of Maine, and by which he would shorten the line of his operations against that of the coasts of New Hampshire and Massachusetts. These forts will secure to the United States a position from which will result the following advantages:

1st. A nearer and better point of departure for operations, in time of war, against the British establishments in New Brunswick and Nova Scotia, and against the commerce of those provinces.

2d. This position will protect, as far as the local circumstances of the country will allow it, the Eastern extremity of the maritime frontiers of the Union, being that nearest the possessions of another Power.

3d. It will secure a port of refuge for our Navy and privateers in the vicinity of a much frequented cruising ground.

From this rapid sketch we may deduce the urgent reasons, and the almost absolute necessity, for fortifying each of the points designated. But we refer to the reports of the commission in 1818, 1819, 1820, and 1821, for ampler information, as well as to give exact ideas of the manner in which these several points depend upon and support each other; of their mutual relations; and, in short, of all the naval and military properties of the frontier, both defensively and offensively considered.

To give, however, an idea of the chain of reasoning by which the commission directed its researches, and which governed its plans, we shall

Report on Fortifications.

select one of the plainest cases of all those which came under its consideration. We will trace for this purpose the attack and defence of one of our cities in its actual state of defence, and then on the supposition that the works projected by the commission have been executed. It matters not where our choice falls, for unhappily all our cities are in the like predicament of total insecurity; and, as to the projected works, we believe they will place every important point of our frontier equally above every species of attack, whether by surprise or by force. We shall select Philadelphia, because its attack in neither case involves any complication in the movements for defence. We suppose an enemy to have arrived at Fort Mifflin, within a very few hours of the annunciation of his appearance off the capes. His attack will be instantly made by one or other of these methods:

1st. He will transfer the troops to the row boats of the squadron, and pass them by the forts, hugging the Jersey shore, while the fire of the forts is engaged by an attack of his numerous heavy ships and bomb vessels; land just below the city; seize and destroy the Schuylkill bridges, and take position north of the city, where he can only be assailed in front. His retreat will be conducted like his advance.

2d. He may land upon the Pennsylvania shore, and, by a rapid march, seize the Schuylkill bridges.

3d. He may land in Jersey, and cannonade the city from Camden; covering his incendiary batteries with his troops.

4th. He may assault the forts in the first place, (and he would hardly fail of capturing them,) and there will remain no further impediment to his advance upon the city, and nothing to interrupt his retreat from it. Arriving suddenly from the ocean, as he may, with an army of 20,000 men, an able enemy must succeed by either of these methods, and perhaps by others more complicated, and his retreat can be effected too before a sufficient force can come in to jeopardize his forces. It must be remembered that an enemy has so many points of attack amongst which to choose on the instant, that our forces, divided upon them all, can offer but a slight resistance at the particular point he may prefer.

We will now suppose the lower defences completed, and an enemy suddenly arrived before them. The numerous and well-covered artillery possessed by these works, and covering the obstructions which it is proposed to fix in the channel during a war, must render hopeless every attempt to force the water passage to Philadelphia, and leave him only the chance of reaching the city by land. His march will be either through Delaware or Jersey, or, by dividing his forces, along both shores of the river. The defence must be nearly the same in all these cases: two corps, one in Delaware and one in Jersey, each of about 2,000 men, will be prepared to meet his advance, under cover of the first natural obstacles. Whether these corps continue to act on different sides of the river, or unite, which, having the navigation of the river secured to them by the forts below, they

are at liberty to do, will depend upon whether or not the enemy divides his forces. These corps will have improved every natural advantage beforehand, by the addition of field works, and they will now defend them vigorously. Every disposition they make for defence, whether feigned or real, will oblige corresponding arrangements for attack, and thus, though too inferior to resist long at any one point, their repeated efforts produce that delay which is finally to defeat the enemy's design. Considering the rapidity with which, by their command of the river, they can send detachments to strike at the rear of the enemy's columns; considering that they have constructed works of strength upon positions naturally strong; that they have destroyed the bridges and obstructed the roads; considering their superiority over the enemy in a perfect knowledge of the country, and that their forces are hourly augmenting; we cannot doubt that the march which would, without resistance, have consumed four days, will be extended to six. The enemy, arrived at last before the city, will find all means of communicating with it destroyed or removed, and if it be not even now too late, must instantly begin his retreat. For, should he attempt the cannonade with incendiary batteries, they can hardly begin to produce effect before he will be surrounded by greatly outnumbered forces. The tables give a concentration at Philadelphia, in six days, of 83,991 militia. (See report of 1820.)

From the general exposition which we have given, it will be seen that all fortifications projected by the board are not of the same pressing necessity, nor of like importance; that some are required immediately, and that the commencement of others may be delayed. In classing them we shall observe, that the works of the most urgent necessity are those which are destined to prevent an enemy, in time of war, from forming a permanent establishment, or even a momentary one, on the soil of the Union; those which defend our great naval arsenals; and those which protect our chief commercial cities.

In the second grade we will place those which defend stations for our navy, and commercial cities of secondary importance, which, either from natural or artificial defences, existing works, &c., are not entirely without protection, and can wait until the chief and more important points are secured, at least against a first attack.

Finally, in the third class, we will range the works which will complete the defensive system in all its parts, but whose construction may, without imminent danger, be deferred until the frontier has received all the successive degrees of strength which the gradual erection of the forts of the first and second class will give to it.

The table A, joined to this report, has been drawn up on this principle, and shows:

1st. That the works to be erected during the first period, will cost $8,010,054; will require two thousand five hundred and forty men at most to garrison them in time of peace, and twenty thousand three hundred and five in case of siege.

2d. That the works of the second class will cost

Report on Fortifications.

$4,711,030; will require one thousand three hundred men at most to garrison them in peace, and eight thousand six hundred and fifteen in case of siege.

3d. That the expense of the works belonging to the third class will amount to $5,073,970; their garrisons, in time of peace, to one thousand one hundred and twenty men, and, in case of a siege, to nine thousand and forty-two men.

4th. That the total expense of completely fortifying the maritime frontier, will amount to $17,795,055; the troops necessary to guard these fortifications in peace, to four thousand six hundred and ninety men at most, and thirty-seven thousand nine hundred and six-two men in time of war; supposing them, which is beyond all probability, all besieged at once.

The time required to construct these works must depend entirely upon the annual appropriations which the nation may grant to this branch of the public service. All that can be said upon this subject is, that, in an undertaking of such vital importance to the safety, prosperity, and greatness, of the Union, there should not be an instant's relaxation of effort and perseverance. A work of such magnitude must, with every possible effort, be the work of years; but each year, with limited means, will produce its fruit, and the final result is to endure for ages. However long it may be before sensible effects are produced the result will be certain; and, should no danger threaten the Republic in our own days, future generations may owe the preservation of their country to the precaution of their forefathers. France was at least fifty years in completing her maritime and interior defences; but France, on more than one occasion since the reign of Louis XIV. has been saved by the fortifications erected by his power, and by the genius of Vauban. However slow the progress of this system may be, from the necessity of a sparing application of the public funds to this purpose, it is essential to disburse something in this way each year, so as to give to the frontier an annual increase of strength. We must, therefore, insist upon the advantage of dividing the construction of works into several periods, according to their more or less immediate urgency, and of beginning them, successively in that order. By these means satisfactory results as to the augmentation of the strength of the frontier will be obtained as early as possible, whilst, if we were to begin them all at once, we should be a great while without defence upon any one point.

We shall now enter into the question of the expense of erecting these forts, and garrisoning them for war, and compare it with the expense of defending the coast in its proper state. To render this question as clear as possible, we shall only examine it with respect to New Orleans, Norfolk, Baltimore, Philadelphia, New York, and Narraganset bay.

Supposing that an enemy had concentrated about twenty thousand men at Halifax or Bermuda; the United States must, on hearing of this force, at once prepare to receive them at all the points mentioned above. As it will be impossible to foresee on which of these points the first blow will be struck, it will be necessary to have troops encamped at each of them, and, to meet an attack with a force at least numerically equal to that of the assailant, the force kept constantly under arms in these camps must be at least equal to one half of the hostile expedition, whilst as many more must be kept in readiness, and within call. The points are so immediately accessible in some cases, and so remote from succor in others, that after the point of attack is known by the appearance of the enemy before it, there will remain no time for reinforcements to arrive. By manœuvering in front of any of these places, he will induce us to concentrate our forces there, when, suddenly, profiting of a favorable breeze, he will sail to another, which he may reach in a few hours and seize, if a force is not stationed there likewise, at least equal to his own. Neither, in such a case, can reinforcements be directed against him in time, for all the forces under march will have received a direction upon the point he has just quitted. Our whole coast will thus, by a single expedition, be kept in alarm, from Louisiana to Maine; and, such is the extent and exposure of the maritime frontier, that any enemy may ruin us by a war of mere threatenings. If our cities are not garrisoned, they will become his prey at once; if they are, the Treasury will be gradually emptied, the credit of the Government exhausted, the wearied and starving militia will desert to their homes, and nothing can avert the direful consummation of tribute, pillage, and conflagration.

The table B, joined to this report, shows that, to be in readiness on every vulnerable point, it will be necessary to maintain sixty-seven thousand men encamped and under arms at the six places above mentioned, and fifty-three thousand ready to march, and within call. This number is really below that which would be required; for these points being exposed, according to our hypothesis, to an attack from twenty thousand regular and disciplined troops, twenty thousand militia would not be able to repel them, unless aided by entrenchments, requiring a time to perfect them which would not be allowed us, and involving expenses which we have not comprised in our estimates. Besides, to have twenty thousand men, and especially new levies, under arms, it will be necessary, considering the epidemics which always attack such troops, to carry the formation of this corps to at least twenty-five thousand men. The State of Louisiana, being more remote from all succor, requires a larger force under arms than the other points; we have fixed this force at seventeen thousand, considering that the State might furnish three thousand within call.

These premises considered, and taking in all expenses, 1,000 regular troops, including officers, cost $300,000 per annum, and $150,000 for a campaign of six months; 1,000 militia, including officers, cost $400,000 per annum, and $200,000 in a campaign of six months, or $200 per man for six months.

But if we take into consideration the diseases which infallibly attack men unaccustomed to a military life, the expense of hospitals in conse-

APPENDIX.

Report on Fortifications.

quence, the frequent movement of detachments from the camp to their homes, and from the interior to the camp, and the first cost in camping utensils, accoutrements, &c., which is the same for a campaign of six months as for a year, this expense cannot be rated at less than $250 for every militiaman, and $250,000 for every 1,000 men for six months.

From these bases, the 67,000 men of the militia necessary to guard the above-mentioned points, in the present situation of our maritime frontier, will cost, in a campaign of six months, $16,750,000.

In strict justice we should add to this expense, which is we believe greatly undervalued, amongst many other things the loss of time, and the interruption of the labor of the citizens who have left their business to assume arms for their defence. This is a real loss to the nation, and a heavy tax on individuals. And while reflecting on the dreadful mortality which rages in the camps of men unaccustomed to the fatigues and privations of a military life, we cannot help remarking how much greater the loss of a citizen is than of a soldier.

The latter is generally an isolated being; he has prepared the sacrifice of his life by entering the Army; it is the peculiar and constant duty of his profession. The former is a man of business—the father of a family—and his loss involves with it a large circle of domestic sorrow and suffering.

The total expense of constructing the works at New Orleans, Norfolk, Baltimore, Philadelphia, New York, and Narraganset bay, will amount to $11,147,695, (see table B, and the reports presented in 1818, 1819, 1820.) Their garrisons might consist of the same number of regular troops in time of war as in time of peace; and the remainder might be furnished by the militia held in readiness to throw themselves into the forts on the first appearance of an enemy. By these means, 2,720 regulars and 21,000 militia, either in the forts or in small corps upon advantageous positions, making 23,720 men, would suffice after the erection of these works, and 36,280 might be kept in readiness to march when called upon. We should have kept only 23,720 to pay and support, instead of 67,000; and the expense would be $5,658,000, instead of $16,750,000. The difference, $11,092,000, being about equal to the expense of the forts—it follows that the cost of their erection will be compensated by the saving they make in a single campaign of six months. It is proper to add, that though the expense of these works be great, that expense is never to be renewed; while with troops, on the contrary, the expense is annually repeated, if not increased, until the end of the war. Besides, the disbursements for fortifications are made in time of peace, slowly, and to an extent exactly correspondent with the financial prosperity of the country. Armies, however, are most wanted, and must be paid in periods of great emergency, when the ordinary sources of revenue are dried up, and when the Treasury can only be kept supplied by a resort to means the most disagreeable to, and the most burdensome upon, the people.

The defence of our maritime frontier by permanent fortifications, and even the expense of erecting these fortifications, will thus be a real and positive economy. The points of attack being reduced to a few, instead of awaiting an attack on every point, and holding ourselves everywhere in readiness to repel it, we shall force an enemy to direct his efforts against these few points, with which we shall be well acquainted beforehand, and which we shall have disposed to withstand all his attempts. There is no doubt but that such circumstances will render an enemy more backward in risking his expeditions, and that we shall not only therefore be better able to resist attack, but that we shall also be less frequently menaced with invasion.

Some prominent military writers have opposed the principle of fortifying an extensive land frontier; but no military or political writer has ever disputed the necessity of fortifying a maritime frontier. The practice of every nation, ancient and modern, has been the same in this respect. On a land frontier, a good, experienced, and numerous infantry, may dispense with permanent fortifications, although they would prove excellent auxiliaries and supports when properly disposed and organized; but though disciplined troops can, rigorously speaking, without their aid, cover and protect a frontier, undisciplined troops never can. On a maritime frontier the case is totally different. Troops cannot supply the place of the strong batteries which are disposed along the important places. The uncertainty of the point on which an enemy may direct his attack, the suddenness with which he may reach it, and the powerful masses which he can concentrate at a distance out of our reach and knowledge, or suddenly, and at the very moment of attack, are reasons for erecting defences on every exposed point, which may repel his attack, or retard it until reinforcements can arrive, or the means of resistance be properly organized. By land we are acquainted with the motions of an enemy, with the movements and directions of his columns; we know the roads by which he must pass; but the ocean is a vast plain without obstacles; there his movements are performed out of our sight and knowledge, and we can receive no intelligence of his approach, until he has already arrived within the range of the eye. In a word, the vulnerable points of a seacoast frontier are left to their fate, if they are not covered by permanent fortifications; and their only chance of safety must then depend upon the issue of a battle, always uncertain, even when regular and well disciplined troops, inured to danger, have been assembled beforehand, and have made all possible preparation for the combat.

If we overlook for a moment the many points of the maritime frontier, which the enemy might invade with the most serious consequences to the United States; if we suppose that there exists no object on that frontier worth the trouble and expense of a great expedition; these fortifications will even yet be highly necessary. For we still have one great object to attain—the security of our Navy: this cannot be protected without fortifications, especially in struggling with an adversary superior in numbers, and jealous of a supremacy

Report on Fortifications.

on which may ultimately depend his political importance. A navy can neither be augmented nor secured without fortifications; nor can it enjoy, without them, the advantages which the localities of the frontier might otherwise afford: accidents may and must happen to it, and it is only in closed and fortified harbors that it can repair the losses and disasters of a course of war; and from them, when refitted and refreshed, recommence its operations. England herself, notwithstanding the great naval superiority which she possesses at this moment over the rest of the world, and the excellent organization of her militia, strengthens and augments the fortifications of her frontier every day: and no nation of Europe, France excepted, possesses a stronger and more complete system of permanent defences along its coast.

Lastly, the defensive system of our seacoast by permanent fortifications being completed, and the Union being protected against all danger of invasion from that quarter, she can direct all her resources towards her navy. Her national quarrels will then all be decided upon the ocean, and no longer upon her own territory: her wars will all be maritime, a species of warfare in unison with the institutions of the country, less costly in men and money; and which, by keeping off all aggressions from her own territory, will preserve untouched her industry, her agriculture, her financial resources, and all the other means of supporting a just and honorable war.

As for the garrisons which these forts will require in time of war, a small portion of them, equal in number to the garrisons necessary in time of peace, may be composed of regular troops: the surplus of militia practised to the manœuvres of artillery; for the greatest part of the troops required for the defence and service of these great coast batteries should be composed of artillery.

To this end, every State might organize a number of battalions of militia artillery proportioned to the exigencies and armament of the forts upon its coast, or within the sphere of activity of its military force. These battalions should be within call of the forts, as long as no invading expedition is announced; but, as soon as some operation of an enemy should menace the frontier, they should throw themselves into the forts, and remain there as long as the precise point of attack should remain uncertain. The system of defence for the coast was established in France, where it succeeded very well: it appears to us to harmonize as well with the institutions and spirit of the country, as with the principle of economy which should direct and govern all the expenses of the Government.

In the present report, we have taken no account of the interior and land frontiers of the Union: they have not yet been sufficiently reconnoitered to enable us to give an exact idea of the system of defensive works which they may require. All that we can say, by anticipation, is, that from their general topographical features, these frontiers can be covered at a very moderate expense by such a defensive system, that no enemy will be able to invade them without exposing himself to disasters almost inevitable; and that the armies of the Uni-

ted States, supposing all her warlike preparations well organized beforehand, will be enabled, at the very opening of the first campaign, to carry the theatre of war beyond her own territory.

If to our general system of permanent fortifications and naval establishments we connect a system of interior communications by land and water, adapted both to the defence and to the commercial interests of the country, if to these we add a well-constituted regular army, and perfect organization of our militia, the Union will not only completely secure its territory, but preserve its national institutions from those violent shocks and revolutions, which, in every age and every nation, have been too often incident to a state of war.

All which is most respectfully submitted.

[Signed by Brig. Gen. BERNARD, J. D. ELLIOTT, Capt. U. S. N., J. D. TOTTEN, Bt. Lieut. Col.]

Division of the proposed fortifications for the defence of the maritime frontiers of the Union in three classes, according to the urgency of their construction; exhibiting the strength of their required garrisons in time of peace and in time of war, and the expense of erecting them.

FIRST CLASS.

To be erected during the first period.

DESIGNATION OF FORTS.	Garrisons.		Expense of construction.
	For a Siege.	For Peace Establishment.	
In Louisiana.			Dolls.
Fort St. Philip - - -	400	80	77,810
Fort at Plaquemines - -	750	100	392,927
Fort at Chef Menteur - -	400	80	260,517
Fort at Rigolets - - -	400	80	264,517
Fort at Bayou Bienvenue -	224	25	94,582
	2,174	365	1,094,353
In Virginia.			
Fort at Old Point Comfort -	2,625	600	816,814
Fort at the Rip Raps - -	1,130	200	904,355
	3,755	800	1,721,169
In Pennsylvania.			
Fort at the Pea Patch Island	1,560	150	258,000
In New York.			
Fort at New Utrecht Point -	1,140	100	424,995
Fort at Tompkins' Point -	970	100	485,988
Fort at Wilkin's Point -	1,336	100	456,845
Fort at Throg's Point - -	1,540	100	471,181
	4,986	400	1,839,009
In Rhode Island.			
Fort at Bronton's Point -	2,400	200	730,166
Fort at Dumpling's Point -	1,850	200	579,946
Fort at Rose Island - -	580	25	82,411
Dyke on the N. W. passage	-	-	205,000
	4,830	425	1,597,523

its citizens in a science indispensable to its independence and safety, and to perfect which instruction, it is necessary that some portion of them (the number to be regulated by the resources of the country and its relation with other Governments) should make arms their profession.

I have thus presented an organization which I deem the most effective, and which, in the future exigencies of the country, may be of the utmost importance. A different one, requiring for the present an expenditure something less than that proposed, might, in some respects, be more agreeable at this moment; but, believing that nothing in our situation or in our relation with other Powers, however pacific at this time, can give a certain assurance of uninterrupted peace, a state which may exist in the imagination of the poet, but which no nation has yet had the good fortune to enjoy, I have deemed it my duty to present that organization which will most effectually protect the country against the calamities and dangers of any future contest in which it may be our misfortune to be involved.

Economy is certainly a very high political virtue, intimately connected with the power and the public virtue of the community. In military operations, which, under the best management, are so extensive, it is of the utmost importance; but, by no propriety of language can that arrangement be called economical, which, in order that our Military Establishment in peace should be rather less expensive, would, regardless of the purposes for which it ought to be maintained, render it unfit to meet the dangers incident to a state of war.

With a single observation, which was omitted in its proper place, I will conclude my remarks. The plan proposed for the reduction of the Army gives six thousand three hundred and sixteen non-commissioned officers, musicians, and privates, instead of six thousand, the number fixed in the resolution. It was found difficult to form an organization on proper principles, which would give that precise number, and, as the difference was not deemed very material, I have ventured to deviate to that extent from the terms of the resolution.

I have the honor to be, &c.,
            J. C. CALHOUN.
Hon. JOHN W. TAYLOR,
  Speaker of the House of Representatives.

REPORT ON FORTIFICATIONS.

[Communicated to the House, February 15, 1821.]
DEPARTMENT OF WAR,
          February 12, 1821.

SIR: In compliance with a resolution of the House of Representatives of the 9th instant, directing "that the Secretary of War report to that House the progress which has been made by the Board of Engineers, in determining the sites and plans of fortifications of the coast of the United States; the sites which may have been selected; the estimates of the expense in completing the several works; the number of troops necessary to garrison them in peace and in war; the progress made in erecting the fortifications; the advantages resulting from the system when completed, particularly in reducing the expense of defending the Atlantic frontier," I have the honor to enclose a report of the Board of Engineers, marked A, and a report of the Engineer Department, marked B, which give the information required by the resolution.

It may be proper to observe that the projected fortifications have been distributed into three classes, according to their relative importance, and that it is determined to erect those of the first class, previous to the commencement of the second and third classes, with the exception of the works at Mobile Point and Dauphin Island. These works were commenced in preference to those projected at Bayou Bienvenue, and Fort St. Philip; for, although the latter are placed in the first class, it was not however deemed proper to commence with them, as they were much less extensive than the two former, and could be completed in a short time, should the state of our relations with other Powers render it necessary.

The contractors for the works at the Rigolets were, by the arrangements with them, to have erected those contemplated at Chef Menteur, but so many impediments have been encountered, that it has been necessary for them to confine their operations wholly to the former.

I have the honor to be your obedient servant,
            J. C. CALHOUN.
Hon. JOHN W. TAYLOR,
  Speaker of the House of Representatives.

CITY OF WASHINGTON,
          February 7, 1821.

SIR: The following summary of the operations of the Board of Engineers, called for by your order, is respectfully submitted:

The commission charged with reconnoitering the frontiers of the United States has completed the three most important sections of the maritime boundaries, viz: The coast of the Gulf of Mexico, the coast between Cape Hatteras and Cape Cod, and the coast between Cape Cod and the River St. Croix. The coast between Cape Hatteras and Cape Fear has likewise been surveyed; and the only section which remains to be examined, to complete the reconnoissance of the coast, is South Carolina and Georgia.

The reports presented in 1818, 1819, 1820, and 1821, to the Hon. Secretaries of the War and Navy Departments, were accompanied by every necessary plan, table, &c., and embrace every naval and military consideration, both as to the attack, and as to the defence of the frontier, as to fixing the sites for the great naval depots, and as to protecting, by the general system of defence, the general system of internal navigation. We must refer to the details of these reports to show the importance of establishing a complete system for the protection of the frontiers, and the necesssity of building this system upon principles har-monizing with the modern system of warfare. It will be seen that most of the existing forts only defend single points, and satisfy only a few essential conditions; and that they have not been planned with a view to the defence of the frontiers, considered as one great and combined system, whose several parts should be connected and should mutually support each other. The navy yards (excepting that of Charlestown near Boston) have all been improperly placed; the conveniences for the erection of the necessary establishments having alone been taken into consideration, while all other requisites for points so important, such as security against attack by sea or land, facility of receiving all kinds of building materials in time of war as well as in time of peace, vicinity to a place of rendezvous, have been overlooked.

A defensive system for the frontiers of the United States is therefore yet to be created; its bases are, first, a navy; second, fortifications; third, interior communication by land and water; and, fourth, a regular army and well organized militia; these means must all be combined so as to form a complete system.

The navy must, in the first place, be provided with proper establishments for construction and repair, harbors of rendezvous, stations, and ports of refuge. It is only by taking into view the general character, as well as the details, of the whole frontier, that we can fix on the most advantageous points for receiving these naval depots, harbors of rendezvous, stations, and ports of refuge.

On these considerations, Burwell's bay, in James river, and Charlestown, near Boston, have been especially recommended by the commission, as the most proper sites for the great naval arsenals of the South and of the North. Hampton Roads and Boston Roads as the chief rendezvous, and Narraganset bay as an indispensable accessary to Boston Roads. (See reports of 1819 and 1820.)

It is also from an attentive consideration of the whole maritime frontier, of the interior, and of the coast wise navigation, that Mobile bay on the Gulf of Mexico, St. Mary's in the Chesapeake, the Delaware, New York bay, Buzzard's bay, New London, Marblehead, Portsmouth, Portland, the mouths of the Kennebeck and Penobscot, and Mount Desert bay, have been fixed upon as stations and ports of refuge, as necessary and essential to our merchant vessels as to our navy.

Smithville and Beaufort, North Carolina; Annapolis and Baltimore, Maryland; New Haven, Connecticut; Salem, in Massachusetts; and Wiscasset, in Maine, have likewise been examined with attention, with a view to secure them from attack by sea or land. (See reports of 1819, 1820, and 1821.)

St. Mary's river and Savannah, in Georgia; Beaufort, Charleston, and Georgetown, in South Carolina, will be examined and surveyed in the course of this year.

After determining the general and connected system of naval depots, harbors of rendezvous, stations, and ports of refuge, the commission, in the next place, traced the scheme of fortifications necessary to protect this system, and at the same time to guard the whole frontier against invasion. The forts projected by the commission for this purpose satisfy one or more of the following conditions:

1. To close important harbors to an enemy and secure them to the navy of the country.

2. To deprive an enemy of strong positions, where, protected by his naval superiority, he might fix permanent quarters in our territory, maintain himself during the war, and keep the whole frontier in perpetual alarm.

3. To cover our great cities against attack.

4. To prevent as much as possible the great avenues of interior navigation from being blockaded by a naval force at their entrance into the ocean.

5. To cover the coastwise and interior navigation, and to give to our navy the means necessary for protecting this navigation.

6. To cover the great naval establishments.

A rapid review of the works which have been projected by the commission, will exhibit, with sufficient distinctness, the advantages which must result from their construction.

In Louisiana, the forts projected at the Turn of Plaquemines, at the Bayou Bienvenue, at the Chef Menteur, at the Rigolets, form altogether a system of defence, not only covering New Orleans, but preventing an enemy from taking and holding his position at the northern point of the Delta of the Mississippi, where, presenting a small front, easily fortified in a few days, and impossible to turn, he might defy all the forces of the West. Supposing even that he were expelled from it, he might, in his retreat, pillage and burn all the habitations, and carry off the slaves from both sides of the river for a length of one hundred and fifty miles. This whole projected system of works will cost a little more than $1,000,000; a sum small indeed to avert such calamities, and which bears no sort of proportion to the effects which it will produce. The fortifications projected at the mouth of Mobile bay, prevent as far as practicable its blockade, secure the communication of the Tombigbee and Alabama with the ocean, as well as that which is proposed to connect these rivers with the Tennessee; protect also the communication between Mobile bay and Lake Pontchartrain by the interior channel, lying between the main and the chain of islands bounded by Cat island to the west, and Dauphin island to the east, and deprive an enemy of a station whence he might act either against New Orleans, or the establishments which the United States may form hereafter in Pensacola. At present, Fort Boyer, at Mobile Point, which could not hold out three days against a regular attack, and Fort St. Philip, which is much too small and weak to defend the Mississippi, are the only protection to Louisiana.

The forts which will be projected at St. Mary's river and Savannah, in Georgia; Beaufort, Charleston, and Georgetown, in South Carolina, will have for object to secure the communication between the sea and the interior, to prevent the blockade of the rivers and harbors of these States, to secure

Application to abolish Privateering.

ENGINEER DEPARTMENT,
February 10, 1821.

. SIR: So much of the information, required by the resolution of the House of Representatives of yesterday's date, as is contained in the following sentence, "the progress made in erecting the fortifications," will be found in the following extract from a report on the same subject, made on the 9th ultimo for the use of the Committee of Ways and Means.

EXTRACT.

Fort Delaware is about five-sixths finished, and will be completed in the course of this year.

Fort Washington is still further advanced, and will be finished in the course of the ensuing Summer.

Fort Monroe has progressed two-fifths towards completion. Its appearance would not indicate that state of advancement, and yet the operations so far have been advantageously conducted. The reason is, that in this work, as in all works of magnitude, the operations have been mostly confined to the collection of materials, depositing them in the places where they will be used, and maturing arrangements preparatory to the commencement of constructions, and therefore make no show. The constructions of masonry were commenced last Summer; in the course of which was completed a casemated work capable of presenting to the channel of entrance a battery of forty 32-pounders. The masonry in future, by reason of the preparations above stated, in which are included immense excavations, part of them applied to the opening of a canal following the course of a ditch around the work, having locks, &c., from the use of which great facilities and economy in transportation of materials, &c., may be expected, will be carried on with rapidity. The fort will be completed in five years.

Fort Calhoun has received one half of the stone intended for the formation of the breakwater, or that part of its foundation to be below the surface of the water; the remainder will be deposited in the course of next year, after which it should be permitted to settle during one or two years before the superstructure be commenced, the completion of which will occupy three years more.

The fort on Mobile Point exhibits but little advancement. The impracticability of procuring the requisite materials by purchase, obliged the contractor to fabricate them, and the means by which even that could be effected were difficult of attainment, in some instances it having become necessary to create them. Under such embarrassments much delay was unavoidable; nevertheless, extensive arrangements for the preparation and transportation of materials have been matured. According to the terms of the contract, this fort should be completed on or before the 1st of next July, but the difficulties above stated will no doubt protract the completion to at least two years beyond that period.

The fort on Dauphin Island, although in all respects situated similarly to that on Mobile Point, is in better condition. The period limited in the contract for its completion will expire on the first December next, but the fort will not be finished until some time in the following year.

The fort on the Rigolets Pass, under circumstances not materially differing from those stated, in reference to the two works last noticed, has been more successfully managed than either of them. The contract will expire on the 1st December next, and the work will probably be completed within that time, or shortly after.

All which is respectfully submitted.
W. K. ARMISTEAD,
Colonel Engineers.

Hon. J. C. CALHOUN,
Secretary of War.

APPLICATION TO ABOLISH PRIVATEERING IN TIME OF WAR.
—

[Communicated to the House, January 26, 1821.]

To the Senate and House of Representatives of the United States in Congress assembled, the undersigned inhabitants of the State of Massachusetts respectfully represent:

That, in common with many of their fellow-citizens in different parts of the United States, they consider it due to natural justice, and to the honor of Christian nations, that the capturing of private property should no longer be authorized by the laws of maritime warfare. Many practices once allowed in war have disappeared, as civilization and christianity have advanced; the same benign spirit calls for this further reform. It seems to be the design and scope of the modern laws of war to exempt, as far as possible, from the effects of hostilities, all persons who bear no voluntary part in the contest. On the land, public possessions alone become a prize to the conqueror. The common consent of nations has attached a deep disgrace to the plunder of an unresisting foe. On the sea, too, certain trades deemed necessary to human subsistence are privileged from capture. Why should not the same immunities be extended to all ships engaged in carrying on the commerce of nations, without agency in the war?

There is a striking inconsistency between the usages of war on the land and on the sea. Goods landed and stored are preserved to the owner, while those which remain on shipboard, though, perhaps, a part of the same cargo, are seized and confiscated. To rifle shops and dwelling-houses in a captured city, would excite a general disapprobation, but it is otherwise when the same wealth is intercepted in its passage over the ocean. Why the same acts which on land are pronounced disgraceful should on the sea escape reproach, it would be difficult to explain.

In exempting commercial property from capture, it would not be necessary to authorize a direct commercial intercourse between the belligerent Powers; this may, perhaps, be incompatible with a state of war. With this exception, the entire neutrality of trade would be far more bene-

Application to abolish Privateering.

ficial to the parties, and to the world, than a mutual exposure to attack and capture. Commerce is the interest of the world; it connects distant regions, multiplies and distributes the fruits of every climate, and makes every country a sharer in the natural, intellectual, and moral wealth of all others. To facilitate commercial intercourse, and multiply the incitements to industry, should be the wish of all nations. Confine any considerable part of the world to the consumption of its own products within itself, and you diminish the resources of all the other parts. Every cause, therefore, which embarrasses and restricts commerce, operates unfavorably to the progress and welfare of the human race.

And what are the effects of maritime war, as it is now carried on, upon commerce? Are they not to render trade unsettled and insecure; to destroy confidence and credit; to build up the fortunes of some, and to ruin others, with equal suddenness; to involve the rich in bankruptcy by unforeseen misfortune, and to load the adventurer, who hazards nothing, with a wealth which he can only abuse? Agriculture is depressed and discouraged; idleness is forced upon many who would willingly be employed in useful labor, and the sufferings of war are increased without any apparent benefit. But your memorialists forbear to insist on the advantages which would arise to commerce from the abolition of this practice. The measure is recommended by other and more powerful reasons. They believe that they speak a language justified by past and recent experience, when they say that the custom of making prize of private property at sea has been a source of great moral depravation, and of individual suffering, the measure and extent of which, it would be impossible to calculate. The habit of preying on the possessions of others, and of growing rich by a violent appropriation of their wealth, can hardly fail to engender, in those who are engaged in this pursuit, a rapacious and avaricious spirit, eager for riches, and little solicitous about the means by which they are acquired; negligent of others' rights, and ready to raise a specious pretext for invading them. This spirit will continue when the war has ceased; and there is too much reason to fear that those who have plundered under the sanction of the laws, may continue to plunder in defiance of their prohibitions.

In the Navy, perhaps, the character and education of the officers, and the elevated, generous feelings they regard as the ornaments of their profession, may, in a good degree, secure them from the dominion of a sordid avarice; but seamen, with no better means of instruction than they ordinarily enjoy, are exposed to these bad influences, on board of public, as well as private, ships. They are not used to nice and accurate distinctions. Once taught to acquire by violence, there is danger of employing the same means, with little reluctance, whenever it can be done under the color, however fallacious, of a lawful authority. It is true, that the practice of privateering is far more pernicious than the predatory warfare carried on by public ships. The private cruiser has no motive but the thirst of gain. He may indirectly contribute to the success of the war, but this is not his principal object. With public ships, the taking of commercial ships is but accessory; with private cruisers it is the moving cause and chief design of the enterprise. Your memorialists, therefore, admit that, though they are unable to distinguish, in principle, between captures by public and private ships of war, it is from the latter they apprehend the most serious and extensive mischiefs. They deem the abolition of all captures of commercial property desirable, and they fear, that to take away privateering alone, would leave much of the evil incurred; but even were the measure thus limited, they believe that an additional provision, that all captures by public ships should be for public use, much would be gained to humanity and peace.

Your memorialists feel, and gladly acknowledge, that the legal sanction given to privateering has concealed from multitudes its real and detestable nature; and that this, like other barbarous customs, has been followed by men who have respected the general and undoubted principles of humanity. But they conceive that the time of this ignorance is past. Christianity and civilization have advanced too far to leave any who reverence moral distinctions blind to the guilt of this flagrant violation of social duty. The voice of religion and humanity has gone forth distinctly, and leaves, without excuses, the man who prowls the ocean to plunder unoffending strangers, to prey upon the weak, to grow rich on the spoils of those who are following a useful and honorable trade, to shed blood for no other ends than private gain. That men calling themselves Christians, and civilized, should ever have justified themselves in a practice so akin to robbery and murder, and should have held, without remorse, what they had extorted from an innocent fellow being with the sword, is indeed wonderful. But the darkness is gone, and the plunderer on the ocean, however sheltered from punishment by law, cannot escape the reproaches of all the friends of public and private virtue.

If war cannot be abolished, your memorialists desire that its evils may, as far as possible, be mitigated; and they rejoice at the general recognition of the principle, that a nation is bound to abstain from inflicting any evils on its enemy, except such as is necessary to the assertion of its just claims. That this humane principle may be more and more infused into national hostilities, it is of great and obvious importance that private passions, and the selfishness of individuals, should be enlisted as little as possible in the prosecution of the war, that its inevitable sufferings should be inflicted by public instruments for public ends.

Your memorialists conceive, that the peculiar facilities for privateering afforded by our maritime situation and habits, will give weight to whatever efforts our Government may employ for the abolition of the practice, and that, at the same time, they impose on us a peculiar obligation to resist it. The fact that, in the event of war, privateering will be the resource of multitudes of our citizens,

Application to abolish Privateering.

ought to alarm us. We are, perhaps, more than any other people exposed to depravation of manners from this source; and a worse evil cannot menace a community. Good morals are the strength of a State, especially of a free one; and policy joins with principle in denouncing a practice which whets the thirst for pillage, and weakens the obligations of humanity in the mass of the people.

The experience of the present moment gives great force to the arguments against the usage of subjecting to capture private property on the ocean: for we see how easily and naturally it becomes a cover for piracy and unauthorized depredation. We learn from the dreadful abuses to which this practice is liable, and which cannot be separated from it, that property at sea should ever be made more sacred, and be guarded by more rigid laws, than on land. We say nothing of the sufferings of the present moment from the capture and destruction of neutral ships. The injury to commerce and to society, from the depravation of seamen, is a wider and more lasting evil. The confidence once placed in that useful class of men is shaken, and with it the intercourse of nations, and the security of property at home are impaired.

The time has been when an application like the present to a Government would have been hopeless; when the civil power was the last resource for the friends of humanity. But we trust that we live in better and brighter times, when Government, instead of being a monopoly for the few, is regarded as a provision for the general good; and when that greatest of all political truths begins to be felt, that the interests of each country are bound up with the general interests of humanity, and that each country owes a debt to the world. A ruler is no longer considered as false to his own country when he seeks its prosperity in connexion with the progress and welfare of the race, and may be honored as a patriot, without ceasing to be a man. We earnestly desire that our Government, founded as it is on the broad principle of the equal rights of men, may lay an early claim to what will hereafter be esteemed the highest glory of a country—that of having introduced into the intercourse of nations those principles of equity and humanity which are now acknowledged to be binding upon individuals.

The practice of granting commissions to privateers is comparatively of modern date, and writers of the highest eminence and authority have concurred in lamenting its introduction. The opinion of Franklin has been quoted by other memorialists; and we would refer to an excellent precedent and guide in the article on this subject, introduced at the suggestion of that distinguished philosopher and statesman into the treaty concluded with Prussia in 1785.

The present state of the world is favorable to the proposed reform. No reasonable objection, it is believed, can be offered on the part of any nation if the laws concerning goods contraband of war, and those relating to blockades, are permitted to remain. The memorialists leave to the wisdom of their Government the course best

adapted to attain the proposed end. Mutual stipulations by treaty seem to be the most obvious means, and, for this reason, your memorialists would have applied to the Executive, had it not seemed to them that the legislative powers may also be properly and usefully exercised upon a subject so nearly connected with commerce and with public morals. The passing of a law, conditional as to its operations, and referring to future stipulations by treaty, may produce the happiest effects, and would be an immediate recognition of this great and humane principle.

Your memorialists therefore pray that Congress may consider the subject, and adopt such measures as may seem to them most wise and expedient.

William Phillips,	Frs. Parkman,
Isaac Parker,	Henry Ware,
John Phillips,	Benj. Dearborn,
Joseph Coolidge,	Lewis Tappan,
Jos. May,	Charles Tappan,
George Cabot,	David Hale,
Redford Webster,	Saml. Worcester,
Josiah Salisbury,	A. Haskell,
A. P. Cleveland,	R. F. Cloutman,
Thomas Dawes,	Thos. Worcester,
Jeremiah Evarts,	Thomas Longby,
Daniel Webster,	Jas. Humphreys,
William Prescott,	J. M. Brewer,
Samuel Hubbard,	Saml. Harkings,
Thad. M. Harris,	Thos. Wallcut,
William Jenks,	Thomas Vase,
W. E. Channing,	J. P. Blanchard,
Charles White,	George Hunt,
Robt. Waterston,	John Gallison,
John Mycall,	John Glen King.

PRIVATEERING.

1. An Appeal to the Government and Congress of the United States against the depredations committed by American privateers on the commerce of nations at peace with us. By an American citizen. New York. 1819.

2. A proposed Memorial to the Congress of the United States. Boston. 1819.

The writers on national law distinguish between rules deduced by just reasoning from certain principles, and those which derive their force from common usage and consent. The former are of universal obligation, and are properly the law of nature applied to communities of men. The latter " are fitted, not so much to the goodness of an uncorrupted nature, as to the wants of one that is depraved;"[*] they are neither binding upon all, nor at all times; they are brought gradually into use, are received by some sooner than by others, and may be changed without any violation of natural justice.

There is not much difficulty in defining the rights of property and the obligations of contracts,

---

[*] *Jus gentium secundarium* dicitur, quod accommodatum [est], non tam incorrupta naturæ bonitati, quam depravatæ necessitatibus.—*Voet ad Pand. L.* i. t. l. n. 18.

Application to abolish Privateering.

as they exist between nations. Public justice differs not essentially in these respects from private. The facts once settled, it is as easy to decide by what acts one nation has injured another in a state of peace, as to determine when the rights of one individual have been invaded or withheld by another ; as easy to pronounce what is a just cause of war, if we allow war for any cause to be lawful, as to judge of the grounds of a lawsuit. In most cases, indeed, it will be found that neither party in a war is entirely right nor entirely wrong, and through the mist of mutual crimination and defence, manifestoes, answers, insults, and aggressions, it will be difficult to discern the first offence. But this is a difficulty not attributable to any defect or uncertainty in the code of public law.

But there is also a law of war, and it forms by far the most important branch of the *jus gentium.* Whence is this to be deduced ? How far are the reciprocal rights and duties of nations at peace destroyed by a state of war, and what are the new obligations that grow out of this state ? What are the limits to the rights of destruction, and how are they to be known ? Who shall say to mad revenge, " It is enough—stay thy hand !" Where is the precise boundary, on one side of which are glory, and honor, and victory : on the other, rapine and murder ? It will be obvious that there must be great uncertainty as to the extent of the power given to enemies over the persons and goods of each other, and that wars will be carried on with more or less cruelty, as nations are more or less advanced in humanity. Reason will afford little aid, and the restraint will be rather the effect of milder feelings than of more correct judgment. The conqueror will be deterred from a passionate and vindictive abuse of his power, more by the fear of being disgraced as a barbarian, than of being condemned as a violator of public law. What was once a theme of applause will in time be followed by reproach and shame. What is fit and right to be done towards an enemy will depend more on usage, varying at different times and among different people, than on any conclusions of reason. We would be understood to speak, as most writers on national law have done, without reference to the commands or the counsels of religion, whether natural or revealed. These writers seem to have adopted as a truth the poetic declaration, " *nulla fides, pietasque viris qui castra sequuntur.*" They have proceeded upon false principles. As some political sophists have derived the principles of the social compact from a supposed natural state of men, when every one stood single and independent, free to give or retain that entire sovereignty which he enjoyed over himself ; so jurists have sought in the condition of savage nature for the rights and relations of political societies. They have therefore considered a state of hostility as a dissolution of all ties, and a license to all mischief. An enemy, in their view, cannot be injured. Charity and humanity may be offended ; the atonement exacted may be greater than would consist with generosity and tenderness which we esteem men the more for possessing ; but the sufferer cannot consider himself wronged,

nor is any positive and binding law broken. " It stands to reason," says Heineccius, " that against an enemy all things are permitted."[*] And Puffendorf thus explains both the rights of belligerents, and the restraints which humanity would impose upon the exercise of them : " From the moment that any one declares himself our enemy, since we have any thing to fear on his part, we are authorized, as far as in us lies, to use acts of violence against him to any extent,[†] and with no other limit than our will ;[‡] but humanity requires, that, as far as the rules of military art allow, we do no more injury to an enemy than is necessary for our defence, for the vindication of our rights, and for our future safety."—" *Non id solum considerari vult, quid hostis citra injuriam possit pati, sed et quid humanum, adde et generosum victorem facere deceat.*" Grotius, indeed, limits the rights of war to what is necessary for attaining the end proposed, whether of self-preservation, just reparation, or merited punishment.—*Lib. 3. cap. i.* But this, however just in theory, is too indefinite to afford any practical rule ; especially when it is considered that hostilities are allowed to be continued until satisfaction is obtained, not only from the original wrong which was the cause of the war, but for all the expense and injury sustained in prosecuting it. And we learn from the same enlightened and benevolent jurist, that, " by the law of nations, the possessions of one party in a war are to the other, in all respects, as things without a proprietor,"[§] and that " all are accounted slaves who are made prisoners in solemn public war,"—" nor is an offence necessary, but the lot of all is the same, even of those who, on the sudden breaking out of war, may be so unfortunate as to be found in the enemy's country."[‖] Cocceius, the commentator of Grotius, goes somewhat further, and maintains that " an enemy is to be regarded as a criminal deserving of death : hence, when the Government declares war against any one, by the very act it gives to every citizen the right to inflict on him any degree of evil, to lay waste and plunder his possessions," &c. Let us not, however, forget what we owe to Grotius. The lessons of moderation and humanity which he gave as admonitions, have so approved themselves to the reason of mankind, that they have acquired the force, if not the character, of laws ; and cruelties, of which he contented himself with saying, " *certe omittantur sanctius, et cum majori apud bonos laude,*" would now cover with disgrace the conqueror who should practise them.

---

[*] Hosti enim in hostem omnia licere rationi consentaneum est.—*De Nav. ob vect. &c. commiss.*

[†] A toute outrance.—*Barbeyrac.*

[‡] Licentiam concedit vim contra ipsum exserendi in infinitum, aut quantum mihi videatur.—*De Jure Naturæ, &c. lib. 8. cap. vi.* § 7, *De Officiis Hom. &c. lib. 2. cap. xvi.* § 6.

[§] Gentibus placuisse, ut res hostium hostibus essent non alio loco, quam quo sunt res nullius.—*Lib. 3. cap. vi.* § 8.

[‖] Par omnium sors est, etiam eorum, qui, fato suo, ut diximus, cum bellum repente exortum esset, intra hostium fines deprehenduntur.—*Lib. 3. cap. vii.* § 1.

Thus have the rights of war been deduced from the assumed position that an enemy cannot be injured; that, by the injustice or violence which gave occasion to the war, he has forfeited all rights and become as an outlaw; that his life, liberty, and property, are at the mercy of the conqueror; that to spare may, indeed, be praiseworthy, but cannot be enjoined as an act of justice. And, as between nations there is no arbiter, each party in the war has all the rights of the injured, and is subject to all the penalties of the guilty. Justice must always be presumed to reside with good fortune or superior strength. Every subject, too, of the warring State, however ignorant he may be of the causes of the war, however peaceful and unoffending, has incurred a daily guilt in the acts of his superiors, and is the object of unsparing vengeance and unlimited punishment. Whatever *temperaments* have been admitted in the conduct of wars, have been the result of feelings and notions of humanity more or less refined, and views of policy more or less enlightened, as different degrees of knowledge and improvement have prevailed. "Every people have a law of nations. The Mohawks even have theirs. They eat their prisoners, it is true, but they send and receive embassies, and acknowledge the rights of war and peace; the mischief is, that their law of nations is not founded upon true principles."—*Montesq. Esp. des Loix, liv.* 1. *ch.* ii. What Barbeyrac, in his eloquent and beautiful discourse on what the laws only permit or allow, has said of civil laws applies with still greater force to national jurisprudence: "We learn from the monuments of antiquity, that the first laws had scarcely any other origin than custom, which is often a wretched master. Rules thus introduced are commonly established with little examination or reflection. Ignorance, prejudice, passion, example, authority, caprice, have manifestly a greater share in producing them than reason. It is rather the opinion and decision of a blind multitude than that of the wise and virtuous."

Had religion and the morality of the gospel been made the foundation of the rights and duties of States, in war as well as in peace, it is probable that many customs derived to us from ruder ages, perhaps even war itself, would long since have disappeared. But rights have been sought for in another source, and religion has been permitted to interpose her counsels, not her authority, to moderate the usage of that power, which reason and nature have been thought to bestow. Is it not probable that some usages yet remain, which habit and prejudice, and an imaginary interest alone, prevent our regarding with the same abhorrence with which we should now look upon the reducing of captives and their posterity to perpetual and irredeemable slavery? Have we yet confined the license of war within those bounds which the law of charity would assign to it? Do we not even receive as principles of justice some things which have no better support than the practice of earlier and less enlightened times, justified by an artificial reasoning, which, taking things as they are found, invents a plausible defence for whatever custom allows?

We have made these remarks more especially with a view to the practice of privateering. It is matter of just astonishment that a species of warfare so repugnant to all our better feelings, so estranged from all that is deemed noble and honorable among men, should so long have prevailed. It is a practice which can boast nothing of the chivalrous spirit which we have been taught to admire in the warrior. It begins and ends in pure unmixed selfishness. It seeks neither fame nor power, but wealth—wealth, not the fruits of patient industry or honest skill, but wrested by the hand of violence, or stolen by surprise and stratagem. It makes every other consideration yield to a sordid avarice. In its greediness it hardly distinguishes between friend and foe, and is ever ready to pounce upon its prey, whether it be the property of an enemy or that of a fellow-citizen, which, by the rigid rules of war, has become the subject of confiscation as prize. The means which it employs are not less cruel and disgraceful than its purpose is unworthy. It can make its way through blood to the treasure it gloats upon, lure by false smiles to destruction, advance securely to its object under the guise of friendship, ensnare by treachery, deceive by perfidy, and secure its unrighteous gains by shameless perjury. Not that every one who engages in this practice is under the influence of the vilest passions, insensible to shame, or stained by the blackest crimes. Many, we doubt not, whose lives prove them to be friends to religion and humanity, and who would scorn to enrich themselves by fraud or dishonesty, have adventured in privateering without reflecting upon its nature and tendency. They have been deceived by the legality of the practice. Perhaps, even they have persuaded themselves that, while they improved their own fortunes, they were displaying a patriotic zeal for the service of their country. As long as privateering is countenanced and encouraged by public authority, there will be many estimable men, who, looking no further than to what the law allows or forbids, are blind to the immorality of preying upon their fellow creatures. A solemn responsibility, then, rests upon those who govern. Nations, by a common consent, should relinquish a custom so inseparable from abuse and licentiousness, so vexatious to commerce, and so little under the control of wholesome laws.

There is no doubt that great antiquity may be pleaded for the practice of plundering. For several ages after the irruption of the northern barbarians, war and plunder might almost be considered as individual rights. Every petty baron enjoyed the privilege of taking up arms, and every vassal was free to seek his fortune in predatory incursions upon the enemy, whether by land or sea. The infidel Powers, which bordered the Mediterranean, covered the sea with small piratical vessels; and the Christian States, whose commerce suffered from their depredations, partly in self-defence and partly in the hope of gain, fitted out small cruisers, or armed their merchant ships. It was most common for many persons to unite for this purpose in a sort of partnership. No public commission was required. Against infidels it was the right and

Application to abolish Privateering.

duty of every Christian to wage incessant hostility, and to do them all possible injury.—*Martens.* At the same time the inhabitants of the North sent their fleets to make descents upon the coasts, and enrich themselves with the wealth and luxuries of the South.[*] They were most often conducted by private adventurers, whose bravery or skill caused them to be selected as chieftains. Piracy was a common trade, and the word was far from carrying with it the ideas of criminality and disgrace which we now attach to it. Selden cites a passage from Asserius, who was the preceptor of King Alfred, in which he says that this " Prince caused long ships to be built for the purpose of defence against enemies approaching by sea—*impositisque piratus in illis vias maris custodiendas commisit ;*" on which Selden remarks, that " this word 'pirates' is not here used for robbers, as it now commonly is, but for such as attacked the enemy's fleets in naval warfare."[†] So the term " corsair," from the Italian *Corso*, is the generic term of pirates and privateers. (*Martens on Privateers, page* 2, *note.*) The truth is, that in an age when the obligations of humanity were neither acknowledged nor understood, and every person might make such use of his strength, or his cunning, as seemed to him best, so as he did not invade the property of those to whom he was bound by the tie of a common allegiance ; and when the sanction of the prince was not necessary to enable private persons to attack and plunder the enemy, there could be no distinction between authorized and unauthorized depredations on the ocean. " The Gauls," says Cleirac, " regarded all strangers as enemies, and not only robbed them of their goods, but put them cruelly to death, offering them as bloody sacrifices to their false gods.[‡] And Boucher : " In the height of the feudal anarchy, that is to say, in the ninth century, every person might act the part both of judge and executioner, without any incompatibility in the two conditions, and without disgrace. At that period mariners were a set of robbers."—*Consulat. de Mer. vol.* 1, *p.* 74. The inhuman law of wreck, first relaxed in England by the act of Henry I, providing that the property should be saved from forfeiture, if any person escaped alive from the ship, is a memorable instance of the same savage state of manners.—*See Hume, reign of Henry II. Black. Com. chap.* 8, *b.* 1. *Boucher, Consul. de Mer. vol.* 1, *p.* 490.

It is in vain, then, for the apologists of privateering to have recourse to these remote ages in support of the assertion that the practice has long

---

[*] The ravages of the Normans are hardly mentioned before Charlemagne. It was then they began those cruises which made them the terror of other nations.— *Boucher Consul. de Mer. page* 494.

[†] Selden's Mare Clausum, lib. 2, cap. 10—quoted Robinson's Coll. Mar. page 21, " and embarking *pirates* in them employed them to guard the approaches by sea."

[‡] Les Gaulois reputaient tous les étrangers pour leurs enhemis, et ne les expoliaient pas seulement de leurs biens, mais en outre ils les mettaient cruellement à mort, et en faisaient de sanglans sacrifices à leurs faux dieux."—*Us. et Cout. de Mer. page* 95.

or always existed.[*] Even were antiquity a less doubtful plea than it is, the argument proves nothing, but that in those benighted ages men robbed of their own head, and that in these more civilized times we have so far improved as to sanction the proceeding by public authority. The modern practice is better than the ancient, inasmuch as some excesses may now and then be prevented by the control of the Government over privateers, and it is convenient to be able to denote piracy by the absence of a lawful commission : but the question remains, whether it is morally right, or politically expedient, for Governments to grant such commissions, or for individuals to act under them ? And this question can never be answered by saying that men were accustomed to rob for a long time before it began to be necessary to have a public commission for doing it. It was found necessary to impose restraint upon private and unauthorized violence, even between the subjects of hostile Powers. This was a declaration, that the ancient practice was only fit for a state of society as barbarous as that in which it existed. Something, doubtless, has been gained by the restrictions of acts of war to those whose hands are armed by the sovereign power ; but whether this gain has been great, or the most essential evils connected with private plunder have been remedied, let history speak. We appeal to the loud and incessant complaints of neutrals, of whose commerce privateers have been just called the scourge ; and to the tortures and cruelties inflicted by these " judges and executioners," of which the annals of privateering, ancient and modern, afford so many examples.

It is probable that the practice of nations, in the disputes arising between them or their subjects, has followed the same course of improvement with their municipal laws. Every one who has attended to the history of criminal jurisprudence, knows that not many ages since every individual possessed the power of punishing, and the avenging of wrongs was left to the injured party or his friends.[†] But as the world grew wiser and more inclined to peace, a check was put on the right of private revenge, and tribunals began to inquire into the fact, and to measure the punishment in proportion to the guilt. So, among nations, the frequent broils occasioned by the hostile attempts of individuals, gave rise, by degrees, to the custom of granting letters of reprisals. At first, doubtless, they were only given in a few instances, and subjects continued to attack and plunder without asking the permission of the sovereign. The *Consolato del Mare* contains an entire chapter regulating, with great precision, the conduct of armed cruisers, and the division of their plunder. Not a syllable appears of any public commission being necessary, or even a judicial condemnation of prizes. The publication of the first Catalan edition of this collection is supposed by Boucher to have been

---

[*] See note to Martens on Privateers, page 20. Willenberg derives privateers from Theute, Queen of Illyria ; and Valin maintains that they have existed at all times.

[†] See Kames's Historical Law Tracts.

Application to abolish Privateering.

about 1494, and he carries the compilation as far back as the beginning of the tenth century. But its origin is fixed with more probability between the years 1250 and 1266.* This code is commonly supposed to have been first compiled in Barcelona; and it is in the Mediterranean, where commerce was preyed upon by the Barbary corsairs, that we should expect to find the practice of private cruising most prevalent. Letters of marque and reprisals were issued upon the petition of a subject, who complained of injustice done to him by some foreign Prince or subject, and they empowered the party receiving them, whether an individual or a community, to obtain satisfaction by seizing the goods of any subject of the offending State. They were limited to the restitution of what had been unjustly taken or withheld, or compensation in damages for the injury suffered. Reprisals are sometimes spoken of as a means of preserving peace, because wrongs were thus remedied by a sort of violence, which is compared to that used in the execution of legal sentences between subjects of the same State, without the extreme resort of war † The earliest instance of reprisals recorded in England, was in 1295, when Edward I. granted to a subject, " licentiam marcandi homines et subditos de regno Portugalliæ et bona eorum per terram et mare."—*Rymer. vol. 2, page* 691; *Anderson, vol.* 1, *page* 136. It does not seem to have been considered necessary to be provided with letters of reprisals until the fourteenth century, and no mention is made of them in treaties prior to that time.—*Martens, note, page* 10. The right of making reprisals is said to have belonged to every magistrate, and even to private subjects, until the reign of Charles VII., in France.‡—*Puffendorf, de Jure Nat., &c., lib.* 8, *chap.* 9, *sec.* 13, *note* 2. A law was made in France concerning them, in 1345.—*Martens.* There are frequent instances in Rymer, in the fourteenth and fifteenth centuries.§ An act of the English Parliament, of the

year 1353, 27 Edward III., provides, " that no foreign merchant shall be troubled or impeded, &c., provided, that if any of our liege subjects, merchants, or others, be injured by any lords of foreign lands, or their subjects, and the said lords, upon due request, refuse to do justice, *we shall have the right of mark and reprisals,* as has been used in time past."—*Martens, page* 12, *note.* An ordinance of Charles VI. of France, of December 7, 1400, forbids any subject to fit out ships at his own expense, for carrying on war against enemies, without license first obtained from the admiral or his lieutenant.—*Code des Prises, tome* 1, *page* 1. *Robinson, Coll. Mar.* 75. *Martens, page* 18.* From this ordinance, and from other documents, it is probable, that in the fifteenth century commissions began to be issued to private subjects, in the time of war, similar to those which were granted for making reprisals in time of peace. They retained and still retain the name of letters of marque and reprisal ;" and, at this day, the issuing of them is often the first declaration of war. It is, however, very certain, that the practice of granting commissions to privateers did not become general before the end of the sixteenth century. The first instance, in which their aid appears to have been considered important in carrying on the war, was, in the contest between Spain and her revolted provinces of the Low Countries, which began in 1569. In 1570, the Prince of Orange, in the hope of replenishing his impoverished finances by seizing on the money sent from Spain to the Netherlands, issued commissions to many of his adherents, authorizing them to cruise against the ships of Spain. A considerable fleet was equipped, and, increasing daily in number, they soon became terrible by their depredations, not only on the commerce of Spain and the Netherlands, but on that of their own and of other countries. It is said that their country suffered from them not less than from the despotism and cruelty of Alva. As the confederated reformists had themselves been called in derision *gueux,* or beggars,† these freebooters were called *gueux de mer,* or sea-beggars.—*English Univ. Hist., vol.* xvii., *page* 388. Many of them were punished by Spain and other nations as pirates, not so much, it is said, on account of their excesses, as of the supposed illegality of their commissions.—*Martens, chap.* 1, *sec.* 7. The French, however, may probably claim the distinction of

---

* Martens, page 6. And this is the assertion of Giannoi, in his History of Naples, book xi., chap 6. But see notes to the preface of Robinson's translations of the prize chapters. The chapters relating to this subject were probably added at a period subsequent to the original compilation.

† Puffendorf defines them, " violentæ executiones in cives aut bona civium alterius reipublicæ, quæ justitiam administrare detrectat."—*De Jure Nat. &c., lib.* 8, *c.* 6, *sec.* 13.

‡ This is probably a mistake for Charles VI. See his ordinance mentioned afterwards.

§ Vol. viii. page 96—Fr. ed. vol. iii. part 4. page 166, year 1399—letters granted by Henry IV. commanding his admirals and other officers to seize the ships and goods of subjects of the Earl of Holland in English ports, reciting, with great care, the previous demands and refusal of justice. Rymer, Fr. ed., vol. iv., part 1, page 161, year 1409—granted, by Henry IV. to the Sieur de Casteillon to enforce the performance of contracts made with him by the subjects of the King of Arragon, commanding all public officers to assist him, and to keep all prizes safe in their fortresses till the contracts are fulfilled. Rymer, Eng. ed., vol. viii., page 717, year 1411—against the Genoese. Rymer, Eng.

ed., vol. viii., page 755, year 1412—against the persons and goods of the French, limited to the satisfaction of the actual damage. Anderson. vol. i., page 239—another instance against the Genoese, limited in sum, year 1413. In the year 1379, Richard II. is said to have granted to the people of Dartmouth a general cruising commission against the French ; and in 1385, the inhabitants of that town took some French vessels.

* An English act of Parliament to the same effect was passed, A. D. 1414, 2 Henry V., c. 6 ; and a law of the Emperor Maximilian respecting the Admiralty of the Low Countries in 1487, ordered " that no person should fit out a ship for a cruise without the express permission of the admiral or his lieutenant." *Martens on Privateers, page* 18.

† De Thou, tome v.

having first sent out, in any considerable numbers, these scourges of the sea. Their code exhibits the most ancient regulations concerning privateers; and, it is well known, that their maritime laws have always been the most severe against the commerce of neutrals. De Thou relates,[*] that, in 1555, the French King, having received advice that several Dutch ships of great burden were returning from Spain, laden with every sort of valuable India goods, gave orders to the inhabitants of Dieppe unquestionably the most experienced mariners in France, to equip such vessels as they could find in the ports on the coast of Normandy, and seize this rich fleet. The privateersmen of Dieppe,[†] having fitted out for cruising nineteen ships and six brigantines, under the command of Epineville, a celebrated mariner, met the Dutch opposite to Dover. A most obstinate battle ensued, which lasted six hours. Many ships on both sides were burned; the flames drove the French from their own ships into those of the enemy, and, having more men, they made many of them prizes. The Dutch lost a thousand men, and the French four hundred.

The English seem not to have been slow in imitating the example set them by the French and Dutch. In the year 1586, we are told by the author last quoted,[‡] before war had been declared between England and Spain, Philip II. seized and confiscated the goods of the English merchants. The English, under pretence of reprisals, set themselves to pirating over the whole ocean, harassing the navigation not only of the Spanish and their allies, but even of the people of the Low Countries, whom they robbed without distinction. The merchants of the United Provinces in vain sought redress in the English admiralty. But the Queen, Elizabeth, wearied by the complaints which came to her from all quarters, made severe regulations, requiring cruisers to give security not to meddle with any ships but those of Spain, and not to dispose of their prizes till they had been regularly condemned in the Admiralty. "The piracies," says De Thou, were checked for a time by these decrees; but means were soon found to evade them, under pretence of privileges, or by means of subtleties, which persons in power connived at."[§] Spain and England, shortly after the

[*] Hist. tome ii., page 633.
[†] *Les armateurs de Dieppe ayant armé en course, &c.*
[‡] De Thou, Hist. tome ix., p. 545.
[§] See in Robinson's Coll. Mar. a proclamation of Elizabeth, of the year 1602, reciting the great extent of the piracies complained of, and forbidding any man of war to be fitted out without license and surety. The preamble refers to other laws and orders lately published, "upon the growing on of these fowl crimes and piracies colored by other voyages." And in the Statuta Admiralitatis of Master Rowghton, printed in Clarke's Praxis, p. 161, we have an ordinance of 1591, requiring presentment to be made of all those that since the late proclamation have had traffic with the leaguers in France, and of all who have set out ships without commission, and to inquire what ships and goods have been taken at sea without commission, and of breaking bulk and disposing of prizes before

depredations committed under the commissions of the Prince of Orange, issued commissions to great numbers of privateers. The expeditions of Drake and Frobisher are said to have been of this nature.[*] In 1625, James I. found it necessary to issue letters patent addressed to the High Admiral, reciting the great losses and damages sustained by many of his subjects, by the surprising and taking of their ships and goods by the subjects of Spain in the Low Countries, and by those of the States General, and that justice having been demanded in vain, his subjects had made humble suit to him for letters of reprisals. He therefore requires the Admiral to grant commissions for taking the ships of the Low Countries and States General to such of his subjects as had been so damnified.[†] In 1627, Charles I. granted reprisals against the French to such of his subjects as had had ships or goods taken by the French, and a war followed in the same year.—*Anderson, vol.* ii. *p.* 27. In that same year, too, we are told that Charles was obliged to fit out an armament to protect the coal trade against privateers from the Spanish Netherlands.—*Anderson, vol.* ii. *p.* 29. The Dutch war for independence ended in 1648. Towards the close of it, in 1643 and 1645, the *placarts* or decrees of the States General held out great encouragement to privateers.—*Martens,* 26. In that long continued contest, the use of these instruments had become familiar. Treaties and laws were made for defining their rights, and preventing the abuses to which they were found to have so strong a tendency.[‡] But new discords kept alive the spirit of

sentence of the admiralty, and what captains, &c., under color of commission of reprisal, have boarded, taken, &c., ships of England, France, &c., Holland, Zealand, &c.
[*] Martens, p. 26. And in the debate upon Pulteney's act for encouraging privateers, 1739, Pulteney argues from this, as an instance of the spirit and power with which private adventurers could act. "It was," he says, "to private adventurers that all the success of Francis Drake was owing."—*Parl. Deb. vol.* xvii. *p.* 415. We have great doubts, however, whether these expeditions are to be classed with cruises of privateers. Drake's was an expedition fitted out for the purpose of attacking Spain in her home dominions. Elizabeth furnished about £30,000 and several ships, and Drake and his associates supplied the residue. The spoils were to be equally divided between the Queen and the fleet.—*De Thou, vol.* x. *p.* 692. There is an important difference between the employment of ships equipped at private expense, but hired by the public, and sailing in fleets with the public forces, under the government of naval officers, and cruises performed by one or more ships under the orders of private adventurers.—*See also Lee on Captures, p.* 199. It seems to have been an ancient practice to use in warlike expeditions ships under the wages of the King, and to give them a part of the prizes. See the ancient articles of the Admiralty subjoined to Clarke's Praxis, p. 163, A. 19.
[†] Rymer, Fr. Ed. vol. vii, part 4, p. 185.
[‡] Martens, p. 26. Voet ad Pand. vol. ii, p. 602, speaks of the "naves privatorum praedatorias permissione ordinum instructas," and cites the Admiralty instructions of the 13th August, 1597, and decrees of

Application to abolish Privateering.

plunder, and privateers still found favor, as a cheap means of carrying on war through the instigation of private avarice. In 1634, disputes began between the English and Dutch. The northern fishing, and the sovereignty claimed by the British in the narrow seas, were the chief subjects of contention. England, in the mean while, was disturbed by civil wars, and the Parliament party was not likely to omit any means of annoyance which had heretofore been employed with success. In 1643, exasperated by the cessation of arms in Ireland, " they forbade all masters of ships to bring over any officers or soldiers, on penalty of the forfeiture of their vessels, and give letters of marque to merchants and others who would fit out ships at their own expense, empowering them to take to their own profit all such ships and goods as they should meet coming over with soldiers or warlike stores for the King."* The friends of the King were not slow in retaliating this measure, for in 1644 the goods of the merchants trading in France were seized, and letters of marque granted against all that adhered to the Parliament.—*Whitelocke, p.*. 130. Of the activity of private cruisers in the hostilities which ensued, the reader may satisfy himself by referring to the book last quoted, where he will find instances of mutual depredation more numerous than we have any disposition to record. Doubtless, the practice was attended with much abuse and licentiousness. In the year 1650, April 16, " an act was passed for preventing wrongs and abuses done to merchants at sea, and prohibiting mariners from serving foreign Princes or States without license.—*Whitelocke, p.* 451. Soon after this, in 1652, the Parliament and the Dutch came to open hostilities, and an active course of privateering commenced between them.† From their near neighborhood and their former habits, there can be no doubt that during this two years' contest they kept up this sort of warfare in its worst form.

The restoration of the King made no alteration in the policy of the English, as it respected their rivals, the Dutch. The scheme of maritime superiority was carried on in the same spirit which had dictated the navigation act. Privateers found great favor in the eyes of the Court,‡ and the passage we

1st April, 1602, and 28th January, 1631, and he adds, that the decrees of the 9th August, 1624, and 22d October, 1627, required all prizes to be brought into port before breaking bulk, " that the republic and others might not be defrauded of their due portion of the plunder."

* Neal's History of the Puritans, ch. 12. Whitelocke says, " they granted letters of marque against all such as had taken up arms against the Parliament, or assisted the Irish rebels."—*Memorials, p.* 76, *year* 1643.

† July 19. New letters of marque granted by the States against the English. 12th August. A Dutch private man of war taken and sunk by two English ketches.—*Whitelocke, pp.* 539, 541, *and see pages* 545, 547.

‡ This may be inferred from the treaty made between the Dutch and Charles II. in 1674, which Postlethwait [*Dict. Art. Privateer*] says " is fit to be a standard to all nations." The preamble runs thus :

are about to quote from the Life of Clarendon will show that this is an important epoch in the history of the practice. It is the more remarkable, as it is from the pen of that virtuous Chancellor himself. It relates to the period, 1864, when the Ministers of Charles II. provoked a new war with the Dutch, in the prosecution of their great design of becoming the exclusive masters of the commerce. " It was resolved, that all possible encouragement should be given to privateers, that is, to as many as would take commissions from the Admiral to set out vessels of war, as they call them, to take prizes from the enemy ; which no articles or obligations can restrain from all the villany they can act, and are a people, how countenanced soever, or thought necessary, that do bring an unavoidable scandal, and it is to be feared a curse upon the justest war that was ever made at sea. Besides the horrible scandal and clamor that this class of men brought upon the King and the whole Government for defect of justice, the prejudice which resulted from thence to the public, and to the carrying on the service, is unspeakable. All seamen run to them, and though the King now assigned an ample share of all prizes taken by his own ships to the seamen, over and above their wages, yet there was a great difference between the condition of the one and the other. In the King's fleet they might gain well, but they were sure of blows ; nothing could be got there without fighting. With the privateers there was rarely fighting. They took all who could make little resistance, and fled from all who were too strong for them. And so these fellows were always well manned, when the King's ships were compelled to stay many days for want of men, who were raised by pressing, and with great difficulty."—p. 242. From this time privateers have been common in all wars between maritime countries, and Governments have endeavored, by the most liberal encouragements, to increase their number and whet their thirst of plunder. At the same time the evils suffered from them, and the loud complaints of neutrals, have caused various expedients to be resorted to for checking their excesses, while their use has been continued. The great increase and wider extent of commerce have added to the opportunities and the temptations for growing rich by this sort of authorized violence ; and it has hitherto been found impossible to impose any effectual restraints upon forces of so low a character, and called into action by motives so unworthy and sordid.*

" and whereas the masters of merchant ships, and likewise the mariners and passengers, do sometimes suffer many cruelties and barbarous usages when they are brought under the power of ships which take prizes in time of war, the takers in an inhuman manner tormenting them, thereby to extort from them such confessions as they would have to be made, it is agreed that both his Majesty and the Lords, the States General, shall, by the severest proclamations or placarts, forbid all such heinous and inhuman offences," &c. There was an article with France to the same purport, in the Treaty of Utrecht.

* Immediately after the war of 1756 had commenced,

Application to abolish Privateering.

From this historical deduction, it appears, 1st. That the practice of privateering is truly what it has been called, "a remnant of the ancient p rac ," and has its root and origin in the general license of plundering, which we justly regard as the vice of a barbarous and lawless age. 2d. That the public commissions, under which it is now carried on, were expedients adopted when the world began to assume a more regular and settled form; the first step towards a state of society more consistent with reason and humanity. 3d. That at first, letters of reprisals authorized the seizing of goods on the land, as well as at sea. * 4th. That the first notice we have of privateering to any considerable extent, is the measure to which, in the outset of the war of the Netherlands, poverty and revenge drove the Prince of Orange; and that these privateers became notorious for their piratical depredations. If, before that it was practised by the French, it was not under circumstances more honorable, nor with less cruelty. 5th. That the practice has always continued to answer well to its original; privateers having been, in earlier and later times, the "scourges of neutral commerce," a continual theme of complaint to neutral Powers, the causes of new wars, subjects of negotiation in treaties, and of frequent restrictive laws; but still eluding all attempts to put a stop to their abuses, and reverting to their primitive character.

It is now time to turn our attention for a moment to the practice of war upon land, and here we are at once struck with a strange difference in conduct and opinions. It would seem that, while we have been growing more refined and generous in hostilities by land, we have certainly not improved, and, it is to be feared, have even become less attentive to considerations of equity and humanity, in our maritime warfare. We can claim, in this respect, no superiority over the men of two centuries ago. Like them, we set upon the peaceful merchant to rob him of his property, and if those to whom he has intrusted it defend it faithfully, we suffer no tenderness for life to keep us from our booty. On the land, do we ever hear of an honorable commander's delivering up to pillage a captured city, unless induced by some extraordinary violation of the rules of honorable warfare in the enemy? Does he ever seize the merchandise of the inhabitants, or disturb them in the exercise of their trades? Why, then, on the sea should captured ships and the goods they are freighted with, pursuing peacefully their course, and engaged in the useful interchange of the products of different lands, become a prey to the rapacious cruiser? The most that is allowed upon the land, is the exaction of a tribute, and even of this

we suspect the instances are becoming rare, and it is regarded as somewhat disgraceful. But even if the commander of an invading army forbears to touch any property, but that of the sovereign, what should we say if bands of private adventurers were commissioned to enter the enemy's borders to rob and pillage for their own profit? Should we not regard it much in the same light as we should the use of poison, or assassination, or infernal machines? *

How, then, shall we reconcile this inconsistency? A late writer has, we think, given the true account of it. The jealousy of commerce has entered much into all the wars between maritime countries from the time of Cromwell's war with the Dutch. To exhaust the commercial resources of the enemy, and so to cripple his trade, that he may not be able to resume it upon fair terms of competition, when peace shall be restored, has been one of the objects proposed by one or the other of the belligerent Powers. Privateers, as the most destructive assailants of commerce, have, for this cause, been encouraged and protected, and the exemption granted upon the land to the property of peaceful subjects has been denied at sea. "From thence arises that striking inconclusiveness,† [inconsistency] which has been so frequently declaimed against, that whilst in wars on the continent, the civilized nations of Europe (so long as they do not betray that character) endeavor to make the burden of it fall as lightly as possible on the peaceable subjects of the enemy, and that they respect their property in consideration of a contribution levied by authorizing pillage only in some extraordinary cases, the barbarous practice has been retained, in maritime wars, of depriving hostile subjects of their ships and their cargoes by prohibiting now, almost universally, the acceptance of a ransom."‡—*Martens on Privateers, p. 22.*

That some cause, like that here suggested, has retarded the progress of civilization in the customs of maritime war, can hardly be doubted, when we consider how many of the most distinguished writers, ancient and modern, have declared their disapprobation of the practice of privateering. To begin with Albericus Gentilis, who was professor of law in one of the English universities, from the year 1582 to his death in 1608. Privateers, as we have seen, had then first began to be used to any considerable extent, and to be recognised by stipu-

---

* As to what are unlawful arms, see Martens, Précis du Droit des Gens, t. ii. p. 351, and also as to the difference in the rules respecting property on land and at sea.

† We copy from the English translation, published in 1801.

‡ It appears that in Holland, by an edict of the Earl of Leicester, of 4th April, 1586, all captures, whether by land or sea, were brought before one tribunal, and the counsellors of the States of Holland formerly, as appears from their ancient forms in 1590, adjudged upon the plunder obtained by the soldiers on the land. But, says Bynkershoek, "I do not find this in their new form, 4th October, 1670, nor is it observed in practice."—*Quest. Jur. Pub. lib. i. cap. 18.*

---

the English privateers began to swarm in the Channel, and to commit depredations upon the commerce of friendly nations. The Dutch complained, and in 1759 an act was passed, prohibiting commissions to any vessel under one hundred tons burden and forty men.—*Smollett's Contin. vol. vi. p. 151—294.*

* See letters granted by Edward I. ante, p. 175, and the form in Rymer, vol. iv. part 1. p. 161, French edition.

Application to abolish Privateering.

lations in treaties. * Gentilis, in his book *De Advocatione Hispanica*, speaks of them under no other name than "pirates," and will not admit them to be entitled to any better consideration. Grotius says it is worth inquiring how far the right of private captures may be carried, without violating internal justice or charity. † And after showing that, by the law of nature, no injustice is done to the enemy, if the plunder be confined to a compensation for the injury which caused the war, he adds that, "although justice, strictly speaking, may not be violated, yet there may be an offence against that moral duty which consists in loving others, as by the law of christianity we are especially commanded; as if it should appear that such depredation will fall, not upon the hostile commonwealth, or the sovereign, or those who are in themselves guilty, but upon the innocent, and that it will reduce them to such a measure of distress as it would not be lawful for us to inflict even upon our private debtors. But if, in addition to this, such depredation will neither be of great effect in putting an end to the war, nor in cutting off the enemy's strength, then, indeed, an honest man, and more especially a Christian, will scorn to profit by the calamity of the times."—*Lib.* 3, *chap.* xviii. § 4. From this and other passages of Grotius it cannot be doubted in what light he regarded privateering as in fact carried on. We have already quoted the opinion of Clarendon, than which none can be entitled to greater respect. The treatise of Molloy, *De Jure Maritimo,* was first published in 1676; many editions have been published since that time, and its reputation is deservedly great. "Most certain," says this writer, "these sorts of capers, or privateers, being instruments found out but of later ages, and it is well known by whom, it were well they were restrained by consent of all princes; since all good men account them but one remove from pirates, who, without any respect to the cause, or having any injury done them, or so much as hired for the service, spoil men and goods, making even a trade and calling of it, amidst the calamities of war."—*Book* 1. *chap.* vii. § 15. The compilation, entitled "Sea Laws," was published early in the last century. We find in it this passage: "Our laws take not much notice of these privateers, because the manner of warring is new and not very honorable, but the diligence of our enemies in this piratical way obliges us to be also as diligent for the preservation of our commerce."—p. 472. So Beawes, whose Lex Merca-

toria was compiled in 1750, "The use of these sort of vessels we were taught by our neighbors, and obliged by their example to encourage them," &c.—p. 207. Loccenius, who was professor at Upsal in 1670, seems, like Gentilis, to have known no distinction between privateering and piracy His words are, "When a naval war is unavoidable, it is far better to assail the enemy with domestic levies or hired marines, under officers and discipline, or to depend on the aid of allies, than to give license to pirates, the vilest of mankind, who, once authorized to plunder, soon forget all restraint, and spare not even friends, nor those who have never injured them or their employers."* If we come down to more modern times, we find Mably † and Galliani ‡ supporting the justice and expediency of exempting commerce from the calamities of war. But especially Linguet, whose essay we would quote entire, if it were possible, has exposed, in the clearest manner, the absurd contradiction in practice, to which we have already referred.§ "It is," to use his words, "one among a thousand proofs of the confusion, barbarism, and extravagance of all our principles, of every sort. Whence comes this difference between fleets and armies, squadrons and regiments, corsairs and hussars?" He thus concludes a glowing description of the circumstances which principally give a character to privateering: "It is cowardly, for *its* object is to attack the unarmed; it is odious, for it has no other principle than a base self-interest ; it is barbarous, for the flying merchant ship is compelled to submit by murderous broadsides; nor is it uncommon for a part of the crew, at the moment of striking the flag, to be slaughtered by the balls that brought the order for striking." Martens has expressed himself in language not less clear and decisive. "Glory and duty call an officer to fight the enemy, whenever the interest of his sovereign is concerned, and honor is the best reward for his labors and its dangers; it is not so with the privateer. Indifferent to the fate of the war, and often of his country, he has no other inducement but the love of gain, no other recompense but his captures and the prizes conferred by the State on his privileged piracies. To encourage individuals to fit out privateers at considerable expense, it is necessary to present them the allurement of a rich booty, and, by prescribing them a moderation, which they are fully determined not to observe, not to intimidate them by imposing on them too many restrictions."—p. 24. The opinion of Dr. Franklin we shall have occasion to quote

---

* Bynkershoek, Q. J. P. lib. i, cap. 18, seems to refer the origin of privateering to the war of the United Provinces with Spain, for he mentions no earlier instance. "Olim in Belgio fœderato fuerunt privati, qui ipsi naves bellicas exercebant, quibusque, præter premia, ex captis et recuperatis navibus redacta, ex publico ærario numerabatur certa pecunia pro modo expensarum, et pro modo temporis, quo operam bellicam præstabant. Illæ naves privatorum dicebantur *Kruyssers,* usque adversus Hispanos cum maxime usi sunt Ordines Generales."

† "Id vero quatenus procedat, illæsa justitia interna et charitate, non immerito quæritur."—*Lib.* 3. *cap.* xviii. § 2.

* "Sed et si belli maritimi necessitas incumbat. præstat delectis domesticis, aut militibus nauticis mercenariis, qui sub duce et disciplina degant, aut sociorum ope, quam colluvie pessimorum hominum, piratis. adversus hostes uti, qui licentiam spoliandi nacti, facile præscriptos fines excedunt ; ut ne quidem amicis aut aliis, a quibus vel ipsi, vel eorum patroni numquam læsi sunt, parcant."—*De Jure Mar. et Nav.* lib. 2, cap. iii. § 4.

† Droit Publique, tome 2, cap. xii.

‡ Lib. 1, cap. 10.

§ See this able paper in Annales Politiques, tom. v. p. 518.

hereafter. The apologists of privateering have, we believe, rested its defence on the sanction given to it by law, and have contented themselves with showing that there is a real and substantial distinction between privateers and pirates. Azuni, one of the latest and most distinguished of these apologists, after mentioning the opinions of Galliani and Mably, adds, that he respects their opinion, and would adopt it "if he were speaking as a mere philosopher."

It is wonderful, when we consider how much the commerce of neutrals has suffered from privateers, that more frequent efforts have not been made to put a stop to the practice by the general consent of nations. Our own history furnishes, indeed, a fact which cannot fail to gratify the feelings of an American. "As early," says the Memorial before us, "as 1785, the celebrated philosopher, Dr. Franklin, in a letter to a friend, observed that the 'United States, though better situated than any other nation to profit by privateering, are, as far as in them lies, endeavoring to abolish the practice, by offering, in all their treaties with other Powers, an article engaging solemnly that, in case of a future war, no privateer shall be commissioned on either side, and that unarmed merchant ships on both sides shall pursue their voyages unmolested.'"—Page 6.[*] It was accordingly stipulated in the twenty-third article of the treaty with Prussia, in 1785, as follows:

"And all merchant and trading vessels employed in exchanging the products of different places, and thereby rendering the necessaries, conveniences, and comforts of human life more easy to be obtained, and more general, shall be allowed to pass free and unmolested; and neither of the contracting Powers shall grant or issue any commission to any private armed vessels, empowering them to take or destroy such trading vessels, or interrupt such commerce."

Martens[†] has taken notice of this article, adding that this "example, worthy of imitation, has not been hitherto followed by other States." Doctor Franklin, to whom, doubtless, the credit of this humane scheme belongs, has elsewhere expressed his opinion in emphatic terms. The author of the Appeal, mentioned at the head of this article, quotes a passage from the propositions relative to privateering, communicated by Doctor Franklin to Mr. Oswald, January 14, 1783, in which the principal reasons of policy for abolishing the practice are forcibly stated.

"It is for the interest of humanity in general that the occasions of war, and the inducements to it, should be diminished. If rapine is abolished, one of the encouragements to war is taken away, and peace, therefore, more likely to continue and

be lasting. The practice of robbing merchants on the high seas, a remnant of the ancient piracy, though it may be accidentally beneficial to particular persons, is far from being profitable to all engaged in it, or to the nation that authorizes it. In the beginning of a war some rich ships, not upon their guard, are surprised and taken. This encourages the first adventurers to fit out more armed vessels, and many others to do the same. But the enemy, at the same time, become more careful, arm their merchant ships better, and render them not so easy to be taken; they go also more under the protection of convoys; thus, while the privateers to take them are multiplied, the vessels subject to be taken, and the chances of profit, are diminished, so that many cruises are made wherein the expenses overgo the gains; and, as is the case in other lotteries, though particulars have got prizes, the mass of adventurers are losers, the whole expense of fitting out all the privateers, during a war, being much greater than the whole amount of goods taken. Then there is the national loss of all the labor of so many men during the time they have been employed in robbing, who, besides spendi g what they get in riot, drunkenness, and debauchery, lose their habits of industry, are rarely fit for any sober business after peace, and serve only to increase the number of highwaymen and housebreakers. Even the undertakers, who have been fortunate, are, by sudden wealth, led into expensive living; the habit of which continues when the means of supporting it cease, and finally ruins them; a just punishment for their having wantonly and unfeelingly ruined many honest, innocent traders and families, whose subsistence was obtained in serving the common interests of mankind."

And in a letter to David Hartley, Esq., May 8, 1783—

"I do not wish to see a new Barbary rising in America, and our long-extended coast occupied by piratical States. I fear lest our privateering success in the two last wars should already have given our people too strong a relish for that most mischievous kind of gaming mixed with blood."— *Private Correspondence, p.* 530. *Appeal, p.* 9.

The motives for abolishing this practice are so many that we hardly know where to begin stating them. If it were not in itself unjust and immoral, we would urge upon nations its inconsistency even with an enlightened policy; we would show that it can never be productive of any real advantage to either party in the war; we would call to mind the many seamen who are thrown by it into prisons, and thus taken from the service of their country; [*] we would speak of the difficulty of procuring sailors to man the fleets, or defend the coasts from invasion, when they are lured by the hope of plunder to embark in long and distant cruises; we

---

[*] Letter to B. Vaughan, Esq. Franklin's works, vol. ii, p. 448.

[†] Essay on Privateers, p. 31, note. The only instance of a similar attempt, mentioned by him, is that of the agreement between Sweden and the United Provinces, when at war in 1675, that neither they nor their allies should make use of privateers, but the agreement was not performed.

[*] It is said that, at the close of the war ending by the peace of Amiens in 1801, there were 30,000 French sailors in English prisons. (Bonnemant's D'Abreu, note, page 27.) It is well known what numbers of our seamen were thus lost to us for the time in the late war with England.

Application to abolish Privateering.

would insist upon the discouragement of the naval service by the higher privileges which are granted to privateers; we would bring into view the loss of life, and the distress and poverty brought upon the families of seamen; we would ask for an instance in which privateers can be fairly said to have given essential aid in the prosecution of the war, or to have produced any serious impression upon the enemy's resources and strength; we would refer to the ill-will and jealousy excited in neutral nations by the vexation to which their commerce is exposed, from the eagerness of these marauders, and their unwillingness to return from a cruise without some evidence of vigilance and success. Lastly, we would leave it to history to decide, and challenge the experience of every nation, that has employed privateers in war, whether, on the whole, the national strength has not been impaired, and its resources diminished, by this expense of its treasure and force in the pursuit of pillage.*

Let these considerations be duly weighed by those, who allow of no rule for the conduct of nations, but the greater or less profit to themselves, or injury to their enemies, which this conduct may seem likely to produce. Let them reflect upon the words of Franklin, and remember that his opinion and his remarks were founded on experience acquired in a war, in which perhaps, if ever, privateering was a powerful means of annoyance in the hands of one of the parties. With those, who believe that the true interests of a nation can never be separated from a strict regard to religion and moral duty, there are other arguments of greater weight, than any which terminate in mere policy. With them it is enough to determine any action to be impolitic, to know that it is unjust.

What judgment, then, must we pass upon privateering, if we test it by the rules of a sound morality? We ask not, what will be its fate if judged of by the high dictates of high and honorable feeling, of that elevated morality, which rises far above the ordinary sense of right and wrong, as it is found in the mass of men; we ask not that it should be condemned or absolved by the sentence of a nice and scrupulous conscience; we are ready to put the question fairly to the grossest and least reflecting of mankind, be they only honest and unperverted; and we doubt not, that when brought to view the subject in its proper light, stripped of the cloak which law and custom may have lent to it, the most uncultivated conscience will pronounce it unjust and disgraceful to grow rich upon the spoils of the innocent, to gather by violence the fruits of another's industry. If upon the breaking out of a war, every debtor should be declared released from debts due to the subjects of the hostile State, would that man be thought to possess common honesty, who would profit by

such an advantage? But how much more palpable is the injustice of attacking, and bearing away as prize, the property of that enemy, not found in our own territory, but upon the ocean, the common highway of nations? Let it not, then, be said that the law of war has made it yours, and annulled the rights of its former possessor. This law is not the law of reason or conscience. It is a custom which has grown out of the selfish and revengeful passions of men, and has been handed down from age to age, receiving now and then some mitigations, by which it has approached nearer to what is suited to a rational nature, but still it is founded in violence, and only one of the few remains of the right of the strongest. Grant that war is not in itself unlawful. Yet, in a ruder age than the present, it was said by one, who admitted the lawfulness of war, 'militare non est delictum, sed propter prædam militare, peccatum est.'* Of the justness of this distinction, who can doubt? It is the motive which determines the character of the action. And what motive has the privateersman but plunder?†

Let us once more try this question by the principles of national law, as they are stated by Grotius and others, whose works are of acknowledged authority. It is in the first place to be observed, that there is no pretence of justice to support the practice of capturing private property in war, but what is founded on one or the other of the following principles: 1. That the wrong done extends to every subject of the injured State, and vests in him the same rights, as if that wrong were personal, and that every subject of the offending State is equally responsible in person and property for the injury done by his Government, or a fellow-subject, as if he were personally guilty. 2. That each party in the war is to be considered, as it respects other nations, to have a just cause of war. 3. That the war being just, every subject, having the authority of his Government, may pursue the enemy in all the modes of lawful warfare,

---

* The French editor of D'Abreu's treatise on Prize Law has strongly expressed the opinion that it is a mistake to ascribe great efficacy to privateers in war. See note, p. 27, Bonnemant's translation.

* St. Augustin. Canon. Militare, 59, 1. "It is not a crime to war, but to war for plunder is sinful."

† In the letter before quoted of Dr. Franklin to B. Vaughan, Esq., (Works, vol. ii. p. 448,) are two instances of the judgment of an impartial conscience upon this subject: one of a Quaker gentleman, who was part owner of a ship, which the other owners thought proper to fit out as a letter of marque, and which took several French prizes. He took his share of booty, but employed an agent to find out by advertisement who were the sufferers, that he might restore what had come to him. The other is of the Scotch presbyterians, who, soon after the reformation, made an ordinance of the town council of Edinburgh, which is extant, "forbidding the purchase of prize goods, under pain of losing the freedom of his burgh forever, with other punishment at the will of the magistrates; the practice of making prizes being contrary to good conscience, and the rule of treating Christian brethren as we would wish to be treated; and such goods are not to be sold by any Christian men within this burgh." This, it will be remarked, extends to all captures.

Application to abolish Privateering.

if he do it at his own expense, may acquire property to his own use.*

But it is not, nor was it in the age of Grotius, pretended, that the right over the person and property of the enemy is unlimited. And, if we mistake not, these limitations will be found to be established as part of the national code : 1. That the right to kill is limited to cases of extreme necessity, for the preservation of life and property, "and even this last," says Grotius, " to put men to death for the sake of perishable and uncertain possessions, though in strictness it may stand with justice, is irreconcilable with the law of charity." 2. That even in a just war, if more is taken than an equivalent for the debt, or the injury is either unjust, or else it is to be kept by way of pledge or security, without any change of property, and to be restored when justice has been obtained. *Grot. lib.* 3. *cap.* xiii. § 1. 3. That certain classes of persons, among whom are cultivators of the earth and *merchants*, are to be spared.—*Lib.* 3. *cap.* xi. § 10. and *cap.* xiii. § 4. 4. That where the object of war is to obtain restitution of what belongs to us, all the subjects are to be considered as sureties one for another; but where the object is to punish, none but the magistrates, who have refused to inflict punishment themselves, and actual offenders, can justly be made to suffer.—*Lib.* 3. *cap.* xiii. § 1. 5. That the right of recourse to the goods of the innocent is only subsidiary, and humanity requires that we should not make use of it as long as there is a hope of obtaining justice without it.—*Lib.* 3. *cap.* xiii. § 4. 6. That we have no right to lay waste or destroy, unless with the design and reasonable hope of thereby promoting peace; and that if the same purpose can be otherwise effected, we have no longer this right.†

Now all these principles are violated by the practice of privateering; it assumes a right to kill, not for defending, but to obtain property; it has no regard to the injury done, but seizes whatever falls in its way, and that, not for the use of those who may have suffered from the depredations of the enemy, but for the profit of those concerned in the cruise; it has nothing to do with restitution, but takes with no other intent than to enjoy a *plenum dominium* over the thing taken, be its value ever so great; it spares no class, much less the merchant, against whom all its attacks are directed; it regards all the enemy's subjects as game to be hunted, without any concern, who may have been the authors of the war; it hears to no distinctions between the innocent and guilty, debtors and sureties, primary or subsidiary rights; it understands nothing, but that as much wealth is to be gotten as can be with impunity.

It would be easy to enlarge upon some of these topics, but the unexpected length of this article obliges us to abridge the argument. The distinction between those who bear arms and those who

are engaged in peaceful occupations, and the principle that the latter are to suffer no more of the evils of the war than may be absolutely unavoidable, are now universally recognised. It is only in maritime warfare that they are not adopted in practice. The exemption, as it prevails in hostilities by land, comprehends all those whose occupations are of a peaceful sort : " quorum quæstus pacem amat, non pellum." It extends, of course, to those whose business it is to supply, by a mutual interchange, the wants of different countries. How it should happen that, the moment the merchant embarks his property upon the ocean—the moment he begins to exercise his trade in the very way in which it yields most benefit to the world, he loses the protection of all laws, and meets the same treatment, as to his property, with the pirate, whose ship is loaded with the gains of violence and treachery, is indeed unaccountable upon any supposition consistent with fairness and equity. " The canon," says Grotius, in enumerating the exempted classes, "adds also merchants; not merely those who have a temporary residence in the enemy's country, but those who owe him perpetual allegiance, 'nam et horum vita abarmis aliena est.'" Many of the opinions we have quoted go to the entire neutrality of commerce; and this would be only extending to the sea the humane principles long since adopted on the land. The article already cited from our treaty with Prussia has been understood as giving protection against public as well as private ships.* Many of the evils connected with privateering are equally to be feared from public captures: the effects upon the habits and morals of seamen will be nearly the same; the cruelty and injustice are the same. A French writer, of the year 1744, has asked "would it not, then, be possible to revive the ancient custom of commercial truces, and to make war without involving in it commerce and mercantile navigation ?†" It may be objected that, the greater the sufferings connected with wars the less ready will nations be to enter into them, and the sooner will they be disposed to return to a state of peace. But surely the experience of the world is against this. Wars were not less frequent, nor less obstinate, when it was thought lawful to enslave prisoners, to sack towns, and to put to the sword a garrison which defended itself to the last extremity. The argument would justify every degree of cruelty; it would justify the poisoning of streams, and the employment of assassins; it would introduce a law no better than that of the Mohawks. But if to make prize of the property of the innocent is in itself opposed to equity and good conscience, it deserves a double reproach when it is allowed to be done by privateers. Powers, in their nature oppressive, ought not to be committed to instruments so certain to make them more odious by abuse.‡ A Russian treaty, of 1801,§ prohibits to

* Grotius, lib. 3. cap. vi. Puffendorf, lib. 8. cap. vi. De Jure Nat. et Gent. lib. 2. cap. xvi. § 10. et seq. De Officio Hom. &c. Martens, Droit des Gens, liv. 8. chap. iii.

† Martens, Précis, &c., tome ii. p. 349.

* Martens, Précis, &c., tome 2, p. 352, note.
† Examen de l'Essai sur la Marine, p. 181.
‡ Jus hoc mutandi per vim dominii odiosius est, quàm ut produci debeat.—*Grotius*, lib. 3, cap 6, sec. 5.
§ Convention with G. Britain, June 17, 1801, art. 4.

Public Lands for Education.

privateers the right of searching ships sailing under convoy. This cures some part of the evil, and it shows the light in which privateers are viewed. But the same reason should induce the entire suppression of them.

In all that we have hitherto said, we have gone upon the supposition that there is a just cause of war. But, in every war, one party or the other must be fighting in support of an unjust cause. Terrible, indeed, is the guilt of the subject who, with no other end than private gain, attacks, kills, and robs the enemy, if, in doing this, he is at the same time abetting injustice and fraud. Grotius holds to complete restitution every general and soldier, who, in an unjust war, has assisted in the work of destruction.—*Lib.* 3, *cap.* 10, *sec.* 3, &c. Who, then, in any war, can feel so assured that his country is in no respect chargeable with injustice or rashness as to be willing, for the sake of plunder, to incur the hazard of so great a guilt? What Government can be excused in encouraging its subjects to put their integrity to so perilous a trial? And if there is guilt in fighting for a cause which we know to be unjust, is there not also guilt in plundering in one which we are not sure is just?

We had something to say of the effects of privateering upon the morals of the community, and more especially of seamen; of the taste which it gives for violence and bloodshed; of its breaking down the barriers by which property is defended; of its tendency to annihilate the distinction of mine and thine. But these consequences are too obvious, and have been proved by too recent experience, to need that we should labor to enforce them. They spring up in our path; they meet our view wherever we go; the land and the sea send forth their reports of murders and piracies, and daring robberies, as if the outcasts of society had become emulous of glory, and resolved to hide the disgrace in the magnitude and boldness of their crimes.

It is the laudable purpose of the writer of the Appeal to call the attention of the proper authorities in the United States to the numberless depredations committed upon the ocean by ships fitted out in our own ports, and sometimes, it is to be feared, by our own citizens. He has diligently collected the statements of writers on the laws of nations, and the provisions of the British and French laws in relation to piracies, and the accepting of commissions from foreign Powers; and he has reviewed our own laws for preventing armaments against nations at peace with us, pointed out their insufficiency, and endeavored to awaken attention to the importance of new restraints and prohibitions, and a more vigilant and thorough execution of those already existing. For all this he deserves the thanks of the public. Whatever may be thought of cruising against the enemies of our own country, there are few, we trust, who will not agree with Vattel, "that for strangers it is a shameful trade to take commissions from a foreign Government, for cruising against a nation perfectly innocent in regard to them. The thirst for gold is their only motive; and the com-

mission they receive, however it may screen them from punishment, cannot wipe off their infamy."[*] It is agreed by all nations that a cruiser furnished with commissions from two different sovereigns is to be treated as a pirate. Much of the reasoning in support of this principle would extend equally to the acceptance of any commission from a foreign belligerent against a nation at peace with us.[†]

The Memorial, of which we have also spoken, contains a concise and impressive view of the character and consequences of the practice of privateering. It was our intention to avail ourselves of one or two extracts from it, but we have already exceeded our limits.

It may be expected that we should say something of the practicability of the measure proposed. We must, however, content ourselves with remarking that there cannot be reason to despair of what all commercial nations must feel it to be their interest, by mutual stipulations, to effect. The United States, as a great commercial people, disposed by habit and interest to peace, have every inducement, however great may be their local advantages for the carrying on a predatory warfare, to enter into such an arrangement. Great Britain can expect no benefit from the continuance of the practice of privateering. Holland, France, and Spain, have too much interest in the *revival* of their fallen commerce not to acquiesce cheerfully in a proposal which takes away one of its greatest vexations. Russia, Sweden, and Denmark, are friends to the freedom of commerce; and it is a remarkable and encouraging fact, that Russia made no use of privateers in the Archipelago in her war with Turkey, 1767 and 1774.

We are disposed to think well enough of mankind to believe that there is something in this practice too harsh and illiberal to be much longer borne in the present improved state of knowledge and manners. We trust the time is coming when the greater part of the civilized world will feel the truth of these words of Clarendon: "Indeed, it must be a very savage appetite that engages men to take so much pains, and to run so many and great hazards, only to be cruel to those whom they are able to oppress."[‡]

REPORT RELATIVE TO APPROPRIATIONS OF PUBLIC LAND FOR THE PURPOSES OF EDUCATION—

Made to the Senate of Maryland, January 30, 1831.

The committee to whom was referred so much of the Governor's message as relates to education and public instruction beg leave to report—

That they concur with his Excellency in believing education, and a general diffusion of knowledge, in a Government constituted like ours, to be of great importance, and that "in proportion

---

* Vattel, liv. 3, ch. 15, sec. 229.
† See, as to double commissions, D'Abreu, part 2. page 2: Bonnemant's translation.
‡ Tracts, page 206.

Public Lands for Education.

as the structure of a Government gives weight to public opinion, it is essential that public opinion should be enlightened." Your committee consider our Government as emphatically a Government of opinion. A general diffusion of knowledge, which is essential to its right administration, cannot be effected, unless the people are educated. No high degree of civilization, of moral power and dignity, or of intellectual excellence; no superiority in science, in literature, or in liberal and useful arts, which constitutes the noblest national supremacy, can be attained without the aid of seminaries of learning. The establishment of literary institutions, then, of all grades, from the common school up to the university, becomes the first duty of the legislature of a free people.

Your committee are well aware of the difficulty, in the present embarrassed state of our pecuniary concerns, of providing the means of making education general. They are fully sensible that, at this time, large appropriations out of the public Treasury for this purpose, all important as it is, cannot be expected. They deem it therefore their duty to recall to your notice a report and certain resolutions, presented to the Senate at the last session by a committee of a like nature with the present, which has been referred to your committee, as a part of the unfinished business. The object of those resolutions was to call the attention of Congress, and the Legislatures of the several States, to the public land, as a fund, from which appropriations for the purposes of education may with justice be claimed, not only by Maryland, but all the original States, and three of the new ones.

One thirty-sixth part of all the States and Territories, (except Kentucky,) whose waters fall into the Mississippi and the Gulf of Mexico, has been appropriated by Congress, wherever the Indian title has been extinguished, and provisions made for further appropriations, according to the same ratio, wherever the Indian title may hereafter be extinguished, for the support of common schools, and other large appropriations have been made for the support of seminaries of a higher grade. Your committee are of opinion that the States, for whose benefit no such appropriations have been made, are entitled to ask them of Congress, not as a matter of favor, but of justice. That this may more fully appear, especially as the right of those States to an equal participation with the States, formed out of the public lands, in all the benefits derived from them, has been doubted, your committee have deemed it proper to take a cursory view of the manner in which they have been acquired.

Before the war of the Revolution, and indeed for some years after it, several of the States possessed, within their nominal limits, extensive tracts of waste and unsettled lands. These States were all, at that epoch, regal and not proprietary provinces, and the Crown, either directly or through the medium of officers, whose authority had been prescribed or assented to by the Crown, was in the habit of granting those lands. The right of disposing of them was claimed and exercised by

the Crown in some form or other. They might, therefore, with strict propriety, be called the property of the Crown.

A question arose soon after the Declaration of Independence, whether those lands should belong to the United States, or to the individual States, within whose nominal limits they were situated. However that question might be decided, no doubt could be entertained, that the property and jurisdiction of the soil were acquired by the common sword, purse, and blood of all the States, united in a common effort. Justice, therefore, demanded that, considered in the light of property, the vacant lands should be sold to defray the expenses incurred in the contest by which they were obtained; and that the future harmony of the States required that the extent and ultimate population of the several States should not be so disproportionate as they would be if their nominal limits should be retained.

This State, as early as the 30th of October, 1776, expressed its decided opinion, in relation to the vacant lands, by an unanimous resolution of the convention, which framed our Constitution and form of Government, in the following words, viz. " *Resolved, unanimously,* That it is the opin- ' ion of this convention, that the very extensive ' claim of the State of Virginia to the back lands ' hath no foundation in justice, and that if the ' same, or any like claim is admitted, the freedom ' of the smaller States and the liberties of Amer- ' ica may be thereby greatly endangered; this ' convention being firmly persuaded that, if the ' dominion over those lands should be established ' by the blood and treasure of the United States, ' such lands ought to be considered as a common ' stock, to be parcelled out, at proper times, into ' convenient, free, and independent governments."

In the years 1777 and 1778, the General Assembly, by resolves and instructions to their delegates in Congress, expressed their sentiments in support of their claim to a participation in these lands, in a still stronger language, and declined acceding to the Confederation, on account of the refusal of the States claiming them exclusively to cede them to the United States. They continued to decline, on the same grounds, until 1781, when, to prevent the injurious impression, that dissension existed among the States, occasioned by the refusal of Maryland to join the Confederation, they authorized their delegates in Congress to subscribe the articles; protesting, however, at the same time against the inference, (which might otherwise have been drawn,) that Maryland had relinquished its claim to a participation in the Western lands.

Most of the other States contended on similar grounds with those taken by Maryland for a participation in those lands.

By the Treaty of Peace in 1783, Great Britain relinquished "to the United States all claim to the government, property, and territorial rights of the same, and every part thereof."

The justice and sound policy of ceding the unsettled lands, urged with great earnestness and force by those States, which had united in conquering them from Great Britain, strengthened by

Public Lands for Education.

the surrender on the part of Great Britain of her rights of property and jurisdiction to the United States collectively, and aided, moreover, by the elevated and patriotic spirit of disinterestedness and conciliation, which then animated the whole Confederation, at length made the requisite impression upon the States which had exclusively claimed those lands; and each of them, with the exception of Georgia, made cessions of their respective claims within a few years after the peace. Those States were Massachusetts, Connecticut, New York, Virginia, North Carolina, and South Carolina, the charters of which, with the exception of New York, extended westwardly to the South Sea or Pacific ocean. This circumstance gave to Massachusetts and Connecticut a joint claim with Virginia, to such parts of what was then called the Northwestern Territory, as came within the breadth of the charter of Virginia. New York, indeed, had an indefinite claim to a part of it. Cessions, however, from all these States, at length completed the title of the United States, and placed it beyond all controversy.

The State of North Carolina ceded its claim to the territory which now constitutes the State of Tennessee.

Georgia (whose charter also extended westwardly to the Pacific Ocean) at length, in 1802, ceded the territory which now constitutes the States of Mississippi and Alabama, except a small part on the south side of them, which was acquired under the treaty ceding Louisiana. The conditions of that cession were, that the United States should pay one million two hundred thousand dollars to Georgia, and extinguish the Indian title within the limits which she reserved.

The United States have, in this manner, acquired an indisputable title to all the public lands east of the Mississippi.

All the territory west of the Mississippi, together with the southern extremity of the States of Mississippi and Alabama, was purchased of France for fifteen millions of dollars. This sum, as well as the sums required for the purchase of the Indian title to the public lands, was paid out of the Treasury of the United States.

So far, therefore, as acquisition of public lands has been made by purchase, it has been at the common expense; so far as it has been made by war, it has been by the common force; and so far as it has been made by cessions from individual States, it has been upon the ground, expressly stipulated in most of the acts or deeds of cession, that the lands should be "considered," in the words of the act passed for that purpose by the State which made the largest cession, "as a common fund, for the use and benefit of such of the States as have become, or shall become, members of the Confederation or Federal alliance of said States, according to their usual respective proportions in the general charge and expenditure, and shall faithfully and bona fide be disposed of for that purpose, and for no other use or purpose whatsoever."

In whatever point of view, therefore, the public lands are considered, whether as acquired by pur-

chase, conquest, or cession, they are emphatically the common property of the Union. They ought to inure, therefore, to the common use and benefit of *all* the States, in just proportions, and cannot be appropriated to the use and benefit of any *particular* State or States, to the exclusion of the others, without an infringement of the principles upon which cessions from States are expressly made, and a violation of the spirit of our national compact, as well as the principles of justice and sound policy.

So far as these lands have been sold, and the proceeds been received into the National Treasury, all the States have derived a justly proportionate benefit from them. So far as they have been appropriated for purposes of defence, there is no ground for complaint, for the defence of every part of the country is a common concern. So far, in a word, as the proceeds have been applied to *national*, and not to *State* purposes, although the expenditure may have been local, the course of the General Government has been consonant to the principles and spirit of the Federal Constitution. But so far as appropriations have been made, in favor of any State or States, to the exclusion of the rest, where the appropriations would have been beneficial, and might have been extended to all alike, your committee conceive there has been a departure from that line of policy, which impartial justice, so essential to the peace, harmony, and stability of the Union, imperiously prescribes.

Your committee, then, proceed to inquire, whether the act of Congress, in relation to appropriations of public lands, have been conformable to the dictates of impartial justice.

By the laws relating to the survey and sale of the public lands, one thirty-sixth part of them has been reserved and appropriated in perpetuity for the support of common schools. The public lands are laid off into townships, six miles square, by lines running with the cardinal points: these townships are then divided into thirty-six sections, each a mile square, and containing 640 acres, which are designated by numbers. Section number 16, which is always a central section, has invariably been appropriated (and provision has been made by law for the like appropriations in future surveys) for the support of common schools in each township.

In Tennessee, in addition to the appropriation of a section in each township for common schools, 200,000 acres have been assigned for the endowment of colleges and academies. Large appropriations have also been made in Ohio, Indiana, Illinois, Mississippi, Alabama, Louisiana, Missouri, Michigan, and the Northwestern Territory, for the erection and maintenance of seminaries of learning, of a higher grade than common schools. Your committee have not had an opportunity of ascertaining the exact amount of those appropriations, but, from such examination as they have been able to make, it is believed that they bear a smaller proportion to those of common schools, than in Tennessee. Tennessee, in Seybert's Statistical Annals, is stated to contain 40,000 square miles, which are equal to 25,600,000 acres. One thirty-sixth part of this number of acres, which is the

Public Lands for Education.

amount of appropriation for common schools, is 711,111. The appropriation for colleges and academies in that State is, as above stated, 200,000 acres, being something less than two-sevenths of the common school appropriation. It is believed that the appropriations in the other States and Territories for seminaries of a higher grade, do not amount to more than two-tenths or one-fifth of the appropriations for common schools. Your committee think they will not be far from the truth in estimating them at that proportion.

The States and Territories east of the Mississippi, which have had appropriations made in their favor for the support of literary institutions; that is to say, Ohio, Indiana, Illinois, Mississippi, Alabama, Michigan, and the Northwestern Territory, are estimated, in Seybert's Statistical Annals, to contain of unsold

lands - - - - -	200,000,000
Of lands sold - - - -	11,697,125
To which add Tennessee - -	25,600,000

And the aggregate number of acres in those States will be - - -	237,297,125

One thirty-sixth part of that aggregate number being the amount of appropriation for common schools, is -	6,591,586
Add one-fifth part of the common school appropriation as the appropriation for colleges and academies - -	1,318,317

And the aggregate number of acres appropriated for the purposes of education in Ohio, Indiana, Illinois, Tennessee, Mississippi, Alabama, Michigan, and the Northwestern Territory, will be - - - - -	7,909,803
At two dollars per acre, which is less, according to Seybert's Statistical Annals, than the average price of all the public lands, which have heretofore been sold, the amount in money will be - - - - -	$15,819 806

Seybert estimates the lands purchased of France by the United States in 1803, at acres	200,000,000

By the laws relating to the survey and sales of lands in Louisiana, Missouri, and Arkansas, appropriations of lands for the purposes of education have been made after the same ratio, as in the new States and Territories on the east of the Mississippi, and it is presumed the same policy will be adhered to in relation to the whole of the public lands on the west of that river. On that supposition the appropriations for common schools, that is, one thirty-sixth part of 200,000,000 acres will be

	5,555,555
Add for colleges and academies one-fifth part of the appropriations for common schools - - - - -	1,111,111

And the aggregate number of acres will be - - - - -	6,666,666⅔
At $2 per acre, the amount in money will be - - - - -	$13,333,333⅓

To the aggregate number of acres appropriated for the support of literary institutions on the east side of the Mississippi - - - -	7,909,903
Add the aggregate number of acres which, if the system heretofore followed should be (as it ought to be) adhered to, will ultimately be appropriated for literary purposes on the west of the Mississippi	6,666,666⅔

And the total literary appropriation, in the new States and Territories, will be - - - - - Acres	14,576,569⅓
At $2 per acre, the amount in money will be - - - - -	$29,153,130⅓

Such is the vast amount of property destined for the support and encouragement of learning in the States and Territories carved out of the public lands. These large appropriations of land, the common property of the Union, will inure to the exclusive benefit of those States and territories. They are appropriations for State, and not for national purposes; they are of such a nature that they might have been extended to all the States; they therefore ought to have been thus extended. All the other States paid their full share for the purchase of the region west of the Mississippi, and for the extinguishment of the Indian title, on both sides of that river. Massachusetts, Connecticut, Virginia, North Carolina, South Carolina, and Georgia, besides paying their proportion of those expenses, ceded all their vacant territory on the east side of the Mississippi. All these States, therefore, might, with great propriety, complain of partiality and injustice, if their applications to Congress for similar appropriations for like purposes should be refused.

But of this refusal they need have no apprehension, if they are true to their own interests, and are united in asserting them; for if, contrary to all reasonable expectation, the States which have already received the benefit of literary appropriations, should be opposed to the extension of them to their sister States, the latter are more than two-thirds in number of all the United States, and have a still larger proportion of representatives in Congress. These States are, Vermont, New Hampshire, Maine, Massachusetts, Rhode Island, Connecticut, New York, New Jersey, Pennsylvania, Delaware, Maryland, Virginia, North Carolina, South Carolina, Georgia, and Kentucky; and together have one hundred and sixty-nine representatives in Congress. The favored States, on the contrary, have only seventeen representatives. The excluded States have therefore an overwhelming majority in Congress, and have it completely in their power to make appropriations for the benefit of their literary institutions, upon the improbable supposition, that the representatives of the favored States would oppose them in Congress; a supposition too discreditable to their character for justice to be admitted.

The magnitude of the appropriation that would be required to place the States which have not yet enjoyed any for the purposes of education, upon an equal footing with those in whose favor they

Public Lands for Education.

have already been made, can afford no just ground of objection. For, superior as the population of those States is, yet if the ratio of appropriation be observed with regard to them which has been adopted in relation to the others, i. e. one thirty-sixth part of the number of acres in the territory of each for common schools, and one fifth part of that one thirty-sixth for colleges and academies, the number of acres required will be much less than has already been given to the favored States and Territories; it will indeed amount to but a very small portion of the public lands. For, according to Seybert's Statistical Annals, those lands, in 1813, amounted to 400,000,000 acres. The amount required for all the excluded States would be less than two and a half per centum of that quantity. To show which more clearly, your committee beg leave to submit the following statement, founded upon calculations made upon the extent of territory in each of those States, as laid down in Seybert's Statistical Annals:

New Hampshire contains 6,074,240 acres.

One 36th part of that extent, being the number of acres of public land to which that State is entitled for the support of common schools, is	168,728	acres.
One 5th part of that 36th to which New Hampshire is entitled for the support of colleges and academies, is	33,745	
Total for New Hampshire		202,473

Vermont contains 6,551,680 acres.

One 36th part, for common schools is	181,999	
One 5th of one 36th, for colleges and academies	36,398	
Total for Vermont		218,389

Massachusetts, including Maine, contains 28,990,900 acres.

One 36th of one 36th, for common schools	805,277	
One 5th of one 36th, for colleges and academies	161,055	
Total for Massachusetts and Maine		966,332

Rhode Island contains 1,011,200 acres.

One 36th part, for common schools	28,086	
One 5th of one 36th, for colleges	5,617	
Total for Rhode Island		33,705

Connecticut contains 2,991,360 acres.

One 36th part, for common schools	83,093	
One 5th of one 36th, for colleges and academies	16,618	
Total for Connecticut		99,711

New York contains 23,800,000 acres.

One 36th part, for common schools	800,00	
One 5th of one 36th, for colleges and academies	160,000	
Total for New York		960,000

New Jersey contains 5,325,800 acres.

One 36th part, for common schools	144,577	
One 5th part of one 36th, for colleges and academies	28,917	
Total for New Jersey		173,494

Pennsylvania contains 29,872,090 acres.

One 36th part, for common schools	829,777	
One 5th of one 36th, for colleges and academies	165,955	
Total for Pennsylvania		995,732

Delaware contains 1,356,800 acres.

One 36th part, for common schools	37,688	
One 5th of one 36th, for colleges and academies	7,537	
Total for Delaware		45,225

Maryland contains 8,960,000 acres.

One 36th part, for common schools	248,888	
One 5th of one 36th, for colleges and academies	49,777	
Total for Maryland		298,665

Virginia contains 44,800,000 acres.

One 36th part, for common schools	1,244,444	
One 5th of one 36th, for colleges and academies	248,888	
Total for Virginia		1,493,332

North Carolina contains 29,720,000 acres.

One 36th part, for common schools	825,555	
One 5th of one 36th, for colleges and academies	166,111	
Total for North Carolina		990,666

South Carolina contains 15,411,200 acres.

One 36th part, for common schools	4528,088	
One 5th of one 36th, for colleges and academies	85,617	
Total for South Carolina		513,705

Georgia contains 39,680,000 acres.

One 36th part, for common schools	1,102,222	
One 5th of one 36th, for colleges and academies	220,444	
Total for Georgia		1,323,666

Kentucky contains 32,000,000 acres.

One 36th part, for common schools	888,888	
One 5th of one 36th, for colleges and academies	177,777	
Total for Kentucky		1,066,665

Total amount of literary appropriation necessary to do justice to the States which have not yet had any	9,370,700

The Senate will perceive, from the foregoing calculations, that, if the ratio of appropriation for the purposes of education which has hitherto been observed be adopted with respect to the sixteen States which as yet have received no appropriations of that nature, a much smaller number of acres will be required than has already been assigned to the western region of our country: it would be an inconsiderable portion of the aggregate of public lands: a much less quantity, indeed, than now remains unsold in any of the States which have been formed out of them, with the exception perhaps of Ohio and Tennessee. The magnitude of the appropriations, then, which equal justice now requires, cannot be considered as a reasonable objection to them; and, as the literary appropriations that have heretofore been made, have been granted for State, and not for National purposes, according to the just principle set forth in the beginning of this report, similar appropriations ought to be extended to all the States.

The circumstance, that the lands which have heretofore been appropriated for the purposes of education are a part of the territory of the States for whose benefit they have been assigned, can furnish no reasonable ground for the preference which has been given them. The public lands are not the less the common property of all the States because they are situated within the jurisdictional limits of the States and Territories which have been formed out of them. Such States have no power to tax them; they cannot interfere with the primary disposal of them, or with the regulations of Congress for securing the title to purchasers; it is, in fact, Congress alone that can enact laws to affect them. The interest which a citizen of an Atlantic State has in them, as a part of the property of the Union, is the same as the interest of a citizen residing in a State formed out of them. But hitherto appropriations of them for State purposes have only been made in favor of such States; and the citizen on the eastern side of the Alleghany may well complain that property, in which he has a common interest with his fellow-citizen on the western side, should be appropriated exclusively to the use of the latter. That this is the fact, in regard to that part of the public lands which have been assigned for the support of literary institutions, and the promotion of education, cannot be denied.

Your committee do not censure the enlightened policy which governed Congress in making liberal appropriations of land for the encouragement of learning in the West, nor do they wish to withdraw one acre of them from the purposes to which they have been devoted; but they think they are fully justified in saying, that impartial justice required that similar appropriations should have been extended to all the States alike. Suppose Congress should appropriate 200,000 acres of the public lands for the support of colleges and academies in New York; and Virginia, who gave up and ceded a great portion of those lands to the United States, on the express condition, that "they should be considered as a common fund for the use and benefit of all of them, according to their usual respective proportions in the general charge and expenditure," should apply for a similar grant, and her application should be refused, would she not have a right to complain of the partiality of such a measure, and to charge the Federal Government with a breach of good faith, and an infringement of the conditions on which the cession was made? It cannot be denied that she would. Congress have

already made a grant of 200,000 acres of land for the support of colleges and academies, not indeed in New York, but in Tennessee. Would not Virginia, if she now made an application for a like grant, and were refused, have the same reason to complain as if New York, instead of Tennessee, had been the favored State?

Your committee beg leave to illustrate, by another example, the equity of the principle which it is the object of this report to establish. Foreign commerce and the public lands are alike legitimate sources, from which the United States may and do derive revenue. Foreign commerce has fixed its seat in the Atlantic States. Suppose Congress should pass a law appropriating one 36th part of the revenue collected from foreign commerce, in the ports of Baltimore, New York, Boston, Norfolk, Charleston, and Savannah, to the support of common schools throughout the States in which they are situated; the other States, every person will admit, would have a right to complain of the partiality and injustice of such an act; and yet, in what respect would an act appropriating one 36th part of the revenue derived from foreign commerce to the use of schools in the six States in which it should be produced, be more partial or unjust than an act appropriating one 36th part of the public land in Ohio, Indiana, Illinois, Tennessee, Mississippi, and Alabama, the six States in which the public lands, on this side of the Mississippi, are chiefly situated, to their exclusive benefit in the maintenance of their schools?

Your committee are aware that it has been said that the appropriation of a part of the public lands to the purposes of education, for the benefit of the States formed out of them, has had the effect of raising the value of the residue, by inducing emigrants to settle upon them. Although, in the preambles of such of the acts on this subject as have preambles, the promotion of religion, morality, and knowledge, as necessary to good government and the happiness of mankind, have been assigned as the reason for passing them, and no mention has been made of the consequent increase in the value of the lands that would remain, as a motive for the appropriation, yet the knowledge that provision had been made for the education of children in the West, though other motives usually influence emigrants, might have had its weight in inducing some to leave their native homes. If such has been the effect, the value of the residue of the lands has no doubt been increased by it. This increase of value, however, has not been an exclusive benefit to the Atlantic States, but a benefit common to all the States, Eastern and Western, while the latter still enjoy exclusively the advantages derived from the appropriations of land for literary purposes. The incidental advantage of the increase in value of the public lands in consequence of emigration, if it is to be considered in the light of a compensation to the old States, must be shown to be an advantage exclusively enjoyed by them. That this, however, is not the case, is perfectly obvious; because the proceeds of the lands thus raised in value by emigration, when sold, go into the United States Treasury, and are applied, like other revenues, to the general benefit; in other words, to national, and not to State purposes.

It is moreover most clear, that this increase of the value of lands in consequence of emigration produces a peculiar benefit to the inhabitants of the new States, in which the inhabitants of the other States, unless owners of land in the new, have no participation. The benefit consists in the increase of the value of their own private property.

On the other hand it is undoubtedly true, that emigration is injurious to the Atlantic States, and to them alone. While it has had the effect of raising the price of lands in the West, it has, in an equal ratio at least, and probably in a much greater, prevented the increase of the value of lands in the States which the emigrants have left. It is an indisputable principle in political economy, that the price of every object of purchase, whether land or personal property, depends upon the relation which supply bears to demand. The demand for land would have been the same, or very nearly so, for the same number of people as are contained within the present limits of the United States, if they had been confined within the limits of the Atlantic States. But the supply in that case would have been most materially different. It must have been so small, in proportion to the demand, as to occasion a great rise in the value of land in the Atlantic States; for it cannot be doubted that it is the inexhaustible supply of cheap and good land in the West which has kept down the price of land on the eastern side of the Alleghany. If the Atlantic States had been governed by an exclusive, local, and selfish policy, every impediment would have been thrown in the way of emigration, which has constantly and uniformly operated to prevent the growth of their numbers, wealth, and power; for which disadvantage the appreciation of their interest in the public lands, consequent upon emigration, can afford no adequate compensation. It appearing, then, perfectly clear to your committee, that emigration is exclusively advantageous to the new States, whose population, wealth, and power, are thereby increased at the expense of those States which the emigrants abandon, the inducement to emigration furnished by the appropriation of public lands for the purposes of education in the West, instead of affording a reason for confining such appropriations to that quarter of the Union, offers the most weighty considerations, of both justice and policy, in favor of extending them to the States which have not yet obtained them.

Your committee beg leave to present one further reflection to the consideration of the Senate, drawn from the effect produced by encouraging learning in the Western States alone, upon the relative moral power of the Atlantic and Mississippi States. They are far from wishing to make any objection to the augmentation of the intelligence and mental improvement of the people of the West. On the contrary, they sincerely desire the advancement of their brethren in that quarter of the Union, in every thing that can strengthen,

dignify, and embellish political communities.— But, while they entertain these sentiments, they cannot shut their eyes to the political preponderance which must ultimately be the inevitable result of the superior advantages of education there, and they must, therefore, ardently desire that the same advantages be extended to the people of the Atlantic States.

Your committee are persuaded that, from the views which they have thus presented, on the subject of appropriations of public lands for the purpose of education, the Senate will be satisfied that Maryland, and the other States which have not yet had the benefit of any such appropriations, are entitled to ask of the General Government to be placed on an equal footing with the States which have already received them. They believe that no one, convinced of the justice of such a measure, can question its expediency; nor can they entertain any apprehension that an application to Congress, supported by the combined influence of all the States which are interested, would fail of success. For the purpose, therefore, of drawing the attention of the National Legislature to this important subject, and of obtaining the co-operation of the other States, your committee beg leave to recommend the adoption of the following resolutions:

Resolved by the General Assembly of Maryland, That each of the United States has an equal right to participate in the benefit of the public lands, the common property of the Union.

Resolved, That the States in whose favor Congress have not made appropriations of land for the purposes of education, are entitled to such appropriations as will correspond, in a just proportion, with those heretofore made in favor of the other States.

Resolved, That his Excellency the Governor be requested to transmit copies of the foregoing report and resolutions to each of our Senators and Representatives in Congress, with a request that they will lay the same before their respective Houses, and use their endeavors to procure the passage of an act to carry into effect the just principles therein set forth.

Resolved, That his Excellency the Governor be also requested to transmit copies of the said report and resolutions to the Governors of the several States of the Union, with a request that they will communicate the same to the Legislatures thereof, respectively, and solicit their co-operation.

All which is respectfully submitted,

         V. MAXCY, *Chairman.*

A PROCLAMATION.

BY THE PRESIDENT OF THE UNITED STATES.

Whereas the Congress of the United States, by a joint resolution of the second day of March last, entitled "Resolution providing for the admission of the State of Missouri into the Union on a certain condition," did determine and declare—" That ' Missouri should be admitted into this Union on ' an equal footing with the original States, in all

Proclamation by the President.

'respects whatever, upon the fundamental condi-
'tion, that the fourth clause of the twenty-sixth
'section of the third article of the constitution sub-
'mitted on the part of said State to Congress, shall
'never be construed to authorize the passage of
'any law, and that no law shall be passed in con-
'formity thereto, by which any citizen of either
'of the States of this Union shall be excluded from
'the enjoyment of any of the privileges and im-
'munities to which such citizen is entitled under
'the Constitution of the United States : *Provided,*
'That the Legislature of the said State, by a
'solemn public act, shall declare the assent of the
'said State to the said fundamental condition, and
'shall transmit to the President of the United
'States, on or before the first Monday in Novem-
'ber next, an authentic copy of said act ; upon the
'receipt whereof, the President, by proclamation,
'shall announce the fact: whereupon, and with-
'out any further proceeding on the part of Con-
'gress, the admission of the said State into this
'Union shall be considered as complete :"—And
whereas, by a solemn public act of the Assembly
of the said State of Missouri, passed on the twenty-
sixth of June, in the present year, entitled "A
'solemn public act declaring the assent of this
'State to the fundamental condition contained in
'a resolution passed by the Congress of the United
'States, providing for the admission of the State
'of Missouri into the Union on a certain condi-
'tion ;" an authentic copy whereof has been com-

municated to me, it is solemnly and publicly enacted
and declared, that that State has assented, and
does assent, that the fourth clause of the twenty-
sixth section of the third article of the constitution
of said State " shall never be construed to author-
'ize the passage of any law, and that no law shall
'be passed in conformity thereto, by which any
'citizen of either of the United States shall be ex-
'cluded from the enjoyment of any of the privi-
'leges and immunities to which such citizens are
'entitled under the Constitution of the United
'States :"—Now, therefore, I, JAMES MONROE,
President of the United States, in pursuance of
the resolution of Congress aforesaid, have issued
this my Proclamation, announcing the fact, that
the said State of Missouri has assented to the fundamental condition required by the resolution of
Congress aforesaid ; whereupon the admission of
the said State of Missouri into this Union is declared to to be complete.

In testimony whereof, I have caused the seal
      of the United States of America to be affixed
      to these presents, and signed the same with
[L. S.] my hand. Done at the City of Washington,
      the tenth day of August, 1821 ; and of the
      Independence of the said United States of
      America the forty-sixth.
                      JAMES MONROE.
By the President:
    JOHN QUINCY ADAMS,
         Secretary of State.

Proclamation by the President.

and are applied, like other revenues, to the general benefit; in other words, to national, and not to State purposes.

It is moreover most clear, that this increase of the value of lands in consequence of emigration produces a peculiar benefit to the inhabitants of the new States, in which the inhabitants of the other States, unless owners of land in the new, have no participation. The benefit consists in the increase of the value of their own private property.

On the other hand it is undoubtedly true, that emigration is injurious to the Atlantic States, and to them alone. While it has had the effect of raising the price of lands in the West, it has, in an equal ratio at least, and probably in a much greater, prevented the increase of the value of lands in the States which the emigrants have left. It is an indisputable principle in political economy, that the price of every object of purchase, whether land or personal property, depends upon the relation which supply bears to demand. The demand for land would have been the same, or very nearly so, for the same number of people as are contained within the present limits of the United States, if they had been confined within the limits of the Atlantic States. But the supply in that case would have been most materially different. It must have been so small, in proportion to the demand, as to occasion a great rise in the value of land in the Atlantic States; for it cannot be doubted that it is the inexhaustible supply of cheap and good land in the West which has kept down the price of land on the eastern side of the Alleghany. If the Atlantic States had been governed by an exclusive, local, and selfish policy, every impediment would have been thrown in the way of emigration, which has constantly and uniformly operated to prevent the growth of their numbers, wealth, and power; for which disadvantage the appreciation of their interest in the public lands, consequent upon emigration, can afford no adequate compensation. It appearing, then, perfectly clear to your committee, that emigration is exclusively advantageous to the new States, whose population, wealth, and power, are thereby increased at the expense of those States which the emigrants abandon, the inducement to emigration furnished by the appropriation of pu l c lands for the purposes of education in the West, instead of affording a reason for confining such appropriations to that quarter of the Union, offers the most weighty considerations, of both justice and policy, in favor of extending them to the States which have not yet obtained them.

Your committee beg leave to present one further reflection to the consideration of the Senate, drawn from the effect produced by encouraging learning in the Western States alone, upon the relative moral power of the Atlantic and Mississippi States. They are far from wishing to make any objection to the augmentation of the intelligence and mental improvement of the people of the West. On the contrary, they sincerely desire the advancement of their brethren in that quarter of the Union, in every thing that can strengthen,

dignify, and embellish political communities.— But, while they entertain these sentiments, they cannot shut their eyes to the political preponderance which must ultimately be the inevitable result of the superior advantages of education there, and they must, therefore, ardently desire that the same advantages be extended to the people of the Atlantic States.

Your committee are persuaded that, from the views which they have thus presented, on the subject of appropriations of public lands for the purpose of education, the Senate will be satisfied that Maryland, and the other States which have not yet had the benefit of any such appropriations, are entitled to ask of the General Government to be placed on an equal footing with the States which have already received them. They believe that no one, convinced of the justice of such a measure, can question its expediency; nor can they entertain any apprehension that an application to Congress, supported by the combined influence of all the States which are interested, would fail of success. For the purpose, therefore, of drawing the attention of the National Legislature to this important subject, and of obtaining the co-operation of the other States, your committee beg leave to recommend the adoption of the following resolutions:

Resolved by the General Assembly of Maryland, That each of the United States has an equal right to participate in the benefit of the public lands, the common property of the Union.

Resolved, That the States in whose favor Congress have not made appropriations of land for the purposes of education, are entitled to such appropriations as will correspond, in a just proportion, with those heretofore made in favor of the other States.

Resolved, That his Excellency the Governor be requested to transmit copies of the foregoing report and resolutions to each of our Senators and Representatives in Congress, with a request that they will lay the same before their respective Houses, and use their endeavors to procure the passage of an act to carry into effect the just principles therein set forth.

Resolved, That his Excellency the Governor be also requested to transmit copies of the said report and resolutions to the Governors of the several States of the Union, with a request that they will communicate the same to the Legislatures thereof, respectively, and solicit their co-operation.

All which is respectfully submitted,

           V. MAXCY, *Chairman.*

A PROCLAMATION.

BY THE PRESIDENT OF THE UNITED STATES.

Whereas the Congress of the United States, by a joint resolution of the second day of March last, entitled "Resolution providing for the admission of the State of Missouri into the Union on a certain condition," did determine and declare—" That ' Missouri should be admitted into this Union on ' an equal footing with the original States, in all

' respects whatever, upon the fundamental condi-
' tion, that the fourth clause of the twenty-sixth
' section of the third article of the constitution sub-
' mitted on the part of said State to Congress, shall
' never be construed to authorize the passage of
' any law, and that no law shall be passed in con-
' formity thereto, by which any citizen of either
' of the States of this Union shall be excluded from
' the enjoyment of any of the privileges and im-
' munities to which such citizen is entitled under
' the Constitution of the United States : *Provided,*
' That the Legislature of the said State, by a
' solemn public act, shall declare the assent of the
' said State to the said fundamental condition, and
' shall transmit to the President of the United
' States, on or before the first Monday in Novem-
' ber next, an authentic copy of said act ; upon the
' receipt whereof, the President, by proclamation,
' shall announce the fact: whereupon, and with-
' out any further proceeding on the part of Con-
' gress, the admission of the said State into this
' Union shall be considered as complete :"—And
whereas, by a solemn public act of the Assembly
of the said State of Missouri, passed on the twenty-
sixth of June, in the present year, entitled "A
' solemn public act declaring the assent of this
' State to the fundamental condition contained in
' a resolution passed by the Congress of the United
' States, providing for the admission of the State
' of Missouri into the Union on a certain condi-
' tion ;" an authentic copy whereof has been com-

municated to me, it is solemnly and publicly enacted
and declared, that that State has assented, and
does assent, that the fourth clause of the twenty-
sixth section of the third article of the constitution
of said State " shall never be construed to author-
' ize the passage of any law, and that no law shall
' be passed in conformity thereto, by which any
' citizen of either of the United States shall be ex-
' cluded from the enjoyment of any of the privi-
' leges and immunities to which such citizens are
' entitled under the Constitution of the United
' States :"—Now, therefore, I, JAMES MONROE,
President of the United States, in pursuance of
the resolution of Congress aforesaid, have issued
this my Proclamation, announcing the fact, that
the said State of Missouri has assented to the fundamental condition required by the resolution of
Congress aforesaid ; whereupon the admission of
the said State of Missouri into this Union is declared to to be complete.

In testimony whereof, I have caused the seal
of the United States of America to be affixed
to these presents, and signed the same with
[L. S.] my hand. Done at the City of Washington,
the tenth day of August, 1821 ; and of the
Independence of the said United States of
America the forty-sixth.
JAMES MONROE.

By the President:
JOHN QUINCY ADAMS,
Secretary of State.

PUBLIC ACTS OF CONGRESS;

PASSED AT THE SECOND SESSION OF THE SIXTEENTH CONGRESS, BEGUN AND
HELD AT THE CITY OF WASHINGTON, MONDAY, NOVEMBER 13, 1820.

An Act to alter the terms of the District Court in
Alabama.

Be it enacted, by the Senate and House of Representatives of the United States of America in Congress assembled, That the first session of the District Court, for the District of Alabama, shall be holden at Mobile, on the third Monday of February, 1821; and, thereafter, the stated sessions of said Court, instead of the times heretofore appointed, shall be holden, annually, as follows: at Mobile, on the first Mondays of January and June, and at Cahawba, on the first Mondays of April and November; any law to the contrary notwithstanding.

SEC. 2. *And be it further enacted,* That all process which may have issued, or may hereafter issue, returnable to the next succeeding terms, as heretofore established, shall be held returnable, and be returned, to those terms to which they are severally changed by this act.

SEC. 3. *And be it further enacted,* That there shall be but one clerk for the District, who shall keep only one set of records; any law to the contrary notwithstanding.

Approved, November 27, 1820.

An Act to provide for paying to the State of Illinois three per cent. of the net proceeds arising from the sale of public lands within the same.

Be it enacted, &c., That the Secretary of the Treasury shall, from time to time, and whenever the quarterly accounts of public moneys of the several Land Offices shall be settled, pay three per cent. of the net proceeds of the lands of the United States, lying within the State of Illinois, which, since the first day of January, one thousand eight hundred and nineteen, have been, or hereafter may be, sold by the United States, after deducting all expenses incidental to the same, to such person or persons as may be authorized by the Legislature of the said State to receive the same; which sums, thus paid, shall be applied to the encouragement of learning within said State, in conformity to the provisions on this subject, contained in the act, entitled "An act to enable the people of the Illinois territory to form a constitution and State government, and for the admission of such State into the Union on an equal footing with the original States," approved April eighteenth, one thousand eight hundred and eighteen, and to no other purpose; and an annual account of the application of the same shall be

transmitted to the Secretary of the Treasury, by such officer of the State as the Legislature thereof shall direct; and in default of such return being made, the Secretary of the Treasury is hereby required to withhold the payment of any sums that may then be due, or which may thereafter become due, until a return shall be made, as herein required.

Approved, December 12, 1820.

An Act to amend the act, entitled "An act to alter the times of the session of the Circuit and District Courts in the District of Columbia."

Be it enacted, &c., That the act passed on the eleventh day of May last, to alter the times of the session of the Circuit and District Courts in the District of Columbia, instead of being limited to take effect on the first day of January next, shall have full operation and effect from and after the passing hereof; and that all the writs and process of the Circuit Court of the District of Columbia, for the county of Washington, shall be returned and continued in like manner as if the said act had taken effect from and after the thirtieth day of July last.

Approved, December 29, 1820.

An Act to amend the act, entitled "An act for the relief of the legal representatives of Henry Willis."

Be it enacted, &c., That the act, entitled "An act for the relief of the legal representatives of Henry Willis," passed on the eighth day of May, one thousand eight hundred and twenty, be so construed as to except from location all town lots and lands now or hereafter reserved by the United States, or which may have been, or may be, appropriated by Congress for the use of any State, or for any other purpose, and that the location be made within two years from the passage of this act.

Approved, December 29, 1820.

An Act to alter the time of holding the District Court in the District of Mississippi.

Be it enacted, &c., That the District Court, in the District of Mississippi, heretofore holden on the first Mondays in May and December, shall hereafter hold its regular terms only on the first Monday in January and July; any law to the contrary notwithstanding.

SEC. 2. *And be it further enacted*, That every writ, process, subpœna, or recognisance, returnable, according to law, or the tenor thereof, to either of the aforesaid terms, holden on the first Mondays in May and December, shall be returnable to the next succeeding term of said court, to be holden on the first Monday in January and July.—Approved, January 11, 1821.

An Act making a partial appropriation for the Military Service of the United States, for the year one thousand eight hundred and twenty-one.

Be it enacted, &c., That the following sums be, and they are hereby, appropriated, on account of the military service for the year one thousand eight hundred and twenty-one, to wit:

For subsistence of the Army of the United States, one hundred and fifty thousand dollars.

For arrearages on the settlement of outstanding claims, twenty thousand dollars.

For the Quartermaster's department, one hundred and fifty thousand dollars.

SEC. 2. *And be it further enacted*, That the said sums be paid out of any moneys in the Treasury, not otherwise appropriated.

Approved, January 17, 1821.

An Act to extend the time for locating Virginia Military Land Warrants, and returning surveys thereon to the General Land Office.

Be it enacted, &c., That the officers and soldiers of the Virginia line on continental establishment, their heirs or assigns, entitled to bounty lands within the tract of county reserved by the State of Virginia, between the Little Miami and Scioto rivers, shall be allowed a further time of two years, from the fourth day of January, one thousand eight hundred and twenty-one, to obtain warrants and complete their locations, and the further time of four years, from the fourth day of January, one thousand eight hundred and twenty-two, to return their surveys and warrants, or certified copies of warrants, to the General Land Office, to obtain patents.

SEC. 2. *And be it further enacted*, That the provisions of the act, entitled "An act authorizing patents to issue for lands located and surveyed by virtue of certain Virginia resolution warrants," passed the third day of March, one thousand eight hundred and seven, shall be revived and in force, with all its restrictions, except that the respective times allowed for making locations, and returning surveys thereon, shall be limited to the terms prescribed by the first section of this act, for the location and return of surveys on other warrants, and that the surveys shall be returned to the General Land Office: *Provided*, That no locations as aforesaid, in virtue of this or the preceding section of this act, shall be made on tracts of lands for which patents had previously been issued, or which had been previously surveyed; and any patent which may, nevertheless, be obtained for lands located contrary to the provisions of this act, shall be considered null and void.

Approved, February 9, 1821.

An Act to incorporate the Columbian College in the District of Columbia.

Be it enacted, &c., That there be erected, and hereby is erected and established, in the District of Columbia, a college, for the sole and exclusive purpose of educating youth in the English, learned, and foreign languages, the liberal arts, sciences, and literature, the style and title of which shall be, and hereby is declared to be, "The Columbian College, in the District of Columbia."

SEC. 2. *And be it further enacted*, That the said college shall be under the management, direction, and government, of a number of trustees, not exceeding thirty-one, to be elected triennially, by the contributors to the said college, qualified to vote, in such manner, and under such limitations and restrictions, as may be provided by the ordinances of the college, on the first Monday in May; and that the first trustees of the said college shall consist of the following persons, viz: Obadiah B. Brown, Luther Rice, Enoch Reynolds, Josiah Meigs, Spencer H. Cone, Daniel Brown, Return J. Meigs, Joseph Gibson, Joseph Cone, Thomas Corcoran, Burgis Allison, Thomas Sewall, and Joseph Thaw. Which said trustees and their successors, shall forever hereafter be, and they are hereby declared to be, one body politic and corporate, with perpetual succession, in deed and in law, to all intents and purposes whatsoever, by the name, style, and title of "The Columbian College in the District of Columbia;" by which name and title they, the said trustees, and their successors, shall be competent and capable, at law and in equity, to take to themselves and their successors, for the use of the said college, any estate, in any messuage, lands, tenements, hereditaments, goods, chattels, moneys, and other effects, by gift, grant, bargain, sale, conveyance, assurance, will, devise, or bequest, of any person or persons whatsoever: *Provided*, The same do not exceed, in the whole the yearly value of twenty-five thousand dollars; and the same messuages, lands, tenements, hereditaments, and estate, real and personal, to grant, bargain, sell, convey, assure, demise, and to farm, let, and place out on interest, for the use of the said college, in such manner as to them, or at least nine of them, shall seem most beneficial to the institution, and to receive the rents, issues, and profits, and interest, of the same, and to apply the to the proper use and benefit of the said and by the same name to sue, commence, prosecute, and defend, implead, and be impl, any courts of law and equity, and in a of suits and actions whatsoever, and ge and in the same name, to do and trans every the business touching or concei premises.

SEC. 3. *And be it further enacted*, That the said trustees shall cause to be made for their use one common seal, with such devices and inscriptions thereon as they shall think proper, under and all deeds, diplomas, certificates, and said college, shall pass and be authen the same seal, at their pleasure, to br vise a new one.

SEC. 4. *And be it further enacted*, That the said

trustees, or five of them at least, shall meet at the college, on College hill, in the said District of Columbia, on the first Monday in March next, for the purpose of concerting and agreeing to such business as, in consequence of this act, shall be proper to be laid before them at the commencement of the work they have undertaken, and shall have power to adjourn, from time to time, as they shall see cause, to any other times or places for the purpose of perfecting the same. That there shall be a stated meeting of the said trustees held twice in every year at least, at such place and time as the said trustees, or a quorum thereof, shall appoint, of which public notice shall be given, after the first meeting, at least twenty days before the time of such intended meeting, whenever the president, to be appointed by them, shall deem the business of the institution to require the same, and give due notice thereof, which he is hereby authorized to do; and if, at such stated or occasional meetings, five of the said trustees shall not be present, those of them who shall be present, shall have power to adjourn the meeting to any other day, as fully and effectually, to all intents and purposes, as if the whole number of trustees for the time being were present; but, if five or more of the said trustees shall meet at the said appointed times, or at any other time of adjournment, then such five of the said trustees shall be a board or quorum, and a majority of the votes of them shall be capable of doing and transacting all the business and concerns of the said college not otherwise provided for by this act; and particularly of making and enacting ordinances for the government of the said college; of electing and appointing the president, professors, and tutors, for the said college; of agreeing with them for their salaries and stipends, and removing them for misconduct, or breach of the laws of the institution; of appointing committees of their own body to carry into execution all and every the resolutions of the board; of appointing a president, treasurer, secretary, stewards, managers, and other necessary and customary officers, for taking care of the estate, and managing the concerns of the corporation; and, generally, a majority of voices of the board, or quorum of the said trustees, consisting of five trustees at least, at any semi-annual, occasional, or ___ ___d meeting, after notice given as aforesaid, ___ ___ ___rmine all matters and things (although ___ ___ be not herein particularly mentioned) wh___ ___ ill occasionally arise, and be incidentally n___ ___ to be determined and transacted by the sa___ch ___: *Provided always,* That no ordinances sh___ Leg ___ force which shall be repugnant to this ch___ ___; ___ to the laws of the District of Columbia. ___ ___ *And be it further enacted,* That the head or chief master for the said college shall be called and ___yled " The President," and the masters thereof shall be called " Professors and Tutors," but n___ ___ ___sident, professors, or tutors, while they r___ission ___ shall ever be capable of the office of ___ting wi ___ ___ ___ ___ ___ ___ti ___ ___ ___d be it further enacted, That the president, pro___ ___rs, and tutors, or a majority of them, shall be called and styled " The Faculty of the

College;" which faculty shall have the power of enforcing the rules and regulations adopted by the trustees for the government of the pupils by rewarding or censuring them, and, finally, by suspending such of them as, after repeated admonitions, shall continue disobedient and refractory, until a determination of a quorum of the trustees can be had; and of granting and confirming, by and with the approbation and consent of a board of the trustees, signified by their mandamus, such degrees in the liberal arts and sciences to such pupils of the institution, or others, who, by their proficiency in learning, or other meritorious distinction, they shall think entitled to them, as are usually granted and conferred in colleges; and to grant, to such graduates, diplomas or certificates, under their common seal, and signed by the faculty, to authenticate and perpetuate the memory of such graduation.

Sec. 7. *And be it further enacted,* That persons of every religious denomination shall be capable of being elected trustees; nor shall any person, either as president, professor, tutor, or pupil, be refused admittance into said college, or denied any of the privileges, immunities, or advantages thereof, for or on account of his sentiments in matters of religion.

Sec. 8. *And be it further enacted,* That no misnomer of the said corporation shall defeat or annul any gift, grant, devise, or bequest, to or from the said corporation: *Provided,* The intent of the parties shall sufficiently appear upon the face of the gift, grant, will, or other writing, whereby any estate or interest was intended to pass to or from the said corporation.

Sec. 9. *And be it further enacted,* That the constitution of the said college, herein and hereby declared and established, shall be, and remain, the inviolable constitution of the said college forever; and the same shall not be altered, or alterable, by any ordinance or law of the said trustees: *Provided,* That it may be lawful for the Congress of the United States to revoke and repeal this act, at any, and at all times whenever they shall think fit so to do.

Sec. 10. *And be it further enacted,* That it shall be the duty of the said board of trustees to keep a regular book or journal, in which shall be entered, under their direction, besides an account of all their ordinary acts and proceedings, all the by-laws, ordinances, rules, and regulations, which may be adopted by the said board, for their own government, and for the government of the institution; also, a schedule of all the property and effects, real, personal, or mixed, which shall or may be vested in the said trustees, for the use of the said college, by virtue of any gift, grant, bargain, sale, will, or otherwise, together with annual statements concerning the accounts and finances of the institution. That it shall, moreover, be the duty of the said trustees, to cause to be enrolled in the said book or journal the names of all the contributors to the institution qualified to vote for trustees, with their respective places of residence, and the said book or journal shall, at all times, be open to the inspection or examination of the Attorney General

Public Acts of Congress.

of the United States; and, when required by either House of Congress, it shall be the duty of the said trustees to furnish any information respecting their own conduct, the state of the institution, and of its finances, which shall or may be so required.

SEC. 11. *And be it further enacted,* That in case any vacancy or vacancies shall happen in the board of trustees aforesaid, by death, inability, resignation, or otherwise, at any time between the stated or triennial elections, that then it shall and may be lawful for the other trustees, or any five of them, to proceed, at any subsequent meeting after the happening of such vacancy or vacancies, to choose by ballot any suitable person or persons to fill the same.

SEC. 12. *And be it further enacted,* That the employment or application of the funds or income of the said corporation, or any part thereof, for any purpose or object other than those expressed and defined in the first section of this act, or the investment thereof in any other mode than is described and provided in the second section thereof, shall be deemed and taken to be a forfeiture of all the rights and immunities derived from this act, and the same shall thenceforth cease, and become null and void.

Approved, February 9, 1821.

An Act for the relief of the purchasers of public lands, prior to the first day of July, eighteen hundred and twenty.

Be it enacted, &c., That, in all cases, where lands have been purchased from the United States, prior to the first day of July, eighteen hundred and twenty, it shall be lawful for any such person or persons, being the legal holder of any certificate, or certificates, of land, on or before the thirtieth day of September, eighteen hundred and twenty-one, to file, with the register of the land office where any tract of land has been purchased, a relinquishment, in writing, of any section, half section, quarter section, half quarter section, or legal subdivision of any fractional section of land so purchased, upon which the whole purchase money has not been paid, and all sums paid on account of the part relinquished shall be applied to the discharge of any instalments which may be, or shall hereafter become, due and payable upon such land, so purchased, as shall not have been relinquished, and shall be so applied and credited as to complete the payment on some one or more half quarter sections where the payments by transfer are sufficient for that purpose: *Provided,* That all divisions, and subdivisions, contemplated by this act, shall be made in conformity with the first section of an act making further provision for the sale of public lands, passed the twenty-fourth day of April, one thousand eight hundred and twenty: *And provided, also,* That the right of relinquishment hereby given shall, in no case, authorize the party relinquishing to claim any repayment from the United States: *And provided, also,* That where any purchaser has purchased, at the same time, two or more quarter sections, he shall not be permitted to relinquish less than a quarter section.

SEC. 2. *And be it further enacted,* That the interest which shall have accrued before the thirtieth day of September next, upon any debt to the United States, for public land, shall be, and the same is hereby, remitted and discharged.

SEC. 3. *And be it further enacted,* That the persons indebted to the United States, as aforesaid, shall be divided into three classes; the first class to include all such persons as shall have paid to the United States only one-fourth part of the original price of the land by them respectively purchased or held; the second class to include all such persons as shall have paid to the United States only one-half part of such original price; and the third class to include all such persons as shall have paid to the United States three-fourth parts of such original price; and the debts of the persons included in the first class shall be paid in eight equal annual instalments; the debts of the persons included in the second class shall be paid in six equal annual instalments; and the debts of the persons included in the third class shall be paid in four equal annual instalments; the first of which instalments in each of the classes aforesaid shall be paid in manner following, to wit: of the third class, on the thirtieth day of September next; of the second class, on the thirty-first day of December next; and of the first class, on the thirty-first day of March, one thousand eight hundred and twenty-two; and the whole of the debt aforesaid, shall bear an annual interest at the rate of six per cent.: *Provided always,* That the same shall be remitted upon each and every of the instalments aforesaid which shall be punctually paid when the same shall become payable as aforesaid.

SEC. 4. *And be it further enacted,* That, in all cases where complete payment of the whole sum due, or which may become due, for any tract of land purchased from the United States aforesaid, shall be made on or before the thirtieth day of September, one thousand eight hundred and twenty-two, a deduction, at the rate of thirty-seven and a half per centum, shall be allowed upon the sum remaining unpaid: *Provided,* That nothing herein contained shall authorize any discount upon payments made by a transfer of former payments under the provisions of the first section of this act.

SEC. 5. *And be it further enacted,* That each and every individual or company, that has laid off, or any lands by him or them purchased of the United States, any town, a part or the whole of the lots whereof have been sold, shall be entitled to the benefits of this act in relation to any half quarter, or quarter section of land, on which such town may be situated, and of all lands by him or them owned, contiguous to and adjoining said half quarter, quarter section, or section, on which said town is situated, upon condition only, that each and every person who has purchased of him or them a town lot, or part of a lot, or land in and adjoining the same, shall be entitled to a remission of all interest that has accrued, and a discount of twenty per centum on the amount unpaid, and to discharge their debt by bonds, with security, in equal annual instalments of four years from the thirtieth day of December next. Nor shall the provisions of this act be construed to extend to any person or persons claiming title to land under the provisions of an act passed the third day of March, eighteen hundred and seventeen, entitled "An act to set apart and dispose of certain public lands for the encouragement of the cultivation of the vine and olive."

SEC. 6. *And be it further enacted,* That, for failure to pay the several debts aforesaid, in manner aforesaid, and for the term of three months after the day appointed for the payment of the last instalment thereof, in each of the classes aforesaid, the land so purchased or held by the respective persons indebted to the United States, as aforesaid, shall, *ipso facto,* become forfeited, and revert to the United States.

SEC. 7. *And be it further enacted,* That no person shall be deemed to be included within, or entitled to, the benefits of any of the provisions of this act, who shall not, on or before the thirtieth day of September next, sign and file in the office of the register of the land office of the district where the land was purchased, or where the residue of the purchase money is payable, a declaration in writing, expressing his consent to the same, and shall pay to the register, for receiving, recording, and filing the same, fifty cents.

SEC. 8. *And be it further enacted,* That it shall be, and hereby is made, the duty of the several registers and receivers of the land offices of the United States, according to the forms and instructions which shall be given in that behalf by the Treasury Department, to assist in carrying this act into execution, to keep full and faithful accounts and records of all proceedings under the same; and, within the term of three months after the said thirtieth day of September next, to transmit to the said department a correct report of the quantity of land relinquished to the United States; the quantity on which full payment shall have been made; and the quantity on which a further credit shall have been given, distinguishing the amount of the debt on which further credit shall have been allowed; and the registers and receivers, respectively, shall be entitled to receive fifty cents from the party relinquishing, for each half quarter section, quarter section, half section, section, or legal subdivision of a fractional section, so relinquished.

SEC. 9. *And be it further enacted,* That no lands purchased from the United States, on or before the first day of July, eighteen hundred and twenty, which are not already forfeited, shall be considered as forfeited to the Government, for failing in completing the payment thereon, until the said thirtieth day of September next; and all the lands which shall be relinquished to the United States, as aforesaid, shall be deemed and held to be forfeited, and, with all other lands which may become forfeited under this act, shall be sold according to the provisions of the act entitled "An act making further provision for the sale of the public lands," passed the twenty-fourth day of April, eighteen hundred and twenty.

SEC. 10. *And be it further enacted,* That no land which shall be surrendered under the provisions of this act, shall be offered for sale for the term of two years after the surrender thereof.

Approved, March 2, 1821.

An Act to reduce and fix the Military Establishment of the United States.

Be it enacted, &c., That, from and after the first day of June next, the Military Peace Establishment of the United States shall be composed of four regiments of artillery and seven regiments of infantry, with such officers of engineers, of ordnance, and of the staff, as are hereinafter provided for.

SEC. 2. *And be it further enacted,* That each regiment of artillery shall consist of one colonel, one lieutenant colonel, one major, one sergeant major, one quartermaster sergeant, and nine companies, one of which shall be designated and equipped as light artillery; and that there shall be attached to each regiment of artillery one supernumerary captain to perform ordnance duty, and that each company shall consist of one captain, two first lieutenants, one second lieutenants, four sergeants, four corporals, three artificers, two musicians, and forty-two privates. That each regiment of infantry shall consist of one colonel, one lieutenant colonel, one major, one sergeant major, one quartermaster sergeant, two principal musicians, and ten companies, each of which shall consist of one captain, one first lieutenant, one second lieutenant, three sergeants, four corporals, two musicians, and forty-two privates; and that to each regiment of artillery and infantry there shall be one adjutant, who shall be taken from the subalterns of the line.

SEC. 3. *And be it further enacted,* That the corps of engineers (bombardiers excepted) and the topographical engineers, and their assistants, shall be retained in service as at present organized.

SEC. 4. *And be it further enacted,* That the ordnance department shall be merged in the artillery, and that the President of the United States be, and he is hereby, authorized to select from the regiments of artillery such officers as may be necessary to perform ordnance duties, who, while so detached, shall receive the pay and emoluments now received by ordnance officers, and shall be subject only to the orders of the War Department; and that the number of enlisted men in the ordnance department be reduced to fifty-six.

SEC. 5. *And be it further enacted,* That there shall be one major general, with two aids-de-camp, two brigadier generals, each with one aid-de-camp; and that the aids-de-camp be taken from the subalterns of the line, and, in addition to their duties, shall perform the duties of assistant adjutant general.

SEC. 6. *And be it further enacted,* That there shall be one adjutant general, and two inspectors general, with the rank, pay, and emoluments, of colonels of cavalry.

SEC. 7. *And be it further enacted,* That there shall be one quartermaster general; that there shall be two quartermasters, with the rank, pay, and emoluments of majors of cavalry; and ten assistant quartermasters, who shall, in addition to their pay in the line, receive a sum not less than ten dollars, nor more than twenty dollars per month, to be regulated by the Secretary of War.

Sec. 8. *And be it further enacted,* That there shall be one commissary general of subsistence; and that there shall be as many assistant commissaries as the service may require, not exceeding fifty, who shall be taken from the subalterns of the line, and shall, in addition to their pay in the line, receive a sum not less than ten, nor more than twenty dollars per month; and that the assistant quartermasters, and assistant commissaries of subsistence, shall be subject to duties in both departments, under the orders of the Secretary of War.

Sec. 9. *And be it further enacted,* That there shall be one paymaster general, with the present compensation, and fourteen paymasters, with the pay and emoluments of regimental paymasters, and that there shall be one commissary of purchases, and two military storekeepers, to be attached to the purchasing department.

Sec. 10. *And be it further enacted,* That the medical department shall consist of one surgeon general, eight surgeons, with the compensation of regimental surgeons, and forty-five assistant surgeons, with the compensation of post surgeons.

Sec. 11. *And be it further enacted,* That the officers, non-commissioned officers, artificers, musicians, and privates, retained by this act, except those specially provided for, shall have the same rank, pay, and emoluments, as are provided in like cases by existing laws; and that the force authorized and continued in service under this act shall be subject to the rules and articles of war.

Sec. 12. *And be it further enacted,* That the President of the United States cause to be arranged the officers, non-commissioned officers, artificers, musicians, and privates, of the several corps now in the service of the United States, in such manner as to form and complete out of the same the force authorized by this act, and cause the supernumerary officers, non-commissioned officers, artificers, musicians, and privates, to be discharged from the service of the United States.

Sec. 13. *And be it further enacted,* That there shall be allowed and paid to each commissioned officer, who shall be discharged from the service of the United States in pursuance of this act, three months pay, in addition to the pay and emoluments to which he may be entitled by law at the time of his discharge.

Sec. 14. *And be it further enacted,* That the system of "General Regulations for the Army," compiled by Major General Scott, shall be, and the same is hereby, approved and adopted for the government of the Army of the United States, and of the militia when in the service of the United States.

Approved, March 2, 1821.

An Act making appropriations for the support of Government, for the year one thousand eight hundred and twenty-one.

Be it enacted, &c., That the following sums be, and the same are hereby, respectively appropriated for the service of the year one thousand eight hundred and twenty-one, that is to say:

For compensation granted by law to the Senate and House of Representatives, their officers, and attendants, three hundred and fourteen thousand eight hundred and sixty-six dollars.

For the compensation of the Senators and Representative elected by Missouri, six thousand dollars.

For the expenses of fire wood, stationery, printing, and all other contingent expenses of the two Houses of Congress, forty-nine thousand dollars.

For the expenses of the Library of Congress, including the Librarian's allowance for the year, one thousand nine hundred and fifty dollars.

For the purchase of books for the Library of Congress, comprehending the statutes and the reports of the decisions of the courts of law and chancery of the different States, with the latest maps of the several States and Territories of the United States, one thousand dollars.

For compensation to the President of the United States, twenty-five thousand dollars.

For compensation to the Vice President of the United States, five thousand dollars.

For compensation to the Secretary of State, six thousand dollars.

For compensation to the clerks in the Department of State, by the act of twentieth April, one thousand eight hundred and eighteen, fifteen thousand nine hundred dollars.

For compensation to the messengers in said department, including the messenger to the Patent office, nine hundred and sixty dollars.

For the contingent and incidental expenses of the Department of State, including expenses of distributing copies of the laws of the second session of the sixteenth Congress, twenty-two thousand and seven hundred dollars.

For compensation to the Secretary of the Treasury, six thousand dollars.

For compensation to the clerks in the office of the Secretary of the Treasury, per act of twentieth April, one thousand eight hundred and eighteen, ten thousand four hundred dollars.

For compensation to the messengers in said office, seven hundred and ten dollars.

For compensation to the First Comptroller of the Treasury, three thousand five hundred dollars.

For compensation to the clerks in the office of the First Comptroller, per act of twentieth April, one thousand eight hundred and eighteen, seventeen thousand eight hundred and fifty dollars.

For compensation to the messenger in said office, four hundred and ten dollars.

For compensation to the Second Comptroller, three thousand dollars.

For compensation to the clerks in the office of the Second Comptroller, per act of twentieth of April, one thousand eight hundred and eighteen, nine thousand seven hundred and fifty dollars.

For compensation to the messenger in said office, four hundred and ten dollars.

For compensation to the First Auditor of the Treasury, three thousand dollars.

For compensation to the clerks in the office of

the First Auditor, per act of twentieth April, one thousand eight hundred and eighteen, fifteen thousand two hundred dollars.

For compensation to the messenger in said office, four hundred and ten dollars.

For compensation to the Second Auditor of the Treasury, three thousand dollars.

For compensation to the clerks in the office of the Second Auditor, per act of twentieth April, one thousand eight hundred and eighteen, seventeen thousand two hundred dollars.

For compensation to the messenger in said office, four hundred and ten dollars.

For compensation to the Third Auditor of the Treasury, three thousand dollars.

For compensation to the clerks in the office of the Third Auditor, per act of twentieth April, one thousand eight hundred and eighteen, twenty-eight thousand six hundred dollars.

For compensation to the messengers in said office, seven hundred and ten dollars.

For compensation to the Fourth Auditor of the Treasury, three thousand dollars.

For compensation to the clerks in the office of the Fourth Auditor, per act of twentieth April, one thousand eight hundred and eighteen, fifteen thousand and fifty dollars.

For compensation to the messenger in said office, four hundred and ten dollars.

For compensation to the Fifth Auditor of the Treasury, three thousand dollars.

For compensation to the clerks in the office of the Fifth Auditor, per act of twentieth April, one thousand eight hundred and eighteen, ten thousand five hundred dollars.

For three clerks, to complete the duties of the Commissioner of the Revenue, transferred to the office of the Fifth Auditor, three thousand seven hundred dollars.

For compensation to the messenger in said office, four hundred and ten dollars.

For compensation to the Treasurer of the United States, three thousand dollars.

For compensation to the clerks in the office of the Treasurer, per act of twentieth April, one thousand eight hundred and eighteen, five thousand two hundred and fifty dollars.

For compensation to an additional clerk, as allowed by act of appropriation, of one thousand eight hundred and nineteen, and one thousand eight hundred and twenty; and also for an assistant to the chief clerk, one thousand two hundred dollars.

For compensation to the messenger in said office, four hundred and ten dollars.

For compensation to the Commissioner of the General Land office, three thousand dollars.

For compensation to the clerks in the office of said Commissioner, per act of twentieth April, one thousand eight hundred and eighteen, twenty-two thousand five hundred and fifty dollars.

For compensation to the messenger in said office, four hundred and ten dollars.

For compensation to the Register of the Treasury, three thousand dollars.

For compensation to the clerks in the office of

the Register, per act of twentieth April, one thousand eight hundred and eighteen, twenty-two thousand three hundred dollars.

For compensation to the messenger in said office, including the allowance for stamping ships' registers, five hundred dollars.

For compensation to the secretary of the Commissioners of the Sinking Fund, two hundred and fifty dollars.

For allowance to the person employed in transmitting passports and sea-letters, for expense of translating foreign languages in the office of the Secretary of the Treasury, for stationery, fuel, printing, and all other contingent and incidental expenses in the Treasury Department, and the several offices therein, forty-eight thousand seven hundred and forty dollars.

For allowance to the superintendent and four watchmen, employed for the security of the State and Treasury buildings, one thousand nine hundred dollars.

For compensation to the Secretary of War, six thousand dollars.

For compensation to the clerks in the War Department, per act of twentieth April, one thousand eight hundred and eighteen, twenty-three thousand four hundred dollars.

For compensation to the messengers in said Department, seven hundred and ten dollars.

For expense of fuel, stationery, printing, and other contingent expenses, in said Department, five thousand dollars.

For maps, plans, books, and instruments, one thousand dollars.

For compensation to the Paymaster General, two thousand five hundred dollars.

For compensation to the clerks in the office of the Paymaster General, per act of twentieth April, one thousand eight hundred and eighteen, nine thousand two hundred dollars.

For compensation to the messenger in said office, four hundred and ten dollars.

For compensation to the Commissary General of Purchases, three thousand dollars.

For compensation to the clerks in the office of said Commissary, two thousand eight hundred dollars.

For compensation to the messenger in said office, three hundred and sixty dollars.

For compensation to the clerks in the office of the Adjutant and Inspector General, per act of twentieth April, one thousand eight hundred and eighteen, two thousand one hundred and fifty dollars.

For compensation to the clerks in the office of the Ordnance, per act of twentieth April, one thousand eight hundred and eighteen, two thousand nine hundred and fifty dollars.

For compensation to the clerks in the office of the Commissary General of Subsistence, two thousand one hundred and fifty dollars.

For compensation to the clerks in the Engineer office, two thousand one hundred and fifty dollars.

For compensation to the clerks in the Surgeon General's office, one thousand one hundred and fifty dollars.

For the contingent expenses of the said office, five hundred dollars.

For compensation to the Secretary of the Navy, six thousand dollars.

For compensation to the clerks in the office of the Secretary of the Navy, per act of twentieth April, one thousand eight hundred and eighteen, eight thousand two hundred dollars.

For compensation to the messengers in said office, seven hundred and ten dollars.

For the contingent expenses of said office, two thousand dollars.

For compensation to the Commissioners of the Navy Board, ten thousand five hundred dollars.

For compensation to the secretary of the Commissioners of the Navy Board, two thousand dollars.

For compensation to the clerks in the office of the Commissioners of the Navy Board, per act of twentieth April, one thousand eight hundred and eighteen, three thousand five hundred and fifty dollars.

For compensation to three clerks and a draughtsman, as allowed by acts of appropriation for one thousand eight hundred and nineteen, and one thousand eight hundred and twenty, in the office of said Commissioners, four thousand dollars.

For compensation to the messenger in said office, four hundred and ten dollars.

For the contingent expenses of said office, two thousand dollars.

For allowance to the superintendent and four watchmen, for the security of the War and Navy buildings, and for the repairs of engine, hose, and buckets, one thousand nine hundred dollars.

For compensation to the Postmaster General, four thousand dollars.

For compensation to two Assistant Postmasters General, five thousand dollars.

For compensation to the clerks in the General Post Office, per act of twentieth April, one thousand eight hundred and eighteen, twenty-two thousand seven hundred dollars.

For compensation to the messengers in said office, six hundred and sixty dollars.

For contingent expenses of said office, four thousand dollars.

For compensation of the Surveyor General, two thousand dollars.

For compensation to the clerks in the office of the Surveyor General, two thousand one hundred dollars.

For compensation to the surveyor south of Tennessee, two thousand dollars.

For compensation to the clerks in the office of said surveyor, one thousand seven hundred dollars.

For compensation to the surveyor in Illinois, Missouri, and Arkansas, two thousand dollars.

For compensation to the clerks in the office of said surveyor, two thousand dollars.

For compensation to the surveyor in Alabama, two thousand dollars.

For compensation to the clerks in the office of the surveyor in Alabama, one thousand five hundred dollars.

For compensation to the Commissioner of the

Public Buildings, at Washington City, two thousand dollars.

For compensation to the officers and clerks in the Mint, nine thousand six hundred dollars.

For wages of persons employed in the different operations of the Mint, nine thousand and fifty dollars.

For incidental and contingent expenses and repairs, cost of machinery, and for allowance of wastage, in the gold and silver coinage of the Mint, eight thousand one hundred dollars.

For compensation to the Governor, Judges, and Secretary, of the Arkansas Territory, six thousand six hundred dollars.

For the contingent expenses of said Territory, three hundred and fifty dollars.

For compensation to the Governor, Judges, and Secretary, of the Michigan Territory, six thousand six hundred dollars.

For the contingent expenses of said Territory, three hundred and fifty dollars.

For compensation to the Chief Justice, the Associate Judges, and District Judges of the United States, including the Chief Justice and Associate Judges of the District of Columbia, seventy-eight thousand two hundred dollars.

For compensation to the Attorney General of the United States, three thousand five hundred dollars.

For compensation to the clerk in the office of the Attorney General, per act of twentieth April, one thousand eight hundred and eighteen, eight hundred dollars.

For the contingent expenses of said office, including compensation to the messenger, five hundred dollars.

For compensation to the reporter of the decisions of the Supreme Court, one thousand dollars.

For compensation to sundry district attorneys and marshals, as granted by law, including those in the several Territories, eight thousand nine hundred and fifty dollars.

For the payment of sundry pensions granted by the late and present governments, one thousand five hundred and ninety dollars.

For making good a deficiency in the fund for the relief and protection of sick and disabled seamen, fifty thousand dollars.

For the support of lighthouses, and other establishments for the protection of navigation, one hundred and two thousand three hundred and forty-one dollars and twenty-eight cents.

For surveying the public lands of the United States, one hundred and fifty thousand dollars.

For additional compensation allowed by the act of the twentieth April, one thousand eight hundred and eighteen, to the clerks in the office of the Superintendent General of Indian trade, four hundred and fifty dollars.

For bringing on the votes of President and Vice President, three thousand one hundred and ninety-five dollars and fifty cents.

For expenses of ships' registers, three thousand seven hundred and fifty dollars.

For the discharge of such miscellaneous claims against the United States, not otherwise provided for, as shall be admitted in due course of settlement at the Treasury, six thousand dollars.

For the salaries of the Ministers of the United States at London, Paris, St. Petersburg, and Madrid, with the salaries of their several Secretaries of Legation, and the salaries of the Chargé d'Affaires at the Hague, Rio Janeiro, and at Stockholm, fifty-seven thousand five hundred dollars.

For an outfit to a Minister at Paris, nine thousand dollars.

For the contingent expenses of those missions, ten thousand dollars.

For the contingent expenses of foreign intercourse, thirty thousand dollars.

For the expenses of intercourse with the Barbary Powers, forty-two thousand dollars.

For salaries of the agents for claims on account of spoliations and for seamen, at London and Paris, four thousand dollars.

For the relief and protection of American seamen in foreign countries, forty thousand dollars.

For opening, under the direction of the Secretary of War, within the Indian country, a road from a point at or near Turner Brashear's Stand, on the old Natchez road, to a point at or near Columbus, on the military road, the sum of five thousand dollars, which, by an act of the twenty-seventh of March, one thousand eight hundred and eighteen, was appropriated for keeping in repair said old road from Natchez to Columbia, in Tennessee, and which remains unexpended.

Sec. 2. *And be it further enacted,* That the several appropriations hereinbefore made, shall be paid out of any moneys in the Treasury not otherwise appropriated.

Approved, March 3, 1821.

An Act making appropriations for the Military Service of the United States for the year one thousand eight hundred and twenty-one.

Be it enacted, &c., That the following sums be, and the same are hereby, respectively, appropriated for the military service of the United States for the year one thousand eight hundred and twenty-one, to wit:

For the pay of the army and subsistence of the officers, nine hundred and fifty-four thousand five hundred and fifty-five dollars eighty-six cents, in addition to an unexpended balance of the year one thousand eight hundred and twenty, of one hundred and eighty dollars and seventy-eight cents.

For three months gratuitous pay for disbanded officers and soldiers, including travelling allowances for the same, sixty thousand dollars.

For subsistence, one hundred and four thousand six hundred and fifty-four dollars and sixty-seven cents, in addition to the sum of one hundred and fifty thousand dollars already appropriated.

For forage for officers, forty-one thousand five hundred and forty-one dollars.

For clothing, two hundred and seventy-six thousand five hundred and sixty-five dollars and twenty-five cents, in addition to an unexpended balance of thirteen thousand nine hundred and three dollars and seventy-two cents.

For the Medical and Hospital department, twenty-four thousand five hundred and five dollars, in addition to an unexpended balance of nine thousand eight hundred and eighty-one dollars and sixty-five cents.

For the Quartermaster General's department, two hundred and two thousand eight hundred and sixty-eight dollars, in addition to the sum of one hundred and fifty thousand dollars already appropriated, to wit:

For regular supplies, transportation, rents, and repairs, postage and courts martial, and contingencies of the department, and pay of soldiers employed in the erection and repairs of barracks, surveys, roads, and other labor, three hundred and seventeen thousand eight hundred and sixty-eight dollars.

To complete the barracks at Baton Rouge, twenty thousand dollars ; and for the transportation of ordnance, fifteen thousand dollars.

For arrearages in the Quartermaster General's department, twenty thousand dollars.

For the Military Academy, seventeen thousand and thirty-six dollars and twenty-two cents.

For fortifications, two hundred and two thousand dollars, in addition to an unexpended balance of one hundred thousand dollars, to be applied to the following fortifications, to wit:

Fort Delaware, fifty-five thousand dollars, to complete the same.

Fort Washington, twenty-two thousand dollars.

Fort Monroe, sixty-five thousand dollars.

Fort Calhoun, fifty thousand dollars.

Rigolets, sixty thousand dollars.

Mobile Point, thirty thousand dollars.

Repairs and contingencies, twenty thousand dollars.

For the contingencies of the army, forty thousand dollars.

For the national armories, three hundred and forty thousand dollars, in addition to an unexpended balance of twenty thousand dollars.

For the current expenses of the ordnance service, an unexpended balance of twenty-three thousand six hundred and sixty-three dollars and seven cents.

For the fulfilment of existing contracts for cannon, shot, and shells, and for the purchase of one thousand sword belts, and of timber for gun carriages, fifty-three thousand two hundred and fifty dollars.

For the annual allowance to the invalid pensioners of the United States, two hundred and thirteen thousand three hundred and twenty-four dollars, in addition to an unexpended balance of one hundred and one thousand six hundred and seventy-six dollars and seventy-five cents.

For the half-pay pensions of widows and orphans, thirty thousand dollars.

For arrearages, prior to the first of January, eighteen hundred and seventeen, fifty thousand dollars, in addition to a former appropriation of twenty thousand dollars.

Public Acts of Congress.   .

For arrearages in the Indian Department, one hundred and thirty thousand two hundred and five dollars and forty-four cents.

For the current expenses of the Indian Department, one hundred thousand dollars.

For the annual allowance to the Revolutionary pensioners of the United States, one million two hundred thousand dollars, being part of the unexpended balance of a former appropriation.

For carrying into effect the treaty concluded with the Creek nation, on the eighth day of January, one thousand eight hundred and twenty, and ratified by and with the advice and consent of the Senate, on the twenty-fourth of February, one thousand eight hundred and twenty-one, forty-eight thousand five hundred dollars.

For carrying into effect the treaty concluded with the Choctaw nation of Indians, on the eleventh of October, one thousand eight hundred and twenty, sixty-five thousand dollars; and for payment of one year's annuity to Mushulatubba, a Choctaw chief, one hundred and fifty dollars.

For completing the road in the State of Georgia, through the Creek nation, under the acts of the twenty-seventh of April, one thousand eight hundred and sixteen, twenty-seventh of March, one thousand eight hundred and eighteen, and fourteenth of April, one thousand eight hundred and twenty, one thousand dollars.

For discharging arrearages incurred in building the arsenal at Augusta, in Georgia, forty thousand dollars.

SEC. 2. *And be it further enacted,* That the several appropriations, hereinbefore made, shall be paid out of any money in the Treasury, not otherwise appropriated.

Approved, March 3, 1821.

An Act making appropriations for the support of the Navy of the United States for the year one thousand eight hundred and twenty-one.

Be it enacted, &c., That, for defraying the expenses of the Navy, for the year one thousand eight hundred and twenty-one, the following sums be, and the same are hereby, respectively appropriated:

For the pay and subsistence of the officers, and pay of the seamen, nine hundred and eighty-three thousand three hundred and twenty-five dollars and twenty-five cents.

For provisions, three hundred and thirty-seven thousand eight hundred and thirty-one dollars.

For medicines, hospital stores, and all expenses on account of the sick, thirty-two thousand dollars.

For repairs of vessels, three hundred and seventy-five thousand dollars.

For improvement of navy yards, docks, and wharves, pay of superintendents, storekeepers, clerks, and laborers, twenty-five thousand dollars.

For ordnance and ordnance stores, twenty-five thousand dollars.

For contingent expenses, two hundred thousand dollars.

For pay and subsistence of the marine corps,

one hundred and sixty-nine thousand three hundred and ninety-three dollars.

For clothing the same, thirty thousand six hundred and eighty-six dollars, and thirty-one cents.

For fuel for the same, six thousand eight hundred and eighty-seven dollars and fifty cents.

For contingent expenses of the same, fourteen thousand dollars.

For completing the equipment of the vessels constructed in pursuance of the act authorizing the building of a certain number of small vessels of war, ten thousand dollars.

For the purpose of enabling the Secretary of the Navy to remove obstructions placed in the river Thames, in Connecticut, by the commander of the American ships during the late war, one hundred and fifty dollars.

SEC. 2. *And be it further enacted,* That the several appropriations hereinbefore made shall be paid out of any money in the Treasury not otherwise appropriated.

Approved, March 3, 1821.

An Act to authorize the President of the United States to borrow a sum not exceeding five millions of dollars.

Be it enacted, &c., That the President of the United States be, and he is hereby, empowered to borrow, on the credit of the United States, a sum not exceeding five millions of dollars, at a rate of interest, payable quarter-yearly, not exceeding five per centum per annum, and reimbursable at the will of the Government, at any time after the first day of January, one thousand eight hundred and thirty-five; to be applied, in addition to the moneys now in the Treasury, or which may be received therein from other sources, during the present year, to defray any of the public expenses which are, or may be, authorized by law. The stock thereby created shall be transferable in the same manner as is provided by law for the transfer of the public debt.

SEC. 2. *And be it further enacted,* That it shall be lawful for the Bank of the United States to lend the said sum, or any part thereof; and it is hereby further declared, that it shall be deemed a good execution of the said power to borrow, for the Secretary of the Treasury, with the approbation of the President of the United States, to cause to be constituted certificates of stock, signed by the Register of the Treasury, or by a Commissioner of Loans, for the sum to be borrowed, or for any part thereof, bearing an interest of five per centum per annum, transferable and reimbursable as aforesaid, and to cause the said certificates of stock to be sold, provided that no stock be sold under par.

SEC. 3. *And be it further enacted,* That the Secretary of the Treasury be, and he is hereby, authorized, with the approbation of the President of the United States, to employ an agent or agents for the purpose of obtaining subscriptions to the loan authorized by this act, or of selling any part of the stock to be created by virtue thereof. A commission of not exceeding one-eighth of one per centum on the amount thus sold, or for which subscriptions shall be obtained, may, by the Secretary of the Treasury, be allowed to such agent or agents; and a sum, not exceeding four thousand dollars, to be paid out of any moneys in the Treasury, not otherwise appropriated, is hereby appropriated for that object, and subscription certificates, and certificates of stock, and other expenses incident to the due execution of this act.

Sec. 4. *And be it further enacted,* That so much of the funds constituting the annual appropriation of ten millions of dollars for the payment of the principal and interest of the public debt of the United States, as may be sufficient for that purpose, after satisfying the sums necessary for the payment of the interest, and of such part of the principal, of the said debt, as the United States are now pledged annually to pay and reimburse, is hereby pledged and appropriated for the payment of the interest, and for the reimbursement of the principal, of the stock which may be created by virtue of this act. It shall, accordingly, be the duty of the Commissioners of the Sinking Fund to cause to be applied, and paid out of the said fund, yearly, such sum and sums as may annually be necessary to discharge the interest accruing on the said stock, and to reimburse the principal, as the same may become due, and may be discharged in conformity with the terms of the loan. And they are further authorized to apply, from time to time, such sum or sums towards discharging, by purchase, and at a price not above par, the principal of the said stock, or any part thereof; and the faith of the United States is hereby pledged to establish sufficient revenues for making up any deficiency that may hereafter take place in the funds hereby appropriated for paying the said interest and principal sums, or any of them, in manner aforesaid.—Approved, March 3, 1821.

An Act for carrying into execution the Treaty between the United States and Spain, concluded at Washington on the twenty-second day of February, one thousand eight hundred and nineteen.

Be it enacted, &c., That the President of the United States be, and he is hereby, authorized to take possession of, and occupy, the territories of East and West Florida, and the appendages and appurtenances thereof; and to remove and transport the officers and soldiers of the King of Spain, being there, to the Havana, agreeably to the stipulations of the treaty between the United States and Spain, concluded at Washington on the twenty-second day of February, in the year one thousand eight hundred and nineteen, providing for the cession of said territories to the United States; and he may, for these purposes, and in order to maintain in said territories the authority of the United States, employ any part of the Army and Navy of the United States, and the militia of any State or Territory, which he may deem necessary.

Sec. 2. *And be it further enacted,* That, until the end of the first session of the next Congress, unless provision for the temporary government of said territories be sooner made by Congress, all the military, civil, and judicial powers exercised by the officers of the existing government of the same territories, shall be vested in such person and persons, and shall be exercised in such manner as the President of the United States shall direct, for the maintaining the inhabitants of said territories in the free enjoyment of their liberty, property, and religion; and the laws of the United States relating to the revenue and its collection, subject to the modification stipulated by the fifteenth article of the said treaty, in favor of Spanish vessels and their cargoes, and the laws relating to the importation of persons of color shall be extended to the said territories. And the President of the United States shall be, and he is hereby, authorized, within the term aforesaid, to establish such districts for the collection of the revenue, and, during the recess of Congress, to appoint such officers, whose commissions shall expire at the end of the next session of Congress, to enforce the said laws, as to him shall seem expedient.

Sec. 3. *And be it further enacted,* That the President of the United States be, and he is hereby, authorized to appoint, during the recess of the Senate, a Commissioner and Surveyor, whose commissions shall expire at the end of the next session of Congress, to meet the Commissioner and Surveyor who may be appointed on the part of Spain, for the purposes stipulated in the fourth article of said treaty; and that the President be, and he is hereby, further authorized to take all other measures which he shall judge proper, for carrying into effect the stipulations of the said fourth article.

Sec. 4. *And be it further enacted,* That a board of three commissioners shall be appointed, conformably to the stipulations of the eleventh article of the said treaty; and the President of the United States is hereby authorized to take any measures which he may deem expedient for organizing the said board of commissioners, and, for this purpose, may appoint a secretary well versed in the French and Spanish languages, and a clerk; which appointments, if made during the recess of the Senate, shall, at the next meeting of that body, be subject to nomination for their advice and consent.

Sec. 5. *And be it further enacted,* That the compensation of the respective officers, for whose appointment provision is made by this act, shall not exceed the following sums:

The commissioner to be appointed conformably to the fourth article, at the rate, by the year, of three thousand dollars.

To the surveyor, two thousand dollars.

To each of the three commissioners to be appointed conformably to the eleventh article of the treaty, three thousand dollars.

To the secretary of the board, two thousand dollars.

To one clerk, one thousand five hundred dollars.

Sec. 6. *And be it further enacted,* That, for carrying this act into execution, the sum of one hundred thousand dollars be, and hereby is, appropriated, to be taken from any moneys in the Treasury not otherwise appropriated.

Approved, March 3, 1821.

Public Acts of Congress.

An Act to establish the District of Pearl River.

Be it enacted, &c., That, from and after the first day of July next, all the bays, waters, and shores, on Lake Borgne and the Gulf of Mexico, and all the rivers emptying into the same, within the limits of the State of Mississippi, shall be a collection district, to be called the district of Pearl river; of which a port near the mouth of Pearl river, at such place as the President of the United States shall designate, shall be the port of entry; and a collector for the district shall be appointed, to reside at such place as the President shall direct, at or near the said port, who shall be entitled to receive, in addition to the fees and other emoluments established by law, the annual salary of two hundred and fifty dollars.

Approved, March 2, 1821.

An Act confirming the location of the seat of government of the State of Illinois, and for other purposes.

Be it enacted, &c., That the four sections of land, including the section number sixteen, in township number six north, range number one east, of the third principal meridian, heretofore selected by commissioners appointed for that purpose, for the seat of government of the State of Illinois, be, and the same are hereby declared to be, confirmed to, and vested in, the said State, for the purpose aforesaid.

SEC. 2. *And be it further enacted,* That the Governor of said State be, and he is hereby, authorized to select any unappropriated section in said township, for the use of the inhabitants thereof, which shall be in lieu of the said sixteenth section.

Approved, March 2, 1821.

An Act further to regulate the entry of merchandise imported into the United States from any adjacent territory.

Be it enacted, &c., That it shall be the duty of the master of any vessel, except registered vessels, and of every person having charge of any boat, canoe, or raft, and of the conductor or driver of any carriage or sleigh, and of every other person coming from any foreign territory adjacent to the United States, into the United States, with merchandise subject to duty, to deliver, immediately on his or her arrival within the United States, a manifest of the cargo or loading of such vessel, boat, canoe, raft, carriage, or sleigh, or of the merchandise so brought from such foreign territory, at the office of any collector or deputy collector which shall be nearest to the boundary line, or nearest to the road or waters by which such merchandise is brought; and every such manifest shall be verified by the oath of such person delivering the same; which oath shall be taken before such collector, or deputy collector; and such oath shall state that such manifest contains a full, just, and true account, of the kinds, quantities, and values, of all the merchandise so brought from such foreign territory; and if the master, or other person having charge of such vessel, boat, canoe, or raft, or the conductor or driver of such carriage or

sleigh, or other person bringing merchandise as aforesaid, shall neglect or refuse to deliver the manifest herein required, or pass by or avoid such office, the merchandise subject to duty, and so imported, shall be forfeited to the United States, together with the vessel, boat, canoe, or raft, the tackle, apparel, and furniture of the same, or the carriage or sleigh, and harness and cattle drawing the same, or the horses, with their saddles and bridles, as the case may be; and such master, conductor, or other importer, shall be subjected to pay a penalty of four hundred dollars.

SEC. 2. *And be it further enacted,* That any deputy collector, stationed in any district of the customs contiguous to a foreign territory, to whom a manifest of merchandise, subject to duty, shall be delivered as aforesaid, is hereby authorized to require of the importer of such merchandise the payment of the duties thereon, or good and ample security, either by bond, with one or more sufficient sureties, for the payment thereof, or by the deposite of a portion of such merchandise, equal, at least, to double the amount of the duties on the whole importation; which bond shall be cancelled, or the merchandise so deposited shall be delivered to the owner, on the producing to the deputy collector a certificate of the collector of the district, that the duties have been duly paid.

SEC. 3. *And be it further enacted,* That all penalties and forfeitures incurred by force of this act, shall be sued for, recovered, distributed, and accounted for, in the manner prescribed by the act, entitled "An act to regulate the collection of duties on imports and tonnage," passed on the second day of March, one thousand seven hundred and ninety-nine, and may be mitigated or remitted in the manner prescribed by the act, entitled "An act to provide for the mitigating or remitting the forfeitures, penalties, and disabilities, accruing in certain cases therein mentioned," passed on the third day of March, one thousand seven hundred and ninety-seven.

Approved, March 2, 1821.

An Act establishing the salaries of the Commissioners and Agents appointed under the Treaty of Ghent.

Be it enacted, &c., That, from and after the first day of January, one thousand eight hundred and twenty-one, each commissioner now appointed, or who may be appointed agreeably to the provisions of the Treaty of Ghent, shall be entitled to receive at the rate of twenty-five hundred dollars per annum; and each agent appointed, or who may be appointed, as aforesaid, shall be entitled to receive at the rate of twenty-five hundred dollars per annum; which said sums, so allowed to said officers, respectively, shall be a full compensation for services, and all the personal expenses incurred while in the performance of the duties of their respective offices: *Provided,* That the compensation by this section allowed, shall not be continued longer than two years from the said first day of January, one thousand eight hundred and twenty-one.

SEC. 2. *And be it further enacted,* That each

Public Acts of Congress.

commissioner and agent shall not be entitled to receive, for services performed in their respective offices, before the said first day of January, one thousand eight hundred and twenty-one, any greater sum than the rate of four thousand four hundred and forty-four dollars per annum, which shall be considered a full compensation for services, and all personal expenses, incurred while in the discharge of their respective duties.

Sec. 3. *And be it further enacted,* That the sum of twenty-five thousand dollars be, and the same is hereby, appropriated for the payment of the salaries of the said commissioners and agents, and for the expenses under the several commissions under the Treaty of Ghent, for the present year.

Approved, March 3, 1821.

An Act to authorize the Collectors of Customs to pay debentures issued on the exportation of loaf sugar, and spirits distilled from molasses.

Be it enacted, &c., That all debentures which have been, or may hereafter be, issued upon the exportation of spirits distilled from molasses, or sugar refined within the United States, shall be payable within thirty days after the passing of this act, or thirty days after the date of their issue, as the case may be, and shall be discharged by the collector of the customs, by whom they may have been, or shall be, issued, out of the product of the duties upon imports and tonnage; any thing in any act or acts of Congress to the contrary notwithstanding.

Approved, March 3, 1821.

An Act making appropriations for the Public Buildings.

Be it enacted, &c., That, for continuing the work on the centre building of the Capitol, and other improvements on the public buildings, the following sums of money be, and hereby are, appropriated :

For continuing the work on the centre building, the sum of eighty thousand dollars.

For covering the roof of the President's house with copper, seven thousand eight hundred and forty-five dollars.

For graduating and improving the ground around the Capitol, two thousand dollars.

For improvements in the Senate Chamber, and in the Hall of the House of Representatives, and in the Library, seven hundred dollars.

Sec. 2. *And be it further enacted,* That the unexpended balances of appropriations to other public buildings, are hereby appropriated to the centre building.

Sec. 3. *And be it further enacted,* That the said several sums of money be paid out of any moneys in the Treasury, not otherwise appropriated.

Approved, March 3, 1821.

An Act extending the time for issuing and locating military land warrants to officers and soldiers of the Revolutionary Army.

Be it enacted, &c., That the time limited, by the second section of the act, approved on the twenty-fourth day of February, one thousand eight hundred and nineteen, for issuing military land warrants to the officers and soldiers of the Revolutionary army, shall be extended to the fourth day of March, one thousand eight hundred and twenty-three; and the time for locating the unlocated warrants shall be extended to the first day of October thereafter.

Approved, March 2, 1821.

An Act to extend the time for unlading vessels arriving from foreign ports, in certain cases.

Be it enacted, &c., That, when the capacity of any vessel arriving with a cargo from a foreign port shall exceed three hundred tons, the term for unlading such vessel shall hereafter be twenty days from the report of arrival, Sundays excepted.

Approved, March 3, 1821.

An Act to continue in force an act, entitled "An act regulating the currency within the United States of the gold coins of Great Britain, France, Portugal, and Spain," passed on the twenty-ninth day of April, one thousand eight hundred and sixteen, so far as the same relates to the crowns and five-franc pieces of France.

Be it enacted, &c., That so much of the act, entitled "An act regulating the currency within the United States of the gold coins of Great Britain, France, Portugal, and Spain," passed on the twenty-ninth day of April, eighteen hundred and sixteen, as relates to the crowns and five-franc pieces of France, shall be, and the same hereby is, continued in force for the further term of two years, from and after the twenty-ninth day of April next.

Approved, March 3, 1821.

An Act to extend the charters of certain Banks in the District of Columbia.

Be it enacted, &c., That the acts incorporating the several banks in the District of Columbia, herein named, that is to say : the Bank of Alexandria, and the Farmers' Bank of Alexandria, in the town of Alexandria; the Bank of Washington, the Bank of the Metropolis, and the Patriotic Bank of Washington, in the City of Washington ; the Union Bank of Georgetown, the Farmers and Mechanics' Bank of Georgetown, and the Bank of Columbia, in the town of Georgetown, be, and the same are hereby, extended and limited to the third day of March, which shall be in the year of our Lord one thousand eight hundred and thirty-six, under, and subject to, such limitations, modifications, and conditions, as are hereinafter enacted.

Sec. 2. *And be it further enacted,* That, if any one of the banks herein named shall, at any time, fail, or refuse to pay on demand, any bill, note, or obligation, issued by such bank, in lawful currency of the United States, when required, or shall neglect or refuse to pay on demand in like currency, if required, any moneys received by such bank on deposite, to the person or persons entitled to

Public Acts of Congress.

receive the same ; then, and in such case, the holder of any such note, bill, or obligation, or the person or persons demanding such deposite as aforesaid, shall respectively be entitled to receive and recover interest on the same, at the rate of twelve per centum per annum, from the time of the demand until the same be fully paid and satisfied. *And further,* It shall be lawful for Congress, forthwith, to revoke the charter of such bank, and to provide for liquidating and settling the accounts and affairs thereof, in such manner as to their judgment may seem expedient.

SEC. 3. *And be it further enacted,* That any president, director, cashier, teller, clerk, or other officer, or servant, of any of the said banks, or of the Bank of Potomac, hereinafter named, who shall withhold, withdraw, conceal, or embezzle, or connive at the withholding, withdrawal, concealment, or embezzlement, of the money or other property of the bank whereof he is an officer or servant, with intent to defraud the said bank, shall be subject to prosecution therefor, in the name of the United States, by indictment, on presentment or information, in the circuit court of the county wherein such offence shall have been committed, and, on conviction thereof, shall be adjudged a felon, and suffer an imprisonment of not less than one year, nor more than ten years, and forfeit and pay a sum not less than one thousand, nor more than twenty thousand, dollars ; one moiety whereof shall go to the United States, and the other to the informer.

SEC. 4. *And be it further enacted,* That, unless the president and directors, for the time being, of each of the banks respectively, whose charters are hereby extended, shall, on behalf of their stockholders, and in virtue of an authority from them, or a majority in interest and number of them, file their declaration, in writing, in the office of the Secretary of the Treasury, within six months from the passage of this act, assenting to and accepting the extension of charter hereby granted, under the terms, conditions, and limitations, contained in this act, such bank shall forfeit all title to such extension of charter.

SEC. 5. *And be it further enacted,* That every stockholder of the Bank of Alexandria, of the Farmers' Bank of Alexandria, and of the Bank of Washington, (being a citizen of the United States, and not otherwise,) shall be entitled to vote by himself, his agent, or proxy, appointed under his hand and seal, at all elections, in virtue of this act, and shall have as many votes as he has shares, as far as thirty shares, and not more than one vote for every five shares thereafter.

SEC. 6. *And be it further enacted,* That a meeting of the stockholders of the Bank of Alexandria, in the town of Alexandria, shall be held on the third Monday of January in every year, during the continuance of this act ; previous notice whereof shall be published in some newspaper printed in Alexandria or the City of Washington, for the space of four weeks successively ; and the stockholders assembled in consequence of such notice shall choose by ballot from among themselves, by a majority of votes of such as shall be present, or

by proxy, ten directors, being citizens of the United States, for the term of one year thereafter, and on the same day annually, for and during the continuance of this act, a like election shall be made; and in case of death, resignation, refusal, or disqualification, of any director, the remaining directors, at their next meeting, or as soon as convenient thereafter, shall elect, by ballot, another person, qualified as aforesaid, in his place, for the residue of the year. The directors, or any seven of them, shall, at their next meeting after every general election, elect, by a majority of members present, by ballot, from among themselves, a president, who shall retain all the powers ond privileges of a director ; and in case of refusal, death, resignation, or disqualification, of the president, the directors shall meet as soon as conveniently can be thereafter, and, after filling the vacancy in the number of directors required by this act, elect another person for president in manner before directed.

SEC. 7. *And be it further enacted,* That it shall not be lawful for any of the said banks, after the first day of January next, to make, issue, or reissue, any bill, note, or obligation, payable to bearer or order, of a denomination under five dollars.

SEC. 8. *And be it further enacted,* That the fourteenth section of the act incorporating the Bank of Columbia aforesaid, passed the twenty-eighth day of December, one thousand seven hundred and ninety-three, be, and the same is hereby, repealed and annulled : *Provided,* That the said fourteenth section shall remain in full force and effect in relation to all debts contracted with the said bank previous to the passing of this act.

SEC. 9. *And be it further enacted,* That it shall be lawful for the Central Bank of Georgetown and Washington to proceed, forthwith, to liquidate and close all the concerns of the corporation, and, after paying and satisfying the debts, contracts, and obligations, of the corporation, to divide the capital and profits which may remain among the stockholders, in proportion to their respective interests ; and for this purpose, and for no other intent or purpose whatever, all the necessary powers, as fully as they are now enjoyed by the said corporation, shall be, and the same are hereby, continued to the said corporation, for the term of five years from the first day of January next, and no longer.

SEC. 10. *And be it further enacted,* That it shall and may be lawful for the stockholders of the Central Bank of Georgetown and Washington aforesaid, at their next annual meeting for the election of directors, to reduce the board of directors for the said Central Bank, to any number not less than six.

SEC. 11. *And be it further enacted,* That the corporation of the Bank of Potomac be, and the same is hereby, continued and extended to the third day of March, in the year of our Lord one thousand eight hundred and thirty-six, during which time it shall hold, and be possessed of all the rights, privileges, and immunities, now secured to it by an act, passed on the sixteenth day of February, one thousand eight hundred and eleven, entitled

Public Acts of Congress.

"An act to incorporate the Bank of Potomac," and shall be subject to all the restraints and limitations expressed in the said act, except so far as the same shall be altered by any provisions hereinafter contained.

SEC. 12. *And be it further enacted,* That an election for directors of the Bank of Potomac shall be held in the town of Alexandria, on the first Monday in November in each year, of which notice shall be given in one or more newspapers published in said town, for four weeks at least before the day of election; and the stockholders shall choose, by ballot, to be given in person or by proxy, by a majority of votes, from amongst the stockholders, thirteen directors, for the term of one year thereafter, and, on resignation, disqualification, or removal, of any director out of the county of Alexandria, or out of the county of Fairfax, in Virginia, the other directors, at their next meeting thereafter, may elect, by ballot, another person, qualified as aforesaid, in his place, for the residue of the year. The directors of said bank shall, at the first meeting after every general election, elect, by ballot, from among their own number, by a majority of their whole number, a president; and in case of his death, resignation, or removal out of the county of Alexandria, or out of the county of Fairfax, or of his refusal to accept his office, the directors shall meet, as soon as conveniently can be thereafter, and elect another person as president, in the manner before described.

SEC. 13. *And be it further enacted,* That every stockholder of the Bank of Potomac, being a citizen of the United States, shall be entitled to vote at all elections to be holden by the stockholders of said bank, in pursuance of this act, and shall have as many votes in proportion to the stock he may hold, as follows, that is to say: For every share, from one to twenty, one vote; for each share, from twenty to fifty shares, one vote for two shares; from fifty to one hundred, one vote for four shares; above one hundred shares, one vote for six shares: *Provided,* That no share, or number of shares, pledged to the said bank as security for any debt due, or to become due, to it, shall be considered as conferring any right to vote at the said elections.

SEC. 14. *And be it further enacted,* That it shall be lawful for the president of the Union Bank of Alexandria, at any time before the first day of April next, with the consent of a majority in interest of the stockholders thereof, to subscribe to the said Bank of Potomac the full amount of the capital stock of the said Union Bank, and, on such subscription being made, to deliver over and transfer to the said Bank of Potomac all the books, papers, money, property, and evidences of debts, belonging to the said Union Bank, and to convey to the said Bank of Potomac the real estate belonging to said Union Bank, for passing the title of which bank in the said estate, to the said Bank of Potomac, the deed of the President of the said Union Bank shall be effectual; on which subscription, delivery, transfer, and conveyance, being made, the stockholders of the said Union Bank shall, forthwith, become stockholders in the said Bank of Potomac, and shall be entitled to the same privileges and advantages, and the stock of the said Union Bank shall, to all intents and purposes, be considered as forming a part of the capital of the said Bank of Potomac; and the proper officers of the said Bank of Potomac shall forthwith issue to the stockholders of the said Union Bank certificates of stock in the said Bank of Potomac, at the rate of one share, or one hundred dollars of Potomac Bank stock, for every hundred dollars of the Union Bank stock so subscribed, according to the respective interests of the said stockholders in the stock so subscribed.

SEC. 15. *And be it further enacted,* That, on the said union being made as aforesaid, all contracts legally made by the said Union Bank shall, forthwith, become obligatory on the said Bank of Potomac, and all debts due by the said Union Bank on notes issued by it, or otherwise, shall become chargeable on, and payable by, the said Bank of Potomac; and the parties to such contracts, and the creditors of the said Union Bank, shall have the same remedies to enforce the performance of such contracts, and the payment of such debts, against the said Bank of Potomac, its property, and effects, as are now, by law, given to them against the said Union Bank; and that the said Bank of Potomac may, in its own name, sustain all actions and suits which may be necessary to enforce the payment of debts due to, and the performance of contracts made with, the said Union Bank, and for the recovery of any lands, tenements, goods, and chattels, belonging to, and improperly withheld from, the said Union Bank.

SEC. 16. *And be it further enacted,* That all bonds, bills, notes, or other securities for money, which, by the terms thereof, have been, or shall be, made payable at the said Union Bank, which shall fall due after the said union shall have been carried into effect, shall, from thenceforth, be considered as if the same had been made payable at the said Bank of Potomac; and that a demand of payment at the said Bank of Potomac shall, to all intents and purposes, be as effectual in law as if the same were made at the said Union Bank.

SEC. 17. *And be it further enacted,* That, from the time the said union of the said banks shall be carried into effect, the twenty-seventh section of the act of Congress, passed on the third of March, one thousand eight hundred and seventeen, entitled "An act to incorporate the subscribers to certain banks in the District of Columbia, and to prevent the circulation of the notes of unchartered associations within the said District, shall be, and the same is hereby, repealed: *Provided,* That such repeal shall not, in any way, impair the right of the said Bank of Potomac to the money, property, debts, and effects, which shall be transferred or conveyed to it, as aforesaid, nor its remedies in its own name for the recovery thereof; nor shall any suit now brought in the name of the said Union Bank, thereby abate, but the same may be carried on and prosecuted for the benefit of the said Bank of Potomac, to final judgment and execution; and that proceedings on such judgments or executions may be instituted and carried on in the name of the said Union Bank, against the bail, securities, and all other persons bound in such suits for the defendants therein.

SEC. 18. *And be it further enacted,* That if any stockholder or stockholders in either of the said banks, who has not heretofore assented to the union aforesaid, shall, within three months from the passing of this act, file his declaration in writing in the said Bank of Potomac, declaring himself dissatisfied with the said union, and his determination to withdraw his interest from the same; and if the said bank cannot agree with such stockholder or stockholders on the amount of such interest, and shall not forthwith pay the same, then it shall be lawful for the circuit court of the District of Columbia, at Alexandria, on the petition in writing of such stockholder or stockholders, to appoint three commissioners, whose duty it shall be to ascertain the value of the interest of such stockholder or stockholders in the bank to which he or they may belong at the time of the said union, for which purpose such commissioners shall, under the direction of the said court, have access to the books, papers, and accounts of the said banks, and on the report of the said commissioners, and such other evidences as may be laid before them, then said court shall proceed to ascertain the value of the stock of such stockholder or stockholders, and shall decree the value, so ascertained, to be paid to him or them by the said Bank of Potomac, and shall have power to enforce such decree by execution, attachment, or other legal process.

SEC. 19. *And be it further enacted,* That it shall and may be lawful for any two or more of the banks, whose charters are hereby extended, by their respective presidents and directors, with the consent of a majority in interest of their respective stockholders, to agree, under written articles of association, to unite and form one bank, by a style and name to be prescribed in such articles; and the subscribers thereto, and their legal representatives, shall, from the day fixed for that purpose in the said articles, be incorporated under the style and name set forth in the said articles, and thenceforth subject to the same rules, duties, regulations, conditions, provisions, and impositions, and be vested with the same rights, privileges, and immunities, as a body corporate, as by this act appertains to the Bank of Potomac, and are prescribed for the union of the Union Bank of Alexandria with the Bank of Potomac.

SEC. 20. *And be it further enacted,* That this act be, and the same is hereby declared to be, a public act, and that so much, and such parts of the said acts incorporating the several banks aforesaid, as may be repugnant to this act, be and the same are hereby repealed and annulled.

Approved, March 2, 1821.

An Act to regulate the location of Land Warrants, and the issuing of patents, in certain cases.

Be it enacted, &c., That the holders, by assignment, of warrants issued under the acts of Congress, of the fifth March, eighteen hundred and sixteen, the third of March, eighteen hundred and seventeen, to Canadian volunteers, may be, and hereby are, authorized to locate the said warrants, and to receive patents therefor in their own names, as had been the practice before the twenty-sixth of December, eighteen hundred and nineteen: *Provided however,* That in no case shall lands be so located until after having been exposed to public sale, shall remain unsold.

Approved, March 3, 1821.

An Act to continue in force, for a further time, the act entitled "An act for establishing trading-houses with the Indian tribes."

Be it enacted, &c., That the act entitled "An act for establishing trading-houses with the Indian tribes," passed on the second day of March, one thousand eight hundred and eleven, and which was, by subsequent acts, continued in force until the first day of March, one thousand eight hundred and twenty-one, shall be, and the same is hereby, further continued in force until the third day of June, one thousand eight hundred and twenty-two, and no longer.

Approved, March 3, 1821.

An Act to amend the act entitled "An act for the gradual increase of the Navy of the United States."

Be it enacted, &c., That the first section of the act entitled "An act for the gradual increase of the Navy of the United States," approved April twenty-ninth, eighteen hundred and sixteen, shall be, and the same is hereby, repealed.

SEC. 2. *And be it further enacted,* That, instead of the appropriation therein contained, there shall be, and is hereby, appropriated, the sum of five hundred thousand dollars per annum, for six years, from the year eighteen hundred and twenty-one, inclusive, to be applied to carry into effect the purposes of the said act.

Approved, March 3, 1821.

An Act to release French ships and vessels, entering the ports of the United States prior to the thirtieth of September, one thousand eight hundred and twenty, from the operation of the act entitled "An act to impose a new tonnage duty on French ships and vessels, and for other purposes."

Be it enacted, &c., That the provisions of the act entitled "An act to impose a new tonnage duty on French ships and vessels," passed May fifteenth, one thousand eight hundred and twenty, shall not extend to, or operate upon, any French ship or vessel that shall have entered into any port within the jurisdiction of the United States prior to the thirtieth day of September, one thousand eight hundred and twenty.

SEC. 2. *And be it further enacted,* That the Secretary of the Treasury, after deducting a tonnage duty equal to that paid by every French ship or vessel which entered the ports within the jurisdiction of the United States prior to the passage and operation of the act entitled "An act to impose a new tonnage duty on French ships and vessels," passed May fifteenth, one thousand eight hundred

Public Acts of Congress.

and twenty, from the tonnage duty collected from French ships and vessels by virtue of the above recited act, between the first day of July, one thousand eight hundred and twenty, and the thirtieth day of September following be, and he is hereby, authorized and directed to pay and refund the remainder of such tonnage duty, free from costs and charges, to any person or persons who shall have authority to receive the same.

SEC. 3. *And be it further enacted*, That, in the event of the signature of any treaty or convention concerning the navigation or commerce between the dominions of the United States and France, the President of the United States be, and is hereby authorized, should he deem the same expedient, by proclamation, to suspend, until the end of the next session of Congress, the operation of the aforesaid act entitled "An act to impose a new tonnage duty on French ships and vessels, and for other purposes;" and, also, to suspend, as aforesaid, all other duties on French vessels, or the goods imported in the same, which may exceed the duties on American vessels and on similar goods imported in the same.

Approved, March 3, 1821.

An Act to establish a port of entry in the District of Sandusky, in the State of Ohio, and for other purposes.

Be it enacted, &c., That, from and after the first day of May next, the town of Portland, in the district of Sandusky, in the State of Ohio, shall be the port of entry for that district; and that from and after that time the present port of entry established at Danbury shall cease to be the port of entry for said district.

Approved, March 3, 1821.

An Act authorizing the Secretary of the Treasury of the United States to sell and convey a certain tract of land in Northumberland county, in the State of Virginia.

Be it enacted, &c., That the Secretary of the Treasury of the United States be, and he is hereby, authorized and empowered to sell and dispose of, at public or private sale, all the estate, right, title, interest, claim, and demand, of the United States of America, of, in, and to, all that certain tract or piece of land, situate in Northumberland county, in the State of Virginia, formerly owned by Presly Thornton, of the said county and State, and late of Sharp Delany, containing about two thousand five hundred acres, be the same more or less ; the same being the premises which William Lewis and Thomas Robinson, by deed of indenture, executed on the second day of June, Anno Domini one thousand eight hundred and nine, granted and conveyed to the United States ; the moneys arising from the said sale to be appropriated towards the payment of a debt due from the late Sharp Delany to the United States, and the residue thereof, if any there be, to be paid over to the legal representatives of the said Sharp Delany.

Approved, March 3, 1821.

An Act to authorize the Clerk of the District Court of the United States for the district of Louisiana to appoint a deputy to aid him in the discharge of the duties of his office.

Be it enacted, &c., That the clerk of the district court of the United States for the district of Louisiana shall be authorized to appoint a deputy to aid him in the discharge of the duties of his office; and that the said clerk shall be, in all respects, liable for the acts of his said deputy.

Approved, March 3, 1821.

An Act to amend an act entitled "An act for regulating process in the courts of the United States."

Be it enacted, &c., That in all suits and actions in any district court of the United States, in which it shall appear that the judge of such court is any ways concerned in interest, or has been of counsel for either party, or is so related to, or connected with, either party, as to render it improper for him, in his opinion, to sit on the trial of such suit or action, it shall be the duty of such judge, on application of either party, to cause the fact to be entered on the records of the court; and, also, an order that an authenticated copy thereof, with all the proceedings in such suit or action, shall be forthwith certified to the next circuit court of the district; and if there be no circuit court in such district, to the next circuit court of the State, and if there be no circuit court in such State, to the most convenient circuit court in an adjacent State ; which circuit court shall, upon such record being filed with the clerk thereof, take cognizance thereof, in the like manner as if such suit or action had been originally commenced in that court, and shall proceed to hear and determine the same accordingly, and the jurisdiction of such circuit court shall extend to all such cases so removed, as were cognizable in the district court from which the same was removed.

Approved, March 3, 1821.

An Act to revive and continue in force "An act fixing the compensations of the Secretary of the Senate and Clerk of the House of Representatives, of the Clerks employed in their offices, and of the Librarian," approved the eighteenth day of April, one thousand eight hundred and eighteen.

Be it enacted, &c., That the act, entitled "An act fixing the compensation of the Secretary of the Senate and Clerk of the House of Representatives, of the Clerks employed in their offices, and the Librarian," approved the eighteenth day of April, one thousand eight hundred and eighteen, be, and the same is hereby, revived and continued in force from the first day of January, one thousand eight hundred and twenty-one, until the first day of January, one thousand eight hundred and twenty-four.—Approved, March 3, 1821.

An Act to alter and establish certain Post Roads.

Be it enacted, &c., That the following post roads be, and the same are hereby, discontinued, that is to say :

Public Acts of Congress.

From Concord, in Rockingham county, by Salisbury, Andover, New Chester, Bridgewater, and Plymouth, thence by New Holderness, New Hampton, Sanbornton, and Salisbury, to Concord, and

From Farmington to Middleton, in New Hampshire.

From Carver to Wareham.

From Northampton, by Southampton, to Springfield, in Massachusetts.

From Herkimer, by Woodworth's, Columbia, by Underwood's, Litchfield, to Laghwaite.

From Vernon to Delhi.

From Little Falls, by Fairfield, Newport, and Russia, to Remsen, in New York.

From Liberty Corner, by Doughty's Mills and New Providence, to Springfield, in New Jersey.

In Morgantown, by Crab Orchard, to Kingwood, in Virginia.

From Milledgeville, to Greensborough, Georgia.

From Pocotaligo, by Hickory Hill, to Augusta, in South Carolina.

From Clinton, in Tennessee, to Pulaski, in Kentucky.

From Washington to Cincinnati ; and

From Lancaster to Washington, in Ohio.

From Falmouth to Grant's Lick, on the east side of the river, in Kentucky.

From Smithton to John Graham's in Missouri.

SEC. 2. *And be it' further enacted,* That the following be established post roads, that is to say :

In Maine.—From Brunswick, by Topsham, Lisbon, Wales, Monmouth, Leeds, Wayne, and Fayette, to Jay ; and thence by Livermore, Turner, and Durham, to Brunswick.

From Green, by Leeds and Wayne, to Winthrop.

From Bangor, by Levant, Corinth, New Charlestown, Atkinson, Sebec, Brownsville, Williamsburg, Foxcroft, Guilford, and Sangerville, to Bangor.

From Warsaw, by Hartland and St. Albin's, to Palmyra.

From Bethel, by Gilead, Shelburne, Durand, Kilkenney, and Jefferson, to Lancaster, in New Hampshire.

In New Hampshire.—From Concord, in Rockingham county, by the McCrillis tavern, in Canterbury, Northfield meeting-house, Sanbornton, Smith's village on the turnpike, across the river near Pine Hill, and Bridgewater, to Plymouth.

From Smith's village on the turnpike, by New Hamptom meeting-house, and the paper mill in Holderness, to Plymouth.

From Concord, by Boscowan, Salisbury village, Andover, New Chester, Bristol, and the Mayhew turnpike, to Rumney.

From Rochester, by Chesnut Hill, in Farmington, to Middleton.

From the post route from Centre Harbor to Plymouth, and the post route from Portsmouth, by Meredith, and New Hampton, to Plymouth, shall be by the post office in Holderness.

In Massachusetts.—From Greenfield, by Bernardstown, Northfield, Warwick, Orange, New Salem, Shutesbury, Leverett, Sunderland, and Montague, to Greenfield.

From Richmond to West Stockbridge.

From Northampton, by East Hampton, South Hampton, Westfield, Southwick, and East Granby, to Hartford, in Connecticut.

From Worcester to Croton.

From Boston, by a turnpike road, to Taunton ; and thence by Wellington, Dighton, Swanzey, Warren, Bristol, Portsmouth, and Middleton, to Newport, in Rhode Island.

From South Hadley, by Granby, to Belchertown.

In Connecticut.—From Mansfield to Willington.

From Stafford, by Union, to Woodstock.

From Brooklin, by South Killingly, to Thompson.

From Bridgeport, by Long Hill, Trumbull, Levi Edwards's, in Huntington, Newtown, and Brookfield, to New Milford.

In New York.—From Utica, by Whitesborough, Floyd, Steuben, and Western, to Rome.

From Cayuga to Montezuma.

From Turin, by Harrisburg, Copenhagen, Tylersville, Pinkney, and Rodman, to Adams.

From Newburgh, by Middletown, Marlborough, Milton, and New Paltz, to Poughkeepsie.

From Upper Red Hook Landing, to the present post road from New York to Albany.

From Watertown, by Le Raysville, to Antwerp.

From Mooresville, by Bovina, in Delaware county, to Delhi.

From Bergen, by Riga, and East Riga, to Rochesterville.

From Ellicottville, by Little Valley, Conewongo Creek, and Gerry, to Mayville.

From Caledonia to Riga.

From Whitehall, in Washington county, by Putnam, to Ticonderoga.

From Southold, in Suffolk, to the village of Oysterponds.

From Utica, in the county of Oneida, to Bainbridge, in the county of Chenango, by New Hartford, Paris Furnace, Bridgewater, Brookfield, Columbus, New Berlin, Norwich, and Guilford.

From Lisle in the county of Broome, through the towns of Berkshire and Carolina, on the Susquehanna, and Bath turnpike road, to Ithica, in the county of Tompkins.

From Manlius, by Oran, Delhi, Fabius, Pompey, and thence to Manlius.

From Utica, by Rome, to Montezuma, and thence to Rochester, upon and near the Great Canal.

From Bennington, Vermont, by White Creek, Cambridge, Easton, and Greenwich, to Saratoga Springs, New York.

From Richfield, by Peltries, in Columbia, by Underwood's, in Litchfield, to Utica.

From Peltries, in Columbia, by Elie Palmer's, to Herkimer.

From Little Falls, Herkimer county, by Eaton's Bush, Middleville, Newport, Naham Daniel's, Russia post office, to Trenton, with a side mail from Middleville to Fairfield post office.

From Canandaigua, in the State of New York,

Public Acts of Congress.

by Manchester, to Palmyra; from thence by South Williamson and Williamson, to Pultneyville.

In New Jersey.—From Chester to Flanders.

From Liberty Corner to Somerville.

From Trenton, by Croswick's tavern, Rickle's town, Julius, and Arny's, to New Egypt.

In Pennsylvania.—From Easton, by Stockertown, to Roscommon.

From Chester, by Village Green, Wilcoxe's mills, Concord meeting-house, and Dilworthtown, to West Chester.

From Clark's Ferry, by Landisburg, Douglass's mills, and Concord, to Fannellsburg.

From Somerset, by Connelsville, Union, Smithfield, Germantown, and Geneva, to Morgantown, in Virginia.

From Hanover, by Berlin, to Dillstown.

From Lambpeter square to Cochransville.

From Gettysburg, by Petersburg, and Dillstown, to Harrisburg.

From Berwick, on the Tioga and Susquehanna turnpike, to Meansville.

From Lancaster, by New London cross roads, Newark, and Christiana bridge, to New Castle, in Delaware.

From Gettysburg, by Lughtersburg, to Hagerstown, Maryland.

From Leditz, in Lancaster county, by Elizabeth furnace and Shuefferston, to Lebanon.

From Beavertown, Jeffriestown and Noblestown, to Cannonsburg.

In Delaware.—From Milford to the village of Milton, a new route.

In Maryland.—That the mail route from Easton to Princess Anne shall pass over Dover Bridge, and by New Market and Cambridge; the route from Easton, by the Trappe, to Cambridge, shall nevertheless be continued.

From Easton to the Trappe, in Talbot county.

From Harford to Michael's store.

In Virginia.—From Kingwood, by Crab Orchard, Hagan's store, to Smithfield, in Pennsylvania.

From Lewis courthouse, by French Creek settlement, Flatwood's, and Elk river, to Nicholas courthouse.

From Woodring's mill, in Preston county, by Goff's ferry, on Cheat river, to Leading creek, in Randolph county.

From the mouth of Fishing creek, on the Ohio, river, by Buffalo, Barnes's mills, Pritchett's settlement, and Smithfield, to Kingwood.

From Springfield to Romney, in Hampshire county.

From Morgantown, by Jackson's iron works, Carlisle's furnace, to Sandy creek glades.

From Charlottesville, by Warren, to Buckingham courthouse.

From Culpeper courthouse, by State mills, to Woodville.

From Staunton, by Little river, to the Panther Gap.

From Jacksonville, in Wood county, by Murphy's settlement, to Lewis courthouse.

16th Con. 2d Sess.—58

That the mail route from Wheeling pass by Sisterville and the mouth of Fishing creek.

That the mail route from Warm springs, in Bath county, by Anthony's creek, to Lewisburg, shall, in returning, pass by Frankford, Locust creek, Barnes's mill, Cackley's, Bradshaw's, and Gatewood, to the Warm Springs.

In North Carolina.—From Salisbury to Fayetteville.

From Wilkesborough, by Mock's Old Fields, Salisbury, Skeen's ferry, Lawrenceville, Wadesborough, and Sneedsborough, to Cheraw, formerly Chatham, in South Carolina.

From Charlotte, by Chester courthouse, and Newberry courthouse, to Edgefield courthouse, in South Carolina.

That the mail route from Fayetteville to Wilmington pass by David Wright's store, in Duplin county.

From Salisbury, by Fulton, to Huntsville.

In South Carolina.—From Columbia, by Ashville and Warm Springs, in North Carolina, to Lexington, in Kentucky.

From Coosawatchie, by Robertsville and King creek, to Augusta.

In Georgia.—From Monticello, by Monroe, in Walton county, and Lawrenceville, in Gwinnet county, to Hall courthouse.

From Jefferson to Fairfield, in Camden county.

From Carnesville, by Habersham courthouse, to Rabun courthouse.

From Powelton, in Hancock county, by Greensborough, to Madison, in Morgan county.

From Carnesville, by Bushville, to Hall courthouse.

In Kentucky.—From Franklin to Nashville, in Tennessee.

From Eddyville, by Iron Banks, to New Madrid, in Missouri.

That the post route from Burkesville to Monticello shall pass by Robert Poage's in Stockton's Valley.

That the post route from Columbia to Glasgow shall pass by Edmonton, in Barren county.

From Scottsville to Cairo, in Tennessee.

From Falmouth, in Pendleton county, passing the three forks of Grassy creek and Gains's, to Burlington, in Boone county.

From Bowling Green, by Litchfield and Hardingsburg, to Corydon, in Indiana.

In Tennessee.—From Clinton to Burkesville, in Kentucky.

From Washington, in Rhea county, by Hamilton courthouse and the new turnpike road, to Morgantown, at the mouth of Sequatchee, by Marion courthouse and Jackson courthouse, to Huntsville, in Alabama.

From McMinville, by Shelby, to Columbia.

From Sparta, by Cookeville, Gainesborough, and Meigsville, to Tompkinsville, in Kentucky.

From Kingston, by Washington, to Huntsville, in Alabama.

That the route from Springfield to Russelville, in Kentucky, shall pass Fort's mills, on Red river.

From Murfreesborough to Statesville.

Public Acts of Congress.

From Vernon, by Perry courthouse, to Reynoldsburg.

In Ohio.—From Lebanon, by Monroe, to Hamilton.

From Washington, in Pennsylvania, by Wellsburg, in Virginia, Steubenville, New Salem, New Philadelphia, Wooster, and Norwalk, to Lower Sandusky.

From Canton, in Stark county, by New Portage, Norton, and Wadsworth, to Medina, in Medina county.

From Lancaster, by Circleville, to Chillicothe.

From Granville, in Licking county, by Worthington, to Dublin, in Franklin county.

From Urbanna, by Troy, to Granville, in Dark county.

From Dover, in Tuscarawas county, by Shanesville and Berlin, to Millersburg, in Coshocton county.

From Dresden, in the county of Muskingum, to Mansfield, in the county of Richland, by the way of West Carlisle, in Coshocton county.

From Aurelius, by Duck creek salt works, in Morgan county, by Senecaville, to Guernsey salt works, and to Washington, Guernsey county.

In Indiana.—From Brownstown to Indianapolis.

From Vernon to Indianapolis.

From Connersville to Indianapolis.

From Lawrencebugh to Aurora, Hanover, and the Rising Sun, to Versailles ; and to return by the way of Vaughan's, in Manchester township.

From Richmond, by Salisbury and Centreville, to Indianapolis.

From Brookville to Indianapolis.

In Illinois.—From Golconda, by Franklin courthouse, and Hinds's, to Vandalia.

From Golconda to Belgrade.

From Shawneetown to Golconda.

The mail from Vincennes, Indiana, to St. Louis, Missouri, shall pass by Vandalia.

From Vandalia, by the seats of justice of such counties as may be established by the Legislature prior to the next session of Congress, north of Madison county, to Edwardsville.

From Fairfield, by John G. Fitch's, to Vandalia.

From Palestine to Vandalia.

The mail from Golconda, by Bloomfield, to Jonesborough, to pass by Vienna.

In Mississippi.—From Columbia, by Fort Alford's, to Monticello.

From Green courthouse, by New Augusta and Monroe, to Covington courthouse.

In Alabama.—From Blakeley to Mobile Point.

From Fort Hawkins, by Fort Gaines and Butler courthouse, to Conecuh courthouse.

In Missouri.—From Shawneetown, by Rood's, Jonesborough, in Illinois, and Bainbridge, in Cape Girardeau county, to Jackson.

From St. Charles, by James Journey's, John Biven's, Isaac Vanbibber's, John Grayum's, and Augustus Thrall's, to Franklin.

From Franklin, by the mouth of Arrow Rock and Mount Vernon, to Fort Osage.

From St. Genevieve, by the Saline, Amos Bird's, John F. Henry's, and Bainbridge, to Cape Girardeau.

From Franklin to Boonsville.

From Smithton to Augusta Thrall's.

From Alton, by the house of Levi Roberts, Jo§ Shaw, and Leonard Ross, to Louisianaville, Missouri.

Approved, March 3, 1821.

An Act to authorize the building of Lighthouses therein mentioned, and for other purposes.

Be it enacted, &c., That the Secretary of th Treasury be, and he is hereby, authorized and em powered to provide, by contract, for building ligh houses and placing buoys on the following site and shoals, to wit : five lighthouses, one on Cro§ Island, near Machias ; one in the harbor of Booth bay, at such place as the Secretary of the Treasury shall designate ; and one on Pond Island, at th§ mouth of Kennebeck river ; one on the Stratford Point, in Connecticut ; and one on Throg's Neck, in New York ; and on the shoals of Nantucket and the Vineyard Sound a number of buoys, not exceeding ten, in the State of Massachusetts. A lighthouse at the mouth of Oswego river, at such place as shall be designated by the Secretary of the Treasury, in the State of New York. And two buoys, one on James's Ledge, and one on the rock called Old Gay , and a spindle on the Brothers, in the State of Rhode Island.

SEC. 2. *And be it further enacted,* That there be appropriated, out of any money in the Treasury not otherwise appropriated, the following sums of money, to wit : For building three lighthouses, one on Cross Island, near Machias ; one in the harbor of Boothbay ; and one on Pond Island, ten thousand five hundred dollars ; for building the lighthouses on Stratford Point, and Throg's Neck, four thousand dollars ; for a lighthouse at the mouth of Oswego river, three thousand five hundred dollars : for ten buoys on Nantucket shoals, and the Vineyard Sound, one thousand five hundred dollars : for two buoys and a spindle for the rocks called James's Ledge, Old Gay, and the Brothers, four hundred and fifty dollars : and for placing buoys, and anchors with buoys, in the Altamaha river, between the port of Darien, and Doboy Sound, in the State of Georgia, a sum not exceeding one thousand five hundred dollars.

SEC. 3. *And be it further enacted,* That no lighthouse shall be built on any site previous to the cession of jurisdiction over the same to the United States.

SEC. 4. *And be it further enacted,* That the President of the United States be and he is hereby authorized and requested to cause such an examination or survey of the Isles of Shoals, on the coast of New Hampshire and Maine, to be made, by proper and intelligent persons, as may be requisite to ascertain the expediency and practicability of repairing the sea-wall at Smutty Nose Island, and building a sea-wall between said island and Cedar Island. And that the President be further requested, in like manner, to ascertain the expediency of erecting a stone pier on Sunken Rocks, in the harbor of Portsmouth, in the State of New Hampshire. And the President of the United States

Resolutions.

is hereby authorized to cause the sea-wall aforesaid to be repaired, and the pier aforesaid to be erected, by contract, under the direction of the collector of the district of Portsmouth, if, on the report of such persons, he shall deem it necessary. And the President is further requested to communicate to Congress, at their next session, the result of so much of the examination and survey, as relates to the expediency and practicability of building the sea-wall aforesaid : *Provided,* That no money shall be expended in erecting the pier aforesaid, until the jurisdiction of the site thereof shall be ceded by the State of New Hampshire to the United States.

SEC. 5. *And be it further enacted,* That a sum, not exceeding two thousand five hundred dollars, is hereby appropriated for the purposes aforesaid ; to be paid out of any money in the Treasury not otherwise appropriated.

Approved, March 3, 1821.

_____

An Act to amend the act, entitled "An act to provide for taking the fourth census or enumeration of the inhabitants of the United States, and for other purposes."

Be it enacted, &c., That, instead of the time prescribed in the above-recited act, in which the marshals and their assistants should perform the various duties assigned them by the said act, the same is hereby enlarged to the first day of September next.

Approved, March 3, 1821.

_____

An Act authorizing the President of the United States to remove the Land Office in the district of Lawrence county, in the Territory of Arkansas.

Be it enacted, &c., That so much of the act, entitled "An act making provision for the establishment of additional land offices in the Territory of Missouri," as requires that the land office for the district of Lawrence county shall be established at the seat of justice in said county, shall be and the same is hereby repealed ; and the President of the United States is hereby authorized to remove and establish said office at any suitable place within the said district.

Approved, March 2, 1821.

_____

An Act to alter the times of holding the District Court in the Northern District of New York.

Be it enacted, &c., That the district court of the United States of America for the northern district of New York, directed by law to be holden at Utica, shall hereafter be holden at the same place on the last Tuesday of August, instead of the third Tuesday of May, in each year ; and that the court directed by law to be holden at Albany, on the second Tuesday of November, shall, instead thereof, hereafter be holden at the same place on the last Tuesday of January in each year.

SEC. 2. *And be it further enacted,* That all ac-

tions, suits, process, proceedings, commenced, or to be commenced, or now pending in said district court, and liable to be discontinued, or suffer prejudice, from the foregoing alterations, may be returned to, and shall be continued to, the district court to be holden in pursuance of this act, in such manner as that the same shall suffer no discontinuance or prejudice by virtue of this act.

Approved, March 2, 1821.

_____

RESOLUTIONS.

Resolution providing for the admission of Missouri into the Union on a certain condition.

Resolved, by the Senate and House of Representatives of the United States of America in Congress assembled, That Missouri shall be admitted into this Union on an equal footing with the original States, in all . respects whatever, upon the fundamental condition, that the fourth clause of the twenty-sixth section of the third article of the constitution submitted on the part of said State to Congress, shall never be construed to authorize the passage of any law, and that no law shall be passed in conformity thereto, by which any citizen, of either of the States in this Union, shall be excluded from the enjoyment of any of the privileges and immunities to which such citizen is entitled under the Constitution of the United States : *Provided,* That the Legislature of said State, by a solemn public act, shall declare the assent of the said State to the said fundamental condition, and shall transmit to the President of the United States, on or before the fourth Monday in November next, an authentic copy of the said act ; upon the receipt whereof, the President, by proclamation, shall announce the fact ; whereupon, and without any further proceeding on the part of Congress, the admission of the said State into the Union shall be considered as complete.

Approved, March 2, 1821.

_____

Resolution providing for jails in certain cases, for the safe custody of persons committed under the authority of the United States.

Resolved, &c., That where any State or States, having complied with the recommendation of Congress, in the resolution of the twenty-third day of September, one thousand seven hundred and eighty-nine, shall have withdrawn, or shall hereafter withdraw, either in whole or in part, the use of their jails, for prisoners commited under the authority of the United States, the marshal in such State or States, under the direction of the judge of the district, .shall be, and hereby is, authorized and required to hire a convenient place to serve as a temporary jail, and to make the necessary provision for the safe-keeping of prisoners committed under the authority of the United States, until permanent provision shall be made by law for that purpose ; and the said marshal shall be allowed his reasonable expenses, incurred for the above purposes, to be paid out of the Treasury of the United States.

Approved, March 3, 1821.

Resolution authorizing the President of the United States to cause astronomical observations to be made, to ascertain the longitude of the Capitol, in the City of Washington, from some known meridian in Europe.

Resolved, &c., That the President of the United States be authorized to cause such number of astronomical observations to be made, by methods which may, in his judgment, be best adapted to insure a correct determination of the longitude of the Capitol, in the City of Washington, from Greenwich, or some other known meridian in Europe, and that the data, with accurate calculations or statements, founded thereon, be laid before Congress at their next session.

Approved, March 3, 1821.

INDEX

TO THE PROCEEDINGS AND DEBATES OF THE SECOND SESSION OF THE SIXTEENTH CONGRESS.

SENATE.

Senate Proceedings and Debates.

Senate Proceedings and Debates.

Senate Proceedings and Debates.

Senate Proceedings and Debates.

HOUSE OF REPRESENTATIVES AND APPENDIX.

House Proceedings and Debates.

House Proceedings and Debates.

House Proceedings and Debates.

House Proceedings and Debates.

House Proceedings and Debates.

Public Acts and Resolutions.

PUBLIC ACTS AND RESOLUTIONS.

Lightning Source UK Ltd.
Milton Keynes UK
UKHW011822261118
332995UK00011B/977/P